DICTIONARY
TELUGU ENGLISH

నిఘంటు
తెలుగు ఇంగ్లీష్

DICTIONARY TELUGU ENGLISH

నిఘంటు తెలుగు ఇంగ్లీష్

Charles Philip Brown

PART – I

అ a TO పై pai

SECOND EDITION

NEW EDITION THOROUGHLY REVISED AND BROUGHT UPTO DATE

BY

M. VENKATA RATNAM
W.H. CAMPBELL
and
RAO BAHADUR K. VEERESALINGAM

GYAN

Published by

GYAN

Gyan Publishing House
5, Ansari Road
Daryaganj, New Delhi-110002
Phone: 011-47034999, 9811692060
E-mail: books@gyanbooks.com

Distribution Network
gyanbooks.com
India, USA, Canada, UK, Australia, France

ISBN : 978-81-212-3070-4 (set)
978-81-212-6588-1 (HB)
First Published, 1903

2nd Impression 2022

Printed at: Gyan Press, Delhi.

నిఘంటు తెలుగు ఇంగ్లీష్

DICTIONARY TELUGU-ENGLISH (Part-I)

Author: Charles Philip Brown

PREFACE.

THIS is a NEW EDITION of the late C. P. BROWN'S well-known Telugu-English Dictionary, thoroughly revised and brought up to date. The chief features of the work are as follows :—

(1) All the latest and best sources of information have been utilised in its preparation, especially as regards the Scientific Terms. Various Government publications such as the Fauna of British India edited by DR. BLANFORD, DR. WATTS'S Dictionary of the Economic Products of India, and the Madras Manual of Administration, have been duly laid under contribution.

(2) All words used in Telugu, both literary and colloquial, from whatever language they may have come, are given in the body of the work, so as to render the use of any other book of reference superfluous.

(3) All the words are given in Romanized spelling, so that the work may be utilised by scholars outside India for indological studies.

(4) Cognate and compound words are grouped together under a head-word so as to afford a greater facility for the study of the Telugu language, and are printed in bold type.

(5) Wherever possible, the derivations of words are given, and similar forms in other languages are indicated. Many words given as native in Telugu Dictionaries are traced to a foreign origin.

(6) Many quotations from the Telugu classics which seemed unnecessary have been left out and several new ones have been added.

In addition to the works named above, the Editors have freely made use of Mr. Brown's own MS. notes kindly lent to the S. P. C. K. by the authorities of the India Office Library. Sitārāmachārlu's Telugu Dictionary published by the Madras School Book and Vernacular Literature Society has also been very largely made use of in preparing this edition. Quotations made from it are indicated by the references given in Telugu characters. The Editors are also indebted to several friends for valuable assistance readily rendered.

26th August, 1903,
MADRAS.

THE EDITORS

INTRODUCTION.

TELUGU, which is one of the South Indian Vernaculars, belongs to the Dravidian group of languages. A semi-circle drawn with Rajahmundry as centre and the distance between it and Madras as radius, covers, roughly speaking, the greater portion of the country in which it is spoken by about 25 millions of people. It is spoken and written in its purity along the coast strip between Nellore and Vizagapatam and in the four districts of the Madras Presidency included within those limits. Beyond this area it contains an admixture of Tamil in the south, of Kanarese in the west, of Mahrati in the west and north-west, and of Uriya in the north.

Telugu is closely allied to Tamil, Kanarese and Malayalam, words of Dravidian origin occurring in all these languages without any great difference of form. The original Dravidian speech seems to have split up into these languages about the time when the modern Teutonic languages such as English, Dutch and German were formed out of their parent tongue. Tamil is probably nearer to the original tongue than any other member of the group, and as it has preserved the older forms of the Dravidian roots a knowledge of it is essential to the proper study of the South Indian languages.

It is doubtful if any of the Dravidian races had a knowledge of the art of writing prior to the Aryan invasion, and certainly none of them can boast of a literature older than the 8th or 9th century A. D. In Telugu there is no work extant older than the translation of the Sanskrit Mahā Bhārata, which is supposed to have been made in the 11th century A. D., but bears traces of having been expanded in subsequent times. The style of this translation, which is quite modern, is accepted as a standard of classical Telugu. As the perfect style of the book could not have been developed all at once, it is hardly possible to avoid the conclusion that there must have been not a few earlier and less polished works which have since perished. There is indeed a tradition that when Vaishnavaism supplanted Saivaism in the country, all the older literature was destroyed.

In the formation of modern Telugu, four strata are distinctly visible. The lowest of these consists of the pure Telugu element. This is of the deepest interest to the student of language at present, as it has as yet been but little worked by scholars. A careful study of the Telugu words reveals to us much of the life and thought of the ancient Dravidians before the Aryan invasion. It shows that the people who spoke the Telugu tongue lived a very simple life, and that, although not ignorant of agriculture and some of the simple industrial arts, they were still only semi-civilized and probably spent much of their time roaming in the forests with which a great part of South India was covered. They lived in communities and had a fairly complicated social system with degrees of relationship carefully recognised and distinguished by significant names. Their religion seems to have been one of a very primitive type. It consisted of a worship of the powers of nature, most of which were regarded as malignant in character. Among these deities the powers that presided over boundaries had special prominence assigned to them, as is seen by the names Anku (అంకు), Ankamma (అంకమ్మ), Ellamma (ఎల్లమ్మ), Pōlēramma (పోలేరమ్మ), &c. The word for 'temple' (కోయిల or కోవెల, Tamil kō-yil) probably points to a worship of the monkey (కో or కోతి). All the higher religious ideas of the people seem to have been derived from Aryan sources, and it is hardly possible to describe any religious ideas or ceremonies without employing Sanskrit terms. Even the ordinary word for God (దేవుడు) is of Sanskrit origin.

The etymology of Telugu words is full of suggestive meaning. The words for father (తండ్రి) and mother (తల్లి) are undoubtedly connected with the root *Ta* (తా) to bring (cf. తెచ్చు), and literally mean 'He who brings' or 'She who brings' respectively. There is thus a very close resemblance, in meaning at least, to the Aryan term *Pitṛi*, father, which comes from the root *Pā* to support or nourish. The Telugu word for son-in-law (అల్లుడు) signifies 'one who weaves' (*i. e.*, relationships between two families). The word for the hand (చెయ్యి) comes from చేయు to do and means 'that which does' (*i. e.*, works), and the word for the right hand (కుడిచెయ్యి) means 'the food (కూడు)-eating hand,' while the left hand (ఎడమచెయ్యి) is the 'distant hand.' The word for house (ఇల్లు) probably shows a connection betwen the Babylonians and the Dravidians at a very early date. Indeed the Dravidians who were probably allied to the Babylonians and had trade connections with them, seem to have spread at one time all over Southern Asia, and the Aryan immigrants appear but to have followed them along their ancient trade-routes into India.

The second element in Telugu is that which has come from Sanskrit. The Aryans have been the great civilisers of the world, and the Indo-Aryans have done for the races that inhabit India what the Greeks and Romans did for the peoples of Europe. It was they who taught the higher arts of life to the South Indian peoples and laid the foundation of the Dravidian literatures. In Telugu the whole of the literature has been their creation, while their Sanskrit speech has influenced the Telugu language as much as, if not more than, Latin has influenced English. All general and abstract terms, and, as has been stated above, even the word for God, are of Sanskrit origin, and now, although some writers have, by employing obscure and obsolete terms, succeeded in writing poems in pure unmixed Telugu, it is in reality hardly possible to write a sentence of ordinary Telugu, without using a Sanskrit word in it. While Sanskrit has thus influenced the Telugu language, it is certain that many Dravidian words have found their way into it and have been naturalised by it. A complete list of such words is given in Kittel's Kannada English Dictionary. In the present work all Telugu words that appear to have been borrowed by Sanskrit have been duly noticed. The attention of scholars has also to be invited to the historical connection between Indo-Aryans and the Semitic races which words like Ambarisha (' 'Ambarice,') Asura (lit: 'Assyrian'), Brahma (Heb: 'Abraham' to suggest.

The third element in Telugu is that which has come from, or at least through, Hindustani. Under the term Hindustani we have included all Persian and Arabic words which have come into use in Telugu. Hindustani words must have begun to find their way into the language in the days of Alla-ud-din, and they can be traced in the literature ever since the times of Krishna Raya of Vijianagar fame, the Macaenas of the Telugu country. In the first edition of this work, a great many Hindustani words were given [*Vide* Brown's Dictionary of mixed Dialects, which was given as an Appendix], but most of these have either gone or are gradually going out of use, their place being taken by English words. especially in the language of the Law courts and of public business.

The fourth element is the English one With the introduction of new ideas consequent upon the British occupation of the country, ready made English words which express these ideas have naturally come into use. At present the influx of such words is very great. In the towns in particular, many people have begun to talk a kind of mongrel Telugu, using English words in their Telugu sentences, even where this is altogether unnecessary. It is impossible to say at present what words will be a permanent gain to the language, but it seems certain that a large number of words such as Road (రోడ్డు), Hospital (ఆసుపత్రి). Mile (మైలు), Ruler (రూలుకర్ర), Quinine (క్వైనా), Rubber (రబ్బరు), Pencil (పెనసలు). Station (స్టేషను). Fiddle (ఫిడేలు). &c., for which there are no equivalents in the vernacular, will retain their place in the common speech of the people.

REFERENCES TO ENGLISH WORKS

Ainslie's Materia Medica.
Blanford's Fauna of British India (quoted as F.B.I.)
Burnell's South Indian Palaeography.
Caldwell's Comparative Grammar of the Dravidian Languages (2nd Edition.)
Cunningham's Inscriptions of Asoka.
Gundert's Malayalam Dictionary.
Jerdon's Natural History.
Kittel's Kannada English Dictionary.
Roxburgh's Flora Indica.
Russell's Indian Snakes.
Taylor's Alphabet.
Dictionary of Economic Products of India (quoted as E.P.)
Sanskrit and English Dictionary (quoted as W.)

ABBR[illegible]VIATIONS.

A or Amuk—Amukta mālyada.
ABA.—Andhra Bhāshārnavamu.
Anir or Anirudh—Aniruddha Charitra.
Anuk—an onomatopœic word.
Appa Kavi—Appa Kāviyamu.
B. or Bhāg.—Bhāgavatamu.
Balarām—Balarāma Charitra.
BD.—Bhāgavatam Daṣama Skandhamu.
Bhar.—Mahā Bhārata.
Bhasc.—Bhāskara Ṣatakamu.
Bmj.—Bhānumad Vijayamu.
Bobbili—Bobbili Charitramu.
BP.—Basava Purāṇamu (Padya Kāvya.)
Charitra—Panditārādhya Charitra.
Dab—Abhimanyu Dvipada.
DB.—Dvipada Basava Purāṇamu.
DR.—Dvipada Ramāyaṇamu.
Drav.—Dravidian.
Eng.—English.
G.—Vikramārka Charitra by Gōpu Rāzu.
Gk.—Greek.
[H.]—Hindustani.
H.—Hamsa Vimsati.
Hari.—Harivamṣamu.
HD.—The Dvipada version of the Tale of Harischandra.
Heb.—Hebrew.
—Ilā Dēviyamu.
Jaim.—Jaimini Bhāratamu.
.—Kanarese.
KP.—Kalā Purnōdayan
KUR.—Uttara Rāmāyat
kanti Pāparāzu.
L.—Prabhu Linga Līla Ch
Lat.—Latin.
M.—Mahā Bhāratamu.
Mand. or Mandhat.—Mandhat tra.
N.—Daṣāvatāra Charitra by Nāga
Naish.—Naishadhamu.
ND.—Nāla Dvipada.
P.—Pancha Tantramu, by Ven, R zu.
Paidim.—Chandrangada Charitra.
Parij.—Pārijātāpaharanamu.
R.—Ramābhyudayamu.
Sar. D.—Sārangadhara Charitra (D pada).
Skt.—Sanskrit.
Suca.—Suca Saptati.
Swa.—Swārōchisha Manu Charitramu.
T.—Tārāṣasankamu.
Tam.—Tamil.
Tel.—Telugu.
UH.—Uttara Harischandra.
UR.—Uttara Rāmāyaṇamu.
Vaij. or Vaija.—Vaijayantī Vilāsamu.
Vasu.—Vasu Charitramu.
Ved. Ras.—Vēdānta Rasayanamu.
Vēma.—Vēmana Ṣatakamu.
Vijaya.—Vijaya Vilāsamu.
VP.—Vishṇu Purāṇamu.
Yayati—Yayati Charitramu.

The Telugu abbreviations used are sufficient to suggest [illegible] [illegible]gu books and the Grammatical abbreviations bein[illegible] [illegible]planatory.

.e on how to consult this Dictionary :—

Derivatives if not found in their proper Alphabetical place are to be looked for either under their primitives or cognate forms. Compound words will be found under one or other of the elements which compose them.

BROWN'S

TELUGU - ENGLISH

DICTIONARY.

అ a

అ *a.* 1. The first letter of the Telugu alphabet as of many others. Hence the phrase అ ఆలు formed like the word 'alphabet' from the first two letters in the series, means the whole of the Tel. alphabet. See ఓనమాలు and వర్ణ మాల. అకారము is the letter or sound of *a*, the term కారము being added to each letter in naming it. అకారాదిగా beginning with the letter అ *seriatim*, i.e., in alphabetical order.

The letter అ has the same shape as the Eng. 'A' reversed, but is quite rounded off, and represents like its Semitic prototype "the horns of an ox" (Taylor.)

The stroke ́ called తలకట్టు *tala-kaṭṭu* and placed over many consonants is popularly, though by mistake as pointed out by Burnell, taken to be the secondary form of అ.

The letter అ has the same sound as the Eng. *a* in 'around,' 'delta', 'Victoria.' It is the 'low-back-wide vowel formed by the jaws, pharynx and lips wide open' and is supposed to be inherent in consonants—*e.g.*, in బ b, ల l, జ j.

అ a

అ *a.* 2. [Drav.] The base of the demonstrative pronoun అతడు, వాడు, అది.

అ *a.* 3. [Tel.] The termination of many pure Tel. words in the fem. and neut. genders, *e. g.*, అమ్మ, అక్క, అత్త, అప్ప, అవ్వ, దండ, కర్ర, కేల, వల, ఓడ. But of a few masculines only; *e.g.*, తాత, మామ, అన్న, బావ, దొర.

అ *a.* 4. [Tel.] A vocative suffix. తమ్ముడ= తమ్ముడు+అ = O (younger) brother! నాయన= నాయనా. Usually the lengthened form is used, as రామా.

అ *a.* 5. [Tel.] An interrogative suffix. నా మాటవినవ, will you not listen to me? "నీ కోర్కి దొడ్డి చెప్పుమ." సర్వ. i. 62.

అ *a.* 6. [Tel.] A suffix meaning 'Only this and no other.'

"దీనిం దెనుగున పాటించి రచింప నీవ ప్రౌఢు డవరయన్." రాఘ. i. 12.

అ *a.* 7. [Tel.] A suffix meaning 'By oneself without the help of another'. సర్వము నీవ తెరుగుదువు. Or, without a rival, *e.g.*,

"శత్రుక్షయంబుచేసి యెవ్వరికి నీక తాన యేలుచుండె మనిరొండె, సాహసంబున." భాగ. vii 10.

అ *a*. 8. [Tel.] A suffix meaning 'Not at all,' 'not in the least.'

"కులమువాడి నడవ దలపడ." శ్రీర. ఉత్త. iii.

అ *a*. 9. [Tel.] A suffix denoting 'absence of interval' తోన=తోడనే = directly afterwards.

అ *a*. 10 [Skt. from న the n sound being elided.] A negative prefix becoming AN before vowels and corresponding to the privatives *á*, *án* (Gk.), *in* (Lat.), and *un* (Eng.) Thus క్రమము regularity, అక్రమము irregularity; ఆదరణ kindness, అనాదరణ unkindness.

అ ఆలు The Telugu Alphabet. See అ. 1.

అంక *anka*. [Tel. √ అంకు = to move in a curve.] Another form of అంక (q. v.)

అంకకాడు *anka-kāḍu*. [Tel. Kan. అంక కాఱ.] n. One who is distinguished by a sign, గురుతుగలవాడు. The leader. One who excites quarrels. కలహప్రియుడు.

"అమరుడు కలహమున కంకకాడయి కాల ద్రన్న." ఆముక్త. v. 84.

అంకణము *ankaṇamu*. [Tel. related to అంగ and అడుగు, the *foot*; borrowed by Skt. from Dravidian languages. Cf. Kittel and Gundert.] n. The act of branding or marking. Intercolumniation. Apartment. The space between any two beams, or pillars. రెండు దూలముల, కేక, స్తంభముల నడిమి ప్రదేశము. నలుచదరపుచోటు; తొట్టికట్టు. అంకణమునకు రూపాయి బాడిగ the rent of each apartment is one rupee. మీ యిల్లు అంకణముల యిల్లు how many apartments are there in your house? how big is it?

అంకపాలి *anka-pāli*. [Tel. Kan. & Skt.] n. An embrace. The lap, hip or haunch. ఆలింగనము. అంకప్రదేశము, తొడ.

"అంకపాలినటద్దుకూలాంచలము." మను. i. 12; and vii. 100.

అంకపొంకములు or **అంకపొంకాలు** *anka-ponkamulu*. [Tel.] n. Fierceness, fury, violence, Enmity, opposition, విరోధము. బిడ్డకు జ్వరము అంకపొంకములుగా వచ్చినది the child was attacked with a violent fever. [Other forms are **అంకాపొంకములు** and **అంకాపొంకాలు**.]

అంకము *ankamu*. [Tel. Drav. word borrowed by Skt. √ అంకు = to move in a curve.] n. A mark, spot, badge. బిరుదాంకము=బిరుదు గురుతు.

"అంకపురాజిలంక." వసు. ii. 11.

The haunch or part above the hip. A chapter or section. An act in a play. Proximity. A numerical figure, a cipher. A military show, a sham fight. బింకపోరు, చిత్రయుద్ధము.

"అంకగతుడైన శైత్యుని నాగ్రహమున." భాగ.

A fault, a sin. Objection, cavil ఆక్షేపము.

"అంకము సేయువచ్చునలయూర్ధ్వుల ముఖ్యు గ ప్ర స్తుతించెదన." హైరా. i.

అంకతలము or **అంకపీఠి** the lap, the part on which an infant sits, as on the lap.

"వసుధీయంకతలంబునన్నిదుర మానంబేయగా జేసెదన." విక్ర. iii. 94.

అంకితుడు n. He who is marked or distinguished గురుతుగలవాడు. మృగాంకుడు the moon.

అంకమ్మ *ankamma*. [Tel. n. అంకు + అమ్మ.] A village goddess, usually worshipped by the Panchamas. అంకచండాలము a filthy mass.

అంకవంక *anka-vanka*. [Tel.] n. Softness, pliability, submissiveness. ఆమె అంకవంకకు రాదు she is stubborn.

అంకవన్నె *anka-vanne*. [Tel.] n. A stirrup, or the strap that supports it అంకువది;

"ఇలబాదద్వయి రాయు నల్కారు నకు రెండేబా రుహా నంకవన్నెలురెండై." ఆముక్త. ii. 29.

అంకవిద్య *anka-vidya*. [Skt.] n. Arithmetic. గణితము.

అంకారము *ankāramu* [Skt.] n. A diminution in music.

అంకారించు *ankārinchu*. [Hind. bankarna.] v. i. To set sail. ఓడవారు లెత్తిపోవు.

అంకాలు, చిట్టి అంకాలు, అంకులు. n. Name of a tree. నందివృక్షము, పాలచెట్టు *Cedrela Tuna*, or, *Mimusops Hexandra*.

అంకాళమ్మ *ankalamma.* [Tel.] n. A village goddess. ఒక గ్రామదేవత. Same as అంకెమ్మ.

అంకించు *ankintsu.* [Tel.] v. t. & i. 1. To raise, take up, lift up. భుజములంకించు shrug the shoulders. 2. To move about, to brandish, ఆడించు, త్రిప్పించు.

"కరవాలంబంకించి యుంగరుభుజాంతరంబు చీల్చు త్రేసి." ద్వి. రా.

3. To turn to one side త్రిప్పు.

"నెమ్మొగమడ్డమంకించి." నిర్వ. ఉ: రా. viii.

4. To hold, పట్టుకొను.

"మారుతిసుతుండు ఘనగదాదండ మంకించి కదిలుటయును." జై. భా. ii. 47.

5. To adopt, take or receive. అవలంబించు.

"ధర్మ మేజయుమనుమాట తెనుగదాయుని కౌంతికై ర్యమంకించి." పారం. 278.

6. To look bright ఉల్లసిల్లు.

"పంకజభవాండమునడమంబు సంకుచేసినపాంకం బునవంకించుచు." వసు. iv. 23.

7. To extol, applaud పొగడు.

"సముచితభాషణంబుల నంకించుచున్న." భాగ. viii. 134.

అంకితము *ankitamu.* [Skt.] a. Marked, spotted. Counted, numbered. **అంకితము** n. A dedication. కృతి. ఆ గ్రంథమును రాజునకు అంకితముచేసినాడు he dedicated that book to the king.

అంకిణీలు *ankinilu.* [Tel.] n. Trappings, ornaments of a saddle. See పట్టాభిరామాయణము.

అంకియ *ankiya.* [Tel.] n. Another form of అంకె.

అంకియము *ankiyamu.* [Tel.] n. Same as అంకెము.

అంకిలి *ankili.* [Tel.] n. An obstacle; impediment. Grief, sorrow.

"శోకోపహతమనంబుల్గల వచనంబులు చెప్పి యంకిలిదేర్చి." భా. శాంతి. i. 288.

అంకిలిపడు *ankili-padu.* v. i. To obstruct, to come in the way. అడ్డపడు. **అంకిలిపెట్టు** v. t. To prevent.

అంకిళ్లు or అంకులు *ankillu.* [Tel. from అంకిలి + కీళ్లు] n. plu. The joints of the cheek bones; the maxillary joints. వానికి అంకిళ్లు పడిపోయినవి he has lock-jaw.

అంకు *anku.* [Tel.] n. A village goddess. Same as అంకెమ్మ.

అంకుటము *ankutamu.* [Skt.] n. The crooked iron-bar used to open the gate of a pagoda, కుంచెకోల.

అంకుడుచెట్టు *ankudu-chettu.* [Skt.] n. A species of *Nerium Antidysentericum.* Also called చిట్టిఅంకుడు and కొండకసుడు.

అంకురము *ankuramu.* [Skt.] n. A germ, a sprout, a bud. మొలక. నఖాంకురములు nail-marks, ప్రేమాంకురము the germ of love. వంశాంకురము నిలిచేలాగు దత్తుచేసికొనెను he adopted a son to preserve the stem of his family. అయనకు అంకురములేనందున as he left no heir.

అంకురించు *ankurintsu.* [Skt.] v. n. To sprout, break forth, emanate, rise as a thought. పెదవిమీదలేనగవంకురింప with a smile on the lips.

అంకురితము *ankuritamu.* [Skt.] a. Sprouted, emanated, arisen. మొలిచిన, ఉద్భవించిన.

"అంకురితస్మితము." ఆముక్త. iv. 35.

అంకుశము *ankusamu,* [Skt.] n. An elephant goad, an elephant driver's hook. Also, a check, a bar, a poser, a ruling case or argument. అంకుశమున నిలిపినాడు he made them stop short. ఇది జ్వరాంకుశము this is a specific against fever, that which arrests the disease. కవిగజాంకుశము (title of a book) a code to guide the poets. అంకుశమునకురాని ungovernable, headstrong, untractable, indocile.

అంకుసంకులు *anku-sankulu.* [Tel.] n. Possibility సాధ్యము.

అంకె *anke.* [Tel.] n. A numerical figure అంకము. Opportunity, time. One pack, half a bullock load. A form of అంకు. Bringing the yoke under the neck, as by a troublesome bullock. ఎద్దులు అంకె దీసికొన్నవి the bullocks turned restive, bringing the yoke under the neck. A command, authority, control, restraint, check. **అంకెకొను** v. i. To cover oneself with కప్పుకొను. **అంకెవేయు** v. t. To obstruct అడ్డగించు. అంకెకురాని (భాస్క. 2.) ungovernable. అంకెకురావు, అనగా అక్కరకురావు they will not be of any use. **అంకెవేసికొను** or అంకవేసికొను v. n. To be restive, as a bullock in the yoke. ఎద్దుకాడి కదుకు తిరుగుట. వాడు తేపతేపకు అంకెవేసికొనును. he turns restive every now and then.

అంకెము *ankemu.* [Tel.] n. A stirrup రికాబు. One pack or pannier, being half a bullock load.

అంకోలము or అంకోడము *ankolamu.* [Skt.] n. The plant called *Alangium Lamarckii.* (Watts) ఊడుగుచెట్టు.

అంక్యము *ankyamu.* [Skt.] a. Fit to be marked or counted. n. A small oblong drum. రెండుప్రక్కలవాయించేమద్దెల.

అంగ *anga.* [Tel.] n. A stride of about three feet. అంగవేయు to stride. అంగకొలత measurement ascertained by striding about.

అంగకము *angakamu.* [Skt.] n. The body. A limb. A bodice or jacket. రవిక, చొక్కా. కాంచనాంగకము a brocade bodice.

అంగజ *angaja.* [Skt.] n. Daughter.

అంగజుడు *angajudu.* [Skt.] n. A son. Cupid మన్మథుడు.

అంగజాల *angazala.* [Tel.] n. Sentinel, పారావాడు.

"అంగజాలలు కావలిగ జాల నిలుప్పు మీర." పారిం. (పద్య) 2. ౩౮.

అంగజాలవాడు *angazala vadu.* [Tel.] A village drudge, one who is at every man's bidding.

అంగడి *angadi.* [Drav.] (Gen. అంగటి Loc. అంగట, plu. అంగళ్లు) n. A shop. అంగడిపెట్టు to open a shop. అంగళ్లవాడ a range of shops. అంగట పోయడము selling in the shop. అంగడివీధి a market place. ఆ సంగతిని అంగడిలో పెట్టినాడు he revealed or exposed the matter.

అంగణము *anganamu.* [Skt.] n. A court or yard. An area, a plain. ముంగిలి.

అంగద *angada.* [Tel.] n. Hunger. Misfortune, trouble, calamity. Mental agony or anxiety. Anger.

"అంగద దేక నిన్నునాతాంబును సంకటలంబు చేస్తి." రామా. v. 319.

అంగదట్టము *anga-dattamu.* [Tel.] n. A petticoat గాగరా, పావడ.

అంగదము *angadamu.* [Skt. from అంగము.] n. A bracelet worn upon the upper arm. కేయూరము, బాహుపురి.

అంగదేశము *angadesamu.* [Skt.] n. An ancient name for the country near the junction of the river Sarayu with the Ganges.

అంగన *angana.* [Skt. from అంగము] n. A woman. పుణ్యాంగన a noble dame.

అంగన్యాసము *anga-nyasamu.* [Skt.] n. Touching various parts of the body as a religious ceremony.

అంగప్రదక్షిణము *anga-pradakshinamu.* [Skt.] n. Rolling the body like a log to the right for a distance or round a temple, as a religious vow or penance. ప్రార్థన చేసికొనువాడు గుడిమొదలుగువాటికి ప్రదక్షిణముగా దొర్లుట.

అంగభవుడు *anga-bhavudu.* [Skt.] n. Cupid. మన్మథుడు.

అంగమచ్చము *anga-mattsamu.* [Tel.] n. Mark, trace, sign, track.

"మార్గంబున ద్రిమ్మరిన యంగమచ్చములు గన్గొని." రామా. v. 264.

అంగమర్దనము *anga-mardanamu.* [Skt.] n. Rubbing or squeezing the body. Shampooing.

అంగమర్దుడు *anga-mardudu.* [Skt.] n. One who shampoos the body or legs.

అంగము *angamu.* [Skt.] n. The body, a limb, member, part, division or branch. **అంగపంచకము**=ఉపాయము, సహాయము, దేశకాలవిభజనము, ఆపదకు ప్రతిక్రియ, కార్యసిద్ధి. అద్భుతాంగులు beings having wondrous forms. **అష్టాంగములు**=the eight forms or stages of meditation, *i.e.*, యమము, నియమము, ప్రాణాయామము, ప్రత్యాహారము, ధ్యానము, ధారణ, మననము, సమాధి. **చతురంగములు** the four divisions of an army, *i.e.*, రథములు, ఏనుగులు, గుర్రములు, బంటులు. **పంచాంగము** the Indian calendar giving particulars of each day, as తిథి, వారము, నక్షత్రము, యోగము, కరణము. **రాజ్యాంగములు** the various departments of Government. **షడంగములు** or **వేదాంగములు** the six sciences dependent on the Vedas. *i.e.*, శిక్ష, కల్పము, వ్యాకరణము, నిరుక్తము, జ్యోతిషము, ఛందస్సు. **సప్తాంగములు** = the seven constituents of a Government. స్వామి, అమాత్యుడు, సుహృత్తు, కోశము, రాష్ట్రము, దుర్గము, బలము. **సాష్టాంగ ప్రణామము** prostrate homage, touching the ground with eight members of the boby, *i. e.*, eyes or chest and forehead, hands, knees and feet.

అంగమొల *anga-mola.* [Tel.] n. Nakedness. దిసమొల, అంగమొలతో ఉన్న naked.

అంగరంగవైభవము *angaranga-vaibhavamu.* [Skt.] n. Enjoyment of riches, pomp, luxury సమస్తభోగములు. రంగడు అంగరంగ వైభవములతో వేంచేయుచున్నాడు he comes with all pomp.

అంగరఖా *angarakha.* [Hind.] A jacket చొక్కాయి.

అంగరక్ష *anga-raksha.* [Skt.] n. A charm for self preservation. **అంగరక్షకులు** [Skt.] n. plu. Guards, attendants. **అంగరక్షిణి** a body protector, a coat of mail.

అంగరాగము *anga-ragamu.* [Skt.] n. Smearing the body. Anointing. A cosmetic. చందనాది లేపనము.

"పొలుపు లేని యంగరాగంబుతో." ఉ. రా. మా. 4. 207.

అంగరుహము *angaruhamu.* [Skt.] n. Hair; down, wool, fleece.

అంగరేకు *anga-reku.* [H.] n. Jacket, చొక్కా. Same as అంగరఖా.

అంగరోల్లెలు *angarollelu.* [Tel.] n. plu. A kind of cakes.

అంగలార్చు *angalartsu.* [Tel.] v. n. To cry or lament. To grieve or sorrow. **అంగలార్పు** n. Grief, sorrow.

అంగవస్త్రము *angavastramu.* [Skt. from అంగము.] n. s. A man's upper vest, a garment.

అంగవించు *angavintsu.* [Tel.] n. To excel; to delight. ఉత్సహించు.

అంగస్పర్శ *anga-sparsa.* [Skt.] n. Touching the body.

అంగహీనము *anga-hinamu.* [Skt.] a. Mutilated, maimed. అంగహీనుడు [Skt.] n. He who is maimed or lame.

అంగారకము or **అంగారము** *angarakamu.* [Skt. Cf. *Lat. ignis.*] n. Fire. Charcoal A live coal. **అంగారక వారము** [Skt.] n. Tuesday, "the day of Mars." మంగళవారము. **అంగారకుడు** [Skt.] n. The planet Mars. కుజుడు.

అంగారదోల్లెలు *angara-dollelu.* [Skt. + Tel.] n. Fried wheat cakes. Same as అంగరోల్లెలు.

అంగారవల్లి *angara-valli.* [Skt.] n. A species of Karanja. (*Galedupa arborea.*) Another plant (*Orieda verticillata.* Rox.) చిరుతేకు, నిప్పవన్నె పుష్పములుగల కానుగభేదము.

అంగారశకటి *angāra-śakaṭi.* [Skt.] n. A stove, a small portable fire pan. కుంపటి

అంగి *angi.* [Skt.] n. Lit. Having a body. లతాంగి, a woman having a body as beautiful and tender as a creeper.

అంగీక or అంగికము *angika.* [Skt. & H.] A bodice. వెనుక ముడివేసే రవిక.

అంగిలి *angili.* [Tel.] n. The palate of the mouth. (Gen. అంగిటి. Ablative అంగిట.) అంగిటిలో వేసికొన్నాడు he swallowed it up. **అంగిటిముల్లు** [Tel.] n. The quinsy, inflammation of the trachea: a sore palate.

అంగీ *angī.* [Skt. & H.] n. A cuirass or quilted jacket worn as armour. More commonly, a long gown. A long jacket.

అంగీకరించు *angīkarinṭsu.* [Skt.] v. a. To consent, agree, admit, approve, receive, accept. **అంగీకారము** [Skt.] n. Consent, admission, acceptance, approval, approbation. అర్ధాంగీకారము half consent, doubtful admission; being half in earnest. **అంగీకృతము** [Skt.] a. Agreed on, accepted, admitted. ఒప్పుకోబడిన.

అంగు *angu.* [Tel.] n. Beauty, agreeableness. అందము, ఒప్పిదము. **అంగు** adj. Agreeable, pleasant, handsome. అందమైన, ఒప్పిదమైన. **అంగుగా** *angugā.* adv. Agreeably. అంగుగానుండే clean limbed, well proportioned. Also helpful, useful, convenient.

అంగుటము *anguṭamu.* [from Skt. అంగుష్ఠము] n. The thumb, the great toe. బొటనవ్రేలు.

అంగుడుతుడుపి *anguḍu-tuḍupi.* [Tel.] n. A backbiter, incendiary. ఇక్కడిమాట అక్కడ అక్కడి మాట యిక్కడ చెప్పేవాడు, కొండెలమారి.

అంగుళము *anguḷamu.* [Skt.] n. The thumb (not used in Telugu). An inch. **అంగుళి** *anguḷi.* [Skt.] n. A finger, or toe. వేలు. **అంగుళిత్రము** or **అంగుళిత్రాణము** *anguḷitramu.* [Skt.] n. A guard of leather or iron worn by archers on the thumb. **అంగుళిమానము** [Skt.] n. A measure with the fingers or arms; such as a span, a cubit, &c. **అంగుళీయకము** [Skt.] n. A finger ring. ఉంగరము.

అంగుస్తాను *angustānu.* [H.] A thimble. తొడుపు or తొడుగు.

అంగుష్ఠము *angushṭhamu.* [Skt.] n. The thumb: the great toe. బొటనవ్రేలు. **అంగుష్ఠమాత్రము** [Skt.] As big as a thumb.

అంగూరు *angūru.* [H.] n. A grape or grapes, ద్రాక్షపండ్లు.

అంఘ్రి *anghri.* [Skt.] n. The foot. పాదము. **అంఘ్రిపము** n. A tree. చెట్టు. **అంఘ్రివల్లిక** n. A plant. (*Hedysarum lagopodioides.*) కోలపొన్న. ముయ్యాకుపొన్న.

అంచత్ *anchat.* [Skt. Used only in compounds.] a. Worshipping, revering, admiring. Adorning. Going.

అంచలము *anchalamu.* [Skt.] n. Selvage, skirt, border.

అంచితము *anchitamu.* [Skt.] a. Worshipped, revered. అంచితముగా adv. Worshipfully, admirably.

అంచియ *anchiya.* [Tel.] n. Another form of **అంచె.**

అంచె *anche.* [Tel. & Kan.] n. The post, a relay of horses or palankeen bearers. తపాలు, టపా. A row of things. అంచెలంచెలను at every station. మను. iv. 87. అంచెలుకట్టు v. n. To be at one's post: to wait as post runners one after another. "అంచెలుకట్టి కాలితోడు సైచనభువుగదమ్మ." వసు. v. 72. See also అంచే.

అంచే *antsa.* [Tel. & Kan.] Also **అంచె.** The post or mail for letters. అంచలంచలుగా పోయినారు they proceeded by relays. అంచెలగుర్రాలమీద పోయిరి they rode post.

అంచ *antsa*. [Vikriti of హంస.] n. A swan. **అంచయాన** a woman that walks as gracefully as a swan. **అంచరవుతు** Brahma who rides on a swan.

అంచ *antsa*. [from అంచు] affix. Near, with, by. వద్ద.

అంచన or అంచనా *antsana*. [Tel.] n. An estimate, a valuation, an appraisement. తూకము; చేసుకోతూకముకు పంట అకవించుటచే యడము. అంచనా చూచు or వేయు to estimate crops, &c. అంచనాదారుడు an appraiser, an officer who estimates the quantity of corn in a field, or of the salt in a heap. నిలువు అంచనా, an estimate of the produce of a field before it is cut. కుప్ప అంచనా an estimate of the produce of a field after it is cut and heaped. అంచనాజాబితా an account of the estimated quantity of each ryot's produce.

అంచపదము *antsa-padamu*. [From Skt. Not in use.] హంసపాదము or హంసపాది n. (lit. a swan's foot.) The mark ʌ used for "caret."

అంచు *antsu*. [Tel.] n. Selvage, skirt, border. ఏటి అంచున on the edge of the river. గిన్నెయొక్క అంచుదాకా brimful. ఆ ఊరి అంచున hard by the town.

అంచు *antsu*. v. a. To send. To command.

అంచు *antsu*. [Tel.] pres. part. of అను to say, think. Saying, calling, considering, thinking.

అంజన *anjana*. [Skt.] n. The mother of Hanumān. అంజనేయుడు Hanumān

అంజనము *anjanamu*. [Skt.] n. Lamp-black, collyrium, eyesalve, the magic ointment used for the purpose of discovering anything that is concealed. కాటుక. అంజనగాడు a conjurer, he who finds that which is concealed by putting this ointment on his hand or on his eyelashes. అంజనము వేసి చూచు to search for hidden things.

అంజనరాయి *anjana-rāyi*. [Skt. అంజనము + Tel. రాయి] n. Antimonium or black antimony. (Watts.)

అంజలి *anjali*. [Skt.] n. The hands joined, palm upwards; అంజలిచేసినాడు he offered a salute with the hands joined, palms upwards. కృతాంజలులై with the hands joined as in prayer. ప్రాంజలియై presenting his joined hands.

అంజిక *anjika*. [Tel.] n. Fear, apprehension. "అంజవేయుడ భీతుకాకృతి నిటకుంజికి మా చందమేయువచ్చితిని." రామా. కిష్కి.

అంజూరు *anjūru*. [H.] n. A fresh or dried fig. సీమ అత్తిపండు, సీమ మేడిపండు.

అంజె *anza*. [Tel.] n. The foot; a footstep; the mark or measure of a foot. A stride. "అట రెండుమూడంజెలరుగునప్పటికాళ్ల బంకి జారీకి దొట్రుపాటునడిరి." మను. iii.

అంజలిగుంజలి *anzaliyunzali*. [Tel.] a. Creating confusion; destroying; causing pain ఛిన్నాభిన్నముచేసిన, గాసిజేసిన.

"తొండముచేపట్టి త్రోచిరాదిగిచి, యంజలి గుంజలియార్చి మైవెంచి, ఛుంజింపుచును." భాగ. iv. 194.

అంజాయించు *anzāyintsu*. [Tel.] v. i. To hesitate, to doubt.

అంట *anta*. Contraction for అనుట they say. Also, to say అనుట.

అంట *anta*. [Tel.] n. A crowd. A platter formed of leaves stitched together విస్తరి. ఒక అంటపొదుచుకొనిరా stitch the leaves as a platter. **అంటగట్టు** *antagattu*. [From అంటు to touch] v. a. To join together, to unite, to tie together చేర్చికట్టు. దీనితో అంటగట్టేపద్దులు the items joined with this. **అంటలుగట్టు** v. To assemble in mobs. గుంపులుకూడు, జతచేరు.

"అంటలుగట్టి చెల్మలకు నాంధ్రులు నక్షలు కూడుకోరు." ఆముక్త. iii.

అంటసిల్లు *antasillu* [Tel.] v. i. To come near, to approach. చేరు.
"అరదంబులరదంబులతో నంటసిల్లిపడుచుచు." ఉ. హరి. iv.

అంటాకు *antāku.* [Tel.] n. A plantain leaf. అరటాకు. అంటిచెట్టు n. A plantain tree.

అంటి *anti,* అనటి *anati.* See అరటి.

అంటించు *antintsu.* [Tel.] v. a. To paste, stick, glue, cause to adhere. To unite, join. To light or set on fire. కాలినమన్ను గాలినమన్ను అంటదు burnt earth will not adhere to moist, *i.e.* we shall never be friends. వాన్ని తేలు అంటించినది a scorpion stung him. వానికి మంచిదెబ్బలు అంటించినారు they gave him a good thrashing. ఆ సమయములో ఒక మాటను అంటించినాడు he put in a word at that moment.

అంటీస or అంటీసా *antīsa.* [Tel.] n. The Bur plant. A kind of grass that sticks to the cloth. Connection. సంబంధము. వానికిని దానికిని కొంచెము అంటీసా ఉన్నట్టు ఉన్నది she has something to do with him.

అంటు *antu* [Tel.] v. t. To touch. అంటించు to cause to touch. అంటీనట్టుగా ఉండే close at hand. ఆ ఊరితో అంటీనట్టుగా ఉండే ఒకపల్లె a hamlet close by the town. వానికి అదురంటినది fear seized him. తెల్ల అంటుతీగె *convolvulus dentatus.*

అంటు *antu.* [Tel.] v. n. To touch, to handle, cleave, stick, adhere. తల అంటుట to anoint the head. వెండ్రుకలను మొదలంట కత్తిరించెను he cropped the head close. చెవులను మొదలంటకోయుట cutting off the ears at the roots. దాని రోగము వానికి అంటినది her disease has infected him. ఆ రోగము అంటుదునా is that disease contagious? ఈ పాపము నిన్ను అంటకపోదు you will certainly be punished for this sin. నీ మాటలు వానిమనసున అంటలేదు your words did not touch him. కుమ్మరపురుగుకు మన్ను అంటదు earth does not adhere to the earthworm.

అంటు *antu.* [Tel.] n. Uncleanness, defilement by touch, impurity, such as is caused by the death of a relative, or by touching a lower caste man. Relationship. అంటుది an unclean woman. అంటుపడ్డాడు he was polluted, he became unclean. అంటుగా ఉండేయిల్లు a house ceremonially polluted. మాకు రేపు అంటు (తేక, పైల) వదలును tomorrow we shall be free from [ceremonial] impurity. వానికినిమాకును మరేమి అంటుసంటులేదు I have no connection with him, I have nothing to do with him.

అంటు, అంటుల or అంట్లు *antulu.* [Tel.] n. A graft, a grafted branch. అంటుమామిడిచెట్టు a graft mango tree.

అంటుకాడు *antu kadu.* [Tel.] n. A gallant. విటకాడు.

అంటుకొను *antu konu.* [Tel.] v. n. To cleave, adhere to, stick, stick as paste. To catch fire. వాడు దాన్ని అంటుకొని పోయినాడు he carried her away, he has run away with her. ఆ యిల్లు అంటుకొన్నది the house has caught fire. వాడు నా పుస్తకమును అంటుకొనిపోయినాడు he stole my book. ఊపిరిమాత్రము అంటుకొనియున్నది his breath just remains in him. వానికడుపు వెన్నుతో అంటుకొనిపోయినది his belly sticks to his back-bone, *i.e.*, he is emaciated.

అంటుజోడు *antu-zōdu.* [Tel.] n. A pair of earrings. అంటుపోగులజత.

అంటుపేను *antu pēnu.* [Tel.] n. A small louse.

అంటుపోగులు *antu-pōgulu.* [Tel.] n.s. plu. close-fitting earrings, small earrings.

అంటుమెడ *antu-meda.* [Tel.] n. A short neck. ఇరుకుమెడ, పొట్టిమెడ.

అంటురాయి *antu-rāyi.* [Tel.] n. in a magnetic stone. సూదంటురాయి.

"దీప్ర. ఇనుమంటురాతికి నెగడినభంగి, ననయం బునామదివారికిగూర్చికడలు." భాగ. vii.

అంటే *anṭē.* Contraction of **అనినట్టయితే** if you say. వద్దంటే don't, I say! **పోయినాడంటే** I tell you, he is gone. **అదేమంటే** if you ask what it is. ఎంత అంటే అంత యిస్తానంటాడు whatever you *ask* he says he will give. ఆయన అంటే నీవు బదులు అంటావా if he *speak*, why should you *answer* him? వాడు నన్ను నీవంటే నీవంటాడు if I say thou to him, he says thou to me; he scorns me.

అంత్రింత *antrinta.* [Tel.] n. Bur-grass.

అంట్లు *anṭlu.* [Tel.] n. plu. Cooking utensils that are not washed clean. ఆ తపెలలో ఇంకా అంట్లుపోలేదు the pot is not yet cleaned (from the stickings, *i.e.,*) from the fragments of boiled rice. నేను యింకా అంట్లు తోమలేదు I have not yet cleaned the cooking utensils.

అండ *anḍa.* [Tel.] n. Nearness; assistance, protection, patronage. ఆసరా, ఆశ్రయము. **అండగోడ** a buttress, a sloping wall, built to support another. ఆయన అండ చేరి ఉన్నాను I am under his protection. ఆయనను అండచేసికొనియున్నాను I look upon him as my supporter, I hold to him.

అండకోశము *anḍa-kōṣamu.* [Skt.] n. The scrotum.

అండగొట్టు *anḍa-goṭṭu.* [Tel.] v. i. To delay. ఆలస్యముచేయు.

అండగొను *anḍa-gonu.* [Tel.] v. t. To seek support in. ఆశ్రయించు.

"ఈతని కౌరవభంగి నండగొని తప్పదుం జావు నకు." Bhar. Ud. iv.

అండజము *anḍajamu.* [Skt.] n. An oviparous creature: lit. "born of an egg," whether a serpent, fish, or bird.

అండబాళ్లవాడు *anḍa-bāḷḷa-vāḍu.* [Tel. Nellore.] n. A sub-renter. లోపాయకారి, లోపాలివాడు.

అండము *anḍamu.* [Skt.] n. An egg. A testicle. The world. The Universe. గుడ్డు, వృషణము, ప్రపంచము. **అండాకర్షణము** castration. **అండాకారముగా** having the shape of an egg, elliptical. **అండాకృతి** an ellipsis. **అండవాయువు** *anḍa-vāyuvu.* [Skt.] n. The disease *orchitis* (swelled testicle.) బుడ్డ. **అండవృద్ధి** *anḍa-vriddhi.* [Skt.] n. The enlargement of the scrotum, hydrocele.

అండా *anḍā.* [Hind.] n. A large metal vessel.

అండి *anḍi.* [Tel.] Sir, O sir, O ye! ఏమండి what, sir! రాకండి please do not come. అట్లు చెప్పకండి please do not say so.

అండెము *anḍemu.* [Tel.] n. One pannier or pack: half a bullock load. కట్లములో సొకభాగము, బరువులో సగము. అంకెము.

అంద్రు *anḍru.* [Tel.] v. contraction of అందురు they will say.

అంత *anta.* [Tel.] n. Whole; adj. So much. adv. Then, afterwards. నీకెంత అడిగితే అంత యిస్తాను I will give you as much as you ask. **అంతకంటె** than that. **అంతకంత** as much again. **అంతకంతకు** by degrees; more and more. అంతకుముందు before that. **అంతమంది** so many men. **అంతమందిలో** among so many persons. **అంతమట్టుకు** so far, thus far. అంతమాత్రము only so much అంతసేపు so long. **అంతలో** in the mean time. **మూడంతలు** three times as much. అక్కడికి పోయినంతలో on his going there. వాడు తనంతటనే వచ్చినాడు he came of his own accord. **అంత** వాడు లేడు. there never was such a man. రాజంతవాడవు thou art equal to the king. నాయంతవాడు my equal, one like me, one as tall as I am. అంతే అవును. that probably is the case నిద్రలేచినంతలో when he rose from sleep, as soon as he awoke. నేను తెలిసికొన్నంత as much as I know. అంతపని such an act.

అంతగా *antaga.* [Tel.] adv. Much, very, urgently, earnestly. అగత్యముగా, అత్యురగా, అంతగా కావలెనంటే యిస్తాను if he wants it much I will give it. ఈ పండ్లు అంతగా లేవు this fruit is not found abundantly.

అంతఃకరణము *antaḥ-karaṇamu.* [Skt.] n. The mind, the heart. మనస్సు. అంతఃకరణ చతుష్టయము the four inward senses. మన స్సు, బుద్ధి, చిత్తము, అహంకారము.

అంతఃకోణము *antaḥ-kōṇamu.* [Skt.] n. The inner corner or angle.

అంతఃకోపము *antaḥ-kōpamu.* [Skt.] n. Inward wrath.

అంతఃపరిధానము *antaḥ-paridhānamu.* [Skt.] n. The innermost garment.

అంతఃపురము *antaḥ-puramu.* [Skt.] n. Seraglio: apartments for women; the inner chamber.

అంతఃప్రకృతి *antaḥ-prakriti.* [Skt.] n. The inner nature of a man.

అంతకము *antakamu.* [Skt.] n. The total, whole, aggregate. మొత్తము. అంతకము వేయు to sum up.

అంతకుడు *antakuḍu.* [Skt.] n. A name of Yama, the god of death. యముడు, మృత్యువు. నరాంతకుడు a homicide. శ్లేష్మాం తకము a remedy against phlegm. In compounds like this అంతకము denotes "anti," as a remedy against.

అంతకురాలు *antakurālu.* [Skt.] n. A fiend, or murderess, a she devil. ఘాతుకురాలు.

అంతట *antaṭa.* [Tel.] adv. Afterwards, and then, in the meantime. Everywhere. వారు చేరినంతట on their arrival. నాలుగుకడియాల దూరము పరుగెత్తి అంతట నిలిచినాడు he ran four miles and then stopped. ఎవరి అంతట వారు పోయిరి every one took his own way. అంతట పోక or అంతట పోవక besides that.

"అంతటపోవక నీవయ్యంతి నెత్తుకొనివచ్చి." T. 4. 820.

అంతటినుంచి from that time thence forward. అంతటికి on the whole. అంతటికి తమ్మును నమ్మియున్నాను I depend entirely upon you for everything. అంతట్లో పారి పోయినాడు meanwhile he ran away. అంత టితో తృప్తిపొందినాడా was he satisfied with this? దాన్ని తాకితే వానివని అంతటితో సరి if he touches it, it will be all over with him. ఈ పండ్లు అంతటా లేవు this fruit is not found everywhere.

అంతము *antamu.* [Skt.] n. End, termination, death, destruction.

అంతరంగము *anta-rangamu.* [Skt.] n. The mind, the heart. కఠినాంతరంగుడు a hard hearted man. సంతుష్టాంతరంగుడు one whose heart is pleased. The middle, midst. Secrecy, privacy. అంతరంగవుమాట a secret.

"కల్యాణవేది కాంతరంగంబున నున్నదొరడ." N. 9. 126.

అంతరంగుడు *anta-ranguḍu.* [Skt.] n. An intimate, a confidant. మిక్కిలి ఆప్తుడు.

అంతరతామర *antara-tāmara.* [Tel.] n. A water plant, without any root to the ground, swimming upon the surface of the lakes, &c. *Pistia stratiotes. Menyanthes cristata (Roxb).* ఆకాశతామర. అం తరతామర also means the itch. గజ్జి.

అంతరపల్లటి *antara-pallaṭi.* [Tel.] n. The pigeon called Tumbler.

అంతరము *antaramu.* [Skt.] n. Interval, intermediate space. Period, term. Difference, disparity. Rank. వాని అంతర మేమి నీ అంతరమేమి consider his rank and yours. అంతరమునందు in the midst. కాలాంతరమందు at another time. గ్రంథాం తరమందు in another book. ప్రత్యంతరము another copy. పాఠాంతరము another reading. వనాంతరమునందు in the forest. స్థలాంతరమందు in another place; elsewhere. భాషాంతరము a translation into another language. అతని ముఖాంతరముగా through him. దేశాంతరముపోయినాడు he is gone to another country, he is in foreign parts. మతాంతరము another opinion or religion. కర్మాంతరము the funeral ceremonies.

అంతరాంతరము *anta-rāntaramu*. [Skt.] n. Difference, distinction of rank. తారతమ్యము.

అంతరాత్మ *antarātma*. [Skt.] n. The Supreme Spirit. The heart or mind. దేవుడు, మనస్సు.

"అంతరాత్మవిదుడు." A. 4. 329.

"కాక్షితదంతరాత్మునిజొనగడె." A. 4. 253.

అంతరాయము *anta-rāyamu*. [Skt.] n. Obstacle, impediment. విఘ్నము.

అంతరాళము *antarālamu*. [Skt.] n. The middle space; interval between the earth and sky.

అంతరాళికము *anta-rālikamu*. [Skt.] n. The apartment in a pagoda, next to the shrine. గర్భగృహమునకును ముఖమంటపమున కును నడిమిచోటు.

అంతరించు *antarinsu*. [Skt.] v. n. To pass over, to cross.

"బహుదేశము లంతరించుచున్." J. Bhar. v.

To perish, die. చచ్చు, నశించు.

"అట్లమైన సత్పుత్రుడుదయించు నకుచిద్దైః గర్భమంతరించు," Vish. 2. 366.

"సుతశోకవిపద్దశ నంతరించినన్." R. 5. 74.

అంతరింద్రియము *antarindriyamu*. [Skt.] n. Internal organ, such as మనస్సు, బుద్ధి, అహంకారము, చిత్తము.

అంతరిక్షము *anta-rikshamu*. [Skt.] n. The sky, atmosphere. Lit. What is seen in the middle, *i. e.*, the space between the earth and the sky.

అంతరీయము *anta-riyamu*. [Skt.] n. A lower garment. కట్టుబట్ట.

అంతరువు *antaruvu*. [Skt.] n. Interval. Difference. తారతమ్యము. A secret place. మరుగుచోటు.

"పెద్దపిన్నయంతరువు లెంగి." విజ. 1. ఆ.

క॥ "ఆయకుసెడ నంతరువున
నరవిందాస్యులయి నారిగి యూరల గదలన్,
గ్రామకును నీవలచోకయుం,
తెరువున జిత్రాంగి చెలులు దానుండంగన్."
సా. 3. ఆ.

అంతరువుపడ్డ *antaruvupadda*. [Tel.] a. Suspended, intermitted.

అంతర్గతము *antargatamu*. [Skt.] adj. Intermediate, internal, inner, hidden. లోపలి లోని. మరుపబడిన. అంతర్గతజ్వరము internal fever, slow fever.

అంతర్గర్భితము *antargarbhitamu*. [Skt.] adj. Internal, concealed.

అంతర్ధానము *antardhānamu*. [Skt.] n. Disappearance, concealment, vanishing. అతడు అంతర్ధానమయ్యెను he disappeared.

అంతర్ధి *antardhi*. [Skt.] n. Disappearance, a covering, a screen. అంతర్ధానొందు to disappear, to vanish.

అంతర్ధ్యానము *antardhyanamu*. [Skt.] n. Inward meditation.

అంతర్భూతము *antarbhūtamu*. [Tel.] adj. Included in, internal, inner. చేరిన, అంతర్గతమైన.

అంతర్మనస్కుడు *antarmanaskudu*. [Skt.] n. He who is sad, or perplexed. వ్యాకులచిత్తుడు.

అంతర్ముఖుడు *antarmukhudu*. [Skt.] n. He who has an inner eye, (that is) wise though seeming dull. నిప్పుగప్పిన నిప్పువలె నుండేవాడు.

అంతర్యాగము *antaryagamu*. [Skt.] n. Mental adoration. మానసికపూజ.

అంతర్యామి *antaryami.* [Skt.] n. (Lit. The indweller.) The soul. The Supreme Spirit. లోపల వసించేవాడు, జీవాత్మ, పరమాత్మ. **అంతర్యామిత్వము** *antaryamitvamu.* [Skt.] n. Indwelling. Abiding. (*vide* శంకరవిజయము.)

అంతర్లంబము *antar-lambamu.* [Skt.] n. Acute-angled triangle.

అంతర్లాపి *antarlāpi.* [Skt.] n. A kind of puzzle, riddle or question which contains the solution or answer in itself, విడికథవలె అతిశయమైన ప్రశ్నలు ఉత్తరములుగా నుండేటిది. *e.g.*

క॥ "శ్రీకాంతుని దివమెన్నడు
రాకొమరునికెద్ది ప్రియము రథతిథియెన్నం
డేకొలదినన్న మఱుగును
ఏకాదశినాడు సప్తమేడేగడియల్."

శ్లో "కాశంభుకాంతాకిముచంద్రకాంతం,
కాంతాముఖంకింకురుతేభుజంగః,
కశ్శీపతిఃకావిషమాసమస్యా,
గౌరీముఖంచుంబతివాసుదేవః."

అంతర్వంశికుడు *antarvamsikudu.* [Skt.] n. The superintendent of a harem.

అంతర్వత్ని *antarvatni.* [Skt.] n. A pregnant woman.

అంతర్వాణి *antarvāṇi.* [Skt.] n. He who is skilled in science.

అంతర్వాహిని *antarvāhini.* [Skt.] n. A concealed river, which runs under ground. నది యిక్కడ అంతర్వాహిని అయినది here the river is lost in the earth.

అంతర్హితుడు *antarhithudu.* [Skt.] n. He who has disappeared, or vanished. **అంతర్హితము** adj. Concealed, covered, hidden.

అంతలపొంతలవాడు *antalapontalavāḍu.* [Tel.] n. A distant relation పరంపరాసంబంధి, దగ్గిరచుట్టాలుకానివారు.

అంతవట్టు *antarattu.* [Tel.] adj. and adv. All, the whole యావత్తు. Till then. **అంతవరకు** అంతవట్టువారు All. అందరు.

క॥ పుట్టినయంత వెన్న ప్రోవుగఁబెట్టితి
కడగికడగియొక్క గసపచేర
నంతవట్టు మ్రింగె. హరి. పూ. 5. ఆ.

"ధాత్రీపతులదోడు
తెచ్చితిపలువుర; వచ్చిరంత
వట్టువారును." భార, శల్య. 2. ఆ.

అంతశయ్య *antasayya.* [Skt.] n. The last bed or the bed of death; death; the burying or burning ground.

అంతశ్శత్రువు *antassatruvu.* [Skt.] n. Inward foe. "ఇంద్రియోత్కరంబు గెలిచి, అంతశ్శత్రులమైన కామాదివర్గంబు." M. XIII. 3. 277.

అంతస్తు *antastu.* [Tel.] n. A secret place a hiding place, a corner. A square compartment. కొట్టికట్టు A storey, or range, one above another, as the decks of a ship. రెండు అంతస్తుల యిల్లు a two storeyed house.

"ఎనుగవలసిన యంతస్తులెల్లజూచె."
పర. 4. ఆ.

"అంతఃపురముహాని యల్లననివలి
యంతస్తునకు వచ్చునంతటిలోన."
విష్ణు. ఉ. 4. ఆ.

అంతస్థ *antastha.* [Skt.] n. Money given secretly; a bribe. రెండవవానికి తెలియకుండా యిచ్చే లంచము.

అంతస్థలు *antasthalu.* [Skt.] n. A name given in grammar to the four consonants y, r, l, v, య, ర, ల, వ. which are considered by the Sanskrit Grammarians to be semi-vowels, and "to be intermediate between vowels and consonants, or because they *stand between* the consonants and the sibilants in the alphabet." *Wms.* అంతస్థముద్గరము in anat. the malleus of the ear.

అంతస్సు *antassu.* [Tel.] n. The heart. మనస్సు. అంతశ్శుద్ధి Purity of heart.

అంతా *anta.* [Tel. Colloquial for అంతయును] adj. All, whole (always used after the noun,) as ఊరంతా all the town. adv. Completely, wholly, altogether. బొత్తిగా; n. యావత్తు, సమస్తము. అంతా ఆయనకు తెలుసును he knows everything.

అంతావసాయి *antāvasāyi.* [Tel.] n. A barber; a low caste wretch. మంగలవాడు, సీచుడు, మాలవాడు.

అంతిక *antika,* [Skt.] n. A fire-place, hearth. పొయ్యి. "చెరకుముక్తియముల్ చిటిలించి క్రొత్తసంబనికముపండునంతికకలాంతికమార్గము చేయునప్పుడిక." D. A. 1. 79.

అంతికము *antikamu.* [Skt.] n. Nearness, closeness. సమీపము.

అంతికలు *antikalu.* [Tel.] n. A (tatty) screen made of grass, (usually of cuscuss.) కట్టివేళ్లచాపవలె అల్లే కసువుతడక, [వట్టు కట్టి గుడిసెకుపైన కప్పుగా గాని ధాన్యరాశికి తేక ఉప్పుకొ రాకుండుకుపైనగాని వేస్తే దూరియదు.]

అంతిపురము *antipuramu.* [from Skt. అంతఃపురము] n. The seraglio. రాణివాసము.

అంతిమ *antima.* [Skt.] adj. Last, final. కడపటి. A. 4. 338.

అంతు *antu.* [Tel.] n. End. చివర.

అంతు *antu.* [Tel.] n. The whole, total. మొత్తము, అంతేకము. అంతు ఏమైనది, అంతు ఎంత what is the total?

అంతేవాసి *antēvāsi.* [Skt.] n. A pupil. శిష్యుడు. One who is near. అంతేవాసిత్వము n. Pupilage. శిష్యత్వము, విద్యార్థిత్వము.

అంత్యము *antyamu.* [Skt.] adj. Final, last, ultimate, concluding. కడపటి. అంత్యనియమము rhyme, the last syllables corresponding. అంత్యదశ the last condition, *i. e.*, death. అంత్యధనము the last member of an arithmetical series. అంత్యమూలము in arith: the last or greatest root in the square. అంత్యకాలము last time, the time of one's end. అంత్యకులుడు or అంత్యజుడు n. A pariah. మాలవాడు.

అంత్యేష్టి *antyēshṭi.* [Skt.] n. Funeral rites.

అంత్రము *antramu.* [Skt.] n. An entrail, a gut. పేగు. అంత్రవృద్ధి inguinal hernia, rupture. అంత్రమాలిక a garland of guts, a necklace of sausages.

అందంద *andanda.* [Tel.] adv. Here and there. More and more. "ఆసలారనందంద సొబగులగ్గలమెసగె." Vish. 1, 178.

అందకత్తె *andakatte.* [Tel. from అందము.] n. A beauty, a lovely girl. సౌందర్యవతి.

అందగాడు *andagāḍu.* n. A handsome fellow. సౌందర్యవంతుడు.

అందగించు *andagintsu.* [Tel.] v. a. To dress, trim, adorn. అలంకరించు "అన్నగకందగించు" Ila. 1. 127. "అలుకదీర్చగంటు నందగించి." ib. 3. 68.

అందగించు *andagintsu.* [Tel.] v. n. To be adorned, to be pretty, to look well. సొగసుగానుండు. ఈ రత్నము ఇక్కడ అందగింపదు this gem does not look well here.

అందగింపు *andagimpu.* [Tel.] n. Adorning, ornamenting, beauty. సొగసు.

అందదుకులుగా *andadukuluga.* [Tel. అదుకు+ అదుకు] adv. About enough, చాలీచాలక. అందదుకులుగాకుండె not sufficient. ఆ చీర ఆమెకు అందదుకులుగానున్నది that cloth is not long enough for her.

అందనుక *andanuka.* [From అంత and దనుక] adv. Until then, up to that time, as far as that place, thus long, thus far. అంతపర్యంతము. అందాక.

అందము *andamu.* [Tel.] n. Beauty. సౌందర్యము. Manner. నానాగందాల or అన్ని అందాల in every way. Carr. 1248. **అందపడు** *andapadu.* [Tel.] v. to become beautiful, handsome. అందపరచు to cause to be beautiful, to adorn.

అందరు *andaru.* [From అంత+వారు] indef. pro. All. plu. gen. అందర or అందరియొక్క of all.

అందలము *andalamu.* [Tel.] n. s. A palanquin. N. 7. 40. A. 4. 6. ఆందోళిక. ప్రక్కలందు మరుగులేని పల్లకీ.

అందహీనము *andahīnamu.* [Tel.] n. adj. Ugly, deformed. వికారమైన.

అందాక *andāka.* [Tel. from అంత+దనుక.] adv. Thus far, so far, so long, till then. అదివరకు.

అందాజు *andāzu.* [H.] Estimate, valuation, తంకము.

అందాయుత్తుగానుండే, or **అందాయుత్తైన** *andāyattu-gānunde.* [Corrupted from అందముగా] adj. Neat, pretty, handsome. సొంపుగానుండే. ఈ బండి అందాయుత్తుగానున్నది this carriage is neat.

అందిక *andika* [Tel.] n. Nearness, proximity. సమీపము.

అందిపొందినవారు *andipondinavāru.* [Tel.] n. plu. Distant relations. దూరపుచుట్టాలు.

అందియ See **అందె.**

అందు *andu.* (a defective pronoun.) There, in that place. అక్కడ. అందుకు or అందులకు thereof, thereto, for that. అందులో therein. అందున or అందుచేత thereby, by that. అందునిమిత్తము therefore. అందుమీదట adj. thereafter. అటుతర్వాత. వాడు వచ్చి చేసినందుమీదట after his arrival. అందులకు (an affix) thereto, for that. వ్రాయుటకలందులకు *ad scribendum,* to write. అందువల్ల (an affix) thereby. పోయినందువల్ల యేమి ప్రయోజనము what is the use of going? ఆయన రాకలందులకు for his coming. నేను వచ్చేటందుకు అయిదు దినములు పట్టును it will take five days for me to come. అట్లా ఉన్నందుకు for its being so. వాడు అట్లా చేసినందుచేత as he has done so. వాడు అట్లా చేసేటందుచేత by his doing so. అందులకు ఒక ప్రతి వ్రాసినాడు he wrote a copy of it. "ఇందు గలడందు లేడని సందేహమువలదు" there is no doubt he is every where. ఇందు అందు both here and there; here and hereafter: in this life and the next. **అందే** in the same place దానియందే; అందలి=అక్కడ ఉండే.

అందు (The locative affix) in, within, on, upon. లో, మీద, నీయందు నమ్మికయుంచి relying upon thee.

అందు *andu.* [Tel.] v. n. To be within reach; (with the Dative) to reach at. అది చేతికందును it is within the reach of the hand. అది చేతికందదు it is not within my reach. తమ జాబు నాకు అందలేదు I have not received your letter. అది నాకందదు I cannot reach it. అందచేయు to cause to be delivered.

అందు *andu.* [Tel.] v. a. To reach, get at. To obtain or gain. To suffer or meet with (joy, grief, death, &c.) చెయ్యి నాచి పుచ్చుకొను, పొందు. అరుదందు feel surprise. భయమందు to be afraid. జన్మమందు to be born. వియ్యమందు to intermarry. అందిచూచు to peep, to look over a wall, &c. దుఃఖమందు to be sorry. కృతి అందినవాడు he to whom it is dedicated కంపమందు to be afraid. మిన్నందిన sky-high, reaching to the clouds. అందిపొందినవారు distant kinsfolk. **అందించు** [causal of అందు to reach.] v. t. To give, hand over, to enable to get.

అందుకొను *andukonu.* [Tel.] v. a. To reach at, to get at, take with the hand. చెయ్యి చాచి పుచ్చుకొను.

అందుకోలు *andukōlu.* [Tel.] n. Nearness, proximity. చేరువ, సామీప్యము. అందుక స్తులముక్తిఁ ద్రోచుకొనందుకోలననందిమా బిందుమాధవదేవునిన్. G. 6. 110.

అందుగు or **అందుగుచెట్టు** *andugu.* [Tel.] n. The clearing nut plant (*Strychnos potatorum*). చిల్లగింజచెట్టు.

అందుపాటు *andupātu.* [Tel.] n. Nearness. adj. Near, close. సమీపమైన. అందుపాటు గ్రామము a neighbouring town.

అందుబడి *andubadi.* [Tel.] n. Nearness Getting, obtaining. ప్రాప్తము. వాడికి ఆ రూకలు యింకా అందుబడి కాలేదు he has not yet got the money. అది అందుబడి అయిన తరువాత after it was received or came to hand.

అందువు *anduvu.* [Skt.] n. A fetter or chain; an ornament for a woman's foot. ఏనుగు సంకిలి, అందె.

అందె *ande.* [Tel.] n. A foot trinket of silver, filled with small pebbles in order to sound and worn by women on their ankles. నూపురము. అందెబందలేని adj. Free from any trouble or annoyance. ఏ చిక్కున్ను లేని, జంజాటములేని.

అందేషా *andēsha.* [H.] n. Doubt, guess, conjecture.

అంధకారము *andhakāramu.* [Skt.] n. Darkness. చీకటి.

అంధకుడు *andhakudu.* [Skt.] n. A blind man. గుడ్డివాడు.

అంధకురాలు *andhakurālu.* [Skt.] n. A blind woman. గుడ్డిది.

అంధకూపము *andha-kūpamu.* [Skt.] n. పాడునుయ్యి a well in disuse, or disrepair.

అంధతమసము *andha-tamasamu.* [Skt.] n. Thick darkness. కటికచీకటి, చిమ్మచీకటి.

అంధము *andhamu* [Skt.] n. చీకటి.

అంధము *andhamu.* [Skt] adj. Blind. గుడ్డి.

అంధస్సు *andhassu.* [Skt.] n. Food, boiled rice. అన్నము. అమృతాంధసులు. nectar-eaters, immortals.

అంధుడు *andhudu.* [Skt.] n. A blind man. గుడ్డివాడు. మదాంధుడు One who is blinded by passion or pride.

అంధువు *andhuvu* [Skt.] n. A well, బావి.

అంధ్రము or **ఆంధ్రము** *andhramu.* [Skt.] n. A Sanscrit name for the Telugu language. తెలుగు. ఆంధ్రదేశము the Telugu country తెలుగుదేశము. "ఆంధ్రమధురమాధవము." A. pref. 12. "ఆంధ్రబలవాక్పటిమలని యాంధ్రోక్తి." ib. pref. 14.

ఆంధ్రుడు *andhrudu.* [Skt.] n. This word in ancient times meant a hunter, who lives by killing game. See the Laws of Manu X. 36. వ్యాధుడు, మృగవధాజీవి, కిరాతుడు.

అంప *ampa* [Genitive singular of అమ్ము an arrow] బాణము. See. అంపకోలు.

అంపకము or **అంపకోలు** *ampakamu.* [Tel.] n. Permission to go; dismission. An entertainment given to a friend on the occasion of his departure. పంపించడము, సెలవు. విందుచేసి సాగనంపడము, బహుమానమిచ్చి పంపడము. అంపకము చేయు to dismiss, send away. అల్లునికి అంపకము చేసి పంపిరి they gave the son-in-law the entertainment preparatory to his departure and sent him away.

> "ప్రస్థానసభకేమబోయి కొంత,
> కాలముండుండి యుజాడంపకంబుసేయ,
> మానవసదంబునకువచ్చి."
>
> H. 4. 7.

అంపకాడు *ampakādu.* [Tel. from అమ్ము.] n. One who carries an arrow. విల్లు చేతబట్టినవాడు, ధానుష్కుడు. A true marksman, a skilful archer. గుఱికప్పక అమ్ముకేయు వాడు, కృతహస్తుడు.

"పాదమువచ్చుదాకనవరాధిపైరోష
మాగిపాదనుగన్న నడపవలయు
లక్ష్యసిద్ధిదాకలావునశరమాగి
కాడవిడుచునంపకాడుపోలె."

Amuk. iv.

అంపకోల *ampa-kōla.* [Tel.] n. An arrow బాణము. "పిలగరులయంప కోలలంపెలవిల్లు గాను కిచ్చి." Swa. 4. 13.

అంపగఱి *ampa-gari.* [Tel.] n. The feather of an arrow. బాణముయొక్క గఱి.

అంపర *ampara.* [Tel. అమ్ము+పర] n. plu. Arrows. అమ్ములు, శరసమూహము. అంపరచిచ్చు అనగా, బాణాగ్ని.

అంపాచారము *ampa-chāramu.* [Tel.] n. Stream. జలప్రవాహము.

"సంపాదిత శరగావలి
దెంపారిన మేఘచయము పృథివియునభమున్
గంపింపగ బెట్టియుచు
సంపాచారంపువానలప్పుడుకురిసెన్."

వి. పు. 7. అ.

అంపు *ampu.* [Tel.] v. a. To send, forward, despatch. పంపు. సాగనంపు to accompany a friend a little way so as to set him on his journey. పిలువనంపు to send for one. అం పించు. same as అంపు or పంపు to send. అం పుడోడు *ampu-dōḍu.* n. A companion in a journey. దారిలో సహాయముగా వచ్చేమ నిషి. వాడు అంపుడోళ్లకు బిడ్డకావ్పులకు తిరుగు తున్నాడు he employs himself as a companion and as a nurse.

అంపెలు *ampelu.* [Tel.] n. Rags, tatters. పీలికలు, చింపిగుడ్డలు. అంపెలు గట్టి చేత నుంక యుప్పిధరింపుచు. G. X. 72.

అంబ *amba* [Skt.] n. Mother; a name of Durga. తల్లి, పార్వతి. అంబాత్రయము=జ్ఞా నాంబ, భ్రమరాంబ, మూకాంబ.

అంబకము *ambakamu.* [Skt.] n. An eye. An arrow. కన్ను, బాణము. Swa. 3. 5. R. 5. 60.

అంబకళము *amba-kaḷamu.* [Tel] n. Porridge. అంబలి. "చెన్నయ్యయింట బలిదుం బకళము చెయిదియ్యకనుజాత్రి." B.D. 3. 750.

అంబడితేకి *ambaḍi-ṭēki.* [Tel.] n. The torpedo fish. See. టేకి.

అంబరము *ambaramu.* [Skt.] n. The sky. Cloth woven of cotton. Clothing, apparel. Ambergris. ఆకాశము, వసనము, వస్త్రము, పరిమళద్రవ్యము. See అంబరు. అంబ రమణి the gem of heaven, *i. e.*, the sun. అంబరచరుడు one who dwells in the sky. అంబరాంబరుడు n. Sky-cinctured, that is, (dik-ambara) "naked," an epithet of Siva. శివుడు.

అంబరసా *ambarasā.* [M.] n. Expressed juice of ripe mangoes. మామిడిపండ్లరసము.

అంబరీషము *ambarīshamu.* [Tel.] n. A fire pot, a portable stove. నిప్పుడుచట్టి. అంబరీషుడు. Name of a king, the Assyrian Ambarice.

అంబరు *ambaru.* [Tel.] n. Amber. Ambergris. "పరిమళద్రవ్యముల చాయశ్రీగంధ మగరుకేసరికదంబ మంబరువుననుజవ్వాది." Hamsa. 5. 162. See అంబరము.

అంబలి *ambali.* [Tel; plu. అంబలులు, అంబళ్లు or అంబళ్లు. Gen. అంబటి] n. Porridge. పిండి నూకలుకలిసి కాచినగాచినది. చింతంబలి paste made of pounded tamarind seeds. అంబటి కుండ a porridge-pot. అంబటిప్రొద్దు breakfast time: about noon.

"పలుచనియంబలుల్ చెఱకుపాలెడనీళ్లు...
వడపిండెలు నీరుచల్లయున్ వెలయగబెట్టు
వేసవిజందనచర్చమున్నుగన్."

Amuk. i. 41.

అంబలిజోరిగాడు or **జోరిగాడు** *ambali-zōrigāḍu.* [Tel.] n. The rufous-tailed finch lark [F. B. I.]

అంబాణపుకాయ *ambāṇapu-kāyā.* [Tel.] n. A tree, *Averrhoa Carambola;* commonly called Kamrak or Bilimbi. A green sour fruit with five sides.

అంబారపిణుజు or **పిడుదు** *ambārapiṇuzu.* [Tel.] n. A tick which infests animals. పశువులను పట్టే పురుగు.

అంబారము *ambāramu.* [H.] A heap of grain. ధాన్యరాశి. Also, the government share in a crop.(Vizag) అంబారముపోయు to heap up grain. అంబారములుగా పడియుండు to lie in heaps. ఉభయరాశి అంబారము a heap of grain containing both the shares due to government and to the landholder.

అంబారి or **అంభారి** *ambāri.* [H.] A howdah; the seat or throne on an elephant's back హౌదా.

అంబాళము or **అంబాళవృక్షము** *ambāḷamu.* [Tel.] The hog-plum (*Spondias mangifera*), the fruit resembling the mango. నోరు అంబాళపుపండు చెయ్యి బలుసుముల్లు. your mouth is like a sweet plum and your hand is like a thornbush. (Carr).

అంబిక *ambika.* [Skt.] n. A name of Parvati, wife of Siva. పార్వతి. Also, తల్లి, ధృతరాష్ట్రుని తల్లి.

అంబు or **అమ్ము** *ambu.* [Skt.] n. An arrow, a dart. బాణము. అంబువేసినట్లు adv. exactly; hitting the mark precisely: straight as an arrow. **అంబులపొది** *ambula-podi.* [Tel.] n. A quiver of arrows. తూణీరము.

అంబుజము *ambujamu.* [Skt.] Lit. water-born. See under అంబువు.

అంబువాసిని *ambu-vāsini.* [Skt.] n. The trumpet-flower, *Bignonia suaveolens.*

అంబువాహిని *ambu-vāhini.* [Skt. Lit. a water-carrier.] A piece of palmyra trunk hollowed out and placed at the well to carry to the fields the water poured into it.

అంబువు *ambuvu.* [Skt.] n. Water. నీళ్లు. **అంబుజము** or **అంబురుహము** a lotus. అంబుజోదరుడు an epithet of Vishnu. అంబుజలోచన or అంబుజాక్షి a lotus-eyed woman. అంబుదము a cloud. **అంబుధి** the sea. **అంబురాశి** the ocean.

అంబేద *ambēda.* [Tel.] n. A simpleton. మొత్తనివాడు. "వేదురుపల్కి నన్నదర వేయగజూచెద నింద్యునంతయంబేదలులేరు." పద్మ. iii. 57.

అంభస్సు *ambhassu.* [Skt.] n. Water. ఉదకము, నీళ్లు. అంభశ్చరము aquatic, moving in water. అంభోయానపాత్రము a boat. Bhag. i.

అంభారము or **అంభారవము** *ambhāramu.* [Skt.] n. The lowing of oxen.

అంభోజము or **అంభోరుహము** *ambhōjamu.* [Skt.] n. A lotus. తామరపువ్వు

అంభోదము or **అంభోధరము** *ambhōdamu.* [Skt.] n. A cloud. మేఘము.

అంభోధి, అంభోనిధి or **అంభోరాశి** *ambhōdhi.* [Skt.] n. The sea. సముద్రము.

అంశకుడు *aṃsakuḍu.* [Skt.] n. He who partakes of the nature. పాలికాపు.

అంశము *aṃsamu.* [Skt.] n. A share, part, portion, a fraction; the denominator of one; a degree of latitude or longitude (Geog.); a subject. భాగము, విషయము. దేవుని యంశమున పుట్టినవాడు he who is born from a portion of the deity, he who is of divine origin; అంశపురుషుడు a fortunate man, a man of talent or parts. వర్ణనాంశము a descriptive part or passage in a poem. ఈ అంశము నాకు తెలుసును I am acquainted with this subject. ఈ అంశమందు in this respect. వాడు అన్ని అంశములు తెలిసినవాడు he knows every thing. అంశచక్రము a table consulted by astrologers in casting nativities, an astrological diagram for ascertaining the degree of the sun in any sign. దశాంశము the tenth part; **అంశసవరణ** = reduction of fractions; అంశనీయము or అంశ్యము = that which is divisible.

అంశుకము *amsukamu.* [Skt.] n. Cloth, a robe. వస్త్రము, పైటకొంగు.

అంశువు *amsuvu.* [Skt.] n. A ray of light, a beam. కిరణము. **అంశుజాలము** *amsu-jalamu.* [Skt.] n. A collection of rays. **అంశుమాల** *amsu-mala.* [Skt.] n. A garland of the rays of light, a halo. అంశుమాలి *amsu-mali.* [Skt.] n. He who is girded with rays. An epithet of the sun. సూర్యుడు. **అంశుమంతుడు** *amsumantudu.* [Skt.] n. The sun or moon. సూర్యుడు. A rich man.

అంసగుడ్డ *amsa-gudda.* [Tel.] n. Polishing cloth (used by carpenters.) కొయ్యకు మెరుగుపెట్టేటట్టు తోమే గుడ్డ.

అంసము *amsamu.* [Skt.] n. A shoulder, భుజశిరస్సు. అంసకూటము, a bull's hump. అంసపాదికొట్ట a small forked prop which supports the woodwork on which a roof is laid. A small forked stake used at intervals to relieve the shoulders of those who bear a car, &c., in procession. **అంసఫలకము**, the upper part of the spine.

అంసలము *amsalamu.* [Skt.] adj. Robust, lusty. బలిసిన. **అంసలుడు** *amsaludu.* n. He who is robust or lusty. బలిసినవాడు.

అంహస్సు *anhassu.* [Skt. √anh=to press together. Gk. ἄγχω.] n. Anxiety, trouble. Sin, guilt. పాపము.

అకంపితము *a-kampitamu.* [Skt.] adj. Unshaken, firm. అకంపితరభసము great speed.

అకంప్యము *a-kampyamu.* [Skt.] That cannot be shaken.

అకట, అక్కటా *akata.* [Tel.] interj. Alas! O! what a pity! అయ్యో.

అకటవికటము *akata-vikatamu.* [Tel.] adj. Adverse, contrary, awkward, inverted, contrariwise. తారుమారైన, విరుద్ధమైన, ప్రతికూలమైన. అకటవికటమైన మాట an incoherent speech, a prevarication, అకటవికటపు మాటలాడుట to shuffle, prevaricate. అకటవికటమైన పని an awkward, confused or troublesome affair.

అకటవికటము n. Opposition, contrariety, awkwardness. విరుద్ధము, ప్రతికూలము. ఎందుకు అకటవికటము చేస్తున్నావు why do you give trouble?

అకము *akamu.* [Skt. from అ = not & క = happiness.] n. Ache, pain, affliction. Sin. దుఃఖము, పాపము. నాకము = న + అకము = heaven, the sinless place.

అకరం *akaram.* [H.] Service Inam land. అకరికుడు a collector of customs. సుంకరి.

అకరు or **అకరువు** *akaru.* [Tel.] n. The stamens of a lotus. తామరదుద్దులోనగువాని చుట్టునుండునది; కింజల్కము.

"ఆకాశమండలంబను నల్లగలువకు
నకరువాద్యుండులోలార్క్యమూర్తి."

కాశి. i.

అకర్మకక్రియ *a-karmaka-kriya.* [Skt.] n. An intransitive verb.

అకర్మము *a-karmamu.* [Skt.] n. Absence of work; improper work; crime, sin.

అకలుషము *a-kalushamu.* [Skt.] adj. Stainless, sinless, unspotted.

అకల్పితము *a-kalpitamu.* [Skt.] adj. Not manufactured. Natural, simple, not artificial, not contrived. సహజమైన, చేయబడని.

అకళంకము *a-kalankamu.* [Skt.] adj. Stainless, spotless, faultless, blameless. నిష్కళంకమైన, నిర్మలమైన, దోషరహితమైన. **అకళంకుడు** a spotless man.

అకస్మాత్తుగా *akasmattu-ga.* [Skt.] adv. By chance, suddenly, unexpectedly. హఠాత్తుగా, without a why or wherefore.

అకస్వారీ *akasvari.* [H.] Spite, malice, ill-will. కసి, అసహ్యము.

అకాంక్షితము *a-kankshitamu.* [Skt.] adj. Undesired.

అకారము *akāramu*. [Skt.] n. The letter అ.

అకారణము *a-kāraṇamu*. [Skt.] adj. Groundless, causeless. నిర్హేతుకమైన. అకారణముగా without a reason. అకారణోత్పన్నము produced spontaneously. అకారణ్ (H. incorrect form of అకారణముగా) without cause నిర్హేతుకముగా, ఊరక.

అకార్యము *a-kāryamu*. [Skt.] n. An evil deed. కార్యాకార్యము right and wrong, just and unjust.

అకాలము *a-kālamu*. [Skt.] n. Untimeliness, unseasonableness. adj. Untimely, unseasonable. అసమయమైన. అకాలమృత్యువు an untimely death. అకాలకుసుమము a flower blossoming out of season.

అకించనము *a-kinchanamu*. [Skt.] adj. Penniless, poor, indigent. దరిద్రుడైన. **అకించనుడు** *a-kinchanuḍu*. n. A penniless wretch, a poor man. దరిద్రుడు, నిరుపేద.

అకిల్బిషము *a-kilbishamu*. [Skt.] adj. Sinless, faultless. నిర్దోషమైన.

అకీకత్ *akīkat*. [H.] Account, narration, explanation, affairs, events. సంగతి.

అకుంఠితము *a-kunṭhitamu*. [Skt.] adj. Not blunted. Fresh, vigorous. Uncurved, unbent. Not checked, not hindered. నిరాటంకమైన.

అకూపారము *a-kūpāramu*. [Skt.] n. The sea or ocean. సముద్రము.

అకృతాస్త్రుడు *a-kritāstruḍu*. [Skt.] n. One unpractised in arms.

అకృత్యము *a-krityamu*. [Skt.] n. That which should not be done. A sinful act.

అకో! or **అకో**! *ako*. [Tel.] interj. Either, or whether; I wonder, I imagine, Query, ఏమి? "మృత్యువు, దాగెనుకోట లేదకో." Swa. iv. 145.

అక్క *akka*. [Tel. a Dravidian word borrowed by Sanskrit, where it is used in the sense of mother. cf. Lat. *acca*] n. An elder sister. అక్కచెల్లెళ్లు elder and younger sisters. పెద్దక్క the eldest sister. Any woman older than oneself is usually styled అక్క elder sister, or, అమ్మ mother, madam: and any man older than oneself is usually styled అన్న elder brother, or, అయ్య father, sir. వంటలక్క a cook or kitchen maid. See అక్కలవాడ.

అక్కజము *akkazamu*. [from Skt.] n. Wonder, surprise, astonishment. ఆశ్చర్యము. **అక్కజపడు** v. i. To wonder, to be surprised at.

అక్కజుడు *akkazuḍu*. [from Skt.] n. A wonderful man. Fem: gender, అక్కజురాలు.

అక్కట. See అకట.

అక్కటికము *akkaṭikamu*. [Tel.] n. Favour, mercy, pity. కారుణ్యము. దయ. కనికరము.

"ఉల్లమునందు నక్కటిక

మూనుట మీకులమందుఁ గంటిమం

చల్లన మేలమాడునచలాత్మజమాటకు

Manu. i. 2.

అక్కడ *akkaḍa*. [Tel. from అ + కడ = that place.] adv. There. ఆ స్థలమందు. అక్కడి of that place. అక్కడక్కడ here and there. అక్కడికిన్ని సమ్మతించనందున as he would not even yet consent.

అక్కర *akkara*. [Tel.] n. Necessity, occasion, want, need, desire. అగత్యము. అక్కరతీర్చు to relieve from want. అది నాకక్కరలేదు I do not want it. దీనితో నీకేమి అక్కర what have you to do with this? నీవక్కడికి రావలసిన అక్కరయేమి what business had you to come there? అక్కరకొద్ది మాట్లాడుట to speak as necessity demands. అది అక్కరకురాదు it will be of no use. వాడికి ఆ పని అక్కరపట్టలేదు he does not care for it. **అక్కరకాడు** one who is in need. అక్కరగలవాడు; **అక్కరగండడు** one who has an interest in an affair. శ్రద్ధగలవాడు; **అక్కరపడు**, **అక్కరగొను** to feel an interest in a thing. అక్కరకలిగియుండు; అక్కర పాటు a state of necessity. అక్కర పడుట.

అక్కరము for అక్షరము *akkaramu*. [Skt.] n. A letter of the alphabet. వర్ణము.

అక్కలకర *akkalakara*. [Tel.] n. A medicinal root. *Anacyclus Pyrethrum*, or, the pellitory of Spain. జ్వరదోషహరమైనపరద్రవ్యము.

అక్కలవాడ *akkala-vāḍa*. [Tel.] n. A street in which cook maids live. వంటచేసే ఆడంగులు ఉండేవీధి. "అక్కలవాడలఁగరకూళ్లు మెక్కి." A. vi. 92.

అక్కలి *akkali*. [Tel.] n. A wave. అల, తరంగము.
"కడలిమొగ యక్కలిందగులు
పడినతోఁకనుండొరె." కా. 2. ఆ.

అక్కలించు *akkalintsu*. [Tel.] v. n. To twist, to contract, used of the muscles of the belly, a condition due to want of food. కడుపువెన్నున అంటుకొని పోవునట్లుగా సగ్గించు. "అక్కలించినపొట్టమక్కలించి." Swa. I. 15.

అక్కసము *akkasamu*. [Tel.] n. Sorrow.
"నీ, వెక్కడనుండి వచ్చితిది యేటికి
నుస్సురుమంటినీకు నీ, యక్కసమేలవచ్చెను."
కా. 3. ఆ.

అక్కసరి *akkasari*. [H.] adj. Neighbouring, near. సమీపములోనుండే. అక్కసరి ఊరు a neighbouring village.

అక్కసు *akkasu*. [H.] n. Spite, malice, anger, opposition. కసి, చలము, ఆగ్రహము, కోపము. **అక్కసుకాడు** or **అక్కసి** an angry man.

అక్కి *akki*. [Tel.] n. A skin disease, eczema. బిడ్డలకు తేచే ఒక గజ్జి.

అక్కిబిక్కిదండ *akki-bikki-danda*. [Tel.] n. A kind of game. ఆటభేదము. హంస. 3. ఆ.

అక్కిలి *akkili*. [Tel. a variant form of అక్కలి n. Confusion. కలత. అక్కిలిపడు to be confused. "అక్కిలిపడి చిక్కబల్ల పొందెను." Bhag. vii.

అక్కు *akku*. [Tel.] n. The breast or chest. రొమ్ము. అక్కుజచేర్చు embracing. వాని అక్కులు చెక్కులు ఎండినవి (lit: his breast and cheeks are dried up.) he is emaciated. అక్కుపక్షి a starveling, a wretch, a fool. అక్కుగొర్రు a spear piercing the heart. "అవనీశులకునెల్ల నక్కుగొర్రగుడు." BD. 4. 1658.

అక్కుళ్లు *akkuḷlu*. [Tel.] n. A sort of grain called అట్రగడలు.

అక్కుసాయి *akku-sāyi*. అక్కుసాయి, అక్సాయి or అక్సాయి. [H.] n. Commission granted to the seller of goods, or to the broker. తరుగు.

అక్కెచెట్టు *akke-cheṭṭu*. [Tel.] n. A tree, the *Ficus Racemosa*.

అక్రమము *a-kramamu*. [Skt.] n. Want of order. Irregularity. Wickedness, crime. క్రమభంగము, దుర్మార్గము, నేరము, దుష్కార్యము. **అక్రమము** adj. Irregular, disorderly, wicked, unjust. క్రమభంగమైన, దుష్ట, దుర్మార్గమైన, అన్యాయమైన. నన్ను గురించి అక్రమముగా మాట్లాడినాడు he railed at me. ఆ రూకలను అక్రమముగా వ్యయముచేసినాడు he wasted the money.

అక్రోటుకాయ, నాటు అక్రోటుకాయ *akrōṭu-kāya*. [Skt.] n. *Aleurites moluccana*, the Belgium or Indian walnut; the candle-nut (Watts.)

అక్రోధనుడు *a-krōdhanuḍu*. [Skt.] n. One who is free from anger.

అక్లేశము *a-klēśamu*. [Skt.] n. Freedom from sorrow or trouble.

అక్షచరణుడు *aksha-charaṇuḍu*. [Skt.] lit. eyefooted; who has an eye in his foot. An epithet of the sage Gautama. గౌతముడు. A follower of the Nyaya Philosophy.

అక్షత *akshata*. [Skt.] adj. Not broken, uninjured. అక్షతయోని a virgin.

అక్షతలు *akshatalu*. [Skt.] vulgarly అక్షింతలు n. plu. (lit. unbroken grains.) Grains of raw rice, made yellow with saffron,

The red mark worn by some Hindus on the forehead formed of saffron and slaked lime. పసుపు రాచిన బియ్యము, సేలాలు. నొసట పెట్టుకొనడమునకై పసుపు సున్నము కలిపిన బొట్టు.

అక్షమాల *aksha-mála*. [Skt.] n. A rosary, especially of the seeds of the *Elcocarpus*. జపమాల.

అక్షము *akshamu*. [Skt.] n. A die to play with; dice; an axle. సొగటాలపాచిక, ఇరుసు. Terrestrial latitude. అక్షకర్ణము=The hypotenuse, especially of the triangle formed with the gnomon of a dial and its shadow; in astronomy, the argument of the latitude. అక్షాగ్రము, the end of an axle. అక్షాగ్రకీలకము, a linch-pin; the pin which fastens the yoke to the pole. రుద్రాక్ష, the seed of *Elcocarpus Ganitrus*, or of Beleric Myrobalan, which is used as a die. అక్షావపనము, a dice-board అక్షతత్వము science of dice. **అక్షవిద్య** *aksha-vidya*. [Tel.] n. Gambling, dice-play. పాచికల ఆట. **అక్షధూర్తుడు** *aksha-dhūrtuḍu*. [Skt.] n. A game master, a gambler. జూదరి.

అక్షము *akshamu*. [Skt.] The eye. హిరణ్యాక్షుడు the golden eyed one.

అక్షపాదుడు *aksha-paduḍu*. [Skt.] n. See అక్షచరణుడు.

అక్షభాగము *aksha-bhāgamu*. [Skt.] n. A degree of latitude.

అక్షయ *akshaya*. [Skt.] adj. Durable, permanent imperishable. నాశనరహితమైన. అక్షయలోకము, the undecaying world, heaven. **అక్షయపాత్రము** *akshaya-pātramu*. [Skt.] n. (lit. the inexhaustible vessel.) A cup for receiving alms, a beggar's dish. బిచ్చమెత్తుకొనే పాత్ర. Alms given to a brahmin beggar.

అక్షరము *aksharamu*. [Skt. lit. Eternal. imperishable.] n. A letter, a single syllable, a character of the alphabet, handwriting. A single syllable, whether of one letter or more. Thus the word సంస్కృతం *Sam-skru-tam* is termed a word of *three letters*. ఏకాక్షరము a monosyllable. సంయుక్తాక్షరము two or more letters united in one syllable, as స్త్రీ wherein four letters are united. త్ర్యక్షరి *try-ak-shari;* the sacred or mystic syllable (ఓం AUM, or O'M a name of the Deity) that contains three letters. అక్షరజ్ఞుడు a man of letters. అక్షరాభ్యాసము beginning to learn the alphabet or the first principles of a language; మంత్రాక్షరము a cypher or syllable used in magic. ఇది ఆయన అక్షరము కాదు this is not his handwriting. నీవద్ద అప్పుగా తీసుకొన్న రూ. 300 అక్షరాల మున్నూరు రూపాయలు i.e., "Rs. 300 (three hundred Rupees.)" here *the same sum* is denoted in writing as well as in figures. వాడు నిరక్షరకుక్షి he is an illiterate man. వానికి నోట్లో అక్షరాలు లేచియున్నవి his mouth is inflamed. అక్షరవిన్యాసము, the array of letters, writing.

అక్షసరము or అక్షసూత్రము *aksha-saramu*. [Skt.] n. A rosary or string of beads to repeat prayers over. జపమాలిక. "అక్షసూత్రము ద్రిప్పనగు లేతలి." T. 4. 223. "అక్షసరంబా ద్రాక్షాంకుశమక్షయకర పాత్రమ మర నతిడప్పారిలోభితాంబరేహి యటంచును." H. 4. 211.

అక్షాంశము *akshāmśamu*. [Skt.] n. A degree of latitude.

అక్షి *akshi*. [Skt.] n. An eye. కన్ను. మదిరాక్షి a woman: (lit.) she who is tipsy eyed. అక్షితార, the pupil of the eye. అక్షిపక్ష్మము, the eye-lash, రెప్పవెంట్రుకలు. అక్షిపటలము a coat of the eye. అక్షిభ్రువము= the eyebrow, **అక్షిగోళము** *akshi-gōlamu*. [Skt.] n. The eyeball.

అక్షింతలు Corruption of అక్షతలు. q. v.

అక్షిగతుడు *akshi-gatuḍu*. [Skt.] n. He who is hateful, hated, disliked. ద్వేషింపబడినవాడు.

అక్షీణము *a-kshīṇamu.* [Skt.] adj. Lasting, permanent. నిరంతరమైన. Vasu. I. 7.

అక్షుద్రము *a-kshudramu.* [Skt.] adj. Not small పెద్దదైన. "అక్షుద్రశరోర్మి క్షుర్ణి." R. 5. 253.

అక్షోడము *akshōḍamu.* [Skt.] n. A walnut. *Pistacio nut* (?) or the nut of *Aleurites Triloba.*

అక్షోభము *a-kshōbhamu.* [Skt.] adj. Unagitated. n. Imperturbability.

అక్షౌహిణి *akshauhiṇi.* [Skt. The anikini (అనీకిని) consists of 27 vahinis (వాహినులు.) and 27 being the cube aksha (అక్ష) of 3, it is probable that akshauhini is a compound of *aksha* and *vahini.* Wils.] n. A host, a complete army, ౨౧౮౭౦ గజములు, ౨౧౮౭౦ రథములు, ౬౫౬౧౦ గుర్రములు, ౧౦౯౩౫౦ భటులుగల సైన్యము.

అఖండము *a-khaṇḍamu.* [Skt.] adj. Whole, entire; abounding; imperishable. సకలమైన, విస్తారమైన. అఖండానందము eternal bliss. అఖండైశ్వర్యము abounding wealth. అఖండకావేరి the main stream of the Cavery. అఖండము n. A permanent lamp in a temple. నిరంతరము నుండే దీపము. అఖండిత adj. Unbroken, undivided. Untorn, undisturbed, uninterrupted, unrefuted, continuous, imperishable. ఖండింపబడని, అనశ్వరమైన. అఖండితలక్ష్మి imperishable riches.

అఖండుకము *akhaṇḍukamu.* [Skt.] n. A short cocoanut tree. చెన్నంగి.

అఖతివాసి *akha-tivāsi.* [Mahr. from akha = whole, and తివాసి carpet.] A large carpet. H. 5. 394. పెద్ద రత్నకంబళి.

అఖర్వము *a-kharvamu.* [Skt.] adj. Much, vast, great. విస్తారమైన.

అఖాతము *a-khātamu.* [Skt.] adj. Not dug (by man), very deep. n. A Bay (Geog.)

అఖిలము *a-khilamu.* [Skt.] adj. All, whole, entire. సమస్తమైన.

అఖ్యాతి *a-khyati.* [Skt.] n. Bad repute. Ill fame.

అగండ్రపాకు *agaṇḍrapāku.* [Tel.] n. A plant called *Ammania Vesicatoria.* (Ainslie. 2. 92.) Rox. 1. 426.

అగచరము or **అగచరుడు** *agacharamu.* [Skt.] n. The hill-ranger, *i.e.*, a monkey. కోతి.

అగచాట్లు *agatsāṭlu.* [Tel. from అగ్గము + చాటులు] n. Evils, afflictions, troubles. కడగండ్లు, తిప్పలు. అగచాట్లుపడుచున్నాడు he suffers great distress. నన్ను అగచాట్లు పెట్టినాడు he brought me into trouble. **అగచాట్లపోతు** *agatsāṭlapōtu.* [Tel.] n. A wretch, a villain. దుష్టుడుగా తిరిగేవాడు. "చిక్కుబిల్లలు మైనవు తేట్లు చిక్కుముళ్లు జమిడాకు చిల్కులు తాళ్లపాములకట యగచాట్లపోతనై దూడుకొంటి." H. iii. 192. **అగచాట్లమారి** *agatsāṭlamāri.* [Tel.] He who has suffered, a martyr, a sufferer. one who is thoroughly practised. నానాకడగండ్లుపడి తిరినవాడు, అరి తిరినవాడు.

అగజాత *aga-jāta.* [Skt.] n. An epithet of Parvati, wife of Siva. పార్వతి.

అగడు or **అగుడు** *agadu.* [Tel.] n. Ill fame, bad name, clamour, disturbance. నింద, అపవాదము, రచ్చ, రట్టు, అల్లరి. దాన్ని అగుడుపెట్టకు you must not blab of this. "అగడుసేయుచటంచు వానబెట్టినగాని." N. 7. 154. **అగడుపడు** v. To be blamed; to be confused. నిందపడు, తొట్రుపడు.

> బెగడుంపలదనుచు బెట్టిద
> ముగుసెవ్వగ నగడుపడుచు వాడుపడుచుమరే
> పగవారికి వలదనవా
> పగవారికి నేలరొమ్ముసగ పద్మజాడనుచుణా.
>
> Vasu. vi.

అగడ్త *agaḍta.* [Tel.] n. A moat, ditch, trench. పరిఘ, కందకము. గచ్చకాయలకు తెచ్చిన గుర్రము అగడ్త దాటునా? (Prov.)

అగణితము *a-gaṇitamu* [Skt.] adj. Inestimable, countless, innumerable, endless, great. అపరిమితమైన, మహత్తైన, విస్తారమైన.

"అగణితాలంకారయుక చంద్రముఖిని." Sar. D. 17. "అగణితమగు మానభంగమునకు తెలిసెగా." H. 1. 140. "అగణితోత్కృష్టి." N. 6. 74.

అగణ్యము *a-ganyamu*. [Skt.] adj. Incalculable, indescribable, vast. n. carelessness, disregard.

అగతా *agata*. [Uriya] An advance of money. బయానా.

అగత్యము *agatyamu*. [Tel.] n. Necessity, need. అవశ్యకత. అగత్యము adj. Urgent, important, needful. అవశ్యమైన, అగత్యములేని unnecessary. అగత్యమైనపని an urgent affair. ఆ మాటనుగురించి నీకేమి అగత్యము what is that to you? అగత్యముగా adv. Urgently, assuredly, positively, by all means. అవశ్యముగా. అగత్యముగా రా you must certainly come.

అగదంకారుడు *agadamkarudu*. [Skt.] n. A physician. వైద్యుడు.

అగప or అబక *agapa*. [Tel] n. A ladle, a scoop made of a cocoanut shell. కొబ్బరి చిప్పగరిటె. A. 1. 39.

అగపడు or **అగుపడు** *agapadu* [Tel. from అగ్గము+పడు.] v. n. To appear, seem. To be found, or perceived. To be seized or apprehended. కనబడు, దొరకు, చిక్కు. వానికి కండ్లు అగుపడవు he cannot see, he is blind. ఉన్నది ఒకటి అగుపడేది ఒకటి it is one thing and appears another. నేను చెప్పినది వానికి అగుపడలేదు he did not understand what I said. **అగపరచు** or **అగుపరచు**. v. n. To show, point out.

అగమము *agamamu*. [Skt.] n. A tree. A mountain. వృక్షము, పర్వతము.

అగము *agamu*. [Skt. అ not, గ=move or walk.] n. A hill, mountain; a tree.

అగమ్యము *a-gamyamu* [Skt.] adj. Inaccessible, impenetrable, impassable. పోవశక్యముకానిది. అగమ్యగమనము (vulgarly అగమ్యాగమనము) incest, prostitution. వ్యభిచారము. అగమ్యగోచరమైన inexplicable. **అగమ్యత** *agamyata*. [Skt.] n. Inaccessibility: impossibility. పొందశక్యముకానిది. A. 2. 29.

అగరు *agaru*. [Skt.] n. A kind of sweet scented wood; a superior kind of sandal. విశేషమైన పరిమళముగలిగి యుండ్రచాలుగానుండే గంధపుచెక్క. *Agallochum*, *Amyris Calambac*, *Aquilaria*, Aloe-wood or Eagle-wood. (Watts). కృష్ణాగరు or కాలాగరు the black species.

అగరుశొంఠి *agaru-sonthi*. [Skt.] The plant *Cissampelos hexandra*.

అగర్హితము *a-garhitamu*. [Skt.] Undespised, unreproached, blameless.

అగలు *agalu*. [Tel.] v. n. To break or go to pieces, be broken, burst. పగులు, విచ్చు, బద్దలగు. "ప్రాణంబులవిడిచె కంసుప్రాణముల గలగా." B. X. 1465.

అగలుచు or **అగల్చు** *agalutsu*. [Tel. causative of అగలు.] v. a. To cause to break, burst. పగులగొట్టు, బద్దలుచేయు. "కేలగలించికొట్టి" P. 4. 374. టీ॥ చెయ్యి చిగబట్టి. "మామాటనలరు తమ్ములతావులగలించు" ib. 4. 132. టీ॥ పోగొట్టు.

అగలుసత్తు *agalu-sattu*. [Tel.] n. A perfume. వాసనాద్రవ్యవిశేషము Swa. 1: 26.

అగవాళ్లు *agavallu*. [Tel. అగ్గము+వారలు] n. Light shoes; slippers.

అగవుతగవులు *agavu-tagavulu*. [Tel.] n. Wedding gifts. పెండ్లిలో అల్లునికి కూతునికి యిచ్చే వస్త్రభూషణాదులు. "అల్లుడని యాడుబిడ్డని యగవుతగవులంపకము కుశశోభనమున." N.9.97.

అగసాలి or **అగసాలెవాడు** *agasali*. [Tel.] n. A goldsmith. కంసాలివాడు.

అగస్త్యుడు *agastyudu*. [Skt.] n. Name of a certain sage. కుంభసంభవుడు. అగస్త్యశాకము the leaves of a leguminous tree which are dressed and eaten, అవిసెచెట్టు; **అగస్త్యనక్షత్రము** the star Canopus. అగస్త్యచారము

the course of Canopus. అగస్త్యోదయము the rise of Canopus. అగస్త్యభ్రాత (lit: the brother of Agastya.) a new-comer, who tries to make out that he is a great personage.

అగాడీ *agāḍī* [H.] adv. Before, in front, forward, further on, ముందర. n. The ropes with which a horse's forefeet are tied. గుర్రముయొక్క మెడకుగాని లేక ముందరి కాళ్లకుగాని కట్టే తాడు. ఆ గుర్రము అగాడిపిచాడీలను తెంచుకొని పారిపోయినది the horse broke its head ropes and heel ropes and ran away.

అగాదు *agādu.* [H.] n. Discharge, explosion. వేటులేవడము. తుపాకిని అగాదు చేయు to discharge a gun. ఒక అగాదు one volley, or, one shot.

> తెరియను లోపూకారకుడు దగ్గర
> బళ్ళిమశైల శృంగముం
> గుగిగొని కేలుపుంజెరువు గొప్ప
> పిరంగిని జాయమందుతో
> గొరలేడువిన్న మానికపుగుండు
> ఘటించియగాదు చేసిన
> దయమగగ్రమ్ము క్రొంబొగలనంగ
> జగంబునబర్వెచీకటుల్ రవి. 4. అ.

అగాధము *a-gādhamu.* [Skt.] n. A hole, a chasm. రంధ్రము. adj. Unfathomable, very deep, bottomless, abstruse, obscure. అతలస్పర్శమైన, అమోఘమైన. అగాధజలము very deep water.

అగారము *agāramu* [Skt.] n. A house, a dwelling. ఇల్లు.

అగావు *agāvu.* [H.]. An advance of money, earnest money. బయానా, కుదవ.

అగిసె or **అగిశె** or **అవిసెచెట్టు** *agise.* [Tel.] n. Common flax, or lint. *Linum usitatissimum;* also, a leguminous tree, *(Coronilla grandiflora* or *Æschynomene grandiflora,* planted as a support for the betel vine.) అడివి అవిసె *Kauchinia parviflora.* అగిసె కూర its leaves which are dressed and eaten. తెమ, అనగా, నూనెతీసే అవిశవిత్తులు. అవిసెనూనె linseed oil. సీమ అవిసె broad leaved Cassia. (Ainslie.) నల్ల అవిసె black flax. See అవిసె.

అగు *agu.* [Tel.] (commonly written **అవు**), v. To be, to become, to prove to be. The present p|| is అగుచు, or అవుచు as అగుచున్నాడు or అవుతున్నాడు he is becoming. మిక్కిలి సిరి అగును. much fortune will result. The past p|| is అయి as దొంగ అయి turned a rogue, become a thief. The root in A of అగు is కా as అట్లా కారాదు it cannot happen so. Aorist p|| అగు, అగునట్టి, అయ్యే, అయ్యేడి as క్రూరుడగు cruel. శాలివాహనశక వర్షంబులు ౧౪౬౬ అగునట్టి క్రోధి సంవత్సర కార్తీకశుద్ధ ౫ శనివారము Saturday the 5th of the bright fortnight of the month Kārtika in the year Krōdhi *"which is"* the year 1466 (of the Salivahana æra.) ఇది దొంగతనము అయ్యేపనిగనుక as this is a matter in which a man might prove a rogue. Past Rel. p|| అయిన as నాది అయిన గుర్రము a horse of mine. The imperatives are కమ్ము plu. కండి. Causal forms కాజేయు or కావించు. Negative aorist కాదు, &c. అగుర=అగును+ర=అవును. It is so.

1. To be, to become, as కాకి కోకిలయగునె can a crow become a cuckoo? వాడు ఏమయినాడు what has become of him? దొంగ అయినాడు he proved to be a thief. వాడు నేరస్థుడైనాడు he was found guilty. ఆ పని అవును కాకపోవును that undertaking may or may not be accomplished. వానికి ఆకలి అవుతున్నది he is hungry. ఇల్లు రాత్రియగుట as it was now night. బాలుడగుట as he is but a child.

2. To be made, to be finished, to be spent or expended, to elapse, as పని శీఘ్రముగా కావలెను the work must be done soon. వివాహమగును marry her. ఆ పెండ్లి అయినది the marriage took place. భోజనమయినది dinner is over. రాజ

చూచుచున్నది I got a sight of the king. అయి నదాన్ని చూపు shew what has been done. ఆ పని అయినది the work is over, it is done. కావచ్చినది it is nearly done. రూకలు అయి పోయినవి the money is expended. సంవత్సరము అయినది a year has passed. నెల అవుతున్నది it is about a month since. అర్థమయినదా do you understand it? నాకు భావముకాలేదు I do not understand it. భావమయినది I understand it. స్నానము కావించు to bathe, or to cause to bathe. తీర్పుకాలేదు no decision has been given. ముచ్చిలితెచ్చుట మగతనం బగునా is it a manly thing to steal?

3. To be proper or fit, to be agreeable, as ఇచ్చట నుండనగునే మనకు is it fit for us to remain here? కాని పని an improper or unbecoming act. అట్లా చేయనవునా is it right to do so? పగలు కాచినపాలు ఆ రాత్రికి అవును milk boiled the same day is fit for use that night. అతనికి నాకు కానందున as we are not on good terms. అయినవాండ్లున్ను కానివాండ్లున్ను friends and enemies.

4. To grow, as ఈ తోటలో ఏమి అవుతవి what is grown in this garden? ఇక్కడ వరి కాదు rice does not grow here.

5. (Governing a dative) To stand in relation, as వాడు నీకేమవుతాడు how is he related to you? నాకు కావలసినవారు my relations. వానికి మేము ఏమీకాము we are in no way related to him.

6. Added to some nouns it gives them a verbal significance, as వారు ఎప్పుడు ప్రయాణమవుతారు when will they start or set out? విభాగాలు అయి వేరింటి కాపురము చేస్తున్నారు they separated and live apart.

అగు *agu.* [Tel.] adj. అయిన which is.

అగుడు *agudu.* [Tel. subjunctive of అగు.] అయ్యేటప్పటికి. "అంతికంతి కగ్గలంబగుడు, నుడి కొంచు." A. v. 166. as it was excessive. Also (Optative.) May it be so.

అగుపడు *agu-padu.* [Tel.] v. n. See అగపడు.

అగుపరచు *agu-paratsu.* [Tel.] See under అగపడు.

అగురువు *'a-guruvu.* [Skt.] adj. Light, not heavy, Small. చులకని, తేలికైన, చిన్న.

అగులు *agulu.* [Tel.] Same as పగులు. "గగ నమగుల" so that the sky rent, cf. "a shout that tore Hell's concave." Milton. P. L. i. 541.

అగోచరము *a-gócharamu.* [Skt.] adj. Not visible to the eye. Inconceivable, imperceptible. గ్రాహ్యముకాని, అగుపడని.

అగౌరవము *a-gauravamu.* [Skt.] n. Disregard, contempt. వారిని అగౌరవము చేసి నాడు he did not show them respect.

అగ్గపడు *agga-padu.* [Tel.] v. n. To bow, yield, to become subject. వశమగు. See అగ్గము.

అగ్గము *aggamu.* [Tel.] n. That which is seen; object, victim. విషయము, స్వాధీనము. "అయోధ్యాధిపతులకారి కగ్గంబుగాక." M. X i. 207.

అగ్గలము *aggalamu* [Tel.] adj. Excessive, vehement, intolerable. మెండు. "తూర్పు వినదమగ్గలమరొజ్జ" Swa. vi. 105. అగ్గల ముగ adv. Excessively, vehemently, cruelly. దుస్సహముగా. "దాపక చెప్పము చెప్పకున్న నగ్గలముగ నిష్టభింతువని." H. iii. 140.

అగ్గలించు *aggalintsu* [Tel. from అగ్గలము]. v. n. To increase, to grow. ఎక్కువగు. "ముచ్చటలగ్గలింప." Vish. vii. 375.

అగ్గలిక *aggalika.* [Tel. from అగ్గలించు]. n. Greatness, power, prowess, pleasure. Wantonness, sportfulness, dalliance. "మదమలందాటించిన ఘోటకంబు విగ్గలించువ మ్రొక్కియు నగ్గలిక చెడక." Swa. iv. 161.

అగ్గి *aggi.* [Tadbhava form of Skt. agni] n. Fire. అగ్ని, నిప్పు. వానిముఖమునకు అగ్గికాశినది he looks flushed or red in the face.

అగ్గించు *aggintsu.* [Tel]. v. a. To praise, commend, applaud. **అగ్గింపు** *aggimpu.* n. Praise, eulogy.

అగ్గు *aggu.* [Tel.] v. n. To be contained. అమరుట. "కొంచెంబైనపైలక్ష్మిక కుచద్వయము నగ్గె." Lâvanya 35.

అగ్గువ *aggura.* [Tel.] n. Cheapness. చవక. అగ్గువగా కొను or తెచ్చు to buy cheap.

అగ్ని *agni.* [Skt. Lat. ignis.] n. Fire. జఠరాగ్ని the gastric juice, the digestive power. ఆగ్నేయమూల the south-east point. అగ్నిష్టోమము a sacrifice to the god of fire. అగ్నిపురము the pudendum muliebre. శోకాగ్ని mental anguish. చింతాగ్ని corroding care. అగ్నివైద్యము the use of a cautery. అగ్నికుండము a fire-pit. అగ్నింధనము kindling or feeding the fire. అగ్నికణము a spark of fire. అగ్నికార్యము kindling or feeding the sacrificial fire with oblations of liquid butter. అగ్నికాష్ఠము *Agallochum* అగరుగంధపుచెక్క. అగ్నిక్రియ funeral rites or other religious acts performed by means of fire. అగ్నిజిహ్వ a tongue or flame of fire. అగ్నిజ్వాల n. flame of fire. త్రేతాగ్నులు the three sacred fires called గార్హపత్యము, ఆహవనీయము and దాక్షిణము. అగ్నినక్షత్రము the Pleiades. అగ్నిపరీక్ష ordeal by fire. అగ్నిపర్వతము a volcano. అగ్నిప్రవేశము entering the fire, self-immolation by means of fire. అగ్నిబాణము an arrow of fire, a rocket. అగ్నిమంథనము production of fire by friction. అగ్నిమయము fiery. అగ్నిమాంద్యము indigestion, dyspepsia. అగ్నిరాశి a heap of fire. అగ్నివర్ణము the colour of fire. అగ్నిసంస్కారము the consecration of fire, the performance of any rite by means of fire. అగ్నిసాక్షికముగా in the presence of fire as witness. ఆగ్నేయాస్త్రము fire thrown as a rocket. అగ్న్యుత్పాతము a fiery portent, meteor. అగ్నిమండలము a large caterpillar that destroys crops and whose touch is supposed to occasion inflammation. అగ్నిమాలి n. The plant called Ceylon leadwort. *Plumbago Zelanica.* చిత్రమూలము. అగ్నిబెండపాకు *ammannia baccifera* or blistering Ammannia (Watts) అగ్నిశిఖ. a flame of fire. Also a plant (*Gloriosa superba*) కలగొట్టచెట్టు, కుంకుమపువ్వుచెట్టు the Safflower plant. అగ్నిహోత్రము fire. అగ్నిహోత్రుడు the god of fire. అగ్నిహోత్రాలు కాల్చుచున్నాడు or చేయుచున్నాడు colloquial for "he is smoking."

అగ్రము *agramu:* [Skt] n. End, point, tip, front, fore-part, top, peak, summit. adj. First, preliminary, chief, principal. అగ్రజ్య (in astron.) the sine of the amplitude. అగ్రభాగము (astron.) degree of amplitude. అగ్రసారము a compendious method of counting immense numbers. అగ్రాంశువు the end of a ray of light, the focal point. జిహ్వాగ్రము the tip of the tongue. Similarly నాసికాగ్రము, కుశాగ్రము, &c. అగ్రగణ్యము adj. Estimable, conspicuous. శ్రేష్ఠమైన, అగ్రగణ్యుడు n. A chief, a leader. కొందరు నెంచదగినవాడు. అగ్రజంఘము the forepart of the thigh. అగ్రజన్ముడు n. A brahmin. Elder brother. అగ్రజుడు n. An elder brother. అన్న. అగ్రణి n. A leader.

అగ్రహారము *agra-hâramu.* [Skt.] n. A street or village inhabited by brahmins. A village of which the old and hereditary cultivators are brahmins. A village granted to brahmins by government for charitable or religious purposes; either rent free, or at a favourable assessment. The conditions on which these villages are held are specified thus, సర్వాగ్రహారము a village free from all tax. శ్రోత్రియాగ్రహారము a village granted at a certain fixed assessment. కోడి అగ్రహారము, or. ఏల్బడి అగ్రహారము or కట్టుబడి అగ్రహారము a village granted at a rent which fluctuates with the produce. అగ్రహారికుడు a brahmin belonging to such a village. అగ్రహారమనుభవించేవాడు he who enjoys a village free from tax.

అగ్రామ్యము *a-grāmyamu.* [Skt.] adj. Not vulgar. పామరోక్తముకాని.

అగ్రాహ్యము *a-grāhyamu.* [Skt.] Unfit to be accepted, deserving to be rejected.

అగ్రిమము *agrimamu.* [Skt.] adj. Chief, principal, best, first. అగ్రిముడు n. A chief, a leader.

అగ్రేదిధిషువు *agrē-didhishuvu.* [Skt.] n. A woman's first husband.

అగ్రేసరుడు *agrēsaruḍu.* [Skt. from అగ్రము.] n. A leader, chief. మొనగాడు, మేటి.

అఘము *aghamu.* Skt] n. Sin, guilt. **అఘమర్షణము** *aghamarshaṇamu.* n. An expiatory prayer. సర్వపాపములను పోగొట్టు మంత్రము.

అఘటనము or **అఘటితము** *a-ghaṭanamu.* [Skt.] adj. Impossible, impracticable. దుర్ఘటమైన. Vasu. iv. 77.

అఘోరము *a-ghōramu.* [Skt.] adj. Terrible, dreadful. అఘోరమైన యుద్ధము a fierce battle. అఘోరప్రమాణము a terrible oath.

అఘోరించు *aghōrintsu.* [Skt. from above] v.n. To be in grief: to lament, be horrified.

అచట or **అచ్చట** *atsaṭa.* [Tel. fr. అ+చోటు.] adv. There, in that place; అక్కడ.

అచరము *a-charamu.* [Skt. lit. not moving.] adj. Immovable. స్థావరమైన.

అచల *a-chala.* [Skt. lit. not shaking.] n. The earth, as being stable. భూమి. **అచలము** n. A mountain, a hill. **అచలుడు** n. He who is firm.

అచింత్యము *a-chintyamu.* [Skt.] adj. Incomprehensible, not to be thought of. అప్రమేయమైన, చింతింప శక్యముకాని.

అచిత్తు *a-chittu.* [Skt.] n. That which has no life or understanding. Matter, as opposed to mind. చిదచిద్జ్ఞానము knowledge of the distinction between matter and mind.

అచిరము *a-chiramu.* [Skt.] adj. Momentary. అస్థిరమైన.

అచుంబితము *a-chumbitamu.* [Skt.] adj. Lit: Not kissed; untouched; unattainable. "అచుంబితభావము." T. ii. 60. ఇది అచుంబితమైన విషయము this is an unattainable subject.

అచేతనము *a-chētanamu.* [Skt. lit. life-less]. adj. Devoid of life. Inanimate, insensible.

అచ్చ *atstsa* [Tel.] adj. Pure, real, unmixed. అచ్చతెనుగు Telugu without foreign words. అచ్చపుగుండ్ల పేరు a necklace of pure beads.

అచ్చట *atstsaṭa* [Tel.] adv. There, in that place. See అచట.

అచ్చనగండ్లు, అచ్చనగాయలు or **అచ్చన గుండ్లు** *atstsana-gunḍlu.* [Tel. singular అచ్చనకాయ] n. Chuck-stones. Pebbles which are tossed up, and caught on the back of the hand, in a game played by girls. "మగువలు కెమ్మోవి గాయలు ముత్యాలదిన్నెపై పైడియచ్చనగండ్లు పాటైచి." Yayati. iii. 149. **అచ్చనలాడు** or అచ్చనగాయలాడు to toss up balls and catch them on the back of the hand. "పొంచి నాకము మదిలో నచ్చ నలాడంగనవియు నమ్మనితోపలా." Jai. Bhar. i. 62.

అచ్చముగా *atstsamu-gā.* [Tel.] adv. Purely, without any mixture. నిర్మలముగా.

అచ్చర *ats-tsara.* [Tadbhava form of Skt. అప్సర.] n. A fairy, a courtezan of heaven. అప్సరస్త్రీ.

అచ్చారము *atsâramu.* [Tam.] Earnest money. సంచేకరువు.

అచ్చాళి or **అచ్చాళు** *atsali.* (K) One who lives a single life, an unmarried person. ఒంటిమనిషి, ఏకాంగిగా నుండేవాడు, సంసారిపు పీకులాటలేనివాడు. అచ్చాళుగానుండు or అచ్చాళిగానుండు to be alone, to be quiet, free from perturbation. "చారుశీలానుకూలజలజ లోచనల, చేకాబంధుల చెలులవీక్షణమెు, నగరికుటేరులౌక బహుదుర్గమార్గ, మగుతోవశమహార్ణ యాత్రమస్థలిని, శేరిచి మనము నిశ్చింత సేతెంచి, యూరూఢిబలయుక్తసచ్ఛాళిగాగ, అనికిసన్నద్ధుల మై యుండవలె." Pativratya. 35.

అచ్చి *acchi.* [Tel.] n. An *Acheen* or Pegu pony.

అచ్చియుండు *acchi-undu* [Tel.] v. i. To be indebted to. వాడికి అది అచ్చియుండ యిచ్చి నాను it was my bad luck and I had to give it to him. See. అచ్చు.

అచ్చిక or **అచ్చికము** *acchika.* [Tel.] n. Deficiency, want, defect. Clearness, cleanness. కొదవ, అచ్చము, ప్రసన్నము, తేటది. "నీకొకందులకు నచ్చికలేక మెలంగ." H. i. 93. "పల్లవులు లేతపచ్చికమచ్చిక చెలులకిందచ్చు నచ్చికములేక." B. viii. 46.

అచ్చికబుచ్చిక or **అచ్చికబుచ్చికము** *acchika-buchika.* [Tel.] n. Familiarity, affability. కలుపుగోలుతనము. "సారెంబులకు విన్యాసాదం బులు తెచ్చియిచ్చుచు నచ్చికబుచ్చికలదరి గొంతి కాలంబు గడపి." P. ii. 69. "అచ్చుగాదీర్చు విూయప్పని కొన్ని యచ్చికబుచ్చికలాడిమత్రములు గెంటకయిచ్చి." H. D. ii. 630.

అచ్చిమట్టము *acchi-mattamu.* [అచ్చి from Acheen; మట్టము is Tel.] An *Acheen*, or Pegu pony. పైగోపుర్రము.

అచ్చివచ్చు *acchi-vattsu.* [Tel.] v. n. To be cheap. To prosper, be advantageous. చౌకను, కలిసివచ్చు. వానికి గుర్రములు అచ్చిరావు he has no luck in horse flesh. ఆ యిల్లు నాకు అచ్చివచ్చినది. we got the house cheap, or we have prospered in that house. See. అచ్చియుండు.

అచ్చు *acchu.* [Skt.] n. A vowel. స్వరము, జీవాక్షరము.

అచ్చు *attsu.* [Tel.] n. A stamp, a form for printing or for any other impression, a type, a printing press. An axle-tree. A mould. The handle of a handmill. A weaver's reed or stay. An image, or picture. ప్రతియాగాయమును కల్పించేటిది, ఇరుసు నాను, తిరగటి పిడి, బట్ట నేసేటందుకు సాధనమైనది, ప్రతిబింబము. పోత అచ్చు the mould wherein clay or metal is cast. ఇటికె అచ్చు the box or mould used in making bricks. అచ్చుక్షరములు printed letters. **అచ్చువేయు** to print. ఇంకా అచ్చువేయని unprinted, unpublished. అచ్చువేసేవాడు a printer. అక్షరాల అచ్చులు types of letters. బెల్లపు అచ్చు a square mould into which boiled treacle is poured, and thus formed into cakes. అచ్చుబెల్లము a lump of jaggery. **అచ్చొత్తు** to seal, impress with a mark, to print అచ్చుకూటము. (a Madras word,) A printing press office ముద్రాశాల. అచ్చుపల్ల the frame on which a weaver's reed is fixed. అచ్చువేసినయెద్దు a "brahminy" bull that is marked or stamped and is allowed to wander at large, as consecrated to the deity. అచ్చుకట్టు or అచ్చుకట్టువేయు v. a. To prepare land for wet cultivation by throwing up banks to divide it into plots, partitions or beds. మళ్లుగా పేర్చను. అచ్చుకట్టించినమడి or అచ్చుకట్టు పొలము a field which is divided into beds for wet cultivation. **అచ్చులువారేయు** to find yarn on the frame for weaving (Cuddapa.) **అచ్చుగా** *attsu-gá.* [Tel.] adv. Precisely, exactly, clearly, evidently. "పిచ్చుకపై బ్రహ్మాస్త్రము నచ్చుగ దొడిగినవిధాన." T. iv. 22.

అచ్చు *attsu.* [Tel.] v. n. To be indebted, suffer loss. బుణపడు, దండుగ పెట్టు. నీకు నే నచ్చియున్నానా am I indebted to you? దానికి పదిరూపాయలు అచ్చినాను I lost ten rupees by that business. See. అచ్చియుండు.

అచ్చుకొను *attsu-konu.* [Tel.] v. n. To pay, pay wrongfully, liquidate. దండుగ పెట్టు. వాడు దివానముకు పది రూపాయలు అచ్చుకొన్నాడు he paid ten Rupees to government. ఆ నేలకుగాను నలభైరూపాయలు అచ్చుకొనియున్నాను I have suffered, on account of that land, a loss of forty rupees. మేము అచ్చుకొనువారము we will make it good.

అచ్చుదల or **అచ్చుబాటు** *attsu-dala.* [Tel.] n. Debt. బుణముతీరుకట. వానికి ఆవులు అచ్చుదలలేదు (lit: the cattle do not owe him anything) he has no luck in cattle.

అచ్చుపడు *attsu-padu.* [Tel.] v. n. To be apparent, evident or plain, to be precise or exact. విశదమగు, స్పష్టమగు, సంగా తుండు. "సొమ్మచ్చుపడంగ జేయుటకు సైయలకొలదినగలు పేరికచ్చెచ్చున నిచ్చు." A. iv. 187.

అచ్చెరువు *accheruvu.* [Tadbhava form of Skt. ఆశ్చర్యం.] n. Astonishment. అచ్చెరువందు, అచ్చెరువొందు to be astonished. అచ్చెరుపాటు or అచ్చెరువుపాటు. n. astonishment.

అచ్యుతము *acchyutamu.* [Skt.] adj. Imperishable. **అచ్యుతుడు** *acchyutudu* [Skt.] n. The eternal one. Vishnu.

అచ్ఛత *achchhata.* [Skt.] n. Clearness. స్వచ్ఛత, తేట.

అచ్ఛము *achchamu.* [Skt.] adj. Clear, transparent. **అచ్ఛముగా** adv. Purely, clearly, plainly. **అచ్ఛాచ్ఛము** *achcha-chchamu.* [Skt.] adj. Perfectly pure. అతినిర్మలమైన. A. vi. 140.

అచ్ఛభల్లము *achcha-bhallamu.* [Skt.] n. A bear. ఎలుగుగొడ్డు. A. iv. 287.

అజ *aja.* See. అజా.

అజ *aja.* [Skt.] n. A she-goat. ఆడుమేక.

అజంతము *ajantamu.* [Skt. అచ్ + అంతము.] A word which ends with a vowel.

అజగరము *aja-garamu.* [Skt.] n. The rock snake, the Boa constrictor. కొండచిలువ.

అజగవము *aja-gavamu.* [Skt.] n. The epithet of the bow of Siva. శివుని విల్లు.

అజమాయిషి *aja-mayishi.* [H.] See. అజ్మాయిషి.

అజము *ajamu.* [Skt.] n. A goat. మగమేక, మేకపోతు.

అజమోద *aja-moda.* [Skt.] n. The seed of Bishop's weed. *Sison Ammi.* ఓమము. Common Carroway, the species called Ajwaen (*Lingusticum Ajwaen*), and especially a species of Parsley, *Apium Involucratum.*

అజశృంగి *aja-sringi.* [Skt.] n. The shrub called *Odina Wodier* used as a remedy for sore eyes. జొప్పుచెట్టు.

అజస్రము *ajasramu.* [Skt. √ jas = to injure.] adv. Constantly, always. ఎల్లప్పుడును, నిత్యమును.

అజా *ajā.* [H.] Amount. The whole, grand total. Also, the gross produce of a land including both the ryot's and government shares. [Vizag.]

అజాండము *aj-andamu.* [Skt. అజ + అండము.] n. Lit. Brahma's egg. The universe. బ్రహ్మాండము. [See. అజుడు]

అజాగ్రత or **అజాగ్రత్త.** *a-jāgrata.* [Skt.] n. Carelessness, heedlessness. అజాగ్రతగా carelessly.

అజాజీవి *ajā-jīvi.* [Tel.] n. A goat-herd. కురుమవాడు.

అజాతశత్రువు. *a-jāta-satruvu.* [Skt.] n. He who has no enemy; an inoffensive man. An epithet of Dharmaraja, the eldest of the Pandavas.

అజితము *a-jitamu.* [Skt.] adj. Unconquered, invincible. అజితేంద్రియులు those whose lusts are unsubdued.

అజినము *ajinamu.* [Skt.] n. Skin చర్మము. కృష్ణాజినము an antelope's skin.

అజిరము *ajiramu.* [Skt.] n. A court or yard. ముంగిలి.

అజీర్ణము or **అజీర్తి** *ajirnamu.* [Skt.] n. Indigestion.

అజుకుంచు *a-zukuntsu.* [Tel.] v. i. To underrate or value unfairly, to embezzle. మొకము తక్కువగాచేసి కొంగిలించు [Guntur.]

అజుడు *ajudu.* [Skt.] n. Lit. not born; the self-existing one. An epithet of Vishnu, Bramha, or Cupid.

అజేయము *a-jēyamu.* [Skt.] adj. Invincible, impregnable. జయింపగూడని.

అజ్జ *azza.* [Tel.] n. Foot. Opportunity. "మాపజ్జనుజేరి యజ్జగనిభక్తి నొసర్చుచు విద్య నేర్చెనా." T. ii. 48. **అజ్జగా** adv. Cleverly, neatly, ingeniously. నేర్పుగా. "అజ్జగా తిలకంబువాపెళించినదుట." Vencatacal. page. 37.

అజ్జము *azzamu.* [Skt.] n. A division of the Veda. అనువాకము.

అజ్జరే or **అజ్జారే** *azzarē.* [Tel.] interj. Well done! శాబాసు.

అజ్జవాలు *azza-vālu.* [Tel.] n. A fowl. కోడి.

"అటులుడించిన జేరగు
మంచునను నేస్తులేని నేర్పడం
కోటానకంగ నూతిలిన
సాగెరుటూరి పుట జవాల్గమల్."
అప్పా. ఆ. కాం.

అజ్జాయించు *azzāyintsu.* [H.] v. n. To doubt, hesitate. సందేహించు.

అజ్ఞత *a-gnyata.* [Skt.] n. Ignorance. తెలివిలేమి. **అజ్ఞాతవాసము** *aynyāta-vāsamu.* [Skt.] n. Living incognito. తాను ఇట్టివాడని తెలియకుండా ఉండడము. ఆ రాజు అక్కడ అజ్ఞాతవాసము చేసినాడు the king lived there incognito. పాండవుల అజ్ఞాతవాసము the life led by the Pandavas in retirement.

అజ్ఞానము *a-gnyānamu.* [Skt.] n. Ignorance, అవివేకము, మూఢత్వము. అజ్ఞానబంధములు the fetters of iguorance. **అజ్ఞాని** *a-gnyāni.* [Skt.] n. An ignorant person, a person without knowledge. "ఆచారమెరుగని అజ్ఞాని నేను."

అజ్ఞుడు *aynyudu.* [Skt.] n. An ignorant person, one without knowledge.

అజ్మాయిషి *ajmāyishi.* [H.] Trial, proof, examination, experience. పరిశోధన.

అట *ata.* [Tel.] adv. There. Then. Afterwards. అటకు పో go there. అటుమున్ను previously, before that.

అట *ata.* [Tel.] or **అంట** (contraction of అంటున్నారు they say) It is said, they say. వాడు వచ్చెనట they say he is come. రావటె for రావటవే, i.e., రావంటావా యేమే what, will you not come? కోపమటే, i.e., కోపమా యేమే what, are you angry? బాలుడటే వాడు what! do you call him a child? అటరా is a contraction for అంటావురా dost thou say so?

అటక or **అటుక** *ataka.* [Tel.] n. A loft under the roof of a house.

అటకమామిడి or **అటికమామిడి** *ataka-māmidi.* [Tel.] n. The spreading hogweed, *Boerhaavia diffusa* (Watts). గలిజేరుపల్లె. Ainslie 2. 205.

అటకలి *aṭakali*. [Tel.] n. A stuff used to rub upon the head to clean the hair. ఒడలు తోముకొనే పిండి. Plu. అటకళ్లు.

అటకాయించు *aṭakāyintsu*. [H.] To prevent, stop, hinder, check. అటకాపు [H.] Prevention, hindrance.

అటతాళము *aṭa-tālamu*. [Tel.] n. Quick time in music.

అటనము *aṭanamu*. [Skt.] n. The act of wandering about. దేశాటనము travel in foreign parts.

అటని *aṭani*. [Skt.] The notched extremity of a bow. వింటికొప్పు.

అటమట or అటమటము *aṭamaṭa*. [Tel.] n. Trickery, guile, fraud. Sorrow, untruthfulness. "అటమట దీరగాదు సుద్దులాడెద వారా." T. iii. 102. "అటమటమ్ముల విద్యల నటులదుండగాక నటనటలు నురువుతో నారయుని" Swa. v. 19. అటమటకాడు, అటమటీడు a cheat. అటమటించు *aṭamaṭintsu*. [Tel.] v. a. and v. n. To deceive, cajole, obtain by fraud. To be troubled మాయచేసి అపహరించు.

"తమ్ముడవని నిన్నేగతి
నమ్మంగా వచ్చునిట్లు నాతోనకక ర
త్న మ్మటమటించుకొంటివి."

Vish. vi. 307.

అటవి *aṭavi*. [Skt. అడవి] n. A forest. అరణ్యము.

అటికె *aṭika*. [Tel.] n. A small earthen pot with a large mouth. చిన్నకుండ.

అటు *aṭu*. [Tel.] adj. That. అటుతర్వాత after that. అటుపూర్వము before that. అటుమొన్న the day before that preceding yesterday. ఏటికి అటువక్క on the other side of the river. అటుపోక యెటుపోయినాడు he did not go there, but is gone I know not whither. తురంగంబటునిటు బడి పారిపోయెను the horse ran this way and that way and escaped. అటు *aṭu*. [Tel.] adv. So, thus, in that way or manner. అట్లు, అరీతిగా. అటువలెనే adv. In like manner. అరీతిగా. అటుగాన adv. Wherefore, therefore: so then: if so.

అటుక *aṭuka*. [Tel.] n. A loft in a house, under the roof.

అటుకులు *aṭukulu*. [Tel.] n. Rice wetted, parched and flattened.

అటులు *aṭulu*. [Tel.] adv. Thus, so that, according to. అట్లా. "నంటిరేని కర్ణులతను తేటుపట్టనటులు లాతిని." T. ii 64. అటులైన *aṭulaina*. [Tel.] adv. If so. అట్లాగైతే.

అటువంటి *aṭu-vanṭi*. [Tel.] adj. Like that, such. అలాగంటి, అట్టి.

అటే or అటా *aṭē* [Tel.] Contraction of అటనే or అటమ్మా (intensive of అట) My good woman! అతను పోయినాడటే is he gone, ma'am? ఇంకా కాలేదటా is it not finished, ma'am?

అట్ట *aṭṭa*. [Tel.] n. The sole of a shoe or slipper: hide; leather. Card, pasteboard. A headless trunk. A part or division. చర్మము, మొండెము, భాగము. ఒంటట్ట చెప్పులు shoes with a single leather for a sole. చెమట్ట a piece of leather put inside a shoe. అట్టపొట్టగా నుండేవాడు a stout pot-bellied man. అట్టలెత్తిన ప్రాతచెప్పులు. A. vi. 103. "అస్త్రంబునందునిమిడుచుతం డదట్ట ట్టలయుదలయును ధరణీతలకరంబుచేసె." M. VII. v. 398. "ఆ రాజులలో పరస్పర వైరంబు బుట్టించిన ఆ దండు రెండట్టలై." G. vi. 92.

అట్టచెమ్మ *aṭṭa-chemma* [Tel. Here అట్ట is from Skt. అష్ట.] n. A certain game played with four shells. నాలుగు గవ్వలు వేసి ఆడే దచ్చి వంటిది ఒక ఆట.

అట్టడి aṭṭaḍi. [Tel.] n. A chamber built over the gate of a fort. కోటవాకిటిమీది యిల్లు. See అట్టము. "అట్టడులయందు గాలి యట్టళ్లగూడె." DRY. 1518.

అట్టము aṭṭamu. [Skt.] n. A gazebo, or top room: a fortified place in front of a building. A palace. An upper roomed dwelling: an upstair house.

అట్టహాసము aṭṭa-hāsamu. [Skt.] n. Violent, phrenzied laughter. Vehement action, exceeding effort or exertion. Toil, pains, laborious efforts. Pomp. "అట్టహాసం బున నడచెదు తెరువుల." N. ix. 31. నా కూతురిని పంపితేనేగాని కూడదని అట్టహాసము చేస్తాడు he protests violently that his daughter shall go with him. రాజు బహు అట్టహాసముతో బయలుదేరినాడు the king set out with great pomp. అట్టహాసకాడు n. A pompous or ostentatious man.

అట్టాణి aṭṭāṇi. n. [Tel.] A stone seat or low wall, built for carriers to place their loads on when resting.

అట్టాయెనా (from అట్టు so; and అయెను it happened.) If it be so. ఇస్తినట్టాయెనా if you were to give it.

అట్టాలకము aṭṭālakamu. n. [Tel.] A room on the top of the house. A house or chamber built over the gate of a fort, an upstair house. A palace.

అట్టి aṭṭi. adj. pron. Such, like that అటువంటి. Such a man అట్టివాడు. అట్టిట్టు n. (lit. that way and this way.) Confusion. అయినవట్టుకు వాడు ఈ ఊరిని అట్టిట్టుచేసి వెళ్లినాడు he ruined this place. అట్టిట్టుగా adv. In a confused state. వానికి ఇప్పుడు అట్టిట్టుగానున్నది he is in a very critical state. అట్టిదా it is such or is it such? అటువంటిదే.

అట్టిడు aṭṭiḍu. [Tel. from అట్టి+వాడు] n. Just such man. అటువంటివాడు. "కీనట్టిడ నగుదురా." M. XII. vi. 244.

అట్టియ aṭṭiya. [Tel.] n. Crowd, multitude. గుంపు, సమూహము.

"అట్టిరుండ దొరిమిశత్రిము
అట్టియలుగనగూడి చేడియలంగనియునిరి."
సింహా. 2. ఆ.

అట్టు aṭṭu. [Tel.] n. A cake roasted or baked (on an iron plate.) పెనముమీద కాల్చినది. ఇందునగురించి ఊరంతా అట్టుడికినట్టు ఉడుకుచున్నది the whole town is in a stir about this. (Homer, Odyss. xx. 10.) The whole town rings with the news. అట్టుకట్టు aṭṭukaṭṭu. v. n. To be formed, as a cake. అట్టువలె చేర్పడుట. అట్టుపుట్టానవాలు aṭṭupuṭṭanavālu. n. An exact description. యూపర్తి వివరము. అట్లతద్దె aṭlataḍḍe. [Tel.] n. Cake-day, a feast that falls on the new moon in the month of Aswija when women offer buns in payment of vows. Plural అట్లు.

అట్టు or అట్టుగా aṭṭu. [Tel.] adv. (A particle) So that, as, according to. అతడు వచ్చేటట్టు వ్రాయుము write a letter *so that* he may come. మీరు చెప్పినట్టుగా చేస్తిని I did as you bid me. ఆయన చెప్పినట్టు according to his order. వాడు ఇంకా అవతలకు పోవునట్టు అగుపడ్డాడు he seemed as though he would go further. నేను చెప్పినట్టు చేసినాడు he did as I said. వారు సాగిపోయినట్టుగా చెప్పెను he said that they had passed on. అట్టుగాక or అట్లుగాక aṭṭugāka. adv. Without being so. అట్టుల aṭṭula. adv. As soon as, soon after. వెంటనే. "చెట్టు దిగి వచ్చినట్టుల." H. ii. 47. Just as. అప్పుడు. అట్టే (for అట్లాగే) aṭṭē. [Tel.] adv. Thus. So. In the same manner, as it was. అట్టే ఉండనీ leave it as it is. నొప్పి అట్టే ఉన్నది the pain is in the same state. అట్టే పోయినాడు he went off straightway. అట్టే మాట్లాడుతూ ఉండినాడు he was talking straight on. ఆ గుర్రములట్టే ఉన్నవి the horses are as they were: they are untouched.

అట్టుక *aṭṭuka* [Tel.] n. A loft under the roof of a house, like a shelf. సామానులు ఉంచుటకై ఉండేటిది. "పతికుండుండెడు నట్టు కప్పై." S. iii. 179. A garret. Same as అటక.

అట్టువ *aṭṭuva.* [Tel.] n. Same as అటక and అట్టుక. "మరియొక్కని నట్టువమీద దాచి." G. xi. 44.

అట్టె See on అట్టే under అట్టు The final long vowel ē is sometimes shortened in metre.

అట్టెడ *aṭṭeḍa.* [Tel.] n. A sieve. తూర్పారపెట్టినధాన్యమును జల్లించే ఒక విధమైన జల్లెడ. A bridge. A part of a fort.

"అట్టెళ్లపైవారు, అట్నాలపైవారు,
కోటకొమ్మలకును జేరుచున్నవారు."
Pal. 461.

అత్థము *atthamu.* [Corrupted from Skt. అష్టకము.] A division of the Veda Ashtaka.

అట్నము *aṭnamu.* [Tel. Plu. అట్నాలు.] n. A tower. బురుజు. See. అట్టెడ.

అట్లు *aṭlu.* [Tel.] (adv.) So, as, according to. **అట్ల** *aṭla.* [Tel.] adv. Like, as. వాడు చెప్పినట్లు as he said. ఎప్పటియట్లు as usual. శత్రువులట్లు like enemies. తనయట్ల పంక్తివారును people like himself. **అట్లా** *aṭlā.* [Tel.] adv. So, thus. అట్లా చెప్పినాడు he said so. అట్లా ఉన్నది it is so. అట్లా పో go there. ఇట్లా రా come here. **అట్లాగంటి**, *aṭlaganṭi.* [Tel.] adj. Such. అలాగంటి, అలాటి. **అట్లాగా** or అలాగా. Is it so? **అట్లాగు** *aṭlāgu.* [Tel. from అట్లు+ఆగు.] adv. Thus, so. అట్లాగే just so, yes, very well, అలాగు. **అట్లాటి** *aṭlāṭi.* [Tel.] adj. Such, like this, like that అలాగంటి. అట్లైన if so.

అత్తావణీబంట్రోతు *atthavani-bantrōtu.* [H.] A revenue peon.

అత్వాడ *atthvāḍa.* [H.] A week, వారము. అత్వాడలెక్క a weekly account.

అడ *aḍa.* [Tel.] n. A lump, clot, mass (as of dates, sugar, hair, &c.) ముద్ద. చింతపండు అడలు lumps of tamarind. **అడకట్టు** or **అడగొను** to become clotted. ముద్దకట్టుకొను. తల అడలుకట్టెను the hair became matted, all the tresses are matted together. **అడచేయు** *aḍa-chēyu.* [Tel.] v. To knead and make into lump.

అడంగు *aḍangu.* [Tel.] n. Home. The original or starting place. ఉత్పత్తిస్థానము. అడంగు వెల cost price, prime cost. పట్టిన వెల, అసలు కరీదు, అయిన వెల.

అడకత్తి or అడకత్తు or అడకొత్తు *aḍakatti.* [Tel. from అడ్డ+కత్తి. lit. cross knife.] n. Nippers for cutting betel-nut.

అడకము *aḍakamu.* [Tel.] a. Included in. Which is contained in. లోపల నణగినది, అంతర్భూతము.

"నానామునీంద్ర బృందము మాయలెల్ల
హరిమాయలోపల నడకముల్."
విష్ణు. పూ. 1 ఆ.

అడకించు *aḍakintsu.* [Tel.] v. t. To laugh at. To scorn. To blame. అపహసించు.

వ॥ "పలికిననట్లయున్న దిదియు
పత్రికలోనడకించెదో నను."
త్రి. భా. 3 ఆ.

క॥ "అకట నీవు నన్ను నడకించిపోజాలె
జేసు మోసపోను." భో. 6 ఆ.

అడకువ or **అణకువ** *aḍakuva.* [Tel.] n. Submission, obedience, politeness, humility. వినయము.

అడగారు *aḍagāru.* [Tel.] v. i. Same as అడగు.

అడగించు *aḍagintsu.* [Tel.] v. a. To keep under, quell, depress, restrain, crush. అణచు, పోగొట్టు. రూపడగించు to slay, ruin, destroy. చంపు. "అరవిందములకొక్కట కడగించు జిగిపొమ్మనాయతంబగు కన్నుదోయితోడ." A. i. 13.

అడగు or **అడుగు** *adagu.* [Tel.] v. n. To sink, be depressed, humbled, abated. To be concealed. అణగు, నశించు, మట్టుపడు, దాగు. "క్షితివాలస్సృష్టిబుట్టి యడగెగా క్షితియందు జనీశ," A. iv. 30. "పొరువుదరువులు నీడల నడంగి." Swa. iii. 46.

అడగోలుకొను *ada-gōlu-konu.* [Tel. అడ+కోలు+కొను.] v. t. To rob.

ఇల్లడపొమ్ము
నడగోలుకొని త్రోచునదనికతిక. భో. 6 ఆ.

అడచిపడు or **అడిచిపడు** *adachipadu.* [Tel.] v. n. To be rash or precipitate. To bounce. ఆత్రపడు, మిట్టిపడు. "దైవోపపన్నంబు లైన కార్యంబులు సిద్ధింపాండుని యడచిపడువలదు విచారించుకొండవలయుటయు." M. X. ii. 43.

అడచు or **అడంచు** *adatsu.* [Tel.] (causative of అడగు.) v. To depress, humble, abate, quench. To ruin, destroy, kill, అణచు, వధించు, కొట్టు, నరుకు.

అడజడి *adazadi.* [Tel.] n. grief. అలజడి. దుఃఖము. అడజడిపెట్టు v. t. To grieve దుఃఖపరచు.

చ॥ నన్నడజడిపెట్టుమాట
యటులాడక గూడుచు
యీయకార్యముల్ విడువులతాంగి.
మార్క. i. ఆ.

అడతి *adati.* [Hindi అఢ్హత్.] n. Agency, commission, business done by an agent, consignment; అడతిదారుడు A broker, ఈ గని; agent.

అడదడి *adadadi.* [Tel.] n. Reign, rule. ఏలడము, ప్రభుత్వము. అయన అ. దేశమును అడదడిచేయుచుండెను he ruled the country. అడదడి or అడావడి ravage, riot. అల్లరి, దడబిడలు, దాడు. అడదడి చేయు to ravage. See అడావడి.

అడపకత్తె or **అడపకత్తియ** *adapa-katte.* [Tel. from అడపము.] n. A woman in waiting, who carries her mistress's betel nut pouch and serves it out. తాంబూలము మడిచియుచ్చే బోటికత్తె. "అడపకత్తియ యిచ్చు విడెము గైకొనగా" Satyabha. iii. 143. **అడ పకాడు** masculine of అడపకత్తె.

అడపట్టె *adapatte.* [Tel.] n. A board used for smoothing a ploughed field after the grain is sown: in effect corresponding with a roller. పొలములో విత్తనము విత్తి మిట్ట పల్లము లేకుండా సరదడమునకై యెద్దులకుకట్టి తోలే మాను, దిండు.

అడపతడప, or **అడపాతడపా** *adapa-tadapa.* [Tel.] adv. Now and then, occasionally. అప్పుడప్పుడు.

అడపము *adapamu.* [Tel.] n A pouch for betel-nut; a barber's case for razors. వక్కలాకుల సంచి, మంగలవానిపొది.

అడపర *adapara.* [Tel.] n. A lump, a clod. ముద్ద, అట్టు. అడపరగట్టు to become a lump.

అడపు *adapu.* [Tel.] v. To be held or contained. పట్టు. "పెడదలుగాగ విష్వచు బ్ర హేశ తటంబులనొగ్గి కోలనొల్లడపక వీపుచిప్ప తొగయుంబడి" Mandhat. vi. 151.

అడపు or **అడంపు** *adapu.* [Tel.] v. a. To depress, humble, abate, quench, ruin, destroy, smite. అణచు, నశింపచేయు, చంపు. "అడపుమాదైత్యుని." Swa. iv. 132.

అడపొడ or **అడాపొడ** *ada-poda.* [Tel.] n. Signs, traces. జాడ, ఆచూకి.

అడబాల *adabala.* [Tel.] n. A cook. వంట వాడు, వంటలక్క.

ద్వి. అడబాలకొనిపోయి యమ్మినుఁజెంది
కడుపులో కొకబాలుగని పెరగంది.
Bhag X.

అడమానము *adamanamu.* [Tam.] A mortgage. కుదువ, తాకట్టు (not used in pure Tel. Districts.)

అడరించు *adarintsu.* [Tel.] v To do, make, perform; to discharge a missile weapon, to shoot an arrow. చేయు, వేయు.

Also, to cause to fear. "ఘూర్ణప్రదక్షిణ మడరింపగబోయి యున్మహామహీరుహముండు పదంపడి." Vijaya Vil. ii. 173.

అడరు *adaru.* [Tel.] n. Grief, sorrow, fear విచారము. అడ రొందు to be afraid.

అడరు *adaru.* [Tel.] v. n. To arise, to issue, to come. To arise, as fear. To be fit or proper: to shine. పుట్టు, కలుగు, జనించు, వచ్చు; భయపడు; ఒప్పు, అతిశయించు, వ్యాపించు, ప్రకాశించు, వ్యాపించు. "అడరునవీన భానుకిరణావలమంటె." Swa. iii. 83. "ఇంపడరబ్రోచు గడప్పు." H. i. 89.

అడరుచు *adarutsu.* [Tel.] Same as అడరించు. Another form is అడర్చు.

అడరుదెంచు *adaru-dentsu.* [Tel.] Same as అడరు.

అడలించు *adalintsu.* [Tel.] v. a. To frighten, bully. To do, make, perform. అదలించు, గద్దించు. చేయు. "ఒండు రెండుగా వారదలించుకేటి నెరవాదితనంబది." P. iii. 205.

అడలు *adalu.* [Tel.] n. Grief, sorrow, misery, fear, terror. అంగద, చింత, విపత్తు. "మనంబునం బొడమియుండునడలు అప్పుడు తలంపునంబాసిన." Swa. vi. 11.

అడలు *adalu.* [Tel.] adj. Grieving, fearing. వ్యాకులపడే, భయపడే. "అడలు రతిమణిచందంబున." Swa. iii. 13.

అడలు *adalu.* [Tel.] v. n. To grieve, be in sorrow, be afraid. దుఃఖపడు, చింతించు, భయపడు, వ్యాకులపడు, బిగ్గరగా శోకము చేయు. "నను నిమువంబుగానక యున్న యూరెల్ల నరయుచు మజ్జనకుడెంతయడలు నొక్కొ." Swa. ii. 18.

అడలుకొను *adalu-konu.* [Tel.] v. i. To grieve, to be grieved. అడలు, శోకించు.

అడలుచు *adalutsu.* [Tel.] v. a. To daunt. భయపెట్టు.

అడవ *adava.* [Tel.] adj. Old, damaged. పాతదైన, బహుదినాలదైన. అడవసరుకులు old damaged goods. అడవ అప్పు a bad debt.

అడవి *adavi.* [Tel. from Skt. అటవి.] n. A forest, wilderness. కాననము. adj. Wild, of the forest, or desert. వనసంబంధమైన. (All wild species of plants or animals are distinguished by prefixing అడవి to their names. e. g., అడవికంద, అడవికాకర, అడవికోడి, అడవిచెరుకు, అడవిపంది, అడవిమామిడి, అడవిమేక, &c.) **అడవి అవిసె** *adavi-avise* [Tel.] n. A tree, the *Bauhinia parviflora.* **అడవి ఆముదపుచెట్టు** *adavi-āmudapu-chettu.* [Tel.] n. A shrub, *the Jatropha curcas.* కొండాముదపుచెట్టు. **అడవి కుక్క** *adavi-kukka.* [Tel.] n. The wild dog. **అడవికోడి** *adavi-kōdi.* [Tel.] n. The jungle fowl. **అడవిచిక్కుడు** *adavi chikkudu.* [Tel.] n. A kind of beans which grow wild. *Dolichos tetraspermus.* **అడవినెల్లికూరచెట్టు** *adavi-nellikūra-chettu.* [Tel.] n. A shrub, *croton repandum.* **అడవిబీర** *adavi-bira.* [Tel.] n. A plant, a sort of Ghosha with white flowers. **అడవిమల్లె** *adavi-malle.* [Tel.] n. *Jasminum angustifolium.* **అడవిమునగ** *adavi-munaga.* [Tel.] n. A plant, *Hedysarum sennoides.* **అడవి మొల్ల** *adavi-molla.* [Tel.] n. A sort of jasmine (*Jasminum auriculatum.*) Globe amaranth.

అడసట్టా *ada-satta.* [Kan.] n. Guess, conjecture. Valuation. An appraiser. అడసట్టాలెక్క. A rough estimate.

అడసాల *ada-sāla.* [Tel.] n. A cook house a cook room, kitchen. వంటయిల్లు.

అడాయించు *adāyintsu.* [Tel.] v.n. To stop, seize, arrest. నిలుపు, పట్టుకొను.

అడావడి or **అడావుడి.** *adāvadi.* (properly హడావడి) [Tel.] n. Confusion, uproar, fright, అల్లరి, దడదడలు. Same as అడదడి.

అడి *adi.* [Tel.] adj. Great, excessive; vain, useless. **అడిబీరపు** *adi-birapu.* [Tel.] adj. Excessively proud. "వదమువి భుజవిక్రమంబు వారలమనమె, పుడమివిన మొక్కలవి విననెయడిబీరపుతులబన గెలమనబె పాండవులకా." M. VII. iv. 171.

అడిగము *aḍigamu*. [Tel.] n. A load. ఎడ్ల మీదవేసే కట్లనులలో భేదము. H. v. iii.

అడిగర్ర *aḍi-garra*. [Tel. from అడుగు+కర్ర.] n. A sandal, a shoe. పాదుక. "పాద గణంబులకెల్ల నడిగర్రవనిన." L. viii. 57.

అడిగెండ్లు మలిగెండ్లు *aḍigenḍlu-maligenḍlu*. [Tel.] n. Little stones and dirt. రాయి, రవ్వ, నూక, నుచ్చు. "చేసిమలచి అడిగెండ్లు మలిగెండ్లు తినెనిమిడెదు కటికకేలవెల్ల." Vema. iii. 84.

అడిగొట్టు *aḍi-goṭṭu*. [Tel.] n. A mean fellow, a sly man.

అడిచిపడు *aḍichi-paḍu*. [Tel.] n. To be in a hurry, to be impatient. త్వరపడు. మిడిసిపడు. "దైవోపహతంబులగు కార్యంబులు సిద్ధింపొందునె యడిచిపడవలదు." M. X. ii. 43. "తడవోర్వక త్వరయమోర్వక తడుకేగిరమడచిపడిన కార్యంబుగునే." Sumati. 27.

అడిచిపాటు *aḍichi-pāṭu*. [Tel.] n. Haste, hurry. త్వర, అతిత్వర.

అడితి *aḍiti*. [Hindi.] n. Premium, commission. తరుగు. same as అడతి. (q. v).

అడిత్రాగుడు *aḍi-trāguḍu*. [Tel. from అడుగు+త్రాగుడు lit. "ask and drink"] n. Famine.

"అడిత్రాగుడునకి యుప్పటి
కడిదికి నేమాంసమైన గ్రక్కునగొనిరం,
కొదనేయుక."

సంచ. నా. 1 ఆ.

అడిదము *aḍidamu*. [Tel.] n. A sword. కత్తి. ఖడ్గము. "అడిదంబుఝళిపించి మెడమీదనైచిన." N. iv. 204. అడిదపుమెకము (Lit. the sword animal.) The rhinoceros.

అడిమె *aḍime*. [Tam.] n. A bond-man; a slave; slavery. దాసుడు, దాసత్వము.

అడియడు *aḍiyaḍu*. [Tel. from అడుగు+అడు. Lit. foot servant.] n. A Servant. పాదసేవకుడు.

సీ. "దండంబుదర్పితోద్దండరక్షో వార్త
కడియంద నారయోపాంబరుడను."

రుక్మాం. 1 ఆ.

అడియన్ *aḍiyan*. [Tam. A Vaishnavaite word.] A slave, a servant. దాసుడు, అడియేన్ I am (your) slave.

అడియరి *aḍiyari*. [Tel. అడుగు + అరి.] n. Servant. A Miser. లోభి.

"అటునటనితోడ నడియరితోడను
వెలకుసెట్టిమాడ వెరపుగాదు"

తి. వా. iii.

అడియరితనము service, slavery.

"ఇంకనడియరితనమున నప్పాండవుల
నాశ్రయింపగజాలనే సెక్కడేని"

భార. సౌప్తిక: i. 7.

అడియాలము *aḍi-yālamu*. [Tel. అడుగు+ఆలము. ఆలము, place.] n. A sign, mark, token. గురుతు, చిహ్నము. అడియాలముపట్టు to recognise. గురుతుపట్టు. "విరులుతోడి, గోడుగులు నడియాలంబులతోడి, సిడంబులు నైపం చుకొని." M. IV. v. 224.

అడియాస *aḍiyāsa*. [Tel.] n. Empty fancy or hope, vain desire. అందని కోరిక. వట్టి ఆశ, దురాశ. "ఆ పైడిమ్మగి మేండ అడియాసలేద." HD. i. 1023.

అడియొత్తులు *aḍi-yottulu*. [Tel.] n. Sandals. పాదుకలు.

"జన్ని దింబులుచిక్కు జడలను
బెట్టియడియొత్తునుంచి"

భాగ. 5 స్కం.

అడివి *aḍivi*. [Tel.] n. See అడవి.

అడిసాటా *aḍi-sāṭā*. [Hindi. అడితి+సాటా.] n. Commission, agency. తరుగుపేచను.

అడుకు *aḍuku*. [Tam.] n. A pile or heap, దొంతి. Also అటుకులు. (q. v.)

అడుగు *aḍugu*. [Tel.] n. The foot, the footstep, a pace, step, the bottom, basis. A foot in length containing twelve inches. A line of verse. Thus four "feet" make one stanza, or quatrain. చెట్టు అడుగు the foot of a tree. అడుగురాయి a stone at the bottom కొండ అడుగుననుండే ఊరు a village at the foot of a mountain. ఆ కథను అడుగునుండి చెప్పు tell the story from the beginning. కుండ అడుగు the bottom of a pot. అడుగంటకోయు to cut off by the root. అడుగుతో పెల్లగించు to eradicate, to root out. అడుగారిపోవు to be utterly ruined. నా మాటను అడుగుదాటకు do not transgress my command. వాని అడుగుల జాడ పట్టుకొని పోయినారు they traced his footsteps and followed him. అడుగడుగున or అడుగడుగునకు step by step, now and then, often. అన్నము అడుగంటినది the rice has burnt at the bottom of the pot.

అడుగు *adugu.* [Tel.] v. To ask, question, beg, solicit, demand. ఇమ్మను, ప్రశ్నచేయు. వారు మా పడుచును అడిగినారు they asked my daughter in marriage.

అడుగు or **అడుగుకొను** *adugu.* [Tel.] v. To beg. To entreat. వేడుకొను, బతిమాలు కొను. అడుగుకొని తిను v. n. To live by alms. తిరిపెమెత్తుకొని జీవించు.

అడుచు *adutsu.* [Tel.] v. n. To close, to shut. మూసివేయు. అందులో నాలుగు వాకిళ్లు అడిచివేయున్నవి four of the gates are closed, ఆ గుడ్డలను ఈ పెట్టెలో అడుచు (here అడుచు is for అణచు) cram the clothes into the box. Also, v. a. To beat, strike, thrash. To destroy కొట్టు, వశింపచేయు. "ఎమ్మెలిరి యుగ శిలతో నడిచిన." P. i. 729. **అడుచుకొను** *adutsukonu.* v. To contract, choke, be stopped. ఆ కాలువలో ఇసుక అడుచుకొన్నది the channel is choked with sand. వాని రొమ్మడుచుకొన్నది he has a contraction of the chest. గొంతు అడుచుకొన్నది, మాట్లాడకూడదలేదు his throat is hoarse, he cannot speak.

అడుపు *adupu.* [Tel.] n. A stroke, blow. దెబ్బ.

అడుసు *adusu.* [Tel.] n. Mire, mud, clay. బురద. ఆ వ్యవహారము అడుసులో నాటిన స్తంభముపలె నున్నది the matter is unsettled. (lit. like a post in a quagmire.)

అడ్డ *adda.* [Tel.] n. A dry measure equal to two manicas. రెండు మానికెలకొలది. సగము కుంచెము.

అడ్డంకి *addanki.* [Tel.] n. Hindrance, obstruction. ఆటంకము.

అడ్డగించు *addagintsu.* [Tel.] v. a. To stop, hinder, obstruct. ఆటంకముచేయు. **అడ్డగింత.** n. Obstacle.

అడ్డణము *addanamu.* [Skt.] n. A shield, buckler. డాలు.

అడ్డపట్టుబాల *addapattu-bala.* [Tel.] n. A child in arms; an infant. శిశువు. "అడ్డపట్టు బాలుడటవేయోయమ్మ." Sar. D. 369.

అడ్డమాడు *adda-madu.* [Tel.] v. n. To contradict. విరుద్ధముగా చెప్పు.

అడ్డము or **అడ్డమైన** *addamu.* [Tel.] adj. Cross. నన్ను అడ్డమైనమాటలు అడినాడు he reviled me. అడ్డమైనకూళ్లు any food that comes to the hand. నాకు అడ్డమైనపని పెట్టుచున్నాడు he employs me in anything that comes to hand. వాడు అడ్డత్రోవలు తొక్కుచున్నాడు he goes the wrong way to work. **అడ్డకట్ట** *adda-katta.* [Tel.] n. A dam or bank, an embankment. సేతువు, చేలకు నీళ్లు నిలిచేటందుకు కట్టిన గట్టు. **అడ్డకత్తి** *adda-katti.* A broad sword. పట్టిసము. **అడ్డకమ్మి** *adda-kammi.* A cross piece, the cross selvage in cloth. **అడ్డకర్ర** *adda-karra.* A cross-piece of timber: an obstacle: a bar. విఘాతము. నా పనికి అడ్డకర్రలు వేయుచున్నాడు he throws difficulties in my way. See అడ్డము. **అడ్డగోడ** *addagoda* a cross-wall. **అడ్డచాపు** *adda-tsapu.* A cross beam. అడ్డవాసము. **అడ్డతల** *adda-tala.* A narrow projecting head: having a narrow fore head. నిడుపు తల. **అడ్డదూలము**

aḍḍa-dūlamu. A cross beam. అడ్డదోవ aḍḍa-dōva. A crossway. అడ్డపలక aḍḍa-palaka. A cross plank. అడ్డపట్టె aḍḍa-paṭṭe. A thick board drawn by two oxen used for smoothing a ploughed field after the grain is sown. మడిసమముచేసే మాను. అడ్డపడు aḍḍa-paḍu. [Tel.] v. n. To interpose, to help; to obstruct, impede. విఘ్నముచేయు, వారించు. నా పనికి అడ్డ పడ్డాడు he threw obstacles in my way. భార్యను కొట్టబోతే కొడుకు అడ్డపడినాడు as he was going to strike his wife his son interposed. నేనడ్డపడకపోతే వాండ్లు చత్తురు had I not interposed they would have died. అడ్డపాటు aḍḍa-pāṭu. [Tel.] n. Obstacle, hindrance, obstruction. అడ్డి, విఘ్నము. అడ్డబాస aḍḍa-bāsa. n. A nose jewel. బులాకి. అడ్డబొట్టు aḍḍa-boṭṭu. A cross mark worn by the Hindus on their fore-head. అడ్డమాను aḍḍa-mānu. A cross bar. వాడు అడ్డవాట్లు వేస్తున్నాడు he throws impediments in the way.

అడ్డము aḍḍamu. [Tel.] n. Obstacle, hindrance, A screen. అభ్యంతరము, అటంకము, చాటు. A pledge తాకట్టు నీ మాటకు అడ్డము లేదు no one will resist you. వాండ్లకు మాకు గోడ అడ్డముగా ఉండినది there was a wall between them and us. ఒక నగను అడ్డముపెట్టి యిరువైరూపాయలు తెచ్చినాడు he pawned a jewel and got twenty rupees. నా పనికి అడ్డమువచ్చినాడు he opposed my endeavours. మొగుణ్ని అడ్డముపెట్టుకొని తానే అన్ని పనులు చూచుకొనిపోయినది she used her husband as a screen and carried on the business. వాడు తండ్రికి అడ్డమాడుతాడు he opposes or contradicts his father. తిరుపతికి పోయేలోగా మూడేర్లు అడ్డమువస్తవి there are three rivers to cross on the way to Tirupati. ఏదో ఒకటివచ్చి అడ్డమువచ్చినది something has got in the way. వానికి అడ్డము తగిలినారు they interrupted him. కొంతదూరము దోవనే పోయి అవతల అడ్డము తిరిగినాడు or అడ్డము తొ క్కినాడు he went along some way and then cut across. "శరాగ్రములు దృష్టులకడ్డమి డుచు." BD. iv. 1532. అడ్డముగా aḍḍamu-gā. [Tel.] adv. Crosswise, across, transversely. చెట్టు కండ్లకు అడ్డముగానున్నది the tree intercepts the view, నేను అడ్డముగా నిలిస్తిని I stood in his way.

అడ్డసరము or అడ్డసరపు చెట్టు aḍḍa-saramu. [Tadbhava from ఆటరూష.] n. A medicinal shrub. Adhatoda Vasica (E. P.)

అడ్డసాలెలు or అడ్డసాళ్లు aḍḍa-sāḷelu. [Tel.] n. plu. Dice. సొగటాల పాచికలు. "ఇవుడిచట పాసనసేయవి, మత్సాయకములడ్డసాళ్లే" M. VII. i. 337. "శకునినేతియడ్డసాలెలు గాపుగాండీ విముక్త బహుంపటిష్టబాణముల్." ib. VII. v.29.

అడ్డాదిడ్డి aḍḍa-diḍḍi. [Tel.] adj. Froward, perverse. అక్రమమైన. నన్ను అడ్డాదిడ్డిపనులకు పంపుతాడు he employs me on idle jobs. అడ్డాదిడ్డిమాటలు ఆడబోకు do not speak perversely.

అడ్డి aḍḍi. [Tel.] n. Delay, hindrance, obstacle, ఆటంకము. అడ్డిపడు to come in the way. అడ్డినేరము the crime of unlawful interference.

అడ్డిగలు aḍḍigalu. [Tel.] n. A jewel worn by women about the neck.

అడ్డు aḍḍu. [Tel.] v. To impede, obstruct. An obstacle. A screen. any thing that affords concealment. చాటు. అడ్డుగర్ర a cross bar; an obstacle. "నీ యడ్డుగర్రమాటల, కేయుడుబనియేమి!" రుక్మాం: v.

అడ్డుగ aḍḍuga. [Tel.] n. A two anna piece. బేడ.

అడ్డుగొను aḍḍu-gonu. [Tel.] v. To come in the way, to interpose. "అడ్డుగొనిపోకు దొరకు బ్రహ్మాస్త్రమనిరయు." అత్రే. యుద్ధకాండ.

అణక aṇaka. [Tel.] n. The act of bringing the yoke under the neck. అణకలు వేసి కొను v. n. To go wrong, turn restive, as a bullock which turns the wrong way in the yoke. ఎద్దుగాని గుర్రముగాని కాఁక కొదురు తిరుగు. "పెనఁగొండదనిచేతకాఁకలఁగట్టుఁబట్టి వా హంబు లనకలుకైదికొనియె." విక్ర. iv. 51. తిన్నగా నడకనీయక మాటిమాటికి అనకలు చేసి కొంటాడు instead of going on smoothly he now and then turns restive.

అణకువ *aṇakuva.* [Tel.] n. Modesty, politeness, humility, submission అడఁకువ.

అణఁగించు *aṇagintsu.* [Tel. Causative of అణఁగు.] v. a. To keep under, quell, repress. అణఁచు, పోఁగొట్టు.

అణఁగు *aṇagu.* [Tel.] v. n. To be suppressed, humbled, abated, quelled or calmed. To be ruined; to be concealed. వెల్లువిరుచు, శాంతించు, నశించు, దాఁగు. **అణఁగఁగొట్టు** *anga-goṭṭu.* [Tel.] v. a. To beat down, suppress, crush. Subdue, keep under, control. కుంగఁగొట్టు, శిక్షించుచేయు. **అణఁచు** or **అణుచు** *aṇatsu.* [Tel.] v. a. To depress, humble, abate, quench. To ruin, destroy. క్రిందికి అదుము, శాంతిపొం దించు, నశింపచేయు.

అణఁగారు *aṇa-gâru.* [Tel. from అణఁగు] v. n. To be extinguished, to be quelled, to subside. చల్లారు, అణఁగు, నశించు.

అణచడము *aṇatsaḍamu.* [Tel.] n. Compression. అదుముడము.

అణా *aṇâ.* [Tel.] An anna, the sixteenth part of a Rupee.

అణిమ *aṇima.* [Skt.] n. A mote. One of the supernatural faculties, extreme minuteness, invisibility, the subtle and invisible state assumable by a deity. అణుత్వము.

అణీయుఁడు *aṇiyuḍu.* [Skt.] n. One who is very small like an atom. అతిసూక్ష్మమైన వాఁడు. "అణుసమూహములకును నణీయుఁడవును." A. vi. 148.

అణుకుఁడు *aṇukuḍu.* [Skt.] n. A low man, అల్పుఁడు. A skilful man. నేర్పరి.

అణుజు *aṇuzu.* [Tel.] n. A kind of hawk. డేఁగ. "ఉడుపథిఁబోకున్న నొక్కట్రయుఁబాజా." Swa. iv. 84.

అణువు *aṇuvu.* [Skt.] n. An atom. లేశము Name of a grain, *Panicum Miliaceum.* నల్లవరి. **అణుత్వము** *aṇutvamu.* [Skt.] Atomic nature, minuteness. **అణుమాత్రము** *aṇumâtramu.* [Skt.] As small as an atom. **అణుజాలము** *aṇu-jâlamu.* [Skt.] A collection or multitude of atoms. **అణుమధ్య** a slender waisted girl. **అణువ్రీహి** *aṇuvrihi.* [Skt.] Name of a fine sort of rice. **అణ్వంతము** *aṇvantamu.* [Skt.] A hair splitting question.

అణ్యము or **అణ్ణెము.** *aṇyamu.* [Tel.] adv. (Sea term) Abaft, that is, behind. వెనుక.

అణ్యము *aṇyamu.* [Tel. An onomatopœic word.] n. అనుకరణపదము. అణ్యము పుణ్యము ఎరుఁగను I know neither good nor bad about it.

అతకరించు *atakarintsu.* [Skt.] v. a. To excel, surpass, transgress. మించు, అతిశ యించు, అతిక్రమించు. "ఇందువదనల మందగమన స్వభావంబు నతిక్రమించు కుటుకద్వయంబునకు ప్రతి కూలంబగుచు." KP. vi. 246.

అతఁడు or **అతను** *ataḍu.* [Tel.] pron. He, that man. అయన. అతనికతనే of himself. **అతగాఁడు** *atagâḍu.* [vulgar Tel.] pron. He, that fellow.

అతగుఁడు *ataguḍu.* [Tel.] n. A miserable creature, a poor wretch. బలహీనుఁడు, దీనుఁడు. "అతిగులచే ద్రుపదుఁడు బలవ్యాకులుఁడైపట్టు బడెఁగటె హీనుఁడై." M. vi. 7.

అతనుఁడు *atanuḍu.* [Skt.] n. The "bodiless," or incorporeal god, i. e., Cupid.

అతర్కణము *a-tarkaṇamu.* [Skt.] n. Transgression, wickedness. అతిక్రమము, దుర్మార్గము. [colloq.]

అతర్క్యము *a-tarkyamu.* [Skt.] adj. Incomprehensible, unsearchable. ఊహింపఁగూడని. "అవాఙ్మనోగోచరమతర్క్యమైనది." Lalito. vii. 27.

అతలము *atalamu.* [Skt.] n. One of the fabled subterraneous regions, supposed to be immediately below the earth. భూలోకము కిందిలోకము. **అతలకుతలము** n. Disorder, confusion. disturbance. అల్లరి, కలిబిలి, తారుమారు. **అతలకుతలమవు** v. n. To be routed, scattered, dispersed. కలిబిలియగు, తారుమారగు, చెదిరిపోవు. **అతలకుతలముచేయు** to make a bustle or great noise, to cause a tumult or confusion. **అతలకుతలముగా** adv. In confusion. అల్లరిగా.

అతలషు *atalashu.* [H.] Satin, formerly called in Europe "Atlas" or Damask. అతలషుకర్ర satin wood, or a sort of timber resembling mahogany.

అతసి *atasi.* [Skt.] n. Common flax: *Linum Usitatissimum;* also, a leguminous tree, the leaves of which are dressed and eaten. (*Coronilla grandiflora.*) అవిసెచెట్టు.

అతి *ati.* [Skt. prefix.] Over, beyond, exceeding, very much; extreme, vast. అధికమైన. A rhyme says అతిదానాద్ధతఃకర్ణః, అతిలోభాత్సుయోధనః, అతికామాద్దశగ్రీవః, అతి సర్వత్రవర్జయేత్. ఎందుకును అతి కారాదు excess is always hurtful.

అతికాయము *ati-kayamu.* [Skt.] n. A gigantic body అతికాయుడు a giant. మహాకాయుడు.

అతికించు *atikintsu.* [Tel.] v. To solder, cement, join, unite. అంటించు.

అతిక్రమము or **అతిక్రమణము** *atikramamu.* [Skt.] n. Transgression, wickedness. దుర్మార్గము. అతిక్రమముచేయు to transgress, to offend. **అతిక్రమించు** *atikramintsu.* [Tel.] v. To transgress, trespass, pass over, pass. ఉల్లంఘనముచేయు, గడుచు.

అతిచారము *ati-charamu.* [Skt.] Accelerated motion, especially of planets.

అతితిమింగిలము *ati-timingilamu* [Skt.] n. The craken or biggest of fish. మహాత్తరమైన చేప.

అతిథి *atithi.* [Skt. . a=not, and *tidhi*—day; hence lit. one who comes unexpectedly;] n. A guest, a stranger. పరగ్రామాగతుడు. అతిథిధర్మము title to hospitality. అతిథిపూజ or అతిథిసత్కారము welcoming a guest, showing respect to a guest by ministering to his wants. అతిథిసేవ attention paid to a guest, hospitality.

అతిదేశము *ati-dēsamu.* [Skt. Lit. making over.] n. Extended application, inference, analogy, substitution.

అతిమధురము *ati-madhuramu.* [Skt.] adj. Very delicious; delightful. నిండా రుచిగల, రమ్యమైన. **అతిమధురము** n. Liquorice, *Glycyrrhiza glabra* or the root of the Abrus precatorius which is used instead.

అతిమాత్ర *ati-matra.* [Skt.] n. A "pill too much," i. e., excess in medicine. అధికమైన మందు. వాడు యిప్పుడు నిండా అతిమాత్రగా నున్నాడు he has now gone wild. **అతిమాత్రము** *atimatramu.* [Skt.] adj. Exceeding; immoderate; excessive. మిక్కిలి, మిక్కుటమైన.

అతిముక్తము *ati-muktamu.* [Skt.] n. A creeping plant, *Gærtnera racemosa.* పుల్లగురివింద.

అతిరథుడు *ati-rathudu.* [Skt] n. A charioteer or warrior in a car. తేరుమీదనుండి అనేకులతో యుద్ధముచేయుటలో గట్టివాడు.

అతిరసము *ati-rasamu.* [Skt.] n. A sweet cake made of rice meal and sugar fried in ghee. పాకముపట్టిన బెల్లము పిండికలిపి నేతిలో పక్వముచేసిన భక్ష్యవిశేషము, అరిసెలు.

అతిరిక్తము *ati-riktamu.* [Skt.] adj Superabounding, excessive. Other, different. అత్యంతమైన, సమధికమైన, హెచ్చు అయిన, ఇతరమైన. అతిరిక్తగృహము the other house.

అతిరేకము *ati-rēkamu.* [Skt.] n. Excess ఆధిక్యము. కామాతిరేకము strong lust.

అతివ *ativa.* [Tel. from అతి+వాయి lit. one that has a big mouth.] n. A woman. ఆడుది.

అతివస *ati-vasa* [Skt. వస from విసం] *Aconitum heterophyllum* or the great sweet-flag. (E.P.)

అతివాసము *ati-vāsamu.* [Skt.] The fast observed on the day preceding the ceremony in which oblations are presented to the manes of departed ancestors. శ్రాద్ధమునకు ముందు ఒక్కపొద్దు ఉండేదినము.

అతివృష్టి *ati-vrishti.* [Skt.] n. Excess of rain. అధికవాన.

అతివేలము *ati-vēlamu.* [Skt.] adj. Much, excessive. మిక్కుటమైన.

అతిశయము *ati-sayamu.* [Skt.] adj. Much, excessive. (In Telugu) Marvellous, wonderful, uncommon. అత్యంతమైన, చోద్యమైన. **అతిశయము** n. Excellence, pre-eminence, pride. ఎక్కువ. ఇదియేమి అతిశయము what great matter is this. **అతిశయిల్లు** v. To be proud of. గర్వించు. **అతిశయించు** or **అతిశయిల్లు** v. To overmatch, surpass. To increase, become augmented. మించు, ఎక్కువ అగు. **అతిశయోక్తి** exaggeration, hyperbole.

అతిసంచయము *ati-sanchayamu.* [Skt.] n. Excessive accumulation of wealth. అతిసంచయేచ్ఛ a desire to hoard money too much.

అతిసారము *ati-sāramu.* [Skt.] n. Diarrhœa or dysentery. పాచనము. వాతాతిసారము a flatulent disease of this kind by which the belly is swollen. పిత్తాతిసారము bilious vomiting and purging. అతిసారము కనుపించు to have diarrhœa.

అతీంద్రియము *atīndriyamu.* [Skt.] adj. Imperceptible to the senses. అప్రత్యక్షమైన.

అతీతము *atītamu.* [Skt.] adj. Past, elapsed. గతమైన. కాలాతీతమైనది the time is gone by. లోకాతీతమైన extraordinary, wonderful. **అతీతుడు** n. He who has passed or gone over. గడిచినవాడు. Thus వేదాతీతుడు he who has perused the Vedas.

అతుకు *atuku.* [Tel.] n. Junction, union patch. జతపడినది. అతుకులబ్రతుకు living in another man's house. **అతుకు** v. n. To join. To agree with, to be fit. అంటుకొను. **అతుకు** or **అతికించు**, v. t. To solder, cement, join, unite to. అంటించు, చేర్చు, జతపరచు. **అతుకుబడి** fixing; posting; the engagement to cultivate taken from the ryot at the commencement of the Revenue year; leasing. అతుకుబడిచేయు to rent out. **అతుకుబాటు** giving or letting out on rent.

అతులము or **అతులితము** *a-tulamu.* [Skt.] adj. Unequalled, unparallelled, matchless. అసమానమైన. **అతులితుడు** *a-tulitudu.* [Skt.] n. He who is matchless. అసమానుడు.

అతుష్టి *a-tushti.* [Skt.] Discontent.

అతృప్తి *a-tripti.* [Skt.] Dissatisfaction.

అతృప్తుడు *a-triptudu* [Skt.] One who is not satisfied.

అత్త *atta.* [Tel. borrowed by Skt. in dramas.] n. Father's sister, mother-in-law, maternal uncle's wife. అత్తమామలు mother-in-law and father-in-law.

అత్తపత్తి *attapatti.* [Tel.] n. The sensitive plant. సిగ్గాకు.

అత్తమిల్లు *attamillu.* [Skt. from. అస్తమించు.] v. n. To sit down, lie down; to lean against. ఒరగు, కూర్చుండు, పరుండు. "పసుపు టాకుల గుత్తుల నత్తమిల్లు పిత్తాఫుల పుత్తడంబులు తాల్పుచుంటబుర్తై." S. iii. 436. "విదురుండు మణిపీఠంబునం గృష్ణునివెన్ను దనరచెదయొన్న దపీఠంబున నత్తమిల్లియుండె." M. V. iii. 253.

అత్తము *attamu.* [Tel.] n. A cluster or part of a bunch of plantains. అరటిపండ్ల గుత్తి.

అత్తరము *attaramu.* [Tel.] n. Haste. త్వర. R. viii. Another form of ఆత్రము.

అత్తరు *attaru.* [H.] Attar, or oil of roses. Perfume, Essence. సుగంధతైలము.

"అత్తరుగబ్బున వలచేపతీవు
మెత్తనిరాయిడు పేడనిగలవా?"

అత్తలము or **అర్తలము** *attalamu.* [Tel.] n. A short spear, a lance with a three sided point.. ఈటె, కొా. "కేతకాశ్వంబు మెలం పుచువింటున, వంత్రకోలలు నడిదంబున నత్తలంబున చేసియు ప్రేసియునడిచియుం జొడిచియు." Swa. iv. 167.

అత్తి *atti.* [Tel.] n. The glomerous fig tree, *ficus glomerata* or country figtree, *ficus racemosa.* మేడిచెట్టు. అత్తికాయ. its fruit. అత్తికల్లు the juice that flows from its root: This tree has no apparent blossoms; hence అత్తిమానుపూచినట్లు denotes "about as likely as milk from a stone.

అత్తు or పత్తు or **అత్తుకొను** *attu.* [Tel.] v. n. To be attached or joined. కూడుకొను. Also to happen. కలుగు. "అత్తిన కువృష్టివలనఁ గ్, విత్తు లకుం బొడమినట్టి విత్తులపోలెన్." పంచ. నా. 1 ఆ.

అత్తెము *attemu.* [Tel. from Skt. హస్తము] n. A hawk's jesses. డేగకాలిగోళ్లు చేతికి తగలకుండా కట్టుకొనే చర్మము, హస్తకవచము. "కనకోరపువల్లని దీర్ఘబాహువై హేలవాలంచె పోలెనిడియత్తెమునందల డెత్తిమాడుబల్ సాళువ మజా వడింబుకళంబుపయిజా విడిచెజా మహోగా ద్ధతిజా." Swa. iv. 82.

అత్తెసరు *attesaru.* [Tel. అత్తు+ఎసరు] n. Rice which has been boiled without having the water poured off.

అత్యంతము *aty-antamu.* [Skt.] adj. Excessive, very much. మిక్కిలి విశేషమైన. అత్యంత వినయపూర్వకముగా with profound respect. అత్యంతసుకుమారము very delicate. అత్యంతాభావము entire non-existence.

అత్యయము *atyayamu.* [Skt.] n. Distress, transgression. అతిక్రమము, దోషము. చేటు. Death, end. "చావు. వర్షాదివాత్యయము." A. iv. 206.

అత్యాశ *atyaṣa.* [Skt. అతి+ఆశ.] n. Covetousness.

అత్యుక్తి *atyukti.* [Skt. అతి+ఉక్తి.] n. Hyperbole.

అథవా *atthava.* [Skt.] adv. Or, or else. లేకుంటే, అట్లు కాకుంటే.

అదంత్రము or **అదంతరము** *adantramu.* [Corrupted from Skt. అతంత్రము] n. Instability, weakness. Dependence, helplessness. అస్థిరత, అస్వతంత్రము.

అడక *adaka.* [Tel.] n. An old shoe. శీర్ణ పాదరక్ష.

అడటు *adaṭu.* [Tel.] n. Pride, presumption, arrogance. గర్వము, పొగరు. "అడటుతో నీక పొడిచియుడటుగాంచెజా." DRY. ii. 1016

అడనబడన *adana-badana.* [Tel.] adv. Safely, without being hurt. Economically. చెక్కుచెదరకుండా, పొదుపుగా. "అంబునిధిత రమున కులాయంబుమర్చికొని కలంగుచు ౘట్టిభి త్రద్దుపెట్టి పాదిగ నేమరిపాటు లేకడనబడనకలచ బడకుండ నొండొంటి గలసికొనుచు." P. i. 616. "అండనబడనసేగూర్చి మాయయప్పదీర్చిపొమ్ము నీవన్న." Sankara H. iv. 37.

అడనము *adanamu.* [Tel.] n. Plenty, abundance. అధికము. **అడనము** adj. Exceeding, much, superior, great, excessive. అధికమైన.

అదను *adanu.* [Tel.] n. An opportunity, season, critical point of time. సమయము. "చెరుపనదనుచూచి." A. iv. 292.

అదభ్రము *adabhramu.* [Skt.] adj. Much, many. విస్తారమైన, మెండు.

అదమాయించు *adamāyintsu.* [Tel.] To reprimand, to admonish. గద్దించు.

అదయత *a-dayata.* [Skt.] n. Unkindness.

అదయుడు *a-dayudu.* [Skt.] n. A cruel man, a merciless man. నిర్దయాత్మకుడు, క్రూరుడు.

అదరు or **అదురు** *adaru.* [Tel.] v. n. To tremble, shake, quake, shiver. To dread. కంపించు, భయపడు. భూమి అదురుచున్నది the earth trembles. దాన్ని చూడగానే వాని గుండెలు అదిరినవి his heart quivered to see this. కుడికన్ను అదురుతున్నది my right eye tingles. వాడు నట్టి అదురుగుండె he is a coward. **అదరు** or **అదురు** n. Concussion, shaking, tremour, trembling, fear, కంపనము, చలనము, కొట్టుకొనడము, భయము. భూమి అదురు a tremour or convulsion of the earth. వానికి తండ్రివద్ద కొంచెము అదురు ఉండవలెను he ought to fear his father. **అదరుగడ** or **అదురుగడ** *adarugada.* [Tel.] n. Daunting, fright. బెదురు. **అదరిపడు** or **అదిరిపడు** *adari-padu.* [Tel.] v. n. To caper about, to curvet. ఉలికిపడు. to be arrogant. **అదరిపాటు** n. Pride. అదరిపాటున adv. Suddenly, unexpectedly. ఏమరిపాటున. "అదరిపాటున వారాశిరయుడుటు చూచి." N. i. 126.

అదలించు or **అదల్చు** *adalintsu.* [Tel.] v. To frighten, menace, rebuke, reprove. బెదిరించు, గద్దించు. "అర్భకుల్ తనదూడనదలించ పాలుమ్మనివలంద కొమ్ములగుమ్మ." N. x. 37. **అదలుపు** or **అదల్పు** n. Menace, threatening. బెదిరింపు, గద్దింపు.

అదవ or **అదువ** *adava.* [Tel.] n. Rent. అద్దె. అదవయిల్లు a house that is hired. వాడు అదవసేద్యము చేస్తున్నాడు he cultivates a rented field.

అదవద *adavada.* [Tel.] n. Confusion, grief; affliction. కలత, దుఃఖము, వ్యాకులము. "ఎందు నున్నను తెత్తునియ్యుండుమదన నదననముజాడుమద వదవదలియుధిప." R. v. 276. **అదవదపడు** v. n. To be in grief, be sorrowful, be troubled. కొందలమందు, విచారపడు, వ్యాకులపడు. "వదవదరాఘవ విలువిలు, మదవదవదవలు దుదశరథాధిపతీకుల." R. iv. 15.

అదాచేయు same as అదాపరుచు.

అదాటుగా or **అదాటున** *adāṭu-gā.* [Tel.] adv. Suddenly, unexpectedly. అకస్మాత్తుగా.

అదాపరుచు or **అదాచేయు** *adā-parutsu.* [H.] v. t. To perform, pay, discharge. అచరించు, తీర్చు, చెల్లించు.

అదాలతు *adālatu.* [H.] Justice, equity. A court of justice. న్యాయము, న్యాయసభ.

అదావత్ *adāvat.* [H.] Enmity, hatred, spite. కార్పణ్యము, చలము.

అది *adi.* [Tel.] Pron. She, it, that. (Genitive దాని, accusative దానిని, Dative దానికి.) అదిమొదలు, or అదిమొదలుగా from that time, ever since. అదివరకు until then, then, as far as that. **అదిగో** or **అదుగో** there! look! lo! behold! to be sure! అదిగాక adv. Besides which. అదిగాన adv. Therefore.

అదీనుడు *a-dīnuḍu.* [Skt.] One who is not poor in spirit.

అదుగో See under అది.

అదుము *adumu.* [Tel.] v. a. To press, squeeze. అణచు. దానిని అదిమి పట్టుకో press it and hold it firmly. **అదముడము** n. Compression. **అదుముడు** n. Squeezing, pressing down. ఒత్తడము.

అదురు *aduru.* [Tel.] v. and n. See అదరు.

అదురువేటు *aduru-vēṭu.* [Tel.] n. A large gun-rocket, fired in processions. పెట్లబిమ్మె.

అదువ *aduva.* [Tel.] adj. Unstable, shifting. అస్థిరము.

అదృశ్యత *a-driśyata.* [Skt.] n. Invisibility. అగుపడమి. అయన అదృశ్యతను పొందినాడు

he disappeared or vanished. అదృశ్యము *a-drisyamu.* [Skt.] adj. Invisible. అగపడని. అదృశ్యుడు *a-drisyudu.* [Skt.] n. One who has disappeared or vanished.

అదృష్టము *a-drishṭamu.* [Skt.] n. Fortune, luck, chance, fate. భాగ్యము. దురదృష్టము bad luck. అదృష్టవంతుడు or అదృష్టశాలి or అదృష్టపురుషుడు a fortunate man. అదృష్టహీనుడు an unfortunate man. అదృష్టఫలము the consequence of (one's) good luck.

అదేవుడు *a-dēvuḍu.* [Skt.] One who is not a god; a godless man. నిరీశ్వరుడు.

అద్ద *adda.* [from Skt. అర్ధ] adj. Half. సగము. అద్దగోడ. a wall that serves as a screen. అద్దరూపాయి a half rupee. అద్దమణుగు a half maund. అద్దపావులా a two anna piece. అద్దమరేయి *addama-rēyi.* n. Midnight. అర్ధరాత్రము, నిశీథి. "అద్ద మరేయద్దానను." A. vi. 10. In revenue phrase, అద్ద means an incomplete heap. Also, a stamp or seal. పట్టిముద్ర. అద్దలవాడు he who stamps or marks the salt heaps. A marker or stamper. Also, a salt manufacturer. ముద్రమనిషి, ఉప్పుచేసేవాడు. అద్ద n. A dry measure, half of a "sola." A small heap of straw not yet thrashed. అర్థసోల, నూర్పుకుండా చేసిన చిన్నకుప్ప.

అద్దకము *addakamu.* [Tel. from అద్దు.] n. Chintz-printing; dyeing with colour. రాతవన్నె. అద్దకపుబట్ట a dyed cloth. వాని అద్దకము మంచిదికాదు his dyeing is not good.

అద్దము *addamu.* [Tel.] n. A mirror, a pane of glass. అద్దాలు or కంటియద్దాలు spectacles. అద్దాలతలుపు a glass door. అద్దాలరవిక a spangled jacket. అద్దపుపోసిలి the fee for the looking glass, a certain allowance of grain granted to the village barber as remuneration for his services.

అద్దించు *addintsu.* [Tel. causal form of అద్దు.] To get dipped or stained, to have a cloth dyed, &c. అద్దకట్టుచేయు. మైనములో అద్దించినగుడ్డ or మైనపుగుడ్డ wax cloth.

అద్దికము *addikamu.* [Tel.] n. Protection, custody. కావలి, రక్షణము.

"వాటివాటిలోనింతకాటోటుచేసి,
యటువమటెంచక యుండలైయద్దికముగ,
నేవదియుగాడుదిక్కానుతెల్పుడుమాకు
జాగిలంబులుకుమ్మమాసామికావ."

పా. i.

అద్దికె [Tel. from అద్ద rent.] Mortgage. తాకట్టు. అద్దికెభూమి mortgaged land. (Cuddapa).

అద్దిర or అదిర *addira.* [Tel. అది+ర] Interj. What a wonder! Wonderful! అద్దిరపాటున *addirapaṭuna.* adv. Suddenly, unexpectedly. అదాటున. "అనిలిలపోయువాని బాలు నద్దిరపాటునజూచి విస్మయంబునుపమరీలదాట్టెన." S. iii. 543. అద్దిరయ్య interj. Bravo! excellent! శాబాసు. "చెప్పక చెప్పెడు నద్దిరయ్యనా కెరుగదరంబెమీమహిమ." Swa. i. 35.

అద్దు *addu.* [Tel.] v. a. To press gently. To dip, to print with colours. ముంచు. "ఇద్ధంబుగా గాలనద్దును నిటునద్దును మాతింకన వ్యథాశేదు." BD. v. 319. సిరా అద్దుము blot the ink. కండ్లను అద్దుకొనుము press it to the eyes as a mark of respect. అద్దుముద్దు n. Sport, play. బిడ్డయొక్క చేష్టలు. ఆ బిడ్డయొక్క అద్దుముద్దు చూడక చచ్చినాడు he died without seeing the child play.

అద్దె *adde.* [Tel.] n. Rent, hire. బాడుగ. అద్దెకు కాపురముండు to dwell in a house for rent. అద్దెకు తీసికొను to hire. అద్దెకు ఇచ్చు to let out. అద్దెచీటి a written agreement to pay rent, a rent bill. అద్దెయిల్లు a rented house.

అద్భుతము *adbhutamu* Skt. n. Marvel, wonder. విస్మయము. **అద్భుతము** adj. Amazing, surprising. ఆశ్చర్యకరమైన. **అద్భుతక్రియ** a wonderful deed, miracle.

అద్రవము *a-dravamu.* [Skt.] Not liquid.

అద్రి *adri.* [Skt.] n. A mountain. పర్వతము. అద్రికాకము n. A hill crow, కొండకాకి. అద్రిజ or అద్రితనయ=Pārvati అద్రిరాజము n. The king of mountains, i. e., the Himalayas. హిమపర్వతము.

అద్రు for అదురు.

అద్వంద్వుడు *a-dvandvuḍu.* [Skt.] n. A philosopher, i. e., he who despises the pairs of opposites, such as heat and cold, good and evil, pleasure and pain, &c. నిస్సంగుడు. "అందుండుఁ ద్వయసక్త సద్మవదనుండద్వంద్వుడ క్రాంతిరోగాంధూబద్ధ మధుద్విషద్వరదుడ స్వర్గాభిధానుండు." A. i. 77."

అద్వితీయము *a-dvitīyamu.* [Skt.] adj. Unparalleled, unequalled. అసమానమైన.

అద్వైతము *a-dvaitamu.* [Skt.] n. Non-duality. The doctrine of the identity of the human soul with the divine essence of the Deity and the universe. జీవేశ్వరులకు అభేదమును చెప్పేమతము. **అద్వైతి** n. One that maintains the Advaita doctrine.

అధఃకరించు *adhah-karintsu.* [Skt.] v. a. To treat with disrespect. తక్కువపరుచు; క్రిందుపరుచు. **అధఃకారము** n. The act of looking down on one. హీనపరచడము. **అధఃకారి** *adhahkari.* [Skt.] n. He who defies or outrivals. తక్కువపరిచేవాడు.

అధనుడు *a-dhanuḍu.* [Skt.] One who has no wealth; a poor man. నిర్ధనుడు.

అధమము *adhamamu.* [Skt.] adj. Inferior; vile, low, despicable. నీచమైన. అధమం సేవకావృత్తిః servitude is the meanest work. **నరాధములు** the vilest of men. **అధమాంగము**,= the lowest member of the body, the foot. **అధమత్వము** n. Inferiority, vileness. నీచత్వము. **అధమాధమము** adj. The basest, the worst, the lowest of the low. అతినీచమైన. **అధమాధముడు** n. He who is the meanest of the mean, or basest of the base. మిక్కిలి నీచుడు. **అధముడు** *adhamuḍu.* n. A low fellow. నీచుడు.

అధమర్ణుడు *adhamarṇuḍu.* [Skt.] n. A debtor. అప్పుపడ్డవాడు. ఉత్తమర్ణుడు a creditor. అప్పిచ్చువాడు (from ఋణము a debt.)

అధరము *adharamu.* [Skt.] n. Lip. పెదవి. The underlip. క్రిందిపెదవి. అధరమధువు the honey of the lip. **అధరము** adj. Low, inferior, vile. దిగువైన, నీచమైన. Lower. "ప్రతతోర్ధ్వాధరభాగపీఠయుగళీ భాస్వత్త్రిసంధి సంస్థితి." Amuk. i. 6.

అధర్మము *a-dharmamu.* [Skt.] n. Injustice, unrighteousness, every thing unscriptural or contrary to principles. అన్యాయము, అనాచారము. **అధర్మపరులు** wicked persons.

అధర్వణకారిక *adharvaṇa-kārika.* [Skt.] n. The name of a certain grammatical treatise written in Sanscrit, regarding Telugu, of which only some fragments remain.

అధర్వవేదము The *Atharva-Vēda.*

అథవా *adhavā.* [Skt.] adv. Or, otherwise. అట్లాకాకుంటే. Same as అథవా.

అధార్మికుడు *a-dhārmikuḍu.* [Skt.] n. One who does not generally give alms.

అధికము *adhikamu.* [Skt.] n. Superiority, greatness. విస్తారము, ఎచ్చు, ఎక్కువ. అందులో ఏమి అధికము what superiority has it? నేను అధికాని కాశపడలేదు I am not greedy. **అధికము** adj. Great, much, excessive, ఎక్కువైన, శ్రేష్ఠమైన, మిక్కుటమైన. **అధికముచేయు**, **అధికపరచు** to increase, augment. ఎచ్చుచేయు. అధికప్రసంగము n. Meddling, officious interposition, impertinence, తనదికానిజోలి. అధికప్రసంగముగా officiously, impertinently. అధికప్రసంగి n. An impertinent fellow. అధికమాసము n. An intercalary month, i. e., an extra month inserted in particular years (like leap years;) the intercalary month precedes the month that bears the same name. ఒక సంవత్సరిములోనే రెట్టింపుగావచ్చే నెల. అధికుడు *adhikuḍu*. [Skt.] n. Superior. ఎచ్చుగానుండేవాడు, దొడ్డవాడు.

అధికరణము *adhi-karaṇamu*. [Skt.] n. Support. ఆధారము. In metaphysics, a substratum, a category; in grammar, government, the dependence of words in a sentence, which agree together. అధికరించు *adhikarintsu*. [Skt.] v. a. and v. n. To excel, surmount, increase. పొడుగగు, ఎచ్చు, అతిశయించు. ఆ పాప మధికరించుచున్నది that vice is on the increase. అధికరించు v. a. (colloq.) To study, acquire a science. చదువు.

అధికారము *adhi-kāramu*. [Skt.] n. Authority, government, power, dominion. దొరతనము, బాధ్యత, అధికారమిచ్చు to invest with power, authorize, empower. అధికారముచేయు to exercise authority. అధికారచ్యుతుడు he who has fallen from office or power. అధికారస్థుడు n. One in power or authority. అధికారి n. A governor, a ruler, one in power or authority. The master of a science, he who has the command of it. దొర, ఏలేవాడు, పరిపాలకుడు. ఈ సొత్తుకు అధికారి యెవడు who is the owner of this property? వాడు పూర్ణాధికారి he has full powers. అధికారితో విరోధము కారాదు it is not proper to be on bad terms with one who is in authority.

అధిక్షేపించు *adhi-kshēpintsu*. [Skt.] v. t. To blame, to frighten, to threaten. అధిక్షేపము n. Act of blaming or finding fault with.

అధిగతము *adhi-gatamu*. [Skt.] adj. Known, found, acquired, obtained, gone through or over, perused, read, studied. అవగతమైన, ప్రాప్తమైన, చదవబడిన.

అధిగమించు *adhi-gamintsu*. [Skt.] v. a. To obtain, attain, assume, to perceive, go through, go over. పొందు, గ్రహించు, చొరబడు, చదువు. "అట్లకాలని మునిచేసమధిగమించె." R. v. 259. "అవటపర్వంబునందుండి యచ్యుతుం డఖిలభూతంబుల నధిగమించి, భువనప్రపంచంబు పుట్టింపమదిగోర." Padma. vi. 20. అధిగమము *adhi-gamamu*. [Skt.] Attainment, acquisition.

అధిజ్యము *adhijyamu*. [Skt.] adj. Strung, as a bow. ఎక్కుపెట్టబడ్డ, అల్లెగల.

అధిత్యక *adhityaka*. [Skt.] n. Uplands. Heights. పర్వతోర్ధ్వభూమి.

అధిదేవత *adhi-dēvata*. [Skt.] A presiding or tutelary deity.

అధిపతి *adhi-pati*. [Skt.] n. A ruler, lord, master, owner. ఏలేవాడు, ప్రభువు.

అధిపుడు *adhipuḍu*. [Skt.] n. Lord, ruler, master. ఏలిక.

అధిరథుడు *adhi-rathuḍu*. [Skt.] A charioteer. One who is mounted on a car.

అధిరాజు *adhi-rāju*. [Skt.] An over-lord. రాజాధిరాజు King of kings.

అధిరోహించు *adhi-rōhintsu*. [Skt.] v. i. To mount up, to ascend, go up as a ladder. అధిరోహణము same as ఆరోహణము. అధిరోహిణి *adhi-rōhiṇi*. [Skt.] n. A ladder. నిచ్చెన.

అధివసించు *adhi-vasintsu*. [Skt.] v. n. To dwell. కాపురము ఉండు. అధివాసము n. An abode. ఉనికిపట్టు.

అధిష్ఠించు *adhi-shthintsu.* [Skt.] v. n. To reside, be in. ఆశ్రయించి ఉండు, ఆవహించి ఉండు. అధిష్ఠానము *adhi-shthānamu.* [Skt.] n. Abode, residence, residing in. The place of abode. ఆశ్రయించి ఉండడము, ఉనికిపట్టు. అధిష్ఠానదేవత n. a tutelary or guardian deity, a presiding deity. విద్యాధిష్ఠానదేవత n. the patron of learning. అధిష్ఠాత n. One who takes up a residence.

అధీతము *adhītamu.* [Skt.] adj. Studied. చదివిన. అధీతి or అధీతుడు n. He who has read or studied the Vedas. వేదములను చదివినవాడు. అనధీతుడు n. He who is unlearned in or ignorant of the Vedas.

అధీనము *adhīnamu.* [Skt.] adj. Dependent on, subject to, subservient. పరాధీనమైన, విధేయమైన. అధీనత *adhīnata.* [Skt.] Subjection, dependence. అధీనము n. Possession, power, charge, control, authority. స్వాధీనము, అధికారము. అది నా అధీనములో లేదు it is not in my possession. నా అధీనములోనుండేవారు those who are under my control. నాన్ని నీ అధీనము చేసినాను I have committed it to you.

అధీరత *a-dhīrata.* [Skt.] Absence of self command, cowardice. అధీరము adj. Cowardly, confused ధైర్యములేని, చంచలమైన.

అధీశ్వరుడు *adhīsvarudu.* [Skt.] A supreme lord.

అధునాతన *adhunātana* [Skt.] Of the present time. అధునాతనకవులు Living or contemporary poets.

అధృతి *a-dhriti.* [Skt.] Want of firmness.

అధైర్యము *a-dhairyamu.* [Skt.] n. Absence of courage. Cowardice. పిరికితనము. అధైర్యపడు to be afraid.

అధోక్షజుడు *adhōkshajudu.* [Skt.] n. A name of Vishnu.

అధోగతి *adhō-gati* [Skt.] n. A low state. Perdition, utter destruction. తక్కువస్థితి, నాశము. అధోగతుడు a ruined man. తక్కువస్థితిని పొందినవాడు.

అధోదృష్టి [Skt.] n. downward look; a down cast look.

అధోభాగము [Skt.] n. The lower side.

అధోముఖము *adhō-mukhamu.* [Skt.] n. The face turned downwards: a downcast countenance. క్రింది వైపుకు తిరిగియుండే మొగము. అధోముఖముగా adv. With the face turned downwards, with a downcast countenance; headlong. తలక్రిందుగా, తలక్రిందుగా. దివటీని అధోముఖముగా పట్టినాడు he held the torch with the flame downwards. అధోముఖుడు [Skt.] n. He who is downcast, ashamed or crestfallen. అతడు అధోముఖుడై ఉండెను he hung his head.

అధోలోకము [Skt.] n. The lower or nether world. పాతాళలోకము.

అధ్యక్షుడు *adhyakshudu.* [Skt.] n. A superintendent, an overseer. A bishop పైవిచారణచేయువాడు, అధికారి. అధ్యక్షత *adhyakshata.* [Skt.] n Superintendence, sway అధికారము.

అధ్యయనము *adhyayanamu.* [Skt.] n. Study, reading, especially of the sacred books. గురుముఖముపూర్వకశ్రవణము, పఠనము, The word అధ్యయనము is commonly used for the study of the Vedas or for the Veda itself thus: ఆ చిన్నవాడు నాలుగేండ్లనుండి అధ్యయనము చేయుచున్నాడు the boy has been studying the Veda for four years. నాకు అధ్యయనము రాదు I have not studied the Vedas.

అధ్యవసాయము *adhyavasāyamu.* [Skt.] n Perseverance, devotedness. ఉత్సాహము, ప్రయత్నము, పట్టు, పూనిక, శ్రద్ధ. In rhetoric, concise and forcible language.

అధ్యాత్మము *adhyatmamu.* [Skt.] n. The soul; individuated spirit or that which belongs to, and presides over the body.

The supreme spirit. జీవాత్మ, పరమాత్మ Also, Knowledge. జ్ఞానము. అధ్యాత్మ adj. Spiritual, belonging to spirit, inherent. ఆత్మసంబంధమైన. అధ్యాత్మజ్ఞానము knowledge of the Supreme spirit. అధ్యాత్మరామాయణము Ramayana explained as an allegory relating to the Supreme spirit. ఆధ్యాత్మికము or అధ్యాత్మికము adj. relating to the soul, spiritual.

అధ్యాపనము *adhyāpanamu.* [Skt.] n. Instruction in sacred knowledge. **అధ్యాపకుడు** *adhyāpakudu.* [Skt.] n. A teacher, one who instructs in the sacred books. వేదములను నేర్పువాడు.

అధ్యాయము *adhyāyamu* [Skt.] n. A chapter, a section. ప్రకరణము. Reading. "సహాధ్యాయుడు" fellow student. Bhar. Adi. i. 25.

అధ్యాహారము *adhyāhāramu.* [Skt.] n. Adding a word or words to complete a sentence, supplying an ellipsis. లోపముగా నుండేచోట ఒకటి రెండు మాటలను తెచ్చుకోవడము. **అధ్యాహృతము** *adhyāhritamu.* [Skt.] Supplied as an elliptical word.

అధ్వము *adhvamu.* [Skt.] n. Road, way, path. మార్గము. **అధ్వగుడు** n. A traveller. దారిని నడిచేవాడు, బాటసారి. అధ్వగభోగ్యము "The Traveller's Tree." The *Spondias Mangifera.* అధ్వగామి a traveller. **అధ్వాధిపుడు** protector of travellers, a police officer on the public roads. అధ్వరథము a travelling car. **అధ్వపతి** in astron. lord of the orbits, i. e., of the Zodiac.

అధ్వరము *adhvaramu.* [Skt.] n. A sacrifice. యజ్ఞము. "అధ్వరవైకల్య మరయుచుండు బ్రహ్మరాక్షసకోటి." భాస్క.: రామా: బాల. 99. **అధ్వర్యుడు** n. A Bramin versed in the Yajur Veda; యజుర్వేదకర్త; the officiating priest at a sacrifice whose duty it is to measure the ground, build the altar, prepare the sacrificial vessels, fetch wood and water, light the fire, bring and immolate the animal. For a description of the sacrifice, *vide* భాస్క. రామా. బాల 114. అధ్వర్యవేదము=యజుర్వేదము.

అధ్వానము *adhvānamu.* [Skt.] n. Desolation, waste, ruin. పాడు. ఆ రూకలను అధ్వానముగా చేసినాడు he wasted the money. అధ్వానముచేయు to ruin, lay waste. అధ్వానమగు to turn to nothing, to become waste. అధ్వానమైనచోటు a waste place. అధ్వానమైన పుస్తకము a bad book, a perplexing book. అరవము అధ్వానము Tamil is a perplexing language. అధ్వానపు అడవి a pathless forest. అధ్వానపుబయలు an open waste. అధ్వానపుజ్వరము a wasting fever. అధ్వానపువాన a troublesome shower; annoying rain.

అన్ *an.* [Tel.] (Aorist p|| of అను to say) Saying. అనే. "బలియన్ దనుజాతుడు" N. il. 501. "కృపయాభోక్తృత్వమున్ పల్కులున్" A. i. 43.

అన *ana.* [Tel.] n. A bank, or dam. అడ్డకట్ట. అనకట్ట. Also, a pliable tender twig:

> క|| "అనలుంగొనలుంబారుచు
> మనమునవాకొర్కి తీగముగుపకుమిగులన్."
> K. P. vi. 126.

అనలుంగొనలుంబారు or అనలుకొనలుగా నుండు to bloom, flourish. తామరదంపరై పెరుగు, కోమలముగా పెరుగు.

అనంగీకారము *an-angīkāramu.* [Skt.] n. Disapprobation, disagreement. అసమ్మతి.

అనంగుడు *an-angudu.* [Skt.] n. The incorporeal one, an epithet of Cupid. మన్మథుడు. అనంగలేఖ a love letter.

అనంటి *ananṭi.* [Tel. pl. అనంటులు] n. A plantain tree. అనటి or అరటిచెట్టు.

అనంతము *an-antamu.* [Skt.] adj. Endless, eternal అంతములేని. **అనంతము** n. The sky.

ఆకాశము. **అనంతత** endlessness; infinitude. **అనంతరాశి** *ananta-rāṣi.* [Skt.] An infinite quantity. **అనంతవిజయము** n. The name of the conch or shell of Dharmaraja. **అనంతవ్రతము** *ananta-vratamu.* [Skt.] A vow or festival observed in honor of Ananta. (Vishnu.) **అనంతశక్తి** *ananta-ṣakti.* [Skt.] n. Omnipotence, boundless strength or power. **అనంతుడు** *an-antudu.* [Skt.] n. The infinite being, an epithet of Vishnu. A name of the great dragon, the king of serpents విష్ణువు, ఆదిశేషుడు. **అనంతశయనుడు** *ananta-sayanudu.* [Skt.] n. An epithet of Vishnu, (lit.) the god whose couch is the king of serpents. విష్ణువు. **అనంత్యము** *an-antyamu.* [Skt.]. adv. Eternally for ever and ever.

అనంతరము *an-antaramu.* [Skt. lit. without interval.] adj. Next, immediately following; in the next place. అనతిరి, వ్యవధాన ములేని. **అనంతరము** adv. Afterwards, after. తరువాత.

అనంతరాయము *an-antarāyamu.* [Skt.] adv. Without a break in the middle.

అనకట్ట or **అనగట్టు** *ana-katto.* [Tel.] n. A bank, or dam. Anicut. కట్ట.

అనగత్యము *an-agatyamu.* [Skt.] adj. Not wanted, unnecessary. See అనవశ్యము.

అనగు *anagu.* [Tel.] v. n. To unite with; to obey. **అనగిపెనగియుండు** *anagi-penagi-yundu.* v. n. To be familiar, easy, affable. కలియుగలుపుగానుండు. "అట్టిజగజంతకే గాని యనగిపెనగియుండుదువెనీవు నూబోంట్ల రొద్దజేరి." N. ix. 393.

అనఘము *an-aghamu.* [Skt.] n. Sinlessness. పాపములేమి. **అనఘుడు** *an-aghudu.* [Skt.] n. He who is sinless. పాపములేని వాడు, నిర్దోషి.

అనటి or **అనంటి** *anaṭi.* [Tel.] n. A plantain tree. అరటిచెట్టు. H. iv. 180.

అనడ్వాహము *ana-dvahamu.* [Skt. Ox, వృషభము.

అనతి *an-ati.* [Skt. neg. అన్+అతి prefix] adj. Not much, not excessive. మట్టుగా నుండే, కొద్దిపాటిగానుండే. **అనతిదూరము** not very distant, near.

అనద *anada.* [from Skt. అనాథ] n. She who is without a master or protector, without a husband. A rake or worthless fellow. అల్పుడు. adj. Destitute, wretched, abject. దిక్కులేనిది, మొగుడులేనిది.

అనధికారము *an-adhikāramu.* [Skt.] Absence of authority. అనధికారచర్య meddlesomeness, officiousness.

అనన్యము *an-anyamu.* [Skt.] adj. One, sole, without any other, same, identical. ఏకమైన, అనితరమైన, అదే. అనన్యవిషయము exclusively applicable. **అనన్యగతికుడు** n. He who has only one refuge or asylum. వేరేగతిలేనివాడు. **అనన్యాదృశము** n. adj. Not seen elsewhere. Unparalleled, prodigious, strange. అసమానమైన, వింతైన.

అనన్వయము *an-anvayamu.* [Skt.] n. Inconsistency, unconnectedness, incongruity. ఇమడమి, అసాంగత్యము, పొసగమి, విరుద్ధము. adj. Unconnected, irrevelant. అసంబంధమైన, అసంగతమైన, పొసగని, ఇమడని.

అనపకారము *an-apakāramu.* [Skt.] n. Harmlessness.

అనపచెట్టు *anapa-chettu.* [Tel.] A leguminous plant (*Dolichos tetraspermus.*) అనుముచెట్టు అనపకాయ A legume, a pod, a kind of pulse (*phaseolus radiatus.*)

అనపత్యుడు *an-apatyudu.* [Skt.] n. He who has no issue. A childless man.

అనపరాధి *an-aparādhi.* [Skt.] n. A guiltless man, an innocent man. అనపరాధిత్వము guiltlessness, innocence.

అనపాయము *an-apāyamu.* [Skt.] adj. Harmless.

అనపేక్ష *an-apēksha.* [Skt.] Absence of desire. అనపేక్షణీయము not to be desired.

అనఫా *anapha.* [Skt. = Gr. ἀναφη.] A particular configuration of the planets.

అనభ్యాసము *an-abhyāsamu.* [Skt.] n. Want of practice or skill.

అనయము *anayamu.* [Skt.] n. Ill-luck, bad fortune; calamity. Vice, transgression. నీతికానిది, అశుభము, వ్యసనము, విపత్తు.

అనయము *anayamu.* [Tel.] adv. Always, eternally; continually. నిరంతరము, సతతము. Much, greatly, అత్యంతము, అవశ్యము, మరిమరి.

అనరులు *anarulu.* [Tel.] n. plu. The vitals, the parts essential to life. ఆయువుపట్టులు, మర్మస్థానములు

అనర్గళము *an-argaḷamu.* [Skt.] n. adj. Resistless, unimpeded, free, unrestrained. నిరంకుశమైన, అడ్డములేని.

అనర్ఘ్యము or **అనర్ఘము** *an-arghyamu.* [Skt.] adj. Costly, invaluable. వెలలేని.

అనర్థము *an-arthamu.* [Skt.] n. Hurt, damage; evil; a prediction of bad luck. కీడు, దుర్దశ. ఇందువల్ల యేమి అనర్థము వచ్చెను what harm has come by this? అనర్థకాలము an evil time.

అనర్హము *an-arhamu.* [Skt.] adj. Unfit, unworthy. తగని, అయోగ్యమైన. **అనర్హుడు** *an-arhudu.* [Skt.] n. An unworthy man.

అనలము *analamu.* [Skt.] n. Fire. నిప్పు. **అనలుడు** *analudu.* [Skt.] n. The god of fire. Vulcan అగ్నిహోత్రుడు.

అనల్పము *an-alpamu.* [Skt.] n. Not little, much. అనల్పఘోషము very noisy.

అనవతిల్లు *anavatillu* [Tel.] v. t. To settle, dry and cool a little so as to be fit for eating, as boiled rice. ఉమ్మగిల్లు. అన్నము ఉడికి చల్లారు.

అనవద్యము *an-avadyamu.* [Skt.] adj. Blameless, faultless, spotless, irreproachable. నింద్యముకాని, దోషరహితమైన.

అనవధానము *an-avadhānamu.* [Skt.] n. Inattention.

అనవరతము *anavaratamu.* [Skt.] adj. Incessant, perpetual, constant. నిరంతరమైన, ఎడతెగని.

అనవసరము *an-avasaramu.* [Skt.] adj. Unnecessary (Madras usage.)

అనవశ్యము *an-avaśyamu.* [Skt] adj. Unnecessary.

అనవుడు, నావుడు or **నాక** *anavuḍu.* [Tel.] adv. On saying this అనగా, అనేటప్పటికి. "స్వపనమ్ము వివాహమ్మగుమనవుడు." Swa. vi. 23.

అనశ్వరము *a-naśvaramu.* [Skt.] n. adj. Eternal, imperishable. నిత్యమైన.

అనశ్రు *an-aśru.* [Skt.] adj. Tearless.

అనసూయ *an-asūya.* [Skt.] n. Absence of spite, ill-will or envy.

అనహంకారము *an-ahamkāramu.* [Skt.] n. Absence of egotism or self-conceit; absence of pride.

అనాకారము *an-ākāramu.* [Skt.] adj. Deformed, ugly. వికారమైన, కురూపియైన. **అనాకారము** n. Deformity, ugliness. వికారము, కురూపము. **అనాకారి** n. An ugly person. కురూపి.

అనాకాలము *an-ākālamu.* [Skt] Unseasonable time. Bad time.

అనాగతము *an-āgatamu.* [Skt.] adj. Not come, not arrived, future. భవిష్యత్తు అయిన. **అనాగతము** n. The future. భవిష్యత్తు. అనాగతమును చెప్పుట to foretell. **అనాగతవేది** n. A prophet; one who "knows that which has not happened." సంభవింపబోవుదాన్ని యెరిగినవాడు.

అనాచారము *an-āchāramu.* [Skt.] n. Improper conduct, Impurity. దుర్నడత,

అనుచి. అనాచరణము *an-ācharaṇamu.* [Skt.] n. Non-observance.

అనాథ *a-nātha.* [Skt.] adj. Without a master or protector, forlorn, unprotected, without a husband. రక్షకలేని, దిక్కులేని, మొగుడులేని. అనాథ *a-nātha.* n. A destitute, a poor helpless wretch. నిరాధరువుగా నుండేవాడు, దిక్కుమాలినవాడు

అనాదరము or అనాదరణ *an-ādaramu.* [Skt.] n. Disrespect, disregard, contempt. తిరస్కారము, అలక్ష్యము. అనాదరణచేయు disregard, to look with indifference, to despise.

అనాది *an-ādi.* [Skt.] adj. Without beginning, eternal. ఆద్యంతములేని, నిత్యమైన. అనాదిబీడు immemorial waste, i. e., land that never has been brought under the plough. అనాదీయము [Skt.] adj. Immemorial, aboriginal, of unknown origin. పూర్వికము. అనాద్యము adj Without origin, of unknown origin, everlasting. నిరంతరమైన, ఎన్నటికిని ఉండే. అనాద్యంతము without beginning and end.

అనామధేయుడు *a-nāmadhēyuḍu.* [Skt.] n. A nameless fellow, an insignificant fellow, a mere cipher. A mere nobody, one of no repute. ఊరుపేరు లేనివాడు, అప్రసిద్ధుడు.

అనామయము *an-āmayamu.* [Skt.] Free from sickness.

అనామిక *a-nāmika.* [Skt. lit. the nameless finger] n. The ringfinger, the one next to the little finger. ఉంగరపువ్రేలు, చిటికెనవ్రేలికి ఇవతలివ్రేలు.

అనాయకము *a-nāyakamu.* [Skt.] adj. n. Being without a leader. Used for అరాజకము. Anarchy, misrule, confusion. అనాయకుడు n. He who is forlorn or helpless. దిక్కుమాలినవాడు, నాథుడులేనివాడు.

అనాయాసము *an-āyāsamu.* [Skt.] adv. Without pains or effort, easily, readily. సులభముగా.

అనారంభము *an-ārambhamu.* [Skt.] Absence of commencement. అనారంభ్యము not fit to be commenced.

అనారతము *anāratamu.* [Skt.] adj. Continual, frequent, eternal. నిరంతరమైన, ఎడతెగని. అనారతము adv. Always. ఎల్లప్పుడు. Same as అనవరతము.

అనారాధ్యుడు *an-ārādhyuḍu.* [Skt.] adj. n. Unhonoured. He who is not worshipped. పూజ్యుడుకానివాడు.

అనారోగ్యము *an-ārōgyamu.* [Skt.] n. Sickness, unhealthiness.

అనార్యుడు *an-āryuḍu.* [Skt.] n. A non-Aryan.

అనాలోచితము *an-ālōchitamu.* [Skt.] adj. Unconsidered, imprudent.

అనావిలము *anāvilamu.* [Skt.] adj. Clear, clean, pure. నిర్మలమైన. Vasu. iii. 153.

అనావృష్టి *anā-vrishṭi.* [Skt.] n. Drought, a failure of rain. వానలేమి, కరువు.

అనాశ్రయము *an-āśrayamu.* [Skt.] Defencelessness. అనాశ్రితుడు having none to depend upon oneself.

అనాస *anāsa.* [Tel.] n. *Ananas sativa* or the Pine Apple, Or, *Bromelia sativa.*

అనాసికము *a-nāsikamu.* [Skt.] adj. Noseless.

అనాహారము *an-āhāramu.* [Skt.] n. Absence of food, abstinence. అనాహార్యము adj. not fit to be eaten.

అనాహూతుడు *an-āhūtuḍu.* [Skt.] n. One who is not called or invited.

అని *ani.* [Tel.] n. War, battle. యుద్ధము.

అని *ani.* [Tel.] (Past p|| of అను to say) Having said. This is translated by the word "That" or "so" or the infinitive mood is used, as వారు అక్కడ ఉండినారని అన్నాడు he told me *that* they were there. అవతల వెళ్లరాదని తిరిగి వస్తిమి we did not think it right to go on *and* returned; we thought we must not go further; *so* we came back. నన్ను పొమ్మని చెప్పెను he told me to go. తన సొమ్మని యెంచి considering it his own. నాన్ని నాకని కొన్నాడు he bought it *for* me. కావలెనని అక్కడికి పోయి నాడు he went there on purpose. పండ్లను పటపటమని కొరికినాడు he gnashed his teeth. ఘుమ్మని fragrantly. తళుక్కుని brilliantly. గడగడమని మాట్లాడినాడు he spoke rapidly. ఈగలు జుమ్మని ము సు రు కొ న్న వి the flies covered it buzzingly. నీవు ఈ శాలువ కప్పుకొంటే గుమ్మని ఉండును if you wear this shawl it feels warm: or, you will feel warm.

అనిందితము *a-ninditamu*. [Skt.] adj. Unblamed. **అనింద్యము** *a-nindyamu*. [Skt.] adj. Unblameable, faultless.

అనిత్యము *a-nityamu*. [Skt.] adj. Temporary, not permanent. అస్థిరమైన. **అనిత్యత్వము** state of not being permanent; transient character of a thing.

అనిదంపూర్వము *anidampūrvamu*. [Skt.] adj. Novel, unprecedented, unheard of. పూర్వమందు లేనటువంటి, చోద్యమైన, ఎన్నడును వినని కనని. "అనిదంపూర్వ పరాక్రమధనుడు." P. i. 113.

అనిపించు *anipintsu*. [Tel. causative of అను.] v. n. To cause one to say. జ్వరములో ఊరక నీళ్లు తాగవలెననిపించును in a fever one is inclined to drink constantly. ఇంత చల్లగాలి కొట్టితే ఎండకాలమనిపించదు while this cool breeze blows it does not seem to be summer (lit.) the heat is not felt. యోగ్యుడనిపించుకొన్నాడు he was considered a good man.

అనిమిత్తము *a-nimittamu*. [Skt.] n. Having no adequate cause, groundless.

అనిమిషము *a-nimishamu*. [Skt.] n. Winklessness. **అనిమిషత్వము** n. Divinity, apotheosis. దేవత్వము. **అనిమిషుడు** or **అనిమేషుడు** n. A god. దేవత. అనిమిషపతి "ruler of the gods" (a title of Indra or Jupiter.)

అనియుక్తము *a-niyuktamu*. [Skt.] adj. Not appointed.

అనిరుద్ధుడు *aniruddhuḍu*. [Skt.] n. The son of Cupid and Usha. మన్మథునికిని ఉషకును పుట్టినవాడు. కృష్ణుని మనుమడును.

అనిర్జితము *a-nirjitamu*. [Skt.] adj. Unvanquished.

అనిర్దిష్టము *a-nirdishṭamu*. [Skt.] adj. Indefinite, unexplained, undefined. నిర్దేశింపబడని, వివరింపబడని.

అనిర్మలము *a-nirmalamu*. [Skt.] n. Not pure, dirty.

అనిలము *anilamu*. [Skt.] n. Wind, breeze. వాయువు, గాలి. అనిలప్రకృతి the nature of wind or air. **అనిలుడు** *aniluḍu*. [Skt.] n. The god of air. వాయుదేవుడు. **అనిలులు** *anilulu*. n. plu. Subordinate deities: forty-nine of these form one class, the Anilas or winds. ఏకోనపంచాశద్వాయు గణము, అష్టవసుభేదము.

అనివారితము *a-nivāritamu*. [Skt.] adj. Unchecked, unforbidden, unimpeded. అడ్డములేని, ఆటంకములేని. **అనివార్యము** *a-nivāryamu*. [Skt.] adj. Unavoidable. అపరిహార్యమైన, పోగొట్టకూడని.

అనిశము *aniṣamu*. [Skt.] adv. Incessantly, constantly. ఎల్లప్పుడును.

అనిశ్చయము or **అనిశ్చితము** *a-niṣchayamu*. [Skt.] adj. Uncertain. అస్థిరమైన, సందిగ్ధమైన.

అనిష్టము *an-ishṭamu*. [Skt.] adj. Unwished, undesirable. Bad, unlucky. అసమ్మతమైన, దౌర్భాగ్యమైన. **అనిష్టము** n. Mischief, ruin, misery, చెరుపు. ఆ అనిష్టమునకు నేనా పాత్రుడను am I to be subjected to that misery? అనిష్టమునకు పాత్రుడుగా నుండేవాడు one who deserves to be ruined. **అనిష్టసూచకము** foreboding evil.

అనీం [from అనీ H.] n. The point or edge. కొన. The bows or front of a ship. ఓడ ముఖముయొక్క చెంపలు.

అనీకము *anikamu.* [Skt.] n. Battle. యుద్ధము. Army. సేన.

అనీకిని *anikini.* [Skt.] n. An army, three Chamus or 1/10th of an అక్షౌహిణి. host. సేన, దండు.

అనీతి *a-niti.* [Skt.] n. Immorality.

అనీప్సితము *an-ipsitamu.* [Skt.] adj. Not desired.

అను *anu.* [Tel.] A prefix like the Latin *con*, or *sub*, or *re* as కోటానుకోట్లు laces upon laces.

అను *anu.* [Tel.] v. n. To say, to think, to suppose. చెప్పు, తలచు, ఎంచు. (Past p.‖ అని. Relative p.‖ అనిన or అన్న, Aor. p. అనే, అనెడి, అనెడు, అనేటి. Neg. p.‖ అనని.) అట్లా అంటాడు so he says. కావలెననే మనసు a desire to have it. తళుక్కుమను to shine or glitter. చేతితో ఇట్లా అన్నాడు he did so with his hand. **అనుటయు** on his saying so. **అనగా** may be translated "or;" thus అచలమనగా కొండ Achalam or hill; Achalam which means a hill. **అనుచు** adv. On (his) saying this. అనగా, అనేటప్పటికి, అనపుడు. **అనుకొను** *anu-konu.* [Tel.] v. n. To say, suppose, think, (middle voice of అను to say or think.) నేను ఇది యిస్తాననుకొన్నాడు he thought that I would give him this.

అనుంగు See అనుగు.

అనుకంప *anu-kampa.* [Skt.] n. Tenderness, compassion, pity. దయ.

అనుకరించు *anu-karintsu.* v. a. To imitate. ఒకనిని లేక ఒకదానిని చూచి ఆ ప్రకారముగా చేయు. **అనుకరణము** *anu-karanamu.* [Skt.] n. Imitation. ఒకనిని లేక ఒకదానిని చూచి అదేప్రకారముగా చేయుటము; చిటచిట, పటపట, దబదబ, గడగడ,—యిట్టివి అనుకరణశబ్దములు these words are onomatopœic words, imitatives. **అనుకారము** *anu-karamu.* [Skt.] n. Imitation. Resemblance. పోలిక. **అనుకారి** *anu-kari.* adj. Imitative. తద్వత్తుగాచేసే, ఒకడు చేసేట్టుగాచేసే.

అనుకర్షము *anu-karshamu.* [Skt.] n. A piece of wood at the end of a cart pole, to which the yoke is fixed. Invoking, summoning by incantation. బండికింది కోడిపీట. ఆకర్షణము.

అనుకు or **అనుకనుగా** *anuku.* [Tel.] adj. Neither thick nor thin. అంత గట్టిగాను అంత పలచనగాను కాని. **అన్కనుకగు** adv. to become neither thick nor thin. కొంచెము పలచగా. ఇంత అనుకుగానుండదేమి? బాగా కలుపు why is this so thin? mix it to a proper consistency.

> "నూనెయు నన్కనుకగు నుడికించియు." P. i. 108.

అనుకూలము *anu-kulamu.* [Skt.] adj. Favourable, friendly, assisting, salubrious. హితమైన, సహాయమైన, ఆరోగ్యమైన, శ్రేయస్కరమైన. **అనుకూలమైనగాలి** a favourable wind. వాని శరీరమునకు అనుకూలమైనస్థలము the place which agrees with him. అనుకూలమైనమాట a friendly word. **అనుకూలశత్రువు** a friendly enemy **అనుకూలకాలము** a suitable time. **అనుకూలము** or **అనుకూలత** n. Favour, goodness, kindness, aid. సహాయము, మేలు, దయ. ద్రవ్యానుకూలము means, resource. దైవానుకూలమున్ను by the grace of God. **అనుకూలించు**, అనుకూలపడు or అనుకూల

మగు *anukūlintsu.* [Skt.] v. n. To be of use ఒదవు. To have effect, to have a good result. సఫలమగు; ఒనగూడు. అనుకూలము కాలేదు it failed, it had not the desired effect. నాకు ఇంకా రూకలు అనుకూలపడ లేదు I have not yet obtained the money ఈ పని నీకు అనుకూలమగును you will succeed in this business. అనుకూలము చేయు or అనుకూలపరచు *anukūlamu-chēyu.* v. a. To shew favour, to bring a thing about, to countenance. సహాయము చేయు, నెరవేర్చు. కార్యమును అనుకూలము చేసినా న్నారు they brought it about, brought it to a conclusion. అనుకూలుడు *anukūluḍu.* n. A friend, ally, patron. హితుడు, సహాయుడు, ఉపకారి. వాడు నాకు అనుకూలుడు he is well disposed towards me.

అనుకృతి *anu-kriti.* [Skt.] n. Imitation, అనుకరణము. "తదవతారకలికలీలానుకృతుల నత్తి లయచుమంచె." A. v. 38.

అనుక్రమము *anu-kramamu.* [Skt.] n. Series, succession, method, order. వరుస. అనుక్రమణిక *anu-kramaṇika.* [Skt.] n. An index, table of contents. సూచీపత్రము, భూమిక, విషయసూచిక.

అనుక్రోశము *anu-krōśamu.* [Skt.] n. Pity. దయ.

అనుగతము *anu-gatamu.* [Skt.] adj. Followed, united to. Determined, defined. పొందబడిన, అధీనమైన, వెంబడింపబడిన, నియతమైన. T. iv. 147. అనుగతి *anu-gati.* [Skt.] n. Going after, following. వెంబడించి పోవడము. "పశానుగతి." A. ii. 28.

అనుగమించు *anu-gamintsu.* [Skt.] v. a. To accompany or follow. వెంబడించు. అనుగమనము *anu-gamanamu.* n. Going after, following. కూడాపోవడము, సహగమనము.

అనుగు or అనుంగు *anugu.* [Tel.] adj. Beloved, dear, desired. ప్రియమైన. "అనుగు చెల్లెలైన." A. iv. 233. "అనుగుచెలికాడు." ib. 542. అనుగు n. A friend. స్నేహితుడు, స్నేహితురాలు. అనుగుతనము *anugu-tanamu.* n. Friendship. స్నేహభావము, మిత్రత్వము. "నన్ను గదురంజిలలేక నితండునచ్చి యున్నమగు తనంబుజూపెడి యటంచు తదుష్ట కతకా బ్రస్తలేక." Raghava Pandav. iii. 110. అనుగుకత్తె a female companion. చెలికత్తె.

అనుగుణము *anu-guṇamu.* [Skt.] adj. Fit, proper, suited to. తగిన, అర్హమైన. అనుగుణ్యము *anu-guṇyamu.* adj. According to, suitable to. తగిన, అర్హమైన. అనుగుణ్యముగా adv. Accordingly, fitly, suitably. తగినట్టుగా. ఆజ్ఞానుగుణ్యముగా according to orders.

అనుగ్రహము *anu-grahamu.* [Skt.] n. Mercy, favour, grace, కృప, దయ, ఏలుకోలుట. అనుగ్రహముపొందు to gain favour. మాయందు అనుగ్రహముంచవలెను have mercy upon us, favour us. అనుగ్రహించు v. a. To favour, shew kindness, help, bless. To grant, bestow. దయచేయు, సహాయముచేయు, మా యింటికి అనుగ్రహిస్తారా will you favour me with a call?

అనుచరుడు *anu-charuḍu.* [Skt.] n. A follower, an attendant, సహాయుడు, తోడు, వెంటనుండువాడు.

అనుచితము *an-uchitamu.* [Skt.] adj. Unfit, unseemly, unsuitable. తగని, అనర్హమైన, అయుక్తమైన.

అనుచు *anutsu.* [Tel.] v. a. To send, dismiss. పంపు. "నిజపురింబునకనిచెనిందిన రాత్రు." Swa. v. 132. Also, to command, to order.

అనుజన్ముడు *anu-janmuḍu.* [Skt.] n. A younger brother.

అనుజాత *anu-jāta.* [Skt. lit. Born together with.] n. A younger sister.

అనుజీవి *anu-jīvi.* [Skt.] n. A dependant, or hanger on. సేవకుడు.

అనుజుడు *anujuḍu.* [Skt.] n. Younger brother. తమ్ముడు.

అనుజ్ఞ *anugnya.* [Skt.] n. Command. Permission, order, leave. ఉత్తరువు, సెలవు. ఆజ్ఞ. **అనుజ్ఞాతుడు** *anu-gnyātuḍu.* [Skt.] n. One who has been commanded to do a thing, one who has obtained permission to do a thing.

అనుజ్యేష్ఠుడు *anu-jyēshṭhuḍu.* [Skt.] n. The next eldest son.

అనుతాపము *anu-tāpamu.* [Skt.] n. Regret, sorrow. పశ్చాత్తాపము. **అనుతాపపడు** or **అనుతాపమునుపొందు** to regret.

అనుత్తమము *an-uttamamu.* [Skt.] adj. Most excellent, very superior. మిక్కిలి శ్రేష్ఠమైన.

అనుత్తరము *an-uttaramu.* [Skt.] adj. Not north. ఉత్తరదేశముకానిది. Unanswerable మారుమాటలేనిది.

అనుత్పత్తి *an-utpatti.* [Skt.] Non-production; non-birth.

అనుత్పన్నము *an-utpannamu.* [Skt.] adj. Unborn, unproduced.

అనుదాత్తము *an-udāttamu.* [Skt. from ఉదాత్తము.] n. Unaccented syllable. తగ్గ స్వరము. (ఇది వేదమునుగురించినమాట.) See స్వరము.

అనుదినము *anu-dinamu.* [Skt.] adv. Daily. ప్రతిదినము, నానాడు.

అనుద్యోగము *an-udyōgamu.* [Skt.] n. Want of exertion, inactivity.

అనునయము *anu-nayamu.* [Skt.] n. Conciliation, consoling, entreaty, begging. సాంత్వనము, ఓదార్పడము. అడుగుకొనడము, మంచిమాటలాడడము, ఊరట. **అనునయించు** *anu-nayintsu.* [Skt.] v. a. To conciliate, console; to entreat, beg. ఓదార్చు, అడుగుకొను, మంచిమాటలాడు.

అనునాసిక *anu-nāsika.* [Skt.] n. Uttered through the nose. In gram. the letter n.

అనుపకారి *an-upakāri.* [Skt.] n. A disobliging person.

అనుపదిష్టుడు *an-upadishṭuḍu.* [Skt.] n One who is uninstructed.

అనుపనీతుడు *an-upanītuḍu* [Skt.] n A person who has not undergone the rite of ఉపనయనము.

అనుపపత్తి *an-upapatti.* [Skt.] n. Inconvenience, want of the means. అసందర్భము. కలిమిలేమి. ఉపపత్త్యనుపపత్తులు చూచుకోవద్దా ought not we to consider, whether we have the means? అనుపపత్తికాలము a season of trial or anxiety, hard times.

అనుపమము *an-upamamu.* [Skt.] adj. Incomparable, unrivalled, unparalleled. అసదృశమైన, ఈడుకాని. **అనుపమితము** uncompared, that cannot be compared, matchless.

అనుపయుక్తము *an-upayuktamu.* [Skt.] adj. Useless. unnecessary, unserviceable. కొరగాని, పనికిమాలిన.

అనుపయోగము *an-upayōgamu.* [Skt.] n. Unserviceableness, uselessness.

అనుపలక్షితము *an-upalakshitamu.* [Skt.] adj. Unseen, unobserved, unnoticed.

అనుపల్లవి *anu-pallavi.* [Skt.] n. The response in a chorus.

అనుపానము *anu-pānamu.* [Skt.] n. A vehicle in medicine, anything taken with medicine to make it less nauseous. మందుతోకూడా తీసుకొనే మధురమైన వస్తువు. "దివ్యవసాపానంబు క్షీరయూషపాన సహితంబై." Anir. ii. 108. యీ మందును పాలను అనుపానముచేసి పుచ్చుకో you must take milk as a vehicle to this medicine, you must take this medicine in milk.

అనుపు *anupu.* [Tel.] n. Toll, customs; ambuscade, ambush. సుంకము. పొంచియుండు చోటు. "తెరవరిటులనిరు పోయుపందిలియుండేరు, యనలగొరగాళ పిచ్చుకుంకైయనంగు, దనుపుగొన జొచ్చి కల్లసుట్టమర." A. ii. 69. టీ॥ సుంకము పుచ్చుకొనుపక్షమించెను. **అనుపు** v. a. To send, dismiss. పంపించు. "నన్ననుపుగాథల చేరనెప్రొద్దు ద్రోయక॥." H. i. 42.

అనుప్రయోగము *anu-prayōgamu.* [Skt.] n. Additional use.

అనుప్రాసము *anu-prāsamu.* [Skt.] n. Alliteration, repetition of similar letters, syllables and words. తుల్యవర్ణవిన్యాసము, వర్ణసామ్యమను ప్రాసతతి. వర్ణావృత్తిరను ప్రాసః పదేపాదేవిధీయతే.

అనుబంధము *anu-bandhamu.* [Skt.] n. Connection, affinity, alliance. చుట్టరికము. అనుబంధక్రియ a defective or auxiliary verb. ప్రకృతి ప్రత్యయాదులచేత చెడెడి అక్షరము. In Arith. the junction of fractions. Also appendix, "that which is added" (to the main part of a book.) **అనుబంధి** or **అనుబంధుడు** n. One who acts in accordance with the wishes of the elders among his relations. A relation, దేహసంబంధముగల వాడు. **అనుబంధించు** *anu-bandhintsu.* v. n. To join, connect, unite. సంబంధించు.

అనుబింబించు *anu-bimbintsu.* [Skt.] v. n. To reflect or throw back an image. ప్రతిఫలించు.

అనుభవము *anu-bhavamu.* [Skt.] n. Experience, suffering, enjoyment. Knowledge obtained by observation and experiment. వాడుకపడడము, పరీక్ష. సుఖానుభవము the enjoyment of pleasure. దుఃఖానుభవము suffering distress or grief. నరకానుభవము the sufferings of hell, falling into hell. వాడు చేసినది వాడికే అనుభవమునకు వచ్చినది he has come in for the fruits of his actions. **అనుభవవేద్యము** that can be known by experience. **అనుభవసిద్ధము** that is confirmed by experience. **అనుభవశాలుడు** or అనుభవికుడు he who enjoys, he who is experienced. అనుభవించేవాడు, అనుభవముగలవాడు. **అనుభవపరుడు** or **అనుభవి** or అనుభవశాలి. n. A man of experience. వాడుకపడ్డవాడు. **అనుభవించు** v. a. To experience, enjoy, suffer, share in, to have, hold, possess, partake of, undergo. పాపము, పాపఫలమనుభవించు to suffer the fruit of sin. పుణ్యఫలమనుభవించు to enjoy the reward of virtue. చేసినది అనుభవించకుంటే తీరునా can you avoid suffering the consequences of your acts?

అనుభావము *anu-bhāvamu.* [Skt.] n. Majesty, dignity, magnanimity. A positive conclusion, decision, firm opinion. Indication of passion or emotion by word or gesture. ప్రభావము, నిశ్చయము, భావబోధక ముఖవికారాది. **అనుభావ్యము** *anu-bhāvyamu.* [Skt.] adj. that which may be enjoyed. అనుభవింపదగినది.

అనుభోగము *anu-bhōgamu.* [Skt.] n. Enjoyment, experience. **అనుభోగి** n. A man of pleasure. మంచిభోగమనుభవించేవాడు.

అనుమంత్రణము *anu-mantraṇamu.* [Skt.] n. Consecration by prayers. అనుమంత్రణమంత్రము formula or prayer used in consecrating.

అనుమడు *anumaḍu.* [Skt.] n. Hanuman. హనుమంతుడు.

అనుమతము *anumatamu.* [Skt.] adj. Allowed, permitted, consented to. సెలవియ్యబడ్డ, సమ్మతింపబడిన.

అనుమతి *anumati.* [Skt.] n. Agreement, consent, permission, leave. The fourteenth day of the moon's age, on which she rises one digit less than full. సమ్మతి, అనుజ్ఞ. నూక్ష్మైకేందుకళాపూర్ణా, చతుర్దశీ యుక్తపూర్ణిమ.

తండ్రి అనుమతిని కొమారుడు రంగయ్యవ్రాలు signed by Rangayya with the consent of his father **అనుమతించు** v. n. To consent.

అనుమరణము *anu-maraṇamu.* [Skt.] n. Death that follows another's death, as in Suttee.

అనుమానము *anu-mānamu.* [Skt.] n. Surmise, conjecture, suspicion, doubt. In logic, inference. సందేహము, యుక్తిచేత నిర్ణయించడము. వానిమీద అనుమానము తోచినది, వానిమీద అనుమానమున్నది I suspect him. **అనుమానఖండము** Induction (logic.) **అనుమానించు** or **అనుమానపడు** *anu-mānintsu.* [Skt.] v. n. To doubt, hesitate, suspect. సందేహపడు.

అనుము or **అనపచెట్టు** *anumu.* [Tel.] n. A leguminous plant, Dolichos catjang (the cultivated species.) అనపకాయ a legume, a pod, a sort of pulse (phaseolus radiatus.) **అనుములు** n. plu. The seeds of అనపచెట్టు.

అనుము *anumu.* [Tel.] n. Fitness. Beauty ఒప్పు.

> "అమ్మానేనిక్నే లిద
> యమ్ముద్దియగానుబుడమినమదలిర్చన్
> బ్రిమ్మను యయాతియుడిగవు గొమ్మన్."
> య. v.

అనుమేయము *anu-mēyamu.* [Skt.] adj. Inferable. ఊహింపదగినది. See అనుమానము.

అనుమోదము *anu-mōdamu.* [Skt.] n. Pleasure, delight. ఆనందము, ఉల్లాసము. **అనుమోదించు** v. n. To consent, agree, approve, to be pleased with. ఒప్పు, సంతోషించు.

అనుయోగము *anu-yōgamu.* [Skt.] n. A question, examination. అడుగుట, ప్రశ్నము. a rejoinder in argument.

అనురక్తి or **అనురాగము** *anu-rakti.* [Skt.] n. Love, attachment, desire. ప్రీతి. **అనురక్తము** *anu-raktamu.* [Skt.] adj. Attached, fond, enamoured. ప్రీతిగల. **అనురక్తుడు** n. He who loves, he who is fond of. ఆసక్తుడు, ప్రీతిగలవాడు.

అనురూపము *anu-rūpamu.* [Skt.] adj. Like, resembling, fit, suitable, corresponding with. సమానమైన, తగిన.

అనులాపము *anu-lāpamu.* [Skt.] n. Repetition. అడినమాటే అడడము, పునరుక్తి. **అనులాపించు** v. a. To repeat the same words. చెప్పినమాటలనే మళ్లీ చెప్పుట.

అనులేపనము *anu-lēpanamu.* [Skt.] n. Smearing; daubing the body with unguents. పూత, గంధాదులయొక్క మైపూత.

అనులోమము *anu-lōmamu.* [Skt. lit. With the hair or grain.] adj. Regular, successive. యథాక్రమము, ఆరోహణాక్రమము గలది.

అనువదించు *anu-vadintsu.* [Skt.] v. a. To re-echo, or repeat. ఒకరు చెప్పినదానినే చెప్పు.

అనువరి *anuvari.* [Tel. from అనువు+అరి] See అనువు.

అనువర్తించు *anu-vartintsu.* [Skt.] v. a. To attend on, serve, follow, court one's favour. అనుసరించి నడచు. **అనువర్తనము** n. Serving or following another.

అనువాకము *anu-vākamu.* [Skt.] n. A chapter of the Veda. An explanatory text or sentence from the Veda. వేదభాగము.

అనువాదము *anu-vādamu.* [Skt.] n. Tautology, repetition. Abuse. పునరుక్తి, చెప్పినదాన్ని మళ్లీ చెప్పడము, కుత్సితార్థవాక్యము.

అనువు *anuvu.* [Tel.] n. Convenience, fitness, propriety, suitableness. ఒప్పు, యోగ్యము, అనుకూలము. "మీకుగాక జలసంచారం బనువగునే మముబోలిన మచరులకు." P. iv. 59. "అనువారిన్వాదరథంబునిచ్చె." T. i. 50. **అనువుగానివేళ** in an inconvenient hour. **అనువరి** n. A man of tact, ఉపాయశాలి, యుక్తిపరుడు. **అనువు** adj. Proper, right, fit, suitable.

convenient. ఉచితమైన, యుక్తమైన, యోగ్యమైన. అనువుగా adv. Conveniently, suitably, fitly, with propriety. అనువుచేయు v. t. To make ready or fit. సిద్ధపరుచు. అనువుపడు v. n. To be suitable or agreeable, or convenient. అనుకూలపడు. అనువైంద or అనువైందగ adv. Duly, well. ఒప్పుగా. "ఈ కథ వినిపించినమీరొందరిల్లు వినూగోత్తంపా." H. i. 233.

అనుశాసనము *anu-śasanamu.* [Skt.] n. A command, order. ఆజ్ఞ, విధి.

అనుశ్రుతము *anu-śrutamu.* [Skt.] adj. In accordance with what is heard or the traditional teaching. Perpetual, continual. నిరంతరమైన. అనుశ్రుతముగా adv. Traditionally. Perpetually, continually. నిరంతరముగా.

అనుషంగము *anu-shangamu.* [Skt.] n. Attachment, love. చేళి, సంబంధము, దయ.

అనుష్ఠానము *anushthanamu.* [Skt.] n. An observance, practice. ఆచారము, నడవడి. అనుష్ఠానక్రమము the order of observing the religious ceremonies. అనుష్ఠించు v. a. To make, do, observe, celebrate. చేయు, ఆచరించు. అనుష్ఠితము *anushthitamu.* [Skt.] adj. Observed, practised (as a religious observance).

అనుష్ణుడు *an-ushnudu.* [Skt. Lit. a man without heat.] n. A man without energy. An idle fellow.

అనుసంధానము *anu-sandhanamu.* [Skt.] n. Reciting, repeating. వేదవిషయమైన గ్రంథములను చదవడము. అనుసంధించు v. a. To unite. To recite, repeat.

అనుసరించు *anu-sarintsu.* [Skt.] v. a. To follow, attend on, hold to serve, court one's favour. అనువర్తించు. న్యాయమును అనుసరించక disregarding justice. అనుసరణము or అనుసారము *anu-saranamu.* [Skt.] n. Following, going after. Serving or attending on another. తెంబడించడము, అనువర్తించడము. అనుసారముగా adv. According to. ప్రకారముగా, అనుగుణ్యముగా. అనుసారణి *anu-sarani.* [Skt.] n. Name of the second string of a lute. రెండోతంతి. అనుసారి n. A follower, a hanger on.

అనుసు *anusu.* [Tel.] n. A metal ring on the end of a stick, a rice pounder, &c. పొన్ను, కడియము.

"తలకుబుత్తడియనుసు కెత్తంపుకర్ర
బట్టి సేనాధిపతి బరాబరులుసేయు."

చంద్రా, i.

అనుస్మరణము *anu-smaranamu.* [Skt.] n. Calling to mind, thinking on తలంచడము.

అనుస్వారము *anu-svaramu.* [Skt.] n. The name of the letter (ం) the nasal character. సున్న, బిందువు.

అనూకము *anukamu.* [Skt.] n. Race, family; peculiarity of race, character. అన్వయము, శీలము.

అనూచానము *anuchanamu.* [Skt.] adj. Well-behaved. సవినయమైన. అనూచానుడు *anu-chanudu.* [Skt.] n. A bramin versed in the Vedas. సాంగవేదవిచక్షణుడు.

అనూనము *an-unamu.* [Skt.] adj. Whole, entire. యావత్తు, అంతయు, వెలితిలేని.

అనూపము *anupamu.* [Skt.] adj. Wet, watery, inundated. జలయుక్తమైన, జలమయమైన. అనూపము n. A fen or marsh. చిత్తడినేల. అనూపదేశము a marshy country.

అనూరుడు *an-urudu.* [Skt.] n. The charioteer of the sun. సూర్యసారథి, అరుణుడు.

అనూర్జితము *an-urgitamu.* [Skt.] adj. Not strong. Not permanent. అస్థిరమైన.

అనృతము *a-nritamu.* [Skt.] n. A falsehood, a lie. అబద్ధము. అనృతవాది a liar.

అనే, అనేడి, అనేటి *ane.* (the indefinite p[illegible] of అను to say) Called, named, termed. కడప అనే ఊరు the town of Cuddapa.

అనేక *an-êka.* [Skt. lit. not one] adj. Several, many. బహు, పెక్కు. **అనేకత్వము** *an-êkatvamu.* [Skt.] n. Abundance, బహుత్వము. **అనేకపము** n. The elephant. ఏనుగ. అనేకాక్షరము a polysyllable. **అనేకమంది** or **అనేకులు** n. plu. Many persons. నానా మంది.

అనోకహము *anô-kahamu.* [Skt.] n. A tree. వృక్షము.

అన్కసకగు or **అనుకసకుగా,** [అనుకు+అనుకగా.] See. అనుకు.

అన్న for అనిన (the past relative pt. of అను to say.) Called, said, termed. రాముడన్నవాడు a man called Ramudu. వాడు యీ మాట అన్నప్పుడు when he said this. ఈ లెక్క వ్రాసినదన్న తేదిని on the date on which this account is said to have been written. నీవన్న దానికిని వారు అన్న దానికిని యేమి భేదము what difference is there between your statement and theirs? ఏమన్నా సరే no matter what they said.

అన్న *anna.* [Tel.] n. An elder brother. Voc. sing. అన్నా. plu. అన్నలారా. పెద్దన్న the eldest of the elder brothers. చిన్నన్న the younger of the elder brothers. అన్నదమ్ములు brothers (both elder and younger.) నీవు వానికి అన్నవే you are even worse than he is. ఇవి లేళ్లన్నలు, అనగా యివి లేళ్లను మించినవి these surpass stags in speed. **అన్నా** or **అన్నన్న** an interjection of grief of admiration, e. g., "కారుకమ్ములన్నన్న కురుల్."

అన్నపూర్ణచెంబు *anna-pûrṇa-chembu.* [Skt+Tel.] n. A sort of bowl. ఒక చెంబు, అన్నపూర్ణ being the name of a goddess, a form of Durga.

అన్నప్రాశనము *anna-prâsanamu.* [Skt.] n. The ceremony of giving an infant solid food for the first time. చంటిబిడ్డకు మొట్టమొదట అన్నము పెట్టే శుభప్రయోజనము.

అన్నభేది *anna-bhêdi.* [Tel+Skt.] n. Green vitriol, sulphate of iron.

అన్నము *annamu.* [Tel.] n. Boiled rice, meat, food. ఓదనము, కూడు, వణ్ణము. **అన్నవస్త్రములు** food and raiment. అన్నదానము the giving of food. **అన్నరసము** essence of food, chyle. అన్నవికారము disorder of the stomach from indigestion. అన్నశేషము leavings of food.

అన్ని *anni.* [Tel.] (Plu. adj. pron.) So many, all. సమస్తము. అన్నినాళ్లు so many days. **అన్ని** *anni.* [Tel.] n. All. (Loc. అన్నిట or అన్నిటిలో in all, in all things. Dative అన్నిటికి to all, on the whole.) వాడు అన్నిటా సమర్థుడు he is clever in every thing. **అన్నిటికి** నేను ఉన్నాను I will be answerable for all. అన్నిటికి నిన్నే నమ్మి యున్నాను you are my all in all. **అన్నిటికి** అన్ని చెప్పుచున్నాడు he gives an excuse for every thing.

అన్ను *annu.* [Tel.] n. A woman. స్త్రీ, ఆడుది. వేలుపుటన్ను a fairy. "కారుమెరుగుచెన్నుగా దేని యీ యన్ను మోహనాకృతినమున మొనపు కొట్టు." N. ii. 379. "అంబుజాక్షుని మోహంపు టన్నుదోడు." T. i. 45. **అన్ను** or **అన్నువు.** *annu.* [Tel.] n. Phrenzy, madness, wildness, intoxication. మదము, మత్తు, పారవశ్యము, ఒళ్లెరుగమి.

> ఉ. "కన్నులనిద్రతేరగ
> నకంపితుడైయటిదెంత చేసినన్,
> నిన్ను నెరుంగక కొక్కుమిగి
> దక్కువిషిస్వచయుంబు బోరవే
> రన్నున మ్రింగబోచ్చి."
>
> భార. అర. vii.

అన్నుకొను *annu-konu.* [Tel.] v. n. To be intoxicated, be inebriated. మత్తిలుట. "మీరమీరంగదిన్న దొరలన్నుకొని" Swa. iv. 30.

అన్నుపన్ను *annu-pannu.* [Tel.] n. Taxes, &c., the word అన్ను is a mere anuk, పన్ను మొదలైనవి. BD. iv. 1959.

అన్నువ *annuva.* [Tel.] adj. Slender, little, small. అల్పము, సూక్ష్మము. "ఇన్నగమునందు గాండీవమున్న దియదిగాని మధ్యజోద్రేకవిలా సోన్నతికోర్వవు పెద్దయునన్ను వలివిండ్లుకురుచలత్యంతంబుగా." M. IV. iv. 100. "అజానుబాహులు అన్నువనడుము." ND. p. 31.

అన్నెము *annemu* [Tadbhav of Skt. అన్యము] adj. Another, other, different. అన్యము. అన్నెము n. Other thing. వేరొకటి, ఇతరమైనది. "మున్నొకనాడు సంగనలముద్దులుద్దు తెరుంగనట్టిచో నన్నెమికేల." T. ii. 112. Also, corruption of అన్యాయము injustice. అన్నెకాడు an unjust man. అన్యాయకారి; అన్నెకారి unjust woman. అన్యాయకారిణి.

అన్యత్ర *anyatra.* [Skt.] adv. In another place, elsewhere. మరియొకచోట.

అన్యథా *anyatha.* [Skt.] adv. Otherwise, in a different manner. మరియొకవిధముగా. దాన్ని అన్యథాచేసినాడు he did it otherwise.

అన్యథాకరించు *anyatha-karintsu.* [Skt.] To separate. వేరుచేయు.

> "గురులలోనపరమగురువు తల్లియటంట్టి
> తల్లివచనమును విధాతకృతియు
> నన్యథాకరింప నలవియె యనిన."
>
> భార. ఆది. vii.

అన్యము *anyamu.* [Skt.] adj. Another, other, different, strange, foreign. ఇతరమైన, వేరే, మరియొక. అన్యదేశము a foreign country. అన్యదేశస్థులు foreigners. **అన్యుడు** *anyudu.* [Skt.] n. A stranger. పరుడు, ఇతరుడు. **అన్యోన్యము** adj. Mutual, reciprocal. పరస్పరమైన. **అన్యోన్యము** n. Friendship, amity, intimacy, mutual attachment, or affection. స్నేహము, విహితము. **అన్యోన్యముగా** adv. On good terms, amicably, in a friendly manner, affectionately. స్నేహముగా, విహితముగా.

అన్యాపదేశము *anyapa-dēśamu.* [Skt.] n. Indirect reference; innuendo. ఒకటిని చెప్పబెట్టుకొని చెప్పడము. అన్యాపదేశముగా by innuendo.

అన్యాయము *a-nyāyamu.* [Skt.] n. Injustice, wrong. అనీతి, అధర్మము. అన్యాయార్జితధనము ill gotten wealth. ఇదేమి అన్యాయము what a shame this is! **అన్యాయము** adj. Unjust, wrong. నీతిలేని, అధర్మమైన. **అన్యాయముగా** adv. Unjustly, wrongfully. అధర్మముగా, నీతిలేకుండా. **అన్యాయస్థుడు** n. An unjust man, a sinner. దుర్నీతుడు.

అన్వయము *anvayamu.* [Skt.] n. Race, lineage. In grammar, the government of words in a sentence. Syntax. వంశము. పదములయొక్క పరస్పరాకాంక్షాయోగ్యత, ఇమిడిక. ఈ శ్లోకమునకు అన్వయము తెలియలేదు I do not perceive the syntax of this verse. దూరాన్వయము a far-fetched allusion. కురువాన్వయుడు one of the Kuru race. **అన్వయజ్ఞుడు** a genealogist. **అన్వయవ్యాప్తి** (in Logic,) an affirmative argument. **అన్వయించు** v. a. To arrange words in their natural order, explain the syntax. పదముల సంబంధమును చెప్పు, పొందికపరచు.

అన్వర్థము *an-v-arthamu.* [Skt.] adj. Descriptive, expressing the properties or attributes. సార్థకమైన. **అన్వర్థనామము** a name which suits one's character. **అన్వర్థసంజ్ఞ** a significant term, a term whose meaning is intelligible in itself.

అన్వవాయము *anvavāyamu.* [Skt.] n. Lineage, descent, race, family. వంశము.

అన్వితము *anvitamu.* [Skt.] adj. Connected, యుక్తమైన, చేరిన, మిళితమైన. ఈ వాక్యము

అన్వితముగానున్నది this is a broken phrase. **అన్వితుడు** n. He who possesses a thing. సకలగుణాన్వితుడు he who is possessed of all virtues.

అన్వీక్షణము *an-ikshaṇamu.* [Skt.] n. Seeing, research. చూడడము, వెదకడము.

అన్వేషణము *anvēshaṇamu.* [Skt.] n. Search, research, enquiry. వెదకడము. **అన్వేషించు** v. t. to look for, to search for. వెదకు. **అన్వేషితము** adj. Searched, sought.

అప *apa.* [Skt.] prefix. Away from, ill, evil. చెడు. అపకీర్తి a bad name, ill-fame.

అపండితుడు *a-paṇḍituḍu.* [Skt.] An unlearned man.

అపకారము *apakāramu.* [Skt.] n. Injury, harm. చెరుపు, కీడు. అపకారముచేయు to do one an ill turn or injury. **అపకారి** n. an ill-doer.

అపకీర్తి *apa-kīrti.* [Skt.] n. Ill-fame. Infamy, an ill-name. చెడ్డపేరు, దుర్యశము, దూరు. వానికి అపకీర్తి వచ్చినది they were disgraced.

అపకృతి *apa-kriti.* [Skt.] n. Same as అపకారము. **అపకృతుడు** one to whom an ill turn has been done.

అపక్రమము *apa-kramamu.* [Skt.] n. Rout, defeat, flight, retreat. పలాయనము. **అపక్రమించు** to run away from a battle.

అపక్వము *a-pakvamu.* [Skt.] adj. Unripe, raw, immature, green. పండని.

అపఖ్యాతి *apa-khyāti.* [Skt.] n. An ill name, evil report, disgrace. అపకీర్తి.

అపగతము *apa-gatamu.* [Skt.] adj. Gone, departed, deceased, dead. మృతము, గతము, అపగతప్రాణులైన deprived of life.

అపచయము *apa-chayamu.* [Skt.] n. Loss, detriment. The act of plucking flowers. హాని, అపహానము, పుష్పముల కోయడము. పుష్పాపచయము (Swa. iv. 116.) gathering flowers.

అపచారము *apa-chāramu.* [Skt.] n. An insult, an affront, incivility, fault. పూజ్యుల మొదల చేసిన నేరము.

అపజయము *apa-jayamu.* [Skt.] n. Failure, defeat. ఓటమి.

అపత్నీకుడు *a-patnikuḍu.* [Skt. from పత్ని.] n. A widower. పెండ్లాములేనివాడు.

అపత్యము *apatyamu.* [Skt.] n. A child (male or female) offspring. సంతానము, బిడ్డ. **అపత్యప్రత్యయము** a patronymical affix. **అపత్యార్థశబ్దము** a patronymic.

అపత్రప *apa-trapa.* [Skt.] n. Shame caused by others. పరులవలన కలిగిన సిగ్గు.

అపథ్యము *a-pathyamu.* [Skt.] n. An error in diet, a deviation from పథ్యము or prescribed regimen. వైద్యుడుకారాదన్న దాన్ని తినడము.

అపదార్థము *a-padārthamu.* [Skt.] n. Non-entity. Nothing. శూన్యత. వాడు వట్టి అపదార్థము he is a mere nothing, he is a cipher.

అపదిశము *apa-diśamu.* [Skt.] n. A half point or quarter point or "airt" of the compass; intermediate space. విదిక్కు, దిక్కోణము, దిక్కులనడిమిమూల, అయిమూల.

అపదూరు *apa-dūru.* [Skt.] n. Calumny, infamy, undeserved blame. అపవాదము. **అపదూరుపడు** v. n. To be calumniated, defamed. అపకీర్తినిపొందు. **అపదూరుచెప్పు** v. a. To slander, spread an ill report of one. ఒకరిమీద తప్పుమాటలుచెప్పు.

అపదేశము *apa-dēśamu.* [Skt.] n. Pretext, pretence. వ్యాజము, సాకు.

అపనమ్మిక or **అపనమ్మకము** *apa-nammika.* [Skt. అప + Tel. నమ్మిక.] n. Incredulity, unbelief, mistrust, diffidence.

అపనయము *apa-nayamu.* [Skt.] n. Taking away, withdrawing, removing, destroying. తొలగించడము, దూరీకరణము, పోగొట్టడము.

అపనయించు *apanayintsu.* [Skt.] v. a. To remove, do away with, dissipate. పో గొట్టు. "ఎన్నిబాధలబెట్టిన నన్ని బాధలమ్మకృస్ణు తి చేత నపనయించబడియుండి." N. iv. 247.

అపనింద *apa-ninda.* [Skt.] n. Undeserved blame, reproach, detraction, slander, false accusation. అపవాదము.

అపనెపము *apa-nepamu.* [Skt.] n. False or unjust accusation. అపదూరు. "అటుబోయునం తలో నపనెపమాయె." Sar. D. 106.

అపనేయము *apa-nēyamu.* [Skt.] adj. That which is to be taken away, that which is to be removed. తీసివేయతగ్గది. "ఈయురగాకం బులు రెండును నీచేత నపనేయంబులుగాకుండవల యును." Vish. vi. 74.

అపనోదము *apa-nōdamu.* [Skt.] n. Removing, taking away. తొలగించుట. Vasu. ii. 57.

అపపాడి *apa-pādi.* [Skt. అప + Tel. పాడి.] n. Injustice. అన్యాయము.

అపప్రయోగము *apa-prayōgamu.* [Skt.] n. Misapplication of a word. దుష్ప్రయోగము.

అపభ్రంశము *apa-bhramsamu* [Skt.] n. Common vulgar talk; a low term. గ్రామ్యభాష, అపశబ్దము.

అపమృత్యువు *apa-mrityuvu.* [Skt.] n. Sudden death, violent death, untimely death. ఆకస్మికమరణము. ఈడూలేని కలిగినచావు.

అపయశము *apa-yaśamu.* [Skt.] n. Ill-fame, infamy. అపకీర్తి.

అపరంజి *aparanji.* [Skt.] n. Fine refined gold. కుందనము, పదివన్నె బంగారు, ఉజిజి.

అపరము *a-paramu.* [Skt.] adj. Other, another, latter. అన్యము, ఉత్తరము. **అపరక్రియలు** n. Obsequies, funeral rites. దినవారాలు, కర్మాంతరము. **అపరధాన్యములు** or **అపరాలు** or **అపరదినుసులు** other kinds of grain, miscellaneous grains, all sorts of grain in pods, such as beans, &c. కాయధాన్యములు. One verse says. "ఉత్తరే పూర్వసస్యాని అపరసస్యానిరేవతా." **అపరనామము** n. A second name. రెండో పేరు. **అపరభాగము** n. The hind part, వెనుకటిభాగము. **అపరమంత్రములు** n. Funeral prayers. అపరరాత్రి, midnight, the latter half of the night. అపరలోకము another world. అపరవారధి the western ocean. వాడు పూర్వాపరములు చేయించగలడు he is qualified as priest to solemnize both the marriage and funeral rites. **అపరాహ్ణము** or **అపరాహ్నము** [Skt. అపర+అహ్నము.] n. The afternoon. రెండుఝాము లకుమీదికాలము.

అపరాజితము *a-parājitamu.* [Skt.] adj. Not conquered. జయింపబడని. Bhār. I. i. 3.

అపరాత్రి *apa-rātri.* [Skt. అప+Tel. రాత్రి] n. The dead of night. Mid-night. నిశీధి, అర్ధరాత్రము.

అపరాధము *apa-rādhamu.* [Skt.] n. A fault, sin, guilt, (commonly) a fine, punishment, penalty. శిక్షార్థమైనకర్మము, పాపము, నేరము, (వాడుకగా) నేరమునకై పుచ్చుకొనే రూకలు. అపరాధమును మన్నించు or కాచు to pardon, overlook. అపరాధక్షమను చేసికొను to beg pardon. అపరాధము వేయు to inflict a fine. అపరాధముతీయు to take a fine. **అపరాధి** n. An offender, delinquent. నేరముచేసినవాడు. **అపరాద్ధము** adj. Criminal, guilty, erring, faulty. అపరాధి యైన, పాపియైన.

అపరిమితము *a-parimitamu.* [Skt.] adj. Boundless, infinite, immense. మితములేని, విస్తారమైన.

అపరిహార్యము *a-pari-hāryamu.* [Skt.] adj. Indefeasible, unavoidable. పోగొట్టకూడని. అపరిహార్యులైన దేహసంబంధులు relations that cannot be neglected.

అపరూపము *apa-rūpamu.* [Skt.] adj. Ugly. deformed. Rare, scarce, uncommon. వికృతాకారము, వికారము, (వాడుకగా) వింతైన, అరుదైన.

అపరోక్షము *a-parōkshamu.* [Skt.] n. Presence. సమక్షము. **అపరోక్షజ్ఞుడు** n. A. prophet; one who knows the past and the future. భూతభవిష్యత్తులను ఎరిగినవాడు.

అపర్ణ *aparna.* [Skt.] n. An epithet of Parvati. పార్వతీదేవి.

అపలపించు or **అపలాపముచేయు** *apa-lapintsu.* [Skt.] v. a. To deny, conceal. ఉండగా లేదను, ఎరిగియుండగా ఎరుగనను, మరుగుచేయు. **అపలాపము** *apa-lāpamu.* [Skt.] n. Denial, concealment of knowledge, evasion. ఉండగా లేదనడము, ఎరిగియుండగా ఎరుగననడము.

అపవర్గము *apa-vargamu.* [Skt.] n. Detachment from matter, final beatitude. మోక్షము. భోగాపవర్గములు the present enjoyment and the final bliss.

అపవాదము *apa-vādamu.* [Skt.] n. Calumny, reproach, slander. నింద, అపఖ్యాతి.

అపవిత్రము *a-pavitramu.* [Skt.] adj. Impure; unclean. అపరిశుద్ధమైన.

అపశకునము *apa-sakunamu.* [Skt.] n. A bad omen.

అపశబ్దము *apa-sabdamu.* [Skt.] n. An ungrammatical word. వ్యాకరణవిరుద్ధమైన పదము.

అపసత్యము *apa-satyamu.* [Skt.] n. Perjury. అప్రమాణము.

అపసవ్యము *apa-savyamu.* [Skt.] adj. Contrary, opposite to, on the wrong side ప్రతికూలమైన, దక్షిణమైన, అనగా కుడిదైన. అపసవ్యలిపి letters written the wrong way as in a seal. **అపసవ్యము** n Putting the braminical thread the wrong way: that is, on the right shoulder and letting it fall on the left side instead of lying on the left shoulder. జందెమును కుడిభుజము మీదనుంచి యెడమభుజమునకు క్రిందికట్టుగా వేసుకొనడము.

అపసాక్షి *apa-sākshi* [Skt.] n. (Not a good phrase) A false witness. తప్పుసాక్షి. అపసాక్ష్యము false evidence. తప్పుసాక్ష్యము.

అపస్మారము or **అపస్మారకము** *apa-smāramu.* [Skt.] adj. Nasty, filthy, nauseous, dirty. అసహ్యమైన, రోతైన. **అపస్మారము** n. Forgetfulness. A confused feeling: violent passion, approaching to madness. Nastiness: Epilepsy, కాకిసోమాల, తెలుపు మరుపుమాటలు, (లోకవాడుకలో) రోత, అసహ్యము. **అపస్మారకుడు** n. A nasty or dirty fellow. రోతమనిషి. **అపస్మారి** n. An epileptic (vulgarly) he who is nasty or filthy. కాకిసోమాల గలవాడు, రోతమనిషి.

అపస్వరము *apa-svaramu.* [Skt.] n. Mispronunciation: a false note or discord in music. తప్పు ఉచ్చారణ, సంగీతములో తప్పుస్వరము. **అపస్వరము** adj. Inharmonious, discordant. శ్రావ్యముకాని, సుస్వరముకాని.

అపహతము *apa-hatamu.* [Skt.] adj. Destroyed, killed.

అపహము *apahamu.* [Skt.] adj. Doing away, with, healing, averting. పోగొట్టె. కల్మషాపహము doing away with sin or impurity.

అపహరించు *apa-harintsu.* [Skt.] v. a. To pillage, plunder, take by violence or deceit, usurp. ముచ్చిలించు, అన్యాయముగా ఎత్తుకొనిపోవు. **అపహరణము** *apa-haranamu.* [Skt.] n. Plundering, purloining, carrying off, stealing. చౌర్యము, ముచ్చిలించడము, అన్యాయముగా ఎత్తుకొనిపోవడము. **అపహర్త** n. One who carries away by force or violence, a thief, rogue. **అపహారము** *apahāramu.* [Skt.] n. Pillage, plunder, taking by violence. దోచుకోవడము. సర్వస్వాపహారము robbing of every thing. దత్తాపహారము taking back a gift. **అపహృతము** adj. that which is robbed or stolen.

అపహసించు *apa-hasintsu.* [Skt.] v. a. To laugh convulsively, to laugh outright

To laugh at, deride. *గేలిచేయు, ఎగసక్కెము చేయు, వెక్కిరించు. అపహాసము or అపహాస్యము *apahāsyamu.* [Skt.] n. Laughter, ridicule, jest. ఎగసక్కెము, వెక్కిరింపు.

అపాంగము *apāngamu.* [Skt.] n. The outer corner of the eye. కడకన్ను.

అపాంపతి *apām-pati.* [Skt.] n. The father of waters, the sea or ocean. సముద్రము.

అపాంక్తేయుడు *a-pāngtēyuḍu.* [Skt.] n. An unfashionable man, one with whom others will not eat. పఙ్క్తిలో నుండదగనివాడు, అర్హుడు కానివాడు.

అపాటవము *a-pāṭavamu.* [Skt.] n. Weakness, infirmity, illness, అశక్తి. వానికి ఒళ్లు అపాటవముగానున్నది he is unwell.

అపాత్రము *a-pātramu.* [Skt.] adj. Unworthy, undeserving, unfit. తగని, అయోగ్యమైన, అర్హముకాని. అపాత్రుడు n. He who is unworthy or undeserving. అయోగ్యుడు, అనర్హుడు. నేను అతని దయకు అపాత్రుడనైనాను I forfeited his favour. I incurred his displeasure.

అపానము *apānamu.* [Skt.] n. The Anus. గుదము, ముడ్డి. అపానవాయువు n. *ventris crepitus.* పిత్తు, ముడ్డిగాలి.

అపామార్గము Same as ఉత్తరేణి. (q. v.)

అపాయము *apāyamu.* [Skt.] n. Peril, danger, mischief. హాని, చెరుపు, చేటు. ప్రాణానికివచ్చిన అపాయము the peril of life, mortal peril.

అపారము *a-pāramu.* [Skt.] adj. Shoreless, boundless, infinite, excessive, abundant. అమితమైన, విస్తారమైన. అపారపారము the shoreless waters, the ocean. అపారముగా adv. Profusely, abundantly. విస్తారముగా.

అపార్థము *aparthamu.* [Skt.] n. Misinterpretation. తప్పు అర్థము. అపార్థముచేయు or అపార్థము చెప్పు to misinterpret or misconstrue.

అపిధానము *api-dhānamu.* [Skt.] n. A covering, screen, concealment. ఆచ్ఛాదనము, తిరోధానము, మరుగు.

అపుడు *apuḍu.* [Tel.] adv. Then. See అప్పుడు.

అపుణ్యము *a-puṇyamu.* [Skt.] adj. Wicked, bad. దుష్టమైన. అపుణ్యజనులు the wicked.

అపుత్రుడు or **అపుత్రవంతుడు** *a-putruḍu.* [Skt.] n. He who is sonless. కుమారులు లేనివాడు.

అపునర్భవము *a-punarbhavamu.* [Skt.] n. Freedom from re-birth, final beatitude, eternal bliss. మోక్షము.

అపురూపము *apu-rūpamu.* [Skt.] adj. Rare, seldom, uncommon, unusual. అరుదైన, వింతైన, అపూర్వము. KP. vi. 232.

అపూపము *apūpamu.* [Skt.] n. A cake. భక్ష్యము.

అపూర్వము *a-pūrvamu.* [Skt.] adj. Novel, uncommon, extraordinary. వింతైన, చోద్యమైన.

> "వీయదివ్యాస్త్రమపూర్వం
> చేయుచు." Bhar: I. i. 29.

అపేక్ష *apēksha.* [Skt.] n. Expectation, hope, wish, desire. ఆశ. తదపేక్షయా than that, with reference to that. అశ్వాపేక్ష యేనుగజము బలవత్తరము as regards the horse the elephant is strong, i. e., the elephant is stronger than the horse. అపేక్షించు *apēkshintsu.* v. a. To covet, long for, wish for. ఆశపడు, కోరు. అపేక్షణీయము or అపేక్ష్యము *apēkshaṇīyamu* [Skt.] adj. Desirable.

అపోహము *apōhamu.* [Skt.] n. An unwarranted inference Inferring the existence of what does not really exist any where లేనిది ఊహించుట. Ascertaining by investigation, decision. నిర్ణయము, నివృత్తి. It commonly means a lie, a falsehood, a false charge. అబద్ధము, కల్ల, తప్పు ఫిర్యాదు. నామీద అపోహము చెప్పినాడు he laid the blame upon me falsely.

అప్డు *apḍu.* [Tel.] adv. (అప్పుడు is occasionally thus spelt to suit the metre.) Then, when, at that time.

అప్ప *appa.* [Tel. cognate with Heb. Abba, father.] n. Papa, a father. An elder sister. తండ్రి, అక్క. (This word is frequently added to the proper names of men; as a term of common respect; thus రంగప్ప, రామప్ప.)

అప్పగించు *appagintsu.* [Tel.] v. a. To entrust, commit, deliver to the charge of another, give over, to put into another's possession. ఒప్పగించు, పదిలముగా నుంచుమని వశముచేయు. **అప్పగింత** n. Delivery, consignment. ఒప్పగింత. ఆ యింటిని నాకు అప్పగింత పెట్టినాడు he made the house over to me.

అప్పచ్చి *appachchi.* [Tel.] n. A cake. అపూపము.

అప్పటము *appaṭamu.* [Tel.] adj. Pure, unmixed. స్వచ్ఛమైన.

అప్పటి *appaṭi.* [Tel.] Again. మరల.

"అట్లకా, కనియలభీమనాధునకు
నప్పటియుం బ్రణమిల్లి వేడుకన్."
రుక్మాం. i.

అప్పడము *appaḍamu.* [Tel.] n. A sort of thin cake which is fried. భక్ష్యవిశేషము.

అప్పతి *ap-pati.* [Skt. అప్ + పతి.] n. Lord of waters, a title of the Indian Neptune. వరుణుడు.

అప్పన *appana.* [Tel. from అప్పగించు] n. Consent, order, command. అనుమతి, ఆజ్ఞ.

అప్పనము *appanamu.* [from Skt. అర్పణము.] n. Offering. అర్పణము, కానుక. Tribute, tax. భాగధేయము, పన్ను. "రాజనీచేత జేయించు రాజనాయ, మప్పనములు నిశ్చితప్పనములు." T. v. 167. **అప్పనచేయు** to offer, to give over the charge of, to hand over. ఒప్పగించు.

"పుత్త్రులకును ఈ రాజ్య మెల్లనప్పనచేసి."
భాగ. v.

అప్పము *appamu.* [Tel.] n. A kind of sweet cake. అపూపవిశేషము.

అప్పళించు *appaḷintsu.* [Tel.] v. a. To tap, touch, slap, strike gently with the open hand. To embrace, To smear, apply. కొట్టు, చరచు, అంటు, మొత్తు, ఆలింగనముచేసి కొను, చరుసు. "దప్పదేనగతోక నప్పళించి." A iii. 27. "జేనుఁగునకుంకుమరసంబప్పళించి." P. iv. 419. To try. యత్నించు. To cover. కప్పు. "లేనగవుబొల్తుక రెప్పలనప్పళించుచున్." Swa. v. To take. గ్రహించు. "పండులనప్ప ళింపగా" సై. 6 ఆ. To wipe as tears అద్దు, తుడుచు. To touch. స్పృశించు. **అప్పళింత** *appaḷinta.* [Tel.] n. Striking gently with the hand. చరపుట.

అప్పసము *appasamu.* [Tel.] n. The cut at which water is let into a field. మడవ. **అప్పసము.** adv. Always.

"పసిరికపాముఁబంటిదని పల్కుదురీ
యలివేణిలేణిస్సప్పసము"
కళ. i.

అప్పు *appu.* [Tel.] n. Loan, debt. ఋణము. అప్పుపుచ్చుకొను to borrow. **అప్పుయిచ్చు** to lend. **అప్పుపడు** to fall in debt. **అప్పుస ప్పులు** debts: here the word సప్పులు is an anuk. అప్పులకోరు a man in debt; a debtor. అప్పు పుచ్చుకొన్నవాడు. **అప్పులవాడు** n. A creditor, lender. ఉత్తమర్ణుడు, అప్పుయిచ్చిన వాడు.

అప్పు *appu.* [Skt.] n. Water. నీళ్లు. plu. అప్పులు Vasu i. Preface 56. "ధరయేయపాం సులత చూపరాకుండ దనకూర్తిరేని నప్పునని యుంచె." Vasu. i. "అప్పులెల్లాబ్ధిచేతబుచ్చుకొని కాళ్లంగైన మన్గొన్నయయ్యప్పులే దానవియుణ నప్పటికిముగా నవ్వార్ధకేకోన్నగా." A. iv. 198.

అప్పుడు *appudu.* [Tel. from అ + పొద్దు] adv. Then, at that time (This is also used as a defective noun.) Dative అప్పటికి at that time. అప్పట్లో (locative) at that time. అప్పటినుంచి since that time. అట్లా చెప్పేటప్పటికి when he said so. మరియొకప్పుడు at another time. In compounds it means 'When', as వాడు వచ్చినప్పుడు when he came. ఒకప్పుడు వచ్చును ఒకప్పుడు రాకపోవును he sometimes came and sometimes stayed away. అప్పుడే (emphatic form) just then, already. అప్పుడే పుట్టినబిడ్డ a child just born. అప్పుడప్పుడు now and then. అప్పటిరాజులు the rulers of those days, the then princes.

అప్రకాశముగా *a-prakasamu-ga.* [Skt.] adv. in secret.

అప్రతికారము *a-pratikaramu.* [Skt.] n. Ingratitude. కృతఘ్నత. "క్రోధంబు ప్రతికార హైమ్ప్రదమును సుంబింమనర్థంత చింతా ధూతాత్మ వశై." M. IV. ii. 281.

అప్రతిద్వంద్వుడు *a-prati-dvandvudu.* [Skt.] n. He who is incomparable or matchless in battle. అసమానుడైనవాడు.

అప్రతిష్ఠ *a-pratishtha.* [Skt.] n. Bad reputation, disgrace. అపకీర్తి, అపవాదము.

అప్రతిహతము *a-pratihatamu.* [Skt.] adj. Irresistible. అనివార్యమైన, అడ్డగింపరానటి. అప్రతిహతరోషుడు he who is irresistible in wrath.

అప్రత్యక్షము *a-pratyakshamu.* [Skt.] adj. Imperceptible, invisible. అగోచరమైన, అగుపడని.

అప్రదక్షిణము *a-pradakshinamu.* [Skt.] n. Walking round (a corpse, &c.) presenting the left hand towards it. ఎడమచెయితట్టుగా చుట్టును తిరగడము.

అప్రధానము *a-pradhanamu.* [Skt.] n. Unimportant, secondary. **అప్రాధాన్యము** *a-pradhanyamu.* [Skt.] n. Inferiority.

అప్రమాణము *a-pramanamu.* [Skt.] n. Perjury, a false oath. అసత్యము, తప్పుప్రమాణము. అప్రామాణికుడు one who forswears himself. A rogue; a liar.

అప్రమేయము *a-prameyamu.* [Skt.] adj. Incomprehensible; inconceivable; beyond human understanding. అగోచరమైన, అగు పడని, మితియెడదగనిది. **అప్రమేయుడు** n. God, the incomprehensible one. దేవుడు.

అప్రయత్నము *a-prayatnamu.* [Skt.] n. Absence of effort, indifference.

అప్రయోజకము *a-prayojakamu.* [Skt.] adj. Unserviceable, fruitless, useless. ఉపయోగముకాని, పనికిరాని. **అప్రయోజకుడు** n. A useless man. పనికిమాలినవాడు.

అప్రశస్తము *a-prasastamu.* [Skt.] adj. Not excellent, worthless, contemptible, not public, secret, hidden. అప్రసిద్ధమైన, రహస్యమైన, ఎవరుఎరుగని.

అప్రసిద్ధము *a-prasiddhamu.* [Skt.] adj. Not known to the world, not public, secret, hidden. అప్రశస్తమైన, రహస్యమైన, ఎవరుఎరుగని. **అప్రసిద్ధి** n. Infamy, అపకీర్తి. Obscurity.

అప్రాప్తవ్యవహారుడు *a-prapta-vyavaharudu.* [Skt.] n. A minor in law; one who is under age. వ్యవహారదశరానివాడు.

అప్రాప్యము *a-prapyamu.* [Skt.] adj. That which is unattainable. పొందశక్యముకానిది.

అప్రామాణికుడు. See అప్రమాణము.

అప్రాశ్యుడు *a-prasyudu.* [Skt.] n. An outcaste, he who is not fit to eat with others. అపాంక్తేయుడు, భ్రష్టుడు.

అప్రియము *a-priyamu.* [Skt.] n. Disagreeableness. Enmity, hatred. ద్వేషము.

అప్సరస or **అప్సరస్త్రీ** *apsarasa.* [Skt.] n. Heavenly nymph: a celestial courtesan. స్వర్వేశ్య, రంభమొదలైనవారు.

అబందర *a-bandara.* [Tel.] n. Disorder, confusion, irregularity. తారుమారు, రసాభాసము.

అబందరగానుండే adj. Disorderly, confused, irregular. కలవరముగానుండే.

అబక *abaka*. [Tel.] n. A ladle, a spoon made of a cocoanut shell. టెంకాయచిప్ప గరిటె.

అబటుచేప *abaṭu-chēpa*. [Tel.] n. A fish, a species of Balistes (Russell, Fishes, plate 21.)

అబద్ధము *a-baddhamu*. [Skt.] adj. False, untrue, erroneous, wrong. అసత్యమైన. నేను చెప్పినమాట అబద్ధము what I said was wrong, or not true. **అబద్ధము** n. A lie, a falsehood. అసత్యము, తప్పు. **అబద్ధికుడు** n. A liar. అసత్యవాది.

అబల *a-bala*. [Skt. lit. the weak one.] n. A woman. ఆడుది.

అబాధితము *a-bādhitamu*. [Skt.] adj. Unobjectionable. నిరాక్షేపమైన. ఇది అబాధితముగానున్నది it is not open to objection.

అబిసీలు *abisīlu*. [Tel.] n. To go for an airing, or for a walk. షికారు, వాహ్యాళి.

అబ్జము *abjamu*. [Skt. అప్+జ lit. waterborn] n. A lotus. A conch. పద్మము, శంఖము. అబ్జరేఖ name of a particular form of the lines in the hand. **అబ్జజుడు** or **అబ్జభవుడు** *abja-juḍu*. [Skt.] Brahma (being born from the lotus.) **అబ్జనయన** *abja-nayana*. [Skt.] The lotus-eyed (one.) **అబ్జబాంధవుడు** n. The sun. సూర్యుడు. **అబ్జారి** or **అబ్జుడు**. n. The moon. చంద్రుడు.

అబ్దము *abdamu*. [Skt.] n. A year. A cloud. సంవత్సరము, మేఘము. అబ్దశతము or శతాబ్దము a century; అబ్దసహస్రము a thousand years.

అబ్ధి *abdhi*. [Skt. అప్ + ధి] n. The sea. సముద్రము. అబ్ధిజ Lakshmi, having been produced at the churning of the sea of milk. అబ్ధిఅగ్ని submarine fire. అబ్ధిపల్లవము n. Coral. పగడము.

అబ్బ *abba*. [Heb. Abba. Aryan *Pa*.] n. A father. తండ్రి. నాయబ్బతోడుగా I swear by my father. వీడు వాని అబ్బ this man is ten times worse than he is. నీయబ్బతో పోయి చెప్పు go and tell your granny. **అబ్బ**, **అబ్బా** or **అబ్బబ్బా**! An interjection of grief or admiration a common exclamation. అయ్యో!

అబ్బకాడు *abba-kāḍu*. [Tel.] n. An ignorant fellow.

అబ్బరము *abbaramu*. [Tel.] adj. and adv. To a surprising degree. n. A wonder, a marvel. ఆశ్చర్యము.

అబ్బాటు *abbāṭu*. [Tel.] n. Closeness, *ennui* as in a crowded room. జనసమ్మర్దము వలన కలిగేదుఃఖము Swa. v.

అబ్బాయి *abbāyi*. [Tel.] n. My lad! అబ్బి, కుర్రవాడు.

అబ్బాలాడు *abbālāḍu*. [Tel. అబ్బాలు+ఆడు] v. n. To grope. తేవులాడు. To get flurried. తడబడు.

అబ్బి or **అబ్బిగాడు** *abbi*. [Tel.] n. My lad! అబ్బాయి, కుర్రవాడు.

అబ్బు *abbu*. [Tel.] v. n. To come into one's enjoyment, possession, or reach; be obtained or gained. చిక్కు, దొరకు, లభించు, ప్రాప్తించు. ఇది వీనికి అబ్బేసొమ్ముకాదు the luck is too good to last; that is, he is not worthy of such good fortune, and it will not stick by him. దీన్ని వానికి అబ్బనియ్యరు they will prevent his getting it.

అబ్బురము *abburamu*. [Tel.] n. Surprise, amazement, astonishment. ఆశ్చర్యము. "అంబురాసు లబ్బురంబుగాగ గ్రాగిపొంగె." N. iii. 211. **అబ్బురపడు** to be surprised. **అబ్బురపాటు** *abburapāṭu*. [Tel.] n. Surprise, amazement. ఆశ్చర్యము.

అబ్బెంద *abbenda*. [Tel.] n. A kind of plant. వృక్షవిశేషము. "అబ్బెందలమా కబ్బెందలిలి." య. 4 ఆ.

అబ్బెసము *abbesamu*. [Tadbhava form of Skt. అభ్యాసము] n. Practice. అలవాటు.

అబ్రము *abramu.* [Another form of అబ్బురము] adj. Wonderful, amazing. అద్భుతమైన. n. Wonder, marvel. అద్భుతము. T. ii. 77. "కువలయాక్షుల కింపొనరించుట బ్రము." N. 1. 167. **అబ్బురపడు** v. n. To wonder. ఆశ్చర్యపడు.

అబ్రహ్మణ్యము *a-brahmanyamu.* [Tel.] n. A deed improper to be done by a Brahmin; an unbrahminical or sacrilegious act; an exclamation meaning 'to the rescue! a heinous sin is about to be committed!' Crying for quarter. మొఱ, ఆపత్కాలో క్తి, చంపవద్దనేమాట. "ఈ వ్యాసుపాటంబు లో భామా రోదనమాచరింతువిధిక బ్రహ్మణ్యముం బెట్టుదురా." Swa. iii. 137. "బలభిన్ముఖ్యులు హాహాహాహాయని యబ్రహ్మణ్యముం బెట్టగజా." N. ii. 490.

అబ్రాశి *ab-rāsi.* [Skt.] అప్+రాశి] n. Ocean, as being the heap of waters. సముద్రము. "దుగ్ధాబ్రాశింబడి." A. vi. 158.

అబ్రాహ్మణుడు *a-brāhmanudu.* [Skt.] A non-Brahmin.

అబ్లింగము *ab-lingamu.* [Skt. అప్ = water]. n. The watery principle Hydrogen.

అబ్లోసు *ablōsu.* [?] n. *Ablōs.* The *wake* of a ship. ఓడపోవునప్పుడు వెనక నీళ్లలో తెలిసేజాడ.

అబ్వాబు *abvābu.* [H.] n. (Lit. Doors, chapters.) Miscellaneous revenue accounts. "The usual heads in Revenue accounts are Mal and Abwab. The Mal or Regular revenue is collected on land and customs, including taxes on liquors, &c The Abwab, or Miscellaneous includes the difference of exchange (often considerable) between that of the market and the fixed rate at which the revenue of the district is paid, casual aid or support of the Government officers, fees to the shroff, and contributions to various feasts." Malcolm, vol. ii. p. 48.

అభంగురము *a-bhanguramu.* [Skt.] adj. Imperishable, eternal. నిరంతరమైన. "అభంగుర స్వాదురసావలంబంబులగు ఫలంబులం." R. ii. 94.

అభముశుభము *abhamu-subhamu.* [Skt. శుభము] n. (Conversational) Evil and good, right and wrong. ఆ పిల్లకాయ అభముశుభము ఎరగకముందు before that boy was old enough to know good from evil.

అభయము *a-bhayamu.* [Skt. lit. fearlessness.] n. An assurance of security: warrant of safety, a promise of shelter, impunity or protection. భయములేదనడము, నీకు భయములేదు నేను ఉన్నానడము, ధైర్యము. ఆయన నాకు అభయమిచ్చియున్నాడు he told me not to be afraid. అభయహస్తము the hand of protection.

అభవుడు *a-bhavudu.* [Skt. lit. the unborn one]. n. God, దేవుడు.

అభాండము *a-bhāndamu.* [Origin not known.] n. False or unjust accusation, slander. లేనిపోనినేరము, అపవాదము. అభాండపు వ్యాజ్యము a false complaint.

అభాగ్యము *a-bhāgyamu.* [Skt.] adj. Unfortunate, luckless, wretched. దౌర్భాగ్యమైన, దురదృష్టమైన.

అభావము *a-bhāvamu.* [Skt.] n. Non-existence, nonentity, want. లేమి. **అభావము** adj. Non-existent. లేని.

అభిక్రమము *abhi-kramamu.* [Skt.] n. Expedition. శత్రువులపై దండెత్తి పోవుట.

అభిఖ్య *abhikhya.* [Skt.] n. Name, title; splendour, glory: fame. పేరు, శోభ, కీర్తి.

అభిగమనము *abhi-gamanamu.* [Skt.] n. Motion towards, a going to. ఎదురుగా పోవడము.

అభిఘరించు *abhi-gharintsu.* [Skt.] v. a. To put a few drops of clarified butter upon rice before eating or before the rice is put into the sacrificial fire to purify the food. నేయిచుక్క వేయడము, భోజనమునకు ముందుగాగాని ఆహుతిచేయుడమునకు ముందుగాగాని అన్నములో నెయిచుక్క వేయడము.

అభిఘారము *abhi-ghāramu.* [Skt.] n. Ghee or clarified butter. నేతిబొట్లు, usually putting a few drops of clarified butter upon rice prior to eating: or putting it in the sacrificial fire to purify the rice.

అభిఘాతము *abhi-ghātamu.* [Skt.] n. Striking together, collision. తగలడము, తాకుడు, దెబ్బ, కొట్టుకోవడము, అడిచడము. అభిఘాతజ్వరము fever caused by exhaustion.

అభిచరించు *abhi-charintsu.* [Skt.] v. n. To roam, stroll. సంచరించు, తిరుగు. **అభిచరుడు** n. A servant, an attendant. దాసుడు, భృత్యుడు. A companion. సహాయుడు, తోడు. **అభిచారము** n. An incantation to injure or destroy, a magical ceremony to procure the death of an enemy. హింసాకర్మ, హింసార్థమైన హోమకర్మము.

అభిజనము *abhi-janamu.* [Skt.] n. The birth-place Caste, A caste-mark as a title. Fame. పుట్టినచోటు, కులము, కులాగతమయిన పెక్కుముల్లోగల బిరుదు, ప్రసిద్ధి. **అభిజనుడు** n. A man of high birth. కులశ్రేష్ఠుడు. **అభిజనమదము** pride of ancestry.

అభిజాతము *abhi-jatamu.* [Skt.] adj. Born, produced. **అభిజాతుడు** a high caste man, a man of a high family. మంచికులమున బుట్టినవాడు.

అభిజిత్తు, అభిజిత్తువేళ or **అభిజిల్లగ్నము** *abhi-gittu.* [Skt.] n. The Zenith, midday, the 24 minutes immediately preceding and the 24 following midday. పగటిలో ఎనిమిదో ముహూర్తము.

అభిజ్ఞానము *abhi-gnanamu.* [Skt.] n. A mark, a sign. చిహ్నము. Intelligence, cleverness. **అభిజ్ఞుడు** n. A learned man, he who is skilled or conversant; a genius. ప్రవీణుడు, నిపుణుడు, గట్టివాడు, తెలిసినవాడు. **అభిజ్ఞురాలు** n. A genius, an apt or sensible woman. ప్రవీణురాలు, గట్టిది.

అభిధ *abhidha.* [Skt.] n. A figure of speech. ఇ.క. శబ్దవృత్తి. సంకేతములను పదపదార్థముల సంబంధము.

అభిధానము or **అభిధేయము** *abhi-dhanamu.* [Skt.] n. A name, an appellation, a title. నామము, పేరు. **అభిధాయకము** adj. Designated. పేరుగానుండే. ఈ శబ్దములు ప్రథమావిభక్త్యభిధాయకములుగావున as these words express the nominative

అభినందించు *abhi-nandintsu.* [Skt] v. n. To be delighted, rejoice. ఆనందించు. n. **అభినందనము** joy.

అభినయించు *abhi-nayintsu.* [Skt.] v. n. To express emotions by looks, gestures, &c., as actresses do. కండ్లు వేళ్లు మొదలైనవాటిని తిప్పి మనోభావమును తెలియచేయు, అంగన్యాసాదులచే అర్థమును సూచించు. **అభినయము** *abhi-nayamu.* [Skt.] n. Action and posture expressive of sentiment, especially the gestures and movements of dramatic representation. వేళ్లు మొదలైనవాటిచేత మనః కార్యమును తెలియచేయడము.

అభినవము *abbi-navamu.* [Skt.] adj. New, modern నూతనమైన, క్రొత్త. అభినవకాళిదాసుడు "The modern Kalidasa." This is equivalent to "The Milton of our days" or, "a Byron, a Moore:" merely denoting an excellent poet.

అభిని *abhini.* [H.] n. Opium. నల్లమందు. అభినిపాలు milk opium, which is sold in leather bags like bladders.

అభినివేశము *abhi-nivesamu.* [Skt.] n. Ardour, zeal, enthusiasm, earnestness. పట్టు, శ్రద్ధ, చొరవ.

అభినుతించు *abhi-nutintsu.* [Skt.] v. a. To praise, applaud, extol. స్తుతించు, కొనియాడు. **అభినుతము** adj. Lauded, celebrated, praised. స్తోత్రముచేయబడ్డ. **అభినుతి** n. Praise. స్తుతి.

అభిన్యాసము *abhinyasamu.* [Skt.] n. A fit. A morbid state of the three humours.

అంతర్భావా బహిస్థితములుగల సన్నిపాతవిశేషము, వాతపైత్య శ్లేష్మదోషాలు ప్రకోపించి మూడున్ను సరి అయి చేష్టలుమాటలు క్రమముతప్పి అవశ్యమా చంపే సన్నిపాతము.

అభిపాతము *abhi-pātamu.* [Skt.] n. Falling. పడడము. Vasu. iv. 12.

అభిప్రాయము *abhi-prāyamu.* [Skt.] n. Opinion, sentiment, notion, idea, thought, design, meaning, signification, import. తలపు, తాత్పర్యము. **అభిప్రేతము** adj. Intended, designed, aimed at. సమ్మతమైన.

అభిభవము *abhi-bhavamu.* [Skt.] n. Insult, dishonour, disgrace. అవమానము, తిరస్కారము. **అభిభవించు** v. To insult. తిరస్కరించు. **అభిభూతము** adj. Defeated, humbled, subdued. తిరస్కరింపబడిన, పరాభూతమైన, గర్వభంగము చేయబడ్డ, అణచబడ్డ. R. i. 79.

అభిమంత్రించు *abhi-mantrintsu.* [Skt.] v. a. To call on, address, conjure, raise by spells, invoke. To consecrate by a formula. పిలుచు, ఆవాహనముచేయు, మంత్రాలుచేత సంస్కరించు. **అభిమంత్రితము** adj. Devoted, consecrated, a certain formula having been pronounced over it. మంత్రించబడ్డ. **అభిమంత్రణము** *abhi-mantraṇamu.* n. Calling to, addressing, inviting, a consecration, benediction by religious formula. ఆహ్వానము, పిలుచుడము, సంస్కారము.

అభిమతము *abhi-matamu.* [Skt.] n. Desire, wish, inclination, consent, approbation. ఇచ్ఛ, సమ్మతము. **అభిమతము** adj. Wished, approved, acceptable. సమ్మతమైన, ఈప్సితమైన.

అభిమానము *abhi-mānamu.* [Skt.] n. Pride, self-esteem, haughtiness Patronage, protection. Affection, regard, care, love, favour. గర్వము, సంరక్షణ, విశ్వాసము. **దేశాభిమానము** love of one's own country, patriotism. వాడు దేహాభిమానము కలవాడు he pays great attention to his own ease, he is luxurious. **అభిమానపుత్రుడు** one who passes for one's son, or is looked upon as a son, or, supposed to be his child. అభిమానపుత్రత్వము an understood or attributed sonship. తమ అభిమానము కావలసినది I beg your patronage. నాయందు నిండా అభిమానముగా జరిగించినాడు he has treated me honourably. ఒకనిమీద అభిమానము ఉంచు to be partial to a person. అభిమానము లేనివాడు one without affection; unkind. **అభిమాని** n. He who loves. విశ్వాసముగలవాడు. మతాభిమాని a bigot. కులాభిమాని one who stands up for his caste. దేశాభిమాని the advocate for his country, he who loves his country, a patriot. **అభిమానించు** v. a. To honor, favour, protect, patronise, regard with kindness. గొప్పచేయు, గారవించు.

అభిముఖము *abhi-mukhamu.* [Skt.] adj. Fronting, facing, having the face towards. (fig.) Propitious, favourable. Allayed or subdued as disease or anger. సమ్ముఖమైన. సూర్యాభిముఖముగా facing the sun. నాకు అభిముఖముగా తిరుగు turn your face to me. **అభిముఖమగు** v. n. To face, turn towards, ఎదురుముఖముగా తిరుగు, దోపకుపచ్చు, శాంతపడు. జ్వరము అభిముఖమైనప్పుడు when the fever was on the turn. **అభిముఖుడు** n. He who faces. సమ్ముఖుడు. మాకు అభిముఖుడై turning towards us. పర్వతాభిముఖుడై పలికెను he turned his face towards the mountain and said. BD. iii. 1855.

అభియాతి *abhi-yāti.* [Skt.] n. A foe, an enemy. శత్రువు. R. v. 128.

అభియోగము *abhi-yōgamu.* [Skt.] n. Application, strong effort; challenging to fight. **అభియోగపత్రము** a complaint made in writing, a plaint. **అభియోగి** *abhi-yōgi.* [Skt.] n. A plaintiff, an enemy.

అభిరక్షితము *abhi-rakshitamu.* [Skt.] adj. Protected, guarded.

అభిరతి *abhi-rati.* [Skt.] n. Attachment, love. ప్రీతి.

అభిరామము *abhi-rāmamu.* [Skt.] adj. Beautiful, engaging, agreeable. మనోహరమైన, రమ్యమైన.

అభిరుచి *abhi-ruchi.* [Skt.] n. Wish, desire, taste, relish, inclination. కోరిక, ఆశ, ఆసక్తి.

అభిరుచిరము *abhi-ruchiramu.* [Skt.] adj. Very pretty.

అభిరూపము *abhi-rūpamu.* adj. Learned, pleasing, handsome. చదువుకొన్న, మనోజ్ఞమైన.

అభిలషించు *abhi-lashintsu.* [Skt.] v. a. To desire, wish. కోరు. **అభిలాష** n. Desire, wish, inclination. ఇచ్ఛ, కోరిక, ఆశ. అభిలాషకలవాడై being inclined. వానికి అభిలాషలేనందున as he was disinclined. **అభిలాషి** n. He who loves. కోరికగలవాడు, ఇచ్ఛగలవాడు. ధర్మాభిలాషి he who loves justice.

అభివందనము *abhi-vandanamu.* [Skt.] n. Salutation, prostration. నమస్కారము, వందనము, మ్రొక్కు. **అభివాదనము** *abhivādanamu.* [Skt.] n. Salutation, prostration, reverence. ప్రణామము, నమస్కారము. గోత్రనామములుచెప్పి పాదములు తాకినట్లు మ్రొక్కుట. అభివాదకుడు one who salutes by falling at one's feet.

అభివృద్ధి *abhi-vriddhi.* [Skt.] n. Increase, improvement, progress, augmentation. పెంపు. వంశాభివృద్ధి, కులాభివృద్ధి increase of a family. **అభివృద్ధిచేయు** v. a. To increase, swell, improve, augment పెంచు, అధికముచేయు. **అభివృద్ధియగు** v. n. To increase, prosper. అధికమగు, పెరుగు.

అభివ్యక్తి *abhi-vyakti.* [Skt.] n. Revelation, declaration, expression, making evident. Reflection. ప్రకాశము, ప్రతిబింబము. "నిజమంటె రాత్రి రత్నమ్మలకెల్లానభివ్యక్తి" Vasu. i. 1.

అభిశస్తము *abhi-sastamu.* [Skt.] adj. Calumniated, falsely accused. నిందమోపబడిన. **అభిశస్తుడు** n. He who was calumniated, or falsely accused. నిందమోపబడినవాడు.

అభిషంగము *abhi-shangamu.* [Skt.] n. A defeat, overthrow, calumny, false accusation. పరాభవము, మిథ్యాపవాదము, అవమానము, తిట్టు.

అభిషేకము *abhi-shēkamu.* [Skt.] n. Installation by anointing, initiation, royal unction, bathing, anointing, inauguration. స్నానము, ముసుక, పట్టముకట్టడము. దేవునికి అభిషేకము అయినతరువాత after the idol was bathed. తైలాభిషేకము anointing with oil. హరిద్రాభిషేకము a particular rite of pouring turmeric powder over the head of an idol on the sixth day of the annual feast called బ్రహ్మోత్సవము. పట్టాభిషేకము coronation of a king. పట్టాభిషేకముచేయు to crown a king. రాజు ఆ కవికి స్వర్ణాభిషేకము చేసినాడు the prince showered bounties upon the poet. అన్నాభిషేకముచేయు to pour boiled rice over an image. **అభిషేకించు** v. t. To bathe, anoint. తలంటు, ముసిగించు. **అభిషిక్తము** *abhi-shiktamu.* [Skt.] adj. Installed by anointing, bathed, anointed. పట్టముకట్టబడిన, స్నానముచేయింపబడిన. **అభిషిక్తుడు** n. He who is inaugurated or installed, he who is bathed or anointed. పట్టప్రాప్తుడు, పట్టముకట్టబడినవాడు, స్నాతుడు. **అభిషేచనము** *abhi-shēchanamu.* [Skt.] n. Sprinkling, inauguration.

అభిసంచారము *abhi-sanchāramu.* [Skt.] n. A wandering about.

అభిసంధానము *abhi-sandhānamu.* [Skt.] n. Cheating.

అభిసంయోగము *abhi-samyōgamu.* [Skt.] n. Close contact.

అభిసరించు *abhi-sarintsu.* [Skt.] v. t. To go after, or follow one another, as lovers, to a particular place previously determined upon. ప్రియులగోశకనాశకి నుద్దేశించి పోవు. "శేయునిజవాధుల నభిసరించిరోయి" కవిక. 4 ఆ. **అభిసారిక** *abhi-sārika.* [Skt.] n. She who keeps or makes an assignation. నాయకునివిరోరి సంకేతస్థానమునకు పోవు నది. A v. 124.

అభిహారము *abhi-hāramu.* [Skt.] n. Robbing; taking up arms against.

అభిహితము *abhi-hitamu.* [Skt.] adj. Said, spoken, declared.

అభీప్సితము *abhīpsitamu.* [Skt.] adj. Desired, wished for. కోరిన. **అభీప్సితము** n. Desire, love. వాంఛ, ఇచ్ఛ, కోరిక.

అభీరువు *a-bhīruvu.* [Skt.] n. The undaunted one. Name of a plant, *Asparagus Racemosus.* పిల్లపీచరచెట్టు.

అభీషువు *abhīshuvu.* [Skt.] n. A ray of light. కిరణము.

అభీష్టము *abhīshtamu.* [Skt.] adj. Wished, desired, beloved. ప్రియమైన, కోరబడిన. **అభీష్టము** n. Wish, desire, inclination. ఇష్టము, కోరిక, కోరబడినది.

అభూతము *a-bhūtamu.* [Skt.] adj. Non-existent. లేని, అవిద్యమానమైన. అభూతకల్పనము. a novel invention.

అభేదము *a-bhēdamu.* [Skt.] adj. Identical, similar, alike. ఆదే. వబయోరభేదః "V and B are alike:" that is, many words use either letter at pleasure: డలయోరభేదః, i. e., L and D are alike: thus we may write నారికేళము *nārikēlamu*, or నాడికేళము *nādikēramu.* **అభేదము** n. Identity, similarity. భేదములేమి, ఐక్యత. **అభేద్యము** adj. Solid, indivisible, impenetrable. దృఢమైన, భేదింపశక్యముకాని.

అభ్యంగము, అభ్యంగనము or **అభ్యంజనము** *abhyangamu.* [Skt.] n. Rubbing the body with an unctuous substance. Anointing, oiling. తలంటు. అభ్యంజనముచేసికొను to anoint one's self. అభ్యంజనస్నానము an oil bath.

అభ్యంతరము *abhyantaramu.* [Skt.] n. Obstacle, delay, hindrance, impediment. A central place, an included place, an interval. మధ్యము, అంతరము, విఘ్నము. **అభ్యంతరముచేయు** v. a. To hinder. విఘ్నముచేయు.

అభ్యనుజ్ఞ *abhy-anugnya.* [Skt.] n. Permission, leave. సెలవు, ఉత్తరువు.

అభ్యర్చన *abhy-archana.* [Skt.] n. Worship, reverence. పూజ. **అభ్యర్చించు** *abhyarchintsu.* v. t. To worship. **అభ్యర్చితుడు** one who is worshipped.

అభ్యర్ణము *abhyarṇamu.* [Skt.] adj. Contiguous, near, close. సమీపమైన.

అభ్యర్థించు *abhyarthintsu.* [Skt.] v. t. To desire, to pray, to beg. **అభ్యర్థితుడు.** who is prayed to, one who is solicited.

అభ్యవహారము *abhy-avahāramu.* [Skt.] n. Eating, food. భక్షణము, ఆహారము.

అభ్యసించు *abhyasintsu.* [Skt.] v. a. To exercise, practise, learn, study. అలవాటుచేయు, వాడుకచేయు, నేర్చుకొను. అభ్యసింపజేయు to cause to practise or learn **అభ్యసితము** *abhyasitamu.* [Skt.] adj. Practised, exercised, skilled. Learned, expert. అలవాటుపడిన, చెయ్యితిరిగిన, పనుపడిన, నేర్చుకొబడిన. **అభ్యసనీయము** *abhyasaniyamu.* n. That can be practised or learned. **అభ్యాసము** *abhyāsamu.* n. Practice, exercise, study, use. వాడుక, అలవాటు. అక్షరాభ్యాసము learning the alphabet. అభ్యాసం కూసువిద్య practice makes perfect.

అభ్యాగతుడు *abhy-āgatuḍu.* [Skt.] n. A guest, a visitor, one who drops in at dinner. అతిథి. అభ్యాగతపూజ or అభ్యాగత సేవ courteous reception of a guest. Welcome given to a guest.

అభ్యుత్థానము *abhy-uthhānamu.* [Skt.] n. Rising, rising to welcome a person. లేవడము, ఎదురుకొనిలేచుట, లేచి మర్యాదచేయుడము, గౌరవము.

అభ్యుదయము *abhy-udayamu.* [Skt.] n. Welfare, happiness, prosperity. మంగళము, శుభము. అభ్యుదయపరంపరాభివృద్ధిగా so that his prosperity may ever increase.

అభ్యుదితుడు *abhy-uditudu.* [Skt.] n. A man asleep at sunrise. సూర్యోదయకాలమందు నిద్రపోవువాడు.

అభ్రకము *abhrakamu.* [Skt.] n. Talc, Mica. భూమిలోనుండు అద్దపు పెంకులవంటి వస్తువు. కాకి బంగారము.

అభ్రము *abhramu.* [Skt.] n. The sky, a cloud. ఆకాశము, మేఘము. అభ్రంకషము heaven-kissing, sky-touching. **అభ్రగము** *abhragamu.* [Skt.] n. A sky-rover. i.e., a bird. పక్షి. అభ్రగపతి the eagle as being the king of birds. గరుడుడు. **అభ్రమణి** *abhra-mani.* [Skt.] n. The gem of the sky, i.e., the sun. సూర్యుడు.

అమ *ama.* [Tel.] n. Mother. తల్లి. Another form of అమ్మ.

అమంగళము *a-mangalamu.* [Skt.] adj. Unhappy, unpropitious, abominable. అశుభమైన, చెడ్డ.

అమంజీ, or **అమింజీ** *amanji.* [Tam.] n. Unpaid labour, work done by people who are impressed for service. Drudgery. వెట్టిపని.

అమందము *a-mandamu* [Skt.] adj. Not slow, violent, not little, great, extreme. అమందవ్యథ deep grief. అమందసౌభాగ్యము great wealth.

అమందారముగ *a-mandāramu-ga.* [Skt.] adv. Abundantly, greatly, plentifully. విస్తారముగా. "మందారమబీజము మందారమున విచ్చు కనకాంబరంబులు కట్టులగట్టి." N. ii. 425.

అమడలు or **అమడబిడ్డలు** *amaḍalu.* [Tel.] n. Twins. కవలలు. అమడయిండ్లు similar chambers, twin rooms. అమడకాయ a twin fruit, two fruits grown into one.

అమరకము or, **అమరము** *amarakamu.* [Tel.] n. A feudal tenure, i.e., land given to a chieftain on the condition that he shall supply the king with certain troops when required. Land. అగత్యమైనప్పుడు కొంత దండును తీసికొని రావలసినదనే నిబంధనమీద చిన్నరాజులకు విడువబడ్డ సీమ, చేడిగలేకుండా యివ్వబడ్డ గ్రామభూములు మొదలైనవి. Krishna Raya Vij. ii. 68. "ఏను బదివాల్గులక్షలకు నెన్నగ కన్నడ రాజ్యమందులో నమ్రుగ దేవరాయ వసుధామరరాయను తెన్నె వేల, నిలచినవరహాలకును గణనచెప్పెద వెయ్యజిరాను రాలకిం బొసరగల క్షవంతున, మహాల్సుతి నిర్వది నాల్గువేలకును. ఇరువదినాలుగులక్షలు, కరికిని వెయ్యింటిలెక్క గలనూరుఘటల్, మెరయగ ద్వాదశలక్షలు, మరహాల్షిగ్గయను సుస్థు వసుధాధీశా. భటులు వేయింటికిన్న నిర్వదియును నాల్గువేలుగా లక్షయర్వ దివేల ప్రజను తెల్లినల్బదిలక్షలు తీరమున ఘనయమరమేలెడి దొరలక్రమమెసుమ్మి." గండికోట సీమ అమరానికి పాలించియుండగాను he held the Gandicota lands on feudal tenure. స్వామివారికి అమరముగా యిచ్చినవనము a grove granted in free gift to the god. **అమరనాయకుడు** he who enjoys a feudal tenure. **అమరనాయంకరము** the lordship of a feudal tenure.

అమరశిలాగంధకము *amara-sila-gandha-kamu.* [Skt.] n. Sulphur or brimstone.

అమరాపగ *amar-āpaga.* [Skt.] n. The Ganges of heaven. ఆకాశగంగ. M. I. v. 5.

అమరు *amaru.* [Tel.] v. n. To be fit or proper, be agreeable, be prepared. ఒప్పు, తగు, తగియుండు. వానికి అన్నము చక్కగా అమరలేదు

the dinner was not such as befitted him. వానికి అన్ని అమరియున్నవి he has every thing right with him, he wants nothing. "అమరదు నీబొత్తుపృథా." P. ii. 49.

అమర్చు or **అమరుచు** or **అమరించు** *amartsu.* [Tel.] v. a. To prepare, make ready. To engage. To provide, supply, furnish. సిద్ధముచేయు, జాగ్రతచేయు. ప్రయాణమునకు కావలసినదాన్ని అమర్చినాడు he prepared every thing for the journey. "సొమ్ములుకొన చేరుకగా వెలయనమర్చి." H. i. 230. "అధమ వృత్తికధికునమరించుచుతి తిట్టుచుడుచుగాదె." P. i. 177. **అమరిక** *amarika.* n. Neatness. అందము. Tranquility, quietness, mildness. శాంతము, నెమ్మది. అమరికగలవాడు he who has presence of mind.

అమరుడు *a-marudu.* [Skt.] n. An immortal, a god. నిర్జరుడు. అమరావతి the Immortal city. Name of Indra's abode. **అమర్త్యుడు** *a-martyudu.* [Skt.] n. An immortal, a deity, a god. నిర్జరుడు.

అమర్యాద *a-maryada.* [Skt.] n. Incivility, disrespect; dishonour. అగౌరవము.

అమర్షము *amarshamu.* [Skt.] n. Rage; wrath. కోపము.

అమలము or **అమలినము** *a-malamu.* [Skt.] adj. Stainless, pure, clean. నిర్మలమైన, పరిశుద్ధమైన, నిష్కల్మషమైన. **అమలినుడు** *a-malinudu.* [Skt.] n. He who is holy, sinless, pure. The Deity. దేవుడు.

అమలు *amalu.* [H.] Authority, reign, sway, government. An office or post, a public charge. Execution, fulfilment, the period of one ruler's government. ఏలుబడి, దొరతనము, పాలన. అతని అమలులో in his reign or sway. ఆ కలెక్టరుగారి అమలులో in that Collector's days. ఆ తీర్పు అమలులోకి తేబడిన తరువాత after the decision was executed. వానిమీద అమలుచేసినారు they took steps against him, they put in force against him. **అమల్దారుడు** = an Amildar, i.e., one who exercises authority. One who puts government orders into force. A Tahsildar or revenue officer in charge of a Taluq.

అమవస *amavasa.* [from Skt. అమావాస్య] n. The new moon.

అమాంతము *amantamu.* [H.] adv. Unexpectedly, all at once. Totally, wholly. ఉన్నట్టుగా, యావత్తున్ను. ఆ రాళ్లను అమాంతముగా ఎత్తినాడు he raised the rocks bodily. **అమాంతగాడు** [H.] n. An interloper, నడిగొల్లగాడు. also, a petty dealer. చిల్లరబేరగాడు. **అమాంతవర్తకము.** Interloping, tricks in trade. బేరములో నడుమవచ్చి కొట్టుకొనిపోవడము. **అమాంతవర్తకుడు.** An interloper in trade. నడిగొల్లగాడైన వర్తకుడు.

అమాంసుడు *a-mamsudu.* [Skt.] n. He who is feeble or thin. దుర్బలుడు.

అమాత్యుడు *a-mātyudu.* [Skt.] n. A king's minister. మంత్రి.

అమాదినుసు *amādinusu.* [H.] n. Goods, market wares, as grain or vegetables.

అమానతు *amanatu.* [H.] Deposit, charge, anything given in trust.

అమాని *amani.* [H.] Land in charge of a revenue collector on the part of the government, as distinguished from that which is farmed out. అమానీగ్రామములు villages under the immediate care of a collector. అయినా అమాని అయినతరువాత after the land was taken into the collector's own charge. ఆ శ్రోత్రియము అమానీబాపతు చేసుకొన్నతరువాత after the land held on private tenure was taxed. అమానిభూములు Crown-lands, lands that are in the hands of a collector on behalf of Government. అమానీబాకీబాబు sundry farms under a Collector's management. పన్ను తేకుండా కొడిపోలు ఇచ్చేభూమి.

అమానుదస్తు *amanu-dastu.* [H] n. A pestle and mortar for pounding betelnut. వక్కలు కొట్టే రోలు రోకలి.

అమానుషము *a-mānushamu.* [Skt.] adj. Beyond the power of man. Supernatural. Inhuman, below human nature. మనిషికి అలవిగాని.

అమారు, అమారుతాడు [Port. *amarra.*] A cable. మోకు, ఓడలంగరు మోకు.

అమావాస్య or **అమాస** *amavasya.* [Skt.] n. The last day of the lunar month on which the moon is invisible. దర్శము.

అమిజీ Same as **అమంజీ** (q. v.)

అమితము *a-mitamu.* [Skt.] adj. Interminable, unlimited, immense. Vast, prodigious, immoderate, 'exorbitant. విస్తారమైన.

అమీనా *amina.* [H.] n. Ameen, a petty revenue officer.

అముద్రితము *a-mudritamu.* [Skt.] adj. Not sealed up, not stamped. ముద్రవేయబడని.

అమూల్యము *a-mūlyamu.* [Skt.] adj. Priceless, invaluable. అనర్ఘ్యమైన, విలువలేని.

అమృతము *a-mritamu.* [Skt.] n. Nectar, ambrosia. Water, milk, clarified butter, the residue of a sacrifice. Final emancipation from matter and absorption in the Deity. సుధ, ఉదకము, దుగ్ధము, ఘృతము, యజ్ఞశేష ద్రవ్యము, మోక్షము, (వాడుకగా) మజ్జిగ. **పంచామృతములు** the five nectars, namely, water, milk, curds, ghee and honey. అమృతమునకు అంటులేదు nothing can defile buttermilk. వానిది అమృతహస్తము. he has a healing hand. వానిది అమృతవాక్కు his tongue is inspired. **అమృతముహూర్తము** n. An auspicious hour. శుభముహూర్తము. **అమృతాంధసుడు** n. One whose food is ambrosia, a god. దేవత. **అమృతాంశువు** n. That which gives forth soft beams of light, i. e., the Moon. చంద్రుడు.

అమేధ్యము *amēdhyamu.* [Skt.] adj. Filthy, foul. అపరిశుద్ధమైన. **అమేధ్యము** n. Nastiness, excrement. అపవిత్రిరి, పురీషము.

అమేయము *amēyamu.* [Skt.] adj. Immeasurable, immense, vast. అపరిమితమైన.

అమోఘము *a-mōghamu.* [Skt.] adj. Fruitful, not vain, unerring, efficacious. సఫలమైన, నిరర్థకముకాని. వానికి అమోఘనిద్ర వచ్చినది he fell into a deep sleep. అమోఘవిక్రముడు a man of unerring valor.

అమ్మ *amma.* [Tel. of. Aryan root 'Ma.'] n. Mother. తల్లి. Madam. అమ్మక్కచెల్ల, అమ్మచెల్ల alas! ah! oho! **అమ్మణ్ణి**, **అమ్మయ్య** or **అమ్మా** or అమ్మల్లి interj. My dear, my love. **అమ్మవారు** *amma-vāru,* [Tel.] n. A Brahmin woman. A village goddess. The small pox. బ్రాహ్మణస్త్రీ, పోలేరు, మసూరికము. ఆ సత్రములోనుండే అమ్మవారిని పిలువు call the Brahmin woman who is in the lodge. అమ్మవారికి పొంగలి పెట్టినారు they offered a sacrifice to the village goddess. వానికి అమ్మవారు పోసినది he has got the small pox. అమ్మవారిచుక్కలు, అమ్మచుక్కలు pock marks. అమ్మవారి చుక్కలుగల or అమ్మచుక్కలుగల pitted with the small pox. అమ్మపాలు పోయించు to inoculate. అమ్మవారిధూము an outbreak of cholera. **అమ్మాయి** *ammāyi.* [Tel.] n. A little girl. పడుచు. **అమ్మి** or **అమ్మాళు** n. Missy, my dear, my love.

అమ్మకము See అమ్ము.

అమ్మనబొంట్లు *ammanu-bōntlu.* [Tel.] n. plu. Cunning jades. దొంగతొత్తులు. "బంకెతల టెంకెతల పళ్ళ క్రాసలు, రొమ్ముసకుంపట్లు రోత ప్రాముల్లు, బ్రహ్మెతకత్తెలు నమ్మనబొంట్లు." Charitra p. 460 line 7.

అమ్మనలు or **అమ్మనములు** *ammanalu.* [Tel.] n. A game wherein a number of balls are thrown into the air, one being caught in the hand descending whilst others are rising:

అగాంగలు గుండ్లను ఎగరవేసి ఆడే ఆట. "గుజ గుజరేకులు గుజ్జనగూళ్లును బొమ్మల పెండ్లిండ్లు వన్న నములు." N. ix. 101.

అమ్ము *ammu.* [Tel.] n. An arrow; a dart. బాణము. విల్లమ్ములు a bow and arrows. అమ్ముచేటు the distance an arrow flies. బాణము బోయి పడునంతదూరము.

అమ్ము *ammu* [Tel.] v. a. To sell. విక్రయించు. **అమ్మించు** (causal of **అమ్ము** v. n. To sell.) To have a thing sold, get it disposed of. విక్రయింపజేయు. **అమ్మకము** *ammakamu.* [Tel.] n. Sale, selling, vending. విక్రయము. **అమ్ముడు** *ammuḍu.* adj. and n. Saleable, that which is to be sold. విక్రయింపదగిన విగానుండే. అమ్ముడుసరుకులు goods which are to be sold. అవి యింకా అమ్ముడుపోలేదు they are not yet sold. **అమ్ముడుపోవు** v. i. To be sold. చెలుపోవు.

అమ్రాయి *amrāyi.* [H.] A garden or grove of mango trees. మామిడితోపు. Also, a tope or garden. తోపు, తోట.

అమ్లము *amlamu.* [Skt.] adj. Acid, sour. పుల్లని. **అమ్లము** n. Acidity. పులుసు. **అమ్లిక** *amlika.* n. A tamarind tree. చింతచెట్టు. **అమ్లవర్గము** *amla-vargamu.* [Skt.] A class of trees with acid leaves or fruits, such as the lime, orange, pomegranate, tamarind, &c.

అమ్లానము *a-mlānamu.* [Skt.] adj. Unfading. వాడని.

అయత్నము *a-yatnamu.* [Skt.] adj. Unintentional, unpremeditated, done without effort. అనుద్యమమైన. n. Absence of intention or attempt.

అయనము *ayanamu.* [Skt.] n. Road, path. Half a year. Motion, course. మార్గము, అర్ధవత్సరము, సూర్యుని ఉత్తరదక్షిణగతి. **ఉత్తరాయణము** or **ఉత్తరాయణము** the sun's course for six months in the northern constellations of the zodiac. **దక్షిణాయనము** the sun's course for six months in the southern constellations of the zodiac. **అయనకాలము** the interval between the equinoxes. **అయనభాగము** the arc between the vernal equinoctial point and the beginning of the fixed zodiac or first point in Aries. **అయనచలనము** deviation of the ecliptic. **అయనవృత్తము** the ecliptic.

అయబు *ayabu.* [H.] n. Fault, defect, infamy. లోపము, దోషము.

అయము *ayamu.* [Skt.] n. Good fortune: a tax. శుభావహకర్మము; పన్ను.

అయశము *a-yaṣamu.* [Skt.] n. Dishonour, disgrace. అపకీర్తి. **అయశస్కరము** *ayasaskaramu.* adj. Disgraceful. అపకీర్తికరమైన.

అయస్కాంతము *ayas-kāntamu.* [Skt.] n. The load-stone, a magnet. సూదంటురాయి. **అయస్కారుడు** *ayaskāruḍu.* n. A blacksmith, one who works in iron. కమ్మరి. **అయస్సు** *ayassu.* n. Iron. ఇనుము.

అయాచితము *a-yāchitamu.* [Skt.] adj. Unasked, unsolicited. అడుగని.

అయి (past p|| of అగు to become.) Having become, turned into. మ్రాను అయి నిలిచినాడు he stood like a post., i. e., he was transfixed with surprise &c. దొంగ అయి తిరుగుచున్నాడు he has turned thief. పోకిరి అయిపోయినాడు he has become a wicked fellow. **అయిన** (past rel. p|| of అగు to become.) Accomplished, becoming, agreeable, suitable. అయినపని a work that is accomplished, a becoming art. అయినపెండ్లాము a good wife. అయినమందు a suitable medicine. అయినమనిషి a useful or proper man. అయినవాండ్లు friends, relations. See కాని. **అయిన** is also used to change nouns into adjectives as సొగసైనపిల్ల, ఆశ్చర్యమైన కార్యము a wonderful deed. For other uses, see under అగు.

అయిను *ayinu*. [H.] Essence, the very thing itself.

అయివజు or అయివేజు *ayivazu*. [H.] Anything substituted for another.

అయుక్తము *a-yuktamu*. [Skt.] adj. Improper, inconsistent, unfit, bad. తగని.

అయుతము *ayutamu*. [Skt.] adj. Ten thousand. Many. పదివేలు, అనేకము.

అయోగ్యము *a-yōgyamu*. [Skt.] adj. Unfit, unbecoming, unworthy, shameful. తగని, కూడని. అయోగ్యత *ayōgyata*. n. Unworthiness, unbecomingness. తగమి, అనర్హత. అయోగ్యుడు *ayōgyuḍu*. n. An unworthy man. అనర్హుడు.

అయోనిజ *ayōnija*. [Skt.] n. She who is of a miraculous birth, not born in the womb. మనిషికడుపులో పుట్టనిది. అయోనిజుడు or అయోనిసంభవుడు *a-yōnijuḍu*. n. A man born in a supernatural manner, not born in the womb. మనిషికడుపున పుట్టనివాడు.

అయోమయము *ayō-mayamu*. [Skt.] adj. Made of iron; abstruse, hard, difficult. ఇనుముతో చేసిన, కఠినమైన. నేను ఈ అయోమయములో పడియున్నాను. I am now in these difficulties.

అయ్య *ayya*. [Tel.] n. Father. తండ్రి. Sir. ఏమయ్య what, Sir. ముసలయ్య an old gentleman. మీ అయ్యలు your fathers: (this word includes the brothers of a father.) బాపనయ్య a Bramin. అయ్యా! O Sir! అయ్యో or అయ్యయో or అయ్యయ్యో interj. Alas! Alas! సంతాపార్థకములు. అయ్యవారు n. A teacher. ఉపాధ్యాయులు. అయ్యరే or అయ్యారే interj. Oh, O thou! హాహా. అయ్యల్ల interj. Sir, father.

అయ్యు or అయ్యును *ayyu* [Tel. from అయి+యు conj. (from అగు] Although. అయినప్పటికిన్ని. నిర్మలుడయ్యు though he be pure.

అయ్యెడిని or అయ్యెడు *ayyeḍini*. [Tel. from అగు] It will be, or it will become. వేగంబె నీకు నిరోగమయ్యెడిని You will soon be well. ప్రసన్నుడయ్యెడును he will become visible.

అర *ara*. [Tel.] n. A room or chamber, గది. అరలపెట్టె a box with partitions. Hesitation, doubt. జంకు, "నాయంతివానిగా నెరిగి లోపలికి, నరతేరరానిచ్చి నందుకుమేలు." Sar. D. 502.

అర *ara*. [Skt. from అర్థ] adj. Half అర్థము, సగము. రెండున్నర two and a half. అరకాని *arakāni*. n. The 128th fraction of a rupee Half a pice. అరపది *arapadi*. n. (half ten) A phrase for five. ఐదు. అరకన్ను a side glance. అరకాలు the sole of the foot. అరగూడు *aragūḍu*. A niche in a wall. గోడలోనిగూడు. అరచూపు a glance. అరచెయ్యి the palm of the hand. కరతలము. అరచొక్కాయి a waistcoat, a half jacket. అరమోము the profile నన్ను అరకంట చూచినాడు he took no notice of me, he neglected me. Also, deficiency. కొరత; difference. భేదము; deception. వంచన; evil. కీడు; rag. చింపిగుడ్డ. అరచావు lit. half-death, swoon. "అతండు నీ మరందికి నరచావొనర్చె." Bhara. Drona. v.

అర *ara*. n. Half, a moiety. అర్థము.

అరక *araka*. [Tel.] n. A plough with bullocks complete. సర్వావయవములుగల నాగటికి ఎద్లను పూనినది. అరకలుకట్టు to harness a team. అరకలువిప్పు to unyoke the cattle. ఒకయెద్దు చనిపోయినది, అరకసాగక తొందరగానున్నది I cannot carry on my ploughing well as one of my bullocks is dead. అరకట్టరక a plough with a pair of bullocks. విడికట్టరక a plough with a change of bullocks. అరకాడు *ara-kāḍu*. (from అరక+కాడు) n. A cultivator, a ryot.

అరకి, అరకడ, అర్కాడ or అరకటము *araka*. [Tel.] n. The hip. తొండి. నితం

బహిఃపార్శ్వము. అది బిడ్డను అరకటబెట్టుకొని వచ్చినది she came with a child on the hip. "జనకుడక్కడ బెట్టుకొని కొలుచునాడు, చనిసకోపరతిరమున కొలుచునిచి" BD. vi. 277. మునిపుత్రుల అరకదనిడి ప్రాణ్ముఖులై. M. V. iii. 307. "మునికొమారునిదివముహూర్తపైనునిచి యరకటంబునకాంత నమువుగానునిచి" HD. i. 1752.

అరకము or **అరుకువ** *arakamu.* [Tel.] n. Indigestion. అజీర్ణి. అన్నాదులం అరగకపోవడము.

అరకొర or **అరగొర** *arakora.* [Tel.] Sticking. అనుమానము, సందేహము. 'కరకంఠభక్తుల కరకొరలేక సెరచిబ్రతుకు పొమ్మనేయును నేల." BD. v. 327. "కానుకొబలియుకొ మునమున నరగొరయొరుగక." Barij. v. 74.

అరగలి *aragali.* [Tel. from అర+కలిమి] n. Hesitation, doubt. సందేహము, అనుమానము.
అరగలిగొను *aragaligonu.* [Tel.] v. n. To hesitate, doubt. సందేహించు, అనుమానించు. "భావవేదివిజాలుబసవయ్యయిప్ప, డావస్త్రమును గొనునరగలిగొనడు." BD. iii. 93.

అరగు *aragu.* See అరుగు.

అరగుండెపసము *ara-gunde-tanamu.* [Tel.] n. Courage, spirit. గుండె, ధైర్యము. "అద్దిరభక్తునియరగుండెతనము." BD. v. 207.

అరగొడ్డెము *ara-goddemu.* [Tel.] n. Violence, quarrel. జగడము, దుండగము, ఆకార్యము.

> "ఎరిగిదొంగిరిసిముండట
> నరగొడ్డెముచేసిపోయిరి." ఉ.హరి. iv.

అరగొర See అరకొర.

అరచు See అరుచు.

అరటి, అరంటి or **అరిటి** *arati.* [Tel.] n. A plantain tree. అరటికాయలు green plantains. అరటాకులు plantain leaves.

అరడ *arada.* [Tel.] n. A kind of boat. ఒకవిధమైన తెప్ప. "ఈడుకొయ్యలు తెప్పలు నీడుకాయలరడలరిగోల్లు పడవలు ఓరులుపుట్లు, వేపడవలోడలాదిగాకెలుసట్టి, యంబురాశులకు నెల్ల నధిపుడరడు." Hansa. iv. 219.

అరడా *arada.* [Tel.] n. The brass or gold mouth of a scabbard. A particular kind of neck jewel. Also, the lion's heads at the ends of the pole of a Hindu marriage palankeen. కర్నాటకపల్లకి కొంగుకొనకుచేసేసింహాలలాటములు.

అరణము *araṇamu.* [Skt.] n. A present given by a father-in-law to his son-in-law or by a father to his daughter, at the nuptials. పెండ్లికొడుకునకు మామలు ఇచ్చే వస్తుసామగ్రి, పెండ్లికూతురికి తండ్రియిచ్చేదిన్ని. "అల్లునికిరైవతుడొసంగెయరణమపుడు." Balarama. vi. 157.

అరణి *araṇi.* [Skt.] n. A piece of dry wood to produce fire by friction at sacrifices. మంథనముచేత అగ్నిని పుట్టించేకాష్ఠము.

అరణ్యము *aranyamu.* [Skt.] n. A forest; a wilderness, thicket. అడవి. అరణ్యసభ a forest court. అరణ్యాధిపతి king of a forest. అరణ్యశునకము the wild dog or the wolf; అరణ్యాని great forest, పెరడవి, పెద్ద అడవి.

అరత్ని *aratni.* [Skt.] n. A cubit, distance from the elbow to the extremity of the little finger. విస్తృతకనిష్ఠాంగుళి ముష్టికహస్తము, మోచేతినుంచి చిటికెనవ్రేలుదాక. The elbow. మోచెయ్యి.

అరదండ *ara-danda.* [Tel.] n. Hand cuffs that slide on a bar of iron. అష్టముగా కొక యినుపకమ్మికేసిన చేతిసంకెల.

అరదము *aradamu.* [from Skt. రథము] n. A car; a chariot. రథము, తేరు.

అరదేవులు *ara-devulu.* [Tel.] n. Consumption, phthisis. క్షయరోగము. "అమ్మహాత్మునొపించియరదేవులంగొనుమని శపించినకొర్యాధినాథుండు నానాటికింగృశుండయ్యె." M. IX. ii. 166.

అరదేశిపరదేశి *aradêśi-paradêśi.* [Skt.] n. A mendicant, a pilgrim. తిరిపెగాడు, యాత్రకు పోయేవాడు.

అరప *arapa.* [Tel.] n. A temporary scaffold in a field. మంచె. "క్రచ్చరనీసంగగాచిచక్కలకు, నిచ్చినయట్లయ్యోగీశితక్తి, మంచెయలవేయుమ సెరయు బండించి, యరపడిగ్గినయట్టు లయ్యె సర్వేశ." BD. vii. 619.

అరపు *arapu* [Tel.] n. Blame, censure. (Vizag).

అరమర or **అరమరిక** *aramara.* [Tel.] n. Hesitation, doubt. సందేహము, సంశయము. "చిరజీవివిన్నరమరలేక కాకరాజామన్నించుమగదా." P. iii. 167. Difference. భేదము.

అరము *aramu.* [Skt.] adj. Swift; speedy. వడిగల, వేగమైన. **అరము** n. The spoke or radius of a wheel, the edge of a weapon: a corner or angle. ఆయుధధార, చక్రపు అంచు. కోణము. "అరపంచకసంయుక్తాస్యస్త్రికా కారికాలిని." Anand. T. xii. 27. "సహస్రారచక్రము." N. vi. 69. A discus or circular missile weapon.

అరమోడ్చు *ara-môdtsu.* [Tel] v. a. To half close. సగముమూయు. **అరమోడ్పు** adj. Half closed. సగముమూసికొన్న. "అరమోడ్పుకనుదోయి రసపారవశ్యవిభ్రమము దెలుప." T. iv 79.

అరమోము *ara-mômu.* [Tel.] n. The side face. **అరమోముచేయు** v. n. To turn away the face, disregard. ముఖముతిప్పుకొను.

అరయు *arayu.* [Tel.] v. a. To search, examine, see, observe, know, understand. వెదకు, విచారించు, విమర్శించు, పరీక్షించు, చూచు, ఎరుగు, తెలిసికొను. "తగువారి నరయంగ బంపు." BD. v. 168. **అరయన్**, **అరయగ**, or **అరయంగ** adv. On examining, or searching for. విచారింపగా. **అరయించు** (causal of అరయు) To cause to search, to have a search made. వెదకించు. "పలుకులు వేయు నేమిటికి పార్థివుదాత్త భుజాగ్నితప్తమారులమున బుట్టుకేడు బహుధా యరయించియుడంచి." A. iv. 296. **అరయిక** *arayika.* [Tel.] n. Examination, search. విచారణ, అరయుట.

అరరము or **అరరి** *araramu.* [Skt.] n. A door. తలుపు. **అరళము** for **అరరము** n A door. "తాళంబులు, మహాత్తాళంబులైన బిష్టనికినష్టంబుగాకకీలూడిపడిన అరళంబులు విరళంబులైన." Bhāga. X. iii. 42.

అరవడి *aravadi* [Tel.] n. A bruise made by attrition. రాపిడిచేత అయినగాయము, ఉరిత్రాటిగొంతుక్రింద నల్లగా అరవడిగానున్నది గనుక, as there was a black mark of a bruise caused by the attrition of a noose.

అరవము *aravamu.* [prob. Skt. అ+రవము without sound, i. e., having no aspirates. See Caldwell] n. Tamil. ద్రావిడము. అరవలు Tamilians, Tamil people. నీకు అరవము వచ్చునా do you know Tamil?

అరవరలు *aravaralu.* [Tel.] n. plu. Bits, fragments. తునకలు, ఖండములు. చిద్రుపలు. తుత్తునకలు. "కావించు దక్షయాగమున శివుని మరచినసయ్యజ్ఞ మరవరలైపోదె." M. XIII. v. 393. అరవరచేయు to divide into small pieces, to destroy.

అరవాయి *ara-vâyi.* [Tel.] n. Hesitation, timorousness. వెనుకదీయుడము. అధైర్యము. **అరవాయిగొను** v. n. To draw back, retract, retire, retreat. వెనుకదీయు, అధైర్యపడు, సంకోచించు. "అట్టిగాంధారులు బోరనరవాయిగొందురె." M. V. i. 263.

అరవిందము *aravindamu.* [Skt.] n. A lotus, *Nelumbium Speciosum* or *Nymphaea Nelumbo.* పద్మము, తామర.

అరవిరి *ara-viri.* [Tel.] adj. Half blown, half opened, as a flower, &c. సగము వికసించిన, అరవిరికంటు (BD i. 221.) with a half opened eye.

అరవీసము *ara-vîsamu.* [Tel.] n. The half of half an anna: the thirty-second part of unity. వీసములో సగము, ఒకటిలో ముప్పదిరెండో భాగము.

అరవ్రుడు or అరువ్రుడు *aravudu.* [Tel.] n. Bit, fragment, rag. తునక, చింపి, పోడి, తూటు. "కురుచెంప్రుకల కోరకోప్పిడి, కావి యుర వుడు కలనిట్టునట్టునుబాట్టి." HD. ii. 1376. "మైమరువరువుల్లగజేసి లిలనంగములెల్ల బరి యులంగజేయు." M. VI. ii. 319.

అరవై *aravai.* [Tel. from ఆరు+పది] adj. Sixty. అరువదులు. అరవైమంది sixty people.

అరసంజె *ara-sanza.* [Tel.] n. The evening twilight. అర్ధాస్తమానము.

అరసికుడు *a-rasikuḍu.* [Tel.] n. One devoid of taste for art.

అరాజకము *a-rājakamu.* [Skt. lit. kinglessness.] n. Anarchy, misrule, confusion. రాజు లేకపోవడము.

అరాతి *arāti.* [Skt.] n. An enemy. శత్రువు.

అరాళము *arāḷamu.* [Skt.] adj. Bent, curved, crooked. కుటిలమైన, వంకరయైన. "అరాళంబులైన కుంతలజాలంబులును." R.v.297.

అరి *ari.* [Tel.] Affix denoting possession. నేర్పు skill, నేర్పరి skilful. సిగ్గు shame, సిగ్గరి timid. **అరి** *ari.* [Tel.] n. A bowstring. Tax, tribute. పంటివారి, ప్రజలవద్ద రాజులు మర్యాదకు పుచ్చుకొనేపాలు. అరిపెట్టు to pay revenue. అరిగోరులు the share both of the government and of the inhabitants, i. e., the total produce. పుల్లరి tax on grazing lands. "అరులంమిగుల గొనిరాజులు, నరులకు నింతెరయును భయముకొనర్తురు." M. III. v. 302.

అరి *ari.* [Skt.] A foe, an antagonist. A wheel. The missile weapon of Vishnu. శత్రువు, చక్రము, సుదర్శనము. అరిషడ్వర్గములు the six classes of foes, i. e., the six sinful lusts, which are కామము lust, క్రోధము anger, లోభము avarice, మోహము longing desire, మదము prid and మాత్సర్యము envy. మురారి the foe of Mura, an epithet of Krishna. బలారి the foe of Bala, an epithet of Indra. అరిందముడు n. A conqueror or slayer of foes. శత్రునాశకుడు.

అరికట్టు *arikaṭṭu.* [Tel.] v. a. To check, stop, hinder. అడ్డగించు. "కాసరమును నవ్వుకొన గోట కొప్పదువ్వ కొంటెనరికట్టెనిలుమంచు కొట్టు బెట్టు." T. ii. 98.

అరికాలు for **అరకాలు** See under అర. అరికాలిమంటు నెత్తికెగసినది he was filled with fury.

అరిగ or **అరిగె** *ariga.* [Tel.] n. A large disk, like a shield, held in processions as a royal ensign. డాలువలె బ్రహ్మాండముగా నుండేటిది, దీన్ని రాజులయెదుట పట్టుకొనెదరు. "తేరులుకలముల తెరగునదిరుగగా గరులు మైనాకా దిగిరుల ప్రోల, నరిగెబిళ్లలుకమలాకృతి మెరయగా నడిదంబులును మీలనుకరింప." G. i. 22.

అరిగాపు *ari-gāpu.* [Tel. అరి+కాపు.] n. Tributary. కప్పము కట్టేవాడు. "నైరేచరాధిరాజ్ఞాది వసుధేశులెవ్వాని కడిమిసొంపున నరిగాపులైరి." M. VIII. i. 20.

అరిగొను *ari-gonu.* [Tel.] v. a. To check, stop, oppose. అడ్డమునిలుచు. "అలుకు బెట్టు లియుగరిగొన్నయట్లు." Pal. 108.

అరిగోలు *ari-gōlu.* [Tel.] n. A basket boat lined with leather. పుట్టి. "అరిగోలు బట్టుక అపగదాటు." L. xii. 118. "అది చంద్రమండలంబకాదు చదలేటి దేలుదంతపుటరిగోలు గాని." P. iv. 251.

అరిజె *ariza.* [Tel.] n. A sort of fish. ఒకవిధమైనచేప. Buch. Mys. iii. 344.

అరిటిచేప *ariṭi-chēpa.* [Tel.] n. A fish like a whiting (సొరంగి). The tucks at the waist in front of a petticoat.

అరిణ or **అరిణె** *ariṇa.* [Tel.] A trough made of a palm tree hollowed like a canoe. దోనె, దోణి.

అరితి *ariti.* [Tel.] n. Love, attachment. **అరితి** Gen. of అఱ్ఱు. Of the neck.

అరిత్రము *aritramu.* [Skt.] n. An oar; a rudder, a helm. ఓడనడపు తెడ్డు, చుక్కాని.

అరిదళము *ari-dalamu.* [Skt. from హరితాళము] n. Yellow orpiment, yellow sulphuret of arsenic. హరిదళము.

అరిది *aridi.* [Tel.] adj. Rare, seldom. అపురూపమైన, అశక్యమైన. "అద్భుతు భీష్ము దెరిగి నట్లరుగగవికలదిశకుపోల." భార: సభా: ii. "అరిదిబంగారు మైయలదునిమైజికి." Ila. iv. 64. **అరిది** n. Wonder, surprise, astonishment. అబ్బురము, ఆశ్చర్యము. "ఎల్లతాపంబులు డిగించుటేమియరిది." N. ii. 330.

అరిపడు *ari-padu.* [Tel.] v. n. To intervene.

అరిపోయు *ari-poyu.* [Tel.] v. a. To set the arrow on the bow. బాణముసంధించు. "ధన్వంబునఁ బ్రహ్మాస్త్రంబరిపోసినేసి." N. viii. 208. See. అరి.

అరిమి *arimi.* [Tel.] n. A disease to which children are subject, tonsilitis. బిడ్డలగొంతు నకువచ్చే ఒక రోగము. "పిలపలుకవు చెప్పవే యున్న దీకు, నరిమియో కోవరోయంగిటి ముల్లో." Bhallana iii. 726.

అరిమురి *ari-muri.* [Tel.] adv. Much, exceedingly, greatly. Quickly, hastily. One after another, repeatedly. అత్యంతము, మిక్కిలి, త్వరగా, శీఘ్రముగా, ఒకటివెంట నొకటి, మాటిమాటికి, ముందువెనుక. "పొరువం బరిమురిగ్రాల పింగళకుడన్నగరాజచరించునచ్చటఁ." P. i. 107. **అరిమురితనము** *ari-muri-tanamu.* n. Haste, hurry. ఆత్రము. అరిమురిని in haste. ఆత్రపడి "మరికదాశివునకు మాకుసం గంబు, అరిమురితనమిప్పుడదియేలనను." BD. iv. 1747. **అరిమురిపడు** *ari-muri-padu.* v. i. To hasten. సంభ్రమించు.

అరిమెనకుండలు *arimena-kundalu.* [Tel.] n. plu. Painted vases used at weddings. పెండ్లిలోపెట్టే బచ్చెనకుండలు, పెండ్లికుండలు.

అరిమేదము *ari-mēdamu* [Skt.] n. The fetid Mimosa tree. కంపుతుమ్మ.

అరివాణము *arivāṇamu.* [Skt. హరివాణము] n. A kind of copper dish. ళోగిలి, గిన్నె.

అరిష్టము *arishṭamu.* [Skt.] n. Misfortune, calamity. అశుభము, ఉపద్రవము. అరిష్టనివారణము removal of calamity.

అరిసె *arise.* [Tel.] n. A sweet rice cake fried in ghee. అతిరసము.

అరు Same as అఱ్ఱు (q. v.) **అరుతెవులు** *aru-tevulu.* n. Consumption. క్షయరోగము. **అరుత** or **అరుతను** Loc. of అఱ్ఱు. On the neck. కంఠమునందు. "అరుతలింగముం దరదనిచూడు." Vema. 1777. **అరుత** or **అర్త** *aruta.* [Tel.] adv. Near, close by. సమీపమందు. రాముడు విశ్వామిత్రునరుత నేగెను Rama went close to Viswamitra. "నవ్వగో ధములయర్తనరుగుచు మసలక దూడయమ్మంబిరం బరుత." BD. viii. 515.

అరు *aru.* [Tel.] v. n. To be lost, be ruined or destroyed, be broken. చెడు, నశించు, ఛేదమగు, తెగు, లేకపోవు. "శ్రమమ్మర." R. iii. 41. "అరగ బాలుండెక్కుడ బండియు క్కుడ పథోభాగంబు పైలెంపరగ కాలందన్ను టయొక్కు డావడుచుల్." BD. vii. 11.

అరుంతుదము *aruntudamu.* [Skt.] adj. Sharp, corrosive. మర్మము నొత్తునది. అరుంతుదుడు, అనగా మర్మపీడకుడు.

అరుంధతి *arundhati.* [Skt.] n. The wife of the sage Vasishtha, celebrated for her virtue. వసిష్ఠునిభార్య. A star in the Pleiades. At marriage ceremonies అరుంధతి is invoked by the bridegroom as a pattern of conjugal excellence and the star in the Pleiades which represents the wife of Vasishtha is pointed out to the bridal pair.

అరుకుర *arukura.* [Tel.] n. Indigestion. అజీర్తి.

అరుగు or **అరగు** *arugu.* [Tel.] n. A terrace, a raised flat terrace, a raised seat, a pial. వేదిక, తిన్నె.

అరుగు *arugu.* [Tel.] v. n. To go, pass, proceed, walk. To digest as food. To be worn away by being used or rubbed; waste away. వెళ్లు, జీర్ణమగు, క్షీణించు, క్షయించు. **అరగతీయు** *araga-tīyu.* v. a. To rub off. **అరుగుడు** *arugudu.* n. The act of wearing away; attrition. శిథిలము. **అరుగుదెంచు** or **అరుదెంచు** *arugu-dentsu.* [Tel.] v. n. To come. వచ్చు. To go. పోవు. "పరమధర్మాత్ముల భార్యాసమేతులనవమానింపదలంచియరుగుదెంచె." M. iii. 5. 455. **అరుదేడు** he will not come. "అయ్యమరులు దివినుండి నేలకరుదేరే." R. iii. 22. **అరుగుపడు** *arugu-padu.* v. i. To wear away. క్షయించు, నశించు, హీనమగు.

అరుచి *a-ruchi.* [Skt.] n. Tastelessness. Disgust. రుచిలేమి.

అరుచు or **అరచు** *arutsu.* [Tel.] v. n. To cry, shout, bawl. బొబ్బలుపెట్టు, కూయు, మొరపెట్టు, ఏడ్చు. **అరుపు** or **అరపు** *arupu.* [Tel. from అరుచు.] n. A great or loud noise, clamour, cry. కూత, కేక.

అరుజు *aruzu.* [Tel.] n. A kind of fish. మత్స్యభేదము. One kind is కల్లరుజు. H. iv. 225. And another పుల్లరుజు. H. iv. 226.

అరుణము *arunamu.* [Skt.] adj. Red. ఎర్రని. **అరుణత** or **అరుణిమ.** n. Pink, dark red. ఎరుపు. ఇంచుకరొఱుపు, కపిలవర్ణము, సంధ్యారాగము. **అరుణుడు** *aruṇuḍu.* n. Sun. The charioteer of the sun. సూర్యుడు, సూర్యసారథి. **అరుణోదయము** *aruṇōdayamu.* n. The dawn of the day. వేకువజాము.

అరుదు *arudu.* [Tel.] n. Surprise, wonder, marvel, rarity. వింత, అద్భుతము, ఆశ్చర్యము, అపురూపము. "అరుదారెభువచ్చరిత్రముల్." N. ii. 33. "వేగిరెలువందగు నీయరుదెల్లవారికిన్." P. ii. 222. "ఒకగుణముస్నచోట మఱియొక్కగుణంబరుదెన్నిచూడగా." N. ii. 311.

అరుదు adj. Rare; scarce; uncommon. Dear. Excellent. అపురూపమైన. **అరుదుగా** *arudu-gā.* adv. Rarely, scarcely, seldom. అపురూపముగా. **అరుదందు** *arudandu.* v. n. To be surprised, be astonished, to wonder. ఆశ్చర్యపడు. **అరుదార** or **అరుదారగా** *arudāra.* adv. Duly, well ఒప్పుగా. "నీ కరుదారం జెప్పెదనిక." P. iv. 347.

అరుపు See అరుచు.

అరుపు or **అరపు** *arupu.* [Tel.] v. n. To remain or be left, to be saved, to be within one's power. దక్కు. అరపరాని unwieldy, not handy. అరపరానికడి a morsel too big to swallow. వాడు అరపరానికడిగానున్నాడు, అనగా, వాడు గుమ్మడికాయంత మత్స్యముగానున్నాడు he is unwieldy.

అరుపుకొను *arupu-konu.* [Tel.] v. a. To digest; to enjoy the possession of. జీర్ణముచేసికొను, దక్కించుకొను. వారిసొమ్మును అన్యాయముగా అపహరించినాడుగాని దానిని వాడు అరుపుకోలేడు he has got the wealth wrongfully and will not be able to enjoy it.

అరుము or **అరము** *arumu.* [Tel.] v. a. To browbeat, to bully, to attack. గద్దించు, గదమాయించు, ఎదిరించు, ఆక్రమించు. "కయ్యమెల్లను దనమీదబెట్టుకొని లావును దీరముతో నపూర్వనియోపునదరి మెకోధవద్విశిఖపుంజములతొ దగటార్చుమీఅనిన్." M. VIII. i. 69. "అరిమురమాకుమారుడపుడగ్రతలంబునవచ్చినిల్చి." Vasu. iii. 240.

అరులు or **అర్లు** *arulu.* [Tel.] n. Tenderness, affection, fondness. వాత్సల్యము. **అరులుమరులు** *arulu-marulu.* n. Dotage, childishness of old age. ముదిమిచేత తెలివితప్పియుండడము.

అరువది or **అరవై** *aru-vadi.* [Tel. అరు+పది] adj. Sixty. అరువదులు. అరువదిగడియలు the 24 hours, that is, day and night. **అరువండ్రు** *aru-vandru* [Tel.] n. Sixty persons. అరవైమంది.

అరువము *aruvamu.* [Tel.] n. Eagerness, fondness. అ. "పరువూనా ధురాశకరువం బునగోఁ." Vish. vi. 266.

అరువు *aruvu.* [Tel.] n. A loan in grains. ధాన్యాదుల అప్పు. అరువుకాపు a tenant. అద్దె కాపు. **అరువు.** [cf. Tamil అఱివు] n. Good sense; judgment; the reasoning faculty. తెలివి. వానికి అరువుచెడినది he has lost his wits. **అరువుతిక్క** *aruvu-tikka.* [Tel.] n. A disease among cattle in which the belly is swollen in consequence of eating green fodder. తంగిడిరోగము, అనగాపశువులకు వచ్చే ఒక వ్యాధి.

అరువుల్లు *aruvullu.* [Tel.] n. plu. Fragments, shivers. పొట్లు. తూటులు. "మైమరు వులరువుల్లు సేయుచు." M. VII. iv. 165.

అరుసము *arusamu.* [from Skt. హర్షము] n. Joy, gladness. హర్షము. ఉ. రా. ii.

అరుసు *arusu.* [Kan.] n. A king. రాజు. "అసందలుసాల్వకోనమరుసునకనడే." Appakavi. iii. 233.

అరోచికము *arōchikamu.* [Corrupted from Skt. అరుచి] n. Disgust, dislike, want of appetite. అన్నముగిట్టకపోవడము. దానికి అరోచికముపుట్టినది she lost her appetite.

అర్కము or **అర్కవృక్షము** same as జిల్లేడుచెట్టు. (q. v.) అర్కక్షీరము the acrid milk of this plant.

అర్కము or **అర్కుడు** *arkamu.* [Skt.] n. The sun. సూర్యుడు. అర్కేందుసంగమము the conjunction of the sun and moon. ఆచంద్రార్కముగా as long as the sun and moon last.

అర్కలి *arkali.* [Tel.] n. The hip. ఓండి. (Loc. అర్కట) On the hip or side. "జనకు దర్కట బెట్టుకొని మొక్కువాడు." BD. vi. 228.

అర్గారా See హర్గారా.

అర్గళము *argalamu.* [Skt.] n. A round wooden bar or bolt for a door. గడియమాను. (Metaphorically) an impediment, hindrance, restraint. విఘ్నము, అడ్డంకి. ను. అన ర్గళముగా irresistibly. వాని అధికారము అనర్గళముగా జరుగుచున్నది his authority is unrestricted.

అర్ఘము *arghamu.* [Skt.] n. Price. Adoration, worship, respect. మూల్యము, వెల, పూజ. అర్ఘబలాబలము the cheapness or dearness of commodities. **అర్ఘ్యము** *arghyamu.* n. A respectful oblation to gods or to venerable men, of rice, darbha-grass, flowers, &c., with water, or of water only. పూజార్థార్హజలాదికము. అర్ఘ్యపాత్ర a vessel for this. అర్ఘ్యపాద్యాదులు the same with the addition of water for the feet, &c. అష్టార్ఘ్యములు the 8 kinds of offerings, viz., పెరుగు, తేనె, నెయ్యి, అక్షతలు, గరిక, నువ్వులు, దర్భ, పుష్పలు. **అర్ఘ్యము** adj. Venerable, deserving worship. పూజకు తగిన, యోగ్యమైన.

అర్చ, అర్చన or **అర్చనము** *archa.* [Skt.] n. Worship, adoration. సపర్య, పూజ. This is of 8 kinds: ముగ్గు, సుగంధము, అక్షతలు, పుష్పము, ధూపము, దీపము, ఉపహారము, తాంబూలము. **అర్చకత్వము** *archaka-tvamu.* [Skt.] n. The office of an officiating priest. నంబితనము, పూజచేయుట. **అర్చకుడు** *archakudu.* n. An officiating priest. పూజచేయువాడు, నంబివాడు. **అర్చించు** *archintsu* v. a. To worship, adore, offer, as flowers. పూజించు. **అర్చితుడు** n. One who is worshipped.

అర్చి or **అర్చిస్సు** *archi* [Skt.] n. Flame, light, radiance, splendour, refulgence. మంట, వెలుగు, దీప్తి, తేజస్సు.

అర్జీ *arji.* [H.] A petition, a letter. అర్జీదారుడు petitioner. అర్జీదాస్తు a written petition.

అర్జునము *arjunamu.* [Skt.] adj. White. తెల్లని. అర్జునుడు one of the five Pandavas.

అర్జు *arzu.* [H.] n. Price, value. అర్జుబాజారు ధర price current, market price.

అర్జు *arzu.* [H.] n. **Breadth.** The measurement of a heap of grain from the bottom to the top. అర్జుపట్టు to search, examine.

అర్ణము *arṇamu.* [Skt.] n. Water. నీళ్లు. అర్ణవము *arṇavamu.* n. The sea or ocean. సముద్రము.

అర్త for అరుత (q. v.)

ఆర్తి *arti.* [Skt.] n. Sorrow. దుఃఖము.

అర్థన *arthana.* [Skt.] n. Asking, begging. యాచన, వేడుకొనుట.

అర్థము *arthamu.* [Skt.] n. Meaning, signification. Thing, stuff. Money, wealth. అభిప్రాయము, వస్తువు. ధనము. ఇదియేమి అర్థమిస్తున్నది what is the meaning of this word? నీకు అర్థమైనదా do you understand this? అర్థము (an affix) For, on account of. నిమిత్తము. ఆ కార్యార్థమై వచ్చినాను I came on account of that affair. ఆ నిమిత్తార్థముగా for that reason. అర్థాంతరము another sense or meaning. అర్థార్థసంబంధము *arth-ārtha-sambandhamu.* n. Pecuniary ties. రూకలతో చేరిన బాధ్యత. వారికి మాకు అర్థార్థసంబంధములేకుండా తీరిపోయినది there are no pecuniary ties between us. ఇంతిమొదలు నీకు నాకు అర్థార్థసంబంధములేకుండా తీరిపోయినది from henceforth your property and mine are separated. అర్థవంతుడు *artha-vantuḍu.* n. A rich man. రూకలుగలవాడు. అర్థశాస్త్రము *artha-ṣāstramu.* n. Political economy; the science of wealth or property. రూకలపోనిమినిగురించిన శాస్త్రము. అర్థవృద్ధి accumulation or increase of wealth; అర్థసంచయము acquisition of wealth. అర్థవ్యయము expenditure of wealth. అర్థాధికారి a treasurer; అర్థాధికారము the office of treasurer. అర్థాంతరన్యాసము antithesis. అర్థోపమ a metaphor. అర్థహీనుడు *artha-hīnuḍu.* n. A penniless fellow, a poor man. పైకములేనివాడు, దుడ్డులేనివాడు, దరిద్రుడు. అర్థాపత్తి *arthā-patti* n. (in logic) Inference of a cause or motive from an effect. కార్యమునుబట్టి కారణమును ఊహించడము. అర్థి *arthi.* [Skt.] n. One who asks, a beggar, (Vulgarly,) eagerness, zeal. యాచకుడు, (వాడుకలో) ఆశ, కోరిక, అన్నార్థి or ఆశార్థి a beggar of food. "అలయుకవచమినవర్థితో వినిన." BD. v. 1458., i. e., with eagerness. అర్థించు *arthintsu.* v. a. To ask, beg, entreat. కోరు, అడుగు, బతిమాలుకొను. అర్థితము *arthitamu.* [Skt.] adj. That which is asked. కోరబడినది, వేడబడినది. అర్థిత్వము *arthitvamu.* n. Beggary. యాచన. అర్థేశుడు *arthēṣuḍu.* [Skt.] The god of wealth. కుబేరుడు.

అర్ధము *ardhamu.* [Skt.] adj. Half; a moiety. సగము. అర్ధచంద్రుడు or అర్ధేందువు the crescent moon, a half moon. అర్ధనారీశ్వరుడు the god Siva, in his form of half man and half woman. అర్ధరాత్రి midnight. అర్ధాంగీకారము half permission, doubtful consent. అర్ధాక్షరము a half letter. (that is) a letter incompletely sounded, as k in పృథక్ *prithak.* అర్ధదృష్టి purblindness. అర్ధగోళము a hemisphere. అర్ధరథుడు a warrior who fights on a car along with another. అర్ధరాత్రార్ధదివసము the equinox. అర్ధవ్యాసము half a circle. అర్ధాశనము half a meal. అర్ధోరుకము *arthōrukamu.* n. A short petticoat. తొడల సగముతోడులదాకా తొడుకుకొనే చల్లడము, లాగు.

అర్పణము *arpaṇamu.* [Skt.] n. An offering, dedication, delivering up. Placing. ప్రదానము, ఉంచడము. అంకురార్పణము the offering of buds to a god. అర్పించు *arpintsu.* v. a. To offer, dedicate. ఇచ్చు. తనసొమ్మునంతా పరులకు అర్పించి కూర్చున్నాడు he gave up all his goods and became a beggar. అర్పితము *arpitamu.* [Skt.] adj. Offered, dedicated. ఇవ్వబడ్డ. కంఠార్పితభూషణము an ornament placed on the neck. ఆ గ్రామము సముద్రార్పితము అయినది the village became the prey of the sea. తన తండ్రికి అర్పితముగా కొంత భూమిని దానముచేసినాడు he gave some land as a gift in memory of his father.

అర్బుదము *arbudamu.* [Skt.] (a numeral adj.) One thousand millions. నూరుకోట్లు.

అర్భకుడు *arbhakuḍu.* [Skt.] n. An infant, a child. శిశువు, బాలుడు.

అర్మిలి *armili.* [Tel.] n. Fondness, affection. ప్రేమ. వాత్సల్యము. "అర్మిలిపెంపుతోనలరుమనంబుతో." M. XV. ii. 162.

అర్యముడు *aryamuḍu.* [Skt.] n. The sun. సూర్యుడు. అర్యమకులము the solar race.

అఱ్ఱ *arra.* [Tel.] n. A division, a partition. A room or chamber. పెట్టెలో యేర్పరచిన ఒకభాగము, అర, గది.

అఱ్ఱము *arramu.* [Tel.] n. A bundle of thorns. ముండ్లమోపు.

అఱ్ఱాకలి *arrakali.* [Tel. అఱ్ఱ+ఆకలి] n. Excessive hunger, torment, fatigue. కడగండ్లు. "ఆకలికాదో, భక్తిలేకుదగలవాడగానో, తినజాలక్రపణో, సాకగదేవన్నిపుడఱ్ఱాకలిబెట్టక పలోకవాసక్తుడనై." Kalahasti. iii. 109.

అఱ్ఱాడు *arraḍu.* [Tel. అఱ్ఱు+ఆడు] v. n. To hesitate, waver, roam about, wander about in distress. తడబడు, అల్లాడు, దేవులాడు. "ఒలువవిదిలలకు నొలిచినతిలలీనఱ్ఱాడు వసుమతీసురభార్యా తిలకమునందు." P. ii. 4. "పరువంబుగాగజోప్పడని మామిడి తోటలానసాసానఱ్ఱాడునవిదియు." Pariz. iii. 97.

అఱ్ఱావు *arravu.* [Tel.] n. A wild cow. అడవి ఆవు. M. IV. i. 95.

అఱ్ఱు *arru.* [Tel.] n. The neck. కంఠము, పశుజాతి మెడవంపు, కుతిక, ఆపద, హాని. A sore on a bullock's neck occasioned by ploughing. ఆ యెద్దుయొక్క అఱ్ఱు కొట్టుకొనిపోయినది the bullock's neck is hurt (by the yoke.) "అందినిఫలముల కఱ్ఱుచాపకజెల." Kalahasti.

అఱ్ఱు *arru.* [Tel.] n. A tree, the *Bauhinia Parviflora*, Roxb ii. 323.

అఱ్ఱెము or **అఱ్ఱియము** *arremu.* [Tel.] n. Indigestion. అజీర్ణి, అరగకపోవడము.

అర్లుపెట్టు for **అల్లుపెట్టు** *arlu-peṭṭu.* [Tel.] v. a. To set a branch for a creeper to spread over. పాకుడుపెట్టు.

అర్వము *arvamu* [Skt.] n. A horse. గుఱ్ఱము. అర్వారోహణము mounting on horseback.

అర్వాచీనము *arvachinamu.* [Skt.] adj Reverse, contrary. Recent, modern. క్రొత్తనుండునది, విపర్యస్తము.

అర్హణ *arhaṇa.* [Skt.] n. Worship, duty. సపర్య, అర్చ, పూజ.

అర్హత *arhata.* [Skt.] n. Worthiness, fitness. యోగ్యత. **అర్హము** *arhamu.* adj. Worthy, proper, fit, liable, acceptable. తగిన. **అర్హుడు** *arhuḍu.* n. He who is worthy. యోగ్యుడు. శిక్షార్హులు those who merit punishment.

అల or **అల్ల** *ala.* [Tel.] adv. There. That. అక్కడ, ఆ. "అలయున్నిద్దరు సూరులందును సముద్యల్లీలగానున్న వెగ్గలపుండాపముమాన్పవా." A. pref. xi. "విల్లిపుత్తూరిలో నల్లవిష్ణుచిత్తుడతులతులసీసుగంధమాల్యంబు." A. ii. 101.

అల *ala.* [Tel.] n. A wave, surge, billow, ripple. తరంగము.

అలంకరించు *alankarintsu.* [Skt.] v. a. To adorn, embellish. సింగారించు. **అలంకరణము** *alankaraṇamu.* [Skt.] Act of adorning; decoration. **అలంకారము** *alankāramu.* n. Ornament, adornment. A jewel. In Rhetoric, a rhetorical figure. భూషణము, శృంగారము. అలంకారశాస్త్రము Rhetoric. వాడు వట్టి అలంకారవిద్యార్థి he is a sham student, he has merely a veneer of scholarship. అలంకారహీనమైన unadorned. **అలంకృతము** *alankṛitamu.* adj. Adorned, ornamented, embellished. శృం

గారింపబడిన. **అలంకృతుడు** *alankritudu.* n. He who is adorned.

అలంగము *alangamu.* [H.] n. The wall of a fortified place, a rampart, a bulwark. ప్రాకారము, కోటగోడపైభాగము. "కోటలమీదబట్టు జని గొప్పయలంగపుటిండ్లు చూడియవ్వీటికిసిల్ల" D. R. vi. 244. "బంగారపుకోటలకుదంగలంగు మానికపు శృంగములకెక్కుచు నలంగములపైకి చంగునదాటుచు." N. vii. 167.

అలంఘనీయము *a-langhaniyamu.* [Skt. from లంఘించు to leap]. adj. Impassable, not to be crossed. దాటకూడని. **అలంఘ్యము** *a-langhyamu.* adj. Impassable, not to be crossed. దాటకూడని. **అలంఘ్యత** *a-langhyata.* n. Difficulty of access, inaccessibility. అసాధ్యత.

అలంత See అలత.

అలంతి or **అలంతులు** See అలతి.

అలందు See అలదు.

అలందురు *alanduru.* [Tel.] n. Grief, sorrow, affliction. ఖేదము, దుఃఖము. "కంద ర్పునిదర్పంబున నలందురుపొందుదుననినవ్వేలంది వెండియునిట్లనియె." M. IV. ii. 73. "మేదిక ల్పులకా గొడుకులనేవ్వరంబమును గొన్ననలందురు గాడ చేర్తునే." M. XII. i. 210. **అలందురు** v. n. To grieve, to sorrow. దుఃఖపడు. "నిలు కడయును, లేమితాల్మికొనగలేక యలందురితనువు నింద్రియములుమనము ధృతియు, తనవశంబుగాక తల్లడపడి." M. IV. ii. 318

అలక *alaka.* [Tel. from అలుగు] n. Displeasure, anger. కోపము. **అలక** [Skt.] n. Kubēra's capital. కుబేరునిపట్టణము. అలకాధిపతి Kubera.

అలకన *alakana.* [Tel.] n. Ease, lightness, సులకన, తేలిక. **అలకనగా** adv. Lightly, easily. తేలికగా. దానిని అలాగ్గా (corrupted from అలకనగా) ఎత్తినాడు he lifted it with ease.

అలకలు *alakalu.* [Tel.] n. plu. Ringlets, curls. ముంగురులు.

అలకాలు, అలగాలు, *alakālu.* [Tel.] n. Brass handles of drawers, &c.

అలకి *alaki.* n. A small vessel. కుండ, కల శము. "దూగనిలయుంబు కలపదయుగలశములును నలకులుగాగులునాదిగాగల భాండములును." M. XIV. iii. 175.

అలకీహిసాబు *alaki-hisābu.* [H.] According to account.

అలక్తము *alaktamu* [Skt.] n. Liquefied lac. It was used by women as an ornament to dye their feet red. లాక్షు, లత్తుక.

అలక్ష్యము *a-lakshyamu.* [Skt.] n. Indifference. Disregard. అగౌరవము, తిరస్కారము. **అలక్ష్యముచేయు** or **అలక్ష్యపెట్టు** v. a. To neglect, disregard. తిరస్కరించు, అగౌరవము చేయు.

అలగా *alagā.* [H.] adj. Separate, unconnected. ప్రత్యేకమైన, అలగాభూమి pasture-land, waste land kept for grazing. అలగా పుల్లరి grazing tax levied on cattle not belonging to the village. అలగా ఆసామి a private individual, one not concerned, not a regular cultivator.

అలగు for--లు—which see.

అలఘు *a-laghu.* [Skt.] adj. Not light. Heavy, large, big. భారమైన. **అలఘువు** *a-laghuvu.* n. A long vowel; a sound equal to two mátras or simple sounds. గురువు, గుర్వక్షరము. **అలఘుడు** *a-laghudu.* n. A man of weight. A respectable man. పెద్ద వాడు, గొప్పవాడు.

అలచంద *alatsanda.* [Tel.] n. A leguminous plant. *Dolichos Catiang.* **అలచందలు** n. The pulse got from this plant.

అలచు or **అలంచు** *alatsu.* [Tel. Causative of అలయు to be tired.] v. a. To tease, harass. బాధపెట్టు.

అలజడి *alazadi.* [Tel.] n. Trouble, misfortune. ఆపద. Grief, affliction, sorrow. దుఃఖము, మనోదుఃఖరూపమైన విచారము. "అల

చేడినచ్చుటకు మాలమతిమయ్యెదినో." భా. అర. vii "స్వపతికి లే వలజల్లగ దయలోక లల యుండుగా." M. XII. ii. 353. **అలజడిదరి** *alazadi-dari*. [Tel.] n. A kind of bird. పక్షివిశేషము. H. iii. 269

అలత or **అలంత** *alata*. [Tel. from అలయు] n. Fatigue, exhaustion, weariness. బడలిక.

అలతి or **అలంతి** *alati*. [Tel.] adj. Little, small. స్వల్పమైన, చిన్న, సూక్ష్మమైన, అల్పమగు, అనగా చిరుచిన్న. "బలుపు చూపిన దేమి యలతినదుము." N. vii. 18. **అలతి** or **అలంతి** n. A trifle, a small thing. అల్పము, స్వల్పము. "అలతులతో పు చెప్పి, యుదితమైన." TUR. vi. 20. **అలతులు** or **అలంతులు** n. plu. Low wretches, mean men. అల్పులు. "అలతులైనవారికంటె నతిపెద్దలకును బాలపెద్దయగుదురా రుగొలుతుగా." M. XII. ii. 26.

అలదు or **అలందు** *aladu*. [Tel.] v. a. To smear, daub, to apply perfumes, &c. పూయు. R. iv. 106.

అలపు *alapu*. [Tel. from అలయు] n. Fatigue, lassitude. బడలిక. Tara. iii. 9.

అలపు *alapu*. [Tel.] a. To cause to be fatigued, to harass or trouble. అలయునట్లు చేయు, బాధించు, తొందరపెట్టు. "వనచరుడైన నలపగజాలడె నోపునుచు." BRS. 325.

అలబలము *ala-balamu*. [Tel.] n. An outcry, a noise. కలకలధ్వని, వ్యాకులము, సద్దు, చప్పుడు, రొద, గోల్లు. "విభునితో వెళ్ళుచుండుక నిలిచినా రులేమగా యుండుసదనంబు పాటలాది యలబలము లేని నిజమందిరాంగణము." T. iii. 128.

అలభ్యము *a-labhyamu*. [Skt. from లభించు] adj. Unobtained; unobtainable; unattainable. Unexpected, casual. పొందబడని, ఆకస్మికమైన. అలభ్యయోగము unexpected good fortune. ఇది అలభ్యయోగముగా ప్రాప్తమాయెను this happened unexpectedly.

అలమట *alamata*. [Tel.] n. Grief, sorrow, affliction. విచారము, దుఃఖము. "కలకాలము లేని లమటకలకాలము లేనుకుపము." P. ii. 26. **అలమటించు** *ala-matintsu*. v. n. To grieve, sorrow, to sink under affliction. వ్యాకులపడు. "అసురుసురంచు మోమువంచు, విధిదెంచుచు క్రుళ్ళునించులో నలమటించు." కళ్లాణచరిత్రి.

అలమరించు or **అలమరు** *alamarintsu* [Tel.] v. n. To be wearied or exhausted. ఆయాసపడు to grieve చింతపడు "ప్లవగంబట్ల మా మీ నవశంబుగటయు త్యజించెనుష్ల" P. i. 137.

అలము *alamu*. [Tel.] n. Weeds that grow in fields of dry grain. జొన్నమొదలైన మెరక చేలలో మొలిచినగడ్డి. ఆకు అలములు leaves and weeds.

అలము *alamu*. [Tel.] v. n. To spread or extend. To happen or occur. To spring, to proceed from. వ్యాపించు. కలుగు, పుట్టు. "పులకలతినగాత్రమునలమగా." A. vi. 189. "చీకటులలమెడివేళ." N. vii. 205. "అమవొందకగాంచి భక్తినలమనుదితోగా." H. i. 196. **అలము** *alamu*. [Tel.] v. a. To seize, lay hold, handle. To put, place, to wash. పట్టు, ఉంచు, కడుగు. "లక్కనీట మమ్ములమినది." A. v. 34. **అలముకొను** same as అలము.

అలయు *alayu*. [Tel.] v. n. To be fatigued or harassed. బడలు, గాసిపడు. "అలయక చదివినస్థితోపనిన." BD. v. 1458. To delay. ఆలస్యముచేయు.

> క॥ "కనుగొనివాతలచిన పని
> యనువుపరచిమరచిర్తైన నలయకవేగం
> బునపట్టు" ఈ. పారి. ii.

అలయించు *alayintsu*. [Tel.] v. a. To trouble, harass, weary, fatigue. శ్రమపెట్టు, బడలించు. "అందరికి సన్నిరూపులై యతు

లగకుల రతులనలయించె." N. ix. 422. "సీతన లయించి వచ్చి నాచేతబాలిక మాయలేడన్న వాచరు మరుగుసొచ్చి." R. vi. 30. **అలయిక, అలత, అలపు** *alayika.* [Tel.] n. Fatigue, harassment, weariness. బడలిక, గాసి.

అలరు *alaru.* [Tel.] v. n. To shine, glitter, be splendid. To rejoice, or be pleased. ప్రకాశించు, సంతోషించు, ఒప్పు. "సురాసురులకు జాలవిచిత్రసైయయులరెగా." N. ii. 208. **అలరు** *alaru.* [Tel.] n. A flower, blossom. పువ్వు, Joy. సంతోషము. **అలరుచు** or **అలరించు** *alaruṭsu.* [Tel.] v. a. To please, gratify. సంతోషపెట్టు. **అలరుబోడి** or **అలరుబోణి** *alarubōḍi.* [Tel.] n. A woman. స్త్రీ. **అలరువిల్తుడు** *alaru-viltuḍu.* [Tel.] n. He who has a bow of flowers, Cupid. మన్మథుడు. **అలరారు** *alarāru.* [Tel. అలరు+అరు] v. n. To shine, glitter. To rejoice, or be pleased. ప్రకాశించు, ఉల్లసించు. "మానసం బలరారె." N. i. 35.

అలర్కము or **అలర్కపత్రము** *alarkamu.* [Skt.] n. A shrub, the three-lobed nightshade. *Solanum trilobatum.* ముండ్లముస్తె, ముళ్లయుచ్చిరిచెట్టు, తెల్లకల్లేడు.

అలవ *alava.* [Tel.] n. A fence woven with twigs, a hedge, an inclosure. మండలతో అల్లిన ఆవరణము.

అలవడు *ala-vaḍu.* [Tel.] v. n. To be accustomed, be practised in. To be mastered. అభ్యాసమగు, పరిచయమగు, సాధ్యమగు. "బ్రహ్మలోకపర్యంతంబుల నలయుచువిహరించి మాంధి తినలవడదిది నీవెలెలుంపు సాంగుబిడ్డా." H. ii. 67. "వీనియందలవడగల్గిన బలుపుహాస్యములకుంద్రియు మెచ్చివ్వదంబునన్." Swa. vi. 74. **అలవరించు** or **అలవరచు** *ala-varintsu.* v. a. To make, celebrate. To put on. చేయు, ధరించు, పెట్టు. "వేదోక్తపద్ధతి వెలయంగ యాగంబులలవరించిన సోమయాజులకును." N. iv. 106. "హరిచందనము పూతలందంబుగా మేననలవరించి." N. ii. 425. **అలవరుచు, అలవర్చు** or **అలవరించు** v. a. To habituate, accustom, exercise, teach. వాడుకచేయు, అభ్యాసపరచు, మసుపరచు, నేర్పు. **అలవాటు** *ala-vāṭu.* n. Use, habit, custom, practice. వాడుక, అభ్యాసము. అలవాటుగానుండే adj. Customary, usual. వాడుకైన.

అలవి *alavi.* [Tel.] n. Possibility, practicability, power, ability. శక్యము, కొలది. అది చెప్పనలవికానిది it is indescribable. **అలవు** *alavu.* [Tel.] n. Power, ability. శక్తి, పరాక్రమము, బలిమి. "తలకడచినదద్రోణుని యలవుబలంబును సహింపక." M. VI. ii. 354. Difficulty. కష్టము, శ్రమము.

అలవోక *ala-vōka.* [Tel.] n. Sport, amusement, playfulness. లీల, వేడుక, విలాసము, ఆట్లాట, **అలవోకగా** *ala-vōka-gā.* [Tel.] adv. Carelessly. అలక్ష్యముగా, అసడ్డగా. "అలవోకగావచ్చి యప్పటప్పటికి పసేలంపుమాటల మేలమాడు." Vish. vi. 19.

అలసట *alasaṭa.* [Tel. from అలయు q. v.] n. Exhaustion, weariness. ఆయాసము, అలపు. **అలసత** *alasata.* [Skt.] n. Inactivity, laziness, idleness. జడత్వము, మాంద్యము. Delay. ఆలస్యము. **అలసము** *alasamu.* [Skt.] adj. Idle, slothful, indolent. మందమైన, జడమైన. **అలసుడు** *alasuḍu.* n. He who is idle or indolent. మందుడు, జడుడు. **అలసురాలు** *alasurālu.* n. A lazy woman, a dawdle. మందురాలు.

అలాతము *alātamu.* [Skt.] n. A fire-brand. Charcoal. కొరివి, అంగారము, బొగ్గు.

అలాదా, అలాహిదా *alāda.* [H.] Separate, apart, distinct. ప్రత్యేకమైన, వేరే.

అలాబువు *alābuvu.* [Skt.] n. The long gourd. *Cucurbita lagenaris.* ఆనపతీగ.

అలామతుకర్ర *alāmatu-karra.* [H. అలామతు a mark] n. A buoy for anchors. తోయాకట్టె.

అలి or **అళి** *ali.* [Skt.] n. A large black bee. A scorpion. అళిని the female scorpion. తుమ్మెద, తేలు.

అలిందము or **ఆళిందము** *alindamu*. [Skt.] n. The terrace before a native house ఇంటిమోసాల, తలవాకిటిఅరుగు, తావ్వారము. Also a small room in the front part of a house, or a room near the passage that leads into a house. తలవాకిటిప్రక్కనుండు ఒక చిన్న గది; లేక, నడవగది.

అలికము or **అళీకము** *alikamu*. [Skt.] n. The forehead. లలాటము.

అలికిడి or **అలుకుడు** *alikiḍi*. [Tel.] n. Noise, sound. ధ్వని, చప్పుడు. వారి మాటల అలికిడి వల్ల మేలుకొన్నాను I was awakened by the sound of their talking.

అలిపిరి *alipiri*. [Tel.] n. A lean man. బక్కవాడు. **అలిపిరిది** n. A lean woman.

అలియు Same as అలయు. (q. v.)

అలివేణి *ali-vēṇi*. [Skt.] n. A woman, (lit. a *bee-tressed* nymph.) స్త్రీ.

అలీకత or **అలీకము** *alīkata*. [Skt.] n. A falsehood, falseness. అబద్ధము, మిథ్య, అలీక శౌర్యము. Feigned courage. Vasu. iii. 103.

అలుక or **అలుకువ** or **అల్క** *aluka*. [Tel. from అలుగు] n. Anger. కోపము. "అలుకచే నుండబుగ్గలనలిచివైచె." H. iii. 180.

అలుకు or **అళుకు** or **అళ్కు** *aluku*. [Tel.] n. Fear; terror; dread. భయము. **అళుకు** *aluku*. v. n. To be afraid, to fear, to scruple, hesitate. జంకు, వెనుకదీయు. **అళుకరి** *alukari*. [Tel.] n. A coward, a man of no courage. భయశీలుడు.

అలుకు *aluku*. [Tel.] v. a. To smear the floor of a house or a mud wall, &c., with cowdung, &c. పేడవేసి శుద్ధిచేయు. (అలుకుమట్ట a besom dipped in cowdung and water used in smearing a floor.) Also, to sow seed in a field prepared for the purpose (Vizag.) **అలికించు** *alikintsu*. (causal of అలుకు.) To have the floor smeared with cowdung, &c.

అలుకుడు see అలికిడి.

అలుగు *alugu*. [Tel.] n. A sluice to carry off water from a pond that overflows. The tip of an arrow, the blade of a sword. పరీవాహము, చెరువునకు నీరెక్కువైనప్పుడు అది పోవుట కేర్పరచినదారి; బాణముయొక్క కొనకు వేసే యినుపముక్క, కత్తిపిడికిపైని ఉక్కుతునక. "కజ్జలాన్వితధూమాసితరేఖపై యలుగుగావిజ్ఞాన దీపాంకురాకృతి." A. pref. 7.

అలుగు *alugu*. [Tel.] v. n. To be angry or annoyed. కోపించు. **అలిగించు** (causal of **అలుగు**.) To irritate, annoy. కోపమువచ్చేటట్టుచేయు. See అలుక.

అలుగులము *alugulamu*. [Tel.] n. Pain, suffering. బాధ. **అలుగులపడు** *alugula-paḍu*. [Tel. అలుగులము+పడు.] v. n. To be crushed. నలుగుడుపడు. To suffer. బాధపడు.

అలుచు *alutsu*. [Tel.] n. A dull or stupid man. మందుడు. భార. విరా. iii.

అలుపము *alupamu*. [Skt. అల్పము.] adj. Small, little, trifling. అల్పమైన, అలుపాలక (=అల్పకార్యములచేత.) భార. ఉద్యో. iii.

అలుపు or **అలసు** *alupu* [Tel. from అలయు.] n. Fatigue, exhaustion, weariness. బడలిక, ఆయాసము. T. iii. 9.

అలువు *aluvu*. [Tel.] Same as అలుగు to be angry. (q. v.)

అలేఖము *a-lēkhamu*. [Skt.] n. A blank book. వ్రాయనిపుస్తకము.

అలోభము *a-lōbhamu*. [Skt.] Absence of cupidity.

అళ్కు *alku*. [Tel.] n. Fear, terror, dread. భయము, అధైర్యము. See అలుకు.

అల్కి or **హల్కి** *alki*. [H.] adj. Light, base. తేలికైన, నీచమైన. అల్కిగుడ్డ inferior cloth.

అల్జడి *aljaḍi*. [H.] n. Confusion. అల్లరి. Grief, affliction, sorrow. దుఃఖము, విచారము. "తా వసించుచోట తగవల్ల జాడెనా." Vema. i. 64. Same as అల జడి.

అల్పము *alpamu.* [Skt.] adj. Trifling, mean, slight, small, little, petty. స్వల్పమైన, నీచమైన, చిన్న. అల్పకార్యము a small matter. అల్పజ్ఞుడు one that knows little, an ignorant man. అల్పదృష్టి short-sightedness, narrow-mindedness. అల్పప్రాణి a weak creature. అల్పబుద్ధి little-mindedness. అల్పవయస్కుడు one who is tender in age, a mere youth. అల్పాశయము Urine. అల్పాయుస్సు Tender age. అల్పాయుష్కుడు A short lived man. అల్పారంభము A small beginning. అల్పాహారము A light meal. అల్పుడు n. A mean wretch. నీచుడు, క్షుద్రుడు.

అల్మారి or **అలమారు** *almāra.* [H.] n. A wardrobe, almirah. అల్మారుగోనేరు a well with steps down into it.

అల్ల *alla.* [Tel.] adj. pron. That. అల్లది. that thing. అల్లవాడు that man. అల్లంతన adj. Then, in the mean time. అంతటిలో. "అల్లనుపట్టి మల్లంతనశైచి." L. XIX. 184. అల్లదిగో or అల్లదుగో interj. Lo! behold! Look there!

అల్లకల్లోలము *alla-kallōlamu.* n. [Tel.] Confusion, disorder. తారుమారు, కలవరము.

అల్లటపెట్టు *allaṭa-peṭṭu.* [Tel. అల్లటము+పెట్టు] v. a. To annoy, harass. "అల్లనమూకేదములెల్ల నన్నింత యల్లటపెట్టెదోయయ్య నేనెరుగ." Bhallā. 1. 455. అల్లటము *allaṭamu.* [Tel.] n. Annoyance. అల్లాటము.

అల్లన *allana.* [Tel.] n. Slowness. మెల్లన, తిన్నన. అల్లన *allana.* [Tel.] adv. Gently, softly. తిన్నగా, మెల్లగా. "తనయాశ్రమమున కల్లనవచ్చి." N. i. 170.

అల్లనల్లన or **అల్లల్లన** *allan-allana.* [Tel.] adv. Very gently. మిక్కిలిమెల్లగా. "అల్లనల్లన నాగురితో." A. iv. 38. అల్లని adj. Slow. అల్లనినవ్వు gentle laughter, smile.

అల్లము *allamu.* [Tel.] n. Green ginger, as distinguished from శొంఠి dry ginger.

అల్లరి *allari.* [Tel.] n. Tumult, commotion, noise, confusion, quarrel, riot. కల్లర, రచ్చ. అల్లరిమనిషి a noisy or troublesome man. అల్లరిచేయు v. a. To trouble, disturb, discompose. కల్లరచేయు, తారుమారుచేయు.

అల్లాడు or **అల్లలాడు.** *allādu.* [Tel. అల్ల+ఆడు] v. n. To shake, move, wave, toss about, to wander about, to be in distress. ఆడు, గాలికి కొట్టుకొను, తిరుగు, సంచరించు, కడగండ్లుబడు. "ధరాచక్రమల్లాడె." N. iv. 288. ధ్వజపటము గాలికి అల్లాడుచున్నది the flag flutters in the wind. కూటికిఅల్లాడుతాడు he is in want of bread. కొలువుకు అల్లాడుతాడు he is in trouble for want of employment. అల్లాటము *allāṭamu.* [Tel.] n. A to-and-fro movement, wandering about. అల్లారుచు or అల్లార్చు *allārutsu.* [Tel.] v. a. To shake, move, vibrate, agitate, wag, wave. ఆడించు, విసురు. "ఘనవాలమల్లార్చు." N. i. 144. అల్లారుముద్దు *allāru-muddu.* [Tel. అల్ల+ఆరు+ముద్దు.] Prettiness, agreeableness, sweetness. జనసమ్మతి, అతిప్రేమాస్పదము. అల్లారుముద్దుగా ad. Prettily, agreeably, sweetly, pleasantly. జనసమ్మతిగా, అందరికి సంతోషముగా, ముచ్చటగా. "పడుచుదనమున నేడుకపడుచునాడు ముద్దరాండ్రకు నల్లారు ముద్దుగాను." N. ix. 102.

అల్లి *alli.* [Tel.] n. The water plant called *Nymphæa alba.* అల్లికాడ its *peduncle* or flower stalk. అల్లిపువ్వు the flower of this water plant. ఉత్పలభేదము. ఆకాశపు అల్లి *Menyanthes cristata,* a water plant. ఎర్ర అల్లి *Nymphæa Lotus,* a variety with a red flower. Rox. ii. 260, says, 'అల్లి is *Memecylon Edule:* a wild shrub, like broom, with beautiful fragrant flowers in bunches.' దాని ఒళ్లు అల్లికాడవలెనున్నది her body is like the stem of a water lily, she is very chilly. అల్లిగాయలు the fruit of the blue lotus.

అల్లించు *allintsu.* [Tel.] (causal of అల్లు) To get it plaited or braided. అల్లేటట్టు చేయు. See అల్లు. అల్లిక *allika.* [Tel. from

అల్లు] n. A twist, a plait, a braid, a netting.

అల్లిచెట్టు *alli-chettu.* [Tel.] n. A kind of wild shrub, with beautiful and fragrant lilac flowers in bunches. ఒక అడవిచెట్టు. అల్లికర్ర the wood of this plant. అల్లివిత్తులు the seed of this plant.

అల్లితెమ్మెర or అల్లిటెమ్మెర *alli-temmara.* [Tel.] n. A cool breeze. చల్లనిగాలి.

అల్లిబిల్లి *alli-billi.* [Tel.] n. Twisting, twining. పెనకువ. "మాపుల్ క్రొవ్వులనల్లిబిల్లిగాను కాం తారంబులన్." Swa. ii. 25.

అల్లిసకర్ర *allisa-karra.* [H.] n. An oar. పడవతెడ్డు, తెడ్డు. (The boatmen usually cry అయిలేస *ayilēsa* and అయిలేసబడియేల when rowing) అల్లిసకర్రలువేయు or కోలలు వేయు to row a boat with oars.

అల్లు *allu.* [Tel.] v. a. To plait, braid, weave, wattle rods or twigs, &c., together. గంపలల్లు to weave baskets. చాపలల్లుతాడు he plaits mats. పద్యములల్లు to compose verses. అబద్ధాలల్లు to fabricate lies. తీగెలు చెట్టుమీదికి అల్లినవి the creepers have crept over the tree. గసవు అల్లినభూమి land overgrown with grass. n. అల్లిక (q. v.)

అల్లుడు *alluḍu.* [Tel. from అల్లు lit. one who plaits, i. e., who is the means by which the family circle is enlarged.] n. A son-in-law. జామాత. మేనల్లుడు the son of a man's sister, or of a woman's brother. అల్లుడుకోమాళ్లు n. plu. Foster brothers or vassals, who feed at the baron's table and form his body-guard. దొరతోదొరగా భోజనముచేసి ఆతనికి అంగరక్షకులుగా నుండేవారు. అల్లువాడు n. A son-in-law. అల్లుడు, జామాత. "అల్లువాని మృతికి నాత్మజలించును, తనయుమృతికి దాపె తలచుచుండు, పూర్వపురుషు మృతికి భూలోకజనులకు నుర్వ కుంటినట్లుండు." Vema. 1288.

అల్లుబచ్చలి *allu-battsali.* [Tel.] n. A plant, called *Basella alba.* తీగబచ్చలి.

అల్లె *alle.* [Tel.] n. A bow-string. మౌర్వి, నారి. అల్లె (a vulgar error for వలె) Like; as బంట్రోతులల్లె వచ్చిరి they came like Police officers.

అల్లెదమ్ము *alle-dammu.* [] n. A sort of fish. మత్స్యవిశేషము. "అల్లెదమ్ములు చేపయు గొల్ల దొండు." Hamsa. iv. 226.

అల్లెము *allemu.* [Skt.] n. The being a son-in-law. జామాతృత్వము. Commonly the invitation given to a son-in-law immediately after the marriage. [Connected with అల్లుడు.]

అల్లోనేరేడు *allō-nērēḍu.* [Tel.] n. A kind of *Myrtus Cyminum* (Roxb.) its fruit being like a black cherry. See నేరెడు or నేరేడు. అల్లోనేరెళ్లు *allo-nērellu.* [Tel.] n. Salutations. నతివిశేషములు, దండములు. "మధురాపురిలో మహిమలు చెందిన, బాల కృష్ణునకు ప్రాణాచారము, మాయాస్థలిలో మధు సూదనునకు నిరతంబల్లోనేరెళ్లనుకొని." Hamsa. iv. 271. అల్లోనేరేడుపాటలు songs sung by women with a chorus అల్లోనేరేళ్లో. "ఇంతి యల్లోనేరెళ్లు గోరికల్యాణము లందు." పాంచా. iv.

ఎల్ల సుఖంబులఁజేకొన
జెల్లెటు యౌవనమునంద చిక్కిన మరిపా
టిల్లునె వెన్నెలదినముల
నల్లోనేరేళ్లుగాక యూవలగలవే.
రామా. సుంద: కాం.

అవ *ava.* [Tel.] Same as అవ్వ (q. v.) Also, a Skt. prefix, meaning Bad.

అవకరము *ava-karamu.* [Skt.] n. Dust, or sweepings. ఊడ్చియుంచినకుప్ప.

అవకాశము *ava-kāsamu.* [Skt.] n. Leisure, opportunity, opening, interval, space, intermission, rest. సమయము, అంతరము, ఎడము, ఎడపు, తెరపి.

అవకీర్ణము *avakīrṇamu.* [Skt.] adj. Scattered, strewed. చల్లబడిన.

అవకుంఠనము *ava-kunthanamu.* [Skt.] n. Veil, a cover. ముసుకు. అవకుంఠితము

avakunṭhitamu. adj. Veiled, covered. ముసుంగిడబడిన.

అవక్తవ్యము *a-vaktavyamu.* [Skt.] Not fit to be said or uttered; improper.

అవక్రము *a-vakramu.* [Skt.] Not crooked, straight.

అవక్షేపము *ava-kshēpamu.* [Skt.] n. The act of discarding a thing after finding fault with it. తప్పు మోపివిసర్జించడము. Sarcasm, irony. పోల్లింతనము, ఆయుములెత్తి ఆడడము, పొడుపుడుమాటలు. **అవక్షిప్తము** adj. Discarded as faulty, sarcastic, ironical, having an insinuation. తప్పుమోపి విసర్జింపబడినది, పోల్లింతనమైన.

అవగడము *ava-gaḍamu.* [Skt.] n. Peril, danger, evil, mischief. అపాయము, చెరుపు. ఆగడము, అకార్యము. "మోసమువచ్చుటయురకే యీమనరద్దవ్వ భావించటిస్సగాలా గ్రసరుల్లై కురేదిను మాసమయముమున్ను దొరలకవగడమురయరా." P. iii. 368.

అవగణితము *ava-gaṇitamu.* [Skt.] adj. Disregarded. అవమానింపబడిన.

అవగతము *ava-gatamu.* [Skt.] adj. Known, understood. తెలియబడినది, పొందబడినది.

అవగాహము or **అవగాహనము** *ava-gāhamu.* [Skt.] n. Immersion: bathing: comprehension. మునగడము, తెలియడము, ఆకళింత. అది నాకు అవగాహనముకాలేదు I do not comprehend it. అది నీకు అవగాహనమైనదా have you understood it? దాన్ని నేను అవగాహనముచేసికొన్నాను I have understood it.

అవగుణము *ava-guṇamu.* [Skt.] n. An evil disposition, a bad temper, a defect. దుర్గుణము, దోషము.

అవగ్రహము *ava-grahamu.* [Skt.] n. Drought, famine. Obstacle, impediment. వర్షప్రతిబంధము, కరువు, వరపు, ప్రతిబంధము.

అవఘళము *ava-ghaḷamu.* [Skt.] adj. Difficult, impossible. కష్టమైన, సంకటము, అసాధ్యము. "సగుణనిర్గుణ యోగసంవిస్తయునకు నల్లమసాధ్యమిక నవఘళంబెట్టి." L. ii. 206. **అవఘళించు** *ava-ghaḷintsu.* [Skt.] v. a. To excel or surpass. To neglect, disregard. మించు, అతిశయించు, తిరస్కరించు. "అర్ధచంద్రునిరేట నవఘళించులలాటపట్టి దీర్చునగంక మట్టితోడ" Swa. iii. 92.

అవఘోటముగా *ava-ghōṭamugā.* [Tel.] adv. Unexpectedly, unawares. ఆకస్మికముగా, హఠాత్తుగా.

"ఖలుడగుకంసునిపంపున
నరిగి తృణావర్తుడవనికవఘోటముగా
సురకరువలియైబిసబిస
నరుదరుదనముసరివిసరిహరిగొనిపోయెన్."
B. X. § 7.

అవజ్ఞ *ava-gna.* [Skt.] n. Disregard, contempt. అనాదరము, తిరస్కారము. **అవజ్ఞత** *ava-gnata.* [Skt.] n. Ignorance, stupidity, folly. అజ్ఞత, తెలివితేమి. **అవజ్ఞుడు** n. An idiot, a fool. అజ్ఞుడు, తెలివితేనివాడు.

అవటము *avaṭamu.* [Skt.] n. A hole in the ground, a cavity, a pit, a well. గొయ్యి, బొక్క, నుయ్యి. **అవటువు** *avaṭuvu.* [Skt.] n. The back of the neck. పెడతల, అవాగా, మెడ వెనుకటిప్రాగము, ఋచ్ఛిలికుంట. "ఉన్నమితానటు విలటద్ఘోరంబుల భేదంబులవాటనోయరా." Vasu. iv. 39. "అవటుకచంబువాని." A vi. 23. టీ॥ పెడ తిలనుమాత్రమే వెంట్రుకలు గలవానిని.

అవతంసము *avatamsamu.* [Skt.] n. A flower put on the ear for ornament; a crest, a ring worn at the tip of the ear. కర్ణభూషణము, సిగబంతి, శిరోభూషణము. స్త్రీపురుషులు చెవికొనమంచే పుష్పపల్లవాదులు, శేఖరము, శిఖయందుకట్టిన పూలదండ. **అవతంసితము** adj. Worn on the ear for ornament. చెవికొనను ఉంచుకోబడిన.

అవతరించు *ava-tarintsu.* [Skt.] v. n. To come down, to get down into. దిగు. To be born. పుట్టు. To appear, to put on a form, to become incarnate. అవతారమెత్తు. విష్ణువు మత్స్యముగా అవతరించెను Vishnu appeared as a fish. కృష్ణుడుగా అవతరించెను he was

born as Krishna, or he appeared as Krishna or he put on the form of Krishna.
అవతారము *ava-tāramu.* [Skt.] n. Incarnation, metamorphosis. The descent of a deity from heaven in a particular shape, the appearance of any deity upon earth, origin. దేవుడు రూపాంతరమును ఎత్తి దము. విష్ణువు ఎత్తిన దశావతారములు the ten incarnations of Vishnu. రామావతారమెత్తి నప్పుడు when he appeared on earth as Rama వాడు గర్వావతారము he is pride incarnate, అది క్షామావతారము she is the genius of famine. (Shakesp. 2. Hen. IV. act 3.) "famine in the abstract, famine embodied, or personified." **అవతారపురుషుడు** *avatāra-purushuḍu.* n. A god-man, a divine being in human form. మహాత్ముడు.

అవతల, అవల or **ఆవల** *avatala.* [Tel. అవల+తల = అవలివోటు] adv. Afterwards, beyond, on the other side, further. తరువాత, అటు, ఆపైన. "అవల నాపొట్టునూరు రవ్వులుగానియె." A. i. pref. 43. **అవతలి** or **ఆవలి** adj. Next, following. తరువాతి. అవతలిసోమవారము Monday after next. అవతలి వైనములు further particulars. అవతలివారు those who are on the other side. అవతలి ఒడ్డు on the other side. అవతలిగతియేమి? what happened afterwards? **అవతలకు** adv. Further off, to the other side. అవట్టుకు.

అవతారము See అవతరించు.

అవతారిక *ava-tārika.* [Skt.] n. A preface. పీఠిక.

అవతీర్ణము *avatīrṇamu.* [Skt.] adj. That into which one descends, as a well or tank. That which is crossed as a river.

అవదంశము *avadamṣamu.* [Skt.] n. A pickle, a preserved fruit. ఊరుగాయ.

అవదగాకి *avada-gāki.* [Tel.] n. An abominable wretch. పలుగాకి. "దాచినొమురుపోయి దక్కినగతి నవ్వునివ్వటిల్లనదననేరజమున, తూచ్చి చెట్టుబట్టుకొని తెచ్చెలోపలి, కవదగాకినారియత్తి లాతి. P. i. 592.

అవదాతము *ava-dātamu.* [Tel.] n. Whiteness. తెలుపు. adj. White. తెల్లని.

అవదూరు *ava-dūru.* [Tel.] n. (a bad phrase) Calumny, defamation. అపదూరు, నింద, అపవాదము.

అవద్యము *a-vadyamu.* [Skt.] adj. Mean, low, servile, inferior. నికృష్టమైన. **అవద్యము** *a-vadyamu.* [Skt.] n. Ruin, harm, loss. చెరుపు. దీనికి అవద్యములేదు this has lost nothing.

అవధరించు *ava-dharintsu.* [Skt.] v. a. To favour with one's attention. To lend an ear, listen. To wear, put on. ఎచ్చరికపడు, విను, ఆలకించు, పెట్టుకొను. "నవపింఛమయూఖా వలుఘరించినటించు." Swa. iii. 25. "దుర్వ సుమంళంబునంబుట్టినకిట్టిశోభనంబులే మద్భుతింబు లవధరింపుము." A. pref. 21. **అవధారు** (the second person singular of the imperative of the verb. అవధరించు.) Oh Listen! O give ear! వినుము, ఆలకించుము, చిత్తగింపుము. "కుబేరశంకరుల్ సరసముగొల్వుమ్రొక్కులిడ స్వామిపరాకవధారుదేవ హెచ్చరికయటంచుకంచుకులు." N. i. 177.

అవధానము *ava-dhānamu.* [Skt.] n. Attention, care, regard. మనోయోగము, ఎచ్చరిక. **అవధాని** or **అవధానుడు** n. He who is attentive or careful. He who is skilled in the Vedas. ఎచ్చరికగలవాడు, జాగ్రతగల వాడు, వేదము వొరుగావచ్చినవాడు. అష్టావధాని a versatile man; one who can attend to eight matters simultaneously. శతావధాని n. One who can attend to a hundred things at one and the same time.

అవధారణము *ava-dhāraṇamu.* [Skt.] n. Certainty, determination, resolution. Emphasis. నిశ్చయము. **అవధారు** See అవధరించు.

అవధి *avadhi.* [Skt.] n. Boundary, period, time, conclusion, end. (Colloq.) Strait, calamity, misfortune. పొలిమేర, కాలము అవసానము, ఆపద. శరీరపతనావధి as long as one lives. వానికి ఒక అవధివచ్చినది a misfortune happened to him. అవధిక్రయపత్రము a mortgage bond with the penalty of forfeiting the mortgage after a limited time. **అవధీరితము** *ava-dhiritamu*. [Skt.] adj. Disregarded, scorned, despised. అవమానించబడిన, తిరస్కరించబడిన. **అవధూతము** adj. Removed, tossed aside, cast away, thrown. తోసివేయబడిన. **అవధూతుడు** *ava-dhūtudu*. [Skt] n. A naked mendicant. One who has renounced all worldly feeling and obligation. దిగంబరుడుగా తిరిగే సన్యాసి.

అవధ్యము *a-vadhyamu*. [Skt. వధ్=to kill] adj. Not meriting death, innocent. చంపరాని, చంపదగని. **అవధ్యుడు** n. One who is not deserving of death. చంపననర్హుడు.

అవనతము *avanatamu*. [Skt.] adj. Bowed, bent. వంగిన.

అవనము *avanamu*. [Skt.] n. Preservation, protection, rescue. రక్షణము. "గజప్రాణావనోత్సాహి" one who hastens to save the life of the elephant.

అవని *avani*. [Skt.] n. The earth. భూమి. అవనీవరుడు or అవనీతలేంద్రుడు a king. అవనీసురుడు a Brahmin.

అవపథ్యము *ava-pathyamu*. [Skt.] n. Violation of prescribed regimen. Error in diet. అపథ్యము.

అవపాతము *ava-pātamu*. [Skt.] n. A pit concealed under leaves and earth to catch elephants. ఏనుగులు మొదలైన మృగములను పట్టుకొనుటకై త్రవ్వి మీద కర్రలను కంపలను పరచి వాటిపైన కొద్దిగా మన్ను వేయబడిన గోయ్యి, ఓదము.

అవభృథము *ava-bhrithamu*. [Skt.] n. Ablution after a sacrifice, a purification made at the termination of a sacrifice or any auspicious ceremony. యజ్ఞాంతస్నానము.

అవమతి *ava-mati*. [Skt.] n. Disgrace, disregard. అవమానము. **అవమతము** adj. Despised, disregarded. అవమానితము.

అవమర్దనము *ava-mardanamu*. [Skt.] n. Beating as a drum. వాయించడము. "మర్దలముఖావమర్దనకుంగ్రుంగుటయు." A iv. 42.

అవమర్యాద *ava-maryada*. [Skt.] n. Incivility, unpoliteness. అగౌరవము, అమర్యాద.

అవమానించు *ava-manintsu*. [Skt.] v. a. To dishonor, to disgrace. అగౌరవముచేయు. **అవమానము** *ava-mānamu*. [Skt.] n. Disgrace, dishonour, disrespect. అమర్యాద. వానికి అవమానము అయినది or వాడు అవమానపడినాడు he was disgraced or treated with disrespect. **అవమానితము** adj. Despised, disrespected. పరిభూతమైన. **అవమానితుడు** *ava-manitudu*. [Skt.] n. He who is disgraced or treated with disrespect. పరిభూతుడు.

అవయవము *ava-yavamu*. [Skt.] n. A limb, a member. అంగము. **అవయవి** *ava-yavi*. n. An organism; that which has limbs.

అవయోగము *ava-yōgamu*. [Skt.] n. A bad sign, an inauspicious omen. అవలక్షణము.

అవరజుడు *avarajudu*. [Skt.] n. A younger brother. తమ్ముడు, అనుజుడు.

అవరోధము *ava-rōdhamu*. [Skt.] n. Obstacle, hindrance. A seraglio. అడ్డి, అడ్డగింత. అంతఃపురము. **అవరోధించు** *ava-rōdhintsu*. [Skt.] v. t. To obstruct, to hinder. అడ్డగించు.

అవరోహము *ava-rōhamu*. [Skt.] n. Descending దిగడము. The root that grows from the branches of trees like the Banyan tree. ఊడ.

అవల Same as అవతల (q. v.)

అవలంబించు *avalambintsu*. [Skt.] v. a. To take hold of any thing; depend on any person or thing. చేపట్టు, ఆశ్రయించు. ఆ మతమును అవలంబించినవారు Converts, those who embraced that creed. ధైర్యము నవలంబించి picking up courage. ఆయనమాట నవలంబించినారు they embraced his opinion, or sided with him. **అవలంబనము** or **అవలంబము** *avalambamu* n. Taking hold of any thing, hanging on or from. Adoption, or profession of certain views. పట్టు, ఆశ్రయము. మతావలంబనము the adoption of a religion. అవలంబితము adj. That which is adopted, as one's own.

అవలక్షణము *ava-lakshanamu.* [Skt.] n. Evil omen, an inauspicious sign. అపరూపము, చెడులక్షణము. **అవలక్షణము** adj. Deformed, inauspicious. వికారమైన.

అవలగ్నము *ava-lagnamu.* [Skt.] n. The waist. నడుము.

అవలీల *ava-lila* [Skt.] n. Ease, facility. సులభము, చులకన. **అవలీలయైన** adj. Easy, facile, ready. సులభమైన. **అవలీలగా** *ava-lila-ga.* [Skt.] adv. Easily, as play. సులభముగా, చులకనగా.

అవలుంఠనము *ava-lunthanamu.* [Skt.] n. Rolling on the ground. పొరలడము. **అవలుంఠితము** adj. Rolled on the ground. పొరలిన, నేలమీద దొర్లిన.

అవలేపము *ava-lēpamu.* [Skt.] n. Pride. గర్వము.

అవలేహనము *ava-lēhanamu.* [Skt.] n. Licking with the tongue. నాకడము.

అవలోకించు *ava-lōkintsu.* [Skt. Root connected with the English word Look.] v. n. To look at. చూచు, వీక్షించు. **అవలోకనము** n. Sight, seeing. చూడడము. పునరావలోకనము re-perusal. సింహావలోకనము retrospection. సింహావలోకనపద్యము a verse in which every line looks back to the beginning. వాని ముఖావలోకనము చేయరాదు one should not look at his face. **అవలోకితము** adj. That which is seen. చూడబడినది.

అవశ *a-vaṣa.* [Skt.] n. She who is out of her senses. స్మారకములేనిది. "అవశచందాన శైవాలునవ్వుధూటి." Swa. vi. 41. **అవశము** *a-vaṣamu.* [Skt.] adj. Unsubjected, unrestrained, independent. అస్వాధీనమైన. "మేనవశంబు గుటదయుతృజించెనసువుల." P. i. 137. అవశముగా not in one's power.

అవశకునము *ava-sakunamu.* [Skt.] n. An evil omen, a bad sign. దుర్లక్షణము, దుశ్శకునము.

అవశాత్ or **అవశాత్తుగా** *a-vaṣat.* [Skt.] adv. Suddenly, unawares, providentially, abruptly. అకస్మికముగా, హఠాత్తుగా.

అవశిష్టము *ava-ṣishtamu.* [Skt. from శేషము] adj. Left, rest, remainder. శేషము, మిగిలినది. వాన్ని ప్రాణావశిష్టముగా విడిచిపెట్టిరి they left him half dead.

అవశ్యము *a-vaṣyamu.* [Skt.] adj. Necessary, indispensable, urgent, requisite. నిశ్చితమైన, నిశ్చయమైన. **అవశ్యముగా** adv. Necessarily, positively. అగత్యముగా. నిశ్చయముగా.

అవష్టంభము *ava-shtambhamu.* [Skt.] n. Support, stay, a post or pillar. ఆధారము, పట్టు, కంబము. నాకు మంచి అవష్టంభములేదు I have no defender, I have no patron. మీ అవష్టంభము ఉండగా వానికేమి తక్కువ as long as he has your support what need he care?

అవసడి *ava-sadi.* [Tel. with Skt. prefix] n. అపవాదము.

అవసత్ *a-vasat.* [Skt.] adj. Indwelling. నివసించియుండే. "అలనాజనాపాంగవలనావసదనంగ." Vasu. i. 141.

అవసథము *ava-sadhamu.* [Skt.] n. A house, habitation. ఇల్లు.

అవసరము *avasaramu.* [Skt.] n. Occasion, opportunity. వేళ, సమయము, కార్యోచితసమయము. ఇది మూడో అవసరము this is the third time. "చేరవచ్చు నయ్యవసరంబున." T. iii. 39. అవసరము also means food offered as a meal to a god, or a kind of mantram said on the occasion. శ్రీరంగములో అరువై అవసరములు ఆరగింపుచేయుదురు they make an offering of sixty meals. Also necessity, urgency, hurry, flurry. అగత్యము, ఆతురము. అవసరమైనప్పుడు నిన్ను పిలిపించుకొంటాను I will send for you when necessary. అవసరము చేస్తే పని చెడిపోవును if you hurry the business will be spoiled. అది నాకు అవసరములేదు I have no occasion for this. అవసరము adj. Necessary, urgent, hurried, hasty. అగత్యమైన, ఆతురమైన. అవసరమైనపని urgent business. అవసరపడు *avasara-padu.* v. n. To hurry, to haste. త్వరపడు. అవసరముగా adv. Urgently, in haste. అగత్యముగా, ఆతురముగా. అవసరించు *avasarintsu.* [Skt.] v. a. To hurry, make haste. త్వరచేయు.

అవసానము *ava-sānamu.* [Skt.] n. End, conclusion, termination, death. Limit. కడ, విరామము, సమాప్తి, శేషము, మృత్యువు, అవసానకాలము the time of death. **అవసన్నము** *ava-sannamu.* [Skt.] adj. That which has reached its end, that which is destroyed. కడముట్టినది, నశించినది.

అవసాయము *ava-sāyamu.* [Skt.] n. Certainty, termination, remainder. నిశ్చయము, ముగింపు, శేషము.

అవస్థ *avastha.* [Skt.] n. State, condition, situation: trouble, difficulty, strait. దశ, సంకటము. వాడు నిండా దురవస్థలోనున్నాడు he is in a wretched state. అవస్థాత్రయము, అనగా జాగ్రత్స్వప్నసుషుప్తులు the three states: viz., waking, sleeping and dreaming. అవస్థాచతుష్టయము, అనగా బాల్యావస్థ the period of childhood. యౌవనావస్థ the period of youth. వార్ధకావస్థ old age. మరణావస్థ the agony of death.

అవహేళనము *ava-hēlanamu.* [Skt.] n. Contempt, disrespect, disregard. తిరస్కారము, అవమానము.

అవాంతరము *avāntaramu.* [Skt.] adj. Included, subordinate. అంతర్భూతమైన, లోని, కింది. అవాంతరదశ a minor distinction: a species, a subdivision of a general term. అవాంతరశ్లోకము a spurious verse: an interpolation. అవాంతరకథ an episode. అవాంతరముగా unexpectedly.

అవాచ్యము *a-vāchyamu.* [Skt.] adj. Unutterable, not fit to be uttered, obscene. అనరాని, ఆడరాని, ఉచ్చరింపగూడని, బండైన, బూతు అయిన.

అవాజా *avāzā.* [H.] n. Report, public talk. పుకారా, వదంతి.

అవాప్తము *a-vāptamu.* [Skt.] adj. Obtained. పొందబడిన. **అవాప్తి** *avāpti* n. Obtaining, attaining. పొందడము.

అవారణము *a-vāranamu.* [Skt.] adj. Unrestrained, resistless. అనర్గళమైన, అడ్డంకిలేని, యథేచ్ఛమైన. "వీరవరనవారణమహిమాఢ్య." A. i. pref. 38. **అవారణ** or **అవారణము** n. Resistlessness, want of restraint. అడ్డులేమి. **అవారణ** or **అవారణగా** adv. Irrepressibly. అనర్గళముగా, యథేచ్ఛగా.

అవారి *avāri.* [Tel.] adj. Abundant, excessive, much, ample. విస్తారమైన. **అవారిగ** adv. Abundantly, excessively. విస్తారముగా, మెండుగా. "అవారిగ తియ్యనిమేడిపండ్లుగొంచు." P. iv. 37.

అవారితము or **అవార్యము** *a-vāritamu.* [Skt.] adj. Inevitable, irresistible. దుర్వారమైన, అప్రతిహతమైన, అడ్డగింపగూడని.

అవి *avi.* [Tel.] pron. Those, (things.) అవి యెవరివి whose things are they?

అవికలము *a-vikalamu.* [Skt.] adj. Entire, perfect, unimpaired. సంపూర్ణమైన, సమగ్రమైన, తారుమారుకాని.

అవిచ్ఛిత్తుగా *a-vichchittu-gā.* [Skt.] adv. Undisturbedly, uninterruptedly. నిరాటంకముగా. **అవిచ్ఛిన్నము** adj. Uninterrupted, unintermitting. ఎడతెగని, నిరంతరమైన. **అవిచ్ఛిన్నముగా** adv. Uninterruptedly. ఎడతెగక, నిరంతరముగా.

అవిటి *aviti.* [Tel.] n. He who is maimed, crippled or deformed. A blind man. అంగహీనుడు, వికలాంగుడు, గుడ్డి, పిచ్చుకుంటు.

అవిద్య *a-vidya.* [Skt.] Want of knowledge, ignorance. అజ్ఞానము.

అవిధి *avidhi.* [Skt.] n. Misfortune, calamity, trouble, distress. తొందర, సంకటము.

అవినీతుడు *a-vi-nītuḍu.* [Skt.] n. A wicked man. దుష్టుడు, వినయము, లేక, నీతిలేనివాడు.

అవిభక్తము *a-vibhaktamu.* [Skt.] adj. Undivided, unpartitioned, unseparated, joint. పంచుకొనబడని. **అవిభక్తులు** *a-vibhaktulu.* n. plu. Those who live together without dividing their inheritance, those who live as one family. భాగాలు తీరనివారు, పాళ్లుపంచుకొననివారు. మీరు విభక్తులా అవిభక్తులా do you live apart from your brothers or not?

అవిముక్తము *a-vi-muktamu.* [Skt.] adj. Unloosed, not delivered. విమోచనముకాని.

అవియు *aviyu.* [Tel.] v. n. To break, burst, be destroyed. బద్దలగు, పగులు. వానికన్నులవిసినవి his eyeballs are destroyed. **అవియించు** *aviyintsu.* v. a. To break. బద్దలుచేయు.

అవిరతము *a-viratamu.* [Skt.] adj. Continual, incessant. సంతతమైన, నిరంతరమైన.

అవిరళము *a-viralamu.* [Skt.] adj. Thick, close, dense. నిబిడమైన, దట్టమైన.

అవిరి *aviri.* n. [Tel.] The indigo plant (*Indigofera tinctoria.*) A certain disease that attacks the pupil of the eye. నీలిచెట్టు, కంటికివచ్చే ఒక రోగము.

అవిలంబనము *a-vilambanamu.* [Skt.] n. Rapidity, swiftness. త్వర, వేగము. **అవిలంబితము** *a-vilambitamu.* [Skt.] adj. Rapid, swift. త్వరగాగల, వడిగల.

అవివాదము *a-vivādamu.* [Skt.] adj. Undisputed, unquestioned. తగవులేని.

అవివేకము *a-vivēkamu.* [Skt.] n. Want of sense or judgment, absence of discrimination, ignorance, imprudence, blindness of heart, folly. తెలివిలేమి. **అవివేకము** adj. Undiscriminating, foolish, blundering. తెలివిలేని. **అవివేకి** *a-vivēki.* n. A fool, a blockhead. తెలివిలేనివాడు.

అవిశ్వసనీయము *a-visvasanīyamu.* [Skt.] adj. Untrustworthy, dishonest. నమ్మదగని.

అవిసెచెట్టు or **అవిసెచెట్టు** *avisi-chettu.* [Tel.] n. Common flax, *Linum usitatissimum,* also a certain leguminous plant. అవిసి. సీమ అవిసె *Cassia alata* (Watts.)

అవు *avu.* [Tel.] Another form of అగు (q.v.) నీవ్యాధికి యిది అవును this will be good for your disease.

అవుడు or **ఔడు** *avuḍu.* [Tel.] n. The under lip. అడుగుపెదవి. అవుడుగరచు to bite the under lip from anger. కోపముచేత అధరోష్ఠమును కొరుకుకొను.

అవుతు *avutu.* [H.] n. A waterspout in which the stream descends; if the stream ascends, it is called పీలుసుడి. **అవుతుఖానా** *avutu-khāna.* [H.] n. A reservoir, a cistern, pond, bath. తొట్టి, గుంట, స్నానవాటిక.

అవును or **ఔను** It is so, yes. 3rd pers. sing. indefinite of అవు v. n. To become.

అవురుగడ్డి See under ఇట్టిపేరు.

అవేలము *a-vēlamu.* [Skt.] n. Boundlessness, unlimitedness. మేరలేమి, మితిలేమి. "విస్మయంబవేలముగాగ." Swa. iv. 28.

అవ్యక్తము *a-vyaktamu.* [Skt.] adj. Indistinct, invisible, imperceptible. అస్పష్టమైన, అగుపడని. **అవ్యక్తగణితము** n. Algebra. బీజగణితము. **అవ్యక్తరాశి** an unknown quantity in algebra. **అవ్యక్తరాగము** n. Dark red; the colour of the dawn. కొంచెము ఎరుపు, అరుణము.

అవ్యక్తుడు *a-vyaktuḍu.* [Skt.] n. A blockhead, one who is ignorant or stupid. మూర్ఖుడు, మూఢుడు, అవ్యక్తులు the ignorant. **అవ్యక్తురాలు** *avyaktu-rālu.* n. An ignorant woman. మూర్ఖురాలు, మూఢురాలు

అవ్యథ *a-vyadha.* [Skt.] n. Freedom from sorrow. దుఃఖములేమి.

అవ్యయము *a-vyayamu.* [Skt.] adj. Imperishable, immutable, eternal. నాశరహితమైన, నిత్యమైన. n. An indeclinable word, a particle. విభక్తిప్రత్యయాదులు లేనిశబ్దము. అవ్యయుడు *a-vyayuḍu.* n. He who is imperishable, i.e., God. నాశరహితుడు, నిత్యుడు, దేవుడు.

అవ్యవధానము *a-vyavadhānamu.* [Skt.] n. Absence of interval. వ్యవధానములేమి. అవ్యవధానముగా adv. Immediately. వెంటనే, తోడుతోనే.

అవ్యవహితము *a-vyavahitamu.* [Skt.] adj. Close, near, adjoining. సమీపమైన.

అవ్యాజము *a-vyājamu.* [Skt.] adj. Not cunning, honest. కపటములేని. Causeless. నిర్హేతుకమైన. అవ్యాజకరుణ free grace.

అవ్యాపకము *a-vyāpakamu.* [Skt.] adj. (In Logic.) Not spreading over the whole, not covering the whole. అవ్యాపకత్వము n. Non-comprehensiveness or generalisation. అవ్యాప్తము that which is not pervaded with. అవ్యాప్తి inadequate extent (of a definition) అవ్యాప్యము not covering the whole ground, not extending over the whole matter. అవ్యాప్యవృత్తి a category of limited application, a partial inference.

అవ్వ *avva.* [Tel.] n. A grandmother, a mother: any old or respectable woman. జననీజనకులతల్లి, తల్లి, పూజ్యురాలు. అవ్వపండు *avva-paṇḍu.* n. A certain scarlet fruit called in Tamil சௌளிப்பழம் కొరపండు. It is boiled in oil to anoint the head. అవ్వరో interj. O madam!

అవ్వల్ *avval.* [H.] adj. First. మొదటి. అవ్వల్‌రకము best quality (of goods.)

అవ్వల *avvala.* [Tel. అ+వల lit. that side.] adv. Afterwards, after, beyond, on the other side further. తరువాత, అవ్వట్టు, ఆపైన. అవ్వలవ్వలి further and further.

అవ్వాయిచువ్వలు or అవాయిచువ్వలు *avvāyi-tsuvvalu.* [H. *hawai*] n. plu. Rockets, sky rockets. ఆకాశబాణములు.

అవ్వారి *avvari.* [Tel. another form of అవారి] adj. Abundant, excessive, much, ample. విస్తారమైన. అవ్వారిగా, అవారిగా, adv. Abundantly, excessively. విస్తారముగా.

అశక్తము, అశక్తత or అశక్తి *aśaktamu.* [Skt.] n. Weakness, inability, illness. దుర్బలము, అసమర్థత, వ్యాధి. నేను అశక్తముగానున్నప్పుడు when I was ill. అశక్తుడు *a-śaktuḍu.* n. An invalid, a patient, a sick man. రోగి. అశక్తులు invalids, patients.

అశక్యము *a-śakyamu.* [Skt.] adj. Impossible. అసాధ్యము. అశక్యుడు *a-śakyuḍu.* n. He who is invincible. అసాధ్యుడు.

అశనము *aśanamu.* [Skt.] n. Food, boiled rice, subsistence. అన్నము. భోజనము. అశనానికిలేనివారై being without bread to eat. మాంసాశనుడు he who eats flesh. అశనాతురుడు n. He who is hungry. క్షుధితుడు, ఆకలిగొన్నవాడు.

అశని *aśani.* [Skt.] n. A thunderbolt. వజ్రాయుధము, పిడుగు.

అశరీరవాణి *a-śarīra-vāṇi.* [Skt.] The speech of an invisible being, a voice from heaven. ఆకాశవాక్కు. అశరీరి *a-śarīri.* n. A spirit, an incorporeal being. దేహము లేనివాడు. "తనకునబ్బాలుచే చావుగలదని యశరీరిచేవిని" (Vish. viii. 78.) being warned by a voice from heaven that this child should cause his death.

అశాశ్వతము *a-śāśvatamu.* [Skt.] adj. Not permanent, temporary. అస్థిరమైన.

అశాస్త్రీయము *a-śāstrīyamu.* [Skt.] Opposed to the Śāstras. శాస్త్రసమ్మతముకాని.

అశీతి *aśīti.* [Skt.] (a numeral adj.) Eighty. ఎనుబది. అశీతిభాగము the eightieth part. అశీతికుడు an octogenarian.

అశుచి *a-suchi.* [Skt.] n. Uncleanness. అపరిశుద్ధత. **అశుచి** adj. Unclean. అపరిశుద్ధమైన.

అశుద్ధము or **అశుద్ధత** *a-suddhamu.* [Skt.] n. Impurity, uncleanness. పారిశుద్ధ్యము లేమి (Colloq:) the human excrement. అమేధ్యము. **అశుద్ధము** adj. Unclean, impure. అశుచియైన.

అశుభము *a-subhamu.* [Skt.] n. Inauspiciousness. అమంగళము. శుభాశుభములు good and evil. వారిని శుభాశుభములకు పిలవనములేదు they never invite them on any occasion either of joy or sorrow.

అశేషము *a-seshamu.* [Skt.] adj. Without a remainder, whole, all, entire. యావత్తు, అంత. **అశేషము** n. The whole, all the people. యావత్తుమంది. ఊరిశేషమును పిలిచినారు they invited the whole village.

అశోకము *asókamu.* [Skt.] n. The Jonesia Asoca, *or, the Uvaria longifolia.* వంజుళము. **అశోకము** adj. Free from sorrow. దుఃఖములేని.

అశౌచము *a-sauchamu.* [Skt.] n. Uncleanness, impurity, defilement. Same as అశుచి.

అశ్మము *asmamu.* [Skt.] n. A stone, a rock. రాయి. **అశ్మరి** n. The disease called stone in the bladder. మూత్రకృచ్ఛ్రము, నీరుకట్టురోగము. **అశ్మసారము** n. Iron. ఇనుము. Metal. లోహము.

అశ్రద్ధ *a-sraddha.* [Skt.] n. Neglect, inattention. ఉపేక్ష.

అశ్రాంతము *a-srantamu.* [Skt.] adj. Eternal, continual. నిరంతరమైన, ఎడతెగని, ఎల్లప్పుడును ఉండే.

అశ్రి *asri.* [Skt.] n. The edge of a sword. అస్త్రాదుల అగ్రభాగము, ఆయుధధార, అంచు.

అశ్రువు, or **అస్రము** *asruvu.* [Skt.] n. A tear. కన్నీళ్లు.

అశ్లీలము *a-slilamu.* [Skt.] n. Rustic language. పామరోక్తి, అసభ్యమైనమాట.

అశ్వగంధ *asva-gandha.* [Skt.] n. A certain medical plant *(Physalis flexuosa)* పెన్నేరు చెట్టు.

అశ్వత్థము *ascatthamu.* [Skt.] n. The holy fig tree *(Ficus Religiosa.)* పిప్పలము, రావిచెట్టు. అశ్వత్థమునుంచి దేవదారుచెట్టువర్యంతము from the cedar to the hyssop. అశ్వత్థపత్రాకారమైన heart-shaped, shaped like a fig leaf. **అశ్వత్థామ.** a certain hero, the son of Drona.

అశ్వము *asvamu.* [Skt.] n. A horse. గుర్రము. అశ్వగతి the pace of a horse. అశ్వదూత a messenger who rides on horseback. అశ్వపాది horsefooted. అశ్వమేధము the sacrifice of a horse, performed anciently by Hindu rajahs. అశ్వరథము a carriage drawn by horses. గుర్రపుబండి, గుర్రాలబండి. అశ్వవైద్యుడు a veterinary surgeon. అశ్వశాల a stable. అశ్వశాస్త్రము veterinary science. అశ్వశిక్ష the training of horses. అశ్వశిక్షకుడు a rough-rider, a horse-breaker. అశ్వారూఢుడు or అశ్వారోహుడు one who is mounted on horseback. రవుతు.

అశ్విని *asvini.* [Skt.] n. The first lunar mansion. మొదటి నక్షత్రము. The twins in the zodiac; the head of the Aries or the 1st of the 28 Nakshatras or lunar mansions.

అష *asha.* [Tel. for అట] v. They say, it is said: as వెళ్లినాడష they say he is gone. (This and the following forms are used chiefly by Vaidiki women among the Brahmins.) **అషు** *ashu.* [Tel. for అట్లు] adv. Thus, so. అషయితే If so. అషుంటు adv. Further or farther. అవతల. **అషువంటి** for **అటువంటి** adj. Such. **అషే** for **అటే** a phrase used in questioning a woman: thus, వాడితో చెప్పినావషే did you tell him? (a word addressed to the wife, &c.)

అష్ట *ashta.* [Skt. cf. Eng. "Eight," Lat. Octo.] adj. Eight.—**అష్టకష్టములు** The eight unpleasant circumstances liable to occur in the course of life. [Viz. దేశాంతర గమనము foreign travel, భార్యావియోగము separation from one's wife, కష్టకాలములో ప్రియబంధుదర్శనము friends and relations arriving in the time of trouble, ఎంగిలితినడము eating the leavings of others, తన శత్రువులతో స్నేహముచేయడము courting one's enemies, పరాన్నమునకు కాచియుండడము looking for food from strangers, సభలో అప్రతిష్ఠవచ్చుట being ignorant in an assembly of wise men, దరిద్రమనుభవించడము suffering poverty.] **అష్టకోణి** an octagon, అష్టదిక్కులు the eight points of the compass.—**అష్టదిక్పాలకులు** the regents of the eight points of the compass, viz. Indra of the East, Agni of the South-east, Yama of the South, Nairriti of the South-west, Varuṇa of the West, Marut of the North-west, Kubēra of the North, and Iṡana of the South-east.—**అష్టదిగ్గజములు** the elephants supporting the eight corners of the earth.—**అష్టనాగములు** the eight serpents supporting the eight angles or points of the world. Their names are as follow :—వాసుకి, అనంతుడు, తక్షకుడు, శంఖపాలుడు, కులికుడు, పద్ముడు, మహాపద్ముడు, కార్కోటకుడు. **అష్టపదులు** a certain set of songs of eight lines in length.—**అష్టపాత్రములు** the eight vessels used in a sacrifice.— **అష్టభాగ్యములు** the eight requisites to the regal state; as రాజ్యము territory, భండారము wealth, సైన్యము an army, ఏనుగులు elephants, గుర్రములు horses, ఛత్రము an umbrella, చామరము a fly fan or whisk, అందోళిక a palanquin.— **అష్టభోగములు** the eight sources of pleasure, viz., ఇల్లు house, పరుపు bed, వస్త్రము raiment, ఆభరణము jewels, స్త్రీలు women, పుష్పము flowers, గంధము perfume, తాంబూలము areca nuts and betel-leaves.—**అష్టమదములు** eight kinds of pride, viz., అన్నమదము luxury in food, అర్థమదము pride of wealth, స్త్రీమదము pride of lust, విద్యామదము pride of learning, కులమదము pride of rank and family, రూపమదము pride of beauty, ఉద్యోగమదము pride of station, యౌవనమదము pride of youth.—అష్టసావ్యములు, the eight respects in which an absolute conveyance is made, viz., విక్రయ, దాన, వినిమయ, జల, తరు, పాషాణ, నిధి, నిక్షేపములు.—**అష్టాంగములు** See under అంగము. సాష్టాంగదండము prostration in worship. — **అష్టాపదము**. an eight legged dragon: a spider. **అష్టావధానము** See under అవధానము. అష్టైశ్వర్యములు complete comfort, every blessing, also eight attributes, viz., అణిమ, మహిమ, గరిమ, లఘిమ, ప్రాప్తి, ప్రాకామ్యము, ఈశత్వము, వశిత్వము.

అష్టమము *ashtamamu.* [Skt.] adj. The eighth. **అష్టమి** *ashtami.* n. The eighth day after the new or full moon, the eighth phase of the moon. ఎనిమిదవ తిథి. **అష్టాదశము** *ashta-dasamu.* adj. Eighteen. పదునెనిమిదవది.

అసంకల్పితము *a-sankalpitamu.* [Skt.] adj. Not thought on, not purposed, not intended. అప్రతిజ్ఞాతము.

అసంఖ్యేయము *a-sankhyēyamu.* [Skt.] adj. Innumerable. లెక్కలేని.

అసంగతము *a-sangatamu.* [Skt.] adj. Incoherent, incongruous, improbable, inconsistent. అసమంజసమైన, పొసగని. **అసంగతము** n. Incoherency, incongruity. పొసగమి.

అసంతుష్టి *a-santushti.* [Skt.] Discontent. తృప్తిలేమి.

అసందర్భము *a-sandarbhamu.* [Skt.] n. Incongruity, inconvenience, unseasonableness. అసంగతము, అసమయము. **అతడు లేనందున అట్లు చేయడానకు అసందర్భమైనది** his absence prevented my doing so. అసందర్భము adj. Unconnected, inconvenient, unseasonable. అసమయమైన.

అసంపూర్తి a-sampūrti. [Skt.] adj. Incomplete. అసమగ్రము.

అసంబంధము a-sambandhamu. [Skt.] adj. Unconnected, incongruous. అసంగతమైన.

అసంభవము a-sambhavamu. [Skt.] adj. Improbable, unlikely, non-existent. సంభవింపనదికాని, కలుగని.

అసడ్డ a-sadda. [Derived from Skt. అశ్రద్ధ] n. Carelessness, negligence. Disdain, scorn, contempt. అలక్ష్యము, ఉపేక్ష, అశ్రద్ధ.

అసత్, అసత్తు or అసత్తైన a-sat. [Skt.] adj. Bad, vile. చెడ్డదైన.

అసతి a-sati [Skt.] n. A faithless wife. కులట, రంకులాడి, రంకుటాలు.

అసత్యము a-satyamu. [Skt.] n. Perjury, falsehood. బొంకు, అబద్ధము.

అసదు a-sadu. [Tel.] n. Slenderness, smallness, minuteness. A wretch, a vagabond. సూక్ష్మము, అల్పము. కొంచెము; అల్పుడు. "అతివితమ్ములువార్తలాలుమునసదుతే." M. V. i. 263. అసదు adj Small, slender, minute. సూక్ష్మమైన, కృశమైన, సన్నని, కొంచెమైన, అల్పమైన. "నీసముడగుగాని యసదుగా తలంపగరాదు." M. IX. i. 100.

అసదృశము a-sadrusamu. [Skt.] adj. Incomparable. అసమానమైన, సాటిలేని.

అసభ్యము a-subhyamu. [Skt. from సభ] adj. Unfit for an assembly. Vulgar, low, base. సభకు యోగ్యముకాని, క్షుద్రమైన, నీచమైన. అసభ్యుడు asabhyudu n. An unmannerly man, a wretch. క్షుద్రుడు.

అసమంజసము a-samanjasamu. [Skt.] adj. Bad, inconsistent. బాగుకాని, అసంగతమైన, అనుపయుక్తమైన.

అసమగ్రము a-samagramu. [Skt.] adj. Incomplete. అసంపూర్ణము.

అసమము a-samamu. [Skt.] adj. Unequal, unequal either in surface or number, uneven, unrivalled: సమముకాని, అసదృశమైన, విషమమైన. అసమనేత్రుడు asama-nētrudu n. An epithet of Siva, the god who has an extra eye. శివుడు. అసమశరుడు asama-șarudu n. An epithet of Cupid. మన్మథుడు.

అసమయము a-samayamu. [Skt.] n. An inconvenient, unfit or unfavourable time. అకాలము. అసమయము adj. Unseasonable. అకాలమైన.

అసమర్థము a-samarthamu. [Skt.] adj. Unable, incompetent. అశక్తమైన. అసమర్థుడు a-samarthudu. n. He who is unable or incompetent. అశక్తుడు, చేతకానివాడు.

అసమాధానము a-samadhanamu. [Skt.] n. Dissent, dislike, aversion, discontent. అసమ్మతి. అసమాధానము adj. Discontented.

అసమానము a-samanamu. [Skt.] adj. Unequal, different. సమముకాని.

అసమీక్ష్యకారి a-sam-ikshya-kari. [Skt.] n. He who acts inconsiderately. చక్కగా ఆలోచింపక పనిచేయువాడు. అసమీక్ష్యకారిత్వము n. Acting inconsiderately.

అసము asamu. [Tadbhava form of Skt. యశము] n. Fame, reputation, renown, power, influence, authority, opportunity. కీర్తి, ఉద్రేకము, యశము, అధికారము, బలము, సందు, ఎడము. "కులగిరిపైనుండి కుంభిని మీదికి సమున నురుకు సింహంబుచందమున." H. D. ii. 2069. తనపనివాండ్లకు అసము ఇచ్చియున్నాడు he has given all his authority to his servants, he has given up the reins to them. మొగుడు అసమిచ్చినందున అది యింత త్రుళ్లుచున్నది she is so conceited as her husband has given the management of things into her hands.

అసరవేయు asara-vēyu. [Tel.] v. n. To delay. ఆలస్యముచేయు.

అసరు asaru. [Tel.] n. The juice of leaves. ఆకుపసరు. భార. శల్య. ii.

అసలారు *asalāru.* [Tel.] v. n. To increase. అతిశయిల్లు. **అసలార** adv. Duly, agreeably, well. ఒప్పుగా. "బసవనిభక్తిసౌభాగ్య మహత్త్వమసలారవిని." BD. v. 850.

అసలు *asalu.* [Tel.] n. Mud, mire. బురద. plu. అసళ్లు. "అడుగున బండివీలియసళ్లై." A. i. 21. "అవనిరేణువులనీరసలుగాగ." P. i. 238.

అసలు *asalu.* [H.] adj. Original, principal, excellent, real, genuine, legitimate. మొదటిదైన, ముఖ్యమైన, స్వచ్ఛమైన, సంకరముకాని. అసలుదావా the original complaint. అసలువాది the original complainant. అసలుజేబీజు the original rents or account. **అసలు** n. The principal, as opposed to the interest మూలధనము. Plu. అసళ్లు originals. అసళ్లు ఉంచుకొని నకళ్లు ఇచ్చినాడు he retained the originals and gave the copies. Also, origin, stock in trade.

అసహాయత *a-sahāyata.* [Skt.] n. Loneliness, solitude, the life of a hermit. ఒంటి. **అసహాయశూరుడు** *a-sahāya-sūruḍu* n. He who fights single-handed. **అసహాయుడు** *a-sahāyuḍu.* n. He who is friendless, he who is single-handed. ఒంటిగాడు, ఒండోమనిషి సహాయము లేనివాడు.

అసహిష్ణుడు *a-sahishṇuḍu.* [Skt.] n. He who is impatient. తాళలేనివాడు. **అసహిష్ణుత** n. Impatience. ఓర్వలేమి, తాళలేమి. **అసహిష్ణువైన** adj. Impatient, unenduring. ఓర్వలేని, తాళలేని.

అసహ్యము *a-sahyamu.* [Skt.] adj. Intolerable, unbearable, hateful, loathsome. తాళగూడని, సహింపగూడని, చీదరైన. **అసహ్యము** n. Loathsomeness, disgust. చీదర, తాళగూడమి. **అసహ్యపడు** or **అసహ్యించు** v. n. To have a dislike for, to be disgusted with. రోతపడు.

అసాక్షికము *a-sākshikamu.* [Skt.] adj. Unattested, unwitnessed. సాక్షిలేని.

అసాదు *a-sādu.* [Skt.] adj. Good, well. మంచిది, బళి.

బుధుల్,
సాదనశాస్త్రవుల్లెల్లన,
సాదన జెగ జెల్లదొడఁసాదనసేయఁగ.
రామా. 3 ఆ.

అసాధారణము *a-sādhāraṇamu.* [Skt.] adj. Not common, special, specific. విశేషమైన.

అసాధువు *a-sādhuvu.* [Skt.] adj. Not mild, not in conformity with the rule. Wicked, bad. సాధువుకాని, చెడ్డ, దుష్ట.

అసాధ్యము *a-sādhyamu.* [Skt.] adj. Impossible. సాధ్యముకాని. **అసాధ్యత** *a-sādhyata,* n. Impossibility. వల్లగామి.

అసి *asi.* [Skt.] n. A sword. ఖడ్గము. adj. Slight. అల్పమైన. **అసిగాయము** *asi-gāyamu.* n. A slight or superficial wound, a slight graze or wound. స్వల్పగాయము. **అసిధారావ్రతము** *asi-dhāra-vratamu* a vow to stand on the edge of a sword; (figuratively) being engaged in any hopelessly difficult task. **అసిధేను** or **అసిధేనుక** or **అసిపుత్రి** *asidhēnu.* n. A knife. ఛురిక, మూరకత్తి. "సంబద్ధాసిధేనుల్." Parij. ii. 118. **అసిపత్రము** *asi-patramu* [Skt.] n. The blade of a sword. కత్తియొక్క అలుగు or the sheath. కత్తి ఒర. **అసిబోవు** *asi-bōvu.* v. n. To glance off, to miss. రవంత తగిలి తప్పిపోవు. "శరజర్ద్రిపి వైచినకూలమసిబోవ." N. iv. 115.

"అసిబోవుటెట్లునాయసిబోవుమొనములఁ
జెంచునాచేయమ్మువిలుకుటమ్ము."
రామా. 2 ఆ.

అసిమి *asimi.* [Tel.] n. A bag placed on the back of a bullock to carry things. ఎద్దు మీదవేయు గోనెవలె కట్టిన సంచి. **అసిమిగొల్లెన** *asimi-gollena.* [Tel.] n. A kind of small tent. ఇరుప్రక్కలను వంపుగా కాలవలె నేర్పరిచిన చిన్నగుడారము. "మనువుగానేగియసిమిగొల్లెనలుపన్ని" కళా viii.

అసియాడు *asi-y-āḍu.* [Tel.] v. n. To tremble, dance, move, dangle; to hang as a pendulum. చలించు, ఊగు, వ్రేలాడు. "ముక్కునసియాడు ముదురుతొమురితాడు."

N. ii. 82. అసివారు asi-rāru. [Tel. అసి+ పారు] n. A gentle walk, a stroll. విహారము "ఎవ్వడునలుకలేకక్కి యస్థాదశద్వీపాళి వడి వారుదిరిగెలు." శా. iv.

అసిలేరు asilēru. [Tel.] n. A vulgar name for ఆశ్లేష the ninth lunar mansion.

అసుఖము a-sukhamu. [Skt.] Want of happiness, misery. సుఖములేమి.

అసున్నతి a-sunnati. [Skt. అ not, + Arabic సున్నతి circumcision) n. Uncircumcision. [Used in Pritchett's Telugu Gospels, 1819]. అసున్నతిగలవారు the uncircumcised.

అసుర or అసురుడు asura. [Skt. lit. "Assyrian".] n. A demon, giant. రాక్షసుడు. The Asuras were such as Rāvaṇa and Bana, who were adorers of Siva. అసుర కృత్యము a horrible deed. అసురధ్రువము asura-dhruvamu n. The south pole. దక్షిణధ్రువము. అసురసంధ్య asura-sandhya n. The dusk, the evening. సాయంకాలము. (In the Vedas and in the cuneiform inscriptions, the word అసుర is used in the sense of (1) a nobleman, (2) a powerful being, (3) a god. In later Skt. literature, it is always used in an evil sense.)

అసురుసురు or అసులుసులు asurusuru. [Tel.] n. (lit. sighing and sobbing.) Exhaustion, waste of strength. మిక్కిలి అలుపు.

అసువు asuvu. [Skt.] n. Life, breath. ఉసురు, ప్రాణము.

అసూయ a-sūya. [Skt.] n. Envy, malignity, intolerance. ఓర్వలేమి.

అసూర్యంపశ్య a-sūryam-pasya. [Skt. lit. she who never beholds the sun.] n. A woman who dwells in a harem. రాణివాసముగా నుండేస్త్రీ.

అసృక్కు a-srikku. [Skt.] n. Blood. రక్తము, నెత్తురు.

అస్ఖలితము a-skhalitamu. [Skt.] adj. Firm, unshaken; chaste. చలింపని. అస్ఖలితబ్రహ్మచారి a youth who has not known a woman.

అస్తమయము or అస్తమానము astamayamu. [Skt.] n. Sunset, evening. ప్రొద్దుక్రుంకడము. ఇసుక కమ్ముకొని లోకమంతా అస్తమానమైనట్టున్నది clouds of sand obscured the face of nature. అస్తమించు astamitsu. v. n. To set, to draw towards evening. ప్రొద్దుక్రుంకు. మబ్బుకమ్ముకొని లోకము అస్తమించినట్టున్నది the world is enveloped in shade. అస్తమితము astamitamu. adj Set, as the sun. క్రుంకిన. అస్తము astamu. [Skt.] adj. Set, cast, thrown, disappeared, lost, gone. క్రుంకిన, పోయిన, మరుగైపోయిన. అస్తబలుడు he who is exhausted. అస్తము n. An imaginary mountain in the west behind which the sun is believed to set. అస్తాచలము, అస్తాద్రి astachalamu. n. The western mountain. అస్తమయపర్వతము.

అస్తరు astaru. [H.] n. The lining of a garment, a patch. అస్తరువేసికుట్టు to line (a coat, &c).

అస్తినాస్తి asti-nasti. [Skt.] adj. Doubtful, partly true and partly false. సందేహాస్పదమైన.

అస్తిభారము or అస్థిభారము asti-bhāramu. [Skt. for హస్తిభారము] n. A foundation. అడుగుమట్టు, పునాది.

అస్తు astu. [Skt.] v. Be it so. తథాస్తు may it be so, amen.

అస్తోకము a-stōkamu. [Skt.] adj. Not a little, not trifling, great. బృహత్తైన, అల్పముకాని. అస్తోకత్వము astōkatvamu. n. Greatness.

అస్త్రము astramu. [Skt.] n. A weapon, a sword, a missile. ఆయుధము, బాణము, కత్తి కటారి మొదలైనవి. ఆగ్నేయాస్త్రము a fiery weapon, a weapon having the power of fire. నాగాస్త్రము a serpent weapon, having a serpent's power. అస్త్రకారుడు a maker of weapons. అస్త్రవిద్య military science.

అస్త్రవృష్టి a shower of arrows. అస్త్రశిక్ష military exercise. అస్త్రాగారము an arsenal, an armoury. అస్త్రి astri. n. A bowman. విలుకాడు. అస్త్రజీవి astrajivi. n. A soldier. బంటు, సైనికుడు.

అస్థి asthi. [Skt.] n. A bone. ఎముక. అస్థిగతము in the bones, అస్థిగతజ్వరము or అస్థిజ్వరము slow fever, an internal fever. అస్థినిక్షేపము the rite of depositing the bones of the dead at a holy place. అస్థిపంజరము a skeleton, lit. a cage of bones. అస్థిభంగము fracture of the bones. అస్థిసంచయనము collecting the bones after the burning of a corpse. అస్థిసారము marrow.

అస్థిరము a-sthiramu. [Skt.] adj. Transient, perishable, unstable. అశాశ్వతము. అస్థిరత a-sthirata. n. Unsteadiness, instability. చాంచల్యము, నిలుకడలేమి.

అస్పష్టము a-spashtamu. [Skt.] adj. Not clear, indistinct. విశదముకాని.

అస్పృశ్యము a-sprisyamu. [Skt.] adj. Not to be touched, intangible. తాకరానిది.

అస్ఫుటము a-sphutamu. [Skt.] n. Indistinct. స్పష్టముకాని.

అస్మత్, అస్మదీయము asmat. [Skt.] (pron.) Mine, my. నా, నాది. అస్మదాగమనము my arrival. అస్మదాదులకు to me and others.

అస్రము asramu. [Skt.] n. Blood. A tear. రక్తము. కన్నీళ్లు. అస్రపుడు a blood-drinker, a fiend. అస్రమాతృక chyle, chyme.

అస్వకీయము a-svakiyamu. [Skt.] adj. Not one's own, belonging to another. తనది కాని. అస్వకీయధనము another's property.

అస్వచ్ఛము a-svachchamu. [Skt.] adj. Not clear, indistinct. అస్పష్టమైన.

అస్వతంత్రము a-svatantramu. [Skt.] adj. Not free, dependent. పరాధీనమైన. అస్వతంత్రుడు asvatantrudu. n. A dependant, one who is not a free agent, not his own master. పరాధీనుడు.

అస్వప్నులు a-svapnulu. [Skt.] n. The sleepless, i. e., the gods. దేవతలు.

అస్వరుడు a-svarudu. [Skt.] n. One who has a harsh voice. వినికింపుగాని స్వరము కలవాడు.

అస్వాదు a-svadu. [Skt.] n. Tasteless, insipid. రుచిలేని.

అస్వాధీనము a-svadhinamu. [Skt.] adj. Dependent, not free. అస్వతంత్రమైన. ఆ సొత్తు వానికి అస్వాధీనముగా నుండెను the property was not in his power.

అహము ahamu. [Skt. cf. Lat. ego. Eng. I.] pron. I, myself. నేను. (Met.) Arrogance, presumption. అహంకారము. వానికి నిండా అహమున్నది he is very proud. అహంకరించు ahan-karintsu. v. n. To be arrogant or over-bearing. గర్వించు. అహంకారము, అహంకృతి or అహంక్రియ ahankaramu. n. Egotism, conceit, arrogance. గర్వము. అహంపూర్విక ahampurvika. n. Emulation. నేనంటే నేననిపైబడడము. అహంభావము ahambhavamu. n. Egotism, pride. గర్వము. అహమహమిక ahamahamika. n. ("Saying, I, I.") Conceit, emulation, vaunting, bragging. పరస్పరాహంకారము. అహమించు ahamintsu. v. n. To be conceited. గర్వించు.

అహము ahamu. [Skt.] n. Day. అహస్సు, దినము. పుణ్యాహము holy day. అహర్నిశలు day and night, continually. అహరహము aharahamu. adv. Daily. ప్రతిదినమున్ను, దినదినము. అహర్నిశములు or అహోరాత్రములు day and night. అహర్ముఖము ahar-mukhamu. n. Morning. ప్రాతఃకాలము. అహర్పతి, అహస్పతి or అహస్కరుడు aharpati. n. The lord of day, the sun.

అహాలెకారులు a-hale-karulu. [H.] n. Public servants, men of business.

అహవాలు ahavālu. [H.] n. The actual state of things, particulars, circumstances.

అహషాంబంట్రోతులు ahashām-bantrōtulu. [H.] Police peons.

అహహ or అహహా ahaha. [Tel.] interj. Ah! aha! implying surprise, fatigue, pain, pleasure. అద్భుతము, ఖేదము, సంతోషము—ఈ అర్థములందు చెప్పేమాట.

అహార్యము a-hāryamu. [Skt.] n. A mountain, a hill. పర్వతము.

అహి ahi. [Skt.] n. A snake or serpent. సర్పము, పాము. అహితుండికుడు ahi-tundikudu. n. A snake catcher. పాములవాడు. అహిపతి ahi-pati. n. The lord of snakes. ఆదిశేషువు. అహిభుక్కు ahi-bhuk ku. [Skt. lit. the serpent-eater.] n. The Eagle. The peacock. గరుత్మంతుడు, నెమలి. అహిభయము ahi-bhayamu. [Skt.] n. Apprehension of treachery, fear from one's own party being like the fear of a lurking snake. రాజులకు స్వపక్షమువల్ల కలిగే భయము. N. ii. 114; A. ii. 48; A. iv. 295. రాజులకు స్వపక్షమువారెవరనగా, 1. army దండు, 2. friends మిత్రులు, 3. courtiers ఆశ్రితులు, 4. relations సంబంధులు, 5. acquaintance కార్యసముద్భవులు, 6. attendants or people భృత్యులు, 7. personal servants ఉపచారము చేయువారు.

అహింస a-himsa. [Skt.] n. Harmlessness. అహింసాపరమోధర్మం harmlessness is the highest virtue.

అహితము a-hitamu. [Skt.] n. Unfriendliness, enmity. వైరము. అహితము adj. Unfriendly, inimical. విరోధమైన, శత్రుత్వమైన. అహితుడు a-hitudu. n. An enemy, a rival. శత్రువు.

అహేతుకముగా a-hētukamu-gā. [Skt.] adv. Causelessly. నిష్కారణముగా.

అహో ahō. [Skt.] interj. Ah! Oh! (expressing compassion, regret, praise, weariness or surprise.)

అహోరాత్రము ahō-rātramu. [Skt.] n. A day and night. A whole day. రాత్రియును పగలును. adv. Continually.

ఆ ā

ఆ The broad vowel A, as in arm, father. [The Secondary form of this letter is ా which is a modified form of the upright stroke । used to denote the long sound of a in Sanskrit.

[The ingenuity of the inventors of the Indian Alphabets is shown by the way in which they formed the long vowels out of the short ones by giving a slightly different turn to their forms. See Taylor.]

2. The demonstrative sign, as ఆ పని that act, ఆ కథలు those stories, ఆ పిమ్మట after that, ఆ తెల్లవారి next morning. ఆ ఆ (or ఆయా) యిండ్లలో in the various houses.

3. As a contraction ఆ. stands for ఆశ్వాసము chapter; also for a certain verse ఆటవెలది of a certain metre.

4. As a Sanskrit prefix it means Up to, Until, As far as: as ఆచంద్రార్కము or ఆచంద్రతారకము as long as the moon and the sun or stars last. ఆజానువు to the knee. ఆపాదమస్తకము from head to foot. ఆబాలగోపాలము up to or including the children and the shepherds. ఆసముద్రము as far as the sea. See ఆకంఠము and ఆదంతాలను.

5. A Telugu affix denoting question, or surprise as అతడా (is it) he?

6. An interjection ఆ, or ఆ ఆ, or అహా Yes, Aye: or Ah! A. iv. 5.

ఆంక్ష ânksha. [Skt.] n. Custody, surveillance. (Vizag.) కావలి, పారా.

ఆంగికము āngikamu [Skt. from అంగము.] n. Gesture, action. శరీరావయవముల చేసే చేష్టలు.

ఆంగిరసుడు āngirasudu. [Skt.] n. Brihaspati. బృహస్పతి, దేవగురువు.

ఆండ్రు ândru. [Tel.] plural of ఆలు. n. Wives, women.

అంతర్యము *antaryamu.* [Skt.] n. Heart, mind. అభిప్రాయము, తలపు. ఇది అంతర్యానికి తేవలెను please to consider this.

అంత్రము *antramu.* [Skt.] n. A bowel. పేగు.

ఆందోళించు *āndōḷintsu.* [Skt.] v. n. To swing. ఊగు. **ఆందోళనము** *āndōḷanamu.* n. Swinging, trembling, oscillation. ఊగడము. **ఆందోళము** or **ఆందోళిక** *āndōḷamu.* n. A palankeen. అందలము, పల్లకి. **ఆందోళితము** *āndōḷitamu.* adj. Moved, swung, agitated. ఊచబడిన.

ఆంధ్యము *āndhyamu.* [Skt.] n. Blindness. Opposition, obstruction, hindrance. గుడ్డితనము, అడ్డి, ఆటంకము.

ఆంధ్రము *āndhramu.* n. [Skt.] The Sanskrit name for Telugu. ఆంధ్రరాజ్యము the Telugu country. ఆంధ్రులు the Telugu people, Telugus.

ఆక *āka.* [Tel. from ఆగు to stop.] n. A check, an order, a command. Custody. అడ్డగింపు, ఆజ్ఞ, చెర. "కినుకరించిచిచ్చిపుచ్చుకొను చోటులవారలాకకులోనుగాకపున్నిక." Swa. iii. 163. **ఆకట్టు** (ఆక+కట్టు) *ākaṭṭu.* v. i. To prevent, hinder, check. నిరోధించు. **ఆకపడు** *āka-paḍu.* v. i. To intervene, to interpose. అడ్డిపడు. రామా: కిష్కిం: **ఆకపెట్టు** *āka-peṭṭu.* v. t. To prevent.

ఆకంఠము *ākaṇṭhamu.* [Skt.] adv. Full, up to the neck. గొంతుమట్టుకు. H. i. 186. ఆకంఠపూర్తిగా భక్షించినాడు he ate to the full.

ఆకంపించు *ā-kampintsu.* [Skt.] v. n. To tremble, shake. మిక్కిలి కంపించు, వణకు. **ఆకంపితము** *ā-kampitamu.* adj. Well shaken. చక్కగా కదిలింపబడినది.

ఆకతాయి *ākatāya.* [Tel.] n. A rascal, a rogue, a wretch. A naughty boy. తుంట. ఆకతాయితనము rascality or naughtiness. తుంటరితనము.

ఆకత్రాడు *āka-trāḍu.* [Tel.] n. The string used to tie the churning rod to a post. కవ్వమును తిరిగించుటకై తెడకంబమునందు కట్టెడు త్రాడు.

ఆకరము *ākaramu.* [Skt.] n. A mine: foundation: basis, authority. గని, ఉత్పత్తిస్థానము, ఆధారము, సాధకము. Also, a crowd, multitude. సమూహము. **ఆకరము** *ākaramu.* [Tel.] n. Anger. ఆగ్రహము.

"ఏకబట్టి తెంచినల్లడ
దాకిన గద్దుఙ్గఘోర ఈటకట వాతిన
మ్రూకలు విరుయగనర్జును
డాకరమున నేసెను గ్రుడయుదిరుధూమిక."

భార: ఆది. viii.

ఆకర్ణించు *ākarṇintsu.* [Tel.] v. a. To listen, attend to. విను. **ఆకర్ణనము** *-karṇanamu.* n. Hearing. వినుట.

ఆకర్షము *ākarshamu.* [Skt.] n. Pulling, hauling: attracting, drawing. ఈడ్వడము. **ఆకర్షకము** *ā-karshakamu* n. That which attracts, a magnet. **ఆకర్షణము** *ākarshaṇamu* n. The act of drawing, or attracting. ఆకర్షణ మంత్రము a magic spell that has power to draw or attract, putting an enemy in our power. ఆకర్షణశక్తి n. The power of attraction. భూమ్యాకర్షణశక్తి terrestrial attraction or gravity. **ఆకర్షించు** *ākarshintsu.* To attract. **ఆకర్షితము** *ā-karshitamu.* adj. That which is attracted. ఆకర్షింపబడినది.

ఆకలనము *ākalanamu.* [Skt.] Wish, desire: counting, reckoning. ఇచ్ఛ, కోరిక, అభిలాష, ఎన్నిక, గణనము. Vasu. pref. 1.

ఆకలి *ākali.* [Tel.] n. Hunger, appetite. Eagerness. క్షుత్తు. G: ఆకటి; or ఆకంటి D. ఆకటికి; L. ఆకట. ఆకలిగొన్నాడు he had an appetite, he was hungry. **ఆకలియెత్తు,** or పెట్టు To be hungry. **ఆకలితీర్చు** To appease or satisfy hunger. వానికి ఆకలి కాలేదా is he not hungry? See ఆకొను.

ఆకల్పము *ā kalpamu.* [Skt.] n. Ornament, decoration. అలంకారము.

ఆకళించు *akalintsu.* [Tel.] v. t. To understand. గ్రహించు. **ఆకళింత** or **ఆకళింపు** *ākalinta.* [Skt.] n. Intelligence; comprehension. అవగాహనము. అది నాకు ఆకళింపు కాలేదు I do not comprehend it.

ఆకసము *ā-kasamu.* [Skt. ఆకాశము] n. The sky: heaven.

ఆకస్మికము or **ఆకస్మికముగా** *ā-kasmikamu.* [Skt.] adv. n. Suddenly. అకస్మాత్తుగా.

ఆకాంక్ష *ā-kanksha.* [Skt.] n. Wish, desire. (In gram.) the government or concord of words in a sentence. ఈ శ్లోకమునకు ఆకాంక్ష చెప్పు regarding this verse state who is meant, what did he do, where, why, to whom, &c. **ఆకాంక్షించు** *akankshintsu.* v. a. To wish, long for.

ఆకాండికము *ā-kāndikamu.* [Skt.] n. Unseasonable, unusual at that season. Vasu. v. 3.

ఆకాకర *ā-kākara.* [Tel. ఆకు+కాకర] n. The wild species of *Momordica Dioica.* అడవికాకర.

ఆకారము *ākāramu.* [Skt.] n. Shape, form. ఆకారపుష్టుడు A fop, a beau. ఆకారవంతుడు or ఆకారి a handsome man.

ఆకారితము *ā-kāritamu.* [Skt.] n. Called, summoned. పిలువబడిన. Parij. iii. 81.

ఆకాశము *ākāsamu.* [Skt. another form of అవకాశము emptiness, empty space, or interval.] n. Ether, sky, atmosphere. ఆకాశగంగ the river of heaven. ఆకాశగరుడ దగ్గ a plant which like the misletoe grows on a tree. Ainslie. 2. 158. *Bryonia Epigœa,* air-living-Bryony. **ఆకాశవల్లి** *ākasa-valli.* n. *Cassytha filiformis* (Watts.) **ఆకాశపంచాంగము** *ākasa-panchāngamu.* n. A fool's chronicle, a pack of nonsense. **ఆకాశబాణము** *ākasa-bānamu.* n. A sky rocket. **ఆకాశరామన్న** *ākasa-ramanna.* Jack Robinson, nobody. **ఆకాశవాణి** *ā-kāsa-vāni.* adj. "Sky-speaking," as the voice of an angel or invisible being.

ఆకీర్ణము *ā-kirnamu.* [Skt.] adj. Sprinkled, scattered. Also dishevelled, loose, as locks.

ఆకు *āku.* [Tel.] n. A leaf of any sort. A petal. పత్రము, దళము. A betel, or palmyra leaf; also the leaf on which the Hindus eat their food. విస్తరాకు. An ear-ring. చెవి కమ్మ. Young rice (paddy) not yet transplanted. Any herb: young sprouts of corn. A flake as ఆకు ఉప్పు a flake of salt. Any filament. The radius or spoke of a wheel. The shutter of a blind. ఆకులతలుపు a venetian door. Also, a chit, note or short letter. చీటి; a loan bond. ఇచ్చిపుచ్చుకోలు పత్రము. This word prefixed to others generally denotes *green;* as **ఆకుతేలు** a green scorpion, and ఆకుమిడత a green cricket. ఆడంగులకంటె మగవారు ఏడాకులు ఎక్కువ చదివినారు men have read seven pages further than women; that is, men are tenfold worse than women; or, are their masters in wickedness. నీ పేరు ఆకుచాటున అంటుకుంటా చెప్పుతాను I shall mention (or use) your name with great caution. **ఆకు అలము** *āku-alamu.* n. Greens, herbs, vegetables. (The word అలము here has no definite sense.) **ఆకుకూరలు** or **కూరాకులు** *āku-kūralu.* n. Potherbs, garden stuff. **ఆకుచాటున** *āku-tsātuna.* adj. In ambush, hidden, veiled, screened. **ఆకుచిరుతపులి** *āku-chirula-puli.* n. A small species of leopard. **ఆకుచిలక** *āku-chilaka.* n. A butterfly, or a green parrot. **ఆకుజెముడు** *āku-jemudu.* n. The oleander-leaved spurge. *Euphorbia Neriifolia.* (See జెముడు.) **ఆకుటిల్లు** *āku-tillu.* n. A booth or hut of leaves, an arbor of leaves. ఆకుటింట in a booth. **ఆకుతీగ** the vine that produces the tamala (or betel) leaf. ఆకుతోట a betel garden: a garden in which plants are reared. **ఆకుపచ్చ** *āku-pattsa.* n. The colour called sap green. **ఆకుపత్రి చెట్టు** *āku-pattri-chettu.* n. The clove tree *Cassia lignea.* **ఆకుబీకలు** a certain game. (H. iii. 190). **ఆకుపురుగు** *āku-purugu.* n.

A green caterpillar. ఆకుపోత *āku-pōta*. n. Transplantation of a green crop. ఆకుపోయు *āku-pōyu*. v. a. To transplant corn. To set the sprouts. ఆకుమడి *āku-madi*. n. A field sown, but the sprouts of which are to be transplanted. (also, called నారుమడి.) ఆకుమడుపు *āku-madupu*. n. A roll of betel leaf. A mode of measurement. ఆకు మొలకాకు The self planting herb. ఆకురాయి *āku-rāyi*. n. A file (i.e., ఆకు a filament రాయు to rub off.) Also the name of a bird, the cuckoo (F. B. I.) బొబుపాకురాయి or ముల్లాకురాయి (from ముల్లు a thorn) a rasp. కత్తి ఆకురాయి a sharp thin file for cutting combs. కమ్మి ఆకురాయి a very small file. పట్టె నాకురాయి a three sided file.

ఆకుంచనము *ā-kunchanamu*. [Skt.] n. Contracting, drawing up, shrinking. Elasticity. ముడుచుట.

ఆకుజెల్ల *āku-jella*. [Tel.] n. A kind of fish.

ఆకులము *ā-kulamu*. [Skt.] adj Troubled, distressed, confounded. ఆకులపడు *ākula-padu*. v. i. To be troubled or confounded. కలతపడు, చెదరు. ఆకులపాటు *ākula-pāṭu*. n. Agitation ఆకులపడుట.

ఆకుసన్నములు *āku-sannamulu*. [Tel.] n. A sort of fine rice.

ఆకూతము or ఆకూతి *ā-kūtamu*. [Skt.] n. Meaning, intention, wish, desire Expression, mien, demeanour. The thought of the heart, manifested by the acts: expression of features. అభిప్రాయము, తలంపు.

ఆకృతి *ākriti*. [Skt.] n. Form, shape, figure, mien. ఆకారము.

ఆకృష్టి *ākrishti*. [Skt.] n. Attraction. ఆకర్షణము.

ఆకె *āke*. [Tel. ఆ+అకె] pron. She, that woman. ఆవిడ.

ఆకొట్టు *ākottu*. [Tel. ఆకు+ఒత్తు] n. Nippers or clippers to cut betel nut with. అడకొత్తు.

ఆకొను *ā-konu*. [Tel. ఆకలి+కొను] v. n. To be hungry, to have an appetite. See ఆకలి.

ఆక్రందనము or ఆక్రందము *ā-krandanamu*. [Skt.] n. Weeping, lamentation. ఆక్రందించు *ākrandintsu* v. n. To lament. ఏడ్చు.

ఆక్రమించు *ā-kramintsu*. [Skt.] v. a. To appropriate wrongfully, to encroach on, usurp. ఆక్రమణము *ā-kramanamu*. [Skt.] n. Surrounding, occupying, usurpation, filling (as smoke.) ఆక్రాంతము *ā-krāntamu*. adj. Appropriated, seized. ఆక్రమింపబడినది. రాజాక్రాంతము seized by the king. ఆక్రాంతి *ā-krānti*. n. Filling, pervading, spreading through. (T. iv. 159.) వ్యాపకము.

ఆక్రోశము *ākrōsamu*. [Skt.] n. Anger, dissatisfaction, malice. Curse, imprecation. తిట్టు. ఆక్రోశించు *ākrōsintsu*. v. n. To grieve, to be displeased, to be malicious. To curse or abuse. తిట్టు.

ఆక్షేపము, ఆక్షేపణ *ākshēpamu*. [Skt.] n. Censure, blame, reproach, criticism, scruple, objection, a question. ఆక్షేపించు *ākshēpintsu*. v. t. To criticise, to object, to question. ఆక్షేపకుడు *akshē-pakudu*. n. One who criticises or objects. ఆక్షేపించువాడు. ఆక్షిప్తుడు *akshiptudu*. n. One who is blamed or censured. నిరాక్షేపముగా above all question, blame or reproach, unquestionably. దురాక్షేపం a groundless cavil.

ఆఖరు *ākharu*. [H.] adj. Last, final. కడపటి. n. End, termination. తుద, అంతము. ఆఖరున, ఆఖరుకు adv. Finally, lastly. నెల ఆఖరుకు at the end of the month. ఆఖరయినది it is finished or expended.

ఆఖువు *ākhuvu*. [Skt.] n. A rat. ఎలుక. a bandicoot. పందికొక్కు.

ఆఖేటము *ākhēṭamu*. [Skt.] n. Hunting; the chase. వేట.

ఆఖ్య *ākhya*. [Skt.] n. A name, or appellation. పేరు. ఆఖ్యాత *ākhyāta*. n. The speaker. చెప్పెడువాడు. ఆఖ్యాతము *ākhyātamu*.

adj. Said, spoken, rehearsed. **ఆఖ్యానము** *ākhyānamu*. n. Telling. చెప్పుట. An episode of a book, a tale or fable, an ancient story. **ఆఖ్యేయము** *ākhyēyamu*. adj. Fit to be said or rehearsed.

ఆగంతుకము *āgantukamu*. [Skt.] adj. Unexpected (as a guest dropping in.) **ఆగంతుకుడు** or **ఆగంతువు** *āgantukuḍu*. n. A guest, a stranger, one who drops in. పరదేశి, అతిథి.

ఆగడము *āgaḍamu*. [Tel.] n. Sport, jesting, fun, wantonness. **ఆగడకాడు** or **ఆగడీడు** *āgaḍakāḍu* n. A scoffer, one who teases. **ఆగడముచేయు** *āgaḍamu-chēyu*. To tease, sport with. ఆగడపుప్రభుడు (P. i. 520.) a troublesome master, a wanton ruler, a tyrant.

ఆగడవలు *āgaḍavalu*. [Tel.] n. A range of clouds. మొగిలుదొంతి, మబ్బులసన్నపు దొంతరలు.

ఆగతము *āgatamu*. [Skt.] adj. That which is come. Gained, realized, obtained, gotten. వచ్చిన, పొందబడిన.

ఆగమనము *āgamanamu*. [Skt.] n. Arrival. వచ్చుట, రాక. **ఆగమము** *āgamamu*. n. Arrival, approach; a treatise on వేదాంతము or divinity describing religious rites. A grammatical augment or letter inserted in any part of the radical word or affix as ఇంచుకాగమము "the causal affix *intsu*" as in the word ప్రాయించు. వర్షాగమము the coming of the rains, the rainy season.

ఆగాడి *āgāḍi*. [Tel.] n. An inferior sort of grain.

ఆగాత్యము or **ఆగాయిత్యము** *ā-gātyamu*. [Tel.] n. Outrageous behaviour, obstinacy, desperation, baseness, villainy. Pretence of agony or injury: threatening to commit suicide.

ఆగామి *āgāmi*. [Skt.] adj. Future.

ఆగు *āgu*. [Tel.] v. n. To stop, to stay, abstain, refrain. To bear (as a cord does a weight.) To be confined, set aside, or reserved. అయుటను ఆగబడియున్న దేవకి (B. X. 75.) Devaki who was *kept in restraint*. దిక్కులేని బాలురు ఆగ నీవు దిక్కు thou art the refuge of the helpless. పసులకు ఆగినభూమి land set aside or reserved for pasture. ఇది లేనిది నాకు ఆగదు I cannot get on without this. నా కోటిలో ఆ మాట ఆగదు I cannot keep that word a secret. **ఆగు, ఆగించు, ఆచు, ఆపు** the causal of ఆగు: *āgu*. [Tel.] v. t. To stop, check, hinder. To keep, tend. To look to, superintend, guard, protect, preserve. To fold or gather as a flock. కోరాచి మాట్లాడిరి they spoke cautiously. చెయ్యి ఆపక (T. v. 22.) without intermission. నిద్ర ఆచుట to refrain from sleep, keep away drowsiness. రాత్రిళ్లు ఇక్కడ మందలు ఆచుకొనియుండేవారు they used to keep cattle here at nights.

ఆగుబ్బతిల్లు or **ఆగుబ్బకొను** *āgubbatillu*. [Tel.] n. To increase. అతిశయించు, వృద్ధి పొందు. to be overjoyed. Swa. ii. See. ఉబ్బతిల్లు. **ఆగుబ్బు** *āgubbu*. [Tel.] n. Greatness, vastness. ఆగుబ్బాగుబ్బై స్వనహూతి with a waxing and still swelling shriek. **ఆగుబ్బుగా** *āgubbu-gā* adv. All at once, heavily, in a thick shower, bitterly (weeping) ఘోరము.

ఆగ్నేయము *āgnēyamu*. [Skt.] n. The south east point, of which Agni is regent. **ఆగ్నేయాస్త్రము** *āgnē-yāstramu*. n. A fiery weapon: a rocket or grenade.

ఆగ్రహము *āgrahamu*. [Skt.] n. Anger, displeasure, rage, wrath. **ఆగ్రహించు** *āgrahintsu*. [Skt.] v. n. To be angry, or enraged. కోపించు.

ఆఘాతము *ā-ghātamu*. [Skt.] n. Striking, a blow. కొట్టుట.

ఆఘూర్ణిత *ā-ghūrṇita*. [Skt.] adj. Rolling (the eyes.) R. vii. 211.

ఆఘోషించు *ā-ghōshintsu*. [Skt.] v. n. To roar, yell. Jaimni Bhar: VI. 220.

ఆఘ్రాణము āghrāṇamu. [Skt.] n. Smelling. The sense of smell. ఆఘ్రాణించు ā-ghrāṇintsu. v. a. To smell. వాసన చూచు, ముక్కుతో పీల్చు.

ఆచండాలము ā-chanḍālamu. [Skt.] adj. High and low, including every rank "down to the pariahs."

ఆచంద్రతారకము, ఆచంద్రార్కము ā-chandra-tārakamu. [Skt.] adv. For ever, as long as the moon and stars or sun endure.

ఆచమనము āchamanamu. [Skt.] n. Sipping water three times before religious ceremonies or meals, or after meals, or after relieving oneself, repeating at the same time the 24 principal names of Vishnu వార్చుట. ఆచమించు āchamintsu. v. a. To sip (water) వార్చు. ఆచాంతము āchāntamu. n. Tasted, sipped.

ఆచరించు ācharintsu. [Skt.] v. a. To practise, to observe, to be used to, to do habitually. To put in practice (the precepts of religion), to perform (bathing, &c.) To celebrate (a religious festival.) ఆచరణము ācharaṇamu. n Doing, performing. ఆచారము, నడత. ఆచారము āchāramu. n. Practice, custom. Rule, fashion, mode, a course of conduct, institute or observance, Religious observance. మతాచారముచొప్పున according to the principles of the creed. ఆచారి āchāri. n. A caste title borne by the Vaishnavite Brahmins, the men of the blacksmith and goldsmith castes. సదాచారి a man of good principles. ఆచార్యత్వము āchāryatvamu. n The office of a priest. ఆచార్యుడు āchāryuḍu. n. A teacher. A priest: a spiritual guide or preceptor: one who invests the student with the sacrificial thread and instructs him in the mysteries of the religion.

ఆచు See అచు.

ఆచూకి ātsūki. [Tel. ఆ+చూడ్కి.] Trace, sign. జాడ.

ఆచ్ఛాదనము āchchhādanamu. [Skt.] n. Lid, cover: clothes, covering, cloak. ఆచ్ఛాదితము āchchhāditamu. adj. Hidden, concealed.

ఆజవంజవము āja-vanjavamu. [Skt.] n. The world, earthly ties. A family. సంసారము. "ఆజవంజవభ్రమాతీతమార్గుడై." (Chenn. iv. 132.) He who is freed from earthly ties. ఆజవంజవమానసమాలిన్యము worldy defilement.

ఆజానుబాహుడు ā-jānu-bāhuḍu. [Skt.] n. *Longimanus*: one whose arms reach to his knees.

ఆజానేయము ājānēyamu. [Skt.] n. One of the best breeds among horses.

ఆజి āji. [Skt.] n. War, battle. యుద్ధము.

ఆజూబాజూ āzu-bāzu. [H.] adv. Around, about, in the vicinity. చుట్టును, ఆ ప్రాంత ములందు.

ఆజ్ఞ āgnya. [Skt.] n. Command, order, sanction, leave, permission. ఆజ్ఞచేయు to command. ఆజ్ఞానుసారముగా according to order. ఆజ్ఞాపనము āgnyāpanamu n. Command, order. T. ii. 2. BD. vi. 120. ఆజ్ఞాపించు āgnyāpintsu. v. t. To command, order. ఆజ్ఞాతుడు āgnyātuḍu. n. He who is ordered. ఆజ్ఞాపితము āgnyāpitamu. adj. That which is ordered.

ఆజ్మాయిషీ or ఆజమాయిషీ āz-mayishī. [H.] n. Trial, proving. పరీక్ష, సరిచూడడము. ఆ జ్మాయిషీచేయు to test, to try.

ఆజ్యము ājyamu. [Skt.] n. Ghee, clarified butter. నెయ్యి.

ఆట āṭa. [Tel. from ఆడు] Play, sport, a game: a dance, acting or stage performance. Jest, joke, gambling. ఆటకత్తె, ఆటది or ఆటవి āṭa-katte. [Tel.] n. An actress or public dancer. ఆటకాడు āṭa-kāḍu. n. An actor or dancer. Also a gambler. ఆటగొర్రు āṭa-gorru. n. A rake used in husbandry. ఆటచిప్పరు A swimming bath. ఆటతోట āṭa-tōṭa.

a park. ఉద్యానవనము. అటపట్టు *āṭa-paṭṭu* n. An abode, residence, scene, place. ఆటసాల A playhouse, a theatre. ఆట విడుపు *āṭa-viḍupu* n. A school holiday or play day. ఆటవెలది *āṭa-veladi*. n. A species of metre ఆటాడు *āṭāḍu*. (ఆట+ ఆడు) v. a. To play a play, to dance a dance, to act.

అటంకము *aṭankamu*. [Tel.] n. Obstacle, prevention, hindrance, resistance, difficulty. అటంకపరచు *aṭanka-paratsu*. v. t. To object, prevent.

అటి Same as అదేలు.

అటు *aṭu*. [Tel.] v. n. To suffice: to last, to be enough దాన్ని పొదిమిగా నాడితే యింకా నెలదినములకు అటివచ్చును with caution it may suffice for a month. అది అటదు or అటి రాదు it is not enough. కట్టెలు ఒకమాటు గా తీసికొంటే అటివస్తుంది, చిల్లరచిల్లరగా తీసి కొంటే అటిరావు if you buy your firewood in the lump it will last; if you buy only a little at a time it will not. అటు n. Striking. కొట్టుట. Shooting, or rheumatic pain: పోటు (M. VIII. i. 218:) throbbing. నాకు అటుపోటుగానున్నది I am in great pain. ఆ పుంటిలో అట్లుపోట్లు ఎత్తినవి the boil throbbed much.

అటోపము *aṭōpamu*. [Skt.] n. Hastiness: excess, pride. సంభ్రమము, వేగిరపాటు, రభసము, అడంబరము, ఔద్ధత్యము, తొందర.

అట్రగడలు *aṭra-gaḍalu*. [Tel] n. A sort of grain. అర్కుల్లు.

అడ *aḍa*. [Tel. corrupted from అడు] adj. Female. అడగుంపు a mob of women. అడ కండ్లవాడను I am a timid woman అడకూతురు a woman. అడతనము *aḍa-tanamu*. n. Womanishness, weakness. అడది *aḍadi* A woman; plural అడవాండ్లు or అడవాండ్రు. అడపడుచు *aḍa-paḍutsu*. A girl, a young woman. అడపాప *aḍa-pāpa*. Girl. A lady in waiting, a handmaid. అడమనిషి *aḍa-manishi*, A woman.

అడ adv. There, in that place. అక్కడ. అడాడ *aḍāḍa*. Here and there. L. ii. 175. Padim. iv. 294.

అడంగి or అడంగి *aḍangi*. [Tel.] n A female. (Usually in the plural alone) అడంగులు, or అంగులు women. అడంగిమాటలు language fit for a woman. అడంగిలేకి a girlish fop.

అడంబరము *aḍambaramu*. [Skt.] n. Pomp, grandeur. Vain display: abortive arrogance. The onset of battle: the charge; the sound of trumpets. యుద్ధవాద్యధ్వని. మేఘాడంబరము the display of clouds. ఆ యింట్లో ఏమో అడంబరముగానున్నది there is some stir in that house.

అడాలు *aḍālu*. [Tel.] n. A herb like cress. (Ainslie 2. 12.)

అడి *aḍi*. [Tel.] n. An affix (derived from అడు) implying 'doer' or 'performer,' as మాయలు tricks, మాయలాడి a rogue: ముద్దులు fondness, ముద్దులాడి a fond girl: కులుకులు graces, కులుకులాడి a lovely woman: టక్కులు pranks. టక్కులాడి a cheat.

అడించు *aḍintsu*. [Tel. causative of అడు.] v. a. To cause to move or play, to amuse.

అడిక *aḍika*. [Tel.] n. Rumour, talk, scandal, infamy. రచ్చ, నింద, రట్టు. అడిక పడు *aḍika-paḍu*. v. n. To be blamed అడికోలు *aḍi-kōlu*. [Tel.] n. Scandal. నింద, అడిపోసికొనుట. అడికోళ్లు *aḍikōllu*. Revilings, abusive words. H. v. 304: P. ii 38.

అడితప్పు *aḍi-tappu*. [Tel.] v. n. To break one's word. అడితప్పనివాడు one who keeps his word. A man of his word.

అడిపోసికొను *aḍi-pōsikonu*. [Tel.] v. n. To scandalize, vilify. నిందించు.

అడు *āḍu*. [Tel.] v. n. 1. To play, dance, work, act, do, move, ply. కాళ్లు అడక నిలిచె he stood stock-still, his feet did not stir. 2. To shake, totter, wag. 3. To beat, as the pulse. ధాతువు అడుచున్నది the pulse beats.

4. To speak, say. ఇట్లు కొందరు అడగా while some spoke thus. అడినది ఒకటి చేసినది ఒకటి he said one thing and did another. ఛీ యాడు to cry Avaunt! ముచ్చాడు to advance or come forward. ఆ పేరు నోట్లో ఆడుచున్నది I have the name at the tip of my tongue.

ఆడు āḍu. [Tel.] v. a. 1. To play, ply, work, move. 2. To use, do, practise, perform. 3. To speak (a language.) తెలుగు మాటలాడుతాడా? does he speak Telugu? నిజమాడు to speak the truth. 4. To say. ఎవ్వరు ఏమి ఆడినా let folks say what they will. 5. To promise. 6. To act a character, personify, represent, personate. 7. To assume, or put on (a manner) గాంభీర్యములాడసాగెను he began to assume an arch manner. 8. To place, put, set. 9. To sound or play on (an instrument) జలకమాడు to bathe; ముద్దు లాడు to kiss. మాట్లాడు to speak. బొంకు లాడు to tell lies. ఆట్లాడు to play. రెక్క లాడు to use the wings, to fly. పోట్లాడు to fight. వేటాడు to hunt. పోట్లాడు struggle, to fight. పిశాచములాడిన possessed by devils. ఈడ్చులాడు to pull. ఈదులాడు to swim. సరసమాడు or సరసములాడు to crack jokes. Other senses will be found under various nouns and verbs. వాడు ఆడినది ఆట పాడి నది పాట all he says is law, all he chooses to do is right (a taunting proverb) 10. It is also added to the *Infinitive in A, or AN*, thus విడు. v. n. To separate. విడనాడు to cast off.

ఆడు āḍu. [Tel.] adj. Female. ఇవి ఆడుమాటలు these are a woman's words. ఆడుచందము āḍuṭsandamu. The female shape, feminine disguise. B. viii. 445. ఆడుబొబ్బ A woman's shriek. R. v. 207. ఆడుతోడు āḍu-tōḍu [Tel.] A female companion. ఆడుది āḍudi. A woman. ఆడుబిడ్డ āḍu-biḍḍa. A little girl. The sister of a woman's husband. ఆడుముండ āḍu-muṇḍa. An abusive word for a woman: equivalent to slut, jade, wretch. ఆడుపేడు woman's town, a place without brave men. See ఆడ adj.

ఆడుకొను āḍu-konu. [Tel.] v. n. To play, to ply about, sport. To say. v. t. To blame. నిందించు.

ఆడేలు āḍēlu. [Skt.] n. A night hawk (HD. ii. 2887.) ఆడేలువలె కదలకుండా ఉన్నావు you are as sluggish as a night hawk. తెరాతి, or రామతొంత *Turdus. Ginginianus*. A species of thrush. The buzzard; gerfalcon See Jerdon's Catal. No. 21.

ఆఢకము āḍhakamu. [Skt.] n. A measure of capacity called తూము.

ఆఢకి āḍhaki. [Skt.] n. The grain called pigeon pea. *Cytisus cudjan*. ఆడవికందులు, పెద్దకందులు. Rox. iii. 325.

ఆఢ్యము āḍhyamu. [Skt.] adj. That which has or possesses. గల. Thus. సంపదాఢ్య possessed of wealth. అమృతాఢ్యకమండలము a cup holding nectar. ఆఢ్యుడు āḍhyuḍu. n. Owner, possessor. సంపన్నుడు.

ఆణంగులు See. ఆణంకి.

ఆణి āṇi. [Tel.] adj. Spherical, round (a term applied to pearls.) ఆణిముత్తెము a rounded or faultless pearl. See on కల్గాణి. ఆణి n. A nail or pin. ఆణికాడు āṇi-kāḍu. n. A confidant, or confidential friend. మర్మజ్ఞుడు. ఆణిపోటు āṇi-pōṭu. n. A stab in the vitals, a deep wound. చావుదెబ్బ.

ఆతంకము ātankamu. [Skt.] n. Obstacle, pain, fear, apprehension. Disease. అటంకము, బాధ, భయము. రోగము.

ఆతగాడు āta-gāḍu. [Tel. అతడు+కాడు.] n. He, that man. అతడు.

ఆతడు ātaḍu. [Tel. ఆ+(త)+డు] another form of అతడు. (ఇక్కడ తెల్గము అగమము.)

ఆతతము ātatamu. [Skt.] adj. Extended, great, large. ఆతతనిష్ఠ with extreme affection or fidelity.

ఆతతాయి āta-tāyi. [Skt.] n. A villain, one who attempts to kill. చంపనుద్యమించు వాడు.

ఆతపము *atapamu.* [Skt.] n. Sunshine. ఎండ. **ఆతపత్రము** or **ఆతపవారణము** *ata-patramu.* n. An umbrella. గొడుగు.

ఆతరము *ataramu.* [Skt.] n. Freight, fare. రేవు, ఓడకిచ్చెడి కూలి.

ఆతల *atala.* [Tel. ఆ+తలు=(beyond) that + place.] n. Further on, away. ఆవల.

ఆతిథ్యము *atithyamu.* [Skt. from అతిథి] n. Entertainment, hospitality, food given to a wayfarer. అతిథిసత్కారము. **ఆతిథ్యము** adj. Hospitable, proper for a guest. అతిథికి యోగ్యమైనది.

ఆతిథేయము same as ఆతిథ్యము. n.

ఆతిథ్యుడు an unexpected guest. అతిథి, విందు.

ఆ, *with* **తు** The pubes. కాలిసందులుక, రొమ్ము.

ఆతురత or **ఆతురము** *aturata.* [Skt.] n. Hurry, eagerness, affection. ఆతురచిత్తుడై being afflicted. గర్భాతురము famishing hunger. క్షుధాతురుడై famishing with hunger. కామాతురుడై eager with lust. **ఆతుర పడు** *atura-padu.* v. n. To hurry or haste. **ఆతురుడు** *aturudu.* n. He who is eager.

ఆతోద్యము *a-todyamu.* [Skt.] n. A musical instrument. వాద్యము.

ఆత్తము *attamu.* [Skt.] adj. That which is got or stolen. పొందబడిన, అపహరించబడిన.

ఆత్మ *atma.* [Skt.] n. The soul, the living principle. జీవుడు. Self, the individual, a person. The body శరీరము. Nature. స్వభావము. Mind, intellect, reason, understanding. బుద్ధి, మనస్సు. పుణ్యాత్ముడు a pious minded man. పాపాత్ముడు a bad hearted man. God, spirit. ఆత్మ. adj. Own; peculiar. **ఆత్మకము** *atmakamu.* adj. Consisting of: as స్థావరజంగమాత్మకమైన consisting of real and personal goods. ఆత్మకార్యములు private affairs, one's own business. **ఆత్మజ** or **ఆత్మతనయ** *atma-ja.* n. One's own daughter. **ఆత్మకుడు** *atmakudu.* [Skt.] adj. Formed of. అమృతాత్మకుడు one who has a sweet nature. **ఆత్మగతమున** *atmagatamu-na.* adj. Mentally, in the heart. **ఆత్మఘాతకుడు** *atma-ghatakudu.* n. A suicide or self murderer. **ఆత్మజుడు** *atmajudu.* n. A son, as springing from oneself. **ఆత్మజ్ఞుడు** *atmagnyudu.* n. A sage, who knows God and his own heart. **ఆత్మనేపదము** *atma-ne-padamu.* n. The grammatical name for the middle voice in కొను; as ప్రాపించుకొను. **ఆత్మవంచన** *atma-vanchana.* n. Self delusion. **ఆత్మస్తుతి** *atma-stuti.* n. Self applause. **ఆత్మార్థము** *atmarthamu.* adv. For oneself. **ఆత్మీయము** *atmiyamu.* adj. One's own. తనది.

ఆత్రము *atramu.* [corrupted from Skt. ఆతురము] n. Haste. త్వర. **ఆత్రగాడు** *atra-gadu* n. A hasty person. త్వరపడువాడు.

ఆద *ada.* [Tel.] n. Sorrow, grief. దుఃఖము, విచారము. **ఆదమరచి** *ada-marachi.* adv. Soundly, well, casually. హాయిగా, నిర్భయముగా, నిశ్చింతగా, నోచుకొని. M. X. i. 53. A. iv. 229 "అనియాదమఱచిపలుకగ." R. vii. 46.

ఆదట *adata.* [Tel.] n. Fulness, satiety, love. ప్రేమము, తృప్తి, తనివి. ఆదటపోయిన. full, satisfied. ఆదటపోక. without satiating his appetite.

ఆదరము or **ఆదరణ** *adaramu.* [Skt.] n. Respect, reverence, kindness. మన్నన. **ఆదరించు** or **ఆదరణచేయు** *adarintsu.* v. t. To be gracious, to relieve, cure. **ఆదరణీయము** *adaraniyamu.* adj. Worthy of respect. సాదరముగా (స+ఆదరముగా) with kindness, graciously. **ఆదృతము** *adrutamu.* [Skt.] adj. Respected. **ఆదృతి** *adruti.* n. Respect, inclination.

ఆదరబాదరగా *adara-badara-ga.* [Tel.] adj. Precipitately, confusedly. అతిత్వరగా, తొందరగా, అవసరముగా.

ఆదరించు *ādarintsu*. [Skt.] v. a. To treat kindly, soothe, comfort, honour, welcome. ఆదరము (q. v.)

ఆదరవు *ādaravu*. [from Skt. ఆధారము] n. A prop, or support. Protection, aid, refuge, subsistence. కడుపులో ఆదరవులేక యుండే with empty stomach.

ఆదర్శము *ādarśamu*. [Skt.] n. A looking glass or mirror.

ఆదా *ādā*. [H from Skt. ఆదాయము.] n. Profit, gain, advantage. ఆదాయము. ఆదా చేయు or ఆదాపరచు *ādā-cheyu*. v. a. To realise or collect the value.

ఆదానము *ādānamu*. [Skt.] v. n. Taking, acceptance, receipt.

ఆదాయము *ādāyamu*. [Skt.] n. Profit, gain, income, emolument, moiety. లాభము, ధనము, వచ్చుబడి, రాబడి.

ఆది *ādi*. [Skt.] n. The beginning. మొదలు. Also, an aim గురి. ఆదిని at the beginning, at first. ఆదిముని an ancient prophet. ఆదిశేషువు *ādi-śeshuvu*. [Skt.] n. The old dragon, who is worshipped as the supporter of the earth. ఆది, ఆదిగా { *ādi*. n. Etcetera. వాని గృహాదులు his house, &c., మన్వాదులు Manu and others. ఉత్తరాదినుంచి వచ్చినారు they came from the north. ఉత్తరాదివాండ్లు people of the north. దక్షిణాది సరుకులు goods imported from the south. ఆదికము *ādikamu*. n. Etcetera. అన్నాదికములు food, &c. ఆదికొను *ādi-konu*. v. i. To have one's eye on కన్నువేయు "పృథివీధమునకాదికొను చెల్పుచియుండెను." భార: విరాట. v. ఆద్యంతములు (ఆది+అంతము) first and last. ఆద్యంతరహితుడు He who is without origin and end. God.

ఆదితాళము *ādi-tālamu*. [Skt.] n. One of the modes by which musical time is measured. ఎనిమిది అక్షరములకాలము.

ఆదిత్యుడు *ādityudu*. [Skt.] n. A name of the Sun. ఆదిత్యవారము or ఆదివారము *āditya-vāramu*. [Skt.] n. Sunday. The 12 adityas are Indra, Dhāta, Parjanya, Twashta, Pūsha, Aryaman, Bhaga, Vivasvat, Vishnu, Amsumat, Varuna, and Mitra.

ఆదిమము *ādimamu*. [Skt.] adj. First, original, primeval. ఆదిమయుణము a primary claim.

ఆదుకొను *ādu-konu*. [Tel.] v. a. To aid, assist, support, treat kindly. ఆదరించు.

ఆదుర్దా *ādurdā*. [Tel.] n. Alarm, distress, trouble. భయము, తొందర. ఆదుర్దాపడు *ādurdā-padu*. v. i. To be troubled about. కలతపడు.

ఆదేశము *ādēśamu*. [Skt.] n. Instruction. Grammatical permutation, a substitute. ఆదేశనకారము the letter N inserted in the place of another letter. ఆదేశించు *ādēśintsu*. v. t. To teach, instruct. ఆదేష్ట *ā-dēshṭa*. n. A teacher, one who gives orders.

ఆదోకగా *ādōka-gā*. [Tel. ఆవు+తోక] adv. Like a cow's tail. Slanting, in a slanting form, taperingly; conical, pyramidical. A. iii. 30. నక్షత్రము ఆదోకపాటుగా పడుచున్నది the shooting star passes in a slanting direction.

ఆద్యము *ādyamu*. [Skt.] adj. Prime, first, initial.

ఆధానము *ādhānamu*. [Skt.] n. The act of keeping, covering or putting on. ఉంచుట, కప్పుట, ధరించుట. A ceremony performed with fire. గర్భాధానము the nuptials.

ఆధారము *ādhāramu*. [Skt.] n. Support, prop, stay. ఆ చేనికి ఈ బావే ఆధారము this well is the sole support of that field; that land depends wholly on this well. జలాధారములేనిభూమి land that has no water convenience.

ఆధి *ādhi*. [Skt.] n. Sorrow. వ్యసనము; anxiety. మనోవ్యథ; pledge, pawn. కుదువ. Also, a residence. ఉనికిపట్టు.

ఆధిక్యము *ādhikyamu*. [Skt. from అధికము] n. Greatness. Increase. accumulation, excess, superiority.. గొప్పతనము.

అధిదైవికము *adhi-daivikamu.* [Skt. from దేవ.] adj. Superhuman, supernatural. దైవముచేత కలిగినది. అధిదైవికతాపములు sufferings due to supernatural causes.

ఆధిపత్యము *ādhi-patyamu.* [Skt.] Government, dominion. దొరతనము.

ఆధిభౌతికము *ādhi-bhautikamu.* [Skt.] adj. Natural, or caused by the operation of the natural elements. పృథివ్యాదిభూతములవలన కలిగినది.

ఆధీన్యము *ādhīnyamu.* [Skt.] n. Possession, trust, charge, control. అధీనత్వము.

ఆధునికము *ādhunikamu.* [Skt.] adj. Modern, not ancient, recent. ఇప్పటిది, క్రొత్తది. **ఆధునికులు** *ādhunikulu.* n. The moderns. నవీనులు.

ఆధేయము *ā-dhēyamu.* [Skt.] adj. Placed, deposited, kept. ఉంచబడిన.

ఆధోరణుడు *ādhōraṇuḍu.* [Skt.] n. An elephant driver. మావటివాడు.

ఆధ్యాత్మికము *ādhy-ātmikamu.* [Skt.] adj. Spiritual. ఆత్మవల్ల కలిగినది. ఆధ్యాత్మికతాపములు sufferings self caused.

ఆన *āna.* [corrupted from the Lat. *Anno.*] In the year, as ఆన ౧౮౩౪ *in the year* 1834 or A. D. 1834; used in correspondence, and only regarding the Christian era.

ఆన *āna.* [from Skt. ఆజ్ఞ.] n. Command or order. ఆజ్ఞ. n. Oath, adjuration. తోడు అని ఒట్టుపెట్టుకొనుట. Protestation. ఆన పూర్వకముగా faithfully, according to oath. ఆనలుకడకండ్లు అప్పు ముప్పు oaths are nonsense and a debt is a plague. నీయాన I swear by thee, నాయాన I swear by myself (as in English *upon my word, upon my honor.*)

ఆనందము *ānandamu.* [Skt.] n. Happiness, bliss, delight. ఆనందబాష్పములు tears of joy. **ఆనందించు** *ānandintsu.* v. i. To be glad, to rejoice..

ఆనక *ānaka.* [Tel. colloquial for అటువెనుక.] adv. Hereafter, afterwards.

ఆనకట్ట *āna-kaṭṭa.* [Tel.] n. Anicut. A dam or embankment across a river to raise its level artificially.

ఆనకము *ānakamu.* [Skt.] n. A large kettle drum, a tabor. తప్పెట, భేరి.

ఆనగోలుపోవు *āna-gōlu-pōvu.* [Tel.] v. n. To fade, perish. వాసిచెడు.

ఆనతము or **అవనతము** *ānatamu.* [Skt.] adj. Bent, humbled. వంగిన, వంచబడిన.

ఆనతి *ānati.* [Tel.] n. An order, permission, leave. సెలవు. **ఆనతిచ్చు** (ఆనతి+ఇచ్చు) v. a. To say, tell or relate, command, desire, instruct. సెలవిచ్చు.

ఆనద్ధము *ā-naddhamu.* [Skt.] n. A drum.

ఆననము *ānanamu.* [Skt.] n. The face, mouth. ముఖము, నోరు.

ఆనపకాయ *ānapa-kāya.* [Tel.] n. A long gourd (*cucurbita lagenaris*). The bottle gourd. సొరకాయ.

ఆనమితము *ānamitamu.* [Skt.] adj. Bowed, weighed down, bent. వంపబడిన.

ఆనయించు *ānayintsu.* [Skt.] v. t. To bring. తెచ్చు. **ఆనయము** *ānayamu.* n. Bringing. తేవడము.

ఆనవాటిపొలము *ānavāṭi-polamu.* [Tel.] n. Disputed land: a field the boundary line of which is questioned. కరకసాపొలము.

ఆనపాలు *ānavālu.* [Tel. ఆన+పాలు.] n. Porridge, rice and milk boiled. కాచిన పాలు, ఇగరకాచిన పాలు. **ఆనవాలు** [Tel.] n. Token, keepsake: a mark in lieu of signature: sign. Presumptive proof, a token or credentials. ఉంగరమానవాలొసగె he gave a ring as credentials. **ఆనవాలుపట్టు** *ānavālu-paṭṭu.* v. t. To identify, recognize. గురుతుపట్టు.

ఆనాయము *ānāyamu.* [Skt.] n. A net. వల.

ఆనించు, ఆనిక See ఆను.

అను ánu. [Tel.] v. n. To rest on, to touch, be contiguous to. వానికి దృష్టి అనదు he cannot see out of his eyes.

అను ánu. [Tel.] v. a. To press on, put on. అరాను, గ్రహించు. To drink. తేంట్లుమధ్వమునాను the bees drink honey. పాలిండ్లవిషమూని putting poison on her nipples. చేతులచెవులూని putting his hands to his ears. అనించు ânintsu. v. a. To cause to rest on. అనిక ânika. n. A support, strength. అనుకర్ర ânu-karra. n. A prop. ఊతకోల. అనుకొను ânu-konu. v. a. To lean against or on. To border on, be contiguous to. అడివిని అనుకొన్నచేనులు lands bordering on the forest. ఓడను అనుకొన్నపడవలు the boats that were alongside the ship. అనుడుబిళ్ల ânudu-billa. n. A cushion to lean on, a semicircular cushion or pillow. ఒరుగుదిండు.

అనుకూల్యము ânukûlyamu. [Skt.] n. Convenience, suitability. అనుకూలముగా నుండుట.

అనుగము or అనుగుతీగె ânugamu. [Tel.] n. The creeper of the long bottle gourd, cucurbita lagenaris.

అనుగుణ్యము ânu-gunyamu. [Skt.] n. Fitness, suitability. The state of being in accordance with anything. అనుగుణముగా నుండుట.

అనుపూర్విగా or అనుపూర్వకముగా ânu-pûrvi-gâ. [Skt.] adv. Invariably. Regularly, in order.

ఆనేత ânéta. [Skt.] n. One who brings. తెచ్చువాడు. ఆనేయము ânéyamu. adj. That which deserved to be brought. తేదగినది.

అన్వీక్షకి ân-vîkshakî. [Skt.] n. Logical philosophy, metaphysics. న్యాయశాస్త్రవిద్య.

ఆపగ âpaga. [Skt.] n. A river, a stream.

ఆపణము âpanamu. [Skt.] n. A market. అంగడి. ఆపణికుడు âpanikudu. n. A dealer or shopkeeper. వర్తకుడు.

ఆపత్తు or ఆపద âpattu. [Skt.] n. Calamity, misfortune, adversity. ఆపన్నము âpannamu. Unfortunate, hapless. ఆపన్నుడు âpannudu. n. One who is afflicted or distressed. ఆపదను చెందినవాడు.

అపము âpamu. [Tam.] n. *Hopper* or Oppas, a kind of rice cake. అప్పము.

అపసోపాలుపడు âpa-sôpâlu-padu. [Tel.] v. n. To be dejected, or grieve, be low-spirited.

ఆపాతము âpâtamu. [Skt.] n. Falling. పడుట.

ఆపాదమస్తకముగా âpâda-mastakamu-gâ. [Skt.] n. From head to foot. నిలువెల్ల.

ఆపాదిల్లు âpâdillu. [Skt.] n. To happen, to arise. కలుగు, పుట్టు. ఆపాదనము âpâdanamu n. Happening. కలుగుట.

ఆపు âpu. [Tel. Causative of ఆగు] v. a. To hold back, restrain, check, stop. ఆపుచేయు, అరించు. ఆపు or ఆపుదల âpu. n. A stoppage. ఆపుట. Support. ఆసరా, సహాయము. ఆపుచేయు âpu-chéyu. v. t. To check, stop, stay, suspend. నిలుపుదలచేయు

ఆపె âpe. [Tel. ఆ+అవ్వ] pron. She, that woman, a woman. ఇంటిఆపె the housewife, the lady of the house.

ఆపేక్ష Same as అపేక్ష.

ఆపోవు âpôvu. [Tel. from ఆ a contraction of ఆకలి hunger and పోవు to go or ఆకటు+పోవు] v. n. To be satisfied. తృప్తినొందు.

ఆపోశనము âpôśanamu. [Skt.] n. The sipping of water from the palm of the hand as a religious ceremony before or after meals, &c.

ఆప్తము âptamu. [Skt.] adj. Obtained, gained, intimate, dear, confidential, trusted, attached. ఆప్తముగా confidentially, in a friendly manner, candidly. ఆప్తజనము, ఆప్తజనులు own people, or relations. ఆప్తి âpti. n. Gain, profit. Joining, attachment ఆప్తుడు âptudu. n. A friend.

అప్యాయనము or **అప్యాయము** *a-pyā-yanamu.* [Skt.] n. Refreshment, comfort, reconciliation. తృప్తి.

అప్లవము *a-plavamu.* [Skt.] n. Bathing, plunging. స్నానము, మునుగు.

అబాదు *ābadu.* [H.] adj. Cultivated, prosperous. n. A town. పట్టణము. అబాదుపరుచు or అబాదుచేయు to cultivate; also, to make a place habitable. ఆ గ్రామమును అబాదుచేసెను he made the village a great town.

అబాలగోపాలముగా *a-bāla-gōpālamu-gā.* [Skt.] adv. Both small and great, one and all. అబాలపండితసహాయము equally useful to the learned and the simple.

అబాలు *ābalu.* [H.] n. Transplantation.

అబిడ, అబిడె *a-biḍa.* [Tel. ఆ+బిడ్డ] Pron. She, that woman. ముసలాబిడ the old woman.

అబుకారి Same as అబ్కారి.

అబోతు *a-bōtu.* [Tel. ఆవు+పోతు.] n. A bull. అబోతును విడుచుట to release a bull at a man's funeral (this being a prescribed rite.) అబోతుగాతు one who rides on an ox, Siva.

అబ్కారి, అబుకారి, or **అబ్కారి** *abkāri.* [H.] n. *Abkari*, tax on spirituous liquors. కల్లు సారాయిలమీద వేసే పన్ను.

అబ్దికము *ābdikamu.* [Skt.] n. Anniversary of a death, annual ceremonies.

అభరణము *ābharaṇamu.* [Skt.] n. Ornament, decoration, jewels. **అభరణుడు** n. He who wears jewels.

అభాషణము *ābhāshaṇamu.* [Skt.] n. Addressing, speaking; a speech, harangue, oration.

అభాసము, అభాసు *ābhāsamu.* [Skt.] n. Fallacy, corruption. అభాసముచేయు to injure, to spoil. అభాసాంధ్రము a coarse low dialect of Telugu.

అభిజాత్యము *ābhi-jātyamu.* [Skt.] n. Lineage, descent.

అభిముఖ్యుడైన *ābhi-mukhyuḍaina.* Skt.] adj. Meeting, fronting.

అభీరుడు *a-bhīruḍu.* [Skt.] n. A herdsman. **అభీరపల్లి** *ābhīra-palli.* n. A hamlet, a village of herdsmen. **అభీరి** *ābhīri.* n. A woman of the herdsmen's caste.

అభీలము or **అభీలత** *ābhīlamu.* [Skt.] n. Fear, terror. భయము. అభీలనేత్రుడు the fierce-eyed one.

అభోగము *a-bhōgamu.* [Skt.] n. Completion. Fullness, plumpness. పరిపూర్ణత.

అమంత్రించు *a-mantrintsu.* [Skt.] v. n. To call **అమంత్రణము** *a-mantraṇamu.* n. Calling. పిలుపు. Adieu; farewell. వీడుకోలు.

అమడ *āmaḍa.* [Tel.] n. A measure of distance equal to four coss: that is, either 8 or 10 miles. అడుగు అమడగానుండినది every step was as wearying as a mile.

అమతించు *āmatintsu.* [Skt.] v. a. To invite. పిలుచు. అమతింపు an invitation to a wedding.

అమతిల్లు *āmatillu.* v. i. To arise. పుట్టు.

అమదను *āmadanu.* [H.] n. Income, revenue.

అమని *āmani.* [Tel.] n. Alarm, fright, annoyance. Also, season, time, harvest time. Plenty. వసంతఋతువు, సమృద్ధి. అన్నం బామనిగానిడుము give them plenty to eat. చేరామని a long time. అమనిచెలికాడు Cupid. మన్మథుడు.

అమము *āmamu.* [Skt.] adj. Raw, unripe, undressed. పచ్చి, పండని, వండబడని. అమశ్రాద్ధము n. A funeral rite celebrated by giving unboiled rice, &c., to Brahmins. **అమము** n. Mucus, bad secretions of the bowels. అమకట్టు a collection of mucus. అమశూలము dysentery.

అమయము *āmayamu.* [Skt.] n. Sickness, disease. రోగము.

అమలకము *āmalakamu.* [Skt.] n. A tree, *Emblic myrobalan.* ఉసిరిచెట్టు. దానికి అది

కరతలామలకముగానున్నది he has it at his fingers' ends.

ఆమవడ *āma-vaḍa.* [Tel.] n. A cake made of pulse (termed *phaseolus radiatus*) soaked in curds.

ఆమిక or హామిక *āmika* [Skt. అహమహమిక] n. Egotism, boasting. Presumption, boldness, vigour. అహంకారము, గర్వము. ఆమిక జాత్ర *āmikajātra.* n. Satiety.

ఆమిషము *āmishamu.* [Skt.] n. Flesh, meat. Enjoyment. భోగము.

ఆమిషము or హామిషము *āmishamu.* [H.] n. Means, property, worth, resources, gross produce. అయివజు. ఆ గ్రామమునకు పోయి ఆమిషముచూచుకొని వచ్చినాడు he went to the village and examined what its resources were. "తనపోమిషము అమ్మి ఆ వెలువలో కొంత దాచికొని" Pritchetts' Acts v. 1.

ఆమీను *āmīnu.* [H.] n. An ameen, a petty revenue officer.

ఆము *āmu.* [Tel.] n. Fatness, lust, desire. మదము. ఆము or ఆముకొనియు *āmu.* v. a. To cover, spread over. వ్యాపించు, నిండు. కళలామినముఖము a face bright with radiance. ఆముకొను *āmu-konu.* v. n. To increase. హెచ్చును, పైకొను.

ఆముక్తము *ā-muktamu.* [Skt.] n. That which is worn or put on as a cloth or armour. కట్టబడిన, తొడుగబడిన.

ఆముదము *āmudamu.* [Tel.] n. Castor oil. ఆముదములు castor oil seeds. ఆముదపు చెట్టు *āmudapu-cheṭṭu.* n. The castor oil tree, *palma christi*, or, *ricinus communis.* పెద్దాముదము a species of castor oil used for lamps. చిట్టి ఆముదము a more gentle purging oil used for infants. కొండ ఆముదము, or అడవి ఆముదము or నేపాళము a plant, *Baliospermum montanum* (Watts.)

ఆముష్మికము *āmushmikamu.*[Skt.] adj. That which is mental, spiritual, or heavenly; as distinguished from ఐహికము that which is material or earthly. ఆముష్మిక సుఖములు spiritual delights.

ఆమూలము *ā-mūlamu.* [Skt.] adv. Radically, to the root. ఆమూలము adj. Entire, root and branch. ఆమూలాగ్రముగా (lit. from the root to the top.) Through and through, completely. ఆమూలాగ్రముగా చెడినది it is ruined root and branch.

ఆమె *āme.* [Tel. ఆ+అమ్మ.] pron. She.

ఆమెత or ఆమిత *ameta.* [Tel.] n. Invitation, banquet, feast. ఆమెతచేయు. to feed on: make a meal. Vasu. iii. 152. ఆమెత పెట్టు to give a dinner. విందుచేయు "కోటి కుమ్మరలకామెతలుపెట్టు." రసి. iv.

ఆమేన్ *āmen.* [Heb.] n. తథాస్తు. అట్లు అగుగాక (ఇది బైబిలులోవచ్చేమాట.)

ఆమోదించు *ā-mōdintsu.* [Skt.] v. n. To be glad; to agree, concur with, assent, consent. సంతోషించు, సమ్మతించు. ఆమోదము *āmōdamu.* n. Sweetness, delight, joy. సంతోషము, సమ్మతము.

ఆమ్నాయము *āmnāyamu.* [Skt.] n. The Veda or Scripture.

ఆమ్రము *āmramu.* [Skt.] n. The mango tree. మామిడిచెట్టు.

ఆమ్రేడించు *āmrēḍintsu.* [Skt.] v. t. To reiterate. Parij. v. 92. ఆమ్రేడితము *āmrēḍitamu.* adj. n. Reiterated; that which is repeated, that which is said twice. In gram. the second form of the repeated word. ద్విరుక్తములొక్క పరరూపము.

ఆమ్లము *āmlamu.* [Skt.] n. The tamarind tree or fruit. Sourness. పులుసు.

ఆయకము *āyakamu.* [Tel.] n. Mortgage. తాకట్టు, కుదువ.

ఆయకాడు *āya-kāḍu.* [Tel.] n. A bailiff or village officer. ఊరి ఉద్యోగస్థుడు.

ఆయతనము *āya-tanamu.* [Skt.] n. Place, home, temple. ఇల్లు, గుడి.

ఆయతము *āyutamu.* [Skt.] adj. Long, fit, proper. నిడుపైన, పొడుగైన, తగిన.

ఆయతి *āyati.* [Skt.] n. Tallness, length. The future రాబోవుకాలము. The space of four months కందాయము, కారు, మాసచతుష్టయము. Income. వచ్చుబడి. **ఆయతికాడు** *āyati-kāḍu.* A tall man; a man of rank; a powerful man, one who acquires wealth. ధనార్జనముచేయువాడు.

ఆయత్తము *āyattamu.* [Skt.] n. Readiness, preparation. **ఆయత్తము** adj. Ready. Inclined for; submitting to. అధీనమైన. కామాయత్తము given up to one's lusts. **ఆయత్తపడు** *āyatta-paḍu.* v. n. To be ready, to be prepared. **ఆయత్తి** *āyatti.* n. Subjection. లోకువ. Friendship. స్నేహము. Boundary. ఎల్ల. Day. దినము.

ఆయన *āyana.* [Tel. ఆ+అన్న] pron. He, ఇంటిఆయన the master of the house.

ఆయపరచు *āya-paratsu.* [Tel.] v. a. To cultivate, bring under the plough. సాగుబడిచేయు.

ఆయపిల్లు *āyap-illu.* [Tel.] n. Closet or inner chamber.

ఆయము *āyamu.* [Tel. and Skt.] n. A vital part of the body. జీవస్థానము particulars, details. Receipt, gain, profit. వచ్చుబడి. ఆదాయము. Toll, tax, customs, income. సుంకము. Rate, standard, fixed number. **ఆయకట్టు** *āya-kaṭṭu.* ఆయము+కట్టు] ఆయము, శేక, ఆదాయముయొక్క నిర్ణయము, ప్రమాణము. A yard, an enclosure. Quantity, extent of land, an account specifying the varieties of kinds of soil in a certain field. ఆ యింటి ఆయకట్టులోగా within the compound of the house. ఆయమునకు వెచ్చమధికమైన if the expense is greater than the income. ఆయంపాటిగాయం or ఆయంపట్టుగాయం a mortal wound. ఆయములసోకగా to the quick.

ఆయల్లకము *āyallakamu.* [Skt.] n. Longing desire. Loving regret. కామచింత, కామాతురము, విరహము, ఎడబాపు.

ఆయవారము *āya-vāramu.* [from Skt. యాయావరము] n. Alms. ధాన్యభిక్షము.

ఆయసము *āya-samu.* [Skt.] n. Iron. adj. Made of Iron, metallic. **ఆయసపట్టిక** *āyasa-paṭṭika.* n. An iron plate or lid placed over a lamp to collect the soot.

ఆయా *āyā.* [Tel.] ఆ+ఆ That and that: those and those; several, various **ఆయా** *āyā.* [H. or Tam.] n. A waiting woman, a maidservant, an ayah. పనికత్తె, దాసిది.

ఆయాసము *āyāsamu.* [Skt.] n. Fatigue, trouble, uneasiness, vexation. శ్రమము. **ఆయాసకరము** *āyāsa-karamu.* adj. Vexatious or troublesome. **ఆయాసపడు** v. i. To toil, be wearied. శ్రమపడు, to grieve. **ఆయాసపెట్టు** v. a. To trouble, to plague, vex, harass.

ఆయిటుదూది *āyiṭu-dūdi.* n. [Tel.] Silk cotton. బూరుగుదూది. A. vi. 75.

ఆయితము or **ఆయిత్తము** *āyitamu.* [Tel.] adj. Ready, prepared. n. Preparation. సన్నాహము. **ఆయితపడు, ఆయితముచేయు** or **ఆయితపెట్టు** *āyita-paḍu* v. a. To prepare, trim.

ఆయత్తము, or **ఆయిత్తు** *āyattamu.* [Tel.] n. Convenience, readiness. **ఆయిత్తు** adj. Ready, prepared, convenient. నాకు రానాయిత్తుకాదు I cannot come.

ఆయుధము *āyudhamu.* [Skt.] n. A weapon, an instrument, a tool. **ఆయుధవిద్య** *āyudha-vidya.* n. The science of arms. **ఆయుధశాల** *āyudha-śāla.* n. An arsenal. **ఆయుధస్థుడు** *āyudhasthuḍu.* n. An armed man. ఆయుధోపజీవి one who lives by his sword, a hired soldier.

ఆయుర్వేదము *āyur-vēdamu.* [Skt.] n. The science of life. Hygiene or medicine. ఆరోగ్యశాస్త్రము. శేక వైద్యశాస్త్రము.

ఆయువు *āyuvu.* [Skt.] n. Age, life, duration of life. ఆయువుతీరి చచ్చినచావు a natural death, death from old age. ఆయుర్దాయము

period of life. ఆయుస్సు. ఆయుష్కరము *ayush-karamu.* adj. Life-lengthening. ఇది నీకు ఆయుష్కరము this will lengthen your days. ఆయుష్కర్మము *ayush-karmamu.* n. A polite term for *shaving,* క్షౌరము, as the "renewing of one's age." ఆయుష్మంతుడు *ayushmantudu.* adj. Long lived. n. One who can live a long life. ఆయుష్యము or ఆయుస్సు *ayushyamu.* n. Life.

ఆయోగము *ā-yōgamu.* [Skt.] n. Intelligence, తెలివి. Work. వ్యాపారము.

ఆయోధనము *ā-yōdhanamu.* [Skt.] n. War, battle యుద్ధము.

ఆర *ara.* [Tel.] n. A shoemaker's awl. మాదిగవానిసూది. ఆర adv. (lit. so as to fill) Much; fully. (From ఆరు.) It is often added to a noun; as చెవులార వింటిని I heard it distinctly: కండ్లార చూస్తిని I saw him plainly with my own eyes. కడుపార భోజనముచేసినాను I ate to the full. ఆర *ara.* [Tel.] A vocative plural suffix as అన్నలార. O brothers!

ఆరంగపువక్క *arangapu-vakka.* [Tel.] n. Areca nut of a certain superior quality.

ఆరండకము *arandakamu.* [Skt.] n. The art of writing in cypher.

ఆరంభము *arambhamu.* [Skt.] n. A beginning, the commencement. మొదలు. ఆరంభించు *arambhintsu.* v. t. To begin, to commence. మొదలుపెట్టు.

ఆరకాటి *arakati.* [Tel.] n. A boatman, a sailor. ఓడనడపువాడు, నావికుడు.

ఆరకూటము *ara-kūtamu.* [Skt.] n. Steel or brass. ఉక్కు, ఇత్తడి. ఆరకూటచ్ఛాయ the hue of steel or brass.

ఆరకూడు *ara-kūdu.* [Tel.] n. A chance dinner. పూటకు ఒకచోట తినడము. A. vi. 92.

ఆరక్షుడు *a-rakshudu.* [Skt.] n. A watchman, తలారివాడు.

ఆరగించు *aragintsu.* [Tel.] v. a. To partake of food or drink. భుజించు, త్రాగు. ఆరగింపు or ఆరగింత *aragimpu.* n. Eating; food, భుక్తి. ఆరగింపుచేయు v. To eat, or, cause to eat.

ఆరజము *arazamu.* [Tel.] adj. Elegant, pretty, bland, fine. ఇంపైన. n. Prettiness, grace, elegance. ఇంపు, సొగసు. ఆరజంబుగా *arajambu-ga.* adv. Elegantly, gracefully.

ఆరటము *aratamu* [Tel.] n. Distress, grief చింత, ఖేదము, పరితాపము. ఆరటించు or ఆరటపడు *aratintsu.* [Tel.] v. n. To grieve. పరితాపపడు, పరితపించు. ఆరటపెట్టు *arata-pettu.* v. a. To distress, to grieve. ఆయాసపెట్టు, పరితపింపచేయు.

ఆరట్టము *arattamu.* [Skt.] n. *Herat* in Khorasan, whence horses were brought.

ఆరడము *aradamu.* [Tel.] n. Effort. పూనిక. Pleasure. ఉత్సాహము.

ఆరడి *aradi.* [Tel.] n. Scandal, disgrace, censure. నింద. ఆరడి adj. Vain, useless వ్యర్థము. ఆరడిపడు *aradi-padu.* v. n. To incur censure, to be blamed. నిందింపబడు. ఆరడిపెట్టు *aradi-pettu.* v. a. To scorn, slight. To grieve, afflict. ఆరడిపోవు *aradi-pōvu.* v. n. To be the sport of scandal, to be slandered. To grieve.

ఉ॥ "మొల్లసుగంధినామనసు
మోహమునారడిబెట్టినీవు న
న్నొల్లకవీడన్నా డెద వయో
తగవా."

V. P. ii. 240.

ఆరతి *arati.* [Tel.] n. An oblation or wave offering, an offering of lights or of water, turmeric and chunam waved over a deity or over any individual to take off the supposed ill effects of the evil looks. హారతి or మంగళహారతి. (This ceremony answers to lustration or sprinkling with holy water.)

ఆరనాళకము *aranalakamu.* [Skt.] n. Water in which rice has been washed, or, kept till it ferments. Sour gruel made by the fermentation of boiled rice. కడుగు, కలి.

ఆరబము *ārabamu.* [Tel.] n. Vegetation, crops, fruit of the earth in general. పైరు. "ఆకీడునకా, వానల్కల్గకమానెనారబములెండం జొచ్చె." V. P. ii. 113. Cultivation, tillage. సాగుబడి; కాడారబము dry cultivation; నీరారబము wet cultivation.

ఆరబ్ధము *ārabdhamu.* [Skt.] adj. That which is begun. ఆరంభింపబడినది.

ఆరభటి *āra-bhaṭi.* [Skt.] n. Valour, manhood. బంటుతనము, ప్రౌఢిమ. R. i. 108. A grand style in Tel. or Skt. Composition. ఒక కావ్యవృత్తి.

ఆరభి *ārabhi.* [Skt.] n. A certain tune in music.

ఆరము *āramu.* [Skt.] n. One side or angle of a polygon. ద్వాదశారము a twelve sided body. అష్టారక eight sided.

ఆరయు *ārayu.* [Tel. another form of అరయు.] v. a. To inquire, look to, search for. విచారించు.

ఆరవము *āravamu.* [Skt.] n. Sound, noise. మ్రోత.

ఆరాటము *ārāṭamu.* [Skt.] n. Distress, grief. పరితాపము. ఆరాటపెట్టు or ఆరాటించు *ārāṭintsu.* v. a. To distress, grieve.

ఆరాత్రికము Same as నీరాజనము. (q. v.)

ఆరాధించు *ārādhintsu.* [Skt. lit. సంతోషపరుచు.] v. a. To worship, to pray, to adore. మొక్కు. ఆరాధకుడు *ā-rādhakuḍu.* n. Worshipper. ఆరాధనము *ārādhanamu.* n. Worship, prayer. ఆరాధితము *ārādhitamu.* adj. That which is worshipped. ఆరాధనీయము or ఆరాధ్యము *ā-rādhanīyamu.* adj. Worthy of reverence. ఆరాధ్యుడు *ārādhyuḍu.* n. His reverence, the venerable, a title given to those Bramins who are of the lingayat caste.

ఆరామము *ārāmamu.* [Skt.] n. A grove, a garden. తోట.

ఆరావము *ārāvamu.* [Skt.] n. Sound, voice. ధ్వని, మ్రోత.

ఆరిందా *ārindā.* [H.] n. A broker, an agent, or merchant on behalf of others. అడితిదారు.

ఆరితీరు *āri-tīru.* [Tel.] v. n. To be perfect, qualified, complete, accomplished or well versed in. ఆరితీరినవాడు he who is well versed or thoroughly practised. ఆరితీరి కూర్చున్నప్పుడు when he was sitting at his ease.

ఆరిపువ్వుచెట్టు *āri-puvvu-cheṭṭu.* [Tel.] n A tree (*Cristea tomentosa.*) ధాతకి.

ఆరివేరము *āri-vēramu.* [from Skt. వైరము.] n. Quarrelsomeness, fretfulness, peevishness, fretting. కలహమునకు త్వరపడి తిరుగుట. ఆరివేరపుకసపి the great mischief maker, i. e., Nārada

ఆరు *āru.* [Tel.] n. A line of hair, extending from the navel up towards the breast. రోమావళి. నూగారు.

ఆరు *āru* [Tel.] Numeral adj. Six. ఆరుగురు, ఆరువురు Six men. ఆరున్నొకటి or ఆర్నొకటి "six and one" which, for euphony, is commonly used for ఏడు seven, because ఏడు means also to cry.

ఆరు *āru.* [Tel.] v. n. To teem with, be full of. నిండు; to be or *have.* సొంపారిన beautiful. ఇంపారిన delightful. నిండారుగానున్నది it is full. అలరారు blooming. చెన్నారిన lovely. పొల్పారిన charming (compare the affix ఆరి as కొల్పరి, సొంపరి, &c.) గోజారు to trouble. సొంపారు to bloom, to be pretty. In such phrases as నూరారు, వెయ్యారు the word ఆరు is not the numeral *six*, but is a form of ఆరు to be full; so వెయ్యారు means full a thousand and నూరారు full a hundred. నూరారుముద్దులు a full hundred kisses. వేయంబరంగ శివుని పూజింపకుండిన if he sacrifice not to Siva with his own hands. చేతులార రూకలు చెల్లిస్తిని I paid the money with my own hands. పని ఆరుమూడు అయినది the work is all in confusion, at sixes and sevens.

ఆరు or ఆరిపోవు *āru.* [Tel.] v. n. To dry, be dried up. To be quenched, or extinguished. To be cooled, to cool. To be appeased, allayed, mollified. To heal or be cured, as a wound. To be blunted. చేతది ఆరదు the hand is yet wet: i. e., I have this moment finished the work. ఆరుచు or ఆరపోయు to put to dry. ఆరవేయు or ఆరపెట్టు to dry or cause to dry by exposure to the sun or air. ఆరని without intermission, unceasing.

ఆరుకలు, ఆరుగలు, ఆరికెలు, ఆరిగెలు or ఆర్లు *ārukalu.* [Tel.] n. A sort of inferior grain. A species of grain, called *paspalum frumentaceum.* కొర్లు is similar but oblong in shape.

ఆరుచు, ఆరుచు or ఆర్చు *ārutsu.* [Tel.] v. To cry, exclaim, roar. To cause to dry. To move. రెప్పలార్చు to wink.

ఆరుదొండ *āru-donda.* [Tel.] n. The plant termed *capparis horrida.*

ఆరుద్రపురుగు or ఆర్ద్రపురుగు *ārudra-purugu.* [Tel.] n. An insect of a bright red colour belonging to the Mite family. Its body resembles silk; so it is also called పట్టుపురుగు or చంద్రమామపురుగు.

ఆరుపు or ఆర్పు *ārupu.* [Tel.] n. (in painting) the *ground* which *sets off* a colour. (Commonly) a cry. కూత, ఏడ్పు.

ఆరుపోరు *āru-pôru.* [Tel.] n. Squabble, (here ఆరు is a mere echo.)

ఆరుమూడు See ఆరు (six).

ఆరులు అనగా ఆరెగదుబ్బులు. A. iv. 130. See ఆరుకలు.

ఆరూఢము *ārūḍhamu.* [Skt.] adj. Ascended, mounted. పంచారూఢపత్రము a bond signed by five persons, viz., the creditor, debtor, writer, and two witnesses.

ఆరె *āre* [Tel]. n. An awl used by cobblers ఆరెలు or ఆరెబొట్లు A cock's spurs ఆరెలు or ఆరెవడ్లు *ārelu.* [Tel.] n. A kind of fine rice.

ఆరెకుడు *ārekudu.* [Tel.] n. Watchman. కావలి. ఆరెకోల *āre-kôla.* [Tel.] v. An elephant goad. ఏనుగును అదిలించే కోల, అంకుశము.

ఆరెచెట్టు *āre-chettu.* [Tel.] n. A tree *(Bauhinia Spicata)* with large leaves and a fruit like cranberries. పెద్ద ఆరెచెట్టు *Bauhinia purpurea.* తెల్ల ఆరెచెట్టు *Bauhinia racemosa.* శ్వేతకాంచనము. కాంచిని ఆరెచెట్టు. *Bauhinia tomentosa.* అడ్డచెట్టు *Bauhinia Vahlii.* చిరు ఇప్పచెట్టు *Bauhinia retusa.* (Watts.) ఆరెకూర Vegetables or curry made of the leaves of the ఆరెచెట్టు.

ఆరెబొట్టె *āre-botte.* [Tel.] n. The sharp claw that is on the back of a cock's leg. కోడి కాలివెనక వెనుకతట్టున నుండెడి ముల్లుగల వాడిగానుండే ఒంటిగోరు.

ఆరెము *āremu* [Mahr.] n. The name for Mahratta. ఆరెకాపులు a certain class of farmers. ఆరెలిపి Mahratta writing ఆరెలెక్కలు accounts written in Mahratta. ఆరెము or ఆరెభాష The Mahratta language.

"ఆరెవిపారెవి గుజరాతియారెను
ద్రవిడతెనుగుకర్ణాటములుగా బదిపిన్నారు
వాడిగన్నట్టిగాడు." య. i.

ఆరెము *āremu.* [from Skt. ఆరామము.] n. Garden, park. తోట.

ఆరోగణము *ārôgiṇamu.* [Skt. ఆరగించు.] n. Eating, the act of taking refreshment. ఆరోగణముసేయు to eat. Swa. ii.

ఆరోగ్యము *ārôgyamu.* [Skt.] n. Health. Freedom from disease. రోగములేమి.

ఆరోపించు *ārôpintsu.* [Skt.] v. t. To impute. లేనిదివారిపు. Imputing. ఆరోపణము. గుణారోపణము attributing any quality. ఇది నీ మీద ఆరోపింపబడినది this is attributed to you. ఆరోపితము *ārôpitamu.* adj. That which is imputed.

ఆరోహణము *ārōhaṇamu*. [Skt.] n. Ascent, a staircase. Elevating, raising. ధ్వజారోహణము a certain rite at the beginning of a feast when the "*flag is raised*." **ఆరోహము** *ārōhamu*, n. Length, ascent, rising, creeping up. The buttocks. పిరుదులు, నితంబము. "ఆరోహభరమునదుగలు తడబడ." B. VIII. 450. స్వరారోహము rising notes, swell in music. **ఆరోహించు** *ārōhintsu*. v. n. To mount upon. **ఆరోహకుడు** or ఆరోహకుడు- a rider. గుర్రపు రౌతు.

ఆర్చు or **ఆరచు** *ārtsu*. [Tel.] v. n. To cry aloud, shout, roar. కూయు, కేకవేయు. **ఆర్చు** or **ఆరుచు** v. a. To dry up, to quench, extinguish, to cool, dry, appease, allay, to heal or cure, destroy, to dry in the sun, to expose to heat, to cause to dry; to move to and fro. ఆడించు. to move the eyelid. పోకార్చు to ruin, destroy. విక్రయమార్చు to sell. BD. v. 526.

ఆర్జనము See under ఆర్జించు

ఆర్జవము *ārjavamu*. [Skt.] n. Straightness. ఋజుభావము, చక్కన.

ఆర్జించు *ārjintsu*. [Skt.] v. a. To acquire or accumulate, to gain, make money. గడించు, సంపాదించు. **ఆర్జన** or **ఆర్జనము** *ārjana*. n. Acquisition, gain, accumulation. గడన, ద్రవ్యార్జన the acquisition of wealth. **ఆర్జకుడు** *ārjakuḍu*. n. He who acquires or procures. గడించువాడు. **ఆర్జితము** *ārjitamu*. adj. Acquired, gained. కష్టార్జితమైన earned by toil.

ఆర్తి *ārti*. [Skt.] n. Distress, pain, affliction. దుఃఖము. **ఆర్తుడు** *ārtuḍu* n. A sorrowful or afflicted man. ఆర్తరక్షకుడు a reliever of the distressed. ఆర్తనాది he who bewails or laments. P. vi. 84. మదనార్తుడై amorous.

ఆర్ద్రము *ārdramu*. [Skt.] adj. Wet, damp, moist, imbued, steeped. తడిసిన. See అశ్రుపూరము. దయార్ద్రదృష్టి with eyes moist with love or full of love. **ఆర్ద్రకము** *ārdrakamu*. n. Undried ginger. అల్లము.

ఆర్పు *ārpu*. [Tel. from ఆరచు] n. A cry. ఆర్పు లనిగుడ uttering cries.

ఆర్భటము or **ఆరాభటము** or **ఆర్భటి** *ārbhaṭamu*. [Skt.] n. Cry, roar, yell, uproar. **ఆర్భటించు** *ārbhaṭintsu*. v. n. To cry, roar.

ఆర్య *ārya*. [Skt. √ ār=to plough.] n. The Skt. form of Tel. అయ్య. **ఆర్యపుత్రుడు** *ārya-putruḍu*. n. (In dramas) Husband. **ఆర్యావర్తము** *āryā-vartamu*. The land of the Aryans, a name applied to northern India, between the Himalayas and the Dekkan. **ఆర్యుడు** *āryuḍu*. n. An Aryan; a good or respectable man, one worthy of reverence.

ఆర్వేరము *ārvēramu*. [Tel. another form of అఱవేరము.] n. Quarrel, enmity. కలహము, ద్వేషము.

ఆర్షము *ārshamu*. [Skt. from ఋషి] adj. Relating to, belonging to or derived from a Rishi. ఋషిసంబంధమైన. Spiritual, prophetical; inspired or revealed by means of a *Rishi*. Archaic. పురాతనము. n. A form of marriage in which a girl is freely given away in accordance with the Sastras, her parents receiving a cow and an ox in return. ధర్మార్థము వరునివలంది ఆవును ఎద్దును పుచ్చుకొని కన్యనిచ్చి శాస్త్రానుసారముగా చేయు పెండ్లి.

ఆలంకి *ālanki*. [Tel.] n. A palankeen which is like a chair. కుర్చీవంటి పల్లకి. **ఆలంకిగుడి** or **ఆలంకులు** *ālanki-guḍi*. n. A boisterous game among boys. Vish. vii. 211.

ఆలంబము *ālambamu*. [Skt.] n. An asylum, prop, receptacle, support. Adj. Hanging from, depending on. అవలంబము. **ఆలంబితము** *ālambitamu*. [Skt.] adj. Pendent, suspended.

అలంభము *ālambhamu.* [Skt.] n. Slaughter, killing. చంపడము.

అలకాపరి or **అలకాపు** *āla-kāpari.* [Tel. అల=అవుల] A herdsman. అవులను కాచువాడు.

అలకించు *ālakintsu.* [Tel.] v. i. To listen, hear, attend to. వినుు.

అలక్షించు *ālakshintsu.* [Skt.] v. i. To see, find out. చూచు, కనుగొను.

అలచిప్ప *āla-chippa.* [Tel.] n. A cockleshell.

అలతి *ālati.* [from Skt. అలప్తి] n. Buzzing, singing mournfully. రాగాలాపము.

"అళులాలతిసేయగ శాడి దాగుదిం
తలం తాఃతోదనాడుదుకు తద్వన
విధులయందు గోపికల్."

నాతి: పూ. viii.

అలనపాలనము *ālana-pālanamu.* [Skt.] n. Care and caution. -See పాలనము. (The word అలన is an anuk.)

అలపదములు *āla-padamulu.* [Tel.] n. Bucolics, madrigals. (Sukas ii. 190.)

అలపించు *ālapintsu.* [from Skt. ఆలాపించు.] v. i. To sing.

అలపొయ్యి *āla-poyyi* [Tel.] n. A furnace with a great boiler or kettle.

అలపోతు *āla-pōtu.* [Tel. అల=అవుల] A bull. ఆబోతు.

అలము *ālamu.* [Tel.] n. War, battle. Plague, trouble, oppression; పోరు, జగడము. Disregard, scorn, despite. అలక్ష్యము, వ్యర్థము. "ఆనిపలుకు నమ్మరాకోలాలనయున పలుకులాలం బుచేసి చక్రవాకి యుట్లనియె." Swa. vi. 72.

అలయము *ālayamu.* [Skt. cognate with ఇల్లు q. v.; borrowed by Skt. from Dra. languages.] n. An abode, home, dwelling; a temple, as being the dwelling of the god. కష్టాలయము the home (or place) of misery. దేవాలయము a temple.

అలరి *ālari.* [Tel.] adj. & n. Unprotected, destitute. అనాథ, నాథుడులేనిది. An ill tempered man, a bad man. దుష్టుడు.

అలరేడు *āla-rēdu.* [Tel.] n. The ox. వృషభము, బసవడు.

అలవ or **అలువ** *āluva.* [Tel.] n. An armadillo, a scaly anteater. See అలుగ.

అలవట్టము *āla-vaṭṭamu.* [Tel.] n. A banner or large fan, like a sun or like a fig leaf, carried in processions.

అలవాలము *āla-vālamu.* [Skt.] n. A garden-bed; a basin for water round the trunk of a tree. పాదు. మాధుర్యాలవాలము a paradise of delights, a sea of sweets.

అలస్యము *ālasyamu.* [Skt.] n. Delay. heedlessness; sloth, idleness. జాగు, సోమరితనము. **అలస్యముచేయు** or **అలసించు** *ālasyamu-chēyu.* v. n. To delay, to idle or trifle time away.

ఆలాగు *ā-lāgu.* [Tel. ఆ+లాగు) n. That way. **అలా** *ālā.* [Tel. ఆ+లాగు] adv. So, thus (contracted from ఆలాగున). **ఆలాగంటి** *ā-lāganṭi.* [Tel. ఆ+లాగు] adj. Such. **ఆలాగు**, **ఆలాగున**, **ఆలాగే**, *ālāgu.* adv. Thus; so, in that manner. **ఆలాటి** *ālāṭi.* adj. Such: like that.

ఆలాతము *ālātamu.* [Tel.] n. A torch. Swa. ii. 138. కొరవి.

ఆలానము *ālānamu* [Skt.] n. The post to which an elephant is tied. A fetter. (R. iv. 51. A. ii. 34.) Also, a rope. త్రాడు.

ఆలాపము, ఆలాపన *ā-lāpamu.* [Skt.] n. Talking, lamentation. మాట. Recitation; the prelude in music; tuning the voice or pitching the note. రాగాలాపము. **ఆలాపించు** *ā-lāpintsu.* v. n. To talk, to grieve. To tune the voice. రాగముమ తిన్నగా తీయు.

ఆలాయము *ā-lāyamu.* [Tel.] n. Readiness, intention, preparedness. **ఆలాయము** adj. Fit. పాత్రము. Ready, prepared, resolved, determined. **ఆలాయమగు** *ālāyam-agu.* v. n. To be ready or prepared.

ఆలావర్తము Same as అలవట్టము. (q. v.)

అలి or **ఆళి** *āli.* [Skt.] n. A line, row, or range, a bank or ridge. A woman's female friend or gossip. చెలికత్తె. **అలి** [Tel.] n. Ridicule, satire. adj. Inferior. హీనమైన. **అలిగొను** *ali-gonu.* [Tel.] To ridicule. అవహసించు. To disrespect or disgrace. హీనపరచు. రామా. అర. నిర్వ. v. భార. శల్య. ii.

ఆలింగనము *ālinganamu.* [Skt.] n. An embrace; **ఆలింగనముచేయు** *ālingana-mu-chēyu.* v. t. To embrace. కౌగిలించు. **ఆలింగ్యము** *ālingyamu.* A sort of drum made like a cow's head.

ఆలించు *ālintsu.* [Tel.] v. a. To listen to, give ear to. ఆలకించు.

ఆలివిప్పు See అలవిప్పు.

ఆలీఢము *ā-līḍhamu.* [Skt.] adj. Stretching, striding. (See ప్రత్యాలీఢము) n. The archer's attitude in drawing the bow when he puts the right foot forward.

ఆలు *ālu.* [Tel.] n. A woman, a wife. (Genitive ఆలి. Pl. ఆండ్రు.) ఆలుమగడు man and wife, a married pair. ఆలివంకవారు a wife's kinsfolk. ఆలిసైదోడు a wife's brother or sister. ఇల్లాలు the housewife.

ఆలు *ālu.* (from ఆవు a cow.) n. plu. Cows, kine. ఆవులు.

ఆలుక *āluka.* [Skt.] n. A small vessel. గిండిచెంబు.

ఆలుకము *ālukamu.* [Skt.] n. An esculent root *(arum campanulatum,)* the sweet potato, *(cucurbita lagenaris.)* చేమగడ్డ, గెనుసుగడ్డ.

ఆలుగ or **ఆలువ** *āluga.* [Tel.] n. A scaly anteater, an armadillo. వజ్రకాయము Same as అలవ.

ఆలుగడ్డ *ālu-gaḍḍa.* [H.] n. Potato. ఉరలగడ్డ, బంగాళాదుంప.

ఆలెగాండ్లు *āle-gāndlu.* [Tel.] n. Servants. పాలెగాండ్లచేతికింది కొలువుగాండ్లు.

ఆలెపొయ్యి or **ఆలెకపొయ్యి** *āle-poyyi.* [Tel.] n. A fire place, whereon three or four pots are fixed in the earth together, with a fire in the centre. Same as అంబపొయ్యి.

ఆలేఖనము *ā-lēkhanamu.* [Skt.] n. Writing, painting. చిత్తరువువ్రాయుట. **ఆలేఖ్యము** *ā-lēkhyamu.* [Skt.] n. Writing, Painting. వ్రాత, చిత్తరువు. See లిఖించు.

ఆలోకనము or **ఆలోకము** *ā-lōkanamu.* [Skt.] n. Sight, view; sun's heat, light. చూపు, ఎండ, వెలుగు. **ఆలోకించు** *ālōkintsu.* v. a. To see, view or look at. చూచు.

ఆలోచన *ā-lōchana.* [Skt.] n. Thought, looking at, or examining. Consultation, consideration, reflection, counsel, policy, deliberation, plan, intent, purpose, motive, imagination, supposition, advice, view, intention. ఆలోచనచేయు to weigh, consider, view, regard. **ఆలోచించు** *ālōchintsu.* v. a. To think, view, consider, consult, deliberate, suppose or reflect.

ఆలోడనము *ālōḍanamu.* [Skt.] n. Churning, a thorough enquiry, rinsing, investigation, sifting, research. కలియబెట్టుట. **ఆలోడించు** *ālōḍintsu.* v. a. To churn: investigate. కలియబెట్టు.

ఆలోన *ālōna.* [Tel.] adv Meanwhile.

ఆలోలము *ā-lōlamu.* [Skt.] adj. Agitated, shaken, fluctuating, tremulous, quivering. ఆలోలుడై eager, desirous. ఆసక్తికల. A. vi. 132.

ఆల్లకోస *ālla-kōsa.* [Tel.] n. A species of crow.

ఆల్లు *āllu.* [Tel.] n. A species of grain. ఆరికెలు చిన్నకుప్ప నేదాల్లు a proverb for 'one who has grown up under one's eyes.'

ఆళ్వారు *āḷvāru.* [Drav.] n. A Vaishnava name for a saint. The Alwars or saints were twelve in number and are considered to have been incarnations of the attendants, arms, or insignia of Vishnu: each of them wrote a portion of the "Dravida Prabandham," or "Tamil Veda" held in greater veneration than the original Sanskrit Veda, of which it is, in fact, an ancient Tamil translation (Ellis.) The భరమరాజీవిలా సము is a history of these personages. A hawk is sometimes called కరుణాశ్వరు.

ఆవ *ava*. [Tel.] n. A flat or marsh glebe, low ground. A lake. Mustard seed. Recollection. **ఆవపారు** *ava-paru*. [Tel.] v. i. To come to recollection. జ్ఞప్తికివచ్చు. అది నాకు అవపారదు I do not recollect it. అన్నా విన కోకనటమటిల్లు they were sick at heart. V. P. ii. 58. **ఆవకాయ** *ava-kaya*. n. Mango pickle made with mustard seed and oil. తెల్లఆవాలు *Brassica alba*, or, the white mustard. నల్లఆవాలు *Brassica dichotoma*. ఆవాలు *Brassica nigra*, the black or true mustard (Watts.) **ఆవంత** *avanta*. [ఆవ+అంత] n. A very little, a mere grain: as much as a mustard seed. రవంత.

ఆవజము *avazamu*. [Tel.] n. A brazen kettle drum. రుంజ. B. ii. 88. A. iv. 36. H. iii. 38.

ఆవటము *avaṭamu*. [Tel.] n. Manner, good style, mode. నూతికట్టకడన అవటమున in peril, *like* a pitcher on the brink of a well. అవటముగశయ్యదీర్చి (G. v. 60.) Arranging his bed properly. "శేతిలీరావటములారొచె ను!" Velag. iii. 95. **ఆవటించు** *avaṭintsu*. To take, live upon. వాడు గాలి ఆవటించి బ్రతికెను. P. iv. 53. He lived upon mere air: he starved. To help (one to food or to drink.) To serve up a meal. See Vasu. iii. 162. **ఆవటిల్లు** *avaṭillu*. v. n. To be confused. కలగు. కలతనొందు.

ఆవడ or **ఏరావడ** *avaḍa*. [Tel.] n. A sort of cucumber. ఆవడదీర a bitter cucumber. చేదుబీర.

ఆవడి or **కోవడి** *avaḍi*. [Tel.] n. Danger, harm, peril. ఉపద్రవము, హాని.

ఆవము *avamu*. [Tel.] n. A potter's kiln. కాళ్ల ఆవము a "kiln on logs," i.e., one built with interstices through which fuel is supplied. వంటిబిరుసావము 'a shed kiln,' one built solid on a layer of fuel, pots or tiles. Vish ii. 58.

ఆవరణము *avaranamu*. [Skt.] n. A precinct, premises, enclosure, compound; space enclosed round a house or garden. **ఆవరించు** or **ఆవరించుకొను** *avarintsu*. v. t. To surround, hem in. To cover all over as a creeping plant or grass does. చుట్టుకొను.

ఆవర్జా *avarza*. [H.] A journal; a diary. దినవహి; a cash book; the distribution of items of account under appropriate heads.

ఆవర్తము *avartamu*. [Skt.] n. A whirlpool; also (metaphorically) a curl of hair. **ఆవర్తనము** or **ఆవర్తము** *avartanamu*. n. Repetition of a lesson, doing again. పాఠముచెప్పుకొను వల్లె.

ఆవర్తి *avarti*. [Skt.] Corrupted from ఆవృత్తి. (q. v.)

ఆవల *avala*. [Tel. ఆ+వలను lit. that side.] adv. Beyond. (See ఆవలిు.) ఎనిమిదియేండ్లకు ఆవలనో యీవలనో eight years ago more or less. ఆవలయీవల both before and after. ఆవలికి ఆవల further and further.

ఆవలి or **ఆవళి** *avali*. [Skt.] n. Range, row, line, assembly. కేశావళి tresses.

ఆవలించు *avalintsu*. [Tel.] v. n. To yawn, to gape. **ఆవలింత** *avalinta*. n. Yawning.

ఆవశ్యకము *a-vasyakamu*. [Skt.] n. Necessity, need. అక్కర. ఆవశ్యకమైనపని an inevitable act.

ఆవహము *a-vahamu*. [Skt.] adj. That which produces. కలిగించునది. భయావహము producing or causing fear. **ఆవహించు** or **ఆవహిల్లు** *avahintsu*. v. n. To arise in the mind, as joy or any passion. To enter as a spirit into the body, the spirit of a deity to possess an idol. వానిని పిశాచము ఆవహించినది a devil seized him.

ఆవాలము or **ఆవాపము** *avalamu*. [Skt.] n. A basin for water round the foot of a tree. పాదు. ఆలవాలము.

ఆవాలు *avalu*. [Tel.] n. Mustard seed. See under ఆవ.

ఆవాసము *a-vasamu*. [Skt.] n. A house. పురుగులకు రత్నకంబళ్లు ఆవాసములు Woollens harbour insects.

ఆవాహనము *âvâhanamu*. [Skt.] n. Calling, attraction (as opposed to విసర్జనము repulsion.) The invocation (of the deity or evil spirits by mystical words, the bringing down the spirit of a god into an image).

ఆవి *âvi*. [Tel.] n. Steam, vapour. ఆవిరి. Heat. తాపము. M. v. iii. 39. To breathe into a handkerchief and put it to the eye to relieve pain. **ఆవించు** *âvintsu*. v. t. To cook in steam. **ఆవిపట్టు** *âvi-pattu*. v. t. To inhale steam or to pass steam over.

ఆవిడ or **ఆవిడె** *âvida*. [Tel. ఆ+ఇద్ది] pron. She, that woman: as opposed ఈవిడ.

ఆవిరి *âviri*. [Tel.] n. Steam, vapour, exhalation, the heat of the breath. **ఆవిరిల్లు** *âvirillu*. v. n. To sweat, to steam, to moisten. చెమర్చు.

ఆవిర్భవించు *âvirbhavintsu*. [Skt.] v. i. To be produced, generated or born. పుట్టు. **ఆవిర్భవము** or **ఆవిర్భావము** *âvirbhavamu*. n Birth, origin. **ఆవిర్భూతము** *âvirbhûtamu*. adj. Produced. పుట్టిన.

ఆవిలము *âvilamu*. [Skt.] adj. Agitated, turbid. కలతనొందినది. మోహావిలుడు eager with desire. కోపావిలుడు agitated with anger.

ఆవిలి *âvili*. [Tel.] n. A still, used by chemists.

ఆవిష్కృతము *âvishkritamu*. [Skt.] adj. Evident, manifest, undisguised.

ఆవు *âvu*. [Tel.] n. A cow. Plu. ఆవులు or ఆలు. Cows, kine.

ఆవురాకులు *âvurâkulu*. [Tel.] n. Bulrushes. Swa. iv. 92.

ఆవురుమను *âvuru-m-anu*. [Tel.] v. n. To weep; literally, to cry 'Alas;' ఆవురుమని యేడ్చె she wept bitterly.

ఆవులించు *âvulintsu*. See. ఆవలించు.

ఆవృతము *â-vritamu*. [Skt.] adj Enclosed, surrounded.

ఆవృత్తి *âvritti*. [Skt.] n. A time, see ఆవృత్తి. ఒక ఆవృత్తి once. రెండావృత్తులు. twice.

ఆవేగము *â-vêgamu*. [Skt.] n. Haste, hurry, anger. కోపము, పాటు

ఆవేదనము *â-vêdanamu*. [Skt.] n. Making known. తెలుపుట. **ఆవేదించు** *âvêdintsu*. v. t. To make known. తెలియజేయు. A. iii. 60. **ఆవేదితము** *âvêditamu*. adj. Made known, communicated. తెలియజేయబడిన.

ఆవేశము *âvêsamu*. [Skt.] n. Possession. Inspiration (by the deity), possession (by evil spirits), fury, demoniac frenzy. వానికి ఆవేశము వచ్చినది he is possessed. **ఆవేశనము** *âvêsanamu*. n. A manufactory or workshop పట్టడ. **ఆవేశించు** *âvêsintsu*. v. a. To enter in, to possess (as a demon does.) ప్రవేశించు, చొచ్చు. **ఆవేష్టకము** *âvêshtakamu*. n. A hedge, fence or enclosure. ముండ్లకంచె.

ఆశ *âsa*. [Skt.] n. Love, attachment, desire, wish, hope, passion, inclination, curiosity, avarice. ఆశాపాశము or ఆశాబంధము the chain of our lusts, fleshly ties. **ఆశకొలుపు** *âsa-kolupu*. v. t. To cause to desire, to allure, tempt, incite, encourage, to hold out prospects. **ఆశపడు** *âsa-padu*. To desire, covet, long for. **ఆశాపాతకుడు** *âsâ-pâtakudu*. n. A covetous man. **ఆశపెట్టు** *âsa-pettu*. To raise hopes or expectations, give hopes, tantalize. **ఆశాబంధము** *âsâ-bandhamu*. n. The bond of love or desire.

ఆశ *âsa*. [Skt.] n. Quarter, region, point of the heavens. దిక్కు.

ఆశయము *âsayamu*. [Skt.] n. Meaning, intention, mind. అభిప్రాయము.

ఆశాసించు *âsâsintsu*. [Skt.] v. a. To bless. ఆశీర్వదించు.

ఆశి *âsi*. [Skt.] n. A serpent's fang. పాము కొక్కి కోర.

ఆశించు *âsintsu*. [Skt. from ఆశ] n. To love, wish for, covet. ఆపేక్షించు.

ఆశీర్వచనము, ఆశీర్వాదము *āsīr-vachanamu.* [Skt.] n. A blessing or benediction. **ఆశీర్వదించు** *āsīrvadintsu.* v. a. To bless, give a benediction. **ఆశీస్సు** *āsīssu.* n. A blessing.

ఆశీవిషము *āsī-vishamu.* [Skt.] n. 'Venom fanged', i. e., a serpent. పాము.

ఆశుగము *āsugamu.* [Skt.] n. Wind, an arrow. గాలి, బాణము.

ఆశువు *āsuvu.* [Skt.] n. Speed. **ఆశుకవిత్వము** or **ఆశుధారాకవిత్వము** *āsu-kavitvamu.* n. Extempore poetry. ఆశుకవిత్వము చెప్పు to improvise verses.

ఆశౌచము *ā-sauchamu.* [Skt. అశుచి] n. Pollution. అంటు. Mourning on the death of a relative; or imaginary pollution proceeding from the birth of a child; మయిల, సూతకము, (శేర) పురుడు. The former is commonly termed మృతాశౌచము the latter జాతాశౌచము. Hence ఆశౌచముపట్టు to go into mourning.

ఆశ్చర్యము *āscharyamu.* [Skt] n. Wonder, admiration. **ఆశ్చర్యము** adj. Miraculous, marvellous. **ఆశ్చర్యపడు** *ascharya-padu.* v. n. To wonder, be surprised.

ఆశ్రమము *āsramamu.* [Skt.] n. Abode, cell, hermitage, retreat (equivalent to a Living, rectory or see). State, stage, period or time of life from a religious point of view. There are four such stages, viz, 1. బ్రహ్మచర్యము bachelorhood or studentship. 2. గార్హస్థ్యము householdership or being head of a family. 3. వానప్రస్థము being an anchorite. 4. సన్న్యాసము being a recluse. ఆశ్రమధర్మము the duties peculiar to each stage of life. ఆశ్రమస్వీకారము *āsrama-svikāramu.* n. Embracing the ascetic condition: bidding farewell to the world.

ఆశ్రయము *āsrayamu.* [Skt.] n. Support, asylum, refuge, retreat, place of safety, protection, patronage, countenance. అండ, బలవంతు నాశ్రయించుట, ఇల్లు. **ఆశ్రయాశుడు** *āsray-āsudu.* n. The god of fire, because he *eats* or destroys one's abode. **ఆశ్రయించు** *āsray-intsu.* n. To take refuge, to depend upon or have recourse to, to court, to follow. అనుసరించు, అండగొను. ఈ ప్రతిభేదమును ఆశ్రయించినాడు he adopted this reading. **ఆశ్రితము** *āsritamu.* adj. Dependent on. **ఆశ్రితుడు** *āsritudu* n. One who is looked up to for help. ఆశ్రయింపబడినవాడు.

ఆశ్లేష, ఆశ్లేషానక్షత్రము *ā-slēsha.* [Skt.] n. The ninth lunar mansion, containing five stars.

ఆశ్లేషము *ā-slēshamu.* [Skt.] n. An embrace. **ఆశ్లేషించు** *āslēshintsu.* v. a. To embrace; to clasp. కవుగిలించు. **ఆశ్లిష్టము** *ā-slishtamu.* adj. Embraced.

ఆశ్వయుజము or **ఆశ్వినము** *āsvayujamu.* [Skt.] n. The name of the seventh month.

ఆశ్వాసము or **ఆశ్వాసనము** *āsvāsamu.* [Skt. lit. taking breath or rest.] n. A chapter or section; a canto. Consolation. ఊరట. **ఆశ్వాసించు** *āsvāsintsu.* v. n. To console, to comfort. ఊరడించు.

ఆశ్వినము *āsvinamu.* [Skt.] n. A day's journey for a horse.

ఆషాఢము *āshādhamu.* [Skt.] n. The name of a month, June—July. The name of a tree called మోదుగు. A iv. 142. **ఆషాఢభూతి** *āshādha-bhuti.* [Skt. from ఆషాఢ= మోదుగకోల.] n. A cheat, a swindler. P. i. 224.

ఆస *āsa.* Same as ఆశ. (q. v.)

"ఆసకుమేఁ లేదు కనకాద్రి
సమానధనంబుకూర్చినన్
కాసును వెంటరాదు, కనికానక
చేసినపుణ్యపాపముల్
వీసరపోవు."

ఆసచేయు or **ఆసపడు** or **ఆసించు** *āsacheyu.* [Tel.] v. i. To desire. ఆశించు.

ఆసకప్పిరగాడు or **ఆసకప్పెరగాడు** *āsa-kappira-gadu.* [Tel.] n. The goatsucker or night-jar, caprimul-gus. F. B. J. Vol. iii. 182. et. seq. గుండుములుపుగాడు.

ఆసక్తి *ā-sakti.* [Skt.] n. Love, attachment, inclination, longing, whim. ఆస. Diligence. శ్రద్ధ. **ఆసక్తము** *ā-saktamu.* adj. Inclined to, devoted to one object, diligent, active, addicted to. **ఆసక్తుడు** *ā-saktudu.* n. An aspirant, devotee, lover. A man of diligence. ఆసక్తికలవాడు.

ఆసనము *ā-sanamu.* [Skt.] n. A seat: a posture or mode of sitting and kneeling, as పద్మాసనము.

ఆసరా or **ఆస్రా** or **ఆసాము** *āsarā.* [H. from Skt. ఆశ్రయము]. n. Shelter, support, protection, patronage. ప్రాపు, అదుపు, ఆధారము. ఆ ఊరికి నీళ్ల ఆసరాలేదు the village has no resources for watering the lands.

ఆసన్నము *ā-sannamu.* [Skt.] adj. At hand, near, proximate, ready, prepared. దాపైన. ఆసన్నప్రసవగర్భవతి on the point of bringing forth, about to be confined.

ఆసవము *āsavamu.* [Skt.] n. Toddy, palm-wine. కల్లు, సారాయి. (a generic term for all spirituous liquors.)

ఆసాదించు *āsādintsu.* [Skt.] v. i. To obtain. పొందు, ప్రాపించు.

ఆసామి *āsāmi.* [H.] n. An individual. ఆసామివారీగా with each individual in order.

ఆసాయము *āsāyamu.* [H.] adv. The live long day, all day long, till evening.

ఆసారము *āsāramu.* [Skt.] n. A hard shower. జడివాన, వడిగలవాన. Vasu. iv. 13.

ఆసీనము *āsīnamu.* [Skt.] adj. Sitting, seated. **ఆసీనుడు** *āsīnudu.* n. He who is seated. ఆసీనులైన they who are seated.

ఆసు [Eng. *ace.*] n. The ace in the game of cards. కాగితాల ఆటలో ఒంటిచుక్కగల కాగితము.

ఆసు *āsu.* [Tel.] n. Three or five sticks in a line, fixed in the ground, on which thread is so wound as to form the figure of 8; (used in preparing the web for the loom.)

ఆసుకోవి *āsu-kōvi.* [Tel.] n. A stick through which the thread thus placed is passed. **ఆసుపోయు** *āsu-pōyu.* v. i. To pass this thread through the ఆసుకోవి: (in so placing it they run backwards and forwards, and hence) ఆసుపోసినట్లు denotes, backwards and forwards: this way and that way. ఇటుఅటుదారము తిప్పినట్లు. **ఆసుమాను** *āsu-mānu.* n. A frame work used to adjust the thread. నూలుపోగు పోయించుటకు వాడేచట్టము.

ఆసురము *ā-suramu.* [Skt. from అసుర.] n. The Asura's fashion: the custom of the Asuras, such as rapine, murder, and violence ఆసురవివాహము. The marriage custom of the Asuras, by which the bride was purchased. **ఆసురి** *āsuri.* n. A female Asura.

ఆసె *āse.* [Tel.] n. Cutaneous and herpetic eruptions. దద్దురురోగము, ఒళ్లంతా దద్దురులు వచ్చురోగము.

ఆసేకము *āsēkamu.* [Skt.] n. Sprinkling water. నీళ్లుచల్లుట.

ఆసేధము *āsēdhamu.* [Skt.] n. Check, restraint. అడ్డగింత. Arrest: legal restraint; limitation of four kinds, viz.; కాలాసేధము limitation of time, స్థానాసేధము confinement to a place, ప్రవాసాసేధము prohibition against removal or departure, కర్మాసేధము restriction from employment.

ఆసోదా *āsōdā.* [H.] n. Rest, refreshment.

ఆస్తరణము *āstaraṇamu.* [Skt.] n. A coverlet, a covering, a seat on an elephant. దర్భాస్తరణము a seat or bed of sacred grass.

ఆస్తి *āsti.* [Skt.] n. Property, effects, wealth, capital, riches, estate. **ఆస్తికాడు** *asti-kādu.* n. A rich person. **ఆస్తికాపు** *asti-kāpu.* n. A substantial farmer. ఆస్తిపాస్తి goods and chattels, స్థిరాస్తి immovable property, చరాస్తి movable property. **ఆస్తిమంతుడు** *asti-mantudu.* n. A man of property; a rich man.

ఆస్తికుడు *āstikuḍu*. [Skt. from అస్ to be] n. A believer in a god, one who acknowledges the existence of God, in opposition to నాస్తికుడు an atheist. ఆస్తిక్యము *āstikyamu*. n. Belief in the existence of God. Theism. ఈశ్వరుడు గలడనడము.

ఆస్థ *āstha*. [Skt.] n. Bent or inclination, Wish, desire, fondness. Effort, diligence. ప్రయత్నము. Studiousness. శ్రద్ధ, ఆశ, ఆసక్తి.

ఆస్థానము *ā-sthānamu*. [Skt.] n. Court, hall: సభ, రాజసభ.

ఆస్పదము *āspadamu*. [Skt.] n. Place, room, situation: basis, ground for a supposition. సందేహాస్పదమైన doubtful. వ్యాజ్యాస్పదమైన disputed.

ఆస్ఫాలనము *ā-sphālanamu*. [Skt.] n. The flapping of an elephant's ears. ఆస్ఫాలితము *āsphālitamu*. adj. Flapped.

ఆస్ఫోటనము *ā-sphōṭanamu*. [Skt.] n. Expanding, blowing. ఆస్ఫోటించు *āsphōṭintsu*. v. t. To give a slap to. చరచు. To butt. పొడుచు. To split. చీల్చు. (రామా: యుద్ధ.)

ఆస్యము *āsyamu*. [Skt.] n. The face, the mouth. ముఖము, నోరు.

ఆస్వాదనము *ā-svādanamu*. [Skt.] n. Feasting, eating, enjoying. తినడము, అనుభవించడము. ఆస్వాదించు *āsvādintsu*. v. a. To taste, eat. రుచిచూచు, తిను.

ఆహా *āhā*. [Tel.] Interj. denoting surprise, Ah!

ఆహాకము *āhakamu*. [Tel. for ఆధకము.] n. Pledge. కుదువ. Harischandra ii. [Skt.] n. A disease that affects the nose. ముక్కునకు కలుగు ఒక రోగము.

ఆహతము *ā-hatamu*. [Skt.] adj. Beaten. కొట్టబడిన.

ఆహరించు *āharintsu*. [Skt.] v. t. To rob. అపహరించు; to attract. ఆకర్షించు. To eat as food. ఆరగించు. ఆహర్త *āharta*. n. One who eats. ఆహరించువాడు.

ఆహవనము *āhavanamu*. [Skt.] n. A sacrifice. యజ్ఞము. ఆహవనీయము *āhavanīyamu*. n. One of the three consecrated fires in the grand Hindu sacrifice. It is lighted from the house-holder's perpetual fire; and is prepared for receiving oblations.

ఆహవము *āhavamu*. [Skt.] n. War, battle. యుద్ధము.

ఆహా *āhā*. [Tel.] Interj. Ah! Aha!

ఆహారము *āhāramu*. [Skt.] n. Food, nourishment. ఆహారములు viands, foods. ఆహారి *āhāri*. The eater: one who feeds on. ఆహారించు *āhārintsu*. v. t. To eat, partake of food. ఆరగించు. ఆహార్యము *āhāryamu*. adj. That which is to be understood or supplied in an ellipsis. తెచ్చుకొనదగిన.

ఆహికము *āhikamu*. [Skt.] n. An intermittent fever. విడిచివిడిచివచ్చు జ్వరము.

ఆహుతి *ā-huti*. [Skt.] n. Offering, oblation. What is offered by means of fire.

ఆహో *āhō*. [Tel.] Oh! A. vi. 5. ఆహోపురుషిక *āhō-purushika*. [Skt.] n. Boasting, vaunting.

ఆహ్నికక్రియలు *āhnika-kriyalu*. [Skt. from అహస్సు.] n. Rites or religious duties, to be done in *the day time*: పగలు చేయదగిన క్రియలు.

ఆహ్లాదము *āhlādamu*. [Skt.] n. Delight, pleasure. సంతోషము.

ఆహ్వ or ఆహ్వయము *āhva*. [Skt.] n. Name, title. పేరు.

ఆహ్వానము *āhvānamu*. [Skt.] n. A summons: calling. పిలుపు.

ఇ i

ఇ The vowel I as in 'ill.' The initial form ఇ is usually changed into యి yi especially when there is no sandhi, thus: ఇల్లు *illu*, a house, is written యిల్లు yillu.

ఇంక *inka*. [Tel.] adv. More, yet more, still yet. As yet, till now, hitherto, hereafter, presently. Henceforth. ఇంకరా come along, come further. ఇంక చూడు look further! ఇంకా Same as ఇంక.

ఇంకి *inki*. [Eng. ink]. n. Ink. మసి, సిరా.

ఇంకు *inku*. [Tel. a form of ఇసుకు.] v. n. To dry up, sink as water. ఇసుకు. ఇంకుడు *inkuḍu*. n. Drying up. ఇంకుటు. adj. Dried up. ఇంకిన.

ఇంగము *ingamu*. [Skt.] n. Hint, sign, indication of sentiment by gesture. అభిప్రాయము.

ఇంగలము or ఇంగాలము *ingalamu*. [Prakrit from Skt. అంగార] n. A coal, charcoal. బొగ్గు.

ఇంగితము *ingitamu*. [Skt.] n. Hint, sign, gesture, symptom. Intention, purpose, inclination. ఆకారైరైవ చతురాస్తర్క్యయంతి పరేంగితం, గర్భస్థం కేతకీపుష్ప మామోదదేనైవ షట్పదాః. From the countenance the wise discover the *disposition* as bees discover the unblown lily by its scent. ఇంగితజ్ఞుడు penetrating, skilful in reading a man's character, one who sees the heart. పరేంగితము knowledge of another's intention.

ఇంగిలము Same as ఇంగలము.

ఇంగిలాయి *ingilāyi* [Tel.] n. A sort of fish, the thorny eel, *(platystachys anguillaris.)* గడ్డియింగిలాయి the fish called *scaurus viridis*.

ఇంగిలికము or ఇంగిలీకము *ingilikamu*. [from Skt. హింగుళము] n. Vermilion, brick-colour. A medicinal drug, levigated cinnabar. (Ainslie.)

ఇంగుడి *inguḍi*. [Tel.] n. The plant called *Terminalia Calappa*. గారచెట్టు, తాపసతరువు.

ఇంగువ *inguva*. [Tel.] n. Asafœtida.

ఇంచిమంచి *inchi-manchi*. [Tel.] n. Sweets. నోటికి రుచిగానుండుటకై తినే చిరితిండి. "తినకు నిమకూలమను నొక్కచాసితోడ, మాటిమియొనర్చి కొని యించిమంచిపెట్టి." శుక: iii. 260.

ఇంచు *intsu*. [Tel. Skt. ఇక్షు seems to be derived from this word.] n. Sugar-cane. adj. Sweet, pleasant. ఇంపైన, మనోజ్ఞమైన. ఇంచుపాలకడలి *intsu-pāla-kaḍali*. n. The sea of sugar. ఇక్షుసముద్రము. ఇంచుబోడి or బోటి *intsu-bōḍi*. n. A beauty, a lady. ఇంచుమాను *intsu-mānu*. n. The sugar-cane. ఇంచువిల్తుడు *intsu-viltuḍu*. n. The Indian Cupid whose 'bow is made of the sugar-cane.'

ఇంచు *intsu*. [Tel.] v. a. To increase. హెచ్చు. P. i. 198. Dasav. ix. 47. Parij. ii. 6. To wish. కోరు.

ఇంచు *intsu*. [Tel.] adj. Small. ఇంచుమించుగా less or more.

ఇంచుక *intsuka*. [Tel.] adj. A little, even the least, petty. కొంచెము.

ఇంజేరు or ఇంజేరుగడ్డ *injēru*. [Tel.] n. A certain root. ఒకవిధమైన కంద.

ఇంట *inṭa*. [Tel. from ఇల్లు. (q. v.) reckoning or counting being made by means of squares.] affix. By, at the rate of. నాలుగింట గుణించుట to reckon or multiply by four. ఇంటికి *inṭi-ki*. At the rate of. అయిదింటికి at five; by fives, five at once. ఒకటింటికి పదిరూకలు ఇస్తిని I gave ten rupees for each. గజమొకటింటికి ఎంత how much is it per yard. నలుబదియింటికి వచ్చిరి about forty men came. నూరింటికి one hundred in number.

ఇంటరము *inṭaramu*. [Tel.] n. Narrowness. Difficulty. ఇరుకు, సంకటము. (భా. ఉద్యో. iv.)

ఇంటి *inṭi*. [Tel. from ఇల్లు] adj. Of the house ఇంటిదియొక్క. ఇంటికాపు *inṭi-kāpu*. n. A householder, a married man. గృహస్థుడు. ఇంటిపట్టు *inṭi-paṭṭu*. n. The place near the house. The state of being a householder or married man. గృహస్థత్వము. ఇంటిపాప *inṭi-pāpa*. n. A slave girl. ఇలుకుత్తుక దాసి. ఇంటిపేరు *inṭi-pēru*. n. The family or house name.

ఇంటియాతడు or ఇంటిఆయన inti-yatadu. n. The husband. పెనిమిటి. ఇంటిల్లిపాది intilli-padi. [ఇల్లు + ఎల్ల + (ప) + అది] n. All the family. కుటుంబమువారందరు. See ఇల్లు.

ఇంత్రము intramu. [Tel.] Same as ఇంబు రము. ఇంత్రుపడు intra-padu. v. i. To be in difficulties, to suffer. సంకటపడు.

ఇండు indu. [Tel.] v. plural imperative of ఇచ్చు. Give ye: ఇయ్యుడు or ఇయ్యండి.

ఇండె inde. [Tel.] n. A crack, a split. చీలిక. ఇండెపోయిన split, cracked. ఇండెపోయు to split. చీలు.

ఇంత inta. [Tel. ఇ+అంత] adj. This much, so large as this. ఇంతమట్టుకు thus far; as yet. ఇంతకు and beside all this. ఇంతలో meanwhile. ఇంతకుమున్ను, ఇంతకుపూర్వము heretofore. ఇకయింత this much more. ఇంతదాక all this while, thus far. ఇంతచెడ్డ so bad. ఇంతపొడుగు so long. ఇంతలేసి కన్నులు eyes so large. ఇంతలేసి పనులు such great works. నాలుగింతలు four times as much. ఇంతా అంతా కాదు it is vastly great, lit. it is not so much nor so much. వాడు పడ్డ ప్రయాసము ఇంతింతకాదు the trouble he is in is beyond telling. ఇంతింత దొంగకాడు he is no common rogue. ఇంతట intata. adv. With this. ఇంతలోగా within this time. ఇంతటి such. ఇంతవట్టు inta-vattu. All this. ఇది అంతే యును. ఇంతమాత్రము. ఇంతేను, or ఇంతే only this much; that's all ఇంతమాత్రమే, ఇంతయినాగాని and notwithstanding all. ఇంతేకాకుండా and besides all this.

ఇంతి inti. [Tel.] n. Woman. స్త్రీ.

ఇండ or ఇండము inda. [Tel.] Lo here! take it, here it is, come and take. ఇదిగో తీసి కొనుము. ఇదండి here it is! take it, sir. రామా. iv.

ఇందరు indaru. [Tel. ఇంత+వారు] pron. So many persons.

ఇందాక or ఇందనుక indaka. [Tel. ఇంత+ వినుక] adv. Thus far, hitherto, just now (past time), already, up to this place, up to this time, until now, so long. ఇంత వరకు. ఇందాక ఉండునా will it be thus far? ఇందాకటి ప్రశ్న the preceding question ఇందాకటివాడు the man that was here just now.

ఇంది, ఇందిర indi. [Skt.] n. Lakshmi. లక్ష్మి.

ఇందిందిరము ind-indiramu. [Skt.] n. A large kind of bee. తుమ్మెద.

ఇందీవరము indivaramu. [Skt.] n. The blue lotus.

ఇందు indu. [Tel.] v. n. To stay, remain, dwell. To be contained in. ఇముడు, అడగు.

ఇందు [Tel.] (pron.) This place. ఈచోటు. (See అందు) ఇందుకు for this ఇందులకు. hither ఇప్పటికి; for this దీనికి. ఇందు in this, herein. ఇందువల్ల by this. ఇందుకింద under this. ఇందుమీద upon this. ఇందు తెమ్ము bring it hither. ఇందునందులేడు he is neither here nor there.

ఇందు or ఇందువు indu. [Tel.] The clearing nut. చిల్లగింజ.

ఇందుడు indudu. [Skt.] n. The moon. చంద్రుడు, చేందమామ ఇందువారము indu-varamu. Monday. సోమవారము.

ఇందుప్పు ind-uppu. [Tel. ఇందు (the Indus) +ఉప్పు] n. Rock-salt. సైంధవలవణము.

ఇంద్ర indra. [Skt.] n. The god Indra. ఇంద్రకీలము indrakilamu. n. A certain mountain మందరగిరి. ఇంద్రగోపము indra-gopamu. n. A cochineal insect, a red insect belonging to the mite family. చందమామపురుగు; same as ఆరుద్రపురుగు. (q. v.) ఇంద్రజాలము indra-jalamu. n. Juggling, conjuring. ఇంద్రజాలవిద్య sleight of hand. కనుకట్టువిద్య. ఇంద్రజాలికుడు indra-jali-kudu. n. A conjurer or juggler. ఇంద్రజిత్తు indra-jittu. n. Name of the son of Rāvaṇa. ఇంద్రధనుస్సు indra-dhanussu. "The bow of Indra." The rainbow. ఇంద్రనీలము or ఇంద్రశిల indra-nilamu. n. A sapphire. నీలమణి, నల్ల

రాయి. Vasu. iv. 129. **ఇంద్రలోకము** *indra-lōkamu.* n. The heaven of Indra. Fairyland. **ఇంద్రాణి** *indrāṇi.* n. Name of the wife of Indra. A sort of bracelet. **ఇంద్రాయుధము** *indr-āyudhamu.* n. The rainbow, a thunderbolt as the weapon of Indra. **ఇంద్రారి** *indr-āri.* (Indra-āri) The foe of Indra. A giant. అసురుడు. **ఇంద్రావరజుడు** *indra-varajuḍu.* Vishṇu.

ఇంద్రియము *indriyamu.* [Skt.] n. An organ of sense. జ్ఞానేంద్రియములు organs of perception, కర్మేంద్రియములు organs of action, and అంతరింద్రియములు the internal organs, the first includes the eye, ear, nose, tongue, and skin; the second, the organ of speech, or larynx, hand, foot, and the organs of generation. The last are మనసు the mind or organ of thought; బుద్ధి the organ of apprehension, అహంకారము the organ of self-knowledge or consciousness, and చిత్తము the heart or organ of feeling. ఇంద్రియవృత్తి the natural propensities. పంచేంద్రియములు the five organs of sense. పంచేంద్రియబద్ధుడు the sensual man, one who is a slave to his lusts.

ఇంద్రుడు *indruḍu.* [Skt.] n. Indra, the god of the sky corresponding to the Roman Jupiter armed with thunderbolts and noted for his amours. In composition the word denotes excellence. గజేంద్రము or గజేంద్రుడు a noble elephant.

ఇంధనము *indhanamu.* [Skt.] n. Fuel, firewood. చిదుగు, వంటచెఱకు.

ఇంపు or **ఇంబు** *impu.* [Tel.] n. Fulness, satisfaction, ease. Fondness, liking. 'కంటికింపైతే కడుపుకింపు' that which pleases the eye pleases the appetite. ఇంపైన pleasing, comfortable. **ఇంపితము** *impitamu.* [ఇంపు+ఇతము] adj. Pleasant. ఇంపైన. **ఇంపుగా** or **ఇంపెసలార** Finely, sweetly, nobly. Suitably, pleasantly. **ఇంపొలయు** *impolayu.* [ఇంపు+ఒలయు] v. n. To suit, to be pleasing.

ఇక or **ఇంక** or **ఇకమీదట** or **ఇగ** *ika.* [Tel.] adv. Yet, still, further, hereafter, henceforth, then, next, in future, presently, soon. ఇకయెందుకు why now? ఇక వెళ్లు now you had better go.

ఇక్క *ikka.* [Tel.] n. Place, home, dwelling. "చక్కదనాలయిక్క" (T. iv. 85.) she was the very home of the graces. ఒక్కయిక్క in one direction. మోవిక్క the lip. అధరమండలము.

ఇక్కట్టు *ikkaṭṭu.* [Tel. ఇరుకు+కట్టు.] n. Difficulty, intricacy. సంకటము.

ఇక్కడ *ik-kaḍa.* [Tel. ఈ+కడ] adv. Here: in this place.

ఇక్కము *ikkamu.* [Tel. another form of ఇరుకటము] n. A narrow place. ఇరుకుచోటు.

ఇక్కరించు *ikkarintsu.* [Tel.] v. n. To blink, look hard at.

ఇక్కుపాటు *ikku-pāṭu.* [Tel. ఇక్కు=ఇరుకు.] n. Difficulty. ఇక్కట్టు.

ఇక్కువ *ikkuva.* [Tel.] n. A place: చోటు. a secret: a secret part. జీవస్థానము. Trace. జాడ. Machination, internal agency. R. ii. 102.

ఇక్తియారు *iktiyāru.* [H.] n. Will, pleasure, choice, liberty. స్వతంత్రత, యిచ్ఛ.

ఇక్షువు *ikshuvu.* [Skt. prob. der. from Tel. ఇంచు. q. v.] n. Sugarcane. చెరుకు. **ఇక్షుఖండము** *ikshu-khaṇḍamu.* n. A bit of sugarcane. **ఇక్షుదండము** *ikshu-daṇḍamu.* n. A stalk or stem of sugarcane. **ఇక్షువనము** *ikshu-vanamu.* n. A sugarcane plantation. **ఇక్షుధన్వుడు** or **ఇక్షుశరాసనుడు** *ikshu-dhanvuḍu.* n. Cupid, the god of love (whose bow is made of the sugarcane).

ఇగము or **ఇమము** *igamu.* [from Skt. హిమము] n. Moisture, dew, frost. శీతము.

ఇగిరిక *igirika.* [Tel. from ఇగురు] n. Boiled rice from which the water is not drawn off but evaporated so that no gruel is formed. అత్తెసరన్నము, అత్తెసరు.

ఇగిలించు *igilintsu.* [Tel.] v. n. To grin. ఇగిలింత or ఇగిలింపు *igilinta.* n. A grin. పండ్లను వెలికిబెట్టుట.

ఇగురు *iguru.* [Tel.] v. n. To evaporate. ఇంకు. ఇగరబెట్టు to cause to dry up by boiling. To dry up.

ఇగురు *iguru.* [Tel.] n. A sprout or young leaf: the red gums of the mouth. చిగురు. ఇగురుకూర *iguru-kūra.* n. A kind of curry. ఇగురుబోడి *iguru-bōḍi.* n. A blooming girl. ఇగురొత్తు *igur-ottu.* v. n. To bud or blossom, to bloom. చిగిరించు. "కోపమిగురొత్తగా" with a burst of displeasure. ఇగుర్చు or ఇగురుచు or ఇగిరించు *igurtsu.* [Tel. from ఇగురు (q. v.) v. a. To dry up, decrease, do away with. నశింపచేయు. "ఈ దవానజ్వర మిగిరించుతండ్రీ." B.D. vi. 351. To sprout, shoot, bud. చిగిరించు.

ఇగో *egō.* Same as ఇదుగో.

ఇగ్గాముగ్గి *iggā-muggi.* [Tel.] n. Hauling about, struggle, violence.

ఇగ్గు *iggu.* [Tel.] v. a. To pull, haul, drag, jerk, struggle. Subh. ii. 30. To incline to a side or backwards. ఒరుగు, వెనుకకు ఒరుగు. ఇగ్గులాడు *iggul-āḍu.* v. To pull, to jerk, to struggle. ఇగ్గులాట *iggu-l-āṭa.* n. Struggling, jerking, pulling backwords. వెనుకకీడ్చుట.

ఇచట *itsaṭa.* [Tel. ఈ+చోటు] adv. Here. ఇచటి *itsaṭi.* adj. Belonging to this place. (Same as ఇచ్చట or ఇక్కడ.)

ఇచ్చ *ittsa.* [Tadbh. from Skt. ఇచ్ఛ] n. Inclination, fancy, love. ఇచ్చకము *ittsakamu.* n. Cajolery, wheedling, trickery. ఇచ్చకాలమారి a rogue, a flatterer. ఇచ్చకుడు *ittsakuḍu.* n. Flatterer. (A. iv. 48.) ముఖప్రీతిమాటలాడేవాడు. ఇచ్చగించు *ittsa-gintsu.* v. a. To like, fancy.

ఇచ్చట *ittsaṭa.* [Tel. ఈ+చోటు] adv. Here, in this place. Same as ఇచట.

ఇచ్చిపుచ్చుకోలు *ichchi-puttsu-kōlu.* [Tel.] n. giving and taking. Traffic, affinity, matrimonial relationship.

ఇచ్చు *ittsu.* [Tel. from ఇయు.] v. t. To give, to permit, let, allow. చేయనిచ్చిరి they let (him) do so. పోనిచ్చిరి they let (him) go. పోనీ or పోనిమ్ము let it pass. చూడనీ or చూడనిమ్ము let me see it. రానీ or రానిమ్ము let it, or them, &c., come నన్ను రానిచ్చినారు కారు they did not let me come. కానీ or కానిమ్ము let it be so, he it so. మరియొక అర్థమిస్తున్నది it gives another meaning. మనసిచ్చు to give the heart, consent, listen. ఇయ్యనా or ఇవ్వనా shall I give? ఇప్పించు *ippintsu.* v. a. (The causal of ఇచ్చు) to cause to deliver bestow or grant.

ఇచ్చో, ఇచ్చోట Same as ఇచట.

ఇచ్ఛ *ichcha.* [Skt.] n. Love, wish. స్వేచ్ఛ *svēchcha.* [Skt. స్వ+ఇచ్ఛ] n. One's own inclination, independence. స్వతంత్రత.

ఇజము, ఇజాలు *ijamu.* [corrupted from Skt. బీజము] n. The testicles. వృషణములు.

ఇజారా *izārā.* [H.] n. Farming, renting, a farming of the revenue customs, contract, monopoly. గుత్త. ఇజారాదారుడు *izārā-dāruḍu.* Farmer, renter, contractor.

ఇజారు *izāru.* [H.] n. Trousers. లాగు.

ఇజుకు *izuku.* [Tel.] n. Puzzle, dilemma, distress. సంకటము, శ్రమము.

ఇజ్యుడు *ijyuḍu.* [Skt.] n. The planet Jupiter. బృహస్పతి.

ఇట *iṭa.* [Tel.] adv. Here, in this place. ఇటురా come hither. ఇటుమునుపు heretofore, already. ఇటునుండి from this ఇది మొదలుకొని.

ఇటిక or ఇటికె or ఇటుక *iṭika.* [Tel.] n. Brick. ఇటికెలుకోయు or ఇటుకచేయు to make bricks. ౧౦౦౦ ఇటుకలు కాల్చిరి they burnt 1000 bricks.

ఇటీవల *iṭivala.* [Tel. ఇటు+ఈవల] adv. Since, that time, lately, recently, latterly. ఇటీవల నుండిపోయినరాజు the late king. ఇటీవలి (in the inflexion) subsequent, as ఇటీవలిపనులు the latter operations. ఇటీవలి వివరములు subsequent particulars.

ఇటు *iṭu.* [Tel. lit. this way.] adv. *Thus;* ఇటుకిరము heretofore. **ఇటువంటి** *iṭu-vanṭi.* [Tel. వంటి=వంటివలెనుండు] Such ఇట్టి. ఇటువంటిపనికి to such an affair. See అటువంటి. **ఇటువలె** *iṭu-vale.* Similarly. ఇట్లు.

ఇటుక See ఇటిక.

ఇట్టట్టు *iṭṭaṭṭu.* [Tel. ఇట్టు+అట్టు] adv. This way and that. Fie! O fie! T. iv. 159. Alas! ఇట్టట్టుపడు (A. iv. 87.) to be surprised or shocked.

ఇట్టలము *iṭṭalamu.* [Tel.] adj. Vast, huge, great, abundant. గొప్ప, తరుచు, అధికము, విస్తారము. **ఇట్టలముగా** or **ఇట్టలమున** *iṭṭulam-u-ga.* Vastly, greatly.

"అట్టిదియేలపుట్టునమరాధిప నీవుజగత్ప్రభుండవై
యిట్టలమైన తేజమునపొంచి సుఖంబునుండు."
M. III. v. 241.

ఇట్టి *iṭṭi.* [Tel.] adj. This, like this: such as this. ఇటువంటి.

ఇట్టిక Same as ఇటిక.

ఇట్టిడు *iṭṭiḍu.* [Tel. ఇట్టి+వాడు] n. Such a man. ఇటువంటివాడు. **ఇట్టిది** *iṭṭidi.* This, this sort of. **ఇట్టు** *iṭṭu.* n. This way, adv. Thus. ఇట్లు. **ఇట్టె** *iṭṭe.* adj. Thus, at once. **ఇట్ల** or (ఇట్లు) **ఇట్లా**, **ఇట్లాగు**, *iṭla.* Thus, in this way. ఇట్లారా come here. **ఇట్లాటి** or **ఈలాటి** *iṭlaṭi.* Such. ఇట్లాటి యిండ్లలో in such houses. **ఇట్లు** or **ఇట్టులు** *iṭlu.* adv. Thus, so, in this way.

ఇడ *iḍa.* [Skt.] n. Ground. నేల.

ఇడాఫలము *iḍa-phalamu.* [Skt.] n. The musk orange: a species of citron.

ఇడి or **ఇడికుడుములు** *iḍi* [Tel.] n. A sort of wheat cake. ఒకసారి ఆవిరియుండును ఒక సారి ఎసటుతుకడిన పిండిని సన్నముగా ఒక అచ్చులో పెట్టి ఒత్తు భక్ష్యవిశేషము. సేవియాలు. "బుడుకులు పడుకులు నిడియు జలిమిడియును." కాశీ. vii.

ఇడియు or **ఇడిసిపోవు** *iḍiyu.* [Tel. విను.] v. n. Split, crack, fall to pieces. చీలు, బద్దలగు. To fall in, as a well. ఇడిసినబావి a ruined well. **ఇడియగొట్టు.** *iḍiya-goṭṭu.* To demolish.

ఇడు *iḍu* [Tel.] v. a. To give, offer, place, put, lay. To set, plant. ముల్లిడె. (A. iv. 265.) he *planted* thorns. కుయ్యిడగా uttering a cry. గొడుగిడు hold an umbrella అడ్డమిడు to interpose, place between. పూజలిడు to offer worship: to worship. తాకట్టిడు to pawn. శబ్దమిడు to sound. గంతులిడు to leap

ఇడుగడ *iḍu-gaḍa.* [Tel.] n. Envy. అసూయ. Difficulty. కష్టము.

ఇడుపు *iḍupu.* [Tel. from ఇడియు] n. A breach or crack, a hole. Parij. ii. 44.

ఇడుము *iḍuma.* [Tel.] n. Trouble, evil, misfortune, hardship ఆపద, దుఃఖము. ఇడుము పాటు to suffer trouble. ఇడుములంపడుట. ఇడుములపెట్టు to torment, grieve, plague.

ఇడ్డెన *iḍḍena.* [Tel.] n. A sort of cake వాసెనకుడుము. H. i. 117.

ఇతఃపరము *itah-paramu.* [Skt.] adv. Henceforth. ఇకమీద.

ఇతకరి *ita-kari.* [from Skt. హితకారి] adj. Agreeable, హితమైన.

ఇతడు *itaḍu.* [Tel.] n. He, this man.

ఇతము *itamu.* [from Skt. హితము] adj. Agreeable. హితమైన.

ఇతరము *itaramu.* [Skt.] n. Another thing. **ఇతరము** adj. Other, different. ఇది అన్యాయము యితరముకాదు this is injustice and nothing else. **ఇతరుడు** *itaruḍu.* n. Another man. అన్యుడు.

ఇతవు *itavu.* (from Skt. హితము) n. Liking, agreeableness: ఇష్టము. **ఇతవరి** *hitav-ari.* n. One who says what is agreeable or good. హితముచెప్పువాడు. **ఇతవుడు** *itarudu.* n. A friend. హితుడు.

ఇతి *iti.* [Skt.] A particle meaning 'This.' It shows like the Telugu 'అని' that the preceding words are a quotation, statement or reflection, and takes the place of inverted commas in English. **ఇత్యాది** *ityādi.* [ఇతి+ఆది] And so forth, etcetera. ఇత్యాదులైన పుస్తకములు = and other books. ఇత్యాదికములైన = and the like.

ఇతిహాసము *iti-hāsamu.* [Skt.] n. Ancient story, legend. History: traditional accounts of former events: heroic history, such as the Mahābhārata and the Rāmāyaṇa. పూర్వవృత్తకథ.

ఇత్తడి *ittaḍi.* [Tel.] n. Brass. పిత్తళి.

ఇత్తము *ittamu.* [Tel. from ఇచ్చు.] v. imper. Let us give. ఇచ్చెదము.

ఇత్తిగ *ittiga.* [Tel.] n. A throw at dice in which a pair of threes comes up. పట్టుము.

ఇత్వరుడు *itvaruḍu* [Skt.] n. A poor man. దరిద్రుడు. A low man. నీచుడు. A wicked man. క్రూరకర్ముడు. A wayfarer. బాటసారి.

ఇది *idi.* [Tel.] pron. She, it, this. The 6th case is దీని and the acc. దీనిని as దీని నెరిగించు declare this. The abl. is దీన or దీనిచేత "hereby." plu. ఇవి నాకు చాలా ఇది గానున్నది I am very much out of sorts. ఆ నడతబహుయిదిగా నున్నది that conduct is not the thing, is so and so. **ఇదిగో**, or **ఇదుగో** *idigō* [ఇది+కొమ్ము lit. take this] interj. Look! do you see! behold! here it is! ఇదుగో యిస్తాను అదుగో యిస్తున్నానని అంటాడు he puts me off with empty promises—Lit. Here I will give it, there I will give it, says he. ఇదుగో వస్తానని చెప్పెను or ఇదుగో వచ్చెదనని he promised to return presently. **ఇదె** Same as ఇదిగో.

ఇద్దరి *id-dari.* [Tel. ఈ+దరి] n. This side, bank, or, shore. See దరి and అద్దరి.

ఇద్దరు *iddaru.* [Tel. ఇరు+వారు] adj. or pron. Two persons, both persons. A negative verb requires this is to be translated *neither:* as ఇద్దరినిన్ని రానియ్యవద్దు let neither of them come in.

ఇద్ది Same as ఇది.

ఇద్దుము *id-dumu.* [Tel. ఇరు+తూము] n. The measure called two తూములు. Marked thus in accounts ౨ ౼.

ఇద్దుగ *id-duga.* [Tel ఇరు+దుగ] n. A throw of dice in which a pair of twos comes up.

ఇద్ధము *iddhamu.* [Skt.] adj. Glowing, shining, pure. ప్రకాశము, శుద్ధము. **ఇద్ధచరితుడు** *iddha-charituḍu.* A man of glorious deeds. **ఇద్ధరూపి** *iddha-rūpi.* One of glorious form.

ఇధ్మము *idhmamu.* [Skt.] n. Fuel. చిదుగు, వంటచెరుకు.

ఇనప *inapa.* [Tel. for ఇనుప] Made of iron. See ఇనుము.

ఇనాము or **ఈనాము** *ināmu.* [H.] Inam; a present or gift; land granted by the Government rent free for ever or subject to a small quit rent. A present by Government. మాన్యము, బహుమానము. ఇనాముదారుడు a holder of an inam. నెత్తురుకట్టు ఇనాము land granted to such as had shed blood in battle. కదీంయినాము an old bequest. దివిటీయినాము a grant of land to a torchbearer. ఇనాయముచేయు to grant.

ఇను *inu.* [Tel.] adj. Two. **ఇనుమారు** *inu-māru.* Twice. రెండుసారులు. **ఇనుమిక్కిలి** *inu-mikkili.* Still more or very much. అత్యధికము. See ఇనుమడి, ఇన్నూరు.

ఇనుక *inuka.* [Tel.] n. Broken rice mixed with husk. ఊకకలిసిన నూకలు.

ఇనుకు *inuku.* Same as ఇంకు. (q. v.)

ఇనుడు *inuḍu.* [Skt.] n. A name of the god Surya. **ఇనసుతుడు** *ina suṭuḍu.* n. The son of Surya. viz., Yama.

ఇనుమడి *inu-maḍi.* [Tel. ఇను+మడుగు] adj. Double, twofold. రెట్టి, ద్విగుణము. **ఇనుమడించు** *inumaḍintsu* [Tel.] v. a. To double or redouble. రెట్టించు.

ఇనుమద్ది *inu-maddi.* [Tel. ఇనుము+మద్ది] n. The Sal tree (*Shorea robusta*) సాలము. Iron wood. నల్లమద్ది. See మద్ది.

ఇనుము *inumu.* [Tel.] n. Iron. ఇనుప made of iron. ఇనుపగొలుసు an iron chain. ఇనుపకచ్చ an iron girdle, i.e., continence, chastity.

ఇన్ని *inni.* [Tel. *from* ఇంత] neuter adj. So many, thus many. ఒకయిన్ని a very few ఇన్నిటికి for all this. **ఇన్నో** *innō.* adj. Of such and such a number.

ఇన్నూరు *innūru.* [Tel. ఇను+నూరు or ఇరు+నూరు] n. Two hundred. రెండువందలు.

ఇపుడు or **ఇప్డు** *ipuḍu.* See ఇప్పుడు.

ఇప్ప *ippa.* [Tel.] n. *Bassia latifolia* or, the Butter Tree or Mahua Tree. చిన్న ఇప్పచెట్టు *Bassia longifolia*, the Mowa or Mahua Tree of South India. సీమ ఇప్పచెట్టు *Achras Sapota*, the Sapodilla Plum of the West Indies. The Bully or Neesberry Tree (Watts.) ఇప్పపిండి the flour made from the seeds. ఇప్పపూరాజనాలు a fragrant sort of rice. ఇప్పసారాయి strong spirit obtained from the ఇప్పచెట్టు.

ఇప్పుడు *ippuḍu.* [Tel. ఈ+పొద్దు] n. Now, this time. **ఇప్పటి** of this time. ఇప్పటిపని the present business. ఇప్పటివాండ్లు the people of these days. ఇప్పుడే వచ్చినాడు he is just come.

ఇబ్బంది *ibbandi.* [Tel. ఇను+బంది]. n. Strait, inconvenience, ambiguity. నిర్బంధము. నీళ్లకు ఇబ్బందిగానున్నది water is deficient or scarce. ఇబ్బందిగానుండే irksome. ఇబ్బందిపని a troublesome affair. ఇబ్బందికాడు a troublesome fellow. Also, a mongrel tiger supposed to be begotten by a tiger on a leopard. ఇబ్బందిగుర్రము a horse of doubtful breed.

ఇబ్బట్టు *ibbaṭṭu.* [Tel.] n. Scarcity, dearness. కాలము ఇబ్బట్టుగానున్నది the times are hard.

ఇబ్బడ or **ఇబ్బెడ** *ibbaḍa.* [Tel.] n. A certain tree. (Hamsa. iv. 18.)

ఇబ్బడి *ibbaḍi.* [Tel. ఇను+బడి, or ఇను+మడి.] adj. Twice as much. **ఇబ్బడించు** *ibbaḍintsu.* Same as ఇనుమడించు.

ఇభము *ibhamu.* [Skt. cf. *elephant.* Gr. *elephas.*] An elephant. **ఇభయాన** *ibhayāna.* n. A graceful woman, *i.e.*, a woman with an elephant's easy and luxurious rolling gait. **ఇభి** *ibhi.* n. A she-elephant **ఇభ్యుడు** *ibhyuḍu.* A ruler, rich man. (A. ii. 125.)

ఇముడు *imuḍu.* [Tel.] v. n. To be contained in, to remain, to stay. ఔషధము అతనికి ఇముడక పోయినది the medicine did not stay on his stomach. ఈ సమాచారము వానిలో ఇమిడి ఉండదు he will not be able to conceal this news. **ఇముడుకొను** *imuḍu-konu.* v. n. To be held or contained, ఇముడ్చుకొను. **ఇముడ్చు** or **ఇముడుచు** *imuḍtsu.* v. a. To contain, hold, include, retrench, contract, abbreviate. ఇముడచేయు. **ఇమిడిక** *imiḍika.* n. Brevity, compactness. అణిగియుండుట, చేరియుండుట.

ఇమ్మడి *immaḍi.* [Tel. ఇను+మడి] Double. See ఇనుమడి. ఇమ్మడించు Same as ఇనుమడించు.

ఇమ్ము *immu.* [Tel. imperative of ఇచ్చు] v. t. Give (thou.) See ఇచ్చు. **ఇమ్ము** n. A place, a home. Opportunity, convenience. State, plight. Beauty. ఇంపు. Expediency ఉపాయము, happiness, ease సుఖము. ఇమ్ములేని inconvenient, pinched. ఇమ్ముగను well, suitably బాగుగా. **ఇమ్ము** adj: Convenient, suitable, opportune, fitting. అనుకూలము, యుక్తము. whole, entire, అమూలము.

Pleasant, fine.-మనోజ్ఞము. Plain, evident. స్పష్టము. ఇమ్మెయి immeyi. adv. Thus. (See మెయి.) ఇమ్ముకొను immu-konu. v. i. To dwell, to live. వసించు. ఇమ్ముతప్పు immu tappu. n. Difficulty. ఇక్కట్టు, సంకటము.

ఇయ్య iyya. [Tel. from ఇచ్చు.] v. t. Giving. ఇయ్యకొను iyya-konu. v. n. To consent. ఇయ్యకొలుపు iyya-kolupu. v. a. To persuade. ఇయ్యకోలు iyya-kōlu. n. Consent. సమ్మతి, అంగీకారము. ఇయ్యచేయు iyya-jēyu. v. i. To consent. అంగీకరించు, సమ్మతించు.

ఇయ్యది iyy-adi. [Tel. ఈ+అది] pron. This one, this. ఈయది, ఇది.

ఇరకటము or ఇరకాటము or ఇరుకటము or ఇరుకాటము irukaṭamu. [Tel. from ఇరుకు] n. A strait, difficulty, narrowness.

ఇరమ్మదము irammadamu. [Skt.] n. Lightning. మెరుపు.

ఇరలవాండ్లు irala-vanḍlu. [Tel.] n. Name of a jungle tribe.

ఇరవు or ఇరువు iravu. [Tel.] n. Place స్థానము. ఇరవారు ira-vāru. [Tel. ఇరవు+ ఆరు] or ఇరవుకొను iravu-konu. v. i. To become settled or fixed. స్థిరపడు, నెలకొను. ఇరవు iravu. [Tel.] adj. Firm, fixed. స్థిరమైన. Fitting, suitable. తగిన. ఇరవొందు or ఇరవుపొందు irav-ondu. (ఇరవు+ ఒందు) v. n. To become firm, to be fixed. నెలకొను, స్థిరపడు.

ఇరస or ఇరుస irasa. [Tel.] n. A grain measure being half a తూము the Indian bushel. రెండుకుంచాలు, అరతూము.

ఇరారు ir-āru. [Tel. ఇరు+ఆరు.] Twice six, twelve. Another form is ఈరారు.

ఇరి iri. [from ఇరియు q. v.] adj. Small, little. సూక్ష్మము, అల్పము. D. A. ii. 42. Squeezed. ఇరిసినది.

ఇరికి iriki. [Tel.] n. A game played by children. ఒకవిధమైన ఆట.

ఇరియు iriyu. [Tel.] v. n. To be squeezed, crushed, powdered. To be jammed as a door. నలుగు. To be thin or narrow. సన్నగిలు. ఇరికౌను thin waist. ఇరిగుబ్బలు hard or firm breasts. A. v. 109. ఇరియబట్టు to seize, to hold fast. గట్టిగా పట్టుకొను. To be broken, to be smashed. ఛిన్నాభిన్నమగు, నుగ్గునుగ్గుచేయబడు.

ఇరివిలి irivili. [Tel.] n. A hole made with a drill or తొలగర.

ఇరు iru. [Tel. cognate with రెండు.] adj. Two, both. ఇరువంకలు or ఇరుగడ both sides. ఇరుగోరు both shares, the whole, the gross crop. ఇరుతెక్కి both sides. ఇరువాల్లదుక్కి a second ploughing. ఇరుమూడు or ఇత్తిగ six at dice: ఇరుతూము or ఇద్దుము two bushels. See తూము. ఇరువసల on both sides, ఇరునాలుగు twice four. ఇరువది or ఇరువై or ఇరవై twice ten. ఇరువంకల on both sides, from side to side. ఇరువురు or ఇరుగురు both persons.

ఇరుకు iruku. [Tel.] n A strait, difficulty, distress, narrowness. Closeness, contact. adj. Narrow, tight, squeezing. ఇరుకు v. n. To be squeezed, stuck in. ఇరుకటము or ఇరుకాటము irukaṭamu. n. A narrow place. ఇరుకుచోటు. ఇరుకుమాను iruku mānu. n. Posts set in a gate-way (i. e., పంగలకర్ర) to exclude cattle but admit men; a turnpike. ఇరికించు or ఇరికించుకొను irikintsu. v. a. To insert, poke in, stick in. ఇరికికొను or ఇరుక్కొను iriki-konu. v. n. To get in; stick, be caught, be inserted, be entangled.

ఇరుగు irugu. [Tel. cf. Tam. ఇరు to be] n. Nearness; the neighbourhood. adj. Neighbouring, near, adjoining. ఇరుగుపొరుగు neighbourhood, neighbouring, adjoining, on both sides, hither and thither.

ఇరుగుడుచెట్టు irugudu-chettu. [Tel.] n. A tree called *Dalbergia Sisu*. శింశుపా. Rox. iii. 223.

ఇరుము *irumu*, [Tel.] n. A covert, hiding place. మరుగు. ఇరుముకొను *irumu-konu*. v. i. To hide, to be hidden. మరుగుపడు.

ఇరులు *irulu*. [Tel.] n. Shades, shadows, darkness. చీకటి, చీకట్లు. ఇరులుకొను *irulu-konu*. v. n. To become dark or obscure చీకటిపడు. ఇరులడొంగ *irulu-gonga*. n. The destroyer of darkness. i. e., the Sun.

ఇరువ *iruva*. [Tel.] n. A sort of fish resembling a wedge in shape. *Platycephalus*. Rox. No. 46. 47.

ఇరువాయికట్టు *iru-rāyi-kaṭṭu*. [Tel. వాయి mouth.] n. Double palsy: a disease in which the excretions are stopped.

ఇరువు *iruvu*. [Tel. same as ఇరుగు. q. v.] n. A neighbouring house, neighbourhood, place. పక్కయిల్లు. adj. Neighbouring. పక్కనుండే.

ఇరువుడు Same as ఇరుగుడు (q. v.)

ఇరువురు or ఇర్వురు See under ఇరు.

ఇరువై or ఇరువది. *iruvai*. [Tel. ఇరు+పది] n. Twenty. ఇరువైమంది twenty persons. "ఇరువైనాలుగుమూర్తులేమి" కాశీ. i.

ఇరుస Same as ఇరస (q. v.)

ఇరుసాలు or ఇర్సాలు *iru-sālu*. [H.] n. Sending, a remittance of money sent with a guard. The government money so sent. ఇరుసాలుచేయు to remit gold or silver. ఇర్సాలునామా an invoice of the sums sent and of the coins in which the payment is made.

ఇరుసు *irusu*. [Tel.] n. An axle. The cross beam in the middle of a picota. ఏతపుమ్రాని నడుమనుండు అడ్డుకొయ్య.

ఇర్ర *irra* [Tel.] n. Side. ప్రక్క, పార్శ్వము. Same as ఇఱ్ఱియ (q. v.)

ఇఱ్ఱి *irri*. [Tel.] n. The male of the Indian antelope, a black buck. A. Bennettii, of Sykes, Elliot. ఇఱ్ఱింక (for ఇఱ్ఱిజింక). A male antelope. మగజేడి. ఇఱ్ఱింకచూపులు wild glances like those of the antelope. "ఈక్షింపగా నేర్చె నిఱ్ఱింకచూపుల, మోవిగా ర్వగనేర్చె మొలకనవ్వు." Matid. iii. 248.

ఇఱ్ఱింకులు *irrinkulu*. [ఇంకులు+ఇంకులు] Drying up altogether. మిక్కిలియింకిపోవుట. Stares, wild looks. Mand. iii. 248. ఇఱ్ఱింకునైన wild, stern, severe, wasting, harsh. ఇఱ్ఱిగోరజము *irri-gōrazamu*. n. Musk. కస్తూరి. (Swa. iv.)

ఇఱ్ఱియ *irriya*. [Tel.] n. Side. ప్రక్క, పార్శ్వము. Same as ఇర్ర.

ఇల *ila*. [Tel.] n. The earth. నేల.

ఇలకరుచు or ఈలకరుచు *ila-karuću*. [Tel.] v. i. and t. To be set, jammed, stuck. వానికి తల యిలకరుచుకొనిపోయినది his head is jammed or sunk between his shoulders. "ప్రాణము ఇలకరుచుకొన్న." P. iii. 196. hard to kill: having stubborn life. ఆతనికి పండ్లు ఇలకరిచినవి his jaws were set, he gnashed his teeth. A. v. 13,

ఇలకోడి *ila-kōḍi*. [Tel.] n. The grey cricket, or cicada. ఈలపురుగు.

ఇలవరము, ఇలారము Same as ఇలువరము. (q. v.)

ఇలాకా *ilaka*. [H.] n. Interference. Relation, jurisdiction, connection by business, charge, possession. సంబంధము, అధికారము లోనైన ప్రదేశము, స్వాధీనము. మా యిలాకాదారులు, మా యిలాకావాళ్లు those who belong to me, my people. adj. Belonging to.

ఇలాయి *ilayi*. [Tel.] n. A torch. దివిటీ. "తక సూర్యప్రభ లాయిలాయులును చంద్రజ్యోతు లున్." హంస. iii.

ఇలి *ili*. [Tel.] n. Food. ఈగకు ఇలి పాముకు బలిదొరకదు or వానియింట్లో యీగకు బలికి తిండిపుట్టదు in his house a fly cannot find a dinner.

ఇలింద or ఇలిందం *ilinda*. [Tel.] A kind of tree. జేదురు, ఇంద్రవల్లి.

ఇలికము *ilikamu*. [Borrowed by Skt. from Drav. languages.] n. Rat. ఎలుక. ఇలిపా

పాణము, ఇల్లిపాపాణము ili-pāshāṇamu. [Tel.] Ratsbane: corrosive sublimate or perchloride of mercury.

ఇలు ilu. (See ఇల్లు.) ఇలుచుట్టు ilu-tsuṭṭu. [Tel. from చుట్టు.] n. Lustration, walking round a house to keep away demons. ఇలురేడు ilu-rēḍu. n. The master of the house. ఇలువడి iluvaḍi. n. Respectable birth. కులీనత. Good conduct. మంచినడత. భార. శాంతి. iii. "ఇలువడిగున్న చేసి." భాగ. 10 స్కం. ఇలువరుస ilu-varusa. Family, race, consanguinity. వంశానుక్రమము. ఇలువరుసగా at each house, from house to house. ఇలువేలుపు or ఇలువేల్పు ilu-vēlupu. A patron saint or god. The household god కులదేవత.

ఇలుకు iluku. [Tel.] n. Cramp, sprain, strain. నరముబెణుకు. ఇలుకుపట్టిన Sprained, cramped. బెణికిన.

ఇలుగు or ఈలుగు ilugu. [Tel.] To die, expire. చచ్చు.

ఇలువరము or ఇలువారము ilu-varamu. [Tel.] n. A hut built without walls. గోడలులేని యొత్తుకుగుడిసె. A portable hut. గోడలులేక అంతా పూరితో కట్టబడిన గుడిసె. See ఇలవరము or ఇలారము.

ఇల్ల illa. [Drav. the basis of such words as లేదు, లేక, &c.] A Kanarese word for లేదు, నాస్తి. Kuchēlo. ii. 118. R. i. 45.

ఇల్లంత్రము See ఇల్లటము.

ఇల్లటము illaṭamu. [Tel. from ఇల్లు.] n. Residence in the house of one's wife's father. ఇల్లటపల్లుడు one who has become a member of his father-in-law's household. ఇల్లటముపెట్టిరి they kept their son-in-law in their family. ఇల్లటకాడు the son-in-law thus kept in their family.

ఇల్లడ illaḍa. [from ఇల్లు] .n. Dwelling. కాపురము; committing, entrusting. అప్పగింత. "ఇల్లడగాచేసి." A. v. 142. Keeping in one's house. నన్ను యిల్లడచేసినాడు he made me dwell with him.

చ. "నన్నిదనమ్ముదేనియు,
ల్లడయిడుధీమనర్జును నలంభుల్గ
బలాఢ్యులవానరంబునన్."

భార: సభా. i. 163.

ఇల్లము illamu. [Tel. ఇరు+పలము] n. Two palams' weight. రెండుపలములు. "ఇల్లమునం గను నెసగుద్విపలి." ఆం. భా: ద్వి: నై.

ఇల్లరి illari. [Tel. ఇల్లు+అరి] n. A house tax or hearth tax, quit rent. ఇంటిపన్ను.

ఇల్లరికము or ఇల్లంత్రికము Same as ఇల్లటము (q. v.)

ఇల్లవ illava [Tel.] n. A sort of fish

ఇల్లామల్లి illa-malli. [Tel.] n. A talebearer. కొండెకాడు. ఇల్లామల్లితనము illamallitanamu. [Tel.] n. Scandal, tattle. ఇల్లామల్లిసుద్దులు illamalli-suddulu. n. Tattle, backbiting, scandal.

ఇల్లాయము Same as ఇల్లరి.

ఇల్లాలు illalu. [Tel. ఇల్లు + ఆలు.] n. A housewife. A wife, an honest woman.

ఇల్లి illi. [Tel.] n. Fast, fasting. ఉపవాసము.

ఇల్లింద See ఇలింద.

ఇల్లిగ్గులు illiggulu. [Tel. ఇగ్గులు+ఇగ్గులు] n. Dispiritedness. అధైర్యము, హృదయము కుంగిపోవుట.

"లొల్లియగువగల త్రొక్కున
నిల్లిగ్గులుగాననచ్చు హృదయములోనన్,
మల్లామడియగు మదముడు
మెల్లనగూర్చుండెబాల్లి మినుమినుకనగన్."

ఉ. హరి. v.

ఇల్లిముక్కు illi-mukku. [Tel.] n. A nose that bleeds. వాని యిల్లిముక్కు పగిలి నెత్తురు కారినది he was bleeding at the nose.

ఇల్లు or ఇలు illu. [Tel. The primitive form is ఇల్ which means 'a house.' ఆలయము (q. v.) borrowed by Skt. from Drav. means (1) house and (2) 'God's abode' or house. cf. కోయిల or కోవెల. In the Chaldee word 'Babylon'

(= bab-ilu), the latter part 'ilu' means 'God' by a transition of ideas.] n. A house, a chamber, room. Home, place, caste, family. A place or space in a table of accounts. A square at draughts or chess. (Genit. ఇంటి Dat. ఇంటికి. Loc. ఇంటిలో or ఇంట. Plural ఇండ్లు or ఇళ్లు.) మీరు ఏయింట్లవారు who are you? of what family are you. "మనయింటి చేటు చూచితే." నిర్వ. ix. ఇంటిగుట్టు a family secret. ఇంటికిదూరమైన ceremonially unclean, i.e., ముట్టుమంతి రైన. In poems మరునిల్లు is the భగము. ఇల్లునింపడము setting up a house, house-warming వధూవరుల నూతన గృహప్రవేశము.

ఇల్లెము *illemu.* [Tel.] n. A kind of fish, H. iv. 225.

ఇల్వడి *ilvadi.* [Tel. another form of ఇలు వడి] ఇంటిపరువు, ఇంటిమర్యాద. respectability, decency. "రాసుతులకెక్కడి యిల్వడి యుంచు దుర్జనస్తోమమునిండచేయు." Padma. IX. 9. What do princes care for their respectability? See under ఇలు.

ఇవక *ivaka.* [Tel.] n. Wetness, damp, a puddle. శీతము.

ఇవతల *ivatala.* [Tel.] adv. Hither, on this side, hereafter, next. ఇవతలి of this side, as ఇవతలివారు those who are on this side. ఇవతలికి to this side: this way.

ఇవతళించు or ఇవతాళించు *ivatalintsu.* [Tel.] v. n. To become cool, to be chill or cool. చల్లపడు, చల్లగానుండు. ఇవతాళింపు *ivatalimpu.* n. Coldness, chillness. చలువకలుగుట.

ఇవము *ivamu.* (from Skt. హిమము) n. Cold frost, dew. మంచు. ఇవముకొను *ivamukonu.* v. n. To become wet. తడియు. ఇవముమేపరి or ఇవముసూడు *ivamu-mēpari.* n. The devourer of the damp. The sun. సూర్యుడు.

ఇవల *ivala.* [Tel.] another form of ఇవతల.

ఇవి *ivi.* [Tel.] pron. These things.

ఇవిరించు *ivirintsu.* [Tel. from ఇవురు.] v. t. To cause to sprout. చిగిరించు.

ఇవుకు *ivuku.* [Tel. same as ఇగురు.] n. Wet, puddle, damp.

ఇవురు *ivuru.* [Tel.] n. A sprout. చిగురు. ఇవురు v. n. To sprout or shoot. చిగుర్చుట. To dry up. ఇంకు. ఇవురుచు or ఇవుర్చు *ivurutsu.* v. t. To cause to dry up.

ఇవ్వల *ivvala.* [Tel ఈ+వల] Hither, this side. ఈవల.

ఇషణము *ishanamu.* [Skt.] n. Desire. ఇచ్ఛ, విత్తేషణము love of money. పుత్రేషణము love of offspring. దారేషణము desire or love towards a wife.

ఇషిరాసి *ishi-rāsi.* [Skt.] n. The rusty soapnut tree: a large timber tree the wood of which is straight, strong and durable. *Sapindus Rubiginosa.* (Ainslie.)

ఇషీక *ishīka.* [Skt.] n. A blade of grass, a reed, a painter's brush.

ఇషువు *ishuvu.* [Skt.] An arrow. ఇషుధి. a quiver. అమ్ములపొది.

ఇష్టక *ishṭaka.* [Skt derived from ఇటుక.] n. A brick. ఇటుక రాయి.

ఇష్టము *ishṭamu.* [Skt.] n. Wish, inclination, liking, pleasure, choice. ఇష్టము. adj. Desired, dear, beloved. ఇష్టమువచ్చినదాకా as long as one liked. ఇష్టదేవత *ishṭa-dēvata.* A patron saint or tutelary god. ఇష్టపడు. *ishṭa-padu.* v. n. To wish. To consent. ఇష్టగోష్ఠిగా *ishṭa-gōshṭhi-ga.* adv. Agreeably, comfortably. ఇష్టాలాపము *ishṭa-lāpamu.* n. Pleasant conversation. ఇష్టి *ishṭi.* n. Wish, inclination. A sacrifice, rite, ceremony. కోరిక, యజ్ఞము. ఇష్టించు *ishṭintsu.* v. a. To desire, wish for. BD. iv. 1051. ఇష్టుడు *ishṭudu.* n. A friend.

ఇష్వాసము *ishvasamu.* [Skt.] n. A bow. విల్లు.

ఇసక Same as ఇసుక.

ఇసడిలు *isadilu.* [Tel.] v. i. To be tired or disgusted, to dislike. విసుగు.

ఇసిరింతలు *isirintalu.* [Tel.] n. Movement. చలనము.

క॥ "భూపాలమెరుగుబోడుల
చూపులకుంజాయనీడు సొబగట్లనుటన్,
మాపిన్నదియిసిరింతల
చూపులనరిగంటవెరచుచున్నిమజాచున్." సై. viii.

ఇసిరింతలుపారు *isirintalu-pāru.* [Tel.] v. i. To move about. చలించు, అదరు.

ఇసీ *isī.* [Tel.] interj. Fie! alas! pooh! pah!

ఇసు *isu.* [Tel.] n. Child, infant, pupil. R. iv. 6.

ఇసుక or ఇసక *isuka.* [Tel.] n. Sand. బంగారు ఇసుక gold dust. ఇసుకపాతర a sand pit, confusion, a puzzle. ఇసుకదాసరికూర *isuka-dāsari-kūra.* n. A certain herb. ఇసుకదిన్నె or ఇసుకదిబ్బ *isuka-dinne.* n. A sand bank. See దిన్నె. ఇసుకదొండు or ఇసుకదొండు *isuka-doṇḍu.* n. The fish called white caboose, or river whiting, dragonet: (it is somewhat cylindrical, with a thick tail.) ఇసుకపఱ్ఱ *isuka-parra.* A sandy waste. ఇసుకబేలు *isukabēlu.* A creeping plant, of great beauty. ఇసుకమాను *isuka-mānu.* A tree (*Tapia cratoeva or capparis trifoliata*) ఉలిమిడిచెట్టు, వరుణవృక్షము.

ఇసుము *isumu.* [Tel.] n. Sand. ఇసుక. ఇసులు or ఇసుమంత *isulu.* adv. A very little, an atom, a particle.

ఇసుళ్లు or ఈసుళ్లు *isullu.* [Tel.] n. Winged ants (termites.) రెక్కచీమలు.

ఇస్తిమిరారి or ఇస్తింరారి *istimirāri.* [H.] adj. Perpetual, in perpetuity, continual. శాశ్వతమైన.

ఇస్త్రి *istiri.* [H.] n. Ironing of clothes. బట్టలు మెరుగువచ్చేటట్టు చిన్న ఇనుపపెట్టెలో నిప్పులుపోసి రాచడము.

ఇస్తిహారు *istihāru.* [H.] n. Proclamation. చాటించడము. ఇస్తిహారునామా a written proclamation. ప్రకటనపత్రిక.

ఇస్తువ or ఇస్తువు *istuva.* [Tel. for ఆస్తి] n. An estate. సొత్తు.

ఇస్పేటు *ispēṭu.* [Eng.] n. The spade in playing cards. ఇస్పేటుశాకితాలు playing cards.

ఇస్సీ or ఇస్సిరో *issī.* [Tel.] interj. Fie! alas! pooh!

ఇహము or ఇహలోకము *ihamu.* [Skt.] adv. Here. Here below. The present world or life; opposed to పరము the future state. ఇహపరాలులేని వెరవక having no fear of god or man.

ఇహిహి *ihihi.* [Tel.] Ha ha ha! (in laughter or derison) R. v. 144.

ఈ ī

ఈ The vowel ī as in *machine*, or *ee*, in *seen*, or *ea* as in *mean*, or *ie*, or *mien*.

ఈ ī. [Tel.] adj. This, these, *as* ఈ చోటున in this place. ఈ కాపులు these farmers.

ఈ ī. [Tel. from ఇచ్చు to give.] ఇయ్యజాలను, or ఈజాలను I cannot give. Also the imperative of the same verb. ఈ or ఇమ్ము Give (thou.) ఈక without giving ఇవ్వక. ఈకుంటేనేని if I fail to give it. ఈకు (for ఇవ్వకుము from ఇచ్చు.) do not give. ఈడు *īḍu.* [Tel. from ఇచ్చు] v. He will not give.

ఈండ్ర *īṇḍra.* [Tel.] n. The toddy-drawer caste. ఈండ్రవాడు a toddy-man. ఈండ్రది a woman of the same caste.

ఈండ్రము *īṇḍramu.* [Tel.] n. Trouble, pest. పీడనము. "ఎన్నడు ననుబెట్టుమనుచు నీండ్రము సేయకు." భా. viii. ఈండ్రించు *īṇḍrintsu.* v. t. To trouble. పీడించు, తొందరపెట్టు.

ఈక Same as ఈకె. (q. v.)

ఈకు *īku.* [Tel.] v. n. To be imbibed: to soak in. ఇంకు. To drop off, as feathers. ఈకువ *īkuva.* n. Dampness, wetness. తడి.

ఈకె or ఈక *īke.* [Tel.] n. A feather. పక్షిరెక్క.

ఈకె *īke.* [Tel. ఈ+అక్క] pron. She, this woman. See ఈమె.

ఈకోను Same as ఇయ్యకోను. (q. v.) ఈకోలు Same as ఇయ్యకోలు. See under ఇచ్చు.

ఈక్షణము ikshanamu. [Skt.] n. Eye, look. కన్ను, చూపు. ఈక్షించు ikshintsu. v. t. To see, to look.

ఈగ iga. [Tel. Tam. ఈ] n. A fly. పోతుటీగ. (from పోతు male and టి inserted) a male fly. చ॥ "నృపాలకులు . . . నిగ్రహాకొంపునగ పోతుటీగయుగా బొలయనీయక్కరంతిపురి." T. iv 17. Princes would, if possible, keep out even male flies from their seraglio. ఈగపులి iga-puli. n. A spider: literally a fly-tiger.

ఈగడ i-gada. [Tel. from ఈను.] n. Trace జాడ, పోబడి.

ఈగి See ఈవి.

ఈగు igu. [Tel. another form of నీగు] v. a. To enter, penetrate. "వాధిసొరంగ వీగి" Vasu ii. 91. To give, bestow. సీ॥ "పానీయమునన ర్ఘ్యపాద్యమీగి" Naish iv. 11. To get rid of. To do away with. పోగొట్టు, తొలగించు, నివర్తించు. "ఋణత్రయం బునీగి." A. iv. 341. ఈగు v. n. To fail, lose: submit, (compare. నీగు.) To perish. ఓడు, డస్సిపోవు, చచ్చు. To be crushed. ఒత్తుడుపడిపోవు. "ఈగెదరాకటిచే." Hari Vams. i. 23. They perish with hunger.

ఈచు itsu. [Tel.] v. n. To shrivel, wither, dry up. ఈచ itsa. adj. Lank, withered, misshapen. ఈచపడు or ఈచపోవు itsa-padu. To fall away, become lean. ఈచుక పోయిన lean, withered, flabby. కుష్కించి చిపోయిన.

ఈటు itu. [Tel.] adj. Useless, empty. వ్యర్థము, శూన్యము. ఈటుపోవు to become useless or empty.

ఈటె ite. [Tel.] n. A dart, a spear. ఈటెగాడు a spearman.

ఈటేరు iteru. [Tel.] v. n. To cool as food.

ఈడ ida. [Tel. ఈ+కడ] adv. Here. ఇక్కడ.

ఈడబోవు ida-bovu. [Tel.] v. i. To retreat, retire. తగ్గు, వెనుకదీయు.

ఈడాడు idadu. [Tel. ఈడు+ఆడు] v. t. To oppose మార్కొను.

ఈడి idi. [Tel.] adj. Small. ఈడికుండ a small cup, a milking pail. పాలుపిటికెకుండ.

ఈడిగవాడు or ఈడిగెవాడు idiga vadu. [Tel.] n. A toddy-man, or toddy drawer.

ఈడిగిలు or ఈడిగిలబడు idigilu. [Tel.] v. n. To halt, be weary, to hang back, linger, be reluctant to move. To sit down immovably through fear, etc., refusing to stir.

ఈడితము iditamu. [Skt.] adj. Lauded, praised, commended. పొగడబడినది.

ఈడిపించు or ఈడ్పించు idipintsu. [Tel.] v. To cause to draw. See ఈడ్చు. To drawl, prolong.

ఈడిబండాడు idibandadu. [Tel.] To ruin, crush, destroy. చిన్నపుచ్చు. L. ii 295.

ఈడు idu. [Tel.] As an affix answering to కలవాడు one who has. కుమ్మరీడు or కుమ్మరి a potter. సాలీడు or సాలెవాడు a weaver. కన్నడీడు a native of the Kanarese country. ద్రావిడీడు a Tamil man.

ఈడు idu. [Tel.] n. 1. Age, time of life. ప్రాయము. ఈడైన equal. రెండేండ్ల యీడుగల two years old. ఈడుచాలిన or ఈడునిండిన full grown, adult. ఈడుచాలని or ఈడురాని not ful grown, minor. ఈడుమీరిన too old. 2. Resemblance, similarity, proportion. A match, a rival. సమానము. ఈడుపడు idu-padu. v. i. To become equal. సమానమగు. ఈడుపరచు idu-paratsu. v. a. To equalize, to compare.

ఈడు idu. [Tel.] v. i. To stretch, to slip, to vanish, to disappear. సాగు, జారు. v. t. To pull, to draw milk లాగు, పిదుకు.

"శ్రద్ధగలిగిలోక సంగ్రహసంగంబు
నెడవిడిచియొవ్వ డీయుపాయ
ములభజించువాడు మోక్షలక్ష్మిపతి
యగునొకింత సందియంబులేదు."

భార. ఆశ్వ. i.

"గోవులకుంగ్రేపుల విడువకయు
విడిచివిడిచి యీడకయు
ఈడీయాడీయాడిన పాలుకాచకయు."
భాగ: 10 స్కం.

ఈడుపు or **ఈడ్పు** *īḍupu*. [Tel.] n. Pulling, dragging, impetus, hard breathing. A stitch in the side, the contraction of a limb. నీళ్లు నిండా యీడ్పుగానున్నవి the water runs here with a great draught. ఈడుపు or పాడికట్టు the sill, the side post of a door.

ఈడుమానిటి Same as ఈడిమంటి. See ఈడి.

ఈడె *īḍe*. [Tel.] n. The name of a certain tree. ఈడెచెట్టు. A core or inner division of an orange, &c. తొన. **ఈడెలి** or **ఇడవలి** *īḍeli*. n. Rushes, bulrushes. The cuscuss roots. వట్టివేళ్లు.

ఈడేరు *īḍēru*. [Tel. ఈడు+ఏరు] v. n. To be effected, completed, fulfilled, attained. నెరవేరు. To come to maturity. ఈడేరిన. ripe, mature. **ఈడేర్చు** *īḍērtsu*. v. a. To effect, complete, fulfil, accomplish. ఈ కష్టమీడేర్చితివా if you will only get me through this distress.

ఈడ్యము *īḍyamu*. [Skt.] adj. Noteworthy, glorious, noble. పొగడదగిన.

ఈడ్గిలబడు *īḍgila-baḍu*. [Tel.] n. To be supine, on the back. Same as ఈడిగిలబడు. (q. v.)

ఈడ్చు or **ఈడుచు** *īḍtsu*. [Tel. causative of ఈడు] v. a. To pull, haul, drag. కన్నులు లోపలికి యీడ్చుకొనిపోయినవి his eyes are sunken.

ఈత or **ఈతచెట్టు** *īta*. [Tel.] n. The wild date tree. ఈతకల్లు date toddy, date wine. ఈతకాయలు wild dates. ఈతపేళ్లు date fibres. ఈతపేళ్లపెట్టె a wicker box. **ఈవాడి** *īvāḍi*. (ఈత+వాడి) the marshy date tree, *Phoenix* or *Elatea paludosa*. పెంటీతలు, ఈతాకుచెట్టు. చిట్టీతచెట్టు the dwarf date tree. పేరీతచెట్టు the common or tall date tree. See also under ఈడు.

ఈతండు, **ఈతడు**, **ఈతగాడు**, **ఈతను**. Same as ఇతడు.

ఈతి *īti*. [Skt.] n. Plague, pest, nuisance, evil. ఈతిబాధలు the (six) plagues, *viz.*, excessive rain అతివృష్టి, drought or failure of rains అనావృష్టి, rats ఎలుకలు, parrots చిలుకలు, locusts మిడతలు, neighbouring kings చేరువరాజులు.

ఈద *īda*. [Tel.] n. Wind, cold wind. ఈద గాలి or ఈదరగాలి or ఈదురగాలి a strong, cold wind; a storm. పెద్దచలిగాలి. **ఈదర** *īdara*. adj. Stormy, violent.

ఈదలు *īdalu*. [Tel.] n. plu. The sides of a pit in salt works.

ఈవాడి. See under ఈత.

ఈదు *īdu*. A kind of tree, కలబంద.

ఈదు *īdu*. [Tel.] v. n. To swim. **ఈత** *īta*. n. Swimming. ఈతకాడు a swimmer. ఈతకాయ a swimming gourd, a float. ఈతకొట్టు or ఈతలాడు or ఈదులాడు to swim or float. క్రీడించు. దారిద్ర్యమనే సముద్రమునందు యీదులాడుచున్నాను. I am struggling in the sea of poverty.

ఈదురు Same as ఈదర. See ఈద.

ఈదృశము *ī-driśamu*. [Skt.] adj. Such-like, similar.

ఈన Same as ఈనె. **ఈనపుడక** or **ఈన పుల్ల** *īna-puḍaka*. [Tel.] n. The long grass of which brooms are made.

ఈనిక *īnika*. [Tel. from ఈను] n. Bearing, calving, foaling. ఈనుట. yeaning, bringing forth young (only applied to brute creatures.) **ఈనికయావు** *īnika-y-āvu*. n. A cow about to calve.

ఈను *īnu*. [Tel.] v. a. To give produce (as fields of grain.) To yean or bear (young.) To give forth, emit (sound, or splendour.) ఈనగాచి నక్కలపాలుచేసినట్టు all one's care is thrown away. మెరుగులీను emitting radiance. నేలయీనినవిధమున as though the earth calved.

ఈనె *ine.* [Tel.] The stem or centric fibre in a leaf or feather. వేపయీనెలు withes or twigs of the margosa tree. **ఈనెగాజులు** *ine-gajulu.* A game played by girls.

ఈపి *ipi.* [Tel.] n. The dung of flies which is supposed to turn into nits. A nit. ఈపికట్టు a lump or mass of nits. ఈపి పెట్టిన fly blown.

ఈపె *ipe.* [Tel. ఈ+అప్పు] pron. This woman, she. See ఆపె.

ఈప్స *ipsa.* [Skt.] n. Will, desire, volition. ఇచ్ఛ, కోరిక. **ఈప్సితము** *ipsitamu.* adj. Desired, hoped.

ఈబరి or **ఈబిరి** *ibari.* [Tel.] adj. Useless, unprofitable. ఈబరిగొట్టు a ninny, a noodle. నిష్ప్రయోజకుడు.

ఈబిడ or **ఈబిడె** *ibida.* [Tel. ఈ+బిడ్డ] pron. She, this woman.

ఈమిరి *imiri.* [Tel.] n. Wet, moisture. తడి.

ఈమె *ime.* [Tel. ఈ+అమ్మ] pron. She, this woman.

ఈయన *iyana.* [Tel. ఈ+అన్న] pron. He, this person.

ఈర *ira.* [Tel.] n. The inner flesh, the core of the heart. A spindle or shank for winding thread. ఈరు.

ఈరగాడు (Vizag.) Same as వియ్యంకుడు. (q. v.) **ఈరకత్తె** Same as వియ్యపురాలు. (q. v.)

ఈరతార *ira-tara.* [Tel.] n. Disorder. తారుమారు. adj. Disordered, confused. తారుమారైన. Here and there, this way and that. తీర్చగూడనిది, ఈడగానిది. హెచ్చుతగ్గులు, ఈరతారలు more or less: some.

"అప్పుడుసస్మైటకోలల నంకురములు
జేరుకొలలదీటుల నీరతారయదలుపుల
వాహానంబులు చెదరిపరచె."

ఈరమి or **ఈరము** *irami.* [Tel.] n. A bush, clump, bower. పొద, పొదరిల్లు. ఆ యీరమిముయుంగన behind the bush. **ఈరమి** or **ఈరము** *irami.* adj. Thick. దట్టమైన, దట్టమైన, సాంద్రమైన.

ఈరలు Same as ఇరలు.

ఈరలు *iralu.* [Tel.] You, yourselves. See ఈరు.

ఈరస or **ఈరసము** *irasa.* [from Skt. ఈర్ష్య] n. Spite, malice, anger. ఈర్ష్య, క్రోధము, కోపము. **ఈరసించు** *irasintsu.* v. i. To be angry, to get angry. కోపపడు; to hate. ద్వేషించు.

ఈరారు *iraru.* [Tel. ఈరు+ఆరు] n. Twice six, twelve.

ఈరిక *irika.* [Tel. A sprout, shoot. చిగురు. ఈరికలుకొను to sprout, to arise (as love).

ఈరితము *iritamu.* [Skt.] adj. Thrown out. త్రోయబడినది. Uttered, said, told.

ఈరు for ఇయ్యరు. [Tel. from ఇచ్చు.] They do not give. See ఇచ్చు.

ఈరు *iru.* [Tel.] n. A nit. ఈపి. **ఈరు** adj. Low, mean అల్పము, హీనము. Slight, gentle. ఈరెలుగు a low note, a gentle voice. హీనస్వరము. ఈరెండ gentle warmth. **ఈరుపెన** or **ఈర్పెన** *irupena.* n. A comb for extracting nits or lice.

ఈరు *iru.* [Tel.] pron. for మీరు You.

ఈరుచు or **ఈర్చు** *irutsu.* [Tel.] v. t. To remove nits from the hair with a comb.

ఈరువారు *iruvaru.* [Tel. ఈరు+వారు.] Same as ఆరివారు. See under ఆరియాడు.

ఈరువు *iruvu.* [Tel.] n. Flesh, meat. ఎరచి, మాంసము.

ఈరె *ire.* [Tel.] n. Thread. వంటెనుచుట్టితీసిన నూలు.

ఈరేడు *iredu.* [Tel.] n. Fourteen. A hurdle on which a corpse, &c, may be dragged.

ఈర్చు See ఈరుచు.

ఈర్పెన See under ఈరు.

ఈర్మము *irmamu.* [Skt.] n. A sore, a wound. పుండు.

ఈర్ష్య *irshya.* [Skt.] n. Spite, envy, ill will, malice, intolerance. ఓర్వలేనితనము. **ఈర్ష్యాళువు** *irshyāluvu.* n. An envious man. An intolerant person. ఈసుబోతు.

ఈల *īla.* [Tel.] n. Whistling. **ఈలకరచు** *īlakarutsu.* v. n. To retain life, to set, or gnash the teeth. పలుకొరుకు. పండ్లు కట్టిగా కరచుకొను. **ఈలగద్ద** *īla-gadda.* A vulture; a kind of hawk; a miser లోభి. **ఈలవేయు** *īla-vēyu.* v. n. To whistle. **ఈలపురుగు** or **ఈలకోడి** *īla-purugu.* n. Moth. చిమ్మట.

ఈలా, ఈలాగు, ఈలాగున *īla.* [Tel.] adv. Thus, so, in this manner. **ఈలాటి,** *īlaṭi.* Such as this.

ఈలుగు *īlugu.* [Tel. from హిలుగు.] v. n. To die, perish. చచ్చు, మరణించు.

ఈలువు *īluvu.* [Tel.] n. Respectability, honour: character, faithfulness to a husband. పాతివ్రత్యము. Modesty. మానము, అభిమానము. Vasu. iii. 106. "ఈలువు టాండ్రు." (A. v. 74.) honourable women. Also, courage. ధైర్యము.

ఈవల *īvala.* [Tel.] n. This side. ఈప్రక్క. adv. Since. ఇటుపిమ్మట. **ఈవలావల** on this side and on that.

ఈవి or **ఈగి** *īvi.* [Tel. from ఇచ్చు] n. Giving, liberality, a gift. **ఈవికాడు** or **ఈగికాడు** or **ఈవరి** *īgi-kāḍu.* n. A liberal man. **ఈవిమాను** or **ఈగిమాను** *īvi-mānu.* n. A fabulous tree which gives everything one desires. కల్పవృక్షము.

ఈబడి Same as ఈవిడి.

ఈవు *īvu.* [Tel.] pron. Thou. See నీవు. The initial N. is here dropped.

ఈవు *īvu.* [Tel. for ఇయ్యవు from ఇచ్చు.] thou dost not give. A. iv. 125. **ఈవుత** or **ఈవుతన్** *īvuta.* May he bestow!

ఈశానము *iṣānamu.* [Skt.] n. Light, brightness. వెలుగు, ప్రకాశము. **ఈశానుడు** *iṣānuḍu.* n. Siva. **ఈశాన్యమూల** *iṣānya-mūla.* n. The north-east.

ఈశిత *iṣita.* [Skt.] n. Master, owner. ప్రభువు.

ఈశుడు *iṣuḍu.* [Skt.] n. A king, a master. Siva. రాజు, శివుడు.

ఈశ్వరవేరు *iṣvara-vēru.* [Skt.] n. The Indian birthwort (*Aristolochia Indica*) (Watts.)

ఈశ్వరి *iṣvari.* n. The goddess Parvati, wife of Siva. ఈశ్వరి or ఈశ్వరిచెట్టు wormwood. నాగదమని. H. iv. 12. **ఈశ్వరుడు** *iṣvaruḍu.* n. Lord, king, the supreme ruler of the universe: GOD A name of Siva, especially in a compound, when the image meant is a *linga*, as Visveswara, Rameswara, &c.

ఈషణము *ishaṇamu.* [Skt.] n. Love, desire. **ఈషణత్రయము** *ishana-trayamu.* n. The three strongest affections of mankind, viz., దారేషణము, విత్తేషణము, పుత్రేషణము, love of one's wife, wealth, and child.

ఈషత్తు *ishattu.* [Skt.] adj. Slight, small, little, trifling. ఈషద్భేదము a slight difference. **ఈషత్** *ishat.* (used only in Skt. compounds) adv. Lightly, slightly, a little.

ఈషిక *ishika.* [Skt.] n. A reed for writing, a painter's bush, a pencil. The eyeball of an elephant.

ఈస or **ఈసకర్ర** *īsa.* [Tel.] n. The wooden cross beam of an anchor. లంగరుమీదటి అడ్డముగాకట్టేకర్ర.

ఈసడము *īsadamu.* [Tel.] n. Blame. అపవాదము. **ఈసడించు** *īsadintsu.* v. a. & n. To hate, abhor, or dislike. To be angry with, to find fault with. కోపపడు, కోపించు, నిందించు. గులాబిపూలనీసడించు outblushing the roses. **ఈసడింపు** *īsadimpu.* n. Dislike, hatred. T. iv. 33.

ఈసపిట్ట *īsa-piṭṭa.* [Tel.] n. The porcupine fish (*Diodon hystrix*). It is nearly globular and is covered with prickles.

ఈసపోవు, ఈసరపోవు *īsa-pōvu.* [Tel.] v. n. To pine, shrink. కుచ్చుకొను. ఈసరపోనీక without omitting anything. కడంతైనా విడువక. "వనితల నూరార్చి వారలచ్చటికి జనిమరలివచ్చినవిధంబీసరపోనీకపూసగుచ్చిన తెరంగునజెప్పెను." HK. ii. 185.

ఈసు *īsu.* [from Skt. ఈర్ష్య.] n. Envy. Dislike, disgust, anger. ఈర్ష్య. "కూలంబు రాఘువుమీద బ్రయోగించినవతండును నదుమున దానిదునియలు సేసిననీసునంబెరిగిసురలైరి." భార. అర: vii. **ఈసుకాడు** *īsukāḍu.* n. an envious man. ఈర్ష్యాళువు.

ఈహ *īha.* [Skt.] n. Wish, desire, inclination.

ఈహీ *īhī.* [Tel.] interj. Fie! ఛీ.

ఉ U

ఉ *u.* [Tel. In common writing the vowel ఉ is shaped like ఈ. Compare with this the Kanarese ಉ and the Skt. उ and Eng. U and W, all having the same origin.] The vowel U, as sounded in *put*, as in *oo foot.* Many Telugu words use A or U at pleasure: particularly in the second syllable, thus: వాటిక or వాటుక, పరచు or పరుచు, కరగు or కరుగు, వరస or వరుస, అటక or అటుక, తరము or తరుము, పలకరించు or పలుకరించు. If one of these forms does not occur we must look for the word with the other spelling.

ఉ. In poetry denotes a stanza in the metre named ఉత్పలమాల. The character ఉ. in common business is used as a contraction for ఉత్తరము an answer, as ప్ర. means a question.

ఉంకించు *unkinṭsu.* [Tel.] v. n. To try, to attempt. ప్రయత్నించు. "ఉరుతరశక్తిమై యురంకించియెగసి" "కనకాంగి తనుతేర చెనకంగనుంకించె." T. ii. 101. To start, as in surprise. ఉలికిపడు.

ఉంకు *unku.* [Tel.] v. i. To fly. ఎగురు. **ఉంకు** n. Consent. సమ్మతి.

ఉంకుటుంగరము *unku-ṭ-ungaramu.* [Tel. from ఉంకువ+ఉంగరము.] A wedding ring. H. iv. 201. వధూవరులు పెండ్లిచేసికొనుట కొప్పపడి ఒండొరులకిచ్చుకొనే ఉంగరము.

ఉంకువ *unkuva.* [Tel.] n. A pledge; money given to the parents of a bride "originally as a purchase price." అల్లుడు కన్యకొరకై మామకిచ్చు ద్రవ్యము, శుల్కము.

ఉంగ Same as ఉగ్గు. q. v.

ఉంగరము or **ఉంగ్రము** *ungaramu.* [Tel.] n. A ring, a finger ring. ఉంగరపువేలు the ring finger, or fourth finger. అనామిక.

ఉంగిడి *ungiḍi.* [Tel.] n. A disease amongst cattle arising from their grazing on the sprouts of జొన్నలు, సాజచేను and అనుప పొలు, as in England they are injured by eating clover.

ఉంగుటము *unguṭamu.* [from Skt. అంగుష్ఠము] n. The thumb. బొటనవ్రేలు.

ఉంచు *unṭsu.* [Tel. Causal of ఉండు] v. t. To place, put, set, lay, let be, keep, deposit, preserve, reserve. ఈ మాటలు అట్టే ఉంచు leave off these assertions. మదిలోనుంచు to bear in mind. తమరు దయ ఉంచవలసినది you must not forget me: ఉంచుకొను *unṭsu-konu.* To keep for himself. To keep a mistress. To entertain in service.

ఉంఛము *unchchamu.* [Skt.] n. Gleanings. To live by gleaning corn in the fields, ధాన్యమేరుకొని బ్రతుకుట. Extreme poverty రేకిబ్రతుకు. **ఉంఛవృత్తి** *unchha-vritti.* Living on alms. పేదబ్రతుకు.

ఉంట *unṭa.* [Tel.] n. Contraction of ఉండుట q. v. చెప్పరాకుంట being unable to tell. Also, a ball. ఉండ. ఉంటగాలము a fish hook to which a ball of lead is tied. సీసపుగుండుకట్టిన గాలము.

ఉండ *unḍa.* [Tel.] n. A lump, a ball, a pellet, a pill or bolus. adj. Round. గుండ్రని. **ఉండకోవి** *unḍa-kōvi.* n. A rod, a staff. చేతికర్ర. **ఉండచిట్లువేయు** *unḍa-chiṭlu-veyu.*

v. n. To ballot. ఉండనూలు *uṇḍanūlu*. n. A ball of thread. See ఉండ్రాయి. ఉండవిల్లు *uṇḍa-villu*. n. A pellet-bow.

ఉండమి *uṇḍami*. [Tel. negative noun from ఉండు.] n. Absence: non-existence. లేమి, ఉండకపోవుట.

ఉండి *uṇḍi*. [Tel. from ఉండు] Past p|| of ఉండు. (An affix) by, through or from చిరకాలమునుండి. బహుకాలమునుండి from a long time. n. A poor's box. హుండి or హూండి. (q. v.)

ఉండు *uṇḍu*. [Tel.] v. n. To be, exist, live. 2. To reside, dwell. 3. To remain, stop, stay. 4. To last, endure, continue. 5. To keep still, stay quiet; 6. To wait. To stand over, remain as a surplus. ఉండిపోవు, శేషించు. 7. To have. నాకు భార్య ఉండగా as I have a wife. "కనకము ఉన్నవాడు" he who possesses gold.—8. To keep a feast. విజయదశమి ఉండినారు they kept the Vijaya Dasami feast. ఉన్న మాటయిది this is the fact. ఉన్నరూపు the true form, the reality. నేను అక్కడ పది దినములుంటిని I remained there ten days, వాడు (ఇంట్లో) ఉన్నాడా is he at home? మీ తండ్రి బాగా ఉన్నాడా is your father well? ఉన్నట్టుండి suddenly, just as they were. ఉన్నారు they are; రేపటిదాక ఉంటారా will they remain till to-morrow? అక్కడ ఉన్నారా are they there?

ఉండ్ర or ఉండ్రన *uṇḍra*. [Tel.] n. The white Mimosa tree. తెల్లతుండ్ర.

ఉండ్రకంప *uṇḍra-kampa*. [Tel.] n. A bush with thorns.

ఉండ్రము *uṇḍramu*. [Tel.] n. A ball. adj. Round. plu. ఉండ్రములు same as ఉండ్రాళ్లు. See ఉండ్రాయి.

ఉండ్రాయి *uṇḍrāyi*. [Tel. ఉండ+రాయి] n. A ball of rice flour boiled in steam. ఉప్పుడుపిండిని ఉండలుగాచేసి వండినభక్ష్యము. ఉండ్రములు, ఉండ్రాలు, ఉండ్రాళ్లు *uṇḍrallu*. n. Cakes offered to the gods and particularly to Ganesa. ఉండ్రాళ్లపండుగ or ఉండ్రాళ్లతద్ది a feast kept by women who pay their vows by such offerings.

ఉంపడము *umpaḍamu*. [Tel. from ఉంచు] n. Keeping. వాని ఉంపడములోనున్న భోగముది the dancing woman kept by him. ఉంపుడు *umpuḍu*. adj. Kept.

ఉంబ *umba*. [Tel. an imitative word.] n. The lowing of oxen.

ఉంబళము, ఉంబళి or ఉంబళిక *umbaḷamu*. [Tel.] adj. Free from taxation. ఈనామైన, పన్నులేని. ఉంబళిగ్రామము a village free of rent. జాగీరుగ్రామము.

ఉంభనము *umbhanamu*. [Skt.] n. Sinking, depressing. A. ii. 75. ముంచడము. Filling. నించుట. ఉంభితము *umbhitamu*. adj. Filled. నింపబడిన.

ఉక్క *ukka*. [Tel. from ఉడుకు.] n. Heat, closeness. ఉష్మ.

ఉక్కడగు See under ఉక్కు.

ఉక్కడము *ukkaḍamu*. [Tel. from ఉడకడము] adj. Much, great. గొప్ప. ఉక్కడీడు *ukkaḍīḍu*. n. A brave man. బంటు, శూరుడు.

ఉక్కణము *ukkaṇamu*. [Tel.] n. A watch, guard. కావలి, రక్షణము.

ఉక్కరి and ఉక్కసు See under ఉక్కు.

ఉక్కలుడు *ukkaluḍu*. [Tel.] adj. Eager, earnest. దురంధరుడు, ఆసక్తికలవాడు.

ఉక్కళము *ukkaḷamu*. [Tel.] n. The vanguard, pickets round a camp. A principal or royal road near a city. పట్టణసమీప రాజమార్గము.

ఉక్కిరిబిక్కిరి *ukkiri-bikkiri*. [Tel.] adj. Close, suffocating, oppressive. ఊపిరి రుకని.

ఉక్కివము *ukkivamu*. [Tel.] n. Baseness, vileness, cunning, cruelty. కపటము, కుత్సితము. adj. Vile, base. క్షుద్ర. ఉక్కివుడు *ukkivuḍu*. n. A cunning man, a wretch కపటముగలవాడు.

ఉక్కిస or ఉక్కిసము *ukkisa.* [Tel.] n. Asthma, gasping for breath. ఉబ్బసము, ఎగ ఊపిరి, కాసము. Dry cough. పొడిదగ్గు.

ఉక్కీడు *ukkīḍu.* [Tel. ఉక్కు+ఈడు] n. A stubborn man. మూర్ఖుడు.

ఉక్కు *ukku.* [Tel.] v. i. To die, to be crushed. చచ్చు, నలగు.

ఉక్కు *ukku.* [Tel.] n. Steel. Strength, courage, pride, vigour, potency. అహంకారము, బలము, శౌర్యము. Steadiness. స్థైర్యము. తెలగ ఉక్కు A very tough sort of steel. R. v. 197. ఉక్కుతీగె *ukku-tige.* n. Steel wire. ఉక్కుతునక or ఉక్కుముక్క *ukku-tunaka.* n. A bit of steel, a brave, sharp or active man. ఉక్కుముఖి *ukku-mukhi.* n. The crimson crested barbet, or coppersmith bird, *Xantholaema haemaxtocephala.* (F.B.I.) ఉక్కుసున్నము *ukku-sunnamu.* n. Ashes of calcined iron, scoriæ, calx. ఉక్కడగించు or ఉక్కడచు *ukkaḍagintsu.* v. a. To crush one's pride, to humble: to dishearten. ఉక్కడగు *ukkaḍagu.* (ఉక్కు+అడగు) v. To sink or faint. To be disheartened. ఉక్కరి *ukk-ari.* (ఉక్కు+అరి) A man, a hero. శూరుడు, ధీరుడు. ఉక్కారు *ukk-āru.* (ఉక్కు+అరు) v. n. To ebb (as strength), to be exhausted, to faint. To lose one's vigour. ఉక్కుచెడు. To die. చచ్చు. ఉక్కరి having lost vigor. సామర్థ్యము లేకపోయి. ఉక్కుమడగు *ukku-maḍugu.* v. i. To lose vigor. To die. ఉక్కుమడచు to kill.

ఉక్కెడ *ukkeḍa* [Tel.] n. An oblong ball of thread for a spindle.

ఉక్కెర *ukkera.* [Tel.] n. A maccaroon, or sugar cake.

ఉక్తము *uktamu.* [Skt.] adj. Spoken, said, uttered. ఉక్తి *ukti.* n. Speech, speaking, a word, an expression.

ఉక్షము *ukshamu.* [Skt.] n. An ox. ఎద్దు.

ఉగము *ugamu.* [Tel.] n. Life. ఆయుష్షు. Ragha. i.

ఉగాది *ugādi.* [Skt. యుగాది] n. The Telugu New Year's day. చాంద్రమాన సంవత్సరాది.

ఉగ్గ *ugga.* [Tel.] adj. Tight, fast. ఉగ్గపట్టు *ugga-paṭṭu.* v. n. To determine. నిశ్చయించు. Kalah. iii. 122. ఉగ్గపోసికొను *ugga-pōsi-konu.* v. a. To resolve. నిశ్చయించుకొను.

ఉగ్గడించు *uggaḍintsu.* [Tel.] v. a. To sound. మ్రోగు, శబ్దించు. To use, to utter (language or expression.) To remember, bring to mind. To mention, speak of.. వచించు To calculate in the head without writing. To utter notes: to trill or harmonize. M. XII. vi. 368. T. iii. 332. ఉగ్గడింపు or ఉగ్గళింపు *uggaḍimpu.* n. Eloquence, voice, argument. ఉగ్గడువు *uggaḍuvu.* adj. Much, great. మిక్కిలి, అధికము.

ఉగ్గము *uggamu.* [Tel.] n. A cord or suspender attached to any thing for the purpose of carrying it about. చేతిలో పట్టుకొనిపోవుటకు వీలునట్లుగా చెంబులు మొద లగువానికి కట్టే తాడు.

ఉగ్గళించు Same as ఉగ్గడించు.

ఉగ్గాడు *ugg-āḍu.* [Tel.] n. To tread to pieces, destroy. పొడుచేయు.

ఉగ్గించు *uggintsu.* [Tel.] v. a. To weave closely so as to be without any interstices between the threads either of the woof or warp. Also, to flatter. పొగడించు.

ఉగ్గు *uggu.* [Tel.] n. A mixture of castor oil and breastmilk given to infants. A wrinkle or plait in cloth. ముడత. Confusion. ఉగ్గుపడు *uggu-paḍu.* v. i. To form into a fold. ముడతపడు. ఉగ్గులుపారు *uggulu-pāru.* v. n. To run into a knot in spinning or twisting, to be entangled, to run into wrinkles. చిలిపడు. To be confused or confounded.

ఉగ్గుడు *ugguḍu.* [Tel.]n. Distance. Respect. మేర, మర్యాద.

ఉగ్మలి *ugmali.* [Tel.] n. A woman. స్త్రీ.

ఉగ్రము *ugramu.* [Skt.] adj. Fearful. Angry, wrathful, fierce, furious, violent, cruel. ఉగ్రము or ఉగ్రత n. Fierceness.

ఉగ్రాక్షుడు *ugr-ākshuḍu*. n. The 'Fierce-eyed,' an epithet of the god Siva. **ఉగ్రుడు** *ugruḍu*. n. A fearful or fierce man. భయంకరుడు.

ఉగ్రాణము *ugrāṇamu*. [Tel.] n. A store house: a pantry, a treasury. ఉగ్రాణపు వాడు, ఉగ్రాణి, ఉగ్రాణికుడు a steward, a butler, a storekeeper, a treasurer.

ఉచితము *uchitamu*. [Skt.] adj. Proper, agreeable. Free, gratis, for charity. **ఉచితముగా** *uchitamu-gā*. adv. Freely, as a gift, of one's own pleasure, without money or price.

ఉచ్చండము *uchchaṇḍamu*. [Skt.] adj. Quick, hasty, sudden in temper. ఉచ్చం డుడు=త్వరపడేవాడు.

ఉచ్చము *uchchamu*. [Skt.] adj. Vertical, high, tall. ఉన్నతము. పొడవు. **ఉచ్చము** n. The zenith, the meredian, the vertical point in the sky.

ఉచ్చయము *uchchayamu*. [Skt.] n. A crowd. A knot formed of a woman's cloth in front. పోకముడి. ఆడుదానికోకకట్టుముడి.

ఉచ్చరించు *uchcharintsu*. [Skt.] v. a. To pronounce, articulate, recite, say. చెప్పు. **ఉచ్చారణ** or **ఉచ్చారణము** *uchchāraṇa* n. Pronunciation, utterance, recitation.

ఉచ్చాటనము *uchchāṭanamu*. [Skt.] n. Routing, driving away. **ఉచ్చాటనము చేయు** *uchchāṭanamu-chēyu*. v. To exorcise, drive out (evil spirits.)

ఉచ్చావచము *uchchā-vachamu*. [Skt.] adj. Diverse: not of one sort, in all sorts of ways. బహుప్రకారములుగలది, అన్నివిధాలు. **ఉచ్చావచముగా** *uchchā-vachamu-gā*. adv. Up and down, high and low. నన్ను ఉచ్చావచముగా తిట్టినాడు he called me all sorts of names.

ఉచ్చి *uchchi*. [Tel.] n. The crown or top of the head. మాడ, బ్రహ్మరంధ్రము. దానికి ఉచ్చి తాకినది she is suffering from the evil (imagined to be) caused by letting the nipple touch the top of her child's head.

ఉచ్చింత or **ఉచ్చిత** *uchchinta*. [Tel.] n. The gigantic swallowwort: a large kind of calotropis. HK. iii. 70. అలర్కభేదము. Rox. i. 571.

ఉచ్చిచ్చిరే or **ఉచ్చిరే** *uchchichchire*. [Tel.] Hey! hiss! a word used in setting a dog on to fight. BD. vii. 55.

ఉచ్చైఃశ్రవము *uchchaiṣravamu*. n. Name of the horse of Indra.

ఉచుకరించు *utsu-karintsu*. [Tel.] v. i. To cry shame (అనాదరముతో) ఉచుక్కు అను. **ఉచుక్కు** *utsukku*. n. An onomatopoeic word imitating the sound ఉచుకు.

ఉచ్చ *uttsa*. [Tel.] n. Urine. కాలుమడి, మూత్రము. **ఉచ్చపోయు** *uttsa-pōyu*. v. n. To make water. **ఉచ్చబుడ్డ** *uttsa-buḍḍa*. The bladder. వస్తి.

ఉచ్చమల్లి *uttsa-malli*. [Tel.] n. A naked or low woman. A jade, a slut.

ఉచ్చు *uttsu*. [Tel.] n. A slip-knot, a noose, a halter. ఉరి.

ఉచ్చు *uttsu*. [Tel.] v. n. To rush. దూరు. v. i. To go, to enter. To send. To drive away. "దుర్రుచ్చు" he cried avaunt.

ఉచ్ఛిష్టము *uchchhishṭamu*. [Skt.] adj. & n. Spittle, the leavings or fragments of the table. ఎంగిలి. మధూచ్ఛిష్టము a bee's leavings, i. e., wax.

ఉచ్ఛూనము *uchchhūnamu* [Skt.] adj. Swollen, turgid, close. దట్టము.

ఉచ్ఛృంఖలము *uch-chhṛunkhalamu*. [Skt.] adj. Self-willed, perverse, unrestrained. అడ్డములేని.

ఉచ్ఛ్రయము or **ఉచ్ఛ్రాయము** *uchchrayamu*. [Skt.] n. Height, the highest point: exaltation. అత్యుచ్ఛ్రాయము పతనహేతువు. Great exaltation leads to downfall.

ఉచ్ఛ్వసితము *uchchhvasitamu*. [Skt.] n. Breathing, Dasav. VII. 91. **ఉచ్ఛ్వాసము** *uchchhvāsamu*. n. Breath, a breathing sigh. ఎగఊపిరి. ఉచ్ఛ్వాసనిరోధము *uchchhvāsa-nirōdamu*, n. A stoppage of the breath from stitch or other bodily pain. ఊపిరికట్టు.

ఉజ్జయిని *ujjayini*. [Tel.] n. Ujjain or Oojein in Malwa.

ఉజ్జి *ujji*. [Tel.] n. A match, a rival. ఉద్ది.

ఉజ్జీవనము *ujjīvanamu*. [Skt. ఉత్+జీవనము] n. Animating, inspiring with life. Revival. జీవనము, బ్రతుకు. ఉజ్జీవించు *ujjīvintsu*. v. a. To live. జీవించు.

ఉజ్జృంభితము *ujjrimbhitamu*. [Skt.] adj. Bursting forth, betrayed, manifested, as any passion.

ఉజ్జ్వలము *ujvalamu*. [Skt.] adj. Radiant, splendid. తెలుగునది.

ఉజాడ *uzāḍa*. [H.] adj. Depopulated, waste, deserted. పాడైన. ఆ గ్రామము ఉజాడైనది the village was depopulated.

ఉజేరుబోడ *uzia-bōḍa*. [H.] n. Starboard. కుడిపక్క. (a sea phrase).

ఉజ్జె *uzza*. [Tel.] n. A guess, estimate. ఊహ. ఉజ్జెగొను *uzza-gonu*. v. t. To guess. ఊహించు.

ఉజ్జెగించు *uzza-gintsu*. [Tel.] v. a. To cease from, lay aside, leave, abandon, desist from. విడిచిపెట్టు. "అగ్నియు నుజ్జెగించి సమ్మదమున నన్నుగొల్వుము." ఉజ్జెగిల్లు *uzza-gillu*. v. i. To avoid. to pass. తొలగు, పోవు.

ఉజ్జెనము *uzzanamu*. [Tel.] n. The act of giving up, abandonment. విడుపు. ఉజ్జెనచేయు *uzzana-chēyu*. v. t. To give up. విడుచు.

ఉజ్జాయించు *uzzāyintsu*. [Tel. from ఉజ్జె.] v. i. To guess. ఊహించు. ఉజ్జాయింపు *uzzāyimpu*. n. Conjecture, guess, estimate.

ఉజ్జువకల్లు *uzzuva-kallu*. [Tel.] n. Pumice stone. A stone thrown up by a volcano.

ఉజ్ఝిత *ujjhita*. [Skt.] adj Left, abandoned.

ఉటంకము *uṭankamu*. [Tel.] n. Summing up, a summary. టూకీ, సంగ్రహము. ఉటంకి *uṭanki*. adj. Clever, active, ready, nimble, brief. ఉటంకించు *uṭankintsu*. v. a. To note, make a note or abstract of; to note down as a memorandum. To state, cite. To sum up or abstract. ఉటంకితనము *uṭanki-tanamu*. n. Vivacity, briskness.

ఉటజము *uṭajamu*. [Skt.] n. A hermitage: a cell formed of leaves. పర్ణశాల, ఆకుటిల్లు, ఇల్లు.

ఉట్టి *uṭṭi*. [Tel. plu. ఉట్లు.] n. A fibrous network sling, in which pots, &c., are suspended from the beams of the house. కలిమిపోయిన వెనుక ఉట్టికెగురనేల why long for little things after losing the *greater?* ఉట్లూడిపడి వచ్చినది it came down by the run, it fell down flat. చింతపండుయొక్క ఉట్లు the fibres inside a ripe tamarind.

ఉట్టిచీల *uṭṭi-chīla*. [Tel.] n. A rivet. రెండు కొనలందును తలగల చీల.

ఉట్టిపడు *uṭṭi-paḍu*. [Tel.] v. n. To start forth. To be manifested, as a passion. ఉన్నట్టుండి కలుగు, అతిశయించు.

ఉట్టు *uṭṭu*. [Tel.] n. Salt land; land fit for the manufacture of salt. ఉప్పుపట్టి, ఉప్పుపర్ర. ఉట్టు *uṭṭu*. [for పుట్టు] v. n. To be born. To flow. కారు, స్రవించు.

ఉట్రవడియము *uṭra vaḍiyamu*. [Tel.] n. A rich dish, a kind of *pilao* of rice and spices. వానిసొమ్ము ఉట్రవడియముగా నోట్లోవేసికొన్నాడు he took that man's property as quietly as he would have eaten his dinner.

ఉట్లతద్దె or ఉట్లపండుగ A feast. See ఉట్టి and తద్దె.

ఉట్లబొడ్డి or బొడ్డి *uṭla-boḍḍi*. [Tel.] n. A. certain plant.

ఉఠాపీ *uṭhāpi.* [Mahr.] adj. Great, high. గొప్ప, ఎత్తైన, ఉన్నతము.

ఉఠావుఠి or **.ఉఠా కుఠి** *uṭha-kuṭhi.* [H.] n. Hastiness. అతిత్వర. ఉఠావుఠిపయనము a forced march. ఉఠావుఠిగా వచ్చిచేరిరి they arrived in a great hurry.

ఉడత same as ఉడుత.

ఉడవ *uḍava.* [Tel.] n. A sort of fish, *Gerres mentosus*, a species of Zues. Russel, plate 67.

ఉడాయించు *uḍāyintsu.* [H.] v. i. To run away.

ఉడికిలించు, ఉడికిలు See under ఉడుకు.

ఉడిగము Same as ఊడిగము. q. v.

ఉడిగిపోవు or **ఉడిపోవు** Same as ఉడుగు.

ఉడుకాడు *uḍu-kāḍu.* [Tel.] v. t. To plague, tease, chaff. ఉడికించు.

ఉడుకు *uḍuku.* [Tel.] v n. To boil, to bubble with heat, to seethe. To be hot, feverish from heat, to boil with rage. **ఉడుకు** *uḍuku.* n. Boiling, ebullition, bubbling, heat. తాపము. **ఉడుకు** *uḍuku* adj. Hot. **ఉడుకుబోతు** *uḍuku-bōtu.* [Tel. ఉడుకు+పోతు] n. An envious wretch ఓర్వలేనివాడు, ఈర్ష్యాళువు. **ఉడికించు** *uḍikintsu.* v. t. To cause to boil, to debase, disgrace. To displease, offend, annoy. నొప్పించు, బాధించు.

> "రక్తయుపచారములచే
> మత్తమువకుధర్మతనయు నుడికించితివు
> ర్వృత్తులకు వాడుకులకు."
>
> M. V. ii. 81.

ఉడికిలించు *uḍikilintsu.* v. t. To irritate, to make one's blood boil. To distress or hurt one's feelings, to annoy. **ఉడికిలు** *uḍikilu.* v. n. To feel sore or hurt, to be annoyed. ఉడికిలునట్లుచేయు.

ఉడుకువ See under ఉడుగు.

ఉడుగర *uḍugara.* [Tel.] n. A gift, a present, any present given to a bride or bridegroom during the celebration of their marriage. A. vi. 190.—కట్నము, కానుక. "గంధర్వులకుడుగరల్ దయనొసగు" N. ii. 126.

> "కలకాంధవులొసగిరవుడు కాంచనభూషలు
> చీరలునరపతికింబొలతికనుడుగరల్యనుదము
> పొడలగనంతక." Swa. v. 120.

ఉడుగు *uḍugu.* [Tel.] v. n. To fall away, grow thin, lean or emaciated, decrease, to be cast off, to be removed as a stone or chain: to be exhausted. To pause, halt, stop. To cease, abate, leave, quit, or relinquish anger. To cease or depart as desire. To be shaken (as a resolution.) M. II. ii. 126. కాపువు ఉడిగినది breeding has ceased. ఉడుగక ceaselessly, incessantly, without intermission. ఎడతెగక. **ఉడుకువ** *uḍukuva.* [Tel. ఉడుగు+వు] n. Cessation. Rest. ఊరట, ఉపశమనము. **ఉడిగించు** *uḍigintsu.* [Tel. causative of ఉడుగు] v. a. To weaken, to lower or starve. To loosen. To turn out, cause to leave, &c., to check, stop, bridle. To remove, do away with. పోగొట్టు.

ఉడుత or **ఉడత** *uḍuta.* [Tel.] n. A squirrel. ఉడుతభక్తి the squirrel's devotion. Kuchēlo. i. 130 (When Rāma was building his bridge between Ceylon and the mainland, the squirrel came to lend his little aid: Rama in approbation stroked the squirrel down the back, which accounts for the white marks seen upon it.)

ఉడుపకుక్క *uḍupa-kukka.* [Tel. ఉడుము+కుక్క] n. A hound that hunts after iguanos. Swa. iv. 78.

ఉడుపము *uḍupamu.* [Skt.] n. A float or raft. తెప్ప.

ఉడుపు *uḍupu.* [Tel.] n. A suit of clothes; a dress.

ఉడుపు *uḍupu.* [Tel. causative of ఉడుగు] v. a. To efface, to turn out, to do away with, to wipe away, remove. To leave, to stop or cease. ఉడుగజేయు, ఉడిగించు.

ఉడుపుష్పము *uḍu-pushpamu.* [Skt.] n. The scentless china rose. *Hibiscus Sinensis.* అశోకము, దాసనము.

ఉడుము *uḍumu.* [Tel.] n. The iguana గోధ; గోధిక. ఉడుముపిల్ల the young iguana. ఉడుముపోయినా చెయ్యి వదిలించుకొని రావ లెను. if you catch an iguana, you are lucky if you get your hand off it.

ఉడుపు another form of ఉడుగు. (q. v.)

ఉడుపు *uḍuvu.* [Skt.] n. A lunar mansion, a star. నక్షత్రము. **ఉడుపతి** or **ఉడుపుడు** *uḍu-pati* n. The lord of the stars, i. e., the moon. చంద్రుడు. **ఉడుగణము** *uḍu-gaṇamu.* n. A constellation. ఉడువీథి. The heavens. **ఉడుతతి** *uḍu-tati.* n. The constellations. **ఉడ్వధిపుడు** *uḍvadhipuḍu.* n. The moon, as prince of the stars.

ఉడుసర *uḍu-sara.* [Tel.] n. A kind of plant. వాయుసి.

ఉడ్డ or **ఉడ్డా** *uḍḍa.* [Tel.] n. Four, a parcel or pack of four, నాలుగు; an assemblage or collection, a heap or pile. రాశి. **ఉడ్డా చేయు** *uḍḍa-chēyu.* v. a. To collect in a heap or crowd.

ఉడ్డాడించు *uḍḍaḍintsu.* [Tel. causative of ఉడ్డాడు] v. t. To palter, play backwards and forwards. Satyab. i. 114. **ఉడ్డాడు** *uḍḍāḍu.* v. i. To be confounded, to be confused. కలతకొను.

ఉడ్డీనము *uḍḍīnamu.* [Skt.] n. Flying, soaring. ఎగురుట.

ఉడ్డుకుడుచు *uḍḍu-kuḍutsu* [Tel.] v. n. To be out of breath, to be suffocated. To be at one's wits' end. ఊపిరి తిప్పకొనలేక బాధపడు. స్నానమందు నీళ్లచలికి ప్రాణములు ఉడ్డుకుడిచినవి the coldness of the water took away my breath. పిల్ల పాలుడ్డుకుడిచి నది the infant was choked with milk.

ఉణుజు *uṇuju.* [Tel.] n. A kind of fish.

ఉతక *utaka.* [Tel.] n. The pivot under a door. ఉతకదొబ్బు to lift a door off its hinges. See ఉత్తరాసి.

ఉతుకు *utuku.* [Tel.] v. a. To wash, as cloth. ఉదుకు. To thrash. ఉతకవేయు కువేయు to send clothes to be washed. **ఉతికించు** *utikintsu.* (Causal of ఉతుకు.) v. To get washed.

ఉత్కంఠ *ut-kaṇṭha.* [Skt.] n. Great eagerness. తహతహ, వేగిరపాటు.

ఉత్కటము *utkaṭamu.* [Skt.] adj. Abundant, excessive. అధికమైన.

ఉత్కరము *utkaramu.* [Skt.] n. A mass or heap. సమూహము, రాశి. మానవోత్కరములు crowds of men.

ఉత్కర్షము *utkarshamu.* [Skt.] n. Excellence, superiority. శ్రేష్ఠత, మేలు.

ఉత్కలము *utkalamu.* [Skt.] n. The country of Orissa.

ఉత్కలిక *ut-kalika.* [Skt.] n. Desire, longing. కోరిక, ఉత్కంఠ. **ఉత్కలుడు** *utkaluḍu.* n. An eager or clever man దురంధరుడు, నిర్వాహకుడు.

ఉత్కలితము *ut-kalitamu.* [Skt.] n. Geometric progression. సంకలితము arithmetical progression.

ఉత్కారము *ut-kāramu.* [Skt.] n. Winnowing ధాన్యమును తూర్పెత్తుట.

ఉత్కృష్టము *ut-krishṭamu.* [Skt.] adj. Superior, great, fine, grand. గొప్ప, శ్రేష్ఠము. ఉత్కృష్టదశ good fortune, high station. గొప్పదశ. ఉత్కృష్టమైన బాధ. terrible suffering.

ఉత్కోచము *utkōchamu.* [Skt.] n. A bribe. లంచము.

ఉత్క్రమణము *ut-kramaṇamu.* [Skt.] n. Going up; setting out. మీదికిపోవుట. ప్రాణోత్క్రమణవేళల at the moment the soul leaves the body.

ఉత్క్రోశము *ut-krōśamu.* [Skt.] n. The ospray, or sea eagle.

ఉత్క్షిప్తము *ut-kshiptamu.* adj. That which is thrown up. ఎగజిమ్మబడిన. **ఉత్క్షేపము** *ut-kshēpamu.* n. Throwing up in fragments. ఎగజిమ్ముట.

ఉత్త *utta.* [Tel.] adj. Empty, mere, bare, plain, actual, just, simple; idle, naked, vain, useless, in jest, not serious, not in earnest, false. ఉత్తప్పుడు on common occasions, in general. ఉత్తదొంగతనము actual theft. ఉత్తగుర్రము a horse without a rider. ఉత్తవారు persons not involved or concerned in a matter. ఇచ్చినప్పుడు ఉంటివా ఉత్తప్పుడు ఉంటివా were you present when he gave it, or *at some other time?*

ఉత్తండములు, ఉత్తండాలు *uttaṇḍamulu.* [Tel.] n. plu. A sort of gold necklace, worn by women.

ఉత్తంభితము *ut-tambhitamu.* [Skt.] adj. Planted, set. పాతుకొన్న, నిలుపబడిన. Lengthened. పొడిగింపబడిన. Vasu. vi. 137.

ఉత్తంసము *uttamsamu.* [Skt.] n. An earring: a tire or tiara. పూగుచ్చ, సిగబంతి. ఉత్తంసితము *uttamsitamu.* adj. Set or worn as a crown. ఉత్తంసుడు *uttamsuḍu.* n. The chief or noblest man.

ఉత్తప్తము *ut-taptamu.* [Skt. ఉత్+తప్తము] adj. Dried. n. Dried flesh.

ఉత్తమ *ut-tama.* [Skt.] n. An excellent good woman.

ఉత్తమము *ut-tamamu.* [Skt.] adj. Excellent, best, virtuous, chief, principal, first. ఉత్తమపురుషము (in gram. lit. ఉత్తమ=last), the first person. ఉత్తమర్ణుడు *ut-tamarṇuḍu.* [Skt. ఉత్తమ+ ఋణము] n. A creditor. అప్పిచ్చినవాడు. ఉత్తమాంగము *ut-tam-angamu.* [Skt. అంగము] n. The principal member, i. e., the head. ఉత్తముడు *ut-tamuḍu.* A most excellent man. ఉత్తమోత్తమము *ut-tamōt-tamamu* [Skt. ఉత్తమ+ఉత్తమ] adj. Superlative, best, excellent.

ఉత్తర *ut-tara.* [Skt.] n. The 12th lunar mansion. The daughter of the King of Virāṭa. ఉత్తరాభాద్ర the 26th mansion.

ఉత్తరంగము *uttar-angamu.* [Skt.] n. An arch over the door frame. గడపమీది కమ్మి.

ఉత్తరక్రియ *uttara-kriya.* [Skt.] n. A funeral rite, obsequies. చచ్చినపోయినవానికి చేసెడి అపరక్రియలు.

ఉత్తరణము *ut-taraṇamu.* [Skt.] n. Passing, crossing. దాటుట.

ఉత్తరము *utt-aramu.* [Skt.] n. An answer, a reply. A letter or epistle. The north. A command. ఉత్తర ప్రత్యుత్తరములు letter and reply, correspondence. ప్రశ్నోత్తరములు question and answer. ఉత్తరఖండము the northern division of the country. ఉత్తరాది *ut-tarādi.* n. The north, northern. ఉత్తరాదిదేశము the north country. ఉత్తరాయణము *uttarāyanamu.* [from ఉత్తర the north and అయనము going.] n. The sun's progress to the north of the equator, the period of the year during which the sun is north of the equator, the summer solstice.

ఉత్తరము *uttaramu.* [Skt.] adj. Secondary, subsequent, following after. మీదిది. ఉత్తరభాగము the sequel or supplement. ఉత్తరరామాయణము the sequel to the Rāmāyaṇa. ఉత్తరసాధనము a further means. ఉత్తరసాక్షి a subscribing witness. పొత్తులుకట్టుసాక్షి. ఉత్తరపక్షము the party who support the affirmative. Also, the affirmative proposition సిద్ధాంతము, the party in opposition being called ప్రతిపక్షము; the hypothesis or affirmative proposition, the second part or deduction from an argument. ఉత్తరార్థము the second half of an argument being the demonstration or exemplification of the పూర్వార్థము or assertion first made. ఉత్తరోత్తర adv. Ever after, at any future time, hereafter, in course of time, gradually.

ఉత్తరవాదము *uttara-vadamu.* [Skt.] n. Responsibility, security. ఉత్తరవాదముచేయు to hold one responsible. ఉత్తరవాది *uttara-vadi.* n. One who is responsible or answerable. A respondent or defendant, a security. ఉత్తరసభ *uttara sabha.* n. An ulterior or superior court.

ఉత్తరాషాఢ *uttarāshāḍha.* [Skt.] n. The 21st of the lunar mansions.

ఉత్తరాసంగము *uttarāsangamu.* [Skt.] n. A cloak: an upper or outer garment. ఉత్తరీయము.

ఉత్తరాసి *uttarāsi.* [Tel.] n. A hole in the lintel and sill or below the doorway, in which are inserted the pivots upon which the door turns. తలుపుటిరోగ కూసము.

ఉత్తరించు *uttarintsu.* [Tel.] v. a. To cross or pass over. To amputate: to divide cloth into separate pieces, to refund, repay, restore. ఉత్తారకుడు *uttārakuḍu.* n. One who helps one to cross. A saviour, a deliverer. దాటించువాడు, రక్షకుడు.

ఉత్తరిగ *uttariga.* [Tel.] n. A kind of necklace. ఒకవిధమైన సరము.

> "అందంపుటుత్తరిగలు
> అలరుచిరుగజ్జెయులు." H. v. 404.

ఉత్తరీయము *uttarīyamu.* [Skt.] n. A cloak, an upper garment. పై బట్ట.

ఉత్తరుడు *uttaruḍu.* [Skt.] n. Name of the son of Virāṭa (See Bhārata). ఉత్తరకుమార ప్రజ్ఞలు vain bragging like that of ఉత్తరుడు. ఉత్తరకుమారప్రజ్ఞలు పలుకువాడు he is a mere braggart.

ఉత్తరువు *uttaruvu.* [Skt.] n. An answer, a reply, an order, a command, permission, leave. ఉత్తరువుచెప్పు *uttaruvu-cheppu.* v. n. To answer or reply. ఉత్తరువుచేయు *uttaruvu-chēyu.* v. t. To order. ఉత్తరువు పుచ్చుకొను to take leave. ఉత్తరువిచ్చు *uttaravittsu.* v. t. To dismiss, give leave, direct.

ఉత్తరేణు or ఉత్తరేణి or ఉత్తరేను *uttarēnu.* [Tel.] n. The plant termed *achyranthes aspera* or, the Prickly Chaff-flower (E.P.) ఉత్తరేణిముల్లు a bur that sticks to the clothes.

ఉత్తలము *uttalamu.* [Tel.] n. Fear, dread, terror, distress, agitation, trouble. భయము, దిగులు, వెరపు, ఆర్తిద్యము. Haste. త్వర. "మత్తారులకు నుత్తలంబిడునుత్తలంబును" Swa. iv. 158. ఉత్తలపడు or ఉత్తలమొందు *uttala-paḍu.* v. i. To be in trouble or agitated. ఉత్తలపాటు *uttala-pāṭu.* n. Disquiet, distress.

ఉత్తానము *uttānamu.* [Skt.] adj. Not deep. Turned on one's back, lying supinely, reclining. లోతులేని, వెల్లకిలబడిన. ఉత్తానశయుడు n. One who lies on one's back.

ఉత్తాలము *uttālamu.* [Skt.] adj. Long: formidable. ఉత్తాలవాలుడు he of the formidable sword. ఉత్తాలపడు to hurry, to be precipitate. తొట్రుపాటుపొందు.

ఉత్తి *utti.* [Tel.] n. An equal. A substitute. ఈడు, ప్రతినిధి. (Jai. Bhār. i.)

ఉత్తీర్ణము *uttīrṇamu.* [Skt.] adj. That which is crossed over. దాటబడిన.

ఉత్తుంగము *uttungamu.* [Skt.] High, tall: big, projecting. పొడుగైన.

ఉత్తుడు *uttuḍu.* [Skt. యుక్తుడు.] adj. A fit person. తగినవాడు. భార. అను. ii.

ఉత్థానము *utthānamu.* [Skt.] n. Rising: effort: an army, war. ఉత్థాపనము *utthāpanamu.* n. Rising: erection. లేపుట. ఉత్థానములేని impotent. మృతోత్థానము resurrection. పునరుత్థానము resurrection.

ఉత్పతనము *ut-patanamu.* [Skt.] n. Flying, soaring. Birth, production. ఎగురుట, పుట్టుక.

ఉత్పత్తి *utpatti.* [Skt.] n. Birth, creation, production, origin. పుట్టుక. ఉత్పత్తిచేయు *utpatti-chēyu.* To produce, create, fabricate. ఉత్పత్తియగు *utpatti-y-agu.* v. n. To be born, created, formed, framed.

ఉత్పన్నము *utpannamu.* [Skt.] adj. Born. పుట్టిన.

ఉత్పలము *utpalamu.* [Skt.] n. A water-lily, a blue lotus. కలువ. ఉత్పలమాల *utpala-māla.* The name of a particular metre in verse.

ఉత్పాటనము *ut-pāṭanamu.* [Skt.] n. Rooting out, eradication. పెరికివేయుట. ఉత్పాటించు *utpāṭintsu.* v. a. To root out or eradicate. పెరికివేయు. ఉత్పాటితము *utpāṭitamu.* adj. Eradicated, rooted up.

ఉత్పాతము *ut-pātamu.* [Skt.] n. A prodigy, a preternatural phenomenon such as an earthquake, a comet, or an abnormal birth. ఉత్పాతపిండము a wonderful genius. త్రివిధోత్పాతములు marvels or signs in air, earth, and heaven. A iv. 300.

ఉత్పాదించుor ఉత్పాదిల్లు *utpādintsu.* [Skt.] v. n. To be born, to rise, to spring from a source. కలుగు, పుట్టు. ఉత్పాదితము *utpāditamu.* adj. Produced, effected, generated, begotten. కలిగింపబడిన.

ఉత్ప్రాసము *ut-prāsamu.* [Skt.] n. Satirical speech. పరిహాసపుమాట.

ఉత్ప్రేక్ష *ut-prēksha.* [Skt.] n. Hyperbole, rhetorical sublimity, high flown language, Poetical ecstacy. Apostrophe. ఉత్ప్రేక్షించు *ut-prēkshintsu.* v. i. and t. To apostrophise, or describe hyperbolically.

ఉత్ఫుల్లము *ut-phullamu.* [Skt.] adj. Expanded, or blown as a flower. వికసించిన.

ఉత్రాసి *utrāsi.* [Tel.] n. The upper hinge of door, a pivot on which the door turns. Same as ఉత్తరాసి. The lower hinge is called ఉటక *utaka.* ఉటకదిమ్మితి దొ మగాను to enter the house as a thief does by lifting the door out of its socket.

ఉత్సంగము *ut-sangamu.* [Skt.] n. The lap, the front of the thigh. Association, union. ఒడి, తొడ, కూడిక.

ఉత్సన్నము *ut-sannamu.* [Skt.] adj. Rooted up, destroyed, decayed, ruined. పెల్లగింపబడిన.

ఉత్సర్గము or ఉత్సర్జనము *ut-sargamu.* [Skt.] n. Yielding, relinquishment, quitting. విడుపు. Common. సామాన్యము.

ఉత్సవము *ut-savamu.* [Skt.] n. A feast, festivity, merriment. నేత్రోత్సవము a feast for the eyes.

ఉత్సహించు or ఉత్సాహించు *ut-sahintsu.* [Skt.] v. i. To attempt. యత్నించు. To triumph, to rejoice. సంతోషించు. ఉత్సాహము *ut-sāhamu.* n. Perseverance. Alacrity. Glee, eagerness, mettle, spirit, jollity, bloom of beauty. ఉత్సాహపురుషుడు a man of mettle. ఉత్సాహసంపన్నుడు sanguine, straight forward, mettlesome.

ఉత్సుకము *ut-sukamu.* [Skt.] adj. Strenuous, zealously active, earnest, zealous. ఉత్సాహముగల.

ఉత్సృష్టము *ut-srishṭamu.* [Skt.] adj. Abandoned, left. విడువబడిన.

ఉత్సేకము *ut-sēkamu.* [Skt.] n. Increase; pride; sprinkling water. అతిశయము, గర్వము, ప్రోక్షణము. ఉత్సేకించు *ut-sēkintsu.* v. i. To be full, to increase. అతిశయించు.

ఉత్సేధము *ut-sēdhamu.* [Skt.] n. Height, elevation, loftiness. పొడవు, ఎత్తు.

ఉదంచనము *udanchanamu.* [Skt.] n. An earthen cover for a pot. మూకుడు.

ఉదంచితము *udanchitamu.* [Skt.] adj. Thrown up, tossed. Worshipped, honoured. Fine, grand, splendid. విజృంభించిన.

ఉదంతము *udantamu.* [Skt.] n. A message. Tidings, intelligence. వృత్తాంతము, సమాచారము.

ఉదక్ *udak.* [Skt.] n. North. ఉత్తరదిక్కు. adj. Northern. ఉత్తరపు.

ఉదకము *udakamu.* [Skt.] n. Water. నీళ్లు.

ఉదగ్రము *ud-agramu.* [Skt.] n. High. Fearful. పొడవైన, భయంకరమైన.

ఉదధి *uda-dhi.* [Skt. ఉద water+ధి place.] The sea. సముద్రము. ఉదపానము *uda-panamu.* n. A well. నుయ్యి.

ఉదయము *udayamu.* [Skt.] n. Birth. పుట్టుక. The rising of the sun or other heavenly bodies, the morning. ఉదయాన in the morning. **ఉదయాద్రి**, *udayādri.* n. The eastern mountain behind which the sun is supposed to be born. ఉదయరాగము Morning carol. A particular sort of red silk. **ఉదయించు** *udayintsu.* v. a. To be born. To rise. To begin or originate, as a quarrel or an opinion. To arise or become celebrated. కుటిలబుద్ధి ఉదయించి crooked thoughts having arisen in the mind.

ఉదరము *udaramu.* [Skt.] n. The belly, the centre; లంబోదరుడు the corpulent being, a title of Gaṇēsa. ఉదరపోషకుడు a glutton, one who cares chiefly to fill his belly. **ఉదరపోషణము** *udara-pōshaṇamu.* n. Nourishing the belly, livelihood.

ఉదరు *udaru.* [Tel.] v. i. To be afraid, to be alarmed. **ఉదరిపడు** *udari-padu.* v. n. To start or be alarmed. అదిరిపడు, ఉలికిపడు. **ఉదరిపాటు** *udari-pāṭu.* n. Startling. ఉలికిపడుట.

ఉదర్కము *udarkamu.* [Skt.] n. Future or remote consequence, భవిష్యత్ ఫలము; future time. రాగలకాలము.

ఉదస్తుడు *udastudu.* [Skt.] adj. He who is expelled, humbled or shamed; an exile; నిరాకరింపబడినవాడు; తొలగింపబడినవాడు.

ఉదాత్తము *udāttamu.* [Skt.] n. A sort of quaver used in reading the Veda. **ఉదాత్తము** *udāttamu.* adj. Generous, liberal, noble, glorious. Exceeding, great, vast. గొప్ప. **ఉదాత్తుడు** *udāttudu.* n. A noble man, a liberal man. గొప్పవాడు, దయగలవాడు.

ఉదానము *udānamu.* [Skt.] n. Air that rises in the throat. కంఠమందలి గాలి.

ఉదారుడు *udārudu.* [Skt.] n. A liberal or splendid man, a generous man ఇచ్చువాడు, గొప్పవాడు.

ఉదాసీనము *udāsīnamu.* [Skt.] n. Bullying, rejection, disregard. ఉదాసీనపుమాటలు, abusive language. దుర్భాషలు. **ఉదాసీనుడు** *udāsīnudu.* n. A stranger. One who is indifferent or unconcerned. నిర్విచారభావముగలవాడు. వాడు దానిలో కలియక ఉదాసీనుడుగానుండెను he was an unconcerned spectator.

ఉదాహరణము *udāharaṇamu.* [Skt.] n. An example, instance, or illustration of any rule or precept. **ఉదాహరించు** *udāharintsu.* v. a. To instance, mention. చెప్పు, దృష్టాంతముగా చెప్పు.

ఉదితము *uditamu.* [Skt.] adj. Spoken, said. Risen, produced. చెప్పబడిన, పుట్టిన.

ఉదియ *udiya.* [Tel. another form of ఉద్దియ] n. An attempt. యత్నము. గామా. అర: ii. **ఉదియగొను** *udiya-gonu.* v. t. To try. యత్నించు.

ఉదిరి *udiri.* [Tel.] adj. Fine, pure. Refined. తప్తము, ఉదిరిబంగారు fine gold ఆహరంశ. R. vii. 184. ఉదిరిసెత్తములు lilies. ఉదిరికౌగిలిట in a sweet embrace. **ఉదిరిగొను** *udiri-gonu.* v. i. To be hot, to melt. తపించు.

ఉదిల *udila.* [Tel.] n. Trouble, grief, regret. పరితాపము. Discouragement, timidity, cowardice. పిరికితనము, అధైర్యము. **ఉదిలకొను** *udila-konu.* v. i. To be afraid. భయపడు; to lose heart, to grieve, to regret పరితపించు.

"పేనరుడుమానసముద్ధృతి,
మానినుచితవృత్తినుండియుదిలగొనక."
M. XII. iii. 166.

ఉదీచి *udīchi.* [Skt.] n. The north. **ఉదీచీనము** or **ఉదీచ్యము** *udīchīnamu.* adj. Northern.

ఉదీర్ణము *udīrṇamu.* [Skt.] adj. Generous, noble, great. ఉదారము, గొప్ప.

ఉదుంబరము *udumbaramu.* [Skt.] The glomerous fig tree, *ficus racemosa.* మేడిచెట్టు.

ఉదుకు Same as ఉతుకు. (q. v.)

ఉదుటు or ఉదుటుతనము *uduṭu.* [Tel.] n. Bigness, vigour, weight. ఉద్దతి. adj. Big, vigorous, fine. ఉద్ధతము.

ఉదురు *uduru.* [Tel.] adj. Insolent. ఉదురు మిండడు a fool. దుర్వినీతుడు.

ఉద్గతి *ud-gati.* [Skt.] n. Birth, production. పుట్టుక. "జగదుద్గతికి నిలయము." ఆము. iii.

ఉద్గమము *ud-gamamu.* [Skt.] n. Birth, production, flight. పుట్టుక, ఎగవు. ఉద్గమించు *udgamintsu.* v. i. To fly. ఎగురు.

ఉద్గాఢము *ud-gāḍhamu.* [Skt.] adj. Much, excessive, deep. అధికము.

ఉద్గాత *ud-gāta.* [Skt.] n. One who directs the Sama Veda ceremonies in a sacrifice. యజ్ఞమందు సామవేదము నడపువాడు.

ఉద్గారము *ud-gāramu.* [Skt.] n. Vomiting, belching, emitting, exuding, gushing. కక్కుట, తేపు. A. ii. 92. R. vi. 24. ఉద్గారించు *udgarintsu.* v. a. To vomit, to belch, emit. కక్కు, తేపు.

ఉద్ఘాటనము *ud-ghaṭanamu.* [Skt.] n. Breaking. భేదించుట. ఉద్ఘాటించు *udghaṭintsu.* n. To break, open. భేదించు.

ఉద్ఘాతము *ud-ghātamu.* [Skt.] n. Beginning. Striking. ఆరంభము, దెబ్బ.

ఉద్ఘోషము *ud-ghōshamu.* [Skt.] n. Cry మొర. ఉద్ఘోషించు *ud-ghōshintsu.* v. i. To cry. మొరపెట్టు.

ఉద్ద *udda.* [Tel.] adj. and adv. Much, very. మిక్కిలి. High or long. ఎత్తైన, పొడవైన.

ఉద్దండము or ఉద్దండత *uddanḍamu.* [Skt.] n. Violence, fierceness, as of heat. ఎక్కువయినది. ఉద్దండముగా fiercely, hotly.

ఉద్దము *uddamu.* [Tel.] n. Height, length. ఉద్దములు or ఉద్దాలు *uddamulu.* n. Shoes, slippers. పాదరక్షలు.

"పాదములకు కెంపు క్రొన్నని పలుకుచుండ
కమ్మటుద్దాలు చేపట్టుకొలువవుర."
H. iii. 121.

ఉద్దరి *uddari.* [Tel. ఉద్ద+దరి] n. A steep bank: నదిలో దిగుటకు యుక్తముకాని దరి. ఉద్దరువు *uddaravu.* (ఉద్ద+అరువు.) n. Mortgage of a crop not yet raised. ఉద్దవడి or ఉద్దవిడి *uddaraḍi.* ఉద్ద+వడి] n. Rapidity, great celerity. Violence, haste. P. i. 134.

ఉద్దాముడు *uddāmuḍu.* [Skt.] n. An irresistible man. నిరంకుశుడైన శక్తిగలవాడు. An independent man. స్వతంత్రుడు.

ఉద్దారి *uddāri.* [H.] n. A superintendent. విచారణకర్త. (Vizag.)

ఉద్దాలు See under ఉద్దము.

ఉద్ది *uddi.* [Tel.] n. A match, an equal, a rival. Rivalry, equality. A bank or dam with a channel on it, into which water is pumped to be conveyed to higher lands. The name of a certain tree. *Bignonia spathacea.* Rox. iii. 103. జత, సమానము. ఉద్దిచూపు to rival. ఉద్దులు equals సమానులు. ఉద్దులుద్దులుగా పోరాడి fighting hand to hand. ఉద్ది *uddi. adj.* Paired, couple, side by side. ఉద్దించు *uddintsu.* v. a. To pair, match, couple. జతపరుచు, పోలు. ఉద్దికాడు *uddikāḍu.* n. A match, an equal. A friend జతగాడు, చెలికాడు.

ఉద్దియ *uddiya.* [Tel.] n. A trial, attempt. యత్నము. ఉద్దియచేయు to try. యత్నించు.

ఉద్దిష్టము *ud-dishṭamu.* [Skt.] adj. Designed, mentioned. ఉద్దేశింపబడినది.

ఉద్దీడు Same as ఉద్దికాడు. See under ఉద్ది.

ఉద్దీపకము *uddīpakamu.* [Skt.] adj. Inflaming, lighting. వెలిగించునది.

ఉద్దీపనము *ud-dīpanamu.* [Skt.] n. Burning. వెలుగుట.

ఉద్దులు *uddulu.* [Tel.] n. The grain called black gram. మినుములు.

ఉద్దేశము *ud-dēsamu.* [Skt.] n Intent, design. గురి. ఉద్దేశించు *ud-dēsintsu.* v. i. To intend, design. ఉద్దేశ్యము *ud-dēsyamu.* adj. That which is intended.

ఉద్ధతి *ud-dhati.* [Skt.] n. Rudeness, arrogance. గర్వము. **ఉద్ధతుడు** *ud-dhatuḍu.* n. An insolent man.

ఉద్ధరణి *ud-dharaṇi.* [Skt.] n. A little spoon used in worship.

ఉద్ధరించు *ud-dharintsu.* [Skt.] v. a. To raise, lift, set up, support, up-hold, re-establish, restore, rescue, deliver, preserve, protect. పైకెత్తు, కాపాడు. వేదములనుద్ధరించు to restore the Vedas. సంసారమునుద్ధరించు to support the family. "నగరగలిసిన గ్రామము నుద్ధరించినాడు" he saved the village which had been sequestrated.

ఉద్ధవము *ud-dhavamu.* [Skt.] n. A festival, a holiday పండుగ.

ఉద్ధారణము or **ఉద్ధారణ** or **ఉద్ధారము** *ud-dhāraṇamu.* [Skt.] n. Lifting up. Protection. Sustaining. Rescuing, delivering, releasing, restoring. మతోద్ధారణచేయు to re-establish a religion. ఉద్ధారాంశము a share granted to the man who re establishes something that has fallen into decay. పోయినదానిని మళ్లీ సాధించినవానికిచ్చే విశేషభాగము. ఉద్ధారముచేయు to sustain: support. **ఉద్ధారకుడు** *ud-dhārakuḍu.* n. He who sustains or nourishes, a saviour, a redeemer రక్షకుడు.

ఉద్ధురము *ud-dhuramu.* [Skt.] adj. Weighty, firm. బరువైన, నిలుకడైన.

ఉద్ధూతము *ud-dhūtamu.* [Skt.] adj. Driven up, shaken off, scattered, removed. మీదికి ఎగరగొట్టబడిన, పోగొట్టబడిన.

ఉద్ధృతము *ud-dhṛitamu.* [Skt.] adj. Raised, drawn up. పైకెత్తబడిన, చేదబడిన.

ఉద్బుద్ధము *ud-buddhamu.* [Skt.] adj. Awakened, excited, reminded తలపునకు వచ్చిన, తెలుపబడిన, లేపబడిన, ఉసికొలుపబడిన, జ్ఞాపకముచేయబడిన. **ఉద్బోధకము** *ud-bōdhakamu.* n. Hinting, suggesting. Association, connection of ideas: exemplified thus: హస్తిహస్తిపకన్యాయము the sight of this elephant reminds one of him who rode it. **ఉద్బోధకుడు** *ud-bōdhakuḍu.* n. One who reminds. తలపునకు తెచ్చువాడు.

ఉద్భటము *ud-bhaṭamu.* [Skt.] adj. Great, exceeding. హెచ్చు అయిన.

ఉద్భవము *ud-bhavamu.* [Skt.] n. Birth, production, emanation. పుట్టుక. **ఉద్భవించు** or **ఉద్భవిల్లు** *ud-bhavintsu.* v. i. To be born or produced. పుట్టు.

ఉద్భాసితము *ud-bhāsitamu.* [Skt.] adj. Splendid, glorious. ప్రకాశితము.

ఉద్భిజ్జము, ఉద్భిత్తు, ఉద్భిదము *ud-bhijjamu.* [Skt.] n. Sprouting, germinating, shooting. A. v. 114. భూమిని భేదించుకొని పుట్టునది. **ఉద్భేదము** *ud-bhēdamu* adj. Breaking or bursting through, as a shoot through the ground. పుట్టిన.

ఉద్యమము *udyamamu.* [Skt.] n. An attempt. యత్నము. **ఉద్యమించు** *udyamintsu.* v. i. To attempt.

ఉద్యానము *udyānamu.* [Skt.] n. A royal garden, or park.

ఉద్యాపనము *udyāpanamu.* [Skt.] n. Sending out. వెడలించుట.

ఉద్యుక్తము *ud-yuktamu.* [Skt.] adj. Attempted. Zealous, resolved, determined. **ఉద్యుక్తుడు** He who is ready or prepared. యత్నించువాడు, సిద్ధముగానున్నవాడు. అక్కడికి పోవలెనని ఉద్యుక్తుడై being about to go. జాబువ్రాయుటకు ఉద్యుక్తుడనై when I was going to write the letter క్రూరమైన పనికి ఉద్యుక్తుడై ready to do a cruel deed.

ఉద్యోగము *udyōgamu* [Skt.] n. An attempt, endeavour, undertaking; enterprise, exertion; activity యత్నము. a profession, employment, occupation, calling, mission, office, or situation; ఉద్యోగముచేయు to exercise an office. **ఉద్యోగస్థుడు** or **ఉద్యోగి** *udyōgasthuḍu.* n. An officer, a functionary. **ఉద్యోగించు** *udyōgintsu.* v. t. To undertake, set to do, to turn one's mind to: to apply oneself to యత్నించు.

ఉద్రేకము *udrêkamu*. [Skt.] n. Increase, excess. అతిశయము. ఉద్రేకించు *udrêkintsu*. v. i. To increase. అతిశయించు. ఉద్రిక్తము *udriktamu*. adj. Distinct: increased.

ఉద్వర్తనము *ud-vartanamu*. [Skt.] n. Any unguent applied to the body before bathing. నలుగుపిండి. B. iii. 1002.

ఉద్వాసనము *ud-vāsanamu*. [Skt.] n. Expulsion, exile. ఉద్వాసించు or ఉద్వాసనముచేయు *udvasintsu*. v. a. To expel. అగ్నిని ఉద్వాసనముచేయుట to banish the regent of fire out of flame. M. XV. ii. 192.

ఉద్వాహము *ud-vāhamu*. [Skt.] n. Marriage. పెండ్లి.

ఉద్విగ్నము *ud-vignamu*. [Skt.] adj. Disturbed, discomposed, disquieted, affected with fear or sorrow. ఆకులితమైన, కలవరము గాకుండే.

ఉద్వృత్తము *ud-vrittamu*. [Skt.] adj. Potent, irresistible, ill behaved, proud గర్వించిన. ఉద్వృత్తి *ud-vritti*. Might; misbehaviour. గర్వము.

ఉద్వేగము *ud-vêgamu*. [Skt.] n. Anxiety. agitation. వెరపు.

ఉద్వేలము *ud-vêlamu*. [Skt.] n. Excess, vastness. అధికము. ఉద్వేలము adj. Extreme, vast, prodigious. ఉద్వేలతరమైన very vast. R. iv. 116.

ఉద్రము *udramu*. [Skt.] n. An otter. నీరు పిల్లి.

ఉనికి or ఉన్కి *uniki*. [Tel. from ఉండు] n. Being, existence. Stay, dwelling, home, place, residence, state, condition. ఉండుట, స్థితి, స్థానము. మాటాడకునికి remaining silent. హితవుగాకునికి his not being friendly. ఉనికి పట్టు *uniki-pattu*. n. Home, dwelling, abode. ఉనుకువ same as ఉనికి.

ఉనుచు Same as ఉంచు.

ఉన్నతము *un-natamu*. [Skt.] adj. Tall, high, lofty. ఉన్నతి *un-nati*. n. Tallness, height. Increase, advancement, prosperity, rising, ascending. పొడవు, అతిశయము, ఔన్నత్యము.

ఉన్నమితము *un-namitamu*. [Skt.] adj. Raised, high, exalted. పైకెత్తబడిన.

ఉన్ని *unni*. [Tel.] n. Wool. గొర్రెబొచ్చు.

ఉన్నా for ఉండునా is it likely to be so?

ఉన్మత్తము *un-mattamu* [Skt.] adj. Mad, foolish, tipsy. వెర్రెత్తిన. ఉన్మత్తుడు *un-mattudu*. n. A madman, a fool. మిక్కిలి మదించినవాడు. ఉన్మదుడు *un-madudu*. adj. Proud, spirited. ఉన్మాదము *unmādamu*. n. Madness, folly. వెర్రి.

ఉన్మాథము *un-māthamu*. [Skt.] n. A trap, a snare. బోను, గాలము.

ఉన్మీలనము *un-mîlanamu*.[Skt.] n. Opening, expanding. వికసించుట, తెరచుట. ఉన్మీలితము *un-mîlitamu*. adj. Opened, blooming, blown as a flower, opening. వికసించిన.

ఉన్ముఖము *un-mukhamu*. [Skt.] adj. Looking up, facing, fronting. ఎదురుచూచునది. ఉన్ముఖత్వము *un-mukhatvamu*. n. Tendency, inclination. మదనోన్ముఖత్వము an amorous feeling.

ఉన్మూలము *un-mūlamu*. [Skt.] adj. Radical, or from the root వేరుతెగిన. ఉన్మూలముగా radically, by the roots. ఉన్మూలించు *un-mūlintsu*. v. t. To root up, eradicate, destroy. పెల్లగించు. ఉన్మూలితము *unmūlitamu*. adj. Eradicated, pulled up by the roots. వేరుతో పెల్లగింపబడిన.

ఉన్మేషము *un-mêshamu*. [Skt.] n. Opening blowing as a flower. వికాసము. నవనవోన్మేషముగా with increasing delight.

ఉపకంఠము *upa-kanthamu*. [Skt.] n. Contiguity, nearness. adj. Near, proximate. దాపైన.

ఉపకథ *upa-katha*. [Skt.] n. An episode.

ఉపకరణము *upa-karaṇamu*. [Skt.] n. An instrument, implement, apparatus, an appendage. సాధనము. **ఉపకరించు** *upa-karintsu*. v. a. To be of use, benefit, do good to. **ఉపకారము** *upa-kāramu*. n. Beneficence, kindness, obligation, aid, help. మేలు **ఉపకారి** *upa-kāri*. adj. Beneficent, kind, charitable, obliging, assisting. n. One who does good. **ఉపకారిక** *upa-kārika*. n. The temporary abode of a king. రాజులయొక్క విడిదియిల్లు, ఉప్పరిగె. **ఉపకృతి** *upa-kriti*. n. Aid, assistance, kindness. మేలు.

ఉపక్రమము *upa-kramamu*. [Skt.] n. Beginning or commencement. A skilful plan. ఉపాయము మొదలైన ప్రారంభించుట. **ఉపక్రమించు** *upa-kramintsu*. v. a. To begin, to proceed to do, commence. ఆరంభించు.

ఉపక్రోశము *upa-krōśamu*. [Skt.] n. Censure, blame. నింద.

ఉపగూహనము *upa-gūhanamu*. [Skt.] n. An embrace. ఆలింగనము.

ఉపగ్రహము *upa-grahamu*. [Skt.] n. A satellite.

ఉపఘ్నము *upa-ghnamu*. [Skt.] n. A prop: a trellis for creepers to grow over. సమీపాశ్రయము, ప్రాపు.

ఉపచయము *upa-chayamu*. [Skt.] n. Increase, heap, excess. వృద్ధి.

ఉపచరించు *upa-charintsu*. [Skt.] v. a. To serve, befriend. To help (at table), to tend, wait upon. సేవించు, సన్మానించు. **ఉపచారము** *upa-chāramu*. n. Service or waiting upon. Kindness, good offices, attendance ఊడిగము. **ఉపచారమైన** *upa-chāramaina*. adj. Civil, polite.

ఉపజాతి *upa-jāti*. [Skt.] n. A sub-class. జాతిలో చేరిన భాగము.

ఉపజీవి *upa-jīvi*. [Skt.] n. A dependent. ఒకరినాశ్రయించి జీవించువాడు, ఆశ్రితుడు. తత్పాదపద్మోపజీవి his humble servant.

ఉపతాపము *upa-tāpamu*. [Skt.] n. Grief, weariness; disease, trouble. సంతాపము, రోగము, రోగము.

ఉపత్యక *upa-tyaka*. [Skt.] n. Low land. The foot of a hill. కొండదిగ్గువ నేల

ఉపద *upada*. [Skt.] n. A present or gift. కానుక.

ఉపదంశము *upa-damśamu*. [Skt.] n. A relish, a pickle or condiment. ఉరుగాయ. A painful venereal disease కొరుకురోగము.

ఉపదేశము *upa-dēśamu*. [Skt.] n. Teaching, instruction, guidance, practical observations. హితవచనము. Initiation, confirmation in the creed: **ఉపదేశించు** *upa-dēśintsu*. v. a. To teach, guide, initiate, prompt. **ఉపదేశకుడు** or **ఉపదేష్ట** *upa-dēśakuḍu*. n. A teacher. ఉపదేశించువాడు.

ఉపద్రవము *upa-dravamu*. [Skt.] n. Trouble, annoyance, plague, affliction. Danger, injury, harm. అపాయము. ఉపద్రవపుపని a dangerous business.

ఉపధ *upadha*. [Skt.] n. (In gram.) the penultimate letter. కడపటి అక్షరమునకు ముందరి అక్షరము.

ఉపధానము *upa-dhānamu*. [Skt.] n. A pillow or cushion. తలగడ.

ఉపనయనము *upa-nayanamu*. [Skt.] n. Investiture with the sacred thread. The initiation rite in the twice-born castes among the Hindus. వడుగు.

ఉపనిధి *upa-nidhi*. [Skt.] n. A secret hoard. మిక్కిలి రహస్యముగా దాచిన సొమ్ము.

ఉపనిషత్తు *upa-nishattu*. [Skt.] n. An Upanishad, a philosophical disquisition attached to the Vedas.

ఉపనీతుడు *upa-nītuḍu*. [Skt.] n. One initiated into the twice born castes. వడుగైనవాడు. See ఉపనయనము.

ఉపన్యసించు *upanya-sintsu*. [Skt.] v. a. To keep. ఉంచు. To detail, inculcate, amplify.

ఉపన్యాసము *upa-nyā-samu*. n. Dwelling on a subject; an exposition, a lecture.

ఉపపట్టణము *upa-paṭṭaṇamu*. [Skt.] n. A suburb.

ఉపపతి *upa-pati*. [Skt.] n. One who keeps a woman. విటుడు, రంకుమగడు.

ఉపపత్తి *upa-patti*. [Skt.] n. Convenience, aid, wealth, acquisition, gain. ద్రవ్యోపపత్తి a fund.

ఉపపదము *upa-padamu*. [Skt.] n. An affix in grammar.

ఉపపన్నుడు *upa-pannuḍu*. [Skt.] n. An opulent man. ఉపపత్తిగలవాడు.

ఉపపురాణము *upa-purāṇamu*. [Skt.] n. A minor Purāṇa. See పురాణము.

ఉపప్లవము *upa-plavamu*. [Skt.] n. A calamity. ఉపద్రవము, ఉత్పాతము, చంద్రసూర్యగ్రహణము, రాహువు.

ఉపబర్హము *upa-barhamu*. [Skt.] n. A pillow. తలగడ.

ఉపబలము *upa-balamu*. [Skt.] n. Aid, assistance. సహాయము. ఉపబలమైన conducive to.

ఉపబృంహణము *upa-brimhaṇamu*. [Skt.] n. Increase, prosperity. చక్కగా పెరుగుట, వృద్ధి.

ఉపభోగము *upa-bhōgamu*. [Skt.] n. Enjoyment, use. అనుభవము.

ఉపమ *upama*. [Skt.] n. A resemblance, a simile. Also, skill నేర్పు. **ఉపమరి** *upamari*. adj. Clever, ready at expedients. **ఉపమానము** *upamānamu*. n. A comparison, simile. The object to which a thing is compared. **ఉపమించు** *upa-mintsu*. v. a. To compare. పోల్చు. **ఉపమేయము** *upa-mēyamu*. n. The object which is compared to another. The antitype or thing meant in a parable or comparison. ఇక్కడ ఇది ఉపమానము, దీనివల్ల ఉపమేయమును గ్రహింపవలసినది here we must understand the thing meant from the figure the poet uses.

ఉపయుక్తము *upa-yuktamu*. [Skt.] adj. Convenient, fit, disposable, serviceable. ఉపయోగమయిన. **ఉపయోగము** *upa-yōgamu*. n. Use, advantage, benefit. వనికి వచ్చుట. ఆ రూకలు ఉపయోగమునకు రావు that money won't pass. **ఉపయోగించు** *upa-yōgintsu*. v. a. To benefit, avail. To be useful or applicable, as an argument. అది ఉపయోగింపదు it is of no use, of no avail.

ఉపరతి See రతి.

ఉపరి *upari*. [Skt. cognate with Eng. Up.] adj. Over, above. **ఉపరిరయితు** *upari-rayitu*. [H.] n. A tenant at will. పాయకారి.

ఉపలక్షణము *upa-lakshaṇamu*. [Skt.] n. Implying something that has not been expressed; implying something in addition or any analogous object where only one is specified; using a term in a generic sense; metaphorical or elliptical expression; synecdoche of a part for the whole. **ఉపలక్షించు** *upa-lakshintsu*. v. t. To survey, to observe. చూచు.

ఉపలబ్ధి *upa-labdhi*. [Skt.] n. Acquirement, gain, knowledge. పొందుట, తెలివి.

ఉపలము *upalamu*. [Skt.] n. A stone, a jewel, a rock. వర్షోపలము a hailstone. భూతలసమోపలము a rock even with the surface of the ground.

ఉపలాలనము *upa-lālanamu*. [Skt.] n. Lulling, coaxing. బుజ్జగము. **ఉపలాలించు** *upa-lālintsu*. v. To lull (a child, &c.) to sleep, to coax. బుజ్జగించు. **ఉపలాలితము** *upa-lālitamu*. adj. Coaxed, lulled. బుజ్జగింపబడిన.

ఉపలేపనము *upa-lēpanamu*. [Skt.] n. Smearing, plastering. అలుకుట.

ఉపవనము *upa-vanamu*. [Skt.] n. A park or demesne, a garden or grove. ఆరామము, తోట.

ఉపవాసము *upa-vāsamu*. [Skt.] n. Fasting, a fast. వస్తు. ఉపవాసముచేయు to go without food, to fast.

ఉపవాహ్యము *upa-vāhyamu*. [Skt.] n. A king's elephant. రాజారెక్కు సవారీయేనుగు.

ఉపవిష్టము *upa-vishṭamu*.[Skt.]adj. Seated, sitting. సుఖోపవిష్టులై seated at their ease.

ఉపవీతము *upa-vītamu*. [Skt.] n. The Brahminical thread. జందెము.

ఉపశమనము or **ఉపశమము** *upa-samanamu*. [Skt.] n. Tranquillity, calmness, patience, alleviation, relief, abatement. ఓర్పు. **ఉపశమించు** or **ఉపశమిల్లు** *upa-ṣamintsu*. v. n. To be calmed or pacified, to be alleviated, to be abated or assuaged. **ఉపశాంతి** *upa-sānti*. n. Calmness, quiet, serenity. అణకువ, ఓర్పు.

ఉపశ్రుతి *upa-sruti*. [Skt.] n. A good or bad omen gathered from overhearing a conversation.

ఉపశ్లోకించు *upa-ślokintsu*. [Skt.] v. t. To applaud. స్తోత్రముచేయు.

ఉపసంహరించు *upa-samharintsu*. [Skt.] v. t. To clear away, get rid of. To kill. To recall. సంహరించు, మరలించు. **ఉపసంహరము** *upa-samharamu*. n. Recalling, annulling, concluding: averting a spell, recalling an enchanted arrow to prevent its taking effect, refutation. తొలగించుట, మరలించుట, ఖండించుట.

ఉపసదనము *upa-sadanamu*. [Skt.] n A neighbouring abode: the neighbourhood.

ఉపసర్గ *upa-sarga*. [Skt.] n. A grammatical particle, a prefix or preposition. **ఉపసర్గము** *upa-sargamu*. n. A portent such as an eclipse, &c. ఉత్పాతము. "ఉపసర్గాధికహీన వృష్టి పటువాయువ్యాజ నానాసరీసృప దుర్భిక్ష జలాగ్ని దుష్టవిమ దాత్రేపాది దోషంబులందు." V. P. vi. 349.

ఉపసర్పణము *upa-sarpaṇamu*. [Skt.] n. Courting, fawning. ఆశ్రయించుట. **ఉపసర్పించు** *upa-sarpintsu* v. a. To court, sue. ఆశ్రయించు.

ఉపస్థానము *upa-sthānamu*. [Skt.] n. Service. సేవ. **ఉపస్థితము** *upa-sthitamu*. adj. Near, that is near. Contiguous. చేరు. **ఉపస్థితి** *upa-sthiti*. n. Nearness.

ఉపస్పర్శము *upa-sparṣamu*.[Skt.]n.Touching, contact. Also ఆచమనము. (q. v.)

ఉపహతము *upa-hatamu*. [Skt.] adj. Struck (by lightning,&c.) hurt,injured,destroyed. కొట్టబడిన. **ఉపహతి** *upa-hati*. n. A blow, calamity, trouble, ruin. ఉపద్రవము, నాశము, ఆపద. దైవోపహతిచేత by the finger of God.

ఉపహారము *upa-hāramu* [Skt.] n. A c plimentary present. కానుక.

ఉపాంగము *upāngamu*. [Skt.] n. In . the accompaniment, as the drone. సుతిపోసెడి తిత్తి.

ఉపాంతము *upāntamu*. [Skt.] n. Nearness. గ్రామోపాంతమునందు in the vicinity of the village సరోవరోపాంతదేశమునందు in the land near the lake.

ఉపాంశు *upāmsu*. [Skt.] adv. Solitary. ఏకాంతము. A iv. 73. **ఉపాంశువు** *upāmsuvu*. n. Muttering a prayer, జపభేదము.

ఉపాకర్మము *upa-karmamu*. [Skt.] n. A rite celebrated by Brahmins on the full moon in the month Sravanam (July, August:) they imagine that this blots out all the sins of the past year, and they put on new threads సంస్కారపూర్వకముగా వేదమును గ్రహించుట.

ఉపాఖ్యానము *up-ākhyānamu*. [Skt.] n. A tale, legend, narrative. ఇతిహాసము. కుచేలోపాఖ్యానము the story of Kuchēla. నలోపాఖ్యానము the life of Nala.

ఉపాత్యయము *upātyayamu*. [Skt.] n. Neglect, transgression. అతిక్రమము.

ఉపాదానము *upā-dānamu*. [Skt.] n. A cause or motive. కారణము. Alms భిక్షము, ఉపాదానమెత్తు to beg.

ఉపాధి *upādhi* [Skt.] n. Meditation ధర్మచింత. One who support his family కుటుంబ

సాధకము. Cause or means. వ్యాజము. An attribute or characteristic. విశేషణము. జీవనోపాధి means of subsistence.

ఉపాధ్యాయుడు upa-dhyāyuḍu. [Skt.] n. A tutor, instructor చదువుచెప్పువాడు. A preceptor in religion. One who teaches the Veda. వేదమును చదివించువాడు. ఉపాధ్యాయ upadhyāya. n. A female teacher. ఉపాధ్యాయాని upa-dhyāyāni. n. A teacher's wife. ఉపాధ్యాయి upadhyāyi. n. A female teacher or a teacher's wife. ఉపాధ్యాయత్వము upa-dhyāyatvamu. n. A teacher's profession. The teaching profession.

ఉపానహము upa-nahamu. [Skt.] n. A shoe. M. XIII. iii. 274.

ఉపాయనము upāyanamu. [Skt.] n. A complimentary gift. కానుక. A iv. 37.

ఉపాయము upāyamu. [Skt.] n. A contrivance, expedient, means, method, agency. నేర్పు. ఉపాయముకల్పించు to contrive. చతురుపాయములు or ఉపాయచతుష్టయము, the four devices, i. e., సామము using gentle or pacific means, దానము giving presents or bribing, భేదము sowing dissensions among the enemy or dividing his force or strength, దండము punishment. ఉపాయముగా upāyamu-gā. adv. Cleverly, artfully. ఉపాయశాలి upāya-śāli. n. A clever man, a man of tact, a man of many devices.

ఉపాలంభము upālambhamu. [Skt.] n. A taunt, irony, innuendo దూషణ. ఉపాలంభించు upālambhinṭsu. a. To taunt దూషించు.

ఉపాసన upāsana. [Skt.] n. Service, worship. సేవ, ఆరాధనము. ఉపాసించు upāsinṭsu. v. t. To wait on, worship. సేవించు,ఆరాధించు. ఉపాసకుడు upāsakuḍu. n. A worshipper, a devotee. ఆరాధకుడు. ఉపాస్తి upasti. n. Service, worship. ఉపాసన. V. P. iv. 143. ఉపాసితుడు upāsituḍu. n. One who is worshipped సేవితుడు.

ఉపాస్యుడు upāsyuḍu. n. One who is fit to be worshipped సేవ్యుడు.

ఉపాసము Same as ఉపవాసము.

ఉపేంద్రుడు upēndruḍu. [Skt.] n. A name of the god Vishṇu.

ఉపేక్ష upēksha. [Skt.] n. Indifference, heedlessness, contempt, disregard అశ్రద్ధ, అలక్ష్యము. ఉపేక్షించు upēkshinṭsu. v. a. To disregard, to contemn. అలక్ష్యముచేయు. ఉపేక్షకుడు upēkshakuḍu. n. One who disregards or treats another with contempt. ఉపేక్షించువాడు ఉపేక్షితుడు upēkshituḍu. n. One who is disregarded. ఉపేక్షింపబడినవాడు.

ఉపోదకి upōdaki. [Skt.] n A kind of spinach. *Basella alba* or *Basella cordifera*. బచ్చలి.

ఉపోద్ఘాతము upōdghātamu.[Skt.]n.Preface, introduction. A commencement. పీఠిక.

ఉపోషణము or ఉపోష్యము upōshaṇamu. [Skt.] n. Fasting, starving పస్తు.

ఉప్ప Same as ఉప్పన. (q. v.)

ఉప్పత uppata. [Tel.]n. Betraying; divulging a secret; dilating on any man's extraordinary prosperity, qualifications or beauty of any person. రద్ది, రట్టు, రవ్వ, ఒకని మేలునకోర్వలేక అడిపోసికొనుట. అది నిండా ఉప్పతిగానున్నది it is the common talk of the town. ఉప్పతికారాదు to be the talk of the town is unlucky. ఉప్పతించు uppatinṭsu. v. a. To abuse through envy. ఓర్వక అడిపోసికొను.

ఉప్పతిలు or ఉప్పతిల్లు uppatilu. [Tel.] v. n. To be born, produced, made. ఉద్భవించు, పుట్టు. "కవికన్నులనిప్పుకలుప్పతిల్ల." N. ii. 29. "కన్నులకోకబాష్పధారాతతులుప్పతిల్లగా." P. ii. 74.

ఉప్పత్తులు uppattulu. [Tel.] n. Shares, portions. ధాన్యము ఉప్పత్తులుచేసినారు they shared the grain.

ఉప్పన or ఉప్ప or ఉప్పదనము uppana. [Tel. from ఉప్పు] n. Saltness.

ఉప్పనబట్టెలు *uppana-battelu.* [Tel.] n. A sort of game. ఉ. హా౩. v.

ఉప్పని *uppani.* [Tel.] adj. Saltish, brackish. ఉప్పనిమాట చప్పనిమాటచెప్పి by fair means or foul.

ఉప్పర or **ఉప్పరి** *uppara.* [Tel.] n. The name of the mining caste who are tank diggers and makers of wells, &c. ఉప్పరవాడు a man of this caste. ఉప్పరది a female of that caste.

ఉప్పరము *upparamu.* [Tel.] n. The sky or atmosphere. ఉప్పరవీధి the path through the sky.

ఉప్పరించు Same as ఉప్పలించు. (q. v.)

ఉప్పరిగ *uppariga.* [Tel.] n. The upper story of a house. మేడ.

ఉప్పలవాయి *uppala-vāyi.* [Tel.] n. The space of flesh between the thumb and the forefinger. బొటనవ్రేలికిని చూపుడువ్రేలికిని నడుమనుండు మేర.

ఉప్పళము *uppalamu.* [Tel. from ఉప్పు] n. A salt marsh. The soil where salt is manufactured. ఉప్పళపువాండ్లు salt manufacturers.

ఉప్పలి *uppali.* [Tel.] n. Harm, evil, danger. కీడు, ఆపద.

ఉప్పలించు or **ఉప్పళించు** or **ఉప్పరించు** *uppalintsu.* [Tel.] v. t. To beat. కొట్టు, తాడించు.

ఉప్పి, ఉప్పిచెట్టు *uppi.* [Tel.] n. A thorny medicinal styptic shrub with a ligneous hollow fruit or gall as large as a nutmeg. *Volkameria Capparis Sepia.* Ainslie. 2. 369. *Monetia Barleriodes.* Rox. 3. 765. మార్జాలఫలవృక్షము. అంతకోటర. తెల్ల ఉప్పిచెట్టు *Azima tetracantha.* కుండలి. నల్ల ఉప్పిచెట్టు *Capparis sepiaria* (Watts.)

ఉప్పిడి *uppidi.* [Tel. from ఉప్పు+ఇడి] adj. Saltless, unsalted. ఉప్పులేని. ఉప్పిడిచప్పిడి మాటలు nonsense. ఉప్పిడినప్పిడి good or bad. ఉప్పిడిచప్పిడిలేనికూడు dry bread: lit. a mess without any flavour.

ఉప్పిరింత *uppirinta.* [Tel.] n. A certain plant. జ్యోతిష్మతి. *Cilastrus paniculata.* The *Olcum Nigrum* plant.

ఉప్పు *uppu.* [Tel.] v. t. To cook or boil. To steam or scald grain. ఉడకబెట్టు, ఆవిరిపోక ఉడకబెట్టు. ఉప్పుడుపిండి flour boiled in steam. **ఉప్పుడు** *uppudu.* adj. Malted. ఉప్పుడు బియ్యము malted rice. ఉప్పుడుపసుపు kiln dried turmeric.

ఉప్పు *uppu.* [Tel.]n. Salt. పెట్లుప్పు saltpetre. రాతి ఉప్పు rock salt. వెదురు ఉప్పు a sort of gum (tabasheer. Ainslie 1. 420) found in the hollows of the bamboo. కప్పురంబుపెట్టి ఉప్పుకొనుట. (A. vi. 75.) To give camphor for salt, that is, what is valuable for what is worthless. **ఉప్పుకండ** *uppu-kaṇḍa.* n. Dried flesh, salt meat. **ఉప్పుకాయ** *uppu-kāya.* n. Salted fruit, pickle. ఉప్పుకాపడమిచ్చు to foment with heated salt. ఉప్పుకల్లు or ఉప్పురాయి a grain of salt. **ఉప్పుచేప** *uppu-chēpa.* n. Salted fish. **ఉప్పుటేరు** *uppu-ṭ-ēru.* n. A salt stream. **ఉప్పుపఱ్ఱ** *uppu-parra.* n. Salt marsh. పఱ్ఱ ఉప్పు salt which effloresces on marshy places. బూడిద ఉప్పు. **ఉప్పుమడి** *uppu-maḍi.* n. A salt pan, salt-bed. **ఉప్పుమిడత** *uppu-miḍata.* n. A kind of large black cricket. **ఉప్పురేవు** *uppu-rēvu.* n. A place where salt is manufactured: **ఉప్పురియు** *upp-uriyu.* v. i. To moulder. ఉప్పురిసిపోయిన mouldering, dilapidated. ఉప్పురిసిన యిల్లు a house that sweats salt or that is going to decay. **ఉప్పుసముద్రము** *uppu-samudramu.* n. The ocean or salt sea.

ఉప్పెన *uppena.* [Tel.] n. The swell of the sea, an inundation.

ఉప్పొంగు *up-pongu.* [Tel. ఉబ్బి+పొంగు] v. n. To swell, burst forth, overflow, to be transported with joy. మిక్కిలి సంతోషించు.

ఉబలాటము *uba-lāṭamu.* [Tel.] n. Inclination, fancy, thought. అభిలాషము, కోరుక. Kindly feeling. జాలి.

ఉబీరచెట్టు *ubīra-chettu.* [Tel.] n. A certain weed that grows on old walls. *Streptium Asperum.* Rox. iii. 90.

ఉబుకు *ubuku.* [Tel.] n. Heaving, swelling. పొంగుట. ఉబుకు v. n. To swell, jut, bulge, be projected, to heave or rise. పొంగు.

ఉబుసు *ubusu.* [Tel.] n. Rest, repose, unemployed time. పనిలేనికాలము. News, intelligence. వృత్తాంతము, సమాచారము. ఉబుసు పుచ్చు *ubusu-puttsu* v. To while away the time, to loiter, to idle, to trifle.

ఉబ్బ *ubba.* [Tel.] n. Warmth, oppressive closeness of weather, excessive heat. ఉక్క. ఉబ్బచేయు to be close. ఈవేళ చాలా ఉబ్బచేయుచున్నది it is very close to-day.

ఉబ్బకము *ubbakamu.* [Tel. from ఉబ్బు] n. Increase. హెచ్చు.

ఉబ్బతిల్లు *ubbatillu.* [Tel.] v. i. To swell. పొంగు, ఉబ్బు.

ఉబ్బనీరు Same as ఉష్ణనీరు. A. iv. 115.

ఉబ్బరము *ubbaramu.* [Tel. from ఉబ్బు] n. Swelling, inflation. Swelling of the belly due to wind. ఉబ్బరించు *ubbarintsu.* v. n. and v. a. To swell, to inflate, to be bloated. ఉబ్బరింపు *ubbarimpu.* n. Swelling (of the belly). ఉబ్బరపోవు to be stunned. నివ్వెరపడు, చేష్టలుడిగి యేమితోచక అట్టెనిలుచు.

ఉబ్బలపడు *ubbala-padu.* [Tel.] v. n. and t. To be fumigated with mercury. ఉబ్బ వేయబడు. "రసధూమముఖిలగాత్రచ్ఛిద్రములబ్రాకనుబ్బలపడి మూర్ఛనుండువారు." P. iv. 724.

ఉబ్బలి *ubbali.* [Tel.] n. Mire, deep mud, a quagmire బురద. బొంగు ఉబ్బలి a bog.

ఉబ్బసము *ubbasamu.* [Tel.] n. Asthma. ఊర్ధ్వశ్వాసరోగము. బాల ఉబ్బసము chincough.

ఉబ్బు *ubbu.* [Tel.] n. Swelling ఉబ్బడము. సంతోషము. Haughtiness. ఉబ్బు v. n. To swell, be puffed up, to be delighted. ఉబ్బిన swollen or proud. నవ్వి కడుపు ఉబ్బినది he burst with laughter. "ఉబ్బి తెలకని వసుదేవుడుత్సహించె." (B. X.) he was overjoyed. అది నాకు దొరికినదని వానికి కడుపు ఉబ్బుచున్నది he is vexed at my obtaining this. కడుపుబ్బు suppression of urine, envy, spite. ఉబ్బున haughtily, fiercely. ఉబ్బించు *ubbintsu.* v. t. To inflate, to puff up with joy, to flatter. ఉబ్బురోగము *ubbu-rōgamu.* n. Dropsy.

ఉభయము *ubhayamu.* [Skt.] adj. and pron. Both. ఉభయకావేరి the two branches of the Cauvery. ఉభయపార్శ్వములు both sides. ఉభయము n. Giving money for the celebration of a feast in a temple. ఉత్సవము జరిగించుటకై సొమ్మిచ్చుట. నేడు ఉభయమెవనిది who gives money for the celebration of the feast to-day? నేడు అతని ఉభయము to day it is his turn to perform the ceremony in the temple. ఉభయకాడు *ubhaya-kādu.* n. The donor, or he who bestows money for the celebration of a particular feast in a temple ఒకనాటి ఉత్సవము జరిగించేవాడు. ఉభయత్ర or ఉభయత్రా *ubhayatra.* adv. On both sides. ఉభయరాశి *ubhaya-rāsi.* n. Both shares: the gross total. A heap of grain containing both the Government and the farmer's share. ఉభయవాదులు *ubhaya-vādulu.* n. Both parties, plaintiff and defendant. ఉభయులు *ubhayulu.* n. Both parties, both of them.

ఉమ *uma.* [Skt.] n. Pārvati the wife of Siva.

ఉమక *umaka.* [Tel.] n. Chaff. ఊక. ఉమక చెరుగుట to winnow paddy after it is beaten.

ఉమాదము Same as ఉన్మాదము.

ఉమియు *umiyu.* [Tel.] v. a. To spit, to spit out.

ఉముక Same as ఉమక.

ఉమేదు or **ఉమేదా** *umēdu.* [H.] n. Hope. ఆశ, కోరిక. ఉమేదుచేయు to live in hope, to be a hanger on, as an expectant. ఉమేదువారి *umēdu-vāri.* n. Expectancy, waiting for an employment. Volunteering for employment ఆశించుకొని యుండడము, ఉద్యోగముకై కనిపెట్టుకొని యుండడము. **ఉమేదువారు** *umēdu-vāru.* n. A candidate for employment, a volunteer, an apprentice.

ఉమ్మ *umma.* [Tel.] n. Heat, warmth, closeness. కాక, ఉక్క, ఉబ్బ. **ఉమ్మగిల్లు** *ummagillu.* v. i. To be hot and close as a closed room. ఉక్కగానుండు "లోనుమ్మగిలిగబ్బువలవని కమ్మతావులుగల" (Swa. iv. 92.) To be distressed or half suffocated with closeness.

ఉమ్మడి *ummadi.* [Tel.] n. Partnership, fellowship. ఉమ్మడిగానుండే common to both: held in common. ఒక్క ఉమ్మడిని at once, in one rush, all at once. ఒక్క సారిగా. ఆ సరుకును ఉమ్మడిని కొన్నాను. I bought it wholesale.

ఉమ్మదము *ummadamu.* [Tel.] n. Closeness. ఉమ్మ.

ఉమ్మనీరు *umma-nīru.* [Tel.] n. The waters that precede childbirth. ఉబ్బనీరు, ప్రసవజలము. A. iv. 115.

ఉమ్మలము *ummalamu.* [Tel.] n. Grief, care. దుఃఖము. M. XII. iv. 382. M. V. ii. 84.

ఉమ్మలి *ummali.* [Tel.] n. Mud, mire. బురద, రొంపి.

> "కనకకపుచ్చుట్టుతోటల
> సుగంధఫలంబులురాలవాటిపై
> పనసలుపండి త్రెళ్లిపడు
> పాటునరొంపులుగట్టివాటిమీ
> దని రసధారలు ప్రోలి
> రసధారలునించగ నైనయుమ్మలిం
> జనువడిపాంథులందుబడ
> సారెవసించురుకాలిపాలికల్."
> H. v. 107.

> "కరులుమ్మలిలోజిక్కిన
> కరులెత్తగజాలియుండు గాదేపుడమిన్."
> P. ii. 172.

ఉమ్మలించు or **ఉమ్మలికించు** *ummalintsu.* [Tel. from ఉమ్మలము.] v. n. To grieve, to cry. దుఃఖించు, శోకించు. **ఉమ్మలింత**, **ఉమ్మలిక** *ummalinta.* n. Heat, warmth, closeness, grief, uneasiness, agitation. ఉష్ణము, వ్యసనము.

> "మదీయాంబులునః క్షీరనిధితంబులు
> ధనవర్ధనంబులుమ్మలికయుంత యేటికిమట
> యుము."
> Swa. vi. 14.

ఉమ్మలికాడు *ummali-kādu.* n. A ruler. అధికారి. "శ్రీమదాదుగాంతిరావరిచక్రము లగ్గలుపట్టుతోడ పుంజేవుడు కనినికావసుధనీమకు నుమ్మలికాడు." P. i. 379.

ఉమ్మాదము Same as ఉన్మాదము.

ఉమ్మాయముత్తెము *ummāya-muttemu.* [Tel.] n. A sort of artificial pearl. క్షుద్రముత్యము.

ఉమ్మి *ummi.* [Tel.] n. Spittle. **ఉమ్మివేయు** *umm-vēyu.* v. t. To spit out. ఉమియు.

ఉమ్మెత్త or **ఉమ్మెత** *ummetta.* [Tel.] n. The thorn apple *(Datura)* or Indian night shade; దుత్తూరము. Ainslie. i. 442. తెల్ల ఉమ్మెత్త *Datura metel.* నల్ల ఉమ్మెత్త *Datura fastuosa.* ఉమ్మెత్తపువ్వుగిన్నె a cup shaped like the flower of this plant. ఉమ్మెత్త పురుగు a clamorous cricket that lives on this plant.

ఉయ్యల or **ఉయ్యాల** or **ఉయ్యేల** *uyyala.* [Tel.] n. A swing. ఉయ్యాలతొట్టి, ఉయ్యాల మంచము a cradle, a swinging bed. ఉయ్యాల జోలపాటలు (Dasav. ix. 243.) Lullabies. **ఉయ్యాలజిట్ట** *uyyala-jitta.* The wagtail ఉయ్యాలపులుగు. See జిట్ట, సారసపక్షి.

ఉరక Same as ఉరుక. (q. v.)

ఉరగము *uragamu.* [Skt. ఉరము+గ=go.] A snake. పాము.

ఉరడించు or **ఉరణించు** Same as ఉరవడించు. See under ఉరవడి.

ఉరణము *uraṇamu.* [Skt.] n. A ram. పొట్టేలు.

ఉరభ్రము Same as ఉరణము.

ఉరమరిక *uramarika.* [Tel.] adv. About రమారమి.

ఉరము *uramu.* [Skt.] n. The breast, bosom. రొమ్ము. విప్పటురము a broad breast. **ఉరసిలుడు** or **ఉరసుడు** *urasiludu.* n. One who has a broad chest. విశాలమైన రొమ్ముగలవాడు. **ఉరస్త్రాణము** *uras-tranamu.* n. Armour for the breast. రొమ్ముకవచము.

ఉరరీకృతము *urari-kritamu.* [Skt.] adj. Granted, agreed. అంగీకరించబడిన. అర్ధోరరీకృతము half allowed, not fully ceded. అర్ధాంగీకృతము.

ఉరలు *uralu.* [Tel. cf. రోలు. Drav. ఉరల్ = a roller.] v. a. To roll down. రాలు, దొర్లు. To flow down. కారు. **ఉరలుకొను** or **ఉర్లుకొను** Same as ఉరలు. **ఉరలన్** *uralan.* adv. Off, over, violently. **ఉరలద్రోచు** *uraladrōtsu.* To roll down, to send bounding. **ఉరలబడు** or **ఉర్లబడు** *uralabadu.* To roll over. దొర్లు. **ఉరలబారు** *urala-baru.* v. i. To move చలించు.

ఉరలించు *uralintsu.* [Tel.] v. i. To shine. ప్రకాశించు, వెలుగు.

ఉరవడి *ura-vadi* [Tel. ఉరవు+వడి] n. Swiftness. అతివేగము. **ఉరవడించు** *ura-vadintsu.* v. i. To be quick, to hasten. తొందరపడు.

ఉరవు *uravu.* [Tel.] n. Beauty, abundance. సౌందర్యము, విస్తారము. adj. Great, large. అధికమైన. "ఉత్తమసౌభాగ్యము గోమటు యురవో ధరగొనుటురవో." A. iii. 65.

ఉరస్యుడు. *urasyudu.* [Skt.] n. A legitimate son. ధర్మపత్నియందు తనకు పుట్టినకొడుకు. See ఔరసు.

ఉరి *uri.* [Tel.] n. A noose or slipping knot: a snare. ఉచ్చు. కాలురి a snare for the feet. **ఉరికోల** *uri-kōla.* n. A rod attached to a noose. **ఉరిత్రాడు** *uri-tadu.* n. A halter, a tether, a rope to tie a cow's legs when it is being milked. **ఉరితీయు** or **ఉరిపోయు** *uri-tiyu.* v. t. To hang: strangle. **ఉరిపోసికొను** *uri-pōsi-konu.* v. i. To hang one self. **ఉరియాడు** *uri-yadu.* To move, tremble, fear. చలించు. భయపడు. M. ix. ii. 105. ఉరియాట moving to and fro. చలించుట, ఊగులాడుట.

ఉరికించు See ఉరుకు.

ఉరిడె *uride.* [Tel.] n. A beetle కుమ్మరపురుగు. రుక్మి. iv.

ఉరిది *uridi.* [Tel.] adj. Steady. Rapid. వడిగల. దృఢము, స్థిరము. adv. Quickly. వడిగా.

> "కదలనీటికిమీనము
> లెదురెక్కి యురిదిబారు నీటికిపోలెన్,
> పదవినిరుద్యోగులబొందదు
> సోద్యోగులకగానితొల్కటమున్ భాగ్య."
> N. ix. 190.

ఉరియ *uriya.* [Tel.] adj. Strong, steady. దిట్టతనముగల. M. XII. ii. 367.

ఉరియు *uriyu.* [Tel.] v. a To sweat or leak. ఉప్పురిసినగోడ a wall out of which salt oozes. ఇల్లు ఉరుస్తున్నది the house leaks. ఆ ఊరు ఉప్పురిసినందున as the land of that village turned saltish. Also, to move చలించు. To turn grey, as hair నెరయు. To ripen పక్వమగు. To pine away పరితపించు. **ఉరుపు** *urupu.* n. Leaking, soaking through. ఉరియుట.

ఉరు *uru.* [Skt. & Tel.] adj. Great, large, valuable. గొప్ప, శ్రేష్ఠమైన. [Tel.] v. i. To be fit, to suit. In A. vi. 32 is rendered ఒప్పు. ఉరుకు, ఒప్పును. ఒప్పు. v. t. To mind. లక్ష్య పెట్టు. " ఉరదునురేంద్రుడైన" భార: ఆది. vi. **ఉరుతరము** *uru-taramu.* More, larger.

ఉరుకు *uruku.* [Tel.] v. i. To run: fly, start. To run out or project. To transgress. ఉరుకుడుకప్ప the flying frog. ఉరుకు బొడ్డు a projecting navel.

ఉరుకొట్టు *uru-kottu.* [Tel. ఉరు+కొట్టు] v. i. To cry like a monkey when angry. కోపముతోనున్న కోతివలె నరుచును.

ఉరుజ *uruza.* [Tel.] n. A sort of fish (*Sparus.*) The gilthead. పొలుసు.

ఉరుజో *uruzu.* [Tel.] n. A sluice or water channel.

ఉరుత *uruta.* [Tel.] n. A squirrel. ఉడుత.

ఉరుపు. See under ఉరియు.

ఉరుమ *uruma.* [Tel.] n. A kind of musical instrument made of leather A. iv. 38.

ఉరుమంజి *uru-manji.* [Tel. హుర్మంజి] n. The yellow water in a pearl. ముత్తెపుపసుపునీరు, హాలి.

ఉరుము *urumu.* [Tel.] v. n. To thunder. ఉరిమిచూచె he looked daggers. **ఉరుము** n. Thunder. A sort of drum. To cry avaunt. వీరహుంకారము. ఉరుముపోయించు to celebrate a feast in honor of a rustic deity when a village is to be founded. జాతరచేయు.

ఉరుముడు *urumudu.* [Tel.] n. A certain forest tree, with delicate blossoms and a fruit as large as a lemon. *Cassia marginata* (Watts.)

ఉరువడి *uruvadi.* [Tel.] n. Violence, impetuosity, speed, haste. ఉరవడి. **ఉరువడించు** *uru cadintsu.* v. n. & a. To be energetic, to bully, to roar or thunder in talking. To flourish, shine forth, display. To gain, win, conquer. విజృంభించు, గెలుచు.

"ప్రజకనురాగమైనమనపాలనకాంతియు
సంగరజయంబున
విజితవిభీతమైయురువడించుట
యున్నవి..."
Appakavi. ii. 483.

ఉరువడు *uru-vadu.* [Tel.] v. i. To be fulfilled. నెరవేరు.

ఉరువిడి *uru-vidi.* [Tel.] n. A collection of things. వస్తుసమూహము. వి.క్ర. ii.

ఉరువు or **ఉర్వు** *uruvu.* [Tel.] v. t. To get rid of. పరిహరించు. n. Form, shape. రూపము. **ఉరువు** adj. Great, big, large. గొప్ప. v. t. To flay. తోలు దోచుట. Also, same as ఉరుగొట్టు. టెంకాయ ఉరువుగా నుండే as large as a cocoanut. ఆ పని యింకా ఉరువు ఏర్పడలేదు that work is as yet in embryo.

ఉరోజము *urojamu.* [Skt. from ఉరము+జ] n. Breast. కుచము.

ఉర్రాడు *urr-adu.* [Tel.] v. i. To hang loose, to dangle.

ఉర్రు, or **ఉర్రట్లు** or **ఉర్రూతలు** (*anuk.*) *urru.* [Tel.] n. The cry of a monkey in anger. కోతిముక్కు విక్రుతిధ్వని. Also, violent movement. **ఉర్రట్లులూగు** or **ఉర్రట్లూగు** or **ఉర్రూతలూగు.** *urrattul-ugu.* [ఉరు+ఊగు] v. i. To totter. మిక్కిలి ఊగు. To move చలించు.

ఉర్రుకట్టు *urru-kattu.* [Tel.] v. t. To tie up a cow's legs while milking. పాలుపిదుకు నపుడు ఆవుకాళ్లను కట్టు.

ఉర్రుత్రాళ్లు or **ఉరుత్రాళ్లు.** See ఉరిత్రాళ్లు and under ఉరి.

ఉర్లగడ్డ *urla-gadda.* [Tel.] n. A potato. Lit. the *crumbling root:* so called because it is farinaceous.

ఉర్లు. Same as ఉరులు.

ఉర్వర *urvara.* [Skt.] n. The earth, fruitful soil. నేల. **ఉర్వి** *urvi.* n. The earth. భూమి. **ఉర్వీశుడు** *urv-isudu.* (ఉర్వి+ఈశుడు) n. A king, a ruler.

ఉలక, ఉలకన *ulaka.* [Tel.] n. Lightness. తేలిక, చులకన.

ఉలచే *ulatsa.* [Tel.] n. An excellent sort of fish, called *Hilsa* in Hindustani. A. ii. 62.

ఉలపము *ulapamu.* [Skt.] n. A creeper, a trellis. తీగ.

ఉలవ *ulava.* [Tel.] n. A kind of pulse, horse gram, *Glycine tomentosa: Linn. Dolichos biflor. Buch.* Rox. iii. 313. అడవి ఉలవలు *Glycinea Suaveolens.* (Rottler.)

ఉలవరము or **ఉల్లరము** or **ఉల్లారము.** *ulavaramu.* [Tel.] n. A drain. Land enriched by drains. The smart caused by the sting of a nettle. **ఉలవరించు** *ulavarintsu.* v. n. To be enriched or fattened as land by manure. ఉలవరించిన rich.

ఉలస Same as ఉలత.

ఉలి *uli.* [Tel.] n. A chisel. adj. (another form of నులి) Little. అల్పము.

ఉలిందచెట్టు *ulinda-chettu.* [Tel.] n. A sort of tree.

ఉలికిపడు *uliki-padu.* [Tel.] v. n. To start, shake. పాటూర్తుగాగలిగిన భయముచేత కంపించు. To be afraid. భయపడు. **ఉలికిపాటు** *uliki-patu.* n. A start, tremor, shudder.

ఉలిపి *ulipi.* [Tel.] adj. Brittle (as glass): touchy, easily irritated, low, mean, wicked. దుర్మార్గమైన. **ఉలిపి, ఉలిపికట్టె** or **ఉలిపిగొట్టు** *ulipi.* n. A touchy person, an irritable person. కోపిష్ఠి. ఉలిపితెవులు itchiness, soreness, irritability.

ఉలిమిడి or **ఉలిమిరి** *ulimidi.* [Tel.] n. The tree named *Cratæva Tapia*; or, *Diospyros Cordifolia* (Rox. 2. 538.) or *Capparis trifoliata.*

ఉలియు or **ఉలివాడు** *uliyu.* [Tel.] v. n. To move. చలించు. To sound, resound. మ్రోయు, ధ్వనించు. A. i. 84. **ఉలివు** *ulivu.* n. Sound, voice. ధ్వని, చప్పుడు. Movement. చలనము.

ఉలుకు *uluku.* [Tel.] v. n. To start, quiver, (See the causal ఉలుచు) ముద్దులుకు కన్నులు eyes quivering with prettiness. "కటిక లేనడుమలికికులికెగా" she wagged her waist at him in derision. **ఉలుకు** n. Timidity, fright. జడుపు.

ఉలుచే Same as ఉలస.

ఉలుచు *ulutsu.* [Tel. causal of ఉలుకు.] v. a. To brandish, wave, whisk, shake వాలంబులులిచె brandished the tail. Also, to pull off. ఊడదీయు. "సత్కావులుత్రుప్పదుల్చు వసంతవేళ." వై. i.

ఉలుప or **ఉలుపా** *ulupa.* [Tel.] n. A gift, present. కానుక.

ఉలుపడు or **ఉలుపి** *ulupadu.* [Tel.] n. కోడి గలవాడు. See కోడి.

ఉలుపు *ulupu.* Same as ఉలుచు to pull off.

ఉలుము *ulumu.* [Tel.] n. Leprosy. కుష్ఠము.

ఉలూకము *ulūkamu.* [Skt. cognate with Eng. owl] n. An owl. గుడ్లగూబ.

ఉలూఖలము *ulū-khalamu.* [Skt.] n. A mortar. రోలు. Vasu. iv. 25.

ఉల్క *ulka.* [Skt.] n. A firebrand, embers. మంటలేని కొఱవినిప్పు, భస్మము. Also, a meteor or an aerolite.

ఉల్టా *ulṭā.* [H.] adj. Reverse, the wrong side, opposite, contrary, turned back లోతట్టు, అడుసుకట్టు. ఆ శాలువను ఉల్టాగా కప్పుకొన్నాడు he wore the shawl the wrong side up.

ఉల్బణము *ulbaṇamu.* [Skt.] n. Excess, increase. అతిశయము. పైత్యోల్బణము excess of bile. **ఉల్బణము** *ulbaṇamu.* adj. Apparent, evident. Gushing, overflowing. పొంగిన, స్పష్టమైన. రసోల్బణముగా with overflowing affection.

ఉల్ముకము *ulmukamu.* [Skt.] n. A firebrand కొఱవి.

ఉల్లంకి *ullanki.* [Tel.] n. A bird of the plover family; a plover, sandpiper, stint.

ఉల్లంగి *ullangi.* [Tel.] n. A sort of tree. H. iv. 13.

ఉల్లంఘనము *ul-langhanamu.* [Skt.] n. Disregard, disgrace, contempt. అతిక్రమించుట. **ఉల్లంఘించు** *ul-langhintsu.* v. a. To disregard, to pass over, transgress, refuse, decline, disgrace, browbeat. అతిక్రమించు, తిరస్కరించు. ఆజ్ఞనుల్లంఘించు to disregard an order.

ఉల్లంచేప *ullam-chēpa.* [Tel.] n. Name of a large fish that is very delicious but full of bones.

ఉల్లకి *ullaki.* [Tel.] n. A sling or hammock of cloth or cradle hanging down from a pole carried on two men's shoulders. ఉల్లకిలోవేసి తెచ్చినారు they slung him in a hammock and brought him.

ఉల్లట *ullaṭa.* [Tel.] n. A hammock. ఉల్లెడ. శవమును ఉల్లటకట్టి తీసికొనిపోయినారు they slung the corpse in a sheet on a pole and carried it away.

ఉల్లడ or **ఉల్లడము** *ullaḍa.* [Tel.] n. An awning or canopy. చాందిని, ఉల్లాభము, మేలుకట్టు.

ఉల్లడి *ullaḍi.* [Tel] n. Confusion, trouble, disturbance. BD. v. 1025.

ఉల్లము *ullamu.* [Tel.] n. The heart. హృదయము. **ఉల్లరము** *ullaramu.* [Tel. from ఉల్లము+అరు] adj. What is painful to the heart or feelings. మనస్సునకు సహింప కూడనిది.

ఉల్లల *ullala.* [Tel.] n. A bubbling noise, ebullition. ఉడుకుటయందు ధ్వన్యనుకరణము.

ఉల్లలము *ullalamu.* [Skt.] n. Movement. చలనము, కదలిక. **ఉల్లలితము** *ullalitamu.* adj. Moved. కదలిన.

ఉల్లసము *ullasamu.* [Skt.] n. Sport, satire, fun, frolic. సంతోషము, ఉపాలంభము. ఎత్తిపొడుపుమాట. M. XII. iv. 388. **ఉల్లసమాడు** *ullasam-āḍu.* v. i. To sport with, to joke. పరిహసించు, ఎత్తిపొడుచు, ఎగతాళిచేయు. **ఉల్లసించు** or **ఉల్లసిల్లు** *ullasinṭsu.* v. i. To exult, rejoice.

ఉల్లాకు *ullāku.* [Tel. ఉలి+ఆకు] n. A ticket or invoice left with goods or grain, specifying the quantity and the owner of the goods. చీటి.

ఉల్లాకుచేప *ullāku-chēpa.* [Tel.]n. The bony hilsa or sable fish.

ఉల్లాభము *ullābhamu.* [Skt.] n. A canopy borne over marriage offerings or over the bride and bridegroom as they go in procession. చాందిని, మేలుకట్టు, ఉల్లడ.

ఉల్లామపిట్ట *ullāmupiṭṭa.* [Tel.] n. A snipe.

ఉల్లారు *ullāru.* [Tel.] n. A saddle-cloth: a particoloured cushion. నర్జు. Fringes. జాలరులు. "మూరకొకకటియు కేనకొకటియుంగా గట్టి నడొల్లటుల్లారుల్లసిల్లంబల్లించిన పల్లంబులపై." A. iv. 36.

ఉల్లాసము *ullāsamu.* [Skt.] n. Joy, delight, amusement. సంతోషము. **ఉల్లాసపురుషుడు** *ullāsa-purushuḍu.* A luxurious man or man of pleasure. A prodigal. **ఉల్లాసి** *ullāsi.* A cheerful man. ఉల్లసించువాడు. "సమిదుల్లాసిధనంజయుండు." T. iv. 136.

ఉల్లి *ulli.* [Tel.] n. The onion. నీరుల్లి the onion. ఎర్రగడ్డ. వెల్లుల్లి garlic, తెల్లగడ్డ. **ఉల్లిపాయ** or **ఉల్లిగడ్డ** *ulli-pāya.* n. An onion.

ఉల్లింకాయ *ullin-kāya.* [Tel.] n. A species of plover.

ఉల్లిపాషాణము *ulli-pāshāṇamu.* [Skt.] n. Corrosive sublimate. సౌవీరము.

ఉల్లె *ulle.* [Tel.] n. The crust at the bottom of pies or tarts.

ఉల్లేఖము *ul-lēkhamu.* [Skt.] n. Uttering, mention, rehearsing. ఉచ్చారణము. A rhetorical trope.

ఉల్లోలము *ullōlamu.* [Skt.] n. A surge, a large billow, or wave. పెద్ద అల.

ఉల్వరము *ulvaramu.* [Tel.] n. Rubbish. sweepings, &c., used for manure (Vizag.)

ఉళక్కి or **ఉళ్లక్కి** *uḷakki.* [Tel.] n. A lie. a joke, a pretence. బొట్టిది. Vasu. iii. 163.

ఉవిద *uvida.* [Skt.] n. Woman. ఆడుది, స్త్రీ.

ఉవ్వ *uvva.* [Tel.] n. A certain tree. *Dillenia speciosa.* Rox. ii. 650.

ఉవ్వన *uvvana.* [Tel.] adv. Unexpectedly, all at once. తటాలున, గుబాలుగా, గొల్లగా. Rukmāngada. iii. 140.

ఉవ్వపిట్ట *uvva-piṭṭa.* [Tel.] n. A sort of bird, a wagtail. గోల్తిక.

ఉవ్వలపోటి *uvvala-pōṭi*. [Tel.] n. A certain game among children. "చిరుకుడుముల్వలపోటి చెండుగట్టిబోటి యల్లికయుప్పనబట్టిలప్పగాలం." శాశ. iii.

ఉవ్వాయి *uvvāyi*. [Tel.] n. Cheerfulness, joy. వికాసము.

ఉవ్విల్లూరు or **ఉవ్విల్లిగొను** *uvvill-ūru*. [Tel.] v. n. To water, as the mouth. To be eager. త్వరపడు, మిక్కిలి ఆశపుట్టు. To hasten త్వరపడు. **ఉవ్విల్లూర్చు** or **ఉవ్విల్లూరచేయు** *uvvillūrṭsu*. v. a. To tempt, to stir or excite the appetite. అభిలషింపజేయు, పురిగొలుపు.

ఉవ్వు *uvvu*. [Tel.] n. Attempt, exertion, effort. పూనిక. **ఉవ్వెత్తు** *uvv-eṭṭu*. adj. All. యావత్తు. "ఒక్కమాత్రలోన నువ్వెత్తు గానరా" M. v. 30. **ఉవ్వెత్తుగా** *uvvettu-gā*. Quite easily. All at once. మిక్కిలి సులభముగా, ఏకకాలమందు. Completely. నిశ్శేషముగా. From the bottom అడుగుతో.

> "మైమత్తిలి మిన్నెరుంగక
> సమస్తరిపుప్రకరంబువచ్చియువ్వెత్తుగనూలెపా
> పమతులెయ్యెడలన్ జయమంద నేర్తురే."
>
> Chenna BP. v. 65.

ఉశనుడు *uśanuḍu*. [Skt.] n. The name of the planet Sukra or Venus.

ఉశీరము *uśīramu*. [Skt.] n. A sort of fragrant root, *Andropogon muricatus* usually termed వట్టివేరు cuss-cuss.

ఉషర్బుధుడు *ushar-budhuḍu*. [Skt.] n. He who awakes with the dawn. An epithet of the god of fire. Vulcan. అగ్ని.

ఉషస్సు *ushassu*. [Skt.] n. Dawn, daybreak. తెల్లవారుటకుముందు నాలుగుగడియలకాలము.

ఉష్ట్రము *ushṭramu*. [Skt.] n. A camel క్రమేలకము, ఒంటె.

ఉష్ణము *ushṇamu*. [Skt.] n. Sunshine, warmth; heat; fever, feverishness. **ఉష్ణము** adj. Hot. ఉష్ణరశ్మి the sun. **ఉష్ణించు** *ushṇinṭsu*. v. n. To be hot. **ఉష్ణీషము** *ushṇīshamu*. n. A turban, a diadem. కిరీటము, పాగా.

ఉసి *usi*. [Tel.] n. A hiss, hissing. **ఉసికొను** *usi-konu*. v. i. To give the chase as a dog does కుక్కకరచుట. **ఉసిగొల్పు** *usi kolpu*. v. a. To hiss a dog on. To excite or stir up anger. ఉసిపోసిన అక్షరములు a quaver or superfluous syllables, used in singing. **ఉసి** n. Dust, powder, నుసి. ఆనలుసి oaths are nonsense.

ఉసిరి or **ఉసిరిక** *usiri*. [Tel.] n. A tree with acid fruit used for pickles. *Phyllanthus Emblica; Emblic myrobalan.* Various species are named in Rox. III. 654—673.

ఉసుక *usuka*. [Tel.] n. Sand ఇసుక. ఉసుకపంటముగాగనుడికింపవచ్చు. పారిశ్చ. ii.

ఉసుము *usumu*. [Tel.] v. a. To scour or wash. పులుము, ఉదుకు, తుడుచు.

ఉసురు *usuru*. [Tel.] n. Breath, life; strength, vigour, grief; a sigh, affliction, plague, hardship, evil result; retribution or result. వాని ఉసురు నీకు తగులును his trouble will come upon you. ఆడదాని ఉసురు తగలకపోదు the sigh of a woman will not fail to bring trouble (to him who caused her grief). వారి ఉసురు తాకి వాడు చెడిపోవును their sorrows shall be visited on his head. **ఉసురుపోసికొను** or **ఉసురుపుచ్చుకొను** *usuru-pōsi-konu*. v. a. To cause sighs. To afflict. నా ఉసురు ఏల పోసుకొంటావు why do you torment me thus? ఇది చేసినందున ప్రజలయొక్క ఉసురు పోసుకొనెను this called down the curses of the people. ఉసురుతోకూడా alive.

ఉసులు *usulu*. [Tel.] n. Ease, facility; convenience అనుకూలము, సౌఖ్యము. వాని శరీరము కొంచెము ఉసులుగానున్నది he is rather better in health. వానికి ఉసులుగాలేదు it was not convenient or easy for him. ఉసులుగా tolerably good, easy, light ఉసులుచేయు to facilitate.

ఉసుళ్లు usullu. [Tel.] n. Winged white ants. ఇసుళ్లు.

ఉసూరను Same as ఉస్సురను.

ఉస్తె uste. [Tel.] n. The gigantic swallow wort. The fruit is called ఉస్తెకాయ ఉస్తెవరుగు is the fruit dried and preserved.

ఉస్సు ussu. [Tel.] n. Ah! alas! "ఉస్సను సూర్పుపోయునట్." P. i. 246. ఉస్సని కూర్చున్నాడు he sighed and sat down. ఉస్సురను ussur-anu. v. n. To sigh, (from ఉస్సు alas! and అను to say; the R being inserted to save elision.) నిట్టూర్చి విడుచు. ఉస్సురనిపించు ussur-anipintsu. (causal of ఉస్సురను.) v. a To grieve, to make one sigh.

ఉహుహు uhuhu. [Tel.] n. Shivering from excessive cold. (Imitative of the noise then made.)

> బహుశీతోపేతంబై
> యుహుహుహూయనినడకె లోకమ్మోన్నాథా.
> భా. x.

ఉహ్హు uhhu. [Tel.] n. The sound produced when a fire is kindled by blowing on it. నిప్పూదేటప్పుడు కలుగుధ్వని. "ఉహ్హని బాహాగ్నినూద నొల్లదుగాని విరహుహ్వ రార్తితో నెప్పునూర్పు." పాండు. iii.

ఊ Ū

ఊ ū. The long vowel Ū or oo, as in flute or shoot.

ఊక ūka. [Tel.] n. The husk of paddy. ఉముక. Also (noun from ఊగు) Swinging ఊగుట. ఊకనబొడ్డు ūkana-boddu. n. A certain plant used in fevers. ఊకబంతి ūka-banti. n. The flower called Bachelor's button. పోకబంతి.

ఊకర ūkara. [Tel.] n. To say ఊ ఊ while listening to what another says. ఊకొట్టుట. ఊకరగొట్టు ūkara-gottu. v. i. To crow or make indistinct sounds, as an infant. G. iii 46. BD. v. 967.

ఊకించు or ఊకు ūkintsu [Tel.] v. n. To shake, egitate or move; to endeavour or make an effort. పూను; to rattle the dice. ఊకు or ఊకువ ūku. n. Effort, exertion. పూనిక, ప్రయత్నము. "ఒక్కూకునందెగడు" (R. v. 6.) moving at a single effort. ఒక్క ఊకునగా at once, all at once. ఒక్కసారిగా. ఊకువగు ūkuvagu. (ఊకువ+అగు) v. n. To try, to undertake. పూను.

ఊకొట్టు or ఊకొను ū-kottu. [Tel.] v. n. To hum or make an indistinct sound, resembling ఊ, ఊ, denoting that one is listening to what another is saying.

ఊగు or ఊగులాడు or ఊగాడు ūgu. [Tel.] v. n. To be agitated or shaken, to swing, to wag, roll. ఊగించు ūgintsu (causal of ఊగు) v. a. To shake, to move, to swing or rock. ఊగులాట ūgul-āṭa. (ఊగులు+ఆట.) n. Swinging: tottering. ఊచు ūtsu. [Tel. causal of ఊగు] v. a. To swing, cause to swing, to wag or shake, rock, nod. ఊగజేయు. చెయ్యి ఊచు to shake or wave (the hand in forbidding) or to say no, to forbid by the hand.

ఊచ ūtsa. [Tel.] n. The soft core of the plantain or similar tree. దూట. A thorn-bush ముండ్లదుబ్బు. ఊచేకోసగా గొంతుకోసివేసినాడు he cut the throat without any trouble. ఊచ ūtsa. adj. Withered. ఊచకాలు a withered leg. ఊచచెయ్యి a withered hand. ఊచపట్టు to grow big enough for the core in a plant to form. ఊచపోవు to become lean. కృశించు. ఊచబియ్యము ūtsa-biyyamu. n. Grain not quite ripe. బాగుగా ముదరనికొన్నలు మొదలైనవి. ఊచముట్టు ūtsa-muṭṭu. adv. To the core, entirely, wholly.

> "ఉల్లమంతగడంచి యూచముట్టుగను
> కల్లలాడించిన గలదెపన్నిదము."
> H. D. i. 252.

ఊచు ūtsu. [Tel.] v. n. To wither. వెంట్రుకలు ఊచిపోవుచున్నవి his hair is falling off. ఊచు causative of ఊగు. (q. v.)

ఊటు *ūṭa*. [Tel. from ఊరు] n. Juice, sap. A fountain, a spring as of water. Marrow. ఎముకలోటు. Pickling liquor. Strength. బలము, సేవ. ఊటకల్లు *ūṭa-kallu*. n. A grain like అల్లు. ఊటగుండు *ūṭa-gunḍu*. n. The stone to which a weaver fastens the cross sticks on which he stretches his web. ఊటనీరు *ūṭa-nīru*. n. A gushing spring. ఊటపుట్టు *ūṭa-puṭṭu*. v. n. To spring (as water.) ఊటబుడ్డిచెక్క *ūṭa-buḍḍi-chekka*. n. Wood that is strong and durable for building purposes. ఊటయెత్తు *ūṭa-yettu*. v. n. To be damp. ఊటయెత్తిన damp, moist. ఆచెట్లు ఊటయెత్తిపో యినవి these trees have been injured by excessive moisture. ఊటయెత్తినయిల్లు a damp house. ఊటగల heavy, abounding in springs. సత్తువగల, బరువైన. ఊటగలకర్ర a heavy piece of wood. ఊటాడు *ūṭāḍu*. (ఊటు + ఆడు) v. n. To shake, totter, waver, be agitated. చలించు, సంక్రమించు. ఊటాడించు. (Vasu. iv. 159.) to shake కదల్చు, ఆడించు, అల్లాడించు.

ఊటించు *ūṭintsu*. [Tel.] v. t. To deceive వంచించు.

ఊటు *ūṭu*. [Tel.] v. t. To thrust through. పొడుచు.

"పులిపులిగాగ బెబ్బులిపిండు నొకనాడు
చెదరగా నూటెనా చేరియూటె."

రామా. ii.

ఊటు *ūṭu*. [Tel.] n. Moisture. చెమ్మ. ఊటు కార్చు to wet.

ఊడ *ūḍa*. [Tel.] n. A root growing down from the branches of the banyan and similar trees. ఊడలుపోసినచెట్టు a tree that has such suckers or roots.

ఊడనిపాడు *ūḍani-pāḍu*. [Tel. ఊడు+అని+పాడు] v. t. To cry ఊడు while running away. To run away. To be put to flight; to be routed. సిగ్గూడనిపాడెను her modesty left her. P. iv. 433. వాల్గెమాయమూడనిపాడెను that fascination is now over.

"ఒకనాడురాత్రి, పడుపడు
కకుకెప్పుకయిల్లువెడలి గాఢరతకూ
నికరమునకరుగకొడుక
నొకరుడు పేరదుత్తో, న నూడనిపాడెన్."

పాండు. iii.

ఊడికూర *ūḍi-kūra*. [Tel.] n. A kind of herb. ఒకవిధమైన కూరాకు.

ఊడిగము *ūḍigamu*. [Tel.] n. Service. Drudgery, task. కొలువు. ఊడిగపుపనులు menial duties. ఊడిగపుడి *ūḍigapuḍi*. n. A maid servant. ఊడిగపువాడు or ఊడిగీడు *ūḍigapu-vāḍu*. n. A manservant, a menial.

ఊడిత *ūḍita*. [Tel.] n. A staff used as a prop by a weaver for his warp. సాలెవాడు పడుగుచేయునపుడు అది వాలకుండ కింద ఊతగా నిలుపుకొయ్య.

ఊడు *ūḍu*. [Tel.] v. n. To part, drop out, slip out. జారు, రాలు. To give way, fail: to be unfastened, loosened, separated. వదులగు, To flee, run away. పారిపోవు. తం డ్రినోట్లోనుండిపడ్డాడు he is the very image of his father. ఊడగొట్టు to take out, root up, remove. ఊడదీయు to pull out, to take off (skin or clothes), to unloose. ఊడదీసు to root out. ఊడలాగు to pull out, to draw out.

ఊడుకొను *ūḍu-konu*. [Tel.] v. n. To become moist, as earth. A. v. 144. To pierce. గుచ్చుకొను.

ఊడుగు *ūḍugu*. [Tel.] n. The plant named *Alangium Lamarckii*. (E.P.) అంకోలము.

ఊడుచు *ūḍutsu*. [Tel.] v. a. To sweep. To slacken, loosen, divest, open, sever, separate. ఊడదీయు To wrest, take by force. To transplant. నారునాటు. To root out, to eradicate. ఊడుపు చేయించిన పొలము a field in which rice plants have been set (by transplanting.) తలలూడ్చె he smote off their heads. R. v. 275. ఊడుపు *ūḍupu*. n. Sweeping: ఊడ్చడము. transplanting. నారునాటుట. ఊడుపుపొలము land in which shoots are transplanted.

ఊడ్పు Same as ఊడుపు.

ఊడెము ūḍemu. [Tel.] n. A fortified place with a few bastions. గడి, చిన్నకోట. Also, ఊడిగము. (q. v.)

ఊఢ ūḍha.[Skt.] adj. Married. పెండ్లాడినది. n. A wife. పెండ్లాము. A married woman వివాహిత.

ఊత ūta. [Tel.] n. A support, a prop. A fishing hook, a basket snare to catch fish. A coop to keep animals in. A pannier. కేలూతచేసి giving the hand as a support. అరటుల యూతగొని leaning against the plantain trees. ఊతగమ్మెగట్టుపట్టినాడు he held the cudgel at my face as close as possible. ఊతగానిలిచి he stood as a support. ఊత కొను ūta-konu. v. n. To support oneself, to rest, lean on. ఊతకోల ūta-kōla. n. A staff to lean on. ఊతము ūtamu. n. Grasp, strength. పట్టు, బలము. ఈ మాట ఊతము చేసినాడు he relied on this statement. ఊతముగా పుచ్చుకొనెను he took it for granted. తన వ్యాజ్యమునకు ఊతము అయిన మాట a circumstance that was in his favour. ఊతముచేయు. to state or declare, to strengthen. బలపరుచు.

ఊద ūda. [Tel.]n.A swelling, tumour. వాపు కడుపూద. Malice, spite, envy. ఈర్ష్య. ఊద కడుపు ūda-kaḍupu. n. A pot belly. ఊద or ఊదర ūda. n. A kind of grass. Tares. H. v. 53. ఒక అల్పధాన్యము. "ఊదలు బలియు పైరొదగబట్టె." L. xiii. 394. ఊదర ūdara. n. Smoke. ఊదరగొట్టు or ఊదరపెట్టు ūdara-goṭṭu. v. a. To smoke an animal out of its hole, or to ripen fruit by passing hot smoke.

ఊదా ūdā. [H.] n. Dark colour, purple or brown.

ఊదిబము ūdibamu. [Tel.] n. Produce, income. ఫలము, ఆదాయము.

ఊదు ūdu. [Tel.] v. n. To blow with the breath or with bellows. To swell వాచు. To press అదుము, నొక్కు. To play on a flute. To purify or refine metal with the blowpipe. To place, ఉంచు. To be swollen. To arise as a thought or feeling. To catch fish. చేపలను ఊతలో పట్టుకొను. ఊదు ūdu. n. A snare for fish made of basket work. Clay, mud బురద. A swelling వాపు. ఊదు ūdu. [H.] n. Frankincense, benzoin. సాంబ్రాణి. ఊదువత్తి a pastille. సాంబ్రాణివత్తి. ఊదించు to cause to blow. ఊదిన వెండి or ఊదు వెండి silver refined with the blowpipe ఊదుగొట్టము ūdu-goṭṭamu. n. A. blow-pipe. ఊదు క్రోవి or ఊదువాద్యము ūdu-krōvi. n. A wind instrument.

ఊధము or ఊధస్సు ūdhamu. [Skt.] n. An udder. పొదుగు.

ఊనము ūnamu. [Skt.] n. Loss, disgrace, injury, defect. లోపము. adj. Less, defective. తక్కువైన, లోపముగల. ఏకోనవింశతి nineteen.

ఊనిక ūnika. [Tel.] n. Resting, support, steadiness. ఆనుట, నిలువు. ఊను ūnu. v. a. To have, take, bear, వహించు, ధరించు. To soften as leather. మెత్తపరుచు. v. n. To lean against, to rest on. ఆను. "అయినను నెచ్చెలిపై మది, నూనినదెయ్యది మునుకేశి" మార్క. ii.

ఊప ūpa. [Tel.] n. An underwood in a forest. అడవిలోని చెట్లగుంపు.

ఊపిరి ūpiri. [Tel.] n. Breath, respiration. ఊపిరివిడుచు to breathe. ఊపిరిపట్టు to hold in the breath. వానికి ఊపిరి వచ్చింది he has revived. నీకు ఊపిరి తిరుగుచున్నదా can you draw your breath? ఊపిరితిరుగక being suffocated ఊపిరిపోయిన dead. ఊపిరి కుట్టు ūpiri-kuṭṭu. n. A stitch in the side. ఊపిరి తీయరాకుండునట్లు బాధించే ఒకవిధమైన వ్యాధి

ఊపు ūpu [Tel. from ఊగు and ఊచు.) v. t. To cause to swing ఊగజేయు. n. Swinging. A push, one oscillation in swinging. ఊచుట.

ఊబ ūba. [Tel.] n. A eunuch. నపుంసకుడు. A corpulent man. బొండు.

ఊబి *ûbi*. [Tel.] n. A slough, or bog, mire. బురద.

ఊయల *ûyala*. [Tel.] n. A swing. See ఉయ్యల.

ఊయు *ûyu*. [Tel.] v. n. To whistle. ఎద్దుల నూసినారు. They whistled the bullocks on.

ఊర See under ఊరు. n.

ఊరక or ఊరకె *ûraka*. [Tel.] adv. Without. For nothing. Silently, merely, idly, in vain. Without cause, of itself, spontaneously, voluntarily, causelessly. Without employment; unoccupied, empty, vacant. ఇల్లు ఊరకె ఉన్నది the house is vacant. ఊరకె పోనిచ్చు to let a thing go free. ఊరకె వచ్చు without any special purpose. ఊరకుండు to submit, be still; to be passive or silent. చ॥ . . . " ఒప్పుత, ప్పురయురసజ్ఞ లూపాదిలి యంగలకేళ కపాలకోత్తముల్, దొరికినగాక యూరకకృతుల్ రచియించుమటన్న శక్యమే." (అల్లసాని పెద్దన్న) i.e., how can a poet compose verse *without* these conveniences?

ఊరగాయ See under ఊరు. v.

ఊరట *ûraṭa*. [Tel.] n. Comforting. ఊరడించుట. Rest. విరామము. Ease, freedom, leisure. Aid, help. సహాయము. ఊరటపడు *ûraṭa-paḍu*. v. n. To be consoled. ఊరటపరచు *ûraṭa-paraṭsu*. v. a. To console. ఊరడించు *ûraḍinṭsu*. v. a. To comfort, console. ఉపశమించు. ఊరడిల్లు or ఊరడు *ûraḍillu*. v. n. To be calmed, appeased, comforted, consoled. శాంతిపొందు. ఊరడబల్కె he spoke consolingly.

ఊరవ్యుడు *ûravyuḍu*. [Skt.] n. A man of the Vaisya caste. కోమటి.

ఊరార్చు *ûrarṭsu*. [Tel. ఊరుపు+అర్చు] v. t. To console, cheer, comfort. ఓదార్చు, ఊరడించు.

ఊరించు *ûrinṭsu*. [Tel.] v. a. To excite appetite, tempt, tantalize. To make one's mouth water. ఊరునట్లుచేయు.

ఊరికె See ఊరక.

ఊరీకరించు *ûrî-karinṭsu*. [Skt.] v. t. To consent, to accept. అంగీకరించు. ఊరీకృతము *ûrîkritamu*. adj. Accepted. అంగీకరింపబడిన.

ఊరు *ûru*. [Tel. In Chaldee Ur=town. of. "Ur of the Chaldees." Genit. ఊరి, abl. ఊర or ఊరిలో, ఊళ్లో. Plu. ఊరులు; ఊళ్లు, ఊళ్లు] n. A village, a town. నేను ఊరిలో లేనప్పుడు when I was absent from home. ఊర *ûra*. (=ఊరియొక్క) adj. Rustic, common, village, belonging to the town or place. Rural, country. ఊరన abl. At home, in the village. ఊరనుండు. ఊరనున్నారు they are at home. ఊరకవి *ûra-kavi*. n. A rustic bard; a country poet. ఊరకంద *ûra-kanda* n. The root of the plant named *Tacca Pinnatifida*. Rox. Vol. 2. p. 172 ఊరజోగి *ûra-zôgi*. n. A wandering beggar. బిచ్చపుసన్యాసి ఊరనుయ్యి *ûra-nuyyi*. n. The common well; the town well. ఊరపంది *ûra-pandi*. n. A village pig. ఊరపిచ్చుక *ûra-pichchika*. n. The village sparrow: that is, the house sparrow. ఊరపిల్లి *ûra-pilli*. n. A domestic cat. ఊరవిందు *ûra-vindu*. n. A feast given to all the town on the occasion of a wedding.

ఊరు *ûru*. [Tel.] v. n. To be full, steeped or soaked. To be puffed or fat. To increase or grow great. To exude, leak out, ooze, or spring as water. To overflow as feelings. To sink as ink into paper. To take effect as a medicine. నోరూరుట the mouth watering. ఊరబెట్టినచెక్క timber left to steep or steam so as to be seasoned. తేటలూరగా full of light. ఊరుగాయ or ఊరగాయ *ûru-gâya*. n. A pickled fruit, a pickle. ఊరుబిండి *ûru-bindi*. n. A paste or *chutney* (used as sauce,) of fried grain and chillies. కూరిమలూర with overflowing love.

ఊరుకొను *ûru-konu*. [Tel.] v. n. To be still, or quiet. ఊరకయుండు.

ఊరుచు *ûruṭsu*. [Tel.] v. n. To sigh, sob. ఊపిరివిడుచు.

ఊరుజుడు *ūru-juḍu*. [Skt. from ఊరువు a thigh and జ=born] n. A man of the Vaisya caste. కోమటి.

ఊరుపు or **ఊర్పు** *ūrupu*. [Tel.] n. Breath. sighing, శ్వాసము. A sort of stew or curry, నిట్టూరుపు a deep sigh.

ఊరువు *ūruvu*. [Skt.] n. The thigh తొడ.

ఊరేగు *ūr-ēgu*. [Tel. ఊరు+ఏగు] v. n. To go (in parade or procession) through a village or town. **ఊరేగించు** *ūr-ēgintsu*. v. a. To parade, to carry through the town. **ఊరేగింపు** *ūr-ēgimpu*. n. A procession.

ఊర్చు *ūrtsu*. Same as ఊరుచు.

ఊర్జము *ūrjamu*. [Skt.] n. Bodily strength, perseverance. బలము, పూనిక. **ఊర్జస్వలుడు** *ūrja-svaluḍu*. n. A strong man. బలాఢ్యుడు. **ఊర్జితము** *ūrjitamu*. adj. Stable, firm. గట్టిగానున్న. ఊర్జితమైన or ఊర్జితమవు stable, confirmed: in force, as a law. ఊర్జితపరచు to confirm, to make stable, to fix. దృఢపరచు. ఊర్జితముగా firmly. గట్టిగా.

ఊర్ణము *ūrṇamu*. [Skt.] n. Wool, felt, &c. ఉన్ని, నూలు. ఊర్ణనాభము a spider. సాలె పురుగు.

ఊర్ధ్వము *ūrdhvamu*. [Skt.] adj. Above, upper, high. ఊర్ధ్వబాహువులై with his arms raised. ఊర్ధ్వరేతసుడు a *Rishi* or Sage. **ఊర్ధ్వలోకము** *ūrdhva-lōkamu*. n. The world above. Heaven.

ఊర్పు *ūrpu*. [Tel.] Same as ఊరుపు (q. v.) ఊర్పోవు (ఊర్పు+పోవు) to breathe. ఊపిరి విడుచు. ఊర్పోక (ఊర్పు+పోక) a pastime ఊసుపోక. ఊర్పుచ్చు (ఊర్పు + పుచ్చు) to cause the breath to go out.

ఊర్మి *ūrmi*. [Skt.] n. A wave. అల; the fold of a cloth వస్త్రపుముడత. Pain నొప్పి. షడూర్ములు the six kinds of pain, *viz.*, hunger, thirst, grief, passion, old age and death. క్షుత్, తృష్ణా, శోక, మోహ, జరా, మరణములు. **ఊర్మిక** *ūrmika*. n. A wave, a plait or fold, a finger ring.

ఊర్మిళ *ūrmila*. [Skt.] n. A woman that has separated from her husband మగని ఎడ బాసిన స్త్రీ.

ఊల or **ఊళ** *ūla*. [Tel.] n. A whistle. The howling of a fox నక్కకూత. ఊలవేయు the fox. ఊలవేయు to whistle.

ఊలమాల *ūlamala*. [Tel.] n. Pain, anxiety తహతహ. ఊలమాలపడు to suffer pain or anxiety. తహతహపడు.

ఊలు *ūlu*. [Tel. for కూలు] v. n. To fall. పడు. "ఈపికకూనిమీద పిడుగూలిన కాయములెంతయు ద్రుళ్లిపా కృతికా." Hurling a thunderbolt to crush a fly.

ఊవు Same as ఊగు. **ఊవాడు** Same as ఊగాడు.

ఊషణము *ūshanamu*. [Skt.] n. The stimulant called త్రికటు, viz., శొంఠి, పిప్పలి, or మిరియాలు ginger, pepper, or long pepper.

ఊషము *ūshamu*. [Skt.] n. Fuller's earth. చౌడు. **ఊషరము** or **ఊసరము**. *ūsharamu*. n. Salt soil.

ఊష్మము *ūshmamu*. [Skt.] n. Heat: sunshine ఉష్ణ, వేసంగి. In Gram: the letters శ, ష, స and హ. ఊష్మకము the hot season. **ఊష్మలము** *ūshmalamu*. adj. Heat, hot.

ఊసరము *ūsaramu*. [Tel.] n. Salt soil. **ఊసరము** adj. Lean: fallen away by disease. ఊసరపిల్లి a lean cat.

> "ఉట్టిమీదకొక్కు లూసరబిల్లులు
> పట్టజేసినన్న బొక్కునట్టు."
> వీరశైవకీర్తనలు. p. 33.

ఊసరవెల్లి *ūsara-velli*. [Tel.] n. A chameleon.

ఊసరిల్లు *ūsarillu*. v. i. To become lean or dry. చిక్కు, కృశించు.

ఊసు *ūsu*. [Tel.] n. Speech. ఊసుపోక. ఊసు లాడు to chit-chat.

ఊహ or **ఊహనము** *ūha*. [Skt.] n. Thought, reasoning, a guess, supposition, idea, contrivance. Probability, prospect. ఊహామీద

on a guess, probably. ఊహచేయు *ūha-chēyu.* v. n. To think, form an opinion. ఊహాపోహలు *ūha-pōhalu.* n. Thoughts and imaginations. (పోహ is anuk). ఊహించు *ūhintsu.* v.n. To think, reason, guess, contrive, consider, reflect on. బుద్ధినూహించుము think within yourself అట్లు ఊహించును man think so.

ఋ ṛi

ఋ The vowel Ri or Ru like ri in *trick* or ru in *fruit;* sometimes wrongly written రు. These vowels ఋ and ౠ in Prosody rhyme to ఇ and ఈ, never to రి, రీ and ఱి.

ఋక్కు *ṛikku.* [Skt.] n. The name of one of the Vedas. A Vedic slōka. ఖిలఋక్కు a supplementary hymn or Rik appended to the Veda.

ఋక్షము *ṛikshamu.* [Skt.] n. A bear. ఎలుగుగొడ్డు.

ఋజువు *ṛijuvu.* [Skt.] adj. Straight. తిన్నని, ఋజుమార్గము rectitude, honesty.

ఋణము *ṛiṇamu.* [Skt.] n. Debt, obligation. A claim, a title or lien. ఇంతేకున్న ఇక్కడి నీళ్లఋణము ఎన్నిరోజులు ప్రాప్తి ఉన్నదో besides I know not how much longer it is my fate to dwell here. ఋణపడు *ṛiṇa-paḍu.* v. n. To get into debt. ఋణముచేయు *ṛiṇamu-chēyu.* v. a. To contract a debt, to borrow. ఋణముతీర్చు *ṛiṇamu-tīrtsu.* To discharge a debt. ఋణత్రయము the three kinds of obligation, viz., దేవఋణము, ఋషిఋణము and పితృఋణము. ఋణవిముక్తుడు *ṛiṇa-vimuktuḍu.* n. One who is free from debt. ఋణస్థుడు or ఋణిక or ఋణిక స్థుడు *ṛiṇasthuḍu.* n. A debtor. ఋణార్ణము *ṛiṇārṇamu.* n. A debt contracted to pay off another debt. అప్పుతీర్చుటకై చేసిన అప్పు.

ఋతము *ṛitamu.* [Skt.] adj. True, real. సత్యమైన. n. Truth, reality సత్యము. అనృతము, falsehood, or a lie అసత్యము.

ఋతువు *ṛituvu.* [Skt.] n. A season. The Hindu year is divided into six seasons, each lasting two months, viz., వసంతము the spring, గ్రీష్మము summer, వర్షము the rainy season, శరత్తు autumn, హేమంతము the dewy season and శిశిరము the cold season. ఋతుకాలము *ṛitu-kālamu.* n. The menstruous period. A. ii. 22. ఋతుమతి *ṛitu-mati.* n. A menstruous woman. ముట్టుది. ఋతుస్నాత *ṛitu-snāta.* n. A woman who has bathed after menstruation. ఋతుస్నానము *ṛitu-snānamu.* n. Bathing after purification.

ఋత్విక్కు, ఋత్విజుడు *ṛitvikku.* [Skt.] n. A priest appointed to perform particular rites at a sacrifice. There are 16 orders of Vedic priests, of whom only three (viz: ఉద్గాత, హోత, అధ్వర్యుడు.) are mentioned in Telugu works.

ఋద్ధి *ṛiddhi.* [Skt.] n. Abundance, సమృద్ధి.

ఋభువు *ṛibhuvu.* [Skt.] n. A deity వేల్పు. Vasu. v. 3. ఋభుక్షుడు *ṛibhukshuḍu.* n. Indra.

ఋశ్యము *ṛiśyamu.* [Skt.] n. The white footed antelope. ఋశ్యవర్ణ శ్యము లు horses having the color of this antelope. Dun horses. ఋశ్యశృంగుడు (lit. one who bears the horn of an antelope.) n. Name of a Rishi or saint.

ఋషభము *ṛishabhamu.* [Skt.] n. A bull. adj. Excellent (in certain Samāsams or compounds.)

ఋషి *ṛishi.* [Skt.] n. A prophet or saint, gifted with supernatural powers. A sage. The author of a spell or prayer. cf. ముని and యోగి. సప్తర్షులు means (1) the "seven sages," viz., మరీచి, అత్రి, అంగిరుడు, పులస్త్యుడు, పులహుడు, క్రతువు, వసిష్ఠుడు; (or) కశ్యపుడు, అత్రి, భరద్వాజుడు, విశ్వామిత్రుడు, గౌతముడు, జమదగ్ని, వసిష్ఠుడు; (2) the constellation of the Great Bear. A proverb says ఋషిమూలము నదీమూలము the origin of a sage is as obscure as that of a river.

ౠ ṝ

ౠ Ṝi, and ౡ Li. No word admitted into Telugu begins with these Sanscrit letters.

ఎ e

ఎ The vowel e short; as in *them*, *set*, or *well*.

ఎ *e* [Tel.] An interrogative affix. "మునికూడు దున్నారె" భాగ. i.

ఎ *e* A negative affix. "నీవంత రమ్మన్నవె, నీరు తక్కవె—కారు అనుట.

ఎ *e* A feminine affix ఏమె O woman!

ఎ *e* An affix denoting "Only that and no other." అవధారణ—అదిమాత్రమే.

ఎ *e* An affix meaning "Look"! "behold!" "వారుడనుడిక్కా" భార. అర. v. "వీడె కృష్ణుడు" పారి. ఆ. ii.

ఎ *e* An affix denoting "By oneself," 'unasked,' &c., తనంతట. "ఎవరునడుగలేదు. వాడె వచ్చిపోయెను."

ఎ *e* As a prefix the long ē is contracted into the short e, while the next consonant is doubled; thus ఏ *what*, and కడ *place*, becomes ఎక్కడ.

ఎంగిలి *engili*. [Tel. gen. ఎంగిటి plu. ఎంగిళ్లు] n. Spittle. Defiled food, leavings. adj. Defiled, nasty. ఎంగిలి అన్నము leavings. ఎంగిలిమాటలు foul language, nonsense. ఎంగిలి ఆకు a leaf on which another has eaten his food.

ఎంగెస *engesa*.[Tel.] *n*. A forest tree. *Pterocarpus marsupium*, (Rox. Ainslie. ii. 264.) the wood of which is of a yellowish orange colour, durable and light. The gum is called dragon's blood.

ఎంచు *entsu*. [Tel.] v. a. To count, reckon, think: to be of opinion, consider, judge: to regard, care for: to believe, imagine: to select or choose. నేను ఎంచినది ఒకటి అయినది ఒకటి I anticipated a result very different from that which has happened. ఎంచుకొను Same as ఎంచు.

ఎండ *enḍa*. [Tel.] n. Heat, sunshine, glare, radiance, ఎండయెక్కినది the sun is high. చిరుఎండ the soft heat of the morning or evening; వెన్నెండ moonshine. వాడు వచ్చినప్పుడు నిండా పొద్దెండయెక్కినది it was late in the day when he arrived. ఎండకాచునప్పుడు when it is hot. నీకు ఎండ తగిలినది, or, నీ ముఖమునకు ఎండతగిలినది you look hot or fatigued, ఎండకన్నెరుగనివాడు one whose "eye knows not the sunbeam," i. e., who lives in the shade. ఎండకాలము *enḍa-kālamu*. n. The hot weather. ఎండగట్టు *enḍa-gaṭṭu*. v. t. To tie up (as a cloth) in the sun to dry. ఆరగట్టు. ఎండగాలి *enḍa-gāli*. n. A burning wind. ఎండగొట్టు *enḍa-goṭṭu*. v.i. To dry up or wither ఎండిపోవు. ఎండదెబ్బ *enḍa-debba*.n. A stroke of the sun. ఎండదొర or ఎండరేడు *enḍa-dora*. n. The sun. ఎండపొద్దు *enḍa-poddu*. n. Noon. ఎండమావి *enḍa-māvi*. n. The mirage మృగతృష్ణ. ఎండబెట్టు *enḍa-beṭṭu*. v. t. To put out to dry. ఎదురెండ the sun against the face.

ఎండు *enḍu*. [Tel.] v. n. To dry up, to become dry, to become lean or withered. తడి ఆరు, నీళ్లు ఇంకు, కృశించు, కృశ్చించు. ఎండిపోయిన dried up. ఎండు *enḍu*. adj. Dry, dried, shrivelling. ఎండుతెవులు a wasting disease.

ఎండుగులు *enḍugulu*. [Tel.] n. Grain put out to dry in sunshine. ఎండబోసినధాన్యము. ఎండుగుతట్ట *enḍugu-taṭṭa*. n. A basket for clothes or grain: a drying basket. ఎండు పులు same as ఎండుగులు.

ఎండ్రకాయ or ఎండ్రి, or ఎండ్రిక *enḍra-kāya*. [Tel.] n. A crab. కర్కాటకము. ఎండ్రిరాశి *enḍri-rāśi*. n. The sign of the Crab

ఎంత *enta*. [Tel. ఏ+అంత] adj. How much. ఇది ఎంతపొడుగు how long is this? ఎంత అన్యాయము what injustice! ఈ బంగారు వెంత ఉన్నది what is the price (or weight) of this gold? అది ఏమంతపని what great matter is that? ఎంతమాత్రము how much?

ఎంతలో within what price? ఎంతమాత్రము కాదు by no means. అట్లు అనడానికి నేనెంతవాణ్ని who am I that I should say so? నీకెంత అతనికెంత? what comparison is there between you and him? నేనెంతచెప్పినా notwithstanding all I could say. ఎంత చెల్లించితే అంత మంచిది the more you pay the better అప్పుడు ఎంత రాత్రియైయుండెను what time of night was it then? ఎంతసేపటికి వచ్చినాడు how long after did he come? ఎంతకు అమ్మినాడు for how much did he sell it? ఎంతమాత్రము కానిపని a thing quite out of the question. నీవెంత నేనెంత అని పోట్లాడినారు they scorned or insulted one another. ఎంతటి వారు what sort of persons? ఎంతమంది how many (persons.) The conjunction యు is sometimes added as an intensive. ఎంతయు రయమున with very great speed

ఎంతేని *enténi*. adv. Ever so much, how much soever. ఎంతైనను. ఎంతైన how vast, how great, ever so great. ఎంతో much. ఎంతోసంతోషముతో with great joy.

ఎందరు *endaru*. [Tel. ఎంత+వారు] adj. How many (persons.) ఎందరేని many, అనేకులు.

ఎందాక or **ఎందమక** *endāka*. [Tel. ఎంత+దనుక] adv. How far? how long? ఎంతదనుక.

ఎందు *endu*. [Tel.] adv. Where? ఎందో somewhere. ఎందుగురించి regarding what or which. ఎందున్ను everywhere. ఎందు పోయినాడు where is he gone? ఎందుమీద whereupon. ఎందెందులకు in what respects. ఎందులో wherein ఎందేని somewhere or other, anywhere. ఎందుండి whence. ఎందుకు or ఎందులకు why? for what? wherefore? అది నాకెందుకు what is that to me, ఎందుచేత whereby. ఎందుచేతనంటే because. ఎందున where. ఎందునిమిత్తము wherefore, why. ఎందునుంచి, ఎందునుండి whence. ఎందైన wheresoever, anywhere.

ఎంబన్న *embanna*. [Tel. ఎంబె+అన్న] n. An idiot, a good-for-nothing fellow. చేతగానివాడు.

ఎకదొట్టు *eka-doṭṭu*. [Tel.] v. t. To excel, increase. అతిశయించు, తిరస్కరించు. A. v. 2.

ఎకరా *ekarā*. [Tel.] n. A court yard, a cock pit; a place in front of a house where an elephant is tied up. ఏనుగును కట్టు కొట్టసాల. (మను i. Intro: 48.). Also the English word Acre.

ఎకరారు *ekarāru*. [H.] n. Confession. ఎకరారుపడు to confess.

ఎకసకెము or **ఎకసక్కెము** *ekasakemu*. [Tel.] n. A prank, trick. పంచన. Mockery పరిహాసము. "చక్కరవింటివానియెకసక్కెములన్ని యుమాగ్ర" indulging in all sorts of amorous pranks.

ఎకిమీడు *ekimīḍu*. [Tel.] n. A ruler, general, lord, owner. అధిపతి, రాజు.

ఎక్కటి *ekkaṭi*. [Tel.] adj. Single ఒక్కటి, single-handed అసహాయుడైన. Noble, great, superior. శౌర్య n. A hero, a warrior. Cruelty, harshness. **ఎక్కటీడు** *ekkaṭīḍu*. n. A hero who is without any assistants. అసహాయుడైనబంటు.

ఎక్కడ *ekkaḍa*. [Tel. ఏ+కడ] adv. Where? ఇది యెక్కడ అది యెక్కడ where is this and where is that, i.e., what comparison is there between this and that? వాడు నీకెక్కడ అచ్చియున్నాడు how is he in debt to you? i. e., what do you mean by pretending he is indebted to you? ఎక్కడి విప్రుడు a pretty sort of a Brahmin! ఇది యెక్కడి సంకటము who ever saw such a business! ఎక్కడనుండి whence. ఎక్కడనో I know not where, somewhere or other. ఎక్కడనైనా anywhere, somewhere or other. ఎక్కడను everywhere. ఎక్కడను లేదు No where. నీవెక్కడివాడవు of what town are you? ఇది యెక్కడిది whence is this? what nonsense this is ఎక్కడి మగడెక్కడి బ్రతుకు what care I for my husband or for life? ఈ పువ్వులు నీకు ఎక్కడివి where did you get these flowers? వాడు ఎక్కడి బుధుడు what sort of a sage is he! నీకెక్కడి తపమెక్కడి what have you to do with penance? ఎక్కడకు whither, to what place. ఎక్కడెక్కడ wherever. ఎక్కడివారు అక్కడికి వెళ్లిరి everybody went home, i.e., all fled.

ఎక్కము *ekkamu.* [Tel.] n A bank or path between fields. గనిమ. In arithmetic, a unit, the place of units. ఎక్కములు n. The multiplication-table.

ఎక్కలమ్మ *ekkal-amma.* [Tel.] n. The name of a village goddess.

ఎక్కలి *ekkali.* [Tel.] n. Sand washed down by a river. ప్రవాహముతో కొట్టుకొనివచ్చిన యిసుక.

ఎక్కసక్కెము *ekkasakkemu.* [Tel.] n. Scorn, derision. ఎకసక్కెము, వికటపుమాట. Swa. ii. 39.

ఎక్కాడు *ekkāḍu.* [Tel.] v. t. To incite, encourage, to egg on. పురికొలుపు.

ఎక్కాలు *ekkālu.* [Tel.] n. The multiplication-table. ఎక్కములు.

ఎక్కించు *ekkintsu.* [Tel. from ఎక్కు] v. a. To raise. To mount. To enter, file or insert: to help up, to place.

ఎక్కిడు *ekkiḍu.* [Tel. ఎక్కు+ఇడు] v.t. To bend or string a bow. Bhāsc § 104.

ఎక్కిరించు *ekkirintsu.* [Tel.] v. a. To make faces at, to mock, to gibe at వెక్కిరించు. ఎక్కిరింపబోయి వెలికిలబడెను he went to gibe but met with a fall. ఎక్కిరింత *ekkirinta.* n. Mockery, making faces. A vehicle. వాహనము. ఎక్కిరింతయెద్దు a saddle bullock. ఎక్కిరింతపక్కి the eagle on which Vishṇu rides. A. vi. 183. R. i. 145.

ఎక్కిలి *ekkili.* [Tel.] n. The hicoup వెక్కి. (plu: ఎక్కిళ్లు.) BD. i. 389.

ఎక్కు *ekku.* [Tel.] v. a. & n. To rise, increase, swell. To appear (by its effects as wine, water, poison, or medicine.) To affect the mind. To prevail as a report; to come to notice వానితలకు మదము ఎక్కినది he is beside himself with pride or lust. వానికి మత్తెక్కినది he is intoxicated. వడ్డియెక్కినది interest has accrued. ఎక్కినవడ్డి the interest that accrued. వానిదుష్టగుణములు నీకు ఎక్కినవి you have caught his bad habits, or, followed his example. వార్తకెక్కు to become the theme or topic of discourse. వన్నెకెక్కినాడు he became celebrated, rose to distinction. వాసికెక్కిన celebrated, honoured. వన్నెకెక్కినవాడు one who has risen to reputation. పదిగంటలపొద్దు ఎక్కిన వేళ when it was ten o'clock, lit. when the sun had mounted (to) ten hours. ఆ పనికి ఎవరును ఎక్కలేదు no one *came forward*, or *volunteered* for the business. ఆతనిమాట యెక్కదు his word will not do, or avail. తలకు నీళ్లెక్కి జలుబుగానున్నది the water has got into the head and I have a cold. To mount on, get upon. మంచమెక్కు to take to one's bed. ఎక్కుకొను *ekku-konu.* v. a. To mount on ఆరోహించు.

ఎక్కు *ekku.* [Tel.] n. A bowstring వింటినారి. Also, encouragement, incitement, goading on ప్రేరణ. ఎక్కుడించినాడు he unbraced or unbent the bow.

ఎక్కుడించు (ఎక్కు (n) + దించు) *ekku-ḍintsu.* [Tel.] v. To unbrace a bow.

ఎక్కుడించు *ekku-ḍintsu.* [Tel. ఎక్కుడు+ఇంచు]: v. t. To increase హెచ్చించు. ఎక్కుడు *ekkuḍu.* [Tel. from ఎక్కు.] n. Ascent, greatness. ఎక్కుట, అతిశయము. A bowstring వింటినారి. ఎక్కుడు *ekkuḍu.* adj. High, great, mighty. అధికము. ఎక్కుడుతనము *ekkuḍu-tanamu.* Superiority. ఆధిక్యము. P. i. 634.

ఎక్కుపెట్టు or ఎక్కుడుపెట్టు *ekku-peṭṭu.* [Tel.] v.n. To brace a bow.

ఎక్కులుపెట్టు *ekkulu-peṭṭu.* [Tel.] v. a. To stir up, to provoke, excite, tempt. పురికొలుపు.

ఎక్కువ *ekkuva.* [Tel.] n. Excess, greatness, eminence. Particularity, peculiarity. ఆధిక్యము, విశేషము. అతనివద్దర పుస్తకాలు ఎక్కువగా లేవు he has not many books. ఎక్కువ *ekkuva*, adj. Great, peculiar, remarkable, singular. అధికము. ఎక్కువపాత దికాదు it is not very old. ఎక్కువశ్రమకాదు it is no great trouble. ఎక్కువతక్కువ *ekkuva-takkuva.* n. More or less, unevenness, irregularity, ups and downs. కొంచెము ఎక్కువతక్కువగా నూరురూపాయలు about 100 Rupees. మాలో చేసినా ఎక్కువ తక్కువ ఉంటే తమరు క్షమించవలెను please to excuse all errors.

ఎక్కువలు *ekkuvalu.* [Tel.] n. News, novelties, singularities. విశేషములు.

ఎక్కొలుపు *ek-kolupu.* [Tel.] v. a. To excite, stir up. పురికొలుపు.

ఎగ *ega.* [Tel. from ఎగయు] adv. Up, upward. ఎగగొట్టు *ega-goṭṭu.* v. a. To throw up, rob, to run away with. ఎగురవేయు, అపహరించు. ఎగగ్రోలు *ega-grōlu.* v. t. To suck up పీల్చు. ఎగజల్లు *ega-zallu.* v. t. To scatter upward. పైకిచల్లు. ఎగజేపు *ega-jēpu.* v. a. To keep in (the milk) or restrain it from flowing (as a cow does unless the calf is with her. ఎగదన్ను *ega-dannu.* v. t. To kick up. ఎగదీయు *ega-dīyu.* v. a. To lift or pull up. To raise. ఎగదువ్వు *ega-duvvu.* v. t. To comb upwards. మీదికి దువ్వు. ఎగద్రోయు *ega-drōyu.* v. t. To lift up, push up. ఎగనూదు *ega-n-ūdu.* v. t. To blow upwards, to disregard. పైకి ఊదు, తిరస్కరించు. ఎగనెత్తు *ega-n-ettu.* v. t. To lift up. పైకెత్తు. ఎగబట్టు *ega-baṭṭu.* v. t. To hold up. ఎత్తిపట్టు. ఎగబిల్చు *ega-bilṭsu.* v. t. To snort aloud. ఎగఊపిరి *ega-ūpiri.* n. A gasp. ఎగబోత *ega-bōta.* n. Spreading upwards, giving bad advice, rumination, a brown study, discontent. ఎగబోత వ్యాపించుట, దుర్బోధనచేయుట. వానికి చెమట తొంగబోత దిగబోతగా నున్నది he was in a sweat from head to foot. ఎగబోయు *ega-bōyu.* v. t. To give bad advice. దుర్బోధచేయు to hint. సూచించు. ఎగబ్రాకు *ega-brāku.* v. i. To creep up, crawl up. మీదికి ప్రాకు. ఎగరోజు *ega-rōzu.* v. i. To breathe hard. ఎగరొప్పు *ega-roppu.* n. Breathing hard. ఎగవిడుచు *ega-viḍuṭsu.* v. t. To let alone. తొలగవిడుచు. ఎగవేయు *ega-vēyu.* v. t. To embezzle, misappropriate. అపహరించు.

ఎగతాళి *ega-tāḷi.* [Tel.] n. Joke, derision hoax. గేలి, పరిహాసము. ఎగతాళిచేయు to deride, mock, to gibe, to crack jokes at పరిహాసముచేయు.

ఎగపు *egapu.* [Tel.] n. Pride, wrath. గర్వము, మండిపడుట.

ఎగయు *egayu.* [Tel.] v. n. To rise, to spring up. To fly or bound. ఎగురు, పైకెగయు. నా కాళ్లలోను చేతులలోను మంటలెగసినవి my hands and feet are burning. ఎగసిపడు To attack, to be proud, to be arrogant, to fly into a passion. ఎగిరిపడు, గర్వించు, మండిపడు. నేను ఈమాట చెప్పినప్పుడు ఎగసి పడ్డాడు he flew into a passion. ఎగసిపాటు *egasi-pāṭu.* n. Arrogance, pride, ఎగసిపడుట, గర్వించుట, మండిపడుట. ఎగసిపో to fly up or away, to fly off. ఎగువు *eguvu.* n. Flying, flight ఎగురుట.

ఎగసన *egasana.* [Tel.] adv. Up, upwards. ఎగువగా. ఎగసనద్రోయు to push up, lift up: to trim the wick of a lamp పైకిత్రోయు.

ఎగాదిగా or ఎగదిగ *egā-diga.* [Tel.] adv. Up and down, backwards and forwards, from head to foot. ఎగువదిగువలుగా. వాడు నూనెను ఒళ్లంతా ఎగాదిగా రాసుకొన్నాడు he anointed himself from head to foot.

ఎగు *egu.* [Tel. for ఎగువ or ఎగురు] adj. High ఎత్తైన. ఎగుబుజములు high or strong shoulders. ఎగుబోద a new fledged bird

లెక్కలువచ్చి తొంగరగల పక్షిపిల్ల. ఎగుచు *egutsu.* v. a. To run after, to chase తరుము. ఎగుడు *egudu.* adj. Up ఉన్నతము. ఎగుడుదిగుడు *egudu-digudu.* Up and down, backwards and forwards. ఈ త్రోవ ఎగుడుదిగుడుగానున్నది this road is uneven. ఎగుడుదిగుడు నేల uneven ground. ఎగుడుదిగుడుమాటలు incoherent words. అసంగతమైనమాటలు. వాడు చెప్పేది యేమీ యెగుడు దిగుడుగానున్నది he shuffled, or spoke incoherently.

ఎగుడల *egudala.* [Tel.] n. The upper portion, increase. పైభాగము, వృద్ధి.

ఎగుమతి *egumati.* [Tel.] n. Shipment, lading, putting goods on board ship, export. ఎగుమతిచేయు *egumati-chēyu.* v. t. To ship or export goods. ఎగుమతిదిగుమతి *egumati-digumati.* n. Export and import. Shipping and unshipping.

ఎగురు *eguru.* [Tel.] v. n. To fly. ఎగయు. ఎగరగొట్టు *egara-gottu.* v. a. To toss up. నామాటను ఎగరగొట్టినాడు he scorned what I said. ఎగురులాడు *egurul-adu.* v. n. To cut capers, to leap or make bounds. గంతులువేయు.

ఎగువ *eguva.* [Tel.] n. The top, the upper part. Uppishness అధికత్వము. ఉ. "తగవా మగవారికినిటు మగువదుందుడుకుదనము" రామా. v. adj. Up, high ఉన్నతము. See ఎగు.

ఎగ్గతము *eggatamu.* [Tel.] n. A lonely or solitary place ఏకాంతస్థలము.

ఎగ్గాడు See ఎగ్గు.

ఎగ్గించు *eggintsu.* [Tel.] v. a. To slight. అనాదరించు. To wrong, injure. ఎగ్గులాడు, ఎగ్గుచేయు.

ఎగ్గు *eggu.* [Tel.] n. Harm, injury. కీడు, అపకారము. Shame, disgrace. అనాదరము, దూషణము. Abuse or evil word కీడుమాట. Fault, sin అపరాధము, దోషము. Loss or evil కీడు, నష్టము. ఎగ్గులాడు, ఎగులుపట్టు. *eggul-adu.* v. t. To find fault, to disgrace. నిందించు. ఎగ్గొందు to meet with ill success, to be baffled.

ఉ. "దగ్గరకొంచెము చెప్పెడు
ప్రెగ్గడపలుకులకురాజు ప్రియుడై మరి తా
నెగ్గుప్రజకాచరించుట
బొగ్గులకై కల్పతరువు బొడుచుటసుమతీ."
సుమతిశతకము.

ఎగ్గురాతు or ఎగ్గుర్తు *egguruta.* [Tel. ఎగు+గురుతు] n. An abstract, a memorandum. ఎగ్గురుతులెక్క an abstract of an account.

ఎగ్గోగిల *eggōgila.* [Tel.] n. The plant called Cowach, *mucuna pruritus* కపికచ్ఛూ.

ఎచ్చిరిల్లు or ఎచ్చిరు *echchirillu.* [Tel.] v. n. To thrive, succeed. R. v. 260.

ఎచట *etsata.* [Tel. ఏ+చోటు]. adv. Where ఎక్కడ.

ఎచ్చరించు or ఎచ్చరికించు *ettsarintsu.* [Tel.] v. a. To warn, challenge, hail, call to. To hint, allude to, advert to. To invoke, remind, or implore. To rally troops. ఎచ్చరికచేయు. ఎచ్చరిక or ఎచ్చరము or ఎచ్చరింత *ettsarika.* n. Hint, caution, warning, challenge, reminder. సూచన. ఎచ్చరికచేయు to caution or warn. ఎచ్చరికతప్పు to be off one's guard. ఎచ్చరికపడు to be on the alert, to be forewarned.

ఎచ్చు or హెచ్చు *ettsu.* [Tel.] n. & adj. Much. అధికము: అధికమైన. ఎచ్చుతగ్గులుగా *ettsu-taggulu-ga.* adv. Insolently. నన్ను ఎచ్చుతగ్గులుగా మాట్లాడినాడు he spoke to me scornfully.

ఎచ్చోటు or ఎచ్చోటు *ettsōtu.* [Tel. ఏ+చోటు] adv. Where.

ఎట *eta.* [Tel. for ఎచ్చట] adv. Where. ఎటకేని somewhere or other. ఎటు *etu.* adv. How. ఎట్లు. ఎటుతోచక not knowing what to think. ఎటుగా where. ఎటులు or ఎట్లు *etlu.* adv. How. ఎటువంటి *etu-vanti.* Like what, of what sort. ఎట్టి. నీవు ఇది చేయడము ఎటువంటిది what is the meaning of your doing this? ఎటువలె *etu-vale.* Like what? ఎట్లు.

ఎట్టకేని *eṭṭa-k-ēni.* [Tel.] adv. Hard, scarcely, with much difficulty అతిప్రయాససముతో. ఎట్టకేలకు *eṭṭa-kēla-ku.* adv. With much difficulty ఎట్టకేని. Shortly after, soon after, after a while. కడకు, చాలాసేపటికి, కొంతసేపటికి, అటుతర్వాత. ఎట్టట *eṭṭaṭa.* (ఎట్టు + అటు+అ) adv. Anyhow ఎట్లాయిన.

ఎట్టపోగు *eṭṭa-pōgu.* [Tel. ఎట్ట for ఎదుటు, పోగు multitude] n. An army దండు.

ఎట్టయెదురు *eṭṭa-eduru.* [Tel. ఎదురు+ఎదురు] adv. Exactly in front మిక్కిలియెదురుగా.

ఎట్టి *eṭṭi.* [Tel.] adj. What like, what kind, however (much or great) ఎటువంటి. ఎట్టిది of what kind is it? ఎట్టిడు *eṭṭi-ḍu.* [Tel. ఎట్టి+వాడు] What kind of man ఎటువంటి వాడు. plu. ఎట్టిరు.

ఎట్టు *eṭṭu.* [Tel.] adv. How ఏ. గను? ఎట్టువలె or ఎట్టులు *eṭṭulu.* adv. What like, of what sort ఏప్రకారము. ఎట్లా Same as ఎట్టు. ఎట్లాగు *eṭlāgu.* (ఎట్లు and ఆగు.) adv. How. ఎట్లాగైనా or ఎట్లాగైన *eṭlāgaina.* adv. In some way or other.

ఎట్లు *eṭlu.* See under ఎటు and ఎట్టు.

ఎడ *eḍa.* [Tel.] n. Place, space, చోటు; Interval, medium, distance. చోటు, అవకాశము, దూరము. An interval of time గడువు. Breach or obstacle విఘ్నము. Business వ్యవహారము. Peace. సంధి. ఎడగా further off. నూరుబారల దూరముగా 100 fathoms off. వాడు బలములేనియెడ while or if he is powerless. రానియెడ on his not coming. ఊరుచేరినయెడ on his arrival at the village. ఎడ *eḍa.* adj. Tender, young, లేత. Middle నడుమ. ఎడదూడ a weaned (i. e., separated) calf. కోడియెడ a chicken. ఎడబిడ్డ the last but one child. తొంటియెడ in the former place. ఎడపోవువాడు a go-between. BD. iii. 737. ఎడతెగని continuous, without interval or break. ఎడను or ఎడల regarding, concerning, of, about. నాయెడ towards me. గురువునెడ towards the teacher. ఇచ్చినయెడ on giving, కానియెడ if it is not so. మీయెడ నాయెడ towards you and me. పట్నప్రవేశము చేయునెడ on arrival at the town. ఎడగాపెట్టు to set aside, reserve. ఎడకట్టు *eḍa-kaṭṭu.* v. n. To find a place for itself. To gather or form as a boil అయినపుండు తల చీముపట్టు, చేరు. ఎడకత్తె *eḍa-katte.* n. A bawd. ఎడకాడు *eḍa-kāḍu.* n. A go-between, a pimp. ఎడకారు *eḍa-kāru.* n. An untimely crop, a crop produced out of season" before the rains. వ్యత్యయకృషి. ఎడకారుగా పుట్టిన forced, grown out of season, succedaneous.

ఎడగిల్లు or ఎడగిలియుండు *eḍa-gillu.* [Tel.] v. n. To stand out of the way, stand aside, get out of the way ఒత్తిగిల్లు. ఎడజేయు *eḍa-jēyu.* v. n. To do away with, abolish. ఎడతాకు *eḍa-tāku.* v. t. To meet, to unite. ఎడతీయు *eḍa-tīyu.* v. a. To remove or abstract. తొలగించు. ఎడతెగు *eḍa-tegu.* v. n. To break off, separate. ఎడతెగకుండ incessantly, without interval. ఎడతెరపి *eḍa-terapi.* n. Interval వ్యవధానము.

ఎడద *eḍada.* [Tel.] n. The heart, the breast. ఎద, హృదయము.

ఎడదవ్వు *eḍa-davvu.* [Tel.] n. A great distance అతిదూరము.

ఎడనీరు or ఎడనీళ్లు *eḍa-nīru.* [Tel.] n. The water of a tender cocoanut. See ఎడ adj.

ఎడనెడ *eḍan-eḍa.* [Tel.] adv. Here and there అచ్చటచ్చట. now and then అప్పుడప్పుడు.

ఎడపడు *eḍa-paḍu.* [Tel.] v. i. To break off, to separate. ఎడతెగు; to be pledged for పూటపడు. ఎడపడకునికి dissent, refusal, division. BD. i. 389.

ఎడపదడప *eḍapa-daḍapa.* [Tel.] adv. Now and then అప్పుడప్పుడు.

ఎడపు eḍapu. [Tel.] v. a. To separate, disunite, break. To shiver or smash. ఎడచుచేయు. ఎడపక eḍapaka. adv. Continually, without break.

ఎడపెట్టు eḍa-peṭṭu. [Tel.] v. t. To remove out of the way తొలగించు. To keep aside for further use, as rice మారువడ్డించుటకొరకు అన్నమును తీరుగానుంచు.

ఎడపోవు eḍa-pōvu. [Tel.] v. n. To go between: to pimp. దౌత్యముచేయు. BD. v. 1480.

ఎడబాయు eḍa-bāyu. [Tel.] v. n. To give up, to stand aloof, to be separated from, be cut off, to abstain. కూటికి నెడబాసి abstaining from food. నీళ్లెడబాసిన చేప a fish out of water. ఎడబాటు eḍa-bāṭu. n. Separation వియోగము. ఎడబాపు eḍa-bāpu. v. a. To cut off, or discontinue.

ఎడమ eḍama. [Tel. (lit.) Distant; from ఎడము distance దూరము] adj. The left. ఎడమచెయ్యి the (distant or) left hand. ఎడమకాలు the left leg

ఎడమడుగు or ఎడమడువు eḍa-maḍugu. [Tel.] n. Delay. ఆలస్యము. Difference. వ్యత్యాసము. adj. Different వ్యత్యస్తము.

డము eḍamu. [Tel.] n. Place, spot, room. చోటు. An interval, occasion, opportunity, leisure, opening. అవకాశము. ఎడమిచ్చు to give an opportunity.

ఎడయు eḍayu. [Tel.] v. n. To stand aside. To separate. తొలగు, ఎడబాయు. ఎడయిక eḍayika. n. Separation ఎడబాటు, వియోగము.

ఎడయెడముగా eḍa-y-eḍamu-gā. [Tel.] adv. Separately, at intervals దూరదూరముగా.

ఎడరు eḍaru. [Tel.] v. i. To break భగ్నము. n. Interval, సందు. An opportunity సమయము. A misfortune ఆపద.

ఎడల eḍala. [Tel. plu: of ఎడ, the final A being the Locative sign.] prep. Towards, regarding, touching, in the matter of. In the event of, in case, if. అట్లు చేసినయెడల in doing so or if it is done so. వాడు నన్ను చూచినయెడల if he saw me. నాయెడల regarding me. ఆయెడల on that occasion, or if so.

ఎడలించు or ఎడలుచు eḍalinṭsu. [Tel.] v. a. To separate, or unravel. To do away with. To remove, clear, loosen. To drive away తొలగించు, వదలించు. ఎడలు eḍalu. v. n. To go, depart. విడలు. To break వికలమగు, విచ్ఛిన్నమగు. To be thrown away విసర్జించు.

ఎడవాడు eḍa-vāḍu. [Tel.] n. The last one కడపటివాడు. A stranger అన్యుడు.

ఎడవు eḍavu. [Tel.] adj. Distant, remote. దూరము. A. vi. 90.

ఎడసాల eḍa-sāla [Tel.] n. A separate room, an antechamber. విడిగానున్నశాల.

ఎడాటము eḍāṭamu. [Tel.] n. Sport, play, ఆట. Matter or subject, విషయము. Sar. Pad. ii. 9.

ఎడారి eḍāri. [Tel.] n. A wilderness, a lonely spot. A desert చెట్లుచేమలులేని పెద్ద నిర్జలభూమి. ఎడారిత్రోవ a lonely path, a bye road.

ఎడి another form of ఎడు affix. (q. v.)

ఎడు eḍu. [Tel.] An affix denoting quantity (like *full* in a cup-ful, a bagful) పరిమాణార్థకము. మూరెడు a cubit, as much as a cubit. బారెడు an ell-long. బుడ్డెడు a bottleful. To this word the affix ఏసి is sometimes added: గంపెడేసి by basketfuls, a basketful at a time. ఎడు or ఎడి an affix applied to participles, does not alter the sense, as పోవు or పోయెడు going.

ఎడ్డ Same as ఎడడ. ఎడ్డవగచు much sorrowing BD. iv. 570.

ఎడ్డము eḍḍamu. [Tel.] n. Folly, stupidity, అవివేకము. Evil, calamity. ఆపద. ఉ॥ "ఎడ్డమిన్నైనయప్పటికి కివ్వరు చేరరు లోకులేమియున్, సడ్డలుచేయునొల్లరు" VP. v. 102.

ఎడ్డము *eḍḍamu.* [Tel.] n. An obstacle; opposition అడ్డంకి, విరోధము.

ఎడ్డె *eḍḍe.* [Tel.] adj. Ignorant మూఢమైన. ఎడ్డెవాడు or ఎడ్డెడు a boor, a fool. Véma. ii. 68. **ఎడ్డెతనము** *eḍḍe-tanamu.* n. Boorishness.

ఎడ్డెన *eḍḍena.* [Tel.] n. A table or high seat on which the dinner service is kept భోజనపాత్రములు నుంచుకొనే ఎత్తైనపీఠము.

ఎడ్లు *eḍlu.* [Tel. Contracted from ఎద్దులు] n. Oxen, cattle దుక్కిటెద్దులు plough oxen.

ఎతడు *etaḍu.* [Tel.] pron. Who. ఎవడు.

ఎత్తనగోల *ettana-gōla.* [Tel.] n. A rod used as a lever to lift up bags of rice, &c., in order to place them on the backs of bullocks గోనెలెత్తి యెద్దులమీదవేసుకొనుటకు సాధనమైన కర్ర. A staff used to support anything ఊతగా నానించిన కోల.

ఎత్తనగోలు *ettana-gōlu.* [Tel.] n. Beginning మొదలు, ప్రారంభము.

ఎత్తరము or **ఎత్తరవు** *ettaramu.* [Tel.] adj. High ఉన్నతము, ఎత్తు. **ఎత్తరతత్తరలు** *ettara-tattaralu.* n. Fragments, bits, shivers. వానికెత్తరతత్తరలుగానున్నది he is silly, or in his dotage.

ఎత్తలి *ettali.* [Tel.] n. A means, instrument, tool కొరముట్టు, సాధనము.

ఎత్తు *ettu.* [Tel.] v. n. To rise పుట్టు. To occur, come about కలుగు. To start బయలుదేరు. To come on (as a disease.) వానికి అతిసారము ఎత్తినది dysentery came on. వానికి వెర్రియెత్తినది madness came on him; he became mad. నాకు ఆకలియెత్తినది I am hungry. గాలియెత్తినది the wind arose. నేను వాంతియెత్తితిని I vomited. **ఎత్తించు** *ettintsu.* [Causal of ఎత్తు] v. t. To lift. To cause to raise, erect, or build. **ఎత్తికొను** or **ఎత్తుకొను** *etti-konu.* v. i. To bear, to carry వహించు. To attempt యత్నించు, v. t. To rob అపహరించు.

ఎత్తికోలు *etti-kōlu.* n. An endeavour, a beginning; striving, effort, intention, purpose. ఆరంభము, ప్రయత్నము, సంకల్పము. **ఎత్తిపొడుచు** *etti-poḍutsu.* v. t. To taunt, jeer, reproach నిందించు. ఎత్తిపొడుపుమాట a taunt, a reproach. నింద. **ఎత్తిలి** *ettili.* adv. Hard. గట్టిగా. **ఎత్తివేయు** *etti-vēyu.* v. t. To throw away, to strike out. కొట్టివేయు, తీసివేయు; to slight, to despise అలక్ష్యముచేయు.

ఎత్తు *ettu.* [Tel.] v. a. To take up, raise, lift up పైకెత్తు. To take, to remove. తీసికొను. To assume or take on oneself, to obtain or acquire (a name.) వహించు, పొందు. మంచిపేరెత్తు to acquire reputation. To cite, quote, mention, adduce, introduce a subject ప్రస్తావించు. మాటయెత్తు. To mention by name, advert to, allude to. To erect (a door or pillar.) To undertake. To raise or levy (an army.) అతడు జన్మమెత్తెను he assumed a mortal body, he was born. ఎత్తివ్రాయు to copy out or extract from a book. గొంతెత్తిచదువు to read aloud. భిక్షమెత్తు to take or receive alms. తళుకులెత్తు to assume lustre or become bright. నోరెత్తు to open the mouth, to speak నేను నోరెత్తలేదు I did not open my lips. గుత్తయెత్తినాడు he undertook the contract. దండెత్తు he raised troops. తూము ఎత్తించు to open a sluice. అలుగెత్తు to open an అలుగు (q. v.) లంగరు ఎత్తు to weigh anchor. పరుగెత్తు to take a run, to run. ఎత్తుకొనివచ్చు to fetch, to bring away. పిల్లను ఎత్తుకొను to take up a child. ఎత్తుకొనిపోవు to carry away or remove, to steal. బిచ్చమెత్తు to take alms, to beg. చిగురులెత్తు to sprout, to send forth shoots.

ఎత్తు *ettu.* [Tel.] n. 1. Height. ఉన్నతము. 2. Weight: బరువు, తూనిక. The weight of a quarter of a maund, *i.e.*, two viss, or, six pounds and a quarter రెండువీసెల తూలము. (A. v. 96.) A wreath of flowers. పువ్వులెత్తు, పుష్పసరము. A move at chess

చదరంగపు ఎత్తు; hence (metaphorically) a contrivance, a trick, ఉపాయము; an effort. ప్రయత్నము. ఎత్తులమారి a clever man. ఎత్తుకట్టు or ఎత్తిచూచు to weigh, to try. ఎత్తుకు ఎత్తు a Roland for an Oliver, one device against another. ఎత్తు *ettu.* adj. High, heavy. ఎత్తుపయనము a sudden journey.

ఎత్తుకొయ్య *ettu-koyya.* [Tel.] n. The fulcrum or rest of a lever.

ఎత్తుగడ *ettu-gaḍa.* [Tel.] n. An endeavour, project. A contrivance. A manœuvre, device, trick. యత్నము, ఉపాయము. ఎత్తుగడచేయు to endeavour.

ఎత్తుగడ్డలు *ettu-gaḍḍalu.* [Tel.] n. The movable earthen cheeks of a fire place. ఎత్తుపొయ్యిగడ్డలు.

ఎత్తుగున్న *ettu-gunna.* [Tel.] n. A young elephant కేల యేనుగుపిల్ల.

ఎత్తుపడు *ettu-paḍu.* [Tel. from ఎత్తు] v. n. To perish, to be abolished or done away with, to fail చెడు. To grow feeble. శేవశేకపోవు. ఎత్తుపడిన bedridden, feeble, helpless. ఎత్తుపడ్డగుర్రము a horse that is worn out. ఎత్తుపెట్టు *ettu-peṭṭu.* v. To raise, to support, to prop up. To urge, stir up, incite. H. i. 128. ఎత్తుపోవు Same as ఎత్తుపడు.

ఎత్తుబరికాడు or ఎతుబరికాడు *ettu-bari-kāḍu.* [Tel.] n. A thief, a rogue దొంగ, చోరుడు.

ఎత్తుభారము *ettu-bhāramu.* [Tel.] n. Plague, harassment, responsibility, business. Ruin. పాడు.

ఎత్తువచ్చు *ettu-vaṭṭsu.* [Tel.] v. i. To counterpoise, to be equal to సరిపోలు. ఎత్తువేయు *ettu-vēyu.* v. t. To weigh. తూచు.

ఎత్తెల *ettela.* [Tel. ఎత్తు+వల] n. A snare for fish (or for birds) చేపలను పట్టేవల (భార. శాం. iii.)

ఎద *eda.* [Tel.] n. The heart. Fear. Growth. ఎదను పెట్టు to keep or cherish in the bosom. ఎదపడు *eda-paḍu.* v. i. To be alarmed. భయపడు. ఎదాన (for ఎదను) కేసికొను to purloin, to abstract or misapply. ఎదాచెదలు dispersed, scattered.

ఎదావు *edāvu.* [Tel. ఎద+ఆవు] n. A cow in heat ఆబోతుచేత పిలుగానున్న ఆవు. ఎదుసుకున్న. A cow ready for the bull. ఎద అయినది it is in heat.

ఎది Same as ఏది.

ఎదిరించు *edi-rintsu.* [Tel. from ఎదురు] v. t. To face, front, resist, encounter. ఎదుర్కొను.

ఎదుగు *edugu.* [Tel.] v. n. To grow పెరుగు. To overtake. వారిని కలిసికొనలేకపోయెను. (Cuddapa) he was unable to overtake them.

ఎదురు *eduru.* [Tel.] v. n. To advance. ఎదురుగు. ఎదురుచూచు Same as ఎదిరించు. (q. v.)

ఎదురు *eduru.* [Tel.] n. The front. An opponent ప్రతివిరోధి. adj. ఎదురు opposite, other, అన్యమైన. ఎదురాడు *edur-āḍu.* (ఎదురు+ఆడు) v. i. To speak against, to oppose. మారాడు. ఎదురీదు to swim against, to resist. ఎదురుకట్టుల or ఎదురుకట్ల *eduru-kaṭṭula.* adv. In front ఎదుట. ఎదురుపట్టుక *eduru-kaṭṭuka.* n. The lock jaw. ఎదురుకొను or ఎదుర్కొను *eduru-konu.* v. n. & a. To go forward to meet. To act against, to disobey. ఎదురగు, ఎదిరించు. ఎదురుకోలు or ఎదుర్కోలు *edur-kōlu.* n. The mutual advances of the relations of the bride and bridegroom during the marriage. Going forward to welcome a guest. ఎదురుగడ *eduru-gaḍa.* n. A joint bond, a reciprocal or mutual agreement. ఎదురు వ్రాసిన ఒడంబడికలోసగము. ఎదురుగడగా వ్రాయు to write off (a sum as balance.) ఎదురుగాలి *eduru-gāli.* n. A head-wind, a contrary wind. ఎదురుచూచు *eduru-tsūtsu.* v. n. To look forward, expect ప్రతీక్షించు. ఎదురుపడు *eduru-paḍu.* v. To come forward to meet. ఎదురుగావచ్చు. To be met.

వారు నాకు ఎదురుపడినారు I met them. ఎదురుపలుకు *eduru-paluku*. v. n. To object, gainsay. ఎదురురొమ్ము *eduru-rommu*. n. The chest or breast. రొమ్ము నడిమిభాగము. ఎదురువడ్డీ cross interest. ఎదురువ్యాజ్యము *eduru-vyājyamu*. n. A cross suit. ఎదురేగు *edur-ēgu*. v. i. To go in the opposite direction to meet. ఎదురుగాపోవు. ఎదురొత్తు *edur-ottu*. n. A return push, shove for shove. మారొత్తు. ఎదురుక్షౌరము shaving against the grain, or, the wrong way.

ఎడ్డడి *eddaḍi*. [Tel.] n. Lack, want, scarcity లేమిడి. adj. Poor దరిద్రమైన. కూన్యమైన. ఎడ్డడినేల a place where there is no water నిర్జలభూమి.

ఎడ్డము *eddamu*. [Tel.] n. A striped border. ఎడ్డపుచీర *eddapu-chīra*. n. A petticoat with a striped border.

ఎడ్డి *eddi*. Another form of ఏడి.

ఎడ్డు *eddu*. [Tel.] n. A bullock, an ox; (plural ఎడ్డులు, ఎడ్లు.) ఎడ్డునాలుక Ox-tongue. a kind of plant, *Phlouns or Bremma esculenta or Elephantopus scaber*. ఠోన్నకము. ఎడ్డుపట్టు *eddu-paṭṭu*. v. a. To geld an ox ఎడ్డునకు వీత్తేలుతీయు. ఎడ్డుబలువు *eddu-baluvu*. n. A bullock load. ఎడ్డుముట్టె *eddu-muṭṭe*. (from ముట్టె a nozzle) a sort of root. ఎడ్డులవాడు or ఎడ్లవాడు *eddula-vāḍu*. n. A bullock driver. ఎడ్డుచాటు (R. ii. 29.) n. The use of a bullock as a screen for the huntsman, like a stalking horse.

ఎద్రుచు *edruṭsu*. Another form of ఎదురుచు or ఎదిరించు. (q. v.)

ఎన *ena*. [Tel.] n. Equality. సమత్వము. adj. Equal సమానము. ఎనలేని matchless. వెండి కెనయు నేరు the silvery stream.

ఎనబది, ఎనభై *ena-badi*. [Tel. ఎనుబది]. n. Eighty.

ఎనమండుగురు or ఎనమండ్రు *enamandu-guru*. [Tel. from ఎనిమిది.] n. Eight persons. ఎనిమిదిమంది.

ఎనమండుము *ena-man-dumu*. [Tel. ఎనిమిది+తూము.] n. The measure of eight tooms.

ఎనమన్నూరు *ena-man-nūru*. [Tel. ఎనిమిది+నూరు] n. Eight hundred.

ఎనయు *enayu*. [Tel.] v. n. & a. To seem, to resemble. పోలు, సరిపోలు. To mingle. coalesce, unite. To accord. To associate, To participate in, enjoy, or suffer (as death.) పొందు. ఎనయమి *ena-yami*. n. Discord. ఎనయించు *ena-yintsu*. v. a. To mix or mingle, join, unite. ఎనయిక *enayika*. n. Mingling, mixture, fitness. పొందిక, సామ్యము.

ఎనిక *enika*. [Tel. another form of ఎన్నిక] n. Counting గణనము. A yarn of 3 or 4 threads united.

ఎనిమిది or ఎనిది. *enimidi*. [Tel. ఇను+పది= ఎనిమిది lit. two less than ten] n. Eight. ఎనిమిదిదినములు '*Eight days*' is used for '*a week*.' నేటికి ఎనిమిదోనాడు this day week. ఎనిమిదినాళ్లనుండి అంకణముగానున్నాడు he has been ill this week.

ఎనియు *eniyu*. [Tel.] v. i. To meet కలుసుకొను.

ఎను or ఎనుప *enu*. [Tel. from ఎనుము] adj. Of the buffalo. ఎనుపపాలు buffalo's milk బర్రెపాలు, గేదెపాలు. See ఎనుము.

ఎనుచు or ఎనుపు *enuṭsu*. [Tel.] v. a. To mix, mingle, stir up. To think ఎంచు. To nip, pluck, twitch off చిదుము.

ఎనుపుడు *enupuḍu*. [Tel.] n. Mixing, mingling, stirring up, nipping, gathering, plucking. ఎనుచుట.

ఎనుబది *enu-badi*. [Tel.] pron. Eighty. ఎనభై.

ఎనుము or ఎనుపెంటి *enumu*. [Tel.] n. A she buffalo. బర్రె, గేదె. ఎనుపోతు *enu-pōtu*. A he buffalo.

ఎన్నడు *en-naḍu*. [Tel. ఏ+నాడు] adv. When, what day. Ever, always. ఎన్నడును for ever, always. ఎన్నడో some time or other. I know not when. ఎన్నటికిని constantly, ever. ఎన్నటికైనా ever, at any time. ఎన్నాళ్లు how many days, how long.

ఎన్ని *enni.* [Tel. from ఎంత] adj. How many. ఎన్నినీళ్లు how much water. ఎవ్వరెన్ని అడినను whatever any body says. ఎన్నితోని many అనేకము. ఎన్నిట in how many (things.)

ఎన్నిక *ennika.* [Tel. from ఎన్ను to count.] n. Reckoning; thought, calculation, esteem, estimation, idea, hope. గణనము, తలంపు. ఎన్నికగలపశువులు cattle of value. ఎన్నికచేయు or ఎన్నికపెట్టు to count or reckon; to rate. ఎంచు, లెక్కపెట్టు, గణించు. ఎన్నికమనిషి a person of distinction. ఎన్నికమాటలు weighty words.

ఎన్ను *ennu.* [Tel. for వెన్ను] n. An ear of corn కంకి.

ఎన్ను *ennu.* [Tel.] v. a. To count, reckon; think, esteem, believe. To care for, regard. To narrate ఎంచు, గణించు. ఎన్నువ *ennuva.* n. Reckoning ఎన్నిక. A song of mourning in which the virtues of the deceased person are extolled. ఆడువారు ఏడ్చినపుడు పాడే చచ్చినవారి చారిత్రము.

ఎబ్బది Same as ఏబది.

ఎపుడు or ఎప్డు Same as ఎప్పుడు.

ఎప్పుడు *ep-puḍu.* [Tel. ఏ+పొద్దు] adv. When. ఏకాలము; ఎప్పటి of what time. ఎప్పటికి at what time, at any time, for ever. ఎప్పటికిని ever, at all times, always. ఎప్పటికైనా at any time. ఎప్పటివలె as usual. ఎప్పటిపని the usual employment. ఎప్పుడెప్పుడని కాచుకొనియుండినాడు he waited impatiently. ఎప్పుడో some time or other, I know not when.

ఎబ్బె *ebbe.* [Tel.] interj. Pish! foh! fye! రోతను తెలుపుమాట. ఎబ్బెట్టు *eb-beṭṭu.* n. Dislike అసహ్యము, అభ్యంతరము. ఎబ్బెరాశి *ebbe-rāsi.* [Tel.] n. A slovenly man, a slut, a slattern. రోతకలవాడు, రోతకలది. ఎబ్బెరికము or ఎబ్బెతనము *ebberikamu.* n. Nastiness, disgust, loathsomeness. రోత, అసహ్యము.

ఎబ్బెర, ఎబ్బెరింత or ఎబ్బెరింత *ebbera.* [Tel.] n. The bird called the grey hornbill. *Buceros Ginginianus,* Jerdon No. 198. *Lophoceros birostris* F. B. I. కొమ్ముముక్కుపక్షి.

ఎమిడికపాములు or ఎమిడికలు *emiḍika-pāmulu.* [Tel.] n. Worms in the bowels. ఏలికపాము.

ఏముక or ఎమ్ము or ఎమ్ముక. *emuka.* [Tel.] n. A bone. A difficulty, a puzzle. మారునిరెముకలు Coral. ఎముకలపరుగు or ఎముకలపుర్రు skin and bone, a starved object. ఎముకలేనిచెయ్యి a liberal heart, (lit. a hand without a bone in it.) ఎమ్మూట *em-mūṭa.* [ఎమ్ము+ఊట] n. Marrow మూలుగ.

ఎముకు *emuku.* [Tel.] v. a. To search. వెదకు.

ఎమ్ము or ఎమ్ముక *emmu.* See ఎముక.

ఎమ్మె *emme.* [Tel.] n. Loveliness, charm, desire, sport, dalliance. విలాసము, మనోహరత్వము. ఎమ్మెకాడు a beau, విలాసవంతుడు. ఎమ్మెలాడి a beautiful woman విలాసిని.

ఎమ్మెయి *em-meyi.* [Tel. ఏ+మెయి] adv. How? in what way.

ఎయిదు *eyidu.* [Tel.] v. t. To follow, to go after వెంబడించు, కూడాపోవు. To attain పొందు.

ఎయ్యది *eyyadi.* [Tel. ఏ+అది] pron. Which ఏది.

ఎర *era.* [Tel.] n. Food. A bait: an incentive. An earthworm, because used as a bait. వానపాము. A sacrifice of flesh. బలి. (M. IX. ii. 120). Sorrow, sadness వ్యసనము. ఆ శబ్దముయొక్క యెర కనిపెట్టినాడు he discovered the recondite sense. ఎరకొను *era-konu.* To take a bait. To devour. To get angry కోపగించు.

ఎర *era.* [Tel.] adj. Red ఎర్రని. **ఎరకందు** *era-kandu.* n. An infant లేతబిడ్డ, శిశువు. ఎరమంటలు redness, red flames.

ఎరక *eraka.* [Tel.] n. Wing రెక్క. A rib. పక్షిరెక్క. Shoulder భుజము.

ఎరగలి *eragali.* [Tel.] n. Wildfire. కార్చిచ్చు, దావాగ్ని.

ఎరగు *eragu.* [Tel.] v. i. To descend దిగు. To salute, to make a bow to, to bow down to, to prostrate oneself నమస్కరించు, మ్రొక్కు. **ఎరగుడు** *eragudu.* n Salutation నమస్కారము.

ఎరచి *erachi.* [Tel.] n. Flesh, meat, మాంసము. ఎరచితిండి *erachi-tindi.* n. One who eats flesh. An Asura అసురుడు.

ఎరపరికము *era-parikamu.* [Tel.] n. Dislike, reluctance. రోత.

ఎరపలి Same as ఎరగలి. (q. v.)

ఎరవు Same as ఎరువు. (q. v.)

ఎరసంజె *era-sanza.* [Tel. ఎర=ఎర్ర] n. The dawn or the sunset time. ప్రాతస్సంధ్య, సాయంసంధ్య.

ఎరికె Same as ఎరుక. (q. v.)

ఎరిగించు or ఎరుగించు *erigintsu.* [Tel. causal of ఎరుగు.] v. t. To make known, declare, notify, proclaim, explain, reveal. తెలుపు చేయు.

ఎరియు *eriyu.* [Tel.] v. n. To burn; to pine, to sorrow. కాలు, మండు, బాధపడు, పరితపించు. **ఎరియించు** *eriyintsu.* v. a. To cause to burn. To inflame, afflict, hurt.

ఎరుక *eruka.* [Tel. from ఎరుగు] n. Knowledge, understanding. తెలివి, జ్ఞానము; acquaintance పరిచయము; notice, information, report, intimation. Fortune-telling సోది, శోధపద్ధము. ఎరుకచెప్పు to tell fortunes. ఎరుకచేయు to make known, to give notice, inform, intimate, signify. తెలియుచేయు. ఎరుకపడు to be plain or evident స్పష్టమగు. ఎరుకమాలిన senseless, foolish, brutish తెలివిలేని. **ఎరుకువ** *erukuva.* n. Knowledge ఎరుక, తెలివి.

ఎరుకు *eruku.* [Tel.] n. A hillman, a wild man కిరాతుడు. A hunter వ్యాధుడు. ఎరుకుల రేడు a highland chief. ఎరుకులవాడు a gypsy. ఎరుకలది, ఎరుకత or ఎరుకలసాని a woman of this tribe: a witch, a gypsy, wench కొరవ్వ.

ఎరుగించు *eruginṭsu.* See ఎరిగించు.

ఎరుగు *erugu.* [Tel.] v. a. To know, be aware of, to understand. తెలిసికొను, గ్రహించు. వాడు దానిని ఎరిగి చేసినాడు he did it on purpose or intentionally, or ఎరుగక చేసిరి they did it unintentionally ఉపకారము ఎరిగినవారై being grateful, feeling one's kindness. మీరు ఎరిగియుండవలసినది I call upon you to be witness or to observe this. సత్తువయెరిగి లంకణముకట్టవలసి నది let the patient be kept fasting in proportion to his strength. ఎరుగని ignorant, innocent. దేహమెరుగక being stupified, or insensible. ఎరుగవా don't you know? ఎరుగను I do not know. మేము కుడిచెయ్యి ఎడమచెయ్యి యెరుగనివారమై as we are such simple people that we do not know our right hand from our left -నేనుబుద్ధియెరుగకమునుపే when I was an infant, before I knew anything. ఎరిగితెచ్చుట గాని యెరుగక కాదు I was well aware of what I was bringing: I did not bring it unknowingly. పాటుయెరుగని భాగ్యము fortune that knows no decline. **ఎరుగమి** *erugami.* n. Ignorance తెలియమి.

ఎరుపు *erupu.* [Tel.] n. Redness, red. ఎర్రదనము.

ఎరువు *eruvu.* [Tel. from ఎండు lit. Dried in the sun.] n. Manure పైరుకై చేర్చిపెట్టిన పేడ. **ఎరువాటు** *eru-vaṭu.* n. Manuring (a field, &c.) ఎరువుకట్టుట.

ఎరువు *eruvu.* [Tel.] n. Lending, loan. బదులు. ఎరువు ఇచ్చు to lend. ఎరువు తీసికొను to borrow.

ఎరుసు *erusu.* [Tel.] n. Jealousy, envy ఈర్ష్య.

ఎఱ్ఱ *erra.* [Tel.] n. An earthworm. Any bait used in fishing. ఎర. గాలమునకు ఎఱ్ఱ వచ్చినట్లు లొంగియుండినాడు he was as submissive as a worm in the hook.

ఎఱ్ఱ, ఎఱ్ఱన *erra.* [Tel.] n. Redness ఎఱ్ఱదనము, ఎరుపు. ఎఱ్ఱ or ఎఱ్ఱని adj. Red, scarlet, crimson. ఎఱ్ఱనివాండ్లు people of fair complexion. కన్ను లెఱ్ఱచేసి పలికినాడు he spoke with eyes inflamed with fury. ఎఱ్ఱనియేగాని నావద్దలేదు I have not even a copper with me. ఎఱ్ఱకాళ్లజిట్ట *erra-kallajitta.* n. A small bird, *Pyctorhis sinensis*, the Yellow-eyed babbler (F. B. I.) ఎఱ్ఱకాళ్లకొంగ *erra-kalla-konga.* n. The painted stork or pelican, ibis, *Pseudotontalus leucocephalus* (F. B. I.) ఎఱ్ఱకోడి *erra-kōdi.* The common spurfowl. The painted sort is చిమటకోడి. Jerdon. No. 74. ఎఱ్ఱగడ్డ *erra-gadda.* An onion, the red garlic. ఎఱ్ఱగొల్లలు *erra-gollalu.* The name of a certain tribe. ఎఱ్ఱగోగిల *erra-gōgila.* [Tel.] n. A large red spider. ఎఱ్ఱచీమ *erra-chīma.* A red ant. ఎఱ్ఱచేమంతి *erra-chēmanti.* Red chrysanthymum. ఎఱ్ఱన *errana.* n. Redness ఎరుపు. ఎఱ్ఱపోతమ్మ *erra-pōtamma.* n. The name of one of the village goddesses, supposed to cure diseases among cattle. ఎఱ్ఱబారు or ఎఱ్ఱవారు *erra-baru.* v. i. To become red. ఎఱ్ఱనగు. ఎఱ్ఱమన్ను *erra-mannu.* n. Red earth. ఎఱ్ఱమంటిగువ్వ *erra-manti-guvva.* n. The rufous-tailed finch lark. *Ammomanes phoenicura* (F.B.I.) ఎఱ్ఱమల్లె *erra-malle.* Red jasmine. ఎఱ్ఱమీను *erra-mīnu.* Red fish. ఎఱ్ఱవేలుపు *erra-vēlupu.* The red god, i.e., fire. అగ్ని.

ఎల *ela.* [Tel.] n. A witness సాక్షి. adj. Young, tender, delicate. లేత; slight స్వల్పము. ఎలదీగబోడి. A young sprig; a maiden ఎలనగవు a smile. adv. Slightly. స్వల్పముగా. ఎలనగుచున్ slightly laughing, smiling. ఎలనీరు the water of a tender cocoanut. ఎలప్రాయము tender age, youth. యౌవనము. A. v. 153.

ఎలకి Same as ఎలుక.

ఎలకోడి *ela-kōdi.* [Tel.] n. The hoopoe, *Upupa indica* (F.B.I.) గొల్లభామ.

ఎలగోలు *ela-gōlu.* [Tel.] n. Uproar, confusion కలకలము. Marching in front ముందు నడచుట. The van or front of an army. The chosen troops. దండుకుముందు పోయే బలము. A. iv. 95. 169. Parij. ii. 62; iii. 98. T. iv. 104; v. 22. ఎలగోలజగడము the shock of battle. ఎలగోలజల్లు. (A. iv. 127.) a rushing gust of rain, a smart shower. మొదట పటపటమని వచ్చువాన. adj. First మొదటి.

ఎలదోట *ela-dōta.* [Tel.] n. A park, a garden ఆరామము.

ఎలనాగ *ela-naga.* [Tel.] n. A nymph, damsel, maid. ఇంతి. Vish. vi. 221.

ఎలమి *elami.* [Tel.] n. Pleasure. Satisfaction. సంతోషము, తృప్తి. ఎలమిని pleasantly. ఎలమికాడు *elami-kādu.* n. A cheerful or jolly man. విలాసవంతుడు.

ఎలయు *elayu.* [Tel.] v. n. To go near. చేరు. To enter ప్రవేశించు. To have కలుగు. To be eager for ఆసక్తిపడు. To enjoy. పొందు.

ఎలరు *elaru.* [Tel.] n. Joy సంతోషము. ఎలరారు *elar-āru.* v. i. To rejoice ఒప్పు. ఎలరుచు, ఎలర్చు *elarutsu.* To arise or appear: to be produced or manifested. అతిశయించు, పొందు. To rejoice సంతోషించు. ఎలరుపు or ఎలర్పు *elarupu.* n. Joy సంతోషము.

ఎలిక *elika.* Same as ఎలుక. (q. v.)

ఎలిసె *elise.* [Tel.] n. A ledge or board placed as a shelf under a roof. అటక, వెలిసె.

ఎలుక or **ఎలిక** *eluka.* [Tel.] n. A rat. ఎలుకచెవి ఆకు a herb like mint eaten in a time of scarcity. Various fish of the species Balista are called by this name. చూరెలుక a mouse. కంపెలుక a musk-rat చెంచే. ఏలికపాములు worms in the bowels. ఎలిక పాషాణము ratsbane.

ఎలుగు or ఎలుంగు *elugu*. [Tel.] n. A voice, cry, note, sound. కంఠస్వరము, కూత. ఎలుగెత్తి యేడ్చెను she raised her voice and wept. ఎలుగించు *elugintsu*. v. n. To cry. కూయు. Vasu. ii. 28. ఎలుగు or ఎలుగుగొడ్డు or ఎలుగుబంటి or ఎలుగుమంటి *elugu*. n. A bear. ఎలుగులు bears.

ఎల్ల for వెల్ల *ella*. [Tel.] n. White-washing as a house. ఇంటికి ఎల్లకొట్టించు to white-wash a house. adj. White తెల్లని. ఎల్లగిసె *ell-agise*. n. White flax.

ఎల్ల *ella*. [Tel.] adj. All సమస్తము. This adjective is generally used after the noun as అక్కరపడినప్పుడెల్ల whenever requisite, lit. at all times when wanted. దానిని నిజ పరచవలసినదెల్ల అతనిపని he must prove every word of it. వాడు అడిగినదెల్ల యిది this was all he asked. రెండుగడియలకెల్లా వస్తాడు he will come in about two hours. అడిగినప్పుడెల్ల whenever (I) asked. ఎల్లప్పుడు *ellappudu*. (ఎల్ల+అప్పుడు) adv. Always, frequently. ఎల్లవాడు every man ప్రతిమనుష్యుడు. ఎల్లరు or ఎల్లవారు *ellaru*. n. All persons, all men.

ఎల్ల *ella*. [Tel.] n. Limit, boundary. ఎల్లరాయి boundary-stone.

ఎల్లమ్మ *ellamma*. [Tel.] n. Ellamma, a Dravidian goddess.

ఎల్లము *ellamu*. [Tel. from ఏడు+పలము] n. Seven *polams* ఏడుపలములు.

ఎల్లాపి *ellāpi*. [Tel. ఎల్ల+ఆపి] n. One who robs people within a certain tract of country. ఒక యెల్లయందుండి దోచుకొనేవాడు. A rogue, a swindler. దొంగ. ఎల్లాపితనము *ellāpi-tanamu*. n Cunning, guile, roguery, swindling. ఎల్లాపికత్తె *ellāpi-katte*. n. A female swindler.

ఎల్లి *elli*. [Tel.] n. To-morrow. The next day. Also, an umbrella గొడుగు, M. XII. iv. 381.

ఎల్లిదము *ellidamu*. [Tel.] n. Strangeness, oddity. Strange behaviour, scorn. చులకన తనము. ఎల్లిదమైరి they were treated strangely. Manu ii. 45. ఎల్లిదుడు *ellidudu*. n. A despicable or low man చులకనివాడు.

ఎల్లుండి *ellundi*. [Tel. ఎల్లి+ఉండి] n. The day after to-morrow. రేపటియెల్లుంట either to-morrow or the day after.

ఎవడు or ఎవ్వడు or ఎవ్వాడు *evadu*. [Tel. ఏ+వాడు] Pron. Who. Plural ఎవరు, ఎవ్వరు. Who. ఇట్లా యెవ్వరున్ను చేయరు nobody does so. ఎవడేనియు whosoever ఎవడైనా any one. ఎవ్వరి సొమ్ము వారికి ఇమ్ము give each his own money. ఎవ్వరికీతము వారికి ముట్టి ఉన్నది all of them have received their wages. ఎవరూలేరు nobody is there.

ఎవతె *evate*. [Tel. fem. sing. of ఎవడు] pron. Who, which woman.

ఎవరు *evaru*. [Tel.] plural of ఎవడు. (q. v.)

ఎవి or ఎవ్వి Same as ఏవి.

ఎవ్వడు See ఎవడు.

ఎవ్వి Same as ఏవి. (q. v.)

ఎస *esa*. [Tel.] n. Greatness. ఆధిక్యము. adj. Very much అత్యంతము.

ఎసకము *esakamu*. [Tel. from ఎసగు] n. Delight, joy. ఉత్సాహము, ఉల్లాసము. Way, manner విధము.

ఎసకొను *esa-konu*. [Tel.] v. i. To be excited పురికొను. ఎసకొల్పు or ఎసపెట్టు *esa-kolpu*. v. a. To stir up, excite, tempt. ప్రేరేపణచేయు, పురికొలుపు.

ఎసగు *esagu*. [Tel.] v. a. To be or happen. To arise, appear, or be felt, as a passion. To increase. తనరు, అతిశయించు. కోపమెసగ angrily. హర్షమెసగ joyfully. వైభవమెసంగ prosperously. సంతసమెసంగ cheerfully. మరులెసగ amorously. కంకణాక్వాణ

మెసగ (her) bracelets ringing aloud. పొలు పెసంగ beautifully పొలుపార.

ఎసరు *esaru*. [Tel.] v. i. To increase. మీరు, అతిక్రమించు. n. Water boiled for the purpose of cooking food వంటకై కాగబెట్టిన నీరు. (infl. ఎసటి, loc. ఎసట.) **ఎసటిపోతలు** *esaṭi-pōtalu*. n. Rice ready to be cooked. ఎసరుచేయదగిన బియ్యము. **ఎసరేగు** *esa-rēgu*. v. i. To increase, to be full విజృంభించు.

ఎసల *esala*. [Tel.] n. A flat earthen vessel.

ఎసలారు *esa-lāru*. [Tel. ఎసలు+ఆరు] v. n. To be full: to teem: to appear. నిండియుండు, ఒప్పు. "చిత్తమునకింపెసలార" M. XII. vi. 581. "మట్టిదుట్టుటయు నొప్పెసలారెను." V. P. i. 137.

ఎసలిక *esalika*. [Tel.] n. Leisure. తీరిక, అవకాశము.

ఎసలు *esalu*. [Tel.] n. Sand. బంగరెసలు gold dust or sand of gold. (Swa. ii. 40.) Also, a melee బొమ్మియుద్ధము.

ఎసవు—another form of ఎసగు. (q. v.)

ఏ ē

ఏ *ē*. The long vowel E. as *a* in fare.

ఏ The pronoun or sign of question; interrogative adjective. Which, what. Thus ఏచెట్టు which tree? ఏపిల్లలు what children? or, if అయినా is affixed to the word with which it is used, it is translated *any:* as ఏచెట్టయినా, ఏపిల్లలయినా any tree, any children.

ఏ *ē*. An affix denoting emphasis: thus, నేనే I myself. వాడే that very man. మేమే we ourselves. This is sometimes doubled. Thus అతడేనే he himself.

ఏ *ē*. An affix denoting 'only'; by oneself, without others' help. నేనే పోతిని I alone went. వానియింటికి మాయింటికి ఒకగోడే అడ్డము there is only a wall between his house and mine. ఆలెక్కను నేనే చేసితిని I did that sum myself.

ఏ *ē*. An affix denoting denial or negation. అది నీకు తగునే does it befit you? no.

ఏ *ē*. An affix denoting that a female is addressed ఏమే. O woman!

ఏ *ē*. An affix having a demonstrative force. అతడే నాయన్న, there! that man is my brother.

ఏండ్లు *ēndlu*. [Tel. plural of ఏడు.] n. Years. **ఏండ్లు పూండ్లు** *ēndlu-pūndlu*. Many years. "ఏండ్లునుపూండ్లునుబట్టు." Swa. i. 35.

ఏకకుడు *ēka-kuḍu* [Skt.] n. An unassisted man. అసహాయుడు.

ఏకచరము *ēka-charamu*. [Skt.] n. The "solitary animal," a name for the rhinoceros or the wild hog. Manu. iv. 52. అడవిపంది, లేక, ఖడ్గమృగము.

ఏకట *ēkaṭa*. [Tel.] n. Prospect, hope. అపేక్ష, మిక్కిలి అపేక్ష.

ఏకతము *ēkatamu*. [from Skt.] n. Solitude. A place fit for consultation ఆలోచనకు తగిన చోటు. Consultation ఆలోచన. ఏకతమాడిరి they talked in secret. Swa. v. 119. Bilh. iii. 65. ఏకతమైన lonely, uninhabited.

ఏకతాళము *ēka-tāḷamu*. [Skt.] n. Harmony. నాలుగక్షరములకాలము, ఏకతాళముకలిగి harmoniously, keeping time together.

ఏకత్వము *ēkatvamu*. [Skt.] n. Oneness, singleness, unity, identity.

ఏకదంతుడు *ēka-dantuḍu*. [Skt.] The single-tusked one, i.e., Gaṇēsa. వినాయకుడు.

ఏకదృష్టి *ēka-drishṭi*. [Skt.] n. One that has only one eye. ఒక్కచూపుగలది. A crow కాకి.

ఏకదేశము *ēka-dēsamu*. [Skt.] n. A part, భాగము. ఏకదేశియమైన of one and the same country. ఏకదేశస్థులు men of the same place, fellow-country-men. ఏకదేశముగా మాట్లాడు to revile, to talk lightly of తిట్టు.

ఏకన *ēkana.* [Tel.] n. Border అంచు. "బద్ద కంచము ఏకనమంచుము."

ఏకపది *ēka-padi.* [Skt.] A narrow path, a way మార్గము, దోవ.

ఏకము *ēkamu.* [Skt.] pron. One. adj. Sole, single, only, general, universal, uniform, combined, matchless, unequalled, chief. Joined, combined. ఏకదీక్షగా unintermittingly, incessantly. ఏకముగా all at once, unitedly. ఏకతిరగడము ceaseless roaming. అతడు ఏకరీతిని ఉండే మనిషి he is a regular or steady person. రాత్రి ఏకముగా మెరిసినది it lightened incessantly all night. ఏకముచేయు *ēkamu-chēyu* v. a. To make one, unite, gather together. ఏకకాలంబున at one time, simultaneously. ఏకకాలీనుడు *ēka-kalīnuḍu.* n. A contemporary. వారున్ను వీరున్ను ఏకకాలీనులైనందున as these men were contemporaries: ఏకకుండలుడు *ēka-kuṇḍaluḍu.* [lit. Having one earring] n. An epithet of Kubera. ఏకగర్భజనితులు *ēka-garbha-janitulu.* adj. Uterine, of the full blood. అతడున్ను నేనున్ను ఏకగర్భజనితులముగనుక as he and I are sons of the same parents or uterine brothers. ఏకగ్రీవము *ēka-grīvamu.* adj. Unanimous, joint. ఏకగ్రీవముగా unanimously, jointly. ఏకచక్రాధిపతి, or ఏకఛత్రాధిపతి *ēka-chakrādhipati.* n. A sole ruler, an absolute monarch. ఏకచింత one sole or engrossing thought or pursuit. ఏకనిష్ఠగా *ēka-nishṭha-gā.* adv. With a single eye or intent, resolutely, faithfully, thoroughly, downright. ఏకపత్నీవ్రతుడు *ēka-patnī-vratuḍu.* n. A monogamist, a man with one wife. ఏకభోగగ్రామము *ēka-bhōga-grāmamu.* n. A village held by one owner, or tenant. ఏకమనస్కులై *ēka-manas-kulai.* adv. With fixed attention, with a single heart. అందరు ఏకమై నామీద పడ్డారు they fell upon me in a body. ఏకవర్ణముగానున్నది it is all of one sort or colour. భువనైకసుందరి an unrivalled beauty. ఏకశిలానగరము *ēka-silā-naga-ramu.* n. (lit. One stone-town.) A town built near a single rock or hill. The Skt. translation of ఒరంగల్లు Warungul a town in the Nizam's Territories. ఏకాధిష్ఠితము *ēkā-dishṭhitamu.* adj. In one hand: in one person's sole power. M. I. ii. 200.

ఏకరా or **ఎకరా** or **ఎకరము** *ēkarā.* [Eng. acre.] n. An acre.

ఏకరి *ēkari.* [Tel.] n. A particular class of gypsies, or aboriginal people. కిరాతభేదము.

ఏకరు or **ఏకారు** *ēkaru.* [Tel.] v. i. To swell. వాచిపోవు.

ఏకలము or **ఏకలిదు** *ēkalamu.* [Tel.] n. A wild hog. అడవిపంది. See Kaliah. Mah. iii. 69. regarding pork chops, and Paidim. ii. 67 describing a herd of swine. Also G. viii. 12. 21. Parij. iii. 31. Suca. i. 186, &c.

ఏకవచనము *ēka-vachanamu.* [Skt.] n. The singular number.

ఏకస్థులు *ēka-sthulu.* [Skt.] adj. Leagued, united.

ఏకాంగి *ēkāngi.* [Skt. ఏక+అంగి] n. A recluse, a solitary. ఒంటివాడు. వారందరున్ను చచ్చి వీడు ఏకాంగిగా నిలిచినాడు he alone survived. ఏకాంగీలోకరక్షకః అని ఒంటివాడుగానున్నాడు he is alone, the last of his race.

ఏకాండము *ēkāṇḍamu.* [Tel.] adj. Solid, made of one piece of wood. అఖండము.

ఏకాంతము *ēkāntamu.* [Skt.] n. Solitude, secrecy. ఏకాంతముగా secretly. నన్ను ఏకాంతముగా పిలిచెను he called me aside, or in secret. ఏకాంతభక్తి unostentatious or unwitnessed piety. ఏకాంతమైనమాట a secret.

ఏకాకి *ēkāki.* [Skt.] adj. A solitary man, a lonely man. ఏకకుడు. ఏకాకిత్వము *ēkākit-vamu.* n. Loneliness.

ఏకాగ్రుడు *ēkāgruḍu.* [Skt. ఏక+అగ్రుడు] adj. Attentive, intent. ఒక్కచోటనిమ్మలుండే మనస్సును నిలిపినవాడు. ఏకాగ్రచిత్తుడు having his heart bent on some one thing.

ఏకాదశము *ēka-daşamu.* [Skt.] adj. Eleventh పదునొకండవది. ఏకాదశి *ēka-daşi.* n. The eleventh day of each lunar fortnight: తొలియేకాదశి another name for ఆషాఢశుద్ధయేకాదశి which is an annual fast. వైకుంఠయేకాదశి a fast held about the 20th of December.

ఏకారు *ēkāru.* [Tel.] v. i. To whimper, whine, fawn, long for. To languish, pine away. కృశించు, ఉడుకు. పాలకు ఏకారి ఉండే a child that is pining for milk "వెలి నేకారుమదినిట్లువిటులలాడి." H. ii. 112.

ఏకావళి *ēk-āvali.* [Skt.] n. A sort of necklace consisting of one string of pearls or beads. ఒంటిపేటహారము. Swa. v. 125.

ఏకాహము *ēk-āhamu.* [Skt.] n. A certain funeral rite held by Brahmins on the eleventh day after a man's death.

ఏకాక్షరము *ēkāksharamu.* [Skt. ఏక+అక్షరము] n. A monosyllable.

ఏకీకరించు *ēkī-karintsu.* [Skt.] v. n. To unite, become one. L. XIX. 316.

ఏకీభవించు *ēkī-bhavintsu.* [Skt.] v. n. To coalesce, unite, harmonise, accord. ఒక్కటియగు. ఏకీభవించి or ఏకీభావముగా unitedly, jointly. ఏకీభావము *ēkī-bhāvamu.* n. Coalescence, uniting, union. ఒక్కటియగుట, ఐక్యము.

ఏకు *ēku.* [Tel.] v. a. To beat కొట్టు. To pick, beat, or clean cotton. ఏకినదూది cleaned cotton. To slander, defame. దూరు, నిందించు. వాణ్ని యేకి కాకులకు పెట్టినారు they defamed him. ఏకించు *ēkintsu.* [the causal of ఏకు] v. t. To cause to pick or clean cotton. అతని చేత దూదిని యేకించినారు they made him clean the cotton. ఏకు n. A flock of cotton or wool. ఏకులువడుకు to spin cotton. ఏకుడు *ēkudu.* n. Cleaning cotton. దూదిని యేకడము.

ఏకె *ēke.* [Tel. ఏ+అక్క] pron. Who? (fem.) ఏస్త్రీ. See ఆకె she.

ఏకోత్తరము *ēkōttaramu.* [Skt. ఏక+ఉత్తరము] adj. More by one, increased by an unit. "ఆకాశాదిభూతంబు లేకోత్తర గుణంబులైయుండు" Padma Puran. VI. 15. the five elements, ether, wind, fire, water, and earth have each one attribute (or quality) more than the one next named. Earth has five qualities as weight, taste, extension, &c., water has only four, fire has only three, &c. Thus each class is more by one than the next. ఏకోత్తరవృద్ధి the addition of one: increase by one unit: one more. ఏకోత్తరశతము one hundred and one.

ఏకోదర *ēkōdara.* [Skt. ఏక+ఉదర] adj. Of the same womb. ఏకోదరన్యాయముగా as brothers and sisters. Affectionately. ఏకోదరులు *ēkōdarulu.* n. Uterine brothers or sisters.

ఏకోద్దిష్టము *ēkōddishṭamu.* [Skt. ఏక+ఉద్దిష్టము.] adj. In memory of a person. ఒకదుద్దేశించబడినవాడుగాగలది. A certain funeral rite ఒక శ్రాద్ధము.

ఏగలి or ఏగిలి *ēgali* [Tel.] n. That which fertilises or enriches land నీలిపైరు నేలకు ఏగలి indigo enriches the land (Cuddapa)

ఏగాని (or యేగాని) *ēgāni.* [Tel.] A halfpenny, called two pies or 6th part of an anna. దుగ్గాని Thus noted in accounts ౯౽.

ఏగు *ēgu.* [Tel.] v. n. To go, resort, repair. పోవు. ఏగించు *ēgintsu.* To send, to make one go. ఊరేగించు To carry (a god, a married couple, &c.) in procession through the town. ఏగుదెంచు *ēgu-dentsu.* [Tel. ఏగు+ తెంచు] v. i. To go, proceed, repair, resort. పోవు. Also, to come వచ్చు. ఏగుపెండ్లి *ēgu-pendli.* n. A procession in which the bride and the bridegroom are carried through the streets of a town at the end of a wedding పెండ్లికడపట వధూవరులను ఊరేగించునట్టివేడుక.

ఏగురు or ఏవురు *ēguru.* [Tel. from ఏను five.] n. Five men అయిదుగురు.

ఏగుస *ēgusa*. [Tel. ఏను+కుంచెము] n. Five *Kunchams*, i.e., ten measures. అయిదుకుంచెములు.

ఏచ or **ఏస** *ētsa*. [Tel. vulgarly వ్యాస] adj. Wild, rude, vulgar, savage, గ్రామ్యము. Crooked or distorted వక్రము. అక్కడిమాట యిక్కడయేచ, ఇక్కడిమాట అక్కడయేచ our language sounds rude to you, and your's sounds rude to us.

ఏచు *ētsu*. [Tel.] v. n. To increase, exceed. పెరుగు, అతిశయించు, అధికమగు. ఏచినభీతి excessive terror. ప్రబలమైనభీతి, అధికమైన భయము. ఏచినచీకట్లు extreme darkness. A. v. 127; v. 56. **ఏచు** or **ఏవు** *ētsu*. v. a. To heat, burn. To vex, torment, grieve, plague, take vengeance on. బాధించు.

ఏట *ēṭa*. [Tel.] adv. Annually, per annum (the abl. of ఏడు a year). రెండవయేట in the second year.

ఏట *ēṭa*. [Tel. for వేట] n. A ram, a he-goat.

ఏట or **ఏటము** *ēṭa*. [Tel.] n. Side పక్షము. "ధర్మంపేటముగా" on the side of justice, in behalf of justice. adj. Much, great. అతిశయమైన. ఏటంపుసంపద great wealth. అతిశయమైన ధనము. (BD. iv. 699-)

ఏటవాలు *ēṭa-vālu*. [Tel. from ఏటి of a stream+వాలు.] n. Slant, slope. వంపు. "ఏటవాలైపడి అనగా వంపుగా వాలి." A. IV. 98. 127. 130.

ఏటి *ēṭi*. [Tel.] adj. The inflected form of ఏరు a river and of ఏడు a year. ఏటిబొట్టె a canal cut from a river (Vizag.)

ఏటికపాములు *ēṭika-pāmulu*. [Tel.] n. Worms in the bowels.

ఏటికి *ēṭiki*. [Tel. for ఏమిటికి] adv. Why? wherefore? ఎందుకు. అది నాకు నేటికి what's that to me? Swa. iii. 6.

ఏటికోలు *ēṭi-kōlu*. [Tel.] n. Salutation, prostration నమస్కారము.

ఏటిరింత *ēṭirinta*. Same as ఏత్రింత. (q. v.)

ఏటిరేడు *ēṭi-rēḍu*. [Tel. ఏటి from ఏరు a stream]. n. The lord of rivers. The Ocean సరిత్పతి, సముద్రుడు.

ఏటు, i.e., వేటు *ēṭu*. [Tel.] n. A blow. దెబ్బ. వారు ఏటు తగిలినది the blow grazed (his head.)

ఏటేట *ēṭ-ēṭa*. [Tel.] adv. Annually, year by year.

ఏత్రింత *ēṭrinta*. [Tel.] n. The bird called a king-crow: or drongo, *Dicrurus ater* (F. B. I.) పసులపోలిగాడు, భారద్వాజము, కాటుకపిట్ట "ఏనుగకు ఏత్రింతరాయభారము" (Prov.) much aid can the king-crow give to the elephant!

ఏత్రింత *ēṭrinta*. [Tel.] n. A certain plant. Rox. iii. 403.

ఏడ *ēḍa*. [Tel.] adv. Where ఎక్కడ.

ఏడక *ēḍaka*. [Skt.] n. A ram.

ఏడము *ēḍamu*. [Skt.] adj. Deaf. ఏడమూకము Deaf and dumb. **ఏడమూకుడు** *ēḍa-mū-kuḍu*. n. A deaf mute. చెవిటిమూగ. A cheat మోసగాడు.

ఏడాకులయరటిచెట్టు *ēḍ-ākula-y-araṭi-chet-ṭu*. [Tel.] n. The seven leaved plantain tree; సప్తపర్ణము. *Alstonia scholaris*, commonly known as *Ditu Bark*. (Watts.)

ఏడాగోడము *ēḍāgōḍamu*. [Tel.] n. Contradiction, confusion. విరుద్ధము. ఏడాగోడముగా in confusion, contrariwise.

ఏడాటలాడించు *ēḍ-āṭal-āḍintsu*. [Tel.] v. t. To annoy, to torment. మిక్కిలిశ్రమపరుచు, సప్తవ్యసనములను కలుగజేయు.

ఏడాది *ēḍ-ādi*. [Tel. ఏడు+ Skt. ఆది] n. A year, సంవత్సరము, ఏడు.

ఏడి *ēḍi*. [Tel.] adv. Where is (he.) ఏడి నీ తమ్ముడు where is your brother? వాడేడి where is he?

ఏడిక ēḍika. [Tel. cf. Tam ఆడు.] n. A ram పొట్టేలు.

ఏడికోల ēḍi-kōla. [Tel.] n. The pole or shaft of a plough. నాగటికోయ్య.

ఏడు ēḍu. [Drav.; Turkish yedi.] n. Seven. ఆరునొకటి. ఏడెనిమిది seven or eight. వాడు నీకంటే ఏడాకులు ఎగచదివినవాడు he is ten times worse than you. Lit. he has read seven leaves further than you (in roguery.) ఏడుగురు seven persons. ఏడుమంది. ఏడు ēḍu. [Tel.] n. A year. (plu. ఏండ్లు or ఏడులు or ఏళ్లు) ఏన్నర్థము [ఏడు+అర్థము] a year and a half. ఏండ్లు పూండ్లు many years. ఏడు ēḍu. [Tel.] pron. Who? ఎవడు.

ఏడుగడ or ఏడ్గడ ēḍugaḍa. [Tel. ఏడు+కడ (lit.) the place where your ఏడుపు complaint is listened to or కడ means end. So ఏడుకడ means the end of sorrow, that is, refuge.] n. Quarter, patronage, refuge. రక్షకము. Protector, patron. రక్షకుడు, దిక్కు. "మన్మథప్రేరితకోటికేడుగడ."

ఏడుచు or ఏడ్చు ēḍutsu. [Tel.] v. n. To weep. To complain. ముక్కుతో ఏడ్చి సమ్మతించినాడు he submitted with a bad grace. ఏడిపించు ēḍi-p-intsu. n. To make one cry or weep.

ఏడుడి ēḍuḍi. [Tel. ఏడు+ఊడి] n. The rite performed on the next anniversary of a death. సంవత్సరీకము, అబ్దికము.

ఏడుడు ēḍuḍu. [Skt.] n. A deaf man. చెవిటివాడు.

ఏడుపు or ఏడ్పు ēḍupu. [Tel. from ఏడ్చు] n. Weeping, complaint, grievance. Longing, strong desire, or bent of mind. నీయేడుపు నీవు చెప్పు tell your tale yourself. ఎవడి యేడుపు వాడు ఏడుస్తాడు every man knows his own troubles. ఇది వారికి ఒకటే యేడ్పు this is what they have set their hearts on.

ఏడ్తెర ēḍtera. [Tel.] n. Fury, anger, perseverance. అతిశయము, సామర్థ్యము, శక్తి, పరాక్రమము. adv. Much మిక్కిలి; at once, quickly శీఘ్రముగా

"అమ్మహీశుపెన్నురముననాటె
నారథుకుడొక్కసముజ్జ్వల బాణమేడ్తెరన్."

M. IX. i. 210.

ఏడ్దుము ēḍ-dumu. [Tel. ఏడు+తూము] n. The quantity of grain, &c., containing seven bushels or తూములు which is ciphered thus ౻౦౾.

ఏణము or ఏణి ēṇamu. [Skt.] n. A gazelle or black antelope. పెద్దకన్నులుగల నల్లయిఱ్ఱి. ఏణనయన ēṇa-nayana. adj. Stag-eyed, dark-eyed. ఏణాంకుడు ēṇ-ānkuḍu. n. The Moon, because his ensign is an antelope. శశాంకుడు. ఏణాక్షి ēṇ-akshi. adj. Stag-eyed, gazelle-eyed, having beautiful eyes.

ఏతడు ētaḍu. [Tel. ఏ+అతడు] Same as ఎవడు.

ఏతత్ ētat. [Skt.] pron. adj. This. ఏతన్నిమిత్తము hence, for this.

ఏతము ētamu. [Tel.] n. A waterlift made on the principle of the sea-saw. ఏతమెత్తు విరోధము a vast difference.

ఏతరి ētari. [Tel.] n. A vile man, a wretch, a miscreant. దుర్మార్గుడు, దుర్జనుడు కుండగొయ్య. A ii. 47. Swa. vi. 52. ఏతరితనము ētari-tanamu. n. Vileness, wickedness.

ఏతాము ētāmu. Same as ఏతము. (q. v.)

ఏతు ētu [Tel.] n. Pride గర్వము, ఉద్ధతి.

ఏతులవాడు ētula-vāḍu. [Tel.] n. A man of the caste who weave mats. చాపల్లు జాతివాడు. ఏతులకొమ్మ (అము iv.) A woman of that caste. చాపల్లునది.

ఏతెంచు ētentsu. [Tel. for ఏగుదెంచు] v. n. To come, go. వచ్చు, పోవు. ఏతేరన్ ētēran. Having come.

ఏత్వము ētvamu. [Skt.] n. The name of the vowel ē long.

ఏడ or ఏడతెట్టు *êḍa.* [Tel.] n. A certain creeper. ఏడాడంటే కోడాడంటాడు (proverb) If I say white he says black.

ఏడర *êḍara.* [Tel.] n. Personal property, that is, property that is distinct from what belongs to the family as a whole. కుటుంబముతో చేరని స్వతంత్రపు సొమ్ము. వాడు కొంత ఏడర కలిగియున్నాడు he has money of his own which does not belong to the family. వానికి తాయాదులతో ఏడర కమతము కలదు he has his own cultivation in the village apart from what his family has.

ఏది *êdi.* [Tel. ఏ+అది] pron. Which (fem. and neut. singular.) ఏదయినా any. ఏదికాని not any. ఏదికానిప్రాయము middle age, neither childhood nor youth; ఏదిన్నిలేదు there is nothing.

ఏడు *êḍu.* [Tel.] v. n. To go, depart, cease, perish; be lost, leave, abandon. విడుచు, నశించు. దిక్కేడిన friendless, helpless. భయ మేడిన fearless. చెలువేడి having lost its bloom. సంశయమేడి not entertaining a doubt. సందేహముమాని.

ఏడు *êḍu.* [Tel.] v. t. To cherish, protect, bring up, nurse. పోషించు, పెంచు. "రఘుకు మారుకేడిరి బాదులు" రామా.- iii.

ఏదు or ఏదుపంది *êdu.* [Tel.] n. A porcupine. ముండ్లపంది. One species is called కోడిఏదు but in the south it is called ఒంటిజాడు. HD. i. 512. ఏదుపెరికినట్లు or ఏదుపంది ముండ్లుపెరికినట్లు like pulling out the porcupines' quills. ఏదువాసన a disgusting smell like that of a porcupine. cf. "It stinks like a badger." ఏదుకర్రలవంకలు (H. iv. 159) a sort of grain. ఏదుగడ్డి *êdu-gaḍḍi.* n. *Andropagon contortus*, or the Spear grass. (Watts.) ఏదువేట *êdu-vêṭa.* n. A kind of chase. వేటలో ఒక భేదము.

ఏదుము *ê-ḍumu.* [Tel. ఏను+తూము] n. Five bushels అయిదుతూములు.

ఏధ *ê-dha.* [Skt.] n. Increase of wealth and of other things. Fulness, full growth. అభి వృద్ధి, సంపూర్ణవృద్ధి. A iv. 20. ఏధస్సు or ఏధము *ê-dhassu.* n. Fuel. వంటచెరకు. ఏధితము *êdhitamu.* adj. Improved, grown. అభివృద్ధి చేయబడిన.

ఏనము or ఏనస్సు *ê-namu.* [Skt.] n Sin, fault. పాపము ఏనఃపట్టణము. (Chenna. v. 72.) The city of Destruction.

ఏనాడము *ênâḍamu.* [Tel.] n. Seashore సముద్రతీరము.

ఏనాది or యానాది *ê-nâdi.* [Tel.] adj. Savage, belonging to a certain tribe. ఏనాదివారు the people of a certain hill tribe; *the* Yânâdis. ఏనాదిమాటలు the hill dialect.

ఏనాళ్లు or ఏన్నాళ్లు *ê-nâḷḷu.* [Tel ఏను+నాళ్లు] n. Five days. Presents sent to each other by the bride's and the bridegroom's parents after the wedding పెండ్లి యయిన తరువాత వియ్యంకులొకరికొకరు పంపే సారె.

ఏని *êni.* [Tel.] An affix denoting question or doubt. If, though, suppose, వాడు పామును పట్టితేని if he catches the snake. నీవు నన్ను నమ్మవేని if you will not believe me. వచ్చెనేని suppose he came, if he comes, should he come. పుట్టిరేని వారు గిట్టిరేని what though they are born or die.

ఏనిక or ఏనిగ or ఏనిగె *ê-nika.* [Tel.] n. An elephant. ఏనికతిండి or ఏనుగుగొంగ *ênika-tinḍi.* n. One that eats or robs the elephant, i. e., the lion సింహము. ఏనికదోమ *ênika-dôma.* n. A mosquito that has a long proboscis తొండపుదోమ.

ఏను *ênu.* [Tel.] n. Five. ఏబలము (ఏను+పల ము) five palams.

ఏను *ênu.* [Tel. from నేను] pron I. నేను. (The initial N. is thus dropped in the nominative.)

ఏనుగ or ఏనుగు *ênuga.* [Tel. Tamil ఆనై. (Here గు is added as an aid in pronunciation.] n. An elephant. ఏనుగుతొమ్ములు

ēnugu-kommulu. n. Elephants' tusks; also, a kind of rice. ఏనుగడుగులు ēnug-adugulu. n. A kind of parti-colored cloth. చిత్రవర్ణ వస్త్రవిశేషము. In compounds ఏనుగు means Big పెద్ద. ఏనుగుకలబంద the large species of కలబంద (q. v) ఏనుగుకాలు ēnugu-kalu. n. A big leg like that of an elephant. Elephantiasis. ఏనుగుగొంగ enugu-gonga. See under ఏనిక. ఏనుగజెలగ ēnuga-jelaga. n. A horse leech. ఏనుగ పల్లేరు ēnuga-pallēru. n. The thorny weed called *Pedalium murex. Ainslie.* ii. 15. ఏనుగుబీర ēnugu-bīra. n. A large kind of బీర or cucumber (q. v.) ఏనుమద్ది ēnu-maddi. n. A certain herb;—called అశ్వకుశి. See మద్ది. ఏనుగుమోముసామి the elephant-faced god, i. e., Vināyaka విఘ్నేశ్వరుడు. ఏనుగుస్వరము ēnugu-sva-ramu. n. One of the seven notes in music సప్తస్వరములలో నొకటి, నిషాదము.

ఏనూరు ē-nūru. [Tel. ఏను+నూరు] pron. Five hundred. అయిదునూరులు.

ఏపరించు ēpa-rintsu. [Tel.] v. t. To cause sorrow దుఃఖపెట్టు; to pain బాధించు, శ్రమపెట్టు.

ఏపారు ē-paru. [Tel. ఏపు+ఆరు] v. n. To increase, to be proud అతిశయించు, గర్వించు. "కదికొండాటపుచెల్వకుమ్మెరుగు కొల్లపారంగ ఉంచెదుగా." P. ii. 21. To bloom, flourish. విజృంభించు. See ఏపు.

ఏపి ēpi. [Tel.] n. A fierce hound. P. i. 121. Velag. ii. 227.

ఏపు ēpu. [Tel.] n. Increase, excess. Pride, arrogance, presumption అధికము, వృద్ధి, గర్వము, విలాసము. Pain బాధ. Bloom, spirit, mettle, ardour, మదము, పెంపు, అతిశయము, ఔద్ధత్యము. వానయేపు excess of rain. M. XII. iii. 295. ఏపున nobly, in excess, in abundance. ఏపుకొను to be ardent, మదమునించు. P. iv. 255.

ఏపె ēpe. [Tel. ఏ+అప్పు] pron. Which (lady.)

ఏపె ēpe. [Tel.] n. A tree like mahogany, the Sal tree (*Shorea Robusta.*) సాలవృక్షము.

ఏబది or యాభై ēbadi. [Tel. ఏను+పది] pron. Fifty.

ఏబలము—See under ఏను.

ఏబిడ ē-bida. [Tel. ఏ+బిడ్డ] n. Which (lady.) ఏపె.

ఏభ్యము ē-bhyamu. [Corrupted from ఎబ్బము] adj. Nasty. ఏభ్యపడు to be disgusted. ఏభ్యరాశి or ఏభ్రాశి A pack of nastiness. A nasty fellow.

ఏమరు or ఏమరిల్లు ēmaru. [Tel.] v. n. To be off one's guard. To blunder, be deceived. To fall into a trap, or overlook a fact ప్రమాదపడు. ఏమరించు ēmarintsu. v. t. To make one forget himself. To ensnare, delude, entrap, as in an ambush, మోసపుచ్చు. ఏమరిక or ఏమరుపాటు ēmarika. n. Oversight, heedlessness, inadvertence, ఏమరుపాటున inadvertently, suddenly, అకస్మాత్తుగా. ఏమరుచు or ఏమార్చు. ēmarutsu. v. t. To trick, delude. ఏమరచేయు.

ఏమి or ఏమీ ēmi. [Tel.] pron. What. నాదగ్గిర యేమిన్ని లేదు I have nothing with me. వాడు ఏమయినాడు what has become of him? ఇంక చేయవలసినది మరి యేమిలేదు nothing further remains to be done. ఏమైనా ఉండును there may be something. నేనిక్కడ ఉండడమువల్ల ఫలమేమి what is the good of my staying here? సొమ్ము ఏమిన్ని పోలేదు nothing has been lost. ఏమికతంబున (i. e. ఎందునిమిత్తము) for what reason. వాడేమి నేనేమి అంతా ఒక్కటే either he or I, there is no difference. వచ్చినాడా యేమి has he come? నా తండ్రియేమి నేనేమి both my father and I, my father as well as I. ఎవ్వరైననేమి no matter who it is. అదియేమి యిదియేమి either this or that. ఆ యిల్లు మీకు చాలదయేమి what do you mean by saying the house is too small for you? వాడు రాకయేమి why should he not come? surely, he will? ఏమివచ్చినావు what have you come for? కుక్క యేమి మొరుగుచున్నది how the dog barks! వాడు ఏమిన్ని యేడవలేదు he did not weep at all. ఏమిటి

ēmiṭi. pron. & adj. What, of which, what kind of. ఆదేమిటి what's that? ఏమిటో I don't know what that is వాడు ఏమిటివాడు of what caste is he? ఏమిటికి wherefore, for what reason. ఏమిటికో I know not why. ఏమిన్ని anything whatever. ఏమిన్ని ఇవ్వడు he will give nothing. ఏమొ or ఏమో *ēmo.* (ఏమి with ఒ added for doubt.) I know not what. రాలేదేమో perhaps they did not come.

ఏము *ēmu.* [Tel. for మేము the initial m being dropt.] pron. We.

ఏమె *ēme.* [Tel. ఏ+అమ+ఎ] pron. (1) Which woman? who? ఏపుణ్యాత్మురాలు (See ఏవె.) (2) Woman, a word used in calling a female servant or a wife.

ఏయు *ēyu.* [Tel. another form of వేయు the initial Y being dropped] v. t. To throw, వేయు, కొట్టు.

ఏర or ఏరా *ēra.* [Tel. for ఏమిరా] interj. O thou! (a word used in calling an inferior.)

ఏరండము *ēraṇḍamu.* [Skt.] n. The castor oil plant (proverbially weak or pithless "నిరస్తపాదపే గ్రామే ఏరండోపి ద్రుమాయతే" (proverb) in a barren spot any shrub is called a tree.

ఏరవంగ *ēra-vanga.* [Tel. probably ఏటివంగ] n. A certain medicinal plant called *Solanum Speciosum.* In Sanskrit గ్రంథి ల. See వంగకాయ.

ఏరా See ఏర interj.

ఏరాది *ērādi.* [Tel ఎరవు+ఆది.] n. Offspring (applied to horses), breed ఒకదానిసంతతి యగు గుర్రము.

ఏరాలు *ērālu.* [Tel. ఎరవు+ఆలు] n. A sister-in-law తోడికోడలు. ఆమె నేను ఏరాండ్లము గనుక as she and I married two brothers. Plural ఏరాండ్రు.

ఏరాళము *ērāḷamu.* [Tel another form of హేరాళము] adj. Much, numberless. అధికము, అసంఖ్యము.

ఏరు *ēru.* [Tel.] n. A plough complete with cattle. ఏరుకట్టు to yoke a plough. ఏరుకలప implements of husbandry, ploughing apparatus.

ఏరు *ēru.* [Tel. for ఎవరు] pron. Who. ఏరికి to whom? ఏరి *ēri.* pron. Whose. ఎవరిరాము క్కు. (Interrogative.) Where are they? (*m. or f. not n.*) వారేరి Where are they?

ఏరు *ēru.* [Tel. Tamil ఆరు] n. A river. నది. (Genitive ఏటి; plural ఏళ్లు) ఏటికిపోవు to go to the river to answer the calls of nature. ఏట్లో కలిసిపోయినది it is completely ruined or shipwrecked. Lit. it is swept away by the river.

ఏరు *ēru.* [Tel.] n. Headache, pain తలనొప్పి, బాధ.

ఏరు *ēru.* [Tel.] v. t. To glean or pick up one after another ఎదుటనుండువస్తువుల నొక టొకటిగా ఎత్తు. To attain age as in ఈడేరు. ఏరించు *ērinṭsu.* v. t. To cause to pick up one after another. ఏరునట్లుచేయు. ఏరుకొను *ēru-konu.* v. i. To pick up. ఏరుపిడక *ēru-piḍaka.* n. A cowdung cake that is picked up and is not mixed with bran, &c., for fuel.

ఏరుచు, ఏర్చు *ēruṭsu.* [Tel.] v. i. To ache (as the head) తలనొచ్చు. v. t. To ignite, set on fire. దహించు. To train, set in order ఏర్పరచు, చక్కబరచు. See ఏరు n. and v.

ఏరునేల *ēru-nēla.* [Tel.] n. Land as much as can be ploughed in a day ఒక్కనాటిలో దున్నగలభూమి.

ఏరుమద్ది *ēru-maddi.* [Tel.] n. A tree called అర్జునము. See మద్ది.

ఏరుమల్లె *ērumalle.* [Tel.] n. A species of Jasmine మల్లె. See మల్లె.

ఏరువ *ēruva.* [Tel.] n. A ship's keel. ఓడవెన్నుపలక. A country దేశము.

ఏరువాక *ēru-vāka.* [Tel.] n. The commencement of cultivation. The sowing season. Seed-time దుక్కిదొక్క ప్రారంభము. ఏరువా

కసాగించు To celebrate a feast at that season.

ఏర్చు *ērtsu*. See. ఏరుచు.

ఏర్పడు *ērpadu*. [Tel.] v. n. To fix, settle, to assume a shape. To be settled or determined. To seem, appear, come to light, to look. To happen. To be declared, to be or become. To be selected, distinguished, separated, arranged, appointed. రూపడు, తేటపడు, బయలుపడు, నిర్ణయింపబడు. కర్తలై యేర్పడినారు they appeared as, or, turned out to be the heirs. **ఏర్పరచు** or **ఏర్పరించు** *ērparatsu*. v. a. (causal of ఏర్పడు) To form, adjust. To choose, select. distinguish. To separate, divide, To set forth, define, declare. To arrange, to settle. ఏర్పడునట్లు చేయు. **ఏర్పాటు** *ēr-pātu*. n. An arrangement, settlement, rule. Fixing, disposal, decision, management. Selection, choice, agreement. నిర్ణయము, నియమము, వివరణము. ఏర్పాటుచేయు to select, arrange, to effect an arrangement. To project or scheme.

ఏర్పు *ērpu*. [Tel. from ఏర్చు] n. Ardour, burning, hotness. మంట.

ఏల *ēla*. [Tel.] n. The cardamom tree. ఏలకి చెట్టు.

ఏల or ఏలా *ēla* [Tel.] interrogative adv. Why, how, wherefore, to what end, for what reason. ఏలను (చేయు+వేల) why say a thousand words?

ఏల *ēla*. [Tel.] n. A hurrah, or hoop. A carol or catch used by rowers of boats. శృంగారపు పాట.

> "ఏటికట్టకుడిపివేతాం
> ఏరువస్తే కూడాపోదాం
> ఓ, ఓ, గొల్లభామా!"

(The books named గరుడాచలము, ఆటభాగవతము, పారిజాతము, &c., contain many specimens of these carols.) Also, a chorus of applause. ఏలపాటలు a kind of play, a game played by children. గొబ్బిపాటలు. See P. ii. 132.

ఏల *ēla*. [Tel.] n. Name of a stream in the Godavery District ఏలేరు.

ఏలకి *ēlaki*. [Tel.] n. The cardamom tree. **ఏలకికాయలు** *ēlaki-kāyalu*. n. Cardamoms in the husk. **ఏలకులు** *ēlakulu*. Cardamoms. పెద్ద ఏలకికాయ or అడవి ఏలకికాయ *Amomum subulatum* or the Greater Cardamom. ఏలకులు (the seeds). *Amomum Xanthioides (Watts.)*

ఏలపదము or ఏలపాట *ēla-padamu*. [Tel.] n. A carol or ballad. See ఏల.

ఏలము *ēlamu*. [Tel.] n. Auction. ఏలముచేయు or ఏలముపాడు to sell by auction, to auction.

ఏలా *ēlā*. See ఏల.

ఏలాము or ఏలాంచేప *ēlāmu*. [Tel.] n. The saw-fish. A shark.

ఏలావాలుకము *ēlā-vālukamu*. [Skt.] n. A kind of plant సూగంధి.

ఏలి *ēli*. [Tel.] adj. Cunning, false కృత్రిమము. "ఏలిమాట" భా. ఉద్యో. iii. "ఏలి సింగము" చంద్రా. ii.

ఏలిక *ēlika*. [Tel. from ఏలు] n. A ruler, a prince, a king. రాజు, ప్రభువు. **ఏలికసాని** *ēlika-sāni*. n. A queen, a lady. రాణి, దొరసాని.

ఏలిచేప *ēli-chēpa*. [Tel.] n. The saw-fish. ఏలాము or ఏలాంచేప. Russel No. 13.

ఏలిదము Same as ఎల్లిదము. (q. v.)

ఏలిసె *ēlise*. [Tel.] n. The common quail. కొక్కురయేలిసె the large quail.

ఏలు *ēlu*. [Tel.] v. i. & t. To rule, govern, manage. To enjoy, to master. To possess or take. పరిగ్రహించు. పాలించు. **ఏలించు** *ēlintsu*. v. t. To cause one to rule. నిన్ను మాచెర్ల యేలింతును I will make you ruler of Macherla. **ఏలినవాడు** *ēlina-vādu*. n. A ruler, lord, your honor. ప్రభు, రాజు, స్వామి. **ఏలుకోటి** *ēlu-kōti*. n.

The people, subjects. Host, assembly. ప్రజాకోటి. సకలమైనవారు. ఏలుబడి *ēlu-baḍi.* n. Government, reign. ఏలేవారు or ఏలువారు *ēlē-vāru.* n. The rulers. ఏలుకొను= ఏలు.

ఏల్త్సె *ēltse.* [Tel.] n. A kind of snipe.

ఏవ or **ఏవము** *ēva.* [Tel.] n. Loathesomeness, disgust, hatefulness, ugliness. రోత, అసహ్యము. R. iv. 123. **ఏవకాడు** *ēva-kāḍu.* n. One who feels disgusted with a thing రోతగలవాడు. An envious man ఓర్వలేనితనముగలవాడు. **ఏవగించు** or **ఏవపడు** *ēva-gintsu.* v. n. To hate, dislike. To be vexed or disgusted అసహ్యపడు. v. a. To blame, abuse, vilify, accuse నిందించు. To abandon, to desert విడుచు.

ఏవాడు *ēvāḍu.* [Tel. ఏ+వాడు] pron. Who, what man. ఎవడు. ఏ పురుషుడు.

ఏవి *ēvi.* [Tel. pl. of ఏది] pron. Which? నీళ్లేవి where is the water?

ఏవురు *ēvuru.* [Tel.] pron. Five persons ఏగురు.

ఏవే *ēvē.* [Tel.] A particle of emphasis as నేనేవే I myself.

ఏషణి *ēshaṇi.* [Skt.] n. A probe పుండులోతు చొప్పించే శలాక.

ఏష్యము *ēshyamu.* [Skt.] n. The future, what is yet to happen. రాగలది. Foretoken, foreboding. జరుగబోవునది; జరుగబోవుదానికి గురుతు.

> "అగస్త్యోర్వీధరమునకు నిర్వాణం
> బొసంగఁగలందు యుట్టి
> యేష్యంబులు మదీయదివ్యబోధం
> బున నెరింగియుందును." A. vi. 85.

ఏస *ēsa.* [Tel. often pronounced యేస or వ్యాస] adj. Wild. Crooked, wrong. గ్రామ్యము, వంకర. ఏసమాట a solecism or blunder.

ఏసరు *ēsaru.* [Tel.] v. i. To exceed, to be in excess మీరుట. ఏసరేగు *ēsar-ēgu.* v. i. To excel, to be proud విజృంభించు, అతిశయించు.

ఏసి *ēsi.* [Tel.] An affix. At the rate of, at. పదేసి at the rate of ten. ఇంతేసి కన్నులు eyes so large. Also, for వేసి (the initial V being dropt); thus, పెట్టేసి for పెట్టివేసి.

ఏహ్యము *ēhyamu.* [Skt.] adj. Abominable.

ఐ ai

ఐ The vowel AI as the i in pride. The shape ఐ is used as an initial in the dictionary and in poetry, but elsewhere the Telugus use a secondary form అయి "AYI" instead: The secondary form అయి *ayi* is used in poetry as a dissyllable, whenever the metre requires two short syllables for AI, which is one long. The Y in అయి is not pronounced. Thus అయిదు is not pronounced *ayidu*, but *ai-du.* In Telugu words there is this liberty of spelling; but the longer form *ayi* ought never to be used in words of Sanscrit origin.

ఐ or **అయి** *ai.* [Tel.] past. part: of అగు. See అయి. మ్రానై నిలిచెను he stood stock still, lit. he became a tree and stood. వచ్చేవాడనైయుంటిని I was about to come.

ఐంద్రజాలికుడు *aindra-jālikuḍu.* [from Skt. ఇంద్రజాలము] n. A magician, a juggler, a conjurer.

ఐకకంఠ్యముగా *aika-kaṇṭhyamu-gā.* [Skt.] adv. With one voice, unanimously ఏకకంఠముతో.

ఐకమత్యము *aika-matyamu.* [Skt.] n. Unanimity, agreement, harmony ఏకమతిత్వము.

ఐక్యము *aikyamu.* [Skt. From ఏకము] n. Union, oneness, coalescence, unitedness ఏకీభావము.

ఐణము, ఐణేయము *aiṇamu.* [Skt. from ఏణము] adj. Pertaining to the skin of a deer. (ఏణము=ఇర్రి, ఏణి=లేడి.)

ఐతి or **అయితి** *aiti.* [Tel.] adj. Able, possible వల్లగయిన, శక్యము. అది వాని అయితిగాలేదు it was not possible for him.

ఐతిహాసకుడు *aiti-hāsakuḍu.* [Skt. from ఇతిహాసము] n. A story-teller, one who knows stories ఇతిహాసము తెలిసినవాడు.

ఐతిహ్యము *aitihyamu.* [Skt.] n. Traditional teaching పారంపర్యముచేసిన ఉపదేశము.

ఐతిహ్యము, *aitihyamu.* [Skt.] n. Tradition.

ఐతే *aite.* [Tel. wrongly used for అయితే the conditional aorist of అగు] conj. If; should it be so, suppose it were so. But, As for, indeed. as నాకైతే తెలియదు I for my part do not know, lit. to me indeed it is unknown. చేను అయితే ఇచ్చెను గాని ఇల్లు ఇవ్వలేదు he gave the field indeed but not the house. వాడయితే రాలేదు as for him, he did not come. పూర్వమందైతే విన్నాను I heard so indeed formerly. వాడైతే తప్పు చేసినవాడు కాని so far as he is concerned he is wrong.

ఐదు *aidu.* [Tel. for అయిదు] adj. Five. ఐదుగురు for అయిదుగురు five persons అయిదుమంది. అయిదుముట్టుచేయు to salute, to bow to. నమస్కరించు. To be defeated, to lose ఓడిపోవు (ఓడిపోవువారు చేతులుకూర్చి మొక్కుదురు గనుక దీనికి ఓడిపోవుట అని అర్థము వచ్చినది.) "హస్తిః ఘుటుక్తై [illegible] దర్శని [illegible]" అను. ii. To throw into confusion, leave a thing at sixes and sevens. ముందు [illegible] పెట్టు.

ఐదువ *aiduva.* [Tel. అయిదువ=అయిదు+వన్నె గలది.] n. A matron, a housewife, a good woman, a woman whose husband is alive. సౌభాగ్యముగల స్త్రీ. (వన్నెయనగా ఇక్కడ సుమంగలియొక్క అలంకారము. అయిదు వన్నెలేవనగా, మంగళసూత్రము, పసుపు, కుంకుమము, గాజులు, చెవ్వాకు.) See ముత్తైదువ.

ఐదువతనము or **అయిదోతనము** *aiduvatanamu.* n. Wedlock, the state of being a wife. ఐదువరాలు or అయిదువరాలు Same as ఐదువ or అయిదువ.

ఐద్దాగలు *aidu-dāgalu.* Tel. for అయిదు దాగలు] n. The "five anvils:" i. e., the five trades, *viz.*, those of a carpenter, a blacksmith, a goldsmith, a brassmith, and a stonemason.

ఐన *aina.* [Tel. for అయిన. relative p of అగు] p. p. 1. Being, existing. One who or which is or has become. యజమానుడైన రామయ్య Ramaya who was (his) master. Becoming, suitable, fit; అయినగుణములు proper principles. అయిన దినము a fit day. అయిన వడ్డి the interest that accumulated. నాకయిన మనిషి my friend. As a conjunction it is thus used ఐన or అయినా or అయినను but though it were so, yet, వాడయినా వీడయినా be it that man or this, either one or the other. It is added to interrogatives as ఎక్కడ, &c., and it gives a strong emphasis as ఎక్కడనైనా wheresoever. ఎవ్వడయినా whosoever. ఎప్పుడయినా whenever. రెండుకోసులయినా at least two miles. ఎవ్వడైననేమి never mind who it was. It turns nouns into adjectives as సొగసైన pretty, having elegance. Elsewhere it is translated who is (and is added to adjective nouns, thus) కవి అయిన భీమన the poet Bhīmana. విద్వాంసుడైన కవి a poet who is a man of learning. Thus also in the plural ధనికులైన వర్తకులు merchants who are rich. ఐనను or ఐనప్పటికిన్ని although, but. అందుకు అయిన క్రయము the price of that. నాకైనను even to me మేనల్లుడైన అంతఃకరణవల్ల through the affection arising from his being a nephew. ఐనట్టయితే See ఐతే. మీది అయినట్టయితే should it be yours. ఐనప్పటికిన్ని conj. When it is so, even then, nevertheless, still, yet.

ఐనిల్లు *ainillu.* [Tel. for అయినిల్లు] n. The inner or middle house నట్టిల్లు, అంతర్గృహము.

ఐపు *aipu.* [Tel. for అయిపు] n. A flaw, a defect, harm, detriment, damage. తప్పు, దోషము.

ఐపోవు *ai-pōvu.* [Tel. for అయిపోవు] v. t. To be done, finished, exhausted.

ఐమూల *ai-mūla.* [Tel. for అయిమూల] adj. Oblique, diagonal. Oblong and crooked. Rhomboidal. మూలవాటు. ఆ యిల్లు అయిమూలగానున్నది that house is crooked, not straight; ఆ యిల్లు అయిమూలనున్నది that house is in a corner.

ఐర *aira* [Tel. for అయిర.] n. Dimness of sight మసకకమ్ముట.

ఐరకొను *aira-konu.* [Tel. for అయిరకొను.] v. i. To be set right, చక్కబడు. To heal, to become better మాను.

క. "ధీనుల మనమున నాయురు
శ్రేష విశేషమున గ్రుళ్లి చిపుకకయుచ్చో
నీవు ద్రుజలేక మహా
ఘోవన్నపంబునకు నైరకొనికాల్ వచ్చెన్.
P. i. 106.

ఐరాజులు *ai-rājulu.* [Tel.] n. A slang word for mice; as donkey for an ass.

ఐరావణము or ఐరావతము *airāvaṇamu.* [Skt.] n. The name of the elephant on which Indra rides ఐరావతి *airāvati,* n. The bolt of Indra. Lightning: forked lightning మెరుపు, కొలమెరుపు, విద్యుత్.

ఐరేణి *airēṇi.* [Tel. for అయిరేణి] n. Painted vases used at weddings. అరివేణి or అరివెు నకుండలు. బచ్చెనపనిచేసిన పెండ్లికుండలు.

ఐలబిలుడు *aila-biluḍu.* [Skt.] n. Kubēra. కుబేరుడు.

ఐలారము *ailāramu.* [Tel. for అయిలార ము.] n. A root used as a medicine in dropsies.

ఐవచ్చు *ai-vaṭṭsu.* [Tel.] v. i. To be agreeable, or profitable. To prosper. To agree with one's health. అచ్చివచ్చు.

ఐశ్వర్యము *aiṣvaryamu.* [Skt. from ఈశ్వర] n. Riches, wealth, prosperity. కలిమి, సంపద. అష్టైశ్వర్యములు the eight supernatural perfections or attributes of the deity as summed up in this verse. అణి మామహిమాచైవ గరిమాలఘిమాతథా । ప్రాప్తిః ప్రాకామ్యమీశత్వం వశిత్వంచాష్టభూతయః. That which is 1, fine as an atom, 2, of prodigious vastness, 3, of great weight, 4, light as ether, 5, omnipotent, 6, free, 7, supreme, and, 8, under control. ఐశ్వర్య వంతుడు *aiṣvarya-vantuḍu.* adj. An opulent or prosperous man.

ఐహికము *aihikamu.* [Skt. from ఇహము.] adj. Pertaining to the present world or this life, temporal. The condition of being here on earth.

ఒ O

ఒ The short vowel O, as in polite, indigo.

ఒ or ఓ An affix of doubt: as నీకో వారికో either to thee or to them.

ఒంకె *onke.* [Tel.] n A hook or peg. చిలుక కొయ్య.

ఒంజిలి *onjili.* [Tel.] n. Sorrow దుఃఖము. Calamity, misfortune. ఆపద, ఒంజిలి. adj. Sorrowful దుఃఖముగల.

ఒంటరము *ontaramu.* [Tel.] n. Enmity, opposition విరోధము.

ఒంటరి *ontari.* [Tel. ఒంటి+అరి.] adj. Alone, single ఏకాకి. ఒంటరి n. One who fights alone. అసహాయుడైన బంటు, ఏకభటుడు. ఒంటరికత్తె *ontari-katte.* n. A lonely woman. A single woman. ఒంటరికము *ontarikamu.* n. Solitude, loneliness, privacy. ఒంటరివాడు *ontari-kāḍu.* n. A solitary person or animal. ఏకాకి. One who fights alone అసహాయుడైనబంటు. A hog or a rhinoceros. అడవిపంది, లేశ, ఖడ్గమృగము. ఒంటరిపాటు *ontari-paṭu.* n. Loneliness, privacy, retirement, solitariness. ఏకాంతము, ఏకాకిత్వము. ఒంటరీడు *ontariḍu* (ఒంటరి+ఈడు) Same as ఒంటరి (n). ఒంటరులు *ontarulu.* n. Foot soldiers, Infantry. కాలిబంట్లు.

ఒంటి *onṭi.* [Tel.] n. One (of a pair or couple). Privacy. ఏకాకిత్వము. ఒంటికపోవు

to go to pass water. ఒంటి adj. Single, only one. ఒంటిపొర a single fold. ఒంటి కొయ్యి a single masted (vessel.) ఒంటిగంటకు at one o'clock. ఒంటి (genitive of ఒడలు or ఒళ్లు) adj. Of the body. ఒంటెత్తు గామండి headstrong, self-willed.

ఒంటింపు *ontimpu.* [Tel.] n. Convenience, aid, help. అనుకూల్యము. వానికి రూకలు ఒంటింపు కాలేదు he had no money at hand. వానికి ఒంటింపు తప్పినది he has no longer the means of doing it.

ఒంటికాడు or **ఒంటిగాడు** *onti-kadu.* [Tel.] n. A single man, a lonely person. A rhinoceros, or a wild boar. ఏకచరము. "అనురక్తి రేమనూతనసారసాటోప మొంటికాండ్రకు కెంపులాసనుసేచటు." వాతిస్బ్రం. ౨౫ ii.

ఒంటిపాటు *onti-pātu.* Same as ఒంటరిపాటు.

ఒంటెరు Same as ఒంటె. (q. v.)

ఒంటు *ontu.* [Tel.] n. A share, division. A village community గ్రామసమూహము. A unit in numeration. సారని ఒంటు the place or square in which a counter stands in a game at draughts. ఒంటు or ఒంటుబావిలి. n. A sort of ear-ring worn by men. పురుషులకర్ణభూషణము. ఒంటు v. i. To agree with one's health, to be wholesome or salubrious. ఇముడు, అనుకూలించు. To touch, to go near, to approach చేరు. ఆ దేశానికిప్పి ఈ దేశమునకున్న ఒంటక అశక్తముగానున్నది or అక్కడి నీళ్లకును ఇక్కడి నీళ్లకును ఒంటనందున వానికి ఒళ్లు కుదురులేదు his health suffered from change of water, (change of air.) See on నీళ్లు. **ఒంటుకొను** *ontu-konu.* v. i. To touch, go near. తాకు, చేరు.

ఒంటె *ontc.* [Tel.] n. A camel. ఒంటె కోడి an ostrich. **ఒంటెపులి** *onte-puli.* n. The camelopard.

ఒంటొల్లె *ont-olle.* [Tel. ఒంటి+ఒల్లె.] n. A thin petticoat. A. ii. 73.

ఒంట్లు *ontlu.* [Tel.] n. plu. Ear-rings, పురుషులకర్ణభూషణము. "ముత్యపు టొంట్లసియాడ." (T. v. 7.) pearl ear-rings dangling about. Figures, numerical signs. ఒకట్లు, అంకెలు. See ఒంటు. n.

ఒండ *onda.* [Tel.] n. Ill, evil. A whitlow, a sore nail. **ఒండరిమిండరిమాటలు** *ondari-mindari-matalu.* n. Nonsense, idle talk.

ఒండు *ondu.* [Tel.] n. Sediment, deposit; mud left on land by a flood. గోదావరి ఒండుపెట్టినది. ఒండుమన్ను alluvial soil or loam used as manure.

ఒండు *ondu.* [Tel.] n. One ఏకము. An individual. ఒకడు. Another. అన్యము. ఒండేమి తెలియక not knowing a single thing. ఒండననేల why should you say anything? **ఒండే** or **ఒండేని** *onde.* (ఒండె+ఏని) if it is not so, అట్లు కానియెడల. **ఒండెడ** *ond-eda.* adv. Elsewhere. **ఒండొండ** *ond-onda.* (ఒండు + ఒండు+అ) adv. One by one, continuously. Gradually. క్రమక్రమముగా. ఒండొండపారుడు flowing on continuously **ఒండొంటికి** *ond-onti-ki.* To one another. ఒకదానికొకటి. **ఒండొరులు** *ond-orulu.* (ఒండు+ఒరుడు) n. Each other. ఒకరొకరు.

ఒందించు for పొందించు. See పొందు. **ఒందిక** *ondika.* [Tel.] n. Convenience ఒద్దిక, అనుకూల్యము.

ఒందిలి *ondili.* [Tel.] n. Sorrow దుఃఖము. Evil, calamity. ఆపద. Epidemic disease, murrain or cattle disease. ఒందిలి. Inconvenience. అసందర్భము. అప్పుడు ఒందిలిచేత పంపలేదు accident prevented (my) sending it.

ఒందు *ondu.* [Tel. from పొందు, the initial ప being dropped.] v. i. To obtain, possess, have పొందు, కలుగు. తెలివినొంది recovering the senses. చలువొంద beautifully.

ఒంపు *ompu.* [Tel.] n. Crookedness, curve, twist. వంపు. A knee of timber. The worm of a still. A small kettle used instead of a still.

ఒక *oka.* [Tel. Not derived from Skt. ఏక, as other words denoting the numerals show, but cognate with it] adj. A, an, one: ఒక్క. ఒక కొందరు a few or some few. కొంచెము some, some little, as కొంచెముసేపు a little time. ఒకరీతిగా after a manner. ఒక పనినిమిత్తము about a certain affair. Adding the intensive ఏ it gives the sense of *only:* thus ఒకేయిల్లు, or ఒకయిల్లే only one house. వారు ఒక చెయ్యిగానున్నారు they are hand in hand, leagued together. ఒకనాడును ఒప్పడు he will never assent. ఇది ఒకలాగున ఉన్నది this is after a fashion, i. e., is odd, such as cannot be defined. నాకు ఒక విధముగానున్నది. I feel very queer, I am out of sorts. ఒకప్పుడు at one time, once. ఒకవేళ at one time, perhaps. ఒకవేళ అట్లా చేసినా if he ever does so, in case he does so. ఒకింత or ఒక్కింత *okinta.* (ఒక+ఇంత) n. So much: a little, some trifle, ever so little.

ఒకటి *okaṭi.* [Tel.] n. and adj. One. ఇందువల్ల ఒకటి వచ్చును from this one thing may result. ఇందులో ఒకటిన్ని తక్కువలేదు there is not a single thing wanting. ఎవ్వరియింట్లోనైనా ఒకటే it is no matter in whose house (he) is. నేను చెప్పినది ఒకటి వాడు చేసినది ఒకటి I told him one thing and he did another. ఒకటివెనుక ఒకటి one after another. దోవకు రెండువక్కలను అడివి ఒకటే గాని దారి మంచిదే there is nothing but jungle on both sides, but the way is good. ఒకటిగా *okaṭi-gā.* adv. Together, unitedly, unanimously, conjointly. ఒకటిచేయు *okaṭi-chēyu.* v. a. To make one, unite, mix. ఒకటియగు *okaṭi-y-agu.* v. n. To be combined. ఒకట *okaṭa.* On or in one. At one time ఏకకాలమునందు. ఒకటొకటిగా *okaṭ-okaṭi-gā.* adv. Separately, one by one, one after another. ఒకటో *okaṭō.* adj. First. ఒకటోసాక్షి the first witness.

ఒకడు *okaḍu.* [Tel.] pron. One man, somebody, anybody. ఒకణ్ని పిలిస్తే ఒకడు వచ్చెను I called one man and another came. వాడు ఒకడు వీడు ఒకడునాడు that man and this man are the same, are not separate. ఒకతె *okate.* pron. One woman, a female.

ఒకరు *okaru.* [Tel. honorific plural of ఒకడు] pron. folks: somebody, anybody, a person. దీన్నిచూస్తే ఒకరు ఏమందురు what will folks say when they see this? ఇది ఒకరిపనిగాదు. అందరికిన్ని కావలసినదే! this is not merely one man's affair, it is of importance to every body. ఒకరు ఉండే చోటు the place where one lives, వారు ఒకరు మేమొకరము they are one and we are one, i. e., they have no connection with us. ఆ ఊరికిన్ని యీ ఊరికిన్ని కరణాలు ఒకరు the clerks of these two villages are the same persons (lit. are one). ఒకరుపోతే ఒకరువస్తారు one goes and another comes. మేము ఒకరమే యిది చేస్తిమి we alone did this.

ఒకళ్లు *okaḷlu.* plural of ఒకడు or ఒకరు q. v.

ఒకానొక *okān-oka.* [Tel. ఒక+ఒక] adj. Some one or other, a certain, some ఒకానొకపట్టణములో in some town or other, in a certain town. ఒకానొకచోట here and there.

ఒకో or ఒకో *oko.* [Tel.] interj. Oh! alas! Perhaps. వాడు వచ్చునొకో will he come?

ఒక్క *okka.* [Tel. The emphatic form of ఒక of. Eng. *a* and *one*] adj. One. ఒక్కుమ్మడిని (ఒక్క+ఉమ్మడిని) all at once, in one rush. ఒక్కపొద్దు A "single meal," i. e., a religious fast: restriction to one meal a day. నిన్న ఒక్కపొద్దు ఉంటిని I ate but once yesterday. ఒక్కెడ (ఒక్క+ఎడ) occasionally, at times.

ఒక్కటి Same as ఒకటి. (q. v.) ఒక్కటను all at once: suddenly ఏకముగా, అకస్మాత్తుగా.

ఒక్కతె Same as ఒకతె. See under ఒకడు.

ఒక్కరుడు or ఒకరుడు *okkaruḍu.* [Tel.] pron. A form of ఒకడు (q. v.)

ఒక్కి *okki.* [Tel. corruption of ఒక్క] adj. Lean, thin, emaciated. వాడు ఒక్కినరసై పోయినాడు he has become very lean.

ఒక్కె or ఒక్కెర *okke.* [Tel.] adj. Terrible. ఉగ్రము. n. Terror ఉగ్రభావము.

ఒగ్గె or ఒగ్గె Same as ఒగి or ఒగి.

ఒగరు *ogaru.* [Tel.] adj. Acrid, astringent, వగరు, కటువు. n. Astringency, acridity

ఒగరుచు or ఒగర్చు *ogurutsu.* [Tel.] v. i. To gasp, to breathe hard. వగరుచు. ఒగర్పు or ఒగరుపు *ogarpu.* n. Gasping, difficulty of breathing, panting. ఒగర్పుమాట *ogarpu-māta.* n. A certain fee or allowance on grain granted to reapers, &c.

ఒగి *ogi.* [Tel.] adv. Duly క్రమముగా. మరి.

ఒగుడు *ogudu.* [Tel.] n. Husk, straw of the great millet (జొన్న). A dry leaf of the millet జొన్నలోనగువానియొక్క యెండిన ఆకు. ఆ యెద్దు ఒగుడు ఒల్చుకొని తిని దంటు పారవేసినది the bullock has eaten the dry leaves and left the stalk. ఒగుడుకడుచు to become thin or lean కృశించు.

ఒగ్గము *oggamu.* [Tel.] n. A pit గొయ్యి, అవపాతము.

ఒగ్గు *oggu.* [Tel.] v. n. To try, undertake పూనుకొను; to yield, submit, లోబడు; to be ready, to stand in order, to be in trim. సిద్ధపడు. To bend, to bow, వంగు. v. a. To spread (as a net) పరచు, ఒడ్డు. To spread చాచు. To lend or give an ear or the hand, to apply (the mind), to apply, to present. ఒగ్గుబల్ల *oggu-balla.* n. A rest or prop in a lathe.

ఒచ్చెము *och-chemu.* [Tel.] n. A defect, a flaw. Fault. An imputation కొరత, న్యూనత, లోపము, అవమానము. disgrace, నింద. ఒచ్చెము లేనికూరిమి love without a flaw.

"మచ్చికమునకొకొనకొన
నొచ్చెమునాయందుగలదె."

Radha. i. 50.

ఒచ్చెల or ఒచ్చెల్ల *ochchela.* [Tel. for ఓచెల్ల] interj. Alas అయ్యో. A. v. 139.

ఒజ్జ *ozza.* [Skt. from ఉపాధ్యాయుడు.] n. A tutor. A priest. ఉపాధ్యాయుడు, పురోహితుడు. యాజకుడు. ఒజ్జదనము or ఒజ్జతనము *ozzanamu.* n. Tutorship, tuition ఉపాధ్యాయత్వము. ఒజ్జబంతి *ozza-banti.* n. A model copy set by a teacher మేలుబంతి. ఒజ్జసాని the wife of a teacher ఉపాధ్యాయునిభార్య.

ఒటుక్కు *otukku.* [Tel.] n. A start, a shock (expressive of starting with fear, &c.) నాకు ఒటుక్కు అనినది I was startled.

ఒట్టు *ottu.* [Tel.] n. A total. ఒట్టుకట్టు or చేసికొను to strike a total.

ఒట్టు *ottu.* [Tel.] n. An oath శపథము. A penalty, curse, ban, interdiction నిరోధము. నిద్రపట్టితే ఒట్టు a curse on me if I slept! ఆ దారిచూపు, నేను పోకపోతే ఒట్టు shew me the way and it shall be my fault if I do not go. See ఆన. ఒట్టుపెట్టుకొను *ottu-pettu-konu.* v. i To take an oath. ఒట్టుపెట్టు *ottu-pettu.* v. t. To adjure, to impose a vow or solemn promise. T. ii. 98. To ban or forbid by a curse. ఒట్టువిడుచు to remove an oath or interdiction. ఆనవిడుచు.

ఒట్టు *ottu.* [Tel.] v. n. To become, to arise కలుగు. v. a. To place ఉంచు; to set (fire) to, రగుల్చు. "చిచ్చొట్టెను." (M. x. ii. 140.) They set fire (to the house.)

ఒడంబడిక or ఒడబడిక *odam-badika.* [Tel.] n. An agreement, engagement, compact, treaty, covenant, consent, assent సమ్మతి; నిబంధన పత్రిక; సమ్మతించి వ్రాసియిచ్చినవ్రాత. ఒడంబడు *odam-badu.* v. t. To agree, engage, consent. To comply with, to concede సమ్మతించు. ఒడంబరుచు *odam-barutsu.* v. t. To persuade, convince. ఒడబాటు Same as ఒడంబడిక.

ఒడప or ఒడప్పు *odapa.* [Tel.] n. A delicate kind of fish with a flat head.

ఒడపి *odapi.* [Tel.] n. A hole, a breach or gap. రంధ్రము, గండి. Same as ఒడిపి. (q. v)

ఒడబడు Same as ఒడంబడు.

ఒడబరువు Same as ఒడంబరువు.

ఒడబాటు Same as ఒడంబడిక.

ఒడము Same as పొడము. (q. v.)

ఒడమి or ఒడామి *oḍami*. [Tel.] n. Wealth, riches. ధనము.

ఒడయడు or **ఒడయుడు** *oḍayaḍu*. [Tel.] n. A king, lord, ruler, master, owner, husband. ప్రభువు, మగడు. ఒడయురాలు wife of a master, యజమానురాలు, స్వామిని.

ఒడలు or **ఒళ్లు** *oḍalu*. [Tel.] n. The body, the person మేను, శరీరము. plu. ఒడళ్లు. L. viii. 50. **ఒడలి** *oḍali*. Of the body. See ఒళ్లు ఒడలిమాపాడయుడు an epithet of Indra (అభ్య: రామా: కిష్కిం.) **ఒడలిమరువు** *oḍali-maruvu*. n. Armour, as a "covering for the body."

ఒడి *oḍi*. [Tel.] n. The lap, the loins: తొడ పైభాగము. A pocket or pouch formed by a fold in a person's vest. Also, same as ఒడుపు. (q. v.). పొకరోవాని. ఒడిలోవేయు to put in one's pocket, to devour. ఒళ్లో or ఒడిలోకూర్చుండు to sit in the lap. ఆవుకు ఒడిజారినది కేదరో దూడవేయును the cow is on the point of calving. **ఒడికట్టు** *oḍi-kaṭṭu*. n. A girdle, as part of female dress. ఒడ్డాణము. ఎంగావి ఒడికట్టు a red petticoat or girdle. **ఒడికట్టు** *oḍi-kaṭṭu*. v. t. To bind up the apron, &c., as a pocket. To be ready or eager to do a thing ఉద్యుక్తుడగు. వాడు పాపానికి ఒడికట్టెను he set himself to commit crime.

ఒడికము *oḍikamu*. [Tel.] n. Propriety, fitness. Prettiness, beauty, elegance మనోజ్ఞము, యుక్తము. A vow, or imprecation. శపథము, పంతము. An expedient. ఉపాయము.

ఒడికారము *oḍi-kāramu*. [Tel.] n. Excess. ఉద్రేకము.

ఒడిదామర *oḍi-dāmara*. [Tel.] A tree also called అతిరసా.

ఒడిదారము *oḍi-dāramu*. [Tel.] n. A string worn round the waist by women స్త్రీల మొలనూలు.

ఒడిపి *oḍipi*. [Tel.] n. A breach, opening, orifice గండి, బొంద. చెరువు ఒడిపికట్టించినందుకు ఈ చేనిని మడియిచ్చినాము we have granted this field on a favourable lease for repairing the breach in the tank.

ఒడిపిలి, **ఒడిపిళ్లు** *oḍipili*. [Tel.] n. Some kind of food. BD. iii. 1319.

ఒడిబ్రాలు *oḍi-brālu*. [Tel.] n. Rice poured into the skirt or lap of a bride at a wedding, &c. See ప్రాలు.

ఒడియు *oḍiyu*. [Tel.] v. n. To run. To drip, drop, trickle. రూకలు ఓడిసిపోయినవి the money is all run out or expended. **ఒడియు** *oḍiyu*. v. a. To snatch, seize or catch. కొంచెము పైకెగిరిపట్టుకొను. To take. To pull లాగు. ఒడిసిచేపట్టుకొనిరాధనూరడించె he caught Rādha by the hand and pacified her. చెవి ఒడియు to pull one's ears.

ఒడిసెగడ్డ *oḍise-gaḍḍa*. [Tel.] n. A bubo.

ఒడిసెల *oḍisela*. [Tel.] n. A sling రాళ్లు విసిరివేయుటకు వాడబడే ఒకవిధమైన తాడు. ఒడిసెలకాడు a slinger.

ఒడుచు *oḍutsu*. [Tel.] v. a. To pierce, to stab, to gore. To attack. పొడుచు. To seize, snatch. To defeat. To overthrow. ఓడించు.

ఒడుదుడుకు or **ఒడుదొడుకు** *oḍu-duḍuku*. [Tel.] n. Unevenness, hardness, difficulty, సమముగాని, సంకటము. ఒడుదుడుకు బేరించు to drive an iniquitous bargain. ఆ రాయి ఒడుదుడుకుగానున్నది that rock seems likely to topple down. ఆ స్థలము ఒడుదుడుకైనందున కుండ పడిపోయినది as the ground was uneven, the pot toppled over.

ఒడుపు *oḍupu*. [Tel.] n. Catching, seizing. "ఒడుపుదప్పినయట్టి యురగంబుపోలె" (HD. i. 372.) like a snake that has missed seizing what it aimed at. An attempt పూనిక. A trick ఉపాయము. Profit, gain, లాభము. ఒడుపుచేయు to use an expedient, to try, to take by trickery, to snatch away, to rob. ఎత్తుకొనిపోవజూచు.

ఒడ్డగ *oddaga.* [Tel.] n. A weapon formed of two antelope's horns fixed one in each end of an ivory handle so as to form a short spear pointed at each end. ఇఱ్ఱికొమ్ములు రెండు జతపరిచి యేర్పరిచిన ఆయుధవిశేషము.

ఒడ్డగిలు or ఒడ్డగిల్లు *oddagilu.* [Tel.] v. i. To incline, lean on one side. ఒరుగు. To increase, to flow in excess అతిశయించు, ఉప్పొంగు. ఒడ్డగెడవు *odda-gedavu.* v. i. To turn upside down. "గీ॥ కడచిహాయము లొడ్డ గెడవయ్యెరథములు." M. VI. ii. 178. తలక్రిందైపోవు.

ఒడ్డనము *oddanamu.* [Tel. from ఒడ్డు] n. A military evolution, an arrangement of troops, a line of battle. వ్యూహము. A wager, anything staked at a game of chance పందెము. A standard or flag కేతనము.

ఒడ్డాణము *oddānamu.* [Tel.] n. A cestus. or belt of gold or silver worn by women over their dresses.

ఒడ్డారము *oddāramu.* [Tel.] n. Obstinacy, jealousy, dislike ద్వేషము. Opposition ప్రతిఘటించుట, మారొడ్డుట. ఒడ్డారమైన obstinate. ఒడ్డారించు *oddārintsu.* v. t. To dislike. To oppose, combat ప్రతిఘటించు.

ఒడ్డిమి *oddimi.* [Tel. from ఒడ్డు] n. A wager, a stake in a game of chance. పందెము, ఒడ్డు.

ఒడ్డీలు *oddilu.* [Tel.] n. Pigeons called Tumblers. ఒడ్డీలుపారావతములు. UR. iv. 254.

ఒడ్డు *oddu.* [Tel.] v. a. To place, put, lay, heap up. To fix, set, cast. To rival. To wager పందెమిడు. To spread (a net), &c. చాచు, పరచు. To oppose అడ్డగించు. To lend an ear to, to listen. చెవియొడ్డు; leap across దాటు. పింఛమ్ములుపురులొడ్డి the peacocks having spread their tails.

ఒడ్డు *oddu.* [Tel.] n. A bank or shore. దరి. The original number; whether multiplicand or dividend. The disposition of an army in a battle field వ్యూహము. A stake in gambling. పందెము. ఒడ్డిమి An attempt ప్రయత్నము. An obstacle. అడ్డపాటు. ఒడ్డుకాచి కొనియుండు to be in wait or ambush. ఒడ్డు విడిచి దానిమీద పడ్డారు they fell upon him tooth and nail. ఒడ్డుచూపు to place one's troops. నీ ఒడ్డు విరుగుగాక may thy greatness perish. ఒడ్డు or ఒడ్డైన *oddu.* adj. Large, great, stout, big. ఒడ్డుగుండ్లు large balls, boulders, or, fragments of rocks hurled from a hill. ఒడ్డోలగము *odd-ōlagamu.* (ఒడ్డు+ఓలగము) n. A great assembly. ఒడ్డుపొడక high and low, ups and downs: unevenness.

ఒడ్డె *odde.* [Tel.] n. Drudgery: mean toil. As a proper name ఒడ్డెదేశము, or ఒడ్రదేశము Orissa. ఒడ్డెవాండ్లు tank diggers, navvies.

ఒడ్డెము Same as ఒడ్డెము. (q. v.)

ఒడ్డోరకము *odd-orakamu.* [Tel. ఒడ్డు+ఒరకము] adj. High and low, up and down, steep. ఎగుడుదిగుడైన, మిక్కిలి ఎత్తైన.

ఒడ్డోలగము *oddōlagamu.* See ఒడ్డు adj.

ఒత్తక్షరము *ott-aksharamu.* [Tel.] n. An aspirated letter, like ఫ, ఖ.

ఒత్తగిల్లు Same as ఒత్తిగిలు. (q. v.)

ఒత్తడము *ottadamu.* [Tel. from ఒత్తు] n. Pressing. Pressure ఒత్తుట. adj. Thick, dense దట్టమైన.

ఒత్తడి or ఒత్తిడి *ottadi.* [Tel.] n. Pressure, trouble, pain సమ్మర్దము, రాపిడి, బాధ.

ఒత్తరము *ottaramu.* n. Raging, excessive, increase ముమ్మరము, ఉద్రేకము. ఒత్తరించు *ottarintsu.* [Tel.] v. t. To excel మించు. To occupy ఆక్రమించు.

ఒత్తిగిలు or ఒత్తిగిల్లు *ottigilu.* [Tel.] v. t. To lie on one's side, to budge, step aside, stand back, get out of the way. To stick to అంటుకొను. ఉదరంబు వీపుతో నొత్తిగిల్లి a starveling with his belly shrunk to his back.

ఒత్తిలి *ottili.* adv. Hard గట్టిగా. Steadily, with perseverance ఒట్టుగా. ఒత్తిలు or ఒత్తిల్లు *ottilu.* v. i. To give way, go aside.

ఒత్తు *ottu.* [Tel.] n. Thickness, closeness of texture, దళసరితనము. Aspiration of a letter. Pressure అదుముడు. A mattress మెత్త. A kind of ring worn by children బిడ్డలచేతులకువేయు ఒకవిధమైన బంగారునగ. ఒత్తులు gold bracelets for children. ఒత్తు పడు to be pressed or squeezed అదుముడు పడు. ఒత్తు adj. Thick దళసరైన.

ఒత్తు *ottu.* [Tel.] v. n. To give way, yield, retire, recede. To be pierced or poked పొడుచుకొను. To lean on one side ఒదుగు. To become heavy ఘనమగు. ఒత్తు *ottu.* v. a. To press, or squeeze. అదుము, పిసుకు. To dry or wipe, to wipe off (sweat), to blot. తుడుచు. To cut or break with teeth or nippers. పొకొత్తు. To thrust away, renounce, cast off త్రోయు. To aspirate a letter. ఆ అక్షరమును బాగా ఒత్తు you must aspirate that letter. To blow as a conch ఊదు. To oppress, బలాత్కరించు.

ఒత్తుకాడు *ottu-kādu.* [Tel.] n. A drone player. శ్రుతిపోయువాడు. M. IV. v. 85.

ఒత్తుడు *ottudu.* [Tel.] n. A thrust, violence. Crowding, squeezing. అదుముడు, పీడనము. A pad used as a rest, on which to place the paper on which one is writing.

ఒత్తొరవు *ott-oravu.* [Tel. ఒత్తు+ఒరవు] n. Great pressure మిక్కిలి అదుముడు. Teasing, vexation సంపీడనము.

ఒదరు *odaru.* [Tel.] v. i. To excel, increase, to be proud, to rejoice, విజృంభించు, సంతోషించు. v. t. To blame నిందించు. ఒదరుచు or ఒదర్చు *odarutsu.* v. t. To detach, separate ఊడదీయు.

ఒదలు *odalu.* [Tel. another form of పొదలు.] v. i. To flourish, prosper వర్ధిల్లు.

ఒదవు *odavu.* [Tel.] v. n. To arise పుట్టు, కలుగు. To serve, be of use. ఉపయోగించు, ఉపయుక్తమగు. To pervade. వ్యాపించు. M. IV. ii. 348. ఒదవుబడి *odavu-badi.* n. Use ఉపయోగము.

ఒదికిలు *odikilu.* [Tel.] v. n. To lie on one side, to incline to one side. To move aside. పక్కకొరగు, ఒత్తిగిల్లు.

ఒదుగు *odugu.* [Tel.] v. n. To make room, to move so as to accommodate తొలగు. To come to hand, to be got or obtained. దొరకు. To become plentiful సమృద్ధమగు. To be of use or convenient. To assist, be at hand or ready. ఈ బియ్యము వండితే అన్నము ఒదుగుబాటవదములేదు on boiling this rice, it does not swell to the proper quantity. ఈ బట్టచలికి ఒదగదు this cloth is of no use against cold. కొంచెము ఒదుగుము, ఆయనను కూర్చుండనివ్వు move a little and let him sit down. ఒదిగి ఒదిగి ఉన్నారు they yielded. నాకు ఇప్పట్లో రూకలు ఒదగలేదు I have not yet obtained the money.

ఒదుగు *odugu.* [Tel.] n. Plenty సమృద్ధి. అన్నము ఒదుగైనది the rice is become plentiful. ఒదుగుపడు Same as ఒదుగు, to move aside ఒదుగుపాటు *odugu-pātu.* n. Moving aside తొలగుట. ఒదుగుబడి *odugu-badi.* n. Plenty సమృద్ధి.

ఒదువు *oduvu.* [Tel.] v. i. To cover, to spread క్రమ్ము. To become plentiful ఒదుగు. n. Plenty సమృద్ధి, ఒదుగు.

ఒద్ద *odda* [Tel.] n. Nearness. దాపు, సమీపము, వద్ద. ఇంటియొద్ద ఉన్నాడు he is at home. నాయొద్దలేదు I have not got it by me. ఒద్ద near, నాయొద్దకి వచ్చిరి they came to me: తనయొద్దిచెలులు her playmates that were near her.

ఒడ్డి *oddi.* [Tel.] n. A kind of a large tree. *Odina Pinnata.*

ఒడ్డిక *oddika.* [Tel.] n. Concord, union, friendship అనుకూల్యము. The weights in a pair of scales, a counterpoise ఒక వస్తువునకు

సరియొత్తుగానుంచి తూచేరొట్లు మొదలైనవి, ప్రతిమానము.

ఒడ్డె *odde.* [Tel.] n. Plenty, abundance సమృద్ధి.

ఒనగూడు *ona-gūḍu.*[Tel.]v. n. To be obtained; to succeed or attain. To be, happen, chance. To prosper. చేకూరు, సిద్ధించు. ఇతనికి ఆమె ఒనగూడినది she is well suited to him. **ఒనగూర్చు** *ona-gūrtsu.* v. n. To effect, attain to, accomplish. To bestow, grant, accede to. సిద్ధించునట్లుచేయు.

ఒనరు *onaru.* [Tel.] v. i. To happen, chance, be. To become, suit, or agree. To be pretty, proper or agreeable. To appertain or belong to, to be attached to. కలుగు, పొసగు, సరిపడు, ఒప్పు. **ఒనరు** n. Convenience, facility, వీలు, వాటము, పొందిక. Elegance, gracefulness ఇంపు. ఆ దుర్గములో ఒనరులుచూచి ఎక్కలెక్కినారు they spied out the convenient places in that fort or hill and then escaladed it. **ఒనరగా** *onara-ga.* adv. Elegantly, becomingly, fitly. **ఒనరజేయు** *onara-jēyu.* v. a. To grace or adorn. To fit or accommodate. పొసగజేయు. **ఒనరుపడు** *onaru-paḍu.* v. i. To agree with పొందుపడు. **ఒనరించు** or **ఒనరుచు** or **ఒనర్చు** *onarintsu.* v. t. To make, form, do, effect, perform. చేయు. To celebrate (as a sacrifice.) To compose or frame, to write (a book). బాగొనరించు to do good, or benefit. ఎగ్గొనరించు to do harm, to injure. నాదమొనర్చు uttering a sound. ఊడిగము లొనరించి having served. యుక్తములుగా నొనర్తువు thou shalt render them acceptable. యుద్ధమొనర్చు to wage war. నగుబాటొనరించును it will make them laugh.

ఒనవెట్టుకొను *ona-veṭṭu-konu.* [Tel.] v. i. To lie in wait పొంచుచేయు, కాచుకొనియుండు.

ఒప్పందము *oppandamu.* [Tel. from ఒప్పు] n. A contract, undertaking, assignment. A debt payable in kind; a bargain. ఏర్పాటు. **ఒప్పందముచేయు** *oppandamu-chēyu.* v. n. To stipulate, to contract. **ఒప్పగించు** *oppa-gintsu.* v. n. To give up charge: to deliver over. అప్పగించు. **ఒప్పగించుకొను** *oppa-gintsu-konu.* v. a. To take charge of. To hear a pupil his lesson. వశముచేసికొను. **ఒప్పగింత** *oppa-ginta.* n. Handing over charge of, delivery of charge అప్పగింత. **ఒప్పచెప్పు** *oppa-cheppu.* v. t. To assign, to put in charge, to deliver over to, to make over.

ఒప్పనము *oppanamu.* [from Skt. అర్పణము] n. An offering. అర్పణము, అప్పనము. **ఒప్పనచేయు** *oppana-chēyu.* To offer అప్పనచేయు, అర్పించు.

ఒప్పమి *oppami.* [Tel. negative verbal noun of ఒప్పు] n. Want of agreement, disagreement, ఒప్పుకొనకపోవుట. Inelegance. harm, fault, impropriety, కీడు, తప్పు.

ఒప్పరము *opparamu.* [Tel.] n. A drain, a gutter. తూము, జలదారి.

ఒప్పరికించు *opparikintsu.* [Tel.]v.t. To slight, disregard. ఉపేక్షించు, ఎదిరించు. **ఒప్పరికము** *opparikamu.* n. Disregard ఉపేక్ష.

ఒప్పారు *oppāru.* [Tel. ఒప్పు+ఆరు.] v. n. To have, to possess. To look, seem, be perceived. To be. To vie with, rival or look like, emulate. ఒప్పు.

ఒప్పించు *oppintsu.* [Tel. from ఒప్పు] v. a. To cause to consent: to prevail on. To assign or make over, commit, entrust స్వాధీనపరచు, వశముచేయు, ఒప్పగించు.

ఒప్పిదము *oppidamu.* [Tel. from ఒప్పు] n. Grace, agreeableness. Consent. agreement, compliance అందము, సమ్మతి, మనోజ్ఞము. ఒప్పిదమైన graceful, agreeable.

ఒప్పు *oppu.* [Tel.] n. Fitness, propriety, right, agreeableness. తప్పు కామి. Elegance, beauty, charm, grace, అందము. Consent సమ్మతి. **ఒప్పయిన** *oppayina.* adj. Due, right, fit. Becoming; agreeable, handsome: beautiful.

ఒప్పు *oppu.* [Tel.]v. n. and t. To be fit or proper, to be agreeable తగు, ఒప్పిదమగు. అది నీకు ఒప్పునా does such conduct become you? To consent or agree. To confess, own, acknowledge సమ్మతించు. అనుగ్రహించొప్పగా graciously. ఒప్పచెప్పిరి they delivered over charge.

ఒప్పుకొను *oppu-konu.* [Tel.] v. a. To confess, own, acknowledge. To agree, consent, abide by, comply with, accept. ఒప్పుకోలు Consent ఒప్పుకొనుట. ఒప్పుగా *oppu-ga.* adv. Duly, well. ఒప్పులాడి *oppul-ādi.* (ఒప్పులు+ఆడి) n. A graceful or beautiful woman. చక్కదనముగల ఆడుది. ఒప్పెసలార *opp-esa-lāra.* adv. Charmingly.

ఒబ్బట్లు *obbaṭlu.* [Tel. ఒబ్బు+అట్లు] n. A kind of sweet cakes. పోళీలు.

ఒబ్బిడి *obbiḍi.* [Tel.] n. Trimness, propriety, thrashing of corn. adj. Trim or clean, as grain; right and tight. చక్కబెట్టడము, నూర్చడము. Ruin నాశము. పని ఒబ్బిడి అయినది the matter is now finished. గరిసె గరిగానున్నది. వడ్లన్ని ఒబ్బిడిక్రైనవి the paddy is all spoiled or ruined.

ఒమ్మచ్చు or **ఒమ్మెచ్చు** *om mattsu.* [Tel.] n. The beazle of a ring, &c., the part of any jewel that holds the stone.

ఒమ్మిక *ommika.* [Tel. from ఒమ్ము] n. Suitability, fitness. ఇమిడిక, పొందిక. ఒమ్మివచ్చు *ommi-vattsu.* v. n. To prosper, to thrive అచ్చివచ్చు. పశువులు ఇతనికి ఒమ్మిరాలేదు he had no good luck in cattle; his cattle did not turn out well. అతనికి జీడి ఒమ్మి ఉంటుంది the *jiḍi* milk agrees well with him.

ఒమ్ము *ommu.* [Tel.] v. n. To agree or suit, సరిపడు. To thrive. వర్ధిల్లు. ఈ భూమి నాకు ఒమ్మలేదు this climate does not agree with me. ఒమ్మి ఉండే salubrious. ఒమ్ము *ommu.* n. Bigness, plumpness స్థౌల్యము, బలుపు. ఒమ్ము *ommu.* adj. Big, plump. ఒమ్మిల్లు to become big, or plump, To swell. "ఒమ్మగానిల్పించెబలుగజనిమ్మపండ్లు." T. iii. 57.

ఒయ్య or **ఒయ్యన** *oyya.* [Tel.] adv. With gentleness, softly, sweetly. "శిరములొయ్యనంచి." Mand. ii. 3. ఒయ్యనొయ్య gently.

ఒయ్యారము or **ఒయారము** *oyyāramu.* [Tel.] n. Bloom, grace, shapeliness, the pride of beauty. సౌందర్యగర్వము. ఒయ్యారపుమాటలు pretty language, bragging. వయస్సుతప్పినా ఒయ్యారముతప్పదు old as he is he has still a sweet tooth in his head. ఒయ్యారకాడు *oyyāra-kāḍu.* n. A fop, a beau. ఒయ్యారి *oyyāri.* adj. Blooming, graceful, shapely, pretty. ఒయ్యారిపిక్కలు pretty legs. ఒయ్యారి or ఒయ్యారకత్తె *oyyāri.* n. A beauty, a graceful woman. A coquette.

ఒర *ora.* [Tel.] n. Touch, rubbing. Trial of metal by touch. Likeness పోలిక. A case, sheath, scabbard. తలగడ ఒర a pillow case. A ring of clay, thus ఒరలనుయ్యి a well built with rings of baked earth. See ఒరగాను & ఒరపెట్టు.

ఒరకటము or **ఒరకము** or **ఒరకాటము** *orakaṭamu.* [Tel.] n. Steepness, inequality. Depth, difficulty. పల్లము, సంకటము. ఒరకటపునేల an uneven spot. ఒరకటపుతోవ an uneven road.

ఒరకట్టు *ora-kaṭṭu.* [Tel.] n. Cloth tied in many folds చుట్టుగా చుట్టికట్టిన వస్త్రపుకట్టు.

ఒరకడుగు *ora-kaḍugu.* [Tel.] n. The water in which rice has been washed a second time.

ఒరగడ్డము *ora-gaḍḍamu.* [Tel. ఒరవ+గడ్డ] n. Difficulty, trouble సంకటము. adj. Uneven విషమము.

ఒరగల్లు *ora-gallu.* [Tel.] n. A touchstone. బంగారును ఒరపెట్టురాయి.

ఒరగాలు *ora-gālu.* [Tel. ఒరగు+కాలు] n. A bent or crooked leg ఒరిగినకాలు.

ఒరగు or **ఒరాగు** *oragu.* [Tel.] v. n. To lean, bend, bow down, slant, be inclined, recline or lie down, to be weighed down, as scales. వంగు, వాలు. ఒరగి crouching, hiding. పడవ ఒరిగెను the boat leant on one side. ఒరిగి పడినాడు he tumbled down. మిన్నొరిగినట్లు crashingly, suddenly, as though the skies were falling, ఆ లెక్కను నామీద నొరగకట్టినాడు he got that debt charged against me. **ఒరగు** n. Crookedness వంపు. ఒరగు, ఒరగుదిండు, ఒరగుడుదిండు, or ఒరగుదిల్లె a cushion or large pillow to lean against. adj. Crooked వంపైన. **ఒరగుపోవు** or **ఒరగబడు** Same as ఒరగు. q. v.

ఒరగొడ్డెము or **ఒరగొడ్డియము** *ora-goḍḍemu.* [Tel.] n. A painful word, a malicious word that pricks the heart మనస్సును నొప్పించే వంకరమాట.

ఒరగోను *ora-gonu.* [Tel.] v. t. To try (gold) by the touchstone ఒరపెట్టు.

ఒరచాలుదుక్కి *ora-tsālu-dukki.* [Tel.] n. A single ploughing ఒకమారు దున్నినపొలము, చాలు తేలికగాపారిన దుక్కి.

ఒరచు Same as ఒరుచు. (q. v.)

ఒరటు *oraṭu.* [Tel.] adj. Wicked దుష్టుడు.

ఒరపదును *ora-padunu.* [Tel.] n. A mere moistening, a slight wetting కొంచెపుతడి.

ఒరపరి *ora-pari.* [Tel. ఒరపు+అరి] n. A fine looking man. సుందరపురుషుడు, సౌందర్యవంతుడు.

ఒరపిడి *ora-piḍi.* [Tel. ఒరపు + ఇడి] n. Pressure, friction రాయిడి, రాపిడి. An unworthy man అయోగ్యుడు.

ఒరపు, ఒరాపు *orapu.* [Tel.] n. Touch, contact, rubbing. Tightness. ఒరయిక, కర్కశము. An expedient ఉపాయము. Fineness, nobleness. విలాసాతిశయము, సౌందర్యము, యోగ్యత. Fault, transgression. An evil effect, mischief కీడు, దోషము. Trouble, anxiety తాపము. **ఒరపు** adj. Steady, firm, fine, noble, beautiful స్థిరము, సుందరమైన, గొప్ప, యోగ్యము. Light. ఒరపుదుక్కి light ploughing, as opposed to బోందుక్కి wet ploughing. ఒరపులాడి a beautiful woman.

ఒరపెంకు *ora-peṅku.* [Tel.] n. A ring of baked earth used in building a well, a tier, నూతిఒర.

ఒరపెట్టు *ora-peṭṭu.* [Tel.] v. t. To test gold by the touchstone ఒరగోను.

ఒరబొమ్మ *ora-bomma.* [Tel.] n. A puppet or doll.

ఒరము *oramu.* [Tel.] v. i. To become hot వేడెక్కు.

"అక్కురములుకరములెకా జిగినొరమెనసన్ రవియుమెరసె." A. iv. 212.

ఒరయు or **ఒరియు** *orayu.* [Tel.] v. n. To rub together, be in contact. To touch or graze, as a bullet. To be bruised. To struggle or compete with. విద్యతో నొరయు to become familiar with (learning.) ఉంగరము వేలును ఒరసికొనిపోయినది the ring has grown into the finger. గుండు ఒరసిపోయినది the ball grazed (my hand.) నేను పడినందున నా మోకాలు ఒరసికొనిపోయినది I fell and my knee was bruised. **ఒరయు** v. a. To rub రాచు, to try on the touchstone ఒరపెట్టు. To test or to examine పరీక్షించు. To consider or enquire into విచారించు. To search for వెదకు. **ఒరయిక** *ora-ika.* n. Rubbing, contact రాపిడి.

ఒరలు *oralu.* [Tel.] v. n. To lament, wail, cry, whimper విలపించు. To sound మ్రోగు.

ఒరవ *orava.* [Tel.] adj. Crooked, sloping. వంకరైన. Different వ్యత్యస్తము.

క॥ "అరపొరదు కురుచచేతులు
నొరవ శరీరంబు."

భార. అర. ii.

ఒరవడి *ora-vaḍi.* [Tel.] n. The Copy set by a teacher కేలుబంతి.

ఒరవబడు *orava-baḍu.* [Tel. from ఒరగు or ఒరుగు.] v. i. To be tilted to a side, to lie on one side ఒరగబడు. **ఒరవు** Same as ఒరగు. (q. v.)

ఒరి *ori.* [Tel.] n. Plunder, spoil దోపిడి. A. vi. 110.

ఒరిగ *origa.* [Tel.] n. A salutation మ్రొక్కు, నమస్కృతి.

ఒరిజె *oriza.* [Tel.] n. A chain tied round the neck of an elephant ఏనుగు మెడగొలుసు. The girth of an elephant made of iron or leather. కచ్చ.

ఒరిబీజము or **ఒరుబీజము** *ori-bijamu.* [Tel.] n. A swelled testicle, orchitis. ఒక్కవైపు బీజము వాచిన రోగము. Also, Hydrocele.

ఒరిమ or **ఒరిమిక** *orima.* [Tel.] n. Friendship, patience ఓర్మి. Unanimity ఏకమత్యము.

ఒరియు Same as ఒరయు.

ఒరుగు Same as ఒరగు.

ఒరుచు *orutsu.* [Tel. from ఒరియు.] v. a. To rub, to try metal by the touchstone. **ఒరుచుబడ్డ** or **ఒరచుబడ్డ** *orutsu-badda.* [Tel. From ఒరయు to be indented.] n. A carpenter's plane, a carpenter's tool to draw parallels with. పలకలోనకునని నునుపు పఱచెడు వడ్లవాని కొరముట్టు.

ఒరుడు *orudu.* [Tel.] n. One ఒకడు. Another: a neighbour or other person, a stranger, అన్యుడు. ఒరులు others.

ఒరుదల *oru-dala.* [Tel.] n. A hole ఎలుక బొక్క. P. ii. 117. Solitude ఏకాంతము. Talebearing, backbiting చాడీలుచెప్పుట, కొండెములుచెప్పుట. కొండెకానితనము. Miserliness పైకున్యము. **ఒరుదలకాడు** *orudala-kadu.* n. A wretch: a miser పిసినుడు. A. iv. 167. A talebearer. A backbiter, a slanderer, a tell-tale, కొండెకాడు.

> "మొదిలన చొరుదిలకానిం
> జెదరంగావాడకాళ్ల జంతింపుపదిం
> బదికమ్మనుయేని మానిడు
> మదముస్తుగజేయకుండు మొక్కపుతమునన్."
>
> A. iv. 267.

ఒరుము *orumu.* [Tel.] v. i. To unite కలియు.

ఒర్ర *orra.* [Tel.] adj. Hot కారము. Bitter కటువు. ఒర్ర or ఒర్రన n. Heat, pungency కారము.

> "తత్ప్రయులవక్త్రవిషజ్వల
> నోష్మనుర్రనై వెలువడ."
>
> A. v. 112.

ఒర్రు *orru.* [Tel.] adj. Large, great పెద్ద, గొప్ప.

ఒర్రె or **ఒర్రియ** *orre.* [Tel.] n. A crack. బీటిక. A rick of corn చిన్నకుప్ప. A low fellow, a black-guard పంద. A bay or inlet. A wild or untamed cow. సాధువు కాని ఆవు. adj. Crooked వక్రము. ఒర్రమాటలు filthy language.

ఒలయు *olayu.* [Tel.] v. n. To appear, seem, or come to light, enter ప్రవేశించు, To take place, to be or happen కలుగు. To spread వ్యాపించు, పొలయు, పొందు, ఒప్పు. చిరునవ్వులొలయ a smile appeared on her lips. పెంపొలయదు no increase took place. **ఒలయు** v. a. To surround, to envelop, to meet చుట్టుకొను, కదియు.

ఒలవు *olavu.* [Tel.] n. Secret intelligence మర్మము, రహస్యము. The neck of a stringed instrument వీణాదండము. ఒలవుగానుండే underhand లోకువైన. ఒలవుగానుండేవాడు an accomplice, a traitor. వారు వానికి ఒలవుగానుండినారు they were leagued with him.

ఒలి *oli.* [Tel.] n. Robbery దోపిడి, అపహారము. ఒలిపడు to be robbed దోపుడుపోవు. ఒలిపుచ్చుకొను To betray, show. బయటపడేట్టుచేయు. To lose, let go పోగొట్టు.

ఒలికి *oliki.* [Tel.] n. A funeral pile ఒలికిమిట్ట the cemetery or burying ground, కాడు, వల్లకాడు, శ్మశానము.

ఒలితామర *oli-tamara.* [Tel. ఒలి+తామర.] n. A certain plant.

ఒలిపించు *oli-pintsu.* [Tel. The causal of ఒలుచు.] v. t. To cause to peel off ఒలుచునట్లుచేయు.

ఒలియు *oliyu.* [Tel.] v. n. To bruise, to abrade or rub off the skin తోలుపోవు. **ఒలియించు** *oli-yintsu.* v. t. To kill (See పొలియించు), చంపు. BD. iv. 400.

ఒలుకు *oluku.* [Tel.] v. n. To spill, చిందు; overflow, to be shed (as tears) or spilt; to flow కారు; To be dropped, పాలలో నెయ్యి ఒలికినట్లు as ghee gushes forth from milk, i. e., luck upon luck. v. a. To sprinkle చల్లు; to pour పోయు.

ఒలుచు *olutsu.* [Tel.] v. a. To peel, shell, flay. To pare off, tear off. తోలూడ్చు. ఒలిచినపప్పు grain cleaned from the husk. ఒలవనిపప్పు grain in the husk. పండు ఒలిచి అరచేత పెట్టినట్టు చెప్పినాడు he said (it) as plainly as a fruit is peeled from its skin and placed in the hand; he gave a graphic description. To rob. అపహరించు See ఒలి.

ఒలుపు *olupu.* [Tel.] n. Peeling, removing the skin, rind, coat or shell. ఒలుచుట. **ఒలుపుపప్పు** *olupu-pappu.* n. Grain freed from the husk.

ఒలె *ole.* Same as ఒల్లె. (q. v.) See A. vi. 100.

ఒల్ల *olla.* [Tel.] adj. Slow, straight అల్లన, తిన్నన.

ఒల్లకాడు *olla-kādu.* [Tel. for వల్లకాడు] n. 'The abominable place,' i. e., the cemetery or place where bodies are burnt. A cremation ground. ఒల్లకాటిమాటలు objectionable language, graveyard jokes.

ఒల్లగిల్లు *olla-gillu.* [Tel.] v. i. To be neglected ఆదరింపబడనిదగు.

ఒల్లన *ollana.* [Tel.] adv. Gently, softly.

ఒల్లబాటు *olla-bātu.* [Tel. ఒల్లమి+పాటు] Same as ఒల్లమి. (q. v.)

ఒల్లబోక *olla-bōka.* [Tel. ఒల్లమి+పోక] n. Disregard అనాదరము.

ఒల్లబోవు *olla-bōvu.* [Tel.] v. n. To faint, మూర్ఛిల్లు. To turn pale వాడు, ఆదరింపబడనిదగు, చిన్నబోవు, తెలతెలబోవు. M. IX. i. 222.

ఒల్లమి *ollami.* [Tel. negative noun of ఒల్లు to love.] n. Hatred, dislike. Refusal, grudge, unwillingness. Dissent, disapproval. Intolerance. కుడువనొల్లమి disinclination to eat.

ఒల్లియు Same as ఒల్లె.

ఒల్లు *ollu.* [Tel.] v. a. and n. To be willing, choose, fancy, wish. To love, like, long for. ఒల్లను I hate, detest, dislike, I will not, I do not choose. ఇంక ఆడనొల్లను I do not choose to play any more. ఎంచనొల్లను I won't think of it.

ఒళ్లు *ollu.* [Tel. another form of ఒడలు] n. The body, person, figure. నీ ఒళ్లు ఎట్లా ఉన్నది how do you do? how are you? వానికి ఒళ్లు తిరుగుచున్నది he is giddy. వానికి ఒళ్లు కుదురుగా ఉండలేదు he is unwell. వానికి ఒళ్లు తెలియలేదు he is out of his senses. ఒళ్లువంచి ఈ పని చేయవలసినది you must bend your back to this work. ఒంటి of the body; ఒంటికి to the body; ఒంట on the body. నీ ఒంటికావరమణచుదును I will crush your pride. వానికి అన్నము ఒంటపట్టినది he digested the food. ఒళ్లుపెట్టు or ఒళ్లుపట్టు to become plump బలియు. మంత్రసానియెదుట ఒళ్లు దాచుతావా will you conceal your form in the midwife's presence, i.e., will you conceal the truth from your lawyer?

ఒల్లె *olle.* [Tel.] n. An upper cloth అంగవస్త్రము, ఒలె. వన్నెయొల్లె colored cloth.

ఒల్లెంక *ollenka.* [Tel.] n. A prickly globular fish with poisonous flesh. *Tetrodon Hispidus.*

ఒల్లెతాడు *olle-tādu.* [Tel.] n. A noose flung at an animal to catch it.

ఒల్లెవాటు *olle-vātu.* [Tel.] n. A scarf, the upper garment gracefully arranged round the neck. The wearing of an upper cloth. పైబట్టను కుచ్చెళ్లుపెట్టి మెడచుట్టి వచ్చునట్లుగా భుజములమీద వేసికొనుట.

ఒల్లో *ollō.* [Tel.] A contraction for ఒడిలో. See ఒడి.

ఒవ్వు *ovvu.* [Tel.] v. i. To agree with, కిట్టు, సరిపడు. To assent, consent. **ఒవ్వమి** *ovvami.* n. Refusal. ఒప్పమి. ఒవ్వనివారు those who hate, or disagree కిట్టనివారు.
ఒవ్వు *ovvu.* n. A sheaf of corn.

ఒసగు or **ఒసంగు** *osagu.* [Tel.] v. a. To give. ముద్దొసగు to give a kiss. ముద్దులొసంగు నీమొగము your beautiful face. **ఒసగు** n. A gift ఈవి, త్యాగము.

ఒసపరి *osa-pari.* [Tel.] adj. Agreeable, pretty, lovely, nice, sweet. **ఒసపరి** n. A fine-looking man సుందరుడు. **ఒసపరితనము** *osa-paritanamu.* n. Agreeableness, prettiness, sweetness. సౌందర్యము.

ఒసవు Same as ఒసగు. (q. v.)

ఒహోహో Same as ఓహో. (q. v.)

ఓ O

ఓ The long vowel Ō.

ఓ Ō. An affix, denoting question, guess or doubt, &c., as నీకో వానికో to you or to him. బిడ్డయో పాపయో either child or baby. అట్లు తలచినారో possibly they thought so. ఎక్కడనో somewhere or other. వాడు వచ్చెనో in case he should come.

ఓ *ō.* [Tel.] Added to cardinal numbers it forms ordinals మూడు three; మూడో third; this is contracted for మూడవ.

ఓ *ō.* [Tel.] The vocative sign O. ఓ తమ్ముడా.

ఓం or **ఓంకారము** *ōm.* [Skt.] The sacred syllable ఓమ. O'M. Om. or A U M being the triliteral name of the Hindu Trinity. ప్రణవము. ఓన్నమశ్శివాయ or ఓం నమశ్శివాయ సిద్ధంనమః. O Siva! I bow to thee for success.

ఓండ్ర *ōndra.* [Tel.] n. The bray of an ass. గాడిద కూత. ఓండ్రించు or ఓండ్రపెట్టు to bay as an ass.

ఓకచెట్టు *ōka-chettu.* [Tel.] n. A small tree called *Carissa Carandas*, bearing an acid fruit. వుల్లకలివె.

ఓకము or **ఓకస్సు** *ōkamu.* [Skt.] n. A house or dwelling place. ఇల్లు, స్థానము.

ఓకర *ōkara.* [Tel.] n. Retching to vomit. Great dislike రోత. **ఓకరించు** *ōkarintsu.* v.n. To retch in vomiting, to hate రోతపడు. **ఓకరింత** *ōkarinta.* n. Retching to vomit: ఓకరించుట.

ఓకస్సు Same as ఓకము. (q. v.)

ఓకిలి, ఓకిలించు, ఓకిలింత Same as ఓకర, ఓకరించు, ఓకరింత, respectively.

ఓకు *ōku.* [H.] n. A telescope దుర్భిని, దుర్బిణి. ఓకువేసిచూడు look with a spy-glass.

ఓగాత్యము *ōgatyamu.* [Tel.] n. Bad taste, impropriety. A bad omen అమంగళము.

ఓగితము *ōgitamu.* [from Skt. యోగ్యము.] adj. Fit, proper, worthy యోగ్యము.

ఓగిరము *ōgiramu.* [Tel.] n. Food, boiled rice అన్నము.

ఓగు *ōgu.* [Tel.] n. Evil, harm, wickedness. కీడు. **ఓగు** n. A fool, a weak creature. ఒంట్లో సత్తిలేనివాడు. A wicked man దుర్మార్గుడు. "ఓగునోగు మెచ్చు." అది బాగో ఓగో ముందుకు తెలియును whether it is good or bad will be known by and bye.

ఓఘము *ōghamu.* [Skt.] n. A crowd, flock or multitude సమూహము. A flood ప్రవాహము.

ఓచెల or **ఓచెల్ల** *ōchela.* [Tel.] Interj. Alas. అయ్యో.

ఓజ *ōza.* [Tel.] n. Order క్రమము. Way, manner విధము. Nature స్వభావము. A command ఆజ్ఞ. Vigor, zeal, joy ఉత్సాహము, ఎచ్చరిక. Fear భయము. Thought, idea, intent. Counsel, wisdom, good sense యోచన. In arithmetic, an uneven or odd number. A row, or range. వరుస. A teacher ఉపాధ్యాయుడు. (another form of ఒజ్జ) "సింగం బాకటితోగుహాంతరముం దీటొప్పటుమ్మైనుండిమా । తంగస్యూధయూధదర్శనసముద్యద్గోధమై వచ్చునో । జేంగాంతారనివాసఖిన్నమతినస్మచ్ఛైన్య పైనీవడవచ్చెకా । కుంతీపుత్రవధార్థమై ..." M. Virata. 93. *Like* a lion bursting forth in rage. "ఓజె గాడిద్లాడనోలిక" L. vii. 7. "ఓజె

గుణము లేర దాచా జేసేర." Vēmana. ఓజేపడు *ōza-paḍu*. v. i. To be settled, to be set right క్రమపడు. ఓజబంతి or ఓజ్జబంతి *ōza-banti*. n. The way shown by the teacher ఉపాధ్యాయుడు చూపినపద్ధతి. A copy set by him నేలబంతి.

ఓజము or ఓజస్సు *ōjamu*. [Skt.] n. Strength, might, renown, light, brilliancy. బిగి, పటిమ, శ్రేష్టత, తేజస్సు.

ఓజు *ōzu*. [Tel. for ఒజ్జ] n. A tutor or master. ఉపాధ్యాయుడు. A goldsmith అగసాలెవాడు.

ఓట *ōṭa*. [Tel.] n. Fear, వెరపు. Hesitation సంకోచము. ఓటమి or ఓటము *ōṭami*. n. Fear భయము. Failure, loss, defeat, భంగము, అపజయము. గెలుపోటములు gain and lose.

"భూమిభృత్సభనోటమైన
గయకొంబులో మీకు రాకుండునే."

A. i. 95.

ఓటరి *ōṭari*. [Tel.] n. Ruin, defeat, the loser at a game. ఓటరు or ఓటారు *ōṭaru*. [Tel. From ఓటు and పారు.] v. n. To be ruined or wrecked; ఓటారిన cracked, broken or gone to pieces. బద్దలయిన.

ఓటి *ōṭi*. [Tel. from ఓడు crack] adj. Cracked ఓటికుండ a cracked pitcher అది ఓటిగొడ్డు it is a mere pack of rubbish. ఓటితిపిరదండె *ōṭi-tipira-daṇḍe*. A kind of guitar. కినాంవాద్యభేదము. A vi. 4. ఓటిల్లు *ōṭillu*. v. i. To hesitate ఓడు, సంకోచించు. ఓటిల్లుబిలచె a kind of game.

ఓటు *ōṭu*. [Tel.] adv. Surely; perhaps. "భోజ ...జేసిన గా ఆనిక, పంటకొంబు లెకుండక చెప్పునటోటుభాగ్యాలా." భాగ్య...

ఓటు *ōṭu*. [Tel.] n. Loss, defeat. అపజయము, భంగము. ఓటుపోవు or ఓటుపడు *ōṭu-pōvu*. v. i. To be defeated. ఓటుపాటు *ōṭu-pāṭu*. n. Defeat. ఓడిపోవుట, ఓడిపోవుట.

ఓడ *ōḍa*. [Tel.] n. A ship, a boat. The word ఓడ prefixed to the names of some drugs, &c., answers to foreign or imported as ఓడచింతపండు imported tamarinds. ఓడ పోక imported areca. ఓడకీలు Pitch. See కీలు.

ఓడించు *ōḍiñtsu*. [Tel.] v. n. To defeat, vanquish. జయించు.

ఓడిక *ōḍika*. [Tel.] n. A stream, a current, a river. ప్రవాహము.

"జేజేనరంబుట్టిక కటికమ్మచికటులు
గానస్రుపజంబోడికల్గట్టన్."

Swa. iv. 104.

ఓడిగిల్లు *ōḍi-gillu*. [Tel.] v. i. To flow ప్రవహించు. To run పరుగెత్తు. To flow out పారు.

ఓడిగించు *ōḍi-giñtsu*. [Tel.] v. a. To empty out, pour out completely.

ఓడినక్క *ōḍi-nakka*. [Tel.] n. A short fox. పొట్టినక్క. See నక్క.

ఓడు *ōḍu*. [Tel.] v. n. or v. a. To fail, lose, to be defeated or worsted, అపజయపడు. To flow or be lost, as blood, పారు. To shrink, hesitate, fall back భయపడు, సంకోచించు. ఆట ఓడినాడు he lost the game. జీవహింసకోడ shrinking or hesitating to take away life. ఓడుపడు to be frightened. వరదు ఓడు అనగా ప్రవాహముగా పారు to rush, as a flood. M. Xiii. ii. 451. మొగమోటమునకోడ unable to look you in the face. ఓడకోడకు fly not! flee not.

ఓడు *ōḍu*. [Tel.] n. Defeat, loss, failure, a forfeit, a crack, chink, hole. ఆ పెనము ఓడుగానున్నది that saucepan is cracked. ఓడుబిళ్ల *ōḍu-biḷḷa*. Pan tiles, such as are used for roofs. T. iv. 202.

ఓఢ్రము *ōḍhramu*. [Skt.] n. Orissa. The Uriya language. ఓఢ్రుడు *ōḍhruḍu*. A native of Orissa.

ఓతువు *ōtuvu*. [Skt.] n. A cat.

ఓత్వము *ōtvamu*. Tel. The name of the vowel O.

ఓదనము *ōdanamu*. [Tel.] n. Food boiled rice అన్నము.

ఓదము *ōdamu*. [Tel.] n. A pitfall for catching elephants. ఏనుగులుపట్టే గొయ్యి.

> "ఊరివిహంగవ్రజంబునకు
> నోదముదంతికిమందుచిల్లకున్."
>
> P. ii. 31.

ఓదారుచు or **ఓదార్చు** *ōdārutsu*. [Tel.] v. a. To comfort, condole with. ఊరార్చు.

ఓదె or **ఓదియ** *ōde*. [Tel.] n. A rick of corn formed of several కుప్పలు or cocks. ఒత్తు. See వామి. **ఓదెకొంగ** or **ఓదెకొంగు** *ōde-konga*. n. The harvest crane. The common crane, *grus communis*; and the demoiselle crane, anthropoides virgo.

ఓనమాలు *ōnamālu*. [Tel.] n. The Alphabet, so named, because it commences with the salutation to God "Ōm Namah."

ఓనికట్టు *ōni-kattu*. [Tel.] n. A narrow pass between hills కొండలనడిమి గొందిదారి.

ఓపమి *ōpami*. [Tel. the negative verbal noun of ఓపు.] n. Inability, indolence, laziness. పాలుమాలిక.

ఓపిక *ōpika*. [Tel.] n. Strength, endurance, patience, toleration. శక్తి, ఓర్పు, సహనము. ఓపికలేని impatient ఓపికపట్టు to exercise patience, to be patient.

ఓపు *ōpu*. [Tel.] v. t. To bear, endure, tolerate. ఓర్చు. చూపోపక A. v. 78. unable to stand before his face. ఇంతకష్ట మోపలేను I cannot bear this trouble. **ఓపరాని** *ōpu-rāni*. adj. Intolerable సహింపకూడని. **ఓపలేని** *ōpu-lēni*. adj. Impatient. ఓర్పులేని; helpless, దిక్కులేని. ఓపలేనివారికి అడ్డున్నవారే బుద్ధిమంతులు those who check the impatient are their best friends. **ఓపు** *ōpu*. v. n. To be fit, to suit; to be worthy: to be able: to be possible or practicable. చాలు, తగియుండు. పోనోపునా can he go? పోనోపడు he cannot go, ఈనోపని unable to give.

ఓబుడు *ōbudu*. [Tel.] n. One of the gods worshipped by the Chentsus, a jungle tribe.

ఓమటి *ōmati*. [Tel.] n. Food అన్నము.

ఓమనకాయలు *ōmana-kāyalu*. [Tel.] n. Pieces such as tamarind seeds, &c., used in a game called ఓమనగుంటలాట. **ఓమనగుంటలు** *ōmana-guntalu*. n. A kind of game అచ్చనగండ్లు. ఓమనపీట a small table which is hollowed out in a number of places, to be used in this game.

ఓమము or **ఓమ** *ōmamu*. [Tel.] n. The seed of bishop's weed, *Carum Copticum*; వాము. ఓమము ఆకు చెట్టు or కర్పూరవల్లి or కొండగచెట్టు *Anisochilus carnosus*: అజమోదవాము *Carum Roxburghianum* (Watts.)

ఓము *ōmu*. [Tel.] v. a. To preserve, to cherish. కాపాడు, పోషించు.

> "ఎప్పుడుసంధ్యలయందు నిలువెల్లనీక
> నిన్నోమెడుతల్లిరొంతోరెలునొక్కా."
>
> Swa. ii. 18.

ఓయారము Same as ఒయ్యారము, (q. v.) **ఓయారి** Same as ఒయ్యారి. (q. v.)

ఓయి *ōyi*. [Tel.] pron. Oh! hallo! O thou! పురుషసంబుద్ధి.

ఓయిరము Same as ఓగిరము.

ఓర *ōra*. [Tel.] n. The side, border, edge. అంచు. A whole day and night అహోరాత్రము. ఒక ఓరను ఉంటిమి we stood on one side. ఓరగా sidelong, sideways. తలుపోరగావేసె or ఓరవాకిలి చేసినది she opened the door a little, or, set it ajar. ఓరపోయి becoming crooked వంకరపోయి. BD. vi. **ఓరచూపు** *ōra-tsūpu*. n. A sidelong glance. కొలకులకొరయారచూపు leeringly. **ఓరంతపొద్దు** *ōranta-poddu*. (ఓర+అంత+ప్రొద్దు) the livelong day, all day long, దినమంతయు, అహోరాత్రము. Also, a little కొంచెము, ఇసుమంత.

> "ఉప్పలేకుండ నోరంతప్రొద్దు
> చెప్పిడితాని పానునే కాల్లి?
> రాలేకొంచుంది రాకయున్నాడు."
>
> Pal. 316.

ఓరగిల్లు *ōragillu*. [Tel.] v. n. To turn aside, to slant. ఒరగు,ఒదుగు. **ఓరగించు** *ora-gintsu*. v. i. To turn aside, కొమ్ములోరగించుచు, pointing its horns, or turning them. BD. v. 241.

ఓరచ్చులు *ōratsulu*. [Tel. ఓర+అచ్చులు.] n. High-soled shoes ఎత్తుగా అట్టలువేసికుట్టిన ఓరట్టచెప్పులు. Also, rough shoes మోటుచెప్పులు.

ఓరణము *ōraṇamu*. [Tel.] n. A hawk. Manu. iv. 84.

ఓరపాక *ōra-pāka*. [Tel.] n. A verandah పంచపాళి. A shed built on the side of a house. ఇంటిపంచనుకట్టిన పాక.

ఓరపాటు *ōra-pāṭu*. [Tel.] n. Leaning against a thing. ఒరగుడు. **ఓరపోవు** *ōra-pōvu*. v. i. To bend, to be slanting వంగు, ఒరిగు.

ఓరసిల్లు or **ఓరసిలు** *ōra-sillu*. [Tel.] v. n. To move sideways. To move aside తొలగు. To be removed or raised as veil. To withdraw oneself. **ఓరసింపు** *ōrasimpu*. n. Moving aside ఓరసిల్లుట.

ఓరి or **ఓరీ** *ōri*. [Tel.] interj. O thou! fellow. లేరోరి up! ఓరీ బాలక my lad!

ఓరిమి *ōrimi*. [Tel. from ఓర్చు.] n. Patience. ఓర్పు, క్షమ.

ఓరు *ōru*. [Tel. from హోరు] n. Sound, noise. Red colour applied to the walls of a house on festive occasions. ఇంటిగోడలయడుగునను మూలలను వేసే ఎర్రమంటిపట్టె. **ఓరు** adj. Large. ఓరుగాలి a great or noisy wind మిక్కిలి బలముగల గాలి. **ఓరుతీయు** *ōru-tīyu*. v. i. To mark red streaks on the walls and corners of a house. గోడలమీదను మూలలను ఎర్రమంటితో పట్టెలు తీర్చు.

ఓరుచు *ōrutsu*. [Tel.] v. n. To bear, endure, suffer, tolerate, pardon సహించు, క్షమించు. (From ఓడు) v. t. To conquer ఓడించు. **ఓరుపు** *ōrupu*. n. Endurance, patience, tolerance. **ఓరుచుకొను** *ōrutsu-konu*. v. n. To endure, to be patient. **ఓరుపరి** Same as ఓర్పరి.

ఓరెము *ōremu*. [Tel.] n. Food. Rice. అన్నము. Ved. Ras. iii. 57. Nila parin. i. 12. ఓయిరము or ఓగిరము.

ఓర్చు Same as ఓరుచు.

ఓర్తు or **ఓర్తుక** *ōrtu*. [Tel.] pron. One (woman). ఒకతె.

ఓర్పరి *ōrpari*. [Tel. from ఓర్పు+అరి.] n. A patient person. ఓర్పుగలవాడు, లేక, ఓర్పు గలది.

ఓర్వమి *ōrvami*. [Tel. from ఓర్చు) n. Impatience, intolerance, envy. సహింపలేమి, ఈర్ష్య.

ఓర్పు *ōrpu*. [Tel. from ఓర్చు.] n. Patience, endurance.

ఓల *ōla*. [Tel.] n. A cry, shout, hurrah! Bathing, playing in water. జలక్రీడ M. vii.iii. 112. **ఓలగందము** *ōla-gandamu*. n. Saffron that is smeared over the body while bathing పూతపసుపు.

ఓలగము *ōlagamu*. [Tel.] n. An assembly, a court. కొలువు, కొలువుకూటము. పేరోలగము, or ఒడ్డోలగము a great assembly. **ఓలగించు** *ōla-gintsu*. v. t. To serve కొలుచు, సేవించు.

ఓలచెంగనాలు *ola-chenganālu*. [Tel. from ఓల] n. Defeat, discomfiture అపజయము.

ఓలపాట *ōla-pāṭa*. [Tel. from ఓల.] n. A song used while bathing or swimming. A boat song.

ఓలము *ōlamu*. [Tel.] n. A covering, screen, shelter, veil. The body as the *covering* of the soul చాటు, నాగస్థలము, మరుగు, రక్ష. ఓలమందు obtaining shelter. "ఓలముల దాగి తలమాపనూడ." P. iv. 258. **ఓలమాసగొను** *ōla-māsa-gonu*. (ఓలము+ఆస+కొను) v. n. To hide. To retreat; flee, draw back మరుగుపడు, చాటుకోరు, పరాఙ్ముఖుడగు.

ఓలలాడు *ōlal-āḍu*. [Tel. ఓలలు+ఆడు.] v. n. To play in water. To bathe. To revel. జలక్రీడచేయు. R. i. 211. **ఓలలార్చు** *ōlal-ārtsu*. n. To cause to play in water.

ఓలాకు *olaku.* [Tel.] n. Exhaustion, fatigue. M. IV. iii. 125. అలయిక, శ్రమము. ఓలాకు పడు *ōlaku-paḍu.* v. i. To be fatigued. అలయు, శ్రమపడు.

ఓలాడు *ōl-āḍu.* [Tel. ఓలు+ఆడు] v. i. To bathe, to sport in water. ఓలారు *ōl-āru.* v. n. To float తేలు. ఓలార్చు *ōl-ārtsu.* v. t. To cause to float, to refresh తేల్చు, సేదదీర్చు.

ఓలి *ōli.* [Tel.] n. A dowry, marriage portion, money paid by a bridegroom to the parents of a bride. ఓంకుము. A line, a row. వరుస. Plu. ఓలులు.

ఓలిమి *ōlimi.* [Tel.] n. A hiding place దాగు కనోటు, ఓలము.

ఓవరి *ōvari.* [Tel.] n. An antechamber లోపలి గది, లోట్టికట్టు. A pavilion, a hall మంటపము, చంద్రశాల. పచ్చతోరణాలు arbours, summer-houses. "పచ్చనిఓవరులు" (R. v. 32.) green pavilions.

ఓవు *ōvu.* [Tel.] v. n. To fit, to be agreeable సరిపడు, ఒప్పు.

ఓషధి *ōshadhi.* [Skt.] n. An annual plant or herb, one that dies immediately after it seeds. ఫలించినతోడనే నశించుచెట్టు. A medicinal plant మందుచెట్టు. ఓషధీశుడు *ōshadh-īṣuḍu.* n. The lord of plants, i. e., the moon.

ఓష్ఠము *ōshṭhamu.* [Skt.] n. The lip పెదవి, అధరము. ఓష్ఠామృతము *ōshṭh-amritamu.* n. The nectar of the lips.

ఓసరు or ఓసరిల్లు *ōsaru.* [Tel.] v. t. To step aside, to get out of the way, to evade. తొలగు. To be tired అలయు. "ఓసరిలెడి కేసరియా పకలీల వాసిగనుండు." A. iv. 52. ఓసరించు *ōsarintsu.* v. n. & t. To turn aside, remove, put aside. To fail, to push aside, move aside తప్పించు. ఓసరిలనుంచు *ōsarila-nuntsu.* v. t. To lay aside ఒక పక్కగానుంచు. ఓసరింత *ōsarinta.* n. Moving aside ఓసరిల్లుట.

ఓసి *ōsi.* [Tel.] interj. Woman! Wife!

ఓహటము *ōhaṭamu.* [Tel.] n. Withdrawal, retreat వెనుకతీయుట. ఓహటించు or ఓహటిల్లు *ōhaṭintsu.* v. t. To retire, retreat, fall back వెనుకతీయు, to give way తొలగు; to be worsted ఓడు, యుద్ధమందు ఓడిపోవు.

> "పంక్తిముఖుండు కంగారునంగా
> రాయసమున మోహటించిపరాజయ
> ప్రాప్తుడాయెను."
>
> Bry. 941.

ఓహరిసాహరి *ōhari-sāhari.* [Tel.] adv. Pell-mell, in a rout, backwards and forwards. వెనుకకునుముందుకు, అటునిటునుగా. చెదరి. ఓహరి ఓహరిగా.

> "ఓహరిసాహరియై...
> ...ఓహరిసాహరి..."
>
> M. VII. iii. 148.

ఓహో. ఓహోహో *ōhō.* [Tel.] interj. Hollo! ho! What! ఏమి. Well done! భళి. ఓహోహో *ohōhō.* Oh, alas! ఓహోరె or ఓహోరే *ōhōre.* interj. Well done! భళి.

ఔ au

ఔ AU, the last vowel, compounded of a and u, and pronounced like ou in out or ow in how, cow, now.

ఔ *au.* [Tel. contracted from అవు or అగు] v. n. Contraction of ఔను or అవును yes. adj. That is, అయిన. "ఔబళుదారితి" T. v. 105.

ఔకాపు *aukāpu.* [Tel.] n. Living in a rented house అద్దెకాపురము (properly written అవుకాపు.)

ఔకు *auku.* [Tel. properly written అవుకు.] n. A fen, morass, bog. అవుకునేల. A. iv. 162.

ఔక్షకము *aukshakamu.* [from Skt. ఉక్షము.] n. A herd of oxen ఎద్దులమంద.

ఔగదే *au-gadē.* [Tel. అవును+కదే] interj. Surely! ఔరా. (Properly written అవుగదే.)

ఔగాక *au-gāka.* [Tel.] "So be it." Still అయినను, అట్లైనను. (Properly written అవుగాక.)

ఔగాములు *au-gāmulu.* [Tel. అవును+కా ములు the 'being and not being.'] n. The hitting or missing, the happening or failing. Prosperity and adversity కలిమిలేములు. Propriety and impropriety యుక్తాయుక్తములు. Good and bad. మేలుకీళ్లు. (Properly written అవుగాములు.)

ఔగు *augu.* [Tel. properly written అవుగు.] n. A kind of cake భక్ష్యవిశేషము.

ఔచిత్యము *auchityamu.* [Skt. from ఉచితము.] n. Fitness, suitability, propriety. యోగ్యత. ఔచిత్యముగా మాట్లాడినాడు he spoke appropriately. అనౌచిత్యప్రసంగము an inappropriate remark.

ఔజు *auzu.* [Tel. also written అవుజు.] n. A servant పనివాడు.

ఔటు See అవు to be or become.

ఔటుగుండు *auṭu-guṇḍu.* [Tel. properly written అవుటు.] n. A bomb shell. చట్టి పిరంగిగుండు.

ఔడు *auḍu.* [Tel. properly written అవుడు.] n. A lip, పెదవి. ఔడుకొట్టు or ఔడుకరచు *auḍu-koṭṭu:* v. a. To bite the lips or gnash the teeth through rage.

ఔత్కంఠ్యము *aut-kanṭhyamu.* [Skt. from ఉత్కంఠము.] n. Cupidity, eagerness. ఉత్కంఠ, కుతూహలం.

ఔత్సుక్యము *autsukyamu.* [Skt. from ఉత్సుకము] n. Anxiety, agitation, passion, emotion, Earnestness. ఉత్సుకత్వము.

ఔదరికుడు *audarikuḍu.* [Skt. from ఉదరము.] n. A gluttonous or voracious man. కర్బ్బ తిండుడు

ఔదరులు *audarulu.* [Tel. properly written అవుదరులు.] n. Plu. Rivulets.

> "క్రొమ్మంచుకౌదరులై ...
> ..." Swa. iii. 38.

ఔదల *audala.* [Tel. properly written అవుదల.] n. The crown of the head నడినెత్తి. The head తల.

ఔదార్యము *audāryamu.* [Skt. from ఉదారము.] n. Bounty, liberality. ఉదారత్వము.

ఔదు Same as ఔజు. (q. v.)

ఔదుంబరము *audumbaramu.* [Skt.] n. Copper రాగి.

ఔద్దాలకము *auddālakamu.* [Skt.] n. The honey in a honey comb పుట్టలో పెట్టిన తేనె.

ఔద్ధత్యము *auddhatyamu.* [Skt. from ఉద్ధతి.] n. Rudeness, roughness. పొగరు, అతిశయము, గర్వము.

ఔను or అవును or అగును [Tel. from అగు to be or become.] v. It may be, it probably is, yes; very well, well done! So be it! ఇది నీకు అవునా will this agree with you? మీరు అట్లా చెప్పవచ్చునా is it proper for you to say so? అది నాచేత నవును I can do it. అవునాకాదా yes or no? అవునవును yes, yes; అది అవునా is it right? అవును కాదనక చేసెను he did it without saying a word.

ఔపనిషద *aupanishada.* [Skt. from ఉపనిషత్తు.] adj. Belonging to the Upanishads. Scriptural, theological. ఔపనిషదుడు *aupanishaduḍu.* n. One who knows the Upanishads.

ఔపవిభక్తికము *aupa-vibhaktikamu.* [Skt. from ఉపవిభక్తి.] n. A noun used in an irregular form.

ఔపాధికము *aupādhikamu.* [Skt. from ఉపాధి.] adj. Temporary, not permanent. That which arises from circumstances. ఔపాధికశక్తి official authority: the power that circumstance or situation gives: ఔపాధికశరీరము a bodily form assumed for a while, as in an incarnation.

ఔపాసనము *aupāsanamu.* [Skt. from ఉపాసనము.] n. The worship of fire enjoined on a married Brahmin every morning గృహస్థుడగు బ్రాహ్మణుడు ప్రాతఃకాలమందు చేయవలసిన అగ్ని యుపాసన. In a comic sense, smoking tobacco.

ఔర or ఔరా *aura.* [Tel. properly written అవుర.] interj. Yea, verily, ah yes, oh indeed, a battle shout.

ఔరడి *auradi*. [Tel. properly written అవురడి.] n. Scorn, despite, slight. Rādha. iii. 72.

ఔరసుడు or ఔరసపుత్రుడు *aurasudu*. [Skt.] n. A son of full blood. ధర్మపత్నియందు పుట్టినకొడుకు.

ఔరు *auru*. [Tel. properly written అవురు.] n. Rushes, bulrush. A fragrant grass, *Andropogon muricatum*. వీరణము, అవురుగడ్డి. Also called విడవలి. అవురు మీటెలు a lever for raising weights. A. iv. 162; vi. 13.

ఔరౌర *aur-aura*. [Tel. properly written అవురవుర.] interj. Oh oh! yes, yes indeed!

ఔర్వము *aurvamu*. [Skt.] n. Devouring flame, fire that will burn under water, unquenchable fire బడబాగ్ని. "మహౌర్వకీలము." Vasu. iv. 23.

ఔల Same as అవుల or అవల. (q. v.)

ఔలు Same as అకులు or అవులు. (q. v.)

ఔలెమ్ము or ఔలే *au-lemmu*. [Tel. properly written అవునలెమ్ము] interj. Yes yes! never mind.

ఔషధము *aushadhamu*. [Skt. from ఓషధి.] n. Medicine. మందు.

ఔష్ట్రకము *aushṭrakamu*. [Skt. from ఉష్ట్రము.] n. A herd of camels. ఉష్ట్రములగుంపు.

ఔసు or అవుసు Same as పౌసు. (q. v.) ఔసుకాడు *ausu-kāḍu*. n. An impassioned lover, a beau. విటకాడు, శృంగారి.

ం sunna

ం The Sunna, *anuswaram*, or circle used for ఙ, న, మ: as అండము *aṇḍamu*, an egg: సంతానము *santānamu*. offspring: కంబు *kambu*, a shell. The half nasal "ఁ" or semicircle is not used in modern Telugu, though some Pundits have made many efforts to introduce it.

ః visarga

ః The H, as in the words దుఃఖము *duh-khamu*, స్వతః *swatah*, or, *swataha*. It is denominated విసర్గ Visarga and pronounced Aha and is used only in Sanskrit words.

క ka

క, The letter K.

కంకటము *kankaṭamu*. [Skt.] n. A cuirass, armour, కవచము, జోడలము.

కంకటి *kankaṭi*. [Tel.] n. A couch or bedstead. మంచము. కంకటిత్రాడు ticken or bed-cord used as a noose. See మలక.

కంకణము *kankaṇamu*. [Skt.] n. A bracelet or anklet. ముత్యాలు మొదలైనవాని సరము. A consecrated thread bound on the wrist at the commencement of a marriage, &c: చేతికి కట్టుకొను తోరము. The trellice or running flowered pattern cut in marble round the walls of a temple. కంకణము వంటి దూడ a thriving calf. బద్ధకంకణుడై bound to execute an act. ఆ పనికి కంకణము కట్టుకొన్నాడు he undertook that work or is wedded to it. ధర్మమునకు కంకణముకట్టుకొని యున్నాడు he is bent on doing justice. కంకణాలయీటె a spear girded with rings of silver or other metal. కంకణగ్రహణము *kankaṇa-grahaṇamu*. n. An annular eclipse.

కంకణము or కంకణాయి *kankaṇamu*. [Tel.] n. A kind of water fowl జలపక్షి. An ibis. కాటికంకణము the glossy ibis, *Plegadis falcinellus*. తెల్లకంకణము the white ibis, *Ibis melanocephala*. నల్లకంకణము the black ibis, *Inocotis papillosus*. (F. B. 1.)

కంకతము or కంకతిక *kankatamu*. [Skt.] n. A comb. దువ్వెన.

కంకము *kankamu*. [Skt.] n. An eagle. గ్రద్దలు. కంకపత్రము *kanka-patramu*. n. An arrow. (Lit: eaglewinged.)

కంకర *kankara*. [H]. n. Gravel. జల్లి. adj. Hard పరుసము. కంకరగాడిద a mule. కంచరగాడిద, అశ్వతరము. కంకరబుర్ర a blockhead.

కంకాళము *kankālamu.* [Skt.] n. A skeleton, అస్థిపంజరము, ఎముకలగూడు. A breastbone డొక్క.

కంకి *kanki.* [Tel.] n. An ear or head of corn: a stem of corn. వెన్ను. కంకి వెడలని బోండు a blasted ear, one that does not sprout.

కంకివాయువురోగము *kanki-vāyuvu-rōgamu.* [Tel.] n. The croup.

కంకు or **కంకులుపెట్టు** *kanku.* [Tel.] v. a. To scold: to abuse. గద్దించు, తిట్టు.

కంకుడు *kankuḍu.* [Tel.] n. One who pretends to be a Brahmin. కపటబ్రాహ్మణుడు. A savage who lives on eagles గ్రద్దలు చంపి తిను బోయవాడు. Yama, the regent of death. యముడు. Yudhishthira యుధిష్ఠిరుడు.

కంగటి Same as కంకటి. (q. v.) **కంగటికాళ్లు** *kangaṭi-kāllu.* [Tel.] adj. Bowlegged.

కంగాణము *kangāṇamu.* [Tam.] n. A watch, a guard. కావలి.

కంగారి *kangāri.* [Tel.] adj. Disorderly or filthy. చిందరగానుండే. **కంగారు** or **కంగిసె** *kangāru.* n. Battle యుద్ధము.

కంగాలీ *kangālī.* [H]. adj. Wretched, miserable దిక్కుమాలిన, కంగాలీ మంచము a wretched bed. కంగాలీబత్తెము paltry batta, a wretched pittance.

కంగు *kangu.* [Tel.] n. A gold armlet of a wavy shape. బంగారుపోగులతో సంకెగా చేసిన చిన కన్ను. A shrill sound as of a bell when struck. **కంగున** *kanguna.* adv. Aloud, resoundingly as a bell. **కంగుమను** *kangum-anu.* v. n. To sound, echo as a bell.

కంగువు *kanguvu.* [Skt.] n. The grain termed *Panicum Italicum,* కొర్రలు.

కంగేలి or **కంగేళి** *kangēli.* [Tel.] n. A large pyramidal tree, *Jonesia asoka.* అశోకము.

కంగోరి *kangōri.* [H.] n. An arch or dome. The moulding in brick-work.

కంగోరు *kangōru.* [Tel.] n. A long waistband. నడుముపట్టి.

కంచి *kanchi.* [Tel.] n. Conjiveram కాంచీపురము. adv. Large పెద్ద. **కంచిమేక** *kanchi-mēka.* n. A goat which has a large udder పెద్దపాదుగుగల ఒక జాతిమేక.

కంచియ Same as కంచె. (q. v.)

కంచుకము *kanchukamu.* [Skt.] n. A woman's waistcoat or jacket. A man's jacket, a piece of armour, a snake's skin. రవిక, కుబుసము, పాముకుబుసము, కవచము. **కంచుకి** *kanchuki.* n. A serpent. An attendant or guard over the women's apartments, an eunuch. పాము. అంతఃపురపు కావలివాడు. Parij. ii. 44. R. i 207. ii. 18. **కంచుకిత** *kanchu-kita.* adj. Armed, in armour విస్తృతకంచుకితమన్మథ blinded by lust.

కంచులిక Same as కంచుకము.

కంచె *kanche.* [Tel.] n. A hedge, pasture land బయలుకేలు. **కంచెకోట** *kanche-kōṭa.* n. The outer hedge or fence round a fort. కంచెనాటుట. To plant a hedge.

కంచెల *kanchela.* [Tel.] n. A woman's jacket. Swa. v. 74.

కంచేము *kanṭsamu.* [Tel.] n. A metal plate or dish. కంచుకంచేము a dish made of bell metal. మా కంచేములో రాయి వేసినాడు he threw a stone into our plate, i. e., took away our bread, he disturbed us. మందకంచేము a dish which has a rim. అకుకంచేము a dish which has none.

కంచేరము *kanṭsaramu.* [Tel.] n. A kind of carriage. ఒకవిధమైన బండి, గాడి. **కంచేరగాడిదె** *kanṭsara-gāḍide.* కంచేరము + గాడిద] n. A mule.

కంచేరవాడు or **కంచరి** *kanṭsara-vāḍu.* [Tel.] n. A brazier, a coppersmith. కంచుపని చేయువాడు. కంచరిది a woman of that caste. **కంచరిపురుగు** *kanṭsari-purugu.* n. A kind of beetle called the deathwatch. **కంచు** *kanṭsu.* n. Bell metal. కంచు కుండ a bowl or vessel of bell metal. కంచు

వాద్యము a cymbal made of bell metal. కంచుతేటనిన్లు as bright or dazzling as the glitter of polished metal. Sunbright. ఆమె కంచుగీచినట్లు పలికె she spoke shrilly or with a voice as clear as a bell.

కంచుకంటు *kantsu-kantu.* [Tel.] n. A frying pan. బాణలి. **కంచుమించు** *kantsu-mintsu.* n. A sort of toe-ring. adj. Invisible, out of sight అగోచరము. In some places it is the name of a hawk. **కంచుమించుగా** *kantsu-mintsu-ga.* adv. Rapidly, like a flash. కంచుమించులై, చెల్లాచెదరై. B. v. 303.

కంజము *kanjamu.* [Skt.] n. Any aquatic product. A lotus. తామర. కంజముఖి bright faced, a fair girl. **కంజజ** *kanjaja.* n. Born from the lotus, a title of Brahma. **కంజాతము** *kanjatamu.* n. A lotus. కంజుడు Brahma.

కంజో Same as గంజో. (q. v.)

కంట *kanta.* [Tel. from కను] n. Seeing. కనుట.

కంటకము *kantakamu.* [Skt.] n. A thorn, a prickle. A pest, plague, evil, inconvenience, besetting sin, stumbling block ముల్లు, విరుద్ధమైనది, రోమాంచము. **కంటకఫలము** *kantaka-phalamu.* n. The Jack tree పనస. **కంటకవృత్తి** *kantaka-vritti.* n. Pestering, plaguing, hatefulness. **కంటకుడు** *kantakudu.* n. A plague, a tormentor, a tyrant. క్షుద్రశత్రువు. ధర్మకంటకుడు he who hates virtue. ధర్మద్వేషి.

కంటగించు or **కంటగిల్లు** *kanta-gintsu.* [Tel.] v. n. or v. a. To feel or cause pain నొప్పు. To oppose, to thwart విరోధించు. To hate, be intolerant, or outrageous. To rave or storm.

కంటలము Same as కంట్లము. (q. v.)

కంటసము *kanta-samu.* [Tel.] n. A disagreeable word or words said in opposition. విరోధోక్తి.

కంటసరి *kanta-sari* [Tel.] n A necklace of gold beads.

కంటాణి *kantani.* [Tel.] n. An awl.

కంటి *kanti.* [Tel. from కన్ను.] n. One who has an eye. ముక్కంటి one who has three eyes. జగడగంటి or కలహకంటి one who has an eye for quarrels, i. e., a quarrelsome woman.

కంటిచేప or **కనుటిచేప** *kanti-chēpa.* [Tel.] n. A kind of fish, a species of *sparus* with a prickly head and large eyes. Russel, plate 104.

కంటు *kantu.* [Tel.] n. The head or top of a pillar. Antipathy, hatred, grudge, unkindness. పగ, విరోధము. కంటుపెట్టు to hate.

కంటె or **కంటెడు** *kante.* [Tel.] n. A carcanet, or gold collar worn by women.

కంటె or **కన్న** *kante.* [Tel.] conj. Than. దానికంటె ఇది మంచిది this is better than that. వానికంటె వేరేమనిషి a different man from him. ఆత్మకంటె వేరు different from spirit.

కంట్లము *kantlamu.* [Tel.] n. A pack-saddle చిల్లరసరకులుంచి యెద్దుమీద వేసే సంచులజత. A pannier or bag made to hold a pack. A saddle-bag. కంట్లపుటెద్దు a pack-bullock.

కంఠము *kanthamu.* [Skt.] n. The throat. కుత్తుక. Sound కంఠధ్వని. Nearness, proximity, సమీపము. గ్రామకంఠము the village common. **కంఠదూలము** *kantha-dūlamu.* n. The beam forming the ridge of a pent roof. **కంఠపాఠము** *kantha-pathamu.* n. A lesson learned by rote. వానికి కంఠపాఠముగా వచ్చిన పద్యములు verses which he had by heart. **కంఠమాల** *kantha-māla.* n. A swelling of the glands of the throat. **కంఠసరి** *kantha-sari.* n. A sort of necklace. **కంఠసూత్రము** *kantha-sūtramu.* n. The marriage thread worn by Hindu wives round the throat. మంగళసూత్రము. దానికి కంఠసూత్రము కట్టినాడు he wedded her. **కంఠస్నానము** *kantha-snanamu.* n. Bathing all but the head, i. e , neckdeep.

కంఠి kaṇṭhi. A necklace. కంటె. కంఠీరవము kaṇṭhī-ravamu. n. A lion. కంఠోక్తిగా kaṇṭhōkti-ga. adv. Specifically, definitively.

కండ kaṇḍa. [Tel.] n. A lump or piece of flesh or pulp. కండకావరమున కన్ను కాన కున్నాడు he cannot see out of his eyes for pride. "కండకన్నులు." (A. vi. 23.) Eyes that are swollen. దుర్మాంసము పెరిగిన నేత్రములు. కండచక్కెర kaṇḍa-tsakkera. n. Sugar-candy. కండచుక్క kaṇḍa-tsukka. n. The liver కాలిజము. కండపట్టు kaṇḍa-paṭṭu. v. n. To grow fat, gather flesh.

కండిగచేప kaṇḍ-iga-chēpa. [Tel.] n. A kind of fish, a species of *Clupea*, Russell No. 203.

కండుబాయిచేప kaṇḍu-bāyi-chēpa. [Tel.] n. The sepia or cuttle fish, from which is obtained the కండుబాయిపలక the bone from which pounce is made.

కండువా kaṇḍuva. [Tel.] n. An upper garment. అంగవస్త్రము. A cross beam or rafter in a roof. అడ్డదూలము.

కండువు or కండూతి or కండూయ kaṇḍuvu. [Skt.] n. Itching, itch దురద, తీట.

కండె kaṇḍe. [Tel.] n. A head or ear of millet or maize. జొన్నకంకి. A ball or roll of thread on a straw, which is put into the shuttle నూలుచుట్ట. A shoulder whose muscles are stiffened by gymnastics సాముచే మిక్కిలి గట్టిపడిన భుజము. (another form in this sense is కండెము.) కండెచేప a fish. A. v. 42. కండెకోటి a skein of thread.

కండ్లు kaṇḍlu. [Tel.] n. The plural of కన్ను an eye: and of కల్లు a stone: బండికండ్లు carriage wheels. కండ్లగంతకట్టు to blindfold. కండ్లబడు to appear, come in view.

కంత kanta. [Tel.] n. A hole, cleft, gap, aperture, fissure, chink. A passage, alley, way. పిల్లకంత a small lane.

కంతి kanti. [Tel.] n. A wen or swelling, a hump, a tumour.

కంతుడు kantuḍu. [Skt.] n. A name of Cupid మన్మథుడు.

కంథ kantha. [Skt.] n. A rag, a patchwork quilt. చింపిగుడ్డ, బొంత.

కంద kanda. [Skt.] n. A bulbous esculent root; *Amorphophallus campanulatus* (Watts). దుంపకంద a species of vegetable grown for food కనుచేదికంద. See Rox. iii. 314, 325, 508, 509.

కందకము kandakamu. [Tel.] n. A ditch, trench. అగడ్త, పరిఖ.

కందనగాయ kandana-gāya. [Tel.] n. The heart. గుండె, హృదయము. అము. iv.

కందపట్టెలు kanda-paṭṭelu. [Tel.] n. Cross pieces of wood at the back of a door.

కందము kandamu. [Tel.] n. A certain metre in prosody. Also, the neck of animals. స్కంధము, పశువులమూపు.

కందరము kandaramu. [Skt.] n. A cave. గుహ. Vasu. v. 54.

కందర్పుడు kandarpuḍu. [Skt.] n. Cupid. మన్మథుడు. కందర్పుని దర్పము అనగా రోగి.

కందళము or కందళికము kandalamu. [Tel.] n. A quilt or rug used as a saddle. ఎద్దుమీద వేసే గంత. కందళము [Skt.] n. A germ or shoot, a sprout. క్రొత్తమొలక. కందళించు kandaḷintsu. v. n. To sprout, germinate, shoot. అంకురించు; to appear or gleam, as a smile. కందళిక kandaḷika. n. Appearance, birth, rising. "రాగరసకందళికగా." (T. ii. 172) as affectionate feelings broke forth.

కందాచారము kandāchāramu. [H and K.] n. The native militia కట్టుబడివాండ్లు. adj. Military దండుసంబంధమైన.

కందాయము kandāyamu. [K.] n. Tribute, tax. కందాయము [Skt.] n. An astrological period of four months.

కంది kandi. [Tel.] n. The grain called red gram తువర. *Cajanus indicus*, Pigeon Pea; No-eye (small form) or Congo-pea (large form) ; Dal or Cadjan Pea. *Cytisus cadjan* (Watts.) కందిపప్పు, See పప్పు. కందిపుల్లలు the stalks of the plant used as fuel. ఆమెముగాలమునాటి కందివిత్తు she is like an old pigeon pea, i. e., she is as sharp as a needle. కందికంప thatch or straw of this plant. **కందిమిడత** *kandi-midata*. n. A locust.

కందిరీగ or **కంద్రీగ** *kandir-iga*. n. A hornet.

కందు *kandu*. [Tel.] n. Blackness, discoloration, as by scorching : a dark shade as in the face of the moon నలుపు. Evil, harm. కీడు. Pain తాపము. "ఇత్తెరంగునగలుగు కందెల్లనోర్చి" M. IV. iv. 60. An infant బిడ్డ. *adj*. Blackish, dark, impure (as silver) కందువెండి base silver. **కందు** or **కందు పోవు** *kandu*. v. n. To scorch, be scorched or charred. మలినమగు. To redden, or be inflamed. To become black నలుపగు. To be annoyed or grieved తపించు. మనసుకందిన వాడై being vexed, or grieved.

కందుకము *kandukamu*. [Skt.] n. A ball to play with చెండు. కందుకమట్లెగసి springing up, bounding or elastic like a ball.

కందుడు *kanduḍu*. [Skt. for స్కందుడు] n. The god of battle. కుమారస్వామి.

కందురీగ Same as కందిరీగ. (q. v.)

కందువ *kandura*. [Tel.] n. 1. A way, path. 2. A place, locality, quarter ప్రదేశము. 3. A season ఋతువు. 4. Fashion, mode, device, trick, peculiarity. 5. Fiction, fraud, మాయ ; archness, a prank, a wrench, or a twist. చమత్కారము, నేర్పు. 6. Finesse, innuendo, a quibble, వక్రోక్తి; refinement, prettiness. 7. A token, or mark, trace, track. జాడ, సంకేతస్థలము, ఏకాంతము. వానకందువ the rainy season. ఇరుకందువ on both sides. "మునుతామునచనిన కందువ నెదకుచు కానలోపలికి." Sar D. vii. 211. "ఇందుబింబముమీది కందువచందంబునకురులు నెమ్మొగమున నెరసిరయుండె." M. IV. ii. 137. "కందువచందమూను." V. P. ii. 51. **కందువ** adj. Peculiar, odd, queer. Pretty, curious. Cunning, false, fictitious. కందువమాటలు a quibble : a play upon words. కందువపద్మము a fairy lily, not a real one. కందువరాజులు mere pretenders : mock warriors.

కందువు *kanduvu*. [Skt.] n. A gridiron పెనము.

కందెన *kandena*. [Tel.] n. Grease for carriage wheels. కందెనబిళ్ల the leather or washer put on an axle tree.

కందెర *kandera*. [Tel. కన్ను+తెర.] n. An eyelid. కనురెప్ప.

కందోయి *kan-dōyi*. [Tel. కన్ను+దోయి.] n. A pair of eyes.

కంధరము *kandharamu*. [Skt.] n. The throat : a cloud. మెడ, మబ్బు. Vasu. v. 54.

కంధి *kandhi*. [Skt.] n. The ocean. కడలి, సముద్రము.

కంప *kampa*. [Tel.] n. A bush of thorns. ముళ్లమండ. **కంపకోట** *kampa-kōṭa*. n. A stockade. వెదురుతోగాని పేముతోగాని చేసిన ఆవరణము. **కంపగోడ** *kampa-gōḍa* n. A thorn hedge. **కంపజిట్ట** *kampa-jiṭṭa*. n. A name given to a number of small birds of the warbler family (sylviidae) Blyth's Reed-Warbler, *Acrocephalus dumetorum*. ఎర్రకంపజిట్ట the paddy-field Warbler (Jerd) or the Paddy-field Reed-Warbler, *Acrocephalus agricola*. పెద్దనల్లకంపజిట్ట the Eastern Orphean Warbler, *Sylvia jerdoni*. చిన్ననల్లకంపజిట్ట The Indian Lesser White-throated Warbler, *Sylvia affinis*. అడవికంపజిట్ట or అడవికంపనల్లంచి The Indian Bush-chat, *Pratincola maura*. (F. B. I.)

కంపణము *kampaṇamu*. [Tel.] n. A kind of weapon. ఆయుధవిశేషము.

కంపతుడుపు *kampa-tuḍupu*. [Tel.] n. A hurdle used as a harrow. రెండు ఎడ్లతో తోలే కంపచీపురుకట్ట.

కంపనము *kampanamu*. [Skt.] n. Tremor motion. Nodding కదలుట, వణకుట. కంపనము

kampamu. n. Trembling, tremor, vibration, agitation. వణకు. భూకంపము an earthquake. శిరఃకంపము nodding the head (in approbation or admiration.)

కంపనల్లంచి kampa-nallanchi. [Tel.] n. *Pratincola caprata*, or, The common Pied Bush-Chat. (F. B. I.) అడవికంపనల్లంచి, తెక, అడవికంపజిట్ట *Pratincola maura*, or, The Indian Bush-Chat.

కంపరము kamparamu. [Tel.] n. A bier for bearing corpses పాడె.

కంపించు or కంపిల్లు kampintsu. [Skt.] v. n. To tremble, shake, be agitated. వణకు. కంపితము *kampitamu*. adj. Trembling, shaking. వణకిన.

కంపిల్లము kampillamu. [Skt.] n. A plant called గోరికూర or కల్యాణాసుకు.

కంపు kampu. [Skt.] n. A smell వాసన. A stink దుర్గంధము. In ancient Telugu this denoted any scent, pleasant or not. P. i. 703. A. i. 87. కంపుకొట్టు *kampu-kottu*. v. n. To smell, to stink. కంపిరుగుడు or కంపుటిరుగుడు *kamp-iruguḍu*. n. The stinking ఇరుగుడు. See ఇరుగుడు. కంపుతుమ్మచెట్టు *kampu-tumma-cheṭṭu*. n. The field Mimosa tree. కంపునాగు *kampu-nāgu*. n. The fetid coluber, a stinking kind of snake. కంపెలుక *kamp-eluka*. n. The musk rat. చుంచు.

కంబడి Same as కంబళి. (q. v.)

కంబము kambamu. [from Skt. స్తంభము] n. A pillar or post. The stem of a tree. దివ్వెకంబము a candlestick. కంబమయ్య or కంబమునాయుడు *kambam-ayya*. n. The god Narasimha who manifested himself to హిరణ్యకశిపు in a pillar. See ప్రహ్లాదచరిత్ర. కంబవల్లి *kamba-valli*. n. Worship of a pillar performed on the last day of an ఉపనయన ceremony. కంబబాణములు *kamba-bāṇamulu*. n. Fireworks fixed on posts.

కంబరునారు kambaru-nāḍu. [Tel.] n. Coir, rope. నారు.

కంబళము or కంబళి kambaḷamu. [Skt.] n. A rug, a blanket: (usually black:) కంబళివలెనల్లని as black as a blanket. రత్నకంబళము a particoloured rug. కంబళికర్ర *kambaḷi-karra*. n. A variegated yellow timber, like satin wood. కంబళిపండు *kambaḷi-panḍu*. A mulberry. కంబళిపురుగు *kambaḷi-purugu*. n. A hairy caterpillar. వాడు ఒక కంబళిపురుగు he is a wretch.

కంబాయి kambāyi. [Tel. from *Cambay*.] n. A kind of cotton cloth.

కంబాలాట kambāl-āṭa. [Tel.] n. A kind of game played by girls. బాలుకస్తంభాలాట.

కంబి kambi. [Tel.] n. Wire: A bar.

కంబు kambu. [Tel.] n. The grain named *Holcus spicatus*: called in Hind. Bajra. సజ్జలు.

కంబువు kambuvu. [Skt.] n. A large shell or conch, pearly white and marked with three ridges across the inner tube. కంబుకంఠి or కంబుగ్రీవ *kambu-kanṭhi*. adj. Fair throated: having a neck as beautiful as a shell.

కంసము kamsamu. [Skt.] n. Bell metal. కంచు.

కంసర or కంసల kamsara. [Tel.] n. Smithery; working in gold: adj. Of the goldsmith caste. కంసలది a woman of that caste. కంసలపని the business of a goldsmith.

కంసారాతి kams-ārāti. [Skt.] n. Slayer of Kamsa, an epithet of Krishṇa.

కంసాలి or కంసాలవాడు kamsāli. [Tel.] n. A goldsmith or silversmith.

కకపాల kaka-pāla. [Tel.] n. A recluse's bag. సన్యాసియొక్క సంచి, కకుపాల.

కకపిక or కకవిక or కకాపికలు kaka-pika. [Tel.] n. Tumult, uproar. కకపికలుగా tumultuously. కకపికలుచేయు to brawl, make an uproar. అల్లరి, గద్దర.

కకుత్తు or కకుదము kakuttu. [Skt.] n. A bull's hump. R. vii. 174.

కకుప్, కకుభ్ *kakup.* [Skt.] n. An *airt* or quarter of heaven. దిక్కు.

కకుభము *kakubhamu.* [Skt.] n. A certain tree మద్దిచెట్టు. (q. v.)

కక్క *kakka.* [Tel.] n. Papa; daddy. Also (vulgarly) flesh, meat; also (childishly) betel nut, dirt, a nasty thing.

కక్కపాలె Same as కకపాలె. (q. v.)

కక్కర, కెక్కర *kakkara.* [Tel.] n. The demoiselle crane, *Anthropoides virgo*, ఓదారుకు. **కక్కరకోడి** *kakkara-kōḍi.* n. The painted Partridge, *Francolinus pictus.* **కక్కర జిన్నాయి** *kakkara-jinnāyi.* The spotted Munia, *Uroloncha punctulata.* (F. B. I.)

కక్కరము *kakkaramu.* [Tel.] adj. Hard, or sharp కరుకు. n. Hardness.

కక్కసము *kakkasamu.* [Tel. for కర్కశము] n. Rigidity, hardness, harshness, hardship, trouble, సంకటము. బాధ. కాఠిన్యము, మనఃక్లేశము. కక్కసములాడు to be rude or cruel. కక్కసపు గుర్రము a stubborn horse. కక్కసపెట్టు to be harsh, to behave cruelly. కక్కసపడు to suffer pain బాధపడు, సంకటపడు. **కక్కసించు** *kakkasiñtsu.* v. a. To beset, harass: to plague. బాధించు. సంకటపరచు. ఆ రూకలకై నన్ను కక్కసించినాడు he harassed me for payment.

కక్కించు *kakkiñtsu.* [Tel.] v. t. To make one vomit. వానివద్ద ఆ రూకలను కక్కించినాను I made him disgorge the money.

కక్కిసచెట్టు *kakkisa-cheṭṭu.* [Tel.] n. A tree called *Posoqueria uliginosa.* Rox. i. 712.

కక్కు *kakku.* [Tel. from కరుకు] n. A notch, roughness: కక్కులు dents, notches: teeth: the rough part of a millstone or of a saw; the toothed part of a file, sickle, or saw. కళ్లెపుకక్కులు teeth of a horse's bit. **కక్కుపెట్టు** *kakku-peṭṭu.* v. t. To set or sharpen a saw, &c. **కక్కువేయు** *kakku-vēyu.* v. t. To roughen, or set (a saw or millstone.)

కక్కు *kakku.* [Tel.] v. a. To vomit. **కక్కు** *kakku.* n. Vomiting: the thing vomited. **కక్కుడు** *kakkuḍu.* n. Vomiting.

కక్కుతెవులు *kakku-tevulu.* Bilious vomiting.

కక్కురితి, కక్కూర్తి *kakkuriti.* [Tel.] n. Want, defect, a whim, idle desire. లోభము. Hard necessity కష్టము, ఇబ్బంది. పొట్ట కక్కూర్తికై for want of food. కక్కూర్తిగా Absurdly, shamefully, hard beset. కక్కూర్తిగాడు one who is in great want.

కక్కువాయి *kakku-vāyi.* [Tel. కక్కు=కరుకు] n. Whooping cough. కాసరోగవిశేషము.

కక్కూర్తి See కక్కురితి.

కెక్కెర *kakkera.* [Tel.] n. A crane. See కక్కర.

కక్షపాలె Same as కకపాలె. (q. v.)

కక్షము *kakshamu.* [Skt.] n. An armpit చంక.

కక్ష్య *kakshya.* [Skt.] n. A belt మొలనూలు, పట్టె. The equator of the earth భూమధ్యరేఖ.

కగ్గము *kaggamu.* [from ఖడ్గము.] n. A sword.

కగ్గు *kaggu.* [Tel.] v. n. To shrink. To be tarnished. వెండికగ్గినది the silver is tarnished. **కగ్గించు** *kaggiñtsu.* v. a. To cause to be tarnished.

కగ్గులు *kaggulu.* [Tel.] n. Sparks. అగ్నికణములు, కగ్గులకాడు a fugitive. Also, (from కాడు a place) the anvil as "the place of sparks." కగ్గులకాటఁగలుపుట to ruin, to destroy. Kalah M. ii. 129.

కచము *kachamu.* [Skt.] n. A hair. వెండ్రుక.

కచిక్కున *kachikkuna.* [Tel.] adv. Slapdash, at once.

కచూరము *kachūramu.* [Skt.] n. A sort of perfume. The plant *Kæmpferia rotunda.*

కచేరీ or **కచ్చేరీ** *kachērī.* [H.] n. An office; cutchery, a place of public business. A public court. A nautch, the ceremony of dancing at a wedding, &c. కొలువుకూటము. కచేరీచేసినారు they had a party.

కచోరము *kachōramu.* [Skt.] n. A plant called Zedoary, *Curcuma zedoaria.* పడీ గ్రంథి.

కచ్చ *kaṭṭsa.* [Tel.] n. A truss. The tuck of cloth, or modesty piece between the legs. గోచి. **కచ్చడము** *kaṭṭsaḍamu.* n. A tuck or truss. గోచి. A large strong cart. కచ్చడపు బండి. ఇనుప కచ్చడాలు కట్టినాడు he was rigorously chaste. Manu. ii. 82.

కచ్చరము *kachcharamu.* [Skt.] n. Dirt, foulness. మయిల.

కచ్చా *kachchā.* [H.] a. Unripe, raw; not good, rough, base. పండని, నీచమైన. కచ్చా సేరు the baser sort of సేరు. కచ్చామనిషి a mean fellow.

కచ్చి *kachchi.* [Tel.] n. A weaver సాలెవాడు. An interstice where a stick is inserted in a warp. కొయ్యలను పడుగునందు చొప్పించే సందు. **కచ్చికొట్టు** *kachchi-koṭṭu.* v. t. To geld. adj. Gelded. కచ్చిచేసిన గుర్రము a gelding.

కచ్చించు *kachchintsu.* [Tel.] v. n. To be raged, to be angry. v. a. To move a piece at chess. To tuck up a cloth కచ్చకట్టు. **కచ్చింపు** *kachchimpu.* n. A move at chess, &c. Also fierceness, emotion. మచ్చరత్వము.

కచ్చిక *kachchika.* [Tel.] n. A burnt cake of dried dung. కాలిన పిడకతునక.

కచ్చితము *kachchitamu.* [Tel.] adj. Strict, correct, exact ఎచ్చుతక్కువలులేక సరిగానున్న.

కచ్చు *kaṭṭsu.* [Tel.] v. t. To move a piece at chess కచ్చించు. To stick out, project. **కచ్చు** n. Stench. The washings of rice. Pride దంభము. గర్వము. "A bunch of flowers. పూగుత్తి, పూబంతి." **కచ్చులాడి** *kaṭṭsu-lāḍi.* n. A jilt, jade, flirt దాంభికురాలు. **కచ్చులు** *kaṭṭsulu.* n. Splendour, glittering, lies, tawdry, frivolous excuses. మిథ్యలు. **కచ్చుకొను** *kaṭṭsu-konu.* v. a. To adhere, cleave, stick. To desire. ఆశించు. **కచ్చువాసాలు** *kaṭṭsu-vāsālu.* n. Rafters inserted in a beam.

కచ్చూరము Same as కచోరము and కచూరము.

కచ్చె *kachche.* [Tel.] n. A quarrel or fight. కచ్చెకు కాలుదువ్వు to bestir oneself for fighting. Lit. to paw the ground preparing for the fight.

కచ్చెర *kachchera.* [Tel.] n. Dirt, that falls from thatch.

కచ్ఛపము *kachchhapamu.* [Skt.] n. A tortoise. **కచ్ఛపి** *kachchhapi.* n. A female tortoise. adj. That which is made of tortoise shell, as a lute.

కచ్ఛము Same as కచ్చ. (q. v.)

కజాయము, కజ్జె, కజ్జెము, కజ్జికాయలు or **కజ్జాయము** *kazzāyamu.* [Tel.] n. A sort of sweet cakes. ఒకవిధమైన భక్ష్యము.

కజ్జలము *kajjalamu.* [Skt.] n. Lampblack. The black part of a wick. Collyrium or black paint for the eyes. కాటుక.

కజ్జా *kajjā.* [H.] n. A quarrel, dispute, altercation. జగడము. కజ్జాలకోరు a quarrelsome person. కల్లికజ్జాలు తెచ్చుకొను to pick quarrels without a cause.

కజ్జూరము *kazzūramu.* [Tel.] n. A date tree. ఖర్జూరము.

కట or **కటకటా** *kaṭa.* [Tel.] interj. Alas. అయ్యో! **కటకటంబడు** *kaṭakaṭambaḍu.* v. t. To feel pity జాలిపడు. To be angry కోపించు. To suffer pain బాధపడు.

కటకటాలు or **కటకటాకమ్ములు** *kaṭakaṭalu.* [Tel.] n. Rails, railings. ఇనుపకమ్ములు మొదలైనవానితో చేసిన అడ్డు.

కటకటమను *kaṭakaṭam-anu.* [Tel.] v. n. To be irritable. **కటకటాత్కారము** *kaṭa-*

kaṭāṭkāramu. n. Grinding the teeth. A. iii. 25.

కటకము *kaṭakamu.* [Skt.] n. A town or city. A capital రాజధాని. The town of Cuttack in Orissa. A ring for the wrist or ankle, a bracelet or anklet. కడియము, పాదకటకము. కళ్యాణకటకము the town of Kalyan. The side or ridge of a hill. కొండనడుము, పర్వతనితంబప్రదేశము.

కటకాముఖము *kaṭakā-mukhamu.* [Skt.] n. The position of the fingers of the right hand when drawing a bowstring. A. v. 150. Anirud. iii. 62.

కటపెట *kaṭa-peṭa.* [Tel.] n. Noise సందడి, ధ్వని. (An onomatopœic word.)

కటము *kaṭamu.* [Skt.] n. A mat: చాప. The temples of the head. చెక్కిలి. The hip మొల.

కటా *kaṭā.* [Tel.] Alas!

కటాక్షము *kaṭākshamu.* [Skt. కట+అక్షము.] n. A look; particularly, a glance or side look; a favourable look; (hence) grace, kindness. క్రూరకటాక్షము an angry glance. కటాక్షము *kaṭākshamu.* interj. You are very good! I thank you! కటాక్షించు *kaṭākshintsu.* v. a. To glance at, to view, to countenance or favour. కటాక్షించవలసినది be pleased to view this with a gracious eye.

కటాకటిగా *kaṭākaṭi-gā* [Tel.] adv. Hardly, with difficulty. అది కటాకటిగా సరిపోయినది. it was just enough.

కటారి or కటారు *kaṭāri.* [Tel.] n. A cross hilted dagger. కటారిగాడు one who carries a dagger. కటారికత్తె a woman who has a dagger with her.

కటాహము *kaṭāhamu.* [Skt.] n. A large vessel: a boiler కడవ, కొప్పెర. బ్రహ్మాండకటాహము the globe of the universe, i. e., space.

కటి *kaṭi.* [Skt.] n. The hip or haunch. మొల. కటిచక్రము the loins, the hips. కటితటము the hip. కటిద్వయము a pair of hips. పిరుదులు. T. ii. 23. కటిసూత్రము girdle. మొలత్రాడు. కటిస్థలము the posteriors.

కటిక or కటికి *kaṭika.* [Tel.] adj. Mere, quite, entire, total, downright, cruel, unfeeling, horrid. కటికపని butchery. కటిక చీకటి utter or thick darkness. నిన్నంతా నేను కటికపస్తు ఉంటిని all yesterday I was absolutely starving. కటిక్కన or కటిక్కున *kaṭikkana.* adv. Sharply, smartly, without making any allowance. కటిక or కటికవాడు *kaṭika.* n. A butcher. మాంస మమ్మువాడు.

కటిత్రము *kaṭitramu.* [Skt.] n. The cavity of the loins, the loins. మొల.

కటుకరోహిణి *kaṭuka-rōhiṇi.* [Skt.] n. Black hellebore, a purging medicine. Ainslie, ii. 310.

కటుక్కను *kaṭukkanu.* [Tel. కటుక్కు + అను] v. t. To crackle (as a nut when broken.)

కటుమరలు or కటుమోరలు *kaṭu-maralu.* [Tel.] n. The cheek bones. చెక్కిళ్లమీది భాగములు, హనువు. కటుమోరలు ఉబ్బుగాగల having high cheek bones.

కటువు *kaṭuvu.* [Skt.] adj. Pungent in taste. కారము. Hard, unpleasant ఇంపుగాని. R. v. 167. కటూక్తి a hard word.

కటోలవీణ *kaṭōla-vīṇa.* [Tel.] n. A stringed musical instrument like the vīṇa. మాలవీణె, కిన్నెర.

కట్ట *kaṭṭa.* [Tel.] interj. Alas! కటకటా, కట్టా.

కట్ట *kaṭṭa.* [Tel. from కట్టు] n. A bank or shore; a dam or embankment. A bundle or pack. నీరుకట్ట a certain water snake, thick, black and harmless. కొంటె పాడెకట్ట a reprobate, a foul mouthed wretch. "కట్టలుకట్టి" (BD. v. 132.) In crowds. గుంపులుగూడి.

కట్టకడ *kaṭṭa-kaḍa.* [Tel. కడ+కడ.] adv. At the very end. See కడ.

కట్టడ *kattada.* [Tel.] n. Order, rule, custom. నియమము. Arrangement, manner, mode తీరు. కావలికట్టడలు or కట్టళ్లు routine or order of guards. మర్యాద. **కట్టడచేయు** *kattada-chēyu.* v. n. To ordain, command, enact, to lay down a rule. ఆజ్ఞాపించు.

కట్టడము *kattadamu.* [Tel.] n. A building or edifice.

కట్టనము *kattanamu.* [Tel.] n. A gift, a present. కానుక. Tying up బంధనము.

కట్టా *katta.* [Tel.] interj. Alas! See కటకటా and కట్ట.

కట్టాణి *kattani.* [Tel.] adj. Fine, first class; కట్టాణిముత్తెము a matchless pearl. See అణి. **కట్టాణిగుండ్లు** *kattani-gundlu.* n. A necklace of small gold beads.

కట్టావి *kattavi.* [Tel.] n. Steam, moisture collected on the lid of a kettle. Stifling heat.

కట్టించు *kattintsu.* [Tel. from కట్టు] v. a. To cause to tie or build. To get built, to have one bound.

కట్టిక or **కట్టికవాడు** *kattika.* [Tel.] n. A macebearer. వెండిబెత్తమువాడు.

కట్టిడి *kattidi.* [Tel. కట్టు+ఇడి] adj. Cruel, merciless; hard. **కట్టిడితనము** *kattiditanamu* n. Cruelty. కట్టిడులు cruel wretches.

కట్టిడు *kattidu.* [Tel.] n. A butcher. BD. VII. 915.

కట్టు *kattu.* [Tel.] v. n. To cease or stop, gather or form as clouds or a boil, or lump; to be with young (used of animals.) భేది కట్టినది the diarrhoea ceased. మబ్బులుకట్టినవి clouds have gathered. నెత్తురు పెల్లువకట్టినది there was a gush of blood. వానికి దెబ్బతగిలి నెత్తురుకట్టినది he received a contusion from a blow. గడ్డలుకట్టిన congealed, become hard. తూటుకట్టినది there is a hole formed.

కట్టు *kattu.* [Tel.] v. a. To tie, bind. బంధించు. To wear, as clothes. ధరించు. To connect, affix, attach. To store up, to lay by. కూడబెట్టు. "క॥ ముకొకట్టిన కర్మఫలంబులు పెట్టనభోగిం పకుండ పేర్చుటెఱుమజాల్." భార. అది. v. To build, erect. నిర్మించు. To fascinate, charm, bewitch. To fabricate, compose, or put a story together. కల్పించు. కట్టుకథ a mere fiction or fable. To impute a sin or offence. దానికి రంకుకట్టిరి they charged her with adultery. తప్పుకట్టు to find fault with, to lay blame on నేరముమోపు. నడుముకట్టు to gird up the loins or be prepared. కనుకట్టువిద్య jugglery, legerdemain. తోటకు నీళ్లుకట్టు to water a garden. గాయముకట్టు to dress a wound. బండికట్టు to get ready a carriage. కత్తికట్టు to put on one's sword or arm oneself. రూకలుకట్టు to pay money. మగ్గములకు పన్ను కట్టినారు they fixed a tax on looms. విలుకట్టు to strike a balance. ధరకట్టు to set a price. పద్యము కట్టు to compose a verse. ఓడకు వాపకట్టు to set sail. వాకట్టు strike dumb by spells, &c. ఈ మాటను కట్టివిడిచినారు they fabricated this story or scandal. దోవకట్టు to stop up the road. దోవకట్టి కొట్టినారు they lay in ambuscade and plundered the wayfarers. కడుపుకట్టు to restrain the appetite. కట్టని (neg. p.) Unbuilt or unbound. కట్టని కల్లుకోట a rock fortress not built with hands. కట్టనిగూడు (P. i. 545.) a natural nest, not constructed.

కట్టు *kattu.* [Tel.] n. A tie, bond, band. A bandage, a knot బంధము, ముడి. A rule, regulation, law. నిబంధనము, నిర్బంధము. A tax or duty. Fascination. వాకట్టు striking dumb. Soil, place ప్రదేశము. ఇసుకకట్టు sandy soil. System, fashion, mode or plot, device. కట్టుగా మాట్లాడు to speak by rule or consistently. A strike. వారు కట్టుకట్టినారు they struck work. Form, shape. Prohibition, restriction, a charm, an enchantment. మితి. A streak. నూనూగు మీసకట్టు the line of his budding whiskers. The hoop or band of a bucket, the tire of a wheel. The water in which any kind of pulse is boiled except rice. ఉలవకట్టు

boilings of horse gram. Season, weather, part of the year. ఋతువు. శీతకట్టు the cold season. A forged coin. సీసకట్టు రూపాయి a leaden rupee. తెండికట్టు a silvered coin. జాతికట్టు the tie of kindred, the custom of the caste. మంత్రకట్టు fascination, charming by spells. నడికట్టు a waistband or girdle, నీరుకట్టు a stoppage of urine. వలకట్టు a weir in a river, posts to fasten a net to. ఈ యింటిలో ముందరికట్టు పెద్దది వెనకటికట్టు చిన్నది the front of this house is larger than the back rooms.

కట్టుక *kaṭṭuka.* [Tel.] n. A miscarriage గర్భస్రావము.

కట్టుకంబము Same as కట్టుగుంజ. (q. v.)

కట్టుకమ్మ *kaṭṭu-kamma.* [Tel.] n. A written agreement.

కట్టుకొంగు *kaṭṭu-kongu.* [Tel.] n. That part of a female's garment, which she ties round her waist. కోకచెంగు.

కట్టుకొను *kaṭṭu-konu.* [Tel.] v. a. 1. To build, to bind, to wear or put on. చీరకట్టుకొన్నాడు he put on his cloth. See కట్టు. 2. To incur (blame or sin) ఇంతపాపము కట్టుకోవలసినదా shall we incur so great a sin? పుణ్యము కట్టుకొను to acquire merit. 3. To marry. దాన్ని కట్టుకొన్నాడు he married her. 4. To conquer. To appropriate, take possession of. వారిదేశమంతా తాను కట్టుకొన్నాడు he conquered all their territories. చేతులు కట్టుకొనుట to fold the hands respectfully. అప్పులు కట్టుకొన్నాడు he took the debts upon him. నూరుకట్టుకొను to refrain from eating.

కట్టుకొమ్మ *kaṭṭu-komma.* [Tel.] n. An embankment, a dyke. ఆనకట్ట.

కట్టుకొయ్య *kaṭṭu-koyya.* [Tel.] n. A tying post, the pole of a plough. నాగటి మేడి.

కట్టుకోక *kaṭṭu-kōka.* [Tel.] n. Ordinary clothes. నన్ను కట్టుకోకతో తెచ్చినారు they brought me just as I was.

కట్టుగడ *kaṭṭu-gaḍa.* [Tel.] n. A store, that which is stored up. చేర్చిపెట్టిన ధాన్యము మొదలైనది. కట్టుగడచేయు to lay up in store. కట్టుగడసరుకులు goods in store. కట్టుగడగుడ్డ cloth that is injured by time while unsold.

కట్టుగుంజ *kaṭṭu-gunza.* [Tel.] n. A post to tie cattle to.

కట్టుగొర్రె *kaṭṭu-gorre.* [Tel.] n. A sheep bound for slaughter.

కట్టుదొన *kaṭṭu-dona.* [Tel.] n. A small tank or cistern కొలను.

కట్టుపకాసు *kaṭṭu-pakāsu.* [Tel.] n. A steady man అచలుడు.

కట్టుపడు *kaṭṭu-paḍu.* [Tel.] v. i. To be tied, to be bound by. To be subject to బద్ధమగు. న్యాయమునకు కట్టుపడి being tied down to justice. **కట్టుపాటు** *kaṭṭu-pāṭu.* n. System, regulation, a code, a byelaw. నిబంధనము. **కట్టుపాటుచేయు** *kaṭṭu-pāṭu-chēyu.* v. a. To ordain.

కట్టుపోతు *kaṭṭu-pōtu.* [Tel.] n. A wizard or necromancer.

కట్టుబండి *kaṭṭu-banḍi.* [Tel.] n. A well equipped carriage. సకల పరికరసహితమైన బండి.

కట్టుబట్ట *kaṭṭu-baṭṭa.* [Tel.] n. A garment. కట్టుబట్టతో విడిచినారు they left him with the skirt on his back. కట్టుబట్టతో పారిపచ్చి నాడు he escaped with nothing but the clothes on his back.

కట్టుబడి *kaṭṭu-baḍi.* [Tel.] n. A settlement: as of permanent revenue. కట్టుబడిబంట్రోతు a serf, a settler; a feudal retainer, who is supported by land settled upon him. a village servant. కట్టుబడిపొలము land assigned to a serf in fee. కట్టుబడి మాన్యము the land assigned to such an officer in perpetuity.

కట్టుమట్టు or **కట్టుముట్టు** or **కట్టు మొదలు** *kaṭṭu-maṭṭu.* [Tel.] n. A stall in a stable. సర్వాదులకుకట్టుచోటు. Place of abode. ఆనికి పట్టు. An arrangement ఏర్పాటు.

కట్టుమాను *kaṭṭu-mānu*. [Tel.] n. A float of timber, a raft. తెప్ప.

కట్టువ *kaṭṭuva*. [Tel.] n A hedge. కంచె.

కట్టువర్గము *kaṭṭu-vargamu*. [Tel. from కట్టు.] A wardrobe or set of clothes.

కట్టె *kaṭṭe*. [Tel.] n. A stick or staff, a piece of wood, fire-wood. నీరుకట్టె a harmless water snake. అడ్డకట్టె a fife. నిడుపుకట్టె a flute. వరాహకట్టె a brush made of hog's bristles. కట్టె *kaṭṭe*. adj. Hard, harsh. కట్టెబుద్ధి a dry or hard disposition. వానికి కట్టెఒళ్లు he is lean but sinewy. కట్టెవిరిచి నట్టుగా severely, rigidly. కట్టెవిరుపుమాటలు severe language.

కట్టెచీమ *kaṭṭe-chīma*. [Tel.] n. A large black ant.

కట్టెడ *kaṭṭeḍa*. [Tel.] n. A kind of snake. కట్లపాము.

కట్టెపండు *kaṭṭe-paṇḍu*. [Tel.] n. Tamarind, with the stone in it.

కట్టెపాపర *kaṭṭe-pāpara*. [Tel.] n. The self planting leaf, indented at the edges and having a seed in each notch.

కట్నము *kaṭnamu*. [Tel.] n. A present giving to a ruler, or given by relations to each other at a marriage, &c. A fee, a gift. కట్నము చదివించుట to proclaim the amount of contributions.

కట్యము *kaṭyamu*. [Tel.] n. A title or name of honour. కట్యపువాడు a herald or crier. కట్యముచెప్పు to proclaim a title.

కట్రాయి *kaṭrāyi*. [Tel.] n. A flagged floor, a floor laid or paved with stone. A. ii. 54. A stall, stable.

కట్ల *kaṭla*. [Tel.] Affix. At (denoting either place or season). తెల్లవారకట్ల in the morning. ఎదురుకట్ల in front.

కట్లగుదియ *kaṭla-gudiya*. [Tel.] n. A club with bands or rings round it. An iron shod, cudgel. ముసుండి.

కట్లతీగె *kaṭla-tīge*. [Tel.] n. A plant called *Cissampelos Hexandria*. పాసతీగె.

30

కట్లదండ *kaṭla-daṇḍa*. [Tel.] n. A necklace of alternate rows of black and gold beads.

కట్లపురుగు or **కట్లపాము** *kaṭla-purugu*. [Tel.] n. A viper or venomous snake barred with black stripes, Russell's viper. (Russell plate xxxv.) Cobra Manilla.

కట్లబల్ల *kaṭla-balla*. [Tel.] n. A camp table or stool.

కట్లమారి *kaṭla-māri*. [Tel.] adj. A thing that is protected by bars of wood or metal కట్లకలది.

కట్లసొర్ర *kaṭla-sorra*. [Tel.] n. A kind of fish, *Galeocerdo rayneri*. (F. B. I.)

కట్లి *kaṭli*. [Tel.] n. A dooly or litter. మంచ పుడోలి.

కట్లు *kaṭlu*. [Tel.] n. The plural of కట్టు. **కట్లు** or **కట్లు** n. Weights, particularly those used by goldsmiths. బంగారుతూనిక గుండు. Plu. కట్లులు.

కట్లెగడ్డిచెట్టు *kaṭle-gaḍḍi-cheṭṭu*. [Tel.] n. A plant, *Chrysopogon aciculatus* చెకర. (Watts.)

కఠము *kaṭhamu*. [Skt.] n. Voice. కంఠస్వరము.

కఠారము or **కఠారి** *kaṭhāramu*. [Skt.] n. A cross hafted dagger. కత్తి, బాకు.

కఠినము *kaṭhinamu*. [Skt.] adj. Solid, hard, severe, difficult, cruel, inflexible. వాడు బ్రతుకడము కఠినము it is hard for him to survive.

కఠిల్లు *kaṭhillu*. [Skt.] v. t. To produce a crackling sound as in striking with a whip.

కఠోరము *kaṭhōramu*. [Skt.] adj. Hard, solid, severe, rigid. కట్టి.

కడ *kaḍa*. [Tel.] n. A place, quarter, or direction. దిక్కు, పార్శ్వము. The end, extremity అంతము. Distance దూరము. Proximity, సమీపము. ఇరుగడ on both sides. కట్టకడ at the very end. కడకు at last చివరకు. నెలకడ dry ground. వరకడ a neighbouring field. తలకడ a pillow, being the place of head. చెట్టుకడ at the tree. అతని కడకు వచ్చిరి they came to him. కడ adj. Last. అంత్యము. కడసారి the last time. కడ (affix) By, near, at. In the hands or possession of. అది నాకడనున్నది I have it by me. వాని పాదాలకడ పడినారు they fell down at his feet మావాండ్లకడ ఆ మర్యాదకద్దు it is the custom with us, or among us. పొద్దుపోద్దుకడ at sunset. పెందలకడ early. రేపకడ in the morning. కడకుపోవు or కడగాపోవు *kaḍaku-pôvu*. To be menstruous. కడకన్ను *kaḍa-kannu*. n. The corner of the eye. క్రేగన్ను, కటాక్షము. కడకంటచూచు *kaḍakanṭa-tsûtsu*. v. n. To glance, view sidelong, to look askance. కడకొరవి *kaḍa-koravi*. n. A fire brand not quite burnt up కాలగా మిగిలిన కట్టె. కడగా *kaḍa-gā*. adv. Aside, away. కడలేని *kaḍa-lêni*. adj. Endless. కడవాడు *kaḍa-vāḍu*. n. A stranger అన్యుడు. The last male child కనిష్ఠుడు. కడసారి *kaḍa-sāri*. adj. & adv. Last, the last time.

కడ *kaḍa*. [Tel.] An affix. (Added to the roots of some verbs it forms nouns or adjectives;) రాకడ arrival, coming. పోకడ going. తేరుకడ settlement. మనుకడ (from మను to live) lifetime.

కడక or కడంక *kaḍaka*. [Tel. from కడగు q. v.] n. An attempt; courage, determination యత్నము, ధైర్యము. ఉద్రేకము, పూనిక.

కడకట్టు *kaḍa-kaṭṭu*. v. n. To scheme, to undertake యత్నించు.

కడగండ్లు *kaḍa-gaṇḍlu*. [Tel. కడ+కండ్లు.] n. Plagues, calamities, evils, dangers, afflictions, miseries, scrapes, troubles. కష్టములు, తొందరలు. శ్రమలు. నానాకడగండ్లుపడ్డారు they were exhausted or knocked up. వానికడగండ్లు పెట్టినారు they handled him roughly. కడగండ్లమారి a troublesome fellow కష్టశీలుడు.

కడగట్టు *kaḍa-gaṭṭu*. [Tel.] v. t. To fix, to settle, to determine నిర్ణయించు, ఏర్పాటుచేయు. కడగట్టురేఖలు *kaḍa-gaṭṭu-rêkhalu*. n. Outlines in drawing, boundaries.

కడగు or కడంగు *kaḍagu*. [Tel] v. n. To venture, dare. To strive or begin యత్నించు.

కడగొట్టు *kaḍa-goṭṭu*. [Tel.] adj. The youngest, the last కడపటి. కడగొట్టుబిడ్డ the last child born; the youngest of a house. v. i. To die చచ్చు. "గిట్టెన్ ఫల్గుణ్ డింక ముల్ కడగొట్టెన్." సా. i.

కడచేను *kaḍa-tsanu*. [Tel.] v. i. To die చచ్చు. To perish నశించు. To end, to be finished ముగియు. v. t. To leap across, to cross దాటు. కడచన్నపసిడి pure gold.

కడచిల *kaḍa-chila*. [Tel.] n. A linch pin.

కడచు or గడచు *kaḍatsu*. [Tel.] v. n. To elapse, pass గడచు. To exceed a limit. మేరమీరు, హెచ్చు. (Metaphorically) to die చచ్చు. To perish నశించు. v. t. To leap across, to cross దాటు. To pass (time), to finish. వానికి గడవకుండానున్నది they have nothing to live on. నాకు అన్నానికి గడవదు I have nothing to live on. ఇది లేకుండ నాకు గడవదు I cannot get on without this. కడవడు Same as కడచు.

కడతెగు *kaḍa-tegu*. [Tel.] v. i. To be finished సమాప్తమగు.

కడతేరు *kaḍa-têru*. [Tel.] v. n. To be concluded or finished. తీరు, సమాప్తమగు. To die చచ్చు. నన్ను కడతేరనివ్వడు he prevents me from succeeding. కడతేర్చు *kaḍa-têrtsu*. v. a. To relieve or save రక్షించు.

కడప or గడప *kaḍapa*. [Tel.] n. A threshold. A gateway. (Metaph.) a house.

కడపచెట్టు *kaḍapa-chettu*. [Tel.] n. *Barringtonia acutangula*, sometimes called the Indian Oak Tree (Watts.) కడంబము.

కడపట *kaḍapaṭa*. [Tel.] adv. At the end, at length. at last. తుదకు.

కడపల *kaḍa-pala.* [Tel.] n. The end. **కడపలి** *kaḍapali.* adj. Last, final, ulterior.

కడపు or **గడపు** *kaḍapu.* [Tel.] v. t. To put off, to send away without giving any thing ఇయ్యకపోవు. To kill చంపు. To drive తోలు. To let go విడుచు. కడపు చెయిక్కి a rudder. చుక్కాని.

కడమ *kaḍama.* [Tel.] n. The rest, remainder. శేషము. A deficit కొరత. Want, defect, deficiency. ఒక నరహా కడమ అయ్యెను there was one pagoda wanting. **కడమపడు** *kaḍama-paḍu.* v. i. To be wanting, to be deficient. కొరతపడు. న్యూనమగు.

కడముంత *kaḍa-munta.* [Tel.] n. A small pot. చిన్నముంత.

కడముట్టు *kaḍa-muttu.* [Tel.] v. i. To be finished, reach the end. సమాప్తమగు, తుద ముట్టు, ముగియు. To accrue to, to come to సిద్ధించు, కలుగు. **కడముట్టించు** *kaḍa-muṭṭintsu.* v. a. To finish.

కడయిల్లు *kaḍa-y-illu.* [Tel.] n. The last house. The next world, heaven. BD. iv.

కడలి *kaḍali.* [Tel.] n. The sea. పాలకడలి the sea of milk. కడలికూతురు Lakshmi. కడలిరేడు the god Varuṇa. కడలిచిన్న the moon. **కడలు** *kaḍalu.* n. A wave. అల.

కడలుకొను or **కడల్కొను** *kaḍalu-konu.* [Tel.] v. n. To gleam, to flash, flicker, as light. "చెక్కులకద్దములవలెకాంతి కడలుకొనగ" B. VIII. 450. The brilliancy of the ear-rings flashed over her polished cheeks. To increase or spread or extend. వ్యాపించు, కడల్కొత్తు. To spread వ్యాపించు.

కడవ *kaḍava.* [Tel.] n. A large water pot or earthen vase. పెద్దకుండ.

కడవటిటు *kaḍava-ṭiṭu.* [Tel.] n. A kind of drum వాద్యవిశేషము, తుడుము.

కడవసము or **కడాసము** *kaḍa-vasamu.* [Tel.] n. A dried skin or mat used by ascetics as a bed. కృష్ణాజినము, తోలు.

క॥ "కడవసములు తోలులు క
ప్పడములు నారలును గలుగ"
భార. అర. vii.

కడవెళ్లు *kaḍa-vellu.* [Tel.] v. n. To be finished, closed, ended. ముగియు. v. t. To cross దాటు. **కడవెళ్ల** *kaḍa-vella.* adv. Completely, throughout, everywhere.

కడవ్రత్తు or **కడవత్తు** *kaḍa-vottu.* [Tel.] n. The beam that lies along the top of the wall and sustains the roof.

కడాని *kaḍāni.* [Tel.] adj. Pure, fine, as gold. Bright, glittering. n. అపరంజి Pure gold.

కడామిచెట్టు *kaḍāmi-chettu.* [Tel.] n. The tree called *Nauclea Cadamba.* బొట్టుకడామి the name of a certain species.

కడారము *kaḍāramu.* [Skt.] n. Dark tawny colour పింగళవర్ణము.

కడాసము Same as కడవసము. (q. v.)

కడి *kaḍi.* [Tel.] n. A mouthful, a morsel. కబళము. పేడకడి cowdung. పెరుగుకడి curds. (plu. కళ్లు.) Smell వాసన. **కడగొను** *kaḍa-gonu.* v. i. To eat in mouthfuls కబళించు.

కడిఖండలు *kaḍi-khandalu.* [from Skt. ఖండ ఖండములు.] n. Bits, fragments. కడిఖండం బులుగా piecemeal.

కడిగించు *kaḍi-gintsu.* [Tel. from కడుగు.] v. a. To cause to wash.

కడితము or **కడితము** *kaḍi-tamu.* [Kan.] n. A folding account book formed of cloth covered with black paste and polished like a slate. On these leaves accounts are written with soap stone. బలపము.

కడితి *kaḍiti.* [Tel.] n. A sambur. కణుజు.

కడిది *kaḍidi.* [Tel.] adj. Extreme, great అధికము. Impossible అశక్యము. Difficult కఠినము. n. Danger అపద.

కడిమి *kaḍimi.* [Tel.] n. Greatness, excess. అతిశయము, ఆధిక్యము. Bravery, gallantry. పరాక్రమము. adj. Vast, great, brave. adv. Greatly, much. మిక్కిలి.

కడిమిచెట్టు See కదంబము.

కడిమిడి *kaḍimiḍi.* [Tel.] adj. Grassy పచ్చికగల (కేలు).

కడియము *kaḍiyamu.* [Tel.] n. A bracelet or anklet. కడియపుట్టు a kind of round ring-like cake చక్కిలము.

కడివెడు *kaḍi-veḍu.* [Tel. from కడవ.] n. A potful.

కడిపోవు *kaḍi-pōvu.* [Tel. కడి+పోవు.] v. i. To be spoiled చెడిపోవు. కడిపోని excellent, unspoiled. చెడని. P. iv. 225.

కడిసెచెట్టు *kaḍise-chettu.* [Tel.] n. A tree called *Cluytia Collina.* Rox. iii. 732.

కడు *kaḍu.* [Tel.] adv. Much, greatly. మిక్కిలి, అత్యంతము.

కడుకొను *kaḍu-konu.* [Tel.] v. i. To excel అతిశయించు. To rejoice తుష్టిపొందు.

కడుగు or **కడ్గు** *kaḍugu.* [Tel.] v. a. To wash, lave, cleanse. n. The water in which rice, &c., has been washed బియ్యము కడిగిన నీరు, కుడితి.

కడుదురు or **కణుదురు** *kaḍuduru.* [Tel.] n. A wild bee. కందిరీగ.

కడుపు or **కడ్పు** *kaḍupu.* [Tel.] n. The belly or stomach. వానికడుపు కాలుచున్నది he is very hungry; కడుపుకట్టుకొను to stint oneself, restrain one's appetite. కడుపుమంట heart burning, malice, envy. ఓర్వలేమి, ఈర్ష్య. వాని కడుపులోనిమాట the thoughts of his heart. నన్ను కడుపులో పెట్టుకొని పెంచెను he reared me tenderly. కడుపుతోనుండు to be pregnant or with child. కడుపుదిగినది she had a miscarriage. కడుపుదించు to effect miscarriage, to cause an abortion. వట్టికడుపు an empty or fasting stomach. పొత్తికడుపు the abdomen. కడుపు చల్లగానుండుట to be happy or blessed. కడుపునొప్పి belly ache, stomach ache. కడుపూద. (కడుపు+ఊద.) a cattle disease in which the belly is bloated; also, envy ఓర్వలేనితనము, ఈర్ష్య.

కడ్డాయము *kaḍḍayamu.* [Tel.] n. Compulsion, force: exaction: forcing people to pay the price set upon articles. బోరము, బలాత్కారము. వడ్లకడ్డాయము, ఉప్పుకడ్డాయము an order to receive grain or salt at a high price.

కడ్డి *kaḍḍi.* [Tel.] n. A stick, an ingot, bar of metal. A tube or catheter. ఫుటిక. నల్లకడ్డి చీరలు cloths with black edges. కడ్డివేయు to pass a catheter.

కణకు *kaṇaku.* [Tel.] n. A firebrand. కొరవి. Fire అంగారము.

కణగు Same as కడగు. **కణక** Same as కడంక.

కణజ *kaṇaja.* [Tel.] n. An embankment or dam.

కణజము *kaṇajamu.* [Tel.] n. A grain cellar.

కణజు or **కడజు** *kaṇazu.* [Tel.] n. A portico with a tiled roof. A wasp. కందిరీగ.

కణత or **కడత** *kaṇata.* [Tel.] n. The temples of the head, the part of the forehead that moves as the jaw moves.

కణము *kaṇamu.* [Skt.] n. A particle or atom. ఘర్మకణము a drop of sweat. అగ్నికణము a spark of fire. ఆనందబాష్పకణములు tears of joy.

కణయము *kaṇayamu.* [Tel.] n. A kind of javelin కంఠదజీవము; a kind of arrow బాణవిశేషము.

కణిక *kaṇika.* [Tel.] n. A bit, piece or stick. లక్కకణిక a stick of sealing wax. నల్లేరుకణిక a stick of the Nalleru plant. కణికరాయి a hard species of black and white marble.

కణితి *kaṇiti.* [Tel.] n. A sambur. కణుజు. Also, a lump, a bump, a wen. కంతి.

కణిసెము *kaṇisemu.* [Tel.] n. An ear of corn: ఎన్ను.

కణుజు *kaṇuju.* [Tel.] n. The deer called Sambur. *Cervus Hippelaphus.*

కణుదురు See కడుదురు.

కత *kata.* [from Skt. కథ.] n. A tale or story.

కతకము Same as చిల్లగింజ. (q. v.)

కతన katana. [Tel.] affix. By, through, on account of, for. కారణముచేత. వేగులకతన by means of spies.

కతము katamu. [Tel.] n. Cause, manner, reason, కారణము. Token, keep-sake, గురుతు. ఏమికతంబున for what cause. అట్టికతమున for that reason. తెగాకి రా గతమిచ్చి he gave a token that he would come soon.

కతాయించు katâyintsu. [Mahr.] v. t. To enter in an account. చేర్చు, ఎక్కించు, ఖాతాలుచేసికొను.

కతిపయ katipaya. [Skt.] adj. Some, a few కొన్ని.

కత్తరి kattari. [Tel.] adj. Of various colors, piebald. కత్తరావు a piebald cow. కత్తరి గుర్రము a piebald horse. కత్తరికలియు to be mixed up in confusion సంకరమగు.

కత్తరిల్లు. kattarillu. [Tel.] v. i. To move, shake చలించు.

కత్తళము kattaḷamu. [Tel.] n. Armour, mail. కత్తళీడు kattaḷîḍu. (కత్తళము+ఈడు) n. One who has put on armour.

కత్తలాని or కత్తళడు kattalâni. [Tel.] n. A black horse with white hoofs and tail.

కత్తి katti. [Tel.] n. A knife. A sword. తిసినకత్తివలె నిలిచినది she stood as a drawn sword. A measure of land, which differs in various districts. It is considered to be as much as a man can reap in one day. In the Government accounts a "cutty" is rated at 40 acres and 14 గుంటలు (q. v.) This phrase, which means a "sword of land" implies that this quantity of land was assigned to a family which furnished the feudal lord one fighting man. కత్తికట్టెదొర katti-kaṭṭe-dora. An officer, a gentleman who wears a sword. కత్తికాసు katti-kâsu. n. A carpenter's tool for squaring. కత్తిపిట్ట katti-piṭṭa. The Cuckoo called *Hierococcyx varius*. చిన్నకత్తిపిట్ట The Indian plaintive cuckoo, *Cacomantis passerinus*. (F. B. I.) కత్తికడి a basket in which a toddy drawer keeps his knives కుండ, పాని కత్తుల బుట్ట. కత్తిపీట katti-pîṭa. n. A large knife standing slantwise in a block of wood upon which vegetables are sliced. కత్తిబల్లెము katti-ballemu. A "sword spear," a scythe-like blade mounted as a spear.

కత్తిరించు kattirintsu. [Tel.] v. a. To cut or crop with scissors; కత్తెరతో కోయు. కత్తిరిల్లు kattirillu. v. i. To split, to be split భిన్నమగు.

కత్తివాటు katti-vâṭu. [Tel.] n. A cut with a knife.

కత్తివాతి అమ్ము katti-vâti-ammu. [Tel.] n. An arrow shaped like a sword. A semicircular arrow అర్ధచంద్రబాణము.

కత్తువ kattuva. [Tel.] n. A wooden spade with a triangular blade. A dam across a stream. A dam, mole or bank ఆనకట్ట.

కత్తె or కత్తియ katte. [Tel.] An affix. Maid, girl. పనికత్తె a servant girl. చెలికత్తె a play-mate among girls. కత్తెతనము katte-tanamu. n. Girlhood.

కత్తెము kattemu. [Tel.] n. An item in an account. అంశం అడ్డబదీ.

కత్తెర kattera. [Tel.] n. Scissors. The constellation or sign called కృత్తిక. The period of time when the sun is between the signs భరణి, రోహిణి and కృత్తిక. కత్తెర కాలు kattera-kâlu. n. The upright cross pieces of wood in a dooly or litter, that connect the bottom with the pole above. కత్తెరగడ్డము kattera-gaḍḍamu. n. A cropped beard. కత్తెరగాయము kattera-gâyamu. n. A certain kind of window కవాటవిశేషము. కత్తెరచీల kattera-chîla. n. A pin on which a lever acts. మీట ఆడే చీల. కత్తెరదొంగ kattera-donga. n. A cut purse. కత్తెరబావిలీలు kattera-bâvililu. n. An ornament of gold and gems worn by women near the top of the ear. కత్తెరయెండ kattera-yenḍa. n. Fierce heat. కత్తెరరాయి kattera-râyi. n. Marble; a kind of black stone, which is sonorous like metal. కత్తెరవాసములు *kattera-vāsamulu*. n. Bamboos arranged against each other like the blades of scissors.

కత్రి *katri*. [Tel.] n. A part or division of a game called ఇక్కిడి. ఈ. రా. vi.

కత్రించు Same as కత్తిరించు.

కథ *katha*. [Skt.] n. A book containing a legendary tale. ఇంచుకసత్యమైన కల్పిత ప్రబంధము. A story, tale, fable, chronicle: a riddle or puzzle. కథవేయు. v. n. To give a riddle to be solved. కథకుడు *katha-kuḍu*. n. A chronicler. A story teller కథచెప్పువాడు. కథనము *kathanamu*. n. Telling చెప్పడము. కథించు *kathintsu*. v. t. To tell, relate, narrate చెప్పు. "కథించుకొని కోలకయుండగ" హరి. ఈ. v. కథితము *kathitamu*. adj. Said, that which is said చెప్పబడిన.

కద *kada*. [Tel.] n. The barb of an arrow or of a fish hook. కద Interj. Is it not so: indeed. n. [from Skt. కథ.] వృత్తాంతము.

కదంబము or కదంబకము *kadambamu*. [Skt.] n. A mixture. మిశ్రము. An assembly, a collection గుంపు, సముదాయము. A garland of various flowers, a mixture of divers things, a miscellany. బాణకదంబకము a flight or cloud of arrows. నృపాలకదంబము an assembly of kings. A certain flowering plant called *Nauclea Cadamba*. కొడుకుల కడిమి. ఆవాలు. రుద్రాక్షకదంబము *Anthocephalus Cadamba* (Watts.) కదంబపొడి *kadamba-poḍi*. n. Pouncet. A fragrant powder compounded of various essences. కదంబించు *kadambintsu*. v. i. To be mixed మిళితమగు. To mix మిళితము చేయు.

కదనము *kadanamu*. [Skt.] n. A battle, combat, encounter. యుద్ధము.

కదన్నము *kadannamu*. [Skt.] n. Vile food, trash. చెడ్డకూడు.

కడపా *kaḍapa*. [H.] n. An agreement, a written bond. ఒడంబడిక, పత్రము. A counter agreement. కడపాబనాయించు to fabricate a counter lease.

కదపు Same as కదుపు.

కదము *kadamu*. [H.] n. A footstep, twelve inches. Trotting (as a horse does). కదము తొక్కు to trot (as a horse).

కదరము *kadaramu*. [Skt.] n. A kind of tree, the *Mimosa Catechu*. తెలిచండ్ర, అంతరతామర. A saw రంపము.

కదలము or కదళి *kadalamu*. [Skt.] n. A plantain tree.

కదలు or కదులు *kadalu*. [Tel.] v. n. To move, stir, move from or removed, to totter or shake, to be displaced or dislocated. To attempt, to try యత్నించు. To set out on a journey. ప్రయాణమగు. మోకాటి చిప్ప కదిలినది the knee joint is dislocated. n. Movement చలనము. Trial యత్నము. కదలుడు *kadaluḍu*. n. A journey ప్రయాణము. కదలించు, కదలుచు or కదల్చు *kadalintsu*. v. t. To move, stir, shake, jog: to mention కదలునట్లు చేయు, ప్రస్తావించు. కదలిక *kadalika*. n. Motion, stirring. చలనము. Trial, attempt. యత్నము.

కదించు Same as కదియించు.

కదియు *kadiyu*. [Tel.] v. n. To approach, to come near దగ్గరకువచ్చు, సమీపించు. To become equal. సమానమగు. v. a. To encounter, to meet, join చేరు. కదిసికొంచిన కార్యనాశనము to begin and then retreat ruins all. కదియించు or కదించు *kadiyintsu*. v. a. To join, to cause to join or unite కదియజేయు.

కదిర *kadira*. [Tel.] n. A slender pipe-shaped fish.

కదిలించు Same as కదలించు.

కదీము *kadīmu*. [H.] n. An old servant, an old inhabitant. పాతకాపు. కదీములు the old and hereditary cultivators of a village మిరాశీకాపులు.

కదుకు *kaduku.* [Tel.] v. n. To eat. BD. vii. 1888.

కదుకొను *kadukonu.* [Tel. కదుము+కొను.] v. n. To be proud అతిశయించు.

కదుగు *kadugu.* [Tel.] v. n. To doubt, fear, hesitate. BD. vii. 58.

కదుపు *kadupu.* [Tel.] n. A herd of cattle or flock of sheep. సమూహము, మంద. ఎనుపకదుపు a herd of buffaloes. పందికదుపు a herd of swine. లేటికదుపు a herd of antelopes. గూబకదుపు a flock of owls. చిలకకదుపు a flock of parrots, తేటికదుపు a swarm of bees.

కదుపు or **కదపు** *kadupu.* [Tel.] v. n. To move. To cause to move. కదులునట్లు చేయు.

కదుము *kadumu.* [Tel.] n. A lump, a swelling, a bump. వాపు, a tumour. గడ్డ. v. a To encroach upon, to occupy ఆక్రమించు. To push away. To rebuke, check. కదుముకొను to struggle.

కదురు *kaduru.* [Tel.] n. A spindle, an awl. A sort of fish.

కదురు *kaduru.* [Tel.] v. n. To extend, spread. విస్తరించు. కలగు. v. a. To frighten. బెదిరించు. సిగ్గుగదిరెడు చూడ్కి eyes full of shame. "మేనబెళ్లిపెను గదిరినదివ్యగంధము." P. iii. 36. In M. Dro. i. 326. కోపంబుగదుర, అనగా కోపమతిశయించగా In T. iii. 88. 'కదురు' అనగా కలుగుట. In Dassav. iv. 250. "శ్వేతాశ్వముల్ కహాకహానినదము గదురుకొనిన." అనగా బెదిరించి.

కదులు See కదలు.

కదుష్ణము *kadushnamu.* [Skt. కత్+ఉష్ణము.] n. Gentle warmth. కొంచెముకాక. adj. Warm.

కదే Same as గదా. (q. v.) (This is used in speaking to a woman.)

కద్దు *kaddu.* [Tel. for కలదు.] It is; it happens usually. It is the case.—See కలుగు.

అట్లా చెప్పుటకద్దు it is usual to say so. అట్లా ఉండుటకద్దు it frequently is the case. అమావాస్య రెండుదినములు కద్దనగా two days before new moon. (Lit. when they said, after two days it will be new moon). It is opposed to లేదు, thus కద్దులేదనక he neither said yes nor no.

కద్దుము *kaddumu.* [Tel.] adj. Thick, dense. దట్టము.

కద్రువ *kadruva.* [Skt.] n. The name of the mythological mother of serpents.

కనకన *kanakana.* [Tel.] adv. Blazingly, intensely, glowingly. తేజస్సుతో. కనకనలాడు or కనకనమను to glow, as a blazing fire. మిక్కిలి ప్రకాశించు.

కనకము *kanakamu.* [Skt.] n. Gold. "కనకంబునకును సౌరభ్యము కలిగినట్లు" (L. XIX. 332. "Marvellous as would be fragrance in gold: it is as strange as though gold were fragrant. (The Telugu poets frequently mention this fancy; that, were gold gifted with fragrance, it would be indeed perfect.)

"భూతిగస్త్రకేల పుట్టించెవాసన,
కనకము తనకేమి కల్లజేసె."

వేమన.

కనకాంగి *kanakāngi.* [Skt.] adj. Bright bodied. Golden-hued (woman). **కనకాంబరము** *kanak-ambaramu.* n. Gold cloth. The name of a beautiful yellow flower. **కనకాభిషేకము** *kanak-abhishekamu.* n. Lavishing wealth. Showering gifts.

కనగర్త *kanagarta.* [Tel] n. A kind of fish, a species of scomber. (Russell, plate 136.]

కనత్ *kanat.* [Skt.] adj. Bright, shining. Vasu. iv. 23.

కనపరాకు *kana-paraku.* [Tel.] n. A kind of arrow. గన్నెరాకులవంటి అలుగు. A. vi. 103.

కనమ or **కనుమ** *kanama.* [Tel.] n. A gap, opening, breach. A defile, pass. సందు, కొండలసందు, దోవ. A scar అమ్మవారుకనములుగల

వాడు one whose face is pitted with the small pox.

కనము or **కనముచెట్టు** *kanamu*. [Tel.] n. A tree called *Saccharum exaltatum*. Rox. i. 245.

కనముచేప *kanamu-chēpa*. [Tel.] n. A fish, a species of *Cyprinus*. Russell, plate 109.

కనరు *kanaru*. [Tel.] n. Acridity, tartness. Bitterness. కంచుగడ్డలోనగువానియందుండెడి దురద, నస, ఒగరు. adj. Unpleasant అసహ్యము.

కనలు *kanalu*. [Tel.] n. Anger. కోపము. A burning sensation. మంట. v. n. To be angry. కోపపడు. To burn, to give pain. మండు.

కనారిలు *kanārilu*. [Tel.] v. n. To be angry, కోపగించు.

కనాలు *kanālu*. [Eng.] n. A canal. కాలువ.

కనికరము *kanikaramu*. [Tel.] n. Kindness, compassion. దయ. Sorrow దుఃఖము.

క॥ "తనమీఁదనదయలేమికి,
కనికరమందుచును."
భల్లా. iii.

కనికరముంచు to be kind to, or favour.

కనిపించు *kanipinchu*. [Tel.] v. n. To seem, appear, be known, to come on. కడుపునొప్పి కనిపించిపండుకొన్నాడు a pain came on and he lay down. వానికి తలనొప్పికనిపించినది he has a headache. దానికి అమ్మవారు కనిపించినది she has got the small pox.

కనిపుతీగ *kanipu-tīga*. [Tel.] A plant called *Roxburghia gloriosoides*. Rox. ii. 234.

కనిపెట్టు *kani-pettu*. [Tel.] v. n. To wait, expect. ఎదురుచూచు. To watch, guard, tend. To find out, discover. మిమ్మును కనిపెట్టుకొని ఉండేవారు your dependants.

కనియు *kaniyu*. [Tel.] v. n. To be overripe మాగు. "ఎట్టిదిపప్పుడుంకనియగ బండియుండు." భార. అర. vii.

కనిష్ఠ *kanishtha*. [Skt.] n. A young sister. చెల్లెలు. The little finger చిటికెనవేలు. కనిష్ఠము the least. కనిష్ఠిక the little finger. కనిష్ఠుడు the youngest brother. కనిష్ఠురాలు the youngest sister.

కనిసిచేప *kanisi-chēpa*. [Tel.] n. A fish, a species of mullet. Russell, plate 181.

కనీనిక *kanīnika*. [Skt.] n. The pupil of the eye. నల్లగుడ్డు.

కనీయసి *kanīyasi*. [Skt.] n. A younger sister. **కనీయుడు** *kanīyuḍu*. n. A very low man మిక్కిలి అల్పుడు. A younger brother తమ్ముడు.

కనీసము *kanīsamu*. [from Skt. కనిష్ఠ.] adj. Smallest, least. అధమము.

కను *kanu*. [Tel.] n. The eye. See కన్ను. v. a. To see, perceive, observe. To know or understand. To bear or bring forth (young or fruit.) "నసలేఁగన." (A. v. 132.) bearing blossoms. To beget. నలుగురిని కన్నతండ్రి one who has four children. To experience, feel, enjoy. ఇందులో స్వర్గమును కన్నవారెవరు who among these has been to heaven. విమలతగనిరి they acquired holiness. కని/ (the past p.) is used adverbially; clearly, distinctly. ఆ సంగతినికని వ్రాసినాడు he wrote his letter with an eye to this point. కనిచెప్పు to specify clearly in words, to particularize. కనిగానమి the seeing and not perceiving. Oversight. Ila. i. 60.

కనుక, గనుక or **గనక** *kanuka*. [Tel.] adv. Therefore, seeing which, so, thereby.

కనుకట్టు or **కనికట్టు** *kanu-kattu*. [Tel.] n. Legerdemain జాలవిద్యావిశేషము.

కనుకని *kanu-kani*. [Tel.] n. Nervousness, సంభ్రమము.

క॥ దినదినమునకు గ్రహించెను
గనుకనియును ద్రపయునిరవకాశతబోలెన్.
కళా. vii.

కనుకను *kanu-kanu*. [Tel.] v. n. To be alert, to have one's senses about one. కర్తతంత్రిగాక కనుకనియుంటోప్పు. Vēma. i. 45.

కనుకలి *kanukali* [Tel.] n. Sight చూపు.

కనుకుట్టు *kanu-kuṭṭu.* [Tel.] n. An oppressor. బాధకుడు. **కనుకుట్టుదనము** *kanukuṭṭu-danamu.* n. Envy.

కనుకూలి *kanu-kūli.* [Tel.] n. Hire paid in kind, i. e., with part of the goods prepared by the workman.

కనుగవ or **కన్గవ** *kanu-gava.* [Tel.] n. A pair of eyes. కన్నులజత.

కనుగీటు *kanu-gīṭu.* [Tel.] v. a. To wink. n. A wink. Dasav. iv. 358.

కనుగుచేప *kanugu-chēpa.* [Tel.] n. A sort of fish.

కనుగుడ్డు *kanu-guḍḍu.* [Tel.] n. The eye-ball.

కనుగుపోతు *kanugu-pōtu.* [Tel.] n. A tailless peacock.

కనుగొను or **కనుంగొను** *kanu-gonu.* [Tel.] v. a. To see, observe, find out, discover, perceive. చూచు. To bring forth young. ప్రసవించు.

కనుచాటు *kanu-tsāṭu.* [Tel.] n. Being out of sight, privacy. కనుచాటుగానుండిరి they were in concealment. ఇది అంతా కాస్త కనుచాటుగా నుండవలెను this should be kept somewhat private.

కనుచీకటి *kanu-chīkaṭi.* [Tel.] n. Twilight.

కనుదోయి or **కందోయి** *kanudōyi.* [Tel.] n. A pair of eyes.

కనుపట్టు *kanu-paṭṭu.* [Tel.] v. n. To come to light, be perceived. గోచరమగు. To seem, look, appear. R. v. 163.

కనుపడు or **కనబడు** *kanu-paḍu.* [Tel.] v. n. To fall under the eye, appear, seem, come to light. **కనుపరచు** or **కనబరచు** *kanu-parutsu.* v. n. To shew, exhibit.

కనుపాప *kanu-pāpa.* [Tel.] n. The pupil of the eye. Lit. the baby (pupillus) that appears in the eye. కంటిలోనిప్రతిమ.

కనుపించు See కనిపించు.

కనుపు *kanupu.* [Tel.] n. A joint of the fingers, or toes, or of the sugar cane, &c. Same as గణుపు. (q. v.) **కనుపులగుండ్లు** *kanupula-gundlu.* n. A sort of bracelet. Suca I. 176.

కనుపుకొట్టు *kanupu-koṭṭu.* [Tel.] v. n. To scatter, defeat. చిందరవందరచేయు, యుద్ధాదులు చేయు. తునకలుచేయు. M. VII. i. 174.

కనుపెట్టు *kanu-peṭṭu.* [Tel.] v. n. Same as కనిపెట్టు.

కనుబంటి *kanu-banṭi.* [Tel.] n. A kind of owl. తెలుగుపక్షి. అముక్త vi.

కనుబడి *kanu-baḍi.* [Tel.] n. Prospect, capability: the productive power of land. Income, fruits, produce. ఉత్పత్తి. **కనుబాటు** *kanu-bāṭu.* n. Sight. దృష్టి. The evil eye దృష్టిదోషము, దిష్టి.

కనుబొమ్మ *kanu-bomma.* [Tel.] n. The eye-brow.

కనుబ్రాము or **కన్బ్రాము** *kanu-brāmu.* [Tel.] v. a. To delude. మాయచేయు, వంచించు.

కనుము Same as కనము. (q. v.)

కనుమబ్బు *kanu-mabbu.* [Tel.] n. Twilight, slight darkness.

కనుము *kanumu.* [Tel.] n. The day after a feast, such as the Pongal feast. మకరసంక్రమణమునకు అవలిదినము. పండుగమరునాడు. **కనుము** *kanumu.* n. A kind of grass. Rox. i. 409. కనువిల్లు A cross bow. M. VIII. ii. 284.

కనుమాయు or **కనుమొరగు** *kanu-māyu.* [Tel.] v. t. To deceive. వంచించు. **కనుమూసిగంటలు** *kanu-mūsi-ganṭalu.* n. The game called a blind man's buff.

కనురెప్ప *kanu-reppa.* [Tel.] n. The eyelid. కనురెప్పపాటులో in the twinkling of an eye. **కనురెప్పవెండ్రుకలు** The eyelashes.

కనువిచ్చు *kanu-vittsu.* [Tel.] v. n. To open the eyes. To open, as grain when boiled.

కనువినికి *kanu-viniki*. [Tel.] n. A snake. పాము, చక్షుశ్శ్రవము. (ఆం. iii.) (So called because it is supposed to hear through its eyes.)

కనువెచ్చ *kanu-veṭṭsa*. [Tel.] n. Slight heat. నులివెచ్చ.

కనుసన్న *kanu-sanna*. [Tel.] n. A sign with the eye: a wink.

కన్గంట *kangaṇṭa*. [Tel. కంటి+కంట.] adv. Right in the face, plainly. ప్రత్యక్షముగా.

కన్గవ See కనుకవ.

కన్న *kanna*. [Tel.] adj. (Contracted from కనిన who begot). "By birth" (a parent) as distinguished from పెంపుడు "by adoption." కన్నతండ్రి one's own father or natural father; కన్నతల్లి one's own mother; కన్నబిడ్డ a child by birth, not by adoption. కన్న (i. e., కనిన seen, perceived.) adj. Any, miscellaneous, indiscriminately taken, vile. కన్నకూడు any food that one could get. కన్నమాటలు vile language. కన్నవాడు anybody, without selection. కన్నవారు strangers, anybody. కన్నచోట anywhere. In Paraj. v. 46. కన్నదిక్కుగా in any way or direction, headlong. కాకి కన్నది తింటుంది the crow eats trash.

కన్న or కన్నా *kanna*. [Tel.] affix. Than. కంటె. దానికన్న యిది నల్లది this is blacker than that. దానికన్న యిది వేరు this is different from that. నీకన్న దొంగలేడు. there is no greater rogue than you.

కన్నగాడు *kanna-gāḍu*. [Tel. from కన్నము.] n. A house breaker.

కన్నడ *kannaḍa*. [Tel.] n. Disregard, neglect. ఉపేక్ష. కన్నడించు *kannaḍintsu*. v. a. To disregard. ఉపేక్షించు.

కన్నడము *kannaḍamu*. [Tel.] n. The Canara or Carnatic; a name including the Telugu and Canarese countries. Canarese language. కన్నడ అక్షరము the Canarese character. కర్ణాటకము. కన్నడికలశము *kannaḍi-kalaṣamu*. n. The 'blessed light' or holy candle. See ఆరతి. కన్నడి or కన్నడీడు *kannaḍi*. n. A native of the Canarese country. కర్ణాటదేశస్థుడు. Also, a contemner ఉపేక్షించువాడు.

కన్నపోవు *kanna-pōvu*. [Tel.] v. n. To be pierced through by a robber as a wall. కన్నము వేయబడు.

కన్నము *kannamu*. [Tel.] n. A hole made by burglars through a wall. సేలకన్నము a way dug under a wall by thieves. BD. v. 701. కన్నపుకత్తి *kannapu-katti*. n. A housebreaker's wrench. A sharpened bar of iron to bore a hole through a wall. కన్నపుముట్టు or కన్నకోల *kannapu-muṭṭu*. A crowbar used in digging such a hole; called in thieves' slang, a jemmy, betty, or a rook. కన్నముపెట్టు or కన్నమువేయు *kannamu-peṭṭu*. v. n. To commit burglary, to dig through a wall.

కన్నయ్య *kannayya*. [Tel.] n. A father by blood (as distinguished from an adopted father). Another meaning is in use. When parents fear an infant may die, they sometimes bore a crevice through the wall and put the babe through it: then they name their son కన్నయ్య "him of the cleft" as received directly from the deity.

కన్నర *kannara*. [Tel.] n. Catastrophe, misfortune. ఆపద. Sorrow, grief దుఃఖము. కన్నరి *kannari*. n. A sorrowful man దుఃఖితుడు.

కన్నలవు *kannalavu*. [Tel.] n. Disregard ఉపేక్ష. Vasu. iv.

కన్నవిటి *kannaviṭi*. [Tel. కన్ను+అవిటి.] adj. Blind. గుడ్డి, చీకు. n. A blind man. గుడ్డివాడు.

కన్నాకు *kannāku*. [Tel. కన్ను+ఆకు.] n. The spoke of a spinning wheel, which, being the last put in, keeps the rest all tight. The outside leaf in a bundle of betal leaves. The finishing bit or corner stone;

that which keeps all the rest right. A noble or excellent person. రక్షకుడు; ముఖ్యుడు, అగ్రేసరుడు. M. VI. i. 92.

కన్నాత kannāta. [Tel.] n. A hug or catch in wrestling. T. iii. 121. Ila. 1. 137. కన్నాతలాగిలు to try a fall in wrestling. (The various words about wrestling, given in ABA. ii. 393 are not explained in any book; and are not understood by wrestlers at the present day.)

కన్నిరు Same as కన్ను.

కన్నీరు kannīru. [Tel. కన్ను + నీరు.] n. Tears.

కన్ను or కను kannu. [Tel.] n. The eye. నేత్రము. Sight చూపు. An orifice, small hole or hollow రంధ్రము. The black mark in the middle of the parchment or of a drum. మద్దెలమీదిఅరువానిలోనుండు గుండ్రని నల్లగురుతు. A trace జాడ. The bush for box in a carriage wheel బండికన్ను. An arch or a span in a bridge వంతెనద్వారము. The eye-like spot in a peacock's train నెమలిపురికన్ను. The mesh of a net వలలోనిరంధ్రము. The eye or joint or knot in a cane or reed చెరుకులోనగువానిగణుపుకింది గుంట. చాటికన్ను the small end of the drum. కన్నువిచ్చు to open the eye. The abl. is కంటు thus కంటబడు to fall into the eye, to be in view. వానికి కండ్లు అగుపడవు he cannot see కన్నుకానపడనివాడు a blind man. కండ్లు తిరిగినవి I turned giddy. పెద్దకండ్లుచేయు to look angry. కన్నుఎఱ్ఱచేసికొను to make one's eyes inflamed with wrath. కన్నుగట్టు kannu-gattu. n. Fascination, deluding. కన్నుకట్టుట to delude, or blind the eyes. కన్నుకట్టువిద్య magic, legerdemain. The art of being invisible. కన్నుగవ or కన్నుదోయి A pair of eyes. కన్నునీరు or కన్నీరు tears. కన్నుద్రాము (R. 1. 107.) To evade, delude. కన్నుమూసిగంత a blindman's buff. కన్నుమూసి గంతకట్టినట్టు as though blind. కన్నుమొరగు or కనుమొరగు to delude వంచించు. కన్నులారచూచు to see with one's own eyes, view distinctly. కన్నువేయు to cast an eye on, to long for ఆశించు. కన్నులవిల్తుడు the sugar cane చెరకు. కన్నులవిలుకాడు. Cupid మన్మథుడు.

కన్నుతిరికి kannu-tiriki. [Tel.] n. A fish called *Trygon kuhlii* (F. B. I.).

కన్నె or కన్నియ kanne. [Tel.] n. A virgin, a young girl, a daughter. Same as కన్య.

కన్నెము or కన్నెముకాలు kannemu. [Tel.] n. A fowl's gizzard.

కన్నెరికము kannerikamu. [Tel.] n. Maidenhood, virginity. కన్యాత్వము. కన్నెరికముతీయు, కన్నెరికముచెట్టు to deflower.

కన్నెలేడి, or కామిలేడిపిట్ట kanne-lēdi. [Tel.] n. The bird called the Bastard Florikin; or stone-curlew, *Œdicnemus scolopax.* (F. B. I.) కారండవము.

కన్య. కన్యక. కన్నియ or కన్నె kanya. [Skt.] n. A virgin, a maiden. పెండ్లికాని పడుచు. Daughter కూతురు. A maiden, a damsel. చిన్నది. The sign Virgo. adj. 1. New క్రొత్త. కన్నెమెరుగు new or fresh flash of lightning 2. Young or small. కన్నెకయ్యము the onset in a battle యుద్ధారంభము. కన్నెబావి a poor well, one not abounding in water. కన్నెబెబ్బులితోలు the skin of a young tiger. కన్నెమావి a young mango tree. కన్యతనము or కన్యాత్వము kanya-tanamu. n. Maidenhood.

కన్యాకుబ్జము kanya-kubjamu. [Skt.] n. The country called Canouj.

కపటము kapaṭamu. [Skt.] n. Hypocrisy, insincerity, cunning, artifice, dissimulation. కపటనిద్ర feigned sleep. కపటకచ్ఛపమైనకైటభారాతి he who wore the form of a tortoise. కపటస్థుడు or కపటి kapa-ṭasthudu. n. A hypocrite కపటించు kapa-ṭintsu. v. n. To be hypocritical కపటముంచు.

కపర్దము *kapardamu.* [Skt.] n. The braided or matted locks of Siva. శివునిజడముడి. కపర్ది *kapardi.* n. A title of Siva.

కపాలము *kapālamu.* [Skt.] n. The skull తలపుఱ్ఱె. కపాలమోక్షము *kapāla-mōkshamu.* n. The bursting of the skull: lit. deliverance through the skull. Breaking the skull of a corpse to allow the spirit to escape. కపాలి *kapāli.* n. The skull-bearing god. Siva.

కపి *kapi.* [Skt.] n. A monkey. కోఁతి. కపిధ్వజుడు a title of Arjuna. కపిముష్టిపాగదము a monkey-like grasp, obstinacy, pertinacity. (This alludes to a mode of catching a monkey, by putting grain into a cocoanut with a hole large enough to admit the monkey's hand: he thrusts it in, and after grasping the grain, his fist is caught in the hole: he obstinately refuses to let the grain go, and thus is secured.)

కపింజలము *kapinjalamu.* [Skt.] n. The Francoline partridge. *Francolinus vulgaris* (F.B.I.). P. iii. 96. చిత్రపక్షి, రెక్కల యందు చిత్రములుంగల పక్షి.

కపిత్థము *kapiththamu.* [Skt.] n. The wood apple. *Feronia elephantum* (*Roxb.*) వెలగపండు. "గజభుక్తకపిత్థవత్" good in appearance but worthless like a wood apple eaten by an elephant.

కపిలము *kapilamu.* [Skt.] adj. Dun, dark brown, tawny గోరోజనమువంటి రంగుగల.

కపిలె *kapile.* [Tel.] n. A water lift consisting of a large leathern bucket which is raised and lowered by a rope passing over a wheel and drawn by bullocks. మోటు. కపిలెతోలు to draw water by means of such a water-lift. కపిలెగుండు the iron ring that forms the lip of the leather bucket in such a well.

కపిలోహము *kapi-lōhamu.* [Skt. from కపిల+లోహము.] n. The "tawny metal," i. e., brass. ఇత్తడి.

కపురము Same as కప్పురము.

కఫోణి *kapōṇi.* [Skt.] n. The elbow. మోచెయ్యి.

కపోతము *kapōtamu.* [Skt.] n. A dove. గువ్వ A pigeon పావురము. కపోతపాలిక *kapōta-pālika.* n. A dove-cot, a pigeon house. పావురపుగూడు.

కపోలము *kapōlamu* [Skt.] n. The cheek, స్వకపోలకల్పితకథ a story made out of one's own head, an original story.

కప్ప *kappa.* [Tel.] n. A frog. ఉరుకుకప్ప or చిఱికప్ప a chunam frog or flying frog. బోదురుకప్ప the bull frog. తలకప్ప a tadpole. బావురుకప్ప a frog that in croaking produces a sound like పప్ప పప్ప. కటాకటికప్ప one that produces a sound like tick, tuck. గాండ్రకప్ప one that produces a sound like ugm, ugm. రాచకప్ప and గోదురుకప్ప are other species. Various species of fish are called కప్పలు. See Russell, plates 19 to 20. కప్పకురుపు *kappa-kurupu.* n. An abscess in the heel. కప్పచిప్ప *kappa-chippa.* n. A bivalve shell. నత్తగుల్ల.

కప్పడము *kappaḍamu.* [Tel.] n. Cloth. కావి కప్పడము cloth dyed red.

కప్పతాళము *kappa-tālamu.* [Tel.] n. A padlock. ముద్రబీగము.

కప్పము *kappamu.* [Tel.] n. Tribute. కప్పము కట్టు to pay tribute.

కప్పరము or కప్పరపాటు *kapparamu.* [Tel.] n. Agitation, emotion. కప్పరపడు *kappara-paḍu.* v. n. To be eager, to be agitated, to be nervous over a thing. సంభ్రమపడు, తొట్రుపడు.

"కాకిపోదొలదమునకప్పరపడనేల." Vēma i. 49.

కప్పరపోలు *kappara-pōlu.* [Tel.] n. A light cloth woven like bunting.

కప్పలి *kappali.* [Tel. cf. Tam. கப்பல்.] n. A boat. ఓడ. నావ.

క॥ "చెప్పుడిదేమిక నోకదో
దప్పిరి మనుమక్కుజీమ దిగినైనిజె
న్నెప్పునిచిలకయుండెడి
కప్పలివిధమునను దేరు కదలకనిలిచెన్."
కు. ii.

కప్పారు *kapparu.* [Tel. కప్పు+అరు.] adj. Bright black, glossy.

కప్పి *kappi.* [Tel.] n. A pulley.

కప్పిరము *kappiramu.* [Tel.] n. A mottled skin, as in leprosy. HD. iii. 1066.

కప్పిరి *kappiri.* [Tel.] adj. Dusky. చీకటికప్పిరిగానున్నది there is still some darkness.

కప్పిరిగాడు *kappiri-gadu.* [Tel.] n. The nightjar or goat-sucker, a bird that flies in the gloaming. There are several species. *Caprimulgus asiaticus. C. indicus* (F. B. I.)

కప్పు *kappu.* [Tel.] n. A covering, a cover; the outside of anything: the husk of grain. The exterior surface or coat. Thatch, roof. Colour, as being a cover. Darkness. Blackness: also the dark colour applied to the teeth by some natives. ఇంటికప్పు or పైకప్పు the thatch. మేలుకప్పు a cover. adj. Black, dark, deep (as colour) కప్పుచాయ dark red. కప్పుకుత్తుక పులుగు a peacock, as its neck is black. కప్పుతెరువరి fire. కప్పుపచ్చ sap green. కప్పురాయి a sapphire నీలము. కప్పుమల the "black hill." కాటుకకొండ. కప్పుమేనిగాము the planet Saturn. (గాము=గ్రహము.). కప్పుకెంపుపొళ్లు crimson rubies. v. n. To spread, extend, come on, to cover, to settle as clouds or smoke. క్రమ్ము. v. a. To cover, to place as a covering. ఆచ్ఛాదించు. **కప్పుకొను** *kappu-konu.* v. a. and n. To cover oneself with. కన్నులకప్పుకొను to greet: or rejoice at the sight of. **కప్పుడు** *kappudu.* n. Covering ఆచ్ఛాదనము. **కప్పుడెంచు** *kappudentsu* Same as కప్పు v. n. **కప్పుబల్ల** *kappu-balla.* n. A plank of wood placed above the lintel of a door ద్వారము మీదనుండునుబల్ల తెప్పునప్పుడు పడుమానుదబెలక.

కప్పురము *kappuramu.* [from Skt. కర్పూరము.] n. Camphor. కప్పురగంధి a woman who wears scented clothes.

కప్పెర *kappera.* [Tel.] n. An earthen dish, trencher or porringer used in begging alms. భిక్షాపాత్రము. A small vessel or jar. బొచ్చె, కమండలువు, సానికె. A skull కపాలము.

కప్రము Same as కప్పురము. (q. v.)

కఫము *kaphamu.* [Skt.] n. Phlegm. తెమడ, శ్లేష్మము. **కఫి** *kaphi.* n. A phlegmatic person. కఫరోగి.

కబంధము *kabandhamu.* [Skt.] n. Water. A headless trunk retaining vitality. క్రియాయుక్తనిశ్శిరస్కకళేబరము.

కబంధుడు *kabandhudu.* [Skt.] n. The name of a demon. ఒక రాక్షసుడు. The moon's ascending node కేతువు.

కబరి *kabari.* [Skt.] n. A braid or fillet of hair. The top knot in which Hindoo females tie their long hair. కొప్పు. కబరీభారము a fine head of hair.

కబళము *kabalamu.* [Skt.] n. A mouthful, a bolus. వానినోరు మూయుటకును ఒక కబళము వేసిరి they gave him a sop to make him hold his tongue. **కబళించు** *kabalintsu.* v. a. To swallow, devour. To snatch, seize. To pervade (as sparks or flashes do the sky.) మింగు, పట్టుకొను, వ్యాపించు.

కబాడము *kabadamu.* [Tel.] n. A bullock load of firewood. కబాడియెద్దులు bullocks carrying firewood. కబాడపువాడు a seller of firewood.

కబాటు or **కబాటుకోడి** *kabatu.* [H.] n. A capon. విత్తులుతీసినకోడి.

కబాయి or **కబాయీ** *kabayi.* [H.] n. A shirt, an ornamental garment. శృంగారార్థముగా అన్నిటిపైన వేసుకొనే చిన్నచొక్కా. అంగీ.

" నవపుష్పవనము నానామణుల్,
స్రుచ్చి వపర్చె పట్టుకజాయిజాగు పెరవు."
K. P. v. 232.

కబురు *kaburu*. [H.] n. A message, news. సమాచారము, వర్తమానము.

కబేలా *kabēla*. [H.] n. A bill of sale, a grant.

కబోది *kabōdi*. [Tel.] n. A blind man. అంధుడు.

కబ్బము *kabbamu*. [Tel.] n. Poetry. An original poem. కావ్యము, ప్రబంధము. కబ్బపు కూరుపరి an author of a poem కావ్యము రచించువాడు, a poet కవి.

కబ్బి *kabbi*. [Tel.] n. Trick, craft, secrecy. (Guntur) కపటము.

కబ్బిలి *kabbili*. [Tel.] n. A toddy seller. కల్లమ్మువాడు.

కమండలువు *kamandaluvu*. [Skt.] n. A bowl or cruise carried by a Hindu ascetic. సన్యాసులుంచుకొనే గిన్నెవంటి మంటిపాత్రము. కమండలి *kamandali*. A hermit: "he who carries a cruise."

కమటము *kamaṭamu*. [Tel.] n. A portable furnace for melting the precious metals. అగసాలెవాని కుంపటి.

"చ॥ కమటముకై గ్లసంచియొక గిల్లను
గత్తెర సుత్తె చీర్ణముల్
ధమనియుపొ వాణంబు మొలత్రాసును
బట్టెడ నీరుకాయ సా
నము పటుకారు మూసు బలునాగె
పరీక్షల మచ్చులాదిగా
సమరగభద్రకారక సమావ్యయూ
డొక్కరుడుండు నప్పరిన్"
హంస. ii

కమఠము *kamaṭhamu*. [Skt.] n. A tortoise. కమఠి a female tortoise, a small tortoise. కమఠేంద్రుడు *kamaṭhēndruḍu*. n. The father of tortoises, or king of turtles.

కమతము or కమ్మతము *kamatamu*. [Tel.] n. Partnership. అనేకులుచేరిచేయుసేద్యము. The cultivation which an owner carries on with his own farming stock. Labour, tillage. కృషి, వ్యవసాయము. కమతకాడు or కమతీడు or కమతగాడు a labourer, or slave employed in tillage.

కమనీయము *kamaniyamu*. [Skt.] adj. Charming, graceful, delightful, lovely. ఇంపైన.

కమనుడు *kamanuḍu*. [Skt.] adj. Lustful, eager. కాముకుడు.

కమరు or కమురు *kamaru*. [Tel.] v. n. To singe, be singed or charred. కాలు. To smell badly. కమరుచు or కమర్చు *kamarutsu*. v. a. To singe or char. కాల్చు. కమరు. adj. Singeing, burning. కమరువాసన a smell that arises from something burning as hair. కాలినకంపు.

కమల *kamala*. [Skt.] n. Lakshmi the goddess of prosperity.

కమలము *kamalamu*. [Skt.] n. The lotus, *Nymphæa nelumboa*, water-lily. తామర, ఎఱ్ఱతామర. Also, water నీరు. కమలదళము the petal of a lotus. కమలదళరూపము a rose pattern, a flower shape. కమలాకరము a tank abounding with the lotus. కమలాకారము heart shaped. కమలాప్తుడు *kamal-āptuḍu*. (from ఆప్త dear) n. The sun, because he is dear to the lotus, which expands as he rises. కమలాసనుడు *kamal-asanuḍu*. (from ఆసన a seat.) n. The god Bramha, because the lotus is his throne. కమలాపండు *kamalā-panḍu*. [from Skt. కమలము water and Tel. పండు. lit. Juicy fruit.] n. The orange called a loose jacket. కమలిని *kamalini*. n. A tank abounding with the lotus: the lotus itself.

కమలు *kamalu*. [Tel.] v. n. To blacken, to be parched, singed or darkened. కందు, కాలు. కమలించు *kamalintsu*. v. a. To parch, scorch, blacken, blast, singe.

కమసాలవాడు Same as కంసాలి.

కమాను *kamānu.* [H.] n. An arch, a bow. The spring of a carriage. విల్లు, విల్లువంపు కట్టడము. **కమానుకఱ్ఱ** *kamānu-karra.* n. The bow of a drill. **కమానుబద్ద** *kamānu-badda.* n. The spring of a watch. **కమాన్‌దస్తా** *kamān-dasta.* n. A large bow for cleaning cotton. **కమాను** (from Fr. *command*) a march or military journey ఒకతుకిడీగా సిపాయిలుపోవడము. **కమానుపోవు** *kamānu-pōvu* (used by servants of Europeans) to go on circuit.

కమాయిషు or **కమాయుషు** or **కమామిషు** *kamāyishu.* [H.] n. Business, public business: affairs, details. Management of affairs. నిర్వాహకము, వ్యవహారపద్ధతి. News. Time of management. అతని కమామిషులో in his time, during his management. మా కమామిషుచూచేవాడు our agent.

కమి or **కమికెడు** *kami.* [Tel.] n. A large handful. కమికెడు as large as the spread hand fingers will contain.

కమిటీ *kamiṭī.* [Eng.] n. A committee, a number of people associated for some purpose, generally a bad purpose.

కమితము *kamitamu.* [Skt.] adj. Loved, beloved. కమనుడు.

కమియు *kamiyu.* [Tel] v. n. To meet, to oppose. కదియు. To be squeezed or reduced to powder నలుగు. To become overripe మాగు.

కముచు *kamuchu.* [Tel.] v. t. To take. పట్టు కొను. గ్రహించు. To swallow మింగు.

కముజు *kamuzu.* [Tel.] n. A partridge, the grey partridge, *Francolinuspondicerianus* (F. B. I.). కౌజు.

కమ్మ *kamma.* [Tel.] n. A branch, or bough of any tree of the palm species. మట్ట. A letter or bond written upon a palm leaf, a bond or agreement. లేఖ. A kind of large drop ear-ring worn by Hindu women. స్త్రీల కర్ణభూషణము. దుద్దుకమ్మ a globular ear-ring: పెద్దకమ్మ or బంగరు కమ్మ an ear-ring formed as a cup which hides the whole ear. **కమ్మ** or **కమ్మ వారు.** n. The name of a class of Telugu Sudras. కమ్మకత్తి a sort of bill-hook used by them. కమ్మది a female of that caste.

కమ్మ or **కమ్మని** *kamma.* [Tel.] adj. Delicious, in odour or taste, sweet. కమ్మనిపసిడి fine gold. కమ్మగా well, in good order, sweetly. కమ్మగాడ్పు a fragrant breeze or wind. కమ్మదనము or కమ్మన [Tel. from కమ్మ adj.] fragrance, deliciousness. మాధుర్యము, సౌరభము. కమ్మని fragrant, pleasant. కమ్మనీరు the nectar or honey of flowers. మకరందము. కమ్మనూనె good sesamum oil or fragrant oil. మంచినూనె. కమ్మపిల్లి the civic cat పునుగుపిల్లి. కమ్మవిల్తుడు or కమ్మవిలుకాడు the sweet or lovely bowman, an epithet of the Hindu Cupid.

కమ్మచ్చు *kammattsu.* [Tel. కమ్మి+అచ్చు.] n. An instrument for drawing out wire. కంసలివాడుకమ్మిలాగేసనిముట్టు.

కమ్మటము Same as కమటము. **కమ్మటీడు** *kammaṭīḍu.* [Tel.] A man of the goldsmith caste.

కమ్మతము Same as కమతము. **కమ్మతీడు** Same as కమతకాడు.

కమ్మరము *kammaramu.* [Tel.] n. Smith's work, iron work. **కమ్మరవాడు,** **కమ్మరి** or **కమ్మరీడు** *kammara-vāḍu.* n. An ironsmith or blacksmith. ఘైటికమ్మరవాడు an itinerant blacksmith.

కమ్మరు or **కమరు** *kammaru.* [Tel.] n. A girdle. మొలనూలు.

కమ్మి *kammi.* [Tel.] n. A wire, bar, beam. Border, a fringe, edging. అంచు. A felloe బండికంటికడకమ్మి, కంటి. బ్రహ్మకమ్మి, ముక్కు కమ్మి, or ముక్కమ్మి a nose ring. కమ్మి ఊడిపోయినది there is a peg loose, i. e., the plot is discovered. కమ్మిచీర a fringed cloth, or one with a border, edging, or selvage. కమ్మిబండి *kammi-bandi*. A cart with wheels having spokes and felloes on the wheels, as opposed to చెక్కబండి a cart with solid wheels.

కమ్మిరించు or కమ్మిచేయు *kammi-rintsu*. [H.] v. t. To cover. మూయు. To conceal దాచు.

కమ్ము *kammu*. [Tel. The sing. imperative of అగు to become.] Be thou: become thou. కృతార్థుడవుకమ్ము may you succeed! సహాయముకమ్మనాకు be thou our aid, assist us.

కమ్ము *kammu*. [Tel.] v. t. To beat out into wire. కమ్మిగా సాగకొట్టు. To overspread or cover మూయు, వ్యాపించు, క్రమ్ము. కమ్ముకొను *kammu-konu*. v. a. To pervade, as smoke; to vail, hide, screen, conceal; to surround. శత్రువులు వానిని చుట్టు కమ్ముకొనిరి the enemy surrounded him on all sides. నాగొంతుకకమ్మినది I became hoarse. మత్తుకమ్మిపడ్డాను a stupor came over me and I fell down. వానికి కావలసినంత బలగము ఉన్నది గనుక వాడు చేసినపనికి వాళ్లు కమ్ముకొన్నారు he had abundance of friends, so they screened him from punishment. కమ్ముదల *kammu-dala*. n. Covering, concealing. తనకృత్రిమమును కమ్ముదలచేసేకొరకు with a view to conceal his roguery.

కమ్మునీళ్లు *kammu-nillu*. [Tel.] n. Water with which cloths after bleaching are tinged bluish.

కమ్మేరాకు *kammer-aku*. [Tel.] n. A strong smelling species of black betel leaf. కారపునల్లతమలపాకు.

కమ్రము *kamramu*. [Skt.] adj. Beautiful, desirable. ఇంపైన, ఇచ్ఛగల.

కయి *kayi*. [Tel. cf. Tam. கை.] n. The hand. చెయ్యి.

కయివారము *kayi-varamu*. [Tel.] n. Praise, worship. స్తోత్రము, మ్రొక్కు.

కయ్య *kayya*. [Tel.] n. A brook, a creek. A bed in a garden or field. మడి. ఉప్పు కయ్య a salt creek.

కయ్యము or కయ్యాటము *kayyamu*. [Tel.] n. A combat, fight, a quarrel. జగడము. కయ్యపుదిండి or కలహాశనుడు one who lives by fomenting quarrels. An epithet of Nārada. నారదుడు. కయ్యాల క్రచ్చు a quarrelsome fellow. సవతుల కయ్యాటము brawls between rival wives.

కయ్యర *kayyara*. [Tel.] n. An inferior sort of pearl. హీనజాతిముత్యము.

కర *kara*. [Tel.]n. The sea shore; an embankment; a sand bank. తీరము. A stain; dirt; blackness. డాగు, మరక. adj. Black, నల్లని; sharp తీక్ష్ణము; rough, harsh బరుసు. కృష్ణకర a bank or dam on the shore of the Krishṇa. కరగట్టు *kara-gattu*. v. n. To be stained or soiled అక్కడ ఉచ్చు కర గట్టినది the place was soiled with urine. కరవాక *kara-vāka*. n. A backwater, or marsh near the sea.

కరంకము *karankamu*. [Skt.] n. A skeleton. లోపల యేమిన్ని లేని బోలుబిచ్చ. The breast డొక్క. The head తల. A roll of betel. తాంబూలపువిడా.

కరంజము Same as కానుగచెట్టు. (q. v.)

కరండము *karandamu*. [Skt.] n. A casket. కరాటము, బరిణె.

కరంభము *karambhamu*. [Skt.] n. A sweet mixture, either of flavours or scents: a mess of food, a pudding or cake. పెరుగుతో తడిపిన పేలపిండి. కరంభితము *karambhitamu*. adj. Mixed: pounded.

కరక *karaka*. [Tel.] n. The yellow myrobalan, *Terminalia chebula*. Ainslie. i. 237. See కరక్కాయ. కరక *karaka*. n. Blackness, darkness. adj. Black, dark, ugly. కరకగడ్డము a shabby beard, like a goat's. కరకనేల rich or fruitful black soil.

కరక *karaka.* [Skt.] n. Hail. A hailstone. వడగల్లు. **కరకము** *karakamu.* A pipkin, or small pot. The cruise of a student or ascetic. గరిగబిడత.

కరకంచు *karak-antsu.* [Tel. కరక+అంచు.] n. A border dyed with the juice of the Myrobalan.

కరకంఠుడు *kara-kanthudu.* [Tel. from కర black.] adj. "Black throated." An epithet of Siva.

కరకండచెట్టు *kara-kanda-chettu.* [Tel.] n. A jungle bush the seed of which is used as medicine.

కరకణి *karakani.* [Tel.] n. A hunting weapon. వేటాడుటకు ఉపయుక్తమగు నొకవిధమైన ఆయుధము. "నొంచె కలత్తికములు కరకణులు" కుక్కు. iii.

కరకర *kara-kara.* [Tel.] n. Sharpness. ఒరయుట. తీక్ష్ణము. A harsh, grating sound. సూర్యుడు కరకర ఉదయించినప్పుడు just as the sun was rising. కరకరమని వ్రాసినాడు he wrote so that the scratching of his pen could be heard. కరకరనమిలినాడు I could hear him chewing. నాకు కరకరమని ఆకలియైనది I felt very hungry.

కరకరి *karakari.* [Tel.] n. Violence, outrage. వేలము, కలత, క్రూరభావము. Anger, dislike ద్వేషము. Pain బాధ. adj. Angry, cruel కఠినుడు. **కరకరించు** *kara-kar-intsu.* v. n. To rage, be violent.

కరకస or **కరకసా** *karakasa.* [Tel.] n. Ill will, contention, jealousy, spite. A contest regarding boundaries of land. A border feud. కరకసభూమి, కరకసాస్థలము disputed land, debatable ground.

కరకు or **కరుకు** *karaku.* [Tel.] n. Sharpness, as of a file or a saw. Roughness, as of a cat's tongue; harshness కాఠిన్యము, వాడి. adj. Sharp, rough, harsh. కరుకు టమ్ములు sharp arrows. **కరకెక్కు** *karak-ekku.* To be rough. వాడికి కరుకెక్కించినారు they made him angry. **కరకుదుమ్ము** *karaku-dummu.* n. Sand. ఇసుక. కరుకు వరహా a four-rupee pagoda. **కరకుగీలు** *karaku-gilu.* v. n. To become harsh or hard. ఎరుసు.

కరకుట్లు or **కరుకుట్లు** or **కర్రకుట్లు** *karakutlu.* [Tel. from కర్ర a spit and కుట్టు to pierce.] n. A rasher of meat; a steak. Kālahas. iii. 69. 72. శూల్యము.

కరక్కాయ *karakkaya.* [Tel.] n. The fruit of the కరక (q. v.) వానినోట్లో కరక్కాయపడ్డది he is ruined: వానినోట కరక్కాయకొట్టినాను I have ruined him.

కరగసము *karagasamu.* [Tel.] n. A saw. రంపము.

కరగు or **కరుగు** *karagu.* [Tel.] v. n. To melt. ద్రవించు. To waste away, to be emaciated. కృశించు. To dissolve away. To be cut, as a bank by the stream. To go down or go off, as a boil. "కరగ కరగ పుట్టు కనకంబునకు వన్నె." (Vēma.) the oftener gold is melted the finer it becomes. అందుకు వానిమనస్సు కరిగినది at this his heart melted. **కరగు, కరుగు, కరగించు,** or **కరిగించు** v. a. To melt. **కరగు** n. Melting కరగుట.

కరగోడ *kara-gōda.* [Tel.] n. A fence. కోట.

కరచు or **కరుచు** *karatsu.* [Tel.] v. a. To bite. కాటువేయు. To teach, instruct. To learn. అభ్యసించు, నేర్చుకొను. **కరుచుకొను** *karutsu-konu.* v. n. To adhere, stick, to catch, as paste. To hold as a hook, lock or button.

కరజము *karajamu.* [Skt.] Lit. "what grows on the hand." n. A finger nail.

కరటము *karatamu.* [Skt.] n. A crow. కాకి

కరటి *karati.* [Skt.] n. An elephant. ఏనుగు. **కరటి** adj. Stubborn, brutish, villainous. మొండి. A cheat, a deceiver వంచకుడు. A bear ఎలుగు. **కరటితనము** *karati-tanamu.* n. Villainy. Deceit. మోసము. **కరటిమూర్ఖము, కరడు**

ముత్యము *karaṭi-mutyamu*. A bad or inferior pearl.

కరడము or కరడు or కరుడు *karaḍamu*. [Tel.] n. A wave. అల. Parij. ii. 59. కరుడ్లు waves, billows.

కరణము *karaṇamu*. [Skt.] n. A village clerk, a writer, an accountant. వాడు మాట కరణముగాని వ్రాతకరణముకాడు he has talents for speaking but not for writing. స్థలకరణము the registrar of a district. కరణము n. Instrument, means. సాధనము. An organ of sense. ఇంద్రియము. Making or causing, as in ప్రియంకరణము endearing. స్థూలంకరణము fattening, శుభంకరణము fortunate. కరణచతుష్టయము the mind, intellect, volition and self-consciousness. మనోబుద్ధిచిత్తాహంకారములు. కరణత్రయము thought, word and deed. మనస్సు, వాక్కు, కర్మము. త్రికరణశుద్ధిగా completely, absolutely, entirely. కరణీయము *karaṇīyamu*. adj. Fit to be performed, worthy to be done చేయదగిన. కరణికము or కరణీకము *karaṇikamu*. Clerkship: the office of a *Karaṇam* or clerk.

కరణి *karaṇi*. [Tel.] n. Manner, way, mode. విధము.

కరతలము *kara-talamu*. [Skt.] n. The palm of the hand. కరతలామలకముగా as easy as possible. అవలీలగా.

కరట *karaṭa*. [Tel.] n. A naughty or wicked deed. దుశ్చేష్ట. Childish desires పోకళ్లు. కరటలాడు *karaṭal-āḍu*. (కరటలు+ఆడు.) n. An evil doer. దుశ్చేష్టుడు.

కరతాళము *kara-tāḷamu*. [Skt.] n. The small leaved palm tree (as distinguished from శ్రీతాళము.) A musical instrument, a cymbal. Beating time by clapping the hands.

కరతిత్తి *kara-titti*. [Skt. కర+ Tel. తిత్తి.] n. A striped bag or wallet. A round bag. వస్త్రపుసంచి.

కరద *karada*. [Tel.] n. Desire. బుద్ధి, కోరిక.

కరదము *karadamu*. [Skt.] n. A gift. కానుక.

కరదివ్వె or కరదీపము or కరదీపిక *kara-divve*. [Skt.] n. A hand lamp, a light borne in the hand. A torch దివిటీ.

కరదూపము *kara-dūpamu*. [Tel.] n. Soot. గృహధూమము.

కరపక్క *kara-pakka*. [Tel.] n. A faded ruby: మాసినకెంపు.

కరపత్త్రము *kara-patramu*. [Skt.] n. A saw. రంపము.

కరపు *karapu*. [Tel. from కరచు.] v. t. To teach "బర్హిస్తంభములకు మురిపెములకరపు." B. X. 52. కరపించు or కరిపించు *kara-pintsu*. v. a. To make a thing bite; to cause one to teach.

కరపోకరాయి *kara-pōka-rāyi*. [Tel.] A counterfeit ruby, resembling a cornelian.

కరఫలము *kara-phalamu*. [Skt.] n. A curry comb. కరారా, గుర్రముమతోమే సాధనము.

కరబట్టావు *kara-baṭṭ-āvu*. [Tel. from కర and బట్ట and ఆవు] n. A striped cow.

కరభము *karabhamu*. [Skt.] n. A young camel. The edge of the hand.

కరమర్దము *kara-mardamu*. [Skt.] n. Same as కలివెచెట్టు. (q. v.)

కరమల *karamala*. [Tel.] n. A blacksmith. కమ్మరి.

కరము *karamu*. [Skt.] n. The hand. చెయ్యి. A ray of light కిరణము. An elephant's trunk తొండము. A tribute or tax కప్పము. కరము adj. Great, much. adv. Much, very. కరవాడిచూపులు very sharp looks. కరవాడిగోరు a very sharp nail. కరశాఖ a finger. వేలు. కరస్థము *karasthamu*. adj. Present, ready to hand. కరరుహము a finger nail. గోరు.

కరమూటిసొర్ర *kara-mūṭi-sorra*. [Tel.] n. *Carcharias menisorrah*. ఒకసొర్ర. (F. B. I.)

కరవ *karava*. [Tel.] n. A sort of parsley.

కరవటము *kararaṭamu.* [Tel.] n A small cup. చిన్నబరిణె.

కరవాడు or కరవడి *kara-vāḍu.* [Tel.] n. Salt fish. ఉప్పుచేప. Dried fish ఎండుచేప.

కరవాయి *kara-vāyi.* [Tel.] n. A curved iron bar which is put inside a small mouthed metal pot to meet the blow of the hammer outside. కంచరవాడు సుత్తితో పాత్రము లను సాగకొట్టునప్పుడు వానిలోపల ఒత్తుకుంగా నుంచే యినుము.

కరవాలము or కరవాలు *kararālamu.* [Skt.] n. A sword. ఖడ్గము.

కరవీరము *karavīramu.* [Skt.] n. The oleander plant. గన్నేరు.

కరవు *karuvu.* [Tel.] n. Same as కరువు.

కరవేరు *kara-vēru.* [Tel.] n. The root of the plant, *Lavendula carnosa.* Heyne.

కరసాన *kara-sāna.* [Tel.] n. A grindstone.

కరహాటము *karahāṭamu.* [Skt.] n. The fibrous root of a lotus. తామరదుంప.

కరా *karā.* [Tel.] adj. Sharp. వాడిగల. కరా మూరకత్తి. కరామూసి or కరామూసి *karatsūra-katti.* n. A sword.

కరాటము *karāṭamu.* [Tel.] n. A pill box. A pouncet box for essences. బరిణె.

కరారు *karāru.* [H.] n. An agreement. కరారుచేయు to enter into an agreement. కరారునామా a written agreement.

కరాళము *karāḷamu.* [Skt.] n. The backbone. వెన్నెముక. adj. High, uneven; horrid, terrible, dreadful. ఉన్నతమైన, ఒక్కువెట్టయిన; భయముపుట్టించే. కరాళించు *karālintsu.* v. n. To cry loud. బొబ్బరించు. To neigh సకిలించు. v. t. To blame నిందించు. To bully, to bluster, or browbeat.

కరి *kari.* [Tel.] adj. Black. కరి n. Blackness. The uterus of animals. పశ్వాదుల యోని, కృష్ణవర్ణము. An illustration నిదర్శ నము. A witness సాక్షి. A limit మేర.

కరి *kari.* [Skt. from కరము.] n. An elephant. కరికర క్రీడ *karikara-krīḍa.* n. Tickling, fingering, handling. చివురుట. కరిణి *kariṇi.* n. A female elephant. కరీంద్రుడు *karīndruḍu.* n. The chief or noblest of elephants.

కరింగోల *karingōla.* [Tel.] n. A kind of leopard.

కరికరి *karikari.* [Tel.] n. Anger, passion, చిరచిర. కరికరి adv. Rapidly, angrily. కరకరిపెట్టు to plague, harrass. కరికోత *kari-kōta.* n. Torment, plague.

కరిఖలము *kari-khalamu.* [Skt.] n. Gambling for pleasure. వేడుకగానాడే జూదము.

కరినెలు *karinelu.* [Tel.] n. plu. A particular caste of weavers.

కరిడి *kariḍi.* [Tel.] n. A kind of musical instrument made of leather. చర్మవాద్యవిశే షము.

కరిదూపము *kari-dūpamu.* [Tel. another form of కరదూపము.] n. Dirt; particularly cobwebs; soot; the blackness produced by wood smoke, as distinct from కాటుక or lampblack.

కరియ *kariya.* [Tel.] n. Black colour. నల్లరంగు.

కరిరె *karire.* [Tel.] n. The bridge of the Viṇa the Indian guitar.

కరివెద *kari-veda.* [Tel.] n. The custom of leaving ploughed land unsown till after rain falls.

కరివేపచెట్టు *kari-vēpa-chettu.* [Tel.] n. A species of వేప (the margosa tree.) కరివేపు ఆకు its leaves. Ainslie ii. 139.

కరివేల్పు *kari-vēlpu.* [Tel.] n. The dark god, i. e., Krishna కృష్ణుడు.

కరిసనము or కర్షణము *karisanamu.* [from Skt. కృషి.] n. Agriculture, cultivation, tillage.

కరిసించు *karisintsu.* [from Skt. ఘర్షణము.] v. t. To oppose, to face boldly. To quarrel.

కరీరము *karīramu*. [Skt.] n. The shoot of a bamboo, *Capparis aphylla* (Roxb.) వెదురు మొలక, వెదురుకుచెట్టు.

కరీషము *karīshamu*. [Skt.] n. A cake of dried cow-dung. పిడక.

కరుకు *karuku*. [Tel.] n. Sharpness, harshness, roughness, medicinal drugs burnt to ashes. కరకు. మందులుకాల్చి చేసినబూడిద. **కరుకు** v. n. To rub. రాచు. కరుకువరహా a coin worth nearly four rupees, commonly called *Behadari*, or Three Swamy Pagoda. కరుకుపెట్టు or కక్కుపెట్టు to set a saw or sickle. To burn or calcine medicinal drugs. See కరకు.

కరుకుట్టు Same as కర్రకట్టు. (q. v.)

కరుకోల *karu-kōla*. [Tel.] n. A firing iron, for cautery.

కరుక్కు *karukku*. [Tel.] n. A sharp noise like that made in cutting or sawing. నరుకునప్పుడు కలుగు ధ్వని.

కరుగు *karugu*. Same as కరగు.

కరుగు *karugu*. [Tel.] n. An unopened ear of corn. పరిపొట్టకర్ర.

కరుడు Same as కరడు.

కరుడు *karuḍu*. [Tel.] n. A lump, mass, clot. ముద్ద. A turf. The snuff of a wick. A wave, a ripple. A daily account or day book. దినవహి. పెంటికరుడు the lesser or female surf, being the one nearest shore. పోతుకరుడు the male surf being the furthest. పిండికరుడు a piece of bread, or dough. **కరుడుకట్టు** *karuḍu-kaṭṭu*. To conglomerate or form in lumps.

కరుణ *karuṇa*. [Skt.] n. Mercy, grace. కని కరము, కృప. కరుణానిధుడు he who is merciful or gracious. **కరుణించు** *karuṇintsu*. v. a. To pity, to have mercy on, to favour. కనికరించు.

కరుడు *karuḍu*. [Tel.] n. Skill. నేర్పు. **కరుడు లాడు** *karuḍul-āḍu*. n. A skilful man. నేర్పరి.

కరుబూజపండు *karu-būja-panḍu*. [H.] n. A melon.

కరుములు or **కరుములవాడు** Same as కరములు.

కరువ *karuva*. [Tel.] n. A hill. కొండ.

కరువలి *karuvali*. [Tel.] n. Wind, air. గాలి, వాయువు. కరువలిపట్టి Bhīma or Hanuman. కరువలిరిక్క The Star Arcturus, స్వాతి నక్షత్రము. కరువలిచెలుడు Fire అగ్ని, వాయు సఖుడు.

కరువు *karuvu*. [Tel.] n. Melting: what is melted. The clay mould for a metal image. A crucible. కరుగు. A lump or clot, as of mud. కరుడు. A. ii. 66. The fœtus in the womb. గర్భము. Scarcity, famine. కరవు. **కరువు** adj. Scarce, as corn in a famine.

కరుసు *karusu*. [Tel.] n. A harsh word. పరుషోక్తి.

కరేకరము *karē-karamu*. [Skt.] n. A blow with the fist. పిడికిటిపోటు.

కరేణువు *karēṇuvu*. [Skt.] n. An elephant. ఏనుగు. A female elephant ఆడేనుగు.

కరేపాకు *karēp-āku*. [Tel.] n. The leaf of the black *vēpa* tree. కరివేప ఆకు.

కరోటకము *karōṭakamu*. [Skt.] n. A clothes' box. బట్టలపెట్టె.

కరోటి *karōṭi*. [Skt.] n. The skull. పుర్రె.

కర్కంధువు *karkandhuvu*. [Skt.] n. The jujube tree. రేగుచెట్టు, గంగరేగుచెట్టు, బదరీ.

కర్కటము or **కర్కటకము** *karkaṭamu*. [Skt.] n. A crab. ఎండ్రి. The sign Cancer. కర్కటిగర్భమువలె like the crab's fœtus. For, like the young of the viper the crabs are supposed to be born by rending and killing the mother.

కర్కము *karkamu*. [Skt.] n. A vase. కుండ. A mirror అద్దము. A white horse.

కర్కరి *karkari*. [Skt.] n. The large cucumber. పెద్దదోస. A small water jar with a spout గిండిబాన.

కర్కశము *karkaṣamu.* [Skt.] adj. Violent, harsh, rough to the feel, rugged. Hard, cruel, unfeeling కనికరములేని, కఠినమైన, నొప్పించే. కర్కశమైనమాటలు harsh words. కర్కశము or కర్కస or కరకసా n. Roughness, want of smoothness: ruggedness. కయ్యము. A feud, an old grudge, particularly between those who dispute about their respective boundaries. కర్కస పొలము debatable land, ground claimed by both parties.

కర్కారుకము *karkārukamu.* [Skt.] n. The plant called *convolvolus punniculatus.* పుచ్చచెట్టు.

కర్కోటకము *karkōṭakamu.* [Skt.] adj. Cruel, hard. కర్కోటకుడు *karkōṭakuḍu.* A snake so named. A cruel wretch.

కర్చు *kartsu.* [H.] n. Expense. Same as ఖర్చు.

కర్జకాయలు *karza-kāyalu.* [Tel.] n. A sort of sweetmeat.

కర్జము *karzamu.* [from Skt. కార్యము.] n. An act, or deed. A good act, propriety. చేయదగినపని.

కర్ణము *karṇamu.* [Skt.] n. The ear. The helm of a ship చుక్కాని. కర్ణధారుడు *karṇa-dhāruḍu.* A helmsman or steersman. ఓడనడపువాడు. కర్ణపత్రము or కర్ణపూరము *karṇa-patramu.* n. A sort of earrings. చెవికమ్మ, పూగమ్మ. కర్ణమంత్రము *karṇa-mantramu.* n. A spell or prayer whispered in the ear of a dying man. కర్ణలత an earring చెవిపొగ్గు. కర్ణాకర్ణి *karṇā-karṇi.* n. From mouth to mouth. వినికిపరుస. (Lit. from ear to ear—a phrase regarding news.)

కర్ణాటకము or కర్ణాటము *karṇāṭakamu.* [Skt. from కరి+నాడు, the black soil or country.] n. The Karṇāṭaka or Kannada language. The Carnatic dance. A comedy: that division of acting which relates to love tales and emotions of amorous passion. కర్ణాటకమేళము Native music, a Hindu band. కర్ణాటకరాజులకథలు Legendary tales, old wives' fables. కర్ణాట క్షత్రియులు the ancient kings or aboriginal princes.

కర్ణిక *karṇika.* [Skt.] n. A trinket for the ear. చెవికమ్మ.

కర్ణికారము *karṇi-kāramu.* [Skt.] n. A sort of hill Cassia. కొండగోగు.

కర్ణేజపుడు *karṇē-japuḍu.* [Skt.] n. A tell-tale, a whisperer, an eaves-dropper. కొండెకాడు.

కర్త *karta.* [Skt. from √kri, to make.] n. Maker, author, doer. చేయువాడు. The nominative case in grammar. గ్రంథకర్త an author. అట్లు చెప్పడానకు కర్తలమా who are we that we should say this? అర్ధాంశకర్త a half owner. విచారణకర్త a superintendent, an examiner. ధనఋణంబులకు కర్తతనయుండుగదా a son is the person concerned in our gains and losses. గ్రామకర్త the head of a village. "వెరపెరుంగక స్వచ్ఛందవృత్తినుందు నాకొకడు కర్తలేడు." I live according to my own inclinations and have no master. వాని ధనఋణములకు కర్త నయినాను I came in for both his goods and debts. క్రతుకర్త he who presents a sacrifice; ధర్మకర్త the warden of a temple. న్యాయకర్త an officer of justice, a ruler. తన ఆస్తికి నలుగురు ధర్మకర్తలను ఏర్పరచిపోయినాడు he died leaving four guardians or executors of his property. స్మృతికర్త a lawgiver, a legislator. క్షేత్రకర్త a mere tenant at will.

కర్తనము *kartanamu.* [Skt.] n. Cutting, severing. కత్తిరించుట. కర్తరి *kartari.* Scissors కత్తెర. కర్తరీముఖము *kartari-mukhamu.* n. A certain position of the hand in dancing.

కర్తలానము *kartalānamu.* [Skt.] n. A black horse having white hoofs and a white tail. కర్తలాని.

కర్తవ్యము *kartavyamu.* [Skt.] adj. Fit to be done. చేయదగినది.

కర్తి *karti*. [Tel.] An inflected form of కఱ్రు, కర్తికాలు One "plough" of land, i. e., as much as one కఱ్రు suffices for.

కర్తృకము *kartrukamu*. [Skt.] n. Doing, agency, action. కర్తృత్వము *kartrutvamu*. n. Agency: the act or property of an agent. Delegated authority: అతనిమీద కర్తృత్వము ఉంచినారు they made him plenipotentiary, they entrusted the affair to him. అది చేయవలసిన కర్తృత్వము నాయందు న్నది the right to do this rests with me.

కర్దమము *kardamamu*. [Skt.] n. Mud, mire. అడుసు.

కర్పటము *karpaṭamu*. [Skt.] n. Rags, dirty clothes. Cloth in general. వస్త్రము. చినిగిన వస్త్రము, మాసినవస్త్రము.

కర్పరము *karparamu*. [Skt.] n. The skull: the cranium. కపాలము, తలచిప్పయెముక. A vessel పాత్ర; a weapon శస్త్రభేదము.

కర్పరి *karpari*. [Skt.] n. A kind of collyrium prepared from saffron. ప్రాని పసుపునందు పండిన అంజనవిశేషము.

కర్పూరము *karpūramu*. [Skt.]n. Camphor. పచ్చకర్పూరము crude camphor. రసకర్పూరము calomel. కర్పూరనూనె camphor oil. కర్పూర అరటిపండు a fragrant kind of plantain. కర్పూరవంకాయ a kind of small brinjal. కర్పూరచెండ a certain vegetable. కర్పూరవల్లి *karpūra-valli*. See under ఓ.మము. కర్పూరశిలాజతు *karpūra-śilā-jatu*. n. A foliated crystallized gypsum, the powder of which, like white alabaster, is used in the preparation of stucco and as a medicine for ulcers. Ainslie. ii. 70.

కర్బురము *karburamu*. [Skt.] n. Gold: బంగారు. Variegated colour. చిత్రవర్ణము.

కర్మంది *karmandi*. [Skt.] n. An ascetic. సన్యాసి.

కర్మ or కర్మము *karma*. [Skt. ✓ kri=to do.] n. An act or deed: action in general. పని. Religious action, such as sacrifice; ablution. Actions, conduct, a course of procedure. Destiny; fate, that is, the allotment, to be enjoyed or suffered in the present life, of the fruit of the good and evil actions performed in former lives. Moral duty; obligation imposed by peculiarities of tribe, occupation, &c. Funeral rites. The object of a verb in Grammar. వాని కర్మము ఎవ్వరు చేసినారు who performed his funeral rites? An art, as శిల్పకర్మము the art of statuary. Doing: ఇది నీకర్మము this is all your doing, it is your own fault. Ill hap, misfortune, hard lot: affliction. అయ్యో కర్మమా O dear! oh what a pity! కర్మము or పాపకర్మము a sinful deed. కర్మజీవి See కర్మఠుడు. కర్మఠము *karmaṭhamu*. [Skt.] n. Ceremonial precision. కర్మఠుడు *karmaṭhuḍu*. n. A formalist, a ritualist: one who is earnest in the performance of the rites of religion. కార్యమును చివరవరకు సాధించేవాడు. కర్మణిక్రియ *karmaṇi-kriya*. n. A transitive verb. అకర్మణిక్రియ an intransitive verb. కర్మరంగము *karma-rangamu*. n. The five sided sour green plum called *Averrhoa Carambola*, or అంబాళపుకాయ. కర్మసాక్షి *karma-sākshi*. n. A witness of all our acts, viz., the sun. కర్మాంతరము *karmāntaramu*. n. Funeral rites, obsequies.

కర్మారము *karmāramu*. [Skt.] n. A bamboo. వెదురు. కర్మారుడు *karmāruḍu*. n. An artisan. కమ్మరవాడు.

కర్మి *karmi*. [Skt. from కర్మ.] n. A doer, an agent, workman, a sinner; a formalist; one bound by the doctrine of works. సాహసకార్యధురుడటువంటి కర్మికాడు he is not a man likely to do this. కర్ముడు *karmuḍu*. n. A doer, an agent. కర్మేంద్రియములు *karmēndriyamulu*. n. The organs of action. The bodily members, or limbs, considered as the instruments of passion and hence agents of sin.

కర్ర *karra*. [Tel.] n. Wood, a piece of wood. A stick or staff. The stem or stalk of grain; any straight rod whether of wood or not. పొగకర్ర or వాలుకర్ర a sunbeam. ఇనపకర్ర a bar of iron. కర్రపచ్చిగాకోసినకోత reaping while the stalks are green. Blackness నలుపు. A dark stain మరక. See కర. కర్రకుట్లు *karrakutlu*. n. A piece of flesh fried over a fire. ఇనుపశలాకయందు గ్రుచ్చి కాల్చే మాంస ఖండము.

కర్రమడ *karramada*. [Tel.] n. A digging instrument. తవ్వే ఆయుధము.

కర్రి *karri*. [Tel.] adj. Dark coloured, dun. కార్యమంటవర్ణముగల. n. A name of the hero Arjuna.

కర్రు *karru*. [Tel.] n. A plough share. (infl. కర్రి.) కర్రిమొన the point of a plough share. కర్రిమొలలు the iron clamps which connect the plough with the share. See కర్రి. గొంతులో కర్రుకాచినట్టున్నది I feel a burning pain in my throat. A stain దాగు.

కర్రుకుట్లు Same as కర్రకుట్లు. (q. v.)

కర్షకుడు *karshakudu*. [Skt. కృషి.] n. A cultivator, a farmer.

కర్షఫలము n. A plant, *Beleric myrobalan*, *Terminalia belerica*. విభీతకము or తాండ్ర చెట్టు. (q. v.)

కర్షము *karshamu*. [Skt.] n. A weight of about half an ounce or 16 palams. ఇరువది చిన్నములయెత్తు. Friction ఒరియుటము, రాయుడము.

కర్షువు *karshuvu*. [Skt.] n. A river. నది.

కల *kala*. [Tel.] adj. (in composition) All, various; actual. కలకాలము at all times. కలగూర various herbs. కలరూపు the actual appearance.

కల *kala*. [Tel.] n. A dream. "కలలోన గ్రా మలకామింపగా నేల" (Bhall. Pad. ii. 50.) Why waste your soul in dreams on the fair? కలగను *kala-ganu*. v. n. To dream.

కల or గల *kala*. [Tel.] An affix. The participle of కలుగు. Possessed of. బుద్ధిగల sensible.

కల *kala*. [Skt.] adj. Harmonious, sweet in sound as కలరవాకలితమేఖల a tinkling girdle. కలధ్వని or కలస్వనము a warbling sound.

కలంకము or కళంకము *kalankamu*. [Skt.] n. A spot, mark, stain. A blemish. దాగు, చిహ్నము, నింద.

కలంకారి *kalankari*. [Tel.] n. A colored cloth. వ్రాతపని వస్త్రము.

కలంగు Same as కలగు. (q. v.)

కలంచు Same as కలచు. (q. v.)

కలంజము *kalanjamu*. [Skt.] n. A drug made of Indian hemp, bhang. గంజాయి.

కలంబము *kalambamu*. [Skt.] n. An arrow. బాణము. Dissension, confusion. గృహకలం బము family feuds, brawls అలకలు.

కలక *kalaka*. [Tel. from కలగు.] n. Turbidity. Trouble, perturbation: foulness: sin: lumbar rheumatism. కంటికలక the disease called country sore eyes, ophthalmia. కలకనీళ్లు turbid water. కలకబారు *kala-ka-paru*. (కలక+పారు.) v. a. To be confused. కలతపడు. కలకపాటు confusion కలత, కలతపడుట.

కలకంఠము *kala-kanthamu*. [Skt.] n. A sweet voice. మధురధ్వని. The black cuckoo so called from its melodious note. కలకంఠి the sweet-voiced one, i. e., a woman.

కలకండ *kalakanda*. [Tel.] n. Sugar candy. పటికబెల్లము.

కలకలము *kalakalamu* [Skt.] n. Buzz, a confused sound. కలకల *kalakala*. adv. Aloud. కలకలనవ్వుట to laugh heartily. పక్షుల కలకలధ్వని the loud notes of birds.

కలకు *kalaku*. [Tel. another form of కలచు.] n. Battle. యుద్ధము.

కలకువ *kalakuva*. [Tel.] n. Confusion. కలత.

కలగలపు or **కలగల్పు** *kalagalapu*. [Tel.] n. Mixture. మిశ్రమము. Friendship. కలుపుకోలుతనము. A mix-up or hotch-potch కలగూర.

కలగుండు *kala-gundu*. [Tel.] n. A large stone or boulder. M. VI. iii. 65. R. v. 313. Confusion కలత, క్షోభము. కలగుండుకొను or కలగుండుపడు to be confused కలగు. కలగుండుపెట్టు to confuse కలచు.

కలగు or **కలంగు** *kalagu*. [Tel.] v. n. To be troubled, disordered, embarrassed, to grieve, to be in distress or broken down. కండ్లుకలగినవి or కలిగినవి his eyes are red or inflamed. కలగబడు or కలగబారు to be confused or embarrassed కలగు, సంక్షోభించు.

కలగూర *kala-gūra*. [Tel.] n. Wild herbs in general: forest herbs, a mixture of herbs, hotch-potch పెక్కుచెనుసులు కలిసిన కూరాకు, కలగూరగంప a medley, a mass of confusion.

కలగొను *kala-gonu*. [Tel. కలుపు+కొను.] v. n. To be agitated. కలగు. To spread వ్యాపించు.

సీ. "పక్షిమృగజాతులెల్లను భ్రమసియుట్టు
నట్టు కలగొనిచెదరి."
భార. విరా. iv.

కలచు *kalatsu*. [Tel. causal of కలగు.] v. a. To trouble, disconcert, disorder. To melt, or agitate with any passion. కలతనొందునట్లుచేయు. **కలత** *kalata*. n. Trouble, perplexity. A dispute, squabble. Indisposition. Turbidity in water. క్షోభము. **కలతపడు** *kalata-padu*. v. n. To dispute, squabble, to quarrel.

కలతెరగు *kala-teragu*. [Tel.] n. Truth. యాథార్థ్యము.

కలధౌతము *kala-dhautamu*. [Skt.] n. A precious metal: silver or gold.

కలన or **కలనము** *kalana*. [Skt.] n. Making, effecting. చేయడము, కావించడము. "తెలిసిధీనవక్త్రంగారకలనములను," Dasav. ix. 416. "ఇష్టమృష్టాన్నకలనసంతుష్టుజేసి." Swa. i. 17.

కలను *kalanu*. [Tel.] n. War, battle, combat. యుద్ధము. A place చోటు. A thrashing floor కళ్లము.

కలప *kalapa*. [Tel.] n. The wood used for a house, or for a plough. Wood in general. A pile of wood. కలపవర్తకము the timber trade. వెదురుకలప bamboos. ఏరుకలప things for ploughing. ఇంటికలప the building materials for a house.

కలపడము *kalapadamu*. [Tel.] n. Mixing. కలుపుట.

రగడ. "కలపడంబులుకలయుచి
కొక్కెంపుగస్తురిరస్తుకీలలు." శుక. i.

కలపనగంప *kalapana-gampa*. [Tel.] n. A quarrelsome fellow. కలహశీలుడు. **కలపనపిండి** (కలపడము+పిండి.) *kalapana-pindi*. n. Confusion. క్షోభము.

కలపము *kalapamu*. [Tel.] n. Mixing. కలుపుట. Perfume, scented paste used by women. పరిమళద్రవ్యములుచేర్చి కలిపిన చందనము.

కలపు *kalapu*. [Tel. Causal from కలయు.] v. t. To cause to unite or mix. n. Mixing. కలియుట.

కలబంద *kalabanda*. [Tel.] n. The aloe-plant. The *Barbadoes aloe*, the Indian aloe, *Aloe vera*. రాకాసికలబంద the American Aloe. *Agave americana*. పెద్దకలబంద or ఎలికతాళి (Bellary) the Bastard Aloe, *Agave vivipara*. చిన్నకలబంద *Aloe littoralis*. ఈరకలబంద *Aloe officinalis* (Watts). కలబందగుజ్జు the pulp of the aloe.

కలభము *kalabhamu*. [Skt.] n. An elephant thirty years old.

కలమ *kalama*. [Tel.] n. A gap, or breach.

కలమము *kalamamu*. [Skt.] n. The finest sort of rice. కలమగర్భము a swelling ear of corn: బరిపొట్టకరుకు: (to which poets compare the calves of the legs) కలమపు కొండుగలు (A. i. 85.) sun-dried grain ఎండబోసిన సన్న ధాన్యము.

కలమయపోతు *kalamaya-pōtu*. [Tel.] n. A fish of the species *Chatodon*. Russell, No. 85.

కలము *kalamu*. [Tel.] n. A ship. M. III. iv. 81. 94. B. X. 6. Also, a measure of capacity containing twelve తూములు. కలమరి *kalam-ari*. (కలము+అరి.) n. A sailor, or boatman. M. XII. v. 566. A passenger on a boat. ఓడనెక్కి పోవువాడు.

కలము *kalamu*. [H. cf. Latin *Calamus*.] n. A pen.

కలముడు *kalamudu*. [Skt.] n. A thief. దొంగ.

కలయ or కలయంగ *kalaya*. [Tel.] adv. Together: on all sides అంతట. All at once. (See కలియు of which this is the *Inf. in* A.) మాతో కలయచూచె he attempted to join us.

కలయంపి *kala-y-ampi*. [Tel.] n. Cow dung dissolved in water and sprinkled on the floors of houses. కళ్లాపు.

కలయుబడు See కలియబడు.

కలయిక *kalayika*. [Tel. from కలియు.] n. Meeting, uniting. కలిసికొనుట, సంగమము.

కలయు Same as కలియు. (q. v.)

కలరవము *kala-ravamu*. [Skt.] n. A sweet note, warbling. Also, a dove. గువ్వ. See కల adj.

కలరూపు *kala-rūpu*. [from Tel. కల existing and Skt. రూపు form.] n. The fact, the very thing, the truth. యథార్థము.

కలవంటకము *kala-vantakamu*. [Tel. కలపు+వంటకము.] n. A hotch potch; a dish containing a number of ingredients. చిత్రాన్నము.

కలవడు *kala-vadu*. [Tel. కలపు+పడు.] v. i. To mix. కలియు.

కలవరము *kalavaramu*. [Tel.] n. Confusion, puzzle. కలవరకంప *kalavara-kampa*. n. A jumble. కలవరపడు or కలవరపోవు *kalavara-padu*. v. n. To be thrown into confusion. కలవరించు *kalavar-intsu*. v. n. To babble. To have the nightmare. To talk in sleep. స్వప్నంలో మాట్లాడు. కలవరింత *kalavar-inta*. n. Babbling. Talking in sleep. నిద్రలో మాట్లాడుట.

కలవాడు *kala-vādu*. [Tel.] n. Lit. 'one who has or possesses.' A rich man ధనవంతుడు. An able man శక్తుడు. A friend ఆప్తుడు.

కలవింకము *kalavinkamu*. [Skt.] n. A sparrow. ఊరపిచ్చుక, కుంకటిమూగ అనే పిట్ట.

కలశము *kalaṣamu*. [Skt.] n. A vase, flagon, or water pot: కుండ. the gilt ornament on the pinnacle of a pagoda or tower. In palmistry, కలశరేఖలు certain lines in the palm of the hand. A. v. 31. కలశమునిలుపు or కలశముపెట్టు or కలశస్థాపనము చేయు the preliminary rite of solemnly placing a vase. కలశపూజ the adoration paid to that vessel, being the principal rite in all religious celebrations. కలశాబ్ధి *kalaṣ-abdhi*. n. The ocean of milk. కలశాబ్ధిజ the goddess Lakshmi. కలశి *kalaṣi*. n. A pot. కుండ. కలశసుతుడు or కలశసంభవుడు The "Vase-born" An epithet of Agastya, who was born, like Orion, in a pot. A. v. 107.

కలహంస or కలహంసము *kala-hamsa*. [Skt.] n. A swan with reddish beak, legs and wings ధూమ్రవర్ణములైన ముక్కు కాళ్లు రెక్కలుగల హంస. A king swan రాజహంస. The best of kings రాజశ్రేష్ఠుడు.

కలహము *kalahamu*. [Skt.] n. A fight, contention, dispute. జగడము, యుద్ధము. కలహాంతరిత *kalah-antarita*. n. A wife who has been vexed and is appeased పతిని విడనాడి తరువాత పశ్చాత్తాపసమన్వితయైన నాయిక. కలహాశనుడు *kalah-aṣanudu*. n. A quarrelsome being, a makebate; an epithet of Nārada. కలహించు *kalahintsu*. v. n. To fight, dispute. జగడమాడు.

కలాచి or కళాచి or కళాచిగా *kalāchi*. [Skt.] n. A sort of cup or bowl. A small metal box. A spittoon. ఉమ్మిపడిగము.

కలాదుడు *kal-ādudu*. [Skt.] n. A goldsmith. అగసాలెవాడు.

కలాపకము *kalāpakamu*. [Skt.] n. A chain that goes round the neck of an elephant. ఏనుగుమెడసంకెల.

కలాపన *kalāpana*. [Tel.] n. Confusion. కలత. హైదరుకలాపన Hyder's invasion or inroad.

కలాపము *kalāpamu*. [Skt.] n. An ornament. నగ. An assemblage. సమూహము. A peacock's tail నెమలిపురి. A quiver అమ్ములపొది. కృష్ణకలాపము కట్టినాడు he wore the dress or played the character of Krishṇa. సోమక్రియాకలాపము the details of a sacrifice or solemn rite. కేశకలాపము ample tresses, fine hair.

కలాపి Same as కలయుంచి (q. v.). A peacock నెమలి.

కలాలుఖానా *kalālu-khānā*. [H.] n. An arrack shop.

కలి *kali*. [Tel.] n. Fermented rice water. పులియబెట్టిన కడుగు.

కలి *kali*. [Skt.] Same as కలియుగము. (q. v.)

కలిక *kalika*. [Skt.] n. A bud. మొగ్గ.

కలికము *kalikamu*. [Tel.] n. An eyesalve. వైక్ల్యనివారణార్థము కంటికిచేసే మందు.

కలికి *kaliki*. [Tel.] n. A lady, a beauty. చక్కని ఆడుది. A charm or grace. adj. Charming, lovely, pretty. మనోజ్ఞము. **కలికితనము** *kaliki-tanamu*. n. Prettiness. **కలికిపిట్ట** *kaliki-piṭṭa*. [Tel.] n. The Darter, or Snakebird, *Plotus Melanogaster*: (F. B. I.)

కలిగెండు See కలుగు.

కలిగొట్టు *kali-goṭṭu*. [Tel.] n. The trumpet flower plant, *Bignonia chelonoides*. Ainsl. ii. 272. పాటలపుష్పచెట్టు.

కలితనము *kali-tanamu*. [Tel.] n. Ability. సామర్థ్యము, గట్టితనము.

కలితము *kali-tamu*. [Skt.] adj. Having, bearing, possessed of. కూడుకొనిన, పొందబడిన. గదాకలితుడైన armed with a mace.

కలితి or **కల్తి** *kaliti*. [Tel. from కలియు.] n. A mixture. adj. Mixed.

కలిమము *kalimamu*. [Tel.] n. Flesh, meat. మాంసము.

కలిమి *kalimi*. [Tel. from కలుగు.] n. Existence, being, possession. కలుగుట. Richness, wealth సంపద. చెలిమికలిమి riches of loving kindness. కలిమిగల rich. కలిమిచెలి the friend of riches, i.e., the goddess of wealth లక్ష్మి. **కలిమిదండుగ** *kalimi-danḍuga*. n. A property tax. నేరములేకున్నను ధనవంతునివద్ద రాజు పుచ్చుకొనే ధనము.

కలియు or **కలయు** *kaliyu*. [Tel.] v. n. To mix, join, mingle. To collect, assemble. To coalesce. To agree, correspond, match. To be included in, to fall under. To set to work, begin to do. దిక్కులు కలయచూచి looking all round. దృష్టి కలిసినప్పుడు when our eyes met. ఆతనిభూమిలో కలిసినస్థలము a spot included in his land. ఆ దారి ఇక్కడ కలియుచున్నది that road meets here. సభ కలిసినది, or సభ కలిసిపోయినది the assembly has broken up or adjourned: **కలియగలుపు** *kaliya-galupu*. n. Familiarity, affability. కలియగలుపుగానుండే familiar, easy, affable. **కలియబడు** *kaliya-baḍu*. v. n. To meddle with. To rush, fall (upon enemies). వాండ్లు మామీద కలియబడ్డారు they rushed upon us. To become entangled. "అరుకసరులకలియంబడుదు." B. viii. 457. **కలియబెట్టు** *kaliya-beṭṭu*. v. a. To mix, to stir.

కలియుగము *kali-yugamu*. [Skt.] n. The *Kali* age, i. e., modern times beginning from the Deluge. The present or Iron age. ఈ కలియుగమున in these hard times.

కలివెచెట్టు *kalive-cheṭṭu*. [Tel.] n. A thorny plant called the Blistering Papaya of Brazil, *Carissa Carandas*, వాకచెట్టు (Watts).

కలు or **కల్లు** *kalu*. [Tel.] n. A carriage wheel. బండిచక్రము. Stone రాయి. Toddy కల్లు. కలుకోట a stone fort. కలుగానుగ

a stone mill. రాతిగానుగ. కలుగుండ్లు boulders, large stones పెద్దరాళ్లు.

కలుకానుగు *kalu-kanugu.* [Tel.] n. A species of sesamum.

కలుగు *kalugu.* [Tel.] n. A hole, a pit. బొక్క. A cave గుహ.

కలుగు or **కల్గు** *kalugu.* [Tel.] v. n. To live, exist. To be. ఉండు. To happen, occur. To become అగు. To endure ఓపు. To be born పుట్టు. To meet కూడు. ఒక రాజు కలడు there was a certain king. అతనికి పిల్లలు కలిగి children being born to him. సొమ్ము కలవాడు one who has money. నాకు న్యాయము కలిగినది I got justice. అట్లా అనడము కద్దు (or కలదు) it is usual to say so. పనికలిగి వచ్చిరి they came about some business. వ్రాయగలడు he can write. అట్లా మేము చెల్లించగలవారము కాము we are not liable to pay this money. వీరాదిరాగలరాజులు (RYD. 2060) these and other princes. తెలివిగలవాడు a man of sense. యాభైయేండ్లుగలవాడు aged fifty. To be sore. వానికి కండ్లు కలిగినవి he has sore eyes. v. t. To have, to show కలిగియుండు, కనుపరచు. "కరుణగలుగుమమ్మ కమలనేత్ర." (భార. ఆది. viii.)

కలుచ *kalutsa.* [from Skt. కలుషము.] n. A fault, defect. దోషము. Confusion కలత. Anger క్రోధము. **కలుచపడు** *kalutsa-padu.* v. i. To be confused. కలతపడు.

కలుజు *kaluzu.* [Tel.] n. Foulness, dirt, rubbish. A sluice, a flood gate. The rim or stone ledge of a well, a stone facing.

కలుపు *kalupu.* [Tel. causal of కలియు.] n. A mixture. Weeds. పైరులోని కసవుకొంది తెగవి. Curds పెరుగు. v. a. To mix. To join, unite. To bring together. To receive (into one's family or caste). దాన్ని కులములో కలుపుకొన్నారు they received or admitted her into the caste అతన్ని కలుపుకొని యెందరు అయినారు including him how many were there? **కలుపుగోలుతనము** or **కలుపుగోలు** *kalupu-kolu-tanamu.* n. Intimacy, friendship. అభేదము.

కలువ or **కలవ** *kaluva.* [Tel.] n. The water lily or lotus. కలువకంటి a lotus-eyed woman, i. e., one that has beautiful eyes. కలువలదాయ the enemy of the lotus, i. e., the sun సూర్యుడు. కలువరేడు the regent of the lily, i. e., the moon. కలువవిందు the moon కుముదబాంధవుడు.

కలువడము *kaluvadamu.* [Tel. కలువ+పడము.] n. A pennon or small flag. "రత్నపుల్యక్రంతలు రాజమార్గంబులు, విపణిదేశంబులువిశదములుగ జేసిరి, చందనసిక్తతోయంబులు కలయంగజల్లిరి, కలువడములు రమణీయవివిధతోరణములుగట్టిరి." B. X. § 53. A garland of lotuses కలువ పూదండ.

కలువము *kaluvamu.* [Tel.] n. An apothecary's mortar in which drugs are rubbed with a pestle మందునూరే రాయి.

కలుషము *kalushamu.* [Skt.] n. Sin, foulness, impurity. పాపము. adj. Foul, sinful. Turbid, muddy. కలకబారిన. **కలుషించు** *kalushintsu.* v. n. To be angry or intemperate, to be agitated కలకబారు.

కలుసుకూర *kalusu-kura.* [Tel.] n. A well-cooked curry. అనుకూరావండిన కూర.

కలెక్టరు *kalectaru.* [Eng.] n. A collector, the chief revenue official in a District.

కల్కము *kalkamu.* [Skt.] n. Foulness, impurity, sediment. పాపము, మష్టి. **కల్కమాత్ర** *kalka-matra.* [Tel.]n. Eyesalve. కల్కద్రవ్యములు drugs used in electuaries.

కల్కి *kalki.* [Skt.] n. The name of the last incarnation of Vishṇu. కలికి అవతారము. **కల్కి** *kalki.* [Tel.] n. Prettiness. A lady. See కలికి. **కల్కితనము** See కలికితనము.

కల్పతరువు or **కల్పవృక్షము** *kalpa-taruvu.* [Skt.] n. The "Wishing tree" in the Hindu Paradise. The cocoanut or palm tree is called కలియుగకల్పవృక్షము.

కల్పన *kalpana.* [Skt.] n. Fabrication, invention, fiction, machination. **కల్పనచేయు** or **కల్పించు** *kalpana-cheyu.* v. a.

To fabricate, devise, invent, or contrive, to produce, form.

కల్పము kalpamu. [Skt.] n. An age. A religious rule. A code or description of religious rites. A legend or pious tale. Thus; వరలక్ష్మీవ్రతకల్పము the legend or book regarding this observance. బ్రహ్మకల్పము an age of Brahma equal to many millions of years. A series of publications as of a journal; as ప్రథమకల్పము first series, ద్వితీయకల్పము second series, &c. adj. That which is equivalent to or that which is almost the same as. సమానమైనది. A word (like ish, in blackish, whitish) denoting similarity. ద్వీపకల్పము a peninsula. కరకల్పము like a hand. తటిత్కల్పమైన resembling lightning కల్పాంతము kalp-antamu. n. The destruction of the world. The end of time. ప్రళయము. A Brahma's day బ్రహ్మదినము. కల్పుడు kalpudu. n. One who is similar to, or equal to. విద్వత్కల్పుడు almost a scholar. అగ్నికల్పుడు he who is similar (in excellence) to the god of fire. M. XIII. ii. 332.

కల్పించు kalpintsu. [Skt.] v. a. To make. To fabricate, devise. కలిగించు, చేయు, సృజించు, లేనిది ఉన్నట్టుచెప్పు. కల్పితము or కల్పితమైన kalpitamu. adj. Made, formed of. Fraudulent. Fictitious.

కల్మషము kalmashamu. [Skt.] n. Sin, taint, dirt. Any impurity, such as pus: foulness. Blackness నలుపు. కల్మాషము kalmashamu. n. Particoloured, variegated colour. చిత్రవర్ణము.

కల్యము kalyamu. [Skt.] n. The dawn. వేకువ. (A. v. 110.) Toddy. కల్లు. కల్యపాలుడు kalya-paludu. n. A toddy-drawer.

కల్ల kalla. [Tel.] n. An untruth, a falsehood, a lie. అబద్ధము. A fault తప్పు. Deception or delusion మోసము. A harsh word పరుషవచనము. The hedge of a garden తోటకంచె. adj. False అసత్యము. Harsh పరుషము. కల్లతనము kalla-tanamu. n. Bad conduct చెడ్డనడత. Deception వంచన.

కల్లచ్చు kallattsu. [Tel.] n. A touchstone, or crucible. "ఇచ్చుచో నెరిగి కల్లచ్చులనూది యచ్చులనొరగాను యగపాలియుతడు." BD. iv. 127.

కల్లము kallamu. [Tel.] n. A couch or bed. పాన్పు. Ila. iii. 135 and 168. A blow on the haunch, in boxing. తొండిపోటు.

కల్లరి kall-ari. [Tel. కల్ల+అరి.] n. A liar, deceiver, rogue. A thief or marauder, a wicked man, or criminal. అబద్ధికుడు, మోసకాడు, దుష్టుడు, తప్పుచేసినవాడు. కల్లరివేషమూని assuming a false shape. కల్లరికత్తె kalari-katte. n. A jilt, a deceitful girl. కల్లరీడు kallar-idu. n. A liar, a rogue.

కల్లరుజు kall-aruzu. [Tel.] n. A kind of fish. See అరుజు. "మిసికల్లరుజొల్లలుమీను"

హంస iv.

కల్లిపాటు or కలవెల పాటు kallipatu. [Tel.] n. Agitation, tribulation, dilemma. Fright, alarm, horror. విభ్రాంతి.

కల్లు kallu. [Tel.] n. Toddy: palmwine: నారికేళపుకల్లు cocoanut toddy: తాటికల్లు palmyra toddy: ఈతకల్లు date tree toddy, పూవుకల్లు. (R. ii. 95.) the nectar or juice of flowers. కల్లుపెంట kallu-penta. n. A toddy shop, a dram shop. కల్లమ్మేకొట్టు. కల్లుకుండ a toddy pot.

కల్లు kallu. [Tel.] A stone. Also, a wheel: (because formerly some cart wheels were made of stone.) A spoke of a carriage wheel. మంచుకల్లు a particle of dew. ఉప్పుకల్లు a crystal of salt. సీ॥ "భానుశితాంశువులు బండికండ్లుగజేసి" (Kotiswara 13.) కల్లుపడు to be stunned స్తంభించు.

"గుండెజల్లుమని కల్లుపడిమునితల్లజాపద
పల్లవంబులంద్రెళ్లియుట్లంటి." స్వా. v.

కల్లెలుక or కల్లెల్క kall-eluka. [Tel. కల్లు+ఎలుక.] n. A field mouse. పొలములలోని కలుగులందుండే ఎలుక. Swa. iv.

కల్లేడి *kall-ēdi.* [Tel. కన్నులేడి.] n. The bastard florikin or stone-curlew, *Oedicnemus scolopax.* (F. B. I.) Jerdon. No. 367. (See Swa. iv.)

కల్లేరు *kall-ēru.* [Tel. కల్లు+ఏరు.] n. A hill-torrent. కొండేరు.

కల్లోలము *kal-lōlamu.* [Skt.] n. A surge, a billow. పెద్ద అల. గృహకల్లోలము family turmoil, household troubles. కల్లోలవతి or కల్లోలిని *kallōla-vati.* n. An eddying stream: a poetical phrase for a river. R. iii. 39. ఏరు, నది.

కల్వ Same as కలువ.

కల్వము Same as కలువము.

కల్వడము See కలువడము.

కల్హారము *kal-hāramu.* [Skt.] n. A reddish fragrant water lily.

కళ or **కల** *kaḷa.* [Skt.] n. A degree, or subdivision. భాగము. That which proceeds by degrees, as effect, virtue, potency, influence, inclination. A ray of light. Look or appearance. A phase of the moon, of which the Hindus reckon sixteen. The degree in which one night's moonlight differs from that of the next. ముప్పది కాష్ఠలకాలము. చంద్రునిలో పదునారవ భాగము In Telugu Grammar, a word that does not end with an N sound. A note, as being a subdivision of music. The nerves or ticklish parts of the body. దీపముయొక్క కళ the brightness of a lamp. అతని ముఖకళ his air, the effect of his features. పిచ్చికళ a look of madness. క్రూరకళ an angry look. నిద్రకళ drowsiness. కళాస్థానములు the nerves. "కళలు చెమ్మగిలగా." (T. ii. 82.) her heart melted: it touched her to the quick. ఈ గాడ్పుకళలు నన్నిటిని పీల్చుచున్నది this burning wind exhausts the spirits కళాకలావ్యత్యయము a morbid affection: an injured constitution. దానికళ బహు బాగా ఉన్నది She has a very pretty air. పెద్దదయ్యేటప్పటికి కళవచ్చినది she is growing very pretty. కళ [Tel.] n. A swoon. మూర్ఛ. A twig కొమ్మ.

కళత్రము *kaḷatramu.* [Skt.] n. A wife శ్రీలక్ష్మీకళత్రుడు he who is wedded to glory and prosperity. ధరిత్రీధరాకళత్రుడు ruler of the land.

కళపెళ *kaḷa-peḷa.* [Tel.] n. Violently boiling. కళపెళలాడు *kaḷa-peḷal-aḍu.* v. n. To boil violently.

కళవళ or **కళవళము** *kaḷa-vaḷa.* [Tel.] n. Anxiety, distress, puzzle. కలత. కళవళపడు *kaḷa-vaḷa-paḍu.* v. n. To be agitated or anxious కలతపడు. కళవళపాటు confusion కలత. కళవళించు to be confused. To be in amazement. To be perplexed. To talk nonsense, to babble. కలతపడు, తొట్రుపడు. Also, to move చలించు.

కళసము Same as కలశము. (q. v.)

కళానిధి *kaḷā-nidhi.* [Skt.] n. An epithet of the moon. చంద్రుడు.

కళాయి *kaḷāyi.* [H.] n. A large vessel for manufacturing indigo. నీలిమందుకాచే గంగాళము. n. The tin coating given to brass vessels.

కళావంతుడు *kaḷā-vantuḍu.* [Skt.] n. An artist: an actor or dancer. A cunning rogue. కళావతి an actress (P. i. 62. A. iv. 36.) వేశ్య.

కళాసము *kaḷāsamu.* [Tel.] n. A skin or hide. చర్మము. ఇర్రికళాసము an antelope skin కృష్ణాజినము. కుక్కకళాసము dogs and curs. (Here it is an Anuk.)

కళాసి *kaḷāsi.* [H.] n. A boatman. A workman on a boat. A tentman.

కళాసించు *kaḷāsintsu.* [Tel.] v. n. To be tired. అలయు.

కళింగ *kaḷinga.* [Tel.] n. A lock in a canal; a surplus sluice.

కళింగము *kaḷingamu.* [Skt.] n. A proper name denoting the *Orissa* (ఒర్యాల) country.

కళింగభూపతి lord of Kalinga. కళింగులు the Kalingas. కళింగరాష్ట్రపుగడ్డ *kalinga-rāshṭrapu-gaḍḍa.* n. A plant that produces febrifuge nuts.

కళిక *kaḷika.* [Skt.] n. A flame.

కళుకు *kaḷuku.* [Tel.] n. Powder. పొడి. Brightness, lustre, brilliancy. కాంతి. adj. Glittering. "కళుకుబంగారుచాయ గాజులల్లన ద్రోయు." T. iv. 81.

కళుక్కుమను *kaḷukku-m-anu.* [Tel. anuk.] v. n. To start, to startle బెదరిపోవు, బెదరు కలుగు. వానికి మనస్సులో కళుక్కుమన్నది he startled, was shocked or confounded.

కళేబరము *kaḷēbaramu.* [Skt.] n. The body దేహము. A corpse. పీనుగు, శవము.

కళ్యాణము *kaḷyāṇamu.* [Skt.] n. Good fortune, weal, prosperity, marriage. కళ్యాణోత్సవము the high day, or anniversary celebrated at any temple as the god's wedding day. కళ్యాణమంటపము a small chapel attached to a temple where the god is placed when celebrating the different festivals.

కళ్ల *kaḷḷa.* [Tel.] n. Phlegm. తెమడ.

కళ్లము or కళ్లాము *kaḷḷamu.* [Tel.] n. A thrashing floor. పంటకళ్లము, ధాన్యములను నూర్చుచోటు.

కళ్లి *kaḷḷi.* [Tam.] n. The plant called milk hedge. *Euphorbia Tirukalli.* Rox. ii. 470. జెముడు.

కళ్లె *kaḷḷe.* [Tel.] n. Thick spittle or phlegm. or శైత్యముచేత గట్టిపడిన ఉమ్మి, తెమడ.

కళ్లెము, కళ్లియము or కళ్యము *kaḷḷemu.* [Tel.] n. A bridle.

కవ *kava.* [Tel.] n. Couple, pair. కవలవారు or కవలపిల్లలు twins. కన్నుగవ a pair of eyes. చన్గవ or చన్నుగవ a pair of breasts. కవలు Kusa and Lava the sons of Rāma; also Nakula and Sahādēva the Pāndava brothers.

కవకవ *kava-kava.* [Tel.] adv. Aloud. కవకవ నవ్వు laughing aloud. "చెవిదొమ్మెగ్గినసుకవకవలు గాలుసు." Dasav. v, 256.

కవచము *kavachamu.* [Skt.] n. Armour, a cover, a leather cover or case. The coating or sheathing of a boat. మంత్రకవచము an amulet, a prayer or phylactery for the safety of the body.

కవటు *kavaṭu.* [Tel.] n. A large branch of a tree. పెద్దకొమ్మ. భార: విరా. i.

కవడె *kavaḍe.* [Tel.] n. A kind of drum. ఒకవిధమైన తప్పెట.

కవణము *kavaṇamu.* [Tel.] n. Gram or other grain given as food to horses and other animals. దాణా. "చేరుదువిదగ్గలకవ గంపుచేసుంగుగములుకదల." UH. iii. 11.

కవనము *kavanamu.* [Skt.] n. Poetry. Composition. వానికి కవనశక్తిలేదు he has no talents for poetical composition.

కవను *kavanu.* [Tel.] n. Grass. కసవు.

కవర or కవరకాయ *kavara.* [Tel.] n. A piece or man, at draughts. పావిక. కవర్లాడు *kavarl-āḍu.* n. To squabble.

కవలు కవలుకొను or కవలుపోవు *kavalu.* [Tel.] n. To take up or catch up the recitation of the Veda from another person without making a break. వేదాధ్యయనమందు కొంత సామ్యముచే నొకటి విడిచి మరియొకటివచ్చి కలయుట.

గీ॥ "పాఠమొనరించుతరి వోడుపడు గురునకు
కవలుపోకుండబుత్రుడోకలుపుకొంటె."
పాండు. ii.

కవాటము *kavāṭamu.* [Skt.] A door. తలుపు.

కవాతు *kavātu.* [H.] n. Drill, parade. కవాతుచేయు to parade, to drill as soldiers.

కవి *kavi.* [Skt. lit. A maker.] n. A poet. A learned man. కవిత్వముచెప్పువాడు, పండితుడు. కవిత or కవిత్వము *kavita.* n. A poem, poetry, composition.

కవియు *kaviyu.* [Tel.] v. n. To join with, be united to. To join in combat, rush upon, fall upon. నీరుగవిసిన నిప్పువోలె like fire under ashes. To spread పర్వు, వ్యాపించు. కవించు or కవ్వించు or కవియించు *kavintsu.* v. t. To cause to rush upon, to chase తరుము, మీదపడు. కవిచేయు or కవియుకొను Same as కవియు.

కవిరి *kaviri.* [Tel.] n. The sediment of boiled betel nut which is made up into balls.

కవిల *kavila.* [from Skt. కపిల.] n. Brown color. కపిలవర్ణము.

కవిలె or **కవిలియ** *kavile.* [Tel.] n. Palm leaves prepared for writing accounts upon. దండకవిలె local archives; the record book, or register.

కవీశ్వరుడు *kav-īsvarudu.* [Skt.] n. A poet; (lit. a prince of bards.)

కవుఁగిలించు *kavu-gil-intsu.* [Tel.] v. n. To embrace. కౌగిలించు.

కవులు or **కౌలు** *kavulu.* [Tel.] n. A written agreement given to the ryot by the landlord regarding the land he takes up to cultivate. మక్తా కవులు an agreement under which land is held at an annual quit-rent for a stipulated period.

కవోష్ణము *kavōshnamu.* [Skt.] n. Warmth, slight heat. adj. Warm, rather hot. కొంచెము వేడియైన.

కవ్యము *kavyamu.* [Skt.] n. The oblation to the spirits (manes) of the deceased. పితృదేవతలకియ్యఁదగిన అన్నము.

కవ్వడి *kavvaḍi.* [Tel. కవ+వడి.] n. One who is a bi-dexter, i. e., has equal strength in his two arms. రెండుచేతుల నడిగలవాడు, i. e., Arjuna.

కవ్వము *kavvamu.* [Tel.] n. A churning staff. కవ్వపుకొండ a phrase for Mount Mandara.

కశ *kaṣa.* [Skt.] n. A whip, a cord. చబుకు.

కశేరుకము *kaṣērukamu.* [Skt.] n. The backbone. వెన్నెముక.

కశేరువు *kasēruvu.* [Skt.] n. A kind of grass. *Scirpus Kysoor.* Rox. i. 230.

కశ్మలము *kaṣmalamu.* [Skt.] n. Foulness, nastiness. మాలిన్యము.

కషణము *kashaṇamu.* [Skt.] n. Rubbing, a trial. ఒరయుట.

కషాయము *kashāyamu.* [Skt.] n. A decoction. An extract. An infusion prepared by boiling or evaporation. adj. Red brown or yellowish red. కషాయాంబరము cloth dyed red. పిచ్చికకషాయము sparrow broth. కోడికషాయము chicken broth. కషాయముకాచు to make an infusion or decoction.

కష్టము *kashṭamu.* [Skt.] n. Difficulty, labour, fatigue, hardship. An affliction, plague, pest. adj. Hard, difficult, abominable, unfortunate. వాడు కష్టములోనున్నాడు he is in difficulty. వాడు అక్కడ పదిదినములు ఉండడము కష్టము he wil hardly be there ten days. కష్టపడు or కష్టించు to take pains, to labour, toil, exert or bestir himself.

కసటు *kasaṭu.* [Tel.] n. Sin. పాపము. Dirt, foulness or foul odour, a bad taste, a nauseating flavour. కసటువోయిన seasoned, rectified, freed from a nauseating taste.

కసమస *kasa-masa.* [Tel.] n Eagerness, greediness. తొట్రుపాటు.

కసరతు *kasaratu.* [H.] n. Exercise. Gymnastics.

కసరు *kasaru.* [Tel.] n. Excess. Ill humour, sharp words, passionate language. కోపము, తిరస్కారము, చిరాకు, చీదర. గాలికసరు, a gale, a squall; a storm వానగాలి. కసరులాడి a peevish woman. కసరాదాయము surplus income. adj. Unripe, raw. కసరుకాయలు raw fruit.

కసరు or **కసరుకొను** *kasaru.* [Tel.] v. n. To move. చలించు. v. a. To scold, to bully, to speak sharply. కోపించు.

కసవు or కసువు *kasavu*. [Tel.] n. Grass, sweepings. కస్తి, ఇంటిలో ఊడ్చిన పెంట. కసవుకుప్ప a midden, a heap of refuse. చీపురితో ఊడ్చిచేర్చిన పెంట. కసవుకోడి A snipe, Ainsl. i. 393. కసవుపిట్ట a sort of sparrow.

కసాయి *kasāyi*. [H.] n. A butcher. కటిక వాడు.

కసి *kasi*. [Tel.] n. Passion, revengeful spite, bitterness, spleen, ill blood, malice. కోపము, పగ. కసితీరగాచేసె he wreaked his anger or passion. Itch దురద. Wish కోరిక. adj. Raw, unripe, unfit for the knife. కసు, పచ్చి, లేత. కసి or కసిడి adj. Petty, small. అల్పము.

కసింద or కసివింద *kasinda*. [Tel.] n. A species of Cassia or Senna. The Negro Coffeetree, *Cassia occidentalis*. నూతికసింద, or పైడితంగేడు, or తగరచెట్టు, *Cassia Sophora* (Watts.) A. vi. 12. కొండకసింద the plant called Prickly Scopolia. Ainsl. ii. 200. కాసమర్దము, మిరసగాండ్ర. Rox. i. 617, ii. 342, 346.

కసినివిత్తులు *kasini-rittulu*. [Tel.] n. The wild or Indian Endive, Chicory, or, Succory, *Cichorium Intybus*. (Watts).

కసిమసగు *kasi-masagu*. [Tel.] v. a. To cut to pieces, slay, torment. ఖండించు, బాధించు. To be eager, or unruly విజృంభించు, చెలరేగు. To kill చంపు. "కింకమున కురంగ సమితింగసిమసంగెడు తెరంగున." R. ii. 11.

కసిమసి *kasi-masi*. [Tel.] n. Eagerness. తొందరపాటు.

కసిమిరి *kasi-miri*. [Tel.] n. Itchiness. తీట.

కసివింద Same as కసింద. (q. v.)

కస్తీసము *kastsamu*. [Skt.] n. Black, dark. నల్లని. A. iv. 10.

కసు *kasu*. [Tel.] A particle denoting "A little:" Raw, young, unripe—used only in composition. కసుకందు *kasu-kandu*. n. A mere child, quite a child. లేతబిడ్డ. (Parrij. iii. 44.) Blackness. నలుపు. కసుగందు *kasu-gandu*. v. n. To fade much మిక్కిలి వాడు. n. Fading much మిక్కిలి వాడుట. కసుగాయ unripe fruit. See కసి adj.

కసుబా or కస్బా *kasubā*. [H.] n. The head station in a district.

కసుమాలము *kasu-mālamu*. [from Skt. కశ్మలము.] n. Rubbish, offal. adj. Vile, wretched, nasty.

కసురు *kasuru*. [Tel.] n. Tender fruit. లేత కాయ.

కసెము or కస్సెము *kasemu*. [Tel.] n. A pool of water, a fountain.

కస్బా See కసుబా.

కస్తి *kasti*. [Tel.] n. Grief. దుఃఖము.

కస్తురి or కస్తూరి *kasturi*. [Skt.] n. Musk. The black spot or line on the forehead, formed of musk. కస్తూరితిలకము a beauty spot or patch of musk. A familiar name for any dog. (Swa. i.) కస్తూరితుమ్మ *kastūri-tumma*. A fragrant species of the Babul tree. See తుమ్మ. కస్తూరిపట్టె *kastūri-paṭṭe*. A kind of flower ప్రియంగుకస్తూరిపట్టెలు the pink species. కస్తూరిపసుపు *kastūri-pasupu*. n. A fragrant kind of turmeric. Turmeric-coloured Zedoary. (Ainslie). కస్తూరిమల్లెచీర a sort of cloth with lines forming squares.

కహాకహా *kaha-kaha*. [Tel.] adv. Hurra, Huzza (the battle shout.) Audibly, with a crash.

కా kā

కా or గా *kā*. the adverbial sign గా. Is it not so, to be sure కదా, కాదా. వాడు న్నాడుకా he is there, I suppose. వాడు వ్రాసినాడుకా you see he wrote it. ఆ యెద్దులు అతనివికావచ్చును perhaps the cattle are his. నగదుగా ఇచ్చినారు they paid it in silver. See గా, and అగు. కాగానే as soon as it is done.

కాంక్ష *kānksha*. [Skt.] n. Wish, desire. ఇచ్ఛ, కోరిక. **కాంక్షించు** *kānkshintsu*. v. a. To wish, desire. ఇచ్ఛించు. **కాంక్షితము** *kānkshitamu*. adj. Wished for, desired. కోరబడినది.

కాంచనము *kānchanamu*. [Skt.] n. Gold. కాంచనవల్లి a piece of gold wire. కాంచనాంబరము tissue, gold cloth.

కాంచెరచెట్టు *kāntsara-chettu*. [Tel.] n. A creeper the seeds of which are used for food.

కాంచి *kānchi*. [Skt.] n. A woman's girdle; ఆడుదాని మొలనూలు. Conjevaram. కాంచీపురము.

కాంచు *kāntsu*. [Tel. from కను.] v. a. To see, view, look at, behold. To possess, enjoy: to have, obtain, receive, acquire. పొందు. సన్నుతిగాంచు to receive applause. To bear, produce, bring forth, generate. కుమారునిగాంచె she bore a son.

కాండపటము *kānda-patamu*. [Skt.] n. A screen or curtain. తెర.

కాండము *kāndamu*. [Skt.] n. Water. నీళ్లు. Opportunity సమయము. An arrow బాణము. A stem or stalk కాడ. A handle. A cluster or clump దుబ్బు. A chapter or section పరిచ్ఛేదము. కర్మకాండము the doctrine of works, the required rites. ఊరుకాండములు the thighs.

కాండ్రదుబ్బులు *kāndra-dubbulu*. [Tel.] n. Bulrushes, high grass.

కాండ్రించు *kāndrintsu*. [Tel.] v. n. To hawk in clearing the throat; to retch in vomiting. వాని ముఖము కాండ్రించుకొన్నది his face is inflamed, or slightly swollen. కాండ్రించుకొన్న ముఖము a grim, gaunt face.

కాండ్రు *kāndru*. [Tel.] n. The roar of a tiger. పులిబొబ్బ. Swa. iv.

కాంత *kānta*. [Skt.] n. A fair one; a lovely woman; a lady.

కాంతము *kāntamu*. [Skt.] n. A stone. రాయి, as in సూర్యకాంతము and చంద్రకాంతము. అయస్కాంతము a lode-stone. కాంతము adj. Pleasing, charming, lovely, friendly మనోహరమైన.

కాంతారము *kāntāramu*. [Skt.] n. A wilderness. అడవి. A pathless desert. పోరాని అడవి.

కాంతాళము *kāntālamu*. [Tel.] n. Anger caused by grief. వ్యాకులముమీదవచ్చేకోపము. Irritation as of anger or the grief of anger. Impatience తాలిమిలేమి. **కాంతాళపడు** *kāntāla-padu*. v. n. To be impatient. ఈర్ష్యపడు.

కాంతి *kānti*. [Skt.] n. Brilliancy, lustre, hue. చిత్రకాంతులు variegated hues.

కాంతుడు *kāntudu*. [Skt.] n. A lover or sweetheart. Lord, a king, a husband.

కాందిశీకము or **కాందిశీకత్వము**. *kāndiśīkamu*. [Skt.] n. Flight, running away. Putting to flight. **కాందిశీకుడు** *kāndiśīkudu*. n. A runaway. భయముచేత పారిపోవువాడు.

కాంబళము *kāmbalamu*. [Skt.] adj. Covered with a blanket, as a carriage. కంబళిచేత కప్పబడిన (బండి.)

కాంబోది *kāmbōdi*. [Tel.] n. A kind of grain. సస్యవిశేషము. V. P. iii.

కాంభోజము *kāmbhōjamu*. [Skt.] n. The country of Cambay. A horse imported from that country. కాంభోజి the name of a sweet tune in Indian music.

కాంస్యము *kāmsyamu*. [Skt.] n. Bell metal. కంచు.

కాక *kāka*. [Tel. imperative of అగు.] v. n. (So) be it. అనుటయునట్లకాకయనె on his saying so, so be it, said he. కాకయేమి why not? నీవు సుఖముగా నుండుదువుగాక mayest thou be happy. పోసిరోకాక probably they poured; they may have poured. కాక (negative imperfect participle of

అను.) Not being so, disliking. కక్షక, సరిపడక. adv. Spitefully, through enmity. నామీదకాక ఇట్లు చేసినాడు he did this through ill will to me. కాక. (affix.), Except, besides, unless, but: ఇదికాక and besides this, further.

కాక *kāka*. [Tel. from కాచు.] n. Heat, warmth వేడిమి. Anger, harshness, ill will, unkindness. కోపము. Fever జ్వరము. Gonorrhea. కాక adj. Hot, warm, angry. కాకకురుపులు boils caused by heat. కాకమాటలు hot words.

కాకము *kākamu*. [Skt.]n. A crow. **కాకతాళీయము** *kāka-tālīyamu*. n. Chance, casualty, accident. "Like the crow and the palm fruit"—a phrase denoting coincidence (అవితర్కితసంభవము): as a palm fruit falling just when a crow has alighted: కాకతాళీయమైన sudden, opportune, unexpected. కాకతాళీయముగా or కాకతాళీయన్యాయముగా suddenly, casually, accidentally.

కాకతుండము *kāka-tundamu*. [Skt.] n. A kind of trumpet. కాహళము.

కాకపక్షము *kāka-pakshamu*. [Skt.]Same as జొంపాలు. (q.v.)

కాకపాల or **కాకుపాల** *kākapāla*. [Tel.] n. A plant named *Zizyphus Trinervius*. Ainslie ii. 69. *Asclepias asthmatica*: used as a substitute for ipecacuanha. Rox. ii. 33. వాతనారాయణకాకు.

కాకపుష్టము *kāka-pushtamu*. [Skt.] n. The Indian cuckoo. కోయిల.

కాకపోవు *kāka-pōvu*. [Tel.] v. t. To fail. ఇది కాకపోయినది this failed.

కాకమారి *kāka-māri*. [Skt.] n. Crows' bane. The *cocculus indicus*, a strong narcotic poison (Ainslie.); *Anamirta Cocculus*. (Watts.)

కాకర *kākara*. [Tel.] n. The creeping plant with a gourd-like fruit, *Momordica charantia*. పొట్టికాకర *Mom. muricata*. బుడ్డకాకర the small leaved heart-pea, *Cardiospermum halicacabum*. (Ainslie and Watts.) బొబ్బకాకర *Momordica operculata*. అడవికాకర. the wild sort. అడవికాకర, తెల్లకాకర, ఎర్రకాకర are other species.

కాకరవత్తి *kākara-vatti*. [Tel.] n. A kind of fireworks which when burnt throws out flowers resembling the leaves of the కాకర creeper.

కాకలము *kākalamu*. [Skt.] n. Paper. కాగితము.

కాకలి *kākali*. [Skt.] n. A trilling note or gentle warble. Melody. సూక్ష్మమైన అవ్యక్త మధురధ్వని.

కాకవెలుగు *kāka-velugu*. [Tel.] n. The Sun. సూర్యుడు. Sunshine సూర్యరశ్మి.

కాకాక్షిన్యాయము *kākākshi-nyāyamu*. [Skt.] n. (In logic.) An argument (zeugma) that cuts both ways. Lit. after the manner of a crow's eye. So called from a crow's peculiar manner of squinting at an object. కాకిచూపువలెనేకైన ఉభయపక్షగామి. This argument is also called అడ్డగోడమీది పిల్లి a cat on a partition wall. A Sanskrit phrase used in illustrating the applicability of one word in two or more senses. See Colebr, on Mitakshara, p. 358.

కాకి *kāki*. [Tel. lit. that which says *ka, ka*.] n. A crow. అడవికాకి the jungle crow or *Corvus macrorhynchus*. ఊరకాకి or ఊరకాకి the Indian house crow, *corvus splendens*. (F. B. I.) This word sometimes denotes depreciation as కాకిబంగారు false gold, tinsel. కాకిదొండపండు the wild cherry. దేశకాకి, or దేశద్రిమ్మరికాకి a wandering wretch or vagrant. సముద్రపుకాకి an osprey. నీరుకాకి a cormorant. ఇనుపముక్కుకాకి the giant vulture or king of the vultures. మాలకాకి a raven. బొంతకాకి a raven. **కాకిచంపు విత్తులు** *kāki-champu-vittulu*. Same as కాకమారి. (q. v.) **కాకిచావు** *kāki-tsāvu*. n. Apoplexy, sudden death. **కాకిఅప్ప** *kāki-*

chippa. n. A bivalve shell. కాకిచెమ్మలు or కాకిదీపు or కాకిపోటుమూల or కాకిపోమ్మ kâki-chemmalu. n. Fainting, epilepsy. కాకిబాతు kâki-bâtu. n. A brown species of wild duck. కాకిరెక్కలు kâki-rekkalu. n. The grain called millet. కాకివెదురు kâki-veduru. n. A reed.

కాకితము Same as కాగితము.

కాకు kâku. [Tel.] n. Confusion. కలత. Pain. గాసి. "గాలిరజోకాక్లిష్టిగాకుజేసి." Vasu. iv. 14. adj. Vain వ్యర్థము, కూగ్లము. కాకుచేయు kâku-chêyu. v. a. To throw into confusion. To outvie or outshine. కాకుపడు to be troubled, startled, or in confusion. T. iv. 153. కాకుపరచు to throw into confusion. "చీకటికాటుకపిట్ట లకాకుపడగా, భాస్కరుండు కరజాలకముల్ బికనికుడింప, తారలు వ్యాకులతందారెఖగములకు టణ్ధిరగా." T. iv. 153.

కాకువు kâkuvu. [Skt.] n. A kind of noise made in grief or fear. శోకభయాదులచేత కలుగునట్టి ఒకవిధమైన ధ్వని.

కాకోదరము kâkôdaramu. [Skt.] n. Snake, a serpent.

కాకోలము kâkôlamu. [Skt.] n. A raven. బొంతకాకి, మాలకాకి.

కాగడా kâgadâ. [Tel. కాగు+కడ.] n. A torch, a lighted wisp. దివిటీ. కుండకొపెట్టిన కాగడావత్తి a dark lantern. (This denotes "Hiding one's lamp under a bushel.")

కాగా kâgâ. [Tel.] adv. Because, seeing that. తమరుకాగా ఇది సాగినది this has been effected through you indeed. The same as అయ్యేటట్టుగా. కరమాశ్చర్యముగాక to their great astonishment. కాగానే as soon as; therefore. ఆ పెండ్లి కాగానే as soon as ever the marriage was over. ఆ సమయములో తమరు వెయ్యి యిచ్చినారు, కాగానే ప్రాణము దక్కినది I owe my life to your aid.

కాగితము, కాకితము or కాగిదము kâgitamu. [H.] n. Paper, a card. ఆటకాగితాలు playing-cards. కాగితాలాట a game at cards.

కాగిస kâgisa. [Tel.] n. The stickleback fish. Gasterosteus aculeatus.

కాగు kâgu. [Tel.] v. n. To be heated (as the earth with sunshine). To boil, simmer, to grow hot, to be feverish. తపించు. To grieve, pine, be in trouble or sorrow. To be angry కోపపడు. "కన్నమోహంబునకాగు నీకు" To thee who burnest with maternal love. కాగు n. A boiler, a kettle, a jar. పెద్దబాన.

కాచము kâchamu. [Skt.] n. Glass. గాజు. P. i. 586. కాచకటకము a bracelet of glass. A. v. 130.

కాచి kâchi. [Tel.] n. A herb with a small lilac flower and black berries, used as a medicine for coughs. One kind is నల్లకాచి the other is ఎర్రకాచి. H. iv. 12.

కాచు kâtsu. [Tel. from కాగు.] v. n. To be hot; to shine, as the sun or moon. To be hot as fever. To wait, dangle in attendance. నాకు జ్వరముకాచినది I had the fever on me. కొంచెము జ్వరముకాస్తున్నది there is a little fever. చలికాచుకొనుట to bask or sit by the fireside, or to warm oneself. ఎండకాస్తున్నది there is sunshine. ఆ చింతచెట్టు కాయుడములేదు that tamarind tree does not bear. To wait for, attend on నాకొరకు కాచుకొన్నాడు he is waiting for me. అతని వద్ద మూడు ఏండ్లు కాచుకొని యుంటిని I was in attendance on him for three years. కాచు v. a. To boil; to heat, to warm. To bear fruit. కాగచేయు. ఆ ఊరంతా కాచి వడపోసినాడు lit. he has boiled and strained off the town, i. e., he has made himself master of the whole town. తేయాకుకాచు to make tea. బెల్లము కాచడము sugar making. రాత్రి అంతా కాకికాచడము కట్టడముతో సరిపోయినది the whole night was passed in fomenting and binding up the limbs.

కాచు *kāṭsu*. [Tel.] v. a. To guard, keep, watch, tend, protect, take care of. To nourish. To spare, have mercy on, forgive, excuse. రక్షించు, కాపాడు. To keep off. అడ్డు. పశువులుకాచడము to tend cattle. పశువులుకాచేవాడు a cow herd. రాత్రియంతా నిద్రకాచినాడు he kept awake all night. నన్నుకాచే దిక్కులేదు I have nobody who cares for me. నేను అట్లా చేసినట్టయితే నన్ను కాయకండి have no mercy on me if I have done so.

కాచు *kāṭsu*. [Tel] n. The extract, or, the medicine called Catechu: the inspissated juice of the చండ్రచెట్టు or ఖదిరము.

కాచికోలు *kāchi-kōlu*. [Tel.] n. Rescue, saving. రక్షణము.

కాచుకొను Same as కాచు v. a. and v. n.

కాజి *kāji*. [Tel.] n. A kind of tree. (పా. ii.)

కాజీ *kājī*. [H.] n. A judge. న్యాయాధిపతి.

కాజేయు *kā-jēyu*. [Tel.] v. a. To accomplish, to finish, to effect, to make away with. సాధించు, అపహరించు. To spend వ్యయముచేయు.

కాటకము *kāṭakamu*. [Tel.] n. Scarcity, famine. కరువు.

కాటమరాజు *kāṭama-rāju*. [Tel.] A rustic divinity like Silenus, worshipped by shepherds. See కాత్రేడు.

కాటా *kāṭa*. [Tel.] n. Scales for large weights.

కాటిపాపడు *kāṭi-pāpaḍu*. [Tel. కాడు+పాపడు.] n. A cowherd. "కాటిపాపడు పసిగాచుచుండ." BD. iv. 157.

కాటిపాపలవాడు *kāṭi-pāpala-vāḍu*. [Tel.] n. A juggler, a conjurer. హస్తలాఘవముచేసే వాడు.

కాటిరేడు *kāṭi-rēḍu*. [Tel. కాడు+రేడు.] n. Lord of the burning ground, i. e., Siva.

కాటు *kāṭu*. [Tel.] n. A bite, notch, cut, scar. కరుచుట, కోతపడినగాయము. Being burnt or singed. మాడి అడుగంటుట.

కాటుక *kāṭuka*. [Tel.] n. Lampblack. Mildew in grain. Eyesalve, or sulphuret of antimony. Collyrium, a paste made of lampblack and oil and applied to the eyes to increase their brilliancy. It is also supposed to assist in conjuring and giving second sight. అంజనము. కాటుక is *lustre* or dark brown. ఎర్రకాటుకలు a species of grain. మందుకాటుక love powders or eyesalve. భూతకాటుక magic powder. కాటుకవలె నూరినాడు he beat it to the consistency of paste. adj. Dark, deep in colour, dark brown, but distinct from black నల్ల. కాటుకపచ్చ dark green. నిడిపచ్చ light green. కాటుకకన్నులు bright black eyes. **కాటుకపట్టు** *kāṭuka-paṭṭu*. v. n. To become black నలుపు పారు. **కాటుకపిట్ట** *kāṭuka-piṭṭa*. n. A wagtail: see జిట్టంగి and దాసరిపిట్ట. **కాటుకరాయి** *kāṭuka-rāyi*. n. Sulphuret of antimony. సౌవీరాంజనము. **కాటుక రేకులపొడ** or **పులిపొడర** *kāṭuka-rēkula-poḍa*. n. A certain venomous snake.

కాటుపెట్టు *kāṭu-peṭṭu*. [Tel.] v. a. To bite. To notch, cut, open.

కాటుపోవు *kāṭu-pōvu*. [Tel.] v. n. To be singed or burnt as milk or food. To be smoked. మాడి అడుగంటు.

కాటులాడు *kāṭul-āḍu*. [Tel. కాటులు+ఆడు.] v. n. To fall out, to quarrel. కలహించు.

కాటువాసన *kāṭu-vāsana*. [Tel.] n. A smoky singed smell.

కాటేరి *kāṭēri*. [Tel.] n. A forest goddess whose power lies in sending diarrhœa or cholera, &c.

కాత్రగడ *kātra-gaḍa*. [Tel.] n. A boundary hedge round a town, a stockade or palisade. కంచుకోట.

కాత్రేడు *kāt-rēḍu*. [Tel. i. e., కాటిరేడు.] The "king of the cemetery." A certain fiend. కాత్రేనిపూజ the worship of this fiend as described in Kālahas. M. iii. 43.

కాడ *kāḍa.* [Tel.] n. A stem, stalk, shoot, handle, shaft. కోడిమె. An arrow బాణము. A. iv. 293.

కాడ *kāḍa.* [Tel. for కడ] adv. At, near, by. ఇంటికాడ at home, at his house. "ఏలయుం టుకాడికేడవు" A. vi. 94. అనగా కల అంటు కాకేపోటి విలంబము. n. State, condition, rate, thus: వానియిల్లు ఈకాడికి వచ్చినది to such a state is his family reduced. ఈగుడ్డ యేకాడికి యిస్తావు at what rate do you sell this cloth?

కాడారంబము *kāḍ-ārambamu.* [Tel.] n. Dry cultivation. See నీరారంబము or మాగాణి.

కాడి *kāḍi.* [Tel.] n. A yoke. కాడిగట్టు the ridge between two fields, a boundary or landmark. ఒకరికొకరికి నేలకుండే హద్దుకట్ట. (gen. కాటి, loc. కాట. plu. కాండ్లు.) **కాడి** n. Vinegar. పులియబెట్టిన కడుగునీరు.

కాడు or **గాడు** *kāḍu.* [Tel. for వాడు.] (an affix.) He, that man. సొగసుకాడు a pretty fellow. వేషగాడు a masker. Added to names, it denotes meanness or low station in life, thus: అబ్బిగాడు, సుబ్బిగాడు, as in English, a fellow named so and so. It is also part of the names of some animals as ఇబ్బంది కాడు a leopard. బావురు గాడు a he cat. పసులపోలిగాడు the bird called a drongo or kingcrow.

కాడు *kāḍu.* [Tel.] n. A funeral pile; a burying ground, or burning ground, శ్మశానము. కాటికి కాళ్లు చాచుకొని యున్నాడు he has one foot in the grave. A forest, a wilderness అడవి. (infl. కాటి.) Ruin నాశము. **కాడుచేయు** *kāḍu-cheyu.* v. t. To ruin, destroy. నాశముచేయు. **కాడుపడు** or **కాడ్పడు** *kāḍu-paḍu.* v. n. To be confused. కలతపడు. To be ruined. To be lost చెడిపోవు. నష్టమగు. కాడుపరుచు to ruin.

కాడు *kāḍu.* [Tel.] v. a. To enter, penetrate, go through, pierce, transfix. నాటు. A. iii. 37. & A. i. 66.

కాణము *kāṇamu.* [Skt.] adj. One eyed. కాణవరాటము or కాణవరాటకము a broken shell. A worthless fragment నష్టికవ్వ. Ved. Ras. iii. 58. The one eyed creature, i. e., a crow. **కాణము** *kāṇamu.* [Tel.] n. Food, provender, fodder. Grass. గ్రాసము, కసువు. "కోటకేమరికపుడు బాటించి కట్టియు గాణంబుగొలుచును." M. XII. ii. 303.

కాణాచి or **కాణయాచి** *kāṇāchi.* [Tel.] n. Inherited right or right of possession మిరాసి. చిరకాలవాసస్థానము. A hereditary right to enjoy a certain office or a piece of land. చిరకాలానుభవముగలది.

కాణాదము *kāṇādamu.* [Skt.] n. Kanada's logic. కణాదుని న్యాయశాస్త్రము.

కాణి *kāṇi.* [Tel.] n. The fraction called $\frac{1}{64}$: or, one quarter of a sixteenth. A measure of land, about an acre. కాణీమంతముకోటి దుఃఖము the smallest folly may cause much trouble.

కాణుడు *kāṇuḍu.* [Skt.] n. A one-eyed being ఒంటికంటివాడు. See కాణము.

కాత or **కావుత** *kāta.* [Tel. from అగు.] An affix in blessing. May it be so! అగుగాక.

కాతరము *kātaramu.* [Skt.] adj. Frightened, perplexed. **కాతరుడు** *kātaruḍu.* n. A timid man. భయశీలుడు, అధీరుడు.

కాతా *kātā.* [H.] n. An account. Dealings with a merchant.

కాతాళము *kātāḷamu.* [Tel.] n. Rashness, hastiness, passion. కోపము. P. iii. 299.

కాత్యాయని *kātyāyani.* [Skt.] n. A name of Pārvati.

కాదంబము n. Same as కలహంసం. (q. v.)

కాదంబరి *kādambari.* [Skt.] n. Wine. మద్య ము. A certain timber tree. *Nauclea kadamba.* Name of a Sanskrit Poem.

కాదంబిని *kādambini.* [Skt.] n. A line of clouds. మేఘపంక్తి.

కాదను *kadanu*. [Tel. కాదు+అను.] v. a. To deny, refuse, reject, forbid to do. To disapprove; to say it is not right. See కాదు.

కాదా *kada*. [Tel. కాదు+ఆ.] v. Is it not? Same as కదా.

కాదాచిత్కము *kādāchitkamu*. [Skt. from కదాచిత్.] n. Scarcity, rareness ఒకానొక ప్పుడు కలుగునది. కాదాచిత్కమైన unusual, infrequent.

కాదారి or కాదారిమూదారి *kadari*. [Tel.] n. Midnight. అర్ధరాత్రము.

కాదు *kadu*. [Tel. from అను.] v. It is not (so). It is not possible. It is out of the question. It is opposed to అవును, i. e., yes, అది మంచిదికాదు it is not good. అవునాకాదా yes or no? ఈయెండచేత పైరుకాదు the crop won't come forward on account of the heat. వారిని పిలిస్తేనేగాని కాదన్నాడు he said nothing could be done unless they were invited. వానికి నాకు కాదు he and I do not agree. ఇది ఒక రాజ్యముకాదు this is a wretched place. కాదే *kade*. [కాదు+ఏ.] Is it not so? కాదా.

కాద్రవేయుడు *kādra-vēyuḍu*. [Skt.] n. A serpent: as being "the child of Kadruva."

కాన *kana*. [Tel.] adv. Then, therefore. కనక. n. A forest. అడవి.

కాననము *kānanamu*. [Skt.] n. A forest. అడవి.

కానబడు or కానబట్టు *kanabadu*. [Tel.] v. n. Appear, seem. See కాను.

కాని *kani*. [Tel.] n. A quarter of an anna.

కాని *kāni*. [Tel.] (neg. part. of అను.) Which cannot be done. కొరగాని useless. చేతకాని unskilled, awkward. అనువుకానివేళ at an inconvenient time. కాని adj. Bad, vile, envious. కానిగుణము a vile temper. కానికులము a low caste. కానివాడు an enemy. కానిపని a vile act.

కాని or గాని *kani*. [Tel.] (conj. denoting an alternative.) But, either, or, except, unless. And not, nor. Rather. Before.

"జాజితియొక్కటియొకాని సకలకుసుమ
వితరసంపదచేనొప్పె వసుధయెల్ల
విరహిణులకుకానిధరిత్రిపై వివిధజనులు
సంతసములొందజేసె వసంతవేళ."

Sunandā Parinyam, iv. 22.

"అలు మగనిమాట కడ్డంబు వచ్చెనా
అలుకాదది వానిపాలుకాని."

(Vēma.)

ఇంతేకాని నేనేమెరుగను I know nothing but this. ఇదియేమోకాని I cannot tell what this may be. అదిగాని యిదిగాని either that or this. ఆపని పది దినములకుగానికాదు that work cannot be finished in less than ten days. రేపుగాని రాడు he will not come here before to-morrow. ఉద్యోగము దొరుకునని ఆశతో ఉంటేగాని నేను అక్కడ ఉండను I would not have remained there had I not hoped to gain employment. ఇది అతని చేతగాని మరియొకనిచేతకాదు he alone can do it, no one else can. ఎల్లవిధములు నిను వధి యించిగాని మరలకపోవుదుము గావున for we will not return without slaying thee. అతడు వస్తేనేగాని యీపనికానేరదు unless he comes we cannot effect this. కాని or కానీ (for కానిమ్ము) imp. verb denoting assent. Let it be done. Be it so. Never mind. Very well. ఆ పని మంచిదికానీ let that be done first. కానీకానీ నీ కావరమణతు very well, I will crush your pride.

కానిక Same as కానుక. (q. v.)

కానితనము *kāni-tanamu*. [Tel.] n. Enmity. See కాని adj.

కానిపించు or కాన్పించు *kanipintsu*. [Tel.] v. n. To be visible, to appear. ప్రత్యక్షమగు, కనబడు. v. t. To show. కనబరచు.

కానీనుడు *kanīnuḍu*. [Skt.] adj. Virgin-born. n. One born to a virgin. కన్యకాసుతుడు. Vyāsa or Karna.

కాను or కానుమజ్జిగ *kānu*. [Tel.] n. Thick buttermilk. చిక్కనిమజ్జిగ.

కాను *kānu*. [Tel. another form of కను.] v. a. To perceive, to see or enjoy, నీ చప్పుడు కానబడలేదు I did not recognize your voice. రవికానని చోటు కవి కాంచును every-thing that the sun sees is seen by the poet. కానవే do you not know. మోక్షము కానలేడు he cannot see or enjoy bliss or heaven. See కానిపించు.

కానుక or కాన్క *kānuka*. [Tel. from కాను.] n. An offering or courtesy, made in homage to a superior, or to a god. A gift on which the lord is supposed to cast his "glance."

కానుగు *kānugu*. [Tel.] n. The tree called *Galedupa arborea* (Roxb.) తరులభ్యక్షము. *Dalbergia arborea* (Ainslie ii. 332.) *Galedupa Punga*, Heyne. "కాలుకాదు కానుగ కాదు" (proverb.)

కానుపు *kānupu*. [Tel. from కను.] n. Breed-ing, bearing, bringing forth. ప్రసవము. Seeing చూచుట. "అది కలలోని కానుపయి" వాసు. ఆ. vii.

కాపట్యము *kāpatyamu*. [from Skt. కప టము.] n. Hypocrisy.

కాపడము *kāpadamu*. [Tel. from కాచు.] n. Fomentation.

కాపథము *kāpathamu*. [Skt.] n. A bad way. కుత్సితపుత్రోవ.

కాపరి *kāpari*. [Tel. from కాచు.] n. A keep-er. రక్షకుడు. ఆలకాపరి or పసులకాపరి a herdsman.

"కాపరిలేని గొర్రెములక్రియను కంటకచోరకోటిచే, నేపడియున్న దీభువన మీశుడు కృష్ణుడులేమి." భాగ. i.

కాపాడు *kāpādu*. [Tel. from కాచు.] v. a. To guard, watch, keep, to preserve, or protect, patronise. To secure from failure. అతనిమాట కాపాడుకొనేటందుకు with a view to verify his statement.

కాపిలము *kāpilamu*. [Skt.] n. The philoso-phy of Kapila. సాంఖ్యశాస్త్రము. "కాపిలము వావలంబు." అను. i.

కాపు *kāpu*. [Tel. from కాచు.] n. Keeping, attendance. Protection, guard. రక్షణము. Heat, warmth (This is from కాగు.) Pro-ductiveness కాయలుకాచుట. The crop or fruit. కాపుడిగినచెట్టు a tree that is past bearing. కండ్లకు రెప్పలు కాపుగానున్నవి the eyelids are a protection to the eyes. కాపు ఉంచు to place a guard. కాపు or కాపువాడు n. A tenant. A farmer, a cultivator. A rustic or countryman. A person, an individual, a dweller. మంచు కొండకాపు or హిమాచలవాసి. Siva రుద్రుడు. సొమ్ముకాపు a holder or owner of property. పాలికాపు a member or shareholder. మహా నాటికాపులు leaguesmen, members of the (Mahanadu) community. కాపుగడ or కాపుదల *kāpugada*. n. Protection. కాచుట, రక్షించుట. కాప *kāpa*. adj. Appertain-ing to the farmer caste. కాపుమాటలు rustic language. The vocative of కాపు a farmer. ఓకాప, నీవెట్లాకో వచ్చితి విటకు O farmer, how did you come here? B.D. iv. 1963. కాపత *kāpata*. n. A country girl, a rustic. The female of కాపు. కాపు తనము *kāpu-tanamu*. n. The rustic condition, the state of farmers. ఈ కాపు తనమును విడిచిపెట్టడము మేలు it would be better to give up the farming business. కాపుది A woman of the farming caste, a female rustic.

కాపురము *kāpuramu*. [Tel.] n. Home, dwelling, abode, residence, lodgings. అక్కడ కాపురముండినారు or కాపురముచేసి నారు they lived there, they made their home there. ఆ కాపురమును చూడుడుపోవల చేసినాడు he has broken up his family. అతడు వేరుగా కాపురము చేస్తాడు he lives separate. కాపురస్థుడు *kāpurasthudu*. n. An inhabitant, a tenant, a native. కాపురస్థు రాలు a female inhabitant. కాపురించు Same as కాపురముచేయు.

కాపురుషుడు kā-purushuḍu. [Skt.] n. A base wretch, a miscreant, an effeminate coward. కుత్సితపురుషుడు.

కాపేయము kāpēyamu. [Skt. from కపి.] adj. Simian, pertaining to monkeys. n. Monkeyhood; the state of being like a monkey. కపిత్వము. "పలుమరు కాపేయంబున దలపకపలికెదవు." BRK. 243. "భూపుత్రి, యునికిదలపక కాపేయముచేసి స్వామి ఘాతుడ నైతిన్." BR. Sundra 555.

కాపోతము kāpōtamu. [Skt.] n. A bevy of doves. కపోతముల సమూహము. కాపోత వర్ణము kāpōta-varṇamu. n. Dove colour. BD. iii. 520.

కాపోతాంజనము kāpōt-āñjanamu. [Skt.] n. Antimony: particularly considered as a collyrium.

కాప్యకారము kāpya-kāramu. [Skt.] n. Hypocritical talk. మనసున పాపముంచి [illegible].

కాబట్టి kā-baṭṭi. [Tel. కాక+పట్టి.] adv. Therefore, consequently. గనుక, అయినందున.

కాబడు kā-baḍu. [Tel.] v. n. To become. అగు.

కాబోలు or కాబోలును. kā-bōlu. [Tel. కా to be+పోలును it seems.] adv. It may be; surely; perhaps, probably. [illegible].

కామ kāma. [Tel.] n. The handle of an axe, hoe, umbrella, &c. దండము, కర్ర. A stalk, staff or shaft కాడ. కూరకామ the stalk of a kind of eatable greens.

కామంచిగడ్డి kāmanchi-gaḍḍi. [Tel.] n. Spice grass, lemon grass or camel's hay. *Andropogon Schænanthus*. Ainslie. ii. 58. కామంచిచెట్టు kāmanchi-cheṭṭu. [Tel.] n. The fox grape, a kind of nightshade, *solanum nigrum*.

కామందు kāmandu. [H.] n. Owner, master. యజమానుడు.

కామధేనువు kāma-dhēnuvu. [Skt.] n. The mythological cow of plenty having the face of a woman and the body of a cow and supposed to give whatever one desires.

కామము kāmamu. [Skt.] n. Love, lust. Wish, desire, concupiscence. ఇచ్ఛ. కామకేళి sexual intercourse. కాముకుడు kāmanuḍu. n. A lustful man. కామచారి kāma-chāri. adj. Sensual, selfish; following one's own pleasure. కామగము kāmagamu. adj. Wish-guided; going at will as an enchanted car. [illegible]. కామరూపి kāma-rūpi. adj. Protean, plastic, able to assume any shape. The heroes Sugriva and Hanuman and all the Rakshasas were *kāmarūpis*, being able to assume various shapes at will. కామాంకుశము kām-ānkuṣamu. n. A stimulant or aphrodisiac. A finger nail గోరు. కామాంధకారము kām-āndhakāramu. n. Blindness of lust. కామాతురుడు kām-āturuḍu. A lustful man. కామానలము kām-analamu. n. The fire of love.

కామర్లు or కామలు or కామాలు kāmarlu. [Tel.] n. The disease called jaundice. ఉబ్బుకామర్లు dropsy. ఎండుకామర్లు consumption.

కామాకు or గండకామాకు kāmāku. [Tel.] n. A sort of Arum.

కామాక్షి kāmākshi. [Skt.] n. The goddess of love. కామాక్షిగడ్డి a kind of grass.

కామాటము kāmaṭamu. [Tel.] n. Rough work. మోటుపని. R. viii. కామాటి kāmaṭi. n. A labourer, a pioneer. మోటుపనిచేయువాడు. adj. Rustic.

కామి kāmi. [Skt.] n. A libertine. కాముకుడు. కామికానివాడు a man free from passion.

కామి kāmi. [Tel. neg. noun from అవు.] n. The not being. That which is not or nil. కొరగాములు evil doings, naughty pranks. "ఇంక చిన్నందు నిట్టి కొరగాములు సేయక బుద్ధిమంతుడవై యుండుమనిన నతండు

లజ్జావనతివదనుండగుచు నచ్చోటువాసి గంగా ద్వారంబున కరిగియుండు" M. III. vi. "క॥ ఏవట్లు మాదిచెప్పితిగాని యది రణంబుపాటిగాని దొరసురుగా" M. IX. ii. 114.

కామించు *kāmintsu*. [Skt.] v. a. To desire, or long for. To like, delight in, love. కామితము *kāmitamu*. adj. Desired: desirable. కామిని *kāmini*. n. A lustful woman. A woman.

కామిలా *kāmila*. [Skt.] n. Jaundice. See కామరులు.

కామిలేడిపిట్ట *kāmi-lēḍi-piṭṭa*. [Tel.] n. The bird called a florikin. *Sypheotis aurita*. (F. B. I.)

కాముకము *kāmukamu*. [Skt.] adj. Lustful, desirous. ఇచ్ఛగల. కాముకుడు *kāmukuḍu*. n. A lustful man. కాముడు *kāmuḍu*. n. A name of Cupid: (In compounds) Desirous, thus: కీర్తికాముడు desirous of glory. కామునిపండుగ the annual *Holi* festival.

కామ్యము *kāmyamu*. [Skt.] adj. Desirable, voluntary, optional, as a work of supererogation. కామ్యార్థములు *kām-yartha-mulu*. n. The lower objects of prayer, all that is short of మోక్షము.

కాయ *kāya*. [Tel. from కాచు.] n. 1. A green unripe fruit. అరటికాయలు green plantains. 2. A nut, berry, pod, bulb, knob, head. 3. Anything round, as the head (తలకాయ) the bob of a plummet: a boss or round piece. 4. The word is used for a thing or article: as a piece at chess తుంటకాయ a wicked thing or creature. 5. A pimple: a wart. త్రవ్వడముచేత వాడిచేతులు కాయలుకాచినవి his hands are callous or hard with digging: he has a wart on his hand. 7. A bottle. రెండుకాయలను ఒకడే తీసుకొన్నాడు he alone drank two bottles. 8. As an affix it often leaves the sense unaltered: thus తల or తలకాయ the head. పిల్ల or పిల్లకాయ a child. గొంతు or గొంతుకాయ the throat. పుస్తె or పుస్తె కాయ a marriage token worn on the neck. మొట్టు or మొట్టికాయ a blow or knock. ఎండ్రకాయ a crab. చెంపకాయ a slap on the cheek. Some fruits are called కాయ even though ripe, thus (from టెంకి shell) టెంకాయ a cocoanut. మిరపకాయ a chillie. ఉల్లికాయ an onion. కూరగాయలు or కాయగూరలు vegetables. కాయధాన్యములు *kaya-dhānyamulu*. n. Pulse: all sorts of grain contained in pods: as పెసలు, కందులు, సెనగలు, &c.,

కాయకన్ను *kāya-kannu*. [Tel.] n. A wall eye; a blind eye. కాయకాచినకన్ను.

కాయకము or కులకాయకము *kāyakamu*. [Tel.] n. Profession, trade, art. జీవనము. See కాయికము. కాయకము (among the Jangams) signifies a prayer or vow. ప్రార్థన, వ్రతము.

కాయజుడు *kāyajuḍu*. [Skt.] n. The god of love: as being "born in our bodies." మన్మథుడు.

కాయమానము *kāya-mānamu*. [Skt.] n. A shed or booth. పందిరి. H. v. 75.

కాయము *kāyamu*. [Skt.] n. The body. అతడు చచ్చినప్పటికిన్ని బహుధర్మాత్ముడని పేరుపడి యశఃకాయముతో యిప్పటికిన్ని జీవించుచున్నాడు though he is dead, through his reputation for charity he still lives in his fame. కాయము [Tel.] n. A certain restorative medecine, administered to a woman in childbed. బాలెంతలకిచ్చే మందు. H. i. 114. కాయపుష్టి *kāyapushṭi*. n. Stoutness. కాయసిద్ధి corporeal perfection imagined to be attainable by religious austerities. కాయసిద్ధుడై ఉన్నాడు he bears a charmed life.

కాయము *kāyamu*. [H.] See ఖాయము.

కాయలము *kāyalamu*. [Tel.] n. A sort of fish.

కాయస్థుడు *kāyasthuḍu*. [Skt.] n. A man belonging to the writer caste. An accountant. కరణము.

కాయికము *kāyikamu*. [Skt.] n. Daily interest నానాటివడ్డి. కాయికములమీద a ro or chest. adj. *Lit.* pertaining to the body. కాయసంబంధమైన. Slight, not strong, బచ్చు, కాయకష్టపుపని not strong work.

కాయు *kāyu.* [Tel.] v. n. To shine as the sun or moon. ఇప్పుడు ఎండకాయుచున్నది there is sunshine now. వెన్నెలకాయుచున్నది there is moonlight. కాచు (another form of కాయు.) v. a. To tend cattle. To spare or acquit. నేను ఇంతపని చేసి ఉంటే నన్ను కాయ వద్దు if I have done this, spare me not.

కాయువు, కాయ్వు *kāyuvu.* [Tel.] n. Love, wish, desire. అనురాగము.

కార, కారా, కారాగృహము or కారయిల్లు *kāra.* [Skt.] n. A prison. చెర, చెరసాల. B. X. 129.

కారండవము *kāraṇḍavamu.* [Skt.] n. A sort of duck. A kind of antelope కన్నులేడి.

కారకము *kārakamu.* [Skt.] adj. Making, causing. సందేహకారకమైన causing doubt or doubtful. సంతాపకారకమైన grievous. దుఃఖకారకమైన grievous, causing sorrow. కారకహేతువు the efficient or active cause. In Telugu it is used to denote heat. కారకజ్వరము a burning fever. కారకదేహము a hot or fervish temperament. మేహకారకము venereal feverishness. పిత్తకారకము bilious feverishness. కారకములు నాలుగువిధములు stimulants are of four sorts.

కారణము *kāraṇamu.* [Skt.] n. A cause, source, motive. హేతువు. కారణశరీరము the fleshly or mortal body as opposed to జ్ఞానశరీరము the spiritual body. ఇందుకు కారణభూతమైన దుఃఖము grief which caused this event.

కారము *kāramu.* [Tel.] n. Pungency, hotness of taste: sauce. Salt earth used in bleaching cloth చవుడు. Tinder: being cloth dipped in saltpetre. A caudle for infants. Caustic, lunar caustic. కారము చచ్చినపొగాకు tobacco devoid of flavour. కారముచచ్చినసున్నము lime devoid of heat. కారముగలసున్నము sharp lime. adj. Pungent, hot to the taste. A particle added to a letter in naming it. Thus కకారము the letter K. An affix denoting, making or doing, thus: ఝంఝంకారము resounding, making a ringing sound.

కారవి *kāravi.* [Skt.] n. The spice called carraways. H. ii. 249. A kind of anise. సదాప.

కారాకు *kār-āku.* [Tel.] n. A withered leaf. పండుటాకు. "గాలిచేసురాలిన కారాకులట్ల." DRAran, 176

కారాకూరము *kārā-kūramu.* [Tel.] adj. Confounded, jumbled, overthrown. కలిసి, ఎడాపెడలయిన. Kalahas. iii. 103.

కారామణి *kāra-maṇi.* [Tel.] n. A black species of pulse called అలచందలు or బబ్బెరలు.

కారావు *kār-āvu.* [Tel.] n. A wild cow. కారావులు forest cattle.

కారి *kāri.* [Skt.] adj. That which causes thus: క్షయకారి destructive, that which causes loss. పిత్తకారి bilious. ఆరోగ్యకారి wholesome. దోషకారి sinful. అన్యాయకారి unjust.

కారించు *kārinṭsu.* [Tel.] v. a. To inflict pain, kill or destroy. బాధించు, గాయపరచు, చంపు. "వారించిమదకరి గారించుసమము." BD. iv. 282.

కారింజా *kārinja.* [Tel.] n. An artificial fountain.

కారిక *kārika.* [Skt.] n. A rule composed in verse: an explanatory verse. సూత్రాది వివరణశ్లోకము.

కారికము *kārikamu.* [Tel.] adj. Brown, unbleached, as cloth. చలువచేయని (బట్ట).

కారిజము *kārizamu.* [Tel.] n. The liver. Manu. iv. 92.

కారిత *kārita.* [Skt.] n. An exorbitant rate of interest offered by a debtor. అప్పుతీసు కొనువాడు తన అక్కరకొద్దీ తానేయిచ్చెదననిన వడ్డీ.

కారియ *kāriya.* [Tel.] n. Pain, trouble, difficulty. బాధ. కారియపడు to grieve, suffer pain. To be in trouble. ఇడుమలపడు, బాధపడు. "అంగదుడనీ ధర్మసూనుండు... కారియపడెనే." M. IV. v. 250. కారియపెట్టు to trouble ఇడుమలపెట్టు, బాధపెట్టు. "నరకంబెట్టిది కష్టకరంబుదుం దెట్టిదంచు గారియపెట్టుగా." M. XIII. v. 159.

కారియము *kāriyamu.* [from Skt. కార్యము.] n. An act, work, deed. కార్యము. In M. IV. v. 251. & XIII. v. 152, the metre proves this spelling.)

కారు *kāru.* [Tel.] v. n. To flow, run, trickle, distil, drop through. స్రవించు. To fall as sparks of fire రాలు. BD. vi. 253. కారుచు or కార్చు to cause to flow.

కారు *kāru.* [Tel.] n. A season, time of the year. కాలము. చిన్నకారు childhood, youth. తొలికారు the opening of the year. కారు మెరుపు or తొలికారుమెరుపు or ప్రొక్కారు మెరుంగు vernal lightning తొలివానకాలపు మెరుపు. నన కారు Spring. ఈ సంవత్సరములో ముక్కారులున్ను పండినవి the three seasons have yielded crops this year. ఒకకారు కోడిపిల్లలను అమ్మివేసినాను I have sold one brood of chickens. కారులెక్క a heifer four years old. కారుకాలము, ఫలకాలము harvest time. కారు పంట. a crop that depends on the rain. వర్షాకాలమందు నీరాసరానుపండే పల్లపుపంట. కారువడ్లు rice grown in the hot season, ఎండకాలమందు పండే వరి ధాన్యము. కారువాటుధర price current of grain at the time of reaping. A plough-share. పటుకారు or నీరుకారు tongs, a pair of pincers. Darkness, jetty blackness. నలుపు, చీకటి. కారుకమ్మెను darkness came on. A forest అడవి. కారుచిచ్చు wild or forest fire. The plu. కారులు, అనగా పరుసలు hard language; reviling. పరుషవచనము; vain talk వ్యర్థవచనము. కారులు lies అబద్ధములు. A stain కఱు. Ignorance అజ్ఞానము.

కారు *kāru.* [Tel.] adj. Black or jet black. కారుమొగులు a black cloud. కారుకమ్ములు black wires. కారునువ్వులు the seeds of the black sesamum. Brackish. చవుడు. కారునీళ్లు brackish water. కారునేల saline soil. కారుసముద్రము the salt sea. కారుప్పు bitter salt. కారుఇంగువ stale asafœtida. Withered. కారాకులు withered leaves. Astringent వగరైన. కసుగాయదెంచిన కారుగాదె if you pluck a fruit raw, is it not sour? Wild. కారెనుము *kār-enumu.* *Bos gaurus.* The Gaur. (F. B. I.) కారుదున్న, కారుపోతు a wild he buffalo, or bison. Great, big. కారుకేక, a loud cry. పెద్దబొబ్బలు. కారు వాసన a strong smell, a stale smell. కారుకూతలు rude language. కారుమొసలి a wild crocodile or alligator. కారుకొను or కార్కొను *kāru-konu.* v. i. To blacken. నల్లబారు. To be noisy సందడించు.

కారుకొల్లి *kāru-kolli.* [Tel.] n. The trumpet flower plant. కలిగొట్టు.

కారుకోడి *kāru-kōḍi.* [Tel.] n. A jungle fowl. అడవికోడి. రసిక. i. 49.

కారుకోడె *kāru-kōḍe.* [Tel.] n. A bull in its prime.

కారుణ్యము *kāruṇyamu.* [Skt.] n. Mercy, pity, favour. దయ, కనికరము. కారుణికుడు *kāruṇikuḍu.* adj. One who is gracious or kind. కారుణికత్వము *kāruṇikatvamu.* n. Tenderness of heart, mercifulness. M. XIII. v. 21.

కారువు *kāruvu.* [Skt.] n. An artist, artificer. శిల్పి. An agent చేయువాడు.

కారూరు *kār-ūru.* [Tel. కారు+ఊరు.] n. A hamlet in a jungle. అడవిపల్లె.

కారెము *kāremu.* [Tel.] n. The hollowed trunk of a palm tree shaped like a canoe and balanced like a see-saw to draw up water. మల్లకు నీళ్లెత్తెడు తాటిదోనె.

కారొడ్డెము *kār-oḍḍemu.* [Tel.] n. A hard word, ridicule. పరుషోక్తి.

కార్కశ్యము *kārkaṣyamu*. [Skt. from కర్కశ.] n. Hardness, cruelty. కఠినత్వము.

కార్ఖానా Same as కారుఖానా.

కార్ఖానా *kārkhānā*. [H.] n. A workshop. An arsenal.

కార్చిచ్చు Same as కారుచిచ్చు.

కార్చు See under కారు.

కార్తాంతికుడు *kārtān-tikuḍu*. [Skt.] n. An astrologer. జ్యోతిష్కుడు.

కార్తికము *kārtikamu*. [Skt.] n. The eighth Hindu lunar month. October-November.

కార్తికేయుడు *kārti-kēyuḍu*. [Skt.] n. The god of war. కుమారస్వామి.

కార్తె *kārte*. [Tel.] n. The particular constellation out of the 27, in which the Sun happens to be. ఇరువైయేడుకార్తెలు అనగా అశ్విని మొదలైన నక్షత్రములలో సూర్యుడు ఉండేదినాలు.

కార్పణ్యము *kārpaṇyamu*. [Skt.] n. Spite, malice, ill-will, pique. కృపణత్వము, పగ. కార్పణ్యమువహించు to bear malice.

కార్పాసము *kārpasamu*. [Skt.] n. A cotton cloth.

కార్ముకము *kārmukamu*. [Skt.] n. A bow. విల్లు.

కార్యము *kāryamu*. [Skt.] n. An act, deed, work, doing, business. An affair. An object. An effect, result. Use, good, profit, advantage. పని, ఫలము. అందువల్ల ఏమికార్యము what is the good of it? The thing to be done or which ought to be. Bhāskara § 41. కార్యాకార్యములెరుగక not knowing good from bad. కార్యవాది one who looks to the main point opposed to ఖడ్గవాది a brawler. కార్యస్థుడు *kāryasthuḍu*. n. A clever man, a man of ability. కార్యస్థానము an office, a place of business. కార్యదర్శి a secretary. గౌరవకార్యదర్శి an honorary secretary.

కాలటక *kāl-aṭaka*. [Tel. కాలు+అటక.] n. A stick resting in the wall at each end, and serving as a shelf to support pots, &c.

కాలము *kālamu*. [Skt.] n. Time, occasion, period. Season, weather. The tense of a verb. Death చావు. Blackness నలుపు. భూతభవిష్యద్వర్తమానకాలములు the past, future, and present tenses. కాలముచేయు to die. వర్షాకాలము the rainy season. శీత కాలము winter. ఎండకాలము summer. వెన్నెలకాలము the bright fortnight or moonlight weather. చీకటికాలము the dark fortnight. కాలముజరుపు to demur: to put off. మీరు ఎట్లా కాలము జరుపుకొంటు న్నారు how do you pass your time, or how do you live? కాలత్రయము at the three times of the day, morning, noon and night, or, the present, past and future. కాలత్రయములందున్ను perpetually. కాలకంఠము *kala-kanthamu*. n. The black-throat, i. e., a sparrow పిచ్చిక. A peacock నెమలి. A wagtail కాటుకపిట్ట. కాల కంఠుడు or కాలకంధరుడు *kāla-kanthudu*. An epithet of Siva. కాలకూటము *kala-kūṭamu*. n. Mortal poison: venom. విషభేదము. కాలక్షేపము *kāla-kshēpamu*. n. Passing or spending time. విద్యాకాల క్షేపము literary pursuits. వట్టికాలక్షేపము mere pastime. గ్రంథకాలక్షేపము reading. కాలక్షేపముచేయు to pass one's time, నీవు ఇప్పుడు ఎట్లా కాలక్షేపముచేస్తున్నావు how do you now live? కాలక్రయము *kāla-krayamu*. n. The price of the day: the present rate; the current price. కాలఖం డము *kāla-khanḍamu*. The liver. కాలిజము. కాలచక్రము *kāla-chakramu*. The circle of time. కాలజ్ఞము *kālagnyamu*. A cock, as knowing the hour. కాలజ్ఞపత్రి *kala-gnyapatri*. n. A cock, also, the cuckoo. "కాలజ్ఞపత్రిరుతం బెట్లువెలంగునమానవపితస్త్రీ కర్ణపుటంబులోకిన్." A. v. 110. కాలజ్ఞానము *kāla-gnyānamu*. n. Knowledge of time.

Predictive knowledge. Certain histories or legends are written under this name, as the విద్యారణ్యకాలజ్ఞానము, the సర్వజ్ఞ కాలజ్ఞానము, the వెన్నబసవకాలజ్ఞానము being the visions or predictions regarding particular saints. కాలజ్ఞుడు *kālagnyuḍu*. n. An astrologer జ్యోతిష్కుడు. కాలధర్మము *kāla-dharmamu*. n. The debt of nature. Death మరణము. అకాలమృత్యువు untimely death. కాలప్రవృత్తి *kāla-pravritti*. n. Evacuation. నేడు నాకు కాలప్రవృత్తికాలేదు I had no motion to-day. కాలయాపనము *kāla-yāpanamu*. n. Delay, loss of time. కాలవహ్ని *kāla-vahni* n. The devouring flames destined to burn up the world. A consuming fire, a conflagration. కాలవిళంబము *kāla-viḷambamu*. n. Tardiness, loss of time, delay. కాలసూత్రము *kāla-sūtramu*. n. A name of a region in the hell of the Hindu Puranas. కాలహరణము *kāla-haraṇamu*. n. Delay, loss of time. కాలాంతకుడు *kāl-antakuḍu*. n. One who brings the end. An epithet of Siva. కాలాంతరము *kāl-antaramu*. n. Another time. కాలాంతరమందు or కాలాంతరేణ through the lapse of time, at another time. కాలాతీతము *kāl-atītamu*. n. Delay, loss of time. కాలాతీతమైనది it is now too late. కాలార్కుడు *kāl-arkuḍu*. The sun that at the last day shall scorch up the world. కాలావధి *kāl-avadhi*. n. The end of a year or season. కాలావసానము *kāl-avasānamu*. n. The end of time, i. e., death. కాలికము *kālikamu*. adj. Regarding time. బహుకాలికమైన of long standing. తాత్కాలికమైన temporary, momentary. కాలోచితము *kāl-ōchitamu*. adj. Seasonable. కాలోచితపుమాటలు such words as suited his purpose.

కాలరి *kālari*. [Tel.] n. A foot soldier. పదాతి, బంటు. A messenger దూత. (భార. ఉద్యో. i.) A poll tax జనపాకీలు.

కాలవ *kālava*. n. Another form of కాలువ.

కాలాయసము *kāl-āyasamu*. [Skt.] n. Iron.

కాలికంచము *kāli-kantsamu*. [Tel.] n. A certain boyish game. H. iii. 165.

కాలియ *kāliya*. [Tel.] n. A devil. పిశాచము.

కాలు *kālu*. [Tel.] n. A leg, a foot, a claw, a talon. మోకాలు the knee. మీగాలు the upper surface of the foot. A pillar. నూరుకాళ్లమంటపము a portico built on 100 pillars. A quarter or fourth part. ముక్కాలు being three legs, or quarters. Bilh. ii. 154. కాళ్లకడ at the feet. కాళ్లజెర్రి a centipede. కంచెకాలు a fence: lit. a fence-foot. కాలిదోవ (A. vi. 16.) a foot path. కాలు త్రవ్వు to paw the ground, to be eager for fighting. M. XII. ii. 301. A. v. 87. సన్నద్ధుడగు. నా కొడుకు పెండ్లాన్ని బిడ్డలను నాకాళ్లకట్టిపోయి నాడు my son died and left a widow and children on my hands. మూడుకాళ్లముసలి (P. i. 322.) a three legged old woman, because leaning on a staff.

తే॥ "మనముశృంగార విధుశేఖర చితనదు
పేరనాక పేటుకట్టి సంప్రీతితోర
గాలమందిన కాలుకంబాలనంగ
కలికియూరులు చెలువు పై కొంచిమెరయు."

Bilh. ii. 154.

కాలుకంబము the side post of a door. కాలి *kāli*. infl. of కాలు the foot. ఎర్రకాలి కొంగ the painted stork, *Pseudotantalus leucocephalus*. (F. B. I.) కాలిదారి or కాలిదోవ or కాలిబాట. *kāli-dari*. n. A foot path. కాలినడ or కాల్నడ walking, going on foot. కాల్నడవాడు *kālnaḍa-vāḍu*. n. A pedestrian, one on foot. కాలిబంటు or కాలుమానిసి *kāli-banṭu*. n. An Infantry man, a foot soldier. పదాతి. కాలుబలము or కాల్బలము Infantry. కాలివేళ్లు *kāli-vēḷlu*. n. The toes.

కాలు *kālu*. [Tel.] v. n. To burn, to be consumed. To be baked, scalded, burnt, or boiled. To shine, gleam. a torch కాగడా. కాలేదుని... కాలుదివిటీ fire —

lit. May his pride be burnt. కాలుచు or కాల్చు kāluṭsu. v. a. To burn, roast, scorch; to fire a gun. కాలుపు kālupu. n. Burning, setting on fire. Baking, boiling, roasting. కాలుపులు burnings. కాల్పించు kālpinṭsu. (causal of కాల్చు.) To have it burnt.

కాలుడు kāluḍu. [Skt.] n. The god of hell. యముడు.

కాలుమడి See కాల్మడి.

కాలువ or కాలవ kāluva. [Tel. cf. Tam. కాలవాయి or వాయికాల్.] n. A canal, a channel; a stream. కాలవకు పోయి ఉన్నాడు or కాలవతట్టుకు పోయినాడు he is gone to the necessary, or to relieve himself.

కాలుష్యము kālushyamu. [Skt.] n. Foulness, dirtiness, turbidness. కలక.

కాలేయము kālēyamu. [Skt.] n. The liver. కాలిజము.

కాల్మడి or కాలుమడి kālmaḍi. [Tel. From కాలు and మడి a bending.] n. Urine. మూత్రము.

కాల్యము kalyamu. [Skt.] n. Dawn, daybreak. వేకువ.

కాల్వురు or కాలువురు kālvuru. [Tel.] n. plu. Infantry, foot soldiers. A. iv. 271.

కాళంజి kāḷanji. [Tel.] n. A spittoon. తమ్మపడుగు.

కాళాంజి kāḷānji. [Tel.] n. Whisks made of peacock's feathers. Also, a spittoon. L. ii. 23. and 40.

కాళి kāḷi. [Skt.] n. The goddess Kali. The Hecate of India. (Sir W. J.) పార్వతి.

కాళింగుడు kāḷinguḍu. [Skt.] n. The name of a serpent which was killed by Krishṇa.

కాళింది kāḷindi. [Skt.] n. A name of the river Jumna. యమున. కాళిందీభేదనుడు kāḷindī-bhēdanuḍu. n. Balarāma.

కాళిక kāḷika. [Skt.] n. The goddess Kali. Blackness నలుపు.

కాళియ kāḷiya. [Skt.] n. A musical instrument. వాద్యవిశేషము.

ఖాళీ kāḷī. [H.] a. Empty, vacant. n. A vacancy.

కావ kāva. [Tel.] Inf. in A. of కాచు. to protect. "జనులనవనిలోన గావ పుట్టితివి" (B. i. 234.) Thou wast born to save the world. కావక without sparing.

కావడము kāvaḍamu. [Tel. from అగు.] n. Becoming.

కావడి kāvaḍi. [Tel.] n. A "bangy" or yoke, carried by men; like that used by milk maids in England. (Infl. కావటి. plu. కావళ్లు.) కంబికావడి a yoke borne about by certain Saiva mendicants. కావడివాడు a carrier. కావటిటపాలు the bangy post. కావటిబద్ద the beam of a yoke. కావటికొమ్ము the tip or end of the yoke. కావటిమట్టు the bottom of the net work attached to each end of the yoke. కావటిఉట్లు the rope net work forming a lodgment at each end of a yoke. కావటి చేర్లు the cords forming this, కావటియుట్ల తాళ్లు. కావడించు kāvaḍinṭsu. v. t. To carry in such a yoke.

కావరము kāvaramu. [Tel.] n. Fat. కొవ్వు, మదము. కండకావరము pride of flesh, arrogance. వయసుకావరము the vigour of youth. కావరి or కావరుడు kāvari. A proud insolent man. దుష్టుడు. BD. vi. 174. కావరించు kāvarinṭsu. n. To become fat or proud. కొవ్వు, మదించు.

కావలము kāvalamu. [Tel.] n. Sin. పాపము.

కావలి kāvali. [Tel.] n. Guard, custody. రక్షణము. చేకావలి an alternative, a thing kept as a stand by; a provision. చెయ్యికావలిగా నుండేస్తంభము a piece of wood kept in reserve. కావలికాడు or కావలివాడు kāvali-kāḍu. n. A sentinel, a watchman.

రక్షకుడు. కావలిబొట్టు a black mark put on the face of children for good luck దిష్టలకు రక్షగానుంచే నల్లనిబొట్టు.

కావా *kâvâ*. [Tel.] n. A peculiar pace of the horse. అశ్వమండలగతి.

కావారి *kâvâri*. [Skt.] n. An umbrella. గొడుగు.

కావి *kâvi*. [Tel.] n. and adj. Red, redness. Russet, tan, pink, salmon colour, fawn colour, terra cotta colour, tawny hue. ఎరుపు, కాషాయవస్త్రము. సంజకావి the red hue of evening. కావి or కావిరాయి red ochre. కావిరోక a tawny robe, worn by ascetics, imitating the colour of the raw hide worn by hermits in old days. కావిగొను to become red ఎర్రనగు. కావితాలుపు an ascetic సన్యాసి, కాషాయధారి.

కావించు *kâvintsu*. [Tel. causal of అగు.] v. a. To make, do, compose, invent, perform.—తునకలుకావించు to break to bits. శిరఃకంపముకావించి shaking the head. తీర్థయాత్రకావించె he went on pilgrimage. ప్రశ్నకావించు to put a question. బాగు కావించు to trim, to set in order.

కావిరి *kâviri*. [Tel.] n. Black vapour, any thing that appears like smoke. పొగ లేకయే పొగవలె మంచుకాసేటిది. కావిరిబొట్టు Same as కావలిబొట్టు.

కావు *kâvu*. [Tel.] n. Cawing, the sound of crows: a hollow booming sound. A well or pit. పాతర. A black mark on the forehead worn for good luck కావలిబొట్టు.

కావుట *kâvuta*. [Tel.] n. The verbal noun form of అగు. "ఇది సిద్ధముకావుటెరింగి" భార. అది. i.

కావుత or **కాత** or **కావుతక** *kâvuta*. [Tel.] imp. v. In poetry, a precative particle derived from అగు similar to వలెను or గాక. q. v. Be it so! may it be so! so be it! సంపదలిచ్చుగాత may he bestow wealth on thee! ఎల్లకాలమునన్నును ప్రోచుగావుతక may he ever support me by his grace! అతనిసంపద శత్రులకేరుగావుతక may his wealth be given to his foes!

కావున *kâvuna*. [Tel.] adv. Therefore, then, whereupon కాబట్టి.

కావుపాతర *kâvu-patara*.. [Tel.] n. A deep pit for grain.

కావేరి *kâvêri*. [Skt] n. The river Caveri.

కావేషము *ka-vêshamu*. [Skt.] n. Spite, malice, ill-will.

కావైరి *ka-vairi*. [Skt.] n. A traitor, a betrayer. A. iv. 293. కుత్సితశత్రువు, కాపురుషుడు.

కావ్యము *kâvyamu*. [Skt.] n. Poetry. A piece of composition, whether in verse or ornamental prose.

కాశము *kâsamu*. [Skt.] n. A sort of reed. రెల్లు.

కాశి or **కాసి** *kâsi*. [Skt.] n. Kasi: a name of the city of Benares. కాశీకోక *kâsi-kôka*. n. A strong girdle of narrow cloth. A fine sort of muslin. కాశీబేడ *kâsi-bêda*. n. A certain pendant worn at the neck. కాశీసంకటము *kâsi-sankatamu*. n. Dysentery.

కాశ్మర్యము *kâsmaryamu*. [Skt.] n. The plant named *Gmelinia arborea*. Roxb. గుమ్ముడుచెట్టు.

కాశ్మీరము *kâsmiramu*. [Skt.] n. Saffron, named *Costus speciosus*. The paint called కుంకుమము, కాశ్మీరజన్మము, కుంకుముపువ్వు. కాశ్మీరము *kâsmiramu*. The land of Cashmere.

కాశ్యపి *kâsyapi*. [Skt.] n. The earth. భూమి. కాశ్యపీసురుడు a Brahmin.

కాషాయము *kâshâyamu*. [Skt.] n. Redness: brick red or tawny: a cloth thus dyed, a hermit's dress: కావివస్త్రము. ఆమె కాషాయముతీసుకొన్నది "she took the veil." కోపకాషాయము redness of the eyes through rage.

కాష్ఠము kasṭhamu. [Skt.] n. Wood. (In Telugu this is the usual phrase for the wood used in the funeral pile.) కాష్ఠగ కాష్ఠ్యి. latent heat. A quarter, region or airt. దిక్కు. A moment, a second. పదు నెనిమిది రెప్పపాట్లకాలము.

కాస See కాసె.

కాసము kāsamu. [Skt.] n. Cough. దగ్గు.

కాసమర్దము kāsamardamu. [Skt.] n. The plant called *Cassia Esculenta.* కసింద.

కాసరతీగె kāsara-tīge. [Tel.] n. A certain thick creeper.

కాసరము kāsaramu. [Skt.] n. A buffalo. ఎనుబోతు. కాసరి kāsari. A she buffalo.

కాసరవడ్లు kāsara-vaḍlu. [Tel.] n. A certain sort of grain. శాలిధాన్యవిశేషము.

కాసా or ఖాసా kāsa. [H.] n. One's own (servant). A personal slave, or hereditary bondman.

కాసారము kāsāramu. [Skt.] n. A pond or lake. సరస్సు, కొలను.

కాసించు kāsintsu. [Tel.] v. t. To wear as a belt కాసెగా ధరించు. "సీ॥ పులితోలుపచ్చడం బుగ కాలగాసించి సర్పాంగములను భూషణంబు లూని." G. VIII. 105.

కాసిబేడ kāsi-bēḍa. [Tel.] n. A sort of neck ornament.

కాసీడు kāsīḍu. [Tel.] n. A mason. రాతి పనివాడు.

కాసీసము kāsīsamu. [Skt.] n. Green vitriol, sulphate of iron. పుచ్చుఉప్పత్తము.

కాసు kāsu. [Tel.] n. A small copper coin, a pie. A coin in general, whether gold, silver or copper, thus బంగారుకాసు a gold coin. వెండికాసు a silver coin (lit. white coin. "అది కుధాకరబింబమా కాదు వెండికానుపన్ని కెంపుటచ్చుపత్తి గాని." P. iv. 251, 551. కాసైనాలేదు there is not even a farthing. (The కాసు or farthing was called cash by the English, and the coin called ten cash was about one halfpenny: "twenty cash" being a penny, and eighty cash a fanam.) కాసంత kāsanta. n. A pie's worth కాసంతలేదు not a bit remains.

కాసె, కాస or కాసెయు kāse. [Tel.] n. The truss of a man's or woman's outer garment, which is passed loosely between the knees and tucked in the waist behind. A girdle దట్టి. కొతుకుంతకాసె a garb worn by masquers, with a monkey's tail. A truss, or modesty piece. గోచి. A truss, the flap of a garment. ఇకుపకాసెకట్టిన straitlaced, severe in chastity. కాసెలం కొని they girded themselves for battle. కాసెపోయు to tuck up the cloth బట్టను గోచివలె వెనుకకుదోపు.

కాసె kāse. [Tel.] adj. Appertaining to the stonecutter trade, masonry, or bricklaying. కాసెవాడు or కాసెభట్టు a mason, a stonecutter, a bricklayer. కాసెపని masonry, building. కాసెయులి a stonecutter's chisel. రాయిచెక్కేది ఉలి, టంకము.

కాసెకోక kāse-kōka. [Tel.] n. A man's girdle. లాగుమీద కట్టుకొనేదట్టి.

కాస్త kāsta. [Tel. for కాసంత or కాస్తయిన.] adj. A little. కాస్తమైనము a little wax. కాస్తకూస్త a mere trifle.

కాహళము or కాహళి kāhaḷamu. [Skt.] n. A clarion, bugle horn, or trumpet. కాహళికుడు one who blows the clarion, a trumpeter కాహళినూదువాడు. HD. i. 1012.

కి ki

కి ki. [Tel.] The dative sign, To or for. See note on కు where the various meanings are given.

కిం kim. [Skt.] pron. What. See కిమ్మను. కిం అంటే కిమ్మనలేడు. he cannot say Bo to a goose.

కింక kinka. [Tel. from కినియు.] n. Anger. కినుక. కింకవాయువు kinka-vāyuvu. n. The croup: convulsions that seize children, or cattle.

కింకరత *kinkarata.* [Skt.] n. Servility. **కింకరుడు** *kinkaruḍu.* n. A servant or drudge, a slave, a base hireling. పరిచారకుడు, దాసుడు. యమకింకరులు the emissaries of death.

కింకిణి *kinkiṇi.* [Skt.] n. A tinkling bell. A small rattle. గజ్జె, చిరుగంట.

కింకిరి *kinkiri.* [Tel.] n. Anger. కోపము. Nastiness: రోత. కింకిరిచేయు to foul or defile చెడ్డ చేయుట. "రోగిపరుని చీర పైకింకిరిచేయు." Navan, 315. **కింకిరిపడు** *kinkiri-paḍu.* v. n. To get angry. కోపగిల్లు. To feel nasty రోతపడు. **కింకిరి పాటు** *kinkiri-pāṭu.* n. Getting angry. కోపపడుట. Feeling disgusted with రోతపడుట. "అతిథినిమనో రసేవియు మతికింకిరి పడకరోలమానగొనక." M. XIII. i. 55.

కింగాణి *kingāṇi.* [Tel.] n. A useless act. కొరగానిపని. "కింగాణిమనుజేయుదంగనమూడు." BD. iv. 1104.

కింగిరి *kingiri.* [Tel.] adj. Trifling. అల్పమైన.

కించు *kinchu.* [Tel.] n. A grudge, ill-will, sorrow, grief. Confusion, disorder. సంజలి, వ్యాకులము. కించగామండే confused, disordered.

కించిత్తు *kinchittu.* [Skt.] n. A very little: a trifle. **కించిజ్జ్ఞుడు** *kinchitgnyuḍu* n. One of a very limited intellect: an ignorant man; opposite of సర్వజ్ఞుడు.

కించులికము *kinchulikamu.* [Skt.] n. An earthworm. ఎర్ర.

కించు or **క్రించు** *kintsu.* [Tel.] adj. Cruel, spiteful, mean. అల్పుడు. "పండితారాధ్య పరసమయాభేద్యవాద్యగ్రించుబౌద్ధుడుధక్కరించి పలుకుచును." Panditárádhya. iv. 959. "అక్కించురక్కసి నుగండుద్దండగతినా ర్చుచు." R. v. 192.

కింజల్కము *kinjalkamu.* [Skt.] n. The filament of a lotus. కేసరము.

కింజుడు *kinjuḍu.* [Skt.] n. A man who fritters away his life. నిరర్థకజన్మముగలవాడు.

కిందు or **క్రిందు** *kindu.* [Tel.] n. The ground. **కింద** *kinda.* (a postposition) Below, under. For, concerning. అకర్పుకింద పది రూపాయలు వ్రాసినాడు he charged ten rupees for it. అప్పుకింద పుచ్చుకొన్నాను he took it in payment of the loan. అతని చేతికింద under his power, subordinate to him; తప్పుకిందపడె it proved erroneous; జిలుగుకిందవచ్చే అక్షరము a handwriting partaking of the illegible. **కింద** *kinda.* adv. Down. On the ground. కింద ఉండేది what is below. కిందపడుండు to lie down on the ground. కిందికి down. కిందికిపోయినారు they went down. **కిందట** *kindaṭa.* n. Formerly, ago. నెలకిందట a month ago. **కిందటి** *kindaṭi.* adv. Last, former. కిందటిసారి last time; also, the former time. కిందటినెల last month. కిందటిశుక్రవారము last Friday. **కిందామీద** adv. Topsy turvy. **కింది** *kindi.* adj. Down. కిందిచూపు a downcast look. కిందిప్రశ్నలో in the following question. కిందిపద్యమందు in the following verse.

కింపచానుడు *kim-pachānuḍu.* [Skt] n. A miser. లోభి, పిసినిగొట్టు.

కింపాకుడు *kim-pākuḍu.* [Skt.] n. A wretch. నిరర్థకుడు, మూఢుడు.

కింపురుషుడు *kim-purushuḍu.* [Skt.] n. A "sort of a man." A kind of fairy, described as a eunuch, employed in the Hindu Olympus as a singer, and an attendant on the goddesses; or represented as a man with a bird's head: or as having a form uniting that of a man, a deer and a bird. నరమృగపక్షిశరీరాకారభేదే. మనుష్యముఖమును, పక్షిశరీరమునుగలవాడు. లేక, అశ్వముఖమును నరశరీరమును గలవాడు.

కింవదంతి *kim-vadanti.* [Skt.] n. Town talk: జనులాడుకొనుమాట.

కింశుకము kimsukamu. [Skt.] n. The tree called *Butea frondosa*. మోదుగుచెట్టు.

కికకిక or **కీకాకిక** *kika-kika*. [Tel.] adv. Laughingly, aloud. (Anuk.)

కికి or **కికిదివి** *kiki*. [Skt.] n. The Indian Roller, *Coracias indica* (F. B. I) erroneously called the blue jay. పాలపిట్ట.

కికిరించు, కికురించు, కిక్కురించు or **కికురు పెట్టు** or **కికురుపొడుచు** *kikirinsu*. v. a. To wheedle, delude, hide from, cheat. మొరగు, కక్కుర్తిచేయు, వంచించు. **కికురింత, కిక్కురింత** or **కికురు** or **కిక్కురు** *kikurinta* n. Deception, cheating. మోసము, వంచన.

కిక్కిటినీస్వనము *kikkitini-svanamu*. [Skt.] n. A chirping sound.

కిక్కిరిబిక్కిరిమాటలు *kikkiri-bikkiri-matalu*. [Tel.] n. Jabber, babble.

కిక్కిరియు or **క్రిక్కిరియు** *kikkiriyu*. [Tel.] v. n. To stand close together, as a crowd or as trees. కిక్కిరిసి standing thick, very close together. కిక్కిరిసిన thickset.

కిక్కిసగడ్డి *kikkisa-gaddi*. [Tel.] n. Bur-grass.

కిక్కురుమనక *kikkurum-anuka*. [Tel.] adv Without opening the lips: silently.

కిక్కెస *kikkesa*. [Tel.] n. Violent shaking. మిక్కిలికదలిక.

కిగ్గాడి *kiggadi*. [Tel.] adj. Inferior, bad (as paper). అంబేడు.

కిచకిచ *kitsa-kitsa*. [Tel.] n. Chirruping, or squeaking: కిచకిచమను to chirp. దాన్ని కిచకిచపెట్టిరి they tickled her. **కిచ కొట్టు** *kitsu-kottu*. n. To chirp. కిచకిచేయు. To tickle చక్కిలిగిలిపెట్టు. Sum. i. 256.

కిచ్చిడి or **కిచ్చడి** *kichchidi*. [Tel.] n. Rice and dhall cooked together in ghee. బియ్యమును పెసరపప్పును కలిపి నేతిలో వండిన అన్నము.

కిచ్చిలిచెట్టు *kichchili-chettu*. [Tel.] n. The orange tree.

కిటకిట *kita-kita*. [Tel.] (Anuk) adv. Creakingly. "కిటకిటపండ్లుకొరుకుచు." Swa. v. 19. **కిటకిటన** *kita-kitana*. n. Spite, ill-will or confusion. క్రోధము.

కిటి *kiti*. [Skt.] n. A hog. పంది, వరాహము.

కిటికి *kitiki*. [Tel.] n. A window, a lattice, గవాక్షము; a gangway, a port hole or window in a ship. కిటికీబావిలి a kind of earring.

కిటుకు *kituku*. [Tel.] n. A trick, device, secret, nicety. కపటము, మర్మము. కిటుకులు intricacies. చిక్కులు.

కిట్టు *kittu*. [Tel.] v. n. To approach, draw near. సమీపించు.

కిణము *kinamu*. [Skt.] n. A wart, scar, or mole, a corn. Hardness of the hands. చేతిలోకాచు కాయ.

కిణకిణలాడు *kina-kinal-adu*. [Tel.] v. n. To tingle or tinkle.

కిత *kita*. [Tel.] n. A heap of three handfuls of grain kept in a field as an offering to God. దేవతార్పణముగా కళ్లమున మొక్కగ వుంచిన మూడుదోసిళ్ల ధాన్యరాశి.

కితనార or **కిత్తనార** *kita-nara*. [Tel.] n. Hemp fibre. Oakum. కిత్తనపీచు, నాగనార. కిత్తనారబట్ట canvas.

కితము *kitamu*. [Tel.] adv. Formerly, before, previously. అంతకితము before that time. ఇంతకితము already, ere this.

కితవము *kitavamu*. [Skt.] n. Mischief, malice. కితవవనిత a wicked jade. కితవ వ్యవహారము mischief, a base pursuit, i. e., gambling. **కితవార్భకుడు** *kitav-arbhakudu*. One who pretends to be a mere child. మాయలబిడ్డ, **కితవుడు** *kitavudu*. A gambler, a cheat. జూదరి, మోసకాడు.

కితాబు *kitabu*. [H.] n. A title.

కిత్తనార See కిటనార.

కిత్తలి *kittali*. [Tel.] n. An orange. కిచ్చిలి.

కిత్తాన Same as కిటనార.

కిత్తి *kitti*. [Tel.] n. Fire. అగ్ని.

కిదుకు *kiduku*. [Tel.] v. n. To fret, or be cross on waking from sleep. "కేలొగ్గి చన్ను దెరగున మెల్లన కనువిచ్చి, క్రేగంటజూచుచు గిదికి నిల్గి, ఆవులించుచు చేతులాదరంబున సాచి." B. X. § VI. 14.

"అమ్మమ్మనీవిపుడగ్నిలోనురుక
నమ్మదంబోదవంగ జనియెదవేని
నత్తుకిదుకుచు న్నుదలకతిగిచి
రొత్తుకొమ్మనుచు బెల్లెసగు దైన్యమున
గిదుకుచుదిన్ని కెంగేలపైకొంగు
గదియంచిబుడిబుడికన్నీరుదెచ్చి."
H. i. 2241.

కినియు *kiniyu*. [Tel.] v. n. To be angry, కోపించు. To approach సమీపించు. కినుక or కిన్క *kinuka*. n. Anger, rage. heat, inflamation. కినుకకాడు an angry man కోపముగలవాడు. కినుపు *kinupu*. n. Anger కోపము. కినుకదు, కినుసదు or కిన్వదు to get angry. కోపపడు.

కిన్నర Same as కిన్నెర.

కిన్నరుడు *kinnarudu*. [Skt.] n. A fairy, a celestial chorister. కిన్నరకంటి fairy-eyed: lovely. Suca. iii. 98. కిన్నరేశుడు Kubera or the lord of కిన్నరులు.

కిన్నెర or కిన్నర *kinnera*. [Tel.] n. A lute. A sort of guitar. కిన్నెరకాయలు the large dried pumpkins that are fixed to the frame of a Hindu lute. కిన్నెరపట్టుచెట్టు the fiddle-bark-tree.

కిఫాయతు *kiphayatu*. [H.] n. Benefit, advantage, profit.

కిమిడి or కిమిడిరాళ్లు *kimiḍi*. [Tel.] n. A sort of flint used in making glass.

కిముక *kimuka*. [Skt.] n. The tree *Costus Speciosus*. Rox. i. 58. పెంకగోష్టు.

కిముడు *kimuḍu*. [Tel.] adj. Petty. అల్పుడు.

కిమ్మతు *kimmatu*. [H.] n. Estimated value, price.

కిమ్మనక *kimm-anaka*. [Tel.] adv. Without hesitation. "Without whats and wherefores." కిమ్మనకుండాచేసినారు they did it without saying a word.

కిమ్మిర *kimmira*. [Skt. cf. Cimmerian.] n. and adj. Dark hue, a mixed hue, the colours of the rainbow. Variegated, particoloured. చిత్రవర్ణములుగల. కిమ్మీరుడు. name of a Rakshasa.

కియ్య, కియ్యవడి or కియ్యావడి *kiyya*. [Tel. కిందు+యు] n. The sign ౣ i. e. అక్షరముకింది యొత్వము. Also, an innuendo for కర్గ్గము.

కిరకిర or కిర్రు, *kira-kira*. [Tel.] n. A creaking sound; a rattling sound. (Anuk.)

కిరణము *kiraṇamu*. [Skt.] n. A ray of light. వెలుగు.

కిరాటుడు *kirāṭuḍu*. [Skt.] n. A merchant. కోమటి. Vasu i. 10.

కిరాత or కిరాతక *kirāta*. [Skt.] adj. Savage, barbarian. కిరాతదేశము the land of savages. కిరాతిని *kirātini*. Indian Spikenard. W. కిరాతుడు *kirātuḍu*. n. A barbarian, a savage. బోయవాడు.

కిరాయి *kirāyi*. [H.] n. Rent, hire, fare.

కిరి *kiri*. [Skt.] n. A hog. వరాహము, పంది.

కిరి *kiri*. [Tel.] adj. Small, little. కిరిపొగ thin smoke. కిరిపిల్లాండ్లు *kiri-pillāndlu*. Small rings worn on the third toe.

కిరిమెట్లు *kiri-meṭlu*. [Tel.] n. Creaking slippers, i. e., leathern sandals. See కిర్రు.

కిరియు *kiriyu.* [Tel.] v. n. To be tight.

కిరస్తాను *kiristānu.* [Eng.] adj. Christian.

కిరీటము *kirīṭamu.* [Skt.] n. A crown. **కిరీటాకృతి** *kirīṭ-ākriti.* adj. Conical, like a cone. **కిరీటి** *kirīṭi.* n. A crowned man: an epithet of the hero Arjuna. **కిరీటగాడు** *kirīṭa-gāḍu.* n. The grey shrike, *Lanius lahtora* (F.B.I.). **కిరీటిపచ్చ** *kirīṭi-paṭtsa.* n. The oriental emerald, a greenish variety of sapphire. మరకతము.

కిరుకు *kiruku.* [Tel.] n. The act of turning anything round త్రిప్పు. **కిరుకుపొడుచు** *kiruku-poḍutsu.* v. n. To turn. తిరుగు.

కిరుడు *kiruḍu.* [Tel.] adj. Inferior. హీనము. కిరుడునేల inferior soil.

కిరుపు *kirupu.* [Tel.] v. a. To twitch, or stretch, as a limb, or the ears, or the eyelids in winking. మైకిరుపు to stretch the body on waking. కిరుపుకొను to wince. కన్నులు కిరుపించుట to wink. M. X. i. 121. A. iv. 222.

కిరుసు or **కిరుసుకత్తి** *kirusu.* [Tel.] n. A small double edged sword. రెండంచులుగల చిన్నకత్తి.

కిర్రు Same as కిరికిరి. కిర్రుచెప్పు a creaking shoe. **కిర్రుకిర్రున** *kirru-kirruna.* adv. Creakingly.

కిర్రుపురుగు or **ఇంతేకిర్రుపురుగు** *kirru-purugu.* [Tel.] n. A cicada, a noisy insect that lives in trees. **కిర్రుమాను** *kirru-mānu.* n. A turn-stile, lit. a creaking bar.

కిలకిల *kila-kila.* [Tel.] n. Din, hubbub, clamour, uproar, as of a marching host. Twittering, as of birds: any confused sound. కిలకిల్లాడు, కిలకిలలాడు to be clamorous కిలకిలధ్వనిచేయు.

కిలకొట్టు *kila-koṭṭu.* [Tel.] v. a. To stir, beat, or whip butter milk, so as to clear it. v. n. To sound. మ్రోగు, చెలగు.

కిలము or **కిలుము** *kilamu.* [Tel.] n. Discoloration of brass or copper. Verdigris.

కిలాటము *kilāṭamu.* [Tel.] n. A horse. గుర్రము.

కిలారము *kilāramu.* [Tel.] n. A herd of cattle. పసులమంద. **కిలారి** *kilāri.* n. A herdsman. గొల్లవాడు.

కిలారించు or **కిలారుచు** *kilārintsu.* [Tel.] v. n. To make a hubbub. కిలకిలధ్వనిచేయు. To play the bully, to swagger. To hoot, halloo, shout. బొబ్బరించు. To laugh in rage. అట్టహాసముచేయు.

కిలాసము *kilāsamu.* [Skt.] n. A blotch, scab. సోబి, సిబ్బెము.

కిలింజకము *kilinjakamu.* [Skt.] n. A mat, a screen. చాప.

కిలికించితము *kili-kinchitamu.* [Skt.] n. Amorous agitation. A conflict of feelings: agitation due to contending passions. Hubbub. తత్తరపాటు. **కిలికించితవతి** *kili-kinchita-vati.* n. A heart-broken damsel.

కిల్బిషము *kilbishamu.* [Skt.] n. Sin, fault, offence; పాపము, తప్పు; disease. రోగము.

కిల్లల *killala.* [Tel.] adv. (anuk) Squeakingly, aloud. కిల్లలబొబ్బలు loud screams or howls. కిల్లలాడు to squeak or howl.

కిల్లాకు *killāku.* [Tel. కిల్లు+ఆకు.] n. A billet, a memorandum. చీటి. Literally కిల్లిన ఆకు a nipped palmleaf, i e, a leaf indented with marks of the finger nail and sent by a messenger. An unequal number of dents agrees to a proposal, but an even number is a refusal. కిల్లపత్రి, ఉల్లాకు.

కివకివ *kiva-kiva.* [Tel.] n. (anuk.) A giggling, murmuring, echoing. Suca i. 256.

కిశోరము *kiśōramu.* [Skt.] adj. Young. n. An infant. A colt గుర్రపుపిల్ల.

కిసక *kisaka* [Tel.] n. A point. కిసకఱ్ఱ. A pointed stick. See గసిక.

కిసకిస *kisa-kisa*. [Tel.] adj & adv. (anuk.) Much, aloud (laughing.)

కిసమస *kisa-masa*. [Tel.] n. Sorrow, pain. వ్యథ.

కిసరు *kisaru*. [Tel.] n. Sharpness, tartness. Bad humours in the body: the evil eye: mischief done to infants by the touch of an impure person. అంటుసోకుటవల్ల బిడ్డలకు కలిగే దోషము. Angriness. కోపము. కసరు చూపు an angry glance. "కస్సరుడు ..." A. iv. 215. కసరుకరు humours in the body.

కిసలము or కిసలయము *kisalamu*. [Skt.] n. A sprout. చిగురు.

కిసికాళ్లుగానడుచు *kisi-kallu-ga-naḍutsu*. [Tel.] v. n. To straddle in dancing.

కిస్తీ or కిస్తు *kisti*. [H.] n. Kist. Stated payment, an instalment of rent. కిస్తీబందీ settlement of instalments of revenue.

కిస్సుమను *kissu-m-anu*. [Tel.] n. To growl.

కీ kī

కీ *kī*. [Tel.] n. (Contracted from కింది) Lower, under; కీగడుపు the abdomen or lower belly. కీతొడ (కింది+తొడ.) n. The inner part of the thigh. కీనీడ (కింది+నీడ.) n. The under shadow, or darkness under a lamp, &c. A glimmer, or gleam through a crevice. కీనీటిభూమి land which has water under it, i. e., where the springs lie close to the surface.

కీకటులు *kikaṭulu*. [Skt.] n. Savages. "... " A. iv. 33. "..." A. iv. 316.

కీకసము *kikasamu*. [Skt.] n. A bone. ఎముక. A. vi. 17.

కీకారణ్యము *kik-araṇyamu*. [Skt.] n. A dark forest, a wilderness.

కీగంటిచూపులు *ki-ganṭi-tsupulu*. [Tel.] n. Downcast glances.

కీచకు *kichaka*. [Skt.] n. The name of a certain tribe of hill people or savages: the name of a certain tribe of robbers.

కీచకము *kichakamu*. [Skt.] n. A hollow bamboo. కీచకరంధ్రములు (Kalahas. Mah. iii. 48.) the pearls of gum (tabasheer) found inside bamboos. కీచకస్వనము a hollow groaning sound, as that of the wind passing the mouth of a tube.

కీచరబాచర *kitsara-batsara*. [Tel.] adv. In confusion, jumbled.

కీచుమను *kitsu-m-anu*. [Tel.] v. n To squeak. కీచుబుర్ర *kitsu-burra*. n. Leathern bellows. "..." Ila. iv. 135. కీచురాయి *kitsu-rāyi*. n. A cicada, or cricket. ఇలకోడి. కీచులాడు *kitsul-āḍu*. v. n. To squabble, brawl, contend, squall or scream.

కీటము or కీటకము *kiṭamu*. [Skt.] n. A worm, an insect. నరకీటకములు wretched mortals, human worms. కీటమణి or కీటరాజము *kiṭa-maṇi*. n. The fire-fly, the glow-worm. HD. i. 1901.

కీటు *kiṭu*. [Tel.] n. A tire, a course, a layer, stratum or range. A line, mark, stroke. గోడ ఒకకీటు పెట్టినాడు he built one layer of the wall.

కీడిసలు *kiḍisalu*. [Tel.] n. The sweepings or refuse of grain.

కీడు *kiḍu*. [Tel.] n. Evil, harm, misfortune, danger. అశుభము, ఆపద. Fault తప్పు, దోషము. Sin పాపము. (plu. కీళ్లు) adj. Bad, evil, base, low. అధమము. కీడుజాతులు low castes. Inauspicious అశుభకరము. Wicked దుష్టము. కీడుపడు, కీడ్పడు or కీడ్వడు *kiḍu-paḍu*. v. n. To be vanquished. తక్కువపడు. కీడుపరచు or కీడ్పరచు *kiḍu-paratsu*. v. a. To vanquish. "... కీడ్పరచినఁ ..." Dab. P. 239. కీడుమేళ్లు *kiḍu-mellu*. Both good and bad: both sides of a question

కిట *kita*. [Tel.] adj. Inferior. అధమము. కిటనేల inferior land. కిటకుంటకేములు *kita-kuntsamulu*. n. Short measure; not heaped up and pressed down.

కిటు *kitu*. [Tel.] n. A cocoanut bough with the leaves plaited so as to form a mat. మట్ట.

కీదృశము *ki-drisamu*. [Skt.] adj. What sort of? like what? ఎటువంటిది.

కీనాశుడు *kinasudu*. [Skt.] n. An epithet of Yama, god of death.

కీర or కీరె *kira*. [Tel.] n. Herb, vegetable, greens. కీరకాయ a cucumber.

కీరము *kiramu*. [Skt.] n. A parrot. కీరవాణి *kira-vani*. n. A sweet voiced woman, having the note of a parrot.

కీర్తి another form of కీర్తి. (q. v.)

కీర్ణము *kirnamu*. [Skt.] adj. Covered. కప్పబడిన.

కీర్తన *kirtana*. [Skt.] n. A hymn, psalm, anthem. A certain class of metres or tunes. కీర్తనము. *kirtanamu*. n. Praise, encomium. కీర్తనీయుడు *kirta-niyudu*. adj. Glorious, praiseworthy. కీర్తి or కీర్తి *kirti*. Fame, glory. యశము. కీర్తించు *kirtintsu* v. a. To praise, laud. పొగడు, స్తుతించు. కీర్తితము *kirtitamu*. adj. Praised, celebrated. పొగడబడినది.

కీలకము or కీలము *kilakamu*. [Skt.] n. A pin, wedge, or bolt, which keeps all fast. మేకు. A master spell: the key to a puzzle or rule. మర్మము. A flame మంట.

కీలడి See under కీలు.

కీలసలు *kilasalu*. [Tel.] n. Paddy, some of the ears of which are empty from disease or want of rain.

కీలారము Same as కీలారము.

కీలారి Same as కీలారి.

కీలాలము *kilalamu*. [Skt.] n. Blood. నెత్తురు. Water నీళ్లు.

కీలి *kili*. [Skt.] n. A title of Agni, the god of fire. అగ్ని, నిప్పు.

కీలించు *kilintsu*. [Tel.] v. a. To put on or in (flowers, shoes, &c. to another,) to deck with, insert, set. తొడిగించు, కట్టు. కలశాగిలించె మద్యఘటమును she put the pail of toddy on her head. కీలితము *kilitamu*. adj. Bound, tied, knotted.

కీలు *kilu*. [Tel.] n. A joint, a hinge. అడెకట్టు. Pitch (or tar.) తారు. The point of a riddle మర్మము. Expedient ఉపాయము. చేతికీళ్లు the joints of the hand. ఓడకీలు (Vema. 628.) Rosin and grease melted together to paint ships with. కీలుచాప a tarpaulin. కీలుగోపురము (Radha. ii. 149.) a castle or chamber that turns on a pivot. కీలు గరుడపక్షి an automaton eagle. కీలుకాడు an engineer, a mechanician or contriver సూత్రధారి. "కీలుగాడెటు లింప గదినిన బొమ్మల క్రియ దిరంగి పృథజము" M. VII. iii. 72. కీలుబొమ్మ an automaton, or puppet. కీలుకత్తి a folding knife or hasp-knife. కీలుకొను or కీలుపడు *kilu-konu*. v. n. To be united, join, be composed. కూడుకొను, తగులు. To be fixed in నాటు. "కెంపులచెక్కడంపుపని కీల్కొనుబంగరు పావలెక్క..." Radha. iii. 13. "కీల పాదుకల్ మలకీల్కొనియున్న నిశాటకోటికిన్." V. P. ii. 304. కీలుకొలుపు or కీలుపరుచు *kilu-kolupu*. v. a. To fasten, unite, to lay, put. కీలుగంటు *kilu-gantu* n. A knot or crest of hair. కొప్పుకలదూముడి. కీల్జడ *kil-zada*. n. A woman's plaited tress of hair.

కీశము *kisamu*. [Skt.] n. A monkey.

కిస *kisa*. [Tel.] adj. Little. కొంచెము; trifling. అల్పము.

కిసర, కిసరతిత్తి or కిసా kisara. [Tel.] n. A purse, a pocket. శేబు. The fourth part of a weight or quantity. H. iv. 194. కిసరమధ్యస్థము dishonesty in arbitration. కిసరిపాలు a small portion.

కు ku

కు ku. [Tel. cf. Turkish and Hindustani: కు and కీ.] To, for. The sign of the Dative case, which when following a final ఇ becomes కి as వానికి, దానికి and elsewhere is కు as మాకు, తోటకు.

కు ku. [Skt.] n. In composition signifies bad, vile కుత్సితము. కుయుక్తి a wicked device. కుమతి a bad disposition. కుచేష్టము a vile prank. So కుతర్కము, కుజనుడు. Also కు= the earth.

కుంక kunka. [Tel.] n. A virgin widow. బాలవిధవ. A wretch, a slut: రండ.

కుంకటి kunkati. [Tel. another form of కూకటి. q. v.] n. A tuft of bair. జుట్టు, పిల్లజుట్టు. adj. Chief. ప్రధానము. కుంకటి మూగ kunkati-muga. n. The fork-tailed shrike కిరీటము. కుంకటివేరు kunkati-veru. n. The tap root from which the others grow. ప్రధానమైనవేరు. కుంకట్లు kunkatlu. n. plu. Curls or ringlets of hair. ముంగురులు.

కుంకు, కూకు or క్రుంకు kunku. [Tel.] v. n. To sink. మునుగు. To set as the sun అస్తమించు. పొద్దుగూకినది or కుంకినది the sun has set.

కుంకుడుచెట్టు kunkudu-chettu. [Tel.] n. The soap nut tree. *Sapindus detergens* or *Sapindus emarginatus*. కుంకుడుకాయలు kunkudu-kayalu. n. Soap nuts. కుంకుడు పురుగు kunkudu-purugu. n. The insect called a lady bird. ఇంద్రగోప పురుగు.

కుంకుమ kunkuma. [Skt.] n. A fragrant cosmetic or rouge, composed of turmeric, alum and lime juice. కూతురికి కుంకుమకు గాను ఇచ్చిన భూమి land granted to the daughter for pin money. కుంకుమ కేసరము kunkuma-kesaramu. n. A certain fragrant cosmetic. కుంకుమపువ్వు kunkuma-puvvu. n. Saffron. కుంకుమపూజిట్ట kunkuma-pu-jitta. n. The small Minivet. *Pericrocotus peregrinus* (F. B. I.) కుంకుమము kankumamu. n. Saffron. జాఫరా, చెందిరము.

కుంగు or క్రుంగు kungu. [Tel.] v. n. To sink, bend, hang down. To give way or yield. To diminish. కుంకుట. వానిజోంకు ఇంకా కుంకలేదు his freshness is not yet gone. ఈ జ్వరము వానిని కుంగగొట్టినది this fever reduced him greatly.

కుంచము kuntsamu. [Tel.] n. A measure of grain, four manikas or one quarter of a toom. కుంచెడు a measureful.

కుంచిక kunchika. [Skt.] n. The key of a lock. కుంచెకోల.

కుంచితము kunchitamu. [Skt.] adj. Crooked. వంకరైన, వక్రము.

కుంచియ kunchiya. [Tel.] n. A painting brush, a brush, or whisk for flies. A carding instrument or teazle for wool.

కుంచి kunchi. [Tel.] n. A cap with a flap behind, worn by boys. A whisk to drive away flies with.

కుంచు kuntsu. [Tel.] v. a. To diminish, do away with, remove. To sink or depress. క్రుంగజేయు. అణాకుంచు to underrate, undervalue. To stint, pinch.

కుంచె or కుంచియ kunche. [Tel.] n. A brush, a whisk; a carding instrument or teazle for wool, a chauri made of peacock's feathers. గుడ్డను కర్రకు కుంచెగా కట్టినాడు he fastened the cloth as a wisp on the pole. కుంచెకోల kunche-kola. n. The crooked pole used in opening the gate of a pagoda.

కుంజడా or కుంజరి kunjada. [H.] n. A huckster, a fruiterer. చిల్లర అంగడివాడు, పండ్లు అమ్మేవాడు, పండ్లమ్మేవాడు.

కుంజము *kunjamu.* [Skt.] n. A thicket, a bower, or arbour. పొదరిల్లు. An elephant's cheek ఏనుగుచెక్కిలి. An elephant's tusk ఏనుగుకొమ్ము. **కుంజరము** *kunjaramu.* n. An elephant. The best of anything శ్రేష్ఠము. కవికుంజరుడు a great poet. మౌనికుంజరులు the noblest of hermits. **కుంజరాశనము** *kunjar-āsanamu.* n. Elephant's food. The poplar leaved fig tree, *Ficus religiosus.* రావిచెట్టు.

కుంట *kunta.* [Tel.] n. A pond. కొలను, చెరువు. A pit, or hole of any kind పల్లము, గుంట. A certain square measure of land, 1/40 of an acre. **కుంటముక్కు** *kunta-mukku.* n. A sort of fish. H. iv. 224.

కుంటి *kunti.* [Tel.] adj. Lame, crooked. గాలికుంట్లు windgalls, rheumatism. **కుంటితనము** *kunti-tanamu.* n. Lameness, a crippled state. **కుంటు** *kuntu.* n. Lameness, crookedness. A lame man కుంటు పిచ్చుక, కుంటివాడు. v. n. To limp, to go lame. **కుంటుపడు** *kuntu-padu.* v. n. To become lame. కుంటిపడు. To fail, or break down as an undertaking. విఘ్నమగు.

> "అపుడుద్దాలకు డాగ్రహించి
> నిజభార్యంజూచి నిర్భాగ్యరా,
> లపవిత్రంబుగుపాపిష్ఠాంబు
> నవగీలంబెంట్లపైవెచి కుం
> టుపడంజేసితి గ్రాద్ధకర్మమని."
>
> Jai. iv. 111.

To be diminished తగ్గు. To be cut off తెగు. **కుంటుపారు** *kuntu-pāru.* v. n. To become weak, బలహీనమగు.

కుంటెండ్లు or **కుంటెనకమ్మలు** *kuntendlu.* [Tel.] n. Large earrings. "కడియాలు కుంటెండ్లుగంట లొడ్డాణంబు" Chand. R. V. ii. 21.

కుంటెన *kuntena.* [Tel.] n. Pimping, procuring. కుంటెనకత్తె A bawd, a procuress. తార్పుడది. కుంటెనకాడు or కుంటెన or కుంటెనీడు. A pimp, a procurer. తార్పువాడు. కుంటెనబోనము or కుంటెనపాట్లు pimping.

కుంటెనకమ్మలు See కుంటెండ్లు.

కుంటెనముడి *kuntena-mudi.* [Tel.] n. A knot in the string that passes through a book of palmyra leaves. తాటాకుల పుస్తకము దారమునకువేయుముడి.

కుంఠనము *kunthanamu.* [Skt.] n. A hindrance, check. Bluntness మొక్కపోవుట. **కుంఠము** *kunthamu.* adj. Blunt. Lazy, dull. మొక్కపోయినది, మొద్దు. **కుంఠితము** *kunthitamu.* adj. Hindered, checked. Blunted మొక్కపోయిన. **కుంఠీభూతుడు** *kunthī-bhūtudu.* n. One who has been defeated. One who has failed. **కుంఠుడు** *kunthudu.* n. An ignorant man. మూఢుడు. A lazy man సోమరి.

కుండ *kunda.* [Tel.] n. An earthen pot. A pot. కంచుకుండ a bell metal pot. A gilt ball on the crest of a tent, &c. కలశము. A bush in a carriage wheel ఇరుసుతిరిగెడుచే బండికంటి నడిమిగుబ్బ. **కుండగోకరి** *kunda-gōkari.* [కుండగోకు+అరి.] n. A cook. వంటవాడు. (నల. ద్విపద, 2 భా.) **కుండపోగులు** Same as కుండలములు. **కుండమార్చు** *kunda-mārtsu.* v. t. To exchange one thing for another. ఒకటినిచ్చి మరొకటిని పుచ్చుకొను.

కుండము *kundamu.* [Skt.] n. An earthen pot. A pit or pot for receiving and preserving consecrated fire. A fire pit నిప్పులగుండము.

కుండబంతి *kunda-banti.* [Tel.] n. The game called hockey.

కుండలము *kundalamu.* [Skt.] n. An earring. చెవిపోగు. **కుండలి** *kundali.* n. One who has earrings. పోగులు గలవాడు. A snake or serpent పాము. A mystic phrase for the spinal marrow. A circular dance కుండలాకారనృత్యము. (భార. విరా. i.) కుండలిస్థానము or కుండలిని or కుండలిశక్తి the pineal gland. సుషుమ్న (Vasu. Pref. 71.) Heyne says, a name of the తెల్ల ఉప్పిడి చెట్టు. కుండలివాడి. **కుండలించు** *kundal-intsu.* v. t. To put or mark a cipher round anything సున్నచుట్టు. (చంద్రా. i.) **కుండలీకరణము** *kundalī-karanamu.* n. To cancel by drawing a circle round an erroneous line. Giving or making a cipher సున్నచుట్టుట.

కుండి or **కుండిక** *kuṇḍi.* [Skt.] n. A student's water pot: a pitcher. కమండలువు.

కుండ్రాయిపొట్టు *kund-rāyi-poṭṭu.* [Tel.] n. A small dried fish. మత్స్యవిశేషము.

కుంతము *kuntamu.* [Skt.] n. A spear, a lance. ఈటె.

కుంతలము *kuntalamu.* [Skt.] n. A hair, a curl, a tress, or ringlet. వెండ్రుక. A country, apparently that about Bombay.

కుంతి *kunti.* [Skt.] n. The name of the mother of the Pāṇḍavas. పాండురాజు పెండ్లాము.

కుందకము *kundakamu.* [Tel.] n. A hindrance. అడ్డంతరము. A defect లోపము. కుందకముగానుండేభూమి waste land ఖాళీ స్థలము.

కుందనము *kundanamu.* [Tel.] n. Solid gold, fine gold. అపరంజి.

కుందము *kundamu* [Skt.] n. The jessamine. *Jasminum multiflorum,* మొల్లపువ్వు. కుందరదన a maiden with teeth like blossoms.

కుందా *kunda.* [H.] n. The butt of a gun.

కుండి or **కుండియున** or **కుందెన** *kundi.* [Tel.] n. A rim, the ledge round a mortar, to prevent the falling of the rice, &c., when beaten in it. రోలికంచు చుట్టునుండే రాతి కుదురు.

కుందించు *kundintsu.* [Tel.] v. a. To grieve, to afflict, to crush. "దెంచుకుందించుగాదు." R. v. 73.

కుందికాళ్లు *kundi-kāllu.* [Tel.] n. Leap frog or a game at hopping. V. P. vii. 211.

కుందు *kundu.* [Tel.] v. n. To pine, to sorrow, to be mortified, dejected. To sink under affliction దుఃఖించు, శోకించు,

కృంగు. n. Affliction, grief, dejection. దుఃఖము. Defect కొరగ్గము.

కుందురుకి *kunduruki.* [Skt.] n. The olibanum tree that produces frankincense. అందుగుచెట్టు.

కుందురువు or **కుందువు** *kunduruvu.* [Skt.] n. A sort of weed that infests corn land. *Saccharum spontaneum.* కుందురుబీడు a waste place covered with such weeds. Also, the resin of the *Boswellia thurifera,* gum olibanum or frankincense సాంబ్రాణి పత్రము.

కుందురెల్లు *kundu-rellu.* [Tel.] n. A reed of which pens are made.

కుందెన See కుంది. **కుందెనగిరి** or **కుందెనగుడి** *kundena-giri.* [Tel.] n. A certain game played by boys.

కుందేలు *kundēlu.* [Tel.] n. The black-naped hare, *Lepus nigricollis.* (F. B. I.) చెవులపిల్లి, చెవులపోతు, శశము. **కుందేటి కొమ్ము** *kundēṭi-kommu.* n. A hare's horn, i. e., a mere nothing, an absurdity. కూన్యము. కుందేటిఖండము land on which hares are found. శశవనము.

కుంపటి *kumpaṭi.* [Tel.] n. A chafing dish, a goldsmith's portable furnace. ఇది కుంపట్లో తామరమొలిచినట్లున్నది this is a perfect oasis in the desert. lit. Like a lotus growing in a furnace. A proverb regarding that which is admirable but of base origin.

కుంపిణి *kumpiṇi.* [Eng. "Company."] n. The East India Company, or a company of sepoys.

కుంపె *kumpe.* [Tel.] n. A tray. తాంబూలపాత్రము.

కుంపెరుగు *kum-perugu.* [Tel. కుండ+పెరుగు.] n. Thin curds, the whey or liquid part of curds. అడుగుపెరుగు.

కుంబ *kumba.* [Skt.] n. A hedge round a place of sacrifice

కుంబీ *kumbī.* [H.] n. Bleaching (cloth). చలవచేయుడము.

కుంభకము kumbhakamu. [Skt.] n. Stopping the breath. ఊపిరిబిగబట్టుట.

కుంభము kumbhamu. [Skt.] n. A small water jar, vase or pitcher. కుండ. The sign Aquarius. The frontal globe on the forehead of an elephant. A heap of boiled rice, prepared in the name of a goddess at her festival. కుంభవర్షముకురిసినది the rain poured down in torrents. కుచకుంభములు large breasts. కుంభసంభవుడు or కుంభజాడు kumbha-sambharudu. n. One born in a vase or pitcher, an epithet of Agastya. అగస్త్యుడు. కుంభాభిషేకము kumbhabhishêkamu. n. Bathing the god in a vessel of water. కుంభి kumbhi. n. An elephant.

కుంభించు kumbhintsu. [Skt.] v. a. To hold the breath. ఊపిరిబిగబట్టు.

కుంభిని kumbhini. [Skt.] n. The earth. భూమి.

కుంభీనసము kumbhi-nasamu. [Skt.] n. A serpent.

కుకరుడు ku-karuḍu. [Skt.] n. One who has a withered hand. ఈడేరోయిన చెయ్యిగలవాడు.

కుకవి ku-kavi. [Skt.] n. A poetaster or bad poet. కుత్సితకవి.

కుకీలము kukilamu. [Skt.] n. A hill or mount.

కుకుందరము kukunduramu. [Skt.] n. The cavities of the loins. కటిమొక్క వెనుకటిభాగ మందలిగుంటు.

కుక్క kukka. [Tel.] n. A dog. ఆడకుక్క a bitch. కుక్కపిల్ల a pup, or whelp, a puppy. కుక్క adj. Inferior. కుక్కగొర్రె kukka-gorre. n The rib-faced deer or barking deer, Cervulus muntjac. (F.B.I.) కుక్కతులసి kukka-tulasi. n. The white basil: (Ainslie. ii. 91.) ocymum album, as distinguished from the proper Tulasi called ocymum sanctum. కుక్కపాల kukka-pala. n. A plant from the fibrous leaves of which bow strings, &c., are made. Aletris hyacinthoides; Sanseviera zeylanica. (Roxb.) చాగచెట్టు. A wild species of the పాలచెట్టు, Periploca Tunicata: అజగంధి, వటపత్రిక. కుక్కముల్లు kukka-mullu. n. An eruption like measles, miliary eruption or nettle rash. కుక్కమూతిపిందె kukka-mūti-pinde. A blasted fruit. A proverb says చెట్టుచెడేకాలానికి కుక్కమూతి పిందెలు పుట్టును producing blasted fruit is a mark that the tree will never thrive again. Metaphorically, wild behaviour portends ruin. కుక్కవావింట kukka-vāpinṭa. n. A plant called the Dog Mustard, Cleome viscosa. గ్రుడ్డిబర్బర.

కుక్కి kukki. [Tel.] n. A poor bed. మంచపు కుక్కి, చిన్నమంచము. adj. Deep. లోతైన. కుక్కిపడు to become loose పల్లమగు. కుక్కిపడ్డ loose, slack. కుక్కిపడ్డమంచము a rickety bed.

కుక్కు or క్రుక్కు kukku. [Tel.] v. a. To stuff, to cram; to crush, to squeeze (lice, &c.) ఇప్పుడు కుక్కివేసినపేనులాగున్నది she is sitting like a crushed louse. ఆ సందులో గుడ్డను కుక్కినాడు he stuffed the cloth into the aperture. వాణ్ని బాదకుక్కినారు they beat him to death.

కుక్కుటము kukkuṭamu. [Skt.] n. A cock: a fowl in general. కుక్కుటధ్వజుడు the god Kumārasvāmi, who has a cock on his banner. కుక్కుటి a hen. కుక్కురుకో the crowing of a cock. కుక్కురుమనక్కురు అనకుండా ఉండినాడు he answered not a word, or he had not a word to say.

కుక్షి kukshi. [Skt.] n. Stomach, కడుపు. Hunger ఆకలి. కుక్షింభరి kukshim-bhari. n. A glutton. పొట్టనింపుకొనువాడు, తిండిపోతు. కుక్షింభరిత్వము kukshim-bharitvamu. n. Gluttony.

కుగ్రామము ku-gramamu. [Skt.] n. A hamlet. A petty or paltry village.

కుచందనము ku-chandanamu. [Skt.] n. The bastard sandalwood tree.

కుచము *kuchamu.* [Skt.] n. The breast. **కుచాగ్రము** *kuchā-gramu.* n. The nipple. the tip of the breast.

కుచేష్ట *ku-chēshṭa.* [Skt.] n. A wicked prank.

కుచోద్యము *ku-chōdyamu.* [Skt.] n. Derision, jesting. కుచోద్యగాడు a jester, a humorist. కుచోద్యముచేయు to jest or joke. కుచోద్యపుమాట a jest or joke.

కుచ్చలి *kutstsali.* [Tel.] n. A species of the herb called the thick leaved sorrel. ఒకవిధమైన పాచలి.

కుచ్చి *kuchchi.* [Tel.] n. Cutch. కుచ్చిగుర్రము a horse brought from Cutch.

కుచ్చితుడు *kuchchituḍu.* [from Skt. కుత్సిత.] n. A rogue. కుత్సితుడు, కుజనుడు.

కుచ్చు *kutstsu.* [Tel.] n. A tassel. The ornament at the tip of a woman's queue. కుచ్చుకట్టినచీర a gown with tassels.

కుచ్చె *kuchche.* [Tel.] n. A heap, a stack, a pile. పిడకలకుచ్చె a heap of cow-dung cakes. కుచ్చెలు or కుచ్చిళ్లు the folds of the lower cloth which the Hindus tie round their loins.

కుచ్చెతీయు *kuchche-tīyu.* [Tel.] v. t. To hollow the back of a jewel so as to increase its lustre when set రత్నములకు సానపట్టు. కుచ్చెతీసినకెంపు a ruby hollowed behind.

కుచ్చెల *kuchchela.* [Tel.] n. A boy's game. K. P. vi. 217.

కుచ్చెల *kuchchela.* [Tel.] n. (plu. కుచ్చెలలు or కుచ్చెళ్లు.) A rick of corn. A heap of cut corn. కోసినధాన్యపుకుప్ప. A land measure which in the Guntur district is twenty nine acres or (33 $\frac{3}{16}$) thirty three guntas (see గుంట) and three sixteenths. One కుచ్చెల is nearly the same as a కత్తి of land, and is equal to eight గొర్రులు or 400 కుంటలు. The land that produces one stack of corn; it varies in various districts, and the above stated quantity is that fixed in the government rates. కుచ్చెళ్లువేయు to lay corn in ricks. కుచ్చెళ్లు See కుచ్చె. కుచ్చెలగంత or కుచ్చెల బొంత a bag of corn.

కుజనుడు *ku-januḍu.* [Skt.] n. A bad man. కుత్సితపురుషుడు.

కుజము *kujamu.* [Skt.] n. A tree. వృక్షము.

కుజుడు *kujuḍu.* [Skt.] n. The regent of the planet Mars. అంగారకుడు. **కుజవారము** *kuja-vāramu.* n. Tuesday, the day of Mars.

కుటజము *kuṭajamu.* [Skt.] n. A tree called *Echites antidysenterica.* అంకుడుచెట్టు. A. iv. 149. కొడిసె, కొడిసెపాల, కొండమల్లె, కోల ముక్కు.

కుటపము *kuṭapamu.* [Skt.] n. A garden attached to a house. ఇంటితోట.

కుటము *kuṭamu.* [Skt.] n. A tree. వృక్షము. A pot కొల్లకడవ. A hut గుడిసె.

కుటి *kuṭi.* [Skt.] n. A hut or cottage. గుడిసె. R. ii. 103.

కుటిలము *kuṭilamu.* [Skt.] adj. Crooked, cross, illnatured. కుటిలకుంతల, or కుటిలాలక a girl with curly locks. కుటిలబుద్ధి a crooked disposition, hypocrisy. **కుటిలత్వము** *kuṭilatvamu.* n. Crookedness. **కుటిలుడు** *kuṭiluḍu.* n. A wicked man: a hypocrite.

కుటీరము *kuṭīramu.* [Skt.] n. A small house, a hut, a cottage. గుడిసె. పటకుటీరము a tent. లతాకుటీరము a bower or arbour.

కుటుంబము *kuṭumbamu.* [Skt.] n. A family. A household. Race. నేను చాలా కుటుంబముగలవాడనుగనుక as I am a man of large family. **కుటుంబి** or **కుటుంబికుడు** *kuṭumbi.* n A householder, the head of a family. **కుటుంబిని** *kuṭumbini.* n. The mother of a family.

కుట్టడము *kuṭṭaḍamu.* [Tel.] n. The act of stitching. కుట్టుపని Also, stinging. కుట్టడిపు

వాడు a tailor. చెవులుకుట్టడము piercing the ears for earrings.

"చవికుట్టిదవు దోరపునిగ్గజెంటీలు
తనులతాద్యుతిక్ నైదండదొయసగ."
కుక. i.

కుట్టనము *kuṭṭanamu.* [Skt.] n. Striking, beating, smiting. ఖురకుట్టనము stamping, prancing.

కుట్టని, కుట్టనిక *kuṭṭani.* [Skt.] n. A bawd, a procuress. కుంటెనకత్తె.

కుట్టమితము *kuṭṭamitamu.* [Skt.] n. Coyness, reluctance. దంతపీడవాదులచేత కోప భావమభినయించినను లోపల మిక్కిలి ఆనందము నపొందునట్టి స్త్రీలయొక్క శృంగారచేష్టావిశేషము.

కుట్టారికె or **కుట్టారూగ** *kuṭṭarike.* [Tel. కురుచ+అరుగ.] n. A small species of the grain called అరుగలు. A. iv. 173.

కుట్టిమము *kuṭṭimamu.* [Skt.] n. A paved floor. రాతికట్టడపునేల.

కుట్టు *kuṭṭu.* [Tel.] v. n. To ache, be sore, to be in pain. వానికి కండ్లుకుట్టినవి he has got sore eyes. Metaphorically, he is envious. కుట్టు. v. a. To prick, bore, pierce: to sting. To sew or stitch. పండ్లు కుట్టుకొను to pick the teeth. మడిచికుట్టు to fold and sew, i.e., to hem. చెప్పులు కుట్టు to make shoes. చెప్పులుకుట్టేవాడు a cobbler, మాదిగవాడు. కుట్టుతేళ్లు scorpions, villains, కంటకులు, దుర్జనులు. కుట్టు. n. A stitch, a seam. Sewing, needlework. A stitch in the side కొంచెము కడుపు నొప్పి. A prick, or puncture, piercing. Spite, grudge, pique. కడుపుకుట్టు belly-ache: spite, grudge. కుట్టుగుగు the last breath, or gasp. **కుట్టుకాడ** or **కుట్టుపోగు** *kuṭṭu-kāḍa.* n. A wire placed in the ear in preparation for an earring. **కుట్టుపోయు** *kuṭṭu-pōyu.* v. n. To stitch or sew slightly.

కుట్టుడు *kuṭṭuḍu.* [Tel.] n. Stitching. కుట్టు వాకు a stitched leaf, విస్తరి.

కుట్టె *kuṭṭe.* [Tel.] n. The anus. గుదస్థానము.

కుట్మలము *kuṭmalamu.* [Skt.] n. A bud. స్తనకుట్మలములు budding breasts.

కుత్ర *kutra.* [from Skt. కృత్రిమము.] n. Fraud, guile, backbiting: a plot or conspiracy కుత్సితమైన ఆలోచన.

కుత్రపువాడు *kutrapu-vāḍu.* [Tel. కుట్టడము +వాడు.] n. A tailor.

కుఠారము *kuṭhāramu.* [Skt.] n. An axe. గొడ్డలి.

కుడతా *kuḍata.* [H. from Tel. కుట్టు.] n. A small jacket. Same as కుడితిని.

కుడి *kuḍi.* [Tel. from కూడు food.] n. Eating. కుడుపు. adj. Right, belonging to the right (dexter.) కుడికన్ను right eye. కుడికాలు right leg. కుడిచెయ్యి right hand. కుడిపక్క right side. కుడినీరు drinkable water, త్రాగదగినజలము. "కుడినీరుమేడలు." వసు. iv. **కుడిదల** *kuḍi-dala.* n. Subsistence, living, land.

కుడితి *kuḍiti.* [Tel. from కూడు.] n. A drink for cattle, made of the washings of rice, &c., left to turn sour. కడుగు.

కుడితిని *kuḍitini.* [H.] n. A small jacket. See కుడతా.

కుడిమివాడు *kuḍimi-vāḍu.* [Tel.] n. A snake catcher; a man who cures the bites of snakes.

కుడుంగము *kuḍuṅgamu.* [Skt.] n. A bower, arbour. లతాగృహము, పొదరిల్లు.

కుడుక *kuḍuka.* [Tel.] n. A scale pan of a balance. తక్కెడపళ్లెము. "గీ॥ తక్కెడపోతమున్న తక్కెడనుడుకచ్చెపైన." శేష. ii.

కుడుచు *kuḍutsu.* [Tel.] v. a. To eat. To suck. To suffer or incur (punishment.) To gain. అనుభవించు, త్రాగు, భుజించు. **కుడుపు** *kuḍupu.* v. a. To feed. To suckle. కుడుపజేయు. ఇది నీకు దేవుడు కట్టి కుడుపును God will reward you with evil for this evil. చన్నుకుడ్పుటకా on giving the child the breast. కుడుపు n. Food, eating. భోజనము. Enjoyment అనుభవము. The tongue of a bell.

కుడుము kuḍumu. [Tel.] n. A bun or cake boiled in steam. మోదకము.

కుడ్యము kuḍyamu. [Skt. prob. derived from Tel. గోడ.] n. A wall. కుడ్యకారుడు one who builds a wall గోడ పెట్టువాడు.

కుణకము kuṇakamu. [Skt.] n. The young of an animal. పిల్ల. "మాతృకుణకము" (కా. v. i.)

కుణపము kuṇapamu. [Skt.] n. A corpse.

కుతపము ku-tapamu. [Skt.] n. Slight heat, warmth. కుతపకాలము midday. కుతపుడు the Sun.

కుతర్కము ku-tarkamu. [Skt.] n. False logic: sophistical reasoning.

కుతలము kutalamu. [Skt.] n. The earth, the world. అతలకుతలముగా topsy turvy: upside down.

కుతాపి kutāpi. [Tel.] Anuk. to కుంటి, thus: కుంటికాదు, కుతాపికాదు neither lame nor limp.

కుతిక, కుతికె or కుత్తిక kutika. [Tel.] n. The gullet. Tone, voice. వానికి కుతిక కవ్వినది he is hoarse. కుతికమట్టుకు neck deep. కుతికంటు kutik-antu. [కుతిక+అంటు] n. A necklace worn close round the throat. కుతికలబడు kutikala-baḍu v. n. To flop down. తేరకలబడు. "మసలక యోగనిమజ్జికట్టుబట్టి కుడియదాకించిన కుతికలబడియె." Pal. 251.

కుతిని kutinī. [Tel.] n. A kind of silk. ఒక దినుసుపట్టు.

కుతిల kutila. [Tel.] n. Pain. బాధ. కుతిలగుడుచు or కుతిలపడు kutila-guḍutsu. v. n. To suffer. బాధపడు. To sob నుటుకలు మింగు. "వినుమృపాలక యూర్లవెంబడి దేవరసుద్దులంచలజేరి కుతిలగుడిచి యుడిగి కెచ్చిన నీరసొమ్ము మరో భూమియుండి." N. Haris. iv. 203. కుతిలపెట్టు or కుతిలపరచు kutila-peṭṭu. v. n. To inflict suffering, to afflict, బాధపెట్టు.

"క॥ అరాజకత్వ,
దోషజాతమైనదురితబాహుళ్యంబు
కుతిలపెట్టభూమియతలమునకు
పోవనెరిగెకశ్యపుడు."
M. XII. ii. 99.

కుతిలపాటు kutila-pāṭu. n. Suffering. కుతిలపడుట.

కుతుక or కుత్తుక Same as కుతిక.

కుతుకము kutukamu. [Skt.] n. Impetuosity, fervour, vehemence. Inclination, curiosity. అనుభవింపని కోరకయుండి ఆశ. కుతుకత kutukata. n. Eagerness, impetuosity. "కుతుకతకూటికి గొలుచువారలకు." Sar. D. vi 468.

కుతూ or కుతుపు kutuh. [Skt.] n. An oil bottle. సిద్దె. కుతూగణము a set of bottles. H. v. 3.

కుతూహలము kutūhalamu. [Skt.] n. Eagerness, impetuosity, overflow of feelings, ecstacy. కుతుకము.

కుత్కీలము kutkīlamu. [Skt.] n. A hill. కొండ. (శై. vi.)

కుత్త kutta. [Tel.] n. A low word for the posteriors.

కుత్తిక kuttika. [Tel.] n. The throat. గొంతు, కుతిక, కంఠము.

కుత్తు or కుత్తుక kuttu. [Tel.] n. The throat, the gullet.

కుత్స kutsa. [Skt.] n. Reproach, contempt, blame. నింద, దూరు. కుత్సించు kutsintsu. v. a. To reproach. దూరు, రోతపడు. కుత్సితము kutsitamu. adj. Vile, base. కుత్సితుడు kutsituḍu. n. A wretch, a contemptible man.

కుథము kuthamu. [Skt.] n. An elephant's housings, or trappings.

కుడప *kudapa*. [Tel.] n. A clot (of curds, of blood, &c.)

కుడరము *kudaramu*. [Skt. cf. Tam. కుదిర.] n. A horse. గుర్రము. See కుదిర. (Tel.)

కుడవ or **కుదువ** *kudava*. [Tel.] n. Pawn, pledge. తాకట్టు.

కుదించు or **కుదిలించు** *kudintsu*. [Tel. from కుదియు.] v. a. To shake violently. కదిలించు, కుదియజేయు. T. iii. 121.

కుదికలపడు or **కుదికిలు** *kudikala-padu*. [Tel.] v. n. To squat down or flop down. Same as కుతికిలపడు. (q. v.)

కుదియు *kudiyu*. [Tel.] v. n. To tighten, contract, become less. అడగు, తగ్గు, క్రుంగు. **కుదియబట్టు** *kudiya-battu*. v. n. To hold fast. "మేకగుదియబట్టి మెడచన్ను గుడిచిన నాకు లేలదీరు నాకగాక." Vêma. 122. See కుదించు.

కుదిర *kudira*. [Tel. cf. Tam. కుదిరై & Skt. కుదిరము.] n. A horse. గుర్రము. కవిస. i.

కుదిరిక *kudirika*. [Tel. from కుదురు.] n. Symmetry, settlement, composure. పొంకము, అమరిక, నెమ్మది. కుదిరికగా నుండే మనిషి a handsome or comely man.

కుదిలించు *kudil-intsu*. [Tel. from కుదులు.] v. a. To shake violently (as water in a bottle), to agitate. To ram down a cartridge in a gun. To jog, jolt, jostle. కుదిలిక shaking కుదులాట.

కుదీలు or **కుదేలు** *kudîlu*. [Tel. a slang word used at cards.] n. An attempt to make five tricks at cards. పేకాట ఆటలో అయిదు పట్లుపట్టుతానని చేసే ప్రతిజ్ఞ.

కుదుచు Same as కుదిలించు.

కుదుటపడు *kuduta-padu*. [Tel. from కుదురు.] v. n. To be settled, or pacified. ఈ గాలి చేత మా ప్రాణము కుదుటపడినది we are refreshed by this breeze.

కుదువ Same as కుడవ. (q. v.)

కుదుపు *kudupu*. [Tel. from కుదియు or కుదులు.] v. a. To shake. n. Shaking. A man born lame. స్వభావమున కాలులేనివాడు, పంగుపు. (నా. v.)

కుదురు *kuduru*. [Tel.] v. n. To settle. స్థిరమగు. To recover (from illness) స్వస్థమగు. To be set, arranged, fixed, settled. To be got, obtained, found, come to hand. To fit or suit. అనుకూలమగు. To be introduced into an employ, to enter on it. To become firm, resolute. To succeed, prosper, flourish. కుదిరిన వ్రాత a settled handwriting అంతా బాగా కుదిరినది all is now right or settled. గణము కుదరలేదు the metre is defective. ఆపని వానికి కుదిరినది he obtained that employment. నాకు ఇల్లు కుదరలేదు. I cannot obtain lodgings. **కుదురుపాటు** *kuduru-pâtu*. n. Settlement, arrangement, cure, remedy. **కుదురుచు** or **కుదుర్చు** or **కుదిరించు** *kudurutsu*. (causal of కుదురు.) v. n. To restore, to settle or arrange, to curl, to heal, to pacify, to calm, to fix or place. **కుదురు** *kuduru*. n. (G. కుదిటి Loc. కుదుట. Plu. కుదుళ్లు) n. Settlement. Symmetry, gracefulness, beauty. Trimness, orderliness. అమరిక. Health, perfection. A family వంశము. One branch of a family. A garden bed. పాదు. A support or prop ప్రాపు. A ledge, or rim, preventing grain falling out of a mortar. A settle or ring of cord to prevent a pot from rolling over. చనుకుదురు a cancer in the breast. వాడు ఒక కుదిటివాడు he belongs to one branch of the family. ఒక్కకుదురైయున్నారు they live as one family. **కుదురుకొను** or **కుదురుపడు** *kuduru-konu*. v. n. To settle, to be settled. కదలకనిలుచు, నిలుకొను, స్థిరపడు.

కుదులు *kudulu*. [Tel.] v. n. To jolt, or shake as a horse does. చలించు, అదురు.

కుదువ *kuduva*. [Tel.] n. A pawn, or mortgage. తాకట్టు. **కుదువపెట్టు** *kuduva-pettu*. v. n. To pawn or mortgage. **కుదువ విడిపించు** v. n. To redeem from pawn.

కుద్దాలము *kuddalamu*. [Skt.] n. A sort of spade. ఒకవిధమైన పార.

కుధరము *ku-dharamu*. [Skt. కు=భూమి.] n. A hill, mountain. కొండ, పర్వతము.

కుని *kuni*. [Tel.] n. An angle, a bit of land. తోకుని a piece or corner of land.

కునుకు *kunuku*. [Tel.] v. n. To nod. తూగు. n. Nodding with sleep, dropping asleep. కునికిపాటు or కునుకుపాటు *kuniki-pāṭu* n. Nodding, dropping asleep, drooping, or winking the eyes. Drowsiness. Ambling.

కున్న *kunna*. [Tel. another form of కూన.] n. The young of an animal: a cub: a child: a sapling, suckling, or young tree. కూన, బిడ్డ. కున్నడు a boy. బాలుడు.

కువసము Same as కుప్పసము. (q. v.)

కుపితము *kupitamu*. [Skt.] adj. Choleric, angry, enraged. కుపితుడు *kupituḍu*. n. A passionate man: an angry man.

కుప్ప *kuppa*. [Tel.] n. A heap or pile, assemblage or collection. కుప్పబండి a scavenger's cart. చక్కదనముల కుప్ప an assemblage of charms. కుప్పతెప్పలుగా abundantly. కుప్పతెప్పలుగా చనిపోవుచున్నారు they are dying in heaps. కుప్పగూరగా or కుప్పనగూరగా all of a heap, in a heap, abundantly. కుప్పలుగా, కుప్పలుపడి. "వత్రో పమానకాండములు వెస కుప్పనగూరగ నేపున." M. VIII. ii. 346. కుప్పవడు or కుప్పతిలు to become a heap, to accumulate into a heap కుప్పగాచేరు. కుప్పకోలుగొన abundantly, plentifully. "అర్థరవంబులు కుప్పకోలుగొన గర్జిల్లుచు తెరంగులెత్తెన్." HK. iii. 61.

కుప్పము *kuppamu*. [Tel.] n. A small village or hamlet; a fisherman's village జెంబడి వారిపల్లె.

కుప్పటుగురిగింజ *kuppaṭa-guri-ginja*. [Tel.] n. A certain boyish game. H. iii. 186.

కుప్పసము or కువసము *kuppasamu*. [Tel.] n. A boddice, coat, or jacket. అంగి, రవిక. The skin of a snake కుబుసము.

కుప్పి *kuppi*. [Tel.] n. The tree called *Acalypha Indica, Anethum Sowa*, a kind of anise. Roxb.

కుప్పించు *kuppintsu*. [Tel.] v. a. To collect, or bring together. To bring the feet together, or take firm footing when about to jump. To hold the breath. ఊపిరిపట్టు. కుప్పిగంతు *kuppi-gantu*. n. A leap. కుప్పిగంతులువేయు to leap, to hop about.

కుప్పె *kuppe*. [Tel.] n. A knob. గుబ్బ. The knot at the root of a tress of false hair. A sort of ornament in masonry. A long-necked bottle మెడనిడుపుగాగల కాచపాత్రము. గాజుకుప్పె a glass bottle. కుప్పెకట్టు ఔషధములు medicine calcined in a bottle. గంగకుప్పె a bottle full of Ganges water.

కుప్పించుచెట్టు Same as కుప్పి చెట్టు. (q. v.)

కుప్పెకోల *kuppe-kōla*. [Tel.] n. A bolt or pointless arrow. "ద్రోణుడుమార్గ్గాన యిరువదేను కుప్పెకోలలనతనిచేత నేటులువడి." M. VII. iii. 276.

కుబుసము *kubusamu*. [Tel.] n. A snake's cast skin. కూసము. The pivot of a door.

కుబేరాక్షి [Skt.] n. A kind of nut. Same as గచ్చకాయ. (q. v.)

కుబేరుడు *kubēruḍu*. [Skt.] n. The god of riches, who is regent of the north.

కుబ్జము *kubjamu*. [Skt.] adj. Hump backed, deformed. గురుగుబ్జైన. కుబ్జవటము the dwarf banyan tree. కుబ్జుడు *kubjuḍu*. n. A cripple, a hump back.

కుమతి *ku-mati*. [Skt. కు=కుత్సిత.] n. An evil mind, a bad heart or temper.

కుమారస్వామి *kumāra-swāmi*. [Skt.] n. A name of Kārtikēya, the god of war. M. III. v. 200.

కుమారి or కుమారిక kumāri. [Skt.] n. A girl, a little maid, a daughter. కూతురు, కన్య.

కుమారిలు kumārilu. [Tel.] n. To glow as fire. కుములు.

" శ్రీ మానవతియుల్లముమానని
మానస్రోధములచే కుమారిలిచింతా
ధీనగతినుండమదిలో
మానినప్రేమమున నంబుజోదరుడనియెన్."
Pariz. i. 87.

కుమారుడు kumāruḍu. [Skt.] n. A son. A name of కుమారస్వామి. In dramas, the heir apparent to the throne యువరాజు.

కుమార్తె or కుమారితె kumārte. [Tel. cf. Skt. కుమారి.] n. A daughter.

కుముఖము ku-mukhamu. [Skt. కు-కుత్సిత.] n. A pig. పంది.

కుముదము kumudamu. [Skt.] n. The white water lily. తెల్లకలువ. కుముదబాంధవుడు or కుముదమిత్రుడు an epithet of the moon (as patron of the lotus.) కుముదిని kumudini. n. A stalk of the white lily.

కుములు kumulu. [Tel.] v. n. To smoulder, burn, consume without flame, glow, pine, waste away with a slow fire of grief or passion. లోలోపల ఏడ్చుట. "కాదు కున్న చందంబు కుములుచుమాడి." Sar D. 421.

కుమ్మకు kummaku. [H.] n. Support, assistance. సహాయము. Abetment, instigation తోడుబడి.

కుమ్మర kummara. [Tel.] n. The potter's caste. కుండలుచేసే జీవించెడుజాతి. adj. Black. నలుపు. కుమ్మరగువ్వ kummara-guvva. n. A wagtail. కుమ్మరత or కుమ్మరది kummarata. n. A woman of the potter caste. కుమ్మరపురుగు kummara-purugu. n. A beetle. కుమ్మరసారె, or కుమ్మరసారె kummara-sāre. n. A potter's wheel. కుమ్మరసారెచుక్క kummara-sāre-tsukka. n. The name of the constellation called విశాఖానక్షత్రము. కుమ్మరస్వరూపములు kummara-svarūpamulu. n. Pots and pans: articles of pottery. కుమ్మరి or కుమ్మరవాడు kummari. n. A potter. కుమ్మరికొకయేడు గుదెకొకపెట్టు one blow of a cudgel will ruin a potter's year's work.

కుమ్మరించు kummarintsu. [Tel.] v. a. To pour out, to empty. "కుండలను కుమ్మరించిన దండి రక్తకాండములుకురియుంచి." T. v. 92. "ఘుమఘుమతావులకుమ్మరించి." T. iii. 10.

కుమ్మరిలు kummarilu. v. n. To be poured out, to gush, to flow. కుమ్మరింపు kummarimpu. n. A downpour as of rain.

కుమ్ము kummu. [Tel.] n. Smouldering ashes. పొట్టునిప్పు. దీన్ని కుమ్ములో కుక్కు push it into the fire. A plague, pest, abomination. ఇదేమికుమ్ము what plague is this?

కుమ్ము kummu. [Tel.] v. a. To butt, pierce, gore. ఆవు నన్ను కుమ్మినది or కుమ్మవచ్చినది the cow butted at me. n. A thrust or poke. కుమ్ముడు to give a poke or thrust. కుమ్ముసుద్ది enigmatical news సంకేతవృత్తాంతము. కుమ్మె kumme. n. A thrust పోటు. A dent సొట్ట. కుమ్మెలుపోవు to be hurt గాయముపడు.

కుయి or కుయ్యి kuyi. [Tel. from కూయు.] n. A cry, yell, vociferation, loud entreaty, or prayer: an exclamation like 'alas'. మొర. Protection రక్షణము. కుయ్యోమొర్రో kuyyō-morrō. interj. Alas! a cry of fright, wailing. కుయ్యక kuyyaka. adv. Without crying, silently.

కుయుక్తి ku-yukti. [Skt. కు=కుత్సిత.] n. Fraud, an evil device. కుత్సితపుయుక్తి.

కురంగము or కురంగమము kurangamu. [Skt.] n. An antelope, an animal of the deer kind. మృగము, జింక. కురంగనయన or కురంగలోచన. n. A gazelle eyed: lady, nymph. కురంగనాభము musk.

కురంగలి or కురగలి kurangali. [Tel.] n. Nearness. సమీపము. కురంగటు or కురగటు

kurangaṭa. adv. Near, hard by. పక్క. "గొం టుకనం పెరుంగక కురంగటనున్న దయ్యపు కురవర కుమారు." Swa. ii. 67.

కురంజి *kuranji.* [Skt.] n. A sort of tune. కురువంజి. H. v. 142.

కురంజీవాము *kuranji-vāmu.* [H. కురింజీ =Khorasani.] Same as కురాసాని ఓమము. (q. v.)

కురంటకము *kurantakamu.* [Skt.] n. Yellow amaranth. పచ్చపెద్దగోరంట, పచ్చ ములు గోరంట. See కురువకము.

కురండము *kuraṇḍamu.* [Skt.] n. Hydrocele. బుడ్డ, అండవృద్ధి.

కురకుర *kura-kura.* [Tel.] adj. Small. అల్పము.

కురగలి *kuragali.* [Tel.] n. Nearness. సమీపము. **కురగట** adj. Near, close, by. "కురగటికేఁగకుండగా దిగొలువఁగవలయుఁ." P. i. 160. కురగటి neighbouring. Same as కురంగటి.

కురచ See కురుచ.

కురము See కురుము.

కురరము *kuraramu.* [Skt.] n. An osprey: లకుముకిపిట్ట, కృష్ణలోహితదండముదరణ కలహంస, పెన్నదవులుగు.

కురవకము *kuravakamu.* [Skt.] n. The crimson amaranth. పుట్టగోక్కు, వసంత కడిమి, ఎర్రపూలపెద్దగోరంట.

కురాడము, కురాళము *kurāḍamu.* [Skt.] n. An awning or canopy. మేలుకట్టు, చప్పరము. "చేర్చికురాళముల్ గలుగు చిల్కకోళ్లదనర్చి పట్టెచేదీర్చినతూగుపాన్పు." H. iii. 119.

కురాసానిఓమము or **కురంజీవాము** *kurāsāni-ōmamu.* [from "Khorasan."] n. Black henbane. *Ligusticum ajwaen.* నల్లఓమము.

కురింజ *kurinja.* [Tel.] n. The plant called *Asclepias Vomitoria.*

కురింజీ *kurinji.* [H.] n. Corundum stone. కురువిందము.

కురిచీ *kurichi.* [H. from Tel. కూర్చుండు.] n. A chair. కుర్చీ.

కురిడీ *kuriḍi.* [Tel.] n. A dried cocoanut. లోపలిటెంకెనకొబ్బరి.

కురిమిడి *kurimiḍi.* [Tel.] n. A bank, dam or embankment. గట్టు, కట్ట.

కురియు *kuriyu.* [Tel.] v. n. To rain, to fall, as dew. వానకురియుచున్నది it is raining. **కురియు** or **కురిపించు** or **కురియించు** *kurip-intsu.* v. a. To shower, to cause to rain. వర్షించు. పువ్వులవానకురిపించిరి they showered down flowers. నిప్పులు కురిపించు to rain coals, i. e., be wroth.

కురు *kuru.* [Tel. from కురుచ.] adj. Small, little, short. పొట్టి. కురుకెంట్రుకలు short hair. కురునువ్వులు small sesamum seed. కురుమాపు slightly soiled. కురుమాపుచీర a rumpled or soiled garment.

"పొరిపొరిఁదనపట్టు పుట్టంబువిడిచి
కురుమాపుమాసిన కోకయుఁగట్టి."

Saranga. 204.

కురుకు *kuruku.* [Tel.] n. A heap, a pile. పోగు, కుప్ప. "పేరాకలిననిముఖంబులకే నరికి కురుకులు పెట్టిన మృగాళంబులనొప్ప." M. IV. iii. 227. "మ॥ విరిగెన్ దెక్కరథంబులొక్కమొకి నుర్విం గూలెకుండాలముల్ తరుపైన్ వ్రాలెతురంగమావళుల సంతానంబులింతింతలై కురుకుల్ గట్టెభటాంగకంబులు." M. VII. iv. 76.

కురుచ or **కురచ** *kurutsa.* [Tel.] adj. Little, short, stumpy, diminutive, dwarfish. **కురుచే** n. A sort of war dance: సాధనభేదమైనవాట్యము, సాముభేదము. **కురుచవేల్పు** *kurutsa-vēlpu.* n. The "stumpy god," Gaṇēsa. **కురుచపడు** *kurutsa-paḍu.* v. n. To become short, to be diminished. తగ్గు. See. కురు.

కురుజు *kuruju.* [Tel.] n. A hawk. డేగ. Honey మధువు. తేనె. A perpendicular post or prop by which a short beam is raised upon larger ones in a pent roof నూలకుమీదిగుజ్జు, ఇంటికప్పులోనుండ నిలువుగానుం

చిన చిన్నకర్ర. "అలమేరువునకోలి యుండంద నందమై కురుజాలు మేరువులై కామరు మిగుల." N. viii. 228. కురుజాతేనె virgin honey, the sweetest honey, లాంటితేనె "కురుజాతే నియతాగాధి కుసుమరసము" T. iii. 64. కురుజా తెలనాకు a fresh light coloured betel leaf.

కురుత *kuruta.* [Tel.] n. A fish, *Sparus Spinifer.* Russell, plate 101.

కురుప, కురుపు or కురువ *kurupa.* [Tel.] n. Long wool. కురుమగొర్రె or కురుపగొర్రె a sheep with long wool. కురుమవాండ్లు, కురుపగొల్ల or కురుమగొల్ల a caste of shepherds who weave blankets.

కురుపంది *kuru-pandi.* [Tel. కురు=short.] n. The Indian Chevrotain or Mouse Deer, *Tragulus meminna.* (F. B. I.)

కురుపు *kurupu.* [Tel.] n. A boil or sore. వ్రణము. Raining, showering. మొన్నకురిసి నదేకురుపు that was indeed a shower.

కురుమట్టము *kuru-maṭṭamu.* [Tel. కురు= short.] adj. Short. పొట్టి. Obedient, humble వినయముగల.

"క॥ మరుగుమమలుకుమదిరదిర
కురుమట్టపుబొట్టినదుకు కొంచెపటించెన్."
భా. viii.

కురుమాడు *kuru-māḍu.* [Tel.] n. The gable end of a house. ఇంటిమూలకప్పు. కురుమాడు దింపు to extend the gable end of a roof.

కురులు *kurulu.* [Tel.] n. A curl or lock of hair. ముంగురులు=ముందుకురులు. Hair కెంద్రుకలు.

కురువ *kuruva.* [Tel. కురు=small.] n. A foot path over a hill. కొండమీదిదారిదోవ.

కురువిందము *kuruvindamu.* [Skt.] n. The stone called Corundum. A ruby కెంపు. A kind of grass తుంగగడ్డి. A small shrub named *Abrus precatorius* or *Gaetnera racemosa.* Roxb. ii. 368. గురువింద.

కురువు *kuruvu.* [Tel.] n. The thigh. పెందొడ, తొడ.

కురువేరు *kuru-vēru.* [Tel. కురు=కురులు.] n. A plant, *Andropogon muricatum.* Roxb. i. 265.

కురుక్షేత్రము *kuru-kshētramu.* [Skt.] n. The battle field of the కురు race. Proverbially, a great slaughter, a sanguinary conflict, a battle-royal.

కురూపము *ku-rūpamu.* [Skt. కు=కుత్సిత.] n. Ugliness, deformity. కురూపి an ugly or deformed person. వికారముగానుండేవాడు.

కుర్కురము *kurkuramu.* [Skt.] n. A dog. కుక్క.

కుర్దనము *kurdanamu.* [Skt.] n. Sport, play. క్రీడ.

కుర్ర *kurra.* [Tel. connected with కురు.] adj. Small, young, little, short. కుర్రవెండ్రుకలు short hair. కుర్రపోటు a little thrust or shove. కుర్ర *kurra.* n. A young one. A child, a boy బిడ్డడు, శిశువు, బాలుడు. A young male buffalo. కోడెదూడపోతు. కుర్రడు or కుర్రవాడు *kurraḍu.* n. A young lad.

కుర్రి *kurri.* [Tel.] n. A milking cow, a heifer. పాడియావు. "పెదమరించియుతనిబొడుగక యావులిప్పుటుక్కభంగి కుర్రినీడి కురికి మనువిదీపు డిప్పమగ గాముసుండిని కొనపిపట్టి యున్నగేండ్రు కనిరి." G. X. 57.

కుర్రు *kurru.* [Tel.] v. n. To cry or yell. కూయు. To groan, draw a deep breath.

కులంగి *kulangi.* [Tel.] n. The Common Crane, *Grus communis.* (F. B. I.)

కులము *kulamu.* [Skt.] n. A caste, class or tribe తెగ. A genus or tribe of animals జాతి. Family. People. Rank. వంశము. బాలికాకులము girls (generically considered.) కులక్రమాగతము hereditary. కులకము *kulakamu.* n. Protraction of the government of the verb through several connected stanzas, contrary to the practice of closing the sense with each verse. ఒక క్రియతో ముగియు పద్యములసమూహము.

కులకాంత *kula-kānta*. n. An honourable wife. **కులకాయకము** *kula-kāyakamu*. n. The trade of one's caste : one's family business. **కులజుడు** *kulajuḍu*. n. One of good caste or honourable descent. **కులట** *kulaṭa*. n. An adulteress. జారస్త్రీ. **కులధర్మము** *kula-dharmamu*. n. A practice or observance peculiar to a tribe or family ; duty peculiar to a caste or race. A caste rule. **కులపర్వతము** *kula-parvatamu*. n. One of the principal mountains, which are మహేంద్రము, మలయము, సహ్యము, శుక్తిమంతము, గంధమాదనము, వింధ్యము, పారియాత్రము. ప్రధాన పర్వతము. **కులపాలిక** *kula-pālika*. n. A girl given away in marriage by her parents తల్లిదండ్రులచేనిచ్చి పెండ్లిచేయబడిన స్త్రీ. **కులవతి** or **కులస్థురాలు** *kula-vati*. n. A woman of one's own caste. ఆమె నా కులవతికాదు she is not of my caste. **కులవిద్య** *kula-vidya*. n. The science or knowledge peculiar to one's caste. **కులసతి, కులస్త్రీ** *kula-sati*. n. An honourable wife. **కులస్థుడు** *kulasthuḍu*. n. A man of the same caste. పదిమంది కులస్థులు neighbours, people of one's caste. కులస్థురాలు a woman of one's own caste. **కులహీనుడు** *kula-hīnuḍu*. n. An outcaste. **కులాచారము** *kulā-chāramu*. n. The proper duty or profession of a caste or family.

కులాయము *kulāyamu*. [Skt.] n. A nest. పక్షిగూడు.

కులాలుడు *kulāluḍu*. [Skt.] n. A potter. కుమ్మరవాడు.

కులాసా or **ఖులాసా** *kulāsā*. [H.] n. Happiness, felicity.

కులిశము *kuliśamu*. [Skt.] n. A thunderbolt. వజ్రాయుధము.

కులీనుడు *kulīnuḍu*. [Skt.] adj. Noble by birth. మంచికులమునందు పుట్టినవాడు.

కులుకరించు *kulukar-inṭsu*. [Tel.] v. n. To expand, to bloom, to grow. విజృంభించు.

"కమనీయకీర్త్యార పాదంబులు కులుకరించుచు." Vasu. iv. 36.

కులుకు *kuluku*. [Tel.] v. n. To move gracefully. To put on pretty airs, or attitudinize. To play tricks. To bloom. To be melodious. శృంగారముగా కదులు. పారావతంబుకులికెడిపలుకులు the melodious notes of the dove. కులుకుపుష్పములు beautiful flowers. ఏమికులుకుతుంది how pretty she is! కరుణారసము కులుకుకన్నులు eyes beaming with kindness, or bright with affection. కులికిన pert, saucy. **కులుకు** v. a. To move, or shake. To rub over పూయు. To pour or sprinkle పోయు, చేయు. n. Grace, elegance, charm, loveliness. Harmony in music, శృంగారచేష్ట, శృంగారపుకులికి, ఒయ్యారము, విలాసము. కులుకులాడి a belle, a pretty woman ఒయ్యారకత్తె. **కులుకు** adj. Fine, pretty, graceful. Harmonious, melodious. సొగసైన.

కులుత్థము or **కుళుత్థము** *kulutthamu*. [Skt.] n. The pulse called horse gram. ఉలవలు.

కులుపురాయి *kulupu-rāyi*. [Tel.] n. A kind of gem. రాజావర్తము. "నీలపుగులుపు చెక్కిన మేలిపసిండి ముద్దుటుంగరము." Paidim. i. 10.

కుల్య *kulya*. [Skt.] n. A canal, a rivulet. కాలువ. A water course. నీళ్లుపోయేత్రోవ.

కుల్యుడు *kulyuḍu*. [Skt.] n. An honourable man. గౌరవింపదగినమనుష్యుడు.

కుల్లిమి, కుల్లిమిపాము, కుల్లెము or **కుల్లెంపాము** *kullimi*. [Tel.] n. A sort of eel. కుల్లెము.

కుళాయి, కుళ్లా, కుళ్లాయి, కుళాయి, కుల్లాయి or **కులాయి** *kulāyi*. [H.] n. A little cap. చిన్నటోపి.

కుళింగము *kuḷingamu*. [Skt.] n. A sparrow : a crow. చటకము, వాయసము. The forktailed shrike, W.

కుళీరము *kuḷīramu*. [Skt.] n. A crab. కర్కాటకము, ఎండ్రకాయ.

కుళుపు *kuḷupu.* [Tel.] n. A stone set in a ring. ఉంగరమునకు పొదిగిన విలువగల మణి విశేషము.

కుళ్లగించు *kuḷḷa-gintsu.* [Tel.] v. a. To loosen or dibble (the earth): to stir (as the fire.)

కుళ్లాయి Same as కుళాయి.

కుళ్లు or **క్రుళ్లు** *kuḷḷu.* [Tel.] v. n. To rot, decay, fret away, become putrid. To pine or rot with envy. నీ అదృష్టము కుళ్లినది you are very lucky. కుళ్లిపోయిన rotten, putrid. మనంబున క్రుళ్లుచు grieving, sorrowing.

కువ Same as కువ్వ. (q. v.)

కువకువ *kuva-kuva.* [Tel.] adv. (Anuk) Trillingly, warblingly.

కువలము *kuvalamu.* [Skt.] n. A lily. కలువ.

కువలయము *ku-valayamu.* [Skt.] n. A water lily, or lotus. కలువ. The earth భూమండలము. కువలయాక్షి fair eyed, having eyes bright as lilies.

కువాడము, కువ్వాడము or **కువాళము** *kuvāḍamu.* [Tel.] n. A cloth cover over a carriage. బండిగూ. Hypocrisy, double dealing కపటము, "నీకువాడమ్ములన్నియు తెలుసు మాకు." HD. 1902.

కువిందుడు *kuvinduḍu.* [Skt.] n. A weaver. సాలెవాడు.

కువిచిలు *kuvichilu.* [Tel.]. n. A kind of saucepan. పాత్రసామగ్రులలో ఒకటి. H. v. 13.

కువేణి *kuvēṇi.* [Skt.] n. A fisherman's basket. చేపలుపట్టివేయుబుట్ట.

కువ్వ or **కువ** *kuvva.* [Tel.] n. A heap. Also a subterraneous granary. పాతర.

కుశంక *ku-ṣanka.* [Skt. కు=కుత్సిత.] n. A false objection, an empty cavil. కుత్సితపు శంక.

కుశము *kuṣamu.* [Skt.] n. A sort of grass which is used in many solemn and religious observances by the Brahmins: hence called sacrificial grass. *Poa Cynosuroides.* దర్భ. plu. కుశలు. కుశాగ్రబుద్ధి a wit as sharp as the point of a blade of grass.

కుశలము *kuṣalamu.* [Skt.] n. Well being, happiness. క్షేమము. కుశలప్రశ్నలడిగిరి they asked him regarding his welfare. adj. Skilful, conversant, expert, clever. నేర్పరి. **కుశలత** *kuṣalata.* n. Cleverness, ability; eloquence. Wellbeing.

కుశాలు *kuṣālu.* [H.] n. Gladness; excessive joy. అతిసంతోషము.

కుశిని *kuṣini.* [Fr.] n. A kitchen, cook-room. వంటయిల్లు, పచనమటిల్లు. కుశినివాడు a cook వంటవాడు.

కుశీలవుడు *ku-ṣilavuḍu.* [Skt.] n. An itenerant dancer, an actor. నానాదేశసంచారకుడైన నట్టువుడు.

కుశేశయము *kuṣē-ṣayamu.* [Skt.] n. A lotus. తామర, పద్మము.

కుషీ or **ఖుషీ** *kushī.* [H.] n. Pleasure, will. ఇష్టము.

కుష్ఠము or **కుష్ఠరోగము** *kushṭhamu.* [Skt.] n. Leprosy.

కుసంధి *ku-sandhi.* [Skt. కు=కుత్సిత.] n. Narrowness, a narrow space. కుసంధియైన adj. Crowded, thickset as houses, restricted or contracted as space. కుసంధిగా adv. Narrowly.

కుసి *kusi.* [Tel.] n. A joint in carpentry. మంచపు పట్టెలకుసి. "కూలినప్పుడేయుకుసులెల్ల విరుగును." Vēma. 247.

కుసిగుంపులు *kusi-gumpulu.* [Tel.] n. Trouble, pain. శ్రమము, బాధ. **కుసిగుంపులబెట్టు** v. a. To plague or tease. రచ్చలబెట్టు or శ్రమపెట్టు. "కూడిదట్టుచేసి కొలువుచేయుచున్న కుసిగుంపులబెట్టి వధింపజాలము." P. i. 435.

కుసిలించు *kusiḷintsu.* [Tel.] v. n. To sulk, to be discontented. అతృప్తిచే దుఃఖించు. **కుసిలింత.** n. Grief caused by discontent sulkiness. అతృప్తిచే దుఃఖించుట.

కుసీదము *kusīdamu.* [Skt.] n. Usury. అన్యాయమైన వడ్డి. Living on the interest got by lending out money వడ్డికిచ్చి జీవనము చేయుట. **కుసీదికుడు** or **కుసీదుడు** *kusīdikuḍu.* n. A usurer. అన్యాయమైన వడ్డితినేవాడు.

కుసుంబాపువ్వు *kusumbā-puvvu.* [from Skt. కుసుంభము.] n. The safflower: *Carthamus tinctorius* (Watts).

కుసుమ *kusuma.* [Tel.] n. Name of a flowering plant. A kind of grain, a kind of fine rice, సస్యవిశేషము, ధాన్యవిశేషము. Also, the safflover కుసుంభపుష్పము.

కుసుమము *kusumamu.* [Skt.] n. A kind of grain. ధాన్యవిశేషము. A flower in general. The safflower. Rose colour. కుసుమవన్నె. **కుసుమగంధి** *kusuma-gandhi.* n. 'Flora,' A poetical word for woman. కుసుమనూనె oil made from the seeds of the safflower. **కుసుమరోగము** *kusuma-rōgamu.* n. A disease connected with menstruation. శ్వేతకుసుమరోగము the disease called whites. Leucorrhea. ఎర్రకుసుమరోగము Menorragia. **కుసుమాస్త్రుడు** *kusum-astruḍu.* n. The god of flowery shafts, Cupid. **కుసుమించు** *kusum-intsu.* v. n. To flower. **కుసుమేషువు** *kusumēshuvu.* n. The god of flowery arrows, Cupid, మన్మథుడు.

కుసులు *kusulu.* [Tel.] n. Plural of కుసి. (q. v.) **కుసుళ్లు** *kusuḷḷu.* n. A gold armlet worn on the upper arm. "సందిటనిరువంకకొందు మైడి కుసుళ్లనందంబుకెందుర్రాకృష్ణా స." Suca. ii. 42.

కుసూలము *kusūlamu.* [Skt.] n. A granary. పాతర, ధాన్యమునుంచుగరిసె.

కుసృతి *kusṛiti.* [Skt.] n. Guile, craft. కపటభావము.

కుస్తరించు *kustarintsu.* [Tel.] v. a. To fondle, cajole, gull, make much of. బుజ్జగించు, ఊరడించు. To pacify సమాధానపరుచు. To arrange సవరించు. To pat చేరుచు.

కుస్తుభుడు *kustubhuḍu.* [Skt.] n. The sea. సముద్రము.

కుహకము *kuhakamu.* [Skt.] n. Juggling, deception, sleight of hand. మోసము. "కుహకమెడతెగకను కుదురులేదు" Vēma. 1349. **కుహకి** *kuhaki.* n. A hypocrite, a cheat.

కుహన *kuhana.* [Skt.] n. Delusion, deception. మాయ. కుహనాకురంగము the fairy hind.

కుహరము *kuharamu.* [Skt.] n. A cave. గుహ. A hole బెజ్జము.

కుహళి *kuhaḷi.* [Skt.] n. A bunch of areca nuts. పోకపొత్తి. "కుహళిదిగళన్నవపోర కావలుల్." Parij. iii. 100.

కుహీకుహీ *kuhi-kuhi.* [Tel.] n. The groaning or whistling sound of reeds. గాలిచేత రెల్లులో కలిగే ధ్వని. "తనరఘనకాస కుహీకుహీధ్వనులవలన." K. P. 392.

కుహూకుహూవు, కుహూకుహూత్కారము, కుహూవు or **కుహూత్కారము** *kuhu-kuhuvu.* [Skt.] n. The cry of the Indian cuckoo. కోకిలధ్వని.

కూ ku

కూ or **కూక** *kū.* [Tel.] n. A cry, a shout. అరుపు. కూకపెట్టు or కూకవేయు to call, to shout. కూకలు scolding, sharp remarks, reprehension, reprimand. కూకలుపెట్టు or కూకలువేయు to reprimand, to blame, to chide, to find fault with, to send one away roughly.

కూకటి *kūkaṭi.* [Tel.] n. Curls, ringlets. పిల్లజుట్టు. adj. chief. ప్రధానము. **కూకటిమాగ** *kūkaṭi-māga.* n. The Indian Roller or the forktailed shrike. పాలపిట్ట. **కూకటివేరు** *kūkaṭi-vēru.* n. The tap root, that from which others shoot out. కంకటిచేరు. "రాజసంశయమున కూకటివేళ్లతో పెరికి." Jai. i. 72.

కూకరించు *kūkar-intsu.* [Tel.] v. n. To scold, or reprimand. కూకలుపెట్టు. "కేదివారిని కూకరించితివో." Satya Bhāma. iv. 58.

కూకి or **కూకీ** *kūki.* [Tel.] n. A dove. **కూకిరవము** *kūki-ravamu.* n. Cooing, the voice of doves, murmuring notes. Satyab. i. 5.

కూకు *kūku,* [Tel. for క్రుంకు.] n. To set (as the sun or moon.) క్రుంకు. పొద్దుకూకినది the sun has set. పొద్దుగూకేవేళకు by sunset.

కూకుండు *kūkuṇḍu.* [Tel. for కూర్చుండు.] v. n. To sit down, to be seated.

కూకుడుగువ్వ *kūkuḍu-guvva.* [Tel.] n. The Indian Hoopoe, *Upupa indica* (F. B. I.)

కూకుడువత్తి *kūkuḍu-vatti.* [Tel.] n. Gossamer. కూకుడువత్తులయ్యె it was driven away like gossamer, i. e., piecemeal, bit by bit. నలినూకలు, తుత్తుమురు. "కంథరద్వ్రహారముల కూకుడువత్తులునైనమిన్ను విశ్వంభరనూలునన్," P. i. 50. See also L. iii. 139. and P. ii. 104.

కూకుదము *kūkudamu.* [Skt.] n. Bestowing a daughter in marriage. సాలంకృతకన్యాదానము. **కూకుదుడు** *kūkuduḍu.* n. He who bestows a girl in marriage. సాలంకృతకన్యాదానముచేయువాడు.

కూకురుగుండంగి *kūkuru-guṇḍangi.* [Tel.] n. The bird called the Gallinule or the Cuckoo. దాత్యూహము.

కూచము *kūtsamu.* [Tel.] n. A pillar, post, prop. స్తంభము.

కూచి *kūchi.* [Tel.] adj. Sharp, sharp pointed. వాడియైన. **కూచిచేయు** *kūchi-chēyu.* v. n. To march as an army. దండుప్రయాణమగు. **కూచిమతము** *kūchi-matamu.* [Tel.] n. Name of a sect among the Satanis. సాతానులలో నొకమతము.

కూచిమారము *kūchi-māramu.* [Tel.] n. Nonsense, mere conceits, lewdness. పోకిరితనము. "కుటిలకుచ్ఛిత్తములు కూచిమారములు, మటుమాయతనములు, మందుమాకులును." L. vii. 278. **కూచిమారుడు** *kūchi-māruḍu.* n. A lewd man.

కూజా *kūza.* [H.] n. A goglet or earthern water bottle.

కూట *kūṭa.* [Skt.] adj. False, fictitious.

కూటపాకలము *kūṭapākalamu.* [Skt.] n. A fever, as a disease which attacks elephants. పిత్తజ్వరము. ఏనుగలకువచ్చే ఒక జ్వరము. A kiln. "ఎవ్వాని క్రోధంబు హీనదుర్జనమశేష పరంపరలకు కూటపాకలంబు." Vēdānta. Ras. i. 16.

కూటబెట్టు *kūṭa-beṭṭu.* [Tel.] n. A sort of serpent. "జాతినాగులుమర్లు పెంజరలును నక్రిపెంజరలును, కూటబెట్టులు చిల్వగుడియలు దాములు" G. viii. 101.

కూటమి *kūṭami.* [Tel. from కూడు.] n. Union, meeting: association. సాంగత్యము. కూడిక society. Criminal connection.

కూటము or **కూటామి** *kūṭamu.* [Tel. from కూడు. n. An assembly, or court. A hall. కొలువుకూటము, చావడి. **కూటము** *kūṭamu.* [Skt.] n. The peak or top of a hill. కొండకొమ్ము. A heap of grain. ప్రోగు. Fraud, trick. కపటము. Conspiracy. కుట్ర. **కూటహర్మ్యము** *kūṭa-harmyamu.* n. The hall of audience. రాజనగరులో లక్ష్మీవిలాసము అనే కూటము. "హరిహయమణి వలయకూట హర్మ్యవిహారి" Manu. iii. 177. **కూటస్థానము** *kūṭa-sthānamu.* n. A focus, centre, place of meeting. See కూటమి. **కూటముత్యము** n. A dead pearl: meaning one without brilliancy. Also, an artificial pearl. మనుష్యులచేత చేయబడునట్టి ఒకవిధమైన ముత్యము. **కూటసాక్ష్యము** *kūṭa-sākshyamu.* n. False evidence.

కూటి *kūṭi.* [Tel.] Genitive of కూడు food. **కూటినీళ్లు** *kūṭi-nīḷḷu.* n. Sour water. Water in which boiled rice has been steeped.

కూటువ or కూటువు *kūṭuva.* [Tel. from కూడు.] n. A crowd. గుంపు. A heap ప్రోగు. A host, an army. కూటువసరులు *kūṭuva-sarulu.* n. A number of necklaces. "కూటుకచెదరి కన్నులలరుచూర, కూటువసరులు చిక్కు-పడగను వాలు మలు ఘనులిమూర్ఛపువొట్టు పడిచూరి చెదర." Padma. iii. 21.

కూడ, కూడను or కూడా *kūḍa.* [Tel. from కూడు.] adv. Together, also, likewise, too, even. సహితము. నీళ్లుకూడ యియ్యరు they do not give even water. అతనితోకూడ together with him.

కూడు *kūḍu.* [Tel.] v. n. To be fit. తగు. To unite చేరు. To be possible. To accrue, be amassed, gained, acquired, come to hand. To agree, be united. v. a. To meet. To add or sum up. ఇందుతో కూడినపని a matter connected herewith. గొబ్బికూడివచ్చిరి they came in a mob. ఇదియును కూడక పోయిన and if this be out of the question. ఇది కూడకుంటే if this is impracticable. అక్కడికి రాకూడక as I could not go there. వారు నోరెత్తకూడకపోరు they could not say a word. కూడని *kūḍani.* adj. Unsuitable, improper. కూడనిమాట an unappropriate word. కూడబడు *kūḍa-baḍu* v. n. To meet, unite చేరు. కూడబెట్టు *kūḍa-beṭṭu.* v. a. To collect. చేర్చు. To save as money. కూడమి *kūḍami.* n. Impossibility. కూడముట్టు *kūḍa-muṭṭu.* v. t. To run after తరుముకొనిపోవు, to overtake or come up with కలిసికొను. కూడలి *kūḍali.* n. Joining, meeting. కూడలిపట్టు a place of meeting. కూడలిదారి *kūḍali-dāri.* n. The place where various roads meet. కూడలిరాయి *kūḍali-rāyi.* n. A corner stone. కూడలిరాయి *kūḍali-rāyi.* n. The gable end of a house. రెండుపంచెలుచేసిన మూలనున్న నీటివారి. కూడిక *kūḍika.* n. Junction, చేరిక. Collocation, juxtaposition. Saving, frugality. Partnership. కూడికవారు partners in merchandise పాలికాపులు (Vizag.) కూడుకొను *kūḍu-konu.* v. a. To associate with, to unite. కూడుదల *kūḍu-dala.* n. Gain, profit. లాభము.

కూడు *kūḍu.* [Tel. from కుడుచు to eat or enjoy.] n. Food, victuals, boiled rice, అన్నము. The pith inside a palm tree: infl. కూటి. plu. కూళ్లు. viands, dishes. పుట్టకూడు the red earth in the heart of a white ant hill, which contains the eggs. వానికి కూటికిలేదు he has not bread to eat. కూటిపేదలు the indigent: those who have no food.

కూనలమ్మ *kūnal-amma.* n. The name of a village goddess. కూనలమ్మకోక a sort of petticoat.

కూత *kūta.* [Tel. from కూయు.] n. A cry కేక. కూతకైదువు a conchshell శంఖము. కూతనేల, కూతవట్టు or కూతవేటు *kūta-vēla.* n. A distance of two miles. కోసునేల. See కూయు.

కూతురు or కూతు *kūturu.* [Tel.] n. A daughter. ఆడకూతురు a woman, a female. పెండ్లికూతురు a bride.

కూతురుబుడమ *kūturu-buḍama.* [Tel.] n. A plant, *Bryonia Scabra.* See బుడమ. Ainslie. ii. 144.

కూన *kūna.* [Tel.] n. A young one, an infant. పిల్ల, బిడ్డ. The cub of an animal. కూనగుంట a small hole చిన్నపల్లము. కూనరాగము *kūna-rāgamu.* n. Whimpering; squeaking. కూనరోగము *kūna-rōgamu.* n. Ophthalmia or country sore eyes. కన్నులలోపెరిగెడుకూనలు fleshy excrescencies in the eyes.

కూని or ఖూని *kūni.* [H.] n. Murder. నరహత్య, హత్య.

కూపకము *kūpakamu.* [Skt.] n. The mast of a vessel. ఓడకంబము. A leather oil vessel. చేతిసిద్దె. The hollow on the loins. పిరిదిమీదిగుంట.

కూపము *kūpamu.* [Skt.] n. A pit, well, or hole. నుయ్యి, బెలము. An orifice. యమకూపము hell. స్మరకూపము the vulva. రోమ

కూపము a pore in the skin. రోమకూపము కూపకూపముగా విచారించుట to examine bit by bit, or minutely.

కూపారము *kūpāramu*. [Skt.] n. The ocean. సముద్రము.

కూపెట్టు *kū-peṭṭu*. [Tel.] v. n. To howl, cry, wail అరచు, మొరపెట్టు. A vi. 93.

కూబరము *kūbaramu*. [Skt.] n. The pole of a carriage connecting the body with the yoke. కూబరం adj. Fine. సూక్ష్మము.

కూయు *kūyu*. [Tel. from కూ anuk] v. n. To cry, exclaim, to make noise. To clamour, yell. To bark, bray, crow, mew, croak, call, sing, shriek, hoot, as an owl. అరచు. **కూయి** *kūyi*. n. A cry. కూత, మొర. Protection. రక్షణము.

"చనుదెంచెకూయిగా జనియెడువాడు"
భార. విరా. ४.

కూర *kūra*. [Tel.] n. A herb, herbs, vegetables, garden stuff. A mess of food, curry even including flesh. ఆకుకూరలు salads or leafy vegetables. కాయకూరలు or కూరగాయలు herbs that bear a fruit or pod, such as beans, peas, brinjals, melons &c. కూరనార herbs and so forth. కూరపసుపు saffron which is added to curries. కూరాకుపురుగు the canker worm that destroys herbs.

కూరట *kūraṭa*. [Tel.] n. Rolling on the ground, పొరలడము.

కూరము *kūramu*. [Skt.] n. Food, cooked food, అన్నము, వంటకము.

కూరముక్కు *kūra-mukku*. [Tel.] n. A sort of fish.

కూరాడు *kūr-āḍu*. [Tel.] n. Vinegar made from rice. కాడికవి.

కూరించు *kūrintsu*. [Tel. from కూరు.] v. n. To cause to cram, thrust or choke.

కూరిచి or **కూర్చి** *kūrichi*. [Tel.] a. Postposition. Concerning. Same as గూర్చి or గురించి.

కూరిమి or **కూర్మి** *kūrimi*. [Tel.] n. Love, charity. ప్రేమ. Friendship, చెలిమి, స్నేహము.

కూరు *kūru*. [Tel.] v. n. To come on, as sleep, or thirst. కలుగు. To collect, as sand in a drain. చేకూరు to accrue or be gained, to happen (as fear) ప్రాప్తమగు, సంభవించు. v. a. To fill, to stuff. To load (a gun), to fill or collect. **కూరువ** or **కూర్వ** *kūruva*. n. The ribs of a ship or boat. Also in carpentry, a bent piece of wood. ఓడకూర్పునకుచేసే వంకర కొయ్య.

కూరుకు or **కూర్కు** *kūruku*. [Tel.] v. n. To slumber, doze or sink in sleep. నిద్రించు. నా కన్నులు కూరుకపోతవి my eyes are closing, I am dropping asleep. n. Sinking to sleep, slumber, dozing. నిద్ర. "కూర్కులేక కూర్కు." R. iii. 93. కూర్కిడు to drop asleep. నిద్రించు.

కూరుకొను or **కూరుకొనిపోవు** *kūru-konu*. [Tel.] v. n. To enter. చొచ్చు. To sink, to be choked. To stuff క్రుక్కు. ఇసుకలో నా కాలు కూరుకొనిపోయినది my foot sank in the sand. కాలువ యిసుకచేత కూరుకొనిపోయినది the channel is choked with sand.

కూరుచు See కూర్చు.

కూరుచుండు See కూర్చుండు.

కూర్చము *kūrchamu*. [Skt.] n. A tuft of hair or grass. The beard గడ్డము, దాడి. A. vi. 21. 94. The top of the nose, being the place where the eyebrows meet. కనుబొమలనడుమ. వరాహకూర్చము a tuft, a brush.

కూర్చి See కూరిచి.

కూర్చిక *kūrchika*. [Skt.] n. A brush. చిత్రము వ్రాసే కూచిక.

కూర్చుండు or **కూరుచుండు** *kūrtsuṇḍu*. [Tel.] v. n. To sit, sit down, be seated. **కూర్చుండబెట్టు** *kūrtsuṇḍa-beṭṭu*. v. a. To seat, make one sit down. కూర్చుండబడు to sit కూర్చుండు.

"క. ఇంత పాపంబుచేయుచుం గౌరవసేనుం
రథ్యధరాజ్యలోభంబున నఖిలబంధు,
జనులవధియించు దొడఁగితివని రథంబు,
మీఁదఁగూర్చుండఁబడితొ జేయూఁదికొనుచు."
భార. భీష్మ. i.

కూర్చు kūrtsu. [Tel.] v. a. To join. కలుపు. To accumulate, heap up, assemble, gather. కూడబెట్టు. To compose or write, put together. గుంపుకూర్చు to raise a mob.

కూర్పరము kūrparamu. [Skt.] n. The elbow. మోచెయ్యి. The knee మోకాలు. A prop, or base ఆసరా.

కూర్పించు kūrpintsu. [Tel. from కూర్చు.] v. a. To cause to join, or to cause to sew.

కూర్పు or కూరుపు kūrpu. [Tel.] n. Joining, uniting. బల్లకూర్పు a seam, a stitch. బల్ల కూర్పుగోడ a wooden wall or screen built of boards.

కూర్మము kūrmamu. [Skt.] n. A turtle or tortoise. తాబేలు.

కూర్మి Same as కూరిమి.

కూలము kūlamu. [Skt.] n. A bank, shore. దరి. కూలంకష a river. నది. కూలంకషము the ocean సముద్రము. కూలంకషముగా the whole from first to last. కూలంకషమైన విమర్శ a thorough enquiry. కూలంక షముగా తెలిసికొన్నాడు he understood it thoroughly.

కూలి kūli. [Tel.] n. Hire, hired labour. Tax పన్ను. కూలికిచేయు to work for hire. కూలి or కూలివాడు, or కూలిమనిషి. n. A hired labourer, a workman, a cooly. Plu. కూలీలు. కూలినాలి kūli-nāli. n. Drudgery, hired labor (నాలి is an Anuk.)

కూలు kūlu. [Tel.] v. n. To fall. పడు. To die చచ్చు. కూలనూకు kūla-nūku. v. a. To knock down. కూలబడు kūla-baḍu. v. n. To fall, to fall down suddenly (a comic word for sitting down.) కూల వేయు kūla-vēyu. v. a. To make one fall, to make one sit down suddenly. కూలుచు or కూల్చు kūlutsu. v. t. To knock down, kill, overthrow, ruin.

కూళ kūḷa. [Tel.] adj. Cruel, vile, wicked. క్రూరము, కుత్సితము. కూళస్వరము a harsh voice. కూళ or కూళుడు n. A wicked man, a wretch. కుత్సితపురుషుడు. An ignorant man మూఢుడు. "కూళకూళమెచ్చుగాని వంతు విడనాడి." Vēma. Plu. కూళలు. కూళతనము kūḷa-tanamu. n. Wickedness, vileness, cruelty. "ప్రేతయన్నములకు ప్రియమతో డుతలిచ్చి, కాకులకును పెట్టుకర్మలార, కుక్కలడుసేమి కూళత్వమున్నది." Vēma.

కూవ kūva. [Tel.] n. A heap, a pile. కుప్ప.

కూష్మాండము or కూశ్మాండము kūshmāṇḍamu. [Skt.] n. A gourd, or pumpkin. గుమ్మడి. A sort of devil or demon. పిశాచ భేదము.

కూసము kūsamu. [Tel.] n. A snake's skin కుబుసము. A coat or jacket చొక్కాయి.

కూసు kūsu. [Tel.] adj. Low, base, trifling. కూసుమతము a miserable sect, a degraded sect. కూసువిద్య idle studies. A proverb says, అభ్యాసముకూసువిద్య Practice makes every thing easy.

కూహకము kūhakamu. [Skt] n. A trick, fraud, semblance. Hypocrisy. Intrigue. adj. Intriguing, fradulent, deceitful.

కృ kri

కృకము krikamu. [Skt.] n. The vertebræ of the neck, the throat. ముచ్చిలిగుంట మీఁదిబుడిపె, కంఠనాళము.

కృకలాసము krikalāsamu. [Skt.] n. A lizard or chameleon. ఊసరవెల్లి, తొండ.

కృకవాకువు krika-vākuvu. [Skt.] n. A cock. కోడి. కృకవాకుధ్వజుడు krika-vāku-dhvajuḍu. n. An epithet of Kumaraswami.

కృకాటిక krikāṭika. [Skt.] n. The nape or back of the neck, పెడతల, ముచ్చికగుంట.

కృచ్ఛ్రము *krichchhramu.* [Skt.] n. Pain. బాధ. Sin పాపము. A vow వ్రతము. Money expended as a mortification or penance for sin. పాంతపనాదివ్రతము.

కృతము *kritamu.* [Skt.] n. An act, a thing done. చేయబడ్డది. దైవకృతము an act of God. **కృతము** or **కృతయుగము** *kritamu.* n. The golden age, the first of the four ages of the world, supposed to consist of 1,728,000 years. **కృతము** *kritamu.* adj. Done, made, accomplished. కృతకృత్యుడు he who has attained his desire. ఇష్టార్థసిద్ధి గలవాడు. కృతాంజలి he who assumes with folded hands a reverential posture before his superiors. అంజలిబంధముకలవాడు. కృతాకృత done and not done. కృతస్నానస్సు having bathed. కృతమతి a prepared mind or set heart. adv. [Used in Vizag. for ప్రకృతము.] At present, just now. **కృతకము** *kritakamu.* adj. Artificial, made. మనుష్యులచేత చేయబడినది. Unreal. కృతకాద్రి or కృతకశైలము an artificial hillock. కృతక కళేబరము a thing made to represent a corpse. **కృతఘ్నము** *kritaghnamu.* [from ఘ్న to kill, destroy.] adj. Ungrateful. **కృతఘ్నత** *krita-ghnata.* n. Ingratitude. కృతఘ్నుడు an ungrateful man చేసినమేలు మరచినవాడు. **కృతజ్ఞుడు** *kritagnyudu.* [from జ్ఞ to know, to recognise.] n. A grateful person. చేసిన మేలు తెలియువాడు. **కృతజ్ఞత** *kritagnyata.* n. Gratitude. **కృతపదు** *krita-padu.* n. To be done or made. నటించు. "దేవావిడుమునగ చినంగృత పడినకార్యంబులు క్రమ్మరంబాడనుచే, గొందంబుగుండు నింతియకాక." M. VIII. i. 232. To be separated విడబడు. **కృతహస్తుడు** *krita-hastudu.* n. An unerring marksman గురితప్పకవేయువాడు. A skilful man నేర్పరి. **కృతాంతుడు** *kritāntudu.* n. He who brings to an end. An epithet of Yama. **కృతార్థత** *kritārthata.* n. Success. కోరిక యీడేరడము. **కృతార్థుడు** *kritārthudu.* n. A gainer, one who is successful. కోరిక యీడేరినవాడు, ధన్యుడు.

కృతి *kriti.* [Skt.] n. An act, an action, doing. చేయుట. Composition, work ప్రబంధము. Dedication. ఈ గ్రంథమును ఆ రాజునకు కృతి యిచ్చినాడు he dedicated this book to that king. **కృతి** *kriti.* n. A learned, successful, fortunate or skilful man. కృతార్థుడు, పండితుడు. నేర్పరి.

కృత్తి *kritti.* [Skt.] n. A hide or skin. తోలు. **కృత్తివాసుడు** *kritti-vāsudu.* n. He whose robe is a hide. A name of Siva.

కృత్తిక *krittika.* [Skt.] n. The Pleiades.

కృత్య *kritya.* [Skt.] n. The goddess of death, corresponding to Cotytto, or Diana Taurica or Hecate. సంహారకదేవత. "భార్గవ నిర్మితమైన కృత్యచేతంజంపించ సమకట్టిన." V. P. ii. 312.

కృత్యము *krityamu.* [Skt.] n. An act, a deed. పని. క్రూరకృత్యము a cruel act. దైవకృత్యము an act of God. నిత్యకృత్యములు daily duties. గృహకృత్యములు domestic matters.

కృత్రిమము *kritrimamu.* [Skt.] n. A trick; craft, art, chicanery. adj. Artificial, made by art. మనుష్యులచేత చేయబడినది. Seeming, apparent, not real, deceitful. కృత్రిమ మత్స్యము an artificial fish. కృత్రిమమిత్రుడు a false friend; a hypocritical ally.

కృత్స్నము *kritsnamu.* [Skt.] adj. All, entire. అంతయు.

కృప *kripa.* [Skt.] n. Favour, grace, mercy. దయ, కనికరము. కృపచేయు to grant, bestow, favour with.

కృపణుడు *kripanudu.* [Skt.] n. A vile person, a miser. లోభి, కుత్సితుడు.

కృపాణము *kripānamu.* [Skt.] n. A sword. కత్తి. **కృపాణి** *kripāni.* n. A knife, a pair of shears or scissors. కత్తి, కత్తెర, పట్టాకత్తి.

కృపాళువు *kripāluvu.* [Skt.] adj. Merciful, compassionate. కనికరముగల.

కృపీటము kripîṭamu. [Skt.] n. Water. జలము, నీళ్లు.

కృమి krimi. [Skt.] n. A worm: an insect in general. పురుగు, క్రిమి.

కృశము kriṡamu. [Skt.] adj. Thin, lank, slender, weak, feeble. చిక్కి, సన్నము. కృశత or కృశత్వము kriṡata. n. Leanness, thinness. కృశాంగి a slender girl.

కృశానువు kriṡânuvu. [Skt.] n. Fire. అగ్ని, నిప్పు.

కృశించు kriṡintsu. [Skt.] v. n. To waste or pine away, to become thin. బక్కచిక్కు, సన్నగిలు. కృశింపచేయు kriṡimpa-chêyu. v. a. To make thin. కృశోదరము a slender waist. M. I. iv. 49. కృశోదరి a slender waisted girl.

కృషి krishi. [Skt.] n. Cultivation, husbandry, agriculture, ploughing, cultivating the soil. సేద్యము. Labour, exertion ప్రయాసము, శ్రమ. కృషీకుడు or కృషీవలుడు krishi-kuḍu. n. A cultivator, a husbandman. సేద్యగాడు.

కృష్టము krishṭamu. [Skt.] adj. That which is drawn. ఈడ్వబడిన.

కృష్టి krishṭi. [Skt.] n. A man of learning. పండితుడు, విద్వాం.

కృష్ణము krishṇamu. [Skt.] adj. Black, dark. నల్లని. కృష్ణ or కృష్ణా krishṇa. n. The river Krishna కృష్ణానది. Draupadi ద్రౌపది. కృష్ణ or కృష్ణపక్షము krishṇa. n. The dark fortnight: the wane of the moon. కృష్ణాష్టమి the eighth day after full moon in the month of Srâvana (August) when Krishna was born. కృష్ణతామర krishṇa-tâmara. n. The flower called Indian reed; also called పెట్టతామర. Ainslie. ii. 534. కృష్ణదోషము krishṇa-dôshamu. n. Typhus fever. కృష్ణలీలలు krishṇa-lîlalu. n. The revels of Krishna. కృష్ణవర్త్మ krishṇa-vartma. n. Fire. అగ్ని. కృష్ణవేణి krishṇa-vêṇi. n. She that has black curls. కృష్ణసర్పము krishṇa-sarpamu. n. A black serpent. కృష్ణసారము a black antelope. నల్లయిఱ్ఱి. కృష్ణాజినము the hide of the black antelope. కృష్ణుడు Krishna, also a name of Arjuna. విష్ణువు, అర్జునుడు.

కృసరము krisaramu. [Skt.] n. A dish of rice and pulse. పులగము.

క్లుప్తము kluptamu. [Skt.] adj. That which is arranged or settled. ఏర్పాటుచేయబడిన. Short, brief. సంగ్రహము.

కె ke

కెం kem. [Tel. in composition, contracted from కెంపు.] adj. Red. కెమ్మోవి a red lip. కెంగేలు ken-gêlu. [కెంపు+కేలు.] n. The palm of the hand, literally the red hand. కెంజడలు ken-jaḍalu. n. Red hair. కెంజాయ ken-zâya. [కెంపు+చాయ.] n. Red colour. కెందమ్మి (కెంపు+తమ్మి) n. Red lotus. కెందామర ken-dâmara. [కెంపు+తామర.] n. The red lotus, the Amaranth of poetry. కెందూళి ken-dûḷi. [కెంపు+దూళి.] n. Red dust. కెందోగ ken-dôga. [కెంపు+తోగ.] n. The red lotus. ఎర్రకలువ. కెందొగరు ken-dogaru. [కెంపు+తొగరు.] n. A kind of scarlet cloth. BD. iii 106.

కెంపు kempu. [Tel.] n. A ruby. పద్మరాగము. Redness ఎరుపు. కెంపు the red metal, i.e., copper (used by goldsmiths in this sense.) కెంపులు the red petals of a plantain flower అరటిపువ్వులోని దుర్రని ముగ్గలు. A. v. 30. కెంపుకంటి kempu-kanṭi. n. The red-eyed bird, i. e., the black Cuckoo కోయిల. కెంపుగాము the red planet (గ్రహము) i. e., Mars. కెంబట్టు kem-baṭṭu. [కెంపు+పట్టు.] n. Red silk.

కెచ్చెలితనము kechcheli-tanamu. [Tel.] n. Riotousness. (Pritchett in Romans XIII. 13.) అల్లరి, దొమ్మి.

కెడ keḍa. [Tel.] n. A side, direction. పార్శ్వము.

కెడయు *keḍayu.* [Tel.] v. n. To fall, to die. కూలు, పడు, చచ్చు. "కడసినగరిపెల," అన గా విరిగికూలినగాడలయొక్క. A. vi. 12. "కేరు రమునవెసనాటినతోరంబగు నారసమునద్రుల్లికెడ సెన్." M. VIII. iii. 42. **కెడపు** *keḍapu.* v. a. To throw down. పడచేయు. To cast off, put aside, push away. త్రోయు. To kill చంపు. "నిర్మూలంబుగళత్రులకాగడపి." వ్యా. viii. 57. **కెడవు** *keḍavu.* n. A fall. పడుట.

కెత్తలముసొర్ర *kettalamu-sorra.* [Tel.] n. A plant, *Galeocerdo rayneri.*

కెన్నడి *kennaḍi.* [Tel.] n. The Sambar or Rusa Deer, *Cervus unicolor.*

కెరకొట్టు *kera-koṭṭu.* [Tel.] v. n. To chirp. కలకలకూయు.

కెరలు *keralu.* [Tel.] n. To be enraged, to cry out from alarm. కోపించు, రేగు, బొబ్బ లిడు. To exceed అతిశయించు, విజృంభించు. To cry as a bird. కూయు.

"గీ॥ ప్రమదమునదేటుకెలుగెత్తిపాడుచోట,
శారికలనంగశాస్త్రముల్ చదువుచోట,
గిరకలకంఠములుకొవ్వికెరలుచోట,
పావురములారజంబులుపలుకుచోట."
వ్యా. iii.

కెరలించు or **కెరలుచు** or **కెరల్చు** *kera-lintsu.* v. a. To make angry, to enrage, to stir up. రేచు, కోపింపజేయు, కెరలజేయు. "నను గెరలింపనాలికభవుడే." L. XIII. 158.

"పాదపాశులుపరిభూతిబడగబడిపి,
కొనుచుబరతెంచిరద్భుతమునగెరల్చి,
రోసరించిన భ్రాతృవ్యయుగళమునకు
దోడుపాటొప్ప."
BRY. 101.

కెరలియాడు *kerali-y-āḍu.* v. n. To dance with pride. చెలరేగు. **కెరలుపొడుచు** *keralu-poḍutsu.* v. n. To be proud. వర్ధిల్లు, విజృం భించు.

కెలకు Same as కెలుకు. (q. v.)

కెలకు or **కెలను** *kelaku.* [Tel.] n. A side, part, quarter. దిక్కు. ఆకెలనికి towards that side. Plu. కెలకులు.

కెలయు *kelayu.* [Tel.] v. n. To be arrogant. విజృంభించు.

"ద్వి. కెలయుచునినునికెక్కించుకొనెదు
కులజాండుతనుదానకొనియాడుకొనునె."
రా. అర. కాం.

కెలవు *kelavu.* [Tel.] n. Amorous desire. సంభోగేచ్ఛ.

"క. పలువురకొకభామినిపై
దలపును కొకవారసతికి దగబలువురపై
వలపునమృగవిహాగాదుల
కెలవురసాభాసమయ్యోటీతెలిసెల్లన్న న్."
కా. iii.

కెలస or **కెలసము** *kelasa.* [Tel. and Kan.] n. Business, work. పని, అక్కర.

"చుట్టమవై భుజాబలముసొంపున
నీకెలసంబుతీర్చెదన్."
M. III. v. 241.

కెలుకుor **కెలకు** *keluku.* [Tel.] v. a. To stir up, dig up or loosen earth. To scratch. మాని పోయినపుండ్లు మరలికెలికినట్లు this is merely stirring an old quarrel, opening a healed sore. "ఇందులకుంబొందుసడు ప్రత్యుత్తరంబుల బెలిగెలంకినబుద్ధిభ్రంశంబుగాక." A vi. 47. To dig up పెల్లగించు. "కోలలగెలికిన గురుములు గెల సె." Pal. 27. **కెల్లగించు** *kella-yintsu.* v. t. To dig up. పెల్లగించు. To rake up, to irritate, to exasperate రేచు.

కెల్లువారు *kelluvāru.* [Tel.] v. n. To rejoice. To rush. "నిష్ఠురబాణవాతంబులేసికె, గప్పెకరాళి నూతుడుదెగకా పారులోటరి కెల్లువారగకా." M. VII. iv. 114. "కెలకులదన్నుచు కెల్లువారు చుండు." BD. v. 961.

కెవకూళి or **కెవాకూళి** or **కెవాకూళి** See కెవా కూళి.

కెవవు *kelavu.* [Tel.] n. Distance. దూరము. "తానుపాడైనకెళవులయుమ్రొల్లకుతి."Manu. v. 28.

కెల్లు or **కెల్లన** *kellu.* [Tel.] adv. (Anuk.) Slapdash. కెల్లునను to gambol. "కెల్లురికెమల కెరేగిలు మల్లడిగానిరంకెలిడిరు మదవృషభం బుల్." Padma. vii. 243. B v. 7.

కెవ్వున *kevvuna.* [Tel.] adv. Resoundingly, aloud. Slapdash, at once. "యుతిదయాంచ్ఛటి కవ్వునవాల్చి పెచ్చి." Anir. iv. 59.

కే kē

కే *kē.* [Tel.] n. A cry. కూత.

"క॥ నాయింటింబదికదనల
నేయి పెరుగుపాలుద్రావి నీస్త్రీయతనయుం
డోయమ్మకదవలన్నియు
నేయునిదొరకిల్లరో చికేయుచునచ్చెన్."
పారి. తృ. v

కేంద్రము *kēndramu.* [Skt.] n. A centre. నాభి.

కేక *kēka.* [Tel.] n. A loud cry. పెద్దకూత. కేకవినబడునేల the distance at which a shout may be heard. **కేకారవము** *kēkaravamu.* [Skt.] n. The peacock's cry.

కేకరము *kēkaramu.* [Skt.] adj. Turned, as an ogling eye; glancing aside. "కేకరాక్షి రుచి" A. ii. 36.

కేకరించు *kēkarinṭsu.* [Tel.] v. n. To cry, to yell. కేకలువేయు. [Skt.] v. t. To look kindly at కటాక్షించు. To hawk in spitting. సకిలించునట్లు శబ్దించు. **కేకరింత** *kēkarinta.* n. The act of hawking in spitting. A. v. 62. To cry కేకలువేయుట.

కేకరుడు *kēkaruḍu.* [Skt. from కేకరము.] n. One who squints. మెల్లకంటివాడు.

కేకస *kēkasa.* Same as కేకస.

కేకి *kēki.* [Skt.] n. A peacock. Vasu. ii. 28.

కేకిసలు or **కేకేసలు** *kēkisalu.* [Tel.], n. Clapping of hands. చేచప్పట్లు. Sounds of merriment, prattle, riot at play. కేకిసలు కొట్టు to shout. "కేకిసలుకొట్టుచు బోటులు దానికవ్వగా." Parij. iii. 13.

కేటత్రాడు *kēṭa-traḍu.* [Tel.] n. A rope of Yama's. యమపాశము.

"॥ కేటిదాటి కేటత్రాటన్
జటకంబునకడియ."
సెూ. i.

కేటికప్పి *kēṭi-kappi.* n. A block; a kind of pulley. ఒకవిధమైనకప్పి.

కేడ *kēḍa.* [Tel.] adj. Harsh, cruel or wicked. దూర్తుడు. **కేడించు** *kēḍinṭsu.* v. n. To part, to turn, to go aside. v. a. To shield off, turn aside, or ward off. "అంతకుపెనే సాయకబలములు ద్రొబుండు గృపుడును ద్రోణసుతుండునుకల్యాంగ కేడించిదనిర యుపుడు." M. VI. i. 75. "కలగక విరుగక మురుగక నలగక కేడింపక తోడింపక." Zakk. iv. 104.

కేడెము *kēḍemu.* [Tel.] n. A shield. డాలు.

కేతకి *kētaki.* [Skt.] n. The tree named *Pandanus odoratissimus.* పచ్చపువ్వుగేదంగి. The female of this plant is called గొజ్జంగి. Roxb. iii. 738.

కేతనము *kētanamu.* [Skt.] n. A flag, standard, banner. టెక్కెము. A sign గురుతు. A house ఇల్లు.

కేతువు *kētuvu.* [Skt.] n. A flag, standard, banner. టెక్కెము. The Dragon's tail or descending node of the moon. ఒకగ్రహము See రాహువు. A. ii. 17.

కేదారము *kēdāramu.* [Skt.] n. A rice field. వరిమడి; a garden bed పాదు. A plot or mound దిబ్బ; a mountain కొండ. **కేదారకంకణము** *kēdāra-kankaṇamu.* n. A kind of bracelet. "అరుదుగాక్రొత్తముత్తెపు నరులంటిపాగాలు కరమున కేదారకంకణములు." Kalah. Intro. 16. **కేదారగౌరీవ్రతము** *kēdāra-gaurī-vratamu.* n. A certain vow performed to the goddess Gauri. **కేదారి, కేదారిగౌళ** *kēdāri.* n. Names of certain tunes.

కేపు *kēpu.* [Tel.] n. Offspring, young. See క్రేపు.

కేపుమారి *kēpu-māri.* [Tam.] n. A rogue a swindler. కైతవకాడు.

కేయూరము *kēyūramu.* [Skt.] n. An epaulet or shoulder knot. అంగదము, బాహుపురి. నాగకేయూరుడు he who wears a snake as an ornament or shoulder knot.

కేరడము kēradamu. [Tel.] n. Indifference. ఉపేక్ష. Derision తిరస్కారము, ఎత్తిపొడుపు మాట, తిరస్కారపుమాట, వంకరమాట. "కలికి నవ్వుచు కేరడమాడి." Abhim. 216. కేరడించు kēradintsu. v. t. To deride. పరిహాసము చేయు.

కేరళము kēralamu. [Skt.] n. The country called Malabar or Malayalam.

కేరిజము kērijamu. [Tel.] n. A kind of bird. "గద్దలుడేగలు కేరిజములును." L. 20. 80. G. i. 108.

కేరు or కేరించు kēru. [Tel.] v. n. To warble. To crow, as a babe. To chuckle with pleasure. To giggle. To cluck, as a laying hen. To make a low inarticulate sobbing sound expressive of joy or grief. కూయు. అరచు, గద్గదస్వరముచేయు. To deride or scorn పరిహాసముచేయు, తిరస్కరించు. To do చేయు. To rejoice ఉత్సహించు, సంతోషపడు; to be proud విజృంభించు. v. t. To slight తిరస్కరించు. To deride పరిహసించు. "కిన్నరిస్వరాలీల కేరుచినాదవిద్య" Pururavas. iii. 89. కేరుగువ్వ a cooing decoy pigeon, or any bird like a pigeon so used. కేరుపు kērupu. n. Pride. విజృంభణము.

కేలు kēlu. [Tel. cognate with చెయ్యి. and Tam. కై.] n. The hand. చెయ్యి. కేలుదమ్మి or కేల్దమ్మి kēlu-dammi. n. A lily-like hand. కేలుమొగ్గ the folded hands చేమోడ్పు. కేల్గవ kēlgava. n. The two hands రెండు చేతులు.

కేళకుళి or కేళకూళి or కేళాకూళి kēla-kuḷi. [Tel.] n. A bath or well with steps. మడుగు, నడబావి, క్రీడాసరస్సు. Vasu. i. 57.

> " లలితమైనట్టికేళాకూళిచాట్టి
> పెల్లలిన ద్రాక్షపందిళ్లచెంత."
>
> T. iv. 195.

కేళి kēḷi. [Skt.] n. Sport, play. ఆట. కేళిక kēḷika. n. Sport, play. Dancing నృత్యము. కేళికాగృహము or కేళీగృహము kēḷika-grihamu. n. A chamber for pleasure or enjoyment; a summer house or kiosk. Dasava. x. 343. కేళికాడు kēḷik-adu. v. n. To dance. కేళీవాదము kēḷi-vadamu. n. A comic quarrel. BD. v. 914.

కెల్లురుకు kell-uruku. [Tel.] adj. & adv. Rapidly, running, making a rush or dash, as a stag. కెల్లువారు to run. M. VII. iv. 114. పరుగెత్తు. See కల్లువారు.

కేవ See క్రేవ.

కేవడము kēvaḍamu. [Tel.] n. A shield. డాలు. "మిహిపసింధిపరంజమెరుగా కేలుమల దాపుగజ్జె సేత కేవడంబు." Manu. iv. 36.

కేవలము kēvalamu. [Skt.] adj. and adv. Pure, mere, simple, unmixed, uncompounded. ఒక్కటేయైన. ఇది కేవలము బంగారు తో చేసినది this is made with gold alone. కేవలము నీళ్లేతాగినాడు he drank nothing but water. వాడు కేవలవైయాకరణుడు he is a mere grammarian. వాడు కేవలనైయాయికుడు he is a mere logician. Altogether, in every respect. అంతయును: as ఈ పట్టణము కేవలము లంకవలెనున్నది this city is in every respect like Lanka. ఇది కేవలమునృతము this is entirely false. కేవలుడు kēvaluḍu. n. The supreme Spirit పరమాత్మ.

కేవు kēvu. [H.] n. Freight. ఓడకూలి, ఓడ మీదవేసే సరుకునకు కూలి. కేవరి kē-vari. (కేవు +అరి.) n. He who hires a ship: the freighter. ఓడను కేవుకు పుచ్చుకొనువాడు.

కేశము kēśamu. [Skt.] n. A hair. వెంట్రుక. కేశపాశము kēśa-pāśamu. n. Beautiful hair. కొప్పు. కేశబంధము kēśa-bandhamu. n. Ornamented tresses. పువ్వులుముడిచిన కొప్పు. కేశవుడు kēśavuḍu. n. One who has fine hair. మంచివెంట్రుకలుగలవాడు. A name of Vishṇu. కేశవేశము kēśa-vēśamu. n. A tress or lock of hair. కొప్పు. కేశిని kēśini. n. She who has fine hair. మంచి వెంట్రుకలుకలది.

కేసరము kēsaramu. [Skt.] n. A lion's mane. సింహముమెడమీదివెంట్రుక. జూలు. The anthers of a flower: a filament: కేసరి

kēsari. n. A lion. కేసరివడ్లు or కేసరాలు n. A reddish sort of rice.

కేసి kēsi. [Tel. for కైసెసి.] (An affix.) Towards, as ఇండ్లకేసి. towards the houses.

కై kai

కై or కేయి kai. [Tel. Cognate with చెయ్యి and Tam. కయి] n. The hand. The ending of the fourth case in gram. చతుర్థీ విభక్తియందువచ్చే ఒక ప్రత్యయము.

కైంకర్యము kain-karyamu. [Skt. from కిం కర] n. Duty, service. Divine service. ఊడిగము, సేవ.

కైకట్టు or కేయికట్టు kai-kattu. [Tel.] n. A connection. సందర్భము.

కైకానుక or కేయికానుక kai-kanuka. [Tel.] n. A present given to a king when one visits him. A nuzzur. రాజులలోనగువారిని చూడబోయినపుడు ఇచ్చేకానుక.

కైకొను or కేయికొను kai-konu. [Tel.] v. n. To undertake. పూను. v. a. To take, receive, గ్రహించు. కైకొలుపు or కేయికొలుపు to cause to undertake or receive కైకొను నట్లుచేయు. కైకోలు or కేయికోలు kai-kōlu. n. Agreement, consent. అంగీకారము. Acceptance గ్రహణము.

కైకోల or కేయికోల kai-kōla. [Tel.] n. A sect among weavers. సాలెజాతిలోభేదము.

కై చాపు or కేయిచాపు kai-tsapu. [Tel. lit. stretching the hand.] n. Salutation. నమస్కృతి. H. iv. 311.

కైజీతము or కేయిజీతము kai-jitamu. [Tel.] n. Wages, daily cooly, batta. బత్తెము.

కైజా or కేయిజా or కేయిజామోర kaiza. [Persian khaiz, bounding, capering.] n. A bridle: bridled up as a prancing horse. A. ii. 31. Vasu. Intro. 30. గుర్రపు ముఖుచేస్తు. వాగెను వెనుకదిప్పికట్టుట.

కైజారు kaizaru. [Tel.] v. n. To slide or slip down. జారు.

కైజు or కేయిజు kaizu. [Tel.] n. A sort of quail.

కైటభారి kaitabh-ari. [Skt.] n. An epithet of Vishṇu, as being the అరి foe or slayer of Kaitabha.

కైడర్యము kaidaryamu. [Skt.] n. The black Margosa tree. వల్లవేప.

కైత or కేయిత kaita. [Tel. for కవిత.] n. Talent for composition. కవిత్వము.

కైతవము kaitavamu. [Skt. from కితవ.] n. Hypocrisy, deceit. కపటము. Gambling జూదము.

కైదండ or కేయిదండ kai-danda. [Tel.] n. The hand. Support చేయూత.

కైదీ or ఖైదీ kaidi. [H.] n. A prisoner. అపరాధి. కైదు or ఖైదు kaidu. n. Prison, imprisonment. కైదుచేయు or ఖైదుచేయు to imprison.

కైదువు or కేయిదువు kaiduvu. [Tel.] n. A weapon or instrument. ఆయుధము.

కైపదము or కేయిపదము kai-padamu. [Tel.] n. A test in poetical composition. కవిశక్తి జ్ఞానపరీక్షార్థము పూరింపనిచ్చే పద్యాంశము. సమస్య.

"ఉ॥ కైపదమిచ్చువారలును
గ్రక్కునబద్యముచెప్పువారలున్"

భో. ii.

కైఫీయ్యతు kaiphiyyatu. [H.] n. Circumstances, particulars. సంగతులు, వైనములు.

కైపు or కేయిపు kaipu. [Tel.] n. Intoxication. మైకము. Grace అందము. Pride విజృంభణము. Manner విధము.

"సీ॥ రాముని చేపట్టినట్టిరాజ్యలక్ష్మి
కైపుతోపెంచులంకపొంకంబుగాంచి."

రామా. vi.

కైముడి or కేయిముడి kai-mudi. [Tel.] n. A kind of drum. వాద్యవిశేషము.

కైమోడుపు or కయిమోడుపు or కైమోడ్పు or కయిమోడ్పు *kai-mōḍupu.* [Tel.] n. A salutation నమస్కృతి.

కైరడు or కయిరడు *kairaḍu.* [Tel.] n. A horse so named.

కైరవడి or కయిరవడి *kairavaḍi.* [Tel.] n. See కరిబిరయండ.

కైరవము *kairavamu.* [Skt.] n. The esculent white water lily. తెల్లకలువ. కైరవబంధువు *kairava-bandhuvu.* n. The moon. కైరవలోచన *kairava-lōchana.* adj. Bright eyed, lily-eyed.

కైరవుడు *kairavuḍu.* [Skt.] n. A gambler జూదరి. An enemy పగవాడు.

కైరి *kairi.* [H.] n. A grey-eyed horse, a wall-eyed horse. పిల్లికన్నుగుర్రము.

కైలాటము or కయిలాటము *kai-l-āṭamu.* [Tel.] n. Deceit, fraud, a trick. జిత్తు, మాయోపాయము. "ఏమిచెప్పినా కైలాటమింక మాన." Vijaya. ii. 210. కైలాటకాడు or కయిలాటకాడు *kai-laṭa-kāḍu.* n. A cheat. మాయోపాయముగలవాడు.

కైలాసము *kailāsamu.* [Skt.] n. Kailasa, a mountain in Tibet. The fabled residence of Kubera and the heaven of Siva. కుబేరుని ఉనికిపట్టు. దక్షిణకైలాసము The Kailas of the South, an epithet of Kalahasti.

కైలు *kailu* [H.] n Measurement of grain after thrashing and before sharing it. A frame shaped like the letter A used in a pent roof పెంకుటింటికిపనికివచ్చే ఒక ముక్కోణపు చట్రము. కైలుకాలము harvest time. కైలుదారుడు a superintendent of measurement.

కైవడి or కయివడి *kai-vaḍi.* [Tel.] n. Manner, likeness, kind, sort. విధము, పోలిక. విషముత్రాగినకైవడిగా just as if he had drunk poison.

కైవర్తుడు *kaivartuḍu.* [Skt.] n. A fisherman. చేపలు పట్టువాడు.

కైవల్యము *kaivalyamu.* [Skt.] n. Beatitude eternal happiness. Heaven మోక్షము. The happy event or ending of a novel.

కైవారము or కయివారము *kai-vāramu.* [Tel.] n. Circumference. Measurement round. చుట్టుకొలత. The description of a circle. Description of beauty, praise, encomium. స్తోత్రము. కైవారముచేయు, to praise స్తోత్రముచేయు. కైవారి an encomiast వంది.

కైవు Same as కవు.

కైవ్రాలు or కయివ్రాలు *kai-vrālu.* [Tel.] v. n. To alight as a bird పక్షులుక్రిందికివచ్చి క్రిందికిదిగు. To fall పడు. To incline to one side ఒరుగు. కైవ్రాలుచు *kai-vrālutsu.* v. t. To cause to be inclined కైవ్రాలజేయు.

కైశికము *kaiśikamu.* [Skt.] n. Tresses, beautiful locks. వెండ్రుకలసమూహము.

కైశికి *kaiśiki.* [Skt.] n. A certain rhetorical figure. ఒక కావ్యవృత్తి.

కైశోరక *kaiśōraka.* [Skt.] adj. Childish, puerile, boyish. కైశోరము boyhood పదియేండ్లవయసు.

కైశ్యము *kaiśyamu.* [Skt.] n. Tresses, a fine head of hair. కైశికము.

కైసేయు or కయిసేయు *kai-sēyu.* [Tel.] v. t. To adorn. అలంకరించు. To worship పూజించు. కైసేత or కయిసేత *kai-sēta.* n. Adornment, trimming. అలంకారము.

కో ko

కొంకనక్క *konka-nakka.* [Tel. from కొంకు timid and నక్క a jackal.] n. A small kind of fox. చిన్నజాతినక్క.

కొంకపర్తిదొండ *konka-parti-donda.* [Tel.] n. A wild plant with green mossy buds. See దొండ.

కొంకర *konkara.* [Tel.] n. Bending. వంపు. కొంకరవంకర all twisted and twirled. కొంకరలుపోవు to become crooked.

కొంకి *konki.* [Tel.] n. A bend, a turn: A hook, a hasp. A drag-hook. పంపుచీల. The bones near the nape of the neck ముచ్చిలిగుంటకు ప్రక్కలనుండు ఎముకలు. Also the knee bones మోకాలిచిప్పకులోతట్టు రెండు ప్రక్కలనుండు ఎముకలు. మెడకొంకులు the collar bones. కాలికొంకులు hooked talons. కొంకివ్రేళ్లు fingers resembling hooks.

కొంకు *konku.* [Tel.] v. n. To be timid, alarmed: to fear, to dread, to hesitate. భయపడు, వెనుదీయు, సంకోచించు. n. Fear. Timidity, shyness. వెనుదీయుట. Hesitation. సంకోచము. Shame, scruple, surmise. Distortion, as that of a cripple. కొంకుగొసరులేని careless and heedless. కొంకుపోవక unterrified. **కొంకుపడు** *konku-padu.* v. n. To fear. భయపడు. To hesitate సంకోచించు. To trip, stumble, blunder. కొంకుపాటు fearing, hesitation. **కొంకుపోవు** *konku-pōvu.* n. To become crooked or bent. కొంకరలుపోవు.

కొంగ *konga.* [Tel.] n. A bird of the heron or stork kind. బకము. **కొంగకాళ్ల** *konga-kalla.* adj. Cranelegged, longlegged. నిడుపుకాళ్లుగల. **కొంగగొడ్డలి** *konga-goddali.* n. A pickaxe (so called by ఉప్పరవాండ్లు.) **కొంగముక్కుచేప** *konga-mukku-chēpa.* n. A sort of fish with a long snout or beak. **కొంగవాలు** *konga-vālu.* n. A sort of sword. (A. VI. 110.) మారికత్తి. **ఎర్రకాళికొంగ** *errakali-konga.* n. The painted stork. *Pseudotantelos leucocephalus.* **గేలుకొంగ** *gēlu-konga.* n. The shell ibis. *Anestomuscoscitans.* **గుడికొంగ** *gudi-konga.* n. The paddy bird or pond heron. *Ardeola glayi.* **దోసికొంగ** *dōsi-konga.* n. The little green Heron. *Pontorides javanica.* **చిన్నతెల్లకొంగ** *chinna-tella-konga.* n. The little Egret. *Heriodias garzetta.* **పెద్దతెల్లకొంగ** *pedda-tella-konga.* n. The large Egret. *Herodias-alba.* **పినిగలకొంగ** *ptnigala-konga.* n. The adjutant *Leptoptilus dubius.* **పూకొంగ** *pūkonga.* n. The Flamingo, *Phœnicopterus roseus* సముద్రపుచిలుక. **సంకుబుద్దికొంగ** *sanku-buddi-konga.* n. The white necked stork. *Dissura Lepiscopus.* (F. B. I.)

కొంగు *kongu.* [Tel.] n. A skirt, a hem. చెంగు, చెరగు, అంచు. **కొంగోడువడు** or **కొంగోడుపోవు** *kankōdu-padu.* v. i. To be inclined, to slant. ఒగ్గిల్లు, ఒరగు. "కుక్షివడిసముగల కొంగోడుపోయిన." Vishnu. iv. 237. కచ్చకొంగు simply means a cloth. కొంగుమాసిన menstruous, unclean.

కొంచె See క్రౌంచము.

కొంచించు *konchintsu.* [Tel.] v. a. To draw back in hesitation. సంకోచించు.

కొంచు *kontsu.* [Tel.] v. n. To hesitate. కొంకు, సంకోచించు. To retreat, draw back. వెనుకదీయు. **కొంచు** *kontsu.* n. Dirty sweat. మురికిచెమట.

కొంచుపోవు *kontsu-pōvu.* [Tel. from కొను.] v. a. To carry away. **కొంచువచ్చు** *kontsu-vatstsu.* v. a. To bring. See కొను.

కొంచెము or **కొంచియము** *konchemu.* [Tel.] n. A little. Littleness మాంద్యత. కొంచెముకొంచెముగా little by little. కొంచెముగా ఎంచు to esteem slightly. కొంచెములో వచ్చినాడు in a little (time) he arrived, i. e., very soon. కొంచెపుబుద్ధి little sense. adj. Little, small, trifling, slight, petty, the least: contemptible, vile, low. కొంచెపువాడు a low fellow. కొంచెముసేపటికి in a short time. **కొంచెముచేయు** or **కొంచెపరచు** *konchemu-chēyu.* v. a. To diminish. To wrong or injure. **కొంచెపుపాటి** *konchepu-pati.* adj. Small, middle-sized. **కొంచెమున** *konchemu-na.* adv. In the least, for a trifle. **కొంచెకత్తె** *konche-katte.* n. A low or common woman. అల్పురాలు, సామాన్యురాలు. **కొంచెకాడు** *konche-kādu.* n. A low or common man. అల్పుడు, సామాన్యుడు. **కొంచెతనము** *konche-*

tanamu. n. Littleness; leanness అల్పభావము, సన్నదనము. కొంచెపడు *konche-padu.* v. n. To be wanting, to lack. తక్కువపడు. To become lean సన్నబడు.

కొంజు *konzu.* [Tel.] v.n. To hesitate. అనుమానించు. "రంజిలితామనుముమ్మన నంజలిపడకిచ్చి చేసి నయముగవారలా గొంజకనిత్తురుగ్రక్కన." Kuchēlo. i. 103.

కొంట *konta.* [Tel. from కొను.] n. Contraction for కొనుట. "ఖర్జూరఫలంబుడాక్షియు ముకొన్నదకొంటభాస్కరా."

కొంటె *konte.* [Tel.] adj. Naughty, indecent, childish, puerile, silly, light, idle, mischievous, tormenting, impertinent, teasing. కొంటె *konte.* n. A naughty person. వలగాడు, తుంటరి. కొంటెబొమ్మలు lewd sculptures. కొంటెతనము *konte-tanamu.* n. Indecency, lewdness; pranks, lasciviousness. కొంటెపాడికట్ట *konte-padi-katta.* n. A lewd fellow.

కొండ *konda.* [Tel.] A hill, hillock, mountain, rock. మల. కొండకాకి a hill crow. కొండకాటిగాడు *konda-kati-gadu.* n. The Indian Tree-pie, *Dendrocitta rufa.*(F.B.I.) కొండకాలువ *konda-kaluva.* n. A mountain stream, or cascade. సెలయేరు, ఝరము. కొండగురుతు a common characteristic సామాన్యలక్షణము. కొండగొర్రె *konda-gorre.* n. A wild sheep, or hill sheep, The four-horned Antelope, *Tetracerus quadricornis.* కొండగోగు *kondagōgu.* A plant, *Hibiscus populneoides.* కొండగోరింక *konda-gōrinka.* n. The Southern Grackle, *Eulabes religiosa.* కొండచిలువ *konda-chiluva.* n. The rock snake. అజగరము, కొండపాము. A sluggard. కొండచీమ *konda-chīma.* n. The hill ant, or tree ant. కొండచూలి *konda-tsūli.* n. A name of Parvati; lit. Daughter of a Mountain. కొండత్రిమ్మరి *konda-trimmari.* n. (Lit. a hill-rover.) A monkey. కోతి. కొండనాలుక *konda-naluka.* n. The uvula. చిరునాలుక. కొండపసులపోలిగాడు *konda-pasula-pōligadu.* The White-bellied Drongo, *Dicrurus cerulescens.* కొండపిండి *konda-pindi.* n. A kind of tree. కొండపిచ్చిక *konda-pichchika.* n. A hill sparrow. కొండపోడు *konda-pōdu.* n. A corn-field on high ground. కొండబూరుగు a species of the silk cotton tree. కొండముచ్చు *konda-mutstsu.* n. The lion-tailed monkey. *Macacus silenus.* నల్లనిమూతికలకోతి. కొండయెంటవ *konda-yentava.* n. The ruddy Mungoose. *Herpestes smithi.* కొండయేనుగు *konda-ēnugu.* n. The Indian Elephant. *Elephas maximus.* కొండలొట్టకన్నుజిట్ట *konda-lotta-kannu-jitta.* n. The Jungle Wren-Warbler. (Jerd.) *Prinia sylvatica.* (F. B. I.) కొండరులు *konda-rulu.* [Tel.] n. Hill people, highlanders. "కొండరుల్ చూరు కొకయింతలేక మనుచుగా." G. xi. 20. కొండరేడు *konda-rēdu.* n. The lord of hills. Himavat. కొండలాటిపక్షి *kondalati-pakshi.* n. The bird called Sultan Bulbul. కల్లాటిపక్షి. కొండవంగపండు *konda-vanga-pandu.* n. The Indian Black headed Oriole. *Oriolus melanocephalus.* (F. B. I.) కొండవలిగాలి *konda-vali-gāli.* n. A sharp cold wind. కొండవీటిచేంతాడు an immensely long rope, as long as a well-rope in Kondavidu near Guntur. కొండశిల *konda-sila.* n. A rock snake, or boa.

కొండాటము *kondātamu.* [Tel.] n. Plague, trouble, squable. "చేడీకొండాటంబు చెల్లదయిత్తునుగద." P. i. 91. Joy. సంతోషము.

కొండాడు *kondādu.* [Tel. for కొనియాడు.] v. a. To praise. స్తోత్రముచేయు.

కొండి or కొండీ *kondi.* [Tel.] n. A sting, ముల్లు. A staple or hook కొక్కెము, కొక్కి. దురదగొండి a nettle. కొండివల a kind of net used for catching fish.

కొండిక *kondika.* [Tel.] adj. Young చిన్న. n. An infant, a little boy. బాలుడు. కొండికది a little girl బాలిక. కొండికవాడు childhood బాల్యకాలము.

కొండికాళ్లు kondi-kāḷḷu. [Tel.] n. The legs that support the stem of a drill plough.

కోండి See కొండి.

కొండె or కొండియ kondc. [Tel.] n. A knot of hair. కొంగు, కొప్పు.

కొండెము or కొండియము kondemu. [Tel.] n. Slander, a slanderous tale, backbiting, a calumny. చాడీ. కొండెకాడు or కొండియుడు or కొండీడు konde-kāḍu. n. A slanderer, a talebearer. కొండెముచెప్పువాడు. కొండెకత్తె konde-katte. n. A woman that slanders. కొండెతనము konde-tanamu. n. Backbiting, slanderous behaviour. "అద్దిరక్షస్తని యురగొండెతనము." BD. v. 207.

కొండొక kondoka. [Tel. కొండు (=కొంచెము) +ఒక.] adj. A little, slight. కొంచెము. Some, some few, కొన్ని. A certain one ఒకానొక. కొండొకకోతి a certain monkey.

కొండ్రు kondru. [Tel.] n. A field. The space included in the widest turn of the plough. ఎదురుదున్ని మళ్లించిన నడిచేలు. కొండ్రుగుపు a plough నాగలి. కొండ్రుచేసికొను kondru-chesi-konu. v. a. To cultivate.

కొంత konta. [Tel.] adj. Some, a little, to a certain extent. కొంతకాలమునకు for some time, for a short time. కొంతమట్టుకు. a little, somewhat, to a certain extent.

కొంతము kontamu. [Tel.] n. A javelin. కుంతము.

కొందరు kondaru. [Tel. కొంత+వారు.] plu. Some, a few persons.

కొందలము or కొందలపాటు kondalamu. [Tel.] n. Perturbation, confusion, anxiety. విచారము, కలత, క్షోభము. "కొందలమొకయింతె తేక" M. VIII. ii. 358. కొందలించు or కొందలపడు to be confused. కలతపడు.

కొందు kondu. [Tel.] v. t. To mince or hash. పక్షైగానరుకు.

కొంప kompa. [Tel.] n. A house: ఇల్లు (used as a term of contempt or reproach.) వాని కొంపపోయినది he is ruined. నా కొంప తీయవలెనని యున్నాడు he seeks to ruin me. నాకొంప అమ్మివేస్తాడు he will sell the house over my head.

కొంపోవు or కొనిపోవు kom-pōvu. [Tel.] v. a. To carry away. తీసికొనిపోవు.

కోకిబికి or కోకిబికి koki-biki. [Tel.] adj. Distorted, twisted, crippled. చక్కనితప్పిన.

కొక్కరాయి kokka-rāyi. Same as కొక్కెర.

కొక్కరించు kokka-rintsu. [Tel.] v. a. To mock, ridicule. ఓహోహో అని వెక్కిరించి నట్టుగా అరచుట. To shout, to cluck, like a hen after laying eggs. To dig up with claws పక్షులు కాళ్లతో కెల్లగించు. కొక్కరింత kokka-rinta. n. Clucking.

కొక్కి kokki. [Tel.] n. A hook, a clasp.

కొక్కిస kokkisa. [Tel.] n. Grappling, hugging with the thighs in wrestling. బట్టపట్లలోనొకటి. H. i. 241.

కొక్కు kokku. [Tel.] n. The bandicoot, or great rat. పందికొక్కు, చేలకొక్కు a mole. కొక్కుపాషాణము kokku-pashāṇamu. n. A sort of arsenic. కొక్కువిభుడు an epithet of Vinayaka.

కొక్కెము kokkemu. [Tel.] n. A buckle, or hook. కొక్కి.

కొక్కెర or కొక్కరాయి kokkera. [Tel.] n. A heron. బకము. కొక్కెరపండ్లు kokkera-pandlu. n. Crooked teeth.

కొక్కెస kokkesa. [Tel.] n. A kind of tree.

కొక్కొరొకో kokkoro-kō. [Tel.] n. Crowing as a cock.

కొచ్చి kochchi. [Tel.] n. Cochin. కొచ్చికుక్క a spaniel.

కొజ్జ kojja. [H.] n. A eunuch.

కొటారు, కొటారము or కొఠారు koṭāru. [Tel.] n. A store, a granary. A place to keep grain, salt, &c.

కొటిక or కొట్టిక koṭika. [Tel.] n. A hamlet or small village. గ్రామము.

కోటికాడు Same as కొట్టికాడు. (q. v.)

కొట్టకొన koṭṭa-kona. [Tel. కొన+కొన.] n. The very end. అన్నిటికన్న కొన.

కొట్టడి koṭṭaḍi. [Tel.] n. A store room. సామగ్రులుంచెడి గది, కొట్టు.

కొట్టము koṭṭamu. [Tel.] n. A pent roofed chamber or house as distinguished from మిద్దె which is flat-roofed. Pounding in a mortar. A stable for elephants or horses, or cattle పశ్వాదులపాక. A. i. 43. A kind of dance నృత్యవిశేషము.

కొట్టరువు koṭṭaruvu. [Tel.] n. A barn, a grain store. కొటారు.

కొట్లాడు koṭṭ-āḍu. [Tel. కొట్టు+ఆడు.] v. n. To quarrel. పోట్లాడు. To suffer pain బాధపడు.

కొట్టాము koṭṭāmu. [Tel.] n. A pent roofed house. కొట్టము. Name of a certain country. "కొనవిట్టగొట్టాననిలె." Swa. i.

కొట్టి or కోటి koṭṭi [Tel.] n. A kind of root. కాకాంచి. *Aponogeton monostachyum.* Watts. Espionage వేగు.

కొట్టిక Same as కోటిక. (q. v.)

కొట్టికాడు or కోటికాడు koṭṭi-kāḍu. [Tel.] n. A spy or watchman. వేగరి.

కొట్టు koṭṭu. [Tel.] v. n. To strike. గంట కొట్టినది the clock has struck. గాలి కొట్టుచున్నది the wind is blowing. కంపు కొట్టినది it smells badly. కొల్లగొట్టినాడు he plundered. పిడుగు ఆ చెట్టును చీలగొట్టినది the thunder bolt struck and split the tree. దాన్ని పురుగులు కొట్టినవి insects have attacked it. వానికి ముఖముకొట్టినది he is surfeited or gorged. వానకొట్టినది there was rain. వానికి ఎండకొట్టినది he was exposed to the sun. కొట్టినపిండి a well bruised flour,—a phrase implying thorough knowledge of any subject. వానికి రామాయణముకొట్టినపిండి he is thoroughly acquainted with the Rāmāyaṇa.

"కోమలినాకు నెట్టిరొద
కొట్టినపిండిసమస్తలోకముల్
నీమదికింపులైనయవి
నిర్భరశక్తినిచేసమర్థుడన్."
KP. vi. 30.

కొట్టివేయు koṭṭi-vēyu. To strike off, exclude, dismiss, cut off. కొట్టుకొనిపోవు to be carried towards by wind or water. కొట్టుకొనిపోవు to be blown away, to be carried off. కొట్టుకొను koṭṭu-konu. To beat oneself. To bewail, to lament. To beat, as the pulse. ధాతువు కొట్టుకొంటున్నది the pulse beats. దానిమీద ప్రాణాలు కొట్టుకొంటవి, or దానిమీద మనసు కొట్టుకొంటుంది his heart is set upon her.

కొట్టు koṭṭu. [Tel.] v. a. To strike, knock, smite, beat, thrash. To attack (as rats do.) To rob, as highwaymen do. To quash, refute, defeat, dismiss, nonsuit. To strike off (the head) or behead. To strike out or rescind (a word). దారులు కొట్టు to rob (on) the high road. గోడను కాగితముకొట్టు to put (or stick) a paper on the wall. చప్పట్లుకొట్టు to clap the hands. అచ్చు కొట్టు to print. కొఱ్ఱుకొట్టు to impale. ఈతకొట్టు to swim. సున్నము కొట్టు to whitewash. నన్ను దొంగలుకొట్టినారు thieves robbed me. చెంపకొట్టు to give a slap on the cheek. బుడ్డికొట్టు to crack a bottle, i.e., drink liquor. తలకొట్టు to behead, to ruin. పిండికొట్టు to pound flour. డేరాకొట్టు to pitch a tent. ఊడగొట్టు to loosen. చెడగొట్టు to spoil or ruin. తేలగొట్టు to set afloat. దిగగొట్టు to drive in. నలియగొట్టు to bruise. పండ్లు రాలగొట్టు to knock out a man's teeth. పగలగొట్టు to break to pieces. పడగొట్టు to throw down. పోగొట్టు to lose. విరుగగొట్టు to break; సాగగొట్టు to beat out (metal). ఊకొట్టు to hum in assent while listening. బుసకొట్టు to hiss. వాడు చేసిన దౌర్జన్యము వాణ్ని కొట్టినది his wickedness has fallen on his own head. వాండ్లు నోట్లో మన్ను కొట్టినారు they have cast earth into my mouth, i. e., cheated or ruined me. కొట్టించు koṭṭintsu. v. t. To cause to beat.

కొట్టు koṭṭu. [Tel.] n. A blow, a stroke. దెబ్బ. A storehouse, a godown. సామగ్రు లుంచెడిగది. A jail. కొట్టుడుబిళ్ల koṭṭuḍu-billa. n. A taw, at marbles. కొట్టుపడు koṭṭu-paḍu. n. To be knocked up or exhausted or spent. స్రుక్కు. కొట్టులాడు or కొట్లాడు koṭṭul-aḍu. v. n. To fight. పోట్లాడు. To dispute or squabble. కొట్టులాట or కొట్లాట koṭṭul-aṭa. n. Fighting, a row. పోట్లాట. కొట్లమారి koṭla-mari. n. An ill-used man. కొట్లుపడు స్వభావము కలవాడు.

కొట్టె koṭṭe. [Tel.] n. The stone of a fruit.

కొట్నము koṭnamu. [Tel.] n. Pounding rice. వడ్లదంపకము. Service ఊడిగము. A marriage rite వివాహతంత్రవిశేషము.

కొట్ర koṭra. [Tel.] n. Water in which flour is boiled. పిండిలోనగువాని నుడుకబెట్టుటకు పెట్టె యెసరు.

కొటారు Same as కొటారు.

కొఠీ koṭhi. [H.] n. A bank. A mercantile house or firm. కొఠీవేయు to set up or open a bank.

కొడమ koḍama. [Tel.] n. A weir or basket in which fish are snared.

కొడము koḍamu. [Tel.] n. A censer or vase for incense. కుంభధూపితి.

కొడవలి koḍavali. [Tel. కొట్టు+వాలు.] n. A sickle, a reaping hook.

కొడి koḍi. [Tel.] n. The tip, top, a mark, or feature. A flame. The snuff of a wick దీపపువత్తికొన. A standard or flag. చవుటి కొడినేల land that bears marks of being saltish. కొడికట్టు to hoist a flag. కొడిస్తంభము a flagstaff.

కొడిమి koḍidi. [Tel.] n. A sort of tree. A subdivision of the farming caste.

కొడిదిలి koḍidili. [Tel.] n. A handful. పిడి, పుడిసిలి.

కొడిపొయ్యి koḍi-poyyi. [Tel.] n. A fire place.

కొడిమె koḍime. [Tel.] n. A ship, a boat. ఓడ. A fisherman's basket చేపలబుట్ట. Blame అపదూరు. Sin పాపము. కొడిమెవాడు a wicked man. పాపాత్ముడు.

కొడిసె koḍise. [Tel.] n. A sort of fish.

కొడిసెపాల or కొడిసెపుత్తులు koḍisepala. [Tel.] n. The plant named *Echites Antidysenterica*.

కొడుకు or కొడుకడు koḍuku. [Tel.] n. A son. పెండ్లికొడుకు a bridegroom.

కొడుపు koḍupu. [Tel.] n. A barrel, a cylinder: the length of a bamboo between two knots. A thimble or guard worn on the finger when playing the guitar తంతివాయించుటకు వ్రేలికి వేసుకొనే గొట్టు. A stick used in striking a gong, a drumstick నగారాకొట్టెకొయ్య, కోణము. A hollow cylinder used in making vermicelli. జంతికలుచేసేసాధనము. అప్పడాలకొడుపు a cylindrical stick used in flattening cakes. బలపపుకొడుపు a slate pencil. జమ్ముకొడుపు the pod or cylindrical head of a bulrush. దాడుకొడుపు or బల్లలకొడుపు (BD. iii. 2240.) a clog fastened to the neck of a bad tempered cow గుదికొయ్య.

కొడుము koḍumu. [Tel.] n. A large pot. వెడల్పాటికుండ.

కొణజము or కొణజా koṇajamu. [Tel.] n. An alley, passage, gallery, balcony, a portico. ద్వారమునుమాత్రము సందియగాచేసే యిల్లు, వాకిటికావలియిల్లు.

కొణత or కొణతము koṇata. [Tel.] n. A puzzle or check. A stick to tie a dog to. కుక్కనుకట్టెకొయ్య. కొయ్యలుకొరతలు wood, sticks, &c.

కొణము koṇamu. [Tel.] n. A reed for playing on the guitar, &c.

కొణిగ or కొణిగె koṇiga. [Tel.] n. The eaves of a slanting roof. చూరు. A heap కుప్ప, దిబ్బ. అమ్ముడుకొణిగెలు the name of a kind of grain.

కొణిద, కొణిదిలి or కొణిదెలి. *konida.* [Tel.] n. The hand held as a cup. కొణిదెడు As much as can be held in the hand held as a shallow cup; a handful "కానిపోయితే కేలఁగొణిదెడంతైన" HD. i. 1328. కొణిద *konida.* n. The name of a certain caste. జాతిభేదము.

కొణుగురు or కొడుగురు *konuguru.* [Tel.] n. The snuff of a lamp. దీపపుచిక్కెము.

కొణుజు *konuzu.* [Tel.] n. A tick or insect in sheep. పిడుజు.

కొతిక *kotika.* [Tel.] n. A plant, *Rymphaca esculenta.* Rox. ii. 578.

కొతిమిరి or కొత్తిమిరి *kotimiri.* [Tel.] n. Coriander plants. కొతిమిరిపురుగు *kotimiri-purugu.* n. A midge or gnat, so called because when it gets into the candle it gives a scent like coriander.

కొతుకు *kotuku.* [Tel.] n. To pine. To hesitate. సంకోచించు, వగ్గలోపముగామాట్లాడు; to grudge. To boil as water. To stifle sighs. కొతికమాట్లాడుట to hesitate in speaking. నీళ్లుకొతుకుచున్నవి the water is boiling. n. Hesitation సంకోచము. కొతుకుపడు to stutter in speaking. వగ్గలోపముగా మాట్లాడు.

కొత్త *kotta.* [Tel.] adj. New, fresh. క్రొత్త. కొత్తనీరు n. The freshes in a river. కొత్తవారు strangers, foreigners.

కొత్తడము or కొత్తళము *kottadamu.* [Tel.] n. A bastion, bulwark or stronghold. బురుజు.

కొత్తమల్లి Same as కొతిమిరి.

కొత్తముట్టు or క్రొత్తముట్టు *kotta-muttu.* [Tel.] n. A mere filament, not yet twisted into a thread. పెనచినదాళ్లపు నూలుపోగు, నూలిపోగు అతుకు. "కళ్ళాలుబడలింబుగాని సుర్ఠిం బుల క్రొత్తముట్టునకే చయ్యకొలుపు పెదవు." M. IV. v. 88.

కొత్తరికము *kotta-rikamu.* [Tel.] n. Newness, novelty, freshness. చేరినకొత్తరికము shortly after he arrived.

కొత్తెము *kottemu.* [Tel.] n. The pulp of the palmyra fruit. తాటిపండులోని విత్తులేని కండ.

కొత్తెమ్మ *kottemma.* [Tel.] n. A lady saint, a female ascetic.

కొత్వాలు *kotvalu.* [H.] n. The chief officer of the police (of a city or town). కొత్వాల్ చావడి a police station.

కొద or కొదవ *koda.* [Tel.] n. The residue, rest or remainder; deficiency, want, defect. లోతక్కువ. "మిన్నింగినవారధికిం గొరత యుకొదరు." A. vi. 67. కొదవపెట్టు to leave unfinished.

కొదమ *kodama.* [Tel.] adj. Young. Hard. దృఢమైన. కొదమసింగము or సింగపుకొదమ a young lion. కొదమతుమ్మెద or తేటికొదమ a young bee. కొదమపిడుగు a fierce flash of lightning. n. A young animal, a cub. పశుపక్ష్యాదులపిల్ల. A female lamb or kid. ఆడుమేకపిల్ల.

కొదరు *kodaru.* [Tel.] v. n. To splutter, as a pen in writing. చెదరు, ఒగు.

కొదవ See కొద.

కొదుకు Same as కొతుకు.

కొదుపు *kodupu.* [Tel.] n. To fascinate, charm, delude. మోహించు.

కొద్ది *koddi.* [Tel. short for కొలది.] n. A little, a trifle, something. adj. Little, small, few. Petty, trifling, slight, mean, base. కొద్దిపిచ్చివాడవుకావు you are no slight fool. కొద్దిగా in a slight degree. కొద్దిగొప్ప less or more. కొద్దిదినాలకు in a few days, in a short time. (Affix) As, up to, according to, in proportion to, as much as, as far as. మీకు తోచినకొద్ది as much as you think proper. సమయముకొద్ది మనిషి a timeserver. వానిబలము కొద్దిచేసినాడు he did it as well as he could. కొద్దిమంది a few people.

కొన *kona*. [Tel.] n. The end, extremity, termination, point, tip. చివర. కొనగోళ్లు the tips of the nails. కొనచెవి the tip of the ear: చంటికొన the tip of the breast, the nipple or teat. adj. Last. కొనవాడు the last man. కొనప్రాణముతో నున్నాడు he is at his last gasp. కొనచుక్క a certain constellation. రేవతీనక్షత్రము. కొనమొదలుగా *kona-modalu-ga*. adv. Throughout, from end to end. కొనమొదలుగాపెట్టు lay them end to end.

కొనకొను *kona-konu*. [Tel.] v. n. To try. యత్నించు.

కొనటి *konati*. [Tel.] adj. Ugly, deformed. అంగహీనమైన, వికారమైన. M. XII. iii. 78.

కొనసాగు or కొనవిడు *kona-sagu*. [Tel.] v. n. To last to the end. To be fulfilled, or accomplished. వర్ధిల్లు, నెరవేరు. కొనసాగించు *kona-saginisu*. v. a. To accomplish, to complete.

కొనిపోవు *koni-povu*. [Tel.] v. a. To carry away. తీసికొనిపోవు.

కొనియాడు *koni-yadu*. [Tel.] n. To praise, to laud. నుతించు, పొగడు. To hail, to cherish ఆదరించు. To protect కాపాడు. To serve కొలుచు. కొనియాట, n. The act of praising, cherishing, protecting or serving.

కొనివచ్చు *koni-vatstsu*. [Tel.] v. a. To bring. తెచ్చు.

కొను *konu*. [Tel.] v. n. To be pierced as an arrow నాటు. "అనిలాస్త్రంబట్లునమ్ముంబవియు గొనక" మార్క. vii. To be agreeable సరిపడు. "కుటిలబుద్ధులిచటగొనవు." భార, విరా. iv. కొను. v. a. 1. To take, to get. తీసికొను. To experience. ఆకలిగొను to be hungry. అనుకంపగొని feeling pity. 2. To buy, purchase. వెలకుతీయు. To rob అపహరించు. To mind లక్ష్యపెట్టు. కొనిపోవు to carry away. కొనిపించు *konipintsu*. v. n. To cause to buy. కొనుగోలు or కొనుబడి *konu-golu*. n. Worth, valuation, the cost price. క్రయము. కొనుమొదలు the price paid for a thing.

కొను *konu*. [Tel.] The sign of the middle voice in the Telugu verb, as తెచ్చుకొను, and తెలిసికొను. ఇల్లు కట్టుకొన్నారు they built a house for themselves. ఇల్లు కట్టించుకొన్నారు they got a house built for themselves. చంపుకొన్నాడు he killed himself. పచ్చబొడిపించుకొన్నాడు he got himself tattooed. కుదువపెట్టుకొనేవాడు he who lends upon mortgage. Wherever self is used in English this middle verb is used. The causal form of కొను is కొలుపు (q. v.).

కొనుజు *konuzu*. [Tel.] n. A tick. పిడుజు.

కొన్ని *konni*. [Tel.] adj. Some, a few. కొన్నాళ్లు a few days. కొన్ని దినములు. కొన్ని మంది certain persons కొందరు. ఒకకొన్ని a few.

కొపుకు, కొప్పరము or కొప్రము *kopuru*. [Tel.] n. A shoulder, the scapula or shoulder blade. The hump of an ox. మూపు, భుజశిరస్సు. కొప్పరించు *kopparintsu*. n. To grin. ఇకిలించు. To heat metal in the fire, to calcine a drug. కాల్చు, పుటముచేయు. To be proud అతిశయించు, విజృంభించు. "రేవెలుంగురాచిప్పలం గప్పరంపు నుప్పలం గొప్పరించిన." Parij. ii. 60. కొప్పరింత *koppar-inta*. n. Pride. అతిశయము, విజృంభణము.

కొప్పు *koppu*. [Tel.] n. The chignon or tuft in which a Hindu female folds her tresses. కేశబంధము. కొప్పు or కొప్పు వాసము the crest of a roof. The tip or end of a bow విల్లుకొన. తిరుపతికొప్పులు bald heads so used because people have their heads shaved when they visit Tirupati. కొప్పుగువ్వ *koppu-guvva*. n. The Indian hoopoe.

కొప్పెర *koppera*. [Tel.] n. A metal cauldron or boiler. కడుపువుగలిగిన పెద్దపాత్రము.

కొప్రము Same as కొప్పరము.

కొబ్బరి or కొబ్బెర *kobbari*. [Tel.] n. The kernel of the cocoanut. కొబ్బరిబెల్లము sugar made from cocoanut tree juice. కొబ్బరికాయ *kobbari-kāya*. n. A cocoanut. కొబ్బరిపువ్వు *kobbari-puvvu*. n. An excrescence inside a cocoanut which is kept too long. ముక్కి-ముదిరిన కొబ్బరికాయలోనిపువ్వు. కొబ్బరిబొండము *kobbari-bondamu*. n. An unopened cocoanut.

కొమ *koma*. [Tel. another form కొమ్మ.] n. A branch. శాఖ. A woman తరుణి.

కొమరు *komaru*. [Tel.] n. Youth, youthfulness, bloom, beauty, loveliness. మనోజ్ఞత. Manner, way. adv. Beautiful, handsome. అందమైన. కొమరుమిగుల gracefully. కొమరార finely. కొమరారు *komarāru*. v. n. To bloom. కొమరాలు *komarālu*. n. A young woman యౌవనస్త్రీ. కొమరుతనము or కొమరుప్రాయము youth. యౌవనము. కొమరుడు or కొమారుడు *komarudu*. n. A son. కొడుకు. కొమరులు or కొమరకొయ్యలు *komarulu*. n. Bressumers or Brest summers, that is, forked pieces of wood used in buildings. ఇంటి నిమ్ము పట్టెకిందనిడుదూలాలు, కొంకి దూలములనియెడి గుజ్జెలు. కొమార్తె or కొమారి *komarte*. n. A daughter. పెండ్లికొమార్తె a bride. [The Skt. కుమారుడు+కుమారి are apparently derived from this Dravidian root.]

కొమిరె *komire*. [Tel.] n. A young woman. యౌవనముగల స్త్రీ. A peg or pin. (Vizag.) "కొమిరెపాక్కిలి బంగారుకుండచేనందు." H. ii. 107.

కొమ్మ *komma*. [Tel.] n. A branch. శాఖ. A damsel, a maiden, a female. తరుణి. A battlement with loop holes, an embrasure. కోటకొమ్మ. పట్టుకొమ్మ a prop, a refuge, reliance. కొమ్మచెట్టు *komma-chettu*. n. A wood resembling pine, used for torches, *Ceropegia tuberosa*. (Watts.) కొమ్మసొర్ర *komma-sorra*. [Tel.] n. A fish, *Zygæna tudes*. (F. B. I.) కొమ్మరటిచెట్టు *kommaraṭi-cheṭṭu*. n. The branchy plantain tree, or Bengal plantain. బంగాళీ రంభ.

కొమ్మి *kommi*. [Tel.] n. A sort of forest tree with rough leaves and fragrant flowers.

కొమ్ము *kommu*. [Tel.] The imperative of కొను to take. కత్తిదూసికొమ్ము take up your sword.

కొమ్ము *kommu*. [Tel.] n. 1. A horn. A bugle or trumpet. A tusk, an elephant's tusk or tooth కోర, దంతము. 2. The secondary form of the vowel ఉ. అల్లపుకొమ్ము a root or bit of ginger. పసుపుకొమ్ము a root or bit of turmeric. A squirt. చిమ్మనగ్రోవి. "కొమ్ము లకరచిచల్ల," A. 118. 3. Anything projecting, as చెరువుకొమ్ము the tongue or end of a tank. అందలపుకొమ్ము the pole of a sedan chair. పల్లకిబొంగు. కాడికొమ్ము one end of a yoke. 4. A horn or crest as a sign of dignity. శిఖరము, కొన. వానికేమి కొమ్ములు మొలిచినవి why does he talk so big? 5. Strength, joy బలము, ఉత్సాహము. కొమ్ముకాకరకాయ a certain vegetable, being a species of కాకర. కొమ్ముకాడు a horn-blower. కొమ్ముజడివాడు a goldsmith. 6. A hog's tusk. పందికోర. కొమ్ముచేప a shark. కొమ్ముగలచేప. కొమ్ము టేనుగు a tusker, a male elephant. 7. A branch శాఖ. The top or end కొన, శిఖరము. కొమ్ములవాండ్లు *kommula-vāndlu*. n. Trumpeters. కొమ్ములాడు or కొమ్మువాడు *kommul-āḍu*. n. A tusker. A male elephant. A wild boar. "ఆ కొమ్ములాడుతొల్లిటి చేకలమారాక." G. VIII. 21.

కొయికండ *koyi-kanḍa*. [Tel. for కొయ్యన కండ.] n. A corn on the toe.

కొయికూర *koyi-kūra*. [Tel. కొయి for కోయు.] n. A kind of potherb that is cropt and grows again. See కొయ్యకూర.

కొయ్య *koyya*. [Tel.] n. Wood. ద్రుమ. A staff or stick. కర్ర. ఓడకొయ్య a ship's mast. కొయ్యకాలు a wooden leg; stubble. కొన్నకంటె నరిపెన్ను కొయ్యగా మిగిలినది, కొర కోసినవాడు. P. iii. 193. బిరుసుబాటుకొయ్య a stubborn wretch. కుండకొయ్య a wretch. కొయ్యతనము *koyya-tanamu*. n. Stubbornness, obstinacy. కొయ్యంగ *koyyanga*. n. A fish like the carp called Khavai by Musulmans.

కొయ్యగూర or కొయ్యతోటకూర *koyya-gūra*. [Tel. from కొయ్య.] n. A sort of pot-herb called *Amaranthus tristis*.

కొర *kora*. [Tel.] n. What remains, balance. కొరత. Profit, use, good, advantage. పని, ఫలము, ప్రయోజనము. Carpentry or masonry శిల్పము. A kind of fish కొరమీను. కొరగాని useless, unprofitable. కొర *kora*. adj. Available, profitable, useful, advantageous. ప్రయోజనకరమైన. Incomplete, unavailing. కొరయిల్లు an unfinished house. కొరనోములు unavailing vows. కొరప్రాణము the last breath, incomplete vitality. కొట్టుకొను, కొనప్రాణము. కొర కామి or కొరగామి *kora-kāmi*. n. Fruitlessness, uselessness, worthlessness. ప్రయోజనము లేమి. A defect దోషము. A bad sign దుర్లక్షణము.

కొరనెల *kora-nela*. n. A half moon. కొరనెలతూపు a cresent headed arrow. Parij. v. 40. కొరమాలిన *kora-mālina*. adj. Useless.

కొరండము *korandamu*. [Tel.] n. An agate or corundum stone. కురువిందము

కొరకంచు or కొరకచ్చు *kora-kantsu*. [Tel.] n. A fire brand. కొరవి.

కొరకు *koraku*. [Tel.] (an affix as a sign of the fourth case). For: for want of: on behalf of, on account of: with a view to: to the end that. నాకొరకు for me. పరలోకసౌఖ్యముకొరకు with a view to obtaining heaven. కొరకు or కొరకు *koraku*. n. A hedge round a place where cattle graze. పసులు మేయుచోటు. A place where birds find their food పక్షులు ఎరతిను చోటు.

కొరకొర *kora-kora*. [Tel.] n. Anger. కోపము. కొరకొరలాడు *kora-kora-l-ādu*. v. n. To be angry. కోపగించు. "కొరకొరమించె దుష్కృతికి" Satya iv. 197.

కొరడా *koraḍa*. [Tel.] n. A whip, scourge, knout. కమ్చి, చాటి, చేబుకు.

కొరడు *koraḍu*. [Tel.] n. A pair of pincers. A gleam or streak of a rainbow in the clouds, portending rain. తున్నని యింద్రధనుస్సు. An owl గుడ్లగూబ. The stump of a tree మ్రానిమోడు. కొరడుకోల *koraḍu-kōla*. n. Pincers. కొరడుపారు *koraḍu-pāru*. v. i. To be streaked or marked with stripes. To be benumbed or become callous. తిమురుపట్టు.

కొరత *korata*. [Tel.] n. Want, defect, fault. వెలితి, తక్కువ. That which is wanting. Incompleteness. A predicament వానికేమి కొరతలులేవు he is in want of nothing. కొరత (Loc. of కొర్రు.) on an impaling stake. కొరతమురుకు *korata-muruku*. v. t. To do a useless or unworthy deed. అకార్యము చేయు. n. One who does a thoughtless or unworthy deed. అకార్యముచేయువాడు.

కొరద *korada*. [Tel.] n. A certain fish.

సీ॥ "కొరద వాలుగ కొయ్య కొర్రమీను మలంకే
మొత్తంగి చేపిన జెల్ల చేరమీను."
H. iv. 225.

కొరనాసిగండు *koranāsi-gaṇḍu*. [Tel.] n. The striped Hyena. *Hyaena striata.* (F. B. I.)

కొరను Same as కొరకు. n. (q. v.)

కొరపడము or కొర్పడము *kora-paḍamu*. [Tel.] n. A blanket. BD, iii. 2278.

కొరపనికొయ్య *kora-pani-koyya*. [Tel.] n. A worthless wretch, a villain.

కొరపము *kora-pamu*. [Tel.] n. A curry comb. (H. v. 49.) గొరపము.

కొరపోవు *kora-pōvu*. [Tel.] v. n. To be choked. సొరపోవు. To swoon. మూర్ఛిల్లు.

కొరమాను *kora-mānu*. [Tel.] n. A large tree, *Briedelia Spinosa*; (Roxb. iii. 736.)

కొరముట్టు *kora-muṭṭu*. [Tel.] n. A tool, an implement, an instrument. పనిముట్టు, ఉపకరణము.

కొరలు *koralu*. [Tel.] v. n. To be full. నిండు, తెరచు. To blaze, shine. ప్రకాశించు. To grow, spread. పెరుగు. "కొన్ని నానా పక్షులాగాడిచిమ్మవటు కొరలెనాదానికిగంపు కొడుముకోయు." R. v. 58. v. a. To fancy, like, try. కోరు. "పవాతేనుడు కాకునుం గొరలితాబిదుముబా గృహాస్థమూర్గము." M. XII. v. 295.

కొరవ *korava*. [Tel.] n. The Koravas, a certain tribe of mountaineers.

కొరవంజి *kora-vanji*. [Tel.] n. A gypsy. A gypsy dance. "ఏకొరవఱు మలదూడిచా వ గొరవంజి" Suca. i. 21.

కొరవి or కొరివి *koravi*. [Tel.] n. A firebrand. The touchwood tree, *Sapindus Tetraphyllus*, or, *Guarea Molinea*. Roxb. ii. 243. ఎర్రకొరవులు. A. v. 133. R. vii. 10. కొరవిచీమ or కొరివిచీమ the red ant, so called because its bite gives a burning sensation. కొరవిదయ్యము an *ignis fatuus* or will of the wisp. "కొరవిదో తలగోరు గొమవాయికలరో" Dab. 201.

కొరసంది *kora-sandi*. [Tel.] n. A vital part of the body. జీవస్థానము, ఆయువు.

కొరి *kori*. [Tel.] n. The middle hair in the eyelash. రెప్పనడిమి వెంట్రుక.

కొరిజె *korije*. [Tel.] n. A hoof. గొరిసె. Also a landmark or village boundary. పొలిమేర. (Vizag.)

కొరితిచెట్టు *koriti-cheṭṭu*. [Tel.] n. A kind of tree, *Batis Spinosa*. Roxb. iii. 763.

కొరిమిడి or ముండ్లకొరిమిడి *korimiḍi* [Tel.] n. A tree, *Barleria longifolia*. Heyne. H. iv. 13.

కొరిమిపాల *korimi-pāla*. [Tel.] n. The touchwood tree, used for torches. కొరివి కర్ర.

కొరివి See కొరవి.

కొరిరింద *koririnda*. [Tel.] n. A certain forest tree. H. iv. 9.

కొరుకు *koruku*. [Tel.] v. a. To bite, gnaw, grind or gnash. పండ్లుకొరుకు to gnash the teeth. కొరుకుడుపుండు a cancer or gnawing ulcer. కొరుకు n. A bite. Food. Also, a venereal disease, syphillis కొరుకురోగము. H. D. i. 1741. కొరుకులు bites, peckings, eating. H. D. i. 1741. కొరుకులు *korukulu*. n. Props, timbers set to prevent the fall of a weight.

కొర్నా or కొర్నాగుండు *korna*. [H. from ఖొరాసాని = Khorassan.] The hyæna, *Hyæna striata*. దుమ్ములగొండి, కొరపోతు

కొర్ర *korra*. [Tel.] n. The grain called Millet, *Panicum italicum*. Heyne. Rox. i. 302. ఈశ్వరకొర్రలు a coarse kind of this grain. A sort of fish, *Silurus boalis*. Ham. పాతినము. కొర్రముట్టు or కొర్రమీను *korra-muṭṭu*. n. A fish found in tanks, thick and shaped almost like an eel, *Gobius Lagocephalus*. (Roxb.) H. iv. 225.

కొర్రు *korru*. [Tel.] n. A spike on which criminals were impaled. శూలము, శూలము. A spear. A hook on which men are suspended. A thorn. A sort of drill plough. That extent of land which requires one plough. కొర్రుతోలు to harrow. కొర్రుపట్టిన threadbare, torn.

కొల *kola*. [Tel.] n. Measure, measurement. పరిమాణము. Guilt: the result of crime. పాపము, పాపఫలము. Retribution particularly that suffered in a subsequent birth. Killing, murder. హింస. పాపముకొల దినగొల. వానిని చంపినకొల నీకు తీరదు you cannot get rid of the guilt of killing him. ఆడుకొల the guilt of causing a woman's death. T. iii. 114. L. iv. 291. P. i. 331. కొలకర్ర *kola-karra*. n. A measuring rod. కొలకాసు *kola-kāsu*. n. Fees for measuring. కొలగాడు *kola-gādu*. n. One who measures grain. కొలగారము *kola-gāra-mu*. n. Measurement, gauging: fees for measuring grain. కొలత *kolata*. n. Measurement. కొలపాత్రము *kola-pātra-mu*. n. A vessel to measure with. కొలారకము *kolā-rakamu*. n. Measuring grain. ధాన్యమును కొలుచుట.

కొలకు or కొలకువు Same as కొలను.

కొలకొల *kola-kola*. [Tel.] adj. & adv. (Anuk) Aloud, screaming, tumultuous, noisy, confusedly, in chorus. కొలకొలలాడిరి they made an uproar. కొలకొలమనుచు noisily. A. i. 81.

కొలది or కొద్ది *koladi*. [Tel.] n. Extent, measure, height, depth, limit. పరిమితి. Means, mode. Power, glory. శక్యము. "తల పుకొలదిబడదు దైవకమేకాని" (Vēma) not according to our will but as god wills. నీకొలదిదెలియంగక in ignorance of thy power. ఏకొలదినైనా by all means. ఆయన చిత్తముకొలదియొసంగి in conformity with his pleasure. L. XVII. 136. "నోటికొలందుల మాట్లాడి." L. VII. 481. saying anything that came into his mouth. As an affix, కొలది or కొద్ది. In proportion to, according to, in conformity to. నాలుగు ఏండ్లకొలది చదివిరి they studied for four years. మోకాలికొలదినీరు water up to the knee. ఈకొలది thus far, so much, such. "కుప్పకొలదిగ కన్నీరు గ్రుక్కుకొనుచు." Suca. iii. 156. R. v. 187. M. XII. i. 242.

కొలను or కొలకు *kolanu*. [Tel.] A lake, a tank. మడుగు, సరస్సు.

కొలము *kolamu*. [Tel.] n. Caste. కులము. Lineage వంశము. Race జాతి.

కొలారము, కొలారు, కొలారుబండి or కొల్లారుబండి Same as కొల్లారము.

కొలి *koli*. [Tel.] n. A small hole made in the ground to play a certain game called గోడుబిళ్ల.

కొలికి *koliki*. [Tel.] n. The tip or end. కొన. A hook or loop కొక్కి. The corner of the eye near the nose ముక్కుకొంటికంటి మూల. దారమునకు కొలికిపెట్టినది she made a loop in the string. ఈ కావ్యమునందు కొలకులు మాత్రము తెలుగు in this poem the terminations of words alone are Telugu. కొలికితెచ్చు to master సాధించు. కొలికికివచ్చు to become subject to one, to come into one's power. వాడు ఏడు ఊళ్లను కొలికికితెచ్చును he will put seven villages on one ring, i. e., he will have them under his thumb. కొలికిపూస *koliki-pūsa*. n. The chief gem in a necklace. కొలికి దగిలించేపూస. కొలికిముడి *koliki-mudi*. n. A noose: a loop. వదులుముడి.

కొలిపించు *kolipintsu*. [Tel. Causal of కొలుచు.] v. a. To cause to measure. కొల చునట్లుచేయు. To cause to do చేయించు. See కొలుపు.

కొలిమి *kolimi*. [Tel.] n. A pit. A fire pit or furnace. ముద్దకొలిమి a smelting forge. నీళ్లకొలిమి a reservoir. కొలిమితిత్తి a pair of bellows.

కొలిరెపిట్ట *kolire-pitta*. [Tel.] n. A small sort of bird spotted with white.

కొలుచు *kolutsu*. [Tel.] v. a. To measure. కొలతవేయు. To serve, to worship ఉపా సించు, సేవించు. n. Grain ధాన్యము. Rice వరి ధాన్యము.

కొలుపు *kolupu*. [Tel.] v. n. To agree, to consent సమ్మతించు. "క॥ మనసుకొలుపదనికి నిపుడు." భార. భీష్మ. iii. To be agreeable సరిపడు. "సీ॥ హీనముగ బుద్ధులెలకొలుపు" పంచ. నా. i. To have an effect on చెల్లు. "ద్వి॥ మలగక నాపన్ను మాయలన్నియును గొలుపవినిశ్శై." పాతిశ్చ. i. కొలుపు v. a. To encourage, to stir up, to set on, to egg on: పురికొలుపు, కన్నుగీటిసైగచేయు. కుక్కలను కొలిపిరి they set the dogs (on the boar, &c.) "ఎవ్వడు నామీద నేనుంగునొల్పె." (BD. iv. 207.) who set the elephant upon me? "గొల్పి." (G. vi. 70) setting his heart on it. "కొలుపని ఉత్సాహము" unexcited passion. Anir. ii. 92. Used as the causal form of కొను. దరికొలుపు to set on fire. మేల్కొలుపు to awaken, to rouse. పురికొలుపు to stir up. మరులుకొలుపు to enamour. ఉసికొలుపు to hiss. కొలుపు n. A rustic holiday: the festival of the Sakti or village goddess.

కొలువడి *koluvaḍi*. [Tel. కొలుచు+వడి.] n. Measurement. కొలత.

కొలువు *koluvu*. [Tel.] n. Service, employment. సేవ. A hall of audience. ఆస్థానము. A feast in honour of any village goddess, as Ammavāru, or Pōlēramma ఉత్సవవిశేషము. కొలువుకూటము *koluvu-kūṭamu*. n. A court. ఆస్థానమండపము. Audience, levee. కొలువుడుకాడు or కొలువుకాడు *koluvuḍu-kāḍu*. n. A servant. కొలువుకొను to take into service సేవకునిగా పరిగ్రహించు.

కొలె *kole*. [Tel.] adv. Beginning with, since. కోలె.

కొల్చి Same as కొలిచి.

కొల్త Same as కొలత.

కొల్తి Same as కొలది.

కొల్వు Same as కొలువు.

కొల్ల *kolla*. [Tel.] n. Plenty. Pillage, plunder. దోపుడు. అరటిపండ్లుకొల్లగానున్నవి plantains are plentiful or dirtcheap. అది నాకు కొల్ల it is more than enough for me. కొల్లకాడు *kolla-kāḍu*. n, A plunderer కొల్లపెట్టువాడు. కొల్లకొట్టు, కొల్లగొను, కొల్లపెట్టు, కొల్లచేయు or కొల్లాడు *kolla-koṭṭu*. v. t. To plunder. దోచుకొను. కొల్లరి *kollari*. n. A bandit, plunderer, or hill robber. కొల్లలిడు *kolla-l-iḍu*. v. t. To plunder.

కొల్లాటిపక్షి or కొండలాటిపక్షి *koll-aṭi-pakshi*. [Tel.] n. The bird called the Sultan bulbul. పిగిలిపిట్ట.

కొల్లారము or కొల్లారు *kollāramu*. [Tel.] n. A square enclosure, with chambers built at the corners. ధవళి. కొల్లారుబండి or కొల్లాబండి a car రథము, గాడీ. "గాలికన్నను వేగ జను చులకనివి యుకెకొల్లారుబండ్లు." S. i. 158.

కొల్లి or అడవికొల్లి *kolli*. [Tel.] n. A plant called మలాపము. కొల్లికొరజము a plant called పాలక్యము.

కొల్లు or కొల్లుగుంట *kollu*. [Tel.] n. A pit of water: Kodand. § 38.

కొల్లు *kollu*. [Tel.] v. a. To kill. చంపు.

కొళ్లు *koḷḷu*. [Tam.] n. Horse gram. H. ii. 135. కొళ్లుగంజి grain-boilings.

కొల్లెత్తువాడు *koll-ettu-vāḍu*. [Madras. Tel.] n. A mason or bricklayer. తాపివాడు.

కొల్లేరు *kollēru*. [Tel.] n. The Kolair lake. కొల్లేటికొంగ a pelican.

కొర్రాళ్లు *korrāḷḷu*. [Tel.] n. A sort of fish. Russell. No. 186.

కొర్విలిపువ్వు *korvili-puvvu*. [Tel.] n. A certain wild creeper.

కొవ్వు or క్రొవ్వు *kovvu*. [Tel.] n. Fat, fatness. Presumption, insolence. HD ii. 1097. v. n. To be fat. To wax fat. To be proud or presumptuous. తలకొవ్విన, or పొట్టకొవ్విన. (UH. iv. 209.) fat-headed, presumptuous, head-strong, కొవ్వి, (BD. iv. 1463.) giddy: heavy, or thick in the head. గర్వించి.

కొస *kosa*. [Tel.] n. A tip or end. The border or selvege. కొసగలముత్తెము a pear-shaped pearl. కొసగా slanting.

కొసరు *kosaru*. [Tel.] v. n. To demand an article over and above, or into the bargain. To be greedy. To be eager for. To hesitate సంకోచించు. v. t. To pray ప్రార్థించు. కొసరించు *kosar-inṭsu*. n. To demand more; to be exorbitant. n. Eagerness, lust, greediness, pruriency, hankering, cupidity; what is demanded over and above; what is asked into the bargain. Desire, cupidity కోరిక. Prayer ప్రార్థనము. Hesitation సంకోచము. "కొంకు కొసరింపుకయుండక" without the least hesitation or fear.

కొసరుచెట్టు *kosaru-chettu.* [Tel.] n. The plant called *Mucuna puritus.* కండూరాప్పలు.

కో kō

కో *kō.* [Tel.] Interj. Oh! oh! Alas, forbear. Huzza! hurrah!

కో *kō.* [Tel. Imperative for కొనుము.] Take thou. తీసికో=తీసికొనుము.

కోక *kōka.* [Tel.] n. A plaid or garment, particularly that of a woman, a robe. ఆమె కట్టుకోకతో వచ్చెను she came with nothing but the clothes she was wearing.

కోకనదము *kōka-nadamu.* [Skt.] n. The red lotus. ఎంకెలువ.

కోకము *kōkamu.* [Skt.] n. The ruddy goose. చక్రవాకము. A wolf. తోడేలు.

కోకిర, కోకిరి or కోగిరి *kōkira.* [Tel.] n. A thick felt, made of shreds of wool beaten together, and used for saddle cushions.

కోకిల or కోకిలము *kōkila.* [Skt.] n. The Indian black Cuckoo. *Endynomis honorata.* కోకిలడేగ *kōkila-ḍēga.* n. The crested goshawk, *Lopho spizia trivirgatus.* (F. B. I.) వానకోకిల the swallow. (Jerdon No. 256)

కోగు *kōgu.* [Tel.] v. t. To shave. గొరుగు.

కోచ *kōtsa* [Tel. from కొంచు to fear.] n. Cowardice; a coward. పిరికి, భీరువు. కోచపారు *kōcha-pāru.* n. To be afraid. భయపడు.

కోట *kōṭa.* [Tel.] n. A fort. కోటకొమ్మలు *kōṭa-kommalu.* [Tel.] n. Battlements of a fort.

కోటరము *kōṭaramu.* [Skt.] n. The hollow of a tree. చెట్టుతొర్ర.

కోటరము, కోటరికము or కోడరికము *kōṭaramu.* [Tel.] n. The state or relationship of a daughter-in-law. కోడంట్రము.

కోటానుకోటి or కోటానుకోటులు *kōṭānu-kōṭi.* [Tel. కోటి+కోటి.] n. Hosts upon hosts; innumerable numbers, myriads. అసంఖ్యములు.

కోటి *kōṭi.* [Skt.] n. A crore or ten millions. A host. జీవకోటి the animal kingdom: వృక్షకోటి the vegetable kingdom: దేవకోటి or సురేంద్రకోటి the army of gods: the host of heaven. బంధుకోటి or సుహృత్కోటి or మిత్రకోటి one's friends and relations, the circle of one's acquaintance. చరాచరకోటి all nature, both animate and inanimate. కోటికందర్పులాకారుడు a thousandfold brighter than Cupid himself. బాలార్కకోటిరుచిరము more beautiful than the morning sun. In astrology, the calculation of a man's nativity. The end or tip. ధనుష్కోటి the end or horn of a bow వింటికొప్పు.

కోటి *kōṭi.* [Tel.] n. Espionage. వేగు. కోటికాడు or కోటీకాడు *kōṭi-kāḍu.* n. A spy. Amuk. iii.

కోటీరము *kōṭīramu.* [Skt.] n. A crown, a crest, a diadem. కిరీటము, బొమిడికము.

కోటు *kōṭu.* [Eng. 'Court.'] n. A love game at cards.

కోటేరు *kōṭēru.* [Tel.] n. A plough. మొదలు పైకెత్తి నాడికి కట్టినవాగిలి. Sar. Pad. ii. 42. కోటేరువంటిసరిగానుండేముక్కు a long sharp nose.

కోట్రము Same as కోటరము.

కోడ *kōḍa.* [Tel.] n. A certain tree, *Sanseviera Zeilanica.* Roxb. ii. 161. H. ii. 9. వింటినారకోడనార the bowstring-hemp.

కోడంట్రము, కోడంట్రికము or కోడరికము *kōḍantramu.* [Tel. కోడలు+రికము.] n. The state of being a daughter-in-law.

కోడలు *kōḍalu.* [Tel.] n. A daughter-in-law. Also, a wife భార్య. మాకోడలు= my wife.

కోడాడు kōḍāḍu. [Tel.] v. n. To be amazed or confounded. To bewail అలరించు. To suffer pain బాధపడు. "కొనుగొను కొలకొల బుద్ధులు కోదలించుకొనికోడాడును." G. v. 223. "కూడియుండక తగనొంటివిచాలు, కోడాడ కొన్నోటు గూర్చుండుమనుచు." Dab. 217.

కోడి kōḍi. [Tel.] n. A fowl, a bird. కోళ్లు poultry, fowls. సీమకోడి a foreign fowl. i.e., a turkey, or Guinea fowl. పిల్లకోడి a brood hen. కన్నెరకోడి the red painted partridge, *Pernix Picta*. ఎర్రకోడి the red spur-fowl, *Francolinus Spadiceus*. చిరుతకోడి the painted spur-fowl. (Jerdon No. 272, 274.) కోడికూత *kōḍi-kūta*. n. Cock-crowing. కోడిజుట్టు *kōḍi-juṭṭu*. n. A cock's comb. Also the flower called by this name. కోడిపందెము *kōḍi-pandemu*. n. Cockfighting. కోడిపట్టి *kōḍi-paṭṭi*. n. A game called "hen and chickens." కోడిపిల్ల *kōḍi-pilla*. n. A chicken. కోడిపుంజు *kōḍi-punzu*. n. A cock. Also a fish called *Gasterosteus*, or *Pterois volitans*, Cuvier. Russell No. 133.

కోడిగ or కోడీ *kōḍiga*. [Tel.] n. A score, twenty cloths, gems, &c.

కోడిగము *kōḍigamu*. [Tel.] n. Ridicule, jesting. పరిహాసము, హాస్యము. Vanity, an empty show, a fleeting scene. దీనాసచ్చ్చ. కోడిగించు *kōḍi-gintsu*. v. a. To gibe at, deride. హాస్యముచేయు. కోడిగీడు one who gibes కోడిగముచేయువాడు.

కోడిపీట *kōḍi-pīṭa*. [Tel.] n. A piece of wood placed at the end of the pole of a carriage. నొగచివరక్రింద పెట్టగానుంచే పీట. బ్రద్దుకొయ్య.

కోడిబడి *kōḍi-baḍi*. [Tel.] n. A kind of cake. భక్ష్యవిశేషము.

కోడిదు Same as కోడె.

కోడివాటము *kōḍi-vāṭamu*. [Tel.] n. A steep pent roof.

కోడు *kōḍu*. [Tel.] n. A rivulet, the branch of a river: an artificial canal. A bed of bulrushes: a marsh. జమ్ముపల్లము. A line రేఖ. A leg of a bed, table, or chair. కాలు. కోడుతారు to become overripe and wither. పండినపయిరు మిక్కిలిలెండు. పయిరైరు కోడుతా రినది the crop is overripe. Ila. ii. 164. v. a. To brandish (the tongue as a snake.) To whisk (rice so as to separate the whole from the broken grains or stones.)

కోడె *kōḍe*. [Tel.] n. A bullcalf. కోడెదూడ. A young bull. కాడిపట్టనిపడుచు. Plumpness, prime. తరుణము. జోడుకోడెలు a pair of bullocks. కోడె adj. Young. కోడెత్రాచు a young snake, one in its prime. "కోడెనాగముం బులుగులరేడుతెచ్చినకోవి దోవృతెరంగు" రామా. vi. కోడెకాడు *kōḍe-kāḍu*. n. A young man. పడుచువాడు. A lover విటుడు.

కోణంగి *kōṇangi*. [Tel.] n. A buffoon, a fool in a farce. కోణంగితనము *kōṇangi-tanamu*. n. Mimicry, buffoonery, foolery, horseplay. కోణంగిదాసరి *kōṇangi-dāsari*. n. A buffoon, dressed like a pilgrim.

కోణము *kōṇamu*. [Skt.] n. An angle. మూల. A bow with which a lute or fiddle is played. A drumstick. కోలు. A. v. 49.

కోత *kōta*. [Tel. from కోయు.] n. Cutting, reaping, parting. Lopping, maiming. కోతకాలము *kōta-kālamu*. n. Harvest time. కోతదోనె *kōta-dōne*. n. A native boat with two keels. ముప్పదోనె. కోతపట్టు *kōta-paṭṭu*. v. n. To begin to cut or reap కోతకోయనారంభించు. కోతపడు *kōta-paḍu*. v. n. To be cut ఛిన్నమగు. కోతపాలు *kōta-pālu*. n. Weaning milk, i. e., milk not sucked, but drawn into a cup.

కోతి *kōti*. [Tel.] n. A monkey. తాను చెడ్డ కోతి వనమెల్లచెరిచినది 'one sickly sheep infects the flock.' కోతిపుండు బ్రహ్మరాక్షసి యైనట్లున్నది it is like making mountains of molehills. కోతికొమ్మంచి *kōti-kommanchi*. [కోతి+కొమ్మ+అంచు or అనుము.] n. A certain game. కోతివన్నె kōti-vanne. n. Monkey colour, i. e., brown. కోతిపుల్లలు kōti-pullalu. n. Certain sticks fixed in a loom. మగ్గపుపలకదారములను మీదికెత్తిగిరించే పుల్లలు.

కోదండము *kōdandamu.* [Skt.] n. A bow. **కోదండమువేయు** or **కోదండముపెట్టు** *kōdandamu-tīyu.* n. To tie up to be flogged.

కోదాడు *kōdādu.* [Tel.] n. A deformed palm tree. తాళవృక్షవిశేషము. A. iv. 193. H. iv. 211.

కోదు *kōdu.* [Tel. from కో a hill.] n. A Khond: a hill tribe in Ganjam.

కోద్రవము *kōdravamu.* [Skt.] n. The grain called *Paspalum frumentaceum.* ఆరికలు or అర్క.

కోన *kōna.* [Tel.] n. A dell or glade or gorge in the hills, a recess. కొండలలోని మరుగు చోటు. కోన or కొన a corner, a narrow place కొన, మూల. A garden. కోనసీమ the delta of a river; a place of gardens.

> "కోనలకెక్కెర్గొట్టానదగిరె"
>
> అను. i.

A forest అడవి. కోనత్రిమ్మరి a forest-rover, i. e., a monkey వనచరము. కోనమనికి a monkey.

కోనెము *kōnemu.* [Tel.] n. The mackarel fish, *Scomber niger.* **కోనెముచేప** *kōnemu-chēpa.* n. The mango fish or *Tupsee Muchchhee.* Russell No. 185.

కోనేరు *kōnēru.* [Tel.] n. A stone-faced tank with steps. చుట్టుమెట్లుగల నలుచదరపు కుంట.

కోప *kōpa.* [Eng. 'Cup.'] n. A cup. కిన్నె.

కోపము *kōpamu.* [Skt.] n. Anger, displeasure, wrath. కినుక. కోపకాడు a passionate man. కోపి. కోపకత్తె an angry woman. **కోపగించు, కోపగిల్లు, కోపపడు, కోపించు, కోపముచేయు** or **కోపముతెచ్చుకొను** *kōpa-gintsu.* To be angry, to be displeased. **కోపన** *kōpana.* adj. Irascible, passionate. కోపముగల. n. A fury, a scold. కోపముగల ఆడుది. **కోపనుడు** *kōpanudu.* n. A passionate fiery man. **కోపి** *kōpi.* n. A passionate man. కోపముగలవాడు.

కోపు *kōpu.* [Tel.] n. A side or quarter. పార్శ్వము. A bit or stick, కడ్డీ. బలపుకోపు a slate pencil. A sort, a kind or variety. A windfall, something out of the direct line. The tip or end of a bow వింటికొన. A salutation నమస్కారము. Manner విధము. An occasion సమయము. A cause నిమిత్తము. A mercantile house or firm. Beauty అందము. Harmony in music or dancing నాట్యము తీర్పు. A fish-hook చేపలనుపట్టుచున్నగాలము. Intoxicating liquor మద్యము. Fatness కొవ్వు, బలము. ఈ వానవల్ల నేలకు కోపు ఇచ్చినది this rain has softened the earth. **కోపుదారుడు** *kōpu-dārudu.* n. One who imports goods for sale సరకులు బయటనుండి తెచ్చి అమ్మువాడు. **కోపుపారు** *kōpu-pāru.* v. n. To look beautiful, to acquire beauty. అందగించు.

కోమ *kōma.* [Tel.] n. The top of an anthill పుట్టచివర. A woman. కొమ్మ, ఆడుది.

కోమటి *kōmaṭi.* [Tel.] n. A man of the merchant caste. A shopkeeper. adj. Belonging to the shopkeeper-caste. కోమటి మనిషి a man or woman of this caste. కోమటి చిన్నవాడు a shop boy. కోమటిసరుకులు wares. కోమటిసాక్ష్యము doubtful evidence, saying neither one thing nor another. See కన్యకాపురాణము.

కోమలము *kōmalamu.* [Skt.] adj. Delicate, soft, bland, blooming, youthful. మృదువైన. n. Water. నీళ్లు. **కోమలాంగి** or **కోమలి** *kōmalāngi.* n. A blooming girl. **కోమలికము** *kōmalikamu.* n. Bloom, beauty. చక్కదనము. "మేనికోమలికంబు." K. P. iv. 50.

కోయ or **కోయలు** *kōya.* [Tel.] n. A certain hill tribe in the Telugu country.

కోయష్టికము *kōyashṭikamu.* [Skt.] n. The lap wing. కొక్కెర, చిఱుకొక్కెర.

కోయిల *kōyila.* [Tel. కో god+ఇల్ house.] n. A temple. గుడి. The black Cuckoo. కోకిల. కోయిలకూర *kōyila-kūra.* n. The herb called *Amaranthus tristis.* Boxb. iii. 604.

కోయు *kōyu.* [Tel.] v. a. To cut. To pluck, gather. To reap. To slaughter (an animal for food). కోసికొనిపోవు to wear away. To take (at cards).

కోర *kōra.* [Tel.] n. A tusk, fang, tooth. దంష్ట్ర. A cup గిన్నె. A tray or dish, పళ్లెము. adj. Sharp, pointed కోరకొమ్ము a sharp horn. కోరపళ్లు the incisors. కోరమీసాలు pointed whiskers. కోరపంది a tusked boar. Unbleached, brown (See కోరా). Base, impure (as metal, &c.) Slanting, lying on a side ఒరిగియుండే, పక్కగానుండే. కోర చెక్కిళ్లు hollow cheeks. కోరకొండె or కోర సిగ a side lock or tuft of hair ముఖపార్శ్వ మునకుండేకొండె. కోరపోవు to go crooked వంకరలఁబోవు.

కోరంగి *kōrangi.* [Skt.] n. Small cardamoms. చిట్టేలకులు.

కోరకము *kōrakamu.* [Skt.] n. A bud. మొగ్గ. కోరకపాళి *kōraka-pāli.* n. A line or chain of blossoms.

కోరగించు *kōra-gintsu.* [Tel.] v. n. To close as a flower or as the hand ముకుళించు. To sprout మొలకెత్తు.

కోరడము *kōraḍamu.* [Tel.] n. Ridicule, mockery, derision. అపహాస్యము.

కోరడి *kōraḍi.* [Tel.] n. A bank or ridge. A hedge. అడ్డముగాచేసిన పొడిమట్టిగోడ. Ridicule కోరడము, అపహాస్యము. The ferule on the butt of a chisel hilt. A statement recorded of a man's descent, character and circumstances. కోరడిగట్టు *kōraḍi-gaṭṭu.* n. A bank, or ridge, an earth-fence.

కోరదూషములు *kōra-dūshamulu.* [Skt.] n. The grain called ఆరికెలు or అర్లు.

కోరముపువ్వు *kōramu-puvvu.* [Tel.] n. The coral flower.

కోరా *kōrā.* [Tel.] adj. Unbleached. కొరికము, అనాహతము. కోరాబంగారు inferior gold, impure gold మట్టుపుబంగారు.

కోరాడు *kōrāḍu.* [Tel.] v. n. To grovel, to throw up the earth with the horns, or tusks. To purr as a cat.

కోరింద *kōrinda.* [Tel.] n. The bramble. A. vi. 12.

కోరు *kōru.* [Tel.] adj. Steep. కోరుకొండ a steep hill. కోరిల్లు a pent roofed house.

కోరు *kōru.* [Tel. for కొనరు.] కైకోరు they will not accept.

కోరు *kōru.* [Tel.] v. a. To desire, ask, propose, pray, demand, beg. ఇచ్ఛించు. కోరిక or కోరికె or కోర్కి *kōrika.* n. A wish, desire. ఇచ్ఛ. Love, hope. అభీష్టము. A vow వరము. కోరు *kōru.* n. A share. The king's or government portion. ధనికర వస్తురూప మైనకప్పము. సంగోరు a half share. ఇరుగోరు both shares, i. e., all the crop. మేటికోరు the share due to the farmer.

కోల *kōla.* [Tel.] adj. Long. కోలముఖము a long face. కోలమెరుగు forked lightning. నిలువుమెరుగు, ఐరావతి. "శిఖిదిక్కునందు తేకువ గోలమెరుఁగులు మెరసె." వసు. పూ. vii. కోలాకు a long leaf. కోలాకుపొన్న a certain tree. H. iv. 11. కోలకోపెర an oblong cup, a sauce boat.

కోల *kōla.* [Tel.] n. A staff. దండము. An arrow బాణము. అంపకోలలు arrows. తవ్వు కోల, పంటికోల or మునికోల a hoe or digging staff. చెరుకుగోల a sugar-cane. కోలవారు staff-bearers వేత్రధరులు. కోలలేనిపెట్టు తాడులేనికట్టు you feel the blow of an invisible rod: you are bound in viewless ties. (Used of a Goverment) "సీ॥ తలఁగ నారాచపంచకమునఁ నొప్పించి, యొకకోలగ్రుచ్చితవర్త నరముగూలించి." M. VI. i. 342.

కోలంకిపిట్ట *kōlanki-piṭṭa.* [Tel.] n. A sort of bird. A swift.

కోలకము *kōlakamu.* [Skt.] n. Pepper. మిరియము.

కోలక్రోతులు *kōla-krōtulu.* [Tel.] n. A game played by boys. కోతికొమ్మంచి అనే ఆట. Vish. vii. 211.

కోలగగ్గెర *kōla-gaggera.* [Tel.] n. A noose or a tether. (A vi. 31.) ఎద్దులను పశువ్రోసి వాలంకుకాళ్లను కలియుకట్టేకట్టు.

కోలదివ్వె or **కోలదివిటీ** *kōla-divve.* [Tel.] n. A torch. కెలుతురుకర్ర్లదివిటీ.

కోలపాలచెట్టు *kōla-pāla-chettu.* [Tel.] n. A sort of tree.

కోలపొన్న *kōla-ponna.* [Tel.] n. The plant called *Haemonites cordifolia.* పృశ్నిపర్ణి, అంఘ్రిపర్ణి.

కోలము *kōlamu.* [Tel.] n. A dance, dancing. నర్తనము. A pan, an earthen basin. (H. ii. 12.) [Skt.] A float or raft తెప్ప. An apple రేగుపండు. A hog పంది. కోలమాంసము Pork. Kalah. iii. 127.

"సీ॥ గగనరంగస్థలంబున మిగుల ప్రౌఢి
మనునగాలికనీలి కోలమునటింప
బోరికెమొగంబునా రాలు నివ్వకలనంగ
గుంపులైరాలె మహీంద్రకోపరతులు."

A. iv. 135.

కోలముక్కిచెక్క *kōla-mukki-chekka.* [Tel.] n. The plant called *Echites antidysenterica.* కుటజము.

కోలవస *kōla-vasa* [Tel.] n. A species of వస. (q. v.)

కోలాటము *kōl-āṭamu.* [Tel. కోల+ఆట.] n. A morris-dance in a ring in which sticks are struck together in harmony. Single stick is also thus named.

కోలాహలము *kōlā-halamu.* [Skt.] n. An uproar, hubbub, buzz. Bloom, blaze of beauty. బహుజనధ్వని, కలకలము. **కోలాహలుడు** *kōlā-haluḍu.* n. An uproarious or noisy person; the trumpeter or preacher of the day. BD. VI. vi. 204.

కోలు *kōlu.* [Tel.] adj. Big, great, huge పెద్ద. కోలుపులి or కోల్పులి a royal tiger. కోలుపడిగెలు lofty banners. adv. Very. మిక్కిలి. See కోలుమసగు.

కోలు *kōlu.* [Tel. from కొను.] n. Taking కొనుట. An affix, which turns verbs into nouns. అడికోలు usurpation. పొగడికోలు applause. కలుపుకోలుతనము sociable nature. Plu. కోళ్లు. పుచ్చికోళ్లు acceptings. కలుపుకోళ్లు minglings. మొత్తుకోళ్లు lamentations. కోలు n. Plunder. కొల్ల. భార. భీష్మ. iii.

కోలుకాడు *kolu-kāḍu.* [Tel.] n. A bailiff. కావలివాడు. A sealbearer. ముద్రమానిసి. A revenue-officer. An exciseman. నియమించెడి అధికారి, సుంకరియొక్క బంటు.

కోలుకొను or **కోల్కొను** *kōlu-konu.* [Tel.] v. n. To recover, be cured, be remedied. To come to good, become ripe. తేరుకొను, వర్ధిల్లు. అమురము తాగితే నెలదాక కోలకొనను if I take oil I do not recover from it for a month.

కోలుతల or **కోల్తల** *kōlu-tala.* [Tel.] n. Fighting face to face. ఎదుటనిలిచి యుద్ధము చేయుట. Preparation for war or battle యుద్ధసన్నాహము. **కోల్తలచేయు** *kōltala-chēyu.* v. a. To encourage: to place in battle array. దళోద్యోగము చేయు, ఎచ్చరికచేయు. M. Salya i. 248. and i. 43. and i. 94. M. III. vii. 96.

కోలుపడు or **కోల్పడు** *kōlu-paḍu.* [Tel.] v. n. To be lost, ruined. చెడు, నశించు. To lose పోగొట్టుకొను. To appear అగుపడు. Vasu. ii. 51. M. R. v. 267. కోల్పడ్డ foiled, worsted, lost పోగొట్టుకొన్న. **కోలుపాటు** or **కోల్పాటు** *kōlu-pāṭu.* n. Loss, deprivation. పోగొట్టుకొనుట. Ruin చేటు.

కోలుపుచ్చు or **కోలువుచ్చు** *kōlu-putstsu.* [Tel.] v. a. To lose, ruin, chase away, forfeit. కోలుపుచ్చుకొన్న lost. పోగొట్టుకొని. M. IV. ii. 269.

కోలుపోవు *kōlu-pōvu.* [Tel.] v. a. To lose. "ఇక్కడ నిమిషములో గెలుపోయెను." BRY. ii. 777. v. n. To be spoiled. చెడు. **కోలుపోక** *kōlu-pōka.* n. Losing. పోగొట్టుకొనుట.

కోలుమసంగు *kōlu-masangu.* [Tel. కోలు+మిక్కిలి.] v. n. To rave, rage, be furious. చెలరేగు, విజృంభించు. M. VII. v. 314; IX. ii. 288; IX. i. 288.

కోలె *kōle.* [Tel.] n. Stubble, a stump of corn. చెన్ను కోసినకాడ, కొలె.

కోలె *kōle.* [Tel.] (Postposition.) Since. మొదలుకొని, మొదలి. నాటగోలె ever since that day.

కోలెమ్ము *kōlemmu.* [Tel. కోలు+ఎమ్ము.] n. Lit. The long bone, that is, the spine or back bone.

కోవె *kōve.* [Tel.] n. A man who is struck with wonder. ఆశ్చర్యమునొందినవాడు.

కోవ or **క్రోవ** *kōva.* [Tel.] n. A string, as of pearls: సరము. A bunch of coral దండ. One step, grade, or remove, in a genealogical table. A throat disease that attacks children. The actual cautery or burning with a hot iron. కోవతేలిన blistered. తాటాకు కోవతేలినది the palm leaf is blistered.

కోవి or **క్రోవి** *kōvi.* [Tel.] n. A tube, గొట్టము. An orifice, opening. A musket తుపాకి. చేతికోవి a pistol (రా. వి. v.) A bottle బుడ్డి. (నీలా. iii.) A waterpipe భూమి లోపల నీళ్లువచ్చుట కేర్పరచినమార్గము. A crucible మూస. (కళా. viii.) A flute. ముక్కుకోవి a nostril. గొంతుకోవి the gullet, పుట్టకోవులు the openings or mouths of a white ant hill. కోవిపుండు a sinus or opening in a boil: a corn on the foot. కర్పూరంపుకోవులు pastiles of camphor. తేనె కోవి a honey comb. కోవులు round tiles used in roofs, which are truncated and bisected cones. కొండెములక్రోవి a mere pack of lies.

కోవి or **క్రోవి** *kōvi.* [Tel.] n. A certain flowering shrub, *Galedupa Arborea.* క్రానుగచెట్టు, కరవీరము, కలచెట్టు. A. v. 146. Manu. ii. 25.

కోవిదత *kōvidata.* [Skt.] n. Skill. ఖడ్గకోవిదత skill in the use of the sword. T. ii. 40. **కోవిదుడు** *kō-vidudu.* n. A skilful or wise man. A learned man. విద్వాంసుడు, చదువరి.

కోవిల or **కోవెల** *kōvila.* [Tel. కో god+ఇల్ house.] n. A temple. గుడి, కోయిల. The Cuckoo. కోకిలము.

కోవు *kōvu.* [Tel. for కావు.] v. కూయు, చేసి కోవు. n. An imitative sound resembling a cry. అరుపునందున ధ్వన్యనుకరణము.

కోవురము *kōvuramu.* [Tel.] n. Ambush. శత్రువులను కొట్టేటందుకు దారిపక్కను దాగి యుండుట.

"గీ॥ ఉదయగిరిమీద గోవురముండినిగుడు
నహితతరవిరక్త చేష్టుడనుచుదోడి
బలగ మైనట్టిచుక్కలవలసక్రోవి
జూపనేతెంచెననకేగుచుక్కపొడిచె."

Swa. iii. 70.

కోశము *kōśamu.* [Skt.] n. A repository, receptacle, place: the inside. A sheath, scabbard. కత్తిఒర. The cocoon or bag containing the silk worm. An egg గుడ్డు. కోశకారి the silkworm. హృదయకోశమునందు within the heart: at the bottom of one's heart. అండకోశము the scrotum.

కోష్టము *koshṭamu.* [Skt.] n. A plant named *Coitus Arabicus.*

కోష్ణము *kôshṇamu.* [Skt.] adj. Lukewarm, tepid. నులివెచ్చగానున్న, గోరువెచ్చగానున్న.

కోస or **కోసు** *kōsa.* [Tel.] adj. Long. కోస ముత్తెము A pear-shaped pearl.

కోసము or **కోసరము** *kōsamu.* [Tel. cf. Kan. గోస్కర.] (Affix) For, on account of; in behalf of; దానికోసము on its account దానికొరకు.

కోసరలు *kōsaralu.* [Tel.] n. A sort of rice. Rox. ii. 205.

కోసలము *kōsalamu.* [Skt.] n. The district around Benares.

కోసు *kōsu.* [Tel.] adj. Slanting, aslant, oblong. See కోస. కోసుగా *kōsu-gā.* adv. Aslant.

కోసు *kōsu.* [Tel.] n. A distance of about two miles. క్రోశము. కరుకు. The ఆమడ or four koss is 8 or 10 miles.

కోసు *kōsu.* [Eng.] n. A cabbage. *Brassica Oleracea.* (Watts.) ఆకుకోసు lettuce. మొగ్గ కోసు cauliflower.

కోస్తా *kōstā.* [Cor. of Eng. 'Coast.'] n. A coast. కోస్తావర్తకము the coasting trade.

కోహళము *kōhaḷamu.* [Skt.] n. A kind of drum. కాహళము.

కోహో *kōhō.* [Tel.] n. A word expressing ridicule. పరిహాసమును తెలియజేయు మాట.

"వ॥ కేలువరచి కోహో యని గేలిసేయుచు
గడెకాకదంబంబులదప్పటలు."
అముక్త. iv.

కౌ kau

కౌ or **కవు** *kau.* [Tel.] n. In composition, stands for కాను or కవును as కౌదీగ.

కౌండిన్య or **కౌండిల్యగోత్రము** *kauṇḍinya.* [Skt.] n. The name of an ancient family.

కౌక్షేయము or **కౌక్షేయకము** *kaukshēyamu.* [Skt.] n. A sword. కౌక్షేయకుడు one who carries a sword.

కౌగిలి or **కవుగిలి** *kaugili.* [Tel. from కాను] n. The breast. భుజాంతరము. కౌగిలిచేర్చు to take in one's arms, to embrace. **కౌగిలించు** or **కవుగిలించు** *kaugilintsu.* n. To embrace. ఆలింగనముచేయు. **కౌగిలింత**, **కవుగిలింత** or **కౌగిలింపు** *kaugilinta.* n. An embrace. ఆలింగనము.

కౌచు or **కవుచు** *kautsu.* [Tel.] n. A scale of a fish. చేపపొలుసు. Fish-smell, stench చేపవాసన.

కౌజు or **కవుజు** *kauzu.* [Tel.] n. The Indian partridge. *Francolinus Ponticerianus.*

కౌటిల్యము *kauṭilyamu.* [Skt. from కుటిలము.] n. Crookedness, curliness as of crisped locks of hair. వంకరతనము.

కౌడు or **కవుడు** *kauḍu.* [Tel. and Tam.] n. Cunning. కపటము. (హ. ii.)

కౌతుకము *kautukamu.* [Skt. from కుతుకము.] n. Glee. సంతోషము. Strong desire, impetuosity. ఆశ, కోరిక, వేడుక, కుతుకము. The marriage thread or cord. పెండ్లితోరము, దీక్షాదులయందు చేతకట్టే కంకణము.

కౌతూహలము *kautū-halamu.* [Skt. from కుతూహలము.] n. Eagerness, vehemence. మిక్కిలి ఆశ, తమి.

కౌను or **కవును** *kaunu.* [Tel.] n. The waist. నడుము. The middle part of a bow. వింటినడుము.

"చ. పిడికెడుకౌను గొప్పగని ప్రేమ
త్రివిక్రమాంఘ్రి జేసితే,
పిడికెడుకౌను గొప్పబయిశేర్చు
కూరంబున గంటిసంచు."
అను. i.

కౌపీనము *kaupīnamu.* [Skt.] n. A modesty piece. గోచి.

కౌమారము *kaumāramu.* [Skt. from కుమార.] n. Youth, bloom.

కౌముది *kaumudi.* [Skt.] n. Moonlight. వెన్నెల. ఆంధ్రకౌముది illustrations of Telugu, the name of a grammatical work.

కౌమోదకి *kaumōdaki.* [Skt.] n. The club or mace of Vishṇu. విష్ణువుయొక్క గద.

కౌరవ *kaurava.* [Skt.] n. Pertaining to the Kuru (కురు) family.

కౌరు or కవురు *kauru.* [Tel.] n. Tint, hue, gleam; a luminous streak. వర్ణాధిక్యము.

కౌలు or కవులు *kaulu.* [H.] n. A writing of assurance, agreement or engagement granted to the cultivator of the soil. A safe guard or warrant to pass (as granted to an enemy.)

కౌలుదిమ్మ *kaulu-dimma.* [Tel.] n. A die or punch, used by goldsmiths, also called పడి అచ్చు.

కౌలేయకము *kaulēyakamu.* [Skt.] adj. Of a good parentage or high birth. మంచికులమున పుట్టిన.

కౌశలము or కౌశల్యము *kauśalamu.* [Skt.] n. Skilfulness, dexterity. నేర్పరితనము.

కౌశికము *kauśikamu.* [Skt.] n. An owl. BD. vii. 1705.

కౌశికుడు *kauśikuḍu.* [Skt.] n. A title of Indra: also of Viswamitra. కాలకౌశికుడు an abject wretch.

కౌశేయము *kauśēyamu.* [Skt.] n. Silk, a silk cloth. పట్టుబట్ట.

కౌస్తుభము *kaustubhamu.* [Skt.] n. A carbuncle. The breastplate or jewel worn at his breast by the god Vishnu. Metaphorically, gem or masterpiece, or the noblest thing. The "jewel" or middle ornament in a collar of knighthood. అద్వైతకౌస్తుభము the masterpiece of Monism (name of a book.)

క్ర kra

క్రంగున *kranguna.* [Tel.] adv. Aloud. కంగున.

క్రంత *kranta.* [Tel.] n. A hole. రంధ్రము. A lane సందు. A court రచ్చ. A present taken to the intended bride by the bridegroom's party.

క్రందనము *krandanamu.* [Skt.] n. Weeping. ఏడ్పు. Shouting, howling. అర్పు, పిలుపు.. క్రందితము *kranditamu.* adj. Wept, cried, called out. ఏడ్చిన, పిలిచిన.

క్రందు *krandu.* [Tel.] v. n. To sound, మ్రోగు. To weep విలపించు. n. Sound, noise. మ్రోత, సందడి. Greatness, excess. ఎక్కువ. Thickness దళము. Danger ఉపద్రవము. adj. Great, extreme, much. క్రందైన. Crowded as in a battle. సాంద్రమైన. క్రందుకొను *krandu-konu.* v. n. To exceed; to be great. To spread, as clouds. To arise, as a noise or hubbub. అతిశయించు, అరుదగు. క్రందున *kranduna.* adv. Vastly, greatly. క్రందిల్లు or క్రందుపడు *krandillu.* n. v. To sound, make a noise. మ్రోగు, శబ్దించు. క్రందుకయ్యము n. A melee or close fight. దొమ్మి యుద్ధము.

క్రంప or కంప *krampa.* [Tel.] n. A branch of dried thorns, a bramble. ఎండినముండ్ల మండ.

క్రకచము *krakachamu.* [Skt.] n. A saw. రంపము.

క్రక్కన *krakkana.* [Tel.] adj. Cruel. కఠినము. (వై. v.)

క్రక్కు Same as కక్కు to vomit.

క్రచ్చు *kratstsu.* [Tel.] n. Wish. కోరిక. క్రచ్చు or క్రచ్చుకొను v. t. To surround. చుట్టుకొను. (చను. iv.) క్రచ్చర *kratstsara.* (క్రచ్చు+అర.) adv. Suddenly: at once: శీఘ్రముగా. Entirely అంతయు. Much మిక్కిలి. BD. vi. 1890. HK. v. 2.

క్రతువు *kratuvu.* [Skt.] n. Sacrifice, burnt offering. యజ్ఞము. క్రతుధ్వంసి *kratu-dhvamsi.* n. The destroyer of Sacrifices; epithet of Siva. క్రతుభుక్కులు or క్రతుభుజులు *kratu-bhukkulu.* n. Those who live on sacrifices, i. e., the gods. దేవతలు. క్రథనము *kradhanamu.* n. Killing. వధ.

క్రన్నన *krannana.* [Tel.] adv. Rapidly, well, duly. At once, immediately. శీఘ్రముగా. Then, afterwards పిమ్మట. Again మరల.

క్రమణము *kramaṇamu.* [Skt.] n. Turning round. తిరుగుట.

క్రమము *kramamu.* [Skt.] n. A series, an order, a line. A mode, a way, a course, a plan, a rule. Regularity, arrangement. ఈక్రమమున thus, in this order. క్రమక్రమముగా adv. One after another, in order, by degrees, day by day. క్రమశః *kramaśah.* adv. Gradually, in order. క్రమస్థుడు *krama-sthudu.* n. An exact, punctilious or precise man. క్రమాలంకారము *kramālankāramu.* n. Poetical description in natural order. క్రమించు *kramintsu.* v. n. To elapse, pass by, as time: to depart, or pass away. అతిక్రమించు. To occupy or spread over or extend to ఆక్రమించు. క్రమేణ *kramēṇa.* adv. Successively, in due succession.

క్రముకము *kramukamu.* [Skt.] n. The areca or betel nut tree. పోక.

క్రమేలకము *kramēlakamu.* [Skt. cognate with Eng. Camel]. n A camel. ఒంటె.

క్రమ్మరు *krammaru.* [Tel.] v. n. To turn, return, go back. మరలు. క్రమ్మరించు or క్రమ్మరుచు *krammarintsu.* v. a. To turn, send back, recall. To revoke, annul, rescind. క్రమ్మరిచేయు. క్రమ్మర *krammara.* adv. Again. క్రమ్మరిల్లు or క్రమ్మరబడు Same as క్రమ్మరు.

క్రమ్ము *krammu.* [Tel.] v. n. To spread. కవియు, వ్యాపించు. To swell పైకి ఉబుకు. క్రమ్ముదల *krammu-dala.* n. Spreading. క్రమ్ముట, వ్యాపించుట. క్రమ్ముకొను to swell పైకి ఉబుకు. క్రమ్ముదనము *krammu-danamu.* n. Duplicity. కపటభావము. క్రమ్మున *krammu-na.* adv. Quickly. త్వరగా. "క్రమ్మునబర తేరగా పేటకాండ్రు." BD. v. 346.

క్రయము *krayamu.* [Skt.] n. Price. వెల. Purchase వెలయిచ్చికొనుట. కాలక్రయము the current price. క్రయముచేయు to dispose of, to sell. క్రయధనము the cost. క్రయపత్రము or క్రయచీటి a sale deed. క్రయవిక్రయములు n. Buying and selling. క్రయవిక్రయికుడు one who buys and sells వేపారి. క్రయించు to buy కొను. క్రయికుడు a buyer వెలయిచ్చువాడు. క్రయ్యము goods exposed for sale క్రయమునకు పరుపబడిన సరుకు.

క్రయ్య *krayya.* [Tel.] n. A canal. కాలువ, కయ్య. క్రయ్యబడు or క్రయ్య to unite కలియు.

క్రల్లపడు *kralla-padu.* [Tel.] v. n. To become dry, to dry up. ఎండు.

క్రవ్యము *kravyamu.* [Skt.] n. Flesh, meat. మాంసము. క్రవ్యాదుడు or క్రవ్యాశనుడు *kravyādudu.* n. A cannibal, a carnivorous giant. పచ్చిమాంసమును తినువాడు. A Rakshasa రాక్షసుడు.

క్రా krā

క్రాంతి *krānti.* [Skt.] n. Turning. తిరుగుట, క్రమణము.

క్రాక Same as కాక heat. క్రాగు Same as కాగు to be hot. క్రాగుడు Same as కాగుడు. క్రాచు Same as కాచు.

క్రానుగు or కానుగు *krānugu.* [Tel.] n. The tree called *Galedupa Indica: or Dalbergia Arborea.* Roxb. iii. 239.

క్రాయు *krāyu.* [Tel.] v. n. To spit. (A. v. 132.) ఉమియు. To rinse the mouth and spit out the water. పుక్కిలించి ఉమ్మివేయు To vomit క్రక్కు.

క్రార or క్రారవడి or క్రారావడి *krāra.* n. The name of the letter R, ్ర in a conjunct letter as in క్రా. Also a conversational word used instead of క్రార్థము.

క్రాలు *krālu.* [Tel.] v. n. To wave. అల్లలాడు. To turn round and round. గిరగిరతిరుగు. To spread about చెదరు. To wander or roam about సంచరించు. To move about సంచలించు. To rejoice సంతోషించు. To behave ప్రవర్తిల్లు. To be long, oblong, or elongated.

"ఉ॥ కాలిక మోదునంటి కొరగానిశరీరము

పల్లవెండ్రుకల్,

"క్రాలెడుబూవిగడ్డమచుషల్ పటికంబున
నీరలంకము
తేలగనమాధవాకృములు చీదదరంబులు
తోడికుడేయరాా,
మాలెడువక్రదంతములు సోరుముగల్గి
యొకందుపుట్టెరా."

V. P. ii. 143. iii. 25.

To shine, to be clear, to extend as a ray. To hang, dangle, as a necklace A. v. 121. BD. iv. 1589. ప్రకాశించు. క్రాలుకంటి or క్రాల్గంటి a woman who has beautiful eyes.

క్రి kri

క్రించు *krintsu.* [Tel.] adj. Vile. అల్పమైన, నీచమైన, క్షుద్రమైన. **క్రించుదనము** or **కించుదనము** *krintsu-danamu.* n. Baseness. నీచత్వము, అల్పత్వము. Spite, cruelty.

"క॥ క్రించుదనంబున విధిదము
పంచించిన యేడుగోపవరనందనులా
క్కొంచుకకాలంబున నీ
కించిరి రాజేంద్ర బాలకృష్ణుని మాయరా."

B. X.

క్రించుడు or **కించు** *krintsudu.* n. A low fellow. క్రోధి, అల్పుడు.

క్రిందు *krindu.* [Tel.] n. The part below. అధోభాగము. The past time. గతకాలము. క్రిందటినెల the last month గతించిననెల. క్రిందిమాటలు the following words. **క్రిందల** or **క్రిందుతల** *krindala.* n. Head downwards క్రిందుగతల. క్రిందుపడు to go to the bottom అడుగుపడు. క్రిందుపరచు to cause to go to the bottom. To disrespect హీనపరచు.

క్రిక్క *krikka.* [Tel.] n. An encomiast. బట్టువాడు, వంది.

క్రిక్కిరియు *krikkiriyu.* [Tel. క్రిక్క+ఇరియు.] v. n. To crowd, to be crowded. ఎడములేక వ్యాపించు. క్రిక్కిరించు to cause to be crowded క్రిక్కిరియునట్లు చేయు. **క్రిక్కు** *krikku.* n. Closeness. కిదుకు.

క్రిమి *krimi.* [Skt.] n. An insect, a worm, an animalcule. పురుగు.

క్రియ *kriya.* [Skt.] n. Doing. చేయుట. Act, action. పని. Manner విధము. Use, advantage, means, an expedient, a contrivance ఉపాయము. A verb. ధాత్వర్థము. Rite, ordinance, ceremony, obsequies, పూజ. Medical treatment or practice చికిత్స. Fact, truth, utility, effect. తేలినక్రియ the result. క్రియమాట the matter in question, the point on which the thing hinges, a word to the purpose. adv. Like, similar to. విధమున, లాగున. **క్రియావంతుడు** *kriya-vantudu.* n. A man of diligence. పనియందు పూనికగలవాడు.

క్రియ్యు *kriyyu.* [Tel.] v. n. To grow lean. కృశించు.

"ఉన్నమీనముల్లెల్లఖిన్నములై
పక్రిస్సియున్న"

భా. 10 స్కం. పూ.

క్రీ krī

క్రీ *krī.* [Tel.] In compounds, is a contracted form of క్రింది. **క్రీచూడ్కి** *krī-chūḍki.* n. A downcast glance. క్రింది చూపు.

క్రీడ *krīḍa.* [Skt.] n. Play, sport, enjoyment. ఆట్లాట, పరిహాసము. Disgrace దూరు. **క్రీడి** *krīḍi.* n. A name of Arjuna. కిరీటి or అర్జునుడు. **క్రీడించు** *krīḍintsu.* v. n. To sport. ఆటలాడు.

క్రీస్తు *krīstu.* [Gk.] n. Christ.

క్రు kru

క్రుంకు *krunku.* [Tel.] v. n. To sink, to drown. మునుగు. To set అస్తమించు. To die చచ్చు. n. A plunge, the act of drowning, immersion. మునుక. క్రుంకుడు, sun-set. క్రుంకించు to give a plunge. **క్రుంకించు** *krunkintsu.* v. a. To dip, wash, steep.

క్రుంగు or క్రుంగబడు or క్రుంగిలు *krungu.* v. n. To be bent. కుంకి ఆడు. To go down. దిగబడు.

క్రుక్కు.. Same as కుక్కు... (q. v.)

క్రుధ *krudha.* [Skt.] n. Anger. కోపము. క్రుద్ధము *kruddhamu.* adj. Wrathful. కోపముగొంటిన. క్రుద్ధుడు *kruddhuḍu.* n. A wrathful man.

క్రుమ్మరు or క్రుమ్మరిల్లు or క్రుమ్మరిలు *krummaru.* [Tel.] v. n. To wander. సంచరించు, తిరుగు.

క్రుమ్ము or కుమ్ము *krummu.* [Tel.] n. To butt. కొమ్ములతో పొడుచు. క్రుమ్ము or క్రుమ్ముడు *krummu.* n. Butting. కొమ్ములతో పొడుచుట. క్రుమ్ముడుపడు *krummuḍu-paḍu.* v. n. To be butted. పోటుపడు. క్రుమ్ములాడు *krummulāḍu.* v. n. To butt each other. క్రుమ్ము కొనిపోట్లాడు.

క్రుయ్యు *kruyyu.* [Tel.] v. n. To grow lean. కృశించు. To retreat వెనుదీయు. క్రుస్సిపోవు *krussi-pōvu.* v. n. To faint, perish, fail. కృశించిపోవు, కుంగిపోవు. Hari vams. Purva. IX. 124. A. vi. 12.

క్రుళ్లు or కుళ్లు *kruḷḷu.* [Tel.] v. n. To rot. కుళ్లిపోవు. To grieve or pine మనస్సులో దుఃఖించు. క్రుళ్లగించు to pine away. క్రుళ్లగింత *kruḷḷaginta.* n. Pining away. మనసులో దుఃఖించుట. క్రుళ్లుపోతు or కుళ్లుపోతు an envious wretch. ఓర్వలేకమనస్సులో దుఃఖించుస్వభావముగలవాడు.

క్రూ krū

క్రూరము *krūramu.* [Skt.] adj. Cruel, wicked. కఠినమైన, చెడ్డ. Terrible, ferocious, భయంకరమైన. Hard, stern. గట్టి. క్రూరబుద్ధి wickedness or cruel nature. క్రూరతిథి an ill starred day. A. v. 116. క్రూరజంతువు *krūra-jantuvu.* n. A wild beast. క్రూరు *krūru.* adj. Sharp వాడియైన. క్రూరుడు *krūruḍu.* n. A hard or cruel man. కఠినమనస్కుంగలవాడు.

క్రే krē

క్రే *krē.* In composition, is short for క్రేవ as క్రేగన్ను. (q. v.)

క్రేంకారము or క్రేంకృతి *krēn-kāramu.* [Skt.] n. A note, voice, sound: the voice of a bird. A ringing, jangling, creaking sound. R. ii. 103. T. v. 49.

క్రేగన్ను *krē-gannu.* [Tel. క్రేవ+కన్ను.] n. The outer corner of the eye. అపాంగము, కడకన్ను. క్రేగంట *krēganṭa.* adv. Askance, with a sidelong glance.

క్రేగయి *krē-gayi.* [Tel. క్రేవ+కయి.] n. The tip of the hand. హస్తాగ్రము.

క్రేటు or క్రేటుకోము *krēṭu.* [Tel.] v. n. To make a noise in clearing the throat. సకిలించునట్లు శబ్దించు. To be agitated తొట్రుపడు.

"క. కాటుకకన్నీరొలుకగ
మాటవెడల క్రేటుకొనుచుమానినిపలికెన్."
స్వా. iii.

క్రేడి *krēḍi.* [Tel.] n. A kind of red rice. ఒకవిధమైన ఎర్రవడ్లు.

క్రేడించు, క్రేడిచేయు or కేడించు *krēḍintsu.* [Tel.] v. n. To step or move aside. తొలగు. (భార. ద్రో. i.) v. t. To disregard. అలక్ష్యముచేయు. (భార. భీష్మ. ii. and జై. v.)

క్రేణి *krēṇi.* [Tel.] n. A high place, a high situation. ఉన్నతపదము. (కవిక. ii.)

క్రేణించు or క్రేణిచేయు Same as క్రేడించు.

క్రేతొట్టు *krē-toṭṭu.* [Tel. క్రేవ+తొట్టు.] v. n. To wear away the bank. గట్టొరయు.

"వ॥ క్రేతొట్టుకడల్లెనాడిగిలయుకొరయు."
ఉ. హరి. iii.

క్రేపు *krēpu.* [Tel.] n. A calf. దూడ. Also, the top of a mountain పర్వతశిఖరము. The knot of a woman's jacket.

క్రేయము *krēyamu.* [Skt. from క్రయము.] adj. That which can be purchased, purchaseable వెలయిచ్చి కొనదగిన.

క్రేయో *krēyō.* [Tel.] n. A noise made in driving away anything. పక్షులగొట్టుట యందగు ధ్వన్యనుకరణము.

క్రేళ్లు *krēḷḷu.* [Tel.] n. Leaps, skips. గంతులు, దాటులు. Pride ఉన్నతి. క్రేళ్లుగ *krēḷḷu-ga.* adv. At once. అంగలుదెంగలుగ. క్రేళ్లుదాటు or క్రేళ్లురుదు *krēḷḷu-dāṭu.* v. n. To bound, to leap ఎగిరిపడు, గంతులిడు. "నల్లదేల క్రేళ్లుదాటుచు." BRK. 552. క్రేళ్లుబ్బు *krēḷḷubbu.* (క్రేళ్లు+ఉబ్బు.) v. n. To excel, to be proud. అతిశయించు. (కొలి. v.)

క్రేవ *krēva.* [Tel.] n. A side. వైపు, పార్శ్వము.

క్రేవున or క్రేవ్వున *krēvuna.* [Tel.] adv. Shriekingly, suddenly aloud. అకస్మాత్తుగా, బిగ్గరగా.

క్రై krai

క్రైలు or క్రైలు or క్రయిలు *krailu.* [Tel.] n. Thrashing and measuring grain. ధాన్యము నూర్చి కొలుచుట. క్రైలువారి or క్రైలువారు *krailu-dāru.* n. An officer who superintends the thrashing and measuring of grain. క్రయిలుచేయించే అధికారి.

క్రైస్తవుడు [Gk.] n. A Christian. క్రీస్తుమతస్థుడు.

క్రొ kro

క్రొ *kro.* [Tel.] adj. The word క్రొత్త is contracted into క్రొ in compounds and the following hard or soft consonants in Telugu words are doubled as క్రొక్కన్ను (క్రొత్త+కన్ను), క్రొక్కారు (క్రొత్త+కారు), క్రొత్తావి (క్రొత్త+తావి), క్రొన్నన (క్రొత్త+నన), క్రొన్నలుపు, క్రొన్నెరుగు, క్రొన్నె త్తురు, క్రొమ్మొల, క్రొమ్ముడి, క్రొమ్మెరుగు, క్రొమ్మొన, క్రొవ్వాడి, క్రొవ్విరి. &c. In some cases, this change is made even when a Skt. word follows, as క్రొమ్మేఘములు (ఫి. iii.) In some cases, again, when a hard consonant follows, క్రొత్త is contracted into క్రొం where the సున్న stands for the letter న but the succeeding consonant is not doubled but changed into a soft one, as క్రొంజోడు, క్రొంజెమట, క్రొందమ్మి, క్రొంబసిడి, క్రొంబొగ, &c.

క్రొంకి Same as కొంకి. క్రొంతె Same as కొంతె.

క్రొక్కారము *krok-kāramu.* [Tel.] n. Cock-crowing. కోడికూత.

క్రొక్కారు *krok-kāru.* [Tel. క్రొత్త+కారు.] n. New season. క్రొక్కారుమెరుగు *krokkāru-merugu.* n. Brilliant lightning. See under క్రొ.

క్రొత్త or కొత్త *krotta.* [Tel.] adj. New. నూతనము, అపూర్వము. See under క్రొ.

క్రొత్తడము or క్రొత్తళము *krottaḍamu.* [Tel.] n. A battlement. కోటబురుజు.

క్రొత్తడి *krottaḍi.* [Tel.] n. A chaste woman. పతివ్రత.

క్రొత్తముట్టు *krotta-muṭṭu.* [Tel.] n. Fresh spun thread. క్రొత్తనూలు, వడికినినూలు.

క్రొన్నార *kron-nāra.* [Tel. క్రొత్త+నార.] n. New fibre.

క్రొబ్బరుపు *krob-barupu.* [Tel.] n. A new bed. క్రొత్తపరుపు. Bahulas. 5. 162.

క్రొమ్మించు *krom-minṭsu.* [Tel.] v. n. To excel. మించు. See under క్రొ.

క్రొమ్ము *krommu.* [Tel.] n. A shrub, *Lawsonia spinosa.* The nail-dye plant. గోరింట.

క్రొమ్ముడి *krom-muḍi.* [Tel.] n. A fresh knot. క్రొత్తముడి. See under క్రొ.

క్రొమ్మెరుగు *krom-merugu.* [Tel.] n. Fresh brilliancy. క్రొత్తమెరుగు. See under క్రొ.

క్రొవ్వాడి *krov-vāḍi*. [Tel.] adj. Re-set, newly sharpened, bright, keen. See or క్రొ.

క్రొవ్విడము *krovv-iḍamu*. [Tel. క్రొవ్వు+ ఇడము.] n. An evil deed. దుష్కార్యము. Freshness. See under క్రొ.

క్రొవ్విరి *krov-viri*. [Tel.] n. A young blossom. క్రొత్తపువ్వు. See under క్రొ.

క్రొవ్వు or క్రొవ్వు *krovvu*. [Tel.] v. n. To become fat or proud. మదించు. n. Fatness, pride. మదము. క్రొవ్వుగొను to become fat or proud. మదించు.

క్రొవ్వెద *krovveda*. [Tel.] n. Fair tresses (a poetical phrase for కొప్పు.)

క్రో krō

క్రోడము *krōḍamu*. [Skt.] n. The middle of the trunk. మధ్యభాగము. The lap ఒడి, తొడ. The breast రొమ్ము. A pig పంది. "వాధి పంకరుహాక్రోడమిరింద బ్రుండ మెదురెక్కడా." Amuk. i. 6. క్రోడపత్రము *krōḍa-patramu*. n. A supplement, codicil, post-script, leaf inserted. క్రోడాడు *krōḍ-āḍu*. v. t. To butt with horns. కొమ్ములతో పొడుచు. To dig up the earth with the snout ముట్టెతో నేలకెల్లగించు. To sprinkle dust on దుమ్మురెత్తి పైకి చల్లు, క్రోడాడు. క్రోడీకరణము *krōḍi-karaṇamu*. n. The act of putting things together into one. ఒకటిగా చేర్చు. Abridgment సంగ్రహము. Sifting; careful investigation; comparing, balancing facts. శోధించుట. క్రోడీకరించు *krōḍī-karintsu*. v. a. To abridge or shorten. To sift, prove, criticise. To take a general view of a subject.

క్రోతి *krōti*. [Tel.] n. A monkey. కోతి.

క్రోధము *krōdhamu*. [Skt.] n. Wrath, anger. కోపము. క్రోధనుడు *krōdhanuḍu*. n. A passionate man. కోపస్వభావముగలవాడు. క్రోధన an angry woman. Also, name of a year. క్రోధి *krōdhi*. n. A passionate person. కోపముగలవాడు. Also, name of a year. క్రోధించు to get angry కోపగిల్లు.

క్రోయు *krōyu*. [Tel.] v. t. To stretch out cunningly. నిమురుముగాచాచు. (భార. అర. vi.)

క్రోలగట్టు *krōla-gaṭṭu*. [Tel.] n. The ichneumon plant, which is supposed to furnish the mungoose with an antidote when bitten by a snake. (Ophioxylon) సర్పాక్షిచెట్టు.

క్రోలు *krōlu*. [Tel.] v. a. To enjoy. అను భవించు. To eat or to drink తిను, త్రాగు. To swallow మింగు. To take గ్రహించు. n. A tube. క్రోవి. క్రోలుము or క్రోల్చు *krōlutsu*. v. n. To cry. కూయు. To make a noise; to sound శబ్దించు. To cause to eat, drink or enjoy క్రోలజేయు.

క్రోవ *krōva*. [Tel.] n. A string of beads. సరము.

క్రోవి or క్రోవి *krōvi*. [Tel.] n. A hollow tube. గొట్టము. A gun, musket or pistol తుపాకి. A bottle బుడ్డి. An underground sluice భూమిలోపలి తూము. A crucible మూస. A flute. పిల్లనగ్రోవి. The plant termed *Galedupa arborea*. కానుగచెట్టు.

క్రోశము Same as కోసు.

క్రోష్టము or క్రోష్ఠము *krōshṭamu*. [Skt.] n. A plant named *Costus Arabicus*. కోష్టు కచ్చచెట్టు.

క్రోష్టువు *krōshṭuvu*. [Skt.] n. A fox. నక్క.

క్రౌ krau

క్రౌంచము *krauñchamu*. [Skt.] n. A kind of heron, *ardea jaculator*, described in Hindu literature as a type of connubial constancy. Name of a certain mountain and island.

క్రౌర్యము *krauryamu*. [Skt. from క్రూరము.] n. Cruelty. క్రూరభావము.

క్ల kla

క్లమము or క్లమథము *klamamu.* [Skt.] n. Exhaustion. శ్రమము, బడలిక.

క్లా klā

క్లాంతము *klāntamu.* [Skt.] adj. Languid, wearied. బడలిన. క్లాంతి *klānti.* n. Weariness. బడలిక.

క్లామ్యత్ *klāmyat.* [Skt.] adj. Wearied, exhausted. బడలిన. P. iv. 331.

క్లి kli

క్లిన్నము *klinnamu.* [Skt.] adj. Moist, wet. తడిసిన. నిత్యక్లిన్న ever moist.

క్లిష్టత *klishṭata.* [Skt.] n. Intricacy, a puzzle, inconsistency, hardship. క్లిష్టము adj. Intricate, hard, puzzling. పూర్వాపరవిరుద్ధమైన. Forced, unnatural, as a sense. Difficult. కఠినము.

క్లీ klī

క్లీబము *klībamu.* [Skt.] n. The neuter gender. నపుంసకము.

క్లు klu

క్లుప్తము *kluptamu.* [for Skt. క్లృప్తము.] adj. Brief, contracted, short. సంక్షిప్తము. Settled, determined. ఏర్పాటుచేయబడిన. "వారక్లుప్తముల్" A. v. 164. క్లుప్తాక్షరము *klupt-aksharamu.* n. A contraction or abbreviation.

క్లే klē

క్లేదము *klēdamu.* [Skt.] n. Wet. తడి.

క్లేశము *klēṣamu.* [Skt.] n. Affliction, distress. దుఃఖము.

క్వ kva

క్వ *kva.* [Skt.] adv. Where? ఎక్కడ? "క్వసూర్యప్రభవోవంశః క్వచాల్పవిషయామతిః" Where is the race descended from the Sun, and where is my weak wit? Where the comparison!

క్వచిత్తు or క్వచిత్ *kvachittu.* [Skt.] adv. Here and there, occasionally, sometimes, a little, some. క్వచిత్కము adj. Trifling. Petty, slight. క్వచిత్కముగా *kvachitkamu-gā.* adv. Barely, occasionally.

క్వణము or క్వణనము or క్వాణము *kvaṇamu.* [Skt.] n. A musical note, sound, tone. వీణాదులయొక్క మ్రోత.

క్ష ksha

క్ష *ksha.* The letter ksh. (The sound of this letter is said to vary between ksh and tsh and therefore all native authorities class it as the final letter of the alphabet.)

క్షంత *kshanta.* [Skt.] n. A patient man. ఓర్పరి.

క్షణద *kshaṇada.* [Skt.] n. Night. రాత్రి. P. i. 302. క్షణదుడు *kshaṇaduḍu.* n. An astrologer. జోస్యుడు.

క్షణము *kshaṇamu.* [Skt.] n. A moment, an instant. పదినిముషములు. A feast. అర క్షణము వాళ్లు, ఉత్సవము. M. I. i. 147. అర క్షణము half a second, for awhile. క్షణప్రభ *kshaṇa-prabha.* n. A momentary flash. మెరుపు. క్షణభంగురము *kshaṇa-bhanguramu.* adj. Frail, perishing, mortal. నశ్వరమైన. "క్షణభంగురములు కాంతలతాల్మల్" (KP. iii. 60.) woman's patience is but momentary. క్షణించు *kshaṇi-yintsu.* v. t. To stop for a moment. క్షణమాగు. To invite for meals. భోజనార్థముకోరు.

క్షతము *kshatamu.* [Skt.] adj. Beaten, hurt. గాయము కొందిన. n. A wound, a sore, a hurt. పుండు, గాయము. క్షతజము *kshatajamu.* (Lit. Produced from a wound.)

n. Blood. రక్తము, నెత్తురు. క్షతి kshati. n. A wound. గాయము. Mischief, harm, damage. చెరుపు, నాశము.

క్షత్త kshatta. [Skt. from క్షత్రియ.] n. A charioteer. సారథి.

క్షత్రియ kshatriya. [Skt. lit. One who strikes.] adj. Appertaining to the Kshatriya caste; lordly. రాచ. క్షత్రియ or క్షత్రియాణి n. A baroness: a woman of the military caste. క్షత్రియస్త్రీ, రాచెడి. క్షత్రియుడు kshatriyudu. n. A baron, one belonging to the military caste. రాచవాడు. Raghu Vamsam, ii. 48. క్షత్రకులము kshatra-kulamu. n. The knightly order, the regal or military caste. రాచజాతి. క్షత్రబంధువు kshatra-bandhuvu. n. One related to a Kshatriya (used as a term of reproach.) క్షత్రము kshatramu. n. The body. శరీరము.

క్షప kshapa. [Skt.] n. Night. రాత్రి. A. v. 36. క్షపాకరుడు kshapa-karudu. n. The moon. చంద్రుడు.

క్షపణుడు kshapanudu. [Skt.] n. A Buddhist. బౌద్ధమతస్థుడు.

క్షమ kshama. [Skt.] n. Patience. ఓర్పు. The earth భూమి. క్షమము kshamamu. adj. Able, adequate, fit, appropriate. సమర్థమైన, తగిన. ఈ గ్రంథము శోధనక్షమము this book will bear examination. క్షమాపణము kshamāpanamu. (for క్షమార్పణము.) n. Pacifying, softening. సమాధానపరచడము, ఉపశాంతిచేయుడము. క్షమించు or క్షమియించు kshamintsu. v. a. To put up with. ఓర్చు. To pardon మన్నించు. M. VII. v. 122. క్షముడు kshamudu. n. One who is able. శక్తుడు.

క్షయము kshayamu. [Skt.] n. Decrease, perishing, wasting, consumption. క్షీణించడము, తక్కువనశించడము, క్షయరోగము, అరుగుతెవులు. క్షయరోగము kshaya-rōgamu. n. Consumption. Phthisis. క్షయించు kshayintsu. v. n. To diminish, waste, wane. క్షీణించు, తగ్గు.

క్షరితము ksharitamu. [Skt.] adj. Oozed, dropped, flowing. కారిన, జారిన.

క్షా kshā

క్షాంతి kshānti. [Skt.] n. Endurance patience. సహనము, క్షమ, ఓర్పు.

క్షాత్రము or క్షాత్రధర్మము kshātramu. [Skt. from క్షత్రియ.] n. The duty of a military man. క్షత్రియధర్మము.

క్షామము kshāmamu. [Skt.] n. A famine, scarcity of provisions. కరువు. దుర్భిక్షము. adj. Slender, slim, emaciated. క్షీణమైన, కృశమైన, సన్నమైన.

క్షారకము kshārakamu. [Skt.] n. An unblown flower or a raw fruit. వికసించని మొగ్గ, పచ్చికాయ.

క్షారము kshāramu. [Skt.] n. Salt, saltness. ఉప్పు. ఉప్పన. Alkali, soda or potash. Hotness. కారము. Ashes భస్మము.

క్షాళనము or ప్రక్షాళనము kshālanamu. [Skt.] n. Cleansing, washing, rinsing. కడగడము. క్షాళితము kshālitamu. adj. Washed. కడగబడిన.

క్షి kshi

క్షితి kshiti. [Skt.] n. The earth; a house; an abode. భూమి, నివాసము. Loss, wane, destruction. నాశము, ప్రళయము N. i. 44. క్షితిదేవుడు kshiti-dēvudu. n. A Brahmin. బ్రాహ్మణుడు. Vish. ii. 218. క్షితిధరము kshiti-dharamu. n. A mountain. పర్వతము. N. D. ii. 505. క్షితిపతి kshiti-pati. n. A king. రాజు.

క్షిప్తము kshiptamu. [Skt.] adj. Sent, thrown, flung, cast, placed. Distracted, mad. ప్రేరితమైన, తోయబడిన, వేయబడ్డ, ఉంచబడ్డ, వెర్రి.

క్షిప్రము kshipramu. [Skt.] adj. Quick, rapid, swift. శీఘ్రమైన, త్వరితమైన, వడిగల. adv. Quickly, speedily. త్వరగా.

క్షీ kshī

క్షీణము *kshīṇamu.* [Skt.] adj. Wasted, emaciated, decayed, exhausted, slender, thin. క్షయించిన, హీనమైన, కృశించిన, నశించిన. మదక్షీణోనాగః an elephant which is emaciated in its rut. క్షీణే పుణ్యే మర్త్యలోకం విశంతి when their stock of merit [enjoyed by good men] is exhausted, they drop [in the shape of falling stars] again into mortal life. క్షీణపుణ్యులు those whose merit is exhausted. అక్షీణ undiminished. Vasu. i. 7. **క్షీణము** n. Decline, decay, decrease. క్షయము, తగ్గు. ఆయుఃక్షీణము the decline of one's age. ధనక్షీణము decrease of wealth. **క్షీణత** or **క్షీణత్వము** *kshīṇata.* n. Slenderness, thinness, emaciation, decay. కార్శ్యము, నాశము. **క్షీణించు** *kshīṇintsu.* v. n. To be wasted, emaciated, decayed. కృశించు, సన్నగిల్లు, నశించు, క్షీణమగు.

క్షీబుడు *kshībuḍu.* [Skt.] n. He who is intoxicated. సురాపానమత్తుడు. క్రొవ్వినవాడు.

క్షీరము *kshīramu.* [Skt.] n. Milk, పాలు. The milky sap of plants. జిల్లేడు మొదలైన వాటిపాలు. Water ఉదకము. క్షీరాన్నము rice and milk boiled together. పరమాన్నము. క్షీరోదకన్యాయము intimate union as milk and water mixed with each other. నీళ్లును పాలును కలిసినట్లు ఒక్కటిగా కలిసియుండు ధర్మము. వారు క్షీరోదకన్యాయముగా ఉన్నారు they are intimately associated or related. **క్షీరాబ్ధి** or **క్షీరసాగరము** *kshīr-abdhi.* n. The sea of milk పాలసముద్రము. క్షీరాబ్ధితనయ the goddess who sprung from this sea, i. e., Lakshmi, లక్ష్మి.

క్షు kshu

క్షుణ్ణము *kshuṇṇamu.* [Skt.] adj. Bruised, pounded. మథితమైన, మర్దితమైన, చూర్ణితమైన, Exercised, practised, skilful. అభ్యస్తమైన, నిపుణమైన.

క్షుతము *kshutamu.* [Skt.] n. Sneezing. తుమ్ము.

క్షుత్తు *kshuttu.* [Skt.] n. Hunger, appetite. ఆకలి. క్షుత్పిపాసలు hunger and thirst.

క్షుద్రము *kshudramu.* [Skt.] adj. Small, little, insignificant, mean, base, sordid. Petty, low, vulgar. సూక్ష్మమైన. అల్పమైన, తుచ్ఛమైన. క్షుద్రవిద్య an inferior art. క్షుద్రోపద్రవములు petty troubles. **క్షుద్రము** n. Slander, a tale, calumny. కొండెము. క్షుద్రములుచెప్పు or క్షుద్రాలుచెప్పు to tell tales. నామీద క్షుద్రములుచేయుచున్నాడు he is plotting against me. **క్షుద్రుడు** *kshudruḍu.* n. A mean wretch. అల్పుడు.

క్షుధ *kshudha.* [Skt.] n. Hunger, appetite. ఆకలి, క్షుత్తు. **క్షుధాతురుడు** *kshudhaturuḍu.* n. He who is hungry, famished or voracious. ఆకలిగొన్నవాడు. **క్షుధితము** *kshudhi-tamu.* adj. Hungry. ఆకలిగొన్న.

క్షుబ్ధము *kshubdhamu.* [Tel.] adj. Agitated, stirred, disturbed, affected. కలవరపడిన, కలతపెట్టబడిన, క్షోభితమైన, వ్యాకులముగల. క్షుబ్ధమానసుడు one who is troubled in mind.

క్షురప్రము *kshurapramu.* [Skt.] n. A crescent shaped arrow.

క్షురకము or **క్షురిక** *kshuramu.* [Skt.] n. A razor, మంగలకత్తి. A knife. **క్షురి** *kshuri.* n. A barber. మంగలవాడు.

క్షుల్లకము *kshullakamu.* [Skt.] adj. Little, small, low, vile, mean, insignificant. అల్పమైన, సూక్ష్మమైన, సన్నపాటి, క్షుద్రమైన, నీచమైన. **క్షుల్లకుడు** *kshullakuḍu.* n. A mean man, a wretch. అల్పుడు, నీచుడు.

క్షే kshē

క్షేత్రము *kshētramu.* [Skt.] n. A field. పంటభూమి. A place, a spot స్థలము. The body శరీరము. A wife భార్య. A sacred spot, a place of pilgrimage పుణ్యభూమి. Starvation పస్తు. (this meaning is peculiar to Telugu.) నిన్న కటికి క్షేత్రముగానుండినాడు he was starving all yesterday. క్షేత్రములు చేయు to starve. క్షేత్రగణితము kshētra-gaṇitamu. n. Mensuration. క్షేత్రజ్ఞుడు kshētragnyudu. n. The soul. ఆత్మ, జీవుడు. A husbandman. కాపువాడు. A. ii. 100. క్షేత్రపాలుడు kshētra-pāludu. n. An inferior manifestation or terrific form of Siva. భైరవుడు. "క్షేత్రపాలుర కుడికిచిరలారు చాలికేవులగములయ్యొసకలధికలు." A. ii. 55. క్షేత్రాజీవుడు a cultivator దున్నుకొని బ్రతుకువాడు.

క్షేపణము kshēpaṇamu. [Skt.] n. Encouragement. ప్రేరేపించుట. క్షేపణి kshēpaṇi. n. An oar, a net, a fishing net. ఓడనడిపే గడ, వల.

క్షేపము kshēpamu. [Skt.] n. Scattering, dismissing, rejection. విసర్జనము. Disrespect, contempt. తిరస్కారము, నింద. Delay, passing time. కాలక్షేపము. Encouraging ప్రేరణము. In astronomy, 'the complement, or sum added to make up a certain number. "A constant number to be added in certain computations to fit a given epoch." Warren, 363, A. v. 154.

క్షేమము kshēmamu. [Skt.] adj. Happy, well, in good health, prosperous, safe. కుశలమైన, శుభమైన, ఆరోగ్యమైన, శ్రేయస్కరమైన, భద్రమైన. n. Good fortune, welfare, happiness, health, safety. Bliss. A safe for money. శుభము, కుశలము, భద్రము, కలిగినది చెడకుండుట. యోగక్షేమములు విచారించుట to enquire after a person's welfare. క్షేమముగానుండు to be happy or well. క్షేమంకరుడు or క్షేమకారి kshēmankarudu. n. A benefactor మేలుచేయువాడు. క్షేమకరము kshēma-karamu. adj. Auspicious, salutary, beneficial, advantageous. శుభకరమైన, శ్రేయస్కరమైన. క్షేమతండులము kshēma-tandulamu. n. The rice provided for a journey. త్రోవకుకట్టిన బియ్యము. "ఎసటిపోతలుగాగ దెప్పించిన చిరంతనపుశాలి క్షేమతండులములు." A ii. 111.

క్షో kshō

క్షోణి kshōṇi. [Skt.] n. The earth. భూమి.

క్షోదము kshōdamu. [Skt.] n. Powder, any thing in a pulverized state. చూర్ణము, పొడుము, పొడి. "సత్తువ్యాఖండక్షోదవిలిప్తకర్ణికముల్." A. iv. 194.

క్షోభ ksōbha. [Skt.] n. Grief, sorrow, distress. వ్యాకులము, దుఃఖము. Agitation, కలత, shaking. కదలడము, అల్లాటము, అల్లోలకల్లోలము, చిత్తక్షోభము trouble of mind. N. ix. 35. క్షోభించు kshōbhintsu. v. n. To be distressed, to grieve or be sorrowful కలతపడు, దుఃఖించు. N. viii. 181. క్షోభితము kshōbhitamu. adj. Agitated. కలతపెట్టబడిన.

క్షౌ kshau

క్షౌద్రము kshaudramu. [Skt.] n. Honey. తేనె. Water జలము.

క్షౌమము kshaumamu. [Skt.] n. Linen cloth. నారచీర. చెట్టునారలతో చేసినవస్త్రము, దుకూలము, కలిపట్టువస్త్రము. Woven silk. A room on the top of the gate of a fort. కోటవాకిటిమీదియిల్లు. H. iii. 85. Vasu. iii. 224.

క్షౌరము kshauramu. [Skt.] n. Shaving. ముండనము, మంగలిపని. క్షౌరకుడు kshaurakudu. n. A barber. మంగలవాడు, మంగలి.

క్ష్మా kshma

క్ష్మా kshmā. [Skt.] n. The earth. భూమి. క్ష్మాజము kshmā-jamu. n. A tree. వృక్షము. క్ష్మాధరము kshmā-dharamu. n. A mountain. పర్వతము. క్ష్మాపతి kshmā-pati. n. A king. రాజు. క్ష్మాభృత్తు kshmā-bhruttu. n. A king, a prince. A mountain. రాజు, పర్వతము. క్ష్మావరుడు kshmā-varudu. n. A king. రాజు. G. v. 60. క్ష్మాసురుడు kshmā-surudu. n. A Brahmin. బ్రాహ్మణుడు. UR. 6. 448.

క్ష్వే kshvē

క్ష్వేడ, క్ష్వేడితము or క్ష్వేళితము kshvēḍa. [Skt.] n. The roaring of a lion. A war whoop, a battle cry. సింహనాదము, రణమున దలి పిలుపు. T. v. 25.

క్ష్వేడము or క్ష్వేళము kshvēḍamu. [Skt.] n. Venom, poison. విషము. క్ష్వేళహారమైన counteracting poison. క్ష్వేళి kshvēḷi. n. A serpent. పాము.

ఖ kha

ఖ The letter kh. The secondary or subjunct form is also ఖ. n. The sky. ఆకాశము. See ఖగము.

ఖంగు or కంగు khangu. [Anuk.] n. Tinkling. లోహములు కొట్టుకొన్నప్పుడు కలుగు ధ్వని. ఖంగుమను or కంగుమను khangu-m-anu. v. n. To sound, resound as a bell.

ఖంజము khanjamu. [Skt.] adj. Lame, crippled, limping. కుంటి.

ఖంజనము khanjanamu. [Skt.] n. A wagtail. కాటుకపిట్ట.

ఖంజరి khanjari. [Skt.] n. A kind of drum. వాద్యవిశేషము. భాను. iv.

ఖంజరీటము khanjarīṭamu. [Skt.] n. A wagtail.

ఖండ khanḍa. [Skt.] n. A paragraph in the Vedas on marriage ceremonies. గర్భాధానాదివిధిప్రతిపాదకగ్రంథము. A vi. 89.

ఖండనము khanḍanamu. [Skt. from ఖడ్=to cut.] n. Breaking, dividing, cutting, reducing to pieces. నరుకుట. Slaying, smiting, destroying, annihilating. Refuting. Rebellion, opposition. Criticism. ఖండనుడు khanḍanuḍu. n. A slayer, a smiter. ఖండము khanḍamu. n. A piece, part, fragment, portion. A chapter, a section. A country, a district, a division. ఉత్తరఖండము the Northern Division. ఖండసంచిత్తు (L. XIII. 32.) శివేశ్వరుడు, శివపరమాత్ముడు. ఖండశర్కర khanḍa-ṣarkara. n. Lump sugar. ఖండశశి khanḍa-ṣaṣi. n. The moon when less than full: the half moon or crescent. ఖండా khanḍā. n. A cross handled dagger. జంతాతికత్తి, పెద్దకత్తి. In poetry కుసుమఖండుడు he whose dagger is a blossom, i. e., the god of love. ఖండి khanḍi. n. The measure called a Kandy. పుట్టి. ఖండించు khanḍintsu. v. t. To cut to pieces, sever, divide, take to pieces, dissect. To tear or break off. To reject, confute, refute. To criticise, to test. To decide, settle, determine. ఖండింపు khanḍimpu. n. A settlement, a bargain. ఖండింపుచేయు to settle a bargain, to bargain, to settle. ఖండిక or ఖండ్రిక khanḍika. n. A grange or farm house. A lot of land, or portion of a village, granted free of rent or on a favourable lease. ఖండితము khanḍitamu. adj. Severed, cut, divided. నరకబడిన. Decided, certain, strict. Absolute, downright. ఖండితముగా decidedly, positively, strictly. ఖండితోత్తరము a decisive answer. ఖండీభూతము khanḍī-bhūtamu. adj. Dashed to pieces. M. VII. iv. 308. ఖండేందుడు khanḍēnduḍu. n. The half moon or crescent. ఖండశశి. ఖండేందుధరుడు he who wears a crescent as his crest, i. e., Siva.

ఖంబు or కంబు khambu. [Skt.] n. The sky. ఆకాశము. The heavens. స్వర్గము.

ఖగము khagamu. [Skt. ఖ+గ=that which goes on the sky.] n. A bird. An arrow. ఖగేశ్వరుడు khagēṣvaruḍu. n. Lit. the Lord of birds, i. e., the eagle. గరుత్మంతుడు.

ఖచరము khacharamu. [Skt. ఖ=sky, and చర moving.] n. The air, a cloud, a bird, &c. ఖచరుడు. khacharuḍu. n. A demigod. దేవుడు. The sun. సూర్యుడు.

ఖచించు or ఖచియించు khachintsu. [Skt.] v. a. To set precious stones. చెక్కు, పొదుగు.

"క॥ ఖచియించినవజ్రంబుల
రుచులనుబోలుపారు సీవురులు బెరయుంగన్."
భార. ఉద్యో. iv.

ఖచితము *khachitamu.* adj. Inlaid, set. చెక్కబడిన.

ఖజానా *khajāna.* [H.] n. A treasury. ఖజాంజీ or ఖజానావాడు *khajānji.* n. A treasurer.

ఖట్వ *khatva.* [Skt.] n. A bedstead, cot or couch. మంచము.

ఖడ్గము *khadgamu.* [Skt.] n. A sword or scimitar: a rhinoceros or its horn. ఖడ్గపాత్రము *khadga-pātramu.* n. A bracelet made of horn and gold. ఖడ్గబంధము *khadga-bandhamu.* n. An arrangement of words in verse forming the shape of a sword. ఖడ్గమృగము *khadga-mrigamu.* n. The rhinoceros. ఖడ్గవాదము *khadga-vādamu.* n. Violence: force of arms: a combat: a duel.

ఖతమాలము *kha-tamālamu.* [Skt. ఖ=sky.] n. Smoke. పొగ. A cloud మబ్బు.

ఖతలము *kha-talamu.* [Skt. ఖ+తలము place] n. The sky. M. XII. i. 32.

ఖతిలకము *kha-tilakamu.* [Skt. ఖ= sky, and తిలకము an ornament.] n. The sun.

ఖదిరము *khadiramu.* [Skt.] n. The tree called *Acacia catechu.* (E. P.) దంతధావనము, చండ్ర, అంతిరతామర, ముదుగుతామర. See చండ్ర.

ఖడ్డి *khaddi.* [Tel.] n. Strength, might. బలము.

"స్రగ్ధర. ఖడ్డింజెందాడు,మ్రాకుల్
కవ్వుగిట్టికాలదుల్
కత్తినాక్కొక్కఘాతన్."
స్వా. iv.

ఖద్యోతము *kha-dyōtamu.* [Skt. ఖ= sky and ద్యోతము a light] n. A firefly. మిడుగురుపురుగు. ఖద్యోతుడు *kha-dyōtudu.* n. The sun.

ఖనకుడు *khanakudu.* [Skt. ఖన్=to dig.] n. One who digs. ఖని *khani.* n. A mine, a quarry. గని. ఖనిత్రము *khanitramu.* n. A pickaxe. A spade or hoe. గడ్డపార, పార.

ఖపురము *khapuramu.* [Skt.] n. The areca nut tree. పోకచెట్టు.

ఖరము *kharamu.* [Skt.] n. An ass. గాడిద. Heat. వేడిమి. Scarcity. Name of a year. adj. Hot, sharp, pungent, cruel, harsh. వేడిగల, వాడిగల. (Figuratively) Dear, scarce. ఖరకరుడు *khara-karudu.* n. The sun. ఖరణసుడు *kharanasudu.* (ఖర+నాసిక.) adj. Sharp nosed, having an aquiline nose. గద్దముక్కువాడు, వాడిముక్కువాడు.

ఖరాగా *kharā-gā.* [H.] adj. Exactly, accurately.

ఖరారము *kharāramu.* [Skt.] n. A currycomb. గుర్రపుగోరపము.

ఖరారా or ఖరారు *kharāra.* [H.] n. An agreement. ఒడంబడిక.

ఖరీఖలము *kharī-khalamu.* [Skt.] n. Gambling. క్రీడాద్యూతము, పందెమువేసి ఆడే ద్యూతము.

ఖరీదు or కరీదు *kharīdu.* [H.] n. Price. వెల.

ఖరుడు *kharudu.* [Skt.] n. A certain demon. ఒకరాక్షసుడు. A fearful being భయంకరుడు.

ఖర్చు or కర్చు *khartsu.* [H.] n. Expense. వ్యయము.

ఖర్జువు *kharjuvu.* [Skt.] n. The itch, any cutaneous eruption. దురద.

ఖర్జూరము *kharjūramu.* [Skt.] n. The marshy date tree. పేరీతచెట్టు, ఖర్జూరపు చెట్టు. Silver వెండి. ఖర్జూరములు (A. i. 75.) A sort of grain. ఖర్జూరనగము "the silver mountain," an epithet of Kailasa. Dasav. iii. 149.

ఖర్పరము *kharparamu.* [Skt.] n. The skull: the cranium. కపాలము, తలపుర్రె; తలచిప్పయెముక.

ఖర్వటము kharvaṭamu. [Skt.] n. A hamlet or village. A market town, a country town. పల్లె, పరిగణాకు ముఖ్యగ్రామము.

ఖర్వము kharvamu. [Skt.] adj. Of little size or stature. Short, dwarfish. పొట్టి. n. A certain very large number. (See Alberuni's India.) సంఖ్యావిశేషము.

ఖలత khalata. [Skt.] n. Wickedness, villainy, filthiness.

ఖలము khalamu. [Skt.] n. A thrashing floor. వంటకళ్లము. adj. Base, cruel, mischievous. నీచము, అధమము, క్రూరము.

ఖలీనము or ఖలినిము khalīnamu. [Skt.] n. A bridle, a bit. గుర్రపు కళ్లెము. "అశ్వా బద్ధఖలీనాశ్వవచుస్తై" Parij. iv. 72.

ఖలు khalu. [Skt.] adv. Verily, surely.

ఖలుడు khaluḍu. [Skt.] n. A vile wretch, a sinner. నీచుడు.

ఖల్వటకము khalvaṭakamu. [Skt.] n. A severe cough. Vish. P. ii. 143.

ఖల్వాటుడు khalvāṭuḍu. [Skt.] n. A bald headed man. బట్టతలవాడు.

ఖలూరిక khalūrika. [Skt.] n. A parade, a place for military exercise. కరడీవాలు, సాము కూటము. A. ii. 48.

ఖసీచేయు khasi-chēyu. [H.] n. To geld, cut, or emasculate. ఖసిచేసినగుర్రము a gelding.

ఖా khā

ఖాండవము khānḍavamu. [Skt.] n. The name of a grove sacred to Indra. ఇంద్రుని యొక్క ఒకానొకవనము.

ఖాణము khāṇamu. [Tel.] n. Food for horses. దాణా. Provender, fodder. Grass. గ్రాసము, కసువు. "కండచేక్కురల ఖాణంబు మనో యుంచరో." Ila. iii. 79. "కోటకేసర కపుడుపాటించిదిగ్గియు ఖాణంబు గొ లు చు ను." M. XII. ii. 303. "మునుపిడ్డగ్రైవబలంబున జని యుంచినవిరుపల సంభూతంబై యొనరినఖాణము మేసెను." M. VII. 170.

ఖాతము khātamu. [Skt. ఖన్=to dig.] n. A hollow, cavern, pit. A pond కొలను. దేవఖాతము a natural cavern, as being formed by God. బంగాళాఖాతము the bay of Bengal. ఖాతకుడు khātakuḍu. n. A digger. త్రవ్వువాడు.

ఖాదకుడు khādakuḍu. [Skt.] n. One who eats. తినువాడు. ఖాదనము khādanamu. n. Eating. తినుట. Food తిండి. ఖాదితము khāditamu. adj. Eaten. తినబడిన. ఖాద్యము khādyamu. adj. Eatable, edible. n. Viands, food, victuals. భక్ష్యము, తినదగిన పదము.

ఖామందు or కామందు khāmandu. [H.] n. An owner, a master. యజమానుడు.

ఖామముగా khāmamu-gā. [H. for ఖాయము గా.] adv. Positively, without fail.

ఖాయము khāyamu. [H.] n. Settled, fixed, permanent.

ఖాయిదా khāyidā. [H.] n. Safety. భద్రము. ఖాయిదాచేయు to make secure, to take care of.

ఖాళీ or కాళీ khālī. [H.] adj. Empty, vacant. n. A vacancy.

ఖాసా or కాసా khāsa. [H.] n. A servant. దాసుడు. adj. Own, one's own. స్వంతము.

ఖి khi

ఖిన్నము khinnamu. [Skt.] adj. Distressed, in pain, troubled, dejected. ఖేదముపొందిన. ఖిన్నత్వము khinnatvamu. n. Dejection. ఖేదము.

ఖిలము khilamu. [Skt.] adj. Waste or unploughed. దున్నని. Dilapidated, ruined. చెడిన. ఖిలపడు khila-paḍu. v. n. To be ruined or laid waste. ఖిలీభవించు khilībhavintsu. v. n. To be ruined. చెడు. ఖిలీభూతము khilī-bhūtamu. adj. Dilapidated, ruined.

ఖిల్లా khilla. [H.] n. A hill fort.

ఖు khu

ఖుద్దున *khuddu-na*. [H.] adv. In person. Personally. Without an intermediator.

ఖురణసుడు *khura-ṇasuḍu*. [Skt. ఖుర+నాసిక.] n. One who has a big nose. బుఱ్ఱముక్కుగలవాడు.

ఖురము *khuramu*. [Skt.] n. A hoof. గుఱ్ఱపుడెక్క, గొరిజ.

ఖురళి or ఖురళిక *khurali*. [Skt.] n. Military exercise: సాము. A parade, a place for evolutions. గరడీసాల. A. iv. 36.

ఖుర్దనము *khurdanamu*. [Skt.] n. Sport, play. క్రీడ, ఆట.

ఖులాసా or కులాసా *khulasa*. [H.] n. Happiness, comfort, felicity. సౌఖ్యము.

ఖుషీ or కుషీ *khushi*. [H.] n. Pleasure, delight. ఇష్టము.

ఖే khē

ఖేచరము *khē-charamu*. [Skt. ఖ=sky.] adj. Aerial, sky-going (a bird, an arrow, &c.) ఖేచరుడు *khē-charuḍu*. n. A demigod. ఆకాశమున సంచరించువాడు.

ఖేటము or ఖేటకము *khēṭamu*. [Skt.] n. A shield. డాలువారు. A suburb. పేట, పంటకాపులుండుపల్లె or వర్తకులుండే పేట.

ఖేదము *khēdamu*. [Skt.] n. Sorrow, grief, regret. శోకము. ఖేదకరము *khēda-karamu*. adj. Grievous. ఖేదించు *khēdintsu*. v. a. To grieve, to be afflicted, to lament, to regret. ఖేదితము *khēditamu*. adj. Afflicted, distressed, pained.

ఖేయము *khēyamu*. [Skt.] n. A ditch, trench or moat. అగడ్త.

ఖేల or ఖేలనము *khēla*. [Skt.] n. Sport, play, pastime. క్రీడ, ఆట. ఖేలి *khēli*. n. A player. ఆత్మఖేలి he who plays in the soul, i. e., God.

ఖ్యా khyā

ఖ్యాతి *khyati*. [Skt.] n. Reputation, renown, fame, celebrity, notoriety. ప్రసిద్ధి, కీర్తి. ఖ్యాతము or ఖ్యాతమైన *khyatamu*. adj. Known, celebrated, famous, notorious. వాసికెక్కిన.

గ ga

గ *ga*. [Tel. & Skt. formed from the shape of the legs in walking.] The letter G as in *great*. Some Telugu words at pleasure change the letter G into V. Thus పగలు or పవలు, తీగ or తీవ. So in English, thus: *guile* and *wile*; *gate* and *way*; *guard* and *ward*; *guise*, and *wise*.

గ or గా *ga*. The adverbial sign, for కాక, as తిన్నగా correctly, slowly, gently. వంకర గా crookedly. It is added to the *Infinitive in A*, as చేయుగ or చేయుగా, చూడగ. It is also added to nouns to give them an adverbial force. పువ్వములను నీకు సాయకంబులుగ జేసె he provided thee with flowers for arrows. నల్లగనున్నది it is black. గ stands for గజము a yard. In prosody గ denotes గురువు a long syllable, and గా or గగము is a spondee. గ also stands for గద్య prose. In music గ is the note called *mi* in European music.

గంగ *ganga*. [Skt. lit. That which goes.] n. The river Ganges. Water in general. ఈబావిగంగ మంచిది the water of this well is sweet. నేను వానియింట్లో కొంచెముగంగనైనా తాగలేదు I did not take so much as a draught of water in his house. గోదావరి గంగ the waters of the Godavery. ఆకాశ గంగ the river of heaven, మందాకిని. పాతాళగంగ the river of the nether world, భోగవతి. గంగోదకము *gang-ōdakamu*. n. Holy water from the Ganges. [Tel.] adj. Large పెద్ద. గంగరావి the large Pepul tree. Venerable పూజ్యము. గంగగోవు a venerable cow

పంచగంగలు the five great rivers, i. e., the Cauvery, the Tungabhadra, the Krishna, the Godavery and the Ganges. గంగచిప్ప *ganga-chippa*. n. A large white cockle-shell. గంగడోలు *ganga-ḍōlu*. n. The dewlap of cows and other animals.

గంగమయిల *ganga-mayila*. [Tel.] adj. Dun, dark, grizzled. నలుపుతెలుపుకలిసిన(అవు.)

గంగమ్మ *gangamma*. [Skt.] n. The name of a village goddess.

గంగరావి *ganga-ravi*. [Tel.] n. A tree called *Hibiscus Populneus*. The leaf has a short tail and the wood is worthless. (Ainslie. ii. 333.)

గంగరేగు *ganga-rēgu*. [Tel.] n. A species of jujube tree with bright yellow fruit. *Zizyphus jujuba*. పెద్దరేగు.

గంగవాడిజల్లులు *ganga-vāḍi-jallulu*. [Tel.] n. An ornament on a horse's breast.

గంగాజలములు *ganga-jalamulu*. [Skt.] n. A kind of grain. శబ. i.

గంగాధరుడు *ganga-dharuḍu*. [Skt.] n. A title of Siva, because the river Ganges was supported on his head.

గంగానమ్మ or **గంగారమ్మ** *gangān-amma*. [Tel.] n. The name of a certain village goddess, wife to the god పోతురాజు.

గంగాళచిప్ప *gangāḷa-chippa*. [Tel.] n. A ribbed cockle-shell. *Pholas costata*.

గంగాళము *gangāḷamu*. [Tel.] n. A large, wide mouthed metal jar for holding water.

గంగి *gangi*. [Tel.] adj. Venerable. పూజ్యము. (భాగ. ix.) గంగిగోవు a cow of an excellent breed, an excellent cow.

"గంగిగోవుపాలు గంటెడైననుచాలు,
కడవెడైననేమి ఖరముపాలు;
భక్తికలుగుకూడు పట్టెడైననుచాలు."
Vēma. i. 103.

గంగిరెద్దు or **గంగెద్దు** *gangi-r-eddu*. n. A bull that is dressed with bells, &c., and taught to dance. గంగెద్దుచేప *gangeddu-chēpa*. n. A star-fish.

గంగుడుచెట్టు *ganguḍu-cheṭṭu*. [Tel.] n. A tree called *Caesaria Tomentosa*. (Rox. ii. 421.)

గంజ or **గంజాదిలయము** *ganja*. [Skt.] n. A tavern. కల్లుపెట్టు ఇల్లు. P. i. 194.

గంజె *ganza*. [Tel.] n. Arable land. కృషికి యోగ్యమైనభూమి.

గంజాయి *ganzāyi*. [Tel.] n. The drug called Gânja or bhang. గంజాయిచెట్టు *ganzāyi-cheṭṭu*. n. The Indian hemp plant, *cannabis sativa*. (Watts.)

"శ్లో. గంజాయితినెనేమి కల్లుత్రావెనేమి
యుంజకధనమిచ్చు నతడె మెచ్చు."
పాంచా. 2. భా.

గంజి *ganji*. [Tel.] n. Gruel, rice-water. అన్నరసము. A trifling meal or subsistence. గంజితాగడమునకుపోతిని I went to get something to eat. గంజిపెట్టినబట్ట starched linen. గంజిబుగ్గ or గంజిపొక్కు a sore, పొక్కు, పొక్కు. గంజితోరక the cream that collects on rice-water. గంజిమీద మీగడ.

గంట *ganta*. [Tel.] n. A stub, a stump of corn stalks. కడ్డిదుబ్బు. పైరు బాగా గంట కట్టుకొనివస్తున్నది the crop thrives well. గంటపిట్ట *ganṭa-piṭṭa*. n. The Grass Warbler, *Chaetornis locustelloides*. (F. B. I.)

గంట *ganṭa*. [Tel.] n. A bell, a gong. An hour. గంటలకడ a staff hung with bells, used in bands or processions. గంటలమ్మ *ganṭal-amma*. n. Name of one of the village goddesses. గంటవేట *ganṭa-vēṭa*. n. Hunting in which lights and low-bells are used. Bat-fowling. గంటసాల *ganṭa-sāla*. n. A tower in which bells are hung. A belfry.

గంటము or **ఘంటము** *ganṭamu*. [Tel.] n. An iron style for writing on palm leaves.

గంటి *ganṭi*. [Tel.] n. A hole or bore (in the ear for an earring). An interstice, or ward of a key. A wound, sore, hurt. గాయము, క్షతి. Sorrow దుఃఖము. plu. గంట్లు.

గంటిపడు *ganṭi-paḍu.* v. n. To be wounded, hurt, or bruised. గంటు *ganṭu.* v. t. To wound, to hurt గాయముచేయు. n. A depression. A joint గనుపు. A knot ముడి; a knot of hair వెంట్రుకలముడి. గంటుపెట్టు *ganṭu-peṭṭu.* v. n. To put on an angry face, to hate. కోపము చే మొగముముడుచుకొను. గంట్లాడు *ganṭlāḍu* v. n. To struggle or wrestle.

గంటుబారంగి *ganṭu-bārangi.* [Tel.] n. A medicinal root, *Siphonanthus Indica.* భార్గి, బ్రాహ్మణయష్టిక.

గంటె *ganṭe.* [Tel.] n. A spoon. గరిటె. A kind of grain, called the little millet, *Holcus spicatus.* సజ్జలు. గంటెపిట్ట or పరిగంటిపిట్ట *ganṭe-piṭṭa.* n. A species of laughing thrush. Jerdon, No. 88.

గంట్లము *ganṭlamu.* [Tel.] n. A wish or hope entertained by a pregnant woman. గర్భిణిమొక్కుకోరిక. (య. iv.)

గండ *ganḍa.* [Tel.] n. A vow. మ్రొక్కుబడి. గండరోలు hair grown on the head under a vow. గండదీపము a lamp offered as a vow to a god; a lamp made of flour paste with ghee placed in a brazen dish, and carried upon the head round a temple, in fulfilment of a vow after recovery from sickness, &c. See *Reeve.*

గండ *ganḍa.* [Tel. and Kan.] n. A male. జగదొబ్బుడగండా a mighty hero. adj. Large. పెద్ద. గండకత్తెర *ganḍa-kattera.* n. Large shears. The shears of destiny. Chenn. iv. 222. KP. iii. 115. (Metaphorically) difficulty, distress, straits, a plague. వాని పెండ్లాము వానికి గండకత్తెరగానున్నది his wife is a perfect plague to him. గండగొడ్డలి *ganḍa-goḍḍali.* n. A bill hook: a sort of battle-axe. పరశువు. గండమృగము *ganḍa-mṛigamu.* n. The rhinoceros. BD. iii. 2170.

గండంగి *ganḍangi.* [Tel.] n. A large black monkey. The Madras Langur, *Semnopithicus priamus.* (F. B. I.) కొండముచ్చు.

గండకము *ganḍakamu.* [Skt.] n. A rhinoceros. ఖడ్గమృగము.

గండడు *ganḍaḍu.* [Tel.] n. A strong man: a brave man. గండరగండడు the bravest of the brave శూరులకెల్లశూరుడు. గండపెండారము *ganḍa-penḍāramu.* (Kan.) n. A badge of honour, bestowed on a hero, worn as a garter on one leg. (R. iv. 104.) బిరుదుఅందె, శూరులు బిరుదుగా కాలి యందు ధరించే అందె.

గండభేరుండము *ganḍa-bhēruṇḍamu.* [Skt.] n. A griphon, a harpy, a two headed eagle.

గండమాల *ganḍa-māla.* [Skt.] n. Scrofula or swelling of the glands about the neck; the mumps; a goitre, a wen on the throat. కుత్తుకమీదివ్రణము.

గండము *ganḍamu.* [Skt.] n. The side of the head. చెక్కిలి. An elephant's temple. ఏనుగుచెక్కిలి. The baleful influence of a star. గ్రహచారము. An evil event, a narrow escape. గొప్పఆపాయము. దినగండము నూరేండ్లాయుష్షు to live long in daily peril of ruin. నాకు దినగండముగా జరుగుచున్నది I am daily living from hand to mouth. గండము గడిచి పిండము బయలుపడ్డది the affair is over and this is the result. Lit. the trouble is over, the child is born. అతడు తండ్రి గండమునకు పుట్టినాడు he was born to be the cause of his father's ruin. గండపాళి *ganḍa-pāḷi.* n. The temple or side of the head. గండమండలము *ganḍa-manḍalamu.* n. The temples of the head.

గండరించు *ganḍarinṭsu.* [Tel.] v. n. To issue, spring, be produced. ఆవిర్భవించు, పుట్టు. v. a. To produce or cause to be born. పుట్టించు.

గండరాలు *ganḍarālu.* [Tel.] n. Fragments, bits. తునకలు.

గండరువు *gandaruvu.* [Tel.] n. A mould. అచ్చు, ప్రతిమగాచేయు అచ్చుపడి.

గండవడము *ganḍa-vaḍamu.* [Tel.] n. A screen. తెర. BD. iii. 103.

గండశిల or గండశైలము *gandaṣila*. [Skt.] n. A boulder, a large stone or fragment of rock. పెద్దరాయి.

గండారు *gandaru*. [Tel.] n. A prison house. చెరసాల. "పత్తేగండార్లలో" (ము. iv.)

గండాలి *gandali*. [Tel.] n. A kind of grass creeper. పిల్లగరిక.

గండి or గండిక *gandi*. [Tel.] n. A hole, a chink, a breach, an orifice, an opening, a gap. రంధ్రము. A chasm, a strait, a fissure కొండ. A pass, or gorge between hills. A lane సందు. గండిదొంగ a housebreaker కన్నపుదొంగ.

గండు *gandu*. [Tel.] n. Bravery. పౌరుషము. Strength బలము. adj. Brave, heroic, great, large, stout. Male. మగ. గండుమూతి a grim face. గండీగ a large fly. గండుచీమ the large black ant. గండుచేప the carp, which is proverbial for vigour and activity. గండుమీలవంటి చికిలి కన్నులు eyes that glance bright like dolphins. గండుపిల్లి a tom cat. పిల్లికూన గండు బారెను the young kitten turned into a tom cat. గండు among tradesmen is a cant word for వరహా a pagoda. Thus in arithmetic గం is one pagoda; గగం౦౦౦ one thousand pagodas. గండడగు *ganḍadagu*. [గండు+అడగు.] v. n. To lose heart or courage పరాక్రమహీనుడగు. (పా. ఈ. ii.) To die చచ్చు. (Vasu. iv.) గండాడు *ganḍāḍu*. [గండు+ఆడు.] v. n. To have sexual intercourse. రమించు. గండుకరణము *gandu-karaṇamu*. n. The bird called the Green Barbet, *Thereiceryx Zeylonicus* (F. B. I.) (Jerdon's Catal. No. 217.) గండుడు *ganḍuḍu*. [Skt.] n. A courageous man, a hero. శూరుడు.

గండూపదము *ganḍū-padamu*. [Skt.] n. A male prawn. గండూపది a female prawn.

గండూషము *ganḍūshamu*. [Skt.] n. Rinsing the mouth. పుక్కిలింత. A mouthful of water for rinsing. గండూషించు to rinse the mouth. పుక్కిలించు.

గండె *gande*. [Tel.] n. A fish. చేప.

గండోలము *gandōlamu*. [Tel.] n. A kind of fish. కుమ్మెలమీను.

గండ్ర *gandra*. [Tel.] n. The species of grass called *Panicum Uliginosum*. Rox. I. 308. A piece, a fragment, తునక. See గండరించు. గండ్ర adj. Large పెద్ద. గండ్రచీమ a large black ant. n. A harsh word పరుషవచనము. A wicked man దుష్టుడు. గండ్రించు *gandrinṭsu*. v. t. To cut to pieces. ఖండించు. గండ్రిక *gandrika*. n. A piece. తునక.

గంత *ganta*. [Skt.] adj. One who goes. పోవువాడు. గంతవ్యుడు *gantavyuḍu*. adj. One who is fit to go. పోదగినవాడు.

గంత *ganta*. [Tel.] n. A packsaddle, a quilt of motley patchwork. బొంత. గంతకోడు bridal presents, being of all kinds, a medley. A. vi. 181. R. iv. 109. A miscellany, a pack, a set of things. కండ్లగంతకట్టు to blindfold. గంతావు *gant-āvu*. n. A cow that carries a packsaddle.

గంతు *gantu*. [Tel.] n. A jump, leap, vault; a step in dancing. దుముకు. గంతుకొను *gantu-konu*. v. n. To leap. దుముకు. To die చచ్చు.

గంత్రి *gantri*. [Skt.] n. A carriage. గాడీ బండి.

గందము *gandamu*. [from Skt. గంధము.] n. Sandal wood. చందనము. గందపుకొయ్య a cross piece of wood fixed on to the back of a door తలుపుమీద నమర్చిన అడ్డుకొయ్య. (A. ii. 9.) or a streak of sandal paste on a door or a wall. గందపుకొండ *gandapu-konda*. n. The fragrant hill, called Malaya. మలయపర్వతము. గందపుమ్రాను the sandal wood tree. గందపొడి sandal wood powder. గంధద్రవ్యములుచేర్చినపొడి.

గందరగోళము *gandara-gōlamu*. [Tel.] n. Confusion. గందరగోళించు or గందరగోళముచేయు *gandara-gōlinṭsu*. v. n. To confuse, to trouble.

గంధకము *gandhakamu*. [Skt.] n. Sulphur, brimstone. గంధకపుకడ్డి a stick of brimstone. గంధకద్రావకము Sulphuric acid, vitriol.

గంధము *gandhamu*. [Skt.] n. Smell, odour. వాసన. శ్రీగంధము or మంచిగంధము sandal wood. రక్తగంధము red sandal wood. కట్టు వస్త్రంబుల గంధంబునలది smearing his clothes with sandal. **గంధకారి** *gandha-kari*. n. A perfumer. బుక్కాపువాడు. A. iv. 36. **గంధగజము** *gandha-gajamu*. n. A proud and fierce elephant or one in rut. మదపు టేనుగు. **గంధతరువు** *gandha-taruvu*. n. The sandal tree. **గంధపట్టెలు** See గంధ పట్టెలు. **గంధపుకొండ** *gandha-pu-konda*. n. A name for Mount Malaya. **గంధపొడి** *gandha-podi*. n. Perfume powder. గంధ పొడి అంగడి a perfumer's shop. **గంధఫలి** *gandha-phali*. n. The Marigold. సంపెంగి. (q. v.) A. v. 139. **గంధమాదనము** *gandha-madanamu*. n. Name of a certain hill. **గంధమార్జాలము** or **గంధమృగము** *gandha-marjalamu*. n. The civet cat. పునుగు పిల్లి. **గంధరసము** *gandha-rasamu*. n. Myrrh బోళము. **గంధరాజము** *gandha-rajamu*. n. Perfume. Civet జవ్వాది. A. iv. 174. **గంధవాహుడు** *gandha-vahudu*. n. The scent bearer, i.e., the air. **గంధ సారము** *gandha-saramu*. n. Sandal. చందనము. **గంధేభము** *gandhe-bhamu*. n. An elephant in rut. **గంధోత్తమము** *gandhottamamu*. n. Wine. మద్యము. Dasav. IX. 149.

గంధర్వము *gandharvamu*. [Skt. from 'Kandahar' which derives its name from Iskander, i. e., Alexander (the Great.) See *Mahaffy*.] n. A mythological animal. మృగవిశేషము. A horse from Gandhāra or Kandahar, a Kābuli horse. **గంధర్వుడు** *gandharvudu*. n. A mythological being, one of the singers and musicians in the Hindu Olympus. గంధర్వునివంటివాడు a very handsome fellow.

గంధిలము *gandhilamu*. [Skt.] n. The polecat or some stinking creature like the stoat. A large or old jackal నక్క, వృద్ధజంబుకము. R. ii. 24. vii. 88.

గంప *gampa*. [Tel.] n. A basket. గంపెడుపిల్లలు a swarm of children. గంపెడుబొంకులు a pack of lies. **గంపపులుగు** *gampa-pulugu*. (So called because sold in baskets.) n. A wild cock or jungle fowl. *Phasianus Gallus*.

గంబుర, **గంబురా**, **గంబురము** or **గంబూరము** *gambura*. [Tel.] n. Camphor. కర్పూరము.

గంభీరము *gambhiramu*. [Skt.] adj. Deep, profound, secret. లోతుగల. Serious, fearful భయంకరమైన. **గంభీరవేది** *gambhira-vedi*. n. A very intoxicated or restive elephant.

గగ or **గగము** See under. గ.

గగనము *gaganamu* [Skt.] n. The sky, firmament, the ether. The empyrean. adj. Impossible, puzzling. దుర్లభము. ఇదేమిగగనము what great marvel is this? గగనకుసుమము lit. 'the sky blossom' a phrase for '*nothing*,' as milk from a stone. గగనప్రయత్నము an impossible or overwhelmingly great undertaking. గగన రత్నము the gem of heaven, i. e., the sun.

"సీ॥ గగనభూచరాపదక్రమణశీల
వశాంతిగగనమయ్యెలతాంగిశానుచేరలు"

వసు. iii.

గగురు, **గగురుపాటు** or **గగురుపు** *gaguru*. n. Tingling, glowing, a thrill. రోమాంచము. గగుర్పాటందినది she was electrified, or a thrill ran through her. **గగురు పొడుచు** *gaguru-podutsu*. v. n. To tingle, to be thrilled. రోమాంచితమగు. **గగురుపాటు** or **గగుర్పాటు** Same as గగురు పాటు.

గగ్గర, **గగ్గిర** or **గగ్గెర** *gaggara*. [Tel.] n.. A sort of quail. కష్టగగ్గర a plant like sweet thyme. కాలగగ్గర a noose, a tether. A. vi. 31.

గగ్గు *gaggu*. [Tel.] v. n. To shrink. జంకు. To hesitate సంకోచించు.

గగ్గులు gaggulu. [Tel.] n. Empty ears of corn. గింజలులేనివెన్నులు. గగ్గులు జల్లెడతో పోసినారు bring the empty ears of corn in a sieve. గగ్గులవాడు a heap of empty ears of corn. ధాన్యములేని వెన్నులసమూహము. (వా. vii.) Also, a fugitive. Also (from వాడు a place) the anvil as "the place of sparks." గగ్గులవాడుకలుపు to ruin, to destroy. Kalah M. ii. 129.

గగ్గోలు gaggôlu. [Tel.] n. Confusion. కలత, క్షోభము. గగ్గోలుగా gaggôlu-ga. adv. Aloud, confusedly, slapdash. గగ్గోలుపడు to be alarmed, or routed. అదలు, క్షోభించు. (V. P. iii.)

గచ్చ gatstsa. [Tel.] n. A thorny plant, గచ్చకాయ, its fruit, Guilandina Bonducella. (Ainslie); the fever nut, the physic nut, Caesalpinia Bonducella. మూసిగచ్చకాయ Caesalpinia digyna (Watts.)

గచ్చు gatstsu. [Tel.] n. Lime plaster. Brilliance, glitter కాంతి. A coating పూత. A coating with plaster గారపూత. Pretence, bragging, boast. The stench of urine. గచ్చుకొను gatstsu-konu. v. a. To adhere, cleave, stick. గచ్చుతనము gatstsu-tanamu. n. Foppery, pretence. గచ్చుపిచ్చగు or గచ్చువిచ్చగు gatstsu-pitstsagu. v. n. To be disordered, confused, or spoiled. కార్యమైకల్లమగు. గచ్చులాడి gatstsu-l-adi. n. A jilt, or flirt. దాంభికురాలు.

గచ్ఛత్ gachchhat. [Skt.] adv. Cursorily. Slightly. గచ్ఛత్తుగాచూచు to dip into a book. To read cursorily.

గజము gajamu. [Skt.] n. An elephant. adj. Large. గజనిమ్మ the horse lime, i.e., the large lime: గజవ్యాళి a huge dragon, గజదొంగ a great rogue. గజము [H.] n. A yard, three feet. గజేంద్రగజము gajêndra-gajamu. n. The measure called "the great yard" equal to ten yards. గజకర్ణము gaja-karṇamu. (Lit. An "elephant's ear.") n. A large fan with a hollow handle wherein it can be turned round rapidly. గజకర్ణముచేతిగా fickle, uncertain as a weathercock. గజగామిని or గజయాన gaja-gâmini. n. A woman with the rolling pace of an elephant, i. e., with a majestic gait. గజనిమిలితము gaja-nimilitamu. n. Wakefulness or lightness of sleep (Literally, an elephant's sleep.) A nap. Cunning కపటము. గజపిప్పలి gaja-pippali. n. Long pepper. గజపుష్పము gaja-pushpamu. n. A plant also called Messua Roxburghi. నాగకేసరము. R. v. 310. గజరాజము gaja-râjamu. n. A sort of cloth. BD. iii. 103. గజరిపువు the enemy of the elephant, i. e., the lion. గజాననుడు gaj-ânanuḍu. "Elephant faced." — an epithet of Gaṇêsa వినాయకుడు.

గజిబిజి gaji-biji. [Tel.] n. Intricacy, a puzzle. Confusion, కలత ; trouble. సంకటు. Noise సందడి. adj. Confused కలసిన. Bruised నలిసిన. గజిబిజించు gaji-bijintsu v. n. To be confused. కలగు. గజిబిజిసేయుపెద్దపులి a horrid tiger.

గజ్జి gajji. [Tel.] n. The itch, or mange: any cutaneous eruption. చిడుకురుపు. గజ్జిపట్టు gajji-paṭṭu. n. To have the itch. గజ్జిపట్టిన infested with itch or mange. వానికి గజ్జిపట్టినది he has the itch. గజ్జిరాయి gajji-râyi. n. Yellow ochre: the same as గోంతరాయి.

గజ్జె or గజ్జియ gajje. [Tel.] n. A little bell, such as dancers wear: a tinkling ornament, a rattle. దానికి గజ్జెకట్టినారు they appointed her as a dancer. గజ్జెకట్టినటపా an express post. గజ్జెగొలుసు gajje-golusu. n. An anklet made of little silver bells.

గజ్జ gazza. [Tel.] n. The groin. The inner part of the thigh తొడసందు, వంక్షణము. ఊరుసంధి.

గజ్జు gazzu. [Tel.] n. Fatness; pride మదము. గజ్జుపట్టిన adj. Fat, plump. కొవ్వుపట్టిన. L. XX. 268.

గజ్జూరము gazzuramu. [from Skt. ఖర్జూర.] n. A date tree. ఖర్జూరపుచెట్టు.

గటక *gaṭaka.* [Tel.] n. Gruel, pudding. అంబలి, పిండితో చేసినజావ.

గట్ట *gaṭṭa.* [Tel.] n. The wooden stopper of a skin oil bottle. సిద్దెమూతికి వేసి గట్టించే బిరడా.

గట్టన or **ఘట్టన** *gaṭṭana.* [Tel.] n. Ramming down, గట్టించుట. ఈ దారికి గట్టన చాలదు this road has not been sufficiently beaten or rammed

గట్టి *gaṭṭi.* [Tel.] adj. **Hard,** firm, strong, substantial. Tight. Able, clever, expert. Brave, courageous, resolute, smart, fine. Loud. గట్టిచెర close imprisonment. గట్టిబొట్టు Full *sunna*, or the circle—Appa C. ii. 27. గట్టిమోపుగానుండేదారి a very heavy road. **గట్టించు** *gaṭṭintsu.* v. a. To load a gun, to beat into a hard mass. గట్టనచేయు. **గట్టిగా** or **ఘట్టిగా** *gaṭṭi-gā.* adv. Well, strongly. Properly, tight, fast. Eminently, especially, seriously, greatly. Loudly, aloud. గట్టిగా రావలెనినది you must positively come. గట్టిగా చదువు read aloud. ఇల్లు గట్టిగానున్నది the house is in good condition or is solid-built. **గట్టిచేయు** *gaṭṭi-chēyu.* v. a. To make firm. పాఠము గట్టిచేయు to get a lesson by heart. వాడు ఇచ్చినన్నమాటను గట్టిచేయుము you should make him keep his promise. **గట్టితనము** *gaṭṭi-tanamu.* n. Cleverness, ability. **గట్టినాణెము** *gaṭṭi-nāṇemu.* n. Bullion. **గట్టినబోడి** *gaṭṭina-bōḍi.* n. A game played by boys. కాశీ. iii. **గట్టివ** *gaṭṭiva.* [గట్టి+వాయి.] n. An insolent man. ధూర్తుడు. **గట్టివాడు** *gaṭṭi-vāḍu.* n. An able or skilful man. సమర్థుడు. **గట్టివాయి** *gaṭṭi-vāyi.* n. A brawling woman. గయ్యాళి, ధూర్తురాలు.

గట్టు *gaṭṭu.* [Tel.] n. A bank, or shore, a dam or mound of earth. తీరము. A hill. కొండ. **గట్టుత్రిమ్మరి** *gaṭṭu-trimmari.* n. A monkey. కోతి, అగచరము. **గట్టుతాలుపు** *gaṭṭu-tālupu.* n. One who carries a mountain, i. e., Vishnu. **గట్టురాపట్టి, గట్టురాపూబోడి** or **గట్రాపూబోడి** *gaṭṭura-paṭṭi.* n. The daughter of a mountain, i.,e. Pārvati. పార్వతీదేవి. **గట్టులరేడు** *gaṭṭula-rēḍu.* n. The king of hills, i. e., the Himalaya Mountain. హిమాలయము. **గట్టువిల్తుడు** *gaṭṭu-viltuḍu.* n. The Mountain archer, i. e, Siva. శివుడు.

గట్టువకాడు or **గట్టువకాను** *gaṭṭuva-kāḍu.* [Tel.] n. A brave man. శూరుడు. M. VI. i. 317; 2. 387. గట్టువనేతలు, (Parij. i. 100.) cunning deeds. కపటకృత్రిమములు. **గట్టువతనము** *gaṭṭuva-tanamu.* n. Wickedness. గొంటుతనము.

గట్టువాలు *gaṭṭu-vālu.* [Tel.] n. A street woman. బజారుస్త్రీ, విచ్చలవిడిగా ఒకచోటనుండి శృంగారించుటలేవకు పనులుచేసేఆడుది.

గడ *gaḍa.* [Tel.] n. A stick, staff, pole. నిడుపుకోల. Bolt గడియ. A mast. ఓడకంబము (For గడ్డ) A lump or clod. A multitude సమూహము. చక్రవాకపుగడలు a flock of swans. A fortress or small tower. జొన్నగడ a stalk of maize. చెరుకుగడ a sugarcane. దొమ్మరులు గడకట్టి ఆడినారు they set up a pole and performed tumbler's tricks. బోలుగడ a hollow female bamboo. గట్టిగడ a male bamboo. చివ్వగడ a lance or javelin. **గడసాదన** *gaḍa-sādana.* n. Gymnastics. సాము, వ్యాయామము. **గడమంచె** *gaḍa-manche.* n. A wooden frame like a bench to keep things on. గంపలు మొదలగువాటిని ఉంచు మంచె.

గడగడ *gaḍa-gaḍa.* [Tel.] adv. Violently. Rapidly. వాడు గడగడవణికెను or గడగడలాడెను he trembled greatly or exceedingly. గడగడచెప్పు to say rapidly.

గడచు or **కడచు** Same as గడుచు. (q. v.)

గడన or **గణన** *gaḍana.* [Tel. from గడించు.] n. Earnings సంపాదనము. Esteem, regard. ఎన్నిక. Praise స్తోత్రము. అతడెవనిని గడనచేయడు he cares for nobody. అతనిగడన యేమాత్రముంటుంది how much is his income or profit? గడనపడతి a prostitute.

గడప or **గడప** *gaḍapa*. [Tel.] n. A threshold. A gateway. (metaph. a house). వాకిటక్రిందిభాగము, ఇల్లు.

గడబిడ or **గడిబిడి** *gaḍa-biḍa*. [Tel.] n. Trouble, difficulty, a puzzle. Confusion, కలత, క్షోభము. Noise సందడి. **గడబిడించు** *gaḍa-biḍintsu*. n. To make a noise, or uproar. గడబిడచేయు.

గడము *gaḍamu* [Skt.] n. A kind of fish. గండశిల. An obstacle విఘ్నము. A cover over a pot కుండలోనగువానిమూత.

గడవు or **గడువు** *gaḍavu*. [Tel.] n. A period, or fixed time. గడువువాటిక when the time for payment, &c.) comes. The fixed time. (3 days, &c.) at which a bill is drawn.

గడి *gaḍi*. [Tel.] n. A limit, a boundary. ఎల్ల. గడికొల్లలు plundering on the borders. గడినేలలు boundary lands. గడిమెకము a cunning animal which evades the hunter వేటకుచిక్కని మృగము. గడితేరు to be expert, నిపుణుడగు, కడతేరు. plu. గళ్లు. గళ్లుచేయు to mark the boundaries. **గడి** *gaḍi*. n. Strength, a stronghold, fortalice or petty fort బలము, కోట, దుర్గము. **గడి** adj. Big, stout. గడిగుండు a big stone. గడితాడు a stout rope. A tether, a couple for two cattle. గడితాళ్లుచేయు to tie up the legs of two animals together with a rope రెండు పశువులను ఒక్కొక్కకాలుచేర్చి లంకెచేయు. గడిదొంగ a great clever thief. గడికరణము the principal writer. గడిపోతు a bull ఆబోతు; a great scoundrel, దుష్టగర్ఘుడు.

గడించు or **గణించు** *gaḍintsu*. [Tel.] v. a. To acquire, amass, earn. **గడించుకొను** *gaḍintsu-konu*. v. t. To acquire or earn for oneself.

గడితము *gaḍitamu*. [Tel.] n. Thickness. మడుపు. A plaited or folded garment. adj. Plaited, folded. పెనిమిటి, రెట్టి. Thick, దట్టమైన, మందమైన.

గడిబిడి See గడబిడ.

గడియ *gaḍiya*. [Tel.] n. A bolt or bar. గడెమ్రాను. గడియవేయు to bolt or fasten a bolt. గడియకన్నము a hole bored by a thief, through which he puts his hand to draw back the bolt. **గడియ** or **ఘడియ** n. A Hindu hour which consists of twenty four English minutes, and thus forms the sixtieth part of a day. గడియకు ఒక మాట చెప్పెను he changed his opinion hourly. గడియ యేడైనట్టుండగా each hour seemed a year. **గడియారము** *gaḍiyaramu*. n. A clock, originally a cup for measuring the hours by sinking in water. జేబుగడియారము a watch.

గడియారుడు Same as గడియ.

గడు *gaḍu*. [Tel. for కడు.] adj. Great, much. గడుగాయ a naughty boy.

గడుచు or **కడచు** *gaḍutsu*. [Tel.] v. n. To pass or elapse, as time. v. a. To pass over, to transgress, to exceed or surpass. To expire. ఇది లేకుండ నాకు గడవదు I cannot get on without this. గడిచిబ్రతికినవారు the survivors. ఇక్కడ గడవనందున దేశాంతర మునకు వెళ్లినాను as I could not get on here I went elsewhere. **గడపుకొను** or **గడుపుకొను** *gaḍapu-konu*. v. a. To manage, transact, effect. **గడిపించు** (Causal of గడచు.) *gaḍi-pintsu*. v. a. To pass. కాలము ఇట్లు గడిపించి passing the time thus. **గడు పు** *gaḍupu*. v. a. To pass (time). To put off or defer, to finish. To cause to pass over. To forward, push on, drive on, urge on. To get over, get through (trouble).

గడులుడు *gaḍuluḍu*. [Skt.] n. A hump backed man. మరుగుజ్జు, కుబ్జుడు. గడువు a hump on the back కంతి.

గడువు Same as గడవు. (q. v.)

గడుసు *gaḍusu*. [Tel.] adj. Hard, difficult. Cruel, reckless, unfeeling, inflexible. Firm, steadfast. Pertinacious, stubborn, intractable, obstinate, bluff, freespoken, bold, sharp, stout. అసాధ్యము, కఠినము. ప్రౌఢ. గడుసునేల hard ground. కర్కశమైన. గడుసుపిక్కలు stout calves of legs. గడుసు

వాన a sharp shower of rain. గడుసు n. Hardness, determination. Shrewdness, bluffness. కాఠిన్యము, ధైర్యము. గడుసరి *gaḍusari*. n. A stubborn man, an unfeeling man, a bold man అసాధ్యుడు, కఠినుడు, ధైర్యముగలవాడు. గడుసరితనము *gaḍusari-tanamu*. n. Stubborness, unfeeling conduct. గడుసుపడు *gaḍusu-paḍu*. v. n. To become bold. ధీరుడగు.

గడె or గడియ *gaḍe*. [Tel.] n. A bolt. గడెకన్నము Same as గడియకన్నము. గడెకాళ్లుగల *gaḍe-kāḷḷu-gala*. adj. Spindle-shanked. గడెమాను *gaḍe-mānu*. n. The wooden bar or bolt of a door.

గడ్డ *gaḍḍa*. [Tel.] n. A lump, mass or clod, మంటిపెల్ల. Any bulbous root. దుంప. An island. ద్వీపము. A continent or part of the earth. A bank, brink, edge. A boil or ulcer, వ్రణము. తెల్లగడ్డ or వెల్లుల్లి garlic. ఎఱ్ఱగడ్డ an onion. గడ్డకట్టు to solidify, to gather into a lump. గడ్డకెక్కు to escape. గడ్డను చేర్చు to rescue. గడ్డపలుగు *gaḍḍa-palugu*. n. A pickaxe, an instrument for breaking clods. గడ్డపార *gaḍḍa-pāra*. A crowbar. గడ్డపొయ్యి a fire place formed by putting three stones or clods of earth together. గడ్డలుగా ఏర్పరిచినపొయ్యి.

గడ్డము *gaḍḍamu*. [Tel.] n. The chin: the beard. గడ్డముపట్టి బతిమాలుట to beseech. గడ్డముపెంచుకొను to grow a beard.

"గడ్డంబుకలిగిన కఠంబున రోమశాడు."

కా. viii.

గడ్డి *gaḍḍi*. [Tel.] n. Grass. కసవు. వరిగడ్డి rice straw. గడ్డిమొలతాడు a small cord made of the darbha or sacred grass worn around the waist by a young Brahmin in the ceremony of investing him with the sacred thread. కామంచిగడ్డి or కామాక్షికసవు the *Citronella, or Andropogon Nardus*. (Watts.) గడ్డితలకాయ *gaḍḍi-tala-kāya*. n. A hair-brained fellow, a soft-headed fool. గడ్డితినిపించు *gaḍḍi-tini-pintsu*. v. n. To dupe. (lit. to make one eat grass) వానిని గడ్డితినిపించినారు they befooled him. గడ్డితిను *gaḍḍi-tinu*. v. n. To eat grass, to be cheated. ఈలాగున గడ్డితిన్నాడు thus was he befooled. గడ్డిపరక *gaḍḍi-paraka*. n. A blade of straw or grass గడ్డిపాము *gaḍḍi-pāmu*. n. A species of snake. గడ్డిపిట్ట *gaḍḍi-piṭṭa*. n. A kind of bird: there are three sorts, named ఎఱ్ఱగడ్డిపిట్ట, చిత్తరిగడ్డిపిట్ట and భూతగడ్డిపిట్ట. గడ్డిబొద్దువ *gaḍḍi-bodduva*. n. A ring of grass rope to set a pot on. చుట్టకుదురు.

గడ్డిగము *gaḍḍi-gamu*. [Tel.] n. The tube of a drill plough, through which the seed drops. చాలువెంటనే గింజలుపడడమునకు సాధనము, గొర్రుసకూర్చియుండే గొట్టపురీతిసీల.

గడ్డు *gaḍḍu*. [Tel.] adj. Hard, rare, scarce. అసాధ్యము. adv. Much. మిక్కిలి. గడ్డుమాట a bold word. గడ్డువాడు a dangerous character. గడ్డు n. Violence, outrage. Difficulty. బలాత్కారము, ప్రయాసము, దుర్ఘటము. గడ్డురుకు to rebel, to be stiff-necked. గడ్డుపనులు bold deeds. గడ్డుకొను *gaḍḍu-konu*. v. n. To excel. అతిశయించు.

గడ్డెనబొడ్డి *gaḍḍenu-boḍḍi*. [Tel.] n. A certain game played by boys. H. iii. 186.

గణకుడు *gaṇakuḍu*. [Skt.] n. An astrologer. జోస్యుడు. An arithmetician.

గణగణ *gaṇa-gaṇa*. [Tel.] n. adj. adv. Tinkling. Aloud, again and again, over and over.

"గణగణగంట
కదుపులోమంట."

గణన *gaṇana*. [Skt.] n. Counting, numbering. ఎన్నిక, ఎంచుట. గణనీయము *gaṇa-nīyamu*. adj. That may be reckoned or counted. ఎంచదగినది.

గణపతి *gaṇa-pati*. [Skt.] n. A name of the god Gaṇêsa. వినాయకుడు.

గణము gaṇamu. [Skt.] n. A flock, multitude, or assemblage, a tribe, class or troop. వర్గము, సమూహము. A prosodial foot, such as భగణము a dactyl. గణములుకట్టు to scan. గణములు పోయినవి or తప్పినవి the metre is imperfect. A troop of inferior deities, considered as Siva's attendants, and under the special superintendence of Gaṇêsa: whence his name గణేశుడు, గణపతి or గణాధిపుడు. A body of troops consisting of 27 war-chariots, 27 elephants, 81 horses and 135 infantry men. గణార్చన gaṇārchana. n. Worship of the demigods attending on Siva.

గణి gaṇi [Skt.] n. One who knows the Vedas completely. సాంగముగా వేదాధ్యయనముచేసినవాడు. A cunning man, an astrologer among the lowest castes. హీన జాతులకు తిథివారాలు చెప్పేవాడు.

గణించు gaṇintsu. [Skt.] v. a. To calculate, or reckon. ఎంచు. To be mindful of, regard లక్ష్యపెట్టు. గణించు [Tel. used for గడించు.] v. t. To acquire, or gain, to make (money): to earn. గణిక gaṇika. n. A harlot, because prostituted for gain. వేశ్య. గణికుడు gaṇi-kuḍu. n. An accountant, a mathematician, a calculator. లెక్కపెట్టువాడు, కరణము. గణితము or గణితశాస్త్రము gaṇitamu. n. Arithmetic, calculation. అంకవిద్య.

గణిల్లు gaṇillu. [Tel.] n. A shrill sound as of a bell. గణిల్లని Clang! Crash! (anuk.) With a clanging sound.

గణుతి ga-ṇuti. [Skt.] n. Reckoning. ఎన్నిక. Esteem లక్ష్యము. Praise స్తోత్రము. గణుతించు ga-ṇutintsu. n. To reckon, count. ఎంచు. To esteem, praise స్తోత్రముచేయు. గణ్యము gaṇyamu. adj. Respectable, estimable. ఎన్నదగిన. గణ్యుడు a man worthy of respect ఎంచదగినవాడు. వారు గణ్యులు కారు they are men of no weight.

గణుపు, కణుపు or గనుపు gaṇupu. [Tel.] n. A joint (of the fingers or toes, or of a sugarcane, &c.) గణుపులోతుగాయము a wound an inch deep.

గణెము gaṇemu. [Tel.] n. Frippery. Ornaments, trappings, horns, &c., worn by maskers. వేషధారులు ధరించే లక్కసామ్ము.

గతము gatamu. [Skt.] adj. Lost, gone, past, over, late. పోయిన. గతదినము the last day. గతఫలము loss of advantage. గతజీవులు those who had lost their lives. గతకాలము the past time. గతకులము a family which is extinct. గతజలసేతుబంధనము banks for a stream that has run dry, a proverb for pains taken too late (shutting the stable door after the horse is stolen.) గతబుద్ధుడు he who has lost his wits. గతాహంకారులై they being stripped of their pride. గతము n. Passing away. పోక. గతపడు gata-paḍu. v. n. To pass away. గడచు. To die చచ్చు. గతపడ్డ dead. గతపదగ్రస్తపద్యము or ముక్తపదగ్రస్తపద్యము gata-pada-grasta-padyamu. n. A poetical conceit, Capped lines wherein the last word of each line is repeated at the beginning of the next.

గతి gati. [Skt.] n. Way. త్రోవ. Going, gait, pace, march, passage. గమనము. Means, resource, fund, contrivance, expedient, remedy. ఉపాయము. Refuge, resort, help, aid. దిక్కు. Fate, lot, destiny, state, hap, condition, situation. విధి. An adventure. (In the Lila, the different cantos are called గతులు.) Salvation, rescue రక్షణము. Ability, power శక్తి. నాగతి ఏమి what is to become of me? ఇందుకు వేరేగతి ఉన్నది for this there is another remedy. దైవగతి divine providence. గతిలేని helpless, destitute, abject. వానికి దానిని చెల్లించుటకు గతిలేదు he is unable to pay it, he is without means of payment. పుత్రులులేనివారికి గతిలేదు the childless have no hope (or prospect) of heaven. పటుగతి strongly దిట్టముగా. గతించు gatintsu. v. n. To pass away, elapse, గడచు. To die. చచ్చు. గతికల్పించు to devise an expedient. గతికుడు gatikuḍu. n. He who has a resource. అనన్యగతికులై having no other resource. గతుడు *gatudu*. n. One who is gone or entered. ఆనందాబ్ధి గతుండనై I plunged in a sea of bliss. గత్యంతరము *gat-y-antaramu*. n. An alternative: an other means, or resource.

గటుకు *gatuku*. [Tel.] v. a. To lap, as a dog. To eat the leavings of food ఎంగిలితిను. గటుకు n. Lapping or eating the leavings of food. ఎంగిలితినడము. గటుకుటుకుపోతే బ్రతుకు పోయినది he took the bait and lost his life. గటుకు=a pit, గొయ్యి, పల్లము.

గత్త or గత్తము *gatta*. [Tel.] n. Manure. గత్తముచేయు to manure.

గత్తర *gattara*. [Tel.] n. Disorder, disturbance, hubbub. కల్లోలం. Danger ఉపద్రవము. A euphemism for Cholera వాంతిభేది. గత్తరగాడు a noisy man. గత్తరపడ్డ *gattara-padda*. adj. Confused, troubled.

గద *gada*. [Skt.] n. A mace or club. కుంతము. గదము *gadamu*. n. Disease, sickness. తెవులు. గదాధరుడు *gada-dharudu*. n. The club bearer, i. e., Vishnu. గదాపర్వము or మాసలపర్వము the name of the 16th book of the Mahā Bhārata.

గదమాయించు *gada-mayintsu*. [Tel.] v. t. To scold. గద్దించు.

గదర *gadara*. n. A sort of dried fish.

గదాగ్రజుడు *gadā-grajudu*. [Skt.] n. An epithet of Krishna as being the "elder brother of Gada."

గది *gadi*. [Tel.] n. A room, closet. అర.

గదుకు or గదుకు *gaduku*. [Tel.] v. n. To eat the leavings of food. ఎంగిలితిను. BD. vii. 1888.

గదుము or గదుముకొను *gadumu*. [Tel.] v. a. To rebuke, check. గద్దించు.

గదురు *gaduru*. [Tel.] n. To increase, to become augmented. హెచ్చు. వ్యాపించు. n. A bad smell, a stink. చెడుకంపు, దుర్గంధము.

గద్గదము or గద్గదస్వరము or గద్గదిక *gadgadamu*. [Skt.] n. A murmur, broken voice, fluttering accents: sobbing or faltering: a choked sound. డగ్గుత్తిక.

గద్ద *gadda*. [Tel.] n. A kite. గృధ్రము. అడవినల్లగద్ద the black eagle. *Ictinaetus malayensis*. తెల్లగద్ద or పిటిగద్ద the white scavenger vulture, *Neophron ginginianus* తేనెగద్ద the crested Honey Buggard *Pernis cristatus*. పాముగద్ద the short toed eagle, *Circaetus gallicus*. నల్లపాముల గద్ద the crested serpent eagle, *Spilornis cheela*. పిల్లిగద్ద the Pale Harrier, *Circus macrurus*. F. B. I. గద్దముక్కు a Roman nose, a sharp nose. గద్దగోరు *gadda-gōru* n. An instrument used by house-breakers; lit. a kite's claw చోరసాధన విశేషము.

గద్దరి *gaddari*. [Tel.] adj. Impertinent, pert గడుసైన, తుంటైన. "గద్దరికొమ్ములగుజ్జు." (G. VIII. 151.) a broad horned beast. గద్దరికాడు *gaddari-kadu*. n. An impertinent man, an insolent man. గడుసు వాడు. గద్దరించు *gaddar-intsu*. v. a. To shudder, tingle all over, be agitated or frightened. గద్దరితనము *gaddari-tanamu*. n. Boldness. గడుసుతనము, తుంటతనము.

గద్దించు *gaddintsu*. [Tel.] v. a. To rebuke, reprimand, bully, chide. కూకలు పెట్టు, బెదిరించు. గద్దింపు *gaddimpu*. n. Chiding, a rebuke.

గద్దియ See గద్దె.

గద్దువ *gadduva*. [Tel.] n. The chin. గడ్డము.

గద్దె or గద్దియ *gadde*. [Tel.] n. A high seat. ఉన్నతపీఠము; a throne సింహాసనము. An obsolete coin వరహా. గద్దెపొంకము *gadde-ponkamu*. n. Eulogy. పరువునకుతగిన గౌరవపు మాట.

గద్య or గద్యము *gadya*. [Skt.] n. Prose. వచనము.

గణక or **గనుక** or **కనుక** *ganaka*. [Tel.] conj. Then, therefore, so, seeing that, thereby. అవినగక for that reason.

గణగణ *gana-gana*. [Tel.] adv. Fiercely. గణగణనిప్పులు glowing fires.

గణప *ganapa*. [Tel.] adj. Large. పెద్ద.

గణయము *ganayamu*. [Tel.] n. The end or tip of a bow. వింటికొప్పు ; కోపుకొన.

గని *gani*. [from Skt. ఖన్ to dig..] n. A mine, a quarry. A hole. రంధ్రము. **గనిపని** *gani-pani*. n. Mining, quarrying. **గనివాడు** *gani-vadu*. n. A miner, a pitman.

గనిమ *ganima*. [Tel.] n. A ridge. చిన్నకట్ట.

గనియ Same as గను.

గంటు *gantbu*. [Tel.] n. A sheath. ఒర.

గనుపు *ganupu*. [Tel.] n. A joint. కణుపు.

గను or **గనియ** *gana*. [from Skt. ఖన్ to dig.] n. A bit, piece, fragment. తునక. గనులుగా piecemeal.

గన్నేరు or **గన్నారు** *gannēru*. [Tel.] n. The Oleander, *Nerium odorum*. Ainslie ii. 23. గులుగన్నేరు, or Balsam (*gul-i-mehndi*) and ఎర్రగన్నేరు are species. The pagoda tree, i. e., దేవగన్నేరు or నాడగన్నేరు is a large tree, with a fragrant white flower pale yellow inside. అడవిగన్నేరు the *Plumieria Alba* (Linn). పచ్చగన్నేరు పూలాలు. (A. i. 57.) a particular kind of rice.

గప్చిప్పు *gapchippu*. [H.] n. Silence. adj. Silent.

గప్తి *gapti*. [Skt. for జ్ఞప్తి] n. Recollection.

గప్పాలు *gappalu*. [H.] n. Bragging, boasting. బడాయిలు. **గప్పాలుకొట్టుకొను** *gappalu-kottu-konu*. v. i. To brag, to boast.

గబుక్కున *gabakku-na*. [Tel.] adv. Horribly, fearfully.

గబగబ *gaba-gaba*. [Tel.] n. Hubbub, tumult. adv. Terribly, violently. గబగబలాడెను there was a tumult.

గబ్బటము, గబ్బాటు *gabbatu*. [Tel.] n. An uproar, buzz. అల్లి. adj. Cheap. కొలకొన్న మైన.

గబ్బి *gabbi*. [Tel.] adj. 1. Full, big, mighty, 2. Hemispherical, swelling. 3. Great. Thick, as darkness. 4. Noble, heroic. 5. Stubborn, hard, unmanageable, headstrong, proud. స్థూల, అధికమైన, గర్వముగల. **గబ్బి** n. A prig, a conceited fellow. A hemisphere: a round object. అర్ధగోళరూపము. A stout hound, a bulldog. Manu. iv. 80. **గబ్బితనము** *gabbi-tanamu*. n. Bigness, wickedness. కొంటెతనము. **గబ్బిలము, గబ్బిలాయి** or **గబ్బిలాయి** *gabbilamu*. n. A bat or flittermouse.

గబ్బిలి *gabbili*. [Tel.] n. A handful. పిడికిలి. గబ్బిలుకూరతే bring a handful of curry.

గబ్బిలివాడు *gabbili-vadu*. [Tel.] n. A toddy drawer.

గబ్బు *gabbu*. [Tel.] n. Orig: any strong smell or savour, good or bad. A bad smell, a stench. కంపు. గబ్బుచెంపమీకము an elephant ఏనుగు. Pride గర్వము, మదము.

గబ్బులుగు *gab-bulugu*. [గబ్బు+పులుగు.] n. A bird of omen. ఒక శకునపుపక్షి.

గభస్తి *gabhasti*. [Skt.] n. A ray of light, సూర్యకిరణము. అమృతగభస్తి "the nectar-rayed god," an epithet of the moon.

గభాలున *gabhaluna*. [Tel. for గబాలున.] adv. Agitatedly, thrillingly. Slapdash. Bang! smack, all at once. **గభిలుమను** *gabhilu-m-anu*. v. a. (anuk) To be violently agitated, to thrill, tingle, shudder.

గభీరము *gabhiramu*. [Skt.] adj. Deep, profound. గంభీరమైన.

గమకము *gamakamu*. [Skt.] n. Increase, fulness: springiness, exertion. పూనిక, యుత్నము. adj. Much, great అధికము. Fine, pleasant. మనోజ్ఞము. **గమకము** or **గమకర్మము** *gamakamu*. n. Connection, in a sentence the word to be understood. తోపపేదయునది. **గమకించు** *gama-kintsu*. v. n. To rise, to spring: to exert one self పూను, యుత్నముచేయు, ఆయుత్తమగు.

"మ॥ తమిదయించుచు గమకించుభీతి మదిలో
దర్పించు గాంచుచు వెతకు."
T. ii. 80.

గమగమ *gama-gama*. [Tel.] adv. (Anuk) Sweetly, fragrantly ఘుమఘుమ. Swa. ii, 59. Eagerly (hungry) గమగమయని ఆకలి అయినది he was very hungry. గమగమించు *gama-gamintsu*. v. n. To smell very sweet. గమగమయని వాసనకొట్టు.

"సీ॥ కప్పురపువిడెయపు తావి గమగమింప."
శేష. iv.

గమనము *gamanamu*. [Skt.] n. Going, a march, journey పోక, ప్రయాణము. Attention. గురి. Intention తలపు. సహగమనము, lit. 'Accompanying.' The burning a Hindu widow alive with her deceased husband.

" ఉ॥ సంగరమందుంగరంబుగమనంబున
భావనసేయక్రై. "
వై. iii.

గమనించు *gamanintsu*. [Skt.] v. a. To go. పోవు. To intend తలచు. "రథికుడు గమనించు నప్పుడె రథమునడుచు." Vēma. 608. To pay attention to, to attend to. గమనిక *gamanika*. n. Way, manner. విధము. Procedure. నడక.

గమము *gamamu*. [Skt.] n. Going. పోక. A journey ప్రయాణము. A way దారి.

గమాయించు Same as గమగమించు. (q. v.)

గమల్ల *gamalla*. [Tel.] n. The Toddy drawers' caste. గమల్లవాడు A toddy drawer. గమల్లది a woman of that caste.

గమి *gami*. [Tel.] n. A flock, crowd, assembly. A cluster. పసిండిమువ్వగమి a cluster of golden bells. గమిగొను *gami-konu*. v. a. To become a heap పోగగు. To assemble or form into a crowd గుంపుకూడు.

గమించు or గమాయించు *gamintsu*. [Skt.] v. n. To go పోవు. To pass, as time. గమికత్తె *gami-katte*. n. A woman in waiting, an attendant maid. గమికాడు *gami-kāḍu*. n. A leader, chief man. అధిపతి, సేనాధిపతి, ముఖ్యజనుడు.

గమేల *gamēla*. [Portuguese, *Camera*.] n. The crow's nest, i. e., the top of a mast in which men stand. ఓడస్తంభములో మనిషి నిలిచేటట్లుగా కట్టిన అంతస్తు.

గమ్మతు *gammatu*. [H.] n. Diversion, amusement. వేడుక, తమాషా.

గమ్ము *gammu* [Tel.] n. Fragrance. సువాసన, పరిమళము, ఘుమఘుమ. గమ్మని Comfortably. ఆ దుప్పటిని గమ్మని కప్పుకొన్నాను I wrapped myself in the rug comfortably.

గమ్యము *gamyamu*. [Skt] adj. Attainable : accessible : desirable, suitable. పొందదగిన.

గయ *gaya*. [Skt.] n. The city of Gaya.

గయాళి or గయ్యాళి *gayāli*. [Tel.] n. A shrew, a scold. ధిక్కరించి దూల్లాడునది. గయ్యాళించు *gayyālintsu*. v. n. To play the scold, to talk insolently. ధిక్కరించి మాటాడు. adj. Peevish, insolent.

గయాళు *gayālu*. [Tel.] n. Waste or uncultivated land. పాడు వేయబడిన నేల. గయాళుపడ్డ deserted, abandoned, waste. పాడువేయబడిన, విడిచిపెట్టబడిన; సేద్యముచేయ డానకు పనికిరాని (పొలము.)

గయావాళి *gaya-vāli*. [H.] n. A pilgrim returning from *Gaya*. A disorderly, licentious profligate.

గర *gara*. [Tel.] n. A lump, a clod, ముద్ద, గడ్డ. గరకట్టు *gara-kattu*. v. i. To curdle, to solidify. గడ్డకట్టు.

గరగ *garaga*. [Tel.] n. A small pot, vessel or pipkin. M. XIII. ii. 397.

గరగడ *garagaḍa*. [Tel.] n. A funnel.

గరగడమువేయు *gara-gaḍamu-vēyu*. [Tel.] n. To mark heaps of grain (to prevent it being stolen) by sprinkling cowdung water over it in wavy lines.

గరగర garagara. [Tel.] n. Hardness, crispness. కాఠిన్యము. Purity నిర్మలము, నిర్మలత్వము. గరగరలాడు to crackle, as a biscuit in the mouth. గరగరిక or గరాగరిక garagarika. n. Neatness, tidiness, cleanliness. నైర్మల్యము. Beauty అందము.

"గరగరిక బాగుమిగుల్చి,
గరుడాంబుధికుండమునను గనబాగున్నా."

గరగరికల gara-gari-kala. [Tel.] n. Active, nimble. బాగరగరికల. L. 3. 269. గరగరిక్షైన, neat, tidy, nice. గరగరిగా or గరాగరిగా tidily, nicely.

గరగొర gara-gora. [Tel.] n. Lack, deficiency, something wanting. కొఱత.

గరడుడు garadudu. [Skt.] n. A poisoner. M. XII. i. 110.

గరపనేల garapa-nela. [Tel.] n. Red sandy soil, barren land.

గరవడు gara-vadu. [Tel.] v. i. To curdle, to become congealed. గడ్డకట్టు.

"సీ॥ గరుగుకొన్నతునక గరవడ్డదానుంచు
దచ్చియున్నతముగా దీర్చిరొక్క."
శ్రీ. vii.

గరళము garalamu. [Skt.] n. Poison.

గరవులు garavulu. [Tel.] n. Offerings, gifts, rarities.

గరసించు garasintsu. [for Skt. ఘర్షించు.] n. To attack. "కంఠీరవముసైనగరసించుటయుగాని దొరసి వెన్నిని ధటోచ్చయంబు" Bahul. i. 31.

గరసులు garasulu. [Tel.] n. Skins. చర్మములు. A. vi. 17.

గరాసు garāsu. [Tel.] n. A wicked man, a wretch. దుష్టుడు, ఖలుడు.

గరి gari. n. [Tel.] A wing. ఱెక్క. The feather of an arrow. బాణముయొక్కఱెక్క. Harshness. గరిమీసాలు whiskers.

గరిక or గరికె or గరికగడ్డి garika. [Tel.] n. A kind of grass called *Agrostis linearis*. దూర్వ. Ainslie. ii. 28. గరికనక్కు garika-nattu. n. The smaller species of grass (q.v.) The largest species being కుందుమనక్కు. గరికసూడులు garika-sūdulu. n. A fine species of rice.

గరిగొను gari-konu. [Tel.] n. To become sharp: to stiffen. గరిగట్టు gari-gattu. v. n. To be manifest, to be before the eyes. మూర్తీభవించు. "కరవస్త్రసంగత ఘనలింగశశిదము, గరిగట్టినటులౌన గనపచ్చెనగ." L. 6. 132. గరికమ్మ gari-kamma. n. A rough bough (of a palm tree) before the serrated edges are removed. గరిగొన్న gari-gonna. adj. Blackened, stained. నల్లగిల్లిన. G. ii. 28.

గరిగె garige. [Tel.] n. A small earthen pot, or bottle with a spout. గరిగెచెంబు A small saucepan.

గరిచిప్ప gari-chippa. [Tel.] n. A cockle-shell, a pearl shell. BD. vi. 173.

గరిటె garițe. [Tel.] n. A spoon, ladle. మట్టిగారిగరిటె a trowel. పారుగరిటె a huge ladle borne in processions. ముద్రగరిటె a long ladle, with a bell at the end.

గరిడి or గరిడీ garidi. [Tel.] n. Fencing, sword play. సాము. A dancing school, a fencing school. సాముకూటము. గరడీలసాము, or గరిడీవిద్య sword play, gymnastics. A place చోటు. Nearness. సమీపము, చెంత. గరిడిముచ్చు a rogue who pretends to be a good man. మంచివానివలె దగ్గిరనుండి సమయముచూచి దొంగిలించేవాడు. (శశి. ii.)

గరిడీయ garidiya. [from Skt. కరండము.] n. A wallet, or basket for food, &c. బుట్ట. M. III. vii. 221. భా. అర. vii.

గరిత garita. [Tel.] n. A damsel, a woman. A faithful wife. ఇల్లాలు, పతివ్రత. గరితతనము garita-tanamu. n. Womanishness, frailty, light-mindedness. Suca ii. 404.

గరిమ or గరిమము garima. [Skt.] n. Heaviness, weight, gravity. Bigness, largeness, greatness. Seriousness, majesty. పెంపు, గరిమ, గాంభీర్యము. H. iv. 211.

గరిమిడి *garimidi.* [Tel.] n. A species of grass, *Panicum Dactylon.* Also, a rat or mouse. అనగా. గరిమిడికొక్కు a bandicoot "శా॥ ఉడుముగరిమిడి కొక్కులదడవచేల" Swa. iv. 25.

గరివించు *garivintsu.* [for Skt. గర్వించు.] v. i. To be proud.

గరిష్ఠము *garishṭhamu.* [Skt.] adj. Weighty, heavy. Venerable. గరిష్ఠుడు *garishṭuḍu.* n. A venerable man: a man of weight, or of influence.

గరిసె *garise.* [Tel.] n. A hamper or large basket or small round building for storing grain. The measure called a garce containing 320 lbs. గరిసెనేల black soil mingled with pebbles or lime stone.

గరు *garu.* [Tel.] n. The bristling up of the hair. రోమాంచము.

గరుకు *garuku.* [Tel.] adj. Rough; indented or having dents. "గరుకులకొల్లబుగాడిద నేల."

గరుజు Same as గజ్జు.

గరుజుతనము *garuju-tanamu.* [Tel.] n. Roughness, harshness, as the knap of cloth.

గరుడుడు, గరుడి, గరుత్మంతుడు, గరుటామంతుడు or గరుటాలమంతుడు *garuḍuḍu.* [Skt.] n. The eagle or sovereign of the feathered race. The Brahminy or Maroon-backed kite, *Haliastur indus* (F. B. I.) గరుత్మంతుడు. గరుడిరవుతు *garuḍi-ravutu.* n. Vishnu. గరుడముక్కువాడు a man with a Roman nose. గరుడధ్వజుడు *garuḍa-dhvajuḍu.* n. An epithet of Vishnu, whose emblem is the kite. గరుడపచ్చ *garuḍa-patstsa.* n. An inferior emerald. మరకతము. గరుడపార్వ *garuḍa-parva.* n. An eagle-glance. A keen, fearless look, like that of an eagle. గరుడవాస్తు *garuḍa-vāstu.* n. A certain plan on which some Hindu houses are built. గరుడసరులు *garuḍa-sarulu.* n. A fine sort of rice. గరుడస్తంభము or గరుడకంబము *garuḍa-stambhamu.* n. A post erected before a temple, with bells at the top. గరుడాగ్రజుడు *garuḍ-āgrajuḍu.* n. An epithet of Anura, as being the elder brother of గరుడుడు. గరుడాచలము *garuḍā-chalamu.* n. The name of a hill in the Cuddapa District: and the subject of a favourite poem. గరుడాళ్వారు *garuḍ-āḷvāru.* n. A name for an eagle. A brahminy kite. గరుడాసనము *garuḍ-āsanamu.* n. Kneeling on one knee: this being the attitude of the griphon Garuda.

గరుత్తు *garuttu.* [Skt.] n. A wing. పక్క. గరుత్మంతము a bird.

గరుపాటు *garupāṭu.* [Tel.] n. Bristling of the hair. గగుర్పాటు. See గరు. గరుపారు *garu-pāru.* v. i. To tingle. రోమాంచితమగు.

గరుబు or గరుగు *garubu.* [Tel.] n. Thick, as a forest. గరుబుకానలు. V. P. vii. 146.

గరువము *garuvamu.* [from Skt. గర్వము.] n. Pride. Affection. గారవము. Ardour, eagerness. ఎండ. గరువపుటెండ ardent sunshine తీక్ష్ణమైనయెండ. గరువతనము *garuva-tanamu.* n. Valour. పరాక్రమ.

గరువు *garuvu.* [Tel.] n. A side. పెంపు. Swa. v. adj. Hard or gravelly as the ground. గులకరాలచే గట్టిదైననేల. "గరువు నేలల గుంటలానకిండి" Swa. iv.

గరుసు *garusu.* [Tel.] n. Gravel. గరువు. గులకరాళ్లు. A skin, hide. చర్మము, తోలు. A. vi. 17. Respect. మర్యాద.

గర్గర or ఘర్ఘర *gargara.* [Skt.] n. Tinkling ornaments: bells on the anklets. పెంచెము. adv. Resoundingly, echoingly.

గర్గరి *gargari.* [Skt.] n. A churning pot. పెరుగుతరిచేకుండ.

గర్జ, గర్జనము or గర్జితము *garja.* [Skt.] n. A roar, thunder. R. vi. 17. గర్జించు or గర్జిల్లు *garjintsu.* v. n. To thunder, to roar.

గర్జు or గరజు garzu. [Tel.] n. Necessity. అక్కర, అగత్యము. నాకేమి గర్జుపట్టినది what necessity have I? what do I care?

గర్తము gartamu. [Skt.] n. A hole or hollow, a pit. పల్లము.

గర్దభము gardabhamu. [Skt.] n. An ass. గాడిద.

గర్భము garbhamu. [Skt.] n. The belly, the stomach, the womb. కడుపు. The inside of any thing, the interior; the middle. A fœtus కడుపులోనివిండము. నదీగర్భము the middle of a river. గర్భగృహము the nave, sanctuary, or shrine of a temple. గర్భము తోనున్న pregnant. గర్భముధరించు to conceive or become pregnant. ఆమెగర్భము కరిగిపోయింది she miscarried. ఆమెను గర్భము నిలిచినది she has not miscarried. గర్భ కణము a swelling ear of corn. వరి పొట్టకరుకు. Vasu. ii. 101. గర్భాగారము a closet or recess. An inner chamber. లోపలిగది. ఏకగర్భజనితులయిన of full blood children of the same womb. గర్భవాసిగా నుండే yet in the womb, unborn. గర్భశత్రువు a secret enemy. గర్భాధానము the nuptial ceremony. గర్భాశయము the womb, the uterus. గర్భాష్టకము the eighth month of uterine gestation. The eighth year reckoning from conception. గర్భిణి garbhiṇi. n. A pregnant woman: చూలాలు.

గర్రనిలి garra-nili. [Tel.] n. Bastard Indigo: a plant, the leaves of which afford a light blue dye.

గర్రు garru. [Tel.] n. Noise made in belching. తేపుటయందు ధ్వన్యనుకరణము. గర్రున aloud as a belch or as rattling in the throat.

గర్రె garre. [Tel.] n. An instrument for catching fish. పెద్దతిర్రి.

గర్వము garvamu. [Skt.] n. Pride, haughtiness. అహంకారము. గర్వభంగము dishonour, degradation, humiliation, disgrace. గర్వించు or గర్వపడు garvintsu. v. n. To be proud. గర్వి or గర్విష్ఠుడు garvi. n. A proud man.

గర్హించు garhintsu. [Skt.] v. n. To blame, revile. నిందించు. గర్హణము garhaṇamu. n. Blame, censure. నింద. గర్హితము garhitamu. adj. Blamed, censured, base. నిందింపబడిన. గర్హ్యము garhyamu. adj. Contemptible, scandalous, base. నిందింప దగిన.

గలంగ చెట్టు See గలంగ.

గలగరచెట్టు or గుంటగలగర ఆకు galagara-chettu. [Tel.] n. A kind of herb. భృంగ రాజము.

గలగల gala-gala. [Tel.] n. A tinkling or clanging sound. గలగలమను to rattle, to tinkle, to clang.

గలబ or గలభా galaba. [H] n. Confusion. కలత. గలబరించు or గలభరించు or గల బరించు galaba-rintsu. v. n. To grumble. కడుపు గలబరిస్తున్నది the belly grumbles. To confuse గందరగోళపెట్టు.

గలాసు galāsu. [Eng. Glass.] n. A glass vessel. గాజుగిన్నె.

గలిజేరు galijēru. [Tel.] n. A plant, hog-weed. *Trianthema monogyna*, పునర్నవ. గుం టగలిజేరు, గుంటగలగర or భృంగరాజము the verbesina plant. *Eclipta erecta*. Heyne. పచ్చపువ్వులగుంటగలిజేరాకు.

గలిబిలి galibili. [Tel.] n. Disorder, confusion, noise. గందరగోళము, సందడి.

గల్ల galla. [Tel.] n. A shallow pot, in which a cobbler moistens leather. తొట్టి.

గల్లంతు gallantu. [Tel.] n. Confusion, tumult, a fray. కలత.

గల్లము gallamu. [Skt.] n. The cheek. గండ స్థలము, చెక్కిలి. Anirud. ii. 75.

గల్లా galla. [H.] n. Grain in general; grain not thrashed. నూర్చనిధాన్యము. Also, a shop-keeper's cash box అంగడివానిపెట్టె.

గల్లి *galli*. [H.] n. A lane.

గల్లు or గల్లుగల్లు *gallu*. [Tel.] n. A loud noise. A tingling noise, as of jewels. సగల మ్రోత.

గళంతిక *galantika*. [Skt.] n. A small pitcher or jug like a tea pot. గిండిచెంబు.

గళకంబళము *gala-kambalamu*. [Skt.] n. The dewlap (of a bull, &c.) గంగడోలు.

గళగళ *gala-gala*. [Tel.] n. A gurgling sound.

గళము *galamu*. [Skt.] n. The throat, the neck. కుత్తుక, మెడ, గొంతు. గళరవము *gala-ravamu*. n. The voice. కంఠధ్వని.

గళితమైన *galita-m-aina*. [Skt.] adj. Fallen, dropped. జారిన. Eaten తినబడిన. గళితము చేయు *galitamu-chēyu*. v. a. To strain through a cloth.

గల్ల or కల్ల *galla*. [Tel.] n. Phlegm.

గవదలు *gavadalu*. [Tel.] n. Glands of the throat.

గవను or గవని or గవను *gavanu*. A city-gate. A ii. 33. గవనులు or కవనులు fort-gates. కోటవాకిళ్లు.

గవయము *gavayamu*. [Skt.] n. A wild ox. కారెద్దు, కురుపోతు. H. iii. 9.

గవరన *gavarana*. [Tel.] n. Redness. ఎరుపు.

గవాక్షము *gav-ākshamu*. [Skt.] n. Lit: A bull's eye. A window. కిటికీ. గవాక్షివృక్షము *gavākshi-vrikshamu*. n. A kind of bitter melon. పుచ్చకాయ, పాపరకాయ.

గవి *gavi*. [Tel.] n. A cavern or grotto. గుహ. "గవిమాటొక్కటునుర్కుడము" R. vi. 10. Swa. iv. 79.

గవిని *gavini*. [Tel.] n. A city gate.

గవిలెము *gavilemu*. [Tel.] n. A fragrant seed like anise.

గవిసెన *gavisena*. [Tel.] n. A cloth case, or cover.

గవుండ్లవాడు *gavundla-vādu*. [Tel.] n. A toddy-drawer.

గవేషించు *gavēsh-intsu*. [Skt.] v. a. To search, seek. వెదకు. గవేషణము *gavēshanamu*. n. Search, enquiry. వెదకుట, అన్వేషణము.

గవ్యము *gavyamu*. [Skt. గౌః=గోవు] adj. Dairy products. What is produced by the cow. పంచగవ్యములు the five products of the cow, viz., milk, butter, ghee, dung and urine. పాలు, పెరుగు, నెయ్యి, పంచితము, పేడ.

గవ్వ *gavva*. [Tel.] n. A shell, a cowry used as money.

గవ్వచౌకము *gavva-chaukamu*. [Tel.] n. Borax. వెలిగారము.

గస *gasa*. [Tel.] n. Asthma or shortwindedness.

గసగసాలు *gasa-gasalu*. [Arabic *khash-khash*.] n. The seeds of the poppy plant.

గసి *gasi*. [Tel.] n. Dregs of oil or melted butter. Also, a nail. మేకు.

గసిక *gasika*. [Tel.] n. A spike or pointed piece of wood, a wedge. A hoe or small spade made of wood. An arrow. గసికరాయి *gasika-rāyi*. n. A pointed stone. వాడు చెప్పినమాట నామనస్సులో గాఢగసికగా నాటి ఉండెను his words were fixed in my heart.

గసిబిసి *gasi-bisi*. [Tel.] n. Confusion. కలత, గజిబిజి.

గస్తి or గస్తు *gasti*. [H.] n. A patrol, తిరుగుడు, నగరశోధన. గస్తుతిరుగు to go the rounds, to patrol. గస్తీలు *gastilu*. (గస్తు+ఈలు) n. Watchmen. కావలివారు.

"క్ష్మా॥ అల్లిలగోడవిదయ్యంబులదివ్వె
కోలలవాండ్రగానొనిగస్తులిరి."
పారిజా. ii.

గస్తు *gastu*. [Tel.] n. Nastiness, a rank smell. adj. Nasty. గస్తుకంపు A stench, a nasty smell.

గహనము *gahanamu*. [Skt.] n. A wilderness, forest. అడవి. A cave గుహ. లతా గహనము a thicket of boughs. adj Wild, impervious. ఘోరమైన. గహనాపణము A crowded market street.

గహి *gahi*. [Tel.] n. Scorn, menace, bullying. గహిచేయు *gahi-chēyu*. n. To browbeat.

గహ్వరము *gahvaramu*. [Skt.] n. A cave, a grotto, a cavern, a recess in a forest. A forest. అడవి.

గా gā

గా *gā*. [Tel.] n. (an adverbial affix being the infinitive కా of అగు) తండ్రిగా ఉండినాడు he was like a father to me దొరగా ఉండెను he was as master, or he was master. మూడుగా తెలుస్తున్నది it looks like three. గుమిగా వచ్చినారు they came in a crowd. నల్లగానున్నది it is black ;. Added to verbs. it means when, while, as or since. ఈ పని కాగానే as soon as ever this is finished. వాడు చేరగా on his arrival, when he arrived. మీరు ఆ పనిని చేయుచుండగా while you are doing that work.

గా *gā*. [Tel.] v. n. A contraction for కదా or కదా ఆ వచ్చినది వాడుగా it was he who came *most likely*, or, I suppose.

గాంగేయుడు *gāngēyudu*. [Skt.] n. One born to the Ganges, i. e., Bhīshma భీష్ముడు.

గాండివము or గాండీవము *gāndīvamu*. [Skt.] n. The name of a bow used by the hero Arjuna. A bow విల్లు. గాండీవమైన శబ్దము a jaw breaking word, a puzzle.

గాండ్రించు *gāndrintsu*. [Tel.] n. To hawk in clearing the throat; to retch, in vomiting. To swell ఉబ్బు. వానిముఖము గాండ్రించు కొన్నది his face is inflamed, or slightly swollen.

గాండ్లవాడు *gāndla-vādu*. [Tel.] n. An oilmonger. నూనె అమ్మి జీవించేవాడు. గాండ్లది a woman of that caste

గాంధర్వము *gāndharvamu*. [Skt. from గంధర్వ.] n. A fairy-wedding. A love match, without the authority of parents It is a fashionable phrase for seduction.

గాంధారము *gāndhāramu*. [Skt.] n. A certain note in music. The Candahar country. గాంధారి *gāndhāri*. n. The mother of Duryōdhana, proverbially, a bold, pert woman. గాంధారికథలు *gāndhāri-kathalu*. n. A kind of ballads or ditties.

గాంభీర్యము *gāmbhīryamu*. [Skt. from గంభీరము.] n. Depth, grandeur. గంభీరభావము.

గాక *gāka*. [Tel.] affix. Except, besides, unless, but. ఇదిగాక and besides this, further.

గాగరా *gāgarā*. [H.] n. A petticoat. పావడ.

గాజరు *gāzaru*. [Tel.] n. A kind of root. (హంస. iv.)

గాజువరుజు Same as వరుజు. (q. v.)

గాజు *gāzu*. [Tel.] n. Glass; any vitrified substance such as chinaware or a bracelet, which is made of glass black as jet. Hence, blackness. A bracelet. బంగారు గాజులు bracelets made of gold. Various kinds of bracelets are called కల్లగాజులు, ఈడిగిగాజులు, మెట్టగాజులు, దుండిగాజులు, and లక్కపట్టెగాజులు. గాజులు the wards of a lock. గాజుకప్పెరలు *gāzu-kapperalu*. [Tel.] n. A certain sort of grain. H. iv. 156. గాజునీలము *gāzu-nīlamu*. n. An artificial sapphire. Also, deep blue or black. NH. v. 46. గాజురొయ్య *gāzu-royya*. n. A crayfish or large prawn. గాజుపారు *gāzu-pāru*. v. n. To blacken or turn black. కాంతిహీనమగు. గాజుప్పు *gāz-uppu*. n. Dross of a glasswork, scoriæ. గాజురాయి *gāzu-rāyi*. n. A glassy stone. Jet. గాజులవాండ్లు *gāzula-vāndlu*. n. A certain caste who deal in glass bracelets.

గాటె See గాది.

గాటము gāṭamu. [Tel.] n. Difficulty, severity, hardness. అధికము, దుడుకు. adj. Much, great, thick, hard, strong, tight. మిక్కుటమయిన, దుడుకైన.

గాటు gāṭu. [Tel.] n. The beazle of a ring: the notch to hold the stone. Strength, virulence, potency of poison, or of liquor. Pungency, acridity, as of pepper. గాటు పొగాకు strong tobacco.

గాడి gāḍi. [Tel.] n. A drinking trough or manger, a ditch, a groove. గాడిబావి a well that is provided with a trough for watering cattle. గాడిపొయ్యి a kitchen range, being a trench containing fire under a line of places for pots.

గాడిద or గాడిదె gāḍida. [Tel.] n. An ass. adj. Wild, or, inferior. గాడిదవేప the worthless kind of *vepa*. గాడిదగడపాకు a certain herb used in medicine. గాడిదకాళ్లుగల adj. Bandy-legged. గాడిదెగడపర gāḍide-gaḍapara. n. The gaudy birth-wort, *aristolochia bracteata*, a plant used in medicine. గాడిదెపులి gāḍide-puli. n. The hyæna. కుక్కలగండి, కొర్నగండి.

గాడీ gāḍī. [H.] n. A carriage. బండి. "చిత్రంబగుగాడీలు." భార. ఆది. viii.

గాడు gāḍu. [Tel.] n. Longing, rage, hankering. Lust. A prank, caprice, proneness itch. నీకేమి గాడుపట్టినది what evil desire drove you to do this? గాడుపట్టినవాడు the lustful libertine. గాడుగల prurient, eager, prone, vicious, rank. గాడు v. a. To enter, penetrate, go through, pierce, transfix. నాటు. A. iii. 37. & A. i. 66. To pierce or pinch with the finger nail. Surabh. i. 97. గాడుపడు to be bewildered దిక్కుతోచకపోవు. A. vi. 11. గాడుచను or గాడుచాను gāḍu-tsanu. v. a. To enter, go through, penetrate.

గాడుపు or గాడ్పు gāḍupu. [Tel.] n. Wind: a breeze. వడగాడ్పు or ఎండగాడ్పు a land wind, a hot wind. A. v. 131.

గాఢము gāḍhamu. [Skt.] adj. Extreme, much Intense, deep. గాఢాలింగనము a close embrace. గాఢాంధకారము pitch darkness. గాఢనిద్ర deep sleep. గాఢమోహము strong love.

గాణ gāṇa. [Tel.] n. A singer. పాటకాడు or పాటకత్తె.

గాణాపత్యము gāṇa-patyamu. [Skt.] n. The worship of Ganapati.

గాణి gāṇi. [Tel.] n. A female singer. పాటకత్తె. గాణుడు gāṇuḍu. n. A male singer.

గాత gāta. [Tel. for గావుత.] v. n. May it be so! గాక.

గాత gāta. [Skt.] n. A singer. పాటపాడు వాడు.

గాతము gātamu. [Tel.] n. A pit, a hole. బొక్క, పల్లము.

గాతి gāti. [Tel.] n. Food. తిండి, గ్రాసము.

"కం॥ పాపములకెల్లనాడికట్టిపాయకెప్పుడు
క్రేపులకుదీతిలంజముగాతిగాకు."
Bhall. iii. 47.

గాదు gādu. [Tel.] n. Courage. ధైర్యము.

గాత్రము gātramu. [Skt.] n. The body, a member, a limb, a part. శరీరము, అవయవము. adj. Big. స్థూలము. గాత్రసంకోచి contractile, drawing itself up, as an animal before making a spring.

గాథ gātha. [Skt.] n. A tale, story, A hymn, a legend, a verse or stanza. పాట, పద్యము. A puzzle, intricacy. గాథగానుండే. Intricate, puzzling.

గాద gāda. [Tel.] n. Thick prickly heat చెమటకాయలతేమ.

గాదము gādamu. [Tel.] n. Knot grass that infests a field of dry grain. పైరులోనికసవు. A leaf. ఆకు.

గాది gādi. [Tel.] n. A cushion or pad: a throne: a pin-cushion.

గాదిలి *gādili*. [Tel.] n. Love, affection. కూరిమి.

గాదె or గాదే *gāde*. [Tel.] n. A large high basket for storing grain. A barn. A. vi. 12. M. Stri. ii. 81.

గాధేయుడు or గాధిసుతుడు *gādhēyudu*. [Skt.] n. Son of Gādhi, i. e., Visvāmitra.

గానము *gānamu*. [Skt.] n. Song, tune, music. పాట.

గానుగ *gānuga*. [Tel.] n. A mill. An oil mill. చెరుకుగానుగ a mill for sugar cane. రాతిగానుగ a stone mill. గానుగపిండి oil cake: the refuse of the seeds after the oil is pressed out. గానుగరోలు the bowl or mortar part of such a mill. గానుగాడు to mill or to use a mill.

గాబ *gāba*. [Tel.] n. Rushes, bulrushes. ఇక్కడ గాబ నిండా పెరిగియున్నది this place is overgrown with bulrushes.

గాబరా *gābarā*. [H.] n. Fright, terror, confusion. భయము, కలవరము. గాబరాపడు to be in a fright.

గాబు *gābu*. [Tel.] n. A jar for storing grain. కాగ్పెర. An iron saucepan or frying pan. Weeds, trash, dirt, separated from grain by winnowing. గాబుతొట్టి a watering trough. గాబుతీయు to weed land.

గామ *gāma*. [Tel.] n. The young of an ant. చిన్నచీమ.

గామిడి *gāmidi*. [Tel.] adj. Cruel, hard. కఠినమైన, క్రూరమైన, కట్టిడి. Excellent శ్రేష్ఠమైన. "గామిడిగొల్లయా తానసంబుసను మాకు నీకైయున్న యూళొమ్మికానిచేళాని పరకంగ కట్టులంలేవో." BD. iii. 562.

గాము *gāmu*. [from Skt. గ్రహము.] n. A planet. A demon. గాముసోకినట్లు as though planetstruck, or possessed by a devil. Swa. iv. 126. "గాముసోకినమాడ్కి నికలున్నదు." Ila. ii. 26. గాములరేడు the sun, the lord of the planets.

గాయకము *gāyakamu*. [Tel.] n. A secret. మర్మము. "అగాయకపుజంత" Swa. ii. adj. Secret. గూఢము. "గాయకపుసుద్దులు." Swa. iii.

గాయకుడు *gāyakudu*. [Skt.] n. A singer. పాటపాడువాడు.

గాయత్రి *gāyatri*. [Skt.] n. A kind of tree. చండ్రచెట్టు. The name of a certain short prayer addressed to the sun by the Brahmins. M. XIII. iii. 115. It is as follows:— ఓంభూర్భువస్సువః తత్సవితుర్వరేణ్యం భర్గోదేవస్యధీమహి ధియోయోనః ప్రచోదయాత్ "Om! Earth! Heaven! Let us meditate on the supreme splendour of the divine sun! May he illuminate our minds!"

గాయమానము *gāya-mānamu*. [Skt.] n. Surgery. శస్త్రవిద్య.

గాయము *gāyamu*. [Tel.] n. A wound. క్షతి. నాకు గాయముతగిలినది I was wounded. గాయగాడు a wounded man.

గాయు or గ్రాయు *gāyu*. [Tel.] v. n. To spit or expectorate. ఉమియు. A. v. 132.

గార *gāra*. [Tel.] n. Plaster, mortar. సన్నగార fine plaster. A. iv. 21. గారపొడి (Vaijayanti. ii. 137.) a drugged paste used by fishermen to intoxicate fish. పల్లగార the crust or tartar on the teeth. గార or గారచెట్టు n. A kind of tree, *Balanites Roxburghii*. ఇంగుదము. (Watts.)

గారడము *gāradamu*. [Tel.] n. Juggling, cunning. A trick. T. ii. 133. గారడిపుమాట a lie, deceit. గారడీ *gāradi*. n. Mountebank tricks, magic, juggling. గారడీడు a juggler, a snake charmer. పాములవాడు.

గారము or గారవము *gāramu* [Skt.] n. Affection, fondness. గారాబము. Fondling, caressing ప్రేమము. చిన్నవాండ్లయందలి ప్రేమ. Greatness గొప్పతనము. గారవించు *gāravintsu*. v. a. To love, be fond of, to fondle: to welcome. గొప్పచేయు, గారవపరుచు. గారవిల్లు or గారవిలు *gāra-villu*. v. n. To be fondled or loved or treated with respect. గారవపడు.

గారాబము or గారాబు *gārābamu*. [Tel.] n. Affection, fondness; fondling or caressing children: indulgence. గారాబముగా

affectionately, fondly adj. Affectionate, fond. నా గారాబుబిడ్డ my pet child.

గారాము gārāmu. [Tel.] n. Same as గారాబము or గారవము.

గారు gāru. [Tel. another form of వారు.] adj. An honorific plural affix to singular nouns as దొరగారు master, తండ్రిగారు my honored father. అయ్యగారు sir, అమ్మగారు madam. It is used in the plural Thus. వెంకమ్మ సీతమ్మగారులు.

గారుడము gāruḍamu. [Skt.] n. An emerald of a dark hue గరుడపచ్చ. గారుడము adj. Of or belonging to Garuda, the king of birds గరుడునిది. గారుడాస్త్రము gāruḍāstramu. n. A magical weapon over which the Garuda mantram has been pronounced.

గారుత్మతము gārutmatamu. [Skt.] n. An emerald. పచ్చ, మరకతము

గారె gāre. [Tel.] n. A kind of round cake made of black gram (మినుములు.) కడుపునిండినవానికి గారెలు చేదు the full belly will scorn cakes.

గార్దభము gārdabhamu. [Skt.] n. An ass. గాడిద.

గార్హపత్యము gārhapatyamu. [Skt.] n. A sacred fire kept by a Brahmin.

గార్హస్థ్యము gārhastyamu. [Skt.] n. The state of being a householder. గృహస్థత్వము. Honesty.

గాలము or గాలాము gālamu. [Tel.] n. A hook. గాలపుమాట a heart-piercing speech. గాలము వేయు to throw a hook into water to catch fish. గాలకాడు gāla-kāḍu. n. A fisherman. చేపలను పట్టువాడు.

గాలి gāli. [Tel.] n. Wind, air, breeze. వాయువు. Scent మృగములదేహవాసన. A devil పిశాచము. plu. గాలులు. వానికి గాలి సోకినది he is possessed by a devil. గాలి విద్య an art that, like painting, depends on genius alone and cannot be taught. గాలిమాట a rumour. Empty talk, nonsense, లోకప్రవాదము. గాలిచుట్టు a spavin, a disease that attacks horses and cattle. పిచ్చుకకుంటి, పశువులకు గొరిసెలందు పుండుపడే వ్యాధి. గాలికల a senseless or empty dream. వారికి గాలిజీవనము they live upon the wind, i. e., they have no settled means of life. గాలికుక్క gāli-kukka. n. A hound: because it follows the scent. గాలిగుడి gāli-guḍi. n. A halo round the sun or moon. పరివేషము. గాలిగాడు gāli-gāḍu. n. An ass; a fool. గాలిగుడ్డు gāli-guḍḍu. lit. A wind egg. A simpleton. Nothing, nonsense. గాలిగూళ్లు (from గూడు.) gāli-gūllu. n. A mode of arranging sheaves so as to be aired. గాలిగొను gāli-gonu. v. n. To be aired. గాలిపోవు. గాలిగోపురము gāli-gopuramu. n. The dome over a temple gate: a steeple. The ornamented gate of a temple. గాలిచక్రము gāli-chakramu. n. A weather-cock. గాలిదిండి gālidiṇḍi. n. A snake. పాము. గాలినెచ్చెలి gāli-necheli n. The friend of wind, i. e., fire. అగ్ని. గాలిపంట gāli-panṭa. n. A precarious crop. గాలిపటము or గాలిపడగ gāli-paṭamu. n. A paper kite. గాలి బిళ్లలు gāli-billalu. n. The disease called mumps. గాలిమంద or గాలిమందపశువులు gāli-manda. n. Cattle herded in the forest, which become half wild. గాలివాన gāli-vāna. n. A tempest, storm, hurricane. గాలితోడివాన, తుపాను, ఝంఝ.

గాలించు gālintsu. [Tel.] v. a. To search, overhaul, sift. జెడలు. To sift grain in water and thus remove the stones in it. గాలింపు gālimpu. n. Clearance, riddance, sifting.

గాళకుడు gāḷakuḍu. [Tel.] n. A clever, ingenious man. ప్రౌఢుడు, ధీరుడు. "ఉ॥ గాళకులప్పుడె ఘటకఘామములెన్నగ నుప్పతుర్గలా." Vijaya. i. 12.

గావు *gâvu*. [Tel.] n. A sacrifice, wherein a goat or buffalo or a fowl is strangled. బలి. గావుపట్టు or గావు ఇచ్చు to offer such a victim. To kill చంపు. To destroy నాశముచేయు. గావుపట్టు *gâvu-pattu*. n. Perseverance పట్టిపట్టు. గావుకోడి *gâvu-kôḍi*. n. A certain plant.

గాసటబీసట *gâsaṭa-bisaṭa*. [Tel.] n. Confusion. గందరగోళము. Rubbish పనికిమాలినసంగతులు,

"ఉ॥ భాసురభారతార్థములభంగుల
నిక్క మెఱుంగ నేరమిన్,
గాసటబీసటంచదివిగాథలు
త్రవ్వు తెనుంగువారికిన్,
వ్యాసమునిప్రణీతపరమార్థము
తెల్లగఁజేసిపెట్టియు,
బ్రాసనకల్పులందలతువారుల
నన్నయతిక్కవారులన్."
లక్ష్మీ. i.

గ్రాసము *grâsamu*. [from Skt. గ్రాసము.] n. Meadow or pasture, grass, food, livelihood, maintenance. ఆహారము, కబళము.

గాసి *gâsi*. [Tel.] n. Fatigue, distress. శ్రమము. గాసిపడు to suffer pain, to sorrow: to labour. బాధపడు. గాసిపడ్డ exhausted, wearied, కష్టపడ్డ. గాసిచేయు *gâsi-cheyu*. v. t. To destroy. నాశముచేయు. గాసియగు to be destroyed. నాశమగు. గాసిపెట్టు *gâsi-peṭṭu*. v. a. To harass, annoy బాధించు. గాసిలు or గాసిల్లు *gâsilu*. v. n. To labour: to be exhausted or harassed. బాధపడు, శ్రమపడు. To get angry కోపపడు. R. II. 36. IV. 23. V. 168. 187. V. P. vii. 253.

గాసించు *gâsintsu*. [Tel.] n. To wear. ధరించు. "సీ॥ పులితోలు పచ్చడంబుగ మొలగాసించి సర్వాంగములను భస్మంబుబూసి." G. viii. 105.

గాహము or గాహనము *gâhamu*. [Skt.] n. Bathing, ablution. గాహితము *gâhi-* . . . Caught. పట్టుకొబడిన. Sunk . . . i. 10.

గి gi

గి *gi*. [Tel.] n. In speaking slightingly, a word is repeated with its initial short syllable changed into గి as అన్న గిన్న, కొకన్న గికన్న, &c.

గింగురు *ginguru*. [Tel.] adv. (Anuk. "saying ging!") Aloud, resoundingly. గింగురుపఱచు to stun or deafen.

"తెగ గింగురనబాపి దృష్టిసంధించి,
తెగ నేయుటయు."
HD. i. 621.

గింజ *ginza*. [Tel.] n. A grain, a seed. విత్తు. గింజలు grain or corn. గింజలు పట్టినతరువాత after the corn is formed in the ear. చింతగింజ a tamarind stone. మిరియపుగింజ a peppercorn: (fig.) a dapper little fellow. గింజలేరు to glean. గింజలేరుమనికి beggary: living upon gleanings. ఈతగింజ నిచ్చి తాటిగింజను ఈడ్చుట to venture a date seed in order to get hold of a palmyra stone, i. e., to stake a trifle in hopes of great gain.

గింజుకొను *ginzu-konu*. [Tel.]v. n. To twitch: to pull suddenly. To writhe, struggle, wallow in pain. గింజుకొంటూ distressed in anguish.

గింటెము *gin-ṭemu*. [Tel.] n. Weaving with a double thread. Cloth woven with a double thread. గింటెపు thick. "పూని బట్టుజిలుగుగింటెముబట్టోడ." Swa. vi. 107.

గిండి *gindi*. [Tel.] n. A narrow necked vessel. సన్నపుమెడగలచెంబు. plu: గిండ్లు. పోతగిండి a vessel with a spout, like a teapot.

గిచ్చు *gitstsu*. [Tel.] v. a. To scratch. గీచు. To pinch గిల్లు.

గిజగిజ *giza-giza*. [Tel.] adv. (Anuk) Violently (fluttering), agitatedly. BD. 3. 1217. గిజగిజలాడు to flutter, be agitated, troubled. తత్తరపడు. గిజగిజతన్నుకొని చచ్చెను it writhed in agony and died.

గిజరు See గిజారు.

గిజిగాడు or **గిజ్జిగాడు** *giji-gadu*. [Tel.] n. The Weaver bird, or *Baya Ploceus Baya*. (F. B. I.) పసుపుపిట్ట, పచ్చపిట్ట.

గిజిలిగాడు *gijili-gadu*. [Tel.] n. The brown spiny mouse, *Mus platythrix*. (F. B. I.)

గిజురు *gizuru*. [Tel.] n. The pulp of a fruit. గుజ్జు.

గిటక *gitaka*. [Tel.] adj. Stumpy, dwarfish, short in size. పొట్టి. గిటకపాటి dwarfish.

గిటగిట *gita-gita*. [Tel.] adv. (Anuk) Creakingly. "గిటగిటమసల్లుకొంకి" Swa.

గిటగిటన *gita-gitana*. [Tel.] n. Spite, ill-will adj. Little, mean అల్పము. Lean, growing lean. కృశము. A. v. 57. **గిటగిటము** *gita-gitam-anu*. v. n. To tremble. వణకు.

గిట్ట *gitta*. [Tel.] n. A hoof, of either horses or oxen. The claws of a crab or scorpion. An arrow. బాణము.

గిట్టు *gittu*. [Tel.] v. n. To die, expire. చచ్చు, నశించు. "పుట్టినేని వారుగిట్టినేని" what though they be born, what though they die (Vema). To suit, agree, match or meet, to be met. అనుకూలించు. to gnash. వాడికి పండ్లుగిట్టుకొనిపోయినవి his teeth were set in agony. వానికిని నాకును గిట్టదు he and I do not agree. నాకు గిట్టనివారు those who hate me, my ill wishers. ధరగిట్టక not agreeing on a price. అది నాకు గిట్టదు I do not like it, I cannot endure it. గిట్టీగిట్టక ఉన్నారు they are hardly on good terms. గిట్టని unsuitable. గిట్టమి disagreement, enmity. గిట్టమితనము spitefulness. v. a. To attack, meet with; లేళ్లనుమిగిట్టుకొల్పుటి the tiger that attacks the deer. M. 9. 1. 260. కలియు, కదియు, పైకొను, తాకు, పొదువుకొను. "శక్తిదండచక్రపాశ పాశములు వీకొనదము కూలముగొని నిశాచరుని గిట్టి" T. v. 111. **గిట్టుబడి** or **గిట్టేంపు** *gittubadi*. n. Profit (in trade): in demand. గిట్టీపైనసరుకులు goods that are profitable to the seller, good articles

గిడస *gidasa*. [Tel.] adj. Short, dwarfed, stumpy. గిటక, పెరుగని, పొట్టి.

గిడిగిల్లు *gidi-gillu*. [Tel.] n. Salutations. నమస్కారములు. "భక్తిసారముసప్రజలుజగత్పతికిని సంధించిరగిడిగిల్లోయని." H. iv. 294. Castanets, or a kind of rattle. చిటితాళ, చిటితాళం. Balram. v. 24.

గిడిగొను *gidi-gonu*. [Tel.] v. n. To tighten, be tight or squeezed గిడిగొన్నచేతులతో with clasped hands. గిడిగొనగా tightly, aloud, resoundingly.

గిడుగు *gidugu*. [Tel.] n. An umbrella with no handle. కామలేనిగొడుగు. Also, a contemptuous use of the word. గొడుగు.

గిడ్డ *gidda*. [Tel.] adj. Dwarfish, little, short. పొట్టి. n. A short person. గిడ్డితనము Shortness, dwarfishness. కొడవటిగిడ్డ a sickle.

గిడ్డంగి *giddangi*. [Malay *gandong*.] n. A godown, a ware house, a store-room.

గిడ్డతోన్న See తోన్న.

గిడ్డి *giddi*. [Tel.] n. A cow. గిడ్డకొడ్డి a cow house. "గిడ్డినినమేటిగిడ్డదొడ్డి." Sucas. ii. 4. 39. "పెల్లలోపొండిగానర్లకొమ్ముల ప్రేలగిడ్డి ముత్తపునేతిలడ్డగలను" ఆవుదెయ్యి పోయడనిన చేయుపాత్రములు. A. ii. 111.

గిడ్డు *giddu*. [Tel.] n. A hawk or falcon. డేగ.

గిత్త *gitta*. [Tel.] n. A young bull.

గిద్ద *gidda*. [Tel.] n. A gill or liquid ounce, one quarter of a సోల weighing four dubs.

గినియ *giniya*. [Tel.] n. A sort of plant. పెద్దగినియ, అనగా మహాశ్వేత, పాలగురుచేల గుమ్మడు. తెల్లగినియచెట్టు same as గిరికర్ణిక.

గినుము *ginumu*. [Tel.] n. Deception, cheating. మోసము, వంచన. **గినుమాడు** *ginum-adu*. v. t. To cheat. వంచించు.

గిన్నె or **గిన్నియ** *ginne*. [Tel.] n. A cup or goblet. గిన్నెకొమ్ము a horn used as a cup.

గిబ్బ *gibba*. [Tel.] n. A bull. గిబ్బరౌతు the rider on a bull—a title of Siva.

గిర *gira*. [Skt.] n. Speech. వాక్కు.

గిరక *giraka*. [Tel.] n. A pulley. నూతిరాట్నము, ఘటయంత్రము. adj. Short, dumpy. పొట్టి. గిరకతనము *giraka-tanamu*. n. Shortness of stature. గిరకతాడిచెట్టు *giraka-tāḍi-cheṭṭu*. n. The short or stumpy palm tree. గిరకపడు *giraka-paḍu*. v. n. To fall back, fail. "కందమూలంబులునిర్ఝాలంబులరయ్య చెరుకు గిరకపడె ఆకులంతిగెలంచికా కరొఙ్గ." Ellana iii. 219. గిరకకుండ without hesitation, at once.

గిరగిర *gira-gira*. [Tel.] adv. Round and round: spinning. గరగర.

గిరజా or గిరజా *girajā* [Tel.] n. Hair grown round the జుట్టు.

గిరవు *giravu*. [Tel.] n. A pledge. కుదువ.

గిరస *girasa*. [Tel.] adj. Stubborn, hard, tough.

గిరాకీ *girāki*. [H.] adj. Dear in price. ఎక్కువవెలగానుండే.

గిరాటువేయు *girāṭu-vēyu*. [Tel.] v. a. To whirl (as a stick at a mark): to hurl or sling a stone. నామీద రాళ్లు గిరాటువేసిరి they flung stones at me.

గిరి *giri*. [Skt.] n. A hill, a mountain. A circle. గిరిక *girika*. n. A mouse చిట్టెలుక. Name of the wife of King Vasu. వసురాజుభార్య. గిరికన్య *giri-kanya*. n. Daughter of the hills; a title of Pārvati. గిరికర్ణిక *giri-karṇika*. n. A certain plant, the camel thorn; or the Persian manna plant, *Alhagimaurorum*. (Watts). తెల్లగిరిజుచెట్టు. H. iv. 20. గిరికొను *giri-konu*. v. n. To surround or encircle. చుట్టుకొను. "అరవరలైన రథంబులు సెరిదప్పం బడినమాశ్వనికరంబులు బెండరుచుగ కూలినకరులును గిరిగొనియెను సమరమున మేదినీతలమెల్లన్." M. VI. ii. 141. గిరిజ *girija*. n. Lit. The "hill-born," i.e., Pārvati. A metal లోహము. గిరిధరుడు *giri-dharuḍu*. n. Lit. The Mountain-bearer, i. e., Krishna "who bore mount" Gōvardhan as an umbrella. గిరిభిత్తు *giri-bhittu*. Lit. The "render of mountains," i.e., a thunderbolt. వజ్రాయుధము. గిరిమల్లిక *giri-mallika*. n. The hill jasmine. కొండమల్లె.

గిరియకము *giri-yakamu*. [Skt.] n. A toy, a plaything. అచ్చనగాయలు.

గిరిసెము *girisemu*. [Tel.] n. A kind of tree, *Acacia sirisa*. శిరీషము, దిరిసెన.

గిరిశుడు *girisuḍu*. [from Skt. గిరి.] n. An epithet of Siva. Lit. The Mountain's son-in-law కొండఅల్లుడు. గిరీశుడు *girīsuḍu*. n. Lit. The lord of hills, i.e., Siva.

గిరుకు *giruku*. [Tel.] n. To write crookedly. వంకరటింకరగా వ్రాయు. To erase, scratch out, to strike through a written line. తప్పువ్రాతను తుడుచు. n. Erasure. తుడుపు.

గిరుక్కున *girukkuna*. [Tel.] adv. Round and round: whisking. గిరుక్కున తిరిగెను or గిరుక్కున మళ్లెను he turned suddenly.

గిరుపు *girupu*. [Tel.] v. a. To twitch, or stretch, as a limb, or the ears, or the eyelids in winking. మైగిరుపు to stretch the body on waking గిరుపుకొను to wink కన్నులను కిరుకించు. A. iv. 222. To cause to move, to shift కదలించు. గిరుపు or కనుగిరుపు To wink. "క్షేత్రజ్ఞులబరులుచేయు గనుగిరుపుసభన్," A. iv. 73. సంకేతచేయుమని సభవారికి నేత్రముచేత సూచించుము. గిరుపు *girupu*. n. A wink. సెనకుచూపు.

గిర్జ *girza*. [Tel.] n. The jungle Bush-quail, *Perdicula asiatica*. (F. B. I.)

గిర్రున *girruna*. [Tel.] adv. Round and round, suddenly round.

గిలక or గిలుక *gilaku*. [Tel.] n. A child's rattle, the wheel of a pulley, a capstan. A small handmill for cleaning cotton. The name of the letter ా. గిలకకర్ర

gilaka-karra. n. A rattle. గిలకతాడి *gilaka-tāḍi.* n. The male palmyra. గిలకబండి *gilaka-banḍi.* n. A low built dray, a creaking cart. గిలకల కోళ్లమంచము a cot with small bells hung on the legs. గిలకచెట్టు *gilaka-chettu.* n. A tree with rattling pods and a yellow papilionaceous flower, called *Crotolaria juncea*: జనుపవృక్షము. నూనెగిలక (Rox. ii. 357.) the tree called *Cæsalpinia Oleosperma.*

గిలకరించు or గిలకొట్టు *gilakarintsu.* [Tel.] v. a. To stir, beat, or whip buttermilk, so as to clear it. చిలుకు, కలచు, కుదిలించు. To sound మ్రోగు.

గిలాబా or గిలాబు *gilābā.* [Tel.] n. Plaster. గచ్చు. Plastering గచ్చుపూయుడము. గిలాబా చేసినగోడ a plastered wall.

గిలి *gili.* [Tel. derived from a slighting use of the word పులి or కేలి.] n. Fear, terror. భయము. పులిపోయినను గిలిపోలేదు though the tiger is gone, the sensation of fear is not past.

గిలికించు *gilikintsu.* [Tel.] v. a. To crowd writing. గిలిగ్రాత scribbling in writing.

గిలిగింత, గిలిగిలి or గిలిగిలింత *gili-ginta.* [Tel.] n. Tickling, giggling. గిలిగింతలుగ జలక్రీడలాడుట sportively bathing. గిలిగించు. గిలిగిలించు or గిలిగింతపెట్టు to tickle.

గిలిగింత *giliginta.* [Tel.] n. The plant called Blue flowered Crotolaria. Ainslie. ii. 305. 478.

గిలుకు *giluku.* [Tel.] v. n. To be crowded, as writing. See గిలికించు. To sound, jingle, as bracelets, or bells, on the ankles. గిలుకుగిలుకు *giluku-giluku.* (anuk.) adv. Aloud, audibly.

గిలుపు See గిరుపు.

గిలుబు or గిలుబాడు or గిలుమాడు or గిలుబుకొను or గిలుబుచేయు *gilubu.* [Tel.] v. n. To filch, pilfer, steal here and there. "గురువిందన దెలిబుకొనిరు సద్యోగడొంగ" Manu. ii. 114. గిలుబు n. Robbing, theft. అపహారము.

గిల్లకన్ను *gilla-kannu.* [Tel.] n. A squint eye. మెల్లకన్ను. గిల్లచూపు *gilla-tsūpu.* n. Peeping; peering, a squint. మెల్లచూపు.

గిల్లు *gillu.* [Tel.] v. a. To pinch, or nip with the nails. To remind by giving a pinch. గిల్లుడు *gilluḍu.* n. Pinching. గిల్లికొను to pinch oneself. గిల్లుపత్రి *gillu-patri.* n. A billet or note. See కిల్లాకు. A religious rite among the Saivas, during which the worshipper nips a leaf.

గిళితము *gilitamu.* [Skt.] adj. Swallowed. Eaten. తినబడిన.

గివ్వు or గివురు *givvu.* [Tel.] v. n. To scratch. గీరు.

గీ gī

గీ *gī.* [Tel.] In speaking contemptuously or slightingly, a word is repeated with the initial long syllable changed into గీ as రాముడు, గీముడు. See on గి.

గీ *gī.* [Tel.] n. (Anuk. of crying or wailing or buzzing) గీపెట్టు to whimper, to buzz.

గీ॥ In poems denotes గీతి a species of metre.

గీక *gīka.* [Tel.] n. An elephant's roar. ఏనుగు కూత.

గీకు *gīku.* [Tel.] v. a. To scrape, scratch, draw lines, erase. గీచు.

గీగాడు *gīgāḍu.* [Tel.] n. The Large Grey Babbler, *Argya malcolmi.* పెద్దసిదపిట్ట.

గీగీ *gīgī.* [Tel.] adv. (Anuk. whining) Shrilly.

గీచు *gītsu.* [Tel.] v. a. To scrape, scratch, erase: to draw a line. గీరగీచు; to tear, lacerate; to lance a palm tree, or tap it for juice. To shave. కంచుగీచినట్టుగా పలికె she spoke shrilly.

గీజు *gīzu.* [Tel.] n. Haggling. గీజుపోరు to haggle. గీజాడు *gīzāḍu.* v. n. To haggle, raise difficulties.

గీటు gîṭu. [Tel.] n. To push away. చిమ్ము. To gnash the teeth పండ్లు కొరుకు. To wink కన్నుగీటు or గిరుపు. కొరుకులాడు grinning with fury. BD. v. 783. n. A line గీత. గీటునపుచ్చు to disregard అనాదరించు. గీటడుగు gîṭ-aḍugu. v. i. To die. చచ్చు. గీటడచు gîṭ-aḍachu. v. t. To kill. చంపు.

గీట్లబద్ద gîṭla-badda. [Tel.] n. A measuring staff, a ruler.

గీత gîta. [Tel.] n. A line: lancing or pricking a tree. గీతగీసేకాలము the season for tapping the palm tree. గీతకట్టె gîta-kaṭṭe. n. A tool used by carpenters for drawing parallel lines, also called కత్తిగాను.

గీత gîta. [Skt.] n. The poem called Bhagavad Gita. భగవద్గీత. గీతము gîtamu. n. Song, music. పాట. Name of a certain Sanskrit metre. గీతి gîti. n. Song, metre. A species of metre: which in poems is abbreviated into గీ.

గీపెట్టు gî-peṭṭu. [Tel.] n. To whimper, wail: to cry. ఏడ్చు, మొరపెట్టు. To roar as an elephant (ఏనుగు) కూయు. To make a noise శబ్దించు. To buzz, as gnats. See under గీ.

గీము gîmu. [Tel.] n. A chamber, a house or home. "వింటారగింప విచ్చేయుడా దను మాగీములందు." R. ii. 136.

గీయమానము gîya-mânamu. [Skt.] adj. Cantabile; what is to be sung: vocal.

గీయు gîyu. [Tel.] v. a. To draw a line గీత గీయు. To scratch, or scrape. To strip off leaves: to tap a palm tree by cutting lines in it. ఆకులుగీసేకత్తి a large knife for stripping off leaves, a pruning knife. గీచు.

గీర gîra. [Tel.] n. A line. గీత.

గీరనగింజలు gîrana-ginzalu. [Tel.] n. A boys' game called అచ్చనగాయలు.

గీరు gîru. [Tel.] v. a. To tear, scratch, scrape, comb or smooth the hair with the fingers.

"వానినరించి నప్పుడుమాగా కూరిమిమీరగీరు,
కొనగోట చిటుక్కున కొక్కుపొక్కుగా."
T. ii. 95.

గీరుడు gîruḍu. n. Scratching. గోకుడు. గీరుకోను gîru-kônu. Same as గీరు.

గీరుగాజులు gîru-gâzulu. [Tel.] n. A sort of bracelets.

గీర్వాణము gîrvâṇamu. [Skt.] n. Sanskrit: the language of the gods. దేవభాష. గీర్వాణుడు gîrvâṇuḍu. n. A god, a deity. దేవుడు, వేలుపు.

గీలు gîlu. [Tel.] v. n. To flow. ప్రవహించు.

గీష్పతి gîshpati. [Skt.] n. An epithet of బృహస్పతి. Brihaspati.

గీసర gîsara. [Tel.] n. A kind of deer.

గు gu

గుంజ gunja. [Skt.] n. The small shrub called *abrus precatorius*. గురిగింజ. Land that produces salt ఉప్పుకయ్య.

గుంజ gunza. [Tel.] n. A post, a prop, a small pillar of wood. స్తంభము. పంగలగుంజ a forked stick used as a prop. పోటుగుంజ the same but larger.

గుంజచీరెలు gunza-chîrelu. [Tel.] n. A sort of red silk petticoat.

గుంజాటన gunzâṭana. [Tel.] n. Grief, regret. వ్యసనము.

గుంజాయిషి gunjâyishi. [H.] n Capacity, profit. లాభము. Defect, incompleteness, imperfection లోపము. ఈ లెక్కలో గుంజాయిషీ యేమిన్ని లేదు there is no defect in this account.

గుంజిలిపెట్టు gunjili-peṭṭu. [Tel.] v. t. To make a secret of, to hide. గోప్యముచేయు.

గుంజిల్లు or గుంజీలు gunjîlu. [Tel.] n. A punishment which consists in making a man sit down and get up a number of times.

గుంజు *gunzu*. [Tel.] v. a. To pull: ఈడ్చు. To wash clothes or to mangle linen ఉతుకు. n. Pulp; pith. గుజ్జు. గుంజుకొను *gunzu-konu*. v. a. To haul, pull, draw by force. గుంజునుసుకు *gunzu-nusuku*. n. Mocking, bear's play; gibing, joking. గుంజుపిట్ట *gunzu-pitta*. n. A sort of mocking bird, like a red owl: also called పిల్లరాజు. గుంజులాడు *gunzu-l-adu*. v. n. To struggle.

గుంట *gunta*. [Tel.] n. A little boy or girl (contemptuously used.) a brat; చిన్నగుంట or చిన్నదాండ. A slip of a girl.

గుంట or గుంట *gunta*. n. [Tel.] n. A pit, a hole of any kind. పల్లము. A pond కొలను. A tank. చెరువు. వానికన్నులు గుంటలుపడినవి his eyes are sunken. A certain square measure of land, ⅛th of an acre. గుంట పెట్టి గంటవాయించు lit. to put in a pit and ring the bell, i. e., to forget మరచిపోవు. గుంటక *guntaka*. n. A harrow. పొట్టిగుంటక a small harrow. గుంటక గుజ్జాలు the two pieces of wood in a harrow that connect the block with the front iron piece. గుంటకదిండు the cross log of wood in a harrow. గుంటకపలుగు the iron part of a harrow. గుంటకపోయు *guntaka-poyu*. v. t. To harrow. గుంటకదుడ్డు the block of wood in a harrow. గుంటకోవి *gunta-kovi*. n. A firepot, a rocket in an iron tube on a pole: a sort of firework fixed on a pole. పెట్లదిమ్మ. A kind of cannon. ఒకవిధమైన ఫిరంగి. గుంటగలగర *gunta-galagara*. n. The shrub named *Eclipta verbesina-prostrata*. Ainslie. ii. 129. గుంటగలిజేరు *guntagalijeru*. n. A kind of hogweed గలిజేరు (q. v.) గుంటచాళ్లు *gunta-tsallu*. n. The game of marbles. గుంటదూలము *gunta-dulamu*. n. A rafter. గుంటనక్క *gunta-nakka*. n. The Indian fox, *Vulpes bengalensis*. (F. B. I.) చిన్న నాఱినక్క. గుంటమాన్యము *gunta-manyamu*. n. A petty field (Vizag.) చిన్న మాన్యము.

గుంటి *gunti*. [Tel.] n. A portion of a field intended for ploughing. దున్నదానికి భాగం చినపాలము, చేనిభాగము.

గుండ *gunda*. [Tel.] n. A cloth. గుడ్డ. Powder. పొడి.

గుండంగి or గుండంగి *gundangi*. [Tel.] n. The whitefaced black ape. A waterhen జాతిపక్షము. A waterfowl. నీటికోడి.

గుండగొయ్య *gunda-goyya*. [Tel. గుండ + గొయ్య.] n. A stubborn ruffian. దుష్టుడు. గుండతనము *gunda-tanamu*. n. A hard or cruel temper.

గుండడు *gundadu*. [Tel.] n. A servant. దాసుడు.

గుండన్న *gundanna*. [Tel.] n. A rustic deity worshipped by potters.

గుండము *gundamu*. [Tel.] n. A pit, a fire pit. నిప్పులగుంట.

గుండవర్ధనము *gunda-varthanamu*. [Skt.] n. A sort of tree. "గుండవర్ధనములను కొండగోగులను." L. iii. 32.

గుండా *gunda*. [Tel.] (Postposition) Through, by, by means of. adj. Brave, courageous, rude, rough. ధీరుడు. గుండాతనము *gunda-tanamu*. n. Rudeness, roughness, abruptness.

గుండిగ *gundiga*. [Tel.] n. A large metal vessel with a large mouth.

గుడిగుడికుంచాలు *gudigudi-kuntsalu*. [Tel.] n. A certain game played by girls. Vish. P. vii. 211.

గుండియ Same as గుండె. (q. v.)

గుండీ *gundi*. [Tel. from గుండు.] n. A button. బొత్తాము.

గుండు *gundu*. [Tel.] n. A round stone. A cannon ball or bullet. ఫిరంగిగుండు. A lump. A weight (or stone) for scales. A hill పర్వతము. గుండుగుఱ్ఱము a stallion or stone horse. కెండిగుండు name of a kind of dog. శైలభము, "కత్తెరసంపంగి, కెండిగుండు" Manu. iv. 42. A polishing stone used by masons in plastering. నునుపుగుండు

the iron hoop that forms the lip of a leathern bucket. adj. Round, globular, spherical. గుండుకొట్టు gunḍu-koṭṭu. n. To smoke the drug called bhang. గుండుకోవి gunḍu-kōvi. n. A small cannon, a swivel. పెట్టెబిస్సు. See గుండుకోవి. గుండుగిలు gunḍu-gilu. v. n. To move in a circle. చుట్టుపడు. గుండుగుత్త gunḍu-gutta. n. An all-round settlement, i. e., a lease which covers all rights and privileges. సమస్త స్వాతంత్ర్యముతో ఇచ్చే గుత్త, చిల్లర. గుండుకొను or గుండుగూడుకొను gunḍu-konu. v. n. To unite, to make one common effort. To surround చుట్టుకొను. "అప్పుడెందరును వారివారలంబుల గుండుగూడుకొని సమరింపంగ." G. ix. 65. గుండుములుపుగాడు gunḍu-mulupu-gāḍu. n. The Nightjar or the goatsucker. గుండువేయు gunḍu-vēyu. v. n. To fire a gun: to die. గుండువేసికాల్చు to fire a ball at. గుండుసూది gunḍu-sūdi. n. A pin. గుండ్రాయి gunḍ-rāyi. n. A round stone or stone pestle. గుండ్లదండ or గుండ్లపేరు gunḍla-danḍa. n. A necklace of beads.

గుండె or గుండెకాయ gunḍe. [Tel.] n. The heart. The breast or chest. Courage. The apple of the throat. గుండెనొప్పిగా నది I have got a pain in my breast. అయ్యయ్యో నాగుండె O, my heart would break! మంచి గుండెలుగల staunch, stout-hearted. గుండెకాయ gunḍe-kāya. n The heart. గుండెలు gunḍelu. n. The heart.

గుండ్ర gunḍra. [Tel.] adj. Round. గుండ్రని. n. The upright roller of a sugar mill. చెరకుగానుగరోలు... A. iv. 197. గుండ్రలుకొలుపు gunḍralu-kolupu. v. n. To hoot as an owl. గుండ్రతుంగగడ్డి gunḍra-tunga-gaḍḍi. n. A sort of bulrush. The round bulrush. గుండ్రము gunḍramu. adj. Round. వర్తులము. గుండ్రదనము gunḍra-danamu. n. Roundness. గుండ్రన or గుండ్రము gunḍrana. n. Roundess. వర్తులత. గుండ్రని or గుండ్రనైన gunḍrani. adj. Round.

గుండ్రాయి gunḍrāyi. [గుండు+రాయి, or గుండ్ర+రాయి.] n. A round stone, a pestle పొత్రము. గుండ్రించు gunḍrintsu. v. n. To turn as the stomach when feeling sick కడుపుతిప్పు. గుండ్రింపు gunḍrimpu. n. Sickness at stomach, nausea, disgust.

గుంట or గుంటు gunta. [Tel.] n. A pit, a hole, a hollow, a dell.

గుంపు gumpu. [Tel.] n. A crowd. సమూహము. గుంపించు gumpintsu. v. t. To heap up. కుప్పచేయు or కుప్పవేయు. To exceed. అతిక్రమించు. గుంపెన gumpena. n. Pride. దిర్పాంధతనము.

గుంభనము gumbhanamu. [Skt.] n. Composition, in verse or prose. Obscurity, secrecy, mystery. అదియింకా గుంభనముగానే ఉన్నది it is still kept secret. పదగుంభనము the art of framing compound phrases. గుంభించు gumbhintsu. v. a. To string, or connect. గుంభితము gumbhitamu. adj. Tied, strung. Puzzling. అర్థగుంభితమైన obscure, difficult in style.

గుక్క or గుక్కు gukka. [Tel.] n. The act of drawing in the breath, a gulp, a mouthful. గుక్క తిరుగకుండా నవ్వెను he was in fits of laughter. గుక్కనిలుపు or గుక్కపట్టు to restrain the breath. గుక్కెడు gukkeḍu. n. A mouthful. గుక్కిలి or గుక్కిలి gukkili. [Tel.] The apple of the throat, a gulp; గుక్కిళ్లు మింగినాడు he swallowed his saliva, i. e., restrained himself, hesitated.

గుగ్గిలము guggilamu. [Tel.] n. Gum Gugal. The gum or resin of *Balsamodendron Mukal*, or *Boswellia glabra* (Watts).

గుగ్గిళ్లు guggiḷḷu. [Tel.] n. Boiled gram for horses or cattle. ఇనుపగుగ్గిళ్లు a jaw-breaker, a puzzling book. L. XI. 117. మినుపగుగ్గిళ్లు కావలె. ఇనుపగుగ్గిళ్లవలదు give me what I can understand. గుగ్గిళ్లగంప a kind of fee paid in harvest time.

గుచ్చు or గ్రుచ్చు *gutstsu.* [Tel.] v. a. To pierce or prick. To thread, string together. పూసలుగుచ్చు to string beads. దారముగుచ్చినాడు he ran the thread through, or inserted it. చేతులుగుచ్చు to join hand in hand, one's fingers being laced between those of his friend. కౌగిటగ్రుచ్చె he embraced her. గుచ్చుకొను *gutstsu-konu.* v. n. To enter, penetrate, pierce. కాలికి ముల్లుగుచ్చుకొనినది a thorn pierced the foot. గుచ్చుకపోయినకండ్లు sunken eyes. కండ్లు గుచ్చుకొనిపోతివి I cannot keep my eyes open.

* గుచ్ఛము *guchchhamu.* [Skt.] n. A cluster, or a bunch of flowers. పూగుత్తి.

గుజగుజ or గుజగుజలు *guzaguza.* [Tel.] n. Whispering. గుజగుజరేకులు *guza-guza-rêkulu.* n. The game called Puss in the Corner. Dasav. ix. 101. గుజగుజలాడు or గుజగుజపడు *guzaguza-l-âḍu.* v. n. To whisper: to agonize or be in trouble. క్లేశపడు. గుజగుంపులు *guza-gumpulu.* n. Whispering: doubt, hesitation, trouble.

గుజరాని *guza-râni.* [H.] n. Livelihood, employment, subsistence, daily bread, వృత్తి, జీవనము.

గుజరాయించు *guzarâ-yintsu.* [H.] v. t. To present, to offer. ఇచ్చు.

గుజరి *guzari.* [H.] n. A kind of Jasmine, *Jasminum multiflorum.*

గుజిలి *gujili.* [H.] n. A bazaar, a market place.

గుజస్తా *gujasta.* [H.] adj. Passed, elapsed. సాలుగుజస్తా last year.

గుజురు *guzuru.* [Tel.] n. Marrow, pulp. గుజ్జు.

గుజ్జు *guzzu.* [Tel.] n. A prop: an upright piece of wood used in supporting a shorter beam on a longer one in a shelving roof. A dwarf. Pulp, thick juice. చింతపండుగుజ్జు the pulp of tamarinds mixed with water. గడ్డికొమ్ములగుజ్జు (G. 151.) a short ox పొట్టియెద్దు. The cotton pod after the flower has fallen. గుజ్జు adj. Short, stumpy, dwarfish. గుజ్జువాడు a dwarf. గుజ్జది a dumpy woman. ఎక్కిన వానికి ఏనుగు గుజ్జటు అనగా వాడుకగా ఎక్కువానికి ఏనుగు అలక్ష్యము Familiarity breeds contempt. గుజ్జుతనము *guzzu-tanamu.* n. Shortness, dwarfishness. గుజ్జుప్రాలు a sort of rice. గుజ్జుమామిడి n. A young or dwarf mango tree. గుజ్జువేల్పు Lit. the plump short god. A name of Gaṇêsa. గుజ్జెన *gujjena.* adj. Infantile, childish గుజ్జెనగూళ్లు doll's dinners, children playing at cookery.

గుటక *guṭaka.* [Tel] n. A single gulp. ఒక్కసారి మింగగలిగినంతటి. గుటగుట *guṭa-guṭa.* adv. (Anuk of a growl, a growling sound.) Aloud. (Also of a gulping, bubbling, simmering sound) Rustlingly, crashingly. "బెబ్బులుల్ గుహలనిద్రించి గుర్కు చు కానఁజెటు కన్న గుటగుటార్భటులబాసగు" Suriya. iv. 60. గుటుకు, గుటుక్కు or గుడుక్కు *guṭuku.* n. A gulp, a sob. గుటుక్కను or గుటుక్కుమను to sob, gulp: to die, expire. దాన్ని గుటుక్కునమింగెను he swallowed it at a gulp.

గుట్ట *guṭṭa.* [Tel.] n. A hill, hillock. A heap రాశి. గుట్టకూల్చు to ruin, destroy. adj. Shrubby, low, stunted. గుట్టగుట్టపొదలు brushwood.

గుట్టు *guṭṭu.* [Tel.] n. A secret. మర్మము. The real state, reputation, honor, public esteem. "పొమ్మగుట్టునఁదుప్పురింబునకును" DRAy. 282. గుట్టుకీడు A secret foe. "పార్థివుడాత్మభుజాభృతతమాతలమున గుట్టు కీడుబహూధాయరయఁచిముదంచి." A. iv. 296. గుట్టుకీడు the revelation of state secrets రాజమంత్రము బయలుపడుట. గుట్టుసాకిరి *guṭṭu-sâkiri.* n. A witness that overbears secretly all the evidence against his party.

గుడక or గుడక *guḍaka.* [Tel.] n. The shell of a fruit prepared to serve as a snuff box, &c. A small metal box or casket. పైడిగుడక a gold box.

గుడము *guḍamu.* [Skt.] n. Molasses, jaggery, coarse treacle. బెల్లము.

గుడా *guḍa.* [Skt.] n. A particular mode of placing the fingers. "తిమురుడాకేళంబు తిమురు వారు." Dasav. iv. 125.

గుడాక *guḍāka.* [Skt.] n. Sleep. నిద్ర.

గుడాకు *guḍāku.* [H.] n. The drug called *gudak*, for smoking. Tobacco treated with treacle.

గుడారము or గుడారు *guḍāramu.* [Tel.] n. A tent. డేరా.

గుడి *guḍi.* [Tel.] n. A circle. The name of the secondary form of the vowel ఇ. A temple. The halo round the sun or moon. గుడివచ్చి మీదపడినట్లు to meet harm where none was expected. గుడికట్టు *guḍi-kaṭṭu.* n. The round or total extent of land under a village: a district. గుడికొను *guḍi-konu.* v. n. To spread. క్రమ్ము.

"క॥ అవిలుము బెదపులుతిరుపుమ
గుడికొనుకన్నిరు గ్రుక్కిళ్ళకొను మక మదిలో
మడుగని కెంజిలి నెమియు
మడువనియమ్మానధను గనుంగొని నే కన్."

స్వా. iii.

గుడిగి *guḍigi.* n. An armour that reaches up to the knees. గుడిగుడి *guḍi-guḍi.* adj. Little, slight. అల్పము.

"ద్వి. గుడిగుడికన్నీరు గ్రుక్కుచు"

పారిజ్. ii.

గుడిగుడిగుంటలు *guḍi-guḍi-guṇṭalu.* n. A game played by boys. H. iii. 186. గుడిచుట్టు *guḍi-tsuṭṭu.* n. A circle or orb, a disc. A halo. చంద్రసూర్యపరివేషము HD ii. 122. గుడిజెల్ల *guḍi-jella.* n. A species of fish. జెల్ల. గుడిప్రదక్షిణము Circumambulating a temple. గుడితిరుగు *guḍi-tirugu.* v. n. To move in a circle.

"క. కన్నులు గుడితిరుగగ నిదుర..."

శై. v.

గుడిత్రిప్పు *guḍi-trippu.* n. To ride round the ring. To lunge a horse. గుడిబ్రాహ్మణుడు or గుడిపడుసు a Brahmin who officiates in a temple. గుడికొంగ *guḍi-konga.* n. The paddy Bird or Pond Heron, *ardeola grayi* (F. B. I.)

గుడిసె *guḍise.* [Tel.] n. A hut, a cottage, a booth, a shed. గుడిసెవేటుకత్తె or గుడిసేటి లంజ a whore.

గుడుగుడు *guḍu-guḍu.* [Tel.] n. A small hookah. చిన్నహుక్కా. గుడుగుడుమని *guḍu-guḍu-m-ani.* adv. With a sound, rattlingly, rapidly. గుడుగుడుమని పరుగెత్తెను (he) ran rapidly. గుడుగుడుగుంచెములు Same as గుడిగుడిగుంటలు. (q. v.)

గుడుగురావిలము *guḍugu-rāvilamu.* [Tel.] n. A kind of bird. పక్షివిశేషము. (చంద్రా. ii)

గుడుసు *guḍusu.* [Tel.] n. A round or circle. A halo పరివేషము. adj. Round. గుడుసుకయిదువు the weapon of Vishnu. విష్ణుచక్రము. గుడుసుపడు *guḍusa-paḍu.* v. n. To form a circle or become round. గుండ్రమగు. M. VII. iv. 218.

గుడ్డ *guḍḍa.* [Tel.] n. A cloth or garment. వస్త్రము.

గుడ్డము or గుడ్డాము *guḍḍamu.* [Tel.] n. A plot of land. A field of corn. చేను.

గుడ్డి *guḍḍi.* [Tel.] adj. Blind. n. The number marked one that is turned upside down in a game అట్టచెమ్మలో వెలికిలపడిన ఒంటికాయ. గుడ్డివెన్నెల pale moon-light. గుడ్డిపారాయణము a blind recital. గుడ్డిదీపము a dim light. గుడ్డివేటుగా by chance, as a windfall, without expectation, undesignedly. గుడ్డిబెదిరింపు an empty threat. గుడ్డిబేరము a blind bargain. గుడ్డీగ a blind or foolish fly that does not go to rest as it gets dark. గుడ్డింగిలాయి *guḍḍingilāyi.* n. A species of fish, called *Scarus viridis* ఇంగిలాయి. గుడ్డికొక్కిరాయి

guḍḍi-kokka-rāyi. n. The blind crane or the bittern. గుడ్డితనము *guḍḍi-tanamu.* n. Blindness.

గుడ్డు or గ్రుడ్డు *guḍḍu.* [Tel.] n. An egg. The eyeball. గుడ్లుపెట్టు to lay eggs. ఆవుగుడ్డుకార్చుకొన్నది the cow miscarried. కోడిగుడ్డుకారము an oval shape. గాలిగుడ్డు lit. a wind egg, i. e., nothing, nonsense అది గాలిగుడ్డుమాట that is all nonsense. గుడ్డంతపిల్ల a little brat. గుడ్లగురివి *guḍla-guriri.* n. A blind abject wretch. గుడ్లగూబ *guḍla-gūba.* n. An owl.

గుణకము *guṇakamu.* [Skt.] n. The multiplier. పెంచెడులెక్క. గుణకారము *guṇa-kāramu.* n. Multiplication.

గుణము *guṇamu.* [Skt.] n. A quality, property, virtue, disposition, temper, character, or attribute. Tendency, effect, purpose, use. A symptom as of disease. వానికి గుణమువచ్చినది he is now come to his senses. నీలగుణము blackness. మంచిగుణము goodness, good temper. కామగుణము the passion of lust. వానికి గుణముగానున్నది he is better, he has recovered. పదిరూపాయలుయిస్తే గుణమే if he gives ten rupees so much the better. అందువల్ల ఏమిగుణము what is the use of it? వానితో మాట్లాడితే గుణములేదు there is no good in speaking to him పదిగుణములుగల or గడియకు ఒకగుణముగల freakish, changeable, whimsical వాంతిభ్రాంతిగుణము an attack or symptoms of cholera. The three Gunas are Rajah (passion) Tamah foulness: and Satvam (Truth). Added to a numeral, thus ద్విగుణము twice as much or two-fold. త్రిగుణము thrice as much, or three-fold. గుణము n. A cord, a string. త్రాడు. A bow string. అల్లెత్రాడు. గుణధ్వని the sound of the bowstring. గుణపడు *guṇa-paḍu.* v. n. To recover, improve, ameliorate. గుణమగు *guṇa-m-agu.* v. n. To recover. వారికి గుణమైనది they have improved. గుణమిచ్చు *guṇa-m-itstsu.* v. n. To affect favourably, as medicine, to improve the health. గుణముచేయు *guṇamu-chēyu.* n. To cure. గుణవంతుడు or గుణయుతుడు *guṇa-vantuḍu.* n A worthy or good man. గుణవతి *guṇa-vati.* n. A good woman. గుణి or గుణాఢ్యుడు *guṇi.* adj. Endowed or gifted with good qualities. "గుణిగుణంబులట్టి కూడియుండి" (Paidimarri. iv. 214.) united as closely as goodness and the good, as the virtuous and virtue. అధికగుణుడు highly distinguished. గుణించు or గుణియించు *guṇintsu.* v. a. To multiply, calculate. To spell. గుణితము *guṇitamu* n. Multiplication, spelling. గుణ్యత *guṇyata.* n. Excellence, goodness, worth. "గుణ్యత యేమైనను సత్ప్రాగల్భ్యము చేయుదము." T. iii. 96.

గుత్త *gutta.* [Tel.] n. Rent, a contract. ఆ గ్రామాని గుత్తచేసికొన్నాడు he took the village on rent. గుత్తకాడు *gutta-kāḍu.* n. A contractor. గుత్తకుతీసుకొన్నాడు. గుత్తకొను or గుత్తయెత్తు to take on contract గుత్తకు తీసుకొను.

గుత్తము *guttamu.* [Tel.] n. Plumpness, tightness. బిగువు. adj. Plump, tight, close-fitting, as bracelets.

గుత్తి *gutti.* [Tel.] n. A bunch or cluster of fruit, flowers, &c. The ankle చీలమండ. గుత్తికవ్వము or చల్లగుత్తికవ్వము a churn staff. గుత్తిపండు a ligneous berry that grows in bunches. గుత్తిమల్లెలు name of a kind of grain. గుత్తిపడు *gutti-paḍu.* v. n. To be closed. ముడుగు.

గుడగుడ *guḍa-guḍa.* [Tel.] adv. (Anuk) Privately, secretly. గుడగుడలాడు *guḍa-guḍa-l-āḍu.* v. n. (Anuk) To sob. డగ్గుత్తికతో ఏడ్చు.

గుదము or గుదస్థానము *gudamu.* [Skt.] n. The anus. The *os coccygis, uropygium* or crupper.

గుడి *guḍi.* [Tel.] n. A bunch or cluster గుత్తి. A staff. A string of dried fish, leaves,

కం. సరము. మచ్చులగుడి a bunch or set of anything as samples. గాజులగుడికి రోకలి బూదినట్లు a bunch of glass bracelets do not require a rice-pounder to break them. గుడికాలు *gudi-kalu.* n. The heel. మడిమె (plu. గుడికాళ్లు). గుడికాళ్లు నరము తెగ గొట్టుట to hamstring. గుడికర్ర *gudi-karra.* n. A clog suspended from the neck of a beast to prevent it from straying. గుడికొను *gudi-konu.* v. a. To excel. అతిశయించు, చెలరేగు. To become close or thick దట్టమగు. To fall down with a thud. మూటపడి కూలబడు. "గుడికొనినెన్నాడు కుసుమపుంజము తోడ." Ila. i. 10.

> "హృదయమునవలంబైతే,
> గుడికొనుసన్మార్గసమునకు కొమ్ములుంగలవా."
> Vema. iii. 197.

గుడిగుంజలు *gudi-gunzalu.* n. Stick planted at the entrance of a pen or fold. పశువుల దొడ్డిద్వారమునకు నిలువుగా పాతినకర్రలు. గుడిగ్రుచ్చు or గుడిగూర్చు *gudi-grutstsu.* v. n. To arrange. సవరించు. "మున్నిటికథలు గుడిగ్రుచ్చుకొనిచెప్పకొని పోవలదు." L. vii. 74. గుడిత్రాడు *gudi-tradu.* n. A halter, a tether. దూడకాలికికట్టేతాడు. గుడిత్రోచు to tie up the legs and push away కాళ్లు కట్టిత్రోచు.

గుడియ *gudiya.* [Tel.] n. A club, a mace, a cudgel. A clog fastened to a cross cow. గుడియకర్రలు *gudiya-karralu.* n. (In house building) small sticks placed across the rafters. గుదిగుంజలు. గుడియతాలుపు *gudiya-talupu.* n. Lit. The mace-bearer, i. e., Yama, the god of death. దండధరుడు. గుడివడు *gudi-padu.* v. t. To be tied up కట్టుపడు. To shudder, shiver, tremble. వణుకు. "గుడివడుచున్న చెన్నడుము." Padma P. iii. 36.

గుడిలకొను *gudila-konu.* [Tel.] v. n. బాధపడు, "ద్రౌపదీరూపమను సుడిగాలి తనదుహృదయమనుమ్రాన మ్రొత్తి గుడిలగొనగ కామమనుబల్లిదపుకేటకానిబారిబడుట కింతయు నాకించుబలుదు తలరి." M. IV. ii. 28.

గుడ్డ *gudda.* [Tel.] n. The anus.

గుద్దలి *guddali.* [Tel.] n. A pickaxe. గుద్దలి. a spade, or small hoe. గుద్దలించు *guddal-intsu.* v. a. To dig up, to hoe.

గుద్దు or గ్రుద్దు *guddu.* [Tel.] v. a. To strike with the fist, to box, to cuff. గుద్దు or గ్రుద్దు n. A thump, cuff, box. గుద్దులాట *guddu-l-ata.* n. Hand to hand fighting, boxing. గుద్దులాడు *guddul-adu.* v. n. To go to blows, to fight together, to box.

గునకలు *gunakalu.* [Tel.] n. A sort of wild grain.

గునగున *guna-guna.* [Tel.] n. (Anuk: of running), tripping along, trotting along ఆచిట్టి ఆకులు గునగున పెరిగినవి the leaves have come out very delicately కోమలముగా. గుండ్రాతికొళ్లువచ్చి గునగునవడిచెను the stones moved slowly. "గునగున చీమలు గుద్దిత్తుకొనిపార." Velag. iii. 4.

గునపము *gunapamu.* [Tel.] n. An iron crow bar. గడ్డపార.

గునామొలనూలు *guna-mola-nulu.* [Tel.] n. A sort of girdle worn by infants. "కెంపుల రావిరేకు జాబిల్లి పులిగోరుమ చందమామసొమ్ముం పుసరాలు గాజులు గునామొలనూల్ రవగజ్జెలరటియల్." Velag. i. 69.

గునియు or గునిసియాడు *guniyu.* [Tel.] v. n. To dangle, play, wag, dance. నర్తించు, తాండవించు. Also, to grumble, mutter, or murmur. To sulk, కులుకు. "గునియుచు కన్నరగుండయ్యగాద్యమునకాడి." BD. iii. 738. "కొడుకునగల్లని గునిసియాడగరాదు." Vema. గునుపు *gunupu.* n. Motion, action. గునుపుకోడి the jungle cock, so called from its gait.

గునుక, గునుకగడ్డి or గునుకు *gunuka.* [Tel.] n. A sort of wild corn which is eaten in times of scarcity.

గునుకు, గునుగునవరుగిడు or గునుకులాడు *gunuku.* [Tel.] v. n. To trot, amble, trip or run gently. "ఘటంపూర్ణమంత్రపుష్పముధారలెత్తించి గునుముగానకతోడి గునికె నొకడు."

P. i. 127. గుణుకునీసము an ambling metre composed in a peculiar mode. గుణుకు n. An amble, trot, or gentle run. గుణుకు పరుగు gunuku-parugu. n. The act of running slowly. "గుణుకుపరువునను దాటె బలుడు తొలంబడియడుగులు." Dasav. ix. 16.

గున్న gunna. [Tel.] adj. Young: as a cub of a young animal or tree. గున్నచింత a low or bushy tamarind tree. గున్నయేనుగు an elephant's cub. గున్నపంది a young pig. n. The young of an animal: a child: a cub: a sapling, suckling or young tree. మామిడి గున్న a young mango tree. "గున్నలప్రక్కనక నేడుగూడుచెబావా." Chenna. iii. 161.

గున్నంగి gunnangi. [Tel.] A medicinal root: the *Salvadora Persica* of Ainslie: ii. 266. Also, a kind of bird.

గుప్తము guptamu. [Skt.] adj. Hidden, concealed, secret. గుప్తకేళి gupta-keḷi. n. Secret pleasures, hidden delights. Name of a game, Hide and Seek. దాగిలిమూతలు. గుప్తి gupti. n. Concealment దాచుట.

గుప్పళించు guppaḷ-intsu [Tel.] v. a. To mangle cloth: to wash it by beating it gently. To rince the mouth. పుక్కిలించు. To place ఉంచు.

గుప్పించు guppintsu. [Tel.] v. a. To diffuse, emit, shed abroad. To rain కురియు, బాణా దులను ప్రయోగించు.

గుప్పిలి or గుప్పిడి guppili. [Tel.] n. The fist. గుప్పిట in the hand or fist.

గుప్పు guppu. [Tel.] v. n. To be diffused, or spread, as a smell. "ఇక్షుదండము ప్రేమ భక్షింపభక్షింప, చప్పనేలకురుచులే గుప్పునాక." Kalah. § 35. "ధూపంబువాసనగుప్పగా." T. ii. 84. గుప్పు v. a. To pound or beat. To throw, fling or toss. గందపొడిగుప్పిరి they threw powder in handfuls. "అరిసులుగుప్పి పతి గుప్పుచున్నాడు పువ్వుగోలలను" L. X. 98. To place ఉంచు. To sprinkle చల్లు. To throw as a missile or an arrow విసిరివేయు, ప్రయోగించు. To thrust as a calf does at the udder పొదుగును పొడుచు. గుప్పు n. A blow, a dash. గుప్పున guppuna. adv. Sweetly, fragrantly. (గుప్పు + అనునట్లు) "గుప్పునమెరితాని సరగుల్కగ కమ్మనికలదిపప్పు మాపప్పన మిూకురాదు." Balaram. Cha. 135. గుప్పున guppuna. adv. Quickly, hastily. Clearly. గుప్పున కనిపిస్తున్నది it is seen clearly or boldly.

గుబక gubaka. [Tel.] n. A brass boss on a door, a knob on a shield.

గుబగుబ or గుభగుభ gubaguba. [Tel.] n. Hubbub. గుబగుబలు లేనికూటమి meeting without tumult. అక్కడ ఏమి గుబగుబలు what is the uproar? వారేమో గుబగుబలాడు చున్నారు there is some stir among them. adv. Tumultuously: with indistinct accents. పిల్లకాయలు గుబగుబ పరుగెత్తిరి the boys ran along noisily.

"గుబగుబమనిపల్కు కోకిలపల్కులు,
విని యువి కేర్తువా యనుచు నవ్వు."
T. ii. 97.

సముద్రము గుబగుబలాడుచున్నది the sea roars aloud. ఊరంతా గుబగుబలాడుచున్నది all the village is up, in a stir, or in a ferment. గుబాటున gubāṭuna. adv. All at once, in a moment. గుబాటు పెడివానలు sudden showers. గుబాడెబ gubā-ḍeba. adv. Bang! slapdash. "గుబాడెబ పిడుగుల పెంటజంటలై" H. v. 191. వాణ్ని గుబాడెబగుద్దినారు they beat him thoroughly. గుబాలు or గుబేలు gubālu. n. A bang! A loud sound. గుబాలను to bang, to make a noise. గుబాలున or గుభాలున all at once, Bang! crashingly. నీళ్లలో గుబాలున దుమికినాడు he leapt slapdash into the water. గుబాలుమన్న ధ్వనివింటిని I heard an explosion or a bang. గుబాళించు gubāḷ-intsu. v. n. To be emitted or burst forth, as scent. "కమ్మతావిగుబాళించు కమ్మికొలను" a pond perfumed with lilies. Vijaya. i. 162.

గుబారు gubāru. [H.] n. Alarm, confusion, a rumour. పుకారా. అది యిక్కడ గుబారుగా నున్నది it is a rumour here.

గుబిరిక *gubirika.* [Tel.] n. A kind of snare. "సరసశకుమలకుకట్టువ, దూపుకాంతముఖ్యవటక సంఘములకుమగుబిరిక." H. ii. 94.

గుబిలి *gubili.* [Tel.] n. The wax in the ear. గులిమి, గుబిలి. Also same as గుబ్బలికాడు See under గుబ్బ.

గుబుకు *gubuku.* [Tel.] v. a. To thump or beat with the fists.

గుబురు or **గుమురు** *guburu.* [Tel.] n. Thickness, as of trees, or foliage. సమూహము. adj. Thick, crowded. దట్టము. A cluster of trees. సమూహము. గుబురుగాపెరిగినచెట్లు thick-leaved trees.

గుబులు or **గుబులుకొను** *gubulu.* [Tel.] v. n. To spread as scent, to be redolent. "జవ్వాదితావి గుబులుకొనంగ." T. iii. 76. **గుబులుగా** *gubulu-ga.* adv. Aloud, thunderingly, (as drums) గుర్రాలమీద నగారాడబ్బులు గుబులుగ మోసెగా the kettle drums sounded dub-a-dub-dub. **గుబులు గుబులు** or **గుభుల్ గుభుల్** *gubulu-gubulu.* adv. Resoundingly, aloud, as thunder. "దుందుభుల్ గుభుల్ గుభులుమనియెం." Vasu. v. 3.

గుబుసు *gubusu.* [Tel.] n. A secret. కిటుకు. Cunning కపటము.

గుబ్బ *gubba.* [Tel.] n. A stud, a knob, a protuberance. A woman's breast. "బంగారుగుబ్బతో ఛాయిల్లు గొడుగు" an umbrella with a gold knob at the top. Pal. 250. "సకలాతుగుబ్బలజోళ్లు" woollen shoes with knobs. Pal. 62. గుబ్బకాయ a long gourd, *Cucurbita laegenaris,* సొరకాయ. **గుబ్బ** *gubba.* adj. Round గుండ్రని. **గుబ్బతిల్లు** *gubba-tillu.* v. n. To spread, as scent, sound or fire. వ్యాపించు. "గబ్బిని వాచరుండు బలుఖడ్గము కేల నమర్చి దిక్కతుల్ గుబ్బతిలంగ పేరుకాని కోయనియార్చుచు." HK. iii. 154. గుబ్బమేకులు large round-headed nails. **గుబ్బతిల్లు** or **గుబ్బతిలు** *gubbatillu.* v. i. To excel అతిశయించు. ఉప్పొంగు. **గుబ్బలాడి** *gubbal-adi.* n. A full breasted woman. A young woman. యువతి. T. iii. 3. **గుబ్బలి** *gubbali.* n. A hillock, a hill, a mount. కొన్నగుబ్బలి a small hillock. గుబ్బలిరేడు, lit. the king of hills, i. e., the Himalaya హిమాచలము. R. i. 77. **గుబ్బలికాడు** or **గుబ్బిలికాడు** or **గుబ్బిలి** *gubbali-kadu.* n. The spotted owlet. Athene brama (F. B. I.) పైడికంటి. గుబ్బలివిలుకాడు lit. the hill archer, i. e., Siva. శైలధన్వుడు. గుబ్బలిపట్టి lit. the "daughter of hills:" or నగజ a name of Parvati. **గుబ్బసరము** *gubba-saramu.* n. A necklace composed of different kinds of gems.

గుబ్బిక *gubbika.* [Tel.] n. A snare for birds. H. ii. 94.

గుబ్బు *gubbu.* [Tel.] n. The beating of the heart. గుండె అదరుట. గుబ్బున suddenly, all at once, swiftly. "గుబ్బునబడుశిరము గుదిపడుశిరము" BD. vi. 99. **గుబ్బుమను** or **గుబ్బురను** or **గుబ్బుగుబ్బురను** *gubbu-m-anu.* v. n. To beat as the heart. గుండె అదరు.

గుబ్బెత Same as గుబ్బలాడి. (q. v.) H. 54. "తగకేయుధపతికి గుబ్బెతలంతరువైనగ." Satya. iv. 209.

గుబ్బోగర *gub-bōgara.* [Tel. గుబ్బ+పోగర.] n. An engraving chisel.

గుమగుమ or **ఘుమఘుమ** *guma-guma.* [Tel.] (Anuk.) adv. Sweetly, fragrantly, melodiously, strong (as scent.) **గుమాయించు** *gumā-yintsu.* v. a. and n. To spread as a perfume, to pervade. To be close or sultry. ఆ అత్తరు ఇల్లంతా గుమాయించుచున్నది the scent of the *attar* pervades the whole house.

గుమాస్తా *gumāsta.* [H.] n. An assistant, a clerk, an agent. లేకరు.

గుమి *gumi.* [Tel.] n. A crowd, a flock, a multitude. పోగు, గుంపు.

గుమిటి or **గుమ్మిటి** *gumiti.* [Tel.] n. A sword stick, a rapier in a cane. "అమ్మగుమ్మిటిగ." T. ii. 79.

గుముకు *gumuku*. [Tel.] v. a. To box, to strike with the fist. పిడికిలితో పొడుచు.

గుముడు or **గుమ్మడు** *gumuḍu*. [Tel.] n. The plant named *Antidesma diandrum*. (Watts.) కాశ్మర్యము. One species is called నేలగుముడు and another కొండగుముడు.

గుమురు Same as గుబురు. (q. v.) **గుమురు గాగ** *gumuru-gāga*. adv. Thickly. "ఒకా నొకకోనలో గానలో గుమురుగాగఁబలిసిన వెదురు జొంపము క్రిందు." Dasav. iv. 84., i. e., under thickly grown bamboos.

గుమ్మ *gumma*. [Tel.] n. A spirt or gush, as of milk. క్షీరధార. A high basket. బుట్ట. A girl, a darling, a little one. ముద్దుగుమ్మ a pretty woman చక్కనిస్త్రీ.

గుమ్మటము *gummaṭamu*. [Tel.] n. A paper lantern. కాగితపుగూడు. A cupola, or dome. గుమ్మటము or పొగగుమ్మటము a balloon.

గుమ్మడి *gummaḍi*. [Tel.] n. A gourd, a pumpkin, *Cucurbita maxima*. గుమ్మడితీగె or గుమ్మడి చెట్టు a gourd vine. గుమ్మడిపువ్వు a gourd flower. గుమ్మడిపండువంటిదేహము a form delicate and fragile as a gourd. పెండ్లి గుమ్మడికాయ or బూడిదగుమ్మడికాయ the white gourd, *Benincasa cerifera* (Watts.) The expression గుమ్మడిపండు is also a tuck or fold in the front of a woman's petticoat. గుమ్మడికాయచెంబు brass pot of a particular shape. గుమ్మడికాయలాగున కూర్చున్నాడు he was sitting at his ease.

గుమ్మడు *gummaḍu*. [Tel.] n. A beau or fop. సొగసుకాడు, అలంకరించుకొన్నవాడు.

గుమ్మతీలు *gumma-tīlu*. [Tel.] n. A jewel worn by women in the lobe of the ear. చెవిలిమ్మెలందుంచేసొమ్ము.

గుమ్మము *gummamu*. [Tel.] n. A door way, gate-way or entrance. వాకిలి, ద్వారము.

గుమ్మి *gummi*. [Tel.] n. A high basket for holding corn. బుట్ట. "పదతుకనిత్యమైదు గురుగ్వజ్ఞలకన్న మొసంగికానివే, కుడువవు నీగ్న పాయు నను నున్నులుగా దలుకొను మెక్కడేక." Chenna. iv. 102. **గుమ్మి** n. Mire, a morass, a swamp. బురద, పఱ్ఱ.

గుమ్మితి Same as గుమితి. (q. v.)

గుమ్ము *gummu*. [Tel.] n. Fragrance గుమగుమ. గుమ్మున adv. Fragrantly. "కెమ్మెనపొదలలో నిండిన విరులగుమ్మున జడివాన గురియుచుదాని." D. Abh. 38.

గుమ్ముడుచెట్టు See గుముడు.

గుమ్మె *gumme*. [Tel.] n. A dent. సొట్ట. "గుమ్మెలంటాకినబంగరుబొంగరములు." Siranga. Padya, ii. 247. A small tent. గుడారు, చిన్న గుడారము.

గుమ్మెట, **గుమ్మెత** or **గుమ్మెతము** *gummeta*. [Tel.] n. A small drum. తమ్మటము, ఢక్కము, డప్పు. A. iv. 38. "గుమ్మెతల్ కిన్నెరల్ గూడి వాయించుచు." H. iii. 238. **గుమ్మెతకాడు** *gummeta-kāḍu*. n. A drummer. గుమ్మెతవాయించువాడు.

గురక *guraka*. [Tel.] n. Snoring. నిద్రయందలిధ్వని. **గురకపెట్టు** or **గురకకొట్టు** *guraka-peṭṭu*. v. n. To snore.

గురగుర *gura-gura*. [Tel.] n. The grunting of a pig. పందికూత. Also, an itching sensation. ఒకవిధమైన దురద.

గురణము or **గూరణము** *guraṇamu*. [Skt.] n. An attempt. యత్నము.

గురి *guri*. [Tel.] n. A mark. An aim, a goal. లక్ష్యము. A clue, a sign గురుతు. An example దృష్టాంతము. A limit మితి. Certainty నిశ్చయత. గురిచెప్పేస్థలము a place where oracles are uttered. గురిలేని aimless, unsteady. Esteem, respect. వానికి ఆమెయందు గురి ఉన్నది. he respects her. గురిచూచు, గురిపెట్టు or గురికొను to take aim. గురితప్పు to miss one's aim. **గురించి** *gurinchi*. (from గురించు.) an affix used with the accusative case. Regarding, looking at, with an eye to. Of, concerning, about.

For, with a view to, for the sake of, on account of. Towards, to. అతనిన్ని గురించి పలికినది she spoke of him. దేవుణ్ని గురించి ప్రార్థించియున్నాను I have prayed to God. **గురించిన** *gurinchina.* adj. Concerning, connected with, regarding. For, on account of. అందుకుగురించిన కర్చుబడి the expense incurred for this. అతనిన్ని గురించిన జాబు a letter regarding him. **గురించు** *gurintsu.* (గురి+ఉంచు.) v. t. To intend. ఉద్దేశించు. **గురికట్టు** *guri-kaṭṭu.* n. Border, edge, bound, limit. **గురికాడు** *guri-kāḍu.* n. A true marksman. కృతహస్తుడు. **గురికొండి** *guri-koṇḍi.* n. A vital part. మర్మస్థానము, జీవస్థానము. ఆయువు.

గురిగి *gurigi.* [Tel.] n. See గురుగు.

గురిగింజ or **గురివెందగింజ** or **గురుగింజ** *guri-ginja.* [Tel.] n. The plant called Indian shot. The Indian or wild liquorice plant. *Abrus precatorius,* or, *Canna indica* (Watts).

గురిచి The same as గూర్చి, కూర్చి or గురించి.

గురిజ *guriza.* [Tel.] n. A certain grain. Same as గురిగింజ or గురివెంద. గురిజ పేరులు. G. xi. 5.

గురిమిడిగడ్డ *gurimiḍi-gaḍḍa.* [Tel.] n. A root resembling వెల్లగడ్డ. నేలగుమిడి.

గురు *guru.* [Tel.] n. Name of a certain animal మృగవిశేషము, గవయము.

గురుక *guruka.* [Tel.] n. A spear. గొరక గ్గె.

గురుకు *guruku.* [Tel.] n. A heap, a pile. పోగు, కుప్ప. "పేరాకలినరిమురిలబ్ధ ... గురుకులుపెట్టిన మృగావళులనొప్పు." M. IV iii. 227.

గురుకొను *guru-konu.* [Tel.] v. n. To attempt. యత్నించు. ఉద్యోగించు. To redouble, as a storm. కమ్ముకొను.

"క॥ గురుకొని కార్యాకార్యము,
లెరుగక దుర్బుద్ధియగు నహితుడగు నేనా,
మరపక గురుడైనను జను,
లెరుగగ శాసించునది మహీశుడు బుద్ధిన్."
M. I. vi. 105.

గురుగు or **గురిగి** *gurugu.* [Tel.] n. A small cup. చిన్నపిడత. A certain pot herb or darnel that grows in rice fields. The sun flower, *Heliotropum Indicum.* Also, *Celosia argentea.* పంచెచెట్టు (Watts).

గురుగుర్రు *guru-gurru.* [Tel.] n. A rolling sound. ఉరుము.

గురుతు or **గుర్తు** *gurutu.* [Tel. from గురి aim.] n. A mark, a sign, a trace, a token. A limit, an extent మేర. కనుగుర్తులెక్క a memorandum. నాకు గుర్తులేదు I do not recollect. గురుతుగా అడుగు to enquire particularly. గురుతుగాచూచు to look into narrowly. గురుతుపట్టు or గుర్తెరుగు to recognise.

గురుదా *guruḍa.* [Tel.] n. A club or mace: (probably from the Persian word *gurz.*) గద అనే ఆయుధము. T. i. 9.

గురుపెట్టు Same as గురకపెట్టు. (q. v.)

గురుపోతు *guru-pōtu.* [Tel.] n. A wild ox or bison. అడవి ఎద్దు.

గురుములు *gurumulu.* [Tel.] n. Seeds. విత్తులు, గింజలు.

గురువు or **గురుడు** *guruvu.* [Skt.] n. A teacher, a preceptor, a master, a superior, a learned man, a father. A title or name of Brihaspati, tutor of the Gods, who was the husband of Tāra. **గురువారము** *guru-vāramu.* n. Thursday. దొంగలగురువు a master thief, a ringleader. **గురువు** *guruvu.* n. Greatness గౌరవము, weight భారము. పూర్వజన్మార్జిత ఘోరకర్మముల గుర్వగుచు నాకొదవక రావయ్య. BD. iv. 218. A long syllable, in prosody. Fast running వేగపు పరుగు. adj. Heavy, weighty, great, large, bulky: difficult, arduous. Reverend, venerable. గురుకార్యము a weighty matter. గురువుగా or గుర్వుగా positively or greatly అధికముగా. "సర్వమాన్యము నీకు గుర్వుగానిత్తు." BD. iv. 490. గురువువేరు guruvu-tēru. v. n. To swell, చిర్రుచిప్పిలు. గురువులుపారు to run very fast వేగవుపరువుగాపారు. To excel అతిశయించు. గురుత్వము gurutvamu. n. Greatness, weight, importance. Esteem. Heaviness, or languor. గురునాథుడు guru-nādhuḍu. n. The name of a certain village god, whose image is usually a mere block of stone, under a tree.

గురువెంద Same as గురిగింజ. బండిగురువెంద or పెద్దగురుగింజ Red wood or red sandalwood, *Adenanthera pavonina* (Watts).

గురువెట్టు or గుర్రెట్టు guru-veṭṭu. [Tel.] n. To snore. "రెట్టు గా ప లు మా రు ని ట్టూ ర్పు బుచ్చుమ భీకరంబుగ గురువెట్టిరాముచు." N. H. v. 62.

గురుసు gurusu. [Tel.] n. The stump, root or stock, of a tail, tooth or tree. The tuft of a tail. తోకచివర పొడుగువెంట్రు కలుండేది. A vital part జీవస్థానము. A limit మేర.

గుర్రము gurramu. [Tel. short for కుదిరము or కుదిరము. (q. v.)] n. A horse, plu. గుర్రములు, గుర్రాలు or గురాలు. ఆడుగుర్రము a mare. గుర్రపుముఖము the shin of a man's leg. వాడు ఇప్పుడు గుర్రము ఎక్కి ఉన్నాడు he is tipsy or slightly intoxicated. గుర్రపుగట్టాకు gurrapu-gaṭṭ-āku. n. Prickly nightshade, *Solanum Jacquini*. వాకుడు. గుర్రపుచేబుకు a horse whip కొరడా; also a slender fish, *Syngnathus Typhlus*, Linn-Russell, No. 30. గుర్రపుపిల్ల a foal, a colt. గుర్రపుపీట a piece of wood on a door with a horse's face carved on it. గుర్రపుపెరజె a kind of snake. G. viii. 101. గుర్రపుమారిజిట్ట gurrapu-mari-jiṭṭa. n. The Indian Pipit, *Anthus rufulus* (F. B. I.). గుర్రపువాడు a groom. గుర్రపు వాసము gurrapu-vāsamu. n. A prop in the roof of a house. గుర్రపుముక్కు a certain star అశ్వినీనక్షత్రము.

గుర్రు gurru. [Tel.] n. Snoring. Growling, gruff speaking, snarling, anger. గుర్రుగామాట్లాడు to speak gruffly or sulkily. వాడు నామీద గుర్రుగానున్నాడు he is surly towards me. గుర్రుపెట్టు or గుర్రెట్టు gurru-peṭṭu. v. n. To snore, groan, draw a deep breath, or growl. గుర్రుమను gurru-m-anu. v. n. To growl, to snarl. గుర్రెత్తు gurrettu. v. n. To sound, as a groan, or rattle (in the throat).

గుల or గులగుల gula. [Tel.] n. An itching sensation, జిల. గులకరించు gulakarintsu. v. n. To be pleasant. రమ్యమగు. గులగులలు pieces, dust, powder నలుగులు, తుత్తునురు, చూర్ణము. ఆ పుంటిలో పురుగులు గులగులలాడు చున్నవి the worms are crawling about in the wound. Manu. iv. 49.

గులక gulaka. [Tel.] n. A pebble, gravel. సన్నగులకభూమి soil mixed with small gravel. గులకరేగడభూమి gravelly cotton soil.

గులాబిపువ్వు gulābi-puvvu. [H.] n. A rose. గులాబిరంగు pink, or rose colour.

గులాము or గులాపువాడు gulāmu. [H.] n. A slave, a servant. దాసుడు.

గులిబి or గులిమి or గులివి gulibi. [Tel.] n. The wax in the ear. గులిమికదురు or గులిమి తీత్త an instrument for cleaning the ear.

గులిమిడి gulimidi. [Tel.] n. A plant, *Capparis spinosa*. కోకిలాక్షము.

గులివింద gulivinda. [Tel.] n. The balsam plant, *Impatiens balsamina*, Rox. i. 651. A sort of fish, a species of *Sparus* or mullet. లాముగులివింద or రాతిగులివింద red mullet; బండిగులివింద the sur mullet.

గులుగు gulugu. [Tel.] n. A tree called *Limnonia Pentaphylla*. (Rox. ii. 381.)

గుల్ఫము *gulphamu.* [Skt.] n. The ankle చీలమండ. గూఢగుల్ఫ slender ankled or light footed.

గుల్మము *gulmamu.* [Skt.] n. A bush, a shrub. పొద, కొంజెలనిచెట్టు. A body of troops consisting of 9 chariots, 9 elephants, 27 cavalry and 45 infantry. గుల్మరోగము *gulma-rōgamu.* n. Enlargement of the spleen. జ్వరగడ్డ. గుల్మిని *gulmini.* n. A spreading creeper. దట్టముగా అల్లుకొనే తీగెచెట్టు, పొదరు.

గుల్ల *gulla.* [Tel.] n. A shell: a husk: a cowry shell. చిప్పచిప్ప. A white pustule బొబ్బ. Anything hollow డొల్ల. Cotton in the pod. The hull of a ship (Vizag.) గుల్లకాసు a farthing: (lit. a shell) or a penny. గుల్లసున్నము shell lime. చింతగుల్ల tamarinds in the shell or husk. గుల్లాగుట్ర trash, rubbish, gewgaws. adj. Hollow, empty. డొల్ల. గుల్లకర్ర a tube. ఇల్లు గుల్లచేసినవాడు or ఊడిచిపెట్టినవాడు he emptied or plundered the house. గుల్ల పుటిక a small basket. గుల్లపొగాకు tobacco that is immature and worthless. గుల్లపడు to be disgraced అవమానపడు. గుల్ల పరచు to empty, to scorn, to disgrace. HD. ii. 168. గుల్లగాడు an empty handed man ఏమున్నిలేనివాడు.

గుల్లించు *gullintsu.* [Tel.] v. n. To frisk, quiver, frolic, move lewdly. To jog along as palankeen bearers. కదిలించు.

గుల్లు or **గల్లు** *gullu.* [Tel.] n. Plague; alarm.

గుళిక or **గుళిగ** *guḷika.* [Tel.] n. A pill, a bolus, a small ball.

గుళుచ్ఛము *guḷutstsamu.* [Skt.] n. A cluster, as of flowers. గుత్తి.

గువ్వ *guvva.* [Tel.] n. A dove or pigeon. పావురాయి. కూకురానిగువ్వ *kūku-rāni-guvva.* n. The Green Imperial Pigeon, *Carpophaga ænea.* కురుకురుగువ్వ the turtle dove. పొడగువ్వ *poḍa-guvva.* n. The Spotted Dove, *Turtur Suratensis.* రా గువ్వ *rā-guvva.* n. The Red Turtle-Dove, *Oenopopelia tranquebarica.* పచ్చ గువ్వ *patstsa-guvva.* n. The Green Pigeon, *Crocopus chlorogaster.* (F. B. I.) కూటి గువ్వ a dove that has moulted. ఈకలు రాల్చినపక్షి. గువ్వగుత్తిగడ్డి *guvva-gutti-gaḍḍi.* n. A sort of grass. *Trichodesma Indicum.* గువ్వకుత్తుక low voice హీన స్వరము. గువ్వకుత్తుకపడిన pigeon breasted, low-voiced. గువ్వకొలుకొను or గువ్వకట్టను to assemble in crowds. గుంపులుకూడు; to surround చుట్టుకొను. "గువ్వకొల్గొంచు దమలోన నవ్వుకొనుచు." Manu. iii. 144. గువ్వరాయి *guvva-rāyi.* n. Gravel, pebbles. మొరపరాళ్లు. గువ్వరాతినేల gravelly soil.

గుసగుస *gusa-gusa.* [Tel.] n. A whisper. గుసగుసలాడు or గుసగుసలుపోవు to whisper.

గుహ *guha.* [Skt.] n. A cave, cavern, grotto. గుహాశయము *guhā-śayamu.* n. An inmate of a cave, i. e., a tiger. పెద్దపులి.

గుహుడు *guhuḍu.* [Tel.] n. Kumāraswāmi. కొడుకు.

గుహ్యము *guhyamu.* [Skt.] n. Mystery, secrecy: the private parts: adj. Secret, mysterious. గుహ్యకుడు *guhya-kuḍu.* n. A kind of demigod, attending on Kubēra. గుహ్యకేశ్వరుడు *guhyak-ēśvaruḍu* n. A name of Kubēra.

గూ gū

గూండ్రు *gūndra.* [Tel.] n. An owl's hoot. గుడ్లగూబకూత. గూండ్రించు to hoot as an owl.

గూటము or **గూటాము** *gūṭamu.* [Tel.] n. A tent-pin or stake, used both as a mallet and as a peg. The roller of a loom. కొయ్యగూటము an iron or wooden hammer shaped like a pestle and used by stone-cutters and cobblers. A wooden or iron wedge. "గూటంపుమిరుగుళ్లు." H. v. 112.

గూడ *gūda.* [Tel.] n. A triangular basket used as a bucket. A mat hood or cover against rain. A basket in which a Vaishnavite devotee keeps his images used in worship. A flower basket. **గూడకట్టు** *gūda-kaṭṭu.* n. Tying a cloth round the waist like a petticoat, without tucking it up between the legs. అడ్డకట్టు. **గూడకొంగ** or **గూడబాతు** *gūda-baṭṭu.* n. A pelican, *Pelicanus Philippensis* (F. B. I.). **గూడవేయు** *gūda-rēyu.* v. n. To water fields with a basket or bucket.

గూడు *gūḍu.* [Tel.] n. A nest. A case. A niche in a wall for a light దీపపుగూడు. A bird cage పంజరము. A basket to keep fowls or lambs under. A cage of gauze placed over a sleeping infant. A hatchway on boardship. The socket of a joint. An insects' cocoon. పాచికగూడు a dice box. రెక్కగూడు సడలిపోయినది his shoulder is dislocated. గుండెగూడుపట్టి his heart being at repose. కంటద్దపుగూడు a case for a pair of spectacles. గూడుబండి a cart with a mat cover, A. iv. 155.

గూడెము *gūdemu.* [Tel.] n. A hamlet or small village. చిన్నపల్లె.

గూఢము *gūḍhamu.* [Skt.] n. A secret. రహస్యము. adj. Hidden, secret, abstruse. దాచబడిన. **గూఢచారి** *gūḍha-chāri.* n. A secret emissary, a spy, an agent or messenger. **గూఢజుడు** *gūḍha-juḍu.* n. One of unknown birth or uncertain parentage. **గూఢపాత్తు** *gūḍha-pattu.* n. Lit. one whose feet do not appear. A serpent, a snake. **గూఢరత్నము** *gūḍha-ratnamu.* n. A game among girls, like 'Hunt the slipper.' గూఢరత్నపికతాన్వేషణంబు. Vasu. iii. 37. గూఢసాక్షి a witness who knows the real secret; or a secretly hired witness.

గూద *gūda.* [Tel.] n. A prolapse of the uterus or anus. అన్నగూదపండు the vegetable called *Trichosanthes incisa.* Ainslie ii. 391.

గూన *gūna.* [Tel.] n. A large pot. పెద్దకుండ A spout to drain off water from a roof. మేడమీదినుండి నీళ్లుపడే సాధనము.

గూను *gūnu.* [Tel.] n. A hump. A crooked back. **గూని** *gūni.* adj. Crooked. గూనిచూపు drooping glances. Internal. గూనిపోటు an inward bruise. గూనివాడు or గూనిది a cripple, a dwarf కుబ్జుడు. **గూనుగిల్లు** *gūnu-gillu.* v. n. To have or get a crooked back. గూనుకలుగు.

గూపనాలగుల్లు *gūpanāla-gullu.* [Tel.] n. A certain game played by boys. Vish. P. vii. 211.

గూబ *gūba.* [Tel.] n. An owl. The drum of the ear. **గూబలుడ** *gūba-luḍa.* n. A kind of tree with yellow flowers, *Sida rhombifolia.* ముహాబల.

గూబు *gūbu.* [Tel.] n. A basin of sea water.

గూళి or **గూళి** *gūli.* [Tel.] n. A vulture.

గృ gri

గృంజనము *griñjanamu.* [Skt.] n. An onion. తెల్లుల్లి.

గృధ్నువు *gridhnuvu.* [Skt.] n. A covetous or greedy man. ఇచ్ఛగలవాడు.

గృధ్రము *gridhramu.* [Skt.] n. A vulture, a kite. గద్ద.

గృష్టి *grishṭi.* [Skt.] n. A cow that has calved only once, a heifer. ఒకసారి యీనిన ఆవు.

గృహము *grihamu.* [Skt. cf. Prakrit గేహము & Eng. 'Home.'] n. A house, abode, dwelling. ఇల్లు. గృహకలహములు domestic troubles or quarrels. గృహకృత్యములు household affairs. **గృహపతి** *griha-pati.* n. A householder, the head of a family. గృహప్రవేశము entering a new house. గృహమృగము a dog కుక్క. గృహస్థుడు, **గృహస్థు, గృహమేధి** or **గృహి**

grihasthudu. n. A householder ఇలురేడు. An honest man, a good citizen. A respectable man. గృహస్థాశ్రమము householdership, the state of being a householder. గృహయోగ్యమైన habitable, used as a house. గృహారామక్షేత్రములు house, grove and field, i. e., one's entire property, one's all. గృహిణి *grihini*. n. A mistress of a house, a wife. ఇల్లాలు. గృహోపకరణములు furniture, chattels, goods, utensils. గృహ్యము *grihyamu*. adj. Dependant, పరాధీనమైన. n. A tame or domesticated animal. పెంపుడుమృగము.

గె ge

గెంటన *gentana*. [Tel.] n. A plant, a species of Clitoria. The black and white species.

గెంటసము *gentasamu*. [Tel.] n. A cross or abusive speech: harshness, crossness. పరుషవచనము. "ఈ నిష్ఠురోక్తులకు మైనసాపలుకు నైనసేనిపింతంబుగాదటీ, గెంటసమేలమీదబలు కీడుసుమీవివరించిచూడగన్." HK. iii. 247.

గెంటిసలాడు *gentisa-l-adu*. [Tel.] v. n. To totter or jog, as a table that has uneven legs. ఊగ్రట్లాగు.

గెంటు *gentu*. [Tel.] v. n. To move, shake, stir, go. చలించు, తొలగు. "ధరణీమండలమున్న పాంబునిధిమీదన్ విల్చినల్దిక్కులన్ ధరణీధ్రమ్ములు గెంటకుండదనిడి." V. P. i. 78. v. a. To thrust, push away, force, cause to totter. To toss aside. త్రోయు. ప్రయోగించు. n. Movement. చలనము. **గెంటుపడు** *gentu-padu*. v. n. To miss. తప్పుట. **గెంటని** *gentani*. adj. Immoveable, not to be shaken (as love), resistless, irrepressible, not to be turned away. స్థిరమైన, ఎడతెగని. "అక్కలకంఠితమ్మరసమంటగ గెంటని ప్రేమ వానినవ్విక్కలముద్దుపెట్టుకొని." T. ii. 96. **గెంటించు** *gentintsu*. v. t. To push. To cause one to be pushed or sent away. యశోద చెయ్యి పాయ్యనవచ్చిన్న నల్లనయ్యనునిచిచేయ్యన నయ్యవ్వకూతుసెత్తుకొని మరల నింటికింగెంటింపక వచ్చి." B. X. iii. 45.

గెంటెన *gentena*. [Tel.] n. The oleander flower.

గెంటెము *gentemu*. [Tel.] n. A thick cloth. జంటనేతవస్త్రము. adj. Thick. దట్టము.

గెండి, గెండియ or **గెండె** *gendi*. [Tel.] n. A sort of fish, the carp, *Cyprinus fimbriatus*; కండకము. One species is called కాకిగెండె or కాకిటిగెండె.

గెగ్గిలి or **గెగ్గెలు** *geggili*. [Tel.] n. Derision. గేలి. గెగ్గిలి కొట్టు to deride.

గెడ *geda*. [Tel.] n. A pair, a couple. జత. Nearness. సమీపము. A hunting instrument వేటకుతగిన ఒకసాధనము.

గెత్తెర or **వలిగెత్తెర** *gettera*. [Tel.] n. A barren soil, principally consisting of a whitish marl.

గెనయు *genayu*. [Tel.] v. n. To become plump, to be nourished. పుష్టియగు.

గెనుసు *genusu*. [Tel.] n. A creeper, the sweet potato plant, *Dioscorea aculeata*. అలుపుమొక్క.

గెబ్బు *gebbu*. [Tel.] v. a. To rob. అపహరించు. To thrust, push away. గెంటు, తిరస్కరించు. "మబ్బునుబ్బుగెబ్బుచిబ్బోకసతిచేతి," Vijaya. Vil. i. 95. To take గ్రహించు.

గెర *gera*. [Tel.] n. A circle. గిరి. "గెరల్పడగిచి." H. iii. 207.

గెల *gela*. [Tel.] n. A bunch of fruit. గొల.

గెలివి or **గెలివిడి** *geliri*. [Tel.] n. Bloom, brightness or clearness of complexion. Ila. III. 27, 77. Joy సంతోషము. వాడు మిక్కిలి గెలివితోనున్నాడు he is beeming with joy.

గెలుచు *gelutsu*. [Tel.] v. a. To gain, win, conquer, overcome. జయించు. To recover in law, win at dice. To outshine, excel. To go పోవు. గెలుపుమను to encourage. గెలుపుమన్నారు they encouraged me. **గెలిపించు** *gelipintsu*. v. a. To cause or enable one to win. To cause one to go, to send పుచ్చు. గెలుపు or గెలుపము *gelupu.* n. Gain, victory. జయము. గెలుపోటములు gain and loss. గెలుపుకొను or గెల్చుకొను *gelupu-konu.* v. t. To win or conquer. జయించు. గెల్పరి or గెలుపుకాడు *gelpari.* n. The gainer, winner, conqueror. Chenna. ii. 172.

గెలెము *gelemu.* [Tel.] n. An agricultural implement of any kind.

గెల్లి *gelli.* [Tel.] n. A heap, particularly a heap of salt. ఉప్పరాశి.

గెల్లిబతుంగ *gelliba-tunga.* [Tel.] n. A plant called *Cyperus tenuiflorus*, Rox. i. 199.

గే ge

గేందుకము *gēndukamu.* [Skt.] n. A ball for playing with. చెండు.

గేటు *gēṭu.* [Eng.] n. A gate, particularly a toll-gate or toll-bar.

గేడికాళ్లు or గేదెకాళ్లు *gēḍi-kāllu.* [Tel.] n. Lank legs, long and lean legs. కొంగకాళ్లు.

గేదగి or గేదంగి *gēdagi.* [Tel.] n. The tree named *Pandanus odoratissimus.* కేతకి, మొగలి.

గేదె *gēde.* [Tel.] n. A she buffalo. బఱ్ఱె. గేదెదూడ a buffalo about three years old. గేదెదూడ a buffalo calf. గేదెపడ్డ or గేదెపెయ్య a young she buffalo.

గేబు, గేబులు or గేంగులు *gēbu.* [Tel.] n. Malted seeds of the palm tree. తేగలు.

గేయము *gēyamu.* [Skt.] adj. That which can be sung. పాడదగిన.

గేరి *gēri.* [Tel.] n. A street, a passage. వీథి. "ఎందు నిలువంటిలంకెర్ల పేరు జూడ, మందు రప్పటి గేరిలో నసురభటులు." Satyabhāma. ii. 39. "తానన్న గేరికంటెటికి గనచాలి." Suca. iii. 15.

గేలి *gēli.* [Tel.] n. Ridicule, derision. అపహాస్యము, పరిహాసము. గేలిగొను *gēli-konu.* v. t. To deride, ridicule. పరిహసించు.

గేస్తు [Corrupted from Skt. గృహస్థు.] Same as గృహస్థుడు. గేస్తురాలు *gēstu-rālu.* n. The wife of a householder. ఇల్లాలు.

గేహము *gēhamu.* [Skt. from గృహము, & cognate with Eng. 'Home'.] n. A house. ఇల్లు. గేహి Same as గృహస్థుడు. గేహిని or గృహిణి *gēhinī.* n. A wife. గేహుడు *gēhudu.* n. He who dwells, the habitant. ఇల్లుగలవాడు. వైకుంఠగేహుడు Vishṇu.

గై gai

గైరికము *gairikamu.* [Skt. from గిరి.] adj. Rocky. Marbled, variegated in colour, parti-coloured; red. n. Gold. బంగారు.— గైరికాదిధాతుశాస్త్రము Mineralogy.

గైరు *gairu.* [H.] adj. Other, besides, excepting. ఇతరమైన. గైరుహాజరు *gairu-hazaru.* adj. Missing, absent, not present.

గొ go

గొ *go.* [Tel. for కొనుము.] An affix used in pointing out any thing, as అదిగో ఇదిగో, &c.

గొంగ *gonga.* [Tel.] n. An enemy శత్రువు. A foe, or scourge. A conqueror. నిర్మూలము చేయువాడు. మృత్యుగొంగ the foe of Death. తోడేళ్లగొంగ the victor over the wolves, a name applied to the antelope, because it beats the wolf in speed.

గొంగడి or గొంగళి *gongaḍi.* [Tel.] n. A rug, a blanket. (G. గొంగటి. L. గొంగట in a blanket. Plu. గొంగడులు, గొంగళ్లు.) గొంగడికాడు a kind of bird. గొంగళిపురుగు *gongali-purugu.* n. A hairy caterpillar. కంబళిపురుగు.

గొంజ *gonza.* [Tel.] n. A barren woman. గొడ్రాలు.

గొంజి *gonji.* [Tel.] n. The Indian myrtle. *Limonia pentaphylla.* గొంజివండు *gonji-*

pandu. n. The fruit of this tree. గొంటు పండు.

గొంటరి, గొంటి or గొంటరికాడు *gontari.* [Tel.] n. A cunning or hard man కఠినుడు, కపటుడు. A rogue, a wretch. **గొంటి** *gonti.* n. A wicked woman. దుష్టురాలు. **గొంటితనము or గొంటరితనము** *gonti-tanamu.* n. Baseness, rascality, vileness. **గొంటు** *gontu.* n. A wicked man. దుష్టుడు. **గొంటుపోక** *gontu-pōka.* n. An inferior kind of areca nut.

గొండి *gondi.* [Tel.] n. Evil. Bane. A wretch. దుమ్ములగొండి the bone eater, i. e., the hyæna. దురదగొండి ఆకు or గొంగడూల గొండి the nettle, the cowach plant.

గొండిలి or గొండ్లి *gondili.* [Tel.] n. Acting, dancing, gambols, sport. నర్తనము. An actress. నర్తకి. A toss, a fling. గొండ్లిపరచు to toss or fling an attitude in dancing, the actress bending back till she rests on her hands. క్రీడింపచేయు. "సీ॥ జలదీవశాఖాస్త చామరానిలములు, కుటిలాలకములకు గొండ్లి గరప." శాకు. V. 66. **గొండ్లిసలుపు** *gondli-salupu.* v. n. To sport, to dance on all fours bending backwards, to indulge in indecent gambols

గొండ్లెము *gondlemu.* [Tel.] n. A bolt or latch. తలుపుచిలుకు.

గొంతి *gonti.* [Tel.] n. A woman. స్త్రీ. "గోపించియూరకుండు గొంతినిల్లనియెదు." BD. iii. 575. The mother of the Pāndavas. కుంతీ దేవి.

గొంతు or గొంతుక *gontu.* [Tel.] n. The throat. కంఠము. The voice, a tone కంఠధ్వని. గొంతుపట్టినది I am choked, i. e., I do not know what to say. నాగొంతురాసినది I am hoarse. వానిగొంతుకమ్మినది he is hoarse. **గొంతుకపోక or గొంతుముడి** *gontuka-pōka.* n. The apple of the throat. **గొంతు కూర్చుండు** *gontu-kūrtsundu.* v. n. To squat down on one's heels. **గొంతుకోత** *gontu-kōta.* n. A cutthroat business. A brawl, a quarrel. **గొంటెమగోరుచెట్టు** *gontema-gōru-chettu.* n. A plant, *Paederia foetida.* సారణి, లంజె సవరము. **గొంటెమ్మ** *gontemma.* n. The name of a certain rural goddess. **గొంటెమ్మకోరికలు** *gontemma-kōrikalu.* n. Whimsical speculations, castles in the air. గొరదగని కోరికలు, వెర్రి యూహలు.

గొంది *gondi.* [Tel.] n. An alley, a lane, a corner. సందు, మూల. విరిగొందులు flowery lanes. గొందిచెట్టు or గొందులచెట్టు to hide, conceal.

గొగ్గి *goggi.* [Tel.] adj Uneven, irregular, up and down, in and out. ఎచ్చుతక్కువైన. **గొగ్గిపండ్లు** *goggi-pandlu.* n. Uneven teeth. A proverb says. కుక్కకువచ్చే వన్ని గొగ్గిపండ్లు all a dog's teeth are crooked, i. e., all one does is wrong, he cannot do any thing properly. **గొగ్గిముత్తెము** *goggi-muttemu.* n. A pear-shaped pearl. గొసగలముత్తెము.

గొజ్జంగి or గొజ్జగి *gojjangi.* [Tel.] n. A tree called *Pandanus odoratissimus.* గేదగి. (q. v.)

గొజ్జెగ *gojjega.* [Tel.] n. A kind of flowering plant. పుష్పభేదము.

గొటగొట *gota-gota.* [Tel.] n. Loudness, uproar. ధ్వని, చప్పుడు.

గొటిక or గొటికె *gotika.* [Tel.] n. A bramble.

గొట్టము *gottamu.* [Tel.] n. A tube, a cylinder, a barrel, of a gun, &c. క్రోవి. నాళగొట్టము a shuttle. అద్దపుగొట్టము a telescope, literally, the tube with glasses. ఊదుగొట్టము a blowpipe. వెదురు గొట్టము a bamboo tube. గొట్టపుతాళము a padlock shaped like a tube.

గొట్టి *gotti.* [Tel.] adj. Wicked, vicious. గొట్టిగడ్డ a very large bulbous root that grows in marshes like truffles and is eaten by the poor.

గొట్టిక *goṭṭika.* [Tel.] n. Famine. కరవు. HD. ii. 527.

గొట్టిచెట్టు or **గొట్టికంప** *goṭṭi-chettu.* [Tel.] n. A thorny plant, *zyzyphus xylopyrus.*

గొట్టు *goṭṭu.* [Tel.]n. Wickedness. దౌష్ట్యము. Obstinacy. మూర్ఖత. గొట్టునపెట్టినక pertinaciously eluding him, freakishly avoiding him. An enemy. విరోధి. A wretch, a creature (in a derogatory sense) as కేడిరిగొట్టు, పాటిగొట్టు, తంత్రగొట్టు a proud wretch, a fool. adj. Hard, difficult, stubborn. కఠినము. Wicked దుష్టము. గొట్టుమాట a hard or difficult word.

గొడ *goḍa.* [Tel.] n. Trouble, plague. గొడవ. గొడగొడలాడు to chatter, make a noise, to jabber.

గొడగ *goḍaga.* [Tel.] n. A plough without the ploughshare. ఏడికోలులేనినాగలి.

గొడగరి or **గొడారి** *goḍagari.* [Tel.] n. A shoemaker, a worker in leather. మాదిగవాడు. గొడగర the cobbler's caste. The name of a tribe.

"మాలకుమాంసంబు మరిగొడారికిని దోలుమనున్నట్లు"
BD. iv. 51.

గొడవ *goḍava.* [Tel.] n. Difficulty. అటంకము, అడ్డి. Puzzle, confusion కలత. Trouble, danger ఆపద. Fault తప్పు. Sorrow దుఃఖము.

గొడిగ *goḍiga.* [Tel.] n. A pebble. గులకరాయి.

గొడితి or **చేగొడ్డి** *goḍiti.* [Tel.] n. A sort of tree.

గొడియ or **గొడె** *goḍiya.* [Tel.] n. A staff. వెదురుగొడియ a bamboo staff. గొడియకట్టె a rafter: a ceiling over rafters.

గొడుగు *goḍugu.* [Tel.] n. An umbrella. ఆతపత్రము, ఛత్రము. కుక్కగొడుగు a toadstool, a fungus, a mushroom. In palmistry, the name of a certain line in the palm. **గొడుగుకామలు** or **గొడుగు కాడలు** *goḍugu-kāmalu.* n. Staves for umbrellas. **గొడుగుబల్ల** *goḍugu-balla.* n. A piece of wood in which the upper hinge of a door turns. తలుపుమీదిదిమ్మనుసమంతితిరుగుకర్ర.

గొడె See గొడియ.

గొడ్డ *goḍḍa.* [Tel.] n. Hardness. బిరుసు. A hard word బిరుసుమాట. A hard man బిరుసువాడు. **గొడ్డగము** *goḍḍagamu.* adj. Troublesome బాధకము. **గొడ్డతనము** *goḍḍa-tanamu.* n. Stubbornness మొండితనము. "గొడ్డతనంబున గోపతిర్వ్యాజము సడ్డచేయక గాంతసన్నంబు గొడ్డ." Mari Basava. 62. **గొడ్డము** *goḍḍamu.* n. Evil, danger, deadly peril. "విమన్నవరాజాగ్రమినుమంగోనమలు చేత ప్రాణగొడ్డంబైయున్నను." M. Santi. ii. 208. "ప్రాణగొడ్డములుగునములు వారలందిర్వగా." M. Udy. i. 232. "నీకు ప్రాణగొడ్డంబు నీకుం దలంచె." M. Udy. iii. 162.

గొడ్డలి *goḍḍali* [Tel. from గొట్టు.] n. An axe or hatchet. గోటవిచ్చేదాన్ని గొడ్డంటపరు కుట to break a butterfly upon a wheel, a trifle becoming a terror.

గొడ్డలు *goḍḍalu.* [Tel.] n. Bragging, nonsense. "గురువుదుతూరించి గొడ్డలాడెదవు." L. XII. 86.

గొడ్డు *goḍḍu.* [Tel.] n. A beast. పశువు. Barrenness గొడ్రాలితనము. adj. Barren, sterile వంధ్యము. గొడ్డావు a barren cow, ఈనని పశువు. ఎనుపగొడ్డు, or ఎనుము a buffalo. ఎలుగుగొడ్డు, or ఎలుగు a bear. గొడ్లు kine, horned cattle. చిరుతగొడ్డు a leopard. **గొడ్డు, గొడ్డురాలు** or **గొడ్రాలు** *goḍḍu.* n. A barren woman. గొడ్డంబలి gruel without any rice in it. మెతుకులేని అంబలి. గొడ్డుకూడ or గొడ్డుసంకటి ragi food without any sauce or curry to be taken with it. గొడ్డుకారము very hot మిక్కిలికారముగానున్న. గొడ్డుచెట్టు a barren tree ఫలించనిచెట్టు. **గొడ్డుపోతు** *goḍḍu-pōtu.* n. A useless man నిష్ప్రయోజనకుడు. **గొడ్డుపోవు** *goḍḍu-pōvu.* v. n. To become barren.

గొడ్డువోవు. To become useless వ్యర్థమగు. To become effeminate. పౌరుషహీనమగు.

గొడ్డేరు *goḍḍēru* n. A dry stream. ఎండేరు. v. a. To rent or farm గుత్తచేయు.

"కు॥ బొడ్డుపల్లెనుగొడ్డేరిమానసపోతి
నెట్లుచెల్లింతుఁటంత యిలేదునూర్లు?" ద.

గొణుగు or **గొణఁగు** *goṇugu*. [Tel.] v. n. To mutter, to mumble, to whisper. To talk nonsense. గొణగొణలాడు *goṇa-goṇal-āḍu*. v. n. To grumble, to mutter.

గొణ్ణెము or **గొణ్ణెము** *goṇṇemu*. [Tel.] n. A hasp or staple ring.

గొతుపు *gotupu*. [Tel.] n. A species of sapphire, Tourmaline. నీలమణిభేదము. ABA. ii. 528.

గొత్తు *gottu*. [Tel.] n. Arrangement, trim, order. Determination. A bunch or cluster గుత్తి. The rotten smell of long standing milk, butter, &c.

గొద *goda*, [Tel.] n. Hunger, appetite. ఆకలి. గొదగొన్న hungry. గొదగొన్నపులి a famished tiger. గొదగొని hungrily. M. iv. 283. గొదగొను to be eager or in a hurry త్వరపడు, ఆతురించు. గొదగొద *goda-goda*. n. Enmity పగ.

గొనకొను *gona-konu*. [Tel.] v. n. To attempt. యత్నించు.

గొనటి *gonaṭi*. [Tel.] adj. Ugly. వికారమైన. M. XII. iii.

గొనప *gonapa*. [Tel.] adj. Small, short. పొట్టి. n. A worn out plough అరిగిననాగలి. గొనపకోడి a small bird.

గొనబు *gonabu*. [Tel.] adj. Agreeable, fine, charming రమణీయమైన. "గొనబుకొమ్మ." T. iii. 64.

గొనము *gonamu*. [from Skt. గుణము.] Same as గుణము.

గొనయము *gonayamu*. [Tel.] n. A bow-string. వింటినారి. The tip of a bow, where the notch is. వింటినారికొలికి. ధనురగ్రము. ABA. iii. 76.

గొప్ప *goppa*. [Tel.] adj. Great in any sense, noble, కొంచెముగొప్ప more or less, some trifle, a certain quantity. గొప్ప n. Greatness, size, respectability.

గొప్పులు *goppulu*. [Tel.] n. Elevated places in a rice field.

గొబ *goba*. [Tel.] n. A cave. గుహ. A lane గొంది.

గొబ్బండు *gobbanḍu*. [Tel. గొప్ప+పండు.] n. A large fruit. గొప్పపండు.

గొబ్బరము *gobbaramu*. [Tel.] n. Manure. ఎరువు.

గొబ్బి *gobbi*. [Tel.] n. Name of a Hindu goddess. The name of a feast or holiday kept by girls in the month Pushyam. గొబ్బెమ్మ a lump of cowdung worshipped as a goddess on this occasion; a dance practised by young girls. గొబ్బికాయలు *gobbi-kāyalu*. n. A sort of grain. H. iv. 156. గొబ్బిచెట్టు *gobbi-cheṭṭu*. n. A plant called *Barleria longifolia*, ఝాటీ లాటకము. One kind is నీరుగొబ్బి. గొబ్బిళ్లు *gobbiḷḷu*. n. Capering: dancing. (V. P. VII. 211.) Dancing in honour of a god. Salutation, respects. దండము, నమస్కారము.

"రగడ॥ వజ్రపుటిలో తావళ మైదిక్కున
గొప్పిరయూనకు గొబ్బిళ్లనుచును."

H. iv. 273.

గొబ్బున *gobbu-na*. [Tel.] adv. Quickly, hastily, at once, instantly. వేగముగా.

గొయ్యాపండు *goyyā-panḍu*. [Mexican through Spanish.] n. The fruit called guava.

గొయ్యి *goyyi*. [Tel.] n. A pit. In Ganjam, a chain. వానగొయ్యి a gully cut by rain. Plu. గోతులు.

గొరక *goraka*. [Tel.] n. A wild buffalo. కారెనుము. An iron arrow ఇనుపబాణము. గొరకకట్టె *goraka-kaṭṭe*. n. A javelin, or slender spear. అలుగుగల చేకర్ర. గొరక

చేప goraka-chēpa. n. A worthless sort of fish. మాలిగొరక the rice fish which is like the Tunny. Russell, plate 132. వాలిగొరక a sort of fish.

గోరకు or గోరగ goraku. [Tel.] n. A wretch, an abject creature. "బిరుదులుగోరగ వాకవడితింక." BD. v. 899. The name of a plant.

గోరగోర gora-gora. [Tel.] n. Swiftness. వేగము.

గోరపము gorapamu. [Tel.] n. A curry comb. H. v. 49.

గోర పెట్టు gora-peṭṭu. [Tel.] v. n. To grunt. A. v. 140.

గోరస gorasa. [Tel.] n. A shoal of fish. చేపలగుంపు.

గోరిజె or గోరిజే goriza. [Tel.] n. A hoof. గొరిసె. "పొందుగావనిడిగొమ్ములుగొరిజెలు." BD. i. 349.

గోరియ or గొర్రియ goriya. [Tel.] n. A sheep. గొర్రె. M. vi. i. 95. గొరియమాంసము mutton. M. XIII. iii. 175.

గోరిసె gorise. [Tel.] n. A hoof.

గోరుగు gorugu. [Tel.] v. t. To shave. క్షౌరముచేయు. గోరిగించు gorigiṇṭsu. v. a. To shave: to have one shaven. గొరిగించు కొన్నాడు he got himself shaved.

గోరువంక Same as గోరింక.

గొర్రు gorru. [Tel.] n. A piece of land measuring 32 guṇṭas (గుంటలు.) A drill plough. దున్నిన పొలమువిూద దున్నే యంత్రము. గొర్రుతోలు to harrow.

గొర్రె, గొరె, గొరియ or గొర్రియ gorre. [Tel.] n. A sheep. గొర్రెపిల్ల a lamb. కుక్కగొర్రె the jungle sheep. కొండ గొర్రె a species of antelope. గొర్రెచెదలు gorre-chedalu. n. The kind of termites or white ants called soldier ants.

గోల gola. [Tel.] n. A bunch of fruit. గెల.

గోలక golaka. [Tel.] n. A confused noise. కలకలధ్వని. Palmyra twigs. తాటిచేన్నులు.

గోలగోల gola-gola. [Tel.] n. Noise, tumult. adv. Aloud, echoingly, screaming confusedly in chorus. గొలగొలలాడిరి they made an uproar. గొలగొలలాడిన tumultuous, noisy. A. i. 81.

గోలిమిడిదుబ్బు golimiḍi-dubbu. [Tel.] n. A sort of tares. Lolium. శృంఖలీవృక్షము.

గోలుగు golugu. [Tel.] n. The Hemp plant. The species called సీమగోలుగు is the cámóni: it bears a very fragrant flower.

గోలుసు golusu. [Tel.] n. A chain. గోలుసు అక్షరము, గోలుసుకట్టు or గోలుసు మోడి golusu-aksharamu. n. Cursive writing, a running hand.

గొల్ల golla. [Tel. from గొర్రెల.] n. A herdsman, a shepherd. A watchman. ద్వార పాలకుడు, ధనపాలుడు. గొల్లమాట rude boorish language. గొల్లకోడి golla-kōḍi n. A kind of bird with a peculiarly sweet trilling note. గొల్లజిడ్డు golla-jiḍḍu. n. The name of a certain plant కూరిని. H. iv. 13. గొల్లడు golladu. n. A herdsman. గొల్లత or గొల్లది gollata. n. A woman of the herdsman caste. గొల్లత్తకొక్కు gollatta-kokku. n. The Indian mole-rat, *Nesocia bengalensis*. (F. B. I.) గొల్లతనము golla-tanamu. n. Boorishness. గొల్లదొండు golla-dondu. n. A sort of fish. గొల్లపల్లె golla-palle. n. A hamlet inhabited by herdsmen. గొల్లభామ golla-bhāma. n. A shepherdess. A *mantis* or leaf insect, the Indian Hoopoe.

గొల్లము gollamu. [Tel.] n. A deep pit. లోతుగలపల్లము.

గొల్లి golli. [Tel.] n. Fun, naughtiness. కొంటెతనము nonsense. *Pudendum muliebre*. Reeve 580. +కాయ, అనగా తూనిలింగము. Vilap. ii. 61.

గొల్లు *gollu.* [Tel.] n. Hubbub, uproar. కలకలధ్వని. గొల్లుమను *gollu-m-anu.* v. n. To yell or roar. ఈ మాట ఊరంతా గొల్లుమనిపుట్టినది the whole town is in an uproar about this.

గొల్లెన or గొల్లియలు *gollena.* [Tel.] n. A tent; a booth built at a fair. చిన్నదేరా. G. vii. 12. Mand. ii. 108. గొల్లెనబండి *gollena-bandi.* n. A cart, a carriage గాడీ.

గోవరు *govaru.* [Tel.] n. Heat. కావము. గోవరుపోవు *govaru-povu.* v. n. To be parched. కమలు, ఎండిపోవు. "మీ కన్ను దోయిలు తెండవే గోవరుపోయె" రా. i.

గోహారు *gohāru.* [Tel.] n. Uproar, confusion. Danger. ఉపద్రవము.

గో go

గో *gō.* [Tel.] adv. There! look there! See on గో. అదిగో, ఇదిగో.

గో *gō.* [Skt.] n. A cow.

గోంగూర *gōngūra.* [Tel.] See గోగు.

గోండుడు *gōṇḍuḍu.* [Skt.] n. One who has a projecting navel. ఉరుకుబొడ్డువాడు.

గోండ్రించు, గోండ్రిల్లు or గోండ్రిలు *gōṇḍrintsu.* [Tel.] v. a. To roar, as a tiger, to bellow, to croak, to retch (in vomiting): to grunt as a hog. గోండ్రు *gōṇḍru.* n. A grunt, bellow, roar, the lowing of cattle. గోండ్రుకప్ప *gōṇḍru-kappa.* n. The bull frog, or bellowing frog. గోండ్రుపెట్టు *gōṇḍru-peṭṭu.* v. n. To bellow, roar, grunt.

గోందు *gōndu.* [Tel.] n. A Khond. Also, gum గోదు.

గోకంటకము *gō-kanṭakamu.* [Skt.]n. A kind of thorny plant. ఏనుగుపల్లేరు, గాజచెట్టు. See పల్లేరు.

గోకరకాణి *gōkara-kāṇi.* [Tel.] n. The fraction of $\frac{1}{256}$; Ciphered thus గో—రెండు గోకరకాణులు or గో— is $\frac{1}{128}$ and thrice the same or మూడుగోకరకాణులు is గో ౩. See కాణి.

గోకరాయి *gōka-rāyi.* [Tel.] n. The Indian Magpie, *Dendrocitta rufa.* (F. B. I.)

గోకర్ణము *gō-karṇamu.* [Skt.] n. A sort of antelope supposed to be the nil ghai. కడితిమృగము. H. iii. 9. An oblong cup made of a divided cocoanut shell కొప్ప. The name of a district lying south of the Konkan. పరశురామక్షేత్రము.

గోకిరయెలిసె *gōkira-yelise.* [Tel.] n. The common or grey quail, *Coturnix communis.* (F. B. I.)

గోకు *gōku.* [Tel.] n. To scratch. గీయు, గీరు. To scribble, as writing. గోకుడుపార a small hoe.

గోకులము *gō-kulamu.* [Skt. గో=cow] n. The caste of herdsmen. A herd of cattle ఆవులమంద. The ox genus or family ఆవుల జాతి. గోకులాష్టమి *gō-kul-āshṭami.* n. The anniversary of the birth of Krishna which falls on శ్రావణబహుళాష్టమి about September.

గోగు or పుంటగోగు *gōgu.* [Tel.] n. The Hemp plant, *Cannabis Sativa:* గోంగు గోగు, కర్పాసము *Hibiscus Cannabinus.* సీమగోగు the Roselle plant. గోగునార *gōgu-nāra.* n. The fibre of the hemp plant. గోగూర or గోంగూర *gōgūra.* n. A dish made of గోగు leaves.

గోచరము *gōcharamu.* [Skt.] adj. Perceptible, known, manifest, evident, apparent. n. An object cognisable by the senses. విషయము. గోచరించు *gōcharintsu.* v. n. To appear, be visible. అగపడు. v. t. To show అగుపరుచు.

గోచర్మము *gō-charmamu.* [Skt.] n. An ox hide. గోచర్మమాత్రభూమి *gō-charma-mātra-bhūmi.* n. A hide of land.

గోచారము *gō-chāramu.* [Skt.] n. The planetary aspect described in a horoscope (జన్మపత్రిక,) గ్రహసంచారము.

గోచి *gōchi*. [Tel.] n. A clout. A truss or flap; a waist cloth. ఇనుపగోచి an iron buckle fabled to be worn by ascetics. వాడు ఇనుపగోచికట్టినాడు he took a vow of chastity. కొంగగోచిపెట్టుకొను to draw the skirt of the petticoat between the thighs, and tuck it into the waist behind. గోచిదరిద్రము nakedness, utter poverty. గోచిపాతై stripped naked. HD. ii. 1050. **గోచికట్టు, గోచిపాతడు** or **గోచిపాపడు** *gōchi-kattu*. n. A bachelor. బ్రహ్మచారి. HK. iv. 179.

గోజు *gōzu*. [Tel.] n. A puzzle or trouble; a dispute. పీడ, తొందర. **గోజు** or **గోజాడు** or **గోజేయు** *gōzadu*. v. n. To dun, pester, harass. పీడించు. **గోజాటు** *gōjata*. n. A plague. పీడ.

గోటాపన *gōtapana*. [Tel.] n. A feather of a bird. పక్షియీక.

గోటి *gōti*. [Tel.] n. A game like hockey. A hockey దీర్ఘశరచ్ఛ్రాకృతక్రీడ.

గోటు *gōṭu*. [Tel.] n. Trimness, foppery. ఒయ్యారము. Trinkets, a sort of broad glass or gold bracelets. Finery. Trimming, fringe, ribbon, edging, hem. సరిగపట్టుగోటు a lace border. **గోటుకత్తె** *gōṭu-katte*. n. A beau. ఒయ్యారి. **గోటుకాడు** *gōṭu-kāḍu*. n. A fop. ఒయ్యారకాడు. గోటుగామంచే fine, flaunting. **గోటుపోక** *gōtu-pōka*. n. An inferior kind of areca nut.

గోటేరు or **గోటేరు** *gōṭēru*. [Tel.] n. The plough share. నాగేటిచాలు. Sar. Pad. ii. 42. గోటేరువలెనా నుంచే ముక్కు a long sharp nose.

గోడ *gōḍa*. [Tel.] n. A wall. అడ్డగోడ a cross wall అడ్డగోడమీదపిల్లి the cat perched on a cross wall: a phrase used to denote a trimmer, one who "sits on the fence." **గోడకాలు** *gōḍa-kalu*. n. A buttress. కరగోడ. **గోడగించు** *gōḍa-gintsu*. v. n. To speak to. మాటాడు. To make a noise శబ్దించు. v. t. To disregard. తిరస్కరించు. **గోడచేర్పు** *gōḍa-chērpu*. n. A booby, a dunce జడుడు. HD. ii. 1497.

గోడా *gōḍa*. [H.] n. A horse. గుర్రము.

గోడాలు *gōḍalu*. [Tel.] n. The rattlins of a ship's shrouds. నూలునిచ్చెనమెట్లు.

గోడి *gōḍi*. [Tel.] n. Way, manner, custom, regularity, likelihood, prospect. ముక్కుగోడి a nostril. adj. Crooked వంకరగల. **గోడిపడు** *gōḍi-paḍu*. v. n. To become crooked or bent. అరుగు or వంపగు. గోడిపెట్టు to bend, వంచు. **గోడిపెట్టు** *gōḍi-pettu*. n. A stunning blow on the head. **గోడిరెప్ప** *gōḍi-reppa*. n. A sty or swelling in the eye.

గోడిగ *gōḍiga*. [Tel.] n. A mare. ఆడుగుర్రము. A iv. 36. Steepness. ఒరగటము.

గోడు *gōḍu*. [Tel.] n. Grief. గోడుగోడని Crying Alas! Alas! గోడుపన్నగోడు a pack of troubles. ఆడనేరక మద్దెలగోడుపోయినది she who cannot dance cries out on the fiddler. **గోడుకూత** *gōḍu-kūta*. n. Whimpering, blubbering. **గోడాడు** *gōḍ-aḍu*. v. n. To grieve. దుఃఖించు. **గోడుబిళ్లలు** *gōḍu-billalu*. n. A kind of game played by children. **గోడుబొట్టిక** *gōḍu-boṭṭika*. n. A certain plant. **గోడనియెడ్చు** *gōḍ-aniyēḍtsu*. v. n. To weep aloud. Kuchēlo. iii. 114.

గోడెము *gōḍemu*. [Tel.] n. A hamlet near the foot of a hill. కొండదరిని వాసినయుండి యుండెడు చోటుపల్లె.

గోణము, గోవణము or **గోణాము** *gōṇamu*. [Tel. cf. Tam. కోమణము.] n. A waist cloth or modesty piece. గోచి. చింకగోణాము "a T bandage."

గోణి *gōṇi*. [Skt.] n. A sack, sackcloth. గోనె. గోనెడు a sackful. [Tel] n. An ox. ఎద్దు.

గోతము or **గోతాము** *gōtamu*. [Tel.] n. A sack, a bag. గోనె, సంచి.

గోతి *gōti*. [Tel.] n. A woman. భార. అను. iii.

గోత్ర gôtra. [Skt.] n. The earth. భూ. గోత్రము gôtramu. n. A mountain. కొండ. A family, tribe or lineage. వంశము. అన్య గోత్రుడు an alien, one of another family or clan. గోత్రభిత్తు gôtra-bhittu. n. Lit. the 'destroyer of mountains', i. e., Indra.

గోద gôda. [Tel.] n. An ox. ఎద్దు. A beast. గొడ్డుగోద kine, cattle.

గోదరి gôdari. [Tel.] n. The river Godavery. A painter చిత్రకారుడు.

గోదారి gôdari. [Tel.] n. The sediment of melted butter. నెయ్యి కాచిన మడ్డి. గోదారి పేలు gôdari-pêlu. n. A kind of lice, pediculi pubis.

గోదావరి gôdāvari. [Skt.] n. The river Godavery.

గోదు or గోందు gôdu. [H.] n. Gum, బంక, జిగురు.

గోదురు gôduru. [Tel.] n. Large. గోదురు కప్ప gôduru-kappa. n. A toad: a bull frog. పెద్దకప్ప. గోదురుగవ్వ gôduru-gavva. n. A large cowry shell.

గోదుమ, గోధుమ or గోధుమములు gôduma [Tel.] n. Wheat.

గోధ or గోధిక [Skt.] n. An iguana. ఉడుము. గోధ or గోధాంగుళి gôdha. n. A finger stall, made of iguana leather, to protect the finger in drawing a bow. An armour for protecting the hand in shooting from a bow అస్త్రాఘాతము తగులకుండుటకై ఉడుముతోలుతో కట్టి చేతికి తొడుగుకొనే కవచము. DRB. 180.

గోధి gôdhi. [Skt.] n. The forehead. నొసలు.

గోనసము gônasamu. [Skt.] n. A very large kind of snake, the Boa. కొండచిలువ.

గోను Same as గోణ.

గోనె or గోనియ gône. [Tel.] n. A sack, a gunny bag. గోనెసంచి; గోతము.

గోపదము gô-padamu. [Skt.] n. The print of a cow's foot.

గోపనము gôpanamu. [Skt.] n. Hiding, concealing. దాచుట.

గోపానసి gôpānasi. [Skt.] n. A piece of wood placed at the eaves to close in the roof. చూరుకర్ర.

గోపాలుడు gô-pāludu. [Skt.] n. A cowherd. గొల్లవాడు. A king రాజు. A name of Krishna.

గోపి gôpi. [Skt.] n. Armenian bole used in making fine plaster for masons. కావిరాయి. గోపిచందనము gôpi-chandanamu. n. Yellow ochre. గోపిమన్ను yellow ochre.

గోపి or గోపిక gôpi. [Skt.] n. A shepherdess, గొల్లది.

గోపీథము gô-pîdhamu. [Skt.] n. A trough near a well. నీటితొట్టె.

గోపుచ్ఛము gô-puchchhamu. [Skt.] n. The cow-tailed monkey. కోతి.

గోపుడు gôpudu. [Skt. గో=cow, ప=to rule.] n. A cowkeeper, a herdsman. గొల్లవాడు, గోవుల కధిపతి. A superintendent of a district. అనేక గ్రామములకధిపతి. A king రాజు.

గోపురము gôpuramu. [Skt.] n. An arch, a dome, a pinnacle. A portal door, a city gate. గవను, వాకిలి. A high pyramidal tower over the gates of a temple. A steeple. (Figuratively) Elysium. స్వర్గము. R. i. 151. గోపురము (in Telugu for మూపురము) is also the hump on a bullock. వాడు తనకు నన్ను గోపురముమీద ఎత్తిపెట్టినాడు he flattered me grossly.

గోప్యము gôpyamu. [Skt.] adj. Secret. దాచబడిన. Cherished, preserved కాపాడబడిన. గోప్యమైనసంధి a secret interview, an assignation. గోప్యముగా gôpyamu-gā. adv. Secretly.

గోమ, పుట్టగోమ gôma. [Tel.] n. The earth or place round about a white ant hill.

గోమతి gômati. [Skt.] n. The river Gumty.

గోమయము, గోమాయువు See under గోవు.

గోమారి *gōmāri*. [Tel. గోవు+మారి.] n The bots, a disease of cattle caused by ticks.

గోమి *gōmi*. [Skt.] n. One who has cows.

గోమిడి *gōmidi*. [Tel.] n. A kind of quail. పూరేడుపిట్ట.

గోము *gōmu*. [Tel.] n. Felicity. సౌకుమార్యము, శ్రమ మెరుగనితనము. Bloom, freshness of hue. గారబము. గోమించు *gōmintsu*. v. t. To make happy, to cause to be happy. గోముచేయు.

గోముఖము *gō-mukhamu*. [Skt.] n. A sort of trumpet. Also smearing with cow-dung. The front or spout of the lingam. The spout for water in the wall of a temple. గోముఖవ్యాఘ్రము *gō-mukha-vyāghramu*. n. A tiger in the disguise of a cow, i. e., a hypocrite. పైకి మంచివాని వలెనుండే దుష్టుడు.

గోమూత్రము *gō-mūtramu*. [Skt.] n. Cow's urine. గోమూత్రకబంధము *gō-mūtra-ka-bandhamu*. n. Verses arranged in the shape imagined to belong to a cow's urine. See an instance in Magha. XIX. 46.

గోమేధము *gō-mēdhamu*. [Skt.] n. The sacrifice of a cow.

గోమేధికము *gō-mēdhikamu*. [Skt.] n. A topaz: an agate.

గోర *gōra*. [Tel.] n. A shopkeeper. S. i. 98. A drill plough. గోరలంకోలు to plough with a drill plough in preparation for making a channel from a river.

గోర or గోరంక or గోరువంక Same as గోరింక. (q. v.)

గోరంచు *gōrantsu*. [Tel.] n. Selvedge.

గోరంటచెట్టు or గోరింట *gōranta-chettu*. [Tel. గోరు and అంటు.] n. The Henna or nail-dyeplant. *Acacia Intsia*. ముల్లుగోరంట చెట్టు. *Barleria prionitis*. (Watts.) గోరింత దగ్గు *gorinta-daggu*. n. The whooping cough.

గోరచెక్క *gōra-chekka*. [Tel.] n. A drag, with which rivers are cleared.

గోరజము *gōrajamu*. [Tel.] n. Ox-gall. గోరోచనము, కస్తూరి. Swa. iv. 13.

గోరము *gōramu*. [from Skt. ఘోరము.] n. Danger. అపద. Ill-health దేహముయొక్క అస్వాస్థ్యము. Hatred పగ. గోరతనము *gōra-tanamu*. n. Naughtiness, wickedness. దౌష్ట్యము. గోరప *gōrapa*. n. A loud sound. గట్టిమోత. గోరపడు *gōra-padu*. v. n. To hate. పగపడు. గోరగింత *gōra-ginta*. n. Fearfulness. timidity, భయంకరత్వము.

గోరసము *gō-rasamu*. [Skt.] n. Milk or buttermilk. పాలు, మజ్జిగ.

గోరక్షకుడు *gō-rakshakudu*. [Skt.] n. A herdsman. A Goorkha.

గోరింక *gōrinka*. [Tel.] n. The common Myna, *Acridotheres tristis*. కొండగోరింక (lit. a hill myna.) the Southern Grackle, *Eulabes religiosa*. పాపటగోరింక the Black-headed Myna, *Temenuchus pagodarum*. కెంబుగోరింక the Pied Myna, *Sturnopastor contra*. (F. B. I.)

గోరించు *gōrintsu*. [Tel.] v. n. To shove, struggle, thrust. ఎదుర్కొను. T. iii. 140. To fly ఎగురు. గోరింపు *gōrimpu*. n. Flight. ఎగురు. A shove or push; a stroke at a ball; a struggle.

గోరీ *gōrī*. [H.] n. A tomb, a grave. సమాధి.

గోరు *gōru*. [Tel.] n. A nail, a claw. In A. v. 30. గోళ్లు is rendered అరటిపువ్వులోనుండే కడ్డగోళ్లు అని వాడుకోబడే మువ్వులవంటివి "Hawk's claws," i. e., the inside of a plantain blossom. adj. Slight, little. అల్పము. గోరుచిక్కు the quick of the nail. గోరుగల్లు or గోరుగిండి or గోర్గిండి. *gōru-gallu*. n. An instrument for cutting the nails. గోరుగాలము *gōru-gālamu*. n. A kind of fishhook made of iron wire. గోరుచిక్కుడుకాయ *gōru-chikkudu-kāya*. n. The bean called *Dolichos fabæformis*. Rox. iii. 316. గోరుచిత్రలము *gōru-chitra-*

pámu. n. A chisel with a bent edge. గోనయుండు నంపుగల ఉలి. గోరుచుట్టు gôru-tsuttu. n. A whitlow. గోరుచుట్టుమీద రోకటిపోటు a blow from a rice pounder on a whitlow, i. e., trouble upon trouble. గోరువలి or గోరు ఉలి gôruli. n. A gouge, or round-bladed chisel. గోరువెచ్చ gôru-vetstsa. n. and adj. Lukewarm, tepid, partly warm. గోరొత్తు gôr-ottu. v. a. To pinch. n. Pinching.

గోరుపడము or గోర్పడము gôru-paḍamu. [Tel.] n. A cloak, a blanket. కంబళి, కప్పాలు. Chenn. iii. 43. P. i. 593.

గోరువంక Same as గోరింక.

గోరోచనము or గోరోజనము gôrôcha-namu. [Skt.] n. Ox-gall. Ainslie. ii. 164. R. ii. 4. Bilhan. iii. 25.

గోర్పడము Same as గోరుపడము.

గోర్పిల్లాడు gôrpilladu. [Tel.] v. a. To toss up balls in play. అమ్మనగాయలాడు, బుట్ట చెండ్లాడు, ఎగరవేయు. "దంతిరథరథ్య [illegible] శ్రేతులా గోర్పిల్లాడుచు వచ్చుచున్నగని." R. vi. 210.

గోర్వంక Same as గోరువంక.

గోల gôla. [Tel.] n. A moan, a howl, a wailing sound; the sound of weeping; కాకిగోల అలగోలబాలగోల a general howl. కాకిగోల a dismal lament, such as crows utter over a wounded crow. గోలపెట్టు to complain. గోలయెత్తు to raise the voice, wail, cry, howl. గోల n. Simplicity, inexperience. A simpleton, one who is ignorant and innocent. ముగ్ధుడు. A simple girl ముగ్ధ. గోలతనము simplicity, silliness. గోలక్రోతులు gôla-krôtulu. n. A game played by boys. P. vii. 211.

గోలగోండి gôla-goṇḍi. [Tel.] n. The plant called *Tradescantia axillaris*. Rox. ii. 118. Ains. ii. 250. 402.

గోలాంగూలము gôlangûlamu. [Tel.] n. A kind of monkey. కొండముచ్చుకోతి.

గోలాకు gôlâku. [Tel.] n. Trouble, confusion. M. iv. iii. 125.

గోలి gôli. [Tel.] n. A slanting verandah.

గోలించు gôlintsu. [Tel.] n. To fry. వేయించు, చమురు పోసి చేయు.

గోలి gôli. [H.] n. A marble to play with.

గోలుగోలు or గోల్గోలు gôlu-gôlu. [Tel.] n. A great noise, an uproar, loud crying. గొల్లుమనుధ్వని, పెద్ద ఏడ్పు.

గోలురించు gôlurintsu [Tel.] v. n. To roar like a tiger (పులి) కూయు.

గోలెము gôlemu. [Tel. for గోళము.] n. A hollow. Centric space: the inside: a basin. A kettle or boiler. బాన, నీళ్లపోసే మంటిపాత్రము, బాను.

గోలెమ్ము or గోళెమ్ము gôlemmu. [Tel. గోలు+ఎమ్ము.] n. Lit. The great bone, i. e, the spine or back bone.

గోళము gôlamu. [Skt.] n. A globe, a hollow, an opening, a round cavity. అండగోళము the hollow or inside of an eggshell. నయన గోళము (R. v. 126.) the eyeball. బ్రహ్మాండ గోళము the area of the inside of a sphere. బంగారుగోళము a gold ring. L. XIII. 38. కర్ణగోళము the orifice of the ear.

గోళికూర gôli-kûra. [Tel.] n. Spinach. H. iv. 166.

గోల్లగోండి gôlla-goṇḍi. [Tel.] n. A kind of grass. తృణవిశేషము. శా. iii.

గోవ gôva. [Tel.] n. The town Goa. గోవ జేవ్వాళ Castor, imported from thence. గోవ తాడు or గోవమొలతాడు a flexible belt, woven of gold or silver. గోవ n. Youthfulness యౌవనము. adj. Fine మనో జ్ఞము. గోవగాము a modesty piece కౌపీనము. గోవసీద gôva-sîda. n. The bird called the Large Grey Babbler, *Argya malcolmi* (F. B. I.) *Thimalia Malcolmi*. Jerdon's Catal. No. 90.

గోవాడు or గోవాడు gô-vaḍu. [Kan.] n. A youthful lover. విటుడు. Manu. iv. 121. Plu. గోవాడ్లు.

గోవిచెట్టు or గ్రోవి *gōvi-chettu*. [Tel.] n. A certain flowering shrub, *Galedupa Arborea*, also called క్రానుగచెట్టు or కానుగచెట్టు A. v. 146. BD. iii. 2068. T. iii. 29. Manu. ii. 25.

గోవిందుడు *go-vindudu*. [Skt.] n. Lit. A cow-herd. A name of the god Krishna. గోవిందగోవిందా Hurrah! huzza!

గోవిల or మూలగోవిల *gōvila*. [Tel.] n. The plant called *Aristolochia Indica*. Heyne; Rox. iii. 489.

గోవు *gōvu*. [Skt.] n. A cow. గోమయము *gō-mayamu*. n. Cow dung. పేడ. గోమసూచకము *gō-masūchakamu*. n. The cowpox. గోమాంసము *gō-mamsamu*. n. Beef. గోమాయువు *gō-māyuvu*. n. A jackal. నక్క. గోశ్రేణి *gō-srēni*. n. A species of Cassia. తంగేడు. గోష్ఠము *gō-shtamu*. n. A cow-pen, a fold for cattle. గోష్పదము *gōsh-padamu*. n. Grazing land; a spot frequented by cows. గోష్పద మైనచేరదు not enough to hold a cow's foot-print. గోహత్య *gō-hatya*. n. Cow-killing.

గోషా *gōsha*. [H.] n. Seclusion. అంతఃవాసము. గోషాస్త్రీ a woman kept in seclusion, a gosha woman, a *purda* woman. రాణీ వాసస్త్రీ.

గోష్ఠి *gōshti*. [Skt.] n. An assembly, or meeting for conversation, a secret assembly of the initiated. సభ. A discourse, conversation or talk సల్లాపము.

గోష్వారా *gōshvārā*. [H.] n. An abstract, an index, a tabular statement, wherein each article in a general account is reduced to its proper head.

గోసంగి *gōsangi*. [Tel.] n. A cobbler, a worker in leather. మాదిగవాడు.

గోసము *gōsamu*. [Skt.] n. Myrrh. బోళము. Dawn వేకువ.

గోసాయి or గోస్వామి *gōsāyi*. [Tel.] n. Gosains: religious mendicants, who are followers of Chaitanya.

గోసు *gōsu*. [Tel.] n. Pride, pretence, vaunting. అగ్గలము. Blame, disgrace అప దూరు, నింద. Fault దోషము. గోసడచు *gōsadatsu*. v. t. To blame. నిందించు. గోసన *gōsana*. n. Proclamation (in a bad sense) చాటించుట. M. IV. ii. 102.

గోస్తనము *gōstanamu*. [Skt.] n. A cow's udder. గోస్తని the purple grape. ద్రాక్ష.

గోహరి *gōhari*. [Tel.] n. Heroism. పరాక్రమము.

గౌ gau

గౌండ్ల *gaundla*. [Tel.] n. The caste of liquor-sellers. కల్లమ్మువారు.

గౌడ, గౌళ or పంచగౌళము *gauda*. [Skt.] n. The Bengali or Odhra language. The generic name for the languages of India north of the Godavery, viz., Hindi, Bengali, Mahrati, Uriya, and Panjabi which are called the పంచగౌళము. గౌడము *gaudamu*. n. Gaur. Bengal proper. The Gangetic countries.

గౌణము *gaunamu*. [Skt.] n. The secondary or figurative meaning of a word. Technicality. ఆ వ్యవహారము గౌణముగా జరిగినది the work went on but so and so, after a fashion. గౌణార్థము *gaunārthamu*. n. Personification అముఖ్యార్థము.

గౌతమి *gautami*. [Skt.] n. A name of the river Godavery. వృద్ధగౌతమి the "main stream" or northern mouth of this river.

గౌద, గవుద or గవద *gauda*. [Tel.] n. The glands of the cheek. The cheek. చెంప గౌదకట్టు, A. vi. 104.

గౌర or గవుర *gaura*. [Tel.] n. A shop-keeper. బేహారి, వర్తకుడు.

గౌరము *gauramu*. [Skt.] n. A fair complexion. A pale straw colour. "కల్హార గౌరగౌరిమహాపూరముల" (A. vi. 136.) Snow white. adj. Fair complexioned.

గౌరవము *gauravamu*. [Skt.] n. Weight. Heaviness. Grandeur, nobleness, respectability గొప్పతనము. గౌరవించు *gaura-*

vintsu. v.n. To treat respectfully, to show honor to గౌరవించు. గౌరవలేఖ *gaurava-lekha.* n. Honorific salutation. కరణములకు దండము రైతులకు వ్రాసిన గౌరవలేఖ salutation to the village writers and the same to the farmers.

గౌరి *gauri.* [Skt.] n. A damsel. A title of the goddess Parvati. A beautiful woman. గౌరీలక్షణము (a description of female beauty) is the title of a chapter in శిల్పశాస్త్రము on sculpture. గౌరీకుంకుమములు *gauri-kunkumamulu.* n. A fine species of white rice. గౌరీగన్నెము or గౌరిగన్నెము *gauri-ganyamu.* n. A sort of cloth. BD. iii. 107. గౌరీపాషాణము See పాషాణము.

గౌరు or గవురు *gauru.* [Tel.] n. A superior sort of elephant. తెల్లగౌరు a white elephant. A certain musical instrument. హంస. H. iii. 38. A. iv. 36. గౌరుకాకి *gauru-kaki.* n. A sea gull or tern. గౌరుతెలుగు *gauru-telugu.* A hoarse cry, a horrid yell. G. i. 254.

గౌలు or గవులు *gaulu.* [Tel.] n. A stink. దుర్గంధము. Scent గంధము.

గౌళ *gaula.* [Tel.] n. The name of a certain caste.

గౌళ or గౌర *gaula.* [Tel.] adj. Harsh-sounding. గౌళగొంతు a big voice. గౌళ కొమ్ము a loud clarion.

గౌళము and గౌళ దేశము Same as గౌడము.

గౌళి or గవుళి *gauli.* [Tel.] n. A kind of lizard called by naturalists Monitor, from its chirping note. శకునములుచెప్పేబల్లి.

గౌష్ఠీనము *gaushthinamu.* [Skt.] n. A cow-yard or pen.

గౌసెన or గవుసెన *gausena.* [Tel.] n. A cloth cover, a sheath ఒర.

గ్య gya

గ్యప్తి or గ్యప్తి *gyapti.* [for Skt. జ్ఞప్తి.] n. Recollection. జ్ఞాపకము.

గ్ర gra

గ్రంథము *granthamu.* [Skt.] n. A book, a volume. Papers, record, proceedings. The text, as distinguished from notes or quotations. A metre 32 syllables in length. Hence మూడు వేల గ్రంథము means a book of about 3000 lines. అది యెంత గ్రంథము what is the extent of that work? ఇక్కడ గ్రంథముపోయి నట్టు సందేహము or ఇక్కడ గ్రంథము లోప మైయున్నది the manuscript appears to be defective in this passage. గ్రంథకర్త *grantha-karta.* n. The author of a book. గ్రంథపుటి a writing room వ్రాసేచోటు. గ్రంథనము *granthanamu.* n. Stringing together, composing, a series. రచన, కూర్పు. గ్రంథభాష *grantha-bhasha.* n. Book language. గ్రంథసాంగుడు *grantha-sangudu.* n. A great genius. A bully, a fierce fellow. గ్రంథస్థము *granthasthamu.* adj. Found in a book, quoted.

గ్రంథి *granthi.* [Skt.] n. A knot or tie. A knot or joint in a bamboo or cane. A joint in the body. గణుపు. Rigidity of the flesh, a swelling or hardening of the flesh or of the blood vessels or nerves. కంతి. There are 24 species, including hæmorrhoids (వ్రణరోగము).

గ్రంథితము *granthitamu.* [Skt.] adj. Strung, tied, connected. కూర్పబడిన.

గ్రంథితగరము or గ్రంథితగరము *granthi-tagaramu.* [Skt.] n. The flowering plant named Whorl flowered Ruellia, *Ruellia strepens.*

గ్రక్కతిల్లు or గ్రక్కతిలు *grakka-tillu.* [Tel.] v. n. To be frightened. బెదరు.

"క. మొక్కెముసామినీదరు
నెక్కడనుండొ ద్దుపోదుము సెలవగకనే నే
దిక్కునియుండుముదాయలు
గ్రక్కతిలంగడుపు జేల్లగదలకయుండన్."
రామా. ii.

గ్రక్కు *grakku*. [Tel.] adj. Much. గ్రక్కడలు *grakk-adalu*. adj. Much afraid. M. I. ii. 13. గ్రక్కదలు *grak-kadalu*. adj. Much shaken. R. v. 303. గ్రక్కున or గ్రక్కన *grakku-na*. adv. Quickly. శీఘ్రముగా.

గ్రథనము *grathanamu*. [Skt.] n Stringing, uniting. Compilation, collection. కూర్పు, గ్రుచ్చుట. గ్రథితము *grathitamu*. adj. Tied, bound. కూర్చబడిన, గ్రుచ్చబడిన.

గ్రద్ద Same as గద్ద.

గ్రద్దన *graddana*. [Tel.] adv. Quickly. శీఘ్రముగా.

గ్రమ్మన *grammana*. [Tel.] adv. Quickly. దబ్బున.

గ్రసించు *grasintsu*. [Skt.] v. a. To swallow, devour. మ్రింగు. To eat తిను. గ్రస్తము *grastamu*. adj. Swallowed; seized; involved in; slurred, as an omitted word. విచారగ్రస్తుడై plunged in grief. అన్యాయగ్రస్తుడైనాడు he is a victim to injustice.

గ్రహము *grahamu*. [Skt. గ్రహ=to seize.] n. A planet. నవగ్రహములు the seven planets and the sun and moon. దశమగ్రహము a tenth planet: being like the Georgium sidus. A spirit, a devil. A proverb says జామాతా దశమగ్రహః A son-in-law is a more pestilent fellow than any one planet! he is the "tenth!" గ్రహచారము *graha-charamu*. n. Disaster, ill luck, fate, misfortune. నా గ్రహచారము చాలక యిట్లు జరిగినది through my misfortune (or, to my sorrow) it so happened. మా గ్రహచారము ఇట్లున్నది this is what has befallen us. గ్రహణము *grahaṇa-mu*. n. Taking, seizure. Reception, acceptance, comprehension. An eclipse. గ్రహణి *grahaṇi*. n. Diarrhœa, dysentery. అతిసారరోగము. గ్రహతారలు *graha-tāralu*. n. The planets and fixed stars. గ్రహపతి *graha-pati*. n. The lord of the stars, i. e., the sun. గ్రహరాజు the sun or moon.

గ్రహించు *grahintsu*. [Skt.] v. a. To seize, to take, to grasp, to hold, comprehend, understand. To accept. గ్రహీత *grahita*. n. One who takes, seizes, or accepts. గ్రహించువాడు.

గ్రా gra

గ్రాంధికము *grāndhikamu*. [Skt.] adj. Classical (as a word), poetical, peculiar to books; bookish. గ్రంథమందలి.

గ్రాజ *graza*. [Tel.] n. A kind of tree. ఉరాగారాకచెట్టు. పాండు. iv.

గ్రాద *grāda*. [Tel.] n. A bump. కణుపు. "మేను పెను గ్రాదలు కట్టగ పెరుగకొంచు." వాసి. ii.

గ్రాది *grādi*. [Bengali] n. A bannister, balustrade, railing or *chevaux-de-frise* కటకటాలు.

గ్రామము *grāmamu*. [Skt.] n. A village. ఊరు. A scale in music. షడ్జాదిస్వరము. గ్రామత్రయము the three tones, treble, tenor and base. A crowd or multitude సమూహము. as గుణగ్రామము or శబ్దగ్రామము. గ్రామకార్యము *grāma-kāryamu*. n. Village affairs: worldly matters. గ్రామకంఠము *grāma-kanṭhamu*. n. The glebe, or pasture land appertaining to a village. గ్రామణి *grāmaṇi*. n. A chief: a head man. గ్రామాధిపతి. గ్రామణి adj. Chief, head, leading. ముఖ్యుడు నరగ్రామణి, the noblest of men. దుర్గ్రామణి a wicked ruler.

గ్రామణ్యము *grāmaṇyamu*. n. The rule or headship of a town. Imperiousness, violence, outrage. గ్రామణ్యముగా scoffingly. గ్రామదేవత *grāma-dēvata*. n. A village god or goddess. These are the original Dravidian deities. Among them the male deities are chiefly these: పోతురాజు, కాట్రేడు, అంకాలు, గంగయ్య, చెన్నడు and మైలారు. The principal village goddesses are పెద్దమ్మ, కాట్రేణి, అంకాళమ్మ,

ఎక్కలేశమ్మ, ఎల్లమ్మ, పోలేరమ్మ, మల్లమ్మ, మారిడమ్మ, మైసమ్మ or మైసూరమ్మ; (i. e. 'మహిషి,') మారెదుమ్మ, మారెమ్మ (who probably is meant for "Maria") దుర్గాలేశమ్మ (that is, Saint Agatha,) and నంకలమ్మ or నంకేశమ్మ, of whom one inflicts the cholera, another the small pox (see అమ్మవారు) another murrain, another blight. None have any beneficent powers, and they are worshipped to avert their displeasure. గ్రామసింహము *grāma-simhamu*. n. The lion of the village, i.e., a dog. గ్రామస్థుడు *grāma-sthuḍu*. n. A villager. స్వగ్రామస్థుడు a fellow citizen or neighbour. గ్రామాంతము *grām-āntamu*. n. The outlying portion of a village, i. e., the Panchama quarter. మాలపల్లె. గ్రామాదులు *grām-ādulu*. n. Villages. Lit. Villages, &c. గ్రామ్యము *grāmyamu*. adj. Village-born; produced in or relating to a village. Vulgar, rude, rustic. Common, colloquial, unclassical, inelegant: The opposite of శాస్త్రీయము. In Grammar the term is applied to conversational forms as వస్తాడు, తెస్తాడు, like they're, I'm, you're, he's, in English, which are supposed to be inadmissible in literature, though they occur in all even the best poets. గ్రామ్యధర్మము *grāmya-dharmamu*. n. Sexual intercourse. సంభోగము. Lit. what is usual or the fashion, or way of the world.

గ్రాయు *grāyu*. [Tel.] v. n. To spit. A. v. 132. To rinse the mouth and spit out the water. ఊమియు, పుక్కిలించి ఉమ్మివేయు.

గ్రావము *grāvamu*. [Skt.] n. A mountain, a rock or stone. కొండ, రాయి.

గ్రాసము *grāsamu*. [Skt.] n. A mouthful. కబళము. Subsistence, board, forage for cattle. గ్రాసవాసములు *grāsa-vāsamulu*. n. Food and lodgings.

గ్రాహము *grāhamu*. [Skt.] n. An alligator. మొసలి.

గ్రాహ్యము *grāhyamu*. [Skt.] adj. Comprehensible, capable of being understood. గ్రహింపదగిన.

గ్రీ grī

గ్రీవము *grīvamu*. [Skt.] n. The neck. మెడ. గ్రైవము or గ్రైవేయము *graivamu*. n. A halter మెడకుకట్టుత్రాడు. గ్రైవేయకము *graivēyakamu*. n. A neck ornament మెడను కట్టుకొనేసొమ్ము.

గ్రీష్మము *grīshmamu*. [Skt.] n. Heat, warmth. వేడిమి. The hot season వేసంగి.

గ్రు gru

గ్రుక్క *grukka*. [Tel.] n. Swallowing. మింగుట. Breath. ఉక్కు. గ్రుక్కగొను *grukka-gonu*. v. a. To swallow or devour. మింగు గ్రుక్కలుమింగు to desire. అపేక్షపడు; to hesitate సంకోచించు. గ్రుక్కిలి or గ్రుక్కిళ్లు *grukkili*. n. A gulp, swallowing, or deglutition. గ్రుక్కిళ్లు మింగు to sob, to lick the lips, expressive of desire. అపేక్షపడు; to hesitate సంకోచించు. గ్రుక్కమిక్కు to open the mouth to speak మాటాడబోవు.

గ్రుచ్చు Same as గుచ్చు. "రాత్రియందునాడి దారంబుగ్రుచ్చంగ క్షేత్రములకుదృష్టిసేకొల్పు మనుడు." BD. iv. 611.

గ్రుడ్డి Same as గుడ్డి. గ్రుడ్డిపాటు *gruḍḍi-pāṭu*. adj. Providential, accidental. దైవికము.

గ్రుడ్డు *gruḍḍu*. [Tel.] n. Blindness. గుడ్డితనము. The eye ball కనుగ్రుడ్డు. An egg గుడ్డు. గ్రుడ్డుకానుపు *gruḍḍu-kānupu*. n. An ovary, a bird పక్షి. A serpent సర్పము. గ్రుడ్లగూబ *gruḍla-gūba*. n. An owl. గుడ్లగూబ. See గుడ్డు.

గ్రుద్దు gruddu. [Tel.] v. t. To give a blow with the fist. గుద్దు. n. A blow with the fist. గుద్దు.

గ్రొ gro

గ్రొయ్యి or గొయ్యి groyyi. [Tel.] n. A pit. గొయ్యి, పల్లము. గ్రొయ్యు groyyu. v. n. To be formed into a hole or pit. పల్లముపడు. గ్రొచ్చు grotstsu. v. t. To dig a hole. పల్లముచేయు.

గ్ల gla

గ్లహము glahamu. [Skt.] n. A stake in gambling జూదమందలి పందెము.

గ్లా glā

గ్లాని glāni. [Skt.] n. Lassitude, weariness, fatigue. శ్రమముచేతకలిగిన దౌర్బల్యము.

గ్లౌ glau

గ్లౌ glau. [Skt.] n. The moon. చంద్రుడు, చందమామ.

ఘ gha

ఘంట ghanṭa. [Skt.] n. A bell. గంట. ఘంటాపథము ghanṭā-pathamu. n. The king's high way; so called because resounding with elephants' bells. పదిబారలు వెడల్పుగల రాజమార్గము, బాట. ఘంటాపథముగా as clear as the day, openly. ఘంటాపథముగా మాట్లాడుట to talk decisively or openly. cf. "They shall say in all the high ways." Amos. v. 16. ఘంటారవము ghanṭā-ravamu. n. Ringing: the sound of a bell. The plant *crotolaria*. W. గిలిగిచ్చ చెట్టు.

ఘట ghaṭa. [Skt.] n. An assembly, a squadron. సమూహము. A troop or herd of elephants. ఏనుగుల సమూహము.

ఘటకుడు ghaṭakuḍu. [Skt.] n. One who effects: an agent. ఘటిల్లజేయువాడు.

ఘటన or ఘటనము ghaṭana. [Skt.] n. Effort, exertion. Effecting, bringing about. కూర్పు. ఈశ్వర ఘటన అట్లా అయినది such was the will of God. దైవఘటన the dispensations of providence. Assembling, joining. అఘటితఘటనము or అఘటనాఘటనము reconciling the irreconcilable. నవరసఘటన mingling various styles in poetry.

ఘటము ghaṭamu. [Skt.] n. An earthen vessel or jar. కుండ. The body శరీరము. A ruined well పాడుగొయ్యి. ఘటవిసర్జన చేసినాడు he left the body. ఈ ఘటముండేవరకు as long as I live. Bringing about, effecting కూర్పు, ఘటనము. దుర్ఘటము impracticable, hard to get or bring about. ఘటచక్రము ghaṭa-chakramu. n. A potter's wheel. ఘటయంత్రము ghaṭa-yantramu. [Skt.] n. A sort of pump. నూతిగిలక, నీరుతోడేగిలక. "గీ॥ పొంతఘటయంత్రసరము ద్రిప్పుచు జనించు" A. v. 90. ఘటశాసి ghaṭa-śāsi. n. A logician. తార్కికుడు. A. vi. 89. ఘటశ్రాద్ధము or ఘటస్ఫోటనము ghaṭa-śrāddhamu. n. The funeral of a pot; a mode of divorce, wherein funeral rites are performed as though the rebellious wife were actually dead. ఘటస్ఫోటనము చేసినాడు he divorced his wife.

ఘటిక ghaṭika. n. An Indian hour of twenty-four English minutes. గడియ.

ఘటిల్లు ghaṭillu. [Skt.] v. n. To befall, to occur, to happen, to come to pass, to be obtained, be laid, attributed or imputed (as blame) కలుగు. అప్పుడుఘటిల్లక not being then possible or attainable. ఘటిల్లజేయు ghaṭilla-jēyu. v. a. To effect, accomplish, do, manage.

ఘటీకారము ghaṭī-kāramu. [Skt.] n. A clock. గడియారము.

ఘటీయంత్రము ghaṭi-yantramu. [Skt.] n. A machine for raising water, a waterlift. ఏతము, నీళ్లుతోడే యంత్రము.

ఘట్టన ghaṭṭana. [Skt.] n. Ramming down: a road, &c., గట్టించుట. ఘట్టనకారుడు one who hardens. ఈ దారికి ఘట్టనచాలదు this road has not been sufficiently beaten or rammed. అశ్వఖురఘట్టనము the prancings of horses.

ఘట్టము ghaṭṭamu. [Skt.] n. A landing place or quay, తీరము. An object or point gained. A lump, a clod. భారతఘట్టము a puzzle or intricacy in the Mahābhārata.

ఘట్టలయము ghaṭṭa-layamu. [Skt.] n. Quick time in music. "ఉదుమద్దలయుంచాలితఘట్ట లయంత్రిమే." Ananda Tantram IX. 81.

ఘట్టితము ghaṭṭitamu. [Skt.] adj. Hardened. గట్టింపబడిన.

ఘనము ghanamu. [Skt.] n. Greatness in any sense, honour, గొప్పతనము. Extension, diffusion వ్యాప్తి. A cloud. మేఘము. The base in music. Thickness, in measurment. Solidity, cubical content. A cube. The cube of a number. దట్టము. adj. Great in any sense, grand, excellent, honourable, noble. Rich, opulent. Famous. Important. Plenteous, abundant, complete. Large, big. Fat, plump, solid, material. Permanent. Hard, firm. Tight, well fitting. ఘనత ghanata. n. Greatness, fame, glory, nobility, respectability. ఘనతకెక్కు ghanata-k-ekku. v. n. To become famous. ఘనతర ghana-tara. adj. Greater, more famous. ఘనత్వము ghanatvamu. n. Greatness. ఘనపుష్పము or ఘనపుష్పము ghana-pushpamu. n. The cloud "blossom:" a poetical word for water. ఘనరసము ghana-rasamu. n. Water. నీళ్లు. Camphor. కర్పూరము. ఘనసారము ghana-sāramu. n. Camphor. కర్పూరము. (Manu. vi. 5.) ఘనాఘనము ghana-ghanamu. n. A floating or rainy cloud. కురియునట్టి మేఘము, కారుమొయిలు. ఘనాఘనుడు ghanā-ghanuḍu. n. Indra.

ఘనీభవించు ghanī-bhavintsu. [Skt.] v. n. To unite in a mass, to curdle, thicken, freeze. To become firm or solid. గడ్డకట్టు.

ఘనుడు ghanuḍu. n. A great man. గొప్పవాడు. ఘనోపలము ghanōpalamu. [Skt. ఘన+ఉపలము. Lit. a cloud-stone.] n. Hail. A hail stone వడగల్లు.

ఘరట్టము gharaṭṭamu. [Skt.] n. A hand-mill. తిరుగలి.

ఘర్ఘరి gharghari. [Skt.] n. A little bell. చిరుగంట. Tingling or clinking ornaments, as a chain of small bells. పెండెము or పెండిదము. One of the tones or notes in music స్వరభేదము.

ఘర్మము gharmamu. [Skt.] n. Heat. వేడిమి. The hot season వేసంగికాలము. Sunshine ఎండ. Sweat, perspiration చెమట. ఘర్మవారి sweat.

ఘర్షణ or ఘర్షణము gharshaṇa. [Skt.] n. Friction ఒరయుట, రాయుట. Tumult, a dispute, contention, argument, altercation రగ్గా, వివాదము. ఘర్షించు or ఘర్షణ చేయు gharshintsu. v. n. To dispute or contend, to squabble, brawl.

ఘల్లు or గల్లు ghallu. [Tel.] adv. Tinglingly, ringingly, aloud. B. viii. 415. D. iv. 260. H. ii. 27. ఘల్లుమని tumultuously, aloud. ఘల్లుమనినది there was a noise or a crash. ఆ చెంబు ఘల్లుమని పడ్డది.

ఘలుఘలుక్కు ghalu-ghalukku. [Skt.] adv. (anuk) Tinklingly, aloud, audibly. B. viii. 420.

ఘస్మరము ghasmaramu. [Skt.] adj. Gluttonous, voracious, devouring, destroying. ఘస్మరుడు ghasmaruḍu. n. A glutton. తిండిపోతు. One who slays నాశకుడు. మురఘస్మరుడు the vanquisher of Mura. M. XIV.; 3. మదనఘస్మరుడు the Amoricide, or slayer of Love. Epithet of Siva.

ఘస్రము ghasramu. [Skt.] n. A day. దినము. B. vii. 110.

ఘా gha

ఘాటీ or ఘాటు ghāṭi [H.] n. A hill pass or police station. ఆ యింటికి ఘాటీ ఉన్నారు they guarded the house.

ఘాటు or గాటు ghāṭu. [Tel.] n. Strength, virulence, potency of poison or of liquor. Pungency, acridity, as of pepper. ఘాటు పొగాకు strong tobacco. ఘాటించు ghaṭintsu. v. n. To be violent.

ఘాతము ghātamu. [Skt.] n. A blow or stroke. దెబ్బ. Killing, murdering, slaughter. -వాత్య. A square reservoir for water. ఘాతకబుద్ధి a murderous intent. ఘాతకారి or ఘాతకుడు or ఘాతుకుడు ghāta-kāri. n. A murderer, a villain, a destroyer, a wretch. ఘాతిని ghātini. n. A murderess. ఘాతుకము ghātukamu. n. Cruelty, ferocity, murder. adj. Mischievous, hurtful, cruel, savage, violent, ferocious.

ఘారిక ghārika. [Skt.] n. A sort of cake. గారె.

ఘాసము ghāsamu. [Skt.] n. Meadow or pasture grass. పచ్చిక. Food, living, maintenance. కబళము.

ఘీ ghī

ఘీంకరించు ghīm-karintsu. [Skt.] v. n. To scream or yell; to roar like an elephant. ఘీంకారము or ఘీంకృతి ghīm-kāramu. n. The roaring or screaming of an elephant. ఏనుగుకేక.

ఘు ghu

ఘుటిక ghuṭika. [Skt.] n. The ankle. చీల మండ. A small ball or pill.

ఘుణము ghuṇamu. [Skt.] n. An insect that is found in timber, under the bark of a tree, a wood louse, నుసిపురుగు. (A iv. 180.) ఘుణాక్షరన్యాయముగా by chance. ఘుణనియందు పురుగు తొలుచగా ఏర్పడిన అక్షరంవలెయొక్క న్యాయము.

ఘుణఘుణత్కారము ghuṇa-ghuṇat kāramu. [Skt.] n. A slight murmur or broken words.

ఘుమఘుమ or గుమగుమ ghuma-ghuma [Tel.] n. (Anuk.) Fragrance. adv. Sweetly, fragrantly, melodiously, strong (as scent.) ఘుమ్మని ghum-m-ani. adv. Fragrantly, melodiously, sweetly.

ఘుర్ఘురము ghur-ghuramu. [Skt.] n. A grunt, grunting. పందికూత. ఘుర్ఘురించు ghurghur-intsu. v. n. To grunt. (పంది) కూయు.

ఘుసృణము ghusṛuṇamu. [Skt.] n. Saffron. కుంకుమపువ్వు.

ఘూ ghū

ఘూకము ghū-kamu. [Skt.] n. An owl. ఘూకి ghūki. n. The female owl.

ఘూర్జరము ghūrjaramu. [Skt.] n. Guzerat.

ఘూర్ణనము ghūrnanamu. [Skt.] n. Turning round, whirling, rolling. గిరగిరతిరగడము, తిరుగుడు. మదఘూర్ణమైన tipsy. ఘూర్ణితము ghūrnitamu. adj. Rolling, turning. తిరుగుడుపడిన. ఘూర్ణిల్లు ghūrnillu. v. n. To roll, turn round, తిరుగుడుపడు. To sound, resound. To ring or tinkle. To roar, or hiss. మ్రోయు, ఘోషించు.

ఘృ ghṛi

ఘృణ ghṛiṇa. [Skt.] n. Favour, compassion, tenderness, pity. కనికరము, కరుణారసము. Dislike జుగుప్స, రోత.

ఘృణి ghṛiṇi. [Skt.] n. A ray of the sun or moon. కిరణము. Light. వెలుగు.

ఘృతము ghṛitamu. [Skt.] n. Clarified butter. నెయ్యి. ఘృతోదధి a sea of ghee నేతిసముద్రము.

ఘృష్టి *ghrishti*. [Skt.] n. A ray of light. కిరణము. A pig సూకరము. Recollection, readiness, memory జ్ఞప్తి. ఇప్పుడు ఆ ఉదాహరణము నాకు ఘృష్టికి రాలేదు that quotation does not now occur to my memory.

ఘే ghē

ఘే .. ఘేయనునాదము Huzza, a shout of joy. ఘేయని జయపెట్టు to utter joyful buzzas. "ఎంతంతజనులు ఘేయనిజయపెట్ట." BD. v. 1420.

ఘొ gho

ఘొటఘొట or గొటగొట *ghoṭa-ghoṭa*. [Tel.] adv. (Anuk.) Aloud, fiercely. "ఘొట ఘొటగొప్పద్వైలుల ఘోషము." &c.

ఘొల్లు or గొల్లు *ghollu*. [Tel.] n. A yell or roar. ఈమాట ఊరిలో ఘొల్లుమని పుట్టినది the whole town is in an uproar about this.

ఘో ghō

ఘోంట *ghōnṭa*. [Skt.] n. The areca palm tree. పోకచెట్టు.

ఘోటకము *ghōṭakamu*. [Skt.] n. A horse. మన్మథఘోటకము Cupid's steed: that is, a parrot. ఘోటకబ్రహ్మచర్యము chastity perforce. ఘోటికె *ghōṭika*. n. A mare. ఆడగుర్రము, గోడిగ. మదనఘోటిక Cupid's steed, i. e., a female parrot.

ఘోట్టణము or ఘోట్టాణము *ghoṭṭaṇamu*. [Skt.] n. *Khutan*, a name of Tartary. Rukmang. i. 19. Hence, a horse of that country. R. i. 86. A iv. 36.

ఘోణ *ghōṇa*. [Skt.] n. The nose. ముక్కు, నాసిక. The nostrils of a horse. దీర్ఘఘోణ long-nosed. ఘోణి *ghōṇi*. n. A wild hog. అడవిపంది.

ఘోరము *ghōramu*. [Skt.] adj. Frightful, horrible, tremendous. భయంకరము. ఘోరదర్శనము lit. horrid to view: cruel-eyed, i. e., a tiger. ఘోరాటవి *ghōrāṭavi*. n. An awful forest. BD. v. 524. ఘోరుడు-*ghōruḍu*. n. A fierce man భయంకరుడు.

ఘోలి *ghōli*. [Skt.] n. Spinach. H. iv. 166. గోలికూర.

ఘోష *ghōsha*. [Skt.] n. A loud noise, a cry, a roar, an exclamation, proclamation, news. వేదఘోషతోకూడా సాగిపోయిరి they set forth in procession preceded by Brahmins who chanted verses from the Vedas. ఘోషాక్షరము an aspirated consonant. ఘోషము n. A hamlet where herdsmen dwell. గొల్లపల్లె. ఘోషకన్య *ghōsha-kanya*. n. A milkmaid. ఘోషణము *ghōshaṇamu*. n. A roaring noise, a clamour, an uproar. చాటించడము. ఘోషించు *ghōshinṭsu*. v. n. To sound, roar, resound, clamour, exclaim, cry. ధ్వనిచేయు, మ్రోయు, చాటించు. ఘోషుడు *ghōshuḍu*. n. A shepherd or herdsman, గొల్లవాడు.

ఘ్రా ghrā

ఘ్రాణము *ghrāṇamu*. [Skt.] n. The nose. ముక్కు. Smelling, A smell. ఘ్రాణోత్సవము *ghrāṇōtsavamu*. n. A treat for the nose, i. e., a sweet savour. ఘ్రాతము *ghrātamu*. adj. Scented, smelled. మూర్కొనబడిన.

చ cha

చ *cha*. [Tel.] A letter. See under చే.

చంక్రమణము *chankramaṇamu*. [Skt.] n. Going tortuously or slowly. Tottering, toddling, as an infant. Clambering. పాకుట. P. i. 297. A. vi. 143. R. ii. 17.

చంగము *changamu*. [Skt.] adj. Beautiful, చక్కని. Dexterous సామర్థ్యముగల, నేర్పుగల.

చంచ *chancha*. [Skt.] n. A mat. చాప. A doll made of grass. గడ్డిబొమ్మ.

చంచత్ *chanchat.* [Skt.] adj. Wavering. చంచజ్జఘనాంగి frisky, skittish, wincing. P. iv. 362.

చంచరీకము *chanchurikamu.* [Skt.] n. The large black carpenter bee, to which poets compare clusters of jetty locks. తుమ్మెద.

చంచలము *chanchalamu.* [Skt.] adj. Trembling, tremulous, unsteady, moving. Mutable, unstable, transient. చలించునది. n. Wind. గాలి. చంచలించు *chanchal-intsu.* v n. To shake, waver, wag, move.

చంచువు *chanchuru.* [Skt.] n. The bill or beak of a bird. పక్షిముక్కు. చంచూపుటము *chanchū-puṭamu.* n. The point of the beak.

చండము *chandamu.* [Skt.] adj. Passionate, violent, terrible, severe, fiery, hot, warm. తీక్ష్ణమైన. చండకము *chanḍakamu.* n. A tiger. పులి. చండశాసనము *chanḍa-ṣāsanamu.* n. Severe or terrible retribution. చండాంశువు *chanḍ-amṣuvu.* n. The Sun. వేడివెలుగు.

చండాలుడు or చాండాలుడు *chanḍaludu.* [Skt.] n. An outcaste. A Chandāla or Pariah. See మాల. adj. Heathen, savage, stubborn, obdurate. చండాలగుణము a nasty disposition, stubborness. కర్మచండాలుడు one who acts as a savage. జన్మచండాలునికి కాలాంతరమునందు మోక్షముకలదు, కర్మచండాలునికి ఏనాడును లేదు the base by birth may in time attain heaven: the base in life never can.

చండి *chanḍi.* [Skt.] n. Lit: The "terrible." A name of the goddess Kāli. A perverse obstinate woman. adj. Horrible. చండించు *chanḍintsu.* v. n. To get very angry. మిక్కిలి కోపించు. చండిక *chanḍika.* n. A virago, a fury. కోపముగలస్త్రీ. A name of the goddess Durga. పార్వతీదేవి. చండిమ *chanḍima.* n. Sharpness. వాడిమి.

చండుడు *chanḍudu.* [Skt.] n. A furious man. మిక్కిలికోపముగలవాడు.

చందనము *chandanamu.* [Skt.] n. Sandal; *Sirium myrtifolium.* చందనగంధి *chandana-gandhi.* n. A sweet maid, a blooming girl. చందనాచలము *chandan-āchalamu.* n. The Malaya mountains in the south west of the Indian peninsula, where sandal is produced.

చందరస or వాలుక *chandarasa.* [Skt.] n. A weed called *Pharnaceum Mollugo.* Heyne.

చందిరుడు Same as చంద్రుడు.

చంద్రకము *chandrakamu.* [Skt.] adj. Dark. Lurid. మేచకము. n. A semicircle. The eyes in a peacock's tail. The semilunar marks left by finger-nails in pinching.

చంద్రకాంతము *chandra-kantamu.* [Skt.] n. The poetical moonstone, or, noble opal, which is fabled to melt in the moonbeams. A crystal. చలువరాయి.

చంద్రము *chandramu.* [Skt.] n. Gold బంగారము. Camphor కర్పూరము.

చంద్రుడు *chandrudu.* [Skt.] n. The moon; the regent of the moon. చంద్రుడు ఉదయించినాడు the moon arose. చంద్రుడు అస్తమించినాడు the moon set. రామచంద్రుడు the moon-like or beautiful Rāma. చంద్రముఖి *chandra-mukhi.* n. A beautiful woman. చంద్రమూల *chandra-mūla.* n. The plant called *Kæmpferia Galanga.* Rox. i. 15. చంద్రవంక *chandra-vanka.* n. A half-moon, or crescent. Also, a kind of jewel worn on the head. చంద్రివంకలు a sort of rice. H. iv. 156. చంద్రవంశము the Lunar Race of Kshatriya kings. చంద్రశాల n. An upper room, on the house top. మేడమీదియిల్లు, మేడమీదటికటి. (A. i. 2.) చంద్రశిల n. Moonstone. See చంద్రకాంతము. చంద్రశేఖరుడు *chandra-ṣekharudu.* n. The crescent-crowned god, i. e., Siva. చంద్రహాసము *chandrahāsamu.* n. Radiance, flashing, sheen. A sword కత్తి. Name of the sword of Kubēra or Rāvaṇa. చంద్రాతపము *chandra-tapamu.* n. Moonlight. T. ii. 30. వెన్నెల. చంద్రాయుధము *chandr-āyudhamu.* n. A crescent headed arrow. NH. v. 160. చంద్రిక chandrika. n. Moonlight: a pale red tint. An illustration, an essay, a treatise. The reddish envelope of a letter written on palm leaves. చంద్రికచీరలు (A iv. 36.) white cloths తెల్లబట్టలు. చంద్రోదయము chandrōdayamu. n. The rising of the moon. An awning used at festivals. A kind of medicine. ప్రబోధచంద్రోదయము "the masterpiece of wisdom"—(the name of a certain work.)

చంపకము champa-kamu. [Skt.] n. The gold-flower or chrysanthemum సంపెంగ. Michelia Champaca, Rox. i. 16. ii. 655. చంపకమాల or చంపకమాలిక champaka-māla. n. The name of a popular metre in Telugu poetry.

చంపూకావ్యము or చంపూప్రబంధము champu-kāvyamu. [Skt.] n. An anthology. A descriptive poem with an admixture of prose.

చకారము chakāramu. [Skt.] n. The letter cha.—hence చాగుడి or చకారగుడి "the word that begins with chi, i. e., ఛీ fie, shame.

చకితము chakitamu. [Skt.] adj. Fearful, timid, bashful. చకితుడు one who is frightened, or timid.

చకోరము chakōramu. [Skt.] n. The bartavelle or Greek partridge: a bird much referred to in poems: corresponding to the nightingale, or turtledove. చంద్రకిరణములకు చకోరపక్షులు ఏ విధముగా నిరీక్షించుకొనియుందునో eagerly as the partridge languishes for the rays of the moon.

చక్రము chakramu. [Skt.] n. A wheel. A discus or sharp-edged plate of steel, hurled at a foe like a quoit: the thunderbolt or weapon of Vishṇu. A realm, region. రాష్ట్రము. A figure, diagram or sign in astrology. The name of a coin. The bird called చక్రవాకము. A region or division of the body. చక్రధరుడు or చక్రపాణి Vishṇu. కటి or కటిచక్రము the loins, the region of the loins. అష్టకోణచక్రము an octagon. చక్రవర్తి chakra-varti. n. An emperor or sovereign. రారాజు, సార్వభౌముడు. చక్రవర్తిని chakra-vartini. n. An empress. సార్వభౌమురాలు. చక్రవాకము. chakra-vākamu. n. The Brahminy-duck or Ruddy Casarca rotila (F. B. I.) జక్కవపక్షి. The poetical swan, always described as being in pairs, to which poets liken fair breasts. చక్రవాళము chakravālamu. n. A range of mountains supposed to encircle the earth. చుట్టుకొండ. చక్రవృద్ధి chakra-vriddhi. n. Compound interest వడ్డీకివడ్డీ. చక్రాంకణము or చక్రాంకితములు or చక్రాంకములు chakrānkanamu. n. Marks branded on the front of the shoulders, representing the disc and shell of Vishṇu. (It is a rite similar to absolution.) చక్రాంగము chakrāngamu. n. A swan. హంస. చక్రాంగి a female swan. చక్రి chakri. n. The discus-wielder, i e., Vishṇu. A snake, because rolled in a ring. A potter, because using a wheel.

చక్షువు chakshuvu. [Skt.] n. The eye. కన్ను. చక్షుశ్శ్రవము lit. that which hears with its eye, i. e., a serpent పాము.

చటకము chaṭakamu. [Skt.] n. A sparrow. ఊరపిచ్చుక.

చటచట chaṭa-chaṭa. [Skt. anuk.] adv. Furiously, brilliantly.

చటాకు chaṭāku. [Tel.] n. The sixteenth part of a seer.

చటులము chaṭulamu. [Skt.] adj. Tremulous. చలించునది. చంచలమైనది. Glancing, flashing, trembling, as a swimming and beautiful eye. Fierce-eyed. Piercing, potent. చటులాంబకములు mighty arrows. చటులకోపము fierce fury.

చణకము chaṇakamu. [Skt.] n. The chick pea, Cicer arietinum, commonly called Bengal gram. సెనగలు.

చణము chaṇamu. [Skt.] adj. Versed, expert, skilful, united with. విద్యాచణుడు, జయశ్రీచణుడు. (A. v. 127.) endowed with riches; rich or noble.

చతుర chatura. [Skt.] adj. Ingenious, dexterous, artful, clever.

చతురము chaturamu. [for Skt. చదరము.] n. Area, square contents, a four cornered place, a square. చతురపుఇంటి a square house. చతురపుగజాలు square yards, square measurement. చతురంగము chatur-angamu. n. Chess. చతురంగబలము chatur-anga-balamu. n. An army complete with the "*four arms*" of infantry, cavalry, elephants and war chariots. చతురంతయానము chatur-anta-yānamu. n. A palankeen. చతురత్వము chatur-atvamu. n. Sharpness of wit, quickness of intellect. చతురస్రము chatur-asramu. adj. Four cornered, quadrangular. చతురాననుడు chatur-ānanudu. n The four-faced; i. e., Bramha. చతురుడు chaturudu. n. A clever man, a genius. సమర్థుడు. చతురోక్తి chaturōkti. n. A soft or pleasing word చతుర్థము chaturthamu. adj. Fourth. చతుర్థి chaturthi. n. The fourth day of the lunar month. చేవితి. adj. Fourth నాలుగవది. చతుర్దంతము chatur-dantamu. n. Four toothed or double tusked, the name of Indra's elephant. చతుర్దశము chatur-daṣamu. adj. Fourteenth. చతుర్దశి chatur-daṣi. n. The fourteenth lunar day, calculated either from the new or full moon. చతుర్భుజుడు chatur-bhujudu. n. The four armed; a name of Vishṇu. చతుర్ముఖుడు chatur-mukhudu. n. The four faced; a name of Brahma. చతుర్వర్గము or వర్గచతుష్టయము chatur-vargamu. n. The four objects of human pursuit, viz. duty, wealth, pleasure, salvation. ధర్మార్థకామమోక్షములు. చతుశ్శాలము chatuṣ-ṣalamu. n. A quadrangular building enclosing an open square. నాలుగిండ్లచావడి. చతుష్కము or చతుష్టయము chatush-kamu. n. A set of four. A collective term. మూర్తిచతుష్టయము. (M. IX. ii. 227.) the four forms. యుగచతుష్కము the four ages. చతుష్పదము or చతుష్పాదము chatush-padamu. n. A quadruped. చత్వరము chatvaramu. n. A yard or enclosure within a house. ముంగిలి. చత్వారము or చత్వారి chat-vāramu. n. The number four. Purblindness, failing sight, presbyopia; lit. the age of 40 years. Used also for Shortsightedness. చత్వారింశము chatvā-rimṣamu. adj. Fortieth. చత్వారింశత్తు chatvā-rimṣattu. adj. Forty.

చపల chapala. [Skt.] n. Lightning, a flash. A. vi. 130. చపలము chapalamu. adj. Glancing, fickle, tremulous, volatile, wavering, unsteady, wanton. కదిలెడు, నిలుకడలేని. చపలత fickleness, a whimsical disposition చపలచిత్తము.

చపాతు chapātu. [Tel.] n. Prickly pear.

చపేటము chapēṭamu. [Skt.] n. The palm of the hand. చాచినవ్రేళ్లుగల అరచెయ్యి.

చమత్కరించు chamat-karintsu. [Skt.] v. a. To refine on (an idea), to play upon (words). To be adroit or accomplished. To play amorous pranks with. Anirud. iii. 84. చమత్కారముచేయు, ఆడు. చమత్కారము or చమత్కృతి chamat-kāramu. n. Skill, adroitness, ingenuity, wit: నేర్పు. a prank or manœuvre. Curiosity, rarity, refinement.

చమరము chamaramu. [Skt.] n. The yak of Tartary, *Bos-grunnicus* the tail of which is made into whisks (చామరము), సవరపుమెకము. A whisk వింజామరము. చమరి the female of this animal, ఆడుసవరపుమెకము.

చమసము chamasamu. [Skt.] n. A square cup out of which all the worshippers at a Yajna drink the juice of the acid asclepias. చతురస్రమైనయజ్ఞపాత్రము.

చమువు *chamuvu.* [Skt.] n. An army, a squadron. సేన.

చమూరువు *chamūruvu.* [Skt.] n. An antelope.

చయము *chayamu.* [Skt.] n. An assemblage, a multitude, a heap or collection, సమూహము; a mound of earth, a pile. కోట కొరడు. This word is even used for a small number; thus నేత్రచయము the three eyes of Siva are called his "set of eyes."

చరణము *charaṇamu.* [Skt.] n. The foot. పాదము; the root of a tree వేరు. A walk or ramble, roaming. తిరుగుట. In poetry, a couplet. చరణాయుధము the heel armed, i. e., a cock కోడి. కృష్ణచరణాలు (lit. the black footsteps) the spectacles on the crest of a Cobra. రథచరణము a wheel. **చరణారవిందములు** *charaṇ-āra-vindamulu.* n. The "blessed feet"—a phrase for any beloved personage.

చరమము *charamamu.* [Skt.] adj. Last, ultimate, final. West, western. చరమ క్రియ the last or funeral rites చరమగిరి the western hill. **చరమశ్లోకము** *charama-ślōkamu.* n. A requiem. An epitaph. **చరమాంగము** *charam-āngamu.* n. The back of a tortoise. Lit. the last member. Swa. v. 56.

చరము *charamu.* [Skt.] adj. Moveable, locomotive, migratory. Trembling, shaking, unsteady. చరాస్తి personal or moveable property. చరస్థిరరూపకములు property, personal and real. దృష్టిచరము visible. శ్రుతిచరము audible. స్పర్శచరము tangible. చరవృక్షములు (Kalah. i. 101.) moving or walking trees. n. An animal or moving creature. చరాచరములు the animate and inanimate creation. తిరుగునదియును తిరుగనిదియునైనది, జగత్తు. **చరుడు** *charuḍu.* n. A spy వేగువాడు. **చరించు** *charintsu.* v. n. To wander, to roam. తిరుగు. To live, conduct oneself, behave. To go on, continue. v. t. To do or observe; to perform. చేయు.

"వ్రతములో చరించెనధికేచ్ఛన్ గుంధకర్ణుండు."
భార. అర. vi.

చరిత, చరిత్ర, చరితము or **చరిత్రము** *charita.* [Skt.] n. History, tale, narrative. Behaviour, conduct. దినచరిత్ర a diary. వ్యాజ్యచరిత్ర the entire details of the dispute. **చరితార్థము** *charit-arthamu.* n. End, advantage, purpose. వినియోగము, ఫలితార్థము.

చరువు *charuvu.* [Skt.] n. A burnt offering. An oblation. హవ్యము. ఆకొన్నవానికి అమృతముచరువు hunger makes dry bread sweet as ambrosia.

చర్చ *charcha.* [Skt : Cognate with Eng. "Search."] n. Searching, research, judgment, deliberation విచారణ, చింత. Daubing పూత. చందనచర్చ the perfuming a person with fragrant unguents. **చర్చించు** *charchintsu.* v. n. To investigate, విచారించు. To dispute or discuss.

చర్మము *charmamu.* [Skt.] n. Skin, hide. తోలు. **చర్మకారుడు** *charma-kāruḍu.* n. A shoe-maker or tanner, a worker in leather మాదిగవాడు.

చర్య *charya.* [Skt. చర్=to move.] n. An act, a deed, conduct, mode, rite, fashion. Perseverance in religious austerities; due and regular observance of all rites or customs దినచర్య.

చర్వణము *charvaṇamu.* [Skt.] n. Chewing. నమలుట. **చర్వితము** *charvitamu.* adj. Chewed. చర్వితచర్వణము ruminating, chewing the cud: frequent recurrence to one topic. చర్వితచర్వణోదాహరణము an old example or story.

చలనము *chalanamu.* [Skt.] n. Shaking, instability, wandering, roaming, agitation, trembling. చిత్తచలనము Whimsicality, oddity.

చలము *chalamu.* [Skt.] adj. Trembling, tremulous, unsteady. వణుకు. **చలచిత్తము** n. *chala-chittamu.* A freak, a whim;

eccentricity. చలచిత్తుడు *chala-chittudu.* n. An imbecile, cracked, silly, insane or eccentric man. చలచ్చంచువు *chaluch-chanchuvu.* n. The Greek partridge చకోరపక్షి. చలదళము *chala-dalamu.* n. The Indian fig tree (అశ్వత్థము) because its leaves like those of the aspen are proverbially tremulous. Suca. iii. 517.

చలాకు *chalāku.* [H.] n. Smartness, dexterity, cleverness. adj. Smart, clever. చలాకుగా skilfully, smartly.

చలానా *chalānā.* [H.] n. A memorandum. An invoice.

చలాయించు *chalā-y-intsu.* [Tel. corruption of చెల్లించు.] v. t. To exercise authority. To make anything current or valid.

చలించు *chalintsu.* [Skt.] v. n. To shake or move, to hesitate. చలింపించు *chalimpintsu.* v. a. To cause to shake. చలితము *chalitamu.* adj. Shaken, trembling.

చవ్యము *chavyamu.* [Skt.] n. The wood of the long pepper plant. *Piper Chaba.* (Rox. i. 156.) చవ.

చషకము *chashakamu.* [Skt.] n. A drinking vessel, a goblet, a wine glass or cup. గిన్నె.

చషాలము *chashālamu.* [Skt.] n. A chalice, or cup used in sacrifice. A ring attached to the sacrificial post in a horse sacrifice. రాజసూయమునందు యూపస్తంభమునకు అడుగున తగిలించేకడియము.

చా chā

చా *chā.* [Skt.] interj. Fie, out upon him! Avaunt!

చాంచల్యము *chānchalyamu.* [from Skt. చంచలము.] n. Agitation, instability, mutability. చపలత్వము. కాలచాంచల్యమువల్ల by the lapse of time: as the world is so transitory, or fleeting. చిత్తచాంచల్యము aberration of the intellect.

చాండాలము *chāndālamu.* [Skt.] adj. Base, vile. Outcast, lowborn. n. Brutality, beastliness, nasty tricks. A filthy mass, also called అంకమ్మచాండాలము, because అంకమ్మ is the goddess to whom bloody sacrifices are offered.

చాందిని *chāndini.* [H.] n. An awning, a canopy.

చాంద్రమానము *chāndra-mānamu.* [Skt.] adj. Lunar. చాంద్రమానసంవత్సరము a lunar year.

చాంద్రాయణము *chāndr-āyanamu.* [Skt.] n. A religious or expiatory observance regulated by the moon's age. It consists in diminishing the daily consumption of food every day by one mouthful for the dark half of the month and increasing it in like manner during the light half. •Expiatory ceremonies performed by the whole city or kingdom in atonement for some heinous sin the consequences of which affect the people.

చాంపేయము *chāmpēyamu.* [Skt.] n. The bud of the Chrysanthemum, చంపకము or సంపెంగ. (q. v.)

చాకచక్యము *chāka-chakyamu.* [Skt. from. చకచక] n. A gleam, glimmer, flash, shimmer, sparkle. A ready wit, a flash of wit. చకచకభావము.

చాకిరి *chākiri.* [H.] n. Menial service.

చాకు *chāku.* [H.] n. A penknife.

చాగుడి or చకారగుడి *chā-gudi.* [Skt.] n. A phrase for ఛీ (for shame!) which word is formed of చా ch and the గుడి.

చాటువు *chātuvu.* [Skt.] adj. Witty, pleasant. ప్రియమైన. చాటుభాషణము rambling talk. చాటుపద్యములు or చాటుధారపద్యములు stray verses: a current epigram, fugitive verses or couplets. చాటువు n. Pleasing or entertaining conversation.

చాతకము *chātakamu.* [Skt.] n. The Indian or black cuckoo. వానకోయిల.

చాతురి *chaturi*. [Skt.] n. Cleverness: skilfulness. నేర్పు, చాతుర్యము, చతురత్వము.

చాతుర్థికము or **చాతుర్థికజ్వరము** *chaturdikamu*. [Skt.] n. Quartan ague. Intermittent fever which appears every fourth day.

చాతుర్మాస్యము *chatur-masyamu*. [Skt.] n. Lit: The four months of the year containing the వర్షఋతువు and the శరదృతువు that is, from ఆషాఢశుద్ధము to కార్తికశుద్ధము, A sacrifice performed during the whole of that period.

చాతుర్యము *chaturyamu*. [Skt.] n. Skill, cleverness. చాతురి, నేర్పు.

చాదస్తము or **చేదస్తము** *chadastamu*. [Tel.] n. Eccentricity, whimsicality, folly, silliness. **చాదస్తుడు** or **చేదస్తుడు** *chadastudu*. n. A simpleton, a dupe.

చాపము *chapamu*. [Skt.] n. A bow. చాపబాణములు a bow and arrows.

చాపలము or **చాపల్యము** *cha-palamu*. [Skt. from చపలము.] n. Fickleness. Inconstancy జిహ్వాచాపల్యము luxuriousness, or gluttony. Whimsicality.

చామరము *chamaramu*. [Skt.] n. A fly brush, or chowri composed of the tail of the Yak, Bos-grunniens. A whisk. వింజామరము.

చాముండ or **చాముండిక** *chamunda*. [Skt.] n. The name of Durga or one of her attendant goddesses.

చారణుడు *charanudu*. [Skt.] n. A dancer, an itinerant actor.

చారిత్రము *charitramu*. [Skt.] n. A story, a tale. చరిత్రము.

చారు or **చారువు** *charu*. [Skt.] adj. Beautiful, charming. చారుతరము more lovely.

చారు *charu*. [Tel.] n. Soup.

చారుడు *charudu*. [Skt.] n. A spy, a secret agent or emissary. వేగువాడు.

చార్వాకుడు *charvakudu*. [Skt.] n. A follower of the sceptical philosopher Charvaka. An atheist, a materialist or sceptic, a seceder from the Hindu creed: చార్వాకమతము scepticism, materialism. "దేవునితోడ నేల చార్వాక మొనర్చితిన్." (Kalah. iii. 193.) why did I act as a freethinker and question the god?

చాషము *chashamu*. [Skt.] n. The Indian Roller, *Coracias indica* (F.B.I.) పాలపిట్ట.

చి chi

చింక or **చింకు** *chinka*. [Tel.] n. A small water channel in a field. చిన్నకాలువ. Empty or pithless grain not quite ripe when reaped, and which therefore sticks to the pods and requires to be twice thrashed. **చింకబెల్లించి** or **పెద్దకీచుటిగాడు** *chinka-bellinchi*. n. The Indian Grey shrike, *Lanius lahtora*. **చింకబాతు** *chinka-batu*. n. The Grey Pelican, *Pelicanus philippensis* (F. B. I.) **చింకలిక్కు** *chinkalikku*. n. A red faced monkey.

చింగిలిమాగిలి *chingili-magili*. [Tel.] n. Confusion. గందరగోళము. Sar. Pad. i. 16.

చింగుడు *chingudu*. [Tel. for చుంగడి.] adj. Petty, trifling. (Nellore.)

చించ *chincha*. [Skt.] n. The tamarind tree. చింతచెట్టు.

చించు *chintsu*. [Tel.] v. a. To tear, to rend. **చించుకొను** *chintsu-konu*. v. a. To tear or rend. To be disgusted or annoyed. ఏల గొంతుచించుకొంటావు why split your throat with roaring?

చింత *chinta*. [Tel.] n. A tamarind tree. చింతగుల్ల tamarind in the shell. చింతకాయ a green tamarind. చింతపండు tamarind. పులిచింత a small acid plant used in medicine and for pickling. *Oxalis corniculata*. Heyne. *Bauhinia malabarica*. (Watts.) సీమచింతచెట్టు, ఎర్రచింత, కారువేగి or చిందుగ

Albizzia odoratissima. (Watts.) See under చిందుగ. పెద్దచింత or దంతిచెట్టు *Celastrus senegalensis*. (Watts.) **చింతనాగు** *chinta-nâgu*. n. A venomous snake. *Coluber naga*, Russell,—so named because the marks on the back resemble a tamarind flower. **చింతపువ్వులు** *chinta-puvvulu*. n. A certain kind of grain. H. iv. 156.

చింత *chinta*. [Skt.] n. Reflection, thought, wish, musing, consideration, recollection, care, sorrow, pity, grief. చింతలేదు never mind, no matter. **చింతకుడు** *chintakudu*. n. He who thinks or ponders. చింతించు వాడు. **చింతన** *chintana*. n. Thinking over. Reiteration, మలుమారుతలంచుట. చింతన చెప్పు to reiterate. చింతనలు investigations, enquiries. **చింతనము** *chintanamu*. n. Thought, reflection, study of a book. Reiteration. చింతనీయము or చింత్యము fit to be considered or thought over. **చింతాక్రాంతుడు** *chintâ-krântudu*. adj. Grieved, sorrowful, swallowed up with grief. **చింతామణి** *chintâ-mani*. n. The wishing stone, a fabulous gem or magic ruby, imagined to yield its possessor all that he wishes. The name of a certain kind of pill. The term is metaphorically used in the titles of many books and may there be explained as a "key, analysis, essay, or treatise." Thus the ఆంధ్రభాషాచింతామణి is a Key to the Telugu language. వైద్య చింతామణి a key to Pharmacy. **చింతించు**, **చింతిల్లు** or **చింతిలు** *chintintsu*. v. n. To think on, to muse, to ponder, to reflect. To be sorry for, to regret, to grieve or be afflicted వగచు. **చింతితము** *chintitamu*. adj. Mused on, considered.

చింతుచెట్టు *chintu-chettu*. [Tel.] n. A shrub called *Celastrus emarginata*. పెద్దచింతు *Celastrus Montana*. Rox. i. 620. 621.

చింతొక్క or **చింతవక్క** *chintokka*. [Tel.] n. The night Heron, *Nycticorax griseus*. (F. B. I.)

చిందపిట్ట *chinda-pitta*. [Tel.] n. A kind of hawk. చిదరపిట్ట.

చిందము *chindamu*. [Tel.] n. A shell, a conch. శంఖము, R. iii. 42. M. VII. v. 347. UR. iv. 256.

చిందర *chindara*. [Tel.] n. Ruin, breaking. A fragment, bit, shattered piece. Dilapidation, ugliness, disagreeableness. "కీచులు చిందరచేసెఝల్లిగా వినదంబు" the crickets chirped with earsplitting shrillness. HD. i. 1745. **చిందర** adj. Ugly, disagreeable, ruinous. **చిందరవందర** *chindara-vandara*. adv. (anuk) Piecemeal; here and there; in pieces, in shatters. Anir. iii. 92. **చిందరవందరచేయు** or **చిందరచేయు** *chindara-vandara-chêyu*. v. n. To shatter or shiver. To hack, to cut to pieces, to spoil. చిందరవందరగాadv. tossed: at random, in confusion: recklessly, dishevelled, flying loose as hair. చిందరపోవు to spring a leak తూటుపోవు. చిందరగొను to be enraged or furious. విభ్రాంతించు. చిందరకొను to be infused with ఆవేశ మొత్తు.

చిందియ or **చింది** *chindiya*. [Tel.] n. A sprinkle or shedding. పిల్లిచింది a sort of cap. కుల్లాయి. G. viii. 9.

చిందిలు *chindilu*. [Tel.] v. n To shake. చలించు. **చిందిలి** *chindili*. adj. Shaken. Disturbed. చలించినది. చిందిలిమందిలిగాక undisturbed. **చిందిలిపడు** *chindali-padu*. v. n. To rejoice సంభ్రమించు. **చిందిలిపాటు** *chindili-pâtu*. n. Hurry, agitation. కలత పాటు.

చిందు *chindu*. [Tel.] v. n. To be spilt, shed or distilled. To spread వ్యాపించు. వెన్నెల గా చిందుచున్నవు a smile that was pleasant like moonlight. v. a. To spend, to lay out. వ్యయముచేయు. n. A dance, hop, jig. చిందాడు or చిందులుతొక్కు to dance, or tread a measure. చిందుపరువు a dance. A drop, బొట్టు. చిందుగా recklessly, wildly, sorrowfully. చిందుగాచేయు to pester, plague, annoy. **చిందుగుప్ప** *chindu-guppa* n. A sort of wolf. **చిందువందు** *chindu-vandu*. adj. Scattered చెదరిన. adv. Recklessly, sportively, prodigally. చిందువందు చేయు to scatter చెదరగొట్టు. to make sport of. చిందువందుగా చేయు to make sport of.

చిందుగచెట్టు *chinduga-chettu.* [Tel.] n. A kind of tree, *Albizzia odoratissima.* తెల్లచిందుగ *Albizzia procera.* కొండచిందుగ *Albizzia stipulata.* See under చింత. (Watts.)

చిందురము *chinduramu.* [Tel. for సిందూరము.] n. Red lead.

చిందువ *chinduva.* [Tel.] n. A sort of logwood for dyeing, imported from Pegu. A small box చిన్నపెట్టె.

చిందె See చిందిజు. **చిందేలుపాము** *chindēlu-pamu.* [Tel.] n. A sort of eel.

చింపి *chimpi.* [Tel.] n. A rent or tear, a rag, a tatter. బొంతగంత. adj. Ragged, tattered. M. vii. v. 138. **చింపిరాళ్లు** *chimpi-rāllu.* n. Gravel, bits of pebbles. An epigram says

"క॥ కొసగలుముత్తెంబొక్కటి
కసుకోర్చిన చింపిరాళ్ల గంపెండేలా
రసికుండొక్కడె చాలును
రసహీనులు పదుగురేల రాయనిబాలా."

చింపిరి *chimpiri.* adj. Curly headed, dishevelled.

చింపు *chimpu.* [Tel.] v. a. To tear or rend. చించు.

చింబు *chimbu.* [Tel.] n. A goat. మేక. **చింబోతు** *chim-bōtu.* n. A he goat (HD. ii. 965.) చింబుపోతు, మేకపోతు.

చికటారి or **చిక్కటారి** *chikatāri.* [Tel. from చిన్న or చిక small, కటారి a dagger.] n. A small dagger.

చికటాలి *chikatāli.* [Tel.] n. A plant called *Euonymus Ventilago* (yerra chiktāli) Roxb. i. 629.

చికపిక or **చికాపిక** *chika-pika.* [Tel.] adv. Piecemeal, scattered, in fragments.

చికమక *chikamaka.* [Tel.] n. Intricacy, confusion, disorder. చిక్కు.

చికాకు or **చీకాకు** *chikaku.* [Tel.] n. Disgust, annoyance. చికాకుపడు to be disgusted or annoyed. చికాకుపరచు to annoy.

చికి or **చికిలి** *chiki.* [Tel.] adj. Small. చిన్న. Sharp. Sweet. చికిమోవి a sweet lip. చికిచూపు a piercing eye.

చికిత్స *chikitsa.* [Skt.] n. The medical art, medical treatment, a prescription. చికిత్సకుడు a physician. వైద్యుడు. **చికిత్సించు** *chikitsintsu.* v. t. To treat a patient, as a doctor does. చికిత్సచేయు.

చికిలి *chikili.* [Tel.] n. Polishing, burnishing. adj. Burnished, ground sharp, bright, bland, smooth, fine, graceful, trim, pretty. చికిలిచూపు a bland glance. చికిలిచేయు or చికిలిచేయించు to burnish or set. చికిలిసాన a smooth whetstone. చికిలిగాడు one who cleans and sharpens knives, &c. **చికిలించు** *chikilintsu.* v. n. To ogle or leer కన్నులు చికిలించి with a leering look. **చికిలింతగడ్డి** *chikilinta-gaddi.* n. Bur grass. Rox. i. 301.

చికిలు *chikilu.* [Tel.] v. n. To cry like a child that is much fondled. చనవుచేసేడ్చు.

చికీర్ష *chikīrsha.* [Skt.] n. Inclination to do any thing. చేయునిచ్ఛ.

చికురము *chikuramu.* [Skt.] n. A tress or small curl, a hair. వెండ్రుక.

చిక్కంటు, చిక్కంటె, చిక్కట్టు or **చిక్కంటల** *chikk-antu.* [Tel. చిక్కు+అంటు.] n. A large comb with only three or four teeth.

చిక్కణము *chikkaṇamu.* [Skt.] adj. Bland, soft, mild, unctuous, emollient, smooth, polished. నునుపైన. P. iii. 73. A. i. 45.

చిక్కన or **చిక్కదనము** *chikkana.* [Tel. from చిక్కు.] n. Thickness, as of milk or syrup. Strength, stoutness బలము, గాఢ్ఢము. **చిక్కని** *chikkani.* adj. Thick as a liquid, plump. Close pressed, as a kiss "చిక్కనిముద్దుపెట్టిన" Ila. ii. 165.

చిక్కని *chikkani*. [Tel.] (neg. participle of చిక్కు.] adj. Not found: not to be had, rare.

చిక్కము *chikkamu*. [Tel.] n. A net. A bag of net work, a purse, a muzzle of wicker work. A net used as a shelf in a house.

చిక్కరిచెట్టు *chik-kari-chettu*. [Tel. చిక్కు=చిన్న+కాడి.] n. The tree called *Mimosa concina*. Rox. ii. 565.

చిక్కు or చిక్కుకొను *chikku*. [Tel.] v. n. To be found, to be caught, or ensnared. దొరకు. To remain, be left మిగులు. అది నాకు చిక్కినది I have got it. To stop or halt, to remain. వెనుకచిక్కు to remain behind, to fall in the rear. To grow thin or lean. కృశించు. చిక్కని సొమ్ముగానున్నది it is unattainable, it cannot be got. చిక్కించుకొను *chikkintsu-konu*. v. a. To get, obtain. చేతిలో చిక్కించుకొను to get into one's hands, to get hold of. వెతలచిక్కు to be seized with sorrow. ధైర్యము చిక్కనందున as I dared not do so. చిక్కినది the rest, the remainder. చిక్కిపోవు *chikki-pōvu*. v. n. To become lean. చిక్కు n. A tangle, మెలి. A puzzle, perplexity, intricacy, confusion, entanglement, difficulty, distress, trouble. సంకటము, ఇబ్బంది. చిక్కులుపడు to be in distress or to get into difficulty సంకటపడు. చిక్కులబెట్టు to entangle, to involve, puzzle, to distress or harass; to pinch or stint. చిక్కుతీయు to disentangle. చిక్కుగానున్నది it is puzzling. చిక్కుపడ్డ tangled or dishevelled as hair, చిక్కైయున్న. చిక్కుపాటు entanglement. చిక్కుపడుట, సంకటపడుట. చిక్కు adj. Puzzling, perplexing, entangled, intricate, confused, difficult, troublesome, baffled. చిక్కుజడలు tangled hair. చిక్కుకంపు a rancid smell (of oil.) చిక్కుతాళము n. A lock with many wards, and which, like a patent lock, can only be opened by those who know it.

చిక్కుడు *chikkudu*. [Tel.] n. The bean called *Dolichos lablab*. చిక్కుడుకాయ the pod of this plant. Different species of this are called ఎర్రచిక్కుడు, తెల్లచిక్కుడు, గోరుచిక్కుడు, అనపచిక్కుడు, ఏనుగుచిక్కుడు, కోడిచిక్కుడు, తొండచిక్కుడు, ఉలవచిక్కుడు and సొనచిక్కుడు. See Roxb. i. 370. iii. 305. 306. 307. 315. 317.

చీకొట్టు *chik-kottu*. [Tel. చీ+కొట్టు.] v. n. To cry shame, to censure. ఛీయను.

చీకొట్టు Same as చిక్కొట్టు. (q. v.)

చిక్రోడము *chikrōdamu*. [Skt.] n. A squirrel. ఉడత.

చిగురు *chiguru*. [Tel.] n. A sprout, or shoot. The gums around the teeth. The quick or tender red part of the flesh under the nail. adj. Young, budding, tender, delicate. లేత. చిగురుబోడి a girl fair and fresh as a young bud. చిగిరించు, చిగురుకొను, చిగురుచు or చిగుర్చు *chigir-intsu*. v. n. To sprout out or to bud. ఎర్రనగు, పల్లవించు. చిగిరింతగడ్డి *chigir-inta-gaddi*. n. Bur grass. చిగురాకు *chigur-āku*. n. A budding leaf. చిగురాకు చిలుక a parrot. చిగురాకువిలుకాడు he who carries a bow of budding leaves, an epithet of మన్మథుడు. చిగుర్కొత్తు *chigur-ottu*. v. n. To bud. చిత్తముచిగుర్చె with a melting heart. To become red. ఎఱ్ఱనగు.

చిచ్చర (చిచ్చు+అర) or చిచ్చుర (చిచ్చు+ఉర) *chitstsara*. [Tel.] adj. Fiery. నిప్పులరాలే. T. v. 141. M. III. vii. 132. అగ్నిమయమైన. చిచ్చరకంటి the fiery eyed (one), i. e., Siva.

చిచ్చి or చిచ్చీ *chichchi* [Tel.] n. Hush, lullaby, bye bye. A word used in lulling babes to sleep.

చిచ్చు *chitstsu*. [Tel.] n. Flame, fire, అగ్ని. Heat తాపము. కడుపుచిచ్చు the flame in the belly, i. e., hunger. చిచ్చుటమ్ము *chitstsu-t-ammu*. n. A rocket or fire pot used in battle ఆగ్నేయాస్త్రము. చిచ్చు

చిచ్చుబుడ్డి *chitstsu-buḍḍi.* n. A kind of rocket called a flower pot.

చిటచిట or చిటపొట *chiṭa-chiṭa.* [Tel.] adv. Cracklingly, sulkily. చటచట. n A crackling sound, as that of wood that is burning. Sulkiness. adj. Vexed, irritated or annoyed: sharp or cross. చిటచిటమాటలు sharp or cross language. చిటచిటమను or చిటచిటలాడు *chiṭa-chiṭa-m-anu.* v. n. To crackle as fire. To be vexed, irritated or annoyed. To look sulky. మండిపడు. చిటచిటలు *chiṭa-chiṭalu.* n. Heat, inflammation. దానికి ఒళ్లు చిటచిటలాడుచున్నది she has the prickly heat, or, is angry.

చిటపొట *chiṭa-poṭa.* [Tel.] n. Irritation, anger. కోపము. A rattling sound as of falling leaves, fruit, &c. adj. Small, delicate. చిటపొటమాటలు trilling accents. చిటపొట లాడే excited, in agitation.

చిటారము *chiṭāramu.* [Tel.] n. Prettiness. సొంపు, సొగసు, ఒయ్యారము. చిటారించు *chiṭār-intsu.* v. n. To be angry. ముఖము చిటారించు to frown.

చిటాలు *chiṭālu.* [Tel.] n. Suddenness. చిటాలుమని suddenly, with a bounce.

చిటి or చిట్టి *chiṭi.* [Tel.] adj. Little. చిటివేలు the little finger. చిటిచాప a small mat. చిటితాళము *chiṭi-tāḷamu.* n. A small cymbal. చిటిపోటి *chiṭi-poṭi.* adj. Little, petty, trifling, trivial. అల్పము. చిటిముత్యాలు *chiṭi-mutyālu.* n. plu. A kind of very fine white rice. (Lit. little pearls.)

చిటిక *chiṭika.* [Tel.] n. A rap with the fingers. A snap with the fingers. A second of time. క్షణము. చిటికరించు *chiṭika-r-intsu.* v. n. To give a rap with the fingers. చిట్టమిడుచు, చిటికవేయు. చిటికంటి same as చిటిక. చిటికెన *chiṭikena.* n. The little finger or toe. చిన్నవేలు. చిటికాడు *chiṭi-kāḍu.* n. A page or attendant. చిన్నవాడు. చిటికెన బొద్దులు *chiṭikena-boddulu.* n. A jewel worn on the little toe. పాదకనిష్ఠికాభరణము. చిటికెలవాడు *chiṭikela-vāḍu.* n. A pedlar, a hawker of small wares. చిటికెలు *chiṭikelu.* n. Castanets. చిటికెగారెలు a sort of cakes. H. i. 114.

చిటుకు, చిటుక్కు or చిటుకుచిటుకు *chiṭuku.* [Tel.] (anuk.) n. A low soft sound, clicking, chirruping: a just audible sound, as the sound of the crack of the finger joints, a splashing, pattering, or dripping sound. చీమ చిటుక్కుమంటే నిద్ర నుండి లేస్తాడు the sound of an ant will awake him. చీమ చిటుక్కుమంటే వినబడును the tread of an ant might have been heard. చిటుక్కను or చిటుక్కుమను *chiṭukk-anu.* v. n. To give a crackling sound like the sparks of a Leyden jar.

చిటులు or చిట్లు *chiṭulu.* [Tel.] v. n. To crack, as plaster or paint. To split, as a hair. వెండ్రుకలకొనలు చిట్లినవి the ends of the hairs are split. "చిటులుకుసుమబొట్టు."

చిట్టు *chiṭṭu.* [Tel.] n. A wonder. అబ్బురము. Trouble చిక్కు, ఆయాసము. BD. vii. 217; v. 735: M. XII. iii. 441. చిట్టు adj. Invented కల్పితమైన. చెప్పచిట్టులు పూబోడి చెలువుకలదు her loveliness is a wonder to tell; or, it would take whole chapters to narrate her charms. చిట్టి a baby or little one.

చిట్టంటు or చిట్టంటులు *chiṭṭ-anṭu.* [Tel. చిట్టి + అంటు.] n. The dent formed by the nails in pinching or by the teeth in biting. చిట్టంటులంటు to handle delicately or touch.

చిట్టకము *chiṭṭakamu.* [Tel.] n. A trick, a roguish prank, a deceitful action. శృంగారచేష్ట, లీల, కపటము, వ్యాజము, మిథ్య, చెల్లాటము, ఎకసక్కెము, కోడిగము. V. P. i. 131. A. ii. 70. Swa. iii. 40. R. iv. 157. 162. చిట్టకంపుతనము *chiṭṭakampu-tanamu.* n. Roguishness, wickedness.

చిట్టచివర *chiṭṭa-chivara.* [Tel. చిట్ట + చివర.] n. The extremity or utmost point, the very end, the very last. See చివర.

చిట్టముమిక or రావణవృక్షము See కుమిక.

చిట్టమిడుము Same as చిటిక వేయు. See under చిటిక.

చిట్టా or చిట్ఠా chiṭṭa. [Tel.] n. A rough daily account. A ledger. A log-book, a day-book.

చిట్టాడు chiṭṭ-āḍu. [Tel. చిట్టి+ఆడు.] v. n. To play about. క్రీడించు. To trifle, sport, frolic. To be teased or anxious: to fret: to waver, to fluctuate, as the mind between shame and pleasure. చలించు, డోలాయమానమగు. To wander సంచరించు. To spread ప్రసరించు. To walk as a baby తప్పటడుగులిడు. చిట్టాడించు chiṭṭ-āḍintsu. n. To teach a child to walk.

చిట్టాముదము or చిట్లాముదము chiṭṭ-āmudamu. The castor oil plant, *Ricinus Christi*.

చిట్టి chiṭṭi. [Tel.] n. A butter-boat. A certain measure, the fourth part of a సోల. A small high vessel made of brass or copper. చిట్టెడు a cupful. చిట్టి adj. Little, young. చిఱ. చిట్టీతచెట్టు chiṭṭīta-cheṭṭu. n. The small date (ఈత) tree. చిట్టడుగులు little footsteps like those of infants. P. ii. 126. చిట్టటుక chiṭṭ-aṭuka. n. A small shelf or ledge, a little cupboard. అటుక. చిట్టట్టు chiṭṭ-aṭṭu. adv. Delicately, softly, gently. చిట్టడవి chiṭṭ-aḍavi. n. A thicket, or brake. An impenetrable thicket, wood, or forest. అడవి. చిట్టిగూబ chiṭṭi-gūba. n. The scops owl, *Scops giu*. పెద్దచిట్టిగూబ the Collared Scops Owl, *Scops bakkamoena*. చిట్టిచిరతపక్షి chiṭṭi-chirata-pakshi. n. The Indian Pigmy Woodpecker, *Iyngipicus hardwickii* (F. B. I.)

చిట్టు chiṭṭu. [Tel.] n. Coarse bran. ఊక తవుడుకలిసినది.

చిట్టుములు chiṭṭ-umulu. [Tel. చిట్టి+ఉముటు.] n. Want of appetite, disinclination for food, caused by pregnancy. Subhad. iii. 253. R. iii. 93.

చిట్టుముట్టాడు or చిట్టుముట్టాడు chiṭṭu-muṭṭ-āḍu. [Tel.] n. To be in disorder. చిట్టుముట్టాడిన disturbed. BD. v. 92. 365.

చిట్టె or చిట్టెయు chiṭṭe. [Tel.] n. The edge of cloth. బట్టల అంచుకమ్మి. A picture, whim, idea, freak, invention, scheme, plot. An incomplete heap of salt. చిట్టెలు, అనగా చిత్రపటములు, తంత్రములు.

చిట్టెము or చిట్టెయము chiṭṭemu. [Tel.] n. The scoriæ, dross or scum of melted metal. చిట్టెపురాయి pumice stone.

చిట్టెలుక chiṭṭ-eluka. [Tel. చిఱ or చిట్టి+ఎలుక.] n. A mouse. పొలి చిట్టెలుక or చిత్తెలుక (Tel. of Yanadis) The common Indian Field-Mouse. *Mus buduga*. (F. B. I.)

చిట్లు or చిటులు chiṭlu. [Tel.] v. n. To snap, split, crack (as a fruit), burst. వెంట్రుక చిట్లినది a hair has split. చిట్లని unblown, unopened. చిట్లుకట్టె a person of a very irritable temper మిక్కిలి కోపము గలవాడు. చిట్లుచిట్ట chiṭla-jiṭṭa. n. The Nilgiri Flower-pecker. *Dicæum Concolor*, or, the Thick-billed Flower-pecker. *Piprisoma squalidam*. (F. B. I.) చిట్లించు chiṭlintsu. v. a. To crack, break. To burst, split. A. i. 23. v. n. To break, snap, crack, split, burst or be chopped, as the ground, the skin, paint, or the lips in fever. T. iv. 85. ముఖము చిట్లించు to frown. ముఖము చిట్లించుకొన్నారు they changed colour, were abashed, they looked sulky. చిట్లింతకూర chiṭlinta-kūra. n. A herb used in curries. *Marselia Minuta*. Heyne.

చిడిగిరింత chiḍigirinta. [Tel.] n. Dislike, disgust, annoyance. HD. ii. 620.

చిడిపి chiḍipi. [Tel.] adj. Little, small, petty. చిన్న, అల్పము. Harsh పరుషము.

చిడిముడి chiḍ-imuḍi. [Tel.] Peevishness, pettishness, vexation, hastiness. తొట్రుపాటు. Agitation, alarm. చిడిముడిపడు chiḍi-muḍi-paḍu. v. n. To be agitated or vexed, to be angry or hasty. BD. iv. 151. తొట్రుపడు. చిడిముడిపాటు chiḍi-muḍi-

paṭu. n. Irritation, pettishness, anger, haste. కోపము. G. i 220.

చిడుగు *chiḍugu*. [Tel.] v. n. To romp, caper, bounce. H. iii. 186. adj. Trifling. అల్పము. చిడుగుడు or చెడుగుడు *chiḍuguḍu*. n. A game played by boys.

చిడుము *chiḍumu*. [Tel.] n. Smarting, such as is caused by the itch, prickly heat or a whitlow. The itch చిడుముదురు.

చిత్ *chit*. [Skt.] n. Intellect, understanding. In compounds T as usual becomes D; as చిదంబరము; and elsewhere N. as చిన్మయ. Thus చిదాదిత్య a seeming sun; that which looks like a sun. L .i. 98. చిద్విలాసము *chid-vilāsamu*. n. Mental enjoyments, literary pleasures. Adventures. చిన్మయము *chin-mayamu*. adj. Spiritual, mental, intellectual. Invisible. Immaterial, impassive. చిన్మాత్రము *chin-mātramu*. n. The spiritual body. The intellectual form. చిన్ముద్ర *chin-mudra*. n. The impress of wisdom జ్ఞానముద్ర. A. v. 170.

చిత or చితి *chita*. [Skt.] n. A funeral pile. సొద, ప్రోగు.

చితచితలాడు *chita-chital-āḍu*. [Tel.] v. n. To be damp. ఈ కోటు తేమచేత చితచిత లాడుచున్నది the humidity of the air renders this place damp.

చితారివాడు *chitāri-vāḍu*. [corrupted from Skt. చిత్రము.] n. A sculptor, a statuary.

చితుకు or చితికిపోవు *chituku*. [Tel.] v. n. To burst (as a ripe fruit or as a sore), to be dashed, smashed, squashed. To be broken or depressed (as the nose.) చితుకు ముక్కు broken-nosed.

చిత్త *chitta*. [Skt.] n. The 14th lunar mansion. చిత్తానక్షత్రము.

చిత్తడి *chittaḍi*. [Tel. చిత్త+అడి.] n. Much dampness. మిక్కిలితడి. Wetness, moisture. Gloomy and sloppy weather. చిత్తడికనుక from the wetness of the weather. adj. Cloudy, rainy, moist. చిత్తడికాలము wet weather.

చిత్తము *chittamu*. [Skt.] n. The mind or intellect; the heart, considered as the seat of intellect: inclination, will, pleasure. మీచిత్తము (or simply చిత్తము) your pleasure! as you please! yes, sir! చిత్తానకు తేవలెను be so good as to consider this. ప్రవేశము చిత్తగించవలెను pray acknowledge the receipt of this letter. చిత్తానుసారముగా according to one's own pleasure or as one sees fit. చిత్తగించు *chitta-gintsu*. v. a. To listen, grant attention, keep or retain in mind, attend to, mind, note, observe, remark, examine, investigate మనస్కరించు. To think, తలచు; to hear a prayer, to consider విచారించు. At the close of a letter the words చిత్తగించవలెను "Please to consider this" are equivalent to the phrase ("I remain, &c"). అట్లు చిత్తగించినాడు he came to this decision (used of a superior.) చిత్తగించవలెను I beg you to or, do me the favor to. చిత్తచాంచల్యము *chitta-chānchalyamu*. n. Aberration of the intellect. Insanity. చిత్తవృత్తి *chitta-vritti*. n. Temper, wish, inclination, disposition. Will, pleasure, determination. చిత్తుడు and చిత్తురాలు *chittuḍu*. adj. Minded. This is used in compound phrases, thus: సంతోషచిత్తుడు a cheerful man. క్రూరచిత్తుగై cruel-hearted. శాంతచిత్తుడు a gentle character.

చిత్తరుచేప or చిత్తెర *chittaru-chēpa*. [Tel.] n. A sort of fish, the white carp.

చిత్తరువు *chittaruvu*. [from Skt. చిత్రము.] n. A wonder, a marvel. ఆశ్చర్యము. A picture, painting or drawing పటము. చిత్తరువు పటము *chittaruvu-paṭamu*. n. A painting. పటమునందు వ్రాసిన రూపము.

చిత్తాట *chittaṭa*. [Tel.] n. A game called Pitch & toss.

చిత్తిని *chittini*. [corrupted from Skt. చిత్రిణి.] n. A flirt, a wanton woman. చిత్రిణి.

చిత్తు *chittu.* [Tel.] n. A rough draft or copy.

చిత్తు *chittu.* [Skt.] n. Intelligence (one of the attributes of God as in the phrase సచ్చిదానందమూర్తి.) The Animate world, as opposed to **అచిత్తు** the inanimate world.

చిత్ర *chitra.* [Skt.] n. The fourteenth lunar mansion. చిత్త.

చిత్రము *chitramu.* [Skt.] adj. Particoloured, speckled, chequered, streaked. నానావర్ణములుగల. Odd, strange, novel, picturesque, pretty. ఆశ్చర్యకరమైన. చిత్రము చిత్రము most wonderful. n Variety, strangeness, singularity. ఆశ్చర్యము. A painting, a picture చిత్తరువు. Variegated colour, నానావర్ణము. A curiosity, a species, a diversity. **చిత్రకంఠము** *chitra-kanṭhamu.* n. A dove, కపోతము, గువ్వ. **చిత్రకథ** an episode, a novel or story. **చిత్రకము** *chitrakamu.* n. A mark on the face బొట్టు. **చిత్రకాయము** *chitra-kayamu.* n. A cheetah చిరుతపులి. **చిత్రకారుడు** or **చిత్రకుడు** *chitra-karudu.* n. A painter. **చిత్రగుప్తుడు** *chitra-guptudu.* n. Name of an accountant of Yama the god of Death. యమునిలెక్క వ్రాయువాడు. Yama యముడు. చిత్రతరము most extraordinary. **చిత్రనేత్రము** *chitra-nētramu.* n. A kind of fine cloth సాగసయినవస్త్రము. A. vi. 131. **చిత్రపక్షము** *chitra-pakshamu.* n. A peacock. నెమలి. **చిత్రపత్రిక** *chitra-patrika.* n. Damasked hue: figures drawn with musk or gold dust on the cheeks or face. **చిత్రపిల్ల** *chitra-pilla.* n. A kind of fresh water fish: another kind is చిత్తరుచేప. **చిత్రభానువు** *chitra-bhānuvu.* n. Fire. అగ్ని. The sun సూర్యుడు. **చిత్రమూలము** *chitra-mūlamu.* n. The plant called Ceylon leadwort; *Plumbaga zelanica:* ఎర్రచిత్రమూలము Rose coloured Leadwort, *Plumbago rosea.* (Ainslie.) నల్లచిత్రమూలము *Plumbago capensis.* **చిత్రరథుడు** *chitra-rathudu.* n. The name of one of the musicians in Indra's heaven. ఒక గంధర్వుడు. The sun సూర్యుడు. చిత్రవధ horrid torture. **చిత్రవాలము** *chitra-valamu.* n. The Indian Roller, *Coracias indica,* (F. B. I.) పాలపిట్ట. **చిత్రవిచిత్రము** *chitra-vichitramu.* adv. Very wonderful, odd, strange, singular. **చిత్రశిఖండి** *chitra-śikhaṇḍi.* n. The constellation called the Great Bear. **చిత్రహింస** *chitra-himsa.* n. Torture. చిత్రహింసచేసి చంపినారు they tortured him to death. **చిత్రాసనము** *chitr-āsanamu.* n. A tiger's skin or small carpet used by Brahmins during prayer. **చిత్రించు** *chit-rintsu.* v. t. To paint a picture చిత్రము వ్రాయు. **చిత్రికగుల్ల** *chitrika-gulla.* [Tel.] n. A carpenter's plane. చిత్రికపట్టు to plane. **చిత్రిణి** *chitriṇi.* [Skt.] n. A woman of genius. **చిత్రితము** *chitri-tamu.* adj. Painted. చిత్రింపబడిన.

చిదక *chidaka.* [Tel.] adj. Flat. సొట్ట. **చిదకముక్కు** *chidaka-mukku.* n. A flat nose.

చిదగోడ *chida-goda.* [Tel.] n. A difference. A disagreement, a quarrel. భేదము, వ్యత్యాసము. Domestic quarrel, brawl, wrangling. adv. In confusion.

చిదచిత్ *chid-achit.* [Skt.] n. Animated and inanimate. Mandh. vi. 182.

చిదచిద *chida-chida.* [Tel.] n. Damp. ఆ నేల చిదచిదలాడుతున్నది that ground is moist.

చిదమ or **కండచిదమ** *chidama.* [Tel.] n. A sort of fish.

చిదర *chidara.* [Tel.] n. A bit or piece. తునక.

చిదియు *chidiyu.* [Tel.] v. n. To be smashed, to be broken into pieces, to burst. నలుగు. చిదియవు కొండపైబడిన they will not be broken though a hill fall upon them. Hari. Pt ii. BK. v.

చిదుకు *chiduku.* [Tel.] v. n. To be smashed: to be flattened. చిప్పిలు. చిదుకులెక్క a confused or jumbled account

చిదుగు *chidugu.* [Tel.] n. A small stick. చిన్నపుల్ల, సమిధ. చిదుగులు firewood.

చిదుపు or **చిదుము** *chidupu*. [Tel. causal from చిదియు.] v. a. To squeeze or pinch. ఇట్లు. To nip, to twitch off త్రుంచు. To beat flat. To dash, smash ఎత్తు. To pluck a flower. కోయు. n. A bud or sprout చిగురు. **చిదుప** *chidupa*. n. A bit, a fragment, a piece.

చిదుర or **చిదుకుర** or **చిద్రుప** *chidura*. [Tel.] n. A piece, bit, fragment, or atom.

చిన *china*. [Tel.] adj. Small చిన్న.

చిని *chini*. [Tel. for చిన్ని or చిన్న.] adj. Little, young. చిన్న. Pleasing, beautiful. మనోజ్ఞము.

చినుకు or **చిన్కు** *chinuku*. [Tel.] n. A drop, a sprinkling చినుకులుపడుచున్నవి it is drizzling. **చినుకు** v. n. To be shed, or diffused, to fall in drops కారు; to be increased as a passion, or desire అతిశ యించు. చినుకుప్పూస a pearl ముత్యము. A drop of rain.

చినుగు *chinugu*. [Tel.] v. n. To be torn. చినిగినది it is torn. n. A rent or tear.

చిన్న *chinna*. [Tel.] adj. Small, little, short, young, mean, trifling, insignificant, narrow: disgraceful. ముఖముచిన్న చేసుకొను to be ashamed, to be downcast or sorrowful. Junior, younger, smaller. చిన్న చూపు humiliation, scorn. దేవుడు చిన్న చూపుచూస్తే యేమి చేయవచ్చును when God withdraws his favour what can man do? **చిన్న అకురాయి** *chinna-akurayi*. n. The Black-headed Cuckoo-Shrike, *Campophaga sykesi*. (F. B. I.) **చిన్న కారు** *chinna-karu*. n. Childhood, youth. చిన్న కారుపిల్లలు young children. **చిన్నతనము** *chinnatanamu*. n. Infancy: littleness, smallness. Disgrace, dishonor. ఇందువల్ల కులమునకంతా చిన్నతనము వచ్చినది this is a disgrace to the whole caste. **చిన్నది** *chinnadi*. n. A little one. A girl, a lass. ఈ చిన్నది అతనిభార్య this girl is his wife. పెద్దచిన్నది the eldest daughter; or, a grown girl. **చిన్ననాడు** *chinna-nadu*. n. Boyhood బాల్యకాలము, బాల్యము. **చిన్నపుచ్చు** *chinna-putstsu*. v. t. To disgrace, slight, contemn, treat lightly. **చిన్నపోవు** *chinna-pōvu*. v. n. To be disgraced, downcast, low-spirited. **చిన్నవాడు** *chinna-vadu*. n. A boy, a young man. పెద్ద చిన్నవాడు the eldest boy, నాకన్న చిన్నవాడు one younger than me నాచిన్నవాడు పెద్దవాడు అయ్యేదాకా until my son grows up. చిన్నవాండ్లు children, offspring.

చిన్నము *chinnamu*. [Tel.] n. A weight, equal to one thirtieth of a Tola (తులము); one eighth part of the coin termed a pagoda. చిన్నమెత్తెక్కుడుసిరులు (L xi 41.) a trifling increase of wealth.

చిన్నంగిచెట్టు *chinnangi-chettu*. [Tel.] n. A tree called *Lagerstrœmia parviflora*. Rox. ii. 505.

చిన్నారి *chinnari*. [Tel. చిన్న+ఆరి.] (a term of affection.) adj. Delicate, pretty. మనోజ్ఞము. చిన్నారిగోళ్లు pretty or delicate finger nails. **చిన్నారిపొన్నారి** *chinnari-ponnari*. adj. Pretty, lovely, charming. ముద్దులుకులికేటటువంటి.

చిన్ని *chinni*. [Tel. an intensive of చిన్న.] adj. Little, Pretty మనోజ్ఞమైన. **చిన్ని ఆకు చెట్టు** *chinni-aku-chettu*. n The Birch-leaved Acalypha. *Acalypha fruticosa*. (Watts.) **చిన్నిచూపు** *chinni-tsupu*. n. Humiliation, looking downcast or foolish. చిన్నిదము a small flower చిన్న పువ్వు, gold బంగారు. చిన్నిపువు a kind of ornament, or, a salutation నమస్కృతి.

చిన్నియ or **చిన్నె** *chinniya*. [altered from Skt. చిహ్న.] n. A sign, token, mark, feature. గురుతు. Foppery, elegance. విలాసము. **చిన్నెలాడి** *chinne-l-adi*. n. A handsome girl. A coquette. విలాసిని. **చిన్నెలాడు** *chinne-l-adu*. n. A fop, a beau విలాసవంతుడు. v. n. To flaunt, to act the fop.

చిపిటము *chipitamu*. [Skt.] adj. Flatnosed. చప్పటముక్కుగల.

చిప్ప *chippa.* [Tel.] n. A shell. పెంకు, గుల్ల. A cup, a saucer of earth, not of metal. గిన్నె. A hemisphere భూగోళమండలార్ధభాగము.

"క్వ. కనకమయాండ మింక్కటిచేసి దాని
బనిపూని యన్నిటిపైని దేలించె
పైచిప్ప క్రిందిచిప్పయు నొప్ప మీఱ."
విష్ణు. పు. iii.

The lip joint, తొడచిప్ప or దొంటచిప్ప. The knee pan, మోకాలిచిప్ప. The shell of a tortoise, తాబేటిచిప్ప. The shell of a cocoanut or half of a broken cocoanut, టెంకాయచిప్ప or కొబ్బరిచిప్ప. The skull, తలచిప్ప. Mother of pearl, ముత్తెపుచిప్ప. చిప్పగుల్లలయి burnt up, dried up, as dry as chips. P. iii. 75. A fragment తునుక. The scale of a fish చేపమీదిపొలుసు. adj. Little, small, trifling. అల్పము. **చిప్పకసువు** or **చిప్పగడ్డి** *chippa-kasuru.* n. A fragrant sort of grass, *Andropogon schœnanthus.* నిమ్మగడ్డి. **చిప్పకుంకటి** or **చిప్పకూకటి** *chippa-kunkaṭi.* n. The small lock of hair either below or above the long lock left upon the crown of the head by all Hindu males. కాకపక్షము, పిల్లజుట్టు. **చిప్పగొడ్డలి** *chippa-goḍḍali.* n. A broad axe for cutting trees చెట్లునఱకేగొడ్డలి. **చిప్పపెణక** *chippa-peṇaka.* n. Either side of a shelving roof. ఇంటిపార్శ్వములకప్పు. **చిప్పముత్తెము** *chippa-muttemu.* n. An artificial pearl కృత్రిమముత్యము. చిప్పమూతి a dull face కళావిహీనముఖము.

చిప్పము or **చిప్పెము** *chippamu.* [Tel.] n. A large bundle. పెద్దమూట.

చిప్పిలు or **చిప్పిల్లు** *chippilu.* [Tel.] v. n. To gush, flow, well forth, break out, spirt, to overflow. ఉప్పొంగు, పైకి ఉబుకు.

చిప్పెవాడు *chippe-vāḍu.* [Tel.] n. A tailor. దర్జీ, కుట్టుపువాడు.

చిబుకము or **చుబుకము** *chibukamu.* [Skt.] n. The chin. గడ్డము.

చిబుకు *chibuku.* [Tel.] v. t. To smack the lips. చప్పరించు.

చిమచిమ *chima-chima.* [Tel.] n. A smarting pain. చిమచిమయను or చిమచిమగొను to smart. చిమచిమకొలుపు to hurt or cause smart.

చిమట or **చిమ్మట** *chimaṭa.* Same as చిమ్మెట.

చిమటా, చిమిటా or **చిముటా** *chimaṭā.* [Tel.] n. An instrument used to remove hair. చిమటాచేయు or చిమటాచేయు to pull out the hair from the face.

చిమిచిమికారము *chimi-chimi-kāramu.* [Skt. anuk.] n. A slight smarting sound, as in pain.

చిమిటు or **చిమిటా** *chimiṭa.* [Tel.] Same as చిమ్మెట. **చిమిటకోడి** *chimiṭa-kōḍi.* n. The Painted Spur-fowl, *Galloperdix lunulata.* (F.B.I.)

చిమిలి *chimili.* [Tel.] n. Oil cake on which cattle are fed. పిణ్యాకము.

చిముకు Same as చివుకు.

చిముడు *chimuḍu.* [Tel.] v. n. To boil over, to be overboiled. To perish, to be blasted, blighted or scorched. అన్నము చిముడినది the rice was overboiled. **చిముడ్చు** *chimuḍtsu.* v. a. To overboil. **చిమిడిక** *chimiḍika.* n. Overboiling చిముడుట.

చిమ్మ *chimma.* [Tel.] n. A drop. బొట్టు, చుక్క, జలకణము.

చిమ్మటు or **చిమ్మెటు** *chimmaṭa.* [Tel.] n. The grave cricket that destroys clothes. ఈలపురుగు. See చిమ్మెట.

చిమ్మిరి, చిమ్మిలి or **చిమ్మికుంటలు** *chimmiri.* [Tel.] n. A sweetmeat made of fried sesamum seeds with dry cocoanut kernel and sugar.

చిమ్ము *chimmu.* [Tel.] v. a. To thrust, butt (with the horns, &c.) to strike with the claws. పొడుచు. To cast, fling, throw, toss విసురు, చిమ్ము. To squirt or spirt. To sweep. To pat or tap. To splutter ink as a pen. (H. ii. 7.) కన్నీళ్లను కొనగోట చిమ్ము చున్న flicking away the tears with the finger tip. చిమ్మిరేగు (Swa. iv. 104.) to be proud మిక్కిలి విఱ్ఱవీగు. చిమ్ము n. A thrust పొడుచుట. Tossing చిమ్ముట. A spirt. A dash in writing, a splutter of the pen. చిమ్ములాడు to spirt. T. v. 45. చిమ్ముడు or చిమ్ముడము chimmudu. n. Tossing. చిమ్ముట. చిమ్ముబిళ్లలు chimmu-billalu. n. A game like quoits. చిమ్ముల సురియ chimmula-suriya. n. A small dagger. చిమ్మచీకటి chimma-chikati. n. Thick darkness, palpable darkness. Gloom. గాఢాంధకారము, అంధతమసము. చిమ్మన chimmana. adv. Whizzingly, pop! with a spirt or dash. చిమ్మనగొ ట్టము, చిమ్మనగ్రోవి chimmana-gottamu. n. A syringe, a squirt. చిమ్మతిరుగు to turn round and round గిరగిరతిరుగు. చిమ్మాద్రి గుల్ల chimmadri-gulla. n. The worm in a shell that bores the planks of ships.

చిమ్మెట chimmeta. [Tel.] n. The grave cricket that destroys clothes. A moth, a bookworm.

చియ్య chiyya. [Tel.] n. Muscle, flesh. కండ.

చిరంటి chiranti. [Skt.] n. A lady. సువాసిని, పేరంటముచేసే ఆడుది, ముత్తయిదువ, పేరంటాలు.

చిరగడము or చిరుగడము chiragadamu. [Tel.] n. A sort of edible root; తియ్యకండ, గెనుసు, ఒకజాతిదుంప. Tearing చినిగిపోవడము.

చిరచిర chira-chira. [Tel.] n. Peevishness. A fume of passion, sullenness. కోపవికా రము. చిరచిరలాడు to be peevish or furious, మండిపడు. వాడు చిరచిరలాడినాడు he was furious.

చిరత or చిరుత chirata. [Tel.] n. A piece of wood, a wedge, a cudgel. చిన్నకోల, కొడియ. Also, the round piece of wood at the end of a native canoe. A castanet. చిరతలు pincers used in pinching the fingers as a torture. చిరతలవేయు to torture with pincers or thumb screws. See under చిరు.

చిరతపక్షి or చిరుతపక్షి chirata-pakshi. [Tel.] (lit. The castanet bird:) n. The Golden-backed Woodpecker, *Brachypternus aurantius.* పచ్చచిరుతపక్షి the Little Scaly-bellied Green Woodpecker, *Gecinus striolatus.* పెద్దచిరుతపక్షి and చిన్నచిరుత పక్షి are other species.

చిరమర chiramara. [Tel.] n. Difference. భేదము.

చిరము chiramu. [Skt.] adj. Long (as regards time.) అలస్యము, కాలవిలంబము. చిర కాలము a long while. చిరాయువు long life. చిరంజీవి or చిరజీవి chiran-jivi. n. What is long lived: (particularly) a crow. కాకి. adj. Long lived. చిరకాలము జీవించువాడు. This is a term of affection, implying a blessing, often used to inferiors, children, younger brothers or other relations. చిరంజీవులైన మాసీతారామయ్యకు my brother Sitarama; చిరంజీవులైన కొల్లా వెంకన్నభార్య గతించిన సంగతి regarding the death of our dear cousin's wife. చిరంతనము or చి రత్నము chirantanamu. adj. Old, ancient, antiquated. బహుదినములది, పాతది.

చిరాకు chiraku. [Tel.] n. Crossness, snappishness, peevishness. కసరు, కోపము.

చిరి or చిరు chiri. [Tel.] adj. Small, trifling, little, delicate, slight. చిరుచెమట gentle perspiration: చిరుయెండ the gentle warmth of the morning or evening sun. చిరికప్ప chiri-kappa. n. A small frog, the wall frog, chunam frog or flying frog. చిరికూర chiri-kura. n. A herb called *Amaranthus polygonoides.* Rox. iii. 602. చిరికొండి chiri-kondi. n. A small knot చిన్నచిక్కు. చిరిట chirita. n. The stopper of a bottle. చిరి తాళము chiri-talamu. n. A small lock or bell. చిరుతాళము. [In all the compounds here, చిరి may be written చిరు] చిరుతొడ the thinner part of the thigh, the leg.

చిరునవ్వు *chiri-navvu*. n. A smile, a smirk or slight laugh. చిరినాలుక *chiri-nāluka*. n. The little tongue, that is, the uvula. చిరిమాను, తిరమాను or ఎల్లమద్ది a plant called *Anogeissus latifolia*. (Watts.) చిరిమిటరటము *chirimi-taraṭu*. n. A whip or scourge. కొల్లినవలుకు. చిరివేరు *chiri-vēru*. n. The chay root which produces a red dye. *Oldenlandia umbellata*. చిరుతాళిబాడు *chiru-ṭāḷi-bāḍu*. n. A tree called *Dalbergia scandens*. Rox. iii. p. 232. చిరుగొమ్మ *chiru-gomma*. n. A cornice, a battlement. Bhanumati. iv. 135. చిరుచాప *chiru-chāpa*. n. A fine silky mat woven of bulrushes. చిరుత or చిరు *chiruta*. adj. Young, little. చిన్న. n. A bit, piece, fragment. Youth, childhood. A young one, a child, a boy. శిశువు, చిన్నది. చిరుత చూపుతో చూచి to look unkindly. చిరుతలు *chirutalu*. n. Dazzling, radiance, swimming of the eyes: మిరుమిట్లు. నా కన్నులకు చిరుతలు కమ్మినవి or చిరుతలు పారినవి my eyes are dazzled. చిరుత, చిరుతపులి or చిరుతగండు n. A hunting leopard, commonly called a Cheeta. *Cynælurus jubatus*. The Leopard or Panther, *Felis pardus*. (F. B. I.) చిరుతిండి or చిరుతిండి *chiru-tiṇḍi*. n. Slight fare, such as cakes, fruit and the like. చిరువాలు *chiru-vālu*. (చిరు+పాలు) n. Boiled milk. చిరోష్మ *chirōshma*. adj. Heated, lukewarm. కొంచెముగ కాచిన. A. iv. 174.

చిరుగు *chirugu*. [Tel.] n. The tree called *Caryota urens*. Rox. iii. 625.

చిరుగు *chirugu*. [Tel.] v. n. To tear, to be torn చినుగు. n. Tearing, as of cloth; a tear or rent. వస్త్రఛిన్నత్వము, చినుగు. చిరుగడము or చిరువడము *chirugaḍamu*. n. Tearing. చిరుగుట. See చిరగడము.

చిరుగుడు *chiruguḍu*. [Tel.] n. Romping, boisterous play. Trouble, a puzzle. A species of ring-worm or leprosy, which causes large round spots all over the body. కోకమానికుష్ఠు, ఎర్రపులుము.

చిరునామా *chiru-nāma*. [H.] n. The superscription on a letter or address. మైవిలాసము.

చిరుము, చిరుమద్దిచెట్టు or చిరుమామిడిచెట్టు *chirumu*. [Tel.] n. The tree called *Terminalia arjuna*. అర్జునవృక్షము, ఏరుమద్దిచెట్టు.

చిరుము *chirumu*. [Tel.] v. t. To squirt. చిమ్ము. v. n. To scorn, to contemn. విజృంభించు, తిరస్కరించు. Kasi. Kh. V. 63. 68. HD. i. 604. 324.

చిర్ర *chirra*. [Tel.] n. A peg, by which two rafters are held together. Anger కోపము. Dishevelled hair చెదరి. చిర్ర, చిర్రని or చిర్రుమని adv. (anuk) Angrily. Suddenly. కటారున. చిర్రచిర్ర *chirra-chirra*. n. Haste సంభ్రమము. చిర్రముర్ర *chirra-murra*. n. Confusion. చిర్రముర్రాడినను though they are agitated. చిర్రులుపోవు to be agitated సంభ్రమించు. See చిర్రు.

చిర్రి *chirri*. [Tel.] n. A plant called *Amaranthus campestris* కొయ్యి.

చిర్రు *chirru*. [Tel.] n. Anger. కోపము. చిర్రుమను to be angry కోపించు. చిర్రు, చిర్రున or చిర్రుమని adv. (anuk) Violently (angry.) At once, audibly, aloud, flashingly. చిర్రుపలక *chirru-palaka*. n. A sliding door, as of a trap or portcullis. చిర్రుబుర్రు or చిర్రుముర్రు *chirru-burru*. adv. (anuk) Angrily, aloud, audibly. చిర్రుముర్రాడు or చిర్రుబుర్రాడు *chirru-murrāḍu*. v. n. To be angry, sullen or morose. చిటచిటలాడు. See చిర్ర.

చిలక or చిలుక *chilaka*. [Tel.] n. A parrot. ముద్దులచిలక my darling! my pet! చిలకపలుకులు sweet accents. తెల్లచిలక a cockatoo. పంచరంగులచిలక the maccaw. మైనాచిలక the maina. పుల్లలచిలక or అడవిచిలక the Sirkeer Cuckoo. Jerdon No. 230. రామచిలక The Rose-ringed Paroquet, *Palaeornis torquatus* (so called because taught to reiterate the name of Rāma) అకుచిలక the Western Blossom-headed Paroquet, *Palaeornis cyanocephalus*. The name is given to some insects, as a moth, thus, అడవిచిలక, నల్లచిలక a moth. కక్షిచిలక, సీతాకోకచిలక a butterfly. A padlock. The bolt or hasp of a door, because these originally had parrot's heads on them. చిలుకలకొలికి a bright-eyed girl or woman. చక్కని స్త్రీ. చిలకకూర or చిలుకతోటకూర *chilaka-kūra*. n A kind of pot-herb, *Amarantus fasciatus*. (Watts.) చిలక, చిలకట or చిలుకడ *chilaka*. n. A saddle buckle; a ring at the end of the rope used as a girth of the bullock saddle through which the other end is passed to fasten the saddle. కాడికముడి. చిలకడతాడు *chilakada-tāḍu*. n. A girth. ఎద్దు మీదికట్టు జీనుకట్టు కంఠిలించేతాడు. చిలకకొయ్య or చిలుకకొయ్య *chilaka-koyya*. n. A wooden pin fixed in the wall, on which articles are suspended. చిలగడ *chilagaḍa*. (చిలుక+గడ.) n. The cord that fastens a dagger, to prevent its falling out of the sheath. చిలకతాళము *chilaka-tāḷamu*. n. A padlock. చిలకతాళి or చిలుకతాళి *chilaka-tāḷi*. n. A gold buckle in the form of a pair of parrots. చిలకదుడుడి *chilaka-duduḍi*. n The name of a certain tree. చిలకపచ్చ *chilaka-patstsa*. n. Bright green, parrot green. చిలకముక్కు or చిలకముక్కు *chilaka-mokka*. n. (lit. Parrot's bill.) A plant called *crotolaria*. శుకనాసము, శుకనాస. Heyne, 130. The purple red and white scentless flower called Balsam. చిలకరౌతు *chilaka-rautu*. n. Lit: He whose steed is the parrot: an epithet of మన్మథ the god of love. చిలుకకోనము *chiluka-kōnamu*. n. A "T bandage," or clout.

చిలకరించు or చిలుకరించు *chilakarintsu*. [Tel.] v. a. To sprinkle. చల్లు.

చిలగడము or చిలగడదుంప *chilagaḍamu*. [Tel.] n. The white potato: called also country potato.

చిలికించు *chilikintsu*. [Tel.] v. a. To sprinkle, bedew. చల్లు. To churn.

చిలిపి *chilipi*. [Tel.] n. A naughty or worthless person. adj. Naughty, mischievous. చిలిపితనము *chilipi-tanamu*. n. Naughtiness.

చిలిబిలి *chilibili*. [Tel.] n. Confusion. చిలిబిలిపోవు to be confused. సందడించు.

చిలుక Same as చిలక. For all compounds with చిలుక see under చిలక.

చిలుకు *chiluku*. [Tel.] n. An arrow: బాణము. A spray, a spirt. A hasp or bolt of a door. గొళ్లెము, గొలికి. A remainder, balance or residue. శేషము. v. n. To be shed: to distil or trickle. చిందు. To be aroused, as love. ప్రసరించు, మీరు. v. a. To sprinkle, to spirt or shed. చల్లు. To churn త్రచ్చు. To instil. కరుణారసము చిలుకు కన్నుదమ్ములతోడ with eyes that distilled the very essence of affection. చిలుకుటమ్ము *chiluku-ṭ-ammu*. n. A sort of fighting cock. A two pointed arrow. చిలుకుడు *chilukuḍu*. n. Churning చిలుకుట. చిలుకుడుగుంజ *chilukuḍu-gunza*. n. A churn staff.

చిలుగు *chilugu*. [Tel.] n. Grief, anguish. బాధ. HD. i. 2420. L. v. 54. Also, a tree.

చిలుప *chilupa*. [Tel.] adj. Little. అల్పము, కొంచెము. చిలుప or చిలుపచిలపనీళ్లు *chilupa-chilapa-nīḷḷu*. n. Sprinklings, drops, spray. చిలుపరాయి *chilupa-rāyi*. n. A fragment of stone. చిలుపాలు *chilu-pālu*. n. Spirtings: the sweetest milk, which bursts forth spontaneously. చిలుపు *chilupu*. v. n. To spirt out, flow, or gush: lie in pools.

చిలుము *chilumu*. [Tel.] n. Verdigris. Any metallic taste in the saliva. చిలుమువరి *chilumu-vari*. n. A sort of rice. Rox. ii. 204.

చిలువ *chiluva*. [Tel.] n. A wild duck. ఎఱ్ఱచిలువ or చిలువబాయి the Whistling Teal, *Dendrocygna javanika*. నల్లచిలువ the Tufted Duck *Nyroca fuligula*. బాపనచిలువ the Brahminy Duck, *Casarca rutila*. జొట్టుచిలువ the Comb Duck, *Sarcidiornis melanonotus*.

చిలువ *chilura*. [Tel. చిలుము (=విషము)+వాయి.] n. A snake. విషధరము. కొండచిలువ a rock snake or python. A sluggard. చిలువదొర or చిలువరేడు *chilura-dora*. n. The chief of the serpent race: the Great Dragon. శేషుడు. చిలువగుడియ *chilura-gudiya*. n. A sort of snake. G. vi. 101.

చిలువాయనము *chiluvāyanamu*. [Tel.] n. Meanness, baseness. చిల్లర, క్షుద్రము.

చిలువాలు *chiluvālu*. [Tel. చిలుపు+పాలు] n. Milk boiled till it thickens. మరగాగాచిన చిక్కనిపాలు. A. i. 91. See చిలుప.

చిల్ల *chilla*. [Tel.] n. The barb of an arrow or fishhook. A bone ఎముక. A bit, a fragment. M. 12. 2. 430. adj. Empty, trifling, useless. చిల్లపెంకు a potsherd. "చిల్ల తలము"=ఇంచుకవసరు. A iv. 36. చిల్లచెవులు ears that are empty, that is, unadorned with earrings. చిల్లకోల or చిల్లకోల *chilla-kōla*. n. A whip with several lashes. కొమరము. A pitchfork. చిల్లచన్గావు a cow, the ends of whose teats are forked. చిల్ల జగడము a vain dispute, a quarrel about nothing.

చిల్లంగి *chillangi*. [Tel.] adj. Mischievous. చిల్లంగిగొండి a quarrelsome person కలహకారి. చిల్లంగిగొండితనము mischievousness, disobedience, misbehaviour. చిల్లంగిచేతలు. (G. iv. 21.) tricks, frauds చిల్లంగిపోతు *chillangi-pōtu*. n. A wizard, a witch.

చిల్లగింజ *chilla-ginza*. [Tel.] n. The clearing-nut, *Strychnos potatorum*. Ainslie. ii. 420. Rox. i. 576.

చిల్లగొండి or చిల్లంగొండి Same as చిల్లంగిగొండి. q. v.

చిల్లర *chillara*. [Tel.] adj. Retail, as a shop. Miscellaneous, sundry, stray, trifling, mean, of no note or importance, subordinate. Vile, base. చిల్లరవాండ్లు a mixed multitude, people of no consequence. చిల్లరరూకలు loose money, change. పదిరూపాయలపైచిల్లర ten rupees and odd. చిల్లరపూజ vain homage, empty adoration చిల్లరభ్రాంతులు empty fancies. చిల్లరవేల్పులు inferior deities. చిల్లరలు *chillaralu*. (Plu.) Sundries, odds and ends.

చిల్లాకు *chillāku*. [Tel.] n. A kind of forest tree the leaves of which form a manure.

చిల్లాడము or చిల్లాణము *chilladamu*. [Tel.] n. A small dagger. ఖుబరిక. Anir. iv. 39.

చిల్లాడిపోవు *chilladi-pōvu*. [Tel.] v.n. To fly, to be scattered or routed.

చిల్లి *chilli*. [Tel.] n. A small hole, a perforation, a fissure, an opening or cleft. కన్నము. చిల్లులుపోవు *chillulu-pōvu*. v. n. To go into holes, i. e., be perforated or be worn out. చిల్లులుపోయిన ragged, worn out.

చిల్ల *chilla*. [Tel.] adj. Bifurcated, forked, double pointed. చిల్లు *chillu*. n. A fork, as that formed by two branches.

చివచివ *chiva-chiva*. [Tel.] adv. (anuk.) Briskly, all at once. Quicker and quicker. Slippery. చివచివలాడు to be slippery (as land after rain.) నా కాళ్లు చివచివలాడుకొని పోతున్నవి my legs ache.

చివర *chivara*. [Tel.] n. The end, tip, extremity or point. adj. Last, final. ఊరిచివర at the end of the village. చిట్టచివర at the very end. చివరలు *chivaralu*. n. plu. Ends. Bits, fragments, shivers, odds.

చివాలున *chivālu-na*. [Tel.] adv. Suddenly. హఠాత్తుగా.

చివుక *chivuka*. [Tel.] n. A quarter rupee. చివుకపిట్ట *chivuka-pitta*. n. A kind of bat. ఒకవిధమైన గబ్బిలము.

చివుకు *chivuku*. [Tel.] v. n. To rot, to be damaged, weakened, wasted or spoilt. పాడైపోవు. To pine with grief or sorrow. చివికిన rotten, damaged, శిథిలమైన, కుళ్లిన; pining కలతనొందిన. చివుకు n. Corruption, spoiling, rotting. Pining మనస్సుకలతనొందడము. చివుక్కు *chivukku*. adv. Impetuously, rampantly, briskly, with agility. చివ్వున at once, suddenly. చివ్వుక్కురుము to be confused or agitated in mind మనస్సుకలగు.

చివురు Same as చిగురు. **చివుళ్లు** *chivullu.* [Tel.] n. Salt places, spots producing salt.

చివ్వ *chivva.* [Tel.] n. An onset, an encounter, battle, an attack కలహము, పోట్లాట, యుద్ధము. R. iv. 127. vii. 55. M. IV. ii. 290. A thin strip or shaving of wood. A twig or small branch. చివ్వయీటెలు slender lances. గాలపుచివ్వ a fishing rod. A nerve. నాలుకచివ్వ the nerve of the tongue. మెడచివ్వ the sinew between the shoulder and the neck, also the nape. A kind of fireworks బాణపుసంచుకం. చివ్వలాడి a quarrelsome woman, కలహకారాలు. **చివ్వగడ** *chivva-gada.* n. A spear, a javelin. **చివ్వము** *chivvamu.* n. An attack, a struggle చివ్వాలాడు to grapple with, to encounter. పులితో చివ్వాలాడు to be in grips with a tiger; i. e., to be in a critical position.

చివ్వంగి or **చివ్వగి** *chivvangi.* [Tel.] n. A Cheetah. The Hunting Leopard, *Felis jubata.* Jerdon

చివ్వని *chivv-ani.* [Tel. చివ్వ+అని.] adv. At once. slapdash! See చివ్వున.

చివ్వాడు or **సివాలాడు** *chivv-adu.* [Tel.] v. n. To ramble, rove. To sport, play. తెలగ్గాడు, చిందులుతొక్కు.

చివ్వు *chivvu.* [Tel.] v. a. To cut thin, or shave. To pare or trim the nails: to make (a pen), to form (a cloth) in a pointed shape. చెక్కు. n. Quickness త్వర.

చివ్వున *chivvu-na.* [Tel.] adv. All at once, briskly. శీఘ్రముగా. See చివ్వు.

చిహ్నము or **చిహ్నం** *chihnamu.* [Skt.] n. A mark, spot or stain, a sign, attribute, quality, characteristic, feature, representation, symptom. గురుతు. వర్షచిహ్నాలు signs of approaching rain. A flag టెక్కెము.

చి chi

చి *chi.* [Tel.] Interj. Poh! fie! చీకొట్టు to scold, చీయను. చీవాట్లు rebuke, reprehension, scolding.

చీకటి *chīkaṭi.* [Tel.] n. Darkness. అంధకారము. కనుచీకటి twilight. చీకటితో లేచితి I arose before dawn. చీకటిగాము Rahu. చీకటిగొంగ the sun. **చీకటి** adj. Dark, obscure, hidden, imperceptible. చీకటితప్పు a latent or hidden offence, i. e., adultery జారత్వము. చీకటిమొటికెల్లు a certain game played by boys. **చీకటిమ్రాకు** *chīkaṭi-mraku.* n. The tree called *Exonthocymus pictorius.* తమాలము. **చీకటీగ** *chīkaṭiga.* n. Lit. the invisible fly. A small mosquito చిన్నదోమ. **చీజీకటి** *chī-jīkaṭi.* n. The lighter twilight, as opposed to చిమ్మచీకటి.

చీకి or **చీకిరి** *chīkari.* [Tel.] adj. Blinking. **చీకరించు**, **చీకిరించు** or **చీకిలించు** *chīkarintsu.* v. n. To blink or twinkle as the eyes do in a glare, మిణుమిట్లుగొను. **చీకిరి కండ్లు** or **చీకరికండ్లు** *chīkari-kandlu.* n. Blinking eyes.

చీకాకు *chīkāku.* [Tel.] n. Vexation, puzzle. disgust, teazing, pestering. చీకాకు ఉడిగిన (i. e. పోగొట్టిన) యోగి a devotee who hath dispelled all those passions that harass the mind. **చీకాకుచేయు** or **చీకాకుపరుచు** *chīkāku-chēyu.* v. t. To displease, vex, trouble, శ్రమపరచు. శత్రుసైన్యమును చీకాకు పరచినాడు he harassed the foe. **చీకాకుపడు** *chīkāku-paḍu.* v. n. To be vexed, harassed, puzzled or tormented.

చీకాయ Same as సీకాయ (q. v.)

చీకిచెట్టు *chīki-chettu.* [Tel.] n. A thorny creeper. H. iv. 14.

చీకిరించుకొను or **చీకిలించుకొను** Same as చీకరించు. See under చీకరి.

చీకిరేణి or **చీకిరేని** *chīkirēni.* [Tel.] n. A certain medicinal tree.

చికిలి *chikili*. [Tel.] n. A broom. చీపురుకట్ట, చికిలిమాకిలి in confusion, or crookedly. కొక్కిరిబిక్కిరిగా.

చికివెలగ *chiki-velaga*. [Tel.] n. The thorny wood apple tree. కెలగ.

చీకు *chiku*. [Tel.] adj. Blind, Sapless చిప్పుకు, నిస్సారము. n. A blind person. Dampness, damp, తడి. చీకాగ్గము a dense forest. చీకులు fools. చీకుముళ్లు minute prickles. v. a. To suck (a mango, &c.) To smack with the lips. చప్పరించు, చుంబించు. v. n. To be damaged, to rot or be spoiled, by damp, &c. See చిప్పుకు. చీకుకొక్కెర, చీకురాయి or చీకువాయి *chiku-kokkera*. n. The Indian Fruit-Bat or Flying-Fox. *Pteropus medius*. (F.B.I.) ఋషిపిట్ట. చీకురు *chikuru*. n. Blindness. A blind man. చీకురువాయి a beetle or cricket కమ్మరపురుగు. చీకువాలు *chiku-ralu*. n. Darkness. తిమిరము

చిటుకము or చిట్టుకము *chitukamu*. [Tel.] n. Sport. కేలి.

చీటి *chiti*. [Tel.] n. A note or small letter, పత్రిక. Painted cloth. తుదచీటి (an expression for farewell) For the last *time*. చీటికి మాటికి or చీటికిమాటికి *chiti-matiki*. adv. Every instant, every now and then, పలుమారు, పదేపదే.

చీడ *chida*. [Tel.] n. An ill or evil. A blight, disease, rot, or murrain. చీడతెవులు applied either to diseases of animals or of vegetables. చీడపాటన పశువు an ox sick with murrain. చీడపురుగు *chida-purugu*. n. A caterpillar or worm that destroys plants. A grub inside a fruit or a seed.

చీడు *chidu*. [Tel.] n. A skein or bundle of seven *punjums* or a hundred threads. చీడుడబ్బ *chidu-dabba*. n. An instrument used by weavers for winding the thread. నూలిచీడు తగిలించుటకు వెదురుబద్దలతో గుమ్మటమువలె కట్టబడిన సాలెవానిసాధనము.

చీడెలు *chidelu*. [Tel.] n. plu. A sweetmeat, composed of sesamum seeds and treacle.

చీద, సీద or చిందె *chida*. [Tel.] n. The bird called a Babbler. గోరచీద or కొండచీద the Large Grey Babbler, *Argya malcolmi*. పెద్దచీద the Jungle Babbler, *Crateropus canorus* చిట్టిచీద or చిన్నచీద the Common Babbler, *Argya caudata*. (F.B.I.)

చీదర *chidara*. [Tel.] n. Nausea, nastiness, unsavouriness, dislike, abhorrence, loathing, perplexity, distraction of mind, chagrin, disgust. అసహ్యము. Danger ఉపద్రవము. A crack కూటు. తలచీదర a headache. చీదరగొను *chidara-gonu*. v. n. To be in danger. ఉపద్రవపడు. To be excited ఆవేశమెత్తు. To spring a leak కూటుపోవు. చీదరపడ్డ *chidara-padda*. adj. Grieved or hurt, disgusted. చీదరపోవు to spring a leak కూటుపోవు. చీదరకు to be infuriated. Parij. iii. 34.

చీదు *chidu*. [Tel.] v. a. To blow the nose.

చీనము *chinamu*. [Skt.] n. Gold. బంగారు.

చీనా *china*. [Tel.] adj. Belonging to or brought from China: as చీనాపంచదార China sugar candy. (This word is used in the poets, just as the word *Indian* was formerly used in English poetry, to denote what was foreign.) చీనాపెట్టె, or చీనాతకుపెట్టె a tin box brought from China. చీనాంశుకము China silk. చీని *chini*. n. China wares either of silk or of gold: filagree work. Sugar. చీనిపని *chini-pani*. n. Chinese gilding.

చీనివాయి Same as చీకువాయి. (q. v.)

చీపర *chipara*. [Tel.] n. A kind of bird. ఆరాయి

చీపి *chipi*. [Tel.] n. A certain disease of cattle. See బొక్క and దొమ్మ.

చీపు *chipu*. [Tel.] v. a. To make a sound with the lips. n. A comb దువ్వెన. Part of a bunch of plantains అత్తము.

చీపురు *chipuru*. [Tel.] n. A broom. చీపురుకడ్డి a kind of grass, *Aristida setacea*. (Watts.) చీపురుపుల్లలు the twigs of which a broom is made. చీపురుముండ్లు bits of a broom like burrs. చీపురుకట్ట rubbish.

చీబోతు or చీంబోతు *chī-bōtu.* [Tel.] n. A he-goat. HD. iii. 965. మేకలపోతు మేకగడి.

చీమ *chīma.* [Tel.] n. An ant. కొండచీమ the forest ant. రెక్కలచీమ a winged ant. పారేచీమను వింటాడు he can hear an ant crawl; i. e., he is all alive. చీమదూరని అడవి a forest impervious even to an ant. నల్లచీమ a black ant; పై పాకేపక్షి కిందపాకే చీమ (proverb) The bird above, the ant below, i. e., I had no chance with him. చీమంత of the size of an ant. చీమపులి *chīma-puli.* n. The ant lion, an ant-eater.

చీమిడి *chīmidi.* [Tel.] n. The mucus of the nose.

చీము *chīmu.* [Tel.] n. Matter from a sore, prurient matter, pus. చీడి తెల్లనైనచెత్తురు. చీముపోయు or పట్టు to suppurate.

చీమంట *chīmunta.* [Tel.] n. A metal vessel. చెంబు.

చీర *chīra.* [Tel.] n. A garment. వస్త్రము. A woman's garment, a petticoat, a skirt or gown కోక. A curtain తెర. A scratch with the nail. తెరచీర a screen used in ambush for wild beasts. చీరరోగము a certain disease. చీరచింపు *chīra-chimpu.* n. A kind of fish. G. i. 111. చీరము *chīramu.* [Skt.] n. Bark, rind, cloth made of bark. నారచీర. చీరచాప or చాపచీర *chīra-tsāpa.* n. A ship's sail. చీరపొరని చీకటి impenetrable darkness. Anir. D. 60. చీరావి (చీర+ఆవి.) warmth. (They breathe into a handkerchief and apply this "steam in a cloth" to comfort an aching eye.) BD. iii. 1548.

చీరణము or చీర్ణము *chīraṇamu.* [Tel.] n. A very small chisel. చిన్నఉలి.

చీరపిట్ట, చీరపేను or చీరదోమ *chīra-piṭṭa.* [Tel.] n. A white louse.

చీరి *chīri,* [Skt.] n. A moth, cricket. చిమ్మెట.

చీరి [Tel.] n. Care, regard. A mark లక్ష్యము. చీరికొనాక heedless: not caring. చీరికొను to regard, care for. తృణముగానెంచు.

చీరిక or చిరిక *chīrika.* [Tel.] n. A remnant or bit of cloth, a slice, a slip. A scratch.

చీరు *chīru.* [Tel.] v. a. To gash, cut in slices, tear, rend, చీల్చు. To scratch గీరు. To hiss like a serpent. To call out, exclaim. To challenge or vie with in excellence. To call or invite. పిలుచు. చీరుడు *chīruḍu.* n. Splitting. చీల్చుట. Calling పిలుపు. BD. iv. 984.

చీల or సీల *chīla.* [Tel.] n. An iron nail, a wooden pin, a linch pin. మేకు. Any fastening: a corner stone. కట్టుచీల a rivet. మెలిపెట్టుచీల a screw. నిడుపుచీల a straight peg. అడ్డచీల a cross peg or pin. నాగటిచీల the pin of a plough. చీలమండ *chīla-manda.* n. The ankle. మడిమెకీలు. చీలమన్ను *chīla-mannu.* n. The luting round a crucible.

చీలి *chīli.* [Tel.] n. A pet term applied to a cat, like 'Pussy' పిల్లి. జోగడపుచీలి a tom cat మగపిల్లి.

చీలు *chīlu.* [Tel.] v. n. To split or crack. విడిపోవు. To withdraw from company. To be scattered. To fall off or drop off as paint. To divide, or branch off, as a road or stream. చీల్పించు *chīlpintsu.* (v. causal) To tear, divide, &c. To sow dissensions. చీలదీయు *chīla-dīyu.* v. n. To split or to tear, to scatter, to divide. To seduce, beguile. To tempt, tamper with, raise dissensions, foment, worm out a secret. చీలిక or చీరిక *chīlika.* n. A slit, a slice. చీలుచు or చీల్చు *chīlutsu.* v. a. To split, crack, tear, divide.

చీవరము *chīvaramu.* [Tel.] n. The tattered garb of a mendicant. సన్యాసులకాటి, భిక్షుకునివస్త్రము.

చీవు *chīvu.* [Tel.] v. a. To scrape. చివ్వు. చీవించు *chīvintsu.* v. a. To carve in wood or marble.

చు chu

చుంబనము *chumbanamu.* [Skt.] n. A kiss: ముద్దు. **చుంబించు** *chumbintsu.* v. n. To kiss. ముద్దుపెట్టుకొను. చుంబకుడు one who kisses; a superficial student.

చుబుకము *chubukamu.* [Skt.] n. The chin. గడ్డము, చిబుకము.

చులుకము *chulukamu.* [Skt.] n. The hand held as a cup to contain a liquid in the palm. A small cupful. చేరు, పుడిసిలి.

చూ chū

చూచుకము *chūchukamu.* [Skt.] n. A nipple or teat. స్తనాగ్రము.

చూడ or **చూడము** *chūda.* [Skt.] n. The lock of hair worn by men on the crown of the head. శిఖ, జుట్టు. ఆమూలచూడముగా from end to end (of the story.) ఆపాద చూడము from head to foot. **చూడాకర్మము** *chūda-karmamu.* n. The ceremony of removing the first hair of a child. పుట్టు వెంట్రుకలుతీయడము. **చూడాకలాపము** or **చూడామణి** *chūda-kalāpamu.* n. A crest, a diadem.

చూతము *chūtamu.* [Skt.] n. A mango tree. చూతాస్త్రుడు n. Manmadha: because his arrows (అస్త్రములు) are mango-blossoms.

చూర్ణము *chūrnamu.* [Skt.] n. Dust, powder. పొడి. **చూర్ణముచేయు** *chūrṇamu-chēyu.* v. n. To beat to dust; to triturate. చూర్ణకుంతలములు curls, ringlets.

చూర్ణిక *chūrṇika.* [Skt.] n. A sort of harmonious prose, not divided into prosodial feet, but with the unbroken sentence running on continuously. గద్యభేదము.

చూలిక *chūlika.* [Skt.] n. The root of an elephant's ear. గజకర్ణమూలము. The tresses or hair. పిల్లజుట్టు, కొప్పు.

చె che

చె *che.* [Tel. Short for చెన్ను (q. v.) in compounds.] adj. Budding, tender, red. Delicate: pretty.

చెంక *chenka.* [Tel.] n. The cheek: a small plot in a field. The gills of a fish. చెక్కిలి, చెంప, కపోలము. **చెంకవేయు** *chenka-vēyu.* v. n. To slap, to strike on the cheek.

చెంగనాలు *chenganālu.* [Tel.] n. Capers, gambols. గంతులు, వాలుక్రీడలు. Salutations. నమస్కారములు, "శ్రీమూర్తికినిచెంగనాలని." H. iv. 317.

చెంగటి *chengati.* [Tel.] adj. Near, neighbouring. సమీపము. **చెంగట** *chengata.* adv. In the neighbourhood, near, close by. సమీపము.

చెంగలించు *chengal-intsu.* [Tel.] v. n. To appear, shine, bloom, rejoice, to beam with a smile ప్రకాశించు. To deride. హసించు. చెంగలింపు derision.

చెంగలువ *chen-galuva.* [Tel. చెన్ను+కలువ.] n. The red water lily. ఎర్రకలువ. **చెంగల్వకోష్టు** *chengalva-kōshṭu.* n. A sort of drug, a species of *costus* పాంథాష్టము. **చెంగల్వగడ్డి** *chengalva-gaḍḍi.* n. A sort of grass.

చెంగావి *chen-gāvi.* [Tel. చెన్ను+కావి.] n. A reddish tint; saffron colour కాషాయం.

చెంగు or **చేంగు** *chengu.* [Tel.] n. Agility. **చెంగున** *chengu-na.* adv. Suddenly. **చెంగుపిల్లి** *chengu-pilli.* n. A wild cat or mountain cat; one that "leaps" at an object.

చెంగు *chengu.* [Tel.] n. A skirt, border, edge. కొంగు, అంచు. In marriage the couple are tied together by the corners of their skirts. Hence, ఈపనికి చెంగుకట్టి నాడు he is wedded to this business. నీకు చెంగుకట్టినాను I am irrevocably thy servant. చెంగుపట్టి అడుగు to seize one by the skirt as a beggar does.

చెంగు *chengu.* [Tel.] v. n. To be loosened (as a knot) విడిపోవు, సోలు. To withdraw, to retreat వెనుదీయు. To lose or fail in a game ఓడిపోవు. చెంగి ఆడు to talk indifferently. అక్కరపట్టనట్టుగా మాట్లాడు. చెంగిచెంగిపోవు to loiter in walking. గాయ చెంగినది (at games with small balls) the ball stopped, or, missed. రెండుగుంటలు చెంగి నవి there are two holes without balls. చెంగగొట్టు to defeat ఓడించు.

చెంచేలిచెట్టు *chentsali-chettu.* [Tel.] n. A kind of herb. *Digera muricata.* తెలుమరి చెట్టు, కురుంజము.

చెంచు or చెంచువాండ్లు *chentsu.* [Tel.] n. A hill tribe, savages, hill folk, highlanders. చెంచెత *chencheta.* n. A woman of this tribe. చెంచు adj. Savage.

చెండు *chendu.* [Tel.] v. n. To rise, or spread, as a scent. v. a. To cut to pieces, mangle, destroy, break, ruin. ఖండించు. ఈయెండ చెండుతున్నది this sunshine is scorchingly hot. n. A cluster or ball of flowers. పూబంతి. A ball to play with. బంతి. చెండాడు *chend-ādu.* (చెండి+ఆడు.) v. a. To cut up into pieces. ఖండించు. To destroy, slay. To play at ball (చెండు ఆడు). చెండాట *chen-lata.* n. A game at ball. చెండుగోరింపులు *chendu-gōrimpulu.* n. Playing at ball. చెండుకొనిపోవు to devour or plunder. చెండుమల్లె *chendumalle.* n. The marigold. బంతిపువ్వు, చేమంతి. చెండుచెండాడు *chendu-bend-ādu.* v. t. To cut to pieces. చెండిపోతు or చేండిపోతు *chendi-pōtu.* n. A wretch.

చెంత *chenta.* [Tel.] n. Nearness. సమీపము, చేరువ. adv. By, at, beside, along. తండ్రి చెంతనుండి కాపాడిరి they screened him from his father.

చెంతలాసి *chental-āsi.* [Tel.] n. The plant called కటుపత్రము.

చెందమ్మి *chen-dammi.* [Tel. చెన్ను+తమ్మి.] n. The red lotus. ఎర్రకలువ.

చెందిరము or చెంద్రము *chendiramu.* [Tel. from Skt. సిందూరము.] n. Vermilion. The red mark worn on the forehead. కుంకుమము.

చెందిరిక or చెంత్రిక *chendirika.* [Tel.] n. Red colour. సిందూరవర్ణము, కుసుంభవర్ణము.

చెందు *chendu.* [Tel.] v. n. To happen, befall, to belong to, to accrue to, to devolve on. To be got, felt, experienced. కలుగు. v. a. To obtain, attain to, enjoy. పొందు. నిదురచెందిరి they enjoyed sleep. చెందిన భయము the terror he suffered. దైవగతిచెందిరి they died: lit. they suffered the will of God. నిన్ను దోషముచెందదా will not the sin be thine? చెందించు *chendintsu.* v. a. To cause to get, attain, obtain or enjoy. చెందించకేయు to assign or apportion.

చెందుగపులి *chenduga-puli.* [Tel.] n. A kind of leopard.

చెందుప్పు *chend-uppu.* [Tel. చెందు+ఉప్పు.] n. Saltpetre. ఇందుప్పు, సైంధవము.

చెందోవ *chendova.* [Tel. చెన్ను+తోవ.] n. The red lotus. The red water lily. ఎర్రకలువ. చెందోవవిందు epithet of Adonis as the friend of this flower. T. iv. 192.

చెంత్రిక Same as చెందిరిక. (q. v.)

చెంప *chempa.* [Tel.] n. The cheek. కపోలము. A side. పార్శ్వము. నీపాపము నిన్ను చెంప కొట్టె thy sin hath struck thee on the cheek. చెంపకల్లి *chempa-kalli.* n. An ornament worn by women. చెంపకాయ *chempa-kaya.* n. A slap on the cheek, a box on the ear. చెంపదెబ్బ. చెంపగిల్లు *chempa-gillu.* v. n. To turn aside, go out of the way. చెంపతల *chempa-tala.* adv. Close by, at, near. P. iii. 170. చెంపదిళ్ల a cushion or pad.

చెంబడివాడు *chembadi-vādu.* [Tel.] n. A fisherman.

చెంబు *chembu.* [Tel.] n. A cup, a jug, an ewer, a cruise, a goblet, a tankard. A vase or globular metal pot of a peculiar form: గుండ్రమూతిగల లోహపాత్రము. దంతపు

తెంబులు ivory cups for perfumes : చెంబు తల chembu-tala. n. A bald head. బట్టతల.

చెకడా chekaḍa. [Tel.] n. A bullock cart. సరుకులుతెచ్చే రెండెద్దులబండి.

చెకపిక, చెకచెక or చెక బెక cheka-pika. [Tel.] n. Fierceness. See చకచక. చెకపెకలాడు to trouble తొందరపెట్టు.

చెకుముకి or చెకుముకిరాయి cheku-muki. [Tel.] n. A flint. చెకుముకితుపాకి cheki-muki-tupaki. n. A flint gun, as distinguished from the common తుపాకి or matchlock.

చెక్క chekka. [Tel.] n. Wood; a bit, a piece, a chip, a plank of wood. A bed, or division in a field. See చెక్కు. చెక్క adj. Wooden. Smooth. చెక్కసున్నము smooth plaster, (So called because polished with a piece of wood.) చెక్కకొనుదురు or చెక్కపిడుజు chekka-konuduru. n. A wood louse, a tick. చెక్కచెట్టు chekka-chettu. n. A kind of tree from the wood of which a red dye is obtained. చెక్కపేలు chekka-pēlu. n. Cattle lice or ticks. చెక్కరంగు chekka-rangu. n. Wood colour; brown or yellowish.

చెక్కిలి n. chekkili. [Tel.] n. The cheek. కపోలము, చెక్కు.

చెక్కు chekku. [Tel.] v. a. To pare, to cut into slices. To engrave. (రత్నములను) పొదుగు. To make a pen. To set jewels. To tuck in, put in, insert, set. To dig slightly or scrape the surface. To cast up the earth, as a worm does. చెక్కుటద్దము chekku-ṭ-addamu. n. A mirror (అద్దము) set in a frame (చెక్కినది.) చెక్కుడుపార chekkuḍu-pāra. n. A sort of spade for cutting turf. చెక్కొను chek-konu v. n. (middle voice of చెక్కు) To adjust, trim, set right. చెక్కించు chekkintsu. v. t. To thrust forward the breast, as a crowing cock does. చెక్కు n. The side, in general. The cheek. The rind or side of a fruit. Half a pack; being as much as is on each side of a bullock. వానికి చెక్కు చెమర్చినది he was quite exhausted. చెక్కులుపక్కలు pranks, roguery. చెక్కుచెదరక unharmed, untouched, intact. అది చెక్కు చెదరకుండ నున్నది it is in excellent order.

చెక్కెము chekkemu. [Tel.] n. The marrow in a bone. ఎముకలోనిమెదడు.

చెచ్చెర chech-chera. [Tel.] adv. Forthwith, at once. శీఘ్రముగా.

చెటాయించు cheṭā-yintsu. [Tel.] v. t. To reject, refuse, disapprove.

చెట్ట cheṭṭa. [Tel.] n. The hand. చెయ్యి. చెట్టబట్టి or చెట్టలుపట్టి catching him by the hand. BD. iv. 1165. P. i. 51. Mischief. కీడు. adj. Mischievous. చెట్టపట్టాలుపట్టుకొను cheṭṭa-paṭṭālu-paṭṭu-konu. v. n. To walk hand in hand. చెట్టపట్టు cheṭṭa-paṭṭu. v. t. To marry. Lit. take by the hand. పెండ్లాడు. n. Marriage పెండ్లి.

చెట్టు cheṭṭu. [Tel.] n. A tree or plant. చెట్టువట్టు or చెట్టుబ్రహ్మరి a monkey, కోతి. చెట్టుకట్టు to be formed into a tree చెట్టుగా ఏర్పడు. చెట్టుప cheṭṭupa. n. A wing. రెక్క. చెట్టుపడు to be turned into a pillar, to become transfixed or stupified స్తంభించు. చెట్టుముట్టి cheṭṭu-muṭi. n. The plant called *Nepeta Malabarica*. మగబీరాకు. Rox. i. 1. Ainsl. ii. 294. చెట్టురుకుపాము chett-uruku-pāmu. n. The tree snake. (Russell.)

చెడగరము cheḍagaramu. [Tel.] adj. Shy, cruel, as a cow, &c., not fit to go near, dangerous, not trustworthy. Gruff, rough. క్రూరము. n. A cruel person క్రూరుడు.

చెడు cheḍu. [Tel.] v. n. To be spoiled or damaged. To become rotten or worthless. To become wicked or bad. To be dispelled, dissipated, or done away with, as darkness. To become bad, damaged or ruined. నశించు, కనబడకపోవు. To change, be altered from its original state. "నకారము చెడి అర్ధబిందువు వచ్చెను (Appa. C. ii. 31.) the letter N is dropt and the nasal sign (sunna) is substituted." అది చెడె it is ruined! వాసిచెడినశాంతి with diminished brilliancy. మీ సంశయము చెడును your doubts shall be dissipated. M. XIII. v. 97. చెడగొట్టు cheḍa-goṭṭu. v. t. To ruin, spoil. చెడనాడు cheḍa-n-āḍu. v. t. To blame. నిందించు. To curse. To say 'Be it ruined'! To scorn. To waste, throw away. చెడిప cheḍipa. (చెడిన+అప.) n. An unchaste woman. రంకులాలు. చెడు adj. Vile, worthless. Horrid, abominable. చెడుచిక్కు a terrible difficulty. చెడుగు cheḍugu. adj. Ruined, vile, worthless. Cruel క్రూరము. n. Evil, a misfortune or calamity. అశుభము. A bad woman దుష్టురాలు. చెడుగడు or చెడుగొట్టు cheḍugaḍu. n. A miscreant, a wretch. క్రూరుడు. P. i. 559. చెడ్డ cheḍḍa. (contracted from చెడిన.) adj. Bad, spoiled ruined, lost. Terrible, awful, tremendous. Hard, cruel. n. Evil. కీడు. మంచిచెడ్డలు good and bad. కులముచెడ్డవాడు one who has lost caste. తలచెడ్డచెట్టు a pollard, a tree that has lost its head. చెడ్డతనము cheḍḍa-tanamu. n. Badness, wickedness, severity.

చెడ్డీ cheḍḍī. [Tel.] n. Short breeches. పొట్టిలాగు మోకాలివరకు వచ్చులాగా.

చెడ్డు cheḍḍu. [Tel.] v. t. To strike or pat the thighs. తొడచరచు.

చెణుకు or చెనుకు cheṇuku. v. a. To stir up, excite, provoke, stimulate. To challenge, incite. To poke, shove. చెణకకుండా కూర్చుండు sit down quietly without meddling with any one.

చెత్త chetta. [Tel.] n. Stuff, dirt, trash, sweepings, rubbish. చెత్తచెదారము chetta-chedāramu. n. Dirt and rubbish.

చెద or చెదపురుగు cheda. [Tel.] n. A termite or white ant. వెదురుకు చెద పట్టినది or చెదలుపట్టినది white ants have attacked the bamboo. లేడిచెద or గొర్రెచెద a large and destructive species of termites.

చెదరు or చెదురు chedaru. [Tel.] v. n. To scatter; to be dispersed, dissipated, or spent. To splash, to be disordered, dishevelled. To fail or wander, as the mind or attention. To be dazzled. చంచలించు. చెదరగొట్టు chedara-goṭṭu. v. a. To disperse, rout, defeat. చెదరబడు Same as చెదరు.

చెదారము chedāramu. [Tel.] n. Trash. తృణలేశము.

చెనకు chenaku. [Tel.] v. t. To touch, తాకు. అంటు, స్పృశించు. To caper, rush, play pranks. A. i. 21. To oppose ఎదిరించు. n. Opposition ఎదిరించుట. Touching తాకుట. A dent or mark left by pinching the skin with the nails గోటినొక్కు.

చెనటి or చెనంటి chenaṭi. [Tel.] adj. Mad, wretched, foolish, silly, wild. క్రూర. Cunning కుత్సితము. Vain, useless వ్యర్థము. Nothing శూన్యము.

చెనయు Same as చెనకు. (q. v.)

చెనుపరి chenupari. [Tel.] adj. Rustic, as speech గ్రామ్యము. చెనుపరిమాటలు rustic accents or dialect.

చెన్నంగి or చెన్నఁగి chennangi. [Tel.] n. A species of rice. A short cocoanut tree. పొట్టిటెంకాయచెట్టు.

చెన్నటి Same as చెనటి. చెన్నటిపోవు to become useless వ్యర్థమగు.

చెన్ను chennu. [Tel.] n. Grace, beauty. అందము. Manner విధము. Redness ఎరుపు. చెన్నుడు a beau or fop, అందగాడు. చెన్నుపరచు chennu-paratsu. v. a. To trim, adorn, adjust. చెన్నారి chennāri. adj. Graceful, lovely. చెన్నారిపొన్నారి delicate, charming, pretty. చెన్నారు chennāru. v. n. To bloom or blaze in beauty.

చెప్పు cheppu. [Tel. of. Tam. చెరుప్పు.] n. A shoe. పాదరక్ష.

చెప్పు *cheppu.* [Tel.] v. a. To say, tell. To teach, to speak of. To write or compose a poem. To describe, tell of. To term, call, name, denominate. నాతో చెప్పెను he told me. చెప్పడుమాట a hearsay word, hearsay, talk, rumour. చెప్పించు *cheppintsu.* v. a. To make one say or tell. వానికి పనిచెప్పించినాను I got him an employment. వాడికి చదువు చెప్పించినాను I got him taught to read. చెప్పిఅంపు *cheppi-ampu.* v. a. n. To send word.

చెప్పుతట్టాకు *cheppu-taṭṭ-āku.* [Tel.] n. The common asarabica or foalfoot plant. *Asarum europoeum* (Watts).

చెమట or చెమ్మట *chemaṭa.* [Tel.] n. Sweat, perspiration, moisture. స్వేదము. కాసలు చెమటకార్చి బ్రతికేవాడను I live by the sweat of my brow. చిరుచెమట gentle perspiration. చెమటకాయలు *chemaṭa-kāyalu.* n. Prickly heat. చెమటపాత *chemaṭa-pāta.* n. A sweaty cloth. The glove worn by falconers, for the hawk to perch on. చెమరుపోతు or చెమటగొట్టు *chemaru-pōtu.* n. One who perspires profusely మిక్కిలి చెమటగలవాడు. చెమర్చు, చెమరించు, చెమ్మరించు or చెమటుపోయు or చెమటుపట్టు *chemartsu.* v. n. To sweat, to perspire. చెమరు *chemaru* n. Moisture, oozing. v. n. To sweat, to ooze.

చెమిక *chemika.* [Tel.] n. Selvedge of cloth.

చెముడు Same as చెవుడు. (q. v.)

చెమ్మ *chemma.* [Tel.] adj. Damp, moist. n. Damp, moisture. తడి. చెమ్మగిలు or చెమ్మగిల్లు *chemma-gillu.* v. n. To be damp, తడికలదగు. చెమ్మఉరుకు=చెమ్మగిల్లు.

చెమ్మరించు *chemmar-intsu.* [Tel.] v.n. To sweat. To be moist. తేమటిలు.

చెమ్మిలిపాము *chemmili-pāmu.* [Tel.] n. A prickly eel found on the sea coast. *Gymnotus catenatus.*

చెయి, చేయి or చెయ్యి *cheyi.* [Tel.] n. A hand The arm. A sleeve. An elephant's trunk. Five (in counting, as three hands, i. e., fifteen.) అరచెయ్యి or లోచెయ్యి the palm of the hand. మీదిచెయ్యి or మీఁజేయి the back of the hand. మణికట్టు the wrist. మోచెయ్యి the elbow. దండచెయ్యి the upper arm. చెయిదము, చెయిది or చెద్దు *cheyi-damu.* [Tel. from చేయు.] n. An act, action, doing. కృత్యము, చేష్ట. "చేతకానివి యుదములు చేయక." M. XII. ii. 415. చెయిపట్టు *cheyi-paṭṭu.* v. n. To adopt, protect, take by the hand. To seize or ravish a woman. To marry. To foster. చెయివ్రాలు or చేవ్రాలు *cheyi-vrālu.* n. Handwriting, a signature. వారందరు ఒక చెయ్యిగానున్నారు they are all hand in hand, hand and glove with each other. ఆ పని చెయ్యికూడివచ్చినది the business turned out well. చేతికిందిమనిషి a servant, a slave. చేతిపని hand-work. చేతిసొమ్ము money in hand, cash. అతని చేతివాడు one of his creatures or hangers on. చెయ్యిబేరి sale for ready money. రొక్కపు బేరి. చెయ్యి సాగినంతలో when your hand is in, when you have the opportunity. In some phrases the word may be left untranslated: as నా చేతికిచ్చెను he gave it to me; lit. to my hand చెయికావలి means a supply of rice, &c., provided for dinner at a future stage in a journey. చెయ్యికావలికి నాలుగురూపాయలు ఎత్తిపెట్టుకొన్నాడు he laid up something to meet contingencies. కరిడిచెయ్యి అద్దము like a looking-glass in the hand of a bear. చేతకాని idle, paltry, incapable. In some compounds it means extra, as చెయ్యికావలి or చెయిమాన్యత a reserve, or extra ground; చెయ్యితడి ఆరకముందు తీర్చుచెయ్యి do it before your hand cools. చెయ్యిఈటె a small spear. తాళపుచెయ్యి a key. నీచేతినుంచి తగులుతుంది, or, చెయ్యికరుచును you will have to lay out some money. చెయ్యిచేసికొను to handle, interfere, meddle with, to use the hand;

to take the law into one's own hands and beat. చెయ్యివిడుచు to abandon, desert, give over (a person). చెయ్యిచూచు to feel the pulse. చెయ్యితిరిగిన *cheyyi-tirigina.* adj. Experienced, expert, handy. చేయువు or చేయువు *cheyuvu.* n. An act, an action.

చెర *chera.* [Tel.] n. A prison. కారాగృహము. Imprisonment, captivity నిర్బంధము. యుద్ధములో బలాత్కారముచేత పట్టుకోబడ్డది, ఖయిదు. చెరబోవు to go to jail. చెరపట్టు or చెరగొను to take one a prisoner, to capture, to carry away by force; to ravish a woman. చెరచూరలు *chera-chūralu.* n. Rape and robbery. చెరచూరలుపట్టు *chera-chūralu-paṭṭu.* v. t. To ransack or overhaul, to sack. చెరసాల *chera-sāla* n. A prison house or dungeon. చెరబడు or చెరబోవు to be taken prisoner, to be captured or carried away.

చెరకడము or చెరకు Same as చెరుకు.

చెరగడ్డము *chera-gaḍḍamu.* [Tel.] n. The plant called *Indigofera enneaphylla.* Rox. iii. 376.

చెరగు or చెంగు *cheragu.* [Tel.] n. The hem or skirt of a garment. అంచు, కొంగు. Direction దిక్కు. కొంగుచెరగునకట్టిన రూకలు money tied in the skirt. చెరగుమాసిన menstruous. బండిచెరుగు the ropes used as traces for a cart.

చెరప *cherapa.* [Tel.] n. A cheek. చెక్కిలి, చెంప. చెరపనచేటు *cherapana-chēṭu.* n. A worthless wretch. పనికిమాలినవాడు, నాశకుడు, నాశకురాలు.

చెరమ *cherama.* [Tel.] n. A hole. A nostril. ముక్కు చెరమలు the nostrils. Swa. iv. 72.

చెరలాడు or చెల్లాడు *cheral-āḍu.* [Tel.] v. n. To move. సంచరించు. To spread (as smoke) వ్యాపించు: To wallow or play in water. To frisk, gambol. To play with, to sport with, క్రీడించు. చెల్లాటముచేయు. చెరలాట, చెరలాటము or చెల్లాటము *cheral-āṭamu.* n. A game, sport. ఆట. Moving about సంచరించుట, విహారము.

"సీ. కుంజమంటపకుటీ క్రోడమున్గ్యంబున
నాథుతో జెరలాడునడవిపిల్ల."
కాశి. ii.

"రగడ. అలముకొని పెంటిచె
రలాటములు గూటములు,
జలిపెనహి పక్షివ్యాగ
ఝాటములు గీటములు."
రాఘు. ii.

చెరలు *cheralu.* [Tel.] v. n. To be eager or emulous. BD. v. 959; vii. 80.

చెరవ or చెరవము *cherava.* n. A kettle. (Commonly called చేరవకుండ).

చెరి *cheri.* [Tel.] adv. Apiece, each. ఒక్కొక్కనికి. చెరిసగము పుచ్చుకొన్నారు each took half.

చెరుకు or చెరకు *cheruku.* [Tel.] n. The sugar cane. ఇక్షువు. Wood కట్టెలు. వంటచెరుకు kitchen fuel. చెరుకుపందెము a feat of skill and strength in sword play or with an axe, which consists in lopping off a stem of sugar cane at a single blow in any proposed manner. చెరుకువిల్తుడు or చెరుకువిలుకాడు an epithet of Manmadha, as his bow is made of sugar cane. చెరుకుపిచ్చిక *cheruku-pichchika.* n. The yellow-throated sparrow. *Gymnorhis flavicollis,* (F. B. I.) చెరుకడము or చెరకడము *cheru-kaḍamu.* n. Jaggery, బెల్లము.

చెరుగు *cherugu.* [Tel.] v. a. To winnow. చేటను చెరిగినట్లువచ్చినది it came as though it were winnowed. ఎండనిప్పులుచెరుగుచున్నది it rains fire.

చెరుచు or చెరచు *cherutsu.* [Tel.] v. a. To spoil, చెడజేయు; to hurt, to ruin, నశింపజేయు; to ravish, debauch. చెరుపు or చెడుపు *cherupu.* n. Damage, harm, ruin, loss, spoiling, dissension. పని చెరుపు hindrance, prevention. పనిచెరుపు కథ

a nonsensical idle story. చెరుపుదల *cheru-pu-dala.* n. Injuriousness, hurtfulness. చెరుపరి one who spoils or ruins. నాశకుడు.

చెరుము *cherumu.* [Tel.] v. n. To rub. రాచు.

చెరువు *cheruvu.* [Tel.] n. A tank or artificial lake. తటాకము. v. a. To insert, stick in, to cut. చెక్కు. To pierce (గ్రుచ్చు). A. v. 152. Kanak iv. 263. n. Cutting into slices చెక్కుట. చెరువు కాకి *cheruvu-kaki.* n. A cormorant.

చెర్లకోల *cherla-kōla.* [Tel.] n. A whip with several lashes.

చెలక *chelaka.* Same as చెలిక. (q. v.)

చెలక *chelaka.* [Tel.] n. A field, particularly when fallow చెలకదూరము a field's length.

చెలగట్లు or చెలగాటలు *chelagatlu.* [Tel.] n. Gambols, capering. చెల్లాటము.

చెలగు *chelagu.* [Tel.] v. n. To appear, arise, occur, befall, take place, happen, ఒప్పు; enjoy oneself. Resound శబ్దించు; break forth, be felt (as a passion,) come to light, be betrayed, to break out (as a sore). పుష్పవర్షముచెలగె. a shower of flowers took place. To flourish, be strong. ఒప్పు. To rejoice ఉత్సహించు. సంతోషించు. To sound శబ్దించు, బొబ్బరించు. చెలగించు *chelagintsu.* v. a. (causal of చెలగు) To betray, give forth, emit (sighs). చెలగిననిట్టూర్పుల చెలగించి చెలగించి more and more plainly were his sobs heard.

చెలపి Same as చెలిమి.

చెలప or గేదెచెలప *chelapa.* [Tel.] n. A buffalo heifer about three years old.

చెలమ *chelama.* [Tel.] n. An orifice or bore; a small pit dug in the dry bed of a stream for drawing water, దొరువు. నాభి చెలమ the pit of the navel. Vijaya. iii. 13. T. ii. 111.

చెలరేగు *chela-rēgu.* [Tel. చెలగి+రేగు] v. n. To burst out, to riot, to rise as a mob, break out as thieves, to be excited, to be put on one's mettle, to be provoked; to xult. విజృంభించు.

చెలామణి *chelāmani.* [H.] adj. Current, as coin.

చెలి or చెలికత్తె *cheli.* [Tel.] n. A girl's companion, a playfellow, a gossip, a playmate, a confidante. చెలియ, స్నేహితురాలు. చెలికాడు *cheli-kadu.* n. A companion, a friend. స్నేహితుడు. చెలికారము *cheli-karamu.* n. Friendship. చెలిబోటి *cheli-bōti.* n. A female companion, a bridesmaid.

చెలిక, చెలక or చెల్క *chelike.* [Tel.] n. A fallow field. బీటినేల. పురిచెలిక (from పురి fresh) a field lately left fallow. పట్టి చెలక a field long left fallow. చెలకనేల or చెలక మేర a field's length. పంటనేలకొలబాటు.

చెలిది, చెల్ది, చెలది or చెలంది *chelidi.* [Tel.] n. A scab, an ulcer, a sore, a syphilitic affection. చర్మరోగము. చెలిదిపురుగు a spider. A. vi. 75. BD. iii. 572. Kalah. ii. 100.

చెలిమి *cheli-mi.* [Tel. చెలి+ఇమి, from చెల్లు to pass or be mutual.] n. Friendship, intercourse, agreeableness, kindness. స్నేహము. చెలిమికత్తె *chelimi-katte.* n. A female gossip or confidante. చెలికత్తె. చెలిమికాడు *chelimi-kadu.* n. An intimate, a companion. చెలికాడు. చెలియ *cheliya.* n. A female friend, a female companion. స్నేహితురాలు.

చెలియలికట్ట *cheliyali-katta.* [Tel. from చెల్లు to cease, అల a wave, and కట్ట a bank.] n. The sea-shore. Lit: The "bank where the wave stops."

చెలియలు Same as చెల్లెలు.

చెలువ *cheluva.* [Tel.] n. A beautiful woman. UH. iv. 267. B. X. 22 : 3. చెలువము or చెలువు *cheluvamu.* n. Manner, way. విధము. Beauty అందము. ఆచెలువము in that manner, thus, so. చెలువుడు *cheluvudu.* n. A beautiful person. సుందరుడు. A friend. ప్రియుడు. A lover. విటుడు. A husband భర్త.

చెల్ల, చెల్లా, చెల్లగో, చెల్లరే or చెల్లరే. *chella.* [Tel. from చెల్లు to pass] interj. Alas! It is all over! it is past.

చెల్ల *chella.* [Tel.] n. The herb *Asparagus racemosus* (Hēyne.). శాల్మలీయవృక్షము.

చెల్లచెదరు or చెల్లాచెదరు *chella-chedaru.* [Tel. చెదరు+చెదరు.] adj. Confused, horrible, ruinous. మిణ్గురు చెదరు. Flying on all sides like sparks from the anvil.

చెల్లాడు *chell-ādu.* [Tel.] v. n. To frolic, to play pranks. చెల్లాటము *chell-āṭamu.* n. Sport, play. పిల్లికి చెల్లాటము, ఎలుకకు ప్రాణసంకటము it is sport to the cat but death to the rat.

చెల్లి *chelli.* [Tel. Contracted from చెలియ, a playmate. n. A younger sister. See చెల్లెలు.

చెల్లు *chellu.* [Tel.] v. n. To pass (as time), కడచు. To be spent or exhausted (as money), తెలవడు. To be over, to terminate అయిపోవు. To die చచ్చు. To pass current (as a story or a coin.) To suffice, to be valid. To belong to, to pertain to, to be appropriate, suit, correspond to, తగు, తక్కు యగు. To happen, to be accomplished కొనసాగు. To be paid or discharged (with reference to debt.) దీనికి నాకు చెల్లినది I have done with it. చెల్లురా well done! చెల్లే or చెల్లిన pp. Valid, current, fit, proper, applicable, efficacious. చెల్లని uncurrent, inapplicable, inadmissible. చెల్లుబడి *chellu-badi,* n. Authority అధికారము. చెల్లించు *chellintsu.* v. a. To pass (time, life, a rule, &c.), to pay, liquidate, to fulfil. To apply or put to a right use. చెల్లు *chellu.* n. Payment. చెల్లుపెట్టుకొను to credit in accounts or strike a balance. చెల్లుచీటి a receipt for payment. చెల్లుచూచుకొను to consider a sum as paid.

చెల్లెలు, చెల్లియలు or చెలియలు *chellelu.* [Tel. See చెల్లి.] n. A younger sister. పెద్దచెల్లెలు and చిన్నచెల్లెలు denote the elder and younger of two junior sisters.

చెల్వు Same as చెలువ. (q. v.)

చెల్వము Same as చెలువము. (q. v.)

చెవి *chevi.* [Tel.] n. An ear. A key. మాట చెవినిపెట్టు to give ear to, to hearken. చెవులు గడియలు పట్టెను his ears were ringing through faintness. పత్రముయొక్క చెవి the tip or margin of a written bond. పత్రపు చెవి చించు to cancel a bond by tearing the leaf so as to disengage it from the cord on which palm leaf volumes are strung. చెవికొన or చెవికొనకు the tip of the ear. చెవిటి *cheviti.* [చెవి+అవిటి.] adj. Deaf. n. A deaf man. బధిరుడు. చెవి చిల్లుపడేపాపము an unspeakable or unutterable iniquity, lit. one which makes one stop one's ears. చెవిటిమూగ *cheviṭi-mūga.* n. A deaf mute. చెవుడును మూగతనమును గలవాడు. చెవినిల్లుగట్టుకొని చెప్పు to reiterate a precept, as though keeping ti always dwelling in the ear. Mrityanjaya Vilasam ii. 38.—40. "నిచ్చలుచెవినిల్లుగట్టుకొని చాటితినన్నుగణింప వైతివెన్నలియుని తోడి పోతివి." Rāghava Pāndavīyam. iv. 52. Vēma iii. 2. P. i. 533. చెవియాకు or చెవ్వాకు *chevi-y-āku.* n. An ear ornament కమ్మ, లక్కాకు. చెవికట్టు *chevi-kattu.* n. The iron ring on an axle tree. చెవుడు (చెవి+అవుడు) *chevudu.* n. Deafness. (The inflected form is చెవిటి.) చెవుడుపడు *chevudu-padu.* v. n. To become deaf. చెవుడుపరుచు to deafen. చెవులపిల్లి *chevula-pilli.* n. The black-naped Hare, *Lepus nigricollis.* (F. B. I.) కుందేలు. చెవులపోతు *chevula-pōtu.* n. A buck hare కుందేలు, శశకము.

చే che

చే *chē.* [Tel. contracted from చేయి or చెయ్యి.] n. The hand. చెయ్యి. An elephant's trunk తొండము. చేసరచు to pat the hand. చేసంజ్ఞ a sign made with the hand. చేసా

మన a present given in person. చేగలమె గము an elephant. చేగలవాడు a charitable person. చేతప్పు a slip of the pen. చేబదులు or చేతియప్పు a simple debt as distinguished from a bond debt. చే like "hand," when used *adjectively* sometimes means Small, as చేపెట్టె a hand box, చేకత్తి a small knife, చేబాడిస a small adze. చే or చేత affix. By, through, with. తనచేతైనంతదూరి abusing them to the utmost in his power. చేకూలి *chē-kūli*. n. Hire. చేకూలివాడు a hireling, a hired servant. B.D. v. 396.

చేంతాడు or చాంతాడు *chēn-tadu*. [Tel. చేదు+తాడు.] n. The rope used for drawing water from a well.

చేకట్లు or చేకటిగుండ్లు *chē-katlu* [Tel.] n. Bracelets made of gold and coral beads alternately. హస్తభూషావిశేషము.

చేకురు, చేకూరు, చేకూడు *chēkuru*. [Tel.] v. n. To come to hand. To accrue, be gained or be found. లభించు, సిద్ధించు, హస్తగతమగు.

చేకొంజు or చేకొందుడు *chē-konuzu*. [Tel.] n. Yellow white-ants పచ్చరంగుగల చెదలు.

చేకొను *chē-konu*. [Tel. చే=చెయ్యి.] v. a. To accept, receive, take, గ్రహించు. To grant, accede to అనుగ్రహించు. To encourage, to console ఆదరించు. To attain or assume power. To conquer జయించు. చేకొలుపు the causative of చేకొను.

చేగ or చేవ *chēga*. [Tel.] n. Strength. బలము. The heart of a tree. BD. ii. 556. చేగగడ్డ *chēga-gadda*. n. The medicinal root called *Vangueria Spinosa*. Rox. i. 536.

చేజేత *chē-jēta*. [Tel. చేయి+చేత.] adv. Hand in hand, hand over hand: rapidly, at once. చేజేతపట్టుకొన్నారు he was caught in the act.

చేట *chēta*. [Tel.] n. A winnowing basket or fan. చేటకూరప్పు or చేటప్పు *chēta-kūr-appu*. n. A loan of grain, grain lent to be paid in grain or advanced on trust to a buyer. చేటకొల్లారు *chēta-kollaru*. n. A sloping roof without side walls, as over a door. A shed. మూడింద్లుకలిపికట్టినది. చేటచేరు *chēta-chēru*. n. A mode of dress worn by women ఆడువారియొక్క ఒకవిధమైన కోకకట్టు. చేటచేరుపు *chēta-chērupu*. n. An easy slope, a gradual rise.

చేటి or చేటిక *chēṭi*. [Skt.] n. A female servant. పనికత్తె.

చేటు *chēṭu*. [Tel.] n. Work, పని. Ill, harm, ruin, waste, spoiling, misfortune, disaster. కీడు, నాశము. చేటుపాటుచెరిసగము sharing the loss and gain. చేటుకాలము a period of misfortune. చేటుమూడు to be ruined or destroyed. చేటుడు *chēṭudu*. n. A man servant పనివాడు. చేట్లకొరివి *chēṭla-korivi*. n. A perfect firebrand, i. e., an unfortunate or useless person. నిర్భాగ్యుడు.

చేడియ or చేడె *chēḍiya*. [Tel.] n. A damsel, a woman or lady, ఆడుది; a woman, a female companion చెలికత్తె, వనిత.

చేడ్పడు *chēḍ-padu*. [Tel.] v. n. To be ruined. To grieve, be in pain. బాధపడు (M. XII. ii. 285.) చేటునుపొందు. చేడ్పరుచు *chēḍ-parutsu*. v. t. To ruin, to rout. M. VII. iv. 166. చేడ్పాటు *chēḍ-pāṭu*. n. Misery, ruin, rout. బాధ.

చేత *chēta*. [Tel. from చేయి or చెయ్యి.] (Locative) In the hand. నాచేత అయ్యేపని చేస్తాను I will do what I can. ఆ పని నీచేత అవునా can you do that work? వారిచేత పుచ్చుకొంటిని I received it from them or at their hands. n. Doing, చేయుట. An act, action. పని. చేతకాని *uncanny*, useless, unprofitable, awkward, vile. చేతకాడు an able man శక్తియుక్తుడు. (As an affix.) By, through, by means of, with. "నిజహస్తంబుచేత." (HD. i. 1612.) with his own hand. చేతగట్టు an artificial mound కృతకాద్రి.

చేతనము *chētanamu*. [Skt.] n. Consciousness. తెలివి. An animal or living creature. ప్రాణముగల జంతువు.

చేతరాసి or **చేతలాసి** *chēta-rāsi*. [Tel.] n. A kind of potherb. *Pharnaceum Mollugo diffusa*. Ainsl.

చేతరికము *chētarikamu*. [Tel. చేయు+రికము.] n. Evil. కీడు.

చేతవులు *chē-tavulu*. [Tel.] v. n. To accrue to, లభించు. To incur a loss నష్టిపడు.

చేతస్సు *chētassu*. [Skt.] n. Consciousness, intelligence. The mind or intellect: the understanding. మనస్సు. **చేతస్కుడు** *chētaskuḍu*. adj. Inclined, willing, desirous, minded. భీతచేతస్కుడై filled with fear, alarmed. మందచేతస్కుడు a blockhead. క్రూరచేతస్కుడు a hard hearted man. **చేతోజాతుడు** or **చేతోభవుడు** *chētō-jātuḍu*. n. The mind-born, i. e., Manmadha. చేతోమోదము gladness of heart.

చేతాకు *chē-tāku*. [Tel. చేయి+తాకు.] n. Daring. సాహసము.

చేతాళము *chē-tālamu*. [Tel. చేయు+ Skt. తాళము.] n. Clapping the hands. **చేతాళము** or **చేతాళియము** adj. Artificial, not natural. చేతాళలింగము an artificial lingam: a truncated cylinder: also called అనాది, in contradiction to the స్వయంభువు or conical form.

చేతి *chēti*. [Tel.] adj. Of the hand. చేతి సొమ్ము money in hand, cash in hand. చేతి బిడ్డ an infant.

చేతి or **చేదు** *chēti*. [Tel.] adj. Bitter. చేదు చూ. **చేతిపొట్ల** *chēti-poṭla*. n. The bitter snake-gourd. **చేతిబీర** *chēti-bīra*. n. The bitter cucumber. **చేతివిత్తు** *chēti-vittu*. n. A raw or bitter fruit. **చేతి** or **చేదు**. n. Bitterness: gall. A wretch.

చేద *chēda*. [Tel.] n. The rope fastened to a bucket for drawing water. Also, a bucket. నీళ్లచేదపాత్ర. చేదనీళ్లు a bucket of water. చేదబావి a draw well.

చేదండ *chē-daṇḍa*. [Tel చే=చెయ్యి.] n. A garland for the hand.

చేదరాసి *chēda-rāsi*. Same as చేతరాసి. (q.v.)

చేదర్థకము *chēd-arthakamu*. [Skt. చేత్+అర్థకము] n. The subjunctive or conditional form of a verb.

చేదర్నవము Same as చేకాముక. (q. v.)

చేదారము *chēdāramu*. [Tel.] n. Loss, waste, diminution (of gold, in making jewels.)

చేదివిటీ *chē-diviṭī*. [Tel.] n. A torch. దివిటీ.

చేదు *chēdu*. [Tel.] v. a. To draw up (as a bucket) hand over hand. ఆకర్షించు, తోడు. To raise (an anchor.) **చేదుడు బావి** *chēduḍu-bāvi*. n. A draw well, in which the bucket is raised by the hand.

చేదు *chēdu*. [Tel.] n. Bitterness. adj. Bitter.

చేదోడు or **చేయుదోడు** *chē-dōḍu*. [Tel. చేయు+తోడు] n. A helper. కార్యసహాయుడు.

చేన *chēna*. [Tel.] adj. Much, long. This is the old spelling, and the rustic pronunciation at this day, of చాన, చేనా or చెనా.

చేను *chēnu*. [Tel.] n. A corn field. పంటచేలు. A forest అడవి. జొన్నచేను a field of maize.

చేప *chēpa*. [Tel.] n. A fish. A sort of torturing pincers to twitch the ears with. చేపజిగురు Pisces, the source of Isinglass. *Acipenser huso*. (Watts).

చేపట్టు *chē-paṭṭu*. [Tel. చే=చేయు.] v. a. To take by the hand. గ్రహించు. To adopt, to patronise అవలంబించు. To help. To marry. పెండ్లియాడు. n. Adoption అవలం

బనము. Kindness అనుగ్రహము. A place స్థానము. చేపట్టుకుంచేను one who tries to please every body. చేపడు chē-paḍu. v. n. To fall into one's hands, to be seized or caught. పట్టుబడు, చిక్కు, లభించు.

చేపు chēpu. [Tel.] v. n. To let the milk flow, to give forth, emit (as a breast does milk). ఎగచేపు to withhold the milk, or keep it from flowing, as a cow does unless her calf is near her. "కరము సంతసిల్లికుమారుం, గనిచన్నులు చేపిమురంబున." (M. I. v. 37.) at the sight of her child the milk sprang from her breast with affection. ఆవు పాలుచేపలేదు the cow withheld her milk. చేపాకు a plant the leaves of which are given to cows to make them give milk freely. చేపు or చేపుడు n. A gush or spirt, as of milk. చేపుట.

చేబాడిస chē-bāḍisa. [Tel. చే=చేయి.] n. A small adze. చిన్నబాడిస.

చేబియ్యము chē-biyyamu. [Tel. చే=చేయి.] n. Rice that is cleaned by the hand.

చేబీర chē-bīra. [Tel. చే=చేయి.] n. The small herb called *Justicia ligulata*. Rox. i. 126.

చేబోడి chē-bōḍi. [Tel. చే=చేయి.] n. A penniless man. నిర్ధనుడు.

చేమ chēma. [Tel.] n. Bur-grass. చెట్టుచేమలు trees and so forth. A plant, the *Arum esculentum* ఆలుకము. Heyne. Rox. iii. 495. A. ii. 62. చేమగడ్డ chēma-gaḍḍa. n. The root termed *Caladium esculentum*. Heyne. చేమదంటు its stock or stump. చేమపూరాజనములు chēma-pū-rāzana-mulu. n. plu. A peculiar sort of paddy.

చేమంతి chē-manti. [Tel. from చేయి+బంతి.] n. The Chrysanthemum, *Indicum* and *Coronarium*. (Watts). A sort of Chamomile. Ainslie. i. 67 Rox. iii. 436. సీమచేమంతిచెట్టు. The common or true Chamomile, *Anthemis nobilis*. (Watts).

చేమటఆవు chēmaṭi-āvu. [Tel.] n. A particolored cow. చిత్రవర్ణములుగల ఆవు.

చేమిరి chēmiri. [Tel.] n. Sour butter milk which is kept to curdle milk with.

చేమోడుచు or చేమోడ్చు chē-mōḍutsu. [Tel. చే=చేయి.] v. n. To salute. మొక్కు, నమస్కరించు. చేమోడుపు a salutation.

చేయలతి chē-y-alati. [Tel.] n. Nearness. సమీపము. adj. Near.

చేయి See under చేయు.

చేయు chēyu. [Tel.] v. a. To do, make, perform. నొప్పిచేయు or నొప్పిపెట్టు to pain. వంటచేయు to cook. జగడముచేయు to quarrel. ఖైదుచేయు to imprison. స్వాధీనముచేయు to put in one's charge. వర్తకముచేయు to trade. మరుగుచేసికొను to take shelter, use as a screen. బేరముచేయు to settle the price. అప్పుచేయు to contract a debt. నన్ను ఆడదాన్నిచేసి looking upon me as a mere woman. ఈ బిడ్డ నెలబిడ్డచేసినది the infant looks a month old already. బిడ్డ మైనా ఒళ్లుచేసినదా is the child picking up flesh? కాజేయు to misappropriate, to settle, to kill. పల్లకి చేసికొన్నాడు he procured a palankeen. పెండ్లిచేసికొన్నది a wedded wife. పిడికిలిచేసికొని కొట్టె he closed his fist and beat them. అండచేసికొను to take refuge. రహస్యంబుచేసికొని చెప్పెను. (M: XIII. ii. 375) he told it as a secret. చేయు v. n. To do, act, behave. To be worth. అది పదిరూకలుచేయును it will be worth ten groats. వానికి జలుబుచేసినది he caught cold. చేయి chēyi. [lit: That which does or works.] n. The hand. చెయ్యి or చెయి. A ray కిరణము. A trunk తొండము. A wing. రెక్క. Two cubit's length రెండుమూరలపొడవు. A hold or grasp పట్టు. చేయించు chēyintsu. v. a. To cause to do or make. To get done.

చేర chēra. [Tel.] n. The hollow of the hand. చేరెడు chēr-eḍu. [Tel.] n. A handful. A proverb says చచ్చినవాడికన్నులు చేరడేసి a dead man's eyes are a hand's breadth, i. e., very fine!

చేరిక *chērika*. [Tel. from చేరు.] v. n. Joining. కూడిక. Nearness. సమీపము. Arrival, entrance, union, approach, familiarity, application. చేరడము, చావునకువచ్చె యుండు యము.

చేరు or **చారు** *chēru*. [Tel.] n. The native soup usually termed mulagatanny, or pepper water.

చేరు *chēru*. [Tel.] v. n. To arrive, reach the destination, come to hand. To be close or in contact. To lean ఒరగు. To draw near or approach సమీపించు. To be connected with, united to. To be added, joined, included. To belong, appertain. To be assembled or collected. ఆపద్దు ఈ లెక్కలో చేరదు that item does not belong to this account. ఇది ఆ చట్టములో చేరదు this does not fall under that rule. వాకిలి చేరవేసినావా have you shut the door? తలుపుచేరవేసి (BD. v. 234.) setting the door ajar. వానిచేరరమ్మని చేరంబిలిచి calling him near or close. చేరపట్టు to bring close (as a boat to ship) n. A string, a cord, a string of pearls or flowers. సరము, త్రాడు, గొలుసు. A row or a string of spawn in fish. ఉట్టిచేరు the cord on which a net hangs. పాలచేరులు the milk glands. కురువిందచేరులు necklaces of Kuruvinda seeds. కనకపుచేర్లు gold chains. **చేరుచు** or **చేర్చు** *chērutsu*. v. t. To put together, to join, unite, mix, combine, include, add. చేకూర్చు. To assemble, accumulate. To admit, as a member, to introduce. కౌగిలిచేర్చు to embrace. **చేరుకొను** *chēru-konu*. v. a. To touch, to lean upon, to join. శత్రువులతో చేరు కొన్నాడు he joined the enemy. **చేరుగడ** *chēru-gaḍa*. n. Nearness సమీపము. A refuge, దిక్కు, శరణము. adj. Near సమీప మైన. **చేరుగొండి** *chēru-gonḍi*. adj. Stray, strayed. Mischievous. దుష్టము. చేరుగొండి పశువు a stray cow; a wife who has been irregularly married. **చేరుచుక్క** or **చేర్చుక్క** *chēru-tsukka*. n. A jewel worn on the forehead. ముత్యాలబొట్టు, పాపట బొట్టు. **చేరుడు** *chēruḍu*. adj. Accidental, what comes by chance, not expected. చేరుడుపశువులు stray cattle. చేరుడు బియ్యము rice that is roughly pounded or bruised. **చేరుపు**, **చేర్పు** or **చేరువడి** *chērupu*. n. Nearness, closeness, connection. చేరుపు దిమ్మ an abutment. **చేరుపాటు** *chēru-pāṭu*. n. Arrival. **చేరువ** or **చేర్వ** *chēruva*. n. Nearness, neighbour-hood; సమీపము. An assemblage, సమూహము. An army, host. సేన. adj. Near. సమీపమైన. **చేరువ కాడు** *chēruva-kāḍu*. n. The leader of an assembly, a chairman, ఒక సమూహమునకధి పతి. A commander of an army సేనాధి పతి. A watchman కావలివాడు. **చేరుమకోల**, **చేరులకోల**, **చేర్కోల** or **చేర్లకోల** *chērura-kōla*. n. A whip. కొరడా, కొరడా. **చేరుబొందు** *chēru-bondu*. n. A strap of leather to beat with కొట్టే తోలు పట్టెడ.

చేరోలి *chērōli*. [Tel.] n. A kind of sea fish.

చేలము or **చేల** *chēlamu*. [Skt.] n. A covering, a garment, clothing. వస్త్రము. పంటి చేలము the lips; as being a covering to the teeth. adj. Low, base. అధమము. **చేలాంచలము** *chēlānchalamu*. The skirt.

చేవ *chēva*. [Tel.] n. Strength; the heart of a tree, the core, సారము. Courage ధైర్యము. పగడాలచేవకంబములు pillars of solid coral. **చేవచెట్టు** or **చేవమాను** *chēva-cheṭṭu*. n. The timber called Redwood, or Amur timber. *Ampora Rohituka*. (Watts). ఎర్రవి శకము.

చేవడి *chēvaḍi*. [Tel. చే(=చేయి)+వడి.] n. Lightness of hand, swiftness. హస్తవేగము. A. i. 71.

చేవలతి *chē-valati*. [Tel. చే=చేయి.] adj. Easy, controllable. అధీనము.

చేవాటు *chē-vāṭu*. [Tel. చే=చేయి.] adj. Near, close. సమీపము. చేవాటునేల a neighbouring place. HD. i. Lit: a stone's throw off.

చేవాడికాడు *chē-vaḍi-kāḍu*. [Tel. చే=చెయ్యి.] n. A sharper, a light fingered or expert fellow; a thief. చెయ్యిచురుకుగలవాడు, దొంగ.

చేవిచ్చు *chē-vitstsu*. [Tel. చే=చెయ్యి.] v. n. To salute. దండము పెట్టు. **చేవిప్పు** *chē-vippu*. n. Salutation. దండము.

చేవెలుగు *chē-velugu*. [Tel. చే=చెయ్యి.] n. A torch. దివటీ.

చేవ్రాలు *chē-vrālu*. [Tel. చే=చెయ్యి.] n Hand-writing, a signature. సంతకము.

చేష్ట *chēshṭa*. [Skt. from Tel.] n. An act, deed or gesture; conduct, manners. క్రియ, పని. పిల్లచేష్టలు childish behaviour. చేష్టించు to play pranks చేష్టలుచేయు.

చేసి *chēsi*. [Tel.] n. An affix: By, through, because of, by reason of. చేత. అరుగు దెంచుటంజేసి by coming. దర్శనంబున జేసి. Swa. v. 3.

చేసేత *chē-sēta*. [Tel. చేయు+చేత.] n. Handiwork చేపని. adv. From hand to hand ఒక రొకరిచేతిమీదుగా. Then and there అప్పుడే.

చై chai

చైతన్యము *chaitanyamu*. [Skt. from చేతనము.] n. Consciousness. తెలివి. Life ప్రాణము. Locomotion, ability to move.

చైత్యము *chaityamu*. [Skt.] n. A temple. గుడి. A Buddhist temple బౌద్ధాలయము. A place of sacrifice యజ్ఞశాల. A tree in a garden where people meet. రచ్చచెట్టు.

చైత్రము *chaitramu*. [Skt.] n. The name of the first month in the Telugu year, answering to April-May. **చైత్రరథము** *chaitra-rathamu*. n. The garden of Kubera కుబేరునితోట. **చైత్రసఖుడు** or **చైత్రసారథి** *chaitra-sakhuḍu*. n. Manmatha the god of love, as delighting in the month of చైత్రము.

చో chō

చోదితము *chōditamu* [Skt.] adj. Sent, directed, commanded. వేదచోదితమైన declared in the Vedas. **చోదితుడు** *choditudu*. n. One who is sent, directed, told, or commanded.

చోద్యము *chōdyamu*. [Skt.] n. Wonder, marvel, singularity, peculiarity. ఆశ్చర్యము. చోద్యమందు being amazed. adj. Wonderful, singular, rare, refined.

చోరుడు *chōruḍu*. [Skt.] n. A thief. దొంగ. **చోరీ** *chōri*. n. Theft. చోరుసక్తి a spy (Vizag.) **చోరభర్త** *chōra-bharta*. n. A paramour, a lover by stealth.

చోలము or **చోళి** *chōlamu*. [Skt.] n. A woman's jacket or boddice. రవిక.

చోళదేశము or **చోడదేశము** *chōla-dēsamu*. [Skt.] n. The Chola country. The ancient name for the country around Conjiveram.

చోష్యము *chōshyamu*. [Skt.] adj. That which may be sucked, as sauce. పీల్చదగిన.

చౌ chau

చౌర్యము *chauryamu*. [Skt. from చోర.] n. Theft, robbery.

చౌలము *chaulamu*. [Skt.] n. The ceremony of tonsure, shaving off the hair of a child, three years old, with the exception of one lock, left on the crown of the head. జుట్టుపెట్టి కొలిచెంత్రుకలు తీయుట.

చ్యు chyu

చ్యుతము *chyutamu*. [Skt.] adj. Dropped down. జారిన. **చ్యుతి** *chyuti*. n. Dropping జారుట. Letting go విడుపు. Destruction నాశము.

చ tsa

చంక *tsanka.* [Tel.] n. The armpit. బాహుమూలము, కక్షము. The gill of a fish. చంక కాళ్లు crutches. **చంకతాళి** *tsanka-tāli.* n. A bundle or load hanging down under the armpit. చంకను తగిలించుకొను మూట.

చంగు *tsangu.* [Tel.] n. Agility. చంగున Lightly, with agility. **చంగలించు** *tsangalintsu.* v. n. To move. చలించు.

చంటి See చన్ను. **చంటిపిల్ల** *tsanṭi-pilla.* [Tel.] n. A suckling, a child at the breast.

చండి *tsanḍi.* [from Skt. చండి.] n. A name of Pārvati పార్వతి. A stubborn man మూర్ఖపుపట్టుగలవాడు. A cruel man క్రూరుడు. **చండితనము** *tsanḍi-tanamu.* n. Stubbornness, obstinacy. **చండిపోతు** *tsanḍi-pōtu.* n. A wretch, an obstinate man. H.D. ii. 1498.

చండ్ర *tsanḍra* [Tel.] n. An acacia tree ఖదిరము. కవిరిచండ్ర or నల్లచండ్ర The Catechu gum tree. *Acacia catechu.* ఆంచండ్ర *Acacia ferruginea.* తెల్లచండ్ర *Acacia suma.* నల్లచండ్ర *Acacia sundra.* (Watts.)

చందమామ *tsanda-māma.* [Tel.] n. The moon. The yolk of an egg సొన. చందమామముక్కిళ్లు or చందమామముద్దులు kissing or smacking the lips as a sign of being stricken with love. అధరామృతము. శబ్దా. ర. **చందమామపక్కె** *tsandamāma-pakke.* n. A kind of fish: a sprat. **చందమామపురుగు** *tsandamāma-purugu.* n. A lady bird: ఇంద్రగోపము, ఆరుద్రపురుగు.

చందము *tsandamu.* [Tel.] n. Manner, way; state, form. విధము.

చందా *tsandā.* [H.] n. A money subscription. చందాదారుడు a subscriber. **చందావేయు** *tsandā-vēyu.* v. a. To subscribe, contribute.

చందురుడు or **చందమామ** *tsanduḍu.* [Tel.] n. The moon చంద్రుడు. చందురిక moonlight వెన్నెల.

చందుకా *tsanduka.* [H.] n. A box or trunk. A drawer.

చందుగు *tsandugu.* [Tel.] n. A kind of tree.

చందురము or **చంద్రము** *tsanduramu.* [Tel.] n. Red lead, సింధూరము, కుంకుమము. **చంద్రకావి** or **చందురకావి** *tsandra-kāvi.* n. Rose colour: pink. చందురుకావిశాలు a scarlet cloth. A. v. 95.

చందురా *tsandurā.* [Tel. రాంరాయి.] n. The moonstone. చంద్రకాంతము.

చందురుడు Same as చంద్రుడు. q. v.

చందువ or **చందువా** *tsanduva.* [Tel.] n. A canopy. T. iii. 133; మేలుకట్టు.

చందువాయి *tsandu-vāyi.* [Tel.] n. The fish termed the black Pomfret. *Stromateus.* Russell (No. XLIII.) A species of turbot. చెందువాయి.

చంకెబల్లింద *tsanke-ballinda.* [Tel.] n. (K) A wretch, a villain. Chenna. v. 33.

చంద్రపొద *tsandra-poda.* [Tel.] n. The elephant creeper, *Argyreia speciosa.* (Watts.)

చంపు *tsampu.* [Tel. casual of చచ్చు.] v. n. To kill. చంపుడుగట్టు a place of execution. వధస్థానము. **చంపించు** *tsampintsu.* v. a. To cause to kill.

చకచక or **చకచక** *tsaka-tsaka.* [Tel. Anuk.] adv. Brilliantly. Fast.

చక్క or **చక్కగా** *tsakka.* [Tel.] adj. and adv. Beautiful సుందరము. Right, straight, correct, due, proper. చక్కపోయినాడు he departed straightway, he went away. చక్కచేయు to repair, amend, set right, settle, సవరించు. To finish ముగించు. చక్కపెట్టు to set right: to perform, finish: to destroy నాశముచేయు; to kill. చక్కపడు to become right. సరిపడు.

చక్కటి *tsakkati.* [Tel.] n. A place, స్థానము: a direction, దిక్కు: neighbourhood; business కార్యము. Fitness, suitability. అర్హము, సామ్యము. చక్కట్లుదిద్దు to settle a matter తీర్చుదిద్దు. అతనిచక్కటికి to him, అతనివద్దకు.

చక్కడచు or **చక్కడుచు** *tsakk-adatsu.* [Tel.] v. a. To quell అణిచివేయు; to outrival: to cut to pieces ఖండించు. To kill చంపు.

చక్కన or **చక్కదనము** *tsakkana.* [Tel.] n. Prettiness, beauty. adv. Prettily, properly. **చక్కని** *tsakkani.* adj. Pretty, nice, fit, right, correct, proper. Straight, not crooked. చక్కనిబుద్ధి good sense. చక్కనిది a pretty woman. చక్కనినిద్ర sound sleep. చక్కనివాసన a nice smell. నా చక్కనిస్వామి my sweet lord. **చక్కనయ్య** *tsakkan-ayya.* n. A name of the god of love. మన్మథుడు.

చక్కాడు *tsakk-adu.* [Tel. చక్కు+ఆడు.] v. a. To finish, end, kill.

చక్కి or **చక్కియ** *tsakki.* [Tel.] n. A side, పార్శ్వము. A part, place స్థానము. అచక్కికి there, to that place: so, thus, that way. ఏచక్కి where. కటిచక్కి the loins. చక్కిచొల్ల every limb or part. చక్కిని, చక్కికి near, close by.

చక్కిలము *tsakkilamu.* [Tel.] n. Biscuit made of twisted rings of paste without sugar.

చక్కిలి *tsakkili.* [Tel.] n. The armpit. చంక. **చక్కిలిగింత** or **చక్కిలిగిలి** *tsakkili-ginta.* n. Tickling. **చక్కిలిగింత పెట్టు** *tsakkili-ginta-pettu.* v. a. To tickle.

చక్కి *tsakki.* [Tel.] n. The frame or bottom of a palankeen or litter. అడుగుపట్టు.

చక్కిపంచదార *tsakki-pantsadara.* [Tel.] n. Refined sugar.

చక్కు *tsakku.* [Tel.] n. Mince meat. కూరచెక్కు. ఖండము. Destruction. adv. Piecemeal. చక్కుగా కోసెను he chopped them up; he destroyed them. M. iv. 183. L. XVI. 223. **చక్కు** *tsakku.* n. Six at dice, &c. **చక్కుపగడ** *tsakku-pagada.* n. Seven, in games. **చక్కుచేయు** *tsakku-chiyu.* v. a. To chop, shiver, crush, smash. ఖండించు.

చక్కెర *tsakkera.* [Tel.] n. Sugar. శర్కర. **చక్కెరతిండి** *tsakkera-tindi.* n. A parrot చిలుక. చక్కెరబుఱడ a kind of sweet cake. భక్ష్యవిశేషము. చక్కెరవిలుకాడు he who carries the sweet bow, i. e., Manmatha the god of love. మన్మథుడు.

చక్కొలుపు *tsak-kolupu.* [Tel.] v. t. To set straight. చక్కగాచేయు. BD. iii. 385. iv. 1776.

చగుడు Same as చవుడు.

చచ్చౌకము *tsats-tsarukamu.* [Tel. చవుకము+చవుకము.] n. Square. నలుచేదరము.

చచ్చు *tsatstsu.* [Tel.] v. n. To die: to expire. చచ్చుమాట a deadly word, a curse. చచ్చుమన్ను solid earth: mere earth: loose dry earth. ఘోరపుచావుచచ్చె he died a horrid death. చచ్చుఅప్పు a bad debt. కారముచచ్చిన ఆవాలు mustard that has lost its sharpness. చచ్చి బ్రతికినాడు he has had a narrow escape. **చచ్చువాయువు** *tsatsu-vayuvu.* n. Paralysis, cramp. వాని కాళ్లు చచ్చుఅయిపోయినవి his legs have become paralysed.

చచ్చుడివాండ్లు *tsatstsudi-vandlu.* [Tel.] n. A particular tribe of scavengers.

చటాలున or **చటేల్లున** *tsataluna.* [Tel.] adv. Suddenly. అకస్మాత్తుగా.

చటులుపడు *tsatulu-padu.* [Tel.] v. n. To become blunt. మొక్కపోవు.

చట్ట *tsatta.* [Tel.] n. The outside of the thigh. తొడకు వెలుపలిభాగము. A jacket, a coat. చొక్కాయి. A small sack. కొంచెము ధాన్యమునుపోసిన చిన్నగోనె. A coating పూత.

చేట్టున or **చట్టున** *tsaṭṭana.* [Tel.] adv. Hastily, quickly. వెంటనే. BD. iv. 338.

చేట్టము *tsaṭṭamu.* [Tel.] n. A frame. A plan, a system, a rule, a regulation, an ordinance, a statute, a law. A cage. A gang or set. A pedestal, a stand. పునుగుచట్టము the gland or bag of musk found in the civet cat. See Suca. i. 186. 7. "పునుగుచట్టముపిండినట్లు" they tortured this meaning out of his letter. అచట్టమైనది it happened just in that manner, such was the case.

చేట్టలుచీరు *tsaṭṭalu-chīru.* [Tel.] v. t. To kill. చంపు. చేట్టలుపాపు to destroy నాశము చేయు.

చేట్టి *tsaṭṭi.* [Tel.] n. A shallow earthen dish.

చేట్టు *tsaṭṭu.* [Tel.] n. A rock. రాయి. చేట్టుమన్ను hard soil. చేట్టునుయ్యి, చేట్టుపడ్డనుయ్యి a well abandoned because found to be over an impenetrable rock. చేట్టురాయి or చేట్రాయి the living rock. చేట్టువాడు. (HK. iv. 864.) a wretch, a villain. A disciple శిష్యుడు. **చేట్టుతనము** *tsaṭṭu-tanamu.* n. Inexorability, cruelty: a stony or rocky stubbornness.

చేట్టుప *tsaṭṭupa.* [Tel.] n. A wing. రెక్క. Swa. iv. 30.

చేట్టుపము *tsaṭṭupamu.* [Tel.] n. A spoon, a ladle. గరిటె, తెడ్డు.

చేట్రము *tsaṭramu.* [Tel.] n. A frame (corruption of చేట్టము.)

చేట్రాయి or **చేట్టురాయి** See under చేట్టు.

చతికిలు, చతికిలబడు or **చదికిలు** *tsatikilu.* [Tel.] v. n. To sink or fall down, from fatigue or weakness, to succumb, yield, give way. To sit flat on the ground, not on the folded legs. పిర్రలు నేలమోపు.

చదర *tsadara.* [Tel.] n. A small mat to sit on. కూర్చుండే చిన్నచాప.

చదరంగము *tsadarangamu.* [Skt.] n. Chess.

చదరము *tsadaramu.* [Skt.] adj. Square, level, even. n. A square. **చదరములు** *tsadaramulu.* n. The beams of the roof, resting on short upright ones.

చదలము *tsadalamu.* [Tel.] n. An army. సైన్యము.

చదలు *tsadalu.* [Tel.] n. The sky. ఆకాశము. **చదలుకాపు** *tsadalu-kāpu.* n. A god, a heavenly being. **చదలుమాణికము** *tsadalu-māṇikamu.* n. The jewel of the sky, i. e., the sun. **చదలేరు** *tsada-l-ēru.* n. The heavenly stream, i. e., Ganges. ఆకాశగంగ. Swa. iii. 143.

చదికిలబడు or **చదికిలు** Same as చతికిలు.

చదియు *tsadiyu.* [Tel.] v. n. To be crushed. నలుగు. To burst, to be broken చేదియబడు. to shrink back కూలబడు, కుంగు. **చదియ** *tsadiya.* n. Crushing. నలుగుడు.

చదుకము *tsadukamu.* [Tel.] n. A way where four roads meet. నాలుగుమార్గములు కలియుచోటు. **చదుకు** *tsaduku.* n. Mud, mire. బురద, పంకము.

చదును *tsadunu.* [Tel.] n. Evenness, levelness సమము. Level ground సమప్రదేశము. adj. Even, level సమము. చదునుచేయు to level.

చదుపు *tsadupu.* [Tel.] v. a. To break to pieces. To make even with the ground. To level or destroy చదియజేయు. చంపు.

చదుము *tsadumu.* [Tel.] v. To strike with the fist. గుద్దు.

చదుర or **చదురాలు** *tsadura.* [from Skt. చతుర.] n. A clever woman. చతురతగలస్త్రీ. HD. ii. 183. **చదురుడు** *tsadurudu.* n. A clever man విద్యావంతుడు.

చదురు *tsaduru.* [Tel.] n. An assembly. The court of a prince సభ. A dance ఆట కచ్చేరి. Skill నేర్పు. A joke, jest. చతురులు,

jests, riddles. చతురోక్తులు. "పెంజదుములు" (R. iv. 157.) మంచినైపుణ్యములు. A. ii. 48. **చదురుచేయు** or **చదురాడు** *tsaduru-chēyu*. v. n. To hold court. To joke, gibe. పరిహాసముచేయు.

చదువు *tsaduvu*. [Tel.] v. a. To read, to study. **చదువు** n. Learning. చదువులు studies. చదువులబడి a school. చదువులయ్య a schoolmaster. **చదువుకొను** *tsaduvu-konu*. v. n. To learn. నేర్చుకొను. **చదువు చెప్పు** *tsaduvu-cheppu*. v. To teach. నేర్పు. **చదువులపులుగు** *tsaduvula-pulugu*. n. The educated bird, i. e., a parrot, Bhasc. § 70. చదువులవేల్పు the god of learning బ్రహ్మ. **చదువరి** *chadur-ari*. n. One who reads, one who can read. A student, a learned man. **చదివించు** *tsadi-vintsu*. v. a. To make one read; to get some one to read. ఆ జాబును చదివించుకొంటిని I got the letter read to me. To get proclaimed what one presents to a bride or bride-groom on the occasion of their marriage. **చదివింపులు** *tsadivimpulu*. n. Homage or adoration accompanied with a certain recited formula.

చద్ది *tsaddi*. [Tel. Contraction from చలిది] n. Cold rice.

చనవు Same as చనువు. (q. v.) **చనవరి** *tsanav-ari*. [Tel.] n. A pet, a favorite. చనవుకలవాడు. Sumati. § 54. చనవురాలు a favorite woman చనవుగల ఆడుది.

చను Same as చన్ను. చనుగవ and చనుకట్టు. See under చన్ను.

చను *tsanu*. [Tel.] v. n. To go, depart, పోవు; to pass కడచు. To be deserving, to be proper, right, fit. చెల్లు, తగు. చూడ చనదు it is not fit to be seen. v. a. To get, to have పొందు. చన్నంతదవ్వు. (BD. i. 869.) as far as he went. చనునే is it right?

"క॥ అనుటయుం బ్రవరుం డిట్లను
వనజేక్షణ యిట్లు పలుక పరుసరొ ప్రమరై
గినముల గడపెదు విప్రుల
జనునే కామింప మది విచారము వలదే."
Manu. ii. 56.

చనిపోవు *tsani-pōvu*. v. n. To die. **చను వెంచు** *tsanu-dentsu*. v. n. To go, proceed. పోవు. To come వచ్చు. **చనుదేరు** *tsanu-dēru*. v. n. To proceed, to go or come.

చనుప *tsanupa*. [Tel.] n. A body of travellers, a caravan. బిడారు.

చనుపకము Same as చంపకము. (q. v.)

చనుపాలు or **చనుబాలు** *tsanu-pālu* [Tel.] n. Human milk. చనుపాలవిత్తులు the seeds of *Cassia Absus* (Watts).

చనుమర *tsanu-mara*. [Tel. మర=మరక.] n. The black circle round the breast A. vi. 25. 104. M. vii. iv. 105. **చనుమొన** or **చన్మొన** *tsanu-mona*. n. The nipple. **చను మోర** *tsanu-mōra*. n. The side of the breast.

చనువు or **చనవు** *tsanuvu*. [Tel.] n. Familiarity, acquaintance. పొలపు. Affection ప్రేమ. Desire కోరిక. Privilege చెల్లుబడి. Authority అధికారము. చనువువాడు a friend or acquaintance. చనువుగాపోవు to frequent, or resort to.

చన్గవ, చన్దోయి The breasts (as a pair), చన్నులు. T. ii. 84.

చన్నీళ్లు *tsan-nīllu*. [Tel. చలి+నీళ్లు.] n. Cold water. చల్లనినీళ్లు.

చన్ను *tsannu*. [Tel.] n. The breast of a woman or man. The tubers of a palmyra or of a mangrove tree. మొగిలి ఊడ, తాటిజేగురు. చంటిపిల్ల an infant at the breast. మేక మెడచన్ను the teat-like appendages at the neck of the Indian goat. చంటిలో ఎముకలు ఏరినట్లు చేసేవాడు he is a keen investigator. చన్నుపాలు or చనుబాలు human milk. **చన్నుగవ, చనుగవ, చన్గవ, చనుదోయి** or **చన్దోయి** *tsannu-gava*. n. The two breasts. చన్నులు. చనుకట్టు,

చన్కట్టు or చన్నుగట్టు *tsanu-kattu*. n. A bodice. రవిక.

చేపచేప *tsapa-tsapa*. [Tel. anuk.] adv. Pleasantly, sweetly. Poorly, weakly.

చేపరాలు *tsapa-rālu*. [Tel.] n. Small beams across the corners of a roof.

చేప్టా *tsapta*. [Tel.] n. Pavement, flooring.

చేప్ప *tsappa*. [Tel.] n. A wedge, a spar of wood placed for the wheels of a car to pass over in a sandy road. Also, a seal. ముద్ర.

చేప్ప or చేప్పని *tsappa*. [Tel.] adj. Vapid, tasteless, insipid. రసహీనము. చేప్పనేల barren land. చప్పనీళ్లు insipid water. చేప్పబడ్డ inactive, passive, spiritless. చేప్పనిపథ్యము a plain diet. ఆ యుద్ధము చేప్పచల్లారినది the battle is entirely calmed down. చేప్పగా *tsappa-ga*. adv. Insipidly. చప్పగానుండే tasteless, unattractive. చేప్ప సొర్ర *tsappa-sorra*. n. A kind of fish *Zygæna blochii* (F. B. I.) చేప్పదనము or చేప్పన *tsappa-danamu*. n. Insipidity. చేప్పిడి *tsappidi*. adj. Flat, not projecting: insipid: void of any taste. చేప్పిడిముక్కు a flat pug nose. చేప్పిడి పిరుదులచిన్నది a thin-flanked girl.

చేప్పట *tsappata* [Tel.] n. A slap or clap. చరచుట. A fruit, &c., pressed flat as a fig. చప్పటకొను or చప్పటలగు (A. v. 21.) to become lean. సన్నగిల్లు. చేప్పట్లు *tsappatlu*. n. pl. The clapping of the hands. Derision. చేప్పట్లుకొట్టు or చేప్పట్లు చరచు to clap the hands. చేప్పటించు *tsappatintsu*. v. n. To slap, చరచు. To chuckle or cluck to a horse or ox to urge it on.

చేప్పరము or చేప్రము *tsapparamu*. [Tel.] n. A frame. చేట్టము. A canopy, a thatched roof, a shed, a covered seat in which a god is carried about: the tilt of a cot, canopy of a bed, the roof of a bower. పందిరి, గుడారము. ద్రాక్షచప్పరము a trellice of vines. చలువచప్పరకోళ్లమంచము a bed of state. (T. iii. 131.) i. e., a bed, with tester and pillars.

చేప్పరించు or చేప్పరించు *tsapparintsu*. [Tel.] v. t. To smack, to suck with a noise. నాలికకైనుంచి రుచిచూచు

చేప్పాతిపురుగు *tsappati-purugu*. [Tel.] n. The cochineal insect, *coccus cacti*.

చేప్పాలు or సన్నలు *tsappalu*. [Tel.] n. Wedges or blocks placed to turn the course of a cart, &c.

చేప్పి Same as చేప్పిడి. See under చేప్ప.

చేప్పుడు or చేప్పిడి *tsappudu*. [Tel.] n. Noise, sound. చేప్పుడించు to make noise.

చేప్పున *tsappuna*. [Tel.] adv. Quickly; entirely.

చేబుకు *tsabuku*. [Tel.] n. A whip. చేబుకుచెట్టు a casuarina tree, or the Beefwood of Australia. *Casuarina equisetifolia*. (Watts.) చేబుకుచేయు to whip.

చేమరు or చేమరు *tsamaru*. [Tel.] v. n. To give a slap with the palm of the hand. అరచేతకొట్టు. To slay. చంపు. v. a. To rub. రాచు. రెండుగట్టులంచేమరుకొని rubbing, or in collision with both banks. n. Grease Clarified butter, any oily fluid or greasy liquid. క్షీరచమరు milk punch. చమురుపోతు (G. i. 102.) a fat beast.

చేమ్మకాయ *tsamma-kaya*. [Tel.] n. The sword bean, or, a Patagonian bean, *Canavalia ensiformis* (Watts.)

చేమ్మగా *tsamma-ga*. [Tel.] adv. Pleasantly. చేమ్మదనము n. Happiness.

చేయ్యన *tsayya-na*. [Tel.] adv. Quickly, speedily, anon, at once, soon.

చేరచేర *tsara-tsara*. [Tel.] adv. Quickly.

చేరచు or చేరుచు *tsaratsu*. [Tel.] v. a. To slap, to clap, to applaud. అరచేత కొట్టు. అరచేతతట్టు. To beat కొట్టు. మల్లచేరచుట to clap the shoulders with the hands in defiance, as boxers do. చేప్పట్లు చేరచు,

(A. iv. 34.) to clap the hands in derision. Parij. ii. 44. చేరపు *tsarapu*. n. The act of giving a slap, or clapping. ఆస్ఫాల నము. A cover ఆచ్ఛాదనము.

చేరి or చేరియు *tsari*. [Tel.] n. A hollow or gorge under a mountain. A precipice. లోయ, పర్వతనితంబభూమి. Starch, gruel used as paste. చేరిపూయు to paste or starch. Some kinds of rice are called మణిచేరులు, కన్నెసరులు, దీవసరులు, &c. H. iv. 156. చేరికుండ a pot of paste used by a weaver. సాలెవానికంజికుండ.

చేరుగుడు or సరపడి *tsarugudu*. [Tel.] n. A hurdle on which a heap is placed to be drawn by bullocks.

చేరుడు Same as చేరు.

చేరుము *tsarumu*. [Tel.] v. t. To apply as wax or ointment. To smear, daub. రాచు.

చేర్రన or చేర్రున *tsarra-na*. [Tel. anuk.] adv. Rushingly, rapidly, quickly.

చేలము *tsalamu*. [Tel.] n. Spitefulness, malice, ill-will. మాత్సర్యము. Insolence, obstinacy. Rudeness, fury, రోషము, మొటము, పొడి. చేలముసాధించు, చేలముకొను, చేలపట్టు or చేలపూను to entertain spite. ఇది చేలమా ఫలమా (a proverb) did you do this with an object or through mere spite? చేలపకారము same as చేలము. చేలపాడి, చేలపకారి or చేలముకి *tsalapadi*. n. A spiteful or illtempered man. మాత్సర్యకలుడు. చేలపాడితనము *tsalapaditanamu*. n. Spite, grudge, crossness. చేలపోరు *tsala-poru*. (చలము+పోరు.) v. n. To wreak a grudge, to fight inveterately చేలముపట్టి పోరాడు.

చేలవాడి *tsala-vadi*. [Tel.] n. A messenger; who carries the news of a death. A beadle, or javelin bearer who attends the *Pedda Setti* or headman of a community, a man who summons the elders of a community to a council.

చేలి *tsali*. [Tel.] n. Cold, coolness, a chill. శీతము, శీతబాధ. చేలిజ్వరము cold and fever, i. e., ague. నాకు చేలిపెట్టినది I felt cold. చేలి adj. Cold, cool. చేలికూడు cold food, breakfast. చేలియుసుక camphor. Vasu. ii. 36. చేలిగరువు *tsali-garuvu*. n. A soil composed of marl or sand covering black earth. మీద ఇసుకగలరాతిపొరనేల. చేలికొండ *tsali-konda*. n. The Himalaya mountains. చేలిచీమ *tsali-chima*. n. A black ant. చేలిది, చేద్ది or చేల్ది *tsalidi*. n. Breakfast. Lit: cold food left over from supper. చేలిపందిలి *tsali-pandili*. n. A place where passers-by are supplied with water to drink. చేలిపండ్లు *tsali-pandlu*. n. The teeth being set on edge. (A. iv. 151. on which the note says "జాపున్నన పులుసు తిన్నందువల్ల తీకుకపొయ్యేకోటిపండ్లు.") చేలిపని a cooling operation, శైత్యోపచారము. చేలిబిండి *tsali-bindi*. n. The name of a certain plant. చేలిమల *tsali-mala*. n. The hill of snow, i. e., హిమాచలము. చేలిమిడి *tsalimidi*. n. A mixture of rice flour and sugar బెల్లము కలిపిన పిండి. చేలిమిరి or చేల్మిరి *tsali-miri*. n. Coolness చేలువ, శైత్యము. A cake. G. i. 114. చేలివాపు *tsali-vapu*. (చేలి+పాపు.) v. n. To warm, to soothe or comfort ఉపశమింపు. చేలివాలు *tsali-valu*. (చేలి+పాలు.) n. A sign ఆనవాలు. చేలివెలుగు *tsali-velugu*. n. The moon. చంద్రుడు, శీతకరుడు.

చేలుప *tsalupa*. [Tel.] n. Marble. చేపరాయి. A stone రాయి.

చేలుపు or సలుపు *tsalupu*. [Tel.] v. t. To do. చేయు. To pass (as time) గడపు.

చేలువ or చేలవ *tsalava*. [Tel.] n. Coolness, coldness, cold, శైత్యము. Any thing of a cooling or refreshing nature, such as beneficence, liberality, benignity. Bleaching, a bleaching green. Clothes newly washed. ఉతికినబట్ట. adj. Cold, cooling, comfortable, bleached, white. చలువ చేయు *tsaluva-chēyu.* v. t. To bleach, as cloth. To cool the body. చలువ వడి *tsaluvaḍi.* n. Coolness, cool air. శైత్యము. చలువమిరియము *tsaluva-miriya-mu.* n. Long pepper, cubebs. తోకమిరియము. చలువరాయి *tsaluva-rāyi.* n. White marble, alabaster. చంద్రకాంతము. చలువరేడు *tsaluva-rēḍu.* n. The moon.

చల్డి *tsalḍi.* See చలి. వానికి చలుపలు కమ్మినవి a chill came over him, i. e., he is deadly cold or in the extremity of death. చలవపందిలి *tsalava-pandili.* n. A canopy, or triumphal arch, an ornamented booth for an idol. చలువచేప్పరపుకోళ్లమంచము a comfortable bed decked out with a cover-let, tilt and pillars. చలువజ్యోతి *tsaluva-jyōti.* n. A poetical word for the moon.

చల్ల *tsalla.* [Tel.] n. Curds beaten with water, buttermilk. మజ్జిగ. చల్లకువచ్చి ముంతదాచనేల, చల్లకు పోయి ముంత దాచడమేమి why conceal your pot when you come for buttermilk, i. e., why do you beat about the bush? or, why mince the matter? చల్ల or చల్లని adj. Cool, cold. శీతము. Benign, merciful, healing. Comfortable. చల్లకము *tsallakamu.* n. Sprinkling. Watering, irrigation. చల్లుట. చల్లకడి *tsalla-kaḍi.* n. Flummery: buttermilk mingled with fenugreek. మెంతిమజ్జిగ. చల్లకవ్వము *tsalla-kavvamu.* n. A churn-staff: The bird called King-fisher: also a name for the insect called గొల్లభామపురుగు *mantis precatoria.* చల్లగడ్డ *tsalla-gaḍḍa.* n. The linear leaved asparagus. *Asparagus sarmentosus, Willden.* Hamsa. iv. 12. Ainslie. ii. 409. Rox. ii. 151. Watts. శతమూలి. చల్లగా *tsalla-gā.* adv. Easily, gently, well, safely, comfortably: in good health, softly, deliberately. చల్లగాచూచు to look at or regard with satisfaction. చల్లగామాట్లాడు to speak coolly or gently. మీదొరతనము చల్లగా నుండవలెను may your reign be peaceful! వానిచెయ్యి చల్లగా నుండవలెను may his hand be blessed! "చెలి అందరికి నన్నివగల వానందమిచ్చి, చల్లచేయుచు." (Ila. i. 79.) with her graces she charmed them all, cheering and refreshing their hearts. కన్నులచల్లచేసె (T. ii. 38.) it cheered his eyes. చల్లని చెయ్యిగల వైద్యుడు a physician with a lucky hand. చల్లనిప్రభువు a kind master. చల్లచేప్పుడు *tsalla-tsappuḍu.* n. A fool జడుడు. చల్లచీమ or చలిచీమ *tsalla-chīma.* n. A black ant, so called because it is benign or merciful in not stinging as the red ant does. చల్లజంపు *tsalla-zampu.* n. One who kills in cold blood. A cruel man ధూర్తుడు. చల్లటి *tsallaṭi.* adj. Cool. Convex. చల్లటిబిళ్ల a convex plate of glass, as distinguished from అద్దపుబిళ్ల a pane. చల్లడము or చల్లాడము *tsallaḍamu.* n. Tight drawers or breeches: short trousers, which reach as far as the middle of the thigh. The loose skirt end of the waist band that hangs in front: ఇజారు, సగముతొడవరకు తొడుగుకొనే కడిని. చల్లదనము or చల్లన *tsalla-danamu.* n. Coolness, coldness. చల్లనీరుకానిటి *tsalla-nīru-kāniṭi.* n. A sort of fish. A species of sparus. Russell's fishes. No. 104. చల్లపడు *tsalla-paḍu.* v. n. To cool. చల్లారు. చల్లపసము Same as చల్లకడి. చల్లరాడు *tsalla-rāḍu.* n. The post (తరికంబము) round which the string passes, which works the churning stick. చల్లవడియము *tsalla-vaḍiyamu.* n. A kind of cake. వడియములలో ఒకభేదము. చల్లచేయు *tsalla-chēyu.* v. t. To cool. చల్లపరుచు. చల్లారు *tsallāru.* v. n. To grow cool. చల్లపడు. To become calm, to be allayed, restrained or pacified ఉపశమిల్లు. To be extinguished. చల్లార్చు *tsall-ārutsu.* v. a. To cool or calm, to allay, restrain or pacify, to extinguish.

చెల్లు *tsallu*. [Tel.] v. a. To sprinkle, to scatter. To water or irrigate, to sow. Also (metaphorically,) of a smile *spreading* over the face. కూటిలో మన్ను చెల్లడము to throw earth in one's food, i. e., to take away one's bread, to ruin one. ఇంటిమీద నిప్పులుచెల్లిరి they scattered fire on the house. మొక్కచెల్లు to transplant corn. తోటకు నీళ్లు చెల్లినారు they pumped water into the garden. ధూళిచెల్లి sprinkling dust. చెల్లుపోరాడు or చెల్లులాడు *tsallu-pōrādu*. v. n. To fling water or dust at each other. R. I. 211. 186.

చేవక, చేవుక or **చేక** *tsaraka*. [Tel.] n. Brackishness. Cheapness adj. Cheap.

చేవచేవ *tsava-tsava*. [Tel.] adv. Bluishly, lividly.

చేవలము *tsavalamu*. [Tel.] n. One eighth of a pagoda, i. e., about half a rupee. వరహాలో ఎనిమిదవభాగము.

చేవి *tsavi*. [Tel.] n. Taste. రుచి. చేవిగాని మాటలు unpleasant words. చేవిమరిగి touched with her loveliness or sweetness. చేవిగొను *tsavi-gonu*. v. n. To taste. రుచిచూచు.

చేవిక or **చేవికె** or **చేవికె** *tsavika*. [Tel.] n. A closet, a cabinet, a bower or chamber. An arbour. Usually, a hut or open room, supported by a pillar in the centre, మండపము.

చేవితి or **చేవుతి** *tsaviti*. [Tel.] n The fourth day of the moon's age.

చేవిలె *tsavile*. [Tel.] n. Four dubs or coins, of the value of twenty cash each. Four çavilehs equal one టంకము. నాలుగు డబ్బులు.

చేవిలె *tsavile*. [Tel.] n. Leanness, thinness. చేవిలెపోయిన lean as an infant.

చేవు See చా.

చేవుకము See చౌకము.

చేవుకు Same as చేబుకు.

చేవ్వ *tsavva*. [Tel.] adv. Insipid. చేప్ప.

చేవ్వంచ *tsavvancha*. [Tel. చేవు+వంచ.] n. Five. అయిదు.

చా tsā

చాకలి or **చాకల** *tsākali*. [Tel.] adj. Appertaining to the washerman's caste చాకలి or చాకలివాడు a washerman. చాకిత or చాకలిది *tsākita*. n. A female of that caste. చాకలవాని పురుగు *tsākala-vāni-purugu*. n. A snail. చాకలసారెగాడు *tsākala-sāre-gāḍu*. n. The Pied Wagtail, *Motacilla maderaspatensis*. (F. B. I.) చాకి *tsāki*. adj. Of or belonging to the washerman's caste. చాకిరేవు the place by the water side where clothes are washed. చాకిబాన *tsāki-bāna*. n. A washerman's kettle. The name of a bird. A certain romping game.

చాకి *tsāki*. [Tel.] n. A metal dinner plate. భోజనపాత్రము, కంచము.

చాగగడ్డ, చాగచెట్టు or **చాగముల్లు** *tsāga-gadda*. [Tel.] n. The plant called Ceylon hemp. *Sanseviera Zeylanica* Ainsl. ii. 192.

చాగము *tsāgamu*. [from Skt. త్యాగము.] n. Liberality, bountifulness. A. iv. 252. M. iv. i. 62. M. xiv. ii. 71. ఈవి. చాగకాడు or చాగి *tsāga-kāḍu*. n. A liberal man. త్యాగి. చాగరతనము a ruby that grants whatever one wishes చింతామణి.

చాగర *tsāgara*. [Tel.] n. Ruin. నాశము. చాగరగొట్టు to kill, to oppress చంపు, బాధించు. చాగరకొను *tsāgara-konu*. v. t. To beat. కొట్టు. To cut to pieces ఖండించు. చాగరలాడు *tsāgaral-āḍu*. v. n. To destroy. నాశముచేయు.

చాగు or **సాగు** *tsāgu*. [Tel.] v. n. To extend or stretch. To fall prostrate: to lie flat, be stretched or extended; to be set or arranged as pearls on a thread. చాగిమొక్కు to worship, to fall prostrate.

See సాగు. చాగుబడిక tsagu-badika. n. Worship పూజ. H. iv. 305. చాగిలింత tsagil-inta. n. Prostration or homage నమస్కృతి. చాగిల్లు or చాగిలు tsagillu. v. n. To bow down to the earth నేలకు వ్రాలు. చాగుతే well done!

చాచి tsachi. [Tel.] n. A child's word for the breast. స్తనము.

చాచు tsatsu. [Tel.] v. t. To cause to extend సాగజేయు. To stretch, extend. కాళ్లుచాచు to stretch the legs.

చాటు tsatu. [Tel.] n. A shelter, or covering, a screen, or shade, a nook, any thing concealing another or preventing its being seen. మరుగు. తల్లిచాటున in her mother's charge. నేను చాటుగా నిలిచితిని I stood behind. చాటుచేయు to use as a screen. చెట్టుచాటున behind the tree. చాటుననుండే hidden, screened, unknown. పెట్టెచాటున దొరికినది I found it behind the box. ఆ కొండ చాటు ఆయినది that hill intercepts the view. చాటుగానుంచు to keep hidden. చాటు v. a. To proclaim, publish. To warn, threaten, declare. To confess, betray, evince ప్రసిద్ధిచేయు, విశదపరుచు. చాటించు tsatintsu. v. a. To proclaim, to publish, advertise, notify, make known, declare, warn, threaten, foretell, denounce. చాటింపు tsatimpu. n. Proclamation, advertisement. చాటుపడు tsatu-padu. v. n. To be hidden from view మరుగుపడు. చాటువ tsatuva. n. Proclamation చాటించుట. Comparison, పోలిక, దృష్టాంతము. చాటుమాటుమనిషి a suspicious character, a skulker.

చాడీ or చాడి tsadi. [Tel.] n. Slander, backbiting, taletelling. కొండెము. చాడీలకోరు a slanderer.

చాదుపు or చాద్పు tsadupu. [Tel.] n. A way or manner. విధము. Similitude. చాద్పున like to, such as. "బిసరుహపత్రలగ్న జలబిందువుచాద్పున" like a raindrop in a lily leaf. M. XII. vi. 202.

చాతు tsatu. [Tel.] v. t. To put on, to wear. ధరించు.

చాదు tsadu. [Tel.] v. a. To macerate, to triturate in water. n. A black colour made by burning rice; discoloration, darkness of the skin, a black spot placed on the forehead. ఎండుచాదు a dark blotch. Vasu. ii. 57. In A. v. 133. కట్టెచాదు the juice that comes out of a log at one end when the other end is burning. కుష్ఠము దగ్ధమయ్యెటప్పుడు చుంయుమని బయలుదేరేనీరు. చాదిక or చాదుచుక్క tsadika. n. A spot, mark, patch. A blotch.

చాన tsana. [Tel.] n. A woman. ఆడుది.

చాప tsapa. [Tel.] n. A mat. A sail: a sheet; a kind of net ఒకవిధమగువల. Any thing flat. చాపరాయి a flat slab of stone. తాటిచాప cakes of the juice of the ripe palm fruit. చాపన్నము, చాపప్రసాదము or చాపమంటకము a heap of boiled rice poured out on a sheet of cloth. చాపకట్టు a flat bank. చాపకట్టు or చాపమట్టుగా పడ్డారు they all fell flat. చాపగద్ద or తెల్లచాపగద్ద tsapa-gadda. n. The harrier-hawk. Jerdon's Catal. No. 25. చాపట్టు (చాప+అట్టు.) tsap-attu. n. A sort of biscuit. పలచని పెద్ద అట్టు.

చాపలు tsapalu. [Tel.] n. Difficulties. చిక్కులు.

చాపు tsapu. [Tel.] v. a. To extend. సాగచేయు. చాపు n. Length, extent. A whole piece of "cloth" పదునుకోరబట్ట.

చామ tsama. [Tel.] n. A young woman. Parij. iv. 18. A boat. ఒకవిధమగుపడవ. చామ an esculent root, Caladium Nymphæifolium. Rottler, Vol. ii. page 378. చామ n. plu. The grain called millet. Panicum miliaceum శ్యామాకములు. One species is కొంకిచామలు panicum frumentaceum. Roxb. i. 304. 309.

చామనము or చామనచాయ tsamanamu. [Tel.] n. A light complexion, a brown or straw colour. Any dark hue whether blue or black. మక్కుచామనము a dark brown. ఎర్రచామనము bistre.

చాయ *tsāya*. [from Skt. ఛాయ.] n A shadow or shade. నీడ. A colour, a hue, a paint, రంగు, కాంతి. A view, a light, a side or quarter వైపు. Prospect, probability. పోలిక. Trace జాడ. Nearness సమీపము. Straightness ఋజుభావము. ఆ చాయను towards that direction. నాచేతిచాయను వెళ్లు go where I point. ఆ పైరు చాయగా నున్నది the crop is flourishing. నీ చాయలు అట్లు ఉండనిమ్ము have done with your nonsense! H.N. i. 73, and v. 52. కొయ్యచాయ the grain of wood. In wood, నిలువుచాయ the straight grain, అడ్డచాయ cross grain. చాయపప్పు bleached pulse. చాయపసుపు fine turmeric. చాయపట్టి lit. the son of ఛాయా the wife of the sun, i. e., Saturn శని. చాయమగడు lit. the husband of shadows. i. e., the Sun. చాయపారు to resemble పోలు. చాయవేయు *tsāya-vēyu*. v. t. To dye or colour, to paint.

చార *tsāra*. [Tel.] n. A line, a streak. చారలచీర a striped petticoat. చారలమెకము lit. the striped beast, i. e., the tiger. చార, చారమామిడి or చారచెట్టు n. A jungle tree, *Buchanania latifolia*. (Watts.) చారపండు is its fruit; and చారపప్పు or చారబియ్యము its kernel. చారకంద *tsāra-kanda*. n. An esculent and medicinal root, described as sweet, cooling and diuretic. *Colocasia nymphaenefolia*. చారలగాడు *tsārala-gāḍu*. The Magpie Robin. *Copsychus saularis*, పెద్ద నల్లంచి. పకలచారలగాడు the Large Pied Wagtail. *Motacilla maderaspatensis* (F. B. I.)

చారిక *tsārika*. [Tel.] n. A line or streak. చార.

చాల or చాలా *tsāla*. [Tel. from చాలు.] adj. Much, abundant. మిక్కిలి. Many అనేకమైన. adv. Enough, very much, plentifully. To a great length or extent.

చాలించు *tsālintsu*. [Tel. from చాలు] v. a. To cease, to leave off, to quit, to desist. నిలుపుదలచేయు. వాడు దేహము చాలించెను he died. (lit. left the body.) వెదచాలించినాను I abstained from sowing corn. చాలించుకొను to resign, to desist from, to give up (as an employment) చాలిక *tsālika*. n. Ability సామర్థ్యము. చాలమి inability అశక్తి.

చాలు *tsālu*. [Tel.] v. n. To suffice, to be enough or sufficient. కావలసినంత అగు, సమృద్ధమగు. To be able. To bear, tolerate, endure ఓర్చు. చాలును (3rd pers. aor.) it is enough. చాలదు (neg. aor.) it is not enough. అనజాలరు they cannot say. బుద్ధిచాలదు నీకు (Dasav. iv. 195.) you have not sense enough. చాలీచాలకయిది జరిగించినాడు he committed this out of dire necessity. చాలీచాలవు these are barely enough. ఈడు చాలిన grown, of full age. ఈడుచాలని under age, immature. జ్ఞాపకముచాలదు I do not sufficiently remember it. నా గ్రహచారము చాలక యిట్లు సంభవించెను through my luck not being good enough it so happened. వావులుచాలు enough of these words about relationship.

> " చాలి నేమను సురల్ వడిచాకవంక
> చాలిరి యొకవంక చాలి రక్కసులు."
>
> T. iii. 117.

On our side we were mighty, and so were our foes. చాలు n. Sufficiency, abundance సమృద్ధి. A line, a row, series, furrow, stripe, track, trace. A flow or stream. Features, తల్లిచాలుపోలిక resemblance to the mother's features. ఈచాలున in this manner. శ్రేణి, సరణి, జాడ. A. v. 122. R. i. 106. 117. చాల్గల, i. e., చాలుగల. (Vasu. i. 57) in a stream. చాలుపు or చాల్పు *tsālupu*. n. A line or row. A series, succession. Length: the longer measurement as opposed to the width. చాలుపుగా in a line, one after another, here and there, occasionally. చాలుబడి ability, చాలిక, సామర్థ్యము. చాలు

వాడు one who is able శక్తుడు, సమర్థుడు. చాలుపారు to be fine or pretty ఒప్పారు.

"శ్రీ మించి కలశేత్తి నిక్కుచు
సలలితగతి చాలుపార సస్యములెల్లను."
భాగ. x.

చావడి or చావిడి or చావిడి *tsavadi.* [Tel.] n. An audience chamber కొలువుకూటము. A lodge: a post house: a portico or court: a porch: a caravanserai or rest house for the use of wayfarers. A hospital. A barrack room. ఎడ్లచావిడి a cowhouse. సూరేకారముచావిడి salt-petre works or a saltpetre manufactory. చావడిమాటలు town-talk, common report: what everybody knows. తల చావిడి a gate house or hall. ఒకచావిడి a reception room.

చావు *tsāvu.* [Tel.] n. Death. తల్లిదండ్రులచావుపిల్ల an orphan. చావుపిట్ట the hooting barn-owl. Jerdon, No. 37. చావుబిడ్డ a still born child. చావుదెబ్బ a mortal blow. చాపరువు (చావు+పరువు.) *tsa-paruvu.* n. A killing rate of speed. Manu. iv. 72.

చు tsu

చుంగు or చెంగు *tsungu.* [Tel.] n. A skirt, the end of a cloth. చుంగులు, అనగా బట్ట కొనల్లు కొంగులు.

చుంగుడి *tsungudi.* [Tel.] adj. Odd (applied to money), not even. చుంగుడు *tsungudu.* n. A trifling or petty sum (balance or arrear) పదిరూపాయలుచుంగుడు ten rupees and odd. నిలువనాసన్న చిల్లరసొమ్ము.

చుంచు *tsuntsu.* [Tel.] n. A projecting ledge on a house. The lock or knot of hair left on a man's shaven head. పిల్లజుట్టు. Strength బలము. A little child, an infant, శిశువు. A muskrat. సుంచెలుక. చుంచుమూతిపెట్టు to pout the lips. Lit. To make a face like that of a muskrat. చుంచు adj. Young. చుంచుబాలుడు a young child. చుంచు మగుబాలు an infant. చుంచుమిద్దె *tsuntsu-midde.* n. An overhanging tower or turret. గోపురమువలెపొడుగుగాకట్టిన కట్టడము. చుంచు రాయి *tsuntsu-rāyi.* n. A sort of slate stone used for roofs.

చుండి, చుడి, చుడీ, చుండీ, చుందు or చుదు *tsundi.* [Tel. for చూడుడు.] interj. Indeed, you see!

చుండు *tsundu.* [Tel.] n. Scurf or dandruff. చుండు v. n. To evaporate or dry up. To be flicked (as water from the finger.) చుండించు *tsundintsu.* v. a. To decoct, or dry up. చుండెలుక *tsund-eluka.* n. A mouse. The grey musk shrew; the musk-rat of Anglo-Indians. *Crocidura caerulea.* (F. B. I.)

చుంబు See చెంబు.

చుకాయించు *tsukāyintsu.* v. t. To complete, settle, adjust or fix a price.

చుక్క *tsukka.* [Tel.] n. Any small mark; a dot or spot: a drop, a small quantity of liquid. బొట్టు. The round mark (తిలకము) worn on the forehead by Hindus. A star, నక్షత్రము. The planet Venus, శుక్రుడు. A pip on the dice or cards. A comet. తోకచుక్క. చుక్కతిరిగెను it is past midnight. చుక్కకాడ *tsukka-kāda.* n. An annual plant, a native of wet rice fields. *Spermacoce stricta.* Rox. i. 370. చుక్కకార *tsukka-kara.* n. A sort of fish. *Sternoptyx diaphana.* Gmelin. చుక్కకూర *tsukka-kūra.* n. A kind of sorrel. చుక్కచేరు a jewel worn on the forehead; a row of stars చుక్కలచాలు. చుక్కపిల్ల *tsukka-pilla.* n. A kind of fish. చుక్కపిల్లి *tsukka-pilli.* n. A tabby cat. చుక్కబొట్టు *tsukka-bottu.* n. An ornamental spot worn on the forehead. తిలకము. చుక్కయెదురు a star full in front ఎదురుచుక్క. చుక్కలము *tsukkalamu.* n. A spot in the eye due to an injury or to disease. చుక్కలి or చుక్కిలి *tsukkali.* n. A tree called *Trophis Aspera.* Rox. iii. 762. బరెంక. చుక్కలతెరువు the sky ఆకాశము. చుక్కలరేడు the moon. చుక్కవాలు *tsukka-vālu.* n.

An evil planet or unlucky star. Particularly of Venus (చుక్క, i.e., శుక్రుడు), for the Hindus believe that every journey will turn out ill if on setting out this star faces them.

చుక్కాని or **చుక్కాను** *tsukkāni.* [Tel. చుక్క+ఆను.] n. A rudder, a helm.

చుక్కిల్లు *tsukkillu.* n. Wrinkles.

చుక్కి *tsukki.* [Tel.] n. A telescope, a spy glass. ఓకు, దుర్భిణి.

చుచ్చు *tsutstsu.* [Tel.] n. A goat. మేక. బర్రెచుచ్చాలమెట్లు slippers made of buffalo, goat or cow hide. A. vi. 91. A sorrowful cry. చుచ్చాయనిపించు to soothe; to silence. చుచ్చుకొట్టు to sigh, to cry in sorrow.

చుచ్చురుకు *tsutsts-uruku.* [Tel. చురుకు+చురుకు] adj. Very sharp. మిక్కిలి తీక్ష్ణమగు. చుచ్చురుకు పలుకులు very sharp or bitter words.

చుట్ట *tsutta.* [Tel.] n. A ring. A roll of anything, anything rolled up as a leaf, a cheroot or cigar. A ring, a pillar. A relation. చుట్టలు relations, చుట్టములు. అలుకుచుట్ట a roll of cloth dipped in cow-dung and water to smear floors with. చుట్టకుదురు a pad placed on the head to support a pail, &c. చుట్టచేసికొను to hem in or surround, to roll oneself into a mass.

చుట్టము *tsuttamu.* [Tel. from చుట్టు] n. Kin, kindred. బంధుత్వము a relation, a kinsman or kinswoman బంధువు. చుట్టపక్కములు kindred, kith and kin—here పక్కము has no meaning. A proverb says తలచుట్టము తోక పగ I like the head but hate the tail, i. e., I avow one kinsman and disavow another. **చుట్టరికము** *tsutta-rikamu.* n. Kinship, relationship

చుట్టు *tsuttu.* [Tel.] v. a. To go about, to go round. To roll, wrap up, to wind up, to encircle or clasp in an embrace. To hem in, surround, to overtake (as sin does). To draw a circle. To make small ciphers, thus: సున్నచుట్టు, క్రారాడిచుట్టు to write ం or ు; పాగాచుట్టు to tie a turban. చుట్టుకొను or చుట్టుపారు to surround, hem in, roll up. To turn, to go round. దోవచుట్టుకొని పోతున్నది here the road makes a sweep. **చుట్టు** n. A turn, a round, a circuit, a circumference. A turn or bout: a time. A toe ring, worn by women కాలియుంగరము. తలచుట్టు a turban. గోరుచుట్టు a whitlow. ఎన్నిచుట్లు చెప్పేది how often am I to tell you? **చుట్టు** adj. & adv. Around, round about, out of the direct way. **చుట్టలుగు**, **చుట్టువాలు** or **చుట్టుకైదువు** *tsutt-alugu.* (చుట్టు+అలుగు.) n. The Discus of Vishnu చక్రమనే ఆయుధము. R. iii. 42. చుట్టిల్లు a round hut without posts or pillars: చుట్టివచ్చు to go round anything; ప్రదక్షిణము చేయు. To surround పరివేష్టించు. **చుట్టుకొల్లారము**, **చుట్టుకొల్లాను** or **చుట్టుమాలె** *tsuttu-kollāramu.* n. A house built round an open area, with a chamber at each corner and a gallery between. **చుట్టుగుల్ల** *tsuttu-gulla.* n. A volute shell. సుడిగ్రుడ్ల శంఖము. **చుట్టుదల** *tsuttu-dala.* n. The act of surrounding చుట్టుట. **చుట్టుతిరుగు** *tsuttu-tirugu.* v. n. To go the rounds, as a patrol. **చుట్టుపట్టు** *tsuttu-pattu.* n. All sides. Roundabout. **చుట్టుపడు** *tsuttu-padu.* v. n. To fall out of the direct route: to go round. **చుట్టుముట్టు** *tsuttu-muttu.* v. n. To encamp around, besiege, hem in, surround. Vish P. viii 64. **చుట్టువేడెము** *tsuttu-vēdemu.* n. Riding a horse round the ring. Dasav. x. 145. గుర్రపుమండలగతి. **చుట్టువేలు** or **చుట్టనవేలు** *tsuttu-vēlu.* n. The forefinger. "చుట్టువేలనచెక్కుచూపంగ గలిగె." R. iv. 167. **చుట్టూరు** *tsutt-ūru.* adv. Roundabout.

చుదుము *tsudumu.* [Tel.] n. A bur, a teazle. The small weaver fish, *Trachinius Draco.*

చునాయించు *tsunāyintsu.* [Tel.] v. t. To fold a cloth. బట్టమడతపెట్టు.

చుప్పనాక or చుప్పనాతి *tsuppa-nāka.* [Tel. from శూర్పణఖ.] n. A syren, a harpy, a cruel selfish wretch.

చుబ్బనచూర *tsubbana-tsūra.* [Tel. చూర+చూర.] n. Great plunder. మిక్కిలి చూర, పెద్దకొల్ల adv. To the full, to the heart's content: utterly. Irresistibly. At pleasure. M. IV. ii. 91.

చుమి, చుమ్మ, చుమా, చుమ్మి, సుమీ *tsumi.* [Tel.] Interj. Indeed: Do you see? Is it not so? Remember, take care. This is contracted from చూడుమీ the imperative of చూచు. చేసు Look! చూడుము. .

చుమ్మ *tsumma.* [Tel.] n. Severe pain, agony. వేదన. చుమ్మలుచుట్టు *tsummalu-tsuttu.* v. n. To retch in the stomach. కడుపులో గాలించు. To be troubled కలగు, వేదనపడు.

చుయ్యంకి *tsuyyanki.* [Tel.] n. A trumpet. A. iv. 36. సానాయి.

చుయి or చుయ్యి *tsuyi.* [Tel.] n. Fizz, hiss, a sound to express a crackling or hissing sound. చుయి, జలాగ్ని సంయోగముచేత పుట్టే ధ్వని.

చురకత్తి or చురి *tsura-katti.* [Tel.] n. A small knife. చిన్నకత్తి, చురియ.

చురచుర *tsura-tsura.* [Tel.] adv. Fiercely (burning) చురచురకాలు, to burn quickly తీవ్రముగా కాలు.

చురుకు or చురుక్కు *tsuruku.* [Tel.] n. Heat, a burning sensation. వేడిమి. Sharpness, fierceness. వాడిమి. Activity, agility, smartness, intelligence. Speed, impetuosity. వేగము. adj. Sharp, hot, fierce, violent. Rapid, impetuous, active, smart: brilliant (as rubies). చురుకుగా or చురుక్కున *tsuruku-gā.* adv. Sharply, hotly, fiercely, actively. చురుక్కును to wince, be sharp, to be hot. చురుకరి *tsuruk-ari.* n. A man with much 'go' in him, an energetic man చొరవగలవాడు. చురుపుచ్చు *tsuru-putstsu.* v. a. To burn. దగ్ధముచేయు. To be sharp, hot, eager. చుర్రు *tsurru.* adj. Hot. వేడి. చుర్రుమను *tsurru-m-anu.* v. n. To hiss or sputter, as the fire, or boiling water. To shudder, to tingle with horror. చుర్రు చుర్రుమనినది it was hot to taste: it made the tongue smart. చుర్రున *tsurru-na.* adv. Fiercely (burning).

చులక, చులుక, చులకతనము, చులకదనము, or చులకన or చుల్కన *tsulaka.* n. Lightness, ease, facility: slight, scorn. చులకనగా చూచు to despise, to treat with contempt, చులకని *tsulakani.* adj. Light, easy, slight, worthless, contemptible. చులకనిపంట a light crop or lesser harvest.

చుల్ల or చుల్లి *tsulla.* [Tel.] n. The male organ. శిశ్నము.

చుల్లజుండు *tsulla-jundu.* [Tel.] n. A blain or indolent sore. మొటిమవంటి చిన్న సెగ్గురు గడ్డ.

చుల్లరము *tsullaramu.* [Tel.] n. A sow. ఎద అయిన ఆడపంది. Swa. iv. 51.

చువక or చువ్వ *tsuvaka.* [Tel.] n. A twig, a switch, a supple cane, a withe, a slender arrow, the stick of a rocket, a shaft, a slip of wood. గాలపుచువ్వ a fishing rod. చువ్వచువ్వ అడుగుచది it throbs painfully, severely, smartly. చువ్వున *tsuvvu-na.* adv. At once, suddenly.

చువ్వె or చువ్వే *tsuvve.* [Tel. Contracted for చూడవె.] adv. Surely, of course.

చూ tsū

'చూ *tsū.* [Tel.] Interj. Look! behold!

చూకురు *tsūkuru.* [Tel.] n. Crying, wailing. శోకము. చూకురుపడు to cry.

చూచా *tsūchā.* [Tel.] (Anuk) n. A trifle. చూచా తప్పకుండచదివి having read it without missing a syllable.

చూచాయ *tsū-tsāya.* [Tel. చూపు+చాయ.] n. A trace. జాడ. Lightness. తేలిక. చూచాయగా adv. Slightly, indistinctly.

చూచు *tsūtsu.* [Tel.] v. a. To see, to look, view, observe, perceive. To consider, meditate, think on. To visit. To wait. To take care, be on one's guard. To regard, care for. To try, to attempt, to see to. To experience, try, prove by any sense. చేతితో చూచితిని I felt it with my hand. చేవిచూచితిని, రుచిచూచితిని I tasted it. To estimate, to judge. రాజూచు to acknowledge the receipt. మరలిపోజూచు to think of going back. అతనిప్రాణముచూడక not caring for his life. సమయముచూచు or తరి చూచు to watch for an opportunity. ఉండజూచు to overhaul, to see that a thing is there. నన్ను చంపజూచిరి they tried to kill me ప్రేమలొలుకు చూపుల జూచి casting glances that beam with love. సరిచూచు to examine, to see if a thing is right, to check. వాసనచూచు to smell. చెయ్యిచూచు to feel the pulse. వాడు చెప్పేమాటలు చూడు attend to what he says. అతనిపని చూస్తున్నాను I am acting for him. నెలదినములవఱకు చూచితిని I waited for a month. చూచుకొను *tsūtsu-konu.* v. a. To see or perceive. To look silently, look for oneself.

చూడి *tsūḍi.* n. Pregnancy of cattle. చూలు, పశుగర్భము. adj. Pregnant. చూలుగొన్న. చూడియావు *tsūḍi-y-āvu.* n. A cow in calf.

చూడికి Same as చూడ్కి.

చూడు *tsūḍu.* [Tel.] n. Heat, sultriness.

చూడు *tsūḍu.* [Tel.] v. a. To burn or brand with a hot iron. కాల్చు, వాతవేయు. To light a match. A. v. 89. R. ii. 93. M. III. vi. 322. n. Branding. వాత. చూడుకొఱ్ఱు an iron for branding cattle with, పశువులకు వాత వేసే కోల.

చూడ్కి *tsūḍki.* [Tel.] n. A view, a sight, a glance. చూపు.

చూపట్టు *tsū-paṭṭu.* [Tel.] v. n. To appear, అగుపడు, కనబడు. To be fair, or beam with beauty.

చూపు *tsūpu.* [Tel. from చూచు.] n. Sight, a look, vision, glance. లక్ష్మి అతనిని చిన్న చూపు చూచినది fortune frowned on him. చిన్నచూపు humiliation, contempt. బ్రతికే చూపు కనిపించలేదు there was no prospect of his living longer. చూపోపు (చూపు+ఓపు.) to endure the sight of. చూచి సహించు. చూపోపక unable to stand before his face. A v. 78. **చూపు** or **చూపించు** v. a. To shew, point out. భయముచూపించు to frighten. అన్నము చూపించు to provide for, give bread to. ఆశ చూపించు to hold out hopes or prospects. చూపుడుకోక a transparent petticoat. **చూపుగుఱ్ఱము** or **చూపుడుగుఱ్ఱము** *tsūpu-gurramu.* n. A block head, a useless man. పనికి ఉపయోగము కానివాడు. **చూపుడువేలు** *tsūpuḍu-vēlu.* n. The forefinger. బొటనవేలు. **చూపకులు** *tsūp-akulu.* n. Spectators, bystanders. **చూపరి** *tsūpari.* n. A handsome woman, or man. చక్కనివాడు, చక్క, చక్కనిది.

చూపెట్టు *tsū-peṭṭu.* [Tel.] v. n. To await, wait for, attend on, watch, to expect. కనిపెట్టు, ప్రతీక్షించు.

చూర *tsūra.* [Tel.] n. Powder, dust పొడి. Plunder, spoil కొల్ల. వజ్రములచూర (for చూర్ణము) Diamond dust. ముత్తెపుచూర pearl powder. "కన్నులుచూరలుగొన్న," అనగా కండ్లపండువుగాచూచిరి. (Satyabh. iii. 22) he thought his very eyes enriched. చూరగా freely, liberally, to the full, to satiety. చూరయిచ్చు to cast to the dogs: to give lavishly. చూరకొను, చూరపుచ్చు, చూరలాడు or చూరాడు to plunder, waste, ravage. చూరవిడుచు to give up to be plundered, as a conquered city. చూరపోతు a scape goat, one let go as a sacrifice. చూరకాడు a plunderer. చూరకోలు plundering చూరపోవు to be plundered.

చూరకత్తి tsūrakatti. [Tel.] n. A knife or small dagger. చురకత్తి.

చూరి or చూరీ tsūri. [Tel.] n. A knife or small dagger. చురి.

చూరు tsūru. [Tel.] n. A cornice, border, ledge: shelf on a wall: the eaves of a roof. కాలుపట్టి యీడ్చినా చూరుపట్టి వ్రేలాడుతాను though you haul me by the legs I will hang on to the eaves, i. e., though thou reject me I will not cease to cling to thee. చూరు v. n. To be charred or smoked. చూరుకర్ర or పొగ చూరినకర్ర, charred wood చూరుకమ్మి or చూరువట్టె tsūru-kammi. n. The lath that closes in a shelving roof మునుగాడుచున పెంకు ఎత్తుగా వేసిన కమ్మి. చూరుకట్టు tsūru-kaṭṭu. n. The roof bands. చూరెలుక tsūr-eluka. n. The eaves' mouse, or house-mouse.

చూలు tsūlu. [Tel.] n. Pregnancy. గర్భము. చూలుకొను or చూలువడు to be pregnant, the womb, embryo, child, foetus గర్భస్థపిండము, శిశువు. చూలాలితనము tsūl-āli-tanamu. n. Pregnancy. చూలాలు tsūl-ālu. n. A pregnant woman. చూలి tsūli. n. A child, offspring, fruit. తమ్మిచూలి he who was born from the lotus. రాచూలి the prince's child. చూలి adj. Pregnant. చూలిగొర్రె a ewe in lamb. ఆ గుర్రము చూలితో నున్నది the mare is in foal.

చూవి Same as చుక్క, చూడుము.

చొ tso

చొంగ tsonga. [Tel.] n. Saliva, spittle. చొల్లు, లాల.

చొకాటము, చొక్కాటము, చొక్కారము or చొక్కారము tsok-āṭamu. [Tel.] n. Excellence, fineness, elegance, beauty. adj. Excellent, fine, beautiful. Very pure. మిక్కిలి స్వచ్ఛమైన.

చొక్కము or చొక్కటము tsokkamu. [Tel.] adj. Excellent, fine, lovely, pure. దోషము లేని, స్వచ్ఛము. (Same as చొకాటము.) చొక్కబాణము tsokka-bāṇamu. n. A bonfire.

చొక్కా, చొకా, చొక్కాయి or చొక్కాయి tsokka. [Tel.] n. A coat, shirt, jacket, vest, tunic. అంగరఖు, అంగరఖా.

చొక్కు tsokku. [Tel.] v. n. To be intoxicated or stupefied. To enjoy oneself to excess. To pine, languish with desire. పరవశమగు. To dry ఎండు. n. Intoxication, stupefaction, faintness. పారవశ్యము, మూర్ఛ. Falling in love, మోహము. చొక్కాకు tsokk-āku. n. A dead or dried leaf. రాలిన ఆకు, ఎండాకు. చొక్కిడు tsokk-iḍu. (చొక్కు+ఇడు.) v. t. To deceive మోసపుచ్చు. చొక్కునీరు tsokku-nīru. n. Intoxicating liquor. కల్లు, మద్యము. చొక్కెత్తు or చొక్కుపెట్టు tsokk-ettu. v. t. To intoxicate. చొక్కుపొడి or చొక్కు మందు tsokku-poḍi. n. Love powder; an aphrodisiac drug. చొక్కించు tsokk-intsu. v. n. To gratify, soothe, please, entrance.

చొచ్చు tsotstsu. [Tel.] v. n. To enter, find one's way into, penetrate, ప్రవేశించు, చొరబడు. To undertake, to begin, to set to work. శరణుచొచ్చినవాడు one who takes refuge with another. ముక్కుచొచ్చి కన్ను ప్రవేశించేవాడు one who would steal the very teeth out of your head. "సత్యచరితుల పరిపాలనముకకు జొరడె యతడు will he not interpose to rescue the righteous? See చొరు.

చొటచొట or చొడచొడ tsoṭa-tsoṭa. [Tel. anuk.] adv. Noisily, hissingly. Greedily, thirstily.

చొటు Same as చోటు.

చొట్ట or **సొట్ట** *tsotta.* [Tel.] n. A dent, a dimple or depression, bend. సొక్కు, పల్లము, వంకర. adj. Withered or lame as a limb, dented, indented. చొట్టమూతి a flat face.

చొత్తెంచు (చొచ్చు+తెంచు.) Same as చొచ్చు.

చొదుకు *tsoduku.* [Tel.] n. Moisture. చెమ్మ, తడి.

చొదుము *tsodumu.* [Tel.] n. A dried plantain fibre. ఎండిన అరటిపట్ట.

చొనుపు or **చొన్పు** *tsonupu.* [Tel.] v. a. To insert, to push in, to put in. చొరజేయు, చొప్పించు. ఇపుడు నాకు చొనుపు సిగ్గున (Padma. iii. 62.) the shame cast upon me.

చొప్ప *tsoppa.* [Tel.] n. The straw of maize and other plants. చొప్పకాడి a bundle of straw చొప్పమోపు.

చొప్పడి *tsoppadi.* n. A kind of cloth.

చొప్పడు *tsop-padu.* [Tel. చొప్పు+పడు.] v. n. To be convenient. సరిపడు, అమరుండు. To proceed, follow a course. To accrue to, కలుగు, దొరకు. మాటలచొప్పడిన if she fell into conversation. కళలం జొప్పడు శశి the moon who is liable to diminution of light. వైల్యమును పాండుచంద్రుడు. "వైద్యుడు చెప్పడు చెవతెగకపారు నేరుమ ద్విజాదుల చొప్పడినయూరినుండుము చొప్పడకున్నట్టి యూరు చొరకుమనుమతి." **చొప్పరచు** or **చొప్పరించు** *tsopparatsu.* v. t. To cause to be convenient చొప్పడజేయు. See చొప్పు.

చొప్పసొర్ర *tsoppa-sorra.* [Tel.] n. A fish called *Zygæna blochii.* See చప్పసొర్ర. (F. B. I.)

చొప్పించు *tsoppintsu.* [Tel.] v. a. To insert.

చొప్పు *tsoppu.* [Tel.] n. A trace. జాడ. A way, a path, మార్గము. Manner, appearance, fashion, విధము. Rate. చొప్పుకట్టు to trace out anything చొప్పుమార్చు to change one's appearance. **చొప్పున** *tsoppu-na.* adv. According to, like, agreeably to, by reason of, through, at the rate of. ఆరురూపాయలచొప్పున at six rupees. మంచితనముచొప్పున by fair means. భయముచొప్పున through the fear of, in the apprehension that. ఆచొప్పున so, in that way, thus, on that account. ఏచొప్పున how? వాడు చెప్పినచొప్పున from what he said. ఈచొప్పున in this manner; accordingly.

చొర *tsora.* [Tel.] n. A shark. సొర, సొర్ర. A. vi. 154. మత్స్యభేదము. A boy బాలుడు. See చోర.

చొరచొర *tsora-tsora.* adj. Very fast.

చొరియ *tsoriya.* [Tel.] n. A precipice.

చొరు *tsoru.* [Tel.] v. n. To enter. ప్రవేశించు, చొచ్చు **చొర** The infinitive of చొరు. (q. v.) **చొరపోతగా** *tsora-pōtaga.* [Tel. చొరవ+పోత.] adj. Continuous. నిరంతరము, ఎడములేని. adv. In an unbroken line, all in one stream. ఒకవరుసగా. **చొరబడు** or **చొరబాఱు** *tsora-badu* v. n. To enter or rush into, to break into, to intrude on. చొచ్చు. ఆ కథ యిందులో చొరబడదు that tale does not form a part of this. **చొరవ** *tsorava.* n. An entrance. ప్రవేశము. Daring సాహసము. Keen-mindedness బుద్ధికుశలత. Use, familiarity, aptitude, introduction. Desire ఇచ్ఛ. చొరవగల easy of access. వ్యాకరణములో వానికి మంచిచొరవ కలదు he has an aptitude for grammar. వానికి అన్నముచొరవేకాని అక్షరముచొరవలేదు he is sharp enough at eating but slow at reading. చొరవకత్తె a forward woman. చొరవకాడు a forward man. మాట చొరని య్యడు he will not let a word be heard: or, he will not listen. చొరకమానె he did not enter. **చొరిగాడు** *tsoriyadu.* n. A hunter.

చోలిమిడి *tsolimidi.* [Tel.] n. The herb called *Amaranthus Polygamus.* అల్పమారిషవృక్షము, చిర్రకూర.

తొల్లు or జొల్లు *tsollu.* [Tel.] n. Saliva, spittle, slaver. జొల్లుమాట, blabbering. తుంపురుమాట.

తొల్లెము, చొల్లియము, తొల్లెము or జొల్లియము *tsollemu.* [Tel.] n. A tire, formed by weaving the tresses in chains and then coiling them up at the back of the head: a wreath of *mogili* flowers. జడతో చుట్టిన చుట్ట.

చో tsō

చో *tsō.* [Tel. Contracted from చోటు.] adv. Where, when, Wherever, whenever, whereupon, on which, in the event of, if, in case, on the supposition that, as, seeing that, because. వచ్చుచో on his coming. ఇచ్చుచో on his giving. కానిచో if not, otherwise. కుమారులులేనిచో in the event of there being no sons, in case there are no sons.

చోటు *tsōṭu.* [Tel.] n. A place. ఆచోటు that place. ఇచ్చోటు this place.

చోడి Same as చోళ్లు. (q. v.)

చోదు See సోదు.

చోద, జోద or జోదము *tsōda.* [Tel.] n. Plague, trouble, puzzle, difficulty. కష్టము, సందరగోళము, గాథ. H. i. 143. Ila. iii. 79. Padma. ii. 285. చోదంబరి a villain, a pestilent fellow.

చోపా *tsōpa.* [Tel.] n. A shed with a slanting roof, a verandah. A lobby, entrance or passage, అలిందము.

చోపు *tsōpu.* [Tel. The causal of చొచ్చు.] v. n. To enamour. v. a. To dissipate or scatter, to confuse, కలచు; to scare away, strike off, do away. తరుము, తోలు. n. Confusion కలత. చోపుడుపెట్టు to drive wild cattle towards the huntsman's ambuscade, to stalk deer. Suca. i. 200. చోపుడు Same as చోపు (noun). చోపుడు కోల a stick to drive cattle with.

చోపుదారు or జోపుదారు *tsōpu-dāru.* [H.] n. A mace-bearer.

చోర or జోర్ర *tsōra.* [Tel.] n. A shark. A. vi. 125. A boy బాలుడు చోరచిరుత. *tsōra-chiruta.* n. A prank, a trick. చేష్ట. చోరబుడుత a young shark: a beautiful eyed woman.

చోళ్లు *tsōḷḷu.* [Tel. చోడి+లు.] n. A grain called రాగులు. *Panicum paludosum.* Rox. i. 307. 343. 345. తమిదెలు.

చోవి *tsōvi.* [Tel.] n. The crumb of bread. బూరెలమీద మూతగా పెట్టెడుపిండి.

చౌ tsau

చౌ or చేవు *tsau.* [Tel.] n. The number four, in counting. చౌకాడిగుడియ or చేవుకాడిగుడియ *tsaukādiguḍiya.* n. An iron rod with four well-turned sides నాలుగుపక్కలుకలిగిన యినుపదండము. చౌగంటి or చేవుగంటి the god of fire అగ్నిదేవుడు. చౌకాలిపీట or చేవుకాలిపీట a chair; lit. a seat with four legs.

చౌక or చేవుక *tsauka.* [Tel] n. Cheapness. అగ్గువ. A. v. 7. చులుకనితనము, హీనత్వము. adj. Cheap, slight, despised. చౌకచేయు or చేవుకచేయు to slight, scorn, undervalue తక్కువపరచు.

చౌకట్టు or చౌకటు or చేవుకట్టు *tsau-kaṭṭu.* [Tel. చౌ=four] n. A window frame. An earring with four pearls set in it.

చౌకము or చేవుకము *tsaukamu.* [Tel.] n. A square. చదరము. adj. Square, four నాలుగు, చతుష్కము, చతురశ్రము.

చౌకళి or చేవుకళి *tsaukaḷi.* n. A square place. చవ్వాకపుటిల్లు. Earrings పోగులజోడు. Suca. i. 161. చౌకళించు or చేవుకళించు *tsaukaḷ-intsu.* v. n. To dance about, skip, leap, bound, vault. నాలుగుకాళ్లు పైకెత్తి దాటు. తెల్లకడపయు భుజముగా చౌకళించు with her milk pail dancing on her shoulder: చౌకళించు or చేవుకళించు jumping on all fours, dancing చౌకళించుట.

చౌకారము or చేవుకారము *tsaukāramu.* n. Soap. సబ్బు.

చౌకి or చేవుకి *tsauki.* [Tel.] n. A custom house. A toll gate సుంకరిమెట్టు. Watching కావలియుండడము. చౌకీదారుడు or చౌకీనుస్తా a custom house officer.

చౌసు or చేవుసు Same as చేయుకు.

చౌడమ్మ or చేవుడమ్మ *tsaud-amma.* [Tel.] n. "Our Lady of the Marsh," a certain village goddess.

చౌడు or చేవుడు *tsaudu.* [Tel.] n. A kind of earth salt, impure carbonate of soda. Saltness, brackishness, salt land. చేవుడు పోయిన destroyed by saltness of the soil, as corn is. చౌడుప్పు *tsaud-uppu.* n. Soda.

చౌడోలు or చేవుడోలు *tsaudōlu.* [Tel. చౌ+డోలి.] n. A howdah or seat on an elephant. చేవ్వరము. హౌదా.

చౌతా or చేవుతా *tsautā.* [Tel.] n. A litter. డోలి.

చౌతి or చేవుతి or చేవితి *tsauti.* [Tel. From Skt. చతుర్థి.] n. The fourth lunar day from the new or full moon. నాగులచవుతి a certain anniversary feast.

చౌదంతి or చేవుదంతి *tsau-danti.* [Skt.] adj. Four tusked. n. The name of Indra's elephant Airavata.

చౌదరి or చేవుదరి *tsaudari.* [Tel.] n. The headman of a village or district.

చౌపటము or చేవుపటము *tsau-patamu.* [Tel.] n. A walled enclosure, a square built yard or compound. ఆవరణము, ప్రహరి.

చౌపదము or చేవుపదము *tsau-padamu.* [Tel.] n. Four corners. నాలుగుమూలలు.

చౌపుటము or చేవుపుటము *tsau-putamu.* [Tel.] n. A leap or bound (as of a deer.) On all fours నాలుగుకాళ్లెత్తి పైకి దాటుట.

చౌరు or చేవురు *tsauru.* [Tel.] n. A peculiar taste such as that of goat's milk. Salt mixed with sugar. చౌరుకొట్టు or చౌరు కొట్టు *tsauru-kottu.* v. a. To devour. తెగతిను. A. ii. 98.

చౌలు or చేవులు *tsaulu.* [Tel.] n. The lustre of a pearl. ముత్తెపుకాంతి.

చౌరంచ or చేవురంచె *tsau-rantsa.* [Tel. from రంచ one] n. Five at games.

చౌషష్టి or చేవుషష్టి *tsau-shashti.* [Tel. చౌ+ Skt. షష్టి.] n. Sixty four. అరువదినాలుగు.

చౌసాల or చేవుసాల Same as లోల్లారము.

చౌసీతి or చేవుసీతి *tsau-siti.* n. Eighty four. చౌసీతిబంధములు the "84 attitudes", all possible ways.

ఛ chha

ఛ *chha.* [Tel.] n. A letter.

ఛందము *chhandamu.* [Skt.] n. Will. Intention. ఇచ్ఛ, అభిప్రాయము. Way, manner, ఛందస్సు *chhandassu.* Harmony. Prosody or metrical arrangement. A rule, principle. A Veda వేదము. స్వచ్ఛందవృత్తి uncontrolled will.

ఛట *chhata.* [Skt.] n. A lock or tuft of hair, &c. గుంపు, సమూహము. రుచిచ్ఛటలు a mass of brilliancy. పక్షచ్ఛట a tuft of feather: a mass (of hair). A series. వరుస. ఛటఛట, ఛటచ్ఛట, ఛటచ్ఛటము. *chhata-chhata.* adv. (anuk) Brightly, hotly, fiercely. ఛటఛటత్కారము *chhata-chhatatkāramu.* n. Splashing, dashing, heat, fierceness. ఛటి *chhati.* n. A crowd, a multitude, an assembly సమూహము. తరుసమూహాన్వితము. A. v. 149.

ఛత్రము *chhatramu.* [Skt.] n. An umbrella, a parasol, a canopy of state. గొడుగు. ఛత్రభంగము *chhatra-bhangamu.* n. Fall, dethronement, deposition. రాజ్య నాశము. Widowhood ముండమోపితనము.

(The umbrella is an ensign of royalty; and denotes any cover or defence, as a husband, &c.) ఛత్త్రాకము or ఛత్త్రాసువు *chhatrākamu.* n A mushroom. పుట్టగొడుగు. A iv. 143.

ఛదనము or ఛదము *chhadanamu.* [Skt.] n. A leaf, a feather, a wing, a covering. ఆకు, ఱెక్క.

ఛద్మము *chhadmamu.* [Skt.] n. A trick, a pretext: fraud. Deceit, a fault, foible, failing. Sarcasm, a taunt. వ్యాజము, మిష, మోసము.

ఛన్నము *channamu.* [Skt.] adj. Concealed, secret. కప్పబడిన, ఏకాంతమైన.

ఛపాయించు *chapā-y-intsu.* [Tel.] v. t. To evade, defraud, conceal.

ఛర్ది or ఛర్దనము *chhardi.* [Skt.] n. Vomiting. వమనము.

ఛలము, ఛలార్థము or ఛలోక్తి *chhalamu.* [Skt.] n. A trick, a stratagem: an innuendo or covert meaning. A double entendre నెపము, వెనుదీయుట, ఒక అభిప్రాయముతో చెప్పినపదమునకు మరొక అభిప్రాయము చేసుకొని ఉత్తరముచెప్పుట.

ఛవి *chhavi.* [Skt.] n. A ray. కిరణము. Brilliancy కాంతి.

ఛా chhā

ఛాందస *chhāndasa.* [Skt.] adj. Free, subject to no rule, sacred: as the style of some ancient books which being inspired, the broken metres cannot be corrected according to prosody. ఛాందసము *chānda-samu.* n. Silliness, the stupidity of a mere bookworm, simplicity, awkwardness. That part of an almanac which lays down the (వైదికము) diurnal rites: ఛాందసుడు *chhāndasuḍu.* n. A textualist, a ritualist: శ్రోత్రియుడు. A mere silly book-worm: a monk.

ఛాందోగ్యము *chhāndōgyamu.* [Skt.] n. Name of an Upanishad. ఒక ఉపనిషత్తు.

ఛాగము *chhāgamu.* [Skt.] n. A goat. మేకపోతు. ఛాగి. *chhāgi.* n. A goat మేక.

ఛాత్రుడు *chhātruḍu.* [Skt.] n. A disciple, a scholar. శిష్యుడు.

ఛాదనము *chhādanamu.* [Skt.] n. Covering కప్పుట. ఛాదితము *chhāditamu.* adj. Covered, concealed.

ఛాపా *chhāpa.* [H.] n. A print or stamp. ఛాపావేయు to print. ఛాపాకాగితము a stamp paper.

ఛాపు *chhāpu.* [H.] n. The cock of a gun. A tune in music.

ఛాయ *chhāya.* [Skt.] n. A shadow, reflected image; colour. ఛాయాచోరకవి *chāyā-chōra-kavi.* n. A plagiarist ఛాయాతరువు *chāyā-taruvu.* n. A large tree useful only for the shade or shelter it gives. నీడచేతనే మిక్కిలి ఉపయోగకరమగానుండే పెద్దచెట్టు. ఛాయాపుత్రుడు *chhāyā-putruḍu.* n. Saturn. శని, చేయపట్టి. ఛాయాదేవి name of the wife of the sun. సూర్యుని భార్య.

ఛి chhi

ఛిద్రము *chhidramu.* [Skt.] n. A hole, a slit, a cleft, a perforation. బెజ్జము. Fault, defect, flaw, schism. తప్పు. గృహచ్ఛిద్రము domestic strife. ఛిద్రితము *chhidritamu.* adj. Perforated, pierced. బెజ్జమువేయబడిన.

ఛిన్నము *chhinnamu.* [Skt.] adj. Cut, divided. ఛేదింపబడిన. ఛిన్నాభిన్నము *chhinna-bhinnamu.* adv. Piecemeal. ఛిన్నాభిన్నముగా నరుకుట to hack, chop, cut to pieces.

ఛు chhu

ఛురిక *chhurika.* [Skt.] n. A knife. చురకత్తి. A surgical knife. శస్త్రి.

ఛుల్లి *chhulli.* [Skt.] n. A hearth or fire-place. పొయ్యి.

ఛే chhe

ఛేకము *chhêkamu.* [Skt.] n. A kind of alliteration; also called ఛేకానుప్రాసము. "శ్రీ. కుదయుంపురవిపింపు, &c." Bhanumati, iii. 68. A tame or domesticated animal. పెంపుడుమృగము.

ఛేదము *chhêdamu.* [Skt.] n. Cutting, a portion, a part, loss. నరుకుడు, తునక. A denominator of a fraction. భిన్నాంకము నందు క్రిందిసంఖ్య. **ఛేదించు** *chhêdintsu.* v. a. To cut up, sever, divide, quarter. **ఛేదనము** *chhêdanamu.* n. Cutting; ఛేదించుట. **ఛేదితము** *chhêditamu.* adj. That which is cut. ఛేదింపబడిన. **ఛేద్యము** *chhêdyamu.* adj. Fit to be cut. ఛేదింపదగిన.

జ ja

జ *ja.* [Tel.] n. The letter J; as in జింక, జెర్రి. In all Sanskrit words it is thus pronounced, as బీజము, జాలము In Telugu words it retains this sound when followed by I, E, or AI as జింకు. But with other vowels it is sounded as Z, or, dz. Thus జోబు సజ్జ. As initials, the letters చ, cha and జ, ja are often used at pleasure. The initial aspirates also are used without rule. In some Telugu words, జ, డ, ద are equivalent, thus: గోజు, గోడు and గోదు are the same.

జః *jah.* [Skt.] adj. Born, produced. మనోజః or మనోజుడు heart-born: a name of Manmadha.

జంగమము *jangamamu.* [Skt.] adj. Moveable, not stationary. తిరుగునది. జంగమ కట్టుబడి a temporary bailiff. జంగమనగము, (Vasu. iii 249.) జంగమగ్రావము, or జంగమాద్రి a rolling rock, a moving hill. P. i. 202; iii. 62. n. A moveable or chattel; property, personalty. Cattle, cows, sheep, &c. **జంగముడు** *jangamudu.* n. A Jangam, or worshipper of Basava. L. XIV. 210. **జంగమత్వము** *jangamatramu.* n. Moveableness, locomotion. G. ix. 121.

జంగలము *jangalamu.* [Skt. from which is derived Eng. "jungle."] n. An uninhabited place. జనము లేనిచోటు.

జంఘ *jangha.* [Skt.] n. The calf of the leg. పిక్క. **జంఘాలుడు** *janghāludu.* adj. Light footed: rapid, swift. మిక్కిలి వడిగా నడచు వాడు.

జంజీరు *janjiru.* [H.] n. A chain. గొలుసు.

జండా or **జెండా** *janda.* [Tel.] n. A flag, a banner.

జంతువు *jantuvu.* [Skt.] n. An animal, brute, beast. ప్రాణముకలది, చేతనము.

జంత్రము *jantramu.* [Skt. another form of యంత్రము.] n. An instrument, a machine. జంత్రవాద్యము instrumental music. జంత్రగాత్రసంగీతము instrumental and vocal music. జంత్రపుబొమ్మ a puppet, an automaton, a splendid image or beautiful figure.

జంపతులు *jam-patulu.* [Skt. జాయ+పతి.] n. Man and wife: partners; దంపతులు.

జంబాలము *jambālamu.* [Skt.] n. Mire, mud, clay. అడుసు, బురద. Moss or water weeds. పాచి.

జంబీరము *jambīramu.* [Skt.] n. The lime tree. నిమ్మచెట్టు. T. iii. 12.

జంబుకము *jambukamu.* [Skt.] n. A jackal. నక్క.

జంబుఖానా or **జెంబుఖానా** *jambukhāna.* [H.] n. A carpet. తివాసీ.

జంబువు *jambuvu.* [Skt.] n. The rose apple tree, *Eugenia jambos.* **జంబూద్వీపము** *jambūdvīpamu.* n. A poetical name of India, which is, according to the Puranas, the central division of the world. **జంబూనది** *jambū-nadi.* n. A river of gold said to flow from the mountain Mêru.

జంభము *jambhamu.* [for Skt. దంభము.] n. Grandeur, pomp. జంభాలు big words, boasts. జంభముగా grandly.

జంభలము *jambhalamu.* [Skt.] n. The lime tree. నిమ్మచెట్టు. A. v. 151.

జంభారి *jambhari.* [Skt.] n. The foe of Jambha, an Asura; an epithet of Indra.

జగ or **జేగ** *jaga.* [Tel.] adj. Noble, fine, matchless. జగజెట్టి a matchless wrestler. జగదొంగ a great thief. జగరౌతు a heroic trooper.

జగతి, జగత్తు or **జగము** *jagati.* [Skt.] n. The world: the earth. ప్రపంచము, భూలోకము. People. Men in general జనము. జగజ్జ్యోతి *jagaj-jyoti.* adj. Bright, radiant, flaring. ఆవజ్రము జగజ్జ్యోతిగానున్నది that diamond is a paragon of brilliancy. జగత్ప్రాణుడు *jagat-pranudu.* n. Air, వాయువు. జగద్విదితము celebrated: known to the world. జగన్నాథుడు *jagan-nadhudu.* n. Lord of the world, an epithet of Vishnu as worshipped at the shrine in Puri in Orissa. జగన్నుతి celebrated. జగచ్చక్షువు *jagach-chakshuvu.* [Skt. జగత్ + చక్షువు.] n. The eye of the world, i. e., the sun.

జగ్ధి *jagdhi.* [Skt.] n. Eating. భోజనము.

జఘనము *jaghanamu.* [Skt.] The haunches: the hip and loins. పిరుదు. The abdomen పొత్తికడుపు. కటిస్థలము. జఘనములు the loins, పిరుదులు. జఘనదఘ్నము the posteriors. జఘన్యము *jaghanyamu.* n. A low state: degradation. adj. Lowest, last. తక్కువది. జఘన్యజుడు *jaghanyajudu.* n. A younger brother. తమ్ముడు. A Sudra శూద్రుడు.

జట *jata.* [Skt.] n. Matted locks, such as monks wear. Plaited hair, జెడ. A fibrous pendant root of the banyan tree. ఊడ. Ringing the changes on words. Reiteration in reading the vedas. జటాధారి wearing matted hair. **జటి** *jati.* n. A hermit. ముని, జడలుగలసన్న్యాసి. **జటిలము** *jatilamu.* adj. Twisted, intertwined. జడలుగలది, కలిసినది. Intricate, obscure. ఆ కావ్యమంతా సంస్కృతజటిలము that poem is stuffed full of Sanskrit words.

జటామాంసి *jata-mansi.* [Skt.] n. Indian Spikenard, a well known drug: *Valeriana jatamansi.* Roxb. i 163.

జఠరము *jatharamu.* [Skt.] n. The belly. కడుపు. జఠరాగ్ని the sensation of hunger. జఠరయాతన the grief of being in the womb, the plight of a child unborn.

జడ, జెడ or **జేడ** *jada.* [Tel.] n. Hair plaited or braided in coils, matted hair. The finishing twist or plait of a straw roof. **జడధారి** for **జటాధారి** *jadadari.* n. A hermit with matted locks. వానప్రస్థుడు. **జడబిళ్ల** *jada-billa.* n. A head ornament, worn by Hindoo women over their plaited hair. **జడముడి** *jada-mudi.* n. The knot of hair behind the head.

జడధి *jadadhi.* [Skt.] n. The sea. జలధి, సముద్రము.

జడము *jadamu.* [Skt.] adj. Cold, frigid, chilly. చల్లని. Stupid, apathetic, idiotic, inanimate. తెలివితేని. Dumb మూగ. **జడత్వము** *jadatvamu.* n. Stupidity. **జడమతి** *jada-mati.* n. An idiot, a blockhead. **జడిమ** or **జడిమము** *jadima.* n. Slowness, tardiness. జడత్వము. **జడుడు** *jadudu.* n. A fool, a simpleton. Dasav. vii. 103.

జతువు *jatuvu.* [Skt.] n. Lac. A red dye analogous to cochineal. లక్క. జతుగృహము a house built of this inflammable gum. లక్కయిల్లు. M. VIII. vi. 134.

జత్రువు *jatruvu.* [Skt.] n. The clavicle or collar bone. M. VII. 148. మెడకొంకి, మూపుయొక్క సంధియెముక.

జనకము *janakamu.* [Skt.] adj Producing, creative, productive. హాస్యజనకమైన causing laughter. ప్రీతిజనకమైన amiable, causing love. జనకుడు *janakudu*. n. A father or progenitor. Also, the name of a certain king.

జనత *janata*. [Skt.] n. People, folk. జన సమూహము.

జననము *jananamu*. [Skt.] n. Birth, production. పుట్టుక. Family, race, lineage, వంశము జననమువుట to be born. జనని *janani*. n. A mother. జననీజనకులు *janani-janakulu*. n. Parents, mother and father. జనయిత *jana-yita*. n. A father or progenitor. జనయిత్రి *jana-yitri*. n. A mother.

జనము, జనములు or జనాలు *janamu*. [Skt.] n. People, folk, persons. Tara. ii. 84. "జనములేరానియెడల" (Vijaya. i. 358.) when nobody was by. జనపతి *jana-pati*. n. A king, a lord of men. జనపదము *jana-padamu*. n. Any inhabited country. దేశము. A village. గ్రామము. జనశ్రుతి *jana-sruti*. n. News, tidings, intelligence, a rumour. జనులుచెప్పుకొనేవృత్తాంతము, వాడుక. జనాంగము *janangamu* n. A household, a family. A nation. జనాభా *janabha*. [H.] n. Population. జనాభాలెక్క a census. జనాభాపిస్తు or జనాభాదస్తు a poll-tax.

జనార్దనుడు *janardanudu*. [Skt.] n. An epithet of Vishnu.

జని *jani*. [Skt.] n. Birth, production. పుట్టుక. A. vi. 117. R. iii. 8. and iii. 87. జనించు or జనియించు *janintsu*. v. n. To be born or produced, to arise. మదముజనించు joy arising in the heart. జనుడు *janudu*. n. A man. జనులు people. జనుస్సు *janusu*. n. Birth. పుట్టుక. జనుషాంధుడు *janush-andhudu*. n. One born blind. పుట్టుగ్రుడ్డి. జన్మము *janmamu*. n. Birth, production. పుట్టుక. నా జన్మములో వాణ్ని చూడలేదు. I never in my life saw him. ఈ దినము నా జన్మము సాఫల్యమైనది this day my life is perfected పునర్జన్మము Re-birth, resurrection. పూర్వజన్మము a former birth. జన్మదేశము or జన్మభూమి *janma-desamu*. n. Native country. జన్మపత్రిక *janma-patrika*. n. The paper containing one's horoscope, or calculation of nativity. కోష్ఠి. జన్మమెత్తు *janmam-ettu*. v. n. To be born. ఆయన జన్మమెత్తిన తర్వాత after he appeared in the body. జన్మాంతరము *janm-antaramu*. n. Another life. A former or future birth, pre-existence. జన్మించు *janmintsu*. v. n. To be born జన్మి *janmi*. n. An animal.

జన్యము *janyamu*. [Skt.] n. A battle. యుద్ధము. జన్యతలము *janya-talamu*. n. The field of battle.

జపము *japamu*. [Skt.] n. A prayer, Repeating charms. మంత్రావృత్తి. Repeating inaudibly passages from the Vedas, వేదాధ్యయనము. Silent prayer, adoration: religious meditation: holy cogitation. (ధ్యానము is silent, without moving the lips: జపము is silent, but moving the lips.) జపాపుష్పము or దాసనచెట్టుపువ్వు *japa-pushpamu*. n. The shoe-flower. *Hibiscus rosa sinensis*. Roxb iii. 194. జపాకుసుమ సంకాశ blushing rosy red. జపించు or జపియించు *japintsu*. v. a. To repeat prayers, &c., inaudibly. జపము చేయు.

జమాదారుడు *jamadarudu*. [H.] n. A Jamadar. A head sepoy.

జయము *jayamu*. [Skt.] n. Conquest, victory, triumph, success. గెలుపు. జయ *jaya*. interj. Hail! Hurrah! జయంతి *jayanti*. n. The anniversary of an Incarnation. Thus నృసింహజయంతి a festival in honour of Nrisimha. కృష్ణజయంతి Krishna's feast. లక్ష్మీజయంతి, &c. జయకాలుడు a victor over time, an immortal. జయఘంట *jaya-ghanta*. n. A bell, the circular plate of mixed metal, used as a gong in Hindoo temples, &c. జేగంట. జయనము *jayanamu*. n. Armour for a horse or other animal. జయపెట్టు *jaya-pettu*. v. n. To congratulate, to hail. జయముజయము అని దీవించు. జయరంజ the name of a kind of silk. BD. iii. 98. జయవార ము *jaya-varamu*. n. Tuesday. మంగళవా రము. జయశబ్దము congratulations: shouts of victory. జయస్తంభము a pillar erected before a temple: or in the centre of a stone pond or basin. ధ్వజస్తంభము. జయించు *jayintsu*. v.n. & t. To conquer, or win; to be successful. గెలుచు. జయుడు *jayudu*. n. The name of Yudhishthira, the eldest of the Pandavas. జయోత్కంఠుడు *jayot-kanthudu*. adj. Sanguine, emulous, long-ing for victory. జయ్యము *jayyamu*. adj. That which can be conquered. గెలువశక్య మైనది.

జర *jara*. [Skt.] n. Old age, decrepitude. debility consequent upon old age. ముదిమి, ముసలితనము. జరఠము *jarathamu*. adj. Old, decayed, infirm. ముదిసిన. Solid, con-firmed, affected by age either well or ill. గట్టియైన. జరత్ *jarat*. adj. Old, decrepit, A. iv. 32 జరద్గవము an old ox ముసలియెద్దు. జరుడు an old man.

జరాయువు *jarayuvu*. [Skt.] n. The womb or uterus. మావి. జరాయుజము *jara-yujamu*. adj. Viviparous, not produced from an egg. మావియందుపుట్టిన. (Manu i. 43.)

జరిబిల్ల or జెరిబిల్ల *jari-billa*. [Tel.] n. A piece of wood like the sheave of a pulley used by weavers in stretching their webs.

జరిమానా *jarimana*. [H.] n. A fine. జులుమానా.

జర్జరము, జర్జరితము or జర్జరీకము *jarja-ramu*. [Skt.] adj. Ruined. శిథిలమైన.

జలము *jalamu*. [Skt.] n. Water; any fluid. జలకము or జెలకము *jalakamu*. n. A bath, ablution, bathing. స్నానము. జల కట్టె or జెలకట్టె *jala-katte*. n. A sort of hawk. Swa. iv. 43. HD. i. 533. HN. ii. 47. జలకమాడు *jalakam-adu*. v. n. To bathe. జలక్రీడ *jala-krida*. n. Romping in water, naked play, any naked exhi-bition or nudity in sculpture. జలగడుగు or జెలగడుగు *jala-gadugu*. v. t. To wash earth for gold, diamonds, &c., small pebbles, జరగడుగు, జెరగడుగు. జలగడుగుల వాండ్లు *jala-gadugula-vandlu*. n. plu. A caste of gold finders, who search for gold in drains and in the sweepings of gold-smith's shops. BD. vii. 844. జల చరము *jala-charamu*. n. An aquatic animal of any kind. జలజము *jala-jamu*. n. Lit: born in water: The lotus. తామర. A conch, a shell, శంఖము. జలజభవుడు The lotus-born, a title of Bramha జల జారి *jala-jari*. n. The moon, as being the enemy of the lotus. జలతస్కరుడు *jala-taskarudu*. n. The evaporator, the drawer off of water, i. e., the sun. జల దము or జలధరము *jaladamu*. n. A cloud. మబ్బు. జలదారి or జెలదారి *jaladari*. [Tel.] n. A drain: the projecting spout of a lingam. జలధార *jala-dhara*. n. A flood, a torrent, a stream. జలధి or జల నిధి *jala-dhi*: n. The sea, the ocean. సముద్రము, కడలి. జలపక్షి *jala-pakshi*. n. An aquatic bird. జలపాయి *jala-payi*. n. A water drinker, a teetotaler. జలబాధకు పోవు *jala-badha-ku-poru*. v. n. To go to make water: or to go to the privy. జలయంత్రము *jala-yantramu*. n. An artificial fountain or jet. జలరాగము *jala-ragamu*. n. A ruby of imperfect water supposed to be unlucky. జలసూ త్రము *jala-sutramu*. n. A *jet d' eau* or artificial fountain. జలాశయము *jala-sayamu*. n. A lake; a piece of water. జలూక or జలౌకసము *jaluka*. n. A leech. జలగ.

జల్పనము *jalpanamu*. [Skt.] n. Prattle, babble. వదరుట, ఉపయుక్తముకానిమాటాడుట జల్పాకి a babbler, a talkative person. మాటకారి. A. vi. 89.

జల్ల or జెల్ల jalla. [Tel.] n. A manger. A long wickerwork basket used to form the body of a cart. A fish; the river mullet. One kind is ఆకు జెల్ల.

జవనిక javanika. [Skt.] n. A screen. తెరచీర.

జవబియ్యము or జెవబియ్యము java-biyyamu. [Tel.] n. A certain grain.

జవము javamu. [Skt.] n. Speed, swiftness, velocity, potency as of a medicine. వేగము, సత్వము. మనోజవంబున with the speed of thought. adj. Swift. వడిగల. జవనము javanamu. n. Swiftness. వడి. A swift horse వడిగలగుర్రము. adj. Swift వడిగల.

జవాది or జవ్వాది javadi. [Skt.] n. Civet: a paste like pomatum. పునుగు. సంకు మదము. కర్రజవ్వాజి stick civet, that is found adhering to twigs. జవాదిపిల్లి javadi-pilli. n. The civet cat. పునుగుపిల్లి.

జపాపుష్పము or జపాపుష్పము java-pushpamu. [Skt.] n. The shoeflower, *Hibiscus Rosa Sinensis*. Rox. iii. 194. లోగ్రపుష్పము. దాసనము.

జవాబు or జేవాబు javabu. [H.] n. An answer, a reply. జవాబుదారీ responsibility. జవాబుదారుడు a responsible person. జవాబునివీసు a writer of orders or replies.

జవాహిరీ javahiri. [H.] n. Precious stones, jewels. Wealth.

జహ్నువు jahnuvu. [Skt.] The name of a Royal Rishi. ఒకరాజర్షి. జహ్నుతనయ his daughter, i. e., the Ganges గంగానది.

జా jā

జాంగలము jangalamu. [Skt. from జంగల ము.] n. A wild, jungle or wilderness, a forest. అడవి, నిర్జలదేశము. The fracoline partridge, *Francolinus vulgaris*. (F. B. I.) adj. Rural, wild, picturesque, jungly. జాంగలామిషము jangalamishamu. (from ఆమిషము flesh.) n. Venison, game, wild animals, as pigs, &c. జాంగలికుడు jangalikudu. n. A snake-catcher. విష వైద్యుడు, గారడీడు.

జాంఘికుడు janghikudu. [Skt.] n. A courier, an express. హరికారా.

జాంత్ర See జంత్ర.

జాంబవము jambavamu. [Skt.] n. The fruit of the Jambu tree. నేరేడుపండు.

జాంబూనదము jambū-nadamu. [Skt.] Gold: so called because found in జంబూనది a river flowing from Mount Sumeru, the Indian Pactolus. W.

జాగా jaga. [H.] n. Place, a piece of land, site. చోటు.

జాగరము, జాగారము or జోగారము jagaramu. [Tel.] n. A vigil: sitting up all night, waking, watching, watchfulness. BD. iv. 1412. Vipra. i. 75 Kalah ii. 134. Vasu. iv. 121. L. i. 363. Armour కవచము. The name of a piece or man, at backgammon. G. X. 86. జాగరించు or జాగరిల్లు jagar-intsu. v. n To wake, watch, sit up all night. జాగరూకత jaga-rūkata. n Heedfulness, waking, watching. జాగరూకుడు jaga-rūkudu. n. One who is wakeful, a careful man.

జాగిలము or జోగిలము jagilamu. [Tel.] n. A hound used for hog hunting. వేటకుక్క.

జాగీరు jagiru. [H.] n. A Jaghire. An assignment of the Government share of the produce of a tract of country to an individual.

జాగ్రత or జాగ్రత్త jagrata. [Skt.] n. Vigilance, carefulness, caution, activity, adj. Vigilant, careful, cautious, active, ready. జాగ్రత్ప్రాయము presence of mind. జాగ్రతగా with care. జాగ్రతచేయు to take care, to be careful, to make ready, to secure.

జాటి or ఝాటి jaṭi. [H.] n. A whip, a scourge. చబుకు, కొరడా.

జాడ్యము *jāḍyamu*. [Skt.] n. Disease, sickness, infirmity. Coldness, apathy. Dulness, folly, stupidity. జడత, జడ్డు. బుద్ధి జాడ్యము inadvertency.

జాణ or జేణ *jāṇa*. [Tel.] n. A wit, a genius. A clever or cunnig woman నేర్పరి. adj. Clever, wise. Roguish, artful, shrewdish. జాణడు or జేణడు. *jāṇaḍu*. n. A genius, a clever man. జాణతనము or జేణతనము *jāṇa-tanamu* n. Sagacity, shrewdness, archness, cunning.

జాతము *jātamu*. [Skt.] adj. Born, produced, occasioned, possessed, felt, collected. n. A living being. Birth, production, origin; a kind or class, a collection forming a group. జాతకము *jātakamu*. n. A horoscope చీటి. The predetermination from a horoscope, &c., of the fortunes and destinies of an individual throughout life. Also, that branch of astrology which teaches how to make a horoscope. కష్టజాతకములు కుదించేవాడు one who can by theory give the data for such a calculation. జాతకర్మము *jāta-karmamu*. n. The ceremony (like christening) by which a child is introduced into his caste. పుట్టినప్పుడు చేయుక్రియ. జాతవేదుడు *jāta-vēduḍu*. n. An epithet of Fire, as being the "source of the Veda." అగ్ని.

జాతి *jāti*. [Skt.] n. A kind, rank, sort, class, tribe or caste. కులము. Birth పుట్టుక. The nutmeg tree జాజిచెట్టు.—adj. Fine, first rate. జాతికస్తూరి fine musk. జాతిస్ఫటికము a fine crystal. జాతివజ్రము a fine diamond. జాతివాడు a European. జాతిది an English woman. జాతిపత్రి *jāti-patri*. n Mace, the membraneous covering of the nutmeg. జాపత్రి. జాతివృత్తములు *jāti-vrittamulu*. n. Uniform metres. See ఉపజాతి. జాతీయము *jātīyamu*. adj. Appertaining to a tribe or caste. Natural. n. A dialect. An idiom. Local pronunciation. The constitutional effect. జాత్యము *jātyamu*. adj. Born in a good caste or family మంచికులమందుపుట్టిన. Fine చక్కని. Excellent శ్రేష్ఠమైన.

జాన or జేన *jāna*. [Tel.] n. A span.

జానపదము *jāna-padamu*. [Skt.] n. A country. దేశము. A village గ్రామము. జానపదుడు *jāna-paduḍu*. n. A villager. గ్రామ్యుడు.

జాని *jāni*. [Skt.] n. Old age. ముదిమి. A wife భార్య. "జానకీజాని కథల్."

జాను or జేను *jānu*. [Tel.] adj. Graceful, bland. జానుతెనుగు pure or sweet Telugu. n. Grace, prettiness. చక్కదనము, ఒప్పిదము, సౌందర్యము. Appa Cavi. II. జానొప్పగా prettily. BD. v. 1075. జానుగా gracefully.

జానుగు or జేనుగు *jānugu*. [Tel.] n. The ear చెవి. An ear of grain. కంకి.

జానువు *jānuvu*. [Skt.] n. The knee. మోకాలు.

జాప్యము or జేప్యము *jāpyamu*. [Tel.] n. Loitering, dawdling delay. Inertness. Languor.

జాఫరచెట్టు or జాఫ్రాచెట్టు *japhara-chettu*. [Tel.] n. The Arnatto or Arnotto Tree, The Rocon Dye Tree, *Bixa orellana*, (Watts.)

జాబాలుడు *jā-bāluḍu*. [Skt.] n. One who tends goats. మేకలనుమేపువాడు. A shepherd కురుబవాడు.

జామాత *jāmata*. [Skt.] n. A son-in-law. A proverb says జామాతా దశమగ్రహః a son-in-law is a Tenth Planet. The nine Planets are astrologically powerful to do evil, each in his hour, and a son-in-law is as pestilent a fellow as a Tenth Planet.

జాయ *jāya*. [Skt.] n. A wife. భార్య. జాయాజీవుడు *jāya-jīruḍu*. n. One who "lives by his wife;" an actor, a dancer.

జాయమానము *jāyamānamu.* [Skt.] adj. Which is got or produced, కలుగుచున్న. నిర్హేతుకజాయమానకటాక్షము unmerited kindness.

జారత్వము *jāratvamu.* [Skt.] n. Incontinence, adultery. జారధవుడు *jāra-dhavu-ḍu.* n. A lover, an adulterer. విటుడు. జారస్త్రీ or జారిణి *jāra-strī.* n. An adulteress. వ్యభిచారిణి. జారుడు *jāruḍu.* n. An adulterer.

జారీ *jārī.* [H.] a. Current, proceeding. జారీ చేయు to set on foot, to put in force.

జాలము or జాలకము *jālamu.* [Skt.] n. A multitude, an assemblage. సమూహము. తీర్థజాలము a confluence of waters. A net. వల. A window, a lattice, a loop or eyelet hole. కిటికీ. BD. iv. 1525. A bud, an unblown flower. మొగ్గ. Deceit మాయ కపటము

జాలికుడు *jālikuḍu.* [Skt.] n. A fisherman.

జాల్ముడు *jālmuḍu.* [Skt.] n. A fool, a blockhead.

జాస్తి *jāsti.* [H.] adj. Extra, additional; in excess. n. Increase.

జాహ్నవి *jāhnavi.* [Skt.] n. Daughter of Jahnu; an epithet of the river Ganges as a goddess.

జి ji

జింక *jinka.* [Tel.] n. The Indian Antelope or Black Buck, *Antilope cervicapra.* See ఇఱ్ఱి, హరిణము. జింకతాల్పు one who carries the antelope on his head, i. e., the moon or Siva చంద్రుడు, శివుడు. జింకపొక్కిలి *jinka-pokkili.* n. Musk కస్తూరి, మృగనాభి. జింకరవుతు *jinka-ravutu.* n. One who rides on an antelope, i. e., the god of wind. వాయువు.

జిగట *jigaṭa.* [Tel.] n. Stickiness, gum, slime, birdlime. జిగటమన్ను clay.

జిగి *jigi.* [Tel.] n. Brilliancy. కాంతి, వెల్లని వెలుగు. T. iv. 200.

జిగిబిగి *jigi-bigi.* [Tel.] adj. Puzzling, surprizing, strange, striking (as beauty).

జిగిలి *jigili.* [Tel.] adj. Plump, fleshy, rounded. చక్కని. Fine, handsome, bright, nice, pretty. చక్కని.

జిగీష *jigīsha.* [Skt.] n. Emulation, wish to excel or overcome. గెలువవిచ్ఛ. An attempt ప్రయత్నము. జిగీషువు one who is ambitious to win.

జిగురు or జిగట *jiguru.* [Tel.] n. Slime, gum, birdlime, clay or paste. బంక. జిగురు కొండె a gummed twig to catch birds with. జిగురుబాయి *jiguru-bāyi.* n. A large kind of cricket or grasshopper.

జిఘత్సువు *jighatsu-vu.* [Skt.] n. He who is hungry. ఆకలిగొన్నవాడు.

జిఘాంస *jighāmsa.* [Skt.] n. Murderous intent. చంపనిచ్ఛ. జిఘాంసువు *jighāmsuvu.* n. A would-be murderer. చంపనిచ్ఛగలవాడు. An enemy శత్రువు.

జిజ్ఞాస *jignyāsa.* [Skt.] n. The wish to know, a wish to ascertain or enquire. తెలియనిచ్ఛ. An enquiry, a search, an investigation. జిజ్ఞాసువు *jignyāsuvu.* n. An enquirer, an investigator.

జిట్ట *jiṭṭa.* [Tel.] n. Sorrow, grief, anxiety. చింత, ఆయాసము. BD. vii. 217; v. 735: M. XII. iii. 441. A prank or strange act. adj. Small. జిట్టజేగిచిట్టు See జేగి. Miscellaneous, of odds and ends, what remains over. జిట్టరాశి a heap formed of odds and ends.

జిట్ట *jiṭṭa* n. The generic name of a class of birds. ఎఱ్ఱకాలిజిట్ట the Yellow-eyed Babbler, *Pyctorhis sinensis.* చెదురుజిట్ట n. The Rufous Fan-tail Warbler, *Cisticola* cursitans. వంటిపిట్ట the small White-throated Babbler, *Dumetia albigularis.* గార్లపిట్ట a new species called *agrobates brunnescens,* Jerdon No. 269. దర్జీపిట్ట the Tailor bird: No 114. అడవిదర్జీపిట్ట the spotted Babbler, *Pellorneum ruficeps.* లొట్టకన్నుపిట్ట (the hollow eyed bird), the Indian Wren-Warbler, *Prinia inornata.* కొండలొట్టకన్నుపిట్ట the Jungle Wren-Warbler, *Prinia Sylvatica.* కంపపిట్ట Blyth's Reed-Warbler, *Acrocephalus dumetorum.* పెదురుకంపపిట్ట the grass Warbler, or meadow Wren-Warbler, a species of Prinia. No. 122. పెద్దనల్లకంపపిట్ట the Eastern Orphean Warbler, *Sylvia jerdoni.* పెద్దకంపపిట్ట the true Warbler, *Sylvia Montana,* No. 123. చిన్నసల్లకంపపిట్ట the Indian Lesser White-throated Warbler, *Sylvia affinis.* చిన్నకంపపిట్ట the Village Warbler, *Sylvia Rama.* No. 124. ఎర్రకంపపిట్ట the Paddy-field Reed-Warbler, *Acrocephalus agricola.* పెదురుపిట్ట the Rufous Fantail Warbler, *Cisticola cursitans.* ఉలుక్కులపిట్ట the Wagtail, *motacilla variegata.* No. 139. The Forest Wagtail, *Limonidromus indicus.* చీకుపిట్ట the Tree Pipit, *Anthus arboreus.* No. 141. పెద్దయీలపిట్ట the great Whistler, a species of Lark. No. 189. మునగపిట్ట the Purple Honey Sucker, No. 224, 232. కుర్రపుమాలపిట్ట the common Titlark of India, *Anthus rufulus.* వడంగాలపిట్ట the common Wood Shrike, *Tephrodornis superciliosus.* నల్లపచ్చపిట్ట the White-winged Black Tit, *Parus nuchalis.* చిన్నపిట్ట the common Babbler, *Argya caudata.* పెరిపిట్ట, గవ్వపిట్ట the Large gray Babbler, *Argya malcolmi.* పెద్దపిట్ట the Jungle Babbler, *Crateropus canorus.* చిలపిట్ట the White-headed Babbler, *Crateropus griseus.* పచ్చపిట్ట the common Iora, *Aegithina tiphia.* కుంకుమపూపిట్ట the small Minivet, *Pericrocotus peregrinus.* ముద్దితిప్పడుపిట్ట the gray Wagtail, *Motacilla melanope.* అడవికంపపిట్ట, కేక, అడవికంప నల్లంచి the Indian Bush-chat, *Pratincola maura.* (F. B. I.) జిట్టంగి *jittangi.* n. The wagtail (so called in the south): the northern word is గాటుకపిట్ట. The female is called దాసరిపిట్ట.

జిట్టాడు *jitt-adu* [Tel.] v n. To play about. To trifle, sport, frolic. To be teased or anxious: to fret: to waver, to fluctuate, as the mind between shame and pleasure. జిట్టాడునట్టుగనుక. v. a. To beat.

జిట్టెడు *jitt-edu.* [Tel.] n. A short span, measured from the thumb to the tip of the forefinger. adj. A span long.

జిడిగింత or జిడిగిరింత *jidigirinta.* [Tel.] n. Dislike, disgust, annoyance. A deceitful word. మోసపుమాట. HD. ii. 620.

జిడ్డ *jidda.* [Tel.] n. Confusion. కలత.

జిడ్డి *jiddi.* [Tel.] n. A coarse cloth. ముతకగుడ్డ. మైనపుజిడ్డి wax cloth. adj. Coarse మోటైన.

జిడ్డు *jiddu.* [Tel.] n. Grease, oil, greasiness. చమురు. ఈ పాలలో జిడ్డు నిండా ఉన్నది in this milk there is a large proportion of grease or butter. adj. Greasy, oily, buttery, unctuous. మైనపుజిడ్డుగల waxy: జిడ్డుగాను to become greasy, జిడ్డగు. జిడ్డుచెట్టు or జిడ్డుపాలచెట్టు *jiddu-chettu.* n. A sort of tree. H. IV. ix. 17. జిడ్డుకడలి or జిడ్డుకడలి the sea of milk. పాండు. iii.

జితము *jitamu.* [Skt.] adj. Conquered, mastered, overcome. జయింపబడిన. జితక్రోధభరక్లేశుడు (Lalito. XI. 9.) free from the passion of anger and the pressure of difficulties. Firm స్థిరము. జితపడు *jita-padu.* v. n. To become firm. స్థిరపడు. To become familiar. వాడుకపడు. ఆ గుణములు దానికి జితపడ్డవి she became accustomed to these whims. జితవారిధి *jita-varidhi.* n. The conqueror of the ocean: a title of Rama or Hanuman or Agastya. జితించు *jitintsu.* v. n. To become familiar, (as a climate). To agree (with the constitution,) తిన్నఅన్నము జితించదు the food does not digest. జితేంద్రియుడు *jitendriyudu*. n. One who is free from lusts, one who is chaste and not a slave to any passion. జితేంద్రియుడై యున్నాడు he has great self-command.

జిత్తు *jittu*. [Tel.] n. A prank, a freak, deceit. మోసము, మాయ. నక్కజిత్తులు fox's tricks. జిత్తులమారి a cunning rogue జిత్తులు చేయువాడు.

జిద్దు *jiddu*. [Tel.] n. Enmity. A quarrel. జగడము, కలహము.

జినుడు *jinudu*. [Skt.] n. A man of Jain religion. Also, the generic name of the chief saints of the Buddhist and Jains sects. The name of the god they worship.

జిబిలిక or జీబిలిక *jibilika*. [Tel.] n. A tree called ఋశ్యగంధ. A kind of cucumber. ఒకవిధమైన దోస.

జిబ్బుడాయి or జిబ్బుడై *jibbudayi*. [Tel.] n. A small kind of bat. గబ్బిలము, చీకురాయి.

జిమ్మ *jimma*. [Tel.] adj. Much, great. మిక్కిలి, అధికము.

జిమ్మా *jimmā*. [Tel.] n. Charge, fidelity, service.

జియ్య *jiyya*. [Tel.] n. God. దేవుడు. A king రాజు.

"తే॥ గీ॥ జియ్యయొకనైన బ్రోనవే చిత్తగించి"
య. ii.

"అపుడప్పక్కినుకందు రక్కసుల జియ్యండాకి"
రామా. v.

జియ్య or జియ్యరు *jiyya*. [Tel.] n. Sir. A general term of respect or affection. A lord or master. A Vaishnava palmer or mendicant. వైష్ణవసన్యాసి.

జిర or జిర్ర *jira*. [Tel.] n. A whirling noise తిరుగుట, త్రిప్పటలయందు కలుగుధ్వని. జిరగొట్టు *jira-kottu*. v. n. To turn suddenly round. గిర్రునతిరుగు.

జిరా or జీరా *jirā*. [Tel.] n. Armour. కవచము. An arrow బాణము.

జిరాయితీ or జిరాయతి *jirayiti*. [H.] adj. Cultivated. n. Cultivation. కృషి. జిరాయితి భూములు lands assessable, as opposed to inam lands.

జిరుకొట్టు *jiru-kottu*. [Tel.] v. n. To shout, in driving cattle: to hoop or halloo. Parij. v. 20.

జిర్ర, Same as జిర. జిర్రతాడు *jirra-tadu*. [Tel.] n. A twisted cord, a halter (HD. i. 1775.) పెరియొక్కించినతాడు.

జిర్రు *jirru*. [Tel.] n. The noise made by the cricket. చిమ్మటకూత. A loud noise. జిర్రున *jirru-na*. adv. Quickly; suddenly. తటాలున, శీఘ్రముగా.

జిల *jila*. [Tel.] n. An itching sensation. దురద. జిలజిలమను *jila-jila-m-anu*. v. n. To itch, to be prurient. To tingle or tickle.

జిలకర or జిలకర్ర, See జీలకర్ర.

జిలమ *jilama*. [Tel.] n. A kind of rice. జిలమబియ్యము. Rox. ii. 204.

జిలి *jili*. [Tel.] adj. Sweet. జిలిపాలు sweet or fresh milk.

జిలిబిలి *jili-bili*. [Tel.] adj. Sweet, fine, nice, delicate, agreeable. మనోజ్ఞమైన. Trifling, petty అల్పము. జిలిబిలి పట్టుచీర watered silk cloth చిన్నచిన్న మబ్బులగల పట్టుచీర. జిలిబిలిజెల్లి a small mark on the forehead బొట్టు.

జిలుగతిరికి *jiluga-tiriki*. [Tel.] n. A kind of fish, *Taeniura melanospilos, Teniura Lymma*, Forskal (F. B. I.)

జిలుగు *jilugu*. [Tel.] n. Fineness. Fine cloth, muslin. సూక్ష్మవస్త్రము. Swa. v. 92. The Hill-Palm (Bombay), the Sago-Palm, *Caryota urens*, (Watts). స్వర్ణపుష్పి. adj. Fine, delicate. Weak, thin. సూక్ష్మము. జిలుగుపని delicate work. A. v. 78. జిలుగుతిట్లు a delicate rebuke, gentle chiding. జిలుగు v. n. To scribble or write a fine minute hand. గొలుసుమోడిగా వ్రాయు. To make a thing intricate చిక్కుగాచేయు.

జిలుగు, జిలువు or జీలుగు *jilugu*. [Tel.] n. The gigantic Swallow wort. జిల్లేడు.

జిల్ల *jilla*. [Tel.] n. A bit of stick. కర్ర ముక్క, బిళ్లగోడాటయందలిబిళ్ల.

జిల్లా or జిల్లా *jilla*. [H.] n. A province or district.

జిల్లు *jillu*. [Tel] n. Coldness, chill. ముక్కులి చేలి. జిల్లుమనే bleak, chill

జిల్లేడు *jillēḍu*. [Tel.] n. The gigantic Swallow wort. *Asclepias gigantea*. Rox. ii. 30. and ii. 7. *Calotropis gigantea* (Watts.) అర్కవృక్షము the red-flowered variety; నల్లజిల్లేడు the lilac-flowered variety. నల్లజిల్లేడువంటిపిల్ల a child that is as lean as a lath. తేటిజిల్లేడేటికి will the bee seek the acrid asclepias? జిల్లేడు కాయలు *jillēḍu-kāyalu*. n. plu. The fruit of the జిల్లేడు. Also, a cake of that shape. భక్ష్యవిశేషము.

జిల్లేదారుడు *jillēdaruḍu*. [H.] n. A certain revenue officer.

జివురు Same as చిగురు.

జివ్విచెట్టు Same as జువ్విచెట్టు.

జివ్వున *jivvu-na*. [Tel.] adv. All at once, briskly.

జివ్వురు *jivvuru*. [Tel.] n. Boiling over. చిమ్ముడుట.

జిష్ణువు *jishṇuvu*. [Skt.] n. A conqueror; an epithet of Indra and Arjuna. ఇంద్రుడు, అర్జునుడు, విష్ణువు. adj. Victorious, triumphant.

జిహాస *jihāsa*. [Skt.] n. Desire to give up. విడువవిచ్చ. Hate. Inveteracy. Disinclination. చలము, క్రౌర్యము.

జిహీర్ష *jihīrsha*. [Skt.] n. Inclination to seize. హరింపనిచ్ఛ.

జిహ్మము *jihmamu*. [Skt.] adj. Crooked. వంకరైన. జిహ్మాక్షి squint eyed. జిహ్మగము *jihmagamu*. n. (Lit.) A crooked goer, i. e., a snake or serpent. A sinner, one who goes astray.

జిహ్వ. *jihva* [Skt.] n. The tongue. జిహ్వ యంత్రము *jihva-yantramu*. n. A hook for fishing. గాలము. జిహ్వాచాపల్యము *jihva-chāpalyamu*. n. A longing to eat. జిహ్వామూలీయము a term applied to *visarga* when it comes before క.

జీ jī

జీంద్రము *jīndramu*. [Tel.] n. A miserable state, a pest, a plague, teasing. పీకులాట, నచ్చు.

జీగురు Same as చిగురు.

జీడి *jīḍi*. [Tel.] n. The sap or milk of the mango, &c. జీడిగింజ *jīḍi-ginza*. n. The marking nut. జీడిచెట్టు or జీడిమామిడిచెట్టు *jīḍi-cheṭṭu*. n. The cashew nut tree, *Anacardium occidentale*. (Rox. ii. 312. and Watts.)

జీడె or జీడియ *jīḍe*. [Tel.] n. A sweatmeat, composed of sesamum seeds and treacle.

జీతము *jītamu*. [Tel.] n. Salary, wages, pay. వేతనము, సంబళము. జీతగాడు *jīta-gāḍu*. n. A paid servant, one who serves for wages.

జీనపటము *jīna-paṭamu*. [Tel.] n. A belt. దట్టి.

జీనము *jīnamu*. [Tel.] n. A pad put under the saddle of a horse. నమ్దా.

జీని *jīni*. [Tel.] adj. Fine. నాణెమైన. జీనిగిరి వాడు *jīnigiri-vāḍu*. n. An artisan; a worker in leather; an upholsterer. ముచ్చి వాడు.

జీను *jīnu*. [Tel.] n. An anchor. లంగరు. A saddle.

జీనుగోవి or జీనుగ్రోవి *jīnu-gōvi*. [Tel.] n. A flute used in charming snakes.

జీనువ or జీనువాయి *jīnuva*. [Tel.] n. The tailor bird, or The White-throated Munia, *Uroloncha malabarica*. నల్లజీనువాయి

nalla-jinuvāyi. n. The Black headed Munia, Munia malacca. కాకెర జీనువాయి kākara-jinuvāyi. n. The Spotted Munia, Uroloncha punctulata. తొర్ర జీనువాయి torra-jinuvāyi. n. The Indian Red Munia, Sporoeginthus amandava. వెదురుజీనువాయి or వెదురుపిచ్చిక veduru-jinuvāyi. n. The common Rose Finch, Carpodacus erythrinus. పచ్చజీనువాయి patsta-jinuvāyi. n. The Red-headed Bunting, Emberiza luteola. (F. B. I.)(Jerdon, No. 114.) "చిక్కసామునంబున జీనువాయి" Tara. ii. జీనువముక్కులు jinuva-mukkulu. n. A sort of grain. H. iv.159.

జీబు jību. [Tel.] n. A woman's cloth. కోక. Anuk. v. A net: lace: a net-like web which surrounds the cocoanut and other similar trees at those parts whence the branches expand. పీచు. జీబుకొను jibu-konu. v. n. To become thick. దట్టమగు.

జీమూతము jī-mūtamu. [Skt.] n. A mountain: కొండ. A cloud మబ్బు. నీలజీమూతసంకాశము like a blue cloud.

జీర jīra. [Tel.] n. A line or stripe, a crack, slit, or flaw (in coin or diamonds) గీర, రేఖ. A kind of fish. G. i. 111.

జీరంగి jīrangi. [Tel.] n. A green beetle, the emerald wing cases of which are fastened on embroidery as an ornament.

జీరకము, జీరణము or జీరము jīrakamu. [Skt.] n. Cummin seed. జీలకర్ర.

జీరా jīra. [Tel.] n. Armour. కవచము.

జీరు jīru. [Tel.] v. n. To hang down, dangle, or trail on the ground. జీరాడు, జీరుకాడు or జీరులాడు jīrādu. [Tel. జీరు+ఆడు.] v. n. To sweep. పందికడుపు నేలను జీరాడుచున్నది the sow's belly sweeps the ground. కొంగు జీరాడుచున్నది the end of the cloth is hanging down on the ground. జీరువారు jīru-vāru. v. n. To spread (as a smile over the countenance) వ్యాపించు. To move, జరుగు. To avoid, go out of the way. తొలగు.

జీరుకు or జీర్కు jīruku. [Tel.] n. Slipperiness. జారుడు. జీర్కుబండలు smooth slippery slabs of stone. (Parij. iv. 43.)

జీర్ణము jīrṇamu. [Skt.] adj. Digested. Tattered, worn, old, ruined, dead, faded, (as leaves). శిథిలమైన. n. Digestion. అరగడము. Ruin, the act of being destroyed. నశించడము. జీర్ణకోశము the stomach. జీర్ణించు jīrṇintsu. v. n. To be digested. To grow old, to waste, to decay, wear away. జీర్ణమగు, అరుగు.

జీలకర్ర or జీరకము jīla-karra. [Tel.] n. Fennel, cummin seed: Cuminum. Rox. ii. 92. నల్లజీలకర్ర or సీమజీలకర the black Caraway, Carum nigrum. (Watts.) This word is used as a term of contempt like "fiddlesticks."

జీలు jīlu. [Tel.] n. A sequel, a supplement, an appendix. ఈ జీలున వ్రాయబడిన hereinafter written.

జీలుగ jīluga. [Tel.] n. A kind of bird: the shrike, or the small owl.

జీలుగ or జీలుగు jīluga. [Tel.] n. A certain tree of pithy substance, like the cork tree. శీతవృక్షము. ఉగజీలుగ the Indian Horse Chestnut. Æschynomene indica. జీలుగబెండు jīluga-beṇḍu. n. A sort of pith, of which toys are made.

జీవము jīvamu. [Skt.] n. Life, existence. ప్రాణము. The vital spirit, the soul ఆత్మ. An animal or creature ప్రాణి. కాకిజీవము one whose life is as long, as vile and as wretched as that of a crow. దుష్టజీవము a despicable being. జీవరూపము the living image. జీవంజీవము jīvam-jīvamu. n. A fabulous bird చకోరపక్షి, వెన్నెలపులుగు, వెన్నెలపులుగు. జీవగర్ర jīva-garra. n. A prop, stay, support. ప్రాణరక్షకము. R. vii. 143. జీవకుడు jīvakuḍu. n. A living man జీవించువాడు. A ప్రాణి. One who lives A servant కొలువుడుకాడు జీవచ్ఛవము jīvach-chhavamu. n. A living corpse. [illegible] జీవదుడు jīvaduḍu. n. [illegible]

One who gives life. జీవముబిచ్చువాడు. A medical man. వైద్యుడు. జీవధనము *jiva-dhanamu*. n. Cattle. గోవులులోనగునవి. జీవ నౌషధము *jivan-aushadhamu*. n. A medicine that revives life. బ్రతుకజేసేమందు. జీవన్ముక్తుడు *jivan-muktudu*. n. One who has become emancipated from all desire. A man who is in the world but not of the world. జీవించియుండియును జ్ఞానముగోని సమస్తబంధములను విడనాడ్టుకొని . ముక్తి నొందిన వాడు. జీవవృత్తి *jiva-vritti*. n. Tending cattle. గోవులు . గుర్రములు మొదలైనవానిని పెంచుకొని చేసే జీవనము. జీవదంతము *jiva-dantamu*. n. Solid ivory; ivory cut from a living elephant. జీవనము *jivana-mu*. n. Life, existence, livelihood, means of subsistence, profession. బ్రతుకు, బ్రతుకు తెరువు. Water ఉదకము. జీవనముచేయు to make a living, to earn a livelihood. జీవనోపాధి *jiva-nōpadhi*. n. Livelihood, means of living. జీవన్మృతుడు *jivan-mritudu*. n. One who though living is yet dead, one who is half dead. జీవించియుండి యును చచ్చినవాడు. జీవరత్నము *jiva-ratnamu*. n. A gem of the first water. శ్రేష్ఠరత్నము. జీవరేఖలు *jiva-rēkhalu*. n. The finishing lines in statuary, the last touches which give a living appearance. జీవశిల *jiva-sila*. n. The living rock. జీవాంతకుడు *jivantakudu*. n. A bird catcher. పిట్టలకొట్టెవాడు. జీవాతువు *jivaturu*. n. Livelihood. బ్రతుకు. A prop or support జీవగర్ర. Cooking వంటకము. జీవాత్మ *jiv-atma*. n. An embodied spirit, the individual soul enshrined in the human body as distinguished from the Supreme Soul (పరమాత్మ). The principle of life. జీవాళము or జీవ *jivalamu*. n. The main point, the chief object. A bit of cord or wire put loose between the cords of a guitar to regulate the sound. ఎంతికిందివాడు. జీవి *jivi*. n. A living creature or animal. ప్రాణి, జీవించువాడు. స్వల్పజీవి a vain foolish brute. కాకజీవి one whose life is as long and wretched as that of a crow. జీవించు *jivintsu*. v. n. To live, exist, subsist. బ్రతుకు. జీవిక *jivika*. n. Livelihood, profession or occupation. జీవనోపాయము, బ్రతుకుతెరువు. జీవితము *jivitamu*. n. Living, existence. బ్రతకడము. Life ప్రాణము. జీవితకాలము *jivita-kalamu*. n. Lifetime. జీవితేశుడు *jivit-ēsudu*. n. "Lord of one's life, i. e.," a husband, a name of Yama, the judge of departed souls. ప్రాణనాయకుడు, యముడు. జీవుడు *jivudu* n. The soul, the sentient principle: a living being. ప్రాణి.

జు ju

జుగుప్స *jugupsa*. [Skt.] n Dislike. Censure, reviling, నింద, రోత, అవమానము.

జూ jū

జూటము *jūtamu*. [Skt] n. Matted hair; such as is worn by hermits. జడముడి. చుట్టచుట్టినజడ.

జృ jri

జృంభము or జృంభణము *jrimbhamu*. [Skt.] n. Gaping, yawning; opening, expansion, spreading. ఆవులింత, శరీరమువిరుచుకోవడము, వికాసము జృంభించు *jrimbhintsu*. v. n. To gape, yawn. ఆవులించుట. జృంభితము *jrimbhitamu* n. A yawn. ఆవులింత. adj. Gaping, yawning; expanded, open, spread. వికసించిన.

జె je

జెండా *jendā*. [H.] n. A flag, banner. Same as జండా.

జెంత *jenta*. [Tel.] n. A cunning woman. కుత్సితప్రౌఢస్త్రీ

జెట్టి *jetti*. [Tel] n. A wrestler, a prizefighter. మల్లుడు, శూరుడు. adj. Best శ్రేష్ఠుడు. జెట్టి

జెట్టిపట్టు jetti-pattu. n. A wrestling match. జెట్టిపెనకువ jetti-penakuva. n. A bout in wrestling. జెట్టిమిడత jetti-miḍata. n. The giant locust.

జెన jena. [Tel.] n. Spawn, roe. The yolk of an egg. గుడ్డులోని పసుపుసొన.

జెముడు jemuḍu. [Tel.] n. A general name applied to plants of the *cactus* family. The plant called milk-hedge. *Euphorbia tirucalli*. Rox. ii. 470. (Ainslie) వజ్రకంటకము. ఆకుజెముడు oleander-leaved spurge. బొంతజెముడు or బొమ్మజెముడు the large species of cactus. మరిజెముడు and కోలజెముడు and other species occur. సీమజెముడు, *Bryophyllum calycinum*. జెముడుకాకి jemuḍu-kāki. n. The common coucal or Crow-Pheasant, *Centropus sinensis*.

జెర్రి jerri. [Tel.] n. A centipede (*scolopendra.*) కాళ్లజెర్రి the same. జెర్రిపోతు jerri-pōtu. n. The whipsnake, erroneously supposed to be the male of the cobra. This name is given to various species of the Sole-fish (*Pleuronectes*) See Russell, Fishes. No. 70. *Solea Commersonii*. J. No. 71. *Solea Jerreus*. 73. *Plagusia Potous*, No. 74. *Plagusia Bilineatus*.

జెల jela. [Tel.] n. A spring of water. నీటిబుగ్గ, భూమిలోనిజలధార.

జెలగ jelaga. [Tel.] n. A leech. ఆకుతోటజెలగ a snail. చిమిడిజెలగ (the slime snail) a slug. జెలగరోగము jelaga-rōgamu. n. The leech evil, that kills cattle, through their paunches being filled with leeches. జెలగవాటు jelaga-vāṭu n. A triangular pattern woven at the end of cloths.

జెల్ల jella. [Tel.] n. A fish like the dragonet: with a broad snout and three large strong prickles, supposed to be venomous, on its forehead and cheeks. చింతజెల్ల *Bagrus China* (Russell Fishes, No. 167.) పిల్లిజెల్ల *Bagrus bilineatus*, J. (No. 167.) నల్లజెల్ల *Pimelodus nella*, J., three species of Silurus. Also జెల్ల (No 174). *Esox sphyræna jellow* and ముగజెల్ల (No. 183) A species of *Polynemus*, *Hemicampus Marginatus*, Swains. Other species are నారజెల్ల and కుడిజెల్ల. H. iv. 225.

జెల్లి or జెల్లికంప jelli. [Tel.] n. The plant called *Arachis fruticosa*. Rox iii. 282.

జెష్ట jeshṭa. [Tel. from జ్యేష్ఠ an elder sister: used to mean an old crone.] n. A plague: a pest: an evil: gibberish: nonsense, rubbish. జెష్టవదలినది I am out of that plague. నాకు జెష్టపట్టినది I was bewitched. వానికి జెష్టపట్టినది he has lost all his luck.

జే jē

జే jē. [Tel.] Interj. Victory! May the victory be yours! May you have victory or success జయజయ అని దీవించుట. A salutation. నమస్కారము.

జేంద్ర jēndra. [Tel.] n. A certain tribe of weavers.

జేగ jēga. [Tel.] n. A sort of crane or heron.

జేగంట jēganṭa. [Tel. for జయఘంట.] n. A gong or bell. గెలుపునకు గురుతుగా వాయించే పెద్దగంట.

జేగురు or జేవురు jēguru. [Tel.] n. Redness. ఎరుపు. adj. Red. ఎర్రని. జేగురుటేరు a red stream. Kalahas. ii. 58. Zacc. iii. 80. గైరికము. జేగురుగండి jēguru-ganḍi. n. An embrasure or loophole for muskets: being a hole coloured red. జేగురుకొండ a red hill. జేగురువేరు jēguru-vēru. n. The root from which a red dye is extracted. జేగురించు jēgurintsu. v. n. To redden, or blush with shame or anger. To grow red. ఎర్రనగు.

"నెత్తురు మేనెల్ల నిండిపారగ,
జేవురుకొండనా చెలువు దీపింప."

Pal. 108.

జేజె or జేజే jēje. [Tel.] n. A god, a goddess, a deity: వేల్పు, దేవుడు. జేజమ్మ jējamma. n. A goddess. నీకు జేజమ్మ నిన్ను పట్టించిన

జేజమ్మకు దొరకవు it will puzzle you and your grand mother too to find them. జేజేచెలి is a wife of a god. దేవత. జేజే jējē. interj. Hurra! huzza! జయజయ అని దీవించుట. జేజేధ్వనులు huzzas, salutations. నమస్కారములు BD. v. 1035. సర్వోత్కృష్టమైన సుందరమైన మంగళము చేయుడము. జేజేగట్టు the mount Mēru. జేజేపట్టు Heaven స్వర్గము, సురాలయము.

జేడె or **జేడియ** *jēḍe*. [Tel.] n. A marshy soil. బురదనేల.

జేత *jēta*. [Skt.] n. One who conquers. జయించువాడు.

జేన *jēna*. [Tel.] n. A span, a length of nine inches.

జేనగితాడు, జానకితాడు or **జానెకితాడు** *jēnagi-tāḍu*. [Tel.] n. A match or fuse for a gun.

జేనచెట్టు *jēna-chettu*. [Tel.] n. A certain tree the fruit of which is eaten. *Adenanthera aculeata*. Rox. ii. 371. అడివిజేన the Arum Sylvatica. Rox. iii. 511.

జేపట్టు or **జేపెట్టు** *jē-pattu*. [Tel.] v. a. To bless. దీవించు.

జేబు *jēbu*. [H.] n. A pocket. సొక్కాయ లోని సంచి.

జేయుడు *jēyuḍu*. [Skt.] n. One who can be conquered. జయింపదగినవాడు.

జేరుబందు *jēru-bandu*. [H.] n. A martingale, a saddle girth.

జేవురు *jēvuru*. Same as జేగురు.

జై jai

జైత్రము *jaitramu*. [Skt.] adj. Victorious, triumphant. జైత్రుడు a victor or conqueror. జయించువాడు.

జైనము *jainamu*. [Skt.] n. The Jain religion. జైనుడు a Jain.

జైవాతృకము *jaivātṛikamu*. [Skt.] n. A drug or medicament. ప్రతికించేకొషధము. adj. Long lived. జైవాతృకుడు *jaivātṛikuḍu*. n. One who is long lived. దీర్ఘాయుష్మగల వాడు. A physician వైద్యుడు. The moon చంద్రుడు.

జో jō

జోక్యము or **జోక్యము** *jōkyamu*. [Tel.] n. Connection; సంబంధము. Risk, peril, hazard.

జోటి *jōṭi*. [Skt.] n. A sheet or blanket. దుప్పటి.

జ్ఞ gnya

జ్ఞప్తి *gnyapti*. [Skt.] n. Understanding, తెలివి, తలపు. Recollection. జ్ఞాపకము. నాకు అప్పుడు జ్ఞప్తి తప్పి ఉండినది I was at that time out of my senses. అది నాకు జ్ఞప్తికి రాలేదు I did not recollect it.

జ్ఞా gnyā

జ్ఞాతము *gnyātamu*. [Skt.] adj. That which is known. తెలియబడినది. అజ్ఞాతము unknown అజ్ఞాతవాసము living incognito.

జ్ఞాతి *gnyāti*. [Skt.] n. A fellow heir: a cousin or kinsman on the father's side. దాయాదుడు. జ్ఞాతిత్వము relationship through common male ancestors. జ్ఞాతివైమనస్యము rivalry such as exists between heirs.

జ్ఞానము *gnyānamu*. [Skt.] n. Wisdom, knowledge. తెలివి. Higher knowledge. Theology. మోక్షవిషయమైన బుద్ధి. Philosophy. In some compounds it may be rendered supernatural. జ్ఞానకాండము *gnyāna-kānḍamu*. n. The doctrinal portion of the Vedas which contains the esoteric teaching relating to the spiritual knowledge. The doctrine of Faith as opposed to that of Works. జ్ఞానదృష్టి *gnyāna-drishṭi.* n. Spiritual vision, supernatural intelligence, the prophetic eye: second sight. Clairvoyance. జ్ఞాననిద్ర *gnyāna-nidra.* n. A deep unnatural sleep, such as occurs in Mesmerism. Ecstasy. A metaphysical delirium which suspends the senses. యోగనిద్ర. జ్ఞానమార్గము *gnyāna-mārgamu.* n. The path of wisdom; the doctrine that salvation is to be obtained by means of meditation on, and the consequent union with the Supreme Spirit. జ్ఞానశరీరము *gnyāna-śarīramu.* n. The spiritual body: as distinguished from the corporeal body. (స్థూలశరీరము, or మాయాశరీరము.) జ్ఞానస్వరూపము *gnyāna-svarūpamu.* n. The spiritual form or image, invisible to the mortal eye. జ్ఞాని *gnyāni.* n One who possesses wisdom, a philosopher, a sage, a prophet, an inspired teacher. జ్ఞానముగలవాడు. జ్ఞానేంద్రియము *gnyānēndriyamu.* n. An organ of perception. A supernatural sense, such as the power of perceiving spirits. See Tantra Rajam. XVII. 4. జ్ఞానేంద్రియములు senses of perception or knowledge as opposed to కర్మేంద్రియములు senses of action. The five senses of man as త్వక్కు Touch, చక్షువు Sight, శ్రోత్రము Hearing, జిహ్వ Taste and ఘ్రాణము Smell.

జ్ఞాపకము *gnyāpakamu.* [Skt.] n. That which makes known. తెలియజేయునది. Memory. జ్ఞాపకముచేయు to remind, to recall. నన్ను జ్ఞాపకముచేసినారా did you remind him about me? అది జ్ఞాపకమా do you recollect it? జ్ఞాపిక *gnyāpika.* n. A reminder. A notice.

జ్ఞే gnye

జ్ఞేయము *gnyēyamu.* [Tel.] adj. Knowable, cognisable, known. తెలియదగిన.

జ్యా jyā

జ్య *jya.* [Skt.] n. A bowstring. వింటినారి. The earth. నేల, భూమి.

జ్యాని *jyāni.* [Skt.] n. Old age, infirmity. ముదిమి. Decay, పాతగిలడము.

జ్యే jyē

జ్యేష్ఠ *jyēshṭha.* [Skt.] n. The month Jyeshṭha, (June, July.) ఒకనెల. adj. Elder. జ్యేష్ఠసంతతి the eldest born. జ్యేష్ఠ n. Misfortune personified as a goddess జేష్ట. జ్యేష్ఠావధి A day in the month Jyēshṭha, on which ploughing time commences. జ్యేష్ఠుడు the eldest man మొదటివాడు. అగ్రజుడు.

జ్యో jyō

జ్యోతి *jyōti.* [Skt.] n. Light, radiance. వెలుగు. In a mystic sense, internal illumination. The lights that dance before the eyes when dazzled or closed. A lump of paste, used as a meat offering. A star నక్షత్రము The eye కన్ను. The sun సూర్యుడు. జ్యోతిర్లత *jyōtir-lata.* n. An *ignis fatuus.* A ray of light. జ్యోతిరింగణము *jyōti-r-ingaṇamu.* n. A firefly or glow-worm మిణుగురుపురుగు. జ్యోతిషము *jyōtishamu.* n. Astronomy, astrology. జోస్యము. జ్యోతిష్కుడు, జ్యోతిషికుడు or జ్యౌతిషికుడు *jyōtishkuḍu.* n. An astronomer: an astrologer, a fortune teller. జ్యోతిష్మతి *jyōtish-mati.* n. A plant, the Balloon vine, or, the Heart-pea, or, the Winter Cherry, *Cardiospermum Halicacabum,* (Watts), also called ముద్దగ్గలత, వెక్కుడుతీగె or ఉప్పురం. జ్యోతిశ్చక్రము an astronomical chart or diagram. సూర్యచంద్రాది నక్షత్ర గ్రహములను చూపేపటము. జ్యోతిస్సు *jyōtissu*. n. Radiance. జ్యోత్స్న *jyōtsna*. n. Moonlight. వెన్నెల. జ్యోత్స్ని *jyōtsni*. n. A moonlight night. వెన్నెలరాత్రి.

జ్వ jva

జ్వరము *jvaramu*. [Skt.] n. Fever. చలిజ్వరము ague and fever. పిత్తజ్వరము bilious fever. జ్వరాంకుశము a specific against fever. (Rox: i. 275 Ainsl. ii. 114.) Quinine. జ్వరపట్ట the Calisaya Bark, the yellow bark of commerce, *Cinchona Calisaya* (Watts.) జ్వరితుడు *jvaritudu*. n. A fever-stricken man, one suffering from fever జ్వరముగలవాడు.

జ్వలనము *jvalanamu*. [Skt.] n. Burning, fire మంట, అగ్ని. జ్వలించు *jvalintsu*. v. n. To burn మండు. To shine ప్రకాశించు. జ్వలితము *jvalitamu*. adj. Burnt. మండిన. Shining, illuminated. ప్రకాశించిన. జ్వాల *jvala*. n. A flame, a blaze. మంట.

జ dza

జ *dza*. [Tel.] n. The letter z.

జంకు *dzanku*. [Tel.] v. n. To fear. భయపడు. To hesitate సంకోచించు. n. Fear, hesitation, fright. నిచ్చెన జంకుచున్నది the ladder is shaking or giving way. జంకించు *dzankintsu*. v. a. To frighten, to intimidate. బెదిరించు. జంకె or జంకెన *dzanke*. n. Fright, alarm, a threat. బెదిరింపు. జంకెన చూపులు timid glances. జంకెయొనర్చు to frighten బెదిరించు.

జంగ *dzanga*. [Tel.] n. The calf of the leg. పిక్క. A stride. అంగ. జంగయిడు, జంగగొను, or జంగపెట్టు to take a stride. దాటు. జంగ వేయు to stride. జంగనడ *dzanga-nada*. n. A certain pace in horses. జంగనడక striding, కాలుచాచినడచునడక.

జంగము *dzangamu*. [Tel.] n. (Lit. a sojourner) A Jangam. Name of a Saivite sect, the members of which wear the lingam.

జంగాళము *dzangalamu*. [Tel.] n. Length. నిడుపాటు. A fictitious or artificial emerald. Charitr., v. 1878.

జంగి *dzangi*. [Tel.] n. The spreading of fire. అగ్నిప్రసారము.

జంగిలి *dzangili*. [Tel.] n. A herd of cattle. పశువుల మంద. A herd of animals జంతుసమూహము. A headman or leader. నాయకుడు. ఏనుగులజంగిలి a herd of elephants. సింహములజంగిలి a herd of lions. ఉ. ii.

జంగు, జంగె or జంగియ *dzangu*. [Tel.] n. A silver ornament or badge, fastened on the leg of a Jangam when he is first sent to receive alms. అందె, మువ్వ, ఒకవిధ మైనగజ్జె.

జంగుపిల్లి *dzangu-pilli*. [Tel.] n. The serval: a spotted reddish wild cat. అడవిపిల్లి.

జంజడ *dzandzada*. [Tel.] n. A nail or screw. చీల.

జంజా *dzandzā*. [Tel.] n. A multitude గుంపు, సమూహము.

జంజాటము *dzandzatamu*. [Tel.] n. Connection, relationship. తగులము, పొత్తు.

"క॥ ఓటమితో నల్లప్పుడు,
పాటవమున బమలుచేసి బాలుడతోనే
యాటలకుబోక యొకజం
జాటంబునురేక ధృతిసలుపుదునఘా."
భాగ. i.

జంజాడి, జేమువాడి, జేముదాలి, జంజాలి or జంజాళి *dzandzadi*. [Tel.] n. A dagger with a gauntlet handle across the blade. పొడుగైనపరుజాగలకత్తి. A swivel-gun.

జంట *dzanṭa*. [Tel.] n. A pair or couple. జోడు, జత. adv. Behind వెనుక; near దగ్గిర. జంటగా with, along with. మూడుతాళ్లు జంటగా మెలిపెట్టుట to twist three cords together. జంటుముక్కాలి (జంటు+మూడు+కాలు+ఇ.) n. That which has twice three legs, i. e., a bee తుమ్మెద, షట్పదము. **జంటించు** *dzantintsu.* v. a. To add or connect, annex, subjoin. జంటించిమాట్లాడు to add word to word, to jabber. **జంటు** *dzantu.* v. n. To be in a string: to be connected together. జంటుపడు. జంటిన joined. **జంటి** or **జంటీ** *dzanti.* n. Lace సరిగపట్టి. జంటిరవిక a boddice trimmed with lace.

జంత or **జంతి** *dzanta.* [Tel.] n. A wicked woman, a hag, a jade. ధూర్తురాలు.

జంతిక *dzantika.* [Tel.] n. A kind of cake. ఒకవిధమైన భక్ష్యము. Also, an instrument for making those cakes. ఆ భక్ష్యమునుచేసే ఒకవిధమైన పనిముట్టు. జంతికపుండు a boil with many openings in it అనేకరంధ్రములు గల పుండు.

జంతె *dzante.* [Tel.] n. A weeding machine. జంతెపట్టు to weed a field with the weeding machine.

జంత్రము *dzantramu.* [from Skt. యంత్రము. n. An instrument, a machine. యంత్రము. A string సూత్రము. A doll moved by a string, a puppet. **జంత్రగాడు** *dzantra-kadu.* n. One who moves dolls at a show by means of strings. సూత్రధారుడు. జంత్రపువాద్యము instrumental music. జంత్రగాత్రసంగీతము instrumental and vocal music. జంత్రపుబొమ్మ a puppet, an automaton, a doll: a splendid image or beautiful figure.

జందెము or **జంధ్యము** *dzandemu.* [Tel.] n. The sacred thread worn by the twice born castes in India. యజ్ఞోపవీతము, జన్నిదము. వానికి జందెమువేసితిని I drew a line across him (with my sword, meaning, I cleft him through the shoulder.) ఉత్తర జందెము a gold thread worn in lieu of a cotton one on solemn occasions.

జంపఖానా *dzampa-khana.* [H.] n. A carpet.

జంపము *dzampamu.* [Tel.] n. A piece of rope or leather thong to which a stirrup is tied. అంకవన్నె తగిలించే దారము లోనగునది.

జంపాడు *dzamp-adu.* [Tel. జంపు+ఆడు.] v. n. To swing. B. X. 281. To move. కదలు.

జంపాలు *dzampalu.* [Tel.] n. A lullaby, a cradle song. జోలపాట.

జంపు *dzampu.* [Tel.] n. Length. పొడుగు. Procrastination. ఆలస్యము. Thinness సన్నదనము. A long gold jewel with pendant pearls worn on the ear. adj. Long. నిడివియైన. జంపుకురులు long tresses. **జంపునడపు** *dzampu-nadapu.* v. a. To procrastinate.

జంపె *dzampe.* [Tel.] n. Slow time in music. *Andante.* వదియక్షరములకాలము.

జంబి or **జమ్మి** *dzambi.* [Tel.] n. The tree called *Mimosa suma*. Rox. ii. 563.

జంబు or **జమ్ము** *dzambu.* [Tel.] n. A bulrush; sedge. జమ్ముగూడ or జంబుగూడు a cope made of this, worn by fisherman and others against rain. **జంబేరు** *dzamb-eru.* [జంబు+ఏరు.] n. The river జంబువు. A river of gold said to flow from the Mountain Mēru.

జక్కర *dzakkara.* [Tel.] n. A river. నది. జక్కరరాయుడు the ocean సముద్రుడు.

జక్కలించు *dzakkalintsu.* [Tel.] v. t. To ridicule. గేలిచేయు. **జక్కలింపు** *dzakka-limpu.* n. Jeering, quizzing.

జక్కవ Same as చక్రవాకము. జక్కవసోగ the moon చంద్రుడు. జక్కవలరేడు the sun సూర్యుడు.

జక్కి *dzakki.* [Tel.] n. A horse. గుర్రము. A grindstone. తిరుగలి.

జక్కించు *dzakkintsu.* [Tel.] v. n. To be bound as regards the law or duty. కట్టుపడు.

జక్కిణి *ḍzakkiṇi.* [Tel.] n. (A term in music) A flourish, a grace. Vish. vii. 292. An actor's garb or masque. Antics: a sort of wild dance. ఒకవిధమైన ఆట. B. ii. 133.

జక్కిని *ḍzakkini.* [Tel.] n. A woman who dies in the matron state, not as a widow. మృతసువాసిని. Name of Kubera's wife కుబేరుని భార్య. జక్కినీడు *ḍzakkin-īḍu.* [జక్కిని+ఈడు.] n. Kubera కుబేరుడు.

జక్కులవాండ్లు *ḍzakkula-vānḍlu.* [Tel.] n. plu. A certain caste of conjurors or wizards, who worship the goddess Kāmēswari or Circe. జక్కులు *ḍzakkulu.* n. plu. Demigods or nymphs, attendants, on Cubera. యక్షులు. జక్కులరేడు Kubera.

జక్కువ Same as జక్కవ.

జగడము *ḍzagaḍamu.* [Tel.] n. A dispute, a quarrel. కలహము. War, a battle, యుద్ధము. జగడగొండి or జగడగంటి *ḍzagaḍa-gonḍi.* n. A scold, a termagant, a virago. కలహశీలురాలు. జగడమాడు *ḍzagaḍam-āḍu.* v. n. To fight: to quarrel, to wrangle. కలహించు. జగడాలమారి a quarrelsome person. జగడించు *ḍzagaḍintsu.* v. n. To quarrel or fight. To fight a battle. యుద్ధముచేయు.

జగతి *ḍzagati.* [From Skt. జగము.] n. A raised verandah. తిన్నె. జగతులు places, parts, ప్రదేశములు. జగము *ḍzagamu.* [from Skt. జగము.] n. The world. లోకము. జగ ముకన్ను the eye of the world, i. e., the Sun సూర్యుడు, జగచ్చక్షువు. జగముచుట్టము the relation of the world, i. e., the Sun సూర్యుడు, లోకబాంధవుడు. జగముతల్లి the mother of the world, i. e., Lakshmi లక్ష్మి, లోకమాత. జగ *ḍzaga.* [Short for జగము.] adj. Noble, fine, matchless. జగదొంగ a great thief. జగరౌతు a heroic trooper. జగజంత *ḍzaga-ḍzanta.* n. A jade, a vile woman. గయ్యాళి. జగజంపు *ḍzaga-ḍzampu.* n. Greatness. Excess. Delight. A row of pearls. పెద్దకుప్ప. జగజెంపుజిగి కెంపు a very brilliant ruby. అధికకాంతిగల కెంపుమణి. T. ii. 107. iv. 60. A. vi. 181. Vasu. iii. 115. జగజెట్టి *ḍzaga-jeṭṭi.* n. A prize-fighter: a wrestler: a hero. M. VII. iv. 179.

జగా Same as జగ.

జగిలె or జగ్గిలె *ḍzagile.* [Tel.] n. A settle or stone bench. అరుగు. Chikk. i. 62.

జగిలేడు or జగిలెకాడు *ḍzagileḍu.* [Tel.] n. A fellow son-in-law. తోడియల్లుడు.

జగ్గు *ḍzaggu.* [Tel.] n. Brightness. తళతళ. Grace, prettiness. అందము. T. iii. 131. H. ii. 169. iv. 179. జగ్గున prettily. T. iv. 159. జగ్గు జగ్గున very prettily. జగ్గని ఉండు to perform grandly. జగ్గుతనము *ḍzaggu-tanamu.* n. Prettiness, grace. H. v. 101.

జజాయి *ḍzaḍzāyi.* [Tel.] n. A kind of cannon. ఒకవిధమైనఫిరంగి.

జజ్జర or జాజర *ḍzaḍzara.* [Tel.] n. Deception. వంచన. జజ్జరకత్తె or జాజరకత్తె a deceitful woman వంచకురాలు. జజ్జరకాడు a cheat, deceiver, వంచకుడు.

జజ్జు *ḍzaḍzu.* [Tel.] n. The state of being much torn. చిక్కిచివికి. A flaw in an emerald. adj. Old, worn, tattered, threadbare, trite. జజ్జుజజ్జులు mere tatters.

జట్టి *ḍzaṭṭi.* [Tel.] n. Price, earnest money; బేరు. A bargain, a contract, an agreement. Sale అమ్మకము. A monopoly. Forestalling. A species of loan on mortgage. జట్టికాడు a middleman, క్రయనిర్ణయము చేసికొన్నవాడు; a buyer కొనువాడు; one who buys in order to sell to profit కొని అమ్మువాడు. జట్టి బేరము a wholesale purchase. జట్టికొను or జట్టితీసుకొను *ḍzaṭṭi-konu.* v. t. To buy బేరము తీసుకొను. జట్టియిచ్చు *ḍzaṭṭi-y-itstsu.* v. t. To sell wholesale. అమ్ము, విక్రయించు.

జట్టింగ *dzuttinga*. [Tel.] n. A thief. దొంగ.

జట్టు *dzattu*. [Tel.] n. A crowd (of men); a party జనసమూహము.

జడ *dzada*. [Tel.] n. Hair plaited or braided in chains, matted hair. The finishing twist or plait of a straw roof. The mane of a lion. జడకట్టు or జడగొను *dzada-kattu*. v. n. To be plaited, to form into plaits. జడధారి *dzada-dari*. n. A hermit or anchorite with matted locks. వానప్రస్థుడు. జడలుధరించిన ఋషి. జడబిళ్ల *dzada-billa*. n. A head ornament worn by Hindoo women over their plaited hair. జడముడి *dzadu-mudi*. n. The knot of hair behind the head. జడలమెకము the maned beast, i e., a lion. సింహము.

జడక *dzadaka*. [Tel.] n. A blanket. కంబళి.

జడను *dzadanu*. [from Skt. జడము.] n. Awkwardness, stupidity, apathy, laziness. మాంద్యము, జడత్వము. జడనుపడు *dzadanu-padu*. v. n. To become dull or lazy. B. viii. 458. బలహీనమై మందపడు.

జడి *dzadi*. [Tel.] n. A flood, a stream, a gush, a torrent of rain, tears or words. వాన. L. ii. 65. iv. 73. Trouble బాధ. ND. pref. 139. adj. Constant, continuous నిరంతరము, ఎడతెగని. జడిగొను *dzadi-gonu*. v. n. To stream, to pour in a sheet or torrent. నిరంతరముగు. జడిగొనికురిసె, జడిబట్టె it rained in floods. To be excessive అతిశయించు. జడిగాడ్పు *dzadi-gadpu*. n. A strong wind.

జడియు *dzadiyu*. [Tel.] v. n. To fear, to be afraid. భయపడు. To move about చలించు. To move aside తొలగు. To sound మ్రోగు. v. a. To push త్రోయు. To parry a blow నివారించు, అడ్డగించు. To beat కొట్టు. Also, to flower. పుష్పించు. A. v. 137. జడిపించు *dzadipintsu*. v. n. To frighten, threaten, or alarm. జడుపు *dzadupu*. n. Fear, fright.

జడ్డ *dzadda*. [Tel.] adj. Near, close by, connected with. ఒకటితోనొకటి కూడిన. n. Terror, fright. సంకటము. Also, in spelling, one consonant written below another; when two come together, without the intervention of a vowel. The mark of an aspirate. జడ్డన suddenly తటాలున.

జడ్డి *dzaddi*. [Tel.] n. A pole, on which a weight bound in the middle is borne by two men. జడ్డిపెట్టె a large box thus borne on a pole. జడ్డియీటె *dzaddi-y-ite*. n. A spear with a handle in the middle.

జడ్డిగము or జడ్డుగము *dzaddigamu*. [Tel.] n. The funnel on the top of a drill plough. Vij. iii. 29. Pride మదము. నీ జడ్డిగము ఊడ కొట్టుతాను I will knock your top off.

జడ్డు *dzaddu*. [Tel.] n. Drowsiness, exhaustion మాంద్యము. Disease జాడ్యము. A lie, a falsehood. అబద్ధము. Connection తగులము, పొందు. జడ్డుతనము connection తగులము, సంబంధము. జడ్డుపడు to become dull or inactive జడతనొందు.

జత *dzata*. [Tel.] n. A pair; a set, జోడు. Similarity, సామ్యము. A match, an equal; a fellow. నా జతను వచ్చినవాండ్లు those who came with me. అవి నాకు దక్కిగా పోయినవాటితో జతే they are as good as lost to me. adj. Equal. జతపడు *dzata-padu*. v. n. To agree, unite, suit, combine. వానికి జతపడినారు they joined him. ఆ పని జతపడలేదు the business did not succeed.

జతనము, జతన or జతను *dzatanamu*. [from Skt. యత్నము.] n. An endeavour, attempt, effort, exertion. ప్రయత్నము. The design or plan of a picture or a carpet. ఉపాయము. జతనపడు or జతను పడు *dzatana-padu*. v. n. To be ready. సిద్ధముగు. To try యత్నించు. జతనుపరచు to get ready సిద్ధపరచు.

జతి *dzati*. [Tel.] n. Harmony in music. గాననాట్యయోగ్య శబ్దసంతతి.

జటిగెలు *ḍzatigelu.* [Tel. జత+తీగెలు.] n. The small ropes that go round bullock's necks and are tied to the yoke.

జట్టు *ḍzattu.* [Tel.] n. An armlet. M. iv. i. 213.

జడ్డు *ḍzaddu.* [Tel.] n. Hard-heartedness, want of feeling. కఠినహృదయత్వము.

జనుము *ḍzanumu.* [Tel.] n. The jute-plant. జనుపనార or జనపనార the jute fibre.

జన్నడు *ḍzannaḍu.* [Tel.] n. The name of a certain horse. ఈ పేరుగలగుఱ్ఱము.

జన్నము *ḍzannamu.* [from Skt. యజ్ఞము.] n. A sacrifice, a ceremony, in which oblations are presented. యజ్ఞము, వేలిమి. జన్నపుచుక్క a star or constellation on whose appearance sacrifices (యజ్ఞములు) are to be performed. మఘానక్షత్రము. జన్నపుతిండి one who eats at a sacrifice, i. e., a god, వేల్పు. జన్నపుగొంగ *ḍzannapu-gonga.* n. One who steals sacrifices, i. e., Siva. క్రతుధ్వంసి. జన్నపుటొజ్జ *ḍzannapu-ṭ-oḍḍza.* (జన్నము+ఒజ్జ.) n. The priest who presides at a sacrifice. ఋత్విజుడు. జన్నావు *ḍzann-āvu.* n. A cow that is consecrated.

జన్ని *ḍzanni.* [Tel.] n. Delirium. A sort of fit, convulsions. సన్నిపాతము. ఆమెకు జన్ని వచ్చి పడిపోయినది she fell down in a fit.

జన్నిదము *ḍzannidamu.* [Tel. from Skt. యజ్ఞము.] n. The sacred thread. యజ్ఞోపవీతము.

జన్నియ or **జన్ని** *ḍzanniya.* [from Skt. యజ్ఞము.] n. A consecrated thing. దేవతాదులకుద్దేశించి యెత్తిపెట్టుకొనినవస్తువు. A cow or ox so dedicated. A vow వ్రతము. adj. Consecrated. జన్నిఆవు a cow that is consecrated. (See under జన్నము.) జన్నిపడుచు a girl that is presented to a temple as a courtezan. జన్నిపట్టు or జన్నియవిడుచు to consecrate and release a bull calf. జన్నియీతచెట్టు a date tree set aside as consecrated.

జప్తి *ḍzapti.* [H.] n. Attachment of property.

జబర *ḍzabara.* [Tel.] n. An areca blossom. పోకపట్ట.

జబురుకొను *ḍzaburu-konu.* [Tel.] v. a. To devour.

జబురుజంగి *ḍzaburu-ḍzangi.* [Tel.] n. A kind of small cannon. ఒకవిధమైన చిన్న ఫిరంగి.

జబ్బ *ḍzabba.* [Tel.] n. The shoulder. భుజము. The hip, or outer part of the thigh. జబ్బయెముక the shoulder blade.

జబ్బు *ḍzabbu.* [Tel.] n. Weakness, sluggishness, inactivity మందము. Disease, illness, sickness రోగము. వానివ్యవహారము జాజబ్బులోకి వచ్చినది his business has decreased or fallen away. జబ్బుచేయు to make one sick, to cause sickness. జబ్బు adj. Weak, slow, stupid, infirm. Flat, spiritless, as bad poetry. జబ్బుకవి a poetaster. జబ్బుకావ్యము a poor poem అది జబ్బుసంవత్సరము that was but a poor year. జబ్బుగా *ḍzabbu-gā.* adv. Slightly weak. జబ్బుపడు *ḍzabbu-paḍu.* v. n. To fall ill, to become sick. మందపడు.

జమ *ḍzama.* [H.] n. A collection of money. Total. జమాఖర్చు income and expenditure. జమాబంది the yearly settlement of accounts made by a revenue officer under the ryotwari system.

జమట or **జంట** *ḍzamaṭa.* [Tel. locative case of జమిలి.] n. Double. జమటపొర a double fold. జమటపాలి a fold of cloth worn as a glove by falconers, when they have a hawk perched on the hand. HK. ii. 64.

జమిలి or **జమలి** *ḍzamili.* [Tel.] n. A pair, a couple. adj. Double, paired, coupled. జమిలిమాటలు stuttering words, stammering. జమిలిమకారము double M: the letter ఴ. జమిలించు *ḍzamil-intsu.* v. n. To redouble or increase (as fear or shame). జమిలిముక్కాలి "the 'double three footed" insect, i. e., a bee. A carpenter bee. తుమ్మెద.

జమిలిక, జమిడిక, జమళిగ or **జమలిక** *ḍzami-lika.* [Tel.] n. A kind of tabor, a drum. ఆనద్ధము. H. iii. 38.

జమి or **జమీను** *ḍzami.* [H.] n. A zemindar's landed estate. **జమీందారుడు** *ḍzamindārudu.* n. A zemindar or landlord. **జమీందారి** *ḍzamindāri.* n. A zemindari estate which has to pay a permanent revenue to Government.

జముకాణము *ḍzamu-kāṇamu.* [Dekhani.] n. A carpet. Swa. v. 47. జంపఖానా.

జముజాలి, జముదాడి or **జముదళము** *ḍzamu-ḍzali.* [H.] n. A large musket, a wall piece or swivel. A broad sword నిడుపుపదునైనకత్తి, యమధార. R. ii. 22.

జముడు *ḍzamuḍu.* [from Skt. యముడు.] n. Yama, the regent of the world below, and the judge of departed souls. జముని కొలువుకూటము Yama's court. జమునెక్కి-రింత A buffalo (because it is the steed of Yama. **జముదెస** the South. యమదిక్కు.

జముదాడి or **జముదళము** *ḍzamu-dāḍi.* Same as జముజాలి. (q. v.)

జమున *ḍzamuna.* [from Skt. యమున.] n. The river Yamuna or Jumna. జమునయ్య The sun, as being the father of Jumna.

జములు *ḍzamulu.* [Tel.] n. A couple. జమిలి.

జమ్మని *ḍzammani.* [from *Yemen* in Arabia.] n. A horse. G. iii. 134.

జమ్మి *ḍzammi.* [from Skt. శమీ.] n. A kind of tree. *Mimosa suma.* Rox. ii. p. 563.

జమ్ము *ḍzammu.* [Tel.] n. A bulrush. జంబు. జమ్మేరు (జమ్ము+ఏరు.) the river Jambu.

జర *ḍzara.* [Tel.] n. The hasp of a knife. కత్తిపిడిజా.

జరగు, జరపు See under జరుగు.

జరజర *ḍzara-ḍzara.* [Tel. anuk.] n. A crashing rustling sound of dragging. adv. At once, quite, entirely. Aloud.

జరత *ḍzarata.* [Tel.] n. Another form of జలతారు.

జరబాజు *ḍzara-baḍzu.* [H.] adj. Woven with silver lace. వెండిజరిగతో చేసిన.

జరబు *ḍzarabu.* [Tel.] n. Fried flour. వేచు పిండి.

జరభి *ḍzarabhi.* [Tel.] adj. Wicked, guileful. కుటిలుడు. M. iv. iii. 16. HD. ii. 1102.

జరి Same as జరీ.

జరిణిపంది *ḍzariṇi-pandi.* [Tel.] n. The mouse deer.

జరిబిల్ల *ḍzari-billa.* [Tel.] n. A piece of wood like the sheave of a pulley, used by weavers in stretching their webs.

జరీ *ḍzarī.* [Tel.] n. Silver or gold lace. సరిగ.

జరిన or **జరిలున** *ḍzarina.* [Tel.] adv. Quickly. శీఘ్రముగా.

జరుగు or **జరగు** *ḍzarugu.* [Tel.] v. n. To slip, creep, or slide. To pass or change the place. To flee. To pass, elapse, expire as time. To move on, get on. To be current or usual. To occur, happen. జరిగినపని a real occurrence, a fact, a thing that happened. ఇది లేక నాకు జరగదు I cannot get on without this. ఆ భూమి నా కింద జరుగుచున్నది that land is in my hands. జరుగుతీరుగా as usual. అతడు జరిగిపోయినాడు he departed, i. e., died. అక్కడ జరగక వచ్చితిని as I could not subsist there I came away. జరిగడి passing, elapsing. (lit: what slides). **జరుగుబాటు** or **జరుగుబడి** *ḍzarugu-baṭu.* n. Living, subsistence. జీవనము. జరుగుబాటుగావుండే substantial; well-to-do. జరుగుడు slipperiness జారుడు. **జరుపు** or **జరపు** *ḍzarupu.* v. a. To pass or spend as time. To put off, procrastinate. To push on, move forward. To do, perform. జరుపుడు procrastination. దినములనుజరుపుట. **జరిగించు** *ḍzarigintsu.* v. a. To conduct, transact, carry on (business, &c.) To execute, fulfil, commit, perpetrate, celebrate, perform. అల్లరి జరి గించు to raise a disturbance.

ౙర్రున dzarru-na. [Tel.] adv. Quickly. శీఘ్రముగా.

ౙలకట్టె or ౙెలకట్టె dzalakaṭṭe. [Tel.] n. A sort of hawk; a goshawk. Swa. iv. 83.

ౙలకము dzalakamu. [Tel.] n. Water. ఉదకము. A bath స్నానము. ౙలకమాడు salakam-adu. v. n. To bathe. స్నానము చేయు. ౙలగడుగు dzala-gadugu. (జలక ము+కడుగు.) v. n. To wash earth for gold, diamonds, &c. ౙలగరి or ౙలగడుగుల వాడు dzalagari. n. One belonging to the caste of gold finders, who search for gold in drains and in the sweepings of goldsmith's shops. BD. vii. 844.

ౙలగ or ౙెలగ dzalaga. [Tel.] n. A leech.

ౙలౙల dzaladzala. [Tel. anuk] adv. Aloud, audibly, clanking, ringing, rippling, &c. ౙలౙలమన్నది it throbbed fiercely.

ౙలతారు dzalutaru. [Tel. జలకము+తారు.] n. Gold or silver lace. జరీ, సరిగె.

ౙలదరము or ౙలవరము dzala-daramu. [Tel.] n. Trembling కంపము. ౙలదరించు or ౙలదరించు dzladar-intsu. v. n. To shudder, tremble. To be in a fright. P. iii. 213. HD, i. 1185. KP. iii. 20. కంపించు, భయపడు. To be set on edge, as the teeth.

ౙలదారి or జల్దారి dzala-dari. [Tel. జల కము+దారి.] n. A drain: తూము.

ౙలపోత or ౙలపోసనము dzala-pōta. [Tel. జలకము+పోసనము.] n. Gilding with gold leaf.

ౙలుగ or ౙలుగు dzaluga. [Tel.] n. A species of fish akin to the Salmon, *Odoe, sciæna lineata*. A sort of tree, called *Æschynomene sesban*. Rox. iii. 333 and 337. The species మంచి ౙలుగ is *Æschyn. procumbens*.

ౙలుబు dzalubu. [Tel.] n. A cold or catarrh. జలుబు. ౙలుబు చేయు dzalubu-chēyu. v. n. To catch cold. నాకు ౙలుబుచేసినది I have caught cold.

ౙలేరి dzalēri. [Tel. జలకము+ఏరి.] n. The trench part of a lingam image. పానవట్టము.

ౙల్ల dzalla. [Tel.] n. A manger. A long, narrow basket used for the body of a cart. A fish; the river mullet: [illegible] is one kind.

ౙల్లను or ౙల్లుమను dzallanu. [Tel. ౙల్లు+ అను.] v. n. To shudder, twitter. To thrill, to tingle or glow all over, to feel a pang, terror, &c. ఆమె హృదయము ౙల్లుమన్నది her heart shuddered. ౙల్లుమనుట a pit a pat, palpitation. ౙల్లనగా thrillingly, like an electric shock.

ౙల్లి dzalli. [Tel.] n. Shivers, small bits. A whisk made of the tail of the cow of Tartary: చమరము, చామరము. That animal itself. చమరీమృగము. A tassel. కుచ్చు. A curtain తెర. Incoherent talk, a farrago of nonsense. అసత్యవచనము. ముత్యపు ౙల్లి powdered pearls. బొంతరౙల్లి బొంత a patchwork. ౙల్లిగానుండే hirsute, as a branching root. adj. Separated, shivered, broken, incoherent. False అసత్యము. ౙల్లి కాడు a liar అసత్యవంతుడు. ౙల్లితోక a bushy tail like that of a horse. ౙల్లినీడ a broken shade as that of leaves. ౙల్లిముత్తెములు seed pearls. ౙల్లిపెండెము a kind of jewel worn on the foot పాద భూషావిశేషము. ౙల్లిమూకుడు a pan with holes బిల్లులుగలమూకుడు. ౙల్లివేరు a tasselated root. ౙల్లిపొల్లు dzalli-pollu. n. Babble, incoherent jabber. ౙల్లించు dzallintsu. v. a. To sift in a sieve శోధించు. To flow కారు. ౙల్లు dzallu. n. A shower, a drizzle, a sprinkling. ౙల్లుమను Same as ౙల్లను. ౙల్లెడ dzalleda. n. A sieve (from జల్లు a sprinkle.) The skirt, of a dress. ౙల్లెడలాగు అయిపోయినది it became very thin. ౙల్లెడె dzallede. n. A whisk. ౙల్లి.

జళిపించు or **జడిపించు** *ḍzalipintsu.* [Tel. from జడియు.] v. t. To frighten. జడియు చేయు. To shake ఆడించు. **జళుకు** *ḍzaluku.* n. Tremulousness, timidity, alarm. The gleam of the eye, జళుకుచూపులు glancing eyes. Vasu. iv. 17. Fright బెదురు. Chaff పొట్టు.

జవ *ḍzava.* [Tel.] n. The edge of a round jewel worn on the head. జవదిబ్బలోనాగు వానికి చుట్టు చెక్కిన చెడి అంచు. **జవకట్టు** *ḍzava-kattu.* v. a. To set or frame. జవ కట్టినపీట a reeded or inlaid stool.

జవజవ *ḍzava-ḍzava.* [Tel.] n. A quivering sound. వణకుటయందగునను కరణము. adv. Tremulously, violently (trembling or shaking.

జవటు or **జవర** *ḍzavaṭa.* [Tel.] n. A net-like substance, which surrounds the palmyra tree. Fibres, the reticulation at those parts whence the branches expand.

జవదాటు *ḍzava-dāṭu.* [Tel.] v. t. To transgress, to disobey. మీరు, అతిక్రమించు. "అన్న మాట జవదాటక." రామా. i.

జవనిక *ḍzavanika.* [Tel.] n. A screen. తెర చీర.

జవర *ḍzavara.* [Tel.] n. The fibres, in a palmyra tree. See జవటు. adj. Straight. ఋజువు. Soft మృదువు. **జవరగా** *ḍzavara-gā. adv.* Straightway, quickly. DRB. 428. **జవరతనము** or **జవరన** *ḍzavara-tanamu.* n. Straightness: smoothness. ఋజుభావము, మృదుత్వము. జేనరిము thickness. కరుకు దనము.

జవరాలు *ḍzava-r-ālu.* [Tel. జవ్వని+ఆలు.] n. A damsel, a young woman. పడుచుది.

జవళి or **జవిళి** *ḍzavaḷi.* [Tel.] n. A new cloth. జవిళి అంగడి a clothier's shop. Drapery, a draper's shop. జవిళివాడు a draper.

జవాజి or **జవాది** *ḍzavāji.* [Tel.] n. Civet: See పునుగు. కర్ర జవ్వాజి stick civet that is found adhering to twigs. సంకుమదము. **జవాదిపిల్లి** *ḍzavādi-pilli.* n. A female civet cat.

జవుకు *ḍzavuku.* [Tel.] v. n. To waggle, to be loose, as a stake, to become soft, as a boil. To rot. జవికిన loosened. Rotten.

జవ్వనము *ḍzavvanamu.* [from Skt. యౌవనము.] n. Youth, juvenility. పడుచుదనము. **జవ్వని** *ḍzavvani.* n. A damsel, a maiden.

జవ్వాజి or **జవ్వాది** *ḍzavvāji.* [Tel.] n. Civet. **జవ్వాజిపిల్లి** *ḍzavvāji-pilli.* n. A civet cat. కర్ర జవ్వాజి See under జవాది. **జవ్వాజివంకెలు** *ḍzavvāji-vaṅkelu.* n. The name of a sort of grain.

జవ్వాడు *ḍzavvāḍu.* [Tel. జవ+ఆడు.] v. n. To shake, quiver. To struggle, toss about, writhe. Swa. iv. 7.

జవ్వి *ḍzavvi.* [Tel.] n. The hair of a horse's tail. Horsehair. గుర్రపుతోకవెండ్రుకలు.

జవ్వు *ḍzavvu.* [Tel.] n. Beauty, bloom.

జా ḍzā

జాగరము, **జాగరణము** or **జాగారము** *ḍzāgaramu.* [Tel.] n. A vigil or wake: sitting up all night. రాత్రి మేలుకొనియుండుట. Waking, watching, watchfulness. Kalah. ii. 134. Vasu. iv. 121. **జాగరించు** *ḍzāgarintsu.* v. n. To wake, watch, sit up all night.

జాగా *ḍzāgā.* [Tel.] adj. Great గొప్ప. n. Room, space, ఎడము, చోటు.

జాగిలము, **జాగిలాయి** or **జాగిలాయి** *ḍzāgilamu.* [Tel.] n. A sort of dog for hog hunting. A hound. వేటకుక్క.

జాగు *ḍzāgu.* [Tel.] n. Delay: ఆలస్యము. ఏడజాగులుపెట్టు to trifle, to idle. జాగుచేయు to be idle.

జాజము or **జాజాము** *ḍzāḍzamu.* [Tel.] n. Different kinds of corn sprouts thrown into a palanquin on marriage occasions. పాలికలందుపోసిన నవధాన్యముల నారు.

జాజర or **జజ్జర** *ḍzāḍzara.* [Tel.] n. Deception వంచన. **జాజాలపాలిక** *ḍzāḍzāla-pālika.* n. A marriage palanquin.

జాజి or **జాజీ** *ḍzāji.* [Skt.] n. A nutmeg tree. The great flowering jasmine.

"సీ॥ జాజిరొయ్యి కొకాని సకలకుసుమ
విరసనంపదచేవెొప్పె వసుధరోయ్ల."
Sunanda Parin. iv. 22.

జాజికాయ *ḍzāji-kāya.* n. A nutmeg. జాజికాయపెట్టె a spice box: జాజికాయపలక or జాజిపలక the name used for dealwood. పేయజాజి a plant called అగ్నిజ్వాల. **జాజిపత్రి** *ḍzāji-patri.* n. Mace. జాజిపుష్పం.

జాజే or **జాజు** *ḍzāḍzu.* [Tel.] n. Redness. Red chalk, red colour made of lac. P. iii. 266. కావిరంగు, కేసరు. జాజే పారు to become red ఎర్రనగు. Swa. ii.

జాటి or **ఝూటి** *ḍzāṭi.* [Tel.] n. A whip, a scourge. కొరడా, కొరడా.

జాడ *ḍzāḍa.* [Tel.] n. A mark, a trace, a sign. గురుతు. A track త్రోవ. Manner విధము. అడుగులజాడ the marks of footsteps. వీడు తండ్రిజాడగానున్నాడు he resembles his father. ఆ జాడ విడువడు he will not leave off those practices. జాడలంటగట్టు or జాడలు విచారించు to trace out. జాడగానూపు to show a trace, to give a hint, to shew secretly or indirectly. జాడగాచెప్పు to give a hint. జాడగాపోవు to steal off. **జాడకాడు** *ḍzāḍa-kāḍu.* n. One who can trace the way త్రోవ గుర్తెరిగినవాడు.

జాడా *ḍzāḍā.* [Tel.] adj. To the root, entire. సమూలము. **జాడాచేయు** *ḍzāḍā-chēyu.* v. t. To exterminate, to root out. నిర్మూలముచేయు.

జాడించు or **ఝాడించు** *ḍzāḍintsu.* [Tel.] v. t. To rinse about in water. To toss, whisk, flap about, fling, clean from mud. To stretch out the arm or leg. To twit, abuse or reprove. రాలుచు, ఇటుఅటు ఆడించు, గుంజే. నిందించు.

జాడీ or **జాడి** *ḍzāḍi.* [Tel.] n. A jar. బంగారు జాడి a golden vase.

జాడు *ḍzāḍu.* [Tel.] n. Unripe maize or Zonna. లంకెపట్టనిజొన్నకర్ర. The tender stalk of the great millet. ఉండనిస్తే పండు తుంది, పీకితేజాడు let it grow and it will fruit: pull it up and it is only a stalk.

జాణ *ḍzāṇa.* [Tel.] n. A clever woman. నేర్పరి. adj Clever, wise. Roguish, artful, shrewd, arch. నేర్పరియైన. **జాణడు** *ḍzāṇaḍu.* n. A clever man. "మృదుండు జాణ డేని మెచ్చంగవలదె." BD. iv. 1257. **జాణతనము** *ḍzāṇa-tanamu.* n. Artfulness, sagacity, cunning, shrewdness, archness. **జాణెత** *ḍzāṇeta.* (జాణ+ఎత.) n. A flirt, a jilt. ధూర్తురాలు.

జాతర *ḍzātara.* [Tel.] n. A merry-making or holiday. ఉత్సవము, పండుగ. The festival of any deity but chiefly of a village goddess Sakti. శక్తిఉత్సవము.

జాది Same as జాజి. (q. v.)

జాదు Same as జాజే. (q. v.)

జాదుకొను *ḍzādu-konu.* v. n. To become black; to become thick. కరుముకొను, దట్టమగు.

జాదురము *ḍzāduramu.* [Tel. from Skt. చాతుర్యము] n. Cleverness. జాదురజాదురము great cleverness.

జానకి *ḍzānaki.* [Tel.] n. A fuse or match to fire guns with. కర్నాటకపు తుపాకులందు నిప్పు ముట్టించుతాడు.

జానము *ḍzānamu.* [Tel.] n. A cushion used on a saddle గుర్రపుపల్లముమీదిమెత్త.

జాను *ḍzānu.* [Tel.] adj. Graceful, bland. జానుతెలుగు pure or sweet Telugu. జాను or జానువు n. Grace, prettiness. అందము, చక్కదనము, ఒప్పిదము, సౌందర్యము. Appa. Cavi. ii. జానొప్పగా prettily. జానుగా gracefully.

జానుగు *ḍzānugu.* [Tel.] n. An ear. చెవి.

జాపత్రి or **జాపత్తిరి** *ḍzāpatri.* [Tel.] n. The spice called Mace. See under జాజి.

జాప్యము, జావ్యము or **జాపితము** *dzapya-mu*. [Tel.] n. Loitering, delay. Inertness. Languor. Dawdling. జాగు, ఆలస్యము.

జాబితా *dzabita*. [H.] n. A list. పట్టీ.

జాబిల్లి or **జాబిలి** *dzabilli*. [Tel. జాబు+పిల్ల, i. e., చెవులపిల్ల.] n. The moon. చంద్రుడు. (The figure seen in the full moon is supposed to resemble a hare; whence in Sanskrit the name శశాంకుడు.) జాబిల్లితాలుపు or జాబిలితాల్పు Siva. జాబిల్లిమేపరి Rahu. **జాబిలిరాయి** *dzabili-rayi*. n. A carbuncle, a moonstone చంద్రకాంతము. జాబిల్లికొక్కు the constellation called మృగశీర్ష. జాబిల్లి a game played by girls. H. v.

జాబు *dzabu*. [from H. *jawab*, a reply.] n. A letter of correspondence. లేఖ, పత్రిక.

జాబుర or **జాబురా** *dzabura*. [Tel.] n. Name of a tree which yields a dye. గంధపొడిచెట్టు.

జామ, జాము or **జేమ** *dzama*. [Tel.] n. The Guava tree జేమచెట్టు.

జామారు or **జామారు** *dzamaru*. [Tel.] n. A piece of new cloth. కొత్తబట్ట. సెల్లా.

జామీను *dzaminu*. [H.] n. Surety, bail హాజరుజామీను personal bail. మాలుజామీను money security.

జాము or **ఝాము** *dzamu*. [Tel.] n. A watch, or space of time equivalent to three English hours. The day from sunrise to sunset, and the night until sunrise is reckoned in four quarters, or watches; the second watch expires at twelve o'clock. Hence రెండుజాములు is midday or midnight, and రెండుజాములున్నర is about 2 p. m. ఎనిమిదిజాములు the eight watches, i. e., 24 hours; or a day and night. తెల్లవారుజామున in the morning. The plural is జాములు or జాలు.

జారి or **జారీ** *dzari*. [Tel.] n. A vessel with a spout, like a teapot: పెద్దగిండి, కమండలువు.

జారు *dzaru*. [Tel.] v. n. To slide or slip, to trip or stumble, to creep. జారును. To slip, open, or become loose. వదులగు. To drop or gush out as water; to flee. కారుట; ప్రవించు. తలకు జారుదెబ్బ తగిలినది the blow grazed the head. To slope, to slant, as జారుకొప్పు her slanting tire. కింద జారిపోయి నాడు he crept under it. జారుముడి a sliding knot: a knot with bows as distinguished from పెట్టుముడి. జారుచు, జారించు, or జార్చు to cause to slide or slip down. జారకొట్టు. **జారుజీరలు** *dzaru-jiralu*. n. A certain game played by children. **జారుడు, జారుపు** or **జారుపాటు** *dzaru-du*. n. Slipperiness. జారుట. A fault స్ఖాలిత్యము. పాపము. జారుపారు Same as జారు.

జాల *dzala*. [Tel.] n. A fishing net. చేపలను పట్టు వల. A window. కిటికీ. A lattice, a loop, an eyelet hole. **జాలికుడు** *dzalikudu*. n. A fisherman.

జాలకర్ర or **జాగకర్ర** *dzala-karra*. [Tel.] n. Open work or tracery in marble.

"ద్వి॥ సొరదిచేసినపాల కున్నంపుమిద్దె
జాళువా బంగారుజాలకర్రలును."

(The bars across the windows (or—the openwork, or tracery) being made of fine gold). Nija Linga Chikkaya Charitra, verse 48. "చుట్టుజాలకర్రలు సొబగుచేయించి." Pal. p. 64.

జాలపల్లిక or **జాలవల్లిక** *dzala-pallika*. [Tel.] n. A tray for betel leaf. చిత్రపుపనిచేసిన తమలపాకులబుట్ట. Rasica. i. 39. Pal. 255. Parij. ii. 24.

జాలము *dzalamu*. [Tel.] n. Delay, loitering a pretext. ఆలస్యము, నెపము. **జాలముచేయు** *dzalamu-cheyu*. v. a. To shuffle off, or delay. జాగుచేయు. **జాలకాడు** *dzala-kadu*. [జాలము+కాడు.] n. An idler, a loiterer. ఆలస్యముచేయువాడు. A fisherman.

జాలరి *dzalari*. [Tel. జాల+అరి.] n. A fisherman. బెస్తవాడు. Raja Sekhara. ii. 117

జాలారివాడు *dzālāri-vāḍu*. n. A fisherman.

జాలరు *dzālaru*. [Tel.] n. Net-work, a fringe. జాలరుకన్ను the mesh (lit. the eye) of a net.

జాలవారు *dzāla-vāru*. [Tel.] n. Guards, spearmen. BD. iii. 1016.

జాలారిచెట్టు *dzālāri-cheṭṭu*. [Tel.] n. The plant called *Shorea laccifera*. పింప్ర. Heyne.

జాలి *dzāli*. [Tel.] n. Pity, regret, love. విచారము, దయ. జాలిగాఁజుంకథ a pathetic story. జాలివరాలి emotion and eagerness, pining and longing. జాలిగొను or జాలిపడు to feel pity. జాలిజాందు. విచారపడు. జాలిపెట్టు to grieve దుఃఖపెట్టు.

జాలిమి *dzālimi*. [Tel.] n. A veil. ముసుఁగు. L. iii. 72.

జాలియము or జాలీము *dzāliyamu*. [Tel.] n. A purse. జాలె సంచి.

జాలు or జాలువు *dzālu*. [Tel.] n. A stream. ఏరు, అల్పప్రవాహము. జాలుకొను or జాలు వాఱు *dzālu-konu*. v. n. To form in, or be as a line. Vasu. ii. 101. To flow. ప్రవహించు.

జాలె, జాలెము, జాలియ or జాలియము *dzāle*. [Tel.] n. A purse, a bag. జాలె or జాలి the cord used in spinning a top. బొంగరపుత్రాడు. జాలెడేగ *dzāle-ḍēga*. n. A kind of hawk. Swa. iv. 84. HD. i. 532.

జాలించు Same as జాడించు.

జాలియ, జాళి, జాళియము or జాళీము *dzāliya*. [Tel.] n. A certain pace of horses. అశ్వగతివిశేషము.

జాలువా or జాళ్వా *dzāluvā*. [Tel.] n. Probably (like Ophir or Potosi) the name of a place. Fine gold. అపరంజి. Thus జాళువపసిడి. (Sar. Dw. ii. 96.) fine gold of Jalwa. జాలువాబంగారు (Nija. L. C. 48.) మేలింవన్నె భేదము.

జావ *dzāva*. [Tel.] n. Gruel, porridge. పేయ, గంజి.

జావడము or జావళ్ము *dzāvaḍamu*. [Tel.] n. A country horse, a hack కుర్రపుకట్టు. A falcon. The Shahin. Jerdon, Catal: No. 29. కుర్రపుజావడము a mule. గాడిద. జావడములు colts, fillies. ఆడుకుర్రపుకట్లు. A. ii. 122, iv. 36. HD. i. 531. Unmanliness. అధైర్యము. Timidity. పిరికితనము.

జావడి *dzāvaḍi*. [Tel.] n. A washerman. చాకలవాడు.

జావళి or జావళి *dzāvaḷi*. [Tel.] n. A kind of song. గీతవిశేషము.

జావాహిరి *dzāvāhiri*. [H.] n. Wealth. సొమ్ము.

జు dzu

జుం *dzum*. [Tel.] n. A hum. జుమ్మనుధ్వని, ఝంకారధ్వని.

జుంజెము, జుంజాము or జుంజాము *dzumdzamu*. [Tel.] n A jest, a joke, a lie. A torch made of leaves and sticks tied together in a bundle for use in dances or on the Dipâvali day.

జుంజు, జుంజురు *dzumdzu*. [Tel.] n. Dishevelled hair. విరియబోసిన వెంట్రుకలు, చింపిరి వెంట్రుకలు. Shagginess. A lion's mane. జుంజురు or జుంజురుకట్ట a torch made like a brush out of any dry sticks.

జుంటితేనె *dzunṭi-tēne*. [Tel. from జున్ను.] Virgin honey. జుంటీగ n. Honey bee.

జుజురు *dzudzuru*. [Tel.] n. A cluster. గుబురు. జుజురుకొను to cluster గుబురుకొను.

జుజివి *dzujivi*. [Tel.] adj. Trivial, petty, common.

జుట్టనవేలు or జుట్టవ్రేలు *dzuṭṭana-vēlu*. [Tel.] n. The forefinger. తర్జని. The thumb or the great toe. జుట్టెడి or జుత్తెడి the distance between the thumb and the forefinger when they are stretched out. చాచబడిన బొటనవ్రేలికిని మూపుడువ్రేలికిని నడిమికొలత.

జుట్టు *dzuṭṭu.* [Tel.] n. A crest, as that of a peacock. The lock worn by Hindu men on the top of the head. ఆవిద్యజుట్టు అతనికి చిక్కినది he has got a good hold of that art. జుట్టుపట్టి సొమ్ము అడిగినాడు he caught him by the hair and insisted on payment. **జుట్టుపిట్ట** *dzuṭṭu-piṭṭa.* n. A peacock. జుట్టుపిట్టతాలుపు an epithet of Kumáraswámi. **జుట్టుబాతు** *dzuṭṭu-bātu.* n. The crested goose.

జుట్టుపు or **జుట్టుపాకు** *dzuṭṭupu.* [Tel.] n. A common milky creeper with heart shaped leaves. *Asclepias echinata.* Rox. ii. 44. Ainsl. ii. 452. Or, *Cynanchum hirsutifolium.* Heyne. ఆజశృంగి.

జుడుగు, జుణుగు, దుడుగు or **సుడుగు** *dzuḍugu.* [Tel.] v. a. To cheat, delude. v. n. To lurk, slink, to lie in wait. దాగుకొను R. vi. 44; viii. 14; HK. iv. 134. To retreat వెనుకదీయు. జుడుగుమాట a sly or cunning expression.

జుత్తు *dzutta.* [Tel.] n. A short span; measured from the thumb to the end of the ring finger. కోకర్ణము, ప్రసృతాంగుష్ఠానామికామధ్యము. జుట్టెన్నేలు Same as జుట్టెన్నేలు. జుత్తెడు a measure of 12 inches. ద్వాదశాంగుళప్రమాణము.

జునపములు or **జులపాలు** *dzunapamulu.* [Tel.] n. Locks of hair left just above and in front of the ears.

జున్ను *dzunnu.* [Tel.] n. Honey, తేనె. Honey comb తేనెతెట్టె. Cheese. జున్నుపలుకులు honeyed accents, sweet words. T. ii. 106. పులిజున్ను a syllabub of tiger's milk, i. e., an unobtainable luxury A. iv. 273. Suca. iii. 8. Ila iii. 131. తేనె, నవప్రసూతగోక్షీరము, వండినదిన్ని. **జున్నుపాలు** *dzunnu-pālu.* n. Biestings: the milk that flows for a week after a cow has calved. ఈనినదినమువాళ్ళ మొదలుదినములలో గా పితికినపాలు. జున్నుగడ్డ cheese.

జుబ్బా *dzubbu.* [Tel.] n. An epaulette. బాహుభూషణము.

జుమలా *dzumala.* [H.] n. The total, the sum. మొత్తము.

జుమాయించు *dzumāy-intsu.* [Tel.] v. t. To hold tight. గట్టిపట్టు.

జుమాలపేరు *dzumāla-pēru.* [Tel.] n. A kind of necklace made of gold beads. (Vizag.)

జుమ్మ or **జుమ్మట** *dzumma.* [Tel.] n. The Weaver Bird, *Picus Baltimorus.* [illegible]

జుమ్ముడు or **జుమ్ముకాడు** *jummuḍu.* n. [Tel.] A lover, or sweetheart (in a bad sense) విటుడు.

జుమ్ము *dzummu.* [Tel.] n. A hum. జుమ్మను *dzumm-anu.* v.n. To hum. జుమ్మని *dzumm-ani.* (anuk.) adv. Aloud: as a humming or buzzing sound. జుమ్ముమనుధ్వని humming, buzzing. జుమ్ముజుమ్మనగా aloud (buzzing or humming.) Kālahas. iii. 220.

జురుకు *dzuruku.* [Tel.] n. Spirting out (as blood), a gush. **జురుజురుకు** *dzuru-dzuruku.* adv. Gushingly.

జుర్రు *dzurru.* [Tel.] v. t. To suck up, or drink with a noise. పీల్చు.

జులపాలు *dzula-pālu.* Same as జునపములు.

జులాయించు *dzulā-yintsu.* [Tel.] v. i. To reel, swing about, to stagger.

జులిమి *dzulimi.* [Tel.] n. Naughtiness. దుండగము.

జులుమానా, జుల్మానా or **జేరిమానా** *dzulumānā.* [H.] n. A fine.

జులుము *dzulumu.* [Tel.] n. Force, violence; tyranny; oppression.

జులువ or **జులువరిపము** *dzuluva.* [Tel.] n. Relief, comfort.

జుల్కి *dzulki.* [Tel.] n. A wrinkle, twisting.

జువ్వరించు *dzuvvar-intsu.* [Tel.] v. t. To excel. విజృంభించు.

జువ్వి *dzuvvi.* [Tel.] n. The wavy-leafed fig tree: *Ficus infectoria.* తెల్లజువ్వి A tree called *Ehretia aspera*. ఎఱ్ఱజువ్వి A tree called *Ochna squamosa*, or, *Ficus benjamina*. పెద్దజువ్వి A tree called *Ficus tsiela*. పుత్రజువ్వి *Ficus comosa*. కొండజువ్వి *Ficus tuberculata*, also called కొండమఱ్ఱి or కొండజువ్వి. (Kalabas. iii. 69.) కురుకుజువ్వి *Nageia putranjiva*. Rox. iii. 540, 550, 598, 643. జువ్విదీవి *dzuvvi-divi*. n. The island called Plaksha.

జువ్వు *dzuvvu*. [Tel.] n. A whizzing noise.

జూ dzu

జూకు *dzūku*. [Tel.] n. Haste, flurry. తత్తరపాటు. జూకొను to be flurried. తత్తరపడు.

జూకురు *dzūkuru*. [Tel.] n. Grief, sorrow. G. vi. 74.

జూజము *dzūdzamu*. [Tel.] n. Gambling, play. మోసము. Deception మోసము. జూజమాడు *dzūdza-m-āḍu*. v. n. To gamble. జూజరి *dzūdzari*. n. A gambler.

జూజి *dzūji*. [from Skt. దూతి.] n. A female messenger. దూతిక.

జూటు or జూఠు *dzūṭu*. [H.] n. Cunning, artfulness. మోసము. జూటుగా cunningly. జూటుతనము *dzūṭu-tanamu*. n. Cunning, craft, guile. జూటాడు to cheat మోసము చేయు.

జూదము *dzūdamu*. [from Skt. ద్యూతము.] n. Dice-play, gambling. జూదకత్తె or జూదకత్తె *dzūda-katte*. n. A gambling woman జూదరి, జూదరి, జూదకాడు or జూదకాడు *dzūdari*. n. A gambler.

జూడు *dzuḍu*. [Tel.] v. n. To burn, or to be hot. M. IX. i. 27. v. a. To burn. (R. ii. 93.) To light a match. A. v. 89. To brand with a hot iron. HD. i. 1229.

జూలు *dzūlu*. [Tel.] n. The mane of a lion or other animal. A cloth or blanket covering the back of any animal, a jhool.

జూవరము *dzūvaramu*. [Tel.] n Sorrow. సంతాపము.

జో dzo

జొంపము *dzompamu*. [Tel.] n. A plot of grass, a grassy field : a thicket or cluster, as of bamboos. Thick matted tresses, hairiness పుష్కలిపటము, గుంపు, గుబురు. A tender twig చిగురు. A constant downpour నిరంతరధార. adj. Thick, thickset. Constant నిరంతరము.

జొంపు *dzompu*. [Tel.] n. A spring on a hill or mountain. కొండలోని ఊటనీరు.

జొగ్గు or జోగు *dzoggu*. [Tel.] n. Alms. భిక్షము. జొగ్గెత్తు to take alms.

జొటజొట *dzoṭa-dzoṭa*. [Tel. (anuk).] adv. Greedily, thirstily. Fast వడిగా.

జొత్తిల్లు or జొత్తిలు *dzottillu*. [Tel.] v. n. To blush or redden, to turn red. ఎఱ్ఱబారు. To look bright రంజిల్లు. జొత్తు *dzottu*. n. Redness. జొత్తుపాప a newborn child. జొత్తురు *dzotturu*. adj. Crimson, red.

జొన్న *dzonna*. [Tel.] n. The great millet, cholam, jowari. There are many species of this, as తెల్లజొన్న, నుదురుజొన్న, లోనపెద్దజొన్న, పచ్చజొన్న, పాలాపుజొన్న, గిద్దజొన్న, ఎఱ్ఱజొన్న. మొక్కజొన్న Indian corn, or maize. See Rox. i. 268, iii. 568. తెల్లజొన్నలు and సజ్జజొన్నలు id. i. 269, 271. కొండజొన్న id. ii. 422. జొన్ననాగు *dzonna-nāgu*. n. A species of snake.

జొబ్బిలు or జొబ్బిల్లు *dzobbilu*. [Tel.] v. n. To flow స్రవించు. To thrive, grow thickly. To be redolent, to smell of. To revel : to enjoy oneself. వినోదించు. To toss about, to writhe, to wallow. To be produced. ఉప్పతిల్లు. తేనియల్ జొబ్బిలుమోవికెంపు the honey dropping lips.

జొక్కరించు Same as జోకొట్టు. (q. v.)

జొల్లు or జోల్లు *dzollu*. [Tel.] n. Drivel, spittle, slaver. లాల.

జొల్లెము or జొల్లిము dzollemu. [Tel.] n. A tire, formed by weaving the tresses in chains and then coiling them up at the back of the head: a wreath of mangrove flowers.

జోహారు, జోహారువు or జోహారు dzohāru. [Tel.]. n. Homage, welcome, salutation, congratulation. నమస్కారము, సర్వోత్కృష్టుడవై యుండుమని మంగళముచేయుటము. interj. Huzza! Hurra!

జో dzō

జో or జోజో dzō. [Tel.] interj. Hush! a word used in lulling a child to sleep. జోకొట్టు dzō-koṭṭu. v. t. To lull asleep.

జోక dzōka. [Tel.] n. Manner, way. విధము. Grandeur, fineness, bloom, prettiness బాగు, సొగసు, ఒప్పిదము. Similarity, resemblance సామ్యము. Delight ఉల్లాసము, ఉత్సాహము. Companionship, friendship జత. Whole; total మొత్తము. adj. Equivalent సమానము. Proper యుక్తము. Possessed, got, obtained అధీనమైన. adv. Thus, in that manner; duly, properly. "అవ డ్రావిన జోక నటునటిల్లు." (Ila. iii. 159.) he was as sick as though he had drunk poison. జోకగా. జోకతో, జోకై, జోకచేసి or జోకపరగ, grandly, finely. జోకచేయు dzōka-chēyu. v. t. To get, earn సంపాదించు. To get ready సిద్ధపరచు. జోకపడు dzōka-paḍu. v. n. To be obtained or got, to be joined జతపడు.

జోకు dzōku. [Tel.] v. a. To weigh. To lay on, to thrash or thump. కొట్టు. To abuse తిట్టు. n. Abuse. తిట్టడము.

జోకొట్టు See under జో.

జోగము dzōgamu. [from Skt. యోగము.] n. Meditation, abstraction. జోగపట్టె or జోగపట్టెయు dzōgu-patte. n. A hermit's belt. యోగపట్టము. జోగి dzōgi. [from యోగి.] n. A beggar. భిక్షుకుడు. A vagrant. A hermit. జోగిని a female rover, or a hermit. అడవిజోగులు roamers in the woods, vagrants. జోగిణి a certain female goddess; a witch సోదకత్తె.

జోగు dzōgu. [Tel.] n. Alms. భిక్షము. A boat. ఏరుదాటుసాధనము. జోగురుతిరుగు to go about the town for alms. జోగు v. n. To stagger. సొక్కు. జోగురాలు dzōgu-r-ālu. n. A nun యోగిని. A female beggar. భిక్షురాలు.

జోజో dzō-dzō. [Tel.] Interj. Hush, be still. n. A lullaby.

జోటము dzōṭamu. [Tel.] n. A sheet. దుప్పటి. G. ii. 69.

జోటి or జోటికె dzōṭi. [Tel.] n. A damsel. అమ్మడి. Vish. P. ii. 30 జోటికత్తె or జోటికత్తెయ a female companion చెలికత్తె.

జోడగి or జోడాగి dzōḍagi. [Tel.] n. A bloodhound. వేటకుక్క, కోనాగి.

జోడు dzōḍu. [Tel.] n. A pair, or couple, a pair of shoes or sandals. Junction, conjunction. జోడుకాడు a match, an equal; a companion. సముడు, కూడా ఉండేవాడు. పల్లకిజోళ్లు a pair of palanquins. వాడు నాకు ఈడా జోడా is he my equal? జోడు కూర్చు dzōḍu-kūrtsu. v. a. To embrace or join. జోడుతపేల dzōḍu-tapela. n. A metal cup or mug. జోడునక్షత్రము the double star called విశాఖ. జోడన dzōḍana. [H. from jorna to join.] n. A couple: a lined vest. Bounding, a curvetting pace, as of a horse, springing with all four legs off the ground: చౌకళించుట. ముక్కుజోడన a double nose, జమిలిముక్కు. A. v. 122. జోడా or జోడీ dzōḍā. [H.] n. A pair. జత. జోడగించు dzōḍa-g-intsu. v. t. To make a horse go at a curvetting pace. జోడన నడతో నడిపించు. జోడించు dzōḍintsu. v. t. To join, couple, unite, combine, plot, plan, compose, lay together, contrive or scheme. జతచేయు, చేర్చు. జోడింపు joining చేర్చుట.

జోల, జోలము or జోలాము *dzōla*. [Tel.] n. A salutation నమస్కారము.

జోతి *dzōti*. [from Skt. జ్యోతి.] n. Brilliancy కాంతి. A light or lamp దీపము.

జోదు *dzōdu*. [from Skt. యోధ.] n. A hero. సమర్థుడు, దిట్ట.

జోదిల్లు *dzōdillu*. [Tel.] n. Salutations. నమస్కారములు.

జోము *dzōmu*. [Tel.] n. Torpidity, stupefaction, or silliness with pride. సొమ్ము, తిమ్మిరి. v. n. To rock backwards and forwards, as Musulmans do while reading.

జోరావరి *dzōra-vari*. [Tel.] n. Force, violence. బలాత్కారము.

జోరిగాడు or అంబలిజోరిగాడు *dzōri-gadu*. [Tel.] A sort of lark: the thick billed or red bellied species. Jerdon, Catal. No. 188.

జోరీగ *dzōr-īga*. [Tel. జోరు violent, ఈగ fly.] n. The gadfly or horsefly. పులిపక్క జోరీగ ఉండినమాడ్కి or సింహముపక్క జోరీగ ఉండినమాడ్కి as the gadfly is near the tiger, or the lion, i. e., safety in the lion's lap, weak in himself but mighty in his protector. ధీరాశ్రితనిరసుడు.

జోరు *dzōru*. [Tel.] n. Force. బలము, ఊతము.

జోల *dzōla*. [Tel.] n. A lullaby.

జోలి *dzōli*. [Tel.] n. A thing, concern, affair, matter, business. A topic, theme, subject. intercourse. సంగతి, వృత్తాంతము. ప్రశంస, ప్రసక్తము, సంబంధము. వానిజోలికి పోవద్దు don't meddle with him. ఆజోలి యెరుగను I know nothing of the matter. ఇది నీజోలికాదు this is not your business. గాలిజోలి తెలుచుకొన్నావు you are merely building castles in the air.

జోలె or జోలియ *dzōle*. [Tel.] n. A pouch or bag that hangs down from the shoulder. జోలెపుచ్చుకొన్న వాండ్లగుంపు జోల వేయగా చేర్చి ముడివేసి కట్టి వేలాడ వేసిన రొండు సంచి.

జోవ Same as జోల. (q. v.)

జోస్యము *dzōsyamu*. [from Skt. జ్యౌతిషము.] n. Astrology. జోసి or జోస్యుడు *dzōsi*. n. An astrologer.

జోహారు or జోహారుగారు *dzōharu*. [Tel.] interj. Well done!. Hurra! నమస్కారార్థము, సర్వోత్కృష్టచేతనుండుమని మంగళము చేయుట.

జౌ dzau

జౌకు or జవుకు *dzauku*. [Tel.] v. n. To become soft or ripe. To give way or yield, to become loose, as a stake. To rot. మిక్కిలి మెత్తగిల్లు. adj. Swampy. Loose. జౌకు నేల swampy ground ఊబినేల. జౌకించు *dzaukintsu*. v. n. To swing down to hang loosely వ్రేలాడవేయు.

జౌజవ్వు or జవుజవ్వు *dzaudzavvu*. [Tel.] n. A rushing noise.

జౌరు or జవురు *dzauru*. [Tel.] v. a. To thrash or lash. To collect any thing scattered. To stroke. A. ii 98. n. A hit దెబ్బ. ఆ వర్తకమునందు ఒక జవురు జవిరినాడు he made a great hit in that transaction. It sometimes implies taking bribes.

ఝ jha

ఝ *jha*. [Skt.] The name of a letter of the Skt. alphabet equivalent to JH.

ఝంకారము or ఝంకృతి *jhankaramu*. [Skt.] n. The buzzing or humming noise of a bee. తుమ్మెదరొద.

ఝంఝ *jhanjha*. [Skt.] n. Wind accompanied by rain. A storm వానగాలి.

ఝంప *jhampa*. [Skt.] n. A certain kind of music. జంపె (తాళము.) Impudence దూకుడు.

ఝడితీ or ఝడ్తీ *jhaditi*. [H.] n. An examination of accounts, &c. ఝడితీచిట్టా or ఝడ్తీ కాగిదా a certificate of examination, a memorandum of search ; an inventory. A rough note book. A memorandum of daily accounts. ఝడ్తీచూచు to examine, to review, పరిచూచు, ఉండజూచు.

ఝరము or ఝరి *jharamu*. [Skt.] n. A mountain stream. A waterfall or cascade. సెలయేరు, నిర్ఝరము. ఝర్ఝరము or ఝర్ఝరి *jharjharamu*. n. A kind of drum. రంయము డియుకు వాద్యవిశేషము. A flaw in a precious stone మణిదోషవిశేషము.

ఝల్లరి *jhallari*. [Skt.] n. A kind of large drum. ఒకవిధమైనపెద్దడోలు. A whirlpool. సుడిగుండి.

ఝషము *jhashamu*. [Skt.] n. A fish. చేప. A crocodile. మొసలి. A forest. అడవి. ఝషకేతుడు one who has the sign of a fish on his flag, i. e., Manmadha.

ఝా jha

ఝాటము *jhaṭamu*. [Skt.] n. A crowd, a multitude. సమూహము. A thick forest. కారడవి. A bower. పొదరిల్లు. A broom. చీపురుకట్ట.

ఝాడాగా *jhaḍaga*. [H.] adv. Completely, finally. బొత్తిగా.

ఝి jhi

ఝిల్లి, ఝిల్లిక or ఝిరుకి *jhilli*. [Skt.] n. A cricket. ఈలపురుగు. The noise made by a cricket ఈలపురుగుకూత. A towel తుడిచేగుడ్డ.

ఝూ jhū

ఝూటా or జూటా *jhūṭa*. [H.] adj. False. అబద్ధము.

ఞ

ఞ The nasal attached to the palatal letters. It has something like the sound of N in the French words Ange, Melange. W.

ట ṭa

ట *ṭa*. The name of a letter. In composition this is sometimes changed into డ thus చేటుపాటు *cheṭu-pāṭu* becomes చేడ్పాటు *cheḍ-pāṭu*. Colloquially it changes into ష. Thus అటుకంటె, అషుకంటె as, in English, intention is pronounced intenshun. This letter ట is sometimes inserted to prevent elision. ఉప్పు+ఏరు *(uppu-ēru)* becomes ఉప్పుటేరు *(uppu-ṭē-ru.)* a salt river. పెంకు+ఇల్లు, పెంకుటిల్లు. This may happen even where the first word is Sanskrit, thus: మదము+ఏనుగు, మదపుటేనుగు.

టంకము *ṭankamu*. [Tel.] n. A piece of money: a coin: బంగారుటంకము a gold coin. A coin, of the value of 16 copper dubs. దీనారము. A composition of copper and pewter. A stonecutter's chisel. కాసెయులి. Borax వెలిగారము. టంకణము or టంకము. *ṭankaṇamu*. n. Borax: subborate of soda. వెలిగారము. టంకసాల *ṭanka-sāla*. n. A mint. టంకవాటు or టంక సాలవాటు the name of a certain gold coin.

టంకారము or టంకృతము *ṭankāramu*. [Skt.] n. The "twang" of a bowstring. టంకరించు to twang a bow.

టంకు *ṭanku*. [Tel.] n. A civilised person, నాగరకుడు. A pretentious person డాంబికుడు. టంకుతనము *ṭanku-tanamu*. n. Refinement, pride. డంబము, గాసెము.

టంగు or టంగువారు *ṭangu*. [Tel.] n. A saddle girth. గుర్రముమీది జీను జారకుండు టకుకట్టే వారు.

టకటంకు or టకటాంకు *ṭaka-ṭanku*. [Tel.] n. A rogue. కుత్సితుడు. Sar. Pad. iii. 231. adj. Roguish. కుత్సితమైన.

టకటక *ṭaka-ṭaka*. [Tel.] (anuk) adv. Agitatedly. Quickly, briskly.

టక్కు *ṭakku*. [Tel.] n. A trick, a pretence, guile. Gamesomeness, a prank. (Hence the word *Thug* or assassin is derived.) v. a. To deceive, to pretend. మాయచేయు.

టక్కు_లాడి ṭakku-l-adi. n. A deceitful woman. టక్కులుచేయునది. టక్కు_లాడు ṭakku-l-adu. n. A cheat. మోసముచేయు వాడు. టక్క_రి or టక్క_రు ṭakk-ari. n. A rogue, a hypocrite. మోసగాడు, మోసకత్తె. adj. Treacherous, wily. టక్కరి వాడు a deceiver మోసగాడు.

టపా or టపాలు ṭapa. [H.] n. The post or mail, the "tappal." A station or stage. టపాలమీదపోయినాడు he travelled by post.

టమటమ ṭama-ṭama. [Tel.] n. A drum, a tom tom, a proclamation by beat of drum.

టముకు or టమ్కు ṭamuku. [Tel.] n. A drum.

టరీపు ṭartpu. [Eng.] n. Tariff. A table of import and export duties.

టవర or తవర ṭavara. [Tel.] adj. Rash, headstrong, precipitate. Skilful, artful, clever. నేర్పరి. గడుసు, నెరజాణ మైన, పేర జము, ధూర్తత్వ్రీ.

టవాయి ṭavayi. [Tel.] n. A foul wind, an unfavourable breeze.

టా ṭā

టాకానా or టికాణా ṭakana. [Tel.] n. A place of residence; a resort, a resource; prospect.

టాకీ ṭakt. [H.] n. A stitch. టాకీవేయు to unite by stitching up, to patch.

టాకీరాయి ṭaki-rayi. [Tel.] n. The key-stone of an arch.

టాకు ṭaku. [Tel.] n. A flat ring used to keep other rings from slipping down from the fingers. An edge, a side అంచు, ఓర. The end or point of a pen. టాకులో వస్తాడు he will come here in a moment.

టాటోటు ṭaloṭu. [Tel.] n. Deceit, pretence, guile. మోసము, కపటము. టాటోటుకాడు a deceiver మోసగాడు.

టాపు ṭapu. [Tel.] n. An island. A place, తావు.

టాలాటోలితనము ṭala-ṭoli-tanamu. [Tel.] n. Knavery, trickery, ill-behaviour.

టి ṭi

టింగు ṭingu. [Tel.] n. A tinkling sound.

టికము ṭikamu. [Tel.] n. The pelvis. ముడ్డి పూస.

టికాణా ṭikana. [Tel.] n. A trace. జాడ. టూపుటికాణాలేదు there is not the slightest trace (of him).

టిట్టిభము or టిట్టిభకము ṭiṭṭi-bhamu. [Skt.] n. The bird called a wagtail. తీయూర్లలపిట్ట, కాటుకపిట్ట.

టిప్పణము ṭippaṇamu. [Skt.] n. A brief glossary or commentary explanatory of hard passages alone. A commentary on a commentary. టీకకుటీక.

టిర్రి ṭirri. [Tel.] n. A cry to cattle, like jee hup! which turns them to the left: the cry పప్పప్ప turns them to the right. A term used in games, like Play! A beast of burthen. మోసేజంతువు.

టిసి ṭisi. [Tel.] n. A bar of wood or metal. కమ్మి.

టీ ṭī

టీక ṭīka. [Skt.] n. A commentary, notes. A practical exposition of a theme.

టీకము ṭikamu. [Tel.] n. A whetstone. ఒరగల్లు.

టీకా ṭika. [Tel.] n. Inoculation, small pox by inoculation. An ornament hanging down the forehead. ఒక దినుసు పతకము. టీకాలువేయు ṭikalu-veyu. v. n. To inoculate.

టీకు ṭiku. [Tel.] n. Walking with airs. నడ మంటమందలినిక్కు.

టీపు ṭipu. [Tel.] n. A money security given to keep the peace. మంచినడవడికకు పూటా కట్టినధనము.

టూ ṭū

టూకి or **టూకీ** *ṭūki*. [Tel.] n. Brevity. సంక్షేపము. టూకీగా briefly. టూకించు *ṭūkintsu*. v. t. To abridge. సంక్షేపించు.

టూకిచెట్టు *ṭūki-cheṭṭu*. [Tel.] n. A certain broadleaved tree that bears a large fruit.

టె ṭe

టెంక *ṭenka*. [Tel.] n. The stone of any fruit. మామిడికాయలోనగువానివిత్తు.

టెంకణము *ṭenkaṇamu*. [Tel.] n. A salutation. నమస్కారము.

టెంకాయ *ṭenkāya*. [Tel. తేన+కాయ cf. (Tam.) తేంగాయ.] n. A cocoanut. కొబ్బరి కాయ. నారికేళము. ఎళనీరుటెంకాయ a tender cocoanut full of water. టెంకాయచెట్టు తుమ్మెద *ṭenkaya-cheṭṭu-tummeda*. n. The cocoanut tree-borer. A kind of large beetle.

టెంకి *ṭenki*. [Tel.] n. A place, house, home: a covert, a den or lair. Swa. iv. 75. H. i. 85. టెంకులు ఇంకిపోయినవి. (HD. i. 1558.) the wells dried up. The fish called a ray. Various species are described by Russell on Fishes. వాలుగటెంకి *Trigon sephen*. తెలు కర్రటెంకి *Pastinacea dorsalis*, P. *brevicaudis*. కంపటెంకి *Pteroplatea annulata*. తప్పుకూతి or మునుగటెంకి *tappu-kūti*. *Pteroplatea micrura*, *Myliobatis*. తెలిటెంకి *Raia ocellata*, *Myliobatis maculata*. ఏరు గుడుటెంకి *a species of cephaloptera*. వాలు వటెంకి *Rhinobatus lævis*. పులిటెంకి *puli-ṭenki*. *Trygon uarnak*. టెంకిసింద్రకి or సింధుకొల్లు *ṭenkisindraki*. *Trygon walga*. టెంకిపసులపోలిగాడు *ṭenki-pasula-pōligāḍu*. The Large Racket-tailed Drongo. *Dissemurus paradiseus* (F. B. I.)

టెంకిపురుగు *ṭenki-purugu*. [Tel.] n. A bug with wing covers like shells, which form its టెంకి or home.

టెంకె, టెంకి or **టెంకియ** *ṭenke*. [Tel.] n. An awl, a borer. ఆర, పిడిసాన, చర్మకారుడు రంధ్రములుచేసే సాధనము.

టెక్కి *ṭekki*. [Tel.] n. A sort of cap. కుల్లాయి. A. vi. 106.

టెక్కు *ṭekku*. [Tel.] n. Grace, charm, elegance. Coquettishness, coquetry, wantonness. Insolence, airs, pride. Blandishment, amorous ways. Fondling, flaunting. గర్వ చేష్ట. టెక్కులు fine airs, తళుకుచెక్కులటెక్కు the charms of her polished cheeks. టెక్కున with a grace, gracefully. టెక్కులాడి *ṭekku-l-āḍi*. n. A coquette. టెక్కులుగలది. టెక్కులాడు *ṭekku-l-āḍu*. n. A beau. టెక్కులుగలవాడు. టెక్కువ Same as టెక్కు.

టెక్కెము or **టెక్కియము** *ṭekkemu*. [Tel.] n. A banner or flag. ధ్వజము. టెక్కెపుగాము the descending node. కేతుగ్రహము.

టే ṭē

టేంకణము *ṭēnkaṇamu*. [Skt.] n. The name of a certain country.

టేకిచేప *ṭēki-chēpa*. [Tel.] n. The skate or ray fish. అంబడిటేకి the electric torpedo. టేకి. Shagreen: a skate's skin, used in polishing.

టేకు or **తేకు** *ṭēku*. [Tel.] n. The teak tree. చిరుటేకు the smaller species. Rox. i. 601.

టేవు *ṭēvu*. [Tel.] n. A noise such as is made when anything burns. మండుట యందు కలుగుధ్వని.

టొ ṭo

టొంకు *ṭonku*. [Tel.] n. Crookedness. A dent or hollow in a stone. నిమ్నోన్నతము. The forehead. A. vi. 161. adj. Crooked. టొంకుమాటలు broken words, as those of an infant.

టొంటిలు *ṭonṭilu*. [Tel.] n. A kind of earrings.

టొంపు or **టొంకరము** *ṭompu*. [Tel.] n. Imputation, a slander.

టో ṭō

టోకు *ṭōku*. [Tel.] n. A wholesale bargain, a lot or lump; మొత్తము. Way, manner. ఈటోకుగా thus, so. Touching each other's shoulders in wrestling.

టోపి or టోపీ *ṭōpi*. [Tel.] n. A cap or hat. కుల్లాయి. టోపీపెట్టు or టోపీవేయు to cap or cheat a person.

టోలి, టోలీ or ఠోలి *ṭōli*. [Tel.] n. Half a pie. Also, a mob or crowd (Vizag.)

ఠ ṭha

ఠ *ṭha*. [Tel.] n. The name of a letter.

ఠంగుఠింగు or ఠంగుఠింగు *ṭhangu-ṭhingu*. [Tel.] n. A tinkling noise.

ఠక్కు Same as టక్కు. ఠక్కుడు *ṭhakkuḍu*. [Skt.] n. A cheat. మోసకాడు.

ఠక్కురుడు *ṭhakkuruḍu*. [Skt.] n. A god. దేవత.

ఠరాయించు *ṭharāyintsu*. [Tel.] v. t. To fix, determine, settle, adjust. ఠరావు చేసిన the fixed assessment of a village.

ఠలాయించు or ఠలాయించు *ṭhalāyintsu*. [Tel.] v. n. To walk about for pleasure. ఇటు అటు తిరుగు. v. t. To make a horse walk about. గుర్రమును ఇటు అటు తిప్పు.

ఠవఠవ *ṭhava-ṭhava*. [Tel.] n. Fatigue, exhaustion. శ్రమము. A hindrance. అడ్డంకి. ఠవఠవలేక swiftly, unweariedly.

ఠవణించు or ఠవణిల్లు *ṭhavaṇintsu*. [Tel.] v. n. To be ఉండు. To redouble, as sound or brilliancy. ప్రకటించు, అమరు, అవరు, ఒప్పు.

ఠవణె, ఠవణి or ఢవణి *ṭhavaṇe*. [Tel.] n. A great drum. ఢంకా.

ఠవర *ṭharara*. [Tel.] adj. Rash, headstrong, precipitate. Skilful, artful, clever. నేర్పరి, నేర్పరి.

ఠవళి *ṭhavaḷi*. [Tel.] n. A trick, guile, prank. కొంటెతనము, మోసము, కపటము. H. v. 126. ఠవళికాడు, a cheat మోసకాడు, కుత్సితుడు. ఠవళికత్తె, a deceitful woman మోసకత్తె, కుత్సితురాలు.

ఠవిణి Same as ఠవణె. (q. v.)

ఠస్సా *ṭhasya*. [Tel.] n. A stamp, a print, a die.

ఠస్సా or ఠుస్సా *ṭhassa*. [Tel.] n. A proud demeanour. గర్వముగలనడవడి. ఠీవి.

ఠా ṭhā

ఠాకు *ṭhāku*. [Tel.] n. A thrust. v. n. To thrust.

ఠాకురు *ṭhākuru*. [Mahrāti.] n. A lord, a baron, a noble. అధిపతి.

ఠాణము *ṭhāṇamu*. [Tel.] n. A place. ప్రాభవ స్థానంబులఠాణము it is the very fountain of excellence, the home of beauty.

ఠాణా *ṭhāṇa*. [H.] n. A police station. ఠాణాదారుడు a local policeman, a station house officer.

ఠాయము or ఠాయి *ṭhāyamu*. [from Skt. స్థాయి n. A word (like do, re, mi.) used in the gamut. స్వరస్థాయి. ఠాయి అని పాడు to sing in a high note; to raise up the voice, or make the notes swell out.

> "చ॥ ప్రమదయొకర్తుమాధవుని
> చాడవిపంచిధరించికేలసం
> భ్రమమునతంత్రిమీటుచు
> దిరంబుగఠాయముచేసియొక్కరా
> గముతగనాలపించి." B. x. 1162.

ఠారు or ఠూరు *ṭhāru*. [Tel.] n. Suddenness. A sudden blow. అకస్మికమైనదెబ్బ. ఠారుమరణము *ṭhāru-m-aranamu*. n. Sudden death. ఠారుఠారగు *ṭhāru-ṭhār-agu*. v. i. To be afraid or alarmed. To be quite tired.

తావు or తాపు ṭhāvu. [Tel.] n. A place, house, lodging or residence. గృహము, స్థానము. తావువిడచిరి they deserted his banners. A sheet of paper. పైతావులు enclosures in a letter.

ఠి ṭhi

ఠింగణా or ఠెంగణా ṭhingaṇā. [Tel.] n. A little boy, a lad. బాలుడు. A short man, a dwarf. పొట్టివాడు. A. iv. 64.

ఠీ ṭhī

ఠీకు ṭhīku. [Tel.] adj. Proper, just, fit, complete.

ఠీవి ṭhīvi. [Tel.] n. Splendour. Fashion, style, manner. వైభవము. రాజఠీవిని in noble style, royally.

ఠే ṭhē

ఠేవ ṭhēva. [Tel.] n. A particular mode in music. రాగాంశము. Grandeur, fineness. ఒప్పిదము. T. iii. 39. Manner. విధము.

ఠేవణి ṭhēvaṇi. [Tel.] n. A monied security, an advance or a deposit of money.

ఠేవనము ṭhēvanamu. [Tel.] n. Bravery. శౌర్యము.

ఠేఠె ṭhēṭhe. [Tel.] n. Words like ta, la, la, used in beating time.

ఠో ṭho

ఠోలా or ఠోలా ṭhōlā. [Tel.] n. A crowd, a multitude. సమూహము, తెగ.

డ ḍa

డ ḍa. The letter D, sounded as a palatal. D sometimes changes into ణ Na, thus: అడగు, అణగు; పడతి, పణతి. In a few words the hard and soft D are used at pleasure: as డాగు or దాగు. Vide Appa C. bk. ii. rule 168. In the colloquial dialect ండ may become ణ్ణ, thus: దండము and ఆడంగులు are written దణ్ణము or దణ్ణము and ఆణంగులు.

డంకి or డంకా ḍanka. [Tel.] adj. Steady, firm, stubborn. దిట్ట. డంకితనము ḍankatanamu. n. Steadiness, firmness, stubbornness. దిట్టతనము.

డంకా or డంకి ḍankā. [Tel.] n. A drum. ఢక్క.

డంగురము ḍanguramu. [Tel.] n. A kind of leathern drum. చర్మవాద్యవిశేషము.

డంబము, డంబరము or డంబు ḍambamu. [Tel.] n. Grandeur, ostentation, gorgeousness. శ్రీకిమించిన వేషము. Fame. ప్రతిష్ఠ. Splendour, brilliancy. ప్రకాశము. Pride గర్వము. Hypocrisy, cunning. కపటము. Manner. విధము. adj. Much, great, అధికము.

డక్క or ఢక్క ḍakka. [Tel.] n. Fear, apprehension. డక్కలేదు no matter, never mind. The drift or rush (విసురు) of wind. A small double drum used as a rattle. B. iv. 86.

డక్కి, ఢక్కి or డక్కియ ḍakki. [Tel.] n. A small drum, shaped like an hour glass. డమరువు.

డక్కు ḍakku. [Tel.] n. Apprehension, fear.

డగర or డగ్గర ḍagara. [Tel.] n. A demon. పిశాచము. adj. Large. గొప్ప.

డగరము or డగరము ḍagaramu. [Tel.] n. Evil. కీడు.

డగ్గర or డగ్గర ḍaggara. [Tel.] adv. Near. (This form is used only in poetry.) డగ్గరు, డగ్గరించు, డగ్గరిలు or డగ్గరు ḍaggaru. v. n. To approach or draw near. BD. v. 125.

డగ్గుత్తిక ḍagguttika. [Tel. డక్కు+గుత్తిక.] n. Fluttering accents, a tremulous voice. The failure of the voice from dryness of the throat, caused by terror, &c. గద్గద

స్వరము. డగ్గుత్తికయైనదియై her voice failing with anxiety.

డప్పాటు ḍappāṭu. [Tel.] n. Suddenness. ఆకస్మికము. A vi. 19. డబ్బరపాటు, తొందర.

డప్పి Same as దప్పి. (q. v.)

డప్పు ḍappu. [Tel.] n. A large drum. డప్పువాడు ḍappu-vāḍu. n. A drummer.

డబడు Same as దబడు. (q. v.)

డబర, డబ్బర or డబ్బర ḍabara. [Tel.] n. A brass bowl. పోగాణి, గిన్నె.

డబ్బర Same as దబ్బర. (q. v.)

డబ్బా Same as డబ్బి. (q. v.)

డబ్బాటు ḍabbaṭu. [Tel.] adv. Suddenly. ఆకస్మికముగా.

డబ్బి or డబ్బీ ḍabbi. [Tel.] n. A little box: a pill box. బరిణ. A treasure chest: a poor's box, a box to hold collections. నగలడబ్బి a casket. ఎర్రడబ్బిచిక్కుడు a sort of grain. పొడిడబ్బి a snuff box.

డబ్బు ḍabbu. [Tel.] n. A copper coin worth either three or four copper pies చిన్నమెత్తురాగిముద్ర. Cash, money దుడ్డు, Wealth ధనము. A colour or streak. Fiction, falsehood, guile. బొంకు. Display, lavishness. డబ్బుగల rich. పాతడబ్బు a coin worth four pies. కొత్తడబ్బు a copper coin worth three pies, a quarter anna. ఈ చీర అంచు డబ్బుగా (or డాబుగా) నున్నది it has a streaked or rich border. v. a. To make up, feign, fabricate. కథడబ్బుడబ్బి making up a story.

డబ్బర See డబర.

డమరము ḍamaramu. [Skt.] n. A national danger. దేశోపద్రవము.

డమరుకము or డమరువు ḍamarukamu. [Skt.] n. A rattle or small drum shaped like an hour glass. Skill చమత్కారము.

డమాను ḍamānu. [Tel.] n. A sail. డమానుమాసము the sailing season. డమానుతాడు the principal rope that supports a sail.

డమారము, డమాయి or డమ్మారము ḍamāramu. [Tel.] n. A kettle-drum.

డమ్మను ḍam-m-anu. [Tel. డం+అను.] v.n. Lit: To say (dham) Oh! To die చచ్చు.

డయనము ḍayanamu. [Skt.] n. Flight in the air. A car. A palanquin. పక్షిపక్కిపోవుట గుంపుగాపోవడము. A toy cart బాలకులక్రీడాశకటము.

డయ్యు ḍayyu. [Tel.] v. n. To sink, to be wearied or exhausted. బలహీనమగు, అలయు. డస్సిన exhausted, faint. డయ్యక untiringly అలయక.

డలాయతు ḍalāyatu. [H.] n. A messenger, a retainer, a peon.

డల్లి or ఢల్లి ḍalli. [H.] n. A lump.

డవాలీ ḍavāli. [H.] n. A peon's belt or badge.

డవిణ Same as డంక.

డా ḍā

డా ḍā. [Tel.] adj. Left ఎడమ. డాకాలు the left leg: డాకన్ను the left eye: డామూపు the left shoulder.

డాండరవము ḍāṇḍa-ravamu. [Tel.] n. The sound of drumming. Chenna v. 413.

డాంబరము ḍāmbaramu. [Skt.] n. War. క్షామడాంబరములలో in times of famine or of war.

డాంబికము ḍāmbikamu. [Skt.] n. Pretence, pride. డాంబికుడు ḍāmbikuḍu. n. A proud or conceited person. A magician. ఇంద్రజాలవిద్యలు చేయువాడు.

డాక ḍāka. n. Greatness, splendour. విభవము. Courage, heroism. శౌర్యము. ఆము. iv. & ప్రభా. v.

డాకడ ḍā-kaḍa. [Tel.] n. The left side. ఎడమపార్శ్వము. The north ఉత్తరదిక్కు.

డాకన్ను ḍā-kannu. [Tel.] n. The left eye; a side glance. BD. iii. 404.

డాకలి Same as డాకలి.

డాకల్లు Same as డాగల్లు.

డాకిని *ḍākini.* [Skt.] n. An ogre or female imp. పిశాచస్త్రీ. శాకినిడాకినులు fairies and elves, sprites and goblins.

డాకురు *ḍākuru.* [Tel.] v. t. To thrust out, project (as the legs.) కాళ్లు తేలగిలవేయు.

డాకేలు *ḍā-kēlu.* [Tel.] n. The left hand.

డాకొను or డాకొను *ḍā-konu.* [Tel.] v. a. To touch. తాకు. To get ready. సిద్ధపడు. డాకొలుపు causal of డాకొను.

డాగరా *ḍāgarā.* [Tel.] n. A large winnowing basket.

డాగిలిమ్రుచ్చులు, డాగనమ్రుచ్చులు or డాగిలిమూతలు *ḍāgilimrutstsulu.* [Tel.] n. A game called Hide and seek. Kalah. ii. 67. డాగిలిమూతలు.

డాగు *ḍāgu.* [Tel.] n. A mark. గురుతు. A stain. మరక.

డాగు or డాగుకొను *ḍāgu.* [Tel.] v. n. To hide or lie hid. డాగించు. v. a. To hide దాచు. To delude, to tempt. వంచించు. డాచు or దాచు *ḍātsu.* v. a. To hide or conceal, to veil.

డాచెయ్యి *ḍā-cheyyi.* [Tel.] n. The left hand.

డార్కూటము *ḍārkūṭamu.* [Skt.] n. A sort of bitter fish. చేదుచేప. A. ii. 74.

డాపల or దాపల *ḍāpala.* [Tel.] n. The left side. ఎడమభాగము. adj. Left, on the left hand. adv. On the left hand. డాపలిసున్న the sunna on the left hand of a letter, that is, preceding it. డాపటి. adj. Sinister, on the left hand. డాపటికెల on the left hand.

డాపలించు *ḍāpalintsu.* [Tel.] v. n. To go round. ప్రదక్షిణించు.

డాపు or దాపు *ḍāpu.* [Tel.] n. Nearness.

డాబ *ḍāba.* [Tel.] n. A small kind of quail. A belt. జందెమువలె వేసుకొనే తోలుపట్టె.

డాబా *ḍābā* [Tel.] n. The cornice of a pillar, the projecting gallery round the top of a tower; the crest of a bastion. పోడిమిద్దె, ఉన్నతముగా కట్టబడ్డ గృహావిశేషము. A terraced roof, opposed to a pent roof.

డాబు *ḍābu.* [Tel.] n. Pomp. డంబము. A list or catalogue: a physician's recipe దినుసులపట్టిక.

డామరము Same as డమరము. (q. v.)

డాయు *ḍāyu.* [Tel.] v. n. To approach. సమీపించు.

డాలు *ḍālu.* [Tel.] n. Brilliancy, lustre of complexion, prettiness, a shield. A banner, a flag. గురుతు, సౌందర్యము, కాంతి, అందము, డెక్కెము. డాలువారు, same as డాలు a shield. డాలుకాడు a standard bearer. డాలించు to be armed with a shield డాలుపూను.

డి ḍi

డింకవేగు *ḍinka-vēgu.* [Tel.] v. n. To die. చచ్చు. Swa. i.

డింకి or డింకీ *ḍinki.* [Tel.] n. A fall in wrestling. A summersault, a feat in gymnastics wherein two players roll themselves up together into a ball.

డింకు *ḍinku.* [Tel.] v. n. To die. చచ్చు.

డింగ *ḍinga.* [Tel.] n. A vessel. పాత్రము. A. ii. 123. లోహపుడింగలు metal vessels. లోహపాత్రములు.

డింగరీడు or డింగరుడు *ḍingarīḍu.* [Tel.] n. A slave. దాసుడు. A servant సేవకుడు. A. vi. 78. A devotee. భక్తుడు.

డింగిల్లు *ḍingillu.* [Tel.] n. Salutations. నమస్కారవిశేషము.

డించు or డించు *ḍintsu.* [Tel.] v. a. To let down, to leave, give up or abandon. To free, release, let go.

డిండిమము *ḍinḍimamu.* [Skt.] n. A small drum. ఢమామా, రాయడిళిడిళి.

డిండీరము *ḍinḍīramu.* [Skt.] n. Froth, foam. నురుగు.

డిందు *ḍindu.* [Tel.] v. n. To sink అడగు, క్రుంగు. To dry up ఇంకు. To be defeated, ruined, quenched, extinguished. ఓడిపోవు. To expire. v. a. To kill, to ruin. n. Defeat, extinguishment, ruin. అపజయము, హీనత్వము, నాశము. adj. Defeated, worsted, ruined, less, inferior. **డిందుపడు** *ḍindu-paḍu.* v. n. To be calmed, or settled. నెమ్మదిపడు. Vaijayanti. iii. 49. **డిందుపరచు** *ḍindu-paratsu.* v. a. To defeat, ruin, do away with, remove. బడలిక డిందుపరచు to do away with fatigue, to allay suffering. **డిందుపాటు** *ḍindu-pāṭu.* n. Alleviation. ఉపశాంతి.

డింపు or **దింపు** *ḍimpu.* [Tel.] n. Misery. దీనత్వము.

డింబము *ḍimbamu.* [Tel.] n. A bag of skin. ఎముకలడింబము. (Dasav. iv. 95.) a bag of bones. A starve ing. Danger ఉపద్రవము. Fear భయము.

డింభము *ḍimbhamu.* [Skt.] n. An infant. పిల్ల. **డింభుడు** *ḍimbhuḍu.* n. A little boy.

డిక్కి *ḍikki.* [Tel.] n. A blow with the head. తలతో కొట్టుట.

డిగియ Same as డిగ్గియ.

డిగు or **దిగు** *ḍigu.* [Tel.] v. n. To alight, to get down. To alight from, to dismount. M. IX. iii. 299.

డిగ్గ *ḍigga.* [Tel.] adv. (the inf. of డిగ్గు) at once, instantly.

డిగ్గి *ḍiggi.* [Tel.] n. Fire. అగ్ని.

డిగ్గియ or **డిగియ** *ḍiggiya.* [Tel.] n. A long pond: a well with steps descending into it. A. i. 8. v. 120. దీర్ఘిక, బొడ్డనబావి, నడబావి.

డిగ్గు *ḍiggu.* [Tel.] v. n. To alight, get down. దిగు. M. III. ii. 41. T. iv. 86. n. Littleness. తక్కువ.

డిగ్గున or **దిగ్గున** *ḍigguna.* [Tel.] adv. Suddenly, at once. Subhad. ii. 84.

డిగ్గుపడు *ḍiggu-paḍu.* [Tel.] v.n. To become less. తక్కువపడు.

డిప్పకాయ *ḍippa-kāya.* [Tel.] n. A sort of large gourd used as a bottle.

డిబ్బెము *ḍibbemu.* [Tel.] n. A fold of cloth, కడితము. A prayer, an offering or gift to the poor.

డిమ్మరి Same as దిమ్మరి.

డిల్లపడు, డీలాపడు or **డిల్లపోవు** *ḍilla-paḍu.* [Tel.] v. n. To be horrified, astounded, unmanned, unnerved. విరాకుపడు, భయాదులచేత సత్వహీనమగు. **డిల్లపాటు** *ḍilla-pāṭu.* n. Horror. BRY. ii. 153. **డిల్లము** *ḍillamu.* n. Enervation. సత్వహీనము.

డీ ḍī

డీ or **ఢీఢీ** *ḍī.* [Tel.] n. A cry like Hurra! huzza! avaunt!

డీకు *ḍīku.* [Tel.] n. Encouragement. ప్రోత్సాహము.

డీకొను *ḍī-konu.* [Tel. డీ+కొను.] v. n. To meet, as two rams in fighting. To butt. To collide. To defy, to bluster or talk big, to cry out upon. R. v. 145. **డీకొలుపు** *ḍī-kolupu.* v. a. To encorrage. పురికొలుపు. To cause to fall on each other కవ్వించు. **డీకోలు** *ḍī-kōlu.* n. Collision. డీకొనుట.

డీనము *ḍīnamu.* [Skt.] n. Flight, flying. మీదికెగురుట, రెక్కకదలకుండా పక్షి ఆకాశములో పోవడము.

డీలు or **డీలైన** *ḍīlu.* [H. dhīla] adj. Loose, lean, thin. కృశించిన, చిక్కిన. డీలించు to loosen, సడలించు, డీలుచేయు.

డీలు or **డీలుపడు** *ḍīlu.* [Tel.] v. n. To be upset. డిల్లపడు. **డీలుపాటు** *ḍīlu-pāṭu.* n. The act of being upset or done up. డీలుపడుట.

డు ḍu

డు *ḍu*. The sign of the first case in some nouns as రాముడు. The sign of the third person in verbs as రాడు. The sign of concession in verbs అనంతరార్థకప్రత్యయము as కొట్టుడు.

దుందుకము *ḍundukamu*. [Skt.] adj. Mean. అల్పమైన. Cruel. క్రూరమైన.

దుందుభము *ḍundubhamu*. [Skt.] n. A griphon, a two headed snake. రెండుతలల పాము.

డుక్కు *ḍukku*. [Tel.] v. n. To be hidden. మరుగుపడు.

డుబాయించు *ḍubāyintsu*. [Tel.] v. t. To ruin.

డుబుడక్క *ḍubu-ḍakka*. [Tel.] n. A small rattling drum. డుబుడక్కలవాడు or బుడబుడక్కలవాడు *ḍubu-ḍakkala-vāḍu*. n. A mountebank or wizard who uses a drum as a sign of his trade.

డుయ్యు or డుయ్యు *ḍuyyu*. [Tel.] v. n. To retire, to retreat. v. a. To open or unfold a cloth or manuscript. To draw a sword. To pierce.

డుర్రు *ḍurru*. [Tel.] An interjection similar to Huzza, avaunt. డుర్రుచ్చు to cry Huzza. డుర్రుచ్చి *ḍurruchchi*. n. A war-cry, a challenge. యుద్ధాహ్వానము.

డుల్లు *ḍullu*. [Tel.] v. n. To fall off, as moulting feathers, or withered leaves. "తారకలెల్లడుల్లినన్." (G. v. 32.) though the stars fall. పల్లూడుచుడుల్లె (G. v. 32.) his teeth fell out. డుల్లపాడుచు to knock down. రాలుచు. డులుచు or డుల్చు *ḍulutsu*. [Tel. causal of డుల్లు.] v. t. To loosen, knock out, slay. వదిలించు, చరిచముచేయు. డులుపు *ḍulupu*. v. a. To cause to fall, to deprive of. విసర్జనచేయు. A. iii. 106.

డూ ḍū

డూయము Same as డూయు. (q. v.)

డె ḍe

డెందము *ḍendamu*. [Tel.] n. The heart, mind. హృదయము, మనసు.

డెక్క *ḍekka*. [Tel.] n. A hoof, a fin, a crab's claw.

డెక్కు *ḍekku*. [Tel.] v. a. To strike, smite; to hinder, arrest. అడ్డగించు, నివారించు, అటకాయించు.

డెక్కొను *ḍekkonu*. [Tel. డెక్కు+కొను.] v. n. To be fixed firmly. నెలకొను.

డెప్ప *ḍeppa*. [Tel.] n. A flat place on a hill. కొండమీది సమమైనచోటు.

డెప్పరము or డెప్పరము *ḍepparamu*. [Tel.] n. A strait, peril. ఆపద. adj. Impossible, impracticable. అశక్యము. M. vi. i. 239. Great, excessive, అధికము, మెండు. Intolerable దుస్సహము. A. vi. 171. డెప్పరపురాళ్ల వర్షము a dreadful shower of stones. డెప్పరించు *ḍepparintsu*. v. n. To become impossible. అశక్యమగు.

డెప్పు Same as డప్పు.

డెబ్బది, డెబ్బయి or డబ్బై *ḍebbadi*. [Tel. ఏడు+పది.] n. Seventy.

డే ḍē

డేగ *ḍēga*. [Tel.] n. A hawk, a falcon. A falconer or huntsman. Swa. iv. 81. కోకిలడేగ the cuckoo Hawk. Jerdon No. 36. పిట్టపట్టుడేగ ibid. No. 40. డేగాట *ḍēg-āṭa*. n. Hawking: sport, play. డేగలతో అయినోనాడు చేసే ఉత్సవము.

డేరా *ḍērā*. [Tel.] n. A tent. గుడారము.

డొ ḍo

డొంక *ḍonka*. [Tel.] n. A coppice, a copse, a thicket, a waste. Bramble, bushes. A narrow path between two fields left as a passage for ca[illegible] త్రోవ, పశువులదారి. డొం

కనల్లంచి or పొదనల్లంచి *ḍonka-nallanchi.* n. The Shama, *Cittocincla macrura.* (F. B. I.)

డొంకియ *ḍonkiya.* [Tel.] n. A foot path.

డొంకు *ḍonku.* [Tel.] v. n. To lie hidden: to hide or disappear, to shrink or retreat. అడగు. To dry up. ఇంకు, ఎండిపోవు. Swa. iii. 73. n. A dent in a stone. Crookedness. వంకర. డొంకునామము a crooked mark on the forehead.

డొంకెన *ḍonkena.* [Tel.] n. A pruning hook. కోటి, వంకర అలుగుగల ఈటె.

డొంగు *ḍongu.* [Tel.] n. A hollow in a tree. చెట్టులోనితొర్ర. v. n. To hide. దాగు.

డొకారము *ḍokāramu.* [Tel.] n. The interior. లోను. The space between the earth and sky అంతరాళము. డొకారముచొచ్చు to fall within లోపడు, లోనగు.

డొక్క *ḍokka.* [Tel.] n. The flanks. The sides. The belly. The peel, husk, as the hard cocoanut coir. డొక్కపట్టిన నొప్పి a stitch in the side. డొక్కలో పొడిచె he smote him under the fifth rib, డొక్కబుర్ర an empty palmyra stone that has sprouted. తేగపాఱ విడిన తాటివిత్తు.

డొక్కరము *ḍokkaramu.* [Tel.] n. A kind of wrestling మల్ల బంధవిశేషము.

డొక్కు *ḍokku.* [Tel.] v. n. To perish, die. చచ్చు. To grow old ముదియు. adj. Old ముదిసిన. డొక్కుపడు *ḍokku-paḍu.* v. n. To be sallow, sunken eyed or pallid.

డొగరు *ḍogaru.* [Tel.] n. A fault, transgression. అపరాధము. Blame, censure నింద.

డొప్ప Same as దొప్ప. (q. v.)

డొలుచు or డొల్చు *ḍolutsu.* [Tel.] v.n. To tumble head over heels as dancing girls do. డొల్లజేయు.

డొల్ల or దొల్ల *ḍolla.* [Tel.] n. A hamper or long basket placed on a cart. A straw band or withe to bind stacks with. The skeleton of a beast. The cheek. A lie or falsehood. adj. Hollow, concave.

డొల్లు, దొల్లు or దొరలు *ḍollu.* [Tel.] v. n. To fall, to roll over. పడు, పొరలు.

డో ḍō

డోకడా *ḍōkaḍā.* [Tel.] n. A cent; one hundredth part of a coin. నూరవపాలు.

డోకు *ḍōku.* [Tel.] v. n. To vomit. n. Vomiting. Nausea, qualm. డోక్కొను *ḍōkkonu.* v. n. To be queasy or qualmish. డోక్కొన్న ముఖముగల haggard, grim, gaunt with leanness.

డోగు or దోగు *ḍōgu.* [Tel.] v. n. To crawl on the hands and knees.

డోరము Same as తోరము. (q. v.)

డోరములు *ḍōramulu.* [Tel.] n. Streaks on a sword. కత్తిమీదిచారలు.

డోల or డోలి *ḍōla.* [Skt.] n. A swing cot. డోలి *ḍōlī.* [H.] n. A litter. తొట్టి. డోలనము *ḍōlanamu.* [Skt.] n. Swinging. ఊచుట.

డోలు *ḍōlu.* [Tel.] n. A drum.

డౌ ḍau

డౌలు or డవులు *ḍaulu.* [Tel.] n. Pomp. డంభము. An estimate మదింపు. Demand or collection of revenue by the Government: డవులుదారు an appraiser. డవులుపట్టీ an account of the estimate of each farmer's produce.

ఢ ḍha

ఢ The letter dh as in hard-hap, pronounced as a palatal.

ఢక్క or ఢక్కా *ḍhakka.* [Skt.] n. A large drum. డంకా. ఢక్కానినాదము the sound of a drum.

ఢక్కా or ఢక్కు *ḍhakkā.* [Skt.] n. A severe blow. పడవఢక్కాతిన్నది the boat received a severe blow.

ధమంధమ *ḍhaman-ḍhama.* [Skt.] adv. Bang! crashingly, thunderingly. **ధమధమార్భటి** *ḍhama-ḍhamarbhaṭi.* n. A bellowing or crashing sound.

ధమ్మను *ḍham-m-anu.* [Tel.] v. n. Lit. To say (dham) Oh! To die. చచ్చు.

ఢా ḍhā

ఢాక *ḍhāka.* [Tel.] n. Violence. ఔద్ధత్యము. An inroad, invasion. A difficulty. గాలి ఢాక a gust of wind. ఢాకచేయు to invade, rush in upon. **ఢాకావాండ్లు** *ḍhāka-vāndlu.* [Tel.] n. Highwaymen.

ఢామ్మను Same as ధమ్మను.

ఢు ḍhu

ఢుంఢి *ḍhunḍi.* [Skt.] n. A name of Ganēsa. గణేశుడు.

ఢులి *ḍhuli.* [Skt.] n. A female tortoise. ఆడుతాబేలు. Swa. v. 62.

ఢో ḍho

ఢోకా *ḍhōkā.* [Tel.] n. An attack, an assault. Fear, apprehension. An injury, a defect, an impediment. See ఢాక.

ఢోకి or **ఢోకిచిప్ప** *ḍhōki.* [Tel.] n. A ladle formed of half a cocoanut shell.

ఢోలము *ḍōlamu.* [Skt.] n. A drum. డోలు.

ఞ ña

ఞ *ña.* The letter N sounded as a palatal. No Telugu word begins with this letter. In some words చ changes into ఞ. Elsewhere ఞ Ṇ and ళ Ḷ are accounted the same: thus మఞిగ or మళిగ. Sometimes ఞ changes into న N as ఞేను or నేను.

ణి ṇi

ణిచ్ *ṇich* In Telugu Grammar. This denotes ఇంచు the sign of the Causal voice.

త ta

త *ta.* The letter T pronounced as a pure dental. A feminine suffix as in ఒకతె, ప్రోడ. త॥ in ordinary writing denotes తరువాత afterwards. In prosody it stands for the foot called తగణము which consists of two long syllables followed by a short one as సంగాతు.

తః *tah.* An adverbial affix used with some Sanskrit words, as అన్యాయతః unjustly, అజ్ఞానతః unconsciously.

తంకర *tankara.* [Tel.] n. Inferior or useless grain. తుచ్ఛధాన్యము.

తంగేడు or **తంగెడు** *tangēḍu.* [Tel.] n. The Tanner's Cassia. *Cassia auriculata.* నేల తంగేడు Ground Cassia or Senna, *Cassia angustifolia.* అడవితంగేడు the wild species used in tanning. పచ్చతంగేడు the yellow flowering species, *Cassia sophora.* See కసింద (Watts). సీమతంగేడు the flower called Peacock's Pride, *Cassia Sophera.* తంగేటిజున్ను wild honey, a proverbial expression denoting the seeking of grapes from thorns, or milk from a stone (R. i. 127 and iv. 158). **తంగేడుగోరింక** *tangēḍu-gōrinka.* n. The Pied Crested Cuckoo, *Coccystes jacobinus.* (F. B. I.)

తంటా or **తంటు** *tanṭa.* [Tel.] n. Trouble. శ్రమము. A quarrel కలహము, పేచీ. Evil కీడు. Deceit మోసము. Slander, a false report చాడీ.

"తంటాలకేమి మచ్చు జడదారుల
దారులు కొంతెరుంగుదున్."

చంద్రా. iii.

తంటెము or **తంటెరయము** *tanṭemu*. [Tel.] n. A medicinal shrub. *Cassia tora*, and *Cassia alata*, దద్రుఘ్నము, త్రపుపాన్నాటము, సిరి కూనలోతేసే విత్తులచెట్టు.

తండ *tanḍa*. [Tel.] n. The bottom of a ship.

తండము *tanḍamu*. [Skt.] n. An assembly, a collection, mass, quantity. కలువతండము a bed of lilies. మృగతండము a herd of cattle, &c. తండములు crowds, swarms, abundance. గుంపులు, సమృద్ధి. A. v. 39. **తండతండముగా** *tanḍa-tanḍamu-ga*. adv. In heaps. BD. v. 228. **తండోపతండములు** *tanḍōpa-tanḍamulu*. n. Crowds upon crowds. తండోపతండములుగా excessively, more and more, prodigiously.

తండసము *tanḍasamu* [Tel.] n. Tweezers for pulling out hairs. మంగలవాడు వెంట్రుకలుతీసే పనిముట్టు. ఎలుగుబంటికి తంటసపుపని a task as endless as pulling out a bear's hairs. A forge కమ్మరకొలిమి.

తండా *tanḍa* [Tel.] n. A caravan, horde, troop, encampment. A collection of men or things. సమూహము.

తండు *tanḍu*. [Tel.] n. The broad part or beazle of a ring. v. n. To ask for the payment of a debt. To collect or raise money. **తండుకోల** *tanḍu-kōla*. n. An oar. A spear used in killing fish. చేపలనుపొడిచే చిల్లకోల.

"సీ॥ మంగులల్లాడుగోములు తండుకోలలు
చెట్టుకొల్పినమీలపుట్టికలును."

పంచ. పం. i.

తండులము *tanḍulamu*. [Skt.] n. Rice. బియ్యము.

తండువు *tanḍuvu*. [Skt.] n. An oar. తెడ్డు కొయ్య.

తండేలు or **తండెలు** *tand-ēlu*. [H.] n. The headman among sailors. A tindal or boatswain. ఓడపెద్దవాడు.

తండ్రి *tanḍri*. [Drav. cf. Tam. తంతై. Lit. One who brings (food, &c.) తెచ్చువాడు. The addition of the రావడి or r sound is a sign of the honorific plural.] n. A father. పెత్తండ్రి (పెద్ద+తండ్రి) a father's elder brother. పినతండ్రి a father's younger brother. తల్లితండ్రులు parents, &c. తండ్రిసైదోడు a father's brother or sister. తండ్రితండ్రి a grandfather తాత.

తంతన్యమాన *tantanya-māna*. [Skt.] adj. Grown, mature. పరిపక్వమైన. Parij. iii. 81.

తంతి *tanti*. [Tel.] n. The wire or string of a musical instrument, a wire. కమ్మి, తీగె. **తంతికురుపు** or **నారిపుండు** *tanti-kurupu*. n. Guinea worm. **తంతివాద్యము** *tanti-vādyamu*. [Tel + Skt.] n. A stringed instrument.

తంతు *tantu*. [Tel.] n. Craft, cunning, subtlety, a device, shift. తంత్రము, ఉపాయము.

తంతువు *tantuvu*. [Skt.] n. A thread or fibre. నూలిపోగు. తంతుకాష్ఠము a spindle నూలువడికే కదురు. తంతుకీటము a silkworm పట్టుపురుగు. **తంతునాగము** *tantu-nāgamu*. n. A polypus or marine serpent supposed to entangle and drown swimmers. సొరచు. **తంతునాభము** *tantu-nābhamu*. [from తంతు a thread and నాభి the navel.] n. A spider. సాలెపురుగు. తంతువాయము a spider. **తంతువాయుడు** *tantu-vāyuḍu*. n. A weaver.

తంతెలు or **తంతియలు** *tantelu*. n. The divisions or bridges in the neck of a guitar, steps. మెట్లు.

తంత్రకము *tantrakamu*. [Skt.] n. A web, a piece of new cloth. కొత్తబట్ట.

తంత్రము *tantramu*. [Skt.] n. A device, contrivance. ఉపాయము. A theory, system సిద్ధాంతము. Scheme, plan, invention. An art. A trick, intrigue, plot. కుట్ర. రాజ్యతంత్రము a system of government, polity, the affairs of state. దుస్తంత్రము a wicked device. ఈశ్వరతంత్రము the interposition of Providence; the finger of God. The పంచతంత్రము or "Five modes," whereby men secure success: the name of a celebrated book. తంత్రగ్రంథములు *tantra-granthamulu.* n. Apocryphal books teaching a secret code of worship, prescribing the adoration of demons and women with magical rites, with the use of flesh and wine, and extraordinary lewdness. తంత్రజ్ఞుడు *tantra-gnyudu.* n. A conspirator, an accomplice. తంత్రవాది *tantra-vadi.* n. A clever, ingenious man.

తండన *tandana.* [Tel.] adj. Lazy, indolent. తండనము or తండనపదములు *tandana-mu.* n. Wretched drawling music. తండన తాన or తండానతాన words used in beating time. P. ii. 132.

తండర *tandara.* [Tel. from Skt. తంత్ర] n. Hesitation, perplexity, confusion, trembling. Drowsiness, కునికిపాటు. Lassitude, exhaustion, weariness. అలసట.

తంపటి *tampati.* [Tel.] n. A bonfire: a great blaze.

తంపర *tampara.* [Tel.] n. A cluster of lotuses. తామరగుంపు. తామరతంపర blooming or basking like a flower.

తంపి *tampi.* [Tel.] n. A fire pit, used for boiling water. దాగుంట. A quarrel or squabble. కలహము. తంపిపెట్టు *tampi-pettu.* v. n. To make a slow fire. To create a quarrel. వానికి వీనికి తంపిపెట్టినాడు he made them quarrel.

తంబ *tamba.* [Tel.] n. The swordbean, *Conavabia gladista.*

తంబళ, తంబళివాడు or తంబళి *tambala.* [Tel.] n. A caste of Saivite priests.

తంబు *tambu.* [Tel. & Tam.] n. A younger brother. తమ్ముడు.

తంబుగ *tambuga.* [Tel.] n. A small brass water pot in the shape of a truncated cone. చిన్నచెంబు గానుండే చెంబు.

తంబుర or తంబూరా *tambura.* [Tel. తంబి+బుర్ర.] n. A kind of stringed instrument like the guitar. A tambourine.

తకతక *taka-taka.* [Tel. (anuk)] n. A ringing sound. adv. Aloud, tremulously, strongly. తకతకతాళము, తకతాళము the action of keeping or beating time in music.

తకపిక *taka-pika.* [Tel. (anuk)] adv. Wildly, loosely, at random. తకపికలాడు *taka-pi-ka-l-adu.* v. n. To dance about, to dangle.

"ఒకానొకతపసిగా మాపించి నన్ను
తకపికలాడింప తలచితివని
క్రూరాత్మ మన్నన భూతకాపాక్షి
నీరాత్మ్మమును నిన్ను నీరుగావింతు."

HD. i. 1315.

తకరారు *takararu.* [H.] n. A dispute, an altercation. జగడము.

తకావి *takavi.* [Tel.] n. An advance of money, given for the purpose of cultivation. వారకము.

తక్క *takka.* [Tel. from తప్పు] adv. Except, save, but. తప్ప.

తక్కటి *takkati.* [Tel.] n. A lamp with three spouts. adj. (from తక్కు) Remaining తక్కిన, మిగిలిన, శేషించిన.

తక్కరి *takkari.* [Tel.] n. A rogue, a deceiver. B. x. 383. టక్కరి.

తక్కలపడు *takkala-padu.* [Tel.] n. To be in trouble. తారుమారుపడు. G. xi. 157.

తక్కిడి *takkidi.* [Tel.] n. A lie. Deceit. మోసము. తక్కిడికాడు *takkidi-kadu.* n. A cheat. మోసకాడు.

తక్కిన *takki-na.* [Tel. from తక్కు] adj. Remaining as a residue. తక్కినవారు the rest, the others. తక్కినది the rest.

తక్కిలి *takkili.* [Tel.] n. The yellow myrobalan. The tomato plant. తక్కిలిగాయ a tomato.

తక్కిసము *takkisamu.* [Tel.] n. A subscription raised among the ryots to defray the village expenses.

తక్కు *takku.* [Tel.] v. n. To miss, to fail. తప్పు. అట్లుచేయుటతక్కితేని if I fail to effect this. v. a. To leave, let go, loose. విసర్జించు, వదలిపెట్టు. A. iv. 258. n. Remainder, residue. Also, jesting: టక్కు. తక్కు పిక్కు దొంగతనము petty theft. adj. Other ఇతరము. తక్కుడు n. Remaining over. తక్కుట.

తక్కువ *takkuva.* [Tel.] n. A want, deficiency, defect; inferiority, baseness. బాకీతక్కువ the balance or remaining sums of money ఎక్కువతక్కువలు or హెచ్చుతక్కువలు difference, irregularity, improper words. adj. Deficient, defective, inferior, mean, contemptible, base, low. With a dative it means less: as కోసుకు తక్కువ less than two miles. ఇది ఒకటే తక్కువ this alone was wanting. అది యేమి తక్కువ what harm? what matter? తక్కువమాటలు low expressions, improper language. ఎక్కువతక్కువగా *adv.* More or less. తక్కువపడు *takkuva-padu.* v. n. To be wanting, to be deficient, to be insufficient. కొఱతపడు. తక్కువపాటు *takkuva-pāṭu.* n. Want, deficiency.

తక్కె *takke.* [Tel.] n. A weight of two viss. రెండువీసెలయెత్తు.

తక్కెడ *takkeḍa.* [Tel.] n. A pair of scales, a balance, a weighing machine.

తక్కొను *tak-konu.* [Tel. తను+కొను.] v. n. To undertake. పూనుకొను.

తక్కోలము *takkōlamu.* [Tel.] n. The name of a certain plant. *Clerodendrum inerme.* Heyne. *Calyptranthes jambolana.* Ainslie.

తక్రము *takramu.* [Skt.] n. Buttermilk diluted with water. మజ్జిగ.

తక్షకుడు *takshakuḍu.* [Skt.] n. The name of a mythological serpent ఒక సర్పరాజు. The name of a race of men called Takshakas. A carpenter, వడ్లవాడు.

తగటు *tagaṭu.* [Tel.] n. Lace, జెరీ, సరిగె. తగటుచీర a lace cloth. తగటు or తగటి *tagaṭi.* adj. Laced సరిగెగల.

తగడు *tagaḍu.* [Tel.] n. A plate or flat piece of metal. Gold leaf, brocade. తగు A. iv. 132. M. VI i. 298. చీనాతగడు a tin plate.

తగర *tagara.* [Tel.] n. A rogue, a deceiver. KP. iii. 206. A tree called *Morinda tinctoria.* Rox. i. 543. సంధివర్ధనపుచెట్టు. See కసింద. తగిరిసచెట్టు the *Foetid Cassia, Cassia Tora* (Watts). The oval-leaved Cassia. Ainslie.

తగరము *tagaramu.* [Tel.] n. Tin. తగరపు పెట్టె a tin box.

తగరిసె, తగిరిసె or **తగర్చె** *tagarise.* Same as తగరచెట్టు. See under తగర.

తగరు *tagaru.* [Tel.] n. A ram. పొట్టేలు. తగరురవుతు the god of fire అగ్ని.

తగవు *tagavu.* [Tel. from తగు.] n. Justice, virtue, uprightness. ధర్మము, న్యాయము. Also, presents given to a daughter by her parents when she is married. A dispute జగడము. A lawsuit వ్యాజ్యము.

"క॥ తనువారలు ధర్మమేలా
తనగురు తెరుగంగలేని తనువదియేలా
తనబుద్ధిగానిదేలా
తనుతినకేగాకయున్న తగవదియేలా."

(Rama Stava Rajam viii. 203, 188.) తగవుగోరి a peacemaker. సంధిచేయువాడు. **తగవరి** *tagavari.* [తగవు+అరి.] n. A judge or arbitrator. న్యాయాధిపతి. **తగవేది** *tagav-ēdi.* [తగవు+ఏది] n. Sacrificing justice, unjust, wicked. తగవుమాలి. M. IV. ii. 40 and 193.

తగాదా *tagādā.* [H.] n. A quarrel. Dunning for payment of money.

తగిరిస *tagirisa.* [Tel.] n. See under తగర.

తగిలించు *tagilintsu.* [Tel. causal of తగులు.] v. a. To apply (paint, a bandage, punishment, a rule, the law, &c.) To fasten (a bolt, &c.) To inflict (pain.) To attach, fix, insert, lock, bolt, hang on, stick into, అగ్నితగిలించు to set fire. నన్ను ఆ పని లో తగిలించిరి they involved me in that business. వానికి సంకెలలు తగిలించిరి they put fetters upon him. తగిలించుకొను *tagilintsu-konu.* v. a. (middle voice) To put on, apply to oneself, to become involved in, to catch, to contract. రోగమును తగిలించుకొను to catch or contract disease. సంకెళ్లు తగిలించుకొన్నాడు he put on fetters.

తగు *tagu.* [Tel.] v. n. To be fit, or proper, to suit or agree, suffice. యుక్తమగు. p|| తగిన or తగ్గ, fit, proper, moderate. Neg. p|| తగని unfit, unsuitable, immoderate, vast, horrid. It is often used impersonally: Thus అట్లు చేయదగునా is it fit to do so? పోదగదు it is not right to go. తెలిసి కొనదగును it is possible to discover it "తపసులకుపురిమునతగదువర్తింప." DRK. 204. తగుమాత్రమైన sufficient, some. తగుమాత్రముగా moderately, well, amply. తగు మాత్రముగొప్ప pretty large. Here తగు is used as a p|| instead of తగిన. తగిన *tagina.* (Rel. p|| of తగు) adj. Fitting, proper, due, right, likely, probable, pretty. తగినమాత్రము pretty well. తగినట్టుగా *tagi-n-aṭṭu-gā.* adv. Fitly, properly.

తగులము, తగులాటము or తగులు *tagulamu.* [Tel.] n. Connection. సంబంధము. P. i. 635. Desire, lust. ఆసక్తి, వలపు, జంఝాటము. A check, hindrance. అడ్డపాటు. Swa. iii. 4. A iv. 121.

తగులు *tagulu.* [Tel.] v. a. & n. To happen, occur, turn up, appear. To belong to, appertain to, to come in contact with, to touch, hit, strike. To be caught; got, found, joined, entangled, understood. To be received (as a blow), incurred (as expense or punishment.) n. See under తగులము. ఆ యింటికి నిప్పుతగిలినది the house caught fire. ఇక్కడ గాలి తగులుచున్నది the wind strikes here, here we get the breeze. పెండ్లితగిలినది there was a marriage. ప్రయాణము తగిలినది he had occasion to make a journey. అక్కడ మంచినీళ్లు తగిలినవి there we found fresh water. వానికి దెబ్బతగిలినది he received a blow. కుండ కాలికి తగిలినది the pot touched my foot. ఓడ మెరకకు తగిలినది the ship ran aground. వానికి రోగముతగుల కుండ to prevent his catching the disease. అతనితిట్లు నాకు తగలలేదు his abuse did not affect me. ఇది వానిమనసునకు తగిలినది this was impressed upon his mind. వెంటతగులు to pursue. తగులుకొనివచ్చిరి they attacked, they followed. అడ్డముతగులు to oppose, to come in the way. పదిరూకలు తగిలినవి it cost ten cash. తగులుకొను *tagulu-konu.* v. n. To be involved or entangled with. చిక్కుకొను. To fall in love with. వలచు. To catch fire. అది వానితో తగులుకొనిపోయినది she has gone off with him. ఆ యిల్లు తగులుకొన్నది the house caught fire. తగలబడు or తగులబడు *tagala-baḍu.* v. n. To burn or be set on fire. ఇల్లు తగలబడ్డది the house was burnt. తగలబెట్టు or తగులబెట్టు *tagala-beṭṭu.* v. a. To set fire to, to kindle, to burn అడివిని తగలబెట్టిరి they burned the forest. తగులుబడి *tagulu-baḍi.* n. Expense, charge, cost, outlay. పెట్టుబడి. తగులుబాటు *tagulu-bāṭu.* n. Charge, cost, expense. తగులుపడు to be caught. చిక్కు, పట్టుపడు.

తగ్గు *taggu.* [Tel.] v. n. To become less, to decrease, diminish fall (in price,) abate, తక్కువవు. To go back, withdraw, retire, వెనుకకుతీయు. తగ్గుమొగ్గులు *taggu-moggulu.* n. Ups and downs. తగ్గించు *taggintsu.* v. a. To lower, debase, degrade, తగ్గింపు *taggimpu.* n. A fall, sinking, diminution, reduction. A fall in price. తగ్గు or తగ్గువల *taggu.* n. Decrease, a diminution, abatement. తక్కువ.

తచ్చ *tatstsa.* [Tel.] n. A joke, a lie.

తచ్చన *tatstsana.* [Tel.] n. Sport, play, jesting, a joke; slander, lying, misrepresentation, coaxing, feigning. కపటము, పరిహాసము, చాతుర్యపుమాట, చేష్ట. ఇచ్ఛకము, తంత్రము. తత్సనలాడు or తత్సనచేయు to sport, jest, to quiz, laugh at పరిహసించు. **తచ్చాడు** *taṭsṭsāḍu.* v. n. To walk about. సంచరించు.

తటుక or **తటుకా** *taṭaku.* [Tel.] n. Stunning. నిశ్చేష్టత. Surprise. ఆశ్చర్యము. **తటుకపడు** or **తటుకాపడు** *taṭaka-paḍu.* v. n. To be surprised. **తటుకపాటు** *taṭaka-pāṭu.* n. Surprise.

తటతట *taṭa-taṭa.* [Tel. anuk] adv. Violently, loudly.

తటమట or **తటవట** *taṭa-maṭa.* [Tel.] n. Deceit, cheating. మోసము. తటవటమాటలు deceitful words. **తటమటించు** or **తటవటించు** *taṭama-ṭintsu.* v. a. To swindle, to cheat, to deceive మోసపుచ్చు.

తటము *taṭamu.* [Skt.] n. A place. ప్రదేశము. Shore, bank. ఏటిఒడ్డు. A valley కొండ చరియ. నిటలతటమున in his forehead.

తటస్థము *taṭa-sthamu.* [Skt.] adj. Present, near, at hand, proximate, approaching, next, impending, imminent. సమీపముందున్న, ఒనగూడిన. Temporary, occasional, for the time being. **తటస్థమగు** or **తటస్థించు** *taṭastha-m-agu.* v. n. To approach, draw near, or be at hand. To occur, happen, turn up. ఒనగూడు. చేటు తటస్థించియున్నవాడు one who is on the brink of ruin. **తటస్థుడు** *taṭasthuḍu.* n. An onlooker, A bystander, a spectator; one who is indifferent or impartial; a just person న్యాయస్థుడు. వాడు నిక్కిచి తటస్థుడు he is very just.

తటాకము *taṭākamu.* [Skt.] n. A tank, reservoir, pond, pool. తటాకముగానుండేనీళ్లు a pond or well that never dries.

తటాయించు *taṭāyintsu.* [Tel.] v. t. To obstruct. అడ్డగించు. To prevent నివారించు.

తటారించు *taṭārintsu.* [Tel.] v. a. To rub, handle, feel, finger. Balram. iv. 117.

తటాలు *taṭālu.* [Tel.] n. Suddenness. ఆకస్మికము. **తటాలున** or **తటాన** *taṭāluna.* adv. All at once, suddenly, abruptly. **తటాన పాటుగా** *taṭāna-pāṭu-gā.* adv. Suddenly, unexpectedly.

తటి *taṭi.* [Skt.] n. A bank, side, edge. దరి, ఏటిఒడ్డు. Place, district, region, ప్రదేశము.

తటిల్ or **తటిత్తు** *taṭit.* [Skt.] n. Lightning. మెరుపు. **తటిత్వంతము** or **తటిత్వతి** *taṭitvantamu.* n. A cloud. మేఘము.

తటిని *taṭini.* [Skt.] n. A river. నది. A stream. ఏరు.

తటుకు or **తటుక్కు** *taṭuku.* [Tel.] n. A pat or tap. adj. Swagging, flabby. Vema. 982. **తటుక్కున, తటుకున** or **తడుకున** *taṭukku-na.* adv. Suddenly, all at once, in a moment. తటాలున.

తట్ట *taṭṭa.* [Tel.] n. A flat thing of any sort, a metal plate used as an ornament. తెటుకు. A flat hamper for drying grain. పల్లెక. A basket చిన్నగంప. తట్టెడు a basketful. పెల్లతో కూడ తట్టెండవలసివచ్చె the frying pan suffers for the grain, *i. e.*, I got into this scrape on another's account. తక్కెడతట్ట one scale of a balance. తట్టముఖము a flat face. తట్టగిల్లు to become flat తట్టయగు. **తట్టచేప** *taṭṭa-chēpa.* n. A sort of fish. H. iv. 225.

తట్టడి, తట్టు or **తట్టువ** *taṭṭaḍi.* [Tel.] n. A small horse, a pony. తేజి. Parij. iv. 74.

తట్టము *taṭṭamu.* [Tel.] n. A leather thong, a belt టంగువారు.

తట్టమ్మ *taṭṭ-amma.* [Tel.] n. Chicken pox. తట్టు.

తట్టస *taṭṭasa.* [Tel.] n. Courage. ధైర్యము.

తట్టాడు *taṭṭāḍu.* [Tel.] v. n. To toss or fluctuate, to totter అడుగులు ఇట్టట్టుపెట్టు. L. vii 379.

తట్టి *taṭṭi.* [Tel.] n. A metal platter. కంచము. A hurdle or screen తడిక.

తట్టు *taṭṭu*. [Tel.] v. n. To occur or happen, to break out. కలుగు. నాకు సంశయముతట్టినది a doubt occurred to me. అది నామనసుకు తట్టలేదు it did not occur to my mind. అది నాకు నిజమని తట్టలేదు it does not strike me as true. v. a. To strike, beat, knock, pat, clap, slap. కొట్టు. To touch, ముట్టు. To do away with, remove, or dispel (as darkness.) కత్తిదెబ్బ కేడెముతో తట్టినాడు he averted the blow. తట్టివేయు to remove. సరితట్టు to compare with the original, to fill up what was wanting. నీళ్లు ఎగదట్టినవి the water rose to the brink, ఆ ఓడ గట్టుతట్టినది the ship ran ashore. తట్టుపునుకు carefully selected musk. n. A side, direction. పార్శ్వము. మీదితట్టు the top: the upper side. క్రింది తట్టు the under side: the bottom. A bank or shore దరి. A swelling, an inflammation. Chicken pox తట్టమ్మ. రాజ్యము వానితట్టు చేసినారు they delivered the kingdom to him. అందరము ఒకతట్టు తిరిగితిమి we all went over to one side. ఆ పని తట్టుపడ్డది that work is laid aside. ఓడ తట్టుపడినది the ship got aground. తట్టుతీయు to flute wood, or make a groove. వానికి తట్టుపోసినది he has got the chicken pox. తట్టుకొను *taṭṭu-konu*. v. n. To go along. దొరికినమట్టుకు తట్టుకొని పోయెను he ran off with whatever he could get. To pause, delay, take time, hesitate. తట్టుపడు to suffer బాధపడు. తట్లాట *taṭlāṭa*. n. A squabble.

తట్టుముట్టు or తట్టుముట్లు *taṭṭu-muṭṭu*. [Tel.] n. Things, utensils, furniture, tools, household stuff. తట్టుముట్టాడు to surround (as poverty) చుట్టుకొను.

తట్టువ or తట్టువము *taṭṭuva*. [Tel.] n. A country bred pony. టట్టు.

తత్తృపువాడు *tatrapu-vāḍu*. [Tel.] n. A goldsmith.

తడ *taḍa*. [Tel.] n. A check, a hindrance. అడ్డి. A charm, a spell. తంత్రము. Nearness. దరి. దానికితడ లేదు nothing can prevent it. ఆ పాము తడకు నిలవదు that snake is deaf to every charm. The name of a tree, the leaves of which (తడాకులు) are used as leaf-platters విస్తరాకులు. The wood is like fir and makes strong bows. తడవిల్లు. M. III. i. 335. ధనుర్వృక్షము. గూబతడ is one species. H. iv. 16.

తడక or తడిక *taḍaka*. [Tel.] n. A frame-work, a screen, a hurdle, what is called a tatty. A gate made of open bars, a mat used as a door. తప్పులతడక a pack of contradictions, a parcel of blunders, a heap or tissue of falsehoods.

తడకట్టు *taḍa-kaṭṭu*. [Tel.] v. t. To bewitch, charm. To stop by charms. అడ్డగించు. To prove or verify a pair of scales.

తడగము See తటాకము.

తడప *taḍapa*. [Tel.] n. A withe or strip of bark, &c. Peel, rind. పట్టగానుండేనార. నడి తడప the thick part of a palm branch.

తడబడు *taḍa-baḍu*. [Tel.] v. n. To be troubled or confused. To fail. తొట్రుపడు. To quiver చలించు. తడబాటు or తడమాటు *taḍa-bāṭu*. n. Confusion, irresolution, fluctuation. Fidgetting, fribbling. తడమాటేవాడు a trifler, a fribbler. తడపెట్టు or తడబరుచు to confuse.

తడయు *taḍayu*. [Tel.] v. n. To loiter or delay. ఆలస్యముచేయు. తడయక without delay, at once, rapidly.

తడవ *taḍava*. [Tel.] n. Time. మారు, ఆవృత్తి. ఒకతడవ once. కొంతతడవ sometime.

తడవాటు *taḍa-vāṭu*. [Tel.] n. Trouble, confusion. HD. i. 206.

తడవు *taḍavu*. [Tel.] n. Delay. ఆలస్యము. A while, period or space of time. కొంతసేపు. రేయితడవుగజరిగెను the night passed slowly. ఎంతతడవు how long a time.

తడవు *taḍavu*. [Tel.] v. a. and n. To touch, feel, handle, stroke, grope. To search about. వెదకు. To talk about. ప్రస్తావించు. To enquire విచారించు. To save రక్షించు. తడవాడు or తడపడియాడు (తడవి+ఆడు) to dance నృత్యమాడు, to totter తడబడు. తడవుడు *tadavudu*. n. Searching. వెదకుట. తడవుడుపడుదు an epithet of the mythological serpent called ఆదిశేషువు.

తడి *tadi*. [Tel.] n. Damp, moisture. శేమ. Water నీరు. భయమువల్ల నోటు తడిలేక through fright my tongue having dried up. చేతడి ఆరదు (P. i. 502.) my hand is not yet dry, i. e., it is this moment done. adj. Wet, damp, moist. తడిబట్ట a wet cloth. తడిగుడ్డతో గొంతుకోసినాడు he cut his throat with a damp cloth, that is, he ruined him by fair and gentle means; hanging a man with a silken halter. తడిపొడి slightly wet. తడిపడు *tadi-padu*. v. n. To be moist. తడియొత్తు *tadi-y-ottu*. n. A towel, a napkin తడితుడుచుకొనుగుడ్డ. తడియు *tadiyu*. v. n. To be wet, to get wet. తడిసినది it is wet. తడిసి ఉన్నాడు he is wet. తడుపు *tadupu*. v. a. To moisten or wet. తడియుకోక. n. A modesty piece or loin cloth. గోచి. తడుపుదాలుపు a bachelor బ్రహ్మచారి. A towel చిన్నగుడ్డ. adj. Wet (as a cloth) తడిసిన (గుడ్డ.) తడిపించు *tadipintsu*. v. a. To cause to become wet, వానిచేత ఈ బట్ట తడిపించు you must make him wet the cloth.

తడిక or **తడికె** Same as తడక.

తడుము *tadumu*. [Tel.] v. t. To grope. తడవులాడు. To pat నిమురు. v. n. To think or consider. ఆలోచించు.

తణగము, **తడగము** or **తణగాము** *tanagamu*. [Tel.] n. A leather bag for water carried on bullocks. తణగాంయెద్దు *tanagam-eddu*. n. A bullock which bears water in a leather bag.

తత్ *tat*. [Skt.] pron. That, the same. తత్పూర్వము before that, beforehand. తత్క్షణము or తత్కాలము instantly, at that moment తత్సమీపము near, close by. తత్సంవత్సరము the same year. తదాశ్రమము that abode తత్కాలము *tat-kalamu*. n. That time, that period. తత్కాలమైన coeval, belonging to that period. తత్కాలానుసారి a time-server. తత్కాలమునకు for the present.

తతగము *tatagamu*. [Skt.] n. Wind. వాయువు.

తతము *tatamu*. [Skt.] n. Any stringed musical instrument. తీగెలుగల వాద్యము. adj. Spread, diffused, expanded, stretched, extended. **తతరతి** *tata-rati*. n. Insatiable or excessive pleasure. తతరతిమ్రొక్కి delightedly saluting him.

తతి *tati*. [Tel.] n. Season, proper time. సమయము. [Skt.] n. A multitude or crowd, a great number, a collection, a line, row or range. సమూహము. మిత్రతతి a host of friends, the circle of one's acquaintance.

తత్తడి *tattadi*. [Tel.] n. A horse. గుర్రము.

తత్తబడ *tatta-bada*. [Tel.] n. A retinue. పరివారము.

తత్తర or **తత్తరము** *tattara*. [Tel. తర+తర.] n. Perplexity, embarrassment, agitation, violent emotion, shuddering, shrinking. సంభ్రమము. Grief. **తత్తరపడు** *tattara-padu*. v. n. To be perplexed or agitated. To shudder or tremble. సంభ్రమించు. **తత్తరపాటు** *tattara-patu*. n. Agitation. తత్తరబిత్తరయ్యె he was at a loss. **తత్తరించు** or **తత్తరపెట్టు** *tattarintsu*. v. a. To perplex, trouble. **తత్తరించు** or **తత్తరిల్లు** v. n. To shudder, tremble. సంభ్రమపడు, చలించు.

తత్తెర *tattera*. [Tel.] n. A leathern vessel in which spirituous liquors are poured. సారాయిపోసే మానిమంత లేక తిత్తి.

తత్పరుడు *tat-parudu*. [Skt.] n. One who is diligent, intent, heedful, assiduous, or bent upon doing anything. ఆసక్తుడు. **తత్పరము** *tat-paramu*. adj. Diligent. **తత్పరత** or **తత్పరత్వము** *tatparata*. n. Inclination, bent, devotedness, diligence.

తత్రత్యము *tatratyamu*. [Skt.] adj. Of that place. అక్కడవున్న, అక్కడ కలిగిన.

తత్వము *tatvamu*. [Skt.] n. The real nature of a thing, the essential nature of anything. స్వభావము. Any living being, or essence. Any element or elementary property. Truth, reality. A first principle. An axiom. ÆON, thing, existent creature. Mind, intellect. Deity పరమార్థ. The true perfection, or highest good of man, as the knowledge of God and holiness. Truth or reality in religion. The quest of truth: Ideology, metaphysics, philosophy. (Vulgarly,) A puzzle, a mystery. శూన్యతత్వము nothingness, nullity, non-existence. **తత్వజ్ఞుడు** *tatva-gnyudu*. n. He who knows the truth, a philosopher. **తత్వయోగి** *tatva-yôgi*. n. The perfected saint, as being one with God. Vema. 1044. **తత్వసంగ్రహము** *tatva-sangraha-mu*. n. A confession of faith: a book giving a synopsis of any creed. A hand-book of philosophy.

తత్సమము *tatsamamu*. [Skt. తత్+సమము.] adj. Lit: Equivalent to that. A term in Telugu etymology used to denote words borrowed from Sanskrit, but with the termination altered, as రాజ్యము *rajyamu* for రాజ్యం *rajyam*. See on తద్భవము.

తథాగతుడు *tatha-gatudu*. [Skt.] n. An epithet of Buddha. బుద్ధుడు.

తథాస్తు *tadhastu*. [Skt. తథ+అస్తి.] Interj. So be it! Amen!

తథ్యము *tathyamu*. [Skt.] n. Truth, fact. సత్యము. adj. True, real, actual. సత్యమైన. తథ్యమయినది it turned out true. **తథ్యముగా** *tathyamu-ga*. adv. In fact; really.

తదనంతరము *tad-an-antaramu*. [Tel. తత్+అనంతరము.] adv. Afterwards. Thereafter, then, subsequently. తదనంతరకర్త the next heir, the heir presumptive.

తదా *tada*. [Skt.] adv. Then. అప్పుడు. **తదాత్వము** *tadatvamu*. n. That time. ఆకాలము.

తదారభ్య *tad-arabhya*. [Skt. తత్+ఆరభ్య.] adv. Thenceforward, since that (time).

తది, ఝుటు, తఝ్ఝ, or థిఝ్ఝ *tadi*. [Tel.] n. Sounds or words used by dancing masters in keeping time.

తదియ *tadiya*. [Skt. తృతీయ.] n. The third day in the light or dark fortnight.

తదీయ *tadiya*. [Skt.] adj. His, her, its, తదీయమైన appertaining to it.

తదేక *tad-êka*. [Skt. తత్+ఏక.] adj. Fixed, uniform. వాడు తదేకనిష్ఠగానుండెను he was bent upon doing it, he fixed his undivided attention on it.

తద్గుణము *tad-gunamu*. [Skt. తత్+గుణం.] n. Lit. That quality. The peculiarity or characteristic of an individual.

> " ఆ॥ పోసగమాయచేత బుట్టు సత్వాది గు
> ణత్రయంబు తద్గుణప్రకాశ
> లక్షణప్రయుక్తలలితదేహంబుల
> జంతుతతి జనించు చంద్రవదన."
>
> ప్రశ్నోత్తరఖండము. v. 37.

తడ్డ *tadda*. [Tel.] n. "Papa"—a child's word for father. BD. i. 590.

తడ్డ or తడ్డము *tadda*. [Tel.] adv. Much, exceedingly. మిక్కిలి, విస్తారము, అత్యంతము.

తద్దినము *tad-dinamu*. [Skt. తత్+దినము.] n. Lit. "That day," i. e., a commemoration anniversary, or annual mourning for deceased persons. తద్దినముపెట్టు to keep or celebrate "that day." తద్దినముకొనితెచ్చుకొను (proverb) to run one's head against a wall.

తడ్డె *tadde*. [Tel.] n. A ceremony or feast. పండుగ, as ఉట్లతద్దె, అట్లతద్దె.

తద్ధర్మము *tad-dharmamu*. [Skt.] n. Lit. That right, that law, that custom. The aorist of a verb. భూతభవిష్యద్వర్తమానము లను చెప్పేక్రియ.

తద్భవము *tad-bhavamu*. [Skt. తత్+భవము.] n. Lit. Proceeding (or corrupted) from Sanskrit, a term applied to Telugu words which are borrowed from Sanskrit, but greatly changed in spelling as బొక్క for యుక్క.

తద్రూపము *tad-rūpamu*. [Skt. తత్+రూపము.] Lit. That (very) form. adv. Exactly, as it was. ఆ పటమును తద్రూపముగా వ్రాసినాడు he drew the portrait to the life.

తద్వారా *tad-vārā*. [Skt. తత్+ద్వారా] adv. Thereby. Through that channel.

తన *tana*. [Tel.] adj. Own, his, her, my. See తాను of which this is the genitive. తనచేతనైనంతమట్టుకు he reviled them to the utmost in his power. తనబుద్ధి his opinion, one's own opinion. తనకుతాను adv. He of himself, of his own accord, voluntarily. తనదు *tana-du*. adj. Own. His, her. See తన.

తనకలి *tanakali* [Tel.] n. A tangle. చిక్కు. తనకలికొప్పు a tangled knot of hair. A difficulty, puzzle, చిక్కు, సంకటము. One who creates difficulties చిక్కులుపెట్టువాడు.

తనంత or తనంతట *tananta*. [Tel. తన+అంత] adv. Of himself. Voluntarily.

తనకా or తనఖా *tanakā*. [H.] n. A mortgage. తనకాపత్రము a mortgage deed. Also, an assignment on the revenue.

తనకుచెట్టు *tanaku-chettu*. [Tel.] n. A species of the sandal tree. Rox. i. 445. Floats (catamarans) are made of its wood.

తనకు or తనుకు *tanaku*. [Tel.] v. n. To sink, fail. To tremble. తనకక not enduring it, not tolerating it. తనకెడుచిత్తము a trembling, sinking heart.

తనము *tanamu*. [Tel.] An affix, added to many nouns and adjectives to give them an abstract or a collective force like త్వం in Sanskrit words, and ness, tion, ment in English words, thus: దొరతనము government, పెద్దతనము greatness, మంచితనము goodness, పిల్లతనము childishness, కఠినతనము solidity, గొప్పతనము largeness, పిల్లకాయతనము playfulness, గొల్లతనము the peasantry, the shepherd class, బల్లితనము the being a lizard: the being born as a lizard, కాపుతనము the farmer class. It is added like-wise to past participles as తెలియనితనము silliness, ignorance. చేతకానితనము awkwardness.

తనయ *tanaya*. [Skt.] n. A daughter. కూతురు.

తనయుడు *tanayudu*. [Skt.] n. A son. కొడుకు.

తనరు, తనరుచు or తనర్చు *tanaru*. [Tel.] v. n. To appear or shine. To extend; to be great or large. To be, live, exist. ఒప్పు, అతిశయించు, విజృంభించు. తనరుపు or తనర్పు *tanarupu*. n. Length, extent, altitude. పొడుగు, ఉన్నతము. Breadth వెడల్పు. Greatness గొప్పతనము, అతిశయము. తనర *tanara*. adv. Fully, to the full. తనరారు (తనరు+ఆరు.) *tanar-āru*, v. n. To shine. అతిశయించు.

తనాబీ or తనాబి *tanābī*. [Tel.] n. A log of wood. A large beam.

తని *tani*. [Tel.] adj. Little, slight. సూక్ష్మము, అల్పము.

తనిఖీ or తనిఖి *tanikī*. [H.] n. Examination, inspection.

తనిమ or తనిమము *tanima*. [Skt.] n. Much. విస్తారము. Corporeality శరీరత. Fineness, thinness సూక్ష్మత. తనిమను *tanima-nu*. [Tel.] adv. Finely, thinly. తనువ్వెమతో*డ. (A. iv. 142.)

తనియు *taniyu*. [Tel.] v. n. To be full, satiated, or content. తృప్తిపడు. To thrive, flourish.

"కనుధనమున విద్యను సంతతి
తనివినొందుచుండరిలో?"

M. Adi.

Whoever thinks he has enough wealth or learning, or offspring? తనియించు *taniyintsu*. v. a. To satiate or satisfy.

తనివి, తనివు or **తన్వు** *taniri.* [Tel.] n. Fulness, satisfaction, content, ease. Repletion. తృప్తి. తనివితీరక not being satisfied. వారికి తనివితీరినది they are satisfied. తనివోవు (తనివి+పోవు) or తనివిచను to be fully satisfied. తృప్తినొందు. **తనిసిన** *tanisina.* (part. of తనియు.) Satiated, contented. See తనుపు.

తను *tanu.* [Tel.] n. In compounds stands for తనువు (q. v.) and తనుపు. (q. v.)

తనుకు or **తన్కు** *tanuku.* [Tel.] v. n. To happen. కలుగు. To burn or shine జ్వలించు, ప్రకాశించు, తపించు. n. Heat, closeness. తాపము.

తనుపు or **తన్పు** *tanupu.* [Tel. causal from తనియు.] v. a. To satisfy: to nurse or nourish తనియజేయు, తృప్తిపొందించు. n. Satisfaction. తనివి, తృప్తి. Coolness శైత్యము, శైత్యోపచారము. Wet తడి. M. XII. iii. 445. తనుపెక్కి the cold having increased, చలువ హెచ్చగా. తనుపడు to cool చల్లబడు. **తనుపారు** (తనుపు+అరు.) same as తనియు.

తనువు *tanuvu.* [Skt.] n. The body. దేహము. The skin తోలు. adj. Small, delicate, fine. చిన్న, బక్క, సన్నము. **తనుత్రము** or **తనుత్రాణము** *tanutramu.* n. A piece of armour. కవచము. **తనుమధ్య** *tanu-madhya.* n. A slender waisted woman. A beautiful woman. **తనూజుడు** or **తనూభవుడు** *tanūjudu.* n. A son. **తనూరుహము** *tanūruhamu.* n. Hair, as "growing on the body." వెండ్రుక.

తన్ను or **తనను** *tannu.* [Tel.] pron. Himself. The accusative of తాను self.

తన్ను *tannu.* [Tel.] v. a. To kick. కోడిని గద్ద తన్నుకొనిపోయినది the hawk pounced upon the fowl and carried it off. n. A kick. వానిచేత తన్నులుతినివచ్చినాడు he got a kicking from him. తన్నుకోల a prop, పోటీపెట్టిన కొయ్య. **తన్నుబల్ల** *tannu-balla.* n. A footboard. తన్నుబిళ్ల a sort of game played by children. H. iii. 183. **తన్నులబడు** *tannula-badu.* v. n. To get kicked, to suffer blows. **తన్నులాడు** *tannu-l-ādu.* v. n. To kick each other, to exchange blows: to fight, as cocks do. ఒకరినొకరు తన్నుకొను.

తన్మయము *tan-mayamu.* [Skt.] adj. Of that form తత్స్వరూపమైన. **తన్మయత్వము** *tanmayatvamu.* n. Corporeality.

తన్మాత్రము *tan-mātramu.* [Skt.] n. A simple element, a subtle particle, rudiment, or atom. According to the Hindus, (sabdam) sound is the tanmatra of (akas) ether; (sparsha) touch is that of (vayu) air: (rupam) form is that of (tejas) fire or light., (gandham) smell is that of (prithvi) earth: and (rasam) taste is that of (jalam) water. These are the five rudiments of the five elements

తన్వి *tanvi.* [Skt.] n. A graceful, lovely or delicate girl. A woman. అతివ.

తపతప *tapa-tapa.* [Tel. (anuk)] n. A fluttering sound. చిక్కులు కొట్టుకొనుచున్నట్లు తపతపమనుచు being in trouble: showing signs of distress.

తపనము *tapanamu.* [Skt.] n. Heat. Sorrow. తాపము. **తపనీయము** *tapaniyamu.* n. Gold. **తపనుడు** *tapanudu.* n. Lit. He who burns, the burner, i. e., the sun. తపించువాడు.

తపము or **తపస్సు** *tapamu.* [Skt. తప= thinking.] n. Meditation. Austerity, penance, self-mortification, self denial. penitence. A life of retirement and study. **తపసి** or **తపస్వి** *tapasi.* n. A recluse, an ascetic, devotee. తపస్విని a female recluse. **తపోధనుడు** *tapō-dhanudu.* adj. Renowned for self-mortification, distinguished in sanctity. తపస్సేధనముగాగలవాడు. **తపము** [Skt. from తప=తాపము] n. The hot season. వేసవికాలము. **తపర్తు** *tapartu.* [తప+ఋతువు.] n. The dewy season. శిశిరఋతువు. A. v. 110. The hot season. వేసంగికాలము.

తపసి *tapasi.* [Skt.] n. The tree called అవిసెచెట్టు or నారచెట్టు. Swa. iii. 100.

తపారము or తపారా. *tapāramu.* [Tel.] n. A sort of cap. కుళ్లాయి, టోపి. A. ii. 86. P. ii. 9.

తపించు *tapintsu.* [Skt.] v. n. To become warm, be heated, burn, be distressed. To be in anguish. KUR. iv. 265. తాపము పొందు. Also, to meditate by oneself. తపస్సుచేయు. See తపము. తప్తము *taptamu.* adj. Heated, burnt, agitated. తపింపచేయబడిన, కాచబడిన. తప్తహేమరుచి bright as melted gold. తప్తముద్రలు marks or stamps burnt on the body with a hot iron.

తపెల or తపేలా *tapela.* [Tel.] n. A brass vessel.

తప్ప *tappa.* [Tel.] adj. Empty, flabby, pithless. n. An empty ear of corn. గింజపట్టనిధాన్యము. తప్పకాయ fruit without any seed formed in it. విత్తుపట్టనికాయ.

తప్ప *tappa.* [Tel. from తప్పు to fail.] adv. postp. Save, but, except, unless, without. మీరుతప్ప except you. మీరువస్తేనేతప్ప అవనిగాదు unless you come the work will not be done.

తప్పరించు *tapparintsu.* [Tel.] v. t. To put down. అణచు. To defeat, deceive, భంగపెట్టు. Chenn. v. 155. 165.

తప్పు *tappu.* [Tel.] v. n. To err, fail, cease. To be lost, broken, changed, made void, or erroneous. దైవానుగ్రహము తప్పినందున through the divine favour being lost. To drop off, as a shackle. To go off, abate, as a pain రేవుతప్పినది the ford is missed. అడుగులో పిడుగుతప్పు a great mistake in a short space. అడుగువుతప్పినవాడయినాడు he declined into the vale of years. v. a. To transgress, to miss. తప్పచేయు, అతిక్రమించు. దినముతప్పిదినము every other day, missing one day in turn. ఒకటితప్పి ఒకటి one now and then; here and there one. తప్పివచ్చినపని a thing that happened unexpectedly, or out of the common way. మాటతప్పు to break one's word or promise. తప్పక *tappaka.* adv. Unfailingly, steadfastly, steadily, certainly, surely. తప్పచూచు *tappa-tsūtsu.* v. t. To disregard. దైవము తప్పచూచినందున as God withdrew his favour. తప్పు or తప్పితము or తప్పిదము (తప్పు+ఇతము or ఇదము.) n. An error, fault, mistake, offence. తప్పుపలుకు to say what is wrong or false. తప్పులుపట్టు to find fault with, to cavil. adj. Erroneous, mistaken, faulty, wrong. Foul or entangled. తప్పుకూడు unlawful food. తప్పుటడుగులు పెట్టు to stagger or totter as an infant. తప్పుదారి or తప్పుద్రోవ a wrong road. తప్పించు *tappintsu.* v. a. To extricate, to set free విడిపించు. To take away, remove, lose, shift, alter. తాడు తప్పించుట to get the cord free, to extricate it. నా జీవనము తప్పించినాడు he took away my living. To elude మఖము తప్పించు to abscond. To cause to cross over, pass by, transgress, depart from (an agreement.) దోవతప్పించినాడు he misled me. తప్పించుకొను *tappintsu-konu.* v. n. To get free, to escape. ప్రాణము తప్పించుకొని వచ్చితి I escaped with my life. తప్పుడు or తప్పుదల *tappudu.* n. Missing, making a mistake తప్పుట. తప్పుడు adj. Wrong తప్పైన. తప్పుడుపడు or తప్పుపడు to make a mistake పరితప్పు.

తప్పుకుత్తి or కంపలకుంకి *tappu-kutti.* [Tel.] n. A kind of fish, *Pteroplatea micrura.* (F. B. I.)

తప్పున *tappu-na.* [Tel.] adv. At once, suddenly.

తప్పెట *tappeta.* [Tel.] n. A large drum. Also, the name of a tree. వేలుతప్పెట, క్రిష్ణ ఘుందరము, వాకుడుచెట్టు.

తప్సీలు *tapsilu.* [H.] n. Particulars or details of an account.

తబము Same as తపము. (q. v.)

తబిసి Same as తపసిపెట్టు. (q. v.)

తబుకు *tabuku.* [Tel.] n. A dish, a platter. పళ్లెము.

తబ్దీలు *tabdilu*. [H.] n. Exchange. Transportation.

తబ్బిబ్బు *tabbibbu*. [Tel.] n. Agitation, flurry. తడబాటు, తొందరపాటు, తడబాటును, భ్రమ, ఒకటిచేయబోయి ఒకటిచేయుట. అయనకు ఇప్పుడు తబ్బిబ్బులుగానున్నది he is in his dotage.

తమకము *tamakamu*. [Tel.] n. Eagerness, ardour. త్వర. Love మోహము, విరహము. తమకి *tamaki*. n. A lover: one who is enamoured. త్వరగల మోహముగలవాడు. తమకించు or తమకపడు *tamakintsu*. v. a. To be moved. చలించు. To be enamoured, ardent or eager. R. i. 212. త్వరపడు, మోహపడు. To be agitated తత్తరపడు. తమకు *tamaku*. v. n. To hesitate, to draw back. To fail or recede వెనుకదీయు, చలించు. n. Way, manner. విధము.

తమగము or తమంగము *tamagamu*. [from Skt. తమఙ్గ] n. A summer house, having no walls but a roof on pillars. మంటపము, చావిడి. A raised platform మంచె.

తమట, తమటము, తమ్మట or తమ్మటము *tamata*. [Tel. & Skt.] n. A large drum. తప్పెట.

తమము *tamamu*. [Skt.] n Darkness. Illusion, mental blindness. Sorrow. శోకము. తమోమయుడు *tamō-mayudu*. n. One who is in darkness or sin. తమోగుణవిశిష్టుడు. తమోమణి *tamō-mani*. n. The gem of night, i. e., a firefly. మెరుగుడుపురుగు.

తమరకము or తమరము *tamarakamu*. [Skt.] n. Tin. తగరము.

తమరు *tamaru*. [Tel.] pron. plu. (used honorifically.) You, yourself. తమరొకరు your honour alone. The genitive is తమ, own, స్వకీయమైన.

తమలము *tamalamu*. [Tel.] n. The Betel vine. తమలంపుటిరులు (A. iv. 175.) Red and bluish tints, తాంబూలపుర్క్తముల చేత నీలకాంతులు. తమలపాకు *tamala-p-āku*. n. The betel leaf.

తమస్సు *tamassu*. [Skt.] n. Darkness. చీకటి. See తమము.

తమాటకాయ *tamāta-kāya*. [Mexican through Span. and Eng.] n. The Tomato fruit. *Averrhoa carambola* (Watts).

తమాయించు *tamāyintsu*. [Tel.] v. n. To stop, to check oneself; to be patient. శాంతించు, క్షమించును.

తమాలము *tamālamu*. [Skt.] n. The Gloomy tree; *Exanthocymus pictorius*. (Roxb.) or *Galedupa*, చీకటిమ్రాను, కానుగ చెట్టు. As a colour, it means dark brown, or dusky, dun, or dark dull red. Dark hued.

తమి *tami*. [Tel.] n. Eagerness. త్వర. Lust, passion, desire. కుతూహలము, అపేక్ష, మోహము. [Skt.] n. Darkness. చీకటి. తమి కొను *tami-konu*. v. n. To be eager. త్వరపడు. To rejoice కుతూహలపడు. To desire అపేక్షపడు. To fall in love మోహపడు.

తమిదలు, తమిదెలు or తవిదెలు *tamidalu*. [Tel.] n. The grain called ragi, *Cynosurus coracanus*. చోళ్లు or రాగులు.

తమిరె *tamire*. [Tel.] n. The pin in the centre of a yoke. కాడినడిమిసీల.

తమిస్ర *tamisra*. [Skt.] n. A pitch-dark night. చీకటిరాత్రి. Thick darkness, gloom. చిమ్మచీకటి. తమిస్రము *tamisramu*. n. Darkness. చీకటి. Anger కోపము.

తముకు or టమ్మకు *tamuku*. [Tel.] n. A drum, a tambourine. డుడుము.

తమ్మ *tamma*. [Tel.] n. A quid. The chewings of the betel leaf which are of a red colour. నములబడిన తాంబూలము. తమ్మతసుకు or తమ్మతొట్టి *tamma-tasuku*. n. A spittoon, తమ్మపడిగము. తమ్మకర *tamma-kara*. n. The red spittle caused by తమలపాకు.

తమ్మంటు *tammantu*. [Tel. తమ్మి+అంటు.] n. An earring. కుండలము.

తమ్మటము See తమట.

తమ్మడి *tammadi.* [Tel.] n. A Tambala or Saiva priest.

తమ్మళి Same as తంబళి. (q. v.)

తమ్మి *tammi.* [Tel.] n. The lotus. పద్మము. A disposition or arrangement of an army in the battle-field in the form of a lotus పద్మవ్యూహము.. కెందమ్మి the red lotus. **తమ్మికంటి** *tammi-kanṭi.* n. A fair eyed person, a translation of the Sanskrit word పుండరీకాక్షుడు, a name of Vishṇu. **తమ్మికెంపు** *tammi-kempu.* n. A sapphire. పద్మరాగము. **తమ్మికేలు** *tammi-kēlu.* n. A lotus-like (i. e., beautiful) hand. **తమ్మిచూలి** or **తమ్మిపుట్టువు** *tammi-tsūli.* n. The god who sprang from a lotus, i. e., Bramha. పద్మగర్భుడు. తమ్మిదొర the lord of the lotus, i. e., the sun. **తమ్మిచెలి** *tammi-cheli.* n. The lover of the lotus, i. e., the sun. తమ్మిచెలికొడుకు an epithet of Sugrīva. R. v. 259. తమ్మిపగతుడు the foe of the lotus, i. e., the moon. **తమ్మిగెలుపువ్యూహము** *tammivyū-haramu.* n. The "lotus evolution", a certain form of military array. తమ్మియింటి గరిత=Lakshmi.

తమ్ముడు *tammudu.* [Tel.] n. A younger brother. Colloquially — "brother," or "friend." పెద్దతమ్ముడు and చిన్నతమ్ముడు denote the elder and the younger of two brothers, both of whom are younger than the person alluded to. **తమ్ములుపిండు** *tammu-pindu.* n. Brethren. తమ్ములసమూహము. M. VIII. ii. 170.

తమ్ముల The plu. infl. of తమ్ముడు. of తమ్మి, a lily, and of తాము themselves. **తమ్ములవిందు** *tammula-vindu.* [Tel.] n. The sun. పద్మబాంధవుడు.

తమ్మె or **తమ్మెలు** *tamme.* [Tel.] n. The soft part, as the lobe of the ear, or gristle of the nose. A halter's knot. చెవియొక్కక్రిందిభాగము.

తమ్మెట *tammeṭa.* [Tel.] n. A sort of drum. A kind of earring. H iii. 38. **తమ్మెటలు** *tammeṭlu.* n. Earrings. పోగులు. A. vi. 106.

తరంగము *tarangamu.* [Skt.] n. A wave, a surge, an undulating swell or surface like waves. అల. **తరంగిణి** *taranginī.* n. A river. This and other expressions for river, sea, stream, are used in the titles of some books, as విద్యాతరంగిణి the Circle of the Sciences.

తరండము *taranḍamu.* [Skt.] n. A ship. ఓడ. A fishing rod.

తరందారి *tarandāri.* [Tel.] adj. Classified. తరగతులుగా ఏర్పరచబడిన. n. A classifier of soils, &c.

తరకటించు *tarakaṭintsu.* [Tel. from Skt. తర్కించు.] v. n. To argue **తరకటింపు** *tarakaṭimpu.* n Arguing. తర్కము.

తరకలు *tarakalu.* [Tel.] n. The chaff of grain. తప్పలు.

తరకసము or **తరకస** *tarakasamu.* [Tel.] n. A quiver. అమ్ములపొది. Swa. iv. 36. A. ii. 30.

తరక్షువు *tarakshuvu.* [Skt.] n. A hyæna or a hunting leopard. సివంగి.

తరగ *taraga.* [from Skt. తరంగ.] A wave, surge. An undulating surface. Dasav. ii. 283. ix. 159. P. ii. 324.

తరగంపె or **తరగంపెరం** *tara-gampe.* [Tel.] n. A kind of saw. ఒకవిధమైన రంపము.

తరగతి *tara-gati.* [Skt. తరము+గతి.] n. A class, grade, rank, order. తరము. తేర్చి భాగము.] తరగతిలెక్కలు classified accounts. తరగతిగా according to (its) class. **తరగతిగుండ్లు** *taragati-gundlu.* n. A kind of necklace worn by women.

తరగరి *taragari.* [Tel. from తరుగు.] n. A broker, an appraiser.

తరగు See తరుగు.

తరచు or **తరుచు** *taratsu.* [Tel.] n. Thickness. బాహుళ్యము. adj. Thick, in various senses, as coarse cloth; frequent, usual, perpetual, plentiful. అధికము. తరచుగావచ్చిరి they came in crowds

తరటు *taratu.* v. n. To strike, to kick, to lash. T. v. 31. కొడించు. adj. Stout, coarse, not fine. తరటుపెద్ది a great fool. Stubborn మూర్ఖము. n. A whip కశ. Stubbornness. మూర్ఖత్వము. తరటుగొను or తరటు చేయు to strike కొట్టు.

తరణము *taraṇamu.* [Skt.] n. Crossing. దాటుట. Deliverance, extrication. A ship or boat: also a raft. ఓడ. H. iv. 219. **తరణి** *taraṇi.* n. A ship. ఓడ. The sun. సూర్యుడు. The sea సముద్రము. **తరణోపాయము** *taraṇō-pāyamu.* n. A means, an expedient.

తరతమభావముగా *tara-tama-bhāvamu-gā.* [Skt.] adv. In proportion to (their) rank.

తరతరము or **తరతరంబు** *tara-taramu.* [Tel.] adv. Gradually, by degrees. క్రమముగా. One after another, in a series. పరంపరగా. **తరతరముగా** *tara-taramu-gā.* [Tel.] adv. Sort after sort, from generation to generation.

తరతర or **తత్తర** *tara-tara.* [Tel.] n. Fright, panic. **తరతరలాడు** *tara-tara-l-āḍu.* n. To be panic-struck, to quake with fright. తత్తరపడు.

తరద్దూదు *taraddūdu.* [H.] n. Exertion, application. తరద్దూదుకోబిరా an account showing the species and quantity of the seed sown, the extent of land under cultivation and the extent of it remaining fallow.

తరపడి or **తరుపడి** *tarapaḍi.* [Tel.] n. A lathe. తిరిమెం. That which is formed on a lathe.

తరపణ్యము *tara-paṇyamu.* [Skt.] n. Boat-hire, freight. కేవు, పడవ నడుపువానికిచ్చుకూలి.

తరపి *tarapi.* [Tel.] n. A calf six months old. ఆరునెలలదూడ. A fat person. Bloom తారుణ్యము. adj. Youthful. యౌవనముగల.

తరపు *tarapu.* [Tel.] v. t. To remove. పో గొట్టు, పాపించు.

తరబడి *tarabaḍi.* [Tel. తరము+బడి] n. Rate. కోట్లతరబడి by millions, millions at a time. వందలతరబడి అప్పులు hundreds of loans. **తరబడిలెక్క** *tarabaḍi-lekka.* n. A record resembling the Domesday-book wherein the values of lands are stated.

తరము *taramu.* [Tel.] n. Sequence, following: that which follows. A class, sort. A number or collective body. A generation. A step, grade or remove in genealogy. Practicability, possibility. Difference. Power, ability. మూడుతరాల నుండి ఉన్న భూమి land which we have held during three generations. తరతరములనుండి generation after generation. తరముఎత్తిన or జిడ్డెత్తిన borne by two on a pole: so called because one man follows another. చెప్పతరమే is it possible to describe it. అది తరమా is it right or possible? adj. Equal సమానము. Possible శక్యము. తరంవారుడు a classifier, one who superintends the classification of the soils under the Revenue Settlement system. తరమిడు to compare, try the respective merits. HD. i. 146. [Skt.] n. Crossing. దాటుట.

తరలచేప *tarala-chēpa.* [Tel.] n. A kind of fish. మత్స్యభేదము. Russell, plates 80, 81.

తరలు or **తెర్లు** *taralu.* [Tel.] v. n. To set out or start. ప్రయాణమగు. To stir, move, proceed. చలించు, సంక్రమించు. In music తర్లు means Da Capo, recommence: again. v. a. To lose, let go. విడుచు. తరలకు ధైర్యము do not lose heart. తరలకచూచు to view steadily, without intermission. "ధనరాశి యిక్కొట తరలకనిత్తు." (HD. ii. 1492) I will give the money here without fail. **తరలించు** or **తర్లించు** *tara-lintsu* v. t. To cause to move, or march. Vasu. iii. 165. Chenna iii. 143. తరలుచు or తెర్లు to set free విడిపించు.

తరళము *taralamu.* [Skt.] adj. Trembling, tremulous, glancing, as the eye. ప్రకాశమానమైన, చంచలమైన. తరళనేత్ర, తరళాక్షి, or తరళేక్షణ lit. bright eyed, i. e., a fair maid

తరవరి, తరవలి or **తరవారి** *taravari*. [Tel.] n. A broadsword. ఖడ్గశక్తి.

తరవాణి *taravāṇi*. [Tel.] n. Sour or fermented rice water. పుల్లనీళ్లు, పులిసినగంజి.

తరవాయి *taravāyi*. [Tel.] n. An opportunity. సమయము. A time తడవ. ఒకతరవాయి once. A sequence అనుక్రమము, వరుస. An examination ఉపక్రమము. A lesson in the Vedas. వేదపాఠము. "ఆతురుడు తరవా యడుగుడు." A. iii. 4. See తరువాయి.

తరవారి or **తరంవారి** *taravari*. [Tel. from తరము.] n. A settled measurement of fields or villages. తరవారి గ్రామములు the villages under the Ryotwari system.

తరసము *tarasamu*. [Skt.] n. Flesh. మాంసము. P. i 509.

తరహా *tarahā*. [H.] n. A kind, sort, species. విధము. పెద్దమనిషితరహాగా like a gentleman.

తరాజు or **తరాసు** *tarāḍzu*. [Tel. corruption of త్రాసు.] n. A pair of scales. తక్కెడ. "రాజేలతరాజేలు."

తరి *tari*. [Skt.] n. A ship. ఓడ. **తరి** *tari*. [Tel.] adj. Churning. n. Time, occasion. సమయము. ఇత్తరి now. ఒకతరి once. Nearness సమీపము. plu. తరులు. Series వరుసలు, ఆళి. **తరి** or **తరీ** [H.] Wet cultivation, irrigated land మాగాణి. తరిగొను to try, యత్నించు. తరిపడు to be oppressed, ఒత్తుడు పడు. **తరించు** or **తరియించు** *tarintsu*. [Skt.] v. a. To cross over, get through (a stream or trouble :) to attain (heaven.) To shake off, cast off, get rid of, free oneself from. **తరింపు** *tarimpu*. [Skt.] n. Rescue, extrication, salvation. **తరికంబము** *tari-kambamu*. [Tel.] n. The post round which the cord passes which works the churning stick. పెరుగుత్రచ్చెడు స్తంభము. **తరికాడు** *tari-kāḍu*. n. One who churns. త్రచ్చువాడు. తరికడవ a churning pot. **తరిగల** *tari-gala*. adj. Rich in butter. తరిగలావు a butter-producing cow. చిక్కని పాలుగల ఆవు. **తరిగొండ** *tari-gonda*. n. A poetical name for Mandaragiri: lit. "The churn-staff-hill." **తరిగోల** *tari-gōla*. n. A churning staff. **తరిచల్ల** *tari-tsalla*. n. Sweet buttermilk. **తరిచుట్టు** or **తరివట్టు** *tari-tsuttu*. v. n. To consecrate or offer curds to the gods. **తరిత్రాడు** *tari-tāḍu*. n. The cord that works a churnstaff. తరిదాలుపు one who wears or carries the churning mountain, i. e., Vishṇu.

తరిగించు *tarigintsu*. [Tel. from తరుగు.] v. t. To cut off, lop, amputate. తరుగకొట్టు చేయు.

తరిగొర్రకూర *tari-gorra-kūra*. [Tel.] n. A certain potherb, "milch-ewe's heal." Pentaplera Arjuna మద్దిచెట్టు, లాంగలి.

తరిటి or **తరిటీ** *tariṭi*. [Tel.] n. A large sack filled at both ends and laid across a bullock. రెండు రెండేలు దిగించే గోనెపట్టా.

తరితీపు *tari-tīpu*. [Tel.] n. Fondness, liking, lust: a fool's paradise. ప్రీతి, ఆడి యాస, సంతుష్టి. Delay, reluctance. కాల హరణము, ఆలస్యము. Indifference ఉపేక్ష. Greatness, pride, ఉద్ధృతి.

తరిపి or **తరిపిదూడ** *taripi*. [Tel.] n. A sucking calf, a calf less than a year old. Plu. తరుపులు.

తరిమిడి, తరిమిణి, తరిమెన or **తరిమెనకాడ్డి** *tarimiḍi*. [Tel.] n. A lathe. In compounds it is contracted into తెర. **తరిమిడిపట్టు** or **తరిమెనపట్టు** *tarimiḍi-paṭṭu*. v. n. To turn in a lathe.

తరియు *tariyu*. [Tel.] v. n. To approach. సమీపించు. To enter. To plunge into. చొచ్చు, తారసిల్లు. M. VII. iii. 196. Parij. iv. 32. v. a. To cross. దాటు. **తరియజొచ్చు** *tariya-zotstsu*. v. a. To enter, to engage in. చేరజొచ్చు.

తరీఖు *tarīkhu*. [H.] n. Manner, way, custom.

తరుగు or **తరువు** *tarugu*. [Tel.] v. a. To be worn away. తగ్గు, క్షయించు. To pass away, to be done or finished. కఠించు. M. XIV. ii. 139. HD. i. 1982. దోవతరగదు the way does not become shorter. ఎంతవ్రాసినాగాని పని తరగదు however long he wrote, the work does not terminate. భాగ్యముతరుగును fortune will cease or depart. కొలిచినదాన్ని మళ్లీ కొలిస్తే తరుగును if you measure grain twice, some of it will be lost. v. a. To cut or sever. To slice or carve, to mince: to wear away. To amputate. Vedanta Ras. iii. 213. n. Wastage. Deficiency, sinking. Brokerage or fees called custom. Tare. Cutting or wearing away. తరగరి or తరుగరి n. A broker. తరుగుబేరగాడు.

తరుచు or **తర్చు** *tarutsu.* [Tel.] v. a. To stir, agitate; to investigate. To churn చిలుకు, మథించు. **తరుచు** or **తరచు** *tarutsu.* n. Thickness. సాంద్రత్వము. తరుచుగా thickly, సాంద్రముగా; often అనేకపర్యాయములు. తరిచిచూచు to investigate or sound.

తరుణము *taruṇamu.* [Skt.] n. Time, an opportunity, an occasion, సమయము, కాలము. adj. Young, tender, blooming. యౌవనముగల. **తరుణి** *taruṇi.* n. A blooming young girl. **తరుణిమ** *taruṇima.* n. Youth. యౌవనము. **తరుణుడు** *taruṇuḍu.* n. A young man, a youth, యౌవనముగలవాడు.

తరుపు *tarupu.* [Tel.] n. A yearling calf. An artificial diamond. Same as తరిపి.

తరుము *tarumu.* [Tel.] v. a. To drive or pursue, to follow. To encroach upon, or, make away with, బలాత్కరించు. To turn wood in a lathe. తరిమెనపెట్టు.

తరులమెకము or **తరులమోరమెకము** *tarula-mekamu.* [Tel.] n. Lit: The tree-beast, i. e., a monkey. కోతి.

తరువడిమాను *taruvaḍi-mānu.* [Tel.] n. A lathe for turnery. తరిమెన.

తరువాణి, తరవాణి or **తర్వాణి** *taruvāṇi.* [Tel.] n. Sour gruel, fermented rice water పుల్లకలి, పులినీళ్లు, పులిసినగంజి.

తరువాయి or **తరువాయు** *taruvāyi.* [Tel.] n. The next time. అనంతరము. A seasonable time, an opportunity తరుణము. A lesson in the Vedas. The rest, the continuation. తర్వాయిసంగతి the next case. **తరువాత** *taruvāta.* adv. Afterwards, next. నాతర్వాత or నాకు తర్వాత after me. It is usually contractedly written తు. Genitive తరువాతి, as తర్వాతివారు those who stood next. తరువాతికథ the next story.

తరువు *taruvu.* [Tel.] v. a. Same as తరుచు. n. An inroad, attack; dunning, నిర్బంధము. A draft. [Skt.] n. A tree. గంధతరువు the sandal-tree. **తరుచరుడు** *taru-charuḍu.* n. A "tree roamer," a monkey. (DRY. 1502.) చెట్లలోసంచరించేది. **తరువుచేయు** *taruvu-chēyu.* v. n. To attack: to press or dun for payment of money due. **తరువుకాడు** or **తరువుకత్తె** *taruvu-kāḍu.* n. One who duns.

తరుసలి *tarusali.* [Tel.] n. A proud man. గర్వితుడు.

తర్కము *tarkamu.* [Skt.] n. The science of reasoning: logic. వాదము. Reasoning, inferring, deducing, guessing. Discussion, disputation. Conjecture, fancy, notion. ఊహ. **తర్కశాస్త్రి** *tarka-sāstri.* n. A logician. **తర్కించు** *tarkintsu.* v. n. To doubt, dispute, argue, investigate, consider. తర్కముచేయు.

తర్జని *tarjani.* [Skt.] n. The index or forefinger, చూపుడువేలు. **తర్జనము** *tarjanamu.* n. Pointing at, blaming. Threatening, bullying. అదలుపు, బెదరించడము. తర్జన భర్జనము the same. **తర్జించు** *tarjintsu.* v. t. To frighten. బెదరించు.

తర్జుమా *tarḍzumā.* [H.] n. A translation, భాషాంతరము.

తర్ణకము *tarṇakamu.* [Skt.] n. A new born calf. అప్పుడుపుట్టిన దూడ.

తర్పణము *tarpaṇamu.* [Skt.] n. Gratification, satisfaction, fulness. తనివి, తృప్తి. A drink offering

తర్ర or తర్రు tarra. [Tel.] n. A wretch. నీచుడు. "తర్రలతో డిపాళ్లిడక." Dasarathi. § 37.

తర్లు Same as తరలు. (q. v.) తర్లించు tarlintsu. v. a. Same as తరలించు. (q. v.)

తర్వాడి tarvādi. Same as తరువాలి. (q. v.)

తర్వాత Same as తరువాత. (q. v.)

తర్షము tarshamu. [Skt.] n. Thirst. దప్పి. Eagerness ఇచ్ఛ.

తల tala. [Tel.] n. The head. శిరస్సు. The hair on the head. తలవెండ్రుకలు. The top కొన. The front ముందుభాగము. Height ఎత్తు. Whole ముత్తము. An occasion, a time సమయము, ఎడ. An attempt, endeavour ప్రూనిక. A field, place రంగము. A side పక్షము. Telugu books were usually written on palm-leaves connected by a cord running through: and to tear out a leaf or rescind a bond, the top is torn. Hence తలచించిన denotes Rescinded. తలతో నడిచి వస్తున్నాను I will come even though I walk on my head. తలకొవ్విన tala-kovvina. adj. Fat-headed, proud, silly. ఇంతపనిచేస్తే వారిలో ఎట్లు తలయెత్తుకున్నను if he did this how could he shew his face among them? తలతో చెల్లించెను he paid for it with his head, it cost him his life. తలమీదికివచ్చిన పని a perilous undertaking. తలకు ఎక్కినది it got into his head, he is intoxicated. తలకొట్టివేయు to decapitate or behead. తల (for తలను) మోయు to carry on the head. శిరసావహించు. BD. v. 309. ఒకతల on the one hand. తలకట్టు tala-kattu. n. The crest, tire, top, head-dress. పాగా. Chief ముఖ్యము. The head or leader. The mark ✓ denoting అ (a) as in క ka, ప pa, స sa. అతివల తలకట్టు she was the crown of her sex. తలకడచు tala-kadatsu. v. n. To excel, outstrip, push before. M. IX. i. 179, 185, 205. తలమీరు, అతిక్రమించు. తలకప్ప tala-kappa. n. A newt. తలకిందు, తలక్రిందు, తలకిందు, తల్ల-కిందు or తల్లక్రిందు tala-kindu. adv. Upside down. Topsy-turvy. తలక్రిందు గాపడు to fall upside down. తలకిందులు tala-kindulu. adv. Upside down. n. Confusion. తలకొట్లమారి tala-kotla-māri. (from తలకొట్లు blows on the head, and మారి a wretch.) n. A brawler, a riotous man. అవినీతుడు. తలకొట్లమారితనము outrageousness, brawling riot, dissipated behaviour. తలకొరివి tala-korivi. n. The fire placed on the chest of a corpse which is to be cremated, the head-torch which the heir applies to ignite the funeral pile. వీడే మనకు తలకొరివి he was our secret foe. తలకొవ్వు tala-kovvu. v. n. To be wilful, stubborn, headstrong, hotheaded, or giddy. మదించు. తలకోల tala-kōla. n. A noose, on a staff (కోల) to hold the head of a mischievous cow. తలగడ or తల్లగడ talagada. n. A pillow for the head. తలగుడ్డ tala-guddu. n. A turban. తలచేమురు tala-tsamuru. n. Oil. నూనె. తలచించు tala-chintsu. v. a. To cancel, to tear the head or beginning of a document, where the seal is. తలచిదర tala-chidara. n. A headache. తలచుంచు tala-tsuntsu. n. Front locks or forehead tresses. ముందరిసిగజుట్టు. తలచుట్టు tala-tsuttu. n. A head-dress. పాగా. తలచూపు tala-tsūpu. v. n. To show the head, i. e., to make its appearance. పొడచూపు. To seem, to appear తోచు. తలతల to every man. తలత్రాడు the head rope. తలతిక్క tala-tikka. n. A headache. Madness, pride, impudence. తలదన్ను tala-dannu. [from తన్ను.] v. n. To excel. Lit: to trample on one's head. నా తల దన్నుకొని పుట్టినవాడు he was born to excel me. తలవాకిలి the chief gate తలవాకిలి. తలనొప్పి tala-noppi. n. A headache: a source of quarrel, a grudge. తలపన్ను tala-pannu. n. A poll tax. తలపారు tala-pāru. v. n. To run, to disperse and flee. తలపారెడు lengthy. తలపారెడయంగల దీర్ఘము a long island. తలపిడుస *tala-pidusa.* n. The name of a plant. H. iv. 14. See తలపెట్టు, తలపాలను, తలబ్రాలు, &c. తలబిరుసు *tala-birusu.* n. Stubbornness. adj. Stubborn. తలమునక or తలమున్క *tala-munuka.* n. Bathing over head. శిరస్స్నానము. Reaching up to the head as water శిరఃప్రమాణము, తలబంటి, తల లోతుగలిగి యుండుట. తలమునకలు *tala-munukalu.* n. Peril, hazard. Tikk. UR. vi. 57. M. vi. iii. 199. తలమునకలగు *tala-muna-kalugu.* v. n. To be in an agitation of joy or sorrow. తలయెత్తు *tala-y-ettu.* v. n. To prosper, వర్ధిల్లు. To sprout up, మొలచు. తలవంచుకొను *tala-vantsu-konu.* v.t. To hang down the head, to be grieved or ashamed. తలవంపు *tala-vampu.* n. Humiliation, hanging down the head. T. iii. 66. అవమానము.

తల or వల *tala.* [Tel.] affix. In the direction of, near; the act or state of వాలుదల slanting ఊరిదల near the town. విడుదల release. దిగుదలపొలము the lower fields. చావుదల the state of dying. కప్పుదల concealment. మోపుదల weight, charge. తిరుగుదల turning. వ్యాధి తిరుగుదలగానున్నది the disease is on the turn. తగులుదల cost. తగులుదలవ్వయము the sum incurred. నిలుపుదల deferring, postponement, suspension. కూడుదల help. దానివల్ల వారికి కొంచెము కూడుదల కలిగినది thereby they had some profit. నదికి ఎగుదల up the river. నదికి దిగుదల down the river.

తలంకు *talanku.* Same as తలకు. (q. v.)

తలంటు or తలగడుగు *talantu.* [Tel. తల+అంటు.] v. a. To anoint the head. తలయంటు మాడికొను. n. Anointing the head. అభ్యంగము.

తలంపు Same as తలపు. (q. v.)

తలంబ్రాలు Same as తలబ్రాలు. (q. v.)

తలకాయ *tala-kaya.* [Tel.] n. The head. The word కాయ (q. v.) is here a mere colloquial affix.

తలకు or తలంకు *talaku.* [Tel.] v. n. To shudder, hesitate, be at a loss. To cease, abstain. To fail, to be afraid, turn away, shrink, draw back. భయపడు. n. Fear, alarm. భయము. తలకించుక లేక without the least fear. తలకించు *tala-kintsu.* v. t. To alarm. భయపెట్టు.

తలకూడు *tala-kudu.* [Tel.] v. n. To be completed, finished: to be verified సిద్ధించు.

తలకొను *tala-konu.* [Tel.] v. n. To happen. కలుగు. To exceed, become great, come to a head: to head or be a leader. To make an effort. యత్నపడు. v. t. To have or get పొందు. To carry వహించు. తలకోలు *tala-kolu.* n. An attempt. తలకొనుట. తలకొలుపు *tala-kolupu.* v. t. To bring about. సంఘటించు. M. XII. iv. 10.

తలగడుగు *tala-gadugu.* [Tel.] Same as తలంటు. (q. v.)

తలగాము *tala-gamu.* [Tel. గాము is corrupted from Skt. గ్రాసము.] n. The ascending node. రాహువు.

తలగు *talagu.* [Tel.] n. A tether or halter for cattle. పలుపు.

తలగు *talagu.* [Tel. another form of తొలగు.] v. n. To move, draw back, remove, destroyed. To fall off, as a vest. To depart or be lost, as honor or character. To rove or go off. To keep aloof. తొలగు. తలగుడు *talagudu.* n. Moving aside తొలగుట. తలగించు *talagintsu.* v. a. To get rid of, cast off. ఎడబాపు.

తలచావిడి *tala-tsavidi.* [Tel.] n. The front hall. ముందరిచావిడి.

తలచు or తలంచు *talatsu.* [Tel.] v. a. and v. n. To think, think of, reflect, imagine. యోచించు, ఊహించు. To intend, propose, plan. ఉద్దేశించు. To consider, or weigh. To seek or plan. To consider or care for. ఎంచు. To meditate ధ్యానించు. స్మరించు, మొ. తలపు (q. v.) తలపించు *talap-intsu.* v. a.

To induce, persuade, convert. To put in mind of, resemble, remind one of.

తలటుతీగె *talatu-tige*. [Tel.] n. A creeper, *Convolvulus dentatus*. Rox. i. 477.

తలపడు *talapadu*. [Tel.] v. n. To commence, to begin. ప్రారంభించు. యుద్ధానికి తలపడినారు they commenced the fight. v. t. To oppose or attack ఎదిరించు. To meet తాకు. తలపాటు *tala-patu*. n. Commencement, beginning ప్రారంభము. Opposition. ఎదిరించుట.

తలపు or తలంపు *talapu*. [Tel. from తలచు.] n. Thinking, considering తలచుట. A thought, idea, అభిప్రాయము. A desire కోరిక. Reflection చింత. Recollection జ్ఞప్తి. Heart హృదయము. Imagination, intention, proposition, plan, supposition. తలపు చేయు *talapu-cheyu*. v. n. To think, consider. ఎంచు, భావించు. తలపుచూలి the child of Desire, i. e., Manmatha మన్మథుడు, భావజుడు. తలపురాయి *talapu-rayi*. n. The stone that grants all wishes. చింతామణి.

తలపెట్టు *tala-pettu*. [Tel.] v. n. To endeavour, take into one's head, to begin or commence. ప్రారంభించు. To think or talk of, ప్రస్తావించు.

తలపొలము *tala-polamu*. [Tel.] n. The glebe or site of a village. Swa. iv. 11. గ్రామకంఠము, పొలిమేరవద్దనున్న పొలము. భార. ఉద్యో. ii.

తలపోటకము *tala-potakamu*. [Tel.] n. The Cassia tree. తంగేడు, స్వర్ణకేశి.

తలపోయు *tala-poyu*. [Tel. తలపు+పోయు.] v. a. To think, plot, devise, contrive, ruminate, be anxious about, investigate, esteem, hold, reflect on, compare. తలపోసి చూచు to think over, to reflect in one's mind.

తలబీకరకాయ or తలబీకనకాయ *tala-bikara-kaya*. [Tel.] n. Confusion: a puzzle, riddle, difficulty. కలత, చిక్కు.

తలబొము *tala-bomu* [Tel.] n. A sort of eel. Russell No. 38. *Muraena cnox serridentata*. (McLelland) Jerdon.

తలబ్రాలు or తలంబ్రాలు *talabralu*. [Tel.] n. The rice (బ్రాలు) poured over the head (తల) of the bride and bridegroom for luck.

తలమాటు *tala-matu*. [Tel.] n. Evil, ruin. చేటు, నాశము.

తలమానికము *tala-manikamu*. [Tel.] n. A ruby worn on the head. అలంకారార్థము శిరమునందుంచుకొనే రత్నము. adj. Excellent, శ్రేష్ఠము.

తలమించు *tala-mintsu*. [Tel.] v. n. To excel, to exceed, to be in excess. మించు మించు.

తలమిగులు *tala-migulu*. [Tel.] v. n. To remain over. మిందుమిగులు.

తలము *talamu*. [Tel.] interj. Stop! stand back! తొలగుము. తలము [from Skt. స్థలము.] n. Site, situation, place. Actuality, subsistence, existence; Essential nature. స్వరూపము. మహీతలము the earth, the place filled or occupied by a body. కరతలము the palm of the hand. పాదతలము the sole of the foot. నభస్తలము the sky, the heavens. ఆకాశప్రదేశము. తలము తప్పు to become impossible అశక్యమగు.

తలముల్లు *tala-mullu*. [Tel.] n. A kind of instrument used by thieves: or hunters. A picklock. HD. i, 472.

తలయంపి *tala-y-ampi*. [Tel.] n. The head of a bedstead. తలాపి, మంచముననుండు తలవైపు. A pillow తలకిందుంచుకొను దిండు.

తలయేరు *tala-y-eru*. [Tel.] n. A headache. Swa. v. 23. M. III. vii. 277.

తలరు *talaru*. [Tel.] v. n. To move. చలించు. To bloom, shine, thrive, rejoice సంతృప్తి మించు, సంతోషించు. A. iv. 138. BD. iii. 1223. M. I. ii. 200. ఒప్పు. To think or consider చింతించు. To be confused కలగు.

తలవరి *talavari.* [Tel.] n. A beadle, porter, guardsman. A watchman. తలారివాడు. తోకతలవరి a certain fish, resembling a sole: a species of ophidium. Russell, plate XXXIX.

తలవాకిలి *tala-vakili.* [Tel.] n. The house door, or street door. Also, the mouth. H. v. 27. See తల.

తలవిడి *tala-vidi.* [Tel.] n. The severed head or top of a tree తలతుండు.

తలవీడు *talavidu.* [Tel.] n. The city gate, పురప్రవేశము. Nearness. Neighbourhood. సమీపప్రదేశము.

తలవు Same as తలగు or తొలగు. (q. v.)

తలసాల *tala-sala.* [Tel.] n. The entrance into a house. తలవాకిలి. P. iii. 46.

తలా *talā.* [Tel. from తల.] adv. Each, apiece, per head. చెరి.

తలాటము *talāṭamu.* [Tel. తల+అటు.] n. A head or crest. తురాయి.

తలాడ or తలగడ *talāḍa.* [Tel.] n. A pillow, a bolster. A. ii. 99.

తలాపి or తల్లాపి *talāpi.* [Tel. తల+అపి] n. The head of a bed. తలదుండి.

తలారి or తలవరి *talāri* [Tel.] n. A watchman, beadle, constable. See తలవరి.

తలారించు *talārintsu.* [Tel.] v. n. To turn back. మరలు.

తలి *tali.* [Tel. for తల్లి.] n. A mother: thus contracted in composition. తలిదండ్రులు *tali-dandrulu.* n. Parents. మీరే తలిదండ్రులు you are my father and mother: you are all in all to me. (This phrase is common in all the languages of India: and denotes gratitude, devotion, and loyalty.)

తలికి or తలికె *taliki.* [Tel.] affix. Before, until. నేను రాకతలికి or నేను వచ్చేతలికి before I arrived, until I come.

తలిపెర *tali-pera.* [Tel.] n. A fountain or pit where a stream arises; the bottom of a canal or drain carried from a river to irrigate the fields.

తలిమము *talimamu.* [Skt.] n. A cotton mattress. దూదిపరుపు.

తలియ *taliya.* [Tel.] n. A plate or vessel to take food in. భోజనపాత్రము.

తలిరు *taliru.* [Tel.] n. A sprout, a shoot. పల్లవము, చిగురు. తలిరుచు or తలిర్చు *talirutsu.* v. n. To sprout, shoot, bloom: to rise, as a feeling in the heart. To rejoice సంతోషించు. చేవతలిర్చ in the pride of his strength, in the freshness of vigour. Suca. ii. 283. కెమ్మితలిర్చగ with overflowing love. Bilh. i. 66. తలిరుటాకు *tali-ru-ṭ-āku.* n. A young sprouting leaf. తలిరుబోడి or తలిరుబోణి *taliru-bōḍi.* n. A blooming maid, a delicate woman, a beautiful woman. తలిరుపు or తలిర్పు *talirupu.* n. Sprouting. Blooming. Rejoicing. తలిరు విలుకాడు an epithet of Manmatha.

తలివము *talivamu.* [Tel.] n. A bed. శయ్య.

తలుకు Same as తళుకు. (q. v.)

తలుగు or తల్గు *talugu.* [Tel.] n. A halter to tie up cattle. పలుపు.

తలుపు *talupu.* [Tel.] n. A door. తలుపుతీయు to open a door. తలుపువేయు to shut a door.

తలుము *talumu.* [Tel.] n. A sort of winch for raising a bucket.

తలేరు *talēru.* [Tel. తల+ఏరు.] n. The leading pair of oxen in a plough or cart, as distinguished from పెంటిపసరు the thill pair.

తలోదరి *talōdari.* [Skt.] n. A slender waisted woman. A lady. వనిత, అదుతి.

తల్గు Same as తలుగు. (q. v.)

తల్చు Same as తలచు. (q. v.)

తల్పము *talpamu.* [Skt.] n. A cotton bed or mattress. దూదిపరుపు. A wife భార్య. తల్పగుడు *talpagudu.* n. Lit. He who violates a bed, i.e., an adulterer. గురుతల్ప గుడు one who commits adultery with his Guru's wife.

తల్పించు *talpintsu.* [Tel. for తలచు] v. a. To characterise. "నన్ను ఏలా వెర్రితల్పించె నీవు." why make me look like a fool? Yayati. v. 17.

తల్లజము *tallajamu.* [Skt.] n. The finest of (anything) the noblest of. శుకతల్లజము a gem of a parrot. కన్యకాతల్లజము the fairest of women. అశ్వతల్లజము a jewel of a horse.

తల్లడము *talladamu.* [Tel.] n. Shaking, tremor చలనము. Trouble. బాధ. పిల్లికి చెల్లా టము ఎలుకకు ప్రాణతల్లడము it is sport to the cat but death to the rat. స్వతంత్రము స్వర్గలోకము, పరతంత్రము ప్రాణతల్లడము Independence is heaven but dependence is hell. ఇది నాకు ప్రాణతల్లడమవును this will be the death of me. **తల్లడించు, తల్లడిల్లు, తల్లడపడుచు, తల్లడమందు** or **తల్లడపడు** *talladintsu.* v. n. To be troubled, to grieve, be harassed. **తల్లడపెట్టు** *tallada-pettu.* v. t. To trouble, బాధపెట్టు, చలింపజేయు. **తల్లడపాటు** *tallada-pattu.* n. Trouble, agitation. తల్లడపడుట.

తల్లి *talli.* [Tel. తాయి+ఉ. The final ల్లి is the sign of the honorific plural and is doubled on account of the preceding long vowel having been shortened. ✓ త = she who brings (into existence) or who brings food, &c., cf. తండ్రి.] n. A mother. కన్నతల్లి one's own mother, as opposed to సవతితల్లి a stepmother. In affectionate address తల్లీ "my dear," is used even to a daughter. adj. Maternal, parent. తల్లిపశువు the parent cow. తల్లియింటనున్నది she lives in her mother's home. Principal, great, chief, main. తల్లిదరి or తల్లిదొంతి the parapet wall round a well. తల్లికాలువ the principal channel which supplies others. తల్లిగోడ the principal wall in a house. మీరే నాకు తల్లిదండ్రులు you are my father and mother, you are all in all to me. See under తం.

తల్లికొండ్ర *talli-kondra.* The first furrow in ploughing మొదటికొండ్ర. **తల్లితల్లి** *talli talli.* n. A mother's mother, i.e., Lakshmi. లక్ష్మికి తల్లి. A grandmother. **తల్లి వేరు** *talli-vēru.* n. The tap root or principal parent root. ముఖ్యమైనవేరు.

తళతళ *taḷa-taḷa.* [Tel.] n. Glitter, brilliance. తళతళలాడే glittering, brilliant.

తళిగ, తళియ or **తళిగె** *taḷiga.* [Tel.] n. A plate or vessel to take one's food in, భోజనపాత్రము. Food that is fit to be consecrated to the god భగవన్నివేదనార్హమైన అన్నము.

తళుకు or **తళ్కు** *taḷuku.* [Tel.] n. A flash, a gleam. మిక్కిలిప్రకాశము, సన్ననిమెరుగుకాంతి. వజ్రపుతళుకులు the name of a kind of rice. H. iv. 158. **తళుకులాడు, తళుక్కుమను** or **తళుకొత్తు** *taḷukul-āḍu.* v. n. To gleam, flash. మిక్కిలిప్రకాశించు. తళుక్కున brightly, brilliantly.

తళ్లు *taḷḷu.* [Tel.] n. A rush (of water.) An inroad, incursion. A wave. A ripple చిన్నఅల.

తవన *tavana.* [Tel.] n. A short time. స్వల్ప కాలము.

తవరము Same as తెవరము (q. v.)

తవళి or **తవళీ** *tavaḷi.* [Tel.] n. Falsehood అసత్యము.

తవాయి *tavāyi.* [H.] n. An incursion, a battle, a contest, a war. A cross wind, a foul breeze. Misfortune, hazard, peril. ఉపద్రవము. ఓడ తవాయిపట్టినది the ship missed stays or fell out of its course.

తవిటిపాము or **తవుటిపాము** *taviti-pāmu* [Tel.] n. A whitish sort of eel. మలుగు

తవిడ or **తవ్విడ** *tavida.* [Tel.] n. The grain called Ragi. రాగిపైరు.

తవు Same as తపు. (q. v.)

తవుకోలు Same as తప్పుకోలు (q. v.)

తవుజి *tavuji.* [Tel.] n. A pension or allowance granted to a Zemindar

తవుడు *tavudu*. [Tel.] n. Bran. బియ్యపు మీదిపొట్టు.

తవులు Same as తగులు. **తవులుకొను, తవుల బడు** or **తవులుచు** See under తగులు.

తవెల Same as తపెల or తపేలా. (q. v.)

తవ్వ *tavva*. [Tel.] n. A gallon or dry measure, equal to two solas (సోలలు), రెండుసోలలకొలదిగల మానవిశేషము.

తవ్వు or **త్రవ్వు** *tavvu*. [Tel.] v. a. or v. n. To dig: కాలుత్రవ్వు to paw or spurn the ground, to be eager for. ఊరక తవ్వుకొన్నట్లు అవుతుంది this is merely beating about the bush. పాతరతవ్వుకొను to open a closed grain pit. **తవ్వకము** or **తవ్వాటము** *tavvakamu*. n. Digging, excavation, breaking up soil. **తవ్వించు** *tavvintsu*. v. n. To cause to dig up. నా యిల్లు తవ్వించి సోదామాడినారు they dug up the floor of my house and ransacked it. **తవ్వుగోల** or **తవుగోల** *tavvugōla*. n. A spade.

తసరఫు or **తస్రఫు** *tasaraphu*. [H.] n. Embezzlement. Unlawful enjoyment. అపహరించడము.

తసి *tasi*. [Tel.] n. A thick line of sprouts. దట్టముగు నారుమడు.

తసుకు *tasuku*. [Tel.] v. n. To play pranks, to coquet. ప్రేమకలిగినట్లు చేష్టించు. n. A trick, a prank, a freak, coquetting. A deceitful promise or action. టక్కు. తమ్మ తసుకు a spittoon. తమ్మపడిగ. లంజరికముకు an amour or intrigue. **తసుకులాడి** *tasukul-ādi*. n. A coquette. తసుకులాకలది.

తస్కరించు *taskarintsu*. [Skt.] v. a. To steal. దొంగిలించు. **తస్కరుడు** *taskarudu*. n. A rogue, a thief. దొంగ, చోరుడు.

తస్స *tassa*. [Tel.] n. Fat. కొవ్వు. Proud flesh. దుర్మాంసము.

తహతహ *taha-taha*. [Tel.] n. Flurry, agitation, flutter. తమకము. Grief, vexation, వ్యాకులము. తహతహపడు to be in distress, to be at one's wits' end, to be vexed, తమక పడు. To be excited with joy, to rejoice కుతూహలపడు. తహతహపెట్టు to distress, to agitate, తమకపరుచు; to cause to rejoice కుతూహలపరుచు.

తహబీలు or **తహవీలు** *tahabīlu*. [H.] n. Comparison.

తహశ్శీలు *tahassīlu*. [H.] n. Revenue, collection of revenue. తహశ్శీలుదారుడు *tahassīlu-dārudu*. n. A Tahsildar or a Revenue officer in charge of a Taluq.

తహా *taha* [Tel.] n. Consent, agreement

తా tā

తా *tā*. [Tel. the root of తాను.] G. తన. D. తనకు. A. తన్ను. Plu. తాము, తారు, or తమరు. G. తమ. See తాను.

తాండవము *tāndavamu*. [Skt.] n. Motion in general, however slight. Violent capering, a war dance. Gesticulation, Dancing, orgies, antics. ఉద్ధతమైననృత్యము. **తాండవించు** *tāndavintsu*. v. n. To caper or dance violently. ఉద్ధతముగా నృత్యముచేయు.

తాండ్ర *tāndra*. [Tel.] n. Jelly or jam; the inspissated juice of any plant మామిడి తాండ్ర mango jelly. తాటితాండ్ర palmyra jelly. **తాండ్రచెట్టు** *tāndra-chettu*. n. A kind of tree, *Terminalia bellerica*. విభీతకము. తాండ్రకాయ the nut of this tree.

తాంతము *tāntamu*. [Skt.] adj. Exhausted, languid. బడలిన. **తాంతి** *tānti*. n. Fatigue బడలిక

తాంత్రికము *tāntrikamu*. [Skt.] adj. Relating to the Tantras or unorthodox scriptures. Unscriptural, apocryphal, sophistical as opposed to వేదాంతము or ఆర్షము scriptural. తాంత్రికపు ఉపనయనము a loose performance of the rite of *upanayanam*. See on తంత్రము. **తాంత్రికుడు** *tāntrikudu*. n. One versed in the Tantras. A sophist, a freethinker or materialist.

తాంబాళము *tâmbâḷamu*. [Tel.] n. A large brass plate. పెద్ద యుత్తడిపళ్లెము.

తాంబూలము *tâmbûlamu*. [Skt.] n. The betel-leaf and areca nut formed into a parcel, ready for use. వక్కాకు. This is also a phrase for a douceur. తాంబూలము పుచ్చుకొను to take betel (which is generally offered ceremoniously to a stranger as a mark of respect.) To take an oath: (because such a ceremony is gone through when an oath or solemn engagement is taken.) The *tambulamu* likewise is given as the final or termination of every meal, every transaction and every religious rite. Thus తాంబూలమిచ్చు and తాంబూలముపుచ్చుకొను is to ratify most solemnly, as a betrothal; to swear an oath. తాంబూలవల్లి or తాంబూలి the betel vine.

తాకట్టు *tâ-kaṭṭu*. [Tel. తాకు+కట్టు.] n. A pledge. Something given as security. తాకట్టువాకట్టు అయినది the pledge is forfeited.

తాకీదు or తాకీదు *tâkîdu*. [H.] n. An order, a command. ఆజ్ఞ. A written order. ఆజ్ఞాపత్రిక.

తాకు *tâku*. [Tel.] n. A touch, contact. తాకుడు. An attack. A toe-ring కాలిబొటు. v. a. & v. n. To touch; to strike, to push, to encounter, oppose, front. To be attached, to join, apply. To strike (as heat does.) తాకుమందు a potent drug. నీవు చేసినపాపము నీ తలకే తాకినది your sin has fallen on your own head. వానికి దిష్టి తాకినది he is suffering from the effects of an evil eye. వానికి రోగము తాకినది he has caught the disease. తాకించు *tâkinṭsu*. v. a. To cause to touch, to put in contact with, to apply. తాకజేయు. To trouble శ్రమపరచు. తాకుడు *tâkuḍu*. n. Touching తాకుట, స్పర్శము. తాకుడువేకి *tâkuḍu-vêki*. n. An intermittent fever మరుసటికి వచ్చు జ్వరము. తాకుదల *tâku-dala*. n. A meeting, shock, encounter in a battle. యుద్ధప్రారంభము. M. XII. iii. 10.

తాగడించు *tâ-gaḍinṭsu*. [Tel. తాకు+గడించు.] v. a. To oppress. నిర్బంధించు.

తాగలి *tâgali*. [Tel.] n. A low bed of soil for growing plants. పల్లపుమడి.

తాగల్లు, తాగాడి or తాగాటి *tâgallu*. [Tel. తాకు+కల్లు or కాడి.] n. The stone beam placed across the mouth of a well: పడుపు తిమ్మ, నూతిమీద వడ్డముగా వేసే కఱ్ఱ, లేక రాయి.

తాగు or త్రాగు *tâgu*. [Tel.] v. a. To drink. చుట్ట తాగు to smoke a cigar. తాగించు *tâginṭsu*. v. a. To cause to drink. తాగునట్లుచేయు. తాగుబోతు *tâgu-bôtu*. n. A drunkard.

తాచు or త్రాచు *tâtsu*. [Tel.] n. The deadly hooded snake called *Cobra de capello*. Various species of it are నల్లతాచు, కోడెతాచు, చింతపువ్వుతాచు, ఆరెగతాచు. cf. కృష్ణసర్పము.

తాచు *tâṭsu*. [Tel.] v. t. To kick. తన్ను. A. v. 138. and vi. 26. Parij. i. 96. iv. 20. To carve or cut. చెక్కు, ఖండించు. To scoop out, తొలుచు. To adopt, అవలంబించు.

తాజా *tâdzâ*. [H.] adj. Fresh; new. తాజాకలము a postscript in a letter.

తాజు *tâḍsu*. [Tel.] n. A jacket. కుళ్లాయి.

తాట *tâṭa*. [Tel.] n. Skin, bark. చెట్టుమీది పట్ట. Deceit మోసము. The Instrumental case of తాడు. "With a cord." తాట తపసి a deceitful or hypocritical recluse తపసము లోరకు సన్యాసివేషమును ధరించినవాడు, దొంగ. తాటమాలలు deceitful base pariahs. BD. i. 605. తాటగానుండే thin.

తాటంకము *tâṭankamu*. [Tel.] n. A sort of earring worn by women. కమ్మ. T. iii. 82.

తాటకి *tâṭaki*. [Tel.] n. The name of a certain hag: a word like fury, hussey, or ogress used in abuse.

తాటాకు *tâṭâku*. [Tel. తాటి+ఆకు.] n. A palm leaf. తాటాకుచేప a certain sea fish. తాటాకు దూటును a patched up job. adj. Spoilt. చక్కన తప్పిన.

"క॥ తోటలు శైస్నిహున్నవి
తాటాదూటుములుకావు తాపసులుండిన్."
అప్ప. iv.

తాటి or తాడి *tāṭi*. [Tel. Infl. of తాడు.] adj. Belonging to the palmyra tree. తాటిచెట్టు *tāṭi-chettu*. n. The Palmyra Palm tree, Brab tree, or Fan Palm tree, *Borassus flabelliformis* (Watts). పోతు (male) and పెంటి (female) తాటిచెట్టు are two kinds. గొడ్డుతాటిచెట్టు or రామతాటిచెట్టు deformed trees of this species supposed to have magic properties. తాటిపిట్ట *tāṭi-pitta*. n. The Ashy Swallow-Shrike, *Artamus fuscus*, (F. B. I.) తాటిబెల్లము sugar made from the juice of the palm-tree. తాటిసన్నులు or తాటిపెన్నులు the flowers of the palm. తాటికట్లెడ or తాటిగిలిపాము *tāṭi-katteḍa*. n. A snake found on the palmyra trees. తాటిపడగ వాడు an epithet of Balarāma or Bhishma. తాటిచుక్క the constellation called శ్రేష్ఠా. తాటిచుక్కనెల the month called శ్రేష్ఠ మాసము.

తాటించు *tāṭintsu* [Tel.] v. n. To flutter, wriggle or flounder: to mouth or move the cheeks in munching. కుక్క చెవులు తాటించినది the dog cocked his ears. పక్షి రెక్కలు తాటించినది the bird fluttered its wings. కాళ్లుతాటించు to kick. v. a. To pat or beat softly, to strike, as a breeze; to slap, buffet. కొట్టు.

తాటోటు *tāṭōṭu*. [Tel.] n. Deceit, knavery. టక్కు, మోసము. adj. Knavish, false.

తాడనము *tāḍanamu*. [Skt.] n. Beating, tapping, patting, కొట్టుట. తాడించు *tāḍintsu*. v. a. To beat. తాడితము *tāḍitamu*. adj. Beaten, flogged, smitten, struck. కొట్టబడిన.

తాడి *tāḍi*. [Tel.] adj. Appertaining to the palmyra or the tree called Beleric Myrobalan, *Terminalia belerica*: విభీతకము. తాడి మీను the spouting whale.

తాడు or త్రాడు *tāḍu*. [Tel.] n. A cord, thread, string. A match for a gun. The palm tree, so called because cordage is made from it. See under తాటి. The cord of marriage, being the string round the bride's neck, from which the పుస్తె or tali is hung. Hence తాడుతెగిన (lit. cord broken) means widowed. అగ్గి తాడు or సిరితాడు a match, made of cord dipped in brimstone.

తాత *tāta*. [Tel. lit. తండ్రికి or తల్లికి తండ్రి.] n. A grandfather. Also, a name for Brahma. Dasav. iv. 104. తాతమ్మ *tāt-ammu*. n. A grandmother.

తాత్కాలికము *tāt-kālikamu*. [Skt. from తత్కాలము.] adj. Present, of that time. తాత్కాలికదాత. (Dasav. viii. 110.) a ready giver.

తాత్పర్యము *tātparyamu*. [Skt. from తత్పర.] n. Intention, import, purport, meaning, drift. Thought, idea, view, design, purpose, inclination. An object, scheme, plan, అభిప్రాయము. (See on తత్పరుడు.) నా తాత్పర్యమేమంటే what I mean is. తాత్పర్యుడు *tātparyudu*. n. He who holds an opinion. ఇందువల్ల సంభవించినదని తాత్పర్యులై ఉన్నారు they are of opinion that this is the cause of it.

తాత్త్వికము *tāttvikamu*. [Skt. from తత్త్వము.] adj. Concerned with final causes, metaphysical. True, real. తాత్త్వికత్వము *tāttvikatvamu*. n. Dialectics, logic. The telestic mode of reasoning. Ananda. xvii. 6.

తాత్సర్యము or తాత్సార్యము *tātsaryamu*. [Skt.] n. Disregard, neglect, scorn. Delay, waste of time.

తాతై or తైతై *tāthai*. [Tel.] n. Words used in beating musical time.

తాదృశము *tā-driśamu*. [Skt.] adj. Such, such like, similar. అటువంటిది.

తాన *tāna*. [Tel. తాను+అ.] adv. Of himself, personally.

తానకము *tanakamu.* [from Skt. స్థానము.] n. An abode, house. గృహము, స్థానము. Posture. Steadfastness, certainty.

తానము *tanamu.* [from Skt. స్నానము.] n. Bathing. [from Skt. స్థానము.] A place. A note, or sound, also, the words used in music like ut, re, mi. తన్నుతానముతో పాడేపాట. ఆది తానములు నేర్చుకొంటున్నది she is learning the gamut.

తానవము *tanavamu.* [Skt. from తనువు.] n. Leanness, thinness. తనుత్వము.

తాను *tanu.* [Tel.] pron. (reflexive). Self, one, oneself. (G. తన. D. తనకు. Acc. తన్ను. Plu. తాము, తమరు. G. తమ). తనకుతాను voluntarily, of itself, of his own accord. తమకుతామే they of themselves. తానుచెడ్డకోతి వనమెల్లచెరచినది one good-for-nothing monkey ruins the whole garden. తననే చూచినారు (B. viii. 421.) they beheld him himself. తన్నుతానదనితెలియడు (Vēma) he will not see that he is the person in question. తన్నుంచిరానట్టితప్పులేలకు. (Ila. iii. 56.) is there any error that does not spring from one's own folly?

తాప *tapa.* [Tel.] n. A step, stairs. మెట్టు, గడప. (A. i. 8. & iv. 185.) A ladder. నిచ్చెన.

తాపటిమేకు *tapaṭi-mēku.* [Tel. from తాపి.] n. A joining nail or spike nail used to join two planks together, a bolt or rivet.

తాపము *tapamu.* [Skt.] n. Burning, heat. (Metaphorically) Corroding care or trouble. The fire of love or fever of grief. తాపంబుటుడుకు heat, warmth, irritation. R. vi. 249. **తాపత్రయము** *tapa-trayamu.* n. Triple cares, all sorts of troubles arising from worldly cares. These are divided into ఆధ్యాత్మికము, ఆధిభౌతికము and ఆధిదైవికము, that is, sorrows caused by, (1) ourselves, (2) others, & (3) by the will of God. R. iii. 31. తాపత్రయపడు to be harassed or vexed, to be in trouble, care and anxiety.

తాపసి *tapasi.* [Skt. from తపస్సు.] n. A nun, a female ascetic, or pilgrim. **తాపసుడు** *tapasuḍu.* n. A hermit, monk, ascetic.

తాపి or **తాపీ** *tapi.* [Tel.] n. Composition, putting or bringing together. A bricklayer, తాపివాడు. A bricklayer's work. A trowel. A secret, a mystery in any trade, a trace; జాడ, మర్మము. The setting of a stone. Ballast, weight in a boat. ఓడ అడుగున బరువుక్కువేసేది. తాపిచేయు to put or bring together, to pimp. **తాపికత్తె** *tapi-katte.* n. A bawd, a go-between. సంధానము చేయునది. A. v. 74. **తాపికాడు** *tapi-kaḍu.* n. A pimp, a panderer. సంధానముచేయువాడు. Satyabha. iii. 115.

తాపించు *tapinchu.* [from Skt. స్థాపించు.] v. t. To set up, establish or fix. నిలుపు, నిలుకొలుపు. To carve చెక్కు. To belabour. మోదు.

తాపింఛము *tapinchhamu.* [Skt.] n. The tree called *Xanthochymus Pictorius.* తమాలము or చీకటిమాను. (q. v.)

తాపిత *tapita.* [Tel.] n. A fine kind of silk cloth. మేలైన పట్టుబట్ట.

తాపితము *tapitamu.* [Skt. from తాపము.] adj. Heated. తపింపజేయబడిన.

తాపు *tapu.* [Tel.] v. a. To inlay, as precious stones in a jewel. చెక్కు. To join or unite. n. A prop. ఆవలంబము. A kick తన్ను, పాదతాడనము.

తాబందు *tabandu.* [Tel.] n. A petticoat. పావడ, గాగర.

తాబేదారుడు *tabē-daruḍu.* [H.] n. A dependant or subordinate man.

తాబేలు *tabēlu.* [Tel.] n. A sea or land turtle. The land species is often called జానంతాబేలు or hermit-tortoise.

తాము *tamu.* [Tel.] n. A bridge-end or the side of a stream.

తామర *tamara.* [Tel.] n. The lotus. Ringworm. కృష్ణతామర the plant called Indian

Reed or Indian Shot. మెట్టతామర a sort of Cassia, the leaf of which cures ringworm. కితితామర a tree called the Indian Reed or Arrowroot plant, *Pontideria hastata* (Rox. ii. p. 122.) తామరచెలి *tāmara-cheli*. n. The sun. తామరతంపము *tāmara-tampamu*. n. Prosperity. అభివృద్ధి. తామరతంపమగు to prosper వృద్ధిపొందు. తామరతంపర *tāmara-tampara*. n. A cluster or multitude of lotuses. Flourishing, the spreading of a people or family (being likened to the spreading stems of the lotus.) తామరతంపరగా flourishingly, prosperously, "like a green bay tree." తామరతూపరి an epithet of Manmadha. తామరసము *tāmarasamu*. [Skt.] n. The lotus. Gold. Copper. తామరసస్ఖుడు *tāmarasa-sakhudu*. n. The lover of the lotus, i. e., the sun.

తామసము *tāmasamu*. [from Skt. తమసము.] n. Tardiness, delay, dulness. ఆలస్యము. adj. Cruel, bloody, malignant. తామసపూజ a bloody sacrifice. తామసగుణము the dark passions. తామసి *tāmasi*. n. A malignant, mischievous person. Darkness. చీకటి. తామసించు *tāmasintsu*. v. n. To be tardy, to dawdle. ఆలస్యముచేయు. తామసుడు *tāmasudu*. n. A malignant or mischievous man. తమోగుణముగలవాడు, దుష్టుడు.

తామా *tāma*. [Tel.] n. Thickness, bulk, as opposed to length and width.

తామిస్రము *tāmisramu*. [Skt.] n. Darkness. చీకటి. A hell of darkness. చీకటిమయమైన నరకము.

తాము *tāmu*. [Tel.] n. The plural of తాను. Selves (used honorifically); your honour, your lordship.

తామేలు Same as తాబేలు.

తామ్రము *tāmramu*. [Skt.] n. Copper. రాగి. Red color ఎరుపు. adj. Red ఎర్రని. తామ్రకుట్టకుడు *tāmra-kuttakudu*. n. A coppersmith. రాగిపనివాడు. తామ్రచూడము *tāmra-chūdamu*. n. The copper-helmed bird, i. e., a cock, కోడి. తామ్రపర్ణి the copper-river. ఒకయేరుపేరు. తామ్రాక్షము the Black Cuckoo (కాకి) as being red eyed.

తాయము *tāyamu*. [Tel.] n. A rare thing, a rarity. అరుదుగువస్తువు. ఇదో ఒకతాయము నీకిస్తాను here, I will give you a rare thing.

తాయి *tāyi*. [Tel.] n. A mother. See తల్లి.

"సీ॥ కన్నబిడ్డలతోవగానంటికుల్బోన
బంగారుతాయి మా రంగతాయి."

పాంచా. i.

తాయితు, తాయెతు or తాయెత్తు *tāyitu*. [Tel. తాయి+ఎత్తు.] n. An amulet, or charm containing things supposed to bring luck. తల్లి బిడ్డలకుకట్టే రక్షరేకు.

తార *tāra*. [Skt.] n. A star. నక్షత్రము. The pupil of the eye, కనుగుడ్డు, కనీనిక, నల్లగుడ్డు. A. v. 13. The wife of Brihaspati. బృహస్పతిభార్య. Vali's wife. వాలిభార్య. తారకము *tāra-kamu*. n. A star. The pupil of the eye. The eye. తారాపథము *tāra-pathamu*. n. The starry path, i. e., the firmament. ఆకాశము. తారావళి *tāra-vali*. n. A constellation, or set of stars. The starry firmament.

తార *tāra*. [Tel. తారు+అ.] pron. They themselves.

తారకజిత్తు *tāraka-jittu*. [Skt.] n. The conqueror of an Asura called తారక; an epithet of the god of war. T. v. 220. కుమారస్వామి.

తారకాణ, తారకాణము, తార్కాణ or తార్కాణము *tārakāṇa*. [from Skt. తర్కము.] n. An example. దృష్టాంతము. Discussion. Proof, evidence. నిదర్శనము. Appa Kavi. ii. 162. తారకాణించు or తార్కాణించు *tārakāṇintsu*. v. t. To illustrate, to prove by an example దృష్టాంతపరచు. To dispute, debate. Swa. ii.

తారకానందము *tāraka-nandamu*. [Skt.] n. The name of a certain tune.

తారకుడు *tarakuḍu*. [Skt.] n. A mediator, a saviour, redeemer, emancipator. తరింపించువాడు, దాటించువాడు.

తారణ *tāraṇa*. [Skt.] n. The name of a certain year in the Hindu Calendar. adj. That which enables one to cross. తరింపచేయునది.

తారతమ్యము or తారతమ్యత *tara-tamyamu*. [From Skt. తర and తమ affixes of the Sanskrit comparative and superlative degrees.] n. Difference, distinction. Proportionate value: comparative merit. Superiority among competitors. తరతమభావము, న్యూనాధిక్యము. భాగ్యవంతులకు గొప్ప చేయుటలోను నాకంటిదీనులను రక్షించడములోను నుండే తారతమ్యము తమ చిత్తానికే తెలియును you well know how far the merit of relieving the poor exceeds that of promoting the rich.

తారము *tāramu*. [Skt.] n. A clear pearl; స్వచ్ఛమైన ముత్తెము. A clear note, గట్టిశ్రుతి, ఉచ్చస్వరము. Crossing, passing over. దాటుట. Silver, వెండి. The segment of a circle. Protuberance, fullness, bulge, swell. Tare in merchandise: the sum allowed for the packing case.

తారసించు or తారసిల్లు *tārasintsu*. [Tel.] v. n. To approach, draw near. To clash or collide సమీపించు. పూర్వపశ్చిమసముద్రములవలె తారసిల్లెనా it was like the eastern and the western seas encountering one another. To spread వ్యాపించు. తారసము *tārasamu*. n. Nearness, contact, touch. సమీపము. Opposition తలపాటు. A. iii. 36. తారసానకు, అరగా తటస్థపడుటకు. తారసపడు *tārasa-paḍu*. v. n. To draw near, to front, engage in battle, to face. తారసపెట్టు *tārasa-peṭṭu*. v. a. To introduce, insinuate, procure, as a bawd. To adduce.

తారాజువ్వ *tārā-juvva*. [Tel.] n. A sort of sky rocket. A firework in water.

తారాడు *tār-āḍu*. [Tel. తారు+ఆడు.] v. n. To move about. తిరుగులాడు. To lurk about, dangle, hang off and on. To dance attendance without coming to the point. తిరాడు. క్రేలాడు. A. iv. 129.

తారాపీట *tāra-pīṭa*. [Tel.] n. The seat on the back of an ox. ఎద్దుమెడమీద వేసేపీట.

తారి *tāri*. [Tel.] n. One who pulls the wires or strings in a theatrical performance ఆటాడించే సూత్రధారి.

తారించు *tārintsu*. [Tel.] v. t. To make one come close. తారకేయు. See తార్చు, and తారు. (R. v. 192.)

తారీఖు *tārīkhu*. [H.] n. The date of the month. తేదీ.

తారు *tāru*. [Tel.] pro. They themselves. You (honorific) తమరు.

తారు *tāru*. [Tel.] v. n. To roam, rove, stroll, saunter, run about, loiter. సంచరించు. To go. పోవు. To meet. కలియు. To lurk, lie in wait. మాటుకొను. To dance attendance. To fall away in flesh, become lean. క్షీణించు. అడగు. తారుకొను. పొందు. తారుకొన్నసిగ్గు lurking shame. L. iv. 202. తారుకొను or తార్కొను *tāru-konu*. v. n. To meet, draw near. తారసిల్లు. R. i. 111. and v. 155. To follow. వెంబడించు. To bear, wear, carry. ధరించు, ధరించు. "విలసిల్లమెన్నెల్ల తార్కొన్నవారు." L. ii. 116.

తారుచు Same as తార్చు (q.v.)

తారుణ్యము or తరుణత్వము *tāruṇyamu*. [Skt.] n. Youthfulness, bloom. యౌవనము. Vasu. ii. 55.

తారుమారు *tāru-māru*. [Tel.] n. Disorder, confusion. గందరగోళము. adj. Disorderly, riotous. Slovenly. క్రమముతప్పిన, వ్యత్యస్తమైన. తారుమారుగా *tāru-māru-gā*. adv. Confusedly, in disorder, upside down. తారుమారుపడు to be confused, గందరగోళపడు.

తార్కాణ or తార్కాణించు See under తార్కాణ.

తార్కికుడు *tārkikuḍu.* [Skt. from తర్కము.] n. A logician, a reasoner.

తార్కొను Same as తారుకొను. See under తారు. **తార్కొలుపు** *tār-kolupu.* v. t. To cause to meet.

తార్చు or **తారుచు** *tārtsu.* [Tel.] v. a. To unite, set together, join, apply, put. To close. To set as precious stones. To introduce, bring people together. To pimp or pander సంధానపరచు. R i. 120. To lure, gull, trick (ప్రతారణము). To egg on, incite. To put (as a child to the breast.) **తార్చేది** *tārchēdi.* n. A bawd. **తార్చేవాడు** *tārchē-vāḍu.* n. A pimp.

తార్తీయము *tārtīyamu.* [Skt. from తృతీయ.] adj. Third. Ternary.

తార్పు or **తారుపు** *tārpu.* [Tel.] n. Application, joining, setting. తార్పడము. A small box. బరణి, చిన్నపెట్టె గానితార్పు. (R. ii. 89.) a copper plate. తామ్రపత్రము, గల్లెము, తాంబాళము. **తార్పులాడు** *tārpu-l-āḍu.* v. n. To fight as cocks, rams, &c.

తాలాంకుడు, తాళాంకుడు or **తాలధ్వజుడు** *tālankuḍu.* [Skt.] n. An epithet of Balrama, the Bacchus of India, whose standard is the palm tree.

తాలి, తాళి, తాలిబొట్టు or **తాళిబొట్టు** *tāli.* [Tel.] n. A small piece of gold which the bridegroom ties round the bride's neck as a sign of marriage. పుస్తె, మంగళసూత్రము.

తాలించు *tālintsu.* [Tel.] v. a. To season food. కూరలను తిరుగబోయు. To slake lime. **తాలింపు** *tālimpu.* n. The seasoning of a dish. తిరుగబోత. Seasoned curry తాలింపుకూర. Slaking lime.

తాలిమి *tālimi.* [Tel.] n. Gentleness. Endurance, patience, steadfastness. ఓర్పు. Fortitude. ధైర్యము. తాలిమికత్తె a patient woman ఓర్పుగలది. తాలిమికాడు a patient man. ఓర్పుగలవాడు.

తాలు or **తాలుగింజలు** *tālu.* [Tel.] n. Empty ears of corn, తప్పగింజలు, ఎన్నుగింజ ఎండిపోయినవి

తాలుము Same as తాల్చు.

తాలువు *tāluvu.* [Skt.] n. The palate. The inside of the cheek. కోటిలోపలిపక్క.

తాలువుబిల్ల *tāluvu-billa.* [Tel.] n. A spindle.

తాలూకా *tālūka.* [H.] n. A Taluk or division of a *zilla* (జిల్లా) or district. Also, applied to the principal town of a Taluq. A subdivision. adj. Belonging to, pertaining to, సంబంధించిన. **తాలూకు** *tālūku.* adj. Belonging to.

తాల్చు or **తాలుము** *tāltsu.* [Tel.] v. a. To take. To hold. To receive, to bear, to wear (as a dress, ornament, or weapon). ధరించు. To take or assume (a shape, &c.) To hold (as a liquid in the mouth). To slake (lime). To twist (thread by the spindle). దారమునుపేను. See తాలువుబిల్ల. To fan or winnow (grain in a basket). గర్భముతాల్చు to conceive (a child). తాల్చనిసున్నము unslaked lime.

తాల్మి Same as తాలిమి. (q. v.)

తాళకము *tālakamu.* [Skt.] n. Yellow orpiment. Yellow sulphuret of arsenic. హరిదళము, సొన్నముసున్నము.

తాళము *tālamu.* [Tel.] n. A lock. బీగము. తాళపుచెవి a key. కప్పతాళము a padlock. తాళముతీయు to unlock. తాళమువేయు to lock up. Time or measure in music. పాడునప్పుడు జంగె కాలనిర్ణయము. A cymbal, because used to keep time with. తాళమువేసే కంచువాద్యము. A palm tree. తాటిచెట్టు. తాళ appertaining to the palm tree. తాళవృక్షము a palm tree. వానితాళము పట్టినాడు he was in a rage or out of humour against him. ఆదితాళము slow time. ఆటతాళము common time. త్రిపుటతాళము quick time. **తాళగించు** *tāla-gintsu.* v. n. To play (the cymbals, &c.), తాళమువేయు. BD. iii. 1237. తాళరి one who plays the cymbals. తాళము వేయు

వాయు. తాళపత్రము tāla-patramu. n. A palm leaf. తాటాకు, పొవ్వాకు. తాళమానము tāla-mānamu. n. Beating time in music. T. iv 77. తాళవృంతము tāla-vrintamu. n. A fan made of palm leaf. విసనకర్ర.

తాళాబందు tāla-bandu. [H.] n. A complete abstract of the actual receipts and expenditure of the revenue for the past year.

తాళి or తాళీ tāli. [Tel.] n. A necklace. పతకము, ఒకవిధమైన హారము.

తాళించు tālintsu. [Tel.] v. t. To shake the dice before throwing them down. జూదమాడునప్పుడు కిందవేయుటకై పాచికలను చేతిలో ఇటుఅటు త్రిప్పుట.

తాళిక or తాలిక tālika. [Tel. from తాళు.] n. Patience, endurance. ఓర్పు, క్షమ. A pastille or little roll, as of paste or of leaf. పొట్టు. The scurf that drops off the skin when rubbed. A flake or scale of earth. Cords of hair: పెంటెక. Tresses smeared with మృత్తిపాలు. Suca ii. 42. తాళికగలవాడు tālika-gala-vādu. n. A man of substance.

తాళు or తాళుకొను tālu. [Tel.] v. a. To bear, suffer, endure, tolerate, have or show patience సహించు. To refrain. To wait, stop. ఆగు, నిదానించు. ఈ బట్ట కట్టు తాళును this cloth wears very well.

తాళ్లు tāllu. [Tel.] n. Ropes. Palm trees. See తాడు and తాటి.

తాళ్వారము tālvāramu. [K.] n. A shelving roof: a verandah or shed. A pent roof. వసారా.

తావక tāvaka. [Skt.] adj. Thine, thy. తావకీనము tāvakīnamu. adj. That which belongs to thee.

తావకాళ్లు, తావకోళ్లు or తావుకోళ్లు tāva-kāllu. [Tel.] n. Pieces of wood used to rest the feet on while working a picota or water-lift, ఏతమెత్తువాడు కాళ్లుంచుకొనుటకు అమర్చిన కట్టెలు.

తావత్ tāvat. [Skt.] adj. That. తావత్పర్యంతము Thus far, so long.

తావరము tāvaramu. [from Skt. స్థావరము.] adj. Firm. స్థిరమైన.

తావలము tāvalamu. [Tel.] n. A place, abode, home. స్థానము, గృహము, నివాసము. A prop ఆధారము, రక్షకము. M. XII. ii. 182. దయకు తావలమైన who is an object of mercy.

తావళము or తావడము tāvaḷamu. [Tel.] n. A necklace of beads, &c; as రుద్రాక్ష తావళము.

తావి tāvi. [Tel.] n. Odour, fragrance. పరిమళము. తావిగట్టు the mountain called Malaya (మలయపర్వతము.) తావినూనె tāvi-nūne. n. Fragrant or scented oil. తావి మోవరి the scent carrier, i. e., the wind, గాలి, గంధవహుడు. తావివిలుకాడు an epithet of Manmadha.

తావు or టావు tāvu. [Tel.] n. A place, locality; a home, room, space. స్థానము. అది నా తావున ఉన్నది I have it by me, in my hands. నా తావున పుచ్చుకొన్నారు they took it of or from me. అతడు నా తావుకు వచ్చెను he came to me. వానితావునకు పంపితిని I sent it to him. తావు, టావు or తావు n. A sheet of paper. తావు కాగితము.

తావు tāvu. [Tel.] v. t. & n. To drink, త్రాగు. M. XIII. iii. 307.

తావుకోళ్లు or తావకోళ్లు Same as తావకాళ్లు. (q. v.)

తి ti

తింట tinta. [Tel. contracted from తినుట.] n. Eating. తినుట.

తిండి tindi. [Tel. from తిను.] n. Food, ఆహారము. An eater. బువ్వతిండి one who lives on rice. తిండిమెతుకు solid food. పసులతిండి a cannibal, a child-eater. కంచితిండి a corpulent beggar at fairs, an uproarious rioter. తిండికాడు, తిండిపంద, తిండిపోతు or తిండీడు tindi-kādu. n. A glutton. Fem. తిండికత్తె or తిండికత్తియ.

తింత్రిణీ *tintrini.* [Skt.] n. The tamarind tree. చింతచెట్టు. **తింత్రిణీకము** *tintri-nika-mu.* n. The tamarind fruit. చింతపండు.

తికమక *tika-maka.* [Tel.] n. Confusion కలత. Tottering. తొట్రుపాటు. adv. Up and down, backwards and forwards. ఇట్టట్టుగా. **తికమకగొను** or **తికమకలాడు** *tika-maka-gonu.* v. n. To be confused కలతపడు. To totter. తొట్రుపడు.

తిక్క *tikka.* [Tel.] n. Madness. పిచ్చి, ఉన్మాదము. తిక్కయజ్వ the Somayâji Tikkanna. (a celebrated poet.) **తిక్కపట్టిన** or **తిక్కతొత్తిన** *tikka-pattina.* adj. Mad. తిక్కగొను to become mad. వెర్రెత్తు.

తిక్కటుమక్కటు *tikkatu-makkatu.* [Tel.] n. Confusion, higgledy piggledy. కలత.

తిక్కడి *tikkadi.* [Tel.] n. A spindle. నూలు వడికే చిప్పకదురు.

తిక్తము *tiktamu.* [Skt.] n. Bitterness. చేదు. adj. Bitter. చేదైన.

తిగ *tiga.* [from Skt. త్రికము.] n. Three మూడు. **తిగకంటి** *tiga-kanti.* n. The three-eyed one, i. e., Siva, త్ర్యంబకుడు. **తిగవంచ** *tiga-vancha.* n. Four.

తిగటు *tigatu.* [Tel.] n. A screen. తెర. M VI. i. 298.

తిగియు, తివియు, తిగుచు or **తివుచు** *tigiyu.* [Tel.] v. t. To pull, draw, take: లాగు, ఈడ్చు, ఆకర్షించు. To rub as in shampooing the limbs. To stroke. **తిగుచుడుపోగులు** *tigutsudu-pogulu.* n. The cords used with a hunter's nets or snares.

తిగ్మము *tigmamu.* [Skt.] n. Heat, warmth, వేడిమి. adj. Hot, warm. వేడిమిగల.

తిట్ట *titta.* [Tel.] n. A heap, a multitude. రాశి.

తిట్టు *tittu.* [Tel.] v. a. To abuse, rate, scold, rail at, curse. To use obscene language. To express anger: to blame, to condemn. శపించు, నిందించు. n. Abuse, scolding, violent language, a violent rebuke, an abusive or obscene expression. నెయ్యంపుతిట్టు a friendly scolding. Blame, censure నింద. తిట్టుపడు to incur blame or censure నిందింపబడు. **తిట్టుపాటు** *tittu-patu.* n. Blame or censure. నింద. **తిట్టుపోతు** *tittu-potu.* n. A scold, a woman who uses obscene language.

తిడిము or **తిడిమ్మి** *tidimi.* [Tel.] n. The rustling noise of carriage wheels. రథము పోవునప్పటిమ్రోత.

తితిక్ష *titiksha.* [Skt.] n. Endurance, steadfastness. క్షమ, ఓర్పు. **తితిక్షువు** *titikshuvu.* A man of a forgiving nature. ఓర్పరి.

తిత్తి *titti.* [Tel.] n. A purse, bag, case, or cover. సంచి, తోలుసంచి. The skin or hide of animals మృగములతోలు. A leathern bag or bottle as సారాయితిత్తి. చనుతిత్తి a loose dangling breast. మూత్రతిత్తి the bladder. ఇఱోలతిత్తి the scrotum. కొలిమితిత్తి a pair of bellows. తిత్తి విడిచినట్లు నన్ను విడిచినాడు he cast me off like an old shoe. చెయితిత్తి a glove. కాలితిత్తి a stocking. **తిత్తికాడు** *titti-kadu.* n. A piper. తిత్తి పోయువాడు.

తిత్తిరి *tittiri.* [Skt.] n. The Francoline partridge, *Francolinus vulgaris.*

తిథి *tithi.* [Skt.] n. A *Tithi*, a lunar day. The date by computation of lunar days, by which all religious and funeral rites (*Parentalia*) are regulated. రేపు నా తండ్రిగారికి తిథి గనుక రాను as to-morrow is the anniversary of my father's death I cannot come.

తిను *tinu.* [Tel.] v. a. To eat. భుజించు. To suffer or undergo (blows, abuse, hardship, or punishment.) వానిచేత దెబ్బలు తిన్నాను I was beaten or flogged by him. గడ్డితిను to eat grass, i. e., to make a beast or fool of oneself. అన్నము తింటారా గడ్డి తింటారా are you men or brutes? తినివేయు to devour (one's property). **తినిపించు** *tini-p-intsu.* (caus. from తిను.) v. t. To cause to eat. వానికి అన్నము తినిపించినాను

I made him eat dirt. తినుబండారములు *tinu-bandāramulu*. n. Eatables. తినుబండారపువస్తువులు provisions.

తినుకు *tinuku*. [Tel.] v. n. To strain. n. Straining.

తిన్న or తిన్నని *tinna*. [Tel.] adj. Proper యుక్తము. Straight. ఋజువు. Fine, beautiful మనోజ్ఞము. Well స్వస్థము. తిన్నగా or తిన్నంగా *tinna-gā*. adv. Fairly, by gentle or fair means, straightway, directly, properly. Gently, slowly. తిన్నగాపో go slowly or gently. Well, in good health. వానికి తిన్నగా వున్నది he is very well. తిన్నన or తిన్నదనము *tinnana*. n. Rightness, straightness, propriety. Gentleness, gentlemanly conduct, ఋజుత్వము, సౌజన్యత. తిన్నని *tinnani*. adj. Gentle, gentlemanly, worthy, proper, correct, slow, straight, direct. Elegant, pretty. తిన్ననినడుము her slender waist.

తిన్నియ or తిన్నె *tinniya*. [Tel.] n. A pial or seat built at a house door; అరుగు, జేజ.

తిపురుకట్టు *tipuru-kaṭṭu*. [Tel.] v. n. To spread. వ్యాపించు.

తిప్ప *tippa*. [Tel.] n. A hillock. చిన్నకొండ, గుట్ట. A mound, దిబ్బ. A stumbling block, a difficulty. కంటకం. A. vi. 17. తిప్పలుపడు. to be distressed or in difficulties. తిప్పలుపెట్టె he threw difficulties in their way. తిప్పలుపడివెదుకు to ransack, to search high and low. తిప్పలమారి *tippala-māri*. n. A drudge. పాట్లమారి. తిప్పకాయ *tippa-kāya*. n. A naughty person. ఆకతాయి, అకతాయి. తిప్పత్రిమ్మరి *tippa-trimmari*. n. A monkey. కోతి.

తిప్పట *tippaṭa*. [Tel. from తిప్పు.] n. Roving, a rambling life.

తిప్పతీగె *tippa-tīge*. [Tel.] n. The Heartleaved Moonseed, *Menispermum cordifolium*. Rox. iii. 811, a plant used in curing snake bites. H. iv. 13. తిప్పసత్తు the extract of that plant. గురూచిలత.

తిప్పు or త్రిప్పు *tippu*. [Tel.] v. n. To turn; to be giddy. తలతిప్పుచున్నది my head turns. I am giddy. v. a. (causal of తిరుగు.) To turn, to reverse. To steer or command (a ship). To wind up (a watch). To wield or brandish. To revoke, rescind, or alter (an order). To lead about. To turn or check (as disease). తిప్పుత్రాళ్లు the cords that turn a churn. n. Turning, a turn తిప్పుట. తిప్పివేయు *tippi-vēyu*. v. a. To turn back or away, to return, reject. తిప్పుకొను *tippu-konu*. v. a. To turn, oppose, check.

తిబిరి *tibiri*. [Tel.] n. A change, alteration. మారుపాటు. adj. Slight, little. అల్పము.

తిమి *timi*. [Skt.] n. A huge fabulous fish, like the leviathan. R. ii. ix. 9, నారాయుడపాడుగు చేప. తిమింగిలము *timingalamu*. n. A huge sea monster, like the kraken, that is supposed to be capable of devouring the తిమి.

తిమితము *timitamu*. [Skt.] adj. Wet. తడిసిన.

తిమిరము *timiramu*. [Skt.] n. Darkness. The shading of a painting.

తిమిరి, తిమిరివాయువు, తిమ్మిరి or తిమురు *timiri*. [Tel.] n. Paralysis, numbness. తిమిరితిక్కి *timiri-tikki*. n. A kind of fish, *Astrape dipterygia*. (F. B. I.) తిమిరిమీను *timiri-mīnu*. n. A fish, a sort of Torpedo. Russell. i. plate 1 and 2. *Narcine timlei* (F. B. I.) తిమిరిస్వనము *timiri-svanamu*. n. A quaver.

తిమురు *timuru*. [Tel.] v. n. To hasten. త్వరపడు. To be proud. గర్వించు. n. Numbness. తిమ్మిరి. Pride గర్వము. తిమురుకొను to pull about in anger కోపముతో పెనగు లాడు.

తిమ్మ or తిమ్మన *timma*. [Tel.] adj. Whole, healthy. స్వస్థము. n. Health. స్వస్థత. v. t. To bless. దీవించు. చేను వానిని తిట్టనులేదు తిమ్మనులేదు. తిమ్మపడు to become well, to be refreshed, స్వస్థపడు, సేదతేరు.

తిమ్మడు or **తిమ్మన్న** *timmadu.* [Tel. from తిరుమల+డు.] n. A name of a monkey, like Jacko or Pug: the feminine is తిమ్మి. **తిమ్మనబంతి** *timmana-banti.* n. A monkey's dinner party, a riotous scene. పొట్టితిమ్మడి కొర్ర the inferior bastard grain that grows rapidly.

తిమ్మనము *timmanamu.* [Tel.] n. A sort of flummery, made of milk, flour and sugar. పాలు పిండి బెల్లము చేసి వండినది. మజ్జిగ పులుసు.

తిమ్మప్పడు *timm-appadu.* [Tel. తిరుమల+అప్పడు.] n. A name of the god Venkatesvara.

తిమ్మరి or **త్రిమ్మరి** *timmari.* [Tel.] n. A wanderer. తిరుగువాడు. దేశదిమ్మరి a vagabond, a vagrant. తిమ్మరితనము the being a vagrant. **తిమ్మరీడు** *timmaridu.* n. A rover or rambler, a vagrant. **తిమ్మరు** or **త్రిమ్మరు** *timmaru.* v. n. To rove, ramble.

తిమ్మి Same as తిమ్మడు. (q. v.)

తిమ్మిరి *timmiri.* [Tel.] n. The cramp, numbness. Tingling స్పర్శము తెలియని వ్యాధివిశేషము. Itching, lewdness. The teeth being set on edge. Any shock.

తియ్య for తీయు. See తీయు.

తియ్య *tiyya.* [Tel.] adj. Sweet. తియ్యమామిడి a sweet mango. తియ్యకూర a sweet dish. **తియ్యదనము** or **తియ్యన** *tiyya-danamu.* n. Sweetness. **తియ్యని** or **తియ్య** *tiyyani.* adj. Sweet. తియ్యనిల్లిమాటలు fair coaxing words. **తియ్యము** *tiyyamu.* adj. Sweet, agreeable, charming. n. Sweetness, పలుకుతియ్యములు (R. ii. 76.) sweet words. తియ్యమ్రాను the sugarcane. చెరుకు. తియ్యవిలుకాడు an epithet of Manmadha.

తిరగడ or **కొండతిరగడ** *tiragada.* [Tel.] n. A certain jewel.

తిరగటివాడ *tiragati-vada.* [Tel.] n. A brig, a two masted vessel.

తిరగబడు or **తిరుగబడు** See under తిరుగు.

తిరగబోతము See under తిరుగు.

తిరగలి See under తిరుగు.

తిరణామలిచెక్క *tiranamali-chekka.* [Tel.] n. Trincomali wood. A wood resembling ash. కమ్మిచెక్క.

తిరము *tiramu.* [from Skt. స్థిరము.] adj. Firm, steadfast. నిలుకడగానుండే, నిబ్బరమైన. **తిరపడు** *tira-padu.* v. n. To become firm. స్థిరపడు.

తిరస్కరించు *tiraskarintsu.* [Skt.] v. a. To despise, scorn, treat with contempt. To outvie, outshine, eclipse. అనాదరము చేయు. **తిరస్కరిణి** *tiraskarini.* n. A curtain, a screen, a guard, a ward. తెరచీర. **తిరస్కారము** or **తిరస్క్రియ** *tiraskaramu.* n. Rejection, scorn, insult, a sneer. Outshining, eclipsing. అనాదరము.

తిరస్తు *tirastu.* [Tel.] n. An alienated village. (Vizag.) A kingdom రాష్ట్రము.

తిరాల *tirala.* [Tel.] affix. Regarding, concerning, in the matter of, towards, against. ఎడల, విషయము. నా తిరాలవాడు చేసిన అపకారము the injustice he committed towards me.

తిరి *tiri.* [Tel.] n. A twist, turn. మెలి, మడి. plu. తిరులు. Kuchelo. ii. 17. తిరికబ్బము base or paltry poetry. Appa. C. ii. 190.

తిరిక *tirika.* [Tel.] n. A twist. మెలిక.

తిరికి *tiriki.* [Tel.] n. A kind of fish.

తిరికె *tirike.* [Tel.] n. Scurf that is rubbed off the skin.

తిరిగ, తిరిగి or **తిరుగ** *tirigi.* [Tel. from తిరుగు.] adv. Again, anew, back. తిరిగియిచ్చు to return or give back. తిరిగివచ్చు to go round to a temple, &c. ప్రదక్షిణముచేయు; to surround పరివేష్టించు.

తిరితిపులాడు *tiri-tipu-l-adu.* [Tel.] v. n. To be fond of, to be silly, to dote upon. H D. ii. 482. To struggle పెనగులాడు.

తిరిపము or తిరెపెము *tiripamu.* [Tel.] n. Alms, what is given in charity. భిక్షము. తిరిపెగాడు or తిరిపరి *tiripe-gāḍu.* n. A beggar. భిక్షుకుడు. తిరిపగొట్టు *tiripa-goṭṭu.* n. A shameless beggar. నిర్లజ్జుడుగాని భిక్షమెత్తువాడు. తిరియు *tiriyu.* v. n. To live by alms. భిక్షమెత్తు, భిక్షించు. HD. ii. 1247. To beg abjectly. దీనవృత్తిని యాచించు. "తొలికమునను దమ తిరిపెకాండ్రల మరలంగ దిరియ నలయుచును జూచ్చి." Kuchēlo. iii. 105.

తిరివడు *tiri-vaḍu.* [Tel. తిరి+పడు.] v. n. To fly, to be routed, worsted, put to flight, or driven back. To be confused. కలతపడు. తిరివెట్టు *tiri-veṭṭu.* v. t. To confuse. కలత పరచు.

తిరీటము *tirīṭamu.* [Skt.] n. A crown. కిరీటము.

తిరు *tiru.* [A Tamil word for Skt. శ్రీ.] adj. Blessed or holy. (This is used in a variety of ways by Vaishṇavites.) తిరుకాపు *tiru-kāpu.* n. Adorning the god. దేవతాలంకరించుట. తిరుకోలను a sacred tank, పుష్కరిణి. తిరుచూర్ణము the sacred powder used to mark the forehead by the Vaishṇavites, శ్రీచూర్ణము, తిరునామము, వైష్ణవబొట్టు. తిరుమణి [మణి=మన్ను] the sacred earth, a kind of white clay used in making the sectarian mark (నామము). తిరుసుగూడ a small basket in which the తిరుమణి and other things are kept. తిరుపతి *tiru-pati.* n A town, Tripati తిరుమల. తిరుమజ్జనము *tiru-majjanamu.* n. The sacred bath given to an idol. దేవతాభిషేకము. తిరుమన్ను same as తిరుమణి. తిరుమాళిగ *tiru-māḷiga.* n. A Vaishṇavite's word for a house (వైష్ణవపరిభాషయందు) గృహము.

తిరుగలి *tirugali.* [Tel.] n See under తిరుగు.

తిరుగు *tirugu.* [Tel.] v. n. To turn, rove, roam, travel. సంచరించు. To be giddy. పరిభ్రమించు. To go back. వెనుకకుమరలు. To come again. మరలవచ్చు. To cease, go off, as disease, be revoked, as an order. To fail, miss, be fruitless, to break one's faith. అతడు ఈ పనిలో తిరిగినాడు he was engaged in this business. వానికి ఒళ్లు తిరిగినది he felt giddy, he was sick, or vomited. మధ్యతిరుగు to intercede, act between others, be an agent. వానికి నోరు బాగా తిరగదు he does not pronounce well. ఆ మాట నా నోట్లో తిరగదు I cannot pronounce that word. కావలితిరుగు to stand sentry. తిరగదీయు to tamper with or corrupt a witness. తమ మాటకు తిరుగులేదు you are supreme: your word is law. హుండీ తిరిగిపోయినది the bill was dishonoured. చుక్కలు తిరిగినవి the stars have turned, i. e., it is past midnight. తిరుగాణి (తిరుగు+ఆణి.) a screw. సందులు తిరిగిరి they went round by the alleys. తిరుగు v. a. To go round, encircle. పరివేష్టించు. తిరుగు or తిరుగుడు. *tirugu.* n. A turning, a turning back, తిరుగుట, భ్రమణము. A change మారుపాటు. A screw, a rivet, a carpenter's vice. మర. A bend, or turn (as in a road). The point on which an affair turns. తిరుగుడుబండి a return cart. లెక్కలో తిరుగుడు వచ్చినది or తిరుగుళ్లుపడినవి there is a difficulty, a question, a point to be cleared. తిరుగుడుచీల or తిరుగుడుసొక్కు a screw, మర. తిరుగుడు పువ్వు *tirugudu-puvvu.* n. The turning flower, i. e., the sun flower. A sort of gold jewel worn by women. తిరుగుడుత్రాడు a noose, ఉరి, ఉచ్చు. తిరుగుదల *tirugu-dala.* n. A turn. మరలుట. వ్యాధి తిరుగుదలగా నున్నది the disease is on the turn. తిరుగుడుపడు to turn, to be giddy పరిభ్రమించు. తిరుగుడుపాటు *tirugudu-pāṭu.* n. Rebellion, resistance. తిరుగబడు or తిరగబడు *tiruga-baḍu.* v. t. To turn against, to rebel against, to oppose, to attack angrily. తిరగబాటు or తిరుగబాటు *tiraga-bāṭu.* n. Disobedience, rebellion, turning against. తిరగబోయు or తిరుగబోయు *tiraga-bōyu.* v. a. To spice, or season (a curry). తిరగమోత or తిరుగమోత *tiraga-*

bōta. n. Seasoning, putting spice, &c., to food. తిరగవేయు or తిరుగవేయు *tiruga-vēyu.* v. a. To turn a thing over. తిరుగ or తిరుగా *tiruga.* adv. Again. తిరుగడ *tirugada.* (తిరుగు+గడ.) n. A pipe which is turned by a screw. మర పెట్టిన గొట్టము. తిరుగలి or తిరగలి *tirugali.* (తిరుగు+కల్లు.) n. A hand mill. (or తిరుగు+కలి.) Turning భ్రమణము. తిరుగుబోతు *tirugu-bōtu.* n. A rambler, rover, giddy fool. తిరుగుమొరుగు or తిరుగుమరుపు *tirugu-morugu.* n. An intricacy, refinement. Ila iii. 16. తిరుగుమొగము *tirugu-mogamu.* n. Turning away the face. విముఖము. తిరుగుపారు *tirugu-pāru.* v. i. To surround. పరివేష్టించు.

తిరుచు *tirutsu.* [Tel.] v. a. & n. To beg alms. తిరుచు.

తిరునాళ్లు *tiru-nāllu.* [Tel.] n. A temple festival. దేవోత్సవము. "తెప్పతిరునాళ్లరా." అను. ii. See తిరు.

తిరునీరు or తిర్నీరు *tiru-nīru.* [Tel.] n. Sacred ashes used by the Saivites for their sectarian marks. శైవులు బొట్టుగాను పెట్టుకొనే గోమయపిండభస్మము, విభూతి. See తిరు.

తిరుపు *tirupu.* [Tel. from తిరుగు.] n. Turning. తిరుగుట. తిరుపులుకట్టు *tirupulu-kattu.* v. n. To spread. వ్యాపించు.

తిరుమల *tiru-mala.* [Tel. తిరు+మల.] n. The sacred hill of Tirupati వేంకటాచలము. Any sacred hill. తిరుమలేశ *tirumal-ēsa.* n. The Lord of Tirumala, a name employed in the chorus used by a poet who wrote a set of riddles: like this one; "మూడుశిరములున్న ముడిమొప్పు పదికాళ్లు గిట్టు; తోకలురెండు కన్నులారు చెలగి కొమ్ములు వాల్గు చేతులు రెండయా, దీనిభావమేమి తిరుమలేశ." The meaning of this is:—"a man ploughing with a pair of oxen." See తిరు.

తిరుమిడి *tiru-midi.* [Tel.] n. A Vaishnavite. వైష్ణవుడు. See తిరు.

తిరువడికోల *tiru-vadi-kōla.* [Tel.] n. A lamp belonging to a mendicant Vaishnavite. దాసరివాని దీపస్తంభము. See తిరు.

తిరువరంగములు *tiru-v-arangamulu.* [Tel.] n. A kind of fine rice. శాలిధాన్యవిశేషము.

తిరువారాధనము *tiru-v-ārādhanamu.* [Tel. తిరు+ఆరాధనము.] n. Divine worship. దేవతార్చన.

తిరువు or తిర్వు Same as తిరుగు. (q. v.)

తిరోధానము *tirōdhānamu.* [Skt.] n. A cover or veil. Concealment, disappearance. మరుగుపాటు.

తిరోహితము *tirōhitamu.* [Skt.] adj. Covered, veiled, invisible. మరుగుపడిన.

తిర్యక్కు *tiryakku.* [Skt.] adj. Moving crookedly, writhing. అడ్డముగా పోవునది. Moving, animate. తిర్యగ్విధముగా tortuously. Turned away, as the face. తిర్యక్పుండ్రము a mark drawn across the forehead. తిర్యగ్జంతువు or తిర్యగ్జీవి *tiryag-jantuvu.* n. An animal, a bird, a snake, &c., as being prone or having the face downwards in distinction from man who stands erect. తిర్యగ్యోనిజము *tiryag-yōnijamu.* adj. Animated, born from the womb of a living being, as distinguished from plants. "తిర్యగ్యోనిజములు." V. P. iv. 3.

తిర్రి *tirri.* [Tel.] n. A wicker work snare for fish. చేపలుపట్టుబుట్ట. A fisherman చేపలుపట్టేవాడు.

తిర్రిగొట్టు Same as తిరుగొట్టు. See under తిరుపు.

తిర్లాడు *tir-l-ādu.* [Tel.] v. n. To attend, be in waiting, to wander about. తిరుగు. కరణముగా తిర్లాడినాడు he was employed as a clerk.

తిర్లిక *tirlika.* [Tel.] n. A lamp. దీపము.

తిలకము *tilakamu.* [Skt.] n. A mark or beauty spot, made on the forehead with black, scarlet or gold paint. బొట్టు. A brooch. A masterpiece, the acme or apex;

a paragon. శ్రేష్ఠమైనది. చోరతిలకము the prince of rogues. శృంగారతిలకము the masterpiece of poetry. నదీతిలకము the prettiest of rivers. A certain tree. బొట్టుగు చెట్టు. **తిలకించు** *tilakintsu*. [Tel.] v. n. To shine. ప్రకాశించు. To be favoured ప్రసన్నతనొందు. v. a. To view, behold. చూచు.

తిలలు *tilalu*. [Skt.] n. Sesamum or gingilly seeds నువ్వులు. **తిలకారకుడు** or **తిలఘాతుకుడు** *tila-kārakuḍu*. n. An oilman. తిలఘాతుకురాలు a female of that caste. వాడు మహా తిలఘాతుకుడు he is a cruel wretch. తిలతండులన్యాయము as sesamum seeds and rice are mixed up together (See the fable in Panchatantramu.) **తిలయంత్రము** *tila-yantramu*. n. An oil press. గానుగ. **తిలరసము** or **తిలభవము** *tila-rasamu*. n. Gingilly oil. నువ్వులనూనె. **తిల్యము** *tilyamu*. n. A field in which a sesamum crop is raised తిలలుపండుపొలము. "కోలదిలల్ గ్రుమ్మ తైలంబుదివిసి." P. ii. 111.

తివ Same as తిగ. (q. v.)

తివాసి, తివాసీ or **తివాస** *tivāsi*. [H.] n. A carpet. రత్నకంబళి.

తివియు or **తిగియు** v. a. To pull, draw, drag. ఈడ్చు "ఏనుగునెఱపంబునకుదివియు కోచి తమిసుమీ." R. ii. 112. "తివియుటదివియుద్రావుడు ద్రవ్వినగొరియు." BD. v. 184.

తివ్యము Same as తిగుచు. (q. v.)

తివుట *tivaṭa*. [Tel.] n. Desire. కోరిక.

తివురు *tivuru*. [Tel.] v. t. & n. To desire. కోరు. To think ఆలోచించు. To try ప్రయత్నపడు. To hasten, త్వరపడు. To rejoice కుతూహలపడు. To be angry కోపపడు. To excel, to resound మ్రోగు. **తివిరి** (past tense of తివురు.) *tiviri*. Having attempted or intended, intentionally, by attempting. ఆలోచించి, ప్రయత్నపూర్వకముగా, త్వరపడి. "తివిరిగోరోచనా తిలకంబు దిద్ది." Sri Nivasa Satsoam 14. "విలుగట్టొనరిచి రదము రఘువరుడ్గం తనఘా తెప్పించుమనుడు" R. iv. 78.

తిస్సాలా *tissala*. [Tel.] adj. Triennial, once in three years.

తీ tī

తీ *tī*. [Tel.] In compounds this stands for తిగ as తీవంచ.

తీండ్ర or **తీండ్రము** *tīndra*. [Tel.] n. Splendour. ప్రకాశము. A. v. 155. Warmth, heat వేడిమి. Light, radiance తేజస్సు. Activity చురుకు. Enterprise చొరవ. **తీండ్రము** *tīndramu*. adj. Hot, warm, ఉష్ణము, ప్రచండము. **తీండ్రించు** or **తీండ్రిల్లు** *tīndrintsu*. v. n. To shine, or be luminous. ప్రకాశించు. **తీండ్రతీగ** *tīndra-tīga*. n. A certain medicinal plant. H. iv. 13.

తీక్ష్ణము *tīkshṇamu*. [Skt.] n. Heat. వేడిమి. Sharpness, haste, keenness, wit. త్వర, చురుకు. adj. Sharp, hot, hasty, keen. చురుకైన, వాడియైన. **తీక్ష్ణగంధము** *tīkshṇa-gandhamu*. n. The tree called పెద్దతుమ్మ, సరవంజి, కండాలచెట్టు. **తీక్ష్ణత్వము** *tīkshṇatvamu*. n. Asperity, pungency. తీక్ష్ణతుండము a mosquito దోమ.

తీగ, తీగె or **తీవ** *tīga*. [Tel.] n. A creeping plant or vine; a tendril or spray. లత. A wire, the string of a lute, తంతి. A necklace of gold wire, a gold or silver belt, మొలనూలు. A gold ornament worn by women, బంగారుపట్టెడ. ప్రేముతీగెలు the rattan lacing in a chair. మెఱుపుతీగె a flash of lightning. పాలతీగె, బంగారుతీగె, &c., are various creepers. **తీగెగరిక** *tīge-garika* n. A creeping species of bent grass, called *Agrostis stolonifera*. తీగచెప్పలి a creeper, *Convolvulus repens*. See చెప్పలి. తీగయిల్లు an arbour పొదరిల్లు. తీగగొంతుక a low voice హీనస్వరము. **తీగబోడి** *tīga-bōḍi*. n. A slight and graceful girl. తీగమల్లె the creeping Jasmine. **తీగమెరుగు** *tīga-merugu*. n. Lightning without thunder ఉరుములేని మెఱుపు. A sort of grain. **తీగమోడి** *tīga-*

mōḍi. n. Patterns of flourishes or carved work in carpentry. త్రాతుని. ముత్తెములు తీగజాడిక్కుట్టె పనులు embroidery in the fashion of sprigs of pearl. తీగసాగు tīga-sāgu. v. n. To increase, to prosper వర్ధిల్లు. గారె బాగా తీగలు సాగేదాకను కలిపిరి they mixed the mortar till it was of a proper consistency. తీగలుసాగు to spread వ్యాపించు. తీగవిలుకాడు an epithet of Manmadha. తీగసరులు a kind of rice ధాన్యవిశేషము.

తీట tīṭa. [Tel.] n. Itching, smarting. దురద. Itch గజ్జి. Inclination, lust, liking. తీటకోపల or తీటుకసింద tīṭa-kōrila. n. Cowach, *Dolichos pruriens*; కండూర.

తీడిరించు tīḍirintsu. [Tel. another form of తిండ్రించు.] v. n. To shine. ప్రకాశించు.

తీడు tīḍu. [Tel.] v. t. To sharpen. వాడిచేయు. To trim or prune, as a bird does its feathers with its beak. To gnash the teeth or bite the lips in rage. మీసాలుతీడి twisting his mustaches.

తీతకోత tīta-kōta. [Tel. from తీయు and కోయు.] n. Gleaning and reaping.

తీతువ or తీతువు tītuva. [Tel.] The yellow-wattled Lapwing, *Sarciophorus malabaricus*. ఎర్రతీతువ erra-tītuva. n. The Red-wattled Lapwing, *Sarcogrammus indicus*. (F. B. I.)

తీనియ, తిన్నియ, తీనె or తిన్నె tīniya. n. A stone bench, a pial అరుగు.

తీపి or తీపు tīpi. [Tel.] n. Sweetness. Love, liking ఇచ్ఛ. A pang, throbbing pain [illegible]. adj. Sweet మధురము. తీపిపుట్టించు tīpi-puṭṭintsu. v. t. To give an appetite, or sharpen the inclination. తీపిఉలవ or తల్లిఉలవి or ఉలవతుంటి tīpi-ulavi. n. A kind of fish, *Rhynchobatus djeddensis* (F. B. I.) తీపుత్రాడు a sweetened string for catching birds with. తీపురము tīpu-ramu. n. A joke. ఆగడము.

తీయన or తియ్యన tīyana. [Tel.] n. Sweetness.

తీయని tīyani. [Tel.] v. Neg. p. of తీయు adj. sweet. తియ్యని, తీపుగల.

తీయము tīyamu. [Tel. another form of తియ్యము.] n. Wish, desire. ప్ర. M. v. i. 40, XII. ii. 8.

తీయు tīyu. [Tel.] v. a. To take. To draw out, take out, extract. తివుచు. To open, excavate, dig. To deduct, take away, subtract. To find (a place in a book), to discover, bring to light. To turn out, discharge, remove. To exact, receive (payment). To collect, gather, levy as a tax, a fine, పన్ను, శిస్తు, అపరాధము మొ॥ తీయు. To pull off, take off. To extinguish or put out. To buy. కొను. See తీసికొను. దెబ్బతీయు to give a blow. చెరువుతీయు, బావితీయు, to sink or dig a well or tank. పాతరతీయు to open a pit or granary. పాలుతీయు to milk. జాడతీయు to trace, detect. చేదీయు to draw towards, to patronise, take into one's service, to embrace. సానదీయు to whet on a stone. గోళ్లుతీయు to cut the nails. త్రోవతీయు to clear the way, to prepare a path. అగౌరవపరచిరి they disgraced him. తాళముతీయు to unlock. తలుపుతీయు to open a door. విడదీయు to loosen or separate. వేరుగాతీయు to separate. ఎండ కంచు తీసినట్టు కాస్తున్నది the sun is as dazzling as (though reflected from) polished metal. తీయు v. n. To go off, cease, diminish, disappear, be dispelled, intermit, desist from. To draw back, withdraw, retire, stand aside. To contract, shrivel, crack, open, split. జ్వరము తీసినది the fever went down. వెన్నుతీయు to come forth, or be produced (as a sprout,) to bud. కాళ్లు తీయుచున్నవి my legs throb or ache. ఏరు తీసిపోయినది the river has gone down. వెనుక తీయు to fail, retire, withdraw, retreat, hesitate, or flinch. నాలుక పీకినది my tongue is dry, I am thirsty. వాని ఒళ్లు మిక్కిలి తీసిపోయినది he is greatly fallen away in flesh. నీళ్లు తీసిపోవు to dry up, sink, diminish, be exhausted. బలమంతా తీసిపోయినది my strength has gone.

తీసె యున్నది the granary was opened. తీరక unintermittingly, without intermission. తెంకతీరక without hesitation. తీరుకుండా unfailingly, uninterruptedly, without intermission. తీరని incessant, unceasing.

తీయించు *tiyinṭsu.* v. a. To cause to remove, get removed. తీసివేయు *tīsi-vēyu.* v. t. To take away. To dismiss. To sever ఖండించు. తీసివేత కాకితాలు *tīsi-vēta-kākitālu.* n. Outside sheets of paper: paper that is taken away. తీసిపోవు *tīsi-pōvu.* v. n. To diminish. తగ్గు. తీసుక for తీసుకొని bringing. తీసుకరా bring. తీసుకపో take away. తీసికొను or తీసుకొను *tīsi-konu.* v. a. To take, &c.; to buy; to eat or drink, &c. పనితీసుకొను to exact service. వాడు చాలాదినములనుంచి తీసుకొంటున్నాడు he has been lingering for a long time. దండముతీసుకొన్నాను he acknowledged or accepted the salutation.

తీరము *tīramu.* [Skt.] n. A shore, bank, edge, brink. దరి.

తీరు *tīru.* [Tel.] v. n. To end, stop, cease, elapse. To be finished, ended, complete, or ready. To be paid, delivered, discharged, avenged. To be qualified, accomplished, finished, adorned, trim, decked. To be gratified, satiated, wreaked (as passion;) to be assuaged or allayed, to go off. ముగియు, చక్కబడు. తనివితీర to the full: so as to satisfy one's desires. తీరలేదు it came to nothing, it was ineffectual. కోరికతీర having gained his end. ఇది నాచేత తీరదు this is out of my power. నాకు తీరికలేక ఉన్నది I am hardly at leisure. తీరిపోవు to die. To be practicable, or possible. అక్కడికి రాతీరదు I cannot come there, I have not leisure to come. రాకుండా తీరదు (you) must positively come. వెళ్లక తీరదు I cannot help going. తీరనకుండాపోగా న్నాడు he is quite hackneyed. తీరా *tīra.* (Root in A of తీరు, with the intensive affix ఆ) adv. Ultimately, at last; fairly; just, merely, in short, simply. తీరా మధ్యాహ్నమయ్యేటప్పటికి when it was high noon. ఆ గోడ తీరా పడ్డది the wall actually fell down. తీరా పండుకొని నిద్రపోయేటప్పటికి when he was fairly asleep. ఆ సంగతి తీరా బయటపడేటప్పటికి when the matter at last became known. తీరా చెల్లించెను he paid it in full. తీరిక or తీరీక *tīrika.* n. Leisure. పనితీరక యుండడుండుట. తీరకలిక్కుక having no leisure. Adorning, trimming, decoration. సిద్ధము. తీరిన *tīrina.* adj. Full, finished, accomplished, cured, settled. తీరు n. Manner, way, mode, fashion, style, arrangement, విధము. Beauty చక్కన. వాడు ఒకతీరుమనిషి he is an odd man. వాడు ఒకతీరుగానున్నాడు he is but so and so, he is not well, he is not at ease. ఈ తీరు thus. తీరుతప్పి ఉన్నాడు it is all over with him. తీరుగా *tīrugā.* adv. Properly, duly, aright. దాని ముక్కుకండ్లు తీరుగానున్నవి her nose and eyes are pretty. తీరుగడ or తీరువల *tīru-gaḍa.* n. Ending. ముగియుట. తీరుపు or తీర్పు *tīrupu.* n. End, finishing. A decision, judgment, sentence, decree. తీర్పుచెప్పెను he gave his decision. Justice. న్యాయము. Setting right చక్కబాటు. తీరుపరి or తీర్పరి *tīrup-ari.* n. A judge. న్యాయాధిపతి. An agent or ambassador రాయబారి. A superintendent. అధికారి, కార్యనిర్వాహకుడు. తీరుపడు to be destroyed నశించు. తీరుబడి *tīru-baḍi.* n. Leisure. సావకాశము. తీరుపాటు *tīru-pāṭu.* n. A settlement, payment. Leisure. తీరుపాటుగానుండే unoccupied, at leisure. తీరుమానము or తీర్మానము *tīru-mānamu.* n. An ending, settlement, rectification. Pause. A decision, resolve. తీరుమానించు or తీర్మానించు to settle, to come to a decision. తీరువ *tīruva.* n. A settlement, discharge, payment. Duty, dues, fees. కడ్డతీరువ levelling the ground. తీరువ వేయు or తీరువకట్టు to levy a fee or contribution. తీరువజాస్తి *tīruva-jāsti.* [H.] n. An additional or supplementary assessment నిర్ణయించబడిన పన్నుకంటె ప్రాగా

కట్టినపన్ను. తీర్చు, తీరుచు, తీరుపు or తీర్చు *tīrtsu*. v. a. To end, finish. To do with, accomplish, perform or play (his part,) go through. ముగించు. To order, arrange. చక్కబెట్టు. To cool, quiet, assuage. To adjust, liquidate (a debt). To trim, deck, adorn, straighten, correct, rectify, regulate. దిద్దు. To set, place, draw (as the mark on the forehead). To pass (time, day, or night). To pay, give or issue (wages or batta). To settle. To determine, to resolve, to decide. To do away with. పోగొట్టు, తొలగించు. To destroy నాశముచేయు. కాకిపనముతీర్చినది the crow gave a good omen (by crossing my path from left to right.) కోపముతీర్చు to revenge oneself, wreak one's anger. చలముతీర్చు, పగతీర్చు to satiate spite. దాహముతీర్చు to quench thirst. కామతీర్చి satiating one's lusts. వాని పని తీర్చినారు they settled his business or they ruined him. తీర్చుకొను *tīrtsu-konu*. v. a. To end, do away with. To settle or pay up as a debt, &c. తీర్పించు *tīrpintsu*. v. a. To cause to decide, or determine.

తీర్థము *tīrthamu*. [Skt.] n. Water. ఉదకము. Holy or sacred water. పుణ్యోదకము. A holy place. పుణ్యక్షేత్రము. తీర్థమాడు to bathe స్నానముచేయు; to be brought to bed. తీర్థము ఇప్పించు to swear a witness; because the oath is administered with holy water. తీర్థయాత్రపోవు to go on pilgrimage. In theological works తీర్థము means salvation, మోక్షము and కుతీర్థము is false doctrine. తీర్థమాడుట or తీర్థమాట *tīrtham-āduta*. n. Bathing. స్నానము. తీర్థవాసి *tīrtha-vāsi*. n. A pilgrim. తీర్థసేవచేయువాడు. తీర్థీకరించు *tīrthī-karintsu*. v. a. To sanctify, hallow, purify.

తీర్పరి or తీరుపరి *tīrpari*. See under తీరు.

తీర్పు or తీరుపు *tīrpu*. See under తీరు.

తీలు *tīlu*. [Tel.] n. The state of being low, lowliness, poorness, deficiency. అడకము.

తీలగు or తీలువడు *tīl-agu*. v. n. To become little or poor, to be humble or lowly అడగు.

తీవ Same as తీగ. (q. v.)

తీవంచ *tī-vancha*. [Tel. తీగ+వంచ] n. (At dice.) Trois ace, i. e., four.

తీవరము *tīvaramu*. [from Skt. తీవ్రము]. n. Haste, speed. Intensity. త్వరితము. adj. Hurried, hasty, rapid. Intense, scorching. తీవరించు or తీవరపడు *tīvarintsu*. v. n. To hurry. త్వరితపడు. త్వరపడు. తీవరుడు *tīvarudu*. n. A fisherman. వలచేత జీవించేవాడు.

తీవియ or తీవె *tīviya*. Same as తీగ. (q. v.)

తీవిరము *tīviramu*. [Tel.] n. Itching. తీట.

తీవ్రము or తీవ్రత *tīvramu*. [Skt.] n. Speed, quickness, sharpness, heat. adj. Much. అధికము. Hot వేడిమిగల, కాకముగల.

తు tu

తుంకి *tunki*. [Tel.] n. A certain tree. H. iv. 18.

తుంగ or తుంగగడ్డి *tunga*. [Tel.] n. A kind of coarse grass or bulrush. adj. Made of bulrush. ఒక తుంగకాడ తీసుకరా bring me a bulrush. Ainslie ii. 162. తేమగడతుంగ *Agrostis tenacissima*. గరిడితుంగ *Cyperus tenuiflorus*. కర్రతుంగ *C. spinulosus*. కోడు తుంగ *C. seminudus*. కొండతుంగ *C. dubius*. పాలతుంగ *C. compressus*. నాగతుంగ *C. rotundus*. కసితుంగ *Scirpus bispicatus*. ముక్కాలితుంగ *S. tridentatus*. బుడ్డతుంగ *S. maximus*. గొందితుంగ *S. articulatus*. ఛత్రతుంగగడ్డి of which the Sanskrit synonym is గుచ్ఛీల్లం. తుంగముస్తె *tunga-muste*. n. A pignut, or earthnut.

తుంగము *tungamu*. [Skt.] adj. Great, lofty. పొడవైన. Large, full. తుంగభద్ర *tunga-bhadra*. n. The river Tungabhadra. తుంగవృక్షము *tunga-vrikshamu*. n. The tree named *Rottleria tinctoria*. వసంతగంధము. Rox. iii. 827.

తుంగు or **త్రుంగు** *tungu*. [Tel.] v. n. To break to pieces. తునకలగు. Waste away, sink, be ruined, నశించు. **తుంచు, త్రుంచు** or **తుంపు** *tuntsu*. v. a. To break. త్రుంగ జేయు. To pluck, nip, pull (as flowers or fruit); slay. తలద్రుంచు to behead, tear చించు. See తుంపు.

తుంట *tunṭa*. [Tel.] n. A bit, piece, fragment, splinter. తునక. A staff or cudgel, A spar or rafter. A sugarcane: చెరకు. ఇనపకట్లతుంట an iron-bound cudgel. మూల తుంటదూలలు short rafters at the corners of a roof. తుంటవిలుకాడు Manmadha, whose bow is made of the sugar cane. తుంటనరికిన చిరువేరు Dye-root cut off from the plant. adj. Wicked, naughty, mischievous. **తుంటతనము** *tunṭatanamu*. n. Wickedness, mischievousness, naughtiness. **తుంటరి** *tunṭari*. (తుంట+అరి.) n. A wicked person. దుష్టుడు.

తుంటి *tunṭi*. [Tel.] n. The hip or loin. కటి పార్శ్వభాగము, రొండి.

తుంటికూర or **తూటికూర** Same as తోటకూర. (q. v.)

తుండము *tunḍamu*. [Skt. & Tel.] n. The face. ముఖము; the mouth నోరు; a bird's beak, పక్షిముక్కు; an elephant's trunk, తొండము. The pipe or hose of a fire engine. A bit, a fragment. ఖండము. Zaco. VI. 93. వానదేవునకుతుండములాగున కురిసినది the rain fell in torrents. **తుండి** *tunḍi*. n. A projecting navel. ఉదరనాభి. తుండిభుడు, తుండిభుడు, తుండిలుడు or తుండిలుడు one who has a projecting navel. **తుండించు** *tunḍintsu*. v. a. To cut to pieces. To sever. ఖండించు, ఛేదించు. **తుండు, తుండె** or **తుండెము** *tunḍu*. n. A bit, a piece. ఖండము, తునక. A plot of ground. A block of wood, a piece of timber, a short beam. తుండుగా విడిచిపెట్టిన unfinished, incomplete.

తుందము *tundamu*. [Skt.] n. The belly. కడుపు, ఉదరము, కుక్షి. **తుంది** *tundi*. adj. Potbellied. బొజ్జకడుపుగలవాడు. **తుందిలము** *tundilamu*. n. A sort of vegetable, *Bignonia indica*. పంచపాకశాకము. **తుందిలుడు** or **తుందిలుడు** *tundiluḍu*. adj. Big-bellied, pot-bellied. దయాతుందిలుడు one who has bowels of compassion.

తుందుడుకు *tunduḍuku*. [Tel. తుదుకు+ తుదుకు.] n. Remorse, పశ్చాత్తాపము. Sorrow విచారము. Confusion కలత, క్షోభము. Temerity, foolhardiness. Tottering, shaking, motion. Uncertainty, changeableness. తొట్రుపాటు, దుడుకు. ఉద్వేగపడము, ఉద్రేకము, ఉల్లాసము. "తుదయుదిగాదటంచనిన, తుందుడుకేటికి పొమ్మయంటికిన్." UH. iv. 183.

తుందునుకలు *tundunukalu*. [Tel. తునుకలు+ తునుకలు.] n. Little bits. చిన్నచిన్న ఖండములు.

తుంపర or **తుంపురు** *tumpara*. [Tel.] n. A little drop, a sprinkling, a splutter. **తుంపిల్లు** *tumpillu*. n. A slight shower of rain. తూరవాన.

తుంపు or **త్రుంపు** *tumpu*. [Tel. from తుంచు.] v. n. To nip, to cut, to pluck. తుంచు. తునుకు నట్లుచేయు. A. vi. 24. n. A bit or fragment. ఖండము.

తుంపెసలు *tumpesalu*. [Tel. Connected with తుంచు.] n. Movement. చలనము. **తుంపెసలాడు** or **తుంపెసలుగునడయు** *tumpesal-āḍu*. v. n. To dance, as tresses; to be agitated, to palpitate, throb or tremble. నటించు, నర్తించు, చలించు, ఆడు, ఊగాడు. "కొరలతొగకుచ్చముల్ తుంపెసలాడ." Parij. ii. 9.

తుంపొడి *tum-poḍi*. [Tel.] n. The bittern: so named from its call, which sounds like *tump, tump*.

తుంబము, తుంబి, తుంబిక or **తుమ్మి** *tumbamu*.

[Skt.] n. A gourd vine. సొరచెట్టు. ఆనుగ చెట్టు. The belly of the lute. వీణకాయ, తుంబీఫలము a gourd.

తుంబిక *tumbika.* [Skt.] n. The central hole in the wheel of a carriage through which the axle passes. బండిచక్రము నడిమిరంధ్రము.

తుకతుక *tuka-tuka.* [Tel.] n. Ebullition. ఉడుకుటయందు ధ్వన్యనుకరణము. Closeness. Sorrow సంతాపము. Anger కోపము. అంబలి తుకతుకమని ఉడుకుచున్నది the porridge is boiling aloud.

తుకము *tukamu.* [Tel.] n. An estimate of the seed sown in a field. విత్తనాలచల్లకపును కింపు, లేక అంచనా. తుకముచూచు to value or estimate a field.

తుకాటము *tukaṭamu.* [Tel.] adj. Very old. మిక్కిలి పాతది.

తుకిడీ *tukiḍi.* [H.] n. A district, a division. A part, piece.

తుక్కు *tukku.* [Tel.] n. Rubbish, trash. Nonsense. తుక్కుగుడ్డలు rags. తుక్కుగడ్డి mouldy hay. తుక్కురేగగొట్టు to beat one black and blue. **తుక్కుడు** *tukkuḍu.* adj. Worthless. పనికిమాలిన. **తుక్కుమూక** *tukku-mūka.* n. A rabble, a mob.

తుచ్ఛము *tuchchhamu.* [Skt.] adj Base, low, contemptible. నీచమైన. Groundless, false. తూన్యము. తుచ్ఛాసనము a mean or degraded seat. **తుచ్ఛుడు** *tuchchhuḍu.* n. A mean or low man.

తుజోగు *tuḍzugu.* [Tel.] n. A hasty man. త్వరపడువాడు.

తుటాయించు or **తుటారించు** *tuṭāyintsu.* [Tel.] v. t. To disregard. అలక్ష్యపరుచు. To scorn. తిరస్కరించు. **తుటారము** *tuṭāramu.* n. Firmness, boldness, forwardness. దిట్టతనము. A harsh word పరుష వచనము. **తుటారి** or **తుటారికత్తె** *tuṭāri.* n. A beauty, a darling. A bold or forward woman. ధీర, తిరస్కరించేస్త్రీ. "భువనపావన నర్తలుబల్లటారి." H. v. 2. **తుటారికాడు** *tuṭāri-kāḍu.* n. A bold or forward man.

తుటుక్కు *tuṭukku.* [Tel.] (anuk.) adv. At once. n. Palpitation of the heart.

తుటుము *tuṭumu.* [Tel.] n. An assembly, a crowd. A flock or flight, a line or series: a clump of trees: a row of houses గుంపు, వరుస. "తుటుములైకుకదంపతులుంచరించు." Vedanta Ras ii. 17.

తుట్ట, తుట్టెయు or **తుట్టె** *tuṭṭa.* [Tel.] n. A crowd or multitude. పుంజము, సమూహము. A. iv. 17. 21. A flake of fire. తుట్టలేయు to breed quarrels.

తుట్టతుద *tuṭṭa-tuda.* [Tel. తుది+తుద.] n. The very end, the finale. కేవలము తుద.

తుట్టమర or **తుట్టుమర** *tuṭṭa-mara.* [Tel.] adv. Wholly, entirely, completely, radically. బొత్తిగా.

తుట్టు *tuṭṭu.* [Tel.] n. Loss, failure in mercantile profits. నష్టి. ఈ వ్యవహారములో నా సొమ్ము తుట్టుపెట్టుకొన్నాను I incurred loss in this business. One who destroys నాశకుడు.

తుట్టె *tuṭṭe.* [Tel.] n. Trash, odds and ends, stuff, rubbish. A lump ఉండ. A cluster గుంపు, సమూహము. ఈ పిండి తుట్టెకట్టిపోయినది this meal has run into lumps. తుట్టెతోడిచేరు rough *chay* root that is uncleaned. See తుట్ట. **తుట్టెపురుగు** *tuṭṭe-purugu.* n. A sort of venomous snake barred black and grey.

"ఈ తుట్టెపురుగులేమను
నీకేటివచ్చినవుడు."
రామా. viii.

తుత్రు or **తుట్టుర** *tutra.* [Tel.] (anuk.) n. A drizzle. తూరవాన. తుక్కుతుత్రు a heap of sweepings, ఊడ్చినకుప్ప. Dirt and rubbish.

తుత్రుమర Same as తుట్టమర. (q. v.)

తుడుచు or **తుడ్చు** *tuḍutsu.* [Tel.] v. a. To wipe away (as water or tears.) To blot తడిపోవనొత్తు. To sweep ఊడ్చు. **తుడుపు** *tuḍupu.* n. Rubbing, wiping, smearing, blotting, erasure, తుడుచుట. cf. "ఎగదుడుపు దిగదుడుపు." తుడుపుబల్ల a wooden plank with which salt is collected into a heap.

తుడుము *tuḍumu*. [Tel.] n. A kind of drum. తుడుముకాడు a drummer.

తుతార *tutāra*. [Tel.] n. A kind of trumpet. ఒక ఊదువాద్యము.

తుత్తము or తుత్తరము. *tuttamu*. [Tel.] n. Vitriol. పాలతుత్తము white vitriol, sulphate of zinc. మైలతుత్తము sulphate of copper, blue-stone.

తుత్తి, తుత్తిచెట్టు or తుత్తిరిచెట్టు *tutti*. [Tel.] n. The country mallow, Marsh mallow. *Sida populifoliis*. నూగుబెండ. (Rox. iii. 179.) అడవితుత్తిరిచెట్టు *Sida kerta*. (Rottler.) తుత్తిరాకు mallow leaf. తుత్తిరిచెల్లపాకు a species of the same. See under బెండ.

తుత్తినాగము *tutti-nāgamu*. [Chinese] n. Pewter. Zinc. లోహవిశేషము.

తుత్తుంభిక *tuttumbhika*. [Skt.] n. A sort of drum. H. iii. 88.

తుత్తునియలు *tuttuniyalu*. [Tel. తునియలు+తునియలు.] n. Very small bits. చిన్నచిన్న తునకలు. తుత్తునియలగు or తుత్తునకలగు v. n. To go to pieces. తుత్తునకలుచేయు *tuttunukalu-chēyu*. v. a. To shiver or smash. తుత్తునకలయిన gone to pieces. తుత్తునియలుగా piecemeal.

తుత్తుమురు *tuttumuru*. [Tel. తుమురు+తుమురు.] n. Bits, fragments. Fine powder ముక్కలిపొడి. తుత్తుమురై broken to pieces or to bits. తుత్తుమురుగాచేయు to break to pieces, to cut to bits.

తుత్థ *tuttha*. [Skt.] n. The indigo plant. నీలిచెట్టు. H. ii. 248. తుత్థాంజనము *tuttha-anjanamu*. n. Blue-stone, sulphate of copper. మయిలతుత్తము.

తుద or తుది *tuda*. [Tel.] n. The end, the point, the tip. చివర, కడ, అగ్రము, అంతము. Death చావు. తుదకు, తుదను or తుద at last, in the end, in short. In the next place. తుదముట్టు or తుదిముట్టు *tuda-muṭṭu*. v. a. To finish, reach the end. To die చచ్చు. తుదముట్ట to the end. తుదిని at the end; తుదిరేయి lit: the last night, i. e., the end of the Kalpa Yuga కల్పాంతము. తుదివాడు the last man. కడపటివాడు, కనిష్ఠుడు.

తునక or తునుక *tunaka*. [Tel. from తునియు.] n. A bit or piece.

తునికోల *tuni-kōla*. [Tel. తూనిక+కోల.] n. A steelyard: తూచుకట్టికోల. Also, a stick used by toddy drawers to sharpen their knives on, or to carry the toddy vessels on.

తునియు *tuniyu*. [Tel.] v. n. To go to pieces, తునుగు. To be cut to pieces, be severed or broken. ఖండితమగు. v. a. To cut or break to pieces. తునియ *tuniya*. n. A bit, a piece, a fragment. See తునుక.

తుంటి *tunṭi*. [Tel. corruption of తునియ] n. A bed in a salt pan. మడి.

తునుగు *tunugu*. [Tel.] v. n. To go to pieces. ముక్కలగు. తునుక or తునక *tunuka*. n. A piece or bit. ముక్క. తునుము, తునుమాడు or తున్మాడు *tunumu*. v. a. To cut or break to pieces. ఖండించు. To smite; to pluck flowers. To slay, rout, or ruin. చంపు. See తునియు.

తుపాకి *tupāki*. [Tel.] n. A gun, a musket, a matchlock. తుపాకికాల్చు to fire a gun. తుపాకికట్టించు to load a gun.

తుపాను *tupānu*. [H.] n. A storm, a cyclone. గాలివాన.

తుపుక్కు *tupukku*. [Tel.] (anuk) n. A sound like that made in spitting. తుపుక్కున ఉమిసినాడు he spat right aloud, audibly.

తుప్ప *tuppa*. [Tel.] n. A bush, a small bush. చిన్నపొద. తుప్పచెట్టు a shrub.

తుప్పతిల్లు *tuppatillu*. [Tel.] v. n. To be satisfied. తనియు.

తుప్పర or తుంపర *tuppara*. [Tel.] n. A drop, a spray. చినుకు.

తుప్పలుదూలు *tuppalu-dūlu*. [Tel. తూలు+ తూలు.] v. n. To shake violently. మిక్కిలి చలించు.

తుప్పు or **త్రుప్పు** *tuppu*. [Tel.] n. Rust (of iron, not of other metals.) Tastelessness. అరుచి. Wool, fleck, worthless hair. గొంగ్రి కోసము. A. vi. 21. (anuk) A noise made in spitting.

తుభము *tubhamu*. [Skt.] n. A ram. మేక పోతు.

తుమికి or **కర్రతుమికిచేవ** *tumiki*. [Tel.] n. Ebony. *Diospyrus glutinosa*. Rox. ii. 533. *Embryopteris glutinifera*. Linn.

తుమురు *tumuru*. [Tel.] n. A small bit, a piece. ముక్కఖండము. తుమురైన broken, shattered, in shivers. See తుత్తుమురు.

తుములము *tumulamu*. [Skt.] n. Confusion, uproar, clamour, a yell. Mass. A melee or mixed fight. కొట్లాయుద్ధము.

తుమ్మ *tumma*. [Tel.] n. The Babul tree. *Acacia arabica*, which produces gum arabic. ముండ్లతుమ్మ the thorny species, Cockspur thorn. నల్లతుమ్మ *Acacia arabica*. తుమ్మజిగురు gum arabic. మురికితుమ్మ, కంపు తుమ్మ or నాగతుమ్మ the Cassia flower tree. *Acacia farnesiana*. పాలితుమ్మ *Acacia latronum*. తెల్లతుమ్మ *Acacia Cucophloea*. కస్తూరి తుమ్మ, చీతుమ్మ *Acacia jamesiana* (E. P.)

తుమ్మి *tummi*. [Tel.] n. A tree, *Phlomis indica*. Rox. iii. p. 9. 10. తుమ్మికూర *tummikūra*. n. A vegetable with a fruit like a mulberry. ఒకవిధమగుకూరాకు. H. iv. 165.

తుమ్మికి Same as తుమికి. (q. v.)

తుమ్ము *tummu*. [Tel.] v. n. To sneeze. n. A sneeze.

తుమ్మెద *tummeda*. [Tel.] n. The large black carpenter bee. భ్రమరము. To clusters of these the poets often compare braided tresses. టెంకాయచెట్టు తుమ్మెద a large beetle that bores holes in the cocoanut tree. తుమ్మెదకొప్పులు a certain game played by boys.

తురంగము, **తురగము** or **తురంగమము** *turangamu*. [Skt. from Turanian √Tur= haste, త్వర. cf. Turk, త్వర & తొర.] n. A horse.

తురంగలించు or **తురగలించు** See under తురగలి.

తురక *turaka*. [Tel. from Turanian √ T =haste, cf. తురంగము, త్వర and తొ .] n. A Turk. A Mahomedan. తురకపిచికపిట్ట a species of పిచికపిట్ట (q. v.) తురకపువ్వు *turaka-puvvu*. n. A sort of flower. The marigold. బంతిపువ్వు. తురకరాయి laterite జాంతిరాయి. తురకవేప a species of margosa tree with very large leaves. తురకాణ్యము *turakāṇyamu*. Musulman rule. తురకాణ్యపువారు the Musulmans. తురికి *turiki*. (from తురుష్కుడు.) n. A horse.

"క. తితికంఠసుతుడు తురగ
స్తుతుడై యాయచ్ఛరూపుతురికిని వాహ్యా-
ళితఘాటితకల్లత కే
చితవల్గితగతుల దరటుసేవిన నడిచెరున్."
పాండు. i.

తురగము Same as తురంగము. (q. v.) **తురగి** *turagi*. [Skt.] n. A horse. R. i. 78. A horseman, a cavalier. W.

తురగలి *turagali*. [Tel.] n. Brightness. ప్రకాశము. **తురంగలించు**, **తురగలించు** or **తురగలించు** *turangalintsu*. v. n. To gleam, sparkle. ప్రకాశించు. Swa. iii. 42. To excel అతిశయించు.

తురా or **తురాయి** *turā*. [Tel.] n. A bouquet, a nosegay, పూబంతి. A feather, a crest. శిఖమందుచెక్కు ధూమా దికేమము.

తురాషాహుడు *tura-shāhudu*. [Skt from Turanian √Tur = haste.] n. A queller of demons. A title of Indra or Jupiter, the "Titan-queller."

తురి *turi*. [Skt.] n. A cotton mill with spindles. కండెలుంచిరోసేయంత్రము, వా.

తురికి See under తురక.

తురితము Same as త్వరితము (q. v.)

తురిమణిచెట్టు *turimaṇi-chețțu.* [Tel.] n. A certain medicinal plant. రాజదూలి or తెల్ల పొన్న.

తురీన or తుర్రున *turina.* [Tel. from Turanian ✓ Tur = haste.] adv. Suddenly. తటాలున. "తురీనలేచునట్టి తోడదోప." దు. iii.

తురీయము *turiyamu.* [Skt.] adj. Fourth, చతుర్థము. ఆయన తురీయాశ్రమ స్వీకారము చేసినాడు he entered upon the fourth estate, i. e., the hermit life.

తురుంభము *turumbhamu.* [Skt.] n. Tresses adorned with flowers. పువ్వులు ముడిచిన కొప్పు.

తురుగు or తురగు *turugu.* [Tel.] v. a. To insert, stick in, as flowers, to cram in. క్రుక్కు. To gag by thrusting a cloth into the mouth. To caulk (a ship.) ఓడకు లప్పము తేరుచు.

తురుటు *turuțu.* [Tel. from Turanian ✓ Tur = haste.] n. Quickness. త్వరితము, చేసరపాటు. adj. Quick. శీఘ్రము. తురుటుగా rapidly, quickly. తురుటుతిర్పు *turuțu-tirpu.* n. Quick time in music. ద్రుతలయ.

తురుపు or తురుఫు *turupu.* [Eng. 'trump' & 'troop.'] n. A trump at cards. A troop of cavalry. గుర్రపుదండు.

తురుము *turumu.* [Tel.] n. Powder. పొడుము. Braided hair or tresses. కొప్పు. v. a. To cram, or stick: to thrust in. To adjust, trim, deck the head with flowers. కొప్పు గాముడుచు, కొప్పునదోపు. To grate, pound, reduce to powder or to chips పొడిచేయు. వాని నోట్లో గుడ్డతురిమి కొట్టినారు they thrust a handkerchief into his mouth to beat him. తురుముపీట *turuma-pīța.* n. A crooked knife with teeth at the end used to scoop out a cocoanut, &c. తురుముటకు కనుపుగా చివరను పండ్లేర్పరచిన వంకర యినుప కత్తిచెక్కిన పీట.

తురుష్కుడు *turushkuḍu.* [Skt. from the Turanian ✓ తూర్ = haste. cf. తురంగము, తురగ. త్వర, and తొర.] n. A "Turk," or Musulman. తురుష్కము *turushkamu.* n. Turkey.

తుర్యము or తురీయము *turyamu.* [Skt.] adj. Fourth. నాలుగవది. తుర్యావస్థ eternal bliss, being the fourth state; death. మోక్షము, సమాధి. తుర్యప్రకృతి *turya-prakriti.* n. Passionateness, hastiness. A jovial jolly disposition.

తుర్రు *turru.* [Tel. inflection తుర్తి.] n. A village or hamlet. cf. మొగిలితుర్రు Mogilitūr. మామిల్లదుర్రు Mamildūr. పొట్లదుర్రు. infl. పొట్లదుర్తి.

తుర్రు *turru.* [Tel.] n. Haste. చేసరపాటు. adv. Quickly. తుర్రుమని *turru-m-ani.* adv. Rapidly, hurriedly.

తుల *tula.* [Skt.] n. A balance, scales. The sign Libra. త్రాసు. Resemblance, similarity. పోలిక. Equality. సమానము. The measurement round a heap of grain. తులాగ్రములు the measurement of a heap of grain with a cord both over the top (తుల) and round the bottom (అగ్ర). తులదూగు *tula-dūgu.* v. n. To weigh, in a balance, be heavy. To be opulent. R. iv. 60. తులాభారము *tula-bhāramu.* n. A royal donation, according to which a prince is weighed against gold and jewels, which he then distributes as charity. తులాయష్టి *tula-yashți.* n. Scales for weighing.

తులకించు *tulakintsu.* [Tel.] v. a. To seem, rival, resemble. To shine. ప్రకాశించు. To rejoice సంతోషపడుచు. తులకింపు *tula-kimpu.* n. Semblance, seeming. Brightness ప్రకాశము.

తులము *tulamu.* [Tel.] n. A weight, (usually called a tola) being the weight of one rupee; or a సవరాకు or palam. The tola of gold is usually worth sixteen rupees.

తులసి or తొలసి *tulasi.* [Skt.] n. The Sacred Basil, *Ocymum sanctum.* This plant is sacred to Vishṇu as the బిల్వ

is to Siva. Various species are called రామతులసి (Ocymum guatissimum), నేల తులసి (Rox. iii. 17 18.), విష్ణుతులసి, భూతులసి, and నిమ్మతులసి, కుక్క తులసి. The wild Basil. Ocymum album. తులసివనము or తులసికోట the name given to a flower-pot containing one or two of these plants.

తులాంబరము *tulāmbaramu.* [Skt.] n. Muslin or cambric. R. ii. 107.

తులాకోటి *tulā-kōti.* [Skt.] n. A bell worn on the ankles. అందె, నూపురము.

తులితము *tulitamu.* [Skt.] adj. Equal, similar, rivalling. సరిపోల్చబడిన. Weighed తూచబడిన.

తులుచ *tulutsa.* [Tel.] adj. Swift. వేగముగల. **తులుచన** *tulutsana.* n. Swiftness.

తులుపర్ర or **తులులు** *tuluparra.* [Tel.] n. A species of fish: *Scomber, Cyprinus chorinemus.* Russell. No. 137, 138, 140, 208. A sort of sprat or Sardine.

తులువ *tuluva.* [Tel.] n. A wretch, a villain, a scoundrel. కుత్సితుడు, తుంటరి, పనికిమాలిన వాడు, తులువమనిషి. n. A rake, a scamp. adj. Vile, abominable, light or worthless. కుత్సితమైన. **తులువతనము** *tuluva-tanamu.* n. Villainy, wickedness. తులువకత్తి a large crooked knife. వంపుచురకత్తి.

తుల్యము *tulyamu.* [Skt.] adj. Equal to, answering to; matching, comparable with. Like, similar to. సమము, సరి. **తుల్యుడు** *tulyuḍu.* n. One who is equal. సమానుడు.

తుళుకరించు, తులుకరించు or **తులుకాడు** *tulukarintsu.* [Tel.] v. n To shine. To be splendid. ప్రకాశించు. Dasav. viii. 103.

తుళువదేశము *tuluva-dēsamu.* [Tel.] n. The ancient name of the country about Vijayanaggur. of. The *Tulu language.*

తుళ్లు or **త్రుళ్లు** *tullu.* [Tel.] v. n. To frisk, to be elated or puffed up. To writhe. To be conceited మిడిసిపడు. తుళ్లినదొడ్డు గంతె మోయదా must not a frisky bull bear a pack? (prov.) i.e., Pride must have a fall. తుళ్లిపడ్డాడు he tossed his head. n. Glee, friskiness, flow of spirits: exultation, pride. **తుళ్లించు** or **త్రుళ్లించు** *tullintsu.* v. a. To spoil with fondness. To cause to boil over (with rage), to be agitated. ఎగసిపడజేయు.

తువరము *tuvaramu.* [Skt.] n. Astringency. ఒగరు. **తువరి** *tuvari.* n. The grain called pigeon pea. కందులు.

తువాల or **తువాలు** *tuvāla.* [Eng. 'towel.'] n. A towel. చేతిగుడ్డ.

తువాళించు or **దువాళించు** *tuvāḷintsu.* [Tel.] v. n. To leap, to dance. తాండవించు, గంతు లువేయు. Kuchēlo. iii. 4. H. i. 71.

తువ్వ *tuvva.* [Tel.] n. A calf. దూడ. A child's word for water. నీళ్లు. **తువ్వ** or **తుస్స నేల** *tuvva.* n. A sandy ash coloured soil. ఒగర్రనేల.

తువ్వర *tuvvara.* [Tel.] n. Drizzling rain, mizzle, sprinkling. తూర, తుపర, తుంపర, తుప్పర.

తుషము *tushamu.* [Skt.] n. Husk or chaff. ఊక. తుషమాత్రము mere chaff.

తుషారము *tushāramu.* [Skt.] n. Dew, snow, mist. మంచు. Small drops, a sprinkling. తుంపర. adj. Cool. చల్లని.

తుష్టి *tushṭi.* [Skt.] n. Satisfaction, fulness. సంతోషము. Profit or advantage. లాభము. ఆ నష్టికి ఈ తుష్టికి సరి this profit and that loss are equivalent. **తుష్టుడు** *tushṭuḍu.* n. One who is full or satisfied. సంతోషము పొందినవాడు.

తుసుకు, తుసుక్కు or **తుస్సు** *tusuku.* [Tel. (anuk.)] n. Suddenness. **తుసుక్కున** *tusukk-ana.* adv. Suddenly.

తుస్స or **తుస్సి** (నేల) Same as తువ్వనేల. (q. v.)

తుహినము *tuhinamu.* [Skt] n. Dew, snow or hoarfrost. హిమము, మంచు. **తుహినకరుడు** *tuhina-karuḍu.* n. Lit. One whose beams are dewy., i. e., the moon. చల్లిబెలుగు.

తూ tū

తూ tū. [Tel.] Interj. Fie! ఛీఛీ. The sound of a trumpet. తూగొమ్ము tū-gommu. n. A trumpet.

తూకము or తూకం tūkamu. [Tel.] n. A make-weight: a poise or balancing weight used to keep a yoke, &c., steady. An attempt, undertaking, trial ప్రయత్నం. See తూగు.

"వాని తూకంబుల్ సడిసేయులాకసమునన్
మూలంబులైతూలగా."

వై. vii.

తూకముచేయు to weigh. తూకుచేయు to hang (a person).

తూకి tūki. [Tel.] n. A sort of wood like ebony. H. iv. 18.

తూకు tūku. [Tel.] n. Time. ఒక తూకు once. Kalah. iii. 66. See తూకము. తూకొను tū-konu. (తూకు+కొను.) v. n. To take, receive, to carry. To undertake, to try ప్రయత్నం. తూకొను (తూరు+కొను.) v. n. To enter. చొచ్చు.

తూగాడు tū-gāḍu. [తూగు+ఆడు.] v. n. Same as తూగు. (q. v.)

తూగు tūgu. [Tel.] v. n. To nod. To bow down, to be weighed down. To weigh తూనికపడు. To move or rock backwards and forwards. ఊగు, చలించు. To be paid or got. To sleep. నిద్రించు. To be carried on నడచు. సరితూగు to be equal in weight, to rival in excellence. పచ్చిమిరపకాయలకన్న ఎండుమిరపకాయలు నిండా తూగును dried chillies weigh heavier than the green ones. ఆ రూకలు తూగిరాక as he could not obtain payment. పనితూగకపోయెను the work was not carried through. n. Nodding: moving backwards and forwards; equipoise. ఊగుట. Weight. బరువు. Drowsiness, sleepiness. కూరుకుపాటు. సరితూగుల చరుకు ten carats weight of diamonds. నాకు తూగువచ్చున్నది I am drowsy. తూగించు tūgintsu. v. a. To accomplish, to carry through. తూగుమంచము or తూగుటుయ్యెల tūgu-mantsamu. n. A swinging cot, a cradle ఊయెలమంచము. తూగుబాదు or తూగుదు the animal called a sloth.

తూచాతప్పకచదువు tū-cha-tappaka-tsaduvu. [Tel. Derived from Sanskrit conjunctions తు if & చ and.] v. n. To read without missing (a single syllable) an *if* or an *and*. ఇది తూచాతప్పక తున్నది this fitted him to a T or exactly.

తూచు tūtsu. [Tel. from తూగు.] v. t. To weigh. తూకవేయు, తూనికవేయు.

తూట tūṭa. [Tel.] n. A bit, a fragment. ఖండము. adj. Wicked దుష్టమైన. తూటకట్టు tūṭa-kaṭṭu. v. n. To be cut into pieces. ఖండితమగు. తూటి or తూటరి tūṭa. n. A wicked man.

తూటి or తూటికూర tuṭi. [Tel.] n. A certain herb, తోటకూర. Rox. i. 482. 500.

తూటు tūṭu. [Tel.] n. A hole. చిల్లి, రంధ్రము. తూటుకట్టు, తూటుపడు or తూటుపోవు tūṭu-kaṭṭu. v. n. To be cracked, to have a hole. తూటాడు tūṭ-āḍu. v. a. To bore, to make a hole. రంధ్రముచేయు. To harass బాధించు.

తూడికూర tūḍi-kūra. [Tel.] n. The aquatic plant named *Pistia stratiotes*. నీరుబుడికి. Rox. iii. 131. వాక ఆకు చెట్టు.

తూడు tūḍu. [Tel.] n. The root of the lotus. తూడుతిండి a swan which is so called because it feeds on తూడులు. One species is called పెట్టతూటిపువ్వు.

తూణము or తూణీరము tūṇamu. [Skt.] n. A quiver. అమ్ములపొది. తూణించు tūṇintsu. v. t. To wriggle the loins in dancing. H. i. 242.

తూతకొమ్ము or తూగొమ్ము tūta-kommu. [Tel. from తూ q. v.] n. A flute. పిల్లనగ్రోవి.

తూతురు *tūturu.* [Tel.] n. A mulberry tree.

తూతూ See తూ.

తూనరతుక్కము *tūnara-tukkamu.* [Tel.] n. The name of a certain game played by children.

తూనిక *tūnika.* [Tel. from తూచు.] n. Weighing. తూచుట. Respect గౌరవము. తూనికచెడె he lost respect గౌరవము పోయెను. తూనికకోల or తూనికదండె *tūnika-kōla.* n. The beam of a balance. తూనికవేయు *tūnika-vēyu.* v. t. To weigh in a balance. తూచు.

తూనిగ or తూనీగ *tūniga.* [Tel.] n. A dragon fly, *Libellula linearis.* తూనీగపక్షి *tūniga-pakshi.* n. A bird like quail. తూనె కొట్లాట *tūne-koṭl-āṭa.* A certain game among boys. H. iii. 188.

తూపరము *tūparamu.* [Tel.] n. A hole, a small hole. చిల్లి, రంధ్రము. తూపరాణ, తూపరాణము or తూపరాణి *tūparāṇa.* n. A water-course, a drain. నీళ్లు బయటికి పొయ్యు తూము.

తూపి *tūpi.* [Tel.] n. A car-like structure over the place where the principal idol in a temple is kept గుడిలో మూల విగ్రహము ఉండే చోటికి పైని విమానమువలె ఎత్తుగా కట్టిన కట్టడము.

తూపించు *tūpinṭsu.* [Tel. causal from తూచు.] v. a. To cause to be weighed, to get one to weigh (a thing.)

తూపు *tūpu.* [Tel.] n. An arrow. బాణము.

తూపురాసి *tūpu-rāsi.* [Tel.] n. A drain, a water course. A. vi. 9. నీళ్లుపారే తూము.

తూపొడుచు *tū-poḍuṭsu.* [Tel.] v. t. To spit. ఉమియు. See తూ. To puff away with the breath: to blow off, to fumigate in order to keep off ill. To "blow upon" or perform a spell (saying తూ) so as to relieve the pain. తూతూ అను.

తూబరుడు *tūbaruḍu.* [Skt.] n. A beardless youth. ప్రాయమున గడ్డము మీసమురాని వాడు. A watchman over a harem అంతఃపురపు కావలివాడు.

తూము *tūmu.* [Tel.] n. A drain, a sluice, a watercourse, an outlet, a fissure, a bore, a hole. ద్వారము. రంధ్రము. The Indian bushel, equal to four Kunchams, నాలుగుకుంచములకొలది, i. e., about fifteen English bushels. A measure of land (See ఎకరు) being $\frac{1}{16}$ (*one anna*) less than acre." The central hole in a wheel through which the axle passes బండిచక్రములోని నడిమిరంధ్రము. The eye of a needle సూది బెజ్జ.

తూర, తువర or తువర *tūra.* [Tel.] n. Drizzling rain, a drop of rain. జానుతొట్టు. A. iv. 169. A porpoise. జలజంతుభేదము.

తూరణగోలలు or తూరణతుంకములు *tūrana-gōlalu.* [Tel.] n. A certain game played by boys.

తూరి *tūri.* [Tel.] n. A time or occasion తడవ. పర్యాయము. ఒకతూరి once.

తూరు *tūru.* [Tel.] v. n. To drizzle, as small rain. (సన్నగా) కురియు. To enter చొచ్చు. To struggle, endeavour ప్రయత్నము చేయు. Mand. 1. 67. T. v. 56. "తూరు తెండెములాడు" dangling wreaths. Anirud. iii. 80. n. Husks of corn, bran. పొట్టు. తూరబడు to enter. చొచ్చు. తూరించు or తూర్చు to cause to enter. తూరజేయు. తూరుపట్టు, తూరు పార వెట్టు, తూరార్చు, తూరుపెట్టు or తూర్పెత్తు *tūru-paṭṭu.* v. t. To winnow grain by scattering it from a fan to the eastern breeze. To expose anything to the wind. తేనైనను గాలివాటముగా ఎత్తి విడుచు. To sift or examine thoroughly: తూరు (bran) పోవునట్టు ఎత్తు, చెరు, పట్టు. తూరుపు or తూర్పు *tūrupu.* [Tel. from తూరు. to enter. Lit. where the sun enters] n. The East. తూరుపుకొండ *tūrupu-koṇḍa.* n. The Eastern Hill, an imaginary hill supposed to be situated where the sun rises. తూరుపుఱేడు lit. the Lord of the East, i. e., Indra.

తూర్ణము tūrṇamu. [Skt.] n. Speed. త్వరితము. adj. Speedy, rapid. త్వరగా. See త్వర.

తూర్పారబట్టు See under తూరు.

తూర్పు Same as తూరుపు. (q. v.)

తూర్పెత్తు See under తూరు.

తూర్యము tūryamu. [Skt.] n. A musical instrument. వాద్యము. Music. Clamour, roar, uproar. వాద్యఘోష.

తూల tūla. [Tel.] n. A kind of fish. ఒకచేప.

తూలము tūlamu. [Skt.] n. Cotton, down. దూది. హంసతూలము swan's down. The sky. ఆకాశము. తూలి or తూలిక tūli. n. A small feather, down. A brush or hair pencil. A paint brush: A. v. 158. చిత్రముల్వ్రాసేకలము, కలాకి. తూలికాతల్పము a feather bed or quilt, a downy bed. తూలిని tūlini. n. Down: silky cotton. బూరుగదూది. తూలి or తూలి కాడు [Tel. తూల+ఇ.] n. A fisherman.

తూలించు See under తూలు.

తూలు tūlu. [Tel.] v. n. To shake. చలించు. To reel, to stagger. To faint, or become giddy. To be overcome with love, &c. To waver, hesitate. To be dazzled, to blink, as the eye. అడ్డముతూలుట to oppose or hinder. To avoid తొలగు. తూల tūla. [from తూలు.] adv. Down, off, roughly. తూలనాడు or తూలబల్కు to use rough language. తూలబుచ్చు to knock down. తూలగొట్టు. తూలబడు tūla-baḍu. v. n. To fall down, to totter. తూలు n. A stumble, a stagger. adj. Prolix, long, tedious. తూలుచు, తూల్చు or తూలించు tūlintsu. [Tel.] v. a. To make one reel, to cause one to stagger, to knock down. To remove తొలగించు. తూలబారు Same as తూలు. తూలపోవు tula-pōvu. v. n. To be chagrined or disappointed. చిన్నపోవు.

తూలపుచ్చు tūla-putstsu. v. t. To cause to be chagrined, to disappoint, to disgrace.

తూలాడు (తూలి+ఆడు.) Same as తూలు.

తూష్ణీం tūshṇim. [Skt.] adv. Silently, in silence. తూష్ణీకుడు a reserved man.

తృ tri

తృటితము triṭitamu. [Skt.] adj. Broken, cut, severed.

తృట్టు triṭṭu. [Skt.] n. Thirst. దప్పి. Desire ఇచ్ఛ.

తృణము triṇamu. [Skt.] n. Grass, reeds. Corn. A straw, a blade of grass, a reed. A mere trifle. తృణగ్రాహి triṇa-grahi. Lit: "drawing straws," as amber. A sapphire, నీలము, మరకతము. తృణజలూకము triṇa-jalūkamu. n. The leaping leech, that jumps along, fixing its head and tail alternately. భా. 10. స్క. ఉ. తృణజలూకన్యాయము is an expression like "a bird in the hand is worth two in the bush," i. e., Securing one object before trying for another. తృణత triṇata. n. Grassiness. తృణధాన్యము. A bow, ధనుస్సు. మరుత్తృణత Indra's bow, i. e., a rainbow. ఇంద్రధనుస్సు A. v. 154. తృణద్రుమము triṇa-drumamu. n. The "grass-bearing tree," i. e., a tree belonging to the grass family. తృణధ్వజము triṇa-dhvaja-mu. n. A bamboo, వెదురు. తృణప్రాయము triṇa-prayamu. adj. Worth a straw, worthless, contemptible. తృణరాజము the palmyra or the cocoanut tree. తృణశూన్యము triṇa-śūnyamu. adj. Having no grass. తృణముకేని. n. The Jasmine. మల్లె. తృణీకరించు triṇi-karintsu. v. a. To look upon (a thing) as grass. To contemn, despise, slight, make light of తృణముగా ఎంచు, అలక్ష్యముచేయు. తృణీకారము triṇi-kāramu. n. Contempt, disregard.

తృతీయము *tritiyamu*. [Skt. Cf. Eng. 'Three',] adj. Third. తృతీయావిభక్తి the third case of a noun, which has తో "with" or చేత "by" as its signs. మూడవ విభక్తి. తృతీయాకృతము *tritiya-kritamu*. adj. Thrice ploughed. మూడుచాళ్లు దున్నిన (శేల.)

తృప్తి *tripti*. [Skt.] n. Fullness, completeness, satisfaction. తనివి. తృప్తము *triptamu*. adj. Full, satisfied, satiated. తృప్తిపొందిన. తృప్తుడు *triptudu*. n. One who is satisfied.

తృష or తృష్ణ *trisha*. [Skt.] n. Thirst. దప్పి. Wish, desire. ఇచ్ఛ. తృషితుడు *trishitudu*. n. One who is thirsty. మృగతృష్ణ mirage.

తె te

తెంకాయ Same as టెంకాయ. (q. v.)

తెంకి Same as టెంకి. (q. v.)

తెంచు or త్రెంచు *tentsu*. [Tel. The causal of తెగు] v. a. To break, snap. తెగకోయు. తాడుతెంచు to break the cord., i. e., to make a woman a widow by breaking the cord which sustains the token of marriage (తాళిబొట్టు). Hence ఒకనితాడుతెంచు to break a man's cord, to ruin a man. This verb occurs in compounds signifying 'to come' or 'go,' as అరుదెంచు, ఏగుదెంచు, ఏతెంచు, చనుదెంచు, పొత్తెంచు, వచ్చెంచు, పారుదెంచు, వత్తెంచు, &c

తెండు *tendu*. [Tel.] v. n. To sleep. నిద్రించు. To lie down, పరుండు. శయనించు.

తెండె *tende*. [Tel.] n. A dish, boat or trough. దోనె.

తెంప *tempa*. [Tel.] n. A heap, a quantity. P. i. 496.

తెంపరి See under తెంపు.

తెంపి *tempi*. [Tel. from తెగు.] n. A widow. విధవస్త్రీ. See తెంచు. A wretch, jade, slut.

తెంపు or తెంపి *tempu*. [Tel. from తెగు.] n. Breaking. తెగటి. Bravery, daring, ardour, తెగువ. Insolence, rashness. An infraction of a rule. An outbreak, a breach of the peace. Harshness of temper. తాడుతెంపు ruin: See తెంచు. తెంపుచేసి వచ్చినారు they plucked up heart and came, they came in desperation. తెంపులతాడు a rope just breaking. తెంపు v. a. To break, to open a sluice, &c. తెంచు తెంపరి *tempari*. (తెంపు+అరి.) n. A brave man. సాహసికుడు.

తెక తెక *teka-teka*. [Tel. anuk.] adv. Hotly, fiercely. Much (referring to sunshine.) తెకతెకలాడుచున్నది it is hot, it is fierce.

తెక తేర *teka-têra*. [Tel.] adj. Quite unconnected. పొత్తిగాసంబంధములేని. తెకతేరగా *tekatêra-ga*. adv. Off, offhand, by accident, causelessly. పొత్తిగా సంబంధములేక. Quite useless by నిక్కలిని వ్యర్థముగా.

తెక్కరము *tekkaramu*. [Tel.] n. A prank. విలాసము. తెక్కరీడు *tekkar-îdu*. n. A rogue. a cheat.

తెక్కలి *tekkali*. [Tel.] n. Theft. దొంగతనము. A trick. వంచన. A fault ప్రమాదము. Severity, difficulty. adj. Deceitful, stealthy. వంచకము. "తెక్కలివృత్తుర్ధయము." భాగ. vi. తెక్కలిగర్భము దాల్చెను she became pregnant by stealth. తెక్కలికాడు *tekkali-kadu*. n. A thief. A swindler. తెక్కలిదైవము delusive destiny! cheating hopes. తెక్కలి కొను *tekkali-konu*. v. a. To steal or plunder. తెక్కలిపాటు *tekkali-patu*. n. Danger, misfortune, calamity, విపత్తు.

తెక్కొను or త్రెక్కొను *tek-konu* [Tel. తెగ+కొను.] v. n. To become fierce, to kill. తెగు, ఉద్రేకించు, అతిశయించు, తెగటార్చు.

తెగ See under తెగు.

తెగచు *tegatsu*. [Tel.] v. n. To be confused or confounded. కలగు.

తెగటారు *tegataru*. [Tel.] v. n. To die, expire, perish. చచ్చు. నశించు. తెగటార్చు *tegatartsu*. v. a. To kill, slay, destroy.

తెగటు *tegaṭu*. v. n. To forget oneself through joy. క్రొవ్వు. n. Pride. క్రొవ్వుట.

తెగడ *tegaḍa*. [Tel.] n. A certain purgative bark. (*Heyne*) త్రివృత్. తెల్లతెగడ *Convolvulus turpethum*. Rox. i. 476.

తెగడు *tegaḍu*. [Tel.] v. a. To scorn, revile, censure, chide. తిరస్కరించు, నిందించు. అద్దంబుతెగడెడుమోము the face that scorned the brilliance of the looking glass. "తే॥ చేసి తెలు చేయుచున్నందు దొనడదగు." Das. vii. 78. "ఒకపదతెగడు తేరొకపదతెగడు." ND. i. 711. v. n. To be scorned. ఉపేక్షింపబడు. n. Scorn, censure. నింద.

తెగి *tegi*. [Tel.] n. Courage. సాహసము.

"సీ॥ తెగితేనివీరముల్ తెచ్చిపెట్టుకులబు
క్రుంగిగ్రొక్కుడువాడు గాడుకురాడు."
R. vii. 73.

తెగించు *teginsu*. v. n. To dare or hazard. సాహసించు. ప్రాణావిశ తెగించినవా రలు desperate men, men with a forlorn hope. అన్నిటికిన్ని తెగించి యింతపనిచేసినాడు in doing this he risked everything, he hazarded his life.

తెగు *tegu*. [Tel.] v. n. To break, burst, sever, snap, or be separated. To be cut or split, as the skin or flesh with a blow. To burst, as a lake. To be parted out, as shares. ఖండితమగు, ఛిన్నమగు. To be sharp, as a cutting instrument. To venture సాహసించు. To be mellowed, trained or broken in, as a musical voice తీర్పగు. దాని గొంతుతెగినది her voice is tuned aright. To be finished or break off, as a work. తీర్పగు. To die చచ్చు. "మార్గాలమునుగ్గి నశకపించబలుబులు తెగె." P. iii. 96. వగతెగను the dispute was terminated. తెగ *tega*. n. A sort, kind, class. సజాతీయసమూహము. A crowd or flock. సమూహము. A sect, branch or division in a sect. A community, family, kin. Manner విధము. Side పక్షము. A bowstring అల్లెత్రాడు. Stringing a bow అల్లెత్రాటిని ఎక్కుపెట్టుట. A length నిడుపు. తెగ్గాను for తెగగాను See above. తెగగొట్టు *tega-goṭṭu*. v. a. To snap off, to cut, or sever నరుకు. తెగకోయు to cut off, to deduct. తెగగొరుకు to bite through. తెగచూచు to stare. తెగనమ్ము to sell off. v. t. To beat soundly. తెగనాడు *teganāḍu*. v. n. To speak rigorously. తెగబట్టు to hold fast. తెగబడు or తెగబారు *tega-baḍu*. v. n. To dare, to venture. తెగించు. తెగవేయు *tega-vēyu*. v. t. To cut off, నరుకు. తెగ మొగమోడి quite out of countenance. మిక్కిలి ముఖ భంగమునుపొందె. "తెగ మొగ మోడియున్నజన నిందితులొందుదు రిందువక్త్రకున్." UR. K. vii. 267. తెగిన gashed, wounded, broken. భూమి తెగిపోయినది the field was cut up, ploughed up or destroyed by the flood. తెగుడు *teguḍu*. n. Breaking. తెగుట. తెగు డల *tegudala*. n. End, termination. అంత ము. Decrease క్షయము. తెగుతెంపు *tegu-dempu*. (తెగు+తెంపు.) n. A decision. తీర్పు. తెగుబడి *tegu-baḍi*. n. Breaking. తెగుట. Ploughing. దుక్కి. Sale అమ్మకము. తెగులు *tegulu*. n. An outbreak (of disease). Disease, sickness, plague, pain, blight, evil, murrain, rot. వ్యాధి, పీడ. తెగులు గొంటు *tegulu-gonṭu*. n. A sick person, an invalid. వ్యాధిగ్రస్తుడు, వ్యాధిగ్రస్తురాలు. తెగులుగొను *tegulu-gonu*. v. n. To become sick, to fall sick. వ్యాధిగ్రస్తుడగు. తెగువ *teguva*. n. Daring, resolution. సాహసము. Sharpness, decision, decidedness, determination. Hastiness, wilfulness. Suddenness, abruptness. Wreaking or satiating passion. Liberality. A charitable disposition దాతృత్వము. తెగువ కే కేంద్రపదవి our daring is a very heaven, i. e., revenge is sweet! వానికి తెగువపుట్టినది he has become courageous, or venturesome. తెగుదారి *tegu-dāri*. (తెగువ+దారి.) n. A courageous person. సాహసికుడు, సాహసికురాలు. A donor, a charitable person దాత. తెగువడు *tegu-vaḍu*. (తెగుడు+పడు.) v. n. To be separated or severed. తెగబడు.

తెచ్చు *tetstsu.* [Tel. ✓ తె to bring, to give.] v. a. To get, to bring. తీసుకొనివచ్చు. To produce. To adduce as an instance. To understand or imply (a word not expressed in a sentence.) To bring about or cause. చిత్తానకు తెచ్చు to observe or heed, to lay to heart. హరింపులోకి తెచ్చు, i. e., హరించు to embezzle. అనుభవములోకి తెచ్చు, i.e., అనుభవించు to enjoy. ప్రసంగమునకు తెచ్చు to introduce or bring up a subject. వన్నె తెచ్చు to give (or produce) a colour. ముత్తెచ్చు to bring forward. పనికి తెచ్చు to use or put (a thing) to use. దోవకు తెచ్చు to bring one into the way, to reform one. తెమ్ము (imperative) bring. **తెచ్చుకొను** *tetstsu-konu.* v. n. To obtain or procure. To earn. కోపముతెచ్చుకొను to feign or put on anger, to put oneself into passion. బుద్ధితెచ్చుకొను to recover one's senses; to form a good resolution. మనసుకు తెచ్చుకొను to bring to mind, to lay to heart, to understand, to recollect. **తెప్పించు** *teppintsu.* v. a. To procure. To send for. To get, obtain, provide.

తెటుకు *tetuku.* [Tel.] n. Shrinking. తెటుకుగానుండే shrunken, shrivelled.

తెట్టగించు, తెట్టగిలబడు or **తెట్టగిల్లు** *tettagintsu.* [Tel.] v. n. To desist, to be exhausted. To flag, be faint. నిస్సారమగు, చేవచెడియుండు.

తెట్టతెరువు *tetta-teruvu.* [Tel. తెరువు+తెరువు.] n. The middle of the street. నడివీధి.

తెట్టు *tettu.* [Tel.] n. Scum. బెల్లపుపాకము మీదితెట్టు molasses. **తెట్టు** or **తెట్టువ్వు** *tettu.* n. The gate of a fort. A hedge or stockade round a city. A reef of rocks above the water. A place begirt with forests, or guarded by woods. వనదుర్గము. రాళ్లతెట్టు a stone fence or loose wall without mortar. తెట్లుతెట్లుగానుండే horizontally.

తెట్టువ *tettuva.* [Tel.] n. A group. సమూహము. తెట్టువకట్టు, తెట్టువలుకట్టు or తెట్టువలు కొను *tettuva-kattu.* v. n. To be grouped, to be drifted to one side as grass, moss, &c., in water.

తెట్టె, తెట్టెయ or **తెట్టువ** *tette.* [Tel.] n. A bee hive, a bees' nest. తేనెపెట్టె. A nest of the red tree-ants. మిాగడతెట్టె cream, the skin of boiled milk సంతానిక, కాగినపాలమిాదకట్టిన తెట్టె. నాచుతెట్టె a mass of scum and weeds on water, పాచి. తెట్టెలు కట్టు or తెట్టెలుకొను *tettelu-kattu.* v. n. To be heaped. రాశిపడు.

తెట్టెము *tettemu.* [Tel.] n. Total, whole. మొత్తము.

తెడ్డు or **త్రెడ్డు** *teddu.* [Tel.] n. An oar, or paddle. A piece of wood, shaped like a racquet used to stir boiling food, a wooden spoon, a ladle. కొయ్యగరిటె. బల్లెపు తెడ్లు spears. తెగించినవానికి తెడ్డే లింగము he is a stubborn man. **తెడ్డుమూతికొంగ** *teddu-mūti-konga.* n. The bird called the Spoonbill. *Platalea leucorodia.* (F.B.I.)

తెత్తు *tettu.* [Tel.] n. A door composed of thorny sticks. వాకిటిముళ్లతలుపు.

తెనసుణు or **తెలసుణు** *tenamanu.* [Tel.] v. n. To lie down. శయనించు.

తెనసువ Same as తెనువ (q. v.)

తెనుగు or **తెనుంగు** *tenugu.* [Tel. from Dravidian root తెన్ = south. Lit: the language of the south.] n. The Tenugu or Telugu language. అయిదువిధాల తెనుగులు ఉన్నవి there are five species of Telugu. M. I. i. 20. **తెనిగించు** or **తెనుగించు** *tenigintsu.* v. a. To translate into Telugu. See తెలుగు.

తెన్ను *tennu.* [Tel.] n. A way, path. దారి, మార్గము. తెట్టతెన్ను right in the way మిక్కిలిదోవలో.

తెన్నుండు *tenn-undu.* [Tel.] v. n. To lie down. పరుండు, శయనించు.

తెపతెప *tepa-tepa.* [Tel. anuk.] n. Backwards and forwards, this way and that. Radha. i. 98.

తెప్ప *teppa*. [Tel.] n. A raft or float, a cattamaran. కట్టుమ్రాను. వానితెప్ప మునిగినది his float is sunk, i. e., he is totally ruined. తెప్ప బయలుదేరినట్లు ఉన్నది it is as if (his) raft has come to the surface, i. e., he has recovered his spirits. తెప్పలతేలు to be rife, to abound, rejoice, revel. పొంగు. తెప్పలతేలగా or తెప్పతెప్పలుగా abundantly. T. ii. 34. అగ్గితెప్ప a flake of fire. తెప్పతిరునాళ్లు the raft feast, when the god is placed on a float and rowed over a pond or reservoir. తెప్పతెరలుగా *teppa-terala-ga*. adv. At pleasure, యథేచ్ఛముగా. At full speed. అతివేగముగా.

తెప్పరిలు, తెప్పరిల్లు, తెప్పిరిలు, తెప్పిరిల్లు, తెప్పరు or తెప్పిరు *tepparilu*. [Tel.] v. n. To recover one's senses. To be roused, aware, alert. To go off, as weariness, or a swoon. అపాయమునుండి తేరు.

తెప్పిల్లు *teppillu*. [Tel.] n. Taunts, reproaches. అగచాట్లు.

తెప్పున *teppu-na*. [Tel.] adv. Quickly, at once. శీఘ్రముగా.

తెబక *tebaka*. [Tel.] n. Total. మొత్తము. A multitude, సమూహము.

తెమడ *temada*. [Tel.] n. Phlegm, mucus. శ్లేష్మము.

తెమలు *temalu*. [Tel.] v. n. To turn, as the stomach, to cause vomiting. వమించు.

"సమలవశముగాని పాకశాకంబు,
తెమలక మ్రింగ దంతికి జీర్ణమైన."

L. xxiv. 204.

తెమలుచు, తెమలించు or తెమల్చు *temalutsu*. v. t. & n. To feel a retching sensation. To shake, to turn the stomach or cause vomiting. కదిలించు. కడుపులో తిప్పు, గొంద్రించు. "తనపైనతెండుంచివకొద్ది మల్చి." T. iv. 143.

తెమ్మ or తేమ *temma*. [Tel.] n. Wetness, moisture. గొజ్జగితెమ్మ the dew of flowers తేనెతెమ్మ honeyed moisture. తెమ్మెర (తెమ్మ+ఎర wind,) *temm-era*. n. A cool breeze. చల్లగాలి. T. iii. 133. A breeze గాలి.

తెర *tera*. [Tel.] n. A screen, curtain, a blind. A veil, a cover of any kind మరుగుచీర, అడ్డము. A plain or space. బయలు. A billow or surge అల. దోమతెర a mosquito curtain. వాతెర the lips. A time, one bout. ఒకతెర once. మరియొకతెర again. తెరమొత్తగా wave upon wave, in waves, tumultuously, "పొంగిరుదురుద్రెత్తగా." Vijaya. ii. 19. తెరతెర wave after wave, a series పరంపర. adj. Spread out, open as a plain. Gaping, open as the mouth. తెరనోరుగల open mouthed. తేనెతెర *tene-tera* n. A honey comb. తెరపారు *tera-paru*. v. n. To curdle, to coagulate, to congeal as water or other liquid. తెరకట్టు. ఎండ తెరతీసి బయలువెడలినది the sun broke through the clouds. వైష్ణవులకు తెరచాటు కద్దు the Vaishnavas always are behind a screen, particularly while eating. తెరలు గాసిన overpowering, terrible, దుర్భరమైన. తెరలాడు *tera-l-ādu*. (A. vi. 142.) v. n. To hide. To gleam or shine through a veil తెరలులోనుండి. తెరలో ప్రకాశించు. తెరగంటి *tera-ganti*. n. A god, or goddess. అనిమిషుడు. Nila Parin. i. 2. తెరనొంటి మెకము a lion. తెరకట్టు *tera-kattu*. n. A screen. ముఖమును తెరకట్టుతో మూయ్చుకొనుట to hold the handkerchief before the mouth while speaking (a custom of Musulman origin.) H. v. 99. తెరకట్టు *tera-kattu*. v. n. To form into flakes, to coagulate. మీగడకట్టు, to harden గట్టిపడు. తెరకాడు *tera-kādu*. n. A thief: a concealed agent. తెరచాప *tera-tsāpa*. n. A screen, or mat. A ship's sail; (lit:) a screen-cloth, or veil. తెరతెరగా *tera-tera-ga*. adv. At intervals, now and then. తెరనాటకము *tera-nāta-kamu*. n. A puppet show or other play in which a curtain is used. P. iv. 255. తెరయీగ *tera-y-iga*. n. A bee. తేనెటీగ. M. VII. i. 236. తెరవేట *tera-vēta*. n.

"Screen hunting," in which the huntsmen use screens to conceal themselves, a hunt wherein hurdles or screens are placed around the hunting ground. A iv. 154.

తెరకువ *terakuva.* [Tel.] n. Sense, prudence. వివేకము. An expedient, cunning ఉపాయము. తెరకువగా cunningly, artfully

తెరగోలు Same as తెరలు.

తెరగంటి See under తెర.

తెరగు, తెరంగు, తెరవు, or తెరువు *teragu.* [Tel.] n. Way, path, manner, style, fashion. విధము. Beauty చక్కన. Order క్రమము. A treaty of peace సంధి. భార. ఉద్యో iii ఇత్తెరంగున thus, in this way. వానితెరవుకు పోవద్దు do not meddle with him. తెలివితోకలగన్నతెరగునుండె he was as though in a waking dream or reverie. "అత్తెరంగెరుగంజెప్పవె." tell me the way of it. M. XIII. iv. 306. తెరగుపడు *teragu-padu.* v. n. To conclude a peace. సంధియగు. తెరగుపరచు to cause to conclude a peace.

తెరచు or తెరుచు *teraṭsu.* [Tel.] v. a. To open, unfasten, uncover. తెరపజేయు.

తెరప, తెరపి or తెరిపి *terapa.* [Tel.] n. Opening. తెరచుట. An interval, cessation, intermission, leisure. అవకాశము, ఉపశమనము. Disclosure, an opportunity. Looseness, i. e., lewdness. జ్వరమునకు తెరపి చిక్కినది there was an intermission of the fever. తెరపలగా or తెరపతెరపగా loosely, here and there, scatteredly. వాన తెరపి యియ్యలేదు the rain did not cease. తెరప adj. Open, సందుగల. తెరపమాటలు down-rightness, plain speaking, plain language. తెరపుమరపు or తెరుపుమరుపు *terapu-marapu.* n. Dementation. మతిత్రిప్పి నప్పుడు కలుగు తబ్బిబ్బు. Sense and nonsense: absence of mind, forgetfulness. ఎవానికిన్ని తెరుపుమరుపుకద్దు every man has his wise and foolish fits.

తెరల *terala.* [Tel.] n. A mouthful. కబళము.

తెరలు or తెర్లు *teralu.* [Tel.] v. n. To move. To toss about. చలించు. To be routed. To set, or disappear. To come or go out or spread, as scent, బయలుదేరు, వ్యాపించు. To overflow, boil over, పొంగి పొరలు. To be agitated. కలగు. To avoid తొలగు. To die, expire. చచ్చు. తెరలుడు *teraḷuḍu.* n. The act of coming out. బయలుదేరుట. A journey ప్రయాణము. తెరలిక *teralika.* n. A crowd. గుంపు, సమూహము. తెరలగా *terala-ga.* adv. Loudly, openly, aloud. తెరలబడు *terala-baḍu.* v. n. To be at a loss: to hesitate. VP. vi 225. తెరలబారు *terala-bāru.* v. n. To avoid. తొలగు. తెరలుచు, తెర్లుచు or తెరలగొలుపు *teraluṭsu.* v. a. To scatter, or put to flight. విచ్చు. M. VIII. vi. 56. Jaim. viii. 40. To give forth (a scent). To smell. To cause to go out of the way, తొలగించు.

తెరవ *terava.* [Tel. తెర open + వాయి mouth.] n. A maid, girl, woman.

తెరవు, తెరువు or తెర్వు *teravu.* [Tel.] n. Way. See తెరగు. తెరవరి or తెరువరి *terav-ari.* n. A wayfarer, a traveller. బాటసారి. తెరువుకాడు or తెరవుకాడు *teruvu-kāḍu.* n. A highwayman. దారులు కొట్టెడువాడు. తెరువాటు *teruvāṭu.* (తెరువు + అటు) n. A wayfarer, traveller. A road మార్గము. A vi. 51. Highway robbery దొంగలు దారికాచి కొట్టుట. తెరువాటుకాడు a highway man. తెరువాటుకొట్టు to rob on the highway.

తెర్ర *terra.* [Tel.] n. A rash, foolish fellow, a blockhead. Also, another form of తెర open.

తెల or తెల్ల *tela.* [Tel.] adj. White. తెల్లని. తెలతెల *tela-tela.* adj. Whitish, pale, more and more bright. తెలతెలనగు to become more and more white; or to smile pleasantly, to be radiant with smiles. **తెలతెలబోవు** or **తెలతెలనాడు** *tela-tela-bōru.* v. n. To whiten, brighten; to turn pale. తెలతెలవారు. తెలతెలగు to dawn gradually. తెలవారు Same as తెల్లవారు (q. v.) **తెలనాకు** *telan-āku.* n. A fair leaf, a whitish betel leaf, a blank page. తెల్లనిఆకు. తెల్లాకు.

తెలగ or **తెలగా** *telaga.* [Tel. from తెలుగు.] n. A certain division of the Sudra caste. This name is generic for the nation, as Briton is for the English: yet is applied specifically to one caste, as ancient Britons is a name given to the Welsh. adj. Of or belonging to the Telaga caste. తెలగయిల్లు a native house. తెలగబలిజెలు a certain caste. **తెలగవుక్కు** *telaga-vukku.* n. A very tough sort of steel. **తెలగాలు** *telagālu.* n. The caste called Telagas. **తెలగాణ్యులు** *telagāṇyulu.* n. A certain caste of *Smarta* Brahmins.

తెలి *teli.* [Tel.] adj. White. తెల్లని. Bright. Pure నిర్మలము. తెలినవ్వు a bright smile. n. Whiteness. తెలుపు. **తెలిగన్నులు** *teli-gannulu.* n. The whites of the eyes: staring eyes: upturned eyes that shew the white. తెలిగంటి a bright eyed woman చక్కని అతివ. **తెలిపువ్వు** *teli-puvvu.* n. A phrase for the moon, as being the "Flower of brilliancy." H. ii. 4. **తెలిగాము** *teli-gāmu.* n. (Lit.) The white or silvery planet, i. e., Venus శుక్రుడు. **తెలిదమ్మి** *teli-dammi.* n. The white lotus. **తెలిదమ్మికంటి** *teli-dammi-kanti.* n. The white-lotus-eyed, i. e., Vishnu, పుండరీకాక్షుడు. **తెలిపిట్ట** *teli-piṭṭa.* n. The white bird, i. e., a swan హంస. **తెలిమెకము** *teli-mekamu.* n. The bright beast, i. e., a lion. **తెలిమొదవు** *teli-modavu.* n. The white cow, i. e., కామధేనువు. **తెలియేరు** *teli-yēru.* n. The white river, i. e., the Heavenly Ganges. ఆకాశగంగ.

తెలిక *telika.* [Tel.] n. The sesamum plant నువ్వులచెట్టు. **తెలికపిండి** *telika-pindi.* n. The stuff that remains after the oil had been pressed from sesamum seed. Oil cake గానుగపిండి. **తెలికవాడు** *telika-vāḍu.* n. An oilman, an oil merchant.

తెలియు *teliyu.* [Tel. from తెలి lit. to become white or plain.] v. n. To appear, come to light. To be known, perceived, seen, felt. To be discovered, or found. విదితమగు, విశదమగు. To wake up మేలుకొను. To become plain or be favoured ప్రసన్నతనొందు. v. a. To know, to perceive. ఎరుగు.

"సర్వముక్ తెలిసితిఅంచు
గర్వితమతిగ విహరించితి."

భ. i. శతకము.

వానికి ఒళ్లు తెలియలేదు he has lost his senses. ఒళ్లుతెలియకుండాపడినది she lay senseless. కన్నులు తెలియనివాడు a blind man. చీకటిలో పిల్లికి కన్నులు తెలియును. a cat can see in the dark. నీకు తెలిసినదా do you see, understand, or know it? తెలిసితెలియక చేసినాడు he did it unwittingly, unintentionally. మతితెలిసికొండి being conscious, recollecting himself. నాకు బుద్ధితెలిసినానాటినుంచి ever since I grew up. ఈ సంగతి నీకు తెలిసియుండవలెనని I call upon you to be a witness of this, I wish you to observe this. తెలిసినవాడు one who knows, a man of understanding. నిద్ర తెలిసినప్పుడు when he awoke from sleep. **తెలియజేయు** or **తెలియజెప్పు** *teliya-jēyu.* v. a. To make known, to tell, explain, advise, inform. **తెలివి** *telivi.* n. Understanding: perception, consciousness, తెలియుడము. Wisdom, వివేకము. Brightness, ప్రకాశము, కాంతి, వికాసము Clearness, (నీళ్లు) తేరుట. Whiteness తెలుపు. "చిత్తముంబులవింత తెలివిచేసె." పార. iii. తెలివినొందగా on coming to oneself, on recovering one's senses. తెలివిలోచెప్పు to tell discreetly. **తెలివికత్తె** *telivi-katte.* n. A wise woman, వివేకముకలది, ప్రాజ్ఞ. **తెలివికాడు** *telivi-kāḍu.* n. A man of sense. వివేకము

కలవాడు, ప్రాజ్ఞుడు. తెలివిడి *teliv-idi.* n. Understanding. The act of making known, తెలియజేయుట. An illustration దృష్టాంతము. See తెలుపు. తెలిగొను *teli-gonu.* v. t. To know, to find out. తెలిసికొను. To extort an oath, ప్రమాణముచేయించు. తెలుసుకొను or తెలిసికొను *telusu-konu* v. a. To learn, find out, ascertain, understand, know, observe, take notice.

తెలుకులవాడు *telukula-vādu.* n. An oil-man. చేవతెలుకులవాండ్లు a sect among them who wear the జంధెము. See తెలిక.

తెలుగు or తెలుంగు *telugu.* [The original form of this word is తెనుగు (q.v.) It literally means "the language of the *South*" Some wrongly derive it from త్రిలింగ. For other attempts to derive it see Caldwell.] [Drav.] n. The Telugu language, ఆంధ్రము. A Telugu man or woman. A Telugu word. thus తెలుగులు Telugu words (Appa C. i. 271.) so called as distinguished from Sanskrit. అచ్చతెలుగు pure Telugu, free from foreign elements. తెలిగించు or తెనిగించు *teligintsu.* v. t. To translate into Telugu. తెలుగులోనికి భాషాంతరముచేయు.

తెలుచు or తెల్చు *telutsu.* [Tel.] v. t. To bow to, to worship. మ్రొక్కు. To clear up, as a doubt తేర్చు. To make clear తెల్లముచేయు. To pray, to request ప్రార్థించు. See తెలియు and తెలుపు.

తెలుపు or తెల్పు *telupu.* [Tel. from తెలియు]. v. a. To make known, tell, say, instruct, inform, suggest. To shew, manifest, reveal, betray. తెలియజేయు, ఎఱిగించు. To wake up మేలుకొలుపు. To calm. తేర్చు. వానికి ధైర్యము తెలిపి having reassured or encouraged him. తెలుపుడు or తెల్పుడు *telupudu.* n. Knowledge, knowing. ఎరుక. తెలుపుడుచేయు *telupudu-cheyu.* v. t. To make known ఎఱిగించు. తెలుపు [from తెల white.] n. Whiteness. Purity పరిశుద్ధి. తెలుపురోగము gonorrhœa. తెలుపువారు or తెలుపారు to become white.

తెలె or తెలియ *tele.* [Tel.] n. A dish or platter. కంచము, భోజనపాత్రము.

తెల్ల *tella.* [Tel. తెల = white] adj. White, pale, pallid. Plain, evident. స్పష్టము. తెల్ల, తెల్లన or తెల్లదనము n. Whiteness, paleness. తెలుపు. తెల్లకాగితము blank paper. తెల్లజనాలు or తెల్లవారు white people, Europeans. తెల్లబంగారు pale gold. తెల్ల యెఱ్ఱవన్నె light red. మొగము తెల్లవై turning pale. తెల్లనికండ్లు bright eyes. తెల్లకాకి a white crow. తెల్లకొక్కెర a white crane. తెల్లగడ్డ an onion నీరుల్లి. తెల్లజాలు మెకము the lion. సింహము. తెల్లబొరవ *tella-bōrava.* n. The white Scavenger Vulture. తెల్లతీగ *tella-tīga.* n. A large woody climbing creeper called *Dalbergia rubiginosa.* Rox. iii. 231. తెల్లదీవి *tella-dīvi.* n. The white island, one of the sixteen divisions of the world. శ్వేతద్వీపము. A. iv. 127. తెల్లన or తెల్లని *tellana.* adj. White, light coloured, pale, sallow, bright. తెల్లనాకు Same as తెనాకు. (q.v.) తెల్లనార *tella-nāra.* n. A kind of fish, a whiting. తెల్లనిదొర *tellani-dora,* n. Lit. the white lord, i.e., Siva or Balarāma. తెల్లబారు *tella-bāru* v. n. To turn white. తెల్లబారిన whitish, glassy or glazed, as an eye. తెల్లబోవు *tella-bovu.* v. n. To turn pale, to be thunderstruck. తెల్లము or తెల్లము *tellamu.* adj. Apparent, evident, obvious, clear. స్పష్టము, స్ఫుటము. తెల్లముగా clearly. తేటతెల్లముగా as clearly as possible. తెల్లవారు *tella-vāru.* (తెల్ల+వారు.) v. n. To dawn. ఉదయమగు. తెల్లవారి నప్పుడు when the day dawned. ఈరాత్రి యెట్లా తెల్లవారునా అని ఉంటిమి we were in a fix, not knowing how this grief would terminate. "తెల్లవారగవచ్చెను" he came at dawn. తెల్లవారకముందు before break of day. To turn white. తెల్లనగు. తెల్లవారిలేస్తే from the hour of awaking. To be ruined or lost పాడుకావడము. అతని పని తెల్లవారినది his affair has lost all colour, i.e., he is ruined. తెల్లవారులు or తెల్లవార్లు *tella-vārulu.* adv. Until morning. తెల్లవారగట్ల *tella-vāra-gaṭla.* adv. At daybreak. తెల్లవారి *tella-vāri.* n. The dawning, morn. (A verbal noun in ఇ as వినికి and పలుకుబడి). అతెల్లవారి the following morning. తెల్లవారించు or తెల్లవార్చు *tella-vārintsu.* v. a. To cause the day to dawn, to watch all night. To clear up, explain, settle. అతనిపని తెల్లవారించినారు they arranged his matter.

తెల్లు *tellu.* [Tel. for తేరలు.] v. n. To boil. త్రెళ్లు. To fall. పడు. కాగిన్నెరలో నూనె తెల్లుచుండగా వాణ్ని దానిలో పడవేసినారు when the oil was boiling they threw him in.

తెవ *teva.* [Tel. another form of తెగ.] n. A crowd. సమూహము.

తెవడు Same as తెగడు. (q.v.)

తెవులు or తెగులు *tevulu.* [Tel. from తెగు to break.] n. A disease, murrain. Evil, mischief. రోగము. కీడు. తెవులుగొంటు or తెవుల్గొంటు Same as తెగులుగొంటు. తెవులుగొను Same as తెగులుగొను. తెవులువడు Same as తెగులుపడు.

తెవ్వ *tevva.* [Tel.] n. A surge or billow, a large wave. A flood, an inundation.

తెవ్వన *tevva-na.* [Tel.] n. Beauty, elegance. సౌందర్యము, చక్కన.

తే tē

తేంట్లు *tēnṭlu.* [Tel. plu. of తేటి.] n. Bees. తేనెటీగలు.

తేకు *tēku.* [Tel. another form of టేకు.] n. The teak tree.

తేకువ *tēkuva.* [Tel.] n. Firmness, bravery, courage. ధైర్యము. Spirit. Freshness, bloom. Fear, భయము.

తేగ *tēga.* [Tel.] n. The edible sprout of the young palmyra tree. తాటిమొలక.

తేగడ *tēgaḍa.* [Tel.] n. Bloom, vigour. ఈ బిడ్డవాడు మంచితేగడగా నున్నాడు this child is healthy and strong.

తేగము *tēgamu.* [from Skt. త్యాగము.] n. Relinquishment. విడిచిపెట్టడము. Munificence. దాతృత్వము, ఈవి. P. i. 119.

తేగాకత్తి Same as చేరకత్తి. (q. v.)

తేజము or తేజస్సు *tējamu.* [Skt.] n. Brilliance, lustre, splendour. Vigour, potency, might. ప్రకాశము, ప్రభావము. *Semen virile.* రేతస్సు. Courage పరాక్రమము. తేజో పార్జనము acquiring reputation. తేజస్వి a brilliant or vigorous man తేజస్సుగలవాడు. తేజరిలు, తేజఱిలు, తేజరిల్లు or తేజఱిల్లు *tējarilu.* v. n. To shine, to be glorious. ప్రకాశించు. తేజితము *tējitamu.* adj. Bright, sharp. వాడిచేయబడిన. తేజుడు *tējuḍu.* n. He who shines, &c.

తేజి or తేజీ *tēji.* [Tel.] n. A steed. గుర్రము. తేజికాశ్వము *tējikaśvamu.* n. A swift horse. Swa. iv. 167.

తేజు *tēdzu.* [from Skt. తేజస్సు.] n. Brightness, brilliance. కాంతి, ప్రకాశము. Heroism, ప్రతాపము.

తేజెట్టు *tē-jeṭṭu.* [Tel. తే=తేన.] n. A cocoanut tree. టెంకాయచెట్టు.

తేట *tēṭa.* [Tel.] n. Clearness, transparency, purity, brightness. Any clear liquid of which the sediment has fallen to the bottom. Whey నీరుమజ్జిగ. adj. Clear, transparent, free from sediment, pure, evident, distinct. నిర్మలము, విశదము. P. i. 19. తేటతెలుగు plain or clear Telugu. తేటగా *tēṭa-gā.* adv. Clearly, plainly, downright. తేటగీతి *tēṭa-gīti.* n. The name of a species of metre. తేటచేయు *tēṭa-chēyu*. v. n. To reveal, explain, clear up. తేటతెల్ల or తేటతెల్లము *tēṭa-tella*. adj. Very clear or plain. మిక్కిలిస్పష్టము. తేటపడు *tēṭa-paḍu*. v. n. To become clear or evident. విశదమగు. తేటపరచు *tēṭa-paratsu*. v. a. To make clear, explain, illustrate.

తేటి *tēṭi*. [Tel.] n. The large black carpenter bee తుమ్మెద. (These are brilliantly black: and jetty ringlets or twisted braids of hair are likened to clusters of these bees.) "కరువంపు తేటిమొంగరులు కెరలి." Dasav. ix. 159.

తేటిక *tēṭika*. [Tel.] n. A raft. తెప్ప.

తేడా *tēḍa*. [Tel.] n. Profit, balance, surplus. లాభము. Difference తారతమ్యము.

తేడు *tēḍu*. [Tel.] v. n. To lie down. శయనించు. అముక్త. v.

తేది *tēdi*. [Tel.] n. A date, i. e., a day of the month. దినము.

తేనీళ్లు *tē-nīḷḷu*. [Chinese through Eng. తే= tea.] n. Tea: a decoction of tea leaves.

తేనుచు or తేన్చు *tēnutsu*. [Tel.] v. n. To belch, to bring up wind. తేనుపు, తేన్పు or తేపు *tēnupu*. n. Belching.

తేనె or తేనియ *tēne*. [Tel.] n. Honey. Various kinds are called జుంటితేనె, పెద్ద తెరతేనె, కొండతేనె, పుట్టతేనె, పెరతేనె, బొర్ర తేనె, ముసరతేనె, చిన్నపువ్వుతేనె and కర్ర పట్టు (which is the best.) A ruddy nut brown complexion is compared to honey. Radha. i. 11; so in Theocritus, *melichroos* is applied to a bright ruddy or nut brown beauty. పూతేనె the nectar of flowers. తేనెచెట్టు *tēne-chettu*. n. A certain tree. తేనెటీగ, తేటీగ, తేనెదోగ or తేనెతిండి *tēne-tīga*. n. A honey-bee. తేనెతెర *tēne-tera*. n. Honey comb. తేనెతోవలు or తేనెతొలులు *tēne-tonulu*. n. Honey comb, also a sort of vermicelli. తేనెపిట్ట *tēne-piṭṭa*. n. The Sun-bird or Honey-sucker, *Arachnechthra asiatica*, or *A. Zeylonica*. (F. B. I.) తేనెపెట్టు *tēne-pettu*. v. t. To make honey. తేనెఅరటి a kind of sweet plantain. తేనెగాజు a kind of bangle. తేనెగద్ద *tēne-gadda*. n. The Honey Buzzard, *Pernis cristatus*. (F. B. I.) తేనెసారాయి *tēne-sārāyi*. n. Mead, brewed from honey.

తేప *tēpa*. [Tel.] n. A time. తడవ. ఒకతేప once. Also, a raft. తెప్ప.

తేపు or త్రేపు *tēpu*. [Tel.] v. n. To belch. n. A belch, an eructation. See తేనుచు.

తేమ *tēma*. [Tel.] n. Moisture, damp. adj. Moist, damp. తేమగిల్లు or తేమగిలు *tēma-gillu*. v. n. To become moist or wet. చెమ్మగిల్లు. ఆర్ద్రమగు. తేమనము *tēmanamu*. n. Batter, thin paste of milk and flour. పాలతిమ్మనము. Buttermilk మజ్జిగ.

తేమానము *tēmānamu*. [Tel.] n. Interest on money, వడ్డీ. Hesitation, delay, sluggishness. తేమానగాడు an idler. తేమానముగా *tēmānamu-ga*. adv. Gratis. తేరగా

తేయాకు *tē-y-āku*. [Chinese through Eng.] n. The Tea leaf. Tea. See తేనీళ్లు.

తేర *tēra*. n. Clearness. తేట. Want of any relationship or connection. సంబంధము లేమి. adj. or adv. Gratis, unpaid for సంబంధము లేని. Uselessly, వ్యర్థముగా. Without any trouble, easily, అనాయాసముగా. తేరకాపు a rent-free lodging. తేరగాడు a stranger, అన్యుడు; a temporary husband కొంచెపు భర్త. An interloper: one who enjoys gratis. పైపైవచ్చినవాడు.' తేరకత్తె a strange woman అన్యస్త్రీలు, a woman of loose character. తేరగుర్రము తంగేటిబడితె when you ride gratis, you use your cudgel well. తేరకు or తేరకుతేర *teraku*. adv. Quite uselessly మిక్కిలి వ్యర్థముగా. Easily,

ఆనాయాసముగా. తేర or తేరగా [from తెచ్చు.] used with various verbs, as వచ్చుతేర, తెత్తేర. వచ్చుతేర while coming, while going. R. iii. 2. కొనితేర while he brought, కొని తెచ్చుచుండగా. తేరకొను *tēra-konu*. v. n. To become clear తేటపడు. To abound, teem. తేరగాను fully. సమృద్ధిగా. స్పష్టముగా. Swa. iii.

తేరలచేప *tērala-chēpa*. [Tel.] n. A fish; a sort of *Chætodon*. Russell. No. 80, 81.

తేరు *tēru*. [Tel.] n. A car, a chariot. రథము. బండి. "తేరుకెంత్రిప్రతిమ." Cuchēlop. iii. 110. పావురలతేరు a car drawn by doves. తేరుకాడు or తేరుపూన్పరి a charioteer, a carriage driver. రథికుడు, సారథి.

తేరు *tēru*. [Tel.] v. n. To become settled or clear (as water.) తేటపడు. To be rescued, allayed or relieved. To pass off, as a fainting fit. To escape. To recover, as from illness or danger. తేరుకొను, తప్పిను. To extend or reach. To shine forth, ప్రసన్నమగు. To happen, come to pass, or come forth, కలుగు. To rise, as cream or scum. To be finished or over, to reach the end. ముగియు, కడతేరు, ముగియు, జిగితేరదుసొమ్ములు glittering jewels. తేరకయుండగా when it was in abeyance. నారికి ఒళ్లు తేరకయుండగా while he was still an invalid. తేరుకొను *tēru-konu*. v. n. To recover (from illness), to gain strength or become convalescent. స్వస్థతనొందు. తేరుగడ *tēru-gaḍa*. n. Finishing, ending. ముగియుట. Recovering consciousness తెలివిడి. తేరుగడలెక్క a settled account. తేర్చు or తేరుచు *tērtsu*. v. a. To make clear, clarify. తేటచేయు. To rectify, to correct. To finish. To cause to rejoice, ప్రసన్నతనొందించు. To relieve, console. To kill చంపు. తేరవారు *tēra-vāru*. v. n. To become clear. To dawn. "తూర్పు తేరవారగా." HK. ii. 34. తేరి *tēri*. adv. To the end, fully, to the full. తేరిచూచు, తేరజూచు, తేరుకొనిచూచు or తేరిపారచూచు to look hard, to gaze earnestly, to look steadfastly; to see clearly. తేరి *tēri*. n. Clarified ghee. కాచితేరిననెయ్యి.

తేలు *tēlu*. [Tel.] n. A scorpion. తేలుమీను a sort of fish. తేలురాసి *tēlu-rāsi*. n. The constellation Scorpio. వృశ్చికరాశి.

తేలు *tēlu*. [Tel.] v. n. To float. To swim. To bathe. To succeed, be done, be settled, ratified, take place. To terminate, end, blow over or end (as a storm), swell, ripen (as a boil), to emerge, పొడచూపు. To fall clear of, so as not to bit. To clear up, become known, or ascertained, be decided, as a question or doubt. To be found, come to light, result, come to pass, to be evident or revealed. To go off or depart, as sleep, sickness, &c. To escape or get off. నేను తేలే ఉపాయము ఇది this is the plan to save myself. ఏ సముద్రమందు పడవేసినా ఇది తేలును in whatever sea you place this boat it will float, i.e., this must prosper whatever may happen. తేలపలుకు (A. iv. 306.) to speak clearly. తేలిన swelling ఉబికిన; large. తేల్చి పలుకు to accent softly, to use the soft accent instead of the harsh one; as పోతన *Pōtana* for పోతన్న *Pōtanna*, and ఇపుడు *ipuḍu* for ఇప్పుడు *ippuḍu*. తేలదీయు to haul ashore, to pull out or drag out. తేలగిల్లు or తేలగిలుబడు *tēla-gillu*. v. n. To rise to the top. పైకితేలు. To roll or swim, as the eyes. తేలగిల్లు swimming of the eyes. తేలవేయు *tēla-vēyu*. v. a. To open (the eyes) wide. కన్నులుతేలవేయు to stop winking. తేలచేప *tēla-chēpa*. n. A kind of fish. H. iv. 225. తేలాడు *tēl-āḍu*. (తేలి+ఆడు) v. n. To float. తేలు, తేలి ఆడు. తేలించు *tēlintsu*. (causal of తేలు.) v. a. To cause to float. To bring up or produce. To accomplish, do, achieve, perform. To fulfil. To glance, as applied to the eyes. తేల్చిపోయు to pour in loosely or lightly. లాలించితేలించు

to fondle and please. తేలిక *tēlika*. n. Lightness, ease. లఘుత్వము. adj. Easy, simple, light. బరువుతేని. వానికి ఇప్పుడు ఒళ్లు తేలికగా నున్నది he is well. తేలుపారు *tēlu-p-āru*. v. n. To arise, to be born పుట్టు.

తేలుమణి *tēlu-mani*. [Tel.] n. A kind of plant. దుష్టాపాప్తి, ధూమ్రపుష్పవృక్షము, చెంచలికిక, తేలుకొండిచెట్టు.

తేవ *tēva*. [Tel.] n. A kind of festival. ఉత్సవ విశేషము.

తేవనము *tēvanamu*. [Skt.] n. A park. ఆట తోట. A game or play ఆట.

తై tai

తైక్క *taikka*. [Tel.] n. An interjection in games like *play!* bang! తైక్కమని fleetingly. ఇదిఇటుక రెండునాళ్లకు తైక్కమని పోయేది గాని శాశ్వతముగా నిలిచేదికాదు this is a thing that vanishes in a couple of days, it has no permanence.

తైనాతీ *tainati*. [H.] n. Attendance, service, waiting. n. A servant.

తైరు or తయిరు *tairu*. [Tel.] n. Curds. పెరుగు, దధి. (పాంచా. iv.)

తైర్థికము *tairthikamu*. [from Skt. తీర్థము.] adj. Appertaining to pilgrims. తీర్థకోటి the pilgrim band or company. తైర్థికుడు *tairthikudu*. n. A pilgrim. తీర్థసేవచేయువాడు.

తైలము *tailamu*. [Skt. from తిలు.] n. Oil, ointment, unguent, salve, essence. మంటి తైలము earth-oil; bitumen. తైలీనము *tailīnamu*. adj. Oily; belonging to oil, producing oilseeds (as land), తిలలుపండునది (పాలను). తైలికుడు *tailikudu*. n. An oilmonger గానుగవాడు.

తొ to

తొంక *tonka*. [Tel. another form of తోక.] n. A tail. తోక.

తొంగలి *tongali*. [Tel.] adj. Slanting, drooping, వాలిన. Flowing, స్రవించిన. తొంగలిరెప్పలు quivering eyelids "వావురుతొంగలిరెప్పల క్రేవలనునిగ్గులంకురింప." Zacc. iv. 167. తొంగలించు or తొంగలిగొను *tongalintsu*. v. n. To gleam, glance, sparkle, flash, shine. ప్రకాశించు. To expand or open. వికసించు. To excel, అతిశయించు, విజృంభించు. To increase, వర్ధిల్లు. To flow. స్రవించు. తొంగలిపాటు *tongali-pātu*. n. A salutation. నమస్కృతి.

తొంగిల్లు *tongillu*. [Tel. from తొంగలి.] n. plu. Drops. బొట్లు. తొంగిల్లుగా *tongillu-ga*. adv. In drops, drop by drop, బొట్లుబొట్లుగా. "తొంగిల్లుకార్చిరుతో సత్తివిరూము" BD. iii. 679. Oil dops, నూనెబొట్లు.

"అనిశము కెల్లమునౌదేవితాను.
జననిస్మైప్రాణేశుడనయు గావించి,
తొంగిల్లుపైనిడి లింగమూర్తికిని,
తుంగికగావించె నక్షరాజునంబు."
BD. iii. 664.

తొంగు *tongu*. [Tel.] v. n. To be inclined, to slant. వాలు. To lie down, శయనించు. తొంగిచూచు *tongi-tsūtsu*. v. n. To peep, to look into తొంగిన *tong-ina*. adj. Lean, thin. బక్కపలచని, సన్నగిల్లిన. తొంగుండు *tong-undu*. (తొంగి+ఉండు.) v. n. To lie down. శయనించు.

తొంట *tonta*. [Tel.] n. The bark of a tree, చెట్టుపట్ట. గడ్డితొంట or తొంటకొన్న a wisp, a torch made of straw. తొంటచెయ్యి *tonta-cheyyi*. n. A withered hand ఈడబోయిన చెయ్యి. తొంటచేతివాడు a man with a withered hand. కుకరుడు.

తొంటి or తుంటి *tonti*. [Tel.] n. The joint of the hip. Plural. తొంట్లు.

తొంటి or తొల్లిటి *tonti*. [Tel. infl. of తొలి.] adj. First, former, earlier. అప్పటితొంటి మూర్తి his original shape. తొంటితెరువునకు to the former road. తొంటి పెద్దలు ancestors.

తొండ *tonda*. [Tel.] n. A chameleon, a bloodsucker: కృకలాసము. When old it is called ఊసరవెల్లి.—తొండలముచ్చుగద్ద (Jerdon No. 22.) The White-eyed Buzzard Eagle or *Teesa, Butastur teesa*. (F. B. I.)

తొండము *tondamu*. [from Skt. తుండము.] n. An elephant's trunk. The neck or hose of a leather bucket. తొండపుదోమ or ఏనుగదోమ a mosquito with a proboscis, the female mosquito (which alone has such a proboscis), ఘోటి. తొండవుల్లంకి *tonda-ullanki*. n. The Black-tailed Godwit, *Limosa belgica*. (F. B. I.)

తొండాడు *tond-adu*. [Tel.] v. t. To tease. బాధపెట్టు, తొందరపెట్టు. To hasten త్వరపరచు.

తొండి Same as తొంటి (q. v.)

తొండు or తొండోడు *tondu*. [Tel.] n. An idle or careless man. సోమరి, ప్రాలుమాలినవాడు.

తొండ్లిచెట్టు *tondli-chettu*. [Tel.] n. A sort of tree. హంస. iv.

తొంద or తొందు *tonda*. [Tel.] n. A corpulent man. బొజ్జపట్టినవాడు.

తొందర *tondara*. [Tel. తొర+తొర.] n. Great haste, hurry. సంభ్రమము. Trouble, embarrassment. బాధ. Disorder, confusion. Danger, peril. Labour, difficulty. Vexation, needless trouble. తొందరగాకావలెను I want it greatly. వాడు తొందరపడలేదు he was not put about, or flustered. తొందరపడు to be troubled, to be in a hurry, to be embarrassed or flurried. ప్రయాణముమీదతొందరను మరచిపోతిని I forgot it in the hurry of the journey. తొందరచేయు, తొందరపెట్టు or తొందరపరచు to trouble, annoy or vex, to interfere with. తొందరపాటు *tondara-patu*. n. Haste, hurry. Troublesomeness.

తొండలము *tondalamu*. [Tel.] n. Tamarind juice boiled with some vegetable as a preserve. చింతపండుపులుసుతోకూరలుకలిపిన దప్పళము.

తొంబది or తొంబై *tom-badi*. [Tel. తొమ్మిది+పది.] adj. Ninety. తొంబండ్రు. Ninety men తొంబదిమంది. తొంబనూరు or తొంబదినూరులు ninety hundreds.

తొకతొక *toka-toka*. [Tel.] adj. Indistinct. అవ్యక్తము.

తొక్క *tokka*. [from Skt. త్వక్కు.] n. Skin, hide, bark, rind, peel. త్వక్కు, తోలు, పట్ట.

తొక్కట, తొక్కటము, త్రొక్కట or త్రొక్కటము *tokkata*. [Tel. from తొక్కు.] n. Distress, grief. కష్టసుఖము. A scrape or hobble. సంకటము. ఆ తొక్కట రెుఱుగను I know nothing of the trouble. తొక్కటించు *tokkat-intsu*. v. a. To grieve, distress, annoy. తొక్కటపడు or త్రొక్కటపడు *tokkata-padu*. v. n. To be troubled. సంకటపడు. తొక్కటపాటు or త్రొక్కటపాటు *tokkata-patu*. n. Distress, trouble. సంకటపాటు.

తొక్కము *tokkamu*. [Tel.] n A kind of plant like fennel, Anethumsowa. శతాపుష్ప.

తొక్కు or త్రొక్కు *tokku*. [Tel.] v. n. & a. To step, tread, or perform a dance. ఆనగద్రొక్కుట (A. ii. 104) to pound, stamp, trample on, crush, macerate. పొరుగిల్లు తొక్కక not entering your neighbour's house. పొలిమేరతొక్కు to lay down or define a boundary line by treading on it. కొమ్మతొక్కు to lay down suckers or branches from a tree. తొక్కిచూచు to go and examine in person: to inspect personally. మిటకొక్కు to blink or put out of view, to suppress. తొక్కు n. Paste, pickle. తొక్కించు or తొక్కించు *tok-kintsu.* v. a. To cause to tread, &c. నాట్యము తొక్కించినారు they made him dance. చింతకాయలు తొక్కించిరి they had the tamarind pounded. తొక్కు or తొక్కుడు *tokkudu.* n. Treading, grinding, dancing, capering, ఇరుకాటము, సమ్మర్దము, రాపిడి, రాయాపు. R. i. 46. Plu: తొక్కుళ్లు. P. iii. 76. adj. Threshed, pounded తొక్కిన. తొక్కుడుకమ్మి *tokkudu-kammi.* n. A threshold. దొడ్డి తొక్కుడుదాటిపోయినది it broke out of the fold. తొక్కుపలుకులు lisping words. బిడ్డలుపల్కెడు అదేమాటలు. తొక్కుడుబిళ్లలు *tokkudu-billalu.* n. A certain game. తొక్కులాడు *tokku-l-adu* v. n. To grieve, to be in trouble. తొక్కులాడుచునడుచుట to trudge on, plod, to get on with difficulty.

తొగ *toga.* [Tel.] n. The purple lotus or water lily. A crowd, multitude, group. సమూహము. Manner విధము. Trouble, difficulty, కష్టము. adj. Troublesome కష్టమౌ. తొగచుట్టము or తొగచెలికాడు *toga-tsuttamu.* n. The moon, as being the lover of the lotus. తొగకంటి *toga-kanti.* n. A lotus-eyed, (i.e., a beautiful) woman, చక్కనికన్నులుగల ఆడుది. తొగమగడు, తొగరేడు or తొగమిండడు *toga-magadu.* n. The moon as being the lord of the lotus. తొగసూడు *toga-sūdu.* n. The enemy of the lotus, i. e., the Sun.

తొగట *togata.* [Tel.] adj. Belonging to the weaver caste. తొగటవాడు *togata-vādu.* n. A weaver. H. ii. 23.

తొగడు *togadu.* [Tel.] n. Leanness, compression. తొపలికగుట. రామా: యు. కాం.

తొగర *togara.* [Tel.] n. Acridity. వగరు.

తొగరు or తొగరుకె *togaru.* [Tel.] n. The Pigeon Pea tree. కందచెట్టు. A certain forest, wood used as timber.

తొగరు *togaru.* [Tel.] n. Red colour, scarlet. ఎఱుపు. Scarlet thread ఎర్రనూలు. (There are three species of red dye. The best sort is called చిరుకొరుతొగరు; the next sort is మారుచెరము తొగరు; and the worst, మడ్డితొగరు.) A certain fragrant flower. adj. Red. ఎర్రని. తొగరుమల్లి *togaru-malli.* n. A sort of crystal. తొగరు ముక్కుపులుగు the scarlet beaked bird, i. e., a parrot. తొగరుచెట్టు *togaru-chettu.* n. A tree from which a red dye is made. Logwood. *Morinda citrifolia.* తొగరు కొను *togaru-konu.* v. n. To become red. ఎర్రనగు.

తొచ్చెము or తొచ్చియము *tochchemu.* [from Skt. తుచ్ఛము.] n. A low or vulgar word. తుచ్ఛవచనము. రామా. v.

తొటతొట or దొటదొట *tota-tota.* [Tel.] adv. (Trembling) violently, perceptibly (shuddering.) అతిశ. "తొడయుడు నధరంబు తొటతొటనదిర." L. iv. 313.

తొట్ట, తొట్టె or తొట్టు *totta.* [Tel.] adj. Thick. తొట్టిపెదవులు or తొట్టిమూతి thick lips. తొట్టిఅక్కరము (A. vi. 75.) broken pronunciation, mispronunciation. తొట్టి నోటివాడు పలికిన అక్షరము. తొట్టగిలబడు *tottagila-badu.* v. n. To be agitated. తొట్రుపడు. తొట్టగిల్లు or తొట్లగిలు *tottagillu.* v. n. To excel, to bloom. అతిశయించు. To happen, occur, to have కలుగు. పొందు.

తొట్టి *totti.* [Tel.] n. A tub, vat, trough, or manger. A sort of seat on an elephant. పల్లకితొట్టి the frame work of a palanquin, under the bedding. తొట్టికట్టు *totti-kattu.* n. A part or division of a mansion. The square left unroofed in the centre of a Hindu house. తొట్టిలి. కూతురికి రెండు తొట్టికట్ల యిల్లు యిచ్చినాడు he gave to his daughter a large house containing two large divisions. తొట్టిబండి *totti-bandi.* n. A bullock cart.

తొట్టియ Same as తొట్టి. (q. v.)

తొట్టిల Same as తొట్ల. (q. v.)

తొట్టు or తొట్టుకొను tottu. [Tel.] v. n. To spread వ్యాపించు. To happen, come on (as thirst), to chance అవిర్భవించు, పుట్టు, సంభవించు. To flow ప్రవహించు, స్రవించు. "పిట్టవునీవు వారినిధి పెద్దలకెల్లను పెద్ద పెల్లిగా దొట్టు నొకానొకప్పుడతి దూరముతుంగ తరంగసంఘముల్ బిట్టడుచుగా" P. i. 546. టీ॥ వెల్లిగాదొట్టు, వెల్లువగా ప్రవహించును. To stop up from flowing ఎగకట్టు. "క॥ ధరిత్రీవిభుడు చేయి చేతుల, నావాహినినీరు తొట్టునట్లుగబట్టె." V. P. vi. 199. To be filled నిండుకొను. "చెక్కులదొట్టిన కన్నీరు వోవ దుడుచుచు బలికెా." Swa. iii. 52. To move జరగు. "పొట్టలుచీలినదొట్టువారు." రా: రము, కాం. v. t. To touch, స్పృశించు. To adopt, అవలంబించు. To begin, మొదలు పెట్టు. "అత్తాపగమున దుత్తురముగా దొట్టిమ ట్టాడి అట్టహాసంబుచేసి." R. v. 191. ఉత్తురముగా దొట్టి=ఉత్తురముచేసి. తొట్టు tottu. n. A field within the bed of a tank. చెరువు కట్టలోపలిపొలము. A side, direction, quarter. పార్శ్వము, వైపు, దిక్కు. "పార్థునకు మేతొట్టున బొరలకుమవుడు." G. v. 257. Profit, gain. ఫలము, లాభము. Connection, relationship సంబంధము, స్పృక్కు. A sudden sound ఠటాలనుధ్వని. Also, same as తెట్టువ. (q. v.) తొట్టున tottuna. adv. Quickly, at once. దబ్బున. తొట్టువ Same as తెట్టువ.

తొట్టె or తొట్టెయ totte. [Tel.] n. A weaver's shuttle. నాడె.

తొట్ర totra. [Tel.] n. A hole. తొర్ర.

తొట్రకోరె totra-kore. [Tel.] n. A sort of tree. H. iv. 9.

తొట్రు or తొట్రుపాటు totru. [Tel.] n. Trottering. Confusion, perplexity, hurry. తొట్రిలు, తొట్రిల్లు, తొట్రిలుడు, తొట్రుపడు or తొట్రుకొను totrilu. v. n. To stagger, totter, stumble, be bewildered or perplexed, to trip, or stumble, as in speech తడబడు. To split భేదిల్లు. Swa. iii. 125.

తొట్ల, తొట్టిల, తొట్టల, తొట్లియ or తొట్లె totla. [Tel.] n. A cradle. ఉయ్యాల తొట్టి.

తొట్లచెట్టు totla-chettu. [Tel.] n. A plant called *Capparis grandiflora*. Heyne, Tracts, p. 130.

తొడ toda. [Tel.] n. The thigh. తొడమీద ఉంచు to place on the lap. పెందొడ the thicker part of the thigh. చిరుదొడ the thinner part of the thigh. తొడమాంసము a leg of mutton. తొడపుట్టువు lit: one born from the thigh, i.e., a Vaisya. తొడ పాశము or తొడబెల్లము toda-pasamu. n. Pinching the thigh. తొడగిల్లుట.

తొడకు Same as తొడుకు. (q. v.)

తొడగు Same as తొడుగు. (q. v.)

తొడయు todayu. [Tel.] v. a. To wipe. తుడుచు. M. iii. 282. To wash కడుగు.

తొడరు todaru. [Tel.] v. n. To happen. కలుగు. To undertake, attempt, పూను, యత్నించు. To desire, సక్తమగు. To be agitated, తొట్రుపడు. To follow, అనుసరించు. To oppose, ఎదిరించు. To obtain, ప్రాపించు. To resemble, అనుకరించు. "క॥ కురుబలము దొడరిగెలువగ, గురుగణములకైనదరిది." M. VII. v. 6.

"క॥ పాపంబు బుద్ధిపూర్వ
వ్యాపారముగాగదొడరినప్పుడు మనుజుం
డేపాటుదానినెంతియు
బాపికొనంజాలు సుజనబాంధవచెపుమా."

M. XII. iii. 321.

"తోకజంతువులను తొడరిగొంతులుకోసి,
మేకపిందుసెల్ల మెడలువిరిచి,
కడమవాటిసెల్ల కాల్చుకతిందురు."

Vema. 319.

"కావిపంచెగట్టి కడుయోగివలెనుండి,
వెలికినోర్చు కల్ల విడిచిపెట్టి,
తొడతిరుగువాడు దొంగసన్న్యాసిరా."
Vêma. 791.

తొడరిక toḍarika. n. Following, courting. అనుసరణము. తొడరువు toḍaruvu. n. An attempt యత్నము. భా: శల్య. i. adj. First మొదటి.

"ద్వి. తొడలమైనున్న యాతొడరువుగొదుకు
దాడిబడ గడబడ దోసియ్యక్రమున."
భాగ. vii.

తొడవు toḍavu. [Tel. from తొడుగు] n. A jewel, ornament భూషణము. చేతులకు తొడవు దానము liberality is the best jewel of the hand.

తొడి toḍi. [Tel.] n. A ferrule or ring of iron round a staff. పొన్ను. Haste, త్వర, సంభ్రమము. తొడితొడి toḍi-toḍi. adv. Instantly, at once. తొడితొడిజాగిలంబడి మొక్కిమొక్కి. Charitr. v. 537. తొడిబడు toḍi-baḍu. (తొడిక+పడు) v. n To move, shake, waver. చలించు. To haste, hurry. To be perplexed or confused. తొట్రుపడు. To be scattered చెదరు. H. i. 307. R. v. 73.

తొడికిలు toḍikilu. [Tel.] v. a. To seize, snatch, bite. ఒడిసిపట్టు, లంకించుకొను. "చిలిపయకమండుతప్పఘన శైలకటాహముకేలుదామరగా, దొడికిలబట్టిరావాలువిధుంగబలించుకేతి." Jaimini. iv. 147. "మృదుకోకిలముల తొడికిలితిని శిష్యర్షి పిడుచు పచ్చిచెక్కల తలుగ లంగనడచి." BD. iv. 238.

తొడిచెప్పు Same as తోడిచెప్పు. See under తోడు.

తొడిమ or తొడిమె toḍima. [Tel.] n. The stalk of a leaf or flower. కాడ. మొదుగతొడిమలు a sort of rice with long grains.

తొడు Same as తొడుగు. (q. v.) తొడిగించు toḍigiñtsu. [Tel.] v. a. To put on, &c. వానికి బట్టలుతొడిగిస్తిని I dressed him.

తొడుకు toḍuku. [Tel.] v. a. To seize, snatch, bite. ఒడిసిపట్టు, లంకించుకొను.

"పాలముతోనదొడికి పులిపట్టుకైనది
వడివెడిర్పుసంస్థవార్పు కేళ
గంగతోనమొసలి మ్రింగెదుసాటి
నసదగారయ్య యయక్షళా."
G. vi. 17.

n. A bullock. ఎద్దు. A cow, ఆవు. Ill-gotten food. దొంగకూడు.

తొడుకోను or తొడికోను Same as తోడు కొను. (q. v.)

తొడుగర or తొడుగఱ్ఱ toḍu-gara. (తొడుగు+కఱ్ఱ) n. A bundle of thorny brushwood. ముండ్లకంపమోపు. "మంచత్రొ తొడుగరలైరక్ట." మంచమునకంటుకొనిపోయిరి. Swa. iii. 166.

తొడుగు, తొడగు, తొడ్గు, తొడవు or తొడుపు toḍugu. [Tel.] v. a. To put on or wear (dress, jewels, a shape, &c.) To place an arrow on the bowstring. To prepare. To begin. M. XII. v. 88. యత్నపడు, ధరించు, ఆరంభించు, బాణమును ధనువునందు సంధానముచేయు. "తొడవింటివాడు" One who has drawn his bow. ఎక్కుపెట్టినవిల్లు తొడ నవలించుకొనిపోవువాడు A. vi. 102. n. An ornament. ఆభరణము. A piece of armour, కవచము. An arrow, బాణము. A sheath, గవిసెన. A drag, a hurdle of bushes, a load of brushwood. ముండ్లకంపమోపు. Swa. iv. తొడుగుకొను toḍugu-konu. v. a. To wear, put on, &c. తొడుపు toḍupu. n. Armour, plate or coat armour. కవచము. బంగారుతొడుపు gold filagree work. Repetition, చెప్పినది మరల చెప్పట.

తొడుసు toḍusu. [Tel.] n. Stuff, household stuff. Trash, rubbish, scoriae or scum of melted metal. Plague, trouble, annoyance. చీకులాట, జంజాటము, తగులాటము, గందరగోళము. Business, affair, connection. సంబంధము.

"తే॥ తపములు యజనంబులు దానంబులును,
ప్రతములును వేదకించినరత్వంబుతోడుకు."
M. XII. v. 306.

ఇవి అన్నిన్ని చీకులాటలని అర్థము. See also P. iv. 120.

తొణకు or తొణుకు *toṇaku*. [Tel.] v. n. To be spilled. నిండుకుండ తొణకదు a full pot does not spill, *i. e.*, a great or strong man is not easily agitated in his mind.

తొత్తు *tottu*. [Tel.] n. A slave girl. దాసి. A servant girl. దాసి. A whore, లంజె. తొత్తులమారి *tottulamāri*. n. A whore-monger.

తొన *tona*. [Tel.] n. A peel. తొల *tola*. adj. That which saves. రక్షకము.

తొనకు *tonaku*. [Tel.] v. n. To spill. చిందు, తొలకు. "కేనియల్ తొనకనివాని." Vasu. iii. 189. n. Haste, flurry. తొట్రుపాటు.

తొమ్మండు, తొంగుండు or తెమ్మండు *tommuṇḍu*. [Tel.] v. n. To lie down. శయనించు.

తొప్పదోగు *toppa-dōgu*. [Tel. తోగు+తోగు.] v. n. To plunge, to be drenched. తొప్ప దోగిన drenched, soaked. Bedewed, moist. వానలో తొప్పదోగ తడిసిరి they were soaked in the rain.

తొప్పరిల్లు, తొప్పరిలు or తొప్పరు [Tel.] *toppa-rillu*. v. n. To be inclined to one side, to slant, bend over. ఒరగు.

తొప్పలుదొరలు *toppalu-dōralu*. [Tel.] n. Myriads. కోటానకోటులు. కాశీ. ii.

తొప్పి or తోపి *toppi*. [Tel.] n. A cap or hat. టోపి.

తొప్పె *toppe*. [Tel.] n. The foreskin or prepuce.

తొబక *tobaka*. [Tel.] adj. Empty, seedless. విత్తులురాలిన, తొక్క.

తొమ్మందుము *tomman-dumu*. [Tel. తొమ్మిది+తూము.] n. The measure of nine తూములు or Marcals.

తొమ్మన్నూరు *tomman-nūru*. [Tel. తొమ్మిది+నూరు.] n. Nine hundred.

తొమ్మరము *tommaramu*. [Tel.] n. The royal table, maintained by a prince for his servants: also called కంబా and కుమ్మారము.

తొమ్మాడు *tomm-āḍu*. [Tel.] n. Ruin, నాశము. దానిని తొక్కి తొమ్మాడుచేసినారు they trampled upon it and ruined it.

తొమ్మిది *tommidi*. [Tel. తొమ్ము or ఒమ్ము+పది Lit. One less than ten.] n. Nine. (This is written ౯ in the east, but ౯ in the west.)

తొయ్యలి *toyyali*. [Tel.] n. A woman, a lady. అంచతొయ్యలి a female swan.

తొర *tora*. [Tel. for త్వర. (q. v.)] n. Quickness. వేగిరపాటు. Danger. ఆపద. తొరపడు *tora-paḍu*. v. n. To hasten. త్వరపడు, వేగిరపడు.

తొర Same as తొ్ర. (q. v.)

తొరక or గంజితొరక *toraka*. [Tel.] n. The scum or skin formed on gruel when cooling.

తొరగు or తొరుగు *toragu*. [Tel.] v. n. To flow, gush, burst out, run. కారు, స్రవించు, ప్రవహించు, జారు, రాలు. To fall, పడు. v. a. To leave, quit. వదలు, విడుచు. "క॥ మనుకొని కన్నీరు తొరుగ మొగి నిల్లు నిడెన్." Vish. v. 237. "తే॥ అదభిషేకంబు నను వారిధారలట్లు, తొరగునన్నట్లు ముత్తెముల్ దొయిలించి." T. v. 188. తొరగుచొచ్చు or తొరగుచొచ్చు *toragu-tsotstsu*. v. n. To escape, as cattle పశువులు తప్పించుకొనిపోవు.

తొరట *toraṭa*. [Tel.] n. A cell or small hole: a cavity. తొర్ర, కోటరము. వెన్నెముక తొరటగా నున్నది the backbone is hollow. తొరటలుపారు *toraṭalu-pāru*. v. n. To be bored, to become full of holes రంధ్రములుపడు. తొరతేనె *tora-tēne*. n. Hive honey. పుట్టతేనె.

తొరపు or **తొరుపు** *torapu*. [Tel.] v. a. To temper water to a certain heat.

తొరలు *toralu*. [Tel.] v. n. To happen, కలుగు. To be changed. మారు. **తొరలుచు**, **తొరల్చు**, **తొరలించు**, **తొరల్చు** or **తొర్లించు** *tora-lutsu*. v. t. To change. మార్చు. To slake hot with cold water. **తొరలనాడు** *torala-n-āḍu*. (causal of తొరలు to slip, &c.) v. n. To set up or trip up.

తొరవు Same as తొరగు. (q. v.)

తొరుగు Same as తొరగు.

తొరుత్రొక్కు *toru-trokku*. [Tel. త్రొక్కు + త్రొక్కు.] n. Great pressure. కట్టిత్రొక్కుడు.

తొరుపు Same as తొరలుచు. (q. v.)

తొఱ్ఱ *torra*. [Tel.] n. A hole or hollow in a tree. సందు, బొక్క, రంధ్రము. adj. Hollow, having a hole. తొఱ్ఱకొప్పు loosely bound tresses. **తొఱ్ఱజీనువాయి** *torra-jinu-vāyi*. n. The Indian Red Munia. *Sporæginthus amandava*, (F.B.I.) **తొఱ్ఱి** *torri*. n. A defect, breach or blemish. కొఱత, తుఱ్ఱి. adj. Wry, crooked. Leaky. Toothless. Deformed, chipped (as china or glass), damaged (as a shattered statue.) Partial, as an eclipse. "తొఱ్ఱియక్కరంబు." ఆము. vi. తొఱ్ఱివాడు or తొఱ్ఱికోటివాడు a man who has lost his teeth.

తొఱ్ఱు *torru*. [Tel.] n. A cow. ఆవు. పాండు. v. **తొఱ్ఱుపట్టు** *torru-pattu*. n. A cow house. గోష్ఠము. A herd of cattle. ఆవుల మంద, ఘోషము. భార. అర. viii.

తొర్లించు Same as తొరలుచు. (q. v.)

తొల *tola*. [Tel.] n. A bit or division, &c., in an orange, jackfruit, &c. తొన. A hole రంధ్రము. కేసతొలలు a sort of cake or vermicelli.

తొలకరి or **తొల్కరి** *tola-kari*. [Tel.] n. The opening of the year, the beginning of the rainy season. R. v. 157. తొలకరి వాన, తొలకరి మెరుపు summer rain and lightning. The rainy season, వర్షర్తువు. **తొలకరించు** or **తొల్కరించు** *tolakarintsu*. v. n. To rain at the beginning of the rainy season. To rain. To arise పుట్టు. తొలకరిమాడు the enemy of the first rains, i. e., the swan.

తొలకు Same as తొణకు. Parij. v. 51. R. v. 40. v. n. To begin, arise (as joy), happen. To exceed, shine. "మారదరచ న్నయ్య మహానీయకీర్తి యాడటమది తొలకాడ." BD. v. 253.

తొలకు or **తొలకాడు** *tolaku*. [Tel. తొలకి + ఆడు.] v. n. To spill. తొణకు. To move చలించు. To excel. అతిశయించు. To shine, gleam, sparkle. ప్రకాశించు. n. Movement. చలనము. A bright mark, మచ్చ, as those on a deer. A wave. తరంగము. A. iv. 185.

తొలగు or **తొలుగు** *tolagu*. [Tel.] v. n. To depart, go off, be removed: to step aside, retire, recede, get out of the way. To sidle or move sideways, to transgress. To be dislocated, as a bone. To vanish, perish. To end, terminate, cease. తొలగక incessantly, continually, steadfastly, unfailingly. తొలగని unfailing, ceaseless. **తొలగబారు** (తొలగక+పారు.) Same as తొలగు. **తొలగుడు** *tolagudu*. n. The act of going out of the way or moving aside. తొలగుట.

తొలగుబాప *tolagu-bāpa*. n. An enemy. శత్రువు. **తొలగించు**, **తొలంగించు** or **తొలగవీయు** *tolagintsu*. v. a. To remove,

తొలచు *tolatsu*. [Tel.] v. t. To wash. Parij. iii. 35. To wipe, తుడుచు. To cause to be removed, తొలగజేయు. To put away.

Pal. 266. తొలతొలమని Crying Stop! stop! ఆగుఆగుమని. BD. iv. 174. తొల తొలండు Up! begone! rise! Contracted for తొలగండి.

తొలసి or తొళసి *tolasi*. [Tel.] n. The Tulasi plant. తులసి. తొళసిపూసలు beads of Tulasi wood.

తొలి *toli*. [Tel.] adj. First, former, ancient, old, previous. తొల్లి. తొలినాడు the day before. ఆ తొలినాడు the day before that. ఆ తొలిరాత్రి the night before that. తొలితొలి the very first. n. The beginning. మొదలు. A socket, a hole. రంధ్రము. కంతము. A. iv. 218. The central hole in a wheel చక్రమధ్యరంధ్రము. తొలిక *tolika*. n. A hole. రంధ్రము. తొలివారము *toli-vara-mu*. n. The first day of the week.

తొలిపించు *tolipintsu*. [Tel. from తొలుచు.] v. a. To hollow out (a thing.) రాతిలోగాని, చెక్కలోగాని పల్లముచేయించు. To get a thing washed. కడిగించు.

తొలు *tolu*. [Tel. short for తొలుత.] adj. First. తొలుకోడి కూయుచుండగా when the earliest cock crows. తొల్నాడు the day before. See తొలుత.

తొలుకరి Same as తొలకరి.

తొలుకారు *tolu-kāru*. [Tel. తొలుత+కారు.] n. The rainy season. వర్షాకాలము. (తొలుత+కారు.) the first crop in the season మొదటి కారుపంట.

తొలుకు *toluku*. [Tel.] v. n. To rain. వర్షించు, కురియు. తొలుమొగులు (తొలుకు+మొగులు.) a raining cloud వర్షించుచున్న మేఘము. To burst forth, overflow, be emitted (as flames, tears, rays, sweat, &c.) తొలుకు నవ్వు a smile playing or beaming over the countenance.

తొలుకుడుపు *tolu-kuḍupu*. [Tel. తొలుత+కుడుపు.] n. The "first meal" given to an infant at weaning. అన్నప్రాశనము.

తొలుగు Same as తొలగు. (q. v.)

తొలుచు or తొల్చు *tolutsu*. [Tel.] v. a. To bore, perforate. To hollow, dig, scoop. To carve wood. To polish, furbish. To cleanse or rinse. కొయ్యతొలుచుపురుగు the wood-boring insect called a death-watch. ఆ పాత్రను తొలిచినాడు he cleaned or polished the dish.

తొలుత or తొల్త *toluta*. [Tel.] n. Beginning. మొదలు, ముందు. adj. First. మొదటి. adv. At first, in the first place. తొలుతటి *tolutaṭi*. adj. First, prior, preceding. Radha, iii. 62. తొలుతటిపదము the preceding word. Appa. v. 151. తొలుతొలుత or తొలుదొల్త *tolu-toluta*. adv. At the first, at the very beginning. Swa. i. 44. తొలుదీవి *tolu-dīvi*. n. The first island, i.e., Jambu dvīpa, Vasu. i. తొలుగట్టు *tolu-gaṭṭu*. (తొలుత+గట్టు.) n. The legendary eastern mountain on which the sun is supposed to rise. ఉదయాద్రి. తొలు చదువులు or తొల్చదువులు the first books, the Vedas వేదము. తొలుపక్కము the first lunar fortnight శుక్లపక్షము. తొలుచుక్క the first constellation, i. e., Asvini. తొలువేలుపు the first god, i. e., Brahma సురజ్యేష్ఠుడు; also, an Asura. అసురుడు, పూర్వదేవుడు. తొలునాడు *tolu-nāḍu*. n. The day before. తొలుబాము *tolu-bāmu*. n. A former birth. పూర్వజన్మము. M. xii. i. 190. "తొలుబాముల నోములు పెక్కునోచు కంగానిమహోన్నతుల్." R. vii. 118.

తొలుసంజ *tolu-sanḍza*. n. The early dawn. ప్రాతస్సంధ్యాకాలము. See తొలు and తొలి.

తొల్చు See తొలుచు.

తొల్త See తొలుత.

తొల్లి *tolli*. [Tel.] n. A former time. ముందు, పూర్వము. adj. Former, foregoing. ముందటి. adv. First, formerly, of old. M. I. i. 109. *Infl.* తొంటి V. P. ii. 241. తొంటికంటె more than before. తొల్లింటి, తొల్లిటి or

తొల్లింటి *tollinti.* adj. Former, old, ancient, of ancient days. M. I. i. 210. తొల్లింటియట్ల like as before.

తొల్లింటు Same as తొల్లిందు. See under తొరలు.

తొల్లిక or తొల్లీక *tollika.* [Tel.] n. A small hoe. తవ్వకోల.

తొల్లుగడ *tollu-gada.* [Tel.] adj. Joint, mutual, as a bond.

తొళక *tolaka.* [Tel.] adj. Thin. పలుచని.

తొళసి Same as తులసి. (q. v.)

తొవ or తొగ *tova.* [Tel.] n. A water lily. కలువ.

తొవర Same as తొగరు. (q. v.) తొవరి Same as తొగరి. (q. v.) తొవరు Same as తొగరు. (q. v.)

తొవ్వ *tovvu.* Same as త్రోవ.

తొస్స, తొస్సి or తొస్సు *tossu.* [Tel.] n. Brokenness. The state of being chipped, as glass. A defect in pronunciation owing to a tooth having fallen away. A slip or mispronunciation. ఉచ్చారణ లోపము. adj. Chipped or broken on the edges. ముక్కి. వాడు మాట్లాడడములో తొస్సులుపోతున్నవి his pronunciation is lisping or imperfect.

తో to

తో or తోడ *tō.* [Tel. from తోడు.] conj. With, together with, accompanied by, accompanying or following. కూడా, వెంబడి. వానిని కత్తితో పొడిచెను he stabbed him with a knife. నాతో చెప్పు tell me. జ్వరముతో నున్నాడు he is in a fever. ఉపవాసముతో నున్నారు they are fasting. సంకటముతో నుండే diseased, sick. నన్ను దయతో చూడుము look on me with favour. తేటతో వెలుగుచున్నది a lamp that has oil burns with clearness. Vēma. i. 43. అతనితో మనవిచేస్తిని I represented this to him. చీకటితో లేచి వెళ్లినారు they set out in the dark, i. e., before dawn.

తోక *tōka.* [Tel.] n. A tail. తోకత్రొక్కిన పాము వలె like a snake whose tail has been trodden on. తోకస్తంభము a slanting post or pillar అడ్డముగా చేర్చబడిన స్తంభము. తోకకప్ప *tōka-kappa.* n. A tadpole. తోకచిచ్చు a trail of fire. నిప్పులు తగిలించిన పిడకలవరుస. తోకచుక్క *tōka-tsukka.* n. A comet: a star with a tail. ధూమకేతువు. తోకతలవరి *tōka-talavari.* n. A long slender fish called *Ophidion* (Russell. No. 39.) తోకపీకుల్లు *tōka-pīkullu.* n. Plagues, hobbles, squabbles. తోకపీకుడుగాడు one who is always stirring up strife కలతగొట్టు. తోకపురుగు an insect with a tail. తోకమిరియములు cubebs, చలువమిరియాలు.

తోకము *tōkamu.* [Skt.] n. A child, offspring. బిడ్డ, అపత్యము.

తోకటువట్టు *tōkata-rattu.* [Tel.] n. A pollard tree. A tree that is half dead. (This meaning is clearly given in the గృహవాస్తు chap. 4. verse 18.)

తోకొను *tō-konu.* [Tel. for తోడుకొను.] v.n. To bring, to bring along with one. వెంటబెట్టుకొనివచ్చు.

తోకోజి *tokōgi.* [Mahr.] n. The crimson-breasted Barbet or Coppersmith, *Xantholaema hematocephala* (F. B. I.)

తోగు *tōgu.* v. n. To sink. మునుగు. To become wet. తడియు.

తోచిగాడు *tōchi-gādu.* [Tel.] n. A male hawk. మగడేగ.

తోచే *tōtsa.* [Tel.] n. A chuckler, a worker in leather. మాదిగవాడు.

తోచు *tōtsu.* [Tel.] v. n. To arise. పుట్టు. To occur to the mind, to seem, appear. To appear, as the sun; to become visible,

ప్రత్యక్షమగు. నాకు తోచుచున్నది I think, conjecture, conceive, fancy, imagine, suppose, intend. నీకు ఎట్లు తోచితే if you think fit, if you please, if it seems good to you. నాకు ఏమి తోచలేదు I knew not what to think. నాకు అనుమానము తోచినది I suspected. నాకు అర్థము తోచలేదు I do not perceive the meaning. అద్దములో తోచు ముడుపువలె like a purse reflected in a glass. వానికి భయము తోచినది he was afraid.

తోట *tōṭa*. [Tel.] n. A garden. తోటకాపు, తోటమాలి, తోటవాడు or తోటీడు a gardener. తోటకూర *tōṭa-kūra*. n. Greens, garden herbs. The green produce of a garden is divided into ఆకుకూరలు or తోటకూరలు vegetables, the leaf of which is eaten, such as spinach and cabbage: and కాయకూరలు of which the pod, fruit, or head is eaten, such as brinjals, cucumbers, &c. కోయదగ్గతోటకూర or కోయదగ్గ కూర is the phrase for all such plants as sprout after being cut, like camomile: and పెరుగుతోటకూర is the class of herbs which do not send forth shoots after being cut. తోటకూర is also a particular herb, called Braid in French. *Amaranthus Tristis*, (Rox. iii. 604.), *Amaranthus gangeticus*, or *Amaranthus oleraceus*. పెద్ద తోటకూర *Amaranthus giganteus*. దొగ్గలితోటకూర *Amaranthus polygamus*. ముళ్లతోటకూర or నల్లదొగ్గలితోటకూర the Prickly Amaranth, *Amaranthus spinosus*. ఎర్రకోడిజుట్టు తోటకూర or మయూరశిఖ, *Celosia cristata* (Watts.) సిగ్గనగా తోట కూరవంటిది modesty grows anew in the heart like a cropped herb. తోటకూరవంటి like mere green stuff, i. e., weak, feeble. తోటకూరవంటిపని a mere greenherb business. తోటకూరగింజవంటిది small as a mustard seed.

తోటి *tōṭi*. [Tel.] n. A Panchama or pariah. మాలవాడు.

తోడ *tōḍa*. [Tel. from తోడు.] a case ending. With. Together with. See తో. తోడ వడ్డీ including interest, the interest likewise. తోడనే *tōḍanē*. adv. Together: at once, as soon as, వారు వచ్చినతోడనే as soon as they came. తోడబుట్టు *tōḍa-buṭṭu*. v. n. To be born with, or be a brother to. తోడబుట్టినవాడు *tōḍa-buṭṭina-vāḍu*. n. A brother. తోడబుట్టినది a sister. తోబుట్టు, తోడబుట్టు, తోడబుట్టుగు or తోడ బుట్టువు *tōḍa-buṭṭu*. n. A brother or sister: lit: a fellow child.

తోడంటు or తోడు *tōḍanṭu*. [Tel. తోడు+అంటు.] n. Sour milk kept to curdle other milk with, చేమిరి. "పొందవులకన్నింటి విడిచిన పాల్గాచి కొనుకతోడంటుతో నుట్టిబెట్టి." Suca. i. 75.

తోడా *tōḍā*. [Tel.] n. A kind of gold jewel worn on the arm. హస్తభూషావిశేషము.

తోడి *tōḍi*. [Tel. from తోడు.] adj. Fellow, joint. తోడికులాంగనలు the ladies who were her fellows. తోడికోడలు *tōḍi-kōḍalu*. n. A fellow sister-in-law. మగని తోడబుట్టినవానిభార్య. తోడియల్లుండ్లు, fellow sons-in-law, the husbands of sisters. షడ్డకులు. తోడివాడు a companion తోడ నున్నవాడు.

తోడు *tōḍu*. [Tel.] n. Swearing an oath. ఆన. An affix, as నీతోడు I swear by you. A sister తోడబుట్టువు. Also, a souring stuff, చేమిరి. తోడుచెల్ల same as తోడంటు. Aid, help, convoy. సహాయము. A helper or companion. తోడుత or తోడ్త *tōḍuta*. adv. With, along with. తోడను. తోడుతోడ, తోడ్తోడ, తోడుతో or తోడ్తో *tōḍu-tōḍa*. adv. Immediately, at once, therewith, together. వెంటనే. తోడుదొంగ *tōḍu-donga*. n. An accomplice. తోడునీడ *tōḍu-nīḍa*. n. Aid and protection. A helper or companion.

సహాయము, సహాయుడు. తోడుపడు or తోడ్పడు *tōḍu-paḍu.* v. n. To be an aid, to assist. సహాయపడు. ఆట్టి ఆపదలో నాకు తోడుపడ్డాడు he stood by me in that calamity. తోడుపాటు or తోడ్పాటు *tōḍu-pāṭu.* n. Assistance, companionship, సహాయము. తోడుపెట్టు *tōḍu-peṭṭu.* v. n. To gather as a swelling. నరముతోడుపెట్టి నట్టు ఉన్నది the sinew has thrown out a lump. v. a. To add souring stuff to milk. చేమిరిపెట్టు. తోడుపోవు *tōḍu-pōvu.* v. n. To be equal, to suffice, సరియగు. తోడుబాలు *tōḍu-bālu.* n. The "fellow of the milk," i. e., the drops of water, put for luck into a pail before milking. పాలకు తోడుచేసిననీళ్లు. తోడుబోతు *tōḍu-bōtu.* n. A wizard or witch. పంపుచేయువాడు.

తోడు *tōḍu.* [Tel.] v. a. To draw or take up (water:) to bale. To dig up. పెల్లగించు. To wind up, as thread. నూలుపోగుకూర్చిచుట్టు. కుంభముతోడు to place the dinner before the goddess. వడ్డించు. తోడికొను, తోడుకొను or తోడ్కొను *tōḍu-konu.* v. a. To bring along with one, to lead; to draw water. వానిని ఇక్కడికి తోడుకొనిరా bring him here. v. n. To curdle as milk. పేరుకొను. పాలుతోడుకొన్నవి the milk curdled. తోడితెచ్చు, తోడుతెచ్చు, తోడ్తెచ్చు or తోతెచ్చు *tōḍi-tetstsu.* v. t. To fetch, to go and bring పిలుచుకొనివచ్చు. తోడించు *tōḍintsu.* v. a. To have drawn, to cause (water) to be raised. తోడ్తేర=కూడా పిలుచుకొని రావడానకు.

తోడెము *tōḍemu.* [Tel.] n. A little, a trifle. కొంచెము, లేశము. వచ్చినదూరము తోడెము the distance we have come is the shortest. adj. Small, little. చిన్న. చిరు. తోడెంపునవ్వులు smiles, gentle laughter.

తోడేలు or తోడెలు *tōḍēlu.* [Tel.] n. A wolf. వృకము. The Indian Wolf, *Canis pallipes*. (F. B. I.) చొప్పతోడేలు a weevil that destroys hay.

తోడ్తెచ్చు, తోడుతెచ్చు or తోతెచ్చు See under తోడు.

తోడ్తో, తోడ్తోడ తోడ్తోన or తోడ్తోనే See under తోడు.

తోడ్పాటు or తోడుపాటు See under తోడు.

తోతెంచు *tōtentsu.* [Tel. తోచు+ఎంచు.] v. n. To be borne, to arise పుట్టు, ఉదయించు. To make its appearance, to become visible కనబడు, ప్రత్యక్షమగు. To come, వచ్చు.

తోత్రము *tōtramu.* [Skt.] n. A goad, a spike. ఏనుగును అదలించేయీటె, ములుగోల.

తోదనము *tōdanamu.* [Skt.] n. A goad. ములికోల. Poking with the fingers; causing pain. నొప్పించుట. పాపతోదనము atonement, doing away with sin. తోయడము.

తోదము *tōdamu.* [Skt.] n. Pain. దుఃఖము. శిరస్తోదము headache.

తోదు *tōdu.* [Tel.] n. A series. వరుసకట్టు.

తోదోపులు *tō-dōpulu.* [Tel. తోపు+తోపు.] n. Exultation, pushing forward. తోదోపులుమీరి in an increasing struggle; ప్రజ విస్తారమువచ్చినది గనుక తోదోపులు నేడు అధికము a great crowd of people came, so to-day there is great excitement. తోదోపులాడు or తోద్రోపులాడు *tō-dōpu-l-āḍu.* v. n. To overflow or burst forth as the feelings. "ఆ పాలతివలపు లల పునదాపక తోద్రోపులాడుటయు." T. ii 100. టీ॥ పైపైకి తోసుకొనివచ్చుట.

తోన *tōna.* [Tel. తోను+అ.] postp. With. Thereupon, immediately. వెంబడి.

తోనిగాడు *tōni-gāḍu.* [Tel.] n. A sort of hawk.

తోప *tōpa.* [Tel.] n. Paste, batter. పిండి యుడకబెట్టినది, పంకటి. A wallet or bag of provisions.

తోప *tōpa*. [Tel. from తోచు.] adv. Apparently, in appearance, seeming, being manifested తోచేటట్లుగా. చిరునవ్వుతోప while a smile beamed over her countenance. దీనతతోప humbly. " క్రౌర్యము పాపకారి అని యీశ్వరుడు నాబుద్ధికి తోపజేసి నందున as God put it into my heart that cruelty was a sin.

తోపడ *tōpaḍa*. [Tel.] n. A carpenter's plane.

తోపమి *tōpami*. [Tel. from తోచు.] n. Non-appearance.

తోపరా *tōparā*. [H.] n. A horse's nose-bag for its food.

తోపాటు *tō-pāṭu*. [Tel.] adv. Like, as వలె.

తోపారము *tōpāramu* [Tel.] n. A leather mask put on the face of a hawk డేగ ముఖమునకు కట్టే తోలుగంత.

తోపి *tōpi*. [Tel. another form of టోపి.] n. A cap or hat. కుళ్లాయి.

తోపు *tōpu*. [Tel.] n. A grove. తోట. Redness ఎరుపు. A paste put over certain cakes కుడుములలోనకువాని మూతపిండి. adj. Red. తోపుచీర a red petticoat.

తోపు *tōpu*. [Tel. causal of తోచు.] v. t. To convey an idea. దీనతదోపనాడుచుగా to give him an idea of her misery. తోపింపజేయు or తోపజేయు *tōpimpa-jēyu*. (causal of తోచు.] v. t. To cause, to think, to suggest. ఈశ్వరుడే అతనికి తోపింపజేసినందున as God put this into his heart. See తోప adv.

తోపు or తోపుడు *tōpu*. [Tel. from తోయు or త్రోయు] n. A shove or push. Rejecting, refusing, thrusting away. తోపుడు or త్రోపుడు *topuḍu*. n. Dismissal, putting away, pushing away. A carpenter's plane; so called because he pushes it from him. తోపుడుకాకితము a cancelled page. కరముచేనితోపుడు loss arising from an unsaleable article.

తోమగరిక *tōma-garika*. [Tel.] n. A sort of grass. *Agrostis tenacissima*. Rox. i. 316.

తోమరము *tōmaramu*. [Skt.] n. An iron club, a lance, a hog spear. ఈటె, చిల్లకోల.

తోమాలె or తోమాలియ *tōmāle*. [Tel. తోట+మాల.] n. A wreath, garland, or string of flowers and leaves. A. v. 39.

తోము *tōmu*. [Tel.] v. a. To rub, rub down, handle, scrape, clean, రాచు, రుద్దు. To set or grind a razor, అరగదీయు. A. iv. 185. To beat or flog. తోమకము *tōma-kamu*. n. Rubbing, polishing, cleaning, తోముట. తోముకొను to rub or clean. పళ్లు తోముకొను to wash the teeth. తోముడు *tōmuḍu*. n. Rubbing రుద్దుట. తోమించు *tōmintsu*. v. t. To cause to be rubbed, &c., to have (it) cleaned, &c.

తోయము *tōyamu*. [Tel.] n. A marvel or wonder. చిత్రమైనవస్తువు. A band, or company తెగ, పరివారము. "తోయజనేత్రుడు హరితోతోయము గోపకులు దాను దోతెంచె నృపా." B. X. § 22. A delicacy, a tit bit, something nice కమ్మనివస్తువు, వింతవస్తువు Manner విధము. A time or opportunity తడవు, సమయము. తోయమువారు companions.

తోయము *tōyamu*. [Skt.] n. Water. తోయజము *tōyajamu*. n. Lit. The water born, i. e., the lotus. తోయజాక్షి *tōyaj-ākshi*. adj. Bright-eyed, having eyes charming as the lotus. తోయదము *tōya-damu*. n. A cloud. మబ్బు. తోయధి *tōyadhi*. n. The sea, the ocean. తోయరాశి *tōya-rāsi*. n. The "heap of water;" i. e., the sea. తోయరుహము *tōya-ruhamu*. n. A lotus. తామర. తోయసూచకము *tōya-sūchakamu*. n. The indicator of water, i.e., a frog.

తోయలి Same as తొయ్యలి. (q.v.)

తోయు or త్రోయు *tōyu*. [Tel.] v. a. To push, thrust, shove, propel. To dismiss, to deduct. కాలముతోస్తున్నారు they pass their time. పడద్రోయు to knock down తోసివేయు to do away with, set aside, dismiss.

తోరణము or తోరణ tōraṇamu. [Skt.] n. A wreath, a garland, a festoon of leaves, &c., hung over a doorway or across a road, &c. A gate. ద్వారము. A pack of tobacco weighing from two to ten seers. మాంసపు తోరణములు strings of mutton chops hung across the room. జ్వాలా తోరణము a bonfire. తోరణపట్టె tōraṇa-paṭṭe. n. The cross bar of a winch. (కపిలి).

తోరమల్లి or తోరమల్లె tōra-malli. [Tel.] n. Tourmaline, crystal. A false diamond.

తోరము tōramu. [Tel.] n. Thread consecrated and worn on the arm in token of a vow. Swa. iii. 119. కంకణము, చేతికట్టేది, వ్రతసూత్రము. తోరము or తోరంపు tōrampu. adj. Great, large, strong, fine, nice, పెద్ద, చక్కని, బలిష్ఠము. తోరంపుపన్నీరు fine rosewater. తోరంపుకోపము great anger. తోరంపుటేరు a full stream. తోరముగా tōramu-gā. adv. Well, properly, aloud.

తోరహత్తము tōrahattamu. [Tel.] n. A feat in wrestling. మల్లబంధవిశేషము.

తోరహత్తు tōra-hattu. [Tel.] adv. In large quantities, amply. సమృద్ధము. "ఉచితంబుల్ ద్రవ్యముల్ తోరహత్తులుగా గూర్చి." R. iii. 14.

తోలు tōlu. [Tel.] n. Skin, leather, bark. నల్లతోలు a dark skin. ఎర్రతోలు a fair skin. తోలుక Same as తోలు. n. తోలుదాలుపు or తోలుదాల్పు tōlu-dālupu. n. Lit. One who wears skins, i. e., Siva. తోలువాద్యము tōlu-vādyamu. n. A drum. వాద్యము.

తోలు or త్రోలు tōlu. [Tel.] v. a. To drive. వాటిని తన మందలోకి తోలుకొన్నాడు he drove them into his flock. కపిలతోలు to draw (water,) with a bucket, raised by oxen, to work (a pump). పారదోలు to drive off. తోలివేయు to drive off, to rout. తోలించు, తోలుచు or తోల్చు tōlintsu. v. n. To cause to drive, &c. తోలుపార tōlu pāra. n. A sort of fish called Scomber. Russell, plate 137: also called కుద్దుపార.

తోవ, త్రోవ or దోవ tōva. [Tel.] n. A way, path. A road, way or means, an expedient. "త్రోవపెట్టి." A. v. 122. టీ॥ దారిచేసి.

తోసిరాజు tōsi-rāḍzu. [Tel.] n. Lit: A king that has to be driven away. A technical phrase in Chess answering to 'Check!,' 'Sheikh' or 'Shah!' "చ॥ కలికి ముఖార విందమను కల్వలరాయనిదోసిరాజనుక." Dasa. i.

తౌ tau

తౌ or తవు tau. [Tel. from తగు.] v. n. To be fit. తగియుండు. Or, from తవ్వు v. a. To dig.

తౌగోల or తవ్వుగోల tau-gōla. [Tel.] n. A spade: a hoe.

తౌడు or తవుడు tauḍu. [Tel.] n. Bran. చిట్టు. తవుడు చల్లినట్టు ఉన్నారు they are as thick as chaff. తౌటిపాము or తవుటిపాము tauṭi-pāmu. n. A kind of fish. మలుగుచేప.

తౌలు or తవులు taulu. [Tel. from తగులు.] v. n. To follow. వెంబడించు. రాఘ. iii. To be caught చిక్కు. భార. అర. i. n. Connection. తగులము మార్క. ii. తౌలుకోలు or తవులుకోలు Same as తగులుకోలు. తౌలుకొలుపు or తవులుకొలుపు Same as తగులుకొలుపు. తౌలుచు or తవులుచు Same as తగులుచు, తగుల్చు or తగిలించు. తౌలువడు or తవులువడు Same as తగులుపడు. తౌలుబడు or తవులుబడు Same as తగులుబడు. See తగులు.

తౌల్యము taulyamu. [Skt. from తుల్య.] n. Resemblance, similitude. సామ్యము.

త్య tya

త్యజించు *tyajintsu.* [Skt. from √త్యజ్ to leave.] v. a. To leave, quit, desert, abandon. విడిచిపెట్టు. త్యజనము *tyajanamu.* n. Abandonment, desertion. విడుపు. త్యక్తము *tyaktamu.* adj. Left, quitted, deserted. విడువబడిన. త్యాగము *tyāgamu.* n. A giving up, or renunciation. Abdication. విడుపు. A gift, donation. ఈవి. ప్రాణత్యాగము suicide. త్యాగి *tyāgi.* n. A giver, donor, bestower. ఈవిగాడు. కర్మత్యాగి a freethinker or philosopher. త్యాజ్యము *tyājyamu.* adj. Fit to be left. విడువదగిన. An unlucky hour, an hour astrologically unpropitious. వర్జ్యము, దోషయుక్తమైనందున విడువదగినకాలము.

త్ర tra

త్రంచి Same as తెంచి. (q. v.) ఉ. హరి. iv.

త్రచ్చు or తరుచు *tratstsu.* [Tel.] v. a. To churn butter, &c. చిలుకు. To examine, investigate, stir, search. శోధించు, పరీక్షించు, పరిశీలించు. త్రచ్చన *tratstsana.* n. Churning. చిలుకుట.

త్రప *trapa.* [Skt.] n. Modesty, shame. సిగ్గు.

త్రమ్ము *trammu.* [Tel.] n. Dust. v. t. To dirty. To cause to be dusty. దుమ్ముచేయు (రాఘ. i.)

త్రయము *trayamu.* [Skt.] n. A trio. Three collectively, మూటిసమూహము. కవిత్రయము వారు the three poets, i. e., the Telugu poets నన్నయ, తిక్కన and ఎఱ్ఱాప్రెగ్గడ. కాలత్రయము at all hours, morn, noon and night. లోకత్రయము the universe, i. e., heaven, earth and hell, పరలోకము, భూలోకము, పాతాళలోకము. (*mundus tergeminus*—Schlegel) త్రయి *trayi.* n. The three. The three Vedas collectively. త్రయీతనువు or, త్రయీమూర్తి he who is the Vedas incarnate,—a phrase for the Sun. త్రయీధర్మము *trayī-dharmamu.* n. The Vedic duties వేదవిహితధర్మము. త్రయోదశము *trayō-daṣamu.* adj. Thirteenth. పదమూడవ. త్రయోదశి *trayō-daṣi.* n. The 13th day of the moon, reckoned either from new moon or full moon. త్రయ్యంతగంధము *trayyanta-gandhamu.* n. The savour, or knowledge of the Scripture. T. i. 5.

త్రవ్వు Same as తవ్వు. త్రవ్వకోల same as తవ్వుకోల. త్రవ్వటము Same as తవ్వడము or తవ్వుట. త్రవ్వటించు Same as త్రవ్వు. త్రవ్వితండము *travvi-tanḍamu.* adj. Innumerable, అసంఖ్యము. (ఉ. iv. and హరి. ఉ. iv.)

త్రసరేణువు *trasa-rēṇuvu.* [Skt.] n. Dust in the balance. An atom, a mote in the sunbeam. ముప్పది పరమాణువులకొలది.

త్రస్తము *trastamu.* [Skt.] adj. Timid, fearful. భయపడిన. త్రస్తుడు *trastuḍu.* n. One who is timid.

త్రస్తరి *trastari.* [Tel.] n. A gibe, a taunt, scorn, ridicule, పరిహాసము. "అట్లుగవయుం దమకించి త్రస్తరుల గుస్తరించ." Swa. vi. 11. "ఈరువహరుచుల త్రస్తరికిదన్న." A. ii. 88. త్రస్తరించు *trastarintsu.* v. a. To laugh at, to ridicule, or chaff. పరిహాసముచేయు. Swa. vi. 37.

త్రస్స *trassa.* [Tel.] n. Drops of saliva that fall out while speaking. నోటినుండి రాలే తుంపర.

త్రా trā

త్రాగు or త్రావు Same as తాగు to drink. త్రాగుడు or త్రావుడు *trāguḍu.* n. Drinking. పానము. ఆము. ii.

త్రాచు Same as తాచు a cobra.

త్రాడు Same as తాడు a rope. A ray of light. కిరణము. త్రాడుదాలుపు an epithet of Varuṇa

వడుచుచు. త్రాడుపడు *trādu-padu*. v. n. To become lean as a thread, to become emaciated, కృశించు, చాలిపడు.

త్రాణ *trāṇa*. [Skt.] n. Strength, nerve, might, vigour. బలము. శక్తి. త్రాణము *trāṇamu*. n. Protection. రక్షణము. త్రాత *trāta*. n. A protector, saviour. కాచు వాడు. త్రాతము *trātamu*. adj. Protected. కాపబడిన.

త్రావు Same as త్రాగు.

త్రాసము *trāsamu*. [Skt.] n. Fear, dread, horror. భయము. త్రాసామయము *tras-āmayamu*. n. Palsy. వణుకురోగము. A. v. 114.

త్రాసు, తరాసు or తరాజు *trāsu*. [Tel.] n. A balance, or pair of scales.

త్రాహి *trāhi*. [Skt.] n. Mercy! Help!

త్రి tri

త్రి *tri*. [Skt. cf. Eng. 'Three.'] pron. Three మూడు. త్రింశత్ or త్రింశత్తు *trimsat*. n. Thirty. ద్వాత్రింశత్ Thirty-two. త్రికము *trikamu*. n. The thigh bone, ముడ్డిపూస. A water wheel. కపిల. త్రికటుకము *tri-katukamu*. n. Lit: The three spices, viz., black pepper, dry ginger, and long pepper. సొంటి, పిప్పలి, మిరియాలు. త్రికరణము *tri-karaṇamu*. n. The three elements of action, i. e., thought, word and deed. త్రికరణశుద్ధి pure in thought, word and deed. త్రికాలము *tri-kālamu*. n. The three times, i. e., morn, noon and night. త్రికాలములయందున్ను always, ever, day and night, at all hours. త్రికూటము *tri-kūṭamu*. n. A certain hill. త్రికోణము *tri-kōṇamu*. n. A triangle. మూలచేరినంపు. త్రికోణకుండలి *tri-kōṇa-kundali*. n. The pineal gland, the part of the brain wherein the soul is imagined to dwell. త్రితయము *tri-tayamu*. pron. Three. మూడు. త్రిత్వము *tritvamu*. n. Lit: Three-ness. Trinity—a term used in Christian Theology. త్రిదండము *tri-dandamu*. n. A staff, formed of three slips of split bamboo, six feet long bound together as one cane, each slip being intended to represent Thought, Word and Deed. మనోదండము, వాగ్దండము, కర్మ దండము అను మూడు దండములు; ఈ మూడు దండములుగల సన్యాసాశ్రమము. త్రిదండి a mendicant bearing such a staff. త్రిదశుడు *tri-dasudu*. [త్రి+దశ = three states or thrice ten (years.)] n. One who enjoys the three stages of life, viz., infancy, youth and manhood, but no old age. A god: so named as being "thirty years old:" this being considered the prime of a man: and the age at which immortals always continue. త్రిదశాలయము *tri-das-ālayamu*. n. Lit: The abode of the immortals, i. e., Heaven, స్వర్గము. త్రిదివము *tri-divamu*. n. Heaven. త్రిదివుడు *tri-divudu*. n. A god. Padma. ix. 86. త్రిదశేశుడు a god; or, Indra, as lord of the gods. త్రిదోషము *tri-dōshamu*. n. Disorder of the three humours, viz., phlegm, bile, and atrabilis. వాత పిత్త శ్లేష్మములు. త్రినేత్రుడు or త్రిలోచనుడు *tri-nētrudu*. n. The three-eyed god, that is, Siva. త్రిపథగ *tri-patha-ga*. n. The stream which runs in "three beds," i. e., the Ganges, fabled to flow through heaven, earth and hades. త్రిపుండ్రము *tri-pundramu*. n. The triple mark worn across the forehead by Saivites. (ఊర్ధ్వపుండ్రము is the upright line worn by the Vaishnavites.) త్రిపుట *tri-puta*. n. The name of a certain musical metre. ఏడుతురములతాళము. త్రిపురము *tri-puramu*. n. The name of a district of Bengal (now called Tipperah) called after its king, *Tripura*, a giant who was vanquished by Siva: who, as "slayer of Tripura derives hence the name త్రిపురహర్త, త్రిపురసూదనుడు, త్రిపురాంతకుడు, త్రిపురారి, &c. త్రిపురదేవి or

త్రిపురసుందరి the Bona Dea, Venus. త్రిఫలము *tri-phalamu*. n. The three species of myrobalan; the *Phyllanthea emblica* ఉసిరి, *Terminalia chebula* కరక, and *Terminalia speciosa* తాండ్ర.

త్రిభంగి *tri-bhangi*. adj. "Three-ways" twisted. The name of a certain graceful attitude in which some statues stand: such as the వేణుగోపాల or Piping Apollo; or that given to the ద్వారపాలకులు or door keepers carved on each side of a temple gate. The word frequently occurs in books on sculpture (Silpi) and in some poems, but is no where precisely defined. త్రిభంగిగా, three fold: in three ways. మూడువిధములవునట్లుగానని Swa. iii. 76. త్రిభాగము *tri-bhāgamu*. adj. Divided into three parts or shares. త్రిభువనము or త్రిలోకము *tri-bhuvanamu*. n. The three worlds: heaven, earth, and hell, i. e., the universe. త్రిమూర్తి *tri-mūrti*. n. The Hindu Triad, consisting of Bramha, Vishnu, and Siva. త్రియామ *tri-yāma*. n. Night. M. VII. v. 317. త్రిరాత్రము *tri-rātramu*. n. Three nights, మూడురాత్రులు. త్రిలింగము *tri-lingamu*. adj. "Three gendered."—a phrase for Sanskrit nouns of the common gender. "Three formed." "త్రిమూర్తులత్రిలింగస్థలుగా." B. vii. 333. Also a fictitious or fanciful name (యౌగికపదము) used for the Telugu language. It is peculiar to Appa Cavi, and a few other modern writers, but is not mentioned in any ancient or classical poet: nor in any Sanskrit Dictionary, in lists of the "fifty six countries." See W. Vish. Pur. p. 193. In some modern lists *Troilinga* is named, but without any authority. త్రివర్గము a collection of three (things) as Duty (ధర్మము), Wealth (అర్థము), and Desire (కామము) or the *Gunas* called సత్వరజస్తమములు, or the three states called Increase (వృద్ధి), Decrease (క్షయము), and Stationariness (స్థానము.). త్రివళి *tri-vali*. n. A threefold corrugation on the stomach considered a beauty in women. "లలితకృశోదరంబు తరళత్రివళీయుత రోమరాజియున్." M. I. iv. 49. త్రివిక్రముడు *tri-vikramudu*. n. He who subjugated the three worlds in three strides, i. e., Vishnu. త్రివిష్టపము *tri-vishṭapamu*. n. Heaven. స్వర్గము. త్రివేణి *tri-vēṇi*. n. Lit: The Triple braided, an epithet of the Ganges which, according to mythology, springs in three streams from the head of Siva. త్రివేణుక or త్రివేణుకు *tri-vēṇuka*. n. The bands of a carriage pole. కాడికట్లు. T. v. 16. M. VIII. i. 302. త్రిశంకువు *tri-ṣankuvu*. n. Name of the father of the hero Harischandra. త్రిశంకుస్వర్గము the Aerial regions, the place of happiness created for త్రిశంకు who could not be admitted into heaven on account of his low origin. త్రిశూలము *tri-ṣūlamu*. n. The three pronged weapon of Vishnu. త్రిషవణము *tri-shavaṇamu*. n. The three ablutions, to be performed at morn, noon and night. M. XII. iv. 102. త్రిషవణస్నాయి he who bathes thrice a day. త్రిసప్త *tri-sapta*. adj. Thrice seven. BRY. iii. 19. త్రిసంధ్యము *tri-sandhya-mu*. n. The meeting times of forenoon, the noon and the afternoon. పూర్వాహ్ణ మధ్యాహ్న అపరాహ్ణ సంధ్యలు.

త్రిక్కు Same as తిక్కు. (q. v.)

త్రిక్కుట Same as త్రికము. "నలువురు నేర్పు తెలియకుండగ నేయుత్రిక్కుట్లలోపలనే తిరుగువారు." R. viii. 15.

త్రిక్కు *trikku*. [Tel.] v. n. To turn. తిరుగు. n. A twist or turn. Mand. iii. 27. తిరుగుట్లు. Trouble బాధ. Difficulty చిక్కు.

త్రిప్పు or తిప్పు *trippu*. [Tel.] v t. To cause to turn. తిరుగగేయు. n. Turning. తిరుగుడు. త్రిప్పట *trippaṭa*. n. Turning, roaming, wearisomeness. తిరుగుట. అయాసము. త్రిప్పరి a roamer త్రిమ్మరి. త్రిప్పుకోను

trippukonu. v. n. To turn. తిరిగికొను. త్రిప్పియాడు *trippi-y-ādu*. v. t. To turn. త్రిప్పు. త్రిప్పుత్రాడు or త్రిప్పుడుత్రాడు a churning rope కవ్వపుత్రాడు.

త్రిమ్మరు *trimmaru*. [Tel.] v. n. To roam about at pleasure. ఇచ్చవచ్చినట్లు సంచరించు. v. t. To go round. చుట్టివచ్చు. త్రిమ్మట *trimmaṭa*. n. Turning. Wandering about, సంచరించుట. త్రిమ్మరి, త్రిమ్మటుకాడు or త్రిమ్మరీడు *trimmari*. n. A rover, wanderer, vagabond, stroller. Suca. iii. 286.

త్రిష్టుప్పు *trishṭuppu*. [Skt.] n. A kind of metre in which the Vedas are composed. ఒక ఛందస్సు.

త్రు tru

త్రుంగు *trungu*. [Tel.] v. n. To break to pieces. తునకలగు. To be ruined, to perish. నశించు. త్రుంగుడు *trungudu*. n. Ruin నాశము. త్రుంగుడుపడు *trungudu-paḍu*. v. n. To be ruined నశించు. (భా. ix.) త్రుంచు or తుంచు *truntsu*. v. t. To break to pieces. తునకలుచేయు, తుంచివేయు. To kill చంపు. త్రుంపు or త్రుంపుడు *trumpu*. n. A piece, a fragment. ఖండము.

త్రుక్కు *trukku*. [Tel.] n. Pride, vanity, conceit. త్రుళ్లు, గర్వము.

త్రుటనము *truṭanamu*. [Skt.] n. Breaking. M. XII. vi. 513. తెగుట. త్రుటి *truṭi*. n. A twinkle, an instant. One fourth the time that it takes to pronounce a short letter. లఘ్వక్షరమునందలి నాలుగోభాగమును ఉచ్చరించునంతకాలము. త్రుటితము *truṭitamu*. adj. Broken. తెగిన.

త్రుట్టె or త్రుట్టియ *truṭṭe*. [Tel.] n. A crowd or multitude సమూహము. త్రుట్టెలు కట్టు to become a crowd or swarm గుమికూడు.

త్రుప్పు or తుప్పు *truppu*. [Tel.] n. Rust. ఇనుముమీది మకిలి. Tastelessness, చవిచెడి. త్రుప్పుడు *truppuḍu*. n. A hair of a bird or animal.

త్రుళ్లు *truḷḷu*. [Tel.] v. n. To rise and fall suddenly. ఎగిరిపడు. To be arrogant or proud. గర్వించు. n. Pride, arrogance, ఎగిరిపాటు, గర్వము. త్రుళ్లగించు *truḷḷa-gintsu*. v. n. To fly. ఎగురు. త్రుళ్లగింత or త్రుళ్లుమింత *truḷḷa-ginta*. n. Flying, ఎగురుట. త్రుళ్లగింతలుపెట్టు to fly, ఎగురు. త్రుళ్లింత *truḷḷinta*. n. Rising and falling suddenly, ఎగిరిపాటు. Pride గర్వము. త్రుళ్లియాడు Same as త్రుళ్లు v. త్రుళ్లుపోతు *truḷḷu-pōtu*. n. An impudent or insolent man.

త్రుస్సు or తుస్సు *trussu*. [Tel. anuk] n. A hissing sound. నిప్పు చిమ్ముటయందగుధ్వని.

త్రె tre

త్రెంచు. త్రెంపు, తెంచు or తెంపు *trentsu*. [Tel.] v. t. To cause to break. తెగునట్లు చేయు.

త్రెక్కొట్టు *trek-koṭṭu*. [Tel.] v. n. To cast away, to drive away. ఎగదొట్టు.

త్రెక్కొను *trek-konu*. [Tel.] v. t. To spoil. చెరుచు. "తపోబలము నిన్ త్రెక్కొనక." భార. అర. vi. To kill, చంపు. "పెంచినవారి నిమ్మెయిన్ త్రెక్కొనదగదు." భార. భీష్మ. iii. To confuse, కలచు. వై. v. To swallow up. మ్రింగు. మాఱ్కొ. vi. To drink త్రాగు. "జలనిధి త్రెక్కొని." భార. విరా. v. త్రెక్కోలు *trek-kōlu*. n. Spoiling, &c. త్రెక్కొనుట. త్రెక్కోలుకొను *trek-kōlu-konu*. v. t. & n. To kill చంపు. త్రెక్కొనగా murderously, destructively, ruinously. A. v. 159.

త్రెగు Same as తెగు. (q. v.)

త్రెడ్డు Same as తెడ్డు. (q. v.)

త్రెయ్యు *treyyu*. [Tel.] v. n. To break. తెగు.

త్రెళ్లు *trellu*. [Tel.] v. n. To die. చచ్చు. To fall పడు.

త్రెవ్వన *trevvana*. [Tel.] n. Beauty. చక్కన, సౌందర్యము.

త్రెవ్వు *trevvu*. [Tel.] v. n. To break, perish, fall, be severed. తెగు, ఖండితము గు. To wear down or be worn away. "తల త్రెవ్వవేసె." he smote his head off. BD. iv. 1973. "చువ్వపడి నెద త్రెవ్వగ." G. x. 44. v. a. To break, sever, split. ఖండనపరచు. HD. i. 2026.

త్రే trē

త్రేగుడు or **త్రేవుడు** *trēguḍu*. [Tel.] n. Sticky saliva. జిగటుగానుండు ఎంగిలి.

త్రేచు, త్రేపు, తేచు or **తేపు** *trētsu*. [Tel.] v. n. To belch. త్రేపు, త్రేనుపు or తేపు *trēpu*. n. Belching. తేపుట.

త్రేను *trēnu* [Tel.] v. n. To come out. బయలువెడలు, వెడలివచ్చు. "అతివ పూర్ణాంగకాకృతి తల్పద్మకాలక్రేణి." A. v. 155.

"పూర్తికాని యొక్కకొండర
నత్తైరువుం గట్టబనిచి యుండన్ క్రియుడా
దిత్తోకటికను గాని త్రేణిమరి
యుత్తరమున్నత్తరమటంచు నెత్రొప్పుకడకా."
A. vi. 96.

త్రేత *trēta*. [Skt.] n. The mythological Silver age, the second age of the world. The three sacred fires called గార్హపత్యము, దక్షిణాగ్ని, ఆహవనీయము.

త్రేనుచు, త్రేన్చు, తేనుచు or **తేన్చు** *trēnutsu*. [Tel.] v. n. To belch. త్రేనుపు, త్రేన్పు, తేనుపు or తేన్పు *trēnupu*. n. Belching. M. I. viii. 188.

త్రేవుడు Same as త్రేగుడు. (q. v.)

త్రై trai

త్రైగుణ్యము *trai-guṇyamu*. [Skt. from త్రిగుణ.] n. The three qualities called సత్వము, రజము, తమము.

త్రైభంగికము *trai-bhangikamu*. [Skt. from త్రిభంగి.] n. Lit: "Three ways." This is the name of a certain attitude. See త్రిభంగి. "సీ॥ కచభారకుచభార కటిభారములచేత కాయంబు త్రైభంగికముగ నిలిచి:" Nirankusa. i. 24.

త్రైలింగ్యము *trai-lingyamu*. [Skt. from త్రిలింగ.] n. A pedantic word for Telugu.

త్రైలోక్యము *trai-lōkyamu*. [Skt. from త్రిలోక.] n. The three worlds, Elysium, Earth, and Hades. The universe. M. I. viii. 192.

త్రైవర్గికుడు *trai-vargikuḍu*. [Skt. from త్రివర్గము.] n. One who seeks after the three objects of desire, viz: ధర్మము, అర్థము and కామము.

త్రైవిద్యుడు *trai-vidyuḍu*. [Skt. from త్రివిద్య.] n. One who knows the Veda. వేదము తెలిసిన వాడు.

త్రొ tro

త్రొక్కు or **తొక్కు** *trokku*. [Tel.] v. n. To tread, to trample. త్రొక్కుడు, తొక్కుడు, త్రొక్కుట, తొక్కుటము or తొక్కుట *trokkuḍu*. n. Trampling. తొక్కుట. Danger ఆపద. త్రొక్కుడుపడు, త్రొక్కుపడు, త్రొక్కటపడు, తొక్కుడుపడు or తొక్కటపడు *trokkuḍu-paḍu*. v. n. To be trampled upon. త్రొక్కటపాటు or తొక్కటపాటు *trokkaṭa-pāṭu*. n. The act of being trampled upon. తొక్కుడుపడుట. త్రొక్కుడుకమ్మి or తొక్కుడుకమ్మి

trokkuḍu-kammi. n. The threshold. గడప. త్రొక్కుడుపట్టె Same as త్రొక్కుడు కమ్మి. Also, a plank of wood which a weaver treads upon while weaving a cloth. త్రొక్కుడుబిళ్ల or తొక్కుడుబిళ్ల *trokkuḍu-billa.* n. A certain game played by children.

త్రో trō

త్రోసు or తోసు *trōsu.* [Tel.] v. n. To hasten. నడిచును. To undertake, పూను. To walk, నడుచు. To chase or follow after, కవియు. To go beyond or transgress, మీరు, అతిక్రమించు. v. t. To push, త్రోయు. To disregard. ఉపేక్షించు. To kill, చంపు.

త్రోటి *trōṭi.* [Skt.] n. The beak of a bird. పక్షిముక్కు. The mouth of a fish, చేపనోరు.

త్రోయు or తోయు *trōyu.* [Tel.] v. t. To push aside or away. తొలగనూకు. త్రోపు or తోపు *trōpu.* n. Pushing, తోయుట. An insult, నిరాకరణము. Refusal, నిషేధము. త్రోదోపు (త్రోపు+త్రోపు.) n. A hard or violent push, మిక్కిలి తోయుట. త్రోద్రోపులాడు *trō-drōpu-l-āḍu.* v. t. To push hard or violently. మిక్కిలి త్రోయు. బలాత్కారముచేసి త్రోయు. త్రోవడు or త్రోపువడు *trōpaḍu.* v. n. To be pushed, త్రోయబడు. త్రోపనంగోరవి *trōpanangoravi.* (త్రోపు+గోరవి.) n. One who is spoilt in every way, ఉభయభ్రష్టుడు, ఉభయభ్రష్టురాలు. త్రోపరి *trōp-ari.* (త్రోపు+అరి.) n. One who pushes, త్రోయువాడు. త్రోపాటు *trōp-āṭu.* n. The act of being pushed. త్రోపడుట. త్రోపాడు (త్రోపు+ఆడు.) v. t. To push, త్రోయు. త్రోపుడు *trōpuḍu.* n. A push. తోపు. A carpenter's plane. చిత్రిక. త్రోపుడుపెట్టు *trōpuḍu-peṭṭu.* v. t. To plane wood as a carpenter does. త్రోపుడుతో చ్రానా నునుపుచేయు.

త్రోపుచేయు *trōpu-chēyu.* v. t. To disregard, to slight. నిరాకరించు.

త్రోలు Same as తోలు. v. t.

త్రోవ, తోవ or దోవ *trōva.* [Tel.] n. A way, road. మార్గము. Means, an expedient. ఉపాయము. త్రోవరి *trōv-ari.* [త్రోవ+అరి.] n. One who knows the way.

త్ర్య trya

త్ర్యంబకుడు *tryambakuḍu.* [Skt.] n. A name of Siva. త్ర్యంబకసఖుడు *tryambaka-sakhuḍu.* n. Kubēra, the friend of Siva.

త్వ tva

త్వక్కు or త్వచము *tvakku.* [Skt.] n. Skin. తోలు. Rind, bark, husk, coat. చెట్టుపట్ట. నార. త్వక్పుష్పము a cutaneous eruption, a blotch, a scab.

త్వదీయ *tvadīya.* [Skt.] pron. adj. Thy, thine.

త్వము *tvamu.* [Skt.] An affix like *tion, ing, ness, ship,* &c., in *action, doing,* signifying the act or state of. మంత్రిత్వము the ministry; శత్రుత్వము enmity, &c. ఋత్వము the vowel ఋ.

త్వర *tvara.* [Skt. See తొర.] n. Speed, rapidity, haste. త్వరగా *tvara-gā.* adv. Speedily, rapidly. త్వరచేయు *tvara-chēyu.* v. n. and v. a. To make haste. త్వరపడు *tvara-paḍu.* v. n. To hasten, to hurry, or be active. త్వరితము *tvaritamu.* n. Speed, haste, rapidity. adj. Quick. త్వరగల. త్వరితముగా *tvaritamu-gā.* adv. Speedily, rapidly.

త్వష్ట *tvashṭa.* [Skt.] n. A carpenter, వడ్లవాడు. The maker of the universe. విశ్వకర్మ. One of the 12 Adityas, ద్వాదశాదిత్యులలో నొకడు.

త్వష్ట్రము or తావ్ష్ట్రము *tvashṭramu.* [Tel. Colloquial.] n. Bluntness, roughness, want of politeness. Clownishness. adj. Vile, brutish. Wretched. వాడు వట్టి తావ్ష్ట్రుడు he is a villain.

త్వా tvā

త్వాదృశము *tvā-driṣamu.* [Skt.] adj. Resembling you. నీవంటి.

త్స tsa

త్సరువు *tsaruvu.* [Skt.] n. A hilt or handle. కత్తిపిడి. A. i. 7. Parij. v. 45.

థ tha

థ *tha.* The name of a Sanskrit letter. No word used in Telugu begins with it.

ద da

ద *da.* [Tel.] n. The letter D pronounced as a dental. The initial T often changes into D as in అన్నదమ్ములు and తల్లిదండ్రులు.

In some words ద and డ are used at pleasure. Thus దించు or డించు, దాచు or డాచు, దిగు or డిగు.

దంగ or దంగా *danga.* [H.] n. Bullying, outrage. Wrangling, mutiny, sedition, rebellion. దంగాపెట్టు to wrong, to outrage. దంగాపడు to be frightened.

దంగు *dangu.* [Tel.] v. n. To be pounded, or cleaned. బియ్యమునాటి పొట్టు తీసివేయబడు. దంగుడు *dangudu.* adj. Beaten, pounded, cleaned; దంచిన. దంగుడుబియ్యము pounded rice.

దంచేన, దంచేనము or దెంచేనము *dantsana.* [Tel.] n. A large gun, a cannon. ఫిరంగి, బాంబుసనిరంగి, తోకటిఫిరంగి.

" దంచనంబులు, ఫిరంగులు
జబర్ జంగులు తుపాకులు."
K. P. viii. 77.

దంచు *dantsu.* [Tel.] v. a. To pound, to bruise, or clean grain in a mortar. దంపు.

దంట *danṭa.* [Tel.] n. A match, or equal, జంట. A rival, a competitor. A couple or pair. A hero, a genius సమర్థుడు. A dashing or spirited man or woman దిట్టతనముగలవాడు, దిట్టతనముగలది, నేర్పరి. adj. Rival: two, coupled, as twins: spirited, unrivalled. ప్రౌఢమైన. దంటతనము *danṭa-tanamu.* n. Rivalry, spirit, noble genius. దంటపడు *danṭa-paḍu.* v. n. To league, or combine. దంటపిల్లలు *danṭa-pillalu.* n. Twins. కవలు. దంటమోములవేలుపు the two-faced god, i. e., Agni.

దంటు *danṭu.* [Tel.] n. A stalk of such plants as cholam. Pith. తెల్లదంట్లు hay, sapless stalks. దంటునమలు to chew cholam stalks. దంట్లకొస్సాట a certain game among boys. అరటిదంటు the pith of a plantain tree. దంటుకూర *danṭu-kūra.* n. A kind of green vegetable the stalks of which are eaten.

దండ *danḍa.* [Tel.] n. Nearness. సమీపము. A side ప్రక్క. A prop. ప్రాపు. నాల్గుదండల on all sides, around. A garland, a collar, or necklace. adj. Big, large. దండకము *danḍakamu.* [Skt.] n. The name of a celebrated forest mentioned in poems. Blank verse; or a poetical passage formed of one short and two long syllables alternately. దండకట్ట *danḍa-kaṭṭa.* n. A hay band round a stack. The outer ring or line of the thrashing floor where the light grains lie. దండకడియము *danḍa-kaḍiyamu.* n. A bracelet worn on the arm. దండకవిలె *danḍa-kavile.* n. Local Archives: a chronicle or book giving the history of a village. గ్రామచరిత్ర పుస్తకపు కట్ట. దండకోల *danḍa-kōla.* n. A prop. ఊత. "నీకటుదండకోలగుదు నిర్భయమొందుము." జై. i. దండచెయ్యి *danḍa-cheyyi.* n. The upper arm. దండచేరు *danḍa-chēru.* n A sacred string tied on the upper arm దండచేతికి కట్టుకొనే తోరము. దండసరిమాటలు *danḍa-sari-māṭalu.* n. Veracity, true assertion.

దండగ See దండుగ.

దండనము See under దండించు.

దండపడు *daṇḍa-paḍu.* v. n. To approach. సమీపించు. To become tough. ఎద్దుమెడ్డమీద ముల్లుకోలతో పొడువగా బొరుసుగా కేర్పడు. **దండపాటు** *daṇḍa-pāṭu.* n. Approaching సమీపించుట, దండుపడుట. రామా. viii

దండము *daṇḍamu.* [Tel.] n. A bow, a salutation made by joining the palms of the hands in front of the breast. నమస్కారము. Respects, obeisance. Remembrance or compliments in correspondence. దండముపెట్టు to make a bow or courtesy, to make obeisance, to adore. ఆయనకు నాదండములు చెప్పవలసినది please to give him my compliments. **దండము** *daṇḍamu.* [Skt.] n. A rod, stick or staff, కఱ్ఱ, కర్ర. The stem of a plant. Chastisement either by killing a person, or by confiscating his property or by oppressing him in other ways, punishment, a fine. చతురుపాయములలో నొకటి, రాజశిక్ష. An army. దండు. A multitude. సమూహము. **దండన** or **దండనము** *daṇḍana.* Punishment. **దండనాయకుడు** *daṇḍa-nāyakuḍu.* n. A leader of an army. సేనాపతి. **దండనీతి** *daṇḍa-nīti.* n. Politics: the principles of government. నీతిశాస్త్రము. **దండయాత్ర** *daṇḍa-yātra.* n. An invasion, an incursion, a campaign, going with troops or in procession. యుద్ధయాత్ర, దిగ్విజయము. **దండలాసకము** *daṇḍa-lāsakamu.* n. A kind of dance నృత్యవిశేషము. దండధరుడు or దండుడు a macebearer, or staff-bearer, an epithet of Yama. యముడు. **దండాధిపతి** *daṇḍ-adhipati.* n. A general. **దండాసి** *daṇḍāsi.* n. A bailiff, a beadle. The name of a caste in Ganjam.

దండసిల్లు or **దండసిలు** *daṇḍasillu.* [Tel.] v. n. To be jammed in. ఇరుకుకొను; to be pressed or squeezed అదుముపడు, అణగు.

దండి *daṇḍi.* [Tel.] n. Strength, power, valor, courage, heroism ప్రతాపము, శౌర్యము. [Skt.] One who carries a staff. A staff-bearer. దండముగలవాడు. Name of a Sanskrit poet. A gate keeper, ద్వారపాలకుడు. Yama the god of death, యముడు. దండిచెనుదండి a fall in wrestling. The name of a certain tree. ఎఱ్ఱదండి. H. iv. 11. adj. Courageous, valorous ప్రతాపముగల. Plentiful సమృద్ధము. Great గొప్ప. దీనికి దండిపైరు జొన్నలు the principal crop is cholum. దండిగుండములు large pits. దండిమూక a great mob. **దండిగా** *daṇḍigā.* adv. Much, thoroughly, constantly. **దండితనము** *daṇḍi-tanamu.* n. Might, vigour. M. viii. v. 109.

దండించు *daṇḍintsu.* [Skt.] v. a. To punish, chastise. దండించిన దండన the punishment inflicted. **దండితుడు** *daṇḍituḍu.* n. One who is punished దండింపబడినవాడు. **దండ్యుడు** *daṇḍyuḍu.* n. One who deserves punishment. **దండనము** or **దండన** *daṇḍanamu.* n. Punishment. దండించుట.

దండిక *daṇḍika.* [Tel.] n. A guitar. కిన్నెర. A part of a necklace హారమందలి పేట.

దండిగ *daṇḍiga.* [Tel.] n. An ornamental palankeen or royal litter.

దండు *daṇḍu.* [from Skt. దండము.] n. An army, a multitude, a swarm, సైన్యము, సమూహము. మిడతల దండు a swarm of locusts. **దండాట** or **దండాడింపు** *daṇḍ-āṭa.* n. Revels, gambols, frolics, merry-making. Tossing red powder over one another at a feast. కేళాట. **దండెత్తు** *daṇḍ-ettu.* (దండు+ఎత్తు.) To raise an army. యుద్ధప్రయత్నము చేయు. To wage war. To invade.

దండుగ, దండగ, దండుగు దండువ or **దండువు.** *daṇḍuga.* [Tel.] n. Loss. నష్టము. A fine. జుల్మానా. **కలిమిదండుగ** *kalimi-daṇḍuga.* n. Lit: A tax on wealth, an income tax.

దండుదారి or **దండుబాట** *daṇḍu-dāri.* [Tel.] n. A high way.

దండుదివ్వె or **దండుదివియ** *daṇḍu-divve.* [Tel.] n. A lampstand. దీపపుబొమ్మ.

దండె or **దండియ** *daṇḍe:* [Tel.] n. A guitar, కిన్నెర, తంబుర. A. iv. 36. R. ii. 88. A pole. కఱ్ఱ, గడ. **The pole of a palankeen.** పల్లకి బొంగు. The beam of a pair of scales త్రాసు కోల. See కళా. vii.

దండెము or **దండియము** *daṇḍemu.* [Tel.] n. A cord line, or pole on which clothes are hung to dry. A kind of gymnastic exercise. దండెములుతీయు to perform a kind of gymnastic exercise, which consists in resting the hands on the ground and moving the body to and fro. కాళ్లు చేతులు నేలను మోపి ముందుకు వెనుకకు ఊగుట. శారం. iii.

దండోరా *daṇḍōra.* [Tel.] n. Proclamation by beat of tom-tom. దండోరావేయు to proclaim by beat of tom-tom or drum.

దంతము *dantamu.* [Skt. Cognate with Eng. 'Tooth.'] n. A tooth. పల్లు. Ivory. జీవదంతము solid ivory. **దంతధావనము** *danta-dhāvanamu.* n. Cleaning the teeth. పళ్లుతోముట. **దంతావళము** *dantā-valamu.* n. An elephant with tusks, a tusker; an elephant. **దంతి** *danti.* n. A kind of tree, *Croton polyandrum.* నాంచవతివృక్షము. H. iv. 9. An elephant, ఏనుగు. One who has projecting teeth కోరపంటివాడు. See దంతురుడు.

దంతురత *danturata.* [Skt.] n. Ups and downs. Unevenness. A. iv. 316. నిమ్నోన్నతము, మిటకపల్లము. **దంతురము** *danturamu.* adj. Uneven. **దంతురితము** *danturitamu.* adj. Up and down, uneven. పులకాంకుర దంతురితాంగుడు he who was in a tremor. V. P. ii. 233. **దంతురుడు** *danturuḍu.* n. One who has projecting teeth. మిట్టపండ్లవాడు.

దంతె or **దంతియ** *dante.* [Tel.] n. A grade of any kind: a fold, a layer of earth. A large rake. పైరుమీదదున్నే యంత్రము, కొయ్యపండ్ల అచ్చు. దున్నుదంతె a harrow. A rafter అడ్డముగా వేసేపట్టె. **దంతెనము** *dantenamu.* n. A large rake. V. P. viii. 411.

దంత్యము *dantyamu.* [Skt. from దంతము.] adj. Dental: of or belonging to the teeth. n. A dental letter.

దండడి *daṇḍaḍi.* [Tel.] adj. Much, great. Thick. దట్టమైన. adv. Thickly, crowdedly, much. దట్టముగా, దొమ్మిగా, మిక్కిలి. **దండడించు** *daṇḍaḍintsu.* v. n. To thicken. దట్టమగు, దట్టమగు. **దండడిపెట్టు** *daṇḍaḍi-peṭṭu.* v. a. To be confused, కలవరపెట్టు. To oppress, to trouble. బాధించేయు.

దండన *daṇḍana.* [Tel.] n. A trick, a delusion, guile. మాయ, జాలము. **దండనకాడు** *daṇḍana-kāḍu.* n. A trickster, a deceiver. జాలముచేయువాడు. **దండనకత్తె** *daṇḍana-katte.* n. A woman who deceives, a gipsy. జాలముచేయునది.

దండశూకము *daṇḍa-śūkamu.* [Skt.] n. A serpent. సర్పము.

దందహ్యమానము *dandahya-mānamu.* [Skt.] adj. Burning.

దంపకఱ్ఱు *dampa-karru.* [Tel. దమ్ము+కఱ్ఱు.] n. The plough share used in wet land. **దంపనాగలి** *dampa-nāgali.* n. A sort of plough used in wet land. అడుసు దున్ను నాగలి.

దంపతులు *dam-patulu.* [Skt. from జాయా+పతి] n. plu. Man and wife. ఆలుమగలు. దంపతిపూజ worship or homage paid to a man and his wife.

దంపు Same as దంచు. v. (q. v.) n. Beating, pounding, bruising. దంపుటిల్లు a room in which rice, &c., are pounded. **దంపుడు** *dampuḍu.* n. The act of pounding. దంచుట. దంపుడుబియ్యము cleaned rice. **దంపించు** *dampintsu.* v. n. To cause to pound.

దంభము *dambhamu.* [Skt.] n. Fraud, cheating, hypocrisy. కపటము. See డంబము and డాంబికము. A pretence, వ్యాజము. Insolence, impudence. A fault తప్పు. adj Pretended, delusive. దంభబ్రాహ్మణుడు a pretended Brahmin.

దంభోళి *dambhōḷi.* [Skt.] n. A thunderbolt. పిడుగు, వజ్రాయుధము.

దంశము *damṣamu.* [Skt.] n. A fly, a gad fly. అడవిఈగ. దంశము or దంశనము a bite, కాటు; a piece of armour, కవచము. **దంశి** *damṣi.* n. A forest mosquito. అడవిదోమ. దంశి pincers, tongs, పటుకారు. **దంశితుడు** *damṣitudu.* n. One who is bitten. కాటు పడ్డవాడు. One who wears an armour, కవచము తొడిగినవాడు.

దంష్ట్ర or **దంష్ట్రము** *damshtra.* [Skt.] n. A tusk or large tooth. కోరపల్లు. **దంష్ట్రాయుధము** *damshtr-ayudhamu.* n. That which is armed with tusks, i. e., a wild boar. వరాహము. **దంష్ట్రి** *damshtri.* adj Tusked, toothed, carnivorous. n. A wild boar.

దక్కినము *dakkinamu.* [for Skt. దక్షిణము.] The South.

దక్కు *dakku.* [Tel.] v. n. To be available for enjoyment. అనుభవయోగ్యమగు. To fall to one's share or lot; to be saved, to escape. adj. Enjoyable. అనుభవయోగ్యము. మీ ప్రాణములు దక్కవు your lives will not be saved. ఈ రూకలు దక్కనిచ్చేటట్టులేదు I have no chance of keeping the money. **దక్కొను** *dak-konu.* (దక్కు+కొను.) v. n. To be independent. స్వతంత్రుడగు. To happen, కలుగు. వి. క. ii. **దక్కించు** *dakkintsu.* v. a. To rescue, preserve, defend, save, get, redeem. దక్కించుకొను. To get into one's possession, appropriate. To have. To secure for oneself. To digest. ఆ యిల్లు తనకు దక్కించుకొన్నాడు he got the house into his own hands. **దక్కోలు** *dak-kōlu.* n. Occurrence. కలుగుట, సంభవించుట. adj. Taken, usurped; స్వాధీనమైన. Possible, feasible, attainable. **దక్కోలుగానిచ్చు** *dakkōlu-ga-n-iṭstsu.* v. a. To offer in sacrifice: to present as a gift to a god. **దక్కోలుపడు** Same as దక్కు.

73

దక్షత *dakshata.* [Skt.] n. Skill, cleverness, ability. నేర్పు. Management, protection. ముందక్షతలేనిది being without any man protector. **దక్షత్వము** *dakshatvamu.* n. Ability, cleverness, dexterity. సమర్థత. **దక్షుడు** *dakshudu.* n. A clever or capable man. నేర్పరి. Name of a Brahma, దక్షప్రజాపతి. కార్ముకదక్షుడు one skilled in archery. మాయాదక్షుడు a clever rogue.

దక్షాయ్యము *dakshayyamu.* [Skt.] n. kite. గద్ద.

దక్షిణ *dakshiṇa.* [Skt.] n. A present given to a priest at a sacrifice. యజ్ఞాంతమందు ఋత్విగాదులకిచ్చే ద్రవ్యము. A present. An offering made in money. An alms. గురుదక్షిణ the money fee or payment offered to an instructor. వారు ఒకరూపాయి దక్షిణయిచ్చిరి they gave a present of one rupee.

దక్షిణము *dakshiṇamu.* [Skt.] n. The right hand side (i. e., while facing the East). The south, కుడిదిక్కు. See under తూర్పు. adj. Pertaining to the right hand, కుడి. Southern, దక్షిణపు. దక్షిణకైలాసము the southern Kailāsa—an epithet given to the town of Kalahasti. **దక్షిణాగ్ని** *dakshiṇ-agni.* n. A name of the sacred fire that has to be kept up by a Brahmin householder. దక్షిణాశాపతి Yama. దక్షిణాపథము the Deccan and South India together. **దక్షిణుడు** *dakshiṇudu.* n. A kind, honest or candid person. కుటిలుడు కాక దక్షిణమైన మనస్సుగలవాడు.

దఖలు or **దాఖలు** *dakhalu.* [H.] n. Insertion, entering. An application. దాఖలుచేయు to present, to file, admit, &c.

దగ *daga.* [Tel.] n. Heat. తాపము. Thirst, అతిదాహము. M. VII. iii. 309. Swa. iv.

దగదగ or **ధగధగ** *daga-daga.* [Tel. (anuk.)] n. Brilliancy, glittering. adj. Bright. **దగదగమను** or **దగదగలాడు** *daga-daga-m-anu.* v. n. To glitter, to flash.

దగర Same as దగర. (q. v.)

దగరము Same as దగరము. (q. v.)

దగరు dagaru. [Tel.] n. Sand. ఇసుక.

"వ॥ కొంకిమన్ను దగరు పెంకులుగాగల సాధనం బులచే శిక్షితులచేయు."

శు. పాణి. iii.

దగా daga. [H.] n. Fraud, deceit, cheating. మోసము. దగాచేయు to deceive.

దగుల్బాజి dagulbaji. [H.] n. A rogue, a cheat. మోసగాడు.

దగ్గలి daggali. [Tel.] n. A kind of plant used for food.

దగ్గిర, దగ్గర or దగ్గెర daggira. [Tel.] n. Nearness. సమీపము. adv. and postposition. By, at, near, close by, at hand, towards, to, with, in possession of. వద్ద, సమీప మందు. ఎవ్వరిదగ్గర కొన్నావు from whom did you buy it? నాదగ్గిర ఉన్నది I have it by me. అతనిదగ్గిరలేదు he has not got it. ఈ పద్యము దగ్గిరనుండి చదివెను he read on from this verse. నేను దగ్గిర ఉంటిని I was by, I was present. దగ్గిరకుతీయు to take (a child) into one's family, to patronise, protect, take into one's keeping. దగ్గిరి or దగ్గరి daggiri. adj. Near. సమీప మందున్న. దగ్గిరించు, దగ్గరించు or దగ్గరు daggirintsu. v.n. To draw near, approach. సమీపించు.

దగ్గు daggu. [Tel.] v.n. To cough. కాసము చేయు. n. A cough. కాసము.

దగ్ధము dagdhamu. [Skt.] adj. Burnt. కాల్ప బడిన.

దచ్చి or దచ్చుపుల్కి dachchi. [Tel. దంట+ కేవు కము.] n. A word used at games, for eight. cf. దుగదచ్చి. దచ్చికాళ్లమెకము a fabulous beast with eight legs. శరభము.

దటాయించు data-yintsu. [Tel.] v. t. To chide, browbeat, snub.

దట్టి Same as దట్టా. (q. v.)

దట్టడుగులు datt-adugulu. [Tel.] n. Toddling, tottering steps like those of an infant.

దట్టన dattana. [Tel.] n. Thickness, closeness, coarseness. Threatening, bullying. అదలుపు, తర్జనము. దట్టించు dattintsu. v. t. To bully, to frighten. అదలించు.

దట్టము or దట్టి dattamu. [Tel.] n. A body or multitude. Crowd, assembly. తురంగదట్టము a troop of horses, అశ్వసమూహము. గుర్రపు దట్టులు crowds of horses. A. iv. 36. A mummy, a dried carcase. Coarse linen, called దంకిడీ. A woman's undervest, పావడ. adj. Thickset, close, tight, coarse, strong, mighty. Thick, as hair. గట్టి, దిట్టమైన, దళమైన. దట్టపులజ్జ deep shame. దట్టాలు dattalu. n. A coarse cloth used for sails, &c. దట్టపడు datta-padu. v. n. To thicken.

దట్టా datta. [Tel.] n. A stopper or cork బిరడా.

దట్టీ or దట్టి datti. [Tel.] n. A sash, belt, girdle, cestus round the waist. నడికట్టు, కాసెకోక. A. vi. 106. దట్టించు dattintsu v. n. To tie up the girdle. దట్టికట్టు.

దట్టుడు dattudu. [Tel.] n. A brave or daring man, a hero; a clever man, a man of ability. చతురుడు, సమర్థుడు, దిట్టతనముగల వాడు, శూరుడు.

దడ dada. [Tel.] n. Tremor, agitation. భయము. Faintness; apprehension. A weight put in a scalepan to rectify a pair of scales, పాసంగము. దడదొట్టిన tremulous, agitated, flurried, distressed. ఒళ్లు దడగా నున్న unwell, faint. దడకట్టు dada-kattu. v. n. To prove or verify a pair of scales. To counterpoise a vessel in a pair of scales.

దడదడ dada-dada. [Tel. (anuk)] adv. All at once, swiftly. వడిగా. దడదడమను dada-dada-m-anu. v. n. To palpitate. దడ దడకొట్టుకొను.

దడము *dadamu.* [Tel.] n. Firmness or thickness. దట్టము. A v. 273. An army, సేన. A multitude, సమూహము.

దడాలన *dadal-ana.* [Tel. (anuk)] adv. Slapdash, at one thrust.

దడి *dadi.* [Tel.] n. A screen of leaves, bamboos, &c., a fence. plu. దళ్లు. **దడి బియ్యము** *dadi-biyyamu.* n. A certain rite observed regarding maidens.

దడిగ *dadiga.* [Tel.] n. A large shield carried as an ensign. "దడిగలుకుంచెలుం గొడుగు దండములున్ విలసిల్లవచ్చినన్." భార. ఆశ్వ. iii.

దడిబము *dadibamu.* [Tel.] n. A bed. పరుపు, మెత్త, తల్పము, శయ్య.

దడిమము *dadimamu.* [Tel.] n. A robe. A bed, పరుపు. adj. Thin, సన్నని.

దడియ *dadiya.* [Tel.] n. Land at the foot of a hill. కొండచేరువనేల. హరి. పూ. vii.

దడియము, దడెము, దడ్డియము or **దడ్డెము** *dadiyamu.* [Tel.] n. A weight equal to five, or ten seers. ముప్పదడియము thirty seers.

దడియు *dadiyu.* [Tel.] v. n. To shiver, tremble. వణకు.

దడ్డి *daddi.* [Tel.] n. A lump or ingot of steel.

దడ్డు *daddu.* [Tel.] adj. Naked. **దడ్డుసన్యాసి** *daddu-sanyasi.* n. An ascetic who goes naked.

దణా *dana.* [Tel.] n. An army. సేన. ఉ. రా. ii. **దణాయుడు** *danayudu.* n. A leader of an army. సేనాధిపతి. **దణి** *dani.* n. A master, a ruler, a king. ప్రభువు, రేడు.

దణ్నము *dannamu.* Same as దండము a salutation.

దణ్నెము *dannemu.* Same as దండెము (q.v.)

దత్తము *dattamu.* [Skt. cf. Lat. *datus.*] adj. Given, presented. ఇయ్యబడిన. Adopted, reared. స్వయందత్తుడు a son self-given, one who being without natural parents or being deserted by them, offers himself for adoption. **దత్తత, దత్తత్వము, దత్తు** or **దత్తువు** *dattuta.* n. Adoption. స్వీకారము. **దత్తకుడు** *dattakudu.* n. An adopted son. దత్తపుత్రుడు. **దత్తి** *datti.* n. A gift. ఈవి, దానము. "దత్తిసేతకు." A. ii. 38. దత్తుడు a man who is given as a hostage. కుదువ ఉంచబడినవాడు. దత్తుతీసుకొను to adopt a son.

దత్తూరము *datturamu.* [Skt.] Error for ధత్తూరము.

దద్దనాళ *dadda-nala.* [Tel.] n. Tumuli, prehistoric tombs, commonly called పాండు వయింద్లు.

దద్దరించు, దద్దరిల్లు దద్దిల్లు or **దద్దరు** *dadda-rintsu.* [Tel.] v. n. To be alarmed, perplexed, confounded. To be scared or inflamed. తత్తరపడు.

దద్దళము or **దద్దడము** *daddalamu.* [Tel.] n. A flat ceiling. A small temple with a flat mud roof. చిన్నగుడి. A flat roofed house. ఇంటిమిద్దె. పర. i.

దద్దు or **దద్దురు** *daddu.* [Tel.] n. A bump. A slight swelling of the skin. బొక్క.

దధి *dadhi.* [Skt.] n. Curds. పెరుగు. దధ్యుదధి or దధిసముద్రము a sea of curds. A. iv. 141. **దధ్యోదనము** *dadhy-odanamu.* n. A pudding of curds, rice and spice with salt.

దనియాలు or **ధనియాలు** *daniyalu.* [Tel.] n. plu. Coriander seeds. కొత్తిమీరవిత్తులు.

దనియు *daniyu.* [Tel.] v. t. To meet, to unite. కూడు. కలియు. **దనివు** *danivu.* n. A meeting, union. కూడిక, సంగమము.

దనుక, దాక or **దాకా** *danuka.* [Tel.] adv. Until. వరకు, పర్యంతము.

దనుకు or **దన్కు** *danuku.* [Tel.] v. n. To kindle or catch fire. నిప్పు అంటుకొను. To shine. v. t. To strike, to touch. తాకు. దోసముదనుకక the sin not having come home to him. దోసము అంటక. M. XII. i 103. To have, పొందు.

దనుజుడు *danujudu.* [Skt.] n. A giant, fiend, demon. అసురుడు, రాక్షసుడు. **దనుజాధిపుడు** *danuj-adhipudu.* n. The king of the giants.

దప్పము *dappamu.* [Tel.] n. Thickness, swelling, a tumour. దట్టము. **దప్పమైన** *dappam-aina.* adj. Thick. దట్టమైన.

దప్పళము *dappalamu.* [Tel.] n. A sour drink made of tamarinds and vegetables. కాయగూరలువేసి పులుసుగా కాచినపులుసు.

దప్పి or **దప్పి** *dappi.* [Tel.] n. Thirst. దాహము. పట్టు. నాకుదప్పి అయినది I am thirsty. Fatigue, శ్రమము.

దఫా *daphā.* [H.] n. Time, occasion, turn. ఒకదఫా once.

దబదబ *daba-daba.* [Tel. (anuk.)] adv. Audibly, noisily, aloud, trippingly. Quickly. దబదబపారిపోయిరి I could hear them running away, pattering or patteringly. దబదబకురిసినది it rained heavily, or, it pattered. దబదబకొట్టుట to beat soundly or with audible blows.

దబలకము *dabalakamu.* [Tel.] n. A disease of the knee joint. The disease of a swelled and carious knee joint.

దబాయించు *dabā-yintsu.* [H.] v. a. To frighten, bully, browbeat.

దబేనా *dabēna.* [H.] n. Hoard, buried treasure.

దబ్బ *dabba.* [Tel.] n. The citron tree. **దబ్బకాయ** *dabba-kaya.* n. A citron. కొండదబ్బ & నారదబ్బ are two species of it. A slip, strip, piece of split wood, a slice. A thin rafter. బద్ద. వెదురుబద్ద. దబ్బతలుపు a door made of strips of wood. వెదురుదబ్బ a piece of split bamboo. A clot of blood. [From దర్భ a sacred grass] దర్భ, దబ్బవేలు the ring finger, అనామిక. దబ్బఉంగరము a gold ring made like a దర్భ ring. **దబ్బకట్టు** *dabba-kattu.* v. n. To clot, as blood does. దబ్బకట్టిన clotted. దబ్బవాడు a mat weaver, మేదరవాడు.

దబ్బడము *dabbadamu.* [Tel.] n. An earthen cover over a pot. మూకుడు. **దబ్బడించు** *dabbadintsu.* v. n. To close or cover the mouth of a cup with a lid. మూకుటితో మూయు. To slap (with the palm of the hand) అరచేతితో చరచు.

దబ్బనము or **దబ్బలము** *dabbanamu.* [Tel.] n. A bodkin, a large packing needle.

దబ్బర *dabbara.* [Tel.] n. A falsehood. బొంకు. Cheating, deception. A delusion మోసము. A calamity, harm, విపత్తు. దబ్బరలాడు to deal in falsehoods. వానికాలికి దబ్బర అయినది his leg has been injured. దబ్బరపాట్లు feigned blows: mere pretence. దబ్బరకాడు or దబ్బరి a liar. దబ్బరకత్తె or దబ్బరి a deceitful woman. adj. False, spurious, apocryphal. దబ్బర వెంట్రుకలు false locks.

దబ్బాటు or **దబ్బాటు** *dabbatu.* [Tel.] adv. Suddenly, unexpectedly. A. vi. 105. అదాటుగా, అదిరిపాటుగా.

దబ్బిచిప్ప *dabbi-chippa.* [Tel.] n. A kind of axe. కాటికట్టు బద్దలుచేసే సాధనము.

దబ్బిరి *dabbiri.* [Tel.] adj. Cross, unsteady, irregular, curst.

దబ్బిలి or **దబ్బిలి** *dabbili.* [Tel.] n. Trouble. A popular ferment or fray. An insurrection. A liar, a makebate, a rascal. **దబ్బిలితనము** or **దబ్బిలితనము** *dabbili-tanamu.* n. Vileness, rascality. **దబ్బిలిపదము** *dabbili-padamu.* n. A jaw-breaker or hard word, a distracting puzzle. దబ్బిలిదేశము a troubled or unsettled district.

దబ్బు *dabbu.* [Tel.] v. t. To tell, చెప్పు. n. A word, మాట. The cover of a jar, మూకుడు; దబ్బడము. The noise made by a blow on anything. A clapping sound, బల్లలు మొదలైనవాటిని గుద్దినచప్పుడు. దబ్బుపెట్టు to cover మూయు.

దబ్బు *dabbu.* [Tel.] adv. Aloud. దబదబ.

దబ్బుడు Same as దబ్బడము (q. v.)

దబ్బున *dabbuna*. [Tel.] adv. Instantly, at once, quickly.

దబ్బర or **దబ్బెర** *dabbura*. [Tel.] n. A cup. గిన్నె.

దభ్రము *dabhramu*. [Skt.] adj. Little, small. సూక్ష్మము. Thin. సన్నము.

దమము or **దమథము** *damamu*. [Skt.] n. Austerities, mortification of the flesh, a self-controlled state. ఇంద్రియనిగ్రహము. Fortitude, క్లేశమునోర్చుటనము. Suppression, అణచుట. **దమనుడు** or **దమి** *damanudu*. n. the queller or subduer. అణచువాడు; as కందర్పదమనుడు Siva who destroyed Manmadha. **దమితుడు** *damitudu*. n. One who is subdued. అణపబడినవాడు. **దమించు** *damintsu*. v. t. To suppress, subdue (as one's passions), అనిగ్రహించు.

దమదమా *dama-damā*. [H.] n. A battery, a fortress. బురుజు.

దమ్మిడి *dammidi*. [H.] n. A pie, one twelfth part of an anna. అరదుడ్డు.

దమ్ము *dammu*. [Tel.] n. Mud, mire, slush. అడుసు, బురద, పంకము. Moisture, wetness. Breath. Wet ploughing. దమ్మునాగలి a plough used to work wet land. మడినీరుకట్టి దున్నేది. దమ్ముపలక. **దమ్ముకొను** *dammu-konu*. v. n. To become miry, or wet. అడుసగు, తడియు. **దమ్ముకొన్న** *dammu-konna*. adj. Moist. Empty, worthless. **దమ్ముచేయు** *dammu-chēyu*. v. n. To plough a field while wet. దమ్ముచేసినపొలము a field ploughed while wet, ఊడ్పుటకు సిద్ధము చేసినపొలము. దమ్ముపట్టు to hold the breath.

దయ *daya*. [Skt.] n. Favour, kindness, grace, regard. Love, affection, attachment. Mercy, pity, tenderness, clemency, compassion. Pleasure, goodness, amiability, a kind heart. కృప, కనికరము. తమ దయ ఎట్లో అట్లు just as your honour pleases. మీదయ thank you. **దయచేయు** *daya-chēyu*. v. a. & n. To grant, bestow, allow, give ఇచ్చు, అనుగ్రహించు. To honor or favour with (something) కరుణించు. To come or to go. అక్కడికి దయచేస్తారా will you be pleased to come (or go) there? ఇది దయచేయండి oblige me with this, be so good as to grant me this. **దయతప్పిన** *daya-tappina*. adj. Displeased, disgraced, out of favour అయన దయ నామీద తప్పినది I lost his favour. **దయారసము** *daya-rasamu*. n. The spirit of love. Loving-kindness, humanity, benignity, indulgence. **దయాళుత్వము** *dayāḷutvamu*. n. Benignity. సర్వదయాళుత్వము universal beneficence, goodness to all creatures. **దయాళువు** or **దయాశాలి** *dayāḷuvu*. n. A kind, gracious, merciful person. కని కరముగలవాడు.

దయిత *dayita*. [Skt.] n. A darling, pet, favourite. ప్రియురాలు. A woman, ఆడుది. **దయితుడు** *dayitudu*. n. A lover, husband. ప్రియుడు, ఇష్టుడు. మదీయదయితుడు my love.

దయ్యము *dayyamu*. [for Skt. దైవము.] n. A deity, a god. దేవుడు, వేలుపు. M. iv. IV. 57. R. ii. 11. Destiny, fate, విధి. A goblin, fiend, demon or evil spirit, పిశాచము. దయ్యముకాదు భూతమే it was not a fiend but a ghost. కొరివిదయ్యము a jack o'lantern, a will of the wisp. వానికి దయ్యముపూనినది he is possessed. దయ్యముపూనినవాడు a demoniac. దయ్యముపట్టు to be possessed. అతనికి దయ్యముపట్టినది a devil has seized him. దయ్యమువదలగొట్టు or దయ్యమునుతోలు to drive out a devil, to exorcise. దయ్యపుస్తంభనము a spell to scare away fiends. **దయ్యాలపోతు** *dayyāla-pōtu*. n. A wizard or a witch.

దర *dara*. [from Skt. ధర.] n. Price. వెల, క్రయము.

దరఖాస్తు *darakhāstu*. [H.] n. A *darkhast*. an application, a proposal, a tender.

దరణము *daraṇamu.* [Tel.] n. A coin of the value of eight dubs.

దరము *daramu.* [Skt.] n. Fear. భయము. A shell, శంఖము. A pit, గొయ్యి. adj. Slight, little, ఇంచుక. **దరదము** *dara-damu.* adj. Fearful, terrible. **దరహాసితము** or **దరహాసము** *dara-hasitamu.* n. A gentle smile, a smile, a slight laugh. దరహాసితాస్యుడై with a smiling face.

దరి *dari.* [Tel.] n. A bound, line, limit. A shore, or side. గట్టు, తీరు. A refuge, a place of safety. "నాకు ఒకదరి చూపవే నారాయణా." (నారాయణశతకము.) Nearness, సమీపము. దరిమేరలేనిబాధ boundless grief. ఇంటిదరిని close to the house. [Skt.] n. A cave, cavern, grotto. గుహ. **దరిగా** *dari-gā.* adv. Aside, apart, at hand, hard by. **దరిచేరు** *dari-chēru.* v. n. To succeed or "reach the shore," to go to heaven. To be finished. **దరితేలిన** *dari-tēlina.* adj. Terminated, ended. కడతేరిన. **దరికొను** *dari-konu.* v. n. To catch fire, be ignited. మండు, కాలు. కడుపుదరికొన్న పట్టున when the belly is inflamed with hunger. **దరికొలుపు** or **దరికొల్పు** *dari-kolupu.* v. a. To set on fire, to kindle. రగులబెట్టు.

దరిద్రము *daridramu.* [Skt.] adj. Poor, needy. n. Poverty. పేదరికము. **దరిద్రుడు** *daridruḍu.* n. A very poor man. బిక్కిరి బీదవాడు. దరిద్రురాలు a poor woman. దరిద్రులు the poor. గర్భదరిద్రుడు a wretched starveling.

దరిబేసి *dari-bēsi.* [Tel.] n. A helpless man. దైన్యముగలవాడు, దీనుడు.

దరిమిలాను *darimilānu.* [H.] adv. Afterwards, subsequently.

దరియాప్తు *dari-yāptu.* [H.] n. An inquiry, investigation. విచారణ.

దరిసించు *darisintsu* [from Skt. దర్శించు.] v. t. To see, to pay a visit. చూచు. To offer as a gift, కానుకగానిచ్చు. **దరిసెనము** *darisenamu.* n. A gift given to a superior when one visits him. A *nuzzur.* నజరు.

దరుజు or **దురుజు** *darudzu.* [H.] n. A cornice, a frieze, a joining, a seam in carpentry or masonry. గోడకొనగాని స్తంభపు కొనగాని చేసియుండే చిత్రపుపని. దరుజుకున్నము plaster made of lime.

దరువు *daruvu.* [Tel.] n. A song in a peculiar metre. కీర్తనభేదము. Beating time to music. తాళము. దరువువేయు to beat time to music. తాళమువేయు.

దరుసు *darusu.* [Tel.] n. A limit, a landmark. ఎల్ల.

దరోబస్తు *darō-bastu.* [H.] adj. All, whole; entirely.

దర్జా *darja.* [H.] n. Rank, grade.

దర్జీ *darji.* [H.] n. A tailor. కుట్టుపువాడు.

దర్పణము *darpaṇamu.* [Skt.] n. A mirror. అద్దము. దర్పణసేవ the rite of viewing an idol in a mirror and thus adoring it.

దర్పము *darpamu.* [Skt.] n. Pride, passion, anger. Irritability, touchiness. గర్వము, కొవ్వు. దర్పమే యశస్సుగా భావించినారు they prided themselves on their fierceness. దర్పముచేయు to boil over, to be furious or proud. **దర్పించు** *darpintsu.* v. n. To become proud, to be insolent, గర్వించు, త్రుళ్లు. **దర్పితము** *darpitamu.* adj. Proud, arrogant. గర్వముగల. **దర్పితుడు** *darpituḍu.* n. A proud man. **దర్పోద్ధతి** or **దర్పోద్ధతి** *darp-ōddhati.* n. The height of insolence or pride. **దర్పకుడు** *darpa-kuḍu.* n. The inflamer: an epithet of Cupid. దర్పకశాస్త్రము the Art of Love.

దర్బారు *darbāru.* [H.] n. An audience-chamber: audience.

దర్భ *darbha.* [Skt.] n. The sacred grass, used in sacrifices. *Poa cynosuroides.* దర్భపోటు See బ్రాద్ధము. A. vi. 92. దర్భ ముద్రిక or దర్భ అంగుళీయకము a ring made of this grass.

దర్వి *darvi.* [Skt.] n. A spoon, a ladle. మిల్లి గరిటె. The hood of a serpent, పాముపడగ. దర్వీకరము *darvi-karamu.* n. A serpent. పాము, సర్పము.

దర్శనము *darsanamu.* [Skt.] n. Sight, view. చూపు. An eye కన్ను. A mirror, అద్దము. The mind, understanding, బుద్ధి, తెలివి. A dream, కల. Science, శాస్త్రము, ధర్మము. పురుషదర్శనము అయినప్పుడు whenever they see a man. దర్శనముచేస్తిని I visited (him.) దర్శనము చేయించు to introduce. నీకు అతనిదర్శనము చేయిస్తాను I will introduce you to him. దర్శనహుండి a bill payable at sight. దర్శకుడు *darsakudu.* n. One who shows. చూపెడివాడు; a gate-keeper, ద్వారపాలకుడు; a skilful man, నేర్పరి. దర్శనీయము *darsaniyamu.* adj. Worthy to be seen, చూడదగిన. దర్శితము *darsitamu.* adj. Shown. చూపబడిన. దర్శించు *darsintsu.* v. a. To see, view. To visit. చూచు. వానికి నూరురూపాయలు దర్శించినాను I lost one hundred rupees to him, i. e., I am a loser of that sum by him. దర్శము *darsamu.* n. A name for the new moon. అమావాస్య.

దల *dala.* [Tel.] an affix. Used to convert verbs, &c., into nouns. వాలుదల slantingly. ఊరిదల near the town. P. ii. 117. విడుదల release. దిగుదలపొలము the lower field. కప్పుదల concealment. తూగుదల weight. వ్యాధి తిరుగుదలగానున్నది the disease is on the turn. అచ్చుదల payable, due. తగులుదలవ్యయములు the sum incurred. నిలుపుదల stoppage. దానివల్ల ఇంటివారికి కొంచెము కూడుదల ఉండినది the family had some profit by it. నదికి ఎగుదల up the river. నదికి దిగుదల down the river.

దలపము *dalapamu.* [Skt.] n. A visor. ముఖత్రాణము.

దలాలి *dalali.* [H.] n. A broker; a salesman. తరగరి. A swindler. Brokerage. Douceur.

దలిమము or దళిమము *dalimamu.* [Tel.] adj. Thin. సన్నము.

దల్లు Same as తెల్లు (q. v.)

దళనము See దళము. [Skt.]

దళము *dalamu.* [Tel.] n. Thickness, solidity. తిరుమందనము. Troops, a host, an army, దండు. A multitude, quantity, number, heap. adj. Thick, solid. దట్టమైన. Much, great. అధికము. దళముగా thickly. దళముకొను, దళకొను or దళగించు *dalamu-konu,* v. n. To become thick, to increase. అధికమగు. దళముకొలుపు *dalamu-kolupu.* v. t. To cause to increase. దళసరి *dalasari.* (దళము+సరి.) n. Greatness. ఘనత. Thickness, solidity, coarseness. దట్టము, తరుచు, మందము. దళసరినేత a close texture. adj. Thick, coarse, substantial.

దళము *dalamu.* [Skt.] n. A leaf. ఆకు. A petal. A part, భాగము. A hemistich, or half verse. A bar in music. దూర్వాదళము a blade of grass. దళకర్త *dala-karta.* n. A general: a magistrate. Satyabh. ii. 88. దళవరి *dalavari.* [Tel. దళము+వరి.] n. Much grain. Substance, property, ఆస్తి. A general, సేనాధిపతి. దళవరిగాడు a man of property or substance. దళవరిలేని poor, indigent. దళవాయి *dala-vayi.* n. A general, a chieftain or minister of state. దళసంచు *dala-santsu.* (దళము+సంచు.) n. A class of troops. దళము జాతి. దళితము *dalitamu.* adj. Split, divided. ఖండింపబడిన, భేదింపబడిన. Blown, expanded (as a flower.) వికసించిన. దళించు *dalintsu.* v. t. To cut, split, divide. ఖండించు, భేదించు. దళనము *dalanamu.* n. Breaking, cutting, severing. ఖండించుట, భేదించుట.

దవ *dava.* [Tel.] n. Dust. దుమ్ము. The tip of a sugar cane. చెరకుకొన.

దవంత్రి *davantri.* [Tel.] n. A moat, a ditch. కందకము, అగడ్త.

దవడ or దవుడ *davada.* [Tel.] n. The jaw; the cheek. నన్ను దవడమీద కొట్టినాడు he slapped me on the cheek. దవడపండ్లు the jaw teeth or grinders.

దవనము *davanamu.* [Tel.] n. Southern-wood, a fragrant leaf like balm, *Artemisia vulgaris.* (Watts.)

దవము *davamu.* [Skt.] n. A conflagration, wildfire. కార్చిచ్చు. Ardent feelings, the consuming heat of hunger or fever. A forest అడవి. దవానలము or దవవానలము *dav-analamu.* n. Wildfire, a scorching blaze, a conflagration.

దవసము *davasamu.* [Tel.] n. Grain. ధాన్యము.

దవిష్ఠము *davishthamu.* [Skt.] adj. Very remote, far distant. మిక్కిలిదూరమందున్న. దవీయము *daviyamu-ga.* adv. Afar. దూరముగా. A. vi. 15.

దవుడు or దౌడు *davudu.* [H.] n. Running, galloping. An inroad, incursion, or invasion.

దవ్వ *davva.* [Tel.] n. A tender shoot. Pith, the soft part of wood. మ్రానిసడిమి మెత్తని భాగము. చెరకుదవ్వ the young shoot of a sugar cane. ఈ చెట్టులో అంతా దవ్వగాని చేవలేదు this tree is all pith and has no wood.

దవ్వు *davvu.* [Tel.] n. Distance. దూరము. A distant place, దూరదేశము. దవ్వనక not thinking it far, adj. Distant, far. దవ్వుగా *davvu-ga.* adv. Afar, from afar. దవ్వున *davvu-na.* adv. Afar off, at a distance. ఎంతదవ్వున్నను however far. దవ్వులు *davvulu.* n. Far-off places or countries. దవ్వులవారు those who are afar.

దశ *dasa.* [Skt.] n. State, condition. అవస్థ. Power, authority, influence. Luck, fortune. బాల్యదశ childhood. వృద్ధదశ old age. క్షామదశవచ్చెను. a time of famine came. నీ జాతక గ్రహచారము రెండు దశలు భాగ్యమును భవించవలసినది రెండు దశలు గ్రహచారము అనుభవించవలసినది your destiny gives you two portions of good and two of evil. అరాజు ఎన్ని దశలు భాగ్యమును అనుభవించినాడు what proportion of the king's life was happy? గ్రహదశ the influence of the stars. మహాదశ the rule or sway of the predominant planet, qualified or modified by అంతర్దశ the several influences of the minor planets. అతడు జీవదశయున్నప్పుడు when he was alive. కష్టదశ లోనున్నాడు he is in difficulties.

దశనము *dasanamu.* [Skt.] n. A tooth. పల్లు.

దశము *dasamu.* [Skt.] n. Ten. పది. దశకము *dasakamu* n. A word for Ten: as we say a dozen for twelve. దశకంఠుడు *dasa-kanthudu.* n. The "ten throated" demon, i.e., Rāvaṇa. Proverbially, a hydra, devil, or monster. దశమము *dasamamu.* adj. The tenth part (of a book, &c.) దశమి *dasami.* n. The tenth lunar day reckoned from new or full moon. పదోతిథి. దశరథుడు *dasa-radhudu.* n. The name of the father of Rāma. దశాస్యుడు *das-asyudu.* n. The "ten faced" demon, i.e., Rāvaṇa. A hydra or devil. దశాహము *dasahamu.* n. The ceremony performed on the tenth day after a death. పదోనాటిశ్రాద్ధము. దశవంధము or దశబంధము *dasa-randhamu.* n. An Inam, or copy-hold, taxed at one tenth of the produce. An inam granted to one who constructs a tank.

దష్టము *dashtamu.* [Skt.] adj. Bitten. కరవబడిన. దష్టించు *dasthintsu.* v. n. To bite or sting. To chide or rebuke.

దసరా dasara. [from Skt. దశ ten + రాత్రులు nights.] n. The name of a feast called విజయదశమి in the month ఆశ్వయుజ (October.) It is the close of the నవరాత్రి anniversary.

దసిలీ dasili. [Tel.] n. A kind of silk. ఒకవిధమగుపట్టు, పెండ్లపట్టు. "దసిలీనూలుపట్టెయుల్లిక పెడంగు." కళా. ii. Looseness, వదులు.

దసువంది dasu-vandi. [Tel.] n. One who gets up wrestling matches. గుద్దులాటకు కట్టెలను కూర్చువాడు.

దసెన dasena. [Tel.] n. A kind of weapon. ఆయుధవిశేషము.

దస్కతు daskatu. [H.] n. A signature. చేవ్రాలు.

దస్తరము or దస్త్రము dastaramu. [H.] n. A bundle of papers tied together in a cloth, a portfolio, a budget. కాగితాలకట్ట.

దస్తావేజు dastavēdzu. [H]. n. A voucher. A document, a bond.

దస్తు dastu. [H]. n. The actual collection of money. Money.

దస్తూరి dastūri. [H]. n. Handwriting. వ్రాత. "కీ॥ సారముగ వ్రాసియున్న దస్తూరి జూచి." కృష్ణ. iii.

దస్యుడు dasyuḍu. [Skt.] n. A thief, a traitor. A. iv. 274. An enemy, శత్రువు.

దస్రులు dasrulu. [Skt.] n. The Asvins. అశ్వినీదేవతలు.

దస్సాలా dassāla. [H. from దస్+సాలు.] adj. Decennial; lasting ten years.

దహనము dahanamu. [Skt.] n. Burning. కాల్చుట. దహనమయిపోయిన burnt. దహనుడు dahanuḍu. n. The god of fire, అగ్ని. దహించు dahintsu. v. a. To burn. కాల్చు.

దహరము daharamu. [Skt.] n. The heart, హృదయము. Intention, అభిప్రాయము. Swa. i. 53.

దా dā

దా dā. [Tel. for రా.] An interjection signifying Come!

దా dā. [Tel. another form of డా.] In some compounds signifies left, or inner as దాకాలు the left leg. దాచెయ్యి the left hand.

దాంతము dāntamu. [Skt.] n. Patience, endurance, fortitude, self-control, moderation. దాంతుడు dāntuḍu. n. One who is temperate, patient, self-controlled, moderate, or master of himself. ఓపిక బడినవాడు, తపఃక్లేశమునోర్చువాడు. దాంతి dānti. n. Self command, repression of the passions. ఇంద్రియనిగ్రహము, బ్రహ్మచర్యాది తపఃక్లేశమునోర్చుతనము.

దాంపత్యము dāmpatyamu. [Skt.] n. Wedlock. దంపతిభావము. అనుకూలదాంపత్యము harmony in a family, mutual affection.

దాంభికుడు dāmbhikuḍu. [Skt.] n. One who is ostentatious or pompous. దంభము గలవాడు.

దాక dāka. [Tel.] n. A pot with a wide mouth. బోగిణె, మూతివెడల్పుగల అటిక. Also, a vine (corruption of ద్రాక్ష.) దాక or దాకా affix. Until, as long as, about. As far as, as much as, to the extent of, వరకు. నెలదినములదాక for a month. ఇంతదాక until now, before this. ఎందాక how long. పదిదాక as many as ten, about ten. The irregular inflection is దాకటి. ఇందాకటి వ్యాజ్యము the late dispute. ఇందాకటిజాబు his recent letter. ఇందాకటివాడు the man who was here till now.

దాకలి dākali. [Tel. దాయు+కలు.] Same as దాగలి. (q. v.)

దాకల్లు dākallu. [Tel. దాపు+కల్లు.] n. A spoke in a carriage wheel. బండికంటికడ కమ్మి, శీల.

డాకొను or డాకొను dā-konu. [Tel.] v. n. To come on, to happen. డాకొన్నకష్టము the evil he suffered. To meet or encounter, సన్నద్ధపడు. R. v. 282. సమీపించు. To be hidden, మరుగుపడు, దాగుకొను.

దాక్షాయణి dākshāyaṇi. [Skt.] n. A name of Pārvati. పార్వతి.

దాక్షిణాత్యము dākshiṇātyamu. [Skt. from దక్షిణము.] adj. Southern. దాక్షిణాత్యులు dākshiṇātyulu. n. Southerners, people of the South.

దాక్షిణ్యము dākshiṇyamu. [Skt.] n. Shyness, kindness, feeling, delicacy. మొగమోటము. దాక్షిణ్యం ధననాశనం a kindly feeling may cause loss.

దాఖలా dākhala. [H.] n. Proof. A receipt. దాఖలాచూచు to verify.

దాఖలు or దఖలు dākhalu. [H.] n. Submitting, as an application or a complaint in writing. దాఖలుచేయు to file or enter. వ్యాజ్యము దాఖలయినది the suit is filed.

దాగర dāgara. [Tel.] n. A wallet or pouch for food. A large winnowing basket. ప్రసేవకము, ఎండుపుట్ట.

దాగలి or దాకలి dāgali. [Tel. దాయు+కలు.] n. An anvil. ఇరుకుదాగలి a carpenter's vice.

దాగిలిముచ్చులు, దాగిలిమూతలు or దాగిలి మూతలు dāgili-mutstsulu. [Tel.] n. The game of Hide and Seek. దాగిలిబూచు లాడు dāgili-būtsu-l-āḍu. v. To play at Hide and Seek.

దాగు dāgu. [Tel.] v. n. To be hidden or concealed. To hide. To escape. మరుగుపడు. దాగురించు dāgurintsu. v. t. To hide. దాచు. To delude, వంచించు. B. viii. 413. దాగుడుమూతలు Same as దాగిలిమూతలు. దాచు dātsu. v. a. To hide, conceal, secrete. దాగజేయు. దాచుకొను dātsu-konu. v. n. To hide, lie hid, be concealed. ఒళ్లుదాచుకొనుట to spare one's body, i. e., pains. See దాపు.

దాటు dāṭu. [Tel.] v. n. & a. To cross over, to pass over, To jump or leap, లంఘించు. To elude. To escape. To go beyond or transgress, ఉల్లంఘించు. To cross or copulate, applied to cattle. నామాట దాటకు transgress not my command. n. A crossing. A jump, గంతు, లంఘనము. A host, an army, సమూహము. చతురంగబల దాటుతేన. Vijaya. i. 174. Parij. iv. 5. A sore due to having crossed some unlucky spot. దాటులుదాటించిరి they made the cattle pass over a ploughshare for good luck. Also, an ordeal; passing or stepping over an idol. దాట్రాయి or దాటురాయి dāṭrāyi. n. A boys' game. దాట్లువేయు dāṭlu-vēyu. v. n. To bound or jump. దాట్లువేసుకొనివచ్చు to come bounding along. దాటుకట్టు dāṭu-kaṭṭu. v. n. To become a crowd. గుంపుకూడు. దాటుకొను Same as దాటు. దాటించు dāṭintsu. v. a. To cause to pass over. To pass over. అక్కడ పది దినములు దాటించి నాడు he passed ten days there.

దాడి dāḍi. [for Skt. ధాటి.] n. An invasion, an inroad, a campaign. దండయాత్ర. A host, సేన. Flight, escape. దాడిపులి lit: the invading tiger, i. e., a royal tiger. దాడి [H.] The beard. దాడికాడు dāḍi-kāḍu. n. A spy. వేగులవాడు. దాడిచేయు dāḍi-chēyu. v. n. To invade. దండెత్తు. To rush on, to charge in battle. దాడి యాడు dāḍi-yāḍu. v. n. To maraud, or rove for plunder. To oppose, మార్కొను. భాగ. vii.

దాడిమిమ్మ, దాడిమ్మ or దాడిమము Same as దానిమ్మ.

దాడుగచెట్టు dāḍuga-cheṭṭu. [Tel.] n. The tree called *Nauclea cordifolia.* Rox. i. 514.

దాఢ dāḍhu. [Skt.] n. A projecting tooth, a tusk. కోరపల్లు. A multitude, సమూహము.

దాణ or దాణా dāṇa. [H.] n. Horse gram, or other gram given to horses for food. ఉలవలులోనగు గుర్రముదాణాహారము.

దాణము dāṇamu. [Tel.] n. A tax, a toll. సుంకము, శుల్కము.

దాత dāta. [Skt.] n. A giver, donor, bestower, or liberal man. ఇచ్చువాడు. దాతృత్వము dātṛitvamu. n. Generosity, liberality, bounty.

దాతికర్ర or దాతిమాను dāti-karra. [Tel. దాయు+కర్ర.] n. A carpenter's block or work bench. A block used by cloth beaters.

దాత్యూహము dātyūhamu. [Skt.] n. The bird called a gallinule. కారుదుకుండేగిపిట్ట. The black cuckoo or the swallow, కాకి కము, వానకోయిల.

దాత్రము dātramu. [Skt.] n. A sickle. కొడవలి, లవిత్రము. Appa. Cavi. i. 22.

దాదాపు dādāpu. [Tel. దాపు+దాపు.] adv. Close at hand. Very nearly, almost. దాదాపు ముప్పదిదినములయినవి about thirty days have elapsed.

దాది or దాదిలి dādi. [Tel.] n. A nurse, a fostermother. పాలిచ్చి పెంచుతల్లి. M. XII. i. 39.

దాదుంగ dādunga. [Tel. దాయు+దుంగ.] n. Same as దాతికర్ర. (q.v.)

దాన dāna. [Tel. ablative of అది.] adv. Thereby, hereby. దాన A feminine form in verbs. I am she who does. ఒంటిదానను I (feminine) am alone. ఒకదానినే ఉన్నాను I am left by myself.

దానము dānamu. [Skt. cf. Latin word donum.] n. A gift, alms. Giving, donation. దానపత్రము an order to bestow a gift, a deed of gift. The fluid that flows from the temples of an elephant in rut. ఏనుగు కపోలమదము. Protection, rule, పాలనము. Subsidising a possible enemy, one of the four Tantrams or methods of Government, లంచమిచ్చుట. దానశౌండుడు dāna-śauṇḍuḍu. n. A munificent or liberal man. మిక్కిలి ఈవిగాడు, వదాన్యుడు.

దానవుడు dānavuḍu. [Skt. from దనువు. The father of the giant race.] n. A demon, fiend, giant, తొలువేల్పు, దనుజుడు. దానవారి dānav-āri. (దానవ+అరి) n. The queller of the giants, a god, దేవత, వేల్పు. దానవి an ogress or a giantess.

దాని dāni. [Tel.] The genitive form of అది దానిని its accusative.

దానిమ్మ or దాడిమము dānimma. [Tel.] n. The pomegranate tree. దాడిమవర్ణము the scarlet hue of the pomegranate.

దాపన dāpana. [Tel. from దాచు.] n. Hiding. దాచుట.

దాపనము dāpanamu. [Skt.] n. The imposition of a fine. దండుగగొనుట.

దాపరము dāparamu. [Tel. from దాచు.] n. Happening, meeting. ప్రాప్తి. Stealing, దొంగిలించుట. Concealment, duplicity. మరుగు, మాయ, మోసము. వానివద్ద మరేమి దాపరములేదు there is no concealment about him. adj. Secret, unseen, రహస్యమైన. G. ii. 16. దాపరమైన happened, chanced, befallen, లభ్యమైన. ఈ మొగుడు నాకు ఎక్కడ దాపరమైనాడు how was I so unhappy as to have this husband? దాపరించు dāparintsu. v. n. a. To happen, to chance, to have or meet, ప్రాప్తము. To steal, దొంగిలించు. దాపరీడు dāparīḍu. n. A thief. దొంగ. దాపరికము dāparikamu. n. Hiding. దాచుట. See దాపు and దాచు.

దాపల or దాపలి dāpala. [Tel.] n. The left side. ఎడమభాగము. దాపలి dāpali. adj. On the left side, left. In the inside, within, along with, in the possession of, near. నాదాపలిసొమ్ము the property in my hands.

ఆమె నాదాపలనున్నది I have her by me. దాపలి ప్రాలు the letters which are inside, that is, which precede. దాపలినున్న the letter N which stands to the left of a consonant, i. e., precedes it. దాపలికన్ను the small end of a drum, which is struck with the left hand. L. iv. 52. దాపలించు or దాప లించు dāpa-lintsu. v. n. To be near, to come near.

దాపు dāpu. [Tel.] n. Nearness. సమీపము. Fear, భయము.

" దాపులేని రణంబు సేసితి
దానవోత్తమచూడగాక." సై. i.

ఆ యిల్లు నాకు దాపు నీకు దూరము that house is near to me and far from you. adj. Neighbouring, next, bordering on. v. a. To hide, దాచు. దాపించు dāpintsu. v. n. To approach. సమీపించు. v. a. To cause to be hidden. To have hidden, to cause to hide. దాపుడు dāpuḍu. n. Hiding. దాచుట. దాపుడుచీర dāpuḍu-chīra. n. Clothes that are laid by, i. e., holiday clothes, as distinguished from కట్టుకోక. దాపున dāpu-na. (abl. of దాపు.) adv. Near, by. దాపుమాపులు dāpu-māpulu. (anuk) n. Hiding and concealing. దాపురము, దాపరికము or దాపరము dāpuramu. n. Concealment. మరుగుపెట్టుట. A hoard, దాచినసొమ్ము. Coming into one's possession or enjoyment, ప్రాప్తి. దాపురమగు dāpuram-agu. v. n. To accrue. ప్రాప్తించు, లభించు.

దాబు dābu. [Tel.] n. Fear, reverence, subjection.

దామము dāmamu [Skt.] n. A cord, a string. త్రాడు. A wreath, a string of pearls, హారము. దామోదరుడు dām-ōdaruḍu. n. A title of Krishna; as bound with a cord in infancy. "Funiger," cord-girt, the cordelier.

దామర dāmara. [Tel.] n. A halter. ఉరి త్రాడు. A species of leprosy.

దామాషా dāmasha. [H.] n. Allotment, division into shares, dividends. దామాషా ఖర్చులు proportionate costs.

దామినపాము dāmina-pāmu. [Tel.] n. A kind of snake.

దామెనతాడు dāmena-tāḍu. [Tel.] n. A cord, a tether: a long cord, fastened to a stake or tree at each end, to which cattle are secured by short halters.

దాయ dāya. [Skt.] n. A cousin. జ్ఞాతి. An enemy, a foe, శత్రువు. "దాయధనంబు" భార. అను. ii. దాయాది or దాయాదుడు dāyādi. n. A kinsman. దాయాదులు kinsmen, cousins, co-heirs. దాయాదత్వము rivalry, kinship, hereditary right.

దాయము dāyamu. [Skt.] n. Heritage. పంచుకోనదగినతండ్రిసొమ్ము. Kinship, heirship, జ్ఞాతిత్వము. A gift, ఈవి. దాయము, దా యలు or దాయాలు dāyamu. [Tel.] n. A certain game among girls. గవ్వలాట; గవ్వలు పాచికలు మొదలగువాని పంక్తి.

దాయి dāyi. [Tel.] n. An anvil, a work-bench, or smith's form, used as a rest or prop. దాగలి.

దాయి or దాయీ dāyi. [Tel.] n. A nurse. Dasav. IX. 206. బాలురకు పాలిచ్చి పెంచుస్త్రీ. A plaintiff. (Vizag.). [Skt.] n. One who gives, ఇచ్చువాడు.

దాయు or దాయు dāyu. [Tel.] v. n. To approach. సమీపించు.

దార dāra. [Skt. from √ ధృ = to support] n. A wife. పెండ్లాము. పరదార a neighbour's wife. [From ధార] A stream, నీటిసోలు. A gift, దానము. Order, క్రమము. దారకొమ్ము dāra-kommu. n. A torchbearer's oil vessel. దివిటీలవాని నూనెబుర్రి. A. v. 4. దారపోయు dāra-pōyu. v. n. To endow, to give by a formal ceremony, in which water is poured from the hand of the donor. To bestow as a solemn gift. To lose, పోగొట్టుకొను. దారాపుత్రాదులు *dara-putr-adulu.* n. A family, a household. Lit: Wives, children, and all.

దారకము *darakamu.* [Skt.] n. That which breaks or causes breaking. బద్దలుచేయునది. A. v. 116. చీల్చునది. దారకుడు *darakudu.* n. One who splits asunder, చీల్చువాడు.

దారణ *darana.* [Tel.] n. Price, value. వెల, క్రయము.

దారణము *daranamu.* [Skt.] n. Splitting. చీల్చుట.

దారబంధము *dara-bandamu.* [for Skt. ద్వార బంధము.] n. The lintel or post of a door.

దారము *daramu.* [Tel.] n. A thread, cord, string, rope. మూలిత్రాడు. A match for fire.

దారి *dari.* [Tel.] n. A way, road, path. A manner, mode, method, మార్గము. దారికి వచ్చినది it is cleared up, it has turned out well, she has come to her senses. [For Skt. ధారి.] One who bears, ధరించువాడు; used in compounds as జడదారి. జడను ధరించినవాడు. దారిక *darika.* n. A harlot. లంజ, వేశ్య. దారికొట్టు *dari-kottu.* v. n. To rob on the high way. దారిబడి *dari-badi.* n. A convoy or guard, an escort.

దారితము *daritamu.* [Skt.] adj. Split, cut, divided. చీల్చబడిన. దారించు *darintsu.* v. t. To split, to cut. చీల్చు.

దారిద్ర్యము *daridryamu.* [Skt. from దరిద్రము.] n. Poverty. పేదరికము.

దారుణము *darunamu.* [Skt.] n. Horror, terror. భయము. A crime or horrible act. adj. Horrid, cruel, భయంకరమైన.

దారున *daruna.* [Tel.] adv. Unexpectedly, suddenly. అకాలున, తెప్పున, శీఘ్రముగా. T. iii. 8. Swa. iv. 68.

దారువు *daruvu.* [Skt.] n. Wood. మ్రాను. adj. Wooden, made of wood. దేవదారువు *dēva-daruvu.* n. Deodar, dealwood. దారుభూతము *daru-bhūtamu.* adj. Ligneous, woody, turned into wood. దారుయంత్రము *daru-yantramu.* n. A wooden engine or machine. దారుహరిద్ర or దార్వి lit: wood saffron, మ్రానిపసుపు. దార్వాఘాటము *darva-ghatamu.* n. The woodpecker. వడ్రంగిపిట్ట.

దారోగా *darōga.* [H.] n. An agent or superintendent. An overseer of any department.

దార్ఢ్యము *dardhyamu.* [Skt. from దృఢము.] n. Hardness, fixedness, stability. Strength, vigour. దిట్టము, గట్టి. Power, reality.

దాలి *dali.* [Tel.] n. A heap of cowdung cakes used for firing. A hole or little pit used as a temporary fireplace, as పాల దాలి. దాలిగుంట *dali-gunta.* n. A smouldering fire, a fire pit, a little pit serving for a hearth.

దాల్చిని *dalchini.* [H.] n. Cinnamon.

దాళ or దాళా *dala.* [H.] n. Overweight in scales, preponderance. వడి యెక్కు- హెచ్చుతక్కువ.

దాళి *dali* [Skt.] n. Split pulse. పెసలు లోనగువానిపప్పు.

దాళిలు or దాళిమ్మ Same as దానిమ్మ. (q. v.)

దాళీకుడు *dalikudu.* [Tel.] n. An agent. కార్యకర్త.

దాళు *dalu.* [Tel.] n. Slight colour, a tinge. వర్ణలేశము. ఎర్రదాళు reddishness.

దాళువ *daluva.* [Tel.] n. A cheek. చెంప.

దాళువా or దాళ్వా *daluva.* [Tel.] n. A wet crop. పల్లపుపంట. adj. Dark-coated: having a black husk. "దాళువాలు." H. iv. 156. దాళువాపంట the black crop, a technical phrase used in Ganjam.

దావంతము *davantamu.* [Tel.] n. Grief, suffering. దుఃఖము.

"ద్వి॥ దైనమూ యాదూరు తప్పించుమనుచు
దావంతమున మది దలకొనుచుండె."
సా. iii.

దావము dāvamu. [Skt.] n. A forest. అడవి. A burning forest, a conflagration, wildfire, కారుచిచ్చు. దావాగ్ని or దావానలము dāv-agni. n. Wildfire, a devouring flame, a conflagration, burning heat.

దావరి or దావరీడు dāvari. [Tel.] n. A hero. వీరుడు.

"క॥ దేవరగారి చెదనవృథ
నీవిధమున శీతమదుగ దేవ్వరుమగరడు
దావరి కాబోలునుచి
డీవిరుడుమలయునని మహ్యదయుంబులరే."

హ. v.

దావా or దావ dāvā. [H.] n. A claim, a law-suit, or complaint. వ్యాజ్యము, తగవు. దావాదారుడు a prosecutor, a complainant. దావా తెచ్చు to make or file a complaint. దావాచేయు to dispute, to quarrel, to claim.

దాశరథి dāśaradhi. [Skt.] n. The son of దశరథుడు, i.e., Rama.

దాశార్హుడు dāsārhuḍu. [Skt.] n. An epithet of Krishṇa.

దాష్టీకము or దాష్ఠీకము dashṭikamu. [from Skt. దుష్ట.] n. Resolution, bravery. Overbearing conduct, insolence, pride.

దాసనము or దాసానపువ్వు dāsanamu. [Tel.] n. The China rose, or shoe flower plant, *Hibiscus sinensis*. జపా పుష్పము. దాసానిపొడి a blackening dye applied to the teeth.

దాసరి dāsari. [from Skt. దాస.] n. A Sudra or Pariah mendicant who is a worshipper of Vishṇu. దాసరికోరచేప or దాసరికొయ్య dāsari-kōra-chēpa. n. A sort of fish called *Zeus equula*. Russell, Vol. i. plate 65. దాసరయ్య, దాసరిగాడు or దాసరితాబేలు dāsa-rayya. n. The hermit-tortoise, found on land in secluded spots. నల్లదాసరిగాడు the black tortoise. దాసరిపాము dāsari-pāmu. n. The hermit or rock snake. దాసరిపిట్ట or దామూలపిట్ట dāsari-pitta. n. The Southern Scimitar Babbler. *Pomotorhinus horsfieldii*; or the White-browed Fantail Fly catcher, *Rhipudura albifrontata*. (F. B. I.)

దాసుడు dāsuḍu. [Skt.] n. A slave, bondsman, serf. వెట్టిగొడ్డు పనివాడు. A fisherman, జాలరి. దాసానుదాసుడు dāsānu-dāsuḍu. n. A servant of servants, an utter slave. BD. iv. 2023. దాసి dāsi. n. A handmaid, a slave girl, వెట్టిగొడ్డు పనికత్తె. దాసితనము dāsi-tanamu. n Slavery. Abject submission, drudgery. దాసేయుడు dāsēyuḍu. (from దాసి.) n. One born to a slave girl. దాసికి పుట్టినవాడు. దాసోహం dās-ōham. n. Lit: I am (thy) servant. A compliment. దండము. అతడు అతనికి దాసోహములు చెప్పినాడు he presents you his compliments. దాస్యము dāsyamu. n. Slavery, drudgery, obsequiousness, abject submission. సేవ, పని. దాస్యత dasyata. n. A state of servility, slavery, bondage.

దాహము dāhamu. [Skt.] n. Burning, ignition. కాలుట. Thirst, దప్పి. Eager desire, ఆశ. దాహము అయినది I am thirsty. దాహానికి పోయినాడు he is gone to drink water, a usual phrase for going to take refreshment. దాహశాంతి చేసికొని after quenching the thirst. దాహముపుచ్చుకొను to quench one's thirst, to drink water. దాహకుడు dāhakuḍu. n. One who burns. కాల్చువాడు. దాహతిరోగము dāhati-rōgamu n. The disease called diabetes.

దాహిరి Same as దావరి. (అము. vi.)

ది di

ది di. [Tel. contracted from అది.] A verbal suffix as వాది, వానిది.

దించు or దింపు dintsu. [Tel. causal of దిగు. v. t. To bring lower, let down, take off, put down, set down. To place, unload, disembark or land. To distil, or extract spirit. దిగేయు. విషముదించు to bring down or dispel poison. గర్భమునుదించు to bring down the womb, i.e., cause miscarriage or abortion. కడుపుదించుకొను to cause abortion. విల్లెక్కుదించు to unbrace a bow. దింపించు the causal of దించు.

దింటెన or **డింటెన** *dinṭena*. [Tel.] n. The flower called Bluebell (*clitorea*) whether blue or red. *Clitorea ternatea* or *Hedysarum alhagi*. శంఖగ్గి.

దిండు *dinḍu*. [Tel.] n. A bundle, pillow, cushion or bolster. తలగడ. A belt, a girdle, దట్టి. A sheaf of corn. A bag of money. The nave or centre of a wheel: A cylinder. గుండ్రని తలగడవలెనుండునట్టిది. Any thing cylindrical. అరటిదిండు or అరటి బోదె the stump of a plantain tree. adj. Much, fiercely: ఆ దిండురుకు to rush furiously. **దిండీడు** *dinḍ-īḍu*. n. One who wears a belt. కాసెకట్టినవాడు. **దిండు పడు** *dinḍu-paḍu*. v. n. To faint, be exhausted.

దిందిం Same as దిమిదిమి. (q. v.)

దింపు *dimpu*. [Tel. from దించు] n. Diminution, setting down, hanging down loose. వ్రేలుట, లంబనము. **దింపులుపోవు** *dimpulu-pōvu*. v. n. To hang down loose. వ్రేలాడు.

దిక్కు *dikku*. [Skt.] n. A quarter, part, side, direction. దిశ. An airt or point of the compass. The ten directions named in Hindu books are the four points. N. E. S. W. and the intermediate four: N.-E. (ఈశాన్యమూల), S.-E. (ఆగ్నేయమూల), S.-W. (నైరృతిమూల), N.-W. (వాయవ్యమూల) to which are added the Zenith and Nadir. దిక్కులుమ్రోయగా while the heavens resounded. Quarter, shelter, asylum, refuge, protection, patronage, శరణము. దిక్కులేని, దిక్కుమాలిన or దిక్కుడిన helpless, resourceless, devoid of any protector; also vile, abominable. దిక్కుగలవాడు a refuge. దిగ్వలయ స్వరూపుడై the loveliest in the world. **దిక్పతి** or **దిక్పాలుడు** *dik-pati*. n. A demigod who rules one airt or point of the compass; the regent or genius that governs that quarter. ఈశానాదిదిక్పాలురు the genii of the north-east and other directions. **దిక్కుమొగములు** or **దిక్కు మొగములు** *dikka-mogamulu*. [from దిక్కు+ముఖము.] n. Faces turned in every direction. People that flee in all directions through fear, భయముచేత దిక్కున కొకరుగా పోయినవారు. దిక్కుమొగముగా timidly, భీతిచే బెదిరియుండినట్లుగా. **దిక్కరి** *dik-kari*. (దిక్+కరి.) n. One of the mythical elephants that support the corners of the world. **దిగంతము** *dig-antamu*. (దిక్+అంతము.) n. An end of the earth. దిగంతవ్యాప్తి world-wide fame. **దిగంబరుడు** *dig-ambaruḍu*. (దిక్+అంబరుడు.) adj. Lit. "Sky vested," having the air as a robe. Naked, stark-naked, undraped. దిసమొల వాడు. n. An epithet of Siva. దిగంబరురాలు she who is naked. **దిగ్గజము** *dig-gajamu*. n. One of the eight elephants (గజ) that guard the cardinal points (దిక్కులు) of the world. A poetical phrase answering to the poles of heaven. దిగ్గజములు మ్రోయ making the welkin ring. కవిదిగ్గజము a leading or classical author. **దిగ్బంధము** *dig-bandhamu*. n. A magic rite, restraining by spells the influence of certain stars. cf. Job. XXXVIII. 31. **దిగ్భ్రమము** *dig-bhramamu*. n. Giddiness, stupor, amazement. దిక్కులుతెలియమి, భ్రమము. దిగ్భ్రమితాత్ముడై bewildered, horrified, amazed. **దిగ్విజయము** *dig-vijayamu*. n. Dominion, empire. Universal conquest. A royal progress or tour. **దిఙ్మండలము** or **దిఙ్మండలి** *diṅ-maṇḍalamu*. n. The horizon.

దిగ *diga*. [Tel. from దిగు.] adv. Down; downwards. దిగబడు to go down, to sink. దిగజారు to slide down. దిగగారు to distil. **దిగదిగ** *diga-diga*. adv. Rapidly, brightly. దిగముగా, ధగధగముగా, "శ్రీ లక్ష్మీదివ్యరూప దిగదిగయుంచుచున్నది." BD. v. 4, 14. **దిగ దీయు** or **దిగదుడుచు** *diga-diyu*. v. a. To take down. To disenchant, to avert a spell, or the evil eye, to expel a fiend. **దిగదుడుపు** *diga-dudupu*. n. Waving a lamp to break a spell. Disenchantment, దృష్టిదోషపరిహారము. **దిగద్రావు** *diga-dravu*. v. t. To drink down; to let go, to leave, విడుచు. v. n. To come down, దిగు. **దిగనాడు** *diga-n-adu*. v. a. To do away with or remove (sin). To put (a fault) out of view. To lay (a vest) aside. To forsake or desert, విడుచు. **దిగబట్టుకొను** *diga-battu-konu*. v. a. To drag down. **దిగబడు** *diga-badu*. v. n. To get down. దిగు. To sink or give way. కూరు; to remain or be left behind, రాలేక దిగబడ్డాడు he stayed behind as he could not come. దిగబడిన సైకము an outstanding balance. ఈ కాగితము నాదగ్గిర దిగబడ్డది this paper remained in my hands. **దిగబెట్టు** *diga-bettu*. v. a. To set out of view, set aside. To leave (a thing behind, through forgetfulness.) **దిగబోట** *diga-bota*. n. Spreading downwards. దిగువకు వ్యాపించుట. వానికి చెమట ఎగబోటలు దిగబోటలుగాపోస్తున్నది he perspires profusely. **దిగరొజ** *diga-rosu*. n. Panting. ఉబ్బసము. వాడు ఎగరొజ దిగరొజలుగా వడుగుచున్నాడు he runs out of breath. **దిగవిడుచు** *diga-vidutsu*. v. a. To throw aside or leave, to leave behind. విడుచు.

దిగసను *digasanu*. adv. Down, below. దిగువగా.

దిగు *digu*. [Tel.] v. n. To come down from a higher place. To alight, drop, come or go down, descend from; to dismount. To be landed, unladen, or disembarked, as goods. దిగుమతియగు. To fail, break down, sink, fall back, fall in debt or arrears, దిగబడు. To lodge, dwell, halt, ప్రయాణమందు నాటిలో విడియు. To distil, or drop down, as any secretion. To settle, as sediment or dregs. To abate, cease, go off, become less, diminish, as fatness. To sink, as ink in paper, or water in earth. To penetrate or go in, as a stab. To come forth, as fruit from the bud, as in మామిడికాయలు దిగుచున్నవి. ఒళ్లు దిగి పోయినది he is reduced by sickness. బుడ్డ దిగినమనిషి a man with a rupture. దానికి నీళ్లు దిగవు she cannot swallow. మదముదిగిన యేనుగు an elephant not in rut. ఆ పనిలో దిగినాడు he went into that business. The causal form is దించు or దింపు. (q. v.) See also దిగ. **దిగుడు** or **దిగ్గుడు** *digudu*. n. A descent, or downward incline. adj. Descending, going down. Mean, base, low. తక్కువ, పల్లము. ఎగుడుదిగుడు up and down, irregular, uneven. దిగుడుబావి a well into which they descend by steps. **దిగుదల** *digudala*. n. Underneath. Descending, decline. క్రిందిభాగము. **దిగుబాటు** *digu-batu*. n. A descent, or downward decline. కొండదిగుబాటుగానున్నది the path is precipitous. Deduction, loss. **దిగుమతి** *digu-mati*. n. Disembarkation, importation, landing of goods, ఓడలోని సరకులను రేవునందు దించుట. దిగుమతిచేయు to land, unship, import. **దిగువ** *diguva*. n. The under side. క్రింద. adj. Lower, inferior, under. adv. Below, under, క్రిందుగా. **దిగువాయి** *diguvayi*. adj. Lower, inferior. తక్కువ. **దిగువారు** *digu-varu*. (దిగు+వారు.) v. n. To fall down. మీదినుండి క్రింది కిదుగు. To flow, పారు.

దిగులు *digulu*. [Tel.] n. Fear, alarm. భయము. Palpitation of the heart, గుండె అదురు. **దిగులుపడు** or **దిగులొందు** *digulu-padu*. v. n. To fear, be alarmed, be frightened. **దిగులుపరచు** *digulu-parutsu*. v. a. To frighten, alarm. **దిగులుపాటు** *digulu-patu*. n. Fearfulness. దిగులుపడుట.

డిగ్గనాడు Same as దిగనాడు See under దిగ.

డిగ్గియ or డిగ్గియ diggiya. [Tel. from దిగు.] n. A lake, a large pond. దీర్ఘిక, బావి.

డిగ్గు Same as దిగు. (q. v.) డిగ్గు diggu. [Tel.] n. Fear. భయము. డిగ్గురను or డిగ్గను diggu-r-anu. v. n. To shudder, to be alarmed. భయపడు. డిగ్గన or డిగ్గున digg-ana. adv. Suddenly, at once. ఉలుకున. డిగ్గనలేచు to start up, to jump up.

డిగ్గోలు dig-gôlu. [Tel.] n. The last crop reaped before the one which is ripening. కోయుపయిరునకు ముందుపయిరు.

దిగ్ధము digdhamu. [Skt.] adj. Smeared, anointed. n. A poisoned arrow.

దిగ్భ్రమము dig-bhramamu. [Skt. n Confusion.

డిచ్చరి ditstsari. [Tel.] n. An adultress. వ్యభిచారిణి.

డిచ్చుమొగము ditstsu-mogamu. [Tel.] adj. Disappeared, vanished. అదృశ్యము. n. Disappearance, vanishing. అదృశ్యము. డిచ్చుమొగమగు to disappear, vanish.

డిటు dita. [Tel.] n. Strength, power. దార్ఢ్యము, శక్తి. "డిటుచెడిలోబడె" భా. iii. డిటము ditamu. n. Courage. Resolution, firmness. ధైర్యము. adj. Strong. దృఢము. డిటమరి ditam-ari. n. A hero, a spirited energetic person. ప్రౌఢుడు, ప్రౌఢ. డిటమరి losing heart. డిటవు ditavu. n. Courage, bravery. Plumpness. దార్ఢ్యము. adj. Strong. దృఢము. డిట్ట ditta. n. A hero, an enthusiast, a brave man. Firmness. Strength, దార్ఢ్యము, శక్తి. డిట్టడు Same as డిట్ట. డిట్టతనము ditta-tanamu. n. Heroism, gallantry, firmness, pluck, spirit. డిట్టకూళ ditta-kûla. n. A wicked man. డిట్టపడు ditta-padu. v. n. To fit, answer. To be stout or trim. To be verified, come true, be fulfilled. డిట్టపరచు ditta-paratsu. v. a. To regulate, order, ordain, trim, establish, ratify. డిట్టము dittamu. n. Firmness, stoutness, tenacity, tightness, good order. దృఢత్వము. A statute or order, నిర్ణయము. డిట్టముచేయు to arrange, settle. అరచు అరవకుండా డిట్టముచేసినారు they took precautions against his crying out. A scheme; a statement showing what land each man cultivates and the respective assessment. డిట్టము adj. Settled, arranged. Firm, stout, tenacious, solid, tight, orderly. డిట్టము an affix. About. అరడిట్టము about half. ముక్కాలు డిట్టము about three quarters.

డిడ్డి diddi. [Tel.] adj. Small. చిన్న. n. A backdoor, a postern or sally-port. A little door, as of a palankeen. గవనిలోనగు వాని ప్రక్కనుండు చిన్నవాకిలి, చిన్నవాకిలి. డిడ్డివాకిలి diddi-vakili. n. A back door, a small side gate, a wicket.

దితి diti. [Skt.] n. The mother of the Asuras. అసురులతల్లి.

దిద్దు diddu. [Tel. Cf. Tam: తిరుత్తు.] v. a. To correct, rectify, set straight. శోధించు, సవరించు. To prepare, make ready, train, సింగారించు. To deck, adorn, trim, mould, dispose, చక్కబెట్టు. To teach, నేర్పు. దిద్దు, దిద్దుగడ, దిద్దుడు, దిద్దుబడి or దిద్దుపాటు diddu. n. Trimming; a correction, alteration. సవరించుట, శోధించుట. దిద్దించు diddintsu. v. a. To make one correct.

దిదృక్ష didriksha. [Skt.] n. A desire to see. చూడనిచ్ఛ. దిదృక్షువు didrikshuvu. n. One who desires to see. చూడనిచ్ఛగలవాడు.

దిద్ధిమికి ధిమికి did-dhimiki-dhimiki. [Tel. (anuk.)] Rub-a-dub-dub. Samud. 145. See ధిమిధిమి.

దిధక్ష didhaksha. [Skt.] n. A desire to burn or to set fire to (a house, town, &c.) కాలుపనిచ్ఛ. దిధక్షువు didhakshuvu. n.

One who desires to set fire to. కాలంచ దిచ్ఛగలవాడు.

దిధిషువు *didhishuvu*. [Skt.] n. A re-married woman. మారుమనువుది. A man who marries a widow, మారుమనువు దాని మగడు.

దినము *dinamu*. [Skt.] n. A day. The day time. దినేదినే *dinē-dinē*. adv. Daily. దినకరుడు *dina-karuḍu*. n. The maker of the day, i.e., The sun. దినచర్య *dina-charya*. n. A diary, day book, or journal. దినదినము *dina-dinamu*. n. Every day. adv. Daily, day by day. దినబత్తెము daily batta or allowance. దినమణి *dina-maṇi*. n. The gem of day, a title of the sun. దినవారము *dina-vāramu*. n. Funeral ceremonies. ఉత్తరక్రియలు or కర్మాంతరము. దినవెచ్చము daily expense. పాండు. iii. దినసరి *dina-sari*. n. A kind of grain or crop. ధాన్యవిశేషము, సస్యవిశేషము. దినాంతము the evening time. సాయంకాలము, మాపు.

దినారి *dināri*. [Lat. Denarius. This word proves the contact of the Romans with India. The Coins of the Imperial period have been found all over the country.] n. A gold coin. Same as దీనారము. (q. v.)

"ఒకానొకచోట సుబుద్ధికాంచె
బెంహొంద దినారిటంకములుండిన
కాంచనకుంభము." పంచ. నా. i.

దినుసు or దినుసు్సు *dinusu*. [H.] n. An article, thing, drug, ingredient. వస్తువు. Manner, kind, sort. ప్రకారము, విధము.

దిన్న or బిన్న *dinna*. [Tel.] n. A kind of tree. అచ్చు: రూ: కాం.

దిన్నె, దిన్నియ or దిన్నె *dinne*. [Tel.] n. A bulk, divan or settle, being a seat built at a house door; commonly called a pial. A high raised embankment. ఇసుకదిన్నె a bank of sand. దిన్నెలు dunes or sand hills.

దిబ్బ, దిప్ప or దివ్వ *dibba*. [Tel.] n. A high land or mount. ఉన్నతభూమి. A heap or mound. కుప్ప. గోరీలదిబ్బ a burying ground. ఎరువుదిబ్బ a manure heap.

దిబ్బడము, దిబ్బట or దబ్బడము *dibbaḍamu*. [Tel.] n. A lid or earthen cover to a jar. A bung.

దిబ్బడ or దిబ్బెడ *dibbaḍa*. [Tel.] n. Slight deafness, casual deafness, a ringing in the ears, caused by cold, amazement, &c. నా చెవులు దిబ్బెడలేసి (or దిబ్బెడ్లుతేసి) ఉన్నవి I was astounded.

దిబ్బెము *dibbemu*. [Tel.] n. A light, a lamp. దీపము.

దిమము or దీమము *dimamu*. [Tel.] n. A decoy, any lure intended to ensnare.

దిమాకు or ధిమాకు *dimāku*. [Tel.] n. Pride, hauteur, arrogance. అధికారము, గర్వము, పోడిమికి.

దిమిదిమి, దిందిం or ధిమింధిమిన్ *dimi-dimi*. [Tel. (anuk.)] n. Ting tang, ding dong. మద్దెలమ్రోత.

దిమిస, దిమ్మిస or దిమ్మెస *dimisa*. [Tel.] n. A paviour's beetle, a rammer. నేలను చదును చేసే పనిముట్టు.

దిమ్మ or దిమ్మె *dimma*. [Tel.] n. A stand or frame (to support a box or a palankeen.) The frame on which the parchment of a drum is fixed. A sort of rocket. A wooden stopple for a leathern bottle. A mound or heap. దిబ్బ, కుప్ప. Giddiness, thoughtlessness. భ్రమము. దిమ్మను *dimmanu*. v. n. To tingle, to turn giddy, to ring in the ears. దిమ్మరి *dimmari*. (దిమ్మ+అరి.) n. A giddy fool. భ్రమకలవాడు, మత్తుకలవాడు, మత్తుకలది. దిమ్మరితనము *dimmari-tanamu*. n. Folly, giddiness. దిమ్మరీడు *dimmar-īḍu*. n. A giddy fool. మత్తుకలవాడు.

దిమ్మరించు *dimmarintsu*. [Tel.] v. t. To upset or pour out (grain, &c.)

దిమ్మస See దిమిస.

దిమ్ము *dimmu*. [Tel.] n. Giddiness. Madness, folly. భ్రమము, మత్తు. A multitude, సమూహము. దిమ్ముపట్టు to become giddy, భ్రమగొను, మత్తుకొను. తల దిమ్ముపట్టినది my head is confused. చెవులకు దిమ్ముపట్టినది there was a ringing in my ears.

దిమ్మె *dimme*. [Tel.] n. A cone. An ingot, or cylindrical lump of gold. A wooden cork or stopple, గొయ్యబిరడ. A candlestick. A sort of rocket. A heap (as of sand.) A hillock. The stamen of a flower, పుష్ప లోనిదుద్దు, మద్ది. A shoemaker's last, which is conical. The beazle of a ring. A piece of wood built into a wall to hook a bracket, &c., on. A stamp or impress. కమ్మలదిమ్మె a steel board with depressions in the surface, used by goldsmiths. See దిమ్మ. దిమ్మెట్లు *dimmetlu*. n. A deafening sensation. దిబ్బెడలు. దిమ్మెట్లుపడు *dimmetlu-padu*. v. n. To become deaf.

దిమ్మెస See దిమిస.

దిరదిర or దిర్దిర *dira-dira*. [Tel.] adv. Round and round: whirlingly.

దిరిసెన, దిరిసెనము or దిరిసెము *dirisena*. [from Skt. శిరీష.] n. A forest tree with delicate woolly flowers, commonly called the Rain Tree, *Mimosa sirisha*. The species called తెకదిరిసెన is a creeper much used in medicine. *Albizzia lebbek*. Rox.ii. 544.

దివటీ or దివ్వటీ Same as దివిటీ. (q. v.)

దివము *divamu*. [Skt.] n. The sky. ఆకాశము. Heaven. స్వర్గము. Day, పగలు. దివసము *divasamu*. n. A day. దినము, పగలు. దివసములు days set apart for funeral rites. దివసములు చేయు or దివసముపెట్టు to perform the obsequies. దివస్పతి *divas-pati*. n. Lit: Lord of heaven, i. e., Indra. ఇంద్రుడు. దివాంధము *div-andhamu*. n. An owl, as being "blind by day." దివాకరుడు *diva-karudu*. n The sun. lit: the maker of the day. దివాభీతము *diva-bhitamu*. n. An owl. దివాభీతి *diva-bhiti*. n. A sneaking wretch, a thief. దివాభీతుడు *diva-bhitudu*. n. A rogue, robber. చోరుడు, దొంగ.

దివాకీర్తి *divakirti*. [Skt.] n. A pariah or man of low caste. మాలవాడు. A. vi. 9. A barber. మంగలవాడు.

దివాణము *divanamu*. [H.] n. An audience chamber; a tribunal. దివాణపువారు persons connected with the Government. Government. న్యాయసభ, సర్కారు. రాజకొలువు కూటము, కొలువు కూటము.

"ఉ: పాండవులదివాణముకు నరయనిరించిన
త్రైలెడుదుర్గబాంధవులక్, బోడిమిగాన్చి."
అను. ii.

దివాలా *divala*. [H.] n. Bankruptcy. దివాలా తీయు or దివాలాయెత్తు to become a bankrupt. దివాలాకోరు *divala-koru*. n. A bankrupt.

దివి *divi*. [Skt.] n. Heaven. స్వర్గము. The sky. ఆకాశము. adj. Dated so and so (of the month.) దివిజుడు or దివిషదుడు *divijudu*. n. A god. దేవత, వేల్పు. దివిజాధిపుడు *divi-j-adhipudu*. n. Indra, as chief of the gods.

దివిటీ or దివిటె *diviti*. [Tel.] n. A torch.

దివిలు, దీవిలు or దివె Same as దివ్వె. (q. v.)
దివ్వెకోల Same as దివిటీ.

దివు Same as దిగు. (q. v.) "భవ్యకల్పద్రుమ ఫలపల్లవములు దివ్యామృతంబులందివుటగావించి." BD. ii. 658.

దివె Same as దివ్వె. (q. v.) దివెదారికొమ్ము *dive-dari-kommu*. n. A lamp stand.

దివౌకసము or దివోకసము *divau-kasamu*. [Skt.] n. A bird. పక్షి. దివౌకసుడు or దివోకసుడు *divau-kasudu*. n. A celestial being, a god. వేల్పు.

దివ్వ Another form of దివిటీ. (q. v.) దివ్వారుపు పురుగు *divy-arupu-purugu*. [Tel. దివ్వ+అరుపు+పురుగు] n. An insect that puts out light.

దివ్యము *divyamu*. [Skt.] adj. Divine, heavenly, supernatural, celestial. Fairy, appertaining to fairies or demigods. Grand, superb, glorious, noble, fine, admirable, bright. దివ్యమది. n. What is divine or done by God, a divine or providential act or event. A calamity sent by Providence, ఉత్పాతము. దివ్యభావము the spiritual sense. దివ్యప్రమాణము a solemn oath. దివ్యదృష్టి *divya-drishti*. n. Second sight, supernatural intelligence, దివ్యపాదుకలు seven league boots worn by hermits on active service. యోగపాదుకలు. దివ్యచక్షువు *divya-chakshuvu*. n. One gifted with spiritual insight. జ్ఞానదృష్టిగలవాడు. A man with a good eyesight, మంచి కన్నులుగలవాడు. A blind man, i. e., one who used the mental instead of the physical vision, గుడ్డివాడు. దివ్యభామ *divya-bhama*. n. A fairy, an angel. దివ్యార్చన or దేవార్చన *divy-archana*. n. Divine worship. దివ్యుడు *divyudu*. n. A god, a demigod.

దివ్వ or దివ్వెలు Same as దివ్వె. (q. v.)

దివ్వటి or దివ్వటీ Same as దివిటీ. (q. v.)

దివ్వు *divvu* [Tel.] v. a. To draw, pull, withdraw. తీయు, తివిచికొను. P. ii. 48. 52.

దివ్వె *divve*. [Tel. from Skt. దివ్యము.] n. A lamp, a light. దీపము. A torch, దివిటీ. Anir. iii. 51. దివ్వెకంబము a candlestick. దివ్వె *divve*. adj. Bright, luminous. దివ్వెసుడి *divve-sudi*. n. A candlestick, దీపస్తంభము. A niche in a wall to keep a lamp in. గూడు.

దిశ *disa*. [Skt.] n. A point of the compass, quarter, direction, region. దిక్కు, దెస.

దిష్టము *dishtamu*. [Skt.] n. Fate, destiny, time. భాగ్యము, సమయము. adj. Taught. ఉపదేశింపబడిన.

దిష్టి *dishti*. [from Skt. దృష్టి.] n. The evil eye.

దిస *disa*. [Tel. another form of దస.] adj. Plain, unadorned. See దస.

దిసంతు *disantu*. [Tel.] n. Reproach, blame, shame, imputation. దూరు. దిసంతుకొట్టు or దిసంతదుడు to revile. నిందించు, దూరు.

"చెలికాండ్రెదిరనిదిసంతులు కొట్టేరేని."
Swa. iii. 143.

దిసమొల or దిస్సమొల *disa-mola*. adj. Naked: stark naked. n. Nakedness of the body. దిసమొలతోనుండే stark naked. దిస్సమొలవేల్పు Bhairava (భైరవుడు), the king of sprites, who are always spoken of as naked.

దిస్సు *dissu*. [Tel.] n. A hissing sound. పాముకొట్టు బుసబుసధ్వని.

దీ di

దీ, దీ, దీకు or దీకు *di*. [Tel.] n. Striking the heads together as rams do. Butting. దీకొను or దీకొను *di-konu*. v. a. To oppose. మార్కొను, ఎదిరించు. v. n. To arouse, to rouse or bestir oneself, to prepare. R. v. 145. దీకొలుపు or దీకొలుపు *di-kolupu*. v. a. To arouse, warn, excite. దీకోలు Same as దీకొను.

దీక్ష *diksha*. [Skt.] n. A vow. Sacrificing, offering oblations. Worshipping, యజ్ఞాదిక్రియారంభమునందు అనుష్ఠింపబూనుకొనే ఆచార నియమము. A marriage vow. వ్రతాదులయందు నియమమును పూనుకొనడము. వానిని చంపకవిడువను అని దీక్ష చేసుకొన్నాడు he vowed he would slay them. గర్భదీక్ష a vow whereby the husband remains unshorn pending a wife's pregnancy. వివాహదీక్ష a marriage vow. ఏకదీక్షగా

uninterruptedly. దీక్షాగురుడు dîksha-guruḍu. n. A spiritual adviser. వానికి అతడు దీక్షాగురువు. దీక్షాలయము dîksh-âlayamu. n. A convent, a hermitage, a cell. దీక్షించు dîkshintsu. v. n. To make a vow. దీక్ష వహించు. దీక్షితుడు dîkshi-tuḍu. n. One who is under a vow. దీక్షవహించినవాడు.

దీటు dîtu. [Tel.] v. t. To arrange, to level. సవరించు. n. Equality, similarity, resemblance. A share or plot of land. A sort. Rate. adj. Equal, similar, like. సమానము. దీటుకొను or దీటుకట్టు dîtu-konu. v. a. & n. To resemble, equal. సరిపోలు. దీటుకొలుపు to arrange, సవరించు. To level. A. iv. 36. To become full, to be filled. నిండుకొను. To bite the lip or gnash the teeth.

దీడు dîḍu. [Tel.] v. n. To trim or prune, as a bird does its feathers with the beak. To gnash the teeth or bite the lips in rage. It is the same word as దిద్దు. మీసాలుదీడి curling his whiskers, twisting them with his fingers (denoting rage).

దీధితి dîdhiti. [Skt.] n. A ray of light. కిరణము, కాంతి, వెలుగు.

దీన dîna. [Tel.] pron. Hereby. (the abl. of ఇది this).

దీనము dînamu. [Skt.] adj. Poor, humble, wretched, low. n. A helpless or miserable woman. దీనురాలు. దీనత or దీనత్వము dînata. n. Poverty, humility, wretchedness. దీనదశ poverty, humiliation. దీన వదనుడు humble in looks. దీనాలాపము a humble tone, a low voice, a pitiful cry. దీనుడు dînuḍu. n. A poor or helpless man. దరిద్రుడు. A timid man, భయపడిన వాడు. A humble man, దర్పముడిగినవాడు.

దీనారము or దినారి dînâramu. [Latin. Denarius.] n. A certain gold coin. పైడి టంకము.

దీపము dîpamu. [Skt.] n. A lamp, a light. దీపముపెట్టు dîpamu-peṭṭu. v. n. To light a lamp. Metaphorically, to sustain a man's household. Also, to offer prayers for blessing on a benefactor; thus, నీ పాదాలకు దీపముపెట్టుకొంటాను (Lit:) I will light a candle (in the chapel) to thy feet, i.e., I will offer thee worship of thankfulness. దీపకము dîpakamu. n. A light. దీపము. adj. That which burns. వెలిగించునది. Omum seeds, ఓమము, వాము. Also, used for దీపము. (q. v.) దీపవల్లి dîpa-valli. n. The wick of a lamp. దీపపువత్తి. దీప వృక్షము dîpa-vrikshamu. n. A candelabrum, a lamp-stand, దీపస్తంభము దీపారాధన dîp-âradhana. n. The rite of offering a light to a god. The lighting up lamps at a shrine. దీపావళి (దీప+ఆవళి.) dîp-âvali. n. Lit: A row of lights, i.e., A feast held on the 14th day of the dark fortnight (bahuḷa) in Aswayuja (answering to Oct. Nov.) wherein is commemorated the నరకాసురవధ. దీపించు dîp-intsu. v. n. To shine, to be evident, to be distinguished or glorious. దీపిక dîpika. n. A lamp, a light. దీపము, ఆంధ్ర దీపిక the Lamp of Telugu, the name of a Telugu Dictionary. నీతిదీపిక lit. "The lamp of Morals." దీప్తి dîpti. n. Lustre, brilliancy. కాంతి, వెలుగు. దీప్యము dîpyamu. n. Cummin seed. ఓమము, జీలకర్ర.

దీమము. దీమ or దీం dîmamu [Tel.] n. A trained bird, a decoy bird. సాకినట్టి పిట్ట. A snare, decoy or trap (for birds, elephants, &c.) A house, ఇల్లు.

దీమసము dîmasamu. [Tel.] n. Courage. ధైర్యము. Cleverness; a contrivance, a stratagem, యుక్తి, ఉపాయము, ప్రజ్ఞ, ఆలోచన, నైపుణ్యము. P. i. 250.

దీర్ఘము dîrghamu. [Skt.] adj. Long, either as regards size or time. n. A long vowel; thus, సకారదీర్ఘము means సా sá. దీర్ఘకాలము a long time. దీర్ఘజంఘము dîrgha-

janghamu. n. The long shanked bird; the Adjutant, *Leptoptius dubius.* (F.B.I.) నిడుపాటిపిక్కలపక్షి, i.e., పెద్దకొంగ. దీర్ఘదర్శి or దూరదర్శి a far sighted man, దూరదృష్టి గలవాడు. **దీర్ఘనిద్ర** *dirgha-nidra.* n. The long sleep, i. e., Death, పెద్దనిద్ర, చావు. **దీర్ఘబాహువు** *dirgha-bahuvu.* adj. Long armed: a mythological metaphor, signifying the possession of extensive power or influence. It denotes a *Hero.* **దీర్ఘసూత్రత** *dirgha-sutrata.* n. Dilatoriness, tediousness, prolixity, spinning a long yarn, wire-drawing. "భావ్యదీర్ఘసూత్రుల్." P. ii. 163. Cautions, prudent, considerate. **దీర్ఘసూత్రుడు** *dirgha-sutrudu.* n. He who is dilatory, slow, tedious. చిరక్రియుడు. **దీర్ఘాయువు** or **దీర్ఘాయుష్షు** *dirghayuvu.* n. A long life. One who has a long life to live, చిరకాలము బ్రతుకువాడు. A crow, కాకి. **దీర్ఘిక** *dirghika.* n. A long or oval pond.

దీర్ణము *dirnamu.* [Skt.] adj. Shivered, smashed, torn, rent. చీల్చబడిన. Frightened, భయపడిన.

దీలు, డీలు or **డిల్లము** *dilu.* [Tel.] adj. Lean, thin, poor, deficient; loose, slack. దీలైన. (A.ii.75.) Emaciated, కృశించిన. దీలు or డీలుపడు to swoon, be wearied or exhausted. సొమ్మసిల్లిపడు, డీలుపడు.

దీవన See under దీవించు.

దీవసము or **దీమసము** *divasamu.* [Tel.] n. Bravery, courage. ధైర్యము. M. IV. iii. 132.

దీవి *divi.* [Tel.] n. An island. (Poetically) a haven, abode, home. మరిపెమ్ములదీవి the very home or birthplace of attraction, a perfect mine of charms.

దీవించు *divintsu.* [Tel.] v. a. To bless. ఆశీర్వదించు. **దీవన** or **దీవెన** *divana.* n. A blessing, a benediction. ఆశీర్వాదము. దీవెన కోలు a farewell. **దీవనపత్రాలు** Same as అక్షతలు or శేసలు (q. v.) **దీవెనకోలు** *divena-kola.* n. A salutation. నమస్కారము.

దీవియ Same as దివ్వె. (q. v.)

దు du

దుంకి, దుంకేము or **దుంకి** *dunka.* [Tel.] n. A hole. రంధ్రము.

దుంగ *dunga.* [Tel.] n. A block, clog, or piece of wood. కర్రమొద్దు. కికి మెసదొడ్డిదుంగలు the bits or side pieces in a lathe. వానికేమి బాగా దుంగవలె ఉన్నాడు he is as stout and strong as a log of wood.

దుండగము or **దుండరికము** *dundagamu.* [Tel.] n. Villainy, dishonesty, crime, wickedness; a crime, a prank. ధూర్తత్వము, దౌష్ట్యము, కీడు. **దుండగీడు, దుండగుడు** or **దుండగాడు** *dunda-gidu.* n. A wretch, scamp, blackguard, villain. కంటకి. **దుండగాయతనము** *dundagaya-tanamu.* n. Dissipated conduct, forwardness.

దుండి *dundi.* [Tel.] adj. Corpulent, big bellied. HN. iii. 199.

దుండివ *dundiva.* [Tel.] n. A fish: being a sort of *Sparus.* Russell, plates 97. 98. and No. 122. అంతికదుండివ a sort of Perch.

దుండు *dundu.* [Tel.] adj. Stout, strong. **దుండు** or **దుండుపాము** *dundu.* n. A sort of eel. A rock snake. **దుండుబలి** *dundu-bali.* n. An idler. సోమరి.

దుంత *dunta.* [Tel.] n. A male buffalo. దున్నపోతు, ఎనుబోతు. దుంతరౌతు or దుంతతజాలి (for వాహ్యాళి) గాడు Yama, the god who rides on the buffalo. మహిషవాహనుడు.

దుంతిలము, దుండిగము, దుందుకము or **దుందుకము** *dundilamu.* [Tel.] n. A sort of vegetable. *Bignonia indica.* H. iv. 17. నక్తగోధనము.

దుందుభి *dundubhi*. [Skt.] n. A drum. ళేట. స్వర్గదుందుభి the drum of heaven; a poetical phrase for thunder in a clear sky, which is considered a happy omen. The name of a year, ఒకసంవత్సరము.

దుందుము *dundumu*. [Tel.] n. A wheel-like torch. చక్రాకారపుదివిటీ.

దుందురు Same as తొంతోరు. (q. v.)

దుంప *dumpa*. [Tel.] n. A root. The wedge-like part of a plough, నాగలిగొరుకు. దుంపకూర any edible root. దుంపవలెనున్నాడు he is very strong. బంగాళాదుంపలు or సీమదుంపలు potatoes. **దుంపనాగు** *dumpa-nāgu*. n. A sort of snake. G. viii. 101. **దుంపనాశనము** *dumpa-nāśanamu*. n. Total ruin, eradication. వానిని దుంపనాశనము చేసినాడు he ruined him root and branch. దుంపబచ్చలి a kind of plant, a species of బచ్చలి (q. v.), *Basella rubra* or *lucida*. ఉపోదకి. దుంపరాష్ట్రము or పెద్దదుంపరాష్ట్రము the Rhizome, the Greater Galangal, or Java Galangal, *Alpinia galanga*. చిన్నదుంపరాష్ట్రము the Lesser Galangal, *Alpinia officinarum*. (Watts.)

దుంబోడి See under దుమ్ము.

దుః *duh*. [Skt.] A negative prefix. Bad, evil, wicked. చెడు, చెడ్డ. In compounds it changes into దుర్, దుశ్ or దుస్ according to the rules of Sandhi. Such compounds as usually occur in Telugu literature are here brought together and explained. **దురంతము** *dur-antamu*. adj. Endless, eternal, without limit, boundless, unfathomable, అంతములేని. **దురదృష్టము** *dur-adrishṭamu*. n. Ill luck, misfortune. adj. Unfortunate. **దురదృష్టుడు** *dur-adrishṭuḍu*. n. An unfortunate man. **దురభిమానము** *dur-abhimānamu*. n. Arrogance, presumption. **దురభ్యాసము** *dur-abhyāsamu*. n. An evil practice, a bad habit. **దురవగాహము** *dur-avagāhamu*. adj. Hard to understand, inexplicable, puzzling. **దురవస్థ** *dur-avastha*. n. Mishap, evil plight. **దురహంకారము** *dur-ahankāramu*. n. Presumption, arrogance. **దురాకృతము** *dur-ākritamu*. n. An evil act, a misdemeanour. దుర్మార్గము. **దురాక్షేపణ** *dur-ākshēpaṇa*. n. A quibble or groundless objection; a finesse. **దురాగతము** *dur-āgatamu*. n. An outrage. **దురాగ్రహము** *dur-āgrahamu*. n. Groundless anger. **దురాచారము** *dur-āchāramu*. n. A bad custom. దురాచారుడు a man of bad habits or conduct. **దురాత్ముడు** *dur-ātmuḍu*. n. A bad hearted man. **దురాపము** *dur-āpamu*. adj. Intolerable, unbearable. దురాపకోపము prodigious rage. **దురాలోచన** *dur-ālōchana*. n. Bad intent, a plot. **దురాశ** *dur-āśa*. n. Covetousness, vain hopes, avarice, greed. **దురాశాపరుడు** *dur-āśa-paruḍu*. n. A covetous, avaricious man. **దురుక్తి** or **దురాలాపము** *dur-ukti*. n. Hard words, harshness of language. **దుర్గంధము** *dur-gan-dhamu*. n. A bad smell, a stink. **దుర్గతి** *dur-gati*. n. Ruin, perdition, నరకము. Poverty, లేదితనము. **దుర్గమము** *dur-ga-mamu*. adj. Inaccessible, impossible. పొందకూడని, పోకూడని. **దుర్గుణము** *dur-guṇamu*. n. An evil nature, a bad quality, a bad symptom. **దుర్ఘటము** *dur-ghaṭamu*. adj. Hazardous, hard, impracticable. **దుర్జనుడు** *dur-januḍu*. n. A bad man, a wretch. దుష్టుడు. **దుర్జయము** *dur-jayamu*. adj. Unconqerable, invincible, invulnerable. **దుర్దశ** *dur-daśa*. n. Misfortune. **దుర్జాతుడు** *dur-jātuḍu*. n. A man of low birth. **దుర్దినము** *dur-dinamu*. n. A cloudy or foul day. మబ్బుకురుపట్టియుండుదినము. **దుర్ధరము** *dur-dharamu*. adj. That cannot be worn. ధరింపకూడని. **దుర్ధర్షము** *dur-dharshamu*. adj. Despicable. తిరస్కరింపదగిన. **దుర్నయము** or **దుర్నీతి** *dur-nayamu*. n. Wickedness, immorality. **దుర్నిరీక్ష్యము** *dur-nirīkshyamu*. adj.

Dazzling, that which dazzles, which is hard to look at. Terrific. దుర్బలము *dur-balamu.* adj. Weak, not valid, unreasonable, groundless. దుర్బలముచేయు to weaken. దుర్బుద్ధి *dur-buddhi.* n. Folly, weak reason; evil intent. దుర్బోధన *dur-bōdhana.* n. Evil counsel, instigation, temptation. దుర్బోధనచేయు to give evil advice, to instigate. దుర్భరము *dur-bharamu.* adj. Insupportable, భరింపశక్యముకాని. దుర్భాష *dur-bhasha.* n. Abuse, reviling, evil words. దుర్భాషలాడు to use foul language, to revile or scold. దుర్భిక్షము *dur-bhikshamu.* n. Dearth, famine. దుర్భిక్షకాలము hard times, a period of scarcity. దుర్మతి *dur-mati.* n. Folly. An evilminded man, దుర్బుద్ధిగలవాడు. The name of a year. దుర్మదము *dur-madamu.* n. Arrogance. దుర్మరణము *dur-maraṇamu.* n. An unfortunate end, a violent or untimely death. దుర్మాంసము *dur-mamsamu.* n. Proud flesh (that grows in a sore or wound.) దుర్మార్గము *dur-margamu.* n. Misconduct, an offence. adj. Wicked. దుర్మార్గుడు *dur-marguḍu.* n. A wicked man, sinner, villain, evildoer. దుర్యశము *dur-yaśamu.* n. Infamy, disgrace. దుర్యోగము *dur-yōgamu.* n. Misfortune, hard circumstances. దుర్లభము *dur-labhamu.* adj. Hard to get, scarce, rare. Difficult. దుర్వచనము *dur-vachanamu.* n. Foul language, abuse. దుర్వర్ణము *dur-varṇamu.* adj. Tarnished (as copper.) దుర్వృత్తుడు *dur-vrittuḍu.* n. He who is wicked, he who leads a low or infamous life. దుశ్చరితుడు. దుర్వారము *dur-varamu.* adj. Inevitable, irresistible. దుర్వ్యాపారము *dur-vyaparamu.* n. Misconduct. దుశ్చరితము *dus-charitamu.* n. Wicked conduct, wickedness. దుశ్చేష్ట *dus-cheshṭa.* n. A wicked deed. దుశ్శకునము *dus-śakunamu.* n. An evil omen. దుష్కరము *dush-karamu.* adj. Difficult, hard. చేయరానిది. దుష్కృతము *dush-kritamu.* n. A sin, an evil deed. పాపము. దుస్తంత్రము *dus-tantramu.* n. Craft, guile. కపటోపాయము. దుస్తరము *dus-taramu.* n. Difficulty. adj. Difficult, bad, vile, inevitable, unavoidable. తరింపరానిది. దుస్సంగము *dus-sangamu.* n. Unlawful intercourse. దుస్సంధి *dus-sandhi.* n. An error in grammatical elision. A base introduction: an acquaintance formed through the medium of vile persons. దుస్సహము *dussahamu.* adj. Insufferable, intolerable. సహింపరానిది. దుస్స్వప్నము *dus-svapnamu.* n. An evil dream.

దుఃఖము *duhkhamu.* [Skt.] n. Grief, trouble, unhappiness, pain, misery. వ్యసనము, మనోబాధ. దుఃఖించు or దుఃఖపడు *duhkintsu.* v. n. To grieve, to suffer pain. దుఃఖితుడైన grieved. దుఃఖోపశమనము consolation. దుఃఖపాటు *duhkha-paṭu.* n. Grieving. దుఃఖపడుట. దుఃఖపెట్టు to grieve, to cause grief.

దుకాణము *dukaṇamu.* [H.] n. A bazaar, a shop. అంగడి.

దుకూలము *dukulamu.* [Skt.] n. A robe, vest, fine or white raiment. సన్ననివస్త్రము, తెల్లనివస్త్రము.

దుక్కి *dukki.* [Tel.] n. Ploughing. దున్నుట. Tillage, కృషి. Ploughed land. ఒక దుక్కివాన a certain measure of rain that fills a furrow of the field, equivalent to one inch of rain. దుక్కిటెద్దు or దుక్కిపోతు a plough bullock. దుక్కిపొలము a ploughed field. రొంపిదుక్కి wet ploughing, పొడిదుక్కి dry ploughing. దుక్కివాలు a plough, నాగలి. దుక్కివాలుతాలుపు an epithet of Balarama.

దుగ *duga.* [Tel.] n. A deuce at games, or in dice. రెండు, ద్వయము. దుగదచ్చి deuce-eight. దుగరవిక *duga-ravika.* n.

A double bodice, a lined jacket, జంటరవిక. దుగాలంగనఘంఘగాలు a fabulous double-faced bird called గండభేరుండపక్షి. అష్ట. ఆ. గాం. దుగుణము du-guṇamu. n. Same as దుగ. త. హరి. iii. adj. Double, రెండింతలు. దుగ్గాణి or దుగ్గాణీ duggaṇi. (దుగ+గాణి.) n. A copper coin, worth two pies.

దుగలము or దుగులము dugalamu. [Tel.] n. One sixteenth of the coin termed a Pagoda (వరహా.)

దుగ్గ or దుగ్గి dugga. [from Skt. దుర్గ.] n. An epithet of Kāli or Pārvati. కాళి, పార్వతి.

దుగ్గు duggu. [Tel.] n. Musty straw. Straw trodden to pieces; రూపము చెడినది (తృణము).

దుగ్ధ dugdha. [Tel.] n. Ill will, displeasure, annoyance.

దుగ్ధము dugdhamu. [Skt.] n. Milk. పాలు. దుగ్ధాబ్ధి dugdh-abdhi. n. The sea of milk.

దుడిదుడి duḍi-duḍi. adv. With eagerness, sharply. చఱ్ఱన.

దుడుకు duḍuku. [Tel.] n. Rashness, folly, wickedness, silliness, hastiness. చాపల్యము, ఉద్ధతి. adj. Rash, intemperate, foolish, wicked. దుష్టము, ఉద్ధతము. దుడుకుమాటలు thoughtless talk, wild language. అది కొం చెము దుడుకుగానున్నది she is rather rash or headstrong. చేయిదుడుకు pilfering. మాటదుడుకు foolish talk. దుడుకరి దుడుకాడు duḍukaḍu. n. A forward, hasty, mischievous or wicked man, దుష్టుడు.

దుడుదుడ duḍu-duḍa. [Tel. anuk.] adv. Bang, slapdash, off, in a trice. జొదజొద.

దుడ్డు duḍḍu. [Tel.] n. A coin of the value, in some places, of four, and in others, of two annas. డబ్బు. Money in general. ద్రవ్యము. Wealth. దుడ్డుగలవారు rich people. A club. గద. గొఱ్ఱెదుడ్డు a shepherd's crook. దుడ్డువలె నున్నాడు he is as strong as a club. v. n. To strike. Vēma. iii. 55. adj Rough. ముతకైన. దుడ్డుకఱ్ఱ or దుడ్డుకోల duddu-karra. n. A club, stick or cudgel. లావుకఱ్ఱ. దుడ్డె dudde. n. A child, a boy, బాలుడు. Kuchēlo. i. 54. ii. 101. A naughty or wicked person. ధూర్తుడు, ధూర్తురాలు.

దుత్త dutta. [Tel.] n. A jug, a jar, a small pot. చిన్నబాన. దుత్తోయి duttōyi. n. A short half jacket. కురుచ అంగీ. దుత్తారి వలువ duttari-valuva. n. A sort of cloth.

దుత్తూరము duttūramu. [Skt.] n. The Thorn apple, a poisonous plant. *Datura stramonium*, Rox. i. 561. ఉమ్మెత్తచెట్టు. Cunning, కపటము.

దుద్దు duddu. [Tel.] n. The *pericarp* or centre bulb of a lotus: తామరపువ్వులోనిదిమ్మె, కర్ణిక. A mark on a letter written on a palm leaf, తాటాకుజాబుమీది చంద్రిక. A sort of ear ornament worn by women. ఒకవిధ మైన చెవికమ్మ. adj. Coarse, not fine. False, అసత్యము. దుద్దుపెట్టు to evade, elude. దుద్దెక్కు duddekku. v. n. To excel. అతిశ యించు. BD. i. 910. ఇట్లు చేయుటకు వానికేమి దుద్దుపుట్టినది (అనగా దురద) what could bewitch him to do this? దుద్దుకంబళి or దుద్దుగొంగళి duddu-kambaḷi. n. A sort of woollen cloth.

దును dunu. [Tel. another form of దున్ను.] v. t. To plough. "కళింపఁదునితెరువు తెలిసెగా." A. iv. 30.

దునుకు or దుముకు dunuku. [Tel.] v. n. To leap. To make haste. n. A leap, a jump, గంతు. Pain. బాధ.

దునెదారి or దునేదారి dune-dāri. [Tel.] n. One who carries a sword in hand. కత్తికట్టి కొనువాడు. A hero, శూరుడు.

దున్నంగి dunnangi. [Tel.] n. A certain plant, a kind of wild croton.

దున్ను *dunnu.* [Tel.] v. a. To plough. దుక్కి చేయు. **దున్న** *dunna.* n. A male buffalo. మహిషము. A male beast, పురుషపశువు. ఏనుగు దున్న a young male elephant. **దున్నపోతు** *dunna-pōtu.* n. A male buffalo. (Applied abusively), a rude, ignorant wretch.

దుప్పటి or దుప్పటీ *duppaṭi.* [H.] n. A sheet cloth, vest. పక్కదుప్పటి a bed sheet. **దుప్పటము** *duppaṭamu.* n. A vest, a robe. వస్త్రము

దుప్పి *duppi.* [Tel.] n. The Spotted Deer, *Cervus axis.* (F. B. I.)

దుబారా *dubārā.* [H.] adj. Extravagant. దుబారాఖర్చు vain or extravagant expenditure.

దుబాసి *dubāsi.* [H. from Skt. ద్విభాషి.] n. An interpreter. A Dubash.

దుబ్బ *dubba.* [Tel.] n. The female organ of generation. ఆడుగుఱి.

దుబ్బు *dubbu.* [Tel.] n. A bunch or tuft of grass. Stubble, తృణస్తంబము. దుబ్బులుకొట్టి వేయు to weed or clean land.

దుమగతికేతు *duma-gati-kētu.* [Tel.] n. A star portending ill-luck. A comet, ధూమకేతువు.

దుమదుమ *duma-duma.* [Tel. anuk.] adj. All wet. మిక్కిలితడిసిన. "దుమదుమగా తడిసినట్టి దుప్పటులవలెతో." K. P. ii. 75. n. Anger, irritability of temper. కోపము. దుమదుమలాడు to be angry.

దుమారము or దుమ్మారము *dumā*, [Tel.] n. Dust, pollen of flowers. దుమ్ము. పుప్పొడి.

దుమాలు *dumālu.* [Tel.] adj. To the root, entire. సమూలము. భా. vi.

దుముకు or దుమకు *dumuku.* [Tel.] v. n. To leap, to jump, to plunge into. గంతువేయు. n. A leap, గంతు. దుముకులాడు to leap about, గంతులువేయు. గోడదుమికి leaping over the wall. కోటదుమికి leaping down from the castle. బావిలోదుమికి leaping into the well. **దుమికించు** *dumikintsu.* [causal of దుముకు.] v. t. To make (a horse, &c.) leap.

దుముక్కు *dumukku.* [Tel.] n. A thud. The sound made in leaping.

దుముదారు *dumudāru* [Tel. దుము+దారు.] n. An army, a host. దండు. Swa. iii. దుముదారుగా in a mob, గుంపుగా.

దుమ్ము *dummu.* [Tel.] n. Dust. దుమారము, ధూళి. దుంపొడి (దుమ్ము+పొడి.) Currystuff, మెంతి జిలకఱ్ఱ చేర్చిచేసిన సున్నని కూరపిండి. A bone, ఎముక. వానినోట్లో దుమ్ముకొట్టిరి they ruined him. దుమ్ములగొండి the bone-eater, i. e., the striped Hyaena, *Hyaena striata.* కొరనాసిగండు, గాడిదపులి. (F. B. I.) దుముదుము thick dust, దుమ్ముదుమ్ము. **దుముదుములాడు** *dumu-dumu-l-āḍu.* v. n. To raise dust or fire. దుమ్ములేచు, నిప్పులురేచు. To be gloomy, దుమదుమలాడు. **దుమ్మాడు** *dummu-āḍu.* v. n. To wear or use powder. "గంధ కొడితోన దుమ్మాడిమందగతుల." Ila. i. 149.

దుయ్యు Same as దూయు. (q. v.)

దుర్ See under దుః.

దురటిల్లు or దురపిల్లు *duratillu.* [Tel.] v. n. To grieve, suffer.

దురద *durada.* [Tel.] n. Itching. జిల, కసరు. **దురదగొండిఆకు** *durada-gondi-āku.* n. The nettle. దూలగొండి.

దురదుర *dura-dura.* [Tel.] adv. Hastily. అతిత్వరముగా.

దురము *duramu.* [Tel.] n. Battle, war. యుద్ధము. Swiftness. వేగము. v. t. To wage war, to fight. "[illegible]." T. ii. 43.

దురాయి, దురా or దురాయీ *durāyi.* [H.] n. A command, conjuration, adjuration, protestation, a caveat or veto. ఆజ్ఞ. నీవు [illegible] you are not the king's friend.

దురాడము *duradamu.* [Tel.] n. A pillow. ఒరుగుదిండు.

దురితము *duritamu.* [Skt.] n. A crime, sin. పాపము.

దురుసు *durusu.* [Tel.] n. Stubbornness, frowardness, impetuosity, hurry, vehemence, boisterousness, bluntness, rudeness. పెళుకు, పెటుకు, కక్కొవిరుపుతనము, పెడసరిగొట్టుతనము. Tartness, harshness in speech. కాఠిన్యము, మూర్ఖతనము. చేదురుసు an itch for fighting. పోరుదురుసు quarrelsomeness. adv. Forward. ముందు. Quickly. శీఘ్రము.

దురోదరము *durodaramu.* [Skt.] n. Gambling. జూదము. దురోదరుడు a gambler. జూదరి.

దుర్గ *durga.* [Skt.] n. One name of the goddess Kali or Pārvati.

దుర్గము *durgamu.* [Skt.] n. A strong-hold or hill fort. కోట. స్వర్ణదుర్గము a golden-citadel. జలదుర్గము a place begirt with the sea, or, whose walls are the ocean. వనదుర్గము a fort fenced by forest, &c. adj. Impenetrable, పోగూడని.

దుర్బిని or దుర్భిణి *durbini.* [H.] n. A telescope. దుర్భిణి.

దుర్యోధనుడు *dur-yodhanudu.* [Skt.] n. The name of a certain hero.

దులదుల *dula-dula.* [Tel.] n. Hurry, agitation. సంభ్రమము. Das. ix. 21 H. i. 155.

దులుచు *dulutsu.* [Tel.] v. a. To knock down, as fruit off a tree. దులుపు *dulupu.* v. a. To shake off, as dust. విదిలించు.

దువ Same as దువు. (q. v.)

దువారము *duvaramu.* [from Skt. ద్వారము.] n. A gate, gateway. వాకిలి.

దువాళము or దువాళి *duvalamu.* [Tel.] n. A trot. ఒకవిధమైన అశ్వధాటి. దువాళించు to trot (as a horse does).

దువ్వ *duvva.* [Tel.] n. Dust. దుమ్ము, ధూళి.

దువ్వటము Same as దుప్పటము. (q. v.)

దువ్వటెల్లు See దూపటెల్లు. HD. i. 1636.

దువ్వలువ *duv-valuva.* [Tel. దువ+వలువ.] n. A cloth, a vest; a garment. దుప్పటము, కట్టుకోక. Das. ix. 304. దువ్వాటముగా *duv-vatamu-ga.* adv. Waveringly, backwards and forwards.

దువ్వు *duvvu.* [Tel.] v. a. To stroke, finger, or handle. To comb. To run the fingers through the hair. కాలుదువ్వుట to draw the foot slowly over the ground, to paw the ground with the foot. మీసాలుదువ్వు to stroke one's mustaches. కయ్యమునకు కాలుదువ్వు or కాలుత్రవ్వు to paw the ground (in fury.) దువ్వి or దువ్వు *duvvi.* n. A tiger, పులి. A leopard, చిరుతపులి. దువ్వెన *duvvena.* n. A comb.

దుశ్శిరము *dus-siramu.* [Skt.] n. A plant, *Menispermum glabrum.* తుద్యకలత, దూసరి తీగ.

దుష్టము *dushtamu.* [Skt.] adj. Vile, evil, bad, cruel, weak, base. చెడ్డది. దుష్టమృగము *dushta-mrigamu.* n. A beast of prey. దుష్టుడు *dushtudu.* n. A bad man. దుష్టపాకు or దుష్టపుచెట్టు *dushtup-aku.* n. The plant called *Odina wodier.* ఒదియ్యంకి. Rox. ii. 293. Ainsl. ii. 486.

దుసికిలు or దుసికిల్లు *dusikilu.* [Tel.] v. n. To slide off. To slip out of the fingers. జారుపడు. A. ii. 88. H. iv. 55. తొలగు. To escape, తప్పించుకొను.

దుస్, దుస్తరము, &c. See under దుః.

దుస్తు *dustu.* [Tel.] n. A cloth. వస్త్రము. A suit of clothes, ఒక జతబట్టలు. Beauty, అందము.

దుస్సర Same as దూసర. (q. v.)

దుహిత *duhita.* [Skt. cf. Eng. "daughter."] n. A daughter, కూతురు.

దూ dū

దూకదూము *dūka-dūmu*. [Tel.] n. A kind of fish, *Calbichrous bimaculatus*.

దూకలి *dūkali*. [Tel.] n. Pain. బాధ.

దూకు *dūku*. [Tel.] v. n. To leap over, get over, cross. దుముకు. దూకుడు *dūkuḍu*. adj. Uneven. ఎగుడు దిగుడు. Forward.

దూకొను *dūkonu*. [Tel. from దూరు.] v. a. To penetrate, pierce. To learn, acquire. Mand. i. 66. To suck up. To have, పొందు, కలుగు, ఆస్వాదించు. To oppose. v. n. To spread, as a scent, వ్యాపించు. దూకొన్న suitable, proper, ఒప్పిదమైన.

దూగర *dūgara*. [Tel. దూపము+కర.] n. Soot. కరదూపము. Dust, dirt; the dust of grain.

దూచి *dūchi*. [Tel.] n. A sort of game among boys. H. iii. 185.

దూట *dūṭa*. [Tel. verbal noun of దూరు.] n. Entering. The interior tender substance of the plantain tree: అరటిదూట.

దూటు *dūṭu*. [Tel.] v. n. & a. To enter, rush into. To push the udder with the head, to butt. పొడుచు B. X. 282 345. దూటి పోవు. To rush, run swiftly, పరుగెత్తు. P. iii. 75 79. R. v. 157. దూటుకొను *dūṭu-konu*. v. n. To fly. ఎగురు.

దూడ *dūḍa*. [Tel.] n. A calf. దూడలు అరిచినవి the calves were bleating. దూడలగొట్టి గాడు *dūḍalu-goṭṭi-gāḍu*. n. The bird called an Adjutant, *Leptoptilus dubius* (F. B. I.) దూడలపోలిగాడు *dūḍalu-pōli-gāḍu*. n. An eagle.

దూడుగ *dūḍuga*. [Tel.] n. A plant called *Uvariya cerasoides*. చిలకదూడుగ a plant called *Unona discolor*. Rox. ii. 667, 669.

దూత *dūta*. [Skt.] n. (masc.) A messenger, an envoy. రాయబారి. దేవదూత (in Christian usage) an angel.

దూతి or దూతిక *dūti*. [Skt.] n. A lady in waiting; a handmaid.

దూది *dūdi*. [Tel.] n. Cotton: which is thus called after being cleaned: విత్తులుతీసిన ప్రత్తి. దూదినిమ్మకాయ *dūdi-nimma-kāya*. The citron, a kind of a large lime. దూదేకు *dūdēku*. (దూది + ఏకు.) v. a. To clean cotton. దూదేకులవాడు a man of the caste who are cotton cleaners. దూదేకులు cotton fluff. దూదేకులపిట్ట *dūdi-ēkula-piṭṭa*. n. The Grey Shrike, *Lanius lahtora*. పెద్దకీచుకి గాడు. (F.B.I.) దూదెర *dūdera*. n. A small kind of field bug which attacks grain in the ear. There are two kinds of it, ఎర్రదూదెర and పచ్చదూదెర.

దూప *dūpa*. [Tel.] n. Thirst. దప్పి. దూప టిల్లు or దూపటిలు *dūpaṭillu*. v. n. To feel thirsty, దప్పిగొను. To be exhausted or wearied. అలయు. Swa. iii. 43. దూపించు, దూపిల్లు or దూపిలు *dūpintsu*. v. n. To thirst, to feel thirsty. దప్పిగొను R. ii. 36. A. iv. 178.

దూపము *dūpamu* [from Skt. ధూపము.] n. Smoke. పొగ. Burning of incense, incense. దూపార్తి *dūparti*. (దూపము+ఆర్తి.) n. A plate or dish in which incense is burned. దూపముచేసెడుతట్ట.

దూబ *dūba*. [Tel.] n. A mean fellow. అధముడు.

దూబరదిండి *dū-bara-dinḍi*. [Tel. దూయు+ పర+తిండి.] n. A prodigal, a spendthrift. సొమ్మును వృథాగా కర్చుచేసి తినువాడు.

దూబిడి *dū-biḍi*. [Tel. దూయు+పిడి.] n. A stick used for keeping the loose pieces of thread in spinning, నూలుతోడునప్పుడు చీడు తగిలించుటకు నిలిపే పిడుముక్కైనకొయ్య.

దూబూచి *dū-būchi*. [Tel. దూయు+బూచి.] n. A game played by boys.

దూము or ధూమము *dūmu*. [Tel.] n. Laying waste, sucking; a disturbance, plague, pestilence, epidemic. పాడు చేయుటము,

కొల్ల, దోపిడి. అమ్మవారిదూము an attack of cholera. హయిదరుదూము the invasion of Hyder.

దూముడి *dû-mudi.* [Tel. దూయు+ముడి.] n. A knot with a loop, a running knot. దుస్సిపోయేముడి.

దూయు or **దుయ్యు** *dûyu.* [Tel.] v. a. To penetrate, go through. దుయ్యికొను. To pull off the scabbard, as a sword. To take palm leaves out of a volume. ఆకుదీయు to strip off leaves or boughs. To pluck, take, as a handful of grass. వరదూసి pulling off the scabbard. దెబ్బ దూసిపోయినది the blow glanced off. పేగులు దుస్సిరా పొడిచి stabbed him so that the bowels came out. Pal. 424. దూయుతీగె Same as దుస్సిరము. (q. v.) **దూయించు** *dûyintsu.* (causal of దూయు.) v. a. To draw across, to pass over. కాలినగడ్డపారచేత దూయించెను he passed a hot iron over the hand. (This is a ceremony of ordeal in oaths, quite distinct from cauterizing.) దూసిపోవు to go through or penetrate. To glance off, as a dart.

దూరము *dûramu.* [Skt.] n. Distance. (Metaphorically) Distance in point of time. ఇంతదూరము all this while. దూరముగా చూడు look before you, consider well. adj. Distant, far. దూరదేశము a distant land. దూరపురాదాయాది a distant heir. ఇది వ్యాజదూరమైయున్నది it is beyond a doubt. **దూరముగా** *dûramu-gâ.* adv. Afar. **దూరగుడు** *dûragudu.* n. One who is far from (anything) బుద్ధిదూరగుడు he who is far from wisdom. **దూరదర్శి** *dûra-darsi.* n. A sage, one who has foresight. దూరపు యోచనకలవాడు. **దూరదృక్కు** *dûra-drikku.* n. Farsightedness. **దూరభారము** *dûra-bhâramu.* n. A great distance. **దూరుడు** *dûrudu.* n. He who is far from. దుష్ప్రవర్తనదూరుడై being far above such wickedness.

దూరు *dûru.* [Tel.] v. a. To reproach, curse, rebuke, abuse. నిందించు. To enter, penetrate, rush in, చొచ్చు. To be introduced or inserted. ప్రవేశించు. చీమదూరని అడవి a forest impenetrable even to ants. n. Rebuke, censure, reviling, abuse, scandal. **దూరుచు** or **దూర్చు** *dûrutsu.* v. a. To thrust in, push in. **దూరుపడు** *dûru-padu.* v. n. To be censured. నిందింపబడు.

దూర్వ *dûrva.* [Skt.] n. Bent grass: Saint foin, cinquefoil. *Poa cynosuroides.* Rox. i. 333. *Agrostis linearis* or *Panicum dactylon.*

దూర్వాసుడు *dûrvâsudu.* [Skt.] n. The name of a Rishi or demigod proverbial for a fierce disposition. దూర్వాసప్రకృతి a violent temper.

దూల *dûla.* [Tel.] n. Itching. దురద, జిల, నవ. **దూలగొండి** *dûla-gondi.* n. The plant called Cowach, *Dolichos pruriens* or *Carpopogon pruriens.* Rox. iii. 283. 575. The hemp-leaved Tragia; *T. cannabina.* Ains. i. 92. ii. 61. దురదగొండి. **దూలగోరెల** *dûla-gôrela.* n. The Indian Birthwort, *Aristolochia indica,* ఈశ్వరివేరు. దురదగోరెల. Ainslie ii. 298. **దూలపోతు** *dûla-pôtu.* n. One who is always scratching his body on account of an itching sensation. ఎప్పుడును దూలగలవాడు.

దూలము *dûlamu.* [Tel.] n. A beam of timber. ముక్కుదూలము the bony division of the nose. P. i. 133.

దూషించు *dûshintsu.* [Skt.] v. a. To revile, abuse, satirize, laugh at. నిందించు, దూరు. **దూషకుడు** *dûshakudu.* n. A reviler, a scoffer. నిందించేవాడు. **దూషణ** or **దూషణము** *dûshana.* n. Disparagement, reproach. Abuse, reviling. In plays and poems చంద్రదూషణము is "disparagement of the moon:" that is, verses extolling a beauty as surpassing that of the moon. cf. 'And with a blush that laughs to scorn The brightness of the ruddy morn'. దూష్యము *dûshyamu*. adj. Reprehensible, contemnable, vile.

దూసరితీగ *dûsari-tiga*. [Tel.] n. A plant called *Menispermum hirsutum*. Rox. iii. 814. దూసరిధాన్యము or దూసరివడ్లు *dûsari-dhanyamu*. n. The seeds of the same plant.

దృ dri

దృంభువు *drimbhuvu*. [Skt.] n. A serpent. పాము. శై. i.

దృక్కు *drikku*. [Skt.] n. The eye. కన్ను. Sight, seeing, చూపు. దృక్చరణ *drik-charana*. n. Lit. One who is "eyefooted." అక్షపాదుడు, an epithet of some demigods or saints as Gautama, Atri and Bhrigu. The Persian poet Jami applies it also to Yusuf. It means that they were gifted with second sight. దృగాయుధుడు *drig-ayudhudu*. n. Lit: One who is armed with the eye, a title of Siva, who has a blasting glance.

దృఢము *dridhamu*. [Skt.] adj. Hard, solid, strong, firm, bulky, massive. Able, mighty, brave, resolute, confirmed, certain, sure, real. గట్టి. బలిసిన. దృఢదంశక *dridha-damsaka*. n. Lit: That which is hard toothed,—an epithet applied to monsters. దృఢమతి *dridha-mati*. n. Steadfast faith. దృఢలోమ *dridha-lôma*. adj. Bristly, shaggy, rough, hairy. దృఢత *dridhata*. n. Firmness, steadfastness, greatness, certainty.

దృతము *dritamu*. [Skt.] adj. Comforted, consoled. ఆదరించబడిన.

దృశ్యము *drisyamu*. [Skt.] adj. Visible. చూడదగిన. దృశ్యుడు *drisyudu*. n. One who is visible, one worth looking at, a venerable person, a respectable person (*Spectabilis*).

దృష్టము *drishtamu*. [Skt.] adj. Seen, visible, apparent. చూడబడిన. దృష్టాంతము *dristantamu*. n. An instance, illustration, example, proof; evidence, testimony; a sample. ఉదాహరణము. An institute or body of learning. శాస్త్రము. దృష్టాంతీకరించు *drishtanti-karintsu*. v. t. To exemplify, illustrate, ఉదాహరించు. దృష్టి *drishti*. n. Sight, seeing. చూపు. An eye, కన్ను. A glance or look. Regard, care. ప్రమాణముమీది దృష్టి ఉంచలేదు he regarded not his oath. జ్ఞానదృష్టి, దివ్యదృష్టి or యోగదృష్టి second sight, prophetical knowledge, intuitive perception, supernatural intelligence. దృష్టితగిలి ఒంటికి వచ్చినది he was smitten by an evil eye. దృష్టించు *drishtintsu*. v. a. To view or see. దృష్టిదోషము *drishti-dôshamu*. n. A baneful influence, as that of an evil eye. దిష్టి.

దె de

దెప్పము *deppamu*. [Tel.] n. A butt, a target. బాణాదులకెదుట నిలిపిన కృత్రిమలక్ష్యము, కూటలక్ష్యము.

> "చ॥ అలికులవేణి దెప్పయుదకా
> నరపాలుడు చూచుచుండెని,
> శ్చలమతి గాముకోపులకు
> బాలగనిల్చిన దెప్పమాయనన్."

పా. viii.

దెప్పరము *depparamu*. [Tel.] n. Difficulty, distress. ఆపద. కష్టము. Speed, quickness, త్వర. adj Perilous, terrible. అశక్యము, దుస్సహము. "చ॥ ఈ కిరీటికిజనుగాక యీవిధము దెప్పగ మనుష్యులకోర్వవచ్చునే." M. IV. v. 338. దెప్పరిల్లు or దెప్పరిలు *depparillu*. v. n. To be hurt, ఆపదనొందు. దెప్పరికము *depparikamu*. n. Unbearableness, intolerableness, దుస్సహత్వము.

దెప్పు *deppu*. [Tel.] v. a. To taunt, quiz, gibe at, slander, tell tales of, satirize.

డెప్పుడు *deppudu.* n. Taunting, gibing. డెప్పట. డెప్పుడుమాటలు sarcasm.

డెబ్బ *debba.* [Tel.] n. A blow, a stroke. డెబ్బలుతిను to suffer blows, to be beaten. మంచిదెబ్బ a good blow. డెబ్బలుకొట్టు or వేయు *debbalu-kottu.* v. t To beat. డెబ్బాటు *debbāṭu.* (డెబ్బ+పాటు.) n. Heavy rain. బలిష్ఠమైనవాన.

డెస *desa.* [from Skt. దిశ.] n. A quarter or side. దిక్కు, పార్శ్వము. Lot, hap, condition. అవస్థ, దురవస్థ. Protection, refuge, దిక్కు, కాపు, ప్రాపు.

దే dē

దేకు *dēku.* [Tel.] v. n. To slide along on the posteriors. ముడ్డితో ప్రాకు.

దేదీప్యమానము *dē-dīpya-mānamu.* [Skt.] adj. Glorious, splendid

దేని *dēni.* [Tel. from. ఏది.] adj. Of which.

దేబిరించు *dēbarintsu.* [Tel.] v. n. To grovel. దేబరిస్తూ ఉండేవాడు a mean wretch.

దేబె *dēbe.* [Tel.] adj. Wretched, pauper, miserable. Dull, insensible, silly. A silly lout. దేబెముఖమునగు careworn, wretched looking.

దేయము *dēyamu.* [Skt.] adj. Fit to be given. ఇయ్యదగిన.

దేరిజె *dēridza.* [Tel.] n. A tent. గుడారము.

దేవ See under దేవుడు.

దేవకము *dēvakamu.* [Skt.] n. A die. (Plu. dice.) పాచిక, అక్షము.

దేవకి *dēvaki.* [Skt.] n. The mother of the god Krishṇa. దేవకీనందనుడు Krishṇa.

దేవనము *dēvanamu.* [Tel.] n. Gambling, sport. జూదము, క్రీడ.

దేవఖాతము *dēva-khātamu.* [Skt.] n. A sluice from a tank. అలుగు.

దేవరాయికొంగ *dēvarāyi-konga.* [Tel.] n. A kind of ibis, probably the Black ibis.

దేవరుడు *dēvarudu.* [Skt.] n. A title applied chiefly by a wife to a husband's brother, మగనితోడబుట్టినవాడు.

దేవాంగి or దేవాంగులు *dēvangi.* [Skt.] n. The name of a certain caste of weavers, జేండ్రలు. దేవాంగి or దేవాంగిపిల్లి a sort of monkey, a Loris. The Slender Loris, *Loris gracilis.* (F. B. I.)

దేవిడీ *dēvidī.* [H.] n. A fort-gate, a palace-gate. కోటవాకిలి, నగరువాకిలి.

దేవు *dēvu.* [Tel.] v. a. To rinse. To take rice, &c., out of water with the hand. To grope for, as with a drag under water, to trample on so as to destroy, as salt. నీళ్లలోనుండి తడవిదీయు, దేవుకు. v. n. To turn, as the stomach when queasy. నా కడుపు దేవుచున్నది I am sickish; my stomach turns. దేవుకొను *dēvu-konu.* v. t. To scrape together. To root up, turn up. To plunder, rifle. "పదార్థంబులు దేవుకొని వచ్చి." BD. v. 696. దేవురించు *dēvurintsu.* v. a. To sue, intreat, plague or beset with petitions, to beg eagerly, to importune. దీనవృత్తిని యాచించు, దైన్యముపొందు. దేవురుగొట్టు *dēvuru-gottu.* n. A sneak, one who sues for favour, a mean beggar. దేబె, దీనుడు. దేవురింపు or దేవురు *dēvu-rimpu.* n. Begging with importunity. Lamentation, bewailing, complaining, ఏడ్పు, మొర. దేవులాడు *dēvul-ādu.* v. n. To dive in water, to search in water. To roam about, to be in trouble, to pine or struggle. దేవులాడి సాధిస్తిని I managed to effect it with a great effort.

దేవుడు *dēvudu.* [Skt.] n. God. A deity, దేవత, వేలుపు. దేవ *dēva.* adj. Of God, దేవుని యొక్క. దేవకాంచనము *dēva-kanchana-mu.* n. A certain tree. *Bauhinia purpurea.* దేవత *dēvata.* n. A deity, generally a goddess; but also a god, వేలుపు, దేవుడు. గ్రామదేవత the village goddess. దేవతమువ్వ

dēva-taruvu. n. A heavenly tree, కల్పవృక్షము. A venerable tree. దేవతాజీవము *dēvata-jīvamu.* n. A godlike or harmless creature. "ఆ॥ తెలిసి దొరుకగనట్టి దేవతాజీవుల, నరికెదచ్చి భిక్షవలెనుపాశి, పాపమెరుగకంతపట్టి చం పుదురయా." Vema. దేవతాడిచెట్టు *dēva-tādi-chettu.* n. The tree called కరాకరి. *Andropogon serratus.* దానవదంగిచెట్టు. దేవత్వము *dēvatvamu.* n. Divinity, deification, apotheosis.

> "అశ్మాపియాతిదేవత్వం
> మహద్భిస్సుప్రతిష్ఠితః."

A stone even attains divinity when consecrated by the noble. (Hitopadesa. i. 45.) దేవదత్తము *dēva-dattamu.* n. Lit. the gift of god. The name of the conch of Arjuna, అర్జునునిశంఖము. దేవదత్తుడు and యజ్ఞదత్తుడు are two names in Sanskrit Law or Logic like John Doe and Richard Roe, or Titius and Seius, or Omar and Zeid in Arabic Law. దేవదారువు *dēva-dāruvu.* n. The Cedar: the Himalayan Cedar. *Cedrus deodara.* (Watts.) commonly called deodar. The *Erythroxylon areolatum* (Linn.) *Uvaria longifolia.* Rox. iii. 664, 666. సురవృక్షము, అమరద్రుమము. Chittagong wood; usually called cedar. బాలదేవదారువు the Trincomalli wood. *Berrya ammonilla* (Watts.) దేవదాసి *dēva-dāsi.* n. A dancing girl employed in a temple. దేవనాగరి *dēva-nagari.* n. The name of the character in which Sanskrit is usually printed. దేవభూతము or దేవసాయుజ్యము *dēva-bhūtamu.* n. Divinity. దేవత్వము. దేవమణి *dēva-mani.* n. A fortunate curl on a horse's neck. గుర్రముమెడసుడి, అశ్వములకు ఉండే సుడివిశేషము. చింతామణి, మహామేద అనే చెట్టు. R. i. 131. Also, కౌస్తుభము. (q. v.) దేవమాతృకము *dēva-mātrikamu.* n. A country or land which is dependent on providence, i.e., watered by rain only, not by streams. వృష్ట్యంబుసంపన్న ప్రీహిపాలితదేశము. వానవల్లనే పండే పైరులుగల దేశము. దేవయజ్ఞము *dēva-yagnyamu.* n. The holy sacrifice called వైశ్వదేవము. A sacrifice, హోమము, వేలిమి. దేవయానము *dēva-yānamu.* n. The car or vehicle of a god, దేవతావిమానము. దేవర *dērara.* n. God. దేవుడు. A lord or master స్వామి. My lord, Sir. A title of respect used in addressing superiors. దేవరవారు your honour. ఇంటిదేవరలు household deities. కులదేవతలు applied particularly to the manes of married women, ముత్తైదువలు. Your reverence, a phrase among Jangams. జంగములకు శ్రేష్ఠనామము. దేవలుడు *dēvaludu.* n. A temporary paid priest or incumbent. A term of contempt, like priestling. A sacristan, beadle, or attendant in a temple, గుడిలో దేవుణ్ని పూజచేసేవాడు, తంబళివాడు, నంబివాడు. దేవళము *dēvalamu.* n. A temple, గుడి, దేవాలయము. దేవవర్ధకి *dēva-varthaki.* n. The "artist of the gods," a title of Visvakarma. దేవసరులు *dēvasarulu.* n. A sort of grain. దేవాంబరము *dēv-ambaramu.* n. A sort of cloth. BD. iii. 120. దేవాజీవి or దేవాజీవుడు *dēva-jīvi.* n. An attendant on an idol, దేవలుడు; a godlike creature, one that does no harm, as a bird. దేవాదాయము *dēv-adāyamu.* n. The income of a temple. An endowment to a temple, land given for the upkeep of a temple free of all rent, గుడిమాన్యము. దేవానాం ప్రియము *dēvānām-priyamu.* n. Lit. The beloved of the gods, i. e., a goat. మేక. దేవానాంప్రియుడు *dēvānām-,riyudu.* n. A foolish or ignorant man. మూర్ఖుడు. దేవాయుధములు *dēv-āyudhamulu.* n. Stones and cudgels. రాళ్లు దుడ్డుకర్రలు. (దేవశబ్దమునకు యజ్ఞము అర్థముచేసి యజ్ఞమందు ఆయుధములు రాళ్లు దుడ్లు మొదలైనవి గలవు గనుక ఆ సంబంధమునుబట్టి యీ పదము ప్రయోగించినారు.) A.vi.100. దేవాలయము *dēv-ālayamu.* n. A temple. దేవళము. దేవి *dēvi.* n. A goddess, particularly Parvati. A queen. Cf. పట్టపుదేవి. Madam. Lady.

దేవేరి or దేవెరి *dēvēri*. n. A queen, a lady. దొరసాని, రాజపత్ని.

దేశము *dēsamu*. [Tel.] n. A country, land, territory; a district or subdivision of a country. రాజ్యము. A part, site, place, situation, seat, region. ప్రదేశము. **దేశకాకి** *dēsa-kāki*. n. A homeless wanderer, a vagrant. **దేశపాండియ**, **దేశపాండ్య** or **దేశముఖ** *dēsa-pāndiya*. n. A recorder. The higher revenue officer, a superintendent. **దేశభాష** n. A vernacular language, as distinguished from Sanskrit; a dialect. దేశభాషాగ్రంథము a book in a vernacular or modern language as distinguished from Sanskrit. **దేశవాడి** or **దేశవాళి** *dēsavādi*. adj. Of or belonging to a country; produced in a country; native. **దేశస్థుడు** *dēsasthuḍu*. n. An inhabitant of a country. **దేశహాశ్శీలు** *dēsa-hāssilu*. n. Inland duty. **దేశాంతరము** *dēs-āntaramu*. n. A foreign country, a strange land. దేశాంతరమందు in another land, elsewhere. దేశాంతరమునకుపోవు to emigrate: to travel in foreign parts. **దేశాంతరుడు** *dēs-āntaruḍu*. n. An emigrant, a foreigner. దేశాంతరుడైపోయెను he emigrated from his country. **దేశాచారము** *dēs-ācharamu*. n. The custom of a country. దేశాచారప్రకారము వ్రాసియిచ్చిన పత్రము a bond written "in the manner of the country:" **దేశాటనము** *dēsaṭanamu*. n. Travelling. **దేశాధిపతి** *dēs-ādhipati*. n. A king: as "lord of the land." **దేశాయి** *dēsāyi*. n. Desāyi, a title borne by a headman among the Balijas. A chief man among the Lingayat merchants, పెద్దసెట్టి. **దేశికుడు** *dēsikuḍu*. n. A tutor, master, instructor, or teacher. గురువు. **దేశీయము** *dēsīyamu*. n. A dialect, a local expression. An obsolete idiom, a provincialism. adj. Idiomatic, provincial. **దేశ్యము** *dēsyamu*. adj. Belonging to the country. Native. n. The language of a country, a vernacular; a vernacular term. Desya words are opposed to foreign words.

దేహము *dēhamu*. [Skt.] n. The body. శరీరము. దేహబాధ a call of nature. **దేహసంబంధి** or **దేహసంబంధుడు** *dēha-sambandhi*. n. A relation by blood. రక్తసంబంధుడు. **దేహయాత్ర** *dēha-yatra*. n. Death. చావు. **దేహి** *dēhi*. n. The corporeal or embodied spirit. One who has a body, a man, దేహముగలవాడు.

దేహళి *dēhali*. [Skt.] n. A threshold: or the landing place before a door. (ఇంటి) గడప.

దేహీ *dēhi*. [Skt.] n. Lit: "give thou" A demand, a request. దేహీ అని అడిగిన నియ్యడా పోవునా? if you say, Give, I pray thee, will he not grant it? అతడు దేహీ అనెడు వానికి నాస్తి అని అనడు if one asks him to give, he will not answer 'I have nothing.' భిక్షాందేహి Oh! bestow an alms, I pray thee.

దై dai

దైతేయుడు or **దైత్యుడు** *daitēyuḍu*. [Skt. from దితి.] n. A demon, giant, or titan. రాక్షసుడు. **దైత్యారి** *daity-ari*. n. The foe of the demons, i.e., Vishṇu. A god. వేలుపు.

దైన్యము *dainyamu*. [Skt. from దీనము.] n. Lowness, meanness, poverty, humility, దీనత్వము, దరిద్రత్వము. దైన్యపడు to be humiliated. **దైన్యపాటు** *dainya-paṭu*. n. Humiliation.

దైర్ఘ్యము *dairghyamu*. [Skt. from దీర్ఘము.] n. Length. నిడుపు, పొడుగు.

దైవము *daivamu*. [Skt.] n. A deity, God. దైవకృతము caused by chance or fortune. దైవగతి providence, the will or act of God: chance, accident. దైవగతిచేత వర్షము రాలేదు it pleased God to give no rain. **దైవజ్ఞ** *daiva-gnya*. n. A witch. **దైవజ్ఞుడు** *daiva-*

gnyuḍu. n. A fortuneteller, a wizard. దైవతము daivatamu. n. A deity. వేలుపు. adj: pertaining to a god, దేవత. దైవదూషణము daiva-dūshaṇamu. n. Blasphemy. దైవయోగము daiva-yōgamu. n. Providence. Chance, accident. దైవవశాత్ daiva-vaṡat. adv. By the act of God. దైవవాక్యము daiva-vākyamu. n. A revelation, gospel, the word of God. దైవవివాహము daiva-vivāhamu. n. A marriage performed according to due rites. దైవాధీనము daiv-ādhīnamu. n. The power or act of God. దైవాధీనముగా providentially. దైవాధీనం జగత్సర్వం the whole universe is in the hands of God. దైవికము daivikamu. n. A visitation, an act of God. An accident. దైవికరాజకములచేత by the act either of God, or of the king. adj. Supernatural, divine, providential. దైవికముగా accidentally, providentially.

దైవారు daivāru. [Tel.] v. n. To excel, be exuberant. ఒప్పు, ప్రకాశించు, పెంపగు. To overflow, పొరలిపారు. "ఠీవియుని విరిచి పఠిశ దయదైవారగా." T. i. 39.

దైహిక daihika. [Skt. from దేహ.] adj. Corporeal, bodily.

దొ do

దొంగ donga. [Tel. ✓ దొ to take lit. One who takes.] n. A thief or robber. A rogue, cheat, or hypocrite. A wretch, or miscreant: a culprit or felon. Any injurious substance as a thief in a candle or a hard core in the heart of a palmyra or plantain shoot. adj. False, delusive, sly, feigned, pretended, hypocritical, dishonest, dishonourable, mischievous, stolen, wicked, sinful. దొంగనేల land unjustly got, మోసముచేసి అపహరించిన నేల. దొంగయిసుక a quicksand, క్రిందినీళ్లు కలిగిన పుండె మీదనుండు ఇసుక. దొంగనిద్ర feigned sleep. దొంగసొమ్ములు stolen goods, దొంగిలించినసొమ్ము. దొంగకూడు food obtained fraudulently, ఇతరులెరుగకుండ మోసముచేసి తిను కూడు. దొంగగొడ్డు a curst cow, a beast, that strays into other's fields to graze there, దొంగతనము మేయుపశువు. దొంగచీకటు a false key, మారుచీకటు. దొంగజాము that part of the midnight which is most favourable for robbers to go about. దొంగభక్తి hypocrisy. దొంగమాట a deceitful word, a lie. "దొంగవాతిట మంచముచేసినట్లిగా" a proverb implying "make friends for the purpose of ruining one." దొంగతనము, దొంగపని or దొంగరికము dongatanamu. n. Theft, robbery, roguery, cunning, craft, a trick, a fraud. దొంగతనము చేసినట్లు this is mere pretence. దొంగతనముగా donga-tanamu-ga. adv. Secretly, by stealth, unawares. దొంగిలించు or దొంగిలు dongilintsu. v. a. To steal. అపహరించు.

దొంగు or దొంగు dongu. [Tel.] v. n. To hide. దాగు.

దొండ donḍa. [Tel.] n. The plant called *Bryonia* or *Bimba*. దొండపండు the ripe fruit which is glossy and of a bright scarlet colour. కాయదొండ *Bryonia grandis*, (Willd.) *Momordica monadelpha*. Rox. iii. 708. తీగదొండ *Bryonia umbellata*. ib. 711. ఆరెదొండ, అడదొండ or అడవిదొండ *Capparis zeylanica* or *Capparis horrida*. పింగదొండ *Bryonia laciniosa*. (Watts.) కాకిదొండ *Trichosanthes palmata*. Rox. iii. 704. కైదొండ or కాకిదొండ *Cephalandra indica*. కుంకుమదొండ *Bryonia pilosa*. బ్రహ్మదొండ is a large sort of thistle with a red fruit. (Watts).

దొండి donḍi. [Tel.] n. A hole. రంధ్రము, తూటు, బొక్క. దొండిపొడుచు to bore, to make a hole, రంధ్రముచేయు.

దొంతర or దొంతి dontara. [Tel.] n. A series. వరుస. A heap, or set of things, as a pile of pots or cups and saucers. adj. Lying in a series, వరుసగానున్న. adv. In a pile or heap. దొంతరముద్దులు kiss upon kiss. డొంతిజల్లిబొంత a patched quilt. డొంతిపిదెము betel leaves strung together. డొంతిగా కేసిన strung, piled. పెంకులను డొంతిలుగాపేర్చు to pile up the tiles in rows. వలపులడొంతి she was a "bundle" of charms. డొంతిగా tier over tier, range over range.

డొండడి *dondadi.* [Tel.] n. A crowd, throng: a squeeze or crush: closeness, crowdedness. దొమ్మి, సందడి, సమ్మర్దము. **డొండడించు** *dondadintsu.* v. n. To become thick or close. సందడించు, సమ్మర్దమగు.

డొండు *dondu.* [from Skt. ద్వంద్వము.] n. A pair. జత. డొంబులిగొట్టు (డొండు+పులి+గొట్టు.) lit: one who kills two tigers. Ironically used to mean a coward, పిరికివాడు.

డొంపు *dompu.* [Tel.] n. A series of beds of flower or other plants. మళ్లవరుస.

డొగ్గలి *doggali.* [Tel.] n. The Broad leafed thorny dock, *amaranthus polygamus.* రక్తబొప్పముసే మొక్క. The small leaved kind is called చిర్రికూర.

డొట్టి *dotti.* [Tel.] affix. With, from తో, కూడా. రాముడుడొట్టి, రామునితోకూడా.

డొడడొడ or **డొణడొణ** *doda-doda.* [Tel. (anuk.)] n. A rush (of water, &c.), a gushing flow. డొణడొణమను or డొనడొనమను *dona-dona-m-anu.* v. n. To be noisy. సందడిచేయు.

డొడవ *dodava.* [Tel.] n. A deformed person. కురూపి.

"క॥ మగతోతిద్దెం డొడవకు
దగునే కన్నియనొసంగ ధరణీశునకున్."
పా. vii.

డొడ్డ *dodda.* [Tel.] adj. Large, great, respectable. Rich, powerful. Pleasing, charming, fine. డొడ్డనీళ్లు delicious water

డొడ్డి *doddi.* [Tel.] n. A yard. A backyard, a stable or byre. పెరడు. adj. Crooked, వంకరగలిగిన. డొడ్డికాళ్లు bandy legs, వంకటికాళ్లు. డొడ్డివల a kind of net, ఒకవిధమువల. కాశీ. iii.

డొడ్డు [Tel.] Same as డొడ్డ. (q. v.). **డొడ్డువారు** *doddu-vāru.* (డొడ్డు+వారు.) v. n. To become great, to increase. అధికమగు.

డొడ్డ *dodda.* [Tel.] n. Plunder. కొల్ల. **డొడ్డకాడు** *dodda-kādu.* n. A plunderer. కొల్లపెట్టువాడు. "సీ॥ డొడ్డకాడ్లచే బరినోయిటూర్పు బిక్కు..." శు. పారి. iii **డొడ్డకత్తె** *dodda-katte.* n. A woman who plunders. కొల్లపెట్టునది. **డొడ్డగొను** *dodda-gonu.* v. t. To plunder, to rob. కొల్లగొను. **డొడ్డవోవు** *dodda-vōvu.* v. n. To be plundered. కొల్లపోవు.

డొద్దు *doddu* [Tel.] n. A pot-bellied man, a corpulent man. బొజ్జపట్టినవాడు.

డొన *dona.* [Tel.] n. A pool on a hill. కొండమీదినీటిపల్లము. A quiver. అమ్ములపొది. The sheath of a toddydrawer's knife, ఈండ్రవానికత్తిపిడి. **డొనయుప్పు** *dona-yuppu.* n. Fuller's earth. చవుటిఉప్పు.

డొన్నె or **డొప్ప** *donne.* [Tel.] n. A dish formed of a leaf pinned up at the corners.

డొపారము *doparamu.* [Tel.] n. The cap used to blind a goshawk or falcon.

"డేగముల తీసి చెంచులు
మారిలవేసినడొపారము లంటిడిచి న
న్నారిగమదువ్వి రెక్కల
వారిజముగ డేగవేటలాడిరి కొల్లన్."
Velag. ii. 243.

చెంచులు మారిలవేసిన డొపారములు, అనగా డేగల ముక్కులకు కండ్లు అగుపడకుండా తోలుతో కుట్టి వేసిన గంతలు.

డొప్ప See డొన్నె. **డొప్పలబోవు** *doppala-bōvu.* [Tel.] v. n. To bag out with wet, as leather does with damp. To shrivel up: to contract as the hands in pain. డొప్పచెవులుగల flap-eared, having large ears. **డొప్పగానుండే** *doppa-ga-nunde.* adj.

Channelled, like a dish. దొప్పదోగు *doppa-dōgu*. v. n. To plunge, to be drenched. దొప్పదోగిన drenched, soaked, bedewed, moist. వానలో దొప్పదోగి తడిసిరి they were soaked in the rain.

దొప్పుదొప్పు *doppu-doppu*. [Tel. (anuk.)] n. A dull thumping noise.

దొబ్బ *dobba*. [Tel.] n. A piece of flesh. A clot of blood. ముద్ద. The outer side of the thigh. A pool or puddle. నెత్తురుకండ.

"తిరుగక విరుగక యూర్థి
కరకీలితములాపాదంబుగాదింపంగా
నరిరెంటెనదయు నెత్తురు
దొరుగక ప్రవహించి నిలిచి దొబ్బలుకట్టెగా." P. i. 240.

టీ॥ దొబ్బలుకట్టెగా అనగా నడ్డలుకట్టెగా.

దొబ్బు *dobbu*. [Tel.] v. a. To shove, poke, push. తోయు. To cohabit, or lie with. To ravish or rape. పడదొబ్బు to knock down. దొబ్బుకొనిపోవు to run away with, ఎత్తుకొనిపోవు. n. A push, a thrust. ఇట్లుచేసినయెడల దొబ్బులుపచ్చును if you do this you will be scolded or beaten. దొబ్బులుపడు to suffer blows, to be abused. దొబ్బులుపెట్టు to abuse, to reprimand. దొబ్బించుకొను *dobbintsu-konu*. v. n. To copulate. దొబ్బుడాయి *dobbu-ḍāyi*. n. Tympany or windy dropsy. Fatness, pride, మదము, గర్వము. దొబ్బులాట *dobbul-āṭa*. n. Hugging, cuddling. Buffets. Fumbling.

దొమదొమ *doma-doma*. [Tel. (anuk.)] n. A loud buzzing. "కీటకముల దొమదొమ మను నీగరుట్టులు." A. vi. 17.

దొమ్మ *domma*. [Tel.] n. The staggers: a fainting disease. మూర్ఛపంటిరోగము. Also, the chest. దొమ్మవ్యాధి pneumonia. A kind of fish.

దొమ్మడోలు or దొమ్మవారి *domma-ḍōlu*. [Tel.] n. A certain tree. *Physalis flexuosa*, అశ్వగంధి, పెన్నేరు, పాయుగంధ.

దొమ్మర *dommara*. [Tel.] n. The name of a certain wandering caste, the members of which are tumblers, ropedancers and buffoons. దొమ్మరి *dommari*. n. A man of this caste. దొమ్మరివాడు.

దొమ్మి *dommi*. [Tel] n. A swarm, rabble, mob, crowd. A melee fight. A fray, a skirmish. A noise, సందడి. దొమ్మిగూడి వచ్చిరి they came in a mob. దొమ్ములాడు to riot, to fight. To be distressed, to suffer; to struggle, పెనగులాడు. దొమ్మియుద్ధము a melee fight. దొమ్మిగా tumultuously, confusedly, noisily, buzzingly; in the lump, indiscriminately. దొమ్మితనము *dommi-tanamu*. n. Riotousness.

దొర or ధొర *dora*. [Tel. from a Turanian root Tur=swift, powerful. The root is found also in *Turk*, *Turannian*, త్వర, త్వరితము, &c.] n. A chief, a baron, a lord, master, owner, ruler, king, governor. ఏలువాడు, రాజు, గొప్పవాడు. A gentleman. మేటిదొర the chief lord. ప్రభువు. A great man, గొప్పవాడు. An equal, సమానుడు. దొరకడలు *dora-kaḍalu*. (దొర+కడలు.) n. A great wave, a surge. గొప్పఅల, కల్లోలము. దొరసాని *dora-sāni*. n. A lady, a queen. ప్రభ్వి, యజమానురాలు, రాణి. దొరసానితనము *dora-sāni-tanamu*. n. The dignity of being a lady. Queenship, ladyship.

దొరకు Same as దొరుకు. (q. v.) దొరకుపడు *doraku-paḍu*. v. n. To be caught or entangled. చిక్కుకొను. దొరకొను *dora-konu*. (దొరకు+కొను.) v. n. and a. To be found. లభించు, చిక్కు. To begin, ఆరంభించు. To try, యత్నించు. "రథసారథి దొరకొనినం, పగతుల సాధించు పెంపునని." M. IV. iv. 10. దొరకోలు *dora-kōlu*. n. The being found or obtained. An attempt, an endeavour. దొరకడము, ఆరంభించడము. "పిడుగ్గైపై దొరకోలర్జునినకు తోంటిసుకృతస్తో మంబుకర్షించెనా." M. VII. iii. 192.

దొరకోలుసన్యాసి or దొరకుసన్యాసి dora-kōlu-sanyāsi. n. A swindler. తేనములు తేసి నమ్మించి వెనుక మోసము చేయు వాడు.

దొరయు dorayu. [Tel.] v. n. & t. To touch. అంటు. To approach, come near, సమీపించు. To be equivalent to, సమానమగు. To resemble, be one with, suit, befit, become. To come to pass, to happen, కలుగు, జరుగు. To obtain, పొందు. "సీ॥ సకల లోకాధినందక్కకళా కలాపంబుదొరయు నెప్పాను." Vasu. i. 2. టీ॥ కళాకలాపంబు దొరయు నెప్పాను, లావణ్యమనెడు భూషణము పొందు చున్న టువంటి చక్క నిముఖము. "సీ॥ నగనవాహిని దొంపి గాడికొండొకదాచు కమలాపురిభరధాం గంబుదొరసి." P. iv. 249. టీ॥ రథరథాంగంబు దొరసి, రథముయొక్క చక్రమునుపమించి.

దొరలు or దొర్లు doralu. [Tel.] v. n. To roll, to be rolled, to be poured forth, to be overturned or upset. Metaphorically, to die. To turn up, as cards or dice. To slide or slip down, to trip. To be admitted, united, or joined, కలయు. To oppose, మారుకొను. To befall. అన్యాయము దొరలదు injustice will never flourish. కీడుదొరలి వచ్చు evil will befall (him.) v. t. To enjoy, అనుభవించు. దొరలించు or దొర్లించు doralintsu. v. t. To cause to roll. దొరలు నట్లుచేయు. To upset.

దొరవి Same as దొరువు.

దొరుకు or దొరకు doruku. [Tel.] v. n. To be got, gained, found, procured, obtained. To accrue, occur, turn up. చిక్కు, లభించు. దొరికించుకొను dorikintsu-konu. v. a. To apprehend, seize, secure.

దొరువు or దొర్వు doruvu. [Tel.] n. A well-spring supplied by a sluice, a large well: a pit of water. A ship's dock. నడబావి. A tank, కొలను. దొరువుపట్టెడ doruvu-patteda. n. A crupper. ఎద్దుముడ్డికి తగిలించే పట్టెడ.

దొలుపు dolupu. [Tel.] v. t. To cause to roll. దొర్లజేయు. (పాంచా. v.) దొల్లించు dollintsu. v. t. To upset. దొరలించు. పాచిక లను దొల్లించినాడు he threw the dice.

దొసగు or దొసవు dosagu. [Tel.] n. Fear, evil, harm. భయము, కీడు, ఆపద. విఘ్నము. "తే॥ అవావంబున బంధుక్షయంబునేయనెల్ల కెల్ల విఘ్నంబుల నుపశమింప, గోరి రప్పాండవేయులు వారి కిట్టు దొసగు వచ్చెనె తలువలతోదబుట్టి." M. V. iv. 54. v. n. To happen, సంభవించు.

దో dō

దోః or దోశ్ dōh. [Skt.] n. The arm. బాహువు. Plu. దోలు.

"ఈ॥ తడియుదంతములు దోలనమర్చిన ఆడనుప్పిరా చెంగట గాలదండములు చేకొనియున్న యమ ద్వయంబనన్."

Vish. P. vii. 435.

దోర్బలుడు dōr-baluḍu. n. One who is strong in the arm: a mighty man. దోర్మూలము dōr-mūlamu. n. The armpit. దోర్లు dōrlu. a plural of దోః. V. P. vii. 435.

దోకు dōku. [Tel.] v. a. To pare or shave the ground, cutting up the turf. To dig slightly so as to loosen the soil for weeding. చేలనుచెక్కు. దోకుడు or దోకీన dōkuḍu. adj. Paring or scraping the ground. దోకుట. దోకుడుపార dōkuḍu-pāra. n. A weeding spade. A sort of instrument like a hoe, for paring the ground and cutting up the turf for fodder. దోకుడుబార dōkuḍu-bāra. n. A game played by children.

దోగు or తోగు dōgu. [Tel.] v. n. To be wet. తడియు. To be bruised, కొట్టుకొనిపోవు. "బాష్పధారావర్షంబున దోగుచు." R. vi. 32. దోగాడు or దోగియాడు dōg-āḍu. v. n. To crawl on the hands and knees like a babe. దోగురు dōguru. n. Theft. దొంగ తనము, చౌర్యము. దోగుకొనిపోవు dōgu-

koni-pōvu. v. n. To be grazed or excoriated. కాలు దోకుకొనిపోయినది the skin was taken off my leg.

దోగ్ధ *dōgdha.* [Skt.] n. A cowherd గొల్లవాడు. దోగ్ధ్రి *dōgdhri.* n. A milch cow. ఈనిన ఆవు, పాలిచ్చే ఆవు.

దోచు or దోచుకొను *dōṭsu.* [Tel.] v. a. To plunder, rob, sack, కొల్లగొట్టు, అపహరించు. దోచిగాడు or దోచిగాడు *dōchi-gāḍu.* n. A bird of prey. A male hawk. మగడేగ.

దోటి *dōṭi.* [Tel.] n. A pruning hook. A hook at the end of a pole. దోటమ్ము or దోటిదమ్ము *dōṭ-ammu.* n. An arrow with a crescent shaped head. దోటిముక్కర a hook-like nose-ring.

దోటు *dōṭu.* [Tel.] v. t. To give. ఇచ్చు.

దోణము or దోణాము *dōṇamu.* [Tel.] n. A dumb-bell or Indian club. భుజములకు బలమునిచ్చుటకై త్రిప్పెడు కట్టివాని యుపకరణవిశేషము. A mallet, గ్రాసు సుకరముగా చీలుటకై అక్కడక్కడ చెక్కిన మేకులను దిగగొట్టెడు ఉపకరణవిశేషము.

దోత్రము *dōtramu.* [Tel.] n. A garment: clothes. దోవతి. "అమల్లులంబమాలాంబుకోగంబైన దోత్రంబునుపవీతసూత్రములను." Kālahas. iii. 114.

దోదసి *dōdasi.* [for Skt. ద్వాదశి.] n. The 12th day in the dark or lunar fortnight.

దోదు *dōdu.* [Tel.] adj. Bulky, slow, heavy, tardy.

దోదుమి, దోదుమ్మి or దోదుముదాడి *dōdumi.* [Tel.] n. A kind of weapon. ఆయుధవిశేషము.

దోనము *donamu.* [Tel.] n. A large mallet. కాటిబద్దలువేసేటప్పుడు దబ్బిచిప్పమీద కొట్టేది.

దోనె or దోని *dōne.* [Tel.] n. A small boat; a single masted ship. A small bucket, జలకడుగుసాధనము. A trough, usually made of a palm tree hollowed as a canoe. The beam, roller or pillow in a loom. A sluice, కాలువకోవ. adj. Slight, అల్పము. దోనమ్ము, దోనయమ్ము or దోనవిల్లు *dōn-ammu.* n. A small arrow. అల్పశరము. దోనెపెంకు *dōne-penku.* n. A pan-tile.

దోపిడి, దోపు or దోపుడు *dōpiḍi.* [Tel. from దోచు.] n. Plunder, devastation, pillage. దోపిచ్చువారు those who submit to be robbed. A. vi. 101. దోపుడుపడు or దోపుడుపోవు *dōpuḍu-paḍu.* v. n. To be robbed. దోపరి, దోపిడిగాడు, దోపుకాడు or దోపుడువాడు a thief, దొంగ. దోపుడు సొమ్ము loot.

దోపు *dōpu.* [Tel.] v. a. To stick in, insert, fasten (a hook or button.)

దోమ *dōma.* [Tel.] n. A mosquito or gnat. మశకము. దోమతెర *dōma-tera.* n. A mosquito curtain.

దోమటి *dōmaṭi.* [Tel.] n. Food. అన్నము.

దోమడి *dōmaḍi.* [Tel.] n. A marriage feast attended by certain peculiar ceremonies, in which only married people whose partners are alive can join.

దోము *dōmu.* [Tel.] n. Diarrhoea in cattle. ఆహారము జీర్ణముకాకపోవుటచే పశువులు పారుకొనుట.

దోయము *dōyamu.* [Tel.] n. A dose, a certain prescribed quantity. "పాలుకుర్కము గ౹౹౦. ఇల్లిపాముదము గ౹౹౦. ఈ రెండు దోయములున్ను." Chikitsa. S. S.

దోయి *dōyi.* [Tel.] n. A couple, a pair. జత. చేతులదోయి a pair of breasts. తొడదోయి the thighs: "రాజపుత్రుడు జేరిచెదొడదోయి పైనునిచి." T. U. R. x. 144. తామరదోయి a pair of lilies. కండోయి or కన్నుదోయి a pair of eyes, the two eyes. దోయికట్టు *dōyi-kaṭṭu.* v. n. To keep company with each other, to go together. జతకూడు. దోయిడి *dōyiḍi.* adj. Empty. శూన్యము, రిక్త. దోయిడిచేతులు empty hands. దోయిలి

dōyili. n. The two hands joined so as to form a cup. అంజలి. దోయిలించు *dōyilintsu*. v. n. To join the hands like a cup.

దోర *dōra*. [Tel.] n. A heap, pile, stack. కుప్ప, పోగు, రాశి. adj. Dun coloured. Reddish, ఎర్రబారిన. Parboiled. Half ripe. Slanting, ఒరిగిన. దోరకాగినపాలు milk that has simmered. దోరగొఱ్ఱెలు brown sheep. దోరపండు or దోరకాయ a half ripe fruit. **దోరగల్లు** *dōra-gallu*. n. A slanting stone. ఒరిగినరాయి "కొనిదోరగల్లునదొబ్బి." Pal. 441. అనగా రాతిబండను జేరిఒత్తి. **దోరగిలు**, **దోరగిల్లు** or **దోరగిలపడు** *dōragilu*. v. n. To be nearly ripe, to approach maturity. To become slightly red, ఎర్రబారు. To be bent down or to slant (as a tree.) **దోరగిల్లపడు** *dōragallu-padu*. v. a. To cause to slant or bend, దోరగిల్లజేయు.

దోరణ or **దోరణము** Same as తోరణము. (q. v.) దోరపాక or ఒరపాక a shed with a pent roof.

దోరము Same as ద్వారము. (q.v.)

దోరు *dōru*. [Tel.] v. n. To die, expire, perish. చచ్చు. To be done away with or removed. తొలగిపోవు. "కొలని నీళ్లనుకడుగు దోరంగకడిగి, తనునీళ్లతో పాత్ర దాల్పినంచి." Pativratya Charitra. p. 80. She washed it so that the dirty water might flow off. To bend down, ఒరగు, వ్రాలు. **దోరుచు** or **దోర్చు** *dōrutsu*. v. t. To kill. చంపు. To cause to bend down, ఒరగించు, వ్రాల్చు.

దోరువ or **దోరువా** *dōruva*. [Tel.] n. A kind of plover. ఒకవిధమైన పక్షి.

దోరెము *dōremu*. [Tel.] n. The string by which hawks are kept tied up. డేగలను కట్టేత్రాడు. "వ॥ బద్ధిభ్రష్టనిబద్ధాగ్రంబులై కొమరారు దోరెపుత్రాళ్లతోడన్ దిరుగుడులన్ పెడంగు వడి." Swa. iv.

దోవ, **తోవ** or **త్రోవ** *dōva*. [Tel.] n. A way, road, path. A way or means, an expedient. దోవపెట్టు to make a way, దారి చేయు. A. v. 122. వాడు పోయినదెల్లను దోవ every way is his way: he has no settled course, applied to a question that is anomalous or beyond all rule. **దోవపిట్ట** *dōva-pitta*. n. The Rufous tailed Finch-lark, *Ammomanes phoenicura*. అంబడిపిట్ట గాడు. (F. B. I.)

దోవతి *dōvati*. [Tel.] n. A man's garment worn round the loins. కట్టువస్త్రము, పరిధానము.

దోష *dōsha*. [Skt.] n. Night. రాత్రి. The arm, భుజము. **దోషము** *dōshamu*. n. Harm, evil. A fault, crime. An error, mistake, తప్పు. Sin, పాపము. A bad sign: a fatal symptom in illness. ప్రమాణముయొక్క దోషము the penalty of an oath. దోషములేదు there is no harm done. దోచుకొన్న దోషము the guilt of robbery. స్పర్శదోషము the defilement caused by a touch. దోషగుణములు పుట్టినవి bad symptoms appeared. **దోషకారి** *dōsha-kari*. n. An evil doer. దోషము చేయువాడు, దుష్టుడు, దుష్టురాలు. **దోషజ్ఞుడు** *dōsha-gnyudu*. n. A physician, one skilled in diseases. వైద్యుడు. A learned man విద్వాంసుడు, దోషముతెలిసినవాడు. **దోషాకరుడు** *dōshākarudu*. n. The moon. చంద్రుడు. **దోషాచరుడు** *dōsha-charudu*. n. A fiend that "walks at night." రాక్షసుడు. **దోషి** *dōshi*. n. A sinner. దోషముగలవాడు. A criminal. **దోషించు** *dōshintsu*. v. n. To turn out ill. To come on (as bad symptoms.) దోషముపుట్టు. అతనికి దోషించినవి bad symptoms appeared in his case.

దోస *dōsa*. [Tel.] n. A cucumber. A melon (Ceded Districts). చేదిదోస or చేదుదోస the bitter cucumber. నక్కదోసకాయ a gherkin. ముళ్లదోసకాయ the prickly cucumber. మాగుడదోస rough bryony. దోసకాయచెంబు a mug, ribbed like a sort of cucumber.

దోసము *dōsamu.* [from Skt. దోషము.] Same as దోషము. (q. v.) **దోసకారి** *dōsakāri.* n. A wicked person, a sinner. దుష్టుడు, దుష్టురాలు. **దోసి** *dōsi.* n. He or she who is a sinner. Suca. iii. 160.

దోసర *dōsara.* n. The name of a certain creeping plant.

దోసిలి or **దోయిలి** *dōsili.* [Tel.] n. The hands held together so as to form a cup. A double handful: as much as can be contained in the two hands held as a cup. దోసిళ్లు handfuls, i. e., tithes or fees levied at various rates. **దోసిలించు** or **దోయిలించు** *dōsilintsu.* v. n. To hold the two hands together as a cup.

దోసె *dōse.* [from Skt. దోషకము.] n. A kind of cake. అపము.

దోహదము *dōhadamu.* [Skt.] n. Wish, desire, longing. ఇచ్ఛ. The desires of a pregnant woman, గర్భిణీలకు కోర్కెలు. Manure, ఎరువు. The art of gardening: the operation of forcing a plant, or bringing out the flowers prematurely. దోహద లక్షణము pregnancy, గర్భము. **దోహదవతి** *dōhada-vati.* n. A longing woman. కోర్కెగలస్త్రీ. **దోహదశాస్త్రము** *dōhada-śāstramu.* n. The art of gardening.

దోహలము *dōhalamu.* [Skt.] n. Desire, eagerness, or longing. Aspiring, ఇచ్ఛ, ఉత్సాహము. **దోహలి** *dōhali.* adj. Expert. నిపుణుడు, సమర్థుడు. "కొన్నిలతలగోపికాచిత్త వృత్తములట సరసి ముచ్చిలి కేర్పు దోహలియు నంచు." M. v. iii.

దౌ dau

దౌ, దవ్వు or **దవ్వుగ** *dau.* [Tel. another form of దవ్వు.] adj. Far, afar, distant. దూరము. "దౌవనిచనిన" even though he went to a distant land. A. iv. 198.

దౌడ, దవుడ or **దవడ** *dauḍa.* [Tel.] n. The cheek. చెంప. ముఖములోపలిభాగము, కౌలుపు.

దౌడు or **దవుడు** *dauḍu.* [Tel.] n. A fast run, a gallop. మిక్కిలివేగపుపరుగు. See దవుడు.

దౌత్యము *dautyamu.* [Skt. from దూత.] n. Agency, ambassadorship. దూతభావము. An act of an agent, దూతకర్మము. The nature of an agent, దూతస్వభావము.

దౌరు or **దవురు** *dauru.* [Tel.] n. Brightness, brilliancy. కాంతి.

దౌరుగోడ *dauru-goḍa.* [Tel.] n. A parapet wall round a well.

దౌర్జన్యము *daurjanyamu.* [Skt. from దుర్జన.] n. Force, violence, wrong, fraud. బలాత్కారము.

దౌర్భాగ్యము *daur-bhāgyamu.* [Skt. from దుర్భగ.] n. Mischance, evil, ill luck. దురదృష్టము. **దౌర్భాగ్యుడు** *daur-bhāgyuḍu.* n. A wretch, a miscreant.

దౌల or **దవ్వల** *daula.* [Skt.] adv. Afar off. దూరమందు.

దౌలత్తు *daulattu.* [H.] n. Fortune; wealth; regal state.

దౌవారికుడు *dauvārikuḍu.* [Skt. from ద్వార.] n. A warder, a porter. ద్వారపాలకుడు.

దౌవు Same as దవ్వు. (ప్ర. ii.)

దౌష్ట్యము *daushṭyamu.* [Skt. from దుష్ట.] n. Badness, wickedness. దుష్టస్వభావము.

దౌహిత్రుడు *dauhitruḍu.* [Skt. from దుహితృ.] n. A daughter's son. దుహితకొడుకు, మనుమడు. **దౌహిత్ర్యము** *dauhitryamu.* (Low Sanskrit) n. The female line: kinship through a daughter: the relationship between a man and his mother's parents.

దౌహృదము *dauhṛidamu.* [Skt.] n Wish, desire, longing (in pregnant woman.) The prospect or symptoms of pregnancy. Compare దోహదము and దోహదవతి. "దౌహృదోదయశుభసంపన్న తనర్చెల్లెడునెడ." R.iii.91.

ద్యు dyu

ద్యుతి *dyuti*. [Skt.] n. Brilliancy, radiance. కాంతి, వెలుగు.

ద్యుమణి *dyumaṇi*. [Skt. ద్యు = the sky.] n. The gem of the sky, i. e., the Sun.

ద్యుమ్నము *dyumnamu*. [Skt.] n. Wealth; power. విత్తము, పరాక్రమము, బలము.

ద్యూ dyū

ద్యూతము *dyūtamu*. [Skt.] n. Gambling, play. జూదము.

ద్యో dyo

ద్యోతకము *dyōtakamu*. [Skt.] adj. Illuminating. ప్రకాశింపజేయునది. Conveying, shewing. స్నేహద్యోతకము what shews friendship. ద్యోతము *dyōtamu*. n. Light, heat. ప్రకాశము, ఎండ. ద్యోతించు *dyōtintsu*. v. n. To shine, or flash. ప్రకాశించు. ద్యోవీధి *dyō-vīdhi*. n. The path of light, i. e., the sky.

ద్ర dra

ద్రప్సము *drapsamu*. [Skt.] n. A drop of water. నీటిబొట్టు. "జలబిందుస్వరంబుల బనసలు గొన్ని తెలిసి ద్రప్సంబులు మీదజలంబు లిచ్చుచును." HD. ii. 815. అతడు నాకు ఒక ద్రప్సమున్ను ఇయ్యలేదు he did not give me even a drop of water.

ద్రబ్బెడ *drabbeḍa*. [Tel.] n. A kind of cake. ఒకవిధమైన భక్ష్యము.

ద్రవము *dravamu*. [Skt.] n. Juice: moisture. తడి. ద్రవద్రవ్యము *drava-dravyamu*. n. A liquid. ద్రవించు *dravintsu*. v. n. To distil, emit (moisture or liquor.) To trickle, as water. కారు. ద్రవిణము *draviṇamu*. n. Wealth ధనము. [illegible]

dravyamu. n. Stuff, a thing, a substance A drug or ingredient, మందు. An element. పృథివ్యాద్యి. (పృథివి, అప్పు, తేజము, వాయువు, ఆకాశము, కాలము, దిక్కు, ఆత్మ, మనస్సు అనునవి.) Wealth, property, ధనము.

ద్రవిడము *draviḍamu*. [Tel.] n. The Tamil country. ద్రవిడాంగన a Tamil lady. Suca. iii. 290. See ద్రావిడ.

ద్రా drā

ద్రాక్ష *drāksha*. [Skt.] n. A grape, a grape vine. పచ్చిద్రాక్ష an unripe or sour grape. ద్రాక్షపండ్లు raisins. ద్రాక్షరసము wine.

ద్రాక్షారామము *drāksh-ārāmamu*. [Skt.] n. The name of a village near Rajamundry.

ద్రాఘిష్ఠము *drāghishṭhamu*. [Skt.] adj. Longest: very long. మిక్కిలిదీర్ఘము.

ద్రాబ *drāba*. [Tel.] n. A blockhead, a fool. అవివేకుడు, అధముడు. A. iv. 262. adj. Silly, worthless, base, trashy. అధమము. ద్రాబసొమ్ము trash, stuff, rubbish.

ద్రావకము *drāvakamu*. [Skt. from ద్రవము.] n. Spirit. An extract, essence. గంధకద్రావకము Sulphuric acid, vitriol. సురేకారద్రావకము Nitric acid. ఉప్పుద్రావకము Muriatic acid. కర్పూరద్రావకము or కర్పూరతైలము turpentine.

ద్రావిడ *drāviḍa*. [Tam.] adj. Dravida; a name usually applied to Tamil. ద్రావిడదేశము the Tamil country. ద్రావిడులు or ద్రావిడ్లు the Tamil people. As a collective term పంచద్రావిడములు the 'Five-fold Dravida' denotes what the English call the South Indian languages, i. e., Canarese, Tamil, Telugu, Guzerati and Mahratta. RKD. gives the list, thus; Dravida, Carnata, Gujarāta, Mahārāshta, and Tēlangah. See Caldwell.

త్రి dri

త్రిండు *drindu*. [Tel.] Another form of దిండు. (q. v.)

ద్రు dru

ద్రుష్ట Same as దుష్ట adj. (q. v.)

ద్రుతము *drutamu*. [Skt.] n. Speed, quickness. త్వర. A name given by Telugu grammarians to the letter (న) N, in particular places. ద్రుతప్రకృతి A grammatical phrase denoting a word which ends in an N sound.

ద్రుమము *drumamu*. [Skt. cf. Greek *Drus.*] n. A tree. వృక్షము.

ద్రొ dro

ద్రొబ్బు Same as త్రొబ్బు to cause to fall, పడద్రోయు.

ద్రో drō

...ణము or ద్రోణము *drōṇamu*. [Skt.] A certain measure of capacity: rather ...ore than 64 lbs avoirdupois. తూము. ...e name of a certain hill. The plant ...led *Phlomis indica*. తుమ్మిచెట్టు. A steel ...y used in gymnastics. A scorpion. ...ద్రోణాచార్యులు *drōṇ-āchāryulu*. n. The ...e of a certain hero renowned for his ...ngth. ద్రోణి *drōṇi*. n. A boat, a small ... చిన్నఓడ. A iv. 147. (Hence the name ...ey or Dhoneu.) దోనె.

ద్రోవది *drōvadi*. [Tel.] n. The daughter of Drupada. ద్రౌపది.

ద్రోహము *drōhamu*. [Skt.] n. Treachery. కీడుతలపు. Harm, offence, wickedness, a sin. రాజద్రోహము treason. స్వామిద్రోహము a sin against God. గురుద్రోహము a sin against a Guru. ద్రోహముచేయు to act treacherously. ద్రోహబుద్ధి an evil heart. ద్రోహి *drōhi*. n. A traitor.

ద్వ dva

ద్వంద్వము *dvandvamu*. [Skt.] n. A pair or couple. రెండు. The name of a certain kind of compound word (సమాసము) in which two nouns if uncompounded would be in the same case and united by a conjunction. Thus, రామలక్ష్మణులు. Rama and Lakshmana. ద్వంద్వయుద్ధము A duel.

ద్వయము, ద్వయి or ద్వాయి *drayamu*. [Skt.] n. A pair, couple. జత, రెండు.

ద్వా dvā

ద్వాదశ *dvā-daśa*. [Skt.] adj. Twelfth. పండ్రెండవ. ద్వాదశాత్ముడు *dvādaśātmuḍu*. n. The god who has twelve phases, an epithet of the sun. ద్వాదశి *dvā-daśi*. n. The twelfth lunar day of either the light or dark fortnight.

ద్వాపరము *dvāparamu*. [Skt.] n. The third or Brazen age of the world, which has preceded the present కలియుగము or Iron age. ద్వాపరయుగపుకథలు old wives' tales, legends.

ద్వారము *dvāramu*. [Skt. cf. Eng. 'Door'.] n. A door. వాకిలి. An opening, orifice, hole. A medium or way, ఉపాయము. ద్వారపాలకుడు *dvāra-pālakuḍu*. n. A porter. వాకిటికావలివాడు, ప్రతిహారి. The figures of "cherubs" put up on each of the gates of a temple. ద్వారబంధము *dvāra-bandhamu*. n. The frame of a gate, a door frame. వాకిటిమ్రానిచట్టము. ద్వారా *dvārā*. prep. By means of, through. అతని ద్వారా వింటిని I learned it from him.

ద్వి dvi

ద్వి *dvi*. [Skt.] n. Two. రెండు. ద్విగుణము *dvi-guṇamu*. adv. and adj. Double, twofold. ధనద్విగుణము cent. per cent. ద్విగుణీకృతము *dvi-guṇa-kṛitamu.* adv. Twice ploughed. ద్విజ *dvija.* adj. Twice born. ద్విజము oviparous, born first from the ovary and then from the egg, as a bird or snake, పక్షి, పల్లి, పాము. Vasu. iii. 32. A tooth: as all teeth are reproduced. ద్విజుడు A Brahmin, a member of one of the three thread-wearing castes, so called because born into the caste by investiture with the sacred thread. A verse says జన్మనా జాయతే శూద్రః, కర్మణా జాయతే ద్విజః, వేదాధ్యయనాద్విప్రస్స్యాత్, బ్రహ్మజ్ఞానాద్బ్రాహ్మణః, by birth he is a Sudra: rites constitute him a Dwija: reading the scriptures makes him a Vipra: and knowledge of deity makes him a Brahmin. ద్విజన్ముడు *dvi-janmuḍu.* n. A twice born man. ద్విజుడు. (q. v.) ద్విజరాజు *dvija-rāzu.* n. An epithet of the moon, and of the eagle (గరుత్మంతు) as king of birds. ద్విజాతి *dvi-jāti.* n. A bird, a snake, a Brahmin. బ్రాహ్మణ, అండజ, బ్రాహ్మణాది జాతిత్రయం. ద్విజిహ్వము *dvi-jihvamu.* n. Lit: the double tongued, i. e., a snake, పాము. ద్విజుడు See under ద్విజ. ద్వితయము *dvi-tayamu.* n. A couple, pair. జత, రెండు. ద్వితీయము *dvitīyamu.* adj. Second. రెండవది. ద్వితీయ *dvitīya.* n. The second day of a lunar fortnight. విదియ. ద్వితీయావిభక్తి *dvitīya-vibhakti.* n. The second case of a noun, being the accusative. ద్వితీయుడు the second person, రెండవ వాడు. ద్విత్వము *dvitvamu.* n. Reduplication of a letter, a double consonant, thus, ద్విత్వతకారము double T. దకార ద్విత్వము double D. ద్విపము *dvipamu.* n. Lit: That which drinks (ప) with two limbs, i. e., an elephant. ద్విపద *dvipada.* n. Lit: A verse of two lines. A couplet, a sort of metre. ద్విరదము *dvi-radamu.* n. Lit: Two-tusked, i. e., an elephant. ద్విరసనము *dvi-rasanamu.* n. Lit: Double tongued, i. e., a snake. ద్విరేఫము *dvi-rēphamu.* n. The large carpenter bee. Lit: "The Double R." so called because its commonest name *Bhramara* uses the letter R twice. ద్విహల్యము *dvi-halyamu.* n. Lit: Twice ploughed, i. e., a field. రెండుసార్లు దున్నిన (పొలము.)

ద్విషుడు *dvishuḍu.* [Skt. cf. ద్వేషము.] n. An enemy. శత్రువు.

ద్వీ dvī

ద్వీపము *dvīpamu.* [Skt.] n. An island. దీవి. A continent. The Hindu mythology reckons seven such. In compounds this means Foreign. Thus, ద్వీపద్రాక్షపండ్లు Raisins, i. e., foreign grapes. ద్వీపాంతర ములు foreign parts. ద్వీపవతి *dvīpa-vati.* n. A river, stream. నది, ఏరు. ద్వీపి *dvīpi.* adj. Pertaining to islands, native of an island, insular. n. A tiger, ounce or leopard, పులి, చిరుతపులి. The sea, సముద్రము.

ద్వే dvē

ద్వేషము *dvēshamu.* [Skt.] n. Enmity, hatred. పగ, శత్రుత్వము. అన్నద్వేషము loathing food, want of appetite. ద్వేషి. *dvēshi.* n. An enemy. cf. ద్విషుడు. ద్వేషించు *dvēshinsu.* v. a. To hate, dislike. విరోధించు, పగగొను. ద్వేష్ట *dvēshṭa.* n. An enemy.

ద్వై dvai

ద్వైతము *dvaitamu.* [Skt.] n. Dualism; the theory that there are two eternal and self-existing substances or principles. Opposed to అద్వైతము which teaches that there is but one substance of which all things are manifestations. Also the name of a forest, ద్వైతవనము.

ద్వైపాయనుడు *dvaipāyanuḍu*. [Skt. from ద్వీపము.] n. Lit: The Island born. An epithet of వ్యాస the celebrated poet.

ద్వైమాతురుడు *dvai-maturuḍu*. [Skt.] n. An epithet of the god Gaṇēsa; who according to mythology had "two mothers;" one being Parvati and the other an elephant.

ద్వైవిధ్యము *dvai-vidhyamu*. [Skt. from ద్వివిధి.] n. Two-foldness: the being in two modes.

ద్య dvya

ద్వ్యర్థి *dvyarthi*. [Skt. from ద్వి.] adj. Having a double sense, as an allegory or a puzzle.

ధ dha

ధ *dha*. The letter Dh, as in Adhere.

ధగధగ *dhaga-dhaga*. [Skt. anuk.] n. Brilliancy, glittering. adj. Bright. "ధగధగద్గళితరత్నము." Dasav. ix. 202. ధగధగమను or ధగధగలాడు *dhaga-dhaga-m-anu*. v. n. To glitter, to flash.

ధటు or ధటము *dhaṭa*. [Skt.] n. A wooden balance, or pair of scales. త్రాసు.

ధటి *dhaṭi*. [Skt.] n. A belt. దట్టి. A modesty piece, గోచి. ధటిని *dhaṭini*. n. A cotton cord used as a belt: మొలత్రాడు.

ధట్ట *dhaṭṭa*. [Skt.] n, An army. సేన. ధట్టము *dhaṭṭamu*. n. A host, a multitude. సమూహము. "తురగధట్టము" ఉ. హరి. iv.

ధట్టుడు or దట్టుడు *dhaṭṭuḍu*. [Tel.] n. A hero, a brave man. శూరుడు. BD. ii. 1315.

ధనము *dhanamu*. [Skt.] n. A herd of cattle. ఆవులమంద. (Cf. Lat. *pecus*.) Treasure, property, resources, wealth. In mathematics, it is the equivalent of the word 'plus.'' (Warren.) (Metaphorically) a talent. "అభిమానము ధనంబుగా" (Bobbili Padya. ii. 129.) surely honour is wealth. క్రయధనము the price paid, the cost price, the purchase money. స్త్రీధనము dowry or pin-money. ధనద్విగుణము అయినది the interest equalled the principal. ధనదయావరులు beneficent persons. ధనంజయుడు *dhanan-jayuḍu*. n. A title of Agni or Vulcan, the god of fire: as being the "vanquisher of wealth." Also, of Arjuna, అర్జునుడు. ధనంజయపురము *dhananjaya-puramu*. n. A volcano. The భూమి, as being the abode of vital heat. అగ్నిమండలము or అగ్నిపురము. ధనదము *dhanadamu*. adj. Beneficent, liberal. ధనదుడు *dhanaduḍu*. n. A beneficent or liberal man. దాత. A name of Kubēra, the god of riches. ధనికుడు, ధనసంపన్నుడు, ధని or ధనుడు *dhanikuḍu*. n. One who is rich, a wealthy man, a rich man. పాండిత్యధనుడు one who has a richly stored mind: a highly accomplished man. తపోధనులు great saints: those who abound in penances. పుణ్యధనులు those who are rich in good works. See ధన్యము.

ధనియాలు or దనియాలు *dhaniyalu*. [Tel.] n. plu. Coriander seeds. కొత్తిమిరగింజలు.

ధనిష్ఠ *dhanishṭha*. [Skt.] n. The name of a constellation. నక్షత్రవిశేషము.

ధనువు or ధనుస్సు *dhanuvu*. [Skt.] n. A bow. విల్లు. The arc of a circle. The sign Sagittarius in the zodiac. ధనురాకారము *danur-ākāramu*. n. The shape of a bow. ధనుర్ధరుడు, ధనుష్మంతుడు or ధానుష్కుడు *dhanur-dharuḍu*. n. An archer. విలుకాడు. ధనుర్మార్గము *dhanur-margamu*. n. A curved line: an arc.

ధన్యము *dhanyamu*. [Skt. from ధనము.] adj. Fortunate, blest, virtuous. n. Wealth. An exclamation like Hurra! Huzza! most excellent! ధన్యుడు a happy or fortunate man, పుణ్యవంతుడు, పుణ్యాత్ముడు. కృతార్థుడు. **ధన్య** *dhanya*. n. A noble woman, a lady ధన్యురాలు, పుణ్యవతి.

ధన్వంతరి *dhan-vantari*. [Skt.] n. A name common to Surya the sun, and to Siva, but usually given to the physician of the gods. దేవవైద్యుడు.

ధన్వము *dhanvamu*. [from Skt. ధనువు.] n. A bow. **ధన్వి** *dhanvi*. n. A bowman. విలుకాడు. An epithet of Arjuna, అర్జునుడు. A skilful man, నేర్పరి.

ధమనము *dhamanamu*. [Skt.] n. Southernwood, a very fragrant herb. దవనము, కిక్కురుస కసవు.

ధమని *dhamani*. [Skt.] n. A vein. నరము, బోలునరము. A tube or pipe, గొట్టము. A flute. R. vi. 10. **ధమనుడు** *dhamanudu*. n. One who blows a pair of bellows, కొలిమితిత్తి నూదువాడు. A cruel man, క్రూరుడు. Fire. అగ్ని.

ధమ్మిల్లము *dhammillamu*. [Skt.] n. Tresses, curls, locks. కొప్పు.

ధర or **దర** *dhara*. [Tel.] n. Price, rate, valuation. ధరప్రలు rates, prices. **ధరావతు** *dhara-vatu*. n. Valuation. A deposit, an advance of a loan.

ధర *dhara*. [Skt.] n. The earth. భూమి, నేల. See ధరణి. **ధరిత్రి** *dharitri*. n. The earth. భూమి, నేల. **ధరాధరము** *dhara-dharamu*. n. A mountain: as being a pillar or prop of the earth. **ధరణము** *dharanamu*. n. Holding, possessing, having. ధరించుట. **ధరణి** *dharani*. n. The earth. భూమి. **ధరణీదేవుడు** or **ధరామరుడు** *dharani-devudu*. n. A terrestrial deity, i. e., a Brahmin. **ధరణీధరము** *dharani-dharamu*. n. A mountain. కొండ, నేల తాల్పు. **ధరణీధవుడు** or **ధరణీశ్వరుడు** *dharani-svarudu*. n. A king. రాజు.

ధరణము *dharanamu*. [Skt.] n. An imaginary coin, of the value of 8 dubs.

ధరించు *dharintsu*. [Skt.] v. a. To wear or put on. To bear, తాల్చు. To hold or contain. ఆజ్ఞ శిరస్సునధరించు to obey (an order), bow to (a command); lit: to bear it on the head. గర్భముధరించు to become pregnant, lit: to bear a womb.

ధర్మము or **ధర్మువు** *dharmamu*. [Skt.] n. Duty. విధి. Virtue, పుణ్యము. Right, న్యాయము. Alms. A rule, precept or principle. విధి. Nature, character, property, స్వభావము. A function or trade. Custom, usage, propriety, ఆచారము. ధర్మశాస్త్రము or ధర్మసంహిత Law, the science of right. సాత్వికధర్మము the conduct that shows meekness. కులధర్మము the rules of caste. వివాహధర్మము conjugal dues, the behaviour proper for a married pair. పండితధర్మము scholarship, that which is to be expected from a scholar. కాలధర్మము death. అతనిదొరతనములో ధర్మము నాలుగు పాదములతో నడిచెను justice was administered with perfect impartiality during his reign: lit: it went on its four feet. ధర్మపత్ని a lawful wife. **ధర్మకర్త** *dharma-karta*. n. A judge or arbitrator. A church warden, or manager of a temple. The executor to an estate. **ధర్మజ్ఞుడు** *dharmagnyudu*. n. One who knows what is right. ధర్మము తెలిసినవాడు. **ధర్మధ్వజి** *dharma-dhvaji*. n. A formalist or one who pretends to be religious from ulterior motives. జీవనార్థముకొరకు జటాధర్మాదులను ధరించినవాడు. **ధర్మరాజు** *dharma-radzu*. n. The "king of justice," a name of Yama, the king of Hell; also, the name of a hero in the Mahabharata. A certain petty village god. ధర్మరాజులు the Pāndu heroes collectively. **ధర్మసత్రము** *dharma-satramu*. n. A charity house, a poor's house. **ధర్మాత్ముడు** *dharm-atmudu*. n. A virtuous or liberal man. పుణ్యాత్ముడు. **ధర్మాసనము** *dharm-asanamu*. n. A judge's seat, "the bench."

ధర్మాధికారి కూర్చుండుచోటు. ధర్మిష్ఠులు *dharmishṭhulu.* n. Charitable or benevolent persons. ధర్మి *dharmi.* adj. Just. ధర్మముగల. ధర్ముడు *dharmuḍu.* n. The Just One. A name of Yama, యముడు. ధర్మువు *dharmuvu.* n. Virtue, justice. న్యాయము, పుణ్యము. ధర్మేతరుడు *dharm-étaruḍu.* n. An unjust or unrighteous man.

ధర్షణము *dharshaṇamu.* [Skt.] n. Contumely, scorn. బెదిరించడము, తిరస్కారము. ధర్షణి *dharshaṇi.* n. An adulteress. జారస్త్రీ. ధర్షించు *dharshinṭsu.* v. t. To treat with contempt. తిరస్కరించు.

ధవళము *dhavaḷamu.* [Skt.] adj. White, bright. తెల్లని. Fine, చక్కని. n. Whiteness, తెలుపు. ధవళములు *dhavaḷamulu.* n. A kind of song. ఒకవిధమైన పాట. ధవళిమ or ధవళిమము *dhavaḷima.* n. Whiteness. తెలుపు.

ధవిత్రము *dhavitramu.* [Skt.] n. A leather fan used in sacrifices.

ధవుడు *dhavuḍu.* [Skt.] n. A master, lord, owner, king. రాజు. A husband, పెనిమిటి. See విధవ and విధవ్యము.

ధా dhâ

ధాటి *dhâṭi.* [Skt.] n. A rush. An attack, an assault. An inroad, incursion, invasion. దండయాత్ర, దాడి. ధాటికల *dhâṭi-kala.* adj. Resolute, firm, decided, decisive, fluent, well versed. ధాటిగా *dhâṭi-gâ.* adv. Decisively, decidedly, resolutely, firmly, trimly, spiritedly, briskly,

ధాణుకపాలు or ధాణుకోపాలు *dhâṇuku-pâlu.* [Marati.] n. A shuffle; a quivering motion in dancing.

ధాత *dhâta.* [Skt.] n. One who saves. రక్షించువాడు. Brahma, the Creator, బ్రహ్మ.

ధాతకి *dhâtaki.* [Skt.] n. A tree called *Grislea tomentosa,* (W.) or *Bauhenia spicata (Heyne.)* అరచెట్టు.

ధాతువు *dhâtuvu.* [Skt.] n. The essence of anything. సారము. One of the constituent elements of the earth, or of the body. A fossil or mineral red chalk, పర్వతధాతువు, కేసరు. మణిశిలలోనుండు ఎర్రనిధాతువు, శిలాదికారము A red mark on the forehead, బొట్టు. The pulse. ధాతువు ఆడు, నడుచు or కొట్టుకొను to beat as the pulse. A grammatical root. A relic. Thus దంతధాతువు is the Tooth-relic, being the tooth of Gautama Buddha. ధాతువాదము *dhâtu-vâdamu.* n. Assaying, in mineralogy. The art of Chemistry. T. iii. 65. రసవాదము. "ధాతువాదంబు కోటు వాదంబు." Amuk. i. ధాతువాది *dhâtuvâdi.* n. A mineralogist. A critic, grammarian. A Chemist రసవాది, A. v. 231. వైయాకరణి. ధాతువుచూచు *dhâtuvu-tsûtsu.* v. n. To feel the pulse. సప్తధాతువులు or మహాధాతువులు the seven great principles of nature, లోమత్వక్మాంస శోణితాస్థి మజ్జా ప్రాణములు.

ధాత్రి *dhâtri.* [Skt.] n. The earth. భూమి. A foster mother, తల్లి. A nurse, దాది. A plant, *Emblic myrobalan,* ఉసిరికచెట్టు. ధాత్రేయి *dhâtréyi.* n. The earth. భూమి. "క॥ పోయిరుదుబోనివ్వదు ధాత్రేయిక." వై. vii.

ధానుష్కుడు *dhânushkuḍu.* See under ధనుస్సు. ధానుష్కస్వాములు expert archers.

ధాన్యము *dhânyamu.* [Skt. from ధనము.] n. Rice in the husk: rough rice. Grain, corn in general: all kinds of grain are spoken of in the plural number, except cleaned rice (బియ్యము.) నవధాన్యములు the nine kinds of grains, *viz.,* గోధుమలు, యవలు, పెసలు, సెనగలు, కందులు, బొబ్బరలు, నువ్వులు, మినుములు and ఉలవలు. ధాన్యాకము *dhânyâkamu.* n. Coriander. దనియాలు.

ధామము *dhâmamu.* [Skt.] n. A house, abode or dwelling. ఇల్లు. A place, చోటు. Light, వెలుగు. Brightness, splendour.

కాంతి. సుగుణధామ O thou abode of noble virtues! గుణధాముడు he who is the home of excellence. ధామనిధి dhāma-nidhi. n. The sun. Lit: The abode of brightness.

ధార dhāra. [Skt.] n. A stream, a current: oozing or issuing of anything; the course of a stream, a course or sequence. ప్రవాహము. The edge, అంచు. Sharpness, కరుకు. A horse's pace, అశ్వగతి. పంచధారలు, the five paces, trotting, cantering, &c. కార్యధార the course of the affair. Water poured into the hand of the accepter of a gift in token of a donation, a ceremony performed when a gift is made. ధారపోయు dhāra pōyu. v. a. To endow, to give by a formal ceremony, in which water is poured from the hand of the donor; to bestow as a solemn gift. చేత నీళ్లుపోసి దానముచేయు. ధారాగృహీతము dhāra-gri-hītamu. adj. Received (as a boon.) ధారాదత్తము dhāra-dattamu. n. A solemn donation. ధారాధరము dhāra-dharamu. n. A cloud. A sword. ధారాసంపాతము dhāra-sampātamu. n. A hard shower of rain.

ధారకము dhārakamu. [Skt.] n. Sustenance, food. A stimulant, made of spices, &c., given to a convalescent before he is put upon diet.

ధారణ dhāraṇa. [Skt.] n. Exchange, barter. "ధారణాసి." A. vi. 93 Difference in exchange.

ధారణము dāraṇamu [Skt.] n. Keeping, holding, having, maintaining, wearing. ధరించుట.

ధారాటము dhārāṭamu. [Skt.] n. A horse. అశ్వము. A cuckoo, కోకిలపక్షి. వానకోయిల.

ధారాళము dhārālamu. [Skt.] n. Freedom from restraint. అడ్డపాటులేమి. Openness, want of hesitation, generosity, liberality. adj. Liberal, free. అడ్డపాటులేని. ధారాళముగా dhārālamu-ga. adv. Easily, plainly, uninterruptedly, with ease, at free will. ధారాళవృష్టి plenteous rain. R. v. 3. and 31.

ధారి dhāri. [Skt. from ధరించు.] n. One who bears or carries. ధరించువాడు, ధరించునది. విషధారి poisonous, venemous; one who carries a poison, విషముకలిగినవాడు. ధారుడు dhārudu. n. A bearer, carrier, supporter.

ధార్తరాష్ట్రము dhārta-rāshṭramu [Skt.] n. A sort of goose or swan with a black beak and legs. నల్లనిముక్కు కాళ్లుగల హంస. ధార్తరాష్ట్రుడు dhārta-rāshṭrudu. n. A son of Dhritarāshṭra.

ధార్మికుడు dhārmikudu. [Skt. from ధర్మము.] n. A good man. పుణ్యాత్ముడు.

ధావనము dhāvanamu. [Skt.] n. Running. పరుగు. Cleanness. శుద్ధి. దంతధావనము cleaning the teeth.

ధావళ్యము dhāvalyamu. [Skt. from ధవళము.] n. Whiteness, brightness, a white colour. తెలుపు.

ధి dhi

ధిక్కరించు dhik-karintsu. [Skt.] v. a. To flout, scorn, disregard, treat contemptuously, cry out against, తిరస్కరించు. ధిక్కారము or ధిక్క్రియ dhik-kāramu. n. Scorn, contempt. తిరస్కారము. ధిక్కారి dhik-kāri. n. A scorner. H. ii. 82. ధిక్కృతుడు one who is scorned, తిరస్కరింపబడినవాడు.

ధిమింధిమి dhimin-dhimi. [Tel. (anuk.)] n. Ting tang, ding dong. ధిమ్మనిమ్రోగు dhimm-ani-mrōgu. v. n. To resound aloud.

ధిషణ dhishaṇa. [Skt.] n. Sense, wisdom, understanding: the intellect. బుద్ధి, మనసు. ధిషణుడు dhishaṇuḍu. n. A name of Brihaspati.

ధిష్ణ్యము *dhishnyamu.* [Skt.] n. A place. స్థానము. A house, గృహము. A star, నక్షత్రము. Strength, బలము.

ధీ dhī

ధీ *dhī.* [Skt.] n. Understanding, intellect. బుద్ధి, మతి. ధీజనము the wise, the sagacious. ధీంద్రియము *dhīmdriyamu.* n. The understanding sense, the knowing faculty, జ్ఞానేంద్రియము. ధీమంతము *dhī-mantamu.* adj. Sensible, intelligent. బుద్ధిగల. ధీమతి *dhī-mati.* n. A clever woman. ధీమంతుడు a wise man. బుద్ధిమంతుడు.

ధీర *dhīra.* [Skt.] n. A heroine, a brave woman. ధీరము *dhīramu.* adj. Brave, firm, steady, wise, sensible. ధీరత్వము *dhīratvamu.* n. Courage Self-command, resolution to bear or endure. ధీరుడు *dhīrudu.* n. A hero. ధైర్యముకలవాడు. A learned man, విద్వాంసుడు.

ధీవరుడు *dhī-varudu.* [Skt.] n. A fisherman. జాలరి.

ధు dhu

ధుత్తూరము *dhuttūramu* [Skt.] n. The Thorn Apple; *Datura stramonium* Rox. i. 561. ఉమ్మెత్తచెట్టు.

ధుని *dhuni.* [Skt.] n. A river. నది. A stream. ఏరు.

ధుర *dhura.* [Skt.] n. A burden. బరువు. ధురంధర *dhuran-dhara.* adj. Bearing a burden, able, clever, talented. బరువు మోయునట్టి. ధురంధరత్వము *dhuran-dharatvamu.* n. Supporting, upholding, patronage, responsibility. ధురంధరుడు *dhuran-dharudu.* n. One who bears a burden, one who is responsible, a clever or able man. భారమువహించువాడు. ధురీణుడు *dhurīnudu.* n. He who bears a burden. బరువుమోయువాడు. An able or clever man. ధుర్యము *dhuryamu.* adj. Bearing a burden, entrusted with, sustaining. Fit to bear a burden బరువుమోయదగిన. ధుర్యుడు *dhuryudu.* n. One who sustains a burden. భారమువహించు వాడు. గర్వధుర్యుడు one who is inflated with pride. వాగ్ధుర్యుడు an eloquent man.

ధూ dhū

ధూ *dhū.* [Skt.] interj. Fie! Poh! avaunt!

ధూకళి *dhūkali.* [H.] n. A sort of tune or dance. BD. iii. 405.

ధూతము *dhūtamu.* [Skt.] adj. Tossed, flowing, dishevelled. ఎగరగొట్టబడిన.

ధూపము or ధూవము *dhūpamu.* [Skt.] n. Incense, fumigation. ధూపకలశము *dhūpa-kalasamu.* n. A censer. ధూపార్తి *dhūparti.* n. A censer. ధూపితము *dhūpitamu.* adj. Fumigated, ధూపముచేయబడిన.

ధూమము *dhūmamu.* [Skt.] n. Smoke. పొగ. ధూమకేతువు *dhūma-kētuvu.* n. A comet, being "smoke-tailed," i.e., having a trail of smoke. Also a name of fire (Agni). ధూమధ్వజుడు *dhūma-dhvajudu.* n. The god of fire, whose banner is smoke. ధూమరేఖ *dhūma-rēkha.* n. A smouldering smoke. ధూమ్య *dhūmya.* n. A pillar, cloud or volume of smoke. A. v. 124. ధూమములసమూహము. ధూమలము or ధూమ్రము *dhūmalamu.* n. & adj. Tawny, dark-red. Smoke-colour, a sort of purple colour compounded of black and red.

ధూర్జటి *dhūrjati.* [Skt.] n. Siva. శివుడు.

ధూర్తము *dhūrtamu.* [Skt.] adj. Outrageous, rude, violent. ధూర్తుడు or ధూర్తు *dhūrtudu.* n. A violent man, a villain. A cheat, మోసకాడు.

ధూర్వహము *dhūrvahamu.* [Skt.] adj. Able to bear or sustain a burden. బరువుమోయదగిన. ధూర్వహుడు *dhūr-*

vahuḍu. n. One who sustains a burden. ధూర్వహత *dhūr-vahata*. n. Sustaining, bearing. బరువుమోయుట.

ధూళి *dhūḷi*. [Skt.] n. Dust. దుమ్ము, పరాగము. ధూళిధ్వజుడు *dhūḷi-dhvajuḍu*. n. Wind. వాయువు.

ధూసరము *dhūsaramu*. [Skt.] adj. Ash-colored, dark, obscure, embrowned as with dust, discoloured, soiled, begrimed. Iron-grey: blackish. బూడిదవర్ణముగల. n. Ash-color. బూడిదవర్ణము. An ass. గాడిద.

ధృ dhri

ధృతము *dhritamu*. [Skt.] adj. Possessed, held, contained. ధరింపబడిన. ధృతకోపము angry. ధృతరాష్ట్రుడు *dhrita-rashṭruḍu*. n. The father of Duryōdhana and uncle of the Pāṇḍu princes. ధృతి *dhriti*. n. Steadiness, firmness, bravery, valour. ధైర్యము. Pleasure, happiness. సంతోషము, సౌఖ్యము. A spirit, extract, essence. లవంగ ధృతి essence of cloves. చందనధృతి sandal oil.

ధృష్టుడు *dhrishṭuḍu*. [Skt.] n. A man of firmness. దిట్టతనముగలవాడు.

ధే dhe

ధే *dhē*. [Tel.] n. A word used in urging a horse on faster.

"వాయువు సదల్చి ధేయనుచు
నాజికి దోలంట రొయుందుసోచె." క. viii.

ధేనువు or ధేనుక *dhēnuvu*. [Skt.] n. A milch cow. లేగటి ఆవు.

ధై dhai

ధైర్యము *dhairyamu*. [Skt. from ధీరము.] n. Steadiness, firmness, reliance, boldness, bravery, self-command. Resolution, courage, gallantry. నాకు ధైర్యము లేకపోయినది my heart failed me. ధైర్యముచేయు to make bold, to pluck up heart. ధైర్యము గొలుపు to encourage, to comfort.

ధో dhō

ధోరణి *dhōraṇi*. [Skt.] n. A series, line, range; వరుస, పంక్తి. A way, style, tradition. పద్ధతి. ధూమధోరణి a volume of smoke.

ధౌ dhau

ధౌతము *dhautamu*. [Skt.] adj. Washed, cleansed. కడుగబడిన, ఉతికిన. n. A washed cloth. ఉతికినబట్ట.

ధౌరంధర్యము *dhauran-dharyamu*. [Skt. from ధురంధరము.] Same as ధురంధరత్వము. (q. v.)

ధౌరితకము *dhau-ritakamu*. [Skt.] n. A horse's trot. అశ్వగతిభేదము, గాపాతిగదము.

ధౌరేయము *dhaurēyamu*. [Skt.] n. A beast of burden. బరువుమోయుజంతువు. adj. Able to bear a burden. బరువుమోయునది. ధౌరేయుడు *dhaurēyuḍu*. n. One who is able to sustain a burden or responsibility.

ధౌర్త్యము Same as ధూర్తత్వము. (q. v.)

ధ్యా dhya

ధ్యానము *dhyānamu*. [Skt.] n. Fixing the attention on God. Meditation, contemplation. A poetical personification. An encomium, panegyric. ఏదేకధ్యానముగాను న్నాడు he has fixed his undivided attention on it. ధ్యానించు or ధ్యానముచేయు *dhyānintsu*. v. a. To meditate on. ధ్యేయము fit to meditate on, ధ్యానింపదగిన.

ధ్రు dhru

ధ్రువము *dhruvamu*. [Skt.] n. Permanency, stability; certainty. నిశ్చయము. The truth;

sure knowledge. adj. Permanent, fixed, enduring, eternal, certain, ascertained. నిలుకడగల, కదలని. ధ్రువగేణి a permanent lease; ధ్రువపైరు a permanent crop, garden produce. ధ్రువకము *dhruvakamu*. n. The Longitude. (Colebr. Essay on Zodiac.) ధ్రువపరుచు *dhruva-parutsu*. v. a. To establish, settle, ascertain or verify. ధ్రువుడు or ధ్రువనక్షత్రము *dhruvudu*. n. The name of the North Pole: the Pole Star.

ధ్వ dhva

ధ్వంసము *dhvamsamu*. [Skt.] n. Destruction, ruin. నాశము. ధ్వంసముచేయు or ధ్వంసః పరచు to ruin, destroy. నాశముచేయు. ధ్వంసితము *dhvamsitamu*. adj. Ruined, destroyed, wrecked.

ధ్వజము *dhvajamu*. [Skt.] n. A flag or banner. టెక్కెము. A flagstaff, టెక్కెపు కంబము. A mark, a sign or symbol, గురుతు. The male organ of generation, లింగము, మగగురి. బర్హిధ్వజ she whose sign is the peacock, i. e., Parvati. ధ్వజస్తంభము a pillar or mast erected before a temple, having a vertical wooden frame of bars at the top to represent a flag. ధ్వజారోహణము a certain rite at the commencement of a festival when the flag is hoisted. ధ్వజిని *dhvajini*. n. An army. సేన.

ధ్వని *dhvani*. [Skt.] n. A sound: a voice. ప్రతిధ్వని an echo. ధ్వన్యర్థము *dhvan-y-arthamu*. n. An allegory. An elliptical meaning. ధ్వనించు *dhvanintsu*. v. n. To sound. శబ్దించు, మ్రోయు, మ్రోగు.

ధ్వా dhva

ధ్వాంతము *dhvantamu*. [Skt.] n. Darkness. అంధకారము, చీకటి.

ధ్వానము *dhvanamu*. n. Sound. ధ్వని మ్రోత.

న na

న The letter N, pronounced as a dental. When followed by some consonants this changes into ం (*sunna*) as అంట *anta*, కొండ *konda*, పెంకు *penku*. As an initial, N is sometimes dropped, but only in a few words. Thus ఏను, ఈవు, for నేను, నీవు.

న *na*. [Tel.] affix: An ending of the seventh case, సప్తమీవిభక్తియందువచ్చు ఒక ప్రత్యయము. వనమున in the forest. గృహమున in the house.

నంకు *nanku*. [Tel.] v. n. To rub on the ground. నేలను కోరాడు.

నంగ or నంగనాచి *nanga*. [Tel.] n. A weevil, or canker worm, a book worm, a round white worm, (also called పత్తిపురుగు and మురికిపొత్తు) which looks harmless but is destructive. Hence, a demure minx, a sly jade, a specious hypocrite. Sometimes used for a mosquito or gnat because it looks harmless దిట్టతనము కలి గియు బయటికి ఏమియు తెలియని దానివలె నుండునది. Swa. iii. 43. నంగనాచితనము *nanga-nachi-tanamu*. n. Feigned simplicity. నంగిమాట *nangi-mata*. n. A nasal sound: a word pronounced through the nose. ముక్కుతో మాట్లాడినమాట. A snuffle, or twang. నంగు *nangu*. v. n. To speak through the nose: to speak with a twang or snuffle. ముక్కుతో మాట్లాడు.

నంజ or నంజె *nanja*. [H.] n. Land artificially cultivated; land in which wet crops are raised; an irrigated field, a field adapted for the growth of wet crops. మాగాణి. The opposite is పుంజ or పుంజె dry land. నంజనేల n. Wet land.

నంజు, నంజుకొను or నంజుకొను *nandzu* [Tel.] v. n. To eat by small morsels, to nibble, to pick at, to eat a little of any thing like pickle, &c., as a relish to the principal food. కూరలోనగువస్తువులను కొద్ది

గొడ్డిగా తినుట. నంజుకొనేవస్తువు a relish or thing so eaten "తద్భాకంబునంజుముం దలంచు కొనిరె." A. iv. 243. టీ॥ నంజుముం=ఆస్వాదిం చుచు, అనగా నంచుకొనుచు. "చంచుపుటంబులనం జనిచ్చుచుగా." Parij. iv. 27. నంజే or నంజు *nandza*. n. A tart. నంజుకొనువస్తువు. A pickle, ఊరుగాయ, ఊరుగాయ. Smacking with the lips, చప్పరించడము. నంజు *nandzu*. n. Poison. విషము. Beri-beri, blood poisoning, నెత్తురుచచ్చి తెల్లపారుట. A lingering, indolent or dormant disease. నంజుపుండు an indolent ulcer. నంజు చిగురు a gum-boil. నంజుడు *nandzudu*. n. Flesh, flesh-meat. మాంసము, ఎరచి. పిల్లకాయకు నంజుడు పెరిగినది the boy has outgrown his age or strength. నంజుడుతిండి *nandzudu-tindi*. n. A flesh-eater, a carnivorous being. మాంసముతినువాడు. A demon, రాక్షసుడు. నంజుపారు *nandzu-paru*. v. n. To become pale, through the blood having deteriorated; to become anaemic, నెత్తురు చచ్చి తెల్లపారు. వాని శరీరము నంజుపారినది he became anaemic. నంజులు *nandzulu*. n. Pickles or any thing eaten as a relish with food. "మోవినంజులం జవిగొనుచుం గ్రోలి సోలి." Parij. ii. 60. her lips being sauce for the dish.

నంటి or **నంటు** *nanti*. [Tel.] n. Friendship. స్నేహము. మాలిమి. **నంటు, నంటికాడు** or **నంటుకాడు** *nantu*. n. A friend, companion, or lover. నేస్తకాడు, స్నేహితుడు. నంటుకత్తె a female friend, స్నేహితురాలు.

నంద *nanda*. [Skt.] n. A small pot. ముంత. Wealth, fortune, కలిమి.

నంది or **నందికేశ్వరుడు** *nandi*. [Skt.] n. The name of the bull of Siva. A bull, వృషభము. పందిని నంది నందిని పంది చేసేవాడు one who can make a pig a bull and a bull a pig.

నందించు *nandintsu*. [Skt.] v. n. To rejoice. **నందకము** *nandakamu*. n. That which rejoices, సంతోషించునది. The sword of Vishnu. **నందన** *nandana*. n. A daughter, కూతురు. The name of a year, ఒక సంవత్సరము. **నందనము** *nandanamu*. adj. That which rejoices. సంతోషించునది. **నందనవనము** *nandana-vanamu*. n. Indra's pleasure garden. Elysium. A park, ఉద్యానవనము. **నందనుడు** *nandanudu*. n. A son. కొడుకు. **నందవనము** *nanda-vanamu*. n. A flowery spot. The name given to Tulasi plants planted in a bed. This word is much used but is of no authority.

నందివర్ధనము or **నంద్యావర్తము** *nandi-vardhanamu*. [Skt.] n. The broad leaved Rose Bay. *Nerium coronarium*. Rox. ii. 23. నగరచెట్టు.

నందివృక్షము *nandi-vrikshamu*. [Skt.] n. A tree, the Toon or Indian Mahogony Tree, *Cedrela toona*. (Watts.)

నందుడు *nandudu*. [Skt.] n. The shepherd king Nanda, the foster father of Krishna.

నంబరు or **నెంబరు** *nambaru*. [Eng. 'number.'] n. A number. Also (colloquially), a law-case. Abbreviated into నెం॥

నంబి *nambi*. [Tel.] n. A Vaishnava priest. విష్ణుపూజకుడు.

నకనక *naka-naka*. [Tel. (anuk.)] n. Hunger. కార్శ్యము. **నకనకబడు** or **నకనకలాడు** *naka-naka-badu*. v. n. To be famished. కృశించు. వానికడుపు నకనకలాడు చున్నది he is famished. M. 123. 476. "కడుపు మహాక్షుధన్ నకనకంబడ." A. vi. 63.

నకరనర్రలు *nakara-narralu*. [Tel.] n. A weed called *Poa ciliata*. Rox. i. 335.

నకలు *nakalu*. [H.] n. A copy of a document or letter; a duplicate. నకలువ్రాయు or చేయు to make a copy of a document or letter.

నక్షా *nakysha*. [H.] n. A map or plan.

నకారపొల్లు *nakara-pollu*. [Tel.] n. The న sign of N final. This is exemplified in the words నాకున్, వానికిన్, ఇంటిలోన్, రైతున్.

నకించనత్వము *na-kinchanatvamu.* [Skt.] n. Nothingness, nonexistence.

నకీబు *nakību.* [H.] n. A herald, a chamberlain or usher. భట్టురాజు, వందిమాగధులు, కొత్తనులు. Swa. v. 50.

నకులము *nakulamu.* [Skt.] n. The mongoose, *Viverra ichneumon.* ముంగి, ముంగిస. నకులుడు *nakuludu.* n. Nakula, the name of a certain hero. యుధిష్ఠిరునితమ్ముడు.

నక్క *nakka.* [Tel. derived from నక్కు to prowl.] n. A jackal. *Canis aureus.* గోంకు నక్క a fox: (derived from గోంకు timidity.) గుంటనక్క, కొండనక్క or పోతునక్క *gunta-nakka.* n. The Indian Fox, *Vulpes bengalensis.* adj. Mean, base, తుచ్ఛము. నక్కమొగముచూచి వచ్చినావు you have come on a jackal in your way, i. e., you are in luck to-day. నక్కగుంట a pitfall. నక్కలపాలుచేయు to ruin, spoil, send to the dogs. నక్కకోర *nakka-kōra.* n. "Fox-fang." A coarse grass called *Panicum glaucum.* Rox. i. 284. నక్కజిత్తు *nakka-jittu.* n. A sneaking trick, guile, craft. నక్కజిత్తులమారి a wily rogue. నక్కతోక *nakka-tōka.* n. Fox-tail; a certain plant. నక్కతోకకసవు or పొన్న *nakkatōka-kasava.* n. A kind of plant. నక్కతోకవడ్లు a kind of grain, ధాన్యవిశేషము. నక్కదోసకాయ *nakka-dōsa-kāya.* n. The wild or small cucumber. నక్కనరము or నక్కముల్లగడ్డ *nakka-naramu.* n. A sort of bulbous plant with stiff woody stalks. Indian squill, *Scilla indica.* ఒకవిధమైనకన్ద. నక్కనేరేడు *nakka-nērēdu.* n. The wild species of నేరేడు. నక్కనైచ్యము *nakka-naichyamu.* n. Fawning, cunning, craft. నక్కపల్లము *nakka-pallamu.* n. False ground: a quicksand. నక్కపిట్ట *nakka-pitta.* n. A certain wild plant. నక్కపులి *nakkapuli* n. A panther, or leopard. నక్కవిరిగి *nakka-virigi.* n. A kind of tree.

నక్కీ *nakki.* [H.] n. Gold or silver lace, brocade, జరి.

నక్కు *nakku.* [Tel.] v. n. To prowl, crouch down. To peep. To conceal or hide oneself, ఒదుగు, దాగు. n. A joint. అతుకు. నక్కుదూలము a beam in which two pieces are joined together. A lump or ingot of gold, iron or any other metal. A notch, గాటు. Reeded or ribbed work in carpentry or in silver. బంగారుపూదిల్లె. "చొక్కపు పసిండిచక్కల తక్కుతక్కు." R. iv. 63. "తెచ్చియిచ్చినబంగారుకడ్డీలు తూచినదియున్న జంకమాణిక్యమునక్కులనక్కుచెన్నుగా సమర్పణ చేసి ప్రొక్కుచుండు." BD. v. 611. ఈ ఒడ్డాణమునకు నక్కులుకొట్టించు double up part of this belt, to make it shorter. See నక్క. నక్కెరు *nakkeru.* (నక్కు+ఏరు.) n. A sort of plant, the roots of which are used in some medicines. *Cordia myna.* నక్కిళ్లు *nakkiḷlu.* (నక్కు+కీళ్లు.) n. The joints of the jaws. The jaw bones. నక్కుపండ్లకీళ్లు. నక్కిళ్లుపట్టినవాడు one who has lockjaw.

నక్తము *naktamu.* [Skt.] n. Night. నక్తంకరుడు *naktam-karudu.* n. An epithet of the moon. A. iv. 36. నక్తంచరుడు *naktam-charudu.* n. A demon, a fiend that prowls at night. రాక్షసుడు, రాత్రించరి. నక్తంచరము *naktam-charamu.* n. A night rover, i. e., an owl, గుడ్లగూబ.

నక్రము *nakramu.* [Skt.] n. A crocodile. మొసలి.

నక్షత్రము *nakshatramu.* [Skt.] n. A star. చుక్క. A constellation. The name of any one of the twenty lunar mansions. అశ్విని మొదలగు నక్షత్రములు. సూర్యుడున్న నక్షత్రము the sign in which the sun is. నక్షత్రేశుడు lit: the lord of the stars, i. e., the moon. చుక్కలరేడు. నక్షత్రమాల a necklace consisting of twenty seven pearls. నక్షత్రవీథి *nakshatra-vīdhi.* n. The Milky Way.

నఖము *nakhamu.* [Skt.] n. A nail, talon, claw. గోరు. A scale, as of an armadillo. నఖమాంసన్యాయముగా inseparable as the skin and the nail. నఖశిఖాపర్యంతము ఒళ్లు నొప్పులుగా ఉన్నది I am in pain to the tips of my nails, i. e., all over. **నఖక్షతము** *nakha-kshatamu.* n. A nail mark made on the skin by pinching. **నఖముఖాలు** *nakha-mukhalu.* n. Lit. The tips of the nails. adv. Dispersedly, up and down, all about, in all directions, all over, on all sides. నఖముఖాలనుండి from every quarter. **నఖరము** *nakharamu.* n. A nail, talon, claw. గోరు. A kind of weapon, ఆయుధ విశేషము. **నఖరాయుధము** *nakhar-ayudhamu.* n. Lit: "Armed with claws;" i.e., a cat, a lion, &c., but usually a cock, కోడి. **నఖరేఖలు** *nakha-rēkhalu.* n. Nail-marks or scratches.

నఖారా *nakhārā.* [H.] adj. Worthless, useless.

నగ *naga.* [Tel.] n. A jewel or ornament. భూషణము. Cattle in general. A metal vessel, లోహపాత్రము. A bullock load of tobacco, &c., that is, two sackfuls. పొగాకు దూది మొదలగువాని కట్లపుమూట. A pair of leathern vessels, కిర్దలజోడు. A man's load: a cooly load. A robe or long gown. (In house building) బండినగలు are the small rafters laid across the [illegible].

నగదు *nagadu.* [H.] n. Ready money, cash. నగదీలెక్క or నగదులెక్క a cash account.

నగము *nagamu.* [Skt.] n. Lit: That which is immovable. A hill, కొండ. A tree, చెట్టు. నగధరుడు lit: one who carries a hill, i. e., Vishnu, విష్ణుమూర్తి. నగారి lit: an enemy to mountains, i. e., Indra, ఇంద్రుడు. నగాధిపుడు lit: the lord of the mountains, i. e., Himalaya, హిమవంతుడు. నగౌకసము a bird, పక్షి.

నగరము or **నగరి** *nagaramu.* [Skt.] n. A town. పట్టణము, పురము.

నగరిలెక్క Same as నగదులెక్క (q. v.)

నగరు or **నగరి** *nagaru.* [Tel.] n. A house, a palace. రాజగృహము. ఆ మాన్యము నగరకపడిపోయినది that land is fallen in to Government. A temple, దేవగృహము. నగరుసాంబ్రాణి benzoin imported from Nugger.

నగవు or **నవ్వు** *nagavu.* [Tel.] n. A laugh, a smile. నగడి one who is laughing, నవ్వగలవాడు. See నవ్వు.

నగారా *nagārā.* [H.] n. A large kettle drum. పెద్దఢంకా.

నగిషీ or **నకాషి** *nigishi.* [H.] adj. Ornamental, variegated, as sculpture. Sathyabhā. iii. 49; iv. 8.

నగు or **నవ్వు** *nagu.* [Tel.] v. n. To laugh. To smile. నవ్వు. **నగించు** or **నవ్వించు** *nagintsu.* v. a. To make (one) laugh. **నగుబాటు** or **నవ్వులపాటు** *nagu-bātu.* n. A joke, a jest: ridicule, mockery. అపహాసము.

నగ్గు or **నుగ్గు** *naggu.* [Tel.] n. Powder. పొడి, చూర్ణము.

నగ్నము *nagnamu.* [Skt.] adj. Naked. నగ్నదేహుడై stripped naked. R. vi. 23. నగ్నత్వము nudity, nakedness. **నగ్నవేషము** *nagna-vēshamu.* n. Nudity, a naked figure or appearance. నగ్నవేషధరుడై assuming the appearance of a naked man. నగ్నుడు a naked man, దిసమొలవాడు.

నచ్చికొట్టు *nachchi-kottu.* [Tam.] n. A drug called *Coccolus indicus.*

నచ్చు *natstsu.* v. a. and v. n. To confide, trust. నమ్ము. To coax, persuade; to harass, pester. n. Delay. ఆలస్యము. Wearisomeness, annoyance; something that gives trouble. బాధ. A knot-grass that infests corn. Waste land, infested with knot-grass. adj. Wearisome, tiresome, annoying, tedious, importunate. Chronic, as an indolent sore. **నచ్చిక** or **నచ్చిగ**

nachchika. n. Faith, confidence, belief, trust. నమ్మిక. **నచ్చుపెట్టు** *natsiu-pettu*. v. t. To annoy, fret, tease. తొందరపెట్టు, బాధించు. **నచ్చుబేరమాడు** *natstsu-bĕram-adu*. v. n. To haggle, chaffer. నన్ను నచ్చుపెట్టి చెప్పినాడు he drummed this in my ears. **నచ్చుకాడు, నచ్చుమన్న** or **నచ్చుగొట్టు** *natstsu-kadu*. n. A make-bate. A troublesome person, a bore.

నజరానా or **నజరు** *nadzarana*. [H.] n. A present. A present offered in homage. A forced contribution, an unjust fine. నజరుగల shapely, handsome, fine.

నజుగుజులుచేయు *nadju-gudjulu-chēsu*. [Tel.] v. n. To hustle, push about.

నజ్జ *nadzdza*. [Tel.] adj. Thick, buttery, greasy, as buffalo's milk.

నజ్జు *nadzdzu*. [Tel.] n. An atom. అణువు. A bit, fragment, నలుసు. నజ్జునజ్జుగా కోయు to mince, cut up into small bits.

నటత్ *natat*. [Skt.] adj. Dancing. "నటదుదగ్రభ్రుకుటీభయంకర." (Anir. iv. 53.) terrible with moving eyebrows. **నటన** or **నటనము** *natana*. n. A dance, dancing. నాట్యము. Motion, agitation; cunning behaviour, కపటప్రవర్తనము. మాయానటనము a course of fraud. **నటి** *nati*. n. An actress. వేశ్య, నట్టువునిపెండ్లాము. **నటించు** *natintsu*. v. n. To dance. To act, as on the stage. నాట్యమాడు to act, manage, conduct oneself, behave. వర్తించు. To behave cunningly, కపటముగా ప్రవర్తించు. **నటుడు** *natudu*. n. A dancer, an actor, నట్టువుడు. **నటువాలు** or **నట్వాలు** *natavalu*. n. A kind of pace of a horse, అశ్వగతివిశేషము.

నట్ట *natta*. [Tel.] n. A die at play. పాచిక. "నట్టలు రెండు దానజరనంబున జేకొని." భా. vii. **నట్ట** Short for నడుమ. The middle part of anything. నట్టడవి (నడుము +అడవి) the heart of the forest, అరణ్యమధ్యము. నట్టనడుమ (నడుము+నడుమ) in the very middle, exactly in the centre, సరిమధ్యమందు. **నట్టకోటి** *natta-koti*. n. A certain game among boys. **నట్టిల్లు** *nattillu*. (నడుము+ఇల్లు.) n. The middle of a house. గృహమధ్యము. The inner apartments of a house, గర్భగృహము. నట్టింట in the middle of the house. **నట్టేరు** *natteru*. (నడుము+ఏరు.) n. The middle of the stream, నదీమధ్యము. నా బ్రతుకు నట్టేటిలో పుట్టి మునిగిన సామెత అయెను. I am utterly ruined, my raft has sunk in the mid stream.

నట్టనము *nattanamu*. [Tel.] adj. Slight, weak, frail.

నట్టాడు *nattadu*. [Tel. నట్టువ+ఆడు.] v. n. To dance. నర్తించు. To move or shake, చలించు. నట్టాడునడుము a trembling waist.

నట్టు *nattu*. [Tel.] n. A spot of ground. A place, abode. స్థానము, వాసస్థానము. Delay, ఆలస్యము. An obstacle, or hindrance; hesitation. అటంకము. Loss, damage. A platform of earth, a terrace. A tape worm. The bent grass that infests corn-fields. సస్యరోగవిశేషము. One species of this called కుదురునట్టు is found in the రేగడ or black soil, another గరిక నట్టు in the *mudub* or mixed soil. The largest species is called పెదనట్టు; the smaller గంటనట్టు. **నట్టుకొట్టు** *nattu-kottu*. v. n. To delay. ఆలస్యముచేయు. **నట్టుపడు** *nattu-padu*. v. n. To hesitate. తడబడు, అడ్డిపడు. **నట్టుకొను** *nattu-konu*. n. To fix (itself) firmly, to be fixed. కుదురుకొను, నిలుచు.

నట్టువ *nattuva*. [from Skt. నటనము.] n. Dancing నర్తనము, ఆట. **నట్టువుడు, నట్టువకాడు** or **నట్టుగుడు** *natturudu*. n. A dancing master. నాట్యము నేర్పువాడు. A dancer, నాట్యకాడు. Suca. iii. 9. **నట్టువచావిడి** *nattuva-tsavidi*. n. A dancing school. **నట్టువపులుగు** or **నట్టుపులుగు** *nattuva-pulugu*. n. The bird that delights to dance, i. e., a peacock, నెమలి. నట్టువొజ్జ nattu-vodzdza. (నట్టువ+ఒజ్జ.) n. A dancing master, నాట్యాచార్యుడు.

నట్లొట్లు natlotlu. [Tel.] n. Drops of water that fall from the leaves of trees. చెట్లాకులమీద నిలిచినవే నీళ్లొట్లు.

నడచు Same as నడుచు (q. v.) నడ or నడక nada. n. A walk, walking, stepping, motion, movement. గమనము. Pace, step, manner of walking, gait. A trip or journey. పడవ మూడునడలు వచ్చినది the boat made three trips. adj. Walking, moving, locomotive. నడకొండలు moving mountains. నడపీనుగు a walking corpse : a fool, a good for nothing man. Sumati. § 69. నడక nadaka. n. A walk, walking. నడగడు nada-gadu. (నడ+కాడు.) n. A horse. గుర్రము. నడగొట్టు nada-gottu. (నడ+కొట్టు.) v. n. To stand, to remain, to be, నిలుచు, ఉండు. నడజోదు nada-dzodu. n. A foot soldier. కాలిబంటు, పదాతి. నడత nadata. n. Conduct, behaviour. నడవడి, ప్రవర్తనము.

నడము nadamu. [Skt.] n. A sort of reed or bulrush. Bur-grass, కిక్కిసగడ్డి.

నడయాడు nada-y-adu. [Skt. నడ+ఆడు.] v.n. To wander about, to roam, సంచరించు. To move, shake or tremble, చలించు. నడవ nadava. n. The entry into a house. నడవలో పండుకొన్నాడు he lay down in the entry or porch. నడవడి or నడవడిక nadavadi. n. Conduct, behaviour. నడత, చరిత్రము. plu. నడవడులు, or నడవళ్లు. నడతెంచు nada-tentsu. (నడచు+తెంచు.) v. n. To come. వచ్చు. నడతెమ్ము (the imperative.) come. To go, పోవు. నడదివియ nada-diviya. n. A torch, దివిటీ. నడపబడు nadapa-badu. v. n. To be managed, or conducted. ఆ పనులు ఎవరివల్ల నడపబడుచున్నవి by whom are those works carried on. నడబావి nada-bavi. n. A well with steps down into it.

నడి, నడిమి or నడు nadi. [Tel. from నడుము.] adj. Middle, mid. నడికాలము the idle time of the year, between the ploughings. నడిదడవ the thick or middle part of a palm branch, దడవ. నడికట్టు nadi-kattu. (నడిమి+కట్టు.) n. A girdle, waistband. నడిరేయి, నడికిరేయి. నడురేయి or నడురే nadi-reyi. n. Midnight. అర్ధరాత్రము. నడికొప్పు nadi-koppu. n. The ridge of a pent roof. నడికొల్లగాడు or నడిమికొల్లగాడు nadi-kolla-gadu. n. An interloper. నడినూకలు nadi-nukalu. n. Grits, half broken grain, what in America is called hominy. In Madras it is called rolong. అర్ధతండులములు. నడినెత్తి or నడునెత్తి nadi-netti. n. The middle of the head, the crown of the head. నడివ్రేలు nadi-vrelu. n. The middle finger. మధ్యమ. నడిమికావడి a hammock slung on a pole. నడిమివాడు a by-stander, a third person. నడుగుంట nadu-gunta. n. The fontonelle or depression in the centre of the head. తలనడిమిపల్లము, బ్రహ్మరంధ్రము.

నడిరి or నడ్రి Same as నడర.

నడుకు naduku. [Tel.] v. n. To tremble. వణకు, కంపించు. నడుకొను (నడుకు+కొను.) Same as వణకు. నడునడు nadu-nadu. adj. Trembling much. మిక్కిలివణకును.

నడుచు or నడచు nadutsu. [Tel.] v. n. To walk, go, move, proceed. To happen, occur, pass, take place. To behave, conduct oneself, ప్రవర్తించు. To take effect, as an order. To live, continue, last. To descend, as an estate. To beat, as applied to the pulse. To act (as a father, servant, &c.) వానికిందనడిచేభూమి the field they hold or enjoy. నడిచేనెల the current month. వానికిని మాకును నడిచిన జాబులు the letters that passed between us. నడిచినజగడము the dispute that took place. శ్లోకము నడవవల్నా surely the verse ought to flow easily. ఆ ఉత్సవము నడుస్తున్నదా is the feast still kept up? నడుపు or నడపు nadupu. v. a.

To make one walk, make a thing proceed. To manage, conduct. To navigate, steer a vessel. To undertake or govern. న్యాయము నడుపు to execute justice. n. Walk, pace, step, gait. Walking, గమనము. Conduct, ప్రవర్తనము. **నడిపించు** or **నడపించు** *nadipintsu*. v. a. To make one walk. పిల్లవాడును నడిపించినది she made the child walk. To conduct, carry on, push on, నడుపు. ఆ మాన్యము వానికి నడిపించితిని I let my field to him free. **నడుచుకొను** *nadutsu-konu*. v. n. To behave.

నడుము *nadumu*. [Tel.] n. The middle, the waist, or loins. కౌను. The middle portion మధ్యభాగము. **నడుముకట్టుకొను** *nadumu-kattu-konu*. v. n. To undertake, to make oneself ready. To gird up the loins, to be ready. సిద్ధపడు. To take a vow of chastity. **నడుమంతరము** or **నడుమంత్రము** *nadu-mantaramu*. (నడుము+అంతరము.) adj. Extraordinary, unprecedented, unthought of, as a windfall. n. The waist, కౌను. An interval, మధ్యకాలము. adj. Middling, neither here nor there. నడుమంతరపేరు an alias. నడుమంతరపు ఐశ్వర్యమునకును నరము మీది పుండునకును దురుకు అధికము those who have recently become rich and an ulcer on a nerve give great trouble. **నడుమంతరముగా** *nadu-mantaramu-ga*. adv. Unexpectedly. **నడుచొచ్చు** *nadu-tsotstsu*. v. n. To come in the middle, to interpose. నడుము ప్రవేశించు. **నడుదింపు** *nadu-dimpu*. n. The flesh in the loins. మాంసవిశేషము. నడుములోచెక్కు to pocket, because they stick a handkerchief, &c., in at the girdle. నడుముపడిన gone in the loins, broken down, debilitated. నడుము పడినది there was an emission of semen. **నడుమ** or **నడమ** *naduma*. adj. Middle, centrical. నడుమను adv. and postp. In the middle, meanwhile, through, between. ఈ నడుమ presently: (also) lately. ఆనడుమ meantime. నడమవచ్చినారు they came between or interposed; they came as messengers or representatives. నడుమవచ్చినవానికి ఇంతి అధికారమా is an interloper to presume thus? నడుము మాట్లాడు to interrupt one while speaking; or to intercede, to mediate. **నడానా** or **నడుమున** *nadana*. adv. In the middle; midway.

నడ్డి *naddi*. [Tel.] n. The bending of the body back-wards. శరీరము వెనుకకు వంగియుండుట. (The bending of the body forwards or being hump-backed is called గూను.) The small of the back, the hollow above the loins. నడ్డినిల్ల గొట్టినాడు or నడ్డివిరగ పొడిచినాడు he gave him a blow that broke his back. adj. Sunk in, depressed in the middle, crooked. నడ్డిముక్కు a turned up nose. నడ్డిగా నిలుచు to stand with the belly pushed out, and the back drawn in.

నడ్వలము or **నడ్వంతము** *nad-valamu*. [Skt.] adj. Reedy, abounding in reeds. R. v. 225. నడ్వప్రాయదేశే, కిక్కిస కసువుగల (దేశము.)

నతము *natamu*. [Skt.] adj. Bent, bowed. వంగిన. Crooked, వంకరైన. Deep, లోతైన. నతనాభి a deeply curved navel. పాదనతులయిన who were humbled before his feet. **నతనాసికుడు** *nata-nasikudu*. n. A flat-nosed man. **నతవైరి** *nata-vairi*. n. An enemy who prays for quarter. శరణాగతుడైన శత్రువు. **నతి** *nati*. n. A salutation, homage. నమస్కారము, మ్రొక్కు. **నతుడు** *natudu*. n. One who is prostrate.

నత్త *natta*. [Tel.] n. A snail, a shell fish. గుల్లయందుండుపురుగు. A pad (like that used by palankeen bearers, so called because somewhat hollow.) **నత్తగుల్ల** *natta-gulla*. n. The shell of a snail, &c. **నత్తగొట్టు** *natta-gottu*. n. A sort of bird. పక్షిభేదము. **నత్తచిప్ప** *natta-chippa*. n. An oyster shell. **నత్తచేపలు** *natta-chēpalu*. n. A small sort of fish. (*Clupea*, Russell No. 187.)

నత్తి *natti*. [Tel.] n. Stuttering, stammering. నత్తివాడు a stammerer, నత్తిలవాడు. **నత్తు** *nattu*. v. n. To stammer, stutter. అది

బయటను ముక్కుపుడక. n. The ring or small jewel worn by women on the left nostril, ముక్కు-పుడక, ముక్కుపోగు.

నత్తెము *nattemu*. [Tel.] n. A sort of glove worn by falconers. HK. ii. 48.

నది *nadi*. [Skt.] n. A river or stream, A river or stream, which flows from west to east. **నదము** *nadamu*. n. A river which flows to the west. పురుష నది. Noise, ధ్వని. **నదీమాతృకము** *nadī-mātrikamu*. adj. Watered by rivers: (land) depending not on rain but on river water, ఏటినీళ్లచేత పండు పైరుగలదేశము.

నద్ధము *naddhamu*. [Skt.] adj. Bound. కట్టబడిన. Lifted up, projecting, పైకెత్తబడిన, నిక్కిన.

నన *nana*. [Tel.] n. A bud, blossom. మొగ్గ. A sprout, చిగురు. A flower, పువ్వు. క్రొన్ననలుపూచెను it bore fresh blossoms. **ననకారు** *nana-kāru*. n. Lit: Blossom time. Spring, the first of the six seasons into which the Hindus divide the year, వసంతఋతువు. **ననబోడి** *nana-bōdi*. (నన+బోడి.) n. A blooming girl. **ననవిలుకాడు**, **ననవిలుతుడు** or **ననవిల్తుడు** *nana-vilu-kādu*. n. Lit: He who bears a bow made of blossoms, i.e., Manmadha.

ననంద or **ననాంద** *nananda*. [Skt.] n. A husband's sister. ఆడుబిడ్డ, మగనితోడబుట్టినది.

ననయు, ననచు or **ననుచు** *nanayu*. [Tel.] v. n. To expand, bloom, blossom, sprout, పూచు, పుష్పించు, పల్లవించు, చిగిర్చు. To be pleasant or fine, ఇంపగు. To excel, అతిశయించు. A. v. 133. **ననుపు** *nanupu*. v. n. To agree with one's health or constitution. ఈదేశము నాకు ననుపులేదు this country does not agree with me. n. Amiability, agreeableness, seductiveness. అనురాగము, ఇంపు, అతిశయము. adj. Agreeable. Swa. ii. 81. **ననుపుకాడు** or **నన్పుకాడు** *nanupu-kādu*. n. A lover. విటుడు. ననుపుకత్తె a sweetheart. ప్రియురాలు, జారస్త్రీ. **ననుపుపడు** *nanupu-padu*. v. n. To become friends with, or be acquainted with, స్నేహపడు.

ననుబ్రాయి or **నన్బ్రాయి** *nanu-brāyi*. [Tel. నాను+ప్రాయి.] n. Ill-boiled food. చక్కగా ఉడుకనియన్నము. **ననుబ్రాయిపడు** or **ననుబ్రాయియగు** *nanu-brāyi-padu*. v. n. To boil badly, as rice.

నన్న *nanna*. [Tel.] adj. Short. కురుచ.

నన్నూరు *nannūru*. [Tel. నలు+నూరు.] adj. Four hundred.

నపుంసకము *na-pumsakamu*. [Skt.] adj. Neuter, neither masculine nor feminine. **నపుంసకత్వము** *na-pumsakatvamu*. n. Impotency. **నపుంసకుడు** *na-pumsakudu*. n. An impotent man, a man devoid of virile powers, a eunuch. **నపుంసకలింగము** *napumsaka-lingamu*. n. The neuter gender.

నప్త *napta*. [Skt.] n. A grandson, either in the male or female line. మనుమడు. A granddaughter, మనుమరాలు. A great grandson, మునిమనుమడు. **నప్త్రి** *naptri*. n. A granddaughter, either in the male or female line.

నఫరు *napharu*. [H.] n. An individual. నఫరువారీగా individually. నఫరుజామీను personal bail. నఫరువారీలెక్క each customer's account at a shop. H. iv. 43.

నఫా or **నభా** *napha*. [H.] n. Profit, gain, advantage. లాభము.

నభము or **నభస్సు** *nabhamu*. [Skt.] n. The sky, or atmosphere ఆకాశము. **నభస్యము** *nabhasyamu*. n. A name of the month Bhadrapada. భాద్రపదమాసము. A. iv. 172. **నభస్వత్తు** or **నభస్వంతుడు** *nabha-svattu*. n. Air, wind. వాయువు, గాలి. నభోమధ్యమందు in mid heaven, in the vault of heaven. **నభోవచనము** *nabhō-vachanamu*. n. A voice from heaven.

నమః *namaha.* [Skt.] n. Hail! వందనము. **నమసితుడు** or **నమస్సితుడు** *nama-situḍu.* n. One who is worshipped, అర్చితుడు. **నమశ్శివాయ** *namaṣ-ṣivāya.* I salute Siva. **నమస్కరించు, నమించు** or **నమస్కారము చేయు** *namas-karintsu.* v. n. To prostrate one's self, salute with folded hands, bow, adore, పూజించు. **నమస్కారము, నమస్కృతి** or **నమస్సు** *namas-karamu.* n. An obeisance or salutation, like *salām*, or *how do you do* and *good bye.* **నమస్య** *namasya.* n. Worship. పూజ, సపర్య. **నమోనమః** *namō-namah.* n. Homage and salutation.

నమకచమకము *namaka-chamakamu.* [Skt.] n. Certain prayers in the Vedas addressed to Rudra.

నమనమలాడు *nama-nama-l-āḍu.* [Tel.] v. n. To thrive, to bloom, as plants.

నమనము *namanamu.* [Skt.] n. Bending. వంగుట. Humility, నమ్రత. **నమితము** *namitamu.* adj. Bent, humble. వంగిన, నమ్రమైన.

నమలు or **నములు** *namalu.* [Tel.] v. a. To chew, masticate or munch.

నమస్కరించు and **నమస్కారము** See under **నమః.**

నమిలి Same as నెమలి (q. v.)

నముచి *namuchi.* [Skt.] n. A demon, so named. **నముచిసూదనుడు** *namuchi-sūdanuḍu.* n. The slayer of Namuchi, an epithet of Indra. ఇంద్రుడు.

నమూదు or **నమోదు** *namādu.* [H.] adj. Shewn, exhibited, entered, mentioned, specified, particularised. అగుపరచబడిన, చెప్పబడిన, వివరించబడిన. నమూదుచేయు to shew, bring to notice, to enter. వానిమాట నమూదుచేయలేదు they took no notice of his statement. నమూదగు to be entered.

నమూనా or **నమోనా** *namūna.* [H.] n. A specimen, sample, model, pattern. మాదిరి.

నమేరువు *namēruvu.* [Skt.] n. The tree termed *Calophyllum inophyllum.* సుర పొన్న. A. v. 135.

నమ్మకు *nammaku.* [H.] n. Salt. నమ్మకు దారోగా a salt superintendent.

నమ్మదుంప *namma-dumpa.* [Tel.] n. A sort of grass. *Scirpus kysoor.* గోరుకము, గుబ్బి గడ్డి.

నమ్మి Same as నెమలి. (q. v.)

నమ్ము *nammu.* [Tel.] v. a. & n. To believe or give credit to. To trust or confide in. To rely on, to have faith in. విశ్వసించు. To suppose, imagine. నమ్మదగు it is believable, విశ్వసింపదగును. **నమ్మకము, నమ్మిక** or **నమ్మిగ** *nammakamu.* n. Trust, reliance, assurance, confidence, belief, faith, dependence. నమ్మకముగా confidently, positively, trustworthily. **నమ్మకమైన** *nammakam-aina.* adj. Trustworthy, faithful. **నమ్మకస్థుడు** *nammaka-sthuḍu.* n. A trustworthy or faithful man, a respectable man. నమ్మిక మాటలు persuasive words; assurance, beguiling. నమ్మినవాణ్ని చెరుపరాదు you should not injure him who confides in you. **నమ్మించు** *namminṭsu.* v. a. To cause to believe or trust. To assure, cheat, promise, persuade. నమ్మించి గొంతుకోసినాడు lit: he made them believe in him and cut their throat, i. e., he ruined them.

నమ్రము *namramu.* [Skt.] adj. Bowed, bent, crooked, curved. వంగిన. Humble, వినయ. శాల్యగ్రఫలోన్నతోనమ్రః the full ear of corn bows (humbly.)

నయ or **నయము** *naya.* [Tel.] n. Beauty. అందము.

నయనము *nayanamu.* [Skt.] n. An eye. కన్ను.

నయము *nayamu.* [Tel.] n. Cheapness. Profit, లాభము. Smoothness, నునుపు, మృదు

శ్రేయము. Beauty, అందము. Welfare, ease, facility. Good health, soundness, safety. Convalescence, improvement, recovery. Kindness, civility. [Skt.] n. Virtue, morality. నీతి. నయములేదు it is no better. నయభయములమూలమున, or నయభయములతోను by fair means or foul, by allurement or alarm, by rough or smooth methods. నయనష్టానికి for either profit or loss, for better or worse. నయమార్గాన civilly, kindly. ఇది వానికి దొరికినది నయము they were lucky in getting this. నీవు రావడము నయము it is well that you came. కొంచెము నయమయినది it is somewhat improved or better. నయముకొప్పు duly, fitly, easily. adj. Smooth. నునుపైన. Soft, మృదువైన. Fine, అందమైన. Cheap, చౌకైన. Well, easy, better in health, convalescent. Malleable, not brittle. High (as a note in music, as opposed to ఘనము or deep notes.) **నయముగా** *nayamu-gā*. adv. Easily, well, kindly, better, cheaply. నయముగానున్నది there is an improvement, it is better. వానికి నయముగానున్నది he is better or convalescent. **నయగారము** *naya-gāramu*. (నయము+కారము.) n. Smoothness, softness. మృదుత్వము. A soft word, మృదువచనము. **నయగారి** *naya-gāri*. n. A gentleman, a courteous man, మృదుత్వముగలవాడు. మృదువచనముగలవాడు. **నయించు** *nayintsu*. v. n. & a. To agree, or hold well together, as a paragraph. సందర్భించు. To cause to have, పొందించు.

నర, నరపు or **నరుపు** *nara* [Tel.] n. Greyness of the hair. పలితత్వము. A grey hair. **నరవెండ్రుకలు** *nara-vendrukalu*. n. Grey hairs. నరగడ్డము a grey beard. నరమీసము grey mustaches.

నరకము *narakamu*. [Skt.] n. Hell. దుర్గతి. **నరకుడు** *narakuḍu*. n. A scoundrel, villain. దుష్టుడు. [illegible] iii. **నరకాసురుడు** *narak-āsuruḍu* n. The name of a giant slain by Vishṇu. **నరకాంతకుడు** *narak-antakuḍu*. n. The destroyer of Naraka, an epithet of Vishṇu.

నరకు Same as నరుకు (q. v.)

నరగ or **నరగచేమ** *naraga*. [Tel.] n. A drum. భేరి. అనక్షభేరి.

నరము *naramu*. [Tel.] n. A vein or artery, a nerve. నాడి. A tendon, or muscle of the body. వానిచేతికి నరములేదు he has no nerves in his hand, i.e., he is a very open handed man.

నరయు Same as నరయు (q.v.)

నరవ *narava*. [Tel.] n. A hill path. కొండ త్రోవ.

నరవంగి *nara-vangi*. [Tel.] n. A kind of tree. H. iv. 14.

నరాజి or **నరాజె** *narāji*. [Tel.] n. A knife or sword. కత్తి. ఖడ్గము. కృష్ణ. iv. ఆ. i.

నరిగి *narigi*. [Tel.] n. A certain colour of sheep. గొర్రెలలో కొన్ని విధమైన రంగు. H. ii. 86.

నరిడి *nariḍi*. [Tel.] n. A certain disease of the heart among the cattle. గుండెదెబ్బ రోగము.

నరియకొక్కు *nariya-kokku*. [Tel.] n. A sort of snake. G. viii. 101.

నరియుడు *nariyuḍu*. [Tel. cf. Tam: నరి.] n. A jackal or fox. నక్క.

"[illegible]
[illegible]."
[illegible] vi.

నరియు, నరయు or **నెరియు** *nariyu*. [Tel.] v. n. To grow grey, as applied to the hair. గడ్డమునరసినవాడు a man with a grey beard.

నరుకు or **నరకు** *naruku*. [Tel.] v. a. To cut, to hew, to fell, to sever, to chop or lacerate. ఖండించు. గంభీరాలు నరుకు to boast. n. A cut, a wound, the wards of a key. **నరుకుకత్తి** *naruku-katti* n. A short sword, or dagger. నరుకుడు or నరకుడు narukudu. n. Cutting. నరుకుట. నరుకుడుపడు narukudu-padu. v. n. To be cut. ఖండితమగు. నరుకుపరువడి naruku-paruvadi. n. A kind of surgery. శస్త్రవిద్యావిశేషము. నరుకులిచ్చుము Same as నఖ్రాయి. నరుకులాడు naruku-lādu. v. t. To cut one another, to inflict wounds on one another, ఒకరినొకరు నరుకుకొను. నరుక్కు narukku. n. A cry uttered in sudden fear. దిగులుపడినప్పుడు పుట్టునట్టి శబ్దము.

నరుడ్జు narudzu. [Tel.] n. An atom. అణువు. adj. Very small. సూక్ష్మము.

నరుడు narudu. [Skt.] n. A man. A name of Arjuna. నరులు human beings. నర nara. adj. Human. నరపతుడు, నరపాలుడు or నరేంద్రుడు nara-dēvudu. n. A king, a ruler. రాజు. నరపశువు nara-paṣuvu. n. A brutish man. నరబలి nara-bali. n. A human sacrifice. నరమాంసము human flesh. నరవాహనుడు nara-vāhanudu. n. Kubera, the god of wealth. నరసింగడు Same as నృసింహుడు. (q. v.) నరాంతకుడు nar-āntakudu. n. A man-slayer, a murderer. నరభక్షకుడు or నరమాంసభక్షకుడు nara-bhakshakudu. n. A cannibal.

నరుము narumu. [Tel.] v. t. To reduce to powder, to triturate. పొడిచేయు. n. Powder. పొడి. భార. ద్రో. iii. నరుమూడు (నరుము+ఊడు.) Same as నరుము.

నర్తనము nartanamu. [Skt.] n. Dancing, gesticulation, acting. నటనము, ఆట. నర్తనశాల a dancing school. నాట్యశాల. M. IV. ii. 326. నర్తనప్రియము nartana-priyamu. n. A peacock. నెమలి. నర్తించు, నర్తిల్లు or నర్తిలు nartintsu. v. n. To dance. నర్తనముచేయు, ఆడు. నర్తకి nartaki. n. An actress, a female dancer. ఆటది. నర్తకదంపతులు an actor and his wife. నర్తకుడు nartakudu. n. An actor, mime, or juggler. A puppet showman. ఆటకాడు, నట్టువుడు.

నర్మము narmamu. [Skt.] n. Sport, pastime, dalliance. పరిహాసము, కేళి. Gladness, సంతోషము. నర్మద narmada. n. Lit: The gladdener, i. e., the Nurbuda river. నర్మాలాపము nar-mālāpamu. n. An allusion, intimation, hint, a tacit reference, an agreeable prattle.

నర్మిలి or అర్మిలి narmili. [Tel.] n. Desire. అపేక్ష.

నర్ర narra. [Tel.] n. A troublesome milch cow. ప్రయాసముచేత పిదుకదగిన ఆవు. An ox. నర్రలు horned cattle, కొమ్ములుగల పశువులు. Cattle, kine. IV. i. 95.

నర్రమామిడి narra-māmidi. [Tel.] n. A plant used in medicine, called *Tomex japonica*, or *Tetranthera monopetala* or *Leea staphylea*. Rox. i. 658; iii. 821. Wight's plates No. 58.

నల Same as నల్ల adj. (q. v.)

నల or నలు nala. [Skt.] n. The name of a king. See నలు.

నలక nalaka. [Tel. from నలుగు or నలుసు.] n. A particle or mote. నలుసు.

నలకు nalaku. [Tel.] n. A kind of vessel. భాండవిశేషము. "దూగనిలయంబు కలశములగల శకులంబు, నలకులు గాగులు నాదిగాగల భాండములును." M. XIV. iii. 175.

నలగు, నలగడము and నలుగు See under నలుగు.

నలకూబరుడు nala-kūbarudu. [Skt.] n. The name of a son of Kubera.

నలగు Same as నలుగు. (q. v.)

నలత See under నలుగు.

నలదము naladamu. [Skt.] n. The root of the *Andropogon muricatus*, called cus-cuss grass. వెట్టివేరు. Rox. i. 265

నలభై or నలుబది *nalabhai.* [Tel. నలు+పది.] n. & adj. Forty. నలభైమంది forty people.

నలి *nali.* [Tel. from నలుగు] n. Dust, powder. పొడి, చూర్ణము. Indisposition, illness, రోగము. Rubbish, weeds, stuff. చిదుగులు. Affection, love. ప్రేమ. నలితీయు to clear, clean, weed. adj. Powdered, bruised, నలిగిన. Trivial, slight. స్వల్పము. Lean, సన్నము. నలితిండి eating trash, చిరుతిండి. adv. Duly, fitly, properly, చొక్కముగా.

నలికండ్లపాము, నలికె, నలికీడు or నలికీడు *nali-kandla-pāmu.* n. The polished shining greenish house lizard with a scarlet tail, that haunts houses. *Lacerta interpunctata.* Linn. బ్రహ్మణి, రక్తపుచ్ఛిక. నలికము *nalikamu.* n. Smallness, minuteness, as dust. సూక్ష్మము, తనుత్వము. సన్నదనము. నలిగులి *nali-guli.* adj. Very much bruised or crushed మిక్కిలినలిగిన. నలిగొట్టు *nali-goṭṭu.* adj. Very thin. మిక్కిలిసన్నమైన. నలినలి *nali-nali.* adv. Fretfully. నలినలిఅగు to be peevish, to fret, నొచ్చు. నలినలిచేయు to harass, torment. నలినూకలు *nali-nūkalu.* n. Dust, powder. అర్ధచూర్ణములు. నలిపొడి *nali-poḍi.* n. Saw-dust, chips, shavings, dirt, fragments. నలిబులి *nali-buli.* n. Confusion, అల్లకల్లోలము. నలిరేగు *nali-rēgu.* v. n. To take fire, to become irritated or enraged. విజృంభించు. నలియు Same as నలుగు. (q. v.)

నలినము or నలిని *nalinamu* [Skt.] n. A lily. తామర. నలినాయతాక్షి or నలినాక్షి *nalin-āyat-akshi.* n. A woman who has fair eyes or lily-like eyes. నలినారి *nalin-ari.* n. The 'Foe to lilies:' i. e., the moon.

నలు or నాలుగు *nalu.* [Tel.] adj. Four. నలుదెసలు the four quarters or sides. నలుగురు, నల్గురు, నలువురు or నల్వురు *naluguru.* n. Four persons. Some persons, several people, as in English we say half a dozen without meaning exactly the number six. నలుచదరము *nalu-tsada-ramu.* adj. Four square. నలుతూము or నల్తూము (నాలుగు+తూము.) four bushels. నలుదిక్కులు or నల్దిక్కులు *nalu-dikkulu.* n. All round: lit: the four sides. నలుగడలు or నల్గడలు (నలు+కడ). నలుదెసలు or నల్దెసలు *nalu-desalu.* adv. On all sides. నలుబది. నలువది or నలభై *nalu-badi.* (నలు+పది.) adj. Forty. నలువండ్రు *nalu-vandru.* n. Forty persons. నలుబదిమంది. నలువ or నల్వ *naluva.* (నలు+వా or వాయి face.) n. A name of Brahma, as the four-faced god. నలువాలు a house with an open space in the middle. చుట్టుకొల్లారు.

నలుగు, నలగు or నలియు *nalugu.* [Tel.] v. n. To break. To be broken, bruised, crushed, crumpled or reduced to powder. నలియు. To rub with a fragrant paste నలుగుపెట్టు. To become easy, smooth, or familiar by acquaintance. To wither, be weakened or debilitated. ఆ పాఠము అతనికి నలిగినది the lesson has become familiar to him. దోవ యింకా నలగలేదు the road is not yet trodden smooth. వారు జగడమాడగా నేను నలిగిపోతిని they were the disputants but I was the sufferer, I was crushed between them. వారు నలిగిపోయి నారు they are in reduced circumstances. ఒళ్లు నలిగియున్నది the limbs are quite tired. నలుగు *nalugu.* n. Rubbing, scrubbing the limbs with fragrant paste made usually of పెసలు. నలుగుపెట్టు to rub the limbs with paste. నలుగు or నలుగుపిండి n. A sort of fragrant paste used as soap. నలుగుడు or నలగుడు *naluguḍu.* n. Difficulty, trouble, pain, suffering. పీడనము. సంకటము, తొందర, ఇబ్బంది. "అలందు నలుగుడుపడియెదో మనసా" Sucn. iii. 333. That which is thrashed or bruised నలిగినది. నలుగుడుపెట్టు to oppress, to harass. నలగగొట్టు *nalaga-goṭṭu.* v. a. To pound, to bruise. వానిని నలగకొట్టినారు they thrashed him severely. నలత or నల్త nalata. n. Debility: a weak state: the remains or constitutional effects of a disease. పురా తీంచినరోగము. Convalescence, a bad state of health, lingering indisposition, a low fever. నలతగొట్టు nalata-gottu. n. A make-bate, a thorn in one's side. నలుకువ or నలకువ nalukuva. n. Ailing, an ill state of health. వ్యాధి. Suffering, శ్రమము, బాధ. Weariness, ఆయాసము. నలుచు, నలచు or నలుపు nalutsu. v. a. To crush. To rub the skin. నొప్పిచేయు, తోము.

నలుడు or నళుడు naludu. [Skt.] n. The name of Nala, a certain hero.

నలుపు nalupu. [Tel.] n. Blackness. నీల వర్ణము. adj. Black. See నల్ల.

నలువ See under నలు.

నలువు naluvu. [Tel.] n. Beauty. ఒప్పిదము. Ability, సామర్థ్యము. adj. Beautiful. ఒప్పిద మైన. నలువొప్ప beautifully, finely.

నలుసు nalusu. [Tel. from నలుకు.] n. A mote or particle: an atom: a mote that gets into the eye, రేణువు. నలుసంత very little, as much as an atom.

నల్ల nalla. [Tel.] adj. Black. n. Blackness. నలుపు. Black stuff: charcoal, బొగ్గు. Blood, నెత్తురు. నల్లంగి nallangi. n. A sort of snipe. నల్లిండ్లు nallindlu. (నల్ల+ఇండ్లు.) n. Brahmin houses. అగ్రహారము. ఔపాసనధూమము చేత నల్లనైనయిండ్లు. నల్లంచిగాడు or నల్లచ్చి గాడు nallanchi-gadu. n. The Black-backed Indian Robin, *Thamnobia fulicata.* పెద్దనల్లంచి or చాకలిగాడు the Magpie Robin, *Copsychus saularis.* పొదనల్లంచిగాడు or తోకనల్లంచిగాడు the Shama, *Cittocincla macrura.* నల్లఉలవి, తీపిఉలవి or ఉలవ కొంకి nalla-ulavi. n. A fish, *Rhynchobatus djeddensis.* నల్లకాత or ఇజ్జనల్లతీగె a certain plant. నల్లకీడు see నలికిరిపాము or నలికిచి. నల్లగిల్లు nalla-gillu. v. n. To blacken, become dark, నల్లబడు, నల్లనగు. నల్లగుండు nalla-gundu. n. An eel. నల్ల గుడ్డు nalla-guddu. n. The pupil of the eye, కనీనిక. నల్లజీనువాయి nalla-jinuvayi. n. The Black-headed Munia, *Munia malacca.* నల్లచీమ nalla-chima. n. A black ant. నల్లజీలకర్ర nalla-jilakarra. n. Black cummin. *Nigella indica.* Rox. ii. 646. నల్లజేమ the black species of జేమ కూర. నల్లటి or నల్లని nallati. adj. Black. నల్లతిమిరిమీను nalla-timiri-minu. n. A fish. *Narcine timlei.* నల్లదనము nalla-danamu. n. Blackness. నల్లదాసరిగాడు nalla-dasari-gadu. n. A tortoise. తాబేలు. నల్లద్రావుడు nalla-dravudu.. n. A demon. రాక్షసుడు. నల్లదిండి or పాత్తిల తొర nalla-dindi. n. A fish, *Rhinchobatus ancylostomus.* (F. B. I.) నల్లన nallana. n. Blackness. నల్లనయ్య lit: the black god, i.e., Krishna. నల్లపూస nalla-pusa. n. A black bead. నల్లపడు nalla-padu. n. To turn black, to blacken. నల్ల మందు nallamandu. n. Lit. the black drug, i. e., Opium. అభిని. నల్లమడుగు a black pond, that is, a deep pond. మిక్కిలి లోతుగలమడుగు. నల్లమాను nallamanu. n. Black wood. A sort of harrow used before or after sowing the seed, to level the ground. మాగాణిభూమి దున్ని విత్తనములు చల్లుటకు ముందుగా చిదుచిదుగ నీరు సర్దుటకొరకు రెండుతాళ్లు కట్టి తోలేది. నల్లవలువ తాలుపు one who wears a black dress; an epithet of Balarama, నీలాంబరుడు.

నల్లవొ or నల్లవో nallavo. [Tel.] Interj. Alas! అయ్యో. ఓరీ!

నల్లా or నల్లి nalla. [Tel.] n The barrel of a gun.

నల్లి nalli. [Tel.] n. A bug. మత్కుణము. నల్లి చెట్టు A shrub, *Grewia carpinifolia.* Rox. ii. 587.

నల్లికి or నల్లికల్లిపాము See నలికిరిపాము.

నల్లె *nalle*. [Tel.] n. A span, జేన. **నల్లెడు** *nalleḍu*. adj. Of the size of a span, or, of four finger's breadth, జేనెడు, జేన, జెత్తెడు.

నల్లేరు or **నల్లేరు** *nalleru*. [Tel.] n. The plant termed *Cissus quadrangularis*, (Rox. i. 407,) a weed used in dyeing, వజ్రవల్లి. గాంఢనల్లేరు samphire.

నల్వము *nalvamu*. [Skt.] n. A furlong or a distance of four hundred cubits or 200 yards.

నళ *naḷa*. [Tel.] n. Name of a year. ఒకసంవత్సరము.

నవ *nava*. [Tel.] n. An itching. జిల. దురద. **నవగొను** *nava-gonu*. v. n. To itch. **నవనవలాడు** *nava-naval-āḍu*. v. n. To flourish, prosper, thrive.

నవటాకు *navaṭāku*. [Bengali.] n. One eighth part of a seer.

నవల్ *naval*. [Tel.] adj. Budding, చిగిరించెడి. "నవ్వనన," A. vi. 60. లేతనల్లనించే బుద్ధిచేతను.

నవత *navata*. [Tel.] n. Languishing illness, decline. దీర్ఘవ్యాధ్యము, నవయుట. Pain. Sorrow, దుఃఖము.

నవనీతము *navanītamu*. [Skt.] n. Fresh butter. అప్పుడు చిలికితీసిన వెన్న.

నవము *navamu*. [Skt.] adj. New, కొత్త. n. Praise, స్తోత్రము. పొగడ్త. Nine, తొమ్మిది. నవంనవం ప్రీతిమావహరతి (Māgha) every moment presented fresh beauties. నవమ ఛుళ్ళ the figure nine: viz. ౯ which the poets say is the form of a beautiful ear. నవమన్మథుడు a second Cupid. నవసుందరి a second Venus, a rival to Venus. **నవకము** *navakamu*. adj. New, fresh, blooming, నూతనమైనది. Nine, తొమ్మిది. n. Freshness, tenderness, మృదుత్వము. Youth. యౌవనము. "చక్కనిదనమునవకంబు నవకంబు నవకంబు," Nagnajit. ii. 27. **నవగ్రహాపిల్ల** *nava-graha-billa* n. A brooch set with nine stones (ruby, emerald, sapphire, &c.) sacred to the "nine constellations." **నవతి** *navati*. n. Ninety. **నవధాన్యములు** *nava-dhānya-mulu*. n. The nine sorts of grains, viz., Rice, wheat, Bengal gram, &c. **నవమము** *navamamu*. adj. Ninth. తొమ్మిదవ. **నవమాలిక** *nava-mālika*. n. The double Jasmine. విరజాజి. **నవమి** *navami*. n. The ninth lunar day either of the light or dark fortnight. తొమ్మిదవతిథి. **నవరంధ్రములు** or **నవద్వారములు** *nava-randhra-mulu*. n. The nine apertures of the body. **నవరత్నములు** *nava-ratnamulu*. n. The "nine gems," a collective phrase: some reckon them as వజ్రము diamond, వైడూర్యము lapis-lazuli (cat's eye), గోమేధికము agate, పుష్యరాగము topaz, నీలము sapphire, మరకతము emerald, మాణిక్యము ruby, ప్రవాళము coral, మౌక్తికము pearl. నవరత్నకిరీటము a gemmed crown. నవరత్నము a particoloured or mottled game cock. నవరత్నకంఠి or కంటె a neck jewel set with four or five sorts of stones. **నవరాత్రి** *nava-rātri*. n. The "Navaratri" or nine nights: an annual festival in honour of Durga: also called Dussarah, దసరా. **నవరాశికము** *nava-rāsikamu*. n. The *rule of nine* in Hindu arithmetic, i. e., the double rule of three: Compound Proportion.

నవయు or **నవియు** *navayu*. [Tel.] v. n. To languish, sink, perish, to fall away in flesh. శోగాదులచేత కృశించు, కృశించుట. నవిసిన worn away, worn out. వాడు నవిసి నవిసి చచ్చుచున్నాడు he is dropping into his grave.

నవరంగము *nava-rangamu*. [Skt.] n. A chamber, or summer house, standing alone in the square of a house. మధ్య రంగము. Vasu. ii. 35.

నవరు Same as నవరు (q. v.) **నవల్లు** for **నగల్లు** *navallu*. n. Palaces. "[illegible]" M. XII. ii. 327

నవల or **నవలా** *navala.* [Tel.] n. A woman. ఆడుది, ఇంతి. A. v. 41. R. i. 126. 204. In the acc. case, నవలాను. R. v. 225.

నవాచారము or **నవాసారము** *navachāramu.* [Tel.] n. Sal ammoniac. Ammonium chloride.

నవాటు *navāṭu.* [Tel.] n. A sort of white loaf sugar. Vijaya Vilas. iii. 63.

నవారు *navāru.* [H.] n. A broad tape. మంచములకు నేసే పెద్దనేత.

నవి *navi.* [Tel.] n. A foundation pit on which a wall is raised.

నవీనము or **నవ్యము** *navīnamu.* [Skt.] adj. New, recent, fresh.

నవిటి *naviṭi.* [Tel.] n. A measure of twelve seers (Ganjam).

నవుకు *navuku.* [Tel.] n. A leak in a channel or sluice.

నవుకరి or **నౌకరి** *navukari.* [H.] n. Service. కొలువు. **నవుకరు** or **నౌకరు** *navukaru.* n. A servant. పరిచారకుడు, కొలువుకాడు.

నవురు or **నౌరు** *navuru.* [Tel.] adj. Soft (as cloth or the temples.)

నవులు, నౌలు or **నములు** *navulu.* v. a. To chew. To shoot or throb. పిక్కలునవులు చున్నవి the calves of my legs ache.

నవ్వు *navvu.* [Tel.] v. n. To laugh. హసించు. v. t. To laugh at, to joke, పరిహసించు, అపహసించు. **నవ్వులాట, నవ్వుటాల** or **నవ్వుటాలు** (నవ్వులు+ఆట.) *navvul-āṭa.* n. Laughter, amusement, fun. **నవ్వుబాటు** or **నగుబాటు** *navvu-bāṭu.* n. Ridicule, a joke, పరిహాసము. **నవ్వులబండి** *navvula-bandi.* n. A laughing creature. నవ్వెడు స్వభావముగలది. **నవ్వు** or **నవు** n. Laughter. Laughing at, joking, jest, fun. plu. నవ్వులు or నవ్వుటాలు. నవ్వులాయెను వాని బ్రతుకు I am become a laughing stock.

నవ్వించు *navvintsu.* v. a. To amuse or cause to laugh.

నశించు *naśintsu.* [Skt.] v. n. To be ruined or destroyed, to lapse, merge, pass away. **నశింపు** *naśimpu.* n. Loss, destruction, ruin. **నశ్వరము** *naśvaramu.* adj. Perishing, perishable. నశించునది. నాశనముగునట్టి. అనశ్వరకీర్తి lasting fame. **నష్టము** *nashṭamu.* adj. Lost, ruined, destroyed. నాశముపొందిన. **నష్టము** or **నష్టి** n. Loss, damage, injury, detriment, destruction, ruin, death. నాశము, ద్రవ్యనాశము. అతని తండ్రి నష్టమైనతర్వాత after the death of his father. **నష్టపరుచు** *nashṭa-parutsu.* v. t. To waste, to ruin. నష్టపెట్టు to make one lose, to injure. వానికి నష్టపెట్టకుము do not do him any damage.

నస *nasa.* [Tel.] n. Irritation, ticklishness, soreness of throat, itching. దురద. A pest: harm, danger, ఉపద్రవము. నసనసగానుండే irritable, ticklish. **నసగూటి** *nasa-gūṭi.* (నసగూడు+ఇ.) n. An amorous woman, an adulterous woman, కాముకురాలైన స్త్రీ, జారిణి. **నసగూడు** *nasa-gū[illegible]* n. Amorous desire. కామాసక్తి.

" తిండికిచేరండిమెండైనదండికిని,
రెసనునసగూటివిన స్త్రీకిసనుకేగి."
H. i. 257.

See నవ. **నసమిరి** or **నసిమిరి** *nasamiri.* n. Irritation, itching. దురద. **నసలించు** *nasalintsu.* v. a. To disturb, to spoil. వికలముచేయు. "నసలించుచొత్తులు నాగరికము లు." L. xxii. 111.

నసుకు *nasuku.* [Tel.] n. Slinking. An innuendo, a hint. A lie. అసత్యపుమాట. adj. Petty, slight, inaudible. False, అసత్యము. v. a. To hint, express by innuendo.

నస్యము *nasyamu.* [from Skt. నాసిక.] n. Snuff; any powder, or liquid which physicians prescribe to be snuffed up into the nose. నస్యముపిడుచు to express the juice of any herb into the nose. నస్యము చేయు to use such a medicine.

నహి *nahi.* [Skt.] (interjection) No! "వావినహి." (T. iv. 17. R. i. 45.) kinship is all nonsense, the cousinship is a mere nullity.

నా na

నా *na.* [Tel. from. నేను.] pron. I adj. My. నా (Contraction for నాకు to lick.) నాచూచు to taste. "విను నాచూచిన మూచూచిన భోజ్యమునిండ్యము" M. XIII. iv. 105. **నాన్** *nān.* Contracted for అనన్ On (his) saying this, అనేటప్పటికి. R. iv. 4. నానిని on his saying so, అట్లు అనగా విని. "అప్పాళి నమస్స నా." Vasu. iv. 6.

నాంచారు *nāncharu.* [Tam.] n. A lady, a goddess.

నాంది *nāndi.* [Skt.] n. A preliminary. The exordium, prelude, prologue dedication, or praise of a deity, recited in benedictory verses at the commencement of a religious ceremony or poem. నాందీ దూరగము the opening rite. Anand. vi. 1. The opening benedictory verses in a drama. నాటకప్రథమాంగము, మొదలుపెట్టేదము. **నాందీకరుడు** or **నాందిపాఠి** *nāndi-karuḍu.* n. One who pronounces the benediction. ఆశీర్వాదము చేయువాడు.

నాకము *nākamu.* [Skt. క = సుఖము; అకము–దుఃఖము; న+అకము=నాకము=దుఃఖములేని.] n. Heaven, Elysium, Paradise, స్వర్గము. The sky, the atmosphere, ఆకాశము. **నాకిని** See నాగవల్లి. Chenn. iv. 213. **నాకారి** *nāk-ari.* n. Lit: "a foe of heaven," i. e., a demon, a titan or giant. అసురుడు. నాకిని a female supernatural being, a goddess, దేవస్త్రీ. **నాకులు** *nākulu.* n. The celestials, the gods. R. v. 35. 176. **నాకేశుడు** *nāk-ēśuḍu.* n A name of Indra.

నాకు *nāku.* [Tel.] v. n. To lick. నాకించు to make one lick. పుట్ట నాకి విడిచినట్లు (proverb) you have had a narrow escape. వానిని పాము నాకినది the snake stung him. A. i. 53.

నాకువు *nākuvu.* [Skt.] n. An ant-hill. పుట్ట.

నాగ or **నాగన్** *nāga.* [Tel.] adv. As though, so called.

"చిత్రాంగి చేష్టలుడింపుడే నాగ,
చిత్రాంగుడస్త్రాద్రి చేరవేసెగ."

నాగవసాని or **నాగవ్వసాని** See under నాగవల్లి.

నాగము *nāgamu* [Skt. from నగ a hill.] n. Lit: That which pertains to a mountain. A serpent, పాము. Particularly, a cobra. An elephant, ఏనుగు. Various species of పాములు are called కంపునాగము, చింత N. దుంప N. పిడి N. శంకు N. గోక్ష N. కృష్ణ N. కోడె N. adj. Large, పెద్ద. When used as the second part of compound, (సమాసము) it means Excellent. శ్రేష్ఠము. **నాగకంకణుడు** *nāga-kankaṇuḍu.* n. Siva who wears a 'bracelet of snakes.' **నాగకేసరము** *nāga-kēsaramu.* n The small tree termed *Mesua ferrea.* Rox. ii. 605. నాగగన్నేరు n large species of Oleander. **నాగగోలంగ** *nāga-golanga.* n. A plant called *Murraya exotica.* Rox. ii. 374. **నాగజెముడు** *nāga-jemuḍu* n. A kind of cactus or prickly pear. **నాగతాళి** *nāga-tāli.* n. The plant called the prickly pear, *Cactus indicus.* Rox. ii. 474. Ains. ii. 217. **నాగదంతి** *nāga-danti.* n. A plant called కుంజర or నాగస్ఫోటము. **నాగపడిగలు** *nāga-paḍigalu.* n. Earrings in the shape of the expanded head of the cobra de capella. నాగపడిగల దండ a necklace. **నాగపాశము** *nāga-pāśamu.* n. The serpentine weapon of Varuna. Nooses twining like serpents. W. on Vish. P. 140. **నాగబంధము** *nāga-bandhamu.* n. The serpent's embrace, i. e., both wound together in an upright position as shown in various sculptures. అధికయసంయుత వస్త్రభేదము. నాగబెత్తము nâga-bettamu. n. A cane with a metal tip at the end. నాగమల్లి nâga-malle. n. The prickly pear; the plant named *Justicia nasuta*, అన్న పత్రిక. Rox. i. 120. నాగలోకము nâga-lôkamu. n. Lit: The serpent world, i. e., the nether world, పాతాళము. నాగవాసము nâga-vâsamu. n. The subterranean world of Nagas or fairies, నాగలోకము. A staple or a ring for a hasp, because shaped like a snake's head. తలుపుగొళ్లెముకైటు తగిలించేది. The iron stays that diverge from the poles of a palanquin. A dancing house or theatre; a set of dancing girls, a troop of strolling players, నాట్యశాల, వేశ్యలగుంపు. నాగస్వరము or నాగసరము nâga-svaramu. n. A hautboy, a kind of clarionet. A pipe used by snake players, పాములవాడు ఊదు బుర్ర. నాగాంతకుడు nâg-ântakudu. n. Lit: The killer of serpents, i.e., the eagle, గరుత్మంతుడు. నాగాననుడు nâg-ânanudu. n. Lit: 'Elephant faced', an epithet of Ganêsa. నాగు, నాగులు, నాగుపాము or నాగుబాము nâgu. n. A cobra. నాగము. నాగులచీర a sort of petticoat woven with red stripes. నాగులచవితి nâgula-tsaviti. n. A festival devoted to serpent worship, held in the month of భాద్రపదము. నాగేంద్రుడు nâgêndrudu. n. The king of the Naga fairies.

నాగరము nâgaramu. [Skt. from నగర a town.] n. Dried ginger, శొంఠి. H. ii. 172. 248. A. v. 98. నాగరము or నాగరి the name of the Devanagiri alphabet as, being elegant or polished. adj. Pertaining to a town, నగరసంబంధమైన. నాగరికత or నాగరికము nâgarikata. n. Lit: Townliness; urbanity, elegance, civility, courteousness, refinement, civilisation నాగరికము nâgarikamu. adj. Genteel, urbane, civil, polite, polished, elegant, refined, civilised నాగరికుడు nâgarikudu n. A gentleman, a man of elegance, a civilised person

నాగలి, నాగేలు or నాగేలు nâgali. [Tel.] n. A plough. నాగటికర్రు a plough-share. నాగటిచిప్ప or నాగటిదుంప the wooden part of the plough on which the share is fixed. నాగటిజోదు an epithet of Balarama.

నాగవల్లి nâga-valli. [Skt.] n. The vine that produces the betel leaf or *tamalapâku*. నాగవల్లి or more correctly written నాకబలి, i. e., దేవతలకుచేయుపూజ. The finishing ceremony of a marriage (wherein a betel leaf is given) which is performed on the fourth day. Betel nut is presented to a parting guest and thus has come to denote taking leave, or dismissal, as well as the opposite sense of *admission* or installation. నాగవసాని or నాగప్పసాని nâgapa-sâni. n. A married lady who conducts the నాగవల్లి ceremony. నావసాని (another form of నాగవసాని.) nâpasâni. n. A matron.

నాగసింధూరము nâga-sindhûramu. [Skt.] n. A red calx of lead.

నాగా nâgâ. [H.] n. Nought, nothing; a cipher: intermission. Remainder. నాగాలేకుండా without fail, without intermission or remainder.

నాచికొను nâchi-konu. [Tel.] v. a. To snatch, usurp, seize. హరించు. "ఈసని లోకనములు నాదుమానము నాచికొనక నయ్యెంతి నమునమనొని." M. Virat. ii. 88. "మూర్ఖుం చేతనున్న రిత్తునుందు నెనసానాచికొనిన కీర్తిరియు బోటి." M. Dro. v. 290. ABA. ii. 554. నాచికోలు nâchi-kôlu. n. Seizure, usurpation, అపహారము.

"ఘల్గునుడంబనిమీరిస్వైంధవుం, బ్రాణము
నాచికోలునకు నాథ తెలుపనమర్థ్యకృత్యమే."
M. Salya. i. 58.

నాచు nâtsu. v. a. To snatch. n. A thief. శైవల. Water-weeds, an aquatic plant called *Vallisneria octandra*. Greenness in water. Mossiness. Rox. i. 143.

నాజరు *nādzaru.* [H.] n. A sheriff in a court of law. An inspector. Nâzir.

నాజూకు *nādzūku.* [H.] adj. Delicate, fine, tender. సున్నితమైన, నాణెమైన.

నాటకము *nāṭakamu.* [Skt.] n. Acting, dancing. నర్తనము. A play, or drama. Conduct, ప్రవర్తనము. వీధినాటకము a street play. సృష్టిజగన్నాటకము the visible course of the world, the order of creation. జగన్నాటకుడు God, the ruler of the universe. నాటకశాల or నాట్యశాల a theatre. **నాటకమాడు** *nāṭakam-āḍu.* v. n. To act a play. **నాటకులు** *nāṭakulu* n. Stageplayers, dramatis personæ. **నాట్యము** *nāṭyamu.* n Dancing, a dance, నృత్యము. నాట్యమాడు to dance.

నాటు *nāṭu.* [Tel. from నాడు a country.] adj. Home-made, country-made. నాటుపురము the country, the mofussil. నాటుపురానికి పోయినారు they are gone up the country. నాటుపురపువాండ్లు countryfolks. నాటుసీమమనిషి a man from the interior. నాటుపురములో నుండడము being away from town. నాటువైద్యుడు a quack doctor. నాటుమందు country-made gunpowder.

నాటు *nāṭu.* [Tel.] v. n. & a. To plant or fix. గుచ్చు. To impress, as with the nails. To prick or pierce, గుచ్చుకొను. To transfix. హృదయంగమముగా నాటంగచెప్పి they represented it most impressively. నా మాట నీ చెవికి నాటచెప్పెద my words shall pierce thine ears. నా మాటలు వానిచెవిలో ములుకులై నాటెను my words pierced his heart. n. Planting, నాటుట. A wound, (G. X. 152.) a dent: the first or preparatory step, as a chop before striking with the axe. The dent sometimes made on a coin in proving it, called also సూలాకి; hence the నాట్లపట్టము is the loss on shroffage. నాటువేసిన rooted. **నాటుకొను** *nāṭu-konu.* v. n. To be fixed in anything. చిక్కుకొను. నాటుకొలుపు to cause to be fixed. నాటుపు. **నాటనము** or **నాట్నము** *nāṭanamu* n. Planting little sprouts or young plants, నారులోనగువానిని నాటుట. **నాటించు** *nāṭintsu.* v. a. To plant, fix firmly.

నాడా *nāḍā.* [H.] n. A ribbon, tape. చేసిన పట్టా.

నాడి *nāḍi.* [Skt.] n. A pipe, tube, blow pipe. గొట్టము. Any tubular organ of the body, as an artery, vein, the pulse. గోలుసరము. A Hindu hour of 24 English minutes, గడియకాలము. నాడిచూచు to feel the pulse. **నాడింధమము** *nāḍindhamamu.* n. Bellows, కొలిమితిత్తి. **నాడింధముడు** *nāḍindhamudu.* n. A goldsmith, అగసాలెవాడు. **నాడిక** *nāḍika.* n. An hour, గడియ. A country, దేశము.

నాడు *nāḍu.* [Tel.] v. a. To plant, నాటు. n. A land, a country, a district. తూర్పునాడు the eastern districts. నాడెల్ల all the land. పల్లపునాడు low-lying land. వేగినాడు the Vegi country. వేగినాటివారు people of the Vegi sect or party.

నాడు *nāḍu.* [Tel.] n. A day. Time. That day, అనాడు. That time, అకాలము. చిన్ననాడు when he was young, in infancy. ఒకనాటికీ వినడు he will never consent. అనాడు at that time. తాతనాడు in my grand-father's time. నాటినుండి since that time. తండ్రినాటనుంచి from the time of his father. సంవత్సరమునాటికి చెల్లించే రూకలు the money payable at the end of the year. నాటివారు the people of that time. నాటిపుస్తకము the book of those times. అది యన్నాళ్లనాడు how long ago was it? నాలుగేండ్లనాడు four years back. నాటికి on that day, by that time, to that day. నాడే oh I dare say! to be sure! నాటిపని the matter you wot of, you know what I mean. ఇది శాశ్వదినములనాటిది this is very ancient. **నానాడు** *nā-nāḍu.* adv. Day by day, now and then. **నానాటికి** *nā-nāṭiki.* adv. Day by day, by degrees

నాడె *nāḍe*. [Tel.] n. A weaver's shuttle. మగ్గముకండెయుంచి త్రోసే సాధనము.

నాణెము, నాడెము or నాణ్యము *nāṇemu*. [Tel.] n. Quality. Fineness, goodness of cloth, metals, &c. వస్త్రాదులయొక్క పరిశీలనము. Character, honesty, యోగ్యత. Polished behaviour. నాగరికత. నీకు వజ్రముల నాణెము తెలుసునా are you a judge of diamonds. A coin or piece of money. నాణ్యమైన or నాణెమైన *nāṇyam-aina*. adj. Fine, honest, good. నాణెంపు వ్రతము noble devotion. నాణెముచూచు *nāṇemu-tsūtsu*. v. n. To try (a thing's) goodness. నాణెగాడు *nāṇe-gāḍu*. n. An appraiser, or valuer. నాడెకత్తె or నాణెకత్తె *nāḍe-katte*. n. A polished woman. నాణెముకలది.

నాతము *nātamu*. [Tel.] n. A daily allowance of money, batta. బత్తెము. వానికి జీత నాతములులేవు he receives neither pay nor batta.

నాతి or నాతుక *nāti*. [Tel.] n. A woman. స్త్రీ.

నాదము or నాదు *nādamu*. [Skt.] n. Sound; a note, a ringing in the ears. A slight headache. నాకు తలనాదుగానున్నది I have a slight headache. ధ్వని, మ్రోత. నాదించు *nādintsu*. v. n. To make a noise, to sound or ring, మ్రోగు. నాదారు *nādāru*. v. n. To cease. T. iv. 39. "నాదారక," i. e., ఎడతెగకుండా incessantly.

నాది *nādi*. [Tel. from నేను.] pron. Mine. నాదు *nādu*. adj. My, my own. నాదుకరంబులు my hands.

నాదూారు or నాదారు *nādāru*. [H.] adj. Poor, helpless.

నాథుడు *nāthuḍu*. [Skt.] n. A lord, king. రాజు, a husband, పెనిమిటి. మునినాథుడు a saint.

నాన *nāna*. [Tel.] n. Shame, modesty. సిగ్గు. నానగేడిపై losing all shame, సిగ్గువడి. "మచ్చటులాస్త్రఘట్టన మునంబున నెంతనకి నానగేడి యై, నచ్చినవానిజూచితివ." Parij. v. 28. నానగండడు *nāna-ganḍaḍu*. n. A shameless man. సిగ్గుమాలినవాడు.

నానపాల *nāna-pāla*. [Tel.] n. The plant called the Thyme-leaved spurge. *Euphorbia thymifolia* (Linn.) Ainslie ii. 75. రక్షివారి నానబాల బియ్యము.

నానా *nānā*. [Skt.] adj. Many, divers, all sorts of, sundry. వివిధములైన. నానాత్వము *nānātvamu*. n. Plurality, diversity. M. XII. vi. 34.

నాను, నానుకోవి or నానుగ్రోవి *nānu*. [Tel.] n. A gold necklace of small beads linked together. కంఠాభరణవిశేషము.

నాను *nānu*. [Tel.] v. n. To soak, to be steeped, to become wet. నానుచు or నాన్చు *nānutsu*. v. t. To cause to soak. నానజేయు. నానుడి *nā-nuḍi*. (నాను+నుడి.) n. A rumour. కింవదంతి. A proverb, సామెత. నానుడు *nānuḍu*. adj. Moist, damp, wet, soaked, sopped, steeped. తడిసిన. నానుడునేల wet land. నానుడువాన soaking rain. విడువకకురియు పొడిపొడివాన. నానుడువాసన a damp smell. నానుపు *nā-nupu*. v. a. To bleach. చలువచేయు. నానుబోర *nānu-bōra*. n. A breast of mutton, మాంసముగలరొమ్ము. Ila. iv. 275. నాన్పించు *nānpintsu*. v. a. To get bleached. నానబెట్టు or నానపోయు *nāna-beṭṭu*. v. a. To soak, to steep. నానబాలు, నానబ్రాలు or నానబియ్యము *nāna-bālu*. n. New rice that is soaked in water or milk. నానబెట్టిన కొత్తబియ్యము. నానవేయు *nāna-vēyu*. v. a. To soak, sop, steep. ఊరక యెందుకు నానవేసి చెరుపుకొంటావు why do you ruin yourself by delay?

నాపకుడు *nāpakuḍu* [Skt.] n. A destroyer. నాశకుడు, నశింపచేయువాడు. కులనాపకుడు the curse of his father's line. R. v. 178.

నాపరాయి *nāpa-rāyi*. [Tel. నాపు+రాయి.] n. A whitish freestone used in lithography. Grey chlorite slate, or potstone. నాపఉప్పు salt that is not crystallized.

నాపసా *nāpusā*. [Eng. 'knapsack'] n. A knapsack. సిపాయీలభిక్షపుమూట.

నాపసాని See under నాగపల్లి.

నాపితుడు *nāpitudu*. [Skt.] n. A barber. మంగలి.

నాభి *nābhi*. [Skt.] n. The navel. బొడ్డు. Musk, కస్తూరి. Poison, విషము. నాభి or వస నాభి aconite. The central hole in a wheel, రథచక్రమధ్యాగ్రము. నాభిక *nābhika*. n. The navel. T. i. 2. నాభిజన్ముడు *nābhi-janmudu*. n. Brahma, as produced from Vishnu's navel.

నామము or నామధేయము *nāmamu*. [Skt. cf. Eng. 'name'.] n. A name, appellation, title. The upright mark drawn in the forehead by the Vaishṇavites. నిలువు పెట్టుకొనే బొట్టు. నామాంకితము placing one's name in a (poetical) dedication, &c. నామకరణము *nāma-karaṇamu*. n. The ceremony of naming a child. Christening. బిడ్డలకు పేరుపెట్టుట. నామకార్థము for name's sake, nominally. నామముడుచు *nāmam-udatsu*. (నామము+ఉడుచు) v. t. To kill. చంపు. భార. స్త్రీ. ii. నామముపెట్టు to leave one's mark upon a man, i. e., to deceive or ruin him. నామము పెట్టుకొను to draw lines upon one's own forehead. నామదుంప *nāma-dumpa*. n. The water plant called *Rumex aponogeton*. Rox. ii. 210. నామాలకోడి or నామంకోడి The coot, *Fulica atra*. నామాలపిట్ట or వాసనపిట్ట *nāmala-pitta* n. The Southern Scimitar Babbler. *Pomatorhinus horsfieldii* (F. B. I.)

నామా *nāmā*. [H.] n. A deed, letters patent. కరారునామా an agreement. రాజీ నామా a deed of an amicable settlement. వకాలతునామా a deed of attorney, a power of attorney given in writing.

నామాలపిల్లి *nāmalapilli*. [Tel.] n. A sort of wild cat with four upright lines on the forehead. *Felis rubiginosa*. Jerdon. నామాలుతీయు *nāmalu-tīyu*. (నాము-నామము.) v. n. To reed wood in carpentry, to carve it with parallel upright lines, resembling the Vaishṇavite marks.

నాము *nāmu*. [Tel.] n. The new sprout springing from the stumps of millet. Empty or blasted ears of corn which are thought to be hurtful to the health of cattle. చిక్కిన జొన్నకొయ్యకాలు. Malice, చలము. "నిందాదురానాముతో బంధుకృత్యుడు రాకుండుటకై బహులంకెలెండినాడు." Nagnijit. ii. 33. నామువాసన a disgustingly strong scent. నాపచేను *nāpa-chēnu*. (from నాము) n. A field of జొన్నలు of which the stalks after being cut, have thrown out sprouts. నాపపంట the crop so produced.

నామోషీ *nām-ōshi*. [H.] n. Disgrace, shame. అవమానము.

నాయకము or నాయకరత్నము *nāyakamu*. [Skt.] n. The central gem or stomacher of a necklace. హారమధ్యమణి రత్నము.

నాయకుడు *nāyakudu*. [Skt.] n. A leader. శ్రేష్ఠుడు. A chief, అధిపతి. కథానాయకుడు the hero of a poem or story. నాయిక *nāyika*. n. The heroine. నాయంకరము or నాయకరము *nāyam-karamu*. (నాయకుడు+కరము.) n. The rank or office of a Naik or headman, chiefdom, lordship. అధిపత్యము. నాయకవాడి or నాయకవాళి *nāyaka-vāḍi*. n. The police force. The militia, కట్టుబడివాండ్లు. ఊరి బంట్రోతులు. A Government peon who has to look after cultivation operations, సేద్యపుపనులను పరామర్శచేసే బంట్రోతు. నాయుడు or నాయుడు *nāyadu*. n. A chief. A title borne by men of a certain Sudra caste.

నాయన *nāyana*. [Tel. నా+అన్న.] n. Father, sir. Used also as an endearing term for any one that is addressed. మీనాయన your father. మానాయనమ్మ my grandmother. నాయనా, నాయనా Alas! alas, oh! oh!

నాయము *nāyamu*. [for Skt. న్యాయము.] n. Justice.

నార *nára.* [Tel.] n. The fibre of plants, fibrous bark of trees. నారవస్త్రము or నారమడి a garment made of bark used by nuns. నారవస్త్రము. అరటినార strings of the fibres of the plantain tree. నారచీర *nára-chíra.* n. A garment of bark worn by sages, a linen cloth. నారజెల్ల *nára-jella.* n. A sort of fish. G. I. 111. నారదబ్బకాయ or నారదబ్బుకాయ *nára-dabba-káya.* n. The citron. See దబ్బ.

నారంగము *náran-gamu.* [Skt.] n. The orange tree. నారింజ.

నారము *náramu.* [Skt.] n. Water. జలము. A crowd of men. నరసమూహము.

నారకము *nára-kamu.* [Skt. from నరకము.] n. Hell. నారకస్థలము the infernal regions.

నారట్టము *nár-attamu.* [Skt] n. Land which has chasms or cracks in it. నెరియలువానినభూమి, బీటకనేల.

నారదంతకము *nára-dantakamu.* [Skt.] n. The side timber of a door frame. ద్వారపు నిడుపుకమ్మి.

నారదము *náradamu.* [Skt.] n. A sort of orange. "కల్లనియారటులు నారకేళములు, నారద పాటలి నాగరింత్రియులు." N.D. i. 10.

నారదుడు *nára-dudu.* [Skt.] n. Nárada, the Mercury or Momus of the Hindu Olympus, represented as the inventor of the lute, and messenger and newsmonger of the gods. A roaming tell tale, a make-bate. నారదసంగీతము divine music. నారదత్వము *náradatvamu.* n. A jeering make-bate temper like that of Narada or Mercury. A. ii. 36.

నారసము *nárasamu.* [from Skt. నారాచము.] n. An iron style or arrow: a pin or spike run through a volume to keep it together. A tool used by housebreakers for boring walls. Proverbially used for a piercing glance. వాని నాలుకమీద నారసము వేసినారు they have put a padlock on his lips. నారసము or నారసగంటము an iron style (గంటము) of which each end is pointed, but with different tips for writing on harder and softer leaves.

నారాచము *naráchamu.* [Skt.] n. An iron arrow. అచ్చయినుపబాణము, గంటము. నారాచి *naráchi.* n. An instrument to cut gold, బంగారుమును నరికే కొరముట్టు, సానము. The balance used by a goldsmith, అగసాలెవాని త్రాసు.

నారాజి or నారాజీ Same as నరాజి (q. v.)

నారాయణుడు *nára-yanudu.* [Skt. నార+అయనుడు.] n. Lit: One who rests on the waters. See Gen. i. 12. A name of Vishnu or Brahma. విష్ణువు, బ్రహ్మ. A name applied by the common people to God as distinguished from the gods. నారాయణమూర్తి the same. నారాయణము *nárayanamu.* n. A part of the Taittiriya Upanishad, తైత్తిరీయమునందొక పన్నము. The sacred fig tree. రావిచెట్టు. Prosperity, మంగళము. నారాయణపక్షి *nárayana-pakshi.* n. The common heron, *Ardea cinerea* (F. B. I.) నారాయణి *nárayani.* n. The name of a certain goddess. పార్వతి, లక్ష్మి, గంగ. Name of a plant. పిల్లిపీచరచెట్టు.

నారి *nári.* [Skt.] n. A woman. పరనారి another man's wife. నారిత్వము *náritva-mu.* n. The being a female: womanhood.

నారి *nári.* [Tel.] n. A bowstring. వింటియల్లె త్రాడు. A gut or muscle, నరము. నారి or నారిపురుపు n. The guinea worm that breeds in the flesh of the leg, కాలపుండు, నారిపుర్రము. నారికాయ *nari-kaya.* n. A scar caused by drawing the bowstring, అల్లెత్రాటి తాకుడువలన చేతియందు కలిగిన కిణము. A wart, కిణము. నారిపక్షి *nari-pakshi.* n. The sea gull, from the entrails of which (నారి) bowstrings are made.

నారింజ *nárindza.* [H.] n. An orange. కిచ్చిలిపండు.

నారికేళము, నారికెడము నారికేళము or నారికేళము nári-kêḷamu. [Skt.] n. The cocoanut tree. నారికేళపాకము a very difficult style used in books.

నారు náru. [Tel.] n. A tender young sprout, or plant. Young plants kept to be transplanted. నారుమడి a field thickly set with grain to be afterwards transplanted. నారునవ్వు a shoot, &c. (anuk.) నారుపాటలు náru-páṭalu. n. Common ballads or ditties regarding a fairy or goddess named నారు which presides over tender plants. నారుపోయు náru-pôyu. v. n. To sow corn thickly, for the purpose of afterwards transplanting it. మిరపనారుపోసినారు they planted chilie seed in beds.

నారుచు or నార్చు nárutsu. [Tel.] v. t. To cause to wither. వాడజేయు.

నారువ náruva. [Tel.] n. A kind of tree. H. iv. 18.

నాలప See under నాలుగు.

నాలి nâli. [Tel.] n. A mean work. కష్టతర పని. కూలినాలి cooly and other low and uncertain kind of work. adj. Sly. కపట ము. Deceitful, వంచకము. Slight, imperceptible, latent, insidious, మందము. నాలి కురుపు a latent or indolent ulcer. నాలి ప్రాయము, నాలికురుపు. నాలిగాలి or నాలితెమ్మెర a zephyr, a slight or imperceptible breeze. మందమైనగాలి. నాలిగ్రహము (Swa. iii. 71) a star which exercises no influence on human life, దుర్బలమైనగ్రహ ము. నాలిచూపు a sly look or glance. నాలి చూపుచూచు to glance at or view cunningly. నాలి ముచ్చు a traitor or imperceptible foe, a hypocrite. నాలిఏడుపు silent weeping; or, crocodile tears, వంచ కపుఏడుపు. నాలిజీవి powerless. నాలిభూ తము a sly being or a ghost. కపటపురుషు డు, లేక కపటస్త్రీ.

నాలి nâli. [Tel.] n. A forest tree called *Ulmus integrifolia*. Rox. ii. 68.

నాలుక, నాలిక, నాలికె or నాల్క náluka. [Tel.] n. The tongue. A tongue of fire, జ్వాల. కొండనాలుక the uvula. నాలుకచేప or మాతినాలుక, the fish called a Sole, a species of Rhombus, or Pleuronectes. Russell, Nos. 75. 76. నాలికచేరు nálika-chêru. n. A kind of grass. A disease which attacks the cattle that eat it.

నాలుగు, నాల్గు or నాలువు nálugu. [Tel.] adj. Four. Often used indefinitely as when we say half a dozen. "అతడు నాల్గు దెసలు చూచినాడు" he looked on all sides, lit: on four sides. నాలుకాళ్లసవారి cantering, running away, పారిపోవడము. నాలుకమొగములు వేలుపు the Fire god, అగ్ని దేవుడు.

నాళము nâḷamu. [Skt.] n. A tube, a hollow or tubular stalk, as the stalk of the water lily. కాడ, గొట్టము. A sort of air gun or syringe, చిమ్మనగ్రోవి. A tube through which pellets or balls of clay (నాళపుఉండ లు) are discharged. M. Udyog. iii. 325. A blowpipe, ఊదుగొట్టము. A horseshoe, లాడము, గుర్రపుడెక్కలకువేసే యినుపచెప్పు. నాభినాళము the umbilical cord. నాళగ్రోలు nâḷa-grôlu. n. A sort of drum. BD. iii. 390. నాళి or నాళిలు nâḷi. n. A vein in the body. "నాళులను నలు వడిబంధింపఁబడును." L. xiii. 7. నాళీకము nâḷî-kamu. n. The lotus. పద్మము. An arrow, బాణము. An arrow head, బాణపుములికి. కుసుమనాళీకము (Das. ix. 356.) an arrow made of a blossom. నాళీకజుడు or నాళీక భవుడు nâḷîkajuḍu. n. Brahma. నాళీక వదన nâḷîka-vadana. adj. Lily faced, fair. నాళీకాకరము nâḷîk-âkaramu. n. A pond covered with lilies. Vasu. ii. 47.

నాళ్లు nâḷḷu. [Tel.] n. The plural of three words: that is, of నాడు a day; నాడి a vein and నాడు a country.

నావ *nâva*. [Skt.] n. A ship, boat, or vessel. ఓడ, తరణి. **నావకన్ను** *nâva-kannu*. n. A fish called *Kuriteh*, also a species of Sparus. Russell, No. 106. **నావికుడు** *nâvikuḍu*. n. A steersman. A sailor, ఓడనడుపువాడు.

నావర *nâvara*. [Tel.] n. A kind of locust that is most destructive to crops.

నావుడు or **అనవుడు** *nâvuḍu*. [Tel.] conj. On his or her saying so, అనిచెప్పగా. Therefore, wherefore.

నావురాకులు *nâvurâkulu*. [Tel.] n. A sort of plant with broad leaves. *Premna tomentosa*. Swa. iv. 92. Rox. iii. 76.

నాశము or **నాశనము** *nâśamu*. [Skt.] n. Disappearance. కనబడమి. Ruin, loss, destruction, death. "కీర్తనం కలినాశనం." to sing his praise shall destroy all sin. **నాశిలు**, **నాశిల్లు** or **నాశిల్లు** *nâśilu*. v. n. To be ruined. నాశముపొందు, నశించు. To be hurt, నవయు.

నాస *nâsa*. [Skt.] n. The nose. ముక్కు. The lintel, or upper timber of a door. ద్వారము మీది ఉత్తరకమ్మి, అడ్డకమ్మి. **నాసాపుటము** or **నాసికారంధ్రము** *nâsâ-puṭamu*. n. A nostril. ముక్కురంధ్రము. **నాసామణి** *nâsâ-maṇi*. n. A nose jewel. ముక్కర. A. vi. 179. **నాసిక** *nâsika*. n. The nose. The sense of smell, ఘ్రాణము.

నాసీరము *nâsîramu*. [Skt.] n The van of an army. అగ్రసైన్యము, ముందర నడచెడు, సేనాముఖము. Pride, దర్పము. **నాసీరుడు** *nâsîruḍu*. n. A leader, a captain. A. vi. 171 సేనాముఖమందు నడచువాడు.

నాస్తి *nâsti*. [Skt.] n. Lit: "It is not." A cipher, nonentity, nullity. **నాస్తికుడు** *nâstikuḍu*. n One who denies the existence of an after-life, పరలోకము లేదను వాడు. An atheist, a heretic. **నాస్తిక్యము** or **నాస్తికత** *nâstikyamu*. n. Atheism.

ని ni

ని *ṇi*. [Tel.] affix. An ending or sign of the second or accusative case, as in ఇంటిని. ని (*ni*) and ను (*nu*). when final may drop the vowel and become న్, thus వానికిని, వాండ్రకును may be contracted (in verse) into వానికిన్, వాండ్రకున్, both to him and to them.

నింకెర *ninkera*. [Tel.] adv. Quickly. శీఘ్రము.

నింగి *ningi*. [Tel.] n. The sky. ఆకాశము. నింగిచూలి the atmosphere, వాయువు. **నింగిపడు** *ningi-paḍu*. v. n. To set, as the sun, అస్తమించు. నింగిసిగ an epithet of Siva, శివుడు.

నించు or **నింపు** *ninṭsu*. [Tel. causal of నిండు.] v. a. To fill. పసిడికుండలు నించి filling the golden vases.

నింజిలి *ninjili*. [Tel.] n. Uneasiness, distress, trouble of mind. మనోదుఃఖము.

నిండు *ninḍu*. [Tel.] v. n. To be filled, to be full. పూర్ణమగు. **నింటు** or **నిండుటు** *ninṭa*. n. Fullness, as of water (జల)పూరము. **నిండ**, **నిండా** or **నిండుగా** *ninḍa*. adv. Fully. Much, entirely, utterly. Perfectly, నిండా దెబ్బలుకొట్టినాడు he struck many blows. నిండావందనములు పెట్టినాడు he offered many compliments. వాన నిండాకురిసినది it rained heavily. నిండా సంతోషించినాడు he was much pleased. నిండాభయపడిరి they feared greatly. **నిండారు** or **నిండబడు** *ninḍ-âru*. v. n. To be full. **నిండారు** or **నిండు** n. Fullness, completion. పూర్ణత్వము. **నిండించు** *ninḍintsu*. v. a. To fill. **నిండు** or **నిండైన** *ninḍu*. adj. Full, abundant, much, నిండుకుండ a full vessel. నిండుకుండ తొణకదు a full pot does not spill. నిండుమనిషి a pregnant woman. **నిండుకొను** *ninḍu-*

konu. v. n. To be filled: (metaph.) to be pacified, to be silent. తినలే కాండ్లు నిండుకొన్నాని చెప్పు a phrase meaning (by rule of contrary) I have nothing to eat or give.

నింద ninda. [Skt.] n. Blame, censure, reproach, dishonour. అపవాదము, దూరు, అపకీర్తి. నిందాస్తుతి ninda-stuti. n. A sneer: ironical praise: irony. నిందాస్పదము nind-āspadamu. adj. Scandalous, slanderous. నిందించు nindintsu. v. a. To blame, abuse, vilify, or accuse. దూరు. నిందితుడు ninditudu. n. One who is censured. నిందింపబడినవాడు. నింద్యుడు one who deserves to be censured. నిందింపదగిన వాడు.

నింపాది nimpādi. [Tel. నింపు+ఆది.] adj. Plenty, సమృద్ధము. Gentle, proper, right, fair. n. Gentleness, quiet, శాంతి. నింపాదిగా by gentle means, gently, fair and softly.

నింపిరి nimpiri. [Tel.] n. Dirt. మురికి.

నింపు See నిండు.

నింబము nimbamu. [Skt.] n. The margosa tree *Ayadirachta indica*. వేపచెట్టు.

నికటము nikaṭamu. [Skt.] n. Nearness. సమీపము. adj. Near, close to. సమీపమైన.

నికము Same as నిక్కము (q. v.)

నికరము nikaramu. [Tel.] adj. What remains after all deductions are made, the net balance. తీరుబడిగా మిగిలినది. Selected, excellent. నికరముబంగారు the net weight of the gold. నికరంబాబతి net income. [Skt.] n. A flock or multitude. A treasure, నిధి. adj. Excellent, శ్రేష్ఠము.

నికర్షణము nikarshaṇamu. [Skt.] n. The backside of a house, &c. ఇల్లులోనగువాని పెరటిభాగము. An open space around a town or city, పట్టణమునకుచుట్టు నాటిన బయలు.

నికష nikasha. [Skt.] n. The name of the mother of the demons. రాక్షసుల తల్లి. నికష్‌ఆత్మజుడు nikash-ātmajuḍu. n. A son of Nikasha. నిరృతి.

నికషణము nikashaṇamu. [Skt.] n. Rubbing. H.D. ii. 2517.

నికామము nikāmamu. [Skt.] adv. Voluntarily, willingly, (implying certainty.) Much: as much as one pleases, యథేచ్ఛము, మిక్కిలియిష్టముగా.

నికాయము nikāyamu. [Skt.] n. A multitude, a congregation. గుంపు. నికాయము నికాయ్యము or నికాయ్యము n. A house. ఇల్లు.

నికాశము nikāśamu. [Skt.] adj. Like, resembling. తుల్యము, సమానమైన, వలె. n. Certainty, నిశ్చయము.

నికుంజము nikunjamu. [Skt.] n. A bower, thicket, arbour. పొదరిల్లు.

నికురుంబము nikurumbamu. [Skt.] n. A multitude, assembly. గుంపు, సమూహము.

నికృంతనము nikṛintanamu. [Skt.] n. Cutting. ఖండనము, నరకుట.

నికృష్టము nikṛishṭamu. [Skt.] adj. Outcast, vile, abject. అధమము.

నికేతనము nikētanamu. [Skt.] n. A house. ఇల్లు.

నిక్కచ్చి nikkachchi. [Tel.] n. Violence, forcing, annoyance. నిర్బంధము. Strictness. adj. Strict, ఖండితమైన. వాడు చాలా నిక్కచ్చి మనిషి he is a very strict man. నిక్కచ్చిచేయు nikkachchi-chēyu v. t. To force, compel. నిర్బంధముచేయు.

నిక్కము nikkamu. [Tel.] n. Truth, reality, certainty, verity. నిశ్చయము, యథార్థము, సత్యము. adj. True, certain, genuine, real, intrinsic, sterling. Unalloyed, pure, సత్యమైన, నిర్మలమైన. నిక్కల nikkala. (నిక్కము+కల.) n. A true dream, a dream that turns out true. నిజమగుకల. నిక్కపు చెలి గాడు a real friend. నిక్కముగా truly, యథార్థముగా.

నిక్కరుడు *nikkarudu*. [from Skt. నిష్+ Tel. కపటము.] n. Simplicity, absence of cunning. నిష్కపటము.

నిక్కాక *nikkāka*. [Tel. నిండు+కాక.] n. Burning heat. నిక్కిచెరాక. Fever.

నిక్కు *nikku*. [Tel.] v. n. To strut, sit upright, erect oneself, stand on tiptoe. To jut out or protrude. To be proud or conceited. ఉన్నతమగు, గర్వించు, అతిశయించు, ఉబ్బు. n. Jutting out, or projecting, as the nose, protrusion, ఉన్నతి. Conceit. గర్వము. నిక్కుపొడుచు to jut out, to stand on end, as hair, నిక్కనిలుచు. నిక్కించు *nikkintsu*. v. a. To stretch, to cause to project. నిక్కుపోతు *nikku-pōtu*. n. A conceited or proud man, గర్వస్వభావముగలవాడు. నిక్కుచెవులు ears that jut out. నిక్కుడు Same as నిక్కు n.

నిక్కువము *nikkuvamu*. [Tel. another form of నిక్కము.] n. Truth, certainty. యథార్థము. నిక్కువముగా truly, నిజముగా; much, మిక్కిలి. P. iii. 281.

నిక్వణము or నిక్వాణము *nikvaṇamu*. [Skt.] n. A musical note. వీణాదిధ్వనివిశేషము.

నిక్షేపము *nikshēpamu*. [Skt.] n. A buried treasure; a treasure, a deposit, a pledge. నిధి. నిక్షేపించు *nikshēpintsu*. v. a. To hide, bury under ground, lay up, store up. పాతు, పూడ్చు, దాచు.

నిఖిలము *nikhilamu*. [Skt.] adj. All, entire, complete. సర్వము, ఎల్ల.

నిగదించు *nigadintsu*. [Skt.] v. a. To tell plainly. స్పష్టముగా చెప్పు. (భా. ii.) నిగదము or నిగాదము. *nigadamu*. n. Plain speaking. స్పష్టముగా చెప్పుట.

నిగనిగ *niga-niga*. [Tel.] n. Brilliancy, gleam. adj. Bright. adv. Brightly నిగనిగమను or నిగనిగలాడు *niga-niga-m-anu*. v. n. To glitter, to be bright, to glow.

నిగమము *nigamamu*. [Skt.] n. The Veda, వేదము. A market, అంగడివీథి. A way, మార్గము. నిగముడు *nigamuḍu*. n. A merchant. వర్తకుడు, వణిజుడు.

నిగరణము, నిగరము or నిగారము *nigaraṇamu*. [Skt.] n. Swallowing, మింగుట. నిగరము or నిగారము *nigaramu*. adj. Excellent, శ్రేష్ఠము.

నిగర్వముగా *ni-garvamu-gā*. [Skt.] adv. Humbly. గర్వము లేకుండ.

నిగళము or నిగడము *nigaḷamu*. [Skt.] n. A fetter, chain. సంకెల.

నిగా or నిఘా *nigā*. [H.] n. View. Attention, superintendence, control, care. చూపు, దృష్టి, గమనము.

నిగాలము *nigālamu*. [Skt.] n. A horse's neck. గుర్రపుమెడ.

నిగుడు *niguḍu*. [Tel.] v. n. To stretch, or be extended, వ్యాపించు, నిక్కు, సాగు. To rise or increase, విజృంభించు. To fly or be discharged, as a dart. To fall upon or attack, కవియు. To hasten, తొందరపడు. To become straight, చక్కబడు. To be fulfilled, తీరు. To be vented, as a sigh. To burst forth, as rage. అర్బులునిగిడె shouts arose, "ఇంద్రియములు విషయములమీద, నిగుడనీక మనంబులో మగుడ దిగిచి." M. XII. v. 90. "నీళ్లలోన నోడ నిగిడి తిన్నగ బ్రాకు బైట మూరెడైన బ్రాకలేదు." Vēma. "నీళ్లలోన మొసలి నిగిడియేనుగు బట్టు, బైట కుక్కచేత భంగపడును." Vēma. నిగుడుదెంచు *niguḍudentsu*. v. n. To jut out. నిక్కు. నిగడ *nigaḍa*. (Root in A of నిగుడు.) adv. Out, long, along. నిగడగొలుచు to overreach in measurement. నిగడ దన్నుతాడు వాడు he will kick you so that you will stand straight. నిగిడారు (నిగిడి+ఆరు.) Same as నిగుడు. నిగుడించు. నివుడించు, నిగిడించు, నిగుడుచు or నిగుడ్చు *niguḍintsu*. v. a. To stretch, extend. To discharge, shoot, cast, emit (light), give (a sigh). To raise up, prop up. నిగుడించు. చూడ్కి నిగుడించు to extend the view over the opening landscape. "అందనినందనవనంబుల నర్తు నిగు డ్చుదవు." HD. i. 2082.

నిగురు or **నివురు** *niguru*. [Tel.] n. Embers. The ashes covering live coal. కప్పినిప్పుమీది భస్మము. నివురుగప్పిన నిప్పు a fire hidden under ashes. సున్నపునివురు lime for making plaster.

నిగూఢము *ni-gūḍhamu*. [Skt.] adj. Quite hidden. మిక్కిలి మరుగుపరచబడిన.

నిగ్గడి *niggaḍi*. [Tel.] adj. Hard. కఠినము.

నిగ్గు *niggu*. [Tel.] v. n. To thrive, flourish; to be effected, to prosper, get through, go on properly. నెగ్గు, నిర్వహిల్లు, సమకూరు. n. Brilliancy. తళ్కు. Extract or spirit. Light color, వర్ణవిశేషము, నిగరమయిన కాంతి. "వసుపునిగ్గుల చెలువసోదర" Lavanya. 27. "పసుపునిగ్గయినదుప్పటి" ib. 131. ఈ భూమి నిగ్గును తీసివేయలేరు they cannot remove the richness of this land.

నిగ్రహము *nigrahamu*. [Skt.] n. Rejection. త్రోపుడు. Aversion, disfavour: blaming; a threat. బెదురుపాటు. Imprisonment, చెర. A limit, మేర. "దుష్టనిగ్రహము శిష్టపరిపాలనము" discountenancing the evil and cherishing the good. T. iv. 17. నిగ్రహానుగ్రహశక్తి despotism. **నిగ్రహించు** *nigrahintsu*. v. a. To neglect, disregard, set aside, quash, refuse. To discountenance, disapprove. Swa. vi. 93.

నిఘంటువు *nighanṭuvu*. [Skt.] n. A dictionary.

నిఘోషణము *ni-ghōshaṇamu*. [Skt.] n. A sound, voice.

నిఘ్నము *nighnamu*. [Skt.] adj. Obedient, docile, facile. అధీనమైన, లోబడిన.

నిచయము *nichayamu*. [Skt.] n. An assembly, heap, mass. సమూహము, గుంపు.

నిచితము *nichitamu*. [Skt.] adj. Spread, వ్యాపించిన.

నిచులము *nitsulamu*. [Skt.] n. The red Oleander tree. ఎర్రగన్నేరు. M. XIII. i. 167. Game, poultry, any bird that may be eaten. "నిచులజరాయువుల్ నిగ్రహ ద్రపములు, మధురనిచులంబులిడెకొక్క మధుర నాశి." Balarama. vi. 127, 146.

నిచోళము *nicholamu*. [Skt.] n. A veil, cloak, covering. కప్పుకొనుదుప్పటి, గవిసెన, పక్క దుప్పటి. A. vi. 134. Parij. iv. 9.

నిచ్చెన *nichchena*. [Tel.] n. A ladder. నిశ్రేణి. **నిచ్చెనపంజు** or **నిచ్చెనదివ్వెపంజు** *nitchchena-panḍsu*. n. A ladder on which a number of torches are arranged. దివిటీలు కట్టబడియుండిన నిచ్చెనవంటిసాధనము.

నిచ్చ *nitsa*. [Tel.] adv. Always. సదా. Every day, ప్రత్యహము. See నిచ్చలు.

నిశ్చయము *nitsayamu*. [from Skt. నిశ్చయము.] n. Certainty. నిశ్చయము.

నిచ్చలము *nitsalamu*. [from Skt. నిశ్చలము.] adj. Firm, immoveable. నిశ్చలము. Pure, faultless, నిర్దోషము. Eternal, lasting, నిరంతరము. n. Certainty, నిశ్చయము.

నిచ్చలు *nitsalu*. [Tel.] adv. Always. నంత తము, సదా. n. Certainty, నిశ్చయము.

నిచ్ఛేదము *nich-chhēdamu*. [Skt.] n. Cutting off.

నిజము *nijamu*. [Skt.] n. Nature, స్వభావము. adj. Own, peculiar, native, సహజ. Perpetual, eternal, శాశ్వతమైన. నిజపోష్యవర్గుడ నైననేను I who am your own dependant: this is a mere phrase like "your most obedient servant." The word నిజ prefixed to names of months, as నిజవైశాఖము denotes the proper month, not the అధికమాసము the intercalary month. నిజ లాభతుష్టుడై being satisfied with his own resources. నిజస్థితి *nija-sthiti.* n. The real fact. నిజస్థుడు *nijasthuḍu.* n. A just upright man. నిజానుచరుడు *nij-anu-charuḍu.* n. A personal attendant. నిజము *nidzamu.* Truth, reality, సత్యము. Certainty, నిశ్చయము. adj. True, certain. సత్యము. Positive, actual. నిజముగా *nidzamu-gā.* adv. Actually, really, positively, truly. నిజపరచు or నిజముచేయు to verify, prove, try. నిజపడు *nidzu-paḍu.* v. n. To be ascertained, verified, identified. ఇది నాకు నిజపడినది I ascertained this. నిజమరి *nidzam-ari.* n. A truthful man or woman. సత్యశీలుడు, సత్యవతి.

"నిజబిజచేసి భూకాంతుని రెండుట
నిజమరవలె నెంత నిలువ నా డెబ్బు."

Sar. D. 586.

నిటునిటు *niṭu-niṭu.* [Tel. anuk.] adv. Very tremulously.

నిటలము, నిటాలము or నిటలపటము *niṭa-lamu.* [Skt.] n. The forehead. నుదురు, ఫాలము. నిటలాక్షుడు *niṭal-akshuḍu.* n. Siva, who has an eye in his forehead.

నిట్ట *niṭṭa.* [Tel.] n. A place. స్థానము, ఇరవు. "మూడుమూర్తుల నిట్ట మ్రొక్కులగుట్ట." H.D. i. 2103. A stream, ప్రవాహము. A pillar, స్తంభము. Tallness, height, పొడుగు, ఎత్తు, నిక్క. adj. Tall, నిడుపైన, నిడిద. నిట్టతాడి a tall palm tree. Proper, సరియైన. నిట్టనిలుచు, నిట్టకనిలుచు or నిట్టనిలుచుండు *niṭṭa-nilutsu.* v. n. To stand erect, to stand properly. నిట్టనిలువు, నిట్టకనిలువు or నిట్టనిల్వు *niṭṭa-niluvu.* n. Being erect, an erect posture. నిట్టపొడుచు or నిట్టక్రక్కు *niṭṭa-poḍutsu.* v. n. To burst out. To boil up. పైకి విజృంభించు, ఉప్పొంగు. To stand on end, as hair, రోమాంచితమగు. నిట్టరాడు or నిట్రాడు *niṭṭarāḍu.* n. The long post that supports the roof (of a house) which does not rest on a beam, a rooftree, దూలములేని యింటివాసము పొడుగుకంబము.

నిట్టలము or ఇట్టలము *niṭṭalamu.* [Tel.] adj. Certain, నిశ్చయము.

నిట్టు or నిట్రు *niṭṭu.* [Tel.] n. Thirst, నీరు వట్టు, దప్పి. A fast, ఉపవాసము. A famine, క్షామము. adj. Dry, శుష్కము. Entire. Intricate, puzzling, obscure. నిట్టుపవాసము or నిట్రుపవాసము *niṭṭupavāsamu.* [నిట్టు+ఉపవాసము.] A strict fast. శుష్కోపవాసము. నిట్రిల్లు *niṭrillu.* v. n. To fast, ఉపవాసముండు.

నిట్టూరుపు, నిట్టూర్పు or నిడూర్పు *niṭṭuru-pu.* [Tel. నిడు+ఊరుపు.] n. Deep sighing, a sigh. నిట్టూర్చు *niṭṭurtsu.* v. n. To sigh, "ఆవచనంబు చెవుల్ విని యాదలయూచి నిడూర్పు పుచ్చి." P. iv. 203.

నిట్టెమ్ము *niṭṭemmu.* [Tel. నిడు+ఎమ్ము] n. The backbone. BD. vi. 1775.

నిట్రు, నిట్రుము or నెట్రుము *niṭru.* [Tel. from నిట్ట and నిడు.] n. Height. నిలువు. కలమునుఅంత నిట్రముగా పట్టుకొనకుము do not hold the pen so high or erect. నిట్రాయి *niṭrāyi.* (నిట్ట+రాయి.) n. A long stone. A post, a prop. The centre post, (or king post) of a building. నిట్రించు *niṭrintsu.* v. t. To keep or hold erect, నిలువుగానుంచు.

నిడు *niḍu.* [Tel.] adj. Long. నిడుమోము a long face. నిడువాలు a long sword. నిడివి *niḍivi.* n. Length. దైర్ఘ్యము. నిడివిమీద by degrees. adj. Long, దీర్ఘము. నిడుద *niḍuda.* n. Length, నిడుపు, దీర్ఘము. నిడుదయగు long. నిడుదపండ్లు long teeth. నిడుదలైనకురులు long tresses. నిడుసాచు *niḍu-tsāchu.* v. n. To stretch. సాగు. నిడుదవెన్ను *niḍudu-vennu.* n. A snake. సర్పము. నిడుపు *niḍupu.* n. Length, నిడివి. adj. నిడివియైన. నిడుపకమ్ములు door posts, ద్వారశాఖలు. నిడుపడు *niḍu-paḍu.* n. A snake, పాము. నిడువెండ్రుక *niḍu-ven-ḍruka.* (నిడుపు+వెండ్రుక.) n. The hair standing on end, a startling sensation, రోమాంచము. నిడు వెండ్రుక పెట్టు nidu-vendruka-pettu. v. n. To be startled, to stand on end, as hair. నిక్కపొడుచుకొను.

నితంబము *nitambamu.* [Skt.] n. The bottom or posteriors. పిరుదు, పెంఉ. నితంబములు the buttocks. పర్వత నితంబప్రదేశము the ridge of a hill, కొండచరియ. **నితంబిని** or **నితంబవతి** *nitambini.* n. A woman with well developed hips, i. e., a beautiful woman, *callipygis.* "నితంబినీమణి" a graceful woman. H. iii. 5.

నితాంతము *nitāntamu.* [Skt.] adv. Extremely, greatly. పెల్ల. అధికము.

నిత్యము *nityamu.* [Skt.] adv. Always, continually, constantly. ఎల్లప్పుడు. adj. Constant, perpetual, permanent. Everlasting, eternal, universal, omnipresent. Regular, fixed, natural, invariable, usual, daily, ordinary, unchanging. Perennial, flowering all through the year, ఎడతెగని. నిత్యమల్లిచెట్టు or నిత్తెమల్లె a species of jasmine. నిత్యహోమము a daily sacrifice, as distinguished from నైమిత్తికము an occasional one. నిత్యకర్మము daily rites. **నిత్యుడు** *nityuḍu.* n. The everlasting one, i. e., God.

నిదర్శనము *ni-darṣanamu.* [Skt.] n. An illustration, example, instance; evidence, proof. దృష్టాంతము.

నిదాఘము *nidāghamu.* [Skt.] n. Summer, hot weather. వేసంగికాలము. Heat, వేడిమి. Sweat, చెమట.

నిదానము *nidānamu.* [Skt.] n. The original cause, origin, source. ఆదికారణము. **నిదానము** [Tel.] n. Steadiness, patience, gentleness, ఆత్రపడక విచారించుట. నిదానముగా మాట్లాడు speak gently. నిదానములేని మాట an uncertainty, a matter about which we are in doubt. పొద్దునిదానము the exact time. **నిదానస్థుడు** *nidāna-sthuḍu.* n. A correct, prudent, thoughtful or patient man. **నిదానించు** *nidānintsu.* v. n. To pause, to deliberate or ponder. ఆత్రపడక విచారించు. **నిదానముగా** *nidānamu-gā.* adv. Steadily, soberly.

నిదుర, నిద్దుర or **నిద్ర** *nidura.* [Tel.] n. Sleep. **నిదురపోతు** or **నిద్దురపోతు** *nidura-pōtu.* n. A drowsy person, నిద్రపోవు స్వభావముగలవాడు. **నిదురించు** or **నిదురపోవు** *nidurintsu.* v. n. To sleep. నిద్రించు.

నిదేశము or **నిర్దేశము** *nideṣamu.* [Skt.] n. An order, command, direction, instruction. సెలవు, చెప్పుట. నిదేష్ట one who gives an order.

నిద్దము or **నిద్దా** *niddamu.* [from Skt. స్నిగ్ధము.] adj. Bright, smooth, polished. నునుపుగల. Loving, dear, స్నేహముగల. **నిద్దావంకి** *niddā-vanki.* n. A dagger, బాకు. S. iii. 109.

నిద్ర *nidra.* [Skt.] n. Sleep. **నిద్రపుచ్చు** *nidra-putstsu.* v. t. To put to sleep, as an infant. జ్ఞాననిద్ర a mesmeric trance. **నిద్రమబ్బు** or **నిద్రమత్తు** *nidra-mabbu.* n. Drowsiness. **నిద్రలేపు** *nidra-lēpu* v. a. To awake from sleep. **నిద్రాణము** *nidrāṇamu.* adj. Sleepy, drowsy. **నిద్రాణుడు** or **నిద్రాళువు** *nidrāṇuḍu.* n. A sleepy fellow, నిద్రపోతు. **నిద్రించు, నిద్రచేయు, నిద్రిలు, నిద్రిల్లు** or **నిద్రపోవు** *nidrintsu.* v. n. To go to sleep, repose. నిద్రింతము let us sleep. M. X. i. 65. **నిద్రితుడు** *nidrituḍu.* n. One who is asleep or reposing.

నిధనము *nidhanamu.* [Skt.] n. Death చావు. Evil, misfortune, చేటు.

నిధానము *nidhānamu.* [Skt.] n. A treasure, a hoard or fund, a treasury. నిక్షేపము. దాచుకొన్నది, పాతర, పాతిపెట్టుకొన్నది.

నిధి *nidhi.* [Skt.] n. A treasure. A repository. పాతర. The poets frequently mention the nine nidhis of Kubera, the god of riches: these are named పద్మ,

మహాపద్మ, శంఖ, మకర, కచ్ఛప, ముకుంద, కుంద, నీల, వర. నిధినిక్షేపము a hidden treasure. గుణనిధి one who is a perfect assemblage of virtues. పరాక్రమనిధి he who is a perfect hero, a mine of valour.

నినదము or **నినాదము** *ninadamu.* [Skt.] n. A sound, note. ధ్వని, మ్రోత.

నినుచు or **నించు** *ninutsu.* [Tel.] v. a. To fill, satisfy, satiate. నిండునట్లు చేయు, తృప్తిపొందించు. M. X. i. 188. **నినుపు** or **నింపు** *ninupu.* n. Filling, fulness, నింపు. **నినుపారు** or **నింపారు** *ninup-āru.* v. n. To become full, to be filled, పూర్ణమగు.

నిన్న *ninna.* [Tel. నిరు+నాడు.] n. Lit: The last day; yesterday. కడచినదినము. నిన్నటిరాత్రి last night. నిన్నటివాడు the man who was here yesterday. వాడు వచ్చినది నిన్ననా మొన్ననా did he come yesterday or the day before?

నిపఠము or **నిపాఠము** *nipaṭhamu.* [Skt.] n. Reading, perusal, study. పాఠము, చదువు.

నిపాతనము *nipātanamu.* [Skt.] n. An overthrow పడద్రోయుట. **నిపాతించు** or **నిపతించు** *nipātintsu.* v. a. To overthrow, పడద్రోయు. **నిపాతము** *ni-pātamu.* n. A fall, పడుట.

నిపాదితము *nipāditamu.* [Skt.] adj. Hidden, sunken, collected, as mud.

నిపానము *nipānamu.* [Skt.] n. A trough or ditch, near a well. నూతిపట్టి నీళ్లతొట్టి, లేక, గాడి.

నిపుణము *nipuṇamu.* [Skt.] adj. Clever, skilful, conversant. Acquired, learnt. **నిపుణత** or **నిపుణత్వము** *nipuṇata.* n. Eminence in any art, skill, mastery. **నిపుణుడు** *nipuṇuḍu.* n. A clever man, నేర్పరి, కుశలుడు. శాస్త్రనిపుణుడు one who is master of a science.

నిప్పచ్చు *nippatstsu.* [Tel. నిరు+పచ్చు.] n. Ruin. నాశము. **నిప్పచ్చరము** *nippatstsa-ramu.* n. Poverty, indigence, దారిద్ర్యము. adj. Penniless, utterly destitute, శూన్యము.

నిప్పటి or **నిప్పట్టు** *nippaṭi.* [Tel. నిప్పు+అట్టు.] n. A sort of cake or biscuit. అడుగులో పెట్టి కాల్చు భక్ష్యము.

నిప్పరలు *nipparalu.* [Tel.] n. A sort of grain.

నిప్పస్తు *nippastu.* [Tel. నిరు+పస్తు.] n. A strict fast. కుపస్త్యోపవాసము.

నిప్పు or **నిప్పుక** *nippu.* [Tel. cf. Tam. నెరుప్పు.] n. Fire. A spark of fire, a live coal. అంగారము, అగ్ని, అగ్నికణము. "పొరిపొరిమింటను నెరాలు నిప్పుకలనంగ గుంపులైరాలె మహీనింద్రగోపతతులు." A. iv. 135. నిప్పుపన్నెగుత్తులకానుగు or అంగారవల్లరి a species of కానుగచెట్టు, commonly called the Flame of the Forest.

నిబంధనము *ni-bandhanamu.* [Skt.] n. A condition, an agreement. ఏర్పాటు. That which is binding on any one, బంధము. adj. Ordered, arranged, కూర్చబడిన. **నిబంధించు** *ni-bhandintsu.* v. t. To bind, to prevent, to restrict, బంధించు, అడ్డగించు. **నిబద్ధము** *ni-baddhamu.* adj. Tied, bound. బంధింపబడిన. Prevented, restricted, అడ్డగింపబడిన.

నిబద్ది, నిబద్ధి or **నిబ్బద్ది** *nibaddi.* [Tel.] n. Truth, certainty, reality. నిజము, సత్యము. వాడు బ్రతుకుట నిబద్దిలేదు it is not certain that he will live. అది నిబద్దికాని true! to be sure, very true, but yet. **నిబద్దించు, నిబద్ధించు** or **నిబద్దిలించు** *nibaddintsu.* v. a. To prove to be true, నిజపరచు. "కలలేదిన్ని నిబద్ధించును చూడకున్న పరితాపించుగా." Radha. i. 25.

నిబర్హణము *nibarhaṇamu.* [Skt.] n. Slaughter, killing. వధము, చంపుట. **నిబర్హితము** *nibarhitamu.* adj. Killed, slain. చంపబడిన.

నిబిడము *nibiḍamu.* [Skt.] adj. Thick, దట్టము. Crowded (as a mob.). Deep, well defined (as a colour); bulky, huge. Gross, thick (as darkness.) నిబిడాంధకారము pitch darkness. **నిబిడీకరించు** *nibiḍī-karinṭsu.* v. n. To become thick, to thicken. దట్టము చేయు. To be crowded. **నిబిడీకృతము** *nibiḍīkṛitamu.* adj. Thronged, crowded, నిబిడముగా చేయబడిన. **నిబిరీసము** *nibirīsamu.* adj. Thick. నిబిడము. Full, plump, big. Crowded, populous. Satyab. iii. 89.

నిబ్బరము *nibbaramu.* [Tel.] adj. Firm, sound, steady, immoveable, hard, plump. నిబ్బరముగానుండినాడు he was firm. n. Firmness. నిశ్చలము. మనసు నిబ్బరముగానుంచుట to restrain the affections, to curb the mind. **నిబ్బరించు** or **నిబ్బరగించు** *nibbarinṭsu.* v. n. To stand firm. నిదానించు. "మదిమబ్బిన నిబ్బరగింపుచుండు." V. P. ii. 316. To excel, అతిశయించు. **నిబ్బరికము** *nibbarikamu.* n. Steadfastness. స్థైర్యము. Favour, kindness. కరుణ. **నిబ్బరికించు** *nibbari-kinṭsu.* v. n. To be kind, to be gracious, కరుణించు. To be elated, ఉప్పొంగు.

నిభము *nibhamu.* [Skt.] n. A pretext. మిషను, సాకు. adj. Equal, సమానము.

నిభాయించు *nibhāyinṭsu.* [Tel.] v. n. & a. To accomplish. To suffer, endure, bear: to manage. భరించు, సహించు.

నిభృతుడు *ni-bhṛituḍu.* [Skt.] n. A firm, steadfast man.

నిమంత్రణము *ni-mantraṇamu.* [Skt.] n. An invitation, bidding guests to the annual ceremony of making offerings to the manes of deceased ancestors. **నిమంత్రించు** *ni-mantrinṭsu.* v. a. To invite, to invite guests to a feast at an annual ceremony held in honor of departed ancestors. **నిమంత్రితుడు** *nimantrituḍu.* n. One who is so invited, నిమంత్రింపబడినవాడు.

నిమజ్జనము *ni-majjanamu.* [Skt.] adj. Sinking, plunging, bathing: a bath. స్నానము, మజ్జనము.

నిమటాయి *nimaṭāyi.* [Tel.] n. The name of a certain creeper. ఒకవిధమైన తీగె.

నిమయము *nimayamu.* [Skt.] n. An exchange (of things.) వస్తువులమార్పు.

నిమితము *nimitamu.* [Skt.] n. An engagement, settling. నియమనము, ఏర్పాటు. **నిమితకాడు** *nimita-kāḍu.* n. One who is engaged to carry a burden or load, బరువుమోసే పనివాడు.

నిమిత్తము *nimittamu.* [Skt.] n. A cause, reason, motive, mark, sign, token, omen. హేతువు, చిహ్నము, గురి, శకునము. దుర్నిమిత్తము a bad omen. As an affix: Respecting, regarding, on account of, because of. అందునిమిత్తము for that reason, therefore. ఉప్పునిమిత్తము పోయినది she is gone for salt. ఆ ఆస్తికిని నాకును నిమిత్తము లేకుండా చేసినారు they cut me off from the estate. దీన్ని అడగడమునకు నీకేమి నిమిత్తము what business have you to ask this? అతని దర్శననిమిత్తమై పోతిని I went to visit him. నిమిత్తముమాలినపని an unreasonable act. నిమిత్తముమాలినమాట a groundless assertion. నానిమిత్తమై నీవు కొంచెము ప్రయాసపడవలెను you must take a little trouble for me, or on my account.

నిమిషము *nimishamu.* [Skt.] n. A twinkling of the eye, an instant, a moment. రెప్పపాటు, రెప్పపాటుకాలము. నిమిషకవి a ready wit, an extempore poet.

నిమీలనము *nimīlanamu.* [Skt.] n. The act of closing the eyes. కన్నుమూయుట. అర్ధనిమీలితనేత్రములు half closed eyes.

నిముకళ *nimukaḷa.* [Tel. నిమురు+కళ్లము.] n. Gleanings of grain found at a threshing-floor. కైలుచేసిన కళ్లమందలి అడుగు ధాన్యము. Remainder, కొరత.

నిముకు or **నెముకు** *nimuku.* [Tel.] v. a. To search for. To suck. స్తనపానముచేయు.

"...గానిచన్ను,
నిముకె నేనిచిన్ని నెత్తురునందు."
HD. ii. 2387.

నిమురు *nimuru*. [Tel.] v. a. To stroke, to fondle, తడవు, తలలోతడవు, బుజ్జగించు. నెమ్మదిగా పొలుపొందు. R. iv. 44.

నిముసము *nimusamu*. [from Skt. నిమిషము.] n. A moment, an instant. **నిమేషము** *nimēshamu*. [another form of నిమిషము.] n. Twinkling. రెప్పపాటు.

నిమ్నము *nimnamu*. [Skt.] adj. Deep, profound. లోతు, గభీరము. నిమ్నలిఖిత under written. **నిమ్నగ** *nimna-ga*. n. lit: "deep flowing." A stream. నది, ఏరు. **నిమ్నోన్నతము** *nimn-ōnnatamu*. adj. Uneven, high and low, up and down.

నిమ్మ *nimma*. [Tel.] adj. Appertaining to the lime tree. నిమ్మకాయ or నిమ్మపండు a lime. నిమ్మచెట్టు the lime tree. అడవినిమ్మ the wild lime. *Atalantia monophylla*. **నిమ్మతులసి** *nimma-tulasi*. n. A species of the Basil which has a scent resembling the lime. **నిమ్మగడ్డి** or **నిమ్మగడ్డి** *nimma-gaddi*. n. Lemon grass. *Andropogon citratus*, (Watts.)

నిమ్మళము *nimmalamu*. [Tel.] n. Ease, comfort, quiet, patience, gentleness. శాంతము. adj. Easy, quiet, happy, well. విశ్రాంతము, స్వస్థము. నిమ్మళముగానున్నాడు he is well in health. నిమ్మళముగానున్నది it is well, proper, right. **నిమ్మళముగా** or **నిమ్మళముగాను** *nimmalamu-ga*. adv. Well, by degrees, gradually, gently. నిమ్మళముగా చేయుము do it at your leisure, do it slowly. **నిమ్మళించు** *nimmalintsu*. v. n. To be at ease, to be quiet or patient. విశ్రాంతము. To become better, స్వస్థము. To rest one-self. వానికి ఇప్పుడు నిమ్మళించినది he is better now.

నియంత *niyanta*. [Skt.] n. A charioteer, తేరు నడుపువాడు, సారథి. A guide, a leader, నడుపువాడు. A ruler, lord, husband. వాణీ నియంత, i.e., Brahma, spouse of Saraswati.

నియతము *niyatamu*. [Skt.] adj. Self-governed, subdued, restrained, నియమము గల. Constant, permanent, certain, నిశ్చయమైన. **నియతముగా** *niyatamu-ga*. adv. Always, constantly. **నియతి** *niyati*. n. Destiny, luck, good or bad fortune, భాగ్యము. A religious duty or obligation, నియమము. **నియతేంద్రియుడు** *niyat-ēndriyudu*. n. A sage or man of subdued passions.

నియమము *niyamamu*. [Skt.] n. A principle, rule, precept. An engagement. "The restriction of a rule to particular cases." (*Colebr.*) That which is invariable. An religious observance. Certainty. The inevitable result of an act. Taking pains. నిర్బంధబుద్ధి, ప్రతిజ్ఞ, ఏర్పాటు, కట్టు. నియమముగా fixedly, statedly. **నియమించు** *niyamintsu*. v. a. To appoint, direct, order, ఆజ్ఞాపించు. **నియమించుకొను** *niyamintsu-konu*. v. a. To agree on, contract for, engage for, determine, decree, undertake. **నియమితము** *niyamitamu*. adj. Commanded, ordered, నియమింపబడిన. **నియామకము** *niyāmakamu*. n. Certainty, an arrangement. **నియామకుడు** *niyāmakudu*. n. A director, a pilot or steers-man. నియమింపువాడు.

నియుతము *niyutamu*. [Skt.] n. A host, or vast number: diversely interpreted as one lac, ten lacs, and one hundred lacs. సంఖ్యావిశేషము.

నియుద్ధము *ni-yuddhamu*. [Skt.] n. A close fight, a hand-to-hand struggle. కల్లబాటు పోటు, బాహుయుద్ధము. **నియోద్ధ** *ni-yōddha*. n. One who fights hand to hand, బాహుయుద్ధము చేయువాడు.

నియోగించు *ni-yōgintsu*. [Skt.] v. a. To engage in a task, send about, employ on, appoint to; to command, to order, ఆజ్ఞాపించు. **నియోగ్యుడు** *ni-yōgyudu*. n. One who is fit to be appointed or sent. నియోగింపదగినవాడు. **నియోక్తుడు**

niyōjyuḍu n. A servant or slave. భృత్యుడు, పనివాడు. నియోగము or నియోగితము *niyōgamu*. n. An order, command, mandate. నియమించుటము, ఆజ్ఞ. L. III. 259. నియోగి or నియోగ్గి *niyōgi*. n. A minister. మంత్రి. The name of a certain sect of secular Brahmins. The Niyōgis and the Vyápáris are two classes of secular Brahmins. The Niyōgis are in several points different from ఆచార్యులు A'cháris. The authors of the Telugu poems are mostly Niyōgis, Sanskrit literature being confined to the Vaidikis who are considered their superiors.

నిర్ *nir*. A Sanskrit particle prefixed to words of that language and implying negation, privation, &c. This prefix varies in accordance with the rules of Sanskrit sandhi. In some cases it becomes నిష్ as నిష్ఫలమైన fruitless. When attached to a word which begins with S, it becomes నిస్, as నిస్సంశయముగా doubtlessly. When it is followed by a vowel, it remains unaltered as నిరాటంకముగా unchecked. The compounds in which this prefix is used are here put together. నిరంకుశము *nir-ankuṣamu*. adj. Unrestrained, free, uncontrolled, resistless. అడ్డములేని. నిరంజనము *nir-anjanamu*. adj. Free, void of passion or emotion, stainless. నిర్మలమైన. నిరంతరము *nir-antaramu*. adj. Continued, continuous, without interval. Interminable, endless. ఎడతెగని, ఎల్లప్పుడు. adv. Always, constantly, frequently, generally. నిరపరాధము *nir-aparādhamu*. adj. Blameless, innocent, harmless. నిరపరాధి or నిరపరాధుడు *nir-aparādhi*. n. One who is innocent. నిరపాయము *nir-apāyamu*. adj. Harmless, అపాయములేని. నిరపేక్షము *nir-apēkshamu*. adj. Undesired, అపేక్షలేని. నిరర్గళము *nir-argaḷamu*. adj. Unobstructed, unrestrained, unimpeded. Resistless. అడ్డములేని. నిరర్థకము *nir-arthakamu*. adj. Vain, fruitless, improfitable, unmeaning. ప్రయోజనములేని. నిరవగ్రహుడు *nir-avagrahuḍu*. n. One who is unimpeded, independent. అడ్డులేనివాడు, స్వతంత్రుడు. నిరవద్యము *nir-avadyamu*. adj. Unobjectionable, unexceptionable. నిర్దోషమైన. Vasu. ii. 99. నిరవధికము *nir-avadhikamu*. adj. Unlimited. మేరలేని. నిరహంకారము *nir-ahankāramu*. n. Humility, modesty. నిరాకరించు *nir-ākarinṭsu*. v. a. To transgress, disobey, disregard, neglect, contemn, తిరస్కరించు. నిరాకారము or నిరాకృతి *nir-ākāramu*. n. Disregard. తిరస్కారము. What is viewless or invisible. The sky, ఆకాశము. adj. Viewless, shapeless, invisible. నిరాకారుడు *nir-ākāruḍu*. n. One who is without form, the Deity. పరమాత్ముడు. నిరాకృతము *nir-ākṛitamu*. adj. Removed, rejected, despised, expelled, disregarded. నిరాక్షేపముగా *nir-ākshēpamu-gā*. adj. Unquestionably, without objection. నిరాఘాటము *nir-āghāṭamu*. adj. Irresistible, మిక్కుటమైన. Easy, unobstructed, without hesitation. నిరాటంకముగా *nir-āṭankamu-gā*. adj. Without scruple or fear, నిర్భయముగా, నిశ్శంకముగా. నిరాదరణ *nir-ādaraṇa*. n. Helplessness. Disregard. నిరాధారము *nir-ādhāramu*. adj. Groundless, helpless. నిరాపనింద *nir-āpa-ninda*. n. Blame, censure, అపనింద. నిరాబారి *nirābāri*. n. A saint, sage. ముని. Nila. i. 29. నిరామయము *nir-āmayamu*. adj. Well, hale, recovered from sickness, free from disease. నిరామయుడు *nir-āmayuḍu*. n. One who is free from disease. నిరాయాసముగా *nir-āyāsamu-gā*. adv. Easily, without difficulty. నిరాయుధహస్తుడు *nir-āyudha-hastuḍu*. adj. Unarmed. నిరాలంబము *nir-ālambamu*. n. Independent, ఆలంబములేని. నిరాశ *nir-āṣa*. n. Despair, despondency. ఆశలేమి. నిరాక్రోశుడు *nir-*

áśrayuḍu. adj. Unprotected, unpatronised, helpless, ఆశ్రయములేని. నిరాసకము *nirasakamu*. adj. Opposing, rejecting, expelling. Antagonistic, as the potency of medicine. n. A specific, or panacea. నిరసించునది. నిరాస్పదము *nir-aspadamu*. adj. Groundless. నిరాహారము *nir-āhāramu*. adj. Fasting. ఆహారములేని. నిరాళుడు *nir-āḷuḍu*. n. One who is unrestrained, ప్రతిబంధకము లేనివాడు. "నిక్కొను తెరువెంగరాని నిర్భయము, నిరాళుండై చెప్పు." L. ii. 210. నిరుద్యోగము *nir-udyōgamu*. n. Unemployedness: the being in a state of idleness. adj. Passive, inert, unengaged, at leisure. నిరుద్యోగి *nir-udyōgi*. n. One who is unemployed. నిరుపద్రవము *nir-upadravamu*. adj. Harmless. ఉపద్రవములేని. నిరుపమానము *nir-upamānamu*. adj. Incomparable, matchless. సాటిలేని. నిరుపహతి *nir-upahati*. adj. Undisturbed, untroubled, unchecked. నిరుపాధి *nir-upādhi*. n. Ease, freedom from pain. నిరుపాధికము *nir-upādhikamu*. adj. Causeless, నిర్హేతుకమైన. నిర్గుణము *nir-guṇamu*. adj. Indescribable, incomprehensible. Devoid of quality or definable attribute. నిర్గుణుడు *nir-guṇuḍu*. n. One (the Deity) who is devoid of properties or qualities. The Indescribable One. నిర్ఘటము *nir-ghaṭamu*. n. A crowded bazaar or shop, బహుజనసమ్మర్దము గల అంగడి. నిర్జనము *nir-janamu*. adj. Devoid of human beings, lonely, private, solitary, జనములేని. నిర్జరుడు *nir-jaruḍu*. n. One who is not subject to decrepitude. An immortal or god. నిర్జరసతి a goddess. నిర్జలము *nir-jalamu*. adj. Waterless, జలములేని. నిర్దయత *nir-dayata*. n. Unkindness, దయలేమి. నిర్దయుడు or నిర్దయాత్ముడు *nir-dayuḍu*. n. An unkind man, దయలేనివాడు. నిర్దోషము *nir-dōshamu*. adj. Faultless, innocent. దోష ములేని. నిర్దోషులు the innocent. నిర్దోషముగా *nir-dōshamu-gā*. adv. Faultlessly, innocently. నిర్దోషత్వము *nir-dōshatvamu*. n. Innocence, faultlessness. నిర్ధనుడు *nir-dhanuḍu* n. One who has no money, a poor man, ధనములేనివాడు. నిర్ధూమధామము *nir-dhūmadhāmamu*. n. Utter destruction: utter ruin and ashes. "మారు తోక్కిపడితేటు నిర్ధూమధామము." Dab. 232. నిర్నిద్రము *nir-nidramu*. adj. Sleepless, awake. నిర్నిమిత్తము *nir-nimittamu*. adj. Needless, causeless. నిర్నీతి *nir-nīti*. n. Immorality. నిర్భయము *nir-bhayamu*. adj. Fearless. నిర్భయముగా fearlessly. నిర్భరము *nir-bharamu*. adj. Unbearable, సహింపరానిది. Much, excessive, great, అధికము. నిర్భాగ్యుడు *nir-bhāgyuḍu*. n. One who is luckless, unlucky, or cursed భాగ్యములేనివాడు, దరిద్రుడు. నిర్భీతి *nir-bhīti*. n. Fearlessness. నిర్మత్సర *nir-matsara*. adj. Tolerant, free from jealousy. నిర్మర్యాద *nir-maryāda*. n. Dishonor, an insult, impudence. నిర్మలము *nir-malamu*. adj. Pure, transparent, clear, clean, free from dirt or impurities. నిర్మలుడు *nir-maluḍu*. n. One who is pure: a good man. నిర్మొగమోటము *nir-moga-mōṭamu*. n. Unkindness. నిర్దాక్షిణ్యము. నిర్ముక్తము *nir-muktamu*. adj. Loosed, set free from, disjoined, sundered, separated. n. A snake that has lately cast its skin. నిర్ముక్తపరిధానయై dropping her petticoat. నిర్ముక్తుడు *nir-muktuḍu*. n. An ascetic, a monk. సన్యాసి. నిర్మోకము *nir-mōkamu*. n. A snake's skin. కుబుసము. నిర్మూలము or నిర్మూలనము *nir-mūlamu*. n. Extirpation, eradication, utter ruin నిర్మూలమైన ruined. నిర్మూలించు *nir-mūlinṭsu*. v. a. To eradicate, నిర్మూలముచేయు.

చేయుటకు పోవున్నట్టు చేయు. To ruin, నాశము చేయు. నిర్లజ్జము nir-lajjamu. adj. Shameless. సిగ్గులేని. నిర్లేపుడు nir-lēpuḍu. n. Devoid of pride. నిరహంకారి. నిర్వంశుడు nir-vamśuḍu. n. One who is childless, barren. నిర్వచనీయము nir-vachanīyamu. adj. Inexpressible, undefinable. నిర్వాతము nir-vātamu. adj. Windless or close, as a place. గాలిలేని(చోటు.) నిర్వికారము nir-vikāramu. adj. Unchanged, unaltered, uniform, changeless, immutable. వికారము లేని. నిర్వికారముగా or నిర్వికారచిత్తుడై steadfastly. నిర్విఘ్నము nir-vighnamu. adj. Unobstructed. విఘ్నములేని. నిర్విణ్ణుడు nir-viṇṇuḍu. adj. Earnest, absorbed, overcome, enrapt, విన్నదినములేని(వాడు.) నిర్వివాదము nir-vivādamu. adj. Undisputed, unquestioned. వాదములేని, నిశ్చయమైన. నిర్విషము nir-vishamu. adj. Venomless, విషములేని. నిర్వైరము without enmity, వైరములేని. నిర్వ్యాజము nir-vyājamu. adj. Without deceit: without obstruction. Honest, కపటములేని. నిర్హేతుకముగా nir-hētukamu-gā. adv. Without cause, causelessly.

నిర్ nir. [Skt.] n. An intensive prefix. Much, మిక్కిలి. Well, బాగుగా. See నిరీక్షించు, నిర్ణయము, నిర్ఘోషము. &c.

నిరతము niratamu. [Skt.] adj. Very eager. మిక్కిలి ఆసక్తిగల. Ever, always. నిరతాన్నదానము daily alms. నిరతి nirati. n. Great eagerness. మిక్కిలి ఆసక్తి. నిరతుడు nira-tuḍu. n. One who is engaged or interested in any thing.

నిరయము nirayamu. [Skt.] n. Hell. నరకము. Adversity, దుర్గతి.

నిరసనము nirasanamu. [Skt.] n. Rejection, denial, contradiction, disallowance. నిరాకరణము, ఆక్షేపము, తిరస్కారము. నిరసించు nirasinṭsu. v. a. To reject, deny, contradict, set aside or disallow. తిరస్కరించు, నిరాకరించు. నిరస్తము nirastamu. adj. Expelled, sent out, thrown out, cast out. Rejected, loosened (as a knot) పోగొట్టబడిన. నిరస్తపాపము sin that is removed.

నిరీక్షించు nir-īkshinṭsu. [Skt.] v. t. To look for, view, watch, long for, hope for, wait for. ఎదురుచూచు. నిరీక్షణ or నిరీక్షణము nir-īkshaṇa. n. Looking for, regarding, seeing, expectation, hope, ఎదురుచూచుట. నిరీక్షితము nir-īkshitamu. adj. Expected, hoped for. ఎదురుచూడబడిన.

నిరు niru. [Tel.] adj. Past. గతించిన. Very, మిక్కిలి. నిరుపేద very poor.

నిరుకడము nirukaḍamu. [Tel.] n. A plant called అపామార్గము, ఉత్తరేణి, ... and also ... and ...

నిరుకళముగా nirukaḷamugā. [from Skt. నిర్గళము.] adj. Without any let or hindrance, easily, నిర్గళముగా.

నిరుకు niruku. [H.] n. Certainty. నిర్ణయము. A price settled upon, నిర్ణయముచేసిన వెల. జీతము నిరుకులేదు there is no fixed salary.

నిరుక్తము nir-uktamu. [Skt.] n. A glossary of obscure phrases used in the Vedas. వేదాంగము. That which is said, చెప్పబడినది. నిరుక్తి nir-ukti. n. The name of a figure of speech, ఒక అలంకారము. Definition of the meaning of a word, అర్థనిర్వచనము.

నిరుక్తికము nir-uktikamu. [Skt.] n. Dumbness. నిరుక్తులు the dumb. ... P. ii. 135.

నిరుడు niruḍu. [Tel. నిరు+ఏడు.] n. Last year. ... నిరుటి of last year. See నిరు.

నిరూఢి ni-rūḍhi. [Skt.] n. A thorough understanding, skill. fluency. Fame, ప్రసిద్ధి. నిరూఢము ni-rūḍhamu. adj. Famous. ప్రసిద్ధికెక్కిన.

నిరూపణము ni-rūpaṇamu. [Skt.] n. Sight, seeing. Investigation, ascertaining, determining. చూపు, అరయిక, తార్కాణ. నిరూపించు ni-rūpintsu. v. a. To ascertain, prove, determine, resolve. నిరూపణచేయు. నిరూపితము ni-rūpitamu. adj. Proved, settled. నిరూపింపబడిన.

నిరూహము nir-ūhamu. [Skt.] n. A completed sentence, a full sentence. ముగిసిన వాక్యము. adj. Not open to a guess, certain, ఊహలేని, నిశ్చయింపబడిన.

నిరృతి nirṛti. [Skt.] n. The demigod supposed to rule the south west quarter of heaven.

నిరోధము nirōdhamu. [Skt.] n. An interdiction, restraint, check, impediment. అడ్డు. Evil చేటు. నిరోధించు nirōdhintsu. v. a. To interdict, to obstruct, to impede. అడ్డగించు.

నిరోష్ఠ్యము nir-ōshṭyamu. [Skt.] adj. Lit: Devoid of labials: a device in versification, wherein the poet discards the letters ప, ఫ, బ, భ, మ.

నిర్గతము nir-gatamu. [Skt.] adj. That which has come out, gone out. బయలువెడలిన. నిర్గతి nir-gati. n. Helplessness, a hard lot. వానికి నిర్గతిగానున్నది he is in misery. నిర్గమము or నిర్గమనము nir-gamamu. n. The act of coming out. బయలువెడలడము. నిర్గమించు nir-gamintsu. v. n. To go out, to come out. వెడలు.

నిర్గలితము nir-galitamu. [Skt.] adj. Loosened. బయటికిజారిన.

నిర్గుండి or వెలినిర్గుండి nirguṇḍi. [Skt.] n. A plant called *Justicia ganderussa*, or *Vitex negundo*. వావిలిచెట్టు.

నిర్ఘాతము nir-ghātamu. [Skt.] n. A gust of wind, a hurricane, a whirlwind, తుపాను. A thunderbolt. పిడుగు.

నిర్ఘోషము nir-ghōshamu. [Skt.] n. A sound, voice. ధ్వని, మ్రోత.

నిర్జించు nir-jintsu. [Skt.] v. n. & a. To conquer, quell. జయించు, గెలుచు. "దనుజ్ఞము చేసిచేసి నిర్జించునగరేశ." Anir. 14. 90.

నిర్ఝరము nir-jharamu. [Skt.] n. A cascade, a waterfall, a torrent. ధార, సెలయేరు. నిర్ఝరిణి nir-jhariṇi. n. A river. నది, ప్రవాహము, ఏరు.

నిర్ణయము nir-ṇayamu. [Skt.] n. Settlement. Certainty, a positive conclusion, a decision. ఏర్పాటు. నిర్ణయమైన nir-ṇayamaina. adj. Stated, definite. నిశ్చయమైన. నిర్ణయముగా nir-ṇayamu-gā. adv. Positively, definitely. నిర్ణయించు nir-ṇayintsu. v. a. To fix, settle, define, specify, resolve, come to an opinion, conclude, decree. ఏర్పాటుచేయు. నిర్ణీతము nir-ṇītamu. adj. Definite, positive. Settled. నిర్ణయింపబడిన. నిర్ణీతి nir-ṇīti. n. Determination, settlement. నిశ్చయము. "వాదాదిశ్రమాదులకెల్ల నిర్ణీతిపుట్టునిశ్చయము." Vasu. iii. 108. నిర్ణేత nir-ṇēta. n. One who settles or decides. నిర్ణయముచేయువాడు.

నిర్ణేజకుడు nir-ṇējakuḍu. [Skt.] n. A washerman. చాకలి. నిర్ణేజనము nir-ṇējanamu. n. Washing, cleansing with water. "హస్తముఖపదనిర్ణేజనాదులెల్లదీర్చి." Balrama vi. 129.

నిర్దగ్ధము nir-dagdhamu. [Skt.] adj. Well burnt. చక్కగాకాలిన.

నిర్దళితము nir-dalitamu. [Skt.] adj. Well cut. చక్కగా ఛేదింపబడిన.

నిర్దహించు nir-dahintsu. [Skt.] v. a. To burn thoroughly. చక్కగాకాల్చు. నిర్దహనము nir-dahanamu. n. A thorough burning. చక్కగా కాల్చడము.

నిర్దారణము nir-dāraṇamu. [Skt.] n. A clean splitting. చక్కగాచీల్చుట. నిర్దారితము nir-dāritamu. adj. Well split. చక్కగాచీల్పబడిన.

నిర్దేశము *nir-dēṣamu.* [Skt.] n. An order or command; an instruction, direction. ఆజ్ఞ. Telling, కథనము, చెప్పుట. Nearness, సామీప్యము, సమీపము. నిర్దేశించు *nir-dēṣintsu.* v.a. To appoint, to command. ఆజ్ఞాపించు. నిర్దిష్టము *nir-dishṭamu.* adj. Commanded, ordered. నిర్దేశింపబడిన. నిర్దేశ్యము *nir-dēṣyamu.* adj. Fit to be ordered or commanded. నిర్దేశింపదగిన. నిర్దేష్ట *nir-dēshṭa.* n. One who gives a command or order. నిర్దేశించువాడు.

నిర్ధారము or నిర్ధారణ *nir-dhāranu.* [Skt.] n. Certainty; ascertainment, determination; a resolution. నిర్ణయము. నిర్ధారణ చేయు or నిర్ధరించు *nir-dhāraṇa-chēyu.* v. a. To determine, or resolve. కాశి. v. నిర్ధారణీయము or నిర్ధార్యము *nir-dhāraṇīyamu.* adj. Fit to be determined or settled. నిర్ధారణచేయదగిన. నిర్ధారితము *nir-dhāritamu.* adj. Settled or determined. నిర్ధారణచేయబడిన. నిర్ధార్యుడు *nir-dhāryuḍu.* n. A man of determination, one who fights his way in spite of difficulties. దుఃఖములు సంభవించిన అటువంటి సమయములో కలిగిన చేసిన కీడులను ప్రాణమైనను నిరసించి ఏదియును చేయువాడు.

నిర్ధూతము *nir-dhūtamu.* [Skt.] adj. Let out, discharged. విడువబడిన.

నిర్బంధము *nir-bandhamu.* [Skt.] n. Force, violence. బలవంతము, బలాత్కారము, కదల మెదలకూడనికట్టు. నన్ను చేవ్రాలు చేయుమని నిర్బంధముచేసినారు they forced me to sign it. నిర్బంధపుకైదు close confinement. నిర్బంధించు, నిర్బంధముచేయు or నిర్బంధపెట్టు *nir-bandhintsu.* v. a. To force, press, to lay violent hands upon. To constrain or oppress: to persist in, or insist on.

నిర్మించు *nirmintsu.* [Skt.] v. a. To create: to erect, build, form, forge; to invent, కల్పించు. నిర్మితము *nirmitamu.* adj. Made, fabricated; artificial. నిర్మాత or నిర్మాతలు *nirmāta.* n. One who makes. చేయువాడు. నిర్మాణము or నిర్మితి *nirmāṇamu.* n. Manufacture, production, creation, invention.

నిర్యత్ *niryat.* [Skt.] adj. Gushing out. S. i. 135.

నిర్యాణము *niryāṇamu.* [Skt.] n. Death, demise. చావు, మరణము, నిర్గమము. నిర్యాణకాలమందు in his last moments.

నిర్యాతనము *niryātanamu.* [Skt.] n. Revenge. పగతీర్చుకొనడము. A gift, దానము. A return of the money held in custody, న్యాసధనార్పణము. Payment of debt, ఋణశుద్ధి.

నిర్యాసము *niryāsamu.* [Skt.] n. Gum exuding from a tree, చెట్టుబంక. An extract, decoction, infusion.

నిర్రనిలుగు *nirra-nilugu.* [Tel. నిలుచు+నిలుగు.] v. n. To throw one's head up. నిక్కినిలుచు. To be proud, గర్వించు. నిర్రనిల్చిన stiff (as a corpse), stiffly set up.

నిర్లీనము *nir-līnamu.* [Skt.] adj. Lost, hidden.

నిర్వచనము *nir-vachanamu.* n. A definition. అర్థనిరూపణముచేసిచెప్పుట. నిర్వచించు *nirvachintsu.* v. a. To define (a term, &c.), నిర్వచనముచేసిచెప్పు.

నిర్వపణము *nirvapaṇamu.* [Skt.] n. A gift.

నిర్వర్ణనము *nir-varṇanamu.* [Skt.] n. Sight, seeing, view, చూడడము.

నిర్వర్తిల్లు *nir-vartillu.* [Skt.] v. n. To be fulfilled. జరుగు. నిర్వర్తించు *nir-vartintsu.* v. a. To achieve, effect, manage, conduct. నిర్వర్తిల్లజేయు.

నిర్వహణము *nir-vahaṇamu.* [Skt.] n. Management, achievement. A vow. నిష్ఠ.

నిర్వహిల్లు *nir-vahillu.* [Skt.] v. n. To be fulfilled. జరుగు. To come to pass, జరుగు.

నిర్వహించు *nir-vahintsu.* v. a. To manage, carry through, perform. To protect, నిర్వహిల్లజేయు. **నిర్వాహము** or **నిర్వాహకము** *nir-vāhamu.* n. Management, power or ability to perform, execute or sustain. జరుగుబాటు, శక్తి. **నిర్వాహకుడు** *nir-vāha-kuḍu.* n. A manager or director; a man of ability. నిర్వహించువాడు. విద్యానిర్వాహకుడు a Director of Learning.

నిర్వాణము *nirvāṇamu.* [Skt.] n. Eternal happiness, ముక్తి, సుఖము. Annihilation, extinction. నాశము. adj. Liberated, extinct, (as a light or fire) చల్లారిన. In Telugu it means Nakedness. నిర్వాణశేషుడు one whose light was put out. **నిర్వాణి** or **నిర్వాణుడు** *nirvāṇi.* n. A beatified soul. ముక్తుడు. ముక్తినొందినవాడు.

నిర్వాదము *nir-vādamu.* [Skt.] n. Censure, blame, imputation. నింద. A decision.

నిర్వృతి *nir-vṛti.* [Skt.] n. Death. చావు. Destruction. నాశము. Happiness. సుఖము.

నిర్వేదము *nir-vēdamu.* [Skt.] n. Humiliation; neglect, disregard; hopelessness. తత్త్వజ్ఞాన దుఃఖాదులచేత కలిగే హేయత్వబుద్ధి, నిరాశ చేసికొనుట. **నిర్వేదించు** or **నిర్వేదపడు** *nir-vēdintsu.* v. n. To renounce, give up, abandon. Vish: ii. 26. నిరాశచేసికొను.

నిలయము *nilayamu.* [Skt.] n. An abode, a dwelling-house or habitation. ఇల్లు.

నిలింపుడు *nilimpuḍu.* [Skt.] n. A deity. వేలుపు. **నిలింపభాష** *nilimpa-bhasha.* n. The language of the gods, i.e., Sanskrit.

నిలు or **నిలునిలు** *nilu.* [Tel.] Stop! Stand! hold!

నిలుగు Same as నిలుచు. (q. v.)

నిల్చు or **నిలుచు** *nilutsu.* [Tel.] v. n. To stand. To remain, exist, last, live, continue. To stay, stop, halt. నిలిచిపోవు. To be still or quiet, as a fluid in a vessel. To be firm or steadfast. To bear, be patient, restrain one's feelings. To be repressed, allayed, slackened. వానిమాట నిలిచినది he kept his word. నిలిచికురియదు it does not rain steadily. ఆ బడి నిలిచిపోయినది the school is now closed. పని నిలిచిపోయినది the work has stopped. M. XII. v. 459. నిలుపాటి or నిలువుపాటి long, పొడుగైన. నిలువబెట్టు to set up, erect. నిలువబెట్టు to set one on his legs. **నిలుచుండు** or **నిల్చుండు** *nilutsu-unḍu.* (నిలిచి+ఉండు.) v. n. To remain standing, to continue to stand. నిలబడియుండు. **నిలుచుకొను** Same as నిలుచుండు. **నిల** used for **నిలువ**. **నిలబడు**, **నిలువబడు** or **నిల్వబడు** *nilu-baḍu.* v. n. To stand. నిలుచుండు. To be stopped, అడ్డుపడు. To be set up, ప్రతిష్ఠితము. **నిలక**, **నిలకడ**, **నిలుకడ** or **నిల్కడ** *nilaka.* n. Standing; steadiness, constancy, firmness. స్థైర్యము. ఈ యేరు నిలక యివ్వదు I cannot keep my footing in the current. కాలునిలకడచేసికొను to gain a firm footing నిలకడయైన ఉద్యోగము permanent (not acting) employment. నిలుకడగానుండే firm. **నిలితము** *nilitamu.* n. Delay; endurance, (Vizag.) **నిలువేడుఎత్తు** or **నిలువుఎత్తు** *niluvedu-y-ettu.* n. A fathom high, lit: one man's stature. **నిలుపు** *nilupu.* v. a. To cause to stand, నిలువబెట్టు. To fix, to set up, to place, to erect, ప్రతిష్ఠించు. To stay, restrain, interrupt, repress, అడ్డగించు. To support, maintain, keep firm, establish, స్థిరపరుచు. To retain, keep back, reserve, నిలిపియుంచు. To set aside, exclude. **నిలుపు** n. Standing, a halt, &c. నిలువుట, ఉండుట. అది నిలుపుగానున్నది it is suspended or in abeyance. నిలుపుచేసినారు they stopped the work, &c. detained (me) &c. **నిలుపు** or **నిల్పు** *nilupu.* adj. That which stops. నిలుపునట. Firm, స్థిరమైన. **నిలుపోపు** *nilup-ōpu.* (నిలుపు+ఓపు.) v. n. To endure, to bear, to put up with, ఓర్చు. సహించు. **నిలుపుదల** *nilupu-dala.* n. Stopping, suspension.

నిలువ or **నిల్వ** *niluva.* n. A remainder, something that is left over. శేషము, నిల్చి యున్న వస్తువు. **నిలువరి** *niluv-ari.* adj. Steadfast. n. A steady man. **నిలువు** *niluvu.* n. Standing. నిలుచుట. Stature, height, ఎత్తు. A fathom or a man's height, మనిషియెత్తు. Form, shape, figure, ఆకృతి. A storey, మిద్దెయంతస్తు. The standing crop. మూడునిలువులనీళ్లు water three fathoms deep. వాని నిలువెల్లావిషము he is a villain from head to foot. నానిలువెల్లదోచుకొన్నారు they fleeced me or stripped me. వానికి నిలువుగుడ్లుపడినవి his eyes are set, he is dying. నిలువాటి, i. e., నిలువుపాటి standing, erected. **నిలువు** adj. Upright, standing. High, tall. నిలువుచెంబు a cup with upright sides, a mug. నిలువుఅంచనా reckoning upon the standing crop. **నిలువుటద్దము** *niluvu-t-addamu.* n. A pier glass, a full length mirror. నిలువుకొలువు or నిలువుసేవకము service in which one has to stand up always and is not allowed to sit. నిలుచుండిచేయు సేవ. నిలువుకాళ్లు stilts. **నిల వరము, నిలువరము** or **నిల్వరము** *niluvaramu.* n. Firmness, steadfastness. The truth, certainty. A deposit, money lodged. adj. True, certain, fixed, firm, stable, sure, స్థిరమైన. **నిలవరించు, నిలువరించు** or **నిల్వరించు** *nilavarintsu.* v. n. To stand firmly. చలింపకనిలుచు. v. a. To cause to stand firmly. చలింపకనిలుపు. To stop, to cause to halt; to support, to manage, to sustain.

నివర్తకము *nivartakamu.* [Skt.] n. Accomplishing, finishing, ending. Deliverance, ముక్తి. In the Yoga Sāstram, the భువిప్రవర్తకుడు is he who still dies and is born over and over again in various bodies: and the భువినివర్తకుడు is he who is delivered from transmigration, and has obtained union with the Deity. BD. vii. 80—90.

నివర్తిలు or **నివర్తిల్లు** *ni-vartilu.* [Skt.] v. n. To turn back. మరలుట. **నివర్తించు** or **నివృత్తించు** *nivartintsu.* v. a. To quit, abandon; to renounce, resign, cease from; to do away with, to quash, నిర్మూలించు. **నివర్తి** or **నివృత్తి** *nivarti.* n. Doing away, removing, abolition. దారిద్ర్యనివృత్తి అగునట్లు so that the poverty might be removed.

నివసించు *ni-vasintsu.* [Skt.] v. n. To dwell, reside, live in. కాపురముచేయు, ఉండు. **నివాసము, నివసతి** or **నివసనము** *ni-vasanamu.* n. A house, dwelling. ఇల్లు. అక్కడ నివాసముయున్నారు they dwelt there. నివాసి a dweller. నివసించువాడు.

నివహము *nivahamu.* [Skt.] n. An assembly society, crowd; a large quantity. సమూహము, గుంపు.

నివాకము *nivākamu.* [Skt.] n. A proclamation. ప్రకటన.

నివాడా *nivāḍā.* [Mahrati.] n. Settlement of accounts with a ryot; settlement, adjustment.

నివాతము *ni-vātamu.* [Skt.] adj. Airless, close, confined. n. A prop. ప్రాపు. నివాతకవచుడు armed in an air-tight panoply.

నివారించు *ni-vārintsu.* [Skt.] v. a. To do away with, cure, avert, dissipate; to put a stop to, dispel, remove, rescue; to appease, satisfy. To prevent ill luck by sprinkling water, &c. To forbid, bar, debar, arrest. నివారణచేయు, అడ్డగించు. **నివారణము** *ni-vāranamu.* n. Prevention. అడ్డగింత. Doing away with, removing, curing, deliverance, termination. **నివారితము** *ni-vāritamu.* adj Hindered, checked, opposed.

నివాళి, నివ్వాళి or **నివాళిక** *nivāḷi.* [Tel.] n. Fumigation, for the sake of good luck. ఆరతి Burning incense. Pal. 126. **నివాళించు** *nivāḷintsu.* v. n. To bless, lustrate or purify by the ceremony of waving a lamp. ఆరతియెత్తు. నివాళి ఇచ్చు to fumigate in order to avert evil

నివీతము *nivītamu*. [Skt.] n. A veil, a mantle, a wrapper. కప్పుకొనేబట్ట, కప్పుకొనే బట్ట. The Brahminical thread, so called when worn round the neck as a necklace, at certain religious rites. చేరు వలె వేసుకొన్న జందెము. దుమాలుగుడ్డను మెడను నివీతముగా వేలాడగట్టి అందులో చెయ్యిగానుండే చేసిని ఉంచుకొన్నాడు he has slung his arm in a handkerchief.

నివీసు *nivīsu*. [H.] n. A letter writer. జవాబు నివీసు one who writes down an answer. ప్రశ్నోత్తరములను వ్రాయువాడు.

నివుడు Same as నిగుడు. (q. v.) **నివుడించు** *nivuḍintsu*. v. a. To stretch, నిగుడించు. "అవయవములెల్లనుకూర్మము నివుడించుచు లోనికిడ చునిశ్చట్టులు." M. XII. v. **నివుడుచు** Same as నిగుడుచు.

నివురు or **నిగురు** *nivuru*. [Tel.] n. Embers. Ashes over coals. నిప్పుపైనుండేకురువు.

నివురు *nivuru*. [Tel.] v. a. To handle, finger, feel, stroke. నిమురు. "కర కిసలయమున రక్తినివురుచునిడి." భా. iv.

నివృత్తి *nivṛtti*. [Skt.] n. Cessation, renunciation, abdication. Removal of an objection or an evil solution. నివారణము.

నివేదించు *ni-vēdintsu*. [Skt.] v. a. To make known. To deliver up, give, offer. సమర్పించు. **నివేదితము** *ni-vēditamu*. adj. Offered as a sacrifice. **నివేద్యము** *ni-vēdyamu*. adj. Fit to be offered as a sacrifice. సమర్పింపదగినది. **నివేదనము** *ni-vēdanamu*. n. An offering, a burnt offering. సమర్పణము. A. vi. 139. The act of making known any thing, ఎరుక.

నివేశము or **నివేశనము** *nivēśamu*. [Skt.] n. A house. ఇల్లు. The site of a house, a spot of ground: a certain measure of land used in Madras, 60 feet by 40 ft. called "one ground." Entrance, ప్రవేశము.

నివ్వచ్చరము or **నివ్వెచ్చరము** *nivvachcha-ramu*. [Tel.] n. Poverty. లేమి.

నివ్వటిల్లు *nivvaṭillu*. [Tel.] v. n. To spread, extend, overflow. వ్యాపించు. To teem, redound, అతిశయించు. To exist or be, కలుగు, ఉండు. To be fulfilled, నెరవేరు, కొనసాగు. **నివ్వటించు** *nivvaṭintsu*. v. a. To prepare, trim, adjust. సిద్ధముచేయు.

నివ్వరి or **నీవరి** *nivvari*. [Tel.] n. Wild corn. నివారము.

నివ్వాళి, నివాళి or **నివ్వాళిక** *nivvāḷi*. [Tel.] n. Fumigation, used as a superstitious rite to avert evil. A wave offering, నీరాజనము plu. నివ్వాళ్లు. **నివ్వాళిపళ్లెము** *nivvāḷi-paḷḷemu*. n. A censer for a wave offering.

నివ్వెర or **నివ్వెరగు** *niv-vera*. [Tel. నిండు+వెర.] n. Great fear. మిక్కిలిభయము. Amazement, surprise. Great surprise or alarm. పారవశ్యము, నిశ్చేష్టత, భ్రాంతి. **నివ్వెరగందు** or **నివ్వెరపడు** *niv-verag-andu*. v. n. To be greatly astonished. To be greatly afraid, మిక్కిలిభయపడు. **నివ్వెరపాటు** *niv-vera-pāṭu*. n. Astonishment.

నిశ్ *niś*. [Skt.] A negative prefix, altered from నిస్ (q. v.) in accordance with the rules of Sandhi. **నిశ్చలము** *niś-chalamu*. adj. Fixed, immovable, firm. **నిశ్చింతుడు** *niś-chintuḍu*. n. A man without care. చింతలేనివాడు. **నిశ్చేతనము** *niś-chētanamu*. adj. Motionless, inanimate. **నిశ్చేష్టుడు** *niś-chēshṭuḍu*. n. One who cannot move. చేష్టలు ఉడిగినవాడు. **నిశ్శబ్దము** *niś-śabdamu*. n. Silence. adj. Silent, mute. నిశ్శబ్దముగా నుండు to be silent or speechless. **నిశ్శేషము** *niś-śēshamu*. adj. Without a remainder, total, entire, thorough, complete, సర్వము, అంతయును. **నిశ్శేషముగా** *niś-śēshamu-gā*. adv. Wholly, utterly, completely.

నిశ *niśa*. [Skt.] n. Night. రాత్రి. Turmeric. పసుపు. A. iv. 155. **నిశాకరుడు** *niśā-karuḍu*. n. Lit: The night maker, i. e., the moon. **నిశాచరుడు** or **నిశాటుడు** *niśā-*

charudu. n. A night rover, i. e., a goblin, fiend, demon. నిశాటి or నిశాచరి *nisati*. n. A female fiend, an ogress. నిశాదర్శి *nisa-darsi*. n. Lit. That which sees by night, i. e., an owl. నిశాపతి *nisa-pati*. n. The lord of night, i. e., Adonis, the regent of the moon. నిశామణి *nisa-mani*. n. Lit: the gem of the night, i. e., the moon. A fire fly. నిశి *nisi* Night. నిశిరాత్రివేళ *nisi-ratri-vela*. n. The dead of night.

నిశాంతము *nisantamu*. [Skt.] n. A house. ఇల్లు. The dawn of day, ప్రభాతము, వేకువ. శయనిశాంతము a bed room. A. vi. 159.

నిశాతము or నిశితము *nisatamu*. [Skt.] adj. Much sharpened. మిక్కిలివాడిచేయబడిన. Sharp, whetted. Clever, keen. నిశితత్వము *nisitatvamu*. n. Keenness, sharpness.

నిశాని *nisani*. [H.] n. A mark, a sign. గురుతు.

నిశీథము or నిశీథిని *nisithamu*. [Skt.] n. Night, midnight. రాత్రి, నడిరేయి. A. vi. 30.

నిశ్చయము *nischayamu*. [Skt.] n. Certainty, reality. Resolution, determination. నిర్ణయము. adj. Real, intrinsic, actual, true, certain. మరణము నిశ్చయము death is inevitable. నిశ్చయించు *nischayintsu*. v. n. To be determined, settled. v. a. To determine, settle, resolve. నిర్ణయించు. నిశ్చయించుకొను *nischayintsukonu*. v. a. To determine for oneself, to come to a conclusion. నిశ్చితము *nischitamu*. adj. Ascertained, settled. నిశ్చయింపబడిన. నిశ్చితాత్ముడు *nischit-atmudu*. n. One who is steadfast in heart. నిశ్చయింపబడిన మనస్సు గలవాడు. నిశ్చితార్థము *nischit-arthamu*. n. Resolution, determination. The formal demanding of a bride: a settlement, a betrothal.

నిశ్రేణి *nisreni*. [Skt.] n. A ladder. నిచ్చెన.

నిశ్వసించు or నిశ్వాసించు *nisvasintsu*. [Skt.] v. n. To draw in the breath, to sigh. నిట్టూర్పువిడుచు. నిశ్వసనము *nisvasanamu*. n. Sighing, నిట్టూర్పుట. నిశ్వాసము *nisvasamu*. n. A drawing in of the breath, a sigh, నిట్టూర్పు.

నిశ్శ్రేయసము *nis-sreyasamu*. [Skt.] n. Final deliverance, beatitude, మోక్షము. Padma. v. 179.

నిష్ *nish*. [Skt. another form of నిర్ q. v.] A particle of negation. నిష్కపటము *nish-kapatamu*. adj. Without cunning or pretence, sincere, simple. కపటములేని. నిష్కల్మషము *nish-kalmashamu*. adj. Pure, free from evil. నిష్కళంకము *nish-kalankamu*. adv. Spotless, stainless; clear, perspicuous, decisive, unquestionable, కళంకములేని, డాగులేని. నిష్కలుడు *nish-kaludu*. n. One who is devoid of qualities: that is, a divine or holy being. నిష్కాంచనము *nish-kanchanamu*. n. Poverty. The being "without a penny," or penniless. నిష్కాముడు *nish-kamudu*. n. One who is "without any desires," i. e., without hope. నిష్కారణము *nish-karanamu*. adj. Causeless, unreasonable. నిష్కారణముగా *nish-karanamu-ga*. adv. Causelessly. నిష్ఖలుడు *nish-khaludu*. n. One who is sinless or harmless. నిష్ప్రయోజనము *nish-prayojanamu*. adj. Useless. ప్రయోజనములేని. నిష్ఫలము *nish-phalamu*. adj. Fruitless, vain. ఫలములేని.

నిషంగము *nishangamu*. [Skt.] n. A quiver. అమ్ములపొది. A. ii. 17. నిషంగి *nishangi*. n. A bowman.

నిషణ్ణము *nishannamu*. [Skt.] adj. Residing, staying, being. ఉండిన. Sitting, seated. కూర్చుండిన. "ఈడనిషణ్ణుడై" Swa. iii.

నిషధదేశము *nishadha-desamu*. [Skt.] n. The Nishadha country. (It does not appear exactly where this country, so often mentioned in poems, was situated. W. in Vish. p. 190.)

నిషా nishā. [H.] n. Intoxication. మత్తు, మైకము.

నిషాదము or నిషదము nishādamu. [Skt.] n. The first of the seven musical notes.

నిషాదుడు nishādudu. [Skt.] n. The name of a certain aboriginal tribe; a mountaineer, a huntsman, a savage, చెంచువాడు, యానాదివాడు.

నిషిందా nishindā. [H.] n. Writing with flourishes.

నిషిద్ధము nishiddhamu. [Skt.] adj. Prohibited, forbidden. నిషేధింపబడిన.

నిషేకము nishēkamu. [Skt.] n. Sprinkling, aspersion, effusion. W. Consummation of marriage. గర్భాధానము. నిషేకముహూర్తము the same.

నిషేధము nishēdhamu. [Skt.] n. Prohibition, stoppage, contrariety to rule, irregularity. adj. Prohibitory, forbidding. నిషేధార్థము nishēdh-arthamu. n. The negative tense, in verbs. నిషేధించు nishēdintsu. v. a. To prohibit, forbid.

నిషేవణము nishēvaṇamu. [Skt.] n. Service, observance, practice, adhering to rule. సేవించడము.

నిష్కము nishkamu. [Skt.] n. A certain gold coin. మాడ. A gold jewel: a weight, used by goldsmiths. W. Vish. 579. ఇరువది చిన్నముల యెత్తు బంగారుమెట్రిక.

నిష్కర్ష nish-karsha. [Skt.] n. Determination, decision. నిశ్చయము. నిష్కర్షించు nish-karshintsu. v. a. To determine, resolve, settle. నిశ్చయించు.

నిష్కుటము nish-kuṭamu. [Skt.] n. A park. గృహారామము, ఇంటితోట.

నిష్కుహము or నిష్కూహము nish-kuhamu. [Skt.] n. The hollow of a tree. కోటరము, తొర్ర.

నిష్కృతి nish-kṛiti. [Skt.] n. Expiation, atonement. ప్రాయశ్చిత్తము. An omission, చేయుమి.

నిష్క్రమము nish-kramamu. [Skt.] n. Going out. వెడలిపోవుట.

నిష్ఠ nishṭha. [Skt.] n. Fixed affection or attention; devotedness or engagedness of heart. Devotion, austerity in religion, firmness. ఏకనిష్ఠగా చదివినాడు he read with undivided attention. నిష్ఠించు nishṭhintsu. v. t. To determine, resolve, స్థిరపరుచు. M. xv. ii. 86. నిష్ఠుడు nishṭhudu. n. One who is firm or steadfast. వాడు దేవుని నిష్ఠుడై యున్నాడు he is devoutly bent.

నిష్ఠీవనము nishṭhī-vanamu. [Skt.] n. Spitting out. ఉమియుట. Rejecting. M. iv. i. 131.

నిష్ఠురము nishṭhuramu. [Skt.] adj. Hard, harsh, cruel, taunting, rude. కఠినమైన, పరుషమైన. n. Rudeness, harshness. A taunt or reproach. నిజముచెప్పితే నిష్ఠురము the truth is harsh or hard to hear. ఎందుకునిష్ఠురము why incur a reproach? నిష్ఠురత్వము nishṭhu-ratvamu. n. Hardness, cruelty.

నిష్ఠ్యూతము or నిష్ఠూతము nishṭhyūtamu. [Skt.] adj. Cast, thrown, sent, vomited. క్రక్కబడిన, వెడలగ్రక్కబడిన.

నిష్ణాతుడు nishṇātudu. [Skt.] n. One who is skilful or learned. నేర్పరి.

నిష్పందము nish-pandamu. [Skt.] adj. Unmoving, stable, still. నిశ్చలము.

నిష్పత్తి or నిష్పాదనము nish-patti. [Skt.] n. Completion, termination. పరిసమాప్తి. Birth, production. సిద్ధి. నిష్పన్నము nish-pannamu. adj. Complete, done. Natural, born, inborn. సిద్ధించిన. నిష్పాదించు nish-pādintsu. v. a. To cause to be completed. సిద్ధింపజేయు. నిష్పాదితము nish-pāditamu. adj. Completed. సిద్ధించిన.

నిష్పావము nish-pāvamu. [Skt.] n. The grain called అనుములు. Jaimini. iv. 102.

నిష్పేషితము nish-pēshitamu. [Skt.] adj. Reduced to powder. నుగ్గుగానూరిన. Thoroughly sifted or investigated.

నిస్ nis. [Skt. a form of నిర్.] A negative prefix like un or in. నిస్త్రాణ nis-trāna. n. Weakness. నిస్పృహము nis-prihamu. adj. Hopeless. ఆశలేని. నిస్పృహత్వము nis-prihatvamu. n. The being without any wish or hope. Indifference, listlessness. Philosophy. నిస్పృహుడు nis-prihudu. n. A philosopher, a calm observer, a man of an equable mind unaffected by ordinary events. adj. Indifferent or listless. నిస్సంగుడు nis-sangudu. n. One who has quitted his family. A recluse, hermit. నిస్సంతు nis-santu. adj. Without children or offspring, without an heir. సంతానములేని. అతనివంశము నిస్సంతు అయిపోయినది his family is without a representative, is extinct. నిస్సందేహము or నిస్సంశయము nis-sandēhamu. adj. Undoubted. n. The absence of doubt. నిస్సత్తువ nis-sattuva. n. Weakness, a want of nerve, debility. Poorness of soil. అశక్తి, బలహీనత. నిస్తంత్రము nis-tantramu. adj. Easy, deliberate. నిస్తంద్రము nis-tandramu. adj. Unwearied, indefatigable. నిస్తరించు nis-tarintsu. v. a. To cross safely. చక్కగాదాటు. To succeed, get through, be delivered. కడతేరు. నిస్తరణము or నిస్తారము nis-taranamu. n. Crossing. దాటుట. నిస్తారకుడు nis-tārakudu. n. A deliverer, redeemer. కడతేర్చువాడు. నిస్సరణము nis-saranamu. n. An entrance. ఇల్లులోనికిపోవు ముందటిద్వారము. Exit, going out. వెడలిపోవుట. నిస్సారము nis-sāramu. adj. Sapless, pithless, dry, exhausted. సారములేని. నిస్సారముచేయు to exhaust. ఈ నిస్సారపు సంసారము in this worthless world.

నిసబు nisabu. [H.] n. Principal; property, a stated estimate or valuation. నిసబుజాబితా a list of the property; a statement of value.

నిసర్గము nisargamu. [Skt.] n. Nature, a natural state. A peculiar character or condition.

నిసి nisi. [from Skt. నిశి.] n. Night. రాత్రి.

నిసుగు or నిసువు nisugu. [Tel.] n. A young one, a child, an infant. శిశువు. నిసువుతనము nisuvu-tanamu. n. Infancy.

నిస్తలము nis-talamu. [Skt.] adj. Moving. కదలునట్టి. Round, వట్రువైన. నిస్తలుడు nis-taludu. n. One who is unequalled or unrivalled.

నిస్త్రింశము nis-trimsamu. [Skt.] n. A weapon, sword. కత్తి. adj. Cruel, కనికరము లేని.

నిస్వనము or నిస్వానము ni-svanamu. [Skt.] n. A tone, note, musical sound. ధ్వని. మ్రోత.

నిస్సాణము, నిస్సానము or నిస్సాహణము nis-sānamu. [Skt.] n. A large double drum.

నిహతము ni-hatamu. [Skt.] adj. Killed. చంపబడిన. నిహతుడు ni-hatudu. n. One who is smitten, struck or killed. నిహతునిగావించు to slay, destroy. నిహతి ni-hati n. Death. చావు. నిహంత ni-hanta. n. A slayer, చంపువాడు.

నిహితము ni-hitamu. [Skt.] adj. Entrusted, deposited, given in charge. ఉంచబడిన.

నిహ్నవించు nihnavintsu. [Skt.] v. a. To conceal, hide. మరుగుపుచ్చు. నిహ్నవము nihnavamu. n. Disbelief. అపనమ్మిక. Cunning, కపటము. Concealment, దాపరికము. A confidential hint, మరుగుమాట.

నీ nī

నీ nī. [Tel. the root of నీవు.] pron. Thou. "నీ చెప్పిన మెయి మాడెద" M. VIII. ii. 417. "నీపోవు తెరువున" M. v. ii. 286. నీ nī. the infl. of నీవు. adj. Thy. "తెలిసి నీలో మాహింపుము" Consider in your heart. M. v. ii. 103. నీది nīdi. adj. Thine. ఇది నీదా is this thine? నీదు nīdu. adj Thy. నీదు నామము thy name.

నికాశము *nikâsamu.* [Skt.] n. Brightness. ప్రకాశము. Certainty, నిశ్చయము. adj. Equal, తుల్యము.

నిగ. *niga.* [Tel.] n. A certain game among boys. H. iii. 187.

నిగు *nigu.* [Tel.] v. a. To get rid of. నివర్తించు. "ఒక్కతపస్వియొక్క ప్రతిరాజేయాజేదే తక్కి పట్టుపుట్టిన్న గద." టీ॥ పుట్టుపుట్ట, నిగడిక, అనగా యీ రాకుసజన్మము పోగొట్టుకొనెదను. A. vi. 65. "వంతిమునంబులోబారదు నావకనిగద నేడునిక్కుపణ." Parij. ii. 94.

నీచము *nichamu.* [Skt.] adj. Low, base. **నీచత** or **నీచత్వము** *nichata.* n. Lowness, baseness, degradation. **నీచుడు** *nichudu.* n. A wretch, a vile creature, a low scoundrel, అధముడు.

నీచు *nitsu.* [Tel.] n. Savour, stench, a fishy smell. Fleshmeat. నీచునీళ్లు soup, meat broth. నీచుకుండ a flesh pot. నీచుకంపు a stench.

నీటు *nitu.* [Tel.] n. Prettiness, elegance, beauty, శృంగారగర్వము, మురిపెము. adj. Fine, pretty, nice, charming. **నీటుకాడు** *nitu-kadu.* n. A fop, a beau. శృంగారపురుషుడు. **నీటుకత్తె** *nitu-katte.* n. A belle. **నీటుగా** *nitu-ga.* adv. Prettily, nicely, finely. **నీటుతనము** *nitu-tanamu.* n. Prettiness, niceness. **నీటువరచు** *nitu-paratsu.* v. a. To adorn, make fine or pretty.

నీడ *nida.* [Tel.] n. Shade, shadow. ఛాయ, ఎండలేమి. An image or reflection in a mirror. కాంతి. వాడోడునీడ he was my very shadow, my constant companion.

నీడము *nidamu.* [Skt.] n. A nest. పక్షిగూడు. P. I. 544. **నీడోద్భవము** *nid-od-bhavamu.* n. A bird, గూటిలోపుట్టినది.

నీడు *nidu.* [Tel. another form of నాయుడు.] n. A title added to the names of men of the Kamma caste: as అంకినీడు, సామినీడు, అప్పినీడు, &c.

నీతము or **నీతకము** *nitamu.* [from Skt. నియతము.] n. A vow, an order. నియమము. Talk, chatter, words, మాటలు. [Skt.] adj. Brought, obtained, తేబడిన, పొందింపబడిన. Trained, punished, శిక్షింపబడిన. "వినుతా యటువంటి నీతములజేకొంబల్" T. iii. 93. "ఓ బాలా బాలాపురుషాతుడెంతటి గృహస్థా నీతముల్ పల్కె." T. iv. 214.

నీతి *niti.* [Skt.] n. Justice, right, morality, righteousness. న్యాయము. Policy, morals, philosophy, good sense. Conduct. దుర్నీతి immorality. ఇదినీతియా is this right? **నీతి శాస్త్రము** Ethics. **నీతిచెప్పు** to advise, counsel. నీతిమాలినవాడు a bad man. **నీతిపరుడు** *niti-parudu.* n. A moral man. **నీతిహీనుడు** *niti-hinudu.* n. A fool, an immoral person.

నీపము *nipamu.* [Skt.] n. A tree called *Nauclea cadamba,* కడిమిచెట్టు, కుంకుల కడిమి, కదంబవృక్షము.

నీయంచె *niyantsa.* [Tel.] n. The stalk on which an ear of corn grows. కంకివాడి.

నీరంధ్రము *ni-randhramu.* [Skt.] adj. Having no holes. సందులేని. Thickset. నీరంధ్రపువెన్నెల bright moonshine. ఆకాశము నీరంధ్రమయ్యె the sky was thick (with flying darts.)

నీరము *niramu* [borrowed by Skt. from Drav. నీరు.] n. Water. **నీరజము** *nirajamu.* n. "Lit. Water-born," నీటిలోపుట్టిన, i.e., a lotus. తామర. **నీరదము** *niradamu.* n. A cloud. నీరదాలక dark tressed, having bright black tresses. **నీరధి** *nira-dhi.* n. The sea. సముద్రము.

నీరసము *ni-rasamu.* [Skt.] n. Weakness. adj. Weak, pithless, strengthless, poor, రసములేని. **నీరసుడు** *ni-rasudu.* n. A weak man. A pauper. బీదవాడు.

నీరాజనము *nirajanamu.* [Skt.] n. Fumigation; waving a lamp, or burning camphor, &c., before an idol in homage or over a person, as a spell to avert an evil eye. ఆరతి, మంగళహారతి, దిష్టి.

నీరిజ *nīridza.* [Tel.] n. The name of a certain forest tree. Rox. i. 646.

నీరు *nīru.* [Tel. cf. Tam. తణ్ణీర్.] n. Water. ఉదకము. Fluid. టెంకాయనీరు cocoanut water. Bad humors in the body. ఒళ్లు నీరుపట్టినది the body is bloated. Urine. మూత్రము. కొత్తనీరు freshes in a river or rain water. కన్నీరు a tear. plu: నీళ్లు water. కంట నీళ్లుపెట్టుకొన్నది she shed tears. మంచినీళ్లు తాగినట్టుగా coolly, as easily as if drinking water. నీరగుట to melt away, perish, turn to water. బంగారునీరు gilding, gold water. బంగారునీరుపోయు to gild, to dissolve gold. **నీటికానుపు** or **నీటిచూలి** *nīṭi-kānupu.* n. Lit. Water born, i.e., Fire, అగ్ని. నీటిమన్ను, నీరుపుప్పు. నీటి రాశి, నీరువాము or నీర్వాము *nīṭi-kuppa.* n. The sea. సముద్రము. **నీటితాత** *nīṭi-tāta.* n. The wind. వాయువు. **నీటిదయ్యము** *nīṭi-dayyamu.* n. A water-sprite. జలగ్రహము. **నీటిపుట్టుగు, నీరుపుట్టుగు** or **నీరుపుట్టువ** *nīṭi-puṭṭugu.* n. A lotus. **నీటియిక్క** *nīṭi-yikka.* n. A jewel worn on the breast of Vishṇu. కౌస్తుభము. **నీటిరిక్క** *nīṭi-rikka.* n. The constellation called పూర్వాషాఢ నక్షత్రము. **నీటిరేడు** or **నీటిరాయుడు** *nīṭi-rēḍu.* n. Varuna, the god of the Ocean. **నీటిరేనిరిక్క** *nīṭi-rēni-rikka.* n. The constellation called శతభిషం. **నీరాకు** *nīrāku.* (నీరు+ఆకు.) n. Moss, water-weeds. పాచి. **నీరాట** or **నీరాటము** *nīr-āṭa.* (నీరు+ఆట.) n. Bathing, a bath. స్నానము. Sporting in water, జలక్రీడ. **నీరాడు** *nīr-āḍu.* v. n. To bathe. స్నానముచేయు, స్రుంకు. n. Hot water poured on a curry while being cooked, కూరాటిలోపోయు వేణ్ణీళ్లు. **నీరామని** *nīr-āmani.* (నీరు+ఆమని.) n. The rainy season. వర్షఋతువు. **నీరాడుచు** or **నీరాడ్చు** *nīr-āḍutsu.* v. a. To cause to bathe స్నానముచేయించు. To create a friendship between, స్నేహము చేయించు. **నీరాటము** *nīrāṭamu.* n. Bathing, స్నానము. "కొయుచేసి స్నానమాచర్ణకరంతో, నీరాటమొనర్చియు శృంగారించి" Bilh. iii. 203. An aquatic animal.

> "క. నీరాటవనాటములు,
> పోరాటంబెట్లుగలిగె పురుషోత్తముచే,
> నారాటమెట్లుమానెను,
> ఘోరాటవిలోన ద్విరదకుంజరముకును."
> B. VIII. 110.

నీరుకట్టు or నీరుపెట్టు to water, to irrigate. నీటికాలువ a watercourse. **నీరావు** *nīr-āvu.* n. The "water cow," i.e., the boat-fly, an aquatic insect called *notonecta.* **నీరుకట్టు** or **నీరుకట్టు** *nīru-kaṭṭu.* n. Ischuria, a stoppage of urine. మూత్రబంధరోగము. **నీరుకట్టె, నీరుకట్టేయు** or **నీరుపాము** *nīru-kaṭṭe.* n. A water snake. **నీరుకాకి** *nīru-kāki.* n. A cormorant. **నీరుకాయ** *nīru-kāya.* n. A sort of jelly or blubber found on the sea beach. A bubble of water, నీటిబుగ్గ. బుద్బుదము. **నీరుకాయవాడు** or **నీరుకాయమాడు** *nīrukāya-vāḍu.* n. A man of the sea, a triton. నీటిమనుష్యుడు. **నీరుకాసు** *nīru-kāsu.* n. Alms given at bathing places. "తర్ధిపన్నిగ మంత్రములుచెప్పి నీరుకాసులగడించి." H. ii. 166. **నీరుకుక్క** *nīru-kukka.* n. The common otter, *Lutra vulgaris* (F. B. I.) **నీరుకోతి** *nīru-kōti.* n. A water monkey. **నీరుకోడి** *nīru-kōḍi.* n. A water-fowl. **నీరుగండి** *nīru-gaṇḍi.* n. A large snake, పెనుబాము, అజగరము. **నీరుగన్నేరు** *nīru-gannēru.* n. A species of oleander, హింజలము. **నీరుగొబ్బి** *nīru-gobbi.* n. A kind of tree, ఇత్కరము. **నీరుగోరంట** *nīru-gōranṭa.* n. A light tinted గోరంట; a species of this plant which has a light, red tint. **నీరుచిచ్చు** or **నీర్చిచ్చు** *nīru-chitstsu.* n. Fire said to exist under the ocean, బడబాగ్ని, బాడబము. **నీరుచురుకు** *nīru-tsuruku.* n. Heat of urine, a disease. **నీరుజిలుగ** *nīru-jiluga.*

n. A plant, *Æschynomene aspera* (E. P.) నీరూట్టుభూమి *nīr-ūṭṭu-bhūmi*. [నీరు+ఊట్టు for ఫుట్టు.] n. Land under which there are springs. నీరుటెంకి *nīru-ṭenki*. n. A lake, జలాశయము. నీరూడి *nīrūḍi*. (నీరు+ఊడు.) n. A disease in which excessive urine is passed, diabetes. Urine. మూత్రము. నీరుడుము a water iguana, నీటిఉడుము. నీరుతాలుపు or నీటితాల్పు *nīru-tālupu*. n. A cloud, మబ్బు. నీరుతిట్ట *nīru-tiṭṭa*. n. The sea. సముద్రము. నీరుతిత్తి *nīru-titti*. n. The bladder, మూత్రకోశము. నీరుతుట్రు. నీరుకొత్త *nīru-tuṭra*. n. A water snake. నీరుదోమ *nīru-dōma*. n. A water mosquito. నీరుద్రిమ్మరి a water animal, జలజంతువు. నీరుపంది *nīru-pandi*. n. The porpoise. వారి కిటి. నీరుపచ్చ *nīru-paččsa*. n. A sort of emerald. నీరుపాడి *nīru-pāḍi*. A plant called కాకోర్కటి. నీరుపాప *nīru-pāpa*. n. A sort of mermaid, described as a dumb monster somewhat resembling a man in limbs. నీటిమనుష్యుడు. నీరుపిల్లి *nīru-pilli*. n. A water cat, an otter. నీరుప్రబ్బచెట్టు *nīru-prabba-cheṭṭu*. n. A kind of plant, the reton plant, *Bolomus rotong*. జలవేతసి. నీరుబొడ్డి *nīru-boḍḍi*. n. A sort of vegetable. See బొడ్డి. నీరుమజ్జిగ or నీరుచెల్ల *nīru-majjiga*. n. Thin buttermilk. చాలా నీళ్లు కలిసిన చల్ల. నీరుమట్టము *nīru-maṭṭamu*. n. Water-level. నీళ్లనిలుచు ప్రమాణము. నీరుమట్టపుపలక an instrument called a water-level. నీరుముంపు *nīru-mumpu*. adj. Watery, జలప్రాయము. నీరుముట్టు *nīru-muṭṭu*. v. n. To touch water, జలస్పర్శము చేయు; to make water, so called because the Hindus afterwards touch water as purification. "నీటిచేరువ కారాదు నీరుముట్ట." వి. పు. iv. నీరుల్లి *nīr-ulli*. n. An onion. *Allium cepa* [Watts.] నీరువంగ or నీటివంగ *nīru-vanga*. n. A kind of brinjal. నీరువట్టు or నీర్వట్టు *nīru-vaṭṭu*. n. Thirst. దప్పి, పిపాస. నీరువట్టుకొను to be thirsty. నీరువత్తిగ or నీరొట్టు *nīru-vattiga*. n. A sort of sweetmeat. H. i. 117. పేణీలు. నీరేనుగు *nīr-ēnugu*. n. A water elephant, నీటిగజము.

నీరు, నివురు or నివ్వరు *nīru*. [Tel.] n. Ashes, ashes lying over live coal. భస్మము, బూడిద. "శమనీయుడై యుష్మరంబులమాటి నివురంబులో నూరినీరుగావించె." DB. 135 line 3. నీరుగాచేయు to burn to ashes. సున్నపునీరు finely powdered lime, భస్మము. సత్యంబునీరుగావించె he made light of his oath. నీరుకారు *nīru-kāru*. n. Tongs for coals, పటకారు.

నీరు *nīru*. [Tel.] adj. Slight. అల్పము. నీరెండ the soft sunshine (ఎండ) of evening. "నీరెండగాయు" A. vi. 129. నిరువదును slight sharpness, కొంచెపువాడి. నీరుపాయము *nīru-pāyamu*. n. Youth, adolescence, యౌవనము. నీరుకావి or నీర్కావి *nīru-kāvi*. n. A reddish tint, the soft tint of fine cloth after its newness has gone off. కొంచెమెరుపు. నీరుకావులు *nīru-kāvulu*. n. A sort of grain. H. iv. 158. నీరుకాళ్లు *nīru-kāllu*. n. Lit: Reddish legs, i. e., the rays of the sun at sunrise and sunset. కొంచెమెర్రని రంగుగలవై రెండుసంధ్యవేళలందును కనబడు సూర్యకిరణములు. "నిదురలైతిలకించె నీరుకాళ్లు." హరి. పూ. vii.

నీలము *nīlamu*. [Skt.] adj. Blue, purple, deep blue, bright black. నల్లని. n. A blue or black stone. పచ్చరాయి, నల్లరాయి. The sapphire. Blue colour, blackness. The Indigo plant, నీలిచెట్టు. నీలంగువు *nīl-anguvu*. n. An insect. పురుగు. నీలడు *nīlaḍu*. n. A black horse. నీలకంఠము *nīla-kanṭhamu*. n. The purple throated bird, a peacock. నెమలి. నీలకంఠుడు *nīla-kanṭhuḍu*. n. The blue throated god, i. e., Siva. శివుడు. నీలబోడికోడి *nīla-bōḍi-kōḍi*. n.

The purple Moorhen, *Porphyris poliocephalus.* (F. B. I.) నీలాంజనము *nil-anjanamu.* n. Blue vitriol, sulphate of copper. నీలాంబరము *nil-ambaramu.* n. A blue vest. The name of a lilac blue-bell. నీలాంబరుడు *nil-ambarudu.* n. A name of Balarâm or Saturn. నీలి *nili.* n. The indigo plant. Blue dye. Rox. iii. 379. వెర్రినీలి or కారునీలి the wild variety of indigo, id. 372. 377. A dark thread. నల్లనూలు. "నీలిదట్టి." (R. ii. 20.) Or, "నీలికచ్చడము." (BD. v. 677). A waist band. కాసెకోక. A black woman, a factious jade, a hussey: one who blubbers at a touch. "నీలి నీళ్లకుపోతే బావి లోతుకుపోయినది (proverb) when the jade goes to the well all the water disappears. నీలి adj. Black, నల్లని. False, hypocritical. నీలి యేడుపు false or crocodile tears. నీలివార్త *nili-vartha.* n. A lie set afloat under the superstitious notion that the indigo crop will flourish better. Nonsense, delusion. Rhodomontade, a hoax. నీలిమ or నీలిమము *nilima.* n. Black color. నలుపు. నీలిమందు *nili-mandu.* n. Indigo. నీలిమబ్బు *nili-mabbu.* n. A thin or rainless cloud. నీలుడు *niludu.* n. The name of a monkey. ఒకవానరుడు. నీలోత్పలము or నీలాబ్జము the blue water lily.

నీరాగము *nil-ragamu.* [Skt.] n. Heartfelt love, secret and deep love. గాఢానురాగము.

నీలుగు, నీల్గు, నీలుగు or నీల్గు *nilugu.* [Tel.] v. n. To stretch, strut, stretch oneself. ఒళ్లువిరుచుకొను. To die, చచ్చు. To be audacious or impertinent. నీవు తెగనీల్గుచున్నావు you are very presumptuous. నీలుగుబోతుతనము or నీలుగు *nilugu-bôtutanamu.* n. Audacity, impudence.

నీళ *nila.* [Skt.] n. The name of a wife of Vishṇu.

నీళ్లు *nillu.* [Tel. plu of నీరు] n. Water. నీళ్లతీయు *nilla-tiyu.* v. a. To bleach cloth. నీళ్లబుచ్చిగాడు *nilla-buchchi-gâdu.* n. The Kingfisher. నీళ్లవరుగు *nilla-varugu.* n. Salt, ఉప్పు. నీళ్లాడు *nill-adu.* v. n. To be brought to bed, to bring forth. ప్రసవించు. To bathe, స్నానముచేయు.

నీవారము *nivâramu.* [Skt.] n. Wild corn. నివ్వరివడ్లు, విత్తకయే పండునట్టి ధాన్యము.

నీవి *nivi.* [Skt.] n. A zone, or cestus, a belt. The knot (of a peculiar kind) which keeps up a Hindu woman's garment. కోకముడి. Swa. ii. 73. Capital, principal, stock. A stake or wager, మొదటిసొమ్ము, అసలుసొమ్ము, పందెముకట్టినద్రవ్యము. నీవిపము a park or garden around a house. చుట్టూరుయుండుతోట

నీవు *nivu.* [Tel.] pron. Thou. gen. నీ. నీది, నీవే or నీకే thou thyself.

నీవ్రము *nivramu.* [Skt.] n. The edge of a thatched roof, చూరు.

నీహారము or నిహారము *niharamu.* [Skt.] n. Frost, hoar frost. Dew. మంచు.

ను nu

ను *nu.* [Tel.] affix. A particle added to నా, the base of the 1st personal pronoun, as నేను I, and to the first person singular in verbs కొట్టుదును. The sign of the second case of nouns as కోటను. (It is changed into ని in some cases as రాముని) The sign of the gerund as కొట్టనున్నాడు he is going to beat. Conj. And, also, కూడా, జనులును *and* for men.

నుంకు *nunku.* [Tel.] n. A fast, fasting, పస్తు, ఉపవాసము.

నుంగు *nungu.* [Tel.] n. A palmyra fruit kernel, while tender.

నుంచి *nunchi.* [Tel. ను+ఉంచు.] affix. From, by. It governs an accusative, as ఇది నన్నుంచికాదు this cannot be effected by me. నెలనుండి యిక్కడ ఉన్నాను I have been here a month. రెండుదినములనుండి for the last two days. అది నన్నుంచి రావలసి నది is this due by me. నన్నుంచి ఒకనల్లియైనను చావదు not even a bug has died by my hand. ఈ రెండుదినములనుండి లేడు he has not been here these two days. గాలినుంచి from the wind. ఎక్కడనుంచి whence?

నుండి *nundi*. [Tel. ను+ఉండు.] affix. From, by. ఎప్పటనుండి whence.

నుక్కటు *nukkaṭu*. [Tel.] n. Movement, motion. చలనము. పాలిక్స. ii.

నుగ్గు *nuggu*. [Tel.] v. n. To be smashed. నలుగు. n. A bit, fragment, తునుక. Powder, పొడి. A cake of cowdung dried for fuel. పిడక. "నుగ్గులకుప్పలు" piles of such fuel. H. ii. 147. నుగ్గగు or నుగ్గులుపోవు to perish, to be dashed to pieces, to be shivered. నుగ్గైన broken to pieces. గుర్రములన్ నుగ్గయ్యె the horses were smashed. నుగ్గుచేయు *nuggu-chēyu*. v. a. To break to pieces, to reduce to dust. నుగ్గునుగ్గయి (beaten) to pieces. M. X. i. 171. నుగ్గునూచ్చలై or నుగ్గునూచేగా *nuggu-nūtsal-ai*. adv. In bits. నుగ్గాడు to cut to pieces, ఖండించు.

నుచ్చిల్లు *nuchchillu*. [Tel.] n. Foam, froth, నురుగు, ఫేనము.

నుటుక్కున *nuṭukku-na*. [Tel.] adv. Suddenly. సహాలున, కిసాలున. నుటుక్కున అనినప్పుడు అనుకారశబ్దము. A. iv. 36.

నుచ్చు *nutstsu*. [Tel.] n. The dung of sheep or goats, మేకలగొఱ్ఱలపేడ. Goat hair, మేక వెంట్రుకలు. నుచ్చుపాతలు *nutstsu-patalu*. n. 'Dug ties;' bits of cloth with which the teats of sheep or goats are tied. మేకలగొఱ్ఱల చండ్లకుకట్టేగుడ్డలు. Pal. 361. నుచ్చు *nutstsu*. v. a. To tie a cloth round the teats of goats. Swa. iv. నుచ్చుమల్లి *nutstsu-malli*. n. A cheetah. చిరుతపులి. HD. ii. 1091.

నుజ్జు *nudzdzu*. [Tel.] adj. Hurt, cut. నొచ్చి నొంటిన. య. ii. ఉ. రా. vii.

నుడి *nuḍi*. [Tel.] n. A word, a thing said, a promise, an expression. మాట. A bad name, అపకీర్తి.

"క॥ పుడమినపప్రథయగునెడ
బడలికదేహంబు విడువబాడియుకాదే,
నుడికంటెజొప్పునేలను
నుడువుపురాతనముకాక నూతనపదమే."

భో. vii.

నుడికారము *nuḍikāramu*. [Tel.] n. Style, mode of speech. వాచకము, మాట, రచనము, మాటచమత్కారము. నుడుగు or నుడువు *nuḍugu*. v. a. To tell. చెప్పు. నుడుగు or నుడువు n. A word or expression, a thing said, a promise; a line in verse: a bar in music. ఊకొనుడునుడులెంచి చెప్పు to sing line upon line, to pester, to dun, to reiterate. నుడుగుఱేడు lit: the lord of speech, Brihaspati. బృహస్పతి, గీష్పతి. నుడువు *nuḍuvu*. v. n. To speak. పలుకు. Suca. iii. 356. నుడువంగా as he said so, పలుకగా. నుడువరి *nuḍuv-ari* n. One who is ready of speech, a talkative person, మాటలమారి, వాచాలుడు. నుడువరితనము *nuḍuv-ari-tanamu*. n. Readiness, fluency of speech.

నుతి *nuti*. [Skt.] n. Praise, eulogium. స్తోత్రము, పొగడిక. నుతించు *nutintsu*. v. a. To praise, laud, sing the praises of. పొగడు, స్తోత్రముచేయు. నుతము *nutamu*. adj. Praised, lauded. నుతింపబడిన. నుత బలారి *nuta-bal-ari*. n. One who is praised by Indra, the "vanquisher of Bala," a title of Krishna.

నుతిక *nutika*. [Tel.] n. A detachment, తెగ, దళము. Total, మొత్తము. "నూరేసిగుఱ్ఱా లనుతికల రెండుసంఖ్యలుగా జేసి పదిలంబుజేసి." Pal. 60.

నుత్తము *nuttamu*. [Skt.] adj. Sent, ordered, despatched, పంపబడిన. Pushed, త్రోయ బడిన.

నుదురు *nuduru.* [Tel.] n. The forehead, నొసలు, లలాటము. infl. నుదుటి abl. నుదుట in the forehead. నెన్నుదురు (నెర+నుదురు.) the middle of the forehead.

నును, నునుపు, నున్, or నున్న *nunu.* [Tel.] adj. Smooth, gentle. నునుగాలి a gentle breeze. Soft, delicate, tender. నునుపగ్గము a smooth cord. A. v. 129. నునుకినుక slight displeasure. నునుమేను a delicate body. నునుపు, నున్నన or నున్నదనము *nunupu.* n. Smoothness. నునుపరి *nunup-ari.* (నునుపు+అరి) adj. Smooth, polished, నును పుగల. నున్నని *nunnani.* adj. Smooth. నున్ననచేయు to smooth, to level; to clear away.

నున్నము *nunnamu.* [Tel.] adj. Sent, despatched, dismissed. త్రోయబడిన.

నుయ్యి, నుయి or నూయి *nuyyi.* [Tel.] n. A well. Gen: నూతి. Plu. నూతులు. నూతకలుపు to throw into a well; to ruin. నూతికట్ట కడవ అనటము like a pitcher at a well: i. e., in danger. See P. i. 546.

నురుగు or నురువు *nurugu* [Tel.] n. Froth, foam, scum. సముద్రపునురుగు sea foam, the bone of the cuttle fish, from which pounce is made. (Ainslie.) నురుగుదబ్బ *nurugu-dabba.* n. The liver. కాలేజము.

నురుచు or నూర్చు *nurutsu.* [Tel.] v. a. To thresh corn by driving cattle over it. త్రొక్కు, నలుపు. To crush, quell. నలుపు. నురిచియాడు *nurichi-y-ādu.* v. a. To ruin, నాశముచేయు. నురిపిడి *nuripidi.* n. Threshing corn. ధాన్యమును నురుచుట. నురుపు *nurupu.* v. a. To thresh corn, నురుచు. To kill, చంపు.

నురుము *nurumu.* [Tel.] v. a. To reduce to powder, చూర్ణముచేయు. To kill, to destroy, చంపు. n. Powder, what is ground. పొడి నురుమాడు or నురుముచేయు *nurum-ādu.* v. a. To reduce to powder, to ruin, destroy. చూర్ణముచేయు, చంపు.

నులక or నుల్క *nulaka.* n. A cord, woven of three strands and used in lacing the bottoms of cots, like ticken. మంచమల్లుదారము. నులకమంచము a bed the bottom of which is made of such ticken.

నులి *nuli.* [Tel.] n. A twist, a tangle, మెలి. A griping or gnawing pain in the stomach. పేగులలోనొప్పి. వానికి నులిపెట్టినది he had the gripes. నులిపురుగులు worms in the bowels. adj. Gentle, slight. Small, స్వల్పమైన, అల్పము. Thus నులికాలువ A small stream. A. ii. 72. vi. 17. నులివెచ్చగా slightly warm, lukewarm. నులినొప్పి a slight griping pain, నులివాల్లు *nuli-vāllu.* n. A slight withering. కొంచెము వాడిపోవుటలు. నులివాల్లువాడు to wither slightly, కొంచెమువాడు. నులిగొను *nuli-gonu.* v. n. To be twisted, to be tangled. చిక్కుపడు. నులిపెట్టు *nuli-pettu.* v. a. To twist. మెలిపెట్టు, చిక్కుపెట్టు. నులిగడ or నులితడ *nuligada.* n. A medicinal plant, having a capsule consisting of fine fibres twisted in the form of a screw, *Helicteres idora.* Linn, ఆవర్తని. నులియు or నులివు *nuliyu.* v. n. To move about, to shake, to tremble. చలించు. ఇట్టట్టు తూలును. To be reduced to powder, to be crushed or powdered, పొడియగు, నలియు, నలుగు. To ring, sound, tinkle. "తే॥ కానునులియంగ కంకణక్వణనమొలయ." చంద్రహాసవిలాసము. i. 896. నులించు *nulintsu.* v. a. To crush, to cause to be powdered. నలియజేయు, నలుచు. నులుచు or నులుపు *nulutsu.* v. a. To tread out, corn with oxen, to thrash corn, నలియజేయు. నులుగు *nulugu.* v. n. To be crushed, ground, trodden. నలుగు.

నులుము, నుల్ము, నులుమాడు or నుల్మాడు *nulumu.* [Tel.] v. a. To roll (cotton between the hands.) To pull (by the ears.) To twist or curl (the whiskers). To twist or pull (a bullock's tail in urging it on.) నానిమెడ నులిమిరి they wrenched or broke his neck. To dig up, to root up. పెల్లగించు.

నులుసు *nulusu*. [Tel.] n. Failure. విఫ్ఫలము. An imperfection, defect, న్యూనత. "నులుసు లేకఫలించె నోచిన నోములెల్లనునీవ్రెయి." B. X. § 3. 28.

నువ్వు or నువు *nuvvu*. [Tel.] n. Sesamum; a crop of sesamum. నువ్వుచేను. నువ్వులు sesamum seeds, తిలలు. నువ్వుపువ్వు *nuvvu-puvvu*. n. The delicate blossom of sesamum: it is proverbially delicate, and to it the poets compare a beautiful nose. నువ్వెత్తు or ఉవ్వెత్తు *nuvv-ettu*. n. Something extremely minute, that which is not worth reckoning. Lit: as much as a sesamum seed, నువ్వుగింజయెత్తు. నువ్వెత్తుగా very little, తూలాయమానముగా. నువ్వెత్తుగాను to become little or nothing, తూలాయమానమగు. "ఒక్క మాత్రలోన నువ్వెత్తుగానకొ, దురోగ్ధనాదిశకము." M. V. i. 30. నవ్వులెల్లా నువ్వులయినవి (proverb) the laughter is turned into grief. నూబిండి or నువ్వులపిండి *nū-bindi*. n. Flour of sesamum.

నుసము *nusamu*. [Tel.] n. Bitterness. కసరు.

నుసరు *nusaru*. [Tel.] v. a. To rub. రాచు.

నుసలింగ *nusa-linga*. [Tel.] n. A plant called బుసచి.

నుసలు See నుసులు.

నుసి *nusi*. [Tel.] n. Powder, dust made by insects. నుసిరాలుకొయ్య pithless dry wood, touchwood. నుసిపురుగులు book worms, insects that perforate timber. adj. Little, petty, trifling, అల్పము.

నుసుగు *nusugu*. [Tel.] v. a. To disregard, despise. తిరస్కరించు.

నుసుమ *nusuma*. [Tel.] n. An eyefly.

నుసుము *nusumu*. [Tel.] v. a. To attract. ఆకర్షించు.

నుసులు or నుసలు *nusulu*. [Tel.] v. a. To stretch the body in or after sleep. ఒళ్లు విరుచుకొను. v. n. To stir, కదలు. To delay, ఆలస్యముచేయు. To undertake, పూను. మైనుసులుచు stretching oneself. "వ్యసనములుడగిలి నుసలబోక." Vēma. iii. 35, నొసల వ్రాయువ్రాత నుసిలితే పోవునా? will mere rubbing your forehead blot out your destiny? Vēma. 1796. "చ॥ వెరవున నంగమల్ నుసులుస్రేటుల వమ్మగదాకే." M. IX. i. 198. n. Lightness, ease. లాఘవము, తేలిక.

నుస్సెలు *nusselu*. [Tel.] n. A sort of fish.

నూ nū

నూ A contraction for నూవు or నువ్వు 'sesamum' and also for నును 'soft.' See నూవు.

నూక or నూకలు *nūka*. [Tel.] n. Grits, pollard, farina, a kind of coarse flour called roulong or soojey in Madras. ఈ బియ్యము నిండా నూకపడిగానున్నది the rice is full of grits. నూకలకూడు gritty meal, a meal prepared from the coarse grits of rice. నూక n. A kind of tree.

నూకు *nūku*. [Tel.] v. a. To shove, push. నెట్టు, తోయు. To drive as a cart, తోలు. To beat soundly, మిక్కిలి కొట్టు. నూకుడు *nūkudu*. n. Thrusting, shoving, తోపుడు. A shove, poke, thrust. నూకించు *nūkintsu*. v. a. To have (it) pushed, నెట్టించు, తోయించు To get (one) thrashed, కొట్టించు.

నూగు *nūgu*. [Tel.] n. Soft down, downiness or hairiness, whether on plants or animals. పరాగము. Efflorescence of salt. The nap on cloth. Bloom, tenderness, లేతదనము. adj. Downy, tender, లేత. నూగు మీసములు downy moustaches. Hairy, rough. నూగుచవరాలు or కరుకువరహాలు coins that are rough to the touch. నూగుదోస or నూదోస the woolly cucumber plant, కూగుమూడునెట్టు. నూగుబెండ a species of

బెండ (q. v.) నూగుదు *nūgudu*. n. Dust, సర్వులోనకువాని రేణువు. నూగారు *nūg-āru*. n. A line of hair up from the navel to the breast. రోమలేఖ, రోమరాజి. నూనూగు *nū-nūgu*. n. Sprouting down, callow fledge, as of a young beard. "నూనూగు మీసకట్టును." Radha. i. 34.

నూచె or నూచేము *nūtsa*. [Tel.] n. Powder. పొడి. సన్నసూచేము very fine powder, మిక్కిలి పొడి.

నూతనము or నూత్నము *nūtanamu*. [Skt.] adj. New, fresh. క్రొత్త.

నూనె or నూనియ *nūne*. [Tel. నూవు+నెయ్యి.] n. Oil. మంచినూనె sesamum oil, or gingelly oil, తైలము. నెమలినూనె the melted fat of peacocks used in medicine. నూనెకట్లపాము *nūne-kaṭla-pāmu*. n. A small venomous snake "barred with black." నూనెబుడ్డి *nūne-buḍḍi*. n. An oil bottle. నూనెబుడ్డిగాడు *nūne-buḍḍi-gāḍu*. n. The Indian Redstart, *Ruticilla rufiventris* (F.B.I.) నూనెముడి *nune-muḍi*. n. A joint. కీలుగంటు. నూనెఅగిసె the black linseed plant.

నూపురము *nūpuramu*. [Skt.] n. An anklet with bells. అందె.

నూయి Same as నుయ్యి. నూతివాయికట్టు the parapet around a well. పశ్వాదులు పడకుండా నూతి చుట్టును కట్టినగోడ.

నూరు *nūru*. [Tel.] v. a. To grind or sharpen. పదునుచేయు. To reduce to powder, పిండిచేయు. వానికి ఇంత నూరిపోసినా రాలేదే, నేనేమిచేతును I cannot beat learning into him, what shall I do? నూరురాయి *nūru-rāyi*. n. A whetstone, a grindstone. సన్నికల్లు, మంగలకత్తి నూరురాయి. నూరు *nuru*, n. A hundred. నూటపది one hundred and ten. నూరారు *nūr-āru*. adj. Numberless, unnumbered (lit. a hundred and six) నూరంచులకయిదువు *nūr-antsula-kayi-duvu*. n. The hundred-edged (or many edged) thunderbolt of Indra, వజ్రాయుధము.

నూరుచు, నూర్చు or నురుచు *nūrutsu*. [Tel.] v. a. To thrash corn: to tread out grain. నూర్పించు the causal of నూరు. నూర్పిడి, నురిపిడి, నూరిపిడి, నూరుపు or నూర్పు *nūrpiḍi*. n. Thrashing. నూర్పిడిమిట్ట a threshing floor.

నూలు *nūlu*. [Tel.] n. Cotton thread. నూలుతాడు a cotton rope, a measuring line. వాడు సన్నసూలు వడుకుచున్నాడు that man is a mere thread paper. నూలునిచ్చెన a rope ladder. "అంపకోలనూలినాజ్ఞ చెల్లునట్టి సార్వభౌముడైన." A. iv. 251. నూలిగరసు *nūli-garasu*. n. A bald head, బట్టతల. నూలుకొను or నూల్కొను *nūlu-konu*. v. n. To own, ఒప్పుకొను. To be fixed, కుదురుకొను. To be righted, చక్కబడు. To be produced, to flourish, పురికొను, పుట్టు, అంకురించు, విజృంభించు. "క్రాలుగ, న్నులనును సిగ్గునూల్కొన గనుంగొనవేల." Parij. i. 90. నూలుకొలుపు or నూల్కొలుపు *nūlu-kolupu*. v. a. To stir up, spur on, పురికొలుపు, ప్రేరేపించు. నూలుకోలు or నూల్కోలు *nūlukōlu*. n. Flourishing, fixing.

నూవు Same as నువ్వు (q. v.)

నృ nri

నృత్తము or నృత్యము *nrittamu*. [Skt.] n. Dancing, నాట్యము.

నృపతి, నృపాలుడు or నృపుడు *nri-pati*. [Skt.] n. Lit: a "lord of men," i. e., a king. నృశంసుడు *nri-samsuḍu*. n. A tyrant. క్రూరుడు. నృసింహుడు or నృహరి *nri-simhuḍu*. n. A lion among men, నరశ్రేష్ఠుడు. An epithet of Vishṇu, విష్ణువు.

నె ne

నె *ne.* [Tel. Short for నిర & నిండు in compounds, the initial consonant of the next word being always doubled.] adj. Full; gentle, soft, sweet; as నెమ్మోము (నిర+మోము), నెత్తావి (నిర+తావి), నెమ్మనము (నిర+మనము), నెమ్మదురు (నిర+మదురు), నెచ్చెలి, నెత్తమ్మి, నెత్తురు, నెమ్మది, నెవ్వగ, &c.

నెం *nem.* An abbreviation for నెంబరు, the English word 'Number.'

నెంజిలి *nenjili.* [Tel.] n. Sorrow, anxiety, anguish. మనోవ్యథ.

నెక్కర *nekkara.* [Tel.] n. A kind of tree, *Cordia myxa.* Ainsl. ii. 466.

నెక్కొను *nek-konu.* [Tel. another form of నిలుకొను.] v. n. To be fixed, to take root, పాదుకొను. To exceed, become vast, swell. వ్యాపించు, అతిశయించు. నెక్కొన్న spread over, extended, అతిశయించిన, వ్యాపించిన. Parij. ii. 42. A. v. 130. నెక్కొలుపు or నెక్కొల్పు *nek-kolupu.* v. a. To extend, cause to swell. వ్యాపింపజేయు. To cause to be rooted in, పాదుకొనజేయు. నెక్కోలు *nek-kōlu.* n. The act of being fixed in a thing. పాదుకొనుట.

నెగడి *negaḍi.* [Tel.] n. A fire lighted either for warmth or to keep off wild beasts. భార. అను. ii.

నెగడు or **నెవడు** *negaḍu.* [Tel.] v. n. To increase, to extend, to spread. వర్ధిల్లు, తెలయు. ఆ గ్రామము నెగడి కసుబా అయినది the village has enlarged and become a town. n. A polypus, or marine animal (మకరము), supposed to entangle swimmers. జలగ్రహము. The red sea weed, (tangle or dulse.) తంతునాగము. నెగడుపడిన clogged, trammelled. నెగడు కొట్టినట్టు ఉన్నారు they appeared to be astounded. **నెగడించు** *negaḍintsu.* v. a. To spread, to extend, as fame, &c.

నెగయు *negayu.* [Tel. for ఎగయు.] v. n. To fly. ఎగురు. To go up, to rise up, పయికిలేచు. **నెగయుదెంచు** *negayu-dentsu.* v. n. To rise up into the sky. పయికిలేచు, నెగయు. **నెగవు** or **ఎగవు** *negavu.* n. A flight. ఎగురుట.

నెగులు or **నెవులు** *negulu.* [Tel.] n. Regret, disquiet, దుఃఖరూపమైనవిచారము. Pain, బాధ. "నెగులెల్లదీర నైనిలిచె ప్రాణములు." Pativratya. p. 361.

నెగ్గు or **నిగ్గు** *neggu.* [Tel.] v. n. To settle, end, thrive, go on well, get on. నిర్వహిల్లు. **నెగ్గించు** *negginṭsu.* v. a. To manage or settle. To ratify, settle, promote, push forward. **నెగ్గడము** *neggaḍamu.* n. Pressure. సమ్మర్దము, త్రొక్కిడి. **నెగ్గురు** *negguru.* n. Palpitation of the heart, గుండె అదరుట.

నెచ్చెలి *nech-cheli.* [Tel. నిర+చెలి.] n. A thick or close friend, a bosom friend. A friend either male or female. స్నేహితుడు, స్నేహితురాలు.

నెత్సు *neṭsṭsu.* [Tel.] n. Fine rice flour. మిక్కిలి సన్ననూకలసమూహము.

నెటిక, **నెట్టిక** or **మెటిక** *neṭika.* [Tel.] n. The knuckles. నెటికవిరుచు to snap the knuckles. అతనిమీద నెటికలు విరిచినది she snapped her fingers at him. **నెటుకురు** *neṭukuru.* n. Snapping the fingers. నెటిక విరుగుట.

నెట్టుకసీల or **నెట్టికసీల** *neṭṭaka-sīla.* [Tel.] n. A well-behaved person, మంచిస్వభావము గలవాడు, మృదులస్వభావురాలు.

"ఊః నెట్టన నల్లలచ్చి యల నీళయుంభూసతి
యుండ నీవు నీ,
నెట్టికసీలపై మనసు నిల్పుట కేమనవచ్చు."

A. vi. 159.

నెట్టన or **నెట్టనము** *neṭṭana.* [Tel.] adv. Immediately. తక్షణమే. Necessarily, అనివార్యముగా. Finely, grandly, much, exceedingly, excessively, entirely, at all, అత్యంతము. "నెట్టనపోనీక" (Rukmang. iv. 126.) not suffering him to go at all, ఎంత మాత్రము పోనీక.

నెట్టపంట *neṭṭa-panṭa.* [Tel.] adv. Without any cause. నిష్కారణముగా.

నెట్టు *neṭṭu.* [Tel.] v. a. To shove, thrust, push. తోయు, నెట్టు. n. A push, or shove. An attempt. పూనిక. Drought, అనావృష్టి. Ruin, నాశము. A game played by boys. నెట్టు or నట్టు a salt pan, or place where salt is made. తావు. నెట్టుతెగిలిన ruined. **నెట్టుకొను** *neṭṭu-konu.* v. n. To be firm, to maintain one's ground, to remain, పాదుకొను, నిలుచు, కాలూనుకొను. To excel, to be proud, అతిశయించు, విజృంభించు. v. a. To push, thrust, shove, ముందరికి తోసికొని పచ్చు. To force, బలాత్కరించు. "పట్టుకల పటికంపు రాచట్టునేలల నెట్టుకొని." Swa. iii. 40.

> "నెట్టుకొని యాత్రయింతురు,
> గట్టిగ ద్రవ్యంబుగలుగుకాలము సుమతీ."
> Sumati. 95.

నెట్టుడుకాయ or **నెట్టుబొట్టనగోలలు** *neṭṭudu-kāya.* n. A certain game played by boys. H. iii. 190. "చీకటిమాటిల్లు చిమ్ము బిల్లల నెట్టుబొట్టనగోలలు, బొమ్మరాలు." Vishnu. v. 211. **నెట్టె** *neṭṭe.* n. A match, an equal, ఈడు. **నెట్టెము** or **నెట్టేయము** *neṭṭemu.* n. A cushion or pad on the head, for carrying baskets on, like a porter's knot. చుట్టకుదురు. "నిసమానములుగాక పసతోడ శిరమెత్తి నెట్టెంబుగాప్రేగు చుట్టినాడు." Swa. iv. 109. ఈ కొవ్వుపాతతో కూడా పెనవేసి నెత్తి చుట్టగా ప్రేగు జుట్టినాడు. **నెట్టెలుకట్టు** or **నెట్టెలుకట్టు** *neṭṭelu-kaṭṭu.* v. n. To form sides, to make matches. ఈడులు యేర్పరచు.

> "శ్రీ. అరయుడ రఘురాము డాప్తులు దాను,
> నిండారుప్రేమతో నెట్టెలు కట్టి,
> కొండుక దండంబు చెలువొప్పఁబట్టి."
> DRB. 154.

నెత్రము *neṭramu.* [Tel.] n. Steepness, abruptness, ఒడుదుడుకు. కలమును అంతనెట్రముగా పట్టుకోరాదు don't hold your pen so upright.

నెత్తము *nettamu.* [Tel.] n. High land, as the crest or terrace of a hill, ఉన్నతభూమి, పర్వతముమీది విశాలప్రదేశము. Gambling, జూదము, పాచికలాట. A bet, పందెము. **నెత్తమాడు** or **నెత్తములాడు** *nettam-āḍu.* v.n. To play at dice. జూదమాడు. **నెత్తపలక** *netta-palaka.* n. A dice board. **నెత్తకమ్మ** *netta-kamma.* n. A stake at dice. పాచికల పందెము.

నెత్తమ్మి *net-tammi* [Tel. నేల+తమ్మి.] n. The meadow lotus, a flower that resembles the aquatic lotus, *Hibiscus mutabiles*, స్థలపద్మము. నెత్తమ్మి [నెర+తమ్మి.] a full blown lotus, a large lotus flower.

నెత్తరులు *net-tarulu.* [Tel. నెర+తరులు.] n. Billows, high waves. పెద్ద అలలు.

నెత్తలు or **నెత్తళ్లు** *nettalu.* [Tel.] n. Sprats, or some other small fish.

నెత్తావి *net-tāvi.* [Tel. నెర+తావి.] n. Fragrance.

నెత్తి or **నెత్తికాయ** *netti.* [Tel.] n. The head. వానినెత్తిమీద రాయియెత్తినాడు he has got him into a scrape. వానినెత్తిమీద తన్నినారు they trampled him under foot. **నెత్తిగోడ** *netti-gōḍa.* n. The gable end of a house. నెత్తిమూట a bundle carried on the head.

నెత్తురు or **నెత్రు** *netturu.* [Tel.] n. Blood. **నెత్తురుగడ్డ** *netturu-gaḍḍa.* n. A boil. **నెత్తురుకందు** *netturu-kandu.* n. A new-born infant. **నెత్తురుత్రావుడు** *netturu-*

travudu. n. An Asura; a demon. రాక్షసుడు. నెత్తురుపోడ netturu-poda. n. A red snake, మాతులాహిసర్పము. నెత్తురుబంక or నెత్తురుబేది netturu-banka n. Dysentery. నెత్తుకొత్తుమాన్యము or నెత్తురుకట్టుమాన్యము nettur-ottu-manyamu. n. A living bestowed on one who (or whose father) shed his blood for the prince. నెత్తురుపారు netturu-paru. v. n. To become red. ఎర్రనగు. నెత్తురుప్రొద్దు sunset.

నెనడు nenadu. [Tel.] n. Marrow in the bones. ఎముకలలోని కొవ్వు.

నెనరు nenaru. [Tel.] n. Affection, love. ప్రేమ. Gratitude, కృతజ్ఞత.

నెపము or నెపము nepamu. [Tel.] n. Blame; an imputation, charge, accusation, aspersion. నింద, తప్పు. A pretext, pretence, excuse, మిష, వ్యాజము. A cause, కారణము.

నెప్పరము or నెప్పళము nepparamu. [Tel.] n. Fastness, swiftness, వేగము. "వ॥ అత్తెరంగిత్తెరంబున దత్తడిం బల్లింప నేరక నెప్పరంబున నెక్కిపోవువారును." Parij. iv. 74. టీ॥ తత్తడింబల్లింపనేరక గుర్రమునకు పల్లము వేయుడమునకు చేతకాక, నెప్పరంబున నెక్కిపోవువారును గ్రక్కున నెక్కి వాయుత్తపడువారును.

నెప్పు neppu. [Tel.] n. A place, home, abode. స్థానము. Firmness, స్థైర్యము. Knack, tact, ఉపాయము. రథము గ్రామముచుట్టు తిరిగి నెప్పున చేరను the car was taken round the town and returned to its old place. నెప్పెరిగి knowing the knack or right way of doing a thing. దుప్పులకు నెప్పు a home for the deer. నెప్పరి nepp-ari. n. One who has knack or tact, ఉపాయశాలి. నెప్పుకొను neppu-konu. v. n. To be established. పాదుకొను. నెప్పుకొని on reaching home.

నెమకు nemaku. [Tel.] v. a. To investigate, search for, look into. వెదకు. నెమకుడు nemakudu. n. A search. వెదకుట.

నెమటాలు or నెమటాము nemataḷi. [Tel.] n. A low creeper, the root of which is a sweet bulb. H. iv. 13.

నెమరు nemaru. [Tel.] n. The cud, rumination. నెమరువేయు, నెమరువేయు or నెమర్చు nemaru-véyu. v. n. To chew the cud. నెమరుకణతలు the temples of the forehead that move when we chew.

నెమలి, నెమిలి, నెమ్మి or నెమ్మిలి nemali. [Tel.] n. A peacock. నెమలి అడుగు a certain plant, పూతికరజము అనే చెట్టు. H. iv. 18. నెమలికన్నులు the eyes in a peacock's train. నెమలిచెట్టు nemali-chettu. n. A tree called త్రిపాది. నెమలిజుట్టుఆకు nemali-dzuttu-aku. n. A certain medicinal plant. నెమలిమొగ్గ nemali-mogga. n. (lit: The peacock's spreading its tail:) An attitude assumed by dancing girls, walking on the hands with the feet in the air. నెమలివడ్లు nemali-vadlu. n. A kind of rice. శాలిధాన్య విశేషము.

నెమురు nemuru. [Tel.] v. a. To rub. తైలము వేసి కాళ్లు నెమిరితే నొప్పులుతీయును anointing the legs with oil and rubbing them relieves pain.

నెమ్మది nem-madi. [Tel. నెర+మది] n. Quiet, ease, comfort, health. adj. Proper, good, right, fine, in good health or order. నెమ్మదిగానుండెను he was well or at ease.

నెమ్మి nemmi. [Tel.] n. Attachment, affection, delight. ప్రేమము, సంతోషము. Quietness, నెమ్మది. Welfare, క్షేమము. A peacock, నెమలి. నెమ్మిక nemmika. n. Affection, love, ప్రేమ. నెమ్మిచెట్టు nemmi-chettu. n. The tree called తినిశవృక్షము or చిత్రమూల. Hamsa. iv. 20. నెమ్మిరవుతు or నెమ్మిరేడు nemmi-ravutu. n. An epithet of Kumáraswámi.

నెమ్ము *nemmu.* [Tel.] n. **Moisture, wet, damp.** కడి. A bush in the wheel of a carriage. బండిచక్రముల రంధ్రములలో నా ప్పించే ఇనుపగొట్టము. A nail used to join two planks of wood together, పలకలలో నడుమ అంటుకోయుటకు లోపల నాప్పించే మేకు. A spike or nail pointed at each end. బందు, రెండుపలకల నంటుకేయు మేకు. నెమ్ముకొను or నెమ్మగొను *nemmu-konu.* v. n. To become damp. నెమ్మగిల్లు.

నెయ్యము or **నెయ్యమి** *neyyamu.* [from Skt. స్నేహము.] n. Affection, tenderness. స్నేహము, ఇంపు. నెయ్యరి or నెయ్యుడు *neyyari.* n. A friend. నెయ్యంపుటలుక *neyyampu-ṭ-aluka.* n. A lovers' quarrel. ప్రణయకోపము. నెయ్యమాడు *neyyam-āḍu.* v. a. To be kind or loving. To fondle, స్నేహించు. నెయ్యపురేడు *neyyapu-rēḍu.* n. Manmadha. నెయ్యురాలు or నెయ్యరి *neyyurālu.* n. A female friend. స్నేహితురాలు. నెయ్యురు *neyyuru.* n. Friends. ఆప్తులు.

నెయ్యి. నేయి or నెయి *neyyi.* [Tel.] n. Butter which has been melted and clarified, ghee. ఘృతము. Any unctuous juice, grease, oil, or fluid: In cookery it is equivalent to "stock," or lard. నేతులు the pus from sores. నేతనడుపు to moisten. "నెయ్యూరాలు" (A. vi. 94.) vegetables that are fried. పందినెయ్యి or పందికొవ్వు lard. నేతి *nēti.* adj. Of the ghee; buttery. నేతిబీరకాయ the sharp-angled cucumber.

నెర, నెరవు, నెరా or **నేరా** *nera.* [Tel.] adj. Full. నిండైన. Fine, grand, excellent; great, large, big. నెరమంట a great flame or a great pain. "కొండలు కోలాహలంబుగా బంటుదై మింటికెగయు నెరమంటలు గనుగొని." S. iii. 269. నెరగొయ్యి a large gully. నెరమాటలు queer speech. "నెరమాటలు కొడిగ ములు నెరమాటలు జాణతనము" H. v. 86. నెరకాడు *nera-kāḍu.* (నెరవు+కాడు.) n. A perfect man. పూర్ణుడు. నెరిక *neraka.* n. A hair. కెంట్రుక. "నెరికలు తాకినయుమ్మల కొరకొర నెత్తురులుపడియు." Hari vamsa. ii. 192. నెరకొను *nera-konu.* v. n. To fill, నిండుకొను. "తమయశు కాలాహిప్రసంగము నెరకొని." Swa. v. 43. నెరదు *neradu.* adj. Rough. గర్గి, చిదుకుడు. ఆ నేల నెర దుగా ఉన్నది that ground is rough or uneven. నెరతనము *nera-tanamu.* n. Respectability "చిలయుబిక్కలిలలవె నసు కూలమును నెరతనము నేర్చి." V. P. ii. 245. నెన్నడుము *nen-naḍumu.* n. A slender waist. నెన్నుదురు or నెన్నొసలు *nen-nuduru.* n. The forehead. నెమ్మనము *nem-manamu.* (నెర+మనము.) n. The heart. నెమ్మొగము or నెమ్మోము *nem-mogamu.* (నెర+మొగము.) n. A fair face. నెరయు or నెరియు *nerayu.* v. n. To fill, నిండు. To be fulfilled, నెరవేరు. To become grey, తెల్లనగు. To extend, grow, swell, వ్యాపించు. To shine, ప్రకాశించు. "శ్రీల కాటుక నెరయంగ కన్నులలరులొప్పు." B. X. 59. 16. నెరయ *neraya.* adv. Fully, much, greatly. గొప్పగా. నెరపు or నెరుపు *nerapu.* v. a. To fill. నించు To fulfil, నెరవేర్చు. To spread, extend, పరచు. To make, చేయు. To enlighten, ప్రకాశింపజేయు. "మధుర భావుల వారిమీద మైత్రి నెరపి." B. viii. 438 adj. Much, great, అధికము. n. The act of spreading. వ్యాపకము. Greyness of hair నెరయుట. నెరయిక *nerayika.* n. Filling, నిండుట. Spreading, వ్యాపించుట. The act of turning grey, as hair, తెల్లనగుట. నెరవంజి or నెరవెంజ *nera-vanji.* n. A kind of plant. అంటిక. నెరవడి or నెరవడి *nera-vaḍi.* n. Full speed. A scrawl or device. నెరవడిగా వ్రాసినాడు he scrawled or flourished in writing. Wit, skill. నెరవాది *nera-vādi.* n. A skilful, or clever man, సమర్థుడు, నేర్పరి. P. iii. 205. నెరవాదితనము much, greatly. నెరవిద్దె or నెరవిద్య *nera-vidde.* n. Conjuring, sleight of hand. హస్తలాఘవము, గారడి. Foppery, conceit. నెరవ

nerava. n. Fulness. పూర్తి. Spreading, వ్యాపనము. A way, మార్గము. Understanding, తెలివి. A contrivance. ఉపాయము. The name of a certain tree. "నెరవుగ లుగువారు నేరుపుగలవారు, విద్యచేత విర్రవీగు వారు పనికి గలుగువారి బానిస కొడుకులో." Vēma. 140. నెరవుగలుగువారు, ఉపాయ శాలులు. adj. Full. పూర్ణము. Much, great, అధికము. Proper, యుక్తము. Broad, spacious, విశాలము. Spreading, spread, వ్యాపకము, వ్యాప్తము. నెరవేరు *nerav-ēru.* [From నెరవు much, and ఏరు.] v. n. To be fulfilled, to prosper, thrive, succeed, నెరవేరిన mature. నెరవేర్చు *nerav-ērtsu.* v. a. To accomplish, effect, manage, discharge. నెరయ *neraya.* adv. Entirely, vastly, extremely. In the least, at all. మిగుల, బొత్తిగా.

నెరము or నెరసు *neramu.* [Tel.] n. A secret. మర్మము. A vital part, జీవస్థానము. plu. నెరములు.

నెరసు *nerasu.* [Tel.] n. A mote, atom, particle. నలుసు A flaw or small defect, కళంకము, దోషము. A stumbling block, defect, puzzle, hitch: a fault, తప్పు. A. iv. 270. వానిసంగతి నాకు బహునెరసుగా నున్నది his affair is a riddle to me. నెరసరి *neras-ari.* n. A hero, శూరుడు. A troublesome person, a plague, a tormentor. ఇబ్బందికర్తృడు. P. i. 354. నెరసులుపట్టు *nerasulu-pattu.* v. n. To boggle, make difficulties, find flaws.

నెరి *neri.* [Tel.] n. Crookedness. వక్రత. Beauty. అందము. Manner, విధము. Custom, ఆచారము. A fold of a cloth, వస్త్రముకుచ్చె. Order, క్రమము. Justice, న్యాయము. Courage, పరాక్రమము. Skill, ప్రజ్ఞ. Fulness, finishing, పూర్తి. A bird's wing, రెక్క. Hair, tresses, వెంట్రుకలు. Curls, చుట్టు వెంట్రుకలు. Greatness, bigness. A streak. నల్లనెరి a dark streak. A sympathetic swelling: such as appears on one side of the neck or arm in consequence of an injury on the opposite side. adj. Great, large. గొప్ప, అత్యంతము. Pretty, fine, excellent. బాగు, యోగ్యము, మంచి. నెరిక *nerika.* n. A petticoat or shift. గాగరా, పావడా. Parij. iv.22. నెరిపడు *neri-padu.* v. n. To become, అగు. To accrue, సిద్ధించు. To flourish, thrive, బాగుపడు.

"క॥ కానిమ్ముటులుండి నెరిపడు,
నైన తెరగు దోచి మాయమగునిబ్బంగిన్."
M. XII. iii. 31.

నెరిడె *neride.* [Tel.] n. The name of a certain tree. H. iv. 16.

నెరియ, నెరె, నెర్రియ or నెర్రె *neriya.* [Tel.] n. A crack, slit, chink, fissure. చీలిక, బీటలు.

నెరుము *nerumu.* [Tel.] v. n. To rub, రాచు. To rankle. To yearn or ache, as the bowels. మిరమిరలాడు.

నెరులు *nerulu.* [Tel. plural of నెరి. q. v.] n. The hair. Cracks, chinks. నెరియలు, ఛిద్రములు. A. v. 19.

నెల *nela.* [Tel] n. A month. మాసము. The moon, చంద్రుడు. The full moon, పున్నమ. A place, నెలవు, స్థానము. Camphor, కర్పూరము. నెలపచ్చిపాగాలు bits of green camphor. పచ్చకర్పూరపు పలుకులు, వాసనకట్లు, వాసనవక్కలు. నెలవంక the crescent moon. నెల నెలకు every month. నెలసరికి at the end of the month. నెలకట్టు *nela-kattu.* n. A pavement, రాతికట్టడపునేల, కుట్టిమము. "పటికంపునెలకట్టు పైపెక్కు తెకడొందు నిండి యుప్పుట నెట్టి తెట్టువాటె." HK. iii. 74. నెలకువ *nelakuva.* n. A place. స్థానము. నెలకూన the crescent moon, బాలచంద్రుడు. A nail mark, నఖక్షతము. వసు. vi. నెలకొను or నెలవుకొను *nela-konu.* v. n. To be, stay, arise. ఉండు, నిలుచుండు, పుట్టు, కలుగు. To become firm or settled, నిలుకడయగు.

"క॥ నేనుం బసుదించెద మూరట,
నెలకొని కృవమతమునస్త్రబదులు
గొలుసనిరా."
M. VII. i. 55.

నెలకొలుపు nela-kolupu. v. a. To place, deposit. ఉంచు. నెలత nelata. [నెల+త = తనవుగలది] n. A woman. నెలచూలి or నెల పట్టి nela-tsūli. n. The planet Mercury. బుధుడు. నెలతాలుపు or నెలతాల్పు nela-tālupu. n. Lit: He who wears the moon (on his head) i. e., Siva, చంద్రశేఖరుడు. నెలత్రావడము or నెలపులుగు nela-tra va-ḍamu. n. A mythical bird called చకోరము, which is supposed to live on the moon's light. నెలపాలు or నెలదినము nela-pālu. n. A phase of the moon. చంద్రకళ. నెలపొడుచు nela-poḍutsu. v. n. To rise, as the moon, చంద్రోదయమగు. నెలపొడుపు nela-poḍupu. n. Moonrise, the rising or appearance of the moon. నెలమేపరి nela-mēpari. n. Lit: One who feeds on the moon, i. e., Rahu, the ascending node. నెలవెలుగు nela-velugu. n. Moonlight. వెన్నెల. నెలబాలుడు nela-bāluḍu. n. The moon, చంద్రుడు. నెలరాయి, నెలఱాయి or నెలశిలయ nela-rāyi. n. Moonstone. చంద్రకాంతశిల. నెలవంక nela-vanka. n. The crescent moon బాలచంద్రుడు. A mark like a half moon; such as is produced by nipping (in fondness) with the nail. నఖక్షతము. నెలవంక కోల a crescent shaped arrow, అర్ధచంద్ర బాణము.

నెలగ nelaga. [Tel] n. Money, wealth, ధనము. Alms, దానము, ధర్మము.

"క॥ కలిమికిని వనితకొలదిని,
నలగల నెరిగినవారున్న నెలవు పెక్కుడిదా,
కలనుగ నిండినదెపుడు,
కలగిడునె నిదురవున్న నాగనిధంబిరా."
G. ii. 152.

నెలవు or నెళవు nelavu. [Tel.] n. A place, abode, home, dwelling, native country. ఉనికిపట్టు, స్థానము. An acquaintance, పరిచయము. రాతినెలవు a stony place. R. v. 97. A secret, మర్మము. నెలవుకొను Same as నెలకొను. See under నెల. నెలవరి or నెళవరి nelav-ari. n. An acquaintance, మర్మము తెలిసినవాడు. R. v. 18.

నెల్లి nelli. [Tel.] n. The tree called Emblic myrobalan, Phyllanthus emblica. ఉసిరి, ఆమలకము. గడ్డనెల్లిచెట్టు the large species. చిరునెల్లి the small species. Rox. iii. 671. నెల్లికాయ its fruit. నెల్లికాయగంధకము nelli-kāya-gandhakamu. n. Medicinal brimstone (Tariff.) నెల్లిపాషాణము See పాషాణము.

నెళినెళి neḷi-neḷi. [Tel.] adv. Crackingly, suddenly. ఫెళుక్కున, హఠాత్తుగా.

నెవడు Same as నెగడు (q. v.)

నెవము Same as నెపము (q. v.)

నెవరు Same as నెగరు or ఎగరు (q. v.)

నెవలి or నెవిలి Same as నెమలి. (q. v.)

నెవులు Same as నెగులు. (q. v.)

నెవ్వ or నెవ్వము nevva. [Tel.] n. Poverty, దారిద్ర్యము. Distress, ఆపద, కష్టము. Drought, famine, కరవు. "ధనం దెవ్వంట తేక బ్రతుకంట, నెవ్వముననుమనింటెరిగులంటిననావా." G. viii. 201. "శా॥ పర్జన్యు నెవ్వరా దుఃఖరా వారిల్లరా." A. iv. 291. టీ॥ పర్జన్యు నెవ్వరా, అనావృష్టిచేతను.

నే nē

నే, నేను, నేము or ఏను nē. [Tel.] pron. of the first person I. n. (Short for నేయి.) Ghee. నేజెల్ల nē-jella. (నేను+చెల్ల) interj. Alas, అయ్యో!

నేజ, నెజ, నేజము, నెజెము, నేజా or నెజా nēja. [H.] n. A short spear, lance, or iron spit. బల్లెము, ఈటె.

నేటు *nēṭu*. [Tel.] n. Certainty. నిశ్చయము. adj. Good, excellent, fine, శ్రేష్ఠము. Firm, దృఢము. నేటుగా well, properly. **నేటించు** or **నేటించు** *nēṭintsu*. v. n. To become fixed, firm or hard, దృఢపడు. To become sure, నిశ్చయమగు. **నేటుచేయు** *nēṭu-chēyu*. v. a. To make certain, to ascertain, నిశ్చయపరచు. To try, prove, weigh, discriminate, వివరించు, పర్వరము, తారతమ్యము విచారించు. "ద్వి॥ పాటితప్పితివటా పాపపుణ్యముల నేటుసేయగలేక, నిష్కారణంబు." Sāranga. v. 65.

నేడు *nēḍu*. n. To-day, this day. ఈదినము. నేడు వత్తురు they will come to-day. నేటి సమాచారము the news of to-day. నేటికి for this day.

నేడు *nēḍu*. [Tel.] n. A baron, petty chieftain.

నేత *nēta*. [Skt.] n. A lord, master, leader. ప్రభువు, ఏలిక.

నేత [Tel.] See under నేయు.

నేత్రము *nētramu*. [Skt.] n. The eye. కన్ను. A garment. Bleached or woven silk. వస్త్రము, వలిపము. "మర్కటకీటకృతమైన మార్గంబు నేత్రసంపదవహించు." A. i. 46. "నేత్రంబుపట్టు" a kind of silk. BD. iii. 110. నేత్రోత్సవముగానున్నది it is a feast to the eyes.

నేదిష్ఠము *nēdishṭhamu*. [Skt.] adj. Very near, close. మిక్కిలి సమీపము.

నేనలి *nēnali*. [Tel.] n. Weeds. కలుపు. నేనలియేరడము removing weeds, weeding. కసువుమొదలైనవి యేరివేయడము, కలుపుతీయడము.

నేను or **ఏను** *nēnu*. [Drav. cf. Tam. నాన్.] n. The pronoun I. నేను పోతిని I went. The Genitive is నా. నాయిల్లు my house. Dative నాకు, to me. Plu. మేము, నేము or ఏము we (excluding the person or persons spoken to) and మనము we (including the person or persons spoken to.)

నేపథ్యము *nēpathyamu*. [Skt.] n. Ornament, embellishment. వేషము, స్వభావవ్యత్యాస వస్త్రాద్యలంకృతశోభ. A stage. రంగభూమి. A curtain. తెర. Vasu. iv. 22.

నేపాళము *nēpālamu*. [Skt.] n. The "Nepaul plant" or Physic nut, (Jack Spratt), *Croton tiglium*. Called also the coral plant from the flowers which look like red coral. See under ఆముదము. Rox. iii. 687. 682. నేపాళబడిత a crabstick (or blackthorn) cudgel. వెర్రినేపాళము the common coral plant, which is worthless. **నేపాళదేశము** *nēpāla-dēśamu*. n. The country of Nepaul.

నేబు *nēbu*. [Tel.] A coin worth twelve cash. Plu. నేబులు coins.

నేమము or **నేమకము** *nēmamu*. [from Skt. నియమము.] n. An appointment, a vow. నియమము. [Skt.] n. Time, కాలము. Extent, మేర. A bit, తునక. **నేమించు** *nēmintsu*. v. a. To determine, fix, appoint. నియమించు.

నేమి *nēmi*. [Skt.] n. A water pump, నూతి మీదిగిలక. The tire of a wheel. బండికల్లు చుట్టును వేసిన యినుపకట్టు. A plant called తినిస.

నేము *nēmu*. [Tel.] v. a. To winnow. pron. Plu. of నేను. We, మేము. **నేమించు** *nēmintsu*. (causal of నేము.) v. a. To cause to winnow.

నేయము or **నెయ్యము** *neyamu*. [from Skt. స్నేహము or న్యాయము.] n. Friendship. స్నేహము. Justice, న్యాయము. "నేయముగాదుసద్ధంశ నిలిచేది మేరగాదు" క్షేత్రయ.

నేలు Another form of నెయ్యి (q. v.)

నేయు *nēyu*. [Tel.] v. a. To weave, as a cloth, అల్లు. మంచమునేయు to lace a bed. గడ్డినేయు to lay thatch on a roof. ఇంటికి ఆ గడ్డి నేయించెను he thatched his house with that grass. గడ్డివేసిన thatched. నేయించు nêyintsu. v. a. To cause to be woven. అతనిచేత రెండుగుడ్డలు నేయించినాను I made him weave two cloths. నేత nêta. n. Weaving, texture. నేతయుంటు. నేతలు fine long cloth, సన్నబారచాపులు. కవిక. iii. నేతకాడు or నేతరి nêta-kâḍu. n. A weaver. నేతపలక nêta-palaka. n. A plank or board every now and then used by a weaver in arranging the warp and the woof evenly. నేతపురుగు nêta-purugu. n. A spider. "పురుహూతునకు నేత పురుగులు పూజచేసి స్థిరమైన సుజ్ఞానశీవమాయు." Vema. iii. 159.

నేరా Same as నేరు (q. v.)

నేరుగా nêru-gâ. [Tel.] adv. Straight, direct. ఆ దోవను నేరుగాపోవలెను you must go straight along that road.

నేరాజు nê-râḍzu. [Tel.] n. A lace-cloth. జరిబట్ట, జరబాజా, సరిగతోనేసినబట్ట.

నేరుచు or నేర్చు nêrutsu. [Tel.] v. n. To learn. Added to other infinitives it is translated by the English verb Can. రానేరను I cannot come. తెలియనేరరైరి they were unable to know. చూడనేర్తునే can I bear to see it? నేర్చినేర్చి మాట్లాడు తాడు he is talkative or chatters. నేరక neraka. adj. Being unable to. రానేరక being unable to come. adv. Unawares, unconsciously, involuntarily. నేర్చినేరక చేసినపని an act committed unconsciously or ignorantly. నేరకచేసినాను I did it unintentionally or unconsciously. నేరరు they cannot do it. "నీవు ఇచ్చినదానిబంబు గ్రహించనేర్తని గ్రహ్మంపుము." M. I. i. 150. నేరబోతు nêra-bôtu. (నేరమి+పోతు.) n. An ignorant man, తెలియనివాడు. నేరమి nerami. n. Ignorance. అజ్ఞానము. A mistake, fault, దోషము. అడనేరమి ignorance of acting, want of power to act. పాడనేరమి inability to sing. నేరము nêramu. n. A criminal offence, a crime. తప్పు, అప రాధము. నేరస్థుడు nerasthuḍu. n. A criminal, an offender. నేరిమి nêrimi. n. Knowledge, skill, dexterity. నేర్పు, సామ ర్థ్యము. నేరుచుకొను, నేర్చుకొను or నేర్చికొను nêrutsu-konu. v. a. To learn. నేరు పరి, నేర్పరి, నేరుపుకాడు, నేర్పుకాడు or నేరుపులాడు nêrup-ari. n. A wit, an ingenious or skilful person, a genius. సమర్థుడు. నేరుపు or నేర్పు nêrupu. v. a. To teach, నేర్పజేయు. n. Art, skill, craft, cunning. A pretext. నేర్పులు arts, wiles, contrivances. నేరుపుగా or నేర్పుగా nêrupu-ga. adv. Artfully, duly, skilfully. నేర్పించు nêrpintsu. v. a. To make one learn, to teach, to cause to teach.

నేరేడు or నేరేడు nerêḍu. [Tel.] n. The tree called *Myrtus cymimum.* Rox. ii. 486. *Ardisia humilis* (Watts). భూతినే రేడు and అల్లోనేరేడు are other species. జంబునేరేడు the roseapple, *Eugenia jambos.* నేరేడుపండువలె as black as a cherry.

నేల nêla. [Tel.] n. Land, earth, soil. భూమి. A country, దేశము. adj. "Of the earth." A prefix (like *ground*, or *dwarf*,) applied to certain plants, as నేలపేము, dwarf rattan, నేలపొన్న dwarf cassia. నేలగలుపు nela-galupu. v. a. Lit: To mix with the earth. To ruin. దానిని నేలగలిపి నాడు he ruined it. నేలకుగోలకుతెచ్చు to turn upside down, కిందుమీదుచేయు. నేల చూపు a downcast look. నేలచూలి nela-tsuli. n. Lit: The earth-born child, i.e., Sita, భూజ. నేలతాడి nela-tâḍi. n. The plant called *Curculigo orchioides.* తాటి మూలి. Rox. ii. 144. నేలతాలుపు nela-tâlupu. n. A mountain. పర్వతము, భూధరము. A king, రాజు, భూధరుడు. నేలనెమలి nela-nemali. n. The bird called a florikin. నేలపట్టి nela-patti. n. Sita. సీత, భూపుత్రి. Mars. అంగారకుడు. నేలపల్లటి nela-pallati.

n. A kind of pigeon called a tumbler. నేలబారుడ పక్షులలోనొక పావురాయి. నేలబావి a well without any wall round it. నేలమాళిగ, నేలమాళె or నేలమాళిగ a room under ground, భూమిలోపలియిల్లు. నేలములక the plant called ఉంద్రము, *Solanum jacquini.* నేలఱేడు *nēla-rēḍu.* n. A king. రాజు, భూపతి. నేలవేము *nēla-vēmu.* n. The plant called *Justicia paniculata.* Rox. i. 118. or *Andrographis paniculata.* (Watts.) నేలవేలుపు *nēla-vēlupu.* n. A Brahman. భూసురుడు, భూదేవుడు. నేలాపు *nēlāpu.* (నేల+ఆపు.) n. A kind of hawk. ఒకవిధమైన డేగ.

నేవము or నేవము *nēvamu.* [Tel.] n. A pretext. వ్యాజము, మిష.

నేవళము, నేవడము or నేవాళము *nēvaḷamu.* [Tel.] n. Bloom, brilliancy. కాంతి, సువర్ణహారము. A necklace. కంఠమాలిక, సరాలు గ్రుచ్చినహారము. "అమరమతుల్ నెవాళమునకు కేవళంబులు కుందనపుఁదీగె మాదిరాగ." Anir. i. 43. HD. ii. 621.

నేస్తము *nēstamu.* [Tel.] n. Friendship, love. స్నేహము. నేస్తకాడు *nēsta-kāḍu.* n. A friend. నేస్తకత్తె or నేస్తురాలు *nēsta-katte.* n. A female frien. or acquaintance.

నై nai

నైకటికము *naikaṭikamu.* [Skt. from నికటము.] adj. Near at hand. "నైకటికంబు లక్ష్మమని నవ్వఁగనోపినవారు." Charu. Chan. v. 110.

నైగనిగ్యము *naiga-niggyamu.* [Skt. from నిగనిగ.] n. Brilliancy, sparkling, నిగనిగలాడుట. H. i. 61.

నైఘంటికము *naighanṭikamu.* [Skt. from నిఘంటువు.] adj. Appertaining to lexicography or a dictionary. నైఘంటికపదములు learned or dictionary words.

నైచికి *naichiki.* [Skt.] n. A milch cow of a fine breed, మంచిదిగనుండేటి ఆవు.

నైచ్యము *naichyamu.* [Skt. from నీచము.] n. Humility, obsequiousness. నక్కనైచ్యములు assumed humility, cringing.

నైజము *naijamu.* [Skt. from నిజము.] adj. Natural, original. సహజమైన, స్వాభావికము. n. Natural disposition, nature, bent, propensity. Actuality, reality. Character; a trait or characteristic: a peculiarity.

నైపథ్యము *naipathyamu.* [Skt.] n. A theatre, నాట్యరంగము. నైపథ్యమందుండేవారు behind the scenes.

నైపుణము, నైపుణి or నైపుణ్యము *naipuṇamu.* [Skt. from నిపుణుడు.] n. Dexterity, cleverness, skill, art. నిపుణత్వము, నేర్పరితనము. నైపుణితో cleverly.

నైమిత్తికము *naimittikamu.* [Skt. from నిమిత్తము.] adj. Occasional (as opposed to నిత్యము constant). Practical; reducible to practice.

నైమిశము *naimiśamu.* [Skt.] n. The name of a forest mentioned in many poems. (Some imagine it to be near Bhadrica, in Orissa: others say, near ప్రయాగ.)

నైయాయికుడు *naiyāyikuḍu.* [Skt. from న్యాయము.] n. A logician. న్యాయశాస్త్రము తెలిసినవాడు.

నైరాశ్యము *nair-āsyamu.* [Skt. from నిరాశ.] n. Hopelessness. ఆశలేనితనము.

నైరృతి *nairṛti.* [Skt. from నిరృతి.] n. The name of the genius who governs the South West.

నైర్మల్యము *nairmalyamu.* [Skt. from నిర్మలము.] n. Spotlessness, purity. నిర్మలత్వము, నిర్మలత.

నైలింప *nailimpa.* [Skt. from నిలింపు.] adj. Heavenly, divine.

నైల్యము *nailyamu*. [Skt. from నీలము.] n. Blackishness, foulness. నీలత్వము, నల్లదనము.

నైవేద్యము *naivēdyamu*. [Skt. from నివేదము.] n. Consecration of food to a god. An oblation or wave offering.

నైషధము *naishadhamu*. [Skt. from నిషధ.] n. The name of a celebrated Sanskrit poem. నైషధుడు *naishadhuḍu*. n. An epithet of the celebrated king Nala, (నలరాజు) as being 'prince of the నిషధ country.'

నైష్కికుడు *naishkikuḍu*. [Skt. from నిష్కము.] n. A master of the mint. టంకశాలాధికారి.

నైష్ఠికము *naishṭhikamu*. [Skt. from నిష్ఠ.] n. Steadfastness in faith. నైష్ఠికుడు *naishṭhikuḍu*. n. One who is faithful, devoted or steady. నిష్ఠగలవాడు.

నైసర్గికము *naisargikamu*. [Skt. from నిసర్గము.] adj. Natural, inborn, constitutional, స్వాభావికము.

నొ no

నొంచు *nontsu*. [Tel.] v. a. To cause pain, to hurt. నొప్పించు, నొవ్వజేయు.

నొక్కము *nokkamu*. [Tel.] n. A sort of dill or fennel. శతాహ్వయము, పెద్దసదాప.

నొక్కు *nokku*. [Tel.] v. a. To press, pinch, compress, squeeze. అదుము. To nip with the nails. To indent. N. IX. 363. రెండుకొమ్ములనుక్కు butting with the horns. నొక్కు or నొక్కుడు n. A squeeze. An impression, or a dent, as with the tooth or nail. The tooth of a saw or clock wheel. A dimple or ripple.

నొగ *noga*. [Tel.] n. The pole that connects the carriage with the yoke.

నొగులు *nogulu*. [Tel.] v. n. To break, నలగు. To grieve, sorrow, be in pain. To be sunken, as the cheeks. ఆవు నొగిలిపోయినది the cow out of condition. n. Pain, నొప్పి. నొగిలించు, నొగిల్చు, నొగులుచు or నొగుల్చు *nogilintsu*. v. a. To distress, grieve, pain, afflict. శ్రమపెట్టు.

నొచ్చిల్లు *nochchillu*. [Tel.] n. Saliva, spittle. ఉమ్మి.

నొచ్చు *notstsu*. [Tel.] v. n. To ache, smart, pain, be grieved. నొప్పికొను. నొచ్చి ఉండు వాడు a distressed man. నొచ్చిపోయిరి they were in reduced circumstances. నొచ్చుకొను *notstsu-konu*. v. n. To ache, repent, grieve, పశ్చాత్తాపపడు. నొచ్చుకోలు *notstsu-kōlu*. n. Repentance. పశ్చాత్తాపపడుట. నొవ్వ *novva*. adv. Achingly, acutely, sharply, painfully, so as to pain, smartingly. నొవ్వనాడుట to speak severely. నొవ్వని *novvani*. adj. Painless, not aching, easy. నొప్పి, నొవ్వి, నోవు or నోవి *novvi*. n. Pain, suffering, వేదన. Disease, sickness, వ్యాధి. నోవరి a sick person, వ్యాధిగలవాడు.

నొడలదొంతి *noḍala-donti*. [Tel.] n. A doubt, suspicion, సంశయము.

నొడి or నుడి *noḍi*. [Tel.] n. A word. మాట. నొడికాడు or నుడికాడు *noḍi-kāḍu*. n. A talkative person. మాటలమారి. నొడికారము or నుడికారము *noḍi-kāramu*. n. Talkativeness. Cleverness in talking. నొడికారపుమాటలు clever words. నొడికారి or నుడికారి *noḍi-kāri*. n. One who can talk cleverly. మాటల చమత్కారముగలవాడు.

నొడుగు, నొడువు, నుడుగు or నుడువు *noḍugu*. [Tel.] n. A word, speech, మాట. v. a. To say, tell, speak, మాటాడు.

నొడుచు *noḍutsu*. [Tel.] v. a. To find fault with. తప్పులుపట్టు. నొడుపు *noḍupu*. n. Fault finding. తప్పుపట్టుట.

నొప్పి or నొప్పము *noppi*. [Tel.] n. Pain or ache. Danger, ఆపద. Harm, ill, hazard. ముప్పము. నేరమునొప్పము a crime is harmful. నొప్పించు *noppintsu*. v. a. To hurt or cause pain to. To afflict or torment, to displease or offend. ఎవ్వరిని నొప్పింపరాదు you should do ill to no one. నొప్పిగుంటి *noppi-gunti*. n. A sick person. వ్యాధిగ్రస్తుడు.

నొల్ల *nolla*. [Tel.] n. A harrow. నొల్లబల్ల *nolla-balla*. n. A broad hoe. నొల్లు *nollu*. v. a. To level land with the plough. To suck the fingers, చిన్నిలు నోటవ్రేళ్లించుకొని చేప్పరించు.

నొవ్వి or నొవ్వు See under నొచ్చు.

నొసలు *nosalu*. [Tel.] n. The forehead. నుదురు, ఫాలము. Gen. నొసటి. Loc. నొసట. Plu. నొసళ్లు. నొష్ట or నొష్ట (corruption of నొసట) on the forehead, లలాటమునందు. నొసట వ్రాసినవ్రాత తప్పగలదా can what is written on the forehead fail of effect?

నో nō

నోచు *nōtsu*. [Tel.] v. a. To perform a meritorious act, as fasting. To undertake a vow. వ్రతమాచరించు. నోత *nōta*. n. The act of undertaking a vow, నోచుట, వ్రతమాచరించుట. నోము *nōmu*. [Tel.] n. A vow. వ్రతము. v. a. To vow, వ్రతము పూను. To lose, పోగొట్టు. వాడును వాని తండ్రియును ఒకటే నోమునోచినారు he and his father had the same fortune. నోమువారము Same as తోరము (q. v.)

నోరు Same as నొచ్చు (q. v.)

నోరు *nōru*. [Tel.] n. The mouth. వక్త్రము, ముఖద్వారము. G. నోటి, నోరి. Abl. నోట. Plu: నోళ్లు. నోట with the mouth. నోరు మూయు hold your tongue. నోరు లేని dumb, unable to talk. నోరు లేనివాడు a simpleton. నోరుకొట్టు to strike on the mouth, i. e., to silence, check, rebuke; to deprive of one's rights or enjoyment, to plunder, spoil. నోరుకాచు to watch one's lips, to keep a secret. నోరుకట్టు to restrain the appetite. నోటిలో ఆడుచున్నది I have it at the tip of my tongue. వానినోరు మంచిదికాదు he is a foul mouthed fellow. పెద్దనోరుచేయు to talk loud or abusively. నోరుపడిన speechless. నోటిచెడ foolish, ignorant, senseless. నోటిమాట a mere word of mouth. నోరుమెంగ *nōru-menga*. n. A dumb man. మూగవాడు. నోటికి వచ్చినట్టు తిట్టెను he gave them all the abuse that he could think of. నా నోట్లో మన్నుకొట్టినాడు he cast earth in my mouth, i.e., he destroyed my hopes or prospects. నోరూరు *nōr-ūru*. v. n. To water (as the mouth). To desire, ఆపేక్షించు. నా నోరూరుచున్నది my mouth waters. వానితో నీవు ఏల నోరుచేసుకొంటావు why do you quarrel with him? నోరెత్తు *nōr-ettu*. v. n. To raise the voice, cry, speak. To try to speak, మాటాడ యత్నించు. నోరాడు *nōr-ādu*. (నోరు+ఆడు.) v. n. To utter. వానికి ఎటుల నోరాడెనో I can't think how his mouth could utter such words. "చెయ్యిప్పలనుచు నిచ్చినవారు కటువుగా నడుగి నుంకించి నోరాడకరుగ." Suca. iii. 203.

నోవు or నోవి Same as నొవ్వు. నోవక See under నొచ్చు.

నౌ nau

నౌ or నవు Same as నవ్వు (q. v.)

నౌక *nauka*. [Skt.] n. A ship, boat. నావ, ఓడ.

నౌకరి or నౌకరు See under నవుకరి.

నౌకు or నవుకు *nauku*. [Tel.] n. An opening. ముర్రి.

"ద్వి. నల్లమబ్బుకింద నవుకుదావున్న
తెల్లనివాల్చుక్క తెగిపడ్డట్టి."
Sar. Dwi. ii. 65.

నాగులు *naugulu.* [Tel.] n. A sort of sweet biscuits made of చెనగపిండి. R. ii. 114.

నాడు or నవుడు *naudu.* [Tel. for నోరు.] n. A lip, అవుడు, పెదవి. నవుడుకొట్టు *navudu-kottu.* v. n. To swallow with difficulty. To hesitate, మిణుకరించు.

నౌబతు or నౌబత్తు *naubatu.* [H.] n. A large kind of drum. (Bobbili. ii. 213.)

నారు or నవురు *nauru.* [Tel.] adj. Soft, smooth. మెత్తని, మృదువైన.

నాలు or నవులు *naulu.* [Tel.] v.a. To chew. నములు. v. n. To throb or shoot, as a boil.

న్య nya

న్యక్కారము or న్యక్కృతి *nyak-kāramu.* [Skt.] n. Disrespect, contempt, flouting. తిరస్కారము.

న్యగ్రోధము *nya-grōdhamu.* [Skt.] n. The banyan tree. మఱ్ఱిచెట్టు.

న్యర్బుదము *ny-arbudamu.* [Skt.] n. Ten thousand millions. పది అర్బుదములసంఖ్య.

న్యస్తము *nyastamu.* [Skt.] adj. Deposited, placed, consigned, delivered, ఉంచబడిన. "కమనీయ పీతాంబరన్యస్తకటిభాగు" wearing a yellow vest about his loins. V. P. viii. 235.

న్యా nyā

న్యాయము *nyāyamu.* [Skt.] n. Propriety, fitness. Justice, equity. ధర్మము. Law, morality. ఆర్షప్రధర్మము. Logic, తర్కశాస్త్రము. A reason, a cause. మీరు నాకు తండ్రియనే న్యాయమువల్ల by reason of your being my father. A relation, connection. వారు నాకు తల్లి తండ్రి న్యాయముగానుండిరి they were as father and mother to me. చంద్రచకోరన్యాయముగానున్నాము we are like the moon and the partridge, i. e., inseparable lovers. తమరు న్యాయము జరిగించవలెను I request that you will do justice. న్యాయ or న్యాయమైన *nyaya.* adj. Right, proper, fit, just. న్యాయతః *nyāyatah.* adv. Correctly, duly, justly. న్యాయ్యము *nyāyyamu.* adj. Just, న్యాయముతోకూడిన.

న్యాసము *nyāsamu.* [Skt.] n. Placing or depositing, ఉంచుట. A deposit, a pledge. Consigning or entrusting any thing to the mind. Mental appropriation or assignment of various parts of the body to tutelary divinites. కరన్యాసము a mode of folding the hands in prayer.

న్యు nyu

న్యుబ్జము *nyubjamu.* [Skt.] adj. Bent, crooked, hump-backed.

న్యూ nyu

న్యూనము *nyūnamu.* [Skt.] adj. Deficient, defective. తక్కువైన. Blameable నిందింపదగిన. న్యూనాంగుడు maimed, mutilated. న్యూనాధిక్యములు faults of omission and commission. ఎచ్చుతక్కువలు. న్యూనత్వము or న్యూనత *nyūnatvamu.* n. A defect, deficiency, detriment. కొరత.

ప pa

ప *pa.* The name of the letter P. The initial P is at times changed by grammatical rule into B as ఆట్టబలికెను, or into V as వాపు, వాటిల్లు, పీఠ్వడి, for పాపు. &c.

పంకము or పంకి *pankamu.* [Skt.] n. Mud, mire, clay. బురద. Sin, పాపము. పంకము [Tel.] n. Milk పాలు.

" సీ॥ లేడిపిల్లలకు బాలెంత చిప్పంగులు
పంకంబు లిచ్చుచు బంచివిల్లు."
జై. iv.

పంకజము, పంకేజము, పంకరుహము or పంకేరుహము *pankajamu*. n. Lit: Mud-born, i.e., the lotus.

పంకా *pankā*. [from H. పంఖా] n. A fan. A punkah.

పంకించు *pankintsu*. [Tel.] v. a. To apply (as oil to the hair.) పట్టించు. v. n. To move, చలించు.

పంకిలము *pankilamu*. [Skt.] adj. Muddy. n. A muddy place, a bog, బురదగల ప్రదేశము.

పంకేన *pankena*. [Skt.] n. Wet. తడి, పదను. Oiling, anointing, smoothing the hair with oil.

" సీ॥ పాపటయిడి నూనె పంకేనతో మన్న గారుదివ్య
నెరులు కెల్లంటునైరు." H. ii. 158.

పంక్తి *pankti*. [for Skt. పఙ్క్తి] n. A line, row; a range. In composition, Ten, పది. పంక్తికంధరుడు a ten headed giant, i. e., Rāvaṇa. **పంక్తిభోజనము** *pankti-bhōjanamu*. n. A feast or dinner party at which guests sit in a line. పంక్తిభోజనము లేనివాడు a person with whom caste, &c., prevents a man from eating.

పంగ *panga*. [Tel.] n. A fork, as the forked branch of a tree. **పంగగా** *panga-gā*. (adv.) Astride, with the legs apart. **పంగటి** *pangaṭi*. adj. Stretching out like the prongs of a fork. "అనుచు వెల్లడిగందమున నాభి నుండి మూపులదాక పంగటిపూతపూసి." Vaija. iv. 57. **పంగటించు** *panga-ṭintsu*. v. n. To straddle or open the legs far apart; to sprawl. **పంగటికాళ్లవాడు** *pangaṭi-kāḷḷa-vāḍu*. n. A bandy-legged man. దొడ్డికాళ్ల గలవాడు. పంగనామము a fork-like mark worn on the forehead by the Vaishnavaites, నిడుపు ఎడము గలుగ పంగనామ తీర్చిన తిరుమణి, as distinguished from ఏకనామము, a mark which has no broad fork-like branches. పంగలకొయ్య a forked post such as rafters rest on. పంగలకర్ర a forked stick. మూడుపంగలయీటె a trident-shaped spear.

పంగము *pangamu*. [Tel.] n. A tax on certain employments, దేవబ్రాహ్మణవృత్తులమీద పూర్వప్రభువర్యాదవారు తీసికొనే చతుర్థాంశమయిన కప్పము.

పంగిడి or **పంగిడ** *pangiḍi*. [Tel.] n. A pit-fall for catching elephants. ఏనుగులనుపట్టే గొయ్యి, ఓదము.

పంగు *pangu*. [Tel.] n. Fear. భయము.

పంగువు *panguvu*. [Skt.] n. A man with a withered leg. ఈడబోయిన కాలుగలవాడు. A lame or crippled man.

పంచ *pancha*. [Skt.] adj. Large, big, as పంచాస్యము or పంచాననము lit: 'huge-mouthed,' i. e., a lion. పంచగడ్డము a great beard. పంచపద్యము a mere fiction. (this name is given to apocryphal poems that are not grounded on any classical tradition as the మైరావణచరిత్ర, శతముఖరామాయణము, కృష్ణార్జున సంవాదము, జైమినిభారతము.)

పంచ *pancha*. [Skt.] adj. Five. **పంచకము** *panchakamu*. n. A set of five things, as of epigrams. భ్రమరపంచకము a set of five epigrams on a bee. యుద్ధపంచకము the five books of the Mahabharata (VI. X.) which deal with the battle. A battlefield, యుద్ధభూమి. **పంచకళ్యాణి** *pancha-kalyāṇi*. n. Black or any other colour with white points; piebald; a horse with a white mark or star in the face and with white legs. **పంచకోణము** or **పంచకోణి** *pancha-kōṇamu*. n. A pentagon. See కోణము. **పంచగవ్యము** *pancha-gavyamu* n. The five articles derived from the cow, viz.: milk, curds, butter, urine, and dung. **పంచగౌడులు** *pancha-gauḍulu*. n. The collective name for the Brahmins of Bengal and the northern provinces. పంచత్వము *panchatvamu*. n. Death, dying, as being the dissolution of the five elements. పంచజనుడు *pancha-janudu*. n. Man in general. మర్త్యుడు. See పాంచజన్యము. పంచజనచర్వణము cannibalism, eating human flesh. A. vi. 70. పంచదశము *pancha-daṣamu*. adj. Fifteenth. పంచదశకము *pancha-daṣakamu*. n. Fifteen. పంచదశి *pancha-daṣi*. n. The fifteenth lunar day, of either the dark or bright fortnight. పౌర్ణమి, తిథి, అమావాస్య. పంచద్రావిడులు The five divisions of the Dravida races, viz. Tamil, Telugu, Malayalam, Kanarese and Mahrati. పంచనఖము *pancha-nakhamu*. n. Lit: "Five clawed," i. e., a tiger. పులి. పంచనఖి *pancha-nakhi*. n. An iguana. ఉడుము. పంచపాత్రము *pancha-pātramu*. n. The "five dishes:" a phrase used for five cups used in worship. Also, a sort of cup. పంచప్రాణములు *pancha-prāṇamulu*. n. The five vital airs of the body. Life. పంచభూతములు the five elements. పంచబాణుడు, పంచశరుడు or పంచసాయకుడు *pancha-bāṇudu*. n. Manmadha the god of love, so named from his five arrows. These are five fragrant flowers, viz., the అరవిందము or lotus, the అశోకము Jonesia asoka, the చూతము or mango blossom, the నవమల్లిక or Arabian jasmine, and the నీలోత్పలము or blue lotus; these are emblems of five passions denominated ద్రావిణి, శోషిణి, బంధిని, మోహిని and ఉన్మాదిని, that is, flurry, pining, enslaving, bewitching and maddening. పంచభక్ష్యములు five sorts of cakes. పంచమము *panchamamu*. n. A tenor note, similar to that of the cock when crowing; also, a note like that of the linnet or cuckoo. The musical treble. The two notes పంచమము and షడ్జము are called the నిత్యస్వరములు or *constant* (pervading) notes: they are also called స్వయంభుస్వరములు the supreme sounds. adj. Fifth, ఐదవది. Fine, melodious, ఇంపైన. పంచమస్థితి *panchama-sthiti*. n. The being a Pariah. The Pariah state or condition. పంచమి *panchami*. n. The fifth lunar day, of either the dark or bright fortnight. పంచముడు *panchamudu*. n. A Pariah, or "man of the fifth class:" as not belonging to any of the four pure Hindu castes. మాలవాడు. పంచరాశికము *pancha-raṣikamu*. n. The rule of five, the double rule of three. పంచలక్షణము *pancha-lakshaṇamu*. n. A Purana. పురాణము. పంచలవణములు *pancha-lavanamulu*. n. Salts in general. The five kinds of salt. See లవణము. పంచలోహము *pancha-lōhamu*. n. A mixed metal, composed of five ingredients, viz., copper, zinc, tin, lead, and iron. పంచపట్టెలు *pancha-paṭṭelu*. n. Five streaks. ఐదు చారలు. పంచవన్నెలు *pancha-vannelu*. n. Five colours. పంచవన్నెలరామచిలుక *pancha-vannela-rāma-chiluka*. n. A paroquet. పంచశాఖము *pancha-ṣākhamu*. n. The hand. చెయ్యి. పంచాంగము *panch-āngamu*. n. An almanac, as specifying five different things, viz., the lunar day (తిథి), the day of the week (వారము), the sign in which the moon is (నక్షత్రము), the conjunction of the planets shewing good and bad days (యోగము), and the horoscopes (కరణము). పంచాంగముచెప్పు to give a forecast of the year or day; to tell lies or false stories. పంచాణము *panchāṇamu*. n. The united five castes of the carpenter, blacksmith, brazier, goldsmith, and stonecutter. పంచాణులు *panchāṇulu*. n. Workmen, mechanics, or handicraftsmen, పంచాణమువారు. పంచామృతము a meat and drink offering formed of cocoanut kernels, plantains, sugar, honey, and ghee. పంచాయతి *panchayati*. n. A court of arbitrators consisting of 'five members.' A Panchayat, an arbitration court. పంచాయతిదారులు arbitrators, referees. పంచా

యుధము the "five weapons" of Vishṇu: also an amulet, being a plate of gold on which these are engraven. విష్ణువుయొక్క అయిదు ఆయుధములు, మరిన్ని ఆ అయిదు ఆయుధములయొక్క రూపులు చెక్కించిన పతకపుబిళ్ల. పంచారూఢిపత్రము a bond duly executed, i. e., bearing "five names" viz., those of the lender, the borrower, the writer, and two witnesses. పంచాస్యుడు, పంచాననుడు or పంచముఖుడు panch-āsyuḍu. n. "The five-faced;" an epithet of Siva. పంచాక్షరి panch-akshari. n. The "five syllables:" that is, a certain spell or holy name "నమశ్శివాయ" Na-mas-Si-vā-ya or "Salutation to Siva," similar to the five syllables "A-ve-Ma-ri-a." పంచేంద్రియములు panch-endriyamulu n. The five senses or organs. "సీ॥ మునిలోకగణ్యనాపాపకృత్యములు కృష్ణాన్వయ పంచేంద్రియములగోష్ఠి." G. v. 13. పంచేంద్రియబద్ధుడైన panch-endriya-baddhud-aina. adj. Carnal, sensual, worldly, given up to one's lusts.

పంచితము panchitamu. [Tel.] n. A cow's urine. గోమూత్రము. పంచితిలు or పంచితిల్లు panchitilu. v. n. To pass urine. (applied only to a cow.)

పంచె or పంచెరు panche. [Tel.] n. A man's lower garment: పంచెచెట్టు panche-cheṭṭu. n. A flowering plant called Cockscomb, Celosia argentea, గురుగుచెట్టు. (Watts.)

పంచె pantsa. [Tel.] n. A porch, a slanting verandah. పంచాడి, పంచెపాళ or పంచెపాళి pantsaḍi. (పంచె+అడి.) n. The pent roof of a balcony. A pent or shelving roof supported by pillars, a verandah. వసారా. "చుట్టు పంచాడికట్టించి కట్టినంత." Vaija. i. 52. Cf. ఏడాడి (ఏడు+అడి.)

పంచెకము pantsakamu. [from Skt. పశ్చాత్ after, hinder.] n. The hinder part of a horse's body. అశ్వమయొక్క పశ్చాద్భాగము. [From Skt. పంచ five.] n. Five bushels. అయిదు తూములు.

పంచెకరము pantsa-karamu. [Tel.] adj. Very much, exceeding great. అత్యధికమైన. పంచెకరపాటులు great sorrows. మిక్కిలి అధికమైన దుఃఖములు.

పంచదార pantsa-dāra. [from Skt. పంచ ధార. Cf. పంచసారము.] n. Sugar. శర్కర. చీనాపంచదార sugar from China. [This word is in common use for 'sugar' in Telugu, Malayalam and Bengali, but not in Tamil or Canarese.]

పంచబంగాళము pantsa-bangāḷamu. [Tel.] n. Distance. దూరము. Disappearance, vanishing, అదృశ్యము. పంచబంగాళము కావించు to put to flight, rout, chase. పంచబంగాళమగు to disappear.

పంచారించు pantsarintsu. [Tel.] v. n. To spread. వ్యాపించు. To increase, excel, అతిశయించు. పంచారము pantsaramu. n. The act of spreading. వ్యాపనము. Increase, అతిశయము.

పంచు pantsu. [Tel.] v. a. To deal, distribute, divide or share. పాల్పరచు, విభజించు. To despatch or send. పంపు. To appoint. To command, నియమించు. పంచిపెట్టు panchi-peṭṭu. v. a. To share out. పంచివేత panchi-vēta. n. Apportionment, sharing. పంపకం.

పంజ panja. [Tel.] adj. Poor, low, mean. క్షుద్రమైన, నీచమైన.

పంజరము or పంజిరము panjaramu. [Tel.] n. A sort of fish. పంజరము or పంజిరము [Skt.] n. A cage, a case or covering. A cloth covering, as that of a palanquin, గవుసెన, బురకా. "రాచచిలుకమూడువంకాలకంచెట్టి శృంగారంబుగకుంజర పంజరంబు పదిలించి యున్నంత లోకోగానాళి." A. vi. 157. టీ॥ పంజరంబు పదిలించి, ముసుగువేసి. పంజరము or అస్థిపంజరము a skeleton, శరీరముయొక్క యెముకలగూడు.

పంజి panji. [Tel.] n. A tax. కప్పము.

పంజె or **పంజీరు** *panje.* [Tel.] n. A tree called బారంగి.

పంజె *pandza.* [Tel.] n. A boddice. రవిక.

పంజేరము See పంజా...

పంజేళము *pandzalamu.* [Tel.] n. A kind of song. గీతవిశేషము.

పంజోలము *pandzōli.* [Tel.] n. A kind of torch. ఒకవిధమైన కాగడా. హం. iii.

పంజా *pandza.* [Tel.] n. A torch. దివిటీ. A sort of fire-work. A pole of a palanquin. A sort of earring. పంజాసేవ a torch dance. పంజాలకమ్మలు large earrings, worn by women.

పంట See under పండు and పల్లె.

పంటి or **పనటి** *panti.* [Tel.] n. A large earthen pot with a wide mouth; a globular vase. మూతివెడల్పుగల ఆటిక.

పంటించు *pantintsu.* [Tel.] v. n. To delay, జాగుచేయు. To be flurried or confused. తడబడు. To hesitate, అనుమానించు.

పంటిగచెట్టు *pantiga-chettu.* [Tel.] n. A tree called *Briedelia montana.* Rox. iii. 735.

పంటె, పంటియ, పంటెకర్ర or **పంటెకోల** *pante.* [Tel.] n. A weaver's whirl (not a distaff) on which the thread is wound. It is of a pyramidal shape. సాలెవాడు నూలుచుట్టే సాధనము.

పంత్రు or **పంత్రుకోల** *pantra.* [Tel.] n. A fish spear, a harpoon. చిల్లులుగలయినుములు మూడువాళ్లుగలకర్ర, చేపలుపొడిచే ఆయుధము. **పంత్రించు** *pantrintsu.* v. a. To spear or harpoon a fish. పంత్రుకోలపొడుచు.

పండ *panda.* [Tel.] n. Simplicity. తెలివి ఉన్నట్టు తెలిసికొనే స్థితి.

పండారము *pandāramu.* [Tel.] n. A devotee of the Siva sect. This word is in *form* neuter: plu. పండారాలు. **పండా వారు** *panda-vāru.* n. Name applied to a certain beggar caste near Cuttack.

పండితుడు *panditudu.* [Skt.] n. A "Pandit" or learned man; a doctor, or professor. See పండితులు.

పండు *pandu.* [Tel.] v. n. To ripen. ఫలించు To be accomplished. To be produced. (as salt from the ground) to effloresce. to crystallize. n. A fruit, a berry. adj. Ripe, mature. వానికి కాలము పండినది this is harvest time for him. పండుకాచు to be red hot. ఆ యినుమును పండకాచినాడు he made the iron red hot. **పంట** *panta.* n. Ripening, పండుట. Cultivation. కృషి. Produce, a crop. **పంటకాపు** *panta-kāpu.* n. A husbandman. **పంటకాపులు** *panta-kāpulu.* n. Farmers. పంటచెరువు a tank for watering rice fields. కల్లుపంట దినములు the toddy season. వలపులపంట my beloved. "పితరుల పంటలు రమణి నిర్వంశ." Vencatach Mah: iii: 203. **పంటపొలము** *panta-polamu.* n. A cultivated field. పండిన పొలము. **పంటమన్ను** *panta-mannu* n. Plough land, good soil. పంటవలతి, పంట చెలి, పంటపొలతి or పంటతొయ్యలి a poetical phrase for 'the earth. పంటవలంతివింటిదొర n. Cupid, i. e., Lord of the earth-born bow, i. e., the bow of sugar cane which grows from the earth: "పంటవలంతివింటి దొరబారికి సోరువవేక." T. iii. 3. **పంటసాల** *panta-sāla.* n. A granary, ధాన్యాగారము, కణజము. **పండబారు** *panda-bāru.* v. n. To mellow or begin to ripen. To grow pale, turn white. **పండించు** *pandintsu.* v. a. To cause to ripen, పండజేయు. పండుకోతి an old monkey. పండుటాకు a ripened leaf. పండువెన్నెల lit: ripened moonlight: full moon light, the brilliancy of the full moon. ముసలిపండు an old crone. (opposed to కాయ in the sense పిల్లకాయ) In shopkeeper's cant పండు means చింతపండు tamarind. There is a bird called పండు పకిడి. మామిడిపండు a ripe mango. **పండు కప్ప** or **పండుకేప** *pandu-kappa* n. The perch or cock-up fish, of which there are many species. Russell No. 131. పండు మీనుకట్టుము dried fish.

పండు or **పరుండు** *pandu*. [Tel. Short for పడి ఉండు.] v. n. To lie down. శయనించు. **పండబెట్టు** *panda-bettu*. v. a. To lay down, put to sleep, put to bed. **పండు కొను** *pandu-konu*. v. n. To go to bed, to lie down or recline. జ్వరముతో పండుకొన్నాడు he is laid up (or in bed) with fever. అతని వర్తకమంతా పండుకొన్నది his business is asleep, or stagnant.

పండుగ, పండుగు, పండువ or **పండువు** *panduga*. [Tel.] n. A feast or festival, a treat. ఉత్సవము. దాన్ని చూడగా వానికన్నులకు పండుగ అయినది the sight of her was a feast to his eyes. ఇల్లలుకగానే పండుగ యగునా? does the decking of a house constitute a feast? చెవులపండువు a treat to the ears.

పండుడు *pandudu*. [Skt.] n. A eunuch. నపుంసకుడు, పేడి.

పండేరము *panderamu*. [Tel.] n. A cake. భక్ష్యము.

పండ్రెండు *pand-rendu*. [Tel. పది+రెండు.] n. Twelve, పన్నెండు.

పంత or **పంతగద్ద** *panta*. [Tel.] n. A vulture. An eagle.

పంతము *pantamu*. [Tel.] n. A bet or wager, పందెము. Determination, perseverance. A vow, ప్రతిజ్ఞ, శపథము. Rivalry, పోటి. Courage, heroism, పౌరుషము. Way, manner, విధము. నీవు వారితో పంతమేల why do you wager against them? పంతము మీరగా emulously, eagerly. **పంతకాడు** *panta-kadu*. n. A man who is under a vow, ప్రతిజ్ఞకలవాడు. A rival, పోటిచేయువాడు. A man of determination, పౌరుషముకలవాడు. **పంతగించు** *pantagintsu*. v. n. To vow, to wager, ప్రతిజ్ఞచేయు. To persevere. To rival, పోటిచేయు. To lay down a rule, to command, విధించు.

పంతు *pantu*. [Tel.] n. Excellence. మేలిమి. adj. Good, excellent, మేలు.

పంతులు *pantulu*. [short for Skt. పండితులు.] n A teacher. చదువులయ్యవారు. A title given to the లౌకిక Brahmins as నరసన్న పంతులు, వెంకన్న పంతులు, &c.

పంద *panda*. [Tel.] adj. Cowardly, base. పిరికి. n. A coward. పోతే. పందమాటలు silly words. తిండిపంద a glutton. "తిండిపంద యోగి తిరుకుముకుండుమ." Vema. 857. **పందతనము** *panda-tanamu*. n. Cowardice. పోతేతనము.

పంది *pandi*. [Tel.] n. A hog. ఊరపంది the domesticated pig. అడవిపంది the wild hog, a boar. ఏదుపంది or ముండ్లపంది a porcupine. నీరుపంది a porpoise. **పందికొక్కు** *pandi-kokku*. [Lit. The pig-rat. The Eng. 'Bandicoot.' is a corruption of this word.] n. A Bandicoot. The Bandicoot-Rat. *Nesocia bandi-cota*. (F. B. I.) సీమపంది కొక్కు a guinea pig. A proverb says పట్టాగారలో పందికొక్కును పెట్టినట్టు, i. e., setting a bandicoot in a granary. cf. Setting the wolf to take care of the sheep. **పందిగడ్డ** *pandi-gadda*. n. The name of a certain edible root. The pignut. శృంగాటకము, వరికందుము. **పందిగోరు** *pandi-goru*. n. A boar's tusk or claw. A weapon used by boar hunters, వేటగాండ్ర సాధనవిశేషము. **పందిజిట్ట** or **పందిపిట్ట** *pandi-jitta*. n. The small White throated Babbler, *Dumetia albigularis* (F. B. I.) **పందిపోటు** or **పందీటు** *pandi-potu*. n. A spear used to hunt boars with. **పందిముక్కు**. **పందిమూతి** or **పందిపీట** *pandi-mukku*. n. A kind of step used in old fashioned carts, గాడీముఖ్యలో ఎక్కుటకు ఎల్లవిరట ను పందిమూతి వలె చెయ్యబడిన పలక. పందిపీఠము.

పందిరి or **పందిలి** *pandiri.* [Tel.] n. A shed made of leaves or wicker work, a porch. "అత్యుచ్ఛ్రితము ముత్యాలపందిరియు." BD. vii. 290. A trellis for vines or creepers to run over: a frame మాటలలో పందిలి పెట్టినాడు all his words ended in smoke. **పందిరి మంచము** *pandiri-mantsamu.* n. A tilt-bed, a bed with a top, tester or canopy.

పందుము (పది+తూము.) See పది. and తూము

పందెము or **పందియము** *pandemu.* [Tel. Connected with పంతము.] n. A wager, stake, bet. A throw of the dice. వానికి మంచిపందెము పడినది he had a lucky throw. గుర్రపుపందెము a horse-race. **పందెగాడు** *pande-kādu.* n. One who lays a wager.

పందేరము *panderamu.* [Tel.] n. A benediction uttered over money or food which is then distributed. ధనాదికములను పంచిపెట్టుట.

పంతొమ్మిది *pan-dommidi.* [Tel. పది+తొమ్మిది.] pron. Nineteen.

పంపరపనస or **పంపరమాస** *pampara-panasa.* [Tel.] n. The shaddock or pomelose tree, *Citrus decumana.*

పంపు *pampu.* [Tel. from పనుచు.] v. a. To send. పుచ్చు, పనుచు. See **అంపు.** To command, ఆజ్ఞాపించు. n. Sending, dismissing. A command, order. ఆజ్ఞ. A share, division. భాగము. A thing ordered to be done, ఆజ్ఞాపింపబడినపని. Delusion, bewitching, మాయాకర్మము. A row of rice-beds in a field, మడుమళ్లవరుస. A weight equal to five-eighths of a seer. అర్ధసేరు వన టాకుఎత్తు నిరూపకము, తులామానవిశేషము. **పంపించు** *pampintsu.* v.a. To send, పంపు. **పంపు పడు** *pampu-padu.* v. n. To be commanded or ordered, ఆజ్ఞాపింపబడు. To be sent. పంపు పెట్టు to command, ఆజ్ఞాపించు. **పంపకము** *pampakamu.* n. Sending, dismissal. **పంపిణి** *pampini.* n. Distribution, allotment, apportioning, division, sharing. పంపుపిడుచు to exorcise or cast out a devil. **పంపుచేయు** *pampu-chēyu.* v. a. Lit: to set a task to. To bewitch or send a devil into a man. To command. To outrival or outshine. ఆభిచారపంపు witchery, sorcery.

పంపెన *pampena.* [Tel.] n. The tree called *Bignonia indica.* Rox. iii. 110. శ్యోనాకము.

పంబ *pamba.* [Tel.] n. A kind of drum. వాద్య భేదము. **పంబలవాండ్లు** *pambala-vāndlu.* n. A class of beggars or gypsies who are fortune-tellers. పంబవాయించువారు.

పంబు *pambu.* [Tel.] v. n. To grow, increase. వ్యాపించు, అతిశయించు, "పంబిన కోపమునా పమురత్ధంగధరుంబును వగ్గలించి యుల్లంబుదెవం గొంగ." M. IV. ii. 139. n. A large leathern vessel carried by a bullock, ఎద్దుమీదవేసే పెద్దపెట్టె. **పంబోతు** *pam-bōtu.* n. A fat bull. బలిసినదున్నపోతు. A vi. 28. పంబు తాళ్లు strong ropes, దేవిషైనను ఊడ్చికట్టే తాళ్లు.

పకపక or **పకాపక** *paka-paka.* [Tel. anuk] n. Giggling, or a loud burst of laughter; ha! ha! **పకపకనవ్వు** or **పకపకలాడు** *paka-paka-navvu.* v. n. To giggle, to laugh very loud, to burst out laughing.

పఖాలి or **పకాలి** *pakali.* [H.] n. A leathern water bag for carrying water on a bullock. తిత్తి, గంగ. A man who supplies water by means of it.

పకిలు *pakilu.* [Tel.] n. A sudden sound caused in striking anything. కొట్టుటయందు కలుగుధ్వని.

పకోడి *pakōdi.* [H.] n. A kind of hot sweet-meat.

పక్క or **ప్రక్క** *pakka.* [Tel. from పడు. & short for పడక.] n. A side, quarter or direction. పార్శ్వము. A bed or bedding, పక్కదుప్పటి a bed sheet. పక్కవేసుకొనే బొంత a bed cloth or quilt. adj. Near, next, neighbouring. పక్కయిల్లు the neighbouring house. పక్కపండ్లు the side teeth. పక్కబలము an auxiliary force; assistance, help. ఇరుపక్కలు both sides. పక్కకుపోవు to go aside పక్కపొట్లుపొడుచు, to tickle one in the ribs; to elbow, to harass. **పక్కయెముక** *pakka y-emuka.* n. A rib. పక్కశూల or పక్కనొప్పి liver complaint.

పక్కణము *pakkaṇamu.* [Skt.] n A gipsy-hamlet, a fishing village. ఎరుకలగూడెము, బోయపల్లె.

పక్కణి *pakkaṇi.* [Tel.] n. A powder box. బరిణె. "జేవాదిపక్కణి" శిలా. iii.

పక్కము *pakkamu.* [from Skt. పక్షము.] n. A side. పార్శ్వము. A fortnight, శుక్లాది పక్షము. చుట్టపక్కములు kith and kin.

పక్కాలి See పకాలి.

పక్కి *pakki.* [from Skt. పక్షి.] A bird. **పక్కిడాలువేల్పు** *pakki-dāl-vēlupu.* n. One whose ensign is the eagle, i.e., Vishṇu. గరుడధ్వజుడు. **పక్కియొడలివాడు** *pakki-y-odali-vādu.* n. A demigod called a కిన్నరుడు. **పక్కిరాయడు** *pakki-rāyadu.* n. The king of birds, i. e., an Eagle, గరుత్మంతుడు.

పక్కియ *pakkiya.* [Tel.] n. A side, quarter, పార్శ్వము.

పక్కు *pakku.* [Tel.] n. A scab. A lump, as of paint. "గంధపుపక్కులు." Vishṇu. vi. 28. A sudden laugh. Suddenness. **పక్కున** *pakku-na.* adv. Startingly, alarmingly, suddenly. ఠటాలున. "పక్కునభాండంబు పగుల గొట్టె" he broke the pot with a crash. N. iv. 241. **పక్కునవవ్వు** *pakkuna-navvu.* v. n. To burst out laughing.

పక్కె or **పక్కియ** *pakke.* [Tel.] n. The Tamarisk tree. ఝూవుకం, పిచులపుచెట్టు. **పక్కెచేప** or **వేడిసచేప** *pakke-chēpa.* n. A sort of carp with forked bones. Some species are called బుడ్డపక్కె, మంగలపక్కె, మోరపక్కె, మాచెనపక్కె, చందమామపక్కె and బొందపక్కె. H. iv. 225.

పక్కెర *pakkera.* [Tel.] n. Armour: mail. కవచము. శిరా. Swa. iv. 36. M. IV. iii. 124. పట్టుపక్కెర silk housings for a horse.

పక్కెరాలు *pakkeralu.* (పక్కెర+ఆలు.) n. A female warrior, a female sentinel, కావలికత్తె. రామా. vi.

పక్వము *pakvamu.* [Skt.] adj. Mature, ripe, పండిన, పరిపాకమునొందిన. పక్వమగు to grow ripe, to mature. పక్వముచేయు to make fit or ready.

పక్షము *pakshamu.* [Skt.] n. A side, flank. పక్క. A wing, as being the side of a bird. ఈక. The feather of an arrow. A side or party. Bias of mind, partiality. A fortnight, as one half of the month. An argument, position or assertion. A hypothesis. పూర్వపక్షము a refutation. A class, or tribe. A group or multitude, సమూహము. కేశపక్షము a lock of hair. అతని పక్షమున on his behalf, behoof or favour. ఆపక్షమందు in that case, on that supposition, supposing so, provided it be so. ఇట్లుచెప్పె పక్షమందు if he says so, upon his saying this. మొదటిపక్షమందు on the first supposition. **పక్షకము** *pakshakamu.* n. A back door, దిడ్డివాకిలి. **పక్షతి** *pakshati.* n. The first lunar day of either the dark or bright fortnight, పాడ్యమి. The root of a wing, ఈకమొదలు. **పక్షద్వారము** *paksha-dvāramu.* n. A back door, a side door. దిడ్డివాకిలి. **పక్షపాతము** *paksha-pātamu.* n. Leaning to one side, i.e., partiality. ఒక పక్క జారుకట. అక్షరపక్షపాతము love of learning. **పక్షపాతి** *paksha-pāti.* n. One who is partial. **పక్షాంతరము** *paksh-antaramu.* n. An alternative. ఈపక్షము కూడనందున పక్షాంతరము చెప్పెదను this view of the question or hypothesis not answering, I shall explain the alternative or the other side. వారు పక్షాంతరమును అవలంబించినారు they adopted another view. **పక్షి** *pakshi.* n. A bird. A poor wretch. A miserable destitute object. పక్షులు poor wretches. నేను పక్షిసంటివాడను or నేనొక పక్షిని I am as helpless or desolate as a homeless bird. పక్షిణి *pakshini*. n. A period of thirty six hours, a night and two days. రెండుపగళ్లు నొకరాత్రియును, సేక, రెండురాత్రులు నొకపగలునుగలకాలము. **పక్షీకరించు** *pakshi-karintsu*. v. a. To be partial to, to countenance. పక్షముంచు. **పక్ష్మము** *pakshmamu*. n. An eyelash. రెప్పవెండ్రుక. **పక్ష్మలము** *pakshmalamu*. adj. Having eyelashes, రెప్పవెండ్రుకలుగల. **పక్ష్మలించు** *pakshmalintsu*. v. n. To wink, రెప్పవేయు.

పగ *paga*. [Tel.] n. Enmity. విరోధము. An enemy, విరోధి. **పగపట్టు** or **పగగొను** *paga-paṭṭu*. v. n. To bear a grudge, to cherish enmity, విరోధపడు. **పగచాటు** *paga-tsāṭu*. n Blaming, censure, దూషించుమట. **పగతుడు** *pagatuḍu*. (పగ+అతడు.) n. An enemy, foe, శత్రువు. పగతురు or పగతులు enemies. M. v. ii. 80. పగతురాలు a woman who is an enemy. **పగదారి** *paga-dāri*. n. An enemy, విరోధము వహించినవాడు. **పగరు** *pagaru*. (పగ+వారు.) n. Enemies, foes, శత్రువులు. **పగలు** *pagalu*. n. Enmities, శత్రుత్వములు. **పగవాడు** *paga-vāḍu*. n. A foe, an enemy. ఇది నా పగవారికైనా రారాదు I would not wish even my enemies to suffer this.

పగటు *pagaṭu*. [Tel.] v. a. To proclaim, ప్రకటించు. n. Brightness, brilliance, దీప్తి, ప్రకాశము. Beauty, లావణ్యము. Joy, మురిపెము. Pride, పొగరు, గర్వము. A quarrel, wrangling. విరోధము.

> "అభినవాలోక సౌఖ్యంబునవధిపు డలర,
> నలరుబోడి సమగ్రలజ్జానుభావ,
> భావమ్ము లెడమాటున పగటుచూపు,
> చూపరకు సోచె పరిణామయుక్తియుప్పుడు."
>
> Vasu. iii. 86.

పగడము or **పవడము** *pagaḍamu*. [from Skt. ప్రవాళము.] n. Coral. పగడంపుతీగెలు a name of a kind of rice. **పగడ** *pagaḍa*. n. An ace; one at dice. ND. iii. 573. నేను పడిపోవుటకు పగడ తప్పెను I was within an ace of falling, I all but fell. **పగడసాల** *pagaḍa-sāla*. n. A gaming table. సొగటాల వలక. Diceplay, a particular game played with dice on a coloured cloth, సొగటాల ఆట.

> "పందెములు సోరి వైచును పగడసాల,
> తాలితో నాడు పాచికాంకురేశిక్రమ్ముక్క.."
>
> T. iv. 79.

పగడపుజిట్ట *pagaḍapu-jiṭṭa*. n. A kind of bird. పక్షివిశేషము. **పగడపురిక్క** *pagaḍapu-rikka*. n. The constellation called ఆర్ద్రానక్షత్రము. **పగడమల్లె** *pagaḍa-malle*. n. A very delicate and fragrant flower, with white petals and a yellow tube. *Nyctanthes arbor tristisi* Rox. i. 86.

పగలు or **పవలు** *pagalu*. [Tel.] n. Day-time. Day. అహస్సు. (Adverbially) by day, in the day time. రాత్రింబగలు day and night. పగటిమీదను అక్కడినుండి తర్లితిమి we set out in the afternoon. **పగటివేలుపు** *pagaṭi-velupu*. n. The god of the day, i.e., the sun. **పట్టపగలు** *paṭṭa-pagalu*. [పగలు+పగలు.] n. Broad day. adv. In full daylight. **పగలువత్తి** *pagalu-vatti*. n. The fire work called a blue light or Roman candle. మతాబు. "పగలొత్తులే బవిటలంచిద్వళిగులుణ." H. iii. 31.

పగిది *pagidi*. [from Skt. ప్రకృతి] n. Mode, feature, likeness. విధము. A tax, కప్పము.

> "ఆ॥ నందుడాదిగాగ గొందరుగొల్లలు
> పగిదిధనము దీర్పబోలు జేమురు
> మలుపగొంచు గొనుచున్న చోటికిబోవు
> వాంగగాంచె ననటదూరముననునను."
>
> V. P. vii. 74.

పగిదిని (ablative) resembling, or in the appearance of, like, విధముగ. **పగిదిగంటు** (for పైడికంటె.) *pagidi-ganṭa*. n. The spotted owlet.

పగులు *pagulu* [Tel.] v. n. To break, crack, or go to pieces; to be broken, fractured, burst, chopped. అద్దము పగిలినది the glass has broken. n. A crack, a break. **పగుళ్లు** *pagullu*. n. plu. Crevices, cracks. **పగులుచు, పగుల్చు, పగిలించు, పగులచేయు** or **పగులగొట్టు** *pagulutsu*. v. a. To break. **పగుళ్లువారు** or **పగుళ్లువారు** *pagullu-baru*. v. n. To break.

పగ్గపత్తి *pagga-patti*. [Tel.] n. A plant *Cyrilla aquatica*. Rox. iii. 115.

పగ్గము *paggamu*. [Tel.] n. A tether, cord, rein, halter. A rope used by a weaver to stretch the warp on. A churning rope, కవ్వపుత్రాడు. A particular measure (as a *chain*) of land. చిన్నపగ్గము నాలుగు మూరల కొలెదు, పెద్దపగ్గము అయిదు మూరలకొలెదు. రెండుపగ్గాలదూరము twice a tether's length off. "పాయలపగ్గములచే నంటితారొప్పంగ." B. x. 20.

పగ్గె or **పగ్గియ** *pagge*. [from Skt. ప్రజ్ఞ.] n. Skill, cleverness. సామర్థ్యము, ప్రజ్ఞ. Bragging. కత్థోక్తి, బడాయి. **పగ్గించు** *paggintsu*. v. n. To brag. ప్రజ్ఞలుపలుకు, బడాయలుకొట్టు.

పఙ్క్తి *pangkti*. [Skt.] n. A row or series, వరుస. Ten, పది. పఙ్క్తులుతీర్చి కూర్చుండిరి they sat down in rows.

పచ or **పచనము** *pacha*. [Skt.] n. Cooking, dressing food, వంటుట.

పచరణ or **పచేరణ** *pacharana*. [Tel.] n. Feigning. నటన. "పచరణకాదుమీపాదంబు లాన." HD. i. 905.

పచరించు, పచేరించు or **పచారించు** *pacharintsu*. v. n. and a. To make, effect. చేయు. To spread, extend, ప్రసరించు, ప్రసరింపజేయు. To spread, as a net (వల), పరచు, చాచు, వ్యాపింపజేయు. To arrange as goods in a shop, అమర్చు, సవరించు. To use or put into effect. ప్రయోగించు. To throw as an arrow, బాణమును ప్రయోగించు. To conduct, నడుపు. To proclaim, ప్రకటించు, చెప్పు. "అర్యులగా, ఘనమతిదివ్యబంధి నయాగారవముల్ పచరించి." Bilh. i. 67. "కులమునురూపముగా మగనికూరిమియుగా గలదానవంచునవ్వల బచరింపగా రవలో పాడ మెగా మరివారికెంతయుగా." Parij. i. 9.

పచారము or **పచారము** *pacharamu*. [Tel.] n. A shop. అంగడి.

పచారీ, పచారు or **పచేరము** *pachari*. [H.] n. An airing, taking a walk. విహారము. పచారీచేయు to walk to and fro for exercise.

పచేలిమము *pachelimamu*. [Skt.] adj. Ripe. పండిన. "రామకృపచేను, పచేలిమరాజ్యసంపద ఫుల్లస్వతే." Satyabh. i. 178.

పచ్చి *pachchi*. [Tel.] adj. Raw, unripe. ముదరని, పండని. Unbaked, unburnt, కాలని, as పచ్చికుండ. Unboiled, ఉడుకని, as పచ్చి ఫలుసు. Green, not dry, (as firewood), ఎండని. Uncured (as a hide,) raw, sore, tender, as పచ్చిపుండు. Colloquially it means palpable, gross, downright, absolute, rank, arrant, open, unveiled, unblushing, broad, coarse. పచ్చిమిరపకాయలు green chillies. పచ్చివిషము rank poison. పచ్చికస్తురి వీసె an unsunned or unbroached scent bottle. పచ్చికర్ర a green stick. పచ్చి ఒళ్లుగల convalescent. "పచ్చిబడి యాలుతిని బడిగొట్టుదినుచు." Charit. i. 2223. పచ్చి నెత్తురు blood just shed. "పచ్చమంగిన జూచి వనుధేశపత్ని, పచ్చినెత్తురుమూతి పరికించిరిరు." Saranga D. v. 280. **పచ్చిక** *pachchika*. (పచ్చి+ఇక.) n. Grass. పచ్చగడ్డి. పచ్చిక లేలేదు the grass is not brought. పచ్చికపట్టు a grassy spot, a meadow, a lawn, a green. **పచ్చితేరు** *pachchi-teru*. v. n. To become green, పచ్చబడు.

పచ్చెము or **పచ్చియము** *pachchemu*. [from Skt. పక్షము.] n. Swindling cheating. చూచుచుండగా దొంగిలించడము. A trick (or cannon) at marbles. **పచ్చెపువాడు** or **పచ్చెపుకాంగ** *pachchepu-vadu*. n. A cheat, a sharper, a swindler. పచ్చికాడు *pachche-kāḍu*. n. A swindler. పచ్చెపు తనము *pachchepu-tanamu*. n. Swindling.

పచ్చ *patsa*. [Tel.] n. Lit: Leaf colour. Green, yellowish green, yellow colour, (a leaf being first green, then fading into yellow.) An emerald, మరకతము. Any figure punctured or tattooed into the skin, because it is coloured green. A green plant or tree. cf. "పైరుపచ్చ" adj. Green, yellow, sallow. (The word పచ్చ radically means Bright, fair-coloured.) పచ్చ పొడుచుకొను to tattoo the skin. ఆకుపచ్చ green. పసుపు పచ్చ or పాలకపచ్చ yellow. కలంకారిపచ్చలు a sort of cloth, or painted chintz. See on పచ్చి. Various shades of green are called కప్పుపచ్చ dark green, తెల్లపచ్చ light green, సన్నీటిపచ్చ a still lighter tint. రాతిపచ్చ emerald green, చిలకపచ్చ bright green, మక్కిపచ్చ dirty dark green. వాని కండ్లు పచ్చపారినవి he has the jaundice. వారు ఇప్పుడు పచ్చగానున్నారు they are now in prosperous circumstances. కాపు పచ్చగా నుంటే రాజు చూడలేడు the king cannot bear to see a thriving farmer. పచ్చనరాలు the blue veins. పచ్చగువ్వ a bright yellow green bird; the green pigeon. పచ్చపైకము a good coin. HD. ii. 153. పచ్చకట్లపాము a green snake. పచ్చకన్నులమెకము *patsa-kannula-mekamu*. n. Lit: The yellow-eyed beast, i.e., a lion, హర్యక్షము. పచ్చకర్పూరము *patsa-karpūramu*. n. Green coloured camphor; crude camphor. This is the name of a brilliant white drug, used to cure the eye, which real camphor injures. It is not in lumps but is a powder. పచ్చకామెరలు *patsa-kāmerulu*. n. Jaundice. పచ్చజిట్ట *patsa-jiṭṭa*. n. The common Iora (a small green and yellow bird), *Ægithina tiphia*. (F. B. I.) పచ్చజీనువాయి *patsa-jinu-vāyi*. n. The Red-headed Bunting, *Emberiza luteola*. (F. B. I.) పచ్చన or పచ్చదనము *patsana*. n. Greenness or yellowness. పచ్చని *patsani*. adj. Green, yellow. పచ్చబంగారు yellow or pure gold. పచ్చగానున్న yellow or golden: prosperous, fortunate. పచ్చబ్రాలు *patsa-brālu*. n. Yellow rice, i.e., rice coated with saffron and used to sprinkle over persons on auspicious occasions. పచ్చరెక్క *patsa-rekka*. n. The Indian Bee-eater, *Merops viridis*. పెద్దపచ్చరెక్క or తోకపచ్చరెక్క *pedda-patsa-rekka*. n. The blue-tailed Bee-eater, *Merops philippensis*. (F.B.I.) పచ్చవలువదారి *patsa-valuva-dāri* n. Lit: One who wears a yellow cloth, i.e., Vishṇu, పీతాంబరుడు. పచ్చవారువపుతోడు or పచ్చవార్వపుతోడు *patsa-vāruvapu-dzōḍu*. n. Lit: One who rides on a green animal, i.e., the sun or Manmadha. హరిదశ్వుడు, శుకవాహుడు. పచ్చవిలుకుడు, పచ్చవిల్తుడు or పచ్చవిలుకాడు *patsa-vilutuḍu*. n. Lit: The green bow-man, i.e., Manmadha, whose bow is green, being made of a sugar cane. పచ్చారె చెట్టు *patsts-āre-chettu*. [పచ్చ + ఆరెచెట్టు.] n. A large forest tree with a very fragrant flower, *Bauhenia spicata*.

పచ్చడము or పచ్చెడము *patsadamu*. [Tel.] n. A bed sheet. Any cloth. A cloth worn round the loins, కట్టువస్త్రము, అంగవస్త్రము. A cloak, a warm covering.

పచ్చడి *patsaḍi*. [Tel.] n. A chutney, a hotchpotch, a sort of broth, or green sauce, made of vegetables, mixed with tamarind juice, salt, and chillies. తొక్కుడు. plu. పచ్చళ్లు. మామిడికాయలపచ్చడి mango chutney. A bit or fragment, తునక. దానిని పచ్చడి చేసినాడు he reduced it to powder.

పచ్చము *patsamu*. [Tel.] n. A whole piece or double piece of long cloth or chintz, twenty four cubits in length; in chintzes it means a double తాను. Diaper or doiley.

పచ్చెముపాడు *patsamu-pāḍu.* (పాడు+పాడు.) adj. Quite empty. కేవలముశూన్యము.

పజీతి *pajīti.* [H.] n. Disgrace, ignominy. అవమానము. A. v. 52. Annoyance, harassment, నిర్బంధము.

పజ్జ *paḍza.* [from Skt. ప్రజ.] n People, జనము.

"గ్ర, దేవర నీవిపజెలను, ట్రోనక."

శిలా. ii.

పజ్జ *paḍḍza.* [from Skt. పశ్చాత్ behind.] n. The back side, behind, వెనుక. Nearness. సమీపము. adv. Near to. H. i. 72. **పజ్జవరించు** *paḍḍzavarintsu.* v. a. To fawn on, fondle, ముదుపర్చుచు.

పటకారు *paṭakāru.* [Tel. పట్టు+కారు.] n. Tongs, great pincers.

పటకారుడు *paṭakāruḍu.* [Skt.] n. A weaver. సాలెవాడు.

పటచ్చరము *paṭachcharamu.* [Skt.] n. An old cloth. పాతబట్ట.

పటపట *paṭa-paṭa.* [Tel. (anuk.)] adv. Crashingly (either as gnashing teeth or as splitting wood), aloud (as wings flapping), audibly.

పటము *paṭamu.* [Skt.] n. A cloth, వస్త్రము. A picture. గాలిపటము a paper kite, పతంగి. The hood of a serpent, పాముపడగ. పటాంతరము a change of linen clothing. వస్త్రాంతరము R. v. 282. **పటవాసము** or **పటవాసకము** *paṭavāsamu.* n. Perfumed powder. బుక్కాయి. పటాంచలము n. The skirt of a woman's dress thrown over the shoulder. B. X. 183. **పటాటోపము** *paṭ-āṭōpamu.* n. Magnificence, gorgeousness of dress.

పటలము *paṭalamu.* [Skt.] n. A roof; thatch, ఇంటికప్పు. A multitude, troop, train, number or retinue, సమూహము, పరివారము. A film over the eye, a cataract in the eye, నేత్రరోగవిశేషము. A flaw in gems, రత్నదోషము. A mark on the forehead, నొసటిబొట్టు. A section or chapter, గ్రంథభాగము. ధూమపటలము a mass or volume of smoke. **పటలి** *paṭali.* n. A multitude, సమూహము.

పటవణి *paṭavaṇi.* [Tel.] n. Spreading, expansion. వ్యాపనము. **పటవణించు** *paṭavaṇintsu.* v. n. To spread, వ్యా.

పటసాల *paṭa-sāla.* [Tel.] n. A hall or courtyard.

పటసాలెవాడు *paṭa-sāle-vāḍu.* [Tel.] n. A silk weaver. A. iv. 56.

పటహము *paṭahamu.* [Skt.] n. A kettle drum, a war drum. తప్పెట.

పటా Same as పట్టా (q. v.)

పటాకి *paṭāki.* [H.] n. A cracker, a kind of firework. టపాకి, టపాకు.

పటాణి *paṭāṇi.* [Afghan.] n. A Pathan horse. పటాణిదేశపు గుర్రము. "చిలుకపటాణి రాతు." కు. రా. iv.

పటాపంచె, పటాపంచేము or **పటాపంచేలు** *paṭāpantsa.* [Tel.] n. plu. Dispersion, defeat, చెదరుపడలు. **పటాపంచలైన** *paṭa-pantsal-aina.* adj. Dispersed, scattered. Parij. v. 46. పటాపంచలైరి they were scattered.

పటాలము or **పటాళము** *paṭalamu.* [Eng. 'battalion'] n. A regiment of soldiers, సిపాయీలదళము.

పటిక, పటికారము or **పటికకారము** *paṭika.* [from Skt. స్ఫటిక.] n. Alum. కటుకసోరింది. Lit: An astringent crystal. **పటికబెల్లము** *paṭika-bellamu.* n. Sugar-candy, కండ చక్కెర, కలకండ. **పటికము** *paṭikamu.* n. Rock crystal, quartz.

పటికిరింత *paṭikirinta.* [Tel.] n. Malice. కేలము.

పటితలించు *paṭitalintsu.* [Tel.] v. a. To beat or strike, కొట్టు, చేరచు.

పటిమ *patima*. [Skt.] n. Cleverness, dexterity, skilfulness, నేర్పు. Vigour, strength, liveliness. Patience, ఓపిక. వాక్పటిమ eloquence. నటనపటిమ cleverness in dancing. పటిమగల clever, dexterous, skilful, strong, vigorous.

పటీరము *patiramu*. [Skt.] n. Sandal, చందనము. The sandalwood tree.

పటీలుమని *patilu-m-ani*. [Tel. anuk.] adv. Bang, slapdash, with a crash.

పటు or **పటుత్వ** *patu*. [Skt.] adj. Clever, dexterous, skilful, able, smart, sharp, firm, hard, strong, vigorous. పటుగతిని soundly, finely, well, దిట్టముగా. **పటుతరముగా** *patu-taramu-ga*. adv. Dexterously; firmly, vigorously, strongly. **పటుత్వము** *patutvamu*. n. Cleverness, dexterity, skilfulness, strength, vigour. వానిపటుత్వము చూచి observing his vigour.

పటుకారు Same as పటకారు. (q. v.)

పటుకు or **పటుక్కున** *patuku*. [Tel.] adv. Slapdash. BD. v. 948.

పటేలు *patelu*. [Mahrati.] n. The headman of a village. గ్రామయజమానుడు.

పటోలము, పటోలి or **పటోలిక** *patolamu*. [Skt.] A plant called *Trichosanthes dioeca*, పొట్ల; or, *Luffa acutangula*, చేదుపొట్ల. Rox. iii. 702.

పట్కా *patka*. [H.] n. A belt or sash, నడికట్టు.

పట్ట *patta*. [Tel.] n. The bark of a tree, చెట్టుమీదితోలు. Sackcloth, గోనెపట్టలోనగునవి. A broad sword, పట్టాకత్తి. కిన్నెరపట్ట the back of a fiddle or lute. "పెద్దగను రామపట్టకె పెట్టువడెను." A.iv. 37. ఈ ఇనురాకు పట్టకె, చిగురాకు అను పట్టాకత్తిచేతనె. **పట్టతీగ** *patta-tiga*. n. The name of a large climbing shrub, with greenish white flowers, *Capparis heteroclita*. Rox. ii. 570. **పట్టసారాయి** *patta-sarayi*. n. Spirit, distilled arrack.

పట్టడ, *pattada*. [Tel.] n. A smithy, a shop. కమ్మరి పట్టడలో కొలిమిలువారు పనిచేయు చోటు.

పట్టణము or **పత్తనము** *pattanamu*. [Skt.] n. A city. ప్రధాననగరము. A town, నగరము. **పట్టణస్థులు** *pattana-sthulu*. n. Dwellers in a city, city people.

పట్టము *pattamu*. [Skt.] n. A gold band or fillet tied on the forehead of one at the time of his coronation as king, పట్టాభిషేకకాలమున నొసటకట్టెడుపట్టె. A diadem. Silk thread, పట్టునూలు. The bark of a tree, చెట్టుమీదిపట్ట. A grant or lease granted by a king to the ryots, రాజు రైతులకిచ్చు పట్టా. A title, బిరుదు. A grade or step in genealogy. A kingdom, రాజ్యము. అతనికి ప్రతాపసింహుడని పట్టము నిచ్చినారు they gave him the title of Pratāpa Simha. ఆ పట్టాధికారి చనిపోయినాడు the head of the state died. అతనికి పట్టముకట్టిరి they crowned him. పట్టపుదేవి a queen. పట్టపు ఏనుగు or పట్టపుటేనుగు a royal elephant, a state elephant. రాజెక్కు ఏనుగు, భద్రగజము. పట్టపుకత్తి a state-sword. పట్టమేలుట to reign. **పట్టాభిషేకము** *patt-abhishekamu*. n. Coronation, installation. పట్టాభిషిక్తుడు he who is crowned. పట్టాభిషేకముచేయు to crown one king. **పట్టభద్రుడు** *patta-bhadrudu*. n. A chief, leader.

పట్టా, పటా or **పట్ట** *patta*. [Tel.] n. The inner bark of a tree. Sackcloth. A sort of girdle cloth. Also, a lease; a grant or lease specifying the land occupied by a cultivator and the assessment due on it. రాజు రయితులకిచ్చేకవులు. పట్టాదారుడు a pattadar, a leaseholder. దిత్తాపట్టా a lease for a gross aggregate rent, one in which the land-tax and all other cesses are consolidated. See పట్ట, and పట్టము.

పట్టి *patti*. [Tel. from పట్టు.] a postposition. A sign of the fifth case of nouns. For, because of, on account of, with reference to. నిన్నుబట్టి యీ పనిచేస్తున్నాను I do this for your sake. It is added to the infinitive of verbs, as ఆ టోపి ఉండబట్టిగాని లేకపోతే అతనితల పగులును had it not been for the cap his skull would have been fractured. కాలము యుక్తముగాయిరబట్టి, (i.e., ఉండినందున) as the season turned out well or proved good. "ప్రభవించబట్టి" (L. XIV. 29.) because he was born. కాబట్టి therefore, it being so, such being the case. పట్టి n. A child, an infant. బిడ్డ, కొడుకు, కూతురు. పట్టిపట్టి a son's son or daughter, మనుమడు, మనుమరాలు. A roll of betel. A list. పట్టితల్లి a woman who has borne a child. తాంబూలపట్టి a roll or mouthful of betel. [Skt.] n. A plate, పలక. Also, a gold band or fillet tied across the forehead at the time of one's coronation, పట్టము.

పట్టిక *pattika.* [Skt.] n. A plate of metal, a board, a frame, the pieces of wood across a door. ఫలకము, పలక, పట్టము, కోడు, గంటపట్టె. An anvil, కమ్మరివాని దాగలి. "లాటుపట్టికలబెట్టిన పట్టెవర్ధనములు." Suca. i. 19. పట్టికామంచము Same as పట్టె మంచము. (q.v.)

పట్టీడు Same as పట్టె (q.v.)

పట్టీయము or పట్టెము *pattiyamu.* [Tel.] n. A large sword. పెద్దకత్తి, "మేటిబలాగా పట్టి యంబులుపండితోలు." R. ii. 20.

పట్టిలి *pattili.* [Tel.] n. A handful. పిడి.

పట్టిసము *pattisamu.* [Skt.] n. A broad sword. అడ్డకత్తి.

పట్టి *patti.* [Tel.] n. A list or inventory, a roll of names, జాబితా. A roll of betel, &c., tied up, చుట్ట. A bandage or plaster applied to a sore; anything pasted over a wound.

పట్టు *pattu.* [Tel.] v. n. To suffice, to last. చెల్లు. To last a long time, బహుకాలము చెల్లు. To begin, ప్రారంభించు. To happen, కలుగు. To cost. To fit or suit. To be possessed by evil spirits. To arrive, as ships. To be imbibed or absorbed, as a dye. To be held or contained. To be affected by disease or pain. v. a. To take, to hold, to catch, to apprehend. గ్రహించు. To take by force, నిర్బంధముచేసి గ్రహించు. దొంగను పట్టి కట్టుము catch and tie up the thief. To adopt, అవలంబించు. To blow as a conch. ఈ గోనె ఎంతబియ్యము పట్టును how much rice will this bag hold. ఈ మురుగు నా చేతికి పట్టదు this bangle will not fit my hand. వాడు నిండాసేపు ఊపిరిపట్టలేడు he cannot hold his breath long. చేపట్టు or చెయ్యిపట్టు *che-pattu.* v. a. Lit: To take the hand; to take to wife, to marry. చెయ్యిపట్టు to seize the hand, to ravish a female. దారము పట్టు, to twist a cord, పేను. గొడుగుపట్టు to hold an umbrella. కాయలు పట్టు to geld. కాళ్లుపట్టు to massage or rub the legs. పగపట్టు to conceive hatred. శంఖముపట్టు to blow a conch. కత్తి సానపట్టు to set or grind a knife or razor. కంపుపట్టు to stink. చుట్టపట్టు to smoke a cigar or cheroot. పొగపట్టు to apply smoke. ఆ బొక్కలో నా చెయ్యి పట్టదు my hand will not go into the hole. వాలు ఒకదారి పట్టినారు each of them went by a separate road. ఇంకా కోతపట్టలేదు the reaping has not yet been put in hand. ఆ వ్యాజ్యమును పట్టలేదు they did not admit the lawsuit. దానిగోళ్లకు గోరింటపట్టదు the colouring does not adhere to her nails. ఆ మందు ఈ రోగానికి పట్టలేదు the medicine has not affected this sickness. ఆ విద్యకు బాగా పట్టినాడు he has taken well to that branch of study. గింజపట్టే సమయము the time when the grain is forming in the ear. ఇందులో ఎవరికేమిపట్టినది who has any thing to do with this? నాలుగుదినములు పట్టును it will take four days. మనిషిపట్టేమాత్రము only large enough to admit a man. ఐదురూపాయిలు పట్టును it will cost five rupees. మూడు గజాలుపట్టును it will take three yards. మన్ని

ముపట్టి ఉన్నారు they betook themselves to the highlands. **ఆనవాలుపట్టు** or **గురూరుపట్టు** *guruta-paṭṭu*. v. a. To identify, recognise, know again, verify. పట్టి పట్టి మాట్లాడెను he spoke in a broken manner. ఎవరినిపట్టితే వారు చెప్పుదురు ask whom you will, and they will tell you. మీరు పట్టిమాట్లాడితే ఆ పని అనుకూలమవును if you speak to the point the matter will be settled. అది నాబుద్ధికి పట్టలేదు I do not take (or comprehend) the meaning. పట్టిచెప్పితే ఆ పిల్లవానికి చదువు బాగావచ్చును if you teach him sedulously the boy will learn well. వాడు దానిని పట్టుకొని పీకులాడుచున్నాడు he is troubling himself about it. వాడు పట్టినదెల్లా బంగారమవుచు వచ్చినది whatever he touched turned to gold. ఆ కోటను పట్టుకొన్నారు they took the fort. ఆ దొంగను పట్టుకొన్నారు they apprehended the thief. నా చెయ్యి పట్టుకొన్నాడు he laid hold of my hand, or, he seized my hand. ఆ వాడుకను పట్టుకొన్నాడు he began the practice. ఒక నెల జీతము పట్టుకొన్నాడు he stopped one month's wages. చెప్పగానే పట్టుకొన్నాడు he understood me the moment I spoke. నడుము పట్టుకొన్నది my loins are strained. [పట్టు is also added to a great number of nouns, to give them a verbal signification and in such cases it takes its meaning from the noun to which it is affixed; thus:] తుప్పుపట్టు to rust. ఇలుకుపట్టు to be sprained. అక్కరపట్టు to be necessary, to be required or to take interest in. కొవ్వుపట్టు to become fat. బూజుపట్టు to grow mouldy, దోవపట్టు to take a road. సత్తువపట్టు to be recovered, as strength. పెట్టుపట్టు to be seized with cramp, &c. వాడు లంచము పట్టుచున్నాడు he takes bribes. వాడికి వెర్రిపట్టినది he has gone mad. నాకు చలిపట్టుచున్నది I feel cold. వానిగుణములు నీకు పట్టుబడినవి you have contracted his habits. వానపట్టినప్పుడు when rain came on. అట్లు చేయుటకు నీకేమిపట్టినది what business had you to do this? what made you do this? గడ్డిపట్టినచేల్లు land covered with grass. వానిమీద తప్పుపట్టినారు they found fault with him. ఆ మందు నోరుపట్టినది the medicine made his mouth swell. వానికి జలుబు పట్టినది he has caught cold. నాకు కూరుకు పట్టినది I became drowsy. ఆ దూడ యింకా గడ్డి పట్ట లేదు the calf has not yet taken to grass. **పట్టించు** *paṭṭinsu*. [causal of పట్టు.] v. a. To cause to hold. To apply oil or ointment, &c. To make one begin. అదిన్ని వాడికి అమరము పట్టించినారు they have made him begin (reading) the Amaram. రేపు నీపని పట్టిస్తాను or నీతాకీము పట్టిస్తాను I will settle your business to-morrow, i. e., I will punish you. ఆ పెట్టెను వానిచేత పట్టించుకొనిరా make him bring the box with you. **పట్టింపు** *paṭṭimpu*. n. Application. Concern. పిల్లకాయలచేత ఒక పుస్తకము ఆరంభించడము, శ్రద్ధ, అక్కర, పాటింపు. అమరము పట్టింపు అయిన మూడునెలలకు three months after setting to work on the Amaram. ఆరాధ్యులకు కర్మమందు పట్టింపులేదు the Aradhyas pay no attention to rites. "జేనిపట్టింపు తల్లనుపూనిచాల." Hu. iii. 39. **పట్టు** *paṭṭu*. n. Holding, a hold. గ్రహణము, పట్టుకొనుట. A handful. Pertinacity, resolution, hold, strength, grip, grasp, seizing. గ్రహణము. An external application to a swelling to allay pain, &c., పూత. Ground, for a proceeding, కారణము. A prop; support, favor; a party or side, ఆధారము. A part or scene in a play, స్థానము, ఓపము. విరహపుపట్టు an amorous scene. యుద్ధపుపట్టు a warlike scene. A feat in wrestling. అది తలకు పట్టు పెట్టుకొని పండుకొన్నది she put a plaster on her temples and went to bed. ఈ వ్యాజ్యములో పట్టులేదు there is no proper plea in this suit. ఒకనిపట్టుగా మాట్లాడుట to speak on a man's behalf. ఒకపట్టుగానుండు to insist pertinaciously. ఉనికిపట్టు a place, a house, an abode. వాడు పట్టినపట్టు వదలడు he will not relinquish his purpose. వాణ్ని పట్టిన పట్టున తీసుకొనివచ్చిరి they brought him as he was. పట్టుస్నానము bathing at the commencement of an eclipse, as opposed to విడుపుస్నానము bathing at its termination. అతను పట్టువిడుపు తెలిసినవాడు he knows where to be lenient and where to be severe. కూతపట్టువేల as far as a cry may be heard. వారికి కర్మములలో పట్టులేదు they do not lay much stress upon ceremonies. వాడు ఎంతమాత్రము పట్టు ఇవ్వకుండా మాట్లాడు చున్నాడు he speaks without giving them any handle. చాలా మంది ఆతనపట్టు అయిరి many followed him, or joined his side. పట్టున (with న the sign of the ablative) at, by, close to. కొండపట్టున along the hedge. గాడిపట్టున at the manger. ఈ పట్టున at present. పట్లు feats in wrestling. వాడు కొట్టపట్లుపట్టగలడు he is able to wrestle. ఆ చుట్టుపట్ల in the adjacent places, in the neighbourhood. చుట్టుపట్ల వాండ్లు neighbours. పట్టు *pattu*. n. Silk. పట్టుబట్ట a silk cloth. పట్టునూలు silk thread, spun silk. పట్టునూలుసాలెవాండ్లు a class of silk weavers. పట్టునూలువాండ్లు a class of silk dyers. పట్టుపురుగు *pattu-purugu*. n. A silkworm. Also, an insect called ఇంద్రగోపము. పట్టంచు *patt-antsu*. (పట్టు+ అంచు.) n. A silk border, a border fringed or trimmed with silk. పట్టుకొమ్మ *pattu-komma*. n. A refuge, stay, support. ఆధారము, ఊతకోల. పట్టుకారు Same as పటకారు (q. v.). పట్టుకొను *pattu-konu*. v. n. & t. To catch, to catch hold of, to seize. పట్టుకోలు *pattu-kōlu*. n. Catching. పట్టుకొనుట. పట్టుజిట్ట *pattu-jitta*. n. A sort of bird. S. i. 187. పట్టెడు *patt-edu*. adj A large handful. Lit. "as much as the hand will hold." పట్టుజీనువు *pattu-jinuvu*. n. A kind of bird, పికిలిపిట్ట. పట్టుడు *pattudu*. n. Persistence, పట్టుదల. adj. Choice, select. పట్టుడుమేక a first rate sheep. పట్టుడావు a picked cow or fine cow. పట్టుదల *pattu-dala*. n. Affection, favor. Perseverance, persistence. వదలనిపట్టు, అభినివేశము. వానికి దానిమీద నిండా పట్టుదల he has a great regard for it. పట్టుబడి *pattu-badi*. n. A sum received or credited in an account, the worth or cost of any thing, charges, expense, outlay. పట్టుబడు *pattu-badu*. v. n. To be seized or apprehended. చిక్కుకొను. To become plain, విశదమగు. పట్టుసారువ *pattu-sāruva*. n. A fork-like beam used to hold by while working a pikota or water-lift మోట త్రొక్కువాడు ఆధారముగా పట్టుకొనే పంగల కొయ్య. పట్లు plu. of పట్టు. పట్ల *patla*. [from పట్టుల.] adv. About, as ఆ చుట్టుపట్ల in that neighbourhood, round-about. With regard to, with reference to, in the event of. వాడు అక్కడ ఉండినపట్ల in case of his being there. ఇంటిపట్ల at home. ఆతనిపట్ల అన్యాయముచేయకు do him no wrong. ఈపట్ల in this respect, in this matter.

పట్టె or పట్టియ *patte*. [Tel.] n. A spar of wood. బల్ల. A piece of wood that forms the frame of a cot. Hair left on the head at the time of tonsure. A fold in a turban or dress. A tape. A stripe or streak of paint, రేఖ. A facet or side of a diamond, పక్క. A gold band or fillet worn on the forehead, at the time of one's coronation, పట్టము. Ceiling, మిద్దె యొక్కమీద పరచే ప్రానుమొదలగునది. A brush, కుంచె. తాటిపట్టె a palmyra rafter. నవారుపట్టె a broad tape. పట్టె మంచము a cot the bottom of which is woven with broad tape. పట్టెతోలు to use the harrow. సున్నపుపట్టె a streak of chunam. పట్టెలు తీర్చినకెంపు a ruby cut into facets. ద్వార బంధపుపట్టె the lintel or top of a door. టంకపుపట్టె a girth. యోగపట్టె a hermit's girdle. ఒకపట్టెనేల a piece of land. నీరుపారేపట్టె a canal or water course.

పట్టెమారువు check-colors in a cloth. వస్త్రములోని ఒకవిధమైన చిత్రవర్ణము. **పట్టె వర్ధనము** *patte-vardhanamu*. n. A broad caste-mark worn in the forehead, వెడల్పు గానుండుబొట్టు.

పట్టెడ *patteda*. [Tel.] n. A broad and strong tape. నవారు. A collar or ornament for a woman's neck, formed of small square plates. A small anvil. దాగలి.

పట్టెము See పట్టెయము.

పట్నము Same as పట్టణము (q. v.) హంస. i.

పత్రు *patra*. [Tel.] n. A village, a hamlet. పల్లెపత్రు villages and hamlets. H. iv. 103. **పత్రువాండ్లు** *patra-vandlu*. n. plu. A certain caste akin to the Boyas. Also called ఏకరివాండ్లు.

పఠించు *pathintsu*. [Skt.] v. a. To read, to learn. చదువు. See పాఠము. **పఠనము** *pathanamu*. n. Reading, learning. చదువు. పఠనముచేయు to commit to memory, to learn. పఠితము that which is read.

పఠాణి *pathani*. [Afghan.] n. Pathan, a certain tribe of Afghans. An Afghan horse.

పఠిల్లున *pathillu-na*. [Tel. anuk.] adv. Aloud.

పడక or **పడుక** *padaka*. [Tel. from పడు.] n. A bed. పరుపు. Repose or reclining. ఇక్కడ పడక చేసినవారు those who lay here. అటేపడకగా పడియున్నాడు or పట్టపడకగా పడియున్నాడు he did not again arise. **పడకయిల్లు** *padaka-y-illu*. n. A bed chamber.

పడకు or **పణకు** *padaku*. [Tel.] n. A crevice. సందు. స్వా. v. A cave, గుహ. అచ్చ. రా. కాం.

పడగ *padaga*. [Tel.] n. A flag or banner, a crest. టెక్కెము. A snake's crest or hood. An ear ornament worn by females. గాలిపడగ a paper kite. పాము పడగ ఎత్తెను the snake raised its hood. "కోటికిపడగ లెత్తె." Swa. iii. 42.

"కూడంబెడిచియు కఠకోటిపడగలెత్తె, మాటిమాటికిదిఱుమంటగలిపి."

Vema. iii. 104.

పడగదారి or **పడగతాలుపు**. *padaga-dari*. n. A snake, పాము, ఫణి.

పడచ్చు or **పడిఅచ్చు** *pad-atstsu*. [Tel.] n. A puncheon or tool having a figure on it with which impressions are struck. కంసాలిపనిముట్టు.

పడత *padata*. [Tel] n. A cheek bone. పానువు. Also, same as పడతి (q. v.)

పడతి or **పడతుక** *padati*. [Tel.] n. A woman.

పడదల *padadala*. [Tel.] n. A belt. "కడ పన్నెజిగిబట్టు నడికట్టు పడదలబిగించుకొనెజయు డాకు." N. x. 143.

పడపు *padapu*. [Tel. from పడయు.] n. Earning, ఆర్జనము. Money earned. ఆర్జితద్రవ్యము.

పడబా *padaba*. [Tel.] n. A piece, fragment, an extract from a document.

పడమర *padamara*. [Tel Dravidian root పడుకు falling + ఞాయిరు sun.] n. Lit: The side in which the sun sets. The West. తూర్పుపడమరలు East and West. **పడమటి** *padamati*. adj. Western. పడమటిగాలి the West wind. పడమటిల్లు the Western apartment, i. e., the cookroom or the dining room. **పడమటికొండ** *padamati-konda*. n. Lit: The Western hill (behind which the sun is supposed to set.) అస్తాద్రి. పడమటిదొర the lord of the West, i. e., Varuna.

పడము *padamu*. [Tel.] n. A carpet. రత్న కంబళము.

పడయు or **పడుచు** *padayu*. [Tel.] v. a. To obtain, gain, acquire, enjoy, possess. పొందు. To get, సంపాదించు. To beget (బిడ్డను) కను "పుత్రులఁబడసె." M. I. ii. 150. "ధర్మం బులమీకు బడయరానిదేమి యునులేదు." Vish. ii. 192. See పడపు.

పడలు *padalu*. [Tel.] n. plu. Heaps. రాసులు.

పడవ *paḍava*. [Tel.] n. A boat. దోనె. War, combat, fighting, యుద్ధము. Imminent danger, peril, a fatal accident, ప్రళయము. ఈ పడవ గడిస్తే if I can only get over this hobble or scrape. "అరదంబు నందుండి తనతనయుండైన భగదత్తుండు ముందు నడువ పడవక్కైవచ్చెనంత." Satyabhama. iv. 134. **పడవరము** or **పడవలము** *paḍava-ramu*. (పడలు+వలము.) n. The vanguard of an army. సేనాముఖము. "గొల్లనల్లభుక పురు కట్టంబు మిక్కిలి గానుకలిచ్చి, పడవలం బులయూల పలుమారు జేసి." Pal. 80. పడవరు to proceed or go before, ముందునడుచు. **పడవాగె** or **పడివాగె** *paḍa-vāge*. adj. Prepared. Bridled. కళ్లెముపెట్టి సిద్ధపరచిన. "ఇమడప్ప డజ్జెదొర మనుమన్న పడవాగెగాని వచ్చు రాయంచకోదమయను." Swa. iii. 74. టీ॥ కళ్లెముపెట్టి సిద్ధపరచి తేబడినటువంటి, అనగా ముస్తీదై వచ్చినటువంటి. **పడవాలు, పడవాలుడు** or **పడాలు** *paḍavālu*. n. A commander of an army. సేనాధిపతి, దళవాయి. "కనకపు లు వేల్పుపడవాలుగన్న వాటు." Swa. ii. 9. టీ॥ వేల్పుపడవాలు, దేవతలకు సేనాధిపతి. "ధనంజయుండు తమలోదంజకుదరదు పరివారంబు సమకట్టం బడవాల్లంబనిచె." M. XIV. iii. 4. **పడసాల** *paḍa-sāla*. (పడలు+సాల.) n. A hall, a portico. కూటము, కూటామ. "పడసాల ముంగిలి పందిలి పసిగాడి." Suca. iii. 469.

పడి *paḍi*. [Tel.] n. A measure of capacity, containing a seer and half or 120 tolas, or one eighth of a marcal. రెండుసోలలకొలది. **పడికట్టు** *paḍi-kaṭṭu*. n. A weight used in scales: a degree: a standard for reference: a stair, or step. సోపానము. plu. పడికట్లు.

పడికాపు or **పడిగాపు** *paḍi-kāpu*. [Tel.] n. A hanger on, an expectant. పంచను కాచుకొనియుండేసేవకుడు.

"పడికాపులుం పడియుండగ,
బడుగులకేలెత్తు కంసభంజనుసేవల్"
Kuchelōp.

పడిగ, పడిగము or **పడికము** *paḍiga*. [Tel.] n. A vessel, పాత్రము. A spittoon. తమ్మపడిగ or తమ్మపడిగము a spittoon used in chewing betel. "పడిగంబుపెట్టించి పాదముల్ గడిగి." BD. iii. 236. "త్రివిధోదకములాగ్నిక్య పడిగంబులోగూర్చి" Charitra. i. 3089. "కున్నపుకాయ మెచ్చులతమ్మపడిగ." Saranga. iii. 141.

పడిగల్లు *paḍi-gallu*. [Tel. పడి+కల్లు.] n. A gunshot, a bullet. తుపాకిగుండు. "డిప్పికొక్కులు పడిగంటుగూలుతేందమున" రా. సుం. కాం.

పడిదము or **పడిదెము** *paḍidamu*. [Tel.] n. A certain decoction. క్రమచూపమగు వ్యంజన విశేషము, ఊర్పు, బోళము. "సీ॥ అప్పడంబులు వడియములు దాలింపులు బలుచని మెఱిచెప్పు పడిదెములును." శై. iii.

పడిదె or **పడిదియ** *paḍide*. [Tel.] n. Borrowed linen, clothes hired from a washerman. పడిదియిచ్చు to lend out clothes.

పడియ or **పడె** *paḍiya*. [Tel.] n. A puddle; a slough, a dirty pond, a fallow, uncultivated waste, నీళ్లునిలిచిన చిన్నపల్లము, నేదలు పొల్లెగుంట. చవుటిపడియ a salt marsh.

పడిసెము *paḍisemu*. [Tel.] n. A cold in the head, catarrh, running at the nose. జలుబు.

పడిసెకాయ *paḍise-kāya*. [Tel.] n. A wild acid berry that grows on a large tree.

పడిహారి or **పళిహారి** *paḍi-hāri*. [Tel.] n. A messenger, a herald, a servant. A doorkeeper, ద్వారపాలకుడు.

"పళిహారులను బిల్వబంచి యూతిగాను,
కడకతో గల్యాణకటకంబునందు."
Charitra. i. 4415.

పడు *paḍu*. [Tel.] v. n. To feel. To fall, పతనము, రాలు. To lie down, శయనించు. To be, to occur, or happen, సంభవించు, కలుగు. To be caught in a snare. To suffer pain. శ్రమపొందు. To be killed in battle. చచ్చు. To be buried, as money, పూడు. To set, అస్తమించు. v. a. To experience, అనుభవించు. To incur, undergo, enjoy, feel, పొందు. నేను పడిన బాధ నాకే తెలుసును I alone know what I have suffered. Added to nouns it forms them into verbs. సమ్మతిపడు to agree. సంతోషపడు to be pleased. సంతాపపడు to feel sorry. చింతపడు to be anxious. తిట్లుపడు to be reviled. తొందరపడు to be in distress. భయపడు to fear. మూనుపడు to be stunned. వానికి నొక్కిళ్లు పడినవి he has the lockjaw. It may be added in a similar way to past participles. ఉలికిపడు to start. కూనికిపడు to slumber. It is also added to adjectives or verbs. ఎర్రపడు to redden, blush or turn red. వేరుపడు to be separated. ఏర్పడు to become. It may even be added to an interjection, కటకటపడు to cry Alas, to pity. తహతహపడు to be in trouble. ఆ యిల్లు పడినది that house is fallen in. ఆ వలలో నాలుగుపక్షులు పడినవి four birds were caught in the snare. అక్కడ ఒక పల్లము పడినది a hollow has formed there. ఆ యుద్ధములో నలుగురు పడినారు or పడిపోయినారు four persons were killed in the battle. వానికి బంకపడుచున్నది he passes slime or mucus. వానికి పురుగులు పడినవి he passed worms. వానికి కుడిచెయ్యి పడినది his right hand has become paralysed. వారు వెనుకపడినారు they fell back, they retired. ఆ మతములో పడినాడు he embraced that religion. పేరుపడిన renowned, celebrated, notorious. తటస్థపడినప్పుడు when an opportunity occurs. మరుగుపడినారు they went out of sight. నాకు వచ్చిన ఆపదకు వాడు అడ్డపడినాడు he stood in the way of the misfortune that happened to me. వారిద్దరికిని పడదు they do not agree, they are on bad terms. దానినోటిలో పడకుము do not put it in her power to abuse you. ఆ బావిలో మంచినీళ్లు పడినవి sweet water broke forth in the well. వానితో పడలేను I cannot get on with him. నాకు ఇప్పుడు పోవడము పడదు I cannot go now. ఇంకా విత్తనము పడలేదు the seed is not yet sown. ఆ చేనిలో అడ్డముగా పడి పారిపోయినాడు he ran away across the field. ఆ యిల్లు ఊరకె పడియున్నది that house is unoccupied. ఆ రూకలు ఊరకె పడియున్నవి that money is untouched, it is lying idle. ఆ సంసారము నా నెత్తిని పడినది that family is now left on my hands. ఆ నష్టము నా తలమీద పడినది I incurred that loss. Added to the root in A it forms the passive voice, thus కొట్టబడు to be beaten; చూడబడు to be seen. It is added at pleasure to some adverbs, thus బోర్లపడిన prostrate. తలక్రిందులుపడు to be topsy turvy, upside down, to be conceited. అది బయటపడినది it came to light. The causal form is పరుచు or పరచు. తొందరపరచు to trouble, torment. **పడగొట్టు** *paḍa-goṭṭu*. v. a. To knock down. **పడదన్ను** *paḍa-dannu*. v. a. To kick down. **పడద్రొక్కు** *paḍa-ḍokku*. v. a. To tread down. **పడద్రోయు** *paḍa-dōyu*. v. a. To thrust down, knock down. **పడవేయు** *paḍa-vēyu*. v. a. To cast or throw down. **పడిపోవు** *paḍi-pōvu*. v. n. To fall down, to die. అతడు పడిపోయినతర్వాత after his decease. **పడుకొను** *paḍu-konu*. v. n. To lie down, recline. **పడువ** *paḍuva*. n. A very low place. మిక్కిలి పల్లమైనచోటు. **పడువరి** *paḍu-vari*. (పడు+వరి.) n. A crop or sprouts produced by seeds of paddy, that fall by chance as the crops are cut. **పడ్డ** *paḍḍa*. [contr. for పడిన.] pp. Fallen, &c., thus, పిలువబడ్డవాడు the man who was called. ఉంచబడ్డవాడు he who was kept there.

పడుకు *paḍuku*. [Tel.] n. A stone, rock. రాయి, శిల.

పడుగు *padugu*. [Tel.] n. The woof or threads which run the whole length of the web. బట్టపొడుగు నిడుపునూలు. A heap of grain, పైకప్పు లేకుండా మిగిలిన పోసిన వడ్లు, లేక, వరికుప్ప. కూలిపడుగులు thread given out to be woven as piece work. **పడుగుచేయు** *padugu-cheyu*. v. a. To dress, teazle or card the woof with a comb.

పడుచు *padutsu*. [Tel.] adj. Young, youthful. పడుచుబుద్ధి a childish whim. (Vish. ii. 28.) పడుచుమాటలు childish language. n. A girl, damsel, maiden, కన్యక. A boy, a youth. పడుచువాడు. ఆడపడుచు a girl. **పడుచుతనము** *padutsu-tanamu*. n. Youth, girlhood, girlishness, boyishness, silliness; puberty. **పడుచుది** *padutsu-di*. n. A young girl. పడుచులతిండి a devourer of innocents, శిశుఘాతిని. **పడుపు** or **పడుపుతేరు** *padupu*. n. Prostitution. పడుపుమేయు to prostitute oneself. పడుపుకూడు food gained by prostitution. పడుపుపడతి a prostitute. **పడుపుకొమ్మ** *padupu-komma*. n. A prostitute.

పడ్డ *padda*. [Tel.] n. A female buffalo or cow fit for breeding, a heifer, తొలిచూలి ఆవు, లేక, గేదె. See also under పడు.

పణకు Same as పనకు (q. v.).

పణత *panata*. [Tel.] n. A certain part of a plough. నాగేటిగొడక, నాగలిలోముక్క మేడి తగిలించే మొద్దువంటిది. **పణతపడు** *panata-padu*. v. n. To suffer from lockjaw. దవడ నరాలుపట్టుకొను.

పణపరము *pana-paramu*. [Skt.] n. (In astrology), a segment of a circle.

పణము *panamu*. [Tel.] n. A feat of strength, &c., as a reward of which the hand of a heroine is bestowed on the victor. [Skt.] n. Price, వెల. Wages, hire. కూలి. The weight of a cowri, గవ్వయెత్తు. Also, a weight of copper, ఒకరాగినాణెము. A stake at play, a bet, a wager, పందెము. Gaming, gambling, playing with dice, జూదము. **పణితము** or **పణాయితము** *panitamu*. adj. Laid as a wager, పందెము గావేయబడిన. Praised, extolled, పొగడబడిన.

పణవము *panavamu*. [Skt.] n. A tabor or small drum. తప్పెట, ఉడుక.

పణిహారి or **పడిహారి** *panihari*. [Tel.] n. A messenger, herald. A doorkeeper, porter. ద్వారపాలకుడు. A bailiff.

పణుకు or **పణక** *panuku*. [Tel.] n. A ledge; a side (of a hill, sea, or pit); a cleft or hiding place. దరి

పణ్యము *panyamu* [Skt.] adj. Saleable, vendible. అమ్మదగిన. **పణ్యవీథి** *panya-vithi*. n. A place where shops are; a market place, అంగడివీధి. **పణ్యస్త్రీ** or **పణ్యాంగన** *panya-stri*. n. A harlot. భోగముది, లంజె. **పణ్యజీవుడు** *panya-jivudu*. n. A merchant or trader. వర్తకుడు, బేహారి. **పణ్యారము** *panyaramu*. n. A cake. అపూపము. "పణ్యారంబు బువ్వంబు కంపుల." A. i. 26.

పతంగచెక్క *patanga-chekka*. [Tel.] n. Sappan wood, *Cæsalpinia sappan*. Rox. ii. 357.

పతంగము *patangamu*. [Skt.] n. Quicksilver, పాదరసము. A grasshopper, మిడత. A bird, పక్షి. **పతంగించు** *patangintsu*. v. n. To apply quicksilver, by burning it and letting the fumes (like smoke) accumulate. రసము పతంగించినది the mercury rose in fumes and accumulated at the top.

పతంగుడు *patangudu*. [Skt.] n. The sun. M. iv. i. 83.

పతకము *patakamu*. [Tel.] n. A solitaire or brooch hung at the breast. A golden number, a logarithm.

పతగము or **పతత్త్రి** *patagamu*. [Skt.] n. A bird. పతగరాజు the king of birds: the eagle. See పతంగము.

పతత్త్రము *patatramu*. [Skt.] n. A wing. **పతత్త్రి** *patatri*. n. A bird.

పతద్గ్రహము *patad-grahamu*. [Skt.] n. A spittoon. తమ్మపడిగము.

పతనము *patanamu*. [Skt.] n. Falling. పడుట. **పతయాళువు** *patayāluvu*. adj. Falling, cadent, deciduous, liable or accustomed to fall. పడెడు స్వభావముగల.

పతాక *patāka*. [Skt.] n. A flag or banner. టెక్కెము. **పతాకిని** *patākini*. n. An army. సేన. **పతాకి** or **పతాకుడు** *patāki* n. A banneret or ensign. One who has a banner, టెక్కెముకలవాడు. మీనపతాకుడు Manmadha whose banner is the dolphin.

పతి *pati*. [Skt.] n. A lord, master, prince, ruler. ఏలిక. A husband, మగడు. పతింవర a woman who selects her own husband, పర్యా, తనంతట మగని వరించుకొన్నట్టి ఆడుది. **పతివ్రత** *pati-vrata*. n. A chaste and virtuous wife, పతిభక్తిగల యిల్లాలు. **పత్ని** *patni*. n. Lit: She who has a husband; a lawful wife. అగ్నిసాక్షిగా పెండ్లాడినభార్య.

పతితము *patitamu*. [Skt.] adj. Fallen, alighted, defeated, overthrown. Wicked, abandoned. **పతితత్వము** *patitatvamu*. n. The state of having fallen from one's office or righteousness. **పతితుడు** *patitudu*. n. A fallen creature, a sinner. పడినవాడు, చెడిపోయినవాడు. ఏమియెరుగని పతితుగా (for పతితుడుగా) ఉన్నాడు he is as innocent as the babe unborn. పతితపావనుడు a restorer of the fallen, a saviour of sinners.

పతిమ [for Skt. ప్రతిమ.] Same as ప్రతిమ (q. v.).

పత్త *patta*. [Tel.] n. The female organ of generation. [illegible].

పత్తనము Same as పట్టణము (q. v.).

పత్తా *patta*. [H.] n. A sign, trace. జాడ.

పత్తి *patti*. [Skt.] n. A foot soldier. కాలిబంటు.

పత్తి or **ప్రత్తి** *patti*. [Tel.] n. Cotton. అడవిపత్తి a shrub, *Hibiscus abelmoschus*. **పత్తిరేకు** *patti-rēku*. n. A thin plate of metal. Solder. లోహములు అతుకుటకులో వేసే రేకు, పొడి. "క॥ తెమమధ్యస్థలీభంగము, లమరూపుగనవియు దత్కులములేయుకుటకు, తుని యుడిన పత్తిరేకన, జమనొప్పారాయున గొనకేను కుజవామనా." A. v. 27. **పత్తిలిక** *pattilika*. n. A cutting instrument used by goldsmiths, కంసాలివాండ్లు వాడే ఒకవిధమైన పనిముట్టు.

పత్తిరి or **పత్త్రి** *pattiri*. [Tel.] n. Leaves used as an offering. **పత్తిరిబొట్టు** *pattiri-bottu*. n. A kind of mark worn on the forehead. తిలకవిశేషము.

పత్ని See under పతి.

పత్త్రము *patramu*. [Skt.] n. A leaf of a tree, or of a book. ఆకు. A written bond, సత్తు వారి పు కెల్లబడికి వ్రాసికొనినది. A vehicle in general, as a car, a horse, a camel, &c. వాహనము. The wing of a bird, రెక్క. An arrow, బాణము. **పత్త్రపరశువు** *patra-parasuvu*. n. A file. ఆకురాయి. **పత్త్రపాశ్య** *patra-pasya*. n. An ornament for the forehead: a sort of tiara. చేరుచుక్కబొట్టు, పాపటబొట్టు. **పత్త్రరథము** *patra-radhamu*. n. Lit: Wing-borne, i. e., a bird. **పత్రార్థము** *patr-arthamu*. n. The value of a bond, that is, the property or money which it deals with. **పత్త్రి** *patri*. n. A bird. పక్షి.

పత్త్రి or **పత్తిరి** *patri*. [Tel. n. Leaves used in worship. "[illegible] పత్రిపూవు" Vēma.

పత్రిక *patrika.* [Skt.] n. A letter of correspondence. A paper, కాగితము. One number of a periodical publication; a newspaper; a tract or little book, చిన్న పుస్తకము. పత్రభంగము, పత్రరేఖ, పత్రలేఖ, పత్రిక or మకరికాపత్రిక damasked hue, marbled figures drawn with musk or gold dust on the cheeks of a woman.

పత్త్రోర్ణము *patr-ōrṇamu.* [Skt.] n. White silk. ధౌతకౌశేయము, తెల్లపట్టుబట్ట.

పథము *pathamu.* [Skt.] n. A road or way. త్రోవ, మార్గము. **పథికుడు** *pathikuḍu.* n. A traveller, a way-farer. బాటసారి.

పథ్యము *pathyamu.* [Skt.] adj. Proper, fit, suitable, agreeing with diet or regimen. హితము. n. Restriction in diet, diet, regimen. అతనిమాటలు ఆమెకు పథ్యము his words are music to her ears.

పద or **పదము** *pada.* [Tel. for పోవుదము.] (plu. పదండి or పదరు) *interj.* Go or come thou. పదరా or పదవే go along, or come along. పోదముపద come, let us go. పదపద (plu. పదపదరు) go, go along; come, come! "ఇదొప్పుట, పదిమంది కేమింక పదపదమనుచు." Saranga. D. iv. 377.

పదంపడి or **పదపడి** *padampaḍi.* [Tel.] adv. And then, afterwards. తరువాత, వెనుక, మరియు. "కానిరప్పుచేసి నిముబట్టి దండనముచేసి పదంపడి సత్కృపామతిశాగనుగొని మెచ్చి." Vij. ii. 173.

పదకము *padakamu.* [Skt.] n. Order. క్రమము. n. Same as పతకము (q.v.).

పదటము or **పదటు** *padaṭamu.* [Tel.] n. Precipitation, hurry. అత్రము, దుడుకు, తత్తరము. "ఇంతేల పదటముచే నిందమైన భాషించెదవు." S. iii. 305. వానికి చెయ్యిపదటము కద్దు he is given to pilfering. దానికి నోరు పదటము she is a foul mouthed woman.

పదడు *padaḍu.* [Tel.] n. Ashes. బూడిద, భస్మము. An empty corn husk: trash, rubbish. "ద్వి॥ పదడు చేపట్టుటకు పనిచిద్రాడు చనరె." Charitra. ii. 2783. పదట in the dirt. "అ॥ పదడుగానిరూపయుండొ దగరికనరిగిన, బాపత్రు తులదానిబదటగలప" M. XII. v. 468. **పదట బుచ్చు** *padaṭa-butstsu.* v. a. To ruin, to waste. బుగ్గిలోకలుపు. "చదువులెనగాడె నీతు లుపదటబుచ్చె." Satya. iv. 57.

పదను Same as పదును (q. v.).

పదపడి Same as పదంపడి (q. v.).

పదము *padamu.* [Skt.] n. A foot. పాదము. అడుగు. A footstep, the mark of a foot, పాదచిహ్నము. A word or a phrase, శబ్దము. An article, thing, వస్తువు. Preservation, defence, రక్షణము. A place, site, స్థానము. Rank, station, degree, ఉద్యోగము. An attempt, ప్రయత్నము. Cunning, కపటము. A line of a stanza or song, పద్యపాదము. పదభ్రష్టుడు he who is degraded. "మనసిజరథపదాంజనకలికలు." A. v. 124. టీ॥ రథపద, బండికండ్లరొక్క. **పరమపదము** *parama-padamu.* n. Lit: the best place, i. e., Heaven. **పదగుడు** or **పద్గుడు** *padaguḍu* n. A foot soldier, కాలిబంటు. **పదచాళి** *padatsāḷi.* n. A kind of dance. నాట్యభేదము. **పదచ్ఛేదము** *padach-chhēdamu.* n. Dividing or separating the words of a sentence from each other. The order in which words are construed. Analysis. **పదతలము** *pada-talamu.* n. The foot.

పదమూడు See under పది.

పదరము *padaramu.* [Tel.] n. A place where betel leaves are kept safe. తమలపాకులు ఉంచే అడపము.

పదరు or **పమరు** *paduru.* v. n. To be over hasty, to be precipitate. అత్రపడు. To speak hastily, అత్రముతో మాట్లాడు. To get angry, కోపించు. To shake, చలించు. v. a. To find fault with, to blame.

అక్షేపించు. "అదిరొట్టులుం జెసితో. పదరుంబని లేదునాకు పక్షభవునివాటులుం గంపవలయు." M. XII. iv. 399. n. Way, manner, విధము. A hasty word, త్వరితపుమాట. పదురు is also another form of పదుగురు ten persons. పద రులు or పదురులు *padarulu*. n. plu. Angry words, hasty words. కోపవాక్యులు. "పట్టితో పట్టిపనులఁగొట్టితిఁదు, పదరులకునింటి బలుకక్కు లఠితలాడు" S. iii. 237. పదరుచు, పదురుచు or గద్రుము to hasten; to hurry on; to cause to speak, hastily, పదురుచేయు.

పదలము *padalamu*. [Tel.] n. A weight equivalent to half a viss.

పదవి *padavi*. [Skt.] n. A road, or path, మార్గము. Station, situation, degree, rank, స్థితి. A place, site, స్థానము. Fortune, luck సంపద. A high station in life, ఉన్నతస్థితి.

పదహారు or **పదారు** See under పది.

పదాతి or **పదాతుడు** *padati*. [from Skt. పదము.] n. A foot soldier. కాలిబంటు. పదాతులు infantry. See పదగుడు under పదము.

పదార్థము *padarthamu*. [Skt.] n. A thing, article, substance; substantial or material form of being. An ingredient or drug. వస్తువు. Property, money, goods. పదార్థ వంతుడు a man of property. The meaning of a word. మాటయొక్క అర్థము.

పది *padi* [Tel.] adj. Ten. పదిమంది ten persons; (metaphorically,) several or many people: as, in English, a dozen. plu. పదులు tens. పదింబదిగ, పదిపదిక or పదికేలకు by all means, on any consideration, at any rate, అన్నివిధాల, గట్టిగా, చక్కగా. "పదురుకుమారెన్నపదిం, బదిగవిచారించిచేయు మంచి దినుమ్మా." Sāranga. ii. 278. **పందుము** *pandumu*. (పది+తూము.) n. Ten tooms or bushels పదితూములు. **పదకొండు** or **పదునొకండు** *padakondu*. (పది+ఒకండు.) adj. Eleven. **పన్నెండు** or **పంద్రెండు** *pannendu*. (పది+రెండు.) adj. Twelve. **పద** **మూడు** or **పదుమూడు** *padamūdu*. adj. Thirteen. **పదునాలుగు, పద్నాలుగు** or **పద్నాల్గు** *padu-nālugu*. adj. Fourteen. **పదిహేను, పదియేను** or **పదునేను** *padihēnu*. adj. Fifteen. **పదహారు, పదారు** or **పదియారు** *padahāru*. (పది+ఆరు.) adj. Sixteen. పదార్వేలు sixteen thousand. పదియార్వన్నెపసిండి fine gold. **పదిహేడు, పదియేడు** or **పదునేడు** *padihēdu* adj. Seventeen. **పద్దెనిమిది** or **పదు నెనిమిది** *paddhenimidi*. adj. Eighteen. **పందొమ్మిది** *pandommidi*. adj. Nineteen. **పందొమ్మండ్రు** *pandommandru*. n. Nineteen persons. **పదువురు, పదుగురు, పదురు, పదుండ్రు** or **పదుగుండ్రు** *paduvuru*. n. Ten persons. **పన్నిద్దుము** *pannid-dumu*. (పది+ఇరు+తూము.) n. The dry measure of twelve tooms. పన్నిద్దరు, పన్ని దుగురు or పన్నిరువురు twelve persons. **పన్ని ల్లము** *panniilamu* (పది+ఇల్లము.) Twelve palams.

పది *padi*. [Skt.] n. A foot, పాదము. పదికుడు. See పదాతి.

పదిలము *padilamu*. [Tel.] n. Steadiness, స్థైర్యము. Care, caution, security, carefulness, జాగరూకత. adj. Careful, steady. పదిల ముగా carefully, భద్రముగా. **పదిలముచేయు** or **పదిలపరచు** *padilamu-chēyu*. v. a. To secure or take care of, to put by. **పదిలించు** *padilintsu*. v. a. To keep safely, to lay up. పదిలపరచు. "పదుపకేదిదిని పదిలింపుముకుచు." Navan. p: 203. **పదిలుడు** *padiludu*. n. One who is careful, జాగరూకుడు. A steady man, స్థిరుడు.

> "మొదటతనమతిమదిదలక,
> తుదనెవ్వరిమతమున్నైన దూషింపకయుండా,
> పదిలుడయుకోర్కిగోరక,
> మదమునజెరియించువాడెముక్తుడువేమా"
>
> Vēma. 158.

పదుగు *padugu*. [Tel. n. A hole in a path.

పదును or **పదను** *padunu.* [Tel. పది+అను]. n. Time, season, సమయము. Temper, sharpness, whetting, వాడి. Moisture, తడి. Goodness of metal. The right degree of softness (in boiled areca nut, &c.) పరిపాకము. ఆ కత్తికి పదునురాలేదు that knife is not properly tempered. దున్నడమునకు ఆ నేల పదునుగా నుండలేదు the ground is not sufficiently moist for ploughing. ఉక్కునకు కాచడములో పదునుతప్పినది he failed in giving the right temper to the steel. "పదునైనబలువాడిమె గములు." HK. iv. 193. **పదనుకొను** *padanu-konu.* v. n. To become wet or moist, తడియు. "పానబట్టినరాపాడిచల్లి మెదవి, పదనుకొన్నదిచేపనోపద్మభవుడు." Swa. ii. 40. టీ॥ పదను, చేతితడి. పదునుపెట్టేరాయి a hone or whetstone. ఒకపదునువాన one moistening of rain, i. e., so much rain as renders the earth fit for ploughing. One పదును or wetting sinks into the ground about the depth of a plough share: equivalent to "one inch of rain." పదునుచేయు to moisten. పొగాకుపదునుచేయు to prepare or cure tobacco in a particular way. పదునుపెట్టు to set or sharpen.

పదుపు, పదువు or **పదుగు** *padupu.* [Tel.] n. A herd, crowd, assembly, collection, flock or flight. గుంపు. "కుక్కపదుపు" a pack of dogs. M. XII. iii. 476. "ఎలదేటి పదుపుజలజంబుపైవ్రాలు," Bhanum. ii. 81.

పదురు See పదరు.

పదే పదే *padē-padē.* [Tel. from పది.] adv. Repeatedly, reiteratedly, again and again, now and then.

పద్దు *paddu.* [Tel.] n. A vow or promise. పంతము, ప్రతిజ్ఞ. An item or article: a head or entry in accounts. అంకెమొత్తము. "బాసలుచేసిచ్చి పద్దుతప్పినవాని" Ila. iv. 46. టీ॥ మాటయిచ్చితప్పిన కృష్ణునిరొక్కి he who has broken his word.

పద్నియము or **పద్నైము** Same as పద్మము (q. v.).

పద్ధతి *padhdhati.* [Skt.] n. A road. త్రోవ, మార్గము. A line, row or range, వరుస. A ritual, or manual: a work upon any act or ceremony, detailing the mode of its performance, and collecting the texts connected with it. Manner, scale, mode, rate, custom. A principle. A bye-law. రాజ పద్ధతి a chronology of kings. న్యాయ పద్ధతిగా according to justice.

పద్మ *padma.* [Skt.] n. A name of Lakshmi. లక్ష్మి. **పద్మము** *padmamu.* n. The lotus or water lily. *Nelumbium speciosum.* తామర. A large number, ten billions. In Tantrica books it means a part or region of the body. **పద్మనాభుడు** *padma-nābhudu.* n. Vishnu, from whose navel (నాభి) sprung the lotus containing Bramha when he was sent to create the world. **పద్మబాంధవుడు** *padma-bandhavudu.* n. The Sun. **పద్మరాగము** *padma-rāgamu.* n. The chrysolite or ruby of the finest class: a gem of a pink colour called కెంపు. మాణిక్యములో కాంతిగలకెంపు. **పద్మవెలమలు** or **పద్మనాయకులు** *padma-velamalu* n. plu. The name of a certain Sudra caste. See వెలమ. **పద్మవ్యూహము** or **పద్మము** *padma-vyūhamu.* n. A certain kind of military evolution. **పద్మసాలెవాండ్లు** *padma-sāle-vāndlu.* n. A certain caste of weavers. **పద్మాకరము** *padm-ākaramu.* n. A place of lilies a pond in which the lotus grows. A tank, కొలను, చెరువు. **పద్మాలయ** or **పద్మావతి** *padm-ālaya.* n. The goddess Lakshmi, so named because her dwelling (ఆలయము) is in the lily (పద్మము). **పద్మాసనము** *padm-āsanamu.* n. A sitting posture used in religious meditation, in which the Bauddha statues are represented; so called because Vishnu is represented in that posture when throned on a lotus. **పద్మి** *padmi.* n. An elephant. **పద్మిని** *padmini.* n. A lovely woman, like a Penelope, or an Eve. The Hindu poets divide all beautiful women into four classes called (1) హస్తిని, (2) శంఖిని, (3) చిత్రిణి and (4) పద్మిని; which answer to Juno, Flora, Venus and Minerva, respectively: See Addison's Spectator No. 209. **పద్మిని** n. A bed of lilies. పద్మినీవల్లభుడు the Sun. as being the lover (వల్లభ) of the lotus.

పద్యము *padyamu.* [Skt.] n. A verse. A stanza, a quatrain. పద్యమో గద్యమో whether it be verse or prose. ఒకనిమీద పద్యము కట్టుట to lampoon a person.

పన *pana.* [Tel.] n. A sheaf of corn. చేలలో కోసినపనపట్టు.

పనటి or **పనంటి** *panati.* [Tel.] n. A cooking pot, వంటకుండ. A pot, కుండ. A large pot or boiler, పెద్దకాగు. మూతివెడల్పుగల యుటికె. "ఘుమ్మని పనన్ని రుదోలికరడు గంటిపేయని గాజుపటులు." S. i. 154. "ఎపరుపెట్టిన పెద్ద పనంటిలోలె." A. i. 10.

పనవు *panavu.* [Tel.] v. n. To grieve, to bewail. ప్రలాపించు. వలవించు. పనవి sorrowfully. "జనకతనయు తన్ను సౌమిత్రి యాడ విలో, విడిచిపోవగాంచి యుడికరాస్తి, జంతము విగివంతజేడ్పడి దులుగెత్తి. పనవిపనవియేడ్చు పతిదలంచి." Padm. ix. 12.

పనస *panasa.* [from Skt. ప్రశ్నాస.] n. A verse in a chapter in the Véda: వేద భాగము. **పనసచెట్టు** *panasa-chettu* n. The jack-fruit tree, *Artocarpus integrifolia.* (Watts.) చెట్టుపనస or వేరుపనస the species of this tree, the fruits of which issue from the root. పనసమాను the outrigger of a boat, పడవపారవకుండ పక్కను కట్టేమాను. **పనసవాండ్లు** *panasa-vandlu.* [Tel.] n. plu. Mountebanks. The name of a caste of men employed in menial offices, particularly to blow trumpets or conches at funerals. శంఖాలులను యూదించే వారు. పనసర్తి fees given to them

పని *pani.* [Tel.] n. Work, a task, కర్మము. Business, employment, వ్యాపారము. Workmanship, శిల్పము. ఈకట్టడమునందు మంచిపనిచేసియున్నారు there is good workmanship in this building. An affair, act, matter. Service, utility, purpose, object, intention, design. ప్రయోజనము. An order, duty, నియోగము. పనిమీద ఉన్నాడు he is busy. మంచిపని very well, well, good. మంచిపనిచేసినావు you did well or right. అతనిపనిచూస్తున్నాను I am engaged in his service: I am acting for him. అతనిపని తీర్చినారు they settled his business, or they killed him. ఇక్కడ నీకేమిపని what business have you here? This word is sometimes omitted in translating; as in నీపనిపట్టిస్తాను I will punish you. ఇంతపనికి నన్నేల వెంటపెట్టుకొనివచ్చినావు why have you brought me for such a trifle or pretence? పనికిమాలి (or) పనివెడ కూర్చున్నాడు he is sitting idle. వారు వ్యాధిచేత పనిచెడిరి they became infirm through illness. వానితో విరోధము పనికిరాదు he will not stand quarrelling. దాన్ని సంపాదించడము ఎంతపని it is no great matter to get it. నాపని చెరిపినారు they spoiled my work. పనిచెరుపుకథలు idle stories. పనికివచ్చే useful. పనికివచ్చే పిల్లకాయ a promising boy. పనికిరాని or పనికిమాలిన useless. అక్కడికి నీవు ఏపనిమీద పోయినావు about what business did you go there? నీపనినీవు చూచుకొనుము mind your own business. అక్కడికి పోవలసినపనిలేదు there is no need of going there. ఇప్పట్లో వానిపని యిట్లు ఉన్నది he is now in this state. అట్లు చెప్పపనిలేదు there is no need of saying so. **పనిగొను** *pani-gonu.* v. a. To undertake a work, to engage in a business. పూనుకొను. To employ, నియోగించు. "పనిగొనవు తెలియగ బట్టించి చూచిన." Vema. **పనితనము** *pani-tanamu.* n. Workmanship, elegance. పనితనముగల ఒకమంచము a handsome bed. పని

తొడవులు pani-todavulu. n. Worked or embossed jewels. పనిపడు or పనిపడు pani-padu. v. n. To busy oneself with, to engage in, పూనుకొను. To concern oneself with, అక్కఱపడు. పనిపడి or పనిపడి pani-padi. adv. Intentionally. కావలెనని, ప్రయత్నపూర్వకముగా. "పరులను పనిపడి దూషించెనేని పాపము వచ్చుగా." V. P. iv. 249. పనిపాటులు jobs, work. పనిముట్టు or పనిముట్టు pani-muttu. n. An instrument, tool, implement. కొరముట్టు, ఉపకరణము. "పనిమటములుగొంచు పయనమై రెండు." Pal. 314. పనివంచు, పని పంచు or పనిగొను pani-vantsu. v. a. To command. నియోగించు. పనివాడు pani-vadu. n. A servant: a good workman. పనివిను pani-vinu. v. n. To obtain permission, to take leave. To proceed, to go or come. "సేవక కీర్తి వెక్కసంబుగ జెప్పుదిని చూడగోరి, పనివిని నేడు మాభాగ్యంబునకరెన." H.D. i. 847.

పనుకు panuku. [Tel.] v. n. To be angry. ఆగ్రహించు. n. A kind of plant. Its species are called నల్లపనుకు *Mansuris*, a native of sand hills; చెరువుపనుకు *Rottbaelia glabra*; కొండపనుకు *R. exaltata*; పెద్దపనుకు *R. corymbosa*. Rox. i. 351, 355.

పనుగొను or పన్నుగొను panu-gonu. [Tel.] v. n. To become hard or firm, గట్టిపడు, దృఢపడు. To happen, కలుగు.

పనుచు panutsu. [Tel.] v. a. To send, to command, పంపు, ఆజ్ఞాపించు. "పాపుర్తనుని బట్టితెమ్మని నన్ను బనిచినవచ్చితి." M. iii.v. 455. పనుపు, పన్పు or పంపు panupu. v. a. To send. n. Sending, a mission; a command, order. నియోగము. పనుపరి panupari. n. One who is sent or commanded.

పనుపడు or పన్నుపడు panu-padu. [Tel.] v. n. To be accustomed, inured, qualified, to fit, to suit. నాడుకపడు, అలవాటుపడు, సరిపడు, ఇముడు, ఒదిగియుండు. To happen, కలుగు. వాడు వ్రాయుటయందు బాగా పనుపడ్డవాడు he is dexterous or skilled in writing. "సద్బుద్ధిదృఢముగసాధనంబుగ గొని మరలిచియుక్తమునమనునిలిపి యుపగతపంకల్పుడై యుడల స్థాణుభంగికి స్థితిబనుపడిదినంబు రాత్రియును." M. XII. vi. 37. ఉపలస్థాణు భంగికి స్థితిబనుపడి, అనగా రాతిస్తంభము రీతిగా చలించకుండా ఉండవలెనుటకు అలవాటుపడి. పనుపరచు panu-paratsu. v. a. To inure, to accustom, drill, train. To trim, rectify, mend, adjust.

పన్న panna. [Tel.] n. A servant, భృత్యుడు. "ఎరుకుబన్నలుగన్నఏతురునిన్ను." BD. iii. 1316. A man of no consequence in the world, అనామధేయుడు. An old man, వృద్ధుడు.

పన్నగము pann-agamu. [Skt.] n. A snake or serpent. పన్నగాశనుడు pannag-asanudu. n. A snake-eater, that is, an eagle. గరుత్మంతుడు.

పన్నము pannamu. [Tel.] n. One verse in a chapter of the Vedas. వేదములో అష్టకములోనిభాగము.

పన్నా panna. [Tel.] n. A frame used in weaving. The frame on which paper is made. The breadth of a cloth. ఆ గుడ్డ కొంచెము పన్నా చిన్నది that cloth is not broad. A strip of cloth cut out as for jacket.

పన్నాగము pannagamu. [Tel.] n. The hood or canopy over an open palanquin, usually made of scarlet cloth, అందలము మీదికప్పు.

పన్నారు pannaru. [Tel.] n. A pot, a vase, కుండ. A child's toy, బాలికలాడుకొనేకుండి. "కుడికెడుదెత్తునాగుజ్జనోగిరము, మూల పన్నారులయా లోవిలోనపోలెలున్న విపంపు పోయి తెచ్చెదము." BD. iii. 850. నూలుపన్నారులు, లోగామండేకుండలు.

పన్నీరు or పన్నీరము panniru. [Tel. పని + నీరు.] n. Cool water. Perfumed water, rose water, &c. హిమాంబువు. పన్నీరుబుడ్డ

the fragrant flower with a white corolla and a long tube, *Guettarda speciosa*. సీమపన్నీరుపువ్వు the rose, గులాబి, గులాబి.

పన్ను *pannu*. [Tel.] n. A tax, rent, dues. కప్పము. పన్నుకట్టు to impose a tax.

పన్ను *pannu*. [Tel.] v. n. To prepare oneself for battle. యుద్ధమునకు సిద్ధపడు. To happen, కలుగు. v. a. To make, form, invent, frame, చేయు, ఏర్పరచు, కల్పించేయు. To yoke cattle or join together instruments of husbandry, to unite, కూర్చు. To prepare, సిద్ధపరచు. మాటలుపన్ను to spin out a story. **పన్నకము** or **పన్నిక** *pannakamu*. n. Yoking cattle, or joining together instruments of husbandry. నాగేలిమొదలయినవానికి అంగములకూర్చడము. **పన్నిదము** or **పందెము** *pannidamu*. n. A bet, wager, stake. **పన్నుగడ** *pannu-gada*. n. Making, an arrangement, రచన. A scheme, device. యుక్తి, ఉపాయము. "ప్రాణసఖియట్లుపన్నిసపన్నుగడయు, తెలియమిని కేని." Prabhavati v. 174. **పన్నుగా** *pannuga*. adv. Properly, nicely, neatly, in good order, ఒప్పుగా. **పన్నించు** *pannintsu*. v. a. To put on, కట్టు, బంధించు "పసిడిపల్లంబులు పన్నించిపసిడిపక్కెరివేసి." Pal. 52.

పన్నుండు *pann-undu*. [Tel. పడి+ఉండు.] v. n. To recline, lie down. శయనించు, పరుండు.

పన్నువడు See పనుపడు.

పన్నె, పన్నియ or **పన్నెకట్లు** *panne*. [Tel.] n. The centre part of a heckle. A weaver's reed-like comb that strikes the threads of the warps together after the shuttle has passed. మగ్గమునందు పడుగు నూలు వేరువేరుగా చొప్పించుటకై నడుమ [illegible] నిలువుగా చెప్పడియుండునట్లు వెదురు ముక్కలతో అడ్డముగా కట్టబడిన సాలెవాని సాధన విశేషము.

పన్నెండు See under పది.

పప్ప *pappa*. [Tel.] n. A cake. భక్ష్యము.

పప్ప *pappa*. [Eng.] n. Papa, father. తండ్రి.

పప్పళి *pappali*. [Tel.] n. A cloth of a variegated color, చిత్రవర్ణవస్త్రవిశేషము.

పప్పాయపండు *pappaya-pandu*. [Tel.] n. The Papaya fruit. బొప్పాయపండు. **పప్పాయగువ్వ** *pappaya-guvva*. n. The black-headed Myna. *Temenuchus pagodarum*. (F. B. I.)

పప్పు *pappu*. [Tel.] n. Split pulse of any kind. A kernel of any kind freed from the shell as పొంపప్పు and జీడిపప్పు, &c. రొయ్యపప్పు prawns or shrimps freed from the coat or shell. పప్పుకూర the white Goosefoot, *Chenopodium album* (Watts). పప్పుచేయు to reduce to powder.

పబువు *pabuvu*. [from Skt. ప్రభువు.] n. Lord. ప్రభువు.

పబ్బము *pabbamu*. [Tel.] n. A feast. పండుగ. A feast at particular periods of the year such as the equinoxes, &c., when offerings are made by the Hindus to the manes of their ancestors. సంక్రాంత్యాదులు. A festival, ఉత్సవము. Hospitality to guests, ఆతిథ్యము.

పమిడి *pamidi*. [Tel.] n. Gold. పయిడి. **పమిడికంటి** or **పమిడికంత్రిక** *pamidi-kanti*. n. The Indian owlet. See పైడి.

పమిదె Same as ప్రమిదె (q. v.).

పముజె Same as పంజె (q. v.) **పముజెలకమ్ములు** or **పంజెలకమ్ములు** *pamudzula-kammulu*. n. Large earrings worn by women.

పమ్ము or **పొదలు** *pammu*. [Tel.] v. n. & a. To excel, to display, to cover, to spread. అతిశయించు. విజృంభించు, కవియు, ఆవరించుకొను. క్రమ్ముకొను. "పొడలుఁటిగ నెల్లపమ్మిపొరలి, బలముతెక్కడుదయ్య ప్రస్తానాయమునకు." Pal. 294. "జలకూర్పు తారివత్రాలబమ్మినకమ్మి ప్రస్తునమణి రథాంగములగమలు." Vasu. i. 63.

పయుటు, పయ్యుటు, పంటు or పైటు Same as పయ్యెద (q. v.).

పయనము payanamu. [from Skt. ప్రయాణః] n. A journey. పయనించు payanin-tsu. v. n. To get ready for a journey. ప్రయాణమగు.

పయర, పయ్యర or పైర payara. [Tel.] n. A zephyr, a cool wind, చల్లగాలి. A south wind, దక్షిణపుగాలి. పయరపంట is a term for those crops which are grown in the season when this breeze prevails. దక్షిణపుగాలిచేత పండేకందులు పెసలు మినుములు మొదలైనవాటి పంట. పయరపొగాకు early tobacco, that which is grown in spring.

పయస్సు payassu. [Skt.] n. Milk. క్షీరము. Water, ఉదకము. పయస్విని payasvini. n. A milch cow. పాలిచ్చే ఆవు. పయోజము payôjamu. n. Lit: water-born, i.e., a lotus, తామర. పయోధరము payôdha-ramu. n. A woman's breast. A cloud. పయోధరత nebulosity, the quality of being a cloud, ఉదకమునుధరించుట, మేఘత్వము. పయోధి or పయోరాశి payôdhi. n. Lit: A place for or a heap of waters, i.e., the ocean, సముద్రము.

పయ్య payya. [Tel.] adj. Dun, sorrel. పయ్యెద్దు a dun bullock.

పయ్యెద or పయ్యెద payy-eda. [Tel. పయి+ ఎద.] n. a woman's veil or mantle (or wimple) formed of her skirt thrown over her shoulder and her breast, పైట.

పయి Same as పై (q. v.).

పర para. [Tel.] n. A measure with which chunam, &c., is measured. A salt marsh, ఉప్పుపండుబయలు, పఱ్ఱి. A plain, బయలు. ఇసుకపర a sandy plain. ఇసుకపరగానుండే sandy. A series, వరుస. A multitude, సమూహము. అంపర ampara. (అమ్ము+పర.) n. A shower or series of arrows. adj. Another. ఇతరము. Much, great, మిక్కిలి, గొప్ప. పరమేఘములు great clouds.

పర para. [Tel.] n. Another form of పొర (q. v.).

"పెరినాల్గుకన్నులనిజదీప్తినంత,
పరగప్పినట్లుండెఘోరలోచనములు."

BD. iii. 1695.

పర para. [Skt.] prep. Alien, other, appertaining to one's neighbour. పరకాయ ప్రవేశము transmigration from one body (కాయము) to another (పర); the magic power of shifting oneself into another body. పరకీయ para-kiya. adj. Alien, belonging to another. ఇతరునిది. n. A neighbour's wife, a strange woman, పరస్త్రీ, నాయికలలోనొకతె. పరజాతుడు para-jâtuḍu. n. A slave, దానిసవాడు. పరతంత్రము or పరతంత్రత para-tantramu. n. Subserviency, obedience, dependence, agency. పరతంత్రము adj. Subservient, obedient, dependent. పరతంత్రుడు, పరవంతుడు or పరాధీనుడు n. A servant. పరదళము para-daḷamu. n. A foe, an enemy's army. పరదేశము n. A strange country. పరదేశి para-dêśi. n. A foreigner, an immigrant. A guest, అతిథి. Also, a wanderer, refugee or homeless wretch. పరధ్యానము para-dhyânamu. n. Absence of mind, reverie. పరనారి para-nâri. n. A neighbour's wife, another's spouse. పరపురుషుడు another man, not one's own husband. పరపుష్టము or పరభృతము para-pushṭamu. n. A cuckoo, so called as being reared (పుష్టము) in another (పర) bird's nest. కోకిల. పరభృత్తు para-bhṛittu. n. A crow. పరమండలము para-manḍalamu. n. A foreign realm. పరమారకయంత్రము para-mâraka-yantramu. n. A foe-slaying engine. A. ii. 8. పరరతి para-rati. n. Fornication, adultery. H. v. 253. పరలోకము para-lôkamu. n. The other or next world. Heaven. పరలోకగతుడు one who is dead or departed to the next world. పరలోకక్రియలు obsequies, rites for the rest of a departed soul. ఉత్తరక్రియలు. **పరవశము** *para-vasamu.* adj. Out of one's control from joy, ecstacy or sorrow, overpowered, seized in a paroxysm, given up to, transported with or overcome with ecstasy, beside oneself with any passion. పరాధీనము. **పరవశత్వము** *para-vasatvamu.* n. Bewilderment, wildness, ecstasy. **పరవశుడు** *para-vasudu.* n. One who is in ecstasy or wild with joy or sorrow. **పరవాది** *para-vadi.* n. A dissenter. A foe, an opponent, శత్రువు. An impetuous or precipitate man, అత్రగొట్టు. Swa. iii. 113. **పరశ్శతము** *paras-satamu.* adj. More than a hundred. పరస్సహస్రము more than a thousand. **పరసతి** *para-sati* n. Another man's wife, a neighbour's wife, another woman. **పర-సదనము** *para-sadanamu.* n. A neighbour's house. **పరస్థలము** or **పరస్థానము** *para-sthalamu.* n. Another place. **పరాధీనము** *par-adhinamu.* n. Possession by another. ఆ పుస్తకము పరాధీనములోనున్నది the book is in another person's hands. ఆ సొత్తు అంతా పరాధీనమైపోయినది the whole property has fallen into the hands of others. పరాధీనముచేయు to divert or turn aside from its right possessor. పరాధీనం ప్రాణసంకటం a life of dependence is a life of misery. adj. Dependent, subject or subservient to another. **పరాధీనుడు** *par-adhinudu.* n. One who is dependent on or subservient to another. అన్యునికి లోబడినవాడు. **పరార్థవాది** *par-artha-vadi.* n. A vakil, వకీలు.

పరంగి *parangi.* [from 'Frank.'] n. A Frenchman. A Feringee. Applied generically to any European. శ్వేతముఖుడు. హంస. i. Also, a root, పరంగిచెక్క, introduced by the Europeans. The China Root, *Smilax china.* Ainslie. i. 70 ఒక వస్తువు పేరు. **పరంగిసాంబ్రాణి** *parangi-sambrani.* n. The foreign or refined myrrh. పరంగిమాణిక్యము a ruby which is red like a European (the Europeans being usually described as a red, not as a white people by the Hindus.) "పర దుర్గ జాతి కీర్తుల నెత్తురు కలంచులు నీ పురముల విద్యచం బులకు దర్పము రాల్లక నురాగ నుల చెంగట పరంగులాని కెంపులపోగులు మెలగు గాక." చంద్ర.

పరంజము *paranjamu.* [Skt.] n. A mill. గానుగ. The edge of a sword. కత్తి యంచు. Foam, నురుగ.

పరంజు *parandzu.* [H.] n. A hilt. కత్తిపిడి. "పసిడిపరంజు" Swa. iv. 36.

పరంపర *param-para.* [Skt.] n. A series, succession, order, race, a lineage. వరుస, సంతానము. Also, killing, హింస. బాణ పరంపర a shower of darts. చింతాపరంపర a series of griefs. పరంపరగా consecutively, in order. శిష్యపరంపర a succession of pupils, tradition. వంశపరంపరగా in the order of lineage or birth, genealogically. **పరంపరాకము** *param-parakamu.* n. Cow-killing for sacrificial purposes, యజ్ఞమందలి పశువధ. **పరంపరుడు** *param-parudu.* n. A great-great-grandson, మునిమనుమడు.

పరక *paraka.* [Tel.] n. The fraction of one eighth of a rupee, or two annas. The cream on curds. A trifle, a bit, a slip. గడ్డిపరక a blade of grass. గడ్డిపోచ.

పరకాయించు or **పరికించు** *parakayintsu.* [Corrupted from Skt. పరికించు.] v. a. To examine.

పరకాలగుడ్డ *parakala-gudda.* [H.] n. Long cloth.

పరగడ or **పరగడము** *paragada* [Tel.] n. Another place, ఇతరస్థలము. A side, పార్శ్వము. A field outside of a village ఊరికివెలుపలిచేను, కత్తను. **పరగడ** *paragada.* adv (affix.) Off, from, aside. ఊరికిపరగడ, outside the village.

కెట్టి, ఆనగా బైటపెట్టి "పరవకుముంచుకేర్చి యుదుపిరుదునల్లడదాడ గట్టుచా, పరగడనిల్చి." N. ix. 138. టీ: కొంచెము ఆవతలగానిలిచి. plu. పరగల్లు A. iv. 54. **పరగడగా** *paragaḍa-gā*, adv. Indirectly, apart. మేము పరగడగా విన్న సమాచారము the news we received indirectly. వారు పరగడగా నిలిచిరి they stood apart.

పరగడుపు *para-gaḍupu*. [Tel. పరము+కడుపు.] n. An empty belly. Fasting. పరగడుపున ఔషధము పుచ్చుకోవలెను it is proper to take medicine fasting or on an empty stomach.

పరగణా *paragaṇā*. [H.] n. A division of a country, a Parganah.

పరగు *paragu*. [Tel.] v. n. To be, exist, remain, చెలగు, ఉండు. To be used, to be applied, ప్రయుక్తమగు. To apply, to be applicable, ప్రవర్తిల్లు. To spread, వ్యాపించు. To become known, to be found, ప్రసిద్ధమగు. To set out on a journey, ప్రయాణమగు. To flow, ప్రవహించు. To roam about, to walk about, విహరించు. "పన్నగపతులు సంతసముల బరిగిరపుడు." V. P. ii. 148. **పరగ** *paraga*. adv. Agreeably, duly. ఒప్పగా. **పరగించు** *paragintsu*. v. a. To emit. To let fly. బయలువిడుచు. To cause to spread, వ్యాపింపజేయు. M. XIV. ii. 218.

పరచి *parachi*. [Tel.] n. A loan, ఎరువు.

పరచు or **పరుచు** *paratsu*. [Tel. causal of పడు.] v. a. and v. n. To cause to fall, పడజేయు. To make or cause. To spread over, as a mat. To expand or spread. To go, to run. To run away. To urge or cause to run. To flow as water. To pass as time. To make one enjoy or suffer. పాటుపడజేయు. విస్తరింపజేయు, చేయు. పోవు. పరుగెత్తు, పరుగెత్తించు, ప్రవహించు, గడుచు, అనుభవింపజేయు "కాల్పనేని యుగము కోల పోవు." Vema. 1341. "దుర్గాత్మ ప్రపద్యేవాడ్రి గరుడుండు వరిత్యక్తరిపగతిం బరచి." M. I. ii. 68. "నీచేకరిగిరయును దలపనొల్లక పరతురథగతులకోడ బద్ధదళాక్షా." B. X. 93. "పెట్టోకడగాక బరచిరి చెందులపుడు." Swa. iv. 143. "విండిపరచు దరచు పిలచేరుల." Swa. iv. 91. It is used with nouns, adjectives, verbs, and postpositions to form verbs with a causal signification. అటంకపరచు to prevent. భేదపరచు to distinguish, to effect a distinction, to separate. సమ్మతిపరచు to persuade, to convince or to make one agree. దృఢపరచు to make firm, to establish. తెలియబరచు to make known. తేటపరచు to make clear. లోబరచుకొను to subdue, to bring under one's control. సిద్ధపరచు to prepare, to make ready. వారిని లోబరచుకొన్నాడు he has got them into his hands. దాన్ని ఉపయోగించినాడు he brought it into use. **పరత**, **పరతి** or **పరద** *parata*. n. A stream, current, ప్రవాహము, వరద. **పరతెంచు** *para-tentsu*. [పరచు + తెంచు.] v. n. To come running. పారివచ్చు.

పరజ *paradza*. [Tel.] n. A kind of bird. Rasics. i. 49.

పరటు [Tel.] n A cowdung cake, ఎరుపిడక.

పరటి Same as పాటి (q. v.) **పరటిపుట్టువు** *parati-puṭṭuvu*. n. Lit. one who is born in a pot, i. e., Agastya.

పరటు Same as పంటు (q. v.).

పరత *parata*. [Skt.] n. Addictedness, devotedness to, love for. **తత్పరత** *tat-parata*. n. Eagerness, devotedness. ఆసక్తి. "పరత్వమొల్లాసు పరతనొంది." M. XIV. ii. 185.

పరతమము *paratamamu* [Skt.] n. A certain large number, ten billions. మహాపద్మంబు సంఖ్యలోని తొంటి.

పరదా *parada.* [H.] n. A purdah, a screen. తెర.

పరపతి or **పరపత్తేము** *parapati.* [Tel.] n. Credit, trust, loan. పరపతిచేసికొను to borrow money. నాకు పరపతిభంగము చేయ దలచినారు they tried to destroy my credit.

పరపర *para-para.* [Tel.] n. The noise produced when a cloth or paper is torn, బట్టలు మొదలయినవి చించితే పుట్టే ధ్వని. Feigning, affectation. "భక్తులకన్నభక్తి జూపి యుండెను, భక్తియుక్తయమును బరపరగా చే." BD. iv. 674.

పరపు or **పరుపు** *parapu.* [Tel. from పరచు or పరుచు.] v. a. To cause to run or fall, &c. పరపజేయు, పడజేయు. To let fly, as an arrow. (బాణమును) ప్రయోగించు. To cause to flow, ప్రవహింపజేయు. To cast, to make, వేయు, చేయు. To remove, పోగొట్టు. To drive away, తోలు. To spread or smear, పూయు. "బహుధారాపాతముదప్పవితతి, బరపి కూల్పనేని రాముని కృష్ణుడు." M. XIV. iv. 103. adj. Spreading, large, broad, విశాలమైన. n. Extent, spreading. విశాలం. Swiftness, వేగము. A bed, పడక. "పూపరపు" (Vasu. i. 58.) a flowery couch. "సరపరి సాలవిశాల భూజముల పరపారునీడల." (HD. iii. 641,) in the spreading shades of large sweet mango trees. **పరపించు** *parapintsu.* v. a. To cause to run or flow, &c.

పరమము *paramamu.* [Skt.] adj. Best, supreme, most excellent, principal, chief. ఉత్కృష్టము, ప్రధానము. పరమగురువు the supreme teacher. పరమపతివ్రత the most virtuous woman. **పరమపదము** or **పరంపదము** *parama-padamu.* n. Heaven. మోక్షము. **పరమపదించు** or **పరంపదించు** *parama-padintsu.* v. n. To depart to bliss, to die, to expire. పరమలుబ్ధుడు a great miser. పరమపావనుడు the great purifier, he who wholly sanctifies. పరమహంస an ascetic recluse, ఉత్తమసన్యాసి. పరమయోగి an absolute ascetic. "సంవత్సర శతంబ్రాయం పరమాయుష్యరూపితం." (B. iii. XI. 12.) one century is the limit of human life. **పరమాణువు** *param-anuvu.* n. An atom, the invisible base of all aggregate bodies, సూక్ష్మములకంటె సూక్ష్మమైన అణువు. **పరమాత్మ**, **పరమాత్ముడు** or **పరమము** *param-atma.* n. The Supreme Being, considered as the soul of the universe. పరబ్రహ్మము. **పరమార్థము** *param-arthamu.* n. The great object or summum bonum of life. Bliss, heaven. **పరమాన్నము** *param-annamu.* n. Rice-pudding, milk boiled with rice and sugar, పాయసము. **పరమేశ్వరుడు** *param-ēsvarudu.* n. The Supreme Lord. One of the names of Siva, శివుడు. **పరమేష్ఠి** *param-ēshthi.* n. Bramha, the Creator. బ్రహ్మ.

పరమానా or **పరవానా** *paramāna.* [H.] n. A grant or letter from one in authority: a firman, an order, a mandate. పన్నరు, రాజాజ్ఞ.

పరమాను *para-manu.* [Tel.] n. The fore yard of a vessel.

పరము *paramu.* [Tel.] n. The frame or upper part of a carriage. కొట్టుబడిమీది పరుపుగూడు. A level surface, చేరుడు. [Skt.] n. Heaven, మోక్షము. adj. Other, అన్యము. Excellent, శ్రేష్ఠము. **పరముపడు** *paramu-padu.* v. n. To last, as a vow or religious observance. అనశనవ్రతమాచరించు.

పరవ Same as పరవి. See under పరచు.

పరవంజు *para-vandzu.* [Tel.] v. a. To spread, surround, envelop, expand, ప్రసరించు, ఆవరించు, కమ్ముకొను.

పరవతిగాడు *paravati-gadu.* [Tel.] n. The kestrel. Jer. Catal. No. 31.

పరవా *parava.* [H.] n. Regard, respect, care for, లక్ష్యము. పరవాలేదు never mind, no matter, చింతలేదు.

పరవు or **పరగు** *paravu.* [Tel.] v. n. To spread, వ్యాపించు. n. Spreading, వ్యాపనము.

పరశువు or **పరశ్వధము** *paraśuvu.* [Skt.] n. A battle axe. గండగొడ్డలి. M. vi. ii. 93. **పరశురాముడు** *paraśu-rāmuḍu.* n. The name of a certain hero. ఆ యిల్లు పరశురాముప్రీతి అయినది the house was burnt: lit: enjoyed the favour of Parasu-Rāma. పరశురామక్షేత్రము the ancient name of the country now called Malabar.

పరస్పరము *paras-paramu.* [Skt.] adj. Mutual, reciprocal, interchanging. అన్యోన్యము. By proxy, circuitous, not in person. Diverted from its proper purpose. పరస్పర విరోధము mutual discrepancy, mutual enmity, a disagreement between one another. **పరస్పరముగా** *paras paramu gā.* adv. Mutually, to each other. By, through (a proxy). Through the medium of others. Indirectly, circuitously.

పరాకు *parāku.* [Tel.] n. Oversight, error. Carelessness, forgetfulness. ప్రమాదము, పరధ్యానము. పరాకున unawares, by error. పరాకులేక heedfully, without inattention. పరాకుచెప్పు to warn, call attention to. (Interj.) Take heed! Take care. Also used as a conversational phrase like "I beg your pardon! please listen to me!" హెచ్చరిక. పరాకుడు [Skt.] a cunning man, కుత్సితుడు. **పరాకుపడు** *parāku-paḍu.* [Tel.] v. n. To forget, be off one's guard. ప్రమాదపడు, భ్రమపడు, పరాకుననుండు.

పరాక్రమము *parākramamu.* [Skt.] n. Valour, prowess. Power, strength, exertion.

పరాగము *parāgamu.* [Skt.] n. The pollen of a flower. పుప్పొడి. Dust, దుమ్ము.

పరాఙ్ముఖుడు or **పరాన్ముఖుడు** *parāng-mukhuḍu.* [Skt.] n. One who turns away his face from a thing. పెడమొగము పెట్టినవాడు.

పరాచితుడు *parāchituḍu.* [Skt.] n. A slave. గారిసవాడు

పరాజయము *parā-jayamu.* [Skt.] n. Defeat. అపజయము, ఓడిపోవుట. **పరాజితము** *parā-jitamu.* adj. Conquered, overcome. ఓడిన.

పరాత్పరుడు *parāt-paruḍu.* [Skt.] n. The Supreme Being, the Almighty. శ్రేష్ఠులకు శ్రేష్ఠుడు.

పరాన్నుడు *par-annuḍu.* n. One who feeds himself at another's table.

పరాపేక్ష *para-apēksha.* [Skt.] n. Dependence on the aid of others. ఈ పని పరాపేక్షలేకుండా చేసినాడు he did this work himself without any help.

పరాభవము or **పరాభూతి** *parā-bhavamu.* [Skt.] n. Defeat, loss, ruin; contempt, disrespect, defiance. తిరస్కారము, అవమానము, నాశము. **పరాభవించు** *parā-bhavintsu.* v. a. To defeat, disgrace. తిరస్కరించు, అవమానించు. **పరాభూతుడు** *parā-bhūtuḍu.* n. One who is defeated or disgraced. పరాభవించబడినవాడు.

పరామరిక *paramarika.* [from Skt. పరామర్శ.] n. Heed, care, attention. నీ పరామరికలేకుంటే కార్యముకాదు unless you attend to it the work will not succeed. పరామరికలేని inattentive, negligent.

పరామర్శ, పరామర్శము or **పరామరిస** *parā-marṣa.* [Skt.] n. Attention, care, examination. చక్కగా విచారించుట. An inquiry. Condolence, consolation. (In logic), inference, conclusion. **పరామర్శించు** or **పరామరిసించు** *parā-marṣintsu.* v. a. To condole with, to pay attention to; to take care of or tend, to console; to investigate, to examine. (In logic), to infer, draw conclusions, చక్కగా విచారించు.

పరాయణము *parāyaṇamu.* [Skt.] n. A prop, support, ప్రాపు. Devotion, addiction to. తత్పరత, ఆశ్రయము. adj. Eager, devoted to, ఆసక్తము. **పరాయణుడు** *parāya-ṇuḍu.* n. An aspirant to, one devoted to, a candidate ఆసక్తిగలవాడు, [illegible] one addicted to chattering. "ఖోగ్రుక పరాయుణుల్." M. IV. iii. 33.

పరాయి *parayi*. [corrupted from Skt. పర.] adj. Another. ఇతరము. పరాయివాడు a stranger.

పరారి *parāri*. [H. corruption of ఫరార.] adj. Fled, absconded. n. A runaway, a defaulter. పారిపోయినవాడు.

పరార్థ్యము *parārthyamu*. [Skt.] adj. Excellent, noble. ముఖ్యమైన, శ్రేష్ఠమైన.

పరాసుడు *parāsuḍu*. [Fr. Francois.] n. A Frenchman. పరాసులు *parāsulu*. n. plu. The French. "పరాసులెల్లను పరాసత్వము పొందిరి." Bobbili. iii. 158.

పరాసువు *par-āsuvu*. [Skt.] adj. Dead, expired. చచ్చిన. n. A dead man. చచ్చినవాడు. **పరాసనము**, or **పరాసత్వము** *parāsanamu*. n. Death, extinction. పరాసత్వము పొందు to perish.

పరాస్కంది *par-āskandi*. [Skt.] n. A thief or robber. దొంగ.

పరి *pari*. [Tel.] n. An army. సేన. A multitude, సమూహము. A series, పఙ్క్తి. The act of surrounding (anything), వేష్టనము. The weight of the yoke, కాడిబరువు. పరి వెలుపలికిట్టు వేయుట throw the weight of the yoke on the outside. A time, an opportunity, ఆవృత్తి, తడవ, సారి. ఒకపరి once. Manner, విధము. "ఆ మనసుపుచుటకిన పరిగస్వప్న ముగన్న తెలిగ." ఆము. iv. **పరిగమి** *pari-gami*. n. A fully equipped army. చతురంగబలముగల సేన.

పరి *pari*. [Skt.] prefix. Around; full, fully, greatly, completely. మిక్కిలి. **పరికరించు** *pari-karintsu*. [corrupted from Skt. పరీక్ష.] v. a. To examine. పరీక్షించు. **పరికర్మము** *pari-karmamu*. n. Cleaning the body. శరీరశుద్ధికరణము, దేహమాలిన్యమును పోగొట్టుకొనడము. Adornment, decoration, అలంకారము. "ధర్మపరికర్మపరిణతిం బను బ్రహ్మరథంబున." A. iv. 37. **పరిక్రమము** *pari-kramamu*. n. Walking at ease. విహారము. **పరిక్రియ** *parik-riya*. n. Walking round a thing, ప్రదక్షిణము, చుట్టుకొనివచ్చుట. **పరిక్షిప్తము** *pari-kshiptamu*. adj. Surrounded on all sides, అన్నిప్రక్కలను చుట్టుకొనబడిన. **పరిక్షేపము** *pari-kshēpamu*. n. The act of surrounding. చుట్టుకొనియుండుట. **పరిక్లేశము** *pari-klēṣamu*. n. Calamity, affliction, misery. కష్టము. "మహాపరిక్లేశంబున కోర్చు." M. II. ii. 328. **పరిగణనము** *pari-gaṇanamu*. n. Estimation. ఎంచడము, ఎన్నిక. **పరిగణించు** *pari-gaṇintsu*. v. a. To think, reckon, consider, ఎంచు, ఎన్ను. **పరిగ్రహించు** *pari-grahintsu*. v. a. To take, accept, admit or receive. ప్రియముతో పుచ్చుకొను. **పరిగ్రహము** or **పరిగ్రహణము** *pari-grahamu*. n. Acceptance, taking, assent, consent, ప్రియముతో పుచ్చుకొనుట. Dependants, a family, a train, పరివారము. **పరిగృహీతము** *pari-grihītamu*. adj. Accepted, received with kindness, ప్రియముతో పుచ్చుకొనబడిన. **పరిఘట్టనము** *pari-ghaṭṭanamu*. n. Thumping, striking, collision. **పరిఘటించు** or **పరిఘాణించు** *pari-ghaṇintsu*. [Tel.] v. n. To vaunt, to boast, to oppose in words. ఎదురాడు.

"చిరుదరూపుల విరసించు హాస్తములు,
గగనంబుతో బరిఘాటించు పదులు."

HD. ii. 352.

పరిఘోషము *pari-ghōshamu*. n. Sounding, noise, ధ్వని. Thunder, ఉరుము. **పరిచరుడు** *pari-charuḍu*. n. A guard or bodyguard, an attendant, a servant. చౌకిదారులు జాగ్రతగాచేసే భటుడు. A sentinel, సేనకావలిభటుడు. **పరిచర్య** or **పరిచారము** *pari-charya*. n. Service, attendance, dependence. సేవ. **పరిచరించు** *pari-charintsu*. v. n. To serve. పరిచర్యచేయు. **పరిచారకుడు** *pari-chārakuḍu*. n. A man servant. **పరిచారిక** *pari-chārika*. n. A maid servant. పరిచార్యుడు pari-char. yudu. n. One fit to be attended on or served. పరిజనము pari-janamu. n. A train of followers, attendants. పరివారము. పరితపించు pari-tapintsu. v. n. To grieve, to be sorrowful. పరితాపము or పరితాపము pari-tāpamu. n. Pain, anguish, sorrow, affliction, సంతాపము. Heat, fever, జ్వరభేదము. Trembling, భయము, కంపము. పరితోషము or పరితుష్టి pari-tōshamu. n. Pleasure, satisfaction, delight, gratification, great joy, మిక్కిలి సంతోషము. పరితోషించు pari-tōshintsu. v. n. To rejoice greatly. పరిత్యజించు pari-tyajintsu. v. a. To abandon, or quit బొత్తిగావిడుచు. పరిత్యాగము pari-tyāgamu. n. Abandonment, quitting, desertion, yielding, relinquishment, giving up. దేహపరిత్యాగము-dēha-pari-tyāgamu. n. Dying, giving up life. పరిత్యాగపత్రిక pari-tyāga-patrika. n. A writ of divorce. పరిత్యక్తము pari-tyaktamu. adj. Abandoned. పరిత్యాజ్యము pari-tyājyamu. adj. Fit to be abandoned. పరిత్రాణము pari-trāṇamu. n. Preservation, protection, fostering, రక్షణము. పరిత్రాసుడు pari-trāsuḍu. adj. Afraid, భయము గలిగిన. "విపరీత జనసంఘ మహోగ్ర కల్పన పరిత్రాసుఁడై." Ved. Ras. iii. 29. పరిదానము pari-dānamu. n. Barter, exchange. వినిమయము, వస్తువులను మార్చుకొనుట. A bribe. పరిదానముపట్టు to receive a bribe. పరిదేవనము pari-dēvanamu. n. A lamentation, విలాపము, కలవరింత. M. II. iii. 35. పరిధానము pari-dhānamu. n. A cloth, or lower garment. కట్టుబట్ట, దోవతి. నిర్ముక్తపరిధాన she who is stripped. పరిపక్వము pari-pakvamu. adj. Ripe, mature. Cooked, dressed. పరిపాకము pari-pākamu. n. Maturity, perfection; the fruit or consequence of actions. పరిపాలకుడు pari-pālakuḍu. n. A good protector, cherisher, or patron. చక్కగా కాపాడువాడు. పరిపాలన or పరిపాలనము pari-pālana. n. Protection, patronage. fostering care, government. పరిపాలించు or పరిపాలనచేయు pari-pālintsu. v. a. To protect or cherish, to govern or rule. ఆయన రాజ్యపరిపాలన చేయుచున్నప్పుడు during his reign. పరిపాలితము. pari-pālitamu. adj. Well protected or ruled. పరిపూర్ణము pari-pūrṇamu. adj. Complete, full, replete, పరిపూర్తి pari-pūrti n. Completeness, completion, fulness, satiety, satisfaction. పరిపోషించు pari-pōshintsu. v. a. To nourish well, చక్కగా పోషించు. The noun forms are పరిపోషకుడు, పరిపోషణము, పరిపోషితుడు. పరిభ్రమణము pari-bhramaṇamu. n. Wandering, roaming, travelling. పరిభ్రమించు pari-bhramintsu. v. n. To travel, roam or wander in all directions. అంతట తిరుగు. పరిమండలము pari-manḍalamu. adj. Perfectly round. అంతట గుండ్రమైన. పరిమర్దనము pari-mardanamu. n. Rubbing, grinding, trampling or destroying. పరిమర్దితము pari-marditamu. adj. Rubbed, ground, trampled. పరిమార్జనము pari-mārjanamu. n. A thorough cleaning or cleansing, అంతట తుడుచుట, పరిశుద్ధముచేయడము. పరిమితము pari-mitamu. adj. Meted, measured, limited. పరిమితి pari-miti. n. A limit పరిమాణము. పరిరంభము, పరిరంభణము or పరీరంభము pari-rambhamu. n. An embrace. ఆలింగనము. పరిలుఠత్ pari-luṭhat adj. Rolling. పొరలుచుండునట్టి. T. i. 5. పరివట్టము pari-vaṭṭamu. [from Skt. పరివేష్టము.] n. A cloth or head band, used on particular ceremonial occasions at a temple. పరివర్జనము pari-varjanamu. n. Entire abandonment, బొత్తిగా విడుచుట. Killing, చంపుట. పరివర్జితము pari-varjitamu. adj. Wholly abandoned, బొత్తిగావిడువబడిన. పరివర్తనము, పరివర్తము or పరీవర్తము pari-vartanamu. n. The act of going round any thing, చుట్టుతిప్పుట. A return, వెనుకకుతిరుగుట. An exchange, వస్తువులమార్పు. పరివర్తించు pari-vartintsu. v. n

To go round, చుట్టివచ్చు, తిరుగు. పరివాదము or పరీవాదము *pari-vādamu.* n. Reproach, censure. నింద. M. XI. i. 197. పరివాదిని *pari-vādini.* n. A lute with seven strings. ఏడుతంతులగలవీణ. పరివారము or పరీవారము *pari-vāramu.* n. Dependants, a train, or retinue. Those who are about a prince, his escort. పరిజనము. పరివారదేవతలు *pari-vāra-dēvatalu.* n. Attendant gods. పరివారాంగన a handmaid, a waiting woman. పరివాసితము *pari-vāsitamu.* adj. Scented, perfumed. Parij. iv. 35. పరివృతము or పరీవృతము *pari-vritamu.* adj. Encompassed, surrounded. చుట్టబడిన. పరివేషము or పరివేశము *pari-vēshamu.* n. A halo encircling the sun or moon, గాలిగుడి. పరివేష్టించు *pari-vēshṭintsu.* v. a. To surround, or encompass. చుట్టివచ్చు. పరివేష్టనము *pari-vēshṭanamu.* n. Surrounding. చుట్టివచ్చుట. Also, పరివట్టము (q. v.). పరిశీలన or పరిశీలనము *pari-sīlana.* n. An enquiry, investigation. శోధనము. పరిశీలించు *pari-sīlintsu.* v. a. To enquire into, investigate, test, examine, మిక్కిలి శోధించు. పరిశుద్ధము *pari-suddhamu.* adj. Sacred, holy, pure, clean. మిక్కిలి శుద్ధమైన. పరిశుద్ధి *pari-suddhi.* n. Purity, holiness. పరిశోధన or పరిశోధనము *parisōdhana.* n. An enquiry. మిక్కిలి శోధించుట. పరిశోధించు *pari-sōdhintsu.* v. a. To examine well, investigate: to try or search thoroughly, మిక్కిలి శోధించు. పరిశ్రమ or పరిశ్రమము *pari-srama.* n. Industry, assiduity, thorough acquaintance. పరిశ్రమించు *pari-sramintsu.* v. n. To be industrious or diligent. మిక్కిలి కష్టపడు. పరిశ్రాంతము *pari-srāntamu.* adj. Fatigued, exhausted, harassed. పరిశ్రాంతి *pari-srānti.* n. Fatigue, exhaustion, harassment. మిక్కిలి అలయుట.

పరింకి (కంప) *pariṅki.* [Tel.] n. A certain thorny shrub.

పరిక *parika.* [Tel.] n. A kind of bird. పక్షి విశేషము. See పరిగపిట్ట. A kind of stone, ఒకవిధమైనరాయి. Also, a pattern or diagram drawn on the floor with lines of flour or coloured powder. ముగ్గులు, పరికలువేయు, అనగా ముగ్గులుపెట్టు.

"చ॥ తిరుమల కంచి పుష్పగిరి
తీర్థములం జని కొంగుముళ్లతో,
పరములు దంపతుల్ వడియు
వారికి కాన్కలు వైచి యుండెటుల్,
పరికలు దృష్టిదీపములు
పన్నిన నగ్గలు వెట్టి యేమిటుల్,
గరమగు భక్తివాంఛ కడ
గానగ లేని విచారభావమున్నదై."

Hamsa. ii. 96.

పరికరము *pari-karamu.* [Skt.] n. An instrument, ఉపకరణము. Furniture, సామగ్రి. A cot, మంచము. "మిరియంపుబోడి మించుటూటుకు, సంభారంపుదింపుసందు, బజ్జలు, కూరలు, మన్నక్కూరబిండ్లూరుగాయలు, మామిడి తొక్కులు మొదలగుపరికరంబులును." H. i. 113. A retinue, పరివారము. A multitude, సమూహము. A waist-band, నడికట్టు. A belt, దొంగపట్టి.

పరికాడు *pari-kāḍu.* [Tel.] n. The leader among a herd of elephants, ఏనుగుల మందకు ముఖ్యమైనయేనుగు.

"చ॥ దంతిమట్టిన పరికాడు
మొత్తముకడిందిగ వెంచినమాడ్కి నాపగా,
కడయడంగ్లోనగానది
దంటను విట్టదరని సమున్నతిన్."

భా. భీష్మ. i.

పరికి *pariki.* [Tel.] adj. Dishevelled. చింపిరి. n. A savage, కిరాతుడు. "పరికి పెండ్రుకలపై పత్రిని దాల్చి." BD. iii. 1402. See పరింకి. పాలపరికి a certain forest tree.

పరికించు *parikintsu.* [from Skt. పరీక్షించు.] v. a. To seek for, search, enquire into, examine, investigate, scrutinise, to prove by trial, వెదకు, విచారించు, పరీక్షించు.

పరికిణి or **పరికిణీ** *parikini*. [Tel.] n. A frock worn by little girls. గాగరా, పావడ, లంగా.

పరికూటము *pari-kūṭamu*. [Skt.] n. A mound of earth raised in front of a gate, to sit on or to plant flower trees on, అరుగు.

పరికె *parike*. [Tel.] n. The root of the aquatic plant termed *Trapa bispinosa* Rox. i. 428. శృంగాటకము. **పరికెముట్టెరొయ్య** *parike-muṭṭe-royya*. n. A sort of cray fish. G. i. 111.

పరిఖ *parikha*. [Skt.] n. A moat, or ditch. అగడ్త.

పరిగ or **పరిగె** *pariga*. [Tel.] n. Ears of corn that drop down when a crop is harvested, gleanings of corn. చేనిలో రాలినవెన్ను. పరిగెలు fragments, shivers, తునియలు.

> "పైమన్ను కోళ్లను పరిగెలు చేసి,
> భామిడికంబులను దుల్లపొడుముచురాగ."
> Pal. 439.

పరిగచేను *pariga-chēnu*. n. A reaped field. సస్యముకోసినచేను. **పరిగరి** or **పరిగవాడు** *parig-ari*. n. A gleaner. పరిగ ఏరువాడు. **పరిగపిట్ట** *pariga-piṭṭa*. n. The Rose-coloured Starling or Cholam bird, *Pastor roseus*. (F.B.I.) **పరిగబ్రతుకు** *pariga-bratuku*. n. An uncertain means of livelihood, పరిగ ఏరుకొని బ్రతికే బ్రతుకు.

పరిగమ్మి *pari-gammi*. [Tel.] n. A crook or stick used by herdsmen.

పరిగె or **పరిగెయ** *parige*. [Tel.] n. A kind of tree. A sprat. చేదుపరిగె the bitter sprat which resembles the silver fish. పాలుపరిగె the white sprat. బెత్తపరిగె a sort of Chœtodon. adv. Quickly, శీఘ్రము.

పరిగొను *pari-gonu*. [Tel.] v. n. To form a line or series. బారుతీరు. v. a. To surround, చుట్టుకొను. To steal, అపహరించు "చ॥ పరిగొని దివ్యగంధఫలభారసమృద్ధదళీపరంపరా పరివృతకాయమానములబర్వ ఫలావళిరాచి పైపయింబరిగొని వచ్చు రాజశుకపఙ్క్తుల చొప్పునకొప్పె నప్పు డ, ప్పురవిపణిప్రమాణముల ధూరిహరిన్మణి తోరణావళుల్." Vasu. v.77.

పరిఘ or **పరిఘము** *parigha*. [Skt.] n. The pin, bolt, or bar of a door. అర్గళము, గడియ. A club, a bludgeon, a stick mounted with iron. A weapon. లాటికర్ర, గుదియ, ముద్గరము. A blow, దెబ్బ. The gate of a fort, కోటగవను.

పరిచయము or **పరిచితి** *pari-chayamu*. [Skt.] n. Acquaintance, intimacy, knowledge. ఎరుక, స్నేహము. **పరిచయించు** *pari-chayintsu*. v.n. To contract friendship. స్నేహించు. **పరిచితము** *parichitamu*. adj. Known, acquainted with. పరిచయముగల.

పరిచాళిక *paritsālika*. [Tel.] n. A mode of wrestling. ఉ. హ. iii.

పరిచ్ఛదము *parich-chhadamu*. [Skt.] n. Court, train, attendants, retinue, family, dependants. పరివారము. A covering cloth, కప్పడువస్త్రము.

పరిచ్ఛేదము *parich-chhēdamu*. [Skt.] n. A division of a book, a section, or chapter. గ్రంథభాగము. A limit, extent, మేర.

పరిజించు or **పర్జించు** *parijintsu*. [Tel. from పరుజు] v. a. To seize the hilt. కత్తికటారి మొదలయినవాటినిపట్టు, పరుజుతోపట్టు. "పరుజించి కటారిపర్జించినిల్చి" A. vi. 100.

పరిటె *pariṭe*. [Tel.] n. A weaver's whirl. A trundle. H. ii. 12. and ii. 25. **పరిటెపురుగు** or **బరిటెపురుగు** *pariṭe-purugu*. n. A large spotted beetle.

పరిఢవిల్లు *pariḍhavillu*. [Skt.] v. n. To shine, to give light. వెలుగు, ప్రకాశించు. To excel, అతిశయిల్లు. To go on, to get on, ప్రవర్తిల్లు, నడచు. "ఎచ్చోటచూచినంబగా, నమత్కృతి నాటపాటలు మాటలుపరిఢవిల్ల." Bilh.

iii. 177. పరిధవించు *paridha-vintsu.* v. a. To carry on. నడపు, పరిధవిల్లజేయు. To excel, అతిక్రమించు. To bear, to carry, ధరించు. "జెవ్వాదివిల్లులు ప్రియుమెలర్ప, బట్టిపది లంబుగాదించెపరిధవించి." Ruckmāng. iii. 104.

పరిణతము *pariṇatamu.* [Skt.] adj. Ripe, mature, పక్వమైన. Bent, bowed. "పరిణతా తపమున్." Vasu. iv. 6. n. A butting elephant, an elephant stooping to strike with his tusks. పరిణతి *pariṇati.* n. Bending, bowing. నమ్రత, వంగడము. "నిజంబరయగ క్షేత్రజ్ఞుడను పరిణతిగల యతడు సర్వపదవిదుడుగుడీ" M. XIV. ii. 228. A technical expression for a set of verbs. భూర్వాదిః, పరిణతి, భూసత్తాయాం, జెజయి అనే ధాతువులు అదిగాగల కొన్ని క్రియలకు పారి భాషికనామము. త్రివిధమైన క్రియలలో నొకటి. పరిణద్ధము *pariṇaddhamu.* adj. Bound, tied, possessed of. కట్టబడిన, కూడు కొన్న. "భయదస్ఫురణాపరిణద్ధమూర్తియై." M. IV. ii. 131. పరిణమించు *pariṇamintsu.* v. n. To be glad. సంతసించు, ఆనందించు. "సీ॥ పరిణమించిరి ధరావరపురంధ్రిహస్తఘటిత చేలాంచలగ్రంథికలన." Swa. v. 117. To become metamorphosed, transformed, changed. వికారమునుపొందు, ప్రకృత్యన్యభా భావము అగుట. "మంజులమంజరీమహిత సౌభా గ్యంబు పరివృత్తకుచవృత్తిపరిణమింప." Swa. vi. 99. v. a. To cause to rejoice, సంతో షింపజేయు. పరిణయము *pariṇayamu.* n. Marriage. పెండ్లి. పరిణామము *pari-ṇāmamu.* n. Metamorphosis, transformation, change of form or state. వికారము, మారురూపు. Maturity, fulness, ripeness, పరిణామదర్శి one who looks forward to the end. Joy, gladness, ఆనందము, సంతోషము. "పొగడియుక్తంచిన పొంగి యూరివికి, బాదిరాయుడు కడుపరిణామమందె." Pal. 85. 10. Health, prosperity, welfare, క్షేమము, సుఖము. పరిణామశూల *pari-ṇāma-śūla.* n. Pain caused by indigestion, gastritis.

పరిణాహము *pariṇāhamu.* [Skt.] n. Extent, breadth, width. వైశాల్యము, వెడల్పు. M. iv. 412. పరిణాహుడు *pariṇāhuḍu.* n. A great man. వైశాల్యముగలవాడు. "సమకీర్తిపరిణా హుండనగా." R. i. 100. cf. "Broad-based, upon her people's will."

పరిణేత *pari-nēta.* [Skt.] n. A husband. భర్త.

పరితము *paritamu.* [Tel.] n. A cuckoo. కోయిల.

పరిధి or పరిది *paridhi.* [Skt.] n. The halo of the sun or moon. పరివేషము. The circumference of a circle, the disc of the sun or moon. The branch of a tree, to which the victim at a sacrifice is tied. పరిధిస్థుడు *paridhi-sthuḍu.* n. A sentinel.

పరిపంథి *pari-panthi.* [Skt.] An enemy, foe, antagonist. శత్రువు. Swa. ii. 90.

పరిపణము *pari-paṇamu.* [Skt.] n. Capital, principal stock, మూలధనము, సంచిమొదలు.

పరిపరి *pari-pari.* [Tel.] adj. Divers, sundry, various. Harassed, పీడితము. పరిపరివిధము అయిన miscellaneous. పరిపరివిధాలుగా in all sorts of ways. "పాటించము కాకినుడినినగతోజెరనరుదవహుదువుదు బరిపరి చేయుటు నీదు పూన్కి పాపం బెడలగా." M. iv. ii. 286. పరిపరియలు *pari-pariyalu.* n. Piecemeal. తుత్తునియలు, తునకతునకలు. See పరియ.

పరిపాటి *pari-pāṭi* [Skt.] n. Order, method, arrangement, క్రమము.

పరిపోవు or పరివోవు *pari-pōvu.* v. n. To be plundered, కొల్లపోవు. To perish, to be ruined, నశించు.

పరిబర్హము *pari-barhamu.* [Skt.] n. A retinue or train, పరివారము. Insignia of royalty, రాజయోగ్యవస్తువు.

పరిభవము, పరిభావము or పరీభావము *pari-bhavamu.* [Skt.] n. Disgrace, disrespect, irreverence, insult, contempt, disregard, reproach, abuse తిరస్కారము. అవమానము. పరిభవించు *pari-bhavintsu.* v.

a. To contemn, slight, scorn, insult. తిరస్కారము చేయు, అవమానించు. పరిభూతము *pari-bhûtamu.* adj. Contemned, disregarded, despised. తిరస్కరింపబడిన, అవమానింపబడిన.

పరిభాష *pari-bhâsha.* [Skt.] n. A technicality, a conventional term in any science, సంకేతము, నియమము.

పరిమళము *parimaḷamu.* [Skt.] n. Fragrance, perfume. **పరిమళించు** *parimaḷintsu.* v. n. To smell, be fragrant, give forth scent.

పరిమాణము *parimâṇamu.* [Skt.] n. A measure, measuring, quantity, capacity. కొలత.

పరిమార్చు or **పరిమాచుచు** *parimârtsu.* [Tel. పరిచు + మారుచు.] v. a. To kill, assassinate. "చేయుచున్న నృత్యముల జీవములం బరిమార్చుచుండు." Vish. vii. 171.

పరియ *pariya.* [Tel.] n. A piece, bit, fragment. తునక, శకలము. "తనయులు నృపులం దరుబడినగాలిని పెక్కుపరియలైపోవక యుట్లునికి యరయవజ్రమయంబనిదలపుడు." M. iv. i. 26. **పరియవాయు** *pariya-vâyu.* (పరియ + వాయు.) v. n. To split, చీలు. **పరియవాపు** *pariya-vâpu.* v. a. To cause to split, to split a thing.

పరియంకము Same as పర్యంకము (q. v.).

పరియాచకము Same as పరిహాసము (q. v.).

పరియు *pariyu.* [Tel.] v. n. To miss, తప్పు. To be spoiled, to spoil. చెడు.

పరివిత్తి or **పరివిత్తుడు** *pari-vitti.* [Skt.] n. An elder brother who remains unmarried while his younger one is married. **పరివేత్త** *pari-vêtta.* n. A younger brother who is married before his elder. అన్నకు పెండ్లికాకమునుపు పెండ్లాడినవాడు. Swa. iii. 171.

పరివృఢుడు, పరీవృఢుడు or **పరిబృఢుడు** *pari-vriḍhuḍu.* [Skt.] n. A master, owner or superior. ప్రభువు. యజమానుడు.

పరివేల్లము *pari-vêllamu.* [Skt.] n. A bulrush. తుంగగడ్డి, భద్రతుంగగడ్డి.

పరివ్రాజకుడు or **పరివ్రాట్టు** *pari-vrâjakuḍu.* [Skt] n. A mendicant, or devotee. సన్యాసి.

పరిషత్తు *parishattu.* [Skt.] n. An assembly, meeting, audience, congregation. గోష్ఠి. సభ, సమూహము. "సమాసమాగతభాగవతపరిషత్ప్రమోదంబుగా." A. vi. 146.

పరిషేచనము *pari-shêchanamu.* [Skt.] n. The rite of sanctifying a meal by sprinkling water round the dish. Lustration, చుట్టూరుతడుపడము.

పరిష్కరించు *parish-karintsu.* [Skt.] v. a. To trim, deck, settle, arrange, adjust. To get through, finish: to make clear or evident; to decree, decide. చక్కబెట్టు. **పరిష్కారము** or **పరిష్కరింపు** *parish-kâramu.* n. A decision, finishing, settlement, adjustment, arrangement. చక్కబెట్టుట. Decoration, decking. తొడవు. అభిరణము. **పరిష్కృతము** *parish-kritamu.* adj. Accomplished, settled, finished, arranged. చక్కబెట్టబడిన. Decorated, అలంకరింపబడిన. **పరిష్కారముగా** *parish-kâramu-gâ.* adv. Clearly, distinctly, decidedly, flatly, definitively, positively, fully, utterly, wholly, completely, entirely, fitly, duly. **పరిష్కారుడు** *parish-kâruḍu.* n. One who is perfect. పూర్ణుడు. "చాపవైపుణపరిష్కారుడు." R. v. 148.

పరిష్వంగము *parish-v-angamu.* [Skt.] n. Embracing, an embrace. ఆలింగనము, కవుగిలింత.

పరిస *parisa.* [Tel.] n. A built well in the bed of a river.

పరిసరము *pari-saramu.* [Skt.] n. Neighbourhood, ground on the skirts of a river or mountain, or contiguous to a town. ప్రాంతభూమి. Death, చావు. **పరిసర్య, పరిసారము** or **పరీసారము** *pari-sarya-*

n. The act of following the track of a hill, a river, &c. కొండలోనగువాని సమీపమార్గము నను సరించి పోవుట. Wandering about, అంతట తిరుగుట.

పరిసెనము *parisenamu*. [Tel.] n. Tumbling head over heels. A leap, గంతు. "వాని నడి దివ్వనల్లు త్రొక్కంగట్టువడి పొట్టలుదొంగి విక్కి పరిసెనంబులు వేయుచునరియెను." Swa. iv. 28.

పరిస్పందము *pari-spandamu*. [Skt.] n. Beating, throbbing. Decoration of the hair with flowers. పూలాలంకరించిన్నూలము.

పరిస్పర్ధ *pari-spardha*. [Skt.] n. Contention. **పరిస్పర్ధాళువు** *pari-spardhaluvu*. adj. Contentious. పోరాడే స్వభావముగల.

పరిస్ఫోటించు *pari-sphôṭintsu*. [Skt.] v. a. To split. చీల్చు. To cause to shine, ప్రకాశింపజేయు. **పరిస్ఫోటనము** *pari-sphôṭanamu*. n. Splitting. చీల్చుట.

పరిహరించు *pari-harintsu*. [Skt.] v. a. To desert, cast off, throw away, quit, discard, reject. To quash, set aside, nonsuit. To remove, abolish, clear away. **పరిహారము** *pari-hâramu*. n. Abandonment, shunning, removal. Doing away, abolition, remedy. దానికి పరిహారము లేదు there is no remedy for it. **పరిహరి** *pari-hari*. n. One who removes, or shuns. పరిహరించువాడు. **పరిహృతము** *pari-hṛitamu*. adj. Got rid off, shaken off. పోగొట్టబడిన. **పరిహార్యము** *pari-haryamu*. adj. Fit to be got rid off. విడువదగిన.

పరిహాసము, **పరీహాసము** or **పరియాచకము** *pari-hâsamu*. [Skt.] n. Joking, satire, jesting, raillery. అపహాస్యము. మోటుపరిహాసము rough joking, bear's play. **పరిహసించు** *pari-hasintsu*. v. a. To scorn, deride, laugh at. నవ్వు, పరిహాసముచేయు.

పరీక్ష *par-îksha*. [Skt. పరి+ఈక్ష.] n. Observation. నిక్కిచూచుట. A trial, examination, test, experiment. శోధనము. పరీక్షయిచ్చు to appear for an examination or pass an examination. పరీక్షకుడు or పరీక్షకారుడు an examiner. **పరీక్షించు** or **పరీక్షచేయు** *par-ikshintsu*. v. a. To examine, to try.

పరీధావి *paridhâvi*. [Skt.] n. The name of one of the Telugu years.

పరీధానము Same as పరిధానము (q. v.).

పరీరంభము Same as పరిరంభము (q. v.).

పరీవాహము *pari-vâhamu*. [Skt.] n. A drain, or channel: a small sluice. అలుగు. A. v. 71.

పరుండు *par-undu*. [Tel. పడి+ఉండు.] v. n. To lie down, recline, repose, sleep. శయనించు, నిద్రించు. **పరుండబెట్టు** *par-unda-bettu*. v. a. To lay down, put to sleep. **పరున్న** *par-unna*. part. Reclining, lying down.

పరుగు or **పరువు** *parugu*. [Tel.] n. Running, a run. The distance a man can run, that is, a *coss*, about two or two and a half miles. క్రోసు. మంచిపరుగుగల గుర్రము a horse with good paces. **పరుగెత్తు**, **పరుగిడు** or **పరువిడు** *parug-ettu*. v. n. To run. పరుగులెత్తు to run about. "అతిసాధ్వస చిత్తుడౌత్తుకొని పరువగా." M. I. i. 187.

పరుచు *parutsu*. [Tel. from పడు.] v. a. To cause to fall. పడజేయు. To spread, to scatter. To make, do. ఆటంకపరుచు to make objections. సఫలపరుచు to bring to use, to effect. వారిని లోబరుచుకొన్నాడు he got them into his hands. Added to nouns it changes them into verbs; thus నిశ్చయపరుచు to ascertain, to certify. దృఢపరుచు to establish. భేదపరుచు to distinguish, separate. See పరుస్తావు. **పరిపించు** or **పరపించు** *parip-intsu*. v. a. To cause to spread. **పరుపు** *parupu*. n. Bedding, a mattress. పరుండుటకు వేసే వస్త్రం. పడక.

పరుడు *parudu*. [Tel.] n. A halt, hilt or handle. కత్తిపిడి. "బంటుచే నపరంజి పరుడు తోడునకత్తి." S. ii. 261.

పరుడు *parudu*. [Skt.] n. Another man, one's neighbour, an alien, a stranger. అన్యుడు. An enemy. శత్రువు. God, పరమాత్ముడు. adj. Addicted to, attached to, a lover of. పరులపాలయిన alienated, given to others. సత్యపరుడు one given to (or addicted to) truth. ముక్తిపరుడు one devoted to holiness, bent upon salvation. చిత్తచాంచల్యపరుడు one addicted to change of mind. శస్త్రాస్త్రపరుడు a lover of arms and weapons. అత్యాశపరులై being very avaricious. సంతోషపరులైరి they were full of joy. యజ్ఞపరుడు bent upon performing a sacrifice. M. XII. v. 479. నీతిపరుడు a righteous man. పాపపరుడు one addicted to wickedness. పరహింసనపరుడు a murderer. పూజాపరుడు one who delights in worship. న్యాయపరుడు a just, upright, or honest man. దానపరుడు a charitable man. భక్తిపరుడు a pious man. ధర్మపరుడు a righteous man. యుక్తిపరుడు a man of tact, a clever or ingenious man

పరుపత్తి *paru-patti* [Tel.] n. The cross sticks to which a weaver fixes his web.

పరువడి *paru-vadi*. [Tel. పరువు+వడి.] adv. Properly, gently, well, fully, duly. క్రమముగా, కుదురుగా, తిన్నగా, అత్యంతము. "పరువడిసూత్రములు దించి పొలిగెనైతుల." H. iii. 183. n. A time, పర్యాయము. Order, క్రమము. Various steps used in fencing. సాములో అడుగులువేయడము. "ఎడమడుగు పరువడి, కుడియడుగుపరువడి, కదలుపరువడి, తోపుపరువడి, దాటుపరువడి, ఒంటిఅడుగుకత్తెర, స్వరబందుకత్తెర, జాగినకత్తెర. చిట్టిఅడుగుకత్తెర. దాటుసాపులు, జాగినసాపులు, మొదలుగాగల పదిరెండు పరువళ్లగల యుగళ్ళ ప్రాచీన్యంబె 68." H. i. 240. ఇది ముప్పదిరెండువిధంబులని తొందరందురు. "సరసతగరడీలసాముచేయుంచి, పరగముప్పదిరెండుపరువళ్లు పేర్చ." Sarang. 647. "జన్యస, వ్యాయామ మేమి చేస్తలనంబడగా పరువళ్లు చుట్టుచుడు." Satyabhama. iv. 140.

పరువము *paruvamu*. [from Skt. పర్వము.] n. Youth, bloom, prime. యౌవనము. Maturity, పక్వము, పరిపాకము. **పరువంపు** *paruvampu*. adj. Blown, blooming.

పరువు *paruvu*. [Tel.] n. The act of running. పరుగు, శీఘ్రగమనము. Ripeness, పక్వము, పరిపాకము. Dignity, rank, respectability, గౌరవము, అతిశయపరిమాణము. Season. కోత పరువుగానున్నది the crop is in the course of ripening. వానిపరువెక్కడ, నీపరువెక్కడ what comparison is there between him and you in rank. **పరువుగోను, పరువుపోరు** or **పరువుపెట్టు** Same as పరుగెత్తు.

పరుషము or **పరుసము** *parushamu*. [Skt.] adj. Harsh, rough, severe, stern. n. A harsh word, పరుషవాక్యము. A harsh letter. In grammar పరుషములు are the five hard consonants, viz., క, చ, ట, త, & ప. **పరుషత్వము** *parushatvamu*. n. Roughness, harshness. కఠినత్వము. **పరుస** *parusa*. n. A severe man, a tyrant. కఠినుడు. "పరుసలతోడి ప్రొక్కులబడ జాలకీవు." BD. iii. 1288. **పరుసన** or **పరుసదనము** *parusana*. n. Harshness, roughness. కాఠిన్యము, పారుష్యము. **పరుసు** *parusu*. adj. Rough, coarse, brutal. పరుసుపోక a dreadful roar. Bmj. ii. 192. n. Roughness, harshness, కాఠిన్యము.

పరుసవేది *parusa-vedi*. [from Skt. స్పర్శవేధి.] n. The philosopher's stone.

పరుసు *parusu*. [Tel.] n. Manner. విధము.

పరేతుడు or **ప్రేతుడు** *parētudu*. [Skt.] n. A dead man, a ghost or spirit. మృతుడు. పరేతనికేతనము a haunted spot, i. e., a cemetery. "మజాపింఛప్పరేతనికేతన ఘోటిత కత్తగాకేనికా నివసించు." HN. v. 101. పరేత

—రాట్టు *parēta-rāttu*. n. The king of ghosts: a name of Yama who corresponds to Pluto in Classical Mythology.

పరోక్షము *par-ōkshamu*. [Skt.] adj. Imperceptible by the senses. Imperceptible, invisible; absent, past. అప్రత్యక్షమైన, ఇంద్రియములకు అగపడని. n. Invisibility, absence, secrecy. నాపరోక్షమందు చెప్పినమాటలు నాకు తాకవు what was said in my absence does not affect me.

పరోఢ *parōḍha*. [Skt. పర+ఊఢ married.] n. A neighbour's wife.

పరోష్ణి *parōshṇi*. [Skt.] n. A cockroach. బొద్దింక. A bat. గబ్బిలము.

పర్జని *parjani*. [Skt.] n. Turmeric. కొయ్యపసుపు, మ్రానిపసుపు. A. v. 94.

పర్జన్యము *parjanyamu*. [Skt.] n. Muttering clouds, thunder. గర్జదంబుదము, మేఘనిర్ఘోషము. పర్జన్యలతిక lightning. "ఇట్లు శృంగారంబుచేసి యమ్ముద్దియకు ముక్తాఫలప్రాలంబమాలికలతోడి గొడుగులబట్టించి యతాగ్రదంబున నమాత్యులు తోడితేర ధారాధరనికర మనోహరయగు పర్జన్యలతికయుంబోలె వచ్చుచున్నకని." M. IV. v. 354 పర్జన్యుడు *parjanyuḍu*. n. The god of rain, i. e., Indra.

పర్ణము *parṇamu*. [Skt.] n. A leaf. ఆకు. పర్ణశాల a hermitage or bower of leaves or grass: a hut, ఆకుటిల్లు, కుటజము.

పర్పాటకము or **పర్పటము** *parpaṭakamu*. [Skt.] n. A tree called *Pharnaceum cerviana*. Rottler. A kind of grass. ఒకవిధమైనగడ్డి.

పర్మానా *parmānā*. [H.] n. A firman, a royal mandate, a command, a warrant, letters patent, శాసనము. పర్మాయించు *parmayintsu*. v. a. To direct or command, to order. పర్మాయిషి *parmayishi*. n. An order to make an article.

పర్యంకము *paryankamu*. [Skt.] n. A cot. మంచము.

పర్యంతము *paryantamu*. [Skt.] adv. Until, as far as, up to, వరకు, దనుక. పదిపర్యంతము as much as ten or to the number of ten. వారు వచ్చుపర్యంతము until they come.

పర్యటనము *pary-aṭanamu*. [Skt. పరి+అటనము.] n. A wandering about for alms. **పర్యటించు** *pary-aṭintsu*. v. n. To wander about for alms.

పర్యవసానము *pary-avasānamu*. [Skt.] n. The end, conclusion, termination, finishing, completion, accomplishment, fulfilment, upshot. ముగియుట. ఇది జగడములో పర్యవసానమయినది this ended in a quarrel. **పర్యవసించు** *pary-avasintsu*. v. n. To end, terminate. ముగించు. **పర్యవస్థ** *pary-avastha*. n. Quarrelling. విరోధించుట.

పర్యస్తము *pary-astamu*. [Skt.] adj. Fallen. పడిన. Beaten, కొట్టబడిన.

పర్యాప్తము *pary-āptamu*. [Skt.] n. That which is obtained or gained. Satisfaction, satiety, తృప్తి. All, completeness, entirety, enough, sufficiency, యథేష్టితము, పరిపూర్ణము, ప్రకామము. Power, ability, శక్తి. Prevention, నివారణము. **పర్యాప్తముగా** *pary-āptamu-gā*. adv. Readily, ably, satisfactorily.

పర్యాయము *paryāyamu*. [Skt.] n. An order, arrangement. ప్రకారము, క్రమము, వరుస, అనుక్రమము. An opportunity, occasion, a time, అవసరము, సమయము, తడవ. Generic or specific character. నాలుగుపర్యాయములు పోయి ఉంటిని I went four times. ఈ రెండుపర్యాయములనుండి జ్వరము కొటకాయడములేదు these two times the fever has not shown itself. adj. Moderate, మితమైన, యథోచితమైన. **పర్యాయపదము** *paryāya-padamu*. n. A synonym. **పర్యాయముగా** *paryāyamuga*. adv. Moderately. అది యిప్పట్లో పర్యాయముగానున్నది it is now pretty well. ఆ తేరములో వర్షము పర్యాయముగానున్నది the rain is but slight there. పర్యా

యతః or పర్యాయేణ *paryāyatah.* adv. Gradually, by degrees. Moderately.

పర్యాలోచనము *pary-ālōchanamu.* [Skt.] n. Deep consideration, pondering. తెక్కగా ఆలోచించుట. పర్యాలోచించు *pary-ālōchintsu.* v. a. To consider deeply, to ponder.

పర్యుదస్తము *pary-udastamu.* [Skt.] adj. Thrown down, rejected, త్రోయబడిన.

పర్యుషితము *pary-ushitamu.* [Skt.] adj. Stale (as yesterday's food), బహుకాలము ఉంచబడిన. పర్యుషితాన్నము cold food, చద్ది అన్నము.

పర్ర *parra.* [Tel.] n. A marsh, bog, fen, swamp, ఉబ్బిలి. A plain, బయలు. ఉప్పు పర్ర a salt marsh. పర్రమన్ను the soil of a salt swamp, చేవుడు. A certain measure of capacity, ధాన్యాదులుకొలిచే కొలను. పర్రమీను *parra-mīnu.* n. A genus of fish, called Scomber, or Zeus, of which there are many species.

పర్రు *parru.* [Tel.] n. The sound caused in tearing a paper, cloth, &c. పర్రున *parru-na.* adv. (anuk.) Aloud. పర్రునచించి పారవేసెను he tore it up and threw it away.

పర్రె or పర్రియ Same as పరియ (q. v.).

పర్వతము *parvatamu.* [Skt.] n. A mountain. కొండ.

పర్వము *parvamu.* [Skt.] n. A knot, a joint in a cane or body, గణుపు. A feast or annual festival at a certain division of the year. A name given to certain days in the lunar month, as the full and change of the moon, and the 8th and 14th of each half month, పండుగ. పంచపర్వములు the five holidays in a month, i. e., అష్టమి, చతుర్దశి, కుహువు, పూర్ణిమ, రవిసంక్రాంతి. పంచపర్వోత్సవము is a feast celebrated in one of these holidays. A sub-division of a book. The Mahābhārata is divided into eighteen (*Parvamulu*) books. నేత్రపర్వము a joyful sight, a feast for the eyes. పర్వసంధి *parva-sandhi.* n. The time that divides a new or full moon and the next day.

పర్వు or పరవు *parvu.* [Tel.] v. n. To spread or extend, as darkness. వ్యాపించు. n. Running. పరువు, పరుగు.

పలంకష *palankasha.* [Skt.] n. A thorny weed, ఏనుగపల్లేరు. A horse radish, ముల్లంగి.

పలక *palaka.* [Tel.] n. Any flat surface or face. స్తంభము మొదలైనవానియొక్క ఒకవైపు. ఎనిమిదిపలకలకంబము an eight sided pillar. A plank, board, table, బల్ల. A board used as a slate in schools. A writing tablet, వ్రాయుపలక. A slab or flat stone. One side of any polygon, as of a lantern. A gambling table. జూదమాడుబల్ల. The bar of wood in a loom that strikes the weft close after the shuttle has passed. A tom-tom. A shield, డాలు. "అనిశర ధల్లములు తన మేనికి రాకుండ బలక మెరయ వేదియుచుణ." M. IX. i. 154. "బలదుర్వారుండు భీముండుక్కంచె మదంబారగవాలునుంబలక యుణ శీఘ్రత్వసందీప్తుడై." ib. IX. i. 304. తామ్రశాసనాలపలకలుమూడు three inscriptions on plates of copper. పలకమాగిన *palaka-māgina.* adj. Over ripe, dropping to pieces. పలకలు gleanings, corn picked up. "చోడ, సరసతి యూరోగణము నెమ్మినలువ, పలక చేరినంత్రాసకుజ్ఞాలు." BD. v. 1228. adj. Flat, as a board. పలకరొమ్ము a flat breast. పలకరాయి a slate-stone; a sort of rock, like slate, that splits into plates. పలకము *palakamu.* n. A small cot, చిన్నమంచము. పలకసరి *palaka-sari.* n. A kind of neck ornament worn by men.

పలకు *palaku.* [Tel.] v. n. To ripen, పండు. To produce a crop, ఫలించు.

పలగండుడు *pala-ganḍuḍu.* [Skt.] n. A brick layer, a plasterer. సున్నపుపూతపూయువాడు. A tank-digger or excavator. ఉప్పరివాడు.

పలగడి, పలుగాడి or పలుగడ *palagadi.* [Tel.] n. Gratings, bars, a door set with spikes: a gate. Vaija. iii. 51. H. ii. 47. and iv. 149.

పలగొర్రు or **పలుగొర్రు** *pala-gorru.* [Tel.] n. A kind of rake. See under పలు.

పలతేము *palatsamu.* [Tel.] n. A tax. కప్పము.

పలచే See పలుచే.

పలనాడు or **పల్నాడు** *palanadu.* [Tel.] n. The name of a country in the Kistna District, Palnad. పల్నాడు. ప్ర. i.

పలపల, పల్పల, పలపలన or **పల్పలన** *pala-pala.* [Tel. anuk.] adv. Scatteredly, here and there, one by one, dispersedly. M. IX. i. 458. Plainly, స్పష్టముగా. adj. Thin. పలుచని. "పలపలని పొందురాయిడు పచ్చిలూరె." A. iv. 197. టీ॥ అనగా పలచనపలచని. **పలపలన** *pala-palana.* n. Plainness, dispersion. వైరళ్యము. Thinness, కార్శ్యము.

పలము *palamu.* [Skt.] n. A weight, eq to that of ten pagodas. పాలుగురక్షలంటిది One-fortieth part of a viss. పలవిందెడు కూపెండు పలదేసాటిభూమి a land whic will produce a bushel for a half handful of seed corn. **పలము** or **పలలము** *palamu.* n. Flesh, meat, మాంసము. "పలలతోరణము." (A. vi. 19.) a string of dried mutton chops. **పలపైతృకము** *pala-paitrikamu.* n. A rite at a funeral (now obsolete) of making flesh offerings. A verse says, అశ్వాలంభం గవాలంభం సన్న్యాసం పలపైతృకం, దేవరేణ సుతోత్పత్తిః కలౌ పంచవివర్జయేత్.

పలవ *palava.* [Tel.] n. A branch, a fork. పలవకర్ర a forked branch or piece of wood. పలవలంగల దుప్పి a deer with forked or branched horns.

పలవర *palavara.* [Tel.] n. The name of a certain tree much cultivated in the neighbourhood of Hydrabad for its fruit. పలవర ఆకులు, its leaves, which are used to manure land. See description in the Kasi Yatra, date 7th September, 1830.

పలవరించు, పలవించు or **పలవు** *palavarintsu.* [Tel.] v. n. To use broken words or exclamations. ప్రలాపించు, కలవించు. **పలవరింత** or **పలవరము** *palavarinta.* n. Prattling, talking confusedly, ప్రలాపించుట. ప్రలాపము.

పలాండువు or **పలండువు** *palanduvu.* [Skt.] n. An onion. ఉల్లి.

పలాశ్ *palat.* [Skt.] n. A demon. రాక్షసుడు. "కృతపలాశ్వర్ధస్వనోద్భవా." A. iv. 343 టీ॥ చేయబడిన రాక్షసులయొక్క వినాశముగల ధ్వనిచేత అత్యద్భుతముగను పొందుచున్న శరము మగలాహ్నమా.

పలాన or **పలాని** *palana.* [H.] adj. Such and such, such a one. ఒకానొక, అట్టి. పలానివాడు such a man. పలానిపని such a work, such and such an affair.

పలాయనము *palayanamu.* [Skt.] n. Flight, rapid progress. పారిపోవడము. పలాయనము చేయు to disperse, to rout. **పలాయితుడు** *palayitudu.* n. One who is routed or put to flight. పారిపోయినవాడు.

పలాలము *palalamu.* [Skt.] n. Straw. చొప్ప, గింజలేనికస్వి, నిష్ఫలకాండము, ధాన్యశూన్యకస్వి. A. i. 88. "పమద్యత్ప్రాగ్య పలాలందుపై." A. vi. 158. టీ॥ ఎత్తబడిన ధూళియనెడు గడ్డిదుమ్ము గలవాసై.

పలాశము *palasamu.* [Skt.] n. A tree called *Butea frondosa.* కింశుకము, మోదుగ చెట్టు. A leaf, ఆకు adj. Green, ఆకుపచ్చని. **పలాశి** *palasi.* n. A tree. వృక్షము. A demon. రాక్షసుడు.

పలాశుడు *palasudu.* [Skt.] n. A demon. రాక్షసుడు.

పలాస్త్రి *palastri.* [Eng. 'plaster.'] n. A plaster for a wound. పొక్కుపలాస్త్రి a blister.

పలిక్ని *palikni.* [Skt.] n. A grey headed woman. ముసలిది. A cow which is for the first time in calf. తొలిచూలిగపెయ్య.

పలితము *palitamu.* [Skt.] n. Greyness. నెరయుట. A grey hair, నెరసిన వెంట్రుక.

పలిసపిట్ట Same as పరిగపిట్ట. (q. v.) పాలపలిస పిట్ట the Greyheaded Myna, *Sturnia malabarica*. పొదపలిసపిట్ట, the Black-capped Black-bird, *Merula nigripileus*, Or, Tickell's Ouzel. *Merula unicolor*. (F. B. I.)

పలు or పల్లు *palu*. [Tel.] n. A tooth. పలు వరుస a row of teeth. పల్గాడ or పలుగాడ *pal-ḍaḍa*. n. The dent or mark of a tooth. "మొల్లకొన్నిర్వులకాంతిం కెందు పల్గాడ సుందరు మై తేనెలుచిల్కు-మోవి." Bilhan. iii. 92. పలుకప్పు *palu-kappu*. n. A lip, పెదవి. పలు కప్పు, పలుకర or పలుగర (పలు+కర.) n. Tooth powder, పండ్లపొడి. పలుగొఱ్ఱు n. A harrow.

పలు *palu*. [Tel.] adj. Many, several, various. అనేకము. పలుతెరువులు various ways. "పలుబల్కులు." A. vi. 52. పలుకొమ్ముల మెకము *palu-kommula-mekamu*. n. An elephant. పలుగురు, పలుగుండ్రు, పలు వురు or పలువుండ్రు *paluguru*. n. plu. Several men, many men. "పలుగురునడిచెడు తెరువున, పులుమొలవదు మొలిచెనేని పొదలదు సుమతీ." Sumati Satakam. పలుదోయం బులు *palu-dōyambulu*. n. Several seas. సముద్రములు. "పలుదోయంబులు జగములు, పలు దోయములందు మించి భాసిల్లెడునా, పలుదోయ గాడు వల్లన, లలనాకర తోయముల కెలుంగుచు డడియుణా." B. X. v. 17. పలుపట్టడ *palu-pattaḍa*. n. A mongrel race. సంకరజాతి జనము. పలుమారు *palu-māru*. adv. Many times, frequently. పలువగల *palu-vagala*. adv. In many ways. R. v. 237. పల్పోకి *pal-pōka*. plu. n. Rascality. పోకిరితనము. adj. Vulgar. "పతియూరికేనియొద నీ పల్పోక సిగారుమల్." T. iii. 81. టీ॥ తుంపోకిరి సొగసులు.

పలుక *paluka*. [Tel.] n. A shield, డాలు. The small bars of a loom, సాలెవాడు నేయు మగ్గములోని అడ్డకమ్ములు. "అడిదముపలుకయునుం గొని." M. VI. iii. 60.

పలుక, పలుకవ or పల్కువ *paluka*. [Tel.] n. Whiteness. తెల్లన. Paleness, వైవర్ణ్యము. పలుకబారు to become white or pale.

పలుకు or పల్కు *paluku*. [Tel.] v. n. & a. To sound, ring, &c. To speak, మాటాడు, అను. To answer, ఉత్తరముచెప్పు. "బాణాసన ప్రౌఢిమజా ద్రోణాచార్యులకైన పల్కుదురు." T. ii. 18. To blame, నిందించు. n. Speaking, utterance, language, a word. మాట. A sound, note, voice. ధ్వని స్వరము. Blame, నింద. A bit, a piece, తునక. తొలుబల్కు or ప్రాబల్కు the primeval word, i. e., the Vedas. సాక్ష్యము పలుకు to give evidence. కుద్దులుపలుకు to tell tales. పలుకు తత్తడి *paluku-tattaḍi*. n. A parrot. చిలుక. పలుకుతోడు *paluku-tōḍu*. n. Company, society. మాటతోడు. పలుకురాయి *paluku-rāyi*. n. A ringing stone or an echoing rock. పలుకుబడి *paluku-baḍi*. n. Pronunciation. ఉచ్చారణము. Influence, power of word. ఆయనకు ఆ ఊరిలో కొంచెము పలుకుబడి కద్దు he has some influence in that town. పలికించు *palikiñtsu*. v. a. To cause to speak. To utter or use (words or notes.) To sound or ring. అందుకు సాక్షులను పలికించి నాడు he proved this by witnesses, he called witnesses to prove it. పలుకుపడతి or పలుకుచెలి *paluku-paḍati*. n. The goddess of speech, Sarasvati, వాగ్దేవి, సరస్వతి. పలుకరించు, పలకరించు or పల్కరించు *palukariñtsu*. v. n. To speak. మాటాడు. To encourage, to challenge, హెచ్చరించు. పలుకరింత or పల్కరింత *palukarinta*. n. Calling. పిలువడము. Challenge, ఎచ్చరించడము.

పలుగాకి or పల్గాకి *palu-gāki*. [Tel.] n. A wretch, a villain, దుష్టుడు.

పలుగాడి *palugāḍi*. [Tel.] n. Gratings or cross bars. "పలుగాండ్లు తెరచింపు నలరుచు పసులు వలిపేక మునవచ్చి." B. D. vii. 1650. "తోటవాకిట పలుగాడికిణా నగా చిరించి." Vaijayanti. iii. 51. Rails, railings, కటు

గరాటులు. plu. పలుగాండ్లు. A cart, బండి. adj. Having many gra ings or cross bars. పెక్కు-గాదెలుగల.

పలుగు palugu. [Tel.] n. A wretch, a villain. దుర్జనుడు. A crow-bar, గడ్డపలుగు. A rock crystal, స్ఫటికము. పలుగుగుంటక a harrow with iron teeth in it. గుంటక పలుగులు the teeth of a harrow. పలుగు రాయి *palugu-rāyi*. n. A white marble stone. Also, a goldsmith's smoothing stone. పలుగురాప్రతిమ *palugu-rā-pratima*. n. A white marble statue.

పలుగుదుంపాము or పల్లుదుంపాము *palugudu-pāmu*. [Tel.] n. A snake, the bite of which is not fatal but causes great pain, సర్పభేదము.

పలుగుపిట్ట *palugu-piṭṭa*. [Tel.] n. An owl. గుడ్లగూబ.

పలుచ *palutsa*. [Tel.] adj. Thin. సన్నని. Light, తేలికయైన. పలుకని. పలుచన, పలుచదనము or పల్చదనము *palutsana*. n. Thinness, leanness. Slight contempt. అడవి పలుచన thinness of the forest. ఇట్లు చేస్తే మనుష్యులలో పలుచనకాదా if you behave so you will be mean in men's eyes. పలుచని *palutsani*. adj. Thin, spare, lean, paltry. Not thickset. Disreputable, contemptible. పలుచనిపలుకులు or పలుచని మాటలు contemptuous words or slighting expressions. మజ్జిగ నిండా పలుచగా నున్నది the buttermilk is very thin. పలుచనిబట్ట a thin cloth. పలుచపడు *palutsa-paḍu*. v. n. To become thin, to melt as butter. పలుచపడు.

పలుపు *palupu*. [Tel.] n. A halter for cattle or horses: the rope collar for oxen in a cart.

పలుమన *palumana*. [Tel.] n. Rubbing or polishing a statue with an ivory point.

పలుమరు, పలుమారు, పలుమారులు, పల్మరు or పల్మారు *palu-maru*. [Tel.] adv. Many times, often, perpetually, frequently, constantly, repeatedly. మాటిమాటికి.

పలుము *palumu*. [Tel.] v. n. To mutter, talk indistinctly, to prattle. ప్రలాపించు. n. Prattle. ప్రలాపము.

పలుమేరు *palu-mēru*. [Tel.] n. A kind of tree. Swa. iv.

పలువ or పల్వ *paluva*. [Tel. పలు+వా(యి)] n. A wicked wretch. కుత్సితపురుషుడు, కుత్సితస్త్రీ. adj. Vile, abominable, wicked, bad.

పలువరేని *paluva-rēni*. [Tel.] n. A sort of tree. "పనసకరకగాబ్బ పలువరేని." H. iv. 19.

పలువలువ or పల్వల్వ *palu-valuva*. [Tel.] n. A lip, పెదవి.

పలువిత్తు *palu-vittu*. [Tel.] n. A bastard, a child of many fathers. పలువురికి పుట్టినవాడు, దుర్జాతుడు. H. v. 129.

పలువురు, పల్వురు or పలువుంద్రు See under పలు adj.

పలుసము Same as పరుసము (q. v.)

పలుసు *palusu*. [Tel.] n. The sable fish. Russell. plate 198. A species of *Clupea*.

పల్యంకము *palyankamu*. [Skt.] n. A cot. మంచము. పల్యంకిక *palyankika*. n. A palanquin. పల్లకి.

పల్యయనము, పల్యాణము or పల్లము *palyayanamu*. [Skt.] n. A saddle. A howdah or seat on an elephant. అంబారి. A. vi. 182. Parij. iv. 78.

పల్ల *palla*. [Tel.] adj. Red, reddish, as hair. తామ్రవర్ణమైన. పల్లెనజడలు red matted hair. M. XIII. v. 26. పల్లచీమ a red ant. A. vi. 21. పల్లమీసములు red whiskers. పల్లచెట్టు a tree called *Mimusops hexandra*. Rox. ii. 238. ఏటిపల్లచెట్టు *Bradleia nitida*. Rox. iii. 699. పల్లకట్టు *palla-kaṭṭu*. adj. Reddish tinted. పల్లకన్నుమూర్తుడు.

పల్లకి or పల్లకీ *pallaki*. [Tel.] n. A palanquin, సుఖాసనము. మానుగా నిపించు. గాదము.

పల్లగించు See పల్లించు.

పల్లటు or పల్లటము *pallaṭa*. [Tel.] n. Movement. చలనము. Difference, వ్యత్యాసము. Confusion, perturbation, perplexity, agitation. తారుమారు, కల్లోలము, కొల్లటము. "చిటిపొటి కొరకు నానాటికి తీసిన వాల్యం తెలసిన పల్లటముల నిచ్చ నక్కాలకు లచ్చికి వచ్చిన వచ్చి తెచ్చెలరో." Bahulas. ii. 85. పల్లటిల్లు or పల్లటిలు *pallaṭillu*. v. n. To move, చలించు. To turn pale, తెల్లబోవు. To redden with anger, ఎర్రబారు. To be in convulsion or disorder, to be perplexed, to be agitated. తారుమారగు, తత్తరపడు, చెదరు, తల్లడిల్లు, కొందలమందు, కలగు, అదరు. "మున్నెడు తలయుచు తునిసెడు, విల్లును ధరకొరగు చేయి విరిగెడు పీడనుల్, బెల్లడొరుగు నెత్తురులై, పల్లటిలం జొడగ నప్పుడు పాండవబలముల్." M. VI. i. 340. "ఇప్పుడు నామనము పల్లటిల్లుట, హింస భావనలబుల తీరుచునది." M. V. ii. 97.

పల్లటి or పల్టి *pallaṭi*. [H.] n. A sumersault. పక్షి సాధన విశేషము. Tumbling (as of a pigeon in the air), bounding or skipping. పైకెగసి పిల్లిమంటిలేయుట. A pigeon called a Tumbler. "తెల్లపావురమిది తెలిసిచిక్కినది, పల్లటీల్ మైన నామంచిదంబు నాడు." Sāranga. 58. "బలవిమానంబుకోళ్లు పల్లటీలు, పావురాయలు బకబాళ్లుబట్టిగాండ్లు." H. v. 166. పల్లటీల్గొను, పల్లటీల్గొట్టు or పల్లటీల్ వైచు *pallaṭil-gonu*. v. n. To tumble, as a pigeon, to throw a sumersault.

పల్లణ, పల్లణము or పల్లము *pallana*. [Tel.] n. A saddle, an elephant's howdah, అంబారి. "కుముదస్తంబేరమంబగ్రతో భూమిగా బల్లణకట్టిరానసిరుచినూపుర్తిల్ విజృంభింప." Parij. iv. 19. "పారశీపల్లణము" సా. iv.

పల్లము *pallamu*. [Tel.] n. A saddle. A ditch. A hole in the ground (however small). A dale, low ground. పల్లంబుమిట్ట, మిట్ట పల్లము hill and dale, rising and falling ground, ups and downs. పల్లపునాడు low ground capable of being ploughed. పల్లపుపంట a wet crop, being the crop that is sown on low land.

పల్లరపులు *pallarapulu*. [Tel. పలు+అరపులు.] n. Several cries, many useless words, much useless talking. వ్యర్థమైన పెద్ద మాటలు, అపరాని పెద్దమాటలు. పల్లరపు *pallarapu*. adj. Simple, innocent. తేలైన. "వానిని యల్లుడొల్లయరుణానుకుపట్టి కొల్లనాకుంట భావముమర్మకర్తమున ప్రాపకనంబున తారకమ్మనుల్ కొవిదకొటికి తెలిసికొనదు నింతియుతాక కానలం గొప్పుల నిపుపల్లరపుగొల్లని కెంచెలియంగ చెప్పితి." Ila. iii. 181.

పల్లవము *pallavamu*. [Skt.] n. A sprout, a shoot. కరపల్లవములు rosy hands. పల్లవగ్రాహిపాండిత్యము superficial knowledge, పైపైచదువులు. పల్లవాస్త్రుడు *pallav-astruḍu*. n. Manmadha, because his arrows are young leaves. పల్లవించు *pallavintsu*. v. n. To sprout or shoot. చిగిరించు, చిగుర్చు. పల్లవితము *pallavitamu*. adj. Sprouted, చిగిరించిన.

పల్లవి *pallavi*. [Skt.] n. The chorus or burden in songs. కీర్తనకటి చరణములందటి అర్థమునను సరించి సంగీతము మొదట చెప్పెడు వాక్యము.

పల్లవుడు *pallavuḍu*. [Skt.] n. A lover, an adulterer, a gallant. విటుడు.

పల్లా *pallā*. [Tel.] n. A certain measure equal to ten *markals*.

పల్లాయనము *pallāyanamu*. [Tel.] n. Relationship, friendship. ఆప్తత. పల్లాయనమువాడు a friend, ఆప్తుడు.

పల్లి, పల్లియ or పల్లె *palli*. [Skt. Cf. Gk. πολις and Celtic 'bally' a town.] n. A small village. చిన్నగ్రామము. A lizard, బల్లి. పల్లికట్టుమాన్యము *palli-kaṭṭu-manyamu*. n. Land held free by the heirs of the founder of a village. పల్లి *palli*. n. A fisherman, a boatman. Local. vi. 33. plu. పల్లెలు.

పల్లించు or పల్లగించు pallintsu. [Tel.] v. a. To saddle a horse. పల్లమువేయు, జీనువేయు. "అశ్వంబు లుత్తరంబున కొత్తడిగా పల్లించు." సా. iv.

పల్లిక or పల్లీక pallika [Tel.] n. A small basket. చిన్నబుట్ట. పల్లికలు pallikalu. n. The scab or herpes (distinct from తామర, కోడి and చెరి). Varieties of this disease are called సుబ్బరాయని పల్లికలు, ఎంగిలి చిరుగుడు పల్లికలు.

పల్లినాడు, పలనాడు or పల్నాడు palli-nadu. [Tel.] n. The Palnad Taluq in the Kristna District. పల్లినాడుడు the Rajah thereof.

పల్లు pallu. [Tel.] n. A tooth. A tooth of a saw. A sort of gold lace, or bits of gold in a necklace. పంటినొప్పి toothache. పంటిపోటు a gumboil. పండ్లమాను pandla-manu. n. A harrow. పని కొయ్యపండ్లుగల దూలము వంటి ఒక సాధనము. ఇది మాగాని కలుపుతీసే సాధనము.

పల్లు, పల్లము or పల్లడు pallu. [Tel.] adj. Low (as land) ఇక్కడికంటె ఆ చేలు పల్లముగానున్నది that place is lower than this. n Low lands. ఆ ఊరు కొండపల్లమున్నది the town is on the side of the hill.

పల్లుగొర్రు pallu-gorru. n. A sort of harrow. See పలుగొర్రు under పలు.

పల్లె palle. [Tel.] n. A small village, a hamlet. పల్లె or పల్లెకూటము a village, school, బడి. పల్లెటూరు a hamlet. adj. Rustic, rude. పల్లెమాట a rustic expression, గ్రామ్యవచనము. పల్లెపుట్టి a measure. పల్లెత palleta. n. A fisherwoman. పల్లెవాడు palle-vadu, n. A fisherman. A rustic.

పల్లెంక or పిలవ పల్లెంకపులుగు pallenka [Tel.] n. The bird called a kingfisher.

పల్లేరు palleru. [Tel.] n. The thorny creeping plant called *Pedalium murex*. ఏనుగుపల్లేరు a large species, *Ruellia longifolia*. Rox. iii. 50, గోకంటకము, వనశృంగాటము. పల్లేరుపల్లెక small caltrops, a weed with a yellow flower. త్రికంటకము. పల్లేరుపువ్వు a nose jewel shaped like the caltrops blossom. పల్లేరుపోగులు earrings of the same shape. పల్లేరుకాయ a thorny seed of the పల్లేరు plant; a certain jewel of the same shape.

పల్వలము palvalamu. [Skt.] n. A pit, a pond. పడియగుంట.

పల్వురు See పలువురు.

పళపళ pala-pala. [Tel] n. Brightness, ప్రకాశము. adv. Brightly, ప్రకాశముగా. పళపళమని pala-pala-m-ani. (anuk) adv. Dazzlingly, brightly. పళపళయించు pala-pala-y-intsu. v. n. To be bright, to be dazzling.

పళ్లెము, పళ్లెరము or పళ్యము pallemu. [Tel.] n. A saucer, like a soup plate, a small metal basin, dish, tray or platter. తాంబాళము, భోజనపాత్రము. అభిషేకపుపళ్లెము a chalice or vessel to bathe an idol with.

పవడము Same as పగడము (q. v.).

పవడుడు Same as పగడుడు (q. v.).

పవనము pavanamu. [Skt] n. Air, wind. పవనతనయుడు pavana-tanayudu. n. The son of the air, i. e., Hanuman (హనుమంతుడు), Bhima (భీముడు), or Agni (అగ్ని). పవనాశనము pavan-asanamu. n. A creature that lives on air, i. e., a serpent. పాము. పవనుడు or పవమానుడు pavanudu. n. The god of the air. Wind, the god of wind.

పవలు Same as పగలు (q. v.).

పవాడము or పావాడము pavadamu. [Tel.] n. A pretended immolation of a human victim who is afterwards resuscitated. A vow or determination to effect an object.

పవి pavi. [Skt.] n. A thunderbolt. పిడుగు. మెరుపు.

పవిత్రము pavitramu. [Skt.] adj. Pure, clean, purified. పరిశుద్ధము. n. The sacred thread of the twice-born castes, జంద్యము.

A ring or knot made of sacrificial grass, worn on the fourth or ring finger at a sacrifice. A gold ring, resembling that knot. A sort of necklace made of silk or thread, worn by Vaishṇavas. పవిత్రోత్సవము a ceremony observed in Vishṇu temples in the month of Āvani or August. పవిత్రపువేలు the ring finger. ఆసనపవిత్రము or భగంధరము the disease called fistula.

పవిఖి Same as పగిది (q. v.).

పవ్వళించు, పవళించు, పవ్వడించు or **పవడించు** *pavvalintsu.* [Tel.] v. n. To lie down, recline. శయనించు. **పవ్వళింత** or **పవళింత** n. The act of reclining or lying down, పవళించుట, శయనము.

పశువు *pasuvu.* [Skt.] n. A beast, an animal, నాలుగుకాళ్లజంతువు. A domestic animal such as a cow, buffalo, goat, or sheep. పశువులకొట్టము a cow house. పశుభావము simplicity. పశుకృత్యము a brutal act. పశుఘ్నుడు a slayer of animals. పశుజనము the profane or brute folk, i. e., the heathen, the heterodox, or uninitiated. **పశుపతి** *pasu-pati.* n. A name of Siva, as the master or ruler of all living creatures. పశుప్రాయుడు a brutish or ignorant man.

పశ్చాత్తాపము *paschat-tāpamu.* [Skt.] n. Remorse, repentance, pity, compassion, commiseration, regret, reluctance. దీనవాని జనులయందు దిక్కుగుడుమను మిక్కిలి పశ్చాత్తాపమును గలిగినవాడు గనుక as you are a man of a charitable disposition and full of pity. పశ్చాత్తాపపడు to repent.

పశ్చిమము *paschimamu.* [Skt.] n. The West. adj. Western. పశ్చిమాంబుధి the Western ocean.

పశ్యతోహరుడు *pasyatō-harudu.* [Skt.] n. A deluder, a beguiler, a swindler, a common cheat. పచ్చిమ్రుచ్చు, చూచుచుండగా కొంపోయువాడు. A goldsmith, కంసాలివాడు.

పస *pasa.* [Tel.] n. Sap, essence, సారము. Bloom, vigour, brilliancy, సత్తు. కాంతి. సత్తి, సారవస్తువు. Abundance, సమృద్ధి. Skill, చాతుర్యము. "పసమీరగను పేరుంగలు వశిరిలంబసలు గొలుచ జిరునవ్వుమెరయ." B. viii. 419. "ఇవ్వేళదులయందు కూర్మిపసపిరికి నేమియులేదు." Swa. vi. 74. టీ. కూర్మిపస. అనురాగాతిశయము. **పసపడు** *pasa-padu.* v. n. To be inclined, addicted to, devoted to, రుచిమరుగు. "పంచేంద్రియముల పసపడసన్న, మంచువిధంబున మాయనామాయ." L.v. 2.

పసందు *pasandu.* [H.] n. Comeliness, beauty; an ornament or decoration. సొంపు. సొగసు. adj. Comely, handsome, pleasing, nice. పసందగు to become handsome. పసందుచేయు to make handsome, pretty or nice; to prefer or like. ఆయన దీనిని పసందుచేసినాడు he liked this. **పసందుగా** *pasandu-gā.* adv. Nicely, agreeably, fashionably.

పసగరకొను *pasagarakonu.* [Tel.] v. a. To tease, to torment. పీడించు.

పసగు *pasagu.* [Tel.] v. n. To become evident. విశదమగు.

పసదనము *pasa-danamu.* [from Skt. ప్రసాధనము.] n. Adornment, embellishment, అలంకారశోభ. A present of a jewel or cloth, &c., పారితోషికము.

పసను *pasanu.* [Tel.] n. Crimson or orange colour. ఎరుపుమించిన పసుపువన్నె. **పసనుగా** *pasanu-gā.* adv. Well, properly, duly. చక్కగా, బాగుగా. "పసనుగా స్నానంబె పట్టగాం బాకటి." DRB. 250. "పసలక తెప్పించి మందు పోయించి, పసనుగా నొనరింపు ప్రాణదానంబు, పసచుమైన్యమునకోప" HD. ii. 1918.

పసపస *pasa-pasa.* [Tel.] n. Raininess, a drizzling rain, వానతుంపర, ముసురు.

పసపు See under పసుపు.

పసరము or **పసలము** *pasaramu.* [Tel.] n. A beast, an animal. గోమహిషజాతి.

పసరించు *pasarintsu.* [Tel. corrupted from Skt. ప్రసరించు.] v. n. To spread, to extend. వ్యాపించు.

"పసవయీకేన్నరే బ్రస్తావ్యభువుని,
పసరింపగానిట్టి భక్తుండుగలడే."
BD. v. 452.

పసరు *pasaru.* [Tel.] n. The juice or sap of leaves. ఆకురసము. A medicinal extract. Sap, రసము. Green color, ఆకుపచ్చన. Bilious vomiting. Spreading, వ్యాపనము. అతనికి పైత్యముచేత చాలా పసరు వెళ్లినది he vomited some bilious stuff. పసరాకు a leaf full of sap. పసరుమొగ్గ a tender sprout. Parij. iii. 97. "పసర్కొనిన." A. v. 122. టీ॥ అనగా పచ్చివాసన రాగాను adj. Green, ఆకుపచ్చని. బుద్ధిలో పసరిడి thinking well. **పసరుకాయ** *pasaru-kāya.* n. A tender or immature fruit. **పసరుగుబ్బి** *pasaru-gubbi.* n. A sort of bird. **పసరుచాయ** *pasaru-tsaya.* n. Green colour, ఆకుపచ్చరంగు. **పసరుపురుగు** *pasaru-purugu.* n. The sap worm, a green caterpillar. **పసరుమొగ్గ** n. A tender blossom, లేతమొగ్గ.

పసాదము *pasādamu.* [corruption of Skt. ప్రసాదము.] n Blessed food. అన్నము, వంటకము. **పసాపడు** *pasāpadu.* (పసాదము+పాపడు.) v. a. To eat. భోజనముచేయు.

పసారము or **పసారు** *pasāramu.* [Tel.] n. A shop. అంగడి. Charms, grace, తళుకు, మినుకు, పస.

పసి *pasi.* [Tel.] adj. Little, tender, young. పసిబిడ్డ or పసిపాప an infant. పసివాడు a little boy.

పసి *pasi.* [from Skt. పశువు.] n. Cattle. పశుసమూహము, గోగణము. The smell of cattle, పశ్వాదులమీదిగాలి, వాసన. **పసిపట్టు** *pasi-pattu.* v. n. To scent or follow by the nose, as a dog does a fox. పసిగొను to trace out or smell out. వాసనకట్టు. మొసలి కుక్కను పసిపట్టి when the crocodile scented the dog. **పసులు** *pasulu.* r. plu. Cattle, గోవులు. **పసిగాపు** *pasi-gāpu.* n. A herdsman, గోపకుడు **పసితిండి** *pasi-tindi.* n. A tiger, పెద్దపులి. **పసులపాలిగాడు** *pasula-pāli-gādu.* n. The Black Drongo or Kingcrow, *Dicrurus ater.* (F.B.I.) ఏట్రింత. Also, the Adjutant. తోకపసులపాలిగాడు the Raquet-tailed Drongo shrike. Jerdon No. 55. 56. 59. కొండపసులపాలిగాడు the White-bellied Drongo, *Dicrurus coerulescens.* జెంటెకపసుల పాలిగాడు the Hair-crested Drongo, *Chibia hottentotta.* టెంకిపసుల పాలిగాడు the larger Racket-tailed Drongo, *Dissemurus paradiseus* (F. B. I.). **పసులవాడు** *pasula-vādu.* n. A herdsman, గొల్లవాడు.

పసిక Same as పస (q. v.).

పసిడి *pasidi.* [Tel.] n. Gold. బంగారు. Wealth, ధనము. adj. Golden. **పసిడికంటె** Same as పైడికంటె (q. v.). **పసిడికాయ** *pasidi-kāya.* n. The fruit of the silk cotton tree. బూరుగుకాయ. **పసిడిరేకు** Same as పైడిరేకు (q. v.).

పసిమి *pasimi.* [Tel.] n. Yellowness. పసుపువన్నె. Greenness, ఆకుపచ్చన. "పసిమిజిత్కొడుముంజేతిపచ్చలవలె." H. iv. 174. **పసిమిడి** *pasimidi.* adj. Green, పసిమిగల. పసిమిరోగము jaundice.

పసిరిక *pasirika.* [Tel. పసరు+ఇక.] n. Green or yellow color, పసరువన్నె. Young or tender grass. లేతగడ్డి, పచ్చిగడ్డి. adj. Green or yellow, పసరువన్నెగల. **పసిరికపాము** *pasirika-pāmu.* n. A certain green snake that is harmless. పచ్చపాము. బొల్లపసిరిక a species of the same. **పసిరికపిట్ట** *pasirika-pitta.* n. The Indian bee-eater, పచ్చపిట్ట, పాలతపుటి. **పసిరికాయ** *pasiri-kāya.* n. A silk worm, cocoon. See పిసినికాయ. A miser. **పసిరికబయలు** *pasirika-bayalu.* n. A lawn or meadow.

పసుపు or **పసపు** *pasupu.* [Tel.] n. Indian saffron or turmeric. *Curcuma longa.* Rox. i. 32. హరిద్ర. కూరపసుపు turmeric used as a spice. అడవిపసుపు the wild species. Rox. i. 23. చాయపసుపు

the species used as a yellow dye. కీలిపసుపు another species, *Curcuma caesia*, Rox. i. 26. కుసుంబపసుపు (or కుసుంభీలు) Safflower, *Carthamus tinctorius*. W. పసుపుటాకులు turmeric leaves. పసుపాడు to use turmeric (by smearing it over the body), that is, to bathe. A. i. 63, and v. 41. ఎండపసుపు or పసుపెండ golden sunshine. అనగా కీరెండవేళ నడిమి పదిమి. A. vi. 75. ఆమె పసుపుకుంకుమ చెరిన్న టికిని పోదు lit: she will never lose her turmeric and red paint, i.e., she will never become a widow. పసుపుకుంకుమ a phrase for pin money, or dower, because it is money given to a bride, nominally to supply her with yellow and red paint for the forehead. పసుపు కుంకుమముపుచ్చుకొను to ratify a marriage by accepting these on behalf of the bride. పసుపుచాయ *pasupu-tsāya*. n. Yellow colour. పసుపుపిట్ట or పసుపుముద్ద n. Lit. The saffron bird. The Baya, or Weaver bird, *Ploceus baya*. (F. B. I.) గిజిగాడు.

పస్తాయించు *pastāyintsu*. [H] v. n. To regret, to be sorry. పశ్చాత్తాపపడు.

పస్తు *pastu*. [Tel.] n. A fast, fasting, a starved condition, starving. ఉపవాసము, ఉపాసము. పస్తుండు or పస్తుగానుండు *past-undu*. v. n. To be fasting or starving.

పా pā

పాంకోడు *pankōdu*. [Tel. for పావకోడు.] n. A weaver's treadle. A sandal for the foot.

పాంచజన్యము *pancha-janyamu*. [Skt. derived from పంచజన a certain giant, of whose bone the conch was made.] n. The conch of Vishnu. విష్ణుశంఖము. Fire. అగ్ని.

పాంచాలము *panchālamu*. [Skt.] n. The Punjab. The country north of Delhi, between the foot of the Himalayas and the Chambal. పంచాలదేశము. పాంచాలి *panchāli*. n. The daughter of the king of Panchāla: a title of Draupadi, the wife of the five Pandu princes. ద్రౌపది. పాంచాలిక *panchālika*. n. A doll or puppet, an image carved on pillars, &c. బొమ్మ, కరువ్యాగాదిరూపము. పాంచాలుడు *panchāludu*. n. A member of any one of the five castes of artificers, viz., the carpenters, weavers, barbers, washermen, painters. వడ్లవాడు, సాలెవాడు, మంగలవాడు, చాకలవాడు, ముచ్చివాడు, ఈ అయిదు జాతులందు దేనిలోనైనను చేరినవాడు.

పాంజేబు *panjēbu*. [H] n. A silver anklet. కాలిగొలుసు.

పాంక్తేయుడు *pangktēyudu*. [Skt. from పఙ్క్తి.] n. A respectable guest, a person received in society.

పాండవులు *pandavulu*. [Skt. from పాండు (రాజు)] n. The Pāndus or princes of the house of Pāndu. The ancient heroes. Aborigines. పాండవులనాటినుండి time out of mind, అనాదిగా. పాండవబీడు land that has never been brought under the plough, an immemorial waste. పాండవ గుండ్లు prehistoric tombs, tumuli.

పాండిత్యము or పాండితి *pandityamu*. [Skt. from పండిత.] n. Learning, scholarship, mastery, perfect knowledge or skill. పండితభావము.

పాండువు, పాండిమ or పాండిమము *panduvu*. [Skt.] n. Paleness. తెలుపు. A pale yellow colour, తెలుపుమించిన పసుపు. Leprosy. పాండురోగము. adj. White, తెల్లని. పాండుడు *pandudu*. n. The name of a sovereign of ancient Delhi, the reputed father of the five Pandu princes who are the heroes of the Mahābhārata. పాండురము or పాండరము *panduramu*. n. Pale or yellowish white colour. adj. Pale or yellowish white. తెలుపు. పాండురోగము *pandu-rōgamu*. n. Leprosy.

పాండ్యము or పాండ్యదేశము pāndyamu. [Skt.] n. A country in the Southern part of the Indian peninsula, comprehending the districts of Madura and Tinnevelly. పాండీడు pānd-idu. n. A king of the Pāndya country. పాండ్యదేశపురాజు.

పాంథుడు pānthudu. [Skt.] n. A traveller. తెరువరి, పథికుడు.

పాంశువు pāmṣuvu. [Skt.] n. Dust. పరాగము, దుమ్ము. Manure, కసాల్వర్ణసంచితగోమయము, ఎరువు. Vasu. iii. 165.

పాంసనుడు pāmsanudu. [Skt.] n. A contemptible, wicked or bad man. దుష్టుడు. కులపాంసనుడు one who is a disgrace to his family. M. IX. ii. 315.

పాంసుల pāmsula. [Skt.] n. An unchaste woman. జారస్త్రీ.

పాంసువు pāmsuvu. [Skt.] n. Dust. పరాగము, ధూళి. పాంసులము pāmsulamu. n. Saltish earth, saline earth. సుగంధిపాంసుల వనికె "మృదుశయ్యాతలముల మెలతలు మెలపుతో, నమరుగా నిద్ర జనుమధవించు కొమ్మలకి యిపుడు సురుకొనిపాంసుల స్థలముల నిద్ర చనికిదియ." M. III. ii. 85.

పాక pāka. [Tel.] n. A hut, shed or hovel of mats, a booth. దూలములులేకుండా కట్టిన యిల్లు, గుడిసె. Also, a small temple, గుడి. BD. iii. 1274.

పాకనాటిరెడ్లు pāka-nāti-redlu. [Tel.] n. A certain sub-caste of Kāpus (కాపులు,) who derive their name from the country named పాకనాడు. Also, a sub-caste of the Mālas (మాలలు.)

పాకము pākamu. [Skt.] n. Cooking, dressing food, boiling, వంట. Maturity, natural or artificial, as the state of being cooked or ripened. పరిపాకము. The style of an author: the chief distinctions of which are కదళీపాకము the plantain style, which is easily comprehended, the plantain being quite soft and without stones; ద్రాక్షాపాకము or grape style, which is very superior and more difficult, to understand, and నారికేళపాకము or cocoanut style, which is puzzling and dry, requiring time and consideration to digest it. దేహపాకము the constitution of the body. ఆమెకు పాకశుద్ధికద్దు she is a good cook. ఔషధపాకము the concoction or preparation of medicine. పాకగేహము pāka-gēhamu. n. A kitchen. వంటయిల్లు.

పాకలము pākalamu. [Skt.] n. A fever in an elephant. ఏనుగులకు వచ్చు జ్వరము. పాకలపుటేనుగు an elephant that has fever. A. vi. 58. A horse, అశ్వము.

పాకారి or పాకశాసనుడు pāk-ari. [Skt.] n. A title of Indra as the slayer of a giant named పాకుడు.

పాకి, పాకీ, పాకివాడు or పాకీమనిషి pāki. [Tel.] n. A scavenger, commonly called at Madras a Tōti. పాకిది a Tōti woman.

పాకు or ప్రాకు pāku. [Tel.] v. n. To creep or crawl. పాకించు pākinsu. v. a. To train, as a vine or other creeper. పాకుడు or ప్రాకుడు pākudu. n. A trellis for a vine or other creeper. Anything that spreads or creeps; mossiness; the scum or greenness on putrid water. Dirt on the teeth. పండ్లపాచి. Dirt, nastiness, మాలిన్యము. పాకులాడు pākul-ādu. v. n. To creep or crawl. To scramble. పరులను పట్టుకొని పాకులాడితే యేమికద్దు why ask the help of strangers. పాకొను or ప్రాకొను pā-konu. v. n. To attach itself to, or to stick to, as dirt or moss. పాకొన్నమడుగు a green pool. "పాకొన్ననూతియుదకము, మేకలపాడియునుకీర్తి మేదినిసుమతీ."

పాకెన, పాకెన్న, ప్రాకెన్న or పాకొన్నము pākena. [Tel.] n. A ceremony performed on the third day of a wedding. పెండ్లిలో మూడవనాటి యుత్సవము.

పాకోడు or పావకోడు Same as పాంకోడు (q. v.).

పాక్షికము *pākshikamu*. [Skt. from పక్షము.] n. An alternative. పక్షమున కలిగినది. Unfairness, partiality, పక్షపాతము.

పాగడము or **పావగము** *pāgaḍamu*. [Tel.] n. A silver anklet పాదములందు ఒంటిగా చేసియుంచే భూషణము.

పాగా or **పాగ** *pāgā*. [Tel.] n. A turban. పాగాచుట్టు to tie on or form a turban. Also, a stable. అశ్వశాల. A troop of horses, అశ్వసమూహము. పాగాలు Same as పాగవాళ్లు (q. v.). పాగాగుర్రము *pāga-gurramu*. n. A livery horse, stalled horse.

పాగిడ *pāgiḍa*. [Tel.] n. Thread that remains after a web has been woven.

పాగు *pāgu*. [Tel.] n. Thick syrup, melted sugar, treacle.

పాగెము *pāgemu*. [Tel.] n. Connection. సంబంధము.

పాచకుడు *pāchakuḍu*. [Skt.] n. A cook. వంటవాడు.

పాచి or **ప్రాచి** *pāchi*. [Tel.] n. Rot, foulness, squalor, staleness, nastiness, scurf, (as of the teeth,) దంష్ట్రమలిక. Green slime produced in stagnant water, moss, water weeds, శైవాలము, నీళ్లలోని పచ్చని మలిక. Also, a baby word for the nipple, breast, or milk. adj. Old, పాతదైన. Dirty, unclean, not fresh. ఇంటిపాచిపని కాలేదు the cleaning of the house is not done. పాచిచేయు or పాచితీయు to sweep and wash a house, to clean a house. పాచితీగె *pāchi-tīge*. n. A certain creeper, also called పాచిమాను. *Anogeissus acuminata* (Watts.)

పాచిక *pāchika*. [Tel.] n. A die in gambling.

పాచితము or **ప్రాచితము** *pāchitamu*. [from Skt. ప్రాయశ్చిత్తము.] n. Compensation, atonement. "పతిసుష్ఠుద్రోహ కల్మషపాచితం బిడి, పసిడిబొట్టు తా నాని బంతిగడిచి." A. vi. 91.

పాచ్చేసము or **పాచ్చసము** *pāṭsanamu*. [Tel.] n. Looseness of the bowels, విరేచనము. plu. పాచ్చేసాలు.

పాచు *pāṭsu*. [Tel. Causal of పాయు.] v. a. To remove out of the way. తొలగించు, పాయజేయు. To disentangle, చిక్కువిడిపించు.

పాజీ *pājī*. [H.] adj. Vile, worthless, despicable, base, contemptible, పనికిమాలిన, క్షుద్రమైన.

పాజేలు, **ప్రాజేలు** or **పాటిజేలు** *pājēlu*. [Tel. పాటి+చేలు.] n. Land under cultivation, as opposed to waste land, (బీడు).

పాట *pāṭa*. [Tel. from పాడు.] n. Music, a song. సంగీతము, పదము. Manner, way, విధము. ఇప్పాట in this way, ఈ విధముగా. వాడు నిత్యమును పాడేపాట యిదే this is his incessant theme. వాడు ఆడినది ఆట పాడినది పాట his authority is all in all, or his word is law. ఎప్పాట how, in what way? ఎప్పాటనైన, in any way, ఏవిధముననైన.

పాటచెట్టు *pāṭa-cheṭṭu*. n. A tree, called *Cissampelos hexandria*. Rox. iii. 842. విశాక్షీలా, అగరుపోంకి.

పాటకము or **పోటకము** *pāṭakamu*. [from Skt. స్ఫోటకము.] n. Small pox. [Skt.] n. A bank of a river, &c., తీరము.

పాటచ్చరుడు *pāṭach-charuḍu*. [Skt.] n. A thief or robber. దొంగ. A. iv. 300.

పాటన *pāṭana*. [Tel.] n. Adornment. అలంకారము. Putting right, making right, righting, సంస్కారము. Regard, ఆదరణము.

పాటనము *pāṭanamu*. [Skt.] n. Splitting. చీల్చుట.

పాటపాట *pāṭa-pāṭa*. [Tel.] adj. Little by little. కొంచెముకొంచెము.

పాటబండి *pāṭa-banḍi*. [Tel.] n. A kind of carriage. ఒకవిధమైనగాడి.

పాటము *pāṭamu*. [Tel.] adj. Proper, fitting. ఇది కెంపులు చూడదగునకు పాటమైన వేళ కాదు this is not a proper time of day to examine the rubies.

పాటరి *paṭari*. [Tel. from పాటు.] n. A hard working man, a drudge. "కూలినాలిచేసి కల్లాపుపాటరి." Vēma.

పాటల or **పాటలి** *paṭala*. [Skt.] n. The flower called the Trumpet flower. *Bignonia suaveolens*. Rox. iii. 104. Ainslie ii. 273. కలిగొట్టుపువ్వు. **పాటలము** *paṭalamu*. adj. Red, rosy, ruddy. n. Flesh colour. పాటలగంధి a rosy maid. పాటలాధరి cherry-lipped. పాటలజటలు red matted locks. నవపల్లవపాటలము ruddy as a young sprout.

పాటవము *paṭavamu*. [Skt. from పటు.] n. Health. ఆరోగ్యము. Strength, vigour, శక్తి, దార్ఢ్యము. Ability, cleverness, నైపుణ్యము. గానపాటవము skill in singing. Brightness, తైక్ష్ణ్యము. Anir. ii. 65. అతనికి దృష్టిపాటవము తప్పినది he is losing his eyesight.

పాటి *paṭi*. [Tel.] n. Degree, extent, quantity, size. ప్రమాణము. Value, character, quality, kind, sort, విధము. Fitness. Resemblance, equality, సామ్యము. adj. Equal, సమము. Common, general, సామాన్యము. Due, fit, న్యాయ్యము. Of such a size or character, గొలది. పాటికొల an exact measurement. ఈపాటిచాలును so far will do, thus much is enough. "పదుగురాడుమాట పాటియై ధరజెల్లు," the words of many people will carry weight. ఈపాటికి వచ్చియుండును by this time he will have arrived. వానిపాటి కలాగ్యత నీకు ఉండినను చాలును it will be enough if you are equal to him. ఏపాటి రూకలు how much money? అది ఒక పాటి గానున్నది it is tolerably good. పాటిరేవు a ford in a river. పాటినేల rich soil (see పాడు). వీడు ఏపాటివాడు what kind of a man is he? సన్నపాటికర్ర a slender stick. తగుపాటి competent, fit, suitable. కొంచెపాటి small. కొంచెపాటివారు base men, low people, అల్పులు. నీకు బుద్ధిచెప్పేపాటివాడు ఇక్కడ లేడు there is no one here fit to advise you. ఇది ఏపాటిపని what sort of business is this? పాటిపాటిగా little by little, కొద్దికొద్దిగా. **పాటిగొను** *paṭi-gonu*. v. a. To consider as equal, సరిచేయు.

పాటించు *paṭintsu*. [Tel.] v. n. To exceed, to be excessive. మించు, అతిశయించు. "కుసుమశరాబాణంబులు గూడనైదు, కరగి నేరుపుపాటించి కరపుగట్టె." M. IV. ii. 31. నేరుపుపాటించి, చాతుర్యముమించి. v. a. To observe, to care for, to regard, to pay attention to, to honour. ఆదరించు, అక్కఱపట్టు, గౌరవముచేయు. To consider, to take into consideration, విచారించు. To expect, hope, ప్రతీక్షించు. To wear or carry, ధరించు. To have, get, పొందు, కలుగు. "పరధనములమీద నాసపాటింపక." Vish. iv. 248. "కవితపాటింపదగిన కర్ణాట భూమికిని." BD. ii. 149. "తనతోడ సమ్మోగలవారియొడ దురాగ్రహమువాటింపక." Vish. iv. 143. **పాటింపు** *paṭimpu*. n. Care, regard, application, పట్టు, ఆదృశ్యము.

పాటితము *paṭitamu*. [Skt.] adj. Split. చీల్చబడిన.

పాటిల్లు or **పాటిలు** *paṭillu*. [Tel.] v. n. To happen, to occur, to be produced, to be brought about, సంభవించు, కలుగు, వచ్చు, ప్రాప్తముగు. "పాండవులకు పాటిల్లిన యనర్థంబుల కెల్లను మూలంబు నీవకాడె." M. VII. v. 123.

పాటీరము *paṭīramu*. [Skt.] n. Sandal. చందనము. పాటీరగిరి Mount Malaya.

పాటీలు *paṭīlu*. [Tel.] n. A sort of gold bracelets worn by women.

పాటు *paṭu*. [Tel. from పడు.] n. A fall. పడుట. Suffering, శ్రమము. Labour. A movement, an action, చర్య. Distress, misfortune, hardship, mishap, ఆపద. Time, occasion. సమయము. Manner, way, mode, విధము. A declining state. The ebb of the tide. సముద్రపునీరు పోటకి తగ్గుట. రెప్పపాటు (lit: eye-lid-fall) a wink or blink. బల్లిపాటు the fall of a lizard. చెవిటివాడు

పెదవిపాటు గ్రహించును a deaf man understands the motions of the lips. వారు పడే పాట్లు చెప్పనలవికాదు the hardships they suffer are indescribable. కుక్కపడేపాట్లు పడుచున్నాడు he leads the life of a dog. ఎన్నిపాట్లు పడినను వాడు చిక్కలేదు though we did all we could we did not find him. వాడు పడ్డపాట్లు వృథాగాపోవునా will all his trouble be in vain. వచ్చినపాటుననే as soon as he comes. అది ఆపాటుననే ఉన్నది it remains as it was, it remains unaltered. అది యేపాటుననున్నదో ఆపాటుననే ఉండనిమ్ము leave it as it is. అడ్డపాటుగానుండేనేల a declivity, slope or descent. పోటుపాటు the ebb and flow of a river or sea. బోర్లపాటులు vile pranks. పొరపాటు an error. Added to some verbs it serves as an affix like *-tion, -ness* or *-ment* and forms a noun, as నగుబాటు laughter. కలుబాటు cost, expenditure. దిద్దుబాటు a correction. కుదురుబాటు settlement. ఒంటరిపాటు loneliness. ఒంటరిపాటున alone, unaccompanied. ఆపాటున whereupon, thereupon, on that occasion. పనిపాటులు jobs. పాట్లమారి a drudge, మిక్కిలి శ్రమపడు స్వభావముగలవాడు. **పాటుపడు** *pāṭu-paḍu.* v. n. To toil, to labour. శ్రమపడు. **పాటుసాగించు** *pāṭu-sāginisu.* v. n. To cultivate, to begin cultivation operations. **పాటునబడు** *pāṭuna-baḍu.* v. n. To come back to the original position. యథాస్థితికివచ్చు.

పాఠము *pāṭhamu.* [Skt.] n. A lesson. Study, reading. చదువడము. **పాఠశాల** *pāṭha-sāla.* n. A school, a college. పఠి. See పఠించు. **పాఠకుడు** *pāṭhakuḍu.* n. A lecturer. A spiritual preceptor. A reader, a student, ఉపాధ్యాయుడు, విద్యార్థి. **పాఠభేదము** or **పాఠాంతరము** *pāṭha-bhēdamu.* n. A various reading, another reading, a deviation found in other manuscripts.

పాఠీనము *pāṭhīnamu.* [Skt.] n. A fish, which has numerous teeth. *Silurus boalis* (W.) The poetical dolphin. చేప.

పాడగము *pāḍagamu.* [Tel.] n. A silver anklet.

పాడర See under పాడు.

పాడి *pāḍi.* [Tel.] n. Justice, propriety, fitness, decency. న్యాయము, ధర్మము, యోగ్యము. Nature. స్వభావము. Business, వ్యవహారము. Abundance of dairy produce. క్షీరదధ్యాదిసమృద్ధి. Milk, పాలు. పాడియావు a cow in milk.

పాడు *pāḍu.* [Tel.] adj. Waste, desolate, dismal, dreary, neglected, ruined, dilapidated. శూన్యము. Cursed, blasted. Horrid, vile, sad. ఇల్లు పాడుచేసిరి they left the house empty. పాడుమాట sad news, a horrid story. పాడుచలి horridly cold. పాడుతోట a neglected garden. పాడుతాగుబోతు an abandoned drunkard. పాడునేల waste ground. పాటిమన్ను or పాటినేల rich soil. పాడునొసలు a blank forehead, i. e., one unadorned with the *tilacam.* పాడుజ్వరము a wasting fever. పాడువాన cursed rain. n. A wreck, waste, ruin, desolation. శూన్యము. A village. పల్లె. **పాడుచేయు** *pāḍu-chēyu.* v. a. To spoil. To waste, ruin, throw away. **పాడుపడు**, **పాడగు** or **పాడుపోవు** *pāḍu-paḍu.* v. n. To become waste or desolate. **పాడునుయ్యి** *pāḍu-nuyyi.* n. A disused well.

పాడు *pāḍu.* [Tel.] v. a. To sing. గానము చేయు. Also, to sell or to bid at an auction. **పాడించు** *pāḍintsu.* (Causal of పాడు.) v. a. To have something sung. To proclaim, sell by auction. నా ఆస్తి వేలము పాడించిరి they sold my property by auction.

పాదు or **పాదుడు** *pādu.* [Tel.] n. A trellis for a vine or other creeper; anything that spreads or creeps; mossiness; the scum or greenness on putrid water. Dirt on the teeth. పళ్లపాచి. Dirt, nastiness. మాలిన్యము.

పాడె *pade*. [Tel.] n. A bier, a funeral pile. శవవాహనము. పాడెకట్ట a wretch, villain; a fool, simpleton, booby. నీపాడెకట్ట perish thou.

పాడ్యమి *padyami*. [from Skt. ప్రతిపత్.] n. The day after the full or new moon, పక్షమందు మొదటితిథి, ప్రథమ.

పాణసి *panasi*. [Tel.] n. A Pariah. మాల. "పాణసిపుణ్యబోధులను" పాణిక్య. ii.

పాణి *pani*. [Skt.] n The water or lustre of pearls. ముత్తెపుతీరు. The hand. పాణితలము the palm of the hand. పాణివాదము clapping the hand. పాణిగ్రహణము *pani-grahanamu*. n. A wedding, nuptials. వివాహము, పెండ్లి. పాణిగృహీతి *pani-grihiti*. n. A wedded wife.

పాణింధమము *panin-dhamamu*. [Skt.] n. A pair of bellows. కొలిమితిత్తి. Darkness, చీకటి. A kind of drum. వాద్యభేదము.

పాణిక *panika*. [Skt.] n. A spoon, a ladle.

పాణిపడము or **పాణివడము** *panipadamu*, [Tel.] n. A quiver. అమ్ములపొది, తూణీరము.

పాత or **ప్రాత** *pata*. [Tel.] adj. Old, decayed, worn out. పూర్వమందుండినట్టిది, పడుకుదిని. పాతకరణము the old clerk, i.e., the former one (not one who is aged.) పాతగుర్రము a horse that has been with the owner for a considerable time. అది పాతసంగతి that is an old story. n. A cloth, clothes, usually conjoined with the word, బట్ట: thus, బట్టపాత clothing and raiment. An old cloth, జీర్ణవస్త్రము. పాతగిలు, పాతగిల్లు, ప్రాతగిలు or ప్రాతగిల్లు *patagilu*. v. n. To grow old. పాతబడును. పాతకాపు *pata-kapu*. n. An old resident. పాతరికము *patarikamu*. n. Oldness. Experience.

పాత *pata*. [Skt.] n. One who takes care of or guards. కాచువాడు.

పాతకము *patakamu*. [Skt.] n. A sin, a crime. పంచమహాపాతకములు the five great sins, viz., killing a Brahmin (బ్రహ్మహత్య), stealing gold (స్వర్ణస్తేయము), drinking intoxicating liquor (సురాపానము), dishonoring a teacher's wife (గురుపత్నీగమనము), and association with such as are guilty of any of these sins (ఇవి చేయువారితోడి సహవాసము). పాతకి or పాతకుడు *pataki*. n. A sinner.

పాతము *patamu*. [Skt.] n. A fall, descent. పతనము, పాటు. నదీపాతభూమి land devastated by a flood, or that has fallen into a river. గ్రంథపాతము a passage that is lost from a book.

పాతర *patara*. [Tel. పాతు+అర.] n. A grain pit or cellar built with a small mouth above, to preserve salt or grain ధాన్యాదుల నిక్షేపము. A treasury. నిధి. ధాన్యము పాతర పెట్టినాడు he stored up the grain in a pit. ఇసుకపాతర a pack of confusion, a puzzle. పాతరతీయు to dig a pit, or to open a grain cellar. ఇసుకపాతర పాతరగా in a full stream. పడుపాతర a pit-fall, పాతరలు grain pits.

పాతరలాడు, పాతర్లాడు *pataral-adu*. [Tel. for పాత్రలాడు. See పాత్రము.] v. n. To dance about. నృత్యము, ఆడు. To be at a loss, to be perplexed or puzzled, to muse, తడబడు. పెంపరిలాడు, వెదుకు, తత్తరపడు. "కి. స్త్రీలింగోపకులందరు, గీతంబులుపాడ దరుల క్కిరందను నగుచుగా, చేతులు త్రిప్పుచు పదపడి. పాతరలాడెను యశోదపాపందడుగా." B. X. ch. 18. 15.

పాతాళము *patalamu*. [Skt.] n. The nether world, Hades, క్రిందిలోకము. ఆ గుంట పాతాళము వలెనున్నది that pond is as deep as Hades. ఈ బావిలో నీళ్లు పాతాళములో నున్నవి the water is very low down in this well. "పాతాళప్రశ్నలుమాని మేల్కొ నుము." A. vi. 77. టీ॥ పాతాళప్రశ్నలుమాని అధోగతి ప్రశ్నలువిడిచిపెట్టి, దూరప్రశ్నలుమాని, నిండా గూఢముగా నుండేవానిని అడగ డము మానుకొని. పాతాళగంగ *patala-ganga*. n. The name of the river that flows through the Hindu Hades. Also, the name of that branch of the Krishna which flows past Sri Sailam. పాతాళభేది pātāla-bhēdi. n. A grappling hook or drag to recover things sunk in a river.

పాతిక or పాతికె pātika [Tel.] n. One-fourth or quarter of any thing. Thus పాతికరూపాయలు twenty-five Rupees. పాతికేండ్లు గలవాడు a person of 25 years of age. పాతికమంది 25 persons.

పాతివ్రత్యము pāti-vratyamu. [Skt. from పతివ్రత.] n. Matrimonial fidelity, faithfulness in a wife. పతివ్రతాత్వము.

పాతు pātu. [Tel.] v. a. To bury, fix, set up or fasten in the ground, పూడుచు. n. The foundation, meaning that portion of a post, &c., which is under ground. కొండపాతు the roots of the hills.

"క్ష్మాధరంబులపాతుగదలంగ వేకేళ.
నోలినసప్తవారాయువులువిరి."

HN. iv. 11.

పాతుకొను pātu-konu. v. n. To become firm. పాతిపెట్టు or పాతివేయు pāti-pettu. v. a. To bury. To plant, to fix. ఒక గుంజను పాతిపెట్టినారు they set up a post. ఆ మొక్క లను పాతిపెట్టినాను I planted those plants.

పాత్రము pātramu. [Skt.] n. A character in a play, an actress. నర్తకి. పాత్ర or పాత్రము n. A utensil, ఉపకరణము. Hardware. పాత్రసామాను or పాత్రసామగ్రి metal vessels. పాత్రలాడు See పాతరలాడు.

పాత్రము pātramu. [Skt.] adj. Worthy, fit, adequate. యోగ్యము. పాత్రత. pātrata. n. Fitness, worthiness. పాత్రుడు pātrudu. n. One who is worthy, deserving or fit. అర్హుడు, యోగ్యుడు. ఆయనదయకు పాత్రుడ నైతిని I was found worthy of enjoying his favour. వారు దండనకు పాత్రులైరి they were guilty, they were deserving of punishment. A king's counsellor or minister. మంత్రి. "కోటలో గజపతివారు తమతట్టునుండిన పాత్రసామంతులను కొందరు మన్నెపువారినిని కాపా ఉంచినారు." పాత్రసామంతులు means principal servants. A title assumed by the members of a particular caste of Sudras in Ganjam and Orissa, as భోగన్నపాత్రుడు, వీరన్న పాత్రుడు, &c.

పాథము or పాథస్సు pāthamu. [Skt.] n. Water. పాథశ్చరము a fish. Vasu. ii. 57. Food, అన్నము. పాథేయము pāthēyamu. n. Provision or provender for a journey. దారిబత్తెము. Parij. ii. 117. పాథోధి pāthōdhi. n. The sea.

పాదట్టు pādaṭṭu. [Tel. పాడు+అట్టు.] n. A cobweb. బూజు.

పాదము pādamu. [Skt.] n. A foot. అడుగు. A root, వేరు. A quarter, పాతిక. A foot or line of verse being a quarter of a stanza. పద్యములో నాలుగవభాగము. A ray of light, కిరణము. A small hill at the foot of a mountain. కొండదిగువ దిబ్బ. తమ పాదా లనే నమ్మివచ్చినాను I came in reliance on your honour as my protector. This is a mere conversational compliment, like 'I kiss your hands' in Spanish. పాదతీర్థము water made holy by washing a saint's feet. పాదపద్మములు lotus-like feet. పాదలాక్ష red paint for the feet of women, పారాణి. తమపాదాలసముఖానకు నా కుమా రుణ్ని తెచ్చి అప్పగిస్తున్నాను permit me to introduce my son to your honour's protection. వాడు తండ్రిపాదాలమీద పడెను he fell on his father's feet. తమపాదా లవద్ద before your honour, in your presence. తమపాదాల శరణుచొచ్చినాను I throw myself on your goodness. పాదచారి pāda-chāri n. A foot passenger. కాలిబంటు. One who goes walking, నడచి పోవువాడు. పాదజుడు pādajudu. n. A Sudra, because born from the feet of Brahma. పాదత్రాణము pāda-trāṇamu. n. A shoe or boot. పైజారు. పాదపము pādapamu. n. A tree. పాదపూర్ణము

pāda-pūrnamu. n. An unnecessary word inserted in verse, to fill up the measure, such as in Sanskrit the words తు, హి, చ, స్మ, హి, వై, or, in Telugu poetry the words, ఒకో, ఔర, మరి, ఇల, మహి, or verbs, చెలగు, ఒప్పు, &c. పాదరసము *pāda-rasamu*. n. Quick-silver, mercury. రసము. పాదలి *pādali*. n. A base or low man, అధముడు.

" పాపపు విప్రుని పనికిరామున్న,
తాపికాడైన పాదలిమందటీడు. "

HD. iii. 110.

పాదలేపనము *pāda-lēpanamu*. n. A salve or unguent for the feet. పాదాంగదము *pād-āngadamu*. n. An ornament for the feet or toes. పాదపట్టము or పాదపట్టము *pāda-paṭṭamu*. n. An anklet. అందె, కాలి అందె, చిరుదు పెండేరము, పాగడము.

పాదిరి or పాదిరి *pādiri*. [Tel.] n. The flower called *Bignonia suaveolens*. See పాటలి. Rox. iii. 105. పాటలి, కృష్ణపాంతా, కుబేరాక్షి, భూతపాదిరి are species.

పాదిరి *pādiri*. [Fr. Padrè, Eng. Father,] n. A Romish priest. A missionary, or clergyman, గురువు, క్రీస్తుమతబోధకుడైనగురువు.

పాదివేట *pādi-vēṭa*. [Tel.] n. Fowling or catching birds by means of a decoy. కాజే పూరేదులోనను పెంపుడు పిట్టలమూలమున ఇతరమైనపిట్టలను పట్టెడు ఒకానొకవేట. పాది గువ్వ *pādi-guvva*. n. A dove used in పాదివేట.

పాదు or పాది *pādu*. [Tel.] n. A garden bed or plot smaller than a మడి. Also, the watered earth round a tree. The area or areola round the nipple or round a sore. Underneath, the nether portion, క్రిందు. Steadiness, నిలుకడ. పాదుకట్టు *pādu-kaṭṭu*. v. n. To divide into beds. పాదుకొను or పాదునిలుచు *pādu-konu*. v. n. To be grounded, established firm. To take root or gather strength, have a footing. నాటుకొను, నెలకొను, తగులుకొను, నిలుచు. పాదుకొన్న being well grounded. పాదుకొలుపు *pādu-kolupu*. v. a. To fix, to ground, to establish. నాటునట్లుచేయు, స్థిరపరుచు. " భక్తియుక్తిప్రసన్నత పంకజాతు, పా దపద్మంబులందునే పాదుకొలిపి. " Vish. i. 3

పాదుకలు or పాదుపులు *pādukalu*. [Skt.] n. plu. Sandals, పావకోళ్లు. పాదుకాసిద్ధి the art of flying by means of seven league-boots. పాదూవాహుడు. *pādū-vāhuḍu*. n. A slipper-bearer, a menial. చెప్పులు తెచ్చు కొనేవాడు. A. iv. 6.

" వాదవయస్తంభ వశ్యాద్యుపధములు,
పాదుకాసిద్ధులు పరుసవేదులును. "

L. xix. 58.

పానొట్టు [Tel. పాదు + ఒట్టు.] Same as పాదట్టు [q. v.] పానొట్టుపురుగు *pādoṭṭu-purugu*. n. A spider.

పాదుషా, పాదుసా or పాదుసాహి *pādushā*. [H.] n. Padshah, an emperor, సమ్రాట్టు. A king, రాజు.

పాద్యము *pādyamu*. [Skt. from పాదము.] n. Water for washing the feet.

పానము *pānamu*. [Skt.] n. Drinking. Also, a draught (of water, &c.) అన్నపానాదులు food and raiment. పానకము *pānakamu*. n. A sweet drink, a beverage made of sugar and water and drunk as sherbet. పానకపూజ a certain rite performed in the hot weather, when they hold a feast of cooling diets and drinks, with amusements. A. ii. 84. 88. పానగోష్ఠి or పాన గోష్ఠిక *pāna-gōshṭhi*. n. A dram shop, a place where people drink together. Vish. P. viii. 45. పానముచేయు *pānamu-chēyu*. v. a. To drink.

పానము *pānamu*. [from Skt. ప్రాణము.] n. Life.

పానలు *pānalu*. [Tel.] n. plu. Doubts, సందేహములు.

" స్త్రీల బసవాయునగవిన్న పానలాందేల,
పసిబాలలకున్నన ప్రబలదేర్పక్తి. "

BD. ii. 584

పానగిల్లు v. n. To doubt, to hesitate.

పానవట్టము pāna-vattamu. [Tel.] n. The base or trench into which libations, poured on the top of an idol, run down and flow to the spout. లింగపీఠము.

పానసము pānasamu. [Tel.] n. A kitchen. వంటయిల్లు. Cookery, వంట. పానసపు బాడబులు Brahmin cooks, వంటబ్రాహ్మణులు. పానసపుది a kitchen maid, వంటలక్క. "అమ్మహీపతి నీకెవ్వరివాడవని యడిగనేని పాండవాగ్రజునకుం బానసంబు సేయుదు నవంగల వాడనని చెప్పి." M. IV. i. 78. పానసీడు pānas-īḍu. n. A cook. వంటవాడు, స్వయంపాకి. M. IV. ii. 12. & i. 72.

పానారము pānāramu. [Tel.] n. An unbroken betel nut. A ripe areca nut. పండుపోక, క్రముకఫలము.

పానీయము pānīyamu. [Skt.] n. Water. నీళ్లు. adj. Drinkable. త్రాగదగిన. See పానము.

పానుకు pānuku. [Tel.] n. A plant called *Rottbœlia perforata*. Rox. i. 356.

పానుపు or పాన్పు pānupu. [Tel.] n. A cot. మంచము. A bed or couch. పరుపు. విరిపాన్పు a flowery couch, a bed of roses. మల్లెల పాన్పు a bed of jasmine buds.

పాప pāpa. [Tel. from పాము.] adj. Of the serpent, serpentine. పాపరేడు the king of serpents, నాగరాజు. పాపపాన్పు a serpent bed, i e., the great serpent on which Vishṇu reclines. R. i. 46. పాపజగము the serpent world, నాగలోకము. పాపజన్నిగట్టు or పాపజంధెముదాల్పు pāpa-dzanni-gaṭṭu. n. One who wears a serpent as his sacred thread, an epithet of Gaṇēsa, వినాయకుడు. పాపతూపు or పాపరమ్ము pāpa-tūpu. n. A serpent arrow, నాగాస్త్రము. పాపమీను pāpa-mīnu. n. A serpent-like fish. ఒకజాతిచేప. పాపమేపరి or పాపమేపుడు pāpa-mēpari. n. One who feeds on serpents, i. e., an eagle, గరుత్మంతుడు; or a peacock, నెమలి. పాపమేతపక్కి pāpa-mēta-pakki. n. The "snake-eating bird," i.e., an eagle. పాపరమ్ము pāpa-r-ammu. n. A serpent arrow. పాపరేలు pāpa-rēlu. n. A sort of fish.

పాప pāpa. [Tel.] n. A child. The pupil of the eye. కంటిపాప. దానికి బిడ్డపాపలులేరు she has neither chick nor child.

పాపట pāpaṭa. [Tel. from పాయు.] n. The parting of the hair on the forehead. సీమంతము. A flowering forest tree, *Ixora tomentosa*. వృక్షవిశేషము. Rox. i. 385. పాపటబొట్టు or పాపటచేరు pāpaṭa-boṭṭu. n. A kind of head ornament, a brooch or locket suspended on the forehead from the parting of the hair. చేరుచుక్క. పాపటగోరింక pāpaṭa-gōrinka. n The Black-headed Myna, *Temenuchus pagodarum*, (F. B. I.) పాపటపోవు pāpaṭa-pōvu. v. n. To get out of the way, దారివిడిచితొలగు. పాపటపుచ్చు pāpaṭa-putstsu. v. a. To remove out of the way. దారివిడిచి తొలగించు.

పాపటము or పాపనము pāpaṭamu. [Tel. from పాయు.] n. A harrow, or hoeing instrument. పాపటతోలు pāpaṭa-tōlu. v. n. To harrow. పాపడము pāpaḍamu. n. Harrowing. పైపాపడాలకూలి the hire for harrowing.

పాపఠ్యమాన [Skt.] adj. Being read aloud or recited. పఠింపబడుచున్న. R. v. 109.

పాపడు pāpaḍu. [Tel.] n. A little boy, a little fellow. బాలుడు. A male infant, పురుషశిశువు.

పాపము pāpamu. [Skt.] n. Sin, crime, evil. అతనిన్నిగురించి పాపము పుణ్యము రెండు ఎరుగను I know nothing about him either good or bad. interj. Alas! O dear! what a pity! unhappily! పాపము, వారుపడినారు alas! they fell down. ఆమె అక్కకు అన్నానికిలేదు పాపము her sister, alas! has nothing to eat. ఆ చిన్నవాణ్ని కొట్టకు పాపము

for shame! don't beat the boy. నువ్వు తెలిసినవాడవు పాపము you are a clever fellow, to be sure! వాడు నమ్మినాడు పాపము he believed it, alas! పాపము ఆ రూకలు అతడు చెల్లించినాడు to do him justice, he paid the money. పాపాత్ముడు, పాప పురుషుడు, పాపి or పాపిష్ఠుడు *pap-atmudu.* n. A sinner, wretch, villain. పాపాత్మురాలు a wicked woman, a sinful wretch. పాపి *papi.* interj. A vocative particle addressed to a woman or man. My dear! ఒరేపాపి my good fellow! పాపికా, ఓపాపిష్ఠురాలా O wicked woman. "కోపించి యారెండు కొంతి కిట్లనిరా, పాపికా బ్రమసితే! ప్రాణవల్లభుని మాపాడ నూడుతే కుంజుల్లనింక." BD. iii. 576. పాపిష్ఠి *papisthi.* adj. Horrid, scandalous, nefarious (a general term of disgust.) పాపిష్ఠుడు *papishthudu.* n. A great sinner, a miscreant. మిక్కిలిపాపి. పాపుడు *papudu.* n. A sinner. A cruel man, హింసకుడు. A wretch, అధముడు. Bhag. X.

పాపర *papara.* [Tel.] n. The bitter apple, or colocynth (*coloquintida*), చిరాలా, ఇంద్రవారుణి. Ainslie. i. 84. పాపరచెట్టు the bitter melon vine. కట్టెపాపర the shrub called the Self-planter, as the indentations on each leaf contain the seeds. పాపరచేప *papara-chēpa.* n. A sort of fish.

పాపాచి *papachi.* [H.] n. Prickly pear.

పాపు *papu.* [Tel. from పాయు.] v. a. To free from or deliver: to do away with or remove; to expiate or efface: to liquidate or pay, పాయుచేయు. To till, దున్ను. కల్మషముల బాపుట to do away with sin. "ఆత్మబిక్కు బాపునతడు." (M. XIII. iv. 371.) he who hath loosed the bonds of the soul. పాపుకొను *papu-konu.* v. a. To get rid of.

పాపోసు or పాయుపోసు *paposu.* [H.] n. A shoe. మెట్టు.

పాబోలము *pa-bolamu.* [Tel.] n. An old field, ప్రాతచేను.

పామ *pama.* [Skt.] n. A cutaneous eruption, herpes, scab or itch. గజ్జి. పామనుడు *pamanudu.* n. One who is scabby or itchy. గజ్జికలవాడు.

పామరము *pamaramu.* [Skt.] adj. Common or ordinary. Low, base, undignified, vulgar, stupid, senseless, illiterate. Lustful, cupidinous, avaricious. n. Nonsense, folly. దానిమీది పామరము వానికి ఇంకా వదల లేదు he has not yet ceased to dote on her. ద్రవ్యముమీది పామరము చెడ్డది it is miserable to have the heart set upon money. A sort of plant. నీర్లపామరము *Myriophyllum tetrandrum.* Rox. i. 451. పామరుడు *pamarudu.* n. A common or ignorant man, an illiterate man, అజ్ఞుడు. A wretch, a sinner. నీచుడు.

పాము *pamu.* [Tel.] n. A snake or serpent, సర్పము. An eel of any kind, called కల్లెం పాము, మలుగుపాము, చెమ్మేనిపాము, తవిటి పాము, కొమ్మురపాము and నక్కపాము Russell on Fishes, No. 31, 35, &c. నలికండ్లపాము the black dotted lizard. వాన పాములు maggots in rain water. పాములగద్ద *pamula-gadda.* n. A sort of heron. Jerd. Catal. No. 13. పాములనారిగాడు *pamula-nari-gadu.* n. The Common Heron, *Ardea cinerea*, or, the purple Heron, *Ardea purpurata.* (F. B. I.) పాముదొండ *pamu-donda.* n. A species of దొండ (q. v.). పాములవాడు *pamula-vadu.* n. A snake catcher or charmer. పామువేలు *pamu-vēlu.* n. A name for the middle finger.

పాము or ప్రాము *pamu.* [Tel.] v. a. To smear, rub, or wash, as a wall, &c. రాచు, రుద్దు. "పదముచేల చెట్టి పాముచుండ." K.H. v. 52.

పాయ *paya.* [Tel.] n. A clove or division of an onion or of garlick, రెబ్బ. The branch of a river. A piece, తునక. A tract or division of a country. Manner or mode. ఓడపాయ the wake of a vessel. మంచిపాయలో పడినాడు he has taken to good ways, వానిపాయవేరు నాపాయవేరు his way and mine are different. పాయగొమ్మ pāya-gomma. (పాయ+కొమ్మ.) n. A forked branch, కంగలకొమ్మ. పాయపడు or పాయపారు pāya-paḍu. v. n. To split, చీలు. To separate, to avoid, తొలగు. To move out of the way, దారివిడిచితొలగు. To be excommunicated, వెలిపడు.

పాయకట్టు pāya-kaṭṭu. [H.] n. A tract of land newly reclaimed from a jungle. A group of small villages that are connected with another important village. పాయకారీ pāya-kāri. n. A temporary or non-resident cultivator, a cultivator without hereditary interest in the soil. A sub-renter or under tenant, a tenant at will. A man who cultivates land lying in another village. పరస్థలపురయితు, భాగప్రకారము భూస్వాతంత్ర్యములేని రయితు.

పాయమాలీ or పాయిమాలి pāyamālī. [H.] n. Remission granted to a renter on account of the depredations of an enemy, cattle, &c.

పాయము pāyamu. [from Skt. ప్రాయము.] n. Age, వయస్సు. Youth, యౌవనము.

పాయలాకు pāyal-āku. [Tel.] n. A plant used in medicine.

పాయవట్టము See పాదవట్టము.

పాయసము or పాయసాన్నము pāyasamu. [Skt.] n. Rice and milk with sugar, rice pudding, పరమాన్నము.

పాయి pāyi. [Tel. singular of పాలు.] n. Milk. పాలు. Breastmilk, చాయి. [Skt.] n. One who drinks. త్రాగెడివాడు. A drunkard, తాగుబోతు.

పాయిఖానా pāyi-khāna. [H.] n. A privy or necessary, మరుగుకొట్టి.

పాయు pāyu. [Tel.] v. n To avoid. తొలగు. To be disentangled, చిక్కుడలు. To become rancid, as rice or butter, &c., పక్వపదార్థము మెత్తపడిచెడు. v. a. To quit, abandon, విడుచు.

పాయక pāyaka. adv. Constantly, without intermission. పాయగిలు or పాయగిల్లు pāyagilu. v. n. To avoid. తొలగు. పాయవారు pāya-vāru. v. n. To become rancid, పాచు.

పాయువు pāyuvu. [Skt.] n. The anus. గుదము.

పార pāra. [Tel.] n. A short hoe, a spade. త్రవ్వనట్టి సాధనము. పారమీను pāra-mīnu. n. A fish called 'Old wife,' resembling a pomfret. పారమ్ము or పారవాలి pārammu. (పార+అమ్ము) n. A broad-tipped arrow. "పారమ్మైదవాటిచట్లు పడెనతడుత్ర్వరన్." G. viii. 9. పారచేతి pāra-chēti. n. A large sort of fish with a big head, a grampus. పారపరిగె a kind of sprat.

పారంపర్యము pāram-paryamu. [Skt. from పరంపర.] n. Succession, order, series. క్రమము. పారంపర్యముగా అనుభవించేభూమి land that is enjoyed from father to son.

పారణ or పారణము pāraṇa. [Skt.] n. Eating after a fast, breaking a fast, ఉపవాసముండి మరునాడుచేయు భోజనము. Metaphorically used for eating. In Telugu it is applied to a peculiar sacrifice in honor of ancestors. అసతాం ధర్మబుద్ధిశ్చ కృతాం సంతాపకారణం, ఉపోషితస్యవ్యాఘ్రస్య పారణాపశుమారణం. "బవరిక తీరనిత్తపువ్వు పారణసేయుము మైత్రిగల్గినన్." A. vi. 63.

పారతంత్ర్యము pāra-tantryamu. [Skt. from పరతంత్రం.] n. Dependence. పరాధీనత.

పారదము or పారతము pāradamu. [Skt.] n. Quicksilver, పాదరసము.

పారమార్థికము pāram-ārthikamu. [Skt. from పరమార్థం.] n. Devotedness, loyalty, భక్తి. పారమార్థికుడు a devout man. భక్తిగలవాడు, పరమార్థబుద్ధిగలవాడు.

పారము pāramu. [Skt.] n. The further or opposite bank of a river, &c. అవలిదరి. The end or extremity. అంతము. Nearness, సమీపము. పారంగతుడు or పారగుడు pāran-gatuḍu. n. One who has crossed or gained the other shore, దరిచేరినవాడు. జ్యోతిషపారంగతుడై skilled in astrology. "కాముకుచేతంగాంచు కొంతచేయుంచి కడమ పారము ముట్టకయ్యుంబుసేయ వచ్చితివి." Sār. D. v.110. అపారము, లేక, పారములేని endless. పారావారము para-vāramu. n. The sea or ocean. సముద్రము.

పారలౌకికము pāra-laukikamu. [Skt. from పరలోకం.] adj. Pertaining to the other world. పరలోకసంబంధమైన. n. Rice and milk with sugar, పరమాన్నము.

పారవశ్యము para-vaşyamu. [Skt. from పరవశము.] n. Ecstasy, rapture. పరవశత్వము.

పారశీకము, పారసీకము or పారసికము pārasīkamu. [Persian.] n. Persia. A Persian horse. పారసీ parasi. n. The Farsee language. adj Pertaining to Persia, పారసీకదేశసంబంధమైన. "పారసీకల్లము" Swa. iv.

పారా pārā. [H.] n. Watching. కావలి. పారావాడు pāra-vāḍu. n. A guard, a sentry, కావలివాడు. పారాయిచ్చు pāra-y-iṭsṭsu. v. n. To stand sentry.

పారాణి pārāṇi. [Tel.] n. Turmeric mixed with chunam smeared by women on their feet at a wedding. Decorating the feet with saffron powder, &c. Red dye applied by women to the instep. పాదముల యందు కుంకుమాద్యలంకరణము. పారాణించు pārāṇintsu. v. a. To decorate the feet by reddening the instep.

పారాయణము pārāyaṇamu. [Skt. from పారము.] n. Whole, అంతయును. Going over, reading or doing any thing completely, అంతయు చదువడము. Reading a Purana, or holy book at daily lessons. వేదపారాయణము the recital of the Vedas. అతడు నిత్యము రామాయణపారాయణము చేయుచున్నాడు he reads the Ramayaṇam daily in regular lessons.

పారావతము pārāvatamu. [Skt.] n. A dove or pigeon. పావురము.

పారాశరి pārāṣari. [Skt. from పరాశర.] n. A name of the poet Vyasa. Also, a monk, సన్యాసి.

పారి pāri. [Tel.] n. Time, season. ఒకపారి once. మరియొకపారి once again. Earth, మన్ను. [Skt.] n. A pail. పాలుపితికేకుండ, గిండి, కడవముంత.

పారిక pārika. [Tel.] n. A maid servant, a slave. పారికాపు pāri-kāpu. n. An attendant, a servant, పరిచరుడు.

పారిజాతము pāri-jātamu. [Skt.] n. Amaranth. The Coral tree, *Erythrina fulgens*. పగడమల్లె. Also, the *Mimusops elengi*. One of the trees in Paradise. కల్పవృక్షము పారిజాతాపహరణము pārijāt-apaharaṇamu. n. The "Rape of the Amaranth." This is the title of a popular poem.

పారితథ్య pāri-tathya. [Skt.] n. A trinket worn on the back of the head. రాగిడి, జడబిళ్ల, చిగపువ్వు, కొప్పున అలంకారార్థమైపెట్టే సువర్ణాది రచితమైన వలయము.

పారితోషికము pāri-tōṣhikamu. [Skt.] n. An honorary gift, a donation. కానుకనము, బహుమానము. A. iv. 3. and iv. 274.

పారిభద్రము pāri-bhadramu. [Skt.] n. A tree called the Coral tree. దేవదారువృ. (The name is given to some other trees.)

పారిభావ్యము pāri-bhāvyamu. [Skt.] n. A plant or tree called చెంగల్వకోష్టు.

పారిమాండిల్యము pāri-māṇḍilyamu. [Skt.] n. An atom invisibly small.

పారివాడు or పారికాపు pāri-vāḍu. [Tel.] n. A servant. పరిచరుడు.

పారిహార్యము pāri-hāryamu. [Skt. from పరిహారము.] n. A bracelet worn by women. కాంకణము. పారిహారికుడు pāri-hārikuḍu. n. A flower-boy, a maker of garlands. పుష్పలావికుడు.

పారీంద్రము pār-īndramu. [Skt.] n. A lion. సింహము. N. ix. 60.

పారిఖత్తు pāri-khattu. [H.] n. An acquittance, a deed of release from all demands; a deed of dissolution of partnership. A bill of divorcement. A receipt, acquittance or release. విభాగపత్రము, అన్నికగాదాలును తీర్చుకొనినట్లు వ్రాసికొన్నచీటి.

పారీణత pārīṇata. [Skt. from పారము.] n. Complete knowledge, expertness. పారీణుడు Same as పారంగతుడు. (See under పారము.) సకలశాస్త్రపారీణుడు he who has thoroughly mastered all the sciences.

పారు pāru. [Tel.] v. n. To run or run away. పరుగెత్తు, పారిపోవు. To purge, పాడేసుకొను, పారుకొను. To fly or rise in the air, ఎగురు. To flow as water, ప్రవహించు. To creep or crawl, పాకు. To grow, or become. To take effect, as a spell or medicine. To begin. n. A ledge of rock, a flat rock under earth. మడుగులు చొరబారు మహిష సంఘంబులు the buffaloes were rushing to enter the pools. కుక్కను కొట్టితే యిల్లంతా పారును if you beat the dog it will befoul the house. ఈ యెండలో పారే పక్షులు మిడిసిపడి చచ్చును in this heat birds on the wing fall down dead. ఆ తోటకు ఈ నీళ్లు పారవు this water does not reach that garden. నీళ్లుపారనియేరు the river which has ceased to flow. నేలబారే నల్లచీమ a black ant that crawls on the earth. నాలుక నల్లబారినది the tongue turned black. నా మంత్రము పారలేదు my spell did not take effect. ఆకులు పండబారుచున్నవి the leaves are turning yellow. అతనిమీద నా దృష్టి పారినప్పుడు when my eye lighted on him. ఆరాతిమీద నీడ పారినప్పుడు when the shadow fell on that stone. వాని మనసు దానిమీద పారుచున్నది his thoughts run or are bent on her. అది పగుళ్లుపారుచున్నది it is splitting. ఎండబారుచున్నది it is beginning to dry up. గడుసుపారు to grow hard. బిగుసుపారు to grow stiff "అట్లు తన చేత పాలితేషులైన జనుల భారగమగాని రథ మెక్కి చటులరయమున." M. X. i. 198. పారచల్లు para-challu. v. a. To sprinkle, or scatter abroad. పారజాచు para-dzātsu. v. a. To extend, as the arms or legs. కాళ్లుపారజాచు to open or straddle the legs. పారజూచు para-dzūtsu. v. a. To look through, go over, view, examine well, వింతవారువేరుకగా యెంచు సదనంబు పారజూచి." T. iii. 128. పారదోలు para-dōlu. v. a. To drive out or away, to defeat, తరుము. పారబట్టు para-baṭṭu. v. a. To winnow in the wind, to let down grain against the wind. ధనధాన్యంబుల పారబట్టినవాడు, అనగా పాపుభీతిని తూలాయమానము చేసినవాడు. L. ii. 29. and ii. 1. పారబోత para-bōta. n. The act of pouring out or throwing away. పారబోయుట. పారబోయు para-bōyu. v. a. To pour away, to pour off, or empty out. కుమ్మరించు. పారమి pāramu. [negative verbal noun from పారు.] n. The act of not flowing or running. ప్రవహించకపోవుట, పరుగెత్తకపోవుట. "పర కించని చెప్పాల్లి పారమిచెప్పి." BD. iv. 1825. అనగా దినములు సుఖముగా జరుగకుండుకు విసికి. పారవేయు or పారవైచు para-vēyu. v. a. To fling or throw away, to lose, విసిరివేయు, వదలివిడుచు, జారవిడుచు. పారాడు pār-āḍu. (పారు+ఆడు.) v. n. To creep or crawl. పారిపోవు pāri-pōvu. v. n. To run away, escape. పారుకాడు paruk-āḍu. (పారుక+ఆడు.) v. n. To run, పరుగెత్తు. To creep, to roam, to ramble. "పారాడతము కొంత బడి పిదులందు పారుకాడెడి ప్కురుహంబు లనగ." Sar. D. 615. పారుటక్క or పారుత pāru-ṭ-akka. n. A Brahmin woman. A. 452. బ్రాహ్మణస్త్రీ. పారుటసురుడు pāru-ṭ-asuruḍu. n. A demon who was formerly a Brahmin, బ్రహ్మరాక్షసుడు. A. v. i. 57. పారుటాకులు pāru-ṭ-ākulu. n. Autumnal leaves. Leaves, which have got a red tinge but are not withered. (This is the clothing of hermits.) "మంచెలమీద నెక్కి కటమువలిచిట్టిన పారుటాకులిం, చిం దుకిచంచలించి." Kalahas. iii. 12. **పారుడు** *paruḍu*. (పారు+వాడు.) n. A Brahmin. బ్రాహ్మణుడు. M. XII. iii. 460. A motion of the bowels, పారే నము. The act of flowing, ప్రవహించుట. A stream, ప్రవాహము. **పారుతెంచు** or **పారైతెంచు** *parutentsu*. v. n. To come running, పరుగెత్తివచ్చు. "నచ్చిరాహవ మొనరం పవారిలోన పడితిరొక్కతె మున్నాడి పారు తెంచి." Jaimini. v. 725. **పారుబోతు** or **పారుమోతు** *paru-bōtu*. n. A fugitive, a coward. పిరికివాడు. **పారువేట** *paru-reṭa*. n. The chase, game that is hunted. A festival, దేవోత్సవము.

పారుపత్తెము or **పార్పత్తెము** *paru-pattemu*. [Tel.] n. The duty or office of a manager or superintendent of a village or temple. Authority, అధికారము. **పారుపత్తి** or **పారుపత్తెకాడు** *paru-patti*. n. The officer in charge of a village or temple. A man in authority. అధికారి.

పారువ *parura*. [Tel.] n. Sight, a glance. A trace, జాడ. అతనికి పారువమట్టు he has not good eyes. అతనికి గరుడపారువ lit. he has an eagle's glance; (used to mean) he has habitually a side glance. గరుడపారువ a spell to remove the venom of a snake. "విషదష్టమైనందువల్ల చనిపోయినాడని తెలిసి గరుడపారువమొదలైన అనేక మణి మంత్ర ఔషధములచేతను..." Local Records. iii. 205. ఇది పారువరోగము this is a disease brought on by magic. "పారువపట్టినేమొ" ఉ. రా. vi. A certain attitude in dancing, ఆటలో నొకరీతి. "పాదిపారువ, హస్తపారువ, దేహపారువ, నయనపారువ, భ్రూంగిపటలము, ఝంపుచెక్కు, కరలాఘవంబులాదియౌ రీతులు నేర్చి." H. i. 247.

పారువము or **పార్వము** *paruramu*. [Tel.] n. A dove. పారావతము "పారువముపొసంగు పోయిన... " సా. ii.

పారుష్యము *parushyamu*. [Skt. from పరుషము.] n. Harshness, roughness. కాఠిన్యము, పరుషవచనము, పరుషత్వము. దండపారుష్యము personal violence. వాక్పారుష్యము violent language.

పార్టీ *parṭi*. [Eng. 'party.'] n. A faction ఇది నిండా పార్టీలగ్రామము this is a most factious village.

పార్థసారథి *partha-sarathi*. [Skt.] n. An epithet of Krishṇa as the charioteer of Arjuna (పార్థుడు).

పార్థివ *parthiva*. [Skt.] n. The name of a Telugu year.

పార్థివుడు *parthivuḍu*. [Skt. from పృథివి.] A king. పృథివీశుడు. **పార్థుడు** *parthuḍu*. n. A king, రాజు. Also, a name of Arjuna.

పార్వణము *parvaṇamu*. [Skt. from పర్వము.] n. A certain funeral rite. పితృదేవతలకొరకు నిచ్చేపిండము, పిండప్రదానము. పార్వణపుముద్దలు the funeral cakes.

పార్వతి *parvati*. [Skt. from పర్వతము.] n. Parvati, the wife of Siva. పార్వతీనందనుడు. the son of Parvati, i.e., Kumarasawmi.

పార్శ్వము *parṣvamu*. [Skt.] n. A side, a part. ప్రక్క.

పార్ష్ణి *parshṇi*. [Skt.] n. The heel. కాలిమడమ. The rear of an army, దండువెనుక, సైన్యపృష్ఠము. The back, వీపు. A violent woman, ధ్వజినీ, ఉన్మత్తనారీ. S. iii. 282. **పార్ష్ణిగ్రాహుడు** *parshṇi-grahuḍu*. n. An enemy behind an invading king. **పార్ష్ణిత్రము** *parshṇitramu*. n. The vanguard of an army, ముందటనుండి రక్షించుసేన.

పాల *pala*. [Tel. from పాలు milk.] n. The bird called the Indian Roller, *boracias indica* (F. B. I.), the flight of which is consulted as an omen. It is erroneously called a blue jay. Various varieties are called గోరపాలపిట్ట and మేకపాలపిట్ట.

See Jerdon No. 243. A treatise on Omens says. "పాలగరుడతిప్ప పక్షిజాతులకెల్ల కెడమునుండికుడికి కెగయువలయు." పాల or పాలతీగ n. A certain tree, ఇక్షుగంధ, క్షీరకాష్ఠవృక్షము; of which there are various species as, అడవిపాలతీగ *Nerium reticulatum*, కాకిపాలతీగ *Asclepias asthmatica*, దూడిపాలతీగ *Asclepias volubilis*, మట్టపాలతీగ *Convolvulus paniculatus*; చిరుపాల, అనగా ఉటని. Q. మున్నుపాల, అనగా ఉత్పల కృష్ణ. Q. పాలపందు, అనగా కపిష్ట. Q. Various species of the "milk plant" are called ఏనుపాలతీగ, కుక్కపాలతీగ, &c. పాల adj. White. పాలవెండి pure silver. పాలకన్ను *pala-kannu*. n. A sort of grain. పాలకూర *pala-kūra*. n. A certain pot herb. *Oxystelma esculentum*. కుక్కపాలకూర a forest plant, *Trianthema crystallina*. Rox. ii. 444. పాలగచ్చు, పాలగార or పాలసున్నము *pala-gatstsu*. n. Fine lime plaster. సన్న సున్నపుపూత. పాలబుగ్గలు (S. iii. 435.) Infant's cheeks, బిడ్డలచెక్కిళ్లు. పాలగరువు or పాలగార *pala-garuvu*. n. A sort of earth, a whitish marl. తెల్లని యుసుకగల తడినేల. పాలగుమ్మ Same as పాలబిట్ట. పాలగొర్రు *pala-gorru*. n. A rake used in husbandry. పాలగోకుడు *pala-gokuḍu*. n. The butter that sticks to the bottom of a milk pot. పాలచెట్టు *pala-cheṭṭu*. n. A species of the *Mimusops* tree. పాలచేప *pala-chēpa*. n. A sort of Salmon. పాలచేరులు or పాలచేర్లు *pala-chērulu*. n. The nerves. దేహములకు పెనగుండునరాలు, గన్నరాలు. "సీ॥ పాలచేరులుపట్టి తూలింప బలిమి నీచ్ఛుకొని డొంకలదూరి చుట్టబెట్టు." Swa. iv. 68. "సీ॥ కటికి నెత్తురులతో గండలుర్లిపడంగ, శేరి వందులపాలచేర్లుకరచు." S. i. 202. పాలటేకు or పాలటేకు *pala-ṭēku*. n. The white wooded teak tree. పాలడ *palaḍa*. (పాలు+అడుగు.) n. A shell used as a spoon or ladle in giving milk to a child. పాలతుత్తము or పాలతుత్తరము *pala-tuttamu*. n. White vitriol. పాలపండ్లు *pala-pandlu*. n. Milk teeth. Also (from పండు,) a sort of sweet white berries. A. iv. 114. పాలపాపడు *pala-papaḍu*. n. An infant at the breast. పాలపెడిస or పాలపరిస *palapedisa*. n. The Grey-headed Myna, *Sturnia malabarica* (F. B. I.) పాలబొంత *palabonta*. n. A fish called the white mullet, *Chanos salmoneus*. పాలమన్ను *pala-mannu*. n. White earth, pipe clay సుద్ద. పాలమానిచెక్క *pala-manichekka*. n. The 'white wood' produced by the పాలటేకు. పాలసుగంధి *pala-sugandhi*. n. A plant called Country Sarasaparilla. పాలసున్నము *pala-sunnamu*. n. Fine lime plaster, సున్నము. పాలసొర or పాలసూర *pala-sora*. n. A fish, *Carcharias laticaudus* and also *Carcharias ellioti* or *Carcharias macloti*. సొరచేప (F. B. I.) The white shark. సముద్రమందు మనుష్యులను భక్షించే పెద్ద చేప. పాలాకు *pal-aku*. n. A certain herb. చిటిపాలాకు is one sort. పాలానుగు *pal-anugu*. n. The white gourd, అనపతీగ, బూడిదగుమ్మడి. See పాలు.

పాల *pala*. [Tel. ablative of పాలు, a side, a part.] adv. On behalf of. మాపాలగలడు దేవుడు God is on our side. See పాలు a snare.

పాలకీ or పల్లకీ *palaki*. [H.] n. A palanquin.

పాలలము *palalamu*. [Tel.] n. A certain creeping plant.

పాలసుడు *palasuḍu*. [Tel.] n. A wretch, a fool. పలువ, మూర్ఖుడు. పాలసురాలు *palasu-r-alu*. n. The feminine of పాలసుడు.

పాలాడు See under పాలు.

పాలాశము *palāśamu*. [Skt. from పలాశ.] adj. Belonging to the tree called పలాశము, i.e., the *Butea frondosa* (మోదుగు), the leaves of which are proverbial for brightness of deep green, and the flowers for a scarlet hue. Green. పాలాశకుసుమవర్ణము red colour.

పాలాసత్రాళ్లు *palasa-trallu.* [Tel.] A horse's leg ropes.

పాలి or పాలిటి *pali.* [Tel. from పాలు a part or share.] adj. Connected with, appertaining to Near. పాలికాపు or పాలివాడు a comrade, a partner. భాగస్థుడు. n. A partner, proprietor or share-holder. A farm-servant. నాపాలిదైవము my tutelary god. వారిపాలి మృత్యువు the death that was doomed them. వారిపాలికేగె he went up to them. ఈ పాలిభాగ్యదేవత అని లోనికి కొంచు పోయె he looked upon the guest as a God and took him in. Vish. P. iv. 222.

పాలించు *palintsu.* [Skt.] v. a. To nourish, cherish, foster, protect. To rule, govern. పోషించు, రక్షించు, ఏలు, కాపాడు. పాలిక *palika.* n. An earthen vessel containing mould in which nine sorts of seed are sown, in accordance with a rite in Hindu weddings. పాలికలు ఓలలాడుదురు the bridesmaids perform a certain ceremony, as the conclusion of the wedding. పాలితము *palitamu.* adj. Protected, cherished, nourished. పాలిని *palini.* n. She who protects or rules. పాలించునది. పాలకుడు *palakudu.* n A guardian, protector. రక్షకుడు. పాలనము *palanamu.* n. Preserving, guarding, cherishing: government. రక్షణము. అలక్ష పాలన caring, heeding, regard.

పాలు *palu.* [Tel.] n. A share or portion. భాగము, వంతు. Possession, charge, వశము. infl. పాలి, or పాలిటి; local ablative పాల or పాలిటి. plu. పాళ్లు. నాయౌవను నీపాలుచేసినాను I yielded up my youth to thee. అతని పాలికి వచ్చినది యిది this is what fell to his share. నీపాలిదైవము or నీపాలిటిదైవము your good angel, your tutelary God. వాడు నాపాలిటికి యముడు he has been a curse to me. తేనులుపండి కాకులపాలైనవి a proverb regarding the wealth of a prodigal. పరుల పాలైన given up to others or sacrificed. దొంగలపాలైన abandoned to thieves. నవ్వుల పాలుకావచ్చు to become a prey to ridicule, to become a laughing stock. అప్పుల పాలయినాడు he has fallen into debt. పాల బాన or పాలుబాన *pala-bana.* n. The ryot's share of the crop, ఉద్యమంలో అంబారములో కాపులకు చేరే వ్యవసాయభాగము. "కృషిచేసి వ్యవసాయం, మున్నిర్మించి, వివాదమునిచ్చాటు, సగ్గిల్లినంపు, పాలుబాన, ఆ అరుగు, ఇవి వృత్తులు." Miscell. iii. 430.

పాల్అడు *pal-adu.* v.a. To divide into shares. To cut, to sever, to separate, ఖండించు. పాలారుచు or పాలార్చు *pala-rutsu.* (పాలు+అరుచు.) v. a. To disregard, to neglect, ఉపేక్షించు. భా. iii పాలుచేయు *palu-cheyu.* v. a. To hand over, give over to, deliver, sacrifice. నన్ను అప్పులపాలుచేసినాడు he plunged me in debt. పాలుపడు or పాల్పడు *palupadu.* v.n. To undertake, to enter upon, to share, to engage in. పూనుకొను, పైనవేసికొను. To be subject to, స్వాధీనమగు. "వివిధచేష్టలకు పాలుపడి." B.X. §. 30. పాలుపుచ్చు or పాలుపెట్టు *palu-putsu.* v. a. To deduct or subtract: to divide or separate, విభాగించు. To decide or settle, నిర్ణయించు. శోకపాలుకాలేను I cannot endure being a prey to grief. పాలగలవాడు a co-heir, a cousin, దాయాదివాడు. "పాలు గలవాడు మా కొరకు కాలియుడక, తానె తానె పానకు వచ్చెన్." A. iii. 39. పాలుపోవు *palu-povu.* v.n. To be divided or shared. విభక్తమగు. To be decided, నిర్ణీతమగు. ఒకరికిని పాలుపోక ఆ పనిని అట్టె పని వేసిపెట్టినారు no one undertook the work, so it was left undone. అది యెటు వ్రాయడానకు పాలుపోక విడిచినాను unable to decide how to write the passage, I omitted it. పాలుభోగగ్రామము *palu-bhoga-gramamu.* n. A village wherein each field is held as one man's separate property.

పాలు *palu.* [Tel.] n. Milk. Milky juice or sap. చనుపాలు or చన్నుపాలు woman's milk, human milk. ఆకుపాలు the juice of the sugar cane. టెంకాయపాలు the white juice expressed from the cocoanut kernel by pounding. (టెంకాయనీళ్లు is the water in the cocoanut.) మర్రిపాలు the milky juice of the banyan tree. పాలవంటివారు, పాల వంటి మనుష్యులు men (or a tribe) like milk, i.e., candid, simple, pure, unspotted, blameless, honourable. పాలవంటి మనసు a pure mind, a simple heart. పాలుగారేముఖము a milk-distilling face, i.e., a face radiant with loveliness. పాల్గారు చెక్కుటద్దములు radiantly polished cheeks, beaming with beauty. పాలకడలి, పాల్కడలి, పాలకుప్ప, పాలమున్నీరు, పాలవాగు or పాలవెల్లి *pala-kadali*. n. The Ocean of milk. క్షీరాబ్ధి. పాలమున్నీటికూతురు Lakshmi. పాలమున్నీటి అల్లుడు Vishṇu. పాలకాయ *pala-kaya*. n A sort of biscuit, భక్ష్య విశేషము. పాలకుండ *pala-kunda*. n. The milk pot, a certain fee claimed by various hangers on on every crop of grain. పాలవన్నె *pala-vanne*. adj. Milky white, whitish, pale. పాటలవర్ణము. పాలవెల్లి *pala-velli*. n. The sea of milk. పాలసముద్రము. The decorated booth or shrine erected in houses for the worship of an idol at certain feasts. పాలావు *pal-avu*. n. A milch cow. పాలుచాలాయిచ్చే ఆవు. పాలిండ్లు *pal-indlu*. [from పాలు milk and ఇల్లు a home.] n. A woman's breasts. పాలేరు *pal-eru*. (పాలు+ఏరు.) n. The river or sea of milk. పాల కడలి. A river in South India, the Palar.

పాలు *palu*. [Tel.] v. n. To be pallid or turn pale. తెల్లనగు, రోగముచేత తెల్లబారు. ఒళ్లుపాలినది the natural complexion faded.

పాలుమాలు, పాల్మాలు ప్రాలుమాలు or ప్రాల్మాలు *palu-malu*. [Tel. from పాలు a share, మాలు to be without, to go without.] v.n. To fail, neglect, slacken in exertion. To be listless or reluctant, బద్ధకించు. To be unwell, out of sorts. To procrastinate or put off for the present.

పాలుమాలిక or పాల్మాలిక *palu-malika*. n. Heaviness, laziness. Listlessness, putting off the evil day, imbecility, want of energy, ill-health. బద్ధకము, కష్టాలస్యము. నాకు దేహము చాలా పాలుమాలికగా నున్నది నేను ఎట్లు వత్తును? I am so heavy or indisposed that I cannot come.

పాలె *pale*. [Tel.] n. A button or round plate of metal. పాలెలమొలతాడు a zone formed of such pieces. See పాళెము.

పాలెము, పాళెము or పాళయము *palemu*. [Tel.] n. Watching or guarding. కావలి. A town ruled by a Poligar or petty baron, పాళెగాని ఊరు. A hamlet, a small village, పల్లె, చిన్నగ్రామము. An army, a force, troops, దండు. A camping ground, దండువిడియుచోటు. Encamping, halting. A barony or county under a petty chief. పాలెమున్నవారు soldiers in garrison. "మెలకువచేని కోటములుకదాటి పాలెమున్న వారిపై కొల్లబూడిదెముక్కజల్లి, పెద్దమగలు గొంతకులద్రవ్వి." G. 120. "వ్యాగయావిహార ముల్ చేసవలిర్ప జేయుటకుశీఘ్రుమపాళియమెత్తి." Kalahas. iii. 71. పాలెగాడు or పాళెగాడు *pale-gadu*. n. A feudal retainer, a petty chieftain called a Poligar. పాళెపట్టు *pale-pattu*. n. Feudal tenure in fee. Villages held by petty chiefs free of assessment. పాళెముపట్టు *palemu-pattu*. n. An encampment. దండువిడిసినస్థలము. A polygar's estate, పాళెగాని రాజ్యము.

పాలేరు *paleru*. [Tel. పాలు+ఏరు.] n. An under tenant, who holds land in fee. An under farmer, a sub-renter, పాయకారీ ధనికిందనుండి దున్ని ఫలపరుమవాడు. A hired cultivator or labourer. పాలేరుతనము *paleru-tanamu*. n. The state of being an under tenant. Vassalage.

పాళ *pala*. [Tel.] n. The husk or outer coat of a bud, as of that a cocoanut. Parij. iv. 18.

పాళము pāḷamu. [Tel.] n. A manner or method. విధము. Season, time. సమయము, A lump, ingot, or mass of metal. కడ్డి. Extent, కొలది. బిడ్డ ఆకలిపాళ మెరిగి guessing when the child would be hungry. ఆ పాళవువారు men of that class. గరిటెపాళముగా as much as a spoonful. ఒక పాళముగా నుండేయిల్లు a moderate sized house. అతడు వచ్చే పాళముగానున్నది it looks as if he will come. పాళా pāḷa. n. An ingot or bar of metal. కడ్డీ. పాళాపుజొన్న pāḷapu-ḍzonna. n. A species of millet (జొన్న), which is of slow growth and has a large head.

పాళి pāḷi. [Skt.] n. A dice board. జూదమాడే పలక. The sharp edge of a sword or cutting instrument, ఆయుధధార. The lobe of the ear, చెవితమ్మె. A line or row, వృక్షాదిపఙ్క్తి. కర్ణపాళి the tip of the ear. ఖడ్గపాళి the edge of the sword. కపోలపాళి the temples of the head. కలముయొక్కపాళి the point of the pen. This word is often omitted in translation, as జఘనపాళి the haunches. పాళిక pāḷika. n. The lobe of the ear. A quantity. సముదాయము. "కమలధూళిపాళికా కలికలితోక్కు." R. i. 162. పాళి or పాలి pāḷi. [Tel.] n. The slit of a pen. A chess table, or cloth marked with squares. జూదమాడేపలక. Dice-play or gambling. జూదము. A slave. A furrow. An assemblage. సమూహము, సముదాయము.

పాళెము See పాలెము.

పావ or పాగ pāva. [Tel.] n. A sandal, a wooden shoe, పావకోడు. పావలు, పాగలు, పావాలు or పాగాలు sandals. పావకోడు pāva-kōḍu. n. A sandal. పాదుక. Plu. పావకోళ్లు.

పావంచ or పావటే pāvancha. [Tel.] n. A stair, a step, సోపానము, మెట్టు. Plu. పావటీలు steps, మెట్లు.

పావకుడు pāvakuḍu. [Skt.] n. Lit: "He who purifies." పవిత్రము చేసేవాడు. An epithet of Fire: అగ్నిహోత్రుడు.

పావడ pāvaḍa. [Tel.] n. A petticoat, a slip worn under a gown, లంగా. A white cloth, ధౌతవస్త్రము. A cloth, వస్త్రము.

పావడము pāvaḍamu. [Tel.] n. A present, gift. కానుక.

పావనము pāvanamu. [Skt.] adj. Pure, clean, purifying, holy. పవిత్రము. నేడు సుదినము నా జన్మము పావనమాయెను this happy day blots out all my sins: (a common phrase of joy). పరముకన్న నేమి పావనమౌసొమ్ము is wealth any object in comparison with heaven? పరమపావనీ O most holy One! పావనముచేయు to purify. ఆయన ఈ రాజ్యమును పావనముచేసెను he reformed this realm. n. Penance, purification. ప్రాయశ్చిత్తము. Water. జలము. A vow, వ్రతము. "పావనశయవారిజాతముల ధన్యగణార్చ్యలొసర్చు నిత్య ముగా." Chenn. v. 264. పావనశయముగా, జలాశయము. పావని pāvani. [from పవనము, wind.] n. A name of Hanuman or Bhima. R. vi. 67. A pure or holy woman, పవిత్రురాలు. పావనుడు pāvanuḍu. n. The purifier: an epithet of Agni, the god of fire. పరమపావనుడు the all-holy one.

పావాడము Same as పవాడము (q. v.).

పావి pāvi. [from Skt. పాపి.] n. A sinner, పాపి.

పావిలి or పావలి pāvili. [Tel.] n. The herb called the Thick-leaved Sorrel. Its species are బంకపావిలి, *Portulacca crystallina*, Rox. ii. 464. and బుడ్డపావిలి *Trianthema monogyna*, (Heyne). Also గొడ్డుపావిలి, ఫుల్లపావిలి, పెద్దపావిలి, సన్నపావిలి, కుక్కపావిలి and బొడ్డుపావిలి.

పావు pāvu. [H.] n. A quarter. ముప్పావు three fourths. పావులా a quarter of a rupee, a four anna piece.

పావుకోడు Same as పావ (q. v.).

పావురము, పావురా or పావురాయి pāvuramu. [Tel.] n. A pigeon. కల్లపావురము the Indian Blue Rock Pigeon, *Columba intermedia.* పచ్చపావురము the Green Pigeon, *Crocopus Chlorogaster.* (F. B. I.) పావురపలుకు pāvura-paluku. n. Cooing, the cry of a pigeon.

పావులూరు pāvul-ūru. [Tel.] n. The name of a village. The పావులూరిగణితము (as we say the Eton grammar) is a well-known system of Arithmetic, mensuration and geometry written by మల్లన.

పాశము pāsamu. [Skt.] n. A cord, తాడు. Metaphorically, a check, a tie, a bond or instrument of curbing. A multitude. సమూహము. కేశపాశము much (or flowing) hair. ధర్మపాశము the ties of rectitude. పాపపాశము the bond of iniquity. ఛత్రపాశము a shabby umbrella, a mere stick of an umbrella, an apology for an umbrella. కర్ణపాశము a strikingly beautiful ear. మృత్యుపాశములు the bonds of death. పాశాష్టకము the eight ties: i.e., the attachment a man has to his wife, child, wealth, cattle, conveyance, land, house and friend. పాశముక్తుడు freed from all earthly ties.

పాశుపతము pāsu-patamu. [Skt. from పశుపతి.] adj. Appertaining to Siva. పాశుపతమతము pāsupata-matamu. n. A name of the Vira Saiva creed. పాశుపతము or పాశుపతాస్త్రము pāsu-patamu. n. A sort of arrow. శైవాస్త్రము.

పాశుపాల్యము pāsu-palyamu. [Skt. from పశుపాలనము.] n. The business of a grazier, rearing and keeping cattle. గవాద్యవిరక్షణము, గొల్లవృత్తి.

పాశ్చాత్య pāschātya. [Skt.] adj. Western. పాశ్చాత్యుడు a westerner, పడమటివాడు.

పాషండము pāshandamu. [Skt.] n. Heresy, heterodoxy. పాషండుడు or పాషండి pāshandudu. n. A heretic, schismatic, unbeliever, blasphemer, freethinker, or heterodox Hindu. వేదబాహ్యుడు. శివపాషండులు the intolerant sect of Saivites, or Jangams. విష్ణుపాషండులు bigoted worshippers of Vishṇu. In the అష్టాదశస్తోత్రరత్నము is this verse, "నాస్తిక, మ్లేచ్ఛ, పాషండ, బౌద్ధ, ప్రాకృత, దుర్జనం" the atheist, the foreigner, the heretic, the Buddhist, the base man and the evil-doer.

పాషాణము pāshāṇamu. [Skt.] n. A stone. (In Telugu), Poison. నా భోజనములో పాషాణము వేయుదువా do you wish to throw a stone (or poison) into my food? శంఖుపాషాణము or తెల్లపాషాణము white arsenic, *Arsenicum album*, (Watts.) There are four drugs known in the shops by these names: తెల్లిపాషాణము corrosive sublimate, వెల్లిపాషాణము, దొడ్డిపాషాణము and గౌరీపాషాణము. పాషాణత్వము pāshāṇatvamu. n. Stoneness, the being a stone. పాషాణదారణము pāshāṇa-dāraṇamu. n. A stone chisel, రాతి ఉలి. పాషాణభేది pāshāṇa-bhēdi. n. A stone cutter, a hewer of stone. "అప్పుడు పాషాణభేదులకిచ్చి, శిలి నాక దేవళంబుగట్టించిరి వుడు." H. i. 208.

పాసంగు pāsangu. [Tel.] n. A kind of good rice. శాలిధాన్యవిశేషము. ళీ. ii.

పాసనము Same as పాతేనము (q.v.).

పాసీగర్లు pāsi-garlu. [Tel.] n. Thugs or professional murderers.

పాసు pāsu. [Tel.] n. Nastiness, filth, foulness. పాచి.

పాసెము pāsemu. [Tel. Corruption of పాయసము.] n. Rice-milk with sugar. పరమాన్నము. "పాసెంబడిగినవారలె దీడలె." A. v. 60.

పాహి pāhi. [Skt.] interj. Save! save us! look upon us mercifully.

పి pi

పింగ *pinga.* [Skt.] n. Oxgall. గోరోజనము. adj. Of the color of oxgall. గోరోజనపు రంగుగల.

పింగటించు *pingatintsu.* [Tel.] v. n. To brag, to give oneself airs.

పింగలి *pingali.* [Skt.] adj. Being behind, following. వెనుకటి. వెనుకట్రియు. నిఘ. vi.

పింగళ *pingala.* [Skt.] n. The name of a Telugu year.

పింగళము *pingalamu.* [Skt.] adj. Brown, swarthy, tawny, red like a lion, or of the colour of honey, the colour of the mongoose or ichneumon. గోరోజనవర్ణము, నీలపీతమిశ్రితవర్ణము. **పింగళాక్షి** *pingal-akshi.* adj. Fiery eyed, red eyed. **పింగళనాడి** *pingala-nadi.* n. An anatomical phrase, used in the Yoga school of philosophy, for a particular vessel of the body, which runs from the os coccygis to the head, and which is the chief passage of breath and air. See సుషుమ్న.

పింగాణి *pingani.* [Mahrati పింగాణి, a butterfly or moth.] n. A china plate, so called because it is sometimes painted with figures of these insects. **పింగాణులు** or **పింగాణిసామాను** *pinganulu.* n. Crockery. "గాజుపింగాణి." రుక్మా. iv.

పించను *pinchanu.* [Eng.] n. Pension.

పించెము or **పించియము** [from Skt. పింఛము.] Same as పింఛము (q. v.).

పించెము *pintsamu.* [Tel.] n. Nerve, manliness, bravery, vigour, pride. మదము. **పించెమణచు** *pintsam-anatsu.* v. a. To crush one's pride, to humble. To kill. చంపు, ఉద్రేకమణచు.

పించుసేయు *pintsu-seyu.* [Tel.] v. a. To scatter, shiver, destroy. ఛిన్నాభిన్నము చేయు. "బిరుదులుగలవారున్న పిండుపించముసేయ, బలితంపు సేర్పులచ్చెరువు వెనుప." M. IX. i. 137. అనగా శూరులయిన సేనాధిపతులను పేర్చిన దండును ఛిన్నాభిన్నము చేయడానకు విశేషమయిన చాతుర్యములు ఆశ్చర్యమును కలుగజేయగా.

పింఛము *pinchhamu.* [Skt.] n. A peacock's tail. నెమలిపురి.

పింజ *pinja.* [Skt.] n. Cotton. దూది. **పింజము** *pinjamu.* n. Strength. బలము. **పింజనము** *pinjanamu.* n. A cotton cleaning instrument. దూదేకువిల్లు. **పింజిక** n. A roll of cotton, దూదిచుట్ట.

పింజరము *pinjaramu.* [Skt.] n. Tawny yellow color. ఎరుపుమించిన పసుపురంగు. adj. Tawny or reddish yellow. "పింజరీభూత మంజరీపుంజ." R. i. 176.

పింజె *pinje.* [Tel.] n. The tuck in front of a Hindu's dress. ముడతలుపెట్టిదోపే చట్టచెంగు. "తడియూరకూరకుండెడుపాటిదోపిబిగ్గి తేమను పింజెలు పెట్టికట్టి." S. ii. 520. "కాసె దోపితి పింజెగట్టి మిగాళ్లపైనొరసి జీరాడంగ." Surabha. 58. **పింజించు** *pinjintsu.* v. a. To tuck up, as cloth into folds, పింజెలు పోయు. To scatter, as water, నీళ్లు చింద చిలుపోయు. పింజనగ్రోవి a syringe, చిమ్మనగ్రోవి.

పింజె *pindza.* [Tel.] n. The feather part of an arrow. బాణపుంఖము. Also, same as పింజనము (q. v.). **పింజారి** or **పింజారి** *pindzari.* [H.] n. A cotton cleaner. దూదేకువాడు. A poor miserable wretch, దిక్కుమాలినవాడు.

పిండము *pindamu.* [Skt.] n. A lump of rice, అన్నపుముద్ద, A ball. చెండు. A body, form, living frame. ఆకారము, శరీరము. The fœtus or embryo, గర్భస్థశిశువు. The oblations that are made to deceased ancestors. పితృదేవతలకిచ్చు అన్నపుముద్ద. ఈ గండము గడిచి పిండము బయటపడితే చూతము when the fray is over we shall see what happens. వాడు ఉత్సాహపిండము he is a perfect hero. వాడు పిండా

పికిలేక చస్తున్నాను I am dying for a bit of bread. పిండముపెట్టు to offer balls of rice to the manes of ancestors. Vēma. iii. 192. **పిండలి** or **పిండలివండు** *pinḍali.* (from పిండము.) n. A lump or mass. ముద్ద, గడ్డ. పిండలివండు or పిండిలివండు mud and slush. గడ్డలుగు నీళ్లును, గడ్డలుకట్టినబురద. "తురగఖురో ద్ధూత ధూళితో శెరసిన, వననిధిపిండలి వండుగాగ." M. IV. iii. 150. **పిండాకూడు** or **పిండాకుడు** *pinḍā-kūḍu.* n. A contemptuous word for food.

పిండారి *pinḍāri.* [Mahrati.] n. A Pindari or plunderer, a freebooter or mosstrooper. పిండారీలు a gang of mounted robbers.

పిండి *pinḍi.* [Tel.] n. Flour. ధాన్యములోనగు వాని పొడి. [Skt.] n. A multitude. సమూహము. వెన్నెల పిండి ఆరబోసినట్టుగానున్నది there is bright moonlight. తెలికపిండి a residue of sesamum seeds after the oil is extracted, oil-cake. ఈ మాట పిండికిని పడును పిడుగునకును పడును this is equivocal, it is neither chalk nor cheese. పిండిబలపము a whitish kind of slate stone. పిండిరాయి a soft kind of stone; also a mica or slate. బలపము. పిండిమిరియము a sauce made of herbs and chillies mixed with rice flour. పేలపిండి flour of parched grain. **పిండికూర** or **పిండిబొద్దికూర** *pinḍi-kūra.* n A kind of vegetable. **పిండిదొండ** *pinḍi-donḍa.* n. The herb called *Aerua lanata.* (Watts.) H. iv. 12. **పిండివంటలు** *pinḍi-vanṭalu.* n. Pastry, cakes.

పిండిక *pinḍika.* [Tel.] n. The nave of a wheel.

పిండితము or **పిండీకృతము** *pinḍitamu.* [Skt.] adj. Squeezed, పిడుపబడిన, ముద్దగా చేయబడిన. Close, దట్టము.

పిండీతకము *pinḍītakamu.* [Skt.] n. The tree called మంగచెట్టు, గ్రంధితగరపుచెట్టు or మరువము.

పిండు *pinḍu.* [Tel.] n. An army, a multitude, crowd, flock. సమూహము, గుంపు, చతురంగ బలయుక్తసేన. R. i. 2. [Skt.] n. A ball. చెండు. **పిండుకట్టు** *pinḍu-kaṭṭu.* v. n. To form or gather in a crowd. గుంపుకూడు.

పిండు *pinḍu.* [Tel.] v. a. To press out, squeeze, wring. రసము పిడుచు. To milk. పాలుపితుకు. అతడు పిండినపాలు పిండినట్లు మాట్లాడినాడు he is no hypocrite, he speaks the simple truth.

పిందె or **పిందియ** *pinde.* [Tel.] n. A tender fruit. చింతపిందె a very raw tamarind fruit.

పింపిణి *pimpiṇi.* [Tel.] n. A woman's hair separated into four tails and then braided into one. "మ॥ జడిగొన్నొప్పెడు క్రొన్నెలనిం తితాను నుగజేసుంబూనినున్విరుపిణీ, జడలగా పాపు టరావికశ జగిపోచ్చుగా గొప్ప పొంకించి." Satyab. iii. 145.

పింపిళ్లు, **పింపిళులు** or **పింపిసలు** *pimpiḷḷu.* [Tel.] n. plu. Antics, skips, leaps. గంతులు, తూతూ అనే ఆటలో భేదము. **పింపిళ్లాడు**, **పింపిసలాడు** or **పింపిళ్లుకూరు** *pimpiḷḷ-āḍu.* v. n. To dance, నర్తించు.

పికపికలు *pikapikalu.* [Tel.] n. Confusion, dispersion, scatteredness, చెల్లాచెదరు. పికపికలగు to be scattered. చెల్లాచెదరగు.

పికము *pikamu.* [Skt.] n. The Cool or Indian cuckoo, కోయిల. **పికవర్ధనము** *pika-varthanamu.* n. A crow.

పికిలి, **పిక్కిలి**, **పికిలిగాడు**, **పికిలిగువ్వ**, **పికిలిపిట్ట**, **పిగిలి** or **పిగిలిపిట్ట** *pikili.* [Tel.] n. The Common Madras Bulbul, *Molpastes hæmorrhons.* తురకపికిలిపిట్ట the Southern Red-whiskered Bulbul, *Otocompsa fuscicaudata.* తోకపికిలిపిట్ట the Indian Paradise Flycatcher, *Terpsiphone paradisi.* తెలపికిలిగాడు the White-browed Bulbul, *Pycnonotus luteolus.* గొంతుపసుపుపికిలిగాడు the yellow-throated Bulbul, *Pycnonotus xanthelœmus.* పికిలిచెండు a tuft made of the feathers of this bird. పికిలిపూసలు *pikili-pūsalu.* n. plu. A kind of beads. "గోరోజన, మిరుతులు, పికిలిపూసల్, పావిపండులు, కుందేళ్లు." R. ii. 4.

పిక్క *pikka.* [Tel.] n. The calf of the leg. జంఘ. A tamarind seed, చింతగింజ.

పిక్కటిల్లు or పిక్కటిలు *pikkatillu.* [Tel.] v. n. To rise, swell, spread; to burst forth, as scent, anger, sound, passion, నిండు, వ్యాపించు, విజృంభించు, పగులు, పర్విల్లు. "దుందుభిరవములు దిక్కులెల్ల పిక్కటిల్ల." Vish. P. iii. 94.

పిక్కారు *pik-karu.* [Tel. పిదప+కారు.] n. The after or next season.

పిక్కు *pikku.* [Tel.] n. A trick, artifice, a secret. వంచన, మర్మము. అందులోనుండె పిక్కు వానికి తెలియలేదు he did not find out the trick of it. v. n. To withdraw. వెనుదీయు. v. a. To cheat, to deceive. ఠగాచేయు, వంచించు.

పిగిలి See పికిలి.

పిగులు *pigulu.* [Tel.] v. n. To burst, పగులు చెరిచినది. దోవతి పిగిలినది the cloth burst or was rent or split.

పిచండము [Skt.] n. The belly, కడుపు. పిచండిలుడు n. One who has a big belly, పెద్దకడుపుగలవాడు.

పిచాడీ *pichadi.* [H.] n. A rope by which a horse's hind legs are tied up.

పిచుమందము or పిచుమర్దము *pichu-mandamu.* [Skt.] n. The tree called the Neem or Margosa, వేపచెట్టు.

పిచువు *pichuvu.* [Skt.] n. Cotton. దూది.

పిచ్చి or పిచ్చె *pichchi.* [Tel.] n. Madness, folly. adj. Fruitless, vain. Foolish, mad. Short, deficient in measure. Applied to plants, it means Wild, uncultivated. పిచ్చిచెట్టు a weed. పిచ్చిబీర a wild cucumber. పిచ్చిమామిడి a wild mango. పిచ్చివాడు one who is mad. పిచ్చిరూపాయి a light or counterfeit rupee. వానిపని అంతా పిచ్చి పిచ్చి అయిపోయినది his business is gone to dogs. పిచ్చివాన rain that does no good. In weights the పిచ్చసేరు, శేర, కచ్చాసేరు means the smaller or false quantity as opposed to పక్కాసేరు the greater or true weight. పిచ్చిపట్టిన or పిచ్చెపట్టిన *pichchi-pattina.* adj. Mad, foolish. పిచ్చిపట్టు selfishness, లుబ్ధత్వము.

పిచ్చిక or పిచ్చుక *pichhika.* [Tel.] n. A sparrow. పిచ్చికకుంటు, పిచ్చికుంటు, పిచ్చుక కుంటు, లేక, పిచ్చెకుంటు one who hops like a sparrow, *i.e.*, a lame man; a cripple. అనూరుడు, కాళ్లులేనివాడు; a beggar, బిచ్చె మెత్తువాడు. వెదురుపిచ్చిక, కొండపిచ్చిక, చెరుకు పిచ్చిక, ఊరపిచ్చుక, పొదపిచ్చిక, పెదపిచ్చుక are different species. పిచ్చికగోళ్లు *pichchika-gōllu.* n. "Sparrow's claws." A sort of grain. H. iv. 156. పిచ్చికమీను *pichchika-mīnu.* n. A flying fish, *Exocetus volitans.* పిచ్చుకకాలు *pitstsuka-kalu.* n. A kind of grass.

పిచ్చికారు or పిచికారు *pichchikaru.* [H.] n. A syringe.

పిచ్చిలు or పిచ్చిల్లు *pichchilu.* [Tel.] v. n. To gush, flow, exude. "పచ్చినకంచుకనిబొడ గని, పిచ్చని నిట్టూర్పుగదురవిహ్వలమతితో రిచ్చపడిబాష్పభారలు, పిచ్చిలవయ్యందుపదన లెక దుచుపలికెన్." Vish. vii. 79.

పిచ్చె *pitstsu.* [Tel.] n. A tamarind seed, చింతగింజ. A skein of yarn.

పిచ్చెటిల్లు *pitstsatillu.* v. n. To quake, shudder, &c. "పచ్చెమురిభేదిగనిపచ్చెటిల పైన్యములు హెచ్చి నడవగా రిపులు రిచ్చపడిమూడెన్." Adilakshimi Vilāsam. iv. 123.

పిచ్చెలించు *pitstsalintsu.* [Tel.] v. n. To be in a stir, to be afraid, భయపడు, తల్లడపడు. To be proud, అతిశయించు. To sprout, to emanate, అంకురించు, పొటమరించు. "చేలంబునపెచ్చరిక

పిచ్చరించ ప్రచ్చుము." R. v. 194. v. a. To talk or converse about, to praise, admire, ప్రశంసించు.

పిత్సు *pitsu.* [Tel.] n. Fat, grease, కొవ్వు. Poison. విషము. పందిపిచ్చు hog's grease, lard. A tamarind seed, చింతవిత్తు.

పిటకము *piṭakamu.* [Skt.] n. A pimple. చెమటకాయ. P. i. 489. A small box, చిన్న పెట్టె.

పిట్ట *piṭṭa.* [Tel.] n. A small bird. A little thing. నక్కపిట్ట a small wild root. This name is applied to some fish, as ఈసపిట్ట. adj. Trifling. పిట్టకథలు idle stories. **పిట్ట పిడుగు** *piṭṭa-piḍugu.* adj. Inevitable, అనివార్యము. **పిట్టకాసు** or **పిత్తడికాసు** *piṭṭa-kāsu.* n. A small kind of fish: what in England is called the Miller's Thumb.

పిట్టు *piṭṭu.* [Tel.] n. Flour boiled in steam, నానినమీద మడక పెట్టివండి.

పిఠరము *piṭharamu.* [Skt.] n. A little earthen pot. కుండ. A cooking pot, వంట కుండ. A churning rod, కవ్వపుకోల.

పిడక or **పిడుక** *piḍaka.* [Tel. from పిడుచు.] n. A cake of cowdung dried for fuel. కత్తిపిడక a toddyman's case, containing his knife, &c. **పిడకముసలి** Same as శింశుమారము (q. v.).

పిడచె or **పిడుచె** *piḍatsa.* [Tel. from పిడుచు.] n. A handful; as much as can be clutched. పిడచెపాత a besom or bit of cloth used in smearing, అలుకుపొట్ట.

పిడత or **పిడుత** *piḍata.* [Tel.] n. A very small earthen pot, మిక్కిలి చిన్నకుండ.

పిడి *piḍi.* [Tel. Lit: to hold.] n. A small handle, hilt, haft. కత్తిమొదలలోనునది, తగరువు. A handful, a fist, పిడికిలి. The female of any animal, ఆడుమృగము. రెండు పిళ్లరంపము a two handled saw. దారపు పిడి a skein or ball of string. కారుపిడి or మనుబిడి the female bison. Kalahas. ii. 83. పిడియేనుగు a female elephant. **పిడికట్టు** *piḍi-kaṭṭu.* n. The middle part of a bow where it is held, లస్తకము, వింటినడుము. **పిడికిలి** *piḍi-kili.* n. A hold or grasp, a fist, ముష్టి. ప్రాణాలుపిడికిటపట్టుకొన్నాడు his life is in his hand, i.e., he is in great distress: he is at the point of death. (Gen. పిడికిటి, Loc. పిడికిట. plu. పిడికిళ్లు). పిడుగువంటి పిడికిటవానిని పొడిచెను he hit him with his fist which was like a thunderbolt. **పిడికిలించు** *piḍikilintsu.* v. a. To hold in the fist. పిడికిట బట్టు. **పిడికిలింత** *piḍikilinta.* n. Closing the hands in homage.

> "వారణాదిక్షై వరదస్వామికి,
> పిడికిలింతలని పెంపుగనడుపుచు."
>
> H. iv. 286.

పిడికెడు *piḍik-eḍu.* n. A handful, as much as can be held in the closed fist. "ఎరుకపిడికెడు ధనము" (a proverb) acquaintance is a handful of money. **పిడికోల** *piḍi-kōla.* n. The handle of a plough staff, నాగేలులోనునాని మేడి. **పిడిగంట** *piḍi-ganṭa.* n. A bell with a long handle. **పిడిగుద్దులు** *piḍi-guddulu.* n. Blows. **పిడిగొట్టు** *piḍi-goṭṭu.* v. a. To geld, as an animal. Literally, to strike the handle (of a chisel, &c., which is placed on the testicle). ఎద్దునట్టులుకొట్టు, విచ్చులుతీయు. **పిడిపిప్పెడాకు** *piḍi-pippeḍ-āku.* n. An acrid gummy weed, poisonous to sheep, also called కొకటితగురు or గాడిదగడపర. **పిడిమూర** *piḍi-mūra.* n. The distance between the elbow and the closed fist. **పిడియము** or **పిడెము** *piḍiyamu.* n. A dagger, బాకు. **పిడివాటు** *piḍi-vāṭu.* n. Taking sheaves of corn up in the hand and beating out the grain from them. An agreement, ఒడంబడిక. పిడివాటుచీటి a note or letter which parties write to each other after an agreement. **పిడివాదము** *piḍi-vādamu.* n. Obstinacy, మూర్ఖము. **పిడివేయు** *piḍi-vēyu.* v. n. To put a handle on to anything. **పిడిసాన** *piḍi-sāna.* n. An auger, a drill. బరమా. పిడిసి or పిడిసె *piḍisi.* n. A Rose colored Pastor or Cholum Bird. "పిడిసెలు చేనిమీద సొకసిస్సురగా ఒకఝాడి." Sri Natha.

పిడుగు or **పిడ్గు** *piḍugu.* [Tel. from పడు.] n. A thunderbolt. అడుగుతప్పినతప్పు పిడుగు చేమ the thunderbolt shall fall innocuous at the foot. "బొంకులపిడుగులు" thundering liars. Charitr. ii. 1549. కల్లలాడు టకు పిడుగువంటివారు. పిడుగుకైదువు *piḍugu-kaiduvu.* n. A thunderbolt. వజ్రాయుధము.

పిడుచు *piḍutsu.* [Tel.] v. a. To wring, squeeze, press. రసముతోనకుపానిని పిండు.

పిడుజు, **పిడుసు** or **పిణుసు** *piḍudzu.* [Tel.] n. A tick or louse that infests cattle, a bott, గోమరి. Various kinds are బుడ్డపిడుదు or అంబారుపిడుదు a cattle tick. ఆకుపిడుజో or చెక్కపిడుసు a woodlouse, and పేనుపిడుదు a body louse.

పిడుత See పిడత.

పిడె or **పిడెము** *piḍe.* [Tel.] n. A bundle or a clump (of bamboos) వెదురుపొద, గుంపుగా మొలచియుండు వెదురులు. See పిడియము. under పిడి.

పిడేరపుగువ్వ *piḍerapu-guvva.* [Tel.] n. A common kind of dove. Jerdon. No. 295.

పిణ్యాకము *piṇyākamu.* [Skt.] n. An oil cake, sesamum seed left after the oil is extracted. తెలకపిండి.

పిత, **పితర** or **పితరుడు** *pita.* [Skt.] n. A father. తండ్రి. పితరదొర *pitara-dora.* n. The lord of our fathers, Yama. పితృపతి. యముడు. పితామహుడు *pita-mahuḍu.* n. A father's father. తండ్రితండ్రి, తాత. Brahma, బ్రహ్మ. ఆంధ్రకవితాపితామహుడు 'the Father of Telugu poesy,' a title of the celebrated poet Allasāni Peddanna. ప్రపితామహుడు great grandfather. పితామహి a grandmother on the father's side, తండ్రితల్లి. పితాళ్లు *pitāḷḷu.* (another form of పితరులు.) n. The manes or ghosts of forefathers. Charitr. i. 1526. పితరులు *pitarulu.* n. Deceased or departed ancestors, పితృదేవతలు.

పితలాటము or **పితలాటకము** *pitalāṭamu.* [Tam.] n. Trickery, cheating, humbug, మోసము, టక్కు.

పితుకు or **పిదుకు** *pituku.* [Tel.] v. a. To milk out, express, squeeze, draw (milk.) పాలుపిండు. ఆవును పాలుపితికినవాడు he milked the cow.

పితూరి *pitūri.* [H.] n. An intrigue, plot, treason, conspiracy. కుట్ర. Tale bearing (Krishna District). Riot or rebellion (Godavery District). పితూరికోరు *pitūri-kōru.* n. A rebel, a traitor, a conspirator, ద్రోహి. A tale-bearer, చాడీలు చెప్పువాడు.

పితృలు *pitṛlu.* [Skt.] n. Fathers, ancestors. పితృతిథి *pitṛi-tithi.* n. A lunar day, on which offerings are made to the manes of ancestors. పితృపతి *pitṛi-pati.* n. The lord of the ancestors, i.e., Yama. పితృవనము *pitṛi-vanamu.* n. A cemetery. శ్మశానము, వల్లకాడు. M. iv. 18. పితృయజ్ఞము or పితృతర్పణము *pitṛi-yagnyamu.* n. An offering or sacrifice to ancestors. పిత్రార్జితము *pitṛ-arjitamu.* adj. Earned by one's ancestors, inherited from one's ancestors, ancestral. n. Ancestral property. పిత్ర్యము *pitryamu.* adj. Paternal, ancestral. తండ్రిసంబంధమైన, తండ్రిది. పితృవ్యుడు *pitṛivyuḍu.* n. A paternal uncle, తండ్రితోడబుట్టినవాడు.

పిత్తము *pittamu.* [Skt.] n. Bile, gall, the bilious humour. పిత్తకాక or పిత్తకారకము bilious heat. పిత్తకాసము a kind of consumption. పిత్తరోగం a kind of jaundice, Leucophlegmatia. పిత్తపుపగుళ్లు choppings of the hands and feet. పిత్తనాడి a bilious pulse. ఈ మందు పిత్తముచేయును గనుక మారు బైటికి పోరాదు this medicine will stir up the bile, so you must stay at home. పిత్తకోశము pitta-kosamu. n. The gall bladder. పిత్తజాడ్యము pitta-jadyamu. n. A bilious disease.

పిత్తలము, పిత్తళము, పిత్తడి or పిత్తళి pittalamu. [Skt.] n. Brass, ఇత్తడి. adj. Bilious, relating to bilious humour. పిత్తముగల. పిత్తడి కాసు pittadi-kasu. n. A sort of fish. H. iv. 224. See పిట్టకాసు.

పిదప pidapa. [Tel.] n. The after or succeeding time, వెనుక. adj. Succeeding, వెనుకటి. Meanspirited, degenerate, base, vile, silly, foolish. తక్కువైన, నీచమైన. adv. Afterwards. పిదపమనుష్యులు, వెనుకటి వారు. పిదపచేను an after crop.

పిదపిద pida-pida. [Tel.] adj. Soft, smooth, మృదువు, అనుకు. పిదపిదన pida-pidana. n. Softness. మృదుత్వము. Fright, భయము. "వ్య. చెదరకయదరక చిడిముడిగొనక, బెదరక పద లక పిదపిదగాక, క్రొవ్వాడినూపక క్రూరతలేక." Charitr. i.

పిదుకు Same as పితుకు (q. v.).

పిధానము pidhanamu. [Skt.] n. A covering, concealment, veil. ఆచ్ఛాదనము, తిరోధానము, ముసుగు, ఏమునుమీద ఉదక గా.

పిన or పిన్న pina. [Tel.] adj. Little, young, చిన్న. పినతండ్రి pina-tandri. n. Literally, a younger father, i.e., a father's younger brother: also, the husband of a mother's younger sister. పినతల్లి pina-talli. n. Literally, a younger mother, i. e., a mother's younger sister, the wife of a father's younger brother. See పిన్న.

పినాకము pinakamu. [Skt.] n. The name of the bow or trident used by Siva. శివుని ధనుస్సు, త్రిశూలము. A rain of mud, మట్టి వాన. పినాకి pinaki. n. An epithet of Siva. శివుడు. పినాకిని pinakini. n. The Sanskrit name of the river Pennar which rises near Nandidroog and falls into the sea near Nellore.

పినుగు or పిలుగు pinugu. [Tel.] n. A selfish or covetous man, లుబ్ధకుడు.

పిన్న, పిన, పిన్నటి or పిన్నటి pinna. [Tel.] adj. Little, small, tiny, diminutive, young, చిన్న. పిన్నపెద్దలు old and young, every body, great and small; also, the elders of a community. పిన్నపెద్దవివారెంచి మాట్లాడవలసినది you should consider who it is you are addressing. పిన్ననవ్వు a slight smile. పిన్నవాడు or పిన్నటివాడు pinna-vadu. n. Infancy. "పిన్నటివాటనే తనకుపేరము లోకమువారు మెచ్చగా." T. ii. 38. "కనికాస్త్రా మున పిన్ననవ్వునొలకగా." Parij. v. 45. పిన్నతనము or పిన్నరికము pinna-tanamu. n. Childhood. పిన్నవాడు pinna-vadu. n. A boy. పిన్నది pinn-adi. n. A girl. పిన్నకక్కెర pinna-kakkera. n. The small partridge, Perdrix sylvatica, చిన్నకక్కెర, కృకణపక్షి. పిన్నగద్ద pinna-gadda. n. A small kind of kite. పిన్నగోరంట a kind of Carleria, the dwarf species of గోరంట (q. v.) పిన్నపాప pinna-papa. n. A virgin, కన్యక. పిన్నమ్మ pinn-amma. n. A mother's younger sister. పిన్నయ్య pinn-ayya. n. A father's younger brother.

పిపాస pipasa. [Skt.] n. Thirst. దప్పి. పిపాసితుడు pipasitudu. n. A thirsty man.

పిపీలిక pipilika. [Skt.] n. An ant. పిపీలికాది బ్రహ్మపర్యంతము from an ant to God.

పిప్పలము pippalamu. [Skt.] n. The sacred fig tree, the Peepul tree. Ficus religiosa. రావిచెట్టు.

పిప్పలి *pippali.* [Skt.] n. Long pepper, *Anthrocnemum indicum.* పిప్పళ్లబియ్యము grains of this pepper. నరుపిప్పలి a plant called *Sphenoclea zeylanica.* Rox. i. 507. గాయ్యపిప్పలి a plant called *Salicornia brachiata.* గజపిప్పలి a plant called *Pothos officinalis,* or *Tomex sebifera.* Rox. iii. 819. అది పిప్పళ్లబస్తావలెనున్నది it (or she) is as strong as a horse: lit: as a sack (బస్తా) of this pepper. పిప్పలికట్టె the dried root of the long pepper. పిప్పలికట్టు the root of long pepper. పిప్పళ్లమోడి the thick or woody part (మోడి) of the long pepper vine.

పిప్పి or **పిప్పిరి** *pippi.* [Tel.] n. Refuse, residue, the stuff that remains after the juice is squeezed out. పిప్పి or పిప్పిటి n. A common weed. **పిప్పిచేయు** *pippi-chēyu.* v. a. To squeeze dry, as fruit, &c. "విరోధిసేనలన్ పిప్పిరిచేసెదన్." జై. vi.

పిమ్మట *pimmaṭa.* [Tel.] adv. Afterwards, subsequently, అనంతరము. Behind, పశ్చాత్, ముందు. పిమ్మటివారు those who come after.

పిమ్మట or **పిమ్మటము** *pimmaṭa.* [Tel.] n. Stupor, grief. మూర్ఛావస్థ, అచైతన్యము, నిస్త్రాణ, మనోవ్యథ, మానుపడడము. "చిట్టుర్మిమూర్ఛిల్లి పిమ్మటబొంది." BD. v. 257. "తనకు పిమ్మటమైన సర్జునిచాపము, లీలయుక్తోయి ద్రోణంగలేకతెగిరెను, సరిపరాపోతు పెల్లుబికగ్గమైన, పరిదియుద్ధ భాండవులకు సగమూరాగ." M. VIII. i. 5.

పియ్యి *piyyi.* [Tel.] n. Human dung, or the dung of any carnivorous animal, as distinguished from పేడ, లొట్ట, &c. చేపపియ్యి cuttle fish bone, used in varnish. **పియ్యితిను** *piyyi-tinu.* v. n. To eat dirt: i. e., make a fool of oneself. పియ్యితినేనాగము the dung-eater, a sort of snake.

పిర *pira.* [Tel.] n. In arithmetic, the two hundred and fifty-sixth part of a Rupee or of any thing.

పిరంగి or **పిరంగీ** *pirangi.* [corruption of 'Frank'] n. A cannon. **పిరంగిచెక్క** *pirangi-chekka.* n. China root, *Smilax china.* Ains. i. 70.

పిరము *piramu.* [for Skt. ప్రియము.] adj. Dear. వెలయెక్కువైన. "పిరమైనకాయకమెనటతేకుండ." Mari. P. 144.

పిరాయించు *pirāyintsu.* [H.] v. a. To change, మార్చు. **పిరాయింపు** *pirāyimpu.* n. Changing, a change. మార్పడము, మార్పు.

పిరి *piri.* [Tel.] n. A twist. మెలి. A cotton-twist, a thread, a rope, తాడు. **పిరిగొను** *piri-gonu.* v. a. & n. To surround, to twist, to twine round, చుట్టుకొను, పెనగొను, మెలిపెట్టు.

పిరిండి or **పిరిది** *pirindi.* [Tel.] adj. Behind, after, following. సూదిపిరిండి త్రాటిక్రియ as a thread that follows the needle. **పిరిండికి** or **పిరిదికి** *pirindi-ki.* adv. Backwards. వెనుకకు. "అగ్నిహోత్రపరులు నాట పిరిండికి నడుగు పెట్టక తెరగుచువారు." M. XII. iii. 55. See పిరుదు.

పిరికి *piriki.* [Tel.] adj. Cowardly. పిరికివాడు a coward. n. A coward, భయశీలుడు. plu. పిరుకులు. "పిరుకులుగానిభూమజనిధీపగులుండక పిరుసర్గమే." Jaimini. vi. 77. **పిరికితనము** *piriki-tanamu.* n. Cowardice, timidity, shyness, bashfulness. సభాపిరికితనము nervousness that disables a man when in public. **పిరికికండ** *piriki-kaṇḍa.* n. Want of courage, అధైర్యము. **పిరికిమేకము** *piriki-mekamu.* n. A gazelle or antelope, హరిణము, జింక.

పిరిమూడి, పిరియూమ See under పిరాదు.

పిరు *piru.* [Tel. short for పిరుదు.] n. The back part or side. వెనుకప్రక్క, వెనుక, పశ్చాద్భాగము. adv. Behind, back. "నరుకుడు

ననవుడు పిరుసనకతడు." BD. vi. 45. పిరుసనక without going back. **పిరుందు** or **పిరుదు** *pirundu*. The back side, the loins, వెనుకటిభాగము. Back, behind, వెనుక. "మాడిపిరుందిదారంబులిల." L. vii. 185. **పిరుందికడ** *pirundi-kaḍa*. adv. Behind, at the back of, after, following, దానిపిరుందగా at her heels. **పిరుదుకొను** *pirudu-konu*. v. a. To follow, వెంబడించు. **పిరుతీయు**, **పిరుతివియు** or **పిరుతివుచు** *piru-tīyu*. v. n. To draw back, shrink back, retreat. వెనుదీయు, పరాఙ్ముఖమగు. **పిరువడు**, **పిరుపోవు** or **పిరుచేను** *piru-paḍu*. v. n. To go back, to retreat, వెనుదీయు. To be afraid, భయపడు. **పిరువెట్టు** *piru-veṭṭu*. v. a. To slight, disregard. అనాదరించు.

పిరుపీకు, **పిరుటీకు**, **పిరువీకు** or **పిర్వీకు** *piru-piku*. [Tel. పీకు+పీకు.] n. Wrangling. పీకులాట, రచ్చ, జంఝాటము. Pain, బాధ. **పిరువీకులాడు** *piru-vikul-āḍu*. v.n. To struggle. పెనగులాడు. పిరుపీకుచేయు to torment, బాధించు; to struggle, పెనగులాడు.

పిరుము *pirumu*. [Tel.] n. Severity, పరుసభావము. adj. Severe, పరుసము.

పిర్యాదు, **పిరియాదు** or **ఫిర్యాదు** *piryādu*. [H.] n. A complaint, మొర. పిర్యాదీ or పిరియాదీ a complainant.

పిర్ర *pirra*. [Tel.] n. A buttock, పిరుదు. పిర్రలు the buttocks.

పిలక *pilaka*. [Tel.] n. A young one, a young shoot. కందపిలక a small root, as that of a radish. See పిలుక.

పిలపిల *pila-pila*. [Tel. anuk.] adv. Suddenly, at once.

పిలుక or **పిల్క** *piluka*. [Tel.] n. A young one, a young shoot. లేటిలేటిపిలుక the young of the antelope. "పులులకు బుద్ధిసేర్పు గొని పూరియగీరియు మేటిలేడికే, పిలుకలవెంట త్రిప్పుకొని పెంచుచు." R. ii. 69. అంచపిలుక a young swan. సింగపుపిలుక the cub of a lion. తేటిపిలుక a young bee. **పిలుకవాటు** *piluka-vāṭu*. n. Bearing young ones, పిల్లలను కనుట. "పిలుకవాటిగోడిగ జాపడిగాము లకు." A. iv. 36. టీ॥ పిలుకవాటి, పిల్లలను ఇచ్చే, గోడిగజాపడములకు, ఆడగుఱ్ఱపుతట్లకు.

పిలుకు *piluku*. [Tel.] n. Pride, conceit, గర్వము. **పిలుకుమారు**, **పిలుకుమాలు**, **పిల్కుమారు** or **పిల్కుమాలు** *piluku-māru*. v. n. To die, చచ్చు. To be destroyed, to perish. నాశమొందు. "కాల్బలముల్ దనమీకనిచ్చియుగా, మరలియుమాలియుగా పిలుకుమారియునల్లడ బారియుగా." M. VIII. i. 4. **పిలుకుమారుచు**, **పిలుకుమార్చు**, **పిలుకుమాలుచు** or **పిలుకుమాల్చు** *piluku-māruṭsu*. v. a. To kill, to destroy. "మనుజనాధయొక్కడవుపూని మహాద్భుత బాహుసంపదగా, మమువడిదాకడగా పిలుకుమార్చె దనంట యుదాత్తమైన ధైర్యమహిమగాడ." M. IX. ii. 102.

పిలుగు or **పినుగు** *pilugu*. [Tel.] n. A selfish man, లుబ్ధుడు. A mere formalist. కపటి, మాయగాడు.

> "క॥ కలదాసన్యాసికిబహు,
> కలధౌతసువర్ణపూర్ణకంథ సదా యా,
> పిలుగుయతిమరపుమోసము,
> కలవేనియులేక దానిగనిరక్షించుగా."
>
> P. i. 222.

పిలుచు or **పిల్చు** *pilutsu*. [Tel.] v. a. To call; to invite. **పిలుచుకొను** *pilutsu-konu*. v. a. To call for (a man), to call near, call upon, invite. పిలుచుక (for పిలుచుకొని) పోవు to take (a man) along with one. పిలుచుకవచ్చు to bring (a man along) with one. **పిలుపించుకొను** or **పిపిపించుకొను** *pilupintsu-konu*. v. a. To send for, to invite. **పిపిపించు** or **పిలువనంపించు** *pili-pintsu*. v. a. To call for, invite, send for. **పిలు** or **పిలువు** *pilu*. (Imperative of

పిలుచు.) v. "Call him." పిలుపు or పిలుపుడు *pilupu.* n. A call; a cry; an invitation, ఆహ్వానము.

పిల్ల *pilla.* [Tel.] n. A child, a babe, a young girl. A young one, offspring. A shoot or young plant. పిల్లలు, children, బిడ్డలు, young ones. పిల్లలుగలవాడను I am a parent. కుక్కపిల్ల a puppy. పులిపిల్ల a tiger's cub. కోడిపిల్ల a chicken. మేకపిల్ల a kid. ఎలుకపిల్ల a young rat. పిల్లలుకను or పిల్లలుపెట్టు to bring forth young ones. పిల్లపెట్టు to throw doublets on the dice. "మారిపిల్లలక, వంచనలేక పాదుకొన్నవైచియు పోవగచేసి పెంపుగా, వించుటతక్కలంబనుభవించుమనె." Radha. i. 74. పిల్ల adj. Small, petty. పిల్లకొండ a small hill. పిల్లపెత్తనము misrule. పిల్లచేష్టలు boyish pranks or tricks. పిల్లగాలి a gentle breeze. పిల్లదూలము a small beam or rafter. పిల్లసంగీతము a humming or low singing. పిల్లకాలువ a small channel or canal. పిల్లబావి or పిల్లనుయ్యి an inside well; a well or hole bored in the bottom of a well. పిల్లయేనుగు the young of an elephant. పిల్లదున్న a young buffalo. **పిల్లేరుగంటు** *pill-ēru-gantu.* (పిల్ల+ఏరు+గంటు.) n. A summersault. **పిల్లంగోడు** *pillan-gōḍu.* n. A hockey stick or bat used in games. See పిల్లగోట్లు. **పిల్లంగ్రోవి, పిల్లనగ్రోవి, పిల్లగ్రోవి** or **పిల్లగ్రోలు** *pillan-grōvi.* n. A flageolet. plu. పిల్లంగోళ్లు. **పిల్లకాయ** *pilla-kaya.* n. A child, a little boy. **పిల్లగడ్డము** *pilla-gaḍḍamu.* n. A very small beard. **పిల్లగాడు** *pilla-gāḍu.* n. A boy or lad పిల్లవాడు. **పిల్లగిరులు** *pilla-girulu.* n. The name of a game. **పిల్లగోట్లు** *pilla-gōṭlu.* n. A boy's game in which hockey sticks are used. **పిల్లచుట్ట** *pilla-chuṭṭa.* n. A noose, ఉరి. H. v. 112. **పిల్లజుట్టు** *pilla-juṭṭu.* n. The lesser lock behind or in front of the principal one, కొలువుముందరి జుట్టు, లేక, చిన్నజుట్టు. **పిల్లడు** *pilladu.* n. A boy, a child. **పిల్లడి** *pilladi.* n. A girl or lass, **పిల్లదీపులు** *pilla-dīpulu.* n. A certain boys' game. **పిల్లపీచర** *pilla-pīsara.* n. A plant, *Asparagus racemosus.* (Ains. and Watts.) H. v. 51. **పిల్లపెసర** *pilla-pesara.* n. A sort of green gram called పెసలు. **పిల్లపేగులు** *pilla-pēgulu.* n. The small intestines. **పిల్లమొరము, పిల్లమొరియము** or **పిల్లిమంతరము** *pilla-meramu.* n. A summersault, తలక్రిందుగా వేసేలాగు, పల్టీ. **పిల్లవ్రేలు** *pilla-vrēlu.* n. The little finger, చిటికెనవ్రేలు. "పిడికాటిపిల్లవ్రేల్." కై. viii.

పిల్లరి *pillari.* [Tel.] n. A kind of song. "పిల్లరిపాడెదు పెనుపకోవముల.." Pal. 271.

పిల్లాణి or **పిల్లాడి** *pillaṇi.* [Tel.] n. A silver ring worn by women on the fourth toe. plu. పిల్లాండ్లు.

పిల్లి *pilli.* [Tel.] n. A cat. ఊరపిల్లి a tame cat. Several different animals go by this name: as కస్తూరిపిల్లి, భూతపిల్లి, నీటిపిల్లి, బావురుపిల్లి, జెంగుపిల్లి and some more. పునుగుపిల్లి a civet cat. పిల్లికండ్లు blue eyes (lit: 'cat's eyes.'). పిల్లికూత mewing. పిల్లికూన a kitten. పిల్లిలాగు like a cat, i. e., demurely, harmlessly. పిల్లిగుణము a feline disposition. కాలుకాలిన పిల్లివలె తిరుగుచున్నాడు he wanders about like a cat whose feet are burnt. పిల్లి n. A corruption of పల్లె as కొండపల్లి, ఈడేపల్లి, &c. పిల్లికన్రతనము (పిల్లికన్ను+రతనము.) a precious stone, a cat's eye, వైడూర్యము. **పిల్లిగడ్డ** *pilli-gaḍḍa.* n. A root called *Urtica tuberosa.* Rox. iii. 583. Musk. పునుగుచెట్టు. **పిల్లడుగుచెట్టు** (పిల్లి+అడుగు+చెట్టు.) *pill-aḍugu-cheṭṭu.* n. Cowach, a certain plant. కపికచ్ఛూ, ఎగ్గోకిలు. Rox. iii. 283. **పిల్లిమీసరగడ్డ** *pilli-misara-gaḍḍa.* n. Cat's whiskers, a sort of plant. Rasica. i. pref.

పిల్లు Same as పుల్లు (q. v.).

పిళ్ల *pilla*. [Tel.] n. A title generally assumed by the members of some of the Sudra's castes. పిళ్లారి *pillari*. n. A name of the god Gaṇésa, గణేశుడు. అచ్చ. కిష్కిం. కాం.

పిళ్లు *pillu*. [Tel.] n. plu. A tuft of grass. కసవుపెంటి. హరి. పూ. v.

పిశంగము *pisangamu*. [Skt.] adj. Tawny, red, as hair. గోరోచనవర్ణముగల, కపిలవర్ణముగల.

పిశాచము *pisachamu*. [Skt.] n. A demon or ghost. A whirlwind or stormy gust. భేతాళాదులు. పిశాచి *pisachi*. n. A female fiend or spirit. కర్ణపిశాచి a familiar demon. ధనపిశాచి a dragon placed as a guard over hidden treasure.

పిశితము *pisitamu*. [Skt.] n. Flesh, meat. మాంసము. పిశితాశనుడు or పిశితాశి *pisitasanudu*. n. A cannibal, a carnivorous being. "కూర్పరులంబుగాదోడగ దుష్టనిశాచరవేశయుయ్యెడుఁగా, మార్పుముగాలయూపనమము ర్పక యుప్పశితాశిబట్టి." M. I. vi. 235.

పిశునము *pisunamu*. [Skt.] n. Reservedness of temper, a saturnine disposition. పిశునుడు *pisunudu*. n. A reserved man, a false friend. A tale bearer, కొండెకాడు. A wicked person, దుష్టుడు.

పిష్టము *pishtamu*. n. Flour or meal. పిండి. Scoriæ, meltings, dross. మధుపిష్టము wax. పిష్టకము *pishtakamu*. n. A cake, a pudding. అపూప సామాన్యము, పిండివంట. పిష్టచక్రము *pishta-chakramu*. n. A round biscuit, గారె. పిష్టాతకము *pishtatakamu*. n. Perfumed powder. బుక్కా. A. iv. 36.

పిస *pisa*. [Tel.] n. Folly, nonsense, అవివేకము.

పిసక or పిస *pisaka*. [Tel.] n. Grease, or dirt in the hair, తలమురికి. పిసకగానుండే or పిసకపట్టిన greasy. పిసపిసలాడే clammy, viscous. పిసవెర్రి, *pisa-verri*. n. Eager desire, strong lust. గాఢము, కామోద్రేకము.

పిసరు *pisaru*. [Tel.] n. Stuff, trash, waste matter. The wash or refuse of grain. Matter in the eye, humour, pus. Any thing worthless, a mere trifle, a small quantity, లేశము. పిసరంతపొడి a pinch of snuff. పిసరువెళ్లగొట్టినారు they beat the stuff out of him. ఆ పనిచేయుటలో వానిపిసరు వెళ్లినది he was quite exhausted in doing the business.

పిసాసి [from Skt. పిశాచి.] Same as పిశాచి. (q. v.)

పిసాళము *pisalamu*. [Tel.] n Brilliance, వికాసము, ప్రకాశము. A jest, పరిహాసము. Spreading, వ్యాపనము. A trick, దొంగయెత్తు. పిసాళి *pisali*. adj. Brilliant, తళతళమనే, ప్రకాశముగల. Spreading, వ్యాపనముగల. Artful, దొంగ యెత్తుగల. "సకియ క్రొందళుకు బిసాళి చూపులకోపు, ముసిదనిద్దపు ముద్దుమోము గోము." Rasica. iii. 133. An artful or cunning person, కుత్సితపురుషుడు, స్త్రీయును. "మెంటసుమోటు పిసాళినామూఢుడు." ABA. iii. 11. పిసాళించు *pisal-intsu*. v. n. To be brilliant, to flash, to be displayed. తళతళలాడు, వెలుగు, విజృంభించు, మించు. To be fragrant, పరిమళించు. To spread, వ్యాపించు. To jest, పరిహాసములాడు. To pretend, దొంగయెత్తువేయు. "సీ॥ సద్యోవినిర్భిన్న సారంగనాభికా వ్యాప్తమై పిసాళించునట్టి కమ్మదనంబు." Swa. ii. 59. "ద్వి॥ కొడుకుకు విలపించుకొనుచు నీవున్న, నెడపకెవ్వరు సేతురీప నులెల్ల, చాలులేరెమ్ము పిసాళింపకనుచు." HD. ii. 1906. టీ॥ పిసాళింపకు, మాయచేయకు. v. a. To ridicule, పరిహసించు.

పిసి *pisi*. [Tel.] n. A pointed end of a stick, &c.

పిసింగి, పిసెంగి or పిసిని *pisingi*. [Tel.] n. A tree called *Clerodendron inerme*. (Watts).

పిసికిల్లు *pisikillu.* [Tel.] n. Rubbing, kneading, friction, rubbing ears of corn. పిసుకుడు ములు. Grains of millet, &c. కొన్నులంకొల్లు మొదలయినవాటి ఊచబియ్యము. A. iv. 172.

పిసిని, పిసిడి or పిసినీ *pisini.* [Tel.] adj. Avaricious, miserly. పిసినిపురుగు *pisini-purugu.* n. A silk worm: literally, the miser worm. పిసినికాయ *pisini-kāya.* n. The cocoon of the silk worm. పిసినిగొట్టు, పిసినిగొట్టు, పిసినివాడు or పిసినారి *pisini-goṭṭu.* n. A miser. లోభి.

పిసుకు *pisuku.* [Tel.] v. a. To squeeze, knead, handle, massage. ఏమితోచక చేతులు పిసుకుకొనుచుండెను he kept rubbing his hands as if he did not know what to do.

పిహితము *pihitamu.* [Skt.] adj. Covered, concealed. కప్పబడిన.

పీ pī

పీకు *pīku.* [Tel.] v. a. To pull out, root up, uproot, wrest. To tear, pull to pieces, destroy, demolish. To turn out, dismiss. నాలుక పీకుకొని చచ్చెను he pulled out his tongue and so killed himself. పీకుపీకాడు *pīku-pīk-āḍu.* v. n. To be agitated, to be in trouble. మిక్కిలి పెనుగులాడు. "తొంటి యుర్వృప్తతత్వంబును దక్కి తక్కి తగబుద్ధిం బీకుబీకాడగా, చేష్టాధీనతబొంది యగ్గురుడు సంకీ ర్ణాంగుడై యుండ్రెడకా." M. VII. v. 386. పీకుకొను *pīku-konu.* v. a. To snatch. పీకులాట *pīkul-āṭa.* n. A squabble, wrangle, quarrel; nonsense; a plague, scrape. పీకులాడు *pīkul-āḍu.* v. n. To wrangle, struggle, పెనగులాడు, లాగులాడు. A. vi. 18.

పీకె *pīke.* [Tel.] n. The wind-pipe, కంఠనాళము. A pipe. The reed used in blowing musical instruments. ఊదువాద్యములలోని క్రోవిపుల్ల. గొంతుపీకె the windpipe. A leaf rolled up like a cigar, కాలిచలెచుట్ట అరచుట్ట. A cigar which is partly smoked and thrown away, తాగి మిగిలినచుట్ట. పీకె బిళ్లలు *pīke-biḷḷalu.* n. A kind of ornament attached to a bed. సకిలెలు. పీకెపారు *pīke-pāru.* v. n. To become flat. చేప్పటయగు. To become lean, కృశించు.

పీగడ్డ Same as పీతిగడ్డ. (q. v.)

పీచము *pīṭsamu.* [Tel.] n. The chin, the lower jaw. కింది పెదవి. A dimple in the chin, పెదవికిందిపల్లము. Pride, మదము. వాడిపీచముదించితిని I brought down his pride. A peacock's tail or train, పింఛము.

పీచర or పిల్లిపీచర *pīṭsara.* [Tel.] n. A certain wild shrub. See under పిల్లి.

పీచు *pīṭsu.* [Tel.] n. The fibre of plants. వారికి మాకు ఉండే సంబంధము బీరకాయపీచుగా నున్నది our relations are not strong at all. Also, used for grass or straw as కొండపీచు hill grass. "పీచుమోసంబులుల్చిన యుల్లి గడ్డంబు." HK. iv. 82.

పీజు [Eng: Fees.] n. Gold. (a secret word used among goldsmiths).

పీట, పీటచెక్క or పీటకోడు *pīṭa.* [from Skt. పీఠము.] n. A seat made of board. కూర్చుండుపలక. బల్లపీట a bench. నాలుగుకాళ్లపీట a stool. ఫిడేలుపీట the bridge of a violin, also called గుర్రము. దూలపుపీట the short cross rafter in the top of a Hindu house roof. చాకలిపీట a washerman's bench on which he beats the cloth. కాడిపీట a short piece of wood under a yoke, నొగకు దిగువచేయు చెక్క. పీటబెట్టు or పీటవేట్టు *pīṭa-beṭṭu.* v. n. To set up one's seat, i.e., take up permanent residence, settle. స్థిరనివాసముచేయు, కదలక ఉండు. పీటముడి *pīṭa-muḍi.* n. A double knot, without bows.

పీఠము *pīṭhamu.* [Skt.] n. A seat. The "chair," diocese, or see of a Guru. పీఠస్థుడు one who sits on a seat or throne, i. e., a Guru. పీఠమర్దుడు or పీఠమర్ద

మర్దుడు pīṭha-marduḍu. n. A lover. పీఠి pīṭhi. Same as పీఠము. పీఠిక pīṭhika. n. A high seat. ఉత్కృష్టపీఠము. A preface, preamble, preliminary note.

పీడ pīḍa. [Skt.] n. Pain, annoyance, suffering, బాధ. పీడపోయినది the plague is gone. adj. Painful, nasty, annoying. పీడకల a bad dream. పీడనము pīḍanamu. n. Paining, gripe, seizure, squeezing, pinching, trouble caused by others. పరులచే కలుగుబాధ. పీడించు pīḍintsu. v. a. To pain, plague, torment, harass. బాధించు. పీడితము pīḍitamu. adj. Pained, distressed, troubled, afflicted. పీడింపబడిన.

పీత pīta. [Tel.] n. A crab. ఎండ్రకాయ. ఎలుగోటిపీత the crab called *Portunus menestho.* (Linn.) పీత [Skt.] n. Saffron. పసుపు. పీతము pītamu. adj. Drunk up. n. Yellowness. adj. Yellow. పీతదారువు pīta-dāruvu. n. A tree called the deodar. దేవదారువు. పీతాంబరము pīt-ambaramu. n. A yellow garment. పీతాంబరుడు pīt-ambaruḍu. n. The god who is clothed in a saffron robe, an epithet of Vishṇu. పీతముండము pīta-muṇḍamu. n. A yellow throated bird. పచ్చతల పిచ్చుక.

పీతి and పీతిరి. See under పీయు and పీయ్యి.

పీనము pīnamu. [Skt.] adj. Plump, big, బలిసిన. పీనోధ్ని pīnōdhni. n. A cow that has a plump udder, పెద్దపొదుగుగల ఆవు.

పీనసము pīnasamu. [Skt.] n. Cold, catarrh. Loss of scent in consequence of cold. పడిసెము. Inflammation of the nasal membrane (with loss of sense of smell). Charaka. p. 55.

పీనిగ, పీనుగ, పీనుగు or పీన్గు pīniga. [Tel.] n. A corpse or carcass. శవము. "మానవులు కోడంగూడ పీనుంగులైన యేమనంగలను." T. v. 37. పీనుగుతిండి a demon, పిశాచము.

పీయు or పీయ్యి pīyi. [Tel.] n. Human excreta, the dung of unclean animals. పీతి pīti. adj. Pertaining to human dung, unclean. పీతిరి pītiri. n. Defilement with ordure. పీతిరిగద్ద pītiri-gadda. n. The white scavenger vulture. పీతిరిగుంట pītiri-gunṭa. n. A dungpit, a cesspool. పీతిరినాగుపాము pītiri-nāgu-pāmu. n. The stinking cobra, lit: the dung snake.

పీయూషము pīyūshamu. [Skt.] n. Nectar, ambrosia. అమృతము.

పీరు, పీలు or పీగులు pīru. [Tel.] v. n. To tear, చినుగు. పీరుచు or పీర్చు pīrutsu. v.a. To tear, పిగులునట్లుచేయు, -చించు.

పీరు pīru. [H.] n. An image of a Mahomedan saint, made in the form of a hand, used by Mussalmans at the Mohurrum, తురకలు ఊరేగించు ప్రతిమ. పీర్లపండుగ pīrla-panḍuga. n. The Mohurram. పీరుసుడి pīru-suḍi. n. A waterspout at sea. If descending, it is called అవురు.

పీల pīla. [Tel.] adj. Slender, lean. బక్క. Poor, spare, scanty: short, not tall. పీలపంట a scanty crop. పీలచేతులు lean arms.

పీలి or పీలిపిట్ట pīli. [Tel.] n. A Bulbul, పికిలిపిట్ట. "పీలికరులయందుపకోలలు." Swa. iv. 13. A helm or rudder, చుక్కాని. M. II. ii. 44. పీలికాడు pīli-kāḍu. n. A steersman, a helmsman, ఓడచుక్కానిని త్రిప్పువాడు.

పీలిక pīlika. [Tel. from పీలు.] n. A rag, బట్టలు మొదలయినవాటి చీలిక. See పీరు.

పీలుచు or పీల్చు pīlutsu. [Tel.] v. a. To suck up, drink up with a noise. To whiff or inhale (smoke from a pipe.) To dry up the vitals, as fear does.

పీలువు pīluvu. [Skt.] n. A kind of forest tree. పిన్నపారిగోగు. An elephant, ఏనుగు. An atom, పరమాణువు. v. n. To tear, చినుగు, పిగులు.

పీవరము pīvaramu. [Skt.] adj. Plump, big, as arms. కొవ్విన, బలిసిన.

పు pu

పు *pu*. [Tel.] n. Contracted for పువ్వు a flower. Thus పుప్పొడి for పువ్వు+పొడి the pollen of flowers.

పుం *pum*. [Skt.] adj. Male. పుమపత్యము *pum-apatyamu*. n. Male offspring. R. ii. 64. పుంభావము *pum-bhāvamu*. n. Manhood, manliness, virility, skill, ప్రౌఢిమము. పుంశ్చలి *pum-schali*. n. A harlot, రంకులాలు. P. i. 275. పుంసవనము *pum-savanamu*. n. The ceremonies observed when a woman perceives the first signs of a pregnancy, in order that a son may be born. పుంస్త్వము *pum-stvamu*. n. Manhood, manliness, virility. ఆచార్య పుంస్త్వము priesthood. A. v. 151.

పుంఖము *pumkhamu*. [Skt.] n. The feathered part of an arrow. వాడిమీద కూర్చేపింజె. పుంఖానుపుంఖముగా one after another, in rapid succession. పుంఖితము *punkhitamu*. adj. Set on the bow. పుంఖితశరము an arrow set on the bow. T. ii. 214.

పుంగవము *pum-gavamu*. [Skt. పుం male + గవము a cow.] n. A bull. పుంగవుడు *pum-gavuḍu*. n. An eminent man, శ్రేష్ఠుడు. This word is only used in composition, in the sense of "pre-eminent, excellent:" thus మునిపుంగవుడు a venerable hermit.

పుంగుడు *punguḍu*. [Tel.] n. White leprosy, తెల్లపొడలకుష్ఠము.

పుంజనేల *punja-nēla*. [H.] n. Dry land, మెట్టపొలము. పుంజధాన్యము *punja-dhānyamu*. n. Dry crops. The generic name for every kind of grain excepting rice. It includes జొన్నలు, ఉలవలు, కొనగలు, తమిదలు, కొర్రలు, చామలు and so forth.

పుంజము *punjamu*. [Skt.] n. A heap, quantity, collection. రాశి, ప్రోగు. "శోకపుంజములో" oceans of sorrows. M. IV. iv. 282. "రత్నపుంజభరిత" full of gems. M. I. v. 36.

పుంజి *punji*. n. Abundance, plenty, సమృద్ధి. adj. Plentiful, abundant, prosperous. ఆ గ్రామమును పుంజిచేసినాడు he promoted the welfare of the village. "భుంజి టంబుల పుంజి తెలుపు." N. ix. 179. టీ॥ బలమును కనుపరచగాను. వారిప్పుడు పుంజిగానున్నారు they are now in good circumstances. Also, a phrase for Four. రెండుపుంజీల రూపాయలు eight rupees. పుంజికొను *punji-konu*. v. n. To be grouped thickly, to collect in a crowd, గుములుగొను. పుంజీభవత్ *punji-bhavat*. adj. Collecting, gathering, పోగయ్యే. "పుంజీభవత్పాటలప్రాభము." A. ii. 65. టీ॥ దట్టమైన కలిగొట్టు పుష్పములు. పుంజీభవించు *punji-bhavintsu*. v. n. To become a heap, రాశిపడు, కుప్పయగు.

పుంజెము *pundzamu*. [Tel.] n. Thirty skeins of thread. ముప్పది యొనికలనూలు. పుంజాలదండ *pundzala-danda*. n. A kind of necklace worn by women.

పుంజు or కోడిపుంజు *pundzu*. [Tel.] n. A cock. కుక్కుటము, మగకోడి. పుంజుతాలుపు an epithet of Kumāraswāmy.

పుంట *punta*. [Tel.] Another form of పొంట. (q. v.)

పుండరీకము *pundarīkamu*. [Skt.] n. The white lotus. తెల్లతామర. A royal tiger. బెబ్బులి. పుండరీకాజినము a royal tiger's skin. పుండరీకాక్షుడు *pundarīk-akshuḍu*. n. He whose eyes are bright as the white lotus, i. e., Vishṇu, తెలిదమ్మికంటి.

పుండలించు *puṇḍalintsu*. [Tel.] v. n. To invent, అభూతకల్పనముచేయు.

పుండు *punḍu*. [Tel.] n. A boil, an ulcer, a sore. A blister. The reddish cake in the middle of a white-ant-hill. నాగొంతు పుండుగానున్నది I have a sore throat. రాచపుండు a carbuncle. పక్కలోపుండు పెంచేవేమి why do you nourish a thorn in your side? Infl. పుంటి (S. iii. 370.) abl. పుంట. plu.

పుండ్లు. పుండుచేయు pundu-chēyu. v. n. To raise a blister, or make a sore. పుండ్లరోగము venereal disease.

పుండ్రము pundramu. [Skt.] n. A mark worn on the forehead. నుదుటినామము. A blackish red variety of sugar-cane, నలుపురకలసిన ఎఱ్ఱచెఱకు. A white lotus, తెల్లతామర. త్రిపుండ్రము the cross mark. ఊర్ధ్వపుండ్రము the upright mark. పుండ్రేక్షువు pundr-ēkshuvu. n. The white sugar-cane. పుండ్రేక్షుశరాసనుడు an epithet of Manmadha.

పుంత punta. [Tel.] n. An alley, path, by-way. పశువులునడిచేదారి. A raised path, a broad ridge between two paddy fields, గనిమ.

పుకారు or పుకారా pukāru. [H.] n. A rumour. An outcry, alarm, uproar.

పుక్కిలి pukkili. [Tel.] n. The inside of the cheek, బుగ్గలోపలిభాగము. పుక్కిటి పురాణము rigmarole, traditional nonsense, an old wives' tale. "వెచ్చనిట్టూర్పు పుక్కిట వెడలకున్నె." (R. vi. 112.) he could not help drawing a deep sigh. Gen. పుక్కిటి. Loc. పుక్కిట. plu. పుక్కిళ్లు. పుక్కిలించు or పుక్కిలించు pukkilintsu. v. n. To gargle or rinse one's mouth. To spirt out. పుక్కిలింత or పుక్కిలింత pukkilinta. n. Gargling, rinsing one's mouth. పుక్కెడు pukk-edu. n. A mouthful. పుక్కెడునీళ్లు a mouthful of water.

పుచ్చె puchche. [Tel.] n. The skull, తలపుర్రె. The young unripe fruit of the palmyra, cocoanut, &c. తాటినారికేళాదుల బొండ్లము. A cap or loose bit under a screw. The loose caps at the ends of a palm fruit. నీతలపుచ్చె పగలగొట్టుతాను I will break your head.

పుచ్చకాయ putstsa-kāya. [Tel.] n. The wild bitter melon, called *Bryonia callosa*, or *Cucumis trigonus*. కలింగము, కర్కారుకము. వెర్రిపుచ్చె the Colocynth plant, *Citrullus colocynthis*, *Cucumis colocynthis*. Rox. iii. 719. ఏటిపుచ్చకాయ the water-melon, *Citrullus vulgaris* (Watts) "ఒజ్జలపుచ్చకాయ విఠమారా." T. iv. 214. టీ॥ పుచ్చకాయ తిన రాదనిగురువు అందరికిన్ని చెప్పి తాను తిన్నరీతి యగును.

పుచ్చటిక, పుచ్చడిక or పుచ్చడికతనము putstsaṭika. [Tel.] n. Modesty, prudishness, shamefacedness, బిడియము, సిగ్గు. "సీ॥ పుచ్చడికతనంబు పోవెట్టి రికరేన్గపతిగొల్వ నాయాసపడినచోటు." Swa. ii. 8. పుచ్చడిక putstsaḍika. n. A modest or shy person. సిగ్గరి.

పుచ్చు putstsu. [Tel.] v. a. To take. తీయు. To send, to remove. పంపు, పోవజేయు. v. n. To decay, mortify, rot. పుచ్చిపోవు puchchi-pōvu. v. n. To be rotten, decayed పుచ్చు putstsu. adj Rotten, decayed. 'గురువునకు పుచ్చకాయైన నియ్యకరయకోర్కెకిత్తురర్థమెల్ల." Vēma. 69. పుచ్చు putstsu. n. The sediment of oil. ఆముదపుమడ్డి. Filth.

"పప్పులోనుప్పు మిక్కిలి పారజల్లి,
నేతిలో నాముదపుపుచ్చు నిండనించి,"
Jagannadha. i. 67.

పుచ్చు is used idiomatically with some nouns to give them an active force. ఆ బిడ్డను నిద్రపుచ్చినది she put the child to sleep. నూరురూపాయలతో ఆయిల్లు కట్టడమును సరిపుచ్చినాడు he finished the building of the house with a hundred rupees. మోసపుచ్చు to deceive, cheat. చిన్నపుచ్చు to disgrace. ప్రొద్దుపుచ్చు to pass or kill time, కాలక్షేపముచేయు. ఇంతప్రొద్దు పుచ్చినందుకు హేతువేమి what is the reason of your making so much delay?

"రాకివాడుకోక చీకాకుపడజేసి,
మరులుబుచ్చి మంచిమదుపుచేయు,
బుద్ధిచెప్పువాడు గుద్దినేమయా."
Vēma. 230.

"పరులసొమ్ముపుచ్చి ధరణీశులార్జించి,
కడుపునించుకొనుటకానిపద్దు."
Vēma. 258.

పుచ్చుకొను putsisu-konu. v. a. To take. This verb like 'To take' in English is used in many senses, thus: To receive; to purchase. To eat, to drink, to take medicine, poison, &c. To exact (service.) సెలవుపుచ్చుకొను to take leave or retire. సమ్మతిపుచ్చుకొను to take (one's) consent. అతడు వైష్ణవము పుచ్చుకొన్నాడు he embraced the Vaishnava creed. పుచ్చుకోలు putstsu-kōlu. n. The act of taking, or receiving, పుచ్చుకొనుట.

పుచ్ఛము puchchhamu. [Skt.] n. The tail, the hinder part. తోక, వెనుకప్రక్క.

పుట puta. [Skt.] n. A page, one side of a leaf. పుటాక్షరము put-āksharamu. n. The heading of a page.

పుటపుట puta-puta. [Tel. anuk.] n. The noise caused by fast running, గుజగుజ. "చిటిపొటిసొమ్ములు పెట్టుక పుటపుటగా బిడ్డ వెంట పొరిగిండ్లబడక." H. v. 25. పుటపుటన puta-putana. n. The act of breaking forth. పొటమరించడము. adj. Much. అధికము, అతిశయము. Grand, fine. ప్రవృద్ధము. "కొంతెరు కసకుమదము పుటపుటన." A. i. 34. "కంకణంబుల రత్నంపుదరులకులు చెదరనుంకించినట్టైము చేమంతి బంతులం బుటబుట్టసై." Swa. iii. 47.

పుటభేదము or పుటభేదనము puta-bhēdamu. [Skt.] n. A city or town. పట్టణము.

పుటము putamu. [Skt.] n. A fold, a doubling. The cup or hollow formed by a fold, as in a flower or leaf or in any roll or in the joined hands, దొన్నె. A flower basket, పూలబుట్ట. A horse's hoof, గుర్రపుకాలిగొరిజ. Burning or refining a metal, calcining a medicinal drug. A kind of horse's pace, అశ్వగతిభేదము. నాసికాపుటము the calix of the nose, i. e., the nose. పుటముపెట్టు or పుటమువేయు to heat metal in the fire, to calcine a drug. "వనిని తీవెలంబునక, పాండుర్మైతి విర్గతిపుటం బనక, దిరీ పుటం బనక, వన్నెయు నారసి." Vasu. ii. 46. పుటముబ్బు putam-ubbu. (పుటము+ఉబ్బు.) v. n. To swell upwards, మీదికుబ్బు. పుటమెగయు putam-egayu. v. n. To fly upwards, మీదికెగయు. To leap over, దాటు.

పుటి puti. n. A cup or concavity made of a leaf folded or doubled, దొన్నె. A flower basket, పూలబుట్ట. పుటిక or పుట్టిక putika. A cup. A. i. 92. A small basket, చిన్నగంప. పుటితము putitamu. adj. Folded, inserted, contained.

పుటిక్కు or పుటుక్కు putikku. [Tel. anuk.] n. Slapdash, a word imitative of plunging or of snapping, as of a cord.

పుట్ట putta. [Tel.] n. An ant hill, వల్మీకము. పాముపుట్ట an ant hill in which a snake lives. నాగులచవితికి పుట్టలో పాలుపోయుదురు they pour milk in a snake's hole on the feastday called Nāgula Tsaviti. A pack, number, collection, lot, heap, crowd. ఆ యిల్లు చీమలపుట్టగా నున్నది the house is a regular ant's nest. ఆ పుస్తకము అబద్ధాలపుట్టగానున్నది that book is a pack of lies. వాని ఒళ్లు పట్టిన యెముకలపుట్ట he is mere skin and bone. పుట్టకాపు or పుట్టకూడుతిండి putta-kāpu. n. Lit: That which feeds on ant hills, i.e., a bear, ఎలుగుగొడ్డు. పుట్టకాలు putta-kalu. n. A leg swollen with elephantiasis, బోదకాలు, ఏనుగుకాలు. "పుట్టకాల్ పొట్టకల్ పట్టిన వ్రేలుంజెవుల్." Jagan. i. 54. పుట్టకాలివాడు one who is afflicted with elephantiasis in the leg. పుట్టకూడు putta-kūdu. n. The heart of an ant hill, the red earth that contains the eggs. A fungus. కుక్కగొడుగు. "ఏ పొట్టకై పుట్టకూటికిం జీవలకుం జెదలుఁకు నెలంగులు గులగులం బుట్టలు విరిచివిజ నఖరకుటిల కోటులంగోరాడ." Swa. iv. 49. పుట్టకొక్కు, పుట్టగొడుగు or పుట్టచేదు putta-kokku. n. A mushroom, toadstool, fungus. M. XII. v. 418. పుట్టకోట putta-kōta. n. A bulwark, a buttress. కోటకు బలముకోసరము కోటలైట చేసిన పుట్టగోడ్లు. పుట్టకొనలు the pointed tops of ant hills, పుట్టమీదిశిఖరములు. పుట్టగోచి putta-gōchi. n. A large modesty piece. పెద్దగోచి, గోచినము. పుట్టచిలుక putta-chiluka n. The sirkeer Cuckoo. Taccocua leschnenaultii, (F. B. I.) పుట్టచూలు or పుట్టపుట్టువు putta-tsūlu. n. He who was 'born of the ant hill.' This is a word translated from the Sanscrit name వాల్మీకి Valmiki. పుట్టతమ్మచెట్టు putta-tamma-chettu. n. A large creeping plant, the fruit of which is used medicinally. పుట్టతేనె putta-tēne. n. Honey found in an ant-hill. పుట్టతేలు putta-tēlu. n. The large black scorpion, so called because found in rubbish. మండ్రగబ్బ. పుట్టముంగి putta-mungi. n. Lit: A mongoose on an ant-hill, used as a type of composure. adj. Demure. అది తిట్టుచుండగా పుట్టముంగివలె నూరకయుండినాడు she reviled him but he stood stock still. పుట్టలమ్మ puttal-amma. n. A village goddess.

పుట్టము puttamu. [Tel.] n. Cloth, a garment or dress. పుట్టచెండు putta-chendu. n. A ball to play with made of cloth. "చెట్టుకోని కట్టినకట్టు పుట్టచెండ్లపట్టికొట్టించు" H. v. 242. పుట్టచెండ్లు putta-chendlu. n. The name of a game.

పుట్టి putti. [Tel.] n. A wicker boat woven of cane and covered with leather. వాని పుట్టి మునిగినది his raft is sunk, i. e., he is shipwrecked or ruined.

పుట్టి putti. [Tel.] n. An Indian measure of capacity equal to twenty tooms. (.తూములు). The putty or candy (ఖండి) is from 800 to 1000 seers. The పల్లెపుట్టి is 80 కుంచాలు but the మలాకపుట్టి or Malacca ton is 200 or 240 కుంచాలు. కంటికి పుట్టెడు నీరునించె she wept in floods. Also, the extent of land that produces this quantity of grain.

పుట్టిక Same as పుటిక. See under పుటము.

పుట్టు puttu. [Tel.] v. n. To be born, produced. To arise, come into existence, (as love, anger, &c.) జన్మించు. n. Birth, జన్మము. adj. Born. తల్లితోడబుట్టినది a mother's sister. (పుట్టినది and పుట్టినవాడు are used where it is uncertain which member of a family is the elder, as the specific Telugu names for these relations denote the precedency or succession of birth.) తోడబుట్టినవాడు a brother. తోడబుట్టినది a sister. పుట్టుదరిద్రము life-long poverty. పుట్టుభోగి one who is rich from his birth. పుట్టుమచ్చ a birth-mark. పుట్టువ్యాధి a congenital disease, a disease born with one. పుట్టుక puttuka. n. Birth, origin; source. జన్మము. పుట్టుకల్లరి puttu-kallari. n. A born liar, పుట్టుక మొదలు అబద్ధములాడువాడు. పుట్టుగట్టు puttu-gattu. n. The mountain out of which the sun is supposed to be born each morning, ఉదయాద్రి. పుట్టుగొడ్డు or పుట్టుగొడ్రాలు one who is hopelessly barren. పుట్టుగ్రుడ్డి or పుట్టుచీకు puttu-gruddi. n. One who is born blind. పుట్టుచేయువులు puttu-cheyuvulu. n. Ceremonies connected with a birth. జాతకర్మము. పుట్టుపాప puttu-papa. n. An albino. పుట్టువు, పుట్టుగు or పుట్టుబడి puttuvu. n. Birth, origin, production, పుట్టుక. తొంటిపుట్టువున in a former birth. పుట్టుమూగ puttu-mūga. n. One who is born dumb. పుట్టువడుగు puttu-vadugu. n. One who is a bachelor all his lifetime. పుట్టువెర్రి puttu-verri. n. One who is insane from his birth. పుట్టించు puttintsu. v. a. To create, generate, form, make, raise, fabricate. పుట్టింట puttinta. (abl. of పుట్టిల్లు.) At home, in her parent's house. పుట్టినిల్లు, పుట్నిల్లు or పుట్టిల్లు *puttin-illu*. n. Birth-place, home; mint, fountain-head. వాడు దుర్మార్గమునకు పుట్టిల్లు he is a mass of wickedness.

పుడక or పుడుక *pudaka*. [Tel. from పుడుకు.] n. A small stick or bit; a pin, a bodkin, a stiletto. పూరిపుడక a bit of straw. ముక్కుపుడక a gold pin worn in the nose. పుడకలు sticks, firewood. పుట్టుకతో పుట్టినది పుడకలతోగాని పోదు that which is born with a person will not leave him till his cremation, it was born with him and he will carry it to his grave. S. i. 492 పుడకబావిలి an earring like a slender stick of gold.

పుడమి *pudami*. [from Skt. పృథివి.] n. The earth, భూమి. పుడమిఱేడు or పుడమిరాజు a king, రాజు. పుడమితాలుపు *pudami-talupu*. n. Lit: One who bears or carries the earth, an epithet of the Serpent ఆదిశేషుడు. A king, రాజు. A mountain. పర్వతము. పుడమిపట్టి *pudami-patti*. n. Lit: Son of the Earth, an epithet of Mars, అంగారకుడు. పుడమిపుట్టువు *pudami-puttu*. n. Lit: 'Born of the Earth', an epithet applied to a tree or to Sita, చెట్టు, భూజము; సీత, భూమిజ. పుడమివేలుపు *pudami-velupu*. n. A terrestrial deity, i. e., a Brahmin, బ్రాహ్మణుడు, భూదేవుడు.

పుడిసిలి *pudisili*. [Tel.] n. The hollow of the hand. పుడిసెడుబియ్యము a handful of rice. Infl. పుడిసిటి. Abl. పుడిసిట. Plu. పుడిసిళ్లు. పుడిసిలించు *pudisilintsu*. v. a. To hold anything (as water) in the hollow of the hand. పుడిసిలింత *pudisilinta*. n. The act of holding anything in the hollow of the hand, పుడిసిలిలో పట్టుకొనుట.

పుడుకు, పుణుకు or పుణ్కు *puduku*. [Tel.] v. a. To pick up, to handle, to take with the five fingers. వ్రేళ్లతో తీసికొను. To pinch. To give a little, కొంచెముగా ఇచ్చు. To give, ఇచ్చు. నేలపుడుకు to grovel on the earth as in grief. ఆమె అన్నము పుడికిపుడికి పెట్టినది she gave food stintingly. n. A gift. దానం. Giving, ఇయ్యడము. పుడుకుదోడుకు or పుడుకుపసి *puduku-doduku*. (పుడుకు+దోడుకు.) n. The cow that grants all that one wishes, కామధేనువు. పుడుకుగల్లు *puduku-gallu*. n. The stone that grants all that one wishes, చింతామణి. పుడుకుమ్రాను *puduku-mranu*. n. The tree that grants all that one desires, కల్పవృక్షము. పుడుకులు or పుణుకులు *pudukulu*. n. A kind of cake, భక్ష్యవిశేషము. పుణికిరించు or పుడికిరించు *punikirintsu*. v. n. To give a little. కొంచెముగా ఇచ్చు. To fumble, to twitch or be convulsed, as the fingers picking the sheets, &c., పుణికిరింత or పుడికిరింత *punikirinta*. n. Fumbling; twitching. పుణికిళ్లు, పుడికిళ్లు or పుణుకులు *punikillu*. n. Poking, shoving. A romping game like Puss in the corner. "మరిదరూయిడికిళ్లు మొదలుగాఁగల నుపచ్చిన్నాటలన్నియును." N. ix. 102.

పుణుజు or పుణుదు *punuju*. [Tel.] n. A tick.

పుణ్యము *punyamu*. [Skt.] n. Virtue, holiness, merit, excellence, purity. ధర్మము. A good deed, a good or meritorious work or action, a work of supererogation, that which is more than required as a matter of duty. సుకృతము. adj. Virtuous, sacred, holy, pure, righteous. పవిత్రము. Good, excellent, మనోజ్ఞము. Charitable, generous. పుణ్యశ్లోకుడు a celebrated man. పుణ్యకథలు godly legends. పుణ్యకాలము an auspicious time. పుణ్యస్త్రీ (corrupted into పునిస్త్రీ) a happy woman, one whose husband is living. నన్ను ఉత్త పుణ్యానికి కొట్టినాడు he beat me without cause, meaning the same as నిష్కారణముగా. నీపుణ్యముచేత తొందరవచ్చినది (ironical) for this trouble we may thank you. ఇది అంతా మీపుణ్యము this is all due to your goodness. నీపుణ్యమువుండును వాని తోలికిమాత్రము పోకు

for goodness' sake do not meddle with him. పుణ్యానికి ఇచ్చినపొలము a field granted in free gift. A well known verse says శ్లోకార్థేన ప్రవక్ష్యామి యదుక్తం గ్రంథకోటిభిః, పరోపకారః పుణ్యాయపాపాయ పరపీడనం. పుణ్యజనుడు *punya-janudu.* n. A man of excellence, a holy man, సుజనుడు. A Rakshasa, an evil spirit, రాక్షసుడు. పుణ్యజనేశ్వరుడు *punya-janēsvarudu* n. Kubēra. పుణ్యభూమి *punya-bhūmi.* n. The Holy Land (of the Hindus), i. e., Hindustan, the land between the Himalayas and the Vindhyas. పుణ్యలోకము *punya-lōkamu.* n. Heaven. పుణ్యవంతుడు *punya-vantudu.* n. One who is holy or virtuous. ధార్మికుడు, అదృష్టవంతుడు. ఈ విషయములో అతడు చాలా పుణ్యవంతుడు in this respect he is very lucky. పుణ్యస్త్రీ or పుణ్యాంగన *punya-strī.* n A good housewife, good woman, lady. పుణ్యాత్ముడు *puny-ātmudu.* n. A holy, pious or charitable person, పుణ్యస్వరూపుడు. పుణ్యాహము *puny-āhamu.* n. A holy or sacred day, పుణ్యదినము. పుణ్యాహవాచనము *puny-āha-vāchanamu.* n. The consecration or hallowing of a ceremony. A ceremonial purification. పుణ్యుడు *punyudu.* n. A holy or virtuous man. పుణ్యులారా O holy men!

పుతపుత *puta-puta.* [Tel. anuk.] n. Tremor. చలనము. పుతపుతపోవు *puta-puta-pōvu.* v. n. To be perplexed, విలవిలపోవు. "పుతపుతపోవుచున్న వ్రతపుంగవు చిత్తమెంచని." Zacca. iv. 237.

పుతికి *putiki.* [Tel.] n. A tree called *Grewia asiatica.* Rox. ii. 587. నల్లపుతికి *nalla-putiki.* n. A tree called *Aristida depressa* (Watts).

పుత్త *putta.* [Tel.] n. The posteriors. పృష్ఠము.

పుత్తడి or పుత్తళి *puttadi.* [Tel.] n. Gold. పుత్తడికాసు a gold coin. "సీ॥ తరతరంబుల నుండి తనయింట వెలయు పుత్తడిపైడిబొట్ట మస్తమునకెలుంగ." S. i. 16. పుత్తళిక *puttalika.* n. An image, a doll or puppet, బొమ్మ.

పుత్తిక *puttika* [Skt.] n. A white ant. పుట్టలోనిచెద. A honey bee, తేనెటీగ.

పుత్తెంచు [పుచ్చు+తెంచు.] Same as పుచ్చు (q. v.).

పుత్రుడు or పుత్రకుడు *putrudu.* [Skt.] n. A son. ఔరసపుత్రుడు or ఔరసుడు *aurasa-putrudu.* n. A legitimate son. దత్తపుత్రుడు or దత్తుడు *patta-putrudu.* n. An adopted son. పుత్రి or పుత్రిక *putri.* n. A daughter. A copy or transcript from an original. పుత్రవాత్సల్యము parental affection, love towards children. పుత్రోత్సవము *putr-ōtsavamu.* n. Rejoicings on account of the birth of a son. పుత్రకామేష్టి *putra-kām-ēshti.* n. A religious sacrifice performed for the purpose of obtaining a son. పుత్రజీవిక *putra-jīvika.* n. A tree, a species of *Nageia.* Rox. iii. 766. పుత్రపౌత్రపారంపర్యముగా *putra-pautra-pāram-paryamu-gā.* adv. From generation to generation. ఈ నేలను పుత్రపౌత్రపారంపర్యముగా అనుభవించవలసినది the land is to be held by him and his heirs for ever.

పుదియబొట్టు *pudiya-bottu.* [Tel.] n. An upright caste mark worn on the forehead. ఊర్ధ్వపుండ్రము.

"సీ॥ నుదుటిపైఁ జేర్చి కస్తూరిని పుదియబొట్టుముఖాలంకృతిమల్లసిల్ల."

రా. అర. ii.

పుదీనా *pudīna.* [Tel.] n. Mint, Indian peppermint, *Mentha sativa.*

పుద్గలము *pudgalamu.* [Skt.] n. Matter, substance, (in a philosophical sense.)

పుద్గలాస్తికాయం matter as comprising all bodies composed of atoms. Colebr. Ess. i. 385. 386.

పునః *punaha.* [Skt.] prep. Again, (in composition.) Thus పునర్విమర్శ or పునర్విచారణ a review, re-trial. ఈ దావా హైకోర్టువారివల్ల పునర్విచారణకు పంపబడ్డది this suit is remanded by the High Court for a re-trial. పునఃచేసినవిచారణ a repeated inquiry. పునఃపునః again and again. పునఃప్రతిష్ఠ re-consecration. **పునరుక్తము** *punar-uktamu.* adj. Repeated. **పునరుక్తముగా** *punar-ukta-mu-gā.* adv. Repeatedly. **పునరుక్తి** *punar-ukti.* n. Repetition. **పునరుత్థానము** *punar-utthānamu.* n. Restoration. In the Telugu Bible it is used for Resurrection. **పునర్జన్మము** *punar-janmamu.* n. A second birth. Metempsychosis. **పునర్నవ** *punar-nava.* n. Hogweed, గలిజేరు. A finger nail, నఖము. **పునర్భవము** *punar-bhavamu.* adj. Lit: Being born again, మరలపుట్టిన. n. A nail. గోరు. Family life, సంసారము, A phase of the moon, చంద్రకళ. **పునర్భూవు** *punar-bhuvu.* n. A re-married widow, మారుమనువుది, దిధిషువు. **పునర్వసు** *punar-vasu.* n. The seventh of the lunar mansions. See పునాస. **పునశ్చరణ** *punaś-charana.* n. The repetition of a certain prayer, or charm, మంత్రమును మరలమరల పఠించుట. **పునస్కారము** *punas-kāramu.* n. A word like "&c." ఆ విగ్రహము పూజా పునస్కారములేక పడియున్నది homage and the like is no longer offered to that image. **పునస్సంధానము** *punas-sandhā-namu.* n. Lit: Bringing together again. మరలకూర్చుట. A preliminary ceremony. Also used for the ceremony performed at the consummation of marriage.

పునాది *punādi.* [Tel.] n. A foundation of a house, &c., a basis, హస్తిభారము.

పునాస or **పునాసలు** *punāsa.* [from Skt. పునర్వసు, the name of a star or constellation.] n. The first crop of the year which consists of grain of an inferior kind, కొర్రలు, జొన్నలు మొదలగు ధాన్యము. ఆము. iv.

పునిస్త్రీ *puni-strī.* [from Skt. పుంస్త్రీ.] n. A woman whose husband is living.

పునీతుడు *pu-nītuḍu.* [Skt.] n. A sinless or holy man, పవిత్రుడు.

పునుక or **పున్క** *punuka.* [Tel.] n. The skull, తలచిప్పయొక్క యెముక, కపాలము. Swa. iv. 109. "చేతిపునుక కప్పెరనిండ, బ్రాతిగోటుల నల్లబట్టినాడు. L. i. 310. "భూత సంఘంబుల పునుక కంచంబు." M. XII. i. 386. **పునుకతాలుపు** *punuka-tālupu.* n. The bearer of skulls, i. e., Siva.

పునుగు *punugu.* [Tel.] n. The perfume called Civet. See జవ్వాది. **పునుగుచెట్టము** *punugu-tsattamu.* n. A civet bag or gland sold as a drug. **పునుగుపిల్లి** *punugu-pilli.* n. The civet cat. The small Indian Civet, *Viverricula malaccensis.* (F. B. I.) **పునుగుబెండ** or **కస్తూరిబెండ** *punugu-benda.* n. A fragrant kind of బెండ. **పునుగురాజనాలు** *punugu-rādzanālu.* n. Musky rice. A fragrant sort of rice called Muradazalli.

పునెము See పున్నెము.

పున్న *punna.* [Tel. another form of పిన్న.] adj. Young. **పున్నతేలు** *punna-tēlu.* n. A young scorpion. వాడు పున్నతేలువలె అంటించి ఊరక ఉండినాడు he played the part of an innocent looking scorpion.

పున్నమ *punnama.* [from Skt. పూర్ణిమ.] n. The lunar day on which the moon is full. పౌర్ణమి.

పున్నాగము *punnāgamu.* [Skt.] n. A white flower like tuberose: the tree termed *Rottleria tinctoria.* సురపొన్న. A white lotus, తెల్లకలువ. A chief, a pre-eminent man, పురుషశ్రేష్ఠుడు.

పున్నెము or పున్నెయము Same as పుణ్యము. (q. v.)

పుప్పము puppamu. [from Skt. పుష్ప.] n. A flower. పుష్పం.

పుప్పి puppi. [Tel. from పుచ్చు to rot.] n. Decay, rottenness, పుచ్చేడము. పుప్పిపురుగు an insect found in rotten timber, పుచ్చిపురుగు. adj. Decayed, rotten. పుప్పిపల్లు a decayed tooth.

పుప్పించు puppintsu. [Tel. Causal of పుచ్చు.] v. a. To send, పంపు.

పుప్పొడి puppoḍi. [Tel. పూ+పొడి.] n. The dust, pollen or farina of a flower. పుష్పపరాగము.

పుబ్బ pubba. [Tel.] n. The name of the eleventh lunar mansion.

పుయిలోడు puyil-ōḍu. [Tel. పుయిలు+ఓడు.] v. n. To draw back, వెనుదీయు. To hesitate, సంకోచించు. To melt, yield, be kind or tender. To blush, be ashamed. దాక్షిణ్యపడు, సిగ్గుపడు. "నరులనేక కోటుల రణంబునదాఁకటాకౌ గాన న, క్కురుపతి నీ సమక్షమునకుం గదియం బుయిలోడెడుంక్." M. XII. ii. 167. పుయిలోటు, పుయిలోడుట, పుయిలోటమి or పుయిలోటకము puyil-ōṭa. n. Hesitation, వెనుకదీయుట, సంకోచించుట. Regard, delicacy or civility, which is inspired only by a person's presence: kindness shewn with an immediate or remote view to one's own interest: shame. మొగమోటము, దాక్షిణ్యము, సిగ్గు.

పుయ్యి or పల్లపుయ్యి puyyi. [Tel.] n. A thorny shrub, called *Capparis sepiaria*. Rox. ii. 568.

పురందరుడు purandaruḍu. [Skt.] n. A name of Indra.

పురంధ్రి purandhri. [Skt.] n. A mistress of a family, a matron, a good woman. కుటుంబిని, కుటుంబమును పోషించు స్త్రీ.

పురజా puraḍza. [Persian.] n. A daily account of the receipts and disbursements of a village; also sea customs. A piece, bit, rag. A note, memorandum. లెక్కచిట్టా. రోజాపురజా a shopkeeper's day book.

పురడించు, పురుడించు or పురణించు puraḍintsu. [Tel.] v. n. & a. To resemble. To vie with, emulate, to contemn, to subdue. పోలు, సరిపోలు, తిరస్కరించు, నిరసించు. To excel, వర్ధిల్లు, విజృంభించు. "సింగంబున్న గుహాంతరాళమునకుఁ శ్రీఘ్రంబునవచ్చుచుమా, తంగంబు పురడించుచుక్." M. IV. ii. 334.

పురటు puraṭa. [Tel.] n. An old form of పుట (q.v.).

పురణించు or పురడించు puraṇintsu. [Tel.] v. n. To excel, increase, వర్ధిల్లు, విజృంభించు.

పురపుర pura-pura. [Tel. anuk.] adv. Much, greatly, మిక్కిలి. పురపురపొక్కు to sorrow bitterly, deeply, inconsolably. "సురలారమీరు నాకై పురపుర పొక్కకుఁడనవలదు." G. v. 235. ఆ దెబ్బకు వానిచెంప పురపురవాచినది his cheek swelled much from the blow. పురపురలాడు purapural-āḍu. v. n. To be eager, మిక్కిలి అపేక్షపడు. ఏదైనను తినవలెనని వానినోరు పురపురలాడుచున్నది he is eager for some food.

పురము puramu. [Skt.] n. A city, or town. పట్టణము. A house, ఇల్లు. A storey, మేడ.

పురవచేప purava-chēpa. n. A fish, a sort of *Clupea*. Russell's Fishes. No. 189, 190, 194. Or, a species of *Thryssa* (Swainson.)

పురస్కరించు puras-karintsu. [Skt.] v. a. To set in front, as a leader, ముందుంచుకొను. "భీష్మునిబురస్కరించుకొనుము." M. v. ii. 134. To worship, to revere, పూజించు. పురస్కృతము puras-kritamu. adj. Placed in front, put forward. ముందుంచబడిన. Worshipped or honored. సన్మానింపబడిన. పురస్కారము, పురస్కృతి or

పురస్కారము *pura-skāramu.* n. The act of setting a person in front; worshipping.

పురస్సరుడు *puras-sarudu.* [Skt.] n. One who walks in front. A leader, a chief, ముందునడచువాడు.

పురహరుడు, పురారి or **త్రిపురహరుడు** *pura-harudu.* [Skt.] n. An epithet of Siva.

పురాకృతము *purā-kritamu.* [Skt.] adj. Formerly done. ముందుచేయబడిన. n. The good or evil acts committed in a former birth. పూర్వజన్మమునందు చేయబడిన శుభాశుభ కర్మము.

పురాణము *purānamu.* [Skt.] adj. Old, ancient, పురాతనము. n. An ancient story, or legend, a mythological tale, a rhapsody or string of stories. The name of a class of books in Indian literature. పూర్వకథ. స్థలపురాణము local archives, a book regarding the origin of a town, &c. పౌరాణికకథ an old tale or romance. పురాణముచెప్పు to chant or read a legend to an audience. పురాణమువిను to be an auditor of a legend which is recited. పురాణభట్టుడు a mere block-head, one who recites a legend without knowing the meaning of it. **పురాణించు** or **పురణించు** *purānintsu.* v. n. To recite a Purāṇa, పురాణము చెప్పు. To become inveterate, chronic, or constitutional, as a disease, వర్ధిల్లు, విజృంభించు. వ్యాధి పురాణించినది the disease became chronic. **పురాణదంపతులు** *purāna-dampatulu.* n. The 'primeval pair,' a phrase for Siva and Pārvati, or Vishṇu and Lakshmi. A phrase like Adam and Eve.

పురాతనము *purātanamu.* [Skt.] adj. Ancient, old. బహుదినములది. **పురాతనులు** *purātanulu.* n. plu. The ancients, పూర్వులు.

పురాయించు *purāyintsu.* [from Skt. పూర again.] v. n. To excel, to increase. వర్ధిల్లు, విజృంభించు.

పురావలోకనము *pur-āvalōkanamu.* [Skt. పుర+అవలోకనము.] n. Looking again, reperusal.

పురావృత్తము *pur-āvrittamu.* [Skt.] n. An ancient story. పూర్వకథ, ఇతిహాసము. M. XIII. v. 371.

పురి [Skt.] Same as పురము (q.v.). **పురి** [Tel.] n. A twist, మెలి. A peacock's tail. పింఛము. Packthread, twine, twist. A straw basket, plastered with clay, in which grain is stored. A wattle thus plastered. గడ్డితో పురికవలెకట్టి ధాన్యముపోసే గంప, గోనెకుట్టె పాడు. Spreading, కవియుట, క్రమ్ముట. Strength; refreshment. Pride. గర్వము. పురులొత్తి (peacocks) having spread their tails. పురిపులుగు or పురిపిట్ట a peacock, నెమలి. పురియెక్కిన, పురెక్కిన twisted, refreshed, strengthened. "నెమ్మినర్తించు పురివిచ్చినెమ్మిగములు." R. vi. 9. **పురికొను** *puri-konu.* v.n. To be refreshed, to regain strength or spirits. To come to mind, to prick the heart. To cover, surround కవియు, క్రమ్ము.

"క॥ ఉభయబలంబులు పురికొని,
యిభతురగస్యందనములు నిల్వరొప్పులుగా,
రథసాశ్వరాశ్వక్షతమై,
రథిశ్వరులు పొగడనీమునం బోరాడెన్."
M. VII. iii. 133.

పురికొలుపు *puri-kolupu.* v. a. To spur on, move, instigate, incite, stir up, rally. మొనయు, ప్రేరేపించు, ఎచ్చరించు, నూలు కొలుపు. పుల్లలుపెట్టు. **పురికొస** *puri-kosa.* n. A large poisonous spider or tarantula. Also, a rough kind of twine. **పురిగట్టిన** *puri-gaṭṭina.* part. Strong, vigorous. **పురిపెట్టు** *puri-peṭṭu.* v. a. To twine or twist. **పురియెక్కించు** *puri-y-ekkintsu.* v. a. To incite. **పురివిచ్చు** *puri-vitstsu.* v. a. To untwist or unravel a thread. v. n. To separate, withdraw, retreat. జారు, విడిపోవు. **పురులోమము** *puru-*

lômu. (పురులు+ఓము.) v. n. To be enraged, క్షాత్రముచెందుంచు.

పురిటితీగె puriti-tige. [Tel.] n. A creeper, *Ipomoea hispida.*

పురిడిపిట్ట puridipitta. [Tel.] n. A quail. ముక్కుపురిడి a snipe. See పూరేడు.

పురీషము purishamu. [Skt.] n. Dung, excrement, fæces, మలము. మూత్రపురీషములు urine and fæces.

పురుగు or పురువు purugu. [Tel.] n. A worm, any insect or reptile that has no wings. క్రిమి, కీటకము. గుల్లపురుగు a shell fish. వారి పురుగు లేకుండా చేసినాడు he exterminated them. వాడు చెడుపురుగు he is a vile wretch. పురుగుపట్టిన infested with insects, decayed.

పురుడించు purudintsu. [Tel.] v. n. & a. To resemble. పోలు, సరిపోలు.

పురుడు purudu. [Tel.] n. Parturition, child birth. Ceremonial uncleanness for ten days after the birth of a child, జాతాశౌచము. పురుడుపుచ్చు to put away a woman's uncleanness. పురిటిల్లు or పురుటిల్లు the house wherein a birth has happened, ప్రసవగృహము. చిలుపురుడు the lesser degree of uncleanness, extending from the 10th to the 30th day. పురిటిపురుగు a reptile, imagined to injure new born children. ఆమెపురుడుపోసినాను I got her through her confinement, I attended on her in her childbed. "పురిటిజెంకలు పెనుపులులగోర్లు." S. i 176. పురిటిజెంకలు అనగా కనిన పదిదినములైనావాని జింకపిల్లలు. పురిటాలు, పురుటాలు or పురుటియాలు purit-âlu. n. A woman in childbed. బాలెంతరాలు.

పురుడు purudu. [Tel.] n. Likeness, similarity. సమానత, సామ్యము. "అప్పుడు ప్రభాకరుండు నభోమధ్యంబునకువచ్చి వెలుంగుచున్న నతనితోడి పురుడునం దేతో మహీమండలమ్మాన్న తెరంగున మెరుంగు వాలమ్ములను కిరణంబులు బరగించును." M. vi ii. 136. "భరతకులరాజు లెల్లను పురుడనగాంచిల్లనగరమున కరిగడరోండొరుల గడవంగనని భూసురవరు లెఱింగిరి పృథు కుతుకథలుల్లసిల్ల." M. I. vii. 34.

పురుదోన puru-dona. [Tel.] n. A tree that is commonly used for fuel, the *Ekebergia.* Rox. ii. 392.

పురువు or పుర్వు. See పురుగు.

పురుషుడు purushudu. [Skt.] n. A man. A husband. నాపురుషుడు my husband. మహాపురుషుడు a great person. పురుషకారము an attempt of man, human effort, పురుషప్రయత్నము. పురుషోత్తముడు purushôttamudu. n. Lit: the best of men. The Almighty. పురుషము purushamu. n. A person in verbs. క్రియలయొక్క విభక్తుల సంజ్ఞ. ప్రథమపురుషము the third person. మధ్యమపురుషము the second person. ఉత్తమపురుషము the first person. పురుషరత్నము or మంగలింగము purusha-ratnamu. n. A species of violet or phallus flower, *Viola suffruticosa.* Ainslie. ii. 267. *Ionidium suffruticosum.* Wight, plate XIX. పురుషాయితము purush-âyitamu. n. Man-fashion; playing the husband. పురుషార్థము purush-arthamu. n. An object of desire. The principal thing or object in life, i. e., ధర్మార్థకామమోక్షములు the gratification of desire, acquirement of wealth, discharge of duty, and final emancipation. ఇదిచేస్తే పుణ్యమా పురుషార్థమా if one does this, does it bring merit or the satisfaction of one's desires?

పురుహూతుడు puru-hûtudu. [Skt.] n. An epithet of Indra.

పురే or పురే purê. [Tel.] interj. Ah! alas! "చాలుబురేరిత్తె సంవాదమేల." HD. i. 246.

పురోగము or పురోగమము purô-gamu. [Skt.] n. Going before, preceding. పురో

గామి, పురోగమడు or పురోగుడు *purō-gami.* adj. and n. One who precedes or goes in front of, a herald, a leader. అగ్రేసరుడు, ముఖ్యుడు, ముందరనడచువాడు.

పురోటీ *purōṭī.* [Mahrati.] n. A short note or letter; a bill; a note of hand. చీటి.

పురోధసుడు *purōdhasuḍu.* [Skt.] n. A family priest. పురోహితుడు.

పురోభాగము *purō-bhāgamu.* [Skt.] n. The front. పురోభాగి *purō-bhāgi.* n. One who is malevolent or censorious. ఎల్లప్పుడును దోషములు వెదకువాడు.

పురోభావి *purō-bhāvi.* [Skt.] adj. Probable, likely to happen.

పురోసూచకము *purō-sūchakamu* [Skt.] n. Prognostication, a foreboding, an omen or portent.

పురోహితుడు *purō-hituḍu.* [Skt.] n. A family priest.

పుర్ర *purra.* [Tel.] adj. Left. ఎడమ, వామము. పుర్రచెయ్యి *purra-cheyyi.* n. The left hand, ఎడమచెయ్యి. పుర్రచెయ్యివాటము గలవాడు a left handed man.

పుర్రు *purru.* [Tel.] n. Mash, slush, ooze, soft mire, a loose motion of the bowels. పలుచని బురద, మలము మెత్తనైనది. The noise made in tearing a cloth. బట్టచినిగే ధ్వని.

పుర్రె, పుర్రియ or పురియ *purre.* [Tel.] n. The skull. The head when cut off. పుర్రెడు *purr-eḍu.* n. A skull-ful, as much as fills a skull. పుర్రెటి n. A quail.

పుర్వు Same as పురుగు. (q. v.)

పుల *pula.* [Tel.] adj. Yellowish white. Also, పుల్ల. adj. (q. v.). పులకండము *pula-kanḍamu.* n. Sugar-candy. కలకండ, కండచక్కెర.

పులకచేయు *pulaka-cheyu.* [Tel.] v. a. To harrow land.

పులకలు *pulakalu.* [Skt.] n. plu. A bristling, a glow, a tingling or glowing of the skin, as in a blush, the hair of the skin being erected. గగుర్పాటులు, గగుర్పాటు. Fever, జ్వరము. పులకాంకితుడు *pulak-ānkituḍu.* n. One who glows or tingles with ecstasy, గగుర్పాటుకలిగినవాడు. పులకాంకురము *pulak-ānkuramu.* n. A bristling, a tingle, glow, shudder, thrill. గగుర్పు. పులకించు *pulakintsu.* v. n. To glow, bristle or tingle. పులకోద్గమము *pulak-ōdgamamu.* n. A bristling, tingle, glow. పులకరము *pulakaramu.* [from పులకలు.] n. Feverishness, aguishness, జ్వరము. Startling, గగుర్పాటు. పులకరించు *pulakarintsu.* v. n. To be feverish or startled.

పులగము or పుల్లము *pulagamu.* [Tel.] n. A dish made of rice boiled with green gram. ఈ భాషలోని వాడుకలన్నియు పులగము వలెనున్నవి this language is a mere hodge-podge.

పులప *pulapa.* [Tel.] n. A mess of various roots, boiled with lime juice. కందగాని వర్లేరుగాని దొనిపి పులుసుపెట్టినవండినది.

పులపొడుచు or పుల్పొడుచు *pula-poḍutsu* [Tel.] v. n. To look without winking the eyes, to stare. రెప్పవేయకచూచు.

పులము n. Same as పులకలు (q. v.). adj. Large, broad. విపులము.

పులస *pulasa.* [Tel.] n. A sort of fish.

పులసరము *pulasaramu.* n. Indigestion. నా కడుపులో పులసరమున్నది I am suffering from indigestion. Enthusiasm, spirit. ఉద్రేకము. పులసరి *pulasari.* adj. Proud. గర్వముగల. పులసరితనము *pulasari-tanamu.* n. Presumption, pride, arrogance. గర్వము.

"ద్విజ కులవానియట్లు నిక్కుచునివొక్కు,
పులసరితనమున బుద్ధిచెడియెదము."

ద్విప. iv. 590.

పులాకము *pulākamu.* [Skt.] n. A grain of boiled rice. అన్నపుమెతుకు. Brevity, సంక్షేపము.

పులావు *pulāvu.* [H.] n. A kind of rich food prepared by Mahomedans.

పులి or **పుల్ల** *puli.* [Tel.] adj. Acid, sour. పులికడుగు sour washings, i. e., water in which raw rice has been washed and is then left to ferment. పులికూడు food that has turned sour. పులికాపు *puli-kāpu.* n. A mixture of tamarinds in water with which copper or brass images are scoured. పులిగంజి sour gruel. పులికడుగు *puli-gaḍugu.* v. a. To wash. (కడుగు) pearls, &c. in (పులి) acid, to restore their brilliancy. To scour, burnish. "నలువురముసు నీకతిమతి, నిలుపుమహాత్ములకు వాక్శనిర్మలముగునో, పులికడిగినట్లురాగా, దుల సంగతి చేతమున్న దూషితమైనగా." Prabōdha Chandrōd. ii. 108. పులిగాయము *puli-gāyamu.* n. A scar. ఆరినమచ్చ, పుండుమచ్చ. పులిచింతలము *puli-chintsa-lamu.* n. A medicinal plant. అగ్నిజిహ్వ. పులిచింత or పులిచెంచలి *puli-chinta.* n. Yellow wood sorrel, *Oxalis corniculata.* Linn. Ainsl. ii. 324. చుక్రిక. పులిచేను a fresh field, one lately left fallow. పులితేపుడు. పులితేన్పు, పులితేపు or పులితేన్పు *puli-tēnupu.* n. Acid belching, అజీర్ణపుతేపు. పులినీళ్లు raw rank fluid, serum that oozes from a sore. పులిమెట్టు *puli-meṭṭu.* n. The sediment of water in which raw rice has been washed. తెల్లకడుగుచొక్కు, అడుగుది. పులియు *puliyu.* v. n. To turn sour. పులియ, పులియాకు or పుల్లాకు *puliya.* n. A leaf on which one's food has been taken, ఎస్తరాకు. పులిరేవకాకు Same as పుల్లాకు. పులివెలగచెట్టు *puli-velagachettu.* n. A species of wood apple. పులివరుగు *puli-varugu* n. Dried and sour fruits, pickled fruit, పులియబెట్టిన వరుగు. పులిహోరు *pulihōru.* [Kan.] n. Rice dressed with acid sauce, పులి అన్నము.

పులి *puli.* [Tel.] n. A tiger. *Felis tigris.* (F.B.I.) పెద్దపులి. చిరుతపులి a cheetah, leopard or panther. *Felis pardus.* (F.B.I.) ఈగపులి the fly tiger, i. e., a spider. పులిజున్ను cheese of 'tiger's milk' equivalent to 'pigeon's milk'' వాడు పెద్దపులి వలెనుండినాడు he was fierce, or, he acted in a manly manner. పులినిచూచి నక్క వాత పెట్టుకొన్నట్లు as a jackal brands itself to look like a tiger: a proverb meaning "to ape another person. పులికోచ *puli-kōtsa.* n. The tarantula, a large venomous spider. పులిగోరు *puli-gōru.* A tiger's claw, used as the central ornament of a necklace. పులిచెవులాకు *puli-cheval-āku,* n. Tiger's ears; a certain medicinal plant. పులిజూదము *puli-dzūdamu.* A game like drafts. One sort is called గుమ్మడికాయపులిజూదము, because played with gourd-seeds H. iv. 148. పులితెంకి *puli-tenki.* n. A kind of fish. పులిపెంజెర *puli-penjera.* n The snake called కాటుకరేకుపాము. పులిమేకము *puli-mekamu.* n. A certain fish, a species of *Squalus or Tigrinus.* Russell, plate, XVII. పులియడు *puliyaḍu.* n. A name given to a dog which looks like a tiger.

పులినము or **పుళినము** *pulinamu.* [Skt.] n. A sandbank; a sandhill, ఇసుకతిప్ప.

పులిపిరి, **పుల్పిరి**, **పులిపిరికాయ**. **పులిపులి** or **పులిపులికాయ** *pulipiri.* [Tel.] n. Callus, hard skin, callosity, as that of a wart. A wart. A villain, a scoundrel. పులిపిరికేమి రోసము, i.e., what feeling has a scoundrel? పులిపులి *puli-puli.* adj. Tormented. పీడితము. పులిపులిగాగ *pulipuli-gā-ga.* adv. Easily, into slices, తేలికయముగానముగా. "పులిపులిగాగ తెబ్బకెత్తించుకొన్నారాతని చేతగానా చేతనంగాక." R. ii. 23.

పులిరూను Same as పుల్లిరుగు. See under పుల్లు.

పులు or పుల్లు *pulu*. [Tel. cf. Tam. పుల్.] n. Grass. కసవు. Also, foulness in gems, రత్నాదులమాలిన్యము. పుల్గృహము a grass house. A. iv. 167. కనకపులు golden grass. adj. Little, mean. పులుమానిసి a little or low man. పులుమ్రాను *pulu-mrānu*. n. A tree which belongs to the family of the Palms. తాటిచెట్టుమొదలైన తృణద్రుమము. పులుకాసిపురుగు *pulu-kāsi-purugu*. n. An insect with green wings, పచ్చరెక్కపురుగు. A low person, అల్పుడు. పాంచాల్పి. ii. పులుకాసిపులుగు *pulu-kāsi-pulugu*. n. A parrot. "తే॥ ఇన్ని దేవుళ్ల గొలిచి నే నేమిగంటి, పోయిపచ్చనిపులుకాసి పులుగుచేత, మోసపోయి తీని కందుమొనయొఖేడ, మూరటమెనర్పు విని వినయమూర్తిఁబనిచి." S. iii. 53.

పులుకుపులుకు or పుల్కుపుల్కు *puluku-puluku*. [Tel.] n. Blinking. పులుకుపులుకునచూచు *puluku-puluku-na-tsūtsu*. v.n. To blink or view with blinking eyes: to look piqued, మిణుకరించుచు చూచు. "తే॥ పులుకుపులుకునఁజూచి యుక్కళికతోడ, బలుకుపలుకున బ్రహ్మంబు దోఁచబలికె." Sāranga. P. ii. 103.

పులుగాకు *pulu-y-āku*. [Tel. పులు+ఆకు.] n. Harm, mischief. ఉపద్రవము. "ద్వి॥ పలు గాకు పై బరాంధింగనులన్నిట, పులు గాకులాసించుబోలదె మాన్ప." HD. i. 1124.

పులుగు *pulugu*. [Tel.] n. A bird. పక్షి. A mark or sign. గురుతు, జాడ. "తే॥ గీ॥ పొలతిరేలుని యునికియు పులుగుగాడె." A. v. 63. పులుగుపిట్ట *pulugu-pitta*. n. An owl, గుడ్లగూబ. పులుగరి or పుల్గరి *pulug-ari*. n. One who understands a sign, జాడయెరిగినవాడు. పులుగుబొల్లడు or పులుగురేడు *pulugu-bolladu*. n. An eagle, గరుత్మంతుడు. పులుగురాయి *pulugu-rāyi*. n. An emerald, పచ్చ, గారుత్మతము. పులుదిండిరాయి or పులుదిండిరాలుగ *pulu-diṇḍi-rāyi*. n. A sapphire, ఇంద్రనీలమణి.

పులుగుడు *pulugudu*. [Tel.] n. A certain medicinal plant. వాతఘ్ని.

పులుచు or పులుసు *pulutsu*. [Tel.] n. A certain tree, perhaps, *Antidesma ghaesembilla*. (Watts). "బోరెము, మంకెన, పులుచు, నంగరెను, తెక్కలి, ములుగు." H. iv. 20.

పులుప *pulupa*. [Tel.] n. An acid chutney, పుల్లని తొరుకుడు. కాశీ. vii.

పులుము or పులుముకొను *pulumu*. [Tel.] v. n. and a. To scour or rub, in washing or bathing. రుద్దు, పలుచు. To beat, కొట్టు. కండ్లుపులుముకొనుచు లేచినాడు he waked up rubbing his eyes. తలపులుముకొను to rub the head in bathing. గుడ్డలుపులుముకొను to wash clothes. వాన్ని బాగా పులిమినారు they thrashed him well. పులుముడు *pulumudu*. n. Rubbing, రుద్దడము. పులిమిపుచ్చు *pulimi-putstsu*. v. a. To evade. అడిగినదానికి ఉత్తరముచెప్పకుండా మాయచేయు. "నందుడదే మన్న నవ్వుచు మిగులగొమ్మంచుకొనెనేలె పులిమి పుచ్చు." N. ix. 344.

పులుసు *pulusu*. [Tel.] n. Acidity, an acid, as the juice of tamarinds. Pride, self-conceit. అతనిపులుసుఅణచిరి they humbled his pride. adj. Acid, sour. పులుసుకూర vegetables dressed with acids, పులుసుపోసి వండినకూర.

పులోముడు *pulōmuḍu*. [Skt.] n. The name of a Rishi, slain by Indra. పులోమజ *pulōma-ja*. n. The daughter of Pulōma who was ravished by Indra and became his wife, శచీదేవి. పులోమజిత్తు *pulōma-jittu*. n. The slayer of Pulōma: an epithet of Indra.

పుల్కసుడు or పుల్కసుడు *pulkasuḍu*. [Skt.] n. A man of the Chandāla or Pariah caste. చండాలుడు, శ్వపచుడు, అంత్యజుడు. పుల్కసి *pulkasi*. n. A female of the Pariah caste, మాలది.

పుల్పొడుము Same as పులపొడుము. (q. v.)

పుల్ల pulla. [Tel.] n. A small bit or piece of stick. పుల్లలు small pieces of wood for fuel. వానిమీద వ్యాజ్యానికి పొమ్మని నాకు పుల్లలు పెట్టినాడు he goaded me on to quarrel with them. కుట్టుడాకుపుల్లలు pins used in making leaf platters. పానకములో పుల్లవలె అడ్డ పడినాడు he came in my way like a twig in a draught of water. ఆ పనికి నీవు పుల్లలు వేయకు do not throw obstacles in its way.

పుల్ల, పుల్లటి or పుల్లని pulla. [Tel.] adj. Sour, acid, unripe, raw. Whitish, pale, dun-coloured, or reddish, yellow, grizzled, like a lion. పుల్లకంద pulla-kanda. n. A certain root, ఒకవిధమైనకంద. పుల్లకలి pulla-kali. n. Sour gruel. తరవాణి. పుల్ల కూర Same as పులుసుకూర. పుల్లగిల్లు or పుల్లగిలు pulla-gillu. v. n. To turn sour. (Metaphorically,) to be afraid, భయ పడు. Pal. 261. పుల్లగోరక pulla-goraka. n. A water fowl, నీరుకోడి. పుల్లతీగె pulla-tige. n. The Soma plant, సోమలత. సొమ్ము. v. పుల్లదానిమ్మ pulla-danimma. n. A sour pomegranate tree. పుల్లన or పుల్లదనము pullana. n. Sourness, acidity. పుల్లని pullani. adj. Sour, acid. పుల్లనీళ్లు pulla-nillu. n. Soured rice-water, కూటినీళ్లు, కలి. పుల్లప్రబ్బ pulla-prabba. n. Sorrel, *Rumex vesicarius*. శరథేధి, చుక్కకూర. Ainsl. i. 398. పుల్లబచ్చలి pulla-batstsali. n. The sour species of బచ్చలి. పుల్లరుజు pull-arudzu. (పుల్ల+అరుజు.) n. A kind of fish. పుల్లావు pullavu. (పుల్ల+ఆవు.) n. A dun cow, కపిలవర్ణమగల ఆవు. పుల్లె, పుల్లెయు or పుల్లాకు pulle. n. A leaf plate, i. e., a platter made of leaves stitched together and thrown away after it is used.

పుల్లటి pullati. [Tel.] n. A club, కర్ర. A butt, సామువేయువారు గురికిపెట్టుకొను కొయ్య.

పుల్లబడు or పుల్లపడు pulla-badu. [Tel.] v. n. To be stunned, మూర్ఛపడు, స్తంభించు, నిశ్చేష్టితుడగు. "క॥ పుల్లపడి వేలమురిగోసము, బో ల్లైనవతండు కొంతప్రొద్దుమొగమునకా, చెల్లదనము గదురనిలిచి, యొల్లజములుదనమగురియు నిట్లనిపలి కెగా." M. III. iv. 371.

పుల్లరి See under పుల్లు.

పుల్లసిల్లు pullasillu. [Tel.] v. n. To turn pale or pallid, వివర్ణమగు. To be confused in mind, కలతనొందు, వెలవెలబోవు. To be dejected, కుందు. "ఉ॥ పుల్లసిల్లగంధి నామమును మోహనమునారండపెట్టినీవున, నొల్లక వీడనాడిన యోగతినామనివారిం చిత్తములోల్, పుల్లసిలంగజేయు భారపొచ్చెములాడగ నాడువారికి, చెల్లనుచెల్ల బో వ్రతము చెప్ప కుబుంబును చిక్కవడియ్యెగా." V. P. ii. 240.

పుల్లింగము or పుంలింగము pullingamu. [Skt.] n. The masculine gender.

పుల్లిరికి [Tel.] n. A kind of shrub.

పుల్లు or పులు pullu. [Tel.] n. Grass. foulness in precious stones. నెత్త, రత్నాదుల మాలిన్యము. adj. Little, small, అల్పము. పుల్లంటురాగి pull-antu-ragi. n. A sapphire, ఇంద్రనీలము. పుల్లురాసు or పుల రాసు pull-urasu. n. The little wheel over which the bottom rope of a water-lift (కపిల) runs to upset the bucket when it reaches the top. పుల్లుడి pull-udi (పుల్లు+ఉడి.) n. Poor land, land productive only at intervals. ఒకానొక సంవత్సరము సేద్యానకు పనికివచ్చు నేల. పుల్లరి pull-ari (పుల్లు+అరి.) n. Tax, a tax on pasture lands. Also, a tax levied on a fishery, or a head-tax on cattle. పుల్లురుకుపాము pull-uruku-pamu. n. A sort of snake which springs out of grass.

పుల్లెన pullena. [Tel.] n. A plant used in medicine, also called లాలద్రిరు.

పుళింద pulinda. [Skt.] adj. Barbarian, savage, rude. పుళిందదేశము a certain country inhabited by savages. Bulinda Devi is the goddess of the Bheels. Tod's Rajasthan. i. 506. పుళిందుడు *pulindudu.* n. A barbarian, savage, cannibal.

పువ్వు. పువు or పూవు *puvvu.* [Tel.] n. A flower. A cock's wattles. The gills of a fish. Albugo, a kind of blindness. A cataract in the eye. కంటిలో పువ్వు కలదు there is a cataract in the eye. An asterisk or star used in printing. Flowers or flower-like flames which are thrown out by certain fireworks. Vish. viii. 399. A thief in a candle. పువ్వుగాయి a golden ball or ornament on a pagoda. BD. vii. 754. A proverb says వానిమీదపువ్వు వేయ వీలులేదు, i. e., no one can lay a finger upon him. P. iii. 91. కొంపువ్వువాడ... before his garland loses its bloom, i. e., with perfect ease. plu. పువ్వులు or పూలు. పూలవాన a slight shower, a few drops. పువ్వాటు *puv-vatu.* (పువ్వు+ఆటు.) n. "Like a flower"—i. e., waving or rocking backwards and forwards, ... పువ్వారు *puv-varu.* (పువ్వు+...) n. The blossoms of a palm tree. The inner part of a fish's gills. పువ్వారుబోడి *puv-varu-bodi.* n. A woman who is as beautiful as a flower. పువ్విలు *puv-vilu.* [పువ్వు+విలు] n. The bow of flowers: Manmadha's weapon. పువ్విలుకాడు or పువ్విలుకుడు *puv-vilu-kadu.* n. An epithet of Manmadha. పువ్వుచిత్పు or పువ్వుచేప *puvvu-chitstsu.* n. A large fish called the *Veral.* A species of *Chetonn:* Russell's plate 78. పువ్వుబోడి or పువ్వుబోటి *puvvu-bodi.* n. A nymph, lady, fair woman. పువ్వుముడుపు or పూలముడుపు *puvvu-mudu-pu.* n. Placing flowers in the hair, a ceremony performed with pregnant women. సీమంతకర్మము. See పూవు.

పుష్కరము *pushkaramu.* [Skt.] n. The tip of an elephant's trunk. ... A lotus, ... The sky, ... The head of a drum, ... The revolution of twelve years. A feast held once every twelve years at certain holy rivers as the గోదావరిపుష్కరము, కృష్ణాపుష్కరము, &c. ఒక పుష్కర సాలగ్రామ ... a dozen holy stones. కరపుష్కరము the lilies of her hands, i. e., her fair hands. పుష్కరిణి *pushkarini.* n. A flowery lake, a pond wherein lotuses grow. A. i. 55. ... A female elephant.

పుష్కలము *pushkalamu.* [Skt.] adj. Excellent, eminent, chief, best. Much, many. శ్రేష్ఠము. ..., ..., ...

పుష్టి *pushti.* [Skt.] n. Fatness, strength, increase. బలపు. సమృద్ధి. మాటలపుష్టి a farrago of words, wordiness. ధాతుపుష్టి fullness of pulse. వారు పుష్టిగానున్నారు or పుష్టిగాగానున్నారు they are well to do. ధాతుపుష్టిలేని impotent. ... పుష్టిగానున్నాడు he has plenty of money. పుష్టము *pushtamu.* adj. Cherished, nourished. ... పుషితము *pushitamu.* adj. Nourished, nurtured, reared, fostered. పోషింపబడిన.

పుష్పము *pushpamu.* [Skt.] n. A flower. పువ్వు. Menses, స్త్రీరజస్సు. పుష్పంధయము *pushpandhayamu.* n. A bee. తుమ్మెద. పుష్పకము *pushpakamu.* n. A chariot, a car, or stately conveyance used by Kubera or Krishna. కుబేరునివిమానము, కృష్ణునిరేయిల... పుష్పకేతువు, పుష్పధన్వుడు or పుష్పకేతుడు *pushpa-ketuvu.* n. An epithet of Manmadha. పుష్పదంతము *pushpa-dantamu* n. The name of the elephant that is supposed to support the earth at the North-West corner. పుష్పపాము *pushpa-pamu.* n. A certain snake: resembling the one given in Russell's serpents. 2. 9. పుష్పమంజరి *pushpa-manjari.* n. A bouquet of flowers. పూగుత్తి. పుష్పమంజరులు *pushpa-manjaru-lu.* n. A sort of grain. A. i. 75. R. i. 111. పుష్పరథము or పుష్యరథము *pushpa-*

rathamu. n. A pleasure chariot, a car or carriage for any purpose excepting war. విమానము, సవారీరథము, క్రీడార్థమైన రథము. **పుష్పరసము** *pushpa-rasamu*. n. The nectar or honey of flowers, పూతేనె. **పుష్పలావిక** *pushpa-lāvika*. n. A flower-girl, a garland maker. **పుష్పవంతులు** *pushpa-vantulu*. n. The 'Luminaries:' i. e., the sun and the moon, సూర్యచంద్రులు. **పుష్పవతి** or **పుష్పిణి** *pushpavati*. n. A menstruous woman. ఋతుమతి, భాండమునకు దూరమైనస్త్రీ, రజస్వల, ముట్టుది. **పుష్పవనము** or **పుష్పవాటిక** *pushpa-vanamu*. n. A flower garden. పూదోట. **పుష్పవర్షము** or **పుష్పవృష్టి** *pushpa-varshamu*. n. Lit: a shower of flowers, a poetical phrase for the strewing or scattering of flowers on joyful occasions. Colloquially, it means a slight or vernal shower: a mere sprinkling of rain. **పుష్పసమయము** *pushpa-samayamu*. n. Spring, the season of flowers. **పుష్పించు** *pushpintsu*. v. n. To flower, to bloom. పూచు, వికసించు. **పుష్పితము** *pushpitamu*. adj. Flowered. పూచిన.

పుష్యము *pushyamu*. [Skt.] n. The lunar month (December—January, or January February,) in which the moon's change takes place when the sun is in Capricorn. **పుష్యమి** *pushyami*. n. The eighth of the lunar mansions. **పుష్యరాగము** *pushya-rāgamu*. n. A topaz.

పుసలాయించు *pusalāyintsu*. [H.] v. a. To coax, persuade. బుజ్జగించు. **పుసలాయింపు** *pusalāyimpu*. n. Coaxing, persuasion.

పుసి *pusi*. [Tel.] n. The rheum of the eyes. కన్నెప్పిపుసి. వాని కండ్లు పుసులుకట్టినవి his eyes are full of gummy rheum. **పుసికాయలు** granulations in a wound or sore.

పుసుకు *pusuku*. [Tel. (anuk.)] adv. Pop! slapdash! suddenly, abruptly. పుసుక్కునపుట్టు to pop out. పుసుకున మాట్లాడు to blurt out, or say heedlessly.

పుస్తకము or **పుస్తము** *pustakamu*. [Skt.] n. A book, a volume.

పుస్తము *pustamu*. [Skt.] n. A cake of flesh. మాంసపుతిత్తి. Plaster, లప్పము.

పుస్తు *pustu*. [Tel.] n. Stinking, a foul scent, a rammish stink. దుర్గంధము, కంపు. "కదియుచు మైపుస్తుకంపుకొడుకు." H.D. ii. 501.

పుస్తె *puste*. [Tel.] n. The mark of marriage, being a small gold disc worn round the neck by married women. తాళిబొట్టు. See మంగళసూత్రము. Any charmed bead, though worn on the wrist. పుస్తెకట్టు the tali string. **పుస్తెముడుపు** *puste-mudupu*. n. A woman married a second time, రెండోబొట్టు. పుస్తెముడుపుకట్టు to marry in an irregular fashion.

పూ pū

పూ *pū*. [Tel. for పూవు.] n. A flower. పుష్పం. **పూగుత్తి** *pū-gutti*. n. A cluster of flowers, a nosegay. **పూగొమ్మ** *pū-gomma*. n. A flowery branch. **పూజెప** *pū-jepa*. n. A large fish with particoloured sides: called veral (వరాల్.) in Tamil. **పూదరి** *pū-dari*. (పూవు+దరి.) n. Spring time. Lit: the flower season. వసంతఋతువు, పుష్పసమయము. **పూతేనె** or **పూతేనియ** *pūtēne*. n. Honey of flowers, మకరందము. **పూనీరు** *pū-njru*. n. Essence, distilled water. అత్తరునీళ్లు, హిమాంబువు, పన్నీరు. **పూనూక** *pū-nūka*. n. Very fine grits of grain, మెత్తని నూక. **పూనూనె** *pū-nūne*. n. The oil extracted from the Champaka flower, సంపెంగనూనె. **పూబాళ** *pū-bāla*. (పూ+పాళ.) n. A bunch of flowers, as of an areca palm, &c. **పూబిందె** *pū-binde*. n. A very tender fruit, with the flower still attached to it. **పూబోడి**, **పూబోణి** or పుష్పబోధి

pū-bōḍi. n. A beautiful woman, lit: one of a flower-like form. పూరేకు pū-rēku. (పూవు+రేకు.) n. The petal of a flower. పుష్పదళము. A jewel worn by women on the head. "చేరుచుక్క చిన్ని పూరేకు పాలి యలుమకరికా పత్త్రభంగంబులు." Naish. vi. 56. పూరేకులు pū-rēkulu. n. A kind of grain.

పూగము pūgamu. [Skt.] n. The areca palm, పోకచెట్టు.

పూచి or పూచికగడ్డి pūchi. [Tel.] n. A sort of long stiff grass of which brooms are made, *Aristia setocea*. తృణభేదము.

పూచీ or పూచి pūchi. [H.] n. Responsibility. పూచీ నామీద లేదు I am not responsible for it. పూచీపడు pūchi-paḍu. v. n. To undertake the responsibility. పూచీలెక్కలు accounts necessary for current business. పూచీపట్టు or పూచిపట్టు pūchi-paṭṭu. v. n. To be bent upon or firmly resolved, to persist. పూనుకొను. "పాండవమధ్యముండు పదమూడుసంవత్సరంబులు పూచిపట్టికయ్యంబునకు నచ్చె నరనిలాపనను దీరంబున లోకంబున కెక్కియున్నయది." M. VI. iv. 206. "సీతె సైంధవుండు దీనిచుట్టునుగ్గ్యప, శల్యగురుకృపాజ సోమదత్త కర్ణ కర్ణసుతులు కావలియున్నారు పోటుమగలు గాన పూచిపట్టి." M. VII. iii. 179.

పూచు pūtsu. [Tel.] v. n. To flower, bloom, blossom, bud, shoot out, open or expand, పుష్పించు. To have a bad mark, as a horse. To become sapless or weak, నిస్సారమగు. నాలుక పూచినది the tongue furred. కన్నులు పూచినవి the eyes became discoloured by disease. పూచిన బట్టలు spotty clothes, which shew old marks although washed, ఆస్తికముగా తెల్ల బట్టలలో బడే నల్లమచ్చలు. A. v. 127. "పూచిన మావులు" horses that have unlucky marks. కొరగానిమచ్చలుగల గుర్రములు.

పూజ or పూజనము pūja. [Skt.] n. Worship, reverence, respect, veneration, obeisance, homage, adoration. అర్చన. ఇది వాడు చేసుకొన్న పూజాఫలము this is an answer to his prayers. పూజకుడు pūjakuḍu. n. A worshipper, a priest, అర్చకుడు. పూజనీయము pūjanīyamu. adj. Venerable, honourable. M. XIII. v. [illegible]. పూజనీయులు the noble. పూజించు or పూజచేయు pūjintsu v. a. To worship, adore, do homage or obeisance to, reverence. అర్చించు. పూజితము pūjitamu. adj. Worshipped, adored, reverend, reverenced. పూజితుడు pūjituḍu. n. One who is honoured or saintly. పూజింపబడినవాడు. పూజ్యత pūjyata. n. Venerableness. పూజ్యము pūjyamu. adj. Venerable, deserving of respect and reverence. n. Nothing. భోజనానకు పూజ్యమున్నది I have nothing to live upon. పూజ్యుడు pūjyuḍu. n. One who is venerable or honourable, పూజింపదగినవాడు, గౌరవమునకు పాత్రుడు. పూజ్యుడైన pūjyuḍ-aina. adj. Venerable, adorable.

పూజె pūje. [Tel.] n. Painting or filagree work on pots. A bead or spangle: particularly, drops or beads of gold attached to golden jewels. Flourishes or ornaments in a manuscript. Illumination. ఘటాదులమీది చిత్రము. కుండకు పూజెలు పెట్టి the pot is painted with chunam, ochre, &c. Metaphorically a flogging. నీకు పూజెలు కావలెనా do you want a thrashing? పూజెకాగులు or పూజెకుండలు pūje-kāgulu. (పూజె+కాగులు.) n. Painted pots, అలంకరించిన కుండలు. పూజెచేయు to paint pots, &c., ఘటాగులమీద చిత్రించు.

పూజె pūdze. [from Skt. పూజా.] Same as పూజ (q. v.) పూజారి, పూజారి or పూజారి వాడు pūjāri. (పూజె+అరి.) n. An officiating Brahmin or priest of a temple. అర్చకుడు. పూజారిసాని pūjāri-sāni. n. A priestess. Zuma. vi. 127.

పూట pūṭa. [Tel.] n. A time. కాలము. A part of a day, సంధ్య. A day, దినము. Security, surety, bail. ప్రతిభూత్వము. One who stands bail for another, పూటకాపు. పగటిపూట in the day time. రాత్రిపూట at night. తెల్లవారుపూట in the morning. నాలుగుపూటలు మందిచ్చినాడు he administered medicine two mornings and two evenings. పూటకాపు pūṭa-kāpu. n. One who stands security. ప్రతిభువు, జామీనుదారుడు. పూటకూడు food obtained by paying for each meal, boarding. ఏపూటకు ఆపూట సొమ్ము ఇచ్చి తినుట, వెలయిచ్చుకొని వేళవేళకు పెట్టెడు అన్నము. పూటకూళ్లయిల్లు an inn or boarding house. పూటకూళ్లమ్మ a woman who makes her living by preparing food for daily wages. పూటపెట్టు or పూటవెట్టు v. n. To give bail. పూటపడు or పూటవడు pūṭa-paḍu. v. n. To stand bail. అతడు నాకు పూటపడినాడు he stood security for me, అతడు నాకు జామీనుగానున్నాడు. పూటసాక్షి a hired or false witness. దొంగసాక్షి, బూటకపుసాక్షి. పూటపూటకును ఇదే రచ్చ this is the daily plague, ఎల్లప్పుడు ఇదే పోరు or రంధి. పూటవాటు pūṭa-vāṭu. n. The act of standing security for another.

పూటము pūṭamu. [Tel.] n. Weight, బరువు, భారము. పడవ పూటమైనది the boat is filled with the due quantity of goods.

పూడ [Tel.] n. The anus.

పూడు pūḍu. [Tel.] v. n. To be filled or closed up: to fall in, as a well or pit. బావి పూడిపోయినది the well has fallen in. కాలువ పూడిపోయినది the canal is filled up with earth. ఎముకలు పూడిపోయినవి the bones are covered with flesh పూడుపాము pūḍu-pāmu. n. A small, fierce and venomous snake called the *cobra manilla.* మట్టిగాని పూడియుండుపాము. పూడుపు or పూడ్పు n. Burying, పూడ్చుట. Buried treasure. నిక్షేపము. పూడ్చు pūḍtsu. (Madras Telugu for పోయించుచు.) v. n. To go పోవు. పూడిపించు or పూడ్పించు pūḍipintsu. v. a. To cause to be buried or filled up. పూడు or పూడిక pūḍu. n. The filling up, stuff, that has fallen in. పూడుచు or పూడ్చు pūḍutsu. v. a. To fill up, to close, as a pit with earth, to inter or bury, to conceal under the ground. To plant, నాటు.

పూడులు or పూండ్లు pūḍulu. [Tel.] adj. Many, అనేకములు. ఏడులు పూడులుగాక for many years.

పూత pūta. (from Tel. పూయు or పూసే). n. Rubbing, besmearing. పూయుట, పర్పు. Sandal which is smeared over the body, చందనము. Mortar, సున్నపుగచ్చు. Blooming, budding, పూచుట, వికసనము. నోటిపూత Aphthae, a disease of the mouth, thrush. Fragrant paste applied to the skin. చందనము. నాలుగు బంగారుపూతలు అయినవి four coats of gilding are applied. ఆ చెట్టు పూతపట్టలేదు that tree has not commenced to flower.

పూతన pūtana. [Skt.] n. The name of an ogress. అది రెండోపూతన she is a perfect fiend.

పూతము pūtamu. [Skt.] adj. Strained, cleaned, cleansed. వడియబోసిన, వడకట్టబడిన, తూర్పెత్తిన. Pure, purified, పవిత్రమైన.

పూతిగంధి pūti-gandhi. [Skt.] n. A stink, a foul smell, దుర్గంధము.

పూదె or పూదియ pūde. [Tel.] n. A bead of gold. బంగారుపూస. Also, పూదె (q. v.).

పూదెకట్టు pūde-kaṭṭu. v. n. To form into a gold bead. బంగారుపూసగాచేయు.

పూనిగొల్లలు pūni-gollalu. [Tel.] n. A particular class of shepherds.

పూను *pūnu.* [Tel.] v. n. To attempt. యత్నించు, ఉద్యమించు. v. a. To take; to **undertake**; to wear; to bear; to feel or suffer. పొందు, వహించు, పైనవేసికొను, ధరించు, ఆరంభించు, అంగీకరించు. "పూనినవిస్మయ రసమున, మానినిమ్రుగ్గైపడించి మరియుంగనసై." Swa. vi. 101. దానికి శివము పూనినది a spirit or goddess has taken possession of her. పూనిక, పూనికి or పూన్కి *pūnika.* n. Assumption, hope, persistence. అవ లంబింపకేయడము, ఆలోచనము, ఆశ. An attempt, endeavour, ప్రయత్నము, ఉద్య మము. పూనుచు, పూన్చు or పూనించు *pūnutsu.* v. a. To cause to bear or wear. ధరింపజేయు, వహింపజేయు. To cause to undertake, పూనుకొనునట్లుచేయు. To tie, కట్టు. బండికి గుర్రములను పూన్చెను he harnessed the horses to the carriage.

పూనె *pūne.* [Tel.] n. A casket, a small box. బరిణె. "రగడలు త్రొక్కినారు పడేసి మరుగులు తొలఁగ నీకుంకుమపుగోనెలు మిక్కుటపు కస్తూరిపలపులుమించు పునుగిడఁగిన పూనెలు." S. i. 159.

పూప *pūpa.* [Tel.] n. A tender fruit just formed, పుష్పపిండ. An infant. శిశువు. The pupil of the eye, కంటిపాప. adj. Tender, young. లేత.

పూపము *pūpamu.* [Skt.] n. A cake. భక్ష్యము, పిండివంట.

పూపు or పూన్పు *pūpu.* [Tel. from పూను.] n. An undertaking, effort, attempt, పూనిక. "ధీరరసావేశంబున విజయాశా సదన శక్యంబునుంజేసి మును పటి పూపు తప్పక." Kalahas. ii 71.

పూయము *pūyamu.* [Skt.] n. Pus or matter from an abscess or sore, చెరిగిననెత్తురు, చీము.

పూయు *pūyu.* [Tel.] v. n. To bear or produce, as flowers. పూచు. ఆ భూమి ఉప్పుపూస్తున్నది that ground produces salt. v. a. To smear, besmear, daub, anoint, lay on, apply (oil, paint, medicine, &c.) ఒంటికి గంధము పూసికొనుట rubbing oneself with sandal paste. పూయించు *pūyintsu.* v. a. To cause to apply or smear, paint, oil, &c. ఇంటికి సున్నము పూయించితిని or వేయించితిని I got my house whitewashed.

పూరము *pūramu.* [Skt.] n. A flood, a flow, the flowing of the tide. ప్రవాహము. adj. Filled, నిండిన. పూరకము *pūrakamu.* adj Filling, completing. n. That which fills or completes, filling up. A citron, *Citrus medica.* మాదీఫలము. Closing the right nostril and drawing up air through the left. ఊపిరిని పూరించుట. పూరకుడు *pūrakudu* n. One who fills, నించువాడు. పూరగించు *pūra-gintsu.* a. v. To fulfil. నెరవేర్చు. To pass, as time, కడపు. పూర ణము *puranamu.* n. Filling, completing; stuffing: the inside of a pie. నిండించుట. adj. That which fills, నించునది. పూరించు *pūrintsu.* v. a. To fill, to fill with air, to sound a horn. నించు. "పాంచజన్యపూరింప దనాన్యమారుత సుగంధాకృష్టమై." పూరి or పూరికె *pūri.* n. A kind of sweet thin cake made of wheat flour. పూరి తము *pūritamu.* adj. Filled, full, complete. నిండబడిన.

పూరా *pūra.* [H.] adj. Full, complete, సంపూర్ణమైన.

పూరి *pūri.* [Tel.] n. Grass. The milk given by animals, మృగముల చేపుబాలు. పూరిమేయు to eat grass, గడ్డితిను. పూరికి రిచెను he ate grass, i.e., he lost the battle. ఆ నేలను పైపూరితోకూడా అమ్మినాడు he sold the ground with all that was on it. పూరియిల్లు or పూరిల్లు *pūri-illu.* n. A thatched house.

పూరుదొన్నె *pūru-donne.* [Tel.] n. A plant called *Ekebergia indica.* Rox. ii. 392.

పూరుషుడు Same as పురుషుడు. (q. v.)

పూరేడు *pū-rēḍu*. [Tel.] n. A bird of the quail genus. A quail. మిాలవల్లంకి, బాబు, గోనిడ.

పూర్ణము *pūrṇamu*. [Skt.] adj. Full, filled, నిండిన. Complete, all, entire. సమస్తము. Strong, powerful, able. శక్తిగల. పూర్ణకము *pūrṇakamu*. n. A filling up; as, పాదపూర్ణకము a peg in a verse: any useless word inserted to fill the measure, as ఒకి, తగన్, ఇల, &c. పూర్ణకుంభము *pūrṇa-kumbhamu*. n. An ornamented vase filled with water and used in marriages, &c. పూర్ణగర్భము *pūrṇa-garbhamu*. n. A sort of cake. బూరె. పూర్ణపాత్రము or పూర్ణానకము *pūrṇa-pātramu*. n. A full cup or vessel, a vessel filled with cloths or ornaments, which are scrambled for at a festival, a vessel full of rice presented at a sacrifice to the superintending and officiating priests. పూర్ణాదుత్సవకాలే యదలంకారాంబరాదికం. కట్టుము కోసరకు వండ్లు పసుపుబట్టలు మొదలైనవి ఉంచి నపళ్లెము; ఉత్సవకాలమందు సంతోషముచేత వస్త్రాభరణాదికమును దోచుకొనుట; వస్త్రసం పూర్ణపాత్రము. పూర్ణమాసము or పౌర్ణమాసము *pūrṇa-māsamu*. n. A sacrifice performed on the day of the full moon. పూర్ణము or పూర్ణము *pūrṇamu*. n. The inside of a pie. The stuffing of a cake. పూర్ణిమ or పౌర్ణిమాసి *pūrṇima*. n. The lunar day on which the moon is full. పున్నమ, పౌర్ణమి. పూర్ణీభవించు *pūrṇī-bhavintsu*. v. n. To become full, నిండు, పూర్ణమగు. పూర్ణుడు *pūrṇuḍu*. n. One who is full or well skilled. వాడు విద్యలో పూర్ణుడు he is an accomplished scholar.

పూర్తి *pūrti*. [Skt.] n. Fullness, భర్తీ, నిండుట. Completion, termination, end, సమాప్తి. పూర్తము *pūrtamu*. adj. Filled, full, complete. నింపబడిన. Covered, concealed, కప్పబడిన. n. An act of beneficence, as digging a well or tank, planting a grove, building a temple, feeding the poor, &c. Nourishing, cherishing. పాలనము.

పూర్వము *pūrvamu*. [Skt.] adj. First, former, prior, preceding, initial, before, in front of; old, ancient. మొదటిది, ముందటి చోటిది, మొదటికాలపుది. East, eastern. మొదటిదిక్కున. adv. Formerly, of old. తత్పూర్వము previously, before which, before that (time or occurrence.) n. Former or ancient times, days of old. పూర్వ *pūrva*. n. The east. పూర్వకము *pūrvakamu*. adj. Originating in, made of, arising from. బుద్ధిపూర్వకమైన intentional, originating in purpose. వ్రాతపూర్వకమైన in writing. When added to many nouns it makes them adjectives as వినయపూర్వకమైన humble, humbly expressed. పూర్వకముగా *pūrvakamu-gā*. adv. As a token of. As, through, by way of, in accordance with. ప్రమాణపూర్వకముగా on oath. దానపూర్వకముగా as a gift, freely, సమాధానపూర్వకముగా willingly, voluntarily. మంత్రపూర్వకముగా by means of spells, magically. వినయపూర్వకముగా humbly. పూర్వగంగ *pūrva-ganga*. n. The river Narbada. పూర్వజ *pūrvaja*. n. An elder sister. అక్క. పూర్వజన్మము *pūrva-janmamu*. n. A former birth. పూర్వజన్మఫలము *pūrva-janma-phalamu*. n. The result of action in a former birth. Destiny, fortune, fate. పూర్వజుడు *pūrvajuḍu*. n. An elder brother, అన్న. పూర్వదేవుడు or పూర్వగీర్వాణుడు *pūrva-dēvuḍu*. n. An elder god, a Rakshasa, రాక్షసుడు, తొలివేల్పు. పూర్వపక్షము or పూర్వసిద్ధాంతము *pūrva-pakshamu*. n. An argument, one side of a question in logic, వాదము. An objection to an argument. నామాటలు పూర్వపక్షములే all my words were mere statements. పూర్వపక్షమైపోయిన refuted, rebutted. పూర్వపర్వతము or పూర్వాద్రి, *pūrva-parvatamu*.

n. The eastern mountain out of which the sun is supposed to rise. పూర్వరంగము *pūrva-rangamu.* n. A commencement, prologue, overture. నాటకమునకు మొదలు. BD. iii. 97. పూర్వాభిముఖుడు *pūrv-ābhi-mukhuḍu.* n. One who faces the east. పూర్వార్ధము *pūrv-ārdhamu.* n. A former half. పూర్వాషాఢ *pūrv-āshāḍa.* n. The name of a lunar constellation. పూర్వాహ్ణము *pūrv-āhnamu.* n. The first part of the day, the forenoon, దినపూర్వభాగము. పూర్వులు or పూర్వీకులు *pūrvulu.* n. Ancestors, forefathers, predecessors. పూర్వోత్తరదిక్కు *pūrv-ōttara-dikku.* n. The north east. పూర్వోత్తరము *pūrv-ōttaramu.* n. The whole of an affair, from the first (పూర్వము) to the last (ఉత్తరము). Particulars, details. దానిపూర్వోత్తరము ఎరుగను I know nothing whatever about it. నీ పూర్వోత్తరములు చెప్పు tell me your antecedents. పూర్వోత్పన్నము *pūrv-ōtpannamu.* adj. Primeval. అనాదియైన.

పూలి or తెల్లపూలి *pūli.* [Tel.] n. A certain plant, *Arinum pratense.*

పూలి *pūḷi.* [Tel.] n. A star pagoda worth 3½ rupees. పూలీలు plu. Star pagodas.

పూవు *pūvu.* [Tel.] n. A flower. పువ్వు. పూలమట్ట *pūla-maṭṭa.* n. A kind of fish. పూలముడుపు *pūla-muḍupu.* n. Adorning the head with flowers. పూవత్తి or పువ్వత్తి *pū-vatti.* n. A kind of fire works, which give a white light. పూవింటిజోదు, పూవింటివాడు, పూవిలుకాడు or పూవిలుతుడు *pū-vinṭi-dzōḍu.* n. An epithet of Manmadha. పూవుబోడి or పువ్వుబోడి (See under పూ. పూవుగట్టు *pūvu-gaṭṭu.* (పూవు+కట్టు.) v. n. To crystallise. పువ్వుకలియుట. పూలగురివెంద *pūla-guriveṇda.* n. The plant termed *Gærtnera racemosa,* or *Banisteria bengalensis.* Rox. ii. 368.

పూవిల్లు *pū-villu.* n. A bow made of flowers, carried by Manmadha.

పూషుడు *pūshuḍu.* [Skt.] n. The sun.

పూస *pūsa.* [Tel.] n. A bead, మణి. A joint of a finger, వ్రేలిలోనగువానికీలు. A bit or piece. వెన్నుపూసలు the joints of the backbone. ముడ్డిపూస the rump, os coccyx. "చిటిచెలిపూసపై ఘటియిల్లు పెడకట్టి చిమ్మలిగుడియ దాల్చున్నదమ్మ." A. vi. 104. వెన్నపూస a bit of butter, i. e., butter. "పుట్టనిబిడ్డలకు పూసలు కట్టుదు రమ్మలక్కలు." (Ahalya. iii. 63.) women call for necklaces for their children before they are born, i. e., they count the chickens before they are hatched. పూసగ్రుచ్చినరీతి (KP. iv. 193.) in regular order. పూసకజ్జెము *pūsa-kajjemu.* n. The sweetmeat called maccaroons. పూసకామంచిగడ్డి or పూసలకామంచిగడ్డి *pūsa-kāmanchi-gaḍḍi.* n. A kind of కామంచి. పూసగురువెంద *pūsa-guruveṇda.* n. A kind of bead. గురుగులు. పూసదిమ్ము or పూసదిమురు the back bone, వెన్నుపూస. "చేతోయుగురుచదై చెవులు విల్వంకలై పూసదిమ్ములు పొంచుకట్టి." Kāsi Khand. vi. 48. పూసలవాడు *pūsala-vāḍu.* n. One who sells beads, one who polishes precious stones, రత్నములు సానబెట్టువాడు.

పృ pṛi

పృక్తము *pṛiktamu.* [Skt.] adj. Joined, united, కూడుకొనిన.

పృచ్ఛ *pṛichcha.* [Skt.] n. Questioning, a question, query. ప్రశ్నము, అడుగుట. పృచ్ఛించు or పృచ్ఛచేయు *pṛichchintsu.* To question. అడుగు, ప్రశ్నించు.

పృతన *pṛitana.* [Skt.] n. An army, host. సేన, దండు. పృతనాధిపతి *pṛitan-ādhi-pati.* n. A commander, a general. M. VII. i.

50. పృతనాషాట్టు *pritanashattu*. n. An epithet of Indra.

పృథ *pritha*. [Skt.] n. The mother of the Pandus, కుంతీదేవి.

పృథక్ *prithak*. [Skt.] adv. Alone, separately. పృథగ్జనుడు *pritag-janudu*. n. An ignorant man, a fool, a man of low caste, a sinner, a wicked man. నీచుడు, మూర్ఖుడు, పాపి. పృథగ్విధము *prithag-vidhamu*. adj. Of different sorts. వెక్కువిధములుగల.

పృథివి or పృథ్వి *prithivi*. [Skt.] n. The earth. పృథివీపతి a king.

పృథు or పృథువు *prithu*. [Skt.] adj. Great, big. పృథుతరువు a big tree. పృథుకంఠము *prithu-kanthamu*. n. A mole cricket. పృథులము *prithulamu*. adj. Big, great, large. గొప్ప, విరివియైన.

పృథుకము *prithukamu*. [Skt.] n. An infant. పిల్లబిడ్డ. Parched corn, first scalded and then bruised to remove the husk. అటుకులు.

పృశ్ని *prisni*. [Skt.] n. A ray of light, కిరణము. A dwarf, మరుగుజ్జువాడు. A savage, కిరాతుడు.

పృషతము or పృషత్తు *prishatamu*. [Skt.] n. A drop of any liquid. బిందువు. The porcine deer. దుప్పి.

పృషదంశకము or వృషదంశకము *prishadamsakamu*. [Skt.] n. A cat. పిల్లి.

పృష్టము *prishtamu*. [Skt.] adj. Asked. అడుగబడిన.

పృష్టి *prishti*. [Skt.] n. A ray of light. కిరణము.

పృష్ఠము *prishthamu*. [Skt.] n. The back. వీపు. The rear, పశ్చాద్భాగము. The posteriors. ముడ్డి.

పె pe

పెం or పెన్ *pem*. [Tel.] n. A contraction for పెను large. పెంబిలువ (పెను+బిలువ) n. A large rock snake. పెంజీకటి *pen-jikati*. Thick darkness. The compounds (సమాసములు) in which it thus appears in an abbreviated form are as follow:— పెంజెమట *pen-jemata*. n. Profuse perspiration. పెంజెర *pen-jera*. (పెను+జెర్రి.) n. A kind of rock snake, the boa constrictor. రక్తపెంజెర a red snake. తుప్పపెంజెర or తుప్పపెంజెర and పొట్టపెంజెర are other species. పెంజడ *pen-dzada*. n. A large tress. పెద్దజడ. పెంజొట్టుచెట్టు *pen-dzutta-chettu*. A jungle shrub. పెంజోర *pen-dzora*. (పెను+జోరు.) n. A certain large fish. The great shark. "మున్నీటం బెంజోరై కనిపోవు చందంబున." See సొర్రి. పెండడి *pen-dadi*. (పెను+అడి.) n. Mud. పెండడి పనిని work done with stone and mud. "ఇందూపలస్యందంబులకు బిందులకు నిందీవరముక రందంబుల పెండడిబడి ఎండగొనువలి మించు క్రొమ్మంచుకొదరుల నిరయూరా." Swa. iii. 38. టీ॥ ఇందీవరమకరందంబుల పెండడింబడి, పల్లగిలుట పూకలనియులకుక్క [illegible] బడి. పెండలకడ or పెండలాడ *pen-dala-kada*. (పెను+దల+కడ). adv. Early, betimes, quickly, hastily. In the twilight. A. i. 20. ప్రొద్దుపోక ముసుపు. ప్రొద్దుగూలుక. పెండిరువడి *pen-diru-vadi*. (పెను+తిరువడి.) n. A Vaishnavite's name for Garutmant. గరుత్మంతుడు. "వింటి గరుత్మదంబరలనిగ్గువలేదొక రెక్కవంత వీచెంగల వార్ధి మాగడల జిడ్డైగిందెదు కష్టగాడ్పు నిందెంగదు [illegible] పెండిరువడింగనిం." A. iv. 10. పెండీగ *pen-diga*. n. A large creeper. పెండురుము *pen-durumu*. (పెను+కురుము.) n. Full tresses. "చెంగల్వపూదండవేర్చి పెందురుముపై ఘనసారము నూపకముఘటించి." Swa. vi. 5. టీ॥ పెండురుముమునుపై, పెద్దకొప్పుమీదను. పెండెర *pen-dera*. (పెను+తెర) n. A billow, a large wave, like a screen. Swa. v 102. A. vi. 186. పెందెరువు pen-deruvu. n. A high way, రాజమార్గము. భా. ఉద్యో. iii. పెందెవులు pen-devulu. n. A dangerous disease. A great plague, S. iii. 200. పెంగోడ pen-doda. n. The upper or thicker part of the thigh. Mand. iii. 46. పెంద్రోవ pen-drova. n. Salvation, ముక్తి. భా x. పెందూళి pen-dhuli. n. Great dust. పెన్జగతి pen-jagati. n. The great universe. పెన్బొగ pen-boga. n. A great smoke. పెన్భూతము pen-bhutamu. n. A great demon.

పెంకితీగ penki-tiga. [Tel.] n. The name of a large climbing woody shrub, called *Gouania tiliaefolia*. Rox. i. 632.

పెంకు penku [Tel.] n. A potsherd or cullet. A tile, a pantile. కుండపెంకు or చిల్లపెంకు a fragment of a pot. అద్దపుపెంకు a pane of glass, a broken bit of glass. తలపెంకు or పుర్రెపెంకు the skull. రవికమీద పెట్టికుట్టే అద్దపుపెంకులు pieces of glass sewn on to parts of women's dress as ornaments. వానిముఖము పెంకువలె పోయినది his countenance fell, వాని ముఖము వాడిపోయినది. పెంకుటిల్లు penku-t-illu. n. A tiled house, one roofed with tiles. బిళ్ల పెంకులు pantiles.

పెంకె penke. [Tel.] adj. Obstinate, stubborn, impudent. మొండికట్టె, మూర్ఖమైన. "పెంకెమునరాదు పట్టినంజగలనీయు." S. iii. 21. n. A stubborn man, మూర్ఖుడు. An impudent or insolent man. పెంకెపురుగు penke-purugu. n. A weevil in grain.

పెంచు or పెంచిక pentsu. [Tel.] n. A potsherd. "అలనాడు చిల్లపెంచోదిగా నాసినలుగురం బంతయును కనుటయునేడు." HD. i. 1417.

పెంచు or పెనుచు pentsu. [Tel. from పెను.] v. a. To nourish, support, take care of. To adopt or rear a child, పోషించు, సాకు. To increase, improve. To extend or swell. To exaggerate, to multiply. మాంసము మాంసమును పెంచును flesh meat increases the flesh. కలహము పెంచినాడు he fomented the quarrel. గ్రంథము దూరక పెంచెను he spun the story (or book) out. గడ్డము పెంచు to grow or wear a beard. తలపెంచు to wear one's hair long, to keep one's head unshorn. చెవులుపెంచు or చెవులు కుట్టించు to bore the ears. Chenn. iii. 145. ముక్కుపెంచు to keep a hole open for a nose-jewel. దుఃఖముపెంచు to indulge in grief, దుఃఖముపొందు, దుఃఖించు. ND. i. 702. రోగమును పెంచినాడు he increased the illness. కథను పెంచు to exaggerate. See పెంపు & పెంపకము. పెంచుకొను pentsu-konu. v. a. To adopt. దత్తతీసికొను.

పెంచెపుదండ penchepu-danda. [Tel.] n. A sort of crook or staff. "చుట్టినయురుద్రాడు సొంపారు చెంపకుట్టిన యుద్దుల కురుచకొయ్యలును మెరుగు పెంచెపు దండ మేటిదెబ్బలు గరవక యుండవాకట్టునదనికెలు." Navan. D.

పెంజెర penjera. See under పెం.

పెంట penta. [Tel.] n. A heap, as of dirt, sweepings or manure. ఎరువు. Ash, a dunghill. పీనుగుపెంటలు heaps of corpses. పెంటకట్టు to manure land, to dung a field by penning sheep or goats in it. పెంటకై మందకట్టు, గొర్రెలుపెట్టు, మందలాపు. పెంటపట్టు or పెంట penta-pattu. n. An enclosure in which a herd of cattle or a flock of sheep are kept, పసులులోనగు వానిదొడ్డి. Also, a suburb or village, పేట; as కోర్లపెంట, తుమ్మలపెంట, గొల్లపెంట. పెంటి penti. n. A female of a bird, animal or plant. పశుపక్ష్యాదులలో నాడుది. adj. Female: smaller. పెంటికోడి a hen. పెంటికెరటము or పెంటిఅల the smaller surf, చిన్న అల. See పోతు. పెంటివిద్య feminine accomplishments. పెంటితాడు the female palm tree, ఆడుతాటిచెట్టు. పెంటికె or పెంటిక pentika. [Tel.] n. The dung of sheep, goats, hares, deer, or rats, &c.

పెంటిపడు *penti-padu*. v. n. To match or equal. To pair, జతగూడు, సరిగూడు. "ద్విజ మృగపక్షి పశువులు పెంటులుపడరి, పగలురేయును పెంటిపడి పాయవయ్యె." L. iii. 136.

పెండ or పేడ *penda*. [Tel.] n. Cowdung, గోమయము. The dung of any clean animal. గేదెపేడ, గుఱ్ఱపుపేడ. The word రెట్ట is used for the dung of fish or birds, as చేపరెట్ట or పక్షిరెట్ట; and లద్దె for the dung of horses or elephants, as గుఱ్ఱపులద్దె or ఏనుగులద్దె.

పెండలము *pendalamu*. [Tel.] n. The yam, *Dioscorea alata*. Rox. iii. 797.

పెండెరము, పెండెము, పెండరము, పెండారము, పెండెరము or పెండేరము *penderamu*. [Tel.] n. An ornament worn like a garter on one leg.

పెండె or పెండెబద్ద *pende*. [Tel.] n. A lath or small rafter, commonly called a reaper, a strip of wood. ఇంటివాసములమీద అడ్డముగావేసికట్టే కొయ్య. A pannier or pack, being half a bullock load. పొగాకు మొదలయినవాటిలో సగము. విభూతి పెండెకట్లు or త్రిపుండ్రకము the triple line of ashes drawn across the forehead by worshippers of Siva, పెండెలవలె పట్టెలుగాదిద్దిన విభూతి రేఖలు.

పెండెము or పెండెరము *pendemu*. [Tel.] n. A door made of strips of bamboo, a wooden gate. పశువులదొడ్డియొక్క ద్వారకవాటము. A wooden bar used to fasten a door. అడ్డకఱ్ఱ. See పెండెరము.

పెండ్లి, పెండిలి or పెళ్లి *pendli*. [Drav: పెణ్ a wife, a woman.] n. Lit: Taking a wife. Marriage. The rite which answers to betrothal between children, the actual marriage being called, శోభనము. పెండ్లి అరుగు or పెళ్లితిన్నె a small hillock upon which the marriage takes place. పెండ్లికూతురు or పెండ్లికొమార్తె n. The bride, వధువు. A daughter-in-law, కోడలు. పెండ్లికొడుకు, or పెండ్లికుమారుడు n. The bridegroom. A son-in-law, అల్లుడు. తోడిపెండ్లికొడుకు a bridesman. తోడిపెండ్లికూతురు a bridesmaid. పెండ్లికూతుగది the bride-chamber. పెండ్లిచేయించు to unite two persons in marriage. పెండ్లిచేయు to marry a couple. పెండ్లిచేసికొను to marry, i. e., become a husband or wife. పెండ్లిండ్లు or పెళ్ళిళ్లు n. plu. Marriages, weddings. పెండ్లికుండలు *pendli-kundalu*. n. Painted pots used at marriages, అయిరేని. పెండ్లిగుమ్మడి the ash gourd used at marriages, బూడిదగుమ్మడి. పెండ్లినడక *pendli-nadaka*. n. A very slow or tedious walk, as people walk in marriage processions. పెండ్లాడు, పెండ్లియాడు or పెండ్లియగు *pendl-adu*. v. a. To marry. వివాహముచేసికొను. To be married, వివాహమగు. పెండ్లము, or పెండ్లాము *pendlamu*. n. A wife.

పెంపు *pempu*. [Tel. for పెను.] n. Greatness. మహత్త్వము, ఆధిక్యము, అతిశయము. Honour, గౌరవము. Rearing, nourishing, fostering, సాకుట. Increase, growth, వృద్ధి. Plenty, సమృద్ధి. Ruin, నాశము, లయము. గ్రామమును పెంపు చేసినవారు those who enlarged the town. v. a. To ruin, నాశముచేయు. పెంపుడు *pempudu*. adj. Fostered, reared, adopted (as a son), brought up, tamed, domesticated, పెంచబడిన. పెంపుడుకొమారుడు or దత్తపుత్రుడు an adopted son. పెంపుడుతల్లి an adoptive mother. పెంపుడుతండ్రి an adoptive father. పెంపుడుచిలుక a pet parrot. పెంపరలాడు *pemp-ara-l-adu*. v. n. To be increased, augmented. మిక్కుటము. పెంపారు, పెంపగు, పెంపుచెందు, పెంపొందు or పెంపుమీరు *pemp-aru*. v. n. To increase, grow, improve. వర్ధిల్లు, గొప్పయగు, అతిశయించు.

పెకలు *pekalu.* [Tel.] v. n. To come up, i. e., be torn up by the roots, పెల్లగిల్లు. To give way, yield. To get ready to travel, ప్రయాణమగు. **పెకలించు, పెకలుచు** or **పెకల్చు** *pekalintsu.* v. a. To root up, root out, tear up, eradicate. పెకలు చేయు. పెల్లగించు. To tear up by the roots.

పెక్కణము or **ప్రేక్కణము** *pekkanamu.* [Tel.] n. Dancing with gestures. అభినయముతో కూడిన నృత్యము.

పెక్కలి *pekkali.* [Tel.] n. A tree like the Love Apple.

పెక్కు *pekku.* [Tel.] *pron.* Many, అనేకము. పెక్కేల why so many? పెక్కులు many (things.) అనేకము. adj. Many, plentiful. పెక్కు ఉపాయములు numerous contrivances. పెక్కుపగల in many ways. పెక్కుమాటలేల why so many words? పెక్కుమారులు many times. **పెక్కువ** *pekkuva.* n. Increase, growth; tallness; greatness, వర్ధనము, ఆధిక్యము. "నీవు పెక్కువాలేక నేను పెక్కువాయుంచు పరినిల్చు వానిభుజంబుపోక." T. ii. 97. టీ॥ నీవు పెక్కువా, నీవు పొడవా, నేను పెక్కువా, నేను పొడవా, అంచు, అని. Prettiness, elegance, సోము. **పెక్కండ్రు** or **పెక్కురు** *pekkandru.* pron: plu. Many persons, several persons. అనేకులు.

పెగడ, ప్రేగడ or **ప్రెగ్గడ** *pegada.* [Tel.] n. An elder, senior; a noble, a gentleman, పెద్దవాడు. Vish. vii. 153.

పెగలు *pegalu.* [Tel.] Another form of పెకలు. (q. v.) అప్పు ఎక్కడను పెగలలేదు I could not borrow money anywhere.

పెగ్గడి or **పెగ్గురు** *peggadi.* Same as బెగ్గురు a crane. "పెగ్గడికదుపుల బెగ్గిలమగ్గించి కొంగలబొంగళ్ల గుంగదొక్కి." G. i. 108.

పెచ్చారి *petstsari.* [Tel.] n. A stubborn man, a stupid or ignorant man, మూర్ఖుడు.

పెచ్చు *petstsu.* [Tel.] n. Peel, peelings, rind. ఫలాదులపైతొక్కు, తొక్క. Surplus, excess, premium, profit in exchange. హెచ్చు, మార్కము. పైపెచ్చులు incidental profits like fees. adj. Much, great, అధికము. adv. Excessively, మిక్కిలి. "ఇట్లుపొటచ్చరులు పెచ్చుపెరిగి విచ్చలవిడి" A. vi. 103.

పెటపెట *peta-peta.* [Tel. anuk.] n. A crashing or gnashing noise, a loud sound. కాష్ఠమొదలైనవి బద్దలగుధ్వని. పెటపెటమను or **పెటపెట లాడు** *peta-peta-m-anu.* v. n. To produce a crashing sound. పెటపెట అను ధ్వనికలదిఅగు. **పెటులు, పెటులు, పెటేలు.** or **పెట్లు** *petulu.* v. n. To crack or split, as paint, or as grain does when roasted. To explode or go off, as a gun. పగుల్లుపారు, చిట్లు. "కల్పాంత దీర్ఘనిర్ఘాతసంఘంబులు పెళపెళ పెళమంచు పెటిలిపడిన." N. iv. 244. **పెట్లుక్రోవి, పెట్లుదిమ్మె** or **పెట్లుకొలికు** *petlu-krovi.* n. A matchlock, a gun rocket or small cannon fired in processions, అదురువేటుగొట్టము. **పెట్లుమారి** *petla-mari.* n. One who makes himself or herself liable to be constantly beaten, దెబ్బలు తిను స్వభావముగలవాడు, లేక, స్వభావము గలది. **పెట్లుప్పు** *petl-uppu.* n. Saltpetre, nitre. **పెట్లుప్పుద్రావకము** *petl-uppu-dravakamu.* n. Nitric acid. **పెటుకు** or **పెటుక్కు** *petuku.* n. A snapping sound, పెటుక్కుమనేధ్వని. Disgust, విరసము. **పెటులు** or **పెట్లు** *petulu.* n. plu. The explosions or reports of a gun rocket. అదురువేట్లు. "సీ॥ పెటులుచప్పుడులార్త భీరుస్వయంగ్రాహ పరిరంభసుఖము. శేచరులకొసగ." Swa. v. 52. టీ॥ పెటులుచప్పుడులు, అదురువేట్లధ్వనులు. **పెటిలించు, పెటలించు** or **పెట్లించు** *petilintsu.* v. a. To explode, to burst. పేలినట్టిక్కులను చెదరునట్లుచేయు. "పేరినలనగంపు ఘట్టములు దృష్టదిరమ్మద దాపముల్ దవుల్కొనిపెటిలించు నార్భటులతోయనగా." A. iv. 122.

పెట్ట *peṭṭa*. [Tel.] n. A female of animals, పశుపక్ష్యాదిస్త్రీజాతి. A hen, ఆడుకోడి. పెట్టకుక్క a bitch. S. ii. 44. "ఎదపదపనుంబోదలు పెట్టలకుంజాట్టంబులై." Swa. iv. 51. టీ॥ పెట్టలకు, ఆడుపందులకు, చుట్టంబులై, తగులాటము గలవై. పెట్టమారి *peṭṭa-māri*. n. A cock that looks like a hen, ఆడుకోడివలెనుండు పుంజు.

పెట్టు *peṭṭu*. [Tel.] v. n. To happen. కలుగు. క్రి. వా. v. a. To put, place. ఉంచు. To lay (eggs), to bring forth (young), కను. To wear, ధరించు. To give, ఇచ్చు. To impute a blame, a crime, &c. మోపు. To raise a wall, కట్టు. To plant, నాటు. To beat, కొట్టు. n. A blow, a thump. దెబ్బ. Bestowal, charity, giving. ఈవి. A time, మారు, తడవ, ఆవృత్తి. When the verb పెట్టు is added to certain verbs like విడుచు, it means Altogether. పూర్తిగా విడిచిపెట్టు to give up entirely. This verb has numerous senses peculiar to certain nouns under which it will be found. పిల్లలుపెట్టు to bear young ones. గుడ్లుపెట్టు to lay eggs. ఆశపెట్టు to give hopes, tantalise. ఆ తప్పును వానిమీద పెట్టిరి they laid the fault on him. ఆమెకు నూరురూపాయిల సొమ్ముపెట్టినాడు he gave her a hundred rupees worth of jewels. అన్నముపెట్టు to serve or help food at dinner. కావలిపెట్టు to put a guard over. అపరాధముపెట్టు to pay a fine. నైవేద్యముపెట్టు to offer an oblation. బొబ్బలుపెట్టు to yell. బాధపెట్టు to torture. కనిపెట్టు to watch, to find out, to wait. చెట్లుపెట్టు to plant trees. అట్లు చేయవద్దని నాకు ఒట్టుపెట్టినాడు he adjured me not to do so. పాళ్లుపెట్టు to divide or separate into shares. గురిపెట్టు to take aim. కఠిన పథ్యము పెట్టినాడు he put him on strict diet. అంగడి or దుకాణముపెట్టు to open a shop. ఈ మాటను అంగడిలో పెట్టవద్దు do not talk of this publicly. గోడపెట్టు to build a wall. It is also added to many verbs sometimes without altering the meaning. Thus, చేర్చిపెట్టు or కూడబెట్టు to accumulate, store up. పరుండబెట్టు to put to bed. దాచిపెట్టు to conceal or hide. "ఎవ్వనియింటికి నేదువారాకులు పెట్టనికోటదై పెరుగుచుండు" Molla. v. 48. దానిని ఒకపెట్టుపెట్టినాడు he gave her a slap. గోడపెట్టు చెంపపెట్టు రెండును వచ్చినవి his luck was had in both ways. పెట్టుపోతలు శాశ్వతములుకావు meat and drink are momentary matters. మాటలు మా అమ్మవి, పెట్టుసవతితల్లివి the words are those of a mother, but the acts are those of a step-mother. నాల్గుపెట్లు four times. ఒకపెట్టున all at once, simultaneously. పెట్టించు *peṭṭinṭsu*. v. a. To have it placed or put, &c. మరొకరు ఉంచునట్లుచేయు. నాకు అన్నము పెట్టించినాడు he had food given me. పెట్టుకొను *peṭṭu-konu*. v. a. To keep, or put, for one's own advantage or use, ఉంచుకొను. కొడుకునకు తనతండ్రిపేరు పెట్టుకొన్నాడు he gave the boy his father's name. ఏముఖము పెట్టుకొని మాట్లాడును has he the face to speak? పెట్టుకోలు *peṭṭu-kōlu*. n. The act of keeping, పెట్టుకొనుట. పెట్టుచెట్టు *peṭṭu-cheṭṭu*. n. An epithet of the కల్పవృక్షము. పెట్టుడు *peṭṭuḍu*. n. Giving, charity, ఈవి, త్యాగము, దానము. పెట్టుబడి *peṭṭu-baḍi*. n. Money advanced or laid out. An outlay. పెట్టుమందు *peṭṭu-mandu*. n. A medicine given to acquire complete influence over another, తనకు లోబడియుండుటకుగాను పెట్టేమందు, వశ్యౌషధము. పెట్టుపడు *peṭṭu-paḍu*. v. n. To receive a blow, to be beaten, దెబ్బతిను.

పెట్టె or పెట్టెయ *peṭṭe*. [from Skt. పేటిక.] n. A box, a chest. A coil, as of a snake. పెట్టెపెట్టు *peṭṭe-peṭṭu*. v. n. To be coiled up as a snake. పెట్టెబండి *peṭṭe-baṇḍi*. n. A palanquin coach, a closed carriage.

పెట్లుడిప్పి, పెట్లు, పెట్లునప్పు, పెట్లుప్రతాపము See under పెటులు.

పెథిల్లు *pethillu*. [Tel. anuk.] n. The noise produced by a blow or thunder, &c. adv. Bang! slapdash! పెథిల్లుపెథిల్లున *pethillu-pethilluna*. adj. Aloud. Bang!

పెడ *peḍa*. [Tel.] adj. Large. పెద్ద. Hinder, back, behind. వెనుకటి. Wrong, erroneous, audacious, విపరీతము. పెడయుక్తులు wicked devices. పెడతల the back of the head, తలవెనుకటిభాగము. పెడకోరికలు wrong wishes. పెడదారి a wrong way, తప్పుదారి. పెడచెయ్యి the back of the hand, మీఁదిచెయ్యి. పెడర్థము a wrong sense. పెడబొబ్బలు a dreadful yell. పెడకచ్చ the back tuck of the modesty piece. పెడరెక్కలు విఱిచికట్టు to pinion. పెడక *peḍaka*. n. The back part or haft of a knife, కత్తియొక్క వెనుకటి భాగము. పెడకంటివారు *peḍa-kanṭi-vāru*. n. The name of a certain subdivision of the Kāpu caste. "పంటమోటాటి పెడకంటి పాపాటి." H. iv. 171. పెడకట్టె or పెడసరకట్టె *peḍa-kaṭṭe*. n. A stubborn person, మూర్ఖుడు, మూర్ఖురాలు. పెడకట్లు *peḍa-kaṭlu*. n. Tying the hands behind the back, చేతులను వెనుకకు విఱిచికట్టుట. పెడకాలు *peḍa-kālu*. n. A leg folded backwards, వెనుకకు మడిచినకాలు. పెడకేలు *peḍa-kēlu*. n. An arm bent backwards. పెడకేలుకట్టు *peḍa-kēlu-kaṭṭu*. v. a. To pinion, పెడరెక్కలు విఱిచికట్టు. "పెడకేలుగట్టిన ప్రియునుతు గాంచి." SD. v. 419. పెడచెవి *peḍa-chevi*. n. The back part of the ear, చెవివెనుకటిభాగము. నామాటలు పెడచెవిని బెట్టినాడు he turned a deaf ear to my words. పెడనెల *peḍa-nela*. n. A clever or skilful man, తిర్పరి (obsolete.) పెడబాయు *peḍa-bāyu*. v. n. To be separated, ఎడబాయు. "వల్లభులు ప్రాణవిభుంబెడబాయనేర్తురే." Parij. iv. 60. పెడబాపు *peḍa-bāpu*. v. a. To separate, &c. ఎడబాపు. M. XII. v. 87. పెడమరలు, పెడమరు or పెడమర్లు *peḍa-maralu*. v. n. To turn back, వెనుకకు తిరుగు. పెడమర్లు *peḍa-marlu*. n. Turning back, fleeing. వెనుకకుతిరుగుట. పెడమరించు *peḍa-marintsu*. v. a. To cause to turn back, వెనుకకు త్రిప్పు. పెడమల్లె *peḍa-malle*. n. A kind of Jasmine tree. H. iv. 21. పెడమోము or పెడమూ *peḍa-mōmu*. n. The face turned away. పెడమోముపడు *peḍa-mōmu-paḍu*. v. n. To be turned away, as the face. పెడరేచు *peḍa-rēṭsu*. v. a. To goad, instigate, egg on, పురికొల్పు.

పెడలు *peḍalu*. [Tel.] n. The backyard of a house, పెరడు.

పెడసరము *peḍasaramu*. [Tel.] n. Stubbornness, obstinacy. మౌర్ఖ్యము. పెడసరకట్టె Same as పెడకట్టె. See under పెడ.

పెడిసెపిట్ట *peḍise-piṭṭa*. [Tel.] n. The Rose-colored Pastor or Cholam bird, *Pastor roseus*. (F. B. I.)

పెడులు Same as పెటులు (q. v.).

పెడ్డ Same as పెద్ద (q. v.).

పెణక or పెడక *peṇaka*. [Tel.] n. A pent roof, one side of a sloping roof. ఇంటియొక్క ఒకభాగపుకప్పు. The back side of a leaf, ఆకుయొక్క వెనుకటిభాగము. చిప్పపెణక the gable end of a roof.

పెతరులు *petarulu*. [from Skt. పితృలు.] n. plu. Forefathers or ancestors. పితృదేవతలు. పెతరులసామి the lord of the ancestors, i.e., Yama, యముడు. పెతరులచుక్క the constellation called మఘానక్షత్రము. "పెతరులన్నమనుచు ప్రీతితో బిలిపించి కాకులకును బెట్టు కర్ములారా." Vēma. iii. 191.

పెత్తల్లి, పెత్తండ్రి, పెత్తనము See under పెద్ద.

పెదవి *pedavi*. [Tel. corrupted into పెదిమ or పెదివి.] n. The lip. అధరము.

పెద్ద or పేద *pedda*. [Tel.] adj. Great, big, large. గొప్ప, అధికమైన. Long, high, tall, పొడుగైన. Loud. Chief, principal, ముఖ్యమైన, శ్రేష్ఠము. Respectable, honest, honourable. Old, aged. Senior. n. An elder, or senior. జ్యేష్ఠుడు, జ్యేష్ఠురాలు పెద్దవాడు. An old man, వృద్ధుడు, ముసలివాడు, ముసలిస్త్రీ. A great man, గొప్పవాడు. An ancestor. A chief ruler or prince, రాజు. adv. Greatly, much. మిక్కిలి, అత్యంతము. "పెద్దమెచ్చి." M. I. v. 272. పెద్దంతరము, పిన్నంతరము the proper distinctions between old and young, respective rank. పెద్దకాలము a long time; also, old age. అతనికి పెద్దకాలము సమీపించినది or సంభవించినది he has become an old man. "కడుపెద్ద దవ్వుపోయి" going a great distance. M. I. i. 190. ఇందుకు పెద్దమాటలెందుకోయి why make such a noise about this? ఇది ఒక పెద్ద పనియా is this a great matter? పెద్దమేలయ్యె so much the better. సురసంఘముల పెద్ద the father or ruler of the gods. బడిపెద్ద a class leader, or head boy. పిన్నపెద్దలు young and old, every body; or village elders. "మాపెద్దలు మునువేల్పులు" my ancestors were the gods. B. X. 6. పెద్దకాపు *pedda-kāpu*. n. The headman among the ryots of a village, a village headman, గ్రామాధికారి, గ్రామమున్సబు పెత్తనముచేసే కాపువాడు. పెత్తండ్రి *pet-tandri*. (పెద్ద+తండ్రి) n. A father's elder brother: the husband of a mother's elder sister. పెత్తల్లి *pet-talli*. (పెద్ద+తల్లి.) n. A mother's elder sister. The wife of a father's elder brother. పెత్తనము or పెద్దతనము *pet-tanamu*. (పెద్ద+తనము.) n. Power, authority, headship. Greatness, rank, respectability, chieftainship. పెద్దమనిషితనము, గొప్ప, గౌరవము. "పెద్దరికము పొడచూపుబుద్ధి పెదరిలుచున్నది." T. iv. 15. Superintendence, అధికారము. Old age, ముసలితనము. పైనపెట్టుకొన్న పెత్తనము assumed superintendence. మొగుడు చావగానే ముండకు పెత్తనము వచ్చినది after the death of her husband the widow became head of the family. పిల్ల పెత్తనము childish management. దొంగపెత్తనము official insolence or swagger. అయినకు పెత్తనము వచ్చినది, బైట తిరుగలేడు he is now aged, he cannot walk about. పెత్తనగాడు *pettana-gādu*. n. A superintendent, a chief. అధికారి. పెద్దకీర్తిగాడు or తింకబెల్లింత *pedda-kirtti-gādu*. n. The Indian Grey Shrike, *Lanius lahtora*. (F. B. I.) పెద్దకోమటి or పెద్దసెట్టి *pedda-kōmati*. n. The head man or leader among the merchants. పెద్దచేయు *pedda-chēyu*. v. a. To magnify, honour, increase. "ప్రియముపుట్టంగ సంతతము పెద్దచేసి." Vish. vi. 36. పదిమందికూడి తెలివిన్ని పెద్దచేస్తే వాడే పెద్ద he is honorable whom all consent to honor. ఆ దీపమును పెద్దచేయుము put the light out. పెద్దతల *pedda-tala*. n. A leader. పెద్దరికముగా గ్రామమును నడిపించువాడు. పెద్దవి *pedd-adi*. n. An old woman: an old animal; a large or great thing. పెద్దనల్లంచిగాడు or తెల పోరలగాడు *pedda-nallanchi-gādu*. n. The Magpie Robin, *Copsychus saularis*. (F. B. I.) పెద్దనిదుర or పెద్దనిద్ర *pedda-nidura*. n. Deep sleep, i. e., Death. చావు, దీర్ఘనిద్ర. పెద్దనిద్రపోవు *pedda-nidra-pōvu*. v. n. To die. చచ్చు. పెద్దనెల *pedda-nela* n. The month called జ్యేష్ఠమాసము. పెద్దన్న *pedd-anna*. n. The eldest brother. పెద్దపులి *pedda-puli*. n. A royal tiger. వ్యాఘ్రము. పెద్దపులుగు *pedda-pulugu*. n. An owl. పెద్దపోల or పెద్దమాంసము *pedda-pola*. n. Cow's flesh, beef. గోమాంసము. పెద్దమనిషి or పెద్దమనుష్యుడు *pedda-manishi*. n. An aged person. A gentleman, an honest man, a man of respectability. చిన్నవాని

పెద్దమనిషివి you are a very fine fellow. ఆ చిన్నది పెద్దమనిషి కాలేదు that girl has not yet reached puberty, or arrived at maturity. పెద్దమనిషితనము *pedda-manishi-tanamu*. n. Manly or respectable conduct, propriety, decency, honesty. పెద్దమాను *pedda-manu*. n. The name of a certain tree called *Ailanthus excelsa*. (Rox. & E. P.). కట్వంగము. దుండిగపుమాను, పెనుమాను. పెద్దమానుచెక్క or పట్ట the bark of this tree, or, of *Ailanthus malabarica*, which is used in medicine. పెద్దమ్మ *pedd-ammu*. n An elder mother, i. e., mother's elder sister or a father's elder brother's wife. పెద్దమ్మ is also the name of జ్యేష్ఠాదేవి a goddess who is the personification of misfortune, and is described as the elder sister of శ్రీ or Fortune. The word is also used to mean a wretched creature, a blockhead. వాణ్ని పెద్దమ్మపట్టు కొన్నది he is out of luck. వాణ్ని పెద్దమ్మ విడిచినది his luck has taken a turn. ఇది బుద్ధిమంతురాలు వాడు పట్టిపెద్దమ్మ she is a sensible woman, but he is a mere blockhead. పెద్దమ్మనేల a wretched bit of land. పెద్దమ్మతనము *pedd-ammu-tanamu*. n. Wretchedness, stupidity. పెద్దయు *pedda-yu*. adv. Very, exceedingly, much. మిక్కిలి. పెద్దరికము *peddarikamu*. n. Greatness, rank, respectability, old age. పెద్దతనము, వృద్ధత్వము, గొప్ప, గౌరవము. పెద్దరోగము *pedda-rogamu*. n. Leprosy. పెద్దలు *peddalu*. n. plu. Elderly people, one's seniors, the wise, తెలిసినవారు. Ancestors, fore-fathers. పెద్దవయస్సు *pedda-vayassu*. n. Old age. పెద్దకాలము. పెద్దవాడు *pedda-vadu*. n. An elder, senior, an old man. పెద్దవాకిలి *pedda-vakili*. n The principal gate of a temple, &c. గోపురద్వారము. పెద్దవారము *pedda-varamu*. n. Wednesday. బుధవారము. పెద్దవినికపము *pedda-vinnapamu*. n. Hardness of hearing. చెవుడు, బధిరత్వము. పెద్దవిన్నపమువి *pedda-vinnapamu-di*. n. A deaf woman. చెవిటిస్త్రీ. పెద్దవిన్నపమువాడు *pedda-vinnapamu-vadu*. n. A deaf man. చెవిటివాడు. పెద్దవీధి *pedda-vidhi*. n. A highway, a public road, రాజవీధి, రాజమార్గము. పెద్దవేలుపు *pedda-velupu*. n. Brahma. బ్రహ్మ, సురజ్యేష్ఠుడు. పెద్దవేలు *pedda-velu*. n. The thumb, బొటనవేలు, అంగుష్ఠము. పెద్దాకుచెట్టు *pedd-aku-chettu*. n. A certain forest tree. పెద్దాపురి *pedda-puri*. n. A fine sort of sugar made at Peddapur, a town near Rajahmundry. పెద్ది *peddi*. (from పెద్ద.) adj. Great. పెద్దింటమ్మ *pedd-int-ammu*. n. A name of a certain village goddess, ఒక గ్రామదేవత. పెద్దేటికొంగ *pedd-êti-konga*. n. The large river heron. The pelican.

పెన్, పెం or పెను *pen*. [Tel.] adj. Great, large, heavy.

పెన *pena*. [Tel.] n. A twist. మెలిక. A cord coupling two animals together. a tie, a band, బంధము. పెనగు *penagu*. v. n. To be twisted, మెలిగొను. To surround, చుట్టుకొను. To join, unite, కలయు. To oppose, మారాడు. To struggle, to fight. గుంజులాడు, యుద్ధముచేయు. n. Same as పెనకువ. See below. పెనగులాట or పెనగులాటము *penagul-ata*. n. Struggling, fighting. పెనగులాడు *penagul-adu*. v. a. To struggle, to fight. పెనగొను, పెనకువలుగొను, పెనగుడు. పెనగువడు or పెనగొను *pena-gonu*. v. n. To be twisted. మెలిపడు. To be mingled, as mixed feelings. "అనిచవిని సంభ్రమఖేదయు విస్మయంబులాపెనగొంతలు మనంబున వెనగొనన." H. i. 103. పెనచు *penatsu*. v. a. To cause to be twisted, to twist, పెనగజేయు. పెనపెట్టు *pena-pettu* v. a. To stir up a quarrel. మెలిపెట్టు, పురికొల్పు. పెనవేయు or పెనపెట్టు *pena-veyu*. v. a. To twist. మెలిపెట్టు. To couple, tie together. చేర్చికట్టు. పెనకువ *penakuva*. n A struggle. పెనగులాట.

The act of surrounding a thing, చుట్టుకొనుట. Joining, కలయిక. A fight, యుద్ధము. A quarrel, వివాదము. "పెనకువ నర్జునుడుంగు పేలవెనూనుము క్రోధనంబునా." M. VIII. iii. 292.

పెనము penamu. [Tel.] n. An iron plate for baking cakes on. చెరకుపెనము a sugar boiler like a great dish. మంటిపెనము an earthen frying pan.

పెనగు penagu. [Tel.] v. n. To twine, కలయు. To struggle, to be implicated. పెనగు. "రూపు పేరు రెండు రూఢితో నరిసిన, పేరురూపు క్రియను పెనఁగియుండు." Vema. 361. పెనపు penapu. v. a. To cause to be entwined, పెనయుచేయు. To unite, కలుపు. To cause to be twisted. పెనచు. To cause to struggle. n. A quarrel, వివాదము. Enmity, విరోధము. పెనపరి penap-ari. n. A quarrelsome person, వివాదశీలుడు. One who is fond of creating enmity, భేదశీలుడు.

పెనిమిటి or పెన్మిటి penimiti. [Tel. Drav. √పెన = woman. Cf. పెండ్లాము & పెండ్లి.] n. A husband.

పెను penu. [Tel.] adj. Great (in any sense); large, chief. పెనుమూల the greatest of villains. పెనువాన a great rain. M. XII. iii. 291. పెనుసిగ్గు great shame. Ha. i. 102. పెన్నురము a broad chest. B. x. 225. పెన్వెంగలి quite mad. BD. iii. 2285. పెనుచు or పెంచు penutsu. v. a. To bring up, to rear, to cause to grow. To nourish, to foster, to fatten. పెరుగఁజేయు, వర్ధిల్లజేయు. "అస్థిరంపుమేని నధికపాటులబడి, పెక్కువిధము లందు పెనిచి పెనిచి, యుగ్నికిచ్చునట్టి యుపవిచక్కలకివ్వ." Vema. 1719. పెనుపారు Same as పెంపారు. (See under పెంపు) పెనుపరి penu-pari. n. One who causes prosperity. వృద్ధిపొందించువాడు. పెనుపడు (పెనుపు + పడు.) penu-padu. v. n. To increase, అతిశయిల్లు, వర్ధిల్లు. పెనుపు See పెంపు. పెనుమసనము penu-masanamu. n. Benares. కాశి. పెనుమాను penu-manu n. A kind of tree called దుండిగము, పెద్దమాను, అయిల, కార్ముక. పెనుముసుకులు penu-musukulu. n. The Veda. వేదము. పెనువెల్లి penu-velli. n. A deluge. ప్రళయకాలపు జలప్రవాహము. పెనువ్రేలు penu-vrelu. n. The thumb, బొటనవ్రేలు. పెన్నిధి pen-nidhi. (పెను+నిధి.) n. A great treasure. పెన్నెరులు pen-nerulu. n. Long tresses, flowing hair. "పెన్నెరుల్ పెనుకకు నొత్తి." T. ii. 71.

పెన్న penna. [Tel.] n. The name of the river Pennar which falls into the sea near Nellore. పినాకినీనది.

పెన్నడపులుగు pen-nada-pulugu. [Tel. పెను +నడపులుగు.] n. A large sort of crane. కురరము.

పెన్నేరు penu-eru. [Tel.] n. The branched winter cherry, *Physalis flexuosa*. అశ్వగంధ. పెన్నేరుగడ్డ the bulbous root of this plant.

పెమ్మె pemme. [Tel.] n. Another form of పెరమె (q. v.).

పెయ్య or పెయ్యదూడ peyya. [Tel.] n. A heifer, a female calf, పాలువిడిచిన ఆడుదూడ. A calf, దూడ. A young cow, పడుచు ఆవు. ఈ. రా. వ.

పెయ్యెర peyyara. [Tel.] n. A certain forest shrub called *Grewia orientalis*, Rox. ii. 586. అల్లిపెయ్యెర a species called *Grewia didyma*. Rox. ii. 591.

పెర pera. [Tel.] n. A honey comb. పెరతేనె honey in the comb, తెట్టతో నుండు మకరందము. "పులిగోరుల్ పెరతేనెలొకస్తురి మొకంబుల్." R. ii. 4. పెర pera. [from Skt. పర.] pron. and adj. Other, another, అన్యము. Strange, foreign. పెరచేయి the other hand. "తప్పు

కలుండ బెరుకు లదించుచుయున్నవు." Amuk. i. 13. పెరయీగ pera-y-īga. n. A honey bee, a working bee, not a drone. పెరరేచు or పెరరేపు pera-rētsu. v. a. To disturb a beehive. To encourage, incite, excite, stir, ప్రేరేపణచేయు. "లేనిపెరలు రేచినయతండు." Vish. iii. 139. పెరగాయ pera-gāya. (పెర+కాయ.) n. A cunning man, కుత్సితుడు. పెరగాయసుద్దులు peragāya-suddulu. n. Nonsense, vain words, idle tattle. "కటకట నరువులతోనే, నటుగుటలా నేమకోరుకొంకవిటగా, నలునిటు ప్రొద్దులుపుచ్చుచు, నటమటు బెరగాయ సుద్దులా డెదవారా." T. iii. 102. టీ॥ పెరకాయసుద్దులు, కొంటెమాటలు. పెరమగడు pera-magaḍu. n. A lover, an adulterer, జారుడు.

పెరక peraka. [Tel.] n. A tile, పెంకు.

పెరజా peradzu. [Tel.] n. A sort of snake.

పెరడు peraḍu. [Tel.] n. The back yard of a house, ఇంటివెనుకదొడ్డి. పాటిపెరడు a piece of ground manured by cattle confined there for that purpose. కూరపెరడు a kitchen garden. పెరటిగుమ్మము or పెరటిదోవ the backyard door, the back door. పెరటిచెట్టు మందుకురాదు (a proverb) Lit: the tree in the backyard is considered to be of no use as a medicine. i. e., familiarity breeds contempt. "నాపెరటిచెట్లుకల్పద్రుమములు." R. v. 176.

పెరవణి peravaṇi. [Tel.] n. Dancing, capers, gambols. పేరణియాట, తాండవము. "పరమేశ్వరుని సత్యభావంబు గరపుపరిపరి బాగుల పరిహాసకథల సంగీతారాతికి నానంద మొదవ భృంగిముందరిపెంక పెరవణిమాడు." L. ii. 150. టీ॥ వంకపెరవణి, వక్రమైననాట్యము.

పెరసు perasu. [Tel.] n. Flesh మాంసము.

పెరిక or పెరికె perika. [Tel.] n. A sack, గోనెమూట. పెరికెసెట్టి perike-seṭṭi. n. A drover of laden cattle. పెరికాటము perikaṭamu. n. Carrying goods on bullocks.

పెరిమ or పెరిమె perima. [Tel.] n. Love, affection. ప్రేమ. Greatness, పెద్దరికము, గొప్పతనము, అతిశయము. "ఏకదా పేర్పుమైనల్ల యది పెరులతోలుపుచుదురిమె, దర్పకునకర్పింపదలప కొంతేటిపెరిమె." Swa. iii. 107.

పెరుకు or పెర్కు peruku. [Tel.] v. a. To tear out, uproot, pluck up by the roots, to pull out. పీకు, పెల్లగించు. To carry, మోయు. To load goods. సామానులు బండ్లు పడవలు వగైరాలపైని ఎక్కించుట. నాలుకపెరుక్కొనిచచ్చెను he tore out his tongue and so killed himself.

పెరుగు, పెర్గు, పెరువు or పెర్వు perugu. [Tel.] v. n. To grow, increase, వర్ధిల్లు, ఎదుగు, విజృంభించు. To accumulate. To grow up, as a child. To bristle up, as a porcupine. To attempt, ప్రయత్నించు. గడ్డము పెరిగిన unshaven, wearing a beard. కొండలు నాలుగుపక్కల పెరిగియున్నవి the hills extended around it on all sides. కామక్రోధంబుల పెరుగనిచ్చె he gave the rein to his passions. Curds: thick curdled milk, దధి. పెరుగుడు peru-guḍu. n. Growth, increase, పెరుగుట, వృద్ధి. పెరుగుతోటకూర, పెరుగుకూర or పెరుగాకు perugu-tōṭa-kūra. n. A certain potherb, Amaranthus oleraceus. (Heyne.) పెరుగుసముద్రము perugu-samudramu. n. The sea of curds, one of the mythical oceans. An old person, ఏండ్లుచెల్లినవాడు, ఏండ్లుచెల్లినది. వానితల పెరుగుబుడ్డివలె నెరసినది his head is as white as a bottle of curds.

పెరుమాళ్లు perumallu. [Tel.] n. A name for Vishnu, విష్ణువు. "పెన్నదాటితే పెరుమాళ్లసేవ." (prov.) పెరుమాళ్ల కోయిల or పెరుమాళ్లకోయిల perumalla-kōyila. n Conjeveram. కాంచీపురము.

పెరె pere. [Tel.] n. A reservoir for water at the salt pans.

పెలిస or పెలిసె pelisa. [Tel.] n. The Rose-colored Pastor or Cholam bird, Pastor *roseus*, పూలిపెలిస the White headed Maina, *Pastor malabaricus*. పెద్దపెలిస the Cholum Bird, *Pastor roseus*. (Jerdon.) పొడపెలిస *poḍa-pelisa*. n. The Black bird, *Merula negri pileus* (F. B. I.)

పెలుకురు or పెల్కుఱు *pelukuru*. [Tel.] v. n. To start, be alarmed. అదరిపడు. To be troubled through fear, &c., భయముచేత విలవిలపోవు, విహ్వలమగు.

పెలుచ, పెల్చు, పెలుచన or పెల్చన *pelutsa*. [Tel.] n. Greatness, అతిశయము, ఆధిక్యము. Anger, wrath, ఆగ్రహము. Hardness, harshness, కాఠిన్యము. adj. Great, అధికము. పెలుచ adv. Excessively, exceedingly, much. "ఆర్తిన్నవాడొఘము ఘోరంబైయురానీక ములను పెలుచంగప్పెనంతాంచి." M. I. ii. 24.

పెల్ల or పెల్ల *pella*. [Tel.] n. A lump, clod; a chip; a flake; a raw brick. పెల్లగించు or పెల్లగించు *pella-gintsu*. v. a. To pull out, root out, draw out. To dig up, unbury, unearth, eradicate. ఆ చెట్టును పెల్లగించి మరియొకచోట పెట్టినాడు, శేక, పాతి నాడు he took up the tree and planted it elsewhere. పెల్లగిల్లు or పెల్లగిలు *pella-gillu*. v. n. To come out by the roots, పాదుతూడిశేచు. To run away, పారిపోవు. వాడు అత్తవారింటినుంచి పెల్లగిలివచ్చు గతిగా నుండలేదు he seems unlikely to stir from his mother-in-law's house. గాలివానకు చెట్లు కుంకటిపెల్లలో పెల్లగిలినవి the trees were torn up by the roots by the storm. ఆ గోడగారె అంతా పెల్లగిలిపోయినది all the plaster of the wall came off or peeled off.

పెల్లు *pellu*. [Tel] n. Excess, greatness. అతిశయము, ఆధిక్యము. పెల్లు or పెల్లుగా adj. Much, great, excessive, adv. Greatly, exceedingly, vastly, much, మిక్కిలి, అతిశయముగా. పెల్లిదము *pellidamu*. (పెల్లు+ ఇదము.) n. Same as పెల్లు n. పెల్లుకొను *pellu-konu*. v. n. To increase, swell. మిక్కుటమగు, అతిశయిల్లు.

పెళపెళ, ఫెళఫెళ, పెళ్లు or పెఠుక్కు *pela-pela*. [Tel. anuk.] n. The noise produced in breaking a thing suddenly. ఆ కొమ్మ పెఠుక్కుని విరిగినది the bough broke with a crash. adv. Aloud, crashingly, echoingly, roaringly, creakingly, resoundingly, "ఫెళఫెళరవాల్ ఫెళిఫెళిల్లాయించి." H. ii. 98. "కొమ్మఫెళఫెళవిరిగెను." Pal. 173. పెళపెళమను *pelapela-m-anu*. v. n. To crash. To make a rustling sound. అతడు ఆ దేశములో పెళపెళ లాడిస్తున్నాడు he is making a great uproar in the country. "పెళపెళనెల్లెడ నురుముగ." Padya L. iv. 77.

పెళుచు or పెళుసు *pelutsu*. [Tel.] adj. Brittle, harsh, విరసమైన. పెళుచుమాటలు harsh words. n. Stiffness, Inflexibility, Brittleness. A mean or stubborn wretch. మూర్ఖుడు.

పెళ్లమ్రాను *pella-mrānu*. [Tel.] n. A harrow. పాపటము, నేలను చదునుచేయుయంత్రము.

పెళ్లి Same as పెండ్లి (q. v.).

పెళ్లున *pellu-na*. [Tel. anuk.] adv. Loudly, aloud. భేరీమృదంగములు పెళ్లునమ్రోగెను the great drums resounded aloud.

పెళ్లెము *pellemu*. [Tel.] n. A flour consisting of a mixture of several substances used in making liquors, మద్యముచేయుటకు అనేక వస్తువులు చేర్చి చేసినపిండి.

పెసలు *pesalu*. [Tel.] n. plu. The pulse called green gram, *Phaseolus radiatus*: Heyne. పచ్చపెసలు. Rox. iii. 295. పెసర *pesara*. adj. Of or belonging to the పెసలు pulse, as పెసరచేను, పెసరపప్పు, &c. One sort is పిల్లపెసర. P. iii. 272. Rox. iii. 299. and 295.

పే pē

పేక *pēka*. [Tel] n. The warp, or cross threads in a web. పట్టులోని అడ్డనూలు.

పేగు or ప్రేగు *pēgu.* [Tel.] n. An entrail, gut, or bowel. Generally used in the plural: పేగులు. పేగులు తెగేటట్టు పరుగెత్తినాడు he ran so fast as to break his wind. పేగులు తెగిన గుర్రము a broken winded horse. అది నా పేగు గనుక నా మనసు తాళలేదు as it was my own child I could not endure to see this. పేగులుతెగ నవ్వినాడు he is ready to split his sides with laughter. పేగుఃపట్టినఃపోటు rankling or piercing pain. మేమందరము ఒకపేగు we are all sons of the same womb. పేగెక్కుట the wringing of the belly. ఆ బిడ్డకు పేగుపడినది the child is suffering from spasms. పేగుతట్టు or తోయు to handle or rub the belly to remove pain. పేగుజారు *pēgu-ḍzāru.* v. n. To have rupture or hernia, బుడ్డదిగు.

పేచకము *pēchakamu.* [Skt.] n. An owl. పైడికంటి. The tip or root of an elephant's tail, ఏనుగుయొక్క తోకమొదలు. "చెంది మ పేచకశీర్షముపైబలెగా." A. v. 95. పేచకి *pēchaki* n. An elephant. గజము.

పేచిక *pēchika.* [Tel.] n. A plant called *Ambrosinia unilocularis.* జోగనిడ్డ. Rox. iii. 493.

పేచీ *pechi.* [prob. corruption of పూచీ.] n. Responsibility, business. Pecuniary embarrassment, trouble, తొందర, తంటా. పేచీకోరు a troublesome fellow. తంటాలమారి.

పేట *pēṭa.* [Tel.] n. A suburb or division of a large city. శాఖానగరము. A city or town. నగరము. A string as of pearls. హారములోనొకసరము. పేటంచు *pēṭ-antsu.* n. The ornamented woven edge of a cloth. పేట. పేటము or పేటకము *pēṭa.* [Skt.] n. A chest. పెట్టె.

పేటనబెట్టు *pēṭana-beṭṭu.* [Tel.] v. n To attempt. యత్నించు.

పేటము *pēṭamu.* [Tel.] n. A large basket. పెద్దగంప.

పేటాడు *pēṭ-āḍu.* [Tel. పేటు+ఆడు.] v. n. To break. ఛేదించు. To prowl about. To play a game with balls tossed up in the air and kept going round. "నీవు అరిమురి వింధ్యాద్రులను మహాగిరుల, బెరికి పేటాడినవిరి నవు." DRK. 171.

పేటి, పేటిక or పేటి *pēṭi.* [Skt.] n. A chest. పెట్టె. లింగ పేటి the small silver box containing the lingam worn on the breast by Jangams. "మానితానూన కురుచపేటి." Ila. i. 42. పేటి n. A waist band, belt, నడికట్టు.

పేటు *pēṭu.* [Tel.] n. A flake, బిళ్ల, పట్టె. ఆ గోడగచ్చు పేటులెత్తినది the plaster of the wall came of in flakes. The top of a hill, పర్వతశిఖరము.

పేడ or పేండ *pēḍa.* [Tel.] n. The dung of cattle. గోమయము. The dung of any animal. పేడగువ్వ *pēḍa-guvva.* n. A species of pigeon. పేడపురుగు *pēḍa-purugu.* n. A beetle. పేడనీళ్లు, పేణ్ణీళ్లు or పేణ్ణీళ్లు *pēḍa-nīḷḷu.* n. Water in which cowdung is dissolved.

పేడి or పేడె *pēḍi.* [Tel.] n. A hermaphrodite, a eunuch, an impotent man. గడ్డము మీసాలులేనివాడు. నపుంసకుడు. పేడివాడు *pēḍi-vāḍu.* n. A beardless man, a hermaphrodite. బృహన్నల. పేడెమూతి a face without a beard or moustaches, an effeminate face.

పేడు *pēḍu.* [Tel.] n. A piece, cutting, chip, or splinter. చెక్కపేడ్లు billets of wood. ఈతపేడ్లపెట్టె a wicker work box. పేడెత్తు *pēḍ-ettu.* (పేడు+ఎత్తు.) v. n. To split, విచ్చు. To slide, తొలగు.

పేడు or పేను *pēḍu.* [Tel.] v. a. To twist, entwine. పేను. తొడమీద దారము పేడు చుండగా while he was twisting the thread on the thigh.

పేణి or పేణీ *pēṇi.* [Tel.] n. A kind of cake made of wheat and sugar

పేద or పేదా pēda. [from Skt. పదాతి.] n. A foot soldier, భటుడు. Also, a pawn (in chess.)

"క॥ చదుదొ పాశికిపేదలు.
కవిదిద్దునశేచి"
సా. ii.

పేద pēda. [Tel.] adj. Poor, indigent, దీన. Timid, పిరికి. Slender, lean, thin, as the waist. కులికిక పేదలైతే కులానికి పేదా if a man happens to be poor, is he to be regarded as contemptible by his fellow-castemen? పేదసాదలు the poor and wretched. నిదుపేదనడుము a slender waist. చెవిపేదలు those that turn a deaf ear to complaints, మొరలాలకించనివారు. "అవశ్యంబు రాజాలు చెవిపేదలని పలికి." P. i. 534. పేద or పేదవాడు pēda. n A poor person. A powerless or weak man, అశక్తుడు. A man of low station in life, అనర్హుడు. పేదలు the poor. పేదరాలు pēda-r-ālu. n. An indigent woman. పేదరికము pēdarikamu. n. Pauperism, poverty. దారిద్ర్యము. పేదరిమి or పేదర్మి pēdarimi. n. Poverty. Timidity, పిరికితనము. నడుముపేదరిమి slenderness of the waist. "తే॥ అట్టిఽ యీ పెద్దతనముమాని, దండి వైలెమ్మ మనసు పేదరిమివిడిచి." M. VI. i. 240. పేదపడు pēda-paḍu. v. n. To be reduced to poverty, to become poor, దారిద్ర్యమును పొందు. To be humbled or humiliated, దైన్యమునుపొందు.

పేనా pēnā. [Eng.] n. A pen. కలము.

పేను pēnu. [Tel.] n. A louse. Plu. పేలు lice. పేనుకొరుకుడు pēnu-koruku̇ḍu. n. A disease arising from lice which destroy the hair. పేనుగుడ్డు or పేనుపిల్ల pēnu-guḍḍu. n. A nit. ఈరు.

పేను pēnu. [Tel.] v. n. and v. a. To twist, or entwine. కలిపిపేను to twist together. See పేడు.

పేపర pēpara. [Tel.] n. A heron: the species called a Tiger Bittern. *Ardea tigrina.*

పేపాళము pēpāḷamu. [Tel.] n. A medicinal plant having a leaf like that of the vine. *Jatropha curcas.* పిచ్చిపేపాళము the wild sort.

పేము or ప్రేము pēmu. [Tel.] n. A rattan or cane. *Calamus fasciculatus; Calamus rotang;* కొండపేము a plant called Dragon's Blood. *Calamus draco.* (Watts.) పేప pēpa. adj. Made of rattan. A. i. 80. "తనమ్రుచ్చున పేపసజ్జ, దండపుబరణిలా." Swa. i. 40. పేపపండ్లు the rattan fruit.

పేయము pēyamu. [Skt.] adj. Drinkable. అపేయము not fit to be drunk.

పేరంటము, పేరంట్రము or పేరటము pēranṭamu. [Tel.] n. Gossiping. The attendance of married women at each other's houses on any domestic festival, such as a wedding. పిలువనిపేరంటము attending a feast without being invited, shameless impertinence. పేరంటాలికూర pērant-āli-kūra. n. A herb called *Corchorus clitorea.* (Heyne.) పేరంటాలు or పేరటాలు pērant-ālu. n. A married woman, the mistress of a house. A lucky woman, i. e., a woman whose husband is alive. పుణ్యస్త్రీ, పునిస్త్రీ. పేరటము pēraṭamu. n. Inviting to a wedding. పెండ్లికి పిలుపడము. "పెండ్లిస్నపాలు నింటనని పేరటముల్ ప్రియమొప్పజెప్పనిం, డ్లిండ్లకు శోభనాక్షతలు పేమపుపాత్రలగొంచు" KP. vii. 62.

పేరణి. పేరవణి or పేరణము pēraṇi. [Tel.] n. A kind of dancing, skipping. భాండీరవతి నృత్యము. Capers, gambolling. నటనము. "అంగనాజాతికి బానందమొదవ, భృంగిముందర నంత పేరణిచూప." L. ii. 152. A long jacket, అంగీ.

పేరము See పేరణము.

పేరస్తు *pērastu*. [H. from పేర+స్థ.] n. A list, catalogue. జాబితా, పట్టీ.

పేరిమి or పేర్మి *pērimi*. [Tel. పేరు+ఇమి.] n. Excess, greatness, eminence. అతిశయము, గౌరవము. Affection, friendship. ప్రేమ, స్నేహము. "... మద్యపానాద్యోగనమదము శక్తి." M. XVI. i. 67. పేరిమికాడు *pērimi-kādu*. n. A great man, గొప్పవాడు, ఘనుడు.

పేరివము *pērivamu*. [Tel.] n. Coolness. శైత్యము. "... పేరివమున, ..." Vasu. vi. 91. టీ. పేరివము, అనగా అధికశీతలభావము.

పేరీడు or పేరీతచెట్టు *pēr-īdu*. [Tel. పేరు+ఈదు.] n. The large date tree. ఖర్జూర వృక్షము.

పేరు *pēru*. [Tel.] n. A name, an appellation. నామము. Fame, celebrity, notoriety, కీర్తి. A long loose necklace, దండ. దొంగయని పేరుపడినాడు he is notorious as a thief. మంచివాడని పేరొందినాడు he is well known as a good man. నిన్ను కొట్టకుంటే నాపేరు రాముడుకాదు if I do not beat you my name is not Rama. నానుపేరుగలసరి a kind of necklace. adj. Great, అధికము. Large, పెద్ద. పేరోడ a large ship. Vish. iii. 393. పేరెండ fierce sunshine. ib. vi. 304. పేరలుక great anger. T. iii. 86. 119. పేరురము a broad breast. పేరెలుగెత్తి పలికిరి they spoke aloud. B. v. 220. పేరాపద a great misfortune, మహాత్తైన ఆపద. పేరలుకు great joy. M. XIII. i. 242. పేరుంగరము *pēr-ungaramu*. n. A ring with one's name cut on it, a signet ring, పేరుచెక్కిన ఉంగరము, శిఖాఉంగరము. పేరు or పేరుకొను *pēru*. v. n. To congeal, curdle, harden or thicken, as melted butter or curds. ఘనీభవించు, దట్టమగు. పాలు పేరబెట్టినది she set the milk to curdle. To increase, అతిశయించు. పేరుకొను or పేర్కొను *peru-konu*. v. a. To call one by his name, to call, to utter. పేరుపెట్టి పిలుచు, పలుచు, ఉచ్చరించు. To praise, స్తుతించు. "... పేర్కొన్న ..." Vish. vi. 220. పేరుకోలు *pēru-kōlu*. n. Calling one by his name, &c. పేరు గ్రుచ్చు or పేరుకొనచ్చు *pēru-grutstsu*. v. a. To call one by his name. పేరుపెట్టిపిలుచు. To tell, to say, to mention. చెప్పు, ఉచ్చరించు. పేర or పేరట *pēra*. adv. In the name of, in one's name. By name. నా పేరట వ్రాసినాడు he wrote to my name, i. e., wrote to me. నాపూర్వులపేరట పుట్టినమాన్యము a grant made to my ancestors. తల్లి పేరట ఒకపల్లె కట్టెను he built a village in his mother's name. In translation into English we omit "name." దినాలపేరట in course of time. పేరి *pēri*. adj. Named, by name, videlicet, id est. పేరుగల. "శాంత పేరికాంతాలలామ" a woman named Santa. R. ii. 139. పేరిటి *pēriti*. adj. Directed to, bearing the superscription of, as అతని పేరిటిజాబు a letter to his address. నీపేరిటి జాబు a letter for you. నీపేరిటివాడు a man bearing your name. పేరుపెట్టు *pēru-pettu*. v. n. To name, to give newly a name or appellation. పేర్వేర *pēr-vēra*. adv. Name by name. ప్రతిమనిషిపేరుచ్చరించుచు పేరుపెట్టి. "పేర్వేరబొమ్మల పెండ్లిండ్లు సేయుచు ... దవిత్తురుంబులుందు." B. X. 1818. (Rukmini Kalyan.) పేరడవి *pēr-adavi*. (పేరు+అడవి.) n. A great forest, a wilderness. మహారణ్యము. పేరాముదము *pēr-āmudamu*. (పేరు+ఆముదము.) n. The large kind of castor oil tree, పెద్దాముదము, as opposed to చిట్టాముదము, a smaller species. పేరోలగము *per-ōlagamu*. n. A great court, or assembly. నిండుసభ. పేరుడు *pērudu*. n. The act of congealing, or thickening. ఘనీభవము, ... పేరుడు or పేర్చు

pērutsu. v. n. To excel, అతిశయించు, విజృంభించు. v. a. To pile, to heap up. To increase, to enlarge; to display. ఒకటిమీద నొకటిని వరుసగాపెట్టు, వికసింపజేయు. చితి పేర్చిరి they prepared a funeral pile. "ఇనుమును రాగియు దగరంబును వెండియు బసిండియును, బ్రభూతములై పేర్చిన సిరిజేయుగ నూపెడు గనులెడనెడ పెక్కుగలవు కౌరవనాథా." M. VI. i. 50. పేరుపు or పేర్పు *pērupu*. n. The act of arranging things one over another, the act of heaping or piling up. ఒకటిమీద నొకటి పేర్పుట. A potsherd, కుండపెంకు. పేరుమాను n. A large tree, పెద్దమాను.

పేరెము or **పేరము** *pēremu*. [Tel.] n. Course, pace, running, a gallop. గుర్రపు నడక, సామాన్యపునడక. **పేరెముపాఱు** or **పేరెముత్తు** *pēremu-paru*. v. n. To run, to gallop.

పేరోజము, పేరోజము or **పేరోదజము** *pērodzamu* [Tel.] n. A kind of sapphire. ఒకవిధమైన మరకతము. "పేరోజంబులమలుకుముట్టు." సా. iv. A kind of inferior precious stone, ఒకవిధమైన క్షుద్రమణి.

పేలవము *pēlavamu*. [Skt.] adj. Soft, meek, easy, మృదువు. Thin, sapless. పలుచని.

పేలా *pēla*. [Tel.] n. A kind of cup for drinking water.

పేలాలు, పేలగింజలు, పేలలు or **ప్రేలలు** *pēla-lu*. [Tel.] n. Malted grain, fried grain, parched corn. **పేలపిండి** *pēla-pindi*. n. Flour made of parched grain. పరుల సొమ్మువానికి పేలపిండి he devours his neighbour's goods like a bit of bread.

పేలిక *pēlika*. [Tel.] n. A rag, a bit or scrap of cloth, a remnant, a tatter, చింపి.

పేలు *pēlu*. [Tel. plu. of పేను] n. Lice.

పేలు or **ప్రేలు** *pēlu*. [Tel.] v. n. To swell out through heat, సెగచేత ఉబుకు. To break out in prickly heat, or any eruption. To be fried, to be parched. To gabble, brag, chatter, to talk nonsense. To fret. జ్వరము పేలిపడజొచ్చుచున్నది the fever is burning hot. చిటచిటప్రేలు to crackle in roasting. "పేల్పులెల్ల చిటచిటప్రేలుచు చటచటబాసె." BD. iv. 621. వానిముఖము చిటచిట పేలుచున్నది he is very peevish, వాని ముఖము ధుమధుమలాడుచున్నది. ప్రేలడము tattling. **పేల్చు** or **పేలుచు** *pēltsu*. v. a. To fry. Metaphorically, to grieve. A. v. 56. పేల్పుచేప a fried fish. **పేలరితనము** *pēlari-tanamu*. n. Talkativeness. వదురుబోతుతనము.

పేళ్లు *pēḷḷu*. [Tel.] n. The plural of పేరు a name, and of పేడు a chip.

పేవు Same as పేగు (q. v.)

పేశలము *pēṣalamu*. [Skt.] adj. Dexterous, clever. నేర్పుగల, చతురము, delicate, soft, smooth. Agreeable. రుచిరము, మృదువైన.

పేశి *pēsi*. [Skt.] n. An egg, a foetus, అండము. A lump of flesh, మాంసపుముద్ద.

పేషిగీ *pēshigī*. [H.] n. An advance of pay.

పేష్కషు *pēshkashu*. [H.] n. Rent paid to the Government by the proprietor of a permanently settled estate under Regulation, xxv. of 1802. Tribute paid by a Zemindar, కప్పము.

పేష్కారు *pēshkāru*. [H.] n. A revenue officer next to an Amaldar.

పేసము *pēsamu*. [Tel.] n. Juice, sap. తాటి or మామిడిపేసరు the yellow juice of the ripe palm or mango fruit. This is spread out and dried, then preserved in cakes called తాటితాండ్ర, మామిడితాండ్ర.

పై pai

పై or **పయి** *pai*. [Tel.] n. The upper part of any thing, the outer part or exterior మీదు, ఉపరిభాగము. adj. Upper, higher, superior. External. Extra. పైముంగిలి petty sums that remain over. వానిపైబట్ట the garment he had on. అప్పైయేడు the next year, either before or after, ముందువేడు. పైవిరోధము seeming enmity. పైపనులు the further acts; also, out-door work. వాడు నాకు పైయెయ్యగానుండును he is my superior. వట్టిపైమాటలు this is mere talk. పైమినుకు mere external beauty. పైవెల్లువ freshes in a river. దానికి అందరును పైబడుదురు all are eager to get it. పైకొను or పయికొను pai-konu. v. n. and a. To exceed, మీరు. To come upon (with hostile intent), మీదికివచ్చు. To get upon, mount on, attack and overcome. కవియు. To attempt, యత్నించు. To happen, కలుగు. పైకొలుపు pai-kolupu. v. a. To cause to happen, to fall upon, &c. "ఈ తరుణీమణుకును కాదోయని సంధియు మందినిక్కమరియనుదుని పైకొను ఘనహరితాపంబుల వలికంకవివచ్చా." HK. v. 53. పైగస్తీ pai-gasthi. [H.] n. A patrol. పైగా pai-gā. adv. Above, up. Into the bargain, besides, above all; in the next place. పైజోడిపసువు pai-dzoḍi-pasuvu. n. A brindled ox. పైన or పయిని paina. adv. On the top, upon, over, above. In future, hereafter. పైనచెప్పు go on, speak on. పైనచేయవలసినదేమి what is to be done afterwards? నిన్ను శిక్షించేవాడు పైన ఉన్నాడు there is one above who will punish you. పైనబడకుము or పైబడకుము do not touch me. పైపక్కపడు pai-pakka-paḍu. v. n. To caress, పక్కలపైనబడు. "ఆయ్యయయ్యయటంచు కియ్యంబుమీరగా వలుమారు పైబక్కబడకయుంట." N. ix. 103. పైపడు or పైబడు pai-paḍu. v. n. To fall upon, attack, పైకొను, కవియు. To exceed మీరు. అశ్వంబునకు అందరును పైబడుచున్నారు all of them are contending for the horse. M. x. i 145. పైపాటు pai-pāṭu n. An attack or encounter, కవియుట. పైపైగా pai-pai-gā. adv. Easily, superficially, cursorily, కుంభముగా. పైయెద్దు or పైపొన్నెద్దు pai-y-eddu. n. An ox with the belly alone white, called a sheeted ox. పైవిలాసము pai-vilāsamu. n. A superscription or address on a letter.

పైంటు or పయింటు paintu. [Eng.] n. An appointment. పైంటుచేయు to appoint.

పైకము paikamu. [Skt. from పికము.] n. A flock of cuckoos, పికములసమూహము. "ముగము నెక్కులు కిర్కుకోర మిసులారి పైకమలలు." A. v. 134.

పైకము or పయికము paikamu. [Tel.] n. A small copper coin, దబ్బులో నాలుగవవంతు, దమ్మిడి. Cash, money. సొమ్ము, ధనము. ఆ హుండీకి పైకము పుచ్చుకొన్నాము we received the value of the cheque. A multitude, సమూహము.

పైకిలిచేప paikili-chepa. [Tel.] n. A fish of the perch kind, ten inches long and with a forked tail, the body striped with yellow and brown fillets and the second anal spine very large. Russell. No. CXXI.

పైజారు or పయిజారు paidzāru. [H.] n. A shoe, slipper. మెట్టు, జోడు, కిర్రు, చెప్పులు. పైజారుమట్ట paidzāru-matta. n. The Remora or sucking fish.

పైట, పయ్యెద or పయిట paiṭa. [Tel. from పయ్యెద. (పయి+ఎద)] n. A woman's mantle, formed by throwing the train or end of the cloth over her breast and head. పైటకొంగు or పైటచెంగు paiṭa-kongu. n. The skirt or end of the same. ఉత్తరీయము, పయ్యెద. పైటకర్ర paiṭa-karra. n. A weaver's whirl.

పైథ paitha. [Skt. borrowed from Tel.] Same as పైట. (q. v.)

పైడి or **పయిడి** *paidi.* [Tel.] n. Gold. బంగారు. Money, ధనము. A dowry, అరణము. adj. Golden, gold coloured, bright yellow. **పైడికంటి** or **పయిడికంటి** *paiḍi-kanti.* adj. Golden eyed, బంగారువన్నె కన్నులుగల. n. The spotted owlet, *Athene brama* (F. B. I.) కనకాక్షి. **పైడిచూలాలు** *paiḍi-tsūl-ālu.* n. Lit: The lady that produces gold, i.e., the Earth. భూమి, వసుధ్ర. **పైడితామర** *paiḍi-tāmara.* n. The land lotus, మెట్టతామర. **పైడినలత** *paiḍi-nelata.* n. An epithet of Lakshmi, లక్ష్మి. **పయిడిపత్తి** *paiḍi-patti.* n. A kind of fine golden colored cotton. **పైడివాసము** or **పసిడివాసము** *paiḍi-bāsamu.* n. Gold and other things. బంగారు మొదలుగాగల వస్తువులు. A. vi. 100. **పైడిముడుచు** *paiḍi-muḍutsu.* v. a. To betroth, నిశ్చితార్థముచేయు. **పైడిముడుపు** *paiḍi-muḍupu.* n. A betrothal, వివాహమునకు ప్రధానముచేయడము, నిశ్చితార్థము. **పైడిరేడు**. **పైడిరాయుడు** or **పైడిదొర** *paiḍi-rēḍu.* n. The lord of wealth, i. e., Kubēra.

పైతృకము or **పైత్రము** *paitṛikamu.* [Skt. from పితృ.] adj. Ancestral, derived from or relating to ancestors. పితృసంబంధమైన. Ancestral acquisition, family property. పిత్రార్జితము. **పైతృష్వసేయుడు** or **పైతృష్వస్త్రీయుడు** *paitṛishvas-ēyuḍu.* n. The son of a paternal aunt. మేనత్తకొడుకు.

పైత్యము or **పైత్తము** *paityamu.* [Skt. from పిత్తము.] n. Bile, biliousness, melancholy, madness, delirium, imbecility. పైత్యచలనము excess of bile, పైత్యాధిక్యము. **పైత్యప్రకృతి** *paitya-prakṛiti.* n. A bilious temperament. పిత్తజ్వరము or పైత్యజ్వరము bilious fever. పిత్తాధిక్యము or పిత్తోద్రేకము accumulation of bile, congestion of the liver. **పైత్యగాడు** *paitya-gāḍu.* n. A fool, a blockhead, a lunatic, or madman.

పైద or **పయిద** *paida.* [Tel.] n. A child, a boy, పిల్లకాయ.

పైదలి or **పయిదలి** *paidali.* [Tel. from పయ్యెద; lit: పయ్యెదగలది.] n. A woman. స్త్రీ. "పడుచులు పైదలులుమేమును, బడిబాయక వెంట తోంటి పనులను విడావెంబడి." R. ii. 7.

పైనము or **పయనము** *painamu.* [from Skt. ప్రయాణము.] n. A journey.

పైమాయిషి *pai-mayisht.* [H.] n. The survey or measurement of lands. నేలలకొలవడము.

పైర or **పయిర** Same as పయిరి (q. v.).

పైరము or **పయిరము** *pairamu.* [Tel.] n. A milch cow. "క్రొన్ననకొండకోర్కులెఱుకలకు కేవలంపంచుపైపయింగొత్రలు పాడిపైరములు గోకులయాకలుముందుముందుగా." Vaijay. ii. 65. టీ॥ పాడిపైరములు, పాడిపసువులు.

పైరు or **పయిరు** *pairu.* [Tel.] n. Growing corn, a crop. వరిమొదలయిన సస్యము. **పైరులయొకిమిడు** *pairula-y-ekimiḍu.* n. The moon. పయిరుపెట్టు to plant or sow corn. పయిరుచేయు to cultivate.

పైలుమాను *pailu-mānu.* [H.] n. A boxer or wrestler. జెట్టివాడు.

పైశాచికము *paiśāchikamu.* [Skt. from పిశాచము.] adj. Pertaining to the demons or fiends. n. A form of marriage in which the bride is carried away by force. An elopement, a rape.

పైశున్యము *paiśunyamu.* [Skt. from పిశునము.] n. Information, espionage, roguery. కొండెము, కొండెకానితనము.

పైష్టికము *paishṭikamu.* [Skt. from పిష్టము.] n. A cake of flour. A kind of beer made from a fermented paste. పిష్టము, అనేకధాన్యసారకృతమద్యము.

పైసరము or **పయిసరము** *paisaramu.* [Skt.] n. Sexual intercourse.

పైసలు or **ఫైసలు** *paisalu.* [H.] n. A settlement, decision, decree. తీర్పు. పంచాయితీ.

DICTIONARY
TELUGU ENGLISH

నిఘంటు
తెలుగు ఇంగ్లీష్

DICTIONARY TELUGU ENGLISH

నిఘంటు తెలుగు ఇంగ్లీష్

Charles Philip Brown

PART – II

పో po TO స్లో slō

SECOND EDITION

NEW EDITION THOROUGHLY REVISED AND BROUGHT UPTO DATE

BY

M. VENKATA RATNAM
W.H. CAMPBELL
and
RAO BAHADUR K. VEERESALINGAM

GYAN

Published by

Gyan Publishing House
5, Ansari Road
Daryaganj, New Delhi-110002
Phone: 011-47034999, 9811692060
E-mail: books@gyanbooks.com

Distribution Network
gyanbooks.com
India, USA, Canada, UK, Australia, France

ISBN : 978-81-212-3070-4 (set)
978-81-212-6586-7 (HB)
First Published, 1903

2nd Impression 2022

Printed at: Gyan Press, Delhi.

నిఘంటు తెలుగు ఇంగ్లీష్

DICTIONARY TELUGU-ENGLISH (Part-II)

Author: Charles Philip Brown

పొ po

పొ *po.* [Tel. from పోవు.] adv. or interj. Certainly. "ఒల్లరుపొ నృపుడొసగుధనము" వర. iv.

పొం *pom.* [Tel. short for పొన్ను in compounds.] adj. Gold. పొంబట్టు a golden cloth. "పులుకురాయనివట్టుగలవస్త్ర నొరబట్టు పొంబట్టు జిలుగు రంటంబులోడ." A. i. 13.

పొంకణము or **పొంకసము** *pongkanamu.* [Tel.] n. A purse, a pouch. "కటితటంబు నందు గట్టినగోచియు, నొలువుచుటివిట్టు లొంటి దిగి, పంకపొంకణమును సడలి నడికట్టైన, కొండ లందు తిరుగకుండు దేవ." BP. iii. 2829.

పొంకము *pongkamu.* [Tel.] n. Proportion, fitness, suitableness, neatness, grace, beauty, trimness, పొందిక, సొగసు. మాటల పొంకము elegance of speech. **పొంకపడు** *pongka-padu.* v. n. To be fit, to be well arranged, పొందికపడు. **పొంకించు** or **పొంకపరచు** *pongkintsu.* v. a. To make fit or beautiful. **పొంకముగా** *pongkamu-ga.* adv. Meetly, duly, fitly, gracefully, elegantly. **పొంకగింపు** *pongka-gimpu.* n. Neatness, tidiness, suitability, elegance, grace.

పొంగలి or **పొంగళి** *pongali.* [Tel.] n. Rice boiled with milk. పొంగలిపండుగ a Hindu festival at which this dish is used, the Pongal feast, సంక్రాంతి, సంక్రమణము, సంక్రమణము. తెక్కెటిపొంగలి a savoury mess of rice, split pulse, spices, and sugar; a sacrifice of a goat or a fowl to a village goddess. పొంగలిపెట్టిరి they offered a bloody sacrifice. H. v. 15.

పొంగిలి *pongili.* [Tel.] n. A flock of birds. పక్షులసమూహము. Food, ఆహారము.

పొంగు *pongu.* [Tel.] v. n. To effervesce; to boil or bubble up, overflow, boil over. To swell. To ferment. To exult, to be overjoyed, elated, to be in ecstasy. సంతోషించు. To become proud, గర్వించు. పొంగి పొర్లిపడు to boil over with pride or delight. ఎండచేత కండ్లుపొంగినవి the eyes are inflamed by the glare. పొంగునీళ్లు boiling water. **పొంగు** *pongu.* n. Effervescence, boiling or bubbling up, overflowing. Excess of joy. సంతోషము. Pride, గర్వము. Eruption of the measles. Boiling water in which rice is to be cooked, ఎసరుకాగినసీళ్లు, చిట్టుడుకునీళ్లు. ఎసరుపొంగి పొర్లుచున్నది the water is boiling over. నీ పొంగుఅణగ may your pride perish. ఇదియేమి చూచుకొన్న పొంగు on what do you pride yourself? పొంగులక్షణము symptoms of an eruption of measles. **పొంగుప్రాలు** *pongu-pralu.* n. A sort of grain. **పొంగలించు** *pongalintsu.* v. n. To stand erect; to be proud, నిక్కు. **పొంగారు** *pong-aru.* (పొంగు+ఆరు.) v. n. To be full, నిండారు. To swell out, ఉబుకు. To rejoice, సంతోషించు. To excel, to be proud, అతిశయించు, విజృంభించు, నిక్కు. "తొలొకవిగ్రహము లపుడుద్భవ మొదరినింగి పొంగారం బత్యంత నిశ్చలంబులయొక్క సైనికనికరం బులవ్యుటముగ." M. VIII. iii. 273. **పొంగించు** *pongintsu.* v. a. To boil. To delight, to please much. చేరెడుబియ్యము పొంగించుకొని నాడు he boiled a handful of rice.

పొంచు *pontsu.* [Tel.] v. n. To lie in wait: to crouch or lurk. పొంచెదరు they will lie in wait. "పులుల తీర్పుమనుము తొలగియొక పొంచెదరు." R. i. 129. **పొంచు** or **పొంచిక** *pontsu.* n. Lurking, eavesdropping, lying in ambush. **పొంచువినేవాడు** an eavesdropper.

పొంజు or **పొజ్జు** *pondzu.* [Tel.] v. a. To split (grass) into filaments. చీల్చు. "కసవులు సన్నంబుగా పొంజి పొంజి, విసువక యుండిచ్చు విశ్వాసమునను." L. ii. 173.

పొంటె or **పొంటెను** *ponte.* [Tel.] adv. By reason of, on account of, for, కొరకు, నిమిత్తము. "పరుసనిమిత కెక్కలకిత్వపుదేవ్యంబు నిన్నియుపొంటె." M. XII. iii. 125.

జగత్త్రయుపితామహుఁ పొంటె, అనగా లోకత్రయమునకు ఉపకారార్థముగాను.

పోండు *pondu*. [Tel. from పోవు.] v. imperative plu. Begone! Go ye.

పొంత *ponta*. [Tel.] n. Neighbourhood, closeness, nearness. సమీపము. A way, path, దారి. A bank, తీరము, దరి. "పులస్త్య మౌనియాశ్రమంబు పొంతకుజని." T. ii. 24. adj. Near, neighbouring. సమీపమైన, దగ్గిరనుండే. **పొంతకడవ** *ponta-kaḍava*. n. A water pot near the oven, పొయ్యిదగ్గిరనుంచిన నీళ్లకడవ. **పొంత** or **పొంతగద్ద** *ponta*. n. A vulture.

పొంతనము *pon-tanamu*. [Tel. పొందు+తనము.] n. A happy conjunction of stars, గ్రహమైత్రి, కూటము. గణపొంతనము euphony in verse, connection by analogy. నాకు వానికి పొంతనములేదు he and I do not agree, నాకు వానికి పడదు, గిట్టదు, సరిపడదు, లేక, సగముఎరుక. **పొంతము** *pontamu*. n. Friendship, స్నేహము. **పొంతకత్తె** *ponta-katte*. n. A pimp, కుంటెనకత్తె.

పొందు or **హొందు** *pondu*. [Tel.] v. n. To wink, (కన్ను)వాలు. v. a. To gain, obtain, get, acquire. To reach, attain to. To have, enjoy. To suffer, experience, meet with joy, grief or death, &c. ప్రాపించు. వానిని లక్ష్మిపొందినది good luck has befallen him. అవమానమును పొందినాడు he incurred disgrace. సంతోషమును పొందినాడు he was pleased. నష్టమునుపొందినాడు he incurred loss. విఘ్నమొందక meeting with no obstacle or check. నరకమును పొందినాడు he fell into hell. కన్నుపొందు to sleep. "ఆ॥ కడుపు నిండనుడుప గానమిరేయెల్ల, గన్నుపొందకున్న కరముడస్సి, యున్న వాడివాడు." M. I. vi. 322. కన్నుపొందకున్న, అనగా నిద్ర లేకుండా ఉండడముచేత. Also, to have intercourse with. **పొందు** n. Fitness, suitability, agreement. పొందిక intercourse, friendship, స్నేహము. Joining, union, సంధి. The act of obtaining a thing. ప్రాప్తి. Sameness, want of difference, అభేదము. Agreeableness, అనుకూల్యము. adj. Friendly, స్నేహితుడు. "రాలుపొందెరింగి రాలుగూర్చినదొంగిలోను పొందెరింగిలోనుపరచి." Vēma. 637. **పొందుకాడు** *pondu-kāḍu*. n. A friend, స్నేహితుడు. **పొందుకొను** *pondu-konu*. v. n. To be fixed or established, నెలకొను. **పొందుపడు** *pondu-paḍu*. v. n. To be agreeable or fit, సరిపడు, అనుకూలించు. **పొందుపాటు** *pondu-pāṭu*. n. Convenience, suitability, aid, help. వానికి ఆ రూకలు పొందుపాటుకాలేదు he could not get the money. పొందుపాటుచేయు to arrange, అనుకూలముచేయు. **పొందించు** *pondintsu*. v. a. To cause to obtain, get, or experience. నన్ను ఈ శ్రమ పొందించినారు they caused me this trouble. "మునుసతి నంబునజగములు తినులను పొందింప గొంతెదడవె యుకుంటా." B. viii. 446. **పొందిక** *pondika*. n. Fitness, agreement, aptness. ఇమిడిక. Intercourse, సహవాసము, కలయిక. "సీతా కాంతమునిస్త్రీల పొందికలుమరగి." R. v. 59.

పొంపిరి *pompiri*. [Tel.] n. Thickness, సాంద్రత. adj. Thick, సాంద్రము. **పొంపిరిగా** *pompiri-ga*. adv. Thickly. **పొంపిరిపోవు** *pompiri-pōvu*. v. n. To thicken, సాంద్రమగు. To excel, increase, grow, spread, అతిశయించు, విజృంభించు, వర్ధిల్లు, వ్యాపించు. To be born, to spring forth. పుట్టు. To rejoice, సంతోషించు. To become famous, to be well known, ప్రసిద్ధికెక్కు.

పొంపు *pompu*. [Tel.] n. The nape or back of the neck. మెడవెనుకటిభాగము, మెడపొంపు. Grace, beauty, ఒప్పు. **పొంపెసలారు** *pomp-esal-āru*. (పొంపు+ఎసలారు.) v. n. To be fine or beautiful. ఒప్పారు.

పొంబనటులు *pom-banaṭulu.* [Tel. పొన్ను + పనటులు.] n. Golden plantain trees, (a phrase in poems.) H. iv. 341.

పొకారు or పోకారు *pokāru.* [Tel.] v. n. To be ruined, నాశమగు. పొకార్చు, పొకారుచు, పోకారుచు or పోకార్చు *pokārtsu.* v. a. To kill or ruin, to render powerless, to strike with stupor. "ఉ॥ కానకకన్నమా నుతుంపొకారిచి యున్నిదయుమిద్ద చేసితే." R. ii. 50.

పొకాలు, పొకాలిపోవు, పోకాలు or పోకాలిపోవు *pokālu.* [Tel.] v. n. To go off, to be freed, వెడలు, పోవు. To perish, to be ruined. నాశమైపోవు. (The use of this word implies hatred or strong aversion.) "శా॥ బ్రాహ్మణమింకోహాచాలుబొకాలిపోదు దరా పోకోనాటిక్రొ వ్వేటికిణా." Swa. vi. 51.

పొక్కలి *pokkali.* [Tel.] n. One of the three legs or projecting lumps supporting the boiler on an earthen fireplace, పొయ్యి మీది ఎత్తుగడ్డలు, మూడురాళ్లు పెట్టినపొయ్యి. A portable oven, ఎత్తుడుపొయ్యి. పొక్కటిగడ్డలు or పొక్కటిరాళ్లు *pokkaṭi-gaḍḍalu.* n. Stones used as a temporary fireplace. పొయ్యిరాళ్లు. వారుముగ్గురు పొక్కటిరాళ్లకిరిగా నున్నారు those three are as inseparable as the three legs of a fireplace.

పొక్కి *pokki.* [Tel.] n. A mark or sign, గురుతు. Danger, అపాయము.

పొక్కిలి *pokkili.* [Tel.] n. The navel, బొడ్డు. A dent, గుంట. పొక్కిలిగోలి, పొక్కిలిపాప or పొక్కిలిపాపడు lit: the navel-born, i. e., Brahma, బ్రహ్మదేవుడు.

పొక్కు *pokku.* [Tel.] v. n. To be blistered or excoriated. బొబ్బలేచు. పొక్కిన scalded. నానోరు పొక్కినది my mouth is burnt or sore. To be afraid, భయపడు, భయపడు. To grieve much or be afflicted. దుఃఖించు. To come off in flakes, as plaster. ఆ మాట విని పొక్కిపోయినాడు on hearing that word he grieved very much. n. A breaking out; a boil, blister, pustule, pock, బొబ్బ. A flake that has come off from a wall or anything else, ఎండిలేచినపెల్ల. Grief, దుఃఖము. పొక్కుడు *pokkuḍu.* n. Grief, అంగలార్పు. A flake, as of mortar, that has come off from a wall. పెల్ల. పొక్కిలు or పొక్కిలేచు to come off in flakes. పొక్కురోగము a chancre. పొక్కులు. పొక్కించు *pokkintsu.* v. a. To fret, blister, excoriate, scorch.

పొగ or పొవ *poga.* [Tel.] n Smoke, steam, vapour. ధూమము. "ఊరుపుపొగల్" the vapour of sighs. Vasu. iv. 10. పొగతాగు to smoke a pipe or cheroot. "అగరు సాంబ్రాణిపొగలుపట్టి." Ila. i. 140. టీ॥ ధూపమిచ్చి. పొగకన్ను *poga-kannu.* n. Siva's eye from which fire issued. పొగకర్ర *poga-karra.* n. A sunbeam. Lit: a stick of smoke, because a beam has that appearance if it falls amid smoke. పొగగూడు *poga-gūḍu.* n. A chimney. పొగచు, పొగుచు or పొగించు *pogatsu.* v. a. To cause to smoke, పొగయజేయు. To fry, to season with spices. ఇగురబెట్టు, తిరగబోతబెట్టు, పోపించు. "కలమాన్నము నొర్రి పప్పునాలంకే నాగిచినకూరలుణ." A. i. 39. టీ॥ పొగిచినకూరలుణా, ఇగురుకూరలుమ. పొగచుట్ట *poga-tsuṭṭa.* n. A cheroot or cigar, పొగాకుగుంట a tobacco field, పొగాకువేసినగుంట చేను. పొగచూరు *poga-tsūru.* v. n. To be smoked, పొగపట్టు, పొగవాసన కలిగియుండు. పొగచెట్టు or పొగాకుచెట్టు *poga-chettu.* n. The tobacco plant. కారుపొగాకు very strong and black tobacco. పొగపు *pogapu.* v. a. To cause to be fried or seasoned, పోపించు. పొగపు or పోపు n. Seasoning, spicery. తిరగబోత. పోపింపు. పొగబాణము *poga-bāṇamu.* n. A smoke-rocket, i. e., a bombshell, ధూమబాణము. కమ్ము

పొగబట్టువేయు ఆకాశమంటును. "పొగబారి ముఱికముల్ నిగిడింపక స్తనం, ధూమంపు పెను మొగుల్ తొంగలింప." Bobbili. iii. 137. పొగయు or పొవయు *pogayu.* v. n. To smoke or emit smoke, పొగలేచు. To be smoked, పొగకలుదును. To be passed through smoke. To burn slowly, కుములు.

పొగడ or పొవడ *pogada.* n. The tree called *Mimusops elengi.* వకుళవృక్షము.

పొగడు or పొవడు *pogadu.* [Tel.] v. a. To praise, laud, applaud. To compliment, flatter. పొగడిక, పొగడు or పొగడికోలు *pogadika.* n. Praise. స్తోత్రము. The act of praising, స్తుతించుట. పొగడిత or పొగడ్త *pogadita.* n. The act of praising, పొగడుట. Praise, స్తుతి. Fame, కీర్తి. పొగడ్తపడు *pogadta-padu.* v. n. To be praised, స్తుతింపబడు.

పొగరు *pogaru.* [Tel.] n. Pride, presumption, arrogance, insolence, గర్వము. Length, దైర్ఘ్యము. A shade or color. A strong stifling smell, తీక్ష్ణగంధము. "ఘనాఘనముల్ పొగరెక్కి." R. vi. 23. పొగరుబోతు *pogaru-bōtu.* n. A proud or arrogant man, గర్వశీలుడు.

పొగులు or పొవులు *pogulu.* [Tel.] v. n. To grieve, to pine with grief, to languish. దుఃఖముచేత తపించు. To burn. రగులు, కుములు. "పువ్వులవాన, కురిసి నవ్వుచు నవ్వి నొల్లునవడికి, నిగుడుకీలల మాని నిప్పువపైకప్పు, పొగులుట లుడిగి నిప్పుకలు చల్లారె." HD. i. 2285. పొగిలించు *pogilintsu.* v. a. To afflict, to grieve. "మయూరాదులుగా పొగిలించె." R. v. 234.

పొచ్చెము *pochchemu.* [Tel.] n. Deceit; a trick, feint. A spot. A fault, defect, న్యూనత, కపటము, వంచన, కల్లము. "తను పొచ్చెములేని నెయ్యమున పూని విపద్దశనొంద కుండగా" M. IX. i. 91. "కల ఇన్నటి బంధులు నీవును, నచ్చెరువడి నిను చనుండ కైమోడ్చిన మా, కిచ్చినను, ఖాలునంటివి. పొచ్చెముగాదింతవట్టు పూర్ణముసుమ్మీ." M. V. iii. 11. పొచ్చెపు *pochchepu.* adj. Deceitful. కపటమైన, వంచనైన.

పొట *pota.* [for Skt. పుటము.] n. A hollow, a cup. దొప్ప. ఆకుపొట a leaf-cup.

పొటకర or పొటకర్ర Same as పొట్టకర్ర. See under పొట్ట.

పొటకరించు *pota-karintsu.* [Skt.] v. n. To shoot out anew, as lopped trees. పైకొల్పు. To excel, అతిశయించు. వర్ధిల్లు.

పొటపొట or బొటబొట *pota-pota.* [Tel. anuk: of tears flowing] adj. Fast, gushingly, welling. "బొటబొట నేలవ్రాలుచుండ, కటకటపడి మేను వడక గనుగవ నశ్రుల్, పొటపొట రాలగ నేడ్చుచు." T. iv. 19.

పొటమరించు, పొటమరిల్లు or పొటమరులు *potamarintsu.* v. n. To rise or swell up, as a young shoot or a boil, బొబ్బు, చిగురులొత్తనుపుట్టు.

పొటము or పొడము *potamu.* v. n. To be born, to rise. పుట్టు.

పొటి *poti.* Another form of పొట్టి. (q. v.) పొటిపొటి *poti-poti.* adj. Trifling, petty. అల్పము.

పొటుకు or పొటుక్కు *potuku.* [Tel. anuk] adv. Suddenly, said of sunset or sunrise, or of leaves falling from a tree. "ప్రొద్దు పొటుక్కునఁబొడుచు ఘూర్జరికూటము లెక్కి డిగ్గ దుమికి." Kalahasti. iv. 63.

పొటేలు, పొట్టేలు or పొట్లేలు *potēlu.* [Tel.] n. A ram. గొర్రెపోతు, మేకపోతు, మేషము.

పొట్ట *potta.* [Tel.] n. The belly, paunch. కడుపు. The tender ear just formed, an unopened ear of corn. కలుమగర్భము. కను పొట్లలు ఉబ్బినవి the eyes are swollen. పొట్టపెంచుకొను to become corpulent. పొట్టకరుకు *potta-karuku.* n. A bulging ear of corn: a swelling pod, ready to burst, to this is compared the bulge of the calf of a well developed leg. పొట్టకఱ్ఱ, పొట్టకర, పొటుకఱ్ఱ or పొటుకర *potta-karra*. n. An unopened ear of corn. పొట్టపట్టెడ *potta-patteḍa*. n. A saddle girth, టంగువారు, టంగు. పొట్టపెంజర *potta-penjara*. n. A sort of snake. పొట్టకూడు *potta-kūḍu*. n. Food given in lieu of wages. కడుపుకూడు. పొట్టకూటివాడు *potta-kūṭi-vāḍu*. n. One who serves for food alone without wages. పొట్టకొవ్వు *potta-kovvu*. n. Pride, conceit, such as come from good living. పొట్టపోసికొను *potta-pōsi-konu*. v. n. To fill one's belly without any regard to self respect. పొట్టవాడు *potta-vāḍu*. n. A pot-bellied man. బొజ్జకడుపువాడు.

పొట్టి or పొటి *potti*. [Tel.] adj. Short, small in size. పొట్టింపుచీరణము a kind of a short chisel. పొట్టికాకర *potti-kākara*. n. The tree called *Momordica muricata*. పొట్టితనము *potti-tanamu*. n. Shortness of stature. పొట్టిపిట్ట or పొట్టిపిచ్చుక *potti-pitta*. n. The Ashycrowned Finch-lark, *Pyrrhulauda grisea*, (F. B. I.) పొట్టివాడు *potti-vāḍu*. n. A little man. కుబ్జుడు.

పొట్టియ *pottiya*. [Tel.] n. A scorpion. తేలు.

పొట్టు *pottu*. [Tel.] n. Husk, bran. ఊక. The scales of fish Vēma. 1364. పొట్టుధాన్యము grain that has a coat or husk, as వడ్లు, అరికెలు, కొఱ్ఱలు, సాములు, వరిగెలు, &c. పొట్టుకఱ్ఱ an empty sprout in a ear of corn. గట్టివిడిచిపెట్టి పొట్టుకు పోరాడెదవా will you give up the real for the false? మీదితోలు పొట్టుపొట్టుగా రాలిపోయినది the skin peeled off in scales. పొట్టుపొరలగు *pottu-poral-agu*. v. n. To be troubled, harassed or tormented. పీడితమగు. "అప్పాపొత్తుండొల్లుచుం బక్కుంబడక తినదలం బులోన పొట్టుపొరలదొక్క కయ్యంబు పొడుచు వాడుగాని." M. V. iv. 88.

పొట్రేలు See పొటేలు.

పొత్రేను *pot-rēnu*. [Tel. పొట్టి+రేను.] n. A kind of tree.

పొట్ల *potla*. [Tel. lit: that which has spots. పొడలుకలది. cf. Tamil పొడలంగాయ.] n. The snake gourd, ***Momordica** charantia*. చేదుపొట్ల or చేటిపొట్ల the bitter Hair flower, *Trichosanthes laciniata* (Ainslie ii. 296.) అడవిపొట్ల (Rox. iii. 702.) and కుక్కపొట్ల are other species. పొట్లపూచుక్క *potla-pū-tsukka*. n. The constellation called పుష్యమి. పొట్లపూరెక్కనెల the month called పుష్యమాసము.

పొట్లము *potlamu*. [Tel.] n. A packet, pack, bundle, little bag, paper or case to hold perfume, powder or medicine: medicine tied up in a cloth for the purpose of fomentation. A crowd, గుంపు. An army, సేన. పొట్లమొత్తు to apply a fomentation. వారందరు నొకపొట్లముగానున్నారు all of them are in one cluster.

పొట్లు *potlu*. [Tel.] v. n. To become mouldy. పాచిపట్టు, బూజుపట్టు.

పొడ *poḍa*. [Tel.] n. Appearance, form, figure, shape. రూపు, చూపు. A mole, speck, mark, a scruff or eruption on the skin. Variegated colour. పొడలపురుగు a spotted worm or serpent. పొడకట్టు *poḍa-kaṭṭu*. v. n. To make an appearance, to seem, appear, be visible, కనబడు, ప్రత్యక్షమగు, తోచు. నాకు అలాగు పొడకట్టినది it struck me so. పొడగను, పొడగాంచు or పొడచూచు *poḍa-ganu*. v. a. To see, view, behold. చూచు. "పుడమిభర్తకుపండు పొడగాన్పవేచి, కదుభక్తి తోడాని క్రమమెల్లదెలుప." Sārang. D. v.

871. ఇది పదిదినాలుగా వాని పొడ కానను I have not set my eyes upon him these ten days. పొడగానుపు *poḍa-gānupu*. n. Seeing, looking. పొడగనుట, దర్శనము. పొడచూపు or పొడచుపు *poḍa-tsūpu*. v. n. To appear, to become visible, to be seen. కనబడు, ప్రత్యక్షమగు. పొడతామర *poḍa-tāmara*. n. White leprosy, తెల్లతామర. పొడతెంచు *poḍa-tentsu*. v. n. To be born, to rise. ఉదయించు, పుట్టు. పొడనీడ *poḍa-nīḍa*. n. Speckled shade. పొడపత్రి *poḍa-patri*. n. A certain drug, *Asclepias vomitoria* (Kœnig), Vomiting Swallow-wort (Ainslie), which is very efficacious in cases of scorpion stings. పొడయెండ *poḍa-y-enḍa*. n. Sun-shine that appears through the clouds. పొడలమారు See తెండ్ర. పొడలమెకము *poḍala-mekamu*. n. The spotted deer. దుప్పి. పొడసుత్తె *poḍa-sutte*. n. A small hammer, చిన్నసుత్తె.

పొడము or పొడ్మ *poḍamu*. [Tel.] v. n. To be produced, to arise. పుట్టు, కలుగు. పొడమించు *poḍamintsu*. v. a. To create, engender. పుట్టించు. "...పొడమించినంబులావు ఘనమైతి." R. vi. 28.

పొడి *poḍi*. [Tel.] n. Powder, dust. చూర్ణము. Solder, rosin, metallic cement. పొడి or ముక్కుపొడి snuff. పొడిపెట్టించు to solder. చెరుకుకట్టెలపొడి pounded sugar, శర్కర. B. D. iii. 324. చొక్కుపొడి love powder. ఆ పిల్లవానిని చొక్కుపొడిచేసి పట్టుకొనిపోయినారు they deluded him with love powder and carried him off, ఆ పిల్లవానిని మరులు గొలుచేల్లి పట్టుకొనిపోయినారు. పొడిమిరియము or మిరియపుపొడి powdered pepper. R. vii. 105. adj. Dry, ఎండిన. Powdered. Small, young. పొడికూర a curry fried without butter in a dry pan. పొడిచినుకు mizzle, drizzling rain. పొడిరాళ్లు bricks broken into pieces, brick-dust. పొడిబెల్లము pounded jaggery. పొడికావ్యము a petty poem. పొడిపిట్ట a kind of bird. "చిట్టువ, మునుగపూ చిట్టువ, గిజిగాడు, ఉల్లెడ, పొడిపిట్ట, వంక పండు." H. iii. 14. పొడిముత్యాలు seed pearl. పొడిమన్ను dry earth. పొడిచెమట imperceptible perspiration. పొడిబియ్యము dry rice. పొడిపట్టినాలుకలు lips parched with grief. పొడిదగ్గు a dry cough. పొడిచీకటి *poḍi-chīkaṭi*. n. Twilight, darkness. పొడిచేయు or పొడికొట్టు *poḍi-chēyu*. v. a. To powder. పసుపుపొడిచేసినది she triturated or pulverized the turmeric. పొడిపొడిగా *poḍi-poḍi-gā*. adv. In pieces, piece meal, in the form of powder. Very dry.

పొడుగు, పొడువు, పొడగు or పొడవు *poḍugu*. [Tel.] n. Height, length, stature, ఎత్తు. వెలపొడుగుచీర an expensive or high-priced cloth, ఖరీదుగల చీర, హెచ్చు క్రయముగలది. సంవత్సరముపొడుగున throughout the year. adj. High, tall, long, lofty. High, as price. v. n. To grow tall, increase, extend, ఉన్నతమగు, పెరుగు. బియ్యము వెల పొడిగినది the price of rice has risen. పొడుగాటి or పొడుగుపాటి *poḍugāṭi*. adj. Long, tall. పొడవడగు *poḍav-aḍagu*. (పొడవు+అడగు.) v. n. To be spoilt, చెడు. To die, చచ్చు. పొడవడచు *poḍav-aḍatsu*. v. a. To spoil, చెరచు. To kill, చంపు. పొడువు *poḍuvu*. n. Shape, form. రూపు. పొడిగించు *poḍigintsu*. v. a. To lengthen, heighten, raise, increase, exalt. To aggravate, swell. To promote in rank. పొడుగుచేయు, ఎక్కువచేయు. పొడుగుమడుగు *poḍugu-maḍugu*. n. The heavenly Ganges, ఆకాశగంగ.

పొడుచు *poḍutsu*. [Tel.] n. To rise (as the sun or moon, a star, or the tide.) ప్రొద్దుపొడుచు, ఉదయించు, ఎదుపోటుపొడుచు. వాని తిట్లు పొడిచేనాటికి when his curses touch you, or fall upon you. ఏటిలో పోటు పొడిచినది the tide has risen in the river. To fight, పోట్లాడు. "పాండవులందేకాదివా క్కెవ్వాలకీ యొత్తింగొరవచ్చినన్ని మీరలుమందుదునుం కోనుచుం అస్త్రశస్త్రమై ఊరకదోడా ఏకతో పొడుచువా మెచ్చుడుపుడ్కీరాదే వర్తించెదరు." M. I. i. 136. ఏకతో పొడుచువా on their making a bold attack, ధైర్యముతో పైబడగా. v. a. To pierce, stab, gore. To prick or cause pain. To sting, కుట్టు. రంధ్రము పొడుచు to bore a hole. గాలముమీదెడ ఎర్ర పొడుచు to put (a worm) on a fish hook. ఇది కండ్లను పొడుస్తున్నది it tries (pricks) the eyes. మోచేతితో పొడుచు to thrust or hit with the elbow, or to elbow. ముద్రపొడుచు to seal, set a seal on. To cut down, or fell, నరుకు. "పొగ్గులై కల్పతరువు పొడుచుమాటకుమరే." Sumati. v. 73. అన పొడుచు to lay a ban or protest, so as to check proceedings, ఒట్టుపెట్టు. A proverb says వానివేలితోనే వానికన్ను పొడిచినారు they pierced his eye with his own finger, i. e., they turned his arts against himself. పొడుపు podupu. n. A stab, పొడుచుట. A pricking pain, as that of a boil. The rising of the sun. The swell of a river. ఉదయము, పోటు. "ఇదుకత్రోవరి మాన్పు పొడుపులు." P. iv. 255. టీ॥ ఇదుకత్రోవరులైన దొంగలు. వెలపొడుపు the rising of the moon. పొడుకథ or పొడుపుకథ a conundrum. పొడుపుమాట or ఎత్తిపొడుపుమాట a taunt or jeer, దెప్పు. Ila. iii. 8. పొడుపుగొండ podupu-gonda. n. A mountain out of which the sun is supposed to rise, ఉదయాద్రి. పొడువ or పొడుపదు poduva, n. One who thrusts or pricks. పొడుచువాడు. A wicked man, దుర్జనుడు.

పొడుము podumu. [Tel.] n. Powder, snuff, పొడుముకాయ or పొడుంకాయ podumu-kaya. n. A snuff box.

పొణక poṇaka. [Tel.] n. A large grain basket. తాటాకులు మొదలైనవాటితో కట్టి ధాన్యాదులుంచేపెద్దబుట్ట.

పొణకకర్ర, or పొణికికర్ర, poṇaku-karra. [Tel.] n. A light kind of wood like deal or fir.

పొతక potaka. [Tel.] n. A bundle of leaves. ఆకులు మొదలైనవానికట్ట. పొత్తర. పొతకగ in a bundle, in a crowd, గుంపుగా. పోట్లముగా.

పొతము Same as పొట్లము (q. v.). A crowd, గుంపు. "చ॥ అతడొకనాడు వేటకొరకై తనుపేరిన వారుచేర్వతో పొతముగ పైనమాటకరి." Bhallāna Charitra iii. 100.

పొతుకు potuku. [Tel.] n. A line drawn round a stack of corn. ధాన్యపురాశిచుట్టు గీచెడు గీర.

పొత్తము pottamu. [from Skt. పుస్తకము.] n. A book. పుస్తకము, గ్రంథము. A poem, కావ్యము.

పొత్తర pottara. [Tel.] n. A pack or bundle of leaves, ఆకులలోనగువానికట్ట. "పిశితపుం డంబులొండొండపియు వెత్తొత్తగా, నాకుపొత్తరలం గట్టియు గుదులంగట్టియు." Swa. iv. 87. టీ॥ఆకుపొత్తరలంగట్టి, అనగా ఆకులతో పొట్లములు కట్టి.

పొత్తరము or పొత్రము pottaramu. [Tel.] n. A roller or pestle for grinding spices, &c. శిలాపుత్రిక, గుండ్రాయి. పొత్తర ముల్లు pottara-mullu. n. A kind of grass. "కారపొత్తరముల్లువత్రింత." H. v. 54.

పొత్తి potti. [Tel.] n. A thin soft, old cloth, మెత్తని సన్నని పాతవస్త్రము. An integument, coat; skin, bark. నార, పట్ట. కొబ్బరిగెలలు మొదలైనవాటిని పొదిగియుండేది. Also, a torch, దివిటీ. పోకపొత్తి the coat or skin covering the upper part of an areca tree. అరటిపొత్తి the coat or skin on a plantain tree.

పొడుముపొత్తి a snuff box, (literally, a piece of bark folded to contain snuff). పొత్తి or పొత్తిగుడ్డ baby linen. పొత్తినారలు fibres used in garments made of bark. M. XII. vi. 221. పొత్తిపంచ bombasine cloth, woven of silk mixed with cotton. పొత్తిక pottika. n. Same as పొత్తి. Doll's clothes, a gaudy dress for an idol or for a little girl. "బొమ్మపొత్తికలడిగితికొమ్మ యుండమనుచునిచ్చె తాదెచ్చిన యంబరములు." M. IV. v. 308. పొత్తికడుపు potti-kadupu. n. The abdomen, or belly below the navel. వస్తి, క్రిందికడుపు. పొత్తిగడ్డ potti-gadda. n. A certain medicinal root called కరికారి, బిళ్ళు, పొత్తిదుంప. పొత్తిచీర potti-chira. n. Cloth made from the fibres of the bark of certain trees. నారచీర. పొత్తితామర potti-tamara. n. A species of the lotus flower which does not open wide, ముడుగుతామర, వమస్కారి. పొత్తినూలు potti-nulu. n. Silk thread. పొత్తినూలికాయ or పొత్తినూలిగూడు potti-nuli-kaya. n. A cocoon. పొత్తిలి pottili. n. Baby linen. పొత్తిగుడ్డలు. "లీలబొత్తిలిమీద లేచి కూర్చుండుచో తద్దయునొక క్రొత్తముద్దుచెలువు." KP. vi. 207. పొత్తిలిసొర or పల్లదిండి pottili-sora. n. A kind of gourd, *Rhynchobatus ancylostomus.*

పొత్తు pottu. [Tel.] n. Friendship, partnership, holding in common. స్నేహము, సహవాసము, విశ్వాసము, ఉమ్మడి, అవిభక్తత. పోరునష్టి, పొత్తులాభము (proverb) quarrelling is a loss, friendship is a gain. పొత్తునగుడుచు to eat together as messmates, చెలిమిగాతిను. వీధులు అందరికిపొత్తు the streets are free or common to all men. ఆ సరుకులు పొత్తునకొన్నారు they bought the goods between them, or as common stock. ఆ పని పొత్తులపోక పడకేసిపెట్టినారు the work is left undone because they could not settle which of them should do it, ఆ పని నీదంటే నీదని పడవేసిపెట్టినారు. "నృపుపొత్తుబాముపొత్తుంగపటుండగు మిత్రుపొత్తుగడుసరిపోత్తుం, విషకీటఖార్యపొత్తుం బవమిడి విడువంగవలయు." Sumati. 129. "ఇట్టి అవమానపుపొత్తు మనంగవచ్చునే." M. IV. iii. 33. పొత్తులవాడు he in whom both parties have an equal right or interest. ఇద్దరికి సమమైనవాడు. "ఏను పొత్తులవాడనై యురువురకును." ib. XII. v. 257. adj. Friendly, united, associated, స్నేహితము, సంగతము. పొత్తుకాడు pottu-kadu. n. A friend, స్నేహితుడు. పొత్తుకత్తె pottu-katte. n. A female friend. స్నేహితురాలు. పొత్తుగుడుచు pottu-gudutsu. v. n. To avail or come to good. వనికివచ్చు. "సత్కర్మములు పొత్తుగుడుచునా సమ్మతాంగి ధరిం సత్కర్మములానబైవచ్చునీకు." Ila. iv. 21. టీ॥ సత్కర్మములు పొత్తుగుడుచునా, వాసలు కలిసివచ్చునా. పొత్తుగుడుపు pottu-gudupu. n. Eating together as messmates. సంక్తిభోజనము. పొత్తుచేయు pottu-cheyu. v. n. To make friends with, to cultivate friendship, to associate with, స్నేహము చేయు. పొత్తూరు potturu. n. An epithet of Sarasvati, సరస్వతి.

పొత్తెము or పొత్తెపుమట్టి pottemu. [Tel.] n. A red earth, sand or dust with which boxers cover the floor of their gymnasium so as not to be hurt, గరిడీసాలయందు క్రిందపరిచే రొఱ్ఱమన్ను. "మఱి గరిడీల పొత్తెపు మట్టిచల్లడము చెంగావిలో కళల దేరుకా, నిరిహీలా మీరగ జొచ్చి మల్లుర కడలు జేసాన లలా సానల్ బరగ బల్విడు గుజ్జిటో బరవు పోటుల గ్రద్దనల్ గ్రుద్దులు ధర మట్టాడిజయించు నాపని కసాగ్యంబెద్ది లేదెదులలా." Kanaka Ranjani v. 153.

పొత్రము or పొత్తరము potramu. [Tel.] n. A roller or pestle used in grinding.

పొద poda. [Tel.] n. A bush, a shrub. గుబ్బిని. A proverb says "విధికిపొదలడ్డమా" can a bush hide us from our fate? పొదకాచిపిట్ట poda-kachi-pitta. n. The blue Rock

Thrush, *Petrophila cyaneus*. పొదనల్లంచి or పొంకనల్లంచి *poda-nallanchi*. n. The Shama, *Cittocincla macrura*. పొదపలిసపిట్ట *poda-palisa-pitta*. n. The Black-capped Black-bird, *Merula nigripileus*, or, Tickell's Ouzel, *Merula unicolor*. పొదపిగిలి *poda-pigili*. n. The White-browed Bulbul, *Pycnonotus luteolus*. (F. B. I.) పొదపెట్టు *poda-pettu*. v. n. To feign, pretend, assume. "అధికారులముగ నతనికి సమృకంబునగురాము నీకు బాలుడు భువిలో, పొదలని పెద్దరికంబులు పొదపెట్టక లేచిపొమ్ము భోజన్నపాలా." G. ii. 53. పొదరిల్లు *pod ar-illu*. (పొదరు+ఇల్లు.) n. A bower or arbour. నికుంజము. పొదరు Same as పొద. పొదరింట్లె చుక్క the constellation called పుష్యమి నక్షత్రము.

పొదక *podaka*. [Tel.] n. A loud cry. పెద్దఎలుగు. పొదకలెత్తు *podaka-l-ettu*. v. n. To raise the voice or shout. పెద్దగొంతుపెట్టు "పొద కలెత్తి యాపుత్రునికి పిలుచును." Navan. 146.

పొదడు *podadu*. [Tel.] n. A short man, a dwarf. పొట్టివాడు. వామనుడు. పొదిటి *podiṭi*. adj. Short. పొట్టి.

పొదము *podamu*. [Tel. for పోదము.] v. imperative. Let us go. "పొదము ద్దేవతియున్న భూమికని యాభూదేవునిగా గూడి సమ్మదలీలం జని." G. iv. 33.

పొదలు *podalu*. [Tel.] v. n. To increase, to flourish or thrive, be generated, be produced. అభివృద్ధియగు, పెరుగు, ఉద్భవించు, చెలగు, విజృంభించు, ప్రకాశించు. "కాంచనమణి భూషలు చీరలు సొంపతికిం, బొలతికి నుదుగిరులు నుదము పొదలనింతిగా." Swa. v. 120. పొదలించు *podalintsu*. v. a. To undertake. పూనుకొను. "మెయినంచి పొదలించి మెడ రొత్తి నిక్కి కొక్కొరకోయని కోటలగొంక, పంచ మస్వరమున పాటించి కూయు." Pal. iv. పొదలిక *podalika*. n. Increase, growth, పెంపు, వర్ధనము. Assumption, persistence, enterprise. పూనిక. "భూదారమున్తైదూరిన, భూదా రుం డదుగు దొలగి పొదలిక చేసెగా, కైదువగొని రంగైవని, మేదిని బడదాని నపుడు మిత్రులు పొగడగా." Bhanumadvijayam. ii. 232. పొదలాడు (పొదలి+ఆడు.) v. n. Same as పొదలు. పొదలుకొను *podalu-konu*. v. n. To increase, to grow, పెరుగు. To become strong, బలియు.

పొదవెట్టు *poda-vettu*. [Tel.] v. a. To hint, సూచించు. To impute, attribute, ఆరోపించు.

పొది *podi*. [Tel.] n. An udder, పొదుగు. Weight, భారము. A quiver, అమ్ములపొది. A multitude, సమూహము. A barber's pouch, మంగలవాని అడపము. పొదిగొను *podi-gonu*. v. n. To become a crowd, to assemble in a crowd, గుంపుకూడు. పొదుల్లు *podullu*. plu. Cases or pouches, used by barbers. "కత్తులపొదుల్లి మంత్రములె కట్టునపురు." H. iii. 264.

పొదికట్టు *podi-kaṭṭu*. [Tel.] n. The ledge of a pandal. పందిరి. The side of a door: a door sill. A pandal or verandah in front of a house, వాకిటిముందరిపంచపాక.

పొదిగిలి *podigili*. [Tel.] n. The side of the entrance or principal door of a house. "పొదిగిట నిల్చిచూచు చెలిబోడి." Dasav. ix. 481. An armpit, ప్రక్కకు సందిటికి నడిమి భాగము, కౌగిలించినచేంక. పొదిగిట (locative case.) By the door post. In the embrace.

పొదుక or పొది *poduka*. [Tel.] n. A parcel or packet. పొది. Weight. భారము.

"తే॥ తొడ్డిపొండువృశ్చితోలుబిని సంజా,
దంతిరయుచుబుచ్చి పొదుకగానమరగట్టి."

M. XII. iii. 470.

పొదుగు *podugu*. [Tel.] n. The udder of a cow. పొదుగుకోసి పాలుత్రాగు to cut off the udder to drink milk; a proverb like that of killing the goose that laid golden eggs. **పొదుగుచేయు** *podugu-chêyu.* v. n. To have a large udder, as a cow about to calve (ఆవులోనగునది యీనబోవు కాలమందు) పెద్దపొదుగుగలదగు. ఆవు పొదుగు చేస్తున్నది the milk is coming into the udder (previous to calving time.)

పొదుగు or **పొదువు** *podugu.* [Tel.] v. a. To cover: to envelope, to surround, to encircle. కప్పు, ఆవరించు. To embrace. To set, as precious stones. చెక్కు. To sit on eggs. కెంపులపొదిగిననగ a jewel set with rubies. **పొదుగుడు** or **పొదువుడు** *podugudu.* n. The act of covering, కప్పుడు, కప్పట. పొదుగుడుకోళ్లు brood hens, hens that are hatching. పిల్లలుచేయుటకు గుడ్లమీదకుండేకోళ్లు. **పొదిగొను**, **పొదిగిగొను** or **పొదివికొను** *podi-gonu.* v. a. To surround, to encircle, చుట్టుకొను, పరివేష్టించు. **పొదుగు** n. Baby-linen. పొత్తిగుడ్డలు. "మెత్తగా బొదుగలరించి కొమారు నుంచి రాధాదులటగా." G. iii. 40. బొదుగలరించి, అనగా పొత్తిగుడ్డలు పరచి.

పొదుపు *podupu.* [Tel.] n. Thrift, moderation, frugality, careful management. Increase, వృద్ధి.

పొదురు *poduru.* [Tel.] v. n. To blossom, పూచు. **పొదిరించు** *podirintsu.* v. a. To cause to blossom, పూచునట్లుచేయు.

పొద్దు or **ప్రొద్దు** *poddu.* [Tel.] n. The sun. Time, period. బారెడుపొద్దు ఎక్కినప్పుడు when the sun was about two yards high, i. e., about 8 A. M. పొద్దుతిరుగుడుపువ్వు the sun flower or heliotrope. రెండుగడియల పొద్దుఉండగా while two hours of daylight yet remained. చాలాపొద్దుపోయినది it is very late. పొద్దున early in the morning. పొద్దుపొడిచెను the sun arose. పొద్దుగూకె (or క్రుంకెను) the sun has set. పొద్దుగూకులు the livelong day, all day long. పొద్దుపుచ్చు to while away time. పొద్దుపోకుండాఉన్నది the time passes slowly, or it is very dull. పొద్దు సరసముగా గడిపితిమి we passed the time merrily. పొద్దుతిరుగుబాటున at noon. చాలాపొద్దుగలుగలేచినాడు he rose very early. ఒక్కపొద్దుఉండు to take only one meal a day, to fast for a period. ఇప్పుడు (lit: ఈ+పొద్దు) now. అప్పుడు (అ+పొద్దు) then. ఆమెకు ఇప్పుడు పొద్దులు she is near her time. దీన్ని పొద్దుపోకచేస్తివి surely you did this out of mere idleness!

పొన *pona.* [Tel.] adj. Visible, అగుపడుచున్న, దృగ్గోచరమైన. **పొనపొన** or **పొనపొనగా** *pona-pona.* adv. Indistinctly, slowly, gently. మాచాయగా, చరంతరవంత, మెల్లమెల్లగా.

"క॥ అల్లదెకంటివెపొనపొన,
తెల్లనిగట్టురితమబ్బు దేరెడుపొలము,
దల్లెడజూచినధరణీ,
వల్లభసీరాముసేనవాలుమెకంబుల్."
Swa. iv. 15.

పొనము *ponamu.* [Tel.] n. Outward show, పైమినుకు.

పొనరు or **ఒనరు** *ponaru.* [Tel.] v. n. To happen, occur, అగు, పొసగు, కలుగు, సంభవించు. "చ॥ అనఘుయపూర్వమైన భవదాగమనంబు దలంపనాక్కటో, బొనరినకయ్యమిప్పుడెగ బోయగవచ్చినయట్లుతోచె." T. iv. 226. n. Happening, కలుగుట. Suitability, harmony, agreement, పొందిక. Pleasantness, ఇంపు. **పొనరారు** *ponar-âru.* v. n. To be fine or agreeable, ఒప్పు. **పొనరుపడు** *ponaru-padu.* v. n. To be agreeable, to suit, పొందుపడు. **పొనరుచు** or **పొనర్చు** *ponarutsu.* v. a. To cause to be done, to accomplish, సాధించు. To cause to happen, పొసగించు. To fabricate, కల్పించు. "క॥

పొనరించియూడిచుమాటల, గొనదలపకదుర్బోధిత కోటిధనంబుగా." M. XII. ii. 199.

పొనలు *ponulu.* [Tel.] v. n. To flame, జ్వలించు. "ధూపవహ్ని కనలుచు బొనలుచు గరగరయుచు." Charitra. p. 535.

పొనిక or **పొనుగు** *ponika.* [Tel.] n. A kind of grass, *Saccharum munja.* ముంజికర్ర.

పొనుగు *ponugu.* [Tel.] adj. Short, పొట్టి. Dull looking, not bright, తేజములేని. పొనుగువడు, పొనుగుపోవు, పొనువడు or పొవ్వడు *ponugu-padu.* v. n. To become dull in color, to grow cool or calm, చల్లారు, నిస్తేజమగు. To come to ruin, నశించు. To be reduced to nothing, శూన్యమగు. "క॥ విమలాకీర్తిజగంబుల, బొనుగుపడితొయనీవు భువన పూజితవృత్తిం, బనుపడితిగానతెగనీ, కనల పడవిమండనాకు వలవదటింకణా." M. III. v. 152. To become useless, వ్యర్థమగు. పొనుగుపరుచు causal of పొనుగుపడు. **పొనుగుచేప** *ponugu-chèpa.* n. A kind of fish.

పొనుపు or **పొంపు** *ponupu.* [Tel.] n. Courage, heroism. పరాక్రమము.

పొన్న *ponna.* [Tel.] adj. Same as పొన (q. v.).

పొన్న *Ponna.* [from Skt. పున్నాగ.] n. A tree called Alexandrian Laurel, *Calophyllum inophyllum,* (Watts.) పున్నాగము. Various species are called నేలపొన్న which is *Cassia senna,* కోలపొన్న *Cassia fistula,* ముద్దూకుపొన్న a sensitive species. కోలాగుపొన్న and సురపొన్న are other species.

పొన్నంగి *ponn-angi.* [Tel.] n. The bird called in Hind: Nao-rangi or nine coloured. The Yellow-breasted Ground-Thrush. (Jerdon.) The Indian Pitta, *Pitta brachyura* (F. B. I.).

పొన్నగంటికూర *ponna-gantikūra.* [Tel.] n. A certain pot-herb called *Achyranthes triandra.* Rox. i. 677. A medicinal plant called *Illecebrum sessile,* Rox. మత్స్యాక్షి.

పొన్నట్టు *ponn-attu.* [Tel.] n. A wooden ladle. అబక.

పొన్నాడ *pon-nāda.* [Tel.] n. A species of leopard, ఒకవిధమైన చిరుతపులి.

పొన్నారి or **పొన్నరి** *ponnāri.* [Tel.] adj. Beautiful, మనోజ్ఞము. n. My darling. చిన్నారిపొన్నారి "My love, my darling."

పొన్ను *ponnu.* [Tel. and Tam. పొన్. Kan. హొన్ను.] n. Gold. బంగారు. A ring, rim, ferrule on a stick or a pestle. రోకటిపొన్ను an iron rim or ring on each end of a pestle. **పొన్నరిదళము** *ponn-aridalamu.* n. Orpiment. (పొన్ను+అరిదళము.)

పొప్ప, పప్ప, వెర్రిపొప్ప, వెర్రిపప్ప *poppa.* [Tel.] n. A fool or simpleton. "పొంగెడు కప్పుముప్పున బొప్పనికినసంగిట ముల్లయ్యోగని నరులనక." BD. iii. 732. "పోవకనిలునిలు బొప్ప యూగోరియదేవాలయము తొొప్పెటాపున కోడి." ib. v. 53.

పొయి, పొయ్యి or **ప్రొయ్యి** *poyi.* [Tel.] n. A fire-place, hearth, oven.

పొర *pora.* [Tel.] n. A fold or plait, as of cloth or of fat. మడత. A coat, as of an onion. A layer or stratum of soil. A film over the eye. The disease called a Cataract. The skin of a snake, పాముకుబుసము. A secret. An error, mistake, ప్రమాదము. A flaw, defect, as in a stone. Deceit, fraud, duplicity, కపటము. పొరలగడ్డ a boil or ulcer of which the successive coats peel off. **పొరపడు** or **పొరబడు** *pora-padu.* v. n. To be mistaken, to make a mistake, to err. ప్రమాదపడు. **పొరపాటు** *pora-pātu.* n. A mistake, error, oversight. ప్రమాదము. **పొరపు** *porapu.* n. Difference. భేదము. adj. Different. భేదమైన.

పొరపొచ్చెము *pora-pochchemu*. n. Fraud, deceit, guile; a trick, feint. కపటకల్పనము. "నీకూరిమి, పొరపొచ్చెముగాకయుండవోపకవల యుణ్ణా," M. VII. iii. 288. ఆనాగా నీ స్నే హముతో కుత్సిత కల్పనములులేక ఉండవలెనిది. పొరపోవు *pora-pōvu*. v. a. To err, mistake. To go the wrong way in drinking or eating. పొరబాటిగనక్కు, పొరబోయక్కు.

పొరంబోకు or పోరంబోకు *porambōku*. [H.] n. Waste land unfit for cultivation. పొసుబడికిరానిభూమి.

పొరక *poraka*. [Tel.] n. A blade of grass. (గడ్డి) పోచే, ఈనెపుడక. A broom for sweeping, చీపురుకట్ట. పొరకచేప *poraka-chēpa*. n. A certain large fish. పొరకటి *poraka-ṭi*. n. The outside wall of a house. వాకిటిచేరువగోడ, ప్రహారీగోడ. పొరకసుడి *poraka-suḍi*. n. A bad or unlucky mark or tuft of hair, (సుడి), found on oxen and other animals.

పొరచి *porachi*. [Tel.] n. A thing borrowed for use. చేబదులు పుచ్చుకొన్న ధనాదికము, ఎరువు అడిగి తెచ్చుకొన్నది.

పొరట *poraṭa*. [Tel.] n. One side or page of a leaf. పుట.

పొరటు or పొరంటు *poraṭu*. [Tel.] v. a. To fry, grill, toast. పొగచు. "చ॥ గుసుగుసంతెంచలితుమ్మి తేరగిరిపాకుంబిం ద్రిలేపల్లవో, క్కరముంగూడబొరంటి మానియులతో గట్టావి కట్టూరి గోగిరముత్తేసి." A. iv. 173. "అప్పుట నుండి యంతరంగంబు నిప్పులంబొరంటి నట్లు ద్యుడు." M XII. i. 11.

పొరడు *poraḍu*. [Tel.] n. A hump. గూని, గూను. పొరడుపోవు *poraḍu-pōvu*. v. n. To become hump-backed. గూనుపడు.

"ద్వి॥ కొరిగూనిపొందుచ్చదన్ని ఖలావనీశు,
పొరడుపోయీవీవు పొరడుపోశేని."
Charit. iii. 1792.

పొరయు *porayu*. [Tel.] v. n. To happen, occur. కలుగు. To lie in wait, పొంచు. To agree with, కలుగు, పొసగు. "కామాతు రులకు, భయమునులజ్జయు బొరయవనఁజానవే." N. vii. 82. v. a. To gain. To feel, (anger, love, surprise.) పొందు. "రాజదండితుడు వారక బాధబొరయుడు." DRK. 164. పొరయించు *porayintsu*. v. a. To cause to obtain. పొందించు.

పొరలు, పొర్లు, పొరలాడు, పొర్లాడు, పొరల బడు or పొర్లబడు *poralu*. [Tel.] v. n. To roll over, to roll on the ground; to wallow. To be in excess, to over-flow. To continue, ప్రవర్తిల్లు. "యదూద్వహులందు పుష్పతల్పంబుపై కేలి పొరలుచుండు." Pal. 233. "పురవాసుడు మున్ను, సాధింపవచ్చిన చందమున నేడు, పొరలినకోపమున పొంగుచున్నాడు." To wish, long for, like, కోరు, ఇచ్చించు. "మస్థిరభుజశక్తి సైదుపదిసేయరు దత్తినతక్కుమట్టి కై, పొరలగధి కుటీకమలబుద్ధి కరిూరిక దక్కు." A. ii. 39. టీ॥ మట్టికై, భూమికై, పొరలరు, అభి లషింపరు. To be crossed or covered, as a cow. ఆవుపొర్లినతర్వాత after the cow was crossed. మాటపొర్లవద్దు do not break your word. ఆ కల్లుకుండ పొర్లిపొర్లి ఉన్నది the toddy pot is overflowing. పొరలు, పొరలిక, పొర్లిక or పొరలాట n. Rolling over or over flowing. పొరలుదండము a bow or salutation made while rolling on the ground. పొరలుపెట్టు Same as పొరలు. పొర్లుకట్ట *porlu-katta*. n. A bank or bund raised to prevent water from overflowing. పొరలించు, పొర్లించు, పొరలుచు or పొరలుచ్చు *poralintsu*. v. a. To roll. To turn over. మాటపొర్లించినాడు he changed his statement or prevaricated.

పొరి *pori*. [Tel.] n. Same as పొలి (q.v.) adj. Strong, great. అత్యంతము. adv. Exceedingly, very much. మిక్కిలి, అత్యంతము. Firmly,

దృఢముగా. Duly, regularly, క్రమముగా. Often, మాటిమాటికి, తరుచుగా. Again, మళ్లీ. "శ్రీనివాసమను క్షేత్రంబునగల పూర్ణమూర్తి పొరి పూజింతును." H. iv. 297. **పొరిగొను** *pori-gonu*. v. a. To kill, slay. చంపు. To ruin, destroy, నాశముచేయు. To conquer, జయించు. "బలవిక్రమధనులకు దొర, లిగ్గిన మనసేన మేదినీశ్వరవినుత, వ్వారలు నెడినట్లున్నది యిట్లాలదిం బొరిగొనుట నరునకు సుకరముగా." M. IX. i. 60. **పొరిచూపు** *pori-tsūpu*. n. A fierce look, భయంకరమైనచూపు. An envious look, an inimical attitude, ద్వేషదృష్టి. **పొరిచూపుమాటలు** *pori-tsūpu-mātalu*. n. plu. Taunting words. **పొరిపొరి** *pori-pori*. adv. (anuk.) More and more, much more. Repeatedly, again and again, over and over. మిక్కిలి, మరీమరీ, మాటిమాటికి. "రమణి పొరిపొరి కన్నీరు క్రమ్మజొచ్చె, మెలగి కాళ్లక్రద్దల దలకి నడచుచున్నయది." M. XI. ii. 67. **పొరిపోవు, పొరివోవు** or **పొరిమాలు** *pori-pōvu*. v. n. To die, చచ్చు. To be confused, to be agitated, కలగు. **పొరిపుచ్చు** or **పొరి పుచ్చు** *pori-putstsu*. v. a. To kill. చంపు. To confuse, కలచు. "అన్యాయపథమునందు నర్తించువారి నెవ్వరి నాహవంబున పొరిపుచ్చినను నదిపుణ్యకృతియ." M. XII. ii. 168. **పొరిమారుచు, పొరిమార్చు, పొరిమాలుచు** or **పొరిమాల్చు** *pori-mārutsu*. v. a. To kill.

పొరివిళంగాయలు *porivilan-gāyalu*. [Tam.] n. A sort of cakes. "భక్ష్యద్రోవకుసాధ్వపరికరం బులు పెట్టి కట్టిన పొరివిళంగాయ గమియు." A. ii. 111. టీ॥ పొరివిళంగాయ గమియు, వేచిన బియ్యపుపిండినిసి బెల్లముపాకముపట్టి యుండలు చేసినవి. "చక్కిలంబులు, సుక్కారలు కరిజాలు పొరివిళంగాయలు తేమనంబులు." H. i. 116.

పొరుగు, పొరువు, పొర్గు or **పొర్వు** *porugu*. [Tel.] n. A side. ప్రక్క. The part or side adjoining the next house, ఇరుగునప్రక్క. The neighbourhood or vicinity. Nearness, సమీపము. The side opposite to one's house, తనయింటికి ఎదుటిభాగము. నీపొరుగున నున్నవారు your neighbours. H. ii. 114. పొరుగిల్లు the next house. ఇరుగుపొరుగు on this side and on that. adj. Neighbouring, fronting. పొరుగింటివాడు or పొరుగు వాడు a next door neighbour. మేము ఇరుగు పొరుగునయుండేవారము we live in each other's neighbourhood, we are neighbours. See ఇరుగు.

పొర్లాడు or **పొరలాడు** *porl-ādu*. [Tel.] See under పొరలు.

పొల or **పొలను** *pola*. [Tel.] n. Flesh, meat. మాంసము. The stench of bad meat. మాంసపు దుర్గంధము. A scale of a fish. చేపమీది పొలుసు. "అనుకీవులు పొలపెట్టులేక నాకట నొందిరియొండెనిరయంబోవ తానెడబడిన." P. i. 214. టీ॥ పొలపెట్టులేక, మాంసము పెట్టులేక. "పొలగాలివీచెదరువు నెడనను." A. vi. 20. టీ॥ పొలగాలి, మాంసగంధము గలిగినగాలి. **పొల తిండి** *pola-dindi*. n. A cannibal, a carnivorous creature, a Rakshasa, రాక్షసుడు, క్రవ్యాదుడు.

పొలకు *polaku*. [Tel.] n. A kind of grass. తృణవిశేషము. A kind of fruit, కట్యంగఫలము.

పొలకువ *polakuva*. [Tel.] n. A trace, జాడ. వానియింట్లో కత్తిఅనే పొలకువలేదు there were no signs of a knife in his house, there was not such a thing as a knife in his house. వారిపొలకువలేకుండాచేసినాడు he exterminated them.

పొలతి or **పొలతుక** *polati*. [Tel.] n. A lady, a fair girl. స్త్రీ.

పొలపము *polapamu*. [Tel.] n. The act of blowing, or spreading as wind, విసరడము, వీవడము, ప్రసరణము, వ్యాపనము. Smell, వాసన. Brightness, ప్రకాశము. adj. Spread, వ్యాపించిన, వ్యాప్తము. "సీ॥ పొలపంబుమెరసి దిక్కుల గాంతిపూరించు క్రొక్కారుమెరుగులను క్కడంచి." M. IV. ii. 87.

పొలపొల *pola-pola*. [Tel.] adv. Much, very much. **పొలపొలపొక్కు** *pola-pola-pokku*. v. n. To be much afflicted.

> "ధారుణిపైఁ బ్రాలి ధైర్యంబు దూలి,
> పోయున నల్లమయక్కటా విడిచి,
> పోయితే నన్ను నిపొలపొలబొక్కు."
>
> L. vii. 178.

పొలమగు *polam-agu*. [Tel.] v. n. To happen, to come into one's possession, దొరకు, కలుగు. "ఆదినారాయణుడొకనికి, విదితమునీపలన సురలు వివిధమునులు, నిర్మలసిద్ధ సాధ్యగణములు మొదలగునర్థుల సుబోధములబోల మయ్యెగా." M. XIII. iv. 182.

పొలమారు or **పొరపారు** *polam-āru*. [Tel.] v. n. To make a mistake, ప్రమాదపడు. To go the wrong way (in swallowing). వానికి పొలమారినది the food got into his windpipe. పొలమార్చు (causal of పొలమారు) to cause to be deceived, to cause to blunder, ప్రమాదపడునట్లుచేయు.

పొలము *polamu*. [Tel.] n. A field, corn land. చేను, పైరుపెట్టుసేల. A rice field, వరిపైరుపెట్టుసేల. Uncultivated land on which cattle graze, పసులుమేయుభూమి. A forest, అడవి. A place, land, ground, ప్రదేశము. ఊరిపొలము the land attached to a village. వెలిపొలము the outlying fields belonging to a village. A village, ఊరు. A trace, జాడ. Manner, విధము. పొలపు కూరలు field herbs, or ordinary herbs, as చెంచలి, చిట్లింత, పెరింత, పొన్నగంటి, మొదలైనవి. (These weeds infest fields sown with జొన్నలు, &c.). "అప్పొలమువరాహపోతములు భూవర తోండముకేనియోమనుకుల్." Swa. iv. 18. టీ॥ ఆప్పొలము వరాహపోతములు, అక్కడ అడవిపందికున్నలు. "గీ॥ ఈపొలములగుమహోధిక ప్రతములుదేవాబాధకములు." M. XII. iv. 361. ఈపొలములగు, ఈవిధములైన. **పొలముపాటు** *polamu-pāṭu*. n. Husbandry, పైరుపెట్టుట, కృషి, వ్యవసాయము. **పొలకట్టు** *pola-kaṭṭu*. n. A ploughed field. Kasi Yatra. 55. **పొలమరి** *polam-ari*. n. A cultivator. పొలముగాపు. "పొలమరులందుమాతలిడ భూసురులన్నదివార్చివార్చి." A. iii. 28. టీ॥ పొలమరులు, పొలముచేయువారు. **పొలపరి** or **పొలమరి** *polapari*. (పొలము+అరి) n. One who knows the signs, జాడతెలిసినవాడు.

పొలయలుక *pola-y-aluka*. [Tel. పొల్లు+అలుక.] n. A lovers' quarrel, ప్రణయకలహము.

పొలయు *polayu*. [Tel.] v. n. To wander, సంచరించు. To blow, as wind. వీచు, విసరు. To spread over. వ్యాపించు, ప్రసరించు. To approach, సమీపించు. To enter, ప్రవేశించు. "చందలదృగంచలప్రభలు నతని ముఖాంబుజం బునంబొలయు." Swa. ii. 68. **పొలసాడు** *polas-āḍu*. (పొలసి+ఆడు) v. n. To wander, సంచరించు. **పొలయించు** *polayintsu*. v. a. To cause to spread, "పొలయింపగావేర్చ భ్రూలతానటనంబు." Kavikarna. iii. 248.

పొలస *polasa*. [Tel.] n. A sea fish like the bream.

పొలసు Same as పొల (q. v.). **పొలసుతిండి** Same as పొల (q.v.).

పొలి *poli*. [Tel.] n. Freshness, bloom. An offering to some village deity, బలి. Profit, gain, లాభము, పస, మేలు. Loss, నష్టి. **పొలికలుగు** *poli-kalugu*. v. n. To gain a profit, లాభముకలుగు. **పొలికలను** *poli-kalanu*. n. A battle field. యుద్ధభూమి. **పొలిపోవు** or **పొలిసోవు** *poli-pōvu*. v. n. To be spoiled or ruined, చెడు. To die, చచ్చు. To become useless, వ్యర్థమగు. To be defeated, భంగపడు. To be weakened, to give up, as an attempt, ఉడుగు. To lose. కించిచ్ఛింగమగు. "తపమంతయుబా లిపోవగ." Swa. vi. 42. **పొలిపుచ్చు** *poli-putstsu*. v. a. To kill, చంపు. M. X. ii. 115. **పొలిపెట్టు** *poli-peṭṭu*. n. Lands and other property made over to a temple for its support, గుడికొప్పరచినస్థితి. **పొలిమేర** *poli-mēra*. n. A boundary or limit, సరిహద్దు.

పొలికిచెట్టు *poliki-chettu.* [Tel.] n. A certain tree of which some species are called కుమ్మరపొలికి and ఎఱ్ఱపొలికి.

పొలియు *poliyu.* [Tel.] v. n. To be spoiled or ruined, చెడు. To die. చచ్చు. **పొలియిక** *poliyika.* n. Ruin, నాశము. Death, మరణము.

పొలుచు or **పొల్చు** *polutsu.* [Tel.] v. n. To appear, seem. అగుపడు. To become visible, ప్రత్యక్షమగు. To be agreeable, ఒప్పు. To become firm, స్థిరమగు. Also, another form of పొడుచు (q. v.). "సీ. అంబుధరజాల ముక్తంబులయినజలక, ణములు సాత్రాజితీకైశికమునబొలిచె, గగనతలలక్ష్మి పోరంచిగాగ నిడిన, జాలసొమ్ముమౌక్తికస్తబకమనగ." Parij. ii. 98.

పొలునోరు *polu-nōru.* [Tel. for పొల్లునోరు.] n. A wry mouth, వంకరనోరు. "మెడగండ్ల మూలయు మిడిపండ్లుబొలునోరు." HK. iv. 143.

పొలుపు or **పొల్పు** *polupu.* [Tel.] n. Beauty, elegance, gracefulness, agreeableness. సొంపు. Manner, mode, స్థితి, రీతి. Firmness, స్థైర్యము. "పొలుపుమీరిన నెలవంకబొమలు జూచి, రమణుడకొత్త బింబాధరంబుజూచి." Rukmang. i. 158. **పొలుపుగా** *polupu-gā.* adv. Duly, rightly. **పొలుపొందు** or **పొల్పొందు** *polup-ondu.* v. n. To be charming. సొంపొందు. **పొలుపారు** or **పొల్పారు** *polup-āru.* v. n. To appear, shine, be beautiful or pleasant, వెలయు. **పొలుపరి** or **పొల్పరి** *polup-ari.* adj. Beautiful, charming. **పొల్పెసలార** or **పొలుపార** *polp-esal-āra.* adv. Charmingly, fully.

పొలువ Same as పలువ (q. v.).

పొలువడు or **పొల్లువడు** *polu-vaḍu.* [Tel.] v. n. To decrease. తరుగు, తగ్గు, క్షయించు.

పొలుసు or **పొలసు** *polusu.* [Tel.] n. A scale of a fish. మత్స్యముమీద నుండేపొలుసు.

పొల్తి or **పొల్తుక** Same as పొలతి or పొలతుక (q. v.).

పొల్ల or **పొల్లకట్టు** *polla.* [Tel.] n. Pithless or blasted grain. గింజకట్టనిధాన్యము. బూగర పొల్లు, నిస్సారమైనధాన్యము. "కల్లావకూర్పనాతి ఘుట్టనలబారి చనుపొల్లకట్టునోలె." A. iv. 14. A useless person, వ్యర్థుడు. adj. Useless, rejected, వ్యర్థము, విసర్జింపబడిన. **పొల్లపడు** or **పొల్లపోవు** *polla-paḍu.* v. n. To become useless, వ్యర్థమగు. To deteriorate or decrease, తగ్గు, క్షీణించు. **పొల్లపుచ్చు** *polla-putstsu.* v. a. To cause to decrease, తగ్గించు, క్షీణింపజేయు.

పొల్లాయి *pollāyi.* [Tel.] n. Certain fees paid on every thrashing floor.

పొల్లు *pollu* [Tel.] n. Pithless grain in an ear. బొత్తిగా గింజలుపట్టని వడ్లసమూహము. Trash, worthless stuff. తాలు, పనికిరానిది. The consonant sound of a letter, etc., A useless word, a slip of the tongue. A lie, a falsehood. అనృతము. "పొల్లురాదిగని దోస్తిని." Pal. 399. అనగా, అబద్ధము రాగూడని స్నేహముగలవాడవు. adj. Useless, వ్యర్థము. Sumati, 29. పొల్లునదంచిన బియ్యము corn beaten out of husk or pined grain. వాని పొల్లు వాడు పోసికొని బ్రతుకుతాడు he keeps his blighted grain to himself, i.e., he keeps all his griefs to himself. బంగారుపొల్లు ఉన్నదిగాని మనిషిపొల్లులేదు gold may prove worthless, but man never can be so. మాట పొల్లుపోకుండా అడుతాడు he speaks without any slips. నకారపొల్లు the letter N. (న్) without the vowel sound attached to it as in the words కలిగెన్, చెలగెన్. **పొల్లుపోవు** *pollu-pōvu.* v. n. To become worthless. చెబ్బరిపోవు. "కాళ్లగోలుసులవారు గడెమన్నబంట్లు, కోళ్లగానున్నట్టి సురభినాయకులు, ఘల్లుమన్నతిరిగి మల్లమనువారు, పొల్లుపోకయువని పోట్లాడువారు." Pal. 107. To lie, tell stories or lies, అబద్ధమాడు. **పొల్లువదనము** *pollu-danamu.* n. Dispiritedness, effeminacy, పౌరుషములేమి. **పొల్లువడు** *pollu-paḍu.* v. n. To become useless, వ్యర్థమగు.

పొల్లు Same as పొరలు. (q. v.).

పొవ Same as పొగ (q. v.).

పొవయు or పొగయు povayu. [Tel.] v. n. To smoke or emit smoke. To grieve, mourn, or be dejected. "లోఁబొవయఁ బ్రాపొ క్కెహృదయముగా." A. iv. 294. టీ॥ లోఁబొవయు, లోపలపొగరాజేయున్న, అనగా మనస్సు లో ఖేదపడుచున్న.

పొసగు posagu. [Tel.] v. n. To agree, fit, suit, be consistent with. To happen, take place, occur, befal. ఉచితమగు, ఒప్పు, పొందుపడు, చక్కబడు, ఇముడు, సరిపడు, అనుకూలించు. To be got, obtained. సంభవించు, దొరుకు, లభించు. వీరికి వారికి పొసగదు they do not agree, they are on bad terms. వానికేమిపొసగినది what happened to him? ఈ కష్టము నీకెట్లు పొసగినది how did you get into this trouble? "భోజనవేళల పొసగునే మాట," Pal. 44. "పరసమిమునుపొకబం గారమైనట్లు, కప్పురంబుజ్యోతికలసినట్లు, పుప్పు మందుతావి పొసగినట్లుగముక్తి." Vēma. i. 81. పొసగ posaga. adv. Duly, fitly. "చంప దగినయట్టి శత్రుడుతనచేత, జిక్కెనేనికీడుసేయ రాదు, పొసగమేలుచేసి పొమ్మను టేచాలు." Vēma. i. 23. పొసగించు posagintsu. v. a. To cause to agree or fit. To bring to terms, to persuade. పొసగుడు posagudu. n. Convenience, aid, help, అనుకూల్యము. Happening, ప్రాప్తమగుట.

పొసపొస posa-posa. [Tel.] adv. Rapidly, one after another, త్వరగా.

పొసరాకు posar-āku. [Tel. పొసరు+ఆకు.] n. A pungent strong smelling leaf used in checking a cough.

పో pō

పో pō. (The infinitive of పోవు) అతడు పోగా-చి seeing that he was gone. పో pō. (Imperative of పోవు.) v. n. Go, పొమ్ము. In many places this is a mere expletive, as Go to. (in English). It denotes certainty or disregard, నిశ్చయమును లేక అనాదరమును తెలుపును. "తెచ్చెదంబో విను దేవవరా." ఉ. హరి. v. పోక pōka. n. Going. పోవడము. Conduct, behaviour, నడవడి. పోకలు n. plu. Evil ways, wickedness. పోకిరితనములు. Foolish wishes, or longings, ముద్దుకోరికలు. "పలోప్పకళ్ళంగాని మలు" (T. iii. 81.) very naughty pranks. పోకిరిపొకములు నీవుపోయినదేపోకా are you to be indulged in every thing? వారేమి అదేపోక పోయిరి I am surprised that they did not come back. పోక pōka. for పోనక (neg. p. of పోవు.) Without going. Also for పోకు, i. e., పోవద్దు don't go. (the final A being intensive.) పోకడ pō-kada. n. Going, departure, going off. గమనము, గతి. Behaviour, conduct, నడత, ప్రవర్తనము. Riddance. Ruin, నాశము. నెలదినాలుగా రాకడపోకడలేదు there has been no intercourse between us for a month (literally, going and coming.) పోకడపెట్టు pōkada-pettu. v. a. To drive away, to remove, పోగొట్టు. To sell, అమ్ము. విక్రయించు. దాన్నిఎట్లైనను పోకడపెట్టు get rid of it in any way. పోకలాడి pōkal-ādi. (పోకలు+ఆడి) n. A coquette, వగలాడి. "క॥ చూపట్టె గోమయంబున, జేపట్టొనరించి ఒడల శెక్కినలిరిగం, బాపోకలాడి కైకొని చెవికదన్నితిరిగక్రిమిరేగయు పోలెగా." S. ii. 49. పోకలాడు pōkal-ādu. v. n. To be coquettish, to flirt. పోకాడు pōkādu. (పోక+ఆడు) v. n. To go, పోవు. To be done away with, to be destroyed, నశించు. పోకార్చు pōkārtsu. v. a. To lose, పోగొట్టు. పోగొట్టుకొను. To destroy, ruin. "రిపుమకుమారుడదీవర్గ ముపోకార్చి." R. iii. 137. పోకాలు pōkālu. v. n. To go, as anger, sorrow, &c. పోవు. పోకిరి pōkiri. n. A wicked man, a villain, rogue, lewd fellow, blackguard, దుర్మార్గుడు.

adj. Naughty, wicked, mischievous, unprincipled. పోకిరిమాట an obscene word. పోకిళ్లు pōkillu. n. plu. Idle wishes, fopperies, whims, freaks, whimsies. పోకిళ్లమారి a fop, an epicure.

పోక pōka. [Tel.] n. The areca or betel-nut-palm, *Areca catechu*, (Watts). An areca nut. పోకంతయన్నము a morsel of food "అనుచు, పోకలకుండ చట్రాతిమీద నుగుల చేయును" Kanyaka Pur. viii. 266. So saying she hurled a jar full of nuts down on the floor. "నిజముపోకచేయు నీకుమేమిము." HD. i. 1527. పోకగంజి pōka-ganji. n. The Catechu. *Terra japonica*, కాచు. పోక పేరు pōka-pēru. n. A kind of cake, భక్ష్య విశేషము. పోకబంతిపువ్వు pōka-banti-puvvu. n. The flower called Bachelor's button. పోకముడి pōka-muḍi. n. The knot that secures a woman's petticoat at the girdle. పోక ముడివదలించె she unloosed her petticoat. పోకొత్తు pōk-ottu. (పోక+ఒత్తు) n. Nippers for breaking the betel nut. అడ కత్తెర.

పోకు pōku. [Tel.] n. Conduct, behaviour, నడవడి. Loss, నష్టి. Bedewed grass, మంచు కప్పినగడ్డి.

పోగండుడు pōganḍuḍu. [Skt.] n. A deformed man. అంగహీనుడు.

పోగర pōgara. [Tel.] n. A graver, or small chisel used by goldsmiths. శలాక, కంసల వాని పనిముట్టు. పోగరపని carved work. గుండుపోగర a rod for making rings. గుబ్బోగర a tapping chisel.

పోగు pōgu. [Tel.] n. A thread, a string. తంతువు, దారము. A heap, a crowd, an assembly. ప్రోగు, కుప్ప, సమూహము. An ear-ring. పురుషకర్ణాభరణము. ముక్కుపోగు a nose-ring. కట్టుపోగు a wire placed in the ear preparatory to an ear-ring. పోగుపోయు or పోగుతీయు to darn. పోగు త్రాడు pōgu-trāḍu. n. A kind of net, composed of lines or cords laid by huntsman as a snare. "పందినచేలకునరాహ పచ్చ్యులు చోరరా, కుంద శైలనివాసరఖండం బులు పోగుత్రాళ్లు కట్టుదు రరుకుల్." Kalahas. iii. 11. పోగుచేయు pōgu-chēyu. v. a. To collect, to accumulate, to put together. పోగువారు pōgu-vāru. (పోగు+పారు) v. n. To surround with a cord. To surround, ఆవరించు.

పోగొట్టు pō-goṭṭu. [Tel.] v. a. To lose. To do away with, to remove. అంధకారమును పోగొట్టెను he dispelled the darkness. నాకన్నులుపోగొట్టుతావా are you going to put out my eyes? చలిపోగొట్టుకొనుటకు to keep off the cold.

పోచాయించు pōchāyintsu. [H.] v. a. To cause to arrive, to cause to convey or conduct. అందజేయు.

పోచి or పోచి pōchi. [Tel.] n. The place near the wrist, the wrist, మనికట్టుమీది చోటు, మనికట్టు. పోచీలు a sort of bracelets worn at the wrists by women.

పోచికోలు pōchi-kōlu. [Tel.] n. Worthlessness, uselessness. పోచికోలుగానిచ్చు to give away as useless. మనిషిపోచికోలుకాదు (a proverb) there is no man of whom you can say he is of no consequence to you.

పోచిల్లు pōchillu. [Tel.] n. A superstitious rite (ఉపశ్రుతి) regarding omens: a few grains of rice (అక్షతలు) put in water are flung on the roof of a neighbour's house: he who so casts them sits in a corner and listens for any words he can overhear in the family: the words are put together and a meaning is elicited. "శకునమ్ముల నడుగుదు రట్ల, యొకరింగ పోచిల్లు పోతురు మరియు, గద్దె చూపింతురు గాలి నోము దురు." L. iii. 105.

పోచ pōtsa. [Tel.] n. A blade of grass, గడ్డి పరక. A bit, లేశము. నారపోచ a bit of hemp. నూలిపోఁచ a bit of thread. గడ్డిపోఁచ a bit of grass. ఆవపోఁచ a grain of mustard. జందెపుపోఁచ a sacred thread.

పోఁచావణీ or పోంచావణీ *pōtsavaṇi*. [H.] n. Insurance on goods.

పోఁజు or ప్రోఁజు *pōdzu*. [Tel.] v. a. To clean or prepare cotton with the hands for spinning. "పత్తిని ప్రోఁజుమా వడికి బ్రాహ్మణు డిచ్చు పవిత్రతంతువుల్ బ్రాత్తగ నేకవింశతియు నూర్చి." UH. iv. 76.

పోట or పోటన *pōṭa*. [Tel.] adj. Large. పెద్ద. [Skt.] n. A woman that has moustaches. మీసముగల ఆడుది. A servant woman, దాసి. పోటకత్తి *pōṭa-katti*. n. A bill-hook, a wood cutter's knife, అడవికడికే కత్తి. పోటకందులు *pōṭa-kandulu*. n. White dhall, తెల్లకందులు. పోటనబంతి *pōṭana-banti*. n. A large ball. పుట్టచెండు. "పోటన బంతి మీటుకరి." Vasu. ii. 201. పోటముంజి *pōṭa-munji*. n. A large modesty piece, పుట్టగోచి.

పోటకము *pōṭakamu*. [from Skt. స్ఫోటకము.] n. Small-pox, మశూచకము. పోటగళము *pōṭa-galamu*. n. A fish, చేప. A kind of grass, కిక్కిసకసవు. A reed, రెల్లు.

పోటి *pōṭi*. [Tel.] adj. Similar, like, resembling, ఈడైన, మారు. "ఈ భూరిభరంబు నూన్ప నసుపోటి కరకష్టము." నాపోటివాడు a man like me. పోటి or పోటీ *pōṭi*. n. Emulation, competition, rivalry. స్పర్థ. A prop. ఆసరా. వారు పోటీచేసినందున వెల పొడిగినది by their rivalry the price was raised. ఆ దూలమునకు పోటీ యిచ్చినాడు he set a prop against the beam. పోటిగాడు *pōṭi-gāḍu*. n. One who has a prop or support, పోటిగలవాడు. A companion, a fellow, an equal, సముడు, మిత్రుడు. పోటి పెట్టు to stir up emulation, to set by the ears.

పోటు *pōṭu*. [Tel.] n. A thrust, a stab, a blow. పోడుపు, కత్తిపోటు. A throb of pain. పోడుపు, నొప్పి. The swell of a river, or of the sea, the flow of the tides, high water, సముద్రోల్బణము, నదాద్యుదకాభివృద్ధి. Heroism, courage, శౌర్యము. A battle, యుద్ధము. వాడు ఇప్పుడు కొంచెము పోటుమీద నున్నాడు he is now drunk. "నాకొడుకు పోటుమాటలు, నీకేటికి పొసగ నాడ." M. IV. v. 258. పోటుమాటలు అనగా ఎత్తిపొడుపుమాటలు. చెవిపోటు *chevi-pōṭu*. n. Ear-ache. ఆ కురుపు పోట్లు పొడుస్తున్నది the boil is throbbing. పోటాపోటీ *pōṭa-pōṭi*. n. Rivalry, emulation, competition, నీకంటె నాకని పంయుబడడము. వానికి నిన్న దర్భపోటు తగిలినది he was invited to the ceremony held on the anniversary of a man's father's death. పోటుపాటు ఎరిగినవాడు one who knows both sides of the question పోటాడు or పోటాగ్గు to get ready for battle. రణోద్యోగము చేయు. పోటుకంబము *pōṭu-kambamu*. n. A post or pillar which is set up as a prop, ఊతగానిలిపినస్తంభము. పోటుకలుపు *pōṭu-kalupu*. n. A second weeding, రెండవమారు తీయు కలుపు. పోటుకాడు, పోటుబంటు, పోటుమగడు or పోటుమానిసి *pōṭu-kāḍu*. n. A hero, a courageous man, శూరుడు. పోటుకోల *pōṭu-kōla*. n. A sharp pointed stick used as a prop. "వలలును దారులు ప్రోగులు చుట్టగాలేదు, పోటుకోలాకటియు బుచ్చలేదు, తెగిన మెకంబు లతేలేదు." Dhurjati. iii. 96. పోటుగంప *pōṭu-gampa*. n. A large basket. పోటుపాటు *pōṭu-pāṭu*. n. The ebb and flow of a tide. Paidim. i. 86. "నీపోటుపాటున నిపు డిట్లు మమ్ము బోధించితివి." HD. ii. 1196. నీపోటుపాటున, నీవెచ్చి తగ్గటచేతను. పోటెక్కించినవాడు *pōṭ-ekkinchina-vāḍu*. n. An assailant, one who attacks, ఎదిరించి పైకి వచ్చేవాడు. "పోటెక్కించినవానిమీద ప్రయోగించినవాని నమరపతి వధియించుననియును పెద్దలవలన వినియుందుము." M. VII. iii. 96.

పోటొడ్డు pōt-oḍḍu. v. n. To face in battle, to oppose. యుద్ధాభిముఖుడగు. "పోడిసింగరాజు పోటొడ్డినాడు." Pal. 410. పోట్లాట pōṭl-āṭa. (పోటులు+ఆట.) n. Fighting; a struggle, dispute, యుద్ధము, కొట్లాట. పోట్లాడు or పోటులాడు pōṭl-āḍu. v. n. To fight, to battle, to struggle, to come to blows. యుద్ధముచేయు. పోట్లావు pōṭl-āvu. n. A cow that butts, పొడిచే స్వభావముగల ఆవు. పోటరి or పోటరికాడు pōṭari. (పోటు+అరి.) n. A hero, a brave man. శూరుడు. "పోటరులైనభర్త కేవురు గలరంటి." M. IV. ii. 264. పోటరితనము pōṭari-tanamu. n. Heroism. శూరత్వము.

పోడి or పోఁడి pōḍi. [Tel.] n. Beauty, grace, ఒప్పు. adj. Beautiful, ఒప్పిదమైన. పోడిగా pōḍi-gā. adv. Well, properly, duly, ఒప్పుగా. "పోడిగావిడ్డల పొరుగిండ్లనుంచి." HD. ii. 2391. పోడిమి or పోఁడిమి pōḍimi. n. A sign or mark, లక్షణము. Brightness, splendour. పస, వన్నె. Proportion, fitness, neatness, సొంపు, పొంకము. Economy, management, prudence. మితవ్యయము. Wealth, సంపద. Happiness, సౌఖ్యము. Manner, విధము. "విలయకృశానుకీలముల వేడిమిపోడిమి మాలి వ్రేల్చెడి." Swa. ii. 10. టీ॥ పోడిమిమాలి, సొమ్ము చెడి. పోడిమిచెడు to die, చచ్చు. పోడిమడంచు to kill, చంపు. పోడిమిగా pōḍimi-gā. adv. Economically. మితవ్యయముగా.

పోడు pōḍu. [Tel.] n. A down, a piece of scrub, jungle covered with bushes, land cleared from jungle for the purpose of cultivation, as కొండపోడ్లు. పోడుకొట్టు to clear away brushwood, to remove underwood, చేనికొరకు చెట్లునరికివేయు. చిరు వేరుపోడ్లు Chayroot grounds, చాయవేళ్లు పైరగుభూమి.

పోత pōta. [Tel. from పోయు.] n. Pouring, పోయుట. Casting, as of melted metal. Bathing, washing. Eruption of the small-pox. ఆకుపోత putting plants into the ground. పెట్టుపోతలు శాశ్వతములుకావు meat and drink (literally, feeding and bathing) are not matters of eternal consequence. పోత pōta. adj. Molten, cast in metal. పోతచెంబు a metal bottle or jug, which has been cast not hammered.

పోతము pōtamu. [Skt.] n. A vessel, boat, ship. ఓడ. The young of any animal, పిల్ల, శిశువు. An elephant ten years old, పదేండ్ల యేనుగు. A cloth, వస్త్రము. శుకపోతము a young parrot. వాతపోతము a young breeze, i.e., a light wind. పోతపాత్రిక pōta-pātrika. n. A vessel, a ship, ఓడ. "సంసార సాగరమతుల ధైర్యపోత పాత్రికనిస్తరింపుమను హర." M. XII. vi. 222. పోతవణిక్కు or పోతవణిజుడు pōta-vaṇikku. n. A sea-faring merchant. ఓడను కేవుకు పుచ్చుకొన్నవాడు, ఓడ బేరగాడు. పోతవహుడు or పోతవాహుడు pōta-vahuḍu. n. A rower, a boatman, a steersman. ఓడనడుపువాడు, తిండేలు.

పోతరము pōtaramu. [Tel.] n. Fatness, pride, hauteur, గర్వము, మదము, కండకావరము, కొవ్వు. "శా॥ ఓరీయొవ్వడవీవుపోతరముతో నున్మాదివైయున్నాడీ, వారించబట్టితి." KP. iii. 174. పోతరి pōtari. n. A tree called *Kydia fraterna*. Rox. iii. 189. పోతరించు pōtarintsu. v. n. To become fat, to fatten, to pick up flesh. To become proud or conceited, కొవ్వు, మదించు. "తే॥ ఎండకాలం బొరలాడు నేకలముల, నెమురుబోరుడుపోరుపులబ లము గ్రొవ్వి, పోతరించిన కారెనుబోతులచట." Paidimarri. ii. 80.

పోతు pōtu. [Tel.] n. The male of certain birds, animals and plants, పశుపక్షులలో మగది. ఆబోతు an ox, వృషభము. ఎనుబోతు a male buffalo. మేకపోతు a he-goat, a ram. నక్కపోతు a male fox. గొడ్డుపోతు a barren woman. పోతుటీగ a male fly పోతుటేనుగు a male elephant

పోతుకెరటము the bigger surf, పెద్దఅల. పోతుతాడు the male palm tree. పోతురాజు, an epithet of Yama, the god of Death, యముడు. పోతుపిల్ల, a male young one. పసులాతిలో. మగపిల్ల. పోతుపిల్లి a tom cat. పోతు sometimes means one who is addicted to, as తాగుబోతు a drunkard. తిండిబోతు a glutton. తొంగుబోతు a sluggard వదురుబోతు a chatter box. పోతుపిచ్చిక or పెద్దపిచ్చిక *pōtu-pichchika.* n. The Ashy-crowned FinchLark. *Pyrrhulauda grisea.* (F. B. I.) పోతురాజు or పోతేరాజు *pōtu-rāḍu.* n. The name of a rustic god, like Pan, worshipped throughout the Telugu, Canarese and Mahratta countries. He represents the male principle associated with the village goddesses Gangammu, Peddamma, &c. A proverb says పాడుఊరికి మంచపుకోడుపోతురాజు in a ruined village the leg of a cot is a god: cf., 'a Triton of the minnows' (Shakespeare.) బమ్మెరపోతరాజు the name of a certain poet. పోతులరాజు *pōtula-rāḍu.* n. A name given to a large hound.

పోత్రము *pōtramu.* [Skt.] n. The snout of a hog. పందిముట్టె. పోత్రి *pōtri.* n. A pig, పంది, వరాహము. పోత్రిత్వము *pōtritvamu.* n. Hoggishness, swinishness. పోత్రిత్వము వహించె he took the form of a pig.

పోని *pōni.* [Tel. for పోలిన.] adj. Resembling, similar, like. వంటి. పోలిన. మన్మథునిబోనివాడు one as handsome as Manmadha. "పాతాళ నిలయంబునందోని తనతండ్రినిలయంబు దరిచి యుండిన పొక్కుపెట్టమ్మని." M. I. ii. 68. See also under పోవు.

పోపు *pōpu.* [Tel.] n. Grass. గడ్డి, కసవు. "అంతటతద్దేనునటవిస్థలంబున పోపు మేయుచు పోలచేపువచ్చి." Chennu. iv. 159.

పోయు *pōyu.* [Tel.] v. n. To arise, to be born or produced, పుట్టు. చెమటపోయు to perspire, చెమటపట్టు. చీముపోయు to suppurate as a boil, చీముపట్టు. వానికి యింకా అమ్మవారు పోయలేదు he has never had the small-pox. v. a. To pour, as water. To cast in metal or found. To fit on, as a halter as ఉరిపోయు. To place an arrow in a bow (బాణమును) సంధించు or కూర్చు. అమ్మవారు నిన్న సేతులంపోసినది the small pox came to a head yesterday. కట్టపోసినారు they built a bank. నారుపోయు to sow seed, which is afterwards to be transplanted. ఆకుపోయు to transplant rice. గోడపెట్టి మదురుపోసినాడు he built a wall and placed a cope upon it. తలబ్రాలు పోసినది she poured the blessed grain upon their heads (in marriage.) ఉచ్చపోయు to make water, to pass urine. వడపోయు or వడకట్టు to strain rice, &c. ఉరిపోయు to cast a noose. వ్యర్థముగా నా ఉసురుపోసుకొన్నాడు he has injured me without any cause. పురుడుపోసేనిమిత్తము దానిని పుట్టింటికి తీసుకొనివచ్చినారు they brought her home to lie in. వాడు దానిని నోట్లో పోసుకొన్నాడు he poured it into his mouth. ఆ చిన్నది వానికి నీళ్లుపోస్తున్నది the girl is bathing him. ఆమె చెట్లకు నీళ్లుపోస్తున్నది she is watering the trees. భిక్షమెత్తి పొట్టపోసుకొంటున్నాడు he fills his belly by begging. ఆసుపోసినది she placed the thread in readiness for weaving. పోయించు *pōyinṭsu.* v. a. To cause to cast or pour; to erect. కట్టపోయించు to raise a bank. విగ్రహములు పోయించిరి they had some statues cast.

పోరంబోకు or పోరంబోకు *pōrambōku.* [H.] See పొరంబోకు.

పోరచ *poracha.* [Tel.] Contempt, disregard, అలక్ష్యము. Intention, design; use, advantage, gain, ప్రయోజనము. A present, కానుక. adj. Useless, vain,

వ్యర్థము, నిస్సారము. "ఉ॥ కోరినకోర్కి కిందగఁ గుంతిసుతత్రితయంబుగాంచెగాం, భారియుఁ గ్ర్కి దర్చాసుతశతంబుముదంబొనరంగ గాంచె నే, బ చి యాడుపుట్టువున బుట్టెనిరర్థకజీవి నైతిసం, సారసు ఖావహంబయిన సత్సుతజన్మముగానబోలమిన్." M. I. v. 161.

పోరడు or **పోరగాడు** *pōraḍu*. [Tel.] n. A youthful person, a youth, పడుచువాడు. A boy, బాలుడు. పోరి *pōri*. n. A girl. బాలిక.

పోరు *pōru*. [Tel.] v. n. To fight, contend, struggle. కలహించు, యుద్ధముచేయు. పోరి సాధించె he mastered it with difficulty. "దర్పముమీరబోరు మదదంతులబోల్కి." N. ix. 191. n. A fight, combat, struggle, quarrel; teasing, troubling, insistence. ఇంటిలోనిపోరు family jars or brawls. ఆ పిల్ల పోరుపెట్టుచున్నది the child is giving a lot of trouble. పిచ్చుకపోరు the uproar that sparrows make. **పోరుట** *pōruṭa*. n. Fighting. **పోరుదిండి** *pōru-dindi*. n. A quarrelsome person, an epithet applied to Nārada, నారదుడు. **పోరుపెట్టు** *pōru-peṭṭu*. v. n. To tease, to plague, తొందర పెట్టు. To cry aloud, as a child. **పోరాడు** or **పోరితేమాడు** *pōr-āḍu*. v. n. To fight, grapple, contend, struggle. కలహించు, యుద్ధముచేయు. **పోరాట** or **పోరాటము** *pōr-āṭa*. n. A combat, a fight, a dispute, కలహము, యుద్ధము. **పోరించు** *pōrintsu*. v. n. To breed a quarrel, to incite to quarrel. జగడానకు ఉసికొల్పు. "నీపోటువాటునవివు డిల్లుమమ్ము, పోరించితివిజంత్రబొమ్మవాయక్క." HD. ii. 1194. **పోరితము** *pōritamu*. (పోరు+ఇతము.) n. War, a battle, a fight. యుద్ధము, పోరాటము. A quarrel, కలహము. Misunderstanding, స్పర్థ.

పోరువ *pōruva*. [Tel.] n. A cloth, sheet. పెల్లా. "పసమించు మాదిరపాకపోరువలచేదడి యూరనొత్తి." T. iii. 15. టీ॥ మాదిరపాకపోరు వలచేనవగా, సన్నరేకులచేతను. A layer పొర.

పోర్కాడించు or **పోరకాడించు** *pōrka-ḍintsu*. v. a. To bathe an infant. నీళ్లు పోయు. "పలుమరుదలయంటితేనగన్, నలుగిడిపో యుళ్లజలములం బోర్కాడించి." KP. vi. 205.

పోలక, పోలంక, పోల్కి, పోలుక, పోలుగ or **పోలువ** *pōlaka*. [Tel.] n. A Sand Grouse, *Pterochurus exnotus*, (F. B. I.) జాంపోల్కి or జాముపోలంక, పెద్దపోలక, సందపోలక or చిన్నపోలక are species. "నేలసెమర్లపోలు గలుకారుకోళ్లు." Rasica. i. 40. "సీ॥ పట్టు జీనువకొంగ పాకేయపిచ్చిక పోలుకపిక్కిలిమిాల ముచ్చు." H. iii. 14.

పోలక or **పోలకమ్మ** *pōlaka*. [Tel. పోలు a town + అక (అక్క)]. n. A certain village goddess. ఒక గ్రామదేవత.

పోలడు, పోలిగాడు or **మాడలపోలడు** *pōlaḍu*. [Tel.] n. An eagle. పసులపోలిగాడు the bird called the Black Drongo. *Dicrurus ater*. (F. B. I.)

పోలానిగంటలు *pōlāni-ganṭalu*. [Tel.] n. Bells tied to the neck of an elephant.

పోలీసు *pōlīsu*. [Eng. 'police.'] adj. Belonging to the Police. పోలీసువాడు or పోలీసు జవాను a policeman.

పోలు *pōlu*. [Tel.] v. n. To be fit or agreeable. ఒప్పు, తగియుండు. To be proper, యుక్తము. To be possible, శక్యము. This word is added to infinitives. చేయబోలునా can it be done? The neg. is పోలదు; thus, అట్లా చేయపోలదు or తగదు it is not proper to do so. ఉండబోలును perhaps they are there, ఉన్న వేమో. "తెగునవుడే పేంద్రునడ వియనదగుబుద్ధిజనింపబోలుతరుణీనికన్." H. i. 140. v. a. To resemble, to be like, సరి పోలు. n. Resemblance, similarity, సామ్యము. పోలుపొందులేకుండా మాట్లాడు or తలా తోకలేకుండా మాట్లాడు to talk without rhyme or reason. **పోలె** *pōle*. adv. Like. రామునిపోలె like Rama. **పోలమి** *pōl-ami*.

n. Dissimilarity, unlikeness. పోలిందు, పోలుచు or పోల్చు pōlutsu. v. a. To compare, or liken. పోలజేయు. పోలిక, పోలికి or పోల్కి pōlika. n. Resemblance, likeness.

పోలుకర్ర pōlu-karra. [Tel.] n. A shaft of a carriage.

పోలుగ See పోలక.

పోలేరు or పోలేరమ్మ pōlēru. [Tel. పోలు+ఏరు.] n. A village goddess.

పోళి pōḷi. [Tel.] n. A cake made of wheat, pulse and treacle. బొబ్బట్లు.

పోళ్లు pōḷḷu. plu. of పోడు (q.v.).

పోవు pōvu. [Tel.] v. n. To go, proceed. To pass, cease, disappear. To be lost, to die. ఇంటికి పోయినాడు he went home. వానిదోవను వాడు పోయెను he went his way. వానితండ్రి పోయినతరువాత after his father's death. పదిదినములు పోయిన తరువాత after ten days had passed. వానపోయినతరువాత after the rain ceased. ఆ పుస్తకముపోయినది the book is lost. వానికండ్లుపోయినవి he lost his eyes. చిల్లులుపోయిన చెంబు a mug that leaks. పదింటిలో నాలుగుపోతే ఆరు deduct four from ten and six remain. వాడు దానితోపోయినాడు he had (sexual) intercourse with her. Added to infinitives in A, it gives the signification of intent or futurity. వ్రాయబోతే వద్దన్నాడు when I was going to write he told me not to do so. దాన్ని కొట్టబోయినాడు he was about to strike her. వారెప్పుడుపోబోతారు when are they going to set out? చెప్పబోయేవు సుమీ take care, you don't mention it. Affixed to the past affirmative participles of many verbs, it denotes completeness: as ఆ గోడ పడిపోయినది the wall has fallen down. ఆ మాటలు ఇప్పుడు ఏటిలో కలిసిపోయినవి those words are now all forgotten; lit: gone into the river. వారక్కడనే ఉండిపోయినారు they settled there. Joined to negative participles it is used to form a past tense negative. రాకపోయెను he did not come. పోకపోయెను he did not go. వినకపోయెను he would not listen. పోవుకొందు Same as పోవు. Also, to pass, as time, కడచు. పోద్రోయు pō-drōyu. v. a. To baffle, to push back, to thrust away. పోదోలు pō-dōlu. v. a. To drive off. పోనాడు pōn-āḍu. v. a. To drive off, to turn away, to abandon. To blame, censure, నిందించు. పోగొట్టు or పోగొట్టుకొను to lose. పోని pōni. (neg. part. of పోవు) who or which goes not. పోని దోషము a sin that cannot be removed or done away. లేని పోని nonsensical. లేనిపోనిమాటలు foolish language. లేనిపోనిపని a foolish thing. లేని పోనిదేవులు gods that are no gods. పోని pōni. [for పోనిమ్ము.] imperative: Let it go, let it pass. Never mind. పోనొత్తు pōn-ottu. v. a. To do away, to remove. "అయ్యంతులు, చిత్తజాబాణములచేత నిగ్గంతయుబోనొత్తి మునిబెండ్లియాడగ తత్తరపడుచుండిరి." Vish. v. 147. పోపడు pō-paḍu. v. n. To go, పోవు. "కాకోదరంబునరాజుకోడుకు సద్దులు రండుం, పోపడునట్లుగగోల్లెన్, పేరెదిరి." M. XII. iii. 243. పోబడి pō-baḍi. (పోవు+బడి.) n. A trace. జాడ. పోబెట్టు pō-beṭṭu. n. A kind of noise expressive of love. అనురాగసూచకమగు ధ్వని. పోము pōmu. (1st. pers. plu. neg. aor. of పోవు.) We will not go. పోరాని pō-rāni. adj. Unavoidable. Friendly, loving, dear, ఆప్తమైన. పోరానిచుట్టము a dear relation. పోరామి pō-rāmi. n. Affection, love, friendship, స్నేహము. "పోరామిపుట్టుటయుగల్గినజనుల్ పోరామిపోబోవునే." Swa. iii. 173. "ఆరాములలో నెవ్వడు, పోరాములచాలనెఱపె పురుషోత్తముడుగా." B. X. §. 59. Hardship, trouble, సంకటము. పోయిన pōyina. (past rel. p of పోవు) Gone, departed, lost. Also, past, last, as పోయినసోమవారము last Monday: పోయిన నెల last month. పోయివచ్చు pōyi-vatstsu. v. n. To take leave, to go, వెళ్లు. పోయి

వస్తాను farewell, goodbye. పోవిడుచు pō-vidutsu. v. a. To abandon, give up, let go. మాను, వదలు.

పోషించు pōshintsu. [Skt.] v. a. To nourish, cherish, maintain, support, patronize. పోషకుడు pōshakudu. n. A patron, protector. ఉదరపోషకులు those who make a god of their belly. పోషణము pōshaṇamu.. n. Nourishing, cherishing; maintenance, support. బిచ్చమెత్తి ఉదరపోషణము చేసుకొంటున్నాడు he fills his belly by begging. పోష్యము pōshyamu. adj. That which is to be cherished, or taken care of. పోషింపదగిన. ఆతనిపోష్యవర్గము his dependants. పోష్యవర్గుడు or పోష్యుడు pōshya-vargudu. n. A dependant, hanger-on, protege. తమపోష్యవర్గులైన రామయ్య, i. e., your humble servant Ramaya. Lit. Ramaya who is one of your dependants.

పోసనము pōsanamu. [Tel.] n. Milk. పాలు. A coating, painting, పైపూత. Brightness, brilliance, కాంతి. "పోసనంబులు బ్రాపు పోసనకాలికిని, వానికొక్కిన యొప్పరాలిడి కడు." Sanand D. 156.

పోసరము Another form of పోతరము (q. v.).

పోసరించు pōsarintsu. v. n. Another form of పోతరించు (q. v.).

పోసరెక్క pōsa-rekka. [Tel.] n. A kind of fish. మత్స్యభేదము.

పోసూడు Same as పాపోసు (q. v.).

పోస్టు pōstu. [Eng: 'post'.] adj. Belonging to the postal department. పోస్టాఫీసు, పోస్టు జవాను, &c.

పోస్తకాయ or పోస్తుకాయ pōsta-kāya. [H.] n. A capsule of the poppy used medicinally. నల్లమందుకాయ.

పోహణ pōhaṇa. [Tel.] n. Joining, uniting, కూర్పు. Skill, నేర్పు. A fact or occurrence, సందర్భము, వర్తమానము, పని. "మనపురికొకానాటి వారిని, దనరిసేవింపించిదరువుగా దనుచారులంపి పోహణముగజెప్పించినదని, వినిపింతురు నడపునకోలు పుట్టిపోధా." Bdj. iv. 67. పోహణించు pōhaṇintsu. v. a. To string together. గుంభనచేయు, కూర్చు. "పీఠ పోసగము శ్రీపురహర పోహణించిన రీతి తమలోనదొరలయొక్క బ్రమలు కూర్చి." KP. i. 88.

పౌ pau

పౌండ్రదేశము paundra-dēsamu. [Skt.] n. The ancient name of a country including the greater part of Bengal. పౌండ్రుడు a native of the పౌండ్ర country. Vish. viii. 236.

పౌగండుడు pau-gandudu. [Skt.] n. A boy, a youth. బాలుడు. పౌగండ paugaṇda. adj. Appertaining to youth. "పౌగండబాలకృష్ణులు, పౌగండవయస్కులగుచు బహుపాలకులౌ పౌగండమునపుణ్యంబాదన, పౌగండవునాదిరంతపుచుపులనధిపా." BX. §. 15. 593.

పౌజు or పవుజు paudzu. [H.] n. An army, troops, దండు. A series, row, బారు, వరుస. పౌజులుతీరు paudzulu-tīru. v. n. To be arranged in a line, to form a line, బారుతీరు. పౌజులుతీరుచు, పౌజుతీర్చు or పౌజులుచేయు paudzulu-tīrutsu. v. a. To arrange in a line, బారుకట్టునట్లుచేయు.

పౌత్రుడు pautrudu [Skt. from పుత్ర.] n. A son's son. కొడుకుకొడుకు, మనుమడు. పౌత్రి pautri. n. A grand-daughter. పుత్రపౌత్రప్రపౌత్రాది through all generations.

పౌనఃపున్యము paunah-punyamu. [Skt. from పునఃపునః.] n. Frequency, repetition, మరలమరలచెప్పుట. పౌనఃపునిక paunah-punika. adj. Repeated. "పౌనఃపునిక ప్రణామవిధానుండై." Kal. i. 80.

పౌరము pauramu [Skt. from పుర.] adj. Belonging to a city or town (పురము.) పౌరసతులు the ladies of the place: citizens' wives. పౌరలోకము paura-lōkamu. n. The townsfolk, a body of citizens. పౌరుడు pauruḍu. n. A citizen. పౌరులు citizens, townsfolk.

పౌరాణము pauraṇamu. [Skt.] adj. Relating to the Puranas. "ఇట్లు విక్రమార్క్యాదిక్షితివిజయుడై శాలివాహనుండులీలతోడ, పౌరుషెల్లబోగడ పౌరాణమున మహారాజు అంగజేసి రాజ్యమునట." G. i. 33. పౌరాణికము pauraṇikamu. adj. Mythological; old, as a story. పౌరాణికుడు pauraṇikuḍu. n. One who knows the Puranas, పురాణము తెలిసినవాడు. A public reader of a Purana. A bard, minstrel.

పౌరుషము paurushamu. [Skt. from పురుష.] n. Manliness. పురుషభావము. Courage, పరాక్రమము. A resolution, effort, attempt. పురుషప్రయత్నము. A vow, ప్రతిజ్ఞ. "అలకేన్నుండుమడన చేసిన పౌరుషంబు ప్రతిహతింబగుట నవిస్మయంబుకొంది." M. III. vii 153. "బ్రహ్మ వ్రాతలను పౌరుషమా దిద్దరు." Vēma. 500. adj. Of, or belonging to man, human: manly. ఊర్ధ్వనిష్ఠ్యతనో పౌరుషప్రమాణె. మనిషి చెయ్యెత్తు పొడుగు. పౌరుషముగా paurushamu-gā. adj. In a manly fashion, bravely; insolently, haughtily. పౌరుషేయము paurushēyamu. adj. Made by human hands, పురుషుడు చేసినది.

పౌరోగవుడు paurō-gavuḍu. [Skt.] n. An overseer of the kitchen. పాకగృహాధ్యక్షుడు. వంటయింటి అధికారి.

పౌరోహిత్యము paurōhityamu. [Skt. from పురోహిత.] n. The office of priesthood. పురోహితకృత్యము.

పౌర్ణమాసి or పౌర్ణిమ paurṇamāsi. [Skt.] n. The lunar day on which the moon is full. పున్నమ. పౌర్ణమి a corruption of పౌర్ణమ.

పౌలస్త్యుడు paulastyuḍu. [Skt. from పులస్త్య.] n. An epithet of Kubera the god of riches. Also, of Ravana. పౌలస్త్యదిక్కు paulastya-dikku. n. The north, as being the quarter of Kubera.

పౌలు or పవులు Same as పగులు to break, (q. v.).

పౌలోమి paulōmi. [Skt. from పులోమ.] n. The name of the wife of Indra, శచీదేవి.

పౌషము paushamu. [Skt.] n. The month called పుష్యమాసము.

ప్యా pyā

ప్యాదా pyāda. [H.] n. A footman or peon. బంట్రోతు.

ప్ర pra

ప్ర pra. [Skt.] prefix, signifying Very, much, excessively.

ప్రంగ or ప్రగ్గ Same as పగ్గ (q. v.).

ప్రకటము prakaṭamu. [Skt.] adj. Public, notorious. ప్రసిద్ధము, వెల్లడి, స్ఫుటమైన. "ప్రకటబలాఢ్యులు." M. VII. ii. 24. ప్రకటన or ప్రకటనము prakaṭana. n. Publication, notification, announcement. ప్రకటన పత్రిక or ప్రకటన కాగితము a notice or advertisement. ప్రకటించు or ప్రకటనచేయు prakaṭinsu. v. a. To make public, proclaim, announce, promulgate. ప్రకటింపజేయు to get it proclaimed. ప్రకటితము prakaṭitamu. adj. Proclaimed, promulgated, announced, ప్రకటింపబడిన. ప్రకటితబలుడు celebrated for strength.

ప్రకరణము prakaraṇamu. [Skt.] n. An introduction, prologue or prelude. A chapter or section in a book. The plot or thread of a story. An affair, case. Connection, ప్రస్తావము. ఆ ప్రకరణమందు on that occasion.

ప్రకరము *prakaramu.* [Skt.] n. A heap; a quantity; a multitude. సమూహము.

ప్రకర్షము *prakarshamu.* [Skt.] n. Good, excellence. మేలు, అతిశయము.

ప్రకల్పితము *pra-kalpitamu.* [Skt. ప్ర+కల్పితము.] adj. Contrived, made, fabricated. ఉత్పాదితము. Vish. ii. 361.

ప్రకాండము *pra-kāndamu.* [Skt.] n. The stem or trunk of a tree, the part between the root and the branches. adj. Excellent, ప్రశస్తము. గోప్రకాండము an excellent cow.

ప్రకామము *pra-kāmamu.* [Skt.] adv. Voluntarily, willingly. యథేప్సితము, ఇచ్ఛవచ్చినట్లు.

ప్రకారము *prakāramu.* [Skt.] n. Way, manner, mode, similitude, likeness. పోలిక, సాదృశ్యము, రీతి, విధము. ప్రకారము or ప్రకారముగా *prakāramu.* adv. According to, accordingly, as, in the same way as అప్రకారము చేసినాడు he did accordingly. యథాప్రకారము as usual.

ప్రకాశము *pra-kāsamu.* [Skt.] n. Sunshine, ఎండ. Light, splendour, lustre, కాంతి. Manifestation. adj. Brilliant, splendid, lustrous. Celebrated, మిక్కిలి ప్రసిద్ధము. Revealed, బయలుపడిన. Similar, సమానము. అతని పేరు నిండా ప్రకాశముగానున్నది his name is celebrated. ప్రకాశించు *prakāsintsu.* v. n. To shine, be splendid, వెలుగు. To be bright, మెరయు.

ప్రకీర్ణము *pra-kīrnamu.* [Skt.] adj. Spread abroad, published, promulgated: expanded, opened, scattered, dispersed. వెదజల్లబడ్డ. ప్రకీర్ణము or ప్రకీర్ణకము *prakīrnamu.* n. A chowri, a cow tail used as a fan, or whisk, వింజామరము. adj. Miscellaneous. ప్రకీర్ణపరిచ్ఛేదము a miscellaneous chapter or section of a book.

ప్రకృతము *pra-kritamu.* [Skt.] adj. Present. ప్రకృతకార్యము the present business. n. The present time. adv. At present, just now, pro tempore.

ప్రకృతి *pra-kriti.* [Skt.] n. Nature, the goddess of nature. The world, the universe. The original or natural condition of a thing. The elementary or root form of a word. Constitution, temperament, disposition. స్వభావము, సహజము, భూతసత్త్వ రజస్తమోగుణములు, పంచభూతములలో నొకటి. పైత్యప్రకృతి a bilious temperament. శ్లేష్మప్రకృతి a saturnine disposition. వాతప్రకృతి an airy or rheumatic humour. జడప్రకృతి (R. vi. 14.) a dull state, stupefaction.

ప్రకోపము *pra-kōpamu.* [Skt.] n. The height or crisis of any affair. ముమ్మరము. జ్వరప్రకోపములో in the height or crisis of the fever. ప్రకోపించు *pra-kōpintsu.* v. n. To be at its crisis. జ్వరము ప్రకోపించినప్పుడు when the fever was at its height.

ప్రకోష్ఠము *pra-kōshthamu.* [Skt.] n. The fore-arm. మోచేతికిందనుండి మణికట్టుదాక నుండు చెయ్యి. ముంజేయి. A part of the frame of a door. A court yard in a house, an open space surrounded by buildings, తొట్టికట్టు.

ప్రక్క Same as పక్క (q. v.).

ప్రక్కి, ప్రక్కె or పక్కి *prakki.* [Tel.] n. A tree so called, *Tamarix gallica.* శిరసము, పిచులము.

ప్రక్రమము *pra-kramamu.* [Skt.] n. Order, క్రమము. Time, అవసరము. Proceeding, going, beginning. కార్యప్రక్రమారంభము. T. ii. 30.

ప్రక్రియ *pra-kriya.* [Skt.] n. Power, అధికారము. A chapter, ప్రకరణము. Word-building, శబ్దసాధనకల్పనవిధము. A rule, నియమవిధి. సమాసప్రక్రియ the chapter in Sanskrit grammar regarding compound words.

ప్రక్వణము or ప్రక్వాణము *pra-kvaṇamu.* [Skt.] n. The note of a lute. వీణాధ్వని.

ప్రక్షాళనము *pra-kshālanamu.* [Skt] n. The act of washing well, చక్కగా కడుగుట. ప్రక్షాళకుడు *pra-kshālakuḍu.* n. One who washes well, చక్కగా కడుగువాడు. ప్రక్షాళించు *pra-kshālintsu.* v. n. To wash well, చక్కగా కడుగు. ప్రక్షాళితము *pra-kshālitamu.* adj. Well washed, చక్కగా కడుగబడిన.

ప్రక్షిప్తము *pra-kshiptamu.* [Skt.] adj. Well thrown, cast or rejected, చక్కగా విసిరివేయబడిన, నిరస్తమైన. Well united, చేర్చబడ్డది. ప్రక్షిప్తశ్లోకము a spurious verse.

ప్రఖ్యాతము *pra-khyātamu.* [Skt.] adj. Much celebrated, very famous, renowned, మిక్కిలి ప్రసిద్ధమైన. ప్రఖ్యాతి *pra-khyati.* n. Celebrity, fame, renown. మిక్కిలి ప్రసిద్ధి.

ప్రగండము *pra-gaṇḍamu.* [Skt.] n. The upper arm. మోచేతికి మీదిభాగము, దండచెయ్యి, సందిలి.

ప్రగల్భ *pra-galbha.* [Skt.] n. A bold woman. ప్రౌఢనాయిక. ప్రగల్భత *pra-galbhata.* n. Energy, confidence, audacity, insolence, ప్రౌఢత్వము, దౌష్ట్యము, ప్రగల్భములాడుట. ప్రగల్భము *pra-galbhamu.* adj. Bold, audacious, daring. ప్రౌఢమైన. ప్రగల్భుడు *pra-galbhuḍu.* n. A bold man. ప్రతిభగలవాడు.

ప్రగాఢము *pra-gāḍhamu.* [Skt.] adj. Much, excessive, అధికమైన. Hard, దృఢమైన.

ప్రగ్గము Same as పగ్గము (q. v.).

ప్రగ్రహము *pra-grahamu.* [Skt.] n. A rein, rope. కళ్లెము మొదలైన కొనుపట్టె పగ్గము, పగ్గము. Confinement, చెర. A prisoner, a captive, ఖైదుచేయబడ్డది.

ప్రగ్రీవము *pra-grīvamu.* [Skt.] n. A window, a lattice, a balcony in a fort wall. ప్రాసాదముందలి కిటికీ. A bolster, అర్ధచంద్రాకారమైన తలగడ, ఒరగుదిండు.

ప్రఘణము or ప్రఘాణము *praghaṇamu.* [Skt.] n. A covered terrace, or a small portico before the door of a house. తలవాకిటి అరుగుమీదిచపారా, హోపా, శేక, చిన్నకవి. Vasu. iv 138. and v. 77. Parij. v. 58.

ప్రచండము *pra-chaṇḍamu.* [Skt.] adj. Fierce, vehement, wrathful, fervid, exasperated, offended. సహింపశక్యముకాని, చేరరాని, వాడిమిగల, సాధ్యముకాని. ప్రచండుడు *pra-chaṇḍuḍu.* n. A fierce, vehement, terrible man, ప్రతాపశాలి. వాడు తర్కములో ప్రచండుడు he is mighty in logic.

ప్రచయము *pra-chayamu.* [Skt.] n. A multitude, assemblage. సమూహము. A long-drawn note in music, అనుదాత్తస్వరవిశేషము V. P. ii. 146.

ప్రచారణము *pra-chāraṇamu.* [Skt.] n. Putting in practice, causing one to act. ఆచరింపజేయుట. "శాస్త్రంబుల వేదకథితార్థంబుల చక్కనాచరణప్రచారణంబులేమి." A. vi. 86.

ప్రచారము *pra-chāramu.* [Skt.] n. Going, proceeding, సంచారము. Custom, usage, ఆచారము. Appearance, manifestation. "వింటివె జనని యేతత్కథా ప్రచారంబెల్లన్." S. iii. 277. "పలుకులుమూ ప్రచారములుమూము భముల్ వినవచ్చె కీలముల్." BX. i. 16. 66.

ప్రచురము *prachuramu.* [Skt.] adj. Excessive, much, many. అధికము, మిక్కుటము. Public, notorious. ఆ సంగతి నిండా ప్రచురమైనది that matter became widely known. ఈమాటను ప్రచురముచేయకు do not let this become public. ప్రచురించు *prachurintsu.* v. a. To publish, make known

ప్రచేతసుడు or ప్రచేతుడు *prachētasuḍu.* [Skt.] n. The god of the sea, i. e., Varuna, వరుణుడు.

ప్రచోదితము *pra-chôditamu.* [Skt.] adj. Prescribed, directed, sent. ప్రేరేపింపబడ్డ.

ప్రచ్ఛన్నము *pra-chchannamu.* [Skt.] adj. Covered, private, secret, concealed, disguised, కప్పబడిన, గూఢమైన, మరుగైన. n. A private door within a house; a lattice, a loop hole. దిడ్డిదోవ, అంతర్ద్వారము, ఇంటిలోపల ఉండేద్వారము, లోవాకిలి.

ప్రచ్ఛాదనము *prach-chādanamu.* [Skt.] n. An upper or outer garment, ఉత్తరీయము, పైబట్ట. A covering, concealing, మూత. **ప్రచ్ఛాదితము** *prach-chāditamu.* adj. Covered, clothed, concealed. మూయబడ్డ. కప్పబడిన.

ప్రచ్యుతము *pra-chyutamu.* [Skt.] adj. Fallen, slipped. జారిన.

ప్రజ *praja.* [Skt.] n. Progeny, offspring, posterity, సంతతి. People, folk, the community, subjects, జనము. Plu: ప్రజలు. people, men. నల్లప్రజ dark folk. P. ii. 203. **ప్రజాపనము** *prajāpanamu.* n. Subjection, the state of a subject. **ప్రజాపతి** *prajā-pati.* n. The lord of men; a name of the Creator, బ్రహ్మ. A patriarch, one of our first forefathers. ఒకబ్రహ్మ. A king or sovereign. ప్రజాపాలనము protecting one's people. ప్రజామారణము a general mortality. **ప్రజావతి** *prajā-vati.* n. A brother's wife, an elder brother's wife, అన్నభార్య.

ప్రజననము *prajananamu.* [Skt.] n. Impregnation: pregnancy of cattle, తొలిచూలు, చూలు. Birth, production. పుట్టుక.

ప్రజ్ఞ *pra-gnya.* [Skt.] n. Intelligence, understanding, good sense, cleverness. **ప్రజ్ఞలు** *pragnyalu.* n. plu. Boasting words. "పట్టి ప్రజ్ఞలుప్రేలునవ్వారిబరికి" she talks big. S. iii. 24. **ప్రజ్ఞానము** *pra-gnyānamu.* n. Knowledge, wisdom. తెలివి, బుద్ధి. A sign, గురుతు, ఆనవాలు. **ప్రజ్ఞాపత్రిక** *pragnya-patrika.* n. A paper stuck in a volume to shew the place. A book mark. **ప్రజ్ఞుడు** *pragnyudu.* n. A learned man. పండితుడు. A bandy-legged man. వంకటి కాళ్లవాడు.

ప్రజ్వలించు *pra-jvalintsu.* [Skt.] v. n. To burn or be inflamed. మండు. To shine or glitter. ప్రకాశించు. **ప్రజ్వలనము** *pra-jvalanamu.* n. Burning, flaming, మండుట. Shining. ప్రకాశించుట. **ప్రజ్వలితము** *pra-jvalitamu.* adj. Flamed, shone, మండిన, ప్రకాశించిన

ప్రడీనము *pradīnamu.* [Skt.] n. The first flight of a bird; flying rapidly. పక్షిగతి భేదము, పక్షియొక్క మొదటియెగురు.

ప్రణతి *pra-nati.* [Skt. ప్ర+నతి] n. A bow, salutation, reverence, obeisance. నమస్కారము. **ప్రణతుడు** *pra-natudu.* n. One who bows or salutes, వంగినవాడు, నమస్కారముచేసినవాడు. **ప్రణమిల్లు** *pranamillu.* v. n. To bow, to prostrate oneself, to bow down. నమస్కారముచేయు.

ప్రణయము *pra-nayamu.* [Skt.] n. Affection, love, friendship, friendly or fond regard, acquaintance. ప్రణయకలహము lover's quarrels, discord between man and wife. స్నేహము, ప్రేమము. మంచిమాటలాడదము, వినయము. **ప్రణయించు** *pranayintsu.* v. a. To kindle, to make a fire burn. ప్రజ్వలింపజేయు. "అలరగసోమయాజులరు కాస్తమయంబుల నల్లనిల్లనగ్నుల ప్రణయింపనూద గను. గుంపునచొప్పడు ధూమజాలముల్ కలయగ బర్వెనోయన." Bmj. ii. 23. **ప్రణయిని** *pranayini* n. A beloved woman. ప్రియురాలు.

ప్రణవము *pranavamu.* [Skt.] n. The name of the sacred syllable O M, the mystic name of God. ఓంకారము.

ప్రణామము *praṇamamu.* [Skt.] n. A bow, salutation; homage. నమస్కారము, ప్రణతి.

ప్రణాళి *praṇāli.* [Skt.] n. A water-course, channel, canal. నీళ్లుపోవుదారి.

ప్రణిధి *praṇidhi.* [Skt.] n. A spy or emissary, చారుడు, హర్కారా. A.iv. 329. Asking, solicitation, ప్రార్థన.

ప్రణిపాతము *pra-ṇipātamu.* [Skt.] n. A Salutation, reverence, అభివాదము.

ప్రణీతము *praṇītamu.* [Skt.] adj. Dressed, cooked. వండబడిన. Made, done, constructed. చేయబడిన.

ప్రణుతము *pra-ṇutamu.* [Skt. ప్ర+నుతము.] Much praised, celebrated. మిక్కిలి స్తోత్రము చేయబడిన. ప్రణుతి *pra-ṇuti.* n. Great praise, మిక్కిలి పొగడిక. ప్రణుతించు or ప్రణుతిచేయు *pra-ṇutiñtsu.* v. a. To praise. స్తోత్రముచేయు. ప్రణుతుడు *pra-ṇutuḍu.* n. One who is much praised, మిక్కిలి స్తోత్రముచేయబడ్డవాడు.

ప్రతతి *pra-tati.* [Skt.] n. A company, crowd, విస్తారము, సమూహము. A creeping plant, లత.

ప్రతలము *pra-talamu.* [Skt.] n. The open hand, with the fingers extended. చాచిన వ్రేళ్లుగల అరచెయ్యి. One of the infernal regions, అధోలోకభేదము.

ప్రతాపము *pra-tāpamu.* [Skt.] n. Splendour, brilliancy, heat. వేడిమి. తేజము. Power, majesty, valor. ప్రతాపించు *pra-tāpiñtsu.* v. n. To show one's valor, ప్రతాపముచూపు.

ప్రతారణము *pra-tāraṇamu.* [Skt.] n. A delusion, trick; cheating, deceiving, deception. మోసము, వంచన, మోసపుచ్చుట. ప్రతారించు *pra-tāriñtsu.* v. a. To deceive, మోసపుచ్చు. ప్రతారకుడు *pra-tārakuḍu.* A deceiver. ప్రతారితుడు *pra-tāritudu.* n. One who is deceived or cheated.

ప్రతి *prati.* [Skt.] A Sanskrit particle, prefixed to words of that language, and implying Opposition or substitution, (instead of, in lieu of, opposed to,) order, distribution, (severally, each by each.) direction, designation, (towards, upon.) possession or inclusion in (as a part, or portion.) exchange, return, (again, back again.) ప్రతివేదము each Veda. ప్రతిదినము every day. ప్రతిసంవత్సరము each year. ప్రత్యేకము one by one. ప్రతిపక్షి the opposite party. ప్రతివాది a defendant. adj. Equal, సమానము మారు. ప్రతి n. The other. A match, an equivalent or substitute. A copy, as of a letter. A bit, section, spot of ground. One twelfth of a కుంట, one part or length of a wall. ప్రతిలేని matchless, unrivalled. మరియొక ప్రతిలో ఇట్లు వ్రాయబడియున్నది it is thus written in another manuscript or copy.

ప్రతీకారము or ప్రతిక్రియ *prati-kāramu.* [Skt.] n. A return of offices, either good, or bad. Revenge, retaliation. Remedying, counteracting. A remedy, an antidote, what averts a spell. మారుచేయుట. ప్రతికారవచనము a contradictory expression. S. iii. 360.

ప్రతికూలము *prati-kūlamu.* [Skt.] adj. Contrary, adverse, unfavorable, reverse, inverted. అనుకూలముకాని, విరుద్ధమైన. ప్రతికూలమైనగాలి an adverse wind.

ప్రతికృతి *prati-kṛiti.* [Skt.] n. An effigy, figure, image. ప్రతిమ.

ప్రతిగృహీతుడు *prati-grihītuḍu.* [Skt.] n. One who receives alms.

ప్రతిగ్రహము *prati-grahamu* [Skt.] n. An acceptance of alms. The act of receiving anything. A gift. ప్రతిగ్రహించు *prati-*

grahintsu. v. a. To accept, or receive alms.

ప్రతిఘటించు *prati-ghatintsu.* [Skt.] v. a. To oppose, ఎదిరించు. ప్రతిఘటితము *prati-ghatitamu.* adj. Opposed, contradicted.

ప్రతిఘము *pratighamu.* [Skt.] n. Anger, wrath, rage: opposition. క్రోధము. ప్రతిఘాతము.

ప్రతిఘాతము *prati-ghatamu.* [Skt.] n. A blow in return, a blow for a blow, మారుదెబ్బ. Wreaking vengeance, పగతీర్చుకొనుట.

ప్రతిచ్ఛాయ *prati-chchaya.* [Skt.] n. Refraction of light. A reflected image. ప్రతిమ. "దివ్యభూషణరత్నదీప్తులుకోటై సకలదిక్కులప్రతిచ్ఛాయలగ" Vish. viii. 93.

ప్రతిజ్ఞ *prati-gnya.* [Skt.] n. An agreement, engagement, undertaking, asseveration, solemn avowal, determination, resolution, vow. శపథము. Assent, అంగీకారము. ప్రతిజ్ఞాతము *prati-gnyatamu.* adj. Acknowledged, admitted. అంగీకరించబడ్డది.

ప్రతిదానము *prati-danamu.* [Skt.] n. The return or re-delivery of a deposit, barter, exchange. దాచనిచ్చినదానిని మరల నిచ్చుట.

ప్రతిద్వంద్వి *prati-dvandvi.* [Skt.] n. An antagonist, or opponent. శత్రువు.

ప్రతిధ్వని *prati-dhvani.* [Skt.] n. An echo. మారుమ్రోత.

ప్రతిన *pratina.* [from Skt. ప్రతిజ్ఞ] n. A vow, determination. ప్రతిజ్ఞ, పంతము. "నేడుదుర్యోధనుని నెత్తురువెలుచుదును. మదనుజు ద్రావుటలాదిగా రత, ప్రతినదీర్చునంతందనిభయము బొందెది." M. IX. i. 74.

ప్రతినామము *prati-namamu.* [Skt.] n. A second name or alias. మారుపేరు.

ప్రతినిధి *prati-nidhi.* [Skt.] n. A resemblance or equivalent: a substitute, deputy, representative. మారు. An image, a statue, a picture, ప్రతిమ. A surety. అతని ప్రతినిధిగా as his representative.

ప్రతిపక్షము *prati-pakshamu.* [Skt.] n. The opposite side or party. ఎదుటికక్షి. ఎదుటికక్షిదారు.

ప్రతిపక్షి or ప్రతిపక్షుడు *prati-pakshi.* [Skt.] n. An enemy, a defendant, an opponent, a respondent. శత్రువు.

ప్రతిపత్తు *prati-pattu.* [Skt.] n. The first day of either lunar fortnight, i. e., the first of the moon's increase or wane. పాడ్యమి.

ప్రతిపదము *prati-padamu.* [Skt.] n. A synonym. పర్యాయపదము.

ప్రతిపాదకము *prati-padakamu.* [Skt.] adj. That which gives, effects, or causes, కలుగజేసే. Explanatory, demonstrating, proving, తెలియజేసే. ప్రతిపాదకత్వము *prati-padakatvamu.* n. Substantiation. Explanatory force or bearing. నిరూపకత్వము. ప్రతిపాదనము *prati-padanamu.* n. Giving, donation. దానము, ఇవ్వడము. Ascertaining, determining. ప్రతిపాద్యము *prati-padyamu.* adj. Substantiated, established. నిరూపించబడ్డ. ప్రతిపాద్యముగా *prati-padyamu-ga.* adv. Determinately, firmly. పట్టుగా.

ప్రతిపాలకుడు *prati-palakudu.* [Skt.] n. One who protects or defends. A king, a protector. రక్షకుడు. ప్రతిపాలనము *prati-palanamu.* n. Protecting, defending, cherishing, రక్షణము. ప్రతిపాలించు *prati-palintsu.* v. a. To protect, defend, cherish రక్షించు, కాపాడు.

ప్రతిఫలము *prati-phalamu.* [Skt.] n. A return, requital, remuneration, reward.

ప్రతిఫలించు *prati-phalintsu.* [Skt.] v. n. To reflect or give the image of. ప్రతిబింబమగు. ప్రతిఫలనము *prati-phalanamu.* n. A reflection of an image. నీడ అగుపడడము. మారురూపముతో మట.

ప్రతిఫలితము *prati-phalitamu.* adj. Reflected, cast back, as an image. ప్రతిబింబితము. "దర్పణంబుచేతికిచ్చినం దత్ప్రతిఫలిత నిజదేహంబుచుంగనుంగొని." B. iii. 1004.

ప్రతిబంధము *prati-bandhamu.* [Skt.] n. An obstacle, impediment, hindrance. ప్రతిబంధకము *prati-bandhakamu.* adj. Impeding, obstructing. n. An obstacle, impediment, hindrance. వర్షప్రతిబంధకము hindrance caused by rain, or delay of rain. ప్రతిబంధించు *prati-bandhintsu.* v. n. To act against, hinder, obstruct, contradict, అడ్డగించు. అందుకీసూత్రము ప్రతిబంధించుచున్నది this rule is against it.

ప్రతిబింబము *prati-bimbamu.* [Skt.] n. A reflection, as in a mirror, resemblance. ప్రతిఫలనము. ప్రతిబింబించు *prati-bimbintsu.* v. a. To reflect back, as a mirror does. ప్రతిఫలించు. ప్రతిబింబితము *prati-bimbitamu.* adj. Reflected, as an image.

ప్రతిభ *pratibha.* [Skt.] n. Understanding, intellect, light, splendour. బుద్ధి.

ప్రతిభటుడు *prati-bhaṭudu.* [Skt.] n. An enemy. శత్రువు.

ప్రతిభువు *pratibhuvu.* [Skt.] n. A surety. పూటబడ్డవాడు. పూటకాపు.

ప్రతిభేదము *prati-bhēdamu.* [Skt.] n. A various reading in a manuscript. పాఠాంతరము.

ప్రతిమ or ప్రతిమానము *pratima.* [Skt.] n. An image, idol, picture. A resemblance. విగ్రహము, పోలిక.

ప్రతిమాల *prati-māla.* [Skt.] n. An exercise analogous to capping verses, reciting verse for verse, as a trial of memory or skill. అంతాదిగ్రంథము.

ప్రతిమోత *prati-mōta.* [Skt.] n. An echo. ప్రతిధ్వని. "కులగిరులెల్ల ప్రతిమోతలిచ్చుగా." Pal. 258.

ప్రతియత్నము *prati-yatnamu.* [Skt.] n. A desire, వాంఛ. An effort, endeavour, పూనిక. A reform, సంస్కారము.

ప్రతిరోధము *prati-rōdhamu.* [Skt.] n. Opposition. ఎదిరించుట. ప్రతిరోధి *prati-rōdhi.* n. An opponent, ఎదిరించువాడు.

ప్రతిలోమము *prati-lōmamu.* [Skt.] adj. Not right, reverse, inverted, contrary to the natural course or order, against the hair or grain. ప్రతిలోమముగా backwards, as reciting (a spell or the alphabet) the wrong way. ప్రతిలోమవివాహము marriage the wrong way, i. e., wherein the wife is superior to the husband.

ప్రతివసించు *prati-vasintsu.* [Skt.] v. n. To live, to be. వసించు, ఉండు. Molli. iii. 2.

ప్రతివాక్యము *prati-vākyamu.* [Skt.] n. An answer. ఉత్తరము, మారుమాట.

ప్రతివాది *prati-vādi.* [Skt.] n. A respondent or defendant. ప్రతికక్షిగానుండువాడు. ప్రతివాదించు *prati-vādintsu.* v. a. To defend in argument, to reply to charges. ప్రతికక్షియై మాట్లాడు, ఎదురాడు.

ప్రతివిధానము *prati-vidhānamu.* [Skt.] n. A preventative, remedy. ప్రతిక్రియ, పరిహారము.

ప్రతిశ్యాయము *prati-syāyamu.* [Skt.] n. Cold, catarrh. పడిసెము.

ప్రతిశ్రయము *prati-srayamu.* [Skt.] n. An assembly, a place of sacrifice. సభ, సత్రశాల, సత్త్రువు.

ప్రతిషేధము *prati-shēdhamu.* [Skt.] n. A prohibition, forbidding. అడ్డగింత. ప్రతిషేధించు *prati-shēdintsu.* v. a. To forbid, prohibit. అడ్డగించు.

ప్రతిష్టంభము *priti-shṭambhamu.* [Skt.] n. An obstacle, impediment; obstruction, ప్రతిబంధము, అడ్డగింత.

ప్రతిష్ఠ *pratishṭha.* [Skt.] n. Staying, standing. నిలుపుట. స్థితి. Fame, celebrity. కీర్తి. Consecration, dedication. స్తంభప్రతిష్ఠ setting up a pillar as a preliminary to a wedding, &c. దేవాలయప్రతిష్ఠచేయు to consecrate a temple. **ప్రతిష్ఠించు** *prati-shṭhintsu.* v. a. To establish permanently or firmly, to dedicate. శాశ్వతముగానిలుపు, స్థాపించు. "యౌవరాజ్యపట్టంబునకు నంగదుం బ్రతిష్ఠించి." R. v. 326. **ప్రతిష్ఠితము** *prati-shṭhitamu.* adj. Firmly or permanently established, dedicated.

ప్రతిసరము *prati-saramu.* [Skt.] n. A thread tied upon the wrist at the time of some particular ceremonies. కంకణము. దీక్షాదుల యందు ముంజేతగట్టిన నూలుసూత్రము, తోరము. The rear of an army, సేన వెనుకతట్టు, సేనాపృష్ఠము. A garland. మాల్యము.

ప్రతిసీర *prati-sira.* [Skt.] n. A screen or wall of cloth. పరదా, తెరచీర.

ప్రతిస్పర్ధ *prati-spardha.* [Skt.] v. Rivalry, పోటి. **ప్రతిస్పర్ధించు** *prati-spardhintsu* v. n. To behave as a rival, పోటిచేయు.

ప్రతిహతము *prati-hatamu.* [Skt.] adj. Disappointed, opposed, obstructed. విరుద్ధమయిన. అందుకు ప్రతిహతమైన ఒకలెక్క a cross account. అప్రతిహతము irresistible. **ప్రతిహతముగా** *prati-hatamu-gā.* adv. Against, in opposition. విరుద్ధముగా. **ప్రతిహతి** *prati-hati.* n. A prevention, obstruction. A repulse, rebound, beating back. Disappointment, అడ్డగింత, విఘాతము, అభ్యంతరము. ప్రతిహతిలేని irresistible. **ప్రతిహతుడు** *prati-hatuḍu.* n. One who is disappointed, opposed or obstructed.

ప్రతిహారము or **ప్రతీహారము** *prati-hāramu.* n. A gate, or door. ద్వారము. **ప్రతిహారుడు, ప్రతిహారి** or **ప్రతీహారుడు** *prati-hāruḍu.* n. A door-keeper, or porter.

ప్రతిహింస *prati-himsa.* [Skt.] n. Revenge, retaliation. కసితీర్చుకొనడము.

ప్రతీకత *pratikata.* [Skt.] n. The body as being 'a system of limbs. "పరిణామశక్తిం దత్ప్రతీకతాధిష్ఠితమహద్భూతాది సూరిపరిపరాత్త్వ కంబులు." A. vi. 132. టీ॥ తత్ప్రతీకత, తత్తదవయవ సమూహములచేతను. **ప్రతీకము** *pratikamu.* n. A limb, a member, a part, a portion. అవయవము.

ప్రతీకారము *prati-kāramu.* [Skt.] n. Revenge, retaliation, vengeance. A remedy. పగతీర్చుకొనడము. చేసినపనికి బదులు చేయడము. "తత్ప్రతీకారముసేర్తు." M. XIII. iv. 419.

ప్రతీకాశము *prati-kāṣamu.* [Skt.] adj. (In composition) Like, resembling. సమానమైన. సూర్యబింబప్రతీకాశము bright as the sun.

ప్రతీక్షించు *prat-ikshintsu.* [Skt. ప్రతి+ఈక్షించు.] v. n. To look for, to hope for, to expect. ఆశతో ఎదురుచూచు. **ప్రతీక్షణము** *prat-ikshaṇamu.* n. Expectation, hope, ఎదురుచూచుట. **ప్రతీక్ష్యుడు** *prat-ikshyuḍu.* adj. A venerable or respectable person. పూజ్యుడు.

ప్రతీచి *pratichi.* [Skt.] n. The west quarter. పడమర. **ప్రతీచీనము** *pratich-inamu.* adj. Western, west. పడమటిది.

ప్రతీతి *pratiti.* [Skt.] n. Knowledge, common report, traditional, belief, a general impression; notoriety, reputation, fame, వదంతి. ప్రసిద్ధి. **ప్రతీతము** *prati-tamu.* adj. Famous, celebrated, renowned, known, ప్రసిద్ధమయిన. **ప్రతీతుడు** *prati-tuḍu.* n. A famous man, ప్రసిద్ధుడు.

ప్రతీపము *pratipamu.* [Skt.] adj. Disobedient, refractory, perverse, cross, contradictory. విరుద్ధమైన. ప్రతీపభూపుడు the leader of the hostile host. శత్రురాజు. "ప్రతీపభూపసంగ్రామముజాజనాలిన్యత్త." R. i. 53. **ప్రతీపుడు** *pratipaḍu.* n. An enemy, adversary. శత్రువు.

ప్రతీరము *pra-tīramu.* [Skt.] n. A shore, or bank. నద్యాదితీరము, గట్టు.

ప్రతోదము *pratōdamu.* [Skt.] n. A goad. ములుగోల, మునికోల. "తోదనశీలదండము ప్రతోదముగా." Mand. ii. 134.

ప్రతోళి *pratōḷi.* [Skt.] n. A high road, the principal road through a town or village. పెద్దవీధి, రథ్య.

ప్రత్తి or పత్తి *pratti.* [Tel.] n. Cotton (used of the plant or of the uncleaned product.) విత్తులతోనుండుదూది. ఎర్రప్రత్తి red cotton. పైడిప్రత్తి golden or silk cotton. జడప్రత్తి cotton that forms into lumps. పుల్లప్రత్తి cotton that forms like sticks.

ప్రత్యంతరము *praty-antaramu.* [Skt.] n. Another copy. A different manuscript.

ప్రత్యక్పుష్పి *pratyak-pushpi.* [Skt.] n. A plant, *Achyranthes aspera.* ఉత్తరేణు.

ప్రత్యక్షము *praty-akshamu.* [Skt.] adj. Perceptible, perceivable; present, cognizable by any of the organs of sense. దాన్ని నాప్రత్యక్షములో చేసినాడు he did it before my eyes. ప్రత్యక్షనరకము death staring one in the face, hell open before him. అతనికి దేవుడు ప్రత్యక్షమైనాడు the god appeared visibly to him. ప్రత్యక్షవాది *pratyaksha-vādi.* n. An agnostic. A Buddhist. A Jain.

ప్రత్యగ్రము *praty-agramu.* [Skt.] n. New, recent, fresh. క్రొత్త.

ప్రత్యపకారము *praty-apakāramu.* [Skt.] n. Returning evil for evil. Tit for tat. M. I. i. 176.

ప్రత్యయము *pratyayamu.* [Skt.] n. Knowledge, apprehension. జ్ఞానము. Trust, faith, belief, confidence, విశ్వాసము. An oath, ordeal, శపథము. A cause, reason, motive, హేతువు. Custom, ఆచారము. Fame, ఖ్యాతి. (In Gram.), An affix to roots and words forming derivatives and inflections.

ప్రత్యర్థి *praty-arthi.* [Skt.] n. An opponent, defendant, rival, ill wisher, enemy. ప్రతివాది. శత్రువు.

ప్రత్యవాయము *pratyavāyamu.* [Skt.] n. Sin. A reverse, a contrary course or proceeding. Disappointment, disagreement. దోషము. దీనిని చేయడమువల్ల ఏమిన్ని ప్రత్యవాయములేదు there is no harm in doing it. "కేషాంచిత్ కరణే ప్రత్యవాయః, కేషాంచిత్ అకరణే ప్రాయశ్చిత్తం."

ప్రత్యహము *praty-ahamu.* [Skt.] adv. Every day, daily. ప్రతిదినము.

ప్రత్యాఖ్యాతము *praty-ākhyātamu.* [Skt.] adj. Prohibited, forbidden, denied, refused. Removed, set aside. Discouraged, నిరాకృతము. ప్రత్యాఖ్యాతుండయ్యె he was discouraged or refused. ప్రత్యాఖ్యానము *praty-ākhyānamu.* n. Rejection, refutation, disallowance, disregard, denial, refusal. నిరసనము, కూడదనడము.

ప్రత్యాదిష్టము *praty-ādishṭamu.* [Skt.] adj. Same as ప్రత్యాఖ్యాతము. (q. v.)

ప్రత్యాబ్దికము *praty-ābdikamu.* [Skt.] n. An anniversary of a death. ఏటేటవచ్చే శ్రాద్ధము.

ప్రత్యామ్నాయము *praty-āmnāyamu.* [Skt.] adj. Instead of, in lieu of, in place of.

ప్రత్యాలీఢము *praty-ālīḍhamu.* [Skt.] n. Standing with one leg advanced, as when drawing the bow; straddling. విలుకాడు ఎడమకాలు ముందరికిచాచి కుడికాలు వెనుకకు ఉంచి నిలుచుట. కుడికాలు ముందరికిచాచి యెడమకాలు వెనుకకు ఉంటే ఆలీఢమనబడును.

ప్రత్యాశ *praty-āsa.* [Skt.] n. Hope. Vain hope.

ప్రత్యాసత్తి praty-āsatti. [Skt.] n. Connection, relation, familiar intercourse or association with. సంబంధము. ప్రత్యాసన్నుడు paty-āsannudu. He who is connected or joined with, సంబంధముగల వాడు, కలిసినవాడు.

ప్రత్యాహారము praty-āhāramu. [Skt.] n. A withdrawal or restraining of the organs, so as to be indifferent to disagreeable or agreeable excitement బాహ్య వృత్తింపరిత్యజ్య అంతస్సుఖతై. ఇంద్రియస్వాయత్త కరణా. స్వస్వవిషయేభ్య ఇంద్రియాణాం, ఉపాహరణము. (In Gram.) abridgment of letters, వర్ణసంగ్రహము.

ప్రత్యుత్తరము praty-uttaramu. [Skt.] n. An answer, reply or rejoinder.

ప్రత్యుత్థానము praty-utthānamu. [Skt.] n. A welcome given to a guest by rising and meeting him. Civility to a guest, polite reception. గృహాగతమునకుత్థానం ప్రకృత వినయే, ఎదురుకొనిలేచుట.

ప్రత్యుద్గమనము praty-udgamamu. [Skt.] n. Going to meet a guest. ప్రత్యుత్థానము. ప్రత్యుద్గమించు praty-udgamintsu. v. n. To go to welcome a guest, ఎదురుకొనిపోవు.

ప్రత్యుద్యాతము praty-udyātamu. [Skt.] adj. Returning, coming back, మళ్లి వచ్చినట్టి. "ప్రత్యుద్యాతమాసేనసంద్రుడై నలుదిక్కులం గొలువగా." G. viii. 84.

ప్రత్యుపకారము praty-upakāramu. [Skt.] n. Doing good in return. A return for good offices; a return of favours.

ప్రత్యూషము or ప్రత్యూషము praty-ushamu. [Skt.] n. Dawn, morning, ప్రభాతము.

ప్రత్యూహము praty-ūhamu. [Skt.] n. An obstacle, impediment, hindrance, విఘ్నము.

ప్రత్యేకము praty-ēkamu. [Skt.] adj. Separate, distinct, వేరువేరు. ప్రత్యేకముగా praty-ēkamu-gā. adv. Separately, distinctly, in private, alone. ప్రత్యేకించు praty-ēkintsu. v. a. To separate, వేరువేరుచేయు.

ప్రథ pratha. [Skt.] n. Fame, celebrity, ప్రసిద్ధి.

ప్రథనము prathanamu. [Skt.] n. A battle, fight. యుద్ధము. M. VII. i. 243, and iv. 293.

ప్రథమము prathamamu. [Skt.] adj. First, initial, prior, original, chief, principal. మొదటి, ముఖ్యము. ప్రథమపురుషము (in Gram.) the *First* person, which is the *third* person according to English Grammar. He, she, it, they. ప్రథమతః prathama-tah. adv. Originally, in the first instance. మొదట. ప్రథమసత్ప్రసాదము the first communion. ప్రథమశాఖవారు the name of a certain sect among Brahmins.

ప్రథి prathi. [Skt.] n. The periphery of a wheel: the tire, బండికల్లుకు చుట్టువేసిన యినుప కట్టు.

ప్రథితము prathitamu. [Skt.] adj. Famous, celebrated; made known, declared, ప్రసిద్ధమైన. ప్రథితి prathiti. n. Fame. ప్రఖ్యాతి.

ప్రథిమ or ప్రథిమము prathima. [Skt.] n. Greatness, bigness, పెద్ది.

ప్రదక్షిణము pra-dakshinamu. [Skt.] n. Circumambulation. Paying homage (to a god, &c.) by solemnly walking round it with the right hand towards it. అప్రదక్షిణావర్తముండే శంఖము a right hand shell (which is considered a curiosity) being the *Perinthium*, the volutes of which turn (what is commonly called) the wrong way.

ప్రదము pradamu. [Skt.] adj. That which bestows. వర్షప్రదమైన మేఘము a rainy cloud.

దేవానాంచ భయప్రదం terrific even to gods. మంగళప్రదమైనశకునము a good omen. జయప్రదమైనకార్యము a fortunate affair. **ప్రదుడు** *pradudu.* n. One who grants. కామితప్రదుడు he who gratifies a wish. జయప్రదుడు he who grants victory.

ప్రదరము *pradaramu.* [Skt.] n. An arrow, బాణము. A fracture, a breaking: చీలుట, విరుచుట. A disease of the womb, menorrhagia. కుసుమరోగము.

ప్రదర్శకుడు *pra-darṣakuḍu.* [Skt.] n. One who shews clearly. A teacher, expounder, prophet. విశదపరిచిచూపువాడు. **ప్రదర్శనము** *pra-darṣanamu.* n. Showing, explaining, విశదపరిచిచూపుట. **ప్రదర్శితము** *pra-darṣitamu.* adj. Clearly shown or explained. స్పష్టముగాచూపబడిన.

ప్రదానము *pra-dānamu.* [Skt.] n. A great gift, donation. గొప్ప ఈవి.

ప్రదేశము *pra-dēṣamu.* [Skt.] n. A place, situation, region, country, district. చోటు. కంఠప్రదేశము the region of the neck or throat. వారు ఈ ప్రదేశములందు లేరు they are not in these parts.

ప్రదేశిని *pra-dēṣini.* [Skt.] n. The forefinger. తర్జని. చూపుడువ్రేలు.

ప్రదోషము *pra-dōshamu.* [Skt.] n. Evening; the first part of the night. The evening of a particular lunar day, in which the recital of the Vedas is forbidden. రాత్ర్యారంభము. A fault, transgression, sin, దోషము.

ప్రద్యుమ్నుడు *pradyumnuḍu.* [Skt.] n. A name of Manmadha. మన్మథుడు.

ప్రద్యోతనుడు *pra-dyōtanuḍu.* [Skt.] n. The sun. సూర్యుడు.

ప్రధనము *pradhanamu.* [Skt.] n. A fight, battle. యుద్ధము.

ప్రధానము *pradhānamu.* [Skt.] n. Nature, the natural state of any thing; the cause of the material world. ప్రకృతి, పరమాత్మ. A betrothal, the betrothal ceremony. adj. Chief, principal. ముఖ్యమైన. వారిలో ప్రధానమైనవానిని పిలువు call the chief man among them. ప్రధానమైన ఆక్షేపణ the principal objection. ప్రధానద్రవ్యము చవుకగానున్నది the principal provision (or staff of life), i. e., rice is cheap. ప్రధానముచేయు to betroth. ప్రధానపు ఉంగరము a ring with which a woman is betrothed. **ప్రధాని** *pradhāni.* A minister. మంత్రి. In chess, the queen. A principal. ముఖ్యుడు. **ప్రధానుడు** *pradhānuḍu.* n. A president, a chief. Also a minister. ముఖ్యమంత్రి.

ప్రన్ననన or **ప్రన్ననము** *prannana.* [Tel.] n. Beauty. అందము. "అధ్వరంబుకంటె నధికంబుతపము. తపమునంక మేని బ్రన్ననము, నిపుర సేతగాదహింసయుసత్యవాక్యంబుదమముదయయుగాన." M. XII. ii. 361. మేనిప్రన్ననము నిపురసేతగాదు. అనగా దేహముయొక్క అందము నశింపచేయుపముకాదు. adv. Beautifully, సొగసుగా. "అపూర్వపు బంతము వింటి వేయునట్, బ్రన్ననవివ్వియోగాలది బంతమువెవ్వరు శేయరట్టిలో." G. xi. 60. **ప్రన్నని** or **ప్రన్న** *prannani.* adj. Beautiful, handsome, సొగసైన. "భాసురచంద్రబింబమున బ్రన్ననివెన్నెల కందునుంబలెన్." Ellana. iii. 190. ప్రన్ననివెన్నెల అనగా సొగసైన వెన్నెల.

ప్రప *prapa.* [Skt.] n. A place for refreshment, where water is given to passers by. చలిపందిరి. A. ii. 77.

ప్రపంచము *prapanchamu.* [Skt.] n. The world, the Universe, భూలోకము. Family life, సంసారము. Extent, expanse, విరివి. A large quantity, abundance. A delusion, trick, మోసపుచ్చుట, దగాచేయడము. Difference, వ్యత్యాసము. Composition, రచన. **ప్రపంచించు** *prapanchintsu.* v. a. To extend, to enlarge, విస్తరింపజేయు, విరివిచేయు.

ప్రపత్తి *prapatti*. [Skt.] n. Seeking or taking refuge. గతిలేకలేదని పాదములను పట్టుకొనుట, శరణుచొచ్చుట. ప్రపన్నము *prapannamu*. adj. Taking refuge with, reaching, arriving at, seeking, adhering to. ప్రపత్తిచేసిన. ప్రపన్నుడు *prapannudu*. n. A votary, one who seeks refuge. శరణాగతుడు.

ప్రపదము *pra-padamu*. [Skt.] n. The point of the foot; the tip of the toes. పాదముచివర. The upper surface of the foot, మీగాలు, మునుగాలు.

ప్రపాతము *pra-patamu*. [Skt.] n. A fall, cascade, cliff, precipice, నద్యాదితటము, కొండచరియ.

ప్రపితామహుడు *pra-pita-mahudu*. [Skt.] n. A great-grandfather. ముత్తాత. ప్రపితామహి a great grand-mother. వృద్ధప్రపితామహుడు a great-grandfather's father.

ప్రపౌత్రుడు *pra-pautrudu*. [Skt.] n. A great-grandson. పౌత్రునికొడుకు, మునిమనుమడు. ప్రపౌత్రి a great grand daughter. పౌత్రునికూతురు. మునిమనుమరాలు.

ప్రఫుల్లము *pra-phullamu*.[Skt.]adj Blown, blooming. వికసించిన.

ప్రబంధము *pra-bandhamu*. [Skt.] n. A treatise, book, work, composition. కల్పించినకథగల గ్రంథము, కావ్యము.

ప్రబలము *pra-balamu*. [Skt.] adj. Mighty, powerful, strong. మిక్కిలిబలముగల. Important, predominant, prevailing. ప్రబలవిరోధి a mighty enemy. ప్రబలమైనగురుతులు evident signs. ప్రబలు, ప్రబలించు or ప్రబలమగు *pra-balu*. v. n. To grow, increase, swell. అతిశయిల్లు, వర్ధిల్లు, వృద్ధిపొందు. ప్రబలుడు *pra-baludu*. A mighty man, a celebrated man. ప్రసిద్ధుడు.

ప్రబుద్ధుడు *pra-buddhudu*. [Skt.] n. One who is awake. మేలుకొన్నవాడు. A man who has become acquainted with reality; an enlightened man, a wise man. A clever man. ప్రబుద్ధులు the wise. ప్రబోధము *pra-bodhamu*. n. Wisdom, Intellect, understanding. మిక్కిలి తెలివి, జ్ఞానము. Caution, vigilance, wakefulness, మేలుకొనుట. ప్రబోధించు *pra-bodhintsu*. v. a. To teach clearly, చక్కగాతెలుపు. To wake up, మేలుకొలుపు. ప్రబోధిక *pra-bodhika*. adj. That which rouses or warns. లేపునది, జ్ఞానమును కలుగజేయునది. సుకుమారుప్రబోధిక the name of a certain Telugu commentary on the Amara Kosha.

ప్రబ్బ or ప్రబ్బలి *prabba*. [Tel.] n. The rattan tree. కేతసి, పేము, వైత్రపుచెట్టు.

ప్రబ్బు *prabbu*. [Tel.] v. n. To spread, వ్యాపించు. To happen, occur, కలుగు, పుట్టు. To flourish or thrive. పెరుగు, హెచ్చు, విజృంభించు, అతిశయించు, వర్ధిల్లు. "క॥ ప్రబ్బిన భక్తినిహరిపై, కబ్బంబుగ చెప్పికవులు కైవల్యశ్రీ, కబ్బుదురట." Bhag. X: 67. v. a. To lengthen a statement, or spin out a story. పెంచు. To blame, నిందించు. To unite, join, కలయు. n. Blame, నింద. ప్రబ్బికోలు *prabbi-kolu*. n. Spreading, &c. ప్రబ్బికొనుట.

ప్రభ *prabha*. [Skt.] n. Light, radiance, brightness, splendour, వెలుగు, తేజస్సు, ప్రభావము. ప్రభాకరుడు *prabha-karudu*. n. The maker of light, i. e., the sun. సూర్యుడు. ప్రభాతము *prabhatamu*. n. The dawn, or morning. ఉదయకాలము, తెల్లవారువేళ, వేకువ. ప్రభావము *pra-bhavamu* n. Majesty, dignity. మాహాత్మ్యము, తేజస్సు. Magnanimity, high spirit; power, strength, influence, force. ప్రతాపము, శక్తి. ఆ దేశపుగాలిప్రభావముచేత by the effect of that climate. మీ ఆశీర్వాద ప్రభావమువల్ల ఇక్కడికి సుఖముగా చేరినాను thanks to your good wishes I have arrived here safely. ప్రభాసితము *pra-bhasitamu*. adj.

Shining, luminous, glorious. తెలిగెడి. Vish. ii. 217.

ప్రభంజనము *pra-bhanjanamu.* [Skt.] n. Lit. That which breaks thoroughly. Wind, a breeze. గాలి, వాయువు. ప్రభంజనుడు *pra-bhanjanuḍu.* n. The god of the winds. వాయుదేవుడు.

ప్రభవ *pra-bhava.* [Skt.] n. The name of a Telugu year. ప్రభవము *pra-bhavamu.* n. Birth, పుట్టుక. ప్రభవించు *pra-bhavintsu.* v. n. To be born or produced. పుట్టు, కలుగు, జనించు. ప్రభవుడు *pra-bhavuḍu.* n. One who is born, పుట్టినవాడు.

ప్రభిన్నము *pra-bhinnamu.* [Skt.] adj Detached, severed, separated. నరకబడిన, పగిలిన, ప్రత్యేకింపబడిన. n. An elephant in rut. మాతెనమత్తగజము. "ప్రభిన్నగజఘోటుచ్ఛన్నగహనాహనములు." Swa. v. 37.

ప్రభువు *prabhuvu.* [Skt.] n. A lord, master, ruler, అధిపుడు. చిత్తము మహాప్రభూ yes, please your honor. ప్రభుత్వము *prabhu-tvamu.* n. Power, supremacy, lordship, sovereignty, government.

ప్రభూతము *pra-bhūtamu.* [Skt.] adj. Much, abundant. అధికము. Produced, సంభూతము.

ప్రభృతి *prabhriti.* [Skt.] n. A beginning, మొదలు. adv. After that, thence, beginning with, &c. బాల్యాత్ప్రభృతి ever since my youth. శివహరిప్రభృతులు Siva, Hari and the rest. మునిప్రభృతిజనములు the ascetics and the rest.

ప్రమ *prama.* [Skt.] n. Knowledge of the truth, true knowledge, యథార్థజ్ఞానము.

ప్రమత్తము *pra-mattamu.* [Skt.] adj. Very intoxicated. మిక్కిలి మదించిన, మిక్కిలి మత్తెక్కిన. Insane, వెర్రి. R. vi. 149. ప్రమత్తుడు *pra-mattuḍu.* n. A very drunk man.

ప్రమథుడు *pramathuḍu.* [Skt.] n. An attendant on Siva. శివభటుడు, పారిషదుడు.

ప్రమథాధిపుడు *pramath-adhipuḍu.* n. Lit: The lord of Pramathas, an epithet of Siva, శివుడు.

ప్రమదము *pra-madamu.* [Skt.] n. Joy, pleasure, delight. ఆనందము, సంతోషము. ప్రమదవనము or ప్రమదావనము *prama-da-vanamu.* n. A ladies' pleasure-ground, or park. అంతఃపురస్త్రీలు విహరించుటకైన ఉద్యానవనము. ప్రమద *pra-mada.* n. A wanton girl, an attractive woman; a maid, damsel, lady, అతికామవతి, అతిగర్వవతి, స్త్రీ.

ప్రమాణము *pra-māṇamu.* [Skt.] n. Measure, scale; standard; limit; quantity, size, bulk, extent, అంగుళీమానము, కొల, మూర, గజము మొదలైనవి. Proof, testimony, authority. A cause, reason, motive. ప్రత్యక్షాదిజ్ఞానకారణము, హేతువు. Truth. An oath, adjuration. సత్యము. ప్రమాణముచేయు to make an oath, to take an oath, to swear. ప్రమాణముచేయించు to administer an oath. వేదము శబ్దప్రమాణముగానున్నది the Veda is the standard of revealed truth. శాస్త్ర ప్రత్యక్షాది ప్రమాణములు the methods of Reasoning or Inference. These are: ప్రత్యక్షము actual perception, అనుమానము inference, ఉపమానము analogy, శాబ్దము authority or revelation, ఐతిహ్యము tradition. ప్రమాణీకరించు *pramaṇī-karintsu.* v.a. To consider as true. సత్యముగానెంచు. ప్రమాణికము *pramaṇikamu.* n. Fidelity, faithfulness.

ప్రమాదము *pramādamu.* [Skt.] n. A mistake, error; neglect (of study, &c.) తప్పుట, ఏమరుపాటు, మరాకుపడుట. Danger, insecurity, hazard, peril. Mischance, unforeseen evil. అనాలోచితవిపత్తు. ప్రమాది *pramādi.* n. The name of a Telugu year. One who is careless or negligent. ప్రమాదీచ *pramādīcha.* n. The name of a Telugu year.

ప్రమిద, ప్రమిదె or ప్రమ్మిద *pramida.* [Tel.] n. A saucer for oil, used as a lamp.

ప్రమిల *pra-mila.* [Skt.] n. Lassitude, enervation, exhaustion from indolence or fatigue. పనికిపాటు, అలసటచేత సొమ్మసిల్లిపోవడము.

ప్రముఖము *pra-mukhamu.* [Skt.] adj. Chief, principal, best, most excellent, first. ముఖ్యమైన, మొదటిదైన. **ప్రముఖుడు** *pra-mukhuḍu.* n. A chief, a principal man, a leader, ముఖ్యుడు.

ప్రముదితుడు *pra-muditudu.* [Skt.] n. One who is very pleased, మిక్కిలి సంతోషించినవాడు.

ప్రమేయము *pra-mēyamu.* [Skt.] n. That which may be known for a certainty, an object of knowledge, subject. యథార్థముగా ఎరుగదగినది. An opportunity, occasion. ఆప్రమేయములో దీనిని చెప్పినాడు he mentioned this on that occasion. ఆప్రమేయమే ఎరుగను I know nothing of the matter.

ప్రమేహ *pra-mēha.* [Skt.] n. Diabetes. Charaka. p. 218.

ప్రమోదము *pra-mōdamu.* [Skt.] n. Joy, delight. ఆనందము. **ప్రమోదించు** *pra-mōdintsu.* v. n. To rejoice, be joyful, ఆనందించు.

ప్రమోదూత *pra-mōdūta.* [Skt.] n. The name of a Telugu year.

ప్రమ్ము *prammu.* [Tel.] v. a. To surround, పరివేష్టించు.

ప్రయతుడు *pra-yatuḍu.* [Skt.] n. A holy or pious person; one purified by austerity and mortification. పురితుడు, పూతుడు.

ప్రయత్నము *pra-yatnamu.* [Skt.] n. A great attempt, endeavour, or effort. మిక్కిలియత్నము. దైవప్రయత్నమువల్ల ఇట్లు జరిగినది it pleased God that matters turned out thus. **ప్రయత్నించు** *pra-yatnintsu.* v. n. To try very hard, strive, make a great effort, మిక్కిలి యత్నించు.

ప్రయాగ or **ప్రయాగము** *pra-yāga.* [Skt.] n. The name of a holy place, Prayag. (Allahabad) తీర్థవిశేషము. **ప్రయాగలు** *pra-yāgalu.* n. A certain sort of grain.

ప్రయాణము *pra-yāṇamu.* [Skt.] n. A journey, departure. మీ ప్రయాణమెప్పుడు when do you set out? **ప్రయాణమగు** or **ప్రయాణించు** *prayāṇam-agu.* v. n. To set out or start on a journey, బయలుదేరు. ప్రయాణముచేయు to travel, to make a journey. ప్రయాణము. "బంగారుపల్లకియెక్కి ప్రయాణించుచెడ." జై. viii.

ప్రయాసము or **ప్రయాస** *pra-yāsamu.* [Skt.] n. Toil, violent effort, trouble, difficulty, pain. శ్రమము. ఆ మాట వినడమునకే ప్రయాసముగానున్నది it is painful even to hear that word. నేను చెప్పేమాటలు అతను వినడమే ప్రయాస it is hard to get him to listen to what I say. **ప్రయాసపడు** *pra-yāsa-paḍu.* v. n. To try hard, to take pains, to incur difficulties, to suffer. శ్రమపడు.

ప్రయుక్తము *pra-yuktamu.* [Skt.] adj Endowed with, associated or connected with, applied, employed. గల, కూడుకొన్న, ప్రయోగింపబడిన. See ప్రయోగము.

ప్రయుతము *pra-yutamu.* [Skt.] n. A million. పదిలక్షలు.

ప్రయోగము *pra-yōgamu.* [Skt.] n. An application, use or employment, as of a weapon, tool, word, or a spell. Administration of a medicine, నడపుట. A usage. In grammar, a voice. కర్తృ కర్మ క్రియలకూడిక. మహాబిల్వాదిప్రయోగము a prescription of Bilwa and other drugs. దీనికి కాళిదాసప్రయోగమున్నది Kalidasa has used this word. యక్షిణీప్రయోగముచేయు to bewitch or send a devil into (a person.) ఈ ఔషధప్రయోగముచేసినాడు he administered this medicine. విషప్రయోగముచేసి చంపినాడు he killed him by means of poison.

బాణప్రయోగముచేసినాడు he used an arrow, i.e., discharged it. ప్రయోగించు *pra-yōgintsu.* v. a. To use, practise, administer; use, as a weapon. ఉపయోగించు. ప్రయోజకుడు *pra-yōjakuḍu.* n. One who uses. The original instigator of any act. A clever man, a genius. కార్యమును నెరవేర్చువాడు. వాడు శుద్ధ అప్రయోజకుడు he is quite a useless person. ప్రయోజనము *pra-yōjanamu.* n. Use, advantage, profit. A thing to be kept or observed, as a holy day, or a feast. పండుగ. An affair, business. కార్యము. A cause, motive. హేతువు. శుభప్రయోజనము a happy occasion (as a wedding). రేపు మాయింట్లో కొంచెముప్రయోజనము గనుక రావడానకు వల్లలేదు I cannot come to-morrow as there are some rites to be observed at home. అక్కడికి నీవు పోయినందున ఏమి ప్రయోజనము what is the use (good, or advantage) of your going there? ప్రయోజనప్రస్తుతములకు వారిని మేము పిలువడములేదు we do not invite them to parties. In Grammar, ప్రయోజ్యకర్త the indirect agent (in the instrumental case.) ప్రయోజకకర్త the direct agent (in the nominative case.)

ప్రరోహము *pra-rōhamu.* [Skt.] n. A bud, a shoot, మొలక, అంకురము.

ప్రలంబము *pra-lambamu.* [Skt.] n. A garland of flowers, &c., worn round the neck. హారము. A branch, శాఖ. The female breast, పయోధరము. adj. Hanging down, depending from, pendulous. వ్రేలాడే. ప్రలంబుడు *pra-lambuḍu.* n. The name of a demon. ప్రలంబఘ్నుడు or ప్రలంబవైరి *pra-lamba-ghnuḍu.* n. He who slew the demon ప్రలంబ, an epithet of Balarama, బలరాముడు. ప్రలంబితము *pra-lambitamu.* adj. Suspended, pendulous, hanging. వ్రేలాడే.

ప్రలాపము *pra-lāpamu.* [Skt.] n. Unmeaning or incoherent speech, prattle, mere ejaculation. విలాపము, పలవరము, పలవరింత, అర్థములేనిమాట, అక్కరలేనిమాట. Lamentation, wailing. ప్రలాపించు *pra-lapintsu.* v. n. To use broken words or exclamations. విలపించు, పలవరించు. To lament, wail.

ప్రలోభనము *pra-lōbhanamu.* [Skt.] n. Tempting, seduction. ఆశపెంచడము. A bait to catch animals with, మృగములను పట్టు కొనుటకు పెట్టు మేపు.

ప్రలోభము *pra-lōbhamu.* [Skt.] n. Great selfishness, covetousness, greed, మిక్కిలి లోభము. ప్రలోభించు *pra-lōbhintsu.* v. a. To make one desire eagerly, to allure, ఆసగొనజేయు.

ప్రల్లదము *pralladamu.* [Tel.] n. Harshness of speech, పారుష్యము. Pride, arrogance; bragging, a vain or wicked word, nonsense. కొవ్వు, గర్వము, పనికిమాలిన మాట, దుర్భాషణము. A wicked act, దుష్కృత్యము. "ఈశ్వరునిపల్లభుండెంతయుం ప్రల్ల దంబ్రల్లదంబాడినా." Parij. iii. 71.

> "తే. వెలదిఁజాడంబుపానంబు వేట పలుకు,
> ప్రల్లదంబునుదండంబు పరుసదనము,
> సొమ్మునిష్ప్రయోజనముగనమ్ముసేత,
> యనెడుసప్తవ్యసనములఁజనదుతగుల."
> M. V. ii. 42.

ప్రల్లదనము or ప్రల్లదము *pral-la-danamu.* n Pride, arrogance. గర్వము, అహంకారము, కొవ్వు. "ప్రల్లదనంబుచే నెరుక పాటొకయింతయులేక." Bhāskara. §. 17. ప్రల్లదపు *pralladapu.* adj. Nonsensical, vain, proud. గర్వపు, పనికిమాలిన. "విం టిరివానిప్రల్లదపు వెంగలిమాటలు." T. iv. 220. ప్రల్లదుడు, ప్రల్లదీడు or ప్రల్లదకాడు *pralladuḍu.* n. An insolent man, a rogue. An empty fellow. పరుషవాక్యములు పలుకువాడు, తలకొట్లమారి, దుష్టుడు. "ముచ్చులు ప్రల్లదుల్ చచ్చువారలె యట్లుగాకున్న బాధలు లోకమునకు బుట్టవేయని." M. XII. v. 276. ప్రల్లదురాలు *pralladu-r-ālu.* n. A wicked woman, దుష్టురాలు.

ప్రళయము *pra-layamu.* [Skt. ప్ర+లయము.] n. Destruction. The final destruction of the world. కల్పాంతము. Danger, calamity, అపాయము. Death, మృత్యువు. ప్రళయకాలము an awful or portentous period. జలప్రళయము the Deluge. **ప్రళయముగా** *pra-layamu-gā.* adv. In a flood, in a deluge. Prodigiously, hugely, grandly. ఇంతటిలో వానప్రళయముగా వచ్చినది the rain came in floods. రాజు ప్రళయముగా బయలుదేరినాడు the king set out very grandly. వానిపని బహుప్రళయముగానున్నది he lives in grand style, his business goes on thrivingly. ప్రళయముగా మాట్లాడుతాడు he talks pompously. ఏరు ప్రళయముగా పారుచున్నది the river is rushing furiously.

ప్రవక్త *pra-vakta.* [Skt.] n. One who talks well, an eloquent man, చక్కగా మాట్లాడువాడు. (In Telugu Christian literature), a prophet, రాగలసంగతులను తెలుపువాడు. **ప్రవచనము** *pra-vachanamu.* n. The venerated text, i.e., the Vedas. వేదము. A great or noble word, గొప్పమాట. Teaching, expounding, ప్రకృష్టవచనము. ఇప్పట్లో పాఠ ప్రవచనములు లేవు at present there is neither teaching nor learning. **ప్రవచనీయము** *pra-vachaniyamu.* adj. That which is fit to be well said, చక్కగా మాటాడదగినది.

ప్రవణము *pravaṇamu.* [Skt.] adj. Bent. bowed. వంగిన. Attached to, adhering to, తత్పరతగల. ఆసక్తిగల.

ప్రవర or **ప్రవరము** *pra-vara.* [Skt.] n. A name, పేరు. Offspring, descendants; family, lineage. గోత్రము, సంతతి, కులము. "The *Gotram* is the tribe, containing several *Pravaras.*" **ప్రవరము** *pra-varamu.* adj. Noble, excellent. శ్రేష్ఠమైన. **ప్రవరుడు** *pra-varuḍu.* n. An excellent man. శ్రేష్ఠుడు, మేటి.

ప్రవర్గ్యము *pra-vargyamu* [Skt.] n. A certain ceremony or sacrifice అగ్నిష్టోమ ద్యంగ భూతమైనయాగవిశేషము. **ప్రవర్గ్యుడు** *pra-vargyuḍu.* n. An officiating priest. పురోహితుడు.

ప్రవర్తకుడు *pra-vartakuḍu.* [Skt.] n. One who carries on or manages, నడపువాడు. The original instigator or author of an act, the doer. A manager, or superintendent. కారకుడు, అధికారి. గ్రామప్రవర్తకుడు the manager or agent of a village. ఉభయవేదాంతప్రవర్తకులయిన he who cultivates both systems of theology. **ప్రవర్తన** or **ప్రవర్తనము** *pra-vartana.* n. Conduct, behaviour, నడత, ఆచారము. **ప్రవర్తమానము** *pra-varta-mānamu.* adj. Current, as a year. నడుచుచున్న. **ప్రవర్తించు** or **ప్రవర్తిల్లు** *pra-vartintsu.* v. n. To behave, go on, conduct oneself. దుర్మార్గముగా ప్రవర్తించుచున్నాడు he behaves very ill.

ప్రవర్తులు *pra-vartulu.* [Tel.] n. Purging, diarrhœa. భేదులు, విరేచనములు.

ప్రవర్ధిల్లు *pra-vardhillu.* [Skt.] v. n. To increase, grow, improve, flourish, prosper, మిక్కిలి వృద్ధిపొందు. **ప్రవర్ధించు** *pra-varthintsu.* v. a. To cause to flourish, మిక్కిలి వర్ధిల్లజేయు. **ప్రవర్ధమానము** *pra-vardha-mānamu.* adj. Flourishing, thriving, increasing. మిక్కిలి వృద్ధిపొందుచుండే.

ప్రవహణము *pra-vahaṇamu.* [Skt.] n. A covered carriage or litter. మనుష్యులుమోయువాహనము. అందలము మొదలయినవి.

ప్రవహించు *pra-vahintsu.* [Skt.] v. n. To run or flow, (as a river). పారు. **ప్రవాహము** *pra-vāhamu.* n. A stream, flood, current, వరద, వెల్లువ. Continuous passage or flow, unbroken succession, continuity. పరంపర. **ప్రవాహిక** *pra-vāhika.* n. Diarrhœa, dysentery, అతిసారరోగము, పారేవాలు.

ప్రవాదము *pra-vādamu.* [Skt.] n. A rumour, report, వదంతి.

ప్రవాళము *pra-vāḷamu.* [Skt.] n. A coral, పగడము. A shoot, sprout, new leaf, అంకురము, చిగురు, నవపల్లవము. The neck of a lute, వీణాదండము.

ప్రవాసము *pra-vāsamu.* [Skt.] n. Absence from one's home or land, living abroad, remaining away from home. పరస్థలావాసము, పరదేశగమనము. ప్రవాసముగానుండువాడు or ప్రవాసగతుడు one who is from home.

ప్రవాహము *pra-vāhamu.* See under ప్రవహించు.

ప్రవిమలము *pra-vimalamu.* [Skt.] adj. Most pure, spotless, perfectly innocent. నిర్మలమైన, స్వచ్ఛమైన.

ప్రవిశ్లేషము *pra-viślēshamu.* [Skt.] n. Separating, parting. ఎడబాయడము.

ప్రవిష్టము *pra-vishṭamu.* [Skt.] adj. Entered, gone in, entered upon (as an affair,) engaged in. ప్రవేశించిన, చొరబడిన. ప్రవిష్టుడు *pra-vishṭuḍu.* n. One who entered or has gone in; one who entered upon, or is engaged in. దుర్మార్గప్రవిష్టుడు a man given to evil courses, దుర్మార్గచింతగలవాడు.

ప్రవీణము *pravīṇamu.* [Skt.] adj. Skilful, versed in, conversant. నిపుణతగల. ప్రవీణత or ప్రావీణ్యము *pravīṇata.* n. Cleverness, proficiency, skill, ability. నిపుణత. విద్యాప్రవీణత scholarship. ప్రవీణుడు *pravīṇuḍu.* n. One who is skilful or clever, an expert, నిపుణుడు, నేర్పరి. ఆంధ్రభాషయందు మిక్కిలి ప్రవీణుడయిన highly accomplished in Telugu.

ప్రవృత్తి *pra-vritti.* [Skt.] n. Pace, manner of walking, నడక. Entrance, ప్రవేశము. Means of livelihood, బ్రతుకుతెరువు. A story, వృత్తాంతము. Activity, occupation; conduct, నడవడి. Inclination, design, disposition. ఉద్దేశము, స్వభావము.

ప్రవృద్ధము *pra-vriddhamu.* [Skt.] adj. Full grown, expanded, diffused: spread abroad or dispersed. వృద్ధిపొందిన, అటొకగా చెదిరిన.

ప్రవేశము *pra-vēśamu.* [Skt.] n. An entering upon or engaging in, entrance. చొచ్చుట; చొరవ. ఆ శాస్త్రములో వానికి ప్రవేశములేదు he has no acquaintance with that science. ఆ దొరవద్ద నాకు ప్రవేశములేదు I have no influence with that gentleman. గృహప్రవేశముచేసినారు they have gone to live in their new house. ప్రవేశముకావలెను please to acknowledge the receipt. వర్షాకాల ప్రవేశమైనది the rainy season has now set in. ప్రవేశనము *pra-vēśanamu.* n. Insertion, entering. ప్రవేశపెట్టడము. ప్రవేశపెట్టు *pravēśa-peṭṭu.* v. a. To introduce, instal, induct, admit, enter, entertain or take into service. ప్రవేశించు *pravēś-intsu.* v. n. To enter; to enter on or upon, to interfere in. చొచ్చు.

ప్రవ్రజ్య *pra-vrajya.* [Skt.] n. A roaming, travelling about, (particularly as a religious mendicant.) Abandonment of the world. కార్యార్థపర్యటనము, సన్యాసాశ్రమము. ప్రవ్రజితుడు an ascetic.

ప్రవ్వ *pravva.* [Tel.] n. A pot, కుండ. భాగ. vi.

ప్రశంస *pra-śamsa.* [Skt.] n. Praise, commendation, eulogy. స్తోత్రము, స్తుతి. A subject, topic: mention. ప్రస్తావము. ఆ ప్రశంస తెచ్చినాడుకాడు he made no mention of the matter. ప్రశంసించు *pra-śam-sintsu.* v. a. To praise, స్తుతించు, పొగడు. To mention, allude to, speak of. ప్రస్తావముచేయు. ఆయన పేరును నిర్నిమిత్తముగా ప్రశంసింపరాదు thou shalt not take his name in vain. ప్రశస్తము or ప్రశస్తమైన *pra-śastamu.* adj. Famous, renowned, celebrated, excellent, superior, ప్రసిద్ధమైన,

శ్రేష్ఠమైన. ప్రశస్తి *pra-sasti.* n. Fame, excellence, eminence, eulogy. ప్రసిద్ధి, పొగడిక. ప్రశస్తుడు *pra-sastakudu.* n. A renowned man, one who is famous. ప్రసిద్ధుడు. "అనవిని సర్వశాస్త్రములయందు ప్రశస్తులైనయార్యులకా." Bilh. i. 66.

ప్రశాంతి *pra-santi.* [Skt.] n. Perfect peace of mind, tranquility మిక్కిలిశాంతి. ప్రశాంతుడు *pra-santudu.* n. One who enjoys a perfect peace of mind, మిక్కిలి శాంతి నొందినవాడు.

ప్రశ్న or ప్రశ్నము *prasna.* [Skt.] n. A question, query, demand, inquiry అడుగుట. Divination, by dipping into the Ramayanam; it is like the *Sortes Virgilianæ.* ప్రశ్నార్థకము the interrogative form. ప్రశ్నించు *prasnintsu.* v. a. To question, to ask a question, ప్రశ్న అడుగు, సవాలు చేయు.

ప్రశ్రయము *pra-srayamu.* [Skt.] n. Respect, courtesy, civility. Solicitation. అనునయము, ఔదార్యము, అడుగడము.

ప్రసంగము *pra-sangamu.* [Skt.] n. Addiction to, connection with. A conversation, talk, discussion. ప్రస్తావము, సల్లాపము, సంగతి. Connected reasoning or argument. విషయ విస్తరము, వాదము. A discourse, speech, sermon, lecture. ఆ పండితులు ప్రసంగముచేయుచుండిరి the Pandits were holding a disputation. ఇకను ఆప్రసంగము మానుకొండి have done with that discussion. ప్రసంగ సంగతాన in the course of conversation. అధికప్రసంగము talkativeness. ప్రసంగించు *prasang-intsu.* v. n. To talk about, to discuss, ప్రస్తావించు, వాదించు. To make a speech. ప్రసక్తి *pra-sakti.* n. A topic, or subject of conversation. ఆ ప్రసక్తి నాకు తెలియదు I know nothing about the matter. ప్రసక్తించు *prasakt-intsu.* v. n. To talk about, to be related to (a subject). ప్రస్తావమునకువచ్చు.

ప్రసన్నము *pra-sannamu.* [Skt.] adj. Clear, clean, bright. నిర్మలము. Complacent, pleased, gracious, benignant, సంతోషించిన, సుముఖమైన. ప్రసన్నవదనుడై looking upon them graciously. ప్రసన్నత *prasannata.* n. Clearness, purity. Complacency, benignity, favour, kindness. నిర్మలత్వము, ప్రసాదము, సుముఖత్వము. ప్రసన్నుడు *pra-sannudu.* n. One who is gracious, pleased or delighted. అఖండలక్ష్మీప్రసన్నుడైన he who shines in changeless glory.

ప్రసరము *pra-saramu.* [Skt.] n. Spreading, extending. వ్యాప్తి. వ్యాపనము. వ్యాపించడము. ప్రసరణము *prasaranamu.* n. Going forth or round, extending, spreading. వ్యాపించడము. Surrounding an enemy, అంతట సేన వ్యాపించుట. ప్రసరించు or ప్రసరిల్లు *pra-sarintsu.* v. n. To spread, extend. వ్యాపించు. ప్రసరింపజేయు *prasarimpa-jēyu.* v. a. To cause to extend. వ్యాపించునట్లుచేయు, వ్యాపింపజేయు.

ప్రసవము *pra-savamu.* [Skt.] n. Bringing forth, bearing (as young), parturition. కానుపు. Birth, production, పుట్టుక. A flower, a blossom, పుష్పము. A fruit, పండు. An offspring, child. బిడ్డ. ప్రసవాయాసము the pains of childbed, పురుడు. ప్రసవించు *prasav-intsu.* v. a. To be brought to bed, to bring forth, give birth to, (బిడ్డ) కను.

ప్రసవ్యము *pra-savyamu.* [Skt.] adj. Pertaining to the right hand, కుడి. Pertaining to the left hand, ఎడమది. Favourable, అనుకూలము. Contrary, reverse, inverted, reverted. ప్రతికూలము.

ప్రసాదము *pra-sadamu.* [Skt.] n. Clearness, వైశద్యము Composure of mind. స్వాస్థ్యము. Favour, kindness, grace, అనుగ్రహము.

Food presented to a god or blest by a priest and then distributed in a temple. The remains of an offering thus presented, భగవంతుడులోనగువారిచే భుక్తశేషమైన అన్నము మొదలగునది. మహాప్రసాదము an exclamation implying, "Your pleasure!" "Thy will is our law." ప్రసాదించు prasād-intsu. v. a. To favour. అనుగ్రహించు, ఇచ్చు. "సదమలభక్తి ప్రసాదింపు నాకు" bestow faith upon me.

ప్రసాధనము pra-sādhanamu. [Skt.] n. Dress, embellishment, decoration. వేషవిశేషము, వస్త్రాద్యలంకృతశోభ.

ప్రసారణము pra-sāraṇamu. [Skt.] n. Stretching. చాచుట. Pulling, ఈడుచుట.

ప్రసారము pra-sāramu. [Skt.] n. The act of spreading. వ్యాపనము. See ప్రసరము.

ప్రసిద్ధి pra-siddhi. [Skt.] n. Celebrity, fame, notoriety. ఖ్యాతి. ప్రసిద్ధిగలవాడు a celebrated man. ఈమాట అంతటను ప్రసిద్ధిగానున్నది this story is known everywhere. ప్రసిద్ధము pra-siddhamu. adj. Known, celebrated, ప్రసిద్ధికెక్కిన. ఇది ప్రసిద్ధమయిన కావ్యముకాదు this is not a classical poem. ప్రసిద్ధపత్రిక or ప్రకటనపత్రిక a newspaper, a proclamation, a notification. ప్రసిద్ధిగా pra-siddhi-gā. adv. Confessedly, avowedly, notoriously. అతడు వచ్చునని ప్రసిద్ధిగానున్నది there is a general talk of his coming. ప్రసిద్ధిచేయు or ప్రసిద్ధపరచు to publish, or make known.

ప్రసూత or ప్రసూతిక pra-sūta. [Skt.] n. A woman in childbed. బాలెంతరాలు. ప్రసూతి pra-suti. n. Childbed, parturition, bringing forth young, labour. బిడ్డకనడము, కానుపు. Birth, పుట్టుక. A child, బిడ్డ.

ప్రసూనము pra-sūnamu. [Skt.] n. A flower-blossom. పుష్పము.

ప్రసృతము pra-sṛitamu. [Skt.] adj. Stretched, lengthened. కొనసాగించబడిన. Dispersed, extended, spread abroad. ప్రవృద్ధము. ప్రసృతి pra-sṛiti. n. The palm of the hand hollowed so as to hold liquids. పుడిసిలి, చేర.

ప్రసేవకము pra-sēvakamu. [Skt.] n. The globes of a lute. వీణకడెలు.

ప్రస్తరము prastaramu. [Skt.] n. A stone, రాయి. A jewel, a precious stone, రత్నము, మణి.

ప్రస్తరించు prastarintsu. [Skt.] v. n. To spread, extend, విస్తరించు. To arrange prosodial feet. ఛందః ప్రస్తారముచేయు. ప్రస్తారము prastāramu. n. A canon, scheme, or formula. A diagram or figure used in magic. గణప్రస్తారము the combination of syllables in forming prosodial feet, ఛందశ్శాస్త్రప్రత్యయభేదము.

ప్రస్తవము pra-stavamu. [Skt.] n. That which concerns one, an object, విషయము.

ప్రస్తావము pra-stāvamu. [Skt.] n. An opportunity, occasion, కార్యోచితసమయము, అవసరము. A conversation, narration, mentioning. Mention. Incidental reference to a person or thing, ఒకనినిగూర్చి మాటయెత్తడము, ప్రకటించుట, చెప్పుట. ప్రస్తావించు prastāvintsu. v. n. To tell in the course of conversation, to talk about, ప్రస్తావమునకుతెచ్చు. ప్రస్తాపము or ప్రస్తాపన prastāpamu. (corruption of ప్రస్తావము.) ఆ సంగతిని నాతో ప్రస్తాపముచేసినాడు he made a mention of this to me. వాడు ఆ ప్రస్తాపమెత్తలేదు he did not mention it.

ప్రస్తుతము pra-stutamu. [Skt.] adj. Much praised, mentioned; present. adv. At present, just now. ప్రస్తుతముజరిగేపనియేమి what is going on at present? ప్రస్తుతపు కార్యము the present affair, the business in hand. ప్రస్తుతము దీన్ని తీసుకో take this for the present. ప్రస్తుతము or శుభప్రస్తుతము pra-stutamu. n. A festive rite. ప్రస్తుతి pra-stuti. n. Great applause or praise. మిక్కిలి స్తోత్రము. ప్రస్తుతించు pra-stutintsu. v. a. To praise or applaud greatly, మిక్కిలి స్తోత్రముచేయు.

ప్రస్థము prasthamu. [Skt.] n. A measure of quantity equal to four Kunchams or forty-eight double handfuls. చతుష్కుడుపప్రమాణము, నాలుగుకుంచములు. A tableland on the top of a mountain, కొండపైతట్టు.

ప్రస్థానము pra-sthānamu. [Skt.] n. A setting out upon a journey. ప్రయాణము, తరలిపోవడము. M. IV. i. 137. M. XII. iii. 307. ప్రస్థానభేరి the great drum sounded when a march commences.

ప్రస్థాపించు pra-sthāpintsu. [Skt.] v. a. To fix well or firmly, to establish, చక్కగా నిలుపు.

ప్రస్ఫుటము pra-sphuṭamu. [Skt.] adj. Blown, expanded. వికసించిన.

ప్రస్ఫురత్ pra-sphurat. [Skt.] adj. Bright, brilliant.

ప్రస్యందము pra-syandamu. [Skt.] adj. Going quick. "సరభస్వర్భటకటుపటుల ప్రస్యందంబైనవానలా." N. I. 115. టీ॥ ప్రస్యందంబైన, అతివేగమైన.

ప్రస్వేదము pra-svēdamu. [Skt.] n. Great sweat, excessive perspiration. మహత్తైన చెమట.

ప్రహతము pra-hatamu. [Skt.] adj. Struck. కొట్టబడ్డ. Wounded, killed, defeated.

ప్రహరము pra-haramu. [Skt.] n. A watch (of about three hours), జాము. A blow, దెబ్బ. ఆ పిల్లవానికి నిండా ప్రహరములు తగిలినవి the boy was well thrashed. ప్రహరణము pra-haraṇamu. n. A weapon. ఆయుధము. ప్రహరించు pra-harintsu. v. a. To smite, beat. కొట్టు.

ప్రహరి or ప్రహరిగోడ prahari. [from Skt.] n. The boundary wall of a house, garden, &c., Parij. iv. 86. ప్రాకారము, చుట్టుగోడ. ప్రహరిచరించు, ప్రహరితిర్గు or ప్రహరితిరుగు prahari-charintsu. v. n. To walk or go round a boundary wall, ప్రదక్షిణించు, చుట్టివచ్చు. వసు. iv. కాశీ. i. ఖి. i. To go the rounds, to patrol, కట్టి తిరుగు.

ప్రహసనము pra-hasanamu. [Skt.] n. Violent or hearty laughter, mirth. ప్రకృష్టహసనము, పెద్దనవ్వు. Ridicule, పరిహాసము. A farce, a burlesque. నాటకగ్రంథభేదము. ప్రహసించు pra-hasintsu. v. n. To laugh out-right, పెద్దనవ్వునవ్వు.

ప్రహారము or ప్రహరము pra-hāramu. [Skt.] n. Striking, destroying. A blow, దెబ్బ. మానమద ప్రహారము annihilation of pride and passion. M. I. 1. 218.

ప్రహి prahi. [Skt.] n. A well. బావి.

ప్రహితము pra-hitamu. [Skt.] adj. Sent, discharged as from a bow. వింటినుండి విడువబడిన.

ప్రహృష్టము pra-hrishṭamu. [Skt.] adj Glad, pleased, delighted.

ప్రహేళిక pra-hēlika. [Skt.] n. A puzzle, a riddle. గూఢార్థవత్ కావ్యము.

ప్రహ్లాదము pra-hlādamu. [Skt.] n. Joy pleasure, సంతోషము.

ప్రా prā

ప్రా prā. [Tel.] adj. In compounds, short for ప్రాత. Old, ancient, పురాతనమైన. Excellent, శ్రేష్ఠమైన. ప్రాయిల్లు an old house. ప్రాయేరు the ancient stream, i. e., the sea, సముద్రము. ప్రాగబ్బము pra-gabbamu. (ప్రాత+కబ్బము) n. The Veda. ప్రాగెంపు an excellent ruby, మంచికెంపు. ప్రాబచ్చ an excellent emerald, శ్రేష్ఠమైనపచ్చ. ప్రాబడు (ప్రాత+పడు) Same as ప్రాతపడు (q. v.). ప్రాబసిడి excellent gold. ప్రామ్రి an old banyan tree. ప్రావేలుపు or ప్రావేల్పు an ancient god, i. e., an Asura, అసురుడు, పూర్వదేవుడు. ప్రావేదము పులు, ప్రాబలుకులు or ప్రాబల్కులు pra-ḍeuduvulu. n. The Veda. ప్రాబూరులు ancient wilds, old grass lands. ప్రాడౌటు pra-ḍautu. n. An old cap. పాతకుళ్లాయి. "బూదిబ్రుంగిన మొగంబుః గొడకట్టు. మైనపుమైలప్రాడౌటునా పెంపగా." A. vi. 104. ప్రామినుకులు or ప్రామిన్కులు pra-minukulu. n. plu. The Vedas: lit: the ancient words, వేదము.

ప్రాంగణము pr-anganamu. [Skt.] n. A courtyard, ముంగిలిప్రదేశము.

ప్రాంచత్ pr-anchat. [Skt.] adj. Brilliant, shining. ప్రకాశించే.

ప్రాంతము pr-antamu. [Skt.] n. An edge, margin, border, bank. సమీపము. Nearness, neighbourhood, సమీపము. A region, district. ప్రాంత్యము prantyamu. (corruption of ప్రాంతము) n. Neighbourhood, neighbouring places or parts. ప్రాంతరము prantaramu. n. A boundary, పొలిమేర. A forest, అడవి.

ప్రాంశువు pramsuvu. [Skt.] adj. High, tall, lofty. ఉన్నతమైన, పొడుగైన.

ప్రాక్ prak. [Skt.] n. The East. తూర్పుదిక్కు. adj. Before, prior, preceding in place or time, past, gone. Eastern. ముందరి, గడిచిన, తూర్పుసంబంధమైన. adv. Formerly, of old. మునుపు, ముందర. ప్రాక్తనము prak-tanamu. adj. Ancient, of old days. పురాతనమైన.

ప్రాక n. Same as పాక (q. v.). ఓరప్రాక a verandah.

ప్రాకటము or ప్రకటము prakatamu. [Skt.] adj. Displayed, manifest, apparent, public, famous, ప్రసిద్ధమైన. "ప్రాకటసత్కవిత్వ పరిపాటిని లోకమువారిరుండగా." T. Intro. 19. ప్రాకటముగా prakatamu-ga. adv. Publicly, notoriously. ప్రసిద్ధముగా.

ప్రాకామ్యము pra-kamyamu. [Skt.] n. Freedom of will; wilfulness, following or obeying one's own will or inclination. An irresistible will or fiat, one of Siva's eight attributes; శివలీలావిభూతి భేదము.

ప్రాకారము pr-akaramu. [Skt.] n. An enclosure, a fence, a rampart, a surrounding wall. చుట్టుగోడ, ప్రహరి. "శ్రీశైలభీమ కాళేశ మహేంద్రగిరిసంయుతం, ప్రాకారంతు మహత్కృత్వా త్రిలింగ్వారాణిచాకరోత్." ఆంధ్రకౌముది, i.e., He made these mountains as a great boundary wall, wherein there were three entrances.

ప్రాకు or పాకు praku. [Tel.] v. n. To mount up, to get up, to climb, ఎక్కు. To creep, crawl, రొమ్ముతో జరుగు. To climb, as a vine. n. A prop for a creeper to climb on, తీగ పాకుటకు దగ్గరపాతినకొయ్య. Dirt, stain, మాలిన్యము. Moss, పాచి. ప్రాకుడు prakuḍu. n. The act of climbing, పాకుట. ప్రాకుడెంచు praku-dentsu. v. n. Same as ప్రాకు. ప్రాకులాడు prakul-adu. v. n. To mount by climbing up, ప్రాకియెక్కు. ప్రాకొను pra-konu. (ప్రాకు+కొను) v. n. To be covered with moss, పాచిపట్టు.

ప్రాకృతము pr-akritamu. [Skt.] adj. Low, common, vulgar. నీచమైన. n. The colloquial or vernacular language derived directly from Sanskrit. ప్రాకృతుడు pr-akrituḍu. n. A boor, clown, or rustic. పామరుడు.

ప్రాకెణ, ప్రాకెన్న or **పాకెన్న** *prākena.* [Tel.] n. A particular ceremony observed on the third day of a marriage. పెండ్లిలో మూడవనాటిచేయుకృత్యము.

ప్రాగల్భ్యము *pra-galbhyamu.* [Skt. from ప్రగల్భము.] n. Skilfulness, cleverness. ప్రౌఢిమ, సామర్థ్యము, ప్రగల్భత్వము.

ప్రాచి *prāchi.* [Skt from పురా front.] n. The East. తూర్పుదిక్కు. Moss, పాచి. Dirt, filth, mouldiness, sliminess, as upon a stone near water. నాచినట్టు. **ప్రాచీనము** *prāchīnamu.* adj. Eastern, placed towards the East. పూర్వదిక్కుది. Ancient, old. పూర్వ కాలపుది. **ప్రాచీనబర్హి** *prāchīna-barhi.* n. An epithet of Indra. ఇంద్రుడు. **ప్రాచీనావీతము** *prāchīn-āvītamu.* n. The sacerdotal thread, worn (contrary to custom) over the right arm, and passing under the left. అపసవ్యముగా వేసికొన్న జందెము. **ప్రాచ్యము** *prāchyamu* adj. Eastern, easterly, తూర్పుదిక్కునందలిది. n. The country south or east of the Sarasvati. శరావత్యవధి ప్రాగ్దక్షిణదేశము.

ప్రాచిత్తము *prāchittamu.* [from Skt. ప్రాయశ్చిత్తము.] n. Expiation. ప్రాయశ్చిత్తము.

ప్రాచీరము *prāchīramu.* [Skt.] n. A bound, hedge, fence, wall, an enclosure, a rampart. కంచె, కోట.

ప్రాచుర్యము *prāchuryamu.* [Skt. from ప్రచురము.] adj. Excessive, enormous. బహుళమైన. Jaganna. I. 40. n. Abundance, plenty, బాహుళ్యము, ప్రచురత్వము.

ప్రాచేతసుడు *prā-chētasudu.* [Skt. lit. Son of ప్రచేతసుడు.] n. An epithet of వాల్మీకి.

ప్రాజాపత్యము *prājā-patyamu.* [Skt. from ప్రజాపతి.] n. Influence, authority, power. అధికారము. A kind of sacrifice, ఇష్టిభేదము. A form of marriage, మీరిద్దరు కూడి ధర్మముచేయుడని పెండ్లికొడుకుతో చెప్పి కన్యనిచ్చి చేయు వివాహము.

ప్రాజ్ఞుడు *prāgnyudu.* [Skt. from ప్రజ్ఞ.] n. A sage, a wise, or learned man. పండితుడు. An able man, సమర్థుడు. **ప్రాజ్ఞ** or **ప్రాజ్ఞి** *prāgnya.* n. A wise or clever woman.

ప్రాజ్యము *prājyamu.* [Skt.] adj. Much, many. విస్తారమైన, అధికమైన.

ప్రాడ్వివాకుడు *prāḍ-vivākudu.* [Skt.] n. A judge. వ్యవహారదర్శి, సభాపతి.

ప్రాణము *prāṇamu.* [Skt.] n. Air, wind, breath, life, vitality, the living soul. గాలి, హృదయమందలిగాలి, ఉసురు. In Grammar, a vowel. ప్రాణముతోనున్నవాడు one who is yet living కొనప్రాణముతోనున్నాడు he is nearly dead. ప్రాణమువిడిచెను he breathed his last, gave up the ghost. **పంచప్రాణములు** *pancha-prāṇamulu.* n. The five vital airs, called ప్రాణము, అపానము, సమానము, ఉదానము, వ్యానము. అతడు దానిమీద ప్రాణములు విడుస్తున్నాడు or వానికి దానిమీద పంచప్రాణములు he loves her very dearly. ప్రాణముమీదవచ్చేపని a most perilous affair. వానిప్రాణము మీదికి వచ్చినది he is in danger of his life. ప్రాణముతో పట్టుకొనిరి they caught him alive. నాప్రాణముపోయినా ఇట్లు చెప్పను I will not say so even if it should cost me my life. వాడు పిడికిట ప్రాణములు పట్టుకొని వచ్చినాడు he arrived half dead. వానికి నేర్పుట ప్రాణసంకటమవును it would cost immense labour to teach him. ఆ విగ్రహమునకు ప్రాణప్రతిష్ఠచేసినారు literally, they gave life to the image, i.e., they performed the ceremony by which the god is supposed to be lodged in the image. ప్రాణత్యాగము suicide, ఆత్మహత్య. ప్రాణాంతకము or ప్రాణసంకటము deadly peril. "ప్రాణాతురమైనచో పరిణయంబులయందును బొల్లు పొంకు సత్యాతిశయంబు." M. III. v. 67.

ప్రాణాపాయము mortal danger. ప్రాణావనము saving the life. ప్రాణావసానకాలమున in his last moments. ప్రాణాహుతి the five morsels offered to the five vital principles. ప్రాణస్నేహము intimate friendship. ప్రాణదానముచేసినాడు he gave them their lives, he spared their lives. నా ప్రాణము ఉండేవట్టుకు as long as I live. ప్రాణగొడ్డము *prāna-goddamu*. n. The loss of life, death. చేవు, ప్రాణహాని, ప్రాణాపాయము. "వినుమపరాజ్యమిమనుంగొనవలవు రచేత ప్రాణగొడ్డంబైయున్నను ధీరుడేమరమినది దనకునుదక్కించుకొను బుధస్తుత్యముగాదా." M. XII. ii. 208. ప్రాణదుడు *prāna-dudu*. n. The giver of life, the creator. బ్రహ్మ. ప్రాణనాథుడు or ప్రాణేశుడు *prāna-nādhudu*. n. The lord of (her) life, i. e., a husband or lover, మగడు. Yama, యమధర్మరాజు. ప్రాణవాయువు *prāna-vāyuvu*. n. Oxygen gas. ప్రాణాచారము *prāna-chāramu*. See ప్రాణోపవేశము. ప్రాణాయామము *prāna-yāmamu*. n. A ritual mode of breathing, while mentally reciting certain prayers, stopping one nostril and inhaling or exhaling with the other: నాసికారంధ్రము లవద్దనుండు వాయువును మంత్రపూర్వకముగా నిరోధించుట. A. iii. 88. ప్రాణి *prāni*. n. A being, or living creature. జంతువు.

ప్రాత or పాత *prāta*. [Tel.] adj. Old, ancient. పురాతనమైన, పూర్వము. Worn out, జీర్ణమైన. ప్రాతందలము an old palanquin, పాతది అయిన అందలము. A. ii. 121. ప్రాత or ప్రాతవాడు. n. A servant. సేవక, భృత్యుడు. "ప్రాతివానినిస్మరాదర్థగృహములు" G. xi. i. 103. A cloth, వస్త్రము, పాత. An old cloth, పాతబట్ట. ప్రాతగిల్లు, ప్రాతగిలు, పాతగిల్లు, పాతగిలు, ప్రాబడు, ప్రాతపడు or పాతబడు *prātagillu*. v. n. To become old, పాతదియగు. See under ప్రా. and పాత.

ప్రాతః *prātaha*. [Skt.] adv. In the morning, at dawn. తెల్లవారి. ప్రాతఃకాలము early in the morning. ప్రాతర్వాయువు a morning breeze. ప్రాతస్స్నానము bathing in the morning.

ప్రాతికూల్యము *prāti-kulyamu*. [Skt. from ప్రతికూలము.] n. Contradiction, opposition. విరుద్ధము, ప్రతికూలత్వము, అనుకూలముకామి.

ప్రాతిపదికము *prāti-padikamu*. [Skt.] n. A crude Sanskrit root, a word in its uninflected form. ధాతువు, ప్రకృతి.

ప్రాథమికుడు *prāthamikudu*. [Skt. from ప్రథమము.] n. The first man, a chief man, ప్రథముడు. ప్రాథమ్యము *prāthamyamu*. n. Importance, ప్రథమత్వము.

ప్రాదుర్భవించు *prādur-bhavintsu*. [Skt.] v. n. To appear, to become manifest. అగుపడు, ప్రత్యక్షమగు. To be born, పుట్టు. ప్రాదుర్భావము *prādur-bhāvamu*. n. Appearing, manifestation. అగుపడడము, ప్రత్యక్షము. Birth. పుట్టుక.

ప్రాదేశము *prādēsamu*. [Skt.] n. The span from the thumb to the fore-finger. జాడితెడు.

ప్రాధాన్యము *prādhānyamu*. [Skt. from ప్రధానము.] n. Supremacy, dominion. ముఖ్యత, ప్రధానత్వము.

ప్రాధేయపడు *prādhēya-padu*. [Skt.] v. n. To beseech, మిక్కిలి ఆశతో వేడుకొను.

ప్రాపించు *prāpintsu*. [Skt.] v. a. To obtain, get, attain to. పొందు. ప్రాపు *prāpu*. n. A prop. A protection, support, a refuge; patronage; a person on whom one depends, ఆసరా, ఆశ్రయము. ఆయనప్రాపున మన్నాము we are under his protection. ప్రాప్తము *prāptamu*. adj. Obtained, gained, acquired, received, procured, caught, as a disease. పొందబడిన. [illegible]

అతనికి ప్రాప్తమైనందున because he caught the leprosy. n. That which is obtained, that which falls to one's lot, luck, fortune. నా ప్రాప్తమింతే this is all I can get, such is my luck. ప్రాప్తి prâpti. n. Obtaining, attaining, . పొందడము. Gain, profit, లాభము. One of the eight superhuman faculties, the power of obtaining every thing one desires. అష్టైశ్వర్యములలో నొకటి. Luck, fortune. అదృష్టము. వానికి అంతే ప్రాప్తి this is all he can get. దాని ప్రాప్తి అట్లు ఉండినది such was her luck. నీకు అది ప్రాప్తిలేదు you were not fortunate enough to get it. ప్రాప్తించు prâptintsu. v. n. To happen or occur; to be gained, obtained, found. కలుగు, లభించు. వానికి రోగము ప్రాప్తించినది he contracted or caught a disease. ప్రాప్తుడు prâptuḍu. n. One who has attained. వారు వైకుంఠ ప్రాప్తులైరి they went to Vishnu's heaven, i. e., they died. ప్రాప్యము prâpyamu. adj. Attainable, procurable, that may be got, పొందదగిన. ప్రాపకము prâpakamu. n. Protection, patronage, refuge. అవలంబము, అవష్టంభము, ఆసరా. ప్రాపకుడు prâpakuḍu. n. One who puts an object within our power or reach. ఘటకుడు. A patron, protector, guardian.

ప్రాబల్యము pra-balyamu. [Skt. from ప్రబలము.] n. Power, vigour, predominance. ప్రబలత్వము. ఇప్పుడు క్రీస్తుమతము ప్రాబల్యములో నున్నది the Christian religion has now the predominance. ప్రాబల్యముగా pra-balyamu-ga. adv. Predominantly.

ప్రాభవము prâbhavamu. [Skt. from ప్రభవము.] n. Pre-eminence, supremacy, dominion. ప్రభుత్వము, దొరతనము.

ప్రామాణికము prâmâṇikamu. [Skt. from ప్రమాణము.] adj. Based on authority, authoritative. Credible. True, just, fair, right, faithful, equitable, యథార్థమైన.

ప్రామాణికుడు prâmâṇikuḍu. n. A veracious man. యథార్థవాది, సత్యముతప్పనివాడు. An authority in any science, శాస్త్రము తెలిసినవాడు. ప్రామాణ్యము prâmâṇyamu. n. Authority, proof, దృష్టాంతము. Evidence, సాక్ష్యము. Authenticity, credibility.

ప్రామిడి prâmiḍi. [Tel.] n. Fraud, deceit. మోసము, భ్రమ. Cruelty, క్రౌర్యము. A cruel person, క్రూరుడు, క్రూరురాలు. adj. Cruel, క్రూరము. "బంకెరంకెలల్, సచ్చిరక్కసులు, రొమ్ములగుంపట్లు, కోరప్రామిడ్లు." Charitr. ii. 1551.

ప్రాము or పాము prâmu. [Tel.] v. a. To rub, రాచు. To daub, పూయు, పులుము, రుద్దు. To cover, మూయు. To wipe, తుడుచు. To trouble, harass, పీడించు. To cut to pieces, ఖండించు. ప్రాముడు prâmuḍu. n. The act of rubbing anything, పులుముట. "ప్రాముజఠరాగ్నిచేకింకరోమియుణచు." H. i. 223. ప్రాముజఠరాగ్ని, మలిబెట్టె ఆకలి.

ప్రాయము prâyamu. [Skt.] n. Age, time of life, జీవితకాలము, ఈడు, వయస్సు. Puberty, youth, prime, bloom. యౌవనము. లేప్రాయము fresh age. ప్రాయపువాడు a young man. ప్రాయపుది a young woman. A preparation for dying దేహత్యాగార్థవ్రతము, ప్రాయోపవేశము. Death, చావు. Exceeding much, a multitude, సమూహము, బాహుళ్యము. adj. (used in composition.) Like, resembling, సమానము. పశుప్రాయుడు a brutish man. మృతప్రాయుడు one who is as good as dead. అది వానికి తృణప్రాయము he values it no more than a straw. వానికి అబద్ధము తీర్థప్రాయము telling lies is all his delight. ప్రాయశః prâyaśah. adv. Frequently, for the most part. బహుళా. ప్రాయశ్చిత్తము prâyaś-

chittamu. n. Expiation, propitiation, penance, absolution, recompense, retribution, పాపపరిహారముకొరకు చేయుకర్మము. అంత్యప్రాయశ్చిత్తము certain expiatory ceremonies performed over a dying person. తనకొమారునికి ప్రాయశ్చిత్తముచేయించినాడు he had his son purified by expiatory rites. ప్రాయోపవేశము or ప్రాయానాహారము *pray-ōpavēṣamu.* n. Fasting in order to die, starving to death voluntarily. పస్తుపడియుండి ప్రాణమును విడిచిపెట్టుట మనేవ్రతము ప్రాయోపవేశముచేయు or ప్రాయానాహారముచేయు *pray-ōpavēṣamu-chēyu.* v. n. To meet death by fasting in fulfilment of a vow.

ప్రాయి *prayi.* [Tel.] n. Manliness, పౌరుషము. Wealth, fortune, prosperity, భాగ్యము, సౌమంగల్యము. ప్రాయుడి *prayiḍi.* (ప్రాయి+ఇడి.) n. One who has no manliness, పౌరుషహీనుడు. A humble or poor man, దీనుడు. Misfortune, భాగ్యహీనము. Poverty, దీనత్వము

ప్రాయికము *prāyikamu.* [Skt.] adj. Frequent, general, usual, ordinary, common. సామాన్యము.

ప్రారంభము *Pr-ārambhamu.* [Skt.] n. Commencement, beginning. మొదలుపెట్టుటము. An attempt, యత్నము. ప్రారంభించు *pr-ārambhinṭsu.* v. n. To begin, ఆరంభించు. To attempt, యత్నించు. ప్రారబ్ధము *pr-ārabdhamu.* adj. Begun, ప్రారంభించబడిన. n. Destiny, luck, fortune, predestination, పురాకృతము. ప్రారబ్ధకర్మానుభవము suffering the consequences of original sin.

ప్రారాజత్ *pra-rajyat.* [Skt.] adj. Shining. వెలుగుచుండే. "మణిగణప్రాసాదాగాళ ప్రారాజత్ప్రభాదిక్కు." Swa. vi. 107.

ప్రారూఢి *pr-ārūḍhi.* [Skt.] n. Fame, notoriety. ప్రసిద్ధి. Determination, resolution. నిశ్చయము. "ధయుక్తిప్పల్లవాగుంబిరాశ్లేషిలను ప్రారూఢికెక్కె." Vasu. iii. 138. టీ॥ ప్రారూఢి, నిశ్చయభావము.

ప్రార్థన or ప్రార్థనము *pr-ārthana.* [Skt.] n. Asking, begging, prayer, supplication. అడుగుట, యాచన. A vow. ప్రార్థనార్థకము the Imperative mood, as showing entreaty. ప్రార్థనచేసికొను *pr-ārthana-chēsi-konu.* v. n. To pray. To vow. ప్రార్థకుడు *pr-ārthakuḍu.* n. One who prays or asks. ప్రార్థించు *pr-ārthinṭsu.* v. a. To ask, beg, pray or supplicate. అడుగు. యాచించు. ప్రార్థనీయము *pr-ārthanīyamu.* adj. Fit to be asked or begged. ప్రార్థితము *pr-ārthitamu.* adj. Asked, begged, solicited. అడుగబడ్డ. యాచించబడ్డ. ప్రార్థితుడు *pr-ārthituḍu.* n. One who is begged, or entreated. అడుగబడ్డవాడు, యాచించబడ్డవాడు.

ప్రాలంబము or ప్రాలంబిక *pr-ālambamu.* [Skt.] n. A garland, necklace. మెడుగా వేసుకొన్న పూలదండ, పేరు, గొలుసు.

ప్రాలు *pralu.* [Tel. plu. of ప్రాయి. (q v.) n. Rice. బియ్యము. Consecrated rice, తలబ్రాలు, అక్షతలు. "ఎసటబ్రాలిడ నుచ్చుటకెగజను.." Chamatkar. iii. "జనము గొల్లగ డందెత్తుమని నిమాట, చీలతిపల్లడి వెన ప్రాలపంగ." Parij. ii. 43. దీవనప్రాలు, అనగా శోభనాక్షతలు.

ప్రాలుమాలు, ప్రాల్మాలు or పాలుమాలు *pralu-malu.* [Tel.] v. n. To be idle, indisposed, unwell. సోమరియగుమూరాదు. ప్రాలుమాలిక, ప్రాల్మాలిక or పాలుమాలిక *pralu-malika.* n. Idleness, indisposition, ill-health, సోమరితనము.

ప్రాలేయము *pralēyamu* [Skt.] n. Snow frost. మంచు, హిమము, నీహారము. ప్రాలేయాద్రి the hill of snow, i.e., Himalaya.

ప్రావ *prāva*. [Tel.] n. Convenience. అను కూలము, సౌందర్యము. Fault, evil influence, దోషము. "సీ॥ త్రిజగజ్జనులకుపరిపతి నాశ్రయు మైసాగిన ప్రావ యాచార్యసేవ." Vaijayanti ii. 109. ఆకవనములో సుకప్రావ తగిలి వాడు చచ్చినాడు the venom of the verse smote him and he died.

ప్రావారము or ప్రావరణము *pr-āvāramu*. [Skt.] n. An upper or outer garment. పైబట్ట, ఉత్తరీయము.

ప్రావీణ్యము *prāvīṇyamu*. [Skt. from ప్రవీణము.] n. Cleverness, skilfulness. నేర్పు, ప్రవీణత్వము. ప్రావీణ్యుడు *pravīnyudu*. n. A clever person. వేటలో ప్రావీణ్యుడై being expert in the chase.

ప్రావు Same as పరివు (q.

ప్రావృట్టు or ప్రావృష *prāvṛittu*. [Skt.] n. The rainy season వర్షాకాలము, వర్షఋతువు. ప్రావృషిజము *pravrishijamu*. n. A frog, as being 'produced by rain.' కప్ప. ప్రావృషేణ్యము *pravrishēnyamu*. adj. Of the rains, produced in the rainy season. వర్షాకాలసంబంధమైన, వానకాలమందుపుట్టే. "ప్రావృషేణ్య జలదానీతవర్ణుడు." M. I. vi. 253. n. A tree called *Nauclea cadamba*. నీపే or మొగులుకడిమి.

ప్రావృతము *pr-avritamu*. [Skt.] n. A veil, cloak, mantle. కప్పుకొనేబట్ట.

ప్రావృషాయణి *prāvrishāyani*. [Skt.] n. Cowach, *Carpopogon pruriens*. దూలగొండి.

ప్రాశనము *prāsanamu*. [Skt.] n. Tasting, eating. Feeding, causing to taste or eat, భోజనము. ఆ బిడ్డకు అన్నప్రాశనముచేసినారు they performed the ceremony of first giving solid food to the infant. ప్రాశించు *prāsintsu*. v. a. To eat, భుజించు. To drink, త్రాగు. ప్రాశితము *prāsitamu*. adj. Eaten, భుజింపబడిన. Drunk, పానముచేయబడిన.

ప్రాశస్త్యము *prāsastyamu*. [Skt. from ప్రశస్తము.] n. Excellence, ప్రశస్తత్వము.

ప్రాశ్నికుడు *prāsnakudu*. [Skt. from ప్రశ్న.] n. One who asks a question, ప్రశ్నచేయువాడు.

ప్రాసగు *prāsagu*. [Tel.] adj. Old, పాతగిలిన. "పలుకలచేరినప్రాసంగుల్లాలు, నలువడను మ్నాట యురువదిపుట్లు." BD. v. 1229. అనగా బల్లలమీద చేర్చబడిన పాతబియ్యము. n. Old grain, పాతధాన్యము.

ప్రాసము *prāsamu*. [Skt.] n. The second letter of each verse, the rhyming letter, పద్యపాదమున రెండవ అక్షరము. Alliteration, a rhyme. A barbed dart or lance, ఈటె.

ప్రాసవము *prāsavamu*. [Skt. from ప్రసవము.] adj. Appertaining to parturition, or childbirth. Pertaining to a flower. ప్రాసవాయాసము the pains of childbirth ప్రసవవేదన. Chenna. i. 210.

ప్రాసాదము *prāsādamu*. [Skt.] n. A temple. దేవళము, దేవతాగృహము. A palace. రాజగృహము, నగరు.

ప్రాహ్ణము *prāhnamu*. [Skt. ప్రా+అహ్నము.] n. The forenoon. పగటియొక్క మొదటిభాగము, తెలగులు.

ప్రి pri

ప్రిదులు *pridulu*. [Tel.] v. n. To break, విరుగు. To decrease, తగ్గు. To become loose, to grow slack. సడలు, వదులగు, To fall off, as a veil. జారు. To separate, leave each other, drop off, విడుచు, ఊడు. To be dislocated, తొలగు "ప్రిదులనికౌర్యసంపదల బెట్టినదండలు త్రిప్పకేకడుజాగరుమును." KP. viii. 109. ప్రిదలక closely, continually. ప్రిదలని unshaken, firm, unbroken.

ప్రియము *priyamu*. [Skt.] adj. Dear, beloved, desired. ఇష్టమైన. Dear or high, in price. ప్రియవచనములు చెప్పి దాన్ని తీసికొని వచ్చినాను by using fair words I brought her. n. Love, desire, affection, friendship, ప్రేమ. Joy, సంతోషము. ప్రియములాడు to be kind, to speak kindly. కరణాలకు సలాములు కాపులకు ప్రియము చెప్పవలెను give my respects to the clerks and kind regard to the farmers; (as in English give my love to, &c.) ప్రియకము *priya-kamu*. n. A tree called *Nauclea cadamba*. కదంబవృక్షము. ప్రియత *priyata*. n. Friendship, love, స్నేహము, ప్రేమ. ప్రియపడు or ప్రియంపడు *priya-padu*. v. n. To like, to be pleased, ఇష్టపడు. ప్రియవాది or ప్రియంవదుడు *priya-vadi*. n. A fair speaker, one who speaks what is pleasing, a flatterer. హితముమచెప్పేవాడు, ఇచ్చకము లాడువాడు. ప్రియాళువు *priyaluvu*. n. A tree called మొరిలిచెట్టు. ప్రియుడు *priyudu*. n. A lover, a husband, a friend, ఇష్టమైన వాడు, పెనిమిటి. ప్రియ *priya*. n. A beloved woman. ప్రియురాలు.

ప్రి pri

ప్రీణనము *prinanamu*. [Skt.] n. Satisfaction, satisfying, gratification. తృప్తిపొందించడము, సంతోషపెట్టడము.

ప్రీతి *priti*. [Skt.] n. Joy, pleasure, delight, happiness, love, affection, regard. సంతోషము, స్నేహము. The name of the wife of Manmadha, మన్మథునిభార్య. దేవునికి ప్రీతిగా చేసిరి they did it in honour of the god, for the purpose of conciliating the god. ముఖప్రీతిమాటలు feigned or flattering words. ఆచార్యులవారికి ప్రీతిగా ఈ గ్రామము ఇచ్చినారు they bestowed this village on him as a compliment. తల్లికి ప్రీతిగా ఈ దానముచేసినాడు he gave this in honour of his mother. శనిప్రీతిచేసినాడు he did this to avert the evil influence of Saturn. విష్ణుప్రీతిభూములు lands consecrated to Vishnu. ప్రీతిదత్తము *priti-dattamu*. n. A dowry given to a bride by her father-in-law or mother-in-law. ప్రీతుడు *pritudu*. n. One who is pleased or satisfied, ప్రీతిపొందినవాడు.

ప్రు pru

ప్రుంగుడు *prungudu*. [Tel.] n. White leprosy, తెల్లకుష్ఠము.

ప్రుచ్చు or పుచ్చు *prutstsu*. [Tel.] v. n. To rot, పుచ్చిపోవు. ప్రుప్పి or పుప్పి *pruppi*. n. Rottenness, rotting, పుచ్చిపోవుట. A flaw in a precious stone, ఒకవిధమైన మణిదోషము.

ప్రువ్వు Same as పురుగు or పువ్వు (q. v.).

ప్రె pre

ప్రెక్కణము or పెక్కణము *prekkanamu*. [Tel.] n. Dancing, a dance, అభినయముతోడి నృత్యము. A wrestling place, మల్లరింగము.

ప్రెగ్గడ, ప్రెగడ or ప్రెవడ *preg-gada*. [Tel. పేరు+కడ.] n. A minister, మంత్రి. A chief man, ప్రధానపురుషుడు. An heir apparent to a throne, యువరాజు.

ప్రెబ్బొత్తి *preb-botti*. [Tel. పేరు+బొత్తి.] adv. Assuredly, positively, certainly. నిశ్చయముగా. "ద్వి॥ ప్రెబ్బొత్తి పెద్దల పెద్ద యొకండు." BD. v. 921.

ప్రే prē

ప్రేంకణము, ప్రేంకదము or ప్రేంకనము *prenkanamu*. [Skt.] n. The tree termed *Nauclea cadamba*. ప్రియకవృక్షము, ప్రియకువుచెట్టు, కడపచెట్టు, కదంబవృక్షము.

ప్రేంఖ *prēnkha.* [Skt.] n. A swing, a sort of hammock or swinging cot, either for travelling or diversion, డోలి, డోల. Dancing, నృత్యము, నాట్యము. Wandering, roaming or travelling about. సంచారము, పర్యటనము. A horse's pace, వాజిగతి, అశ్వగతి. **ప్రేంఖణము** *prēnkhaṇamu.* n. A kind of dance, ఒకవిధమైన నృత్యము. Wandering, roaming, travelling, పర్యటనము. Entrance, ప్రవేశము. A drama, నాటకము. **ప్రేంఖత్** *prēnkhat.* adj. Touching, being in contact with, reflecting. Scattering, diffusing, shaking, moving. వ్యాపించెడి. "దిశాప్రేంఖత్కటాక్షాంచలద్యుతి జాలుండును." Swa. iv. 100. టీ॥ దిశా ప్రేంఖత్, దిక్కులయందు వ్యాపించుచున్న టువంటి. **ప్రేంఖితము** *prēnkhitamu.* adj. Shaken, moving, set in motion, కదిలింపబడిన. Swung, ఊచబడిన.

ప్రేక్షితము *prēkshitamu.* [Skt.] adj. Seen, చూడబడిన.

ప్రేగు, ప్రేవు or **పేగు** *prēgu.* [Tel.] n. An entrail, a bowel.

ప్రేపు Same as ప్రేరేపు. See under ప్రేరించు.

ప్రేతము *prētamu.* [Skt.] n. A ghost, spirit, shade. The spirit before the obsequial rites are performed. ఒకవిధమైన భూతము. A corpse, పీనుగు. A soul that is thrown into hell. నరకస్థితప్రాణి. **ప్రేతకర్మములు** *prēta-karmamulu.* n. Funeral or obsequial rites. దినవారములు. **ప్రేతత్వము** *prētatvamu.* n. Ghostliness, the state of being a ghost. **ప్రేతపురి** or **ప్రేతపురము** *prēta-puri.* n. Hell, the land of ghosts. యమపట్టణము. **ప్రేతవనము** *prēta-vanamu.* n. A graveyard, cemetery. శ్మశానము. **ప్రేతవస్త్రము** *prēta-vastramu.* n. A shroud. శవమునకుకప్పుబట్ట.

ప్రేపు *prēpu.* [Tel.] n. The dawn, తెలవారు, ఉషఃకాలము.

ప్రేమ or **ప్రేమము** *prēma.* [Skt.] n. Love, affection, kindness, tender regard, స్నేహము. Joy, హర్షము. **ప్రేమించు** *prēmintsu.* v. a. To love, to have an affection for. **ప్రేమిడి** *prēmuḍi.* n. Love, affection, ప్రేమ. M. III. vi. 440. A vi. 136. **ప్రేముడించు** *prēmuḍintsu.* v. n To love, ప్రియపడు. To grieve, ఖేదపడు. శోకించు. To suffer pain, బాధపడు. M. IX. i. 12. **ప్రేయసి** *prēyasi.* n. A loved woman, a sweetheart. ప్రియురాలు. **ప్రేయసుడు** *prēyasu-ḍu.* n. A lover, a friend, ప్రియుడు.

ప్రేము or **పేము** n. Rattan. See పేము.

ప్రేరించు, ప్రేరేచు, ప్రేరేపు or **ప్రేరేపించు** *prērintsu.* [Skt.] v. a. To urge, induce, incite, spur, instigate, excite, prompt, urge, encourage. ప్రేరణచేయు, పురికొల్పు, ప్రేరేపణచేయు. **ప్రేరకుడు** *prērakuḍu.* n. One who incites or encourages, ప్రేరేపణచేయువాడు. **ప్రేరణ, ప్రేరణము** or **ప్రేరేపణ** *prēraṇa.* n. Inducement, encouragement, temptation, excitement, instigation, urging. పురికొలుపడము. "ప్రేరణమున లేనిలేమ." Sumati. 65. **ప్రేరణి** *prēraṇi.* n. A kind of dance, ఒకవిధమైననృత్యము. **ప్రేరణీయము** *prēraṇīyamu.* adj. Fit to be encouraged, ప్రేరణచేయదగిన. **ప్రేరితము** *prēritamu.* adj. Encouraged or incited, ప్రేరేపబడిన. **ప్రేరితుడు** *prērituḍu.* n. One who is induced instigated or encouraged, పురికొల్పబడ్డవాడు. **ప్రేరేపకుడు** *prē-rēpakuḍu.* (for ప్రేరకుడు.) n. One who urges, or instigates. ఉద్బోధకుడు, పురికొలుపువాడు. In Grammar, ప్రేరణార్థకము the Causal voice.

ప్రేలిక Same as పేలిక or పీలిక (q. v.).

ప్రేలు or **పేలు** *prēlu.* [Tel.] v. n. To prattle or tattle, to chatter, talk in a silly manner. వదరు. To be roasted and swollen, పేగు, పేలియుబుకు. **ప్రేలరి** *prēl-ari.*

n. A talkative person, a chatter-box, వదరుబోతు. ప్రేలలు, పేలలు or పేలాలు prēlalu. n. Roasted rice. ప్రేలుచు or ప్రేల్చు prēlutsu. v. n. To fry or roast, ప్రేలకేయు, వేచు. ప్రేలుడు or ప్రేలడము prēludu. n. Talkativeness, ప్రేలుట. ప్రేలరితనము prēlari-tanamu. n. Talkativeness. వదరుబోతుతనము. "అన్న ప్రేలరితనము నడివివడుగులాడు మాటల కేవింతయు నెరిగెదేల." Chenn. iii. 139.

ప్రేవు Same as పేగు. (q. v.)

ప్రేషణము prēshanamu. [Skt.] n. Sending. పంపుట. ప్రేషకుడు prēshakudu. n. One who sends, పంపువాడు. ప్రేషణీయుడు prēshaniyudu. n. One who is fit to be sent, పంపదగినవాడు. ప్రేషితుడు prēshitudu. n. One who is sent, పంపబడినవాడు. ప్రేష్యుడు prēshyudu. n. One who is fit to be sent, పంపదగినవాడు. A servant, పరిచారకుడు.

ప్రేష్ఠము prēshthamu. [Skt.] adj. Very dear, మిక్కిలిప్రియమైన. ప్రేష్ఠుడు prēshthudu. n. One who is very dear, మిక్కిలి ప్రియుడు.

ప్రొ pro

ప్రొద్దు or పొద్దు proddu. [Tel.] n. The sun, సూర్యుడు. Time, కాలము. A day, దినము. Half a day, పూట. The dawn, తెలవారము. The morning, ఉదయకాలము. ప్రొద్దువాలినతర్వాత after the sun began to decline, in the afternoon. పెద్దయుంబ్రొద్దు a long time. ప్రొద్దిటిపూట the morning time. ప్రొద్దుటెండ the morning sunlight. ప్రొద్దులు proddulu. n. plu. The days near the time of the confinement of a woman, ప్రసవదినములు. ప్రొద్దులనెల the month during which a confinement takes place, ప్రసూతిమాసము. ప్రొద్దుకల్లు or ప్రొద్దుటాయి proddu-kallu. n. Lit: the sun-stone, i. e., a focussing lens, సూర్యకాంతశిల. ప్రొద్దుగొడుకు. ప్రొద్దుపట్టి or ప్రొద్దుపూవి proddu-goduku. n. The son of the sun; an epithet applied to Yama, Sani, Karna or Sugriva, యముడు, శని, కర్ణుడు, సుగ్రీవుడు. ప్రొద్దుతిరుగుడు proddu-tirugudu. n. The sun-flower, సూర్యావర్తపుష్పము. ప్రొద్దుపుచ్చు proddu-putstsu. v. a. To pass the time, కాలక్షేపముచేయు. ప్రొద్దురిక్క proddu-rikka. n. A constellation called ఉత్తరఫల్గునీనక్షత్రము. ప్రొద్దురిక్కనెల proddu-rikka-nela. n. A name of the Telugu month called ఫాల్గుణమాసము.

ప్రొయ్యి. ప్రొయి, పొయ్యి or పొయి proyyi. [Tel.] n. An oven. గడ్డపొయ్యి gadda-poyyi. n. An oven constructed with bricks or three pieces of stone placed like a triangle. గాడిపొయ్యి gadi-poyyi. n. An oven which is made by digging a long narrow pit in the ground. గుంటపొయ్యి gunta-poyyi. n. An oven formed by digging a pit in the ground.

ప్రో pro

ప్రోక, ప్రోగు, ప్రోవు or పోగు prōka. [Tel.] n. A heap, multitude, or assemblage, రాశి, సమూహము. "పుణ్యములను పాపములను రెండు ప్రోకలైయుండు." M. XIII. i. 47. ప్రోగగు prōgagu. v. n. To gather, assemble, come together. ప్రోగుచేయు prōgu-chēyu. v. n. To gather, bring together, accumulate.

ప్రోక్తము pr-ōktamu. [Skt. ప్ర+ఉక్తము.] adj. Told, said, declared. చెప్పబడిన.

ప్రోక్షణము prōkshanamu. [Skt.] n. Sprinkling. నీళ్లు చిలుకరించుట. Consecration of an idol by sprinkling. Killing an animal in sacrifice. ప్రోక్షించు prōkshintsu. v. a. To sprinkle, as water. చల్లు, చిలుకరించు.

Sacrifice. ప్రోక్షితము prōkshitamu. adj. Sprinkled, shed (as water), wetted (as earth.) చెలకరింపబడిన. Killed, slaughtered, offered in sacrifice. వధింపబడిన.

ప్రోగు or పోగు prōgu. [Tel.] n. A thread, a string, A heap. See పోగు, and ప్రోవ.

ప్రోచిళ్లు Same as పోచిళ్లు (q. v.).

ప్రోచు prōchu. [Tel.] v. a. To nourish, support, maintain, protect, preserve, save. ఆకోన్నదకముల్చిచ్చి పోషించు. రక్షించు. ప్రోవుతగా O may he bless! రక్షించునుగాక. ప్రోచికోలు or పోచికోలు prōchi-kōlu. n. The act of feeding, bringing up a cow or other animal, బలహీనత్వమునుపొందిన ఆవు మొదలగు జంతువు లను కాపాడి అనుభవించుట. వానికి ఆ యావును పోచికోలుగా ఇచ్చినాడు he gave him the cow to feed and enjoy its milk. adj. Useless, వ్యర్థము. గడ్డిపోచయు ప్రోచికోలుకాదు even a blade of grass is not useless.

ప్రోజ్ఝితము prōjjhitamu. [Skt.] adj. Abandoned, shunned, avoided, విసర్జింపబడ్డ. మానుకోబడ్డ.

ప్రోజే Same as పోజే (q. v.).

ప్రోడ prōḍa. [from Skt. ప్రౌఢ.] n. A wise or skilful person. నిపుణుడు, వివేకి, ప్రౌఢ పురుషుడు, ప్రౌఢస్త్రీ. "నయశాస్త్రములాదిగ నన్నియు నెరిగిన ప్రోడవీవ." R. vii. 227. ప్రోడడు prōḍaḍu. n. A wise or skilful man. ప్రౌఢుడు, చతురుడు.

ప్రోతము prōtamu. [Skt.] adj. Sewn, stitched, కుట్టబడిన. n. A cloth, వస్త్రము.

ప్రోత్తుంగము prōttungamu. [Skt. ప్ర+ఉత్తుంగము.] adj. Elevated, high. ఉన్నతమైన.

ప్రోత్థితము prōtthitamu. [Skt. ప్ర+ఉత్థితము.] adj. Risen, produced, happened. బయలుదేరిన. "ప్రాదాంఘ్రిప్రోత్థితక్రోడనాయకము." Swa. iv. 64.

ప్రోత్సారితము prōtsāritamu. [Skt.] adj. Relinquished, ejected, expelled, got rid of. విసర్జితమేయబడిన.

ప్రోత్సాహము prōtsāhamu. [Skt. ప్ర+ఉత్సాహము.] n. Stimulus, incitement, excitement, encouragement. Alacrity. ఉద్రేకము. ప్రోత్సాహకుడు prōtsāhakuḍu. n. One who urges or incities. An adviser. ప్రేరకుడు.

ప్రోథము prōthamu. [Skt.] n. The nose of a horse, గుర్రపుముక్కు. The loins or hip. కటి.

ప్రోడి prōḍi. [Tel.] n. Nourishing, cherishing, support, పోషణము. Prosperity, grandeur, వైభవము. "రమణీయమందిరా రామదేశంబుల బూవుడీగలకును ప్రోడిసేయు." B. X. 1818. adj. Graceful, pleasant. పొలుపారెడి, ఒప్పారుచున్న. ప్రోడిని prōḍini. adv. Gracefully, pleasantly. పొలుపారగా, ఒప్పారగా. "ముత్తైదువలారతులీగా ప్రోడింబదన నగరుచొచ్చి పూనికమెరయగా." Yayati. iv. 184. ప్రోడిగా prōḍi-gā. adv. In support of, as an aid. ఉపబలముగా. "పల్లభులంటాడి యల్లనను నభిసారికలవెడందకన్నుల చెన్నునన్నుకొనిపొదలు మదనోన్మాదంబునకు ప్రోడిగాకాదంబరికంపొసంచి." Swa. iii. 45. ప్రోడిగొను or ప్రోడిచేయు prōḍi-gonu. v. a. To nourish, పోషించు.

ప్రోద్దామము prōddāmamu. [Skt. ప్ర+ఉద్దామము.] adj. Set free, unbound, unconstrained, self-willed. విచ్చలవిడియైన, నిరంకుశమైన. "మహావృక్షముల్, ప్రోద్దామస్థితి పెల్లగించి నచటగా బోల్పొందుమత్తేభముల్." Tara. ii. 27. ప్రోద్దామత prōddāmata. n. Unconstrained power, a self-willed disposition. విచ్చలవిడి, నిరంకుశత.

ప్రోద్ధతము prōddhatamu. [Skt. ప్ర+ఉద్ధతము.] adj. Excited, intense. రేగిన, అగ్గ

సాముగల. "ధమ్మిల్లమునద్క్షోక్తము వివాదప్రోద్ధత." B. viii. 110.

ప్రోద్ధుతము *pr-ōddhutamu.* [Skt. ప్ర+ఉద్ధుతము.] adj. Shaken. కదిలింపబడ్డ. "ఆద్రిస్థితిక్రీడలక్ష్మీశాగ ద్రాక్ష్యాప్రోద్ధుత తమస్తత్సూజము గ్రత్రిపురధీశ్వుడుగ్రత్వరోద్ధుత." H. v. 60.

ప్రోద్బలము *prōd-balamu.* [Skt. ప్ర+ఉత్+బలము.] n. Support, aid, assistance. సహాయము. Encouragement, instigation. పురికొలుపుట. ఇది వానిప్రోద్బలముపైని జరిగినది this was done at his instigation.

ప్రోద్భిన్నము *prōdbhinnamu.* [Skt. ప్ర+ఉద్భిన్నము.] adj. Opened, burst, proceeded forth or from. వికసించిన, పుట్టిన, కలిగిన.

ప్రోద్యత్ *prōdyat.* [Skt. ప్ర+ఉద్యత్.] adj. Increased, born, produced. Endeavouring. వృద్ధిపొందే, పుట్టిన, బయలుదేరిన. "ప్రోద్యత్పుత్రాపారణీ." Swa. iv. 107. "ఆరీతిరాజనుదెంచి యాభునుడుప్రోద్యద్దాన ధారాధునీపూరంబుల్ సెలయేరులై." T. v. 5.

ప్రోపు *prōpu.* [Tel. from ప్రోచు.] n. Protection, saving. సంరక్షణము. Nourishing. పోషణము. ప్రోపడు *prō-paḍu.* (ప్రోపు+పడు.) v. n. To be fed or nourished, పోషింపబడు. ప్రోపరి *prōp-ari.* n. One who nourishes, పోషకుడు. A saviour, రక్షకుడు.

ప్రోయాలు *prō-y-ālu.* [Tel. ప్రోలు+ఆలు.] n. A housewife, ఇల్లాలు. A woman, స్త్రీ.

ప్రోలు *prōlu.* [Tel.] n. A city. పట్టణము. ప్రోలుగుదుపు or ప్రోల్గుదుపు *prōlu-guḍupu.* v. a. To provoke, rouse, excite. ప్రేరేచు, పుల్లలుపెట్టు. "రాజునకెంతవెర్రియప ప్రసిద్ధమది రాజితమూర్తులు శైలవారలాపైజగతిం రావువారలవ్యాజముగాగ ప్రోల్గుదుపుకుటయశంబటు గావునం." Bobbili. ii. 113. ప్రోలుదిరుగు *prōlu-dirugu.* v. n. To go in procession about a city. ఊరేగు. In marriage ceremonies it signifies a fictitious procession round the city represented by some objects placed in the house.

ప్రోవ *prōva.* [Tel.] n. A trick; gibing; quizzing.

ప్రోవు Same as ప్రోగు and పోగు (q. v.) ప్రోవుకొను *prōvu-konu.* v. n. To lie in a heap, రాశిపడు.

ప్రోషితము *prōshitamu.* [Skt.] adj. Abroad, absent, away from home. దేశాంతరగతుడైన. ప్రోషితభర్తృక a woman whose husband is absent. ప్రోషితుడు *prōshituḍu.* n. One who is gone to a foreign land దేశాంతరగతుడు.

ప్రౌ prau

ప్రౌఢ *prauḍha.* [Skt.] n. A woman in the flower of youth, a lady, dame, గడితేరినస్త్రీ, ప్రగల్భురాలు. "పరవశదైన్యమందుకొను ప్రౌఢలగాదు." Swa. v. 76. adj. Full grown, mature. Respectable, great, grand, fine, noble. ఎదిగిన, దిట్టమైన, గంభీరమైన. ప్రౌఢనాయిక a full grown girl. ప్రౌఢవాక్కు a grand style. ప్రౌఢకావ్యము a noble poem. ఆ చిన్నది ప్రౌఢ అయినతర్వాత after the girl grew up. ప్రౌఢత్వము *prauḍhatvamu.* n. Skilfulness; ability; grandeur. ప్రౌఢి or ప్రౌఢిమ *prauḍhi.* n. Dignity, skilfulness, ability, సామర్థ్యము, ఉత్సాహము, ప్రగల్భత. ప్రౌఢుడు *prauḍhuḍu.* n. One who is mature, wise, skilful, vigorous, clever. ప్రగల్భుడు, ఘనుడు. ప్రౌఢురాలు *prauḍhuralu.* n. She who is mature, skilful, wise, vigorous, clever. ప్రగల్భురాలు.

ప్రౌష్ఠపదము *praushṭha-padamu.* [Skt.] n. The name of the sixth lunar month. భాద్రపదమాసము.

ప్ల pla

ప్లక్షము plakshamu. [Skt.] n. The waved-leaved fig tree. *Ficus infectoria.* జువ్వి, కలజువ్వి. Also, same as రావి.

ప్లవ plava. [Skt.] n. The name of a Telugu year. ప్లవము plavamu. n. A raft, a float, తెప్ప. A frog, కప్ప. A monkey, వానరము. ప్లవంగ plavanga. n. The name of a Telugu year. ప్లవంగము, ప్లవంగమము or ప్లవగము plavangamu. (lit: the leaper.) n. A monkey, కోతి. A frog, కప్ప. ప్లవగుడు plavagudu. n. The charioteer of the sun. సూర్యసారథి, అనూరుడు. ప్లవుడు plavudu. n. A Chandāla or pariah, చండాలుడు, మాలవాడు. A. vi. 57 and 99.

ప్లహ్లాదము plahladamu. [Skt.] n. Joy, rejoicing. హర్షము.

ప్లి pli

ప్లీహము plīhamu. [Skt.] n. The spleen. Enlargement of the spleen, spleen disease, హృదయ వామభాగస్థపీతమాంసము, రోగభేదము. ప్లీహోదరుడు plīh-ōdarudu. n. A man suffering from spleen disease, కడుపులో బల్ల కలిగినవాడు. ప్లీహశత్రువు plīha-śatruvu. n. A tree called ములుమోదుగు.

ప్లు plu

ప్లుతము plutamu. adj. Wetted, soaked. తడపబడిన, తడిసిన. "గీర్వాణవిలాసినీమృదుకరప్లుత మానరసప్లుతాంగుడై." Anirud. v. 53. n. Bounding, curvetting, as a horse. వేగమున అంతటి మేరయము సమముగాపోయే అశ్వధారావిశేషము. A steady pace, నిబ్బరపుగమనము. Steadiness, నిబ్బరము. A long drawn out vowel. మూడు మాత్రలకాలముగల స్వరము. A note, a quaver. స్వరభేదము, తాళమానభేద త్రయము, తాళప్రాణాంగభేదము.

ప్లుష్టము plushtamu. [Skt.] adj. Burnt. కాల్చబడిన.

ప్లో plō

ప్లోషము plōshamu. [Skt.] n. Burning, combustion. కాల్చుట.

ఫ pha or fa

ఫ pha. [Skt.] The aspirated P pronounced like ph. in *Up-hill.* This letter occurs in Sanskrit or foreign words only. The F sound in English and other languages is also represented by this letter.

ఫకీరు fakiru. [H] n. A *fakir*, an ascetic.

ఫక్కి phakki. [Skt.] n. Manner. రీతి, ప్రకారము.

ఫక్కిక phakkika. [Skt.] n. A single treatise. ఏకగ్రంథము.

ఫక్తు faktu. [H.] adj. & adv. Only, merely, simply. మాత్రము.

ఫణి phaṇi. [Skt.] n. A serpent or snake. A hooded serpent. ఫణితల్పగుడు phaṇi-talpagudu. n. A name of Vishnu who reclines on Adi Sēshu, the chief of snakes.

ఫణిజ్జకము or ఫణిర్జకము phaṇijjakamu. [Skt.] n. A delicate sweet smelling plant, apparently a sort of Basil with small leaves. మరువము శేక తులసి.

ఫణితము phaṇitamu. [Skt.] adj. Told, said, cited, adduced, praised. ఫణితి phaṇiti. n. Speech, a word, వాక్యము. Mode, way, course of conversation. ఫక్కిక, పద్ధతి. "హా మాత్సుడ్ల విష్ణునిసాపలమలన్ని యును స్వ

పాదంబున విస్తరఫలితి బడగనిగాక." Vishņu. viii. 323.

ఫయిసలా or **ఫైసలా** *fayisală*. [H.] n. A decision, settlement. నిమిత్తు, తీర్పు.

ఫర్మానా or **ఫర్మానా** *pharmana*. [H.] n. A firman; a command, warrant, royal mandate. **ఫర్మాయించు** *pharmayintsu*. v. a. To command, direct, order, appoint. **ఫర్మాయిషి** *pharmayishi*. n. An order, a commission. An order to make an article. ఆజ్ఞ, వినస్తువున్నైనను ఇట్లు చేయవలసినదనే ఆజ్ఞ.

ఫలకము *phalakamu*. [Skt.] n. A shield, కేడెము, డాలు. A die or round piece of metal, బిళ్ల, పలక. కపోలఫలకము the orb of her cheek, her plump cheek. The wooden bottom or frame of a bed. ఊరుఫలకమందు on the lap.

ఫలము *phalamu*. [Skt.] n. A fruit. A crop. Fruit, profit, use, advantage, benefit, a reward, result, consequence. దుస్స్వప్న ఫలము the fulfilment of a portentous dream. **ఫలపడు** *phala-padu*. v. n. To bear fruit, to avail, turn to good, turn out well. **ఫలపరచు** *phala-paratsu*. v. a. To make fruitful, to realize, to turn to profit, to use. **ఫలపూరము** *phala-puramu*. n. The citron. **ఫలవంతము** *phala-cantamu*. adj. Fruitful, as a tree, పండ్లు గల. **ఫలరాజము** *phala-rajamu*. n. A certain red fruit, *Momordica monadelpha*. **ఫలాహారము** *phal-aharamu*. n. A refection, refreshments, a slight meal of parched corn, cakes, fruit, &c. **ఫలించు** *phalintsu*. v. n. To be fruitful, yield fruit, పండు. To be of advantage, profit, turn out well, to be accomplished, be fulfilled, నెరవేరు. **ఫలితము** *phalitamu*. adj. Ripened, fruitful, profitable, advantageous. నా యత్నము ఫలితముగాలేదు my endeavour came to no good. n. Profit, fruit. **ఫలితార్థము** *phalit-arthamu*. n. The ultimate import, purport, result, or point of a passage, the tendency as distinguished from the literal sense. **ఫలినము** *phalinamu*. n. A fruit tree. విరుల్గూన ఫలనద్వృక్షము. G. iii. 146. **ఫలిని** *phalini*. n. A tree called ప్రియంగువు, కరిగొర్రచెట్టు. **ఫలోదయము** *phal-odayamu*. n. Success, enjoyment, gain, profit; heaven, paradise, joy, happiness. **ఫలోన్ముఖము** *phal-onmukhamu*. adj. Fruitful, effective, efficacious. అది యిప్పుడు ఫలోన్ముఖముగానున్నది it is now coming to good.

ఫలానా or **ఫలాని** *phalana*. [H.] adj. Such, such and such a one. ఫలానివాడు such and such a man. ఫలానిపని such and such a work. ఫలానికార్యము such and such an affair.

ఫల్గునుడు *phal-gunudu*. [Skt.] n. An epithet of Arjuna.

ఫల్గువు *phalguvu*. [Skt.] adj. Pithless, sapless. Vain, unmeaning, empty, useless. నిస్సారమైన. తుచ్ఛమైన, వట్టిది.

ఫసలి *fasali*. [H.] n. Lit: a crop or harvest. Hence, a season, one year. Fasli, the Fasli or Official year.

ఫా phā or fā

ఫాయిదా *fayida*. [H.] n. Profit, gain, లాభము.

ఫారము *faramu*. [Eng. 'Form'] n. A tabular statement, పట్టీ. In printing, a form of printed matter equivalent to eight pages octavo.

ఫాలము *phalamu*. [Skt.] n. The forehead. The share of a plough. A cotton cloth. **ఫాలాక్షుడు** or **ఫాలనేత్రుడు**. *phal-akshu-*

du. n. The 'Cyclops,' an epithet of Siva, who has an eye in his forehead. R. v. 332.

ఫాల్గునము or ఫాల్గునికము *phalgunamu.* [Skt.] n. The twelfth lunar month, that in which the moon's change takes place, when the sun is in Pisces.

ఫి phi or fi

ఫిరంగి or పిరంగి *phirangi.* [From French, 'Frank,' Feringee] n. A European. A cannon (being imported by the Europeans). ఫిరంగిచెక్క *phirangi-chekka.* n. The bark imported by the Europeans, China root, *Smilax china*, a certain medicinal drug. Ainslie. i 70.

ఫిరాయించు or పిరాయించు *phirayintsu.* [H.] v. a. To change, మార్చు. ఫిరాయింపు or పిరాయింపు *phirayimpu.* n. A change, మార్పడము.

ఫిర్యాదు or పిర్యాదు *firyadu.* [H.] n. A complaint, a charge, మొర, నేరము మోపడము. ఫిర్యాది or పిర్యాది *firyadi.* n. A complainant, a plaintiff. ఫిర్యాదు చేయు *firyadu-cheyu.* v. a. To lodge a complaint.

ఫు phu

ఫుల్లత్ *phullat.* [Skt.] adj. Blooming.

ఫుల్లము *phullamu.* [Skt.] adj. Blooming, opened, expanded, వికసించిన.

ఫూ phū

ఫూత్కారము *phūt-karamu.* [Skt.] n. A sound of sobbing, hissing or panting.

ఫె phe

ఫెళఫెళ or పెళపెళ *phela-phela.* [Tel. anuk.] n. A crash or smash; an uproar. అతడు ఆ దేశములో ఫెళఫెళలాడిస్తున్నాడు he is making a great uproar in the country. adv. Aloud, crashingly, echoingly, roaringly, creakingly, resoundingly, "ఫెళ ఫెళవిరచాలు ఫెళ ఫెళమాయెంచి." H. ii. 98. "కొమ్ము ఫెళ ఫెళవిరిగెను." Pal. 173. ఫెళఫెళమను *phela-phela-m-anu.* v. n. To crash.

ఫే phe

ఫేనము *phenamu.* [Skt.] n. Scum, froth, foam. నురుగు.

ఫేనిలము *phenilamu.* [Skt.] n. The Soap nut plant, *Sapindus detergens.* కుంకుడు చెట్టు. Rox. ii. 280. "ప్రాతిఫేనిలములకగ్గిన జలములుగాపు (?)గ్ధములకు." Vish. iv. 302. adj. Foamy, frothy. నురుగుకల.

ఫేరవము or ఫేరువు *pheravamu.* [Skt.] n. A jackal. నక్క.

ఫై phai

ఫైసలా or ఫైసలు *phaisala.* [H.] n. A settlement, decision, sentence, decree, తీర్పు, పరిష్కారము.

బ ba

బ *ba.* The name of the letter B. బకారము.

బంక *banka.* [Tel.] n. Slime, mucus, gum, glue, gluten, gelatine, any thing glutinous, sticky or clammy like jelly or like clay. Stinginess, avarice. బంకలుసాగు *bankalu-sagu.* v. n. To be gummy or sticky. వానికి పెత్తురుబంక పడుచున్నది he has got dysentery. బంక చెట్టు banka-chettu. n. A tree from which gum arabic is obtained. బంకతుత్తర a kind of shrub. బంక తెవులు banka-tevulu. n. The 'gum evil,' a disease of corn. బంకపిట్ట banka-pitta. n. A name applied to various kinds of Swallows because they build their nests of mud. బంకపురుగు banka-purugu. n. A snail, lit: the 'sticky insect.' బంకభేది banka-bhēdi. n. Dysentery. బంకమన్ను banka-mannu. n. Clay. రేగడమన్ను. బంక ముచ్చు banka-mutstsu. n. An avaricious man, a miser. పిసినారి, లోభి.

బంకు banku. [Tel.] n. A lane, సందువీధి. A guard, పారావాడు, కావలివాడు. One who pretends to be a hero, శూరునివలె నటించు వాడు. బంకెత banketa. (బంకు+ఎత.) n. A miserly woman. లుబ్ధురాలు.

బంకోలు bankōlu. [Tel. Name of a place.] n. Bencoolen, whither criminals used to be transported. బంకోలుకుపంపు to transport, to sentence to transportation.

బంగనబయలు bangana-bayalu. [Tel. బయలు+ బయలు.] n. An open plain. బట్టబయలు. బంగ నబయలుగానుండే యిల్లు a house upon a plain, not in an enclosure, a lonely house.

బంగల bangala. [Tel.] n. An oven. కుంపటి.

బంగారము, బంగరము, బంగారు or బంగరు bangarumu. [Tel.] n. Gold. నీ యిల్లు బంగారు ముకాను or నీబుద్ధి బంగారముకాను bless your innocent heart! you silly creature! కాకి బంగారు tinsel. ముచ్చిబంగారు tinsel, gilding, as distinguished from మంచిబంగారు real gold. బంగారు bangaru. adj. Golden. The various names of gold are used (as in other languages) to denote Fine, noble, beautiful, admirable, thus: బంగారు కొండ or బంగరుకొండ the golden mountain, మేరుపర్వతము; my darling. నా బంగారుదొర my beloved lord! బంగారుపిట్ట sweet bird! Also, used to express contempt. బంగారు మర్యాద vastly polite! బం గారువాక్యము a precious reason! బంగారు పని a very pretty business! బంగారు చిన్న వాడు a hopeful lad. వాడు పట్టినది అంతా బంగారు అవుచువచ్చినది all he did prospered. బంగారుగా bangaru-ga. adv. Grandly, vastly, well, preciously. As easily as possible. As you please! with all my heart! by all means! బంగారుకంటి bangaru-kanti. n. (Lit:) Golden-eyed: A name of the Little Owl, పైడికంటి; and also of a sort of rice. బంగారుతీగలు bangaru-tigalu. n. (Lit: Gold-sprouts.) A sort of rice. శాలిధాన్యము. బంగారునీరు bangaru-niru. n. Gilding. బంగారుపాము bangaru-pāmu. n. A very venomous kind of snake. బంగారుపిచ్చిక bangaru-pichchika. n. The Weaver-bird, *Ploceus baya*. బంగారుపూత bangaru-pūta. n. Gilding. బంగారుపూతలు a kind of grain.

బంగాళము bangalamu. [Bengali.] n. Bengal, వంగదేశము. బంగాళా bangala. [H.] n. A bungalow or house standing alone. బంగాళి bangali. n A species of plantain, గొడ్డుపటి. adj. Bengali.

బంగి or భంగి bangi. [H.] n. Bhang, or Indian hemp, *Cannabis sativa*. గంజాయి. Also, the bangy or parcel post or mail. A parcel. బంగిముచ్చు bangi-mutstsu. n. One who smokes *bhang* బంగితాగువాడు.

బంజారి banjari. [H.] n. A tribe of gypsies, లంబాడివాండ్రు.

బంజేరు or బంజరు bandzaru. [H.] n. A waste land, uncultivated land, బీడునేల. ఆనాదిబంజరు land which is immemorially waste. adj. Waste, uncultivated. బంజరు భూమి waste land.

బంటి banti. [Tel.] affix: As high as; up to. లోతుమొక్క ప్రమాణము. మొలబంటినీరు

water up to one's waist. మోకాలిబంటి knee-deep. పుక్కిటిబంటి deep as far as the cheeks. ఈతబంటి deep enough for swimming.

బంటు *banṭu*. [from Skt. భటః.] n. A soldier, an armed attendant, a police officer, a servant; a pawn at chess. సేవకుడు. A devotee, భక్తుడు. A disciple, శిష్యుడు. A brave man, శూరుడు. **బంటుతనము** *banṭu-tanamu*. n. Soldiership, bravery. **బంట్రౌతు** or **బంట్రౌతు** *banṭ-rōtu*. (From బంటు, a soldier, and రౌతు a trooper.) n. A peon.

బండ *banḍa*. [Tel.] n. A rock, a block or slab of stone. రాయి, పెద్దబ్బరాయి. A short pounder or pestle without a ferrule, పొన్నులేనిరోకలి, పొట్టిరోకలి. A much used block, a worn out stone. అరిగినది. (Metaphorically), a block head, an obstinate, stubborn man. adj. Shameless, importunate. Mischievous, naughty, wicked, obscene, indecent, ఆకతాయి. **బండాట** *banḍāṭa*. (బండ+ఆట.) n. Mischief, naughtiness, ఆకతాయితనము. బండవ్యాజ్యము a litigious case. **బండడు, బండ** or **బండగుడు** *banḍaḍu*. n. A dullard, a mischievous person, a stupid man. **బండవాడు** *banḍavāḍu*. n. A class of beggars, who go with a stone in their hands with which they threaten to beat out their brains unless relieved, రాయియెత్తుకొనివచ్చి అడుగుకొనేవాడు.

బండగు *banḍagu*. [Tel.] n. A cage for catching wild beasts, &c. బోను.

బండము *banḍamu*. [Tel.] n. A thing. తినుబండములు eatables.

బండారము or బండారు *banḍāramu*. [from Skt. భండారము.] n. A treasury, ఖజానా, ధనగృహము, సంచికట్టు, బొక్కసము. "తక్కినబండారులెక్కలుచూడు." BD. v. 800. See also ఆముక్త. iv. **బండరు, బండరాడు** or **బండారి** *banḍāri* n. A treasurer, కోశగృహాధ్యక్షుడు, బొక్కసమున కధికారి. "హితులుభృత్యులు బురోహితులునురాజసుతులు, బండరులురాహుతులులెంకలును." Charitr. iii. 108. **బండరువు** *banḍaruvu*. n. A treasury. ఖజానా, సంచికట్టు, బండారము. **బండవలము** or **బండాలము** *banḍavalamu*. n. Stock, capital, funds, treasure. సంచిబలము. Means, capacity, strength, సామర్థ్యము. దానిబండవలము బైటపడినది the secret came to light. అందులో బండారము ఏమిన్ని లేదు there is nothing in that.

బండారు *banḍāru*. [Tel. బండ+అరు.] n. Saffron ground on a stone. రాతిమీదరాచి పూసుకొనేపసుపు. **బండారుకఱ్ఱ** *banḍāru-karra*. n. A hard yellow wood like mango wood. The Karum timber tree, *Adina cordifolia* (F. P.) **బండారుపిచ్చుక** *banḍāru-pitstsuka*. n. "The golden head," a kind of bird, probably *Loxia philippenses*. పీతముండము.

బండారుడు *banḍāruḍu*. [Skt.] n. One who tends buffaloes. బర్రెలను కాచువాడు.

బండాలము See బండారము. (q. v.)

బండి *banḍi*. [Tel.] n. A cart, gig, carriage, coach, waggon, శకటము. A car, రథము. The four kinds of బళ్లు are గూడుబండి or చాపబండి a cart covered with a mat. పెట్టెబండి a palanquin coach, or a bullock coach. విల్లుబండి a carriage on springs. కోచిబండి an English "coach." The piece of wood round which gold lace or cotton lace is rolled: so called because shaped like an axle between two wheels. **బండికల్లు** *banḍi-kallu*. n. The wheel of a carriage or cart. కల్లు, రథచక్రము. (కల్లు is a stone, as the wheels were originally made of stone. Such are still seen in remote towns.) **బండికల్లురూపాయి** or **బండిరూపాయి** *banḍi-kallu-rūpāyi* n. A milled rupee: lit: one like a wheel. బండిగిల్లు *bandi-gillu.* v. n. To suffer difficulties. కడగండ్లుపడు. బండిగురిగింజ or బండిగురువెంద *bandi-guri-gindsa.* n. The vine called *Dalbergia volubilis.* Rox. iii. 231. శాంభోజలత. బండిమొగ్గరము *bandi-moggaramu.* n. A certain military evolution called శకటవ్యూహము, which is shaped like a cart. బండిరిక్క *bandi-rikka.* n. The star called రోహిణి. బండిరేఫ *bandi-rēpha.* n. "The great R." The letter ఱ; which is so named from బండి a wheel. శకటరేఫ. (The Pandits have made fruitless efforts to introduce this obsolete letter into modern Telugu.) బండిరేవు *bandi-rēvu.* n. A ford in a river where carts cross it. The great shore. బండిరొట్ట *bandi-rotta.* n. A sort of fodder.

బండు *bandu.* [Tel.] adj. Indecent, uncouth, obscene, gross. బండుతిట్టు coarse abuse. బండుమాటలు or బండుబూతు gross language, ఆకతాయిమాటలు.

బంతి *banti.* [Tel.] n. A ball to play with. చెండు, కందుకము. Any ball whether formed of cloth or of flowers, &c. The flower called a marigold. A flower, called Bachelor's button. ముద్దబంతి మొదలైనవి. బంతి (for Skt. పఙ్క్తి) n. A row, line, rank. A row of bullocks driven abreast to thrash out corn. బంతిత్రాడు the rope used to yoke a row of bullocks together to thrash corn. బంతికుడుపు *banti-kudupu.* n. A dinner party, ఒకటిగాకూడి భుజించుట. బంతితోలు to drive bullocks to thrash corn. బంతి విడుచు to release bullocks after thrashing corn. బంతులాడు *bantul-ādu.* v. n. To play at ball. బంతులాట playing at ball.

బండ *banda.* [Tel.] n. A small tank.

బండకము Same as బందలము (q. v.).

బందన *bandana.* [from Skt. బంధన.] n. Slime, bird lime, gum, paste, glue, cement, any viscous matter, anything sticky. జిగట, బంక. బందనఅయిన viscous, glutinous. బందనగొను *bandana-gonu.* v. n. To become gummy or sticky జిగటగలదియగు.

బందము or బందాము *bandamu.* [from Skt. బంధము.] n. A tie or band to keep the legs together; hobbles or trammels used to confine cattle. Knee-haltering. The rope which connects the feet of a man who climbs a palmtree. బందా *bandā.* n. One who is put in prison, చెరబడ్డవాడు.

బందరు *bandaru.* [Tel.] n. A sea port. The ordinary name of Masulipatam, also called మచిలీబందరు.

బందలము or బందడము *banda-lamu.* [Tel.] A wide-mouthed jar. వెడల్పునోరుగల కుండ.

బందారుచెట్టు *bandāru-chettu.* [Tel.] n. The Karum timber tree, *Adina cordifolia.* (E. P.)

బంది *bandi.* [from Skt. బంధము.] n. Imprisonment, confinement. చెర, కయిదుచేయడము, నిర్బంధము. That which is imprisoned, చెరబడ్డది. "భావించుమనమాడ బందిచిక్కితిమి." (BD. ii. 800.) behold we have fallen into his hands. బందికాడు *bandi-kādu.* n. A marauder, a high-way-man, బందిపోటుదొంగ. "బందికాండ్రైనపోరుపులు ప్రబలక గనుకొని." Swa. iii. 157. బందిగము *bandi-gamu.* n. A dungeon, a prison, చెరసాల. "బందిగములోన శృంఖలబద్ధుజేసి." Vish. ii. 202. బందిపోటు *bandi-pōtu.* n. Gang robbery, a predatory incursion, a dacoity. "బందిపోటులు తరుచయ్యె పాపకాల." Ellaya. iii. 210. బందీకృతము *bandī-kritamu.* adj. n. Imprisoned. Vasu. vi. 109. బందీఖానా, బందిఖానా *bandi-khānā.* [H.] n. A prison, చెరసాల. See బందము.

బందు *bandu.* [for Skt. బంధువు.] n. A vulture; also called రామబందు and బోరువ. [Also, from Skt. బంధము.] A tie, a band; a hoop, clasp, clamp, or hinge. An iron clamp for joining boards together. తలుపు కుశీ సేయుమునకట్టులు. The bank of a reservoir or tank. The act of surrounding, ఆవరణము. Secrecy, గోపనము. Obstruction, నిరోధము. **బందుకట్టు** *bandu-kattu.* n. A conspiracy, league, cabal, plot, plan, scheme. జాతికట్టుపాటు. బందుకట్టుకట్టుకొను to be leagued together, to have a private agreement. బందుకట్టుమాటలు slang, such as gypsies use. **బందుగుడు** or **బందువుడు** *bandugudu.* (for Skt. బంధువు) n. A relation. **బందె** *bande.* n. Imprisonment, చెర, కయిదు. Confinement of cattle. పశువు లచెర. Poundage fine: a fine for a trespass by cattle. పశువులవందుక. బందెదీసికొను to exact a fine for stray cattle. బందెదొడ్డి a cattle pound. **బందెకాడు** *bande-kadu.* n. One who puts in prison. చెరలోవేయువాడు. **బందెకత్తె** *bande-katte.* n. A woman who puts in prison, చెరలో వేయునది. **బందెగొను** *bande-gonu.* v. a. To imprison, చెరబెట్టు. **బందెలపోతు** *bandela-potu.* n. One who is given to imprison people. చెరశేయు స్వభావముగలవాడు. **బందెవేయు** *bande-veyu.* v. a. To impound cattle. To exact a fine for cattle that have trespassed.

బందెడ, **బందేడుచెట్టు** or **బంజేడుచెట్టు** *bandeda.* n. Touchwood: a pithy wood that ignites easily. *Nyctanthes arbor-tristis.*

బందోబస్తు *bandô-bastu.* [H.] n. Security, భద్రము. A settlement, arrangement, a system of regulations.

బంధము *bandhamu.* [Skt. Cf. Eng. "Bind."] n. A binding, tie, or fetter. కట్టు. A position or attitude. Confinement, imprisonment. చెర. A pledge, కుదువ. A kind of poetical composition, శ్లోకాద్యాదనావిశేషము. A knot, ముడి. **బంధకరణము** or **బంధకవిత్వము** *bandha-karanamu.* n. A poem composed in a fantastic form: either in the shape of a sword (ఖడ్గబంధము), or, a serpent (నాగబంధము), &c. చౌరాసీతిబంధములు 84 ways, i. e., sorts of attitudes. సంసారబంధములు the ties of family. **బంధకము** *bandha-kamu.* n. Binding, tie, confinement, చెరసాల. **బంధకి** *bandhaki.* n. An unchaste wife. రంకులాలు. బంధకీపతి a cuckold. **బంధనము** *bandhanamu.* n. Binding, tying, a knot, కట్టు. Imprisoning, confining, చెర. దిగ్బంధనము the tying up or imposing restriction upon the quarters of the world, so as to prevent the intrusion of evil spirits, &c. **బంధనాలయము** *bandhan-alayamu.* n. A prison house, చెరసాల. బంధస్తంభము a post to which an elephant is tied. **బంధించు** *bandhintsu.* v. a. To tie, bind, tighten. కట్టు, బంధనము చేయు. v. n. To be bound or stopped, as urine, &c. మలము బంధించినది there was a stoppage of the *fæces.*

బంధురము *bandhuramu.* adj. Uneven, undulating, wavy. ఎగుడుదిగుడు. Bowed, bent, వంగిన. Pleasing, delightful, handsome, beautiful. ఉప్పిదమైన. Thick, దట్టమైన. n. A swan. కలహంస.

బంధులుడు *bandhuludu.* [Skt] n. A bastard. కులటాసుతుడు, నడిసెపేటురానికొడుకు, రంకులాలికొడుకు.

బంధువు or **బంధుడు** *bandhuvu.* n. A kinsman or relation. Particularly used for more distant kinsfolk. A. v. 90. కులబంధువు a fellow casteman. **బంధుజీవకము** or **బంధుజీవము** *bandhu-jivakamu.* n. The flower termed *Pentapetes phœnicea.* Rox. i. 376. మంకెన, పీతసారకము **బంధుత** *bandhu-ta.* n. A family party: kinsfolk, a circle of relations. బంధుసమూహము. **బంధుత్వము** *bandhu-*

tvamu. n. Relationship, affinity, consanguinity. బంధూకము bandhū-kamu. n. A certain red flower to which beautiful lips are compared, మంకెనపువ్వు, జేగిస.

బంపు bampu. [Tel.] n. Dirt on the teeth, పండ్లపాచి, పాకుడు. చంద్రా. i.

బంబ bamba. [Tel.] n. The sound of a conch. శంఖాధ్వని. adj. Large, స్థూలము. "భవ్య హస్తముల బంబలింగంబుల దాపనిదారు." L. xxiii. 8. బంబోతు bambōtu. (బంబ+పోతు.) n. A fat bull. పోతరించినయెద్దు. A very fat person, మిక్కిలి బలిసినవాడు. "బంబోతద్దాసరి, యడుపుం, బదవాతులం, గపోతిపోటులు." A. vi. 28.

బంభరము bambharamu. [Skt.] n. The large black carpenter bee. భ్రమరము, తుమ్మెద.

బకదారి baka-dari. [Tel.] n. A dove or pigeon. పావురాయి, పారావతము.

బకము bakamu. [Skt.] n. A heron. కొక్కెరొంగ. బకధ్యానము hypocrisy. (The heron seems to stand praying or meditating, while in truth he is aiming at his prey the fish.) బకవైరి baka-vairi. n. A title of Krishna or Bhima, who slew the demon named Baka. కృష్ణుడు, భీముడు.

బకానుచెక్క bakānu-chekka. [Tel.] n. The Sappan wood or Sampfen wood, *Caesalpinia sappan*. (Watts). The chay root which produces a red dye. Redwood. ఎర్రనాయచేసేచెక్క.

బకాయి or బకాయా bakāya. [H.] n. Arrears, balance due.

బకోటము Same as బకము (q. v.)

బక్క bakka. [Tel.] adj. Thin, lean, meagre. Poor. బక్కవాడు or బక్కపలచనివాడు a lean thin person. బక్కటిల్లు bakkatillu. v. n. To become lean, to become emaciated, శుష్కించు, కృశించు. బక్కడొక్కు or బక్కటొక్కు bakka-ḍokku. n. A lean thin person బక్కమజ్జిగ buttermilk mixed with too much water. బక్కికిబక్కి or మక్కికిమక్కి bakkiki-bakki. n. Tit for tat.

బగబగ or భగభగ baga-baga. [Tel. (anuk.)] n. The noise made by a blazing fire. అగ్నిజ్వాలాధ్వని. "బగబగయనిపించెనతడు వాన్ప్రాదయుంబుల." KP. ii. 97.

బగళము bagaḷamu. [Tel.] n. Avoidance, the act of moving aside, తొలగుట. బగళముసేయు bagaḷamu-seyu. v. n. To remove, తొలగించు.

"తే॥ బెరసిభద్రమహాకాళీభృంగిరిటులు
పాయబగళంబుతొలగనిచ్చేయుడనుచు
భార్గవములయందుమిగులవార్భటముసేయు."

భీ. v.

బగి bagi. [Tel.] n. A side, direction, ప్రక్క.

బగిసి or బగిస bagisi. [Tel.] n. A kind of tree. బగిసి, బవిసి or బైసి n. Wealth, riches, భాగ్యము. Respect, గౌరవము.

బగిలు bagilu. [Tel.] n. A sudden fear.

బగ్గముపాడు baggamu-pādu. [Tel. పాడు+పాడు.] adj. Quite ruined or waste, మిక్కిలిపాడు.

బగ్గు baggu. [Tel. (anuk.)] n. A blaze. The noise produced by a blazing fire, మండుటయందగు ధ్వన్యనుకరణము. బగ్గి n. Ashes, బూడిద. బగ్గున baggu-na. adv. Blazingly, suddenly. బగ్గుమను baggu-m-anu. v. n. To blaze forth suddenly, బగ్గనమండు. బగ్గరి bagg-ari. (బగ్గు+అరి) n. A very irritable person, a hot tempered man. బగ్గని మండిపడువాడు. బగ్గుండి baggundi. n. Red powder, రక్తవర్ణచూర్ణము.

బగ్గె or వగ్గె bagge. [from Skt. ప్రజ్ఞ.] n. Skill, cleverness.

బచాయించు bachayintsu. [Tel.] v. a. To preserve, save or rescue. బచావు protection, preservation, security. (Vizag.)

బచ్చెన bachchena. [Tel.] n. Paint, colour. వర్ణము. The act of applying paint, పూత. adj. Painted, lacquered. బచ్చెనపెట్టె a lacquered box. బచ్చెనబొమ్మ a painted doll or puppet.

బచ్చలి or బచ్చలికూర batsṭsali. [Tel.] n. Indian Spinach, *Basella alba*. ఉపోదకి. తీగబచ్చలి, అల్లుబచ్చలి or పొలముబచ్చలి the plant termed the Creeping Purslane. దుంపబచ్చలి *Basella indica*. Rox. ii. 104. ఎర్ర అల్లుబచ్చలి *Basella rubra*. (Watts).

బచ్చు or బచ్చువాడు batstsu. [Tel.] n. A Vaisya, Chetty or Komati, వైశ్యుడు. A treasurer, బొక్కసమునకధికారి. One who tests silver and gold, వెండి బంగారముల వానెముచూచువాడు. A money changer or shroff. సరాబు. H. ii. 54. A. iv. 317. S. i. 469. "నిచ్చలురత్నపరీక్షయెరిగి చెప్పు బచ్చులు బోరె." BD. 2. 511.

బజంత్రీ or భజంత్రీ bajantri. [H.] n. Music. A musician, మేళము, మేళగాడు.

బజగడగు or బజగడుగు baja-gadagu. [Tel.] adj. Unsteady, నిలుకడలేని. బజగడుగుది an unsteady woman. నిలుకడలేని ఆడుది.

> "బజగడగుదానిమాటలు,
> నిజమనిగురుభక్తినిరతునిర్మలచరితుం,
> సుజనుకుమారునిలీలాం,
> గజానింబోనాడుకొంటెగదచేసెనుమతా."
>
> Sāranga. Pad. iii. 241.

బజాయించు bajāyinṭsu. [Tel.] v. a. To beat soundly.

బజీతు bajitu. [Tel.] n. Disgrace, భంగము. బజీతుచేయు to disgrace, భంగముచేయు.

> "తే॥ ఆటదానిబజీతుసేయుంగవలెనె."
>
> ఆము. ౫.

బజ్జి bajji. [Tel.] n. A dish of vegetables, a chutney. పచ్చడి.

బజారు badzāru. [Tel.] n. A shop, అంగడి. The merchant's quarter, a market, అంగడివీధి. బజారుమాట badzāru-māṭa. n. A rumour, town-talk, వీధులలో చెప్పుకొనుమాట. బజారము badzāramu. n. Adultery, వ్యభిచారము. బజారి badzāri. (బజారము+ఇ.) n. An adulteress, వ్యభిచారిణి. బజారించు badzārinṭsu. v. n. To commit adultery, వ్యభిచరించు.

బజ్జెడి badzḍaḍi. [Tel.] n. A kind of pace or gait, పాదవిన్యాసవిశేషము.

> "ద్వి॥ బహువిచిత్రగతులతోబజ్జెడ్లుత్రొక్కు."
>
> పల్నాటిచరిత్ర. 2. భా.

బటమరులు baṭamarulu. [Tel.] n. Nostrils. ముక్కుచర్మములు. "ముఖజనితహుతాశనుతోతప్పఖండగు గంధవహాంగురూర్పనిక్కనని నొక్కింత నిక్కి చొక్కంపుబటమరులంజూపట్టు తిలకుసుమవిలసనావహనిని యుగునాసఖాసమానుండగువాని." A. vi. 138. టీ॥ చొక్కంపుబటమరులు, సుందరమైన ముక్కుచర్మములచేతను.

బటాకబయలు, బటాబయలు or బట్టబయలు baṭāka-bayalu. [Tel.] n. A quite open place. adj. Broadly open, quite naked or evident. UH. iv. 168.

బటానీలు baṭānīlu. [Tel.] n. Peas. *Pisum sativum*.

బటారము baṭāramu. [Tel.] adj. Great, large, గొప్ప, పెద్ద. "లోలొటారముబయలు బటారము." showy in outward appearance but worth nothing intrinsically. బటాబారము baṭā-bāramu. (బటా+బారము.) n. Gentlemanliness, greatness, పెద్దరికము.

> "తే॥......... ....కొనినియ్యా
> ముల బటాబారముకనెముట్లగెలుచు."
>
> దా. హా. iii.

బటు or బటుక baṭu. [Tel.] n. A Brahmin bachelor. బ్రహ్మచారి. బటువస్త్రము, a bachelor's cloth. బడుగువస్త్రము.

బటువు baṭuvu. [Tel.] adj. Round, circular, spherical. గుండ్రని. Firm, దృఢము. n. Roundness, గుండ్రన. A thin ring, సన్నని ఉంగరము. బటువు or బటువుదిళ్లి baṭuvu. n. A small round pillow, a round bolster, దిళ్లకలగడ. "బటువులూరుగులుగల పూలపాన్పు మీద." A. i. 67. బటువుకైదువు or బటువువాలు baṭuvu-kaiduvu. n. (Lit.) The round weapon, i. e., Vishṇu's discus.

బట్ట baṭṭa. [Tel.] n. Cloth, clothes. వస్త్రము. తడిబట్టతో గొంతుకోయడము to cut the throat with a wet cloth, i. e., to kill by slow torture. adj. Dappled, mottled with white and black or red. బట్టావు a dappled cow. Bald, బెంద్రుకలూడిన. బట్టతల a bald head. బెంద్రుకలూడినతల. బట్టతలవాడు a bald headed man. బట్టగుడ్డ baṭṭa-guṭṭu. adj. Shameless, సిగ్గుమాలిన, లజ్జలేని. బట్టగెనుపుచెట్టు baṭṭa-genupu-chettu. n. A certain forest tree. బట్టపువ్వు or కవ్వె రిమలపాము baṭṭa-puvvu. The caricature plant, on the variegated leaves of which there are white marks like faces.

బట్టబయలు baṭṭa-bayalu. [Tel. బయలు+ బయలు.] n. An open plain, an open country, an expanse. బట్టబయలుగా openly, బాహాటముగా. See బటాబయలు or బటాక బయలు.

బట్టమేక baṭṭa-mēka. [Tel.] n. The great Indian Bustard, *Eupodotis edwardsi*.

బట్టి baṭṭi. [Tel.] n. A still for drawing spirits, &c., సారాయి మొదలగునవి కాచేబాన. A kiln, ఆవము. Talkativeness. వాచాలత. బట్టికాడు baṭṭi-kāḍu. n. Lit. One that is talkative, i. e., a parrot or a myna. The Red-backed Shrike.

బట్టినకోల baṭṭina-kōla. [Tel.] n. A stick with the aid of which bags of corn are lifted and placed on the backs of oxen.

బట్టు, బట్టువాడు or బట్రాజు baṭṭu. [Tel.] n. A bard, herald: a chanter of titles and praise. వంది. బట్రాజులు a caste of Sudras who as a rule are eulogisers by profession.

బట్టువాసంచి baṭṭuva-sanchi. [H.] n. A wallet, తోలా.

బట్టె baṭṭe. [Tel.] n. A water-course fed by a river, a streamlet. కాలువ. తొట్టిబట్టె the trough of a well.

బట్లె baṭle. [Tel.] n. A kind of an earthern cover over a pot, ఒకవిధమైన మూకుడు.

బటువాడా or బట్టువాడా baṭvāḍa. [H.] n. Distribution, disbursement. బటువాడా చేయు to disburse, or pay out, as money or goods.

బడ or బడా baḍa. [H.] adj. Large, పెద్ద. adv. Very, మిక్కిలి. "బడబాకిసోరు." భల్లా. ii. బడకొండ a large hill.

బడప baḍapa. [Tel.] n. A difficulty, a source of trouble or danger, a calamity, ఇడుము, ఆపద.

బడబ baḍaba. [Skt.] n. A mare. ఆడగుర్రము.

బడబడ baḍa-baḍa. [Tel.] n. A rumbling or gurgling noise, పారుటవుండగు ధ్వన్యనుకరణము.

బడబాగ్ని or బడబానలము baḍab-agni. [Skt.] n. An inextinguishable flame: fire that burns under water.

బడలు baḍalu. [Tel.] v. n. To be weary, or fatigued, to tire, to flag, to be exhausted. ఆయాసమునొందు, అలయు. n. Fatigue, అలసట. బడలువడు or బడల్పడు Same as బడలు (verb). "వట బలంబులుబడలువడంబోరు చున్నవాడు." M. VIII. iii. 66. బడలించు

badalintsu. v. a. To fatigue, to exhaust. బడలిక *badalika*. n. Fatigue, weariness, exhaustion, అలసట. బడలికతీర్చుకొను to rest oneself. బడలిన *badalina*. adj. Wearied, fatigued, exhausted. డస్సిన.

బడవా *badava*. [Tel.] n. A pimp, తార్పు వాడు, తార్చువాడు. A base wretch, లుచ్ఛా.

బడాయి *badāyi*. [H. from బడా q. v.] n. Boasting, bragging, బింకాలు. బడాయికోరు a boaster, braggart.

బడి or బది *badi*. [Drav. √ పడు = to read. Cf. Tam. పడి. Skt. పఠించు is cognate with it.] n. A school. పాఠశాల, పల్లెకూటము. Order, క్రమము. Firmness, స్థైర్యము. బడికోలు *badi-kōlu*. n. Resemblance, an example. పోలు, పోలిక. A. v. 139. బడిచేయు *badi-chēyu*. v. a. To warn one to be mindful of any thing, దిట్టముచేయు. బడిపెట్టుకొను *badi-pettu-konu*. v. n. To open or start a school. బడివేళ అయినది the school time is up. బడికలిసిపోయినది or బడిముగిసినది the school is over. బడియెత్తివేయు to abolish a school. బడిపెద్ద *badi-pedda*. n. A class leader, monitor. బడితపాఠము *baditu-pāthamu*. n. A lesson that has been read, an old lesson, చదివినపాఠము.

"ద్వి॥ . . . . ఒజ్జలకు
బడితపాఠము తొంగపడిరులన్నియును."
పాతిశ్చ. ii.

బడి *badi*. [Tel. from పడు to fall.] adj. Slight, petty, "బడిపనులేమేనిపనుపుచు నంబిక దుకాణిపిలువంగ నడుచున్నేచ్చితిని." BD. iv. 1267. బడిపనులు servitude. కొలువుడుపనులు. బడిగుర్రము an unsaddled horse. బడి adv. Along with, కూడ. "అఖిలజనంబులునుంబడి చేసికొని వెడలియాతండు యుక్తిగాపాదంబుడిద్దు కెడ." M. vi. ii. 348. అందరినిన్ని వెంటబెట్టుకొని. Like, as, conformably to, according to. దీని బడి చేయుంము make it like this one. బడికోడి or కోడిబడి *badi-kōdi* n A barn door fowl. A large fowl. బడి *badi*. An affix forming nouns. Thus దారిబడి along the road. తీరుబడి leisure. తెగులుబడి expense. పెట్టుబడి money advanced or laid out. వచ్చుబడి income. ఏలుబడి a reign. So many times as much, గుణాధ్ధము. ఇబ్బడి as much again, twice as much. ముబ్బడి thrice as much. బడిబడి *badi-badi*. adv. Repeatedly, one after another. మాటిమాటికి. "ప్రమదంబున బంధుజనులు బడిబడిరాగా." Sunanda. v. 155. బడివారడి *badi-varadi*. n. Apportionment, allotment, lot. The share of revenue levied on each farmer. ప్రతిమనుష్యునకు వేసినపన్ను.

బడిత or బడిద *baditu*. [Tel.] n. A stake, thick stick, cudgel. గుదియ.

బడితపాఠము See under బడి. n.

బడిమి *badimi*. [Tel.] n. A circular movement. A ceremony performed to remove the effects of the evil eye, బడియుట. Going round in a circle. చక్రాకార భ్రమణము. A sacrifice to a demon, an animal sacrifice, భూతబలి. బడిద్రిప్పు or బడింద్రిప్పు *badi-drippu*. v. a. To parade, to carry a prisoner around the town in procession before execution. To take away the evil eye. దిష్టితీసివేయు, దిగదుడుచు.

బడియ or బడిద *badiya*. [Tel.] n. A stake or short thick stick. A cudgel. చిన్నదుడ్డు కర్ర. పిచ్చిబడియ a fool. See బడిత.

బడియు *badiyu*. [Tel.] v. n. To remove the effects of the evil eye. (దృష్టిదోషపరిహారార్థము) దిగదీయు. వై. iii. See బడిద్రిప్పు. బడిసి *badisi*. n. A charm or amulet, రక్ష. బడిసివాటు *badisi-vatu*. n. Taking away the effects of the evil eye, దిగదీసివేయుట. That which is thrown away to remove the effects of the evil eye on a person, దిగదీసి వేసినది.

"తే॥ ప్రొద్దుకొంకయు కాంక్ష బడసినాటు."
కాశీ. vii.

బడిలి *badili*. [Tel.] n. A hole, కంతలు, బెజ్జము, రంధ్రము.

బడిశము *badiṣamu* [Skt.] n. A fishhook. చేపలుపట్టేగాలము.

బడుగు or బడుపు *badugu*. [Tel.] adj. Weak, lean, skinny, కృశము, అశక్తమైన. Poor, necessitous. బడుగురాక్షసుడు a gaunt demon. బడుగునడుము (B. viii. 421. and Amuk. vi.) a slender waist. బడుగుపనులు (BD. iv. 628.) drudgery, servitude. బడుగుపీనుగు (BD. v. 1098.) a wretched corpse. బడుగుభక్తులు poor saints. (BD. v. 623.)

బడువ Same as బాడువ (q. v.).

బడె Same as బడియ (q. v.).

బడ్డు *baḍḍu*. [Tel.] n. The male organ of generation, మగగురి.

బణాతు See బనాతు.

బణ్ణము or బణ్ణము *baṇṇamu*. [Tel.] n. A pile of new brass pots. కొత్తయిత్తడిపాత్రముల సమూహము.

బతము *batamu*. [from Skt. వ్రతము.] n. A vow, వ్రతము. కళా. iii.

బతిని *batinī*. [Tel.] n. A kind of silk cloth. కవిక. iii.

బతిమాలు or బతిమాలుకొను *batimālu*. [Tel.] v. a. To pray, beseech, importune, beg. దైన్యముతో వేడుకొను. బతిమాలిక *batimālika*. n. Beseeching, బతిమాలుట. బతిమాలుచు *batimālutsu*. v. a. To cause to beseech, బతిమాలజేయు.

బతుకు, బ్రతుకు or బ్రదుకు *batuku*. [Tel.] v. n. To live, subsist. To survive: to be delivered or saved. నేనుమాత్రము బ్రతికినాను I alone survived. n. Life. Means of life, support. Subsistence, mode of life, trade or profession, జీవనము. బతుకుతెరువు or బ్రతుకుతెరువు means of life, జీవనోపాయము. బతికించు, బ్రతికించు or బ్రతికించు *bratikintsu*. v. a. To cause to live, save, rescue.

బత్తడి, బత్తళి, బత్తడిక or బత్తళిక *battaḍi*. [Tel.] n. A quiver. అమ్ములపొది.

బత్తాయి *battāyi*. [Corruption of 'Batavian.'] n. Batavia. బత్తాయినారింజపండు a Batavian orange.

బత్తి *batti*. [for Skt. భక్తి.] n. Faith. బత్తిగల faithful. "అంగనయొంటిని పుణ్యమూర్తినో, బత్తిజనింపనాదుచెర బాపితి." S. iii. 63. See on భక్తి. బత్తుడు *battuḍu*. n. A worshipper. భక్తుడు. The caste title of all the five castes of artificers as వడ్లబత్తుడు a carpenter. కడుపుబత్తుడు one who makes a god of his belly. L. xvi. 230.

బత్తిస *battisa*. [H.] n. Thirty two. "రమణబత్తిసాది రాగంబులకును." BD. iii. 1836.

బత్తెము or భత్తెము *battemu*. [H. from Skt. భృతి.] n. Subsistence, allowance, batta. Daily allowance in money or food. దినబత్తెము daily bread. బత్తెకర్చు daily expense.

బదనిక *badanika*. [Tel.] n. Any parasitic plant. H. ii. 45. S. i. 18. Rox. ii. 185. "పాముకుబదనికచూపితే ఎంత అలుగునో" (proverb) as disconcerted or irritated as a snake if you shew it the misletoe.

బదర *badara*. [Tel.] n. A crack, పగులు. కుండ బదరపోయినది the pot is cracked.

బదరి *badari*. [Skt.] n. The jujube tree. రేగుచెట్టు. బదరము the jujube fruit.

బదరికము *badarikamu*. [Tel.] n. A box. పెట్టె.

బదులు *badulu*. [Tel.] n. Exchange, a substitute. మారు. (కవి. iii.) A loan. చేబదులు or చేబదులు a loan given without a bond being executed. adj. & adv. Instead, in the place of. బదులుజాబు a reply to a letter. బదులుమాట a word in reply. బదులు పలుకు or బదులు చెప్పు to reply. బదలా యించు badalā-yintsu. [H. from బదులు.] v. a. To change, exchange, transfer, మార్చు. బదిలి n. A substitute.

బద్ద or బ్రద్ద badda. [Tel.] n. A piece, bit, fragment, slice, a flat thin bit, split wood. చిలిక, తునక. దూదేకులబద్ద a cotton beater's bow. ఈ భాష మహాకష్టమని బద్దలుకట్టుతారు they figure this language as very difficult. బద్దలుకట్టి మాట్లాడినాడు he arranged his arguments to much advantage. కావటిబద్ద the wooden part of a yoke (కావడి.) See బద్దె. బద్ద or బ్రద్ద adj. Lean, lank. పలచని. "బద్దపిక్కలునంటుబలసిన తొడలు." HD. ii. 1087. "పొదిపట్టినకండ్లు బద్దచేరులును." BD. iii. 558. బద్దలగు badda-l-agu. v. n. To break in pieces, to go to shivers, to crack.

బద్దకము or బద్ధకము baddakamu. [Tel.] n. Laziness, indolence, sloth. Heaviness, పొలుమారిక. Delay, ఆలస్యము. బద్దకించు baddakintsu. v. n. To flag, tire, become lazy. పొలుమారు. బద్దకముగానుండు or బద్ద కించు to feel heavy, or lazy. బద్దకుడు baddakudu. n. An idle man.

బద్దపరి See బ్రద్దపరి.

బద్ది baddi. [Tel.] n. A certain plant. చిరి బద్దితేరు.

బద్దించు baddintsu. [Tel.] v. a. To test a previous measurement (of land, &c.), to check, verify. సరిగానున్నదో లేదో చూచు టకు కొలిచినదే మరల కొలుచు. To rate, settle price, set a value on. To prune a tree. బద్దింపు baddimpu. n. The arithmetical process called Reduction. బద్దింపు తీర్చు to appraise or estimate.

బద్దు or బద్దుర baddu. [Tel.] n. A lie, అబ ద్ధము.

బద్దె badde. [Tel.] n. The fag end or selvage of a web, వస్త్రముమొదలు, వత్తి, బట్టకొనదిభాగము. A slip of cloth. వస్త్రఖం డము. బద్దె మెడకువేసుకొని కర్మను జరిగించెను he performed the funeral rites putting on a slip of cloth round his neck as a mark of mourning. Also, a thin or flat piece of wood as వింటిబద్దె or కావటిబద్దె. నవారుబద్దె a tape. బద్దెగుండ్లు badde-gundlu. n. Little balls like marbles flicked from the finger-ends.

బద్ర badra. [Tel.] n. Twelve. పండ్రెండు.

బద్రము badramu. [from Skt. భద్రము] n. Safety, పదిలము. interj. Beware! Take care, be on your guard. పదిలము.

బధిరము badhiramu. [Skt.] adj. Deaf. చెవుడు. బధిరుడు badhirudu. n. A deaf man, చెవిటివాడు. బధిరితము badhiritamu. adj. Made deaf, బధిరముగాచేయబడిన. "బధిరి తదిఙ్ముఖుండు." భార. భీష్మ. i.

బద్ధము baddhamu. [Skt.] adj. Tied, bound. కట్టబడిన. బద్ధవైరము rancour, fixed hatred. బద్ధాంజలులై with clasped hands, i. e., very humbly. బద్ధము or బద్దము baddhamu. [Tel. Colloq.] n. A boundary, limit. వానికి ఒకబద్దమా is he bound by any conditions? బుద్దిబద్దములేనివాడు an unprincipled man. బద్ధుడు baddhudu. adj. Bound, obliged. కర్మబద్ధుడు one who is addicted to religious rites. ఆజ్ఞాబద్ధుడు bound to obedience.

బనాతు or బనాతు banātu. [H.] n. Broadcloth, woollen stuff. సకలాతు.

బనాయించు banāyintsu. [H.] v. a. To attach, to add. To fabricate, make up. బనాయింపు banāyimpu. n. Fabrication.

బన్నారసు banārasu. [from Skt. వారణాసి.] n. Benares, కాశి.

బన్నము bannamu. [from Skt. భిన్నము.] n. Disgrace, అవమానము, మోసపోవడము. Difficulty, trouble, misfortune. ఇడుము, ఆపద. "పన్నగభూషణులు బడినబన్నములెన్నగరాదు." HK. ii. 12. బన్నపడు. n. To be disgraced, భంగముపొందు. బన్నసరము or బన్నసరి banna-saramu. n. A necklace of coral and gold beads or plates, or of pearl chains and gold plates alternately. పగడములు గుండ్లు మొదలైనవి గుచ్చిన పేరు. A necklace, హారము.

బభ్రువు babhruvu. [Skt.] adj. Ruddy, tawny, red, iron grey, like the colour of the ichneumon. Brown, పింగళవర్ణము. Yellowish green. బభ్రుని. n. A brown cow, కపిలగోవు. Siva, శంభుడు. Vishṇu, విష్ణువు.

బమ్మ bamma. [from Skt. బ్రహ్మ.] Brahma. బమ్మగుడ్డు bamma-guḍḍu. n. The globe, sphere, mundane egg. బ్రహ్మాండము. "బమ్మగుడ్డు ఆనెడు పట్నంబులోపల, బమ్మ మొదలకేలని బాపడేల." Vēma. i. 232.

బమ్మరించు or బమ్మరిల్లు bamma-rintsu. [from Skt. భ్రమ.] v. n. To err, to go wrong, భ్రమించు. To be confounded, to be afraid or amazed, బెదరు, తొందరపడు. "కోరలు గలవాని, గోళ్లుగలవాని, కొమ్ములుగలవాని నమ్మవలదు, బమ్మరించె నేని బ్రతుకంగవచ్చునే, దొలుగుటొకటె చెలిమి యొనరుటకు." G. i. 284. "పొడ సూపినట్లైన వడిబట్టుపమకట్టి. పరికించి కావక బమ్మరించు." M. IV. ii. 303. బమ్మెర or బమ్మర bammera. n. Confusion. భ్రమ, భ్రాంతి, కళవళపాటు. బమ్మెరపోవు v. n. To be in fright or confusion, భ్రమపడు, కళవళపడు. "ఎలదేటిపాటులకా బమ్మెర పోవదోలు దెగబారడుబెంట్రుకలు." Swa. iii. 5. బమ్మెరపోక bammera-pōka. n. The act of being confused. బమ్మెరపోవుట.

బయకాడు baya-kāḍu. [Tel. బయలు+కాడు.] n. A musician, గాయకుడు, గానవిద్యోపాధ్యాయుడు. "చతురతభుయపూర్వమైన భావరాగము సంబు తలంపున గొల్చుచో, బాలికలకెల్ల మిక్కిలి దెగబోయగవచ్చిన యట్లతో చెలి, పనుపమదేవదాసి మనోహరనాటక సూత్రధారియై, ఘనముగ నీటిమీటు బయకాడవునీయొకపేరు గాంచెనే." Tara. iv. 226. బయకారము baya-kāramu. (బయలు+కారము.) n. A youthful prank, యౌవనమందు బయలుపడు శృంగారచేష్ట. బయకారి baya-kāri. n. A sprightly woman, విలాసవతి.

బయలు, బయిలు or బైలు bayalu. [Tel.] n. The outside. An open place, open country, బహిఃప్రదేశము, చెట్లుచేమలులేని చోటు. The sky, ఆకాశము. adj. Empty, unoccupied, శూన్యము. బయలుతామర bayalu-tāmara. n. The land lotus, మెట్టతామర. బయలుదేరు or బయలువెడలు bayalu-dēru. v. n. To come out, to go out, to start, నిర్గమించు. To come to light, to be discovered. బయలుపడు, బయల్పడు, బయలుపోవు or బయలుపెరయు bayalu-paḍu. v. n. To make its appearance, to become visible, ప్రకాశించు. To be found out or discovered, to become publicly known.

బయానా bayānā. [H.] n. An advance of money, earnest money, సంచకరువు.

బయ్యంకలు Same as పేకిల్లు (q. v.).

బయ్యడు bayyaḍu. [Tel.] n. A dull man. మందుడు.

బరక baraka. [Tel.] adj. Rough, sharp, కరుకైన. పిండి బరకగానున్నది the flour is rough to the touch. బరకభూమి baraka-bhūmi. n. Saline soil. బరకము barakamu. n. A load or bale of cotton. దూది బరువు. బరకల్లాపి or బరగడ bara-kallāpi. n. A seal or mark set on heaps of grain to prevent theft.

బరగడము *baragaḍamu.* [Tel.] n. A tree called *Indigofera glandulosa.* Rox. iii. 373.

బరటు *baraṭu.* [Tel.] v.a. To scratch, to scrape, గోకు. To scratch so as to call one's attention to anything, సైగగాగోకు.

బరడు or బెరడు *baraḍu.* [Tel.] n. The rough bark of the tamarind and certain other trees, చింతలు మొదలైనవాటి పైబెరడు. adj. Skinny, lean, as the ribs. "గుజ్జెలుడిగి బలుసు దోప్పచెప్పులుమబోడు ప్రక్కలు." BD. iii. 2231.

బరణి, బరిణ, బరిణె or భరిణ *baraṇi.* [Tel.] n. A casket, small jewel-case, snuff box, pill box. కరండము. పాచికలబరిణ a dice-box. బరణిచుక్క or భరణి *bharaṇi-tsukka.* n. The second lunar mansion consisting of three stars in a triangle.

బరతపిట్ట or భరతపిట్ట *barata-piṭṭa.* [Tel.] n. A species of wagtail: Chendūl.

బరతరపు or బర్తర్ఫ్ *baratarapu.* [H.] n. Discharge, dismissal. బరతరపుచేయు *baratarapu-chēyu.* v. a. To dismiss from service.

బరపట *barapaṭa.* [Tel.] n. A kind of grass or its grain. తృణవిశేషము, తృణధాన్యవిశేషము.

బరబర *bara-bara.* [Tel. anuk.] n. The noise made in dragging anything along the ground. వానికాళ్లుపట్టుకొని బరబరయీడ్చినారు they dragged him violently along the ground.

బరమా or బర్మా *barama.* [H.] n. A bradawl, a drill, a kind of auger or gimlet worked with a string. తొరపరము.

బరవసము *bara-vasamu.* [from Skt. భారవశము.] n. Courage, ధైర్యము. Perseverance, persistence. పూనిక. బరవసముతో with importunity. "పూనికచేతన్ బరవసమున్ [illegible]." Swa. iv. 79

బరాతము *barātamu.* [H.] n. An assignment, a written order for payment, a cheque or draft. బరాతముచెప్పు to transfer the responsibility to another, to ask another to pay for one.

బరాబరి or బరాబరిక *barābari.* [H.] n. Alertness, హెచ్చరిక. "సీ॥ కరదండములుగట్టి యనుచరులుగట్టి ప్రతిహారులు బరాబరికచేసి" చంద్రా. iii. adj. Right, just, proper, సరియైన. బరాబరిచేయు to make equal.

బరి *bari.* [Tel.] n. A side. పార్శ్వము. "పక్కలు వాటించి బరులంటెంగాడి." Pal 108. బరులుబ్బు to bloat, as the belly or the sides of the belly. A line drawn on the ground in a circle, గిరి. An elephant goad, ఏనుగుప్రక్కలు పొడిచి నడిపించుటకై అర్ధచంద్రాకారముగా ఉక్కుతో చేసిన అంకుశవిశేషము. A thief, దొంగ. An enemy, శత్రువు. adj. (for బరిక). Naked. బరిమేను=దిగంబరదేహము. "తోడబుట్టుల కాలు దొరకచుపుట్టెస." B. D. i. 514. బరికొట్టె or బరికట్టె *bari-kaṭṭe.* A spear without a handle, అలుగులేనిఈటె. A crook or stick used by herdsman, కోల. "[illegible]." BD. iii. 2244. బరివాడు *bari-vāḍu.* n. An elephant driver, మావటివాడు. బరికోల n. An elephant goad. An arrow, బాణము. బరిజోగి *bari-dzōgi.* (బరి+జోగి.) n. A snake-charmer, పాములవాడు. బరియెముకలు *bari-y-emukalu.* n. The ribs, పక్కయెముకలు. బరిశూల *bari-śūla.* n. Liver complaint. పక్కశూల. See బరిక.

బరికె *barike.* [Tel.] n. A small stick or bough, a switch. A dried rough palmyra bough, గరుకులుగల యెండిన తాటిమట్ట. adv. Rough, dishevelled చింపిరి.

బరిగి *barigi.* [Tel. another form of బరి.] adj. Empty. ఏమియులేని, శూన్యము. బరిగిరవుతు *barigi-ravutu.* n. One who rides a horse without a saddle, జల్లుపరుపు లేకుండ [illegible].

బరిగె baripe. [Tel.] n. A small kind of grain, like fine rice.

బరిచి barichi. [Tel.] n. A spear, ఈటె, కుంతము.

బరిణ or బరిణె bariṇa. [Tel.] n. A little box. పొడిబరిణె a snuff box. బరిడెగవ్వ or బరిడెగవ్వ bariḍe-gavva. n. A kind of cake, భక్ష్యవిశేషము. హంస. i. బరిణపురుగు or బరిడెపురుగు bariṇa-purugu. n. A cockroach. బొద్దింక. బొద్దిక.

బరివొంక bari-vonka. [Tel.] n. A certain tree with small leaves. G. v. 299. ఖరపత్రి, పక్కిచెట్టు.

బరిస barisa. [Tel.] n. A club with iron bands, ఇనుపకట్లుగలదియు, పరిఘము.

బరుకు baruku. [Tel.] v. a. To scratch. To lacerate, tear. గీరు. To scribble in writing.

బరుజు baruḍzu. [Tel.] n. A small bell, గజ్జె. కింకిణి.

బరువడి baru-vaḍi. [Tel.] adv. Again, మరల.

బరువు or బరువు baruvu. [Tel.] n. Weight, heaviness. A load or burden. భారము. adj. Heavy. బరువుబండ్లు laden carts.

బరుసు barusu. [Tel.] adj. Rough, coarse, కఠినమైన. కరుకైన. Brutal. బరుసుకూత a dreadful roar.

బరెంక barenka. [Tel.] n. A kind of tree, కపిలకవృక్షము.

బర్బరుడు barbaruḍu. [Skt. Cf. Gk. 'Barbarian'.] n. A blockhead, or fool, పామరుడు. బర్బరము barbaramu. n. The name of a country, ఒకదేశము. A sort of drum, కంటిడోలు.

బర్బూరము barbūramu. [Skt.] n. The Babul tree which produces gum arabic. Mimosa arabica, తుమ్మచెట్టు. యుగంధరవృక్షము.

బర్ర barra. [Tel.] n. A switch, sapling.

బర్రింక barrinka. [Tel.] n. A plant, the stiff stalks of which are used as tooth brushes. Rox. iii. 553. 761.

బర్రె or బర్రెగొడ్డు barre. [Tel.] n. A female buffalo. ఎనుము, గేదె. మహిషి. A simpleton or blockhead. బర్రెగొంతు a hoarse deep voice.

బర్హము barhamu. [Skt.] n. A peacock's tail. నెమలిపింఛము. బర్హి barhi. n. A peacock. నెమలి. బర్హిష్ఠము barhishṭhamu. n. The plant called Peacock's Pride. A perfume extracted from its root. H. ii. 176. కేసవారుబంకతో చేసిన ధూపద్రవ్యము.

బర్హిస్సు barhissu. [Skt.] n. Fire, అగ్ని. The sacred grass, used like hyssop, in sacrifices. కుశ, దర్భగడ్డి. బర్హిర్ముఖుడు barhir-mukhuḍu. n. He whose mouth is fire, i. e., a god. వేల్పు. బర్హిశ్శుష్మ or బర్హిశ్శుష్ముడు barhis-sushma. n. A name of the god of fire. అగ్ని.

బల bala. [Skt.] n. A spell or charm విద్యావిశేషము. "బలయతిబలలనంబరగుమంత్రములు" DR. Bala : page 182.

బలపము balapamu. [Tel.] n. Potstone, *Lapis ollaris*, a whitish chalk like a slate pencil. A slate pencil.

బలబల or వెలవెల bala-bala. [Tel. (anuk.)] adv. Brightly : more and more. బలబలతెల్లవారెను it was dawning rapidly.

బలభిత్తు, బలభేది, బలసూదనుడు. బలారాతి, బలారి or బలధ్వంసి bala-bhittu. [Skt.] n. Epithets of Indra, as being the slayer of the demon Bala.

బలము balamu. [Skt.] n. Strength, might, power, influence. Efficaciousness, potency. Force, rigour, severity. సత్త్వము, సారము, బలువు. A force, army, host, folk, people, a crowd, number, party. సేన. బలవితానము a host. దైవబలము the finger of God, Divine assistance. బలము

చేయు to strengthen; to enforce, aid, assist. వాన మరీమరీ బలము చేయుచున్నది the rain is increasing. దానిని ఒక బలముచేసు కొని relying on it as a ground or reason. adj. Strong, mighty, much, అధికము. Potent, efficacious. బలకరము *bala-karamu.* adj. Forcible, violent, strengthening. బలకరమైన సాక్ష్యము strong evidence. బలకరము or బళకరము *balakaramu.* n. Force, violence, strength. Watching, కావలి. A guard, or watch, కావలి, పారా. R. v. 43. బలకరించు *bala-karintsu.* v. n. To spread, వ్యాపించు. v. a. To strengthen. బలకాయించు (బలము+ఇంచు) *balakayintsu.* v. n. To flourish, prosper. వృద్ధి అగు, అతిశయించు. బలకొట్టు *bala-kottu.* v. n. To sing, ah, ah అ అని శ్రుతి పట్టు. బలకొను *bala-konu.* (బలము+కొను.) v. n. To flourish, అతిశయించు. బలగము or బల్లము *balagamu.* n. Attendants, retinue, పరిజనము. A party, set: a troop, army, host: a family circle. జ్ఞాతి బంధు సమూహము. "చెంచు బలగము నేలెను." (Garudach. 113,) he ruled a troop of foresters. Swa. iii. 75. బలదేవుడు, బలభద్రుడు or బలరాముడు *bala-dêvudu.* n. Balarâma, Krishna's brother. బలదేవుడు n. Wind, వాయువు. బలపడు *bala-padu.* (బలము+పడు.) v. n To increase, అధికమగు. బలపరచు *bala-paratsu.* v. a. To strengthen, support, confirm. బలయు *balayu.* v. a. To surround, పరివేష్టించు. బలవంతము *bala-vantamu.* n. Strength, force, violence, compulsion. బలాత్కారము. adj. Strong, violent, బలముగల. adv. Forcibly, బలవంతముగా. బలవంతుడు or బలశాలి *bala-vantudu.* n. A strong man, a violent man, a mighty man. బలవంతులతో విరోధము కారాదు do not contend with the mighty. బలహీనత *bala-hînata.* n. Weakness, debility. బలహీనము *bala-hînamu.* n. Weakness, debility. adj. Weak, strengthless. powerless. బలక్షయము *bala-kshayamu.* n. Loss of strength; weakness, impotence. బలాత్కారము *balât-kâramu.* n. Violence, force, severity, exaction. బలాత్కరించు *balât-karintsu.* v. a. To force, press, compel. బలాత్కారముచేయు

బలే, బళా, బలారా or భళా *balâ.* [Tel.] interj. Well done! well well! very good.

బలాక or బలాకము *balâka.* [Skt.] n. A sort of crane, or curlew. తెల్లకొక్కెర.

బలి *bali.* [Skt.] n. Tax, royal revenue, tribute, కానుక, పన్ను. An oblation. A religious offering in general, presentation of food, &c. పూజోపహారము. The sacrifice of an animal, an animal sacrificed. భూతబలి. నరబలి a human sacrifice. బలి *bali.* n. The name of a giant vanquished by Vishnu who hence is styled బలిధ్వంసి. A strong man, బలముగలవాడు. బలిపుష్టము or బలిభుక్కు *bali-pushtamu.* n. The "devourer of the sacrifice:" i. e., a crow. P. i. 480. బలిపీఠము *bali-pîthamu.* n. An altar. బలిపెట్టు or బలియిచ్చు *bali-pettu.* v. a. To sacrifice, to kill, చంపు. బలిసద్మము *bali-sadmamu.* n. The infernal regions. రసాతలము, పాతాళలోకము.

బలిజె *balije.* [Tel.] n. The name of a caste among Telugu and Canarese Sudras. బలిజెవాడు a man of that caste. బలిజెది a woman of that caste. లింగబలిజెవాండ్లు that portion of this caste who are Lingaites. పంచమబలిజెవాండ్లు another sect. తెలుగుబలిజెలు another sect. బలిజెరికము *balije-rikamu.* n. The community or tribe of the బలిజెలు.

బలితము *balitamu.* [Tel.] adj. Strong, బలిష్ఠము. Stout, స్థూలము. నడుముబలితమయ్యె the waist became stout. బలితపు or బలితంపు *balitapu.* adj. Thick, strong, mighty. బలితపుటురి a strong halter. బలితుడు *balitudu.* n. A strong man. బలవంతుడు.

బలియు *baliyu.* [from Skt. బలము.] v. n. To become corpulent, or strong, to grow fat, big, thick, stable, firm: స్థూలించు.

To increase, thrive, prosper, multiply or be augmented, అధికమగు. అరణ్యము బలిసి పోయినది the forest spread over the place. అడవిబలిసినచోటు a spot overgrown with shrubs. బలియుడు *baliyuḍu*. n. A strong man, బలవంతుడు. బలిపించు *balipintsu*. v. a. To fatten or strengthen. బలిమి or బల్మి *balimi*. n. Strength, power. దేహబలము. Force, బలాత్కారము. బలిమికాడు *balimi-kāḍu*. n. A strong man, బలవంతుడు. బలిష్ఠము *balishṭhamu*. [Skt.] adj. Very strong, most powerful, మిక్కిలిబలముగల. బలిష్ఠుడు *balishṭhuḍu*. n. A very strong man. బలిసిన *balisina*. [Tel.] adj. Big, plump, large. బలీయము *baliyamu*. [Skt.] adj. Very strong, exceedingly powerful. బలీవర్దము *bali-vardamu*. n. A bull, or ox. ఎద్దు. బలుడు *baluḍu*. n. A strong man: one who is powerful. బలముగల వాడు. బలుపు or బల్పు *balupu*. [Tel.] n. Bigness, fatness, plumpness. strength, పుష్టి, బలము. Well being, క్షేమము. "అనీక మునంగడుమంచియోధులంగలయగ నొందునయ్యు యుత్తరి రము వారల నిల్వ బల్పుగా" M. XII. iii. 9. బలుపుకొను or బల్పుకొను *balupu-konu*. v. n. To increase, prosper, అతిశయించు. బలుపాకురాయి *balup-āku-rāyi*. (బలుపు + ఆకురాయి) n. A carpenter's rasp.

బలు or బల్ *balu*. [Tel. short for బలుపు.] adj. Big, strong, mighty, great, exceeding, large, much, very. బలుగాయము a deep wound. బలుమూర్ఛ a deep swoon. బలుతే డవాయె it grew late, much time has passed. R. v. 95. బలుముల్లుమి a cluster of large thorns. T. pref. 43. బలుకెంపుతేల డింపుజేగిమోవి a lip which reminded one of a noble ruby. బలుకెంపు = శ్రేష్ఠమైన కెంపు. బలుగుత్తి *balu-gutti*. (బలుపు+గుత్తి.) n. A sort of rice. "గొబ్బికాయ లబలుగుత్తులు పాలమీగడలు శ్రీరంగాలు కామ ధ్నాలు." H. iv. 156. బలురక్కసి, బల్రక్కసి, బలురక్కసి or బలురక్కసి *balu-rakkisu*. n. A plant called *Arum macrorhizon*, (Reeve), గజకర్ణము, గజాసనము, బ్రహ్మరాకాసిచెట్టు, బృహచ్ఛదము. బలువిడి or బల్విడి *baluvidi*. n. Way, manner, విధము. adv. Much, vehemently, severely, strongly. అత్యంతము. "తేరుగదలనీక వైరులు బలువిడి పొదివిపట్టి రాచపోట్లనైన." M. VIII. ii. 270. బల్దూరము *bal-dūramu*. n. A great distance. బల్మక్కువ (బలు+మక్కువ.) *bal-makkuva*. n. Strong love, great affection.

బలుగు *balugu*. [Tel.] n. A twig, a switch.

బలుపు See under బలియు.

బలువు or బరువు *baluvu*. [from Skt. బలము.] n. Weight, a load or burden; బరువు. Strength, బలము. A charge, or obligatory duty; *onus*; oppression; anguish; acuteness (as of a boil), heaviness, severity of sickness. Importance, consequence. భారము. మీచిత్తమునకు బలువు తోచును you would be displeased. బరువుకరువు ఎరుగని వాడు one who knows no care. దానిని నెర వేర్చే బరువు తమది it is your business to settle this. తలబరువు ఇంకా తీయలేదు the heaviness or stupor is not yet gone off. నా నెత్తిబరువు తీరినది there is a weight off my mind. ఆకురుపు నానాటికి బరువుచేస్తున్నది the boil becomes more painful day by day. adj. Heavy, onerous; obligatory; difficult, acute, severe (as illness), irksome, indisposed. అధికము, ముఖ్యము. Large, పెద్ద. See బలు. వాడు బలువైన పనిచేయలేడు he cannot do any heavy work. బలువుగా or బరువుగా *baluva-gā*. adv. Heavily. అతనికి ఒళ్లు బలువుగానున్నది he is very ill. ఆ ఊరు బలువుగా కోసెడు ఉన్నది the village is fully two miles off. బలువుడు *baluvuḍu*. adj. Strong, బలముగల. n. A strong man, బలవంతుడు, బలియుడు.

బలుసు or బలుసుచెట్టు *balusu*. [Tel.] n. The plant called *Canthium parviflorum*. Rox. and Watts, *Webera tetrandra*.

(Willd. Ainsl. ii. 63.) అజరిచెట్టు. The thorny Caray. బలుసాకు the leaves, eaten as a wretched diet. బలుసుకూర. నల్లబలుసు the black species, *Canthium umbellatum*.

బలె *bale*. [Tel. another form of వలె. and comes from పోలు to resemble.) Adj. Like, resembling, పోలె. బలె or బళే adj. Much, very. బలెబాగా ఉన్నది that's very good. Interj: Very good! fine!

బల్బజము *balbajamu*. [Skt.] n. A sort of grass, మెదవకడ్డి. adj. Pithless, sapless, useless, vain.

బల్ల *balla*. [Skt.] n. A bench, plank, board, table. A ship's deck. The disease called spleen. గుల్మము. వారు బల్లమీద కూర్చుండిరి they were sitting on a bench. రెండుబల్లలను ఏకముచేయుము join the two planks together. అతనికడుపులో బల్లకట్టుకొన్నది or బల్లపెరిగినది he has an enlargement of the spleen. నీరుబల్ల the dropsy. బల్లకట్టు *balla-kattu*. n. A large flat bottomed boat, a raft. వెడల్పైన అడుగుగల పడవ. బల్లకూర్పు *balla-kūrpu*. n. Wainscotting, planking, joiner's work. బల్లకూర్పుయిల్లు a house built of boards. బల్లకోల *balla-kōla*. n. A sort of spear or harpoon. పంట్రకోల. "క్రమిఠేంద్రియములను బలునిర్చేసి, ఖానప్రణీతమన్బలంబల్లకోల, నిమగ్నత్వము వెలుగుకన్నెడిచి." BD. v. 1443. బల్లగోలలవారు *balla-gōlala-vāru*. n. Lancers. "పరుసనుబహుపృప్పవాటికలో నాటి, జాలవారిని దివ్వటీలను బల్లగోలలవారిని సుడిపూజరులను." BD. iii. 1016.

బల్లాడదట్టి or బల్లడదట్టి *ballaḍa-datti*. [Tel.] n. A kind of belt. ఒకవిధమైనదాసె. "ఇవ్విధంబునం దిరిగివీడు పీనుంగుపెంటలైన, వాంఛాలురవిడుదులు వెడలి జకొట్టామువగు. నశ్వత్థామ బల్లాడదట్టి మొదలగు పరికరంబులంబొటించియున్న ఘనవులొగిల్లకుంజని." M. X. i. 173.

బల్లి *balli*. [Tel.] n. A lizard. పాలబల్లి the white kind. మాలబల్లి the mottled kind. చింతబల్లి the speckled kind. బల్లికోక or బల్లిమొట్ట *balli-kōka*. n. A sort of fish, a species of Gobius. Russell's, plate 52.

బల్లిదము *ballidamu*. [from Skt. బలము.] n. Great strength, మిక్కిలి బలము. బల్లిదము or బల్లిదపు *ballidamu*. adj. Strong, mighty. బల్లిదముగా *ballidamu-ga*. adv. Strongly, mightily. "మల్లియు మెకవల్లియు కూడ బల్లిదముగనల్లినికలుప్పటిటమాపెక." Babulas. ii. 76. బల్లిదుడు *ballidudu*. n. A vigorous or strong man. A hero. బలవంతుడు.

బల్లు or భల్లు *ballu*. [Tel.] n. Suddenness, a sudden sound, తెల్లవారుటయందగుధ్వన్యనుకరణము. A crackling sound, విరుగుటయందగు ధ్వన్యనుకరణము. బల్లున or భల్లున *ballu-na*. adv. Suddenly, పెళ్లున. Broadly, brightly. బల్లున తెల్లవారె it dawned brightly, or, it was now broad day.

బల్లెము *ballemu*. [Tel.] n. A spear. ఈటె. వారికి వీడు పక్కలోనిబల్లెమువలె నున్నాడు he is a thorn in their side. బల్లెమునల Same as బల్లెము.

బళా, బళారె, బళారే, బళి, బళిర బళిరయ్యా, బళిరె, బళిరే or బళి *bala*. [Tel.] adv. (Interjection expressive of praise or commendation.) Good! well done! very well, very good, (a word used in argument.)

బళాయి *balayi*. [Tel.] n. A strong man, బలవంతుడు. కా. vii.

బళుకుబళుకు *baluku-baluku*. [Tel. (anuk.)] adv. Tremulously, waveringly, (as a slender waist) "బళుకుబళుకున నతులయుం దళికిబెళుకు, కులుకుగొనునాళువా తెరుపులాలుకు మేటిపద్దానము." H. ii. 5.

బవంతము *bavantamu*. [Tel.] n. Deceit, cunning. కపటము, మోసము.

బవంతి. *bavanti.* [Tel.] n. A house, containing an open area with rooms built at the corners and roofs between. నాలు గిల్లుకలిపి కట్టిన కట్టడము. Variegated colors, చిత్రవర్ణము. బవంతిబట్ట a cloth which has flowers printed on it, చిత్రవర్ణములుగలచీర. ప్ర. iv.

బవని or **బవిని** *bavani.* [Tel.] n. A kind of dance accompanied by story telling. కథలుచెప్పుచు ఆడేనృత్యము. బవనీ, బవనీడు, or బవినీడు *bavani.* n. A kind of dancer, వేషగాడు, జోకరలో వేషమువేసే మాలదాసరి. "వాళట్టుబవనీలపొముకూన, యనగవిఖ్యాతిగాంచె నరయ్యాడుబు-చి." Suca. iii. 19. "నెయ్యం బునాటిలనీపాలిక గేవుడింక బవనీడేయంచుతా నాడగా." ib. ii. 451.

బవణిక Same as బదనిక (q. v.).

బవరము *bavaramu.* [Tel.] n. Battle, war. యుద్ధము.

బవరి, బవిరి or **బవ్రి** *bavari.* [Tel.] adj. గుండ్రము. n. Riding a horse round a ring. వేడెము. బవరి, బవ్రి, బవిరి, బవరి గడ్డము or బవిరిగడ్డము n. A well trimmed beard. దిద్దినటువంటిగడ్డము. "బవిరిగడ్డమువాడు, పన్నిదంబిడిడాగవచ్చునందంపు వెన్నుమచ్చువాడు." Vijayavilāsam. ii. 271. "ఎంతగడ్డంబైన జింతలేదొనపరి తీరుగా బవిరిదిద్దింపవచ్చు." R. ii. 109. "నసనింపునిద్దంపు బవరిగడ్డముసొంపు." Rasikajana. i. 114. **బవిరిటాకు** or **బవరి టాకు** *baviri-ṭ-āku.* n. An emerald, cut in a certain way. "ఊదిరిబంగరుబవిరిటాకుల పచ్చలచంబుమీనుదిన్నెలు." T. iv. 202.

బవిర or **బవిరె** *bavira.* [Tel.] n. An ornament worn from the tip of the ear. కొనచెవియందుంచుకొను భూషణము.

బవిసి or **భవిసి** *barisi.* [Tel.] n. Prosperity, welfare, respectability, భాగ్యము, గౌరవము.

బస *basa.* [Tel.] n. A temporary abode, ఒకడు వచ్చి దిగినచోటు. Home, abode, lodging. వాసస్థానము, ఉనికిపట్టు. **బసచేయు** *basa-cheyu.* v. n. To lodge.

బసవడు, బసవన్న, బసవడు, బసవయ్య. బసవేశుడు or **బస్వేశుడు** *basavaḍu.* [Tel.] n. A bull. వృషభము. The name of a bull sacred to Siva. అచ్చువేసిన ఆబోతు. A proper name much used among worshippers of the Lingam. The name of a Hindu Reformer, Brahmin by birth, the founder of the Jangam sect.

బసివి or **బసవరాలు** *basivi.* [Tel.] n. A female dedicated in infancy to Siva as a prostitute. స్వైరిణి.

బసుమము Same as భస్మము (q.v.).

బస్తము *bastamu.* [Skt.] n. A he-goat. మేక పోతు. H. iii. 9.

బస్తా *bastā.* [H.] n. A bale of goods.

బస్తీ *bastī.* [H.] n. A town; a large town

బహాదరు or **బహద్దరు** *bahadaru.* [H.] n. A nobleman, a lord.

బహిః *bahih.* [Skt.] n. The outside. బహిని on the outside. బయట. "బహినిసూత్రత తిక బరగలింగముగట్టి." Vēma. 940. **బహిత్రము** *bahitramu.* n. A kind of boat, యాన పాత్రవిశేషము. **బహిపడు** *bahi-paḍu.* v. n. To be expelled, to be excommunicated, to be outcast. వెలివేయబడు. "బహిష్కృతులైన కల్పవుపాచిరంబిడి." A. vi. 91. టీ॥ వెలిబడిన బ్రాహ్మణునికి స్వల్ప ప్రాయశ్చిత్తము చేసి. **బహిపెట్టు** *bahi-peṭṭu.* v. a. To excommunicate, to put out of caste, వెలివేయు. **బహిరంగము** *bahir-angamu.* n. An external organ, వెలుపటి అవయవము. Publicity, notoriety, exposure, publication. adj. Made known, made public, బయలుపడిన. **బహిరంగముచేయు** *bahir-angamu-*

chēyu. v. a. To make known or public. బహిర్ద్వారము bahir-dvāramu. n. An outer door, or principal gate. తలవాకిలి. బహిర్దేశము or బహిర్భూమి bahir-dēsamu. n. The skirts (of a village:) used as a necessary in the villages, hence the word denotes a privy. బహిర్భూమికిపోవు bahir-bhūmiki-pōvu. v. n. To go to stool. బహిర్లాపి bahir-lapi. n. An elliptical question which suggests the answer in other words, ఉత్తరము వేరుమాటలందు అగపడునట్లు అడుగునట్టి విధము సమస్య. "సీ॥ రా జులకెటువంటి రత్నములో ప్రియముకు గాయకేచెట్ల వికరులు మ్రింగు." బహిర్వాసము or బైరవాసము bahir-vāsamu. n. A cloak or upper garment. బహిష్కరించు bahish-karintsu. v. a. To expel from a caste or sect: to degrade or excommunicate. బహిష్కారము or బహిష్కరణము bahish-kāramu. n. Expulsion, degradation: excommunication from sect or caste. వెలివేయుటము. బహిష్కృతుడు bahish-kritudu. adj. Expelled from caste, excommunicated. వెలివేయబడిన (వాడు.)

బహు bahu. [Skt.] adj. Very much, very numerous, plenty, abundant, విస్తారమైన. Many, అనేకమైన. బహుకాలము a long time. అది బహుబాగానున్నది that is very fine or good. బహుత్వము bahutvamu. n. Plurality. బహుధా bahudhā. adv. In many ways, అనేకవిధములచేత. బహుధాన్య bahu-dhānya. n. The name of a year. బహునాయకత్వము or బహునాయకము bahu-nāya-katvamu. n. Anarchy. అరాజకము. Authority vested in many chiefs. బహుపాదము or బహుపాద bahu-pādamu. n. The banyan tree, మర్రిచెట్టు. బహుప్రదుడు bahu-pradudu. n. A very liberal or charitable man, మిక్కిలి యీవిగాడు. బహుమతి or బహుమానము bahu-mati. n A present, donation, reward, gratuity, premium. పారితోషికము. Honor, సన్మానము. వానికి అవమానమును అక్కరలేదు బహుమానమును అక్కరలేదు he regards neither disgrace nor honor. బహుమూత్రము bahu-mūtramu. n. Diabetes. బహురూపము bahu-rūpamu. n. A blood-sucker, a lizard. ఊసరవెల్లి, తొండ. బహురూపుడు bahu-rūpudu. n. One who assumes many forms, అనేకరూపములుగలవాడు. బహుళము bahulamu. adj. Abundant, plenty, అధికము, తరచు. n. The waning or dark fortnight. కృష్ణపక్షము. బహుళముగా abundantly. బహువచనము bahu-vachanamu. n. (In Grammar) the plural number. బహువిధము bahu-vidhamu. adj. Various, diverse, multiform. వివిధమైన, అనేకవిధములుగల. బహువు bahuvu. adj. Much, అధికము. Many, పెక్కు. బహువ్రీహి bahu-vrīhi. n. One of the forms of Sanskrit grammatical composition in which two or more words are compounded to furnish an epithet or attributive, as ముక్కంటి. అన్యపదార్థప్రధానమైనసమాసము. బహుశః or బహుశా bahusah. adv. Generally, probably, usually, at large. బహుసుత bahu-suta. n. A woman who is the mother of many children. బహుస్వనము bahu-svanamu. n. Lit: that which is clamorous: i. e., an owl. గుడ్లగూబ. బహూకరించు bahū-karintsu. v. a. To bestow honour, to pay respect to. సన్మానించు, గౌరవించు. "జనకతనయాన్వేషణక్రియారంభం బునీయదియనుమ్మని బహూకరించి పిలుకొలిపి." R. v. 330. బహూకృతి or బహూకరణము bahū-kriti. n. Showing respect, సన్మానించుట.

బా bā

బాండుర bāndura. [from Skt. పాండుర.] n. A pot, కుండ, సాలె[illegible].

బాంధకినేయుడు *bāndhaki-nēyuḍu.* [Skt.] n. The son of a prostitute. కుడిసెకత్తెకొడుకు.

బాంధవము *bāndhavamu.* [Skt.] n. Relationship, చుట్టరికము. **బాంధవుడు** *bāndhavuḍu.* n. A relation, చుట్టము.

బాకా, బాంకా or **భాంకా** *bākā.* [H.] n. A long trumpet, ఒకవిధమైన ఊదువాద్యము.

బాకి *bāki.* [Tel.] adj. Wide, విశాలమైన, పెద్ద. **బాకినోరు** *bāki-nōru.* n. A wide mouth. బాకినోటిమెకము a lion, సింహము.

బాకీ *bākī.* [H.] n. A debt. ఋణము. బాకీ ఉన్నాడు he is in debt. బాకీపడు to incur a debt, to be indebted to. బాకీచెల్లించు to pay a debt. బాకీదారుడు a debtor.

బాకు *bāku.* [H.] n. A dagger, కటారి.

బాగములు, బాగలు or **బాగాలు** *bāgamulu.* [Tel.] n. Areca nut ready cut into pieces for eating. వక్కపొడి. "కప్పురగంధపు బాగములు వడిచ్చి." T. iii. 134.

బాగు *bāgu.* [Tel.] n. Good, well being, a good state, or condition; health. క్షేమము, సుఖము. Beauty, charm, attraction, అందము. Benefit, use, advantage. Manner, విధము. adj. Good, safe, sound, correct. క్షేమముగా. Beautiful, అందముగా. అట్లాచేస్తే ఏమిబాగు what is the use of doing so? మహాబాగు very well, yes. **బాగరి** *bāgari.* (బాగు+అరి.) n. A beautiful or handsome woman or man. అందగాడు, అందకత్తె. "తెల్లనికమ్మలయందు మెలచేటివలెను దనుకొక్క బాగరియాల్లనివాని." R. iii. 44. **బాగా** or **బాగుగా** *bāgā.* adv. Well, properly, duly, satisfactorily, in good health. బాగానే ఉన్నది it is all right or safe. ఈబట్ట బాగా ఉండలేదు this cloth is not good. వానికి బాగా ఉన్నది he is well. వానితలిదండ్రులు బాగానే ఉన్నారు his parents are alive and well. వెన్నెల బాగా ఉండెను the moonshine was bright. చిన్నది బాగా ఉన్నది the girl is pretty. **బాగుచేయు** *bāgu-chēyu.* v. a. To do good to, to ameliorate. To mend, trim, repair. To cure. To clean. To set right, rectify, make fit, చక్కబరచు. **బాగుదార** *bāgu-dāra.* n. A small knife, చిన్నకత్తి. **బాగుపడు** *bāgu-paḍu.* v. n. To be benefited, to thrive, to prosper. To recover health. To be reformed. బాగులోకివచ్చు to prosper or thrive. బాగులోకితెచ్చు to benefit, ameliorate, rectify. **బాగులాడి** *bāgu-lāḍi.* n. A beau, అందకత్తె. **బాగులు** *bāgulu.* n. Gestures, acts. వెర్రిబాగులు foolish gestures. వెర్రిబాగులవాడు or వెర్రిబాగులమారి one who acts as a mad man. "బాలెప్పుడు బాగులుమాయకన్నానగపట్టక వచ్చితిమయ్యా." Satya. iv. 9. బాగాలు (బాగు+ఆలు) the lovely wife, "గురుని బాగాలు కమలోటగోడ బాటి." T. iv. 145.

బాగెము *bāgemu.* [From Skt. భాగ్యము.] n. Wealth, fortune. Good, సుకృతము.

బాజా *bājā.* [H.] n. Music, beating of drums, &c. బాజాభజంత్రీలు musicians, a musical band. Music, drums and trumpets.

బాజారు or **బజారు** *bāḍzāru.* [H.] n. A shop. అంగడి. A market, అంగడివీధి.

బాజు *bāḍzu.* [H.] n. A kind of hawk, శ్యేనవిశేషము. Brightness, brilliancy, కాంతి. **బాజుబందు** or **బాడుబందు** *bāḍzu-bandu.* n. An ornament worn on the arm, an armlet.

బాట *bāṭa.* [Tel.] n. A road, way. దారి, మార్గము. **బాటసారి** *bāṭasāri.* n. A wayfarer, a traveller, దారినడచువాడు.

బాడబము *bāḍabamu.* [Skt.] n. A devouring flame, consuming fire, a tremendous conflagration. బడబాగ్ని. A collection of mares. అడుగుర్రములసమూహము. బాడబుడు bāḍabuḍu. n. A Brahmin, బ్రాహ్మణుడు. Swa. ii. 81.

బాడవ or బాడవపొలము bāḍava. [Tel.] n. A low lying moist land into which water drains, a boggy spot. A piece of low, swampy ground, వాకపొలము లేక చిరువాక.

బాడసము or బాడసపుచెట్టు bāḍasamu. [Tel.] n. A certain plant which has a red flower.

బాడిగ, బాడిగె or బాడుగ bāḍiga. [Tel.] n. Hire, rent. అద్దె.

బాడిత or బాడిద Same as బాడిస. (q. v.)

బాడిదెపుచెట్టు or బాడిసెచెట్టు bāḍidepu-cheṭṭu. [Tel.] n. A large thorny forest tree. *Erythrina indica.* బంధత్రిక. Rox. iii. 249.

బాడిస or బాడిసె bāḍisa. [Tel.] n. A carpenter's adze.

బాడు bāḍu. [Tel.] n. A veil or covering, ముసుగు. బాడుగోలు bāḍu-gōlu. (బాడు+కోలు.) n. A low or mean man, మానహీనుడు. బాడుదల bāḍudala. (బాడు+తల కొను.) n. Putting one to shame, అవమానించుట.

బాడువ or బాడవ bāḍuva. [Tel.] n. Marshy land, పల్లపుచేలు.

బాడె or బాడి bāḍe. [Tel.] n. Mud, mire, slush, ooze, అడుసు, బురద. బాడెపుండు bāḍe-puṇḍu. n. A sloughing ulcer.

బాఢము bāḍhamu. [Skt.] n. A vow, ప్రతిజ్ఞ. adj. Much, excessive, అతిశయమైన. Hard, firm. adv. Very, మిక్కిలి.

బాణము bāṇamu. [Skt.] n. An arrow. A rocket. బాణాలచీర a sort of striped cloth like a plaid. ఆ పుస్తకములో బాణముపడ్డది that book is worm eaten. బాణాసంచి or బాణసంచి a bag containing fireworks, fireworks. బాణవిద్య bāṇa-vidya. n. The pyrotechnic art. Fireworks. బాణా bāṇā. n. A cudgel. దండాయుధము. బాణాకత్తి a two handed sword. బాణాకర్ర a quarter staff, a cudgel or pole used in gymnastics. బాణాసనము bāṇ-āsanamu. n. A bow. విల్లు. "పినాకపాణి బట్టెను విరుంగని కన్యబాణాసనంబెల్లు పట్టనేర్చు." B. X. 59. 32.

బాణలి bāṇali. [Tel.] n. A metal frying pan with handles.

బాతలించు or బాతళించు bātalintsu. [Tel.] v. n. To be perplexed, to be puzzled, తత్తరపడు. "ద్వి॥ పాదుకొనియుండె బలువిడినడిచి, పడక నెలంగనిబాతలింపగను." Navanadha. iii. 530.

బాతాఖానీ bāta-khānī. [H.] n. A loquacious person. Vain talking.

బాతి or బ్రాతి bāti. [Tel.] n. Likeness. resemblance A great matter or affair. Greatness, గొప్ప, విశేషము. "పాండునందనుల దుర్దమతంరియొంగి ధర్మతత్పరులకుగెల్పుబాతిబాతి భక్తులబొంద నెపూనికసంపదల్." M. IX. i. 335. "ధనమేమి బాతినాకిది." Jag. ii. 31. "మానముకన్నం గన్యప్రాణమేమిబాతికు." Ila. iv. 124.

బాతు or బాతువు bātu. [H.] n. A duck. పొట్టిబాతు a duck. పెద్దబాతు a goose. గూడబాతు the smaller pelican. చింకుబాతు the larger pelican.

బాద Same as బాధ. (q. v.)

బాదము or బాదాము bādamu. [H.] n. The almond tree. బాదంకాయలు almonds.

బాదరము or బాదరు bādaramu. [Tel.] n. The match of a matchlock. జానకితాడు. జానకితాడుతుంచే కర్రాటకపు తుపాకిచెవి.

బాదరాయణుడు or బాదరాయణి bādara-yaṇudu. [Skt.] n. An epithet of the sage Vyāsa. వ్యాసముని. A mad man, వెర్రివాడు. A useless man, నిష్ప్రయోజకుడైనమనుష్యుడు.

బాదరా *bādarā.* [Tel.] n. Hurry. బదరా బాదరాగా in a great hurry.

బాదరించు *bādarintsu.* [Tel.] v. n. To be equal, సమానము.

బాదు *bādu.* [Tel.] v. a. To thrash, beat, cudgel. పడబాదు to knock down. n. Fees in grain paid to the village servants before the division of a crop. బాదుమాన్యము an allowance of grain given to the village servants in those Parganas where more ground was formerly given away by the local authorities than existed in reality. (Vizag.) బాదుకొను *bādukonu.* v. a. To beat oneself. బాదుగా *bādu-gā.* adv. From time immemorial.

బాధ *bādha.* [Skt.] n. Pain, trouble, affliction, plague, annoyance, grief. దుఃఖము. బాధకము *bādhakamu.* n. An obstacle, hindrance, what hinders, opposes, or pains. బాధకము లేదు never mind, no matter: there's no *must* in the case. adj. Troublesome, hindering, awkward, opposing. బాధపడు *bādha-paḍu.* v. n. To be in pain, to grieve. బాధించు or బాధపెట్టు *bādhintsu.* v. a. To vex, trouble, oppress, torment, plague, force. బాధితుడు *bādhituḍu.* n. One who suffers or is afflicted. బాధ్యము *bādhyamu.* adj. Responsible, liable. Connected with, related to, having a right or claim to. బాధ్యత or బాధ్యత్వము *bādhyata.* n. Responsibility, liability. Relationship, heirship. Right, claim. బాధ్యస్థుడు or బాధ్యుడు *bādhya-sthuḍu.* n. One who is responsible or liable. An heir. A rightful owner. దానికి నేనా బాధ్యుడను am I responsible for that? బాధ్యపడు *bādhya-paḍu.* v. n. To be obliged or bound, to be under obligation, to be responsible or liable. బాధ్యపరచు *bādhya-paratsu.* v. a. To oblige, put under obligation, cause to be responsible.

బాన *bāna.* [Tel.] n. A kettle, a boiler, a large pot. కడవ. చాకిబాన a washerman's vat or large earthen vessel.

బానగిల్లు or **బానగిలు** *bānagillu.* [Tel.] v. n. To be forced, compelled or obliged, బలాత్కృతమగు.

బానసము *bānasamu.* [Tel. from బాన.] n. Cooking, వంట. A cookroom, kitchen, వంటసాల. బానసీడు *bānas-īḍu.* n. A cook. వంటవాడు.

బానిస or **బానిసె** *bānisa.* [Tel. probably from బానసము & బాస.] n. A female slave, or maid-servant, దాసి. బానిసము *bānisamu.* n. Slavery, బానిసతనము, దాస్యము. బానిసీడు or బానిసవాడు *bānis-īḍu.* n. A male slave, a servant, దాసుడు.

బాపడు or **బాపనయ్య** *bāpaḍu.* [from Skt. బ్రాహ్మణ.] n. A Brahmin. బ్రాహ్మణుడు. బాపన *bāpana.* adj. Brahmin, Brahminical, appertaining to Brahmins. బాపనక్క, బాపత or బాపనది *bāpan-akka.* n. A Brahmin woman. బాపనచీమ n. A large red ant found on trees. బాపనబాతు or బాపనకోడి *bāpana-bātu.* n. The Brahminy duck or Ruddy Sheldrake, *Casarca rutila* (F.B.I.) బాపనవాడు or బాపడు *bāpana-vāḍu.* n. A Brahmin. బాపనికము (బాపన+ఇకము) n. The state of being a Brahmin, Brahminhood, బ్రాహ్మణత్వము.

బాపతు *bāpatu.* [H.] n. An item, a head or section. adj. Relating to, సంబంధించిన.

బాపు or **బాపురే** *bāpu.* [Tel.] interj: Well done! Huzza! ఓరీ. O dear!

బాబా *bābā.* [Tel.] n. A horse. An elephant. "పొద్దుబాబాలు." (R. i. 108.) the horses of the sun. చిలుకబాబాజీరు the parrot-knight, i. e., Manmadha. బాబారవుతు

a horseman, rider, knight; an epithet of Kubēra. తెలిబాబా the white elephant of Indra.

బాబు *bābu.* [Tel. Cognate with Eng. 'Papa', Skt. "Pita", Heb. "Abba"] n. Father, తండ్రి. A venerable man, పూజ్యుడు.

బాము *bāmu.* [Tel.] n. Birth, production. జన్మము. Grief, దుఃఖము. Embarrassment, entanglement. చిక్కు, తొందర, భంగము. తొలుబాము a former birth. "రఘూద్వహానే నపరాధినైననీ, పాదములం జనింపతొలుబాముల నోములుపెక్కునోమ గం, గాదిమహానదుల్." R. vii. 118. తొలుబాములనోములు, అనగా పూర్వజన్మములందు చేసిన వ్రతములు. బాముబెడు to harass. Ila. iv. 81. బాములపెట్టు to torture, torment, plague. "కుంటెనబాములకైయొసగు వీడుబహూవిత్తంబుల్." Sananda Gan. iii. 55.

బాయి *bāyi.* [Tel.] n. A woman's breast, mother's milk, స్తన్యము.

బార *bāra.* [Tel.] n. A fathom, the length of the two arms extended. చాచిన రెండుచేతు లనడిమిపొలత, నాలుగుమూరలు. పదిబారలు twenty yards. బార or బారా *bāra.* [H.] Twelve పండ్రెండు. బారచాచు *bāra-tsātsu.* v. a. To extend (the arms, so as to embrace.) "గారవమున బారచాచి గౌగిటచేర్చెన్." T. iv. 146. బారచాపు *bāra-tsāpu.* n. The cloth called Long cloth. చాలానిడివిగలబట్ట. బారదూలము, బారుపట్టె or బారుదూలము a very long piece of timber, నిడుపాటిదూలము. బార పోయు *bāra-pōyu.* v. a. To spin, with the arm fully stretched. చెయ్యిసాగునంతవరకు నూలునడుకు. ఏకులుబారపోయు to spin thread. బారాడి *bār-āḍi.* (బార+అడి) adj. A great deal. అధికము. A great many. అనేకము, బహుళము, చాలా.

"ఓగోరరానవాడా,
రారా నావెంటదిరుగగా దానుపక్షి,
బారాడిమూడకేచ్చెద
కోరానీయువ్వెదీర్చుకోరాయనుమన్."
HN. iv. 233.

"వారిరువురుగుటమలోపల
నైరముగా నిరాజ్యకాంక్షవిజిగీషువులై,
హోరాహోరిందోరిరి,
బారాడిదినంబులవనిప్రజలుతలంకన్."
A. iii. 21.

బారంగిచెట్టు *bārangi-chettu.* [Tel.] n. A certain tree, అంగారవల్లి.

బారకము or **భారకము** *bārakamu.* [from Skt. భారము.] n. Weight, heaviness; a burden, load. బరువు. A crisis, ముమ్మరము. జ్వరము నిండా బారకముగానున్నది the fever is at its height or crisis. **బారకించు** or **భారకించు** *bārakintsu.* v. n. To become severe, as fever. భారమగు. నాకు ఒళ్లు బారకించులాగున్నది I have a prospect of illness. బార కాడి *bāra-kāḍi.* n. A break, or yoke in which bullocks are trained. క్రొత్తయెద్దులను పాటయెడ్లతోకట్టేకాడి. బారపట్టెorవారపట్టె *bāra-paṭṭe.* n. A chief beam lying on pillars.

బారకాసు *bārakāsu.* [Eng.] n. Barracks. సిపాయీలు ఉండే ఇండ్లవరుస.

బారము *bāramu.* [from Skt. భారము] n. Weight, బరువు. adj. Heavy, బరువైన.

బారసాల *bārasāla.* [Tel.] n. A ceremony or festival, held on the eleventh day after the birth of a child.

బారసి *bārasi.* [Tel.] n. The twelfth day of a fortnight. ద్వాదశి, పండ్రెండవదినము. "ద్వి. బారసిదాకదుభయమునసరిల, పారణగావించెబాష్పవుండంత" భాగ. ix.

బారి *bāri.* [Tel.] n. Annoyance, trouble. ఉపద్రవము, తొందర, వ్యథ, హింస, నిర్బంధము. The slope at the side of a great well for bullocks to run down in drawing up water, by a rope running over a pulley. కపిలెద్దులు నిర్బంధముగా దిగి నడిచే దారి. An elephant's tether, ఏనుగుకాలుకట్టెడు గొలుసు. బారివిడుచు to gallop, పరుగెత్తించు. బారిగొర్రె a sheep let go at a feast to be run for, as a victim or prize.

"గోమునవిశ్వాస్తుల్లోడుకవిశ్రాంచి,
కోమలికినిబారిగొరియగానోపగ,
వలచెలోమల్లెపూవంటిరుమాలు,
కొలగింపవెండ్రుకల్ తూగించిందాడ,
నించువిల్తునిబారినిగాసేల."

Sār. D. v. 295.

why sacrifice yourself to love? మన్మథుని బారి పడినాడు he fell a victim to love. పులిబారిక్రిప్పనలేడికైవడిగా like a fawn escaping from a tiger. బారి or భారి bāri. adj. Great, large, big. బారివాండ్లు well to do people, rich folks.

బారికివాడు bāriki-vāḍu. [Tel.] n. A village watchman.

బారిముద్రరూక bāri-mudra-rūka. [Tel.] n. A forged coin. A light coin, one of an old coinage. There is a proverb, "బారిముద్ర బాసుముద్రే, కరుకుకరుకే" cf. 'A shilling's a shilling but a crown's a crown'

బారిసమరు bāri-samaru. [Tel.] v. a. To kill. చంపు. To annoy, trouble.

బారిసము bārisamu. [Tel.] n. A mask, a masquerade, a disguise, వేసము.

బారీ or బారి bārī. [Tel.] n. An elephant's tether, ఏనుగుకాలుకట్టెడుగొలుసు.

బారు bāru. [Tel.] n. A line, row, range, series, వరుస. A multitude, troop. సమూహము. చీమలబారు a line of ants. బారుతీరి standing in a line.

బారుచాపు Same as బారచాపు.

బారుచేయు bāru-chēyu. [from Eng. 'Bar.'] v. a. To load a gun. తుపాకిలో మందుగుండు వేసికట్టించు.

బారువ bāruva. [from Skt. భారము.] n. A certain weight equal to twenty maunds. ఇరువైమణుగులుగల పరిమాణము.

బార్డపుచెట్టు bārḍapu-chettu. [Tel.] n. The tree called Moochy wood. See బాడిదపుచెట్టు.

బార్లాగా bārlā-gā. [Tel.] adv. Wide open. బార్లాగాతీసినతలుపు a door wide open.

బాల bāla. [Skt.] adj. Young, tender, fresh. బాలసంసారము an infant family, a family of orphans. n. A damsel, maid, virgin, పదునారేండ్లకులోబడినపిల్ల. A stubborn woman, మూర్ఖురాలు. బాలకాండ bāla-kāṇḍa. n. The name of the first book of the Rāmayaṇa. బాలకుడు bālakuḍu. n. A youth. పదునారేండ్లకు లోబడిన పిల్లవాడు. బాలగ్రహము bāla-grahamu. n. An ogre or fairy that frightens infants. B. X. 254. బాలబోధ a child's instruction; a child's primer. బాలనాయకము the follies of a young heir. బాల లత a tender creeper. బాలింత, బాలెంత, బాలింతరాలు or బాలెంతరాలు bālinta. n. A woman in childbed. "ఆబాలస్వాంతనిని గొంటుకట్టెడివసగా బాలింత చందంబునగా బాలిండ్లగావిమమూని." B. X. 209. బాలింతబోళము bālinta-bōḷamu. n. A particular medicine given to a woman in child-bed. బాలింతరోగము or బాలెంతరోగము bālinta-rōgamu. n. Puerperal fever. బాలిక bālika. n. A lass, or maiden. బాల. బాలికాకులము young women. మత్తాళిబాలికలు young female bees. బాలిశము bāliśamu. adj. Silly, childish, puerile. పసి, మూర్ఖమైన, జ్ఞానశూన్యమైన. M. VII. iv. 234. బాలిశుడు bāliśuḍu. n. A fool, a simpleton, అవివేకి, మూర్ఖుడు. M. XII. vi. 111. బాలుడు bāluḍu. n. A youth, a lad. నెలబాలుడు the new moon when one day old. Plu: బాలురు. బాలేయము bālēyamu. adj. Agreeable to a child. బాలునికి హితమైన. Soft, మెత్తని.

బాల్యము *bālyamu.* n. Childhood. పసితనము.

బాలబంద *bāla-banda.* [Tel.] n. Rabbit weed, a plant with very deep roots. *Ipomea pescaprae.*

బాలీసు *bālīsu.* [H.] n. A large pillow to recline against, ఒరుగుదిండు.

బాళి *bāḷi.* [Tel.] n. Concern; affection, emotion, passion, love, desire, lust. కాంక్ష, విచారము; ఆశ, ఆసక్తి, మోహము. "చూడకుండంగనూడదీమదిసొబగు చూచినంత నెమదిలోనకళొచ్చెబాళి." T. iii. 75.

బావ *bāva.* [Tel.] n. A sister's husband, if older than oneself. అక్కమగడు. The son of a mother's brother, or of a father's sister, if older than oneself, పెద్దవాడైన మేనత్త మేనమామలకొడుకు. A woman's brother-in-law, if older than her husband. మగనియన్న. See మరది. బావమరది a man's brother-in-law, either older or younger than himself.

బావనాలు *bāvanālu.* [from Skt. భావనలు.] n. Outlines: the first lines drawn, when carving a statue.

బావి *bāvi.* [Tel.] n. A well, నుయ్యి. A tank, చెరువు. A spring, దొరువు. A pit, పల్లము. లంకెలబావులు, గొలుసులబావులు, సంగడిబావులు or జోడుబావులు wells dug side by side.

బావిలీ *bāvilī.* [Tel.] n. A gold earring. One kind is called పుడకబావిలి.

బావుకొను *bāvu-konu.* [Tel.] v. a. To gobble, devour, swallow, gulp. నోటినిండా కుక్కుకొను.

బావుటా *bāvuṭā.* [H.] n. A flag. జెండా.

బావుడోరు *bāvu-ḍōru.* [H.] n. A horse's leading rein.

బావురుగాడు or **బావురుపిల్లి** *bāvuru-gāḍu.* [Tel. Literally, "one that makes a caterwauling."] n. A tom cat, or wild cat. బావురు నిడూసే గండుపిల్లి, గండుపిల్లి.

బావురుమను *bāvuru-m-anu.* [Tel. anuk.] v. n. To be dreary. To echo, to resound as an empty house.

బాష్పము *bāshpamu.* [Skt.] n. A tear. కన్నీరు. ఆనందబాష్పములు tears of joy.

బాస *bāsa.* [from Skt. భాష.] n. A language, భాష. A slang dialect. A word or phrase. An oath; a command or adjuration, ప్రమాణము. A vow, ప్రతిజ్ఞ, వ్రతము. A sign or mark, సంకేతము. భూమికొట్టి బాసచేయు to swear by laying your hand on the earth. "పాలతోతలయంటిబాసచేసినను" even though they wash their heads in milk and then swear. **బాసపత్రిక** *bāsa-patrika.* n. A written promise, a solemn declaration, in writing. **బాసపలుకు** or **బాసచేయు** *bāsa-paluku.* n. To take an oath, to swear. **బాసాడు** *bās-āḍu.* v. n. To talk, to converse. మాటాడు.

బాసట *bāsaṭa.* [Tel.] n. Assistance, aid, help. ఉపబలము, సహాయము. "బృహద్బలుమే నముప్పదినాగసంబులు నాటించివారలకు బాసటయైకవిసిన సైనికులంబెక్కుతెరంగులతూపులజెక్కుపరచి." M. VII. ii. 99.

బాసము Same as బాసె. (q. v.)

బాసవాలు *bāsa-vālu.* [Tel.] n. A penitent, a sage, ఋషి, మునీశ్వరుడు. A god, గీర్వాణుడు, దేవత. **బాసవాలుదొర** *bāsa-vālu-dora.* n. An epithet of Indra, ఇంద్రుడు. A sage, యోగి. "వారలనుచితసల్లాపంబుల పిడ్కొలిపి యురోగ్యగిపుంగవుండువిశేచ్ఛంబనిరుసబ్బాసవాలుగమియు వేతక్కొశాస్త్రగాం బొవరింపుచు నెప్పటియట్లమృదంబునసుండిరి." Chenna. v. 432.

బాసికము *bāsikamu.* [Tel.] n. A nuptial crown worn on the forehead of the bride and bridegroom. A. i 66. బాసికదండ

a garland worn on the forehead. బాసికపట్టు bāsika-paṭṭu. n. A sitting posture in which the legs are placed over each other, పద్మాసనము.

బాహా bāha. [Skt.] n. The shoulder, బాహువు, భుజము. The upper arm, చెయ్యి.

బాహాటము bāhāṭamu. [from Skt. బహిః.] adj. Public, open, loud, notorious, undisguised. n. Publicity, openness. బాహాటముగా bāhāṭamu-gā. adv. Openly, publicly, notoriously, undisguisedly.

బాహిరము bāhiramu. [from Skt. బహిః.] adj. Made public, బయలుపడిన, బాహ్యము. Excommunicated, వెలియైన. "తే॥ వలయునన్నపానములఁ బలుకెరగుల, నేర్పువిధమున నేమెండసూర్య వేద్య, నున్న నీవుపదొరాగింపకుల్లకునికి, బాంధవమున కునికికి బాహిరంబు." M. V. iii. 212. బాహిరపోవు bāhira-pōvu. v. n. To become public, or open, బయలుపడు. To faint, to lose the senses. మూర్ఛిల్లు. "క॥ కావున వంచన బాహిర, పోవక యుండంగ మనరి పుంబరి మార్పం, గావచ్చు నేనియట్టిది, భావలపటుగాక తక్కెనసువలదు సుమీ." M. IV. ii. 91. "అతండు సోలియును బాహిరపోవక తేరియుద్విగ్ధుం, గట్టినిశాత బాణచయకీలితదేహుని జేసె." M. IX. i. 424. బాహిరుడు bāhiruḍu. n. One who is outside, or excommunicated, బాహ్యుడు. "అటుగాక కర్మఫలలంపటుఁడగుడు నేని యుల్బణ లభోగితమై, నటనిటు దిరుగుచు, జంతునికటప్రత్తికి బాహిరుండగా నెకుమారా." M. XII. i. 73.

బాహుకము bāhukamu. [Skt.] n. A raft. సంగడి.

బాహుల్యము bāhulyamu. [Skt. from బహుళము.] n. Abundance.

బాహువు bāhuvu. [Skt.] n. The arm. బాహుజుడు bāhujuḍu. n. A Kshatriya. బాహుపురి or బాహుదము bāhu-purī. n. An ornament worn on the upper arm కేయూరము. Swa. pref. 35. బాహుపురులు bāhu-purulu. n. The name of a sort of grain. H. iv. 158. బాహుమూలము bāhu-mūlamu. n. The armpit, చంక, కక్షము. Swa. v. 107. బాహుయుద్ధము bāhu-yuddhamu. n. A struggle, a hand to hand fight.

బాహ్యము bāhyamu. [Skt.] adj. Lying outside, that which is excluded, outer, external, public. వెలుపలిది, వెలియైనది. బాహ్యుడు bāhyuḍu. n. One who is outside, an outsider, an outcaste. శ్రుతిబాహ్యులు those who are not allowed to hear the Vedas, excommunicated people.

బాహ్లీకము or బాహ్లీకము bāhlīkamu. [Skt.] adj. Brought from Balkh. n. Saffron, కుంకుమపువ్వు. కుంకుమము. Asafoetida, ఇంగువ. A horse from Balkh. బాహ్లీకకిశోరాశ్వము. A. ii. 34.

బి bi

బింకము or బింకెము binkamu [Tel.] n. Tightness, stiffness. Pride, presumption, arrogance. బిగువు, గర్వము, బడాయి. A proud word, గర్వోక్తి. బింకములాడు to be saucy. "ఇక నీబింకంబులాగింతుము." N. iv. 198.

బింగిపారు bingi-pāru. [Tel.] v. n. To send forth a lot of unhealthy shoots (used of grain).

బింగురాజు bingu-rāḍzu. [Tel.] n. A sort of mocking bird, which is black and smaller than a crow.

బింజరము binjaramu. [Tel.] n. A certain plant. H. iv. 12.

బిందము bindamu. [from Skt. బృందము.] n. A multitude. సమూహము.

బిండీ bindī. [Tel.] n. A jewel worn by children or by women on their forehead, చేరుచుక్క.

బిందువు *binduvu.* [Skt.] n. A drop. (చిల్ల) బొట్టు. A dot, చుక్క. A small circle or cipher representing the letters ం, న, or మ, సున్న. An epigram says చింతాచితాశ్చ చితాయాశ్చ బిందుమాత్రంవిశేషణం, చితాదహతి నిర్జీవం చింతాజీవంతమప్యహో. చిత the funeral pyre, and చింత, grief, differ only in a (bindu) cipher: the former consumes the dead, the latter the living body.

బిందె or **బిందియ** *binde.* [Tel.] n. A metal vase, or pot, of a large size and with a narrow neck.

బింబము *bimbamu.* [Skt.] n. An image, figure, shape, form, shadow, reflection. ప్రతిమ, ప్రతిబింబము. An orb or disc, as of the sun or moon. (సూర్యచంద్ర)మండలము. A scarlet fruit in colour like a cherry, the *Momordica monadelpha,* దొండపండు (to which lips are compared in poetry.) బింబోష్ఠి or బింబాధర a rosy or ruby-lipped maid. **బింబితము** *bimbitamu.* adj. Imaged, reflected, as in a mirror, ప్రతిబింబించిన.

బికారి or **బికాసి** *bikari.* [from Skt. భిక్షము.] n. A beggar, బిచ్చకాడు. A useless person, అప్రయోజకుడు. **బికిరము** *bikiramu.* n Alms, భిక్షము. బికిరాలమారి one inclined to begging, భిక్షమెత్తు స్వభావముగలవాడు.

బిక్కి *bikki.* [Tel.] n. A certain jungle tree. అడ్డోటము.

బిక్కిరించు *bikkirintsu.* [Tel.] v. a. To erect or cock up, as the ears, రిక్కించు.

బిక్కు *bikku.* [Tel.] n. Fear, fright, trembling, భయము. బిక్కుబిక్కుమని ఉన్నది she is all in a fright.

బిగ or **బిగియ** *biga.* [Tel.] adv. Tightly. **బిగతొక్కు** *biga-tokku.* v. a. To tread in or tread down tight. **బిగపట్టు** or **బిగబట్టు** *biga-pattu.* v. a. & n. To stop, to withhold, keep back, check, suspend. ఊపిరి బిగబట్టు to hold the breath in. వాన బిగబట్టినది the rain held off. నా జీతమును బిగబట్టినాడు he kept back my pay. **బిగాది** *bigadi.* adj. Penniless, destitute. n. A beggar. "సీ॥ అకటాయని గాదియడిబండ గుదెదరు సుంచి కొక్కె సులాము జెయ్యుగోవు." H. v. 128. **బిగి** *bigi.* n. Tightness. Firmness of flesh or body. Rigidity, austerity, superciliousness. దృఢత్వము. బిగువు. adj. Tight, hard, firm. Rigid, austere, proud, arrogant. బిగిబద్ద a stick that holds any two things tight. **బిగించు, బిగియించు, బిగుచు** or **బిగియుచేయు** *bigintsu.* v. a. To tighten, to fasten: to stop, suspend. To be stubborn. అత్తవారింటికి పోనని బిగించుకొనియున్నది she stayed at home refusing to go to her husband's house. **బిగింపు** *bigimpu.* n. Rigidity, stiffness. Austerity. నీ బిగింపులు పనికిరావు your stiffness will do no good. **బిగితము** *bigitamu.* (బిగి+ఇతము.) adj. Firm, దృఢము. **బిగిమానము** *bigi-manamu.* n. Tightness, firmness. Rigidity. Austerity. Superciliousness. "ఈయుండజరాజయాన కానయోపురుషుండు మదమ్మదీజగమ్మండలి నివ్వడంచు బిగిమానముతో బురికొనంటటా." N. vii. 67. **బిగియు** *bigiyu.* v. n. To be tight. బిగువగు, బిగువుచేయు. To be proud or arrogant. "చెలువలవిడిదిలోవిచ్చేసియుండి, పిలువబంపినవేళ బిగియకవచ్చి." L. v. 132.

బిగుతు *bigutu.* n. Tightness, tension, adj. Tight. **బిగువు** *biguvu.* n. Tightness, Rigidity, stiffness, austerity. Superciliousness, బింకము. **బిగువుకొను** *biguvu-konu.* v. n. To become tight, బిగువగు. **బిగువులు** *biguvulu.* n. A stays, or rafter in a building. A bundle, sheaf, pack, bale. నీలిదూకు రూ ఒకి౧౬ బిగువుల వంతున వేస్తున్నారు they sell indigo stalks at sixteen bundles a rupee. గొప్ప వరాకి ఒకి బిగువులు ౩౦ వంతున thirty packs or bundles of straw per pagoda. **బిగ్గ** or **బిగ్గన** *bigga.* adv. Tightly. All at once. Vijaya. iii. 24. **బిగ్గర, బిగ్గర** or **బిగ్గిర** *biggara.* adv.

Tightly, firmly. Aloud. బిగ్గరగా నవ్వు to laugh out. బిగ్గరగా మాట్లాడు to speak loudly. **బిగ్గిలి** *biggili*. adv. Tightly (said of an embrace).

బిచానా *bichānā*. [H.] n. A mattress, bedding, పరుపు.

బిచ్చము *bitstsamu*. [from Skt. భిక్షము.] n Alms. బిచ్చమెత్తుకొను to beg. బిచ్చముపెట్టు to bestow alms. ఇది తమరు పెట్టినబిచ్చముగా తలంచుకొంటాను I shall consider this as a piece of charity to me. **బిచ్చగాడు** *bitstsa-gāḍu*. n. A beggar. భిక్షమెత్తుకొనువాడు.

బిడొగు *biḍugu*. [Tel.] v. a. To tell lies, బొంకు.

క॥ "బిడొగడిమాటలుచెవినిడి,
నిజమని గురుభక్తినిరతునిర్మలచరితున్,
కుజనుగుమారునిగేలాం
గజానింబోనాడుకొంటిగడనేడిమనున్."

సా iii.

బిటారము *biṭāramu*. [Tel.] n. A coquettish prank, విలాసచేష్ట. **బిటారి** *biṭāri*. n. A coquette. **బిటికి** or **బిటుకులాడి** *biṭiki*. n. A gad-about. "భిత్తికచెంతకంకటికి వరుసు బిటికి వీక్షించియొప్పటిపెద్దపెట్టి." A. ii. 203. "బిటుకులాడివాని పెండ్లాముగరుబమ్ము పేటిమేటి మేటిపీధులందు, కోడెకాంత్రదిక్కు చూడదు పెం పెత్తి రయాకిబైటనలుసురున్నచోట." Samagamam. iii. 31. **బిటికితనము** *biṭikitanamu*. n. Incontinence.

బిట్టబిర్రు or **బిట్టబిర్ర** *biṭṭa-birru*. [Tel. బిరు+బిరు.] adj. Very tight or stubborn, మిక్కిలిబిగువు. **బిట్టబిర్రుగా** *biṭṭa-birru-gā*. adj. At once, suddenly. BD. VI. 500.

బిట్టు *biṭṭu*. [Tel.] n. Excess. A great action. హెచ్చు, అధికము. Firmness, tightness, దృఢత్వము. "నిన్నుపట్టెదమనిచలముగానిన పట్టుబట్టగా." B. X. 359. **బిట్టు** or **బిట్టుగా** *biṭṭu*. adv. Greatly, much, మిక్కిలి. Often, తరుచుగా. Quickly, శీఘ్రముగా. "ఎనుములుగాలు ముట్టెయెత్తి బిట్టారించె." Swa. iv. 68. "జంబుకంబులు కొరవిదయ్యంబులట్ల, బిట్టు రాత్రులుకూతలు పెట్టుచుండు." Vish. ii. 48. బిట్టవిరియు to burst with a crash. బిట్టులికి పడు to be astonished or frightened. బిట్టోరలు to wail, to howl. Rukmāngada. v. 92. **బిట్టుబిల్లు** *biṭṭu-billu*. (బిట్టు+బిట్టు.) adv. Suddenly, తటాలున.

బిడ *biḍa*. [Tel. another form of బిడ్డ.] n. A child. ఆబిడ or అబిడ that woman. ఈబిడ this woman. ఏబిడ which woman?

బిడము *biḍamu*. [Tel.] n. A cake of salt, ఉప్పుకట్టి, అట్టుప్పు.

బిడాయించు *biḍāyintsu*. [H.] v. a. To fold up a letter; to enclose in a letter; to join. ఒకదానిని మరొకదానిలో పెట్టు.

బిడారము or **బిడారు** *biḍāramu*. [Tel.] n. A caravan. వర్తకులసమూహము, దేశము. A drove of loaded cattle. A load. A heap. వక్కలబిడారు a heap of sacks of areca nut. A camp or halting place. విడిది, బస, వాసస్థానము. కంచరబిడారము a tinker's camp. "ఆరాజులను మారి వాదినాధుండు కూడింతో నెదుర్కొనుచురప్పించి తనదు బిడారులందరికినొసంగె." Vencata. P. 35. టీ॥ తనదుబిడారులు అనగా తనవిడుదులు.

బిడాలము *biḍālamu*. [Skt.] n. A cat. పిల్లి. M. IV. ii. 127. **బిడాలి** *biḍāli*. n. A female cat. R. vi. 135.

బిడియము or **బిడెము** *biḍiyamu* [Tel.] n. Shame. సిగ్గు. A dagger. కటారి. "పదిలంబుగ కట్టినమట్టికాసిలం, బిడియములంటదో పి." Swa. iv. 39. టీ॥ బిడియములంటదోపి, బా కులంపిడిలంటదోపి. "చుట్టుబంగారుసురియుల పరుజాతెపసుబిడియములు." Navan. p. 58.

బిడువు *biḍavu*. [Tel.] n. An interval, leisure. అవకాశము. adj. Having an interval, అవకాశముగల.

బిడౌజుడు *biḍaujuḍu*. [Skt.] n. An epithet of Indra. H. ii. 67.

బిడ్డ *biḍḍa*. [Tel.] n. An infant శిశువు. A child. A son or daughter. ఎత్తువారిచేతిబిడ్డ a compliant simpleton. బిడ్డకుట్టు *biḍḍa-kuṭṭu*. n. The pains of parturition, labour pains. ప్రసవవేదన. "తెలుపకుబిడ్డకుట్టు విల పిల్లగభిల్లపురంధ్రులంతలో బిలువ రెమంత్రసాని దలపెట్టరకాయము." Kalahas. iii. 31. బిడ్డడు *biḍḍaḍu*. n. A little boy, a youngster. A son. Dative: బిడ్డనికి. Kalahas. iii. 32. బిడ్డతనము *biḍḍa-tanamu*. n. Infancy, childishness. బిడ్డతల్లి a woman in childbed, a woman with an infant in arms, బాలెంతరాలు. బిడ్డె another form of బిడ్డ.

బిత్తరము *bittaramu*. [Tel.] n. A flash of light. తళుకు. Brightness. A coquettish prank, an amorous gesture, శృంగారచేష్ట, ఒయ్యారము. "తెలుకుచేవసమీరాలబిత్తరంబులుకంకు" N. ix. 404. బిత్తరముగ *bittaramu-ga*. adv. Flashingly. ప్రకాశముగా. Gracefully, సొగసుగా "సరగమెరుంగుబంగరువు చెందురు కావిపటంబులాడ్చిబి, త్తరముగ చల్ల పాపపలు దాల్చి." N. ix 401. బిత్తరమలాడు to be bright, ప్రకాశించు. బిత్తరి *bittari*. n. A coquette, a flirt. A beautiful woman. ప్రౌఢస్త్రీ, శృంగారచేష్టలుగల ఆడుది. A woman, ఆడుది. "బిత్తరులాహాలాయుధునిబిల్వగ." Balrama. vi. 123. adj. Flashing, sparkling, తళుక్కైన, ప్రకాశమైన. Beautiful, సొగసైన. "శరముఖ కెంజడల్ నురుటి బెన్నుసబిత్తరిబొట్టువాతెరల్." T. iv. 122. బిత్తరించు *bittarintsu*. v. n. To flash, to sparkle, మెరయు, తళుక్కుమను. To move about, చలించు, ఊగాడు. To crack jokes. సరసమాడు. "తెలుకుచేవసమాపుబిత్తరిం చ." N. ix. 159. బిత్తరపు *bittarapu*. adj. Flashing, sparkling, తళుక్కైన, ప్రకాశించే. "సోమునిరీతి నెమ్మొగము సుంపర మాదర హాస చంద్రికా, స్తోమముచిన్నబిత్తరపు చూపులుదిక్కుల పిక్కటిల్ల." Surabha. 18.

బిత్తల *bittala*. [Tel.] n Nakedness. దిసమొల. బిత్తలి *bittali*. adj. Naked. "అత్తరిబిత్తలైభయ ముదాత్తసుచిత్తపుమత్తుపాత్తులో, బిత్తరి తత్తరించ కను." H. ii. 70.

బిత్తెడ *bitteḍu*. [Tel.] n. A metal spoon, a ladle.

బిద్దము *biddamu*. [from Skt. భిన్నము.] adj. Broken, భిన్నము.

బిద్దు *biddu*. [Tel.] v. n. To die, చచ్చు. "కులెపెద్దనిద్దురబోయిబిద్దిరక్తై." ABA. iii. 134.

బిద్దె *bidde*. [Tel.] n. Distress, misfortune, దుర్గతి. Hell, నరకము.

బినామి *binami*. [H.] n. A purchase in the name of another.

బినుగు *binugu*. [Tel.] n. A sportsman or hunter. (an obsolete word) "జీవురుగందెలు గాలపుచిన్నలెదురు, లాదియగుసాధనంబులుంటవ ంచు, కొనిహుటాహుటి నవలతోబినుగులెల్ల, గదిసినడిచిరియమ్మహికాంతునరుత." S. i. 187.

బిన్న *binne*. [Tel. short for బిరాన.] adv. Quickly, త్వరగా.

బిబ్బరిల్లు, **బొబ్బరిలు**, **బిబ్బరించు** or **బొబ్బరించు** *bibbarillu*. [Tel.] v. n. To howl, as a tiger, (పులి) కూయు. బిబ్బరింత or బొబ్బరింత *bibbarinta*. n. Howling, (పులి) కూత.

బిబ్బిలికాయ *bibbili-kaya*. [Tel.] n. A jewel worn by women on the third toe.

బిబ్బి *bibbi*. [Tel.] n. A garland of leaves, flowers, &c., tied across a doorway or street. తోరణము.

బిబ్బీ *bibbī*. [H.] n. A lady, "సీమదలపైబొదలు వయ్యెదలుఁజేరగబాఱు, బిబ్బీలకుముకుంగులబ్బకేసి." Vasu Charitra. Preface. 68.

బిబ్బోకము or బివ్వోకము *bibbōkamu*. [Skt.] n. Coquetry, blandishment, playfulness. శృంగారచేష్ట.

"లలితబిబ్బోకవిలాస భావముల,
కలితవిభ్రమభావగతుల నేమిటను,
వదను గావింపనోపక సిగ్గువిడిచి."
Navanatha. 73.

బిబ్బోకవతి or బిబ్బోకిని *bbibōka-vati*. n. A coquette, or a flirt, విలాసవతి.

"ఆబెబ్బులియిదివచ్చెన్,
తబ్బిబ్బులకేమిసేయుదానని చుమున,
బిబ్బోకవతిమనంబున,
నబ్బురముగ భయమునొక్కు లాడగనుండెన్."
S. ii. 280.

"నీకతగభయంబురా, నీకమెలంగుదునటంచు హితముగరపి బి, బ్బోకినియతనికి వ్యయమున, కైకొంతపదార్థమిచ్చి యనిచెంబుకికన్." Vish. ii. 339.

బిమ్మట, బిమ్మటము or బిమ్మిటి *bimmaṭa*. [Tel.] n. Stupor, grief. మూర్ఛావస్థ, అచైతన్యము. వివశత, నిశ్చయజ్ఞానశూన్యత, మ్రానుపడుట. Doubt, suspicion, misgiving, సంకోచము. "తనకుబిమ్మటమైనసర్జునునిబాహు, లీలయుమ్మెయి క్రొంగరేక తెగియు, నధిపయూతోడు బెబ్బులిక గ్గమైన, వగిచియుయ్యో పాండవులకు పగయుంగె." M. VIII. i. 5. adj. Being in a state of stupor, వివశము. బిమ్మిటిగొను or బిమ్మిటిపోవు *bimmiṭi-gonu*. v. n. To be in a state of stupor, వివశత్వముపొందు. To swoon, మూర్ఛిల్లు.

బియ్యము *biyyamu*. [Tel.] n. Rice when cleared from the husk. లక్క బియ్యము grain lac, i. e., gum lac sold in grains. సగ్గుబియ్యము sago.

బిరడ or బిరడా *birada*. [Tel.] n. A stopple, plug, cork. వీణెబిరడాలు the pegs of a lute.

బిరబిర, బిరాన, బిరాలున, బిరీన or బిరీలున *bira-bira*. [Tel. anuk.] adv. Hastily, hurriedly, rapidly, round and round. Quickly, immediately. అతిత్వరితముగా. Radha. iii. 112. "కల్పుబిరాలునమూకిళ్ళపైనిన్." Radha. i. 98.

బిరికి or బిరికిలసజ్జ *biriki*. [Tel.] n. A kind of necklace. మెడనుకట్టుకొనేసొమ్ము.

బిరుదు or బిరుదము *birudu*. [Tel.] n. A badge resembling a medal. An honorary distinctive mark. శౌర్యలాంఛనము. బిరుదుగల honored with a badge. Courage, శౌర్యము. Resolution, a vow, ప్రతిజ్ఞ. An able man, సమర్థుడు. A hero, a brave man. శూరుడు. బిరుదువాద్యము the *naubat* of Muhammadans, being music which a distinguished person is privileged to use at his abode. "బిరుదులమైనను బిరికివారలమైన." B. viii. 418. బిరుదులాడు *birudul-ādu*. n. A man of determination, ప్రతిజ్ఞావంతుడు. బిరుదుకెట్టి a champion, a wrestler who has received an honorary badge. బిరుదావళి *birud-āvali*. n. The heading of a letter, or the address in correspondence. Titles. "ఇట దిబ్బుండు పరిపూర్ణమానకంపాదివిధబిరుదావళీ ప్రబంధ బంధురేగ." Bharata Champu.

బిరుబిర్రు *biru-birru*. [Tel. anuk. of stones falling.] adv. Quickly. "బిరుబిర్రురాలుచు కెన్." A. v. 97.

బిరుసు *birusu*. [Tel.] adj. Hard, firm, coarse, harsh, rough. అన్నము బిరుసుగా నున్నది the rice is hard, not being sufficiently boiled. తలబిరుసుమనిషి a stubborn man. n. Briskness, hardness, firmness, roughness, harshness to the touch. కాఠిన్యము. బిరుసుగ *birusu-ga*. adv. Harshly, roughly. బిరుసులు *birusulu*. n. A sort of fire work called flowerpots. బాణాసంచు విశేషము. "బిరుసులు తుపాకులు బాణాలులున గ్గి మట్టించి." Sūrya Tanaya. iv. 122.

బిర్ర *birra*. [Tel.] n. Tightness. బిగువు. బిర్రబిగియు *birra-bigiyu*. v. n. To become very tight. To stop completely. మాట్లాడక బిర్రబిగిసికొనియున్నాడు he is stubbornly silent. బిర్రు *birru*. n. Tightness, hardness, stiffness. దృఢత్వము. Haste, speed. వేగము. Heat, as of the sun. Strictness. Peremptory inflexibility. ఉద్ధతి. A bar, as securing a door. adj. Tight, hot, &c. ఉద్ధతము. బిర్రెండ fierce sunshine. Vish. vi 220.

బిలము *bilamu*. [Skt.] n. A hole, aperture, chasm, cavern, cave. రంధ్రము, గుహ. మహాబిలము the great expanse, the sky. బిలేశయము *bilē-śayamu*. n. Lit: The dweller in a hole, i.e., a serpent. పాము. A rat, ఎలుక.

బిలింబిచెట్టు *bilimbi-chettu*. [Tel.] n. The Bilimbi tree, *Averrhoa bilimbi*. (Watts.)

బిలిబిలి *bili-bili*. [Tel.] adj. Sweet, delicate, nice. ముద్దైన, ముద్దు పెవు. "ములుకనిపద్యమైన గడు చోద్యముచేయుచు విన్నవానిపెద్దలు గొని యాడగాను వినితప్పలుబట్టడలంతురత్కుమల్ బిలి బిలిమాటలాడ దను తెంచినవాంకే ముద్దుగాకయా పలికెదుచిల్కా పిల్లకని బావురుబిల్లలుపంచిసిల్లుతే." G. i. 17.

"రమణీనివుప్పయంపన మనస్త్రీరాము,
క్రమమొప్పనైకొన్న కథజెప్పుమనిన,
బిలిబిలినవ్వునుసిగ్గునుదోలుక,
పలికెజానకి మత్తిభార్యనిత్తించి." DRU.

బిలుకుమారు *biluku-maru*. [Tel.] v. n. To die. To be destroyed, to perish. "కాల్బలముతోడనవీకవచ్చియుండా, మదలియయుడాలితుండా బిలుకుమారియున్నల్లడబారియుండా." M. VIII. i. 4. బిలుకుమార్చు *biluku-martsu*. v. a. To kill, to destroy. "మహాజనాధ్యరయొక్క-పెవ్వులని మహాద్భుతబాహుసంపదా, మిమునవి దాకడా బిలుకుమార్చుచుంట యుగాత్తిమైంధ్ర్య మహిమగాడ." M. IX. ii. 102. బిలుకురబట్టు *bilukura-battu*. v. a. To strangle. "ఒక్కరుడుమధుగాంత్రి పుస్కట్టి, పీకరక్షమాగింతుపేడి పట్టి, పెడ కేలుడిక బట్టిబిలుకురబట్టి, పడద్రోచి తా మీదబడి గుద్దుచుండె." Dab. 216. బిలుకురబట్టి, అనగా ఊపిరాడకుండాపట్టి. బిల్కురు *bilkuru*. v. n. To be suffocated or strangled. ఉక్కుకుడుచు

బిలుగు *bilugu*. [Tel.] adj. Hypocritical. కపటమైన, మాయమైన.

"కలవారునవ్వాసికిబహు,
కలథాలిసున్నపూర్ణకంఠసనా,
బ్బిలుగునుతితిమనువువెరాసము,
కలనేనియూరేకదానిగాని కిత్తించుదా."
P. i. 222.

బిల్మక్తా *bil-makta*. [H.] n. A fixed annual rent, payable in all seasons; a consolidated lease; a fixed quit-rent or revenue assessed at a lower rate than the standard one. బిల్మక్తాగా *bilmakta-gā*. adv. By the bulk, in general, మొత్తముగా.

బిల్వము *bilvamu*. [Skt.] n. The Bael or Bel Fruit Tree, *Ægle marmelos*, (E. P.) మారేడుచెట్టు.

బిళ్ల or బిల్ల *billa*. [Tel.] n. Any small, round and flat thing, a disc or tablet. పలుచగానుండి గుండ్రముగానుండేవస్తువు. బంట్రౌతుబిళ్ల a peon's badge. అత్తరుబిళ్ల a cake of rose paste. వెండిబిళ్ల a plate of silver. ఒరుగుబిళ్ల a round cushion. రాగిబిళ్ల a gold tire. అదిపెంకు బిళ్లవేసినాడు he put a patch on the metal vessel. మొలబిళ్ల a bit or piece of metal tied on a string around the loins of a female infant. బిళ్లపెంకు or ఓడుబిళ్ల a tile. ఓడుబిళ్లముచ్చు a tiled roof. బిళ్లబొట్టు a round mark on the forehead. బిళ్లకట్టు *billa-kattu* v. n. To have a blood boil formed on any part of the body, శరీరముపైకట్టు గానిగడ్డ

బిల్లకట్టినది he has buboes. బిళ్ల గోళ్లు or గోడుబిళ్లలు a name of game played by children. బిళ్లచెప్పులు thin, flat shoes. బిళ్లవాలు the flat round discus of Vishnu, చక్రాయుధము. బిల్లి another form of బిళ్ల. బిళ్లగన్నేరు billa-gannēru. n. The jalap plant which has lilac flowers. బిళ్లపురుగు billa-purugu. n. The red winged stinging beetle, one of the Cantharides.

బిళ్లు or బిల్లు billu. [Tel.] n. The Indian Satin wood tree; whose wood resembles the box wood. *Swietania chloroxylon.* (Roxb. and Watts.)

బిస bisa. [Tel.] n. The spring, as of a watch, &c. యంత్రపుకీలు. A machine, యంత్రము. A contrivance, device, ఉపాయము. "అప్పు టం(గ్రు)చ్చి కావరాకుండ మునుమున్న మ్మగదుండు బిసయుక్తిసంఘటించిన కాలిబోనులంబడి." Swa. iv. 55. ఆగ్రంథమును తెప్పించడానకు మరియొక బిసపెట్టి ఉన్నాను I have laid another plan for obtaining that book. బిసబిస bisa-bisa. adv. Rapidly, with a spring. B. X. 257.

బిసము bisamu. [Skt.] n. Fibres, film, as of the water lily. మృణాళము, తామరతూడు, తామరతీగె. "బిసములారటనందరు చెంకిరొంపి, సోనవీళ్లవిదల్చి మోపుగనమ్పి." M. XIII. iii. 238. బిసకంఠిక bisa-kanthika. n. A small crane or water bird. పెద్దపెంటికొక్కెర. బిసప్రసూనము, బిసకుసుమము or బిసజము bisa-prasūnamu. n. The water lily: literally, that which has sprung from fibres. తామర, పద్మము. బిసభుక్తి bisa-bhukti. n. Lit: That which feeds on lotus films, i. e., a swan. Paidim. iv. 45. "పసుపుల నలుగిడ్డిరైదున బిసరుహలోచనలు పెండ్లిపెద్దల యాజ్ఞన." Swa. v. 67.

బిసాతు bisatu. [H.] n. Power. Breadth. Capital, stock. (Vizag) adj. Worthless, worth but a trifle.

బిసి bisi. [Tel.] n. A tie between a tatty or screen and a stick placed across to fasten it. తడకకుకట్టేది, తడికబిర్రు. బిసిపోవు bisi-pōvu. v. n. To loosen one's hold. పట్టువదలు.

బిసిని bisini. [Skt.] n. A pond abounding with lilies. A lotus plant. తామరకొలను. తామరచెట్టు. బిసినీకాంతుడు bisinī-kantudu. n. The 'friend of the lily,' i.e., the sun.

బిసిబిసి bisi-bisi. [Tel. anuk.] adj. Sweet and savoury. లకుముకిపులకల, ముద్దుగానున్న. బిసిబిసిమాటలు charming prattle. ముద్దుమాటలు. "మరియును కన్నెయుం బిసిబిసిమాటల మర, ప్రియమునుచెప్పియు వైచియు హితాను, ప్తి బలిసియు నాకకొంతి మెత్తివడగ, జేసి." ప్రభావతీ ప్రద్యుమ్నము. v. 18.

బిస్తి bisti. [H.] n. A waterman, who loads an ox that carries water in skin bags, పకాలి.

బిస్తు or బిస్త bistu. [Tel.] n. Adversity, దుర్గతి. Hell, నరకము.

బిస్సు bissu. [Tel. anuk.] n. A buzzing sound, a burst as of steam. వానిలోబిస్సు లేదు there is no 'go' in it. బిస్సున all at once, in a flight, as pigeons, in a crowd, whizzingly, buzzing, aloud. "పిడిపెలుచేనిమీద నెకబిస్సునవాలగజాలి."

బీ bi

బీగము bīgamu. [Tel.] n. A padlock, తాళము. బీగపుచెవి a key, తాళపు చెవి. బీగముతీయు bīgamu-tīyu. v. a. To unlock. బీగమువేయు bīgamu-vēyu. v. a. To lock up, as a box.

బీజము bījamu. [Skt.] n. A seed. విత్తనము. A testicle, ముష్కము. బీజాక్షరము or బీజము the essential part of a spell or charm. బీజావరి bīja-vari. n. Paddy seeds sprouted and ready for sowing, మొలకవడ్లు. బీజకోశము bījakōśamu. n. The seed vessel of the lotus. తామరపూస. బీజపూరము bīja-pūramu. n. A citron. మాదిఫలము. బీజాకృతము bīja-kṛitamu. n. A field ploughed or harrowed after sowing. విత్తిదున్నినపొలము.

బీటు or బీటిక *bīṭa.* [Tel.] n. A chink, crack, cleft, split. బీటలు వారిన పెదవులు chapped lips. బీటగిల్లు, బీటగిలు, బీటలువారు or బీటపోవు *bīṭa-gillu.* v.n. To be cracked, పగులు. "నిట్టూర్పు గాడ్పుల నధరపల్లవంబు బీటలు వారె." T. iv. 120.

బీడు *bīḍu.* [Tel.] adj. Waste. Base, low, inferior, poor, second-rate, as rice, or a colour. నా పని యిప్పుడు నిండా బీడుగా వచ్చినది my affairs are in a very bad condition. బీడుది యొద్దు I don't want the worst. బీడుభూమి waste land. n. A waste, uncultivated land, barren land. Worthless iron. మట్టుపుఇనుము. చేనిలో పుట్టిన బీడు ఎక్కడికి పోవును shall I not do what I will with my own? వెదురుబీడు bamboo jungle. గడ్డిపట్టినబీళ్లు grass commons, meadows kept for grass.

బీతు *bītu.* [from Skt. భీతి.] n. Fear. భయము. బీతుకొను *bītu-konu.* v. n. To be afraid, భయపడు. బీతుకొలుపు *bītu-kolupu.* v. a. To frighten.

బీద *bīda.* [from Skt. భీతి.] adj. Poor, needy, downcast, dejected, wretched. n. A poor or destitute person. plu బీదలు. బీదనరాలు lean sinews. బీదపిట్టకు దోమతెవులు a fly can torment a starved bird. బీదగిల్లు *bīdagillu.* v. n. To become poor. బీదగిల్లి పోయిన impoverished. బీదరికము or బీదతనము *bīdarikamu.* n. Poverty.

బీభత్సము. బీభత్స or బీభత్సు *bībhatsamu.* [Skt.] n. Bewilderment, amazement. Horror, disgust, abhorrence, loathing. Rancour, ruthlessness. Distress, harassment. నానాబీభత్సు చేస్తున్నాడు he harasses us in various ways. బీభత్సుడై routed, overthrown. బీభత్సుడు *bībhatsudu.* n. A cruel man, క్రూరుడు. A name of Arjuna. "బీభత్సుండునిర్భర స్నేహంబు కలిమునవిడువక గాండీవంబుగొని వచ్చుచున్న." M. XVII. i. 30.

బీమా *bīma.* [H.] n. Insurance. Money paid for insurance.

బీర *bīra.* [Tel.] n. The sharp angled cucumber. నేతిబీర the butter cucumber. చేతిబీర or చేదుబీర the bitter kind. మగబీర *Anisomeles malabarica.* (Watts.) adj. Large, పెద్ద. బీరెండ hot sun-shine. బీరజడలు luxuriant tresses. బీరనరాలు large veins. అడవిబీరాకు or గోడలబీరాకు Betony-leaved black Horehound, *Ballota disticha.* బీరపండ్లు *bīra-pandlu.* n. A sort of scarlet berries, that are eaten, but quite distinct from బీరకాయ.

బీరము *bīramu.* [from Skt. వీర.] n. Prowess, పరాక్రమము.

బీరాజు *bīrādzu.* [Tel.] v. a. To heap up, కుప్పవేయు.

బీరిజము *bīridzamu.* [from Skt. బీజము.] n. A testicle. ముష్కము.

బీరు *bīru.* [Tel.] adj. Useless. వ్యర్థము. బీరుపోవు, బీరుపాఱు or బీరువడు *bīru-pōvu.* v. n. To become useless, వ్యర్థమగు. To be ruined or spoiled, చెడిపోవు. To become weak, బలహీనమగు. బీరుపోక without losing one's pride. మతిబీరుపోయి overwhelmed with fear, అతిశయముపోయి.

బీరువ *bīruva.* [Eng. 'Bureau'] n. A bureau, a chest of drawers, an almirah, అలమారు.

బు bu

బుంగ *bunga.* [H.] n. The baggage belonging to a camp, సరంజామా.

బుంగ *bunga.* [Tel.] n. A pot with a narrow mouth. చిన్నమూతిగలకుండ. "కల్లుబుంగ." పాంచా. iv. "పొంగుచుమీరెడి కృపారాజ భూరు హాములయుగ్రములనన్న బుంగలయూసకంబు." Surabh. 45. బుంగనామము *bunga-nāmamu.* n. A variety of the Vaishnava mark on the forehead. See పంగనామము. బుంగమూతి *bunga-mūti.* n. An ugly face.

బుంగుడుపరచు *bungudu-paratsu* [Tel.] v. n. To cause to fall down. కూలునట్లుచేయు. "కరములు తునకలుగాజేసి జేసి, భుజములు నేలపై బుంగుడుపరచి, తొడలును గెండలును తునకలుచేసి." Pal. 439.

బుక్కడము or బురదబుక్కడము *bukka-ḍamu* [Tel.] n. An eel.

బుక్కనము *bukkanamu.* [Skt.] n. The barking of a dog. మొరగడము.

బుక్కము *bukkamu.* [Skt.] n. Excellent meat. ప్రసిద్ధమైనమాంసము.

బుక్కా, బుక్క or బుక్కాయి *bukka.* [Tel.] n. A fragrant powder formed of various ingredients. పిష్టాతకము, పటవాసకము. బుక్కాము *bukkāmu.* n. The pollen of flowers. పుప్పొడి. "రగడు నెలతయాగే దెంగి నీకప్పెబుక్కాము, చిలుకనీపుప్పొళ్లు చెంచెల బుక్కాము." Swa iii. 112. బుక్కావాడు *bukka-vāḍu.* n. A perfumer. సుగంధద్రవ్యము లమ్మేవాడు.

బుగడ *bugaḍa.* [Tel.] n. A gold pin worn in the tip of the ear.

బుగబుగ *buga buga.* [Tel.] n. A bubbling sound.

బుగులు or గులులు *bugulu.* [Tel.] n. A bubble, swelling, rising to the surface. బుగులుకొను or బుగులుదోచు *bugulu-konu.* v. n. To become visible. బయలుపడు. To gush forth, చిప్పిలు. To increase, spread, విజృంభించు, వ్యాపించు. బుగులుపుచ్చు *bugulu-putstsu.* v. n. To make plain or evident, to show, బయలుపరచు. బుగులు బుగులు *bugulu-bugulu.* n. The noise made in rushing forth, as by water. A retching noise.

బుగ్గ *bugga.* [Tel.] n. The cheek: the inside of the cheek. A bubble. A spring of water, a fountain. బుగ్గరించు *buggar-intsu.* v. n. To smell, as flowers about to bloom. "క్రొగ్గాలిదూలబాకిచెంగి కుదలు బుగ్గరించినయట్టి మొగ్గపువ్వులను." BD. iv. 250. అనగా వికసించడమునకై పొట్లలుబ్బిన కోరకములు.

బుగ్గి *buggi.* [Tel.] n. Ashes, dust. బూడిద భస్మము.

బుచ్చి *buchhi.* [Tel.] adj. Little, small. చిన్న. బుచ్చిగాడు *buchchi-gāḍu* n. A little fellow, చిన్నవాడు. The white-breasted King-fisher, *Halcyon smyrnensis.* చిన్న నీళ్లబుచ్చిగాడు or నీళ్లబుచ్చిగాడు the common King-fisher, *Alcedo ispida.* బుచ్చిపారు *buchchi-pāru.* v. n. To look a small or disappointed, చిన్నపోవు.

బుజ *bud̤za.* [Tel.] n. A little cross denoting a caret. హంసపాదము. A cipher, సుండాకార ము, సున్న.

"కలనజభపుడపయమవములు,
లనరారస్పృశించిసావధానమతిన్గ,
స్థానికానక్క బెదిబ్బర,
జనిబుజెయిదుసగిరి సాభియంగనకలరుణా."

Paidim, iv. 163.

బుజపత్తిరిచెట్టు *buja-pattiri-chettu.* [from Skt. భూర్జ. Cf. Eng. 'beech' or 'birch'] n. A certain tree. భూర్జపత్త్రము.

బుజము *bud̤zamu.* [from Skt. భుజము.] n. The shoulder. ఒకబుజమునేల the distance bearers carry a palanquin at one run, without halting to change shoulders; that is, about a furlong. బుజమునుపుట్టువు *bud̤zamu-putturu.* n. A Kshatriya.

బుజ్జగించు *budzdzagintsu.* [Tel.] v. a. To caress, or fondle. To pacify, console, calm, lull. To cajole, wheedle, persuade, ఊరడించు. బుజ్జగింపు, బుజ్జవము, బుజ్జగింత or బుజ్జగము *budzzagimpu.* n. Flattering, soothing, consolation. సాంత్వనము, ఓదార్పు. బుజ్జగింపుమాట a consoling or flattering word, సాంత్వనవాక్యము. "అన్నాడు నాదుకుండు. సంప్రీతి మెయిన్ [illegible] [illegible] [illegible]." M. xiii. i. 38.

బుటుక్, బుటుకు, బుటుక్కు or బుడుక్కు *butaku.* [Tel. anuk.] n. A plunge. Same as బుడుక్కు.

బుటా or బూటా *buta.* [H.] n. Flowered pattern in a cloth. బుటాపని flower-work.

బుట్ట, బుట్టి or బుట్టికె *butta.* [Tel.] n. A basket. A hamper, a small basket. కరండము.

బుడకోడి *buda-kodi.* [Tel.] n. A waterfowl. Particularly, a teal. నీరుకోడి.

బుడబుడ *buda-buda.* [Tel.] n. Gurgling: the sound a bottle makes when sinking in water.

బుడమ *budama.* [Tel.] n. The plant named *Bryonia callosa,* or *Cucumis utilissimus.* Ainsl. ii. 428. కూరుబుడమ and కోడి బుడమకాయ are various species. బుడమ కాయలాగు తిరుగుతాడు he is running about here and there; (a phrase regarding a dumpy little man, who goes poking about.) బుడమపండ్లు the ripe fruit of the *Bryonia.* బుడమవరుగు the *Bryonia callosa* cut and dried for pickling. బుడమచేప *budama-chepa.* n. A sort of fish.

బుడము *budamu.* [Tel.] n. The beginning, source, root. [illegible] వానికి నాలుక బుడముతో తెగిపోయినప్పుడు his tongue fell off from the root. నీచెవులు బుడముతో తెగకోసెదను I will cut off your ears to the root.

బుడాలున *budalu-na.* [Tel. anuk.] adv. At once. బుడాలున మునుగు to sink like a shot.

బుడికిళ్లు or బుడికిళ్ళు *budikillu.* [Tel.] n. A kind of game. "[illegible] బుడికిళ్లు [illegible] [illegible]." N. ix. 109.

బుడిగి or బుడుగు *budigi.* [Tel.] adj. Small, squat, short and thick. పొట్టి. బుడిగి, బుడిగె or బుడిగె *budigi.* n. A small pot. పిడత, సిద్దె. "[illegible]." H. ii. 84. A pack or pannier, also a leathern oil bottle (సిద్దె), two of which form a bullock load. ఎద్దులమీది ఒకనైపుసిద్దె.

బుడిపి or బుడ్పి *budipi.* [Tel.] n. A bump or swelling. Callus; an excrescence, బొప్పి. A knot or joint in a cane. కణుపు, [illegible]. The stump of an amputated hand, &c.

బుడిబుడి *budi-budi.* [Tel. anuk.] adj. Easy, gentle. Trifling, petty, అల్పము. బుడిబుడినడ a gentle pace. బుడిబుడిమాటలు muttered words. బుడిబుడికన్నీరు trickling tears. బుడిబుడిరొదవు whimpering. బుడిబుడివేల్పులు petty gods. "[illegible] బుడిబుడివేల్పులను, [illegible]." BD. iv. 648. n. Haste, hurry, flurry. తొట్రుపాటు. బుడిపడు *budi-padu.* v. n. To be agitated, తొట్రుపడు. బుడిబుడిక్కులవారు or బుడుబుడుక్కులవారు *budi-budikkula-varu.* n. A certain class of mendicants. బుడిబుళ్లుపోవు *budi-bullu-pova.* v. n. To be surprised, or astonished, ఆశ్చర్యపడు.

"[illegible]
[illegible]
[illegible]
[illegible] బుడిబుళ్లు [illegible]
[illegible]." BD. v. 388.

బుడుక buḍuka. [Tel. anuk] n. A plunge into water, మునక. A bath, స్నానము.

బుడుకు buḍuku. [Tel.] n. A kind of cake. భక్ష్యవిశేషము.

బుడుక్కున buḍukku-na. [Tel.] adv. Slap-dash, suddenly.

బుడుత or బుడత buḍuta. [Tel.] n. A little one, a child. శిశువు, బిడ్డ, బాలుడు. "ఒక పాటిబుడత, యాకుమడుపులందియ్య." H. i. 134. A. vi. 159. adj. Little. Short, పొట్టి. బుడుతగాడ్పు a gentle breeze. "భూరిభుజంగాస్యకుహరంబునవచ్చి వెడలుపావనిర్గమన బుడుతగాడ్పు." Bmj. iii. 132. బుడుతడు buḍutuḍu. n. A male child. బాలుడు.

బుడుబుడక్కలవాడు or డుబుడక్కలవాడు Same as బుడుబుడుక్కలవాడు See under బుడిబుడి.

బుడుములు buḍumulu. [Tel.] n. A species of grain. One species is called వంగాకు బుడుములు. "చంద్రవంకిలుజేనసరులు, కాంభోజలు, వంగాకుబుడుములుపొంగుప్రాలు." H. iv. 156.

బుడుసు buḍusu. [Tel.] n. Hollowness. బుడుసుపోయిన lean, thin, fallen in. "వెడగొంగమెడయును కడుగూనివీపును బుడుసుబోయినరొండిబొక్కిరొమ్ము." NH. iv. 184.

బుడ్డ buḍḍa. [Tel.] n. A bubble. నీరుబుగ్గ. The disease called rupture, hernia, or hydrocele. అండవృద్ధి. బుడ్డవాడు one who is suffering from rupture or hydrocele; one who has a hydrocele. బుడ్డబెదిరింపులు a mere bugbear. ఉచ్చబుడ్డ the bladder. బుడ్డకాకర buḍḍa-kakara. n. A species of heart pea (కాకర) which is smooth leaved. *Cardiospermum halicacabum.* (Watts.) బుడ్డగించు buḍḍa-gintsu. v. n. To bubble up. v. a. To rout up or stir up the earth as with tusks, కెల్లగించు, (పంది)ముట్టెతో గొరాడు. A. iv. 22. బుడ్డగింపు buḍḍa-gimpu. n. Bubbling up. బుడ్డతుమ్మ buḍḍa-tumma. n. A kind of babul tree. బుడ్డపక్కె buḍḍa-pakke. n. A kind of fish. బుడ్డపినుడు or బుడ్డపినుజు buḍḍa-pinuḍu. n. A tick or round louse. పశువులనుపట్టెక్రిమివిశేషము. బుడ్డబుడుసు or బుడ్డమినిరి buḍḍa-buḍusu. n. The Brazil cherry, a fruit enclosed in a loose dry pod.

బుడ్డి buḍḍi. [Tel.] n. A bottle, a flask. plu. బుడ్లు. బుడ్డిచెంబు a sort of metal bottle. బుడ్డిముకాకు a sort of spear. బుడ్డిగ Same as బుడ్డి.

బుత్తి butti. [from Skt. భుక్తి.] n. Enjoyment. "నిచ్చలపుబత్తిగా బుత్తియుగా ముత్తియుగా." Nila. i. 21.

బుద్ది buddi. [from Skt. బుద్ధి.] n. Sense. "బుద్దులుతెల్పబోవుగతిబూనుకకన్గవబుల్లుకొంచునుగా." Radha. i. 28.

బుద్బుదము budbudamu. [Skt.] n. A bubble. నీరుబుగ్గ.

బుధుడు budhuḍu. [Skt.] n. The regent of the planet Mercury. The planet Mercury. A wise or learned man, a sage. పండితుడు. బుధవారము budha-varamu. n. Wednesday. సౌమ్యవారము.

బుద్ధ buddha. [Skt.] adj. Known, understood. ఎరిగిన, తెలిసిన.

బుద్ధి buddhi. n. Intelligence, intellect, understanding, mind, judgment, sense, wisdom, intention, inclination. judgment, advice. ఇప్పుడు బుద్ధివచ్చినది I have been taught a lesson, I am convinced of my fault. పడుచుబుద్ధి a childish whim or notion. బుద్ధిపుట్టించు to suggest an idea. బుద్ధి పుట్టినది the thought occurred. ఇది నీకు బుద్ధికాదు it is not wise on your part to do so. బుద్ధి (like చిత్తము) is a colloquial reply, equivalent to 'as you please.' బుద్ధిచెప్పు buddhi-cheppu.

v. a. To admonish, exhort, advise. To reprimand or chastise. నాకు ఏమి బుద్ధి చెప్పుతారు what would you advise me to do? కొడుకునకు బుద్ధిచెప్పినాడు he reprimanded his son. బుద్ధిపూర్వకముగా intentionally, on purpose, advisedly. నేను బుద్ధియెరిగిననాటనుండి as long as I can recollect. బుద్ధియెరిగినతర్వాత after he grew to be a man. బుద్ధితెచ్చుకొను *buddhi-tetstsu-konu.* v. n. To come to one's senses or recover one's wits. బుద్ధిమంతుడు *buddhi-mantuḍu.* n. A sensible person, a wise man. బుద్ధిగలవాడు. బుద్ధిహీనత *buddhi-hīnata.* n. Stupidity, folly. అవివేకము. బుద్ధిహీనుడు *buddhi-hīnuḍu.* n. A fool, a man devoid of sense.

బుద్ధుడు *buddhuḍu.* n. A generic name for a deified teacher of the Buddhist sect. The name is especially applied to Gautama, the founder of Buddhism, who has been treated in the Puranas as the ninth incarnation of Vishṇu.

బుధ్నము *budhnamu.* [Skt.] n. The root of a tree. చెట్టువేరు. An aerial root of a tree. ఊడ.

బుబ్బిలి *bubbili.* [Tel.] n. The whispering larch tree. See బొబ్బిలి.

బుభుక్ష *bubhuksha.* [Skt.] n. Hunger. భుజింపవలెననుకోరిక. ఆకలి. బుభుక్షితుడు *bubhukshituḍu.* n. A hungry man. ఆకలిగొనినవాడు.

బుభుత్స *bubhutsa.* [Skt.] n. A desire to learn or to be taught. బోధగొనవలెనను ఇచ్ఛ.

బుయ్యారము *buyyāramu.* [Tel.] n. A prison. చెరసాల.

బురకా *burakā.* [H.] n. A cloth cover. బురకావేసికొను *burakā-vēsi-konu.* v. a. To cover oneself with a cloth. కప్పుకొను.

బురజె *buradza.* [Tel.] n. A small bell. చిరుగజ్జె.

బురటకొమ్ము or బుర్రటకొమ్ము *buraṭa-kommu.* [Tel.] n. A syringe, a squirt, చిమ్మనగ్రోవి.

బురడా *buraḍā.* [Tel.] n. A kind of cloth. "ఘనవిచిత్రపుసకలాత్ కలంకారీలు చినారు పూలీలు తగినకల్బరిగేలు, తరుకొత్తగలుసుకువ్వ తాష్టాలుబురడాలు." H. v. 408.

బురడిజింక *buraḍi-jinka.* [Tel.] n. The Indian Gazelle, *Gazella bennetti.* పొట్టిజింక.

బురద *burada.* [Tel.] n. Mud. అడుసు, పంకము. బురదకమ్మి *burada-kammi.* n. A stepping stone, a threshold or plank at a door. గడపకిందికమ్మి. బురదగుంట *burada-gunṭa.* n. A puddle. గలిజుపాళ్లగుంట. బురదదుక్కి *burada-dukki.* n. Ploughing in an irrigated field. ఊడ్పుటకు సిద్ధము చేసినపొలము. బురదపాము *burada-pāmu.* n. A water-snake. నీరుపాము.

బురినిపంది *burini-pandi.* [Tel.] n. A small animal resembling the guinea pig in shape.

బురుక or బురుకడు *buruka.* [Tel.] n. A child, బిడ్డ. A hound, వేటకుక్క. adj. Short, పొట్టి.

బురుజు *buruḍzu.* [H.] n. A bastion, a tower or fortalice, కోటగోడపట్టె కొత్తడిబ్బ, గడి, చిన్నకోట.

బురుడా *buruḍā.* [Tel.] n. A lie. అబద్ధము.

బురుడుడు *buruḍuḍu.* [Skt.] n. A basket-maker. మేదరవాడు.

బురుమా Same as బరమా (q. v.)

బురులు *burulu.* [Tel.] n. plu. Meanness, inferiority. న్యూనత. BD. iv. 400.

బురుసా *burusā.* [Tel.] n. Red silk. ఎర్ర పట్టు. Silk, పట్టు.

బురుసు *burusu.* [Eng. 'brush'] n. A brush. కుంచె, తూలిక.

బుర్ర *burra.* [Tel.] n. A nutshell: the shell or nut of any fruit. Any small box as a snuff box, or case. The skull or head. తలపుర్ర. బుక్కాబుర్ర a pouncet box. ఇత్తడి బుర్ర a brass box. సొరబుర్ర the empty shell of a long gourd. సొరబుర్ర or కాయబుర్ర a swimming gourd or a float. కిరుబుర్రలతల గడ a creaking pillow. HD. i. 1668. కొంటె బుర్రలకాయ a cocoanut or other shell of a peculiar indented shape. adj. Large, పెద్ద. బుర్రకత్తి *burra-katti.* n. A broad knife, a hatchet చెట్లకొమ్మలునరుకు మోటుకత్తి. బుర్ర కాయ *burra-kaya.* n. The head, the pate. తలకాయ. Also, same as సొరబుర్ర. బుర్ర జింక *burra-jinka.* n. A kind of antelope: the Open nosed deer. బుర్రముక్కుగల జింక. బుర్రటకొమ్ము *burrața-kommu.* n. A squirt. చిమ్మనగొట్టము.

"పెంత్తములంకట్టి తెచ్చిరి.
ముత్తెపుఋఘల్లరులతో డబుర్రటకొమ్ముల్." హైజ.

బుర్రతలము or బుర్రఏతము *burra-talamu.* n. A kind of water-lift. బుర్రపిట్ట *burra-pițța.* n. The Grey Quail, *Coturnis communis* (F. B. I.) ఒకవిధమైన పొపురము. బుర్రబాడిసె *burra-badise.* n. An adze used by stonecutters. బుర్రముక్కు *burra-mukku.* n. A large nose. పెద్దముక్కు. బుర్ర ముక్కువాడు a bulbous nosed man. బుర్ర లావుక *burra-lavuka.* n. The sand grouse.

బుర్రి *burri.* [Tel.] n. A heifer or young cow.

బుర్రు *burru.* [Tel. anuk.] n. A loud and sudden noise such as is made when a bird flies.

బులాకీ *bulaki.* [H. from Boulak, a suburb of Cairo.] n. A jewel worn on the middle of the nose between the nostrils.

బులియు *buliyu.* [Tel.] v. n. To enjoy happiness, to be happy, సుఖించు. బులుపు *bulupu.* n. Happiness, glee, joy, సుఖము. Fancy, liking, whim; a hobby horse, or pet. వేడుక, వాంఛ, ఉబలాటము.

బువ్వ *buvva.* [Tel.] n. Food, అన్నము. బువ్వ కుడుపు *buvva-kuḍupu.* n. The ceremony used on first giving solid food to an infant. అన్నప్రాశనము. బువ్వము or బువ్వ ముబంతి *buvvamu.* n. A marriage feast. పెండ్లిలో మగవారును ఆడువారును ఏకపంక్తిపా టలు పాడుకొనుచు భోజనముచేయుటము. తొలి బువ్వము the feast on the first night of a marriage. నాలుబువ్వము the feast on the fourth night of a marriage. బువ్వముబంతి పాటలు ballads such as are used at marriages. "బువ్వమున మోవి తేనియబువ్వంబున దినిపెంచుట పొలతుకదనియుక." Satya. iv. 273. బువ్వమ్మ *buvvamma.* n. The rustic name for the goddess అన్నపూర్ణ (Anna Purna.)

బుస *busa.* [Tel. anuk.] n. A puff, or whizz. Hissing, snorting, snoring, deep breathing. A sigh, నిట్టూర్పు. వాని ఒళ్లు బుసబుస లాడుచున్నది he is puffed up and strengthless. బుసకొట్టు or బుసలుకొట్టు to breathe, hiss, or puff audibly as a cobra does, or as an elephant does with its trunk, ఫూత్కారముచేయు. To sigh, నిట్టూర్చు. బుస బుస *busa-busa.* n. A bubbling sound, as of boiling water. Ebullition. బుసబుసలాడు *busa-busa-l-aḍu.* v. n. To boil, to hiss, బుసపెట్టు.

బుసము or బుసము *busamu.* [Skt.] n. Chaff, husk. ఊముక, పొల్లు. The thick part of curds. కుండ అడుగుపెరుగు, మీగడతీసినపెరుగు.

బుసి *busi.* [Tel.] n. Embers, ashes, నివురు. అతడు బుసికప్పిననిప్పు he is a fire hidden under ashes, his face conceals his thoughts. బుసిపోవు *busi-povu.* v. n. To be under a cloud, or in slight disfavour. To be spoiled, చెడిపోవు.

బుసుకుజొన్న *busuku-dzonna.* [Tel.] n. A kind of great Millet, *Holcus saccharatus.*

బుస్సు Same as బుస (q. v.). **బుస్సున** *bussu-na.* (anuk.) Puff! (in blowing.) Chenna. v. 332. **బుస్సుమను** *bussu-m-anu.* v. n. To hiss as a snake, to sigh, to groan.

బూ bū

బూక *būka.* [Tel.] n. Hypocrisy. బూటకము, మాయ.

బూగర *būgara.* [Tel.] n. Grain thrashed but not yet winnowed. Trash, dirt, cobwebs, dust, mould. కళ్లమలోనిది పొల్లుకలిసిన ధాన్యము, ఇండ్లలోపలి వాసములకు పట్టినబూజి, బూజు.

బూచి or **బూచము** *būchi.* [from Skt. భూతము.] n. A ghost, spirit, devil. A monster. ఆడుబూచి a hag, an ogress. "పాతకులకొఱు పట్టువుపాలియుదురు, గ్రోవిధరకంపుటయగారి గుండెదిగులు, బట్టువాకట్టుబడినలపాముకూనయు నగవిభ్రాంతిగాంచెనయ్యెడుబూచి." S. iii. 19. మిణుగురుబూచి a firefly. **బూచిగాడు** or **బూచివాడు** *būchi-gāḍu.* n. A hobgoblin. బూచేలేడు Lit. The Lord of demons, i. e. Siva.

బూజకాగులు *būḍza-kāgulu.* [Tel.] n. Painted vases used in marriage processions. అయిరేనికడవలు.

బూజు *būḍzu.* [Tel.] n. Mildew, mould, dirt, as cobwebs. బూజుపట్టు to become mouldy.

బూటకము *būṭakamu.* [Tel.] n. A trick, guile, prank. మాయ, వంచన. adj. False, delusive. **బూటకాలమారి**, **బూటకీడు** or **బూటకుడు** *būṭakāla-māri.* n. A cheat, a liar, rogue, pretender. "బూటకులను మాయలాడినొచ్చుచుండు." L. xxiv. 188.

బూడిద, **బూడిదె** or **బూడ్డ** *būḍida.* [another form of బూది q. v.] n. Ashes. బూడిదగుమ్మడి a white grey or ash-coloured gourd melon, *Benincasa cerifera.* పెండ్లిగుమ్మడి కాయ. **బూడిదవర్ణము** *būḍida-varnamu.* n. Ash-colour. బూడిదఉప్పు or మాముఉప్పు Potash, or Pearl-ash. Carbonate of Potash. (Watts). **బూడిదపండు** *būḍida-panḍu.* n. A ball of ashes. విభూతిపండు. **బూడిదెపన్ను** *būḍide-pannu.* n. A tax levied for burning a corpse on the cremation ground.

బూతము *būtamu.* [from Skt. భూతము.] n. A ghost. పిశాచము. A soul, ప్రాణి. **బూతపిల్లి** *būta-pilli.* n. A civet cat. పూతికము.

బూతి *būti.* [from Skt. భూతి.] n. Ashes, బూది. Food, తిండి.

బూతు *būtu.* [Tel.] n. Foul language, obscenity; slang: nonsense, పలువత్తు, పలువమాట. A flatterer, బట్టువాడు. **బూతాటము** the act of using foul language బూతులాడుట.

బూద *būda.* [Tel.] n. A milk-vessel. పాలకుండ. "మునుపదరోలూఖలమెక్కి నిక్కి నవాజాంకోపేంద్రసంయుక్తుడై, చదలకొబూదకకాంతసేకరవిస్తారంబులంబట్టి." Vasu. iv. 25. టీ. చదలకొబూద, ఆకాశముననుండు బూదకుండను ఆనగా ఉట్టిపైనున్న పాలకుండను.

బూది *būdi.* [from Skt. భూతి.] n. Ashes. బూడిద. బూదిచేచు to become mouldy, ash-coloured, pale, బూజుపట్టు. బూదివన్నె whiteness, paleness, తెల్లనివర్ణము, ధూసరవర్ణము. **బూదె** *būde.* n. Lit: "Ash-day." The name of a day (Siva-rātri) sacred to Siva in the month of Magha. శివరాత్రి. The fourteenth day of a lunar or dark fort-night. చతుర్దశితిథి.

బూను Same as బూజు (q. v.).

బూనుపాసు Same as బూజుపట్టు (q. v.).

బూబు or **బూబుసాని** *būbu.* [H.] n. A Mussulman woman. తురకస్త్రీ.

బూమి *būmi.* [from Skt. భూమి.] Same as భూమి (q. v.).

బూమె or బూమిరము būme. [Tel.] n. A fib, fiction. మారువేషము, మాయ, వంచన. "తెలిసె నెంగిదీర్పమితభుక్తిసలిపి, కెంటబూమెలెరుగని యొకపాటిబుడుత, యూకుమడుపులందియ్య." H. i. 134. బూమెలెరుగని, మాయలెరుగని. బూమెకత్తె or బూమెలాడి būme-katte. n. A tricksy woman. బూమెలాడు or బూమెకాడు būmel-āḍu. n. A tricksy man.

బూర būra. [Tel.] n. A trumpet. adj. Stout, స్థూలము. బూరకాలు būra-kālu. n. A swollen leg. A leg which is affected by elephantiasis, ఏనుగుకాలు. బూరకాలి వాడు būra-kāli-vāḍu. n. One who has elephantiasis. ఏనుగుకాలివాడు. బూరగడ్డి or పిట్టికబూరగడ్డి būra-gaḍḍi. n. A herb called *Ambrosinia unilocularis*. Rox. iii. 493. బూరడు būraḍu. n. One who excels or is proud, విజృంభించినవాడు. బూర దిప్పకాయ būra-dippa-kāya. n. A plant called *Leea integrifolia*. Rox. i. 659. బూరగ or బూర būraga. n. A trumpet. కాహళి, తార. "క్రూరంబులైన బూరగలర వంబులును." T. v. 26. A sort of white vulture. బూరగొమ్ము būra-gommu. n. A trumpet horn, ఊదుకొమ్ము. A conch-shell. శంఖము. బూరట būraṭa. n. Swelling. ఉబ్బరము. బూరటిల్లు or బూరటలు būraṭillu. v. n. To be spread. To swell, ఉబ్బు. To be full, నిండు. "కీల కలము పైగిలించి గాలిత్రాగినచాపపోల్కి మిన్నంత యుబూరటిల్లె." M. V. iv. 120. బూరటించు būraṭintsu. v. a. To cause to fill, బూరటి ల్లజేయు.

బూరగ, బూరుగ, బూరుగు or బూరువు būraga. [Tel.] n. The silk cotton tree. *Bombax heptaphylla*, Rox. iii. 167. శాల్మలి. Its wood is like the poplar or sallow proverbially large and useless. వాడు వట్టి బూరగమాను he is a mere log, he is a stupid booby. One species is called కక్కబూరగ; another is దుంకిబూరగచెట్టు *Briedelia scandens*. Rox. iii. 737. బూరుగ దూది the cotton found in these pods, which, steeped in nitre, is used for tinder. ముండ్లబూరగమాను *Bombax malabaricum*. (Wight, plate 297 and Watts). బూరుగు దీవి the name of an island, శాల్మలిద్వీపము.

బూరె or బూరియ būre. [from Skt. పూరి.] n. A kind of sweet cake, a bun. భక్ష్య విశేషము బూర్లమూకుడు a frying pan. బూరెచెట్టు or కావడిబూరె būre-chettu. n. A tree called *Ehretia buxifolia*. Ainsl. ii. 81.

బూర్నీసు būrnīsu. [H.] n. Flannel. A blanket or thick woollen cloth. మెత్తని కంబళి.

బూల būla. [Tel.] n. Pith, as the centre of wood. దుక్క. బూలతీసివేసిన hollowed, pithless. బూలి pithless, sapless, నిస్సార మైన.

బూసము būsamu. [Tel.] n. Grain, ధాన్యము. "బూసంబుబరపి పేర్చున నమ్ముకొనుటకు." P. i. 773.

బూసరకాయ or బుడ్డబూసర būsara-kāya. [Tel.] n. The berry called Brazil cherry.

బూసి būsi. [Tel.] n. Dirt, మురికి. Cobwebs, ఇండ్లలో వాసాలకుపట్టే సాలీళ్లమగ్గాలు.

బృ bri

బృంద brinda. [Skt.] n. The sacred Basil plant. *Ocimum sanctum*, తులసి. బృందా వనము brindā-vanamu. n. A raised piece of ground, inside of a house, within which Hindus of the Vishnu sect raise and preserve this plant.

బృందము brindamu. [Skt.] n. A multitude, సమూహము. బ్రాహ్మబృందము a circle or number of Brahmins.

బృందారకుడు brindārakuḍu. [Skt.] n. A beautiful or excellent being. సుందరుడు,

త్రిదశుడు. A god, a demigod, a deity, an immortal. వేలుపు, దేవుడు. బృందారకాద్రి *brindarak-adri*. n. A name of Meru, the hill on which the gods abide.

బృంహితము *brinhitamu*. [Skt.] n. The roar of an elephant. ఏనుగుకేక.

బృహత్తు or బృహతి *brihattu*. [Skt.] adj. Great, large. గొప్ప. బృహద్గంగ *brihad-ganga*. n. The main (stream of the) Ganges. బృహద్బీజము *brihad-bijamu*. n. Swelled testicle, Orchitis, అండవృద్ధి, బుడ్డ. బృహద్భానువు *brihad-bhanuvu*. n. An epithet of the god of fire. అగ్ని. బృహద్వ్యాధి *brihad-vyadhi*. n. Leprosy. బృహన్నల *brihannala*. n. A name assumed by Arjuna in his exile.

బృహస్పతి *brihas-pati*. n. The name of the priest of the gods, సురగురువు. The planet Jupiter; also a certain lawgiver. In mythology he answers to Thor, or Vulcan. బృహస్పతివారము *brihaspati-varamu*. n. Thursday.

బె be

బెంగ *benga*. [Tel.] n. Anxiety, sorrowing, pining. మనోవ్యథ, ఏకారికపోవడము. A cry, కూత. బెంగగొను or బెంగపడు *benga-gonu*. v. n. To pine for, to sorrow for. మనోవ్యాధినిపొందు. బెంగలిడు *bengal-idu*. v. n. To yell, to cry out or shriek in alarm. "ఉ॥ బెంగలిడంగ గొంటియటు పెంటిని గానక కెలిపోయి." Sarang. ii. 3.

బెండ *benda*. [Tel.] n. The vegetable called *Hibiscus longifolius*. Rox. iii. 210. ఎద్దువాలికచెట్టు. కర్పూరపుబెండ *Hibiscus esculentus*. తుత్తురబెండ, తుత్తిరిబెండ or నూగుబెండ Country Mallow, *Abutilon asiaticum* or *Abutilon indicum*. (E. P.)

బెండగిల్లు *bendagillu*. [Tel.] v. n. To start on a journey, వెళ్లగిల్లు, ప్రయాణమగు.

బెండు *bendu*. [Tel.] n. Cork, pith. A float used in angling. The shrub termed *Aschynomine aspera*. జీలుగు. adj. Sapless, నిస్సారమైన. బెండ్లదంట్లు sapless stalks. "బెండుబొమ్మవలెనుండెడి సందిటజాల్కనై." A. v. 66. ఈ శాకగాలి శరీరమును బెండుచేయుచున్నది this burning wind dries up the body. బెండుపడు *bendu-padu*. v. n. To be alarmed, to be dejected or disheartened, to become weak, బలహీనతనొందు. "దండిగానార్చినిర్జరుల్ బెండుపడగ." T. v. 92. బెండుపరచు or బెండుచేయు *bendu-paratsu*. v. a. To frighten, to render powerless. నిస్సారముగునట్లుగాచేయు. బెండుమానిసి a weak man, బలహీనుడైన మనుష్యుడు.

బెక్కువా *bekkuva*. [Tel.] n. A sort of silk cloth. "వారణాశియు, బెక్కువాయు, కెంజాకరు, గౌరికనిచయమంబు, కడిగొడకంబు, పట్టును, రత్నంభపుపట్టును, శంఖపట్టును." BD. iii. 106.

బెక్కొట్టు *bekkottu*. [Tel. బెంగ + కొట్టు.] v. n. To pine, వాపోవు.

బెగటికంద or బెగ్గటికంద *begati-kanda*. [Tel.] n. A certain weed called *Athanasia indica*. Rox. iii. 417.

బెగడు, బెగ్గడు, బెగ్గడిల్లు, బెగ్గడిలు or బెగడుపడు *begadu*. [Tel.] v. n. To be alarmed, to fear. భయపడు. బెగడు n. Fear, terror, భయము.

"నీవుతోడిబడజచ్చినతోడనేబెగడి,
విడివడ్డబ్రాహ్మణుల్ విడుచునీశకువు."

HD. i. 2197. బెగడుపరచు *begadu-paratsu*. v. a. To frighten, intimidate. "శకునిమైనరువదియమ్ములు నాటించియనుచరులను బెగడుపరచెవాఖ్రీముడు." M. IX. i. 438. "సింహానివాదంబాలించి దెగడినయేనుంగు తెరంగున బెగ్గడిల్లి." Ila. iii. 6.

బెగ్గలము or బెగ్గలికము beggalamu. [from Skt. విహ్వలము.] n. Fear, concern. భీతి. బెగ్గిలు, బెగ్గిల్లు or బెగ్గిలించు beggilu. v. n. To fear, dread, be alarmed. భయపడు, బెదరు. "మానంబులేగిరమావిభునకు నిట్టులనిరిబెగ్గిలుచు." BD. iv. 364.

బెగ్గురు or వెగ్గురు bagguru. [Tel.] n. The bird called the Adjutant crane, *Leptoptilus dubius*. కరటి, పొడవుపక్షి.

బెగ్గోడి beggōḍi. [Tel. పెద్ద+గోడి.] n. A sort of wild fowl. ఒకజాతికోడి.

బెగ్గోలుపడు beg-gōlu-paḍu. [Tel. పెద్ద+గోలు.] v. n. To be ruined. భ్రాంతిగాచెడు. "వాళ్ళు అందరు తెగడిబోరలికలసుకుబహ్లతకుబండిపడంగి బెగ్గోలుపడికమకించుచున్నారు." Pal. 27.

బెచ్చకాయ betstsa-kāya. [Tel.] n. A fruit resembling the ఉసిరికకాయ.

బెజ్జము beḍzḍsamu. [Tel.] n. An orifice, bore, a small hole. సన్నరంధ్రము. బెజ్జము పొడుచు or తొలుచు to bore a hole.

బెట్ట or వెట్ట beṭṭa. [Tel.] n. Heat. తీవ్రము. బెట్టకిస్తు revenue charged on a summer crop. బెట్టించు beṭṭintsu. v. a. To free from restraint, నిర్బంధమునుండి మరలించు. To set free, విడిపించు.

బెట్టిదము beṭṭidamu. [Tel. బెట్టు+ఇదము.] n. Arrogance. ఉద్ధతి. Harshness, cruelty, క్రౌర్యము. A harsh expression, abuse. క్రూరోక్తి, తిట్టు, నిష్ఠురవచనము. "అనుచుబెట్టిదంబులాడనవనివాధకుతులసై, కినిసి." V. P. v. 265. adj. Proud, ఉద్ధతము. Cruel. క్రూరమైన. Harsh, కఠినము. Hard, గట్టి, దృఢము. బెట్టిదముగా beṭṭ-idamu-gā. adv. Violently, severely. బెట్టిదుడు beṭṭiduḍu. n. A proud or cruel man, ఉద్ధతుడు, క్రూరుడు. A hard man, కఠినుడు. బెట్టిదురాలు beṭṭidu-r-ālu. n. A proud, cruel or hard woman.

బెట్టు beṭṭu. [Tel.] n. Hardness, difficulty, trouble. Respectability, esteem, regard. గౌరవము, పెంపు, ఉద్ధతి, అతిశయము. "నిన్ను వద్దేదమనిచలముతోనినన్నుటబెట్టా." B. X. 359. నీవు అక్కడికిపోతే బెట్టుదక్కదు if you go there you will not meet with honor, you cannot go there with credit. adj. Hard, trying, కష్టము. Proud, ఉద్ధతమైన. adv. Excessively, violently, much. మిక్కుటముగా, మెండుగా, అత్యంతము. Firmly, గట్టిగా, దృఢముగా. నంటాబెట్టుగానున్నది it is very hard (on us), మిక్కిలికష్టముగానున్నది. బెట్టుడుత beṭṭ-uḍuta. n. The large or great squirrel. "పికిలిపిట్టలు, జేగలు, బెట్టుడుతలు." S. i. 187.

బెడక beḍaka. [Tel.] n. An empty sack. ఉత్తగోను.

బెడకు or బెలకు beḍaku. [Tel.] v. n. To move, చలించు. To move aside, తొలగు. To disperse, dissipate, చెదరు. దిశలుబెడకె the quarters of heaven shook. n. Movement, చలనము. Moving aside or away from, తొలగుట.

బెడగు beḍagu. [Tel.] n. Fineness, prettiness, handsomeness, prime, grace, comeliness, elegance, prettiness, foppish airs. కులుకు, సొగసు, అందము, విలాసము, ఒప్పిదము. adj. Great, large, అధికము. Pretty, మనోజ్ఞము. v. n. To be beautiful or pretty, అందగించు. బెడగుతనము beḍagu-tanamu. n. Strength, greatness: fineness, గొప్పతనము, ఔద్ధత్యము, సొగసు. "ఒడలిబడలికందడమున బెడంగుదనంబునిగుడదాడిని" R. v. 196. బెడగారు beḍag-āru. (బెడగు+ఆరు.) v. n. To shine, to be beautiful, అందగించు. adj. Brilliant. "తొడలబెడగారు సన్నపువలువతోడ." Zacca. v. 64. "జాళువాకెంపులకట్టు బెడగారునెర్కాపిడించెతోడ." Swa. iii. 93.

బెడద *beḍada*. [Tel]. n. Evil, misfortune. కీడు, చెరుపు. Pain, బాధ. Danger, ఆపద. A kind of cake, ఒకవిధమైనభక్ష్యము.

బెడలి or **బెడలికె** *beḍali*. [Tel.] n. A sort of plant used in hedging, *Posoqueria fragrans*. Rox. i. 717.

బెడిదము or **బేడిదము** *beḍidamu*. [from Skt. ఖేదితము.] n. Horror, terror, dread. భయంకరత్వము. Cruelty, కఠినత్వము. Evil, కీడు, చెరుపు. "తాను చేసినయెడు తప్పులోబెడిదంబు, మానికడు వివేకమహిమదనరి, యూరకున్న వాడుసుత్తమోత్త ముడురా." Vema. 1027. adj. Horrible, dreadful, terrible. భయంకరమైన, ఘోరమైన. Great, అధికమైన. Hard, కఠినమైన. "తాకి నరాధముండు బెడిదంబగునమ్ములనెల్లి దెల్పనక్కాక కనోక్కువాడు." Padma. viii. 162. **బెడిదముగ** *beḍidamu-ga*. adv. Horribly, dreadfully, terribly. ఘోరముగా. **బెడిదుడు** *beḍi-duḍu*. n. A fearful or cruel man. భయంకరుడు, కఠినుడు. **బెడిదురాలు** *beḍidu-rālu*. n. A fearful or cruel woman.

బెడియు *beḍiyu*. [Tel.] v. n. To separate or fly off as a splinter or a bit. తెప్పు, విరుగు. వానికివానికి బెడిసినది they are now on bad terms.

బెడుసు See బెణకు.

బెడ్డ *beḍḍa*. [Tel.] n. A small stone.

బెణకు, **బెణుకు**, **బెడకు** or **బెడుకు** *beṇaku*. [Tel.] v. n. To be sprained. To totter, to quake. వణుకు. "కొన్ని చిన్ని పన్నిదంబులు చేసి కొనిబడుగు నడుము బెడికి." B. viii. 457. n. A sprain. బెణుకు.

బెణుగులు *beṇu-gulu*. [Tel.] n. Rafters in a roof or shed. పందిరికి అడ్డముగావేసే కర్రలు.

బెత్త or **బెత్తెడు** *betta*. [Tel.] n. The width of the four fingers, a hand-breadth. A hand, or measure of four finger-breadths. **బెత్తెడు** *bett-eḍu*. n. A hand-breadth or measure of four inches.

బెత్తము *bettamu*. from [Skt. వేత్రము.] n. A cane, a rattan. *Calamus fasciculatus*. Rox. iii. 770. పేము. కుర్చీకి బెత్తము అల్లించు to rattan a chair: i. e., to plait thin strips of rattan so as to form a seat. **బెత్తాలచాప** *bettālu-tsāpa*. n. A rattan mat.

బెత్తిక *bettika*. [Tel.] n. A flake, that which comes off in flakes as plaster. ఎండిన పెచ్చు, తేక, మంటిపెళ్ల.

బెత్తు Same as బెత్తిక. Respectability. గౌరవము. A cane, బెత్తము. **బెత్తుపరికె** *bettu-parike*. n. A sort of sprat. *Chetodon*, ఒకచేపపేరు. **బెత్తులెత్తు** *bettul-ettu*. v. n. To come off in flakes. "సర్వతిక్కలుదూరంబుకొత్తాగముల్ బెత్తులెత్త." T. v. 11.

బెదరు, **బెదురు** or **బెదరుపడు** *bedaru* [Tel.] v. n. To start, be alarmed, be frightened. భయపడు. **బెదరు** or **బెదురు** n. Fright, alarm. బెదరిన or బెదిరిన frightened, timid, alarmed. adj. Timid, పిరికి. **బెదురుపెట్టు** *bedaru-peṭṭu*. v. a. To threaten, to intimidate. **బెదురుపోతు** *bedaru-pōtu*. n. A timid person. భయశీలుడు. **బెదరించు** or **బెదిరించు** *bedarintsu*. v. a. To threaten, bully, frighten. **బెదరింపు** or **బెదిరింపు** *bedar-impu*. n. A threat, intimidation, frightening, threatening, bullying.

బెబ్బులి *beb-buli*. [Tel. పెద్ద+పులి] n. A royal tiger. కస్తి బెబ్బులి a tiger's cub.

"వన్నెలుగలయొగ్గఁబట్టిధరించి,
కన్నెబెబ్బులిలోలంకాపెదరించి."
Saranga. v. 22.

బెరడు *beraḍu*. [Tel.] n. The bark of a tree, చెట్టుపట్ట. The shell or coat of a tamarind. చింతలుమొదలైనవాటిపైపెచ్చు.

బెరయు *berayu*. [Tel.] v. n. To be or exist. ఉండు, కలుగు, కలుగు. To spread, వ్యాపించు. To unite, చేరు. To be pleased, సంతోషించు. To be wet, తడియు. To be touched, contaminated, affected. పొందు. "మాయమువెరపొలమునసుమగొలుసు భేదముపెడు బొందవెరపడియుండు." Vêma. i. 171. "అంధ తమసరాసులు వెర పెజా." Swa. iii. 24. టీ॥ కారుచీకటిగుంపులు అవరించెను. "కనుదోయిరె ప్పలలనకుమిగులంచలతవెరసె." ib. iii. 125. టీ॥ చంచలతవెరసె, చాంచల్యమును పొందెను. వెరయించు berayintsu. v. a. To dip, to wet. "మందరధరుండు తమునందరగృపాంబునిధి యందు వెరయించెననిడెందములనత్యానంద రసపూ రములకెందగ." Vish. i. 173. కృపాంబునిధి యందు ముంచె, అనగా కరుణాసముద్రములో ముంచెను.

వెరసు berasu. [from Skt. విరసము.] adj. Cruel, క్రూరము. Coarse, ముతక.

వెరాన or విరాన berāna. [Tel.] adv. At once, hurriedly. త్వరగా, వడిగా. "అడివిని కొరిబాధకరమల్లనబట్టి విరానచేసరాల్." Ila. i. 195. "అడియజా అనిశొక్రమసాని క్రొమ్ముక్కగా కొంగువిరానపట్టి." Chatu. 310.

వెరికి beriki. [Tel.] n. Want, defect. కొరత. న్యూనత.

వెరుకు beruku. [Tel.] n. Difference. భేదము. Use. ప్రయోజనము. Indifference, contempt. అలక్ష్యము. "నీకుమారునిపెంచినట్లాకుమారు నెరసి రక్షింపుమీమది వెరుకులేక." Vish. vii. 99. adj. Indifferent, contemptuous, అలక్ష్యము గల. "వెరుకువానిమదినివింకెమిలాగురా." Vêma. 174.

వెలంచి or వెల్లించి belanchi. [Tel.] n. The bird called a Shrike. చిన్నవెలంచిగాడు the Bay-back Shrike, *Lanius vittatus*. సంకు వెలంచి the large Grey Shrike, *Lanius lahtora*. ఎర్రవెలంచి the Rufous-backed Shrike, *Lanius erythronotus*, (F. B. I.)

వెలము Same as విలము (q. v.).

వెలయు belayu. [Tel.] v. n. To spread, వ్యాపించు.

వెల్లము bellamu. [Tel.] n. Jaggery, molasses, treacle. వెల్లపుసారాయి rum, being extracted from treacle. చెరుకుపాకమువండినసారాయి. వెల్లంకంద a certain plant, *Morea chinensis*. Rox.

వెల్లి belli. [Tel] adj. Coquettish, deceitful. n. Coquettishness, వంచకము. A fop, or coquette. వగలాడి, వంచకుడు, వంచకురాలు. "ఓసివెల్లియిమ్మనటవ్వనీకు దొకై వచ్చెదో." KP. iii. 128. వెల్లించు bellintsu. v. a. To coax, or wheedle. వంచించు. వెల్లింపు. bellimpu. n. Coaxing, wheedling. బుజ్జగింపు, వంచన.

"క॥ అల్లుదుకందుకొనిని,
వెల్లింపులబడిన మొదలు పెనుకొమ్ములకే,
యుల్లైతి." Ila. iv. 104.

వెల్లిమాటలు or వెల్లింపుమాటలు bellimatalu. n. Coaxing talk, sweet words, సాంత్వనవాక్యములు, ఇచ్చకపుమాటలు. "వెల్లిమాటలు వట్టివిగువును దమకు సహజంబులగు." Lila. xx. 113.

వెల్లు or పెల్ల bellu. [Tel.] n. A flake of earth, &c. వెల్లుతప్పించు bellu-tavvintsu. v. n. To dig or break up ground. వెల్లు దుక్కి digging in lieu of ploughing. వెల్లు విరవడము to break up fallow ground. (These phrases are used in the western part of the country.)

వెళకు Same as వెదకు (q. v.).

వెళగు or వెళంగు Same as వెదకు (q. v.). v. a. To cleanse or clean, పరిశుద్ధముచేయు. "కొంచెళంగనోకుంచెడులేవా." BD. iii. 840. అనగా గిన్నెను శుద్ధిచేయకపోయి నావో; కుంచెడులేవో, నాలుగుమానికలయినా లేక పోయినవో.

వెళవ, వెళగువ్వ or వెళ్లగువ్వ belava. [Tel.] n. A dove. Various species are తిండివెళగువ్వ the Bronze-winged Dove, *Chalcophaps indica*; ఎర్రవెళగువ్వ the Red Turtle dove, *Cenopopelia tranquebarica*; చిటివెళగువ్వ

the little Brown Dove, *Turtur cambayensis.* బూడిదబెళగువ్వ or పెద్దబెళగువ్వ the Indian Ring-dove, *Turtur risorius.* పచ్చ బెళగువ్వ the Green Pigeon, *Crocopus chlorogastor.* (F. B. I.). పిదేవృబెళగువ్వ a large species.

బెలుకు *beluku.* [Tel.] n. Polish, brightness, a gleam, radiance, brilliancy. తళతళ, ప్రకాశము. v. n. To shine brilliantly, తళ తళమని ప్రకాశించు.

బెసుకు *besuku.* [Tel.] v. n. To miss the mark, or glance aside. To slip through the fingers. జెసిగిను.

బెస్త or బెస్తవాడు *besta.* [Tel.] n. A man that belongs to the caste of fishermen and palanquin bearers. బోయీలు. బెస్తపెత్తనముచేయు to swagger, lord it, brag (because a head bearer is a jack in office.)

బెహారి and బెహారము See under బేహారు.

బే bē

బే or అంబే *bē.* [from Skt. అంభా.] n. The lowing of a cow. "బేయను" భా. vi.

బేగడ *bēgaḍa.* [Tel.] n. Talc. కాకిబంగారు, అభ్రకము. A filament or very thin plate, as of talc, stone, or gold leaf. A kind of jewel. "కట్టుదండ బేగడమురువులు." H. iv. 100. The name of a certain tune.

బేగి *bēgi.* [H]. adv. Quickly. త్వరగా. బేగిరారు *bēgir-āru.* n. A dromedary, ఒంటె, పెద్దలొట్టిపిట్ట.

బేజరారు *bē-dzarūru.* [H] adj. Useless, unnecessary.

బేజారు *bēdzāru.* [H.] n. Fatigue, weariness, annoyance, అలసట. బేజారగు *bēdzār-agu.* v. n. To become fatigued, or disgusted. బేజారుచేయు *bēdzāru-chēyu.* v. a. To tease, fatigue, torment.

బేటము *bēṭamu.* [Tel.] n. A mask. కనుబేటము a mask for the eyes, కంట్లకుమరుగు.

బేటు *bēṭu.* [Tel.] n. A flake of dried earth or of stone. పెల్ల. A crack in a rock, కొండలోనిగుహానిలోని చీలిక.

బేడ or బేడరూక *bēḍa.* [Tel.] n. A coin worth two annas. బేడలు *bēḍalu.* n. Split pulse, పప్పు; as కందిబేడలు. బేడకొమ్మి a peahen.

బేడిగ *bēḍiga.* [Tel.] n. Rent, a tax, పన్ను.

బేడిజెము *bēḍidzemu.* [Tel.] n. Pretence, feigning, affectation. మాయ. టక్కు.

బేడిదము *bēḍidamu.* [Tel.] n. Another form of జెడిదము. (q. v.)

బేడిస or బేడిసము *bēḍisa.* [Tel.] n. The silver fish, a sort of carp. *Cyprinus chrysopareius;* the poetical dolphin, శఫరి. చంగబేడిస the sprat.

బేదౌలు *bē-daulu.* [H.] adj. Clumsy, ugly, wretched, వికారమైన.

బేతాళము *bētālamu.* [Skt.] n. A demon, పిశాచము. బేతాళకథలు or విక్రమార్క కథలు *bētāla-kathalu* n. A set of fables related by a goblin who is described as the captive of Vikramârka. బేతాళిక *bētālika.* n. A she-devil or sprite; a wicked woman. పిశాచస్త్రీ. "బలవిట్లబేతాళిక లెంపాటదిట్టువారి." A. vi. 23. బేతాళుడు or భేతాళుడు *bētāluḍu.* n. The name of a servant of Yama, a goblin, imp, demon, or fiend similar to Puck, యమకింకరుడు.

బేది or భేది *bēdi.* [from Skt. భేద.] n. A purge, or purging, looseness of the bowels. పాడుచేయు, విరేచనము. భేదిమందు a purgative. భేదికరమైన purgative.

బేపరాకుగా *bē-parāku-gā.* [H.] adv. Heedlessly, carelessly.

బేపి or వేపి *bēpi.* [Tel. from వేగు.] n. Lit: That which wakes up. A hound. A dog.

బేబాకీ *bē-bakī.* [H.] n. Absence of debt.

బేబేఅను *bē-bē-anu.* [Tel.] v. n. To look foolish, or disconcerted.

బేమరమ్మతు *bē-marammatu.* [H.] adj. Out of repair, damaged. శిథిలమైన, చెడిపోయిన.

బేరడ్జము *bēraḍsamu.* [Tel.] n. Fraud, deceit, మాయ, ధౌర్త్యము, కుత్సితపునడత, పరుష వాక్యము. "అమ్మసలిది బేరజేమది రమ్మనెనసుమాట నమ్మరా దెప్పటికిరా." Vijayanti. iv. 40. adj. Fraudulent, deceitful. మాయలమారి అయిన. బేరజంపుమణులు sham gems, మాయరత్నములు.

బేరము *bēramu.* [Skt.] n. An image. ప్రతిమ. "వంకములోని హైమబేరము." పర. v.

బేరము *bēramu.* [Tel.] n. Trade, dealing, a bargain, బేరముసారము or బేరసారము trade, &c. (సారము being a mere expletive.) బేరకాడు *bēra-kāḍu.* n. One who makes a bargain, a purchaser, buyer. కొనువాడు. బేరమాడువాడు. బేరకత్తె *bēra-katte.* n. A woman who bargains or purchases. బేరమాడు or బేరముచేయు *bēram-āḍu.* v. n. To bargain. బేరముపోవు to go on a trading journey. బేరి *bēri.* n. A man of the Beri or merchant caste.

బేరి *bēri.* [from Skt. భేరి.] n. A kettle drum. దుందుభి, నగారా.

బేరీజు *bērīdzu.* [H.] n. An account. A total sum, మొత్తము.

బేల *bēla.* [Tel.] n. One who is simple, or ignorant. మూఢుడు, ముగ్ధపురుషుడు. ముగ్ధస్త్రీ.

బేలు *bēlu.* [Tel.] n. A trick, guile, మోసము, వంచన. బేలరి *bēl-ari.* n. A deceiver, a cheat. మోసకాడు, వంచకుడు. బేలుపెట్టు or బేలుపుచ్చు *bēlu-peṭṭu.* v. a. To deceive, మోసపుచ్చు. "తానటమాంసముదినడట, యీనక్కయబేలుపెట్టె నిన్నాళ్లును." M. XII. iii. 75. బేలుపోవు, బేలువడు or బేల్పడు *bēlu-pōvu.* v. n. To be tricked, or beguiled.

బేవారసు *bē-vārasu.* [H.] adj. Without heir or claimant.

బేషకు, బేషక్కు or భేషక్కు *bēshaku.* [H.] adv. Undoubtedly. నిస్సంశయముగా.

బేషు or భేషు *bēshu.* [H.] adj. Best, superior. శ్రేష్ఠమైన. Interj. Well done! good!

బేసము or వేసము *bēsamu.* [Tel.] n. Juice, sap, తాండ. తాటిబేసము the yellow juice of the ripe palm fruit.

బేసరి *bēsari.* [H.] n. A ring worn by a woman in the right nostril. నాసాభరణ విశేషము.

బేసి *bēsi.* [Tel.] adj. Odd (as applied to numbers.) సరిబేసి odd and even. బేసికంటి *bēsi-kanṭi.* n. Lit. The odd eyed one, i. e., Siva. బేసికయిదువుజోదు *bēsi-kayiduvu-dzōdu.* n. A title of Manmadha.

బేస్తవారము *bēsta-vāramu.* [for Skt. బృహస్పతివారము.] n. Thursday.

బేహారము or బేహారము *bēhāramu.* [from Skt. విహారము.] n. Trade, commerce, వాణిజ్యము, వర్తకవ్యాపారము, బేరము. "అంగళ్లనిలిపె బేహారముల్ మాన్పి." BD. iv. 61. బేహారి or బెహారి *bēhāri.* n. A merchant. వణిజుడు, వర్తకుడు.

బై bai

బైకలు *baikalu.* [Tel.] n. The vomiting and other signs of pregnancy. వేవిళ్లు. "చెలువబైకలైనచెప్ప వేటికిన్నా సిగ్గుపడుచు చెలువచెంతడలగు." G. iii. 29.

బైజే or బయిజే *baidza.* [Tel.] n. Ignorance, అజ్ఞానము. Nonsense, stuff, trash, ఉచ్ఛిష్టని

" ఈ॥ కల్లలు వేవిమల్ ప్పుతులు
కల్లలు కల్లలుయజ్ఞకర్మముల్,
కల్లలు పైతృకక్రియలు
కల్లలు ఘోరతపఃప్రభావముల్,
కల్లలు దేవకార్యములు
కావున బైలమానివివాహితం,
బెల్లవిధంబులకానదుపు
డిమ్మల ముక్తికిబోవగోరినన్. "
V. P. iv 345.

బైడాలము or **బయిడాలము** *baiḍālamu.* [Tel.] n. Anger, కోపము.

బైబిలు *baibilu.* [Gk. through Eng.] n. The Bible, the Christian Scriptures.

బైరవాసము or **బయిరవాసము** *bairavāsamu.* [from Skt. బహిర్వాసము.] n. A cloak, an outer garment. ఉత్తరీయము.

బైరాగి or **బయిరాగి** *bai-rāgi.* [for Skt. విరాగి.] n. A hermit or religious beggar. విరాగమున్నవాడు. cf. వైరాగ్యము.

బైరి, బయిరి, **భైరి** or **భైరవి** *bairi.* [Tel.] n. The Peregrine Falcon, *Falco peregrinus.* జుట్టుబైరి. the Crested Hawk Eagle, *Spizaetus cirrhatus* (F.B.I.)

బైలు, బయిలు or బయలు *bailu.* [Tel.] n. An open field, plain, area. మైదానము. The outside, the exterior. The sky, the expanse of heaven. ఆకాశము. "పండిన చేలెల్ల బయలుగా మేసి." (HD. i. 398.) they devoured the corn fields and reduced them to a bare plain. బయలుమాట a voice uttered (or heard) from heaven. "ధారుణిబడిబయలు దన్ను చున్నేడ్చు." (BD. iii. 878.) the baby was kicking with its legs upwards. adj. Open, clear. **బైలుదేరు**, **బయిలుదేరు**, or **బయలుదేరు** *bailu-dēru.* v. n. To come forth, break out; to begin, start, set out; to come to light, result, appear, be discovered; to prove true or false. To be shed, or to burst forth as tears, తానును ఒక మనిషాడుగా బైలుదేరినాడు he set out as if he was a big man. సెగ్గడ్డబైలుదేరినది a boil rose. వెన్న బైలుదేరినప్పుడు కుండపగిలినది when the butter was coming the churn burst. ఇల్లువిడిచి బైలుదేరగానే on leaving the house. ఆప్రాంతములలో దొంగలు బైలుదేరిరి thieves broke out in that neighbourhood. **బైలుదేర్చు** *bailu-dērcu.* v. a. To bring out, elicit, bring to light, exhibit. **బైలుపడు** or **బైలగు** *bailu-paḍu.* v. n. To fall out, come to light, be disclosed. ఆ మర్మము బైలుపడినది the secret came to light **బైలుపరచు**, బయలుపరచు or **బైలుపుచ్చు** *bailu-parcu.* v. a. To bring to light, to reveal. **బైలువెళ్లు** or **బయలువెడలు** *bailu-vellu.* v. n. To start. **బైళ్లు** or బయళ్లు *baiḷḷu.* n. plu. Plains. **బైట** or **బయట** *baiṭa.* adv. On the outside, on the plain. Out. **బైటపడు** or **బయటపడు** *baiṭa-paḍu* v. n. To come out, come to light. To become public. **బైటపెట్టు** or **బయటపెట్టు** *baiṭa-peṭṭu.* v. a. To put forward, to reveal, బహిరంగము చేయు, వెల్లడిచేయు. **బైటపోవు** or **బయటకిపోవు** *baiṭa-pōvu.* v. n. To go out. To go to the necessary. **బైటఉండు** or **బయటఉండు** *baiṭa-unḍu.* v. n. To be outside: to be menstruous, (because excluded from the family.) **బైటవేయు** or **బయటవేయు** *baiṭa-vēyu.* v. a. To cast out. To bring to light, to let a secret out. దీన్ని బైటవేస్తేచూడు take care you don't let this be known. **బైటి** or బయటి *baiṭi.* adj. Outer, exterior; strange, foreign. బైటిఊళ్లు the circumjacent villages.

బైసణ or బయిసణ *baisaṇa.* [Tel.] n. The bridge of the Vina, or Indian lute. వీణ కాయ మఖమందుండే బంధనము.

బైసి, బయిసి or బవిసి *baisi.* [from Skt. విభూతి.] n. Fortune. భాగ్యము. Respect, గౌరవము. Shame, modesty బైసిమాలిన shameless, నిర్గమించిన, disgraced, ruined. Swa. iv. 109. బైసిమాను చెట్టు a tree called *Odina pinnata*, which in the hot weather is naked of leaves.

బైసుక or **బయిసుక** *baisuka*. [Tel.] n. A resolution, a vow, నియమము, ప్రతిజ్ఞ.

బొ bo

బొంకణము, బొంకెనము or **బొక్కెనము** *bongkanamu*. [Tel.] n. A purse, a pouch. "ఆ॥ కటికటంబునందుకట్టినగోచియు, బొఱవ బడితె విట్టుగొంటెదిరి, చంకబొంకణమును సడలి నదికొనైన, కొండలందుదిరుగకుండుకేన." BD. iii. 282.

బొంకప్ప *bong-kappa*. [Tel.] n. A sort of fish, the genus *Tetrodon*, particularly the species termed *Hispidus*. This fish is nearly spherical and is covered with spikes.

బొంకి Same as బొకి (q. v.).

బొంకు *bongku*. [Tel.] v. n. To lie or speak falsely. n. Fraud, guile, deceit. A falsehood. అబద్ధము. adj. False, అసత్యము. **బొంకరి** or **బొంకులాడు** *bongk-ari*. n. A liar, a man who tells lies. బొంకులాడి a woman who tells lies. **బొంకమి** *bongkami*. Lit. The not lying, i. e., veracity. **బొంకించు** *bongkintsu*. v. a. To cause to tell a lie, బొంకజేయు. To deceive, trick, delude, tempt, mislead, మోసపుచ్చు. "క్రియమాలి యేమిటికైనను బొంకించువాని." M. XII. iii. 374.

బొంగరము *bongaramu*. [Tel.] n. A top, బొమ్మరము. **బొంగరాలు** *bongaralu*. n. A kind of cakes.

బొంగు *bongu*. [Tel.] n. A large hollow bamboo. బోలు వెదురు. పాలకీబొంగు a palanquin pole. డేరాబొంగు a tent pole. వెదురుబొంగు a bamboo pole. Adj. Hoarse. వాడికంఠము బొంగుపోయినది he is hoarse.

బొండ, బొండమాను or **బొండకొయ్య** *bonda*. [Tel.] n. The stocks or light fetters of wood. బొండమువేయు or బొండ మీదొట్టు to put in the stocks. "భేదములేకను బొండ బెరసియుండు." Vema.

బొండము, బొండాము, బొండలము or **బొండ్లము** *bondamu*. [Tel.] n. A cocoanut with the husk on. "ఎలనీటిబొండలంబులు వాలె మెఱదెల్లజాత్రి నైవిసడోల్లు పుత్రకములు." A vi. 17.

బొండరగాళ్లు *bondarag-allu*. [Tel.] n. The flower heads of the oil seed plant.

బొండిగ *bondiga*. [Tel.] n. A stalk of a leaf, the petiole, తొడిమ.

బొండు *bondu*. [Tel.] adj. Round, globular, గుండ్రని. బొండుగంటలు round bells. **బొండుమల్లె** *bondu-malle*. n. A species of Jasmine.

బొండుగ or **బొండువ** *bonduga*. [Tel.] n. The throat or gullet. గొంతుకోవి, కంఠనాళము. "రండేండ్లచిరుతపాపల బొండుగలొత్తించి ప్రాణములగొనియెగా." Ved. Ras. ii. 200. టీ॥ బొండుగలొత్తించి, గొంతులుపిసికించి.

బొండెము *bondemu*. [Tel.] n. A tatty or screen; a hurdle. తడిక.

బొండ్లము or **బొండ్లాము** Same as బొండెము (q. v.).

బొంత *bonta*. [Tel.] n. A quilted cloth, a patched rug, a ragged patched cloth. The mullet fish, *Mugil cephalus*. Russell. No. 56. &c. "గుఱ్ఱముకుతగినబొంతలాగే." Vaija. ii. 90. like horse, like saddle. adj. Large, పెద్ద. **బొంతఅరటి** *bonta-arati*. n. A large kind of plantain. **బొంతకాకి** *bonta-kaki*. n. A raven, the large Cormorant. కాకోలము. **బొంతగంధకము** *bonta-gandhakamu*. n. A sort of brimstone in flakes. **బొంత జెముడు** *bonta-jemudu*. n. A cactus of a large size used as a medicine. బొంత

-రాయి bonta-rāyi. n. A kind of pebbly rock, a conglomerate.

బొంతు bontu. [Tel.] n. Yellow ochre. Saffron colour. The chaff or husk of seeds. బొంతులు bontulu. n. plu. The seeds of the great millet while in the husk. పొట్టు తోనున్న జొన్నలు.

బొంద bonda. [Tel.] n. A hole, a bore, a fissure. రంధ్రము. A pit, a grave. గొయ్యి. A small palmyra or wild date tree. చిన్నతాటిచెట్టు. A little boy. పాడుబొంద a desolate pit or grave. బొందలుపడ్డకుండ a leaky pot. బొందలుపడ్డకండ్లు sunken eyes. బొందపొడుచు to bore. రవంతబొంద a mere stripling, రవంతపిల్లగాడు. బొందకోల bonda-kōla. n. A weapon used in duelling. బొందపక్కె bonda-pakke. n. A kind of fish. బొందపువ్వు bonda-puvvu. n. The film or cotton which is found on young Palmyra leaves. తాటిమువ్వను పట్టియుండేపువ్వు.

బొందళము, బొందడము or బొందలము bonda-ḷamu. [Tel. బొంత+దళము.] n. A piece of armour. కవచము. "పొగడయిజాలు చెంగలువ బొందల మేలకి పువ్వుపట్టె." H. iv. 107. బొందడీడు bondaḍ-īḍu. n. One who has put on armour. కవచముతొడిగినవాడు.

బొంది bondi. [Tel.] n. The (human) body. దేహము.

బొందియ bondiya. [Tel.] n. A ferrule. పొన్ను, కట్టు. "పసిడిబొందియకోలపట్టె గ్రాలుచు తిప్పుచు సోలుచు గతులడ ఎద్రొక్కుచు." BD. iv. 1113. పసిడిబొందియకోల. అనగా బంగారుపొన్ను వేసినకర్ర.

బొందిలి bondili. [Tel.] n. The name of a certain caste or race.

బొందు bondu. [Tel.] n. A skein, a bundle of fibres or thread. A thread, దారము. A tape, నాడా. The string for fastening a jacket, the tie of a boddice. Growing corn dried up, from want of moisture. కంకిపట్టనిపైరు. Flowers woven into a garland, పుష్పసరము. మాలెబొందు or సిగబొందు a piece of cotton or silk thread, with which the tresses are tied. బొందుకంకి a pithless ear. బొందుదొప్ప or బొందుగడ్డి a blasted crop. "పుష్పములకు కోవిసేద్యమిగా బలుతెరంగులవింటివింటికి మాలికలనుబొందులు కందుకంబులరచించి." KP. iv. 69. బొందులనగా లావాటిదండలు, తంతుసమూహము. adj. Big, plump, fat-fleshed. పుష్టిగానుండే, లావాటి. అబిడ్డకాళ్ళు చేతులు బొందుగానున్నవి the child's limbs are plump. వానిది బొందు శరీరము he is plump. "చాలదరంబుగాపృథుల చంపకకోలబాల్పు బొందుతో మాలెలనంగ." A. i. 23. టీ॥ బొందుతో మాలెలనంగ, కట్టుమాలెలోయనగాను. బొందుపోవు bondu-pōvu. v. n. To pine or become pithless, as a ear of corn; to wither, as a crop.

బొందె bonde. [Tel.] n. The edible inner substance or pith of the plantain tree, అరటిదూట.

బొంబాసు bombāsu. [Eng. 'Bomb.'] n. A name given to a mortar because it discharges 'bombs,' గోళీలువేసెడిఫిరంగి.

బొక్క bokka. [Tel.] n. A hole, a pit, an orifice, రంధ్రము. A grave, సమాధి.

> "ద్వి॥ ఎడనెడబొక్కలనిడినబాలకుల
> వెడలించిభక్షించుబేతాళతతులు."
> హరిశ్చ. ii.

అపుంటిచేత దానిచెవడలో బొక్కపడినది the sore made a hole in her cheek. నిన్ను బొక్కపెట్టుతాను I will bring you to your grave, I will ruin you. నేనే బొక్కలో దూరుదును where can I hide my head? బొక్కలాడు bokka-l-āḍu. n. A snake, సర్పము. A house-breaker, thief. కన్నగాడు. బొక్కబెరడు bokka-beraḍu. n. A kind of snake. సర్పభేదము.

బొక్కణము or **బొంకణము** *bokkaṇamu.* [Tel.] n. A pouch, a purse. సంచి. "ద్వి॥పాదలకగొంగ సంబొబూదిబొక్కణమె." HD. i. 1383. టీ॥మూదిబొక్కణమెు,విభూతిసంచితో.

బొక్కవిరుం Same as బొక్కసం (q. v.)

బొక్కసము *bokkasamu.* [Tel.] n. Money, ధనము. A money bag. ద్రవ్యముంచుసంచి. A treasury, ధనాగారము, భాండాగారము.

బొక్కి *bokki.* [Tel.] adj. Defective, deficient in teeth, toothless. బొక్కినోటివాడు one who has lost his teeth. Fleshless, emaciated. బొక్కిరొమ్మువాడు a hollow-chested man. **బొక్కిసొర్ర** *bokki-sorra.* n. A sort of shark. Russell, No. XVI.

బొక్కిస, బొక్కిసా, బొక్కెస or **బొక్కెసా** *bokkisa.* [Tel.] n. A small parcel, a bundle, wallet, knapsack, budget. బట్టలపెట్టె, బట్టలమూట, చిన్నమూట.

బొక్కు *bokku.* [Tel.] v. a. To eat greedily, to gobble. నోటినిండా చేసికొని తిను. n. A mouthful. **బొక్కించు** *bokkintsu.* v. a. To cram. **బొక్కులాడు** *bokku-l-āḍu.* v. a. To eat greedily, gobble, devour. **బొక్కెడు** *bokk-eḍu.* adj. As much as a mouthful.

బొక్కెన *bokkena.* [Tel.] n. A bucket for drawing water from a well or for baling a boat. ఓడలో నీళ్లుదేవి పారబోయు పాత్రము, నూతిలో నీళ్లుతోడేది. A nosebag for horses, the corn bag put on a horse's nose. గుర్రములకు దాణాపెట్టేది, తోబరా. **బొక్కెనాకు** *bokken-āku.* n. The Creeping Vervain, *Verbena nodiflora,* తోయపిప్పలి. Linn. Ainsl. ii. 313. బొక్కెనకాయలు its berries.

బొగడ *bogaḍa.* [Tel.] n. A golden ornament which women wear on the upper part of the ear. The peg or key of a lute. The knob on the top of the leg of a cot. Any knob, గుబ్బ. బొగడచెవి a hole bored in the ear, in which the gold ornament is worn. A chink or leak. నీళ్లువచ్చురంధ్రము. ఆచెరువుకట్టలో బొగడపడినది there is a leak in the bund of the tank.

బొగ్గు *boggu.* [Tel.] n. Carbon, charcoal. సీమబొగ్గు or రాతిసబొగ్గు, coal, భూమిలో తవ్వియెత్తేబొగ్గు.

బొచ్చె *bochche.* [Tel.] n. A sherd or potsherd. The upper part of a skull. The fish called Roball, మీను. Russell. No. 105.

బొచ్చు *botstsu.* [Tel.] n. Hair, down, fledge, downy hair, wool, రోమము. కేశము.

బొజుగు or **బొజుంగు** *boḍzugu.* [Tel.] n. A paramour. విటుడు. S. ii. 605. **బొజుంగుబోటి** *boḍzungu-bōṭi.* n. A licentious woman.

బొజ్జ *boḍzḍza.* [Tel.] n. The belly, a paunch. కడుపు, పెద్దకడుపు. బొజ్జపెరిగిన or బొజ్జసట్టిన corpulent, fat bellied. బొజ్జమడుతులు folds of fat across the belly. **బొజ్జవాడు** *boḍzḍza-vāḍu.* n. A corpulent man, పెద్దకడుపువాడు.

బొటకచెట్టు *boṭaka-cheṭṭu.* [Tel.] n. A thorny bush.

బొటనవ్రేలు, బొటవ్రేలు, బొట్టవ్రేలు, బొట్టనవ్రేలు or **బొటమనవ్రేలు** *boṭana-vrēlu.* [Tel.] n. The thumb, the great toe. అంగుష్ఠము, పెద్దవ్రేలు. కాలిబొటనవ్రేల నేలవ్రాసినది she drew lines on the ground with her great toe.

బొటిమ or **మొటిమ** *boṭima.* [Tel.] n. A wart. మొటిమె.

బొట్ట *boṭṭa.* [Tel.] n. A hamper, a large high basket for storing grain, &c. గాదె. **బొట్టకడపచెట్టు** *boṭṭa-kaḍapa-cheṭṭu.* n. A kind of tree, *Nauclea cadamba.* కదంబవృక్షవిశేషము. **బొట్టపెంజర** *boṭṭa-penḍzura.* n. A sort of snake.

బొట్టడి or బొట్టుడి *bottadi.* [Tel.] n. A stone roller, కొల్లంచెడిరాయి.

బొట్టనగోలలు *bottana-golalu.* [Tel.] n. The name of a game played by children.

బొట్టము *bottamu.* [Tel.] n. A modesty piece. గోచి.

బొట్టియ or బొట్టియుడు See under బొట్టె.

బొట్టు *bottu.* [Tel.] n. A drop. A sectarian mark on the forehead, white, yellow, black or scarlet, long or round. A gold spangle or patch in general. The gold piece attached to the marriage cord. (మంగళసూత్రము.) A three-pie piece. The grammatical *sunna* or circlet, representing N. or M. నిలువుబొట్టు or నామబొట్టు the upright line or streak in the forehead which denotes the Vaishnava sect. అడ్డబొట్టు the cross mark which denotes the Saivites. తాళిబొట్టు the sign of marriage, being a bit of gold tied on the bride's throat. బొట్టుకట్టు to tie the తాళిబొట్టు, i. e., to marry. కట్టిబొట్టు full *sunna.* నేతిబొట్టు a little ghee. "తిరుపతి కొప్ప లందముగదిద్దిన బూడిదబొట్టు, మంచిదొర్పు దబినమిం చునట్టి దుదురా క్షలు పేరులు." S. iii. 99. ఎక్కడ ఉన్నా సరిగా బొట్టుపెట్టినట్టు చిక్కుచున్నది wherever it is, he finds it in a moment. బొట్టువారము *bottu-daramu.* n. The string round the neck from which the *tali* is suspended, మంగళసూత్రము.

బొట్టె or బొట్టియ *botte.* [Tel.] n. A child, బిడ్డ. A son, కొడుకు. A daughter, కూతురు. బొట్టియుడు or బొట్టెడు a son, కొడుకు. నాబొట్టెలు my wife and children, బొట్టెలబేరము the slave trade. బొట్టెకోల *botte-kola.* n. A kind of sharp pointed arrow.

బొట్లచేప *botla-chepa.* [Tel.] n. A sort of *Sparus, cauda bifida.* Russell, 99.

బొట్లు or భొట్లు [for Skt. భట్టు.] n. A title assumed by certain Smarta Vaidika Brahmins. (The three titles Botlu, Sastri, and Dikshitulu closely resemble the titles Bachelor of Arts, Doctor of Laws, and Doctor of Divinity. These are used among Smartas alone.)

బొడబొడ *boda-boda.* [Tel.] n. A gushing noise, as of swiftly flowing water. A loud noise.

బొడిగ *bodiga.* [Tel.] n. A boy. బాలకుడు.

బొడిప, బొడిపి or బొడిపె *bodipa.* [Tel.] n. A knot or excrescence on the trunk of a tree. చెట్టుమీదిబుడిపి.

బొడిమ or బొడిమె *bodima.* [Tel.] n. The peg of a sandal. పావకోళ్లబిరడ.

బొడియ *bodiya.* [Tel.] n. A string, twisted round two leathern jars, కుండునిర్దులకు వేయు పెన.

బొడ్డ *bodda.* [Tel.] n. The Sycamine or glomerous fig tree, *Ficus glomerata,* అత్తి.

బొడ్డనబావి *boddana-bavi.* [Tel.] n. A well with steps descending into it. A. v. 129. నడుచు పిల్లనుయ్యిగల దిగుడుబావి.

బొడ్డసరము *boddu-saramu.* [Tel.] n. A weed called *Stemodia.* Rox. iii. 94.

బొడ్డి *boddi.* [Tel.] n. A plot of ground. మడిబొడ్డి a bed of earth for plants. బొడ్డికడుముకట్టు to form a row of small beds, ఒకవరుసను కొన్ని చిన్నమళ్లుకట్టు.

బొడ్డు *boddu.* [Tel.] n. The navel. నాభి. బొడ్డు or బొడ్డుతీవ a bolt, a pointless arrow. బొడ్డుకొంగు the knot of a man's cloth at the navel. బొడ్డుకోయు to cut the navel string. adj. (In composition) Centrical, interior, inner, middle; as బొడ్డుచావడి the centre court. బొడ్డుబండ or బొడ్డురాయి the middle stone Vish ii. 67. బొడ్డుకిట్టు *boddu-kittu.* n. The coping of a wall. బొడ్డుగిలకలు *boddu-*

gantalu. n. The large bells hung on each side of an elephant. "కరులబొద్దుగంటలు ఘల్లుమని మ్రోయ." Pal. 30. బొద్దుచేవిక boddu-tsavika. n. A central hall. నడిమి చావడి. బొద్దుపుడక boddu-pudaka. n. A double headed wooden instrument, used by cotton beaters. ఏకవిధమైన ముద్దిగర ముట్టు. బొద్దుమల్లె boddu-malle n. The double jasmine. వృత్తపుష్పి.

బొణగ or బొణిగె bonaga. [Tel.] n. A small leather bottle filled with any liquid. నరుకుతో నున్న చిన్న సిద్ది. బొణిగెలు bonigelu. plu. n. A kind of parched corn: a kind of cakes. కాయధాన్యములు, సెనగలు మొద లైనవి, పొట్టుపోయి బద్దలు కానివి.

బొత్త botta. [Tel.] n. A hole. రంధ్రము.

బొత్తాము or బొత్తాను bottamu. [Eng. 'button']. n. A button, గుండి.

బొత్తి botti. [Tel.] n. A pack or bundle in which things are arranged in order. బొత్తిపట్టు బొత్తిపెట్టు or botti-pattu. v. a. To set straight, arrange, put in order.

బొత్తిగా, బుత్తిగ or బొత్తుగా botti-ga. [Tel.] adv. Entirely, wholly, quite, completely, perfectly, utterly, totally, మొదలంటు, ఆమూలము, సంపూర్ణముగా, పూర్తిగా.

బొత్తు bottu. [Tel.] n. Husk or chaff. (Ganjam dialect.) బొత్తుబొత్తుమని bottu-bottu-m-ani. (anuk) adj. Dead, dull, not sharply.

బొడ or బొడ boda. [Tel.] n. A kind of grass, a common hill grass, తృణవిశేషము.

బొడి bodi. [Tel.] n. A dockyard. ఓడలు చేయు చోటు.

బొడ్డి boddi. [Tel.] n. The plant called Osyris peltata. Rox. iii. 755. Cissampelos. (Rottler) త్రిపర్ణి, మహాశ్యామ

బొద్దు boddu. [Tel.] n. A rick or bundle of grass, a skein or bunch of threads. A kind of ornament for the hand. adj. Stout, corpulent, లావైన. బొద్దుకీటు boddu-kitu. n. The coping of a wall. See బొందు. బొద్దిగ, బొద్దిక or బొద్దింక bodd-iga. (బొద్దు+ఈగ.) n. A cockroach. బరిగెపురుగు.

బొనము bonamu. [Tel.] n. Outward show. మెరుగు, పైమినుకు. "నాతినగవారినమ్మటకోరగా ద, వారమేలనమర్దంబులో నిముడువు, గచ్చుపైకు న్నమేమేడికాయబోనమె, యెరుగాలి రోవారికి మే లుగలదే." Miscell. i. 557. line 10. మేడికా యబోనమె, అత్తికాయపైమినికే మేగదా.

బొనుగుచేప bonugu-chepa. [Tel.] n. A kind of fish.

బొప్పడు boppadu. [Tel.] n. An ignorant man. మూఢుడు.

బొప్పాయి boppayi. [Foreign word.] n. The Papaw, or Papaya tree, Carica Papaya; మదనఆనపకాయ. (Watts.)

బొప్పి boppi. [Tel.] n. A bump or weal arising from a blow. బుడిపి. A kind of mug. "నూకలతో పపొగానుతత్త బొప్పి మస్గిన ముంత." H. ii. 84.

బొబ్బ bobba. [Tel.] n. A cry, roar, squealing, bellowing. కేక, పెద్దఅరుపు. A blister or pustule. పొక్కు. అగ్గిబొబ్బలు pustules. A. ii. 66. బొబ్బమెకము a lion, కంఠీరవము, సింహము. బొబ్బరించు, బొబ్బలుపెట్టు, బొబ్బ రిడు or బొబ్బలువేయు bobbarintsu. v. n To shout, scream, bellow, roar, బొబ్బ వేయు. బొబ్బరింత or బొబ్బాటము bobba-rinta. n. Shouting, roaring. బొబ్బలగు or బొబ్బలేచు bobbal-agu. v. n. To blister, to rise in pustules.

బొబ్బడాయి bobbadayi. [Tel.] n. A small bat (vespertilio.) గబ్బిలము or [illegible]

బొబ్బర bobbara. [Tel.] n. Rind or bark. చెట్టుతోలు. బొబ్బరలు or బొబ్బర్లు bobbaralu. n. A kind of beans. plu. A black species of the pulse termed *Dolichos catiang*. Rox. iii. 304. నల్ల అలచందలు.

బొబ్బిలికాయ bobbili-kaya. [Tel.] n. An ornament worn by Hindu wives on the great toe. పాదాంగుష్ఠాభరణము.

బొబ్బిలిచెట్టు bobbili-chettu. [Tel.] n. The whispering larch tree.

బొమ or బొమ్మ boma. [from Skt. భ్రూ.] n. An image, a doll, ప్రతిమ. The eye-brow. కనుబొమ్మ. A. v. 6. బొమముడి or బొమ్మముడి boma-mudi. n. A frown; (lit: a knot of the eye-brows.) "మోముత్రిప్పలు బొమముడి రొమ్ముతాటింపు." S. iii. 320. బొమముడిపెట్టు boma-mudi-pettu. v. n. To frown. Satyab. iv. 165. బొమముడిపాటు boma-mudi-patu. n. Frowning, బొమముడిపడుట. See బొమ్మ.

బొమిక or బొమికె bomika. [Tel.] n. A bone. ఎముక.

"సీ॥ ముంగాళ్ల పైజోగి ముచ్చెచూపులుపర్వ
బొమిక లెత్తుక పారిపోవుకుడులు."
అము. vi.

బొమిడిక, బొమిడికము, బొమిడీకము, బొమ్మిడికము or బొమ్మిడీకము bomidika. [Tel.] n. A tiara or elegant head dress: a helmet. కిరీటము, కవచముధరించి పెట్టుకొనే కుళ్లాయి.

బొమ్మ or బొమ bomma. [from Skt. బ్రహ్మ.] n. The god Brahma. బ్రహ్మదేవుడు. An image, idol, puppet, doll. ప్రతిమ. ఆ పడుచు బొమ్మవలెనున్నది she is as beautiful as a statue. An eyebrow, కనుబొమ్మ. A badge of a title, బిరుదచిహ్నము. A mark of disgrace, అవమానచిహ్నము. adj. Little, trifling, అల్పము. బొమ్మంచు bomm-antsu. adj. Broidered, figured. Dyed in figures on the edges. Red, ఎఱ్ఱని. "ఘుల్లుమంచు ముల్లుగుల్కా బొమ్మంచుచూపికి గుక్కిళ్లు మింగని మంచి వన." N. ix. 287. n. Redness, ఎరుపు. బొమ్మంచులు bomm-antsulu. n. A red-bordered cloth. బొమ్మకట్టు or బొమ్మపెట్టు bomma-kattu. v. a. To deride, to scoff at, to disgrace, to insult. తిరస్కరించు. అవమానపరచు. "బహుధనధాన్య సంపదల సొంపువహించి, పేదలమీద బొమ్మపెట్టువారు." Zacca. v. 134. బొమ్మడు bommadu. n. A Brahmin. బ్రాహ్మణుడు. బొమ్మచారి Same as బ్రహ్మచారి. (q. v.) బొమ్మజెముడు bomma-jemudu. n. The tree called *Euphorbia antiquorum*. సింహుండము. బొమ్మడాయ bomma-daya. n. A kind of fish, మద్గురమనే మత్స్యము. బొమ్మపెండ్లిళ్లు or బొమ్మలపెళ్లిళ్లు bomma-pendlillu. n. Toy marriages, a game played by children, playing at marrying dolls. బొమ్మమేడి bomma-medi. n. The opposite leaved fig tree, *Ficus oppositiolia*, కాకోదుంబరము. బొమ్మరాకాసి bomma-rakasi. n. A devil or fiend, being the ghost of a Brahmin who was skilled in the Vedas, బ్రహ్మరాక్షసి. బొమ్మరాయి bomma-rayi. n. A brick bat, a large pebble. plu. బొమ్మరాలు. బొమ్మరిల్లు bomma-r-illu. n. A doll house, or baby house. R. iii. 35. బొమ్మలాట bommal-ata. n. A puppet show, a show of puppets moved by springs. బొమ్మలాటవాడు bommal-ata-vadu. n. A puppet showman.

బొమ్మరము bommaramu. [Tel.] n. A spinning top. బొంగరము. బొమ్మరములు bommaramulu. n. plu. A game played by children. "చీకటిమాటిర్లు చిమ్ముబిల్లలపెట్టుబొట్టన గోలలుబొమ్మరాలు కుప్పిగంతులుచిరుగుద్దులాటలు." Vish. vii. 211. గొడుగుబొమ్మరము a spinning top shaped like an inverted umbrella, తలకిందుగాతిప్పిన గొడుగు ఆకారముగానుండే బొంగరము. బొమ్మరపోవు bommara-povu. v. n. To turn giddy, భ్రమించు.

బొమ్మికము or బొమ్మిడికము Same as బొమిడికము (q. v.).

బొమ్మిడము or బొమ్మిడాయిచేప bommidamu. [Tel.] n. The great loach, or tobacco-pipe fish, which has a very long head and a body like an eel.

బొమ్మె bomme. [Tel.] n. Faintness. మూర్ఛ. "బొమ్మెలమైమఱచుచు." Ila. i. 178. టీ॥ సొమ్మసిలుటచేత శరీరము మఱచియుండుట.

బొరిగ boriga. [Tel.] n. A small spade, (గడ్డిని) గోకుడుపార. తవ్వుగోల.

బొరియ or బొర్రె boriya. [Tel.] n. A hole or burrow such as is made by foxes, &c. రంధ్రము. A pit, గొయ్యి. A cave, గుహ, పర్వతబిలము. A dried cocoanut. నీరింకిపోయియెండిన కొబ్బరిబొండము. "అంతట నొక్కనొక్కెడొరయంబున బాంధవుడస్తపర్వతో పాంతముజేరుదాక బొరియగా జొరానలకీలకింతయుగా జింతిలుచుండి." S. iii. 350. బొరియచూలి boriya-tsūli. n. Lit. One born in a hole, i. e., Vālmiki.

బొరుగులు or బొరువులు borugulu. [Tel.] n. Parched grain, parched corn. పేలాలు, లాజలు. H. i. 113.

బొరుసు borusu. [Tel.] n. An earthen pan, usually made by breaking off the upper part of a pot. A potsherd, పెంకు, చిప్ప. A tumor, కంతి.

బొర్ర borra. [Tel.] n. A pot-belly. బొజ్జ. బొర్రజిట్ట borra-jitta. n. The Great Reed Warbler, *Acrocephalus stentoreus* (F.B.I.)

బొల్లడు bolladu. [Tel.] n. A horse brought from the Bōlānī country. బోలాందేశపు గుఱ్ఱము. "క॥ ఒనరించిరనీలనినడ, గనిబొల్లని గర్తగాని." G. iii. 134. A white spotted or speckled horse, బొల్లిగుఱ్ఱము.

బొల్లి bolli. [Tel.] adj. White spotted, white. తెల్లపొడగల. "బొల్లిమొదలగువచ్చియావులు." Parij. ii. 113. బొల్లిఆవు a white spotted cow. n. The white leprosy. శరీరమందుండేతెలుపు. A man with the white leprosy. బొల్లివాడు, బొల్లిగలపురుషుడు. బొల్లికోడి bolli-kōdi. n. The coot, *Fulica atra.* (F. B. I.) "ముక్కైకోడియుబోడ బొన్నంగికకోటి బొల్లికోడి." H. iii. 18. బొల్లిగద్ద or బొల్లిమోముపులుగు bolli-gadda. n. The white-faced kite, గరుత్మంతుడు. బొల్లితనము bolli-tanamu. n. Whiteness. శరీరమందుండే తెలుపు. Disgrace, dishonor, చిన్నదనము. "మర్మభేదులయినమార్గణములకోవ, టెంచిసిగ్గుజలముడిగ్గనాడి, యెల్లజనులు చూడ బొల్లితనంబున, గొబ్బియక్కుమారుడోడిపారె." M. xiii. i. 14. బొల్లిమోరమేకము bolli-mōra-mekamu. n. A bear, ఎలుగు.

బొల్లు bollu. [Tel. for బొల్లు.] v. n. To tell a lie. అబద్ధమాడు. n. A lie, a falsehood, అసత్యము. "బొల్లురాదగనిదోస్తివి." Pal. 399. అనగా అబద్ధమురాకూడని స్నేహముగలవాడవు.

బొళుకు బొళుకు boluku-boluku. [Tel.] n. The retching noise made in vomiting.

బొసబొస bosa-bosa. [Tel.] adv. With a gushing noise. Rapidly, one after another.

బొసిక bosika. [Tel.] n. The rind of a fruit like the cocoanut, టెంకాయమొదలగువాని పైతోలు.

బొసుక bosuka. [Tel.] adj. Fat. బలిసిన. n. One who is fat, బలిసినవాడు.

బో bō

బోక bōka. [Tel.] n. The belly, "బొజ్జకడుపు పొట్టబోకయు డొక్కయనసుదరంబోసంగు." Venkatēs-andhram. 76.

బోకి bōki. [Tel.] n. A pot (a word of contempt). A native ship or vessel. డోగీ. బోకిబొచ్చె (anuk) pots and pans.

బోకె bōke. [Tel. for బొమికె.] n. A bone, ఎముక.

బొక్కణము bŏkkaṇamu. [Tel.] n. A bucket. బొక్కెన.

బోగము bōgamu. [from Skt. భోగము.] adj. Appertaining to the dancing or theatrical caste. n. Price, వెల. బోగముదాన or బోగముది (బోగము+అది) a dancing girl, వెలయాలు. బోగమువాండ్లు dancing girls, actresses. బోగమాట dancing. బోగమాడు to dance. బోగి bōgi. n. The name given to the eves of some particular feasts. పండుగకు ముందటిదినము. A serpent. One who lives in splendour or luxury. భోగముగలవాడు, భోగముగలవాడు.

బోగు bōgu. [Tel.] n. An attempt, resolution, పూనిక. బోగుబడి bōgu-badi. n. A glutton. దూబరతిండి.

బోటి bōṭi. [Tel. from బోడి q. v.] n. A damsel, a woman. స్త్రీ. A female companion, చెలికత్తె. adj. Like, resembling. వంటి, వంటివాడు. బోటికత్తె bōṭi-katte. n. A female companion, చెలికత్తె. బోటితనము bōṭi-tanamu. n. Female wit, woman's wisdom. బాలాతనము. "నాటకంబులు బూటకంబులు బోటితనంబులునీటులు." Jaganna. ii. 9.

బోటు bōṭu. [Tel.] n. A projection in a hill, &c. కొండమొదలగువానియందు ఉబ్బుగానుండు చోటు. adj. Clever, ప్రౌఢమైన. Forward, సాహసుడైన.

బోటు bōṭu. [Eng. 'boat'] n. A boat, పడవ.

బోడ bōḍa. [Tel.] n. (In sea language) a board, i. e., a side. ఉజియబోడ starboard. డాపుబోడ larboard.

బోడ, బోడి or బోడు bōḍa. [Tel.] adj. Bald, bare, hornless, cropped. n. A monk, సన్యాసి. బోడితల bald-head. బోడితలతో వచ్చినాడు he came with his head bare or uncovered. బోడిఆవు a hornless cow. బోడిఅమ్ము a blunt arrow, an arrow without a point. [illegible] he stripped them bare, or plundered them. బోడియేనుగు a tuskless elephant. బోడిచెట్టు a pollard or a tree with the boughs cut off. బోడిసిరి a gross tax (as on a crop) without deducting charges. "అసువడిబోడనైన సేసుకుందుగాని యుంటి సామ్ముక్కుకాసైనదియ్య." S. ix. 3. బోడడు a bald headed man, బోడివాడు. బోడతరము bōḍa-taramu. n. A plant, *Sphæranthus indicus.* బ్రాపడి, ముండినిచెట్టు. Ainslie. 167. బోడలు bōḍalu. n. Hornless cattle. కొమ్ములులేనిపశువులు. బోడసరము Same as బొడ్డసరము. (q. v.). బోడికోడి bōḍi-kōḍi. [Tel.] n. A coot, *Fulica atra* (F.B.I.). బోడించు or బోడిచేయు bōḍintsu. v. a. To make bald, to crop the hair on the head entirely, to shave the head entirely bare. బోడింపు bōḍimpu. n. The act of removing the hair on the head entirely, బోడిచేయుట.

బోడి bōḍi. [Tel.] n. One that has a body. మేనుగలది. as చిగురుబోడి, పువ్వుబోడి.

బోడిక bōḍika. [Tel.] n. A companion, చెలికాడు. A pupil, శిష్యుడు. A servant, సేవకుడు. A boy, బాలకుడు.

> "సతతంబుసేయాడు సఖులుసేవింప,
> బొంగరాలాడును బోడికల్ దాను,
> సంగతిబాయకచరియించుచున్న."
>
> Sar. D. 12.

బోణి bōṇi. [H.] n. Handsel or the first money a seller receives towards the price of a thing. The luck-penny. బోణిచేయు to take handsel.

బోద bōda. [Tel.] adj. Swollen, as a leg. బోదకాలు a swollen diseased leg. "శ్లేపదు బొజ్జగలబోదకాలివాని." A. vi. 22. బోదవారు to swell. "పాడిచెడుబోదవారి చిన్న యిల్లాళ్లో." Swa. iv. 21. ఈ బోదవారి చిం, [illegible] n. The young or chick of a bird or tree. పక్షిపిల్ల. [illegible] "[illegible]"

P. i. 291. టీ॥ ఎగుబోదలై, పెద్దపిల్లలై, అవగా ఎగసేమాత్రపు పిల్లలనుట. "నైనికంబునగూడు దప్పి కేలుబడ్డ రాచిల్క-బోదల క్రోచుపిల్లి." Kalahasti ii. 83. పోకబోద a tender areca nut tree, లేతపోక. అంచెబోద a young swan, ఎలుకబోద a young rat.

బోదన bōdana. [for Skt. బోధన.] n. Advice, బోధన. Evil advice, దుర్బోధనము.

బోదు bōdu. [Tel.] n. The sacking in which oil bottles are packed on a bullock, సొగసుమునూనెసీసాలుద్దుకుకంటమీదవేసేది. A sack. గోనె.

బోదె, or బోదియ bōde. [Tel.] n. The trunk of a tree, ప్రకాండము. The bulging part of anything. The pediment or chapter of a pillar, స్తంభముమీద దూలముకిందనుండేది. Also, a runnel or small channel for watering trees. మళ్లకుకట్టేకాలువ. "పూచిన రెమ్మపోకనునబోదియజేరి." Swa. ii. 33. "అరుగులునున్నంపు పెరమంటె వట్టేలుతీర్చినగోడలుకేజిల్ల. నిండుసున్న పుపూతసెటాలుబోదెలు దిద్దినదేవరమిద్దెదనర." H. i. 167. "మిద్దెలో బోదియమీదినున్న కులపొందుగదీసుకరమ్మటంచు." ib. i. 224. బోదకొయ్య a piece of wood for a doorstep, గడపకిందికమ్మి.

బోధ or బోధము bōdha. [Skt.] n. Wisdom, intellect, understanding, awaking, arousing; teaching, instruction, doctrine. తెలియడము, తెలివి, జ్ఞానము. "బోధకళ మూస్పెక మోహవిభ్రాంతి." Swa. ii. 37. టీ॥ బోధకళ, నిరంతరజాగ్రత. "పుత్రకునివాక్య విస్ఫురద్బోధమునకు, తల్లిదండ్రులుసంతోషమున్ల పిల్ల." H. i. 208. బోధకుడు bōdhakuḍu. n. A teacher, preacher, instructor: బోధించువాడు, ఉపాధ్యాయుడు, గురువు. బోధపడు bōdha-paḍu. v. n. To be known, to be understood, to become intelligible. అగపడుచు. అది నాకు బోధపడినది or బోధలయినది I understand it. బోధపరచు bōdha-parutsu. v. a. To teach, explain, or make intelligible. బోధన or బోధనము bōdhana. n. Teaching, informing, awaking, arousing, counsel. వాని బోధన వినవద్దు do not listen to his counsel. బోధ్యము or బోధనీయము bōdhyamu. adj. Fit to be taught. బోధింపదగిన. బోధించు or బోధచేయు bōdhintsu. v. a. To teach, to explain, to inform, తెలియజేయు. To persuade, advise, admonish, induce, నేర్పు. వానికి బోధచేసేశక్తిలేదు he is unable to convey his knowledge, i.e., to teach. బోధితుడు bōdhituḍu. n. One who is taught. బోధింపబడినవాడు. బోధిద్రుమము bōdhi-drumamu. n. The sacred fig tree: *Ficus religiosa*. రావిచెట్టు.

బోనము bōnamu. [from Skt. భోజనము.] n. Food, meat, భోజనము, అన్నము. "వీరా పొంగులు ముట్టకబట్టగిట్టక బోనంబుసేయక." Jaganna. ii. 63. A meat offering, an offering of food to a god, నైవేద్యము. బోనకత్తె, బోనకత్తియ, బోనపుకత్తె or బోనముకత్తె bōna-katte. n. A cook woman, వంటకత్తె. A housemaid or slave girl. దాసీది. బోనకాడు bōna-kāḍu. n. A cook. బోనకావడి bōna-kāviḍi. n. A yoke (కావడి) on which baskets containing food are carried. "కర్పూరగమూటగా వాసనలమరు పెట్టెలును భక్ష్యసంబుసు బలుబోనగావిళ్లు." Pal. 256. బోనపుటిక bōna-puṭika. n. A basket of food.

"వింతగానన్నంబు వివిధభక్ష్యములు,
పొసగనించినబోనపుటికచేబూని."

DRY. 112.

బోనాంపెట్టె bōnam-peṭṭe. [H.] A round box or basket covered with leather, తోలుతోకప్పిన గుండ్రనిపెట్టె.

బోను bōnu. [Tel.] n. A trap. దుష్టవ్యాఘ్రములను పట్టుకొను కపటయంత్రము. A cage, పెంపుడు వ్యాఘ్రముల నుంచుటకైనపంజరము. "కస్తూరిగొను కాపురము కామిని నీతలపొప్పదీయుటకా."

Chenna. iv. 279. బోముపొయ్యి *bōmu-poyyi*. n. A portable oven shaped like a bowl.

బోము *bōmu*. [Tel.] n. Compulsion. బలాత్కారము, బలవంతము.

బోయ *bōya*. [Tel.] n. A forester, or mountaineer. A huntsman or fowler. A man of the hunter caste, కిరాతుడు. "బోయమరునకు." T. iii. 113. టీ. దయలేని మన్మథునికి. బోయకులము the fowler caste. **బోయుడు** or **బోయవాడు** *bōyaḍu*. n. A savage, a man of the hunter caste, **బోయత** or **బోయెత** *bōyata*. n. A woman of this tribe. కిరాతస్త్రీ. R. ii. 15. **బోయి, బోయీ** or **బోయీవాడు** *bōyi*. n. A palanquin bearer, పల్లకిమోయువాడు, బెస్త. A man of the cowkeeper's or shepherd's caste. గొల్లబోయడు a shepherd.

బోర *bōra*. [Tel.] n. The breast, the chest. రొమ్ము, అక్కు, ఎద, వక్షము. **బోరగించు** *bōragintsu*. v. a. To turn upside down. బోరగిల్లజేయు. "కడుపుబోరగించి కన్నులును కులించి బిర్ర బిగిసికొన్న పీడదయ్యాలి." Vēma. 1624. **బోరగిల్లు, బోరగిలు** or **బోరగిలబడు** *bōragillu*. v. n. To lie on one's face or breast. రొమ్ము భూమివాను నట్లు పరుండు. "పారలుబోరగిలబడి జారినముడి..." Bmj. i. 68. **బోరప్రాకుడు** *bōra-prakuḍu*. n. A snake, ఉరగము. **బోర్ల** *bōrla*. adv. Upside down, topsy-turvy. బోర్లదోయు to upset, overthrow. బోర్లపడు to lie prostrate: to be overset. దీన్ని చూచి బోర్లపడుతావు what do you pride yourself upon? బోర్లబొక్కలుపడు to fall on one's breast or face. **బోర్లించు** *bōrlintsu*. v. a. To upset, lay a thing on its face.

బోరిగము *bōrigamu*. [Tel.] n. A broom to sweep with, చీపురు. "అమ్మనెసబోరిగంబదిసిన దంచుబోనియు, ... మంగికి ... మునిమునిదిని." Mari BP. page 149.

బోరు *bōru*. [Tel.] adj. Great, large. బోరుతలుపులు or బోర్తలుపులు large doors, పెద్దకవాటములు. "వారలంతము తమవాకిటి, బోరుతలుపులుబెట్టిసమయములదొనక తా, రారవిపదలను సేయుచు, వారూఢస్థితిని పెంచిరాసౌధములోన." KP. vi. 130. n. A rush or downpour, as of heavy rain, వానకురియునట్టియందుగు ధ్వన్యనుకరణము. **బోరున, బోరన, భోరున** or **భోరన** *bōruna*. adv. Quickly, rushingly, శీఘ్రముగా. Much, grandly, greatly, heavily (as rain.) వాన బోరున కురిసినది it rained heavily. బోరున ఏడ్చినది she wept bitterly. "మునికేశ్వరులెల్లనుబోరన దమయంతి స్వయంవరమునకు నెప్పం, జను దెంచి." M. III. ii. 28. **బోరుకలగు, బోరుకలుగు** or **బోరుకల్లు** *bōru-kalugu*. v. n. To sound loud, మ్రోగు, ధ్వనించు. **బోరుకొను** *bōru-konu*. v. n. To resound, sound aloud. "భేరిమొదలగువాద్యములు బోరుకొనగ." Ila. i. 104. **బోరుకొలుపు** *bōru-kolupu*. v. a. To sound, ధ్వనించునట్లుచేయు. "బూరుగల్ కంచుకొమ్ములు కాహళములు బోరు కొలుపుటకునబుధులెల్లగలగ." ND. ii. 552.

బోరుక *bōruka*. [Tel.] n. A bath. స్నానము. **బోరుకాడు** or **బోర్కాడు** *bōruk-āḍu*. v. n. To bathe, as children. **బోరుకాడించు** or **బోర్కాడించు** *bōruk-āḍintsu*. v. a. To cause to bathe. బోరుకాడజేయు.

బోరువ or **బోరవ** *bōruva*. [Tel. బోరు+వా.] n. A vulture, also called బోరువగద్ద or బందు. పెద్దబోరువ the large vulture. తెల్ల బోరువ also called పీతిగద్ద the White Scavenger Vulture, *Neophron ginginianus*. నల్లబోరువ The Black Vulture, *Otogyps calvus*. (F. B. I.)

బోరెము *bōremu*. [Tel.] n. A bundle or load, as of cotton, దూదిలోనగువానిమూట. మూట. v.

బోలము *bōlamu*. [Tel. for బోళము.] n. A certain decoction. ... బోళము a certain medicine.

బోలు bōlu. [Tel.] adj. Hollow. బోలుగాజులు hollow bangles. మట్టిని బోలుగాపోయించిరి they heaped the earth lightly without pressing it solid.

బోకి bōki. [Tel.] n. A pot, pipkin; a contemptuous word for a vessel. ఓటి కుండ, కుండబొచ్చె. నాకు తాగుటకు ఒకబోకి యైనాలేదు I have not got even a pot to drink out of. బోకెడు అన్నము a bowl of rice.

బోలెము bolemu. [Tel.] n. Swiftness. వేగము.

బోలెవాటు bōle-vāṭu. [Tel.] n. A wretch. తెలగొట్లమారి. "కొండికట్టెగులాము మొప్పె గోవుబోలెవాటగచాట్లపోతుదుర్మార్గుండు." H. v. 128.

బోళము bōḷamu. [Tel.] n. Myrrh, Balsamodendron myrrha (Watts).

బోళా bōḷa. [Tel. from బోలు.] adj. Hollow. Frank, unreserved. కపటముకాని, మనస్సులో దాచని. బోళామనిషి one who is not a reserved man.

బోషాణము or భోషాణము bōshāṇamu. [H.] n. A large chest. పెద్దపెట్టె.

బోసి bōsi. [Tel.] adj. Toothless, పండ్లులేని. Defective, empty. ఒకపెట్టె అరలుగలది ఒక టిబోసిది one box has partitions, the other has none. బోసినోరు bōsi-nōru. n. A toothless mouth. బోసిపడు or బోసిపోవు bōsi-paḍu. v. n. To become toothless. బోసియగు.

బోసేయు bō-sēyu. [for Skt. భోజనముచేయు.] v. a. To eat. "సవరేయువేళబోసేసిపోవు." H. iv. 47.

బౌ bau

బౌద్ధము bauddhamu. [Skt. from బుద్ధ.] n Buddhism. బౌద్ధులు. Buddhists.

బ్ర bra

బ్రక్క or బక్క brakka. [Tel.] adj. Slight, thin, సన్నని. Poor, దీనుడైన. "ఈ బ్రక్కక ద్విజాజాదరయ్యసభవాకు." ఆము. vi.

బ్రతుకు, బ్రదుకు, బ్రతికించు or బ్రదికించు See under బతుకు. బ్రదిమి Same as బ్రదుకు. n.

బ్రద్ద Same as బద్ద. (q. v.). బ్రద్దలవారు or బద్దలవారు braddala-vāru. n. Officers, footmen, personal attendants. బంట్రౌతులు, వేత్రధరులు. "బ్రద్దలవారికగ్గాని పురంబున వారి సీమప్రసిద్ధులా, పెద్దలనెల్ల నిచ్చలిటు బిల్వదు పాండవవారికేశి." Chenna. v. 247. బ్రద్దపరి bradda-pari. n. A shield made of wickerwork. పేములతోనల్లినకేడెము. బ్రద్దర bradd-ara. (బ్రద్ద+అర) n. A piece, bit, తునక, చీలిక.

బ్రధ్నము bradhnamu. [Skt.] n. A root, వేరు. బ్రధ్నుడు bradhnuḍu. n. The sun, సూర్యుడు. Siva, శివుడు.

బ్రమయు bramayu. [from Skt. భ్రమ.] v. n. To err, be deceived. To be confused, perplexed, భ్రమించు. బ్రమరితిరుగు, బ్రమరితిపారు or బ్రమరులువారు bramari-tirugu. v. n. To go round, చుట్టివచ్చు.

బ్రమ్మి brammi. [Tel.] n. A tree called సోమిదచెట్టు.

బ్రమ్మెత brammeta. [for Skt. బ్రహ్మహత్య.] n. Brahmin-slaying, the act of slaying a Brahmin "బ్రమ్మెతకత్తెలంసమ్మనపోండ్లు." Charitra. ii. 1552.

బ్రల్లు or బల్లు brallu. [Tel.] n. A sudden noise, as of any thing that falls from a height.

బ్రహ్మ brahma. [Skt. బృహ్. (brih) to increase, Probably, the Indianised form of the name of 'Abraham', as బ్రహ్మము

is of 'Abram,' the పితామహ of the Jewish race. Compare their storeis. | n. The god Brahma, the operative creator of the world. ఇది బ్రహ్మకేన్యముగానున్నది this is invincible even to Brahma. వాడు వట్టి యుంబ్రహ్మ he is a mere simpleton. There are said to be *nine* Brahmas, *viz.*, భృగువు, పులస్త్యుడు, పులహుడు, అంగిరసుడు, అత్రి, క్రతువు, దక్షుడు, వసిష్ఠుడు, మరీచి. బ్రహ్మము *brahmamu.* n. The deity, పరమాత్మ. The Veda, వేదము. Meditation, తపము. బ్రహ్మకమ్మి *brahma-kammi.* n. The seam that goes down the middle of a sheet. బ్రహ్మచర్యము *brahma-charyamu.* n. The bachelor state. Abstinence from sexual intercourse. బ్రహ్మచారి *brahma-chāri.* n. A bachelor or novice: the title borne by a Brahmin during the period of religious instruction, which extends from childhood up to manhood, when he is married. బ్రహ్మచారిణి *brahma-chārini.* n. A maiden that remains unmarried, a female novice: a woman leading a life of continence. బ్రహ్మచర్యమును అనుష్ఠించు స్త్రీ. బ్రహ్మణ్యము Same as బ్రహ్మదారువు. గంగరావిచెట్టు, (q.v.). adj. Relating to, or connected with a Brahmin. బ్రాహ్మణహితము. బ్రహ్మత్య *brahmatya.* (correctly, బ్రహ్మహత్య) n. Brahmin-slaying, బ్రాహ్మణునిచంపడము. బ్రహ్మత్వము *brahmatvamu.* n. Identification with Brahma, or God. Godhead. బ్రహ్మసాయుజ్యము, బ్రహ్మస్వరూపము. బ్రహ్మదండి *brahma-dandi.* n. The Mexican or Prickly Poppy. (Watts); a plant called *Argemone mexicana.* (Wight.) వారాహి. బ్రహ్మనాడి *brahma-nādi.* n. The cerebral nerves. Hari Vams. i. 11. బ్రహ్మనాభుడు *brahma-nābhudu.* n. An epithet of Vishnu. బ్రహ్మపుత్రము *brahma-putramu.* n. The river Brahmaputra. A sort of poison. మకరాక్షజాతిసర్పవిషము. బ్రహ్మపుత్రుడు *brahma-putrudu.* n. A name of Narada. నారదుడు. Ketu, కేతుగ్రహము. బ్రహ్మబంధువు *brahma-bandhuvu.* n. A wretch, a miscreant infamous as a false witness. అబద్ధపుసాక్ష్యము పలికినందువల్ల నిందింపబడ్డవాడు. కూటసాక్షి అయిననిందితుడు. బ్రహ్మబిందువు *brahma-binduvu.* n. A drop of saliva. బ్రహ్మభూతుడు *brahma-bhūtudu.* n One who has become one with the Supreme Spirit. బ్రహ్మత్వముపొందినవాడు. బ్రహ్మభూయము or బ్రహ్మసాయుజ్యము *brahma-bhūyamu.* n. Brahmanhood, బ్రహ్మత్వము. బ్రహ్మయజ్ఞము *brahma-yagnamu.* n. The name of a certain rite among Brahmins. వేదపాఠము. బ్రహ్మరథము *brahma-rathamu.* n. A vehicle or car borne on the shoulders of Brahmins. P. i. 14. Vulgarly, a bier. పాడె, శవవాహనము. బ్రహ్మరంధ్రము *brahma-randhramu.* n. The fontanella, in anatomy: the quadrangular aperture found betwixt the *os frontis* and *ossa sincipitis,* in children just born; మాడపట్టు, నడినెత్తి. At death the soul is supposed by the Hindus to quit the body by this crevice. బ్రహ్మరాకాసిచెట్టు *brahma-rākasi-chettu.* n. The giant-aloe used in fences. బ్రహ్మరాక్షసి *brahma-rākshasi.* n. A ghoul, ogre or she-sprite. కొరివిపుండు బ్రహ్మరాక్షసి అయినది this made matters worse than before. బ్రహ్మరాక్షసుడు *brahma-rākshasudu.* n. A fiend of the Brahminical class: a priest's ghost. బ్రహ్మలిపి or బ్రహ్మవ్రాత *brahma-lipi.* n. An unintelligible scrawl, a bad scribble. Originally applied to the lines or the sutures of the skull, which are supposed to be hieroglyphics, the mysterious writing of destiny. తలపుర్రమీది వ్రాత. చిక్కుగానుండే వ్రాలు. బ్రహ్మవాది *brahma-vādi.* n. A Vedantist, వేదాంతి. బ్రహ్మవిద్వాంసుడు *brahma-vidvāmsudu.* n. An illustrious doctor or professor.

బ్రహ్మవేళ *brahma-vēla.* n. Dawn. అరుణోదయకాలము. A vi. 2. బ్రహ్మవ్రాలు *brahma-vrālu.* n. The handwriting of God: a name given to the crooked lines on the skull. బ్రహ్మసూత్రము *brahma-sūtramu.* n. The sacred thread worn by Brahmins. యజ్ఞోపవీతము, జంధెము. బ్రహ్మసువు *brahma-suvu.* n Manmadha, మన్మధుడు. బ్రహ్మస్వము *brahma-svamu.* n. A Brahmin's property or wealth. బ్రాహ్మణసొత్తు Kod. §. 5. Jain 1. 77. బ్రహ్మహత్య *brahma-hatya.* Brahmin-slaying. Also (vulgarly) any killing: thus పిల్లిబ్రహ్మహత్య cat slaughter. బ్రహ్మహత్యగాడు *brahma-hatya-gāḍu.* n. A Brahmin-slayer, a man of blood. బ్రాహ్మణునిచంపినవాడు. బ్రహ్మాంజలి *brahm-anjali.* n. Joining both hands together while reading the Vedas. వేదాధ్యయనకాలమందలిమ్రొక్కు. బ్రహ్మాండము *brahm-āṇḍamu.* n. The globe, the universe, the world. adj. Huge, vast, immense, awful. బ్రహ్మాండముగా *brahm-āṇḍamu-gā.* adv. Vastly, prodigiously. బ్రహ్మాణి *brahmaṇi.* n. The female energy of Brahma. సరస్వతి. బ్రహ్మానందము *brahm-ānandamu.* n. Divine bliss. Great joy. మహాసంతోషము. బ్రహ్మారణ్యము *brahm-āraṇyamu.* n. A place where the Veda is studied. వేదపాఠభూమి. బ్రహ్మావర్తము *brahm-āvartamu.* n. Brahmāvarta, the land first occupied by the Brahmins to the north-west of Delhi. బ్రహ్మాసనము *brahm-āsanamu.* A sacred seat. బ్రహ్మ్యము *brahmyamu.* n. Divineness. నాదబ్రహ్మము divine harmony, heavenly tones. See బ్రాహ్మము.

బ్రా brā

బ్రాతి *brāti.* [Tel.] n. Love, ప్రేమ. adj. Much, great. అధికము, హెచ్చు, అతిశయము, గొప్ప. Hard to get, impossible, దుర్లభము. Dear, beloved, ప్రియము. See బాతి. "భవదధీనులకు విజయంబుబ్రాతె." M. VII. v. 8. is it any great matter for thy favourites to be conquerors? నీప్రాపుగలిగినవారికి జయము కలుగుటయరుదియా?

బ్రాహ్మణము *brāhmaṇamu.* [Skt. from బ్రహ్మ.] n. An assembly of Brahmins. The Brahmanas of the Vedas. వేదభాగము. బ్రాహ్మణ్యము *brāhmaṇyamu.* n. An assembly of Brahmins, బ్రాహ్మణసమూహము. The state, quality, or business of a Brahmin, Brahminhood. బ్రాహ్మణభావము. బ్రాహ్మము *brāhmamu.* n. The rite of marriage performed in accordance with the Vedas by Brahmins, కన్యాదానము. adj. Pertaining to Brahma. బ్రహ్మసంబంధమైనది. బ్రాహ్మణుడు or బ్రాహ్మడు *brāhmaṇuḍu.* n. A Brahmin. విప్రుడు. బ్రాహ్మణాయనుడు *brāhmṇ-āyanuḍu.* n. A Brahmin of a good family. బ్రాహ్మణబ్రువుడు *brāhmaṇa-bruvuḍu.* n. A Brahmin who does not act according to rules of his caste. తాను బ్రాహ్మణుడై అన్యజాతికర్మముచేత బ్రతికేవాడు. బ్రాహ్మణి *brāhmaṇi.* n. A Brahmin woman. బ్రాహ్మణస్త్రీ. The lizard called నలికండ్లపాము. బ్రాహ్మి *brāhmi.* n. An epithet of Saraswati, spouse of Brahma. సరస్వతి. See బ్రహ్మ.

బ్రు bru

బ్రుంగు *brungu.* [Tel.] v. n. To be buried, పూడు. To hide, మరుగు. To sink; to die, perish. మునుగు, చచ్చు, నాశమగు. "పెనురొంపిలోపలను బ్రుంగిన ధేనువు వెత్తుపోలికన్." M. IX. i. 172. "పోకలకావిరి బ్రుంగెడు పులుగృహంబులు." A. iv. 167. బ్రుంగుడు *brunguḍu.* adj. Hidden, concealed, మరిగిన. Sunk, మునిగిన. బ్రుంగుపడు or బ్రుంగుడుపడు *brungu-paḍu* v n.

To be hidden, to be diminished, to be in reduced circumstances. మరుగుపడు, దాగిపోవు, మునిగిపోవు. నష్టమగు. "ఆ విభుడు రాజ్య సుఖరేఖావిముఖత చెదరిబంధులం దొరగి యన్నీ, సౌవాసల బ్రుంగుడుపడినోపల డాగొట్టి కదుపు బ్రోతుకొందుచుజా." M. IV. i. 249. బ్రుంగుడుపాటు brungudu-pātu. n. Concealment, బ్రుంగుడుపడుట. బ్రుంచు bruntsu. v. a. To cause to sink, to submerge, బ్రుంగజేయు. బ్రుంగు brungu. v. n. To perish, నశించు.

బ్రుషి or బ్రుసి brushi. [Skt.] n. A seat, throne, couch, as that of a hermit, made of grass. యతీశ్వరులు కూర్చుండే ఆసనము.

భ bha

భ bha. [Skt.] n. The name of a Skt. letter, ఒక అక్షరము. భ or భగణము bha. n. In Prosody, a dactyl or foot composed of a long syllable followed by two short ones as Bhārata.

భంగము bhangamu. [Skt.] n. Breaking; a break, breach, hindrance; prevention, defeat, loss, disappointment, discomfiture, failure, అవమానము, ఓటమి. A breach or chasm. A wave, అల. Overwhelming destruction. చెరుపు. కార్య భంగము disappointment. భ్రూభంగము a frown or contraction of the brow, knitting the brows. A bit, piece, తునక, ఖండము. భంగత bhangata. n. Defeat. అవజయము. "అలనవరుణెప్పుడును తారునిలచియుండు, నిలకడ చెడుకింతయును లేక చలన మొందుచుండు నందును బలిమిరాయునల్లసమున, భంగతొడినట్టి జలధితరంగములకు." Raja Sekh. i. 51. భంగపడు bhanga-padu. v. n. To be disappointed, disgraced, defeated. అవమానపడు. భంగపరచు. భంగించు or భంగపెట్టు bhanga-paratsu. v. a. To disappoint, defeat, disgrace. భంగపడ్డ disappointed, defeated. భంగపాటు bhanga-pātu. n. Defeat, disappointment.

భంగి bhangi. [Skt.] n. Manner, mode, way. విధము. ఏభంగి how? Also, the drug called Bhang. Indian hemp, *Sativa indica*, గంజాయిచెట్టు.

భంగురము bhanguramu. [Skt.] adj. Crooked, bent, వంకరైన. Frail, fragile, perishable, unsteady, fleeting. నశించునది. "స్త్రీలధైర్యంభంగురములు కాంతలతోల్త." KP. iii. 60. women's patience is fleeting.

భంజకము bhanjakamu. [Skt.] adj. That which breaks, dissipates or destroys. భంజనము bhanjanamu. n. Breaking, విరుపు. Dissipating, doing away, destroying. భంజించు bhanjintsu. v. a. To break, విరుచు. To dissipate, to do away with, పోగొట్టు. భంజితము bhanjitamu. adj. Dissipated, scattered.

భండనము bhandanamu. [Skt.] n. A battle. యుద్ధము. A piece of armour, కవచము. A wicked or cruel deed, దుష్కృత్యం.

భండారము, బండారము or బండారు bhandāramu. [Skt.] n. A treasury. భండారం, ధనగృహము, బొక్కసము, సంచికట్టు. "శక్తిని బండారు లెక్కలుంచూడు." BD. v. 800.

భండించు bhandintsu. [Skt.] v. n. To play pranks, బండాటలాడు.

> క॥ "ఒంటరైనదేయకూరక
> భండించిన కలదె పరమపదవిన్నపాలా."
> రుక్మాం. v.

భండుడు bhandudu. [Skt.] n. A wicked man, దుష్టుడు, అకతాయి.

భంబు bhambu. [Skt.] n. A star, నక్షత్రము. The sky, ఆకాశము. A ray of light. కిరణము.

భక్తము bhaktamu. [Skt.] n. Food. అన్నము. adj. Divided, భాగింపబడినది.

భక్తి *bhakti.* [Skt.] n. Attachment, devotion, reverence, piety, loyalty. Faith, belief, శ్రద్ధ, సేవ. Friendship, affection, love, స్నేహము. A part or division of a thing, భాగము. పూర్వాత్పరయోగే భక్తిః is a well known canon. భయభక్తులతో with reverence and love. భక్తుడు a devotee, a pious man, భక్తిగలవాడు, డింగరీడు.

భక్షించు *bhakshintsu.* [Skt.] v. a. To eat, to feed on, తిను, భక్షణముచేయు. భక్షణము *bhakshaṇamu.* n. Eating, తినుట. భక్షకుడు *bhakshakuḍu.* n. One who eats. తినువాడు, తిండిపోతు. భక్షణీయము *bhakshaṇiyamu.* adj. Fit to be eaten, తినదగినది. భక్షితము *bhakshitamu.* adj. Eaten, తినబడిన. భక్ష్యము *bhakshyamu.* adj. Fit to be eaten, తినదగిన. n. An eatable, తినుబండము. A cake or sweetmeat. పంచభక్ష్యములు five kinds of eatables, viz. భక్ష్యము, భోజ్యము, లేహ్యము, చోష్యము, పానీయము. భక్ష్యకారుడు one who makes sweetmeats, పిండివంటచేయువాడు.

భగణము *bha-ganamu.* [Skt.] n. The circumference of a circle. Warren. p. 357. An assemblage of stars. భ, నక్షత్రముల యొక్క, గణము, సమూహము. "గగనగమునైన భానులే చిగురాకులపొగడచాలు చెలిగనగొంటే, భగణంబుపోలుపువులుం, దగుమొగ్గలు సద్గుణాశ్రితములైనవలా." Also, in Prosody, a dactyl.

భగభగ or బగబగ *bhaga-bhaga.* [Tel.anuk.] adv. Blazingly. అగ్నిజ్వాలాధ్వని. "భగభగ మనిమించెనతడు నా హృదయంబున్." KP. ii. 97. భగాలను *bhagal-anu.* v. n. To explode, to be terrible. "గుండెభగాలన" heart-brokenly. HD. ii. 1104. భగ్గరి *bhaggy-ari.* n. An irritable, passionate man or woman. భగ్గుమనిమండిపడేటిది. భగ్గున *bhaggu-na.* adv. Flashingly, suddenly, all at once (applied to fire or anger). వానికోపము భగ్గున మండినది he was all on fire with rage. భగ్గుమను *bhaggu-m-anu.* v. n. To be violent, to explode, as flame.

భగము *bhagamu.* [Skt.] n. The female organ of generation. యోని. భగిని *bhagini.* n. A sister. తోడబుట్టినది. భగందరము *bhagandaramu.* n. An ulcer or sore in the genital parts. మర్మస్థానమందలి వ్రణము.

భగవత్ *bhagavat.* [Skt.] adj. Respectable, worshipful, adorable. భగవద్గీత "the Divine Song," the name of a celebrated poem. భగవద్ధ్యానము meditation on the Deity. భగవచ్ఛాస్త్రము the sacred text. భగవతి *bhaga-vati.* n. A respectable woman. పూజ్యురాలు. భగవతీందేవి the blessed goddess. భగవంతుడు or భగవానుడు *bhaga-vantuḍu.* n. Almighty God. The Supreme Being. The Lord.

భగిని See under భగము.

భగీరథుడు *bhagī-rathuḍu.* [Skt.] n. A certain king whose exertions brought the Ganges from heaven to earth. భగీరథప్రయత్నము a phrase similar to "Herculean labours."

భగ్నము *bhagnamu.* [Skt.] adj. Broken, shattered. భంగముపొందిన.

భజించు or భజియించు *bhajintsu.* [Skt.] v. a. To worship, adore, pray to; to serve. సేవించు. భజనము *bhajanamu.* n. Worship, homage. సేవించుట. భజనము or భజన worship accompanied by music. రామభజనము the rite of singing the praises of Rāma. భజంత్రీలు *bhajan-trilu.* n. Musicians.

భటుడు *bhaṭuḍu.* [Skt.] n. A servant. పనివాడు. A soldier, కాల్బంటు.

భట్టాచారి *bhaṭṭ-achāri.* [Skt.] n. A title given to a learned man, equivalent to *Doctor*, His Reverence (thus used in

Bengal.) In the south this is applied to a mere temple Brahmin (*sacrificulus,*) a priestling. అర్చకుడు, నంబివాడు. A showy person, డాంబికుడు.

భట్టారకుడు *bhattārakuḍu.* [Skt.] n. A sage, a saint. ముని. The Sun, సూర్యుడు. Also, a theatrical phrase for 'a king,' రాజు.

భట్టిగాడు or భట్టీకిటిగాడు *bhatti-gaḍu.* [Tel.] n. The Brown Shrike. *Lanius cristatus.* (F. B. I.)

భట్టిని *bhattini.* [Skt.] n. A theatrical phrase for a king's secondary wife, as distinguished from దేవి the crowned queen.

భట్టీయము *bhattīyamu.* [Skt.] n. The name of an ancient brief treatise upon Telugu grammar, written by నన్నయ భట్టు.

భట్టుడు *bhattuḍu.* [Skt.] n. A title equivalent to 'Doctor,' as లింగాభట్టుడు, కృష్ణ భట్టుడు. భట్టుమూర్తి *bhattu-mūrti.* n. The Minstrel; or he who wore "the form of a Minstrel." This is the title of the celebrated author of the Vasu Charitra, whose original name was Rama Razu.

భట్రాజు or భట్టు *bhat-rāju.* [Skt.] n. A bard, minstrel, herald, chanter of titles.

భద్రము *bhadramu.* [Skt.] Blessedness, prosperity, welfare, శుభము. Care, attention. భద్రమా నీకు is it well with thee? I hope you are well. interj. Beware! take care, be on your guard! adj. Fine, noble. శ్రేష్ఠము. Happy, blessed. శుభకరమైన. Safe, secure. Careful, watchful. భద్రేభము a fine elephant. భద్రాస్త్రము a supernatural or celestial weapon. భద్రముగా carefully. భద్రముచేయు to take care of, to lay up, store up, secure. భద్ర *bhadra.* n. A name of Sri or Venus. భద్రకాళి *bhadra-kāli.* n. An epithet of Parvati, పార్వతి దేవి. భద్రలు *bhadralu.* n. Sixes, at dice. భారకుంకములు. భద్రసురము *bhadra-suramu.* n. A dagger, చేకటారి. భద్రాకరణము *bhadra-karaṇamu.* n. A phrase for shaving. క్షౌరము. భద్రాసనము *bhadr-āsanamu.* n. A king's seat, a throne. రాజు కూర్చుండు పీఠము. భద్రుడు *bhadruḍu.* n. One who is blessed or fortunate. పట్టభద్రుడు the lord of the land. "పలికెడిది భాగవతమట, పలికించెడివాడు రామభద్రుండట." B. i. 21.

భము or భంబు *bhamu.* [Skt.] n. A star, నక్షత్రము. The sky, గగనము. "భంబుగదే నభంబునకు భంబుగదేతోడయానము మహేభంబు గదే." Ratnâvali. iv. 146.

భయము *bhayamu.* [Skt.] n. Fear, fright, terror, alarm. భయంకరము *bhayankaramu.* adj. Frightful, alarming, terrible. భయదము *bhayadamu.* adj. Frightful, terrific. భయపడు *bhaya-paḍu.* v. n. To be afraid. భయపరచు *bhaya-paratsu.* v. a. To frighten, alarm, intimidate. భయపెట్టు *bhaya-pettu.* v. a. To frighten, alarm. భయస్థుడు *bhayasthuḍu.* n. A timorous or timid man; one who fears to do evil; a god-fearing man. భయస్థురాలు a timid woman. భయానకము *bhay-ānakamu.* adj. Fearful, frightful, alarming. భయావహము *bhay-āvahamu.* adj. Frightful, alarming, terrible. భయోత్పాతము *bhay-ōtpatamu.* n. A fearful prodigy or phenomenon.

భరంతు, or భరంతుమిద్దె *bharantu.* [Tel.] n. A terrace or raised floor.

భరటుడు *bharatuḍu.* [Skt.] n. A potter. కుమ్మరివాడు.

భరణము *bharaṇamu.* [Skt.] n. Cherishing, maintaining, nourishing, supporting. పోషణము. Dowry, స్త్రీధనము. Wages, hire.

కూలి, జీతము. భుక్తికైనాపాటిభరణము కష్టపడి
చేసితి I did it to the best of my ability to get my bread. భత్యభరణములు batta and wages. Also, a land measure in Ganjam equal to about one-fifth of an acre.

భరణి *bharani.* [Skt.] n. The second lunar mansion, being three stars in a triangle.

భరతపిట్ట *bharata-pitta.* [Tel.] n. A species of Titlark or Pippit called in Dakhini Chendul.

భరతుడు *bharatudu.* [Skt.] n. The name of a younger brother of Rāma. The name of a celebrated writer on dramatic composition. An actor, dancer. భరతంపుటొజ్జ *bharatampu-t-odzdza.* n. A dancing master. నాట్యశాస్త్రోపాధ్యాయుడు. "భరతంపుటొజ్జకు వచ్చుటంబోలెనప్ప." H. v. 156. భరతశాస్త్రము *bharata-sastramu.* n. Theatrical learning, the art of acting and singing.

భరద్వాజము *bharadvajamu.* [Skt.] n. The King-crow or Drongo-shrike, *Dicrurus ater* (F. B. I.) ఏట్రింత, వ్యాఘ్రమూటపక్షి. Radha KD. (It has been wrongly taken to be the sky lark: it never rises into the sky and is commonly seen on the backs of cattle and hence is called పసులపోలిగాడు. It will even perch on the tiger and hence is called వ్యాఘ్రమూటము.)

భరవసా *bharavasa.* [H.] n. Confidence, trust, belief, pledge. నమ్మకము, తాకట్టు.

భరించు *bharintsu.* [Skt. from భృ to bear.] v. a. To bear, sustain, maintain, support, endure, tolerate. మోయు, ప్రోచు, రక్షించు. భరము *bharamu.* n. Weight, బరువు. Excellence, అతిశయము. భరితము *bharitamu.* adj. Filled with, full, పూరితము. See భృ, భారము and భార్య.

భర్గుడు *bhargudu.* [Skt.] n. A title of Siva

భర్జనము *bharjanamu.* [Skt.] n. Frying. వేయించడము. భర్జించు to fry. To beat, కొట్టు.

భర్త *bharta.* [Skt. from భృ to bear.] n. A husband, lord, master. అవనీభర్త a king, as lord of the earth.

భర్తి or భర్తీ *bharti.* [H.] n. Fullness, completion, filling up. భర్తీచేయు *bharti-cheyu.* v. a. To fill up a deficiency.

భర్త్సనము *bhartsanamu.* [Skt.] n. A threat, menace. బెదిరించడము, బెదిరింపుమాట.

భర్మము *bharmamu.* [Skt.] n. Gold. బంగారు. "భర్మపుటంచుల్" tissue, gold cloth. భర్మదేశము *bharma-desamu.* n. The "land of Gold," Burma. The king has as a title భర్మపదుడు Golden footed.

భల్లము *bhallamu.* [Skt.] n. A bear. ఎలుగుబంటు. A. iv. 255. A broad headed arrow such as cuts through a cord. A spear, బల్లెము.

భల్లాతము or భల్లాతకి *bhalla-tamu.* [Skt.] n. The marking nut, జీడిగింజ.

భల్లూకము or భల్లూకము *bhallukamu.* [Skt.] n. A bear. ఎలుగుబంటి.

భళా, భళి, భళీ, భళిర. భళిరా or భళారే *bhala.* [Tel.] interj. Well done! bravo! Very good! సెబాసు. "ప్రాయపు వాడుగద్దె భళిరాయిటిదంచునొక్కైన పేటికలా." K. P. iv. 68.

భవంతి or బవంతి *bhavanti.* [Tel.] n. A house containing an open area in the middle. నాలుగిండ్లుకలిసికట్టినది. భవంతిబట్ట a handkerchief which has flowers at the corners.

భవదీయము *bhavad-iyamu.* [Skt.] adj. Yours, belonging to you, నీది.

భవనము *bhava-namu.* [Skt.] n. A house, dwelling.

భవము *bhavamu.* [Skt.] n. Being, existence, subsistence. Earthly or corporeal existence. The condition of being on earth. Birth as a mortal, పుట్టుక. భవదూరుడు immortal, released from the bonds of the flesh; free from mortal birth. In theology, sin, the sinful state, or mortality as subject to sin, సంసారము. భవబంధములు earthly ties, as those of kindred. భవదుఃఖములు the ills of human life. భవమోక్షణము a release from mortal life. M. XIII. v. 410. adj. In composition, arising from, produced or caused by. **భవాండము** *bhav-andamu*. n. The world. బ్రహ్మాండము.

భవాదృశుడు *bhavā-drusudu*. [Skt.] n. One like you. నీవంటివాడు.

భవాని *bhavāni*. [Skt.] n. A name of Parvati, the spouse of Siva.

భవించు *bhavintsu*. [Skt.] v. n. To happen, occur. A verb used only in certain compounds, as ఉద్భవించు, మూర్ఛభవించు, &c.

భవిష్యత్తు *bhavish-yattu*. [Skt.] adj. Future, about to be, కాగలది. భవిష్యత్కాలము the future tense.

భవిష్యము *bhavi-shyamu*. [Skt.] n. Prosperity, welfare. శుభము, భాగ్యము.

భవుడు *bhavudu*. [Skt.] n. A title of Siva, adj. Sinful, ignorant. ప్రాకృతుడు, సంస్కారహీనుడు, ప్రాకృతుడు.

భవ్యము *bhavyamu*. [Skt.] adj. Prosperous, శుభమైన. Beautiful, handsome, మనోజ్ఞమైన. Holy, శ్రీమత్.

భషకము *bhashakamu*. [Skt.] n. A dog. **భషితము** or **భషణము** *bhashitamu*. n. Barking, కుక్కమొరుగు.

భసలము *bhasalamu*. [Skt.] n. A wild bee, the large black carpenter bee, తుమ్మెద.

భసితము *bhasi-tamu*. [Skt.] n. Ashes. భసితవర్ణమైన ashy, gray. Suca. iii. 53.

భస్త్ర, భస్త్రి or **భస్త్రిక** *bhastra*. [Skt.] n. A pair of bellows, used in a forge. కొలిమితిత్తి. A leather bag. **భస్త్రికుడు** *bhastrikudu*. n. A bellows-blower.

భస్మము *bhasmamu*. [Skt.] n. Ashes, calx. బూడిద. తామ్రభస్మము calx of copper. Ainslie. i. 513. **భస్మీకరించు** *bhasmi-karintsu*. v. a. To reduce to ashes. భస్మముచేయు.

భా bhā

భా *bhā*. [Skt.] n. Sunlight, సూర్యుని వెలుగు. A ray of light. కిరణము. Splendour. ప్రకాశము.

భాండము *bhandamu*. [Skt.] n. An earthern pot or vessel. Any vessel. కుండలోనగు మంటిపాత్రము, పాత్రము. Capital, principal. ముదలిసొమ్ము, అసలు, మూలధనము, బండారము. Harness, trappings అశ్వభూషణము. ఏకభాండాశనులుగా నున్నారు they eat out of the same dish, i. e., they form one family. పృథగ్భాండాశనులైనారు they began to eat food prepared in separate vessels, i. e., they formed a separate family. భాండశ్రాద్ధము or ఘటశ్రాద్ధము a ceremony used in divorce, when some funeral rites are performed as though a relation was dead. **భాండాగారము** *bhand-agaramu*. n. A treasury. ధనగృహము, ఖజానాకొట్టు, బొక్కసము. **భాండాగారికుడు** *bhand-agarikudu*. n. A treasurer. కోశాధ్యక్షుడు. G. ii. 50.

భాండీరము *bhandiramu*. [Skt.] n. A banyan tree. "పొచ్చుదాటినవారిని దాటజాలని వారు వహించి, భాండీరవటమునదాక, నరిగి రానిచెంచు." N. iv. 10. టీ॥ భాండీరమనే మర్రిచెట్టుదాకా.

భాక్కు *bhakku*. [Skt.] n. One who has obtained. ఫలభాక్కు he who has obtained an advantage.

భాగము *bhāgamu.* [Skt.] n. A portion, share, part, quarter, side. దక్షిణభాగమందు on the south side. సమభాగములుగా in equal shares. భాగంబుగావచ్చిన భూమి land that fell to his share. భాగధేయము *bhāga-dhēyamu.* n. Luck, భాగ్యము. A royal revenue, పన్ను. భాగరి *bhāg-ari.* n. A sharer, partner, fellow. భాగస్వామి *bhāga-swāmi.* n. A shareholder. భాగహారము *bhāga-hāramu.* n. Division in Arithmetic. భాగించు *bhāgintsu.* v. a. To divide or distribute, to share. పంచు.

భాగవతము *bhāga-vatamu.* [Skt.] n. The name of a celebrated Hindu poem describing the life of Krishna. Any Puranic story, a story, పురాణకథ, కథ. "ఆ చెలివిధము ప్రియురాంగన తెల్లక, బాలిమనంబుల శోకమునిగ రక్, రోచనకేళిర రోయించిరిచేశా, బామువుభాగ వతంబుగా నించుక." భరతాభ్యుదయము. ii. 8, 10. A stage play, acting. A comedy. భాగవతుడు *bhāga-vatuḍu.* n. A religious man. A monk or friar. భాగవతులు *bhāga-vatulu.* n. Religious or pious men: fellow scholars in divinity. Stage-players, actors.

భాగినేయి *bhāgi-nēyi.* [Skt. from భగిని.] n. The daughter of a sister, మేనకోడలు. భాగినేయుడు *bhāgi-nēyuḍu.* A sister's son, మేనల్లుడు.

భాగీరథి *bhāgī-rathi.* [Skt. from భగీరథ.] n. The Ganges. గంగ.

భాగ్యము *bhāgyamu.* [Skt.] n. Luck, fortune, riches, wealth. అదృష్టము, ధనము. అదియేమి భాగ్యము what great matter is it? భాగ్యముగలవాడు a man of fortune. భాగ్యరేఖ a line on the palm of the hand, &c., that portends good luck. భాగ్యవంతుడు a fortunate man, a rich man. భాగ్యవతి or భాగ్యశాలి a fortunate woman; a woman (sometimes used contemptuously.)

భాజనము *bhājanamu.* [Skt.] n. A dish, platter, cup, భోజనముచేయుపాత్రము. An object of mercy or anger. Worth, యోగ్యము. భాజనత *bhājanata.* n. Worthiness, desert. పాత్రత, యోగ్యత.

భాట or బాట *bhāṭa.* [H.] n. A road, way. A quarter, దిక్కు. A resource.

భాటకము *bhāṭakamu.* [Skt.] n. Rent. బాడిగ.

భాణము *bhāṇamu.* [Skt.] n. A kind of drama. నాటకభేదము. A short poem or novel. A dramatic monologue. ధూర్తవిట భావాదిరసంభాణమిత్యభిధీయతే.

భాతి *bhāti.* [Skt.] n. Light, brilliance, కాంతి. Way, manner, విధము. (affix) Like, like to. వలె, వలెను. "సాక్షాత్కరించిన శోభను భాతి." Ila. iii. 14. "కాంతమానసమున జల్లనై శీతల భాతినున్నవాడు వరమయోగి." Vēmana. 908.

భాద్రపదము *bhādra-padamu.* [Skt.] n. The sixth month of the Hindu year, that in which the moon's change takes place when the sun is in Virgo.

భానుడు, భానుమంతుడు or భానువు *bhānuḍu.* [Skt.] n. A name of the god Sūrya, the sun, "భానుడుదయించెవెబట్టిచెడ కపోతి." Vēma. iii. 210. భానువారము *bhānu-vāramu.* n. Sunday. భానువు *bhānuvu.* n. A ray of light, కిరణము.

భామ *bhāma.* [Skt.] n. A woman. ఆడుది. భామిని *bhāmini.* n. A woman.

భారతము or మహాభారతము *bhāratamu.* [Skt. from భరత.] n. The name of a celebrated poem called by Sir W. Jones the 'Iliad of India.' పెద్దభారతము an Iliad of woes, an interminable tale of distress. ఆ భారతమంతా యెందుకు నీవు కావలసినదేమో చెప్పుము leave out those long stories and come to the point.

భారతి *bhárati*. [Skt.] n. A name of Sarasvati the Goddess of Speech.

భారద్వాజగోత్రము *bháradvája-gótramu*. [Skt.] n. A certain ancient family up to which many Brahmins trace their genealogy.

భారద్వాజము *bhára-dvájamu*. [Skt.] n. The bird called the King crow: it is the Drongo shrike, *Dicrurus ater*. (F. B. I.) పసులపోలిగాడు, ఏట్రింత.

భారము *bharamu*. [Skt.] n. Weight, heaviness, a burden. బరువు. Responsibility, incumbent or bounden duty. Hardship. A certain weight. బారువ. "భావునవాకుండలములు గైకొనుమని సంభావనముతో నిత్యము మహీవర సౌవర్ణ భారమిచ్చుచుండుఙా." G. vii. 142. నాకు ఒళ్లు భారముగానున్నది I am unwell. నావంటి దీనులరక్షించే భారము తమదే it rests with you to relieve poor men like me. దూరభారములో నున్నాడు he is afar off. **భారకము** *bharakamu*. n. A crisis. ముమ్మరము. జ్వరము నిండా భారకముగానున్నది the fever is at its height or crisis. **భారకర్త** *bara-karta*. n. One who sustains or is responsible. Thus, దేవుడు మా భారకర్త God is our refuge. **భారకించు** *bhara-kintsu*. v. n. To become severe, as fever. నాకు ఒళ్లు భారకించేలాగునున్నది I have a prospect of illness. భారవాహుడు or భారకుడు one who carries a burden, బరువు మోయువాడు. **భారి** *bhari*. adj. Big, high, stout, bulky. Rich, respectable.

భార్గవి *bhargavi*. [Skt.] n. A goddess: usually denoting Párvati or Lakshmi, పార్వతి, లక్ష్మి.

భార్య *bharya*. [Skt. భృ to carry, maintain.] n. A wife. భార్యాబిడ్డలుగలవాడు one who has a wife and children. భార్యాభర్తలు husband and wife, a wedded pair. **భార్యాటీకుడు** *bharyatikudu*. n. A hen-pecked husband. పెండ్లాము మాట జవదాటనివాడు.

భావము *bhavamu*. [Skt.] n. Mind, soul, heart, ఆత్మ. Thought, idea, feeling, disposition, nature. Import, meaning, drift. Motive, aim, view. అభిప్రాయము. Temperament, humour, passion, sentiment, state or condition of being. మనోవికారము. A property or power of matter. స్వభావము. An act, gesture. భావవ్యర్థరూపక్రియ. A learned man, (వాట్య మంభావితాయాం) పండితుడు, విద్వాంసుడు. నన్ను తల్లిభావముతో చూచిరి they looked upon me as a mother. అవి దొంగసొమ్ము అని మీ భావమా do you mean that these were stolen goods? **భావగర్భము** *bhava-garbhamu*. adj. Having a secret import or a mysterious meaning: intelligible, as a glance conveying a certain impression. **భావజారి** *bhavajári*. n. The "*Amoricide*" or slayer (అరి) of Cupid, i.e., Siva. **భావజుడు** *bhava-judu*. n. Lit: "Born in the heart," an epithet of Manmadha. **భావన** *bhavana*. n. Mental perception, recollection, consciousness of past ideas or preceptions, imagination. తలపు. Observing, investigating. వాసనపట్టుట. Steeping, maceration of a drug in a liquid. Thus భావనశొంఠి, భావనకరక్కాయ are ginger or aloes prepared by being repeatedly dipped in certain fluids and dried again. అల్లపురసాన ఏడు భావనలుచెయ్యి let these drugs be steeped seven times in the juice of ginger. **భావనచేసుకొను** *bhavana-chesu-konu*. v. n. To imagine or figure to oneself. **భావభవుడు** *bhavabhavudu*. n. One who exists (భవ) in the heart (భావ): i. e., Manmadha. **భావార్థము** *bhav-arthamu*. n. Implication, inuendo, a sense not expressed, an affirmative sense. The affirmative form of the verb. **భావ్యము** *bhavyamu*. adj. What must, will, or ought to be, కాదగినది. Likely, probable, befitting. ఆ యుంటకోటకి పోవడము నాకు

భావ్యమువాడు you must not have anything to do with that house. భావ్యుడు *bhāvyudu*. n. One on whom they meditate.

భావి *bhāvi*. [Skt.] adj. Future. Later, subsequent, భవిష్యత్తు.

భావించు *bhāvintsu*. [Skt.] v. n. To fancy, imagine, feel. ఎంచు, తలచు.

భావుకము *bhāvukamu*. [Skt.] n. Good fortune, luck. శుభము, భవితవ్యము, మంగళము.

భావుకుడు *bhāvukudu*. [Skt.] n. A sister's husband. బావమరది.

భాష *bhāsha*. [Skt.] n. A language, speech, dialect. A word, phrase, expression. మాట. A solemn undertaking, vow, engagement: what one gives his word for, an oath, ప్రతిజ్ఞ, ప్రమాణము. దేశభాష the vernacular of a country. భాషణము *bhāshanamu*. n. Speaking, speech. మాటాడుట. భాషాంతరము *bhāsh-āntaramu*. n. Another language: a translation. భాషాగ్రంథము *bhāsha-granthamu*. n. A poem in a modern or vernacular language, not in Sanskrit. భాషామంత్రము *bhāsha-mantramu*. n. A spell or charm, written in any *vernacular* language, not in Sanskrit. భాషించు *bhāshintsu*. v. n. To speak, use language, converse, talk, మాటాడు. భాషితము *bhāshitamu* n. Speech, language. మాట. adj. Spoken, మాటాడిన. భాష్యము *bhāshyamu*. n. A commentary, a paraphrase or exposition either of scripture or a work on science, సూత్రవ్యాఖ్యానగ్రంథము. భాష్యకారులు or భాష్యకార్లు *bhāshya-kārulu*. n. A commentator or expounder of technical texts; commonly applied as an epithet to two authors named పతంజలి, and ఎంబెరుమానారు. This last is one of the chief legislators of the Vaishnavite Brahmins. His disciples subsequently separated into the two Sects called Tengala and Vedagalu. భాష్యకార్లు is also vulgarly used for బాసికములు fillets worn at weddings.

భాసము *bhāsamu*. [Skt.] n. Light, brilliancy. భాసి *bhāsi*. adj. Bright, radiant. Pleased. "అప్పరమేశ్వరుఁడనియాడదగుదంచు నిరాసభాసిద్ధు." Vish. ii. 76. భాసిల్లు *bhāsillu*. v. n. To shine. ప్రకాశించు. భాసురము *bhāsuramu*. adj. Bright, shining. భాస్కరుడు *bhāskarudu*. n. A name of the sun or of fire, సూర్యుడు, అగ్నిహోత్రుడు. భాస్వంతము *bhāsvantamu*. adj. Luminous, bright. Solar, భాస్వంతుడు *bhāsvan-tudu*. n. The sun. భాస్వరము *bhāsva-ramu*. adj. Shining, radiant. n. Phosphorus. భాస్వరత *bhāsvarata*. n. Glory, splendour, ప్రకాశము. భాస్వరుడు *bhāsvarudu*. n. One who shines, ప్రకాశించువాడు; the sun, సూర్యుడు.

భి bhi

భిండివాలము or భిందిపాలము *bhindivālamu*. [Skt.] n. A slender arrow or dart, which is thrown from a tube, ఇనుప అలుగు కఱ్ఱపాఱ, హస్తప్రమాణమైన విడిచివాటుకఱ్ఱ.

భిక్ష or భిక్షము *bhiksha*. [Skt.] n. Alms. దీవ్యము. Hire, wages, కూలి. A boon, a great favour. దీన్ని భిక్షముగా అడుగుతున్నాను I entreat this as a boon or particular favour. పతిభిక్ష entreaty for the restoration of a husband. BD. iv. 1347. వాడు పెట్టినది భిక్షగానున్నది his pleasure is law, he is all powerful. భవతి భిక్షాందేహి give me an alms. భిక్షకుడు *bhikshakudu*. (corruption of భిక్షుకుడు). n. A beggar. భిక్షించు *bhikshintsu*. v. n. & a. To beg, take alms. "నరసింహభుజదర్పజన్నిదంబులకు, బరగభిక్షించిన బ్రాహ్మణుండనగను." BD. iv. 119.

భిక్షుకుడు *bhikshu-kuḍu*. n. A mendicant ascetic or monk. A beggar, mendicant, pauper. భిక్షువు *bhikshuvu*. n. A celibate, బ్రహ్మచారి. An ascetic or monk, సన్యాసి. "అచటివాలయజాతి హాలముఖాత్తి విభూతి నాదిభిక్షువు శైత్యమైనమాన్పు." Swa. i. 3. టీ॥ ఆదిభిక్షువు. మొదటి భిక్షుకుడైన శివునియొక్క, శైత్యమైన, భిక్షాన్నాహారము నైనప్పటికిని.

భిత్తము *bhittamu*. [Skt. from భిద్, ఛేద్, to cut, divide.] n. A bit, piece, fragment. "మిగులమెత్తనివలల్భిత్తంబులు." Swa. iv. 93. భిత్తి *bhitti*. n. Dividing, cutting. ఛేదనము. A wall. గోడ. భిత్తిక *bhittika*. n. A wall, గోడ. A thunderbolt, పిడుగు. భిదు *bhidu*. n. The act of tearing or rending. ఛేదనము, బద్దలుచేయడము. "భూభిదాపాదిదిక్పరాంభోధరంబునది." A. iv. 128. భిదురము *bhiduramu*. n. A thunderbolt, వజ్రాయుధము. M. XII. iv. 399. భిదువు *bhiduvu*. n. A thunderbolt. వజ్రాయుధము.

భిదేలిమము or భిదేళిమము *bhidē-limamu*. [Skt.] adj. Frangible, that may be broken.

"తెవిలెలాంతాలందామా సూచికకలిలా దాహాగ్నిది
కాలిరా,
ఘనలాలారుల్పలలా లునింకననలంలాగోపుర్తోత్సం
కత్సం,
గనిటంకంబుల లోకళింపెనపుడిల్లా వైద్యున
కుంబులి,
ట్లెవిగోపిలెలాలా భిదేళిమములయ్యెన్గండ పాషాణ
ముల్."

Parij iv. 101. R. vii. 163.

భిన్నము *bhinnamu*. [Skt. from భిద్, ఛేద్, to cut.] adj. Separated, divided. Broken, maimed (as a statue); distinct, separate. బొమ్మ భిన్నమైనది the image was broken. Blown, opened. Other, different. భిన్నగృహములు separate houses. భిన్ననామములు separate names. భిన్నముగా distinctly, separately. భిన్నోదరులు step-brothers, children by different mothers, as opposed to ఏకోదరులు or సోదరులు children by the same mother. భిన్ని *bhinni*. n. A wound. గాయము.

భిల్లుడు *bhilluḍu*. [Skt.] n. A highlander or 'Bheel,' a savage. చెంచువాడు, బోయవాడు. Kalahasti. iii. 60.

భిషక్కు *bhishakku*. [Skt.] n. A physician. వైద్యుడు, చికిత్సకుడు.

భిస్స *bhissa*. [Skt.] n. Food, boiled rice. అన్నము. భిస్సట *bhissaṭa* n. Burnt grains of rice, stickings, i. e , grain which sticks to the bottom of the kettle. మాడిన అన్నము, మాడు.

భీ bhī

భీ *bhī*. [Skt.] n. Fear, భయము. "అతులితాంతకభీతిభీమితచిత్తాంభోజ." Swa. v. 133. భీకరము *bhīkaramu*. adj. Fearful, frightful, horrid, భయంకరము. భీతము *bhītamu*. adj. Frightened. బెదిరిన. భీతి *bhīti*. n. Fear, alarm. వెరపు, వడకు. భీతిలు or భీతిల్లు *bhītilu*. v. n. To fear, be afraid, be frightened, భయపడు. భీమము *bhīmamu*. adj. Horrible, frightful. భీమాటవి a dreadful forest. భీమరాజు *bhīma-rāḍzu*. n. A song bird with a fine mellow voice *Lanius malabaricus*. Bucha. E. I. iii. 578. భీమసేనుడు or భీముడు *bhīma-sēnuḍu*. n. The name of a certain hero, the Indian Hercules. Also, a name of Siva. adj. Terrible, భయంకరుడు. దృగ్భీమ thou of terrific form. HK ii. 161. భీరువు *bhīruvu*. n. A timid woman. Swa. v. 52. భీరుకుడు or భీలుకుడు *bhīrukuḍu*. n. One who fears, a timid man. భయపడువాడు, పిరికి. భీషణము or భీష్మము *bhīshaṇamu*. n. Horror, dreadfulness. adj. Horrible, dreadful. భీష్ముడు *bhīsh-*

muḍu. n. A terrible man. భయంకరుడు. The name of a hero in the Mahábhárata.

భీష్మించు or భీష్మకరించు bhishmintsu. v. n. To declare or protest as Bhishma did in the affair of Satyavati.

భు bhu

భుంభుం bhumbhum. [Tel. anuk.] n. Bom! Bom! The sound of a conch or shell.

భుక్కనము bhukkanamu. [Skt.] n. The barking of a dog. మొరగడము.

భుక్తము bhuktamu. [Skt.] adj. Eaten, enjoyed, భుజింపబడిన, అనుభవింపబడిన. n. That which is enjoyed, possession. నాభుక్తములోనుండేచేను the field which is in my enjoyment. భుక్తి bhukti. n. Enjoyment, use, possession, అనుభవము. Eating, food, a meal, భోజనము. భుక్తిముక్తి happiness both temporal and eternal, lit: possession (of good) and freedom (from evil.) భుక్తిముక్తియీయనిచ్చు he will teach you to enjoy good and avoid evil. భుక్తిముక్తి దాయకుడు he who gives sustenance here and happiness hereafter.

భుగభుగ or బుగబుగ bhuga-bhuga. [Tel. anuk.] adv. Fragrantly, redolent, breathing forth, or rising, as a scent; sweetly. ఘుమఘుమ. భుగభుగలు bhuga-bhugalu. n. Fragrance. "మృగనాభితిలకంబు భుగభుగల్ గులుకొటము." Subhadra. ii. 84. టీ॥ పరిమళములు. భుగాలున bhugāluna. adv. Slapdash, suddenly. భుగులుకొను bhugu-lu-konu. v. n. To spread, as a smell. "పొలయుసెత్తావి భుగులుకోనలరుదీగె." A. ii. 85. టీ॥ ప్రకాశించుచున్న పరిమళము వ్యాపించగా. భుగులుపుచ్చు bhugulu-putstsu. v. n. To noise abroad, lab.

"పుట్టుమున్న దిమాకు భూపాలపుత్రి,
పుట్టినిముజ్జగంబగాని పరచెరటంచు,
భుగులుపుచ్చిరోమీరు పురలోనసనుము."

HD. p. 245.

భుగ్గురన bhuggu-r-ana. adv. Fragrantly. గుప్పున. "క్రొన్ననతావి భుగ్గురన క్రమ్మడిలరా." Charu Chandr. iv. 21.

భుగ్నము bhugnamu. [Skt.] adj. Curved, bent. వంగిన, వంచబడ్డ, వంకరైన. Broken, విరిగిన. "కృకవాటుల్ మెరసిరా గ్నువాటాపత్రి భంగిరా భుగ్నకంఠధ్వనిరా." Ewa. iii. 75.

భుజ bhuja. [Skt.] n. A hand, చేయి. A little cross denoting a caret. హంసపాదము. "వనాళభవుండనయవములు, తనరారసృజించిపొన భానమతిం, కర్ణాదికాకోక్కటి దబ్బరయని భుజయుమనిరి నా భి య ం గ న క ల రు గా." Paidim. iv. 163.

భుజపత్రము Same as భూర్జము (q. v.).

భుజము bhujamu. [Skt.] n. The shoulder, the arm. భుజంగభుక్కు bhujanga-bhukku. n. The snake-eater, i. e., a peacock, నెమలి. భుజగము, భుజంగము or భుజం గమము bhujagamu. n. A snake. పాము. భుజంగుడు bhujangudu. n. A libertine, a lover. భుజంగ పదజాడలు భుజంగ చరణసఖే the feet of a snake and the tricks of a lecher, are known to himself alone. "పరరాజుల భుజంగుబ్రహ్మినాయుడు" Pal. 291. Brahmi Náyak who hast dishonoured all his foemen. భుజకీర్తి bhuja-kirti. n. A certain ornament for the arm. బాహుపురి. భుజాంతరము the breast, chest, రొమ్ము. Balaram. v. 71. భుజశిరస్సు bhuja-sirassu. n. The shoulder, మూపు.

భుజించు or భుజియించు bhujintsu. [Skt.] v. a. To eat. తిను. To enjoy, అనుభవించు. భుజిష్య bhujishya. n. A handmaid, concubine, prostitute. పరిచారిక, వేశ్య. భుజిష్యుడు bhujishyuḍu. n. A servant. భృత్యుడు.

భువి bhuvi. [Skt. from భూ, the earth.] n. The earth. భూమి. భువనము bhuvanamu. n. The world, the universe, జగము. Water, ఉదకము. The sky, ఆకాశము. "భువనత్రయము." Ellanna. i. 254. భువ

శ్వరము bhuvan-ēṣvaramu. n. An ark or shrine wherein an idol is kept. A casket. "కలిమిచెలువంగలిమలసి యులసి కాంగనిద్రంగూరి తెలిగొలుప్రకటించిల్లటివి భువనేశ్వరంబుగా నచ్చటుంబలుకుచిలుకలకొలికిసంగడీడుమ." R. iii. 41. భువనేశ్వరి bhuvan-ēṣvari. n. An epithet of Lakshmi or Párvati.

భూ bhū

భూ bhū. [Skt.] adj. (In composition) Of the earth. భూకంపము bhū-kampamu. n. An earthquake. భూగతము bhū-gatamu. adj. Buried in the earth. భూచంపకము bhū-champakamu. n. A tree called *Kœmpferia rotunda*. Rox. i. 16. భూచక్రము bhū-chakramu. n. The earth, or terrestrial sphere. Also, a certain tree. "కంకేళు, తక్కలి, ములుకు, శేకి, భూచక్రము, ముక్కిప్ప కొక్కిస, మొల్లమ్రానుం." H. iv. 20. భూచక్రగడ్డ bhū-chakra-gaḍḍa. n. A large bulbous root, like truffles, dried and used in medicine. భూచ్ఛాయ bhū-ch-chāya. (From భూ and ఛాయ.) n. Darkness. చీకటి. భూజము bhūjamu. [lit: born (జ) of the earth (భూ).] n. A tree, వృక్షము. భూజాని bhū-jāni. n. A king. రాజు. భూతలము bhū-talamu. n. The earth, the globe. భూతిలకము bhū-tilakamu. n. A sort of silk. "మంచు, పూజంబు, మణిపట్టు, భూతిలకంబు, శ్రీవన్నియయు, మహాచీనిజీనియును." BD. iii. 99. భూతులసి bhū-tulasi. n. A species of the sacred Basil tree (తులసి) which keeps off insects from clothes. నేలతులసి. భూదారము bhū-dāramu. n. A hog. పంది. భూదేవి bhū-dēvi. n. Mother earth, regarded as a goddess. భూదేవుడు bhū-dēvuḍu. n. A god of this world, i. e., a Brahmin. భూధరము bhū-dharamu. n. A mountain, as being a prop or stay of the earth. పర్వతము. భూపతి, భూభుజుడు or భూపుడు bhūpati. n. A king, రాజు. రసభూపతి a certain quack medicine. H. i. 284. భూపతిరుద్రతిలకము bhū-pati-rudra-tilakamu. n. A particular sort of silk. ఒకవిధమైనపట్టు. BD. iii. 116. భూపాళము bhū-pāḷamu. n. The name of a certain tune. రాగవిశేషము. శివభూపాళము a variation of this tune. భూపురము bhū-puramu. n. A diagram used in magic. భూభృత్తు bhū-bhrittu. n. A king. రాజు. A mountain, కొండ. భూరుహము bhū-ruhamu. n. A tree. భూరూపకము bhū-rūpakamu. adj. Landed (property). భూవరుడు bhū-varuḍu. n. A noble person: a venerable man. A king, రాజు. భూసురుడు or భూసురోత్తముడు bhū-suruḍu. n. A lord of earth, i. e., a Brahmin. భూతృణము bhū-triṇamu. n. A fragrant kind of grass, *Andropogon schœnauthus*. W. చిప్పగడ్డి. భూస్థాపనము bhū-sthāpanamu. n. Burying, inhumation. భూస్వాస్థ్యము bhū-svāsthyamu. n. Landed property. See భూమి.

భూతము bhūtamu. [Skt.] n. A ghost, a demon, a powerless sprite supposed to haunt a cemetery, being the spirit of a bad man. పిశాచము. A living being. ప్రాణి. An essence, or element, పంచభూతములు the five elements, viz: Earth, fire, water, air and ether. "క్షోణిపానీయ తేజోవాయుగగనాఖ్యపంచభూతాంశసంబంధమైన, మేనిలోగర్జనాపాదేశ్రజిహ్వాక్షిగాత్రపంచేంద్రియములగోష్టి,శబ్దగంధాంగరసస్పర్శ సంజ్ఞికపంచవిషయముల బొలుపరచు." G. v. 13. Universal nature. భూతగుణములు elemental qualities. దయ్యమూకాదు భూతము it was not a fiend but a miserable ghost. adj. Past, elapsed. కడచిన, గతించిన. (In composition), Equal, సమానమైన. భూతఅద్దము bhūta-addamu. n. A magnifying glass. భూతకాలము bhūta-kālamu. n. The past tense in verbs. భూతకి bhūtaki. n. An ogress.

రాక్షసస్త్రీ. భూతచికిత్స *bhūta-chikitsa.* n. Remedies against witchcraft. భూతదయ *bhūta-daya.* n. Humanity, kindness. భూతధాత్రి *bhūta-dhatri.* n. The nurse of living beings, i. e., the earth, భూమి. భూతబలి sacrifice of a living animal. భూతనాథుడు *bhūta-nadhudu.* n. An epithet of Siva. భూతవైద్యుడు *bhūta-vaidyudu.* n. One who drives away spirits. భూతశుద్ధి *bhūta-suddhi.* n. Consecration of food at a sacrifice. భూతసంప్లవము *bhūta-samplavamu.* (from సంప్లవము the drowning of భూతములు living creatures.) n. The deluge. యుగాంతప్రళయము. భూతాత్మము *bhūt-ātmamu.* n. The body. దేహము. భూతాత్ముడు *bhūt-ātmudu.* n. Brahma. భూతాంకుశము *bhūt-ānkusamu.* n. A kind of tree, *Croton obliquifolium.* "భూతాంకుశమహీజ భూర్జపత్రమ్ములు." H. iv. 20. భూతావాసము *bhūta-vāsamu.* n. The tree called *Terminalia belerica,* Rox. ii. 431. కర్షఫలము, విభీతకము, or తాండ్రచెట్టు. This tree is said to be haunted, and it is shunned, even its leaves being considered unlucky. భూతుడు *bhūtudu.* n. He who became, he who is. (Used in composition) కృశీభూతుడైనవాడు a lean wretch. సహాయభూతులైనవారు allies. భూతేశుడు *bhūt-ēsudu.* n. The lord of demons, i. e., Siva.

భూతి *bhūti.* [Skt] n. Wealth, prosperity. అణిమాద్యైశ్వర్యము, సంపద. Superhuman power, an attribute of Siva. Ashes, భస్మము. భూతిగడ్డ a ball of white ashes.

భూమి *bhūmi.* [Skt.] n. The earth, land; place, site. Ground, soil. నేల, చోటు. భూమిజెముడు *bhūmi-jemudu.* n. A species of Euphorbia, *Euphorbia antiquorum,* Rox. ii. 468. భూమిజుడు *bhūmijudu.* n. Son of Earth, a title of the planet Mars. కుజుడు. అంగారకుడు. భూమిజ *bhūmi-ja.* n. Sita. సీత.

భూమిక *bhūmika.* [Skt.] n. A garb, costume, theatrical dress, trim. వేషము. A spot, place, situation, land. ప్రదేశము, స్థలము. "తానికట్టినభూమిక వాల్ప్రమాణ." A. vi. 169. "మృంగాంకమండలంబు సగముగ బలించిన రాహుగ్రహభూమికల చందంబునం దండదిరుగు బొల్లిమోరలభల్లూకంబులును." Parij. ii. 113.

భూయిష్ఠము *bhū-yishthamu.* [Skt.] adj. Much, పరిపూర్ణము, ఎక్కువ, అధికము, మిక్కుటము. భూయిష్ఠమర్దనము much rubbing.

భూరి *bhūri.* [Skt.] adj. Much, many. అధికము. n. Gold; బంగారు. భూరిమాయువు or భూరిమాయుడు *bhūri-ma-yuvu.* n. A jackal.

భూరుండి *bhūrundi.* [Skt.] n. A sort of sunflower, *Heliotropium indicum,* నరుకుచెట్టు.

భూర్జము *bhūrjamu.* [Skt. cf. Eng. 'birch.'] n. The Indian Birch Tree. The Indian Paper Birch. *Betula bhojpatra,* (Watts.) బహుత్వచి, భుజపత్రిచెట్టు.

భూష or భూషణము *bhūsha.* [Skt.] n. Ornament, embellishment. An ornament, a jewel. అలంకారము, తొడవు, సొమ్ములు. "ఒక్కయెడనిక్కపైనచో దానివాడితోన్ని జ్వాల భూషలాడ్చుకొని యానందంబుతో డగుపురింకేరగా." S. iii. 507. Flattery, praise. భూషించు *bhūshintsu.* v. a. To praise, laud. స్తుతించు. భూషితము *bhūshitamu.* adj. Adorned, decorated, dressed. భూషితుడు *bhūshitudu.* n. One who is adorned, అలంకరింపబడినవాడు.

భృ bhri

భృంగము *bhringamu.* [Skt.] n. The large black carpenter bee. తుమ్మెద. భృంగరాజము *bhringa-rājumu.* n. A male carpenter bee, గండుతుమ్మెద. The bird called *Dicrurus retifer.* కోకయములపోలిగాడు.

భృంగారము or **భృంగారుకము** *bhringāramu.* [Skt.] n. A golden vase or chalice. A gold vase placed at a royal gate. బంగారు గిండి. బంగకూజా. "బంగారుబొమ్మెరగను భృంగారుజలంబు." T. iii. 20. టీ॥ సాకస్సైబంగారపు బిందెలో పలిదముదకము చెంబులోపటి సంచియున్నగా. "భృంగారుకంబున కఃకధా జనవిక్షిప్తంబులను తుకేశముపేరలవజ్రి సలయుంబులంగడిగి." A. vi. 185. టీ॥ భృంగారుకంబున. బంగారుపు కూజాచేతను.

భృంగి *bhringi.* [Skt.] n. A three legged griphon like a seal or sea calf; a figure carved on temples of Siva, as representing one of his train: a figure with only a head and legs, or a human figure with three legs. **భృంగినాథుడు** *bhringi-nathudu.* n. An epithet of Siva.

భృగువు *bhriguvu.* [Skt.] n. A precipice, cliff. పర్వతతటము, కొండచరియ. A name of Sukra. శుక్రుడు. భృగువాసరము Friday. **భృగుపతనము** *bhrigu-patanamu.* n. A fall from a precipice. "కవిభలనాయకత్వం కర్తవ్యై భృగుపతనం బొనర్చెనవిందుబుతో బడినట్టిమాంబుధిగా." K. P. iv. 220.

భృతము *bhritamu.* [Skt.] adj. Carried, maintained. భరింపబడ్డది. Filled, నిండబడిన. Hired, paid. **భృతకుడు** *bhritakudu.* n. A hired servant. కూలివాడు. **భృతి** *bhriti.* n. Support, భరింపడము. Wages, hire, జీతము, కూలి. Price, వెల. **భృత్యుడు** *bhrityudu.* n. A servant, a slave. పనివాడుకుడు, పనివాడు, బంటు.

భృశము *bhrisamu.* [Skt.] adj. Much, great, extreme. adv. Exceedingly. అతిశయము.

భృష్టము *bhrishtamu.* [Skt.] adj. Fried. వేయించిన.

భే bhe

భేకము *bhēkamu.* [Skt.] n. A frog. A certain slender creeper. **భేకి** *bhēki.* n. A female frog. ఆడుకప్ప.

భేటి *bhēti.* [H.] n. An interview, a visit.

భేదము *bhēdamu.* [Skt.] n. Dividing, separating, tearing, rending, breaking. భేదనము. Distinction, difference, variation. భేదము. A sort, kind, species. Change, alteration, మార్పు. Disagreement, dissension. వైమనస్యము. R. vi. 8. **భేదనము** *bhēdanamu.* n. Dividing, separating, tearing, breaking, discriminating. భేదించుట. **భేది** or **బేది** *bhēdi.* n. That which breaks or penetrates. A purge, or purging. భేదమందు a purgative medicine. భేదకరమైన purgative. **భేదించు** *bhēdintsu.* v. n. To vary, differ, deviate. భేదిం. To split, చీలు. వారిమనసు భేదించినది they now differ in their opinions. v. a. To break, split, divide, separate, pierce. To penetrate a secret, resolve a riddle, explain, open. **భేదిలు** or **భేదిల్లు** *bhēdilu.* v. n. To be rent, as the heart. చీలు, బద్దలు. To become different, భేదిం. "భేదిల్లక స్త్రీంద్రమున." Kasikh. iv. 283. **భేదకుడు** *bhēdakudu.* n. One who cuts or divides. One who sows enmity among friends. భేదించువాడు. **భేదితము** *bhēditamu.* adj. Cut or divided, భేదింపబడిన. **భేద్యము** *bhēdyamu.* adj. That which can be cut or divided, భేదింపదగిన.

భేరి *bhēri.* [Skt.] n. A kettle drum. దుందుభి, నగారా. జయభేరులు వాయించినాడు he sounded the drums in triumph.

భేరుండము *bhērundamu.* [Skt.] n. A fabulous double headed eagle. పక్షివిశేషము. "శరభశార్దూలాది జరమృగావళులు, గండభేరుండపక్షులు." BD. iii. 2175. adj. Formidable, horrible. భయంకరమైన.

భేలుడు *bhēluḍu.* [Skt.] n. An ignorant man. మూర్ఖుడు, మూఢుడు. A timid man, పిరికి. An unsteady man, చలించువాడు.

భేషజము *bhēshajamu.* [Skt.] n. Medicine. మందు. Imposture, deceit. వంచన.

భేషక్కు, బేషక్కు, భేషు or **బేషు** *bhēshakku.* [Tel. anuk.] interj. Excellent! Capital!

భై bhai

భైక్షము *bhaikshamu.* [Skt. from భిక్ష.] n. Mendicity, begging. "అతిథిత్వము భైక్షమై నమాన్పు." Swa. i. 3. టీ॥ భైక్షమైన, భిక్షావ్యాపారమునైనప్పటికిని. బిచ్చమెత్తిన పదార్థము యొక్కగుంపు, భిక్షాసమూహము.

భైరవము *bhairavamu.* [Skt.] n. Frightfulness. భయానకరసము. Darkness, or swimming of the eyes. కన్నులకు భైరవముకమ్మినది a darkness came over my eyes, I was dazzled. adj. Terrible, frightful. **భైరవకత్తి** *bhairava-katti.* n. A large heavy two edged sword. "భైరవకత్తులు పట్టుకరాగా." Pal. 259. **భైరవి** or **భైరి** *bhairavi.* n. The Peregrine Falcon, *Falco peregrinus.* జుట్టుభైరవి the Crested Hawk Eagle. భూతభైరవి an epithet of the goddess Kāli or Durga who is the same as Isis or Venus. పార్వతి. A shrub called *Premna serratifolia.* Rox. iii. 77. **భైరవుడు** *bhairavuḍu.* n. A name of Siva, but more especially an inferior manifestation or form of the deity, eight of which, are called by the common name భైరవుడు, and are severally termed అసితాంగభైరవుడు, రురుభైరవుడు, చండభైరవుడు, క్రోధభైరవుడు, ఉన్మత్తభైరవుడు, కపిలభైరవుడు, భీషణభైరవుడు, సంహారభైరవుడు, ఆకాశభైరవుడు, (a form of Siva, corresponding to *Anubis* or *Osiris.*)

భైషజ్యము *bhaishajyamu.* [Skt. from భేషజము.] n. Medicine. ఔషధము.

భో bhō

భో *bhō.* [Skt.] n. A vocative particle. "Oh!" Fowls are called together by this cry.

భోంచేయు *bōn-chēyu.* [Tel. short for భోజనముచేయు.] v. n. To feed, eat, take a meal, dine.

భోక్త *bhōkta.* [Skt.] n. One who eats, భుజించువాడు. One who enjoys. అనుభవించువాడు. కర్తాభోక్తాజనార్దనః the creator and enjoyer is God, all things are created by God for his good pleasure. **భోక్తవ్యము** *bhōktavyamu.* adj. Fit to be eaten or enjoyed, తినదగిన, అనుభవింపదగిన.

భోగట్టా *bhōgaṭṭa.* [H.] n. An enquiry. విచారణ. భోగట్టాచేయు *bhōgaṭṭa-chēyu.* v. a. To inquire into, విచారించు.

భోగము *bhōgamu.* [Skt.] n. Enjoyment, possession, అనుభవము. Happiness, సుఖము. Food, భోజనము. A snake's body or crest. పాముశరీరము, జెక, పాముపడగ. అష్టభోగములు the eight kinds of enjoyment as Home గృహము, Bed శయ్య, Clothes వస్త్రము, Ornaments ఆభరణము, Woman's company స్త్రీ, Flowers పుష్పము, Scent గంధము and Betel తాంబూలము. ఏకభోగము undivided possession. ఏకభోగగ్రామము a village in the hands of one single person. పాలిభోగము separate possession. పాలిభోగగ్రామము a village whereof the land is the property of several persons, each of whom holds his land as a separate property and always retains the same fields. ఈ సంవత్సరము ఒక భోగము పండినది ఒక భోగము పోయినది one crop turned out well, one crop turned out ill. భోగగృహము *bhōga-*

grihamu. n. A bed room. పడకగది. భోగ బంద bhōga-banda. n. A mortgage in which the article pledged or mortgaged may be converted to use, as land, houses, cattle, &c., the profits of which are to be appropriated by the lender or mortgagee in lieu of interest. భోగమంటపము bhōga-mantapamu. n. An open hall or porch of a temple, in which festivals are celebrated. కళ్యాణమంటపము. భోగవతి bhōga-vati. n. The name of the Capital of the Nagas or serpents, పాతాళము. శేషసర్పపట్టణము. The name of the infernal Ganges. పాతాళగంగ. A fashionable lady, భోగముగలది. భోగస్త్రీ bhōga-stri. n. A kept woman, mistress or concubine, a prostitute. "విచిత్రవీర్యుని భోగస్త్రీయందు బిడ్డను నింబుట్టించె." Vish. vi. 425. భోగాశిపత్రి bhōgāsi-patri. n. A name of Garuḍa. "భోగాశిపత్రిరథస్యాక్షత్రము." Swa. v. 133. టీ॥ పన్నగాశనపత్రి, గరుత్మంతుడు. భోగి bhōgi. n. A happy man. భోగముగలవాడు. One who lives in splendour or luxury. అనుభవశాలియైనపురుషుడు. A serpent. పాము. The name given to the eves of some particular feasts. పండుగతొలినాడు. భోగించు bhōgintsu. v. a. To enjoy, అనుభవించు. To be happy, సుఖించు. భోగించుట bhōgintsuṭa. n. Enjoyment. Plu. భోగించుటలు. "మనమూనాడుమనోవినోదములు ప్రేమంబ్ మీరభోగించుటల్ వినుము." Radha. iii. 25. భోగిని bhōgini. n. A royal concubine. రాజు ఉంచిన భోగముది. An inferior wife of king. పట్టాభిషిక్తురాలుకాని రాజుభార్య. A female serpent. ఆడుపాము. భోగ్యత bhōgyata. n. Deliciousness, sweetness. దీనిభోగ్యత దీనికిలేదు nothing is more delicious than this. భోగ్యము bhōgyamu. n. Use, usufruct, enjoyment, or something given in pledge or on mortgage. భోగ్యపత్రము a mortgage bond, wherein the lender assumes the temporary use of the property mortgaged. adj. Enjoyable, fit to be enjoyed, delicious, agreeable as food. అనుభవింపదగిన. ఆ ప్ర, పాదము భోగ్యముగానుండలేదు that food was not agreeable. భోజనము bhōjanamu. n. Food, a repast or meal, ఆహారము. Eating, కుడుపు. భోజనముచేయు to eat, to dine. భోజనకస్తూరి small oranges pickled. భోజరాజు or భోజుడు bhōja-rāju. n. The name of a king celebrated by Sanskrit poets as a bountiful patron. భోజ్యము bhōjyamu. adj. Edible, fit to eat, eatable. భుజింపదగిన n. Food, ఆహారము.

భోటు bhōṭa. [Skt.] n. The name of a country, perhaps Bootan. "కర్ణాటమహారాటభోటసింధు, వంగ కాశ్మీర కళింగ బర్బరాంధ్ర." Balr. v. 22.

భోరున or భోరన bhōruna. [Tel.] adv. Much, grandly, greatly, heavily (as rain.) వాన భోరున కురిసినది it rained heavily. భోరున ఏడ్చినది she wept bitterly. భోరున వెడలెను he proceeded in great pomp. "భోరున కురిసె పుష్పవర్షములం." DRY. 2268. "మునుజే స్వారుతెల్లను భోరన దమయంతీస్వయంవరమునకు నెప్పం, జను దెంచెను." M. III. ii. 28. భోరుకొను bhōru-konu. v. n. To resound, sound aloud. "భేరీమొదలగునాద్యములల్ భోరుకొనగ." Ila. i. 104. టీ॥ మిక్కిలి ధ్వనిచేయుచుండగా.

భోషాణము bhōshāṇamu. [Tel.] n. A large wooden box.

భౌ bhau

భౌంక్రియ bhaun-kriya. [Skt.] n. The yelping of a dog. Vish. vii. 147.

భౌతికము bhautikamu. [Skt. from భూతము.] adj. Elementary, appertaining to the elements. పాంచభౌతికము composed of the five elements.

భౌముడు bhaumuḍu. [Skt. from భూమి.] n. Lit: Earthborn. A name of Mars. అంగారకుడు.

భౌరికుడు bhaurikuḍu. [Skt. from భూరి gold.] n. A treasurer, భాండాగారికుడు.

భ్ర bhra

భ్రంశము *bhramsamu.* [Skt.] n. Slipping, moving. Falling, declining from a height, or from propriety: falling from or off. జారుట, చలించుట.

భ్రమ or **భ్రమము** *bhrama.* [Skt.] n. Whirling round, gyration. గిరగిరతిరుగడము. Error or obliquity of judgment. Delusion, misapprehension. Misconception, illusion. Desire, wish, fondness, longing. భ్రాంతి, వానికి కొడుకును చూడవలెనని నిండా భ్రమగానున్నది he wishes very much to see his son. adj. Erroneous. తప్పైన. భ్రమపుమాటలు nonsense. **భ్రమణము** or **భ్రమి** *bhramaṇamu.* n. Whirling, turning, going round, wandering. **భ్రమపడు** *bhrama-paḍu.* v. n To err, be mistaken, be deluded. **భ్రమపరచు** *bhrama-paratsu.* v. a. To mislead, delude. **భ్రమప్రమాదము** *bhrama-pramādamu.* n. A blunder, oversight. **భ్రమగు**, **భ్రమియు** or **భ్రమియు** *bhramagu.* v. n. To err, be deceived. To be confused, perplexed. **భ్రమరము** *bhramaramu.* n. The large black carpenter bee, తుమ్మెద. The poets compare braids of black hair to clustering bees. A large kind of wasp. భ్రమరకీటన్యాయము like the caterpillars which the wasp places in its nest as food for its grubs; these are supposed to change into wasps; the similitude is used to point out the entire change produced in the mind of a pupil. **భ్రమరకము** *bhramarakamu.* n. Hair curled upon the forehead, నొసట చుట్టలుచుట్టలుగా జీరాడే ముంగురులు. A top. బొంగరము. **భ్రమరి** *bhramari.* n. A female bee. ఆడుతుమ్మెద. **భ్రమరించు** *bhramarintsu.* v. n. To circle round, భ్రమణముచేయు. **భ్రమించు** or **భ్రమియించు** *bhramintsu.* v. n. To turn round, to spin round. To be confused, misled, deluded, M. I. i. 157. భ్రమవడు, తిరుగు.

భ్రష్టము *bhrashṭamu.* [Skt.] adj. Fallen, lost, depraved, fallen from virtue. జారిన. **భ్రష్టు** or **భ్రష్టుడు** *bhrashṭu.* n. One who has fallen from. కులభ్రష్టుడు one who is excommunicated, an outcast. దేశభ్రష్టుడు one who has lost his kingdom, one who is driven from his country.

భ్రా bhrā

భ్రాంతము *bhrāntamu.* [Skt.] adj. Whirled, revolved; perplexed, deluded; blundering, mistaken. గిరగిరతిరుగబడ్డ, పొరపాటుబడ్డ, భ్రమచెందిన. భ్రాంతదృష్టి giddiness. **భ్రాంతి** *bhrānti.* n. Fancy, whim, error, delusion, whirling. భ్రమ, గిరగిరతిరుగడము, మిథ్యామతి, ఉన్నది లేనట్టును లేనిది ఉన్నట్టును తలచుట.

భ్రాజిల్లు *bhrājillu.* [Skt.] v. n. To shine. ప్రకాశించు. **భ్రాజితము** *bhrājitamu.* adj. Brilliant, shining. ప్రకాశించే. B. X. §. 38.

భ్రాత *bhrāta.* [Skt. Cognate with Eng. "Brother."] n. A brother. తోడబుట్టినవాడు. **భ్రాతృజుడు** or **భ్రాత్రీయుడు** *bhrātri-juḍu.* n. The son of a brother. తోడబుట్టినవానికొడుకు. **భ్రాతృస్నేహము** *bhrātri-snēhamu.* n. Brotherly love. **భ్రాతృవ్యుడు** *bhrātri-vyuḍu.* n. The son of a brother, తోడబుట్టినవానికొడుకు. An enemy, పగవాడు. **భ్రాత్రీయము** *bhrātrīyamu.* adj. Fraternal, appertaining to a brother. తోడబుట్టినవాని సంబంధమైన.

భ్రామరము *bhrāmaramu.* [Skt. from భ్రమరము.] n. Pure honey. భ్రమరములచేకూర్చిన తేనె. adj. Pertaining to bees, భ్రమర సంబంధమైన.

భ్రామిక *bhrāmika.* [Skt. from భ్రమ.] n. Wish, longing. కోరిక. ఆశ. "భ్రామికలేక నవోగ్రకోపభరాంబుజాగ్నికాంతులుబ్బగా దొరసి శరములొరి." H. ii. 129.

భ్రాష్ట్రము bhrāshṭramu. [Skt]. n. A frying-pan. మంగలము, వేపుడుచట్టి.

భ్రు bhru

భ్రుకుంసుడు bhrukumsuḍu. [Skt.] n. A man who puts on a woman's garb. A male actor or dancer in female apparel. స్త్రీవేషధారి, స్త్రీవేషముకట్టికొని ఆడేపురుషుడు, నాట్యపురుషుడు. "హారికోల్లసనవ్వవినలాస్యస్ఫుర్తి సుభ్రూ భ్రుకుంసలవాముల్సరిదీర్పుచ్చి." A. iv. 61. టీ: భ్రుకుంసల, నర్తకులయొక్క.

భ్రుకుటి, భృకుటి or భ్రూకుటి bhrukuṭi. [Skt.] n. A frown. కనుబొమ్మలుముడువడము, బొమముడి.

భ్రూ bhrū

భ్రూ bhrū. [Skt.] n. The eye-brow. కనుబొమ్మ. భ్రూభంగము or భ్రూవిక్షేపము moving the eyebrows as in winking. బొమముడి. "వరికోపమలుల కన్నుసన్నలను భ్రూభంగంబులంగా నర్తముల్." T. iv. 13. టీ: భ్రూభంగంబులంగా, కనుబొమ్మసన్నలను. భ్రూకుటి Same as భ్రుకుటి. (q. v.)

భ్రూణము bhrūṇamu. [Skt.] n. An embryo, fœtus: a child. అర్భకుడు, కడుపులోబిడ్డ, మూలం, గర్భము, బిడ్డ.

భ్రే bhrē

భ్రేషము bhrēshamu. [Skt.] n. Dereliction of duty. తనకు ఉచితమైన ధర్మమునుండి చలించుట.

మ ma

మ ma. The letter M. It stands, like the English letter M for the hieroglyphic sign representing the horns of an owl. (See Taylor.) This letter when an initial is sometimes dropped in poetry. Thus ఏను is written for మేను Sometimes it is inserted to prevent elision as in ఉన్నమనుచు, నినమనము.

మంకు manku. [Tel.] adj. Vile, abominable; stubborn; dull, stupid. మొండి, గడుసు. n. A fool, a stubborn man, a wretch, a jade. దుర్జనుడు, దుష్టస్త్రీ. మూర్ఖుడు, మూర్ఖురాలు. మంకుతనము manku-tanamu. n. Stupidity, brutishness, stubbornness. చండితనము.

మంకెన mankena. [Tel.] n. A hamper, pannier. ఎద్దుమీద నిర్లడింటిలు తెచ్చుటకు కెత్తముతోకట్టినది. A certain tree, Pentapetes phœnicea. జపా, బంధూకము, వాసానిచెట్టు.

మంగ or మ్రంగ manga. [Tel.] n. The tree called Vangueria spinosa, or Randia dumetorum. పిండీతకము, మంగాచెట్టు.

మంగల mangala. [Tel.] n. The barber caste. మంగలకత్తి mangala-katti. n. A razor, క్షురము. మంగలకత్తిరూపు the constellation called కృత్తికానక్షత్రము. మంగలపక్కె mangala-pakke. n. A kind of fish. మంగలపిట్ట or మంగలకత్తిపిట్ట mangala-piṭṭa. n. The bird called a Palm Swift, Tachornis batassiensis (F. B. I.) Also, applied to some species of Martins. మంగలి, మంగలవాడు or మంగి mangali. n. A barber. నాపితుడు. మంగలికొల్లు mangali-kollu. n. plu. The clarionet used by the barbers, సన్నాయి. మంగలిపని mangali-pani. n. Shaving, క్షౌరము.

మంగలము mangalamu. [Tel.] n. A pipkin. An earthen vessel to roast grain in, అంబరీషము, భ్రాష్ట్రము, వేపుడుచట్టి.

మంగళము mangaḷamu. [Skt.] n. Happiness, good fortune, well-being, welfare, prosperity. శుభము, క్షేమము. The lines at the opening of a poem in praise of some deity adj. Happy, lucky, fortunate, auspicious, prosperous, faring well. శుభమైన. నీకు మంగళముగాక blessings upon thee. **మంగళదేవత** *mangala-dēvata.* n. Lakshmi. **మంగళవారము** *mangala-vāramu.* n. Tuesday. అంగారకవారము. **మంగళసూత్రము** *mangala-sūtramu.* n. The cord or necklace with which the తాళిబొట్టు or token of marriage is fastened on the neck of the bride. బొట్టుదారము. **మంగళహారతి** or **మంగళారతి** *mangala-hārati.* (మంగళ+ఆరతి.) n. A lamp used for waving before an idol, శుభకరమైన ఆరతి. Also, the closing verse of a play, the denouement. మంగళాష్టకము a particular kind of song. **మంగళశాసనము** *mangala-śāsanamu.* n. A benediction, ఆశీర్వాదము. **మంగళుడు** *mangaḷuḍu.* n. A name of Angāraka, who corresponds to Mars, అంగారకుడు. **మంగల్యము** *mangalyamu.* n. The peepul tree. రావిచెట్టు, జెమ్మిచెట్టు.

మంగు or **మంగుడు** *mangu.* [Tel.] n. Crow's feet, marks of age in the face. ముఖముందలి నల్లనిపొడ, మొటిమలు.

మంచము *manchamu.* [Skt. borrowed from Drav.] n. A couch, cot, bedstead. మంచెము. A scaffolding, మంచె.

మంచి *manchi.* [Tel.] n. Good, మేలు. మంచిచెబ్బరలు good and evil. adj. Good, excellent, best; sound, fine, fair; much, great, severe (as a blow, a fever), heavy (as rain.) adv. Very, మిక్కిలి. వాడు మంచివాడు he is a good man. మంచివారితో చెలిమిచేయుము seek the company of good men. మంచిపేరు a good name, i. e., reputation, character. వాడు మంచిపేరెత్తినాడు he gained good repute మంచినీళ్లు good or drinkable water. వానితో మంచిమాటలాడి ఆ పుస్తకమును తెచ్చితి. I spoke him fair, and brought the book. దీనితొక్క మంచి చెడుగులు వానికి నిమిత్తములేదు, లేక, దీని మంచి చెడ్డలతో వానికి ప్రసక్తిలేదు he has nothing to do with its good or evil fortune. మంచిగంధము sandal, శ్రీచందనము. మంచిగాయము a severe wound. మంచిచేయి the right hand. మంచిదెబ్బ a sound or severe blow. మంచినిద్ర sound sleep. మంచినూనె sesamum oil. మంచిపాము a venomous snake, i. e., the cobra. మంచిపగడము real coral. మంచిపాలు pure milk, i. e., unmixed with water. మంచిముత్యము a true pearl. మంచివాన heavy rain. ఇది మంచిబంగారా, కాకిబంగారా is this real gold or tinsel? ఒకటి మంచికుక్క ఒకటి వెఱ్ఱికుక్క one dog is sound, the other is mad. వానిమీద మంచితిత్తు మోపినారు they have brought a serious charge against him. మంచిది పో well, you may go! మంచిది కానీ well, be it so! **మంచితనము** *manchi-tanamu.* n. Goodness, friendliness, gentleness. వానిని మంచితనముచేసికొన్నారు they spoke him fair or got him over. మంచితనాన అయ్యేది చెడుతనాన కాదు you may do that by fair means, which you cannot do by violence.

మంచె or **మంచియ** *manche.* [Tel.] n. A shelf, stand, or platform. A shed or scaffolding erected on posts for persons who watch crops. అరప, తెప్పరము వంటి పందిరి.

మంచెము [Tel.] n. A cot. See మంచము.

మంచు *mantsu.* [Tel.] n. Dew, fog, mist. Snow. హిమము. మంచుగడ్డ ice. మంచుకురుస్తున్నది dew is falling. మంచుపుంజము a sort of cloth. BD. iii. 98. **మంచుకొండ** or **మంచుగుబ్బలి** *mantsu-konda.* n. The Himalaya Mts. మంచుతెర the dewy season, హేమంతఋతువు.

మంచు or **మనుచు** *mantsu.* [Tel. from మను v.] v. a. To preserve, maintain, nourish, or cherish. పోషించు.

మంజరి *manjari.* [Skt.] n. A tender branch of a tree with sprouted leaves, చిగిరించిన

తీగొమ్మ. A posy, bunch of flowers or leaves, nosegay. పూగుత్తి, చిగురుగుత్తి. (Used of a collection of proverbs or poems, as నీతిమంజరి.) A large pearl, పెద్దముత్తెము.

మంజిడి or **మంజిడి** *manjidi*. [Tel.] n. A kind of horse's pace, అశ్వగమనభేదము. A parti-colored cloth, చిత్రవర్ణవస్త్రము. A blue cloth, నీలవస్త్రము. "మంజిష్ఠపరిపాటి మరిగినవటన, రంజిల్లుచున్న సాంధ్యరాగ తేజము." Navan. D. p. 310.

మంజిమ or **మంజిమము** *manjima*. [Skt.] n. Beauty, elegance. సౌందర్యము.

మంజిష్ఠ *manjishta*. [Skt.] n. Madder, a plant used in medicine and in dyeing, *Rubia cordifolia*. A very brilliant red colour. మంజిష్ఠచీర a red petticoat. మంజిష్ఠపటరమ్య పీఠావళి a crimson cushion. మంజిటి (from మంజిష్ఠ.) Same as మంజిష్ఠ.

మంజీరము *manjiramu*. [Skt.] n. A ring and bells worn round the ankle or toe; an anklet, అందె, నూపురము.

మంజులము *manjulamu*. [Skt.] adj. Sweet, delicious, pleasing. Pretty, మనోజ్ఞమైన. **మంజువు** *manjuvu*. adj. Beautiful, pleasing, agreeable. మనోజ్ఞమైన. మంజుభాషిణి or మంజువాణి a sweet voiced girl. మంచిమాటలాడేస్త్రీ.

మంజూరు *manjūru*. [H.] n. Approval, sanction. మంజూరుచేయు to approve, admit, sanction.

మంజూష *manjūsha*. [Skt.] n. A large basket or box. పెద్దపెట్టె. **మంజోస** or **మండసము** *mandasa*. [from మంజూష.] n. A box or ark.

> "సూతుడదియుగుబెంచి మాలిరక్ష,
> పుంజభరితమైన మంజసలోనున్న,
> గొడుకుబానితోనగొనుచువచ్చి."
>
> M. I. v. 36.

మంజాడి or **మంజాలి** *mandsadi*. [Tel.] n. A certain weight (in diamonds,) a carat. వజ్రములదిమ్మ, రత్నములతూనిక.

మంట *manta*. [Tel. from మండు.] n. A blaze, flame, burning. A hot or burning sensation. జ్వాల. Heat, acute pain, inflammation. మరుమ్మనుపేగొను. Fury, wrath, కోపము. దానిని చూస్తే నాకు మంటవస్తున్నది I am provoked at seeing it. కడుపుమంట envy. కడుపుమంట తీర తిట్టినాడు he cursed till his rage was exhausted. కడుపుమంటమాటలు ఎందుకు వింటావు why do you listen to envious language? **మంటతేమురు** or **మంటనూనె** *manta-temuru*. n. Burning oil. మంటనెయ్యి hot ghee. మంటమారి or మంటబుమారి a peevish or pestilent fellow, కోపిష్ఠుడు; an envious man, ఓర్వలేనివాడు.

మంటకము *mantakamu*. [Skt.] n. A biscuit, a sort of wheaten cake without sugar. పంచదారలేనటువంటి గోధుమరొట్టె.

మంటపము Same as మండపము (q. v.).

మంటి *manti*. [Tel.] n. Genitive of మన్ను earth. **మంటినూనె** *manti-nūne*. n. Earth oil.

మంటి or **మంటిని** *manti*. [Tel. from మను to live.] I lived, బ్రతికితిని, జీవించితిని. "నిన్నుగంటిమంటిగనకర్చుమై" Parij. iii. 27. I am alive again.

మండ *manda*. [Tel.] n. A twig with leaves on it. చిగురుకొమ్మ. A small branch, తరుశాఖ, the back of the hand. మీదిచెయ్యి. A frying brush, తిరగమోతకుచ్చు. An ankle, చీలమండ.

మండనము *mandanamu*. [Skt.] n. Adorning, dressing, decorating, decoration. An ornament, jewel, భూషణము, అలంకారము. **మండనుడు** *mandanudu*. n. One who is dressed or ornamented. "ఏకాంతభక్తి మహిత మండనుడు" he who is adorned with faith. BD. v. 1.

మండపము *manḍapamu.* [Skt.] n. A porch, a portico, స్తంభములమీద కట్టిన కట్టడము. A bower, pavilion, చావడి, సభాభేదము. నాలుగు కాళ్లమండపము a four pillared portico. ముఖమండపము a porch of a temple. మండపి or గర్భమండపి *manḍapi.* n. A shrine, a sanctuary. గర్భగృహము. A small portico, చిన్నమండపము. "గర్భమండపి నడిగిన కలశజలము." A. vi. 7.

మండము or మండాము *manḍamu.* [Skt.] n. Scum, skimming, froth, foam, barm, సర్వౌషధద్రవ్యసారము, మీగడ, సారము. An ornament, భూషణము. మండకంచము *manḍa-kantsamu.* n. A platter that has a rim like a soup plate. అంచుకట్టిన కంచము. అంచుకంచము a platter that has no rim. మండగంజి *manḍa-ganji.* n. Gruel strained clear of rice. మెరుకులులేని గంజి. మండహారకుడు *manḍa-hārakuḍu.* n. A distiller. కల్లువాడు, కల్లివాడు.

మండలము *manḍalamu.* [Skt.] n. The disc (of the sun, moon and stars.) సూర్యచంద్రాదులబింబము. An orb, బింబము. A circumference in general; or the circle which bounds the view, the sensible horizon. A halo, పరివేషము. A province, district, country or empire; a region, place. దేశము. ముఖమండలము the face. A heap, a quantity. A multitude, an assembly. సమూహము. A division of the Rig-Veda. The period of forty days. మండలార్ధము twenty days. ఈ ఔషధము ఒకమండలము దినములు పుచ్చుకో వలసినది, లేక, సేవించవలెను you should take this medicine for forty days. Standing with the legs apart, as an archer sometimes does. ధన్వివిశేషస్థానస్థితిభేదము. Leprosy, కుష్ఠము. మండలాగ్రము *manḍal-agramu.* n. A sword, a scimitar, కత్తి. మండలి *manḍali.* n. Society, an assembly, సమూహము. A dog, కుక్క. A cat, పిల్లి. A serpent, పాము. మండలేశ్వరుడు *manḍal-ēśvaruḍu.* n. An independent sovereign, a monarch. చక్రవర్తికి లోబడని భూపాలకుడు, గ్రామాధిపతి, ద్రువదాడ్.

మండాడు *manḍ-āḍu.* [Tel.] v. a. To beg, beseech, pray. బతిమాలుకొను. గోజాడు, దైన్యముతో యాచించు. "ద్విజ ఆవేశిభయకంపితాత్ముడైవాడు. చండికి నీశ్వరేశ్వరయనకుమారికి. మండాడలోయన మరియుండుతిరిగె." చండి: ప్ర. i. మండాటము *manḍ-āṭamu.* n. The act of begging with great humility. దైన్యముతో యాచించుట.

మండి or మండీ *manḍi.* [Tel.] n. Kneeling down with one leg, an attitude in archery, ఒకకాలితో నేలమీద మోకరించుట, ఆలీఢపాదము. [H.] n. A wholesale shop, ధాన్య సరుకుల అమ్మేచోటు. మండీలు *manḍīlu.* n. A sort of sweet cakes. మండిగంద్రలు *manḍi-gandralu.* n. A sort of grain. "మండిగంద్రలు, నాగమల్లెలు, తిలమల్లెలు." H. iv. 155.

మండిగము *manḍigamu.* [Tel.] n. A threshold. గడప.

మండిగె or మండెగ *manḍige.* [Tel.] n. A very thin cake made of fine flour, milk, sugar, &c. భక్ష్యవిశేషము. "కుడుములగారెలుబెల్లపుమండిగెలు."

మండితము *manḍitamu.* [Skt.] adj. Dressed, decorated, decked. అలంకరింపబడ్డ. మండితుడు *manḍituḍu.* n. One who is dressed, arrayed, or decorated. అలంకరింపబడినవాడు.

మండిలూటి *manḍilūṭi.* [Tel.] n. An abscess. లోపలనే అణిగియుండు వ్రణము.

మండు *manḍu.* [Tel.] v. n. To burn, blaze, flame. జ్వలించు. To smart, or give acute pain. చురుక్కుమని నొప్పిపెట్టు. To be in a fury or violent rage. కోపము మొదలగు వానిచేత తపించు. నా కండ్లు మండుచున్నవి my eyes are smarting or burning. అయ్యో నా కడుపు మండుచున్నదే alas! I am much grieved. ఈమాట వింటే వానికి ఒళ్లు మండవా

if he hears of this, will he not be in a fury? **మండునెల** *mandu-nela.* n. A hot month, the hot weather, ఎండకాలము. **మండించు** *mandintsu.* v. n. To provoke, irritate, stir up.

మండువా *manduva.* [Tel.] n. A courtyard. A booth. A stable for horses, గుర్రపుశాల, గుర్రపుసాల. హ్రా. i.

మండూకము or **మండుకము** *mandūkamu.* [Skt.] n. A frog. కప్ప. **మండూకపర్ణము** *mandūka-parṇamu.* n. A plant. *Bignonia indica.* దుండిగపుచెట్టు. **మండూకపర్ణి** *mandūka-parṇi.* n. The madder plant, మంజిష్ఠ. **మండూకి** *mandūki.* n. A female, or small frog. ఆడుకప్ప, చిరుకప్ప.

మండూరము *mandūramu.* [Skt.] n. The rust of iron, or refuse of melted iron, used as a medicine. ఇనుపచిట్టెము, ఇనుపచిట్టెముతో చేసిన సిందూరము.

మండె or **మండెము** *mande* [Tel.] A stock or heap of the unthrashed ears of the great millet, or of cut tobacco. జొన్నకుచ్చెలను దించి కంకిలోని ప్రోగుచేసిన ఆకుకోసిన పొగాకుకుప్ప.

మండోదరి *mand-ōdari.* n. Ravana's first wife. A prudent woman, బుద్ధిమంతురాలు.

మండ్ర *mandra.* [Tel.] n. A kind of thorny tree. H. iv 10.

మండ్రగబ్బ *mandra-gabba.* [Tel.] n. A large black scorpion. పుట్టతేలు, నల్లనిపెద్దతేలు.

మండ్రాడు *mandr-ādu.* [Tel.] v. n. To be grieved, సంతాపించు. **మండ్రాటము** *mandr-āṭamu.* n. Grief, సంతాపము. ఉ. హరి. ii.

మండ్రె *mandre.* [Tel. for మనుదురా.] v. inter. Will they live! జీవింతురా. "భూపతిలేకున్న మండ్రె." M. XII. ii. 273.

మంతి *mantu.* [Skt.] n. One who considers, a thinker. ఆలోచించువాడు. **మంతనము** *mantanamu.* n. Secrecy, a secret place, a place of concealment, రహస్యము, ఏకాంతస్థలము. ఏకాంతము. A secret consultation, secret advice, రహస్యాలోచన. "కలసియుండి కొంతసేపు శృంగారాలాపములు. నాగిండసమాయిచుక మంతనంబులాడిచని విద్యాంగులిద్దఱు." A. iv. 8. **మంతరసాని** Same as మంత్రసాని (q. v.) **మంతిరి** Same as మంత్రి. (q. v.) **మంతిరించు** Same as మంత్రించు (q. v.). **మంతవ్యుడు** *mantavyuḍu.* n. One who is fit to be consulted with, ఆలోచింపదగినవాడు.

మంతు *mantu.* [Tel.] n. Greatness, glory, nobility. ఘనత. ప్రసిద్ధి. "వెలగలమగరా, సంతసలమంతుకెక్కిన. దంతపువనిచవికెలోన." Ila. i. 113. [From Skt.] n. A minister, మంత్రి. The Queen in chess. Also, same as మంత్రము (q. v.).

మంతువు *mantuvu.* [Skt.] n. A fault, offence, transgression, అపరాధము. Understanding, intellect. బుద్ధి. తెలివి.

మంతుడు *mantuḍu.* [Skt.] An affix, denoting One who has. బుద్ధిమంతుడు one who is wise.

మంత్రము *mantramu.* [Skt.] n. A sacred text or hymn. A verse sacred to some deity, used as a prayer. A spell, a charm, incantation. జాలవిద్య. Secret consultation, secret counsel. రహస్యము, గూఢోక్తి. రహస్యపుమాట. Help in a woman's confinement, ప్రసవోపాయము. మంత్రపుష్పము consecrated flowers. మంత్రాక్షతలు blessed rice, i. e., rice over which incantations have been pronounced. నీదివ్యనామమంత్రముచేత by the force of thy blessed name. **మంత్రణ** or **మంత్రణము** *mantraṇa.* n. A secret consultation, రహస్యాలోచన. **మంత్రకాడు** or **మంత్రవాది** *mantra-kāḍu.* n. A magician, conjurer. మాంత్రికుడు. ఇంద్రజాలవిద్యనెరిగినవాడు. **మంత్రసాని** or **మంతరసాని** *mantra-sāni.* n. A midwife, **మంత్రసానితనము** *mantra-sāni-tanamu.* n. Midwifery. మంత్రసానికి ఒజ్జబొంతగలవా

can you conceal the truth from your midwife? **మంత్రాంగము** *mantr-āngamu*. n. Machination, trickery. తంత్రము. **మంత్రి** *mantri*. n. A minister, a counsellor, or adviser, బుద్ధిసహాయుడు. The queen at chess. **మంత్రించు** or **మంతిరించు** *mantrintsu*. v. n. To charm, or perform magic spells over. మంత్రముచేయు.

మంథము. మంథానము or **మంథరము** *manthamu*. [Skt.] n. A churning staff, కవ్వము. **మంథము** n. An emulsion of medicine in fine powder with four parts of cold water. ఒకమూతుడులో 4 పలములనీటితో నొకముపాలని అందొక పల్లమానము ఔషధ ద్రవ్యములను చేక్కి దంచిప్రైది చిలికి వడియకట్టు: శా. శార్ఙ్గధరసంహిత, p. 151. **మంథనము** *manthanamu*. n. Churning, త్రచ్చుట. **మంథని** *manthani*. n. A churn. మజ్జిగచిలికే కుండ, తరికడవ, గర్గరి. **మంథరజ్జువు** *mantha-rajjuvu*. n. A churning rope, తరిత్రాడు. **మంథాద్రి, మంథాచలము, మంథశైలము** or **మందరగిరి** *manth-adri*. n. The name of a mountain which served as a churning rod for the Ambrosia. కవ్వపుగొండ.

మంథర *manthara*. [Skt.] n. The name of a female slave of Kaikeyi. A scheming woman. తాంత్రికురాలు.

మంద *manda*. [Tel.] n. A flock or herd of cattle. పశుసమూహము. A place where the flocks or herds are kept outside a village, ఊరిబయట పశువులుండుచోటు. A hamlet, inhabited by herdsmen, గొల్లపల్లె. కుక్కల మంద a pack of dogs. మందకట్టు or మందకట్టుబాటు the bye-laws of shepherds. గొల్లలు ఏర్పరచుకొన్న ఏర్పాటు. ఆ చేలకు మందకట్టిరి they manured the field by penning sheep or goats on it. **మందగొను** *manda-gonu*. v. n. To come together in a crowd, మందగాకూడు. **మందపిచ్చిక** *manda-pichchika*. n. The name of a little white breasted bird with a black-head. పసుపుపిచ్చిక a species with a yellow breast. **మందప్రొయ్యాలు** *manda-proyālu*. n. A shepherdess, గొల్లది.

మందట *mandaṭa*. [Tel.] n. Nearness, సమీపము. Weakness, బలహీనత. adv. Near, along with, at, before.

మందటిల్లు or **మందటిలు** *mandaṭillu*. [Tel. from మందము.] v. n. To subside, to grow weak, అడగు.

మందడి *mandaḍi*. [Tel.] n. A stable, గుర్రపుశాల. మందడిగోడ a partition wall. **మందడీడు** *mandaḍ-īḍu*. n. A groom, a horse-keeper గుర్రపువాడు.

"తే॥ లాయములనున్న,
యపుడుదౌసగించుకరయు లేనియట్లుగాగ,
మాటిమాటికిబరికించి మందడీల.
కల్లమారటయగుచున్నల్ల నేర్తు."
M. IV. i. 89.

మందము *mandamu*. [Skt.] adj. Slow, tardy, dull, stupid, heavy, foolish; gentle, soft, not violent, మెల్లని. మందమారుతము a gentle breeze. మందగమనము a gentle pace. మందబుద్ధి dull intellect. మందమతి a block-head. మందస్వరము a low tone. మందాహారము generous diet. n. Thickness, slowness, indigestion, loss of appetite. మాంద్యము, దళము. వానికి కడుపులో మందముగానున్నది he suffers from indigestion. **మందగామి** *manda-gāmi*. n. One who walks slow, మెల్లగానడచువాడు. **మందగమన** or **మందగామిని** *manda-gamana*. n. The 'gentle mover,' an epithet of a graceful woman. **మందగించు** *manda-gintsu*. v. n. To become dull, to lose one's appetite. To fall, as price. మందమగు. ఇప్పుడు ధర మందగించినది the market is now dull, ధరతగ్గినది. **మందస్మితము** or **మందహాసము** *manda-smitamu*. n. A smile, a gentle laugh, చిరునవ్వు. **మందాగ్ని** *mandagni* n. A slow fire. Want of appetite.

(hunger being considered as fire.) అగ్నిమాంద్యము. మందాక్షము mand-ākshamu. n. Modesty, bashfulness, shame. సిగ్గు,లజ్జ. మందోష్ణము mand-ōshnamu. n. Slight warmth, lukewarmness, gentle heat. నులివెచ్చన, ఇంచుకవేడి. adj. Warm, tepid, lukewarm. నులివెచ్చని, గోరువెచ్చని.

మందరము *mandaramu.* [Skt.] n. The mountain Mandara, the Indian Olympus. The gods are said to have churned the ocean with it and it now lies at the foot of Mount Meru. మందరధరుడు (A. v. 172.) an epithet of Vishnu.

మందల *mandala.* [Tel.] n. A limit, boundary, extent. మేర. Manner, విధము. Life, జీవము. The act of living, మనుగడ. Nearness, సమీపము.

మందలించు *manda-lintsu.* [Tel.] v. a. To tell, చెప్పు. To suggest, warn, allege, mention, remonstrate. ఎచ్చరించు, మనవి చేయు. To command, order, ఆజ్ఞాపించు. To think, తలచు. To pacify. "తే॥ ఇంత యలుకకు కారణంబిదియటంచు, మందలింపుచు నాయానమందయాన." Ila. iv. 65. **మందలింపు** *mandalimpu.* n. Business. వ్యవహారము. A suggestion, remonstrance.

మందస or **మందసము** *mandasa.* [from Skt.] n. A chest, a large bin, an ark or great box. పెట్టె.

మందాకిని *mandākini.* [Skt.] n. The Ganges of heaven. A woman sixty years old. "అమందాకిని మాళిబూని." Vasu. Intro. vi.

మందారము *mandāramu.* [Skt.] n. One of the five celestial trees, ఒక కల్పవృక్షము. The Gigantic Swallowwort, or Coral tree, *Callotropis gigantea.* జిల్లేడుచెట్టు. దీనజనమందారుడు he who is to the wretched a tree of life.

మందారము *mandāramu.* [Tel.] n. Cloudy or gloomy weather. మేఘావృతమైనము, మబ్బుకేసినదియైనదినము. ఇప్పుడు మబ్బుమందారముగా నున్నది the weather is now gloomy.

మంది *mandi.* [Tel.] n. People, జనసమూహము. A retinue, పరిజనము. Infantry, కాలుబలము. అయిదుమంది five persons. కొంతమంది a few persons. సగముమంది half the people. ఎంతమంది how many persons? పదిపదిహేనుమంది ten or fifteen persons.

మందిరము *mandiramu.* [Skt.] n. A house, గృహము. A town. పట్టణము. A temple, దేవాలయము. రామమందిరము Rama's temple.

మందు *mandu.* [Tel. cf. Tam. మరందు.] n. Medicine, physic, a drug. ఔషధము. A love powder, వశ్యౌషధము. An antidote, ప్రతిక్రియ. An expedient, ఉపాయము. దీనికొక మందుచెప్పెదను I will tell you a device for this. Poison, విషము. Gunpowder, తుపాకిమందు. A rarity, a scarce thing. ఇంట్లో బియ్యము మందుకైనా లేవు there is no rice to be had for love or money. మంచివానికి మాట్లాడని దేమందు if you are silent towards a good man it is a punishment to him. నీలిమందు indigo. నల్లమందు opium. మందుభాయీ or నల్లమందుభాయీ an opium eater. వలపుమందు or పెట్టుమందు love powder. మందుగాటుక eye salve. మందుపెట్టు to drug, to infatuate a person by administering to him or her a love powder, to poison. మనోవ్యాధికి మందులేదు there is no cure for the heart-ache. దానిమందు వానితలకెక్కినది the love powder administered by her has turned his head. adj. Impossible, దుర్లభము. "కూడుదానగల్గదేని కూరకుటమందు." Amu. iv. **మందుపట్టెడ** *mandu-pattada.* n. A place where fireworks are prepared, బాణసంచుచేసెడుశాల. **మందుమల** *mandu-mala.* n. A hill on which drugs are found, an epithet applied to a hill called ద్రోణము. **మందులమారి** *mandula-māri.* n. One who administers love powders. మందాకు *mand-āku*. n. A medicinal herb, ఓషధి. "కోటబంగారుగా జేయుకొరకుమున్ను, బ్రహ్మపిడిచిన మందాకు పసర వంక." A. ii. 8. మందులవాడు *mandula-vāḍu*. n. A druggist.

మందుడు *manduḍu*. [Skt.] n. A blockhead, a fool. మూఢుడు.

మందుర *mandura*. [Skt.] n. A stable. వాజిశాల, లాయము. మందురకుడు *mandura-kuḍu*. n. A horsekeeper. హయపాలుడు. గుర్రపువాడు.

మందెమేలము *mande-mēlamu*. [Tel.] n. Over-familiarity leading to insolence, meddling, impertinence. మించినచనువు, అధికప్రసంగము, అధికప్రసంగము. Disregard, carelessness, ఉపేక్ష. "నాసికచ్చత్రచామరకంఠికిరీటవిచిత్రశయ్యాసౌధ సింహాసనంబులు కైకొనుట మందెమేలంబునంగాదె." B. X. ii. 666. "చిన్ననాటిది మన చెలిమినూహించి, మన్నింపవలెనే మందెమేలంబు." Sārang D. ii. 238.

మంద్రము *mandramu*. [Skt.] n. A base, or low sound, such as that of muttering thunder. హృదయజాతి గంభీరధ్వని.

మంపు *mampu*. [Tel.] n. Drowsiness, intoxication, tipsiness, heaviness, నిద్రమబ్బు, మత్తు, మైకము. "ఈ మంపెసగంగటాక్షులవమాత్రముచేతనె మజ్జగంబు తో. హింపగజేయుభూరిమిక నీవునహించితిగాన." Vijaya Vilasa. i. 92. మంపిల్లు, మంపిలు or మంపుగొను *mampillu*. v. n. To be heavy, to be drowsy. నిద్రమబ్బుగానుండు. To be intoxicated, మత్తిల్లు. "క్రొల్ పులుల్ మంపిల్లి గొటగొటమనియార్చి, బలుసింగములైన బట్టజాచు." Sārang. i. 70.

మంబరము *mambaramu*. [Tel.] n. Burning, దహనము. మంబరముచేయు *mambaramu-chēyu*. v. a. To burn, దహించు.

మకమక *maka-maka* [Tel.] n. Dimness, as of the light of a lamp. మకమకలాడు *maka-maka-l-āḍu*. v. n. To be dim, obscure, or dull. నిస్తేజస్కముగానుండు, కుడ్డిగానుండు, మకిలగానుండు.

మకరందము *makarandamu*. [Skt.] n. The nectar or honey of a flower. పూదేనె.

మకరము *makaramu*. [Skt.] n. An alligator. మొసలి. The sign of the Zodiac called Capricorn, రాశిభేదము. మకరసంక్రమణము or మకరసంక్రాంతి, the passing of the sun into Capricorn. This is observed as the Pongul feast, పొంగలిపండుగ. మకరకంఠి *makara-kanṭhi*. n. A necklace shaped like an alligator. మొసలిమూతులుగల కంఠాభరణము. మకరకుండలము *makara-kuṇḍalamu*. n. An earring bearing the figure of a crocodile's head. మొసలిముఖము గల కర్ణభూషణము. మకరతోరణము *makara-tōraṇamu*. n. A festoon of cloth shaped like a crocodile, మొసలిమొదలైనరూపములను చిత్రవిచిత్రముగా కుట్టి వీధులలో కట్టే తోరణము. మకరాంకుడు, మకరకేతనుడు or మకరధ్వజుడు *makarāṅ-kuḍu*. n. An epithet of Manmadha, whose banner is an alligator. మన్మథుడు. మకరాలయము *makar-ālayamu*. n. The sea. సముద్రము. మకరి *makari*. n. A crocodile, or alligator. మొసలి. మకరిక or మకరికాపత్రము *makarika*. n. Figures of crocodiles drawn in gold dust on the cheeks or breasts of women, చెక్కిళ్లమీదను రొమ్ములమీదను వ్రాసే మొసలిఆకారము. "మకరీమృగరేఖ లురస్థలంబున భావజచిహ్నముద్రలయి భాసిల." Vij. Vil. xi. 97. మకరివల *makari-vala*. n. A snare to catch crocodiles.

మకరతము Same as మరకతము (q. v.).

మకాము *makāmu*. [H.] n. A halting place, lodging, station. మకాముగా settled permanently.

మకిల *makila*. [Tel.] n. Dirtiness, soil, dirt. మాలిన్యము. మకిల మకిలగానున్న dirty, dim, tarnished, unclean, impure, మలినముగానున్న.

మకుటము makuṭamu. [Skt.] n. A crest, tiara, crown, head dress. కిరీటము. బాసికము.

మకురము makuramu. [Skt.] n. Glass, a mirror. అద్దము.

మకురు or మకురుతనము makuru. [Tel.] n. Obstinacy, stubbornness. మూర్ఖత్వము, మొండితనము. పెంకితనము.

మక్క, మక్కపగాలు or మక్కల్లము makka. [Tel.] n. A boil on the abdomen, పొత్తికడుపునందలి పుట్టుపుండు.

మక్కళించు makkaḷintsu. [Tel.] v. n. To come back, to reappear, as intermittent fever, మళ్లు. మళ్లుకొను. తిరుగుకొను. To agree, సరిపడు. To resemble, సరిపోలు. v. a. To cause to come back or reappear. తిరుగుకొనజేయు. మళ్లుకొనజేయు. To jut out, as the belly, ఉబ్బునట్లుచేయు. To cause to be contained, సరిపరుచు, ఇముడ్చు. To cause to resemble, సరిపోల్చు. "సీ॥ బిసేయు మైనయొడ్డాణంబులవలచే నక్కళించిన పొట్టమక్కళించి. Swa. i. 15. "సీ॥ నా సెమ్మిచ్చిరాగా మక్కళించుమకరంద నర్తిత నంద్రశేఖరుము వెలయు." H. i. 212.

మక్కా makka. [Arabic.] n. Mecca.

మక్కు makku. [Tel.] v. n. To fade, spoil, lose colour. కాంతివిహీనమగు, వసయు. To die, చచ్చు. To scratch, గీరు. n. Dirt, మాలిన్యము. "వెలవెలనైనభోగిధారలుమక్కు." Kanyaka viii. 315. మక్కించు makkintsu. v. a. To kill. చంపు. Parij. iii. 45. మక్కి makki. adj. Weak, fleshless, emaciated, thin, నిస్సారము. "తే॥ మందగతి వృష్టిగొరిపెలుమక్కిగొడ్లు." H. v. 36. మక్కెక్కు makk-ekku. v. n. To become dim or dull. మకిలగు. "సీ॥ గంపలమత్తెలెడుగరసుల ధూళి మక్కెక్కిమంగళుల తిప్పలుకేసువడువుగ." A. vi. 17.

మక్కువ makkuva. [Tel.] n. Affection, love; desire, lust; wish, inclination, ప్రేమ, ప్రేమము.

మక్కె or మక్కి makke. [Tel.] n. A bone. ఎముక. The hip-joint, the part of the body just above the hip-joint.

మక్తా makta. [H.] adj. Fixed. n. A fixed rate or rent. A contract. మక్తాగాలు a special agreement given to a tenant. మక్తాకత్త a contract or lease of land occupied at a fixed rate, and not liable to extra cesses. మక్తాదారుడు makta-dāruḍu. n. A contractor.

మక్షిక makshika. [Skt.] n. A fly. ఈగ.

మఖము or మఘము makhamu. [Skt.] n. A sacrifice, or oblation. యజ్ఞము. శతమఖుడు an epithet of Indra, who performed a hecatomb. మఖవాజి a horse fit for being sacrificed in the అశ్వమేధయాగము. మఖవంతుడు, మఘవంతుడు, మఖవుడు or మఘవుడు makha-vantuḍu. n. Indra as being the god who offered sacrifices. మఖి makhi. n. A sacrificer, one who celebrates a sacrifice. యజ్ఞముచేయువాడు.

మఖములు or ముఖమలు makhamulu. [H.] n. Velvet.

మగ maga. [Tel.] adj. Male. మగపోడిమి తొలుగవి a pure maid. మగలమగడు a phrase meaning the chief of men, a hero. గండరగండడు. "నయనయగపిలిచి దామరలను గెలుమగలై, దాటెగయు." Swa. iv. 169. మగకరువు want of men. మగటిమి or మగంటిమి magaṭimi. n. Manliness. పౌరుషము, పుంస్త్వము. మగతనము. శౌర్యము. మగడు or మగండు magaḍu. n. A male, a man, పురుషుడు, మగవాడు. A husband, పెనిమిటి. A ruler, a king. రాజు. A hero, a courageous man, శూరుడు. "మగువలుమగలనిరెలుగడు." R.ii.112. "మన్నె రాజులకెల్ల మగడవైయుండు, నన్నెనదల చకనామిద్దకూన." L. viii. 30. మగతనము maga-tanamu. n. Manliness, potency. పుంస్త్వము. పౌరుషము. మగది magadi. n. The male of any animal. మగనాలు magan-ālu. (మగని+ఆలు.) n. A woman whose husband is alive. మగదుంగలస్త్రీ. A good woman. మగపాడి maga-pādi. n. Courage, manliness, శౌర్యము. మగబీర maga-bīra. n. Malabar Cat-mint, *Anisomelos malabarica*. మగమాణిక్యము or మగరాలు maga-mānikamu. n. A diamond. వజ్రము. మగమాణిక్యపువాలు or మగరాతివాలు maga-mānikapu-vālu. n. Indra's thunderbolt, వజ్రాయుధము. మగరూరి magarūri. [H.] n. Haughtiness, arrogance. మగలింగము maga-lingamu. n. A common plant called 'the stinker.' Rox. i. 109. మగవాడు maga-vāḍu. n. A man, a male, పురుషుడు. A hero, శూరుడు.

మగిడి magiḍi. [Tel.] n. A snake charmer, పాములవాడు. A snake charmer's flute, పాములవానినాగసరము.

మగుడు or మగుడబడు maguḍu. [Tel.] v. n. To return or turn back. మరలు. మళ్లుకొను. మగుడ or మగుడి maguḍa. adv. Again, anew, in return మళ్లీ, తిరిగి, వెనుకకుమళ్లి. మగుడించు, మగుడుచు or మగుడ్చు maguḍintsu. v. a. To turn back, to avert. మళ్లించు, త్రిప్పు, మగుడజేయు. "మరణంబునొందిన మగుడించుభాస." BD. v. 842.

మగులు or మమలు magulu. [Tel.] n. The coping of a wall. మదురు. మగులుగోడ a wall that has a cope or crown, మదురుగోడ.

మగువ maguva. [Tel.] n. A woman. స్త్రీ. అతివ. మగువమగని కొలకుమంత్రి a wife is a minister to her husband. మగువతనము maguva-tanamu. n. Womanhood. స్త్రీత్వము. "మగువతః చులజగ ములు తిరుగుచుజొంగిరిచగొంతి పెడి వెనుకుమంగా." B. viii. 446.

మగ్గము maggamu. [Tel.] n. A loom, నేతయంత్రము మగ్గముపెట్టు to set to work, మొదలుపెట్టు, ఆరంభించు. నా మగ్గము చెడగొట్టినాడు he baffled my efforts. మగ్గరి maggari. (మగ్గము+అరి) n. A weaver, సాలెవాడు.

మగ్గు maggu. [Tel.] v. n. To become mouldy by dampness and heat ఉక్కచే చెమ్మగిలి చెడు. అది మానానికి మగ్గుచున్నది she is too proud to stoop to her present condition. మగ్గుడు magguḍu. n. The act of becoming mouldy, మగ్గుట. మగ్గుడుపారు magguḍu-pāru. v. n. To become mouldy.

మగ్దూరు magdūru. [H.] n. Power, authority, అధికారము, శక్తి.

మగ్నము magnamu. [Skt.] adj. Plunged, immersed, sunk, drowned. మునిగిన. మగ్నుడు magnuḍu. n. (In composition,) One who is immersed. మునిగినవాడు.

మఘ magha. [Skt.] n. The name of the tenth lunar mansion. మఘానక్షత్రము.

మఘవ See మఘవు. మఘవాత్మజుడు Arjuna, as son of Indra. మఘోని maghōni. n. The wife of Indra. శచీదేవి.

మచర్చిక macharchika. [Skt.] adj. Best, excellent. శ్రేష్ఠమైన, తిల్లజము. మతల్లిక.

మచిలీమాపు machili-māpu. [from Skt. మత్స్య a fish, and Arabic మావా abode.] n. A fishery. మచిలీపన్ను or మచిలీసము a tax levied on a fishery.

మచ్చిక or మచ్చిగ machchika. [Tel.] n. Love, attachment, affection, liking, fondness, familiarity, tameness. ప్రేమ, ఆసక్తి, స్నేహము. మచ్చికపడు machchika-paḍu. v. n. To become tame or used to, to love, మరలుకొను, మరగు, అలవాటుపడు.

మచ్చెము machchemu. [from Skt. మత్స్యము.] n. A fish, చేప మచ్చెకంటి machche-kanti. n. A woman with eyes as lovely as those of a fish.

మచ్చె matstsa. [Tel.] n. A mole, freckle, stain, scar or spot on the skin. పుట్టుమచ్చలు natural marks on the skin, birthmarks. మచ్చెమాయు matstsa-māyu. v.

n. To be ruined or destroyed, నశించు. మత్సేమాపు matstsa-mapu. v. a. To ruin, destroy. నిను మత్స మాపుతానుచూడు look out, I will certainly ruin you. మత్సేము matstsamu. n. A mark, గురుతు.

మత్సేరము matstsaramu. [from Skt. మత్సరము.] n. Malice, hatred, envy, spite. మత్సరము, కేలము, ద్వేషము, అసూయ, ఓర్వలేనితనము. "మత్సేరముమీరకొండొరు, జిచ్చరపిడుగులనుబోలె నిరతరిశిఖములజా." M. III. vii. 138. మత్సేరికము matstsarikamu. n. Malice, envy, కేలము, ద్వేషము. Rivalry, పోటి. మత్సేరికించు matstsari-kintsu. v. n. To be spiteful, or envious. అసూయపడు, కేలపట్టు, ద్వేషించు. మత్సేరి or మత్సేరీడు matsts-ari. n. A spiteful person, కేలగాడు. An enemy. ద్వేషి. మత్సేరించు or మత్సేరపట్టు matstsarintsu. v. n. To be spiteful. కేలముపట్టు. To hate, dislike. ద్వేషించు. "వాడు నీతోడనెప్పుడు మత్సేరించును." Hari Vams. Pt. II. Bk. i. 171.

మత్సు maistsu. [Tel.] n. A model, standard, sample, pattern, specimen. మాదిరి, నమూనా. An upstair-house. A terraced house, మిద్దెకట్టడముగేని మిద్దెయిల్లు. A shelf. A bait, మృగాదులు వలలో తగులుటకు ఉంచబడే ఆహారము. Love powder, సొక్కుపొడి. Manner, way. "మేల్మత్సులు చేరి" going upstairs. UH. iv. 25. మత్సులగుడి a bunch of samples of gold or silver. మత్సుచల్లు to sprinkle with love powder, i. e., to bewitch. మరులుమందుచల్లు. ఆ బియ్యమంతా ఒకటేమత్సుగానున్నది all the rice is alike. ఆరోగము అదేమత్సునున్నది the disease is in the same state. మత్సుకత్తి matstsu-katti. n. A bill-hook or large wood knife. కొట్టెలునరికేకత్తి. మత్సుపొడి matstsu-poḍi. n. A love powder, an aphrodisiac. మరులమందు.

మచ్ఛము machchhamu. [Skt. another form of మత్స్యము.] n. A fish. మీనము.

మజిలీ majili. [H.] n. A stage in a journey.

మజుకూరు or మజ్కూరు majukūru. [H.] adj. Before mentioned, aforesaid.

మజుబూతు majubūtu. [H.] adj. Strong, powerful.

మజుమూను majumūnu. [H.] n. The purport or contents of a letter.

మజూరి majūri. [H.] n. Hire, the wages of a day-labourer, కూలి.

మజూరు or మజ్దూరు majūru. [H.] n. A workman, a labourer.

మజ్జ majja. [Skt.] n. Marrow, pith, sap. సారము, చేవ, ఎముకలలోనిక్రొవ్వు.

మజ్జనము majjanamu. [Skt.] n. Bathing, ablution. A bath, స్నానము. మజ్జనశాల A bath room. మజ్జనమాడు to bathe

మజ్జిగ majjiga. [Tel.] n. Butter-milk. తేట. మజ్జిగతెవులు mildew in corn which turns it white. నీరుమజ్జిగ whey.

మజే, మజో, మజ్జే, మజ్జో, మజ్జెరె, మజోరె or మజ్జోరె madza. [Tel.] interj. Hail! Huzza! Hurrah! ప్రశంసావాచకశబ్దము. "మజెబాపురె జంగమకులావార్ధ్య." Charitra. i. 4559.

మజా madza. [H.] n. Taste, flavor. రుచి.

మజాకా madzaka. [H.] n. A jest, a joke.

మటమట maṭa-maṭa. [Tel.] n. Boiling, rage. మలమల ఉడుకుట. మటమటలాడు maṭa-maṭal-āḍu. v. n. To burn, to flame forth, మండు, జ్వలించు. To fume, or be enraged. దుమదుమలాడు.

మటుమాయ maṭu-māya. [Tel. మాయ+మాయ.] n. Disappearance, vanishing. ఉన్నట్టుగానుండి అగుపడకపోవడము. మటుమాయము maṭu-māyamu. adj. Very deceitful, మిక్కిలిమాయయను. మటుమాయలాడు maṭu-māyal-āḍu. n. A very deceitful or artful person. మిక్కిలి మాయలుగలవాడు.

మట్ట maṭṭa. [Tel.] n. A bough or stem (of the palm, cocoanut, or date tree.) తాళ నారికేళాదులకొమ్మ. కలబందమట్ట the stem of the Aloe plant. The tail of an animal, అవులలోనగువానితోక. The sucking fish, called the *Echeneis*, or *remora*. Several species of this are called కొర్రమట్ట, పలు పేరుమట్ట, మట్టగుడిసె or మట్టగొరిసె, పూలమట్ట, మాలమట్ట and కడిచమట్ట. See Russell, Plates. 83 and 84. మట్టగిడుసు *maṭṭa-gidusu*. n. A sort of fish.

మట్టము maṭṭamu. [Tel.] n. Measure, extent, level, కొలది. A pony. పైగోమట్టము a Pegu pony. A goldsmith's secret term for Silver. adj. Small, scanty. కురుచగా నుండే. Low, తక్కువ. Short, పొట్టి. "నజ్జాలే మాపులుదాని కంజవురుమట్టపు పొట్టలు నిండమేసి." Sūrya. ii. 10. మట్టగించు *maṭṭa-gintsu*. v. a. To lessen, diminish, or depress. తగ్గించు. మట్టపలక *maṭṭa-palaka*. n. A flat ruler, a bricklayer's level. మూలమట్టపలక a carpenter's rule. మట్టపాటి *maṭṭa-pāṭi*. adj. Small, petty, scanty. కురుచగానుండే. మట్టసము *maṭṭasamu*. adj. Small, petty, scanty. కురుచగానుండే. Limited, మితమైన. మట్టసి *maṭṭasi*. n. A short man, పొట్టివాడు.

మట్టమధ్యాహ్నము See under మధ్యాహ్నము.

మట్టి maṭṭi. [Tel.] n. Earth, soil, mud. Scurf or dandruff. మట్టితిన్నపాములాగె పడి యున్నాడు he is as stupid as a snake gorged with mud. మట్టిగుర్రమును నమ్మి యేటిలోదిగుట to rely on a mud horse and go into a river, i. e., to trust to appearances. మట్టితైలము or మట్టిమానె maṭṭi-tailamu. n. Earth oil, kerosine or petroleum. మట్టాడు *maṭṭ-āḍu*. (మట్టి+ఆడు.) v. n. & a. To walk. నడచు. To wander, roam, సంచరించు. To spread, వ్యాపించు. To cut to pieces, తునుమాడు. "అస్త్రాపుగములు తుత్తుమురుచేసి మట్టాడి అట్టహాసంబుచేసె" R. v. 191. మట్టెరు Same as మట్టె and మట్టె (q. v.). మట్టు *maṭṭu*. v. a. To tread or trample, to crush, తొక్కు. n. Trampling, walking over, త్రొక్కుడు. Limit, bounds, measure, restriction, extent; moderation. పర్యంతము, ప్రమాణము, మితి, కొలత, తగ్గుదల. A settle or ring of cord, fibre, &c., to prevent a pot from rolling over, కుదురు. A place, ప్రదేశము. పైమట్టు the upper place or part. అడుగుమట్టు the bottom. ఆ బల్లమట్టుపట్టి తీసుకొనిరా measure the plank కావడిమట్టు the frame or bottom of the slings in a Kavadi. వానికి తెలివిమట్టు he is wanting in sense. వానితో చెప్పినది నాబుద్ధిమట్టు I was a fool to tell him this. ఈ సంవత్సరము జనము మట్టు this year the assembly is but small. వానికి పుణ్యగతులుమట్టు he has no chance of heaven. మట్టుచీర a kind of చీరకాయ (q.v.). మట్టుగిన్నె a cup with a foot or base attached to it. adj. Limited, small. మితము. తక్కువ. మట్టుకు as far as, up to, as much as, in regard to, until, as long as. దీనికి ఒకమట్టుమితిములేదు there is no end or limit to it. మట్టుమర్యాదలేనివాడు he who has neither modesty nor moderation. మట్టుమీరవద్దు you must not go beyond bounds. అతడు వచ్చువరకు అని దీనికి ఒకమట్టు పెట్టిరి they laid it aside until his arrival, "మనసుచెదరనీక మట్టుపెట్టి." (Vēma. ii. 278.) curbing and restraining the mind. ఈ మట్టున లేచిపోయిరి with this they went away or thereupon they went away. పిడుగుపడి అంతమట్టున వాన విడిచినది there was a thunderbolt and then the rain ceased. వానికి అంతమట్టుకు తెలియదు he does not know so much. ఎంతమట్టుకు పోయినావు how far did you go? గొంతుమట్టుకు నీళ్లువస్తున్నవి the water is up to the neck. వాడు ఎంతమట్టుకుండే అంతమట్టుకు సంతోషిస్తాడు he contents himself with as much as he gets. నా ప్రాణాలు ఉన్నంతమట్టుకు as long as

I have life. నామట్టుకు నేను ఉంటాను నీమట్టుకు నీవు ఉండు I shall keep to myself, you keep to yourself. బియ్యము కావలసిన మట్టుకు చిక్కును you can get as much rice as you want. సొమ్ములమట్టుకు నాకు వద్దు as for the jewels I do not want them. అంతమట్టుకు మంచిపని చేస్తివి so far you did well. ఇంతమట్టుకు వచ్చిన తరువాత ఇకనేమి దాక్షిణ్యము when the matter has come to such a push what is the use of delicacy? వానికి తిండి మట్టుకు బాగా కావలెను he cares for nothing but his dinner. నేనుమట్టుకు పోతిని I alone went. వాని ఒళ్లు కానామట్టుకు వాసిగానున్నది his health is in a great measure recovered. మట్టుఅగు, మట్టుకొను or మట్టుపడు maṭṭu-agu. v. n. To lessen or be diminished. తగ్గు, అడగు. కుదురుపడు. రోగము మట్టుపడినది the disease is moderating. వానికి దాహము మట్టుపడినది his thirst was slackened. మట్టుగా maṭṭu-gā. adv. Moderately, మితముగా. వర్షము మట్టుగానున్నప్పుడు when the rain is moderate. దగ్గు మట్టుగానున్నది the cough is now moderate. మట్టుగా తిన్నాడు he ate moderately. మట్టుచేయు or మట్టుపరచు maṭṭu-cheyu. v. a. To lessen, moderate, diminish. తగ్గించు. వానికి జీతము మట్టుచేసినారు they diminished his pay, వానికి జీతము తగ్గించినారు. మట్టుపెట్టు maṭṭu-peṭṭu. v. a. To keep down, suppress, అడచు. To kill, చంపు. మట్టుమిగులు or మట్టుమీరు maṭṭu-migulu. v. n. To exceed the limits, అతిక్రమించు.

మట్టె or మట్టెలు maṭṭe. [Tel.] n. A ring worn on the toe. కాలివేలియందు పెట్టేటిది. చెప్పుమట్టె a shoe-heel, చెప్పుమడిమ. adj. Dappled. బట్టనాగలుగల. మట్టెఆవు a dappled cow, బట్టావు. H. ii. 88.

మట్ర maṭra. [Tel.] n. An unploughed piece of land between two furrows, మెట్టచేలు దున్నినప్పుడు కొంచెము తిరుగక నడుమనుండు కొండెముగా.

మఠము maṭhamu. [Skt.] n. A monastery, convent. సన్యాసులు మొదలైనవారు ఉండే గృహము. మఠమువేసుకొనికూర్చుండు to squat as the images of Buddha are seated.

మడ maḍa. [Tel.] n. A small opening out of a channel into a field. మడిలోనికి నీళ్లు పోయేతోవ, ప్రవాహమార్గము. "పొదలవృక్షములు నీడలను మడలకేలంబులమడువుల మేటిపడియుండు." Navana. D. 59. మడచెట్టు maḍa-cheṭṭu. n. The mangrove. తెల్లమడచెట్టు the white mangrove, *Avicennia officinalis*. నల్లమడచెట్టు *Avicennia tomentosa*. (Watts.)

మడక maḍaka. [Tel.] n. A plough with bullocks complete. నాగటికి ఎడ్లనుపూన్చిన యుంటక, అరక, ఏరు. A folding, a fold, మడుపు. A promontory of land, ఏటిమలకసందు. వానికి నాలుగుమడకలు సాగుచున్నవి he has four ploughs in use. రెండుమడకలనేల as much land as requires two ploughs. మడకలు కట్టినతర్వాత after he yoked the cattle to his ploughs. మడకలువిప్పినారు they loosed the cattle from the plough.

మడకర్ర maḍakarra. [Tel.] n. A stout piece of wood. లావుకట్టె.

మడగు or మడుగు maḍagu. [Tel.] v. n. To bend, to be folded, వంగు, మడతపడు. To turn, మరలు, తిరుగు. మడతొక్కు maḍa-tokku. (మడగక్+తొక్కు.) v. a. To pile palm leaves and then trample them flat. మడచు or మడుచు maḍaṭsu. v. a. To fold, to plait, to bend To slay. To abolish. "ఇహపరాదులకును ఇదిసాధనంబని, వ్రాసినదిది విన్నవారికైన, మన్నుకన్నులను మహిమతో మడచును పెరులకైన ముక్తిపదము వేమ." Vema 1398. మడత maḍata. n. A fold, plait, crease. A kind of cake. "పేణీలునిరుపత్తిగలు మడతలుపప్పుబూరెలు." H. i. 117. మడతకత్తి a clasp knife. మడతతడిక a folding screen. మడతతీయు maḍata-tīyu. v. a. To unfold. మడతపెట్టు

or మడతపెట్టు maḍata-peṭṭu. v. a. To fold, to double up, to crease. See మడుచు.

మడతి. మడంతి or మడతుక maḍati. [Tel.] n. A woman, స్త్రీ.

మడమ, మడిమ or మడెమ maḍama. [Tel.] n. The heel. మడికాలు. పారమడమ the back of a hoe. గొడ్డలిమడమ the back of an axe. తుపాకిమడమ the butt end of a gun or musket, కుందా. మడిమెత్తుపరుగు running quickly. "మడిమెత్తుపరువుతో మంత్రాక్షతము లియ్య." S. i. 369. "మడిమలుద్రొక్కగా మైల చీరలుకట్టి." Mand. iv. 104.

మడవ or మడువ maḍava. [Tel.] n. A small dam or dike to stop water; a small opening out of a channel into a field. అడ్డకట్ట. మళ్లకు పాదులకు నీళ్లుపోయేదోవయొక్క మొదటిభాగము. "మళ్లకు మడవలుమార్చిమార్చి." KP. iv. 105. మడవచేప maḍava-chepa. n. A kind of fish, మత్స్యవిశేషము.

మడవు maḍavu. [Tel.] v. n. To turn away, as the face, to turn back, to withdraw from, విముఖుడగు. To become useless, నిష్ఫలమగు.

మడి maḍi. [Tel.] n. A field, a sub-division of a field, a garden-bed or plot. వరిపొలము. కాలుమడి urine. మళ్లయెలుక the field mouse. మళ్లచీర muslin woven in little lattice-like squares. మడిపెసలు maḍi-pesalu. n. A kind of green gram, ఒకవిధమైన నల్లపెసలు.

మడి maḍi. [Tel. from మడచు.] n. Purity, an unpolluted cloth, clean clothes. శుచి, ధౌతవస్త్రము. మడితోనుండు to be dressed in clean garments, as a Brahmin, when he takes his meals. ఎక్కడికిపోయినా నా మడితప్పను go where I may, I will not break the rule of purity. adj. Pure, clean. శుచిగానుండే. మడిబట్ట a clean cloth. మడికాసు maḍi-kāsu. n. Silver, వెండి. (Thus, white money was an old English word for silver.) మడికొండ the hill of silver, i. e., రజతగిరి. "అదిసుధాకరబింబమా కాదు మడికాసువన్నె తెలుపుటమ్మ పత్తిగాని." P. iv. 251. మడిచీర maḍi-chīra. n. The end of a woman's cloth tucked up behind. మడివేలు maḍi-velu. n. A washerman. చాకలి. మడిసంచి maḍi-sanchi. n. A pure or sacred bag. మడివస్త్రములను ఉంచుసంచి. మడిసంది maḍi-sandi. n. The arm pit, చంక. కక్షము.

మడిమంచె or మడిమంచెము maḍimantsu. [Tel.] adj. Weak, బలహీనము.

"చ॥ చెట్టుపట్టినమాత్రదళంబులతో డదోలెనా,
మనితోరమంచురాజా మడిమంచగనో
యులగంటబ్రోవగన్."
సాన్వ. vi.

"ద్వి॥ బలదేవుడుద్ధతిబరిఘంబుబూని,
మలయురుక్మిని మడిమంచంబుచేసె."
భాగ. x.

మడియడు maḍiyaḍu. [Tel. from మడ్డి.] n. An ignorant person, a blockhead, మూఢుడు.

మడియు maḍiyu. [Tel.] v. n. To die, perish, చచ్చు. To break to pieces, కూలు. మడియించు maḍiyintsu. v. a. To kill, assassinate, destroy, చంపు.

మడుగు, మడువు, మడ్గు or మడ్వు maḍugu. [Tel.] v. n. To be kept down, అడగు. To be bent, వంగు. n. A proportion, ratio, గుణము. దీనికంటె అది యెన్నిమడుగులు హెచ్చు how many times is it larger than this? A basin, pond, lake, a deep or hollow place, a hole or pool in the bed of a river or tank. నదీమధ్యమందున్న హ్రదము. కొలను. A clean cloth. ధౌతవస్త్రము. Purity, శుచి, పరిశుద్ధి. A weight of eight viss, మణుగు. Humility, submissiveness, suppression of the desires, moderation. అడకువ, ఉపశాంతి. A fold of a leaf, ఆకుమడుపు. adj. Pure. పరిశుద్ధము. "నిండారు కమ్మతేనియ మడుగంగా దే. కె మొగ్గపూపొన్న పేరు కన్నె వాడుకనుక్కొ."

P. iv. 243. అక్కడ నెత్తురు మడుగు కట్టియుండినది the blood was standing in pools. **మడుచు** *maḍutsu*. v. a. To fold, plait, bend, crease, clasp. To shut, or close (as a hook). మడుగ జేయు. See మడచు. కాలు మడుచు lit. to sit down to pass water. **మడుపు** *maḍupu* n. A fold or plait, మడత. A fold of betel leaf, ఆకుమడ్చు. Clean linen fresh from washing, మడుగువస్త్రము. "మాకమునకే తెంచి మడుపులన్నియును కళిం మాల్గాకుండ ఘట్టించిమడువ." BD. iv. 35. **మడుపుకత్తి** *maḍupu-katti*. n. A folding or clasp knife.

మడ్డి *maḍḍi*. [Tel.] n. Dregs, lees, sediment మడ్డిస్తంభము a pole or mast smeared with lees, up which boys climb, on festival days, for prizes placed on the top. ఆముదపుమడ్డి the dregs of castor-oil. adj Foul, dull, stupid, awkward, clumsy. మడ్డిరొదుపు a dull red. మడ్డితిండి foul feeding. మడ్డినిద్ర deathlike sleep, dead sleep. వాడు వట్టిమడ్డి he is a blockhead. **మడ్డికాగితము** *maḍḍi-kāgitamu*. n. Coarse paper, ముతకకాగితము. **మడ్డిచెక్క** *maḍḍi-chekka*. n. A sort of forest wood used for dyeing cloth red. *Morinda citrifolia*. Ainsl. ii. 254. *Morinda bracteata*. Rox. i. 544. Wight's Plate, 126. మలగచెక్క. **మడ్డితనము** *maḍḍi-tanamu*. n. Rudeness, rusticity, clownishness, stupidity, ఎడ్డెతనము, మోటుతనము, బుద్ధిలేకుండడము. **మడ్డిమైనము** *maḍḍi-mainamu*. n. Bees-wax. ముతకమైనము.

మడ్డు *maḍḍu*. [Tel.] n. An iron ball, ఇనుపగుండు. "ఉ॥ ఎర్రగా. కాలినమడ్డు వండె మొనగంగను పట్టి సినుండునున్నవిరా." Prabhavati. v. 62. Great heat, అత్యుష్ణము. వానికడుపులో మడ్డు పోసినట్టు ఉన్నది he is in bitter grief. adj. Red hot. **మడ్డుకత్తి** *maḍḍu-katti*. n. A bill hook, మచ్చుకత్తి.

మడ్డువు *maḍḍuvu*. [Skt.] n. A sort of small drum. తుడుము, కుచ్చెట.

మణగు, మణుగు. మడగు or **మడుగు** *maṇagu*. [Tel.] v. n. To be bent, to bend. మేకులు మణగగొట్టు to clinch nails. మణగగొట్టినమేకు a rivet. **మణచు** or **మణుచు** *maṇatsu*. v. a. To bend. మడుపుకత్తిని మణచు close the clasp knife. See మడగు, మడుగు and మణగు.

మణి *maṇi*. [Skt.] n. A gem, a precious stone. పచ్చరాయిలోనగునది. A pearl, ముత్తెములోనగునది. In compounds this denotes Unrivalled excellence, as నాయికామణి a woman who is a gem of her sex. విప్రమణి the noblest of Brahmins. సుందరీమణి the loveliest of women. అంగనామణులు lovely women. దినమణి the gem of day, i. e., the sun. నవమణులు nine precious stones, viz., గోమేధికము Onyx, నీలము Sapphire, పగడము Coral, పుష్యరాగము Topaz, మరకతము Emerald, మాణిక్యము Ruby, Carbuncle; ముత్యము Pearl, వైడూర్యము Cat's eye, lapis lazuli; వజ్రము Diamond. మణులుచెక్కినసంకెళ్లు jewelled fetters, i. e., disguised difficulties. **మణికంఠము** *maṇi-kanṭhamu*. n. The Indian Roller, *Corracia indica*, చాషము, పాలపిట్ట. **మణికట్టు, మునికట్టు** or **మణిబంధము** *maṇi-kaṭṭu*. [Tel.] n. The wrist: మణికట్లను తెగగొట్టు to cut off the hands. **మణికారుడు** *maṇi-kāruḍu*. n. A jeweller. A lapidary, or worker in precious stones. రత్నములు సానబట్టువాడు. **మణిపట్టు** *maṇi-paṭṭu*. n. A sort of flowered silk. ఒకవిధమైనపట్టు. **మణిప్రవాళము** *maṇi-pravāḷamu*. n. A doggerel verse: or a mixed language, part Sanscrit, part Telugu or Tamil. రెండుభాషలుకలిసిన కవిత్వము. **మణిభిత్తు** *maṇi-bhittu*. n. A diamond. Lit. "the ruby cutter." వజ్రము. **మణిమాల, మణిమాలిక** or **మణిబింబమాలిక** *maṇi-māla*. n. An impression left by a bite. పంటినొక్కువిశేషము. A necklace. హారము. "కమనీయమణిమాలికా శశ ధరచంద్రరేఖాంకమాలికా రేఖలో." T. iii. 126.

మణికము *maṇikamu*. [Skt.] n. A water jar, or pitcher. పెద్దబాన, కాగు. A small pot, ముంత.

మణిగ or **మళిగ** *maṇiga*. [Tel.] n. A wholesale shop. మండి. A shop, దుకాణము.

మణిగాసనము *maṇi-gāsanamu*. [Tel.] n. A thin coating of whitewash or lime, సన్ననిసున్నపుపూత.

మణితము *maṇitamu*. [Skt.] n. A low murmuring sound, కళరవము. A cuckoo's cry, కోకిలధ్వని.

మణియగాడు or **మణెగాడు** *maṇiya-gāḍu*. [Tel.] n. The Superintendent of a village or temple. పారుపత్తి.

మణీవము or **మణిగము** *maṇi-vamu*. [Tel.] n. Authority. అధికారము. **మణీవకాడు** *maṇiva-kāḍu*. n. One who is in authority or power, a superior officer, అధికారి.

మణిశిల or **మణిసిల** *maṇi-sila*. [Skt.] n. Realgar; red sulphuret of arsenic. ఒక విధమైన ఎర్రమన్ను.

మణుగు or **మడుగు** *maṇugu*. [Tel.] v.n. To be folded, bent. To die, to expire. అణగు. n. A clean cloth. ధౌతవస్త్రము, బట్ట. "ఏకా గ్రవంబైనయెడ నహామ్మతుల, శేకొనకదికేడు చాకి యునరడు, మహిలిధక్షాళికి మణుగులకాత, మహి పెళ్ళుమడివాలు మాచయ్యయునగ." BD. iv. 145. **మణుగు** or **మణువు** *maṇugu*. n. A maund or weight of eight viss., i. e., forty seers or twenty-five pounds. ఎనిమిదివిసెల యెత్తు. **మణుగుబువ్వలు** *maṇugu-buvvulu*. n. Vermicelli. సేమియలను భేదమైనభక్ష్యములు. H. i. 117. **మణుచు** or **మడుచు** *maṇutsu*. v. a. To fold or bend. See మడుచు.

మత్ *mat*. [Skt.] adj. Mine, my. మద్వాక్యము my word. మత్కథ my history. మద్భృత్యులు my servants. మచ్ఛునకము my dog. మన్నామము my name. మన్నియమము my custom, my order. మన్నియామ్యులు those who obey me.

మతంగుడు *matanguḍu*. [Skt.] n. The name of a Rishi. A man of the chuckler or shoe-maker caste. మాదిగవాడు. **మతంగజము** or **మతంగము** *matanga-jamu*. n. An elephant. **మతంగస్త్రీ** *matanga-strī*. A chuckler woman. మాదిగది.

మతకము *matakamu*. [Tel.] n. Deception, illusion, delusion. మాయ. "మనమునపా మాయ మతకమంతయును, గనుగొన్నధర్మజుండుగా ననిట్లనియె" L. iii. 295. **మతకరి** *matak-ari*. (మతకము+అరి.) n. A deceitful person, a deluder. మాయలమారి, మాయావి. "మతకరి చిత్రాంగిమత్సరంబునను, సుతునిపై కపటంబుసుద్ది కల్పించె." Sar. D. 350.

మతము *matamu*. [Skt.] n. Opinion. అభిప్రాయము. wish, idea. A doctrine, creed, sect, religion, శాస్త్రము. Consent, సమ్మతి. త్రిమతములు the three creeds, i. e., the Vaishnava, Madhwa and Smarta creeds. షణ్మతములు the six creeds, viz. వైష్ణవము, శైవము, శాక్తము, గాణాపతము, సౌరము and కాపాలికము. కాదిమతము (in magic) is the *mode* wherein the alphabet is recited the right way while హాదిమతము is reciting the alphabet backwards, the wrong way, beginning with హ which is the last consonant.

మతలబు *mata-labu*. [H.] n. Purport, meaning. A topic, subject, contents, as ఆజ్ఞ మతలబు.

మతల్లిక *matallika*. [Skt.] n. (In composition,) the best or most excellent of all things. మిక్కిలిశ్రేష్ఠమైనది. వధూజనమతల్లిక the gem of her sex. Vasu. vi 84.

మతాబు or **మహతాబు** *matābu*. [H.] n. A blue-light, చంద్రజ్యోతి.

మతి *mati.* [Skt.] n. Understanding, intellect, consciousness, judgment; sense, memory, recollection; wish, desire, inclination, బుద్ధి, తెలంపు, ఇచ్ఛ. మతిభ్రమ mental aberration, perplexity, పిచ్చి, వెర్రి. మతి తప్పినవాడు one out of his senses. **మతిమంతుడు** *mati-mantudu.* n. A man of sense, a clever man, బుద్ధిశాలి. **మతిమరుపు** *mati-marupu.* n. Forgetfulness, absence of mind, పారపాటు. **మతిహీనుడు** *mati-hīnudu.* n. A senseless or foolish man. బుద్ధిహీనుడు.

మతించు *matintsu.* [H.] v. a. To estimate, appraise. మతింపు same as మదింపు (q.v.).

మత్కుణము *matkunamu.* [Skt.] n. A bug. నల్లి.

మత్తము *mattamu.* [Skt.] adj. Intoxicated, drunk, tipsy. Infatuated, wanton, lustful. Mad, insane. Proud, gay, merry. మత్తగజము. మత్తవారణము or మత్తేభము an elephant in rut. మత్తచకోరము the amorous dove, the lovelorn nightingale. **మత్తకాశిని** or **మత్తకాసిని** *matta-kāsini.* n. A wanton woman. మదించిన స్త్రీ. **మత్తకోకిల** *matta-kōkila.* n. The name of a certain Telugu metre. **మత్తి** *matti.* n. Intoxication, amorous desire. కామము. **మత్తికాడు** *matti-kādu.* n. A lewd wretch. కాముకుడు. An impudent fellow. అలకోర్వి వవాడు. "చిక్కాబోనేడునా చేమత్తికాడు, చిక్కులబెట్టి కాకుని మెప్పింతు." HD. ii. 535. **మత్తు** or **మత్తా** *mattu.* [from Skt.] n. Intoxication, drunkenness, pride, arrogance. కైపు, మయికము, మదము. మత్తౌషధము an intoxicating drug. **మత్తిలు, మత్తిల్లు** or **మత్తుగొను** *mattilu.* v. n. To be intoxicated, to be inebriated. నిషాచేరు, మదించు, కైపెక్కు. **మత్తుడు** *mattudu.* n. A drunkard, a lustful man. A proud man. మత్తుగొన్నవాడు, మదించినవాడు. **మత్తేభము** *mattēbhamu.* n. The name of a Telugu Metre.

మత్సరము *matsaramu.* [Skt.] n. Envy, impatience of another's success or prosperity, jealousy, passion, anger. ఈర్ష్య క్రోధము. adj. Envious, inimical, ఈర్ష్యగల క్రోధముగల.

మత్స్యండి *matsyandi.* [Skt.] n. Coarse or unrefined sugar. Molasses, బెల్లము. Crystallised sugar. కండచక్కెర.

మత్స్యము *matsyamu.* [Skt.] n. A fish, చేప. **మత్స్యధ్వజుడు** *matsya-dhvajudu.* n. An epithet of Manmadha. మన్మథుడు. **మత్స్యాక్షి** *matsy-ākshi.* n. The moon plant, *Asclepias acida.* పొన్నగంటికూర.

మథనము *mathanamu.* [Skt.] n. Churning. చిలకడము, త్రచ్చుట. **మథించు** *mathintsu.* v. a. To churn, చిలుకు, త్రచ్చు. **మథితము** *mathitamu.* n. Butter-milk. మజ్జిగ. adj. Stirred, churned, agitated, distressed, grieved. త్రచ్చబడిన.

మదట *madata.* [from Skt. మదము] n. An intoxicated person, మత్తుడు, మత్తురాలు. A clownish boor, a stupid rustic. మందుడు, జడుడు. **మదటతనము** *madatatanamu.* n. Stupidity, clownishness, rusticity. జడత్వము, మట్టితనము. "ఇదినాయిదివాకిలి సదనము నీకెందునిలువ జనుని దురాత్మా మదటతనముడిగిరెండె కదలుముతెమ్మనిన." P. iii. 108.

మదనుడు *madanudu.* [Skt.] n. Manmadha. **మదనము** *madanamu.* n. The Thorn Apple, *Datura fatuosa.* ఉమ్మెత్త చెట్టు, దుత్తూరము. Wax, మయినము. "మందారమకరంద మాధుర్యమున దేలు మధుపంబుపోలునేమదనములకు." B. vii. 17. **మదనగ్రంథి** *madana-grandhi.* n. A plant called *Spermatoce hispida.* తాటిగరి. Ainslie. ii. 259. **మదనచేతులు** *madana-chētulu.* n. The wooden frame work over the beams in the roof of a Hindu house. క్రేకి, దంతెలు, దూలములమీది అంక

బాణములు, ఇంటిపనులుజాలమీదచేయు పక్షులు. "మదనచేతులజాతుని బెయ్యకుంపురుంజాడిదలు వార్చు విష్ణుపదమొత్తుపురికృపాలక్ష్మినూత్న కళా." A. ii. 17. "సీ॥ తనువెల్లవేల్లగాదనయునినక్కున బోదుఎనిచేతులుమదనచేతులనయంబు." Paidi. i. 129. **మదనపత్రిక** *madana-patrika*. n. A billet doux, or love-letter, విరహవేద నాదులను తెలియచేయుచు వ్రాసినలేఖ. **మదని** *madani*. n. A civet cat, జవ్వాదిపిల్లి.

మదము *madamu*. [Skt.] n. Fat, కొవ్వు. Pride, arrogance, lust, frenzy, madness. గర్వము. Musk, కస్తూరి. మదాంధత the blindness of pride, haughtiness. విద్యామదము the pride of learning. ధనమదము the pride of wealth. ధనమదాంధుడు he who is blinded by riches. కులమదము the pride of caste or birth. ఉద్యోగమదము the pride of office. రూపమదము the pride of beauty. యౌవనమదము the pride of youth. అన్నమదము the pride of plenty. స్త్రీమదము the pride of passion. మదాలస indolent, heavy as with tipsiness or lust. అతని మదమణిగినది his lustful arrogance has gone, he has sown his wild oats. adj. Proud. మదగజము an elphant in rut. "మదనైరిద్విపసింహమూర్తి." G. viii. 4. **మదించు** *madintsu*. v. n. To become fat, proud, or arrogant, to be in rut. కొవ్వు, అహంకరించు, మత్తిలు. **మదపుటేనుగు** *madapu-t-enugu*. n. An elephant in rut. (The ట is inserted to prevent elision.) **మదమడచు** *madam-adatsu*. v. n. To put down pride, to kill. చంపు. **మదవతి** *madavati*. n. A wanton woman. **మదావళము**, **మదహస్తి**, **మదహత్తి** or **మదకలము** *madakalamu*. n. An elephant in its prime.

మది *madi*. [from Skt. మతి.] n. The mind. మనస్సు, బుద్ధి. మదించు to think, తలచు. **మదిమది** *madi-madi* n. Great calmness, ఏకాగ్రత. Steadiness, నిశ్చలత. "మదిమదిరాక్షు మునీవిడిచి వింకుతిరంబున కెందరానిమేల్, పడి పులుగోరకల్గుచె జనంబు ఘటించుపుము." UK. iv. 183. **మదింపు** or **మతింపు** *madimpu*. n. An estimate, valuation. **మదించు** or **మతించు** *madintsu*. v. a. To make an estimate. మదింపుచేయు.

మదిర *madira*. [Skt.] n. Spirituous or fermented liquor. సుర, కల్లు. మదిరాక్షి or మదిరేక్షణ a wanton eyed girl, a giddy woman, మదముకప్పిన కన్నులుగల అదంది. మదిరాయతేక్షణ one who has drink-swollen eyes.

మదిర *madira*. [Tel.] n. A heap of earth or gravel.

మదీయము *madiyamu*. [Skt.] adj. Mine, appertaining to me.

మదుగు, **మడుము** or **మదుపు** *madugu*. [Tel.] n. A sluice, a flood-gate. తూము.

మదుపు *madupu*. [Tel.] n. Green color, ఆకుపచ్చ.

మదురు or **మదులు** *maduru*. [Tel.] n. Coping, the cope or crown of a wall; or thatch placed on the top of a wall. గోడపైకప్పు. మదురుగోడ an enclosing wall. HD. ii. 1038. మదురు పోయు to put a coping on a wall. మదురుమీదిపిల్లి a cat on the roof, i. e., a calculating man; one who "sits on the fence."

మదురువు *maduruvu*. [from Skt. మధు.] n. Intoxicating liquor, మద్యము. Intoxication, మత్తు.

మద్గువు *madguvu*. [Skt.] n. An aquatic bird: the cormorant, నీరుకాకి, కంకాకప్పి. A kind of fish. మత్స్యభేదము.

మద్దతు *maddatu*. [H.] n. Assistance, help, abetment. **మదద్గారు** *madadgaru*. n. An assistant.

మద్ది *maddi*. [Tel.] n. The tree calle[d] *Mentaptera arjuna*. అర్జునము. Rox. ii. 438 *Terminalia alata*. Kœnig. Ainsl. ii. 193. *Ailanthus malabarica*. (Watts.)

There are various species called ఇనుమద్ది, పూడుమద్ది, ఏరుమద్ది, ఎల్లమద్ది or చిలిమాను and దూదిమద్ది, *Briedelia retusa.* మద్దికాయలు *muddi-kayalu.* n. The fruit of the tree. A kind of earrings worn by boys.

మద్దెల *maddela.* [from Skt. మృదంగ.] n. A small drum. మృదంగము. మద్దెలరూపురిక్క *maddela-rūpu-rikka.* n. A constellation called ధనిష్ఠానక్షత్రము.

మద్యము *madyamu.* [Skt.] n. An intoxicating drink, toddy, liquor. కల్లు, సారాయి, సుర. మద్యపాయి a wine-bibber, a drunkard, మద్యపానము wine drinking. మద్యపానము మానుము give up drink.

మధురము *madhuramu.* [Skt.] adj. Sweet, delicious, agreeable. సుందరమైన, స్వాదువైన, ప్రియమైన. n. Sweetness, తియ్యన. మధురస *madhu-rasa.* n. The vine tree, గోస్తని, ద్రాక్షచెట్టు. మధురిమ or మధురిమము *madhurima.* n. Sweetness, తియ్యన.

మధువు *madhuvu.* [Skt.] n. Wine, spirits. కల్లు. Honey, తేనె. The sweet juice or nectar of flowers. మకరందము, పూదేనె. The spring time of the year. చైత్రమాసము, వసంతఋతువు. మధువ్రతము *madhu-vratamu.* n. A bee. తుమ్మెద. మధుసఖుడు *madhu-sakhudu.* n. An epithet of Manmadha. మధుకరము *madhu-karamu.* n. A bee, as the *maker of honey* (మధువు.) తుమ్మెద. Also, boiled rice given as alms, భిక్షాన్నము. మధుపము *madhupamu.* n. A bee, as 'sucking honey.' తుమ్మెద. మధుపర్కము *madhu-parkamu.* n. Honey mixed with curds. దధిసంయుక్తమధువు. A bridal dress. పెండ్లిలో వధూవరులకు ఇచ్చే వస్త్రము. మధుయష్టిక *madhu-yashtika.* n. Liquorice, అతిమధురము. మధులిహము *madhu-lihamu.* n. The honey bee, తేనెటీగ. మధువారము *madhu-vāramu.* n. Tippling, drinking frequently. మద్యపానక్రమము. మధూకము or మధుకము *madhūkamu.* n. The tree called *Bassia latifolia.* ఇప్పచెట్టు. మధూచ్ఛిష్టము *madhū-chhishtamu.* n. Bees wax. Lit: the refuse of honey. మైనము. మధూలకము *madhūlakamu.* n. The lesser species of *Bassia latifolia.* నీరుఇప్ప. కొండయిప్ప. మధూలిక or మధూళిక *madhūlika.* n. The pollen or dust of flowers. పుప్పొడి. A stream of honey. మకరందధార. "నిడుద మధూళికల్ నడుమ నేకొని దీవలు సాగజొట్టుకొం, చదికి కడారకాచకటకాకృతి నుల్లమెలంగ గాడుపుల్, జడగతిఁ ద్రవ్వి నవ్వెమత్తటువిశ్వసితానలం బెరుప్పడమరిసార్యులై నుడి నుడి యంగుడ నుల్లఁగసు క్రానోయిక." A. v. 130. టీ॥ మధూళికల్, మకరందధారలు.

మధుసూదనుడు or మధురిపుడు *madhu-sūdanudu.* [Skt.] n. An epithet of Vishnu, as having slain the giant Madhu.

మధ్యము *madhyamu.* [Skt.] n. The middle, the waist, the middle part. నడుము, నడిమిభాగము. adj. Middle, that which is in the middle, centric; mean, as opposed to extreme. Middling, that is neither good nor bad, poor, indifferent. నడిరకము, నడుమునుండే. మధ్యమపువెండి inferior silver, much alloyed. మధ్య *madhya.* n. A girl of from 13 to 18 years of age. A youthful maiden. మధ్య adv. affix: Between, in the midst, amongst, amidst, meanwhile. ఆమధ్య thereabouts, during that interval. తొమ్మిదో మాసము ఆమధ్య about the ninth month. జనవరిఆమధ్య about January. ఈమధ్య lately, recently. మధ్యమధ్య here and there, between whiles, now and then, at times, occasionally, అప్పుడప్పుడు, అక్కడక్కడ. మధ్యదేశము *madhya-dēsamu.* n. The central portion of the Bharata Varsha, i. e., of Northern India. మధ్యమ *madhyama.* n. The middle finger. నడిమివేలు. మధ్యమము *madhya-mamu.* n.

The fifth note of the Hindu gamut: Tenor. adj. Middle, centrical, intervening. Mean, ordinary, middling, నడిమిది. మధ్యమమైన వెండి base or ordinary silver. వానికిదృష్టి మధ్యమముగా నున్నది his eyes are not good. మధ్యమ పురుషము *madhyama-purushamu*. n. The second (or middle) person in Grammar. Thou, you. ఎదుటివానిని తెలుపు మాట. మధ్యముడు *madhyamudu*. n. One who is middling, i. e., neither good nor bad. నడిమివాడు. మధ్యరాత్రము *madhya-rātramu*. n. Midnight. అర్ధరాత్రము, నడిరేయి, నిశీథము. మధ్యవర్తి *madhya-varti*. n. An arbitrator, a third person, a mediator, referee, nominee, umpire. మధ్యవర్తిత్వము or మధ్యస్థము *madhya-vartitvamu*. n. Mediation, arbitration. మధ్యస్థుడు *madhya-sthudu*. n. A third person, umpire, referee, mediator. మధ్యవర్తి, నడుమనుండి పక్షపాతములేక యిరువెరగల వారికి న్యాయముచెప్పువాడు. మధ్యాహ్నము *madhy-āhnamu*. n. Mid-day, noon. పట్టపగలు.

మనము *manamu*. [Tel.] pron. We, (including the person or persons addressed,) as distinguished from మేము which excludes the person addressed. మనము చూడలేదే neither you nor I saw it.

మననము *mananamu*. [Skt.] n. The mind. మనస్సు. మననము *mananamu*. n. Minding, understanding, thinking, reflecting, ధ్యానము.

మనవర్తి *mana-varti*. [Tel.] n. Corruption of మధ్యవర్తి. (q. v.)

మనవి *manavi*. [Tel.] n. A request, solicitation, petition, విజ్ఞాపనము.

మనసు or మనస్సు *manasu*. [Tel.] n. The internal organ of cognition, the intellect, understanding, mind. Inclination, wish, will, pleasure, ఇష్టము. adj. Liking, ఇష్టము.

మనసగు *manas-agu*. (మనసు+అగు.) v. n. To like, ఇష్టమగు. మనోవేగముగా పోయినాడు he went as quick as thought. మనోవ్యాధికి మందులేదు there is no cure for the heart-ache or for a mental disease. వాణ్ని పిలవడానకు నీకెట్లామనస్సువచ్చినది how could you find it in your heart to call him? నీకు మనస్సువచ్చినదానిని తీసికొనవచ్చును you may take which you choose. దానిని చేయడానకు వానికి యింకా మనస్సురాలేదు he is not yet inclined to do this. తమరు మనస్సుపట్టితే అవును if you once set your heart upon it it will be done. వానికిమనస్సునస్తే ఒకటి, మనస్సురాకపోతే ఒకటి he is guided by fancy or whim. మనస్సే వైకుంఠము heaven is in the heart. వానిమనస్సు అగోచరము his thoughts are inscrutable. వానిమనస్సును ఎందుకు నొప్పించినావు why should you grieve him or his heart? వానిమనస్సు విరిగినది he is heart-broken. ఈమాట నీమనస్సులో ఉండనీ you must keep this to yourself. అది యేడ్చితే వానిమనస్సు తాళలేదు he could not endure to see her weep. వాని మనస్సు తిరుగలేదు he has not altered his opinion. వానికి మనస్సులో ఒకటి, బయట ఒకటి he has one thing in his heart and another in his mouth. నామనస్సు ఒకవిధముగానున్నది I know not what to think, my mind is confused. "ఇంద్రియములుమనస్స్థములు" the senses are dependent on the mind. M. XII. v. 596. మనస్స్థమైన మాట the thought of his heart. మీమనస్సు as you please, your pleasure. వానిమనస్సువచ్చినట్లు as he chose, as he pleased. మనవిచ్చిచెప్పలేదు he did not tell his real thoughts. నీమనస్సు వచ్చినట్లా or నీమనస్సుపోయినదే దోవా what! are you to do as you like! మనస్సునించు to give close attention. మనస్సులోనిమాట one's real opinion. తనమనస్సువచ్చిన పనులు whatever jobs he pleased. ఇల్లుచేరుటకు మనస్సురాకగా as (he) could not find it (his) heart to do this. నామనస్సున పట్టినది it was impressed on my mind. నాలుగు దినాలు మనస్సుపట్టుకొని (లేక, నిలుపుకొని) ఉండుము you must keep yourself quiet or restrain yourself for a short time. మనస్పతి *manas-vari*. (మనసు+అతి.) n. A wise man. బుద్ధిమంతుడు. "క॥ అనఘుడు మనిజ ప్రవారం, బనయము గాకుండ నచట నతిశోభిలము నగా. మనసరిదేశోపరిమని, మనసరిరంగా మరు పూశ మనుమనుతించా." R. i. 123. మనసా *manasa*. adv. Mentally, in the heart. హృదయమునందు. మనసార *manas-āra*. adv. Sincerely, willingly. మనసిజుడు, మనః ప్రభవుడు, మనోజుడు or మనోభవుడు *manasijudu*. n. Lit.: The mind-born. An epithet of Manmadha, మన్మథుడు. మనస్కరించు *manas-karintsu*. v. n. To be inclined. మనఃపూర్తిగా చేయు, మనస్సు ఉంచు. In correspondence మనస్కరించేది denotes 'please to consider the above: this is equivalent to "yours truly." మనస్కరించి willingly, మనఃపూర్వకముగా. మనస్కారము *manas-karamu*. n. Fixed attention, profound meditation మనఃపూర్తి, మనఃప్రసన్నము, చిత్తపరిపూర్తి. మనస్కుడు *manaskudu*. adj. "Minded;" a word used in compounds, thus సుమనస్కుడు a right minded man, a good hearted man. దుర్మనస్కుడు an evil minded man. భిన్న మనస్కుడయి heart-broken. భిన్న మనస్కులయి being of various minds. ప్రసన్న మనస్కులయి light hearted, pleased. మనస్తాపము *manas-tāpamu*. n. Mental distress displeasure, anger, vexation. ఆమెకు మనస్తాపముగానున్నది she is annoyed or grieved at this. మనస్ఫూర్తిగా or మనఃపూర్వకముగా *manas-phūrti-ga*. adv. Willingly. మనస్వి *manasvi* adj. Attentive, fixing the mind upon anything. Intelligent. ఉదారుడు. Good-hearted. మంచి మనస్సుగల. మనోజ్ఞము *manōgnamu*. adj. Agreeable, pleasing, captivating, lovely, handsome, సొగసైన, సుందరమైన. మనోరంజని *manō-ranjani*. n. (Lit. that which delights the mind.) The name of a certain flower with a rank smell, apparently a sort of arum. మనోరథము *manō-rathamu*. n. A wish, desire. ఇచ్ఛ. నామనోరథము తమరు త్వరగా నెరవేర్తురని నమ్మియున్నాను I trust that you will soon grant what I so earnestly wish. మనోమాలిన్యము *manō-malikitamu*. n. Misunderstanding. మనోహరము *manō-haramu*. adj. Heart-stealing, i. e., charming, lovely, alluring, captivating, fascinating. ఇంపైన. n. Vermicelli.

మనా or మన్నా *mana*. [H.] n. A prohibition, hindrance, prevention. వానికి దేవిడీమన్నా అయినది he is banished the court.

మనాక్ *manāk*. [Skt.] adv. Little, slowly. అమనాక్ not a little. "పునఃపునరుదంచద్ధంత చేలుపత, వ్యపనావిష్కృతపత్కృతంబుల నూనాగ్ఘస్ఫుటదీర్ఘితై." N. vii. 157. టీ॥ అమనాక్. అధికముగనుట్లు గాను.

మనికట్టు Same as మణికట్టు. (q.v.)

మనికితము *mani-kitamu*. [Tel.] n. Grief, affliction, sorrow. వ్యాకులము, దుఃఖము, విచారము. "క॥ తనయురాగము విన్ను మనేచే, పినికితునవ క్రియింత చేసినవిగాకొ, ధనములవిద్యుత్ గానిదె, మనికితములు మానుడనుచు సాధిక్య వెనిరయకా." Vish. vii. 260. మనికితపడు *manikita-padu*. v. n. To be sorry, to grieve. దుఃఖపడు. మనికితపాటు *manikita-pātu*. n. The act of being sorrowful, దుఃఖపడుట.

మనిషి *manishi*. [for Skt. మనుష్యుడు.] n. A man or woman, a person. వానికి రూకలున్నూలేదు మనిషికట్టూలేదు he has neither money nor men. మనిషికొక మాయకొకచుట్టు a proverbial expression, meaning, all men are subject to disease. మనిషికి ఒక రూపాయి చొప్పున యిచ్చినాడు he gave each man a rupee. మనిషికొక్క మాట చెప్పినారు each man gave a different opinion. మనిషికొక మాట చెప్పుతాడు he talks differently to different people. ఒక మను

మనిషి a woman. ఆమె లావాటిమనిషి she is a stout person. నీవేమిమనిషివి what a strange man you are! మనిషివా, పశువువా? are you a man or a brute? do you call yourself a man? నామనిషిని పంపుతాను I will send my man. ఆ దేశపుమనుషులు people of that country.

మనీష *manisha.* [Skt.] n. Mind, understanding, intellect. బుద్ధి, మతి, ప్రజ్ఞ. మనీషి *manishi.* n. A learned man, a teacher. ప్రాజ్ఞుడు, పండితుడు, బుద్ధిమంతుడు.

మను *manu.* [Tel.] v. n. To live, exist. జీవించు. To conduct oneself, వర్తించు. "కంటిని శ్రీపాద కమలంబులేను, మంటినింకేటికి మనుడుదునని." BD. iii. 2220. n. Earth, soil, మట్టి, నేల. మనికి or మన్కి *maniki.* n. Existence, living, జీవించడము, జీవనము. Home, an abode. నివాసము, ఉనికిపట్టు, వాసస్థానము. A place, స్థానము. "మనుకులయు రాచవారల, మనుకులకిరవగుచుకలిమిమనువకు నెలవై, తనరునయోధ్యానగరము." R. i. 102. మనుకులకిరవగుచు, అనగా ఇండ్లకు ఉనికిపట్టైనదగుచు. మనికిపట్టు *maniki-puttu.* n. Home, an abode. గృహము. మనుకువ *manukuva.* n. An abode, house, residence. వాసస్థానము. మనుగడ *manugada.* n. Life, living. జీవనము, జీవించడము. Means of livelihood, జీవనోపాయము. "మనుగడదప్పవొక్క మునిమాట యుచేకొనవైతి." M. XII. iii. 370. మనుచు, మంచు, మనుపు or మన్పు *manutsu.* v. a. To cause to live, to nourish, to take care of, bring up. మనజేయు, పోషించు, ప్రతికించు. మనువిండి or మన్దిండి *manudindi.* n. Lit: That which eats earth, i.e., a kind of snake, ఒకవిధమైనపాము. మనుపరి *manup-ari.* n. A guardian, కాపరి, రక్షకుడు. మనుపీనుగు *manu-pinugu.* n. A living corpse, జీవచ్ఛవము. మనువృత్తి, మనోవర్తి or మనువర్తి *manu-vritti.* n. Maintenance, support; pension, allowance, stipend. మనువు *manuvu.* n. Life, living, జీవనము, బ్రతుకుట. Conduct, వర్తనము. Choosing a husband, the choice of a husband, మగని వరించుట. A husband, మగడు. A fitting match, implying a proper or respectable son-in-law. వివాహనిశ్చయము. అతడు కూతుల్లకు మనువులుచిక్కక అల్లాడుచున్నాడు he is at a loss for a suitable match for his daughters. మంచిమనువుచిక్కితే కూతురికి పెండ్లిచేస్తాడు. if he meets with a suitable match he is ready to give his daughter in marriage. మారుమనువు a second marriage of a woman, ఆడదానికి రెండవవివాహము. మనుగుడుపు *manu-gudupu.* n. A final entertainment given by the bride's parents to the bridegroom, after the conclusion of the whole marriage ceremonies.

మనుగు or మనువు *manugu.* [Tel.] v. n. To die, చచ్చు.

మనుపాల *manu-pala.* [Tel.] n. A certain medicinal tree with oval leaves, *Nerium antidysentericum.* కుటజము, కొడిసెచెట్టు, పాలకూర, జీవంతి.

మనుబోతు, మన్నుబోతు, మను or మన్ను *manu-bōtu.* [Tel.] The Gayal, commonly called the Bison. బుర్కము. మనుపెంటి, మన్నెంటి, మనుబిడి or మన్బిడి *manu-penti.* n. A female bison. ఆడుబుర్కము. HD. i. 511. plu. మన్బిళ్లు.

మనుమడు *manumadu.* [Tel.] n. A grandson. మనుమరాలు *manumarālu.* n. A granddaughter.

మనువు *manuvu.* [Skt.] n. A mystical verse or formula. మంత్రము. A legislator and saint called Manu. There are said to be fourteen of these Manus, viz., స్వాయంభువు, స్వారోచిషుడు, ఉత్తముడు, తామసుడు, రైవతుడు, చాక్షుషుడు, వైవస్వతుడు, సూర్యసావర్ణి, దక్షసావర్ణి, బ్రహ్మసావర్ణి, ధర్మసావర్ణి, రుద్రసావర్ణి, రౌచ్యుడు, భౌచ్యుడు. మనుజుడు or మనుష్యుడు *manujudu.* n. A man, a human being. మనుజాశనుడు *manuj-āsanudu*. n. Lit. An eater of men, i. e., a demon, రాక్షసుడు. మనుజేంద్రుడు *manuj-endrudu*. n. A king, రాజు. మన్వంతరము *manv-antaramu*. n. An age or period of time supposed to be under the sway of one Manu, ఏకసప్తతిదివ్యయుగములు, మనుకాల మన్వచరిత్రము. (Vulgarly) Time, a rule, reign; thus చందులాలు మన్వంతరములో or హయాములో in the time of Chandulala a former governor of Hyderabad. అతని మన్వంతరము తీరినది his days are ended.

మనోజ్ఞము or మనోహరము and మనోరథము See under మనస్సు.

మన్న *manna*. [H.] n. Prevention, an obstacle, అడ్డగింపు, విఘ్నము. See మనా.

మన్నన or మన్నిక *mannana*. [Tel.] n. Respect, regard, grace, favour, సన్మానము, గౌరవము, గొప్పచేయుటము. "మనుజనాథునివలన మన్ననలుగనిరి." V. P. ii. 18. adj. Dear, beloved. ప్రియమైన. "పాలవెల్లికిణా మన్నన యన్నునైతిపనిమంతిచవుం బెరయైనతో య్యలికా." R. v. 17. మన్నించు *manninṭsu*. v. a. To respect, మన్ననచేయు, గొప్పచేయు, సన్మానించు. To excuse, forgive, to pardon. నా తప్పు మన్నించవలెను I pray you to excuse my fault. మన్నింపు *mannimpu*. n. Respect. గౌరవము. Forgiveness, క్షమాపణ. వానికి దెబ్బలు మన్నించు వుచేసినారు they excused him the flogging, i. e., he was not punished.

మన్ని *manni*. [Tel.] n. Life, జీవము. A certain muscle in the back of the head. పిపిలిలు యందుండునట్టి ము. మన్నిగొను *manni-gonu*. v. a. To kill, or slaughter. చంపు. "మన్నిగొన్న విఖ్యాతిమహాప్రతాపముసకు." Kalahas. iii. 234.

మన్నీడు, మన్నియుడు or మన్నియ *mannidu*. [Tel. మన్ను + ఈడు.] n. A lord, a chieftain, ప్రభువు, మన్నెపుదొర. "మాళవజేశబలు మన్నీలగొలన." Pal. 52. "ఎన్న నామనుజునకిట్టిక తన్నెనుతికూర్పుధనము ధరలో నెపుడుణా, మన్నీలకుజాదరులకు, కన్నె లకుమబోపుచుండుగదరా." Sumati s. 49.

మన్ను or మను *mannu*. [Tel.] n. Earth, mud, soil, dirt. మంటబెట్టు to inter or bury. పూడ్చు. పాతపెట్టు. వానికి మన్నుమిన్నుకానరాలేదు. he is too proud to care for anything in heaven or on earth. మన్నుతిండి, మనుతిండి or మన్దిండి *manu-dindi*. n. Lit. that which feeds on earth, i. e., a kind of snake. మన్నురేడు *mannu-rēdu*. n. A king, భూపతి. మన్నులపాము *mannula-pāmu*. n. A harmless species of serpent, extremely thick. Russell on Snakes, Vol. ii. No. XVI.

మన్ను *mannu*. [Tel.] n. A wild animal of the ox tribe, the Gayal or the Bison. ఋశ్యము. See మనుబోతు.

> "తే॥ పంకిమగోరజదిని బడిపఁనలేవు,
> మన్నునిచ్చేరతగటివన్నులందు."
> Swa. iv. 20.

A kind of military weapon, యుద్ధసాధనవిశేషము.

మన్నెము or మన్యము *mannemu*. [from Skt. మాన్యము.] n. Land given as a token of respect. సన్మానించి యిచ్చిన కొంతభూభాగము. High-lands, hilly land, hill-country, uplands. Agency tracts. మన్నెపుజ్వరము jungle fever. మన్నెపుదేశము highlands. లోమన్యము the interior of the hills. "అనయంబు రజతాద్రి యట్టి దుర్గంబు మనకు గల్గగ నేల మన్నెములో." BD. iii. 1093. మన్నెకాడు, మన్నెదొర or మన్నెపుదొర *manuekadu* n. A highland chieftain. మన్నెపువారు hill people. మన్నెపుగొడ్డలి a broad axe, a woodman's axe, a highlander's axe. మన్నెముల్లు *manne-mullu*. n. A large needle used to remove thorns from the feet of goats. "మందులపాడిబుర్ర మన్నెముల్లులతో లుసుల్లాయు." H. ii. 85. మన్నెరికము *manne-riku-*

mu. n. Chieftainship, the state of being a lord among the hill people. మన్నెపుదొరతనము. "వలపుల మన్నెరికంబు" Vijayanti. ii. 66. టీ॥ కొండవాండ్లయొక్క ప్రభుత్వము.

మన్మథుడు *manmathudu.* [Skt.] n. Manmadha, the Hindu Cupid, అనంగుడు. మన్మథ *manmatha* n. The name of a Telugu year. ఒక సంవత్సరముయొక్క పేరు. మన్మథబాణాలు the arrows of Love, the name of a particular kind of rice, or flower. "మన్మథబాణాలం మరువంపు మొలకలు." H. iv. 155. మన్మథపత్రిక *manmatha-patrika.* n. A billet doux or love letter.

మన్యువు *manyuvu.* [Skt.] n. Sorrow, grief, distress, indigence, displeasure, anger. శోకము, పుత్రమరణాదిజాత మనోవ్యథ. క్రోధము. A sacrifice. క్రతువు.

మప్పు *mappu.* [Tel. contracted from మరపు.] v. a. To break in, or train (any animal). అలవరచు, అభ్యాసము చేయించు. అలవాటుచేయు. మప్పవచ్చునుగాని తిప్పలేము it is easy for us to teach but not to correct. మప్పితము adj. Limited, tolerable, మితము, పరిమితము.

మబ్బు *mabbu.* [Tel.] n. A cloud, మేఘము. Obscurity, darkness, dimness, laziness, dullness, heaviness, మాంద్యము, చీకటి. కనుమబ్బు dimness of sight. వానిచెవులకు మబ్బువచ్చెను his ears are dull of hearing. నిద్రమబ్బు drowsiness or heaviness. ఆ సంగతికి మబ్బుతాళము వేసినాడు he eluded or evaded the question. మబ్బుమందారముగానుండే దినాలు cloudy days. మబ్బురంగు a dark tint in colour, మేఘవర్ణము. మబ్బుకొను *mabbu-konu.* v. n. To become cloudy. To be intoxicated, మత్తిల్లు. మబ్బుత్రోవ *mabbu-trōva.* n. The sky, ఆకాశము. మబ్బుపెట్టు *mabbu-pettu.* v. a. To delude, to evade, conceal. మబ్బుమేపరి *mabbu-mēpari.* n. The wind, వాయువు. మబ్బురవుతు *mabbu-ravutu.* n. An epithet of Indra, ఇంద్రుడు.

మమత or మమత్వము *mamata.* [Skt.] The interest or affection entertained for objects, from considering them as belonging to, or connected with oneself. అభిమానము. "పేటుగాదంబు పానంబు మాటచిరుకు, కఠినదండంబుగటలాటికానియావి, యనెడివ్యసనంబులేడింటి యందుమమత, తగదుగావింపధారుణీతలవిభునకు." M. V. ii. 42. మమకారము *mama-kāramu.* n. Egoism, self regard, pride, arrogance, self-sufficiency, అహంభావము. Attachment, love, ప్రేమ.

మమ్మా *mammā.* [Tel. for అమ్మ.] n. A mother. An old woman in general. మమ్మారె, మమ్మారే, మమ్మారి, మమ్మరె, మమ్మ or మమ్మా *mammare.* interj. Oh! Oh! O dear me! ఆశ్చర్యపుమాట. "క॥ అమ్మడినాగేంద్రంబును, కమ్మనిపొరగతిచుట్టు కొనినడిచిరుగఖా, మమ్మారయనుచుమోవరు. మమ్మారుణ బొగడిరొక్క మొగినవ్వోళా." T. v. 58.

మమ్మాయి *mammāyi.* [Tel.] n. A kind of medicine, లేహవిశేషము.

మమ్ము *mammu.* [Tel.] n. An adverse wind on the sea, a kind of whirlwind that is adverse to sailing ships, సముద్రముమీద ఓడలకు విఘాతముగావచ్చెడు సుడిగాలివిశేషము. pron. The plu. accusative of నేను.

మయనము, మయినము or మైనము *mayanamu.* [Tel.] n. Wax. మయినపువత్తి a wax-candle. A. v. 161.

మయము *mayamu.* [Skt.] adj. Composed of, made of, formed of, full of. This is an affix denoting quality or substance. జలమయమైన aqueous, watery. అగ్నిమయమైన fiery. రత్నమయమైన jewelled, set with gems. త్రయి the Vedas; త్రయీమయమైన scriptural. తృణమయసర్పము a snake made of grass. చిన్మయుడైన spiritual, formed of spirit. సత్యమయుడైన full of truth. ఆ ఊరు తురకలమయముగానున్నది the town swarms with Mussulmans. మయత or మయత్వము *mayata*. n. Identity, unity, oneness, sameness. తాదాత్మ్యము. ఉదకమయత్వమొందె she was united or mingled with the water. KP. iv. 94. "కమంగవరెల్ల పెంపొంద్బయుం దలపున మంత్రవ్యా మయతంగనుపట్టెన్." Mand. i. 2. టీ॥ మంత్రమయతన్, మంత్రవర్ణతా సాక్షి...తేరకు.

మయిల, మైల or మకిల *mayila*. [Tel.] n. Dirt, foulness, uncleanness, actual or ceremonial impurity, dirty clothes. మురికి, అశుచి, కట్టివిడిచినగుడ్డలు. చాకలవాడు ఇంకా మయిల యెత్తుకొనిపోలేదు the washerman has not yet taken away the dirty clothes. వారియింట్లో మయిలవచ్చినది their house has been defiled. adj. Dirty, foul, unclean, impure. మురికిగానుండే, అశుచియైన.

మయిలుతుత్తము or మయిలుతుత్తము *mayila-tuttamu*. [H.] n. Blue vitriol, sulphate of copper. Verdigris, subacetate of copper. మయూరతుత్థము.

మయుడు *mayudu*. [Skt.] n. The name of the architect of the *Asuras*, అసురశిల్పి.

మయూఖము *mayūkhamu*. [Skt.] n. Light, brightness, flame. జ్వాల, ప్రభ. A beam of light, కిరణము.

మయూరము *mayūramu*. [Skt.] n. The peacock. నెమలి. మయూరారి lit: the enemy of the peacock, a chameleon, a lizard. ఊసరవెల్లి. కొండమయూరము (Rox. i. 580.) a small tree or large shrub: *Ardisia solanacea*. మయూరశిఖ or మయూరశిఖండి *mayūra-sikhi*. n. The plant called *Adiantum melanocaulum*.

మయ్యచేప *mayya-chēpa*. [Tel.] n. A sort of fish.

మర *mara*. n. [Tel.] n. A spiral, a screw, a joint or hinge. కీలు. adj. Made of wood, wooden. కొయ్యతోచేసిన. మరకట్టు *mara-kattu*. n. A sort of spell called స్తంభనము. "వాకట్టు మరకట్టు పతికడికట్టు, పొట్టపొంగడు కట్టు పొంగులకట్టు." Pal. 93 మరకాడు *mara-kāḍu*. n. A sailor, నావికుడు. A skipper, the commander of a vessel. A ship-owner. ఓడకాడు. "మరరాజునకు పొందుకరి తేర్పుమరకాడు." Swa. v. 56. టీ॥ మరకాడు. ఓడనడ్తకుడు. మరగాలు *mara-gālu*. n. A stilt or wooden leg, కృత్రిమపాదము. మరగొమ్ము *mara-gommu*. n. A stilt. The pommel of a saddle, గుర్రముమీదిపల్లమునకు ముందు వెనుకలవానికై యెత్తుగా నేర్పరచియుండు భాగము. "వెనుకమరగొమ్మునూతగానొనుచు నరిగెను." KP. iii. 69. మరచేప *mara-chēpa*. n. A sort of shark. సొర్లిమర or పొట్లమర the Squatina or Angel Shark. మరచుట్టు *mara-tsuttu*. n. A toe ring secured with a screw, తిరుగుడు. "శ్రీమద్గురురౌమరచుట్టులో యుదశా." A. v. 131. A turnscrew, తిరుగాలి. మరమేకు *mara-mēku*. n. A screw, lit: a spiral nail, ఇస్కూరాణి. మరసాన *mara-sāna*. n. An instrument for polishing stones, రాళ్లనుపదునుపాదునవిశేషము.

మరందము or మకరందము *marandamu*. [Skt.] n. Nectar, the honey of flowers. పూదేనె.

మరక *maraka*. [Tel.] n. A stain, spot, or blot. కరె. A female-kid, ఆడుమేకపిల్ల. చూడు. నా. v.

మరకతము or మరతకము *marakatamu*. [Skt.] n. An emerald. పచ్చ, గారుత్మతము. A. i. 34.

మరకము *marakamu*. [Tam. మరక్కాల్.] n. A certain measure called a markal, i. e., 8 measures or seers.

మరకువ *marakuva*. [Tel. from మరచు.] n. Ignorance, forgetfulness, అజ్ఞానము.

మరగు or **మరూగు** *maragu.* [Tel.] v. n. and a. To use, to be used, accustomed, or addicted to. అలవాటుపడు, పరిచితమగు. To desire, covet, ఆశించు, ఆశపడు. To boil fiercely, మసలకాగు. To fall in love with, to be enamoured of, మోహించు, ఆసక్తుడగు. వాడు దానిని మరగినాడు he fell in love with her. తాగమరిగినవాడు one who is addicted to drink. మరుగుచున్న నేయి boiling oil. మరగకాగు to boil fiercely. "కరుగు చుమరగుచు కటకటాయనుచు, కందుచుగుందుచు కళవళించుచును." L. viii. 52. "వాలిమ్మ్రుకుడోట పోలగనాలో లక్ష్మణుడొంగి యుర్వ్యాజలోడం, బా లుడువోరెంగాలిమి మాలియుదేమిటికినట మరగెద వింక." BRK. x. 343. **మరపడము** or **మరపుట** *mara-paḍamu.* n. Training, breaking in. అలవాటుచేయడము. **మరపు** *marapu.* v. a. To train, break in. అలవాటుచేయు. మరప రాని untameable, indomitable. **మరగించు** *maragintsu.* v. a. To enamour. మోహింపచేయు. To cause to boil. కాగించు.

మరచు, మరుచు, మరచిపోవు or **మరిచిపోవు** *maratsu.* [Tel.] v. n. To forget. **మరపించు** or **మరిపించు** *mara-pintsu.* v. a. To cause to forget, to blot out from one's memory. వాడు దాతృత్వములో తండ్రిని మరిపించినాడు he out-shone his father in liberality. ఆ బిడ్డను చనుమరిపించినది she weaned the child. "కృపాకృత్యవర్తనలవ్మర పించు." T. ii. 161. **మరపు, మరుపు** or **మరువు** *marapu.* n. Forgetfulness, ignorance, delusion. విస్మృతి, అజ్ఞానము, పారవశ్యము, ప్రమాదము.

మరణము *maraṇamu.* [Skt.] n. Death. చావు. **మరణించు** or **మరించు** *maranintsu.* v. n. To die, చచ్చు.

మరదలు or **మరందలు** *maradalu.* [Tel.] n. A wife's younger sister; also a younger brother's wife. పెండ్లాముచెల్లెలు, తమ్ముని భార్య. "నీమఱందలికొమ్మ." T. i. v. 49.

మరది or **మరిది** *maradi.* [Tel.] n. A husband's younger brother, పెనిమిటితమ్ముడు. A younger sister's husband. చెల్లెలిమగడు. A brother-in-law, భార్యతోబుట్టువు.

మరమ్మతు *marammatu.* [H]. n. Repair.

మరల or **మరలి** *marala.* [Tel. from మరలు.] adv. Again, anew, in return. "ప్రా దానముజేసితివీవు మేల్మరలజేయుగనే నమస్కరించితిగా." Anirudh. iii. 59.

మరలు or **మళ్లు** *maralu.* [Tel.] v. n. To turn, return, go back. తిరుగు. వెనుకకు తిరుగు. To be rescinded, abrogated, annulled. "సముద్రంబుప్రవేశించిరాదేరుల నం దంబున మరలనెరుంగక." Vish. ii. 272. **మరలబడు** or **మరలంబడు** *marala-baḍu.* v. n. To return, మరలు, తిరుగు. To rebel. తిరుగబడు. వానినాలుక మరలబడియున్నది his tongue is tied. "వారల, మతిమయమనుష్ఠించు గాకమరలంబడునే." M V. i. 308. **మరలబాటు** *marala-bāṭu.* n. The act of turning back, మరలబడుట. **మరలుకొను** *maralu-konu.* v. n. To turn. **మరలుచు, మరల్చు, మరలించు, మళ్లించు** or **మళ్లిచు** *maralutsu.* v. a. To turn back, to cause to return, to recall, to rescind, abrogate, annul. To ward off, elude, evade. "భక్తవత్సలుండు, గోపాలబాలకులమరలించి మరియు పెక్కువిధంబుల జరియించుచుండె." N. ix. 254. **మరలుపు** or **మరల్పు** *maralupu.* n. Changing, turning, మరల్చుట, మళ్లించు కొనడము. "మక్కువమరల్పునేర్పులు." T. iii. 124.

మరవ or **మరువ** *marava.* [Tel.] n. A sluice, or outlet. తూము.

మరాటు or **మరాటి** *marāṭa.* [from Skt. మహారాష్ట్ర.] n. A Mahrāti man, adj. Pertaining to the Mahrati country or nation. **మరాటితీగ** *marāṭi-tīga.* n. A plant called *Spilanthus acmella.* Rox. iii. 410. **మరాటిమొగ్గ** *marāṭi-mogga.* n. A certain drug. Rox. iii. 410. మరాటీలు *maraṭīlu*. n. plu. The Maharattas.

మరాళము *marālamu*. [Skt.] n. A species of waterfowl, with red legs and bill; commonly supposed to be a swan. హంస.

మరి *mari*. [Tel.] n. A time, season, తడవ. ఒకమరి or ఒక్కమరి once. adv. More, further, still, else, again, then, so, మరియు, పిండియు, ఇంకను, అనంతరము. మరేమిలేదు there is nothing else, or nothing more. మరేమి what else? what more? మరి ఎప్పుడు వచ్చేది then when shall I come? మరి మంచిది so much the better. మరి లేదు there is nothing else. మరియొకడు another. మరియొకటి another thing. మరియొకడు another man. మరిన్ని or మరియును besides, also, moreover. మరియెట్లు in what other way? మరికొన్ని a few more. మరినాలుగు four more. వాడు ఎవడు who is that man? మరియెవరులేరు nobody in particular. మరేమి లేదు there is nothing further. ఇది మరింత దుర్ఘటం this is more troublesome. మరిమరి *mari-mari*. adv. Very much, మిక్కిలి, అత్యంతము. Again and again, more and more, మరియుమరియును.

మరిగ *mariga*. [Tel.] n. A cup cut out of soft soapstone. రాతిచిప్ప. "మరిగపట్టిమూడుడు మరిగంటునాము." BD. iii. 829.

మరిగొమ్మ *mari-gommu*. [Tel.] n. An overflow channel. చెరువునకు నీరు ఎక్కువైతే పోవు తూము అలుగు.

మరిడి or మరిడీ *mariḍi*. [Tel.] n. Cholera, మరిడీజాడ్యము, విషూచి. The name of the goddess of cholera.

మరిది See మరఁది.

మరియాద *mariyāda*. [from Skt. మర్యాద.] n. Order, క్రమము. Extent, limit, boundary, [illegible]. Respectability.

"[illegible]
[illegible]
[illegible]
[illegible]."
భార. విరా. i.

మరీచము or మరిచము *marichamu*. [Skt.] n. Pepper. మిరియము.

మరీచి *marīchi*. [Skt.] n. A ray of light, కిరణము. plu. మరీచులు. Swa. v. 98. Also, the name of a certain rishi. ఒకఋషి.

మరీచిక *marīchika*. [Skt.] n. A mirage. ఎండమావి, మృగతృష్ణ. H. ii. 169.

మరు *maru*. [Tel.] n. In composition, short for మరుగు, మరల, and మారు. adj. Other, next, in return. మరునాడు or మర్నాడు (మరు నటినాడు) next day. మరుమాట (మారు+మాట) a word in return, contradiction. వేమారు or వేమారు a thousand times. మరుపడు *maru-paḍu*. (మరుగు+పడు) v. n. To be concealed, to disappear or vanish, మరుగగు, అదృశ్యమగు. "భూమండలంబు మరు పడియుండెను." M. VII. iv. 315. మరుపెట్టు *maru-peṭṭu*. v. a. To conceal, hide. మరుగుచేయు. మరుమ్రోత *maru-mrōta*. (మారు+మ్రోత) n. An echo.

మరుగు *marugu*. [Tel.] v. n. To be concealed or hidden, చాటగు. To be dejected, to be in deep sorrow, కుందు. సంతాపించు. మరుగు or మరువు *marugu*. n. Privacy, cover, shelter, a screen, concealment, the hidden part of any thing, అగోచర స్థానము. చాటు. తమమరుగుజొచ్చినాను I have sought shelter with you. ఆతోట నిండా మరుగుగానున్నది that garden is very private. మరుగుగోడ a curtain or screen placed before a door. మరుగుపెరడు or మరుగుదొడ్డి a privy or necessary. ఆమాటను మరుగుచేసినారు they kept that word secret. adj. Hidden, unseen, invisible, imperceptible, obscure, sheltered. మరుగువడు

marugu-paḍu. v. n. To disappear, to be hidden. కానరాపోవు. **మరుగుపరుచు** *marugu-parutsu.* v. a. To conceal, keep secret. **మరుకువ** *maruknva.* n. Sorrow, grief, సంతాపము. **మరువ** *maruva.* (మరుగు+వా.) n. A pot, కుండ. adj. Dumb, మూగైన. **మరువకొండు** *maruva-kandu.* n. An epithet of Agastya, కుంభసంభవుడు. **మరువవాడు** *maruva-vāḍu.* n. A dumb man. మూగవాడు.

మరుగుజ్జు *marugudzdzu.* [Tel. మారు+గుజ్జు] n. A dwarf. కుబ్జుడు.

మరుచు or **మరచు** *marutsu.* [Tel.] v. a. To forget. ఒళ్లుమరుచు or మైమరచు to forget oneself, to lose consciousness, to swoon.

మరుడు *maruḍu.* [from Skt. స్మరుడు.] n. Manmadha. మరుసైన్యము the host of Manmadha, i. e., parrots, cuckoos, &c. మరుకాక the fire of love. మరుచిహ్న. or మరుపని the union of the sexes. మన్మథయుద్ధము, రతి. H. ii. 268. మరుతేజీ a parrot. Ila. i. 34. మరువిల్లు *Mons veneris, pudendum muliebre,* మదనగృహము.

మరుత్తు *maruttu.* [Skt.] n. Wind, air, వాయువు. A sort of demigod. వేలుపు. **మరుత్వంతుడు** or **మరుత్వాలుడు** *marut-vantuḍu.* n. An epithet of Indra as lord of the demigods. **మరుత్సఖుడు** *marut-sakhuḍu.* n. An epithet of Fire and of Indra. అగ్నిహోత్రుడు, ఇంద్రుడు.

మరులు *marulu.* [From Skt. స్మర.] n. Love, desire, lust, మోహము. కామము. A demon, పిశాచము. మరులెత్తినట్లైనది as if love stricken. **మరులుకొను** *marulu-konu.* v.n. To fall in love, మోహించు. **మరులుకొలుపు** *marulu-kolupu* v. a. To allure, enamour, to cause to love, మోహింపజేయు మరులుజేయు. **మరులుతీగె** or **మరులుమాతంగి** *marulu-dzaḍa.* n. A creeper or plant which, as soon as touched, makes one fall in love with another, Orris root: a kind of bent grass. "మరులుతీగె మెట్టియురులన్నతో యువి రొండు తమ్మిస్త్ర గాడుపడి." A. vi. 11. మరులుమందు or మరులమందు a love potion. మెట్టిన తోడనే మరులుపుట్టించు ఓషధి, భూతికేశము, లోమివృత్తము. మరులురేడు the lord of the demons, పిశాచములరాజు. ఉ. హరి. ii.

మరువము, మరువకము or **మరువపుచెట్టు** *maruvamu.* [Skt.] n. The plant called the Sweet Marjoram. ప్రస్థపుష్పకము. మరువపుమొలక a slender girl. lit: a sprig of that plant. మరువపుమొలకలు plu. a kind of grain. H. iv. 155.

మరువు *maruvu.* [Tel. another form of మరుగు.] n. A cover, shelter; privacy, solitude. చాటు. మరుగు, అగోచరస్థానము. A piece of armour. కవచము. "మద్రవిభుడు స్వర్ణమారుత మరువులమైమరువులూక, సరికెమగ్గిము." M. IX. i. 295. **మరువుచేయు** *maruvu-chēyu.* v. a. To hide, చాటుచేయు, దాచు. **మరువుపడు** *maruvu-paḍu.* v. n. To disappear, vanish. కానరాపోవు. "ఇల మరువుపడ్డ నిర్జలశివభక్తి." BD. i. 568.

మరువు *maruvu.* [Skt.] n. A desert, waste, barren country. నిర్జలప్రదేశము. A mountain, పర్వతము. **మరుభూమి** *maru-bhūmi.* n. A dry waste, a desert spot. ఊసరక్షేత్రము.

మరుసటి or **మరుస** *marusaṭi.* [Tel.] adj. The next. మరుసటిసంవత్సరము the next year. మరుసటిదినము next day. **మరుసంజె** *maru-sanja.* (మరుస+సంజె) n. Evening.

మర్కటము or **మర్కటకము** *markaṭamu.* [Skt.] n. A monkey, కోతి. A spider. సాలెపురుగు. A. i. 45. మర్కటకిశోరన్యాయము, "like the monkey and its cub," i. e., the weaker adheres to the stronger by instinct, కోతిపిల్ల కోతిని తానుగాపోయి పట్టుకొని

పడము. అనగా శిష్యుడుగాపోయి గురువును ఆశ్ర యించడము. మర్జాల కిశోర న్యాయము like the cat and kitten, i. e., పిల్లి తన పిల్లను కరుచు కొని తీసుకొని పోవడము, that is, the instinct which leads the stronger to protect or carry the weaker, గురువు తానై అభిమానించి శిష్యుని ఏలుకోవడము. The latter instance is used to illustrate the free grace of God: and the former is of man seeking divine aid.

మర్తబు *martabu*. [H.] adj. Closed, settled, as an account, concluded, finished.

మర్త్యము *martyamu*. [from Skt. మృత.] adj. Mortal. n. The visible world, the earth. ప్రపంచము, భూలోకము. "తనకోర్కి కనుమాపరమైన యుట్టికన్యాగాదపరమ్య మర్త్యమున." M. I. ii. 172. మర్త్యుడు *martyudu*. n. A man, a mortal. మనుష్యుడు.

మర్దనము *mardanamu*. [Skt.] n. Rubbing, handling, grinding, pounding. పిసకడము, నూరడము. అంగమర్దనము massaging, rubbing or pressing the limbs.

మర్దలము *mardalamu*. [Skt.] n. A kind of drum. మృదంగము.

మర్దించు *mardintsu*. [Skt.] v. a. To rub, handle, grind, pound, crush, పిసుకు, నూరు. మర్దితము *marditamu*. adj. Rubbed, ground. పిసకబడిన. నూరబడిన.

మర్మము *marmamu*. [Skt.] n. A vital part, ఆయువు, జీవస్థానము. A secret, a mystery, రహస్యం. Secrecy, mystery, dissimulation, hypocrisy, కపటము, వంచన. మర్మముగా in full detail, minutely. మర్మస్థానము a private part, vital part. మర్మాన్వేషి one who investigates or tries to discover. మర్మజ్ఞుడు *marma-gnyudu*. n. An intimate. Lit: One who knows a secret. మర్మ మెరిగిన వాడు. మర్మి *marmi*. n. A hypocrite.

మర్మరము *marmaramu*. [Skt. cf. Eng. 'murmur'.] n. A murmur, a rustling sound. వస్త్రములయొక్కయు పర్ణములయొక్కయు ధ్వని.

మర్యాద *maryāda*. [Skt.] n. A limit, boundary, మేర. పొలిమేర. హద్దు. Respect, civility, సన్మానము. Manner, way, fashion, decency, custom, rule. కట్టుబాటు. ఆయుర్మర్యాద the limit of life. మర్యాదమాట a civil expression. మర్యాదస్థుడు a gentleman, a respectable man. ఇది నీకు మర్యాదా is this manners? is this proper for you. మర్యాదైన *maryād-aina*. adj. Honourable, respectable.

మర్రపాకు Same as మరుదిండి. See under మరు.

మర్రి *marri*. [Tel.] n. The Banyan tree, *Ficus indica*, వటవృక్షము.

మర్షము *marshamu*. [Skt.] n. Patience, endurance. క్షమ. ఓర్పు.

మల *mala*. [Tel.] n. A mountain, కొండ. The axle bar on which the lever (మీట) of a ఏతము turns. పిల్లతోడి దోసకు తోడ అడ్డకర్ర. మలగొంగ *mala-gonga*. n. An epithet of Indra, ఇంద్రుడు. మలమణికి or మలముచ్చు *mala-maniki*. n. A monkey. మలయమ్మ *mala-y-amma*. n. The mountain goddess, i. e., Parvati.

మలక *malaka*. [Tel.] n. A tangle, twist, bend; a spiral, a serpentine line; crookedness, వంకర, చిక్కు, చుట్టు. మలకలు tricks, guiles. The twisting or turns of a channel. మలకజడ a wily monk, కపటముని. "మలకజడ మూప్రచారముల మాయలు మూల్ విమెర్చు కొనుదుర్." B. X. § 16, 66. A Mahomedan, తురక. An earthen lid over a pot, మూకుడు. adj. Crooked, వంకర. మలకతూము *malaka-tūmu*. n. A measure (*toom*) containing ten కుంచములు, పదికుంచములప్రమాణము. **మలకపుట్టి** *malaka-puṭṭi.* n. A measure of grain, about a ton, being from 200 to 240 కుంచములు or 960 seers. ఇన్నూరుకుంచెములకొలదిగల మానికేము. **మలకమెరుపు** *malaka-merupu.* n. A bow-shaped flash of lightning, ధనురాకారమగు మెరుపు. **మలగొను** or **మెలిగొను** *mala-gonu.* v. n. To be twisted, మెలికగొను. **మలపుగొను** *malapu-gonu.* v. n. To dance, నర్తించు.

మలకడము *malakaḍamu.* [Tel.] n. A shoe, పాదరక్ష. "చెలివాడపని త్రొక్కి మలకడాల్గొని నూనెయిడి." A. vi. 94. టీ॥ మలకడాలు, చెప్పులు.

మలగ *malaga.* [Tel.] n. A double bullock load. ఎద్దుపైకంతతోడి సరకుగోనె.

మలగు or **మలుగు** *malagu.* [Tel.] v. a. and v. n. To wander, to roam about, to turn, to quit. తిరుగు, మర్లు, మరలు, విడ్చి త్రిప్పు. To be bent, వంకరగు. "సొరిదిమలంగిచూచుమఱి." A. iii. 28. "వినుముజ్ఞానంబునగర్వనిరూఢతగలుగు, వానమలగవుజననంబుమరణము." M. XII. vi. 163. **మలచు, మలుచు, మలపు** or **మలుపు** *ma-latsu.* v. a. To cause to turn, మలగజేయు, త్రిప్పు, మళ్లించు. To chip, to cut stone with a chisel, to engrave a stone. చెక్కు-చేయు, ఉలితోచెక్కు. To winnow grain so as to remove pebbles, dirt, &c. బియ్యములోని రాళ్లు తీసివేయు. మలచినబియ్యము winnowed grain. ఎద్దులమలచు to turn the oxen. To fold, to bend. మడుచు. "కొమ్మావులుమలచి లోలోన నవ్వుగా మెయ్యక మడచక్కను." A. iv. 45. టీ॥ మలంచి అవగా మడిచి, చెదవివిడిచి. "పాదములు పిక్కలునొక్కటిగామలంచి." T. iii. 120. టీ॥ మలంచి, చుట్టి. **మలపు** *malapu.* n. Acting, dancing, నర్తనము. "మ॥ ఎడనెడంబడకులకలు మలపుగొన." A. iv. 38. టీ॥ మలపు, ఎదురుతిరిగి ఆడే ఆట. Greatness, అధికత్వము.

మలచేము *malatsemu.* [Tel.] adj. Great, much, గొప్ప, అధికము.

మలప *malapa.* [Tel.] n. A cow or buffalo which gives milk after her calf is dead. దూడ చచ్చినను పాలిచ్చే ఆవు మొదలైనవి.

మలమల *mala-mala.* [Tel.] adv. Fiercely, violently. **మలమలమరుగు** *mala-mala-marugu.* v. n. To boil violently. **మలమల మాడు** *mala-mala-māḍu.* v. n. To burn fiercely, "మలమలమరుగుచునిలఁబడసేల, కాల చెరిప్పిన కూడుతుకువంగ సేల." BD. iii 760. ఎండలో చీమలు మలమలమాడును the ants are scorched or burned up in the sun.

మలమాసము *mala-māsamu.* [Skt.] n. An intercalary month. అధికమాసము.

మలము *malamu.* [Skt.] n. An excretion, especially applied to the fæces, dung, dirt, filth, dregs, sediment. Sin, pollution. మూత్రము, పురీషము, కలిబి, చీమిడి, పుసి, ఉమ్మి మొదలైనవి; పాపము, మాలిన్యము, దోషము. మలహరుడు the remover of defilement. ఆణవమలము original sin, అనుసంబంధమైనమలము. మలత్రయము or ముమ్మలము three kinds of defilement or evil passions, viz., గర్వము, మాయ, కామము, pride, confusion of mind and lust. మలమూత్రములు dung and urine, మూత్రపురీషములు. మలబంధనము costiveness, obstruction of the bowels. మలబాధకు వెళ్లు to go to stool.

మలయము *malayamu.* [borrowed by Skt. from Drav. మల.] n. Malabar, మలయాళదేశము. Mount Malaya, a hill range in the southern part of Western India. A garden, తోట, ఆరామము. మలయగిరి (literally,) the sandalwood mountain, i. e., the Indian Hymettus, a mountain celebrated for its fragrant sandal groves. మలయమారుతము a gentle, fragrant breeze, a zephyr.

మలయజము *malayajamu.* n. The Sandalwood tree, చందనవృక్షము. Sandalwood. చందనము. మలయజసిరి *malaya-ja-siri.* n. A kind of cloth. వస్త్రవిశేషము. "శృంగారమున్నునభూసతిరుద్రతిలకంబు, సరిగమ్మి, మలయజసిరిదుప." BD. iii. 117. "మూండోళి భూసతిమలయజసిరి." BP. iii 25.

మలయు *malayu.* [Tel.] v. n. To wander, roam, తిరుగు. To be entangled, to form a tangle, పెనగు, చిక్కుపడు. To spread, వ్యాపించు. To attempt, ఉద్యమించు. To be eager for, ఉత్కంఠించు. To long for, కోరు. To rejoice, be pleased, eager, or delighted. To shine, be splendid. To unfold or display. ఉల్లసించు, వెలయు, విజృంభించు. To blow, as wind. విసరు. "ఇలలోనివిద్దరురాజులు మలయుచుమదదరంగమాడి మాపటివేళ బల పెత్తికట్టమరచిన వెలుకలు తమకలుగులోని కేవ సడిపెదా" చాటుపద్యము. "మాణిక్యదీపముల్ మలయుకోట." Swa. iii. 146. "మలపెనుదా రమయమలయుసమీరము." T. ii. 149. మలయిక *malayika.* n. Rambling, jaunting, junketting. విహారము.

మలవతి *malavati.* [Tel.] n. Extra assessment, an increased demand or cess. (Vizag.)

మలామి or మొలామి *malāmu.* [H.] n. Plating, gilding.

మలారము *malāramu.* [Tel.] n. A rake (used in a garden.) గాజులమలారము a string or bunch of glass bracelets.

మలికితము *malikitamu.* [Tel.] n. Doubt, hesitation, సందేహము. Sorrow, వ్యాకు లము. మలికిత పడు to sorrow. "మనసులోన గాదుమలికితపడము." L. xi. 118. మనోమలికి తము mental grief.

మలిగండ్లు *mali-gandlu.* [Tel. మలి+గండ్లు.] n. Stones separated from grain by winnowing. Light grains which are worthless. తాలుగింజలు, మాకదుప్పు.

"ఆర్లుచేసిమలచి యాలిగండ్లుమలిగండ్లు, [illegible] పెరికి కేరెల్ల, నెలమిమన్ను దనెదు వెర్రితోదురుకుమా."
Vēma. iii. 34.

"ద్వి॥ మలిగండ్లుదీసిన మంచిబియ్యంబు, నిలంమువిధంబున నిష్పారదుష్ట, వాసనవెంతియునడిశదికొత్త, భాసురజ్ఞానసంపద వృద్ధిబొందు."
L. xxiv. 57.

మలినము *malinamu.* [Skt.] n. Dirt, blackness; a fault, defect, మురికి. దోషము. adj. Dirty, soiled, foul, black. మాసినది, నల్లని. Sinful, wicked, abominable, దూషితమైన. మలినముఖుడు blackfaced, an epithet of the god of fire, of a ghost, of a monkey, or of a bad man; the large black wild bee. అగ్ని, పిశాచుడు, దుర్జనుడు, చచ్చినవాడు, కొండముచ్చు, తుమ్మెద. మలీమసము *mali-masamu.* adj. Foul, dirty, మాసిన.

మలు *malu.* [Tel. a form of మరు from మరుస.] adj. The second. మలుకారు *malu-kāru.* n. The second crop produced within the year, the [illegible]ht crop. రెండో మారుపెట్టినపంట. Also, winter, శీతకాలము. మలుచూలు or మలుచూలు the second child. తొలిచూలు first child. మలుపక్షము the second fortnight, కృష్ణపక్షము. మలుసంజె *malu-sandza.* n. The evening time, eventide, సాయంసంధ్య. మలుతుట్టు *malu-tsuṭṭu.* n. A screw, a screw driver, a wrench, తిరుగాలి.

మలుకు or మలుక్కు *maluku.* [Tel.] n. A turn, twist, fold. A slip-knot. దారము మొదలయినవాటిని ఎదురెదురుగా తగిలించి మళ్లీ పెడమర్లతిప్పినది. కొండమలుకుగాలి an eddy of wind round a point of land. "మలుక్కు తో. దామెలివెట్టికట్టినకడానిజగాజిగిపాగమీద." T. v. 7.

మలుకువ *malukuva.* [Tel.] n. Dirt. మలి నము.

మలుగు malugu. [Tel.] v. n. To be extinguished, go out. అణగారు. To perish, నశించు. మలుపు malupu. v. a. To extinguish or put out a lamp. ఆర్పు. To turn, త్రిప్పు. To destroy, నశింపజేయు. n. A turning. తిరుగుడు. మూలమలుపున in turning a corner. మలుచు or మల్చు malutsu. v. a. To winnow grain in order to remove stones and grits from it, ధాన్యమునందలి గులకరాళ్లుపోవుటకు చెరుగు. To turn in a lathe, తెరమెడపెట్టు. To cut stone with a chisel, to engrave a stone, రాతిని తొలుచు. See మలచు. మలుగు or మలుగులు malugu. n. The small of the back above the loins, the sides of the loins. కటిమొక్క ప్రక్కలు, ముక్క. మలుగులు the back of the hip, కుంటి. మలుగు or మలుగుపాము malugu. An eel. పాపమీను.

మల్కాంగిని or మాల్కాంగిని malkāngini. [Tel.] n. The black oil plant, *Celestrus paniculata*, or *Oleum nigrum*. (Watts.) జ్యోతిష్మతి, పెక్కుడుతీగె. పిన్నమాలేరు.

మల్కుడు malkudu. [Tel.] n. A Mussulman "మల్కువిరోధన." Vasu. iii. 251.

మల్మలు or మొమలులు malmalu. [H.] n. A kind of fine silk.

మల్లకుడు mallakudu. [Tel.] n. An obstinate man, a forward man. కఠినుడు, గడుసరి.

"క॥ తల్లికిదండ్రికిగురులకు
పెల్లవిధంబులనువలయు హితములుచెప్పన్.
మల్లకుడుంగాకకర్జము
చెల్లావమునాగజాంచి సౌజన్యమునన్."
భార. అను. iv.

మల్లము or మల్లకము mallamu. [Skt.] n. A vessel holding oil whether for culinary purposes or for burning as a lamp. నూనెచిప్ప, ప్రమిద, సానిక. మల్ల or మల్లె malla. (from మల్లము.) n. A shallow earthen vessel. మంటికంచము. సానిక.

మల్లచేరము, మల్లటు, and మల్లడి See under మల్లు.

మల్లరము mallaramu. [Tel.] adj. Fat, proud, క్రొవ్విన, మదించిన, గర్వించిన. మల్లరపు టాబోతు a fat ox.

మల్లసాల or మల్లెసాల malla-sāla. [Tel.] n. A dining room. భోజనశాల.

మల్పాపు malpāpu. [H.] adj. Covered, enclosed. n. An enclosure. మల్పాపు చేయు malpāpu-chēyu. v. a. To enclose (a letter in a cover).

మల్ల malla. [Tel.] n. A certain grain-fee allowed to potters. మల్లామడి mallamadi. adj. Plagued, troubled, troublesome, distressful. పీడితము, తొందరమానా.

మల్లాటు and మల్లాడు See under మల్లు.

మల్లారము or మలారము mallāramu. [Tel.] n. A cluster of bracelets. A cord on which bracelets (గాజులు) are strung by venders.

మల్లిక mallika. [Skt.] n. The Jasmine plant. మల్లెచెట్టు, మల్లెపువ్వు. నవమల్లిక the double jasmine, విరజాజి. Rox. I. 95. మల్లికాక్షము mallikākshamu. n. A kind of heron or swan with dark legs and light eyes. Ananda. ix. 59. మలినచరణచంచు శ్వేతహంసము. A white-eyed horse, శ్వేతనేత్రాశ్వము.

మల్లె or మల్లియ malle. [Tel.] n. The Jasmine plant. మల్లెపూలు jasmine blossoms. అడవిమల్లె *Jasminum angustifolium*, a shrub which grows to the height of ten feet. ఒలాందామల్లె the tuberose jasmine. బొండుమల్లె or బొడ్డుమల్లె a variety with luxuriant flowers. నాగమల్లె a plant, *Justicia grandiflorum*, prickly pear. నీటిమల్లె a water creeper, *Persicaria madraspatana*: Rox. ii. 287. Other kinds are called కంపటిమల్లె, పేడమల్లె, సూదిమల్లె, మల్లెలగుడి malle-lagudi, n. A name given to a beautiful dog. మల్లెపురుగు *malle-purugu*. n. A parasitic worm that is generated in the flesh of cattle. మల్లెలు *mallelu*. n. Jasmine flowers. Also, pustules produced in the pox. మల్లెతెవులు the disease called Cancer. "విసములయ్యెను చేర్చిన విసములన్ని మల్లెలయ్యెను జిగిబొందుమల్లె లంచ." Ila. iii. 93. మల్లె *malle*. [Tel.] n. A twig. చువ్వ. మల్లెజంగురు or మల్లెజెగురు *malle-janguru*. n. A heron. లోహపృష్ఠము, రాపులుగు.

మల్లు *mallu*. [Tel. from మల and also Skt.] n. A name (like Pug, or Jack) for a monkey. కోతి. A wrestler or boxer. జెట్టివాడు, వస్తాదు. Wrestling, a struggle. జెట్టిపెనకువ. మల్లట, మల్లాట or మల్లాడుట *mall-aṭa*. n. Struggling, wrestling, పెనగులాడుట. మల్లచరచు *malla-tsaratsu*. (మల్లట+చరచు) v. n. To clap oneself on the breast or shoulder (as wrestlers do in challenging their opponents.) భుజాస్ఫాలనముచేయు. "దుర్యోధనునిం దగినవానినికాకని తన్ననప్పుడు కృతార్థునిం గాదలంచుచు మల్లచరచినం." M. IX. i. 412. మల్లచరపు *malla-tsarapu*. n. Clapping the shoulder with the hands in token of a readiness to fight. మల్లడి *malladi*. n. A struggle, పెనకువ. Grief, పరితాపము. A crowd, గుంపు. మల్లడించు or మల్లడిగొను to rise or gather in a mob, గుంపుకూడు. To unfold or display, విజృంభించు, అతిశయించు. To grieve or be afflicted, సంతాపమునుపొందు, పరితపించు. "తేంట్లుమల్లడిగొని చుట్టి రా మనసలరా." A. i. 21. "మనమునజయు కాంతి మిగులమల్లడిగొనగా." BKY. ii. 773. మల్లాడు *mall-āḍu*. v. n. To struggle, పెనగులాడు. మల్లుడు *malluḍu*. n. A wrestler. జెట్టివాడు. మల్లుకట్టు *mallu-kaṭṭu*. v. a. To oppose, obstruct, అడ్డగించు. మల్లుపెనగు *mallu-penagu*. v. a. To struggle like a wrestler, జెట్టిపెనకువగా పెనగులాడు. మల్లగుల్లము *malla-gullamu*. n. A discussion, a dispute. మల్లగుల్లాలుపడుచున్నారు they are disputing or wrangling.

మళయాళము *maḷa-yāḷamu*. [Drav. మల (hill)+ఆలము (place)] n. Lit. The hilly country. Malabar and Travancore, మళయాళదేశము.

మళిగ *maḷiga*. [Tel.] n. A wholesale shop.

మళ్లి or మళ్లీ *maḷḷi*. [Tel. from మళ్లు.] v. adv. Again. తిరిగిన్ని. మళ్లించు *maḷḷintsu*. v. a. To turn, to return, to get back.

మళ్లు *maḷḷu*. [Tel. plural of మడి.] n. Fields. పొదులు.

మళ్లు or మరలు *maḷḷu*. [Tel.] v. n. To turn, తిరుగు. మళ్లుముఖముగానున్నది it is on the turn. మళ్లుకొను *maḷḷu-konu*. v. n. To turn back or return. మళ్లవేసికొను *maḷḷa-vēsi-konu*. v. a. To turn or stop a thing, as a cat or dog does a rat. దోవలో దొంగలు నన్ను మళ్లవేసుకొన్నారు or అడ్డుకొన్నారు the thieves beset me in the road.

మవ్వము *mavvamu*. [Tel.] n. Beauty, comeliness, elegance. సొగసు, కోమలత, సోము. మవ్వము, మవ్వంపు or మవ్వపు *mavvamu*. adj. Beautiful, handsome, neat, comely, pretty. సొగసైన, సుందరమైన, కోమలమైన. "కడుబెట్టిదపుగాలి సుడిసినసెందప్పు దిరిగినమవ్వంపుతీగెమాడ్కి..." URT. vi. 78.

మశకము *maśakamu*. [Skt.] n. A gnat, or mosquito; any stinging fly. దోమ.

మశానము *maśānamu*. [for Skt. శ్మశానము.] n. A cemetery.

మశూచి or మశూచికము *maśūchi*. [from Skt. మసూరి.] n. Small pox. పిల్లకు మశూచికముపోసినది, కనిపించినది, లేక, చూపినది the child has got the small pox.

మషాకత్తు *mashākattu*. [H.] n. The measurement of land. కొలుచుట.

మషాలు *mashálu.* [H.] n. A torch. మషాల్జీ a torch-bearer, a lamp lighter.

మషి or మసి *mashi.* [Skt.] n. Ink. ఇంకి, కాటుక. Blackness, a stain, నలుపు, డాగు.

మష్టు or మస్టు *mashṭu.* [Tel. from మసటు.] n. Sediment, dross. కల్మషము. వెండిమష్టు silver dross.

మస *masa.* [Tel.] n. Delirium, perplexity, భ్రమ, మాయ. A love powder. మచ్చు. Beauty, విలాసము. "జిగిబిగిసగబిన్నెలమస చూచి వలచుచిత్తజాదైన." Hams. ii. 105. మసజేసితెచ్చినాడు he conjured it out of their hands.

మసక or మసకన *masaka.* [from Skt. మషి.] n. Blackishness, ఇంచుకనలుపు. Dimness of the eyes. Dimness, slight darkness, మునిచీకటి. మసమసకన *masa-masakana.* (మసకన+మసకన) n. Great dimness, మిక్కిలి మసక. adj. Very dim, మిక్కిలిమసకగానున్న. Very little, మిక్కిలి కొంచెము, ఇంచుక.

మసకము *masakamu.* [Tel.] n. Sexual intercourse or desire, సంభోగము, సంభోగేచ్ఛ. మసకొను *masa-konu.* (మసకము+కొను) v. n. To yield, melt, be charmed. భ్రమపడు. "మసకొని రేకుపండ్లకును మ్రొక్కిక మల్ వెలబోసినట్లు." Dasaradhi § 12. To desire sexual intercourse. మసకొలుపు to excite such a desire.

మసగు *masagu.* [Tel.] v. n. To be enraged, to rage, to increase, swell. విజృంభించు, రేగు.

మసటు or మసడు *masaṭu.* [Tel.] n. Dirt. మురికి, మాలిన్యము. A stain, మరక, మచ్చ. "నిరవారువములమేనుల మసటువోనెలపుతోడు డిం." Pal. 70.

మసనము *masanamu.* [from Skt. శ్మశానము.] n. A cemetery, or place for burning or burying.

మసర *masara.* [Tel.] n. Grey colour. ధూసరవర్ణము. adj. Grey, ధూసరవర్ణముగల. మసరలు or మసరవడ్లు *masaralu.* n. A sort of rice. H. v. 59.

మసరు *masaru.* [Tel.] n. Fatness, jollity. కొవ్వు. Inspiration, force, energy, ఆవేశము, బలము. "ఒడలెరుంగక తిని మసరుకెక్కి వాడు కావరముపట్టియున్నాడు." NH. v. 59.

మసలు or మసులు *masalu.* [Tel.] v. n. To delay, to tarry, తడవుచేయు, తిరుగు. To roam, wander, walk or go about for pleasure, విహరించు, జాగుచేయు, తిరుగు. To hesitate, సంకోచించు, అనుమానించు. To be gorged, or heavy with eating, వెక్కసముగా తిని బాధపడు. To boil violently, నీళ్లు మిక్కిలికాగు. To turn back, వెనుకకుతిరుగు. దానికి నెలమసలినది a month has passed with her, i. e., she has been a month pregnant. పాము కప్పను తిని మసలుచున్నది the snake is sluggish being gorged. నీళ్లు మసలుచున్నవి లేక, మరుగుచున్నవి the water is boiling violently. "తమకము మానిచనుండన్న నదియు మసలకచని తొలగ." Swa. vi. 85. "పసరపుమాంసముబెట్టితము, మసలకసుల్తాను మసలమానులకెల్ల, పసచెలులయధరమాంసము, గుసుమాస్త్రుడు పెట్టిచెనిచె గులములకేమా." Vēma 814. "కసిగాయ గరచిచూచిన, మసలకమరియొగ రౌకా మధురంబగునే." Sumati 62. మసలుకొను Same as మసలు. మారుమసలు *māru-masalu.* v. n. To rival, match, to oppose, to front, సరిగా ఎదిరించు.

మసారము *masāramu.* [Skt.] n. An emerald, or sapphire, ఇంద్రనీలము.

మసాలా *masālā.* [H.] n. Spicery, curry-stuff, సంభారము. Horse physic. గుర్రానికి ఇచ్చేమందు.

మసి *masi.* [from Skt. మషి.] n. Ink. కాటుక. Blackness, నలుపు. Dirt, a stain, మయల. Charcoal, బొగ్గు. adj. Dirty, black. మసిపాతమాణిక్యము a jewel hidden in a dunghill. మసికట్టు *masi-kaṭṭu* n. The scoriæ of precious metals. బంగారులోనగువాని చిలుము. మసికోతి *masi-kōti.* n. A black monkey. నల్లకోతి. మసిబుడ్డి *masi-buddi.* n. An inkstand. సిరాబుడ్డి.

మసీదు masidu. [H.] n. A mosque, తురకల గుడి. యా. i.

మసూరి or మసూరిక masuri. [Skt.] n. Small pox. మసూచికారోగము. జ్వరము దురద గాత్రభంగము అరుచి భ్రమ వాపు తేజోహీనము నేత్రరోగము ఇవికలిగి మినుములు పెసలు పిటీరూకారముగలకురుపులు కలుగుట. శార్ఙ్గధర. p. 80.

మసృణము masrinamu. [Skt.] n. adj. Glossy, smooth, soft, mild, polished, unctuous. నున్నని, చిక్కని. మసృణత్వము masrinatvamu. n. Smoothness. నున్నన.

మసెల masela. [Tel.] n. A loft or garret near the roof of the house, అటుక.

మస్కరము maskaramu. [Skt.] n. A bamboo. వెదురు. A. v. 146. మస్కరి maskari. n. A mendicant, as using a bamboo staff. P. i. 236. A. i. 45, 48.

మస్టు, మష్టు or మసటు See under మష్టు.

మస్తము or మస్తకము mastamu. [Skt.] n. The head, the skull. శిరస్సు, తల. మస్తిష్కము mastishkamu. n. The brain. మెదడు. మస్తి masti. n. An overfed or disobedient or proud elephant, an elephant in rut, మదించినఏనుగు. మస్తు mastu. n. Plenty, abundance, సమృద్ధి. Fat, pride, మదము. మస్తువు mastuvu. n. The cream on the top of curds, పెరుగుమీదిమీగడ.

మస్తరించు mastarintsu. [Tel.] v. a. To overcome, subdue. లోబరచు. మస్తరు mastaru. n. Subjection, dependence. లోకువ, అధీనత.

మహంతు mahantu. [Skt. మహాంతః nom. plu. of మహత్.] n. The chief of a monastery. A religious superior, like the manager of the temple at Tripati.

మహాజరు mahadzaru. [H.] n. A memorial, a petition, signed by a number of people.

మహత్ mahat. [Skt.] adj. Great, గొప్ప. మహతి mahati. n. The name given to the Vina or lute, of Narada. The feminine gender of Telugu nouns. మహత్తరము mahattaramu. adj. Greater, more. మిక్కిలి. మహత్తు mahattu. n. Glory, greatness. బుద్ధితత్వము, ప్రభావము. The masculine gender of Telugu nouns. మహత్తైన mahattaina. adj. Great, large, bulky. గొప్ప. Best, excellent, illustrious. శ్రేష్ఠము. మహత్వము mahatvamu. n. Greatness, celebrity, glory. మాహాత్మ్యము mahatmyamu. n. Greatness, glory. A legend or chronicle regarding a town. మహదాశ్రయము dependency on the great, బలమైన ఆధారము. మహద్దశ a lofty position, a high station in life, గొప్పదశ. మహనీయము mahaniyamu. adj. Holy, sacred, blessed, excellent, celebrated. శ్రేష్ఠమైన, దివ్యమైన. మహనీయుడు maha-niyudu. n. A great man, గొప్పవాడు. మహర్షి maharshi. (మహత్+ఋషి.) n. A great saint. మహస్సు or మహము mahassu. n. Light, lustre. తేజస్సు. మహేంద్రము mah-endramu. n. A mountain. కొండ. మహేంద్రుడు mah-endrudu. n. A name of Indra, ఇంద్రుడు. మహేశ్వరుడు mah-esvarudu. n. The 'great Lord.' గొప్పప్రభువు. An epithet of Siva. శివుడు. మహోత్పలము the lotus, తామర. మహోత్సవము a high day, a great feast. మహోత్సాహుడు or మహోద్యముడు an extraordinarily enterprising man, an adventurer, అద్భుతకార్యారంభము Kavadu. మహోదధి the great sea, మహాసముద్రము. మహోదయము auspiciousness, prosperity, అభివృద్ధి. మహోదరము dropsy, బల్లచేత కడుపువాచేరోగము. ప్లీహోదరము. మహోద్యోగము great energy, great exertion. అధికప్రయత్నము. మహోన్నతము highly elevated, very high; noble, great. అత్యున్నతమైన.

మహోష్ట్రము a dromedary. See ఉష్ట్రము. మహోక్షము a large bull or ox. ఆబోతు. మహౌషధము a great medicine, a panacea, an epithet applied to Strychnine (అతి విష), onion (తెల్లుల్లి), or dry ginger, (సొంఠి.)

మహాసూలు mahassūlu. [H.] n. Reaping a crop, harvesting. The produce of land, a crop.

మహ maha. [Skt. for మహా in compounds.] adj. Great, much, eminent. మహా క్షుద్రుడు a base wretch. adv. Exceedingly, vastly, excessively, much, very, abundantly, frequently. మహాచెడ్డ very bad. మహామంచి very good. ఉప్పు మహా వేసినావు you have put too much salt. మహా అరిచినాడు he roared out loud. మహా వచ్చినారు they have come in great numbers. ఏటిలో నీళ్లు మహాపారుచున్నవి the water flows abundantly in the river. మహాంగము mah-angamu. n. A camel, ఒంటె. మహాకాయుడు maha-ka-yudu. n. A bulky or stout man. మహాకాళి maha-kali. n. The name of the wife of Siva; a terrific form of Durga. మహాకాలుడు maha-kaludu. n. A name of Siva. శివుడు. మహాకులము maha-kulamu. n. A good or respectable family. మహాకులుడు maha-kuludu. n. A man of a respectable family. సత్కులప్రసూతుడు, కులీనుడు. మహాగ్రీవి maha-grivi. n. (Lit. Long necked.) A camel. లొట్టిపిట్ట. మహాజనము maha-janamu. n. The upper classes, the higher ranks of society. The principal people; a multitude of people, the masses. జనసామాన్యము. మహాదేవుడు maha-dēvudu. n. Lit. the great god. A name of Siva: మహాధనము maha-dhanamu. n. Gold, బంగారు. Cultivation, tillage, husbandry, కృషి. మహానందము mah-anandamu. n. Bliss, eternal emancipation or beatitude. మహానటుడు maha-natudu. n. The great dancer, i. e., Siva. మహానది maha-nadi. n. The name of a river near Cuttack. మహానవమి or మహార్ణవమి maha-navami. n. The name of a feast called the Dasara, which falls on the ninth day of the bright fortnight in the month of Aswayuja, (October.) At this time all tools, arms, books, &c., are worshipped. మహానసము mahanasamu. n. A kitchen, వంటయిల్లు. M. III. i. 50. A. vi. 83. మహానాడు or మహానాడు maha-nadu. n. A council held by headmen. మహానిశ or మహారాత్రము maha-nisa. n. Midnight. అర్ధ రాత్రము. మహానుభావుడు mahanubhavudu. n. An exalted personage, a great man, a gentleman. మహాపద్మము maha-padmamu. n. A certain very high number, a million of millions. మహాపురుషుడు maha-purushudu. n. A hero, a heaven-born personage, a supernatural being. మహాప్రళయము maha-pralayamu. n. The end or destruction of the world, లోకనాశనము. మహాబలుడు maha-baludu. n. A very strong man. Wind, వాయువు. మహాభాగుడు maha-bhagudu. n. A pure or holy man. మహాభారతము maha-bharatamu. n. The Maha-Bharata, a celebrated poem. మహామృగము maha-mrigamu. n. An elephant, ఏనుగు. మహాయుగము maha-yugamu. n. Eternity, a great age or revolution of ages. చతుర్యుగకాలము. మహారజతము maha-rajatamu. n. Gold, బంగారు. మహారజనము maha-rajanamu. n. The Safflower. కుసుంభపుష్పము. Gold, సువర్ణము. మహారణ్యము mah-aranyamu. n. A great forest, గొప్పఅడవి. మహారథుడు maha-rathudu. n. A great charioteer, one who can fight single-handed against 11000 bowmen. మహారాజు maha-radzu. n. A sovereign, or emperor. మహారాజా O mighty Sire! O great king! మహారాజులైన మా ప్రభువు my gracious lord. మహారాజులొగు

by all means! of course! నీవు మహారాజాగా నుండవలెను I wish you all good fortune! వాడు మహారాజాయినాడు he became opulent. మహారాజరాజశ్రీ the usual ascription at the beginning of a letter. మహారాష్ట్రము the Maharata Country. మహారౌరవము *maha-rauravamu.* n. The name of a particular hell, నరకభేదము. మహార్ణవము or మహోదధుడు *maha-rṇavamu.* n. The great ocean. మహాలక్ష్మి *mahala-kshmi.* n. The goddess of fortune. A good woman. మంచియాడుది. మహాలయము *maha-layamu.* n. Offerings made to the manes of departed ancestors, for the fifteen days from full moon to new moon in the month of Bhadrapada. మహావిద్య *maha-vidya.* n. Magic, as being 'the great knowledge. Byron in Manfred. ii. 2. మంత్రశాస్త్రము. మహాశూద్రుడు *maha-sūdrudu.* n. A shepherd, గొల్లవాడు. మహాసేనుడు *maha-sēnuḍu.* n. One who has a large army; an epithet of Kumaraswami. మహాలు or మహాలు *mahalu.* [H.] n. A house, mansion, seraglio, రాజాగారి, లేక, నవాబుగారిమహాలు.

మహి *mahi.* [Skt.] n. The earth. భూమి. మహీపతి or మహీశుడు a king. మహిసాక్షి a sort of frankincense. BD. iv. 766. Charitra. ii. 2101. మహీధ్రము or మహీధరము *mahidhramu.* n. A mountain. పర్వతము. మహీరుహము *mahiruhamu.* n. A tree, as produced (రుహము) from the earth. వృక్షము. మహీలత *mahi-lata.* n. An earthworm, గండూపదము, ఎఱ్ఱ. మహీసుత *mahi-suta.* n. Lit. Earth-born. An epithet of Sita, the wife of Rama, సీత. మహీసుతుడు *mahi-sutuḍu.* n. Mars. అంగారకుడు. The Asura named Naraka, నరకాసురుడు.

మహితము *mahitamu.* [Skt.] adj. Great, గొప్ప. Proper, right, agreeable, fit. Worshipped, reverenced.

మహిమ or మహిమము *mahima.* [Skt.] n. Greatness in general (literal, or figurative), గొప్పతనము. All-pervasiveness, as one of Siva's attributes; illimitability, omnipotence, majesty, grandeur. ఒక ఐశ్వర్యము. The power of working miracles. మాహాత్మ్యము.

మహిళ *mahiḷa.* [Skt.] n. A lady, a female, a maiden. స్త్రీ. మహిళాపురము the name of a town. P. ii. 5.

మహిషము *mahishamu.* [Skt.] n. A he-buffalo, దున్నపోతు, ఎనుపోతు. మహిషి *mahishi.* n. A she-buffalo, గేద, ఎనుము. A queen, consort. పట్టాభిషిక్తరాజభార్య, పట్టపుదేవి. మహిషవాహనుడు *mahisha-vāhanuḍu.* n. One who rides on a he-buffalo, an epithet of Yama, యముడు.

మహిష్ఠము *mahishṭamu.* [Skt.] adj. Great, extreme. విశేషమైన. "ఇరువదాంబారి మహిష్ఠ భక్తికిని." BD. iv. 305. మహిష్ఠత *mahishṭatha.* n. Greatness, ఘనత.

మా mā

మా *mā.* [Skt.] n. A title of Lakshmi. లక్ష్మి.

మా *mā.* [Tel. infl. of మేము.] pron. Our. మా తలిదండ్రులు our parents. మా తండ్రి, my father.

మా [for Skt. మహా.] adj. Great, మిక్కిలి. మా బాగు very well.

మా *mā.* [Tel.] interj. Heigh ho! To be sure! ఐశీ.

" తే॥ చిరమహైశ్వర్యరాచారపారగునకు.
దనకుశశిమ ఫియుచ్చినకనకరథము,
కామగమనంబునైమధిత్మానరునకు,.
మామియిచ్చెనుమాయనిమహిమతింప."

సై. vi.

మాంగల్యము *mangalyamu.* [Skt. from మంగళము.] n. Auspiciousness, మంగళత్వము. The marriage token, తాళిబొట్టు. మాంగల్య

ధారణము tying the marriage knot, i. e., performing the ceremony of attaching the Tali to the neck of the bride.

మాంజిష్ఠము *mānjishṭhamu*. [Skt. from మంజిష్ఠ.] adj. Coppery red, orange red, తామ్రవర్ణమైన. n. A coppery red or orange red colour. తామ్రవర్ణము, ఎరుపు పసుపు కలిసిన గులాలుపొడిచాయ. రక్తాధికపీతము.

మాండవ్యుడు *māṇḍavyuḍu*. [Skt.] n. The name of a certain sage. మాండవ్య మతము 'Mandavya's maxim', i. e., prepossession of victory, confidence (మనో ధాటి.) It is used of those who disregard superstition and act of on their own judgment.

మాంత్రికుడు *māntrikuḍu*. [Skt. from మంత్రము.] n. A magician, conjurer, మంత్రవిద్య తెలిసినవాడు.

మాందాళి *māndāḷi*. [Tel.] n. A green silk cloth, పచ్చపట్టుచీర. "సీ॥ జిలుగుపావడమీద జిరు రక్తిక్కృత్తమింపొందాళి రొయిక్క తివ మాందాళిగ కట్టి." P. iv. 364. మాందాళిపచ్చ a kind of false emerald. కృత్రిమమరకతము.

మాంద్యము *māndyamu*. [Skt. from మంద ము.] n. Dullness, sluggishness, torpor, apathy, stupidity, అలస్యము, జడత్వము. Sickness, indisposition.

మాంసము *māmsamu*. [Skt.] n. Flesh, meat. నంజుడు, పలలము. మాంసలము *māmsalamu*. adj. Strong, stout, lusty, fleshy. మాంసలుడు a strong man. మాంసాశనుడు *māms-āśanuḍu*. n. A meat-eater, an eater of flesh. మాంసికుడు *māmsikuḍu*. n. A meat-seller, మృగపక్ష్యాదుల మాంసము విక్రయించి జీవించువాడు.

మాకందము *mākandamu*. [Skt.] n. The mango tree, చూతము, మామిడిచెట్టు.

మాకు or **మ్రాకు** *māku*. [Tel.] n. A tree,

మాకొను *mā-konu*. [Tel.] v. a. To bite, కరచు.

"శేతోలుకుబుత్రుని పెచటికో తొలగబెట్టి,
యడవిలోబాము మాకొన్న దనుచుపెంరగి."
పారిజా. v.

మాక్షికము *mākshikamu*. [Skt. from మక్షిక.] n. White honey, తెల్లతేనె.

మాగ, మాగకెల్లి or **మాగబొచ్చె** *māga*. [Tel.] n. A fish called Roball. ఎర్రమాగ the Mango fish, *Polynemus*, *paradiseus*, Russell plates 183, 184. There are other species.

మాగధి *māgadhi*. [Skt. from మగధ.] n. A sort of wild jasmine, అడవిమొల్ల. The Magadha dialect. మాగధుడు or మగధుడు *māgadhuḍu*. n. A bard or minstrel whose duty it is to recite the praises of sovereigns. స్తుతిపాఠకుడు, భట్రాజు.

మాగాణి *māgāṇi*. [Tel.] n. Wet land irrigated for cultivation, wet cultivation. వరిపొలము, వరిపంట పెట్టునేల. మాగాని or మాగిలి *māgāṇi*. n. A country, దేశము. తూర్పుమాగాని the east country.

మాగాయ See under మామిడికాయ.

మాగు *māgu*. [Tel.] v. n. To mellow, or ripen fully (as a fruit, or a boil), పండు బారు. n. Dirt, మాలిన్యము. A black spot, నల్లనిపొడ. A disease marked with black spots, నల్లనిపొడలుపుట్టే రోగము. మాగిలు *māgilu*. v. n. To become dim, మసిలజుకు. మాగుడు *māguḍu*. n. Blackness, నలుపు. Dirt, మాలిన్యము. మాగుడుపారు, మాగుపడు or మాగుపారు *māguḍu-pāru*. v. n. To become dim, or dull, to become soiled or black. మాయు, మలినమగు. "పెరుంగిడంగి యుండురాజముంటెలంబు మాగుడుబారికానిపించె." Prabhavati Prad. v. 53.

మాఘము *māghamu*. [Skt.] n. The name of the eleventh Telugu month, answering to February—March. మాఘము

māghuḍu. n. The name of a Sanskrit poet. మాఘ్యము *māghyamu.* n. A sort of jasmine. మొల్లపుష్పము. A. v. 116.

మాచి *māchi.* [Tel.] n. A kind of tree. A gall nut. **మాచిపత్రి,** *māchi-patri.* n. A plant, *Artemisia indica.* (Watts.) నాగదమనము.

మాచెనపక్కె *māchena-pakke.* [Tel.] n. A kind of carp fish. ఒకవిధమైనచేప.

మాచేకమ్మ *māṭsa-k-amma.* [Tel. మాచే+అక+అమ్మ.] n. A woman of a masculine appearance. మీసముగలిగి రొమ్ములులేని ఆడుది.

మాజీ *mājī.* [H.] adj. Cancelled. Former, late, last, past, మునుపటి, గడచిన. ఈచట్టము మాజీఅయినది this law is repealed. మాజీతహశ్శీలుదారు the late Tahsildar. **మాజూలు** *majūlu.* adj. Dismissed from office.

మాట *māṭa.* [Tel.] n. A word, పదము. A promise, వాగ్దత్తము, ప్రతిజ్ఞావచనము. Slander, నింద. Opinion, rumour, వృత్తాంతము. అతడునీ మాటచెప్పలేదు he did not speak of you. ఇదివేరే మాట this is another affair, another thing. వానిమాటకాదు this is not about him, I am not talking about him. గడియకు ఒకమాట చెప్పినాడు he changed his mind every hour. మంచిమాట (interj.) Very well. దాన్ని గురించి రెండోమాటలేదు there is no alternative. వారివద్ద మాటలుపడినాడు he was reproached or reprimanded by them. In some phrases the word మాట need not be translated. Thus, ఆమె తిరిగీ వస్తున్నదనేమాట తెలిసి knowing that she would return. నేను దానిని కొన్నమాట రూఢి it is very true I bought it. ఆమాటే తెలియను I know nothing of it. ఇందుచేతమాటవచ్చును by this you will get into disgrace. అతడు మాటతప్పలేదు he did not fail in his promise. మాట తప్పినవాడు మాలవాడు a promise breaker is a pariah, i. e., is a mean wretch. నేను పోయినమాట వానికి ఎట్లాతెలిసినది how did he know that I was gone? అతడు పోయేమాటా ఉండేమాటా does he propose to go or stay? వాడు ఉండేమాట యింకా తెలియలేదు I do not as yet know that he will remain. మాటకుమాట word for word, literally. నా మాట అడుగుదాటకు transgress not my command. తనమీద మాటరాకుండా ఇట్లాచేసెను he did this to avoid blame. మాటవినుట to obey. ఎంతమాట what nonsense! వానిమాట వాని ఒడిలోవేసినాను I acted as he desired. నీకు మాట నాకు మాట a command is easy to give but hard to perform, or a word from you will make me rich. నెయ్యమాటలేల why discuss it at length, in a word. ఆ పెండ్లి మాట యీ గ్రంథములో లేదు there is no mention of the marriage in this book. నామాటవేరు, నీమాటవేరు I say one thing you say another, my opinion is different from yours, my case is quite different from yours. వానికి నాకు మాటలు లేవు he and I are not on speaking terms. వానితోనీకేమిమాటలు why do you speak with him? ఈమాట వింటే అతడు ఏమనును if he hears of this what will he say? కడపటిమాటయేమి what was the upshot of the business? ఇప్పట్లోవాని మాట సాగదు he has now no influence. కడకు వానిమాటే ముందుకువచ్చినది at last his words proved true. దానిని గురించి ఇంకా ఏమాటా తెలియలేదు I do not yet know the result. మాటలకు పట్టుకొంటే విడవడు if he begins talking he will never stop. అదెక్కడిమాట what nonsense! such a thing is impossible. మాటలు మంచివేకాని మనసు మంచిదికాదు he talks well but has a bad heart. ఇంకా మాటలు రాని బిడ్డ a child that cannot yet speak. వానికి ఆ ఊరిలో మాట వానికద్దు లేక మాట సాగుతుంది he has influence in the town. అతనిమాటకు ఎదురులేదు his word is law. మాటలకుమాత్రము లేదనికములేదు as far as words go he is rich enough. ఒకమాటయిచ్చి పదిమాటలు తీసుకొన్నాడు his reproaches were returned ten-fold. మాటకారి

māṭa-kāḍu. n. A good public speaker, సభయందు భయములేక మాటాడువాడు, వక్త. మాటకారి *māṭa-kāri.* n. A skilful speaker, యుక్తిగా మాటాడువాడు. A talkative person, వాచాలుడు. మాటలమారి *māṭala-māri.* n. A talkative person, ముక్కాలి మాటాడువాడు. మాటలాడు, మాటాడు or మాట్లాడు *māṭa-l-āḍu.* v. n. To speak, talk, converse, to reproach. నన్నెందుకు ఊరక మాటలాడుతావు why reproach me for nothing? S. iii. 41.

మాటినంగ *māṭi-nanga.* [Tel. మాటిన+నంగ.] n. A lustful person, కాముకి.

మాటీ *māṭi.* [Tel.] n. Dirty grain. మాటిపోకలు sweepings of grain.

మాటీడు *māṭīḍu.* [Tel. for మావటీడు.] n. An elephant driver. ఏనుగువాడు. "దంతిదు స్తైన మాటీనితప్పు." Narasim. § 12.

మాటు *māṭu.* [Tel.] v. n. To get entangled, తగులుకొను. "తోడరి యడిగినవిల్లాంత్రతోడ మాటు." T. iv. 31. v. a. To conceal or hide. దాచు, మరుగుచేయు. n. Concealment, మరుగు. A remedy, విరుగుడు. An ambush, screen, covering. నుంకాడుదాగె గొయ్యి, మరుగు. A menstruum in which a metal is dissolved. Time, period, occasion. వేళ. Connection, తగులము. An instalment of payment. A patch of metal put on to mend a vessel, తపెలలకువేసే అతుకు. పొదల మాటున behind the bushes. మాటుకట్టు, మాటుపెట్టు or మాటుకిగ్గు *māṭu-kaṭṭu.* v. a. To set a trap. మాటికి *māṭiki.* adv. Often, every now and then, అడుగడుగునకు. మాటిమాటికి *māṭi-māṭi-ki.* n. Time after time, again and again, frequently. మాటుగొయ్యి *māṭu-goyyi.* n. A hidden pitfall. మాటుపడు *māṭu-paḍu.* v. n. To disappear, vanish, అగుపడక పోవు, మరుగుపడు. Also, to get entangled, to get caught, తగులుపడు. మాటుమణుగు or మాటుమణుగు *māṭu-maṇugu.* v. n. To be hushed, still or silent. వెంపోటము ఉడిగి నిశ్శబ్దముగు. ఊరంతా మాటుమణిగి ఉండినది the whole town was in dead silence. మాటుమణిగిన రాత్రి in the dead of the night.

మాడ *māḍa.* [Tel.] n. Half a pagoda, that is, about two rupees. అరవరహా. Money in general. శ్రీరామమాడ an ancient medal imagined to be lucky and worshipped by the wearer.

మాడపట్టు *māḍa-paṭṭu.* [Tel.] n. The crown of the head. బ్రహ్మరంధ్రము, సోడు.

మాడి *māḍi.* [Tel.] n. The wild species of horse gram. అడవివులవ.

మాడు *māḍu.* [Tel.] v. n. To be burnt or scorched. కాలు, కాలిపోవు. అప్పుడు మాడిపోయినది the boil dried up. n. Rice or any other food burnt in cooking. అడుగున బొగ్గైపోయిన అన్నము. The gable end of a house, ఇంటి యొక్క భాగపు కప్పు. మాడుచు, మాడ్చు or మాడించు *māḍutsu.* v. a. To burn, scorch, blacken, మాడజేయు. వాండ్ల పుటము మాడ్చినాడు he burnt their fining pot, i.e., he broke up their scheme. వాడు ముఖము మాడ్చుకొని నాడు he looked sulky. మాడుచెక్క *māḍu-chekka.* n. Burnt rice. అడుగున చెక్కలుగా మాడిన అన్నము.

మాడుగు or మాడుపు *māḍugu.* [Tel.] n. An upstair house. మిద్దెయిల్లు, మేడ, హర్మ్యము.

మాడెము *māḍemu.* [Tel.] n. The territory of a king, మండలాధిపతుల భూమండలము. "కేళిగే మాడెములు క్రేల్చినొడ్డాదిమనిరొయనర్చె." ప్వా. i.

మాడ్కి or మాడికి *māḍki.* [Tel.] n. Manner, likeness. రీతి, విధము. అమ్మాడ్కి in that manner. చెప్పినమాడికి in the manner said.

మాడ్పు *māḍpu.* [Tel.] n. A kind of tree. H. iv 10.

మాణవకము māṇavakamu. [Skt.] n. A necklace of twenty strings. ఇరువదిపేటలు గలహారము. మాణవకుడు māṇavakuḍu. n. A child, boy, lad, బాలుడు.

మాణిక్యము māṇikyamu. [Skt.] n. A ruby. కెంపు. A term of admiration, as "a perfect jewel, a gem." మాణిక్యమువంటివాడు he is a perfect jewel. మాణిక్యమువలె or మాణిక్యముగా as fine as possible. మాణిక్యమైనకాగితము superfine paper, a fine specimen of paper. మాణిక్యమువంటి ఆడపిల్ల a darling, a pet.

మాత māta. [Skt.] n. Mother, తల్లి. An epithet of Parvati or Lakshmi, పార్వతీదేవి. లక్ష్మీదేవి. పంచమాతలు five ladies who are to be looked upon with as much respect as one's own mother, viz. (1) the king's wife, రాజభార్య; (2) an elder brother's wife, అన్నభార్య; (3) a teacher's wife, గురుభార్య; (4) a mother-in-law, అత్త; (5) one's own mother, కన్నతల్లి. మాతాపితలు mātā-pitalu. n. Father and mother, parents, తల్లిదండ్రులు. మాతామహి mātā-mahi. n. A maternal grandmother. తల్లియొక్కతల్లి. మాతామహుడు mātā-mahuḍu. n. A maternal grandfather. తల్లియొక్కతండ్రి. మాతృశ్రీ mātu-śri. adj. 'Dear' a phrase used regarding elder female relations, as మాతృశ్రీ మా తల్లిగారు my dear mother. మాతృక mātṛika. n. A mother, తల్లి. The original writing from which a copy (ప్రతిక) is made. అసలు గ్రంథము.

మాతంగ mātanga. [Skt.] adj. Outcaste, pariah. చండాల. మాతంగము mātangamu. (born from మతంగుడు a Rishi.) n. An elephant, ఏనుగు. మాతంగత్వము mātanga-tvamu. n. The Pariah state. చండాలత్వము. మాతంగత్వముదాల్చి assuming the form of an outcaste. మాతంగి mātangi. n. The goddess Pārvati పార్వతి. The wife of Vasishṭha, వసిష్ఠునిభార్య. A syren, fairy nymph; a she-devil. A Pariah woman, చండాలస్త్రీ. HD. ii. 2561. A woman who sells or serves wine. The name of the tutelary goddess of the Madras boatmen. మాతంగి mātangi. n. A kind of shrub. మాతంగుడు or మతంగుడు mātanguḍu. n. A pariah, మాలవాడు.

మాతగొరక māta-goraka. [Tel.] n. A fish called Old Wife or Rice Fish, resembling the Pomfret, చందువాయి.

మాతరిశ్వుడు mātar-iśvuḍu. [Skt.] n. An epithet of వాయువు the god of the winds.

మాతలి mātali. [Skt.] n. The name of the charioteer of Indra, ఇంద్రసారథి.

మాతు mātu. [Persian.] n. In chess, checkmating with any piece other than a pawn, చదరంగములో బంటుతోగాక తక్కినకాయలతో రాజుకు చెప్పుమాట.

మాతుల mātula. [Skt.] n. The wife of a mother's brother, మేనమామభార్య. Also, the Datura plant, ఉమ్మెత్త. మాతులపుత్రకము mātula-putrakamu. n. The thorn apple, or fruit of the Datura. ఉమ్మెత్తకాయ. మాతులపుత్రకుడు mātula-putrakuḍu. n. The son of a maternal uncle. మేనమామకొడుకు. మాతులాని or మాతులి mātulāni. n. The wife of a mother's brother, మేనమామభార్య. మాతులుడు mātuluḍu. n. A maternal uncle. మేనమామ. మాతులేయుడు mātulēyuḍu. n. The son of a maternal uncle. మేనమామకొడుకు.

మాతులుంగము mātu-lungamu. [Skt.] n. A citron. మాదీఫలవృక్షము.

మాతుశ్రీ, and మాతృక See under మాత.

మాత్ర mātra. [Skt.] n. Measure, extent, కొలత. A little, కొంచెము. A short time, a moment, క్షణకాలము. Also (in Telugu), a pill. చిన్నమందుతిత్తి. A bag, అసిమిసంచి. A. vi.

మాత్రము *mātramu.* [Skt.] n. Quantity, measure, proportion, computation, whether by number, rate, weight, extent, or capacity. పరిమాణము. వాడు అట్లు చెప్పిన మాత్రమున or మాత్రాన as soon as he said so. అమాత్రపుదేవళము so large a temple. ఆ గ్రంథము ఉండేమాత్రపువాడు a man likely to have that book. ఒకమాత్రపుమనిషి a sort of fellow, not much of a man. ఏమాత్రము or ఎంతమాత్రము how much, how far, to what amount, in what degree. ఆమాత్రము so far. నాకు తెలిసినమాత్రము as far as I know. ఎంతమాత్రముకాదు far from it, by no means, not in the least. అది యేమాత్రము న్యాయముకాదు it is anything but right. ఎంతమాత్రము హేతువులేదు there is not the smallest reason. మనుష్యమాత్రులకు అలవి కాదు it is impossible for mortals. adj. & adv. Only, merely, alone, simply, exclusively. నేనుమాత్రము వచ్చినాను I alone came.

మాత్సర్యము *mātsaryamu.* [Skt. from మత్సరము.] n. Envy, malice. ద్వేషము, పగ.

మాదళము, మాదాళము, మాదవళము or **మాదావళి** *mādalamu.* [Tel.] n. Tawny color, కపిలవర్ణము. A tawny colored cloth. కపిలవర్ణముగలచీర.

మాదిగ *mādiga.* [from Skt. మతంగ.] n. The cobbler or shoe-making caste. మాదిగవాడు a man of that class, చెప్పులుకుట్టువాడు. **మాదిగది** *mādig-adi.* n. A woman of the cobbler caste.

మాదీఫలము *mādi-phalamu.* [Skt.] n. A citron. మాదీఫలము (?) మాదులుంగము.

మాదిరి or **మాద్రి** *mādiri.* [Tel.] n. A pattern, sample, model, type, specimen. మచ్చు, సామ్యము. A sort, kind, variety. adj. Similar, like. సమానమైన.

మాదృశము *mā-driśamu.* [Skt.] adj. Like me, resembling me. నావంటి. **మాదృశుడు** *mā-driśuḍu.* n. A man like me. నావంటి వాడు.

మాధవమతము *mādhava-matamu.* [Skt.] n. A Dwaita sect of Vishnu worshippers who adore Hanuman as the one God and look upon Vyasa as their great prophet. Their tenets are explained in the పరాశరసంహిత. See మాధవుడు.

మాధవము *mādhavamu.* [Skt.] n. A poetical name of the second Telugu lunar month. The spring season, వైశాఖమాసము, వసంతఋతువు.

మాధవి *mādhavi.* [Skt. from మధువు.] n. Sugar. The large creeping plant termed *Gærtnera racemosa.* బండిగురివెంద. A bawd, కుంటెనకత్తె.

మాధవుడు *mādhavuḍu.* [Skt.] n. A name of Vishṇu; also of Vasanta, the spring season. విష్ణువు, వసంతుడు.

మాధుకరము *mādhu-karamu.* [Skt. from మధువు.] n. Begging from house to house as a bee gathers honey from flower to flower, మధుకరవృత్తి.

మాధుర్యము or **మాధురి** *mādhuryamu.* [Skt. from మధురము.] n. Sweetness, తీపు.

మాధ్యస్థ్యము *mādhya-sthyamu.* [Skt. from మధ్యస్థము.] n. Arbitration, mediation, the decision of an arbitrator, మధ్యస్థుడుచేయు తీర్పు.

మాధ్వి *mādhvi.* [Skt. from మధువు.] n. Spirituous liquor. మద్యము, సారాయి.

మాన *māna.* [from Skt. మానము.] n. One sixteenth part of the measure called a తూము. నాలుగుకుంచములు(?) ఒక్క (?) కొలత.

మానము *mānamu.* [Skt.] n. A measure of any kind, కొలత, ప్రమాణము. Pride, arrogance, or indignation, చిన్నెన్నెత్తిము, గర్వము. Civility, honor. గౌరవము, Self-respect, a sense of honor or dignity, modesty. The pudenda. స్త్రీ పురుషులయొక్క మరుగైన అవయవము. A system or method. సౌరమానము the solar system of astronomy. బార్హస్పత్యమానము the system described by బృహస్పతి. "రత్నకటకరఘురాంరఘురా న్యూత్రికాలమానములంగోలప." Swa. ii. 31. టీ॥ కాలమానములు, కాలప్రమాణములు. కాలమానము the state of the weather, the nature of the season. అతనిమానముతీసిరి they disgraced or exposed him. మానముపోయిన తర్వాత ప్రాణమెందుకు what is the good of living after losing one's "character?" మానధనులు those whose good name is their wealth. మానహీనులు those who are devoid of character or of self respect. మానస Same as మన్నన (q. v.) మాననీయము mána-nīyamu. adj. Venerable, honourable, పూజ్యమైన, మన్నింపదగిన. మానభంగము mána-bhangamu. n. Disgrace, dishonor, అవమానము. మానవతి mána-vati. n. A modest woman, మానముగల ఆడుది. మానస్థానము mána-sthānamu. n. The pudendum muliebre. మర్మస్థలము. మానస్థుడు mána-sthudu. n. A man of respectability or character. మర్యాదగలమనిషి. మాని máni. adj. Respectable. మానస్థుడైన.

మానవ mánava. [Skt. from మను.] adj. Written by Manu. మనువుచేత వ్రాయబడిన. మానవధర్మశాస్త్రము the Laws of Manu. Human, మనుష్యసంబంధమైన. మానవబలము human strength. మానవస్త్రీ a mortal woman, i. e., not a goddess. మానవాశనుడు mánav-āsanudu. n. A cannibal, మనుష్యులను తినువాడు. మానవుడు mánavudu. n. A man, మనుష్యుడు. మానవేశ్వరుడు mánav-ēsvarudu. n. A king. రాజు. M. I. i. 111.

మానసము mánasamu. [Skt. from మనస్సు.] n. The mind, the seat or faculty of reason and feeling. The name of a lake, మానస సరోవరము. adj. Mental, మానసికమైన. మానస పూజ mental prayer. మానసించు mána-sinchu. v. n. To think, consider. తలచు. మానసౌకసము mána-saukasamu. n. A swan. హంస.

మానిక mánika. [Skt. from మానము.] n. A dry measure; one fourth of a కుంచము, or one-sixteenth of a తూము. నాలుగుకుంచములయొక్క పరిమాణము. పొట్టి మానిక a stumpy figure.

మానికము mánikamu. [Skt. from మాణిక్యము.] n. A ruby, కెంపు. A diamond, రత్నము. మానికపు mánikapu. adj. Set with gems, jewelled, రత్నఖచితమైన. మానికదాసి a prostitute, భోగముది.

మానితము mánitamu. [Skt. from మానము.] adj. Respectful. గౌరవింపబడిన. మానిని mánini. n. A respectable woman, మానముగలయాడుది. A lady, damsel, maid, స్త్రీ.

మానిసి mánisi. [from Skt. మనుష్యుడు.] n. A man or woman, a person. మానిసికోతి a baboon, "కొచ్చివేపులమానిసి కోతులాడి యైనవన్నియు." S. i. 130. మానిసితిండి a demon, రాక్షసుడు. మానిసిరాయడు mánisi-rāyadu. n. An epithet of Kubera, కుబేరుడు. మానిసిరేడు mánisi-rēdu. n. A king, రాజు. మానిసిసింగము mánisi-singamu. n. A Telugu substitute for Nrisimha, నృసింహుడు.

మాను mánu. [Tel.] adj. Fit, proper, worthy, యోగ్యము. Pleasant, fine, మనోజ్ఞము. ప్రకాశముతో మానై beautiful with brightness. n. Pleasantness, మనోజ్ఞత. మానుగ mánuga. adv. Duly, fitly, truly, బాగుగా. మాను or మ్రాను mánu. [Tel. cf. Tam.

మరము.] n. A tree. Wood. ప్రాను or అడుగు మాను the trunk of a tree. మానువడు, మాన్పడు, ప్రానువడు, ప్రాన్పడు or మానైయుండుడు *manu-padu*. v. n. Literally, to turn into wood. To be astounded, or stunned with horror: to stand aghast, to be struck dumb. అడ్డమ్రాను. the cross bar of a door. కట్టుమాను (cf. Tam. Catamaran), a float. or raft. మానుఉప్పు or బూడిదఉప్పు Potash, Pearl-ash, Carbonate of Potash, (Watts.) మాని or మ్రాని *mani*. adj. Wooden, vegetable. మానిపసుపు *mani-pasupu*. n. Wood turmeric, a medicinal drug. *Curcuma xanthorrhiza*. Rox. i. 25. Ainsl. ii. 188. పర్జని, దారుహరిద్ర. మానిముంత *mani-munta*. n. A wooden pail. S. ii. 391. మడంతె కొయ్యతో చేసినపాత్ర.

మాను *manu*. [Tel.] v. a. and v. n. To forbear, refrain, abstain, or desist from, leave off, విడుచు. To heal, be healed or cured, కుదురు. To be laid aside or left off, to be got rid of. చెప్పకమానెను he stopped without saying it. అక్కడ ఉండకమానరు they will not fail to be there. చేయకేలమాను how should he fail to do this? చేయక మానెను he desisted from doing so. This verb implies a general negative as రాకమానెను he did not come. చొరకమానెను he did not enter. కొట్టితే కరవకమానునా if you strike it, will it not bite you? చెప్పినాడో మానినాడో whether he spoke or not: lit. whether he spoke or whether he forbore. అక్కడ అది లేకుంటే మానెను I don't care if it is not there. రాయివేతునా మానుదునా shall I throw the stone or no? తడివారించినా మానినా whether they mentioned it or no. చింతమానుము abandon your grief. It is even applied impersonally to mean 'Never mind,' పరవాలేదు, as బట్టలుతడిసినా మానె it does not matter if the clothes got wet. ఇయ్యకపోతే మానె if you won't give it, never mind, no matter, it is of no consequence. మానిపించు or మాన్పించు *mani-pintsu*. v. a. To cause to stop; to prevent. To cause to heal. అతనిప్రయాణము మాన్పితిని I made him stop his journey. మానుకొను *manu-konu*. v. a. To relinquish, forego, resign, lay aside, desist from, abstain from. పని మానుకొను to give up or resign an employment. మానుచు, మాన్చు, మానుపు or మాన్పు *manutsu*. v. a. To stop, heal, cure. మానకేయు. మానిపోయిన పుండ్లను మళ్లీ రేపుట to stir up old sores, to revive old quarrels. మామా *mamu*. [Tel. short for మానుమానుమా.] v. imp. Oh! please give up (anger, &c.)

మానుషము *manushamu*. [Skt. from మనుష్యుడు.] n. Honor, respect. మర్యాద, గౌరవము. మానుషస్థుడు *manusha-sthudu*. n. A respectable man. మర్యాదవరుడు. మానుషుడు *manushudu*. Same as మనుష్యుడు. (q. v.) మానుషి *manushi*. n. A woman. మానుషీక్షీరము *manushi-kshiramu*. n. Woman's milk. చేను బాలు. M. XII. i. 358. మానుష్యము *manushyamu*. n. Manhood, manliness. Kindness, humanity, కరుణ.

మానెరు or మానేరు *maneru*. [Tel.] n. A climbing plant, ఎక్కుడుతీగె.

మానేజరు *manejaru*. [Eng. 'manager.'] n. A manager. నిర్వాహకుడు.

మాన్యము *manyamu*. [Skt.] adj. Respectable, venerable. పూజ్యమైన, సన్మానింపదగిన. n. A living: a glebe-land granted by a ruler on quit rent or on various favourable tenures. సర్వమాన్యము land entirely free of rent. అర్ధమాన్యము land which pays only half the usual rent. వినిమయమాన్యము a glebe-land granted in exchange for another. మాన్యగాడు or మాన్యవారు one who enjoys a మాన్యము. మాన్యుడు *manyudu.* n. A respectable or honorable man. పూజ్యుడు. One worthy of respect.

మాపు *mapu.* [Tel. causal of మాయు.] v. a. To dirty, make foul. మలినముచేయు, మురికిచేయు. To destroy, efface. మాయజేయు, పోగొట్టు. మాపుమాపు to ruin, destroy. n. Evening, సాయంకాలము. Night, రాత్రి. Infl. మాపటి. Dative మాపటికి at night. రేపుమాపు morning and evening. మాపటివేళ the night time. మాపటియెండ the evening sunshine. మాపుడు *mapudu.* n. Foulness, మాలిన్యము, మాయిలి.

మాపుచేయు *maphu-cheyu.* [H. + Tel.] v. a. To pardon, forgive, excuse.

మాబాగు *ma-bagu.* [from Skt. మహాబాగు.] Interj. Very well! మంచిది.

మాబీర *ma-bira.* [Tel.] n. The plant called *Ajuga disticha.* Rox. iii. 2.

మాభేరి *mabheri.* [Tel.] n. Malabar batmint, *Anisomeles malabarica.*

మామ *mama.* [from Skt. మామక.] n. A father-in-law. Also, a mother's brother, మేనమామ. The same title is bestowed equally on the brothers of a father-in-law, as పినమామగారు, పెద్దమామగారు. The phrase శకునిమామ denotes 'Uncle Sakuni,' i. e., an evil counsellor. Sakuni was the maternal uncle of Duryódhana. మామమామ an epithet of Vishṇu, as he married Lakshmi the daughter of the Sea (సముద్రుడు) whose wife (Ganges) is related to him as a daughter, లక్ష్మీదేవిని పెండ్లాడినందున తనకు మామయైన సముద్రునికి పెండ్లామగు గంగాదేవి తనకు కూతురువరుస అగుటచేత విష్ణువు సముద్రునికి మామ అయ్యెను.

మామకము or **మామకీనము** *mamakamu.* [Skt.] adj. Mine, నాదైన. మామకీనులు my people, people of my caste.

మామకుడు *mamakudu.* [Skt.] n. A mother's brother, మేనమామ. adj. One belonging to me, నావాడు.

మామా See under మామ.

మామిడి *mamidi.* [Tel.] n. A mango tree, *Mangifera indica.* Rox.i.641. చూతవృక్షము. మామిడిపండు a ripe mango. మామిడికాయ a green mango. మామిడిచెట్లు mango trees. మామిడివనము a mango garden or grove. మామిళ్లు mango trees. పుల్లమామిడి the sour species. తియ్యమామిడి the sweet kind. గుజ్జుమామిడి the low (or small) mango tree. కట్టుమామిడి a tree which bears a fine species of fruit which are usually tied up to preserve them. అడవిమామిడి the wild mango tree, *Spondias mangifera.* చిలుకముక్కుమామిడికాయ a mango fruit terminating in a crooked point like a parrot's bill. Various trees are called చారుమామిడి *Buchanania latifolia.* Rox. ii. 385. బ్రహ్మమామిడి *Ficus glomerata.* Rox. iii. 558. బొడ్డుమామిడి *Ficus racemifera.* Rox. iii. 561. అటికమామిడి, నర్రమామిడి, ముంతమామిడి and so on. తొండ్లమామిడి a jungle shrub. మామిడిగుత్తులు *mamidi-guttulu.* n. A sort of grain. వడ్లలోభేదము. A. i. 75.

మామకోడి or **మాంకోడి** *mamu-kodi.* [Tel.] n. A turkey.

మామూలు *mamulu.* [H.] n. Usage, established custom. మామూలుగా usually, according to custom.

మామెన *mamena.* [Tel.] n. A fragrant root like *Sarsaparilla.* దూడిపాలతీగె. P. i. 703. Ainslie ii. 177. నేలమామెన is another kind. "మామెనయును నేలమామెనయుటె కమామిడి." H. iv. 14.

మాయ *maya.* [Skt.] n. Fraud, trick, deceit, delusion, illusion, diplomacy. Conjuring, ఇంద్రజాలవిద్య. Ignorance, అవిద్య.

Philosophical illusion, the phenomenal world, unreality of all worldly existence. This is personified in mythology as Lakshmi, the consort of Vishṇu, she being the immediate and active cause of creation. మాయాప్రపంచము the delusive world. 'Vanity' in the theological sense: materiality as distinguished from intellectuality. మాయలాడి a deceitful woman. వనితలు మయావినోదులైనందున as women are deceivers. M. XIII. ii. 189. మాయాస్వరూపము a fictitious form. మాయగొల్లడు a seeming herdsman, i.e., Krishna, who bore the appearance of a rustic. మాయదారిగా unexpectedly, by stealth or trick, cunningly. మాయకాడు, మాయగాడు, మాయదారి or మాయపోతు a deceiver, మాయావి. **మాయాదేవి** *māyā-devi.* n. Nature, regarded as a goddess. మాయాదేవి సుతుడు a name of Buddha. మాయానగరము the place called Haridvāra. **మాయము** *māyamu.* n. Same as మాయ. Disappearance, అదృశ్యము. adj. Vanished, disappeared. మాయమగు to vanish. ఉంగరము మాయమైపోయినది the ring disappeared. వారు మాయమైపోయిరి they vanished. ఆ పాము మాయమైపోయినది the snake disappeared. ఇది యేమిమాయము this is a strange trick. **మాయలాడు** *māyal-āḍu.* n. A rogue. మాయలుచేయుపురుషుడు. **మాయావి, మాయి, మాయలమారి** or **మాయికుడు** *māyāvi.* n. A cheat, a deceiver, a juggler, a conjurer. ఐంద్రజాలికుడు. మాయలుచేయు పురుషుడు. **మాయి** *māyi.* n. Concealment. మరుగు. Blackness, నలుపు.

మాయు *māyu.* [Tel.] v. n. To become dirty or foul, to be unwashed, మలినమగు, మాసిపోవు. To perish, be destroyed, or effaced. లేకపోవు, నశించు. అది మాసినది it is dirty. మాసినపాతలు dirty clothes. జాడలు మాసిపోయినవి the vestiges are destroyed, or effaced. వానితల మాసినది his head is dirty, i. e., he is unshaven. తలమాసినవాడు a man of beggarly appearance. దాని కొకనెల మాసినది she is menstruous. చుక్క కనుమాసిపోయినది the star faded away (at dawn.) **మాసిన** *māsina.* adj. Dirty, foul. మురికిగానున్న. **మాయు** or **మాయురె** interj. Alas! ah! అయ్యో, బాపురే. **మాయించు** or **మాపు** *māyinṭsu.* v. a. To do away with, abolish, annihilate. పోగొట్టు. "తవదుగాంధర్వమాయ, నాదము జవరుల మాయ మాయించి." T. v. 76.

మారంకము *māraṅkamu.* [Tel.] n. Opposition. ఎదురు మారంకమగు to oppose. ఎదిరించు. "అసమానశక్తి దమారంకమై గెలిచె. BD. ii. 1021.

మారకము or **మార్కము** *mārakamu.* [Tel. from మారు.] n. Exchange, మార్పు.

మారకుడు *mārakuḍu.* [Skt.] n. A slayer, or destroyer. చంపువాడు.

మారట *māraṭa.* [Tel.] adj. and adv. Other, another, counter. ప్రతి, ప్రతికూలము. Altered, changed. ప్రతి. ప్రతిరూపమైన. In lieu of. మారటరతి a second Venus, a perfect beauty. మారటమారుడు another Cupid. మారటరూపు an exact likeness. "మాటిమాటికి … మారటగద్దె … నిలుపుదునంటే." HD. ii. 2816. "భాగ్యవతులు రూపున మారట రతులు." Raja Sekhara. i. 40. "మారటవారు దాననయి మాటలు చిత్తమునందు నిల్పకే తారులు ప్రేలెదరా విభుడు." M. V. iii. 93. మారటతల్లి or మారటతమ్ముడు, &c., step-mother, step-brother, &c.

మారణము *māraṇamu.* [Skt. of మరణము.] n. Killing, slaughter. చంపుటము.

మారాకు *mār-āku.* [Tel.] n. A prop, a post for a plant to creep on, ప్రాకుడుకొయ్య.

మారాడు *mār-āḍu.* [Tel. మారు + ఆడు.] v. a. To speak against. To oppose in words. ఎదురాడు, మారుమాటలాడు. **మారాట** or **మారాటము** *māraṭa.* n. Opposition in speech, ఎదురాడుట. A quarrel, కలహము.

మారాము or **మారమము** *mārāmu* [Tel.] n. Teasing, plaguing, annoying. గోజాలాట. A secret, మర్మము. A joint, కీలు. A trick, knavery, టెంటా. మారాములమారి a rogue. "ఓ రాముడిలాగ మాకీమారాములు తెలియుటకును మగవాండ్లము." S. ii. 40. **మారాముచేయు** *mārāmu-chēyu*. v. a. To tease, to plague. గోజాలాడు.

మారి *māri*. [Skt.] n. The name of a goddess like Durga, supposed to preside over certain epidemics. A plague, epidemic or pestilence, slaughter, బహుమంది చచ్చే రోగము, మహామారికాదిరోగము. జాడ్యము. మారియమ్మప్రసరము cholera. "ప్రాణాలమారి వచ్చినది." G. i. 276. [Tel.] A noun affix. A doer, one who commits, one who is accustomed to. తిప్పలమారి. or కడగండ్లమారి one who troubles or torments. మందులమారి a poisoner. ముండలమారి one who is given to women. **మారించు** *mārintsu*. v. a. To destroy. నాశముచేయు. "మారింతుసర్వముగా." Kuchēlo. iii. 49. **మారిమసంగు** *mārimasangu*. v. a. To slaughter, ruin, destroy, వధించు. "ఒకరొకడమార్తురు మేల్కాని మార్కొనిన మారిమసంగినట్లు మృత్యుదేవతకాలిని చావ్వ." M. X. i. 174. "గ్రామములమారిమసంగినట్లయ్యె సమస్తము మార్గముజేసి." Rukmangada. iii. 84. "మొసవదొరికొంటె బ్రజమారిమసగినట్లు." Swa. v. 28.

మారిషుడు *mārishudu*. [Skt.] n. The principal actor or the manager in a theatre. (నాటకపరిభాషయందు) పూజ్యుడు, ఆర్యుడు.

మారీచము *mārīchamu*. [Skt.] n. Pretence, feigning, hypocrisy, dissembling. మారీచుడు a giant who was a friend of Rāvana; a deceiver, మోసగాడు.

మారీఫత్తు *mārī-phattu*. [H.] n. Trust, charge, possession. మారీఫత్తుచేయు to entrust to one.

మారు *māru*. [Tel.] v. n. To be changed. మారుపడు. To be transmuted, altered. వ్యత్యస్తమగు, ఒకటిమరియొకటియగు. ఆనాణెము మారదు that money will not pass. To be ruined, నశించు. n. Opposition, ఎదురు. A time, తడవ, ఆవృత్తి. ఒకమారు once. ఈమారు this once, or this time. ఇరుమార్లు twice. ముమ్మారు thrice. పలుమారు many times. Buttermilk, మజ్జిగ. A course or remove at dinner, వండినతూర్పు పెట్టుటకు భోజ్యపదార్థము. **మారు** adj. Other, వేరొక. అన్యము. Opposite, opposed, ఎదురైన. ప్రతి. Turned, averted, పెడ. Replying, answering. మారుమనిషి a substitute. మారుమాట a reply. మారుతాళము a false key. మారుమొగము an averted countenance. మారుమూల a bye-place. **మారుకొను** or **మార్కొను** *māru-konu*. v. a. To attack, front, face. ఎదురు కొను. To oppose, to be adverse to. ఎదిరించు. **మారుగా** *māru-gā*. adv. Instead of, in lieu of, ప్రత్యామ్నాయముగా. నాకు మారుగా పోయినాడు he went in my place, instead of me. **మారుచు** or **మార్చు** *mārutsu*. v. a. To change, మారిచేయు. **మార్పు**. **మారుపు**. **మారువల** or **మారు పాటు** *mārpu*. n. Changing, మారుట. **మార్పు** *mārpu*. n Exchange, change. A kind of fish. కుండమార్పిళ్లుకూడదు or కుండమార్పులుకూడదు marrying a man's son and daughter with another man's daughter and son, is wrong. **మారుతల్లి**, **మారుడు తల్లి** or **మారటితల్లి** *māru-talli*. n. A step-mother. సవతితల్లి. **మారుతాళము** *māru-tālamu*. n. A picklock, a false key. దొంగచీకము చెవి. **మారుపుడు** or **మార్తుడు** *māru-tudu*. n. An enemy. pln. మారుతురు enemies, శత్రువులు. **మారువడు** *māru-padu*. v. n. To be changed or exchanged. భేదపడు. To disappear, vanish, అదృశ్యమగు. **మారుపు** *mārupu*. n. A kind of fish. Russell. 168. "మారుపులును జనుగారు." G. i.

111 మారుపెట్టు or మార్పెట్టు *māru-peṭṭu.* v. a. To oppose. ఎదిరించు. మారుబేరగాడు *māru-bēra-gāḍu.* n. A retail dealer. చిల్లర వర్తకుడు. మారుబేరము *māru-bēramu.* n. Retail trade. చిల్లరవర్తకము. మారుమనువు *māru-manuvu.* n. A woman's second espousals. ఆడదానికి రెండవ వివాహము. మారుమనువుది a woman who is married a second time, బిడివుపు, రెండవపెండ్లాడిన స్త్రీ. మారుమగడు a woman's unlawful husband, ఉపపతి. మారుమలయు, మార్మలయు, మారుమసలు or మార్మసలు *māru-malayu.* v. n. To rival, to match. సరిగా ఎదిరించు. "మార్కొని శౌర్యమున దీని మారుమలయుచున్న శమం తకంబు." Vish. vi. 263. "తానుసంచరించు తన్నుత్పన్నరూపమానవాక్యములతో మారుమలయు చును." L. xiii. 130. మారుమాట or మార్మాట *māru-māṭa.* n. An answer, ఎదురుత్తరము, ప్రతివచనము. మారుమొగము or మార్మొగము *māru-mogamu.* n. An averted face. పెడమొగము. మారుమ్రోత *māru-mrōta.* n. A echo. ప్రతిధ్వని. మారుమూల *māru-mūla.* n. The opposite side, ఎదురుమూల. An out of the way corner or retired place. మారుమ్రోయు *māru-mrōyu.* v. n. To echo. ప్రతిధ్వనిచేయు. మారురూపు *māru-rūpu.* n. A new appearance, a change of form. రూపాంతరము, మారిపోయినరూపు. మారొడ్డు *mār-oḍḍu.* v. a. To oppose, ప్రతిఘటించు. మారువర్తకుడు *māru-vartakuḍu.* n. A retail dealer, చిల్లరవర్తకుడు. మారుమెడ or మార్మెడ *māru-meḍa.* n. A twisted neck. మెలిపడి పోయిన కంఠము. A. iii. 23.

మారుడు or మరుడు *māruḍu.* [Skt.] n. Manmadha, the g ‹ ' o flov మన్మథుడు. మారాంతకుడు *mār-āntakuḍu.* n. An epithet of Siva as the *Amoricide,* or slayer of lust, శివుడు.

మారుతము *mārutamu.* [Skt. from మరుత్తు.] n. Air, wind, గాలి, వాయువు. మారుతి or మారుతాత్మజుడు *māruti.* n. Son of the wind, an epithet of Hanuman and Bhima. హనుమంతుడు, భీముడు. మారుతాశనము *mārut-āśanamu.* n. A snake; (lit. that which lives on air.) సర్పము.

మారుడుడు See under మారు.

మారువ *māruva.* [Tel.] n. A sluice from a tank.

మారువు *māruvu.* [Tel.] n. A sort of fish.

మారేడు or మారెడు *māreḍu.* [Tel.] n. The Bael or Bel Fruit-tree, *Ægle marmelos.* (E. P.) బిల్వవృక్షము.

మార్కండేయుడు *mārkaṇḍ-ēyuḍu.* [Skt. from మృకండ.] n .The name of a certain sage who lived for ten centuries. తమరు మార్కండేయుని ఆయుస్సుకలుగుగాక may you live a thousand years.

మార్కము or మారకము *mārkamu.* [Tel. from మారు.] n. Exchange.

మార్కొను See under మారు.

మార్గణము *mārgaṇamu.* [Skt.] n. Search, research, వెదకడము. Begging, యాచించడము. An arrow, బాణము. మార్గణుడు *mārgaṇuḍu.* n. A mendicant, యాచకుడు. A. i. 30.

మార్గము *mārgamu.* [Skt.] n. A way, road, path, means, manner, method. మార్గదర్శి *mārga-darśi.* n. A guide. మార్గుడు *mārguḍu.* n. A word used only in composition, as దుర్మార్గుడు an evil doer. సన్మార్గుడు he who does good. దుర్మార్గురాలు she who does evil. "అజనంజమార్గితిమార్గుడై" he who is freed from earthly ties. Chenn. iv. 132.

మార్గశిరము or మార్గశీర్షము *mārgaśiramu.* [Skt. from మృగశీర్ష.] n. The ninth lunar month (December—January), wherein the moon's change takes place when the sun is in Sagittarius.

మార్చు *mārtsu.* [Tel. causal of మారు.] v. a. To change, to alter, to exchange. To serve, as food, వడ్డించు. To transmute metals. పరివర్తనచేయు, వ్యత్యయముచేయు, ఒకటియిచ్చి మరియొకటి పుచ్చుకొను. To kill, slaughter, destroy, నాశముచేయు, చంపు. దినముమార్చి దినము every other day. మార్చుకొను *mārtsu-konu.* v. a. To exchange or barter. పరివర్తనచేసికొను.

మార్జనము *mārjanamu.* [Skt.] n. Wiping, తుడుచుట. Rubbing, తోముట. కేశమార్జనము, a comb, దువ్వెన. Parij. iii. 105. గృహసమ్మార్జనము cleaning the house. మార్జని *mārjani.* n. A broom, చీపురు. మార్జించు *mārjintsu.* v. a. To wipe. తుడుచు.

మార్జాలము *mārjālamu.* [Skt.] n. A cat. పిల్లి.

మార్తాండుడు *mārtānḍudu.* [Skt. from మృతండము.] n. The sun. సూర్యుడు.

మార్త్యుడు See under మారు.

మార్దంగికుడు *mārdangikudu.* [Skt. from మృదంగము.] n. A drummer, మద్దెలవాయించువాడు.

మార్దవము *mārdavamu.* [Skt. from మృదువు.] n. Softness, మృదుత్వము, మెత్తన. Smoothness. Grace. మార్దవయుక్తమైన gracious, కరుణాకలవాడైన.

మాల *māla.* [Tel. from మయిల.] n. A Pariah, an outcaste, చండాలుడు. adj. Pariah, outcaste. Vile, base. చండాల. మాలకాకి the jungle crow. In some compounds it is equivalent to dog (as dog-rose), thus: మాలతులసి the wild tulasi. మాలడేగ an inferior sort of hawk. మాలతాచు the lesser sort of viper. మాలసతి a Pariah woman. మాలకూతలు base language. మాలపల్లె a Pariah village. మాలడు *māladu.* n. A Pariah. చండాలుడు, మాలవాడు. మాలది or మాలెత *māladi.* n. A Pariah woman. చండాలస్త్రీ. మాలనూలు *māla-nūlu.* n. Fine thread spun by Pariahs, and used in weaving muslin. మాలరికము *mālarikamu.* n. The being a Pariah. చండాలత్వము. "ఉద్దండ తేమాలరికంబున దండిగనటించెద." UH. iv. 91.

మాల *māla.* [Skt.] n. A garland, wreath, necklace or heraldic collar: a coronal or coronet of flowers. A series or string of verses or songs. జపమాల a rosary or string of beads. కంఠమాల scrofula about the neck. వర్ణమాల the alphabet. మాలకరి or మాలాకారుడు *māla-kari.* n. A garland maker, a flower seller. A gardener, వనపాలకుడు. "పురబాహ్యమున గట్టె మాలెత్తులంగజేసి ముదముమాలకరివోలె." G. vi. 49. మాలి *māli.* n. One who has a garland. A gardener. Radha. i. 74. మాలిక *mālika.* n. A chaplet, garland of flowers, a wreath. A line, or row. పూదండ, పూమాలె, పఙ్క్తి, రూపమైనసమూహము. "తరుణవిద్యుత్మాలికాలతోదారంబై." R. vi. 12.

మాలతి *mālati.* [Skt.] n. The great flowering jasmine, *Jasminum grandiflorum.* Rox. ii. 11. జాజి.

మాలిన్యము *mālinyamu.* [Skt. from మలినము.] n. Foulness, turbidness, filth, మలినత, మలినత్వము, మురికి.

మాలిమి *mālimi.* [Tel.] n. Familiarity, love, attachment, affection. వాత్సల్యము, చిన్ననాంతో చేయు స్నేహము, మచ్చిక. The science of navigation, ఓడనడపు శాస్త్రము. మాలిమి or మాలిమికాడు a navigator, ఓడనడపు శాస్త్ర మెరిగినవాడు.

మాలీసు *mālīsu.* [H.] n. Grooming or rubbing down (a horse). మాలీసుచేయు to groom a horse.

మాలు *mālu.* [Tel.] v. n. To be laid aside, to be desisted from. To be spoiled or ruined, చెడు. నశించు. మాలిన *mālina* adj. Devoid of, విహీనమైన. పనికిమాలిన or కొర మాలిన useless. పాలుమాలిన idle. సిగ్గుమాలిన shameless. పనికిమాలి (or పనిలేక) దీన్ని చేసి నావా did you do this for want of something to do or out of mere idleness? ఈ మాటలు పనియోగముమాలినవి these statements are useless. కరుణమాలిన relentless, merciless. "కరుణమాలినయట్టి కైకసబలిచి." DRyo. 136. దిక్కుమాలిన helpless. ఎరుక మాలిన devoid of wisdom, senseless. వావి మాలిన incestuous. మాలుచు, మాల్చు, మాలుపు or మాల్పు malutsu. v. a. To set aside, stop. మానుచు. వాని బయిటి మాలిచిరి they humbled her.

మాలు malu. [Tel.] n. The pad or cushion placed on the shoulder of a palanquin bearer. బోయీలు మాలుమీదిబెట్టిపోత్తురు. Also, property, wealth; the rent or revenue obtained from land. మాలీ pertaining to the revenue. మాలుకచేరిపను a revenue clerk. మాలుసిబ్బంది the establishment of revenue peons. మాలుగుజారీ paying land tax.

మాలుగు or మాల్గు malugu. [Tel. from మాలు.] v. n. To become or grow idle, సోమరితనముగనుపొందు. n. Idleness, సోమరితనము. Also same as మాలు a pad or cushion placed on the shoulder of a palanquin bearer. మాలుగుపోతు malugu-potu. n. A sluggard, a lazy wretch. సోమరి గొడ్డు, సోమరి. "ఊరికూలికిపచ్చి యూడువరిగో యుంచు, మాలుకుజెండటొచ్చెని, మాలుగుపోతుననిని కనుమానముచేసెర." Chenn. iii. 447.

మాలూరము maluramu. [Skt.] n. The Bael tree, Ægle marmelos. మారేడు చెట్టు, శ్రీఫలము, బిల్వము. Also, the Wood-apple tree, వెలగచెట్టు.

మాలె or మాలియ male. [Tel.] n. A house, dwelling, మాడుగు. హర్మ్యము. నేలమాలె a cellar. "ధరనిబాలుని నేలమాలెలో క్రితి పతించి నాడి." G. I. 90. [Also, for Skt. మాల.] n. A garland, పూదండ. A line, పఙ్క్తి.

మాలెప See under మాల.

మాల్యము malyamu. [Skt.] n. A wreath, chaplet, garland. పూదండ. మాల్యవంతము malya-vantamu. n. The name of a certain mountain. ఒకపర్వతము.

మాళయము malayamu. [Tel.] n. Vulg. for మహాలయము.

మాళవము or మాళవదేశము malavamu. [Skt.] n. The country called Malwa, దేశభేదము.

మాళిగ maliga. [Tel.] n. A house, abode, dwelling. ఇల్లు. నేలమాళిగ a subterranean chamber. తిరుమాళిగ a phrase among Vaishnavas for a house: lit. a blessed tabernacle.

మావంతుడు or మావతుడు mavantudu. [from Skt. మాహత్.] n. An elephant driver, మావటివాడు.

మావటము mavatamu. [Tel.] n. A small roll or packet of betel, areca nut, lime, and other ingredients, made up in order to be distributed among guests. తమలపాకులపట్టీ. "బంగారు చిలుకలనుసమించు తమలపాకుల మావ టాలుకొంచులనిచ్చెది." KP. vii.

మావటి, మావటీడు or మావటివాడు mavati. [from Skt. మహాత్.] n. An elephant driver, or mahout. ఏనుగును తోలు వాడు.

మావి mavi. [Tel.] n. A mango tree. మామిడి చెట్టు. మావిడి or మావిపండు a mango. The after birth, the placenta. గర్భస్థపిండమునకు సుట్టుకొనియుండు పొర. మావిచేప mavi-chepa. n. A kind of fish. ఒకవిధమైనచేప.

మావు mavu. [Tel.] n. A horse. గుర్రము. The covering a mare. అశ్వసంగమము. A snare for fish. వల్లెవాటు చేపలుపట్టు సాధనము. A numerical fraction, one twentieth.

మంచిమావుకు ఇస్తే మంచిపిల్ల పుట్టును if the sire is good the foal will be good. R. i. 8. పాలుమనీరు వేరుపరుపంగలమావులు vehicles that can separate water from milk, that is, swans. క్షీరనీరములను విడదీయు శక్తిగలవాహనములు, అనగా, హంసలు. మావుపిడిబాకు a sort of dagger. మావుమోమువాడు *mâvu-mômu-vâdu*. n. Lit: "Horse faced." A kind of mythological being. కింపురుషుడు.

మావురము *mavuramu*. [Tel.] n. A kind of fish. ఒకవిధమైనచేప. "రాతిజోరుకు, మావురములకుకుంటుమన్క్యా." H. iv. 225.

మాషము *mâshamu*. [Skt.] n. Black gram. *Phaseolus radiatus*. Rox. iii, 296. మినుములు. రాజమాషములు a kind of bean, *Dolichos catjang*. Rox. iii. 303. అలసందలు, commonly called అలచందలు. Jaim. iv. 201. A small weight equal to five seeds.

మాసటి, మాసటీడు or మాస్టీడు *mâsati*. [Skt.] n. A hero, a gymnast, a fine fellow. శూరుడు, మల్లుడు, సాముకాడు, వస్తాదు; శ్రేష్ఠుడు. "కటారి మాస్టీనిచెలువునగూర్చండి." T. iii. 140. "చెరుకువిల్మాస్టీని విరుచుడింది మరీల." ib. iii. 25. "మైనాకు నొరసినమాసటీడు." Swa. v. 56.

మాసము *mâsamu*. [Skt.] n. A month, either of the lunar, solar, or any other computation of the year. నెల. The Telugu months are చైత్రము, వైశాఖము, జ్యేష్ఠము, ఆషాఢము, శ్రావణము, భాద్రపదము, ఆశ్వయుజము, కార్తికము, మార్గశిరము, పుష్యము, మాఘము, ఫాల్గునము. అధికమాసము an intercalary month. క్షయమాసము a lost month. నిజమాసము the month proper. నక్షత్రచంద్రమాసము the time wherein the moon moves through a sidereal revolution. Also, same as మాషము a small weight.

మాసకమ్మ or మాచకమ్మ *mâsak-amma*. [Tel.] n. A woman with male characteristics. See మాచకమ్మ.

మాసరము *mâsaramu*. [Skt.] n. The scum of boiled rice. అన్నమువార్చినగంజి, గంజిమీది మీగడ. adj. Spread, వ్యాప్తము, Long, దీర్ఘము. మాసరముగ or మాసరమై *mâsaramu-ga*. adv. Being mingled or mixed, unitedly, మిశ్రముగా, కలిసినట్టుగా. "చెంగల్వకొలనులకు దిగ్గి కాసరీదధిమండమాసరం బులంగాచినకి యొూరంబెట్టిన సారంగశ్యంత్ర చే ధంగంబులతో." A. iv. 37. టీ॥ మాసరంబులుగా, మిశ్రములుగాను. "ప్రేమసంప్రీతి వినయ భూరితరవిలోకనంబు గృష్ణునిముఖకమలంబునందు మాసరంబుగ వికసనమధుపునకు మధువ్రతంబులు నిగుడునాకుప్రక్కుండు." M. XII. i. 435.

మాసి *mâsi*. [Tel. from మాయు.] n. Dirt, మురికి. Also, another form of మానిసి. (q. v.)

మాసిక *mâsika*. [Tel.] n. A patch. అతుకు. A jumble, a pack of nonsense. చిక్కు. మాసికలు odds and ends. మాసికవేయు or పెట్టు to patch up; to raise false claims.

మాసికము *mâsikamu*. [Skt. from మాసము.] adj. Monthly. మాససంబంధమైన, నెలనెలకు వచ్చే. n. A monthly ceremony for a deceased relative, continued for a year after the death. ఏకాదశికాలోగా. నెలనెలకు పెట్టే శ్రాద్ధము.

మాసూలు or మహసూలు *mâsûlu*. [H.] n. Produce, a crop, పంట, ఫలము. That which is collected, income.

మాహాత్మ్యము *mahâtmyamu*. [Skt. from మహాత్మ.] n. Might, efficacy, greatness. The peculiar efficacy or virtue of any divinity or sacred shrine. A work giving an account of the merits of any holy place or object. శ్రీరంగమాహాత్మ్యము the legend of Sri Rangam. ఈ మంత్రముయొక్క మాహాత్మ్యము the might or efficacy of the spell. రామమాహాత్మ్యము the adventures of Râma or the miracles of Râma.

మాహేశ్వరులు mahêṣvarulu. [Skt. from మహేశ్వరుడు.] n. Worshippers of Siva, a title assumed by the Jangams.

మి mi

మింగు or మ్రింగు mingu. [Tel.] v. a. To swallow, devour. కబళించు. గుక్కిళ్లుమింగు to swallow one's saliva, to stand speechless, to smother one's grief; to water, as the mouth, ఆపేక్షించు. గుక్కిళ్లు ఎందుకు మింగుతావు చెప్పు why do you falter so in speaking. "కన్నవుడొంగలువచ్చిరి, మిన్నక యూళ్లోనివారి మింగిరటంచున్." Vaij. iv. 54. the people inside have devoured it. మింగ పగొండి, మింగగొడ్డి or మ్రింగపగొండి minga-na-gondi. n. A glutton. తిండిపోతు. "మనవిజారిరుము మింగగొండియుత్యే." BD. iv. 1281.

మించు mintsu. [Tel.] v. a. To surpass, excel; to transgress. అతిశయించు, అతిక్రమించు. చదువులో వారిని మించినాడు he surpassed them in learning. అతడు ముందు మించిపోయినాడు he is already gone on. మించిమాట్లాడకు do not talk rashly. పని మించిపోయినది it is now too late, the thing is gone by. చెయ్యిమించవద్దు do not lay a hand upon him, do not take the law into your own hands. ఇంతకుమించి యెరుగను I know nothing more than this. పెదవికిమించినపల్లు a projecting tooth, i. e., a scapegrace, a disobedient fellow, మించిమించియుండేటి, లేక, మహా ఉంటే పదిరూపాయీలు ఉండవచ్చును at the utmost there may be ten rupees. ఆరూకలను మించి ఇచ్చివేసినాడు he had already paid the money. "ఉత్తరంబుమించి యరిగిన" M. III. i. 2; when they first went northwards, ఉత్తరానికి ముందుగా పోవునప్పటికి. మించుకాలు the right leg, కుడికాలు. n. A kind of ring worn on the second toe, కాలిమెట్టు. Excess, అధిక్యము. Lightning, మెరుపు. Brightness, ప్రకాశము. మించూసె it flashed, మెరుపుమెరసెను, మెరసెను. "తోలుబొమ్మకుదయూత్రి కిలాకిమించూని." A. i. 43. మించుబోడి or మించుబోణి mintsu-bôḍi. n. A beautiful girl. మెరుపువలెనుండెడికన్య నిస్త్రీ. మించుదల mintsudala. n. Transgression. అతిక్రమణము. Excess, greatness, అధిక్యము.

మింజుమల mindzumala. [H.] n. A part, payment.

మిజాజు or మిజాజు mijâju. [H.] n. Pride.

మింట minta. [Tel.] n. (Abl. of మిన్ను.) in the sky. మింటి minṭi. Gen. of మిన్ను, of the sky. మింటితెరువరి minṭi-teruvari. n. Lit. a traveller in the sky, i. e., the sun, సూర్యుడు, or an Asura, అసురుడు.

మిఠాయి mithâyi. [H.] n. A sweetment, పిండివంట.

మింఠుడు minṭhuḍu. [Skt.] n. A paramour, విటుడు, మిండగాడు.

మిండడు, మిండగాడు or మిండగీడు minḍaḍu. [from Skt. మింఠ.] n. A paramour. విటుడు. A person, పురుషుడు. A great man, అధికుడు. మిండజంగము minḍa-dzangamu. n. A buck, a lascivious zangam. మిండతపసి a lascivious monk. "కీ॥ కడుపుటు భుజంగ పేముఱు నవసిపప్పు, దుండుపో గండుమీరి యూ మిండతపసి." R. ii. 110. మిండతుమ్మెద minḍa-tummeda. n. A male carpenter bee. "మిండతుమ్మెదల్ మెట్టనిపువ్వు మంజరులు." Kalahas. iv. 54. మిండప్రాయము the bloom of youth, యౌవనము. మిండవడ్డి a high or exorbitant interest on money lent, అధికమగువడ్డి. మిండమేఘము a great cloud, పెద్దమబ్బు. మిండతనము or మిండరికము minḍa-tanamu. n. Whorishness, rakishness, adultery, జారత్వము. మిండత or మిండలోతి minḍata. n. A harlot, an adulteress, an unchaste woman. లంజ, జారిణి. మిండవి minḍavi, adj. Loverlike, appertaining to a paramour విటసంబంధమైన. మిండవిమాటలు the words of a paramour

మిక్కుటము or **ముక్కుటము** *mikkuṭamu.* [Tel.] n. Excess, abundance, greatness, extremity. "కాంతి మిక్కుటమై పర్వి తారకావళులు నష్టోదయ్యోగమైనట్టుండగా." Chenn. ii. 287. **మిక్కుటము, ముక్కుటము** or **ముక్కుటపు.** adj. Excessive, extreme, great, much. దుస్సహము, అధికము, మిక్కిలి.

మిక్కిలి *mikkili.* [Tel.] n. Much, abundance, greatness. అధికము. విస్తారము. "మిక్కిలియైన కీర్తి." భార. అర. vi. adj. Great, much, vast, అధికము. Excellent, fine, best, శ్రేష్ఠము. మిక్కిలికన్ను an extra eye, అధికమైనకన్ను. "క॥ మిక్కిలిచేతులును వాని మిక్కిలికన్నున్." భార. సభా. ii. "సీ॥ అఖిలదక్షుప్పదములకు గోమువు మిక్కిలి, మానవులకు బ్రాహ్మణుండు వరిష్ఠుండు, పక్షులందు శ్యేనమధికంబు." భార. అశ్వ. ii. మిక్కిలికంటివేల్పు Siva. మిక్కిలి దిక్కు the sky. ఆకాశము. "రెక్కలువిదల్చి లావులు ముక్కుకొనం దువ్వి కొందమున కంధరమిక్కిలి దిక్కునకుంగొని కొక్కొక్కో యనుచు కోళ్లు కూయగదొడగెన్." S. i. 173. మిక్కిలి ఉప్పు too much salt. adv. Very, greatly, much, vastly, extremely, excessively, too much, more than. మిక్కిలి అవాస్తవమైన utterly false. మిక్కిలి రహస్యముగా very secretly. గోడలు మిక్కిలి పడిపోయినవి the walls are much ruined. **మిక్కిలివాడు** *mikkili-vāḍu.* n. A great person, అధికుడు. "పాండవుల్ మిక్కిలివారు." భార. ద్రోణ. v. **మిక్కిలు** *mikkilu.* v. n. To exceed, excel, మీరు, అతిశయించు.

"క॥ తెలిదలతో దాటించిన
దలమీరున్ గాలుగాలదాటించిన మి
క్కిలుగాలు గేలుసేతుల
గలిగినదనచేయిమీదుగా జ్రేటుగొనన్."
ఉ. హరి. vi.

Also, to come from left to right, అప్రదక్షిణముగావచ్చు. "మిక్కిలుచున్నవి మెకసిక వాడులు." B. i. §. 14.

మిగులు *migulu.* [Tel.] v. n. To remain over, to be over and above; to be left as a residue, to survive. శేషించు. To excel, అతిశయించు. To expire, as a period. To pass a limit, మట్టుమీరు. సమయముమిగిలినది it is now too late. మిగిలినది the rest, the remainder. మిగిలినవారు the rest of the people. n. Remainder, balance, remnant మిగత, శేషము. **మిగిలిన** *migilina.* adj. Remaining. **మిగుల** *migula.* adv. Much, exceedingly, excessively, greatly; already. మంచి, మిక్కిలి, అత్యంతము. అతడు మిగుల వెళ్లిపోయినాడు he is already gone, it is too late, he is gone. మిగులమాటలాడకు do not use improper language, i.e., do not be rude. **మిగిలించు. మిగులుచు** or **మిగుల్చు** *migi-linṭsu.* v. a. To cause to remain over, మిగులజేయు. To save or lay up, కూడబెట్టు. **మిగులుచుకొను** or **మిగుల్చుకొను** *migulutsu-konu.* v. a. To save or lay up. **మిగత** *migata.* n. That which remains over. Remainder, remnant, surplus, balance. Desideratum, deficit మిగులు, శేషము.

మిటమిట *miṭa-miṭa.* [Tel.] adv. Fiercely, hotly, brightly, మిక్కిలి ఉష్ణముగా, ప్రకాశముగా. "మిటమిటకాండ కాయగ." Padma. iv. 62. **మిటమిటన** *miṭamiṭana.* n. Fierceness, brightness. **మిటమిటని** *miṭamiṭani.* adj. Fierce, bright. **మిటమిటలాడు** *miṭa-miṭa-l-āḍu.* v. n. To leap, to be insolent or arrogant, ఎగిరిదుమికిపడు. **మిటారము** *miṭāramu.* n. Beauty, coquetry, foppery. ఒయ్యారము, బిక్కు, అతిశయము. "అలసితిరంచు, పైకొనులతొంగి మిటారిమ జూచినవ్వుచుగా." N. ix. 55. **మిటారి** *miṭāri.* n. A belle, a pretty woman. కులుకులాడి, సొగసుకత్తె. "కులుకుమిటారి నీవు కొలకొన్న ఫలంబును నీకు హానంబు." Radha. iii. 104. **మిటారి** or **మిటారపు** adj. Graceful, pretty, attractive; charming, beautiful, coquettish, foppish, ఒయ్యారమైన, సొగసైన. "దానిమిటారిపోయగపు పట్టపు పాపాపులతో

చూపులతో." H. v. 26. "చిన్నిమిటారిపు గోటిమొక్కులక్." T. iii. 10. మిటారిచూపు a coquettish look. మిటారించు mitā-r-intsu. v. n. To move gracefully, కులుకు, నిక్కు, విజృంభించు, అతిశయించు. To bound, jump, leap. దుముకు.

మిట్ట miṭṭa. [Tel. from మిడియు.] n. A high or rising ground, a small hill. ఉన్నతభూమి. adj. High, elevated; raised (as ground), jutting out (as teeth.). మిట్టపండ్లు projecting teeth. మిట్టపల్లములు ups and downs, uneven ground. మిట్టమధ్యాహ్నము high noon. మిట్టవరహా a kind of gold pagoda worth four rupees. మిట్టమిర్రు (మిట్ట+మిర్రు.) very high ground, అత్యున్నతభూమి. "ఏటికాల్వ మిట్ట మిర్రుగాబ్రవిచ్చి." HD. i. మిట్టు or మిట్టించు miṭṭu v. n. To fly, ఎగురు. మిట్టాడు miṭṭ-āḍu. (మిట్టి+ఆడు.) v. n. To roam, to walk about. సంచరించు. "మనుజులుమిట్టాడని యొకఘనకాననము." P. i. 292. a forest unfrequented by men. మిట్టిపడు miṭṭi-paḍu. v. n. To jump, hop along, bound. ఎగిరిపడు. To be puffed with pride or insolence. మిడిసిపడు. మిట్టిపాటు miṭṭi-pāṭu. n. Insolence, మిట్టిపడుట.

మిడత or మిడుత miḍata. [Tel. from మిడియు.] n. A grasshopper, locust, or cricket. శలభము. ఆకుమిడత a green grasshopper. మిడతంభట్లజోస్యము a happy hit. వెదురుమిడత the cricket that bores the bamboo. ఉప్పుమిడత a large kind of cricket. గొల్లమిడత or గొల్లభామ a grasshopper. జెట్టిమిడత the wrestler locust, so named from its strength.

మిడమిడ miḍa-miḍa. [Tel. anuk.] adv. Fiercely. మిడమిడమిడుకు miḍa-miḍa-miḍuku. v. n. To be enraged. "మిడమిడమిడుకుచు మినుమిండదనియె." BD. iv. 1460.

మిడి miḍi. [Tel. from మిడియు.] n. Pride, insolence, మిడిసిపాటు, గర్వము. adj. Proud, insolent, మిడిసిపాటుగల. High, raised, ఉన్నతము. మిడిపండ్లు projecting teeth, మిట్టపండ్లు. Sharp, hot, తీక్ష్ణము. మిడిమధ్యాహ్నము midday, noon. మిడిముల్లు spurs. మిడికించు miḍi-kintsu. v. n. To blink (the eyes), మిణుకరించు. "కనులుమిడికించుచుగుడ్లగూబకీ." S. iii. 32., blinking like an owl. మిడిగుడ్లు miḍi-guḍlu. n. Large prominent eyes. మిడిగుడ్లవాడు a man with large eyes. మిడిగొను miḍi-gonu. v. n. To glitter, to flash. మెరయు. "మిడిగొనుపైడిచేకటులు, మేలిమిసూలుదండ." H. iv. 101. మిడినాగు or మిణ్నాగు miḍi-nāgu. n. A springing serpent. The adder. చివుక్కున ఎగిరిపడే సర్పము. మిడిసి మిణ్నాగువలె పడుతాడు he is as proud as a serpent. మిడిపోవు miḍi-pōvu. v. n. To lose brilliance, become blunt, to be spoiled, చెబ్బుపడు. To become less. To be an exception, తప్పు. To avoid, తొలగు. "మిగులనొచ్చియు వాడు మిడిపోవకడిమి." HD. i. 2019. మిడినల్లి or మిణ్నల్లి miḍi-nalli. n. A flea. మిడిమేలపు miḍi-mēlapu. adj. Pragmatic, hot headed, haughty. తలకొట్లమారియైన. తలకొవ్విన. "అడిగినఁజెరంచియ్యని మిడిమేలపుదొరనుగొలిచి మిడుకుటకంటెన్, వడిగలయెద్దులగట్టుక మడిదున్నుక బ్రతుకవచ్చు మహిలో సుమతీ." Sumati Satakam. మిడిమేలము miḍi-mēlamu. n. Insolence, haughtiness, మిడిసిపాటు. "మనుపలుమగలని యెనుకగడు. మృగములకోరిసిలజేసి మిడిమేలమితం డగపడుననితలచితిమే." R. ii. 112. మిడియ miḍiya. n. A word of the Veda. వేదవాక్యము.

"కని తెలిచియుపుడింటోకింతియును
తొలుతటెలివాతి మిడియునో.కనరిచి
వ్వెలనరపిన్రతుతత్వము
పలుకునకుక్ గాకి వినిదుటా.చినాలకకే."
పా. ii.

మిడియు miḍiyu. v. n. To flash or fly off as a chip of wood or a drop of water. ఎగురు. ఆ రాతిచెక్క మిడిసిపడినది the chip of the stone leaped out and fell down. మిడివిల్లు miḍi-villu. n. A pellet bow, ఉండవిల్లు. "తడియము మక్కళవాతిరుణిదొక్కొన మిడివింటికతివన్న మెలతలరాసి." Dah. 170. మిడిసిపడు miḍisi-paḍu. v. n. To bounce, leap: to be insolent, మిట్టిపడు. త్రుళ్లిపడు. మిడిసిపడి చచ్చినాడు he suddenly fell down dead. మిడిసిపాటు miḍisi-pāṭu. n. Bouncing, exultation, pride, త్రుళ్లిపాటు.

మిడుకు miḍuku. [Tel.] v. n. To live, బ్రతుకు. To be insolent, త్రుళ్లు. To move, చలించు. కదలు. To wander, roam, move about, సంచరించు. To grieve, mourn, or lament. దుఃఖపడు. To dry. ఎండు. "అడిగిన శీతలదియ్యని మడిమేలపుదొరనుగోలిచి మిడుకుటకంటెన్." Sumati Satakam. n. Life, జీవము. మిడుకుమిడుకను to grieve, పరితపించు. మిడుకుమాలగా miḍuku-māla-gā. n. adv. Insolently, మిడిసిపడగా. మిడుకరించు miḍu-karintsu. v. n. To blink (the eyes) in fear. See మిణుకరించు. "మెడసాంచుముకొనికన్ను మిడుకరించెదవు" Dab. 217.

మిడుగు or మిణుగు miḍugu. [Tel. from మిడియు.] n. A hard stone. కఠినశిల.

మిడుగురు, మిడుగు or మిణుగురు miḍuguru. [Tel. from మిడియు.] n. A spark, a gleam. అగ్నికణము. "మిడుగురులుపరంగనిమ్నం బినప్పా." HD. i. 2228. A firefly or glowworm, మిణుగురుపురుగు.

మిడుచు miḍutsu. [Tel. from చిడియు.] v. a. To drop or pour by drops. "మృతిబొందు కెడనీరు మిడుచునెప్పటికి." DRU. 1112. To crack the knuckles, మెటికవిరుచు.

మిడుత. Same as మిడత. (q. v.)

మిణుకరించు miṇukarintsu. [Tel.] v. n. To blink (the eyes) as in fear, to hesitate, to be at a loss. అతడు మిణుకరిస్తున్నాడు he is at a loss, he knows not what to do. మిణుకరము miṇukaramu. n. Perplexity, ఏమిన్నితోచక భ్రమించుట.

మిణుకు or మినుకు miṇuku. [Tel.] n. Glimmering, sparkling. తళుకు. మిణుకుమిణుకుమని ఒకదీపము ఉండినది there was a glimmering lamp. మిణుకు మిణుకుమన్నది it gleamed, or was just perceptible. మిణుకు చేయు to polish or burnish. మిణుకుచేసి కొను to be gay in dress. మిణుకుకాటుక black eyesalve. v. n. To be bright, to glimmer. మిణుగురు Same as మిడుగురు (q. v.). Plu. మిణుగురులు or మిణుగుర్లు. మిణుగురుపురుగు or మిణుగురుబూచి miṇuguru-purugu. n. A fire fly or its larva. A glow-worm. ఖద్యోతము.

మిన్నాగు See under మిను.

మితము mitamu. [Skt.] adj. Moderate, temperate. Few. మితజనముతో with a few followers. మితభాషి one who is moderate in language, not talkative. మితజ్ఞులు the ignorant. n. A bound, measure, limit, term; moderation, limitation. మితములేని or అమితమైన countless, endless, immoderate. మితి miti. n. End, limit. పరిమాణము. హద్దు, కొలది. గడువు. మితిలేని unlimited, endless, huge, vast. "అన్నకాముని తోడ ఆడినమితులు." Pal. 120. ఆడినమితులు the terms proposed.

మిత్త mitta. [from Skt. మిత్ర.] n. A friend, స్నేహితుడు.

మిత్తి mitti. [from Skt. మృత్యువు.] n. Death or dying. చావు. మృత్యువు. "సింహంపుమిత్తిగా చేతికర్త." R. ii. 32. మిత్తిక mittika. [from Skt. మృత్తిక.] n. Earth, మన్ను. మృత్తిక. మిత్తికూడు rice offered to the dead. "మిత్తి కూడ్లుకొనగ మేలునకెక్కునా." Vema. 76

మిత్తిగొంగ *mitti-gonga.* n. The conqueror of Death, i. e., Siva. మృత్యుంజయుడు, శివుడు. మిత్తిచూలు *mitti-tsūlu.* n. Lit. the child of death, an epithet applied to the descending node of the moon, కేతుగ్రహము. మిత్తివేటకాడు *mitti-vēṭa-kāḍu.* n. Siva, మృత్యుంజయుడు.

మిత్రము *mitramu.* [Skt.] n. A friend, స్నేహితుడు. మిత్రుడు *mitruḍu.* n. A friend. అప్తుడు. The sun, సూర్యుడు. మిత్రత్వము *mitra-tvamu.* n. Friendship. మిత్రభేదము a breach of friendship. మిత్రలాభము the making of friends. అమిత్రుడు lit. not a friend, i. e., an enemy.

మిథము *mithamu.* [Skt.] adj. Reciprocal, పరస్పరము. అము. iv.

మిథునము *mithunamu.* [Skt.] n. A couple, a brace, a pair: particularly male and female. ఆలుమగలు జత. The sign Gemini. "తెరువున కొకమిథునము జూదరులంగనుగొంటె." M. XIII. ii. 220. ఒక మిథునము జూదరులు a pair of gamblers. మిథునకర్మము sexual intercourse, సంభోగము, రతి. "మిథునకర్మంబు చేసెగాని ప్రజావృద్ధి లేదనుచు." Vish. ii. 270.

మిథ్య *mithya.* [Skt.] n. A lie. అసత్యము, అబద్ధము. adj. False, unreal, deceptive, delusive. అబద్ధమైన. మాయయైన. మిథ్యాదృష్టి *mithya-drushṭi.* Atheism, heresy, materialism. పరలోకనాస్తికత, నాస్తికత్వము. మిథ్యామతి *mithya-mati.* n. Error, mistake, ignorance. భ్రమ, భ్రాంతి.

మిద్దె or మిద్దియ *midde.* [Tel. from మాడు.] n. A flat roof, an upper story. A flat roofed house or a storeyed house. The pistil of the lotus, తామరపువ్వులోనునాని లోపలి దిమ్మ. The beazle of a ring, ఉంగరపు మీదిదిమ్మె. మిద్దెటిల్లు or మిద్దెయిల్లు a terraced house, a house that has a flat roof, or a storeyed house. మూడుమిద్దెలయిల్లు a three storeyed house. మిద్దెయుంగరము a ring with a beazle.

మినమిన *mina-mina.* [Tel.] n. Brightness, twinkling, sparkling. తళతళ. "మినమినల్ పెడుననుమేను." H. iv. 178. మినమినలాడు to sparkle, మెరయు. adv. Twinklingly, sparklingly, brightly. తళతళమని. "మినమినలకురు మెరుపుచంటివాని." Sar. D. 464.

మినహా *minahā.* [H.] n. A deduction, remission, an exception. మినహాయించు *minahā-yi-ntsu.* v. a. To subtract, deduct; to make an exception.

మిను Same as మిన్ను (q. v.).

మినుకు or మిన్కు *minuku.* [Tel.] n. Glittering, flashing, brightness, తళుకు. A ray of light. కిరణము. A marriage token, తాళిబొట్టు. "ఇమ్ము నీకంఠసూత్రము మున్ను మినుకుగలకొంకు ముడిచి." "మదీయగళంబున మున్ను మంగళసూత్రంబునమినుకు పతిపురుషులుకన్నడు లోచన గోచరించు గాదు." HN. v. 102. A small gold coin. చిన్న బంగారు నాణెము. మినుకులు or మిన్కులు *minu-kulu.* n. The sciences, the scriptures. విద్యలు, శాస్త్రములు, వేదములు. "ఉడివోనిమిన్కులరినెడు పేరు లిరుదిస." Vasu. Pref. 7. టీ. ఉడివోని మిన్కులు, వేదములు. మినుకుచేడియ *minuku-chēḍiya* n. An epithet of Sarasvati. మినుమినుకను. మినుకుమినుకుమను or మినుక్కురను to twinkle, to sparkle. మినుకులబరణి or మినుకులయిక్కి *minukula-baraṇi.* n. An epithet of the sun, సూర్యుడు.

మినుము *minumu.* [Tel.] n. Black gram, *Phaseolus mungo, or Phaseolus minimus.* మాషము. మినప or మినుప *minapa.* adj. Made of or belonging to the grain called మినుము. మినపనీళ్లు water wherein this gram has been steeped. మినపగింజలు black gram. మినపపప్పు split black gram.

మిన్కు See మినుకు.

మిన్న *minna*. [Tel.] n. A gem, a jewel. రత్నము. That which is noble or preeminent. మేటి, శ్రేష్ఠము, తల్లజము. "కాంతల కాపులు మిండలైనట్టి వేదనరు, కాపులకుసెల్ల మిన్నయకన్యా పుకాడుకు." H. iv. 171. "తేలకన్ను పూదూండ్లకు మిన్నలైయున్న జిగిదొత్యాడుచేతులు." ib. i. 64. adj. Noble, superior, high. శ్రేష్ఠమైన. పొడుగైన. "ముందుకేగొక్కా లెమిన్న పొమ్మునిక." N. ix. 417.

మిన్నక *minnaka*. [Tel.] adv. Sedately, silently, coolly. ఊరక.

మిన్ను or **మిను** *minnu*. [Tel.] n. The sky or heaven, ఆకాశము. (G. మింటి. D. మింటికి Abl. మింట). మింటికెగసె it flew up into the sky. మిన్నున in the sky. మిన్నువిరిగి మీదపడినట్లు as if the skies were falling. Swa. iv. 115. **మినుచూలు** *minu-ṭsūlu*. n. Lit. the offspring of the sky, an epithet applied to the wind, వాయువు. మినుసిగవేల్పు, lit. the sky-tressed god, an epithet of Siva. **మిన్నుకాలువ, మిన్నువాక, మిన్నేరు** or **మిన్నేరు** *minnu-kolaku*. n. The heavenly Ganges, ఆకాశగంగ. **మిన్నుమన్ను** *minnu-mannu*. n. Heaven and earth, ఆకాశమును భూమియు. The space between heaven and earth, రోదసి. **మిన్నువాకతాలుపు** *minnu-vāka-talupu*. n. An epithet of Siva, as carrying the heavenly Ganges on his head. గంగాధరుడు, శివుడు.

మిన్నుటము *minnuṭamu*. [Tel.] adj. Much, మిక్కుటము.

మిమ్ము, మిము or **మిమ్ముల** *mimmu*. [Tel. accusative plural of మీరు.] n. You.

మిర *mira*. [Skt.] n. Extent, a limit, మేర.

మిరపకాయ, మిరెపుకాయ or **మిరియపుకాయ** *mirapa-kāya*. n. Chilly, or red pepper. *Capsicum annuum*. సూదిమిరపకాయ *Capsicum minimum*. గోలకొండమిరపకాయ or సీమమిరపకాయ a very small hot chilly, Bird's eye Chilly, Spur pepper, Cayenne pepper or Goat pepper. *Capsicum frutescens*. [Watts.] **మిరపకాంద్ర** *mirapa-kāndra*. n. A plant called *Scopolia aculeata*. See మిరియము. **మిరప** *mirapa*. adj. Appertaining to chilly. మిరపపొడి chilly powder.

మిరాసి or **మీరాసి** *mirāsi*. [H.] adj. Hereditary. n. Hereditary right, hereditary property, వంశపరంపరగావచ్చినవాడ్యత లేక ఆస్తి. మిరాసీదారుడు a mirasidar, a man possessing landed property.

మిరిచూపు *miri-ṭsūpu*. [Tel.] n. An upward look. పైచూపు, ఊర్ధ్వదృష్టి.

మిరియము or **మిరెము** *miriyamu*. [Tel.] n. Black pepper. మిర్యాలపొడి or పొడిమిరియము black pepper powder. ఆది మగనితల మీద మిరియాలు నూరుచున్నది she grinds pepper on her husband's head, i. e., she wears the breeches.

మిరు *miru*. [Tel.] adj. Dazzling. **మిరుమిట్లు** *miru-miṭlu*. n. Dazzle. మిరిమిట్లుగొనడము the feeling of being dazzled. **మిరుమిట్లుగొను** *miru-miṭlu-konu*. v. n. To be dazzled, కన్నులు చిరుతలువారు, దృష్టిచెదరు, చీకట్లుకమ్ము.

మిర్రు *mirru*. [Tel.] n. An acclivity, swell, rising ground, knoll, bulge. ఉన్నతభూమి. మిర్రుమోము a face with a projecting forehead. Infl. మిర్తి. మిర్తిచేను high lying land మెరకపొలము. మిర్రుపల్లము high and low ground. **మిరుత** *miruta*. (Locative of మిర్రు) n. On high ground. "కోకనద్రోడియల్లనపెడలిమిరుత, కొకవనస్ఫూర్తిజొంపమైయున్న." M. XII. iii. 292.

మిలమిల *mila-mila*. [Tel.] n. Glittering, sparkling. మెరుగుకాంతి. **మిలమిలలాడు** *mila-milal-āḍu*. v. n. To glitter, sparkle. To abound, swarm, be rife. ఆకలిచేత మిలమిలలాడుచున్నారు they are exhausted with hunger. ఆ నీళ్లలో చేపలు మిలమిలలాడుచున్నవి fishes are swarming or are abundant in that water. మిలమిలన *mila-milana.* adv. Wrigglingly, మెదలుచు. "సంజనితమునై పురుగులు, నేకానమిలమిల మెదలునందు గురుకుల ముఖ్యా." M. XVI. i. 27.

మిళిందము *milindamu.* [Skt.] n. The wild bee. తుమ్మెద.

మిళితము *militamu.* [Skt.] adj. Mixed, conjoined. మిశ్రితమైన, కలిసిన.

మిల్లి or మిల్లిగరిటె *milli.* [Tel.] n. A very small spoon like a tea spoon. మిక్కిలి చిన్న గరిటె.

మిప్పులు Same as మిగులు (q. v.).

మిశ్రము, మిశ్రమము or మిశ్రితము *misrama.* [Skt.] adj. Mixed, mingled, blended. కలిసిన. మిశ్రీకరించు *misri-karintsu.* v. a. To mix, మిశ్రముచేయు, కలుపు. మిశ్రుడు *misrudu.* n. A gentleman, a man of consequence. It is an affix to some proper names, as ఆర్యమిశ్రుడు.

మిష or మిషము *misha.* [Skt.] n. Fraud, a trick, pretext, excuse, pretence. నెపము. ఏదో ఒక మిష పెట్టి నన్ను తిట్టినాడు he got a pretext to abuse me. "నెత్తమ్మిచూపులీనెడు నీ మొగంబని మార్కొ_ను మిషమునను ద్దుబెట్టె." P. iv. 432.

మిస or మిసమిస *misa.* [Tel.] n. Sparkle, flash, brilliancy. మిలమిల, మెరుగుకాంతి. "మిసమిసలుతేరు మనమైనమేనిసొబగు." T. ii. 58. మిసమిసమను, మిసమిసలాడు or మిసమిసను to be bright, మెరయు.

మిసి *misi.* [Tel.] n. A sort of fish.

మిసిమి *misimi.* [Tel.] n. Brilliancy, lustre, polish, మెరుగు. కాంతి. adj. Brilliant, polished, మెరుగైన. మిసిమిగలమామిడిపండులు mangoes that shone as if polished. మిసిమి పిండొడలు thighs that shone as if polished. "మిసిమిచేటు" R. ii. 76. మిసిమింతలు *misi-mintalu.* n. Fading, decrease of brightness. Want of lustre, gloom, gloominess. కాంతితరుగుటలు, కసుగందుటలు. మిసిమింతుడు *misi-mintudu.* n. One who is gloomy, or fallen in countenance. One who is tired, అలసినవాడు. మిసిమింతురాలు *misi-mintu-r-alu.* n. A woman who is gloomy or, in her decline, or past her bloom She who is tired, అలసినది. "రాలెన్ని చేసినను, మిసిమింతుడవుకావు వృద్ధదేవరవైన వినిపించితివే." BD. vi. 532. "లోలలోచన మిసిమింతురాలుగాక, పచ్చి కీలలో నిట్లు వచ్చె చెడక." HN. iii. 149.

మిసుకు or మిసుగు *misuku.* [Tel.] v. n. To move, stir. కదలు. "పసిడి దిమ్మనుమునే బలు మారు కేడ, మిసుక కేనుగు గవ్వమీటినయట్లు." HD. ii. 162.

మిహి *mihi.* [Tel.] adj. New, novel. కొత్త. Excellent, శ్రేష్ఠము. "రహిమీరిన మురళితపు తొణ్ణెల. మిహిపైడిజగామేలిమిగిన్నెల." Satyabh. iv. 98.

మిహిక *mihika.* [Skt.] n. Frost, hoar frost, snow. మంచు, హిమము. A. v. 107. మిహికాకరుడు *mihika-karudu.* n. The moon, "whose rays are frosty." చంద్రుడు. Vijaya. ii. 115.

మిహిరుడు *mihi-rudu.* [Skt.] n. The sun. సూర్యుడు. Jaim. vi. 96.

మీ mi

మీ *mi.* [Tel. Gen: of మీరు.] adj. Your. మీ అన్న your brother.

మీ *mi.* [Tel. contracted for మీది or మీదు.] adj. Upper, above. మీగడ or మీపడ *mi-gada.* (మీదు+కడ.) n. Cream, కాచినపాల మీదికట్టె. మీగడకట్టినది the cream has formed. పాలమీగడలు a name given to a fine sort of rice. H. iv. 156. మీగడపెరుగు curds with the cream on it. మీగాలు *mi-galu.* (మీదు+కాలు.) n. The upper part of the foot, పాదముమీది పైభాగము. మీజెయ్యి *mī-jeyyi.* (మీదు+చెయ్యి.) n. The back of the hand. కరపృష్ఠము, చేతిమీది పైభాగము.

మీట *mīṭa.* [Tel.] n. A lever. A door-latch. A see-saw. బోనుమీట the bar of a trap on which the door hangs.

మీటు *mīṭu.* [Tel.] v. a. To fillip, fling, toss. వీణెమీటు to touch the lute. గోటమీటు to flick away or fling from the nail. గుర్రము మీటు to spur a horse. చెక్కుమీటు to touch or scratch (the cheek) with the nail. తేలు మీటినది the scorpion stung (him) "విజాంగుష్ఠంబున గోని పరిరోజాన ములు పోవగమీటెన్." R. v. 293. "చెక్కుమీటిన వసకారుకొనుచు." Vish. ii. 62. "తేలను మునిగిరియబట్టిన మేలెరుగని మీటుగాక." Vema 1087. "తోదోపులమీన మేటరివుతుల్ కుటంగం బులమీటెపిల్లి." T. v. 22. "విరుమందుమకీర్తి తోగోటజెక్కుమీటు." N. vii. 158. మీటు n. A touch, fillip, toss. Greatness, grandeur. ఉద్రేకము. పెంపు. గొప్ప. "అలంతోల కరతరి పేరదూటువాడు. మీటుగాటల్ల వలరాజము మ్మవదన." R. vi. 18.

మీదు *mīdu.* [Tel.] n. The upper surface; top, head. ఉపరిభాగము. ఊర్ధ్వము. Futurity. భవిష్యత్కాలము. What is vowed, or set aside for sacrifice, దేవతకు నియమించిన ముడుపు. That which is next, the next thing, పరము. మీదుకట్టు *mīdu-kaṭṭu.* v. a. To devote, sanctify, set aside in the name of God. మీద or మీదను *mīda.* postposition. Above, on, upon, on the top of, at, against. నామీదవచ్చినతప్పు a fault laid on me. ఆ పనిమీదనున్నాడు he is engaged in that business. వారిని ఈపనిమీద పంపెను he sent them upon this business. ఇక మీద in future. ఉపాయముమీదచేసిన effected by stratagem. పనిమీదపని task after task. మధ్యాహ్నము మీద in the afternoon. మాటమీదమాట word upon word. నామీదకోపముచేసి being angry with me. టపాలుమీదపంపు send a letter by post. గడియలమీదనున్నది it is hourly expected. మీదట *mīdaṭa* adv. or prep. After. ఇకమీదట in future. అటుమీదట after which, then. వారు పోయినమీదట after they went away. ఇకమీదట నీకు వారితోవాసమువద్దు do not have any thing to do with them hereafter. మీదటి *mīdaṭi.* (Irreg. infl. of మీదు. See మీది.) adj. Subsequent. ఆమీదటిపనులు the subsequent acts. మీదటికి *mīdaṭiki.* adv. In future, next year. మీదటికి వాన లేకుంటే if there should be no rain next year. మీది *mīdi.* (infl. of మీదు) adj. Upper, higher, the next, above, on. మీది కొమ్మ the top branch. నామీది ప్రేమ (her or his) love towards me మీదిమాట the next word. మీదిపనులు what is to be done afterwards. మీదిమన్ను the upper layer of earth. మీదిగుడ్లు staring eyes: (as in the song దొప్పచెవులు, దోనెకడుపు. చుట్టనాసలు. మీదిగుడ్లు.) దానిమీది సొమ్ములు the jewels which were on her. పాలమీదిమీగడ the cream upon milk. మీదికి *mīdiki.* (Dative of మీదు) Upon, against. ఆదండు ఏయూరిమీదికి పోయినది against which village is the army gone? ఆ తప్పు మామీదికి వచ్చినది that fault was laid upon us. మీదుమిక్కిలి *mīdu-mikkili.* adj. Very much, కడు మిక్కిలి.

మీను *mīnu.* [Tel. A Drav: word common to all South Indian languages.] n. A fish. చేప. మీనుకూరుపుక్కి a constellation called రేవతీనక్షత్రము. plu. మీలు. మీనము *mīnamu.* [borrowed by Skt. from the Drav. languages.] n. A fish, మత్స్యము. The sign *Pisces.* మీనరాశి. మీనకేతనుడు a name of Manmadha, మన్మథుడు. మీనవల్లంకి మీనవల్లిక or మీలునాద్రు *mīna-vallanki.* n. A bird that lives on fish: probably, a kingfisher or a tern. [illegible]

తెలిసి వేదము పట్టుకొనిన శాకవిధమైనవది.

మీనాంకుడు *min-ānkuḍu.* n. Manmadha so called because this god has a dolphin in his banner. మన్మథుడు. మీనాక్షి *min-ākshi.* adj. Bright-eyed, having swimming or glancing eyes. శ్రీ [illegible] n. The name of a goddess.

మీమాంస *mimāmsa.* [Skt.] n. A discussion or disputation held to find out the truth regarding anything. ప్రమాణార్థవిచారణ, ప్రమాణములచేత నిజమును గ్రహించడము. Polemical divinity. Theological criticism. The name of one of the six great Indian philosophical systems, పూర్వమీమాంస is a system of ritualism. ఉత్తరమీమాంస is a system practically the same as the వేదాంతము, జ్ఞానకాండ. పుత్రీకరణమీమాంస is a 'treatise' (or essay) on adopting a daughter. మీమాంసచేయు to dispute, argue. మా యిద్దరికి ఇందును గురించి చాలా మీమాంస జరిగినది we had a great discussion about this matter. మీమాంసకుడు *mimāmsakuḍu.* n. One who knows the Mimansa system of philosophy, మీమాంస శాస్త్రము తెలిసినవాడు.

మీరు or మీరలు *miru.* [Tel. plural of నీవు.] pron. You. మీది *midi.* pron. Yours. ఈయిల్లు మీదేనా is this house yours?

మీరు *miru.* [Tel.] v. n. and a. To exceed, transgress, pass, excel, అతిశయించు, కడచు, అతిక్రమించు. ఈడుమీరినపడుచు a grown up girl. మీరక excessively, extremely. రూఢిమీర certainly. సొగసుమీర prettily. వలపుమీర affectionately. బాగుమీరంగ healthfully, cheerfully, i. e., well. చింత మీరంగ sorrowfully. Vish. iii. 290.

మీలనము *milanamu.* [Skt.] n. Closing the eyes, కనుమూయుట. మీలితము *militamu.* adj. Closed, as the eye.

మీలు See మీను.

మీసము *misamu.* [Tel.] n. A moustache or whisker. An insect's feelers, horns, or antennæ. Plu. మీసములు, మీసలు or మీసాలు. "మిన్నక పచ్చివచ్చి పులిమీసలను [illegible]." (Padm. iii. 37.) to beard a lion in his den. వానికి ఇంక మీసకట్టు ఏర్పడలేదు his whiskers have not yet appeared.

మీసరము *misaramu* [Tel.] adj. Excellent, fine grand, శ్రేష్ఠమైన. "మీసరముతో నీ [illegible]." T. iv. 144.

ము mu

ము *mu.* [Tel.] n. An affix of neuter nouns and of masculine nouns that take a neuter form as కళత్రము, అపత్యము. In composition, it is a contraction for మూడు three, and the first consonant of the next word is usually doubled. Thus మారు a time, ముమ్మారు three times, thrice. పాతిక a quarter, ముప్పాతిక three quarters. ముక్కన్ను (మూడు+కన్ను) the third eye, మూడవకన్ను. ముక్కాక threefold heat. ముక్కాని (మూడు+కాని) three quarters of an anna. ముక్కారు (మూడు+కారు) three seasons. ముక్కాలు (మూడు+కాలు) three legs or three quarters of anything. ముక్కాలిపీట a three-legged stool. ముక్కోలు (మూడు+కోలు) a trident, త్రిదండము. ముజ్జగము or ముల్లోకములు the three worlds, viz., earth, heaven and hell. మువ్వన్నె the three (primary) colors. See మూడు.

ముం *mun.* [contracted for Tel. ముందు.] adj. First, fore, front, as ముంగురులు the front locks of hair. ముంగడ *mun-gaḍa.* (ముందు+కడ) n. The front place, ముందు చోటు, ఎదురు, ముందు. ముంగల *mungala.* n. The front, ఎదురు. adv. In front, opposite, before, ఎదురు. ముంగలి *mungali.* adj. Fronting, opposite, being in front. ఎదుటనుండే. Next, తరువాతి,

మీరదటె. "సేనాపతియగుసాత్రుపదపండముండు, ముంగలిదైయనడపించుచుండ." M. VI. i. 147. n. One who goes before, ముందునడచువాడు. **ముంగలు** *mun-galu*. v. n. To walk before, ముందునడచు. **ముంగారి** or **ముంగరి** *mungari*. adj. Pertaining to the beginning of the season, ముంగారిపైరు the early crop. **ముంగాలు** *mun-galu*. (ముందు + కాలు.) n. The fore leg, the tip of the foot. ముందరికాలు, పాదాగ్రము. "ముంగాళ్లపై కేగి." A. vi. 17. **ముంగురులు** *mun-gurulu*. (ముందు+కురులు.) n. Front-locks. అలకలు. **ముంగేలు** *mun-gelu*. (ముందు+కేలు.) n. The fore arm. **ముంగొంగు** *mun-gongu*. (ముందు+కొంగు.) n. A fringe or trimming. The front tuck of a woman's girdle, ముందరిచెరుగు, చెంగుకొన. ముంగొన the front end, ముందటికొన. **ముంగోపము** *mun-gôpamu*. n. Sudden passion, unreasoning anger. ఎందుకును ముందరివచ్చు కోపము, ఓర్పులేక తటాలునవచ్చు కోపము. **ముంగోపి** *mun-gôpi*. n. A passionate man or woman, a peevish man or woman, ముందర కోపముచేయువాడు. **ముంగోలు** *mun-gôlu*. (ముందు+కోలు.) adj. First, మొదటి. **ముంజెయ్యి** *mun-jeyyi*. (ముందు+చెయ్యి.) Same as ముంగేలు. ముంజేతికంకణము a bracelet on the wrist; metaphorically, plain as a bangle on the fore-arm, మిక్కిలి స్పష్టమైనది. **ముంజూరు** *mun-dzûru*. (ముందు+చూరు.) n. The eaves of a house. ఇంటిచూరుచివర.

ముంగ *munga*. [Tel.] n. A certain forest tree called *Crotolaria stricta*. Rox. iii. 265. A bundle of sheaves. ఎన్నులమోపు. adj. Dumb, మూగ. **ముంగతనము** *mungatanamu*. n. Stubbornness, obstinacy, మూర్ఖత్వము. "మనుమట్టనిదియేల ముంగతనంబు." Charita. ii. 523.

ముంగట *mungaṭa*. [Tel. from ముంగడ.] adv. First, at first, in front. **ముంగటి** *mungaṭi*. adj. First, prior. See under ముం.

ముంగమురుగు, **ముంగాముమురుగు**, **ముంగామురువు**, **ముంగమురము**, **ముంగమురాము**, **ముంగామురము**, **ముంగమురారి**, **ముంగామురాసి**, **ముంగయమురాతి** or **ముంగిమురాసి** *munga-murugu*. [Tel. ముందు+కయి+మురుగు.] n. A kind of bangle worn at the wrist, ముంజేతిధరించెడు ఒక విధమైన కటకము.

ముంగర *mungara*. [Tel. another form of ముక్కర.] n. A nose ring, worn by women. నాసాభరణభేదము.

ముంగాము *mungamu*. [Tel.] n. A palmyra leaf folded like a packet, పొట్లముగా మడిచిన తాటాకుముట్టు. Half a packetful of anything, బెల్లముపొట్లమునిని నించిన బరువులో సగము. **ముంగాముచీర** or **ముంగాచీర** *mungamu-chîre*. n. A kind of cloth worn by women.

ముంగి or **ముంగిస** *mungi*. [Tel.] n. The ichneumon or mongoose, a kind of weasel. *Viverra ichneumon*. నకులము. **ముంగి** or **పిల్లిముంగిటీగె** *mungi*. A tree called *Phaseolus madraspatensis*. Rox. iii. 311. Compare ముసగ. **ముంగిమునీడిచేప** *mungi-musidi-chepa*. n. A certain fish: a sort of *Sparus*. (Russell, plate 110.)

ముంగిలి *mungili*. [Tel. ముందు+కలు+ఇల్లు.] n. A courtyard. అంకణముయొక్క మధ్యప్రదేశము, ఇండ్లముందరిచుంకణము. The space between two beams in a house, an apartment, అంకణము. The middle part of anything, మధ్యప్రదేశము. "ముప్పనకాలకింకరులు ముంగిటనిల్చినవేళ." Dasaradhi. § 29. ముంగిటినిధానము a treasure lying at your own door, a windfall. R. iv. 158.

ముంగిసమాను *mungisa-manu*. [Tel.] n. The upright staff of a waterlift (ఏతాము) which suspends the bucket. ఏతామునకడ. "అలరి. ముంగిసమ్రాను దోవానియుండ, కుండ నిండారగాముంచి కూడుండిన. నింటికేగెను." H. i. 319.

ముంచు *muntsu.* [Tel. causal of మునుగు.] v. a. To dip, plunge, immerse. To plunge in ruin. నన్ను పూర్తిగా ముంచివేసినాడు he ruined me entirely. **ముంచుకొను** *muntsu-konu.* v. a. To surround, to cover, ఆక్రమించుకొను. సిరాలో కలమును ముంచుకొని వ్రాసినాడు he dipped the pen in the ink and wrote it. See ముంపు.

ముంజము *munjamu.* [Skt.] n. A fine silky grass called *Saccharum munja.* (Rox.) ముంజగడ్డి. **ముంజకేశుడు** *munja-kēsudu.* n. An epithet of Vishṇu. విష్ణువు. **ముంజి** *munji.* n. The Brahminical girdle made of the *Munja* grass, బ్రహ్మచారులు మొలను కట్టుకొనే గడ్డిదారము. "రెండిల్లు పెనుబొజ్జు ముంజి వాని." A. vi. 21. **ముంజికాడు** *munji-kadu.* n. A bachelor. బ్రహ్మచారి. **ముంజికోక** *munji-kōka.* n. A garment woven of fibres. నారచీర. Vēma. 904.

ముంజె *munje.* [Tel.] n. The kernel of the unripe palm fruit. లేత తాటికాయలోని ముంజె గిజారు.

ముంజెరము *mun-jeramu.* [Tel. ముందు+చెరము.] n. A nostril, నాసాపుటము.

ముండము *muṇḍamu.* [Skt.] n. The head cut off from the neck. దేహములేనితల. A shaven pate, a bald head. బోడితల. The trunk of a lopped tree. కొమ్మలులేనియున మోటుచెట్టు. "ధనమ్ముండవృథాలోన్లము." A. vi. 29. **ముండము** or **ముండితము** *muṇḍamu.* adj. Shaved, bald, having no hair on the head గొరగబడిన. **ముండ** *muṇḍa.* n. Lit: One whose head is shaven. A widow, విధవ. A wretch. A whore. వేశ్య. **ముండమోయు** *muṇḍa-mōyu.* v. n. To become a widow, వైధవ్యముపొందు. To become useless, వ్యర్థమగు. అది చెడ్డముండ she is a wretched slut. ఆడముండ a miserable creature. పాతకిముండ an immoral wretch. పేదముండ a poor wretch. ముండమోపి a widow. పిచ్చిముండ a simpleton. అది రాక్షసి ముండగనుక as she is a horrid wretch. ముండలమారి, ముండరి or ముండలముఠాకోరు a whoremonger. ముండను పెట్టుకొన్నాడు he keeps a concubine. **ముండనము** *muṇḍa-namu.* n. Shaving, shearing, cutting. క్షౌరము. **ముండి** *muṇḍi.* n. Bald-pate: one who has a shaven head. బోడితలవాడు. A barber, మంగలవాడు. **ముండుడు** *muṇ-ḍuḍu.* n. A bald headed man, బోడితలవాడు. A monk. సన్యాసి. "పత్రిగ్రాహివిముఖుస్త్ర ముండుండు వనికేతనుండు వ్యాతమూలవానిదయగ పాలధరుండు." M. XII. v. 133.

ముండ్లు, ముండులు or **ముళ్లు** *muṇḍlu.* [Tel. plu. of ముల్లు.] n. Thorns. కంటకములు. ముండులవాన a shower of prickles (discharged by a porcupine, &c.) KP. vi. 9. **ముండ్ల** *muṇḍla.* adj. Thorny, prickly. కంటకమయమైన. **ముండ్లకంచె** or **ముళ్లకంచె** *muṇḍla-kanche.* n. A prickly-pear fence. **ముండ్లపంది** or **ముళ్లపంది** *muṇḍla-pandi.* n. The porcupine, ఏదుపంది. **ముండ్లముస్తె** *muṇḍla-muste.* n. A shrub, the Three lobed Nightshade, *Solanum trilobatum.* అలర్కము.

ముంత *munta.* [Tel.] n. A lōṭa or small water pot. చెంబు. A wooden bowl, a small pot or cup. A varying measure of grain, commonly two seers. చల్లకువచ్చి ముంత దాచనేల why do you conceal the pot having come for buttermilk? i. e., why conceal your real intention? ముంతపొగపెట్టు to burn chillies, &c., in a pot and apply it to the face as a torture, కాల్చి ముంతలో వేసిన మిరపకాయల పొగను మూతికి కట్టు. **ముంతగజ్జనము** *munta-gaj-janamu.* n. A certain shrub called *Echites frutescens.* సహదేవి. **ముంతమామిడి** *munta-māmidi.* n. The Cashew nut tree. *Anacardium occidentale,* అక్రోడిజము. ముంతమామిడి పప్పు Cashew nuts.

ముండడి *muṇḍaḍi.* [Tel. a word peculiar to the West.] n. A wretch, a miscreant.

"భూపతియాదరోక్తముని పాంకముకొద్దినితేగ మిడుక్కగా నేపికిబుట్టుముందడి సహింపకవిఘ్నము సేదరు." Samudap. ş. 78. plu. ముందర్లు.

ముందు *mundu.* [Tel.] n. The front. ఎదురు. adj. Fronting, fore. Previous, former, preceding, early. After, next. ముందువెనుకలు before and behind, what comes before and what comes behind. adv. In front, in the beginning, at first, first. ముందుపని ముందర చేయవలెను you must first do what is first wanted. దానిముందుమాట కేమి అర్థము what is the meaning of the preceding word? ముందువెనుకలుగా పోవుచుండిరి they were going along, some before, some behind. కారణమైనా ముందువెనుక చూడక without considering causes or consequences. ముందుకు వెనుకకు backwards and forwards, to and fro. Postposition: Before. వారు రాకముందు before they come. **ముందుపడు** or **ముందగు** *mundu-paḍu.* v. n. To go before, to lead. **ముందర** or **ముందల** *mundara.* n. The front, ఎదురు. A former time, మును పు. Beginning, మొదలు. adv. Before, in front. First, in the first instance. Formerly, previously. Hereafter, next, in future. After, following, next. అంతకుముందర before that. ముందటి or ముందటి fronting, opposite, former, previous. ముందటికాలమునందు in former times. ముందరిపోటు a wound in front. "ముందరిపోటులుమాననుమందు౦౦డినసుకలదు." Vema. ముందరిమాట lit. the word before, i.e., the following word; also, the *preceding* word ముందటికి forwards. ముందర నుయ్యి వెనుక గొయ్యి a ditch before, and a hill behind, i.e., to be in a fix, to be caught in the horns of a dilemma. ముందటికి తెచ్చు to bring forward, promote. ముందటికి వచ్చు to come to the front, to be promoted, to prosper. **ముందల** *mundala.* (ముందు+తల.) n. The front part of the head, శిరస్సు యొక్క ముందుభాగము. "గట్టించిముందలల్ బట్టియీడ్చి" URK. iv. 112. **ముందట** *mundaṭa.* adv. In front, before ఎదుట.

ముంపు *mumpu.* [Tel. from ముంచు.] n. Immersion, plunging, dipping. నీటిముంపుగలమంచేపొలము lands under water. ఈ చెరువు యీ పత్తు నీటిముంపుగానున్నది this tank is full. A multitude, గుంపు. **ముంపుగొను** *mumpu-gonu.* v. n. To form a crowd. గుంపుకూడు.

ముకు *muku.* n. Another form of ముక్కు (q. v.).

ముకుందము *mukundamu.* [Skt.] n. The Red lotus. **ముకుందబల్లెము** *mukunda-ballemu.* n. A halberd or broad bladed spear. ఒకయాయుధము. **ముకుందుడు** *mukundu-ḍu.* n. A name of Vishṇu.

ముకుటము *mukuṭamu* [Skt.] n. A crest, diadem, or tiara. మకుటము, కిరీటము. **ముకుటము** or **ముక్కుటము** *mukuṭamu.* [Tel.] n. Linen, నారబట్ట.

ముకురము *mukuramu.* [Skt.] n. A mirror. అద్దము.

ముకుళము *mukuḷamu.* [Skt.] n. A bud: a half opened flower. మొగ్గ, అరవిరిమొగ్గ. **ముకుళించు** or **ముకుళీభవించు** *mukuḷintsu.* v. n. To shut, or close as a flower, the eyes or the hands. మోడ్చు. **ముకుళితము** *mukuḷitamu.* adj. Closed as a bud (used of the eyes, the hands, &c.) మోడ్చబడ్డ, ముకుళించిన. **ముకుళీకృతము** *mukuḷī-kṛtamu.* adj. Closed. మోడ్చబడ్డ, ముకుళింపబడిన.

ముక్క *mukka.* [Tel.] n. A bit, piece, fragment. రెండుముక్కలు వ్రాస్తాను I'll write a line or two, or, two or three words. ఒక గుడ్డముక్క a bit of cloth.

ముక్కంటి *muk-kaṇṭi.* [Tel. from ముక్కన్ను (మూడు+కన్ను).] n. The three-eyed one; a title of Siva. త్రినేత్రుడు. త్రిలోచనుడు. **ముక్కంటిచుక్క** *muk-kaṇṭi-tsukka.* n. A constellation called ఉత్తరభద్రపద. **ముక్కంటిపండు** *muk-kaṇṭi-paṇḍu.* n. A cocoanut, so called because it has three eyes. See under ము.

ముక్కడి *mukkaḍi.* [Tel. మూకు+కాడి.] n. A heap of ploughs, అరకలకాండ్లయొక్క మొత్తము. An epidemic disease. ఆ దేశములకు ఒక్కపెట్టున తగిలేరోగము.

ముక్కపురుగు See under ముక్కు.

ముక్కాడి *mukkāḍi.* [Tel.] n. The timber tree called 'Weaver's beam.' *Schrebera swietenoides.* Ainsl. Rox. i. 109.

ముక్కాలి, ముక్కారు, ముక్కాలు See under ము.

ముక్కిడ or ముక్కిడి *mukkiḍa.* [Tel.] n. A snipe.

ముక్కు or ముకు *mukku.* [Tel.] n. The nose. నాసిక. The bill or beak of a bird, పక్షిముఖము. The point or tip. చేనుముక్కు a nipple. ముక్కుకోదనలు a double nose, జెమిలిముక్కు. "మునుకనలేదమిబట్టి ముంగాళ్ల ముక్కుకోదనలచీలిచి." A. v. 122. ముక్కుడుస్సిన uncurbed, broken loose, rampant, ముక్కుతాడుతీసిన. "వసుధేశముక్కుడుస్సిన పసరముక్రియ." A. vi. 53. ముక్కుబంటి ఘ్రైవదముగ satiating his nostrils with fragrance to the full. P. iii. 224. చిలుకముక్కులు and జీనువముక్కులు two sorts of grain. రెండుముక్కులపిట్ట (the double beaked bird) also called మూడుముక్కులపిక్క and ఎద్దెరపిక్క the Hornbill, or Toucan. Jerdon No. 198. "ముందరగోష్ఠికిముక్కుమొంగ చేదరనకు." HD. ii. 1059. ముక్కుమొగము ఎరుగనట్టు మాట్లాడినాడు he talked as if I was a perfect stranger to him. ముక్కుపట్టనిముత్తెము a pearl not suited to the nose, i. e., a round man in a square hole. ముక్కుకమ్మిక a certain useless forest tree. ముక్కు *mukku.* v n. To moan, groan. To mould or turn musty. To spoil or become half rotten. To strain or press, (as in pain.) ముక్క *mukka.* (Root in A of ముక్కు to be musty or mouldy, &c.) ముక్కపురుగులు weevils in spoilt grain, తపుటిపురుగులు. ముక్కకంపు a frowzy smell. తరాయ్రత తోం దూరిగ్రామము ముక్క ఊరికిసందున ఆ జైత్తము విడిచిరి a disease has appeared which is peculiar to that place. ముత్యాలు ముక్కిపోయినవి the pearls were spoiled. ముక్కు గ్గోళ్లు, ముకుగోళ్లు, ముకుగ్రోళ్లు, ముక్కు జెరములు, ముక్కుచెరములు or ముక్కు రంధ్రములు *mukkugōḷḷu.* n. plu. The nostrils. నాసాపుటములు. ముక్కుత్రాడు or ముకుత్రాడు a nose-rope used for curbing oxen. ముక్కుదొమ్మ or ముకుదొమ్మ *mukku-domma.* n. A sort of fish. H. iv. 225. ముక్కద్దము *mukk-addamu.* n. A pair of spectacles, సులోచనము, కంటిఅద్దము. ముక్కమ్మి or ముక్కుకమ్మి *muk-kammi.* (ముక్కు+కమ్మి.) or ముక్కర *mukka-ṟa.* (ముక్కు+రాయి.) n. A nose ring. నాసాభరణము. ముక్కరమాను *mukkara-mānu.* n. The frame in which the roller (పుల్లిరుగు) of a కపిల well rolls. ముక్కరము *muk-karamu.* (ముక్కు+కారెము.) n. A nostril, నాసికారంధ్రము. ముక్కిడి *mukkiḍi.* (ముక్కు+ఇడి) adj. Noseless. ముక్కులేని. ముక్కిడిరోగము caries of the bones of the nose. "ముక్కిడితొత్తుకు ముత్తెంపునత్తేల." రామలింగశతకము. ముక్కిడి or కొండముక్కిడి n. A certain large tree, *Schrebera swietenoides.* Rox. i. 109. ముక్కుదూలము or ముకుదూలము *mukku-dūlamu.* n. The bridge or division of the nose. ముక్కునడిమిదొలుముక. ముక్కుపురిడి or ముక్కుపూరేడుపిట్ట *mukku-puriḍi.* n. The common snipe. (Jerdon.) ఉకపక్షి. ముక్కుపొడి *mukku-poḍi.* n. Snuff. నస్యము, పొడుము. ముక్కుపోగు *mukku-pōgu.* n. A nose ring, ముక్కమ్మి, నత్తు. ముక్కుబంతి or ముకుబంతి *mukku-banti.* n. A disease that attacks the nose of a cow through cold. ముక్కుముంగర *mukku-mungara.* n. A certain useless forest tree. ముక్కులు

mukkulu. n. Rice flour. మిక్కిలి చిన్న నూకలు. A kind of cake.

ముక్కుటము or **ముక్కుటుపువంతె** *mukkuṭa-mu*. [Tel.] n. A kind of garment, also called దసలిపట్టు or నారమడి.

ముక్కుస *mukkusa*. [Tel. మూడు+కుంచెము.] n. A measure of grain, &c., equal to five ముంతలు, మూడుకుంచములప్రమాణము. "ముత్తో లపాడిమాకు ముక్కుసవలయు." BD. ii. 869.

ముక్కూరు *mukkūru*. [Tel.] v. n. To become ignorant, అజ్ఞానమునుపొందు. "వ॥ ఈ యొక్కువతక్కువలు విచారింపక వలవనివెరపు కట్టుకొని ముక్కూరి యూరక వగచుచున్నవాడవు." భార. ఉద్యో. ii.

ముక్కొను *muk-konu*. [Tel. ముసు+కొను.] v. n. To come forward, ముందుకొను.

ముక్కొమ్ముమెకము *muk-kommu-mekamu*. [Tel. ముందు+కొమ్ము+మెకము.] n. The white-footed antelope, the Gayal. మనుబోతు, ఋశ్యమృగము.

ముక్కోణము *muk-kōṇamu*. [Tel. మూడు+కోణము.] n. A triangle. త్రికోణము.

ముక్తము *muktamu*. [Skt.] adj. Freed, released, liberated, discharged, sent (as a weapon). ముక్తకవచుడు disarmed, freed from his armour. **ముక్తత్వము** *mukta-tvamu*. n. Freedom, release, liberty. విమోచనము. **ముక్తపదగ్రస్తము** *mukta-pada-grastamu*. n. Reiteration somewhat similar to caffing verses. అంతాది. **ముక్తాఫలము** *mukta-phalamu*. n. A pearl, ముత్యము. ముక్తాఫలములవలెనుండు లిపి a pearly hand in writing, i. e., round, clear, and beautiful. ముక్తాయించు to finish (in music.) ముక్తార్థము a summary, the purport. **ముక్తావళి** *mukt-āvali*. n. A pearl necklace. ముత్యాలహారము. **ముక్తాస్ఫోటము** *mukta-sphōṭamu*. n. A pearl oyster.

క్షుక్తి. ముక్తిప్పచిప్ప. **ముక్తి** *mukti*. n. The delivery of the soul from the body, and its exemption from further transmigration, liberation, deliverance, emancipation, మోక్షము. సంసారముక్తి or భవముక్తి release from all earthly bonds or mortal ties. "మనుగభవముక్తి గలుగు మహిలో." Vema. 481. **ముక్తుడు** *muktuḍu*. n. One who is freed, emancipated or released from the body. మోక్షమునుపొందినవాడు.

ముక్తసరు *muktasaru*. [H.] adj. Abridged, brief. సంగ్రహమైన.

ముక్త్యారు *muktyāru*. [H.] n. A free agent, a superintendent.

ముఖము *mukhamu*. [Skt.] n. The mouth, నోరు. The face, countenance, ఆనను. The commencement, ఆరంభము. The front, ముందటిభాగము. The external appearance, the look of the face, ముఖవిలాసము. దినాముఖము nightfall, evening. సేనాముఖము the front of the army. నఖముఖములు the points of the nails. ముఖమిచ్చు to indulge. అతడు వారితో ముఖమిచ్చి మాట్లాడలేదు he did not speak with them as a friend. "బల్లాదంబైన శ్లోకానవాటి ముఖమాలోకింపగ." Bilh. iii. 25. అధోముఖుడుగానుండినాడు he was hanging with his head down. ఆ దివిటీని అధోముఖముగాపట్టినాడు he held the torch with the flaming end downwards. "అనఘకథాముఖంబున హితాహిత బోధమొనర్తురింపుగా." Mand. i. 8. ఏక కథాముఖంబున by means of a story, కథచేతను. అర్ధముఖము the profile or half face. తమరు రామునిముఖముచూచి నన్ను రక్షింపవలెననది I pray that for the sake of Rama you will relieve me. పడమటిముఖముగా towards the west. పడమటిముఖముగానుండేయిల్లు a house facing the west. ఆడదానిముఖమెరుగనివాడు a youth that as yet knows not the face of a woman, i. e., entirely chaste. అందరును ఏకముఖముగా నుండలేదుగనుక as they were not unanimous or were not all of one mind. "బాణఖడ్గాదిముఖాస్త్రశస్త్రములు," M. VII. ii. 275; arrows, swords, and other weapons. ముఖముమాడ్చుకొనియున్నాడు he looked sulky or angry. వానికి ముఖము వెల్లనైనది he turned pale, he looked blank or ashamed. ముఖదాక్షిణ్యము complaisance. వానిముఖములో కళ లేదు he was all in a pucker. ఆ రూకలను వానిముఖముమీద పారవేయుము fling the money at his face. అది వానికి ముఖపాఠముగానున్నది he has got it by heart. వాడు ముఖప్రీతి మాటలాడును he talks plausibly. ముఖమెరుగనివాడు a stranger. ముఖమెరుగనిదేశము a strange land, a land where one has no acquaintance. ముఖవాసికలవాడు he is a winning man. వానికి ముఖవర్చస్సుకద్దు he is a very taking man. ముఖము తప్పించుకొని పోయినాడు he has absconded or disappeared. ముఖస్తుతి flattery. ముఖస్తుతిచేయు to flatter. వాని శ్లోకము ముఖస్థముగానున్నది he knows the verse by heart. **ముఖద్వారము** *mukha-dvāramu.* n. The mouth. నోరు. నదీముఖద్వారము the mouth of a river. **ముఖపట్టి** or **మొగపట్టా** *mukha-paṭṭa.* n. The headstall of a horse, గుర్రము యొక్క ముఖమునకు వేసే తోలుపట్టా. **ముఖమంటపము** *mukha-manṭapamu.* n. The porch or pillared entrance of a Hindu temple. ముందరిమండపము. **ముఖవచనము** *mukha-vachanamu.* n. Verbal communication, word of mouth. నోటిమాట. **ముఖవస్త్రము** *mukha-vastramu.* n. A veil. A pall, ప్రేతవస్త్రము. **ముఖశాల** or **మొగసాల** *mukha-sāla.* n. A hall at the entrance of a house, an antechamber, తలవాకిటిచావడి. **ముఖాంతరముగా** *mukh-antaramu-gā.* adv. By means of, through, ద్వారా. నా తమ్ముని ముఖాంతరముగా పంపించినాను I sent it by my brother. **ముఖాముఖి** *mukha-mukhi.* adv. Face to face. ఎదురెదురుగా. "వినుముఖాముఖిబల్కెడ." T. iii. 84.

ముఖుడు *mukhuḍu.* n. A word used in compounds, thus అధోముఖుడై hanging with his face down. సుముఖుడుగా మాట్లాడినాడు he spoke graciously. దుర్ముఖుడైయుండినాడు he was cross. పరాఙ్ముఖుడైయుండెను he turned his face away.

ముఖరము *mukharamu.* [Skt.] adj. Noisy, resounding, loud, uproarious. మ్రోయునది. ముఖరఝరి a roaring cataract. ముఖరాళులు humming bees. R. viii. 93. **ముఖరుడు** *mukharuḍu.* n. A jabberer. అక్కరలేని మాటలు ప్రేలువాడు.

ముఖ్యము *mukhyamu.* [Skt.] adj. Chief, primary, particular, principal, eminent, urgent, indispensable. ప్రధానమైన. Excellent, prime, శ్రేష్ఠమైన. ముఖ్యార్థము the chief purport. ముఖ్యమైనభాగము the bulk of the work, the chief portion. ఇది ముఖ్యము this is the chief point. ఇది ముఖ్యము కాదు this is no great matter. **ముఖ్యముగా** *mukhyamu-gā.* adv. Chiefly, in a great measure, for the most part, particularly, especially, principally, విశేషించి, ప్రధానముగా. **ముఖ్యుడు** *mukhyuḍu.* n. A chief, a leader, a principal man, a man of weight. ప్రధానమైనవాడు.

ముగితి *mugiti.* [from Skt. ముక్తి.] n. Deliverance, salvation, heaven. ముక్తి. మోక్షము.

ముగియు *mugiyu.* [Tel.] v. n. To come to an end, close, be finished. సమాప్తమగు. **ముగించు** *mugintsu.* v. a. To end, close, terminate, finish, conclude. సమాప్తముచేయు. **ముగింపు** or **ముగింపు** *mugimpu.* n. The end, close, conclusion. సమాప్తి.

ముగుద *muguda.* [from Skt. ముగ్ధ.] n. A simple, innocent woman, ముగ్ధస్త్రీ. A maid, damsel, a lady, a woman, ఆడుది. **ముగుదుడు** *mugudуḍu.* n. A simple man, a simpleton. ముగ్ధుడు.

ముగురు or ముగ్గురు *muguru*. [Tel.] pron. Three persons. "ముగురాడువారు కూడిన, మగువాకారంబట్టుమగలె చుక్కలుంపోదురు."

ముగ్గ *mugga*. [Tel.] n. The name of a particular tree. ఒకచెట్టు.

ముగ్గు or ముగ్గు *muggu*. [Tel.] n. A pattern or diagram (రంగవల్లి) drawn with lines of flour or coloured powder. ముత్తియపుముగ్గు a pattern made in seed pearl. ముగ్గుచెరుపు to spoil one's plans, to break the spell. ముగ్గురాయి a limestone, a pebble. ముగ్గువేయు to set a pattern. ముగ్గులువేయు to perform certain magic rites, seating the patient on a magic square drawn on the floor.

ముగ్గు *muggu*. [Tel.] v. n. To be musty or mouldy, to be damaged or spoiled. బూజుపట్టు, ఆవిసిపోవు. To become overripe. ముగ్గవేయు *mugga-veyu*. v. a. To ripen fruit in baskets in a house. మాగవేయు.

ముగ్గురు *mugguru*. [Tel. మూడు+గురు.] pron. Three persons. మూడుమంది.

ముగ్గొయ్య *mug-goyya*. [Tel. ముందు+గొయ్య.] n. A gag: a difficulty or puzzle. వసుచరిత్ర విద్వాంసులకెల్ల ముగ్గొయ్య the Vasu Charitra is so hard as to puzzle the best scholars. adj. Difficult, అసాధ్యము.

ముగ్దరు *mugdaru*. [H.] n. An Indian club used by wrestlers.

ముగ్ధ *mugdha*. [Skt.] n. A blooming simple girl. ఉదయించుచున్న యౌవనముగలది. A girl of twelve years of age, పన్నెండేండ్ల యీడుగలది. A simple girl. తెలివిలేనిది, మాయలేనిది, కపటములేనిది. adj. Lovely, beautiful, చక్కని. Stupid, ignorant, తెలివిలేని. New, inexperienced, క్రొత్తది. ముగ్ధేందువు the new moon, బాలేందువు. Sananda. 266. ముగ్ధుడు *mugdhudu*. n. A handsome man, అందమైనవాడు. An ignorant man, మూఢుడు.

ముచ్చి or ముచ్చివాడు *muchchi*. [H.] n. A painter. చిత్రకారుడు.

ముచ్చిక *much-chika*. [Tel. ముందు+చిక.] n. Husk or scales like those at the stalk part of a cocoanut or palm fruit. తాటిపండ్లు మొదలయినవాటి తొడిమెకిందనుండే చిల్ల. A basket, గంప.

ముచ్చికొను *muchchi-konu*. [Tel.] v. a. To cover, to swarm upon as flies. ముసురుకొను. "అనిపలుకఁ బెరుకు మదిలోఁ గొనగా మేసెల్ల ముచ్చికొనుచుఁ బులిమెల్ల వెయ వలికి జని." S. ii. 288.

ముచ్చిచ్చు *much-chitstsu*. [Tel. మూడు+చిచ్చు.] n. plu. Three fires, త్రేతాగ్ని.

ముచ్చిబంగారము Same as ముచ్చెబంగారము (q. v.).

ముచ్చిరు *muchchiru*. [Tel.] v. n. To grieve, శోకించు, దుఃఖించు, వ్యాకులపడు. ముచ్చిరనేల why grieve or sorrow? "ముచ్చిరనేల చేకలుగ ముద్దియ నాకు వృకోదరుండు విష్వక్సేనుడు తోడుగాన." M. V. iii. 104. ముచ్చిరి *muchchiri*. n. An aggrieved man, a sorrowful man, దుఃఖముపొందినవాడు. ముచ్చిరితనము *muchchiri-tanamu*. n. Grief, sorrow. మనోదుఃఖము. BX. 239.

ముచ్చిలి *muchchili*. [Tel.] n. A small winnowing fan, used by children as a toy. చెరిటిచేట.

ముచ్చిలి or ముచ్చిలిగుంట *muchchili*. [Tel.] n. The nape or hollow at the back of the neck, అవటువు, కృకాటిక, పెడతలయందలిగుంట.

ముచ్చిలించు or ముచ్చిలు See under ముచ్చు.

ముచ్చిలికా or ముచ్చిలిక *muchchilika*. [H.] n. An agreement in writing, a deed. వాదిప్రతివాదులు వ్యాజ్యములను వ్రాసియిచ్చు

ఒడంబడిక, కార్యలు కేలగలవారికి వ్రాసియిచ్చిన ఒడంబడిక.

ముచ్చిలిపాటు muchchili-pātu. [Tel.] n. Drowsiness, sleepiness, కునికిపాటు.

ముచ్చివుక much-chivuka. [Tel. మూడు+చివుక.] n. Three quarters of a rupee, మూడు పావలాలు.

ముచ్చె muchche. [Tel.] n. A shoe. పైజారు. ముచ్చెలు shoes, పైజారులు. adj. Appertaining to the Moochee caste, who are generally painters, bookbinders, paper cutters, makers of saddles, toys, trunks, &c. చర్మకారసంబంధమైన. ముచ్చెకర్ర muchche-karra. n. A spongy wood, *Erythrina indica*. బాడిదచెక్క. Rox. iii. 249. It is so called because much used by Moochees or cabinet-makers. ముచ్చెపని muchche-pani. n. Lacquer work. ముచ్చెపెట్టె muchche-pette. n. A lacquered box. ముచ్చెబంగారము or ముచ్చిబంగారము muchche-bangāramu. n. Tinsel. రేకు బంగారు, ఇత్తడిలోహభేదము. ముచ్చెవాడు muchche-vādu. n. A man of the ముచ్చె caste, చర్మకారుడు.

ముచ్చె mutstsa. [Tel. ముడ్డి+పూస] n. The base of the spine, the os coccyx.

ముచ్చెంగి mutstsangi. [Tel.] n. A sort of fish. H. iv. 225.

ముచ్చట mutstsata. [Tel.] n. Conversation, discourse, talk. సల్లాపము. A story; news, tidings, వృత్తాంతము. Wish, desire, longing, కోరిక. Love, ప్రేమము, వేడుక. వెర్రిముచ్చట prattle, tattle. మనకువచ్చినసష్టము వట్టిముచ్చటకాదు the loss we suffered is no mere talk, or is no trifle. అది నాకు ముచ్చటగున్నది I am fond of it. వానికి మాట్లాడడమే ఒక ముచ్చట he is fond of conversation. "ఒచ్చెంబులేనికూరిమి ముచ్చటలాడుచును." T. iii. 7. "వచ్చి నా ముచ్చటలదీర్పు మెచ్చు గాను." N. vii. 182. ముచ్చటగానుండే elegant, handsome, attractive, charming, pleasing, ముద్దుగానుండే. ముచ్చటకాడు mutstsata-kādu. n. One who desires, కోరికగలవాడు. ముచ్చటపడు mutstsata-padu. v. n. To fall in love with, be enamoured of, to wish, long for, desire, ఆశపడు, కోరు. ముచ్చటించు, ముచ్చటలాడు or ముచ్చటాడు mutstsat-intsu. v. n. To converse, to talk. సంభాషించు.

ముచ్చట్లు mutstsatlu. [Tel. మూడు+చోట్లు.] n. Three places, మూడుచోట్లు.

ముచ్చముడుగు mutstsa-mudugu. [Tel. ముడుగు+ముడుగు.] v. n. To be entirely folded, మిక్కిలిముడుగు. To become unable to act, చేష్టలుడుగు.

ముచ్చవలము mu-tsa-tsavalamu. [Tel. మూడు+చేవలము.] n. Three tsavalas or three-eighths of a pagoda. మూడుచేవలములు.

ముచ్చు or ముచ్చు mutstsu. [Tel.] n. A rogue, a thief. దొంగ. గొర్రెలముచ్చు a sheep stealer. నరుముచ్చు a cannibal, a flesh eater. మునిముచ్చు a pretended saint. నాలిముచ్చు a sneak. లొట్టిముచ్చు a toss-pot or tippler. adj. Roguish, thievish. ముచ్చుచూపులు roguish glances. A vi. 19. ముచ్చిలు or ముచ్చిలించు muchchilu. v. a. To steal. దొంగిలించు. ముచ్చిలి muchchili. adv. By stealth. దొంగతనముగా. "ముచ్చిలి నత్తురువారలు." BX. 164. ముచ్చుతనము mutstsu-tanamu. n. Roguishness, roguery, thievishness. దొంగతనము. Satya. iv. 232. ముచ్చుప్రొద్దు mutstsu-proddu. n. Midnight, అర్ధరాత్రి. ముచ్చుబొడుపు mutstsu-bodupu. n. A petty thief. అల్పదొంగ. "తడుకద్రోపరిముచ్చుబొడుపులు." P. iv. 255.

ముచ్చుకొను mutstsu-konu. [Tel.] v. a. To cover, to swarm. ముసురుకొను.

ముజ్జగము muj-jagamu. [Tel. మూడు+జగము.] n. The three worlds, viz., earth, heaven and hell, the universe. లోకత్రయము.

ముజేరా Same as ముదరా (q. v.).

ముటము muṭamu. [Tel.] n. Cowdung found dried in woods. ముద్దపిడక.

ముట్టు muṭṭu. [Tel.] v. a. and v. n. To touch, తాకు. To attack as an enemy, శత్రువును తాకు. To touch or strike a sensitive part of the body, మర్మమునుతాకు. To besiege, ముట్టడించు. To be ended or finished, కడముట్టు. To arrive, be received, obtained. నాకు రూపాయిలు ముట్టలేదు I did not receive the rupees. ముట్టగొలుచు to worship to the end, or with unfailing devotion, కడవెళ్లగొలుచు. "ముట్టగొలిచినఫలం బిట్టుండ వలదె." BD. v. 457. రాత్రి కడముట్టగానే (Vasu. iv. 170) as soon as night came to its close. ఇది కడముట్టేదెన్నటికో when will this be finished? వానిని సర్పము ముట్టినది a snake bit him. n. Contact, touching, తాకడము. Defilement by contact. Hence, the menses. A tool or instrument, ఉపకరణము. వానికి అంటుముట్టులేదు he does not care about being touched. పనిముట్టు or కోరముట్టు a tool. కన్నపుముట్టు (B. v. 807.) a house breaker's tool for boring walls. adj. Defiling, foul, unclean, menstruous. ముట్టయిన menstruous. ముట్టుకొను muṭṭu-konu. v. a. To touch, తాకు. To besiege, ముట్టడించు. To surround, encroach upon, ఆక్రమించు. ముట్టుకొలుపు muṭṭu-kolupu, v. a. To cause to touch or besiege. రామా. vi. ముట్టుకోలు muṭṭu-kōlu. n. A siege, ముట్టడి. ముట్టుకోలుగొను, ముట్టుకోల్గొను, ముట్టుకోలువట్టు, ముట్టుకోల్పట్టు or ముట్టుకోలుపెట్టు Same as ముట్టడించు. ముట్టుది or ముట్టుత muṭṭudi. n. A menstruous woman. ముట్టచెప్పు muṭṭa-cheppu. v. a. To assign. వెల్లగట్టు. నాకు పదిరూపాయలసొమ్ము ముట్టజెప్పినాడు. he paid or gave me ten rupees. ముట్టడి muṭṭaḍi. n. A siege, blockade. ఊరుచుట్టుకొని అరికట్టడము. ముట్టడించు or ముట్టడివేయు muṭṭaḍ-intsu. v. a. To besiege. ఊరుచుట్టుకొని అరికట్టుకొను. ముట్టడము or ముట్టుదము muṭṭaḍamu. n. Compulsion, oppression, నిర్బంధము. The act of laying siege to a place, ముట్టడించుట. ముట్టించు muṭṭintsu. v. a. To cause to touch. To light a candle, to kindle, i.e., communicate (fire) తాకించు. ముట్టికాళ్లు muṭṭi-kāḷḷu. n. Knees that touch. ముట్టికాళ్లవాడు a knock-kneed man. ముట్టికాళ్లువేసికొను to kneel down. ముట్టుపడు muṭṭu-paḍu. v. n. To be troublesome, సంకటపడు. ముట్టుపాటు muṭṭu-pāṭu. n. Trouble. సంకటము. ముట్టుసందు muṭṭu-sandu. n. A blind alley. అవల పోవుటకు దారిలేనిది.

ముట్టె muṭṭe. [Tel.] n. A snout, పందిముక్కు. A fruit stone. మామిడిముట్టెవంటిముఖము a haggard face. ముట్టెచేప muṭṭe-chēpa. n. A sort of fish called Gobius. Russell No. 49. అలముట్టె a sort of Salmon: *ibid* No. 171. Other sorts are called కోరముట్టె (plate 50), నూనెముట్టె (plate 52), పొట్టిరంగ్ల ముట్టె (plate 54.) ముట్టెమేకము muṭṭe-mekamu. n. A pig, పంది. ముట్టెగించు muṭṭe-gintsu. v. a. To rout up earth with the snout (as a pig.) పందిమూతితో కల్లగించు.

ముఠా muṭha. [H.] n. A subdivision of a district.

ముడర muḍara. [Tel.] n. A place where platforms for heaping up salt are raised (Vizag.)

ముడి muḍi. [Tel.] n. A knot. గ్రంథి. A knot of hair, వెండ్రుకలముడి. A knot or joint in wood, చెట్టులోనగువానిబుడిపి. The hump of an ox, ఎద్దుమూపురము. A quarrel, కలహము. A form of a letter written like ౘ.

knot as కొముడి the letter ొ. గాముడి the letter ౖ. తాముడి the secondary form of the letter త, i. e., ౖ. An union, joining, సంధి. Also, another form of ముష్టి. (q. v.) వాడు దానిని ముడిపెట్టుకొన్నాడు he tied the nuptial knot to her, he married her. ముష్టికత్తిరించేవాడు a pick-pocket. ఆమె తలముడి విడినది her hair fell loose, the knot being untied. ముడివిప్పు to untie or open a knot. ఆ దారముతో ముళ్లుపడ్డవి that string has formed into knots. ముడివక్కలు unbroken (or whole) areca nuts, గుండుపోకచెక్కలు. బొమలుముడిపెట్టు to knit the eye-brows. ఒకవాళ్లకు మనసు ముడివేసి విడిచిపెట్టినాడు he cast a bone of dispute between them. "సదంతిమది ముడిసడలగా." Bhadra Parin. iii. 297. దాని మనసుచేగ్రంథి విడునప్పటికి. ముడి muḍi. adj. Closed, వికసించని. Entire, whole, unbroken, ఖండముకాని. ముడిపూలు unblown flowers. "ముడిపూలబొట్లముల్." Illa. ii. 163. ముడిజొన్నలు the great millet enclosed in its husk. ముడినువ్వులు sesamum seeds which are not cleaned. ముడిపోక an entire areca nut. ముడిబియ్యము rice that is not well cleaned, చేడిబియ్యము. ముడికట్టు muḍi-kaṭṭu. n. Certain fees on a crop for the benefit of the landlord. A truss of straw, a sheaf. v. a. To tie a knot. To tie a knot in a man's cloth to remind him that you call upon him to be a witness. అందునుగురించి పెద్దలు ముడికట్టినారు our ancestors have laid down this rule or held this doctrine. ముడికాడు muḍi-kāḍu. n. One who ties a knot, one who unites, సంధానముచేయువాడు. ముడికాళ్లు muḍi-kāḷḷu. n. Knock-knees. ముడికాళ్లవాడు a man who is knock-kneed. ముట్టికాళ్లవాడు. ముడికాళ్లది a woman who is knock-kneed. ముడికొక్కు muḍi-kokku. n. A weevil. పంకవాడి. ముడికొను, ముడిగొను or ముడిపడు muḍi-konu. v. n. To be tied in a knot. ముడికొన్న or ముడిగొన్న muḍi-konna. adj. Tied, bound. బద్ధమైన. "ముడిగొన్న సంసార మహాబంధములు విడదన్ను సుజ్ఞానవిదలివకూర్చి..." DRK. 372. ముడికొలుపు muḍi-kolupu. v. a. To cause to be tied in a knot. ముడిగిబ్బ muḍi-gibba. n. An ox, a bull, ఆబోతు. ముడిపంచె or ముడిపట్టు. muḍi-panche. n. A plain cotton cloth without any coloured border. పెల్లాగుడ్డ. ముడిపడు or ముడివడు muḍi-paḍu. v. n. To be tied in a knot, ముడికలుగు. To be united, సంధించు. To be entangled, పెనగొను. To be confounded, puzzled. చీకాకుపడు. "ముడిపడెననితొడదండిడి, ముడివడకుడు." N. vii. 312. "మనక మున చీకట్లుముడివడ." HD. ii. 1380. To increase, excel, అతిశయించు. To happen, కలుగు. ముడిపెట్టు or ముడివేయు muḍi-peṭṭu. v. a. To tie a knot. ముడిబొమ్మ. muḍi-bomma. n. A kind of fish, *Mastacembelus aennatus.* ముడియ muḍiya. n. A knot. A bundle of straw or young plants ready to set. కట్ట, మూట. A wager. పందెము. ముడియవిడుపు muḍiya-viḍupu. n. A pick-pocket. ముళ్లువిప్పు దొంగ. ముడివాటు muḍi-vāṭu. n. The act of being tied in a knot, &c., ముడిపడుట.

ముడుగు muḍugu. [Tel.] v. n. To be drawn in, as one's limbs, to shrink, shrivel, or close, ముకుళించు. To be diminished, తగ్గు, సంకోచించు. To be unable to act, చేష్టలుడుగు. ముడుగుతామర muḍugu-tāmara. n. The plant called *Hibiscus mutabilis,* పాత్తితామర, నమస్కారి. See ముచ్చేముడుగు. ముడుచు muḍuṭsu. v. a. To cause to fold, ముడుగజేయు. To tie into a knot, ముడివేయు, ముడిపెట్టు. To set flowers in the tresses. To bend the limbs. "వక్త్రంబు నొముడుచు." (S. iii. 399.) the doves looked downcast. దానికి పూలుముడిచినదెవరు who set the flowers in her hair? ముడుచుకొను muḍutsu-konu. v. a. To contract as limbs. To wear flowers in one's hair. అది పూలుముడుచుకొన్నది she wore flowers in her hair. మొగముడుచుకొని ఉన్నది her features are contracted, pensive or downcast. ముడత or ముడుత muḍata. n. A wrinkle, crumpling, knot in spinning or twisting. వలి, ముడివి. ముడత తెవులు a transient blight in corn that goes off again. ముడుపు or ముడ్పు muḍupu. n. A rouleau, bag or purse. ముల్లె, ధనము ముడుపు, ధనపుమూట, ధనము. పూలముడుపు a ceremony of setting flowers in the head dress of a pregnant woman. వెంకటేశ్వరులముడుపు money or jewels promised by a vow to the god Venkatesa. ముడుపు కట్టుకొను to vow money or jewels to a god. దివాణపుముడుపు money payable into the Government treasury. "అద్దములోనిదోమ ముడుపు." (Ahal. iii. 48.) a purse reflected in the mirror. ముడుపరి muḍup-ari. n. One who vows to offer some money to a god. ముడుపుపట్టినవాడు.

ముడుము muḍumu. [Tel.] n. The knee, మోకాలు, జానువు. ముడుపుచిప్ప the knee-cap.

ముడుసు muḍusu. [Tel.] n. A bone. ఎముక, అస్థి, కీకసము. The base of the spine, ముడ్డిపూస.

ముడేకము muḍēkamu. [Tel.] n. A half penny, called ten cash. ఏగాని.

ముడ్డి muḍḍi. [Tel.] n. The breech, rump, anus. వానిని ముడ్డివెనుక తిట్టినారు they reviled him behind his back. ముడ్డిమీద కొట్టితే నోటిపండ్లు రాలెను (i. e., పృష్ఠతాడనాత్ దంతభగ్నః) the teeth were dislodged by a slap on the back. ముడ్డికిందికి నీళ్లు వచ్చుట to get into a scrape. దీపము ముడ్డి కింద చీకటి under the lamp it is dark., i. e., roguery hides under the judgment seat. వాని ముడ్డవెంట తిరుగుచున్నారు they are dancing attendance upon him. ముడ్డి తిప్పుడుపిట్ట muḍḍi-tippuḍu-piṭṭa. n. The Grey Wag-tail, *Motacilla melanope* (F. B. I.) ముడ్డిపూస muḍḍi-pūsa. n. The rump bone. వెన్నెముకచివరిపూస.

మునుగు munugu. [Tel.] v. n. To sink, become immersed, submerged; to dive, drown; to be lost, ruined. ఆపని మునుగుతూ తేలుతూ ఉన్నది that affair is still in uncertainty. నాకేమిన్ని మునిగిపోలేదు it is no loss to me. నాసొమ్ము మునిగిపోయినది my money is lost. మునక munaka. n. Immersion, submersion. నీళ్లలో మునుగుట. ఒకమునకలో వాని ప్రాణము పోయినది he died in one immersion. మునకరాములు munaka-rāmulu. n. A puzzle, hesitation, being at a loss. ఎటుతోచనిస్థితి. ఇంతలో పులికి మునకరాములయినది the tiger was now at bay. మునకరాములుగానుంటిని I was in a fix. ముంచు muntsu. v. a. To sink, immerse, drown. నీళ్లలో మునిగిపోవునట్లు చేయు. మునుగలాగుకొను or ముడుగలాగుకొను munuga-lāgu-konu. v. n. To crouch or lie coiled up. దేహమును చుట్టలో కాళ్లుచేతులు ముడుచుకొని పండుకొను.

ముతక, ముతుక or ముడుక mutaka. [Tel.] adj. Coarse. మోటైన. ముతకమాటలు coarse language, abuse.

ముత్త mutta. [Tel.] adj. Old, వృద్ధ. వృద్ధుడు. See ముత్తవ్వ, ముత్తాత, ముత్తైదువ, &c.,

ముత్తరంగులు or ముత్తరాలు mutta-rangalu. [Tel+Skt. మూడు+తరంగములు.] n. The three folds that appear above the navel, మూడైన కడుపుమీది సన్నపుముడతలు, త్రివళి. "పెనుపైముత్తరగులంతరాతిలుగ నాభిస్థానమందొప్పగా." Bilhan. ii 153.

ముత్తరాచే or మురరాచే, ముత్తిరాచేవాండ్లు or ముత్తిరాచోలు *mutta-ratsa*. [Tel.] n. The name of a certain Sudra caste, the members of which were originally feudal retainers. The people of this caste.

ముత్తవ, ముత్తవ్వ or ముత్తవతల్లి *muttava*. [Tel. ముత్త+అవ్వ.] n. A great grandmother, an old woman, వృద్ధ పితామహి, వృద్ధస్త్రీ. ముత్తవపులగము *muttava-pulagamu*. n. A tree called *Pavonia odorata*. (Willd.) The root of the sweet smelling *Pavonia*. Ainsl. ii. 297. సహదేవి, చిట్టాముదపుచెట్టు.

ముత్తాత *muttata*. [Tel. [ముత్త+తాత or మూడు+తాత.] n. A great grandfather. మూడోతాత, వృద్ధపితామహుండు, ప్రపితామహుడు.

ముత్తి *mutti*. [from Skt. ముక్తి.] n. Salvation. "నిచ్చలభుక్తియు ముక్తియు ముత్తియును." Nila Parin. i. 21.

ముత్తిగ *mut-tiga*. [Tel. మూడు+తిగ.] n. Nine, తొమ్మిది.

ముత్తుము *mut-tumu*. [Tel. మూడు+తూము.] n. The measure of three తూములు.

ముత్తెము, ముత్తియము or ముత్యము *muttemu*. [from Skt. మౌక్తికము.] n. A pearl. Any gummy drop resembling a pearl. See ముత్యము. ముత్తెపుబంట *muttepu-banta*. n. Lit: a crop of pearls, an epithet applied to a sugar cane, చెరకు. ముత్తెపురిక్కనెల *muttepu-rikka-nela*. n. An epithet applied to the month, చైత్రమాసము. ముత్తెపుసవతు *muttepu-savatu*. n. The lunar mansion called చిత్రానక్షత్రము. ముత్తెసరి *muttesari*. n. A pearl necklace, ముక్తాహారము. A kind of grain, ధాన్యవిశేషము. Any bead or concretion resembling a pearl, such as is found in bamboos. ముత్తెమువంటి లిపి a pearly (i. e., delicate) handwriting.

ముత్తెపుచిప్ప *muttepu-chippa*. n. A pearl oyster, mother of pearl. శుక్తి. ముత్తెపుచిప్పలు a sort of cake. H. i. 118.

ముత్తైద, ముత్తైదువ or ముత్తయిదువ *mutt[illegible]da*. [Tel. ముత్త+అయిదువ.] n. A woman whose husband is living. A good woman, mistress, dame. The brides-women who are always wives (not maids nor widows.) సుమంగలి.

ముత్తో [Tel. ముత్తి+తోడుది.] Same as ముత్తైదువ (q. v.).

ముత్యము or ముత్తెము *mutyamu*. [from Skt. మౌక్తికము.] n. A pearl. మౌక్తికము. చిప్పముత్యము an artificial pearl. వానికి అమ్మవారు పోసినప్పుడు ముత్యాలు బాగా లేవలేదు the pustules did not rise properly when he had small pox. ముత్యాలమ్మ *mutyal-amma*. n. A certain local goddess.

ముదము *mudamu*. [Skt.] n. Delight, pleasure, joy, సంతోషము. హర్షము. ముదశ్రువులు *mud-asruvulu*. n. Tears of joy. ఆనందబాష్పములు. ముదితుడు *muditudu*. n. He who is pleased or delighted. ప్రహృష్టుడు.

ముదముద *muda-muda*. [Tel.] n. Doubt, hesitation, సంకోచము.

ముదరా or ముజరా *mudara*. [H.] n. An allowance, deduction, remission, compensation.

ముదల *mudala*. [Tel.] n. An order, command, ఆజ్ఞ. An example, లక్ష్యము. Land near a hill, గనిమచేరికనేల. ముదలపెట్టు *mudala-pettu*. v. a. To command, ఆజ్ఞాపించు.

ముదలకించు or ముదలించు *mudala-kintsu*. [Tel.] v. a. To attack, to resist, to oppose. ఎదిరించు, మార్కొను "ఎదురుదురిన ముదలిం

జగ, మదిగొంకి పిరిందివలన మందగిలిగా కేలదిని కేమవిదియున్నాడ, బట్టైదనపువుగ వుష్పకంబుదగ వచ్చుతరిగా." UR. vii. 78. "కన డింపుగా జరగాంచలముల. కింపుదనంబెచ్చి ముదలకింపుగా మంచుగా, సెంచుగా విడకెనమంపూ, దంచచ్చం మాపుటస్ఫుటాఘూతముగా." R. v. 190. To ask, question, అడుగు.

ముడి *mudi*. [Tel.] adj. Old, ancient. ముసలి. వృద్ధ, ముదిరిన. "అచ్చుటనోటవచ్చు సముయంబుకు వేళ దొరయంగ చెప్పితే ముచ్చటదీర్తునంచు ముదిముద్దియ తో వివరించిపంపగా." H. ii. 53. "ఎక్కడ దప్పించపనిదిముదిపోరు." n. Old age, ముసలి తనము, వార్ధకము. **ముడిగారము** *mudi-garamu*. n. Stubbornness, వార్ధక్యము. **ముదిమి** or **ముదిమితనము** *mudimi*. n. Old age, decrepitude. వృద్ధత్వము. **ముదియు** *mudiyu*. v. n. To grow old. "ముదిసిన ప్పనరింత ముదిమరుల్ పొంది." BD. iv. 1249. **ముదివాడు** *mudi-vadu*. n. An old man. వృద్ధపురుషుడు. **ముదుక** or **మొదుక** *muduka*. adj. Coarse. నాణెముగాని, ముదురైన. Old, వృద్ధ. **ముదుక** or **ముదుకడు** *muduka* n. An old man. వృద్ధుడు. "ముదుకండయ్యును కుమారమూర్తివహించెగా." M. VII. i. 134.

ముదిత *mudita*. [Tel.] n. A maid, damsel, lady. వనిత, అడుది. [Skt.] adj. Pleased.

ముదిరము *mudiramu*. [Skt.] n. A cloud. మేఘము.

ముదుగు *mudugu*. [Tel.] adj. Coarse. నాణెముగాని.

ముదురు *muduru*. [Tel.] v. n. To be mature, to arrive at full growth or maturity, to reach its full height. To increase. పక్వమగు, వర్ధిల్లు. ఎండలు ముదిరినవి. the summer or heat is now at its height. కలహము ముదిరినది the battle is raging. To be chronic or established అరోగము ముదిరినది the disease has become chronic. adj. Mature, ripe, elder, senior, old, వృద్ధము. ముదురాకు a leaf that is ripe and brittle. ముదురుముఖము or ముదురు మూతి the face of mature age, set features. ముదురు అక్షరములు a fixed hand, or a formed or settled text.

ముదుసలి *mudusali*. [Tel.] adj. Old, ancient. వృద్ధుడైన. "ముదుసలిబాపనయ్య." R. ii. 108 "ముదుసలితలపిరెండ." Parij. iv. 48. n. An old man or woman. **ముదుసలితనము** *mudusali-tanamu*. n. Old age. వృద్ధత్వము. **ముదుసలిది** *mudusali-di*. n. An old woman. వృద్ధస్త్రీ.

ముద్గము *mudgamu*. [Skt.] n. The pulse called green gram. పెసలు.

ముద్గరము or **ముద్గలము** *mudgaramu*. [Skt.] n. A mace or club, a weapon formed like a hammer. కురుచయినపరుగుదియ. A hammer. కమ్మరవానిసమ్మెట.

ముద్ద *mudda*. [from Skt. ముగ్ధ.] n. A girl, a simple maid. ముగ్ధస్త్రీ. **ముద్దరాలు** *mudda-r-alu*. n. A maiden, lass; a simple girl, ముగ్ధస్త్రీ. **ముద్దుడు** *muddudu*. n. An idiot. ముగ్ధుడు.

ముద్ద *mudda*. [Tel.] n. A lump, mass, morsel. కబళము, పిండము, ఉండ. ముద్దకావడము to form or collect in a mass. వారు తడిసి ముద్ద అయినారు they are soaking wet, or are a mass of wet. నెత్తురు ముద్దగానున్నది. it is a mass of blood ముద్ద ఖర్జూరము a species of date. ముద్దపప్పు pease pudding, యూషము. తడి ముద్దగానుండే బట్టలు a wet wisp of clothes. **ముద్దకమ్మరలు** *mudda-kammaralu*. n. Smelters, smiths who work at smelting iron. రాయి కరగి యినుముచేసేవారు. **ముద్దకవ్వము** *mudda-kavvamu*. n. A sort of churning staff, with a heavy mass at the end కొద్దిబిళ్లకట్టిలించినకవ్వము **ముద్దకూడు** *mudda-kudu* n A lump of boiled rice

A paste of rice and ashes applied to the eye of a drum forming the black spot in the centre of the head, for the purpose of regulating the tone. అన్నపిండము, పుష్కరలేపనార్థమైన భస్మమిశ్రితాన్నము. **ముద్దకొలిమి** *mudda-kolimi.* n. A forge for smelting iron. రాతిలోనున్న యినుము కరిగే కొలిమి. **ముద్దీటె** *mudd-īṭe.* n. A stout spear. **ముద్దవాయువు** *mudda-vāyuvu.* n. The cramp. కాళ్లుచేతులు ముద్దలుగా కట్టుకొను వాతరోగము.

ముద్దతు *muddatu.* [H.] A period or time. **ముద్దతుకౌలు** *muddatu-kaulu.* n. A temporary or conditional agreement. **ముద్దతుక్రయము** *muddatu-krayamu.* n. A foreclosed mortgage, a conditional sale with a penalty attached. **ముద్దతుహుండీ** *muddatu-huṇḍi.* n. A bill payable after a stipulated interval.

ముద్దాయి *muddāyi.* [H.] n. A defendant in a suit. A prisoner at the bar, the accused.

ముద్ది *muddi.* [Tel.] n. A calamity, peril, misfortune, danger, ఆపద, ఇడుము.

ముద్దియ *muddiya.* [from Skt. ముగ్ధ.] A lady, dame, woman. స్త్రీ. ముదిముద్దియ an old woman.

ముద్దు *muddu.* [Tel.] n. A kiss. చుంబనము. Sweetness, fondness, delight; caressing, toying. మనోజ్ఞత, చిన్నవాండ్లయందలి ప్రేమ. ముద్దుచూపు to show love. **ముద్దుపెట్టుకొను** *muddu-peṭṭu-konu.* v. a. To kiss, చుంబనముచేయు. **ముద్దాడు** or **ముద్దులాడు** *mudd-āḍu.* v. a. To caress, to fondle, లాలనముచేయు, ఆడించు. ముద్దిచ్చు, ముద్దిడు or ముద్దుపెట్టు to give a kiss. దాన్ని చూస్తే ముద్దువస్తున్నది I am delighted to see her, she is very charming. ఆబిడ్డ ముద్దులు మూటకట్టుచున్నది the child is a lump of charms, a perfect beauty. ముద్దులతమ్ముడు my darling little brother. ముద్దయ్య an epithet of Kumaraswami. ముద్దులయ్య my sweet lord. ప్రయోగముల ముద్దు కనుగొననెడిది మహాకష్టము it is very difficult to perceive the niceties (or delicacies) of local adaptation or meaning. కాకిపిల్ల కాకికి ముద్దుకాదా surely the crow's chick is dear to the crow, i. e., every beggar will love her brat. adj. Darling, pet, sweet, charming, lovely, dear. నాముద్దుకుమారుడు my beloved son, my darling boy. ముద్దుపేరు a pet name. ముద్దుటుంగరము or ముదుటుంగరము a pet ring, worn on the little finger, a signet ring. ముద్దుమాటలు sweet words. ముద్దుమొగము a sweet face. **ముద్దుగా** *muddu-gā.* adv. Charmingly, tastily. అందముగా. **ముద్దులగుమ్మ** *muddula-gumma.* n. A beauty, a charming woman. **ముద్దులాడి** or **ముద్దురాలు** *muddul-āḍi.* n. A charming woman, ముద్దులుగులికే స్త్రీ, మనోజ్ఞురాలు. **ముద్దులాడు** *muddul-āḍu.* n. A charming or pleasant man, మనోజ్ఞుడు.

ముద్దుగులము *mud-dugulamu.* [Tel. మూడు+దుగులము.] n. The fraction of three *dugulams*, i. e., three-sixteenths of a pagoda.

ముద్దె *mudde.* [Tel.] n. The pistil of a lotus. కర్ణిక. "కొమ్మలలోడివాస్తములు గుత్తపు ముద్దలుముద్దునెయ్యపొందమ్ములు." P. iv. 154.

ముద్ర *mudra.* [Skt.] n. A seal: a seal ring, or signet. The stamp, print, or impression of a seal. A distinguishing mark impressed or burned upon a man or beast. Coinage. మునుపటిముద్ర రూపాయి a rupee of the old coinage. Gesticulation, attitude. మౌనముద్ర the seal of silence, i. e., silence. నిద్రాముద్ర the seal of sleep, i. e., sound sleep. జ్ఞానముద్ర a particular position of the fingers used in religious ceremonies. ముద్రలు marks impressed upon sand or clay placed on heaps of grain, the permanent marks made on the shoulders representing the insignia of Vishnu which are the shell and the wheel, &c. వాడు ముద్రాధారణము చేసికొనినాడు he received the seals, i. e., his shoulders were sealed with the shell and wheel of Vishṇu. మధ్వులు గోపిముద్రలు వేసికొందురు they wear patches of brown clay. వానికి కుక్కముద్ర వేసినారు they stamped him with the figure of a dog. ముద్రకర్త *mudra-karta.* n. An apparitor, the lowest local officer attached to a Guru or priest, ఆయాస్థలములలో గురువుయొక్క తాబేదారుగానుండేవాడు. ముద్రకోల *mudra-kōla.* n. A stamp to mark or seal with. The insignia of Vishnu, being the shell and wheel made in copper. ముద్రవేయు సాధనము, ముద్రధారణముచేయు సుదర్శన పాంచజన్యములు. ముద్రగద *mudra-gada.* n. A sceptre, a royal staff. "తన ముద్రగడ వేరుతలగ బట్టించి." Pal. 450. A wooden stamp. ముద్రగరిటె *mudra-gariṭe.* n. A ladle-shaped mace or large spoon borne in state before a person in authority, దేవాయీలు మొదలైనవారుముందర బిరుదుగా తీసికొనిపోవు గంటెలుగల యుత్తడిగరిటె. ముద్రణము *mudraṇamu.* n. Setting one's seal to, ముద్రించుట. Dooming, giving a decision, సిద్ధాంతప్రతిపాదనము. "శరకాద్రిముద్రణగ్రంథకర్త." A. ii. 45. టీ॥ మేరువునందుకు తనముద్ర చెల్లించువాడు. ముద్రతీసివేయు *mudra-tīsi-vēyu.* v. a. To unseal. ముద్రాధారణము *mudrā-dhāraṇamu.* n. Sealing, i.e, the act of impressing the shell and wheel of Vishnu on either shoulder. చక్రాంకనము చేసికొనుట. ముద్రపలక *mudra-palaka.* n. A wooden stamp for sealing a heap of corn. ధాన్యరాశిమీద ముద్రవేసేపలక. ముద్రమనిషి *mudra-manishi.* n. A sealer, i. e., a bailiff who seals heaps of corn. అంబారములకు ముద్రవేయు బంట్రౌతు. ముద్రవేయు *mudra-vēyu.* v. a. To seal. ఈ భోగముండ్లు అందరూ ముద్రవేయబడినారు these dancing girls are dedicated to that temple. ముద్రాంకితము *mudr-ankitamu.* adj. Sealed, marked with a seal. ముద్రవేయబడిన. ముద్రాంకితుడు *mudr-ankituḍu* adj. One who is impressed with the shell and wheel of Vishnu on either shoulder. సమాశ్రయణము చేసికొన్నవాడు. ముద్రాక్షరశాల *mudr-akshara-ṣāla.* n. A press or printing office. అచ్చుయిల్లు, అచ్చుకూటము. ముద్రించు *mudrintsu.* v. a. To seal. ముద్రవేయు. అచ్చువేయు. "మృషావాదంబేయుదు నమతలంపుముద్రించి." HN. v. 176. ముద్రిక *mudrika.* n. A seal ring, శిఖాంగుళీయకము. ముద్రితము *mudritamu.* adj. Sealed, marked, stamped, closed. ముద్రవేయబడిన, మూసికొనిన, ముకుళితమైన.

మున్ *mun.* [Tel. for ముందు.] adv. Formerly, in old times.

మునక See మునుక.

మునగ *munaga.* [Tel.] n. A plant resembling the horse radish, *Hyperanthera moringa.* శిగ్రువు. [Ainslie.] కారుమునగ a wild species of the same. The *munaga* is proverbially weak and brittle. నేను పట్టినది మునగకొమ్మకాదు చింతకొమ్మ what I rely on is a tamarind branch, i. e., is no broken reed.

మునస *munasa.* [Tel.] n. A piece of wood, fixed on the top of a water lift. ఏతపుమ్రానిమీద అరభాగము. See మీట.

మునసబు *munasabu.* [H.] n. A munsif, native judge. గ్రామమునసబు a village magistrate.

ముని *muni.* [Tel. for ముందు.] n. The point, tip. కొన. adj. Former, front. మునిపల్లు the point of the tooth. మునినాలుక the tip of the tongue. మునికాళ్లు the points of the toes. మునికొంగు *muni-kongu.* n. The tip of the skirt. ముంగొంగు. "మునికొంగొకయించుకయొత్తి." S. i. 330. మునికోల or ములుకోల *muni-kōla.* n. The point of a goad. మునియేడు the year before the last, నిరుటికి తొలిసంవత్సరము. మునిచీకటి the early twilight. "మునిమునిచీకటిం నడుమముంగిటవాకిట." N. IX. 286. మునిగుత్త muni-gutta. n. Usufruct of land in satisfaction of a debt. A forestalled rent: money wrongfully collected by anticipation. మునిమనుమడు or మున్మనుమడు muni-manumadu. n. A great grandson. మునిమనుమరాలు or మున్మనుమరాలు muni-manumarālu. n. A great grand daughter. మునిమాపు muni-māpu. n. A great fault, evil, ప్రదోషము.

ముని muni. [Skt.] n. Lit: a man of silence. A hermit, monk, or recluse. A prophet, seer or sage. A saint or holy man. ఋషి. మునిపుంగవుడు muni-pungavudu. n. A great hermit. Vish. iii. 371. మునిముచ్చు muni-mutsṭsu. n. A pretended saint, a hermit who is a rogue, కపటసన్యాసి, వఱ్ఱతోపరుడు. Swa. ii. 82.

మునిముట్ట muni-muṭṭa. [Tel.] adv. Much, excessively. మిక్కిలి. "ఈతెవ్వనైరింపుమంకె దొంగిలబోవకేనవిమునిముట్టనేద్భువాని." B. X. ix. 16.

మునిషీ munishi. [H.] n. A writer, a secretary. లేఖకుడు, గుమాస్తా. A teacher or tutor in a language. ఉపాధ్యాయుడు.

మునీశ్వరుడు or మునీంద్రుడు mun-īsvarudu. [Skt. from ముని.] n. A venerable saint or hermit.

మును or మున్ను munu. [Tel.] n. The former time, పూర్వము. The beginning of any thing, మొదలు. The end, కడి. మును ముట్టగ to the end, కడపటకు. మునుకట్టు the first or former hill, తొలుకట్టు, పూర్వపర్వతము. adj. First, former, ancient. adv. Formerly, previously, first, పూర్వము. మునుకోసినపైరు the crop first reaped, ముందరిపంట. మునుకొను, మున్కొను, మునుకొను or మున్కొను munu-konu. v. n. To place or have in front, ముందు ఉంచుకొను. మునుకోలు munu-kōlu. n. The act of keeping in front, ముందు ఉంచుకొనుట. మునుమాపు munu-māpu. n. The earlier part of the night. ముంజామము. BD. iii. 269. మునుమును or మునుమున్ను munu-munu. adv. At first. మొట్టమొదట.

మునుకు munuku. [Tel.] v. n. To hesitate, to be at a loss, ఎటులోచకరయుండు, మిరాకరించు. To grieve, సంతాపించు. "మెంగము ప్రాలగనైదిమునుకుచున్న." HD. ii. 2675. To speak in reply, మారుపలుకు. To speak, పలుకు. మునుకువ munukuva. n. An attempt, పూనిక.

మునుగు or మున్గు munugu. [Tel.] v. n. To sink, to be immersed, to plunge; to dive, to go under water. మున్గును. To be depressed, అడగు. మునిగినముక్కు a depressed or snub nose. To perish, to be ruined, నశించు. To be hidden, మరుగుపడు. మునుగుకోడి munugu-kōḍi. n. A water fowl. The little Grebe, *Podiceps albipennis* (F. B. I.). మునుచు or మునుంచు munutsu. v. a. To cause to sink, ముంచివేయు. మునుక munuka. n. Immersion, a plunge or dive. మునుగుట, ముంచివేయుట, మజ్జనము, మునగడము. నీరుమునుకచేలు land liable to inundation.

మునుపు or మున్పు munupu. [Tel.] n. A former time, ముందు, పూర్వము. adv. and postposition. Formerly; before, పూర్వము. వాడు రాకమునుపు before he came. మునుపటి munupaṭi. adj. Former. ముందటి. మునుపే formerly, ముందరనే.

మునుము or మున్ము munumu. [Tel.] n. A field of grain, of which part has been cut. కోయగా మిగిలినచేను. The extent of a crop selected to be reaped, పైరుకోతకొల్ప

రుముకొన్న మిది. The front or van of an army; any thing opposite. సేనాముఖము, ఎదుటిది, ఎదురు, ఎదుటికోటు. Thickness, తరుచుదనము. A series, వరుస. adj. Thick, తరచైన. మునుముకొను *munumu-konu*. v. n. To form a series, వరుసపెట్టు. మునుమిడి *munumi-idi*. adv. Well, properly. తేట్పగా, బాగుగా. "మూడులోకంబుల మునుమిడిమీరు. చూడనియట్టిరాజులుమరిలేరు." HD. i. 113.

మున్నీరు *mun-nīru*. [Tel. మును first + నీరు.] n. The sea, ocean. సముద్రము. మున్నీటి అగ్గి volcanic fire, submarine flame. బడబానలము. ఆమె కన్నీరు మున్నీరుగా వేర్చెను she shed a torrent of tears. "యోష్పప్తి ప్రవృత్తి రాజ్యా." కావ్యాగాను. మున్నీటిచూలి the ocean born, an epithet of Lakshmi.

మున్ను *munnu*. [Tel.] n. A former time, ముందు, మునుపు. The beginning, ఆరంభము. adv. Formerly, erst, before, of old. మునుపు. ఇంతకమున్ను just now, lately. మున్నటియట్ల *munnaṭi-yaṭla*. adv. As usual. మునుపటివలెనే. మున్నడి or మున్నాడి *munn-aḍi*. (మున్ను+అడుగు.) adv. First, at first, before anything else, ముందుగా. "వారిలోన పదతిమొక్కితె మున్నాడి పారుతెంచి." Jaim. v. 125. మున్నరక *munn-araka*. n. The front plough, followed by others. ముందరిదుక్కి. Courage, ధైర్యము.

మున్నూరు *mun-nūru*. [Tel. మూడు+నూరు.] n. Three hundred.

మున్నెరిక *munnerika*. [Tel. మున్ను+ఎరిక.] n. Shrewdness, archness. Outrage, horror. జాణతనము, పూర్వోగాగముపలు కలిగిన విచారము.

ముప్పటిల్లు or ముప్పతిలు *muppaṭillu*. [Tel.] v. n. To cool after boiling. కాగిచల్లారు. "క్రమముగావాడులక్కడను ముప్పటిలిపజలకంబు దివ్యయోచెలుపునుతంచకు." G. iii. 42.

ముప్పది *mup-padi*. [Tel. మూడు + పది.] n. Thirty. త్రింశత్. ముప్పదిరెంటిగుంపు an epithet applied to a lunar mansion called రేవతీనక్షత్రము. ముప్పండ్రు or ముప్పదుగురు *mup-pandru*. n. Thirty persons. ముప్పందుము *mup-pan-dumu*. (మూడు+పది+తూము.) n. Thirty tooms (of grain). ముప్పైతూములు.

ముప్పాతిక *mup-pātika*. [Tel. మూడు+పాతిక.] n. Three quarters.

ముప్పావు *mup-pāvu*. [Tel. మూడు+పావు.] n. Three fourths of anything.

ముప్పావులా *mup-pāvulā*. [Tel. మూడు+పావులా.] n. Three-fourths of a Rupee.

ముప్పిడి *mup-piḍi*. [Tel. మూడు+పిడి.] n. A dagger. బాకు. "పైడిదుప్పటిరయును మొల ముప్పిడియును మణిభూషలయుబొడ్డుమానికంబు." KP. ii. 143.

ముప్పిరి *mup-piri*. [Tel. మూడు+పిరి.] n. Three folds. మూడుపిరులు. adj. Threefold, triple. Of three twists or strands (పురి), as a cord. ముప్పిరిదారము a threefold cord. ముప్పిరిగొను *mup-piri-gonu*. v. n. To redouble or swell. మూడుమార్లు పెనగొను, అతిశయించు. ముప్పిరిగొన్న three-fold, redoubled, vehement. ముప్పిరిగొన్న మోహము redoubled love. ముప్పిరిగొన్న వేడుక exceeding joy. "చలము కోపంబు రోషంబు నీమూడు ముప్పిరిగొనగ" annoyance, anger, and spite united to spur him on. Nala. D. iii. 58. ముప్పిరిచేప or మూంగి ముప్పిరి *muppiri-chēpa*. n. A kind of fish, a species of Sparus, *Mesoprion quinque lineatus*.

ముప్పు *muppu*. [Tel.] n. Old age, వార్ధకము. Danger, peril, మోసము, విపత్తు. "ఇప్పనికిం బోవుట ముప్పొగదాయని." S. iii. 184.

ముప్పూట *mup-pūṭa*. [Tel. మూడు+పూట.] adv. At the three (పూటలు) times; viz., morning, noon, and night: continually. మూడుకాలములయందు, "ముప్పూటనిష్ఠాగ్నిమున జరియించి." BD. vi. 26.

ముప్పై or ముప్ఫయి Same as ముప్పది (q. v.).

ముప్పొంగు *mup-pongu.* [Tel. మూడు+పొంగు.] v. n. To boil over three times, మూడు పొంగులుపొంగు. To be elated (with joy), ఉప్పొంగు.

ముప్పోకలాడు *mup-pokal-āḍu.* [Tel. మూడు+పోకలు+ఆడు.] n. One who manifests the three *gunas* or characteristics, viz., సత్వ, రజస్, తమోగుణములు, i. e., the Universal Spirit, త్రిగుణాత్మకుడు, భగవంతుడు.

ముప్ప్రొద్దు *mup-proddu.* [Tel. మూడు+ప్రొద్దు.] adv. All day long, the livelong day, త్రికాలములయందు. BD. v. 1223.

ముఫస్సలు *muphassalu.* [H.] n. Up-country, provincial, mofussil.

ముబ్బడి, ముమ్మడి or ముమ్మడుగు *mubbaḍi.* [Tel. మూడు+మడుగు.] adj. Threefold, treble, triple. త్రిగుణము. ముబ్బడించు or ముమ్మడించు *mub-baḍintsu.* v. n. To become threefold or trebled. మూడింతలు అగు, ముమ్మడియగు.

ముభావము *mubhavamu.* [H.] adj. Unknown, doubtful, indeterminate.

ముముక్షువు *mumukshuvu.* [Skt.] n. One who desires to give up the world. A sage abstracted from all human passion and feeling. One who is pious, heavenly minded, or devout. మోక్షేచ్ఛగలవాడు.

ముమ్మడి or ముమ్మడుగు See ముబ్బడి.

ముమ్మరము *mummaramu.* [Tel.] n. Vehemence, excess. ఉగ్రము. జ్వరముయొక్క ముమ్మరము the crisis of the fever. జ్వరముయొక్క ముమ్మరము తగ్గినది the vehemence of the ver is now past. అతనికిని యిప్పుడు నిండా ముమ్మరముగానున్నది his star is now in the ascendant. adj. Vehement, excessive. మిక్కిలి అతిశయమైన, ఉగ్రమైన. ముమ్మరముగా *mummaramu-gā.* adv. Vehemently, excessively. మిక్కిలి అతిశయముగా, ఉగ్రముగా. ముమ్మరించు *mummarintsu.* v. n. To grow stronger, redouble, exceed, become violent, to come to its height or crisis. ఉగ్రమగు. జ్వరము ముమ్మరించినది the fever reached its height, maximum, or crisis.

ముమ్మాకు See under మూడు.

ముమ్మొనవాలు *mum-mona-valu.* [Tel. మూడు+మొన+వాలు.] n. A trident, a three pronged weapon. త్రిశూలము. ముమ్మొనవాలు దాలుపు an epithet of Siva.

ముమ్మోటు *mummoṭu.* [Tel. ముమ్+మోటు.] adj. Very rude, coarse or ignorant, మిక్కిలిమోటైన.

మువ్వూరు &c., See under మూడు.

ముర *mura.* [Skt.] n. The name of an Asura. మురారి or మురధ్వంసకుడు *mur-ari.* n. The 'vanquisher of 'Mura' an epithet of Krishṇa, కృష్ణుడు. Also, the name of a Sanskrit poet.

మురకటము *murakaṭamu.* [Tel.] n. The act of turning the face away from or towards a thing, త్రిప్పట. మురకటించు *muraka-ṭintsu.* v. a. To turn, as the face. త్రిప్పు.

మురకము *murakamu.* [Tel.] n. Pride, conceit, నిక్కు, ఉద్ధతి.

మురజము *murajamu.* [Skt.] n. A tabor or small drum. మృదంగము, మద్దెల.

మురబ్బా *murabba.* [H.] v. A conserve, confection.

మురమురలాడు or మురమురమను *mura-mural-āḍu.* [Tel.] v. n. To fume, to evince anger. కోపవికారమునుచూపు.

మురళి *muraḷi.* [Skt.] n. A flute, a pipe. పిల్లనగ్రోవి. A kind of a horse's pace. అశ్వధారావిశేషము. **మురళించు** *muraḷintsu.* v.a. To scorn, set at naught, తిరస్కరించు. "ద్వి॥ ముత్తెపుచిప్పలమురళించుమోము." HD. i. 571.

మురాళించు *muraḷintsu.* [Tel.] v. a. To remove the evil eye or an evil spirit by waving round the head some chilies, &c., and throwing them away, దిగదుడుచు. **మురాళము** *muraḷamu.* n. The act of removing the evil eye, &c. మురాళించుట.

మురి or మురియ *muri.* [Tel.] n. A bit, a piece. A half piece of cloth. "మొగిదమ్మిశరములు మురియలైచెదర." DRY. 1576. adj. Little, small, అల్పము. **మురిమొండెము** *muri-mondemu.* n. A little or small trunk. **మురికోయు** or **మురియకోయు** *muri-konu.* v. a. To cut to pieces, to cut, ఖండించు. **మురిబొంత** *muri-bonta.* n. A sort of sword-fish with an elongated head. **మురిమురి** *muri-muri.* adj. Very little, inconsiderable. కొంచెము కొంచెము. మురిమురిచీకటి slight darkness, చీకటి.

మురి *muri.* [Tel.] n. Pride. గర్వము. A coquettish manner of walking, నడకయందలి కులుకు. **మురించు** or **మురియించు** *murintsu.* v. a. To turn the face about. "వికటభ్రుకుటీయాననముల్ మురింపుచు." P. iii. 159. "కరముగ్రముగ మొగమిటు మురిపించుచుండె." M. X. i. 15. **మురికాడు** *muri-kāḍu.* n. A proud or conceited person, గర్విష్ఠుడు.

మురికి *muriki.* [Tel.] n. Dirt, nastiness, filth, impurity, మాలిన్యము. adj. Dirty, foul. మలినమైన. **మురికినాడు** *muriki-nāḍu.* n. The name of a country.

మురిడీగొలుసు *muriḍi-golusu.* [Tel.] n. A kind of gold chain worn at the wrist, ముంజేతపేనికొను బంగారుగొలుసు.

మురియు *muriyu.* [Tel.] v. n. To exult while walking, నడుచునప్పుడు కులుకు. To exult, rejoice in hope, to evince a strong desire. ఉల్లసించు, ఆశపడు. To turn, తిరుగు. Sar. D. 376. "తొట్రుపల్కులు ముద్దుదొల్కు నవ్వులుగాంచి ముఃపియశోద సమ్మోదమందె." Radha. i. 10. To turn, as the face (మొగము) త్రిప్పు. To break, as the point of a spear, &c. తెగు, విరుగు, తునియలగు. **మురియబడు** *muriya-badu.* v. n. To excel, rejoice, be proud, అతిశయించు. **మురిపము** or **మురిపెము** *muripamu.* n. A proud manner of walking, నడకయందలి కులుకు. Exultation, joy, gladness, gaiety, gracefulness. ముద్దు, ముద్దుతనము. Caressing, fondling, coaxing. ఉల్లాసము, లాలన, శృంగారము, సరసత. Pride, గర్వము, శృంగారగర్వము. **మురిపపు** or **మురిపెపు** *muripapu.* adj. Graceful. సొగసైన. "మురిపపువిరుదవువ్వు." Padma. iii. 13.

మురు *muru.* [Tel.] n. A piece or bit. తునక, as మురుమొండెము. Also same as ముఱ్ఱు (q. v.).

మురుగు *murugu.* [Tel.] n. A bangle, a bracelet: కడియము. కమ్మమురుగులు a wire twisted and worn as an earring.

మురుగు *murugu.* [Tel.] v. n. & a. To putrefy, mortify, rot, decay, కుళ్లు. To pine, languish. **మురుగుడు** *muruguḍu.* adj. Rotten, putrid, putrefied, stinking, మురిగిన, కుళ్లిన, కంపెత్తిన. మురుగుడువాసన a stench, stink. మురుగుడునీరు stagnant water. మురుగుడు నెయ్యి rancid butter. మురుగుడుబోలము land filled with foul water. "మట్టినంటిరులమురుగునెపెపుమ." BD. iv. 84. **మురుగుడుచేప** *muruguḍu-chepa.* n. The Indian flying-fish. Russell. 161. *Trigla volitans.* **మురుత్రోవ** *muru-trova.* (మురుగు+త్రోవ.) n. A dirty stinking road. దుర్గంధపుత్రోవ. **మురగడ** *muragada.* n. Putrid matter.

మురుపు *murupu*. [Tel. from మురియు.] n. Delight, glee, liking. సంతోషించుటయు. See మురయు.

మురువు *muruvu*. [Tel.] n. Beauty, loveliness, grace. సౌందర్యము. Pride, గర్వము. Also, a bangle, మురుగు, కడియము. adj. Beautiful, సుందరమైన.

ముఱ్ఱు or ముఱ్ఱుపాలు *murru*. [Tel.] n. Beestings; milk given by a cow during the first week after calving. ముఱ్ఱుబాము *murru-bāmu*. n. A kind of snake.

ములక *mulaka*. [Tel.] n. The plant called Solanum, or Nightshade. నేలములక *Solanum jacquini*. తెల్లములక *Solanum indicum*. బృహతి.

ములికి or ముల్కి *muliki*. [Tel.] n. An arrow; an arrow head; the peg of a top. బాణము, బాణపుటలుగు, బొంగరమునిముక్కు. "వెండిములికితోడ వెలయుబొంగరము." Pal. 312.

ముల Same as ముల్లు (q. v.). adj. Thorny. ములుకత్తి *mulu-katti*. n. A short knife used for removing thorns. ములుకోల or ములుకోల *mulu-kōla*. n. A goad, ఎద్దులపొడిచేకోల. ములుగోగు *mulu-gōgu*. n. A plant, *Hibiscus suratensis*. ములుగోలిమిడి *mulu-golimidi*. n. A plant bearing a dark black flower, *Capparis spinosa*. కోకిలాక్షము, ఇక్షురము. ములుగోరంట *mulu-gōranta*. n. The plant called *Barleria cristata*. ఝింటి, సైరేయకము. ములుచిత or ముల్లుచిత *mul-uchita*. (ముల్లు+ఉచ్చిత.) n. The name of a herb. ఒకవిధమైన కూరాకు, ముల్లుముస్తె. ములుతారు or ములుతారు *mulu-taru*. n. A kind of snare. "ఆ మృగంబులు మెలగు చోటపట్టులరసి ములుతారుకోయించి, పోనివా రించి." H. N. ii. 16. ములుదోస *mulu-dōsa*. n. The prickly cucumber. *Cucumis muricatus*. కోమశి. ములుబంతి *mulu-banti*. n. See under ముల్లు. ములుమోదుగు *mulu-mōdugu*. n. A tree called *Andersonia rohitaka*. రోహితకవృక్షము. Rox. ii. 213. ములువెంపలి *mulu-vempali*. n. The tree called *Trephosia spinosa*. శరపుంఖ. ములువెలగ *mulu-velaga*. n. The thorny wood-apple tree, దధిత్థకవృక్షము. ములుసూపు *mulu-sūpu*. (ముల్లు+చూపు) v. n. To excel, మీరు. అతిశయించు. ముల్గమి *mul-gami*. n. A cluster of thorns. కంటకసముదాయము.

ములుగు *mulugu*. [Tel. another form of మూలుగు.] v. n. To groan. n. Groaning, a groan. A treasury, a purse, బొక్కసము. ములుగుడు *mulugudu*. n. The tree called *Morinda umbellata*. Ainsl. ii. 253. ములుగుమీను *mulugu-mīnu*. n. A sort of fish.

ములుచ or ముల్చ *mulutsa*. [Tel.] adj. Mean, trifling, slight. తక్కువైన, అల్పమైన. "ఏలవామెయిగమాట మేమియులేక, ములుచ మాటలనన్ను ముదుకజేసెదవు." Dab. 39. n. A mean wretch. అల్పుడు. క్షుద్రుడు. "క॥ చిలుకచదువనుచు చదివిన, ములుచల దృష్టాంతమట్టి మూఢపు దుర్గా, కుల జిలుకలదరిచిన దయు, గలదేమది చెదరవదరుగాక నికేచ్ఛగా." KP. vi. 301. ములుచదనము *mulutsa-danamu*. n. Slightness, meanness. పలుచదనము. "కుల గోత్రములవారి నిలిపి కట్టెలు నీళ్లు మోయించు చుండెదు ములుచదనము." H. ii. 259.

ములుము *mulumu*. [Tel.] n. A stubble field. కోతకోసినపొలము. A field irrigated from wells.

ముల్కి See ములికి.

ముల్కీ *mulkī*. [H.] adj. Pertaining to revenue, as ముల్కీటపా.

ముల్లంగి *mullangi*. [Tel.] n. The radish. *Raphanus sativus*, Rox. i. 569. అడవిము ల్లంగి or కారుపొగాకుచెట్టు. *Blumea lacera*. (Watts.) మూలకము.

ముల్లు *mullu.* [Tel.] n. A thorn, a spur, a prickle. A fish bone, a spine. The tongue of a balance. A small needle or pin, as the hand of a watch or clock. ముల్లిడు to plant thorns. A. iv. 265. ముల్లిడి setting up a hedge. చుట్టూకంపవేసి. ముండ్లు పోయిన గడియారము a clock that has lost its hands. ముల్లాడించు *mull-adintsu.* v. a. To chip (stone with a chisel). To chisel. వడ్లముండ్లు the beards of grain. ముంటికత్తి a sharp instrument to extract thorns with. ముండ్లపంది a porcupine. ముండ్లబంతి or ములుబంతి a cluster of prickers used by thieves. "కత్తెరనిడుము నఖతలు ముండ్లబంతియు నీలికవ్వడమును." BD. v. 676. ముల్లుచూపు or ములుచూపు *mullu-tsūpu.* v. n. To excel, అతిశయించు. To turn the balance, i. e., be superior. ముల్లాకురాయి *mull-āku-rāyi.* (ముల్లు+ఆకురాయి.) n. A rough file. ముల్లుచిత, ములుచిత or ముండ్లమున్తై *mull-uchita.* n. The name of a thorny plant whose leaves are eaten. ఒకవిధమైన కూరాకు.

ముల్లె or ముల్లియ *mulle.* [Tel.] n. A bag, or bundle, (of money, or jewels), a purse or rouleau. Wealth, money, property. మూట, ధనముముడి, ముడుపు.

ముల్లోకము *mul-lōkamu.* [Tel. మూడు+లోకము.] n. The universe, i. e., the three worlds, heaven, earth and hell.

ముల్లయతి *mulla-yati.* [Tel. ముల్లు from ముడి a knot. Skt. యతి.] n. lit. One who ties knots. A hermit who is fond of breeding quarrels, ఒకరొకరికికలహములుముడిపెట్టుముని. An epithet of Nārada.

మువురు or మువ్వురు Same as ముగ్గురు. See under మూడు.

మువ్వ *muvva.* [Tel. మువు+వా.] n. A small bell (such as dancers and post office runners wear). An anklet with small bells. గజ్జె. "మురుగులుకాలిపెండెరలును మువ్వలు మ్రుచ్చినవల్లడాలు." Chenn. ii. 229. మువ్వటపా an express or postal mail carried by runners. Also, a single masted vessel. (Vizag.) మువ్వకోడె *muvva-kōḍe.* n. A bullock in training. కొత్తగా కాడికిగంటకు నలవరచేయెద్దు. మువ్వదోనె *muvva-dōne.* n. A vessel with one keel (as distinguished from కొలదోనె or సంగడిదోనె a shoe dony, which has two keels.) ఒంటి అడుగు పలక గలదోనె.

మువ్వంచె *muv-vantsa.* [Tel. మూడు+పంచె.] n. Three sides. adj. Three-sided. మూడు పంచెలుగల.

మువ్వంటు *muv-vanṭu.* [Tel. మూడు+అంటు.] n. Three pollutions caused by child-births in the same month, నెలకులోపలి మూడు పురుడులు.

మువ్వన్నె *muv-vanne.* [Tel. మూడు+వన్నె.] n. Three colors. మువ్వన్నెమెకము *muv-vanne-mekamu.* (మూడు+వన్నె+మెకము.) n. A royal tiger (literally the tri-colored beast.) పెద్దపులి. మువ్వన్నెవిల్లు *muv-vanne-villu.* n. A rainbow.

మువ్వీసము *muv-vīsamu.* [Tel. మూడు+వీసము.] n. The fraction of three-sixteenths.

మువ్వురు *muvvuru.* [Tel.] pron. Three persons. ముగ్గురు.

మువ్వెట్టి *muv-vetti.* [Tel. మూడు+వెట్టి.] n. Three plagues, all sorts of drudgery. మూడు విధములైన పరిచర్యలు. "కనుముయ్య నెడములేదనగ మువ్వెట్టిగావించెను." BD. iii. 964.

ముషితము *mushitamu.* [Skt.] adj. Stolen, robbed. దొంగిలబడ్డ.

ముష్కము *mushkamu* [Skt.] n. A testicle. వృషణము.

ముష్కరము *mushkaramu.* [Skt.] n. Obstinacy, persistency. మూర్ఖత. adj.

Hard, obstinate, severe, of a sullen saturnine disposition, మూర్ఖమైన. ముష్కరి or ముష్కరుడు mushkari. n. An obstinate, stubborn man, a ruffian, a violent man. మూర్ఖతగలవాడు, క్రిక్కిరిసిన గలవాడు, కుటిలుడు.

ముష్టి mushṭi. [Skt.] n. A fist. The hilt or handle of a sword, పిడి. A handful. పిడికిలి. A handful of grain given as alms, పిడికెడుబియ్యము. ముష్టిపెట్టు to give alms. భిక్షము వేయు. ముష్టియెత్తుకొని బ్రతుకుట to live by alms. ముష్టిమధ్య mushṭi-madhya. n. A slim girl: (lit. slenderwaisted.) "her waist was a handful." (Addison.) ముష్టిచెట్టు the tree called *Strychnos nux vomica* sometimes called the poison nut tree. Rox. i. 575. ముష్టికాంతకుడు mushṭi-kāntakuḍu. n. A name of Balarāma. Dab. 69. ముష్టికాయ mushṭi-kāya. n. The *Nux vomica* or poison unut. ముష్టికాయముచ్చు mushṭi-kaya-mutstsu. n. The Hoopoo: lit. The poison-nut-eater. ముష్టింపచుడు mushṭim-patsuḍu. n. A poor man. ముష్టిచణుడు mushṭi-chaṇuḍu. [Skt.] n. A boxer. జెట్టివాడు.

ముసద్దీ musaddī. [H.] n. A writer, a clerk.

ముసనాబు musanābu. [H.] n. A screen, తెర, తడక. "గొడియ, లలరారు కురువేరుతెరు కుబల్ ముసనాబుపరువంపు పొగడపూబటువు బిండ్లు." Paidim. iii. 77.

ముసముస musamusa. [Tel. anuk.] n. A buzzing noise, ముసురుటలోనగువానియందగు ధ్వని. Sharp anger, చిరచిరలాడుకోపము. ముసముసమను to fume, to be angry; to rustle, as hair. చిరచిరమను, వెండ్రుకలవల్లకల్గుచుప్పుట్టు "ఆరాజు మోముమార్చుచు ముసముసమనుచు రోషాసంబునబలికె." Dab. 139.

ముసర musara. [Tel.] n. Foot and mouth disease in cattle.

ముసరు musaru. [Tel.] v. n. To collect, gather, crowd, settle upon (any object, as flies, or insects): to surround. మూగి కొను, చుట్టుకొను, క్రమ్ము, కవియు.

ముసలము musalamu. [Skt.] n. A club, a pestle. రోకలి, రోకలివంటి ఆయుధము. ముసలాయుధుడు he who is armed with a club. ముసలకిసలయము musala-kisala-yamu. n. "Club blossoms", (an expression similar to "milk from a stone"), the name of a certain book.

ముసలి or ముసిలి musali. [Tel.] adj. Old. ముసలిమనిషి an old person. ముసలిపండు a decrepit person. ముసలివాన the latter rain. n. An old man or woman. మూడుకాళ్లముసలి a crone that hobbles on three legs, i. e., with a staff. plu. ముసల్లు old people. Swa. vi. 57. Pal. 454. ముసలమ్మకథలు an old wife's tales. ముసలితనము musali-tanamu. n. Old age. వృద్ధత్వము.

ముసల్మాను musalmānu. [H.] n. A Mussulman, a Mahomedan.

ముసి musi. [Tel.] adj. False, feigned. బొంకు, అసత్యము. ముసిముసినవ్వు a feigned laugh, a smile, చిరునవ్వు.

ముసించు musintsu. [Tel.] v. n. To become silly or foolish, to be silly, play the fool. చెడు. నీకు ఏల ఇట్లు బుద్ధిముసించినది why are you so silly? వానికి బుద్ధిముసించినది he has lost his wits. వానికి బుద్ధిముసించి ఆ కాగితము ఎత్తి చూచినాడు he was off his guard and took the letter and read it.

ముసిడి, ముసిడికి or ముసిని musiḍi. [from Skt. ముష్టి.] n. The tree called *Strychnos nux vomica*, Rox. i. 573. ముష్టిచెట్టు. "ముసిడిమాకున, నైతమను బండ్లుగల్గించి తెరుకు నంటేల స్పృశింపదగొల్ల." Vaij. iii. 108.

ముసుండి musuṇḍi. [Skt.] n. A wooden club, రొమ్ముగుదియ.

ముసుగు, ముసుకు, ముసువు or ముసుగుగుడ్డ *musugu.* [Tel.] n. A veil, a covering for the head, తలమీదికప్పడము. ముసుకువేసి కొను. ముసుగిడు or ముసుగుపెట్టుకొను to put on a veil, to cover with a veil. "కనకోత్తరీయంబు మేలిముసుంగుగాకేలుంగొల్చ." Ahalya. i. 23. **ముసుగుడు** *musugudu.* n. Covering, కప్పడము, కప్పట. **ముసుగుపడు, ముసుగుడువడు** or **ముసుగుపారు** *musugu-padu.* v. n. To be covered up, కప్పఁబడుట. **ముసుగుబొండ** *musugu-bonda.* n. A small tree of the palm species whose leaves are never cut off, మట్టలు ఊడని తాడిలోనగు చిన్నచెట్టు.

ముసురు *musuru.* [Tel.] n. A constant or continued rain; drizzle, or mizzling rain, విడువకకురియువాన. ముసురు, ముసురు కొను or ముసురుకొనియుండు v. a. & n. To cover as flies or ants do. To surround, to swarm or crowd together, చుట్టుకొను. **ముసురుమూతి** *musuru-mūti.* n. An angry-looking face. ముసురుమూతితనము crossness, ill-humour, peevishness. కోపిష్ఠితనము. ముసురుమూతివాడు a captious, or peevish man, a cross creature. కోపిష్ఠుడు. ముసురుమూతిమాటలు peevish talk.

ముస్త or **ముస్తకము** *musta.* [Skt.] n. A sort of grass, *Cyperus rotundus.* Rox. i. 197, తుంగముస్తె.

ముస్తాబు or **ముస్తీబు** *mustābu.* [H.] n. Equipment, accoutrement. Dressing.

ముస్తీదు *mustīdu.* [H.] n. Readiness. సిద్ధము, అయితము. "స్వారీదరలెడు వేన్కతో సాదిజూచి తెమ్మముస్తీదు ఘటియించితేజనక." UH. iv. 22. adj. Prepared, ready, capable, worthy. **ముస్తీదుగా** *mustidu-gā.* adv. In readiness, ready. సిద్ధముగా. "ఎలదేటికమి మేటి యొలుగోలుమూకల, నెల్లముస్తీదుగా నెచ్చరించి." T. iv. 104. ఔం ముస్తీదుగా, సిద్ధముగా.

ముస్తె *muste.* [Tel.] n. A tree of the *Cyperus* family. మంచిముస్తె or అల్ల్యాము the white Swallow-wort, the Three-lobed Nightshade, *Solanum trilobatum.* (*Linn.*) సముద్రముస్తె *Cyperus speciosus.* (*Heyne.*) తుంగముస్తె *Cyperus rotundus.* (*Heyne.*) తీగముస్తె *Menispermum polycarpon.* Rox. iii. 816,

ముహుః *muhuh.* [Skt.] adv. Again. మాటిమాటికి, మరలమరల. ముహుర్ముహుః, ప్రతిముహుః reiteratedly, over and over. పునఃపునః. ముహుర్భాషః reiteration. మరలమరలపలుకుట.

ముహూర్తము *muhūrtamu.* [Skt.] n. Time; a division of time; a moment; the thirtieth part of a day and night, an hour of forty-eight minutes. కాలము, అల్పకాలము, సం రెండుఘడియలకాలము, ద్వినాడికాకాలము, రెండుగడియలకాలము.

మూ mū

మూ *mū.* In composition, short for మూడు as ముక్కంటి, the next consonant being doubled in such cases.

మూక *mūka.* [Tel. from మూగు.] n. An assembly, a crowd, గుంపు. An army, host, సేన. మూకమీద indiscriminately, in the lump, without details. "కేవిధంబులమూక విరుపులమాటలే చేకొని చెప్పెదరు." Dab. 104. మూకవిరుపులమాటలు, అనగా గుంపు చెదిరిపోతగ్గ మాటలు. **మూకవిప్పు** *mūka-vippu.* adj. Scattering. చెదరగొట్టునది. స్వా. iv.

మూక *mūka.* [Skt.] adj. Dumb. **మూకీకృత** *mūkī-krita.* adj. Stricken dumb. మాట్లాడకుండాచేయబడిన. R. ii. 130. **మూకు** or **మూకుడు** *mūku.* n. A dumb person a miserable wretch. మూగవాడు, దీనుడు.

మూకుడు *mūkudu.* [Tel. మూయు+కుడుక.] n. An earthen platter used as a cover. A cover. మూత. H. v. 12. శరావము. కుండలమూకి కొప్పు మంటిచిప్ప. An earthen cup.

మూకొను mū-konu. [Tel. మూచు or ముక్కు + కొను.] v. n. To smell, to scent. వాసన చూచు. To abscond, to hide oneself. దాగు. "మలికేడ్పుమున్నన మట్టాడెముగనుక, మూకొని పేటికి మూన్నెళ్లువెళ్లె, ఏడబోయిరో యెరుగనో యున్న." Pal. 322.

మూగ mūga. [Tel.] n. A mosquito, దోమ. A kind of bird. Hamsa iii. Dumbness. మూకత్వము. adj. Dumb, మూకఅయిన. మూగవాడు a dumb man. మూగది a dumb woman. మూగయెండ dull, sultry heat. మూగసంజ్ఞలుచేయు to use dumb gestures. కంకటిమూగ the Fork-tailed Shrike. ధూమ్యాటము. మూగెలు mūgalu. n. A sort of cakes. "అటుకులు మూగలలా జలు." H. i. 114. మూగో mūgu n. A dumb man. మూగవాడు. "మూగు, భారతపర్వంబు పఠింపబూనుటసుమీ." G. viii. 2.

మూగు mūgu. [Tel.] v. a. To surround: to settle upon any object (as flies or insects do.) ముసురుకొను, చుట్టుకొను, కవియు. "ఈగలుచీమలుమూగి, మైగలిగిన, చర్మంబురక్త మాంసములుమెసన." N. iv. 95. మూగతీట thick-set itch, దట్టముగాపేలినతీట. మూగా కొను same as మూగు.

మూగుడు Same as ముగ్గురు (q. v.).

మూగెలు mūgelu. [Tel. మూచు+ఎలి.] n. A musk-rat, చుంచు, గంధమూషిక.

మూచూచు mū-tsūtsu. [Tel. మూతి+చూచు.] v. a. To smell, put to the nose. ఆఘ్రాణించు. "వినువాచూచినమూచూచినభోజ్యము నింద్యము." M. XIII. iv. 105.

మూట mūṭa. [Tel.] n. A bundle, a pack. బట్టలలో మెదలైనవాటిముడుపు. ఏమిమూటకట్టుకొని పోబోవుచున్నాము at death what can we carry away with us?

మూడమంచు mūḍa-mantsu. [Tel.] n. Thick or heavy dew, దట్టమైనమంచు.

మూడి mūḍi. [Tel. another form of ముడ్డి.] (q. v.)

మూడు mūḍu. [Tel.] adj. pron. or n. Three. infl. మూటి as అమూటికి to the three. మూట mūṭa. n. ablative. Thirdly, at the third. మూటియందు, మూడవదానియందు. plural మూళ్లు, as పదిమూళ్లు ten times three. మూడుఎత్తులుగాచేసి laying the garland in three festoons. G. xi. 49. మూడుసరములుగాచేసి. ముక్కాక muk-kāku (మూడు+కాక.) n. Oppression, trouble, distress. నిర్బంధము. శ్రమ. "మునులారి మీకింత ముక్కాకలేల సులభంబుగనుముక్తిచొప్పు దెలిపెదను." L. xx. 256. ముక్కాకలుతీరిన thrice proved, thrice tried in the fire, inured; well versed, or experienced. బాగాజతపడి యుండు. ముక్కాని muk-kāni. (మూడు+కాని.) n. The fraction of three కానులు; 9 pies or three sixty-fourths. ముక్కారు muk-kāru. (మూడు+కారు.) n. Three seasons or crops (in a year.) మూడుపంటలు. మూడుభోగములు. "ధరణిని ముక్కారు దరిగనికలిబందె." T. v. 215. ముక్కాలిపీట or ముక్కాలిపీట muk-kāli-pīṭa. (మూడు+కాలి+పీట.) n. A three legged stool or table. A tripod. "ముక్కాలిపీటమీద సొంపలరవసింపజేసి." Rasica. i. 52. ముక్కాలు muk-kālu. (మూడు+కాలు.) n. Three quarters. ముప్పాతిక. Three legs, మూడుకాళ్లు. ముక్కోటిక muk-koṭika. (మూడు+కోటిక.) n. Three cities, త్రిపురములు. ముక్కోటిఏకాదశి muk-kōṭi-ēkādaśi. n. A fast held in honor of Vishnu in the month Margasira. మార్గశిరశుద్ధ ఏకాదశి నాడు తిరుపతిలో స్వామిపుష్కరిణిలో మూడుకోట్ల తీర్థములువస్తున్నవనే ఐతిహ్యమువల్ల ఈపేరువచ్చినది. ముజ్జగము muj-jagamu. (మూడు+జగము.) n. The 'three worlds,' the universe, లోకత్రయము. ముత్తుము mut-tumu. (మూడు+తూము.) n. The measure of three తూములు. మున్నూరు mun-nūru. (మూడు+నూరు.) n. Three hundred. ముప్పది or ముప్పై mup-padi. (మూడు+పది.) n. Thirty. ముప్పందుము mup-pandumu. (మూడు+పది+తూము.) n. Thirty tooms. (తూములు.) ముప్పాతిక mup-pātika. (మూడు+పాతిక.) n. Three quarters. ముప్పావు mup-pāvu. (మూడు + పావు.) n. Three quarters. ముప్పిడి mup-piḍi. (మూడు + పిడి.) n. 'Three handles,' a dagger. ముప్పిరి mup-piri. (మూడు+పిరి.) n. Three twists or strands. adj. Threefold, triple. ముమ్మడి mum-maḍi. (మూడు +మడుగు.) n. Three times as much, threefold, treble, triple. ముమ్మనుమడు mum-manumaḍu. (మూడు+మనుమడు.) n. A great grandson. ముమ్మారు mum-māru. (మూడు +మారు.) n. Three times. ముమ్మూడు mum-mūḍu. (మూడు + మూడు.) n. Three times three, మూడుమూళ్లు, తొమ్మిది. ముయ్యేరు muy-yēru. (మూడు+ఏరు) n. Three streams, an epithet of the Ganges. "ముందరనున్నది ముయ్యేరుచేల." HD. ii. 3. ముల్లోకము mul-lōkamu. (మూడు+లోకము.) n. Three worlds, i. e., the earth, heaven and the nether world. మువ్వీసము muv-vīsamu. (మూడు+వీసము.) n. The fraction of three-sixteenths. మువ్వురు or ముగ్గురు muv-vuru. (మూడు+వారు.) n. Three persons. మూడో or మూడవ mūḍō. adj. The third. మూడోదినము the third day, i. e., the next day but one.

మూడు mūḍu. [Tel.] v. n. To happen, to befall. కలుగు, సరిపడు. To end, close, terminate, అంతమగు. వానికి చావుమూడినది he is sure to die. వానికి ఆయువుమూడినది his days are ended. "ఈమునివృత్తులకిప్పుడు మూడె." HD. i. 1629. మూడించు or మూడ్చు mūḍutsu. v. a. To cause to happen, మూడజేయు, కలిగించు. మూడుపు mūḍupu. n. The name of a certain plant. H. iv. 11.

మూఢము mūḍhamu. [Skt.] adj. Dull, stupid, foolish, ignorant. అవివేకమైన. మూఢభక్తి superstition, blind faith, simple reliance. మూఢభక్తుడు a superstitious man. మూఢత్వము mūḍhatvamu. n. Dullness, stupidity. అవివేకము. మూఢుడు mūḍhuḍu. n. An ignorant man, తెలివితేలనివాడు. A fool, simpleton. అవివేకి. A boy or child, బాలుడు.

మూత mūta [Tel. from మూయు.] n. Shutting, closing, covering, మూయుట. A cover, lid, top. A valve, any little door as that of a lantern. The cover or parchment of a drum. మూయునది. మూతపడు or మూతలుపడు mūta-paḍu. v. n. To be closed, మూసికొనిపోవు. అతనిచెవులు మూతలుపడినవి his ears were stunned, his ears tingled. మూతపోడువు mūta-poḍuvu. n. A kind of game. ఒకఆట. "దాయాలుసొగటాలు చాత్రాయి చదరంగములు కోటురాళ్లును, మూతపోడువు, వామనగుంటలు." H. iii. 191. మూతబల్ల mūta-balla. n. A sheathing plank that closes up the ends of the rafters of a pent roof. ఇంటిముంగారును మూయుబల్ల, వాసోరుపట్టె.

మూతము mūtamu. [Skt.] n. A pillow used by a king to rest his arms on, రాజులు చేతిక్రిందనుంచుకొను తలగడ. adj. Tied, bound, కట్టబడిన.

మూతి mūti. [Tel.] n. Mouth, నోరు. Face, ముఖము. పిరంగిమూతి the muzzle of a gun. మూతిమీదకొట్టు to give a slap on the mouth.

మూత్రము *mūtramu.* [Skt.] n. Urine. ఉచ్చ. నీరు, కాలుమడి. **మూత్రకృచ్ఛ్రము** *mūtra-krichchhramu.* n. The disease of stone in the bladder. Diabetes. అశ్మరి, మూత్రద్వారమందు రాయి పెరిగెడి రోగము, నీరుడి రోగము. **మూత్రించు** *mūtrinchu.* v. n. To pass urine.

మూదల or **మూదలిక** *mūdalu.* [Tel. మూల+ తెలు.] n. Proof, ascertainment. నిరూపణము, తార్కాణ. **మూదలించు** *mudalinchu.* v. a. To prove, to ascertain. నిరూపించు, తార్కాణించు, ముదలకించు, ఎచ్చరించు. "ఉ॥ పాండునృపాగ్రనందనుడు పావనియుం గవలుంగొజలంబులై, కొండొరులమూదలించుకొని యొక్కటదాకిన." M. VIII. ii. 20. **మూదలింపు** *mūdalimpu.* n. Proof, assertion. తార్కాణము.

మూన *mūna.* [Tel.] n. The chaff of castor oil seeds, &c., the larger particles that will not pass through in straining. వస్త్రగాలితము చేయగా రాలక నిలిచినది. రాగులు ఆముదాలు మెలురాని కాగా మిగిలినపొల్లు. **మూను** *mūnu.* v. a. To strain, as flour through a piece of cloth, వస్త్రగాలితము చేయు.

మూపు *mūpu.* [Tel.] n. The shoulder. భుజము. "కుడిమూపుపైచిన్నిగొడుగు చెన్నొదవ డాపల గమండలుదండములు వెలుంగ." Padma. vii. 176. "నీవలమూపులావు. ముమ నేలవహించిన నాగకూర్మగోత్రావనిభృద్దిశాకరుల కారెయమూరట పట్టుగాద." M. IV. ii. 191. **మూపురము** *mūpuramu.* n. A bull's hump. ఎద్దుయొక్క భుజశిరము, కకుదము.

మూయు *mūyu.* [Tel.] v. a. To shut, close, cover. To close in, as darkness. తలుపు మూయుము shut the door. వాని కన్నులు మూయుము shut his eyes. పెట్టె మూయుము shut the box. నేనేనతప్పు మూసిపెట్టిన దాగునా? will a fault remain concealed, however much we may try to do so? రెప్పలుమూసి యుమూయక with half closed eyelids. అంధకారము మూసికొనినది darkness gathered. తోలుమూసినపెట్టె a box covered with leather. **మూయించు** *mūyinsu.* v. a. To cause to shut or close. మూయునట్లుచేయు. **మూసికొను** *mūsi-konu.* v. a. To close. కండ్లుమూసికొను to close the eyes: to die, నోరుమూసుకో hold your tongue.

మూర *mūra.* [Tel.] n. The lower arm. The length of the forearm, a cubit. ఆ గుడ్డను మూరలు వేసినాడు he measured the cloth with his arm or in cubits. ఈబట్టకు మూరాలేదు వెడల్పూలేదు the cloth is deficient both in length and width. మూరకోక long cloth, బారుచీర. **మూరకోల** *mūra-kōla.* n. A measuring rod, గజపుకోల.

మూరు *mūru.* [Tel.] v. n. To be full, to teem. నిండారు. "సారాస్వాదనప్రాప్తమించు కముదృష్టింబొసిసంకీర్ణచాగా మూరింబోనిక్రించి పొంగెడు ధనప్పుందంపుధారోష్ణమింపారంగ్రోలి." A. vi. 29. టీ॥ మూరింబో, అనగా సంపూర్ణమగు నట్టుటికి. To excel, increase, అతిశయించు. **మూరిపోవు** *mūri-pōvu.* v. n. To excel, increase, అతిశయించు, వర్ధిల్లు. విజృంభించు. To succeed, be successful, సఫలమగు. To be ruined, నశించు. **మూరుకొండ** *mūru-konda.* n. The name of a certain tree, రూపగంధచెట్టు.

మూరుతము or **మూర్తము** Same as ముహూర్తము. (q. v.)

మూర్కొను or **మూరుకొను** *mūr-konu.* [Tel.] v. a. To nose, put to the nose, smell. ఆఘ్రాణించు. To smell a child's head, (equivalent to kissing it).

మూర్ఖము *murkhamu.* [Skt] adj. Irrational, brutish, senseless, stupid, stubborn, obstinate, అవివేకమైన, పిచ్చిపట్టుగల. **మూర్ఖత** or **మూర్ఖత్వము** *mūrkhata.* n. Stubbornness, stupidity, senselessness. అవివేకము, పిచ్చిపట్టు. **మూర్ఖుడు** or మూర్ఖు

mūrkhuḍu. n. A fool, an obstinate blockhead. అవివేకి.

మూర్ఛ *mūrchha*. [Skt.] n. A swoon, fainting, an epileptic fit. సొమ్మ, స్మృతి తప్పుట, స్మారకము తప్పడము. మూర్ఛపోవు *mūrchha-pōvu*. v. n. To swoon. మూర్ఛ తెలిసినది the swoon went off, he recovered his senses. మూర్ఛన *mūrchhana*. n. Fainting, swooning. A cadence or dying fall in music. సంగీతమందు క్రమముగా స్వరారోహణావరోహణములు. HD. i. 865. మూర్ఛరోగము *mūrchha-rōgamu*. n. Fainting, a fit. స్మారకము తప్పు రోగము. మూర్ఛాలుడు *mūrchhaluḍu*. n. One who is subject to fits, మూర్ఛరోగము గలవాడు. మూర్ఛితుడు *mūrchhituḍu*. n. One who has fainted, మూర్ఛిల్లినవాడు. మూర్ఛిల్లు or మూర్ఛిలు *mūrchhillu*. v. n. To swoon or faint, స్మారకముతప్పు, సొమ్మసిల్లు.

మూర్తి *mūrti*. [Skt.] n. The body, శరీరము. A figure, form, body in general, or any definite shape, or image. ప్రతిమ. Matter, substance, a divine hypostasis or person. త్రిమూర్తులు the Hindu Triad, i. e., Brahma, Vishṇu, and Siva. కృష్ణమూర్తి the god Krishna, or an image of Krishna. అతడు న్యాయమూర్తి he is justice in human form. వాడు భీకరమూర్తి he is an absolute fright or horrible figure. వాడు సౌందర్య మూర్తియైయుండెను he was beauty personified. వాడు పాపమూర్తి he was all sin. మూర్తిమంతుడు *mūrti-mantuḍu*. n. One who has bodily form. శరీరి. మూర్తిమత్ *mūrti-mat*. adj. Material, corporeal, substantial, solid, having shape. మూర్తీకరించు *mūrti-karintsu*. v. n. To assume a visible form, శరీరముగు. మూర్తము *mūrtamu*. adj. Solid, material, endowed with form or shape. స్వరూపముగల, కఠినమైన.

మూర్ధము *mūrdhamu*. [Skt.] n. The head. తల. మూర్ధాభిషిక్తుడు *mūrdh-abhishiktuḍu*. n. One who is anointed, i. e., an enthroned king: an emperor. పట్టాభిషిక్తుడైనరాజు.

మూల *mūla*. [Tel.] n. A corner, దిక్కు. An angle. కోణము. A retreat. గొంది. A braid, or tress. కొప్పు. కేశబంధము. An airt or point of the compass, దిక్కు. మూల యిల్లు a corner house. మూలవేయు *mūla-rēyu*. v. a. To lay aside, put by, throw aside, neglect. ఇది యేమూలకు వచ్చును this will not suffice at all, ఎంతమాత్రము చాలదు. మూరు మూలను in a bye place. మూలనుండేవానిని నడిమంటికి లాగుడునెందుకు why draw a man out of his corner into the centre of the court, i. e., why pick a quarrel with a quiet man who is sitting still. మూల or మూలా నక్షత్రము [Skt.] n. The nineteenth of the lunar mansions. మూలమట్టము or మూలమట్టపుపలక *mūla-maṭṭamu*. [Tel.] n. A carpenter's square కట్టవానిఅరుగుధము, గోడలమూలలందు సరిచూచు మట్టపలక. మూలమాను *mūla-mānu*. n. A bracket (fixed in the wall and used as a stand), కుండలు మొదలైనవాటిని పెట్టుటకు గోడ మూలలో ఇరికించినమాను. మూలరాయి or మూలరా *mūla-rāyi*. n. A diamond. "అందలి మూలరావసుల యందదు చిత్రములో." Satya. i. 6. మూలరేడు *mūla-rēḍu*. n. The lord or king of the S-W. corner, an epithet applied to Kubēra. కుబేరుడు, నిరృతి.

మూలగ *mūlaga*. [Tel.] n. The marrow in a bone. ఎముకనడిమి సారము. మజ్జ.

మూలము *mūlamu*. [Skt.] n. A root, వేరు. Origin, commencement, beginning మొదలు. Capital, principal, సంచిమొదలు. A text, as opposed to its commentary. శాకలమూనకు మూలమెవరు who was the beginning of this quarrel? ఆది సమూల నాశనమైనది it is ruined, root and branch. ఋషిమూలము నదీమూలము విచారింపరాదు you must not inquire into the origin of a Rishi or of a river. ఆసంగతిని ఆమూలాగ్రము గా విచారించినాను I examined it thoroughly. Means, an instrument. In Algebra, the root of a quantity. adj. Radical, main, principal, primeval. ప్రధానమైన. మూల విగ్రహము the chief image in a temple. మూలకము mûlakamu. n. The horse radish. ముల్లంగి. మూలదుంప the principal root. మూలముగా mûlamu-gâ. adv. Through, by means of, ద్వారా. మూలధనము mûla-dhanamu. n. Capital, principal, stock. పెట్టుబడి. మూలబంధము mûla-bandhamu. n. A foundation, పునాది. మూలభూతము mûla-bhûtamu. adj. Original. ప్రధానమైన. మూలభూతుడు mûla-bhûtuḍu. n. One who is the origin. ప్రధానుడు. మూలముట్టు or మూలముట్టు mûla-muṭṭu. adv. Entirely, ఆమూలముగా. మూలవ్యాధి or మూలశంక mûla-vyâdhi. n. The disease called piles. రక్తమూలము bleeding piles, hæmorrhoids. Ainslie. మూలస్థానము mûla-sthânamu. n. The shrine in a temple. మూలవిగ్రహము ఉండు స్థలము. మూలాధారము mûl-âdhâramu. n. The basis or source. The bottom. The chief support. The Sacrum. The coccyx.

మూలిక mûlika. [Skt.] n. A root. Any medicinal root. మందువేరు. See మూలము.

మూలుగు or మూల్గు mûlugu. [Tel.] v. n. To groan, to moan, to make a noise or sound. రోగి ఆశక్తివల్ల ముక్కులుగుండా చప్పుడు చేయుట. విత్తము పెక్కుసముగా మూలుగుచున్నది the money is lying idle. Vasu. ii. 11. n. A groan, moan, grunt. రోగి ఆశక్తివల్ల ముక్కులగుండా చేసే చప్పుడు మూలుగుమాను mûlugu-mânu. n. A tree, called *Morinda bracteata*. Rox. i. 544. Wight, plate 126. అంబుడపలి.

మూల్యము mûlyamu. [Skt.] n. Price, wages, hire. వెల, ధర, కూలి, జీతము.

మూవ Same as మువ్వ or మూగ (q. v.).

మూవురు Same as ముగ్గురు (q. v.).

మూషకము or మూషికము mûshakamu. [Skt.] n. A rat, or mouse. మూషకేంద్రతురంగుడు he whose steed is the rat, i. e., Gaṇêsa.

మూస mûsa. [from Skt. మూష.] n. A crucible. లోహములుకరిగేపాత్రము.

మూసా mûsâ. [Fr.] n. Monsieur, Mr. మూసాబూసీ Monsieur Bussy.

మూసాంబరము mûsâmbaramu. [Tel.] n. The Socotrine Aloes of commerce. (Watts.) *Aloe succotrina* (Lam). & *A. perryi* (Baker.)

మూసిక mûsika. [Tel.] n. A tube of gold on either side of the Tali (తాళిబొట్టు), through which the string passes.

మృ mri

మృగము mrigamu. [Skt.] n. An animal in general, పశువు. A wild animal. క్రూరమగు జంతువు. A deer, gazelle, antelope. జింక, లేడి. పశుపక్షిమృగములు cattle, birds, and beasts. మృగగ్రీవుడు a certain demon, having the neck of an antelope. మృగనయన a gazelle-eyed girl, having eyes bright and black as those of fawn. మృగతృష్ణ mriga-trishṇa. n. A mirage; vapour that looks like water in the distance. ఎండమావి. మృగదంశకము mriga-damśakamu. n. The deer-seizer, i. e., a dog. కుక్క. A bear, ఎలుగుగొడ్డు. మృగధూర్తకము mriga-dhûrtakamu. n. The deer-snarer, i. e., a fox. నక్క. మృగ

నాభి or మృగమదము mriga-nābhi. n. Musk, produced by the muskdeer. కస్తూరి. మృగపతి or మృగరిపువు mriga-pati. n. The lord of beasts: a lion, సింహము. మృగయ mrigaya. n. The chase: hunting. వేట. మృగయుడు mrigayudu. n. A huntsman, a man of the woods. వేటకాడు, బోయడు. మృగవాహనుడు mriga-vāhanudu. n. The deer-bearer, i. e., a breeze, as bearing the deer along. వాయువు. జింకరవుతు. మృగశిర or మృగశీర్షము mriga-sira. n. The name of the fifth lunar mansion. అగ్రహాయణి, మృగశిరానక్షత్రము. మృగాంకుడు mrig-ankudu. n. The 'fawn bearer': he who has a deer for his banner or ensign, చంద్రుడు. మృగాజీవము, మృగాదనము or మృగాదము mrigā-jīvamu. n. The fawn-eater, i. e., a leopard. సివంగి. చిరుత. "హరిపుండరీక మృగాదభల్లూక." SD. vi. 15. మృగాజీవుడు mrigā-jīvudu. n. A huntsman, బోయవాడు. మృగాక్షి or మృగేక్షణ mrig-ākshi. n. A woman with eyes like a gazelle, a beautiful lady, లేడికండ్లవంటి కండ్లుగలది. మృగి mrigi. n. A female antelope, పెంటిలేడి. మృగీమదము mrigi-madamu. n. Musk, produced by the మృగి, కస్తూరి. H. iv. 1. మృగేంద్రము or మృగేంద్రుడు mrig-ēndramu. n. The lord of beasts, i. e., the lion, సింహము.

మృగ్యము mrigyamu. [Skt.] adj. Fit to be sought, or inquired for. వెదకదగినది. మృగ్యతముడు mrugya-tamudu. n. He who is eminent, not to be overlooked. "మృగ్యతముఁడువానివెదకి పెద్దగొంచితెచ్చుఁగాక." KP. v. 250.

మృడుడు mridudu. [Skt.] n. A name of Siva. శివుడు. మృడాని mridāni. n. An epithet of Pārvati. పార్వతి.

మృణాళము mrinālamu. [Skt.] n. The stem of a lotus. తామరతూడు.

మృతి mriti. [Skt. mri = to die.] n. Death. చావు. మృతిబొందు mriti-bondu. v. n. To die. చచ్చు. మృతుడు mritudu. n. One who is deceased, or dead. చచ్చినవాడు. జీవన్మృతుడు dead while alive. మృతము mritamu. adj. Dead, expired. చచ్చిన. మృతమనుష్యుడు a dead man. మృతనష్టము mrita-nashtamu. adj. Dead, merged, extinct, as a family or heirship. వారు మృతనష్టమైపోయినారు the family became extinct. మృత్యువు mrityuvu. n. Death. మరణము. The god of death, కృతాంతుడు, మరణాధిదేవత. మృత్యుంజయుడు mrityunjayudu. n. The victor over death, i. e., Siva. మృత్యుసూతి mrityu-sūti. n. That which bears young, and then dies, i. e., the crab, which, like the viper, is supposed to be destroyed by its young. పీత.

మృత్తు or మృత్తిక mrittu. [Skt.] n. Earth, clay, soil, మన్ను. మృత్స or మృత్స్న mritsa. n. Rich soil, fine soil, sweet earth. మంచిమన్ను.

మృదంగము mridangamu. [Skt.] n. A tabret, tabor, small drum, double drum. మద్దెల.

మృదువు mriduvu. [Skt.] adj. Soft, smooth, mild, gentle, tender, మెత్తని. మృదుస్వభావముగలవాడు a gentle or mild man. మృదులము mridulamu. adj. Soft, smooth. మెత్తని.

మృద్వీక mridvika. [Skt.] n. A grape. ద్రాక్ష.

మృధము or మృథము mridhamu. [Skt.] n. A battle, యుద్ధము.

మృష mrisha. [Skt.] n. A falsehood, an untruth, అనృతము, అసత్యము, అబద్ధము. మృషామృధము mrisha-mridhamu. n. A tournament or mock battle, a sham fight

మృష్టము *mrishtamu.* [Skt.] adj. Cleaned, cleansed. మృష్టాన్నము *mrisht-annamu.* n. Pleasant food, a delicate morsel, సుభోజనము.

మె me

మెంగ *menga.* [Tel.] n. An affix used with the word నోరు as నోరుమెంగ mouthless, నోరులేని.

మెంచె *mentsa.* [from Skt. మ్లేచ్ఛ.] n. A foreigner, మ్లేచ్ఛుడు. A Turk. తురక.

మెంఢము *menthamu.* [Mahrati.] n. A ram. పొట్టేలు. "రణములో సైనికులకు కాలంబు రెల్ల. దెస తలకుళమించెవర్ధ్దేపుకరుణ, బాల్పెదక్షుండు వీరవ్యధా బలమున, గండనాశాగ్రమునమండ మెంఢశిరము." Kasi Khand. vii. 139.

మెండు *mendu.* [Tel.] n. Abundance, excess. ఆధిక్యము, అతిశయము. కల్లపనిండిక కాంతిమెండు tinsel is abundantly bright, false gold glitters finely. adj. Much, abundant, అధికము. మెండుకొను *mendu-konu.* v. n. To abound, exceed, redound, overflow; to grow, swell. అతిశయించు, నిండుకొను, అధికమగు. "మెండుకొనుఘీంకృతులు." Anirud. iv. 61. మెండుకొలుపు *mendu-kolupu.* v. a. To cause to abound. మెండుగా *mendu-ga.* adv. Much, excessively, greatly. మెండొడ్డు *mend-oddu.* v. n. To rebel. ఎదిరించు, అలస్యముచేయు. "మాటిమాటికిమగనితో మెండొడ్డిచలపాదితనమున వలికియుండు." T. iv. 35.

మెండెము or మెండీడము *mendemu.* [Tel.] n. A ring worn on the index finger. మెండీడు *mend-idu.* n. The index finger, చూపుడువ్రేలు.

మెంతి or మెంతులు *menti.* [Tel.] n. The herb called Fenugreek. *Trigonella fœnum græcum.* మెంతిమజ్జిగ *menti-majjiga.* n. Buttermilk seasoned with fenugreek. తేమనము, తిరుగబోతచేసినమజ్జిగ.

మెకము or మెగము *mekamu.* [from Skt. మృగము.] n. A beast. See మృగము. An antelope, జింక. జడమెకము the long tressed beast, i. e., the lion, సింహము. మెకములతిండి *mekamula-tindi.* n. A leopard, సివంగి. మెకములరేడు *mekamula-rēdu.* n. A lion.

మెకమెకపడు *meka-meka-padu.* [Tel.] v. n. To be puffed up with pride. ఉల్లిపడు, గర్వపడు, ఉద్ధతినొందు. "క॥ ఒకనాడుపాండునీ సి, దకుడబ్బాటరుసుదండుముటయుచమ్మేలా, త్రైతు త్రైగమున్నించిన, మెకమెకపడతెల్లపలుకుమీాతిగ రే ఫుణా." M. XIII. iii. 369. మెకమెకపాటు *meka-meka-pātu.* n. Pride, elation. ఉబ్బు, గర్వము, ఉద్ధతి. "చ॥ ఒకపెను జాపరేడు తేలమొప్పరసాతలసీమకుంజకో, రక ములభూతధాత్రికిసురల్ దివికిం బగదీయనట్టుగా, మెకమెకపాటుతోడ నిను గ్రింగకపోరెవ్వడుం త్రిలోకకంటకుడవు గానసీయొడలునజ్జగ సేవకురం గలాంగనా." Swa. iii. 59. టీ॥ మెకమెక పాటు. మిడిసిపాటు.

మెక్కు *mekku.* [Tel.] v. a. To eat. To swallow, gobble, తిను.

మెగము See మెకము.

మెచ్చు *metsu.* [Tel.] v. a. To applaud, commend, praise, approve, శ్లాఘించు. ఒప్పుకొను. అపనికి మెచ్చి approving that act. "శ్రీవహించపలుకుల శివుడు మెచ్చండు." Raghava Pandav. iii. 25. n. Praise, approbation, applause, commendation. మెప్పు, శ్లాఘనము, అనుగ్రహము, ప్రీతి, బహుమానము. మెచ్చుపడెను he was applauded. adj. Praiseworthy, శ్లాఘ్యము. మెచ్చుకొను *metsu-konu.* v. a. To praise, approve, commend. శ్లాఘించు, కొనియాడు. మెచ్చులపెట్టు *metsula-*

chettu. n. The admirable tree, an epithet applied to the కల్పవృక్షము. మెచ్చులాడి metstsul-ādi. n. A woman who is fit to be admired, మెచ్చుకొనదగిన ఆడుది. మెచ్చులాడు metstsul-ādu. n. One who is fit to be admired, మెచ్చుకొనదగినవాడు. మెరమెచ్చు mera-metstsu. (మెచ్చు+మెచ్చు.) n. Great praise or approbation, entire satisfaction. మిక్కిలిమెచ్చు. See మెచ్చు.

మెటిక or మెట్టిక meṭika. [Tel.] n. A snap or crack (of the fingers, toes, &c.) చిటిక. A step, సోపానము. మొగనిచూచి మెటికలు విరిచినది she snapt her fingers at her husband.

మెట్ట or మిట్ట meṭṭa. [Tel.] n. Rising ground, high lying land, uplands. A hill, a rock. ఉన్నతభూమి, గుబ్బ, పర్వతము, దిబ్బ. The foot, పాదము. Dry land as opposed to మడి or మాగాణి land artificially irrigated. సారంగమెట్ట the hill at Rajahmundry on which Sārangadhara was slain. "ఇట్ట లంబుగమీదబుట్టలు పెరిగి మెట్టలక్రియనున్న యుట్టిసన్నములు." BD. iii. 2141. మెట్టజీలుగు meṭṭa-jīlugu. n. A species of జీలుగు. (q. v.). మెట్టతామర meṭṭa-tāmara. n. The plant called *Cassia alata*, or *Senna alata*. Rox. ii. 349. మెట్టపంట a dry crop, a crop raised on land which is solely dependent on rain. మెట్టమడుగు a lake among hills, or on rising ground, కొండమడుగు. మెట్టమార్గము the upper road, మెరకమార్గము. A land route (in opposition to సముద్రమార్గము "by water.") మెట్టనాలుపిట్ట or మెట్టవాల్పిట్ట meṭṭa-vālu-piṭṭa. n. A fowl, కోడి.

మెట్టెయు See మెట్టె.

మెట్టు meṭṭu. [Tel.] v. a. & n. To step, walk, tread. అడుగుపెట్టు, నడుచు, త్రొక్కు. "మెల్ల మెల్లన మెట్టుమడుగులకి అల్లనల్లనతలుపులందడు కేల." BD. iv. 1523. To tread on, to trample on. To kick, to thrust with the foot. To wear, as sandals. తొక్కు, కాలితో తన్ను, పాదుకలుధరించు. "పదయుగ్మములందు క్రుంకిడిత రేయుద్వీపముల్ మెట్టినారు." Swa. i. 26. "నీళ్లమునుగనేల జలధిమెట్టగనేల మునిగి తేల్పులకును మొక్కనేల." Vema. iii. 259. n. Treading, త్రొక్కుట. A step of a ladder or stair, సోపానము. A step, grade, degree, rank. A mount, a hill, తిప్ప, కొండ. The total, పెరసి. A custom house, సుంకముపుచ్చుకొనుచోటు. A stop on the lute, వీణెపరకట్టు. Curds mixed with water, as పులిమెట్టు sour curds, పుల్లనిమజ్జిగ. మెట్టు a shoe, slipper. పాదరక్ష. plu. మెట్లు sandals, పావకోళ్లు. మెట్టించు meṭṭintsu. v. n. To lead, to make one walk, to cause to be trampled. To suggest, to stir the mind. నడిపించు, తొక్కించు. To kill, చంపు. "మింటికెగ్రా సినమ్రాత కాలిమిని లో మెట్టించినమున్నీవునా యింటికి బుట్టెదవంచుకంసుడులో డికిహింసించె నియున్నలిక." B. X. 102. మెట్టిక meṭṭika. n. A step, మెట్టు, సోపానము. See also మెటిక. మెట్టిమల్లాడు meṭṭi-mall-ādu. v. a. To trample down or all over, to ruin, నాశనముచేయు, ధ్వంసముచేయు. "కర్షంబుల కట్టడలకులోనుగాక మాయలను మెట్టి మల్లాడి నిర్గలలింగసేవ నెట్టికక్షిభుటించు." L. xvi. 229. మెట్టుకు meṭṭu-ku. adv. On the whole, altogether. In fact, in all, at the most, at least, at any rate. In short, at the best or worst, once for all, finally, at last, in the end, after all, withal, yet still. తుదకు. మెట్టుకుపోయినాడు of course he is gone. మెట్టినిల్లు (మెట్టిన + ఇల్లు). the mother-in-law's house, ఆడుదాని అత్తగారిల్లు. మెట్టుబ్రాలు sacred rice, తలబ్రాలు.

మెట్టె, మెట్టెయు or మట్టె meṭṭe. [Tel.] n. A ring worn on the toe, a toe ring, కాలివేలికిపెట్టేసొమ్ము.

మెట్లు See under మెట్టు.

మెడ or మెడకాయ meḍa. [Tel.] n. The neck, కంఠము, గళము. మెడమీదిజంధెము the Brahminical cord worn over the shoulder. మెడగోంకులు the collar bones. మెడమకట్టు to tie on the neck, i. e., to oblige, to constrain. ఈ ముసలిదానిని నా మెడమ కట్టిపోయినాడు he left the old woman as a weight upon my neck. మెడబట్టినూకు to push by the neck. మెడమలిగాడు meḍa-muli-gāḍu. n. The bird called the Wryneck. మెడనూలు meḍa-nūlu. n. A necklace made of gold threads plaited together. మెడవిరుపుప్రశ్నలు teasing questions. నీకు మెడవాచినదిమొదలు ever since I took you for my husband. మెడవెంపు the back of the neck. మెడవిరుకు n. A neck-break, i.e., a puzzle or jaw-breaker. మెడ పిసుకు v. To press the neck, to throttle. మెడపిసికి చంపినాడు he strangled him. మెడ మలుచు, i.e., to twist the neck. మెడేవాలు, మడివాలు or మడివేలు meḍa-vālu. n. A washerman, a washer-woman, చాకలవాడు, చాకలిది.

మెడిదము meḍidamu. [Tel.] n. Noise, sound. ధ్వని.

మెదుడ meḍuḍa. [Tel.] n. Sour buttermilk. పులిమజ్జిగ.

మెణకరి meṇakari. [Tel.] n. A bachelor, బ్రహ్మచారి.

మెణత meṇata. [Tel.] n. A twig. మెల్లె. "మెండుగాపసులకు మెణతల్లించి." Pal. 460.

మెతక or మెతుక metaka. [Tel.] adj. Slack, loose, soft, free from gravel (as soil). మెతకనేల soft soil. మెతకమనిషి a soft creature. మెతకయెద్దు a dull ox.

మెతుకు or మెదుకు metuku. [Tel.] n. A grain of boiled rice, food, a morsel. దానికి మెతుకుదొరకదు she cannot eat a bit. మింగమెతుకు మెతుకులేదు మీసాలకుసంపెంగనూనె, i. e., he has fragrant oil for his whiskers while he has not a morsel to eat. రెండుమెతుకులుతిన్నారు they took a mouthful, they ate a morsel.

మెత్త metta. [Tel.] adj. Soft, mild, gentle, మెత్తని, మృదువైన. n. Bedding, a mattress, cushion, pad. పరుపు, సాగరముగాచే రొద్దు. గంతమీదిపరుపు. A saddle or numdah, గుర్రపుపల్లము. మెత్తగా metta-gā. adv. Softly, slowly. మృదువుగా. మెత్తగా పిండికొట్టు to pound or beat fine. మెత్త గిల్లు metta-gillu. v. n. To become soft, మెత్తనగు. మెత్తడి mettaḍi. n. A sprat, a small inferior fish. ఒకచేప. మెత్తన mettana. n. Softness, మృదుత్వము. Mildness, slowness. శాంతి. "చిత్తంబు లోగల శత్రుచేయుంచు, కత్తికిమెత్తనగలదెరుంగరైన." Sar. D. 584. చెయ్యిమెత్తనచేయు to grease one's palm or to bribe. adj. Soft, gentle, మృదువైన. adv. Softly, straight, తిన్నగా. మెత్తని mettani. adj. Soft, mild, slow, yielding, meek, మృదువైన. మెత్తనివాడు a soft, patient man. మెత్తపడు or మెత్తబారు metta-paḍu. v. n. To soften. మృదువగు. To be mollified, yield, శాంతపడు. అణగు. మెత్తపాటు metta-pāṭu. n. Softness, మృదుత్వము. Delay, ఆలస్యము.

మెత్తు mettu. [Tel.] v. a. To lay on or apply, to daub, as plaster or mud, &c. దళముగాపూయు, దట్టముగాపూయు. "పట్టెవేల్ల మడచికట్టె శ్రీగంధంపుటడుసుమెత్తి." KP. vi. 284. గోడకు మన్ను మెత్తిరి they plastered the wall with mud. "మదదులింపపురోంపిమెత్త నాడు." Swa. iv. 109. n. Plaster, plaster put over grain pits. దళముగాపూసినపూత. మెత్తడము mettaḍam. n. Daubing, మెత్తుట. "మంటిమెత్తడము." వి. పు. vii.

మెదడు meduḍu. [from Skt. మేధస్సు.] n. The brain. తలలోనికొవ్వు, మస్తిష్కము Infl. మెదటి. Loc. మెదట.

మెదపు Same as మెదుపు. (q. v.)

మెదలు or **మెదులు** *medalu.* [Tel.] v. n. To move a little, to stir. కొంచెముచలించు. To wander, rove, go about. సంచరించు. To walk, behave, conduct one self. మెదిలితే చంపుతాను if you stir I will slay you "[illegible]." T. iv. 115. మెదలుడు, మెదల్పు, మెదలించు, or మెదిలించు *medalutsu.* v. a. To cause to move, మెదలజేయు. To stir, to shake, కదలించు. కోరమెదలించు to move the lips.

మెదిలించు See under మెదుగు.

మెదికాళ్లు *medi-kallu.* [Tel.] n. Stilts. మానికాళ్లు.

మెదుక *meduka.* [Tel.] n. Coarseness, mattedness, as of hair, పిసర. One who is coarse or dull, మందుడు. adj. Coarse, dull, మందము. మెదుకగొను *meduka-gonu.* v. n. To become coarse or matted, as hair. పిసకట్టు.

మెదుగు *medugu.* [Tel.] v. n. To be pounded or triturated. చక్కగా నలచినము [illegible] దాగుపడు, నలుపడు, చక్కబడు. నలుగు. To be familiar with, inured to, well versed in. To become old. "[illegible]." వి. పు. iv. మెదుగుడు *medugudu.* n. The state of being pounded, as rice, మెదుకుట. An old cloth, పాతవస్త్రము. మెదుపు, మెదిలించు or మెదుచు *medutsu.* v. a. To pound, grind, triturate. [illegible] కస్తూరి మెదిచి triturating musk or grinding it. "[illegible]." G. iv. 186. వాణ్ని లెస్సగా మెదిచి విడిచినారు they thrashed him properly "[illegible]." HK. iv. 149. "[illegible]." Rasica. iv. 4.

మెదుకు See మెదుగు.

మెదువు *meduvu.* [from Skt. మృదువు.] adj. Soft, మృదువు. Coarse, dull, మందము.

మెనుపు *menupu.* [Tel.] v. a. To stir as with a churning rod, (కవ్వముతో) చిలుకు.

మెప్పు *meppu.* [Tel. from మెచ్చు.] n. Approbation, approval, commendation. శ్లాఘనము. Love, ప్రీతి. A boon, వరము. మెప్పించు *meppintsu.* v. a. To gratify, persuade, talk over, conciliate. మెచ్చుకొనునట్లుచేయు. మెప్పించుకొను *meppintsu-konu.* v. a. To gain one's good word, acquire a good character. To hymn or celebrate. మెచ్చునట్లుచేసికొను. పదిమందితో [illegible] మెప్పించుకొన్నాడు he obtained the applause of many.

మెయి or **మేయి** *meyi.* [Tel.] n. Manner. రీతి, విధము. The body, శరీరము. A side, పక్క, పార్శ్వము. Time, opportunity, సమయము. "[illegible]." M. VIII. ii. 417. "[illegible]." Vema. 885. "[illegible]." N. ix. 350. "[illegible]." M. VII. v. 334. మెయి postp. With, along with. తో, చేత. అలుకమెయి angrily, అలుకచేత. "[illegible]." M. XV. ii. 78. "[illegible]." T. iv. 129.

మెయికొను, **మేయికొను** or **మేకొను** *meyi-konu.* v. n. and a. To wish, desire, want. To consent, to comply with. కోరు, అపేక్షించు, సమ్మతించు, అంగీకరించు, ఒప్పుకొను, అనుకూలించు. To happen, కలుగు. "[illegible]." Jaimini. vii. 36. మెయికొని.

అశించి. "సర్వ సర్వంసహాచక్రంబు గెల్ల నా శాశకునకిచ్చి యతనికిమున్న కేకొన్నధనముకై మెలతనమ్మెదను." HD. టీ॥ కేకొన్న, ఒప్పుకొన్న. మెయికోలు or మెయికోలు meyi-kōlu. n. Consent, సమ్మతించుట, అంగీకారము. మెయితాలుపు meyi-tālupu. n. A corporeal being, a living creature, శరీరి, ప్రాణి. మెయిపాలు meyi-pālu. n. An equal share, సమభాగము. మెయిమరపు or మెయిమరపు meyi-marapu. n. Forgetfulness of oneself, ecstasy, rapture, a trance, పరాకుపడుట. మెయిమెయి or మెయిమెయి, meyi-meyi. adv. Easily. సులభముగా. మెయిమరువు or మెయిమరువు meyi-maruvu. n. A piece of armour కవచము.

మెరక meraka. [Tel.] n. Raised ground, a high spot. మిట్ట. ఉన్నతభూమి. ఆచోటు మెరకగానున్నది it is an elevated spot. మెరకపల్లములు irregularities in the surface, ups and downs. ఆ పడవను ఈడ్చి మెరకను చేసినారు they drew the boat ashore, they hauled up the boat on the beach.

మెరచు meraṭsu. [Tel.] v. n. To flash, as lightning. తళుక్కని ప్రకాశించు. మెరపు, మెరుపు. మెరము or మెరుము merupu. n. Lightning. తటిత్తు. Brightness, brilliance, ప్రకాశము. మెరపుతీగ merapu-tīga. n. A streak of lightning, తీగవంటి మెరుపు. మెరము or మెరుము meramu. v. n. To rankle, or fester. మెర మెరలాడు. కంటిలోగాని పుంటిలోగాని లేక మనసులోగాని మెదులు. కంటిలో నలుసుపడి మెరముచున్నది the mote fell into his eye and pain was caused. "మెర మెరభావంబులోన మెరముగమతి యుండగా." T. ii. 85. టీ॥ మెరముగ, అనగా బెదిరింపచేయుచునుండగాను. v. a. To cause pain or mortification. మెర మెరలాడించు, నొచ్చునట్లు మెదలించు. "మెరుగుగైదువుగ్రుచ్చి మెరముగ్లైన." HD. ii. 314. మెర మెర mera-mera. n. Rankling. కంటిలోగాని పుంటిలోగాని మెదలడము. Mental agony, anxiety. మనోవ్యథ. Doubt, suspicion. సంశయము. Difference, భేదము. "మీసత్యములునమ్మి మెర మెరమాని, పంతము చేసాసపట్టిన దాన." P. ii. 97. మెర మెరపడు mera-mera-paḍu. v. n. To doubt, hesitate, సంశయపడు. మెర మెరపాటు mera-mera-pāṭu. n. Impetuosity of hunger. Mental distress, మెర మెరపడుట, ఆకటికపాటు. మెర మెరమను or మెర మెరలాడు mera-mera-manu. v. n. To rankle, or fester. మెరము, కంటిలోగాని పుంటిలోగాని లేక మనసులోగాని మెదలు. To suffer pain, బాధపడు. "తనుమున్న పలుకుట తద్దయునప్పుడు, మెదులుచు మదిలోన మెర మెరమనగ." Dabh. 224. మెరయు merayu. v. n. and a. To lighten, to gleam: to glitter, to shine, ప్రకాశించు. To come to light, బయలుపడు. To cause to be seen, to show, బయలుపరచు. మెరపించు mera-pinṭsu. v. a. To enlighten or make bright, to illume. మెరయునట్లు చేయు.

మెరవడి or మెరవణి mera-vaḍi. [Tel.] n. Courage, ability, energy. Increase, greatness, excess. Pride. ధైర్యము, శక్తి, ఉద్రేకము, ఆధిక్యము, అతిశయము, గౌరవము. A procession, ఊరేగింపు. Skill, నేర్పు. Respect, గౌరవము. adj. Bright, ప్రకాశముగల. మెరవడిరాయునర్చు to show respect. "తమతమజేగల మెరవడిక్రమమున నేర్పడగాంచి, ప్రభువులు మెచ్చగా కుమిపిట్టలపైకైచిరిప్రమదింబున రాజసుతులు పంతములలరగా." Surya Tanaya. iv. 144. జేగల మెరవడి, శ్యేనముల ధైర్యము, శక్తి

మెరయు or మెరియు meraya. [Tel.] n. A mortar, గుండ్రాయి.

మెరిక or మెరికె merika. [Tel.] n. Grits, that which remains in the sieve after sifting; the finest and hardest particles which resist the pestle. మెరికలు నిలిచిన ధాన్యము. మెరికబియ్యము the rice which in pounding resists the pestle, పొట్టు నిక్కి నిలిచియున్నది. మెరికవంటివాడు a man of grit, a choice favourite. మెరికలవంటి మాటలు choice phrases. ఈగ్రంథము రత్నాలమెరికలు this book is a perfect gem, a galaxy of beauties. మెరియుడు meriyudu. n. A steady man, చలింపనివాడు. మెరియత meriyata. n. A steady woman, చలింపనిది. A victress, heroine, she who escapes with impunity.

"క॥ నిదివొప్పె మెరియతనై,
కావరమునవలసినట్లుగదయ్యాళింపక,
గావరచి చేసి మెరిగా.
నేటికినివాటిదరిలి తేలవచింతుకా."

K. iii. 243.

మెరుకు meruku. [Tel.] v. n. & a. To rankle. మెరము. To pull up by the root, పెరుకు, ఉత్పాటించు.

మెరుగు or మెఱుంగు merugu. [Tel. from మెరయు.] n. Polish, lustre, brightness. కాంతి. Lightning. మెరుపు. Grease, oil, melted butter. నెయ్యి మొదలగువానిజిడ్డు. "మెరుగుచేయకగాని మృదువుగాదన్నంబు." Kōdanda. §. 33. adj. Polished, bright, luminous. మెరుగుసున్నము fine plaster. మెరుగురాయి a polishing stone. మెరుగుపోటు the final pounding of rice. మెరుగుడు నూనె merugudu-nūne. n. Varnish. మెరుగుడుపురుగు or మెరుగుపురుగు merugudu-purugu. n. A lady bird. ఇంద్రగోపము. A firefly or glowworm. మిణుగురుపురుగు. మెరుగుతీగె merugu-tīge. n. A necklace worn by women. ఒకకంఠాభరణము. మెరుగుపెట్టు merugu-pettu. v. a. To polish. కాంతివచ్చునట్లుచేయు. మెరుగుబోడి merugu-bōdi. n. A beautiful woman, మెరుపువలె మనోజ్ఞమైన అవయవములుగల ఆడుది. మెరుగురిక్క or మెరుగుడు రిక్క merugu-rikka. n. Coral. పగడము. A bright star, కాంతిగలచుక్క.

మెరుపు See under మెరయు.

మెరుము merumu. [Tel.] n. Lightning. విద్యుత్తు. ఉరుములు మెరుములు విస్తారముగా నుండినవి there was much thunder and lightning. v. n. To lighten. మెరుపు మెరుము. "ఉరుమును మెరుమును ఉడిగినను, వరలుచునలుగడల, బడినవారికన్నప్పుడు." M. I. iii. 328. v. a. To thrust, పొడుచు.

మెలక melaka. [Tel.] n. A trick, fraud. కపటము, వంచన.

మెలకు melaku. [Tel.] v. n. To burn, to be bright, జ్వలించు.

మెలగు melagu. [Tel.] v. n. To wander, to roam about. సంచరించు. To behave, to conduct oneself carefully, జాగరూకతతో నడుచుకొను, వర్తించు. To move, జరుగు. "కాంతనేపునకాయిరి కొడమలేచి, యుల్లసల్లన మెలగుచువాకటికిని." Vish. iii. 287. మెలచు melatsu. v. a. To cause to behave, మెలగజేయు. మెలకువ, మెలంకువ, మెలుకువ or మెళుకువ melukuva. n. Waking from sleep, మేలుకొనుట. Watchfulness, జాగరూకత. Conduct, వర్తనము. Life, living, livelihood. జీవనము. Wandering, సంచారము. మెలకువకాడు melakuva-kādu. n. A watchful or careful man, జాగరూకుడు. మెలత, మెల్త, మెలతుక or మెల్తుక melata. n. A lady, woman, maid. స్త్రీ. మెలన melana. n. Conduct, behaviour. నడత, ప్రవర్తన. "పాటిమగవాని నమ్మటదొకటి, వానిమెలన తారద్దంబులోని ముడుపు." Miscell. i. 567, line 9. మెలపు or మెల్పు melapu. v. a. To conduct, to lead, to manage. నడిపించు, ప్రవర్తింపజేయు. మెలగజేయు. "పురోహిత ప్రధానుల ప్రాప్తయావనుండగు నతనినిరుగా మెలపుకొంచని నియమించి." A. iii. 109. n. Watchfulness, జాగరూకత. Conduct, behaviour. Dexterity, cleverness, skill, నేర్పు. Steadiness.

చలింపమి. Softness, dullness, మాంద్యము. "దండనీతి విధానమంతటికి రత్నయర్థమును మెలపు తో జేయునది వెలుంగు." M. XII. ii. 182. కనుమెలపు (M. IX. i. 24.) అనగా నేత్రచ మత్కృతి.

మెలయు or మెలియు *melayu* [Tel.] v. n. To mix, be united. To be entangled or twisted, పెనగు. This verb is only used as a rhyme in the phrase కలిసిమెలిసి mixing and mingling. Also, same as మెలగు (q. v.). మెలి, మెలిక or మెలికె *meli*. n. A turn, a twist. పురి, పెన. మెలి గొను or మెలిపడు *meli-gonu*. v. n. To be twisted, to get twisted. పురిపెట్టు... మెలిపెట్టు or మెలివేయు *meli-pettu*. v. a. To twist, పురిపెట్టు. మెలుచు *melutsu*. v. a. To twist, to cause to be twisted, మెలియజేయు, పెనచు. మెలుములు *melu-mulu*. [Tel.] n. Certain ropes used in a కపిల pump. తాళ్లు. మెలుసు *melusu*. n. A twist. మెలిక.

మెల్త, మెల్తుక See under మెలగు.

మెల్ల or పంటిటిమెల్ల *mella*. [Tel.] n. A hall. మధ్యశాలంగము, శాల.

మెల్ల *mella*. [Tel.] n. A squint, squinting. కేకరత్వము. లోమెల్ల a squint inwards. వెలి మెల్ల a squint outwards. adj. Squinting. ఓరకన్నుగల. Excellent, మేలైన. Gentle, soft, తిన్నని. మెల్లకంటి *mella-kanti*. n. A squint-eyed person, కేకరాక్షుడు, కేకరాక్షి. A crow, వాయసము. మెల్లకంటిది *mella-kantidi*. n. A squint-eyed woman. ఓరకంటిది. మెల్లకంటివాడు *mella-kanti-vadu*. n. A squint-eyed man, a man who squints. కేకరుడు. మెల్లగా *mella-ga*. adv. Gently, softly, slowly, gradually. తిన్నగా. మెల్లచూపు *mella-tsūpu*. n. A squint, a side-look, a glance. ఓరచూపు. మెల్లన *mella-na*. n. Gentleness, softness, slowness. మాంద్యము, తిన్నన, అల్లన. మెల్లని *mella-ni*. adj. Gentle, soft, slow. తిన్నని. మెల్లిగా or మెల్లగా *melli-ga*. adv. Slowly, softly, gently. తిన్నగా. మెల్లి మెల్లిగా *melli-melli-ga*. adv. Very gently, gradually.

మెల్లమెల్ల, మెలమెల్ల *mella-mella*. adv. Gently. తిన్నగా.

మెల్లె *melle*. [Tel.] n. A withe, twig, switch, tendril: a withe used as a cord. ఐటెక, చివక.

మెళుకువ *melukuva*. [Tel.] n. Same as మెలకువ q. v.) మెళుకువయొర an allurement, bait, delicacy. మెళుకువపడు *melu-kuva-padu*. v. n To be aroused, to awake, to be alert.

మెసగు or మెసవు *mesagu*. [Tel.] v. a. To eat, feed on. తిను.

మెహదా *mehada*. [H.] n. A kind of sword, "మిహిపసిండిపరుంజు మెహదాకెలంకుల తావు గుజ్జరిసేతకేవడంబు." Swa. iv. 36.

మెహనతు *mehanatu*. [H.] n. A present, gift. (Also,) trouble, difficulty, toil, labour.

మే mē

మే *mē*. [Tel. for మేను.] n. The body. శరీరము. "విధినామేర్త్రాణముల్ నిల్పె." భా. శల్య. ii. మేపూత a perfume, unguent. విలేప నము. Manner, విధము. "నీతలపుమేగలుపక వలెను." భా. ద్రో. v. A side, పార్శ్వము. "ఇరుమేల." భా. viii. adj. Upper. మీది. మేకోట the upper fort. పైకోట. అనగా కోటలో పైనిభాగము. మేతాలుపు or మేను తాలుపు *mē-talupu*. n. A corporeal being, శరీరి.

మేండము *mēndamu*. [Skt.] n. A ram, పొట్టేలు.

మెండ్రించు meṇḍrintsu. [Tel.] v. a. To divide, cut, sever; ఛేదించు.

మెంథి menthi. [Skt.] n. The herb called fenugreek or saintfoin. మెంతి.

మేక mēka. [Tel.] n. A goat. మేకపిల్ల a kid. మేకవన్నె పులి a tiger of the color of a goat. i. e., a wolf in sheep's clothing. పెంటిమేక a she-goat. మేకపోతు a he-goat. పిల్లలు మేకలు కలవాడను I am the head of a large family containing many individuals of both sexes. The Indian goat has excrescences like teats on the neck: as these are useless, వాడు మెడచన్ను మేక మెడచన్ను denotes He is a mere useless burden or appendage. మేకతిండి mēka-tiṇḍi. n. That which feeds on goats, i. e.. a wolf, తోడేలు. మేకము [borrowed by Skt. from Tel.] n. Same as మేక. మేకమేయనాకు mēka-mēyan-āku. n. A certain poisonous herb. H. iv. 14. (As Shakespeare says, 'The green sour ringlets whereof the ewe not bites.')

మేకు mēku. [H.] n. A wooden or iron peg, a nail, a stake or spike, గూటము. మేకును పెరికిన కోతి the monkey that drew out the wedge, i. e., one who brings injury on himself by too much meddling.

మేకొను or మెయికొను mē-konu. [Tel.] v. n. To consent, సమ్మతించు. To happen, కలుగు. To undertake, పూను. v. a. To have, obtain, పొందు. మేకొలుపు mē-kolupu. v a. To fit or suit. పొసగునట్లు చేయు. "పులితో లివిడి పెంచిజిలుగు దువ్వలిరా రెంగులు నల్లెవాటు మేకొలుపవచ్చు." R. ii. 109. మేకోలు, మెయికోలు or మేగలి mē-kōlu. n. Undertaking, an attempt, పూనిక.

మేఖల mēkhala. [Skt.] n. A zone or girdle. The silver girdle worn by women. మొలనూలు, వడ్డాణము. The central part of a hill, కొండనడుము. A sword knot. A string or chain fastened to the hilt. A sword belt. కాంచిదాము, క్రరునిబంధనము మేఖలకన్యక mekhala-kanyaka. n. An epithet of the river Narbada.

మేగ See మేవ.

మేగు or మ్రేగు mēgu. [Tel.] v. a. To smear, besmear. పూయు, దళముగాపూయు, దట్టముగా చేయు, దళసరిగామెత్తు. "వెన్నలుపు మెందికంచు, మేగినట్లున్నమూపె మెగమున చీకట్లుముడివడ." HD. ii. 1388. To surround, ఆవరించు.

మేఘము mēghamu. [Skt.] n. A cloud. మొయిలు. మేఘద్వారము mēgha-dvāramu. n. The gate of clouds, i. e., the sky. ఆకాశము, మింటివాకిలి. మేఘనాదము mēghanādamu. n. Thunder, ఉరుము. మేఘనాదుడు mēgha-nādudu. n. The son of Ravaṇa, ఇంద్రజిత్తు. Also, Varuṇa, వరుణుడు. మేఘపుష్పము mēgha-pushpamu. n. The flower of clouds, i. e., water, or drizzle, ఉదకము, తూర. మేఘవన్నె mēgha-vanne. n. A sort of silk. "మేఘువన్నెలయు, రుద్రాక్ష వన్నెలయు, కాంభోజ పులిగోరుపట్టులును." BD. iii. 114. మేఘాడంబరము mēgh-āḍambaramu. n. The lowering or threatening of clouds. మేఘుడు mēghuḍu. n. A cloud, personified as living. Bhāso. §. 1.

మేచకము mēchakamu. [Skt.] n. Darkness, చీకటి. Dark hue, నలుపు. The eye of a peacock's feather, నెమలిపురికన్ను. adj. Dark, black, నల్లని.

మేజా or మేజీ mēja. [from Eng. 'Mess.'] n. A table, dinner, mess; బల్ల, భోజనము.

మేజిస్ట్రేటు mējistrēṭu [Eng. 'magistrate'.] n. A magistrate. గ్రామపు మేజిస్ట్రేటు a village magistrate or Munsif.

మేజోడు mējōḍu. [H.] n. Stockings.

మేట mēṭa. [Tel.] n. Accumulation, alluvial soil, మేటవేసినమన్ను a deposit of earth.

మేటీ mēṭi. [Eng. 'Mate'.] n. Lit: a helper. A servant, a cook, a menial who cleans plates, dishes, lamps and shoes, &c.

మేటి or మేటరి mēṭi. [Tel.] n. A chief, leader, head man, lord, శ్రేష్ఠుడు, అధిపుడు. adj. Chief, excellent, noble. శ్రేష్ఠమైన. మేటిదొర a noble lord. Bilh. ii. 50. మెర యుచునుండెడి మేటిరంబులు. మేటిరంబులు, అనగా మేటి, గొప్పలైన, ఈరంబులు, పొదలు large bushes. "కేళైనపన్నీట తీర్థంబులాడి, మేటికస్తూరి మేనెల్లబూసి." Misc. iii. 322. మేటిగా=మెండుగా. మేటిల్లు mēṭillu. v. n. To excel, అతిశయించు.

మేడ mēḍa. [Tel.] n. A mansion or large house: an upper chamber, a storey, హర్మ్యము, సౌధము.

మేడము mēḍamu. [Tel.] n. Joining, union, కూడిక. A fight, battle, యుద్ధము. మేడము పొడుచు mēḍamu-poḍutsu. v. n. To fight a battle, యుద్ధముచేయు. కోడి మేడము a cock fight.

మేడి mēḍi. [Tel.] n. The Glomerous Fig tree. *Ficus racemosa.* అత్తి, ఉదుంబరము. మేడిపండు the fruit of this tree. One species is బ్రహ్మమేడి and another is రాతిమేడి which grows parasitically on other trees. మేడికాయపైమిసిమి outward bloom, mere show.

మేడి mēḍi. [Tel.] n. A plough staff, or plough tail. నాగటిదుంపవెనుక నిలిపినకొయ్య. మేడితలక్రిందుగాపాతు or పాతిపెట్టు to bury a plough staff upside down as a signal (గురాయి) to warn people that the land is under ban. మేడికర్ర mēḍi-karra. n. The pole or shaft of a plough. మేడికోరు or మేడిపాలు the farmer's share of the crop. మేడితాడు mēḍi-tāḍu. n. The plough bands. మేడితోక or మేడిపోగ mēḍi-tōka. n. The plough tail. మేడిసీల or మేడిగీల the nail or pin which fastens the plough the handle.

మేడుపడు or మేడ్పడు mēḍu-paḍu. [Tel. for మూడుపడు.] v. n. To become unconscious or senseless, అజ్ఞానమొందు.

మేడెము or మేడియము mēḍemu. [Tel.] n. A spear or dagger. ఈటె, బాకు. The rim of a bell-shaped earring, set with gems. రాళ్లుచెక్కినజోమికి అంచుచొక్కపనితర ము. "కః ఓడిరిదిన్నగా వారల మేడెముపాదు తురి." BD. vi. 116.

మేఢ్రము mēḍhramu. [Skt.] n. The penis. శిశ్నము. పంచమేఢ్రుడు (P. 163.) the name of a giant. Polyphemus.

మేత mēta. [Tel. from మేయు] n. Food, meat, provender, forage. A lure or bait. పశుగ్రాసము. మేతరి mēt-ari. n. A head man, a head labourer or 'maistry'. చిల్లరకులములకు కులశ్రేష్ఠనామము, కొందరు శిల్పులలో ముఖ్యుడు. మేస్త్రి. An eater, తినే వాడు. A glutton, తిండిపోతు. గడ్డిమేతరి a grass eater. విసపు మేతరి he who eats venom, i. e., Siva. మేతమేయు, మేతాడు or మేతలాడు mēta-mēyu. v. a. To eat, graze, feed on.

మేదకుడు mēdakuḍu. [Tel.] n. A meek, mild man. సాత్వికుడు. An artless or simple man, కపటములేనివాడు. మేదకురాలు mēdaku-r-ālu. n. A meek mild woman. సాత్వికురాలు. మేదతనము mēda-tanamu. n. Plainness, a harmless, quiet, simple disposition. సాత్వికత.

మేదర mēdara. [Tel.] n. The basket maker caste. గంపలల్లే ఒకజాతి. మేదరది or మేదరసాని a woman of that caste. మేదరకులము the basket weaver's caste. మేదరపెట్టె a bamboo box. మేదరి or మేదరవాడు a basket maker. మేదరచాప a bamboo mat.

మేదస్సు mēdassu. [Skt.] n. Marrow. మేదః సంకషము triturated marrow, i.e., the brain, మెదడు.

మేదావి *mēdāvi*. [Tel.] n. The ashes obtained from a sacred fire, ఔపాసనాగ్నిమసి. మేదావిబొట్టు *mēdāvi-boṭṭu*. n A black spot of ashes worn by a Brahmin between his eyebrows after the termination of a sacrifice.

మేదించు or మెదించు *mēdinṭsu*. [Tel.] v. a. To soften, make soft, triturate. మర్దించు. "కలియునూనెలో డ కాటుక మేదించి వెలయు బూనికట్టివిధముతో ప." HK. iv. 177.

మేదిని *mēdini*. [Skt.] n. The earth. భూమి.

మేదు *mēdu*. [from Skt. మేదస్సు.] n. Marrow. మేదస్సు. "పొరలెడు మేదుపప్పును దొప్పలందు." DRA. 168.

మేదురము *mēdurāmu*. [Skt.] adj. Thick, compact. సాంద్రమైన, దట్టమైన. Smooth, soft, bland, unctuous, saponaceous. సాంద్రస్నిగ్ధ, చిక్కనైననునుపుగల. "బహురత్న ద్యుతిమేదురోదర దరీభాగంబులంబొల్చు." Swa. ii. 49.

మేధ *mēdha*. [Skt.] n. Wit, understanding, apprehension, conception. బుద్ధి, ధారణ వద్బుద్ధి, మరపులేనిబుద్ధి. "మీకు సర్వంబునెరిగెడి మేధగలదు." B. I. § xiii. 33. మేధము *mēdhamu*. n. A sacrifice, offering, oblation. క్రతువు, యజ్ఞము. మేధావంతము *mēdhavantamu*. n. Fineness of grain, something excellent, distinguished or rare. adj. Sensible, prudent. మేధావి *mēdhavi*. n. A wit, a man of intellect, a genius. మేధగలవాడు, సూక్ష్మబుద్ధిగలవాడు, ధీమంతుడు. మేధావిధిపము pregnancy of wit, cleverness. బుద్ధికౌశల్యము. మేధ్యము *mēdhyamu*. adj. Fit for a sacrifice, pure, purified, nice, delicate. పరిశుద్ధమైన. అమేధ్యము impure.

మేన *mēna*. [Tel.] n. Relationship through a paternal aunt, or a maternal uncle, or through a sister. adj. Connected or related through a maternal uncle or paternal aunt, or through a sister. మేనకోడలు *mēna-kōḍalu*. n. A niece, the daughter of a man's sister or of a woman's brother. భగినీపుత్రిక. తోడబుట్టినవానికూతురు. మేనత్త *mēn-atta*. n. An aunt, a father's sister, or the wife of a maternal uncle. తండ్రితోడబుట్టినది, మేనమామభార్య. మేనబావ *mēna-bāva*. n. The son of a father's sister, or of a mother's brother, who is thus called if older than oneself. మేనత్తమేనమామలకొడుకు. మేనమరదలు *mēna-maradalu*. n. The daughter of a father's sister or of a mother's brother, who is thus called if younger than oneself. మేనత్తమేనమామలకూతురు. మేనమరిది *mēna-maridi*. n. The son of a father's sister or of a mother's brother, who is thus called if younger than oneself. మేనత్తమేనమామలకొడుకు. మేనమామ *mena-mama*. n. A maternal uncle. తల్లితోడబుట్టినవాడు. మేనరికము *mēna-rikamu*. n. The relationship that exists between a man and his father's sister's or his mother's brother's family, మేనత్తకూతురు మేనమామ కొడుకులుగా నుండడము. మేనల్లుడు *mēn-alluḍu*. n. A nephew, son of a man's sister or of a mother's brother. తోడబుట్టినదానికొడుకు, ఒకతెకు తోడబుట్టినవానికొడుకు. మేనవదినె *mēna-radine*. n. The daughter of a father's sister or of a mother's brother, who is thus called if older than oneself. మేనత్తమేనమామలకూతురు.

మేనక *menaka*. [Skt.] n. A goddess (answering to Hebe), wife of Himalaya and one of the courtezans in heaven. స్వర్వేశ్యభేదము, హిమవంతునిపత్ని. మేనకాత్మజ *mēnak-ātma-ja*. n. The daughter of Menaka; an epithet of Parvati. wife of Siva. పార్వతి.

మేని *mēni*. [Tel.] n. Brightness, కాంతి.

మేను, మే, మేయి or మై *mēnu*. [Tel.] n. The body, శరీరము. Birth, జన్మము. A side, పార్శ్వము. "ఇరుమేసంపొందుమము." ఆము. vi.

ఒకమేల on one side. ఒకపక్కనుండు. మేను తాలుపు or మేతాలుపు one who has a bodily form, శరీరి. మేనుపుట్టువు or మేను పుట్టువు mē-puṭṭuvu n. A daughter, కూతురు, తనూజ. A son, కొడుకు, తనూజుడు. మేనుమరువు or మెయిమరువు mē-maruvu. n. Armour, a piece of armour, కవచము.

మేపు mēpu. [Tel. from మేయు.] v. a. To feed, graze, మేయునట్లుచేయు. To herd or tend cattle, పశువులను కాచు. వాడు పశువులను మేపు తాడు he grazes cattle. n. Food, fodder, pasturage, grazing, forage. పశుగ్రాసము, తిండి, మేత. మేపరి mēp-ari. n. Eater, feeder. తినువాడు, భక్షకుడు. మేపించు mēpintsu. v. a. To make (one feed on): to make (one) tend (cattle) తినిపించు, మేయునట్లు చేయు.

మేమను memanu. [Tel.] n. Consent. సమ్మతి, మేకోలు.

మేమెయి or మైమై me-megi. [Tel.] n. Ease, అనాయాసము. adv. Easily, అనాయాసముగా.

మేయు mēyu. [Tel.] v. a. & n. To feed, graze, eat, as cattle, పశ్వాదులు మేతమేయు. మేఘములు కొండమీద మేస్తవి the clouds hang over the hill.

మేర mēra. [Tel.] n. A limit, boundary, space, distance. ఎల్ల, హద్దు, మితి, మట్టు, ఎడము. An instalment, వాయిదా. Order క్రమము. An arrangement, ఏర్పాటు. "దశ మేరలేని బాధకు తాళలేను." SD. vi. 95. "మీరు నుర్వరుణ్ణి దగవుమేరయుడిప్పక." B. X. 73. 12. Respect, మర్యాద మేరయరుగి, మర్యాదనుశెరిగి. A fee in money, in goods or in grain. మేరలేని దుఃఖము boundless grief. మేరతప్పు to transgress. నాలుగుమూర మేర a space of four feet. మేరకు mēra-ku. prep. Up to, according to. ప్రకారము. బుద్ధిమేరకు according to reason. ఆజ్ఞమేరకు according to orders.

మేరువు or మేరు mēruvu. [Tel.] n. A pyramid, a cone. శిఖరము, కూచి. The centre jewel in the top of a necklace. A carboy, jar, or great bottle of rose water. The top or ridge of a pent roof. [Skt.] The name of Mount Mēru, a mountain of gold (the Olympus of India), హేమాద్రి.

మేలము mēlamu. [Tel.] n. Jeering, joking, fun, sport, ridicule. పరిహాసము, కోడిగము, హాస్యము. మేలమాడు mēlam-āḍu. v. n. To joke, కోడిగమాడు.

మేలు mēlu. [Tel.] n. Good, kindness. ఉపకారము. Good fortune, prosperity, favour, happiness, క్షేమము, శుభము. Profit, advantage, లాభము. Righteousness, పుణ్యము, సుకృతము. Excellence, superiority, విశేషము. Love, మోహము. Pride, మదము. "పదువులమేలులేదా." P. iv. 119. అక్కడికి పోతే మేలు it would be better to go there. అదేమేలు so much the better. మేలెరుగు to be grateful, remember kindness. కీడుమేలు తెలిసినవాడు one who knows good and evil. మేలుకలిగినవాడు in time of prosperity. "తిర్యక్తతతిరంబులందు మక నూన్నతవాక్యము మేలుభూవరా." Bharat. మేలు or మేల adj. Upper, higher. ఉపరి, అధికము, పై. Good, better. Noble, fine, excellent, superior, శుభమైన, శ్రేష్ఠమైన. మేలుమిద్దె an upper storey. "లోపలిదంత స్థులోని మేల్మిద్దె." Sārang. D. 113. మేలుగోడ the top wall, battlement, parapet or rail wall. మేలుముసుకు the outer cover. మేలు మాట or మేలువార్త happy news. adv. Up, above, over, మేలు or మేలుమేలు interj. Well done! excellent! better and better! జయ, జయ జయ. మేలుకట్టు mēlu-kaṭṭu. n. An awning, a canopy. వితానము. "మేలిమిమీరగా మేలుకట్టులుగట్టి. దమనీయ చీనాంబరములుగట్టి" N. ix. 124. మేలు కమ్మచీర mēlu-kammi-chīra. n. A cotton cloth woven with a coloured border three inches broad. మేలుచెయ్యి mēlu-cheyyi. n. Superiority, హెచ్చు, ఆధిక్యము. adj. Superior, హెచ్చైన. Victorious, గెలుపుగల. మేలుచెయ్యిగానుండు to prevail, to have the advantage. "అట్లు తమవారు మేలుచెయ్యి న భంగికిని." M. VI. ii. 2. మేలిమి mēlimi. n. Fineness, excellence. Pure gold. అపరంజి. మేలిమి or మేలి adj. Fine, excellent. B. X. 207. మేలిల్లు mel-illu. n. An upper storey, మేడ, సౌధము. మేలుకొను, మేల్కొను, మేలుకను, మేల్కను, మేలుకాంచు or మేల్కాంచు mēlu-konu. v. n. To awake, rise. To be aroused, stand on one's guard, be alert. నిద్ర తెలియు. జాగ్రత్తపడు. మేలుకొలుపు mēlukolupu. v. a. To awaken. నిద్ర లేపు. మేలుకొలుపులు mēlu-kolupulu. n. Matin-song, reveille, music in the dawning. సుప్రభాతములు. cf. "the dulcet sounds at break of day, &c. మేలుకోలు mēlu-kōlu. n. The act of awaking, మేలుకొనుట. మేలుదురంగి or మేల్దురంగి mēlu-durangi. [H. dorungi] n. Fine velvet. Fine shot silk. ఒకవిధమైన చేక్కనిపట్టు. "పటికంపు మెట్లును జిలిబిలి మేల్దురంగి." T. iv. 202. మేలుపడు or మేల్పడు mēlu-padu. n. To fall in love, be enamoured, మోహించు, ఆశపడు. "ఎవ్వనిచూచి మేలుపడితే యరవింద దళాక్షి." Vijaya. iii. 37. మేలుబంతి mēlu-banti. n. The top line, the copy set to a schoolboy learning to write. A pattern, మాదిరి. One who is or sets an example; a paragon of excellence, an example, ఉదాహరణము. adj. Excellent, శ్రేష్ఠము, శ్రేష్ఠుడు, శ్రేష్ఠురాలు. "మేదినివాసులకెల్ల మేలుబంతిగా బ్రవర్తింపకేల, దుష్కృత్యైతి." Vish. ii. 116. "నిజచరిత్రంబు భావిభూభుజులకెల్ల మేలుబంతిగా నమతియొనర్చుండెడు." ib. vi. 63. మేలుమచ్చు mēlu-matstsu. n. An upper storey, చంద్రశాల. మేలుమచ్చులు a kind of game played by boys. మేలురాసి mēlu-rasi. n. The top part of a heap of winnowed grain. తూర్పారబట్టిన ధాన్యపుపోగు. మేలువాడు mēlu-vadu. n. A lover, విటుడు, వలపుకాడు, మంచివాడు. "అంతరంగపు మేలువాడైయుండె." A. v. 56.

మేళనము mēlanamu. [Skt.] n. Meeting, union, coming together. Connection, affinity, as of two languages. కలయుడము, కూడిక. మేళము mēlamu. n. Union, కూడిక. A set of musical instruments, వాద్యములజేత. A band of musicians, a set of dancers or singers. The music used by them. మేళగాండ్రయొక్కయు నటుల యొక్కయు గుంపు. పాటగాండ్రగుంపు. ఆ పెండ్లికి నాలుగుమేళములను పిలిపించినారు they sent for four bands to come to the wedding. అది యిప్పుడు మేళానికి పోవడములేదు she does not now dance. పోకిరిమేళము a pack of rascals. మేళతాళములు instrumental music. మేళించు or మేళగించు mela-cintsu. v. n. To unite, be joined, జతగూడు, కలియు. v. a. To mix, unite in harmony, as the sound of various instruments. కలుపు, జతకూర్చు, శ్రుతికూర్చు. "ఆతడు నప్పుడు పాటకాయి తముగ, వీణమేళవించి వెలపలి మోసలనునిలిచి నికరిగి." KP. ii. 98. "విరిశృంగారములు మేళవించుచుట్టి, చెలువమునవిందుముఖులు." Jaimini. v. 125.

మేవ mēva. [Tel.] n. A fish called White Pomfret, a species of turbot; Stromateus argenteus; also called చావ్వ.

మేవడి mēvadi. [Tel.] n. Humility, gentleness, నమ్రత. An expedient, tact, ఉపాయము. adj. Proper, fit, ఉచితము. మేవడికాడు mēvadi-kādu. n. A gentleman, a humble man, నమ్రతకలవాడు. A man of tact, ఉపాయశాలి.

మేవు Same as మేను (q. v.)

మేషకము mēshakamu. [Skt.] n. A kind of plant, *Amaranthus campestris*. తెల్లకేము, చూరిమము, నీరుచిర్ర.

మేషము mēshamu. [Skt.] n. A ram. The sign *Aries*. పొట్టేలు, మేషరాశి. మేషాక్షికుసుమము mesh-akshi-kusumamu. n. A sort of Cassia. మేషి mēshi. n. A female sheep, an ewe, ఆడగొర్రె.

మేస్త్రీ mēstri. [Eng. 'Master.'] n. A master workman. A head-workman.

మేహము mēhamu. [Skt.] n. A urinary disease, especially, an inflammatory affection of the urethra, gonorrhœa. A venereal disease, gleet. Cachexiæ. స్త్రీసంభోగాధిక్యముచేత కలిగేరోగము. మేహగ్రంథి mēha-granthi. n. Venereal herpes. మేహరోగము mēha-rōgamu. n. A venereal disease. మేహవాయువు mēha-vāyuvu. n. A venereal affection. A complaint wherein the limbs are stiff and contracted.

మై mai

మై or మయి mai. [Tel.] n. The body. శరీరము. Manner, విధము. A side, పార్శ్వము. A time, తడవ. "కత్తుకకత్తుకజుట్టి పోరుచిల్ల లక్ష్మియుగానరానికతులా మైమై బెను చుట్ట నించు." Swa. iii. 83. మైగాపు a body guard. మైతీగ a slender figure. ఇరుమైల on both sides. "తిద్దాసరియయుపుం బరవాతలంగి పోటి పోటులనిరు మైలంబొడుచుచు బెనుచు బోవంబట్టి వటంబుజేర్చివాడిల్లనియొకా." A. vi. 28. "ఇను మైనరిగెలు నెట్టికమ్ముంగ." Pal. p. 277. Prep. With, తో. "నిమ్ము గొల్చెదభక్తి మైనీరజాక్ష." "కాంతు దైత్రి భువనఖ్యాతి మైమండె." BD. v. 336. adv. Equivalent to గా, as ఒంటిమై alone, ఏకాకిగా. వేడుకమై joyfully, ఉల్లాసముగా. "కటకటమమ్ము నెకత్యటికాలమునాటియు గదాని వొంటిమై నెటులెడనిచ్చితమ్మ చెలీ." Vasu. iii. 147. మైతాలుపు or మయితాలుపు mai-tālupu. n. A corporeal being, a living creature, ప్రాణి, శరీరి. మైపూత mai-pūta. n. The act of smearing the body with anything, such as saudal paste, &c., అంగరాగము. మైపోక mai-pōka. n. Lightness, తేలిక. మైమరపు or మయిమరపు mai-marapu. n. Forgetfulness of oneself, ecstasy, a trance, పారవశ్యము. మైమరువు or మయిమరువు mai-maruvu. [from మరుగు.] n. Armour, mail. కవచము. మైమై, మైమయి or మయిమయి mai-mai. n. Ease. అనాయాసము. Freedom from danger, అనుపద్రవము. adv. Easily, without any difficulty, అనాయాసముగా.

మైకము or మయికము maikamu. [Tel.] n. Intoxication, insensibility, drowsiness. మత్తత, మత్తు.

మైకొను or మయికొను mai-konu. [Tel.] v. n. To agree, consent. సమ్మతించు, ఒప్పుకొను. మైకొలుపు or మయికొలుపు mai-kolupu. v. a. To cause to consent or agree with. సమ్మతింపజేయు. మైకోలు or మయికోలు mai-kōlu. n. The act of consenting, మయికొనుట.

మైజారు or మయిజారు mai-dzāru. [Tel.] n. The skirt or selvage of a garment. చీరకొంగు.

మైత్రావరుణి maitra-varuṇi. [Skt.] n. An epithet of the sage Agastya, అగస్త్యుడు.

మైత్రి maitri. [Skt. from మిత్ర.] n. Friendship. మిత్రభావము, స్నేహము.

మైథునము maithunamu. [Skt. from మిథునము.] n. Coition, sexual intercourse, కూడిక, సంగమము, గ్రామ్యధర్మము, రతి.

మైద or మయిద maida. [Tel.] Same as మైకము. (q. v.)

మైదు or మయిదు maidu. [Tel.] n. Deception, deceit, delusion. మాయ.

Intoxication, మయికము. Love-powder, magic-powder made to enamour one. మోహనభస్మము, వలపుమందు, కొక్కుపొడి.

మైనము or **మయినము** *mainamu*. [Tel.] n. Wax. మధూచ్ఛిష్టము. తెల్లమైనము virgin wax, white wax. మడ్డిమైనము bees' wax which is not purified. మైనపువత్తి a wax candle. మైనపుజిడ్డి or మైనపుగుడ్డ wax cloth.

మైరేయము *mairēyamu*. [Skt.] n. Spirituous liquor, made from sugar. చెరుకురసమునచేసినకల్లు. ఒకవిధమైనమద్యము. Wine made from the blossoms of a tree, *Lythrum fruticosum*. Rox. ii. 233.

మైల or **మయిల** *maila*. [from Skt. మలినము.] n. Uncleanness, foulness, impurity, dirt, pollution, ceremonial defilement, మాలిన్యము, అశుచిత్వము. A dirty cloth, మలినవస్త్రము. adj. Dirty, unclean. మైలవస్త్రములు dirty clothes. మైలావు or మయిలఆవు a cow of a grizzled colour. పొగచాయగలఆవు. మడి మైల clean and dirty, foul and fair. **మైలక్రోచి** *maila-krōci*. n. A kind of musical instrument, మురళి. **మైలచాయతొండ** *maila-tsāya-tonda*. n. A kind of lizard or bloodsucker. **మైలతుత్తము** or **మయిలతుత్తము** *maila-tuttamu*. n. Blue vitriol or sulphate of copper. తుత్థము. **మైలపడు** *maila-padu*. v. n. To become dirty or unclean, to become polluted, మలినమగు, అశుచియగు.

మైలారు or **మయిలారు** *mailāru*. [Tel.] n. The name of a petty goddess, ఒకక్షుద్రదేవత.

మైవడి or **మయివడి** *mairaḍi*. [Tel.] n Consent, సమ్మతి Suitability, convenience, అనుకూల్యము. Manner, విధము. Propriety, beauty, సొమ్మత. adj. Convenient, suitable, అనుకూలము.

మైసాక్షి *maisākshi*. [from Skt. మహిషాక్షి.] n. A drug used in fumigation. Indian bdellium గుగ్గిలము. *Balsamodendron mukul*, *Balsamodendron agallocha*. మేసాక్షికసుమము a sort of cassia.

మొ mo

మొ *mo*. [Tel.] n. A contraction for మొదలయిన; that is, etcetera, ఇత్యాది.

మొంటె Another form of మొరిటె (q. v.).

మొండి *mondi*. [Tel.] adj. Maimed, crippled, defective, imperfect. చేతులు కాళ్లు తెగిన, అంగహీనమైన. Bare; lopped. Blunt, blunted, మొక్కపోయిన. Stubborn, obstinate, perverse, pertinacious, impertinent, incorrigible, unmanageable, ungovernable, refractory, unruly, మూర్ఖమైన. మొండిమాటలు stubborn or rude language. మొండిపిల్లకాయ an obstinate or refractory boy. మొండిగోడలు bare walls. మొండిగంటము a blunt stylus. మొండిచెయి a maimed hand. మొండిచేతులు bare hands, i.e., hands without any ornament. మొండితోక a docked tail. మొండిమెడ a bare neck, i. e, without any necklace. వానిది మొండిప్రాణము he is tenacious of life. **మొండికట్టె** or **మొండిదరి** *mondi-katte*. n. A stubborn wretch. మూర్ఖుడు. **మొండిచేయు**, **మొండివాడు** or **మొండివాడులాడు** *mondi-cheyu*. v. n. To be unruly; to oppose. అశ్వము మొండిచేస్తున్నది the horse is stubborn. **మొండితనము** *mondi-tanamu*. n. Stubbornness, obstinacy. మూర్ఖత్వము. **మొండిపారిన** *mondi-parina*. adj. Callous. కాయకాచిన. **మొండిపురుగు** *mondi-purugu*. n. The 'stumpy' snake, or *Amphisbæna*, which looks as if the tail was lopped off. **మొండు** Another form of మొండి. **మొండెము** or **మొండేరుము** *mondemu*. n. A stump. The trunk of a body after the head is lopped off. శిరస్సులేని శరీరము, కబంధము.

A fragment, a limb lopped off, a separated member, ఖండము. **మొండెపుగాము** *mondepu-gamu*. n. An epithet of Rāhu. రాహువు.

మొకద్దమా *mokaddamā*. [H.] n. An affair, business.

మొకమాలు Same as ముఖమల్ (q. v.).

మొకము See మొగము. **మొకమాటము** or **మొగమాటము** *moka-māṭamu*. Corruption of మొగమోటము. See under మొగము.

మొకరము Same as మొక్కరము (q. v.).

మొకరి *mokari*. [Tel.] adj Sounding, మ్రోయునట్టి. Noisy, prattling, అసంబంధముగ పలుకునట్టి. **మొకరితుమ్మెద** *mokari-tummeda*. n A large black bee. ధ్వనిచేసే తుమ్మెద. "నిస్తాపులకు వెకలు నైగాడు మొకరితుమ్మెదలురొదలుగల మెరుగుదుంబురుపులట్లు." Swa. iii. 37. టీ॥ మొకరితుమ్మెదలు, గండుతుమ్మెదలు.

మొక్క *mokka*. [Tel. short for మొలక from మొలకే.] n. A germ, shoot, young plant, నారు, చిన్నచెట్టు. Bluntness, disgrace. నాడిమికేమి. భంగము. A stub of wood. చెట్టు నరకగా మిగిలిన మోడు. మొక్కనగవు a budding smile, a slight laugh. "గ్రక్కునంబొడము మొక్కనగవుల మోముదమ్ములకు వేరొక్కవింత." A. iv. 45. మొక్కపైరు young corn. మొక్కకట్టు to transplant. వాణ్ని మొక్కపరచినారు they disgraced him. **మొక్కచెడు** *mokka-chedu*. v. n. To be disappointed or disgraced, భంగపడు. అవమానపడు. మొక్కచెడి వచ్చినాడు he returned home disgraced. **మొక్కచేరుచు** *mokka-cherutsu*. v. a. To disgrace, disappoint. భంగపరచు. **మొక్కచేయు** *mokka-chēyu*. v. a. To blunt. పదును చెరచు. **మొక్కజొన్న** *mokka-dzonna*. n. Maize, Indian corn, a large species of the Great Millet. Rox. i. 263. **మొక్కడి** or **మొక్కడీడు** *mokkadi*. n. An obstinate man. మూర్ఖుడు. An elephant without tusks. కొమ్ములులేనియేనుగు. **మొక్కడు** *mokkadu*. n. A firm or determined man, a strong man. బలిష్ఠుడు, బలిసినవాడు. **మొక్కడుగు** *mokk-adugu*. n. The stumps of corn which yield a second crop. **మొక్కపడు** *mokka-padu*. v. n. To be disgraced. మొక్కపడుచు. **మొక్కపరుచు** or **మొక్కపుచ్చు** *mokka-parutsu*. v. a. To disappoint, disgrace. భంగపరచు, అవమానము చేయు. **మొక్కపోవు** or **మొక్కలుపోవు** *mokka-pōvu*. v. n. To become blunt, వాడిచెడు. To be disgraced, to be disappointed, భంగపడు. **మొక్కమామిడి** *mokka-māmidi*. n. The Cashew nut, జీడిమామిడి.

మొక్కట్టు *mok-kattu*. [Tel. మొకము+కట్టు.] n. Features, lineaments, face, likeness. ముఖకవళిక.

మొక్కము or **మొక్కపుచెట్టు** *mokkamu*. [Tel.] n. The name of a tree.

మొక్కరము or **మొకరము** *mokkaramu*. [Tel.] n. A post, స్తంభము. A prop. A bar set against a door to keep it shut. తలుపుకు మోటిచ్చినమాను. గడియ, గడెమ్రాను.

మొక్కలము or **మొక్కలితనము** *mokkalamu*. [from Skt. మూర్ఖత్వము.] n. Obstinacy, stubbornness, మూర్ఖత్వము. Bravery, courage, valor, heroism, శౌర్యము, ధైర్యము. Spiritedness, enthusiasm, joy, ఉత్సాహము. మొక్కలములు stubborn language. adj. Stubborn, obstinate, మూర్ఖమైన. Irresistible, అప్రతిహతము. "ఎక్కడిదర్పరహస్యం బెక్కడి చుట్టరికమింక నేటివినయముల్, మొక్కలపుక్రొవ్వొంటిం జిక్కిన జంపుటయె సిరులు సలిసీ." Vish. viii. 446. "వ॥ నకుగవియెుండుపత్త్రములనంబున బెగ్గిలి రాయేకప్పడి. మ్రొగిసరు. శిల్లపోకల్పయ మొక్కలపై కుకొంబుగానకోయరోర్." M. XII. iii. 100.

కృపమొక్కలిమై, అనగా దయామిపేంకుడై. మొక్కలి or మొక్కలిక *mokkali*. n. The flash or sparkle in a ruby. కెంపులోని అధికకాంతి. మొక్కలి, మొక్కలికాడు, మొక్కలీడు, or మొక్కలుడు n. An obstinate man. ముక్కరి, మూర్ఖుడు. A guard, a sentry, కావలివాడు. A hero, a courageous man, శూరుడు, కోపగాడు. "పీః మంత్రినిద్వే షంబు మాన్యపరాధనంబును ప్రజాపీడనంబులును కలిగి, మొక్కలీడగుటయు ముచ్చిలిమంత్రులా, కని బాపియతనినందమనిరాజ్య." M. XIV. i. 23.

మొక్కు or మ్రొక్కు *mokku*. [Tel.] v. n. To prostrate oneself, to bow, to make an obeisance, నమస్కారముచేయు. మొక్కబోయిన దేవుడు ఎదురుగావచ్చినట్లు the god I came to worship has met me in the way. n. An obeisance, a vow, దండము. వ్రతము. మొక్కుబడి or మ్రొక్కుబడి *mokku-badi*. n. A vow. దేవతాప్రార్థన, వ్రతము. మొక్కుబడి వాండ్రు those who are under a vow. మొక్కుకొను or మ్రొక్కుకొను *mokku-konu*. v. n. To vow or to make a vow. ప్రార్థనచేసికొను.

మొఖమల్ or మొకమాలు *mokhamul*. [H.] n. Velvet.

మొఖాసా *mokhasa*. [H.] n. A village held on service tenure. A village granted at a favourable assessment or no assessment, to any person for past or expected service. మొఖాసాదారుడు a person holding the above.

మొగ *moga*. [from Skt. ముఖము.] n. The tip, point, end; the beginning, మొదలు. The mouth of a river, &c. మొన, నదీ సముద్రాదుల ముఖము. An entrance, ద్వారము. ఆ మొగను at the beginning. A blossom, మొగ్గ. మొగకొను *moga-konu*. v. n. To begin, commence. మొదలుపెట్టు. To meet, turn the face towards, అభిముఖమగు. "వి పక్షీముఖోద్యముల నివర్తమూలాగాన నాని యొగ కుతూలంబున మదము శోకము మొగకొననీయవి యమరపులాంతిగోరుజములకుక." M. XII. i. 196. See మొగదల.

మొగ or మగ *moga*. [Tel.] adj. Male. పురుష. మొగజెంపలు side locks. మొగతనము *moga-tanamu*. n. Manhood, virility, పుంస్త్వము. మొగవాడు *moga-vadu*. n. A man, a male, a husband. పురుషుడు.

మొగకట్టు *moga-kattu*. [Tel.] v. n. To sound, మ్రోగు.

మొగడ *mogada*. [Tel.] n. A bud. A boss or knob on a shield or door. మొగ్గ, గుబక. "విత్తులేనియట్టి పృథ్వి మొక్కలేర్పట్టె ఫలముపువ్వు మొగడమత్రిలేదు, స్వాదులేదుమాడ సాపాటునకు లెస్స, దీనిభావమేమి తిరుమలేశ." Tirumalesa. "పూమొగడతో తులదూగులతాంగిముక్కు." R. iv. 60.

మొగడు *mogadu*. [Tel.] adj. Stubborn, obstinate. ముక్కరమైన, మొండి. "అనిశమిలు కయు కలికినివపుడుమంచి, మొగడు సాహసమె లిగినీమగడుచేక, నమ్మకముగేటివచ్చి క్షణంబులోన నీతెరువుమూన్చ చేయనగ్గష్టుడపుడు." N. ix. 359.

మొగడు *mogadu*. [Tel.] n. The ridge of a roof, ఇంటిచూరికొప్పు. plu. మొగళ్లు or మొగడులు and మొగలు. Gen. మొగటి.

మొగము or మొకము *mogamu*. [from Skt. ముఖము.] n. The face. ముఖము. Front, ఎదురు. An entrance, door, ద్వారము. adj. Chief, ముఖ్యము. మొగచాటు *moga-tsatu*. n. Surfeit, disgust in eating, ముఖముకొట్టడము. "తీపితినతినవ్వాకు తీపైన మొగచాటు, సారెకుబలు కుట చేప్పనగను." Venkatésware. §. 16. మొగతప్పు or మొగతిరుగు *moga-toppu*. v. n. To have the face turned away, విముఖమగు. మొగదల *mogadala*. n. The end or butt (of a wall.) ఎదురు, ముందటిభాగము. మొగపట్టు or మొగమాట్లు

moga-paṭṭa. n. An ornament for a horse's head something like a cavesson, ముఖపట్ట. "మణులమొగపట్ట పన్నిపాపాణిరొయికండం." Swa. iv. 37. మొగపడు *moga-paḍu*. v. a. To see, చూచు. మొగసాళము or మొగవాళము *moga-pāḷamu*. n. The front portion of a house, &c. ఇల్లు లోనగు వాని ముందటిభాగము. మొగపిరికి *moga-piriki*. (మొగము + పిరికి.) n. A tortoise, తాబేలు. మొగము తప్పించు to abscond, disappear. మొగపు *mogapu*. (మొగ+పూస.) n. The front portion of a necklace, హారాదులముఖభాగము. A buckle. కంఠభూషణములయొక్క ముఖభాగము. "ధాత్రీమహాదేవి తాల్చినమున్నీటి మొలనూలిరత్నంపు మొగపునంగ." Prabhavati Pradyumnam, i. 3. మొగమిచ్చు *moga-mitstsu*. v. n. To show the face, to favour, to be pleased, సుముఖుడగు. మొగమోటమి, మొగమోటము, మొగమోట or మోగమోటమి *moga-mōṭami*. n. Partiality, pity, compassion, దాక్షిణ్యము. Hesitation, doubt, సంకోచము. మొగమోడు *mogam-ōḍu*. v. n. To be ashamed. సిగ్గుపడు. "మంగిటికేతెంచి మొగమోడనగునె." Abhim. 47. To be partial, దాక్షిణ్యపడు. To hesitate, సంకోచించు. మొగవాడ *moga-vāḍa*. n. The front door of a temple. గోపుర ద్వారము. "అరిమురిమొగవాడ జరచిపిక్షింప." BD. iv. 661. మొగవీణె *moga-vīṇe*. n. A kind of వీణె, ముఖవీణె. మొగసరి *moga-sari*. (మొగము + సరి.) Same as మొగముట్టు (q. v.). మొగసాల, మొగసల or మోసాల *moga-sāla*. n. An entrance hall. నడవ. ముఖమంటపము, నగరితల వాకిటిచావడి. "వీరమ్మందు పెద్దమొగసాలం జాలు మానసులం గావలి కట్టి." M. ix. ii. 34. A porch in front of a house, తలవాకిటిపంచే.

మొగరంబము *moga-rambamu*. [Tel.] n. The large black bee, భ్రమరము. షట్పద.

మొగరము See మొగ్గరము.

మొగరించు *mogarintsu*. [Tel.] v. a. To surround, to seize, ఆక్రమించు.

మొగలాయి *mogalāyi*. [H.] adj. Mogul. కర్ణాటకపు.

మొగలి or మొగిలి *mogali*. [Tel.] n. The Screw Pine, or Mangrove, *Mandanus odoratissimus*. (Rox. iii. 738.) కేతకి. మొగలిచాప a mat made of its leaves. మొగలాకుగొడుగు an umbrella made of its leaves. మొగలి చండ్లు the drooping tips of the branches. మొగలిపువ్వు the fragrant flower of this tree. మొగలినాగు a snake said to be found in its flower. మొగలిరేకు a petal of its flower, or an ornament worn by women on the head. మొగలికోడి *mogali-kōḍi*. n. A watercock. ఉకపక్షి. మొగలిపనస *mogali-panasa*. n. The pineapple, అనాసచెట్టు. మొగలేరు *moga-lēru*. (మొగలి+ఏరు.) n. The celestial river. ఆకాశగంగ. The name of a stream, also called సువర్ణముఖి. "మొగలేటిమడుపున" Kālahas. ii. 161. BD. iii. 349. మొగలివాకిలి *mogali-vākili*. n. An entrance to a town. తలవాకిలి. A town hall where criminal cases are tried. కచ్చేరి, హజారము. "పతిహారులు వేగను పిరచోదునింటను వెలుగొందుగిన్నె కపటంబునస్త్రీ నిదొంగవంచు నవ్వన జదలా డి నిం మొగలి వాకిటికీడిచి చోరదండనమొనరింప జూడగ." Valeswara. v. 85.

మొగవడము *mogavaḍamu*. [Tel. మొగ+ వడము.] n. A black blanket thrown over an elephant, ఏనుగుమీదకప్పు నల్లనికంబళి.

మొగాళము *mogāḷamu*. [Tel.] n. The head of a canal carried from a river to irrigate the fields. ఏటికాలువయొక్క మొగదల, ఆరంభము.

మొగి *mogi*. [Tel.] n. An attempt, ప్రారంభ. "సీ॥ ద్వాదశవార్షికోత్తమసత్రయాగంబు మొగిచే యుచున్నయమ్మునులకడకు." భా. ఆది. i. Total a group. ముత్తము, గుంపు. సమూహము. Joint property, ఉమ్మడి. ఇది వారికి మాకు మొగి or మొగినియున్నది this is held jointly by us. "ధీమంతుడు . . . అతిబలుండు ననువారొక్క మొగి యును, సుమిత్రుండును మిత్రవర్మయు ననువారొక్క మొగియును, సువీరుండును సువర్చుండు ననువారొక్క మొగియును నిట్లు మూడు ముత్తంబులై." భార. ఆది. Manner విధము. A time, ఆవృత్తి. ఒక్కమొగి or ఒక్కమొగిన at once. ఒక్కపెట్టున. "ఉక్కుమిగిలి యొక్కమొగిన విక్కటిల్లి." adv. At first, ముందుగా, ముందర. "తనునిదిరెగదనియెడలో నగుపడి సాధులకు పేదవారికెల్లను మొగిచేయుదుర్వినీతుల కనునిమిత్తాక మనుమైవధియంబుల్." M. I. i. 130. మొగిచియు mogiyu. v. n. To attempt, to undertake, పూను. To spread all over, to surround, as darkness, కవియు.

మొగిలి See మొగలి.

మొగుటము moguṭu. [Tel.] n. The ridge of a roof. మొగుటివాసము the ridge pole of a roof. ఇంటినడికొప్పు.

మొగుడు moguḍu. [Tel. from మొగడ. See మొగ్గ.] v. n. To be closed, as a flower, the hands, etc. ముకుళించు. మొగుచు, మొగుడుచు, మొగుడ్చు. or మొగిడించు mogutsu. v. a. To cause to be closed, as a flower, &c. To close, shut (the eyes), fold (the hands.) ముకుళించు. "సాష్టాంగదండప్రణామంబుచేసి నిలిచి కేలుమొగిచి." Vish. ii. 72. "చనిమంత్రులెల్ల వాస్తుములమొగిడ్చి యున్నరసాధు నకంఠియుచెలువ." Sar. D. 283. "కేల్మొగిడించిభక్తినమస్కరించి." Parama Yōgi Vilāsa. Dwip: page 238. మొగుడు moguḍu. [Tel. for మగడు.] n. A husband. భర్త.

మొగులు, మొగిలు, మొయిలు or మొయులు mogulu. [Tel.] n. A cloud. మేఘము. "కాలమునువాడమొగులుల కాలాక్కృతిపొంగలిన నెలుగవినిబలసి." R. vi. 10. మొగులుకడిమి mogulu-kaḍimi, n. The tree called *Nauclea Orientalis*. కదిమిచెట్టు, నీరుకడిమిచెట్టు. మొగులుదారి mogulu-dāri. n. The cloudy road, i. e., the sky, ఆకాశము.

మొగ్గ mogga. [Tel. another form of మొగడ.] n. A bud. ముకుళము. A feat performed by gymnasts in falling back. మొగ్గవాలడము or మొగ్గవేయడము the feats or contortions practised by acrobats; as that of falling back and dancing on the feet and hands. మొగ్గవాలు to bend backwards touching the ground with the hands. మొగ్గవిచ్చు mogga-vitstsu. v. n. To unfold as a flower, వికసించు To be scattered. యుద్ధాయుధులు.

మొగ్గలము Same as మొక్కలము (q. v.).

మొగ్గు or మొగ్గు moggu. [Tel.] v. n. To incline, to lean on one side. To be depressed, as a scale in weighing, to bow down under a burden, to show an inclination toward, to be inclined to, వంగు, వాలు, తూలు. "అంబరంబిలమొగ్గి నిహమతిప్రస్థ." BD. v. 268. n. Leaning, inclination. ఒకతట్టుకై తూలడము, వంగడము, వాలడము. "విగ్గిరేచియొరబసవధుమతి విమతిదోమమొగ్గమొ మొగ్గగుగాను పోదిమని మందిపొరనిలచు." Chenna. iv. 358. మొగ్గను, విశేషముగానున్నది, ఘనముగానున్నది మొగ్గటలు. మొగ్గటిల్లు మొగ్గతిలు or మొగ్గతిల్లు moggatilu. v. n. To bend down, to stoop. వంగు. To kneel down, మోకరిల్లు. "చరితలఁదిగ్గెముఖలసరి మొగ్గతిలగ." BRY. ii. 437. "ముందటికార్లతునిని మొగ్గతిలంబడియును, మిందులపందియరై, సెరిదప్పుగూలియు." M. VI. iii. 218. మొగ్గరము moggaramu. n. An array, వ్యూహము. "అరిసంవేశంకోటయుక్ ముతు మొగ్గరముగై కనుపట్టునిల్లాలాగ్రముల దూలు." R. v. 112. M. IX. i. 318.

మొటిక or మొట్టిక moṭika. [Tel.] n. A sprout, మొలక A fragment, తునక.

"ఏమి సేరని నిన్న టింబంత మొటికె." Ila. iii. 25. టీ॥ మొన్న టిరవంతపిల్లవని భావము:

మొటిమ or **మొటిమె** *moṭima*. [Tel.] n. A pimple. యౌవనమందు ముఖమునిమీదలేచేకాయ, తారుణ్యపుపిటిక. adj. Short, పొట్టి.

మొట్టమొదట See under మొదలు.

మొట్టు *moṭṭu*. [Tel.] v. a. To rap with the knuckles. తలమీదవ్రేళ్లకణుపులతోకొట్టు. **మొట్టికాయ** or **మొట్టు** *moṭṭi-kāya*. n. A rap with the knuckles, a buffet, a cuff. వ్రేళ్లకణుపులతో కొట్టుదెబ్బ. **మొట్లమారి** *moṭla-mari*. n. One who often gets cuffed, మొట్టికాయలుతినువాడు.

మొట్ట *moṭṭa*. [Tel.] n. A kind of fish. బడిమొట్ట and వానమొట్ట are its species.

మొడికట్టు *moḍi-kaṭṭu*. [Tel.] n. Fashion, mode. విధము. "ముత్తియంబులతోగ మొడికట్టుప నులచేపట్టు మేల్కట్టులవరలవిరుల." Ila. ii. 13.

మొత్త *motta*. [Tel.] n. A side. ప్రక్క. The end, origin. మూలస్థానము. The side way at a door way. వాకిటిమూల. The corner or end of a wall. ప్రక్కగోడ. A bank thrown across a stream. బలిసినమొత్త a fat side or paunch. మొత్తబలిసిన having heavy hips. కనుమమొత్తసుకాచుకొన్నారు they lay hid in the side of the hill pass. **మొత్తపిరి** *motta-piri*. n. A straw cushion placed under the bucket that works in a water-lift.

మొత్తము *mottamu*. [Tel.] n. The total, whole; a flock, multitude, heap, or collection. సమూహము, గుంపు. శూరులమొత్తము a multitude of heroes. కోతిమొత్తము a herd of monkeys. వింటిమొత్తము a heap of bows. మంటమొత్తము a mass of flames. "మంచుమొత్తములోన మార్తాండుడు న్నట్టు." Kalahas. §. 22. మంచుమొత్తములోన, in a mass of clouds, మేఘసంచయమందు. "మెరుపుమొత్తంబులు మీరెనుత్తరమున." Zaccs. iv. 26. మొత్తముగాచెప్పినాడు he spoke in general. మొత్తపువ్యయము the total expenditure. మొత్తపుమాట a generic word. మొత్తముచేయు to make a total. మొత్తములై in mobs. "పులులుమొత్తంబులై పొదరిండ్లలో దూరు." B. VIII. adj. Thick, దళసైన. మొత్తపుదీపములు big lights.

మొత్తు *mottu*. [Tel.] v. a. To beat, smite, thrash. కొట్టు. "కర్తులకేడెముల్ కరముల దాల్చి, మొత్తిరెక్కులతిరణములునుల్లగొట్టి." Venkatachala Maha. page. 171. To cut, నరుకు. n. A blow, దెబ్బ. మొత్తించు to cause to beat, కొట్టించు. **మొత్తులాడు** *mottu-l-āḍu*. v. n. To fight, dispute or quarrel. కొట్లాడు. "పుణ్యాఘపాతండులములకు మొత్తులాడి." A. vi. 91. **మొత్తువడు** *mottu-paḍu*. v. n. To be beaten, కొట్టుపడు, కొట్టబడు. **మొత్తికొను** or **మొత్తుకొను** *motti-konu*. v. n. To beat one's own head or mouth in despair. To lament or wail. అక్కడికి పోవద్దని మొత్తుకొంటిని I entreated him not to go there. "అసురుసురనుచు నడునెత్తిమొత్తుకొనుచు." Jagann. ii. 63. **మొత్తుకొళ్లు** *mottu-koḷḷu*. n. Lamentations, howling, outcries, wailing. ఏడ్పు, పెడబొబ్బలు.

మొదలు *modalu*. [Tel. infl. మొదటి or మొదలిటి. abl. మొదట. plu. మొదళ్లు.] n. The beginning, origin, source. ఆది, మూలము. The root, stock. వృక్షమూలము. Principal, capital as opposed to interest. మూలధనము, అసలు. The chief, the head; the foundation of a thing, the basis. The foot of a mountain. చెవిమొదలు the lower tip of the ear. వడ్డీమొదలు interest and principal. వాడు మొదలే మంచివాడుకాడు in fact he is not a good man. మొదల, అనగా మూలమునందు at the root. మొదలు, మొదలుగ, మొదలైన. మొదలు

గా or మొదలుగాగల modalu. adv. Et cetera. భేరిమొదలుగ drums, &c. (literally, beginning with the drum.) వాడు వచ్చినది మొదలు or మొదలుగ since his arrival. మొదలుకొను or మొదలుగొను modalu-konu. v. a. To begin. ప్రారంభించు. ఇది మొదలుకొని henceforth, beginning from this. వాడు వచ్చినది మొదలుకొని since his arrival. మొదలుచెడు modalu-chedu. v. n. To be ruined, root and branch. తుత్రుమూచెడు. మొదలుపెట్టు modalu-pettu. v. a. To begin. ఆరంభించు. మొదట modata. adv. At first, at the beginning, in the first place. మొట్టమొదట motta-modata (మొదలు+మొదలు.) adv. At the very beginning, at first, first of all, ప్రప్రథమమందు. మొదటి modati. adj. First, earliest, original, primary, principal, capital, chief. వాడు అబద్ధాలకు మొదటిపాడము he is the father of lies, వాడు కలహానికి మొదటిపాదము he was the beginner of the quarrel.

మొదవ modava. [Tel.] n. The grass named *Saccharum cylindricum*. పల్లజము.

మొదవు modavu. [Tel.] n. A milch cow. పాడియావు.

మొదుక moduka. [Tel.] adj. Sharp. కరుకైన. Thick, దట్టమైన. మొదుకన modukana. n. Sharpness, కరుకుదనము. Heaviness, బరువు. మొదుకని modukani. adj. Heavy, బరువైన.

మొద్దడు moddadu. [from Skt. ముగ్ధ.] n. A booby, a blockhead, a great hulking fellow, గండడు, మూఢుడు. A stout man, లావైనవాడు.

మొద్దు moddu. [Tel. from మోడు.] n. A block, stump, pollard, lump, mass. స్థాణువు, మోడు. A blockhead. జడుడు, జడురాలు. "వెర్రిమొద్దుకేల వేదశాస్త్రములు." Vêma. 1073. ఎద్దుమొద్దు స్వరూపముగానుండేవాడు a mere brute, a blockhead. adj. Blunt, not sharp, పదునులేని. Stout, thick, లావైన. మొద్దుపెదవులు thick lips. Stubborn, uncouth, lumpish, dull, stupid, callous. మోటుగానుండే. చేవలేని. మొద్దుగా moddu-ga. adv. Stupidly. మొద్దుపోవు moddu-poru. v. n. To become blunt, వాడిలేనిదగు.

మొన mona. [Tel.] n. The point, end, extremity. అగ్రము. శిఖాగ్రము. An army, or detachment, సేన. A tube, తెగ. A military array, వ్యూహము. A tribe, తెగ. The front, ముందు. "మన మొనలకుపశమగాడు మరలు పుమిండకా." M. VI. ii. 97. "లోమొన, వెలిమొన, ఉపిమొన, ముమ్మొన, చతురమొన, వ్యూహపుమొన. పావపుమొన, దాటుడునుమొన, కదలుమొన, అరమాటుమొన, సెరమాటుమొన, పకిలౌకంపుమొన, లాదిగాగల పదిరెండుమొనల వాసితెలిసి." H. i. 245. మొనలాడిపోయినకత్తి a knife with a blunt point. adj. Last, furthest, utmost. కడపటి. మొనకట్టు mona-kattu v. n. To attempt with enthusiasm, ఉత్సహించు. n. Joy, rejoicing, enthusiasm, ఉత్సాహము. An amulet or drug used as a charm, కట్టుమందులలో ఒకటి. ఒకానొక సంధనమూలిక. "ఇదిదారికట్టు మొనకట్టది, కాంతా వశ్యకారణమది." S. i. 18. "జలాగ్నిస్తంభముల, మొనకట్టును నాకట్టును." H. i. 174. adj. Rejoicing, enthusiastic, ఉత్సాహకరమైన. మొనకాడు or మొనగాడు mona-kadu. n. A leader of an army, a hero, a principal; a ringleader, శూరుడు, సేనాధిపతి, ముఖ్యుడు. దొంగలమొనగాడు a ringleader among thieves. మొనకోను Same as మొనదల. (q. v.) మొనచేయు mona-chêyu. v. n. To face or front in battle. కూపారించు. మొనచన్ను mona-tsannu. n. A nipple. Lit. the tip of the breast. చూచుకము. మొనతప్పు mona-tappu. v. n. To be turned away as the face, to turn away from, విముఖమగు. " మొనరప్పితిమి రణమున మన మకటా ముప్పురము." భార. సౌ. i. **మొనయు** *monayu.* v. n. and v. a. To be, appear, happen, కలుగు. To busy oneself, to engage in. To prepare, be ready, attempt, పూను, పనిపడు. To prepare for battle, రణోద్యోగముచేయు. To cover, to rest upon, ఒప్పు, కమ్ము. అలుము. " మొండి మాటలాడి మొనసిచేయుచుండువిరక్తి యనుమనిగెల్వనె ఎట నలవిగాదు." Vēma. 864. " మొనయు చింతాక్రాంతిమూలా విప్పు." Swa. iv. 148. టీ॥ మొనయు, కమ్ముకొనునట్టి. **మొనపు** or **మొన యించు** *monapu.* v. a. To cause to attempt, పూనజేయు. To cause to happen, కలుగజేయు. To put, place. పొర్చు, ఉంచు. " అనిశా గైటభదైత్య వైరి, దుమహాసంతాపమున్ బాపి మై, మొనపంగొం డొక నిర్వ్యయవ్యసనమునన్." Parij. iv. 12. **మొనపు** n. An attempt, పూనిక.

మొనరు *monaru.* [Tel.] v. n. To be pretty, ఒప్పు.

మొన్న *monna.* [Tel. మొదలు+నాడు.] n. The day before yesterday, ప్రగతదినము, నిన్న టికినిన్న. adv. The other day, lately. అటు మొన్న the day before that, three days ago. మొన్నటిసంవత్సరాది last New Year's day. మొన్నటిబృహస్పతివారము last Thursday (though five days ago.)

మొప్ప *moppa.* [Tel.] n. The dragonet, *Callionymus lyra,* a fish with a projection like a switch from its shoulders. **మొప్పలు** *moppalu.* n. A fish's gills. చేపయొక్క పువ్వార.

మొప్పె or **మొప్పియ** *moppe.* [Tel.] n. An idiot, a head-strong, obstinate fool. మూర్ఖుడు, మూర్ఖురాలు. మొప్పెకు మూరెడు నోరు a fool has a mouth a cubit wide. adj. Stiff, బిరుసైన. " మొప్పెతనము." ఛిల్లా. iv. **మొప్పెతనము** *moppe-tanamu.* n. Idiocy, stubbornness, pertness. కాఠిన్యము, మూర్ఖత్వము.

మొయిలు or **మొయియలు** *moyilu.* [Tel. another form of మొగులు.] n. A cloud. మేఘము. Vasu. ii. 40. plu. మొయిళ్లు.

మొర *mora.* [Tel.] n. A cry, scream, lamentation, complaint, plaint. A declaration, statement. అర్థవాదము. Also, another form of మోర (q.v.) **మొరపెట్టు** *mora-pettu.* v. n. To scream, cry, yell, lament, wail, cry aloud, complain. ఆర్తధ్వనిచేయు, అరుచు, పడిన అన్యాయము మనవిచేసుకొను. మొరపెట్టుకొను to howl, make a complaint, complain, తనకు కలిగిన అన్యాయమునుగూర్చి చెప్పుకొను. స్త్రీలకు స్వాతంత్ర్యములేదని శాస్త్రములు మొరపెట్టు చుండగా while the Sastras declare that women have no independence.

మొరకు or **మొరకుడు** *moraku.* [from Skt. మూర్ఖ.] n. An idiot, a blockhead, an obstinate fool. మూర్ఖుడు, మూర్ఖస్త్రీ, మోటువాడు, జడుడు. " మొరకులగుటప్రతాప భాషణంబులకు వెరవరు." M. V. iii. 233. adj. Stubborn, brutish. Too hard to bite, కఠినమైన, పరుష మైన, కొరికితే గరగరమనియుండెడి కఠినముగా నుండే, మూర్ఖమైన, మొండి. " మొరకుగరకను గారాకు, గాయుండజాలది." BD. iii. 1388. **మొరకుతనము** *moraku-tanamu.* n. Stubbornness. మూర్ఖత్వము. Anger, rage, కినుక. **మొరకు** *moraku.* n. Harm, mischief, damage, defect, deficiency. కలిమి, న్యూనత. adj. Defective. న్యూనము. **మొరకడము** *morakadamu.* n. Wickedness, mischief. దౌష్ట్యము.

మొరగు or **మొరంగు** *moragu.* [Tel.] v. n. To hide. దాగు, పొంచు. v. a. To delude the eyes, to deceive, వంచించు, దాచు, మరుగుచేయు. కను మొరగు to wink, to connive at, to shut the eyes. "మొరగినదురించుచో విని తరియుకుటం జంపబోయెదం బదనుచుణ్." P. iii. 243. టీ॥ మొరగి, కనుమరుగై. "నీడక దునబోరనేలకువెలిగాగ నడుగు పెట్టితిరుగవార్త మొరగి, యొకటిదలపవరులకొడవినరొదవజే, కరణిమ్ము క్కు దేవికమ్ము ల్రాము." Swa. iv. 146. టీ॥ ఆత్మ మొరగి, మనస్సుమవినా చేసి, మనస్సునకు ఎరుకలే కుండా. n. Hiding, concealment; delusion, deception, వంచన. One who deceives, a cheat, వంచకుడు. adj. Deceptive, cheating, వంచకమైన.

మొరటు moratu. [Tel.] n. An obstinate fool. మూర్ఖుడు. "మొరటువానిగిరిచ్చి మొరయగ యూర్చకు." Vēma. 1965. మొరటుతనము morata-tanamu. n. Stubbornness. మూర్ఖత్వము. మొరడు or మొరటి moradu. adj. Hard, hardened, rough, knotty, stubborn. గడుసుపారిన, కఠినమైన, ముడిగానుండే. "మొరడువంగినపెట్టిమడుకకు." P. iii. 193. టీ॥ గడుసుపారిన, ముదిమిచేత అవనతమైన. మొరడు n. A block, a stump; a knot. మొద్దు, ముడి, మోడు. "మట్టువాకిలేరు మొరడుకమ్మరిజేరు." Vēma. 2084. మొరడుపారిన moradu-parina. adj. Hard, grown hard by age, having the limbs contracted by disease. గడుసుపారిన, మద్దులుకట్టుకొనిపోయిన.

మొరప morapa. [Tel.] adj. Stony, gravelly; గులకరాళ్లుగల. మొరపరాళ్లు gravels, pebbles. మొరపనేల a gravelly soil. మొరము or మొర్ము moramu n. A pebble, gravel, గులకరాయి. జెల్లిరాయి. మొరపము or మొరవము morapamu. n. A sound, noise. మ్రోత, ధ్వని, రవము. "అందియలమొరపంబున కరుగుచెంద్రు బ్రోదిరాజుంచదివిధమున." M. IV. iv. 24 మొరవ morava adj. Blunt, మొనలేని, మొక్కపోయిన, మొనమడిగిన, మొక్కయైన. మొరవపోవు morava-pōvu. v. n. To be blunt. To be disregarded, or disused. మొక్కపోవు. మొరవపోయిన morava-pōyina adj. Blunted, మొక్కపోయిన, మడిగిన.

మొరమొర mora-mora [Tel.] n. A noise, murmur, ధ్వని, మ్రోత. మొరమొరలాడు moramora-l-adu. v. n. To crackle, మొరమొరయని మ్రోయు. To be enraged or furious. కోపపడికొని మనుమూపు.

మొరయు or మ్రోయు morayu. [Tel. another form of మ్రోగు.] v. n. To sound, resound. ధ్వనించు. మొరయించు morayintsu. v. a. To sound, cause to resound, roar. ధ్వనిచేయు. వాయించు. "మొరయించె మణుజాల్యవాదము." R. iv. 82.

మొరలి morali. [Tel.] n. The tree called *Celtis orientalis*. Heyne. ప్రియాలవృక్షము, మోరపప్పుచెట్టు.

మొరసదము mora-sadamu. [Tel.] n. A kind of dog, a terrier. ఉడుపుకుక్క. మోటుకుక్క. "జోగిలములు మొరసదములు జాగిలజి చావముత్తరగతి." Swa. iv. 67.

మొరసు or మొరాసు morasu. [Tel.] n. Gravel, a pebble, మొరము. మొరసునేల a gravelly soil. adj. Rugged, stubborn. మోటు. "పాకనాటిరెడ్డి పరగమోటూరెడ్డి యొసగు కటోటపెద్ద యొఱ్ఱరెడ్డి. మొరసులుంచిరుఘని వారువొవ్వున్నింట ప్రతిథకెక్కిరట్టువడగిసేమ." Vēma. 1322. "పంటమోటాటిపెడకంటి పాకనాటి యుగనలమలాదికొండారె మొరసుగోన కొలిచికాపులుమొదలైన." H. iv. 171.

మొరి or మొరికె Same as మొఱ్ఱ. (q. v.)

మొరిటె moritе. [Tel.] n. A little winnowing basket, చిన్నచేట.

మొరుగు or మొరాగు moruga. [Tel.] v. n. To bark, as a dog. కూయు. n. The bark of a dog, కుక్కకూత. A cry, కూత మొరుగుడు morugudu. n. Barking, (కుక్క) కూయుట.

మొఱ్ఱ or మొర morra. [Tel.] n. A cry, scream, outcry, wailing, lamentation, complaint [illegible]

తెగడముచు తా మొఱ్ఱనిరగ." BD. iv. 1961. దొంగలువచ్చిపడగానే కుయ్యోమొఱ్ఱో అని అరిచినారు on being attacked by the thieves they screamed out. మొఱ్ఱోయనిచెప్పు to howl, cry, vociferate. నేను మొఱ్ఱో వద్దని చెప్పితిని I cried 'Alas! do not do this.'

మొఱ్ఱి *morri*. [Tel.] n. A fault, want, defect, broken edge, as that of the moon in an eclipse. ("*Defectus Lunæ.*" Virgil) కొఱత, తొఱ్ఱి, అంగన్యూనత. adj. Defective, maimed, imperfect, damaged. Partial, as an eclipse. తొఱ్ఱి, తొస్సి. ఇప్పుడు గ్రహణముపట్టి చంద్రునిలో కొంచెము మొఱ్ఱిపోయి ఉన్నది as the eclipse came on, the edge of the moon appeared broken. వాడు వెక్కిరిస్తే నీకు ఎక్కడ మొఱ్ఱిపోయినది what harm does his gibing do you?

మొల *mola*. [Tel.] n. The waist, the middle, కటిప్రదేశము. A wedge, pin, large nail, or spike. The pin or needle of a balance, త్రాసుముల్లు, చీల. మొలత్రాసు a balance which has a tongue. "గమనియు త్రాసులంబు మొలత్రాసునుపట్టెడ నీరుకారు." H. ii. 200. దిసమొల or మొండిమొల stark-nakedness, utter nudity. మొలకట్టు *mola-kattu*. n. A girdle or waist-band. నడుముకు కట్టుకొనే త్రాడు, మొలనూలు. A waist cloth, కట్టుకోక. మొలకత్తి *mola-katti*. n. A dagger, బాకు. మొలకులికి or మొలకొలికి *mola-kuliki*. n. A kind of grain, ధాన్యవిశేషము. మొలతాడు *mola-tādu*. n. The small string tied round a Hindu's waist whence is suspended the bit of cloth which serves as a modesty piece. కటిసూత్రము. బంగారుమొలతాడు a woven cord of golden wire. మొలతాటిగోడ *mola-tāti-gōda*. n. A parapet, or rail wall. పిట్టగోడ. మొలనూలు *mola-nūlu*. n. A girdle, a zone: a cestus of gold or silver, worn by women. అడువాలికటిసూత్రము.

మొలచు, మొలుచు or మొల్చు *molatsu*. [Tel.] v. n. To sprout, germinate, vegetate, grow. To rise, to appear, as a star. మొలక, మొలప or మొల్క *molaka*. [from మొలచు.] n. A germ, a sprout. అంకురము. The core, or centre of a boil. దుర్మాంసవిశేషము. Piles. ఆసనములోని మొలక ఉపద్రవము. adj. Young, tender. లేత. టెంకాయలోని మొలక a substance that rises like a knob in an over-ripe cocoanut. మొలకచ్రొన్నెల the new moon. మొలకనవ్వు a budding smile, i. e., a gentle smile. ఆ వంశమునకు వాడొక మొలక ఉన్నాడు he is the only remaining individual or scion of that family. మొలకపండుగ a vernal festival, the feast of the sprouts. మొలకకట్టు *molaka-kattu*. v. a. To put moistened seeds into a basket to germinate with a view to sow them. మొలకెత్తు or మొలకయెత్తు *molak-ettu*. v. n. To sprout up, మొలచు. మొలకబంగారు *molaka-bangaru*. n. Fairy gold, supposed to grow in snake-holes, &c. పుట్టలలో పుట్టుకలుగు పుట్టే బంగారు. మొలకకాయ *molaka-kāya*. n. A small kind of Egg plant. A kind of prickly Night shade, *Solanum hirsutum*. బృహతి. క్షుద్రవార్తాకి. నల్లమొలకాకాయ the black kind. తెల్లమొలకాకాయ the white kind. మొలవేయు *mola-vēyu*. v. a. To sow (corn), to cast seed in order to sprout. మొలిచేలాగు చేయు, నాటు. మొలిపించు *moli-pintsu*. v. a. To cause to sprout. మొలిచేట్టుచేయు. మొలతెంచు or మొలతేరు *mola-tentsu*. v. n. To sprout, shoot, grow. అంకురించు, పుట్టు, కలుగు. "మొలతెంచు సంతోషము నెట్టుదు." Dab. 299.

మొలామపండు *molāma-pandu*. [Eng. 'Melon.'] n. A sort of melon.

మొలాము or మొల్లాము *molāmu*. [H.] n. Gilding, బంగారులోనగువాని పూత. adj. Gilded, plated.

మొలుగు or మోలుగు molugu. [Tel.] n. A certain drug used in dyeing. నల్లవాయిచెక్క. "మొలుగుమడ్డిందోచి మూరగాకటియు శేసగా కటియుంగా కట్టినడొల్లుటుల్లారులు." A. iv. 55.

మొల్క See మొలక. మొల్పు See మొలచు.

మొల్ల or మల్లె molla. [Tel.] n. A kind of jasmine. *J. multiflorum* or *pubescens.* కుందలత. అడవిమొల్ల or యూథిక. wild jasmine, gold amaranth, *Jasminum auriculatum.*

మొల్లము or మొల్లమి mollamu. [Tel.] n. Thickness, సాంద్రత. Abundance, plenty. విస్తారము. అనేకము. adj. Thick, సాంద్రము. Abundant, plentiful. "కంఠకన్యాప్రాపలు మొల్లంబులము గుంగనవడు పల్లంబులును." Swa. iv. 57. మొల్లము n. Money, ధనము. "ఈ యెల్లధనంబునోటుపడి తిందుకులేశ్వర యుంక నొడ్డగా, మొల్లమునాకుజూపుము." భార. సభా. ii. మొల్లమిగా or మొల్లముగా mollamiga. adv. Thickly, దట్టముగా. In abundance, plentifully. విస్తారముగా. అనేకముగా. దండిగా. "తెల్లతెల్లనై మొల్లమిగా నంతకంతకుదికంతటను లందీరిచిన యిదుపులంబోలెందీంద్రింప." Swa. iii. 39. మొల్లమైన mollam-aina. adj. Abundant, plentiful. విస్తారమైన. అనేకమైన. "మొల్లములైనసంపదలు మోచివెలుంగు చున్నవాడు." Vish. ii. 11.

మొవుడు Same as మొగుడు, to close as a flower.

మొవ్వ, మొవు or మోవు movva. [Tel.] n. A sprout or shoot in a palm, cocoanut or plantain tree.

మొసలి mosali. [Tel.] n. A crocodile. మకరము, వక్రము. A monster. Capricorn in the zodiac. మొసలికట్టు, మొసలిచేమ or మొసలికాస్తి mosali-kattu. n. The liver of a crocodile. మొసలిరాశి the sign of the zodiac called Capricorn, మకరరాశి.

మొసలివాపోగు mosali-vā-pōgu. n. An earring with the face of a crocodile engraved on it. మొసలివా, మొసలివాయి or మొసలివాతి mosali-vā. n. The hilt of a sword shaped like a crocodile, మకరముఖాకృతిగల ఖడ్గవక్రము.

మొహదా mohadā. [H. or Mahr.] n. A broadsword, అడ్డకత్తి, పట్టిసము. "మిహిరపనిండ పరుంజొమొహదా." స్వా. iv.

మొహరము moharamu. [H.] n. The first Muhammadan month. The feast celebrated on the first ten days of that month, in honor of the death of Hasan and Hussain. The Mohurrum. పీర్లపండుగ.

మొహరించు moharintsu. [Tel.] v. n. To face or front in battle. మొనచేయుంచు.

మొహరి mohari. [H.] n. A Mohur, a gold coin.

మొహరు moharu. [H.] n. A seal.

మొహాలము mohalamu. [Tel.] n. The name of a certain garden herb, ఒకవిధమైన కూరాకుచెట్టు.

మో mo

మోక mōka. [Tel. another form of మొక్క.] n. A sprout, మొలక. మొక్క. "అత్తరిం భానుడు పశ్చిమాద్రి గనుపట్టెదరిద్రునమూవిలాకిన కా." M. IV. iii. 185.

మోకాలు mōkālu. [Tel. మోద + కాలు.] n. The knee, జానువు. మోకాటిచిప్ప the knee-cap. మోకరించు, మోకరిల్లు, మోకరిలు, మోకరిల్లుదు, మోకారించు or మోకాలించు mōkarintsu. v. n. To kneel, to squat down and sit on the knees.

మోకు mōku. [Tel.] n. A thick rope, a cable. మిక్కిలి లావుతాడు.

మోక్షము mōkshamu. [Skt.] n. Lit. Liberation, that is, of the soul from the body.

Deliverance from the bonds of sense. Exemption from sin and punishment. Beatitude. Final and eternal happiness. ముక్తి. Heaven, కైవల్యము, పరలోకము. మోక్ష రాజ్యము the kingdom of heaven.

మోగు or మ్రోగు *mōgu*. [Tel.] v. n. To sound, ring, resound, echo. ధ్వనిచేయు.

మోఘము *mōghamu*. [Skt.] adj. Empty. vain, fruitless. వ్యర్థమైన. Humble, దీనము.

మోచ *mōcha*. [Skt.] n. The plantain tree, అరటిచెట్టు. The silk cotton tree. బూరుగు చెట్టు. మోచాస్తంభము the trunk of a plantain tree. మోచకము or మోచకము *mōchakamu*. n. The tree called *Hyperanthera morunga*. మునగచెట్టు.

మోచనము *mōchanamu*. [Skt.] n. Liberation, release, deliverance. విముక్తి, విడుపు. సంసారమోచనము release from worldly ties. విమోచనము entire liberation, salvation. మోచితము *mōchitamu*. adj. Liberated, విడిపింపబడిన.

మోచెయ్యి, మోచేయి or మోచేయి *mō-cheyyi*. [Tel. మోడ+చేయి.] n. The elbow. కఫోణి. మోచేతివంపు triangular, having a projecting angle. మోచేతిపోటు a thump or poke with the elbow. మోచేతిముద్దుపుటిల్లు two houses built as one, రెండిండ్లుకలిపి కట్టినకట్టడము.

మోచు *mōtsu*. [Tel.] v. n. To rest on, ఆను. To happen, occur, కలుగు, సంభవించు. "మాకునధికకైన, మోహరసమునూరి మోచి యున్నదిరా కా, మదిండో కృ.. రూపమాకు నీకు." Vish. vii. 98. "మట్టినకర్మములం మూరి మోచినకతన గా." ib. viii. 413. v. a. To bear, to carry, మోయు, వహించు. ధరించు. To begin with, మొదలుకొను. "భూతేశ్వరు నియోజ్య దలమోచియుల్లాలు దానుగి వని." Kulahasti 1. 502.

మోజా *mōjā*. [H.] n. A boot.

మోజు *mōdzu*. [H.] n. An ardent desire, great liking, fancy, taste. ఆశ. ఆ గుఱ్ఱము మీద వాడు మోజుగానున్నాడు he has a great fancy for that horse. మోజుసరుకులు favourite or fashionable goods. "మోజైన సేకురు కొనసి చూడంగ." Vema. 1524.

మోట *mōṭa*. [Tel.] n. A water pump, a water wheel for drawing water from wells to irrigate the fields. మోటకొట్టు to drive the bullocks that draw up water with a మోట. కపిలమోటబాన the large bucket in which the water is drawn up from a well. మోటు [from Skt. మూఢ.] adj. Dull, stupid, simple. మూఢమైన. మొద్దు. మోటుకత్తి *mōṭa-katti*. n. A hunting knife, a cutlass. ముష్టికత్తి. సా. iv. మోటుపారు *mōṭa-pāru*. n. The slope at a well down which the cattle run while drawing water. మోటుబరి *mōṭa-bari*. n. A pack bullock, బరువుమోయుఎద్దు. మోటాటిరెడ్లు or మోటుపాటి రెడ్లు *mōṭaṭi-reḍlu*. n. plu. The name of a subdivision among the Kāpūs (a class of farmers). రెడ్లలో భేదము.

మోటించు *mōṭintsu*. [Tel.] v. a. To prop up, to lean. పోటిగానిలుపు, ఏదైనను పడిపోకుండా ఆధారముగా నిలుపు, ఆనించు.

మోటిక or మొంటిక *mōṭika*. [Tel.] n. A sprout, such as springs from a cocoanut or a potato in a warehouse. మొలక.

మోటు *mōṭu*. [Tel.] n. An obstinate person. మూర్ఖుడు, మ్రొండు. A stupid person, or blockhead. మూఢుడు. మూఢస్త్రీ. A male horse, మగగుఱ్ఱము. A country bred horse, కట్టువగుఱ్ఱము. A stump, block, trunk. మోడు, నరికినా మిగిలిన కొమ్మచేరులు మొండిదైనది, మొద్దు. "కాలినమోటువంటి కొగనాని శరీరము." Vish. ii. 143. A false human figure placed before a sow, పందికాపులు మనుష్యాకారముగా నిలిపిన కపటబొమ్మ.

adj. Dull, stupid, simple, rude, coarse, boorish, uncivilised, vulgar, మడ్డి, మూఢమైన, మూర్ఖమైన. మోటుసరసము bear's play, practical jokes, rough romping. **మోటాసపడు** *mōṭ-āsa-paḍu.* (మోటు+ఆసపడు.) v. a. To aim at. "సీ॥ పటురెత్తుగా నిరుమొత్త కెటైనమోటాసపడిరేయుబోడుకునీపాదవగన." Swa. iv. 44. టీ॥ మోటాసపడిరేయు, మోటు చేసికొని బాణములచేత కేయుట.

మోట or **ఉప్పరమోట** *móḍa.* [Tel.] n. A salt pan, where the salt is made from fuller's earth.

మోడము *móḍamu.* [Tel.] n. Cloudiness, haze, thick weather. ఆకాశము మేఘములచేత మేదురముగానుండడము, మబ్బుకట్టియుండడము, మేఘావరణము, మందారము.

మోడి *móḍi.* [Tel.] n. The act of picking up a thing (kept at one's feet) by bending back like an acrobat, గడిగాడు లుప్పమిక్కిలి కాలికిసమీపముండుంచిన వస్తువు నెత్తుట. Way, manner, air, style, విధము, రీతి. A whim, pettishness, crossness, ill-humour, pique, malice. బింకము. Handwriting, దస్తూరి, వ్రాలు, వ్రాతయొక్క సైఖరి. రాజమోడి royal style, pomp, grandeur. A kind of craft, enchantment, connected with the concealment of a jewel or money, మంత్రగాడు పంతముచేసికొనిపెట్టిబడి. మోడికట్టు to draw magic lines. మోడివిడుచు to break such a spell. మోడిఅక్షరములు or గొలుసుకట్టు a running hand. "మోడికాని సేగబెరుని తెల్పు మంచనిన." Radha. i. 70. టీ॥ మోడిమానిసిగాబలె, మూర్ఖుడైనమనిషివలెనే.

మోడు or **మ్రోడు** *móḍu.* [Tel.] n. The stump of a tree. మొద్దు, స్థాణువు. The stump of an arm or leg which has been amputated. కోయగా మిగిలిన కాలుచేయియొక్క మొదలైనవి. A stumbling block. A knoll or rising ground, the crest of a hill. మిట్ట. **మోడుచేరుచు, మోడువడు** or **మోడ్పడు** *móḍu-tsarutsu.* v. n. To become blunt, మొక్కవోవు. To become hardened or coarse, మోటగు. To break to pieces, తునుకు, ఖండితమగు. **మోడుపరుచు** *moḍu-paruṭsu.* v. a. To cut. ఖండించు. To reduce to a stump. To be motionless, నిశ్చేష్టితమగు.

మోడుచు or **మోడ్చు** *móḍuṭsu.* [Tel. another form of ముకుడుచు.] v. a. To close (as the eyes or a flower), fold (the hands.) మూసికొను, కోడించు. మోడ్చినకన్నుల half closed eyes. "చేతులు మోడ్చినర్తకితో." Vish. ii. 76. **మోడుపు** or **మోడ్పు** *móḍupu.* n. The act of folding or closing, as of a flower or of the hands, ముకుడుట.

మోత *móta.* [Tel. from మోయు.] n. A load. మోయవలసినబరువు. [From మోగు or మ్రోగు.] A roar, a yell, ధ్వని. ఈ ఆవు ఈనెటిమోతలోనున్నది this cow is on the point of calving. మోతయెద్దు a bullock to carry loads.

మోతాదు *mótádu.* [H.] n. A charge (of powder). ఒకకూటుకు గావలసినమందు. A dose (of medicine, &c.) మోతాదుగా moderately, in due proportion.

మోతుబరి *mótubari.* [H.] adj. Trustworthy, honest; respectable, substantial, నమ్మదగిన, ధీరవాడుగాని.

మోద *móda.* [Tel.] n. A small packet or parcel of betel leaves. తమలపాకులకట్ట. Also, see under మోదు.

మోదము *módamu.* [Skt.] n. Pleasure, joy. సంతోషము. **మోదకము** *módakamu.* n. A sort of sweet cake. కుడుము. గణపతి ప్రియమైన వినాయకుడు. **మోదమానము** *móda-mánamu.* adj. Rejoicing, సంతోషించుచున్న. **మోదించు, మోదిల్లు** or **మోదిలు** *módintsu.* v. n. To rejoice, be happy, సంతోషించు.

మోదు *módu.* [Tel.] v. a. To hit, smite, strike, beat, కొట్టు, మొత్తు. "ముద్దునివలె

మరల్ మోదుగాంచి." M. XIII. v. 304. n. A blow or stroke. మోడ *moda.* n. A swelling or stiffening of a joint, callosity formed where a bone was broken. మోడకట్టినది the joint has become stiff.

మోదుగ, మోదుగు or మోదుగ్గు *mōdugu.* [Tel.] n. The tree called Bastard Teak. *Butea frondosa.* పాలాశము, కింశుకము. తీగమోదుగు *Butea superba.* (Watts.) ముండ్లమోదుగు a thorny species. మోదుగు తోడిమెలు *mōdugu-tōḍimelu.* n. The name given to a kind of fine rice, having long grains, ఒకజాతివడ్లు. "మోదుగతోడి మెలు మరుమల్లెసరులు." H. iv. 157. మోదుగు మాడలు *mōdugu-māḍalu.* n. A kind of rice. ఒకజాతివడ్లు. The seeds of the Bastard Teak tree, మోదుగవిత్తులు.

మోదేన or మోదేనము *mōdenu.* [Tel.] n. The name of a tree called also అంబురా, తెల్లవ్వర, రవమల్లి or పిప్పళి.

మోపు *mōpu.* [Tel. from మోయు.] v. a. To load, place a burden on (another), మోయజేయు. To lay (a fault) upon (a person.) To impute, or charge (against another), ఆరోపించు. To prop up, ఆనించు. చేతులు నేలమోపెను he laid or rested his hands on the ground. "నాకిచేసినతప్పు నామీదమోపి." Sār. D. 545. "వాడినూడిమోపినయంతటిభూమి ధర్మసందనునకునీక" as much land as the point of a sharp needle can cover, or rest on. Kanyaka Puran. vii. 116. n. A bundle, load, burden. కట్టెమొదలైనవాటికట్ట, భారము. A bowstring. వింటినారి. adj. Much, heavy, అధికము. ఉత్తరమున వాన నిండా మోపుగానున్నది there is rain impending in the north. దెబ్బలు మోపుగాపడినవి the blows fell thick. మోపుగానుండేగాయము a severe wound. "నరో సకలంతలబునను మోపువైచి." B. P. v. 413. మోపరి or మోపుకాడు *mōp-ari.* n. A sustainer, a supporter, one who props. మోయువాడు, భారవాహకుడు. మోపాడి *mōpaḍi.* (మోపు+అడి.) n. Danger, risk. అపాయము, సంకటము. మోపి *mōpi.* A widow, విధవ, ముండమోపి. ముండమోపినది she wears a shaven pate. మోపించు *mōpinṭsu.* v. a. (Causal of మోయు.) To cause to bear a burden. To impose. మోయునట్టుచేయు, నిందపెట్టు. ఆ కట్టెలను వానిచేత మోపించిరి they made him carry the fagots of wood. ఆ తప్పును వానిమీద మోపించిరి they caused the fault to be laid upon him. "మోపరికనుకర్గుమొగ్గలధరము, మోపించుకొను నట్టిముద్దునికను." BD. page 129. మోపిక *mōpika.* n. Weight, భారము. Help, aid. కాండ్లమోపికచేసి by the help of the plough. మోపిడు *mōp-iḍu.* (మోపు+ఇడు.) v. a. To string a bow, విల్లు ఎక్కుడు. మోపుకొను *mōpu-konu.* v. a. To take upon one's-self. మోపుదల *mōpu-dala.* n. A charge or accusation. ఆరోపణము. A load, భారము. ఈనమోపుదలగానుండే ఆవు a cow on the point of calving. ఇవ్వ మోపుదలయ్యినరూకలు money still due, బాకీయున్నసొమ్ము. చాలామోపుదలగా చెప్పెను he spoke very impressively. వానిమీద నేరము మోపుదల అయినది he was charged with the offence. మోపుదలచేయు *mōpudala-cheyu.* v. a. To lay, charge, to bring as a charge, impose. ఆ రూకలను నేను ఇచ్చేటట్లు మోపుదలచేసిరి they made the money payable by me. మోపెట్టు *mōp-eṭṭu.* (మోపు+పెట్టు.) v. a. To place a weight upon, బరువుపెట్టు. ఆ కాగితములపైని ఈరాయి మోపెట్టు put this weight on those papers. To brace a bow, విల్లు ఎక్కుపెట్టు. "అర్జునుడు గాండీవంబు మోపెట్టె." M. v. i. 261.

మోము *mōmu.* [From Skt. ముఖము; and another form of మొగము.] n. The face, or countenance. "మోమురసేయువాడు మరుముక్తని గాంచునె దున్నిభంగులన్." Vēma. 1455. వాని మోము చిన్నపోయినది he was abashed, his countenance fell. See ముగము. మోమోమా

డు *mōm-ōḍu.* (మోము+ఓడు.) v. n. To yield, fall into temptation; to comply wrongly, దాక్షిణ్యపడు. "ఏదండంబునం దల్పి పొమ్మను మోమోడక యుంచినక బతిని బాయక జేసితే బైనమా." URK. vi. 384. మోమోటు or మోమోటము Same as మొగమోటము. See under మొగము.

మోయు *mōyu.* [Tel.] v. a. To bear, sustain, bring, convey, take or carry as a burden, వహించు. ఆ పాము ముక్కు మోయ తిని మసలుచున్నది the snake is gorged. ముక్కు మోయ తాగెను he drank till the milk ran out at his nose. See మోపు and మోత. మోయించు *mōyinṭsu.* v. a. To cause to bear a burden, to load (with a burden.) మోయ నట్లుచేయు.

మోర *mōra.* [Tel.] n. The projecting face of animals. Phiz, a word of contempt for face, మూతి. (నింద్యముగు) మనుష్యముఖము. మోరచుప్పు చెప్పులు shoes put on the wrong way so as to deceive those who trace the wearer. చనుమోరలు the tips of the breasts. కటుమోరలు the cheek bones. "ఓడెకి ముందర నొకసారి మేయుంబు మురుగుచున్నది మోర యెత్తి." B. 1. § 14. 7. మోరపలుపు the head stall. మోరకొట్టులు *mōra-koṭṭulu.* plu. Rebukes. మూతికొట్టడము. S. i. 490. మోరయెత్తు or మోరయిడు *mōrayettu.* v. n. To turn the face upwards, మోముమీదికెత్తు. మోరతోపు, మోరత్రోపు or మోరతోపుతనము *mōra-tōpu.* n. Aversion, turning away or averting the face. మూతులుత్రిప్పడము, పరాఙ్ముఖత్వము. "పూనకొని మోరతోపున బోవపోనీను సేను." N. ix. 404. టీ॥ మోరతోపున, తల త్రిప్పుకొనిపోవుటకొని. మోరతిరుగా in profile. మోరపక్కి *mōra-pakke.* n. A sword fish. మోరపాక *mōra-paka.* n. A hut thatched with leaves, దూలములులేకుండా గడ్డి తాటాకులతో కట్టినది. A temporary shed, ఓర పాక.

మోరకము *mōrakamu.* [from Skt. మూర్ఖ.] n. Stubbornness, మూర్ఖత్వము. adj. Stubborn. మూర్ఖము. మోరకకత్తె *mōraka-katte.* n. A stubborn woman, మూర్ఖురాలు. మోరకుడు, మోరకీడు or మొరకు *mōraku.* n. A stubborn man, మూర్ఖుడు.

మోరలి or మొరలి *mōrali.* [Tel.] n. A kind of fruit tree. ధనుఃపటము, సన్నకద్రుమ. "నేరేడుపండ్లు మోరలిపండ్లు పనస ఖర్జూరపం డ్లును." Charitra. 1549.

మోరా *mōrā.* [H.] n. A footstool, పీట.

మోరు *mōru.* [Tel.] n. A weal, coagulated blood under the skin, after a bruise. మోకాటిమోరు a node on the shin. వాడి కదుముకట్టడము. A mountain peak, పర్వతశిఖరము. Buttermilk, మజ్జిగ. "గారెలుబూరెలు చారులు మోరులు." ఉ. రా. vi. మోరుండ *mōr-unḍa.* n. A sort of cake. ఒకపక్వాన్నము. "గారెలుబూరెలు మోరుండలు." H. i. 117.

మోలము or మోళము Same as మొలాము. (q. v.)

మోలుగు *mōlugu.* [Tel.] n. A kind of wood from which a black dye is extracted. నల్లరంగుచెక్క.

మోవి *mōvi.* [Tel.] n. The lip. పెదవి, అధరము. A kind of wild fruit tree. ఒకజాతి అడివి పండ్లచెట్టు. "దేవదారు, గుమ్మడు, మోవి, తప్పిస." H. iv. 19.

మోవు or మోవ్వు *mōvu.* n. A sprout, or shoot, the unopened sprout of a plantain tree, &c. "అనామోవులదూసిపోసి తమ ముందటి యూరిముల్లెల్లబోవి." Nagnajit. ii. 113.

మోష *mōsha.* [Skt.] n. Theft. దొంగతనము. మోషకుడు *mōshakuḍu.* n. A thief, or robber. చోరుడు. మోస *mōsa.* [from మోష.] n. Theft. దొంగతనము. A fault, ప్రమాదము. Deceit, వంచన. మోసగాడు *mōsa-gāḍu.* n. A deceiver, rogue. వంచకుడు.

మోసగించు or **మోసపుచ్చు** *mōsagintsu.* v. a. To deceive, delude, or betray. వంచించు. **మోసపోవు** *mōsa-pōvu.* v. n. To be ruined, duped, deluded, or deceived. వంచింపబడు. To make a mistake, ప్రమాదపడు. **మోసము** *mōsamu.* n. Deceit, fraud, a trick, duping. వంచన, దగా, ప్రమాదము. Danger, detriment, peril, mischief. ఇక్కడ ఉంటే మోసమువచ్చును remaining here is dangerous. నాబుద్ధికి మోసము వచ్చెను I was deluded. ఆమందు పెట్టితే కండ్లకు మోసము if you apply that medicine it will injure the eyes. మోసకత్తె a cunning jade. మోసముచేయు to deceive.

మోసల, మోసాల or **ముఖశాల** *mōsala.* [from Skt. ముఖశాల.] n. The front hall. A terrace with seats, before a house. నగరి తలవాకిటిచావిడి. "అత్తరుపతిసొచ్చి యచ్చక్రధరు నగరి మోసలనిలుచుటయు, నవ్విష్ణుచిత్తుండు తద్ద్రభావతరణంబుచేసి, ధరణీధవసమూహస్థానికప్రూహంబుపెంటరానప్పుడుం బుపేవించి." A. iv. 59. టీ॥ మోసల, ముంగిసాల, అనగా ఇక్కడ గోపురద్వారము.

మోసు *mōsu.* [Tel.] n. A shoot, sprout. అంకురము, దుంపజాతిచివురము, మొలక. పొగమోసులు curls of smoke. "పైపైపొగమోసులెత్తె." P. ii. 232. టీ॥ మోసులెత్తె, మొలకలెత్తగా. "సీ॥ పొలవమూర్ఛ దళితకంజాభది ర్ఘల్పుకాసారమున గోమ్మకటిమోసగన్నుంగ." A. iv. 192. మోసునగా, అకువిప్పని అరిటిమొలకపలెను. Also, a kind of fish, *Labeo.*

మోహము *mōhamu.* [Skt.] n. Love, fascination, infatuation, distraction, ignorance, weakness of intellect, loss of consciousness, a swoon. వలపు, అజ్ఞానము, మూర్ఛ, చిత్తవైకల్యము. మోహదృష్టి బేరము buying blind-fold, or without an inquiry into the real value, or on a cursory glance. **మోహనము** *mōhanamu.* n. A sword-hilt. కప్పువు, కత్తిపిడి. "అలఘుమోహనమున హస్తంబుచేర్చి, బలిమించికొననాం నలి లేకరూర్చి." BD. v. 893. **మోహనము** *mōhanamu.* n. A swoon, మూర్ఛ. Enamourment, allurement, fascination, the over-powering of reason, వ్యామోహము. An arrow of Cupid's. మన్మథ బాణవిశేషము. adj. Fascinating, stupefying, depriving of sense or of understanding. వ్యామోహకరమైన. మోహనరాయి the stone beam across the top of a temple gate. రాతిదూలము. **మోహనము** or **మోహనపుదుంప** *mō-hanamu.* n. The red sweet potato. చిలగడ దుంపలలోభేదము. The Thorn apple or Datura fruit. **మోహి** *mōhi.* n. A deceiver, a cheat. వంచకుడు. "పాముకన్న లేదుపాపిష్ఠిజీవము అట్టిపాముచెప్పినట్లవినును, ఖలుమోహిచెప్పునవ్విధినవినదు." Vēma. 1474. **మోహించు** *mōhintsu.* v. a. To fall in love with, to become enamoured of, వలచు. v. n. To lose one's reason, అజ్ఞానముపొందు. To swoon, మూర్ఛిల్లు. **మోహితుడు** *mōhituḍu.* n. One who is fascinated, మోహముపొందినవాడు. **మోహిని** *mōhini.* n. A syren: a name of the queen of the fairies, ఒకదేవత. మోహినివేషము a captivating form, the guise of a syren.

మోహరము *mōharamu.* [Tel.] n. Battle-array; a manœuvre. దండుయొక్కవ్యూహము. "ధనంజయుండును తక్కినవారికి దుర్నిరీక్షుండగుచు, పశ్చాద్భాగంబు దెసనాదరంబుచేసి." M. IV. iv. 266. **మోహరించు** *mōharintsu.* v. n. To array, prepare for battle. మొనపేర్చు, రణోద్యోగముచేయు, వ్యూహముపన్ను. "నీవు రణస్థలి మోహరించినగా." Chatu. ii. 52. line 21. "ఏడక్కొహిణులబలంబుతో మోహరించె." Padma. x. 283. v. a. To face an enemy, ఎదుర్కొను. To oppose, ఎదిరించు.

మౌ mau

మౌంజి *maunji.* [Skt. from ముంజ.] n. The girdle worn by a Brahmin bachelor made of three strings of Munja grass.

బ్రహ్మచారులు కట్టుకొనే ముంజకడ్డి మొలతాడు. మౌంజీధరుడు one who wears this girdle, a bachelor.

మౌక్తికము *mauktikamu.* [Skt. from ముక్త.] n. A pearl. ముత్యము.

మౌఖరి or **మౌఖర్యము** *maukhari.* [Skt. from ముఖరము.] n. Crossness, a scolding disposition, talkativeness. "మౌఖరిమించనిట్టులను." Vijaya i. 137.

మౌఢ్యము *maudhyamu.* [Skt. from మూఢ.] n. Ignorance, folly. మూఢభావము. మూఢత్వము.

మౌనము *maunamu.* [Skt. from ముని.] n. Silence, taciturnity. మాట్లాడక ఉండడము. విభూషణం మౌనమపండితానాం silence does credit to the ignorant. మౌనం సర్వార్థసాధనం silence will conquer every difficulty. **మౌనవృత్తి** *mauna-vritti.* n. Silence, the state of being silent. మౌని *mauni.* n. A hermit, recluse, ascetic, మౌనముగలవాడు, ముని, సన్యాసి.

మౌరజికుడు *maurajikudu.* [Skt.] n. A drummer. మద్దెలకాడు.

మౌరి or **మవురి** *mauri.* [Tel.] n. A clarionet. నాగసరము. A. iv. 38.

మౌర్ఖ్యము *maurkhyamu.* [Skt. from మూర్ఖ.] n. Stubbornness, stupidity, మూర్ఖభావము, మూర్ఖత్వము.

మౌర్వి *maurvi.* [Skt.] n. A bowstring. వింటినారి, అల్లెత్రాడు.

మౌళి *mauli.* [Skt.] n. A crest or top-knot, a lock of hair on the crown of the head, hair ornamented and braided round the head. సిగ. కొప్పు. A diadem, కిరీటము. తాపసమౌళి the venerable hermit, the crown of hermits. Bhanu. iv. 137. నృపాలమౌళి or భూవరమౌళి the noblest of kings.

మౌష్టము *maushtamu.* [Skt. from ముష్టి.] n. Boxing, sparring. పిడికిగ్రుద్దులాట.

మౌహూర్తికుడు or **మౌహూర్తుడు** *mauhürtikudu.* [Skt. from ముహూర్తము.] n. An astrologer. జ్యోతిష్కుడు, జోస్యుడు.

మ్ర mra

మ్రంగ or **మంగ** *mranga.* [Tel.] n. A kind of tree.

మ్రంగు or **మ్రంగుడు** *mrangu.* [Tel.] v. n. To decrease, be abated, be humbled. క్రుంగు, వ్రాలు, తగ్గు, మట్టుపడు. Ellana. iii. 366.

మ్రందు *mrandu.* [Tel.] v. n. To die, చచ్చు. To break, పగులు To be hurt, నొచ్చు. To be tired, fatigued, or withered, వాడు. To burn, consume. దహించు. **మ్రందించు** *mrand-intsu.* v. a. To kill, or cause to be killed. చంపించు. M. VIII. i. 36. **మ్రందిలి** *mrandili.* adj. Hurt. నొచ్చిన.

మ్రగ్గు *mraggu.* [Tel.] v. n. To die. చచ్చు. To incur a loss, నష్టపడు. To be dejected, క్రుంగు. విచారించు. To decrease, to soften (as fruit), to be overboiled.

లసైవానివానికంబులందు, బొదివినవానికములు గాలిపోదొ." DRK. 320. మ్రగ్గు, కమిలిపోవు.

మ్రబ్బు Same as మబ్బు (q. v.).

మ్రా mra

మ్రాకు, మ్రాను, and మ్రింగు, &c. These words may be found in the Dictionary without the R which is used or dropped at pleasure, thus for మ్రాకు; see మాకు or మాను, &c.

మ్రాగు *mrāgu.* [Tel.] v. n. To be tired or fatigued. సొలు. మ్రాగన్ను *mrā-gannu.* (మ్రాగు+కన్ను) n. A dejected eye, a downcast look. మ్రాగన్నిడు, మ్రాగన్ను వేయు, మ్రాగన్నుగు or మ్రాగన్నువడు *mra-gann-iḍu.* v. n. To look dejected. To blink or to have the eyes half closed. అర్ధనిమీలితేక్షణమగు. "అందులఘనికులముసవన చందనసందష్టనిజభుజంగీవదనానందానందకకరమగు మందానిలమానుచుండు మ్రాగన్నిడుచు జా." G. viii. 50.

మ్రాను Same as మాను a tree (q. v.). మ్రానుకోయిల a wood pecker, వడ్రంగిపిట్ట. మ్రానుత్రిమ్మరి, మ్రాద్రిమ్మరి, మ్రానుమనికి or మ్రానుమద్రిమ్మరి *mrānu-drimmari.* n. A monkey, కోతి. మ్రానుపాటు or మ్రాన్పాటు *mrānu-pāṭu.* n. Stupor, the state of being stunned. నిశ్చేష్టత. మ్రానుపడు, మ్రాన్పడు, మ్రానుపొందు, మ్రానుతేరు, మ్రానువిల్లు or మ్రానుపిలు *mrānu-paḍu.* v. n. To be stunned, or become motionless. నిశ్చేష్టితుడగు. "జిక్కకుల్లమ్రాన్పడియొస్తిరయు జేయుగాలికే చిత్తరుబొమ్మలోయనవిచ్చేతకిపొందిన." T. v. 144. మ్రానుపెట్టు *mrānu-peṭṭu.* v. a. To cause to be stunned, మ్రానుపడ జేయు.

మ్రాలు or మ్రాలుకొందు *mrālu.* [Tel.] n. To be fatigued, to be downcast, as the looks, సొలు. మ్రాలుచు or మ్రాల్చు *mrāluṭsu.* v. a. To cause to be downcast. మ్రాలజేయు.

మ్రి mri

మ్రింగు Same as మింగు to swallow. మ్రింగుడు *mringuḍu.* n. The act of swallowing, కబళించుట. మ్రింగుడుపడు *mringuḍu-paḍu.* v. n. To be swallowed, కబళితమగు.

మ్రు mru

మ్రుక్క or ముక్క *mrukka.* [Tel.] adj. Spoiled (as grain), చెడిపోయిన (ధాన్యము.) మ్రుక్కడి *mrukkaḍi.* adj. Petty. trifling, mean, base, అల్పము, క్షుద్రము. మ్రుక్కడిమూక the baser sort of people, the mob.

మ్రుగ్గు Same as ముగ్గు. n. (q. v.)

మ్రుచ్చు or ముచ్చు *mruṭsṭsu.* [Tel.] n. A thief, దొంగ. See ముచ్చు. మ్రుచ్చిలు or మ్రుచ్చిలించు *mruchchilu.* v. a. To steal, దొంగిలించు. To deceive, వంచించు. మ్రుచ్చిలి or మ్రుచ్చిమి *mruchchili.* n. Theft, దొంగతనము, చౌర్యము. మ్రుచ్చిలిపోటు *mruchchili-pōṭu.* n. Attacking or stabbing a person when he is asleep. నిద్రపోవుచుండగా పైబడిచేయుయుద్ధము. మ్రుచ్చుగొర *mruṭsṭsu-gŏra.* (మ్రుచ్చు+కొర.) n. A notorious thief, పెద్దదొంగ. మ్రుచ్చుప్రొద్దు *mruṭsṭsu-proddu.* n. Midnight, అర్ధరాత్రము.

మ్రుదమ్రుద *mruda-mruda.* [Tel. anuk.] n. Loitering, shuffling, hesitation, సందిగ్ధము. మ్రుదమ్రుదగానుండు to be in doubt, సందిగ్ధముగానుండు. మ్రుదమ్రుదచేయు to keep in doubt, shuffle off, సందేహములోనుంచు. "ఈయర్థంబునగిన్నియు, యూయను యూనలయు

గాని యెరుగుటయు పృథా, లోయురగాలకమ్రుస్సు, వ, నేయకవిదిర్గమని పచింపుదు పెట్టెల్." Vaijayanti. iv. 93.

మ్రే mrē

మ్రేగు, మ్రేవు, మేగు or మేవు *mrēgu*. [Tel.] v. a. To smear, పూయు. To surround, ఆవరించుకొను.

మ్రొ mro

మ్రొక్కు. Same as మొక్కు. (q. v.) మ్రొక్కు. మ్రొక్కుడు, మ్రొక్కు or మ్రొక్కుడు *mrokku*. n. A bow, salutation, నమస్కారము. మ్రొక్కుబడి or మొక్కుబడి a vow.

మ్రొగ్గ, మ్రొగ్గుటకు. మ్రొగ్గతిల్లు మ్రొగ్గతిలు or మ్రొగ్గతిల్లుటకు *mroggu*. Same as మొగ్గ. (q. v.) మ్రొగ్గు n. Much, ఎక్కువ.

మ్రో mrō

మ్రోగు or మ్రోవు *mrōgu*. v. a. Same as మోగు. (q. v.) మ్రోగుడు *mrōgudu*. n. Noise, sound, ధ్వని. మ్రోత. మ్రోత *mrōta*. n. A noise, ధ్వని.

మ్రోడు, మొరడు or మోడు *mrōḍu*. [Tel.] n. The stump of a tree. స్థాణువు. Bluntness, మొండి, మొక్క. మ్రోడువడు or మోడువడు to become stumpy. మోడుబారు. "అకుదెల్ల రెండిరాళ్లావిరానమున్ ద్రుంచినైన మ్రోడువడి యుండె." S. iii. 414.

మ్రోయు or మొరయు *mrōyu*. [Tel.] v. n. To sound, ring, resound. To roar. ధ్వనించు, మ్రోగు, మొరబెట్టు. To proclaim, denounce, say, declare, (as a law or book denounces.) "అని యట్లు నిఖిలాగమములు మ్రోయుగ న." Mari. BP. page 175. మ్రోయించు *mrōyintsu*. v. a. To sound or cause to resound. ధ్వనింపజేయు. ధనువుమ్రోయించి twanging his bow. Kusalava, page 129.

మ్రోల *mrōla*. [Tel.] n. The front, ఎదుట. adv. Before, in front. ఎదుట, ముందర.

మ్లా mlā

మ్లానము *mlānamu*. [Skt.] adj. Faded, withered, languid. వాడిన. మ్లాని *mlāni*. n. Fading, వాడుట. Fatigue, అలసటము, బడలిక.

మ్లే mlē

మ్లేచ్ఛము or మ్లేచ్ఛితము *mlēchhamu*. [Skt.] adj. Barbarous, foreign. మ్లేచ్ఛదేశము a country outside the Bharata-varsha or Northern India. మ్లేచ్ఛభాషలు foreign words. మ్లేచ్ఛముఖము *mlēchha-mukhamu*. n. Copper, రాగి. మ్లేచ్ఛము *mlēchhamu*. n. Cinnabar. ఇంగిలీకము. మ్లేచ్ఛుడు *mlēchhuḍu*. n. A foreigner, a stranger by nation or religion.

య ya

య *ya*. [Tel.] n. The consonant y as in Youth, beyond.

యంత *yanta*. [Skt.] n. A charioteer. An elephant driver. Any person or thing that restrains. రథసారథి, మావటీడు. "ఈమైర థంబుపై యంతపయుండరగ నీరహితు పయనింప జేక్రుంచుమా." T. v. 90.

యంత్రము *yantramu*. [Skt.] n. A contrivance, machine, implement, instrument, apparatus. A diagram or figure of a mystical nature, an astrological character; a talisman, or amulet. A pump. సాధనము, యుక్తియుక్తమైనపనిరాము. "లేంగునోయ్రు

లయంత్రములమేలంటిక చాలనో లుచుతూలు వాలికలను." Ila. iv. 58. ఇక్షుయంత్రము a sugarcane mill. A. ii. 94. "కలయంత్రధారలకప్పికప్పి." Zaccaya. v. 47. **యంత్రకారుడు** *yantra-karuḍu.* n. *l.* maker of engines, an engineer, an artillery man, a gunner. యుక్తియుక్తమైనసాధనకారుడు. "కందళితా హస్తుయంత్రకారుడు." A. v. 89. టీ॥ యంత్రకారుడు, ఫిరంగులుకాల్చేవాడు. **యంత్రధారకుడు** *yantra-dhārakuḍu.* n. An engineer, one who manages an engine. యంత్రమును త్రిప్పేవాడు. L. xv. 126. **యంత్రపాతితము** *yantra-patitamu.* n. A kind of cake. జంతికలు. **యంత్రించు** *yantrintsu.* v. a. To contrive: to plan: to make a diagram or figure of a mystical nature, to put under a spell, యంత్రముచేయు. "యంత్రించినయంత్రించి యంత్రించుచుంచు." Pal. 98. **యంత్రితము** *yantritamu.* adj. Spell bound, కట్టబడిన.

యకాయకి or **ఏకాయెకి** *yakā-yaki.* [H.] adj. Sudden, speedy, solitary, ఆకస్మికమైన, త్వరితమైన. adv. Straightway, suddenly, all at once, దిగ్గన.

యక్షుడు *yakshuḍu.* [Skt.] n. A demigod. దేవయోనివిశేషము, కుబేరాదియక్షజాతుడు. Kubēra, కుబేరుడు. **యక్షకర్దమము** *yaksha-kardamamu.* n. A perfume made of powdered sandalwood mixed with camphor, agallochum, musk, and saffron in various proportions. పరిమళద్రవ్యములు కలిపినచందనము. **యక్షగానము** *yaksha-gānamu.* n. A melody, a chant. Poetry written rather to suit an air than according to the strict rules of prosody. There are several poems written in this style as the సీతాకల్యాణము, ఉషాపరిణయము, గరుడాచలము, &c. **యక్షాక్షి** *yaksh-ākshi.* n. A thorny plant. *Guilandina bonducella.* గచ్చకాయచెట్టు, గచ్చ. **యక్షిణి** *yakshiṇi.* n. An art by which events that have happened elsewhere are revealed, జరిగినవృత్తాంతమును తెలిపే ఒకవిద్య. A female fiend attached to the service of Durga, and frequently maintaining (like a sylph or fairy) intercourse with mortals. యక్షిణిపంపు bewitching, sorcery. మాంత్రికుడు పంపిన పనులు చేసే దయ్యము.

యక్ష్మము or **రాజయక్ష్మము** *yakshmamu.* [Skt.] n. Pulmonary consumption, phthisis, క్షయరోగము.

యజనము *yajanamu.* [Skt. from యజ్ to sacrifice.] n. An offering or sacrifice. యజ్ఞము. Vish. v. 363. **యజించు** *yajintsu.* v. n. To perform or offer a sacrifice. యజ్ఞముచేయు. v. a. To worship, అర్చించు. **యజమానుడు** or **యజమాని** *yaja-mānuḍu.* n. One who offers a sacrifice, a sacrificer, యజ్ఞకర్త. A lord, a master, ప్రభువు. An owner or proprietor, సొంతగాడు. A husband, గృహస్థుడు. An employer of priests at a sacrifice; the person who institutes its performance and pays the expense, ఋత్విగాదులనియమించుకయజ్ఞకర్త. గ్రామయజమానులు the headmen of a village. **యజమానురాలు** *yaja-mānu-r-ālu.* n. A wife; a lady, good woman, or mistress of a family. **యజమానత్వము** or **యాజమాన్యము** *yaja-mānatvamu.* n. Mastership, lordship, dominion, ఆధిపత్యము. **యజుర్వేదము** or **యజుస్సు** *yajur-vēdamu.* n. The name of one of the four Vedas. **యజ్ఞము** *yagnyamu.* n. The rite of offering a sacrifice; a sacrifice or offering. The sacrifice in which a goat is smothered and the inside fat is dressed and eaten by Brahmins. (The person who celebrates this sacrifice assumes the honorary title of సోమయాజులు.) **యజ్ఞసూత్రము** or **యజ్ఞోపవీతము** *yagnya-sūtramu.* n. The sacred thread, worn by the three principal classes of the Hindus. జంధెము. యజ్ఞ

or యజ్వుడు *yajra.* n. A sacrificer in due form, agreeably to the Vedas. విధ్యుక్తముగా యజ్ఞముచేయువాడు.

యతనము Same as యత్నము. (q. v.)

యతి *yati.* [Skt.] n. A sage whose passions are completely under subjection; a hermit or religious mendicant. సన్యాసి, జితేంద్రియుడు. A syllable rhyming to the initial of a line of poetry. వళ్ళవిశ్రమస్థానము, తాళప్రాసము. See ప్రాసము.

యత్నము *yatnamu.* [Skt.] n. An effort, exertion, endeavour; a method, measure, step, plan, scheme, intention, design, purpose. చేతనము, ఉద్యోగము, కడక, ఉపాయము. దైవయత్నము a decree or interposition of Providence, the finger of God. **యత్నించు** or **యత్నపడు** *yatnintsu.* v. n. To endeavour, attempt, try, intend, design, ప్రయత్నముచేయు. యత్నపడి ఉన్నాడు he intends or is about to do it. See ప్రయత్నము.

యథా *yatha.* [Skt.] adv. As, according to, to the extent of, యథాకాలము a reasonable time. **యథాక్రమముగా** *yatha-kramamu-ga.* adv. In order, orderly, duly. క్రమప్రకారముగా. **యథాజాతుడు** *yatha-jatudu.* n. A fool, blockhead. మూఢుడు. **యథాతథా** *yatha-tatha.* adv. In any way, in like manner, ఎట్లాగైనా, ఎట్లో అట్లు. **యథార్థము** *yath-arthamu.* (యథా+అర్థము.) n. Truth, reality, verity, the case or fact. నిజము, సత్యము. యథార్థుడు a veracious man, a conscientious man. adj. True, correct, real, actual, నిజమైన. **యథార్థత** *yath-arthata.* n. Rectitude, veracity. నిజము. యథాప్రకారముగా as usual. యథాభిమతముగా జరిగించినారు they did as they pleased. **యథాయథలు** *yatha-yathalu.* adv. Dispersedly. యథాయథలై పోవు to run away in various directions or at random, to flee or disperse on all sides.

యథావిధిగా *yatha-vidhi-ga.* adv. According to rule. విధివత్తుగా, శాస్త్రప్రకారముగా. **యథాశక్తిగా** *yatha-sakti-ga.* adv. To the extent of one's capability, as much as possible. చేతనైనమట్టుకు. **యథాస్థితిగా** or **యథాస్థితిని** *yatha-sthiti-ga.* adv. As it was before. ఎప్పటివలెనే. **యథేచ్ఛముగా** *yath-ēchchamu-ga.* adv. At pleasure, as you please, arbitrarily, ఇష్టమైనట్లు. **యథేష్టముగా** *yath-ēshtamu-ga.* adv. According to will or inclination, freely, abundantly. కోరినట్లు, కోరినంత. **యథోచితము** *yath-ōchitamu.* adj. Suitable, proper, right. యుక్తమైన. **యథోచితముగా** *yath-ōchitamu-ga.* adv. As much as may be fit, precisely what is required, neither more nor less. యుక్తముగా. యథోచితముగా మాట్లాడు to speak to the purpose, or pertinently; to say just what is proper.

యదృచ్ఛ *yadṛichcha.* [Skt.] n. Wilfulness, independence, freedom. స్వేచ్ఛ. **యదృచ్ఛగా** *yadṛichcha-ga.* adv. Wilfully, according to one's own fancies, voluntarily, యథేచ్ఛముగా.

యద్భవిష్యుడు *yad-bhavishyudu.* [Skt.] n. One who resigns himself to whatever may happen, without putting forth his own exertions. తాను ఏ ప్రయత్నము చేయక జరుగునది జరుగనిమ్మని యూరకుండువాడు.

యమకము *yamakamu.* [Skt.] n. A pair, a brace, వస్తుద్వయము. Twins. కవలవారు. A kind of a figure of speech in Sanskrit. A kind of alliteration. ఏకాక్షరయుగ్మోక్తద్వయము.

యమము *yamamu.* [Skt.] n. Restraining or controlling the passions. A pair, a brace. "యమనియమాది" A. ii. 113. **యమి** *yami.* n. A sage, an ascetic. సన్యాసి. A swan, హంస. "యమిశ్రేణులు." ఆము. iv. **యమించు** *yamintsu.* v. a. To subdue, as one's passions. విజ. iv.

యమళము *yamalamu.* [Skt.] n. A pair, brace, or couple. యమళులు twins, కవలలు. "భీమార్జునయమళులదిత్యిజయంబునేను." M. II. i. 251.

యముడు *yamudu.* [Skt.] n. Yama, the ruler of Naraka or hell, and judge of departed souls; "the genius of death:" also, the guardian of the southern point of the heavens. He is often identified with death, and corresponds with the Grecian Pluto or Minos. దండధరుడు. ఇది యమగండముగానున్నది this is terribly difficult. యమకింకరులు messengers of death, angels of death. **యమఘాటి** *yama-ghati.* n. A kind of weapon, జమదాడి. యమధారము *yama-dharamu.* n. A double edged sword.

యమున *yamuna.* [Skt.] n. The river Jumna. కాళింది.

యవనిక *yavanika.* [Skt.] n. A screen, or curtain. తెర, తెరచీర, జవా.

యవనుడు *yavanudu.* [Skt. corruption of Gk. 'Ionian.'] n. A Greek. An Arab. యవనదేశస్థుడు.

యవలు *yavalu.* [Skt.] n. plu. Barley, *Hordeum hexastichon.* బార్లిబియ్యము. "మనుష్యులకు జీవనోపాయంబులుగా వ్రీహులును గోధుమంబులును, యవలును, మినుములును, తిలలు." Vish. i. 103.

యవసము *yavasamu.* [Skt.] n. Grass. తృణము, గడ్డి.

యవాని or యవానిక *yavani.* [Skt.] n. Bishop's weed, *Sison ammi, Linn.* ఓమము. Of this two sorts are mentioned in H. ii. 250. "యవానికద్వయంబుకచ్ఛురములు, మరాటిమొగ్గలు." adj. Swift, వడిగల.

యశము or యశస్సు *yasamu.* [Skt.] n. Prosperity, celebrity, glory, reputation. కీర్తి. యశస్కరము *yasas-karamu.* adj. Rendering famous. కీర్తినికలుగజేయునట్టి. యశస్కాముడు *yasas-kamudu.* adj. Emulous, desirous of renown. యశస్సునుకోరువాడు. **యశస్వి** *yasasvi.* n. A man of fame. **యశులు** *yasulu.* n. They who are glorious; this is used merely in compounds; thus, మహాయశులు the most glorious. విదితయశులు the most celebrated people. "పేరువిశ్వాలురు విదితయశులు." M. III. ii. 34.

యష్టి *yashti.* [Skt.] n. A staff, a stick, a staff armed with iron, &c., used as a weapon. దండము, చేతికర్ర. A necklace, a string or thread, especially of pearls, ముత్యాలహారపుపేట. తులాయష్టి the beam of a pair of scales. BD. iv. 1924. **యష్టిమధుకము** *yashti-madhukamu.* n. Liquorice, the root of the *Abrus precatorius*, అతిమధురము.

యా ya

యాగము *yagamu.* [Skt.] n. A sacrifice, యజ్ఞము.

యాచకము *yachakamu.* [Skt.] n. Begging, asking, అడుగుట. **యాచకుడు** *yachakudu.* n. A beggar or mendicant. అడిగెడువాడు. తిరిపెమెత్తుకొనేవాడు. గ్రామయాచకుడు a village mendicant. యాచన or యాచ్ఞ *yachana.* n. Begging, asking, requesting. అడుగుట. **యాచించు** *yachintsu.* v. a. To beg, solicit, request. అడుగుకొను, అడుగు. **యాచితకము** *yachitakamu.* n. A thing borrowed for use. ఎరవు.

యాజకుడు or యాజ్ఞికుడు *yajakudu.* [Skt.] n. An officiating priest, a Brahmin who conducts any part of a sacrifice. ఋత్విక్కు. యాజనము *yajanamu.* n. A sacrifice.

యాజుషము *yajushamu.* [Skt.] adj. Pertaining to the Yajur Veda.

యాత *yata.* [Skt.] adj. Going, పోయెడు. n. One who goes. పోవువాడు. యాతము *yatamu.* adj. Gone, పోయిన. Past, గతము.

యాతాయాత (యాత+అయాత) going and coming.

యాతన yātana. [Skt.] n. Torment, agony, acute pain. తీవ్రవేదన, బాధ. యాతనా శరీరము the body created to bear the torments of hell, as దివ్యశరీరము is for heaven. గర్భయాతన the prison of the womb, i. e., the misery of the child in the womb.

యాతుధానుడు yātu-dhānudu. [Skt.] n. A giant or goblin, an evil spirit. రాక్షసుడు.

యాత్ర yātra. [Skt.] n. Going, moving, proceeding, marching, travelling, పోవుట. A journey, march, expedition, voyage. Going on pilgrimage, a pilgrimage, తీర్థయాత్ర. Whiling away the time, కాలము పుచ్చుట, యాపనము. దేహయాత్ర subsistence. "దివ్య నీ దేహయాత్ర ..." Vish. iv. 181. నీ చేతి మాత్ర వైకుంఠయాత్ర, a pill from you is a pass to heaven.

యాదము or యాదస్సు yādamu. [Skt.] n. Any cruel aquatic or amphibious animal. క్రూరజలజంతువు. యాదః పతి, యాదసాంపతి or యాదోనాథుడు yādah-pati. n. The king of the sea-monsters, i. e., Varuna or Neptune. వరుణుడు. The Ocean, సముద్రుడు.

యాదాస్తు yādastu. [H.] n. A memorandum or note.

యాదృశము yā-driṡamu. [Skt.] adv. As like, how like, what like, like which, of what kind. ఏలాటి, ఎటువంటి.

యానము yānamu. [Skt.] n. Going. పోవుట. Invading, దండెత్తిపోవుట. Marching, రాజ షాడ్గుణ్య భేదప్రయాణము, దండెత్తిపోవడము. A vehicle, conveyance. వాహనసామాన్యము. యానపాత్రము yāna-pātramu. n. A vessel, ship, boat. ఓడ. యానాం yanam. [Tel. from యానము.] n. The sea beach; also called యానాంది. Hence the town of Yanam in the Godavery district is so named.

యాపనము yāpanamu. [Skt.] n. Spending or passing the time, as కాలయాపనము = కాలముగడపడము, కాలక్షేపము. యాప్యము yāpyamu. adj. Low, vile, contemptible. నికృష్టమైన. యాప్యుడు yāpyudu. n. A wretch, a base person. నికృష్టుడు.

యాబై or యాభై yābai. [Tel. for ఏబది (ఏను+పది.) adj. and n. Fifty. యాభైమంది fifty men.

యామము yāmamu. [Skt.] n. A watch or space of three English hours. జాము. యామవతి or యామిని yāma-vati. n. Night. రాత్రి. యామికుడు yāmikudu. n. A patrol, తలారి, ఆరకుడు, గస్తీబంట్రోతు.

యామళము or యుమళము yāmalamu. [Skt.] n. A pair, a couple, a brace. యుగళము.

యామునము yāmunamu. [Skt.] n. Antimony.

యామ్య yāmya. [Skt. from యమ.] adj. Pertaining to Yama. యమసంబంధమైన. "యామ్యకింకరహేతువై మహాభయంబుతోడ." Vish. ii. 58.

యాయవారము, యాయావారము, యాయావరము or అయావారము yāyavāramu. [Skt.] n. Alms. భిక్షము, తిరిపెము. యాయవారమెత్తు to beg alms. "పాయక ... యాయవారముఎత్తి ..." HD. ii. 492. "మార ... యాయావృత్తి ..." KP. vi. 167. "పంచాంగములజెప్పి ... యాయవారంబులెత్తి." H. ii. 166. యాయవారుడు yāya-vārudu. n. A vagrant, mendicant. భిక్షుకుడు.

యాయి yāyi. [Skt.] n. One who goes. పోవువాడు.

యాలము, వేలము or ఏలము yālamu. [Arabic *Ni'lam*, notification, proclamation.] n. An auction.

యావత్తు yāvattu. [Skt.] n. The whole. సమస్తము adj. All, entire. సమస్తమైన. adv. Wholly, entirely, altogether సమస్తముగా.

యావనాళము yāva-nāḷamu. [Skt.] n. A kind of grain. సస్యవిశేషము.

యావము yāvamu. [Skt.] n. The red animal dye called Lac, sealing wax. లక్క.

యు yu

యు yu. [Tel.] conj. And, also. (Added like que in Latin) With a verb it has the force of 'although'; as వచ్చియు and having come, even though he came. "మణిచయంబులయు తన కుసుచియుకా జూచును." Vish. iv. 147. Added to an interrogative pronoun followed by a negative verb it has a distributive force. వాడేమియు చెప్పలేదు he said nothing whatever. It sometimes has ను added, as అదియును. "బుద్ధియు చిత్తశాంతియును." M. I. i. 218. It is also added to infinitive forms of verbs to denote a participial construction, as "అనుటయు మహేంద్రుడిట్లనియె." భార. శాం. iv.

యుక్తము yuktamu. [Skt.] adj. Joined, combined, united, కూడుకొనిన. Right, fit, proper, ఉచితమైన, న్యాయమైన. యుక్తమైనమనిషి a proper person. n. Fitness, propriety, justice. ఉచితము, న్యాయము. రూక్కనీవు చెల్లిస్తేయుక్తము it will be better for you to pay the money. నీవు యుక్తాయుక్తము విచారింపవలెనది you must look on both sides of the question. యుక్తపడు yukta-paḍu. v. n. To fit or suit. అనుకూలపడు. యుక్తి yukti. n. Union, కూడిక. Wit; a contrivance, expedient, stratagem, artifice; a plot, a happy thought. ఉపాయము, యోచన. యుక్తుడు yuktuḍu. An affix meaning Accompanied by, possessed of, characterised by. కూడుకొన్నవాడు. భార్యాయుక్తుడై being accompanied by his wife. పాపయుక్తులు sinners. దోషయుక్తురాలు she who is sinful, a sinner.

యుగము yugamu. [Skt.] n. A pair, couple, or brace. జత. A measure of length equal to two yards, బార. A yoke, బండికాడి. An age of the world, or long period of time; as సత్యయుగము the Golden Age: కలియుగము the Iron Age. All time is divided into four ages, named the Kṛita, Trēta, Dvāpara and Kali Ages, corresponding with the Golden, Silver, Brazen and Iron Ages. యుగధర్మము the fashion of the day. ఈ కలియుగమునందు in this Iron Age. యుగళము, యుగళి or యుగ్మము yugaḷamu. n. A pair, brace, or couple. ద్వయము. యుగాంతము yug-antamu. n. The end of the Age or World. ప్రళయకాలము. యుగాది yug-ādi. n. New Year's day. సంవత్సరాది. యుగ్యము yugyamu. n. Any vehicle or conveyance; a yoked animal. వాహనసామాన్యము, కాడిపూనినయెద్దు.

యుగ్మలి yugmali. [Tel.] n. A woman. ఆడుది. "ఇట్టినెలవన్నతి చేర్పనోపునను యుగ్మలియుం గుణనాతునారయుచు." M. III. vi.

యుతము yutamu. [Skt.] adj. Joined, united, combined, connected. కూడుకొన్నది. యుతుడు yutuḍu. adj. Endowed with or possessed of. దారిద్ర్యయుతుడు a poor man, one in poverty. మదయుతులు those who are snared in their lusts.

యుద్ధము yuddhamu. [Skt.] n. War; a battle, combat, contest. జగడము. యుద్ధరంగము a battle field.

యువ yuva. [Skt.] n. The name of a Telugu year. adj. Young, youthful. ప్రాయమందున్న. యువతి yuvati. n. A young woman, maiden. యౌవనస్త్రీ. యువరాజు yuvavādu. n. A young prince, especially the heir apparent to the throne. రాజాతర్వాతి రాజు. యువరాజత్వము yuva-rājatvamu. n. The state of being the heir apparent.

యుష్మత్ yushmat. [Skt.] n. Yours. మీ యొక్క. Vish. ii. 211.

యూ yū

యూకము yūkamu. [Skt.] n. A louse. పేను.

యూథము yūthamu. [Skt.] n. An assemblage of beasts or birds, a herd, flock, multitude. సమూహము.

యూథిక yūthika. [Skt.] n. A species of jasmine. అడవిమొల్ల. A. i. 120.

యూపము yūpamu. [Skt.] n. A post to which the victim is bound, at a sacrifice. యజ్ఞపశువుకట్టు స్తంభము.

యూషము yūshamu. [Skt.] n. Pease-soup, or porridge. పప్పుకట్టు.

యొ yo

యొక్క yokka. [Tel.] postpos. Of. The sign of the sixth or genitive case. నాయొక్క గుర్రము my horse.

యో yō

యోక్త్రము or యోత్రము yōktramu. [Skt.] n. The tie of a yoke. పలుపు.

యోగము yōgamu. [Skt.] n. Junction, meeting, union, కూడిక, కూర్పు. Fortune, అపూర్వవస్తుప్రాప్తి. సద్యోగము a lucky conjuncture, good fortune, or luck. దుర్యోగము misfortune. దైవయోగము Divine Providence. దైవయోగముతప్పి unhappily, unfortunately. Accession of property, or wealth. ప్రయోగము. A prescription, a recipe. ఔషధము. మహాబిల్వాదియోగము a prescription including Bilva roots. Devotion, spiritual worship, the practice of abstraction and meditation. ధ్యానము. Of these forms of worship there are eight named (a) యమము restraining the passions, (b) నియమము providing a proper place, &c, for worship, (c) stopping the breath in three modes called రేచకము, పూరకము or కుంభకము, (d) ప్రత్యాహారము withdrawal from sense perception, (e) ధ్యానము meditation, (f) ధారణము repression of all physical movements, (g) మననము fixing the mind on the deity, and (h) సమాధి complete immersion in thought so that the thinker is dead to the world. ధ్యానయోగము an act of faith or meditation. మంత్రయోగము a magical operation. యోగపట్టె or యోగపట్టము yōga-paṭṭe. n. A magic girdle worn by ascetics. యోగదృష్టి the second sight, obtained by devotion, superhuman sagacity or perspicacity. యోగాభ్యాసము the keeping the body in a fixed posture for spiritual worship, the practice of abstract contemplation. యోగనిద్ర or జ్ఞాననిద్ర the divine sleep, or supernatural stupor which yōgis or saints strive to attain. యోగమూర్ఛ supernatural stupor. యోగవాగలు, యోగవాగములు or యోగవాగాలు yōga-vāgalu. n. Magical boots supposed to be worn by hermits. తలచినచోటికి తిరిగిపోవు మంత్రశక్తిగలవారు కలరు. "యోగవాగలు మెట్టి యొకపాదమూద." HD. ii. 135. "యోగపట్టెలవారు జోస్యారు యోగ, వాగలవారును." L. xxiii. 31. యోగక్షేమము yōga-kshēmamu. n. Welfare, well-being, good circumstances. యోగి yōgi. n. A devotee, hermit; an ascetic in general. ముని. యోగాభ్యాసముచేయువాడు. యోగిని yōgini. n. A woman who practises Yoga, a female mendicant. A nymph or fairy, attendant on Durga the good goddess. తాపసస్త్రీ. క్షుద్రదేవతావిశేషము. యోగురాలు yōgu-r-ālu. n. A female mendicant. జటిని.

యోగ్యము yōgyamu. [Skt.] adj. Worthy, fit, proper, suitable, competent, clever, skilful. మంచి, తగిన, నేర్పుగల, శక్తిగల. యోగ్యత yōgyata. n. Ability, cleverness, skill, merit, worthiness, fitness, capacity, desert, respectability, అర్హత. యోగ్యుడు yōgyuḍu. n. One who is fit, proper, worthy, or deserving; an honest, respectable man. మంచివాడు, తగినవాడు, అర్హుడు. వ్యవహార యోగ్యుడు one who is legally of age, a free agent, వయసు వచ్చినవాడు. యోగ్యురాలు yōgyu-r-ālu. n. A woman who is fit, proper, or worthy; a decent, respectable woman. మంచిది, తగినది.

యోచన yōchana. [Skt.] n. Consideration, deliberation, reflection; an idea, supposition, conjecture; counsel, advice; an expedient, means, plan. ఆలోచన. H. v. 272. యోచించు yōchintsu. v. n. & a. To consider, regard, deliberate, plan, devise. ఆలోచించు. ధర్మము యోచించక regardless of justice.

యోజనము yōjanamu. [Skt.] n. Joining, union, junction. చేర్పడము, కూర్పు. A measure of distance equal to four క్రోసులు, that is about ten miles, ఆమడ. యోజించు yōjintsu v. a. To join, unite. కూర్చు.

యోధ, యోధుడు or యోద్ధ yōdha. [Skt. from యుద్ధము.] n. A warrior, soldier, combatant. బంటు. "ఒక్కట దిక్కులో విబుధయోధులతో శశిజుట్టుముట్టి పేరుకున్న." T. v. 89.

యోని yōni. [Skt.] n. The female organs of generation, the vagina, the uterus, place of birth, origin, భగము, కారణము. యోనిజాలు such as are womb-born, as distinguished from egg-born (అండజము). అయోనిజుడు a person born in some supernatural manner.

యోష, యోషిత or యోషిత్తు yōsha. [Skt.] n. A woman. స్త్రీ, వనిత.

యౌ yau

యౌగపద్యము yauga-padyamu. [Skt. from యుగపత్.] n. Simultaneity, ఏకకాలము. "యౌగపద్యాధిరోహణంబున." P. ii. 14. టీ. ఏక కాలమందెక్కుటచేత. "సర్వేషామేవపాపానాం యౌగపద్యేన నాశనం." Lalit. iii. 33.

యౌగికము yaugikamu. [Skt. from యోగము.] adj. Resulting from union or usage. Customary, usual, common, proper, regular (as the sense of words depending upon their derivation or construction.), యోగమువలనకలిగిన, సాధారణమైన, శబ్దవ్యుత్పత్తి నిష్పన్నమైన.

యౌతకము yautakamu. [Skt.] n. A wedding gift, or present. పెండ్లిలో కూతురికి అల్లునికి యిచ్చినసొమ్ము, అరణము.

యౌవతము yauvatamu. [Skt. from యువతి] n. A bevy of maidens, యువతీసమూహము, పడుచుపడుచుల సమూహము. "జిగ్గె తక్కునగు యౌవతమెల్లను బుట్టకుండునట్లుగా." A. i. 70.

యౌవనము yauvanamu. [Skt. from యువ.] n. Youth, manhood. పదియారువేండ్లుమొదలు కొని యేబదియేండ్లదాకనుండువయస్సు. యౌవనస్థుడు yauvanasthuḍu n. A young man. యౌవరాజ్యము yauva-rājyamu. [from యువరాజు.] n. Heirship, the state of being the heir apparent, the rule of the heir apparent, యువరాజు దొరతనము.

ర ra

ర ra. [Tel.] n. The letter R, called రేఫ repha, or రకారము ra-kāramu. When it is a subjunct letter, it is written underneath and shaped, thus, ◡ or L, and is called kravaḍi క్రావడి or క్రావడి krāvaḍi; thus, కర్ర karra, చక్రము chakramu

In many Telugu words this r is used optionally after the initial, as in మాను, పక్కు, కింద, తోవ, సుక్కు which are, in bookish Telugu, written మ్రాను, ప్రక్కు, క్రింద, త్రోవ, స్రుక్కు respectively.

The letter ర is sometimes inserted to prevent elision, as పొదరిల్లు, గంగిరెద్దు, బొమ్మరిల్లు, ఊకస్వరనామము.

ర in prosody, stands for రగణము, a foot composed of a short between two long syllables.

ర ra [Tel. short for రమ్మా.] In addressing intimate friends or very low class persons, this is used as a suffix; thus, ఏమిర, ఎందుకుర, ఏమిరా, ఎందుకురా.

In ancient Telugu, when it was under influence of the Kanarese literature the letter ఱ was used, but it is now obsolete. It is called శకటరేఫము, అలఘు రేఫము or బండి 'ఱ' while the ర is called మంచి 'ర' or లఘురేఫము. The ఱ is never used in Sanskrit words. It is said to have been pronounced hard, and to have had the force of two ర sounds; so that in ఱ్ఱ there are supposed to be four R sounds included, which is absurd on the face of it. According to the ancient spelling తరచు means to churn, తఱచు thick. పెర is a bee hive, పెఱ other, strange. పెరుగు is curd, పెఱుగు to grow. వేరు means a root, వేఱు different. మరుగు means to hide, మఱుగు to boil. In modern Telugu the ఱ is unknown and thus both sets of words are spelt alike. The ancient poets distinguished these sounds, never allowing ర to rhyme with ఱ. Modern Telugu poets such as the translator of the Bhagavata disregard this distinction. In recent years attempts have been made to revive the use of this obsolete letter, but without success.

రంకు or రంకుతనము *ranku*. [Tel.] n. Adultery, whoredom, fornication. జారత్వము. Trouble, ill. రంకుకట్టు to accuse one of adultery. To slander. నూరు నోములు ఒకరంకుతో పోయినవి one act of impurity will ruin a hundred years' penance. నాకెటు పోయినా రంకే whichever way I go I get into trouble. "రంకులాడిగరితలు" loose women. P. iv. 255, 256. రంకాట *rank-āta*. n. Committing adultery, రంకాడుట, జారత్వముచేయుట. రంకాడు or రంకుపోవు *rank-ādu*. v. n. To commit adultery, జారత్వముచేయు. రంకుబోతు *ranku-bōtu*. n. An adulterer or adulteress. జారుడు, జారిణి. రంకుమగడు *ranku-magaḍu*. n. A gallant, a man of loose conduct. జారపురుషుడు. రంకుటాలు, రంకులాడి or రంకెత *ranku-ṭālu*. n. An adulteress, a loose woman. వ్యభిచారిణి. రంకుతెవులు or రంకుజాడ్యము a venereal disease, మేహరోగము. రంకులరాట్నము or రంకులరాట్నము *rankula-raṭṭamu*. n. The machine called a merry-go-round, పిల్లకాయలను కూర్చుండబెట్టి తిప్పెడుయంత్రము.

రంకువు *rankuvu*. [Skt.] n. A sort of deer, the Spotted Axis. తెల్లదుప్పి.

రంకె *ranke*. [Tel.] n. A roar, cry, bellow, as of an ox. ధ్వని, కేక, వృషభధ్వని.

రంగము *rangamu*. [Skt.] n. A theatre, a stage. నాట్యస్థానము. A field of battle, రణభూమి. A name of Trichinopoly, శ్రీరంగము. A colour, రంగు. వారికి రంగముచెడినది they have quarrelled among themselves. రంగడు *rangaḍu*. n. The god శ్రీరంగనాథుడు worshipped at Srirangam near Trichinopoly. రంగమంటపము *ranga-manṭapamu*. n. An ornamented hall in a temple. కళ్యాణమంటపము. రంగవల్లి *ranga-valli*. n. Ornamenting the floor with white lines or figures. ముగ్గు.

రంగు *rangu*. [Tel.] n. Colour, paint, tint, dye, lustre, shining. వర్ణము. కాంతి.

రంగుగా rangu-gā. adv. Finely, gallantly. దివ్యముగా. రంగుచేయు to paint. రంగరించు or రంగరిందు rangarintsu. v. a. To blend or mix together, with the finger, any solid and liquid substances. వేలితో కలుపు. సున్నమును ఆముదమును రంగరించినాడు he mixed the lime and oil with his finger. రంగరి. రంగారి rangari. n. A painter, రంగుచేయువాడు, చిత్రకారుడు. రంగాయించు ranga-y-intsu. v. a. To colour, to paint. రంగుచేయు.

రంజకము ranjakamu. [Skt.] n. Vermillion, levigated cinnabar. ఇంగిలీకము.

రంజని ranjani. [Skt.] n. The Indigo plant. నీలిచెట్టు.

రంజిల్లు or రంజిలు ranjillu. [Skt.] v. n. To be reddened, ఎర్రనగు. To shine, to be splendid, వెలయు. To be glad or pleased, to rejoice, be charmed or delighted. రంజనము ranjanamu. n. Gladdening, rejoicing; excitement. రాగజనకము, సంతోషమును కలుగజేయుటము. Red sandal. రక్తచందనము, ఎర్రగంధము. రంజించు ranjintsu. v. a. To gladden, charm, delight, please. సంతోషము కలుగజేయు. రంజకుడు ranjakuḍu. n. One who causes joy. రంజించువాడు.

రంజేకము randzakamu. [Tel.] n. A fuse used to fire a gun with, the priming of a gun. తుపాకిచెవిని కాల్చుటకుపెట్టేమందు.

రంజేన or రంజేణి randzana. [Tel.] n. A large boiler. గాదిపంటికాగు.

రండ randa. [Skt.] n. A widow. విధవ.

రండి or రండు randi. [Tel. from వచ్చు.] v. imp. plu. "Come ye." రండని saying 'come ye'

రంత ranta. [Skt.] n. One who sports, క్రీడించువాడు.

రంతు rantu. [Tel.] n. A sound, noise; clamour, disturbance, trouble, annoyance. ధ్వని, అరుపు, సందడి, గల్లరు, తొందర, బాధ. "అతిథ్యముగాని పాడికనచేకొనజాలదు, రంతు సేయుననివద్ద ద్రావకలంబులాడి." A. iii. 4. "ఏలా రంతులే." A. vi. 52. టీ॥ కూసందడులేల, ఈరచ్చ సేయుట. Lewdness, sexual intercourse. Sport. క్రీడ, రతి. రంతుకాడు rantu-kāḍu. n. A lewd man, a man of pleasure, క్రీడాపరుడు. రంతిలు or రంతిల్లు rantilu. v. n. To brawl, ధ్వనిచేయు, అరుచు

రంధి randhi. [Tel.] n. A scrape, hobble, evil, heat, lust. చేటు, గాదు. Annoyance, పోరు.

రంధ్రము randhramu. [Skt.] n. A hole, aperture, orifice, fissure, opening, cavity, chasm. బొక్క, బెజ్జము, సందు. నవరంధ్రములు the nine apertures of the body; being the nostrils, ears, eyes, mouth, anus, and the private parts. వాడేవేళను నామీద రంధ్రాన్వేషణము చేయుచున్నాడు he tries to pick holes in my conduct.

రంపము rampamu. [Tel.] n. A saw. క్రకచము, కరపత్రము. రంపగాడు or రంపకాడు a sawyer. రంపానకోసిన రాతిపలకలు sawn slates.

రంపు rampu. [Tel.] n. A squabble, wrangle, plague, scrape. పీకులాట, రచ్చ, కలకలము, పోరు. ఏవేళ యిదేవానిరంపు this is his constant theme. ఏవేళను దీనిరంపేరంపు she has an endless tongue, she is a constant plague. రంపిల్లు or రంపిలు rampillu. v. n. To contend. వాపోవు, పోరాడు. "సీ॥ తెలిసి సోకుడుమూకమునిగి వాలుబిద్దపెంపున బ్రదికించిల్లము ండ." Yayati. iii. 107. To spread, extend, వ్యాపించు. To increase. వర్ధిల్లు, అతిశయించు, విజృంభించు. To chatter, prattle, make an uproar.

రంపె or రంపెయ rampe. [Tel.] n. A cobbler's knife for cutting leather. చర్మకార సాధనము. తోలుకోసే కత్తి. రంపెలాడి rampel-āḍi. (రంపెలు+ఆడి.) n. A slut, vixen, termagant. రాక్షసప్రకృతిగలస్త్రీ, పోరుపెట్టేది. "నీవు చించివైచుకొని చీరలిచ్చినకటిముసన్నై సేయదా రంపెలాడి." P. iii. 190.

రంభ rambha. [Skt.] n. A plantain tree. అరటిచెట్టు. రంభానిభాకృతిరంభోజఘ్నలు her thighs were as smooth as plantain trees. A name of one of the courtezans of Elysium. ఒక అప్సరస్త్రీ. A very beautiful woman.

రంహస్సు ramhassu. [Skt.] n. Speed, haste, velocity. వేగము, వడి.

రకము rakamu. [H.] n. Shapeliness, grace, elegance. అందము సొగసు. Sort, kind, class, style, quality. విధము, మచ్చు. తీరు, దినుసు. ఆ బియ్యములో నాలుగురకములున్నవి of that rice there are four kinds. "చికిలి చొక్కట్లు సరిపెట్టి రకమెసంగు, సుంగరించుటలు సుకవిందియొరపుపెంప." S. ii. 263. adj. Graceful, elegant, handsome, beautiful. సొగసైన, సుందరమైన. "మకుటంపుజిగిసొంపు రకమైనపెలపంపు." T. i. 29. రకముగ rakamu-ga. adv. Gracefully, beautifully, elegantly. సొగసుగా, సుందరముగా.

రక్కసుడు, రక్కసీడు or రక్కసి rakkasuḍu. [from Skt. రాక్షసుడు.] n. A giant, an evil spirit, demon, fiend. రక్కసము rakkasamu. n. Shrewdness, archness, జాణతనము, రాక్షసితనము, రాక్షసము. రక్కసి, రక్కెస or రక్కసురాలు rakkesi, n. An ogress, giantess, a female fiend. రాక్షసస్త్రీ. రక్కెసులగొంగ rakkesula-gonga. n Vishṇu, the foe of the demons, దైత్యారి రక్కిస or రక్కెస rakkisa. n. The thistle, *Cyperus elatus*, Rox. i. 204. రక్కిస నూనె the oil of thistles, used medicinally. రక్కిస గడ్డి matted grass, spear grass. రక్కెస rakkesa. adj. Improper, అయుక్తమైన. రక్కెస మాటలు fiendish or improper language. "రక్కసజాత్రి." భార. ఉద్యో. iii.

రక్కు rakku. [Tel.] v. a. To scratch or tear with the nails or talons. గీరు, గిచ్చు, గిల్లు, బరుకు. n. A scratch, tear, &c.

రక్కొను or రెక్కొను rak-konu. [Tel.] v. n. To extend, grow, thrive, prosper. వృద్ధిపొందు. వర్ధిల్లు, వ్యాపించు. To recover. తేరుకొను, To happen, కలుగు.

రక్తము raktamu. [Skt.] n. Blood. నెత్తురు. Redness, ఎరుపు. adj. Bloody, red. నెత్తురుగారుచుండే, ఎర్రని. రక్తముతీయు to bleed or draw blood. రక్తచందనము red sandal wood. రక్తమాల్యములు purple or red garments. రక్తవాహిక rakta-vahika. n. A blood vessel. రక్తపము raktapamu. n. A blood-drinker. A leech. జలగ. రక్తపుచ్ఛిక rakta-puchchhika. n. A green lizard with a red tail. వలికర్ణిపాము. రక్తపుడు raktapuḍu. n. A blood-drinker, a vampire, a devil. రాక్షసుడు. The ghosts are described in the Odyssey as drinking blood. రక్తపెంజెర or రక్తపింజర rakta-penjera. n. The boa, or rock snake. పెద్దవిషము. రక్తమంచు చెట్టు a kind of shrub. రక్తాక్షి rakt-akshi. n. The name of a Telugu year. రక్తిక raktika. n. A plant, *Abrus precatorius*, the seeds of which are used as weights. గురుగింజ. రక్తిమ or రక్తిమము raktima. n. Crimson, blood colour, రక్తవర్ణము. రక్తోత్పలము rakt-otpalamu. n. The red lotus. కెందమ్మి, ఎర్రతామరపువ్వు. Rox. ii. 647.

రక్తి rakti. [Skt.] n. Affection, attachment, love. Melody in Music. అనురక్తి, ప్రేమ

యము, ప్రాస్యత. "మిగులఁ దద్భక్తి పొల్చు." A. v. 156. టీ॥ రక్తి=గానమాధుర్యము. రక్తుఁడు raktuḍu. n. A lover of, ప్రేమాతిశయముగలవాఁడు. రామ కథానుభూతరసరక్తుఁడు he who loves the story of Rāma.

రక్ష raksha. [Skt.] n. Preservation, salvation, protection, రక్షణము. An amulet. రక్షణముకొరకు పిల్లలు మెడలకువారికి కట్టబడు మూలికలోనగునది. Ashes worn on the forehead for protection against evil, రక్షణముకొరకు నొసట పెట్టుకొను భస్మము. Cautery, branding. పాదరక్ష a shoe. రక్షకము rakshakamu. adj. Preserving, protecting, saving, కాపాడునట్టి. రక్షకుఁడు or రక్షకుడు rakshakuḍu. n. A preserver, protector, saviour, రక్షించువాఁడు. రక్షణము or రక్షణ rakshaṇamu. n. Salvation, protection, రక్షించుట. రక్షరేకు raksharēku. n. An amulet. మంత్రాక్షరములు వ్రాసినరేకు. రక్షించు rakshintsu. v. a. To save, protect, preserve, కాపాడు. రక్షించుకొను rakshintsu-konu. v. a. To preserve, protect, save, keep for oneself. రక్షితము rakshitamu. adj. Protected, saved, preserved, కాపాడబడిన. రక్షితవ్యము or రక్ష్యము rakshitavyamu. adj. Fit or worthy to be saved or protected, రక్షింపబడిన. రక్షివర్గము rakshi-vargamu. n. A body guard, అంగరక్షకసమూహము.

రక్షస్సు rakshassu. [Skt.] n. A giant, a demon, రాక్షసుడు.

రగడ ragaḍa. [Tel.] n. A melody. A species of (dithyrambic) verse used in sportive amorous compositions. రగడ in old English was called an Ecstasy. It is called in French verse a descant or tirade.

రగులు ragulu. [Tel.] v. n. To be kindled, to take fire, burn or flame. రాజు, మండు. రగులుకొను or రగులుకొను ragulu-konu. v. n. To be on fire, to take fire, to burn. నిప్పు అంటుకొను. రగిలించు, రగులుచు or రగుల్చు ragilintsu. v. a. To kindle, light a fire, inflame. నిప్పుముట్టించు, రాజవేయు, రగులజేయు.

రచన or రచనము rachana. [Skt.] n. Making, composing, arranging, preparing, చేయుటము, నిర్మాణము. Decoration, dressing of the hair. Stringing flowers, weaving wreaths: దండలు గుచ్చుటము మొదలైనది. The arrangement of troops. Literary composition. గద్యపద్యాదిరచన, కవిత్వముచె ప్పుటము. "భారుణీవట్టిచిత్రసభారచనవిధనగణాడ బడచెన్నరికిఁ." M. XI. ii. 156. రచించు or రచియించు rachintsu. v. a. To make, compose, frame, arrange, చేయు, కావ్యాదులు చెప్పు. రచితము rachitamu. adj. Made, composed, రచింపబడిన.

రచ్చ ratstsa. [Tel.] n. A public way, a highway, రాజమార్గము. A portico, మండపము. A court of audience, a public place, a place of meeting. సభ, గోష్ఠి. Publication, betraying or divulging a secret. Plague, torment, trouble, quarrel. కలకలము, రట్టు, తొందర, పోరాటము, కలహము. రచ్చచేయు or రచ్చపెట్టు to plague, tease, తొందరపెట్టు. ఇంటగెలిచిరచ్చగెలువవలెను establish your influence at home before trying to do so abroad; master a smaller difficulty and then a greater one. దానితో నీకేమిరచ్చ why do you quarrel with her? ఇంటికి పిలుచుకొనిపొమ్మని రచ్చపెట్టినాడు the child plagued me to carry him home. "రచ్చలు క్రంతలు రాజమార్గంబులు." B. X. § 53. "మెచ్చి రయ్యంతిపొబగురచ్చలఁగూర్చున్న రసికులెల్ల." Surabh. 51. A. iv. 148. రచ్చకీడుచు or రచ్చకీడ్చు ratstsaku-diyu. v. a. To challenge, defy. జగడానకుపిలుచు, వాదునకీడ్చు. రచ్చకొట్టము, రచ్చపట్టు or రచ్చమంటపము ratstsa-koṭṭamu. n. A place where the village authorities sit, a debating room. A court, a hall of audience. కొలువుకూటము, కచ్చేరి. "నానావనీపమూర్తాభిషిక్తులమునిగనుపట్టు రచ్చకొట్టముపకరిగ." S. iii. 158. రచ్చగొను *ratstsa-gonu.* v. n. To assemble. కుంపుకూడు. To plague. బాధించు. "వి॥ఆచ్చెరువుపడినియచ్చరలు వచ్చిరచ్చగొనిచూడ." R. v. 195. "నెమ్మనము ననిచ్చేరచ్చగొనుమచ్చరము." Satyabh. iv. 200. వ్యాధియములలో చెల్లప్పడు బాధించుచున్నటువంటి శ్వాసము. రచ్చబండ, రచ్చబల్ల or రచ్చరాయి *ratstsa-banda.* n. A stone bench in a street or meeting-place. The village bench, where the elders hold council, నలువురుకూర్చుండేబల్ల. H. iv. 148. రచ్చమాను or రచ్చరావి *ratstsa-mânu.* n. A great tree under which a council is held. రచ్చలబెట్టు *ratstsalu-bettu.* v. a. To publish, divulge, expose. రట్టుచేయు. To plague, annoy. బాధపెట్టు.

రజకుడు *rajakudu.* [Skt.] n. A washerman. చాకలవాడు.

రజతము *rajatamu.* [Skt.] adj. White, silvery, argent. తెల్లని. n. Silver. వెండి. రజతాద్రి *rajat-adri.* n. The silver mountain, i.e., Mount Kailasa. వెండికొండ.

రజని *rajani.* [Skt.] n. Night. రాత్రి. Turmeric, పసుపు. రజనీచరుడు *rajani-charudu.* n. A night-rover, i. e., a goblin, a thief. పిశాచము, దొంగ. రజనీవల్లభుడు the lord of night, i.e., the moon.

రజము *rajama.* [Skt.] n. A tree called *Celosia corymbosa.* Rox. i. 681.

రజము or రజస్సు *rajamu.* [Skt.] n. Dust, దుమ్ము, ధూళి. Filings, రంపపుపొడి. The dust or pollen of flowers, పుప్పొడి. The menses, ముట్టునెత్తురు. రజస్సు or రజోగుణము *rajassu.* The second of three *gunas*, or qualities, i.e., passion; the earthly nature, the natural man, the flesh, that which produces sensual desire, worldliness, coveting and falsehood, and is the cause of pain. రజస్వల *rajasvala.* n. A menstruous woman, ఋతుమతి యగుచుండే స్త్రీ, ముట్టుది. రజస్వలఅగు *rajasvala-agu.* v. n. To become adolescent. రజస్వల అయినది the maiden is come to puberty.

రజ్జువు *rajjuvu.* [Skt.] n. A string, cord, rope, తాడు.

రడన *radana.* [Tel.] n. Earning, గడన, సంపాదనము.

రజా *radza.* [H.] n. Leave of absence.

రజాయి *radzayi.* [Tel.] n. A blanket, దేహిక కప్పుకొను దుప్పటి.

రజ్జన *radzdzana.* [Tel.] n. Self-praise, ఆత్మస్తుతి. రజ్జు *radzdzu.* v. n. To be talkative, to prattle, ప్రేలు. n. A boast, వ్యర్థశ్లాఘనము. Self praise, ఆత్మస్తుతి. "కన్నుట్టునలు కనేటికి, నిన్నుచెనటిరజ్జులనికిని తోడ్పడుగే." M. VII. v. 112. "కల్లమంబులెల్లవాపెద నిరజ్జతేచనిరు." M. IX. ii. 142. రజ్జులాడి *radzdzul-adi.* n. A woman who is fond of vain boasting or of self praise, వ్యర్థశ్లాఘనురాలు, ఆత్మస్తుతిపరురాలు. రజ్జులాడు *radzdzul-adu.* n. A vain boaster. ఒట్టిప్రజ్ఞలు పలుకువాడు, వ్యర్థశ్లాఘనుడు. A vain-glorious person, ఆత్మస్తుతిపరుడు. "జామదగ్న్ని బ్రాహ్మణులశాపంబులు భూపాలురు విన నగ్గడించెనిక్కులంత యేని రజ్జులాడికిసర్జునకుగాని శేవంబు తెలిసెంగి చి." M. VIII. ii. 104.

రటత్ *ratat.* [Skt.] adj. Resounding. మోగే, వాగే, ధ్వనించే. రటనము *ratanamu.* n. A sound, ధ్వని, మ్రోత. రటితము *ratitamu.* n. The crackling of fire, అగ్నిజ్వాలాధ్వని. నిప్పుమంటమ్రోత, రవరవ.

రట్టు *rattu.* [Tel.] n. Publication, betraying or divulging a secret. రచ్చ, గచ్చ. Ill-fame, disgrace, అపకీర్తి. Blame, నింద, దూఱు. Danger, ఉపద్రవము. రట్టుచేసిన or రట్టువడిన rattu-chēsina. adj. Notorious, buzzed abroad. రచ్చపడ్డ. రట్టాడి ratt-adi. adj. Blameworthy, నిందర్హము.

రడ్డు raddu. [from Skt. రాష్ట్ర.] n. A kingdom. రాజ్యము. "రాజోరడ్డుగనునని." A. vi. 108. టీ॥ రాజా, ప్రభువుసుగాని, రడ్డు, రాష్ట్రమునుగాని.

రణము raṇamu. [Skt.] n. War, a battle. యుద్ధము. రణగృహము raṇa-grihamu. n. A house built over the gate of a fort. కోటవాకిటమీదియిల్లు. రణనము raṇanamu. n. Noise, ధ్వని.

రతనము ratanamu. [from Skt. రత్నము.] n. A gem, రత్నము. రతనపుగని ratanapu-gani. n. The Ocean, సముద్రము, రత్నాకరము. రతనపువిల్లు ratanapu-villu. n. A rainbow, ఇంద్రధనుస్సు.

రతము ratamu. [Skt.] n. Coition, copulation. adj. Intent on, actively occupied or engaged in. ఆసక్తము. ఇచ్ఛగల. రతి rati. n. Desire, passion, inclination, attachment, ఆసక్తి. Coition, copulation, సంగమము. The name of the wife of Manmatha, మన్మథునిభార్య. A weight used in weighing diamonds. రవలు పచ్చలు తూచే పడికట్టు. "సన్నంపురతిజాతివన్నెపచ్చలసరం బొరయనాతినూగారు తీరు." UH. ii. 55. One twenty-fifth part of a Maund. రతిపతి or రతిరాజు rati-pati. n. Manmadha. రతుడు ratuḍu. n. A lover of, enjoyer of, delighter in. ఆసక్తుడు. పాపరతుడు a lover of sin.

రత్నము ratnamu. [Skt.] n. A jewel, precious stone, gem. మణి. A masterpiece or fine thing, the best of its kind or species స్వజాతి శ్రేష్ఠము. నవరత్నములు the nine precious stones, viz., మౌక్తికము a pearl, పచ్చ రాగము an emerald, వజ్రము a diamond, ప్రవాళము a coral, మరకతము, an emerald నీలము a sapphire, గోమేధికము an agate. పుష్యరాగము a ruby, వైడూర్యము a cat's eye. అశ్వరత్నము a jewel of a horse, i.e., a noble steed. స్త్రీరత్నము an unrivalled woman. గగనరత్నము the sun, as the gem of heaven. అప్సరోరత్నములు the most lovely of nymphs. రత్నకంబళము ratna-kambalamu. n. A carpet. తివాసి. రత్నగర్భ ratna-garbha. n. The earth; as producing gems. భూమి. "వైశ్యకన్యకలోగిరపుకింజలాడుతఱి క్రిందనుపడిన దివ్యరత్నముల్ పాయలుద్రొక్కుచుమణి జనకపాతుకోసంధరణి పురంధ్రికివ్వారెకరత్నగర్భ యనునామమువెట్టిరి సత్యవిశ్వరుల్." T. ii. 20. రత్నగర్భుడు ratna-garbhuḍu. n. Kubera, the god of wealth, కుబేరుడు. The god of the sea, సముద్రుడు. రత్నసానువు ratna-sānuvu. n. An epithet of Mount Meru as having "gems in its slopes." మేరుపర్వతము. హేమాద్రి. రత్నాకరము ratn-ākaramu. n. The abode of gems, that is, the ocean. సముద్రము. రత్నావళి ratna-vali. n. A necklace of gems.

రథము rathamu. [Skt.] n. A car, a chariot, a wheeled vehicle. తేరు. "రథిన ములలోనరథయానపాత్రముల్." M. VI. ii. 400. రథకారుడు ratha-kāruḍu. n. A coach builder. తేరులు చేయువాడు. రథాంగము rath-angamu. n. A wheel. తేరుయొక్కచక్రము. Any part of a carriage. The globular breasted swan. చక్రవాకము. T. i. 14. రథి. రథికుడు or రథసారథి rathi. n. A warrior fighting from a car, a charioteer. రథముమీద యుద్ధము చేయువాడు. రథిని rathini. n. An army. సేన. M. IX. i. 49. రథోత్సవము rath-ōtsavamu. n. The annual festival at a Hindu temple when the god is taken round in his car. హిందువుల దేవుడు తేరుమీదనెక్కేడి సంబరము. రథ్య

rathya. n. A cavalcade, a line of coaches. రథసమూహము. A high road, రాజమార్గము, వీథి. **రథ్యము** *rathyamu* n. A carriage horse. రథమును ఈడ్చే గుర్రము.

రదనము or **రదము** *radanamu*. [Skt. cf. Lat. 'rodent.'] n. A tooth, a tusk. పల్లు, దంతము. **రదనచ్ఛదము** *radana-ch-chadamu*. n. A tooth covering, i. e., a lip. పెదవి.

రద్ది or **రద్దు** *raddi*. [Tel.] n. Tumult, అల్లరి. A great noise, గొప్పధ్వని. Ill-fame, betraying or divulging a secret, అపకీర్తి, రట్టు, రచ్చ.

రద్దు *raddu*. [H.] n. Repeal, abrogation. రద్దుచేయు, to strike out, to rescind, or repeal, as a law, rule or order. **రద్దైన** *radd-aina*. adj. Annulled, quashed, set aside, కొట్టివేయబడిన.

రపణము *rapanamu*. [Tel.] adj. Great, గొప్ప.

రపము or **రపణము** *rapamu*. [Tel.] n. Festivity, joy, delight, pleasure: సంబరము, సంతోషము, ఉల్లాసము. **తనరపమై** or **తమరపంబై** *tana-rapam-ai*. adv. As one pleases, gladly, delightfully. తనవశంబై, యథేచ్ఛముగా, ఉల్లాసముగా. "అపుడాకీర్తము ఖండు ... రెపాంబుప్రతిలం ... యచ్చపులాతీ, మణికిరా వివాహము నరింపంగార్వముగాంపు మగా." S. i. 412. "గర్జించుకరంకి రపములు, నక్కాదరిమరపంబైయున్న విభుడు, పిక్కటిల్లగద్దిపెట్టినయట్లు." Navanatha, page 56. రపాలు ridicule, అపహాస్యము, అపహాస్యము

రప్ప *rappa*. [Tel.] n. A small stone, చిన్నరాయి.

రప్పించు See under రమ్ము.

రప్పు *rappu*. [H.] n. Darning, పోగుపోయడము. రప్పుతీయు to darn.

రబ్బు *rabbu*. [Tel.] n. Brightness, కాంతి. "ఒక్కప్రబ్బు బిరబ్బు నగుమబ్బు జోగిమబ్బులను త్రొబ్బునననబ్బుతరిమపుతోడ." Ila. i. 10. టీ: బిరబ్బునకు, దట్టమైనటుబంటి కాంతినిచ్చు.

రభసము *rabhasamu*. [Skt.] n. Speed, velocity, hurry. ఆతురము, వేగము, విచారింపక త్వరపడడము. Joy, delight. హర్షము, సంతోషము, సమ్మదము. "రభసదరభసమునంగాపు త్రుడు సేనగూర్చి" M. VI. ii. 100. రభసముగా speedily, rapidly. త్వరగా, ఆతురముగా.

రమ *rama*. [Skt. from రమ్ to sport.] n. A name of the goddess Lakshmi. లక్ష్మి. **రమణ** *ramana*. [from రమ.] n. Elegance, beauty. ఒప్పు, ఒప్పిదము. Love, ప్రీతి. Manner, విధము. "రాధికామణికైదండ రమణబూని." Ila. i. 11. **రమణి** *ramani*. n. A beauty, a lovely woman, a grace. సుందరమైన స్త్రీ. **రమణించు** *ramanistu*. v. n. To be beautiful, ఒప్పిదమగు. **రమణీయము** *ramaniyamu*. adj. Pleasing, gratifying, charming. సుందరమైన. **రమణుడు** *ramanudu*. n. A beautiful person, మనోజ్ఞుడు. A husband, మగడు.

రమారమి *rama-rami*. [Tel.] adv. More or less, about, on an average, ఇంచుమించు, సుమారు.

రమించు or **రమియించు** *ramintsu*. [Skt. from రమ్ to sport, play.] v. n. To sport, క్రీడించు. To cover, cress, copulate, lie with, అనుభవించు. సంగమముచేయు.

రమ్ము *rammu*. [Tel. imp. of వచ్చు. వచ్చు is in Tamil వా. The first part of this word being dropped, we get in Tel. the forms రమ్ము and రా in the imperative mood.] v. imp. Come (thou.) **రప్పించు** or **రావించు** *rappintsu*. v. a. To cause to come, to call, summon. పిలిపించు. **రండి** or **రండు** *randi*. (plu. of రమ్ము.) Come (ye).

రమ్యము *ramyamu*. [Skt. from రమ్ to sport.] adj. Charming, pleasing, delightful, agreeable. మనోహరమైన

రయము *rayamu.* [Skt.] n. Speed, velocity, quickness, precipitation. వేగము. అతిరయముగా with great speed. రయత *rayata.* n. Speed, quickness. త్వర, వేగము. సరయత వచ్చి coming with speed. T. iv. 193.

రయితు, రయిత, రహితు or రైతు *rayitu.* [H.] n. A ryot. కాపు. రయితాంగము or రహితాంగము the agricultural body, the peasantry, కాపులు. రయితువారి *rayitu-wari.* n. The Ryotwary system, i. e., the system under which each cultivator holds direct from Government. An individual farmer's settlement of rent, or of the Government demands. రయితువారిలెక్క an account showing the holding, &c., of each cultivator.

రవ or రవ్వ *rava.* [Tel.] n. A small particle. అణువు. A bit, తునక. A diamond. వజ్రము. A kind of horse's pace, అశ్వగతి విశేషము. గోదుమరవ soojee or roulong, i. e., coarse wheat flour. రవలు small shot, తుపాకిగుండ్లచేసేకొళ్ళే సన్నగుండ్లు. adj. Thin, fine, సన్నము. రవసెల్లా *rava-sella.* n. A fine woven vest of transparent muslin. సన్నసెల్లా, తల్లిపొరవంటిగుడ్డ. రవంత or రవ్వంత *rav-anta.* n. A little, just a trifle. కొంచెము, స్వల్పము. adj. or adv. Tiny, a little, somewhat, rather. రవంతకష్టము it is a little difficult. రవగాలు or రవాలు *rava-gâlu.* n. The name of a certain pace in horsemanship. అశ్వగమనభేదము. "సీ॥ రవగాలునకుసాటిరాకగాడ్పుపటాణి పొడలు పిస్తసబోయి పొదలుసాచ్చె." URK. i. 78. రవన్ని or రవ్వన్ని *rav-anni.* adj. A few, కొన్ని. రవపాళము *rava-pâlamu.* adj. Very thin, as cloth, మిక్కిలి సన్నపాటి. రవమంచేము Same as పకినలమంచేము. (q. v.).

రవడి *ravadi.* [Tel.] n. A debt. అప్పు, ఋణము.

రవణ *ravana.* [Skt. for రమణ.] n. Beauty. Also, a handbell, చిడిగంట. "ఢక్కాహుడుక్కారవణానక, ఒటవా, పటహా, కమఠ." H. iii. 38. రవణము *ravanamu.* n. A jewel, an ornament. భూషణము. "వేల్పుటింతులలోన విర్రవీగుచునేమిన, నవరత్నరవనల రమణమెరిగె." Swa. ii. 11. [Skt.] adj. Sonorous, sounding. ధ్వనిచేయుచున్నది. రవణించు or రమణించు *ravanintsu.* v. n. To bloom, flourish. అందముగానుండు. "సీ॥ అమరేంద్రముక్తమేఘములదిమ్ము క్రమంబురవణించి మించివాయువులు విసరె." N. viii. 103.

రవము *ravamu.* [Skt.] n. Sound in general, a noise. ధ్వని. A voice, కంఠధ్వని. ఆర్తరవము a cry of distress. కింకిణీరవము the tinkling or jingling of small bells. రవళి, రవళి or రవాళి *ravali.* [from రవము.] n. Sound, noise. ధ్వని. "రవళిమస్తైల మ్రోతరాయడింప." Vish. vi. 13. "తాబాముసన్న రవళిపాటలరిఘుంకృతి, శ్రుతిబాడుకొనగ." Swa. vi. 38. రవళించు or రవాళించు *ravalintsu.* v. n. To make a noise, resound. ధ్వనించు. "జిగి రవళించి దాటుసామ్రాణి కేళలు." HD. i. 32. రవళించి neighing, సకిలించి. adj Sounding, sonorous. మ్రోగే, ధ్వనించే.

రవరవ *rava-rava.* [Tel.] n. A clamour, disturbance, noise. కూత, రచ్చ, ధ్వని. Brightness, dazzling, కాంతివిశేషము. Distress of mind, anxiety, స్పర్థ. Anger, కోపవికారము. "కులమును రూపముగానిన్ని కూరిమియుగా నెలగానానంచునవ్వులబచుంచగా రవ రవలోబడమెలగ మనవారికెంతయును." Parij. i. 48. "రవలకంకణములు రవరవలెసగ." HD. i 86. రవరవ adv. Precipitately, quickly, hastily, శీఘ్రముగా.

రవాణా or రవానా *ravâna.* [H.] n. Despatching, పంపుట. రవాణాచేయు to despatch, as goods, &c.

రవాయి *ravāyi.* [Tel.] n. A false ruby, కృత్రిమపుష్యరాగమణి.

రవి *ravi.* [Skt.] n. The sun. సూర్యుడు.

రవిక *ravika.* [Tel.] n. A bodice, or corset. N. vii. 229.

రవులు Same as రగులు. (q. v.)

రవేసు or రవీసు *ravēsu.* [H.] n. Customary fees, దుసుము. Grandeur. adj. Best. రవేసు ఆకులు the best betel leaves, రేతాకులు.

రవ్వ *ravva.* [Tel. another form of రచ్చ.] n. Ill fame, a bad name. Clamour, disturbance, అపకీర్తి, రట్టడి. రవ్వాడు *ravv-āḍu.* v. a. To blame, censure, నిందించు.

రశన or రసన *rasana.* [Skt.] n. A woman's zone or girdle, usually set with little bells. పదియారుపేటలుగల ఆడుదాని మొలనూలు.

రశీదు See రసీదు.

రశ్మి *rasmi.* [Skt.] n. Light. వెలుగు. Lustre, కాంతి. A ray of light, కిరణము.

రసము *rasamu.* [Skt.] n. Juice, fluid, liquid, extract, essence. Taste, flavour, రుచి. Taste, sentiment, emotion, passion, affection, humour. Quicksilver, పాదరసము. The షడ్రసములు or six flavours are మధురము or తీపి sweet; ఆమ్లము or పులుసు sour; కషాయము or వగరు astringent; లవణము or ఉప్పు salt; కటువు or కారము pungent; కసాయము or చేదు bitter. రసఘంటమైనభూమి or రసవత్తైనభూమి strong soil, which is not exhausted. నీరసమైనభూమి land that is exhausted. క్రోధరసము the spirit of wrath. దయారసము the spirit of love, kind feelings. ఈ పద్యములో రసములేదు this is a tasteless verse. విరసమైనమాటలు rude language. The nine రసములు or humours produce the following స్థాయీభావములు (symptoms.) 1. శృంగారరసము (love) produces రతి enjoyment. 2. వీరరసము (honour) produces ఉత్సాహము daring. 3. కరుణారసము (mercy) begets శోకము pity. 4. అద్భుతము (credulity) begets విస్మయము marvel. 5. హాస్యరసము (merriment) produces హాస్యభావము laughter. 6. భయానకరసము (timidity) leads to భయము fright. 7. బీభత్సరసము (austerity) begets జుగుప్స sarcasm. 8. రౌద్రరసము (wrath) leads to క్రోధము cruelty. 9. శాంతరసము (gentleness) produces శమభావము calmness. రసకర్పూరము *rasa-karpūramu.* n. A white sublimate or muriate of mercury, కర్పూరరసము. రసగుండు *rasa-guṇḍu.* n. A ball coated with quicksilver, రసముపూసినగుండు. రసజ్ఞ *rasa-gnya.* n. The tongue, నాలుక. రసజ్ఞత *rasa-gnyata.* n. Skill, judgment, taste, critical discernment, తెలివి. రసజ్ఞుడు *rasa-gnyuḍu.* n. A man of taste, a critic. గుణదోషములనెరిగినవాడు. రసదాడి or రసదాళి *rasa-dāḍi.* n. Sugar cane. చెరుకు. "కుముదుగ్న స్థూలగాడిమబీజములతోడ, ఘనరాజరసదాడిగొలతోడ." A. ii. 85. A fine sort of plantain. అరటిగాత భేదము. రసదాళిక *rasa-dālika.* n. A kind of sugar, చెరుకుదినుసు. రసన *rasana.* n. The tongue. నాలుక. రసనేంద్రియము *rasan-ēndriyamu.* n. The sense of taste. రసవతి *rasa-vati.* n. A kitchen. వంటయిల్లు. రసవర్గములు *rasa-vargamulu.* n. plu. The various condiments or ingredients such as salt, pepper, &c., సంబారములు. రసవాదము *rasa-vādamu.* n. Alchemy, chemistry, పాదరసమునుకట్టి బంగారుచేయువిద్య. రసవాది *rasa-vādi.* n. An alchemist, a chemist, రసమునుకట్టి బంగారుచేయువాడు. రససిందూరము *rasa-sindūramu.* n. A sort of factitious cinnabar, made with zinc, mercury, blue vitriol and nitre, ఔషధవిశేషము. రససిద్ధి *rasa-siddhi.* n. Alchemy, రసవాదము. "ధనమునిమ్ముఖంబున, గ్రాలింపిమెరుంగుపసిడిగాజేరసిద్ధిన." R. vi. 10.

రసాంజనము a kind of collyrium, అంజనవిశేషము. రసాతలము *rasa-talamu.* n. A name of Hades. పాతాళలోకము. రసాభాసము *ras-âbhasamu.* n. Bad taste, inelegance. adj. Disagreeable, disgusting. విరసమైన. ఆ శ్లోకమును దిద్ది రసాభాసము చేసినాడు in correcting the verse he has spoiled it, he showed bad taste in correcting it. రసాభాసముగా మాట్లాడినాడు he spoke coarsely. ఆయిల్లు నిండా రసాభాసముగానున్నది that house is very disagreeable. ఊరేగుచుండగా వాన వచ్చి అంతా రసాభాసమైపోయినది when the marriage procession was going on, there was a shower and everything was upset. రసాయనము *ras-âyanamu.* n. A panacea, a medicine preventing old age and prolonging life, జరావ్యాధినాశౌషధము. Butter milk, sweet curds, గోరసము, చల్ల. Poison, విషము. "తినవచ్చో మాధుర్యమెనయ నా యువి మాడు మున్నట్లు మేలిరసాయనములు, ఒప్పుగా గిన్నియలమంచి యుపచరించి." T. iii. 18. టీ॥ రసాయనములు, తీపిగలిగినపదార్థములు. రసాల *rasala.* n. A pudding or mess of curds, mixed up with sugar and spices. పెరుగులో నవేక ద్రవ్యములువేసి చేసినది. రసాలము *rasalamu.* n. The sugar cane, చెరుకు. Also, the sweet mango tree, తియ్యమామిడిచెట్టు. రసావళ్లు *ras-avallu.* n. A kind of cakes. "తినయింటనప్పుడాయితెమెనరించినకమ్మదావులొలంకురసావళ్లుమిసుపపడలు జాపట్లునుగోధుమపిండివంటలంకా గలవనినకా." Vish. iii. 377.

రసి or రసిక *rasi.* [Tel.] n. The pus, or matter of a sore, serum, పుంటిచీము.

రసిక *rasika.* [Skt.] n. A woman of taste రసికురాలు. రసికత or రసికత్వము *rasikata.* [Skt.] n. Good taste or judgment. రసజ్ఞత. రసికుడు *rasikudu.* A man of taste. శృంగారాదిరసములను గ్రహించువాడు, రసజ్ఞుడు. రసితము *rasi-tamu.* n. Sound noise, thunder. ధ్వని, ఉరుము.

రసీదు or రశీదు *rasidu.* [Eng. 'Receipt'.] n. A receipt, an acknowledgment in writing.

రసోనకము *rasônakamu.* [Skt.] n. Garlic. వెల్లుల్లి.

రస్తా *rasta.* [H.] n. A road. బాట. A high road, రాజమార్గము.

రస్తాళి *rastali.* [Tel. for రసదాళి.] n. A kind of plantain, ఒకవిధమైన అరటిపండు.

రస్తు *rastu.* [H.] n. Food, provisions, commissariat supplies. వస్తుసంభారము. "చ॥ పరగెడురస్తుకొట్టములు భద్రముగానొగిబీగముద్రలన్, గరిమనొనర్చి." హంస. i. "కస్తురిపేటి పదారువన్నెబంగారము రస్తుకుప్పతెలిగంబుగ విన్నెలనోనితోట." S. i. 112.

రహటము *rahatamu.* [Skt.] n. A spinning-wheel. రాట్నము.

రహటు, రట్టు or రాటు *rahatu.* [Tel.] n. Ravages, mischief, plague, trouble, annoyance. ఉపద్రవము. ఈ యింటిలో ఎలుకల రహటు మెండుగానున్నది in this house rats have made great havoc.

రహదారి or రావారి *raha-dari.* [H.] n. A public way. A passport. The collection of tolls or taxes on roads

రహస్యము *rahasyamu.* [Skt.] n. A secret, a mystery; secrecy, privacy. ఏకాంతము. adj. Secret, mysterious; private; abstruse, recondite, obscure. ఏకాంతమైన, దాచదగిన.

రహి *rahi.* [Tel.] n. Joy, ఆనందము. Beauty, elegance, harmony. సొంపు. సొగసు. Lustre, కాంతి. Affection, love, ఆశ, రక్తి, ప్రియము. Eagerness, ఆసక్తి. Understanding, తెలివి. Welfare, బాగు. Manner, విధము. "గుజరాతి అగిసిస్తు గోట్లుదాపినదాలు రహిమించుమైతిణీ దవికదాడిక" H. 133. "సీ॥ రహిపుట్టజంత్రగాత్రములరాగ్గరించు విమలగాంధర్వయువిద్య మాకు." Swa. ii. 46. రహి or రహిగా adv.

Eagerly, affectionately. ఆశతో, ప్రియముగా. This word is often used as a mere peg to fill the metre. రహించు or రహియించు *rahintsu.* v. n. To bloom, flourish, to be pleasant, to be agreeable, to shine. వెలయు, చెలగు, ఒప్పు, వర్ధిల్లు. "మెరుపుతునుకెంచ జడివాన మెలుపుగాంచ కరక లురహించ నిరులువర్ణిలుమించ." Paidimarri vi. 29.

రహితము *rahitamu.* [Skt.] adj. Destitute, bereft, abandoned, left. విహీనమైన, విడువబడిన. రహితుడు *rahitudu.* n. One who is without or devoid of, one who is free from, విహీనుడైనవాడు. విద్యారహితుడు one who is devoid of learning, or is unlearned.

రా rā.

రా *rā.* [Tel.] n. and adj. Short for రాయి a stone; and also for రాచ (kingly adj.) Pertaining to a stone. రాతిసంబంధమైన. Pertaining to a king, of the king, royal, రాచ. ఆ నూతికి రాకట్టు కట్టించిరి they built the well round with stone. "వచ్చురా జగతిప్తె, పసిడికంబములు మెచ్చుగానిలిపి, యామీద నిలుపుబోదలు." DRB. 550. రాకులము the royal race, రాజవంశము, రాచకులము. కొండరా the king of hills. రారాజు the king of kings. రాకుమారి a king's daughter. రాజపుత్రి. రాకొమరుడు a king's son, a prince, రాజకుమారుడు. M. IV. i. 173. రాచందము *ra-tsandamu.* n. Kingly style or dignity. రాచూలి *ra-tsūli.* n. A prince, or princess. రాజకుమారుడు, లేక, రాజపుత్రి. రామొలిబాణము a rocket.

రా *rā.* [Tel. short for రమ్ము.] A particle expressive of contempt, disrespect or familiarity (in poems రే, as in Swa. iii. 128. "ఏలా యూచేలంబుచేరితోయా, బాలా సాల మాలుంబాలుములో.") "రా గానంచినుమారెరా రాజ నవరిరా రాకన్నమ్మరారారాగాలగుములరా." అట్లు చేయుము రా come, you must do this? వాన్ని పిలువురా call him, will you? దానిని తేరా come, bring it here. పోరా come, begone.

రా *rā.* [Tel.] The infinitive or imperative of వచ్చు. See note under రమ్ము. మాయింటికిరా come to my house. రాదలచినాడు he thought of coming. రాలేను I cannot come. "దగ్గిరరామొగ్గెని." (T. iv. 173.) when he drew near, (she) turned towards him. రాక, రాకడ or రావడము *rāka.* n. Coming, arrival, approach. వచ్చుట. రాకపోకలు coming and going. రాక adv. Without coming. రాకపోవు or రాకయుండు *rāka-pōvu.* v. n. Not to come or arrive. రాకు or రాకుము *rāku.* v. imp. negative. Come not, do not come, రావద్దు. రాబడి *ra-baḍi.* n. Income, వచ్చుబడి. రాగాపోగా *rāgā-pōgā.* (lit: coming or going.) adv. In the end, finally, at last, one way or another, with one thing or another. రాగాపోగా నిలిచినదియిది after all this is the remainder. రాదు *rādu.* (3d. pers. sing. masc. neg. aorist of వచ్చు.) He will not come, he does not come. రాదు *rādu.* (3rd. pers. sing. neut.) It does not come. It is used as an auxiliary signifying prohibition: కోపపడరాదుగాని చెప్పుతాను you must not be angry but I will tell you. నిరాశకారాదు we should not give up hope. అట్లు చేసెనట్లు ఎంచరాదుగాని we must not imagine he has done so, but yet. నేను ఇక్కడ ఉండరాదు I must not stop here రాని *rāni.* (neg. rel. participle of వచ్చు.) Which has not come, which shall not come or does not happen. పనికిరాని or అక్కరకురాని useless. చెప్పరానిమాట what is not fit to be said. వచ్చీరానిమాటలు a half formed pronunciation as that of a child beginning to speak. వాడు వచ్చినప్పుడు నాతోచెప్పె his coming is as useless as if he were absent. చదువురానివాడు one who cannot read, an illiterate man. చదవరానిజాబు an illegible letter, or a letter that should not be read. "వచనములురానికడుచిన్నవానినిన్ను" thee, a child unable to speak. Yamuna Charya Charitra i. 73. రాను *rānu*. (first person neg. aor. of వచ్చు) I will not come or I do not come. Also, a noun meaning coming, as రాకపోక both coming and going. రాకపోక పదిదినములుపట్టును to go and return will take ten days. రానున్నది that which is to come or to happen. "రానిదికోరినరాదది రానున్నదికోరకున్న రాకుండదుగా" (Sumati. 137) what cannot happen cannot happen though desired: that which will happen though undesired will not fail to come to pass. రాబట్టు *rā-baṭṭu*. v. a. To receive, receive back, recover, regain. వచ్చినదానిని రాబట్టు receive that which is sent to you. రామి *rāmi*. (negative verbal noun of వచ్చు.) The not coming, non-arrival, రాకపోవడము. plu. రాములు. చేయరామి impracticability. తిప్పరామి the difficulty of turning (it.) కానరామి the not seeing, the impossibility of seeing. "అక్కడుడు రామినప్పుడు పొక్కుచునిజనరాజు" (Yayati. iii. 126) grieved at his not coming or at his non-arrival.

రాంకవము *rānkavamu*. [Skt.] adj. Woollen. n. Any thing manufactured of wool or hair. సకలాతులు శాలువులుమొదలయు నవి. A. v. 114.

రాంబోందు or రాబందు *rāmbondu*. [for Skt. రామబంధు.] n. The White Scavenger Vulture. పసుపుపచ్చగాముండే ముక్కుకలిగి చచ్చినగొడ్లమాంసతినేపక్షి.

రాంభము *rāmbhamu*. [Skt.] n. The bamboo staff of a monk or friar. చేతికర్ర, వెదురుదండము. "త్రిదండధారుపు ముంథరాంధుః కుండికలాసంగనంశిక్యతాంతిమూర్త్ముండై." A. vi. 82.

రాక *rāka* [Skt.] n. The day of full moon. పూర్ణచంద్రుడుగలపున్నమ. రాకాచంద్రుడు the full moon. రాక See under రా.

రాకాసి or రక్కసి *rākasi*. [from Skt. రాక్షసి.] n. A Rākshasa, a demon, రాక్షసి. రాక్షసుడు.

రాకించు *rākinṭsu*. [Tel.] v. a. To thrash, కొట్టు.

రాకొట్టు *rā-koṭṭu*. [Tel. See under రా from వచ్చు.] v. n. & a. To address scornfully using thou and thee, tutoyer. రా రా పోరా అని ఏకవచనాంతముగాపిలుచు, రారా పోరా అని అమర్యాదగా అను, తిరస్కరించు. "కలవాకంటకుడెయిది, సిగ్గొకానాదు శత్రునింద్యగ్గరుకో, రాకొట్టి పిలిచిమదిను, క్రేకను ఉట్టించిపోటుకెలుపనికలుడుక." G. vii. 68.

రాక్షస *rākshasa*. [Skt.] n. The name of a Telugu year.

రాక్షసము *rākshasamu*. [Skt.] n. A form of marriage in which the bride is carried away by force. adj. Pertaining to the Rakshasas, రాక్షససంబంధమైన. Devilish, cruel, inhuman. రాక్షసకృత్యము an inhuman act, a horrible deed. రాక్షసత్వము *rākshasatvamu*. n. The condition of being a Rakshasa, cruelty. రాక్షసి *rākshasi*. n. A Rakshasa, a demon. రాక్షసుడు. An ogre or she-demon, a female fiend. రాక్షసుడు *rākshasuḍu* n. A giant, demon, fiend.

రాగ *rāga*. [Tel.] n. A bad creature, దుష్టుడు. రాగదాగుడురాగ a serpent, సర్పము. "రాగదాగుడురాగి ప్రోగుడిడెడు ప్రోడ." (Atstsa Telugu Rāmayan,) i. e., Siva, the hero who wears as an earring a serpent that hides in a hole. An adulteress, జారిణి. A proud or wicked man, ఉద్ధతుడు, దుష్టుడు. adj. Shrewish wicked.

గయ్యాళి, దుష్ట, చెడుగైన. "కూతురురాగైన మాత్రమే అర్వంబు చెడుగైన వారోపావనితిప్పు." Nrisim. § 12. రాగతుంగ a kind of grass called భద్రముస్తకము. రాగతనము *rāga-tanamu*. n. Envy, malice. మాత్సర్యము. "లోగవించుకైన రాగతనంబున రోచినలువ లెల్ల వాడివాపు గీజాపోక కిమ్ము చేజనన లెన్న." Appa kavi. ii. 36. రాగంట్లమారి *ragantla-mari*. n. A blackguard, a villain. పోకిరి, గంటాగుండి. "వాడు నానాటికి భిన్నబుద్ధిచలబెరిగి, కాకలమరిగి గడిమారిగట్టిసారి, రాలుగాయితనాన తేరజపువాని నారికేరికేరాగంట్లమారియయ్యె." H. v. 126.

రాగము *rāgamu*. [Skt.] n. A tune. పాట. పరిగమాద్యాలింగిరిగితము. Affection, love, delight, desire, ప్రేమాతిశయము, అనురాగము. Sorrow. Colour, tint, dye, hue, రంగు. Envy. రాగద్వేషములు envy and hatred. మదనరాగము agitation of love. మన్మథవికారము. ఆ పడుచు రాగములు పెట్టు చున్నది, లేక, రాగములు పెట్టి యేడ్చుచున్నది the girl is screaming away.

రాగి *rāgi*. [Tel.] n. Copper. తామ్రము. plu. రాగులు. n. The grain called Natcheny, *Cynosurus coracanus*. కొర్లు, తివిదలు. రాగిచెట్టు (for రావిచెట్టు) *ragichettu*. n. The Poplar-leaved Fig tree, *Ficus religiosa*. పిప్పలము.

రాగిడి *ragidi*. [Tel.] n. A round golden tire embossed with flower-patterns, worn by Hindu females on the back of the crown of the head. జడబిళ్ల.

రాగిలు. రాగిల్లు or రాగిలు *ragintsu* [Skt.] v. n. To shine, to be glad, rejoice ప్రకాశించు, ప్రియమందు, సంతోషించు, రంజిల్లు. "బసవనియసమప్రాభవభక్తి, రసవార్ధకల్లినిసిన్నట్టి వాదనరాగిల్లికన్నగ ప్రస్తుత్యుచనిరు." BD. ii. 33.

రాచ *ratsa*. [from Skt. రాజ.] adj. Of or belonging to the king, రాజసంబంధ, క్షత్రియసంబంధమైన. రాచవారు persons belonging to the kingly caste. క్షత్రియులు. రాచపుడమిరేడు a Kshatriya king. రాచపీనుగు తోడులేక పోదు a king's corpse will not fall alone; a proverb denoting that every great man's fall ruins many persons. రాచమాల a Pariah who was formerly a క్షత్రియు. రాచపని or రాజకార్యము *ratsa-pani*. n. A public affair, politics, a transaction, business. వ్యవహారము. రాచకొమరుడు or రాకొమరుడు *ratsa-komarudu*. n. A king's son, a prince. రాజపుత్రుడు. రాచకొలము or రాచకులము *ratsa-kolamu*. n. The Kshatriya caste, క్షత్రియకులము. రాచకోడి *ratsa-kodi*. n. A wild fowl with a beautiful purple plumage, and scarlet beak and crest; probably, the Black Ibis. రాచపుండు *ratsa-pundu*. n. A carbuncle. రాజవ్రణము. రాచపుట్టువు *ratsa-puttuvu*. n. A Kshatriya, క్షత్రియుడు. రాచయుసిరిక *ratsa-yusirika*. n. A kind of Emblic Myrobalan. ఉసిరికభేదము. రాచరికము *ratsa-rikamu*. n. Government, రాజరికము. రాచవాడు *ratsa-vadu*. n. A Kshatriya. రాచవీడు *ratsa-vidu*. n. The capital of a king. రాజధాని. రాచిలుక *ra-chiluka*. n. The large red parrot. రాజశుకము.

రాచు *ratsu*. [Tel.] v. n. To be rubbed, ఒరసికొను. v. a. To rub. ఒరయు. కల్పించు. To cover (with any substance;) to whitewash, రుద్దు. శరీరమును గంధాదులచేత లేపనము చేయు, ఇల్లు గోడలుమొదలైనవానిని అలుకు. To rub out. To file. రాచుకొను *ratsu-konu*. (reflexive form of రాచు.) To rub one's self (against any thing.) రుద్దుకొను, ఒరసికొను.

రాజ *raja*. [Skt.] adj. Royal; belonging to a king. Lunar, belonging to the moon. Chief, eminent. రాజసంబంధమైన, చంద్ర సంబంధమైన, శ్రేష్ఠమైన. ముఖ్యమైన. "ఆరాయ రాజానుగ్రహాముగ్లగాకమి. కలువలదరమూలగ

లబనో్భ." R. i. 124. రాజకము rājakamu. n. An assembly of kings. రాజులసమూహము. adj. Pertaining to Government. రిజాలావు వారివల్ల సంభవించునది. An act of oppression by the government or by the king, as opposed to దైవికము evil regarded as a visitation of God. రాజక దైవికములు casualties. రాజము rājamu. In composition denotes superiority (శ్రేష్ఠత్వము.) చాపరాజము a noble bow. "జమదగ్ని కతడిచ్చె చాపరాజంబు." DRB. 603. "మఖరాజము" (N. ix. 200.) a noble sacrifice. రాజకార్యము rāja-kāryamu. n. A royal deed, politics. రాజుయొక్క పని, రిజాలావుపని. రాజగృహము rāja-grihamu. n. A palace. రాజుయొక్క నగరు. రాజత్వము rājatvamu. n. Royalty. రాజైయుండడము. రాజదంతము rāja-dantamu. n. A bright or chief tooth, i.e., a fore tooth. ముందరిపల్లు. రాజధర్మములు rāja-dharmamulu. n. The duties incumbent on a king. రాజనీతులు, విధివత్తుగా రాజా చేయవలసినపనులు. రాజధాని rāja-dhani. n. A metropolis or royal residence. A presidency. రాజుయొక్క ప్రధాననగరము. రాజబంధువులు the king's kinsmen. రాజభాగము the king's share, Government's share of produce. రాజనీతి rāja-niti. n. Royal polity, civil and military government. రాజుయొక్క ధర్మము. రాజన్యుడు rāja-nyudu. n. A man of the royal or military caste, క్షత్రియుడు. రాజన్వంతము rājan-vantamu. adj. Having a good king (as a country). రాజపత్ని a queen. రాజుయొక్క భార్య. రాజపురోహితుడు a king's household priest. రాజబీజి raja-biji. n. One of royal descent. రాజవంశమునందు పుట్టినవాడు. రాజమార్గము rāja-margamu. n. The king's high way, a public road, ఘంటాపథము. పెద్దబాట. రాజమాషము rāja-mashamu. n. The pulse termed *Dolichos catjang*. అలచందలు. రాజయక్ష్మము rāja-yakshmamu. n. Pulmonary consumption. క్షయరోగము. రాజయోగము rāja-yōgamu. n. A simple and easy mode of abstract meditation, as distinguished from the austere and rigorous modes. రాజయోగి rāja-yōgi. n. One who practises the రాజయోగము. రాజయోగ్యము rāja-yōgyamu. adj. Proper or suitable for a sovereign. రాజార్హమైన. రాజరాజు or రారాజు rāja-rādzu. n. An emperor, or universal monarch. రాజులరాజు. The god of riches, కుబేరుడు. Also, an epithet of Duryodhana, దుర్యోధనుడు; and of the moon, చంద్రుడు. రాజరీతి rāja-riti. n. Royal style. Also, Tinsel, బంగారు తగడు, కాకిబంగారు. రాజర్షి rājarshi. n. A man of the క్షత్రియ caste who by religious austerity has become a saint. రాచవాడై యుండినముని. రాజవంతము having a king, as a country. రాజవల్లభము rāja-vallabhamu. n. A kind of cloth. B.D. iii. 102. రాజవీథి rāja-vidhi. n. The main street of a town. పెద్దవీధి. రాజశేఖరము rāja-sekharamu. n. A sort of cloth. BD. iii. 102. రాజశ్రీ rāja-sri. adj. A title like Mr. prefixed to names, రాజసర్పము rāja-sarpamu. n. A large species of snake. రాజసూయము rāja-sūyamu. n. A hecatomb or sacrifice performed by a monarch, after subduing other kings as in the case of Yudhishtira and others. ఒకవిధమైనయజ్ఞము. రాజహంస or రాజహంసము rāja-hamsa. n. A white goose or swan with red legs and bill; perhaps the flamingo. ఎర్రనికాళ్లు ముక్కులుగల తెల్లహంస. Also, a phrase for an excellent king, రాజశ్రేష్ఠుడు. రాజాంకుడు rāj-ankudu. n. Siva: who has the moon as his emblem. శివుడు. రాజాంగము rāj-angamu. n. Government. ప్రభుత్వము. ఇప్పుడు ఆ రాజాంగము తలక్రిందులైనది that government is now upset. రాజాసనము rājāsanamu. [from

రజస్ dust.] adj. Impetuous. రజోగుణము వల్ల కలిగిన, ఐహికమైన, రజోగుణప్రధానమైన. రాజసయజ్ఞము or రాజసపూజ worship offered to obtain a particular object such as fame, కామ్యార్థముగాగాని దంభార్థముగాగాని చేయు పూజ. n. That which is of the earth, worldly, earthly. Passionateness, heat of temper. Hauteur, pride, arrogance. వారిద్దరిలో వొకడు రాజసుడు ఒకడు సాత్వికుడు one man is haughty, the other man is meek. వాడు పలుకకుండా రాజసముగానుండినాడు he haughtily refused to reply. రాజాదనము raj-adanamu. n. A name applied to three different trees. *Butea frondosa*, *Buchanania latifolia*, and *Mimusops kauki*, మోదుగుచెట్టు, ప్రియాళువు, పాలచెట్టు, చారమామిడిచెట్టు, పాలచెట్టు. రాజావర్తము raj-avartamu. n. A sort of *lapis lazuli* having a sky blue or lilac tint. This stone is ground down into powder which painters use for a delicate light blue tint. రాజార్హము worthy of a king, రాజునకుతగిన. రాజోపచారము raj-opacharamu. n. Attendance on a king, homage of servants to their master. రాజునకుచేయుసేవ.

రాజి raji. [Skt.] n. A line or row. పంక్తి. A line, రేఖ. పుష్పరాజి a heap of flowers.

రాజితము rajitamu. [Skt.] adj. Illuminated, adorned, embellished, ప్రకాశింపబడిన. అలంకరింపబడిన, రాజిన.

రాజిలము rajilamu. [Skt.] n. A snake equally thick at each end as if it had two heads, *Amphisuena*. రెండుతలల పాము, సర్పము, సర్పభేదము. "ఉక్కునుకోపానవడి కిని రాజిలంబునకు నుదగవిభునకు కలదింకముఖకు సుభుగకులాధిపునకు." BRY.ii. 223. ఈ ప్రయోగమువల్ల ఇది విష్ణుమాలినపాముని తెలుస్తున్నది.

రాజిల్లు rajillu. [Skt.] v. n. To shine. ప్రకాశించు.

రాజీ raji. [H.] n. Consent. Reconciliation, a settlement of a quarrel or dispute. ఇష్టము, సమ్మతి, సమాధానము. రాజీనామా resignation of an office. రాజీచేయు to satisfy, reconcile, appease. నాకు రాజీగానున్నది it is agreeable to me, I consent to it. రాజీనామాఇచ్చు to resign an office.

రాజీవము rajivamu. [Skt.] n. A lotus, పద్మము, ఎర్రకలువ. Also, a large fish called *Cyprinus niloticus*. చిరాలనేచేపమీనము.

రాజ్ఞి ragnyi. [Skt. feminine gender of రాజు.] n. A queen, రాజుభార్య. A female ruler, రాజ్యము చేసేటిది, రాణి.

రాజ్యము rajyamu. [Skt.] n. Rule, government. Administration of government, sovereignty. ఏలుబడి, ఏలుబడి, ప్రభుత్వము. A kingdom, principality, country, ఒక రాజు ఏలే దేశము. అతడు రాజ్యముచేయుచుండగా while he reigned. మారాజ్యమునకు వెళ్లుచున్నాను I am going to my own country. ఇది అడవి రాజ్యము this is a forest country or land. రాజ్యభ్రష్టుడై being expelled from the kingdom.

రాజనములు or రాజనాలు radzanamulu. [Tel.] n. A superior kind of rice of a reddish colour. వడ్లలోభేదము. "పోతకంటిరాజనాలు, బూడిదపోకరాజనాలు, కలిగిరాజనాలు, పొన్నపూరాజనాలు, గాలిరాజనాలు, వాసనరాజనాలు, నల్లరాజనాలు." H. iv. 154.

రాజు radzu. [Tel.] v. n. To take fire, flame, begin to burn. పొగరాజు, ప్రజ్వలించు. "దినదినమునకు దేవునిముందు కొలువుకు పోయిరాజుదుగా." S. iii. 212. unless I go every day to work I cannot keep the pot boiling.

రాజు radzu. [from Skt. రాజన్.] n. A king, prince, ruler. A lord, baron, earl, count, nobleman, ప్రభువు. ఏలువాడు. క్షత్రియుడు, క్షత్రియకులశ్రేష్ఠుడు. The moon, చంద్రుడు.

రాజావారిసీమ Government land, సర్కారు భూమి. రారాజు or రారేడు rā-rāḍu. n. A king of kings. రాజులకు రాజు. An epithet of Kubēra and Duryōdhana, కుబేరుడు, దుర్యోధనుడు.

రాటుకము Same as రాట్నము (q. v.).

రాటు or రాటుము rāṭu. [Tel.] n. Overcrowding, as of people. (జన) సమ్మర్దము. Appearance, breaking out, as of rats or thieves. A plague, pest, danger, ఉపద్రవము, రచ్చ, కొట్టు, రంపు. ఆ యింటిలో ఎలుకలరాటుగానున్నది the rats broke out in the house. "నోటికూటికి రాటు తెచ్చుకొంటికదా యని" (S. iii. 340.) I saw that I had got into a scrape which might cost me my bread. రాటువడు or రాట్పడు rāṭu-paḍu. v. n. To be troubled, teased, pestered, plagued, ఉపద్రవపడు.

రాట్టము, రాట్నము or రాటుకము raṭṭa-mu. [from Skt. రహాటము.] n. A spinning wheel. నూలువడుకుయంత్రము. "వడిబారముచె వులుచా త్రొక్కుడుపలకయుడిందు కదురుగుంజ లనుంద్రొక్కుడు బొమ్మయునంద్రిప్పుచు ద్రుడక యునుంగలుగు రాట్నములనైకొనుచుచు." S. ii. 455. రంకులరాట్నము a merry-go-round (lit. the prank wheel), a whirligig.

రాట్టు rāṭṭu. [Skt.] n. A king. రాజు. "కృష్ణమంత్రిరాట్టిలకుడు." T. i. 51. రాట్తనయుడు rāḍ-tanayuḍu. n. A king's son. రాజపుత్రుడు. రాడ్వంశము rāḍ-vamṣamu. n Royal race or lineage, రాజాన్వయము. "రాడ్వంశపయోధివిధుడు." R. v. 225.

రాడు rāḍu. [Tel.] n. A post or pillar. గుంజె, స్తంభము. "కొదలుమాలి రాడుచిక్కినే తాలపాడదె సీమజనుచు." A. vi. 13. కొదలు మాలి, మిటలుపడిపోయి, రాడుచిక్కి, మలరాడు మాత్రము అవశిష్టము గానున్న టువంటి. (Also, 3rd pers. neg. sing. of వచ్చు See under రా.)

రాణ rāṇa. [Tel. another form of రమణ.] n. Brightness, lustre. ప్రకాశము. Cheerfulness. ఉల్లాసము. Beauty, సొంపు. Love, liking. ప్రీతి. "రాణసొప్పారుపైతారాంబు పిం గిడి." Swa. iv. 36. టీ॥ రాణసొప్పారు, శృంగారముచేత కొప్పుచున్న. "ప్రాణేశుడులేమిదుఃఖ పరవశయగుచుం రాణచెడియుంటుగని యుద్యోగా కులాంధి." Vish. viii. 181.

రాణి rāṇi. [from Skt. రాజ్ఞీ.] n. A queen, రాజుభార్య. A wife, భార్య. రాణివాసము rāṇi-vāsamu. n. The female apartments, the queen's house, a zenana. అంతఃపురము. "క్షోణీనాథులరాణివాసములు చతురాశులకాపా డిని క్రేడలాలితవార్ధ్యవాటికల." HN. iv. 64. రాణివాసి or రాణివాసము rāṇi-vāsi. n. A gosha lady, a lady. అంతఃపురస్త్రీ. A wife, భార్య.

రాణించు rāṇinṭsu. [from Skt. రమణ.] v. n. To shine, be illustrious, be splendid. ప్రకాశించు. To be beautiful or fine. ఒప్పు.

రాణువ rāṇuva. [Tel.] n. An army, militia, yeomanry, సేన. A retinue, పరివారము.

రాతి rāti. [infl. Tel. of రాయి.] adj. Made of stone. రాతితోచేసిన. రాతిఉప్పు rāti-uppu. n. Rock salt. రాతిఉలి rāti-uli. n. A stonecutter's chisel. రాతిగుండె a hard heart, కఠినహృదయము. వానిది రాతిగుండె he is a hard hearted man. రాతిగొరక rāti-goraka. n. A kind of fish. రాతినార rāti-nāra. n. Stone hemp, an article like asbestos. ఒకమందుదినుసు. రాతిపాచి rāti-pāchi. n. A lichen or rock moss, used in medicine, *Lichen rotundatus* (Rottler.) ఒకమందుదినుసు. రాతిపువ్వు or రాపువ్వు rāti-puvvu. n. A fabulous coral or flower on rock imagined to distil quicksilver. శిలాపుష్పము, అశ్మపుష్పము. "రాతిపువ్వుచేత రసముగట్టె." Vēma. 159. రాతిబొమ్మ rāti-bomma. n. A stone image, a stone statue, శిలాప్రతిమ. రాతివాలు rāti-vālu. n. A thunder bolt, వజ్రాయుధము. రాతిసున్న ము or రాసున్నము rāti-sunnamu. Quicklime.

రాత్రి rātri. [Skt.] n. Night. As an adverb, at night. This means to night or last night according as the verb is past or future. రాత్రివచ్చిరి they came last night. రాత్రివెళ్లుతాడు he goes to night. అర్ధరాత్రి midnight. రాత్రియిల్లుచొచ్చి entering the house at night. "రాత్రికాదిదికాలరాత్రిగా బోలు" (Dab. 206.) this is not night but the shadow of death. Plural రాత్రులు or (vulgarly) రాత్రిళ్లు. రాత్రించరుడు or రాత్రిచరుడు rātrin-charudu. n. A night wanderer, i. e., a goblin or fiend. రాక్షసుడు, దయ్యము. A thief, a patrol, తలారి, రాత్రిళ్లనగరశోధనచేయు తలారివాడు. రాత్రింబగళ్లు rātrim-bagallu. n. Night and day. అహర్నిశము, రేయింబగలు. రాతిరి Same as రాత్రి. "పగలురాతిరి రాతిరిబగలుకాదె." A. iv. 146. రాత్రము rātramu. n. Night. A word only used in compounds as త్రిరాత్రము three whole days. అర్ధరాత్రము midnight. అహోరాత్రము a day and night, i. e., a whole day.

రాధ rādha. [Skt.] n. The name of a shepherdess. ఒకగొల్లది. Also, the name of the foster mother of Karna. రాధేయుడు rādhēyudu. n. The name of Karna, a hero celebrated in the Mahabharata. కర్ణుడు.

రాద్ధాంతము rāddhāntamu. [Skt.] n. An axiom, demonstrated truth: a proved and established fact. ప్రకటముగా నిర్ణయించబడినది, సిద్ధాంతము. Colloquially, an oft-repeated saying, a truism. L. x. 36.

రాపడు rā-padu. [Tel. రాయి+పడు.] v. n. To be turned into a stone, రాయియగు, స్తంభించు. To become firm, or hardened. దృఢపడు. To be stunned, become senseless, జడుడగు.

రాపాడు rāp-ādu. [Tel. రాపు+ఆడు.] v. a. To rub, collide, రాయు. To plague, torment. బాధించు. "వాతూర్పుపట్టి రాపాడించిరా రాజాతో చెప్పి కరకుతాడులచెడకట్టుకట్టించె." Sar. D. 339.

రాపిడి, రాపు or రాయిడి rāp-idi. [Tel. from రాచు.] n. Rubbing, filing, friction. Collision. Plague, torment. ఒరయుట, రాయిడి, బాధ, ఉపద్రవము. రారాపిడి (రాపిడి+రాపిడి) or రారాపు (రాపు+రాపు) rā-rāpidi. n. Great friction or rubbing, మిక్కిలి ఒరయుట. Great annoyance, బాధ. రాపుడు rāpudu. n. Friction, rubbing. రాచుట. రాపుడురాయి a stone used to polish the surfaces of walls, &c. రాపొడి rā-podi. n. Filings, the dust of any metal produced by filing. అరురాయితో రాయగా పడే రజము.

రాపులుగు or రాబందు rā-pulugu. [Tel. రాచ+పులుగు.] n. Lit. the royal bird. A heron, or possibly the Black Ibis or king-curlew. కంకము.

రాబడి rā-badi. [Tel.] n. Income, వచ్చుబడి, ఆదాయము.

రాబోవు rā-bōvu. [Tel.] v. n. To be at hand, వచ్చునట్లుగానుండు. వానరాబోవుచున్నది rain is at hand, rain is approaching, or is expected.

రామ rāma. [Skt. lit. 'Beautiful.'] n. A woman, స్త్రీ. రాముః or రాముడు rāmah. n. Rāma a celebrated hero. This name is also applied to Balarāma and Parasurāma. రామకీర్తన a hymn to Rāma. రామచంద్రుడు or రామభద్రుడు rāma-chandrudu. n. The glorious Rāma. రామచిలుక rāma-chiluka. n. A species of parrot. రామతమ్మ rāma-tamma. n. A parrot, చిలుక. రామతాడు rāma-tādu. n. A gigantic palmyra tree, బ్రహ్మాండమైన తాటి

చెట్టు. plu. రామతాళ్లు. రామదాసు or అడవిరామదాసు *rāma-dāsu*. n. The Black-winged Kite, *Elanus caeruleus*. (F. B. I.) రామప్రతాపము or రామమాడ *rāma-pratāpamu*. n. An ancient gold coin (నిష్కము) weighing ten pagodas. రామఫలము or రామాఫలము *rāma-phalamu*. n. The great red custard apple called Bullock's Heart, or Sweet sop, *Anona reticulata*. The true Custard apple of the West Indies (Watts.) See సీతాఫలము. రామబాణము *rāma-bānamu*. n. A bookworm (*tinea*). Lit. the arrow of the hero Rāma; as these worms spare no volume whatever, being indiscriminate in destruction; equivalent to "the bolts of Jove." పుస్తకములనుకొట్టేపురుగు. రామభజన *rāma-bhajana*. n. Worship of Rama, chanting or reciting the Rāmāyaṇa. రామము *rāmamu*. n. A large species of deer. పెద్దదుప్పి. రామములక *rāma-mulaka*. n. A small plant resembling the brinjal with a white fruit. రామరామ *rāma-rāma*. interj. Alas! alas! రాములు *rāmalu*. n. plu. A sort of fish. మత్స్యభేదములు. రామవరము or రామవాక్యము *rāma-varamu*. n. Lit. the word of Rāma, a phrase for a sacred promise, an irrevocable word, absolute truth, "God's truth." రామసాగరములు *rāma-sāgaramulu*. n. plu. A species of rice. వడ్లలోభేదము. రామానుజులు or రామానుజాచార్యులు *rām-anujulu*. n. The name of a certain reformer among the Vaishnavites. రామామణి *rāma-mani*. n. A jewel among women, i. e., a superior woman. స్త్రీరత్నము. రామాయణము *rām-āyanamu*. n. The Rāmāyana, an epic poem of the Hindus, recording the adventures of Rama, the son of Dasaradha. రామార్పణముగా నిచ్చు *rām-arpanamu-gā-n-itstsu*. v. a. To give in solemn donation. రామునివాడి or రాముండాడి *rāmuni-dādi* n. Lit. Rāmā's invasion. An innumerable number, అసంఖ్యము. వీధిలో జనులు రామునిదాడిగా తిరుగుచున్నారు the people are going about in the streets in vast crowds.

రామఠము *rā-mathamu*. [Skt.] n. Assafoetida. ఇంగువ.

రాయంచ *rā-y-antsa*. [Tel. రాచ+అంచ. from Skt. రాజహంస.] n. The fabulous swan.

రాయడు or రాయుడు *rāyadu*. [from Skt. రాజ.] n. King, master, lord, రాజు. (A word used only in compound phrases.) పులుగులరాయడు the king of birds, i.e., Garuda. తెనుంగురాయడు or ఆంధ్రనాయకుడు the name of the god worshipped at Chicacole. కొండలరాయడు the king of hills, i. e., the Himalaya. A title (like Mr.) assumed by certain Hindus as రామరాయడు, గోవిందరాయడు. రాయలు (plu.) was the title assumed by the last Telugu dynasty, the kings of Vijayanagar.

రాయబారము or రాయభారము *rāya-bāramu*. [for Skt. రాజభారము.] n. A negotiation, message, embassy. Intercession. సంధిచేయుటము, దౌత్యము. రాయబారి or రాయభారి *rāya-bāri*. n. An ambassador. సంధిచేయువాడు, దూత.

రాయసము *rāyasamu*. [for Skt. రాజసము.] n. Authority. Clerkship, secretaryship. జాబులువ్రాయు ఉద్యోగము. రాయసగాడు *rāyasa-gādu*. n. A secretary. జాబులువ్రాయువాడు.

రాయి *rāyi*. [Tel.] n. A stone, rock, శిల. ఇటికరాయి a brick. రాయిరప్పు stone and rubbish. (here రప్పు is an anuk.) (Gen. రాతి, Instr. రాత. Plu. రాళ్లు.) రాతికట్టుభూమి stony soil. చిట్టెపురాయి a lump of dross. ఉప్పురాయి a crystal or bit of salt. ఉప్పురాయివలె నేను ఒకకొడుకును పెట్టుకొన్నాను I have one single son whom I have kept as a pet. ఉప్పురాయివలె ఒకచిన్న

ఉన్నాను I am left solitary. A proverb says చలిపందిటికుండలో రాళ్లువేయుడము to dissuade one from a good deed. See రాతి.

రాయిడి râyiḍi. [Tel. from రాయు.] n. Rubbing, friction; plague, trouble, annoyance, ravages. ఒరయిక, ఉపద్రవము. "రాయిడికేకసరాళంబులైనత్రోవల జను గృహస్థులు." L. xiv. 26. "రాపాడుత్తులప్పటి రాయిడిమాన్పి." Pal. 74. రాయిడించు râyiḍ-intsu. v. n. To rub together. ఒకటితో నొకటి ఒరసికొను. To make a noise, to cause a disturbance. ధ్వనిచేయు, సందడిచేయు, అల్లరిచేయు. "నానాకిరీటవిన్యస్తప్రసూన సౌరభములాండొంటితో రాయిడింప." Vish. iii. 113. "తే॥ క॥ రవలిముక్కైలమ్రోతలు రాయిడింప." V. P. v. 13. రాయిడికాడు râyiḍi-kâḍu. n. A tormentor. ఉపద్రవము చేయువాడు. రాయిడికత్తె râyiḍi-katte. n. A troublesome woman. రాయిడిగిడిగిడి a kind of drum, డిండిమము.

రాయితీ, రాయితు, రాహితు or రాహితీ râyiti. [H.] adj. Cheap. n. Cheapness Remission, abatement of a demand, indulgence, favour.

రాయు râyu. [Tel.] v. n. To rub, to be rubbed, roughened, or frayed, ఒరయు. To become hoarse, as the throat (గొంతు) కమ్ము. To oppose, ఎదిరించు. To quarrel, కలహించు. వానిగొంతు రాసినది he is hoarse.

రాయుడు Same as రాయడు. (q. v.)

రారాజు, రారేడు. See under రాజు.

రాలు or రాళ్లు râlu. [Tel plu. of రాయి.] n. Stones. మణిరాలు diamonds, వజ్రములు.

రాలు râlu. [Tel.] v. n. To fall off or down, to drop, to run or flow off, as tears, &c. పతనమగు, పడు. ఆకులు రాలును leaves fall. వానికండ్లలో నిప్పులు రాలినవి fire flashed from his eyes. ఈ కరువులో జనము ఎండాకులు రాలినట్టు రాలిపోయినది in this famine the people dropped down like withered leaves. "వాలిన యుటురొత్తి వెళ్లనివిక రాలి యుట్టియుర బాణ్గంతరి మున." BD. v. 854. రాలుగాయ râlu-gâya. n. A wicked or mischievous boy. తుంటపిల్లకాయ. రాలుగాయతనము râlu-gâya-tanamu. n. Wickedness, mischief. తుంటతనము. "తే॥ వాడు నానాటికభివృద్ధి వడలబెరిగి, కాకలనుదీరిగడిమిగట్టిపాకి, రాలుగాయతనానచేరబడువాని, జాతిచేరనెరాగంట్ల మాకియయ్యె." H. v. 126. రాలుచు, రాల్చు, రాలగొట్టు, రాలిచేయు or రాల్పివేయు râlutsu. v. a. To knock off, beat down, shed, రాలజేయు. అది కండ్ల నీళ్లు రాల్చినది she shed tears. రాలుపు râlupu. n. Falling off, dropping, as leaves, రాలుట.

రావడము râvaḍamu. [Tel. from వచ్చు.] n. Coming. వచ్చుట. రావడి râvaḍi. n. Danger, ఉపద్రవము, హానిడి.

రావడు Same as రాపడు. (q. v.)

రావము or రవము râvamu. [Skt] n. Sound, voice, noise. ధ్వని.

రావణుడు râvaṇuḍu. [Skt. literally, he who afflicts or injures.] n. Râvaṇa, the Asura lord, the sovereign of Lanka, or Ceylon, లంకేశ్వరుడు. A very cruel man హింసకుడు. A learned fool, తెలిసినమూర్ఖుడు. "దైవతిమిలారత్రిజగద్రావణు రావణుని దాశరథిస్మైదుర్తుంటుకా." R. iii. 69. రావణుని కోట a labyrinth, a great puzzle. రావణహస్తము râvaṇa-hastamu. n. A kind of fiddle. వీణాభేదము. "కావాళిక దోర్దండముఖలు రావణహస్తములు డిండిమంబులు మురిలికలును." Balrama. v. 24.

రావి or రాగి râvi. [Tel.] n. The Poplar leaved Fig tree, *Ficus religiosa*, అశ్వత్థము, పిప్పలము. రావి ఆకురీతిగా వణికినది she trembled like an aspen leaf, the leaves of the fig tree being proverbial for quivering. గంగరావి the Portria tree. *Hibiscus populneus*, ప్రస్తారివృక్షము.

రావించు *rāvinṭsu.* [Tel. from వచ్చు. and another form of రప్పించు.] v. a. To cause to come, to send for, వచ్చునట్లుచేయు. పిలిపించు.

రావిరేక, రావిరేకు, రావిరాకు or రాత్రేక *rāvi-rēka.* [Tel.] n. A jewel worn by children or women on the forehead. బిడ్డలుగాని ఆడవారుగాని నొసట పెట్టుకొను భూషణము. "కాళేందుశోభిత ఫాలంబున రావి రేకదలగ." N. iv. 165.

రావు *rāvu.* [Tel. another form of రాయడు.] n. An honorific title like (Mr.) assumed by Vyapari Brahmins or by the Velama caste in the North ; as రామరావు, కృష్ణరావు. అప్పారావు, మాణిక్యరావు. "కేళి రావు."

రావుతు or రావుత్తు Same as రౌతు or రవుతు. (q. v.) భార. స్త్రీ. ii.

రాశి or రాసి *rāśi.* [Skt.] n. A heap, pile ; a collection, quantity, multitude, mass. ధాన్యాదులప్రోగు. A constellation or sign of the Zodiac, మేషాదిరాశులు. These are మేషము (Aries), వృషభము (Taurus), మిథునము (Gemini), కర్కాటకము (Cancer), సింహము (Leo), కన్య (Virgo), తుల (Libra), వృశ్చికము (Scorpio), ధనుస్సు (Sagittarius), మకరము (Capricornus), కుంభము (Aquarius), and మీనము (Pisces). Plu. రాశులు, జలరాశి or అంబురాశి the collection of waters, i. e., the ocean. జీవరాశి or జీవకోటి the animal kingdom, animated nature. ఉభయరాశిధాన్యము the gross produce of a field before the Government share is deducted. తూర్పురాశి a heap of winnowed grain. మాగరరాశి a heap of unwinnowed grain. రాశిఅడుగు a small quantity of grain remaining after a heap has been measured. త్రైరాశికము the rule of three. పంచరాశికము the double rule of three. బహురాశికము, compound proportion. రాశిపోయు *rāsi-pōyu.* v. a. To heap or pile up. పోగుగాపోయు.

రాష్ట్రము *rāshṭramu.* [Skt.] n. A realm, country, దేశము, A public calamity, such as plague or famine. ఉత్పాతము. మధ్యరాష్ట్రము the middle kingdom, that is, Central India.

రాసభము *rāsabhamu.* [Skt.] n. An ass. గాడిద. రాసభి *rāsabhi.* n. A she ass or jenny. రాసభోక్తి *rāsabh-ōkti.* adj. Braying, harsh-voiced.

రాసము *rāsamu.* [Skt.] n. Frolics, pastime, rustic dances. గోపకులక్రీడ, గొల్లవాండ్రఆట. "రాములతోడను రాసము రామానుజాదిజాతి రాకిల్లిమసారాములమీద విహరించ్చిర రాములు మూర్ఛిల్లిపడిరి రామవినోదా." B. x. 1159.

రాసి *rāsi.* [from Skt. రాశి.] n. A heap. See రాశి.

రాస్న *rāsna.* [Skt.] n. A plant called *Smilax china, or Alpinia galana.* A water plant without any root in the ground. సన్నరాష్ట్రము, పరంగిచెక్క. దుంపరాస్న, అంతర తామర. *Mimosa octandria.* Rox. ii. 564. The Serpent ophioxylon, a sort of perfume. సర్పాక్షి.

రాహిత్యము *rāhityamu.* [Skt. from రహితము.] n. Non existence. రహితభావము, అభావము, లేమి. Absence of, want of, freedom from. దోషరాహిత్యము freedom from fault, the being without fault. గుణరాహిత్యము unqualifiedness, i. e., the absence of any good quality. "దేవాది శేషపీఠంబై తద్భేదరాహిత్యమున." A. iii. 96.

రాహుతు, రాహుత్తు, రాహుత్తుడు or రౌతు *rāhutu.* [Skt.] n. A trooper, a horseman. గుర్రపురౌతు. "ఆపడిశేవురు రాహుత్తులుకొక్కి పెట్ట." M. VI. iii. 217.

రాహువు *rāhuvu.* [Skt.] n. The name of the ascending node of the moon, తలగాము. The name of a certain demon.

రి ri

రి *ri.* [Tel.] n. A note in music called B.

రింఖ *rinkha.* [Skt.] n. A horse's hoof. గుర్రపుడెక్క, అశ్వఖురము. "రింఖాసంఘాతజాతా వృత విశదధరారేణుపంక్తి ర్బభౌల్." Anirud. iv. 62. A certain pace. Dancing, నృత్యము.

రింఖణము or రింగణము *rinkhaṇamu.* [Skt.] n. Slipping, stumbling. జారుట, స్ఖలనము. తొట్రుపాటు. "తురంగతురంగ రింఖణజధూళి పరీతపతంగ." Balaram. v. 109. రింఖత్ *rinkhat.* adj. Slipping, stumbling. Skipping. గంతులువేయు, స్ఖలితమైన, తొట్రుపడే. Shining, ప్రకాశించే, "రింఖత్కనకమణిపుంఖశరములు." T. v. 62. టీ॥ రింఖత్ = ప్రకాశించెడి. "కంధరాకాంతిదూర్వా, ఘనతర్షోత్కర్షరింఖత్కరపదమ వ్యాగ్రాసవిత్రాసలోల." ib. v. 126. టీ॥ రింఖత్ = ఎగురుచున్నటువంటి. "సైంధవరింఖాసంఘాతజాతరేణూగ్రతమోరింఖద్రిపునృప." Swa. preface. 53. టీ॥ రింఖత్ = తొట్రుపడుచున్న.

రింగు *ringu.* [Tel.] n. The fluttering of wings. పక్షిపక్షధ్వని, రెక్కలగాలిచప్పుడు. రింగులు *ringulu.* n. plu. The ends of a garment. చెంగులు, వస్త్రపుకుచ్చెళ్లు. "బలు వైనవిలువచే జలువైనసన్నంపు వలువ రింగులుగాగ వారగట్టి." Raja Sêkhara. i. 24. "పులితోలు విడిపించి జిలుగుదువ్వలువ రింగులు వల్లెవాటుమై గొలుపవచ్చు." R. ii. 109.

రించోళి *rinchhôḷi.* [Skt.] n. A multitude, crowd, mob. సమూహము. "మారురాణుచరగండ పెండేరమణిమరీచిరించోళికలయువాన్పాతము లగుచు." Swa. preface 15. టీ॥ రించోళి = గుంపు.

రింజ *rinḍza.* [Tel.] n. A certain feat in wrestling.

రికము *rikamu.* [Tel.] An affix like 'hood' or 'ness' signifying state or condition, as పెద్దరికము greatness, మేనరికము cousinhood, దొంగరికము thieving, కన్నెరికము virginity, చుట్టరికము relationship, కొత్తరికము newness. మాలరికము (UH. iv. 191) the being a pariah.

రిక్క *rikka.* [Tel.] n. A star. నక్షత్రము. A constellation, a lunar mansion. A peculiar noise made in driving cattle. పశువులను తోలునప్పుడు చేయు ధ్వని. A pustule, weal, blister. బొబ్బ. రిక్కించు *rikkinṭsu.* v. a. To prick up the ears, &c. నిక్కించు, నిక్కపొడుచు. "చిగుపక్ట్లర్లమరించి కటుకథటుల్ కేళ్వర నంకించిమందుగదిల్లక మురిదయక బయల్ పసిగొను దాటుక దిశల్ నిక్కి వీలిగికొల్లద్దవ్వ పెలంగిడుక చెవిగవల్ రిక్కించిమై ప్రాకుపొల్పుగడద్దొల్పుచు పోవుదిస్స పెలవెల్పల్ దత్తిడుక మెత్తమిక." R. ii. 19. రిక్కవెట్టు or రిక్కవిడు *rikka-veṭṭu.* v. n. To stretch the body through drowsiness. ఒళ్లువిరుచుకొను. "పక్కలదిల్పు చురిక్కవెట్టుచును, వెక్కనవొరగాలనిల్పుచుంజను." BD. iii. 2244. రిక్కు *rikku.* n. The noise made by waving a cane or whip, etc.

రిక్తము *riktamu.* [Skt.] adj. Empty, void, poor, indigent. శూన్యమైన, వట్టి, ఉత్త. రిక్తహస్తము *rikta-hastamu.* n. An empty hand. ఉత్తచెయ్యి. One verse says "రిక్తహస్తేనసోపేయా ద్రాజానం దైవతంగురుం." రిక్తహస్తుడు *rikta-hastuḍu.* n. One who is empty-handed. శూన్యహస్తుడు, చేత ఏమిన్ని లేనివాడు. రిక్తుడు *riktuḍu.* n. A poor man, a pauper. దరిద్రుడు. రిక్తురాలు *riktu-r-âlu.* n. A poor woman. దరిద్రురాలు.

రిక్థము *rikthamu.* [Skt.] n. Wealth, property. ధనము. రిక్థహారి *riktha-hâri.* n. An heir, one who succeeds to the property of the deceased and gives the funeral cake. దాయాది, పిండప్రదాత.

రిఙ్ఖము Same as ఋక్షము (q. v.)

రిచ్చ or రిచ్చపాటు *ritsa.* [Tel.] n. Horror, terror, stupefaction. విభ్రాంతి, ఏమియు తోచకయుండడము, బెగులు, బెదరు, భ్రమపాటు. "మింటమండుటగాదని యంటిస్రైక, దిచ్చుకొంటినటంచు పెజా రిచ్చవెడలు." A. v. 155. రిచ్చగొను or రిచ్చవడు *ritsa-gonu.* v. n. To be horror-struck, to be stupefied. బెగులువడు, బెదరుపడు, భ్రమపడు. "అప్పటివార లాబాలగోపాలంబుగా వచ్చి రిచ్చలుపడి చేయుచుండిరి." Vish. vii. 139.

రిత్త *ritta.* [from Skt. రిక్త.] adj. Empty, fruitless, vain, unprofitable, mere. False. శూన్యమైన, ఉత్త, వట్టి, కల్ల. "జగముల లోత్తనడివచ్చెనిదు." BD. v. 178. రిత్తమాటలు empty words. Adv. Without cause, ఊరక. రిత్తదూషించి abusing without any cause. రిత్తకాడు or రిత్తకత్తె Same as రిక్తుడు and రిక్తురాలు. రిత్తపోవు *ritta-povu.* v. n. To become useless, వ్యర్థమగు. రిత్తపుచ్చు *ritta-putsu.* v. a. To cause to become useless. వ్యర్థపుచ్చు.

రిపుడు or రిపువు *ripudu.* [Skt.] n. An enemy, foe. శత్రువు.

రిప్పు *rippu.* [Tel.] n. A defect, something wanting, a flaw, కొరత. Also, same as రివ్వు (q. v.)

రిమ్మ *rimma.* [Tel.] n. Giddiness, perturbation, ఉన్మాదము, దిమ్మ. "జ్ఞానమెన్న గురువు జ్ఞానహీనముబుద్ధి రెంటిపొందునుండు రిమ్మదూడ, రిమ్మతెలిసి చేని నచ్చికానుండరా." Vema. iii. 39. వాని రిమ్మతీరినది his giddiness is gone off.

రిమ్ము *rimmu.* [Tel.] v. a. To scatter, disperse, splash, as water from a syringe, చిమ్మనగ్రోవితో జలాదికమును చిమ్ము.

రిరంస *ri-ramsa.* [Skt.] n. Desire for sensual pleasure, lust, amorousness.

రిరక్ష *ri-raksha.* [Skt.] n. A desire to save or protect, రక్షింపనిచ్ఛ. రిరక్షువు *ri-rakshuvu.* n. One who has a desire to save. రక్షింపనిచ్ఛగలవాడు.

రిల్లు *rillu.* [Tel.] n. A bookworm, a cricket. చిమట.

రివట or రివ్వ *rivata.* [Tel.] n. A branch growing from a large branch, ఉపశాఖ. A small branch, a twig, రెమ్మ.

రివాజు *rivadzu.* [H.] n. Currency, usage, custom. రివాజాస్తి excess (in taxation) above what is usual.

రివ్వు *rivvu.* [Tel.] n. A flutter. పక్షిపక్షాదిధ్వని. The name of a gregarious waterfowl with a grey body and a black head. రివ్వుమని fluttering. రివ్వున *rivvu-na.* adv. Suddenly, abruptly, quickly, speedily. శీఘ్రముగా.

రీ rī

రీఢ *rīdha.* [Skt.] n. Irreverence, scorn. తిరస్కారము.

రీతి *rīti.* [Skt.] n. Manner, mode, method, way, state, condition. ప్రకారము, విధము. Practice, custom, extent, మర్యాద, తీరు. A style in Rhetoric. ఏకరీతిగానుండే regular, correct, steady.

రు ru

రు *ru.* [Tel. short for వారు.] The sign of the plural termination in certain nouns and verbs, as వారు they, బాలురు boys. విలుకారు archers, వేటకారు huntsmen, etc. వత్తురు they will come.

రుంజ *rundza.* [Tel.] n. A brazen drum. అనద్ధవిశేషము, అవజము. "ఘనమైనరుంజలుకనకకళాప్పెట్టు." Pal. 258.

రుండము *rundamu.* [Skt.] n. The head separated from the trunk, దేహవిముక్త

శిరస్సు, తెగినతల. "రుండంబొమ్ముల నొక్కి రుండంబు గాడ ప్రాణవిరోగతాపమునభక్షించు." BD. iv. 66.

రుంద్రము *rundramu.* [Skt.] adj. Large, great, విరివియైన, గొప్ప.

రుక్కు *rukku.* [Skt.] n. Sickness. రోగము. Splendour. తేజస్సు, కాంతి

రుక్మము *rukmamu.* [Skt.] n. Gold. బంగారము. రుక్మకారకుడు a goidsmith.

రుక్మి *rukmi.* [Skt.] n. The brother of Rukmiṇi. రుక్మిణీదేవితమ్ముడు. **రుక్మిణి** *rukmini.* n. The name of the principal wife of Krishna. కృష్ణుని పట్టపుదేవి. రుక్మిణీకళ్యాణము the marriage of Rukmiṇi, the name of a particular episode in the Bhāgavata.

రుగ్ణము *rugnamu.* [Skt.] adj. Bent, crooked, curved. వంగిన, విరిగిన. Sick, రోగమునుచెందిన. **రుగ్ణత** *rugmata.* n. Sickness, disease, వ్యాధి.

రుచకము *ruchakamu.* [Skt.] n. An ornament for the neck or breast. కంఠభూషణము, మాల్యము.

రుచి *ruchi.* [Skt.] n. Taste, flavour, relish, చవి. Desire, wish, inclination, ఇచ్ఛ. A ray of sunlight, సూర్యకిరణము. Lustre, light, splendour, రాగము, ప్రభ, కాంతి. **రుచించు** or **రుచియించు** *ruchintsu.* v. n. To be agreeable, to be sweet. ఇష్టమగు. అది నాకు రుచింపలేదు I did not like it. "ఇప్పుని నాకున్ సరిపోదు మీకురుచియింపక పోలునిప్పట్టునన్." S. iii. 368. **రుచికరము** *ruchi-karamu.* adj. Delicious, fine, sweet, agreeable. చవిగల, సారముగల. **రుచిగల** or **రుచి అయిన** *ruchi-gala.* adj. Tasty, of good flavour, delicious. చవిగల. **రుచిచూచు** *ruchi-tsutsu.* v. a. To taste. చవిచూచు. **రుచిరము** or **రుచ్యము** *ruchiramu.* adj. Tasty, sweet, pleasing. Chraming, beautiful, మనోహరమైన, చక్కని, ఒప్పిదమైన.

రుజ *ruja.* n. [Skt.] Disease, destruction. రోగము. "దుఃఖరుజాపరీతము." P. iv. 213.

రుజువు *rudzuvu.* [H.] n. Proof. **రుజువు చేయు** *rudzuvu-cheyu.* v. a. To prove, to establish. **రుజువైన** *rudzuv-aina.* adj. Proved, established.

రుటము or **రుటంపు** *rutamu.* [from Skt. రూఢము.] adj. Hard, firm. దృఢము. "వానిరుటంపు పెండోడలు." T. ii. 74. **రుటముగ** *rutamu-ga.* adv. Firmly, certainly. గట్టిగా, రూఢిగా. "కట అటుగాను నీవు నిరయ్యెడ, కుటిలాలకనిమ్మనిత్తు గురువర్యవకుం, రుటముగనింతకుమిక్కిలి, ఘటితోపాయంబులేదు కలలోనైనన్." Valeswara v. 116.

రుట్టు *ruttu* [Skt.] n. Wrath, anger. క్రోధము, కోపము, కినుక.

రుతము or **రుతి** *rutamu.* [Skt.] n. The cry of birds. Any cry or noise, ధ్వని, రొద.

రుత్త *rutta.* [Tel.] n. Destruction, ruin, నాశము. వానిరూపు రుత్తాయిమపో he is totally ruined.

రుత్తు *ruttu.* [Tel.] v. a. To beat, కొట్టు.

రుదితము *ruditamu.* [Skt.] n. Weeping, crying. ధ్వనిగా కేడవడము, ఏడ్పు, రోదనము.

రుదురక్క, రుదురాక్ష or **రుదురాచ్చ** *rudu-rakka.* [for Skt. రుద్రాక్ష] n. The berries of the *Elæocarpus*, of which rosaries are usually made. మాలాఫలవృక్షమురొయొక్క విత్తు. "సన్నంపురుదురాక్ష పరములు మెడబూని." Chenn. iv. 206.

రుద్దు *ruddu.* [Tel.] v. a. To rub, scrub. తోము. **రుద్దుడు** *ruddudu.* n. Rubbing. తోముట.

రుద్రుడు *rudruḍu.* [Skt] n. A name of Śiva. శివుడు, Also, a name given to certain lesser deities. ఏకాదశరుద్రులు. ఈశానుడు మొదలగువారు. **రుద్రజడ** or **రుద్రజేడ** *rudra-jaḍa.* [from Skt. రుద్రజట.] n. A plant termed Sweet Basil. *Ocymum basilicum.* తులసి. రుద్రపాము *rudra-pāmu.* n. A certain venomous snake. సర్పవిశేషము. రుద్రభూమి *rudra-bhūmi.* n. A cemetery or place where the dead are burnt or buried. శ్మశానము, వలకాడు. రుద్రవీణె or రుద్రవీణ *rudra-vīṇe.* n. A sort of lute. వీణావిశేషము. "పిల్లగ్రోవియు గాంధారి దలపుటద్దము రుద్ర, వీణెకిన్నెర వట్టి వెల్లసురటి." Surabh. 102. రుద్రాణి *rudr-āṇi.* n. The wife of Rudra, i. e., a name of Durga or Parvati. పార్వతి, రుద్రునిభార్య. రుద్రాక్షము *rudr-ākshamu.* n. The tree termed *Elæocarpus ganitrus,* the seeds of which named రుద్రాక్షలు are much used for rosaries by the Saivites. రుద్రాక్షపిల్లి a hypocrite, lit. a cat with a rosary in her hand.

రుధిరము *rudhiramu.* [Skt.] n. Blood. రక్తము, నెత్తురు. రుధిరోద్గారి *rudhir-ōdgari.* n. The name of a Telugu year.

రుద్ధము *ruddamu.* [Skt.] adj. Obstructed, అడ్డగింపబడిన. Surrounded, begirt, ఆవృతము, పొదగబడిన, చుట్టబడిన.

రుప్పు or రువ్వు *ruppu.* [Tel.] v. To fling, toss, throw. విసరివేయు. n. A fluttering noise, రెక్కలగాలిచప్పుడు. A sudden noise caused by anything that falls down, కూలుటవల్ల కలుగుధ్వని. రువ్వుయిలుగు *ruvu-y-ilugu.* n. A kind of bird.

రుబ్బు *rubbu.* [Tel.] v. a. To grind in a mortar any thing first moistened in water. రోటిలోవేసి పొత్తరముతో మెదుపు. రుబ్బుపొత్తరము, రుబ్బుపాత్రము, రుబ్బుగుండుము or రుబ్బుగుండ్రాయి *rubbu-pottaramu.* n. The stone pestle used in a mortar, రాతిరోటిపాత్రము. రుబ్బురాయి *rubbu-rāyi.* n. A grindstone. రుబ్బురోలు *rubbu-rōlu.* n. A mortar for grinding. రాతిరోలు.

రుమాలు, రుమాలువు or రుమాలి *rumālu.* [H.] n. A handkerchief, a towel, చేతిగుడ్డ. తలరుమాలు a headkerchief or turban, తలగుడ్డ, పాగా. పాగా. i.

రురువు *ruruvu.* [Skt.] n. A sort of spotted deer. నల్లచారలు తెల్లమచ్చలుగలదుప్పి.

రువాణము *ruvāṇamu.* [Tel.] n. Brightness. కాంతి.

రువారము *ruvāramu.* [Tel.] n. Beauty, elegance, grace. అందము, సొగసు. "పీలి కొనలలో వసీదగాడి రువారమిట్టారయనవాడు కొట్టమర్రు." S. iii. 323. రువారపు *ruvārapu.* adj. Beautiful, elegant, graceful. అందమైన, సొగసైన. "ఇంతిపూబో ణులమే, బ్బంతిచేమంతిబిబి రువారపుబంతి, కంతుని పట్టపుదంతి." Ila. iv. 81.

రువ్వ *ruvva.* [Tel.] n. A pie, one twelfth part of an anna. దమ్మిడి.

రువ్వు *ruvvu.* [Tel.] n. A lesson given to a boy in the Vedas. పిల్లకాయలు వసను వల్లె వేయుడమునకై ఉపాధ్యాయులుముందర నొకపర్యాయము చెప్పడము. Repetition, వల్లె. A time, తడవ. "వినుము రెండవరువ్వువిని." పాలి. x రువ్వము *ruvvamu.* n. A time, తడవ. ఆవృత్తి. రువ్విచ్చు *ruvv-itstsu.* v. n. To give a lesson to a boy in the Vedas; making him repeat it a set number of times. చిన్నవాండ్రు వసను వల్లెవేయుడమునకై ఉపాధ్యాయులుముందర నొకపర్యాయము చెప్పు. "సీ. పదవర్ణసౌష్ఠవప్రకటనం బెంతయునింపువీరరంగ రువ్విచ్చియిచ్చి, రిగుమదాత్తాది భేదములుగెంటక పర్వగమబావుచేష్టల గరపికరపి." KP. iv. 46.

రువ్వు *ruvvu.* [Tel.] v. a. To fling, throw, toss. విసరివేయు. "లతావనితాళిరువ్వు లేమరు వవుబంతులట్ల." Vasu. iii. 165.

రుష *rusha.* [Skt.] n. Anger, wrath, passion. రోషము.

రుసి *rusi,* [for Skt. ఋషి.] n. A hermit, monk, saint. "రుసివంటివాన్ని వన్ని

పసిగుంపుల బెట్టి రేమిసుడిచెదు పాపంబని బో లె తాకు నిమ్మ నేనుకురన్న ఱాలుజాలు నో హూరాయు నడుగా." P. i. 259.

రుసుము *rusumu.* [H.] n. A fee, a bribe; commission, brokerage. Customs, taxes, dues.

రూ rū

రూ॥ *ru.* [Tel.] (in accounts) a contraction for Rupees. See on రూపాయి. Thus రూ॥ ౨౫౦=Rs. 250.

రూక *rūka.* [Tel.] n. A silver coin, sometimes equal to two and sometimes to four annas. A two-anna piece. A small coin of silver or gold, చిన్న మెత్తు కెండిబం గారములనాణెము. రూక or చిన్నరూక a single two-anna piece. పెద్దరూక the coin called a quarter of a Rupee. బంగారురూక a small gold coin. కంఠీరవరాయరూక a coin named after a king whose proper name was Canṭirava or "the Lion," valued at nearly three Rupees. రూక or రూకలు *rūka* n. Money in general, wealth, ధనము. రూకలు గల moneyed, having money. రూకలులేని penniless.

రూక్షము *rūkshamu.* [Skt.] Adj. Harsh, rough, not smooth, నిరుసుగామండే, కరుకు గానుండే. Unkind, unfriendly. అవిశ్వాసమైన, ప్రేమలేని.

రూడి Same as రూఢి. (q. v.)

రూఢము *rūḍhamu.* [Skt.] adj. Sure, certain, true, నిశ్చయింపబడిన. Public, notorious, well-known, ప్రసిద్ధమైన. Opened, blown, as a bud, వికసించిన. రూఢముగా *rūḍhamu-gā.* adv. Positively, certainly. రూఢి *rūḍhi.* n. Certainty, truth, నిశ్చయము. Fame, notoriety, ప్రసిద్ధి. రూఢి or రూఢిగల adj. Certain, established, famous, usual or customary. నిశ్చయమైన, ప్రసిద్ధమైన. లోకరూఢిఅయిన universally known. Peculiar, as opposed to యౌగిక (etymological or radical), అసాధారణమైన. The రూఢ్యర్థము or usual meaning of పంకజము is a lotus but the యౌగికార్థము or literal sense is mud-born. రూఢిగా *rūḍhi-gā.* adj. Positively, certainly. నిశ్చయముగా అది నాకు రూఢిగానున్నది I am confident of it, I know it for certain. రూఢిచేయు or రూఢిపరచు *rūḍhichēyu.* v. a. To ascertain, confirm, establish, prove, resolve, determine, నిశ్చయించు, స్థిరపరచు. రేపువెళ్లేటట్టు రూఢిచేసినారు they have determined on going to-morrow. తమరుచెప్పినదాన్ని రూఢిచేసినారు they have confirmed your statement.

రూణించు *rūṇinchu.* [Tel.] v. a. To wrestle in a particular way. రూణింపు *rūṇimpu.* n. A certain feat in wrestling, మల్లబంధ విశేషము.

రూపకము *rūpakamu.* [Skt.] n. An allegory, a parable. A metaphor. Also, same as రూపము. రూపము *rūpamu.* Figure, form, shape, appearance, semblance, ఆకారము. Nature, స్వభావము. Beauty, సౌందర్యము. నిజరూపము, ఉన్నరూపము or కలరూపము the real form, the fact, the very truth, reality. అర్ధరూపము and పూర్ణరూపము are terms in statuary for the profile and front figure. మారురూపము metamorphosis, another shape, a disguise. రూపకముగా or రూపముగా *rūpakamu-gā.* adv. In the shape of. రొక్కముగా రూపకముగా చెల్లించినాడా సరుకురూపకముగా చెల్లించినాడా? did he pay it in money or in kind? రూపకమైన *rūpakam-aina.* adj. In the form of, in the shape of: (a word only used in compounds,) thus, భూరూపకమైన జీవనము subsistence derived from land. రూపాంతరము *rup-antaramu.* n. Metamorphosis, another form. మారురూపు,

రూపవంతుడు *rūpa-vantudu*. n. A handsome man. అందగాడు. రూపవతి *rūpa-vati*. n. A beauty or beautiful woman. అందకత్తె. రూపవతి or రూపసి *rūpavi*. n. A beauty. వేశ్యానిపురుషుడు, వేశ్యాని స్త్రీ. రూపాజీవ *rūpa-jīva*. n. One who lives by her beauty, a harlot. వేశ్యస్త్రీ. రూపించు *rūpintsu*. v. a. To show, అగుపరచు, చూపు. To prove, ascertain, confirm. నిరూపించు. రూఢిచేయు.

రూపాయి or రూపాయు *rūpayi*. [from Skt. రూప్య silver.] n. A rupee. పొట్టిరూపాయి, సిద్దరూపాయి or గుండురూపాయి a narrow thick rupee of the old coinage. డాలరు రూపాయి (i. e., dollar rupee) is a rupee of the broad flat coinage introduced by the English government. ముప్పదిచిన్నములు ఎత్తుగల వెండినాణెము.

రూపు *rūpu*. [from Skt. రూపము.] n. Form, figure, shape, ఆకారము. Beauty, అందము. Manner, mode, way, విధము. రూపగు *rūpagu*. v. n. To prosper, వర్ధిల్లు. రూపుచెడు or రూపుమాయు *rūpu-chedu*. v. n. To perish. నశించు, చచ్చు. రూపడచు *rūp-adatsu*. v. a. To kill, destroy, చంపు. రూపరు or రూపడగు *rūp-aru*. (రూపు+అరు or అడగు.) v. n. To perish. స్వరూపనాశమగు. "తన్వరుదైజనియించిరూపరెన్." Swa. preface. 29. రూపుమాపు *rūpu-māpu*. v. a. To blot out, kill, destroy. చంపు, నాశముచేయు. రూపురూపున *rūpu-rūpu-na*. adv. In one's presence, సమ్ముఖమున.

రూప్యము *rūpyamu*. [Skt.] n. Silver. వెండి. Also, a rupee, రూపాయి.

రూలుకఱ్ఱ *rūlu-karra*. [Eng. 'Rule' + Tel. కఱ్ఱ] n. A ruler.

రూవు Same as రువ్వు. (q. v.)

రె re

రె *re*. [Tel.] An affix denoting approbation, surprise, wonder, &c. భళిరె or బాపురె well done!

రెంచె *rentsa*. [Tel.] n. (In gambling,) Two. రెండు.

రెంట *renta*. [Tel. from రెండు.] n. The state of being two, రెండగుట, జత, ద్విత్వము. ద్వివిధము. Severing, a division. "లోరెంట ఐడిచెడునమును. వారునిజార్జనముజేయువారికి నిజే." A. v. 23. టీ॥ లోరెంటలు, లోపలరెండు గామండుటలు. రెంటద్రావుడుతిండి a lion, సింహము. రెంటద్రావుడుమెకము an elephant, ఏనుగు.

రెంటము *rentamu*. [Tel.] n. A fold, as of cloth, folding, మడుపు. రెంటాన *rentana*. adj. Double folded, folded. రెండుగామడిచిన. Thus, మృతమర్త్యురెంటానవెట్టి on doubling up the corpse. A. vi. 21. రెంటెము *rentemu*. n. A cloth woven with a double thread. జెమిలిపోగుచేత వస్త్రము. "పులుగు రాయునిచట్టుపలనిన్నె మెరసట్టుపోయుంట్టుజిలుగు రంటెంబుతో డ." A. i. 13. టీ॥ దుప్పటితోడను.

రెండు *rendu*. [Tel.] pron. and adj. Two. n. Difference, భేదము. "చ॥ పతియెడ రెండులేక కులధామలు . . . సత్కళిజీయించుచుటొప్పు." రా. అ. కాం. ఆకుండ రెండాయెను the pot broke in two. వాడు ఉన్నదిలేనిది రెండు తెలియలేదు I do not know whether he is there or not. రెండుమాట్లు twice. రెండుతలచు *rendu-talatsu*. v. n. To think both ways, i. e., to be double minded or treacherous. ద్రోహముచేయు. రెండుతలచేవాడు a treacherous man. రెండవ or రెండో *rendava*. adj. Second, other. ఇందుకు రెండోపేరు ఏమి what is the other name of this? గండోవాడు లేడు

nobody else was present. రెండోమనిషితో చెప్పలేదు I told nobody else. అతడు రెండవ కృష్ణుడు in beauty he was a second Krishna. రెండింట *rend-inta.* adv. By two, రెంటితో. రెండింటగుణించు multiply by two.

రేలు Another form of రమ్ము. (q. v.)

రేకరేకలాడే *reka-rekal-adē.* [Tel.] adj. Slender, thin, wizened. పలచని. రేకరేకలాడువాడు a thin lean man.

రెక్క *rekka.* [Tel.] n. A wing, పక్షము. Also, any thing resembling a wing as the shoulder blade, or a leaf of a door. చేపరెక్కలు pieces of smoked fish. అంచెరెక్కలసెజ్జ a downy bed. రెక్కలతలుపు a door which has two leaves, a folding door. రెక్కలాగునున్నది she is very slender. వెనరెక్కలు విరిచికట్టు to pinion a man. రెక్కలువిరిగినపక్షి a bird with broken wings, i. e., a helpless person. రెక్కచాపు *rekka-tsāpu.* n. A long cloth, containing an under and an upper garment. దోవతి ఉత్తరీయము కలిసియుండునది. రెక్కపాయలు or రెక్కపాలలు *rekka-payalu.* n. A sort of grain. H. iv. 157.

రెక్కములు *rekkamulu.* [Tel.] n. A sort of grain. ధాన్యవిశేషము. H. iv. 156.

రేకొను *rek-konu.* [Tel. రేగు+కొను.] v. n. To increase, prosper, thrive, వర్ధిల్లు. రేకొలుపు *rek-kolupu.* v. a. To cause to prosper. వర్ధిల్లజేయు. రేకోలు *rek-kōlu.* n. Prospering, thriving, రేకొనుట.

రెగ్గుత్తి *reg-gutti.* [Tel.] n. A tree called *Capparis grandis* (Watts.)

రెచ్చెల *rechchela.* [Tel. from రేగు.] n. A quarrelsome person, జగడాలమారి.

రెచ్చు *retsisu.* [Tel.] v. n. To low, as cattle. అఱచు. To increase, swell, to be proud. విజృంభించు.

రెట్ట *retta.* [Tel.] n. The upper part of the arm భుజము. Filth, the dung of birds or fish, పక్షిమలము. A certain tint of carmine used in painting, వర్ణవిశేషము. వానిరెట్ట సడలినది his shoulder is dislocated. కోడిరెట్ట fowl's dung. రెట్ట is also the name of an astronomer whose school is called రెట్టమతము. రెట్టనాడి *retta-nadi.* adj. Double muscled, strong. బలిష్ఠమైన. రెట్టనాడిగుర్రము a strong horse. రెట్టి *retti.* n. and adj. A double or twofold. ద్విగుణము. మూడురెట్లు threefold. రెట్టించు *rettintsu.* v. a. To double, redouble, repeat. To oppose. ఇనుమడించు, ఎదురాడు. "సీతాకారంబు రెట్టింప." N. ix. 365. టీ. ఇబ్బడింపగా. "ఘనసామర్థ్యంబు రెట్టించెను." Ila. iv. 33. మాటలు రెట్టించినవి it came to high words. రెట్టింపు *rettimpu.* n. and adj. Twice as much. ఇనుమడి, ఇబ్బడి. Opposing, adverse. రెట్టింపుమాటలు arguing against.

రెట్టు *rettu.* [Tel.] n. A coarse cloth. ముతక గుడ్డ.

రెడ్డి *reddi.* [Tel.] n. A title annexed to the proper names of the members of the farmer caste. The head man of a village. రెడ్డిపాలవంకలు *reddi-pala-vankalu.* n. A sort of grain "మోదుగతోడి మెంటెముదక సరులు, పచ్చసరుల్ రెడ్డిపాలవంకలు సుఖభోగసరులు పచ్చకర్పూరసరులు." H. iv. 157. రెడ్డివారినానబ్రాలు *reddi-vari-nana-bralu.* n. A plant. *Euphorbia thymifolia* or *E. hypersifolia.* Rox. రక్తబిందుచ్ఛదము. చిటుకొర్ల.

రెడ్డిగము *reddigamu.* [Tel.] n. Sitting on the floor, with one knee up and a cloth round it and round the body in a knot. ఒకకాలు మడుచుకొని దానికి అంగవస్త్రముతో నడుమునకు బిగియగట్టుకొని కూర్చుండుట. రెడ్డిగము వేసికొను to sit in this posture.

రెపరెప repa-repa. [Tel. (anuk)] n. The flickering noise made by a flame. అగ్ని జ్వాలధ్వని. A faint flutter (of leaves, &c., as when a wind blows.) దనంతకొట్టుకొను దము, కొనప్రాణముతో నుండుదము. రెపరెపమను or రెపరెపలాడు repa-repa-m-anu. v. n. To be faint or fluttering with weakness. దనంతకొట్టుకొను, కొనప్రాణముతో నుండు. To be hungry, దనంత ఆకలి యగు.

రెప్ప reppa. [Tel.] n. An eye-lid. పక్ష్మము. రెప్పలు మూసి తెరచుచు with quivering eye-lids. "కంటికి రెప్పయునుగాచినభంగి" he kept her as the apple of his eye. Pal. 25. రెప్పపాటు reppa-pāṭu. n. A wink. నిమేషము, రెప్పవాల్పుదము, రెప్పవేయుదము. A second of time, నిమిషము. రెప్పవేయు or రెప్పవాల్చు reppa-vēyu. v. n. To wink. కన్నుమూయు.

రెప్పము reppamu. [Tel.] adj. Full. పూర్ణము. రెప్పముగా reppamu-gā. adv. Fully, పూర్ణముగా.

రెమ్మ, రెమ్మ or రెంబ remma. [Tel.] n. A small branch, a sprig or twig. చిన్నకొమ్మ. "వలదునొజ్జకికొమ్మసురద్రుంపు రెమ్మ" Ila. iii. 172.

రెమ్ము remmu. [Tel.] v. a. To pull out, పెరుకు. "రెలమ్మతాంతులోశశము రెమ్మెదమందు వలంచి." Vijaya Vilas. i. 9.

రెంబ Same as రెంబు (q. v.)

రెల్ల rella. [Tel.] n. A particle of boiled rice, మెతుకు.

రెల్లు rellu. [Tel.] n. A reed, used to write with. *Saccharum sara*. Rox. i, 244. శరము. తృణవిశేషము. రెల్లుచూలి rellu-tsūli, n. Lit. Reed-born; an epithet of Kumāraswāmi. రెల్లుదీవి rellu-dīvi. n. The name of a certain island, శరద్వీపము.

రే rē

రే or రె rē. [Tel.] An affix, • బాపురే alas!

రే, రేయి or రేయి rē. [Tel.] n. Night. రాత్రి, "రేయెల్లజనుదెంచి." UH. iii. 120. రేచీకు rē-chīku. n. A blind man. గుడ్డివాడు. "రేచుకన్నులుకేని రేచీకుచేత." L. vii. 85. రేచీకటి rē-chīkaṭi. n. Purblindness, night blindness. రాత్రులందు కండ్లుకానరాము. రేదొర rē-dora. n. The lord of Night, i.e., the moon, చంద్రుడు, నిశాపతి. రేత్రిమ్మరి or రేత్రిమ్మరీడు rē-drimmari. n. Lit. A night rover, i.e, a Rakshasa, రాక్షసుడు. See రేయి.

రేక rēka. [Tel.] n. A vessel made of palm leaf or tin for drawing water from a well. తాటాకుతోకట్టినబొక్కె. [from Skt. రేఖ.] A line, stripe, streak. రేఖ, గీత. A row, series, పఙ్క్తి. A letter, జాబు. రేకచిత్రణము rēka-chitraṇamu. n. A small chisel used for drawing lines on wood, రేఖలు తీర్చుటకు ఉపయోగించుచుండు చిన్నఉలి.

రేకంటు rēkanṭu. [Tel.] n. The sun. సూర్యుడు.

రేకు rēku. [Tel.] n. A petal of a flower. పుష్పదళము. A strip, plate, or thin piece of metal. తగడు, పలుచనిలోహపుతునక. A sheet of cloth called *Dangri*, అంచులేక్కములు లేనిబట్ట. One half of a sheet of cloth, దుప్పటిలోసగము. A feather of a bird, రెక్క, ఈక. బంగారు రేకు a strip of gold leaf used in setting gems. ఈ పాది రేకుఎత్తును this ruby will look well with a piece of gold leaf under it. తగరపు రేకు పెట్టె a tin box. రేకుమడచు rēku-maḍatsu. v. a. To put down, to suppress, అణగద్రొక్కు. రేకెత్తు rēk-ettu. v. n. To increase, prosper, వర్ధిల్లు.

రేఖ *rēkha.* [Skt.] n. A line, streak, stripe. గీత, గీరు. A row, పఙ్క్తి. A line upon the palm, or on the sole of the foot, కరచరణాదులయందుండెడిగీత. Fortune, one's lot or destiny (in connection with Palmistry), అదృష్టము; as in వాని రేఖ యెంతకాలమునకు తెలుపబడదు. Beauty, grace. శరీరసౌష్ఠవము, సౌందర్యము, కళ, అందము. దైన్యరేఖ the sign of poverty, దారిద్ర్యలక్షణము. Anirud. ii. 148. "రేఖావైభవంబు" great beauty. సౌందర్యాతిశయము. H. i. 94. విలాసరేఖలు graces, శృంగారచేష్టలు. Swa. iv. 6. చంద్రరేఖ a gleam of moonshine. రేఖ *rēkha*, adv. Like. వలె. "గోరేఖ." Swa. iv. 32.

రేగడ, రేగడి, రేవడ or **రేవడి** *rēgaḍa.* [Tel.] n. Clay, బంకమన్ను. రేగడనేల clayey soil, called also cotton soil, కృష్ణమృత్తిక. **రేగటి** *rēgaṭi.* adj. Clayey, loamy. కృష్ణమృత్తికగల. **రేగడిదూల** *rēgaḍi-dūla.* n. A certain plant. లఘుఫలము, కమ్మర.

రేగు *rēgu.* [Tel.] v. n. To rise, as dust. దుమ్మురేగి పైకి ఎగురు. To be excited or aroused, to rage, be angry, విజృంభించు, ఉద్రేకించు, ఆగ్రహపడు. వానికి ఒళ్లు రేగినది he was incensed. వాడు రేగిపడినాడు he was in a rage. **రేగు** *rēgu.* n. A tree called *Zizyphus jujuba.* బదరీవృక్షము. నల్లరేగు *Albizzia amara.* కమ్మరేగు the sweet species.

రేగుప్తిరాగము *rēgupti-rāgamu.* [Skt.] n. The name of a certain tune. రాగవిశేషము.

రేగుడు or **రేగుచె** *rēguḍu.* [Tel.] n. A climbing shrub, called *Hiraea indica.* రెంగపొట్ల.

రేచకము *rēchakamu.* [Skt.] n. Respiring, emission of the breath. ప్రాణాయామమునందు వాయువును విడిచిపెట్టడము, ఊపిరివిడుచుట.

రేచితము *rēchitamu.* [Skt.] n. A particular pace of a horse. అశ్వగతిభేదము, నట్టావులో కప్పడము. A fast trot. వంకరగతి నేగమునా పోవు అశ్వధారావిశేషము.

రేచు or **రేచుకుక్క** *rēchu.* [Tel.] n. A hound or wild dog. రేచులాగు like a wild dog. "సవతిరేచునుబట్టి చంపించదలచి." Navanadna, page 97.

రేచు or **రేపు** *rēchu.* [Tel. causal of రేగు.] v. a. To irritate, excite, set on. రేగజేయు, కోపముపుట్టించు, పురికొలుపు. అతిశయింపజేయు.

రేటుము Same as రెంటుము. (q. v.)

రేడు *rēḍu.* [Tel.] n. A king, lord, husband. రాజు, దొర, నాథుడు. చిలువలరేడు the king of serpents. కొండరేడు lord of hills, the Himalaya.

రేణము *rēṇamu.* [Tel.] n. The dung of young cattle, దూడపేడ. "పెయ్యలరేణంబులు" హరి. పూ. v.

రేణి or **రేని** *rēṇi.* [Tel.] An affix to the names of certain trees, as చీకురేణి, ఉత్తరేణి.

రేణుక *rēṇuka.* [Skt.] n. A sort of perfume. The name of the wife of the saint Jamadagni and mother of Parasurama, పరశురామునితల్లి. [Tel.] n. A sort of cucumber, దోసకాయ.

రేణువు *rēṇuvu.* [Skt.] n. Dust, పరాగము, దుమ్ము. An atom.

రేతస్సు or **రేతము** *rētassu.* [Skt.] n. The seminal fluid. వీర్యము. Quicksilver, పాదరసము.

రేనాడు *rē-nāḍu.* [Tel.] n. The old name of a district containing the lands of జమ్మలమడుగు, ప్రొద్దుటూరు, కామము, and దువ్వూరువాడ, which now form part of the Cuddapah district. Also, the old name of the country on the banks of the Pennēru west of the Gandikota hills.

రేని See రేణి.

రేము Same as రేగు (చెట్టు). (q. v.)

రేపు *rēpu.* [Tel.] n. The dawn, the morning, ప్రాతఃకాలము. To-morrow. మరునాటిదినము. Gen. రేపటి. Loc. రేపటు. రేపటుఎల్లుంటు either to-morrow or the next day. నేటరేపటు to-day or to-morrow. రేపటిపని to-morrow's business or work. రేపుమాపు day and night. రేపటి సోమవారము next Monday. రేపకడ or రేపాడి *rēpa-kaḍa.* n. The morning or dawn. ప్రాతఃకాలము. adv. In the morning, at dawn. "రేపకడమత్స్యయతివృక్షలబంచి." HK. ii. 226.

రేపు *rēpu.* [Tel. causative of రేగు.] v. a. To raise, provoke, irritate, incite, excite. రేచు, ఉసికొలుపు. See రేచు.

రేఫము *rēphamu.* [Skt.] n. The letter R. రవర్ణము. రేఫుడు *rēphuḍu.* n. A low or base man, అధముడు. నికృష్టుడు.

రేయి, రే or రేయు *rēyi.* [Tel.] n. Night, రాత్రి. plu. రేలు. రేయిటి *rēyiṭi.* adj. (Gen. of రేయి.) Nocturnal, nightly, రాత్రిటి. "చల్లని రేయిటిచెట్టుపుష్పలక్ బిందులబేలనూకెముడికెంట్రుకలందడితాపులెనగా." A. v. 95. టి॥ రేయిటి, రాత్రియందుపూసికొన్న. రేయెండ *rē-y-eṇḍa.* n. Moonlight. వెన్నెల. "అడరెరేయెండ లప్పుడద్భుతముగ." N. ix. 145. రేరేడు or రేరాయుడు *rē-rēḍu.* n. The moon, as "lord of night." రేరేనితోబుట్టు a name of Lakshmi. లక్ష్మి. రేపగలు *rē-pagalu.* (రే+పగలు) n. Day and night. అహోరాత్రము. See రే. రేవెలుగు, రేవెల్లు or రేవెలుంగు *rē-velugu* n. The moon. చంద్రుడు. "కొంగకెన్న రేవెలుంగొప్పుగానట్లు." Vēma 274.

రేగు *rēgu.* [Tel.] v. n. To increase, to be proud, అతిశయించు, విజృంభించు. v. a. To cut, sever, ఖండించు. "తరుక్రశరంబులరేచినేసి." రాఘ. iv.

రేల *rēla.* [Tel.] n. The Purging Cassia, Indian Laburnum, *Cassia fistula.* (Watts.) శమ్యాకము, ఆరగ్వధము.

రేవ *rēva.* [Skt.] n. The river Narbada, నర్మదానది. The Indigo plant, నీలిచెట్టు.

రేవంతుడు *rēvantuḍu.* [Skt.] n. A horse breaker, a horse trainer. అశ్వశిక్షకుడు. "రేచిబొట్టగరేరురేవంతులైన." Pal. 53.

రేవడ or రేవడి Same as రేగడ (q. v.)

రేవడు *rēvaḍu.* [Tel. రేవు+అడు.] n. A washer-man, చాకలివాడు. A rogue. కృపణుడు. కుత్సితుడు. "ఇవానరంబులకూరకదూరమైనయట్టిచన రెంటికించెడినరేవడనాడుగా నిరీక్షణా." Swa. iii. 140.

రేవతి *rēvati.* [Skt.] n. The name of the wife of Balarāma, బలరామునిభార్య. The twenty-seventh lunar mansion. ఇరువైయేడవ నక్షత్రము.

రేవల్చిని *rēvalchini.* [H. from చీని China.] n. Rhubarb.

రేవు *rēvu.* [Tel.] n. A landing place, port, harbour; a shore, beach or bank; a ford, a ferry. నద్యాదులయందు మనుష్యులు దిగుటకు యుక్తమైనచోటు; నదులందుగాని సముద్రతీరమునగాని సరకులు ఎగుమతి దిగుమతిచేయుటకు యుక్తమైనచోటు. A seaport కరిపాకపట్టణము. Also, same as రేగు (చెట్టు.) (q. v.) రేవుorచాకిరేవు a washing green or whitster's yard. ఓడరేవు a harbour or sea-port. బండిరేవు a wharf or common shore. రేవుతప్పినది the ford is not now passable, the water is not fordable. చల్లగడ్డలుతిత్తేవారికిగాని దానిరేవు మరి యొకరికి తెలియబడదు the place that produces this root is known only to those who live by digging for it. రేవుబోయ *rēvu-bōya.* n. A boatman, a sailor, ఓడనడపువాడు.

రేసు *rēsu*. [Tel.] n. Ease, lightness, తేలిక. adj. Easy, light. తేలికని. "నీపుణ్యమున జనించిన, దోసము మోసమును చేటెతో పనగలిగెం, గోసఱకు సోకి క్రొన్ననయ్యె రేసోయట్లాపెవిన్యాశకని చేరుగా." P. i. 748. **రేసుగుడ్డ** *rēsu-guḍ-ḍa* n. A handkerchief. చేతిగుడ్డ.

రై rai

రై *rai*. [Skt.] n. Wealth. ధనము. **రైవేశ్మ** *rai-vēsma*. n. A treasury. కోశగృహము. "రైవేశ్మాంతరపద్ధతిక్కెగిరి." A. iv. 3. టీ॥ రైవేశ్మ, భాండాగారము.

రైక Same as రవిక. (q. v.)

రైతు Same as రయితు. (q. v.)

రొ ro

రో *ro*. [Tel.] The vocative sign in some feminine nouns, as చెలియరో O woman. "ఇంతిరో పాలంతెకులమీపుజనించినది." T. iii. 90. It is also added to some other nouns, as అన్నరో, ఏనుగురో, etc

రొంజేడు or **రొండుడు** *rondzuḍu*. [Tel.] n. A wail, ప్రలాపము.

రొండి *ronḍi*. [Tel.] n. The haunch, the side between the ribs and loins. నడుము యొక్క పార్శ్వభాగము, కటిప్రదేశము. "అష్టంబు తిరిగి తలాహతిబడి రొండి హస్తంబులిడ యెంగ లారుప్పక పులు." A. vi. 19. "చీకము చెయ్యిరొండిజెక్కు కొన." S. iii. 317. రొండిన చేతులుపెట్టుకొను to stick the arms akimbo. రొండిపేటు a kind of feat in wrestling. **రొండు** *ronḍu*. n. Asthma. రోజు. శ్వాసరోగము.

రొంప *rompa*. [Tel.] n. A cold, a catarrh. పడిసము, సెలరోగము;

రొంపి *rompi*. [Tel.] n. Mud, mire. పంకము. అడుసు, బురద. గంధపురొంపి sandal paste. "మెదడు గంధపురొంపి మెత్తినాడు." Swa. iv. 100. రొంపిలోనాటిన స్తంభమువలెనున్నాడు he is unstable as a post set up in a bog. రొంపిదుక్కి (opposed to పొడిదుక్కి) wet cultivation: lit. mireploughing. **రొంపిమాను** *rompi-mānu*. n. A piece of wood used for levelling a miry field.

రొక్కము *rokkamu*. [Tel.] n. Cash, money. చేతిపైకం, ధనము. A crowd, multitude, సమూహము. "రొక్కముగన్నకల్లియయును రుద్రుని జెల్లియునమ్మి." URK. ii. 341. "అక్కటికిపోవ నెంచి రొక్కము పూవారుడుదాని సొమ్ము దిగా చక్కటి నిలుకుడు వెరపుగ మొక్కలి తినువాడు తిన్న ముంపనగుండెగా." S. iii. 27. **రొక్కపుదొర** *rokkapu-dora*. n. Kubēra. ధనాధిపుడు. **రొక్కారొక్కములు** *rokka-rokkamulu*. adv. In various ways. బహువిధములుగా, ఉచ్చావచము. "రొక్కారొక్కము కొట్టి, శాస్త్రాల క్రొద్దమ్ము గాదులగా నలుకగా దొంగ" Kālahasti. iii. 68. రొక్కించు or **రొక్కవచ్చు** *rokkinsu*. v. a. To give ready money, to pay down cash.

రొచ్చు *rotstsu*. [Tel.] n. Mud, mire. బురద. Contempt, disregard. పరిభవము. తిరస్కారము. Blame, ill-fame. Noise, సందడి. "నిజరఘువరులసచ్చరిత రొచ్చుయుంబులచ్చింపు చు, రొచ్చెంబులొచ్చుసేయుము." R. v. 194. "రొచ్చొర్వకటులోగితెచ్చి మేము." A. v. 6. రొచ్చుకంపు a foul stench.

రొట్ట or **రొడ్డ** *roṭṭa*. [Tel.] n. A small bough. మండ.

రొట్టె or **రొట్టియ** *roṭṭe*. [H.] n. Bread, a loaf. భక్ష్యభేదము. రొట్టెవిరిగి నేతిలోపడెను (proverb) the bread broke and fell into the butter. Used of a happy occurrence, to denote one's luck.

రొడ్డ *rodda*. [Tel.] adj. On the left hand side. ఎడమ. రొడ్డచెయ్యి *rodda-cheyyi*. n. The left hand. ఎడమచెయ్యి.

రొద్దు or రొండు *roddu*. [Tel.] n. Hard breathing, dyspnœa. రోజు, శ్వాసరోగము. adj. Much, అధికము. రొద్దుపులుసు very sour.

రొద్దుము Same as రొంతోసము. (q. v.)

రొద or రొదాళము *roda*. [Tel.] n. A noise, a cry, an outcry. A sound, voice, note. ధ్వని, కలకలధ్వని. "అమ్మ వనమునందుండి రొద పన్నిరంటు." Swa. iii 152. రొదాలించు *doddalintsu*. v. n. To make a noise, to sound. ధ్వనించు.

రొప్పు *roppu*. [Tel.] v. n To roar, yell. కూయు, అరచు. To get angry. రోపించు v. a. To abuse, revile. తిట్టు. To drive away, turn off. త్వరగాతోలు, పరుగెత్తించు. తరుము, కొట్టు. "వారులుపగ్గములుచేసెంది రొప్పదొడంగె." B. X. 20. "క్షత్రధరుల్ రొప్పగజనిరెటుల్ నిలువక." K. P. ii. 85. "కప్పకునూరగాటైనట్లు, రొప్పడుపులిరుపుఘటికిరోగములైనట్లు." Sumati. §. 120. n. Panting, hard breathing: asthma. ఎగరొప్పు hard breathing.

రొమ్ము *rommu*. [from Skt. ఉరము.] n. The breast, chest or bosom. వక్షము. The female breast. మంచిరొమ్ముగలవాడు one who has a good chest or lungs. రొమ్ముపగిలిన broken-winded. రొమ్ముఎముక *rommu-emuka*. n. The sternum, or breast-bone.

రొయ్య *royya*. [Tel.] n. A prawn, shrimp. గాజురొయ్య the larger kind of prawn, a cray fish. చేపవిశేషము. రొయ్యపొరచెట్టు *royya-pora-chettu*. n. A species of the jujube tree. ఒకచెట్టు.

రొయ్యి or రొయి *royyi*. [Tel.] n. The ashes on live coal. కప్పినిప్పుమీదినివురు. రోయిబూడిద ash used in scouring pearlash, alkali.

రొల్లు *rollu*. [Tel.] v. n. To bewail, ప్రలాపించు. రొల్లుడు *rolludu*. n. Bewailing, a wail. ప్రలాపము, రొంతోసము.

రొష్టు or రొష్టు *roshtu*. [Tel.] n. Confusion, annoyance, outrage, రొంపి.

రో ro

రో *rō*. [Tel. another form of రూక.] n. Wealth, money. Value, price. ధనము. విలువ. రోయీవి *rō-y-īvi*. n. A gift of money. రోవెల *rō-vela*. n. The money value, the sum bargained for, ఎంతకు ఇస్తావని చెప్పకొన్నమూల్యం. రోవెలది *rō-veladi*. n. A woman that has her price, a harlot.

రో *rō*. (affix) A vocative particle, as అక్కరో O sister. అన్నరో Oh brother. This is for the vocative sign ఓ with R inserted to save elision. See రా.

రోండు or రవుండు *rōndu*. [Eng. 'Round.'] n. A round, circuit, journey, a policeman's beat.

రోక *rōka*. [Tel.] n. A corner. "మూల, కోణము."

రోకము *rōkamu*. [Skt.] n. A hole. బెజ్జము. రంధ్రము. Light, దీప్తి. వెలుగు.

రోకమ్మిసజ్జ *rō-kammi-sadzdza*. [Tel.] n. A kind of grain. సజ్జలలోభేదము.

రోకలి *rōkali*. [Tel.] n. A wooden pestle, a rice-pounder, ముసలము. "వెర్రితీర, రోకలి తలచుట్టు." (KP. ii. 116.) my madness is over, so I will make a turban of the poker. In D. Abhim, page 42 is a proverb, "గాజులుగదికిరోకలిబూచివట్టు." రోకటికిచిగురు పట్టుట a strange thing. రోకటిబండ or రోకలిబండ *rōkali-banda*. n. A large brown millepede that rolls itself up like a spring on being touched. శతపది. క్రిమివిశేషము. A small wooden pestle without iron ferrules at the ends. పొన్ను లేని చిన్నరోకలి.

రోకు *rōku*. [Tel.] n. Greenness. పచ్చదనము. Brightness. వికాసము.

రోకొమ్మ *rō-komma*. [Tel.] n. The name of a certain part of a pikota (కపిల).

రోగము *rōgamu*. [Skt.] n. A disease, sickness, ailment. వ్యాధి, తెగులు. తాళపుచెవికి రోగము వచ్చినది the key has got something the matter with it. నీకేమి రోగము వచ్చినది what was the matter with you that you did this? పెద్దరోగము leprosy, in which the limbs drop off. దేహరోగములు the ills of the flesh, the ills or sorrows that flesh is heir to. రోగకారి *rōga-kāri*. adj. Insalubrious, unhealthy. వ్యాధిని కలుగజేసే. రోగహారి *rōga-hāri*. n. Lit. 'The disease-destroyer.' The ash gourd. బూడిదగుమ్మడి. రోగి *rōgi*. n. A patient, a sick person, a sufferer, వ్యాధిగ్రస్తుడు. దేహరోగి one who is subject to the ills of the flesh, one who is not yet released from earthly ties.

రోచన *rōchana*. [Skt.] n. Ox gall. గోరోజనము.

రోచిస్సు or రోచి *rōchissu*. [Skt.] n. Light, brilliancy, splendour. కాంతి. వెలుగు. A ray of light, సూర్యకిరణము. రోచులు *rōtsulu*. n. Splendour, glory. "తారకల రోచులు చెక్కుటద్దములలో తెలిమిసేయు." B. iv. 86. రోచమానము *rōchamānamu*. adj. Splendid, shining, brilliant, ornamented, ప్రకాశమానమైన. n. A curl or swirl of hair round the neck of a horse, or on the lower part of it. అశ్వకంఠమందుండే సుడి. రోచిష్ణువు *rōchishṇuvu*. adj. Splendid, brilliant. ప్రకాశమానమైన. n. One who shines, ప్రకాశించువాడు.

రోజముచెట్టు *rōjamu-chettu*. [Tel.] n. The Dammar tree. *Canarium strictum*. (Watts.) నల్లరోజముచెట్టు' the black species, the Black Dammar tree.

రోజాపువ్వు *roja-puvvu*. [Eng. 'rose'.] n. A rose.

రోజు *rōḍsu*. [Tel.] v. n. To pant or breathe hard. ఎగఊపిరిపడుచు, నిట్టూర్చు, నిశ్వసించు. n. Panting, hard breathing, asthma. ఉగర్పు, అత్యుచ్ఛ్వాసము, నిశ్వాసము, ఉచ్ఛ్వసము. రోజుడు or రొంజుడు *rōdzudu*. n. Wailing. ప్రలాపము.

రోజు *rōdzu*. [H.] n. A day. దినము. నాడు.

రోటు *rōṭu*. [Tel.] n. Thinness, emaciation. కృశత. రోటుపోవు *rōṭu-pōvu*. v. n. To become very thin, or emaciated. కృశించిపోవు.

రోడ్డు *rōḍḍu*. [Eng.] n. A road. మార్గము, బాట. రోడ్డుపన్ను *rōḍḍu-pannu*. n. Road cess.

రోత *rōta*. [Tel. from రోయు.] n. Foulness, filth, nastiness. అసహ్యము, ఏవము, జుగుప్స. adj. Foul, nasty, squalid, disgusting. Disgraceful, abominable, hideous, horrid, vile. అసహ్యమైన. రోతలు *rōtalu*. n plu. Abuses, తిట్లు. రోతగించు *rōtagintsu*. v. n. To feel a disgust for, రోతపడు

రోదనము *rōdanamu*. [Skt.] n. Weeping, wailing, lamentation, ఏడ్పు. ఏడవడము. రోదించు *rōdintsu*. v. n. To cry loud, రోదనముచేయు.

రోదసి or రోదస్సు *rōdasi*. [Skt.] n. The Earth, భూమి. The sky, heaven, మిన్ను. Heaven and earth as one, మన్నుమిన్ను, పృథివ్యంతరిక్షాంతరాళము "భుజిల్లనిరంకశమైచినరో దసీకుహరంబు భేదిలంగ." B. X. ii. 434.

రోదా *rōdā*. [H.] n. A wheel of a cart.

రోధము or రోధస్సు *rōdhamu*. [Skt.] n. A shore, bank. నద్యాదులతీరము, గట్టు, దరి.

రోధించు rōdhintsu. [Skt.] v. a. To obstruct, oppose. అడ్డగించు, నిరోధించు. To quarrel.

రోపణము or రోపము rōpaṇamu. [Skt.] n. Putting on as a load or weight, imputing. మోపుట. రోపము rōpamu. n. An arrow, బాణము. రోపితము rōpitamu. adj. Placed in or upon. ఉంచబడిన.

రోమంథము rōmanthamu. [Skt.] n. Rumination, chewing the cud. నెమరు.

రోమము rōmamu. [Skt.] n. Hair (growing on the body), a hair. శరీరమందుండే వెంట్రుక. రోమకర్ణము rōma-karṇamu. n. Lit: Hairy-eared, i. e., a hare or rabbit. చెవుల పిల్లి. రోమకూపము or రోమరంధ్రము rōma-kūpamu. n. A pore in the skin, a sebaceous gland. "ఘోటకోత్తమరోమకూపంబులం దెల్లనొక్కటఘునధూమము ద్భవించె." M. XIV. iii. 118. రోమరాజి, రోమలత or రోమావళి rōma-rāji. n. A line of hair extending to the navel. నూగారు. రోమవిక్రియ or రోమహర్షణము rōma-vikriya. n. Horripilation. Tingling, a shudder or thrill as when electrified, or blushing, or in a flush with ecstasy. రోమాంచము, గగుర్పు, గగుర్పాటు. రోమశము rōmaśamu. adj. Hairy, woolly. రోమములుగల. రోమశుడు a hairy man, శరీరమందు ఎలుగుబంటివలె నిండువెండ్రుకలుగలవాడు. రోమహర్షణుడు rōma-harshaṇuḍu. n. An epithet of సూత the hermit. ఒకఋషి. రోమాంచము rōm-ānchamu. n. Horripilation, tingling, an electric thrill. "ఆనందాశ్రులుకన్నులఁ గాఱెడు రోమాంచంబుల్." B. i. 200.

రోయి rōyi. [Tel.] n. A stake at play. జూదమందు ఒడ్డినసొమ్ము, పందెము. A pledge, కుదువ. A loan, ఎరవు, చేబదులు. Value, price, వెల. Money, ధనము. రోయిడు rōy-iḍu. v. a. To pawn, pledge. తాకట్టుపెట్టు. రోవెలది rō-veladi. A concubine, a prostitute, వేశ్య, వారకాంత.

రోయు rōyu. [Tel.] v. n. To dislike, abhor, be disgusted with, అసహ్యపడు, రోతపడు. "ఇట్టిదిక్రూరకర్మమని యెంచుకరోయక." M. ix. ii. 140. v. a. To search, seek, look for. వెదకు. "పాదసరసిజంబని రోయుచుదట్టిరోసి తొడ్కొ..డ గాంచుటేమివలదా యభిమానమొకింత యుంటికిన్." A. v. 73. To blame. నిందించు. To leave, give up, quit. త్యజించు, విడుచు, మానుకొను, వదలుకొను. "రోతనైనవారి రోయకవిలుతురో." Vēma. 1945.

రోలంబము rōlambamu. [Skt.] n. The large black bee. తుమ్మెద.

రోలు rōlu. [Tel.] v. n. To weep or cry aloud. రోదనముచేయు, విలపించు. "రోలుచుబోరగిలబడి వాలుకవెడలంగబెట్టి యవ్వడు గరచుచుఁగా లాలల గ్రమ్మగరఁతు సొలుదు విక్రొమ్మడగుచు బ్రాణముబడిచెగా." M. VII. v. 276. n. A mortar for pounding grain in. ఉలూఖలము. (cf. Tam. ఉరల్.) Plu. రోళ్లు. G. రోటి. Loc. రోట. రోలుమాను a door hinge, a piece of wood on which a door turns.

రోషము rōshamu. [Skt.] n. Anger, wrath, irritation. కోపము. రోషగాడు or రోసగాడు rōsha-gāḍu. n. A passionate man. కోపిష్ఠి. రోషించు or రోషపడు rōshintsu. v. n. To be irritated, incensed or annoyed. కోపించు, ఆగ్రహపడు. రోషితుడు rōshituḍu. n. A passionate, irascible man. ఆగ్రహపడినవాడు. రోసము Vikriti of రోషము. "చలముసాధించుదిట్టరోసాలపుట్ట." S. iii. 16. రోసించు Same as రోషించు.

రోసుబడి rōsu-baḍi. [Tel. from రోయు.] n. Disgust. A disgusting man. రోతగొట్టు. A drudge, wretch. Adj. Loathsome, disgusting, shameless. రోతైన, సిగ్గు

మాలిన. రోకుబడితనము rascality, shamelessness, impudence.

రోహణము or రోహము *rōhaṇamu.* [Skt.] n. Mounting, ascending, ఎక్కుట. రోహణము the name of a certain hill, Adam's Peak in Ceylon. ఒకకొండ. రోహము *rōhamu.* n. A bud, a blossom. మొగ్గ, కోరకము.

రోహిణి *rōhiṇi.* [Skt.] n. The fourth of the lunar mansions, personified as the wife of the moon, రోహిణీనక్షత్రము. Also, the mother of Balarāma. బలరామునితల్లి, A medical plant, *Helleborus.* కటుకరోహిణి.

రోహితము *rōhitamu.* [Skt.] adj. Red, ఎర్రని. n. Redness, ఎరుపు. A red streak in the clouds. ఋజుమైనింద్రధనుస్సు, కొరడు. Swa. v. 123. రోహితాశ్వుడు *rōhitaśvuḍu.* n. The god of fire. అగ్నిహోత్రుడు. Also, the name of Harischandra's son. రోహిత్తు *rōhittu.* n. The female white-footed antelope. మన్నుబిడి, ఆడుమన్నుప్పుగము.

రోహిషము *rōhishamu.* [Skt.] n. A species of wild deer. కొండగొర్రె.

రౌ rau

రౌతు or రవుతు *rautu.* [for Skt. రాహుత్తు.] n. A trooper, rider, horseman. గుర్రము నెక్కువాడు. రౌతుకొద్దిగుర్రము like rider like steed.

రౌద్రము *raudramu.* [Skt. from రుద్ర.] adj. Terrible, terrific, fearful, sharp, acute, wrathful, violent. భయంకరమైన, తీక్ష్ణమైన. n. One of the nine feelings or emotions called రసములు. An emotion of fear, ఒకరసము. Terror, wrath. రౌద్రి *raudri.* n. The name of a Telugu year.

రౌప్యము *raupyamu.* [Skt. another form of రూప్యము.] n. Silver. వెండి. adj. Made of silver, argentine. వెండితోచేసిన. T. i. 5.

రౌమకము *raumakamu.* [Skt. from 'Rome.'] n. Salt obtained from Rome, సంభరదేశమున రుమయనెడు గనియందుపుట్టిన ఉప్పు.

రౌరవము *rauravamu.* [Skt.] n. One of the divisions of Naraka or Hell ఒకనరకము. adj. Fearful, terrible, భయంకరము.

రౌలు or రవులు Same as రగులు. (q. v.) రౌలుకొను *raulu-konu.* v. n. To take fire, to flame forth, కాలుమొదలుపెట్టు. రౌలుకొలుపు *raulu-kōlupu.* v. a. To set on fire. మండునట్లుచేయు. రౌలుకోలు *raulukōlu.* n. The act of burning, రవులుకొనుట. రౌలుము or రవులుము Same as రగుల్చు.

రౌహిణేయుడు *rauhiṇ-ēyuḍu.* [Skt.] n. A name of Balarāma or of the planet Mercury. బలరాముడు, బుధగ్రహము.

రౌహిషము *rauhishamu.* [Skt.] n. A sort of wild deer. కొండగొర్రె.

ల la

ల *la.* [Tel.] The letter L(ళ) is the same letter with a harsher sound. These two are separate and one cannot always be used for the other. The harsh sound has been introduced into some Sanskirt words. Thus, the nouns కల, కలేబరము. are in Telugu invariably written కళ, కళేబరము. Authority or custom is the only rule, and it never varies. వేళ time. వేల gen. plu. of వేయి a thousand.

లంక *lanka.* [Skt.] n. An island in general. దీవి. ఏటినడిమిదిబ్బ. The capital of Ravana. Ceylon, రావణాసురునిపట్టణము.

లంకణము *lankaṇamu.* [for Skt. లంఘనము.] n. A day passed without eating any food when one is attacked with fever and other diseases. జ్వరము మొదలైనరోగముల...

వచ్చినప్పుడు ఆహారములేకుండా ఉండేదినము, ఉపవాసము.

లంకించు *lankintsu.* [Tel.] v. a. To join, unite. తగిలించు, చేర్చు. To link or couple together, as two bullocks, పెనవేయు. "నుక్షేత్రోదేలబట్టుకొని ప్రీతిలంకించియుండ లంకియుతో దకందుమీరి పారిజాక్కుడియల్." M. XII. iv. 39. To disgrace. అవమానించు. **లంకించుకొను** *lankintsu-konu.* v. a. To seize, or take by artifice. చెరపట్టుకొను, తంత్రముగా వలలోవేసికొను. **లంకె** or **లంకియ** *lanke.* n. Coupling or tying two animals together. A link, connection. రెండుపశువుల మెడకు తాడుకట్టడము, పెన, కూడిక, సంబంధము, తగులుపాటు, కూర్పడము, సంగము. "నీకును నాకుఁ గాదైవంబులంకె వేసెను." Vish. vi. 31. ఆరెండు చెరువులు లంకెలుగా నున్నవి those two tanks are connected, lit: are as 'links,' వానికి దుడ్డుకులంకె he is much attached to money. "భార్గవకులమున భర్గస్వామికి కేలించెద లంకెగ కేల్తు మతలు." H. iv. 303. **లంకె** or **లంకెమానిసి** *lanke.* n. A slave, vassal. బంటు, దాసుడు. **లంకెపలుపు** *lanke-palupu.* n. A tether that ties two animals together. **లంకెపాటు** *lanke-paṭu.* n. Clinging together. ఒకటితో నొకటి కరుచుకొనియుండడము. Connection, తగులము. "సీ॥ లలిత పాదంబున లంకెపాటై యుండి రాజను పేనూపురంబులార." R. v. 280. **లంకెపీట** *lanke-pīṭa.* n. A wooden plank used in linking cattle together. పశువులను పెనవేయుపలక. **లంకెపెట్టు** or **లంకెవేయు** *lanke-peṭṭu.* v. a. To link together, తగులుపరుచు, పెనవేయు.

లంగ *langa.* [from Skt. లంఘనము.] n. Same as లంఘనము. (q. v.) **లంగగొను** *langa-gonu.* v. a. To leap across, cross over. లంఘించు, దాటు.

లంగరు *langaru.* [H.] n. An anchor. లంగరుఖానా a poor house or hospital where food is dispensed. అన్నసత్రము. లంగరువేయు to cast anchor. లంగరుతీయు or ఎత్తు to weigh anchor.

లంగా *langa* [H.] n. A woman's petticoat. పావడ.

లంగోటి *langoṭi.* [H.] n. A piece of cloth worn like a truss. గోచి.

లంఘనము *langhanamu.* [Skt.] n. Going over, leaping, springing, jumping over or beyond, transgressing, going beyond proper bounds. ప్లవనము, దాటడము. Fasting, abstinence, a day passed without food when one is attacked with fever, &c. అభోజనము, రోగి భోజనము లేకుండా ఉండడము, లంకనము. **లంఘి** *langhi.* n. A transgressor. అతిక్రమించినది. "కన్యాగవత్రి లంఘిన్యైకలిమిగులంగ." Ila. i. 3. **లంఘించు** *langhintsu.* v. n. & a. To pass, or cross over, leap, jump. దాటు, దూకు.

లంచము *lantsamu.* [Tel.] A bribe; bribery. కార్యార్థముగాను అక్రమముగాను రహస్యముగాను ఇచ్చినసొమ్ము. "అనివినతిపముల నర్థంబులంచంబుగానిచ్చి." M. IX. ii. 276. **లంచగొండి** *lantsa-gondi.* n. One who is given to taking bribes.

లంజ *lanja.* [Skt.] n. A whore, a harlot, a concubine or kept woman. జారస్త్రీ, వేశ్య. **లంజె**, **లంజియ** or **లంజెత** [from లంజ.] Same as లంజ. **లంజెకాడు** *lanje-kāḍu.* n. A whoremonger. విటుడు. **లంజెబేడిస** *lanje-bēḍisa.* n. A kind of fish. ఒకవిధమైన చేప. **లంజెరికము** *lanje-rikamu.* n. Whoredom. పడుపు. **లంజెసవరము** *lanje-suvaramu.* n. A medicinal plant. H. v. 52. ఒకమందాకు, గొంతెమగోరుచెట్టు.

లండి, **లండు** or **లండుకోరు** *landi.* [Tel.] n. A wretch: an obstinate or wicked person. కుత్సితపురుషుడు, లేక, కుత్సితస్త్రీ. "లండులైయుద్ధంబు లావుగానడుగు మిండబంగములకు మితిమీఱరదు." L. ix. 186.

లండ *landa*. [Tel.] n. A very stout person, మిక్కిలి లావుమనిషి.

లంపట or లంపటము *lampaṭa*. [Tel.] n. Pain, trouble, weariness, బాధ, తొందర, ఆయాసము. Danger, ఆపద. "మూర్ఛదక్కినలః శోషిల్లుచున్న పద్మాకరింబులెల్లఁ దెరయిల్లె. పెక్కులంపటములజిక్కిమనుత్వముల్ మాకున్న జను లమనసుల్లు." Vish. vii. 228. లంపటపడు *lampaṭa-paḍu*. v. n. To take pains. శ్రమపడు. లంపటుఁడు *lampaṭuḍu*. n. One who loves, one who is given up to or eager for, ఆత్యాసక్తికలవాఁడు, మిక్కిలి ఆశగలవాఁడు. స్త్రీలంపటుఁడు a whoremonger, a libertine, a gallant. "రాజ్యసుఖలంపటుఁడై." URT. iii. 111. "అటుగాక కర్మగతిలంపటుఁడనగుచు నేని." M. XII. i. 37.

లంపతా or లంపతావాఁడు *lampata*. [Tel.] n. A son of a slave. దాసీపుత్రుఁడు.

లంపు *lampu*. [Tel.] n. Stolen food, దొంగమేత. లంపులమారి *lampula-māri*. n. An animal that is fond of stolen food, దొంగమేత మేయునది. "లంపులమారిదానవినులాచుక మాడిక వాడుగోయు." H. v. 80.

లంబము *lambamu*. [Skt.] adj. Long. పొడుగైన. Great, large, spacious, capacious, broad, expanded either in breadth or length or both. విశాలమైన, విరివియైన. Pendulous, depending, వ్రేలాడునట్టి. లంబకర్ణము *lamba-karṇamu*. n. Lit: The long eared, i.e., a hare, చెవులపిల్లి. లంబనము *lambanamu*. n. Depending, descending, falling. వ్రేలాడడము, A necklace. హారము. లంబిక *lambika*. adj. n. The uvula, or soft palate. కొండనాలుక. లంబితము *lambitamu*. adj. Hanging down. వ్రేలాడుచున్న. లంబు *lambu*. [from Skt. లంబము.] n. Largeness, bigness. స్థౌల్యము. Greatness, గొప్పతనము. "నీలంబుజెరికాంచినీలంబులలిదను." T. iii. 71. లంబోదరుఁడు *lamb-ōdaruḍu*. n. Lit. The big bellied god, i. e., Gaṇēśa, విఘ్నేశ్వరుఁడు.

లంబాడి or లంబాడి *lambāḍi*. [Tel.] n. A certain tribe of gypsies called Lambadies or Brinjaris, who trade in bullocks, salt, grain, &c. లంబాడితండా a troop or camp of these vagrants.

లంబి or లంబీ *lambi*. [Tel.] n. A family. కుటుంబము.

లంభనము *lambhanamu*, [Skt.] n. Reviling, abuse. తిట్టడము, దూషించడము. లంభించు *lambhiñtsu*. v. a. To abuse, revile. దూషించు, తిట్టు.

లకుచము *lakuchamu*. [Skt.] n. A species of the bread-fruit tree, *Artocarpus lacucha*. (Rox. and Watts.) కమ్మరేగు. A large species of lemon. గజనిమ్మచెట్టు.

లకుముకి *laku-muki*. [from Skt. లక్కముఖి, so called from its red bill.] n. The White-breasted. King-fisher. *Halcyon smyrnensis*. (F. B. I.) బుచ్చిగాడు.

లకోటా *lakōṭa*. [Marati.] n. An envelope. Sealing. A post parcel.

లకోరి or లకోరీ *lakōri*. [Tel.] n. A sharp arrow. తూగబాణము. "తరుకులకోరులకరకసంబు." Swa. iv. 36. టీ॥ లకోరులకరకసంబు, అంబులపొది. A kind of pigeon, పారావతవిశేషము. "మేలైనలకోరీలు." సా. i.

లక్క *lakka*. [from Skt. లాక్ష.] n. Lac, sealing wax. లాక్ష, జతువు. ఆటుకులలక్క shell-lac. కొయ్యలక్క stick-lac. లక్కతెవులు *lakka-tevulu*. n. The weevil or the blight caused when corn turns rusty. ఒకవిధమైన చీడ. లక్కపెట్టె *lakka-peṭṭe*. n. A lacquered box. చిత్రపేటిక. లక్కబియ్యము or లక్కపొడి *lakka-biyyamu*. n. Powdered lac, grain lac. పొడిలక్క. లక్కయిల్లు a house built with lac, seeming like mortar, intended by Duryodhana to be set on fire to procure the death of the Pāndavas. లక్కపగడాలు false coral. లక్కాకు *lakk-āku*. (లక్క+ఆకు.) n. A roll of palm leaf reddened with *lac* and worn in the ear instead of an earring, కెంపాకు. లక్కకమ్మ a sort of pale red colour.

లక్కణము *lakkaṇamu*. [from Skt. లక్షణము.] n. The science of Grammar, వ్యాకరణశాస్త్రము. A sign, గురుతు, ఆనవాలు.

లక్కిమి *lakkimi*. [From Skt. లక్ష్మి.] Same as లక్ష్మి. (q. v.) లక్కిమనుడు corruption of లక్ష్మణుడు.

లక్ష *laksha*. [Skt.] n. A lac, one hundred thousand. నూరువేలు.

లక్షణము *lakshaṇamu*. [Skt.] n. A sign, mark, token. గురుతు. A symptom, an indication; a characteristic, attribute, quality; a predicate, any thing by which an object is designated, or distinguished. తీరు. A rule of art or science. విధి. The Science of Grammar, &c. వ్యాకరణాదిశాస్త్రము. Perfection, comeliness, beauty, correctness, precision. వర్షలక్షణములు the signs of rain. జ్వరలక్షణములు the symptoms of fever. అక్షరలక్షణము the description of letters in grammar, i. e., Orthography. ఛందోలక్షణము prosody. ఆ రోగలక్షణములను చెప్పుచున్నాను I will now describe the symptoms of that disease. లక్షణయుక్తమైనకావ్యము a classical poem, a book written according to the rules. లక్షణమైన *lakshaṇam-aina*. adj. Handsome, beautiful. అందమైన. లక్షణయా *lakshaṇayā*. adv. Metaphorically. లక్షము *lakshamu*, n. A butt, mark, or aim. గురి. లక్షించు or ఆలక్షించు *lakshintsu*. v. a. To aim at, to see, గురిపెట్టు. చూచు. లక్ష్మము *lakshmamu*. n. A mark, token, or sign. చిహ్నము, గురుతు "మానలక్ష్మాకృతి." T. iii. 140.

లక్ష్మి *lakshmi*. [Skt.] n. Lakshmi, the wife of Vishṇu, the goddess of prosperity. Wealth, fortune, సంపద. Beauty, splendour. శోభ. Turmeric. పసుపు. "శుభశాశ్వతలక్ష్ములనొసగదు." Rukmāngada. iii. 129. లక్ష్మణుడు *lakshmaṇuḍu*. n. The younger brother of Rāma. సౌమిత్రి. A fortunate man, శ్రీమంతుడు. లక్ష్మీపతి *lakshmī-pati* n. The husband of Lakshmi. లక్ష్మీమనోహరాలు *lakshmī-manōharālu*. n. A certain kind of rice. H. iv. 158. లక్ష్మీవంతుడు *lakshmī-vantuḍu*. n. A man of wealth. భాగ్యవంతుడు, సంపదగలవాడు. లక్ష్మీవారము *lakshmī-vāramu*. n. Thursday, గురువారము, బృహస్పతివారము. శేసవారము.

లక్ష్యము *lakshyamu*. [Skt.] adj. Observable, perceptible. చూడదగిన, విచారింపదగిన. n. A mark, or butt, an aim. Care, regard, respect, esteem. గురి, ఉద్దేశము, గౌరవము. వాడునందు వానికి లక్ష్యములేదు. he does not care for me, or mind me. An instance or example adduced in proof. దృష్టాంతము. ఇందుకు లక్ష్యము for instance. అది లక్ష్యము కాదు that is no great matter. లక్ష్యపెట్టు or లక్ష్యము చేయు *lakshya-peṭṭu*. v. a. To aim. To esteem, take notice of, regard, value, care for, respect. గురిపెట్టు. గౌరవముచేయు.

లగడ *lagaḍa*. [Tel.] n. Overboiled rice. చిమిడిన అన్నము.

లగనము [from Skt. లగ్నము.] Same as లగ్నము. (q. v.)

లగాము *lagāmu*. [H.] n. A horse's bridle.

లగాయతు *lagāyatu*. [H.] n. Beginning, commencement. adv. Since, from the commencement of, from the beginning. ఈనాటి లగాయతు beginning from this day.

లగించు *lagintsu*. [Tel.] v. n. To agree or coincide in sense or meaning. ఇముడు. To suit, సరిపడు.

లగుడము *lagudamu.* [Skt.] n. A club bound with iron or made of it, a staff or stick. ఇనుప అలుగుగల దండము. "చిక్కినలగుడంబున తలవ్రక్కలుగావేసి." P. i. 614.

లగుడు *lagudu.* [Tel.] n. A kind of hawk; the Laggar Falcon, *Falco jugger.* (F.B.I.) ఒకజాతిడేగ. "నింగికై కుంచెయెత్తివెసంగోయని యూర్ధ్వపక్షసంహతిగాడ్పులిరింగని మ్రోయుచు బాగ్రుపుకొంగలనోకలగుడుడిగ్గి కొట్టెనిలబడగా." Swa. iv. 86.

లగువు [from Skt. లఘువు.] Same as లఘువు. (q. v.)

లగ్గ *lagga.* [Tel.] n. An escalade, scaling, (ముట్టడించి) కోటపైకెక్కుట. లగ్గకెక్కు, లగ్గపట్టు or లగ్గలుపట్టు to scale a fort, ముట్టడి చేసి కోటనెక్కు. **లగ్గడింపు** *lagga-dimpu.* n. Assault bafflers; (these were stones kept upon fortresses to be rolled down upon the besiegers.) కోటమీదనుంచి శత్రువులపైకి దొర్లించేబండలు.

లగ్గము Same as లగ్నము. (q. v.)

లగ్గు *laggu.* [Tel.] n. Welfare, prosperity, happiness. శుభము, మేలు. **లగ్గులు** *laggulu.* n Obsequies, ఉత్తరక్రియలు. దినవారాలు. "అనంతరంబు దక్షిణభుజాస్పందనం బుపలక్షించి మీదలగ్గగునని." M. III. iv. 110. "దుర్యోధనాదులకు సంతసంబువిధివంబెసగగా ధృతరాష్ట్రదౌర్గ్వాదిహితవిధు లాచరించునట్లుగా నొసర్చి తానెలింగివారికెల్లలగ్గులు సేయుటకుండగు బంధులు లేరని వసుంధరావల్లభుల నెల్లనుద్దేశించియుంచిరదానంబులతో ధామ్యనిరంబనిచె." M. XII. i. 438.

లగ్నము *lagnamu.* [Skt.] n. The rising of a Sign or Constellation. That portion of the equator, which rises in succession with each Sign in an oblique sphere. A period astrologically selected for any auspicious ceremony, such as a marriage, &c. రాశియొక్క ఉదయము. adj. Attached to, adhering to, in contact with, joined to, connected with, intent on, తగులుకొన్న.

లగ్నకుడు *lagnakudu.* n. A security, or surety. పూటకాపు. పూటపడినవాడు. ప్రతిభువు. **లగ్నపత్రిక** *lagna-patrika.* n. A wedding notice.

లఘిమ or **లఘిమము.** *laghima.* [Skt.] n. Ethereality, volatility, subtility, buoyancy. Excessive lightness; absence of weight, especially as an attribute of supernatural power. చులకదనము, లఘుత్వము. **లఘిష్ఠము** *laghishthamu.* adj. Lightest, very light, very small, least, మిక్కిలి చులకనైన, మిక్కిలి తక్కువైన. **లఘుత్వము** *laghutvamu.* n. Lightness, triviality. చులకదనము. **లఘుబ్రహ్మి** *laghu-brahmi.* n. A plant called *Trigonella corniculata* **లఘులయము** *laghu-layamu.* n. The root of a fragrant grass, usually called Cuss-cuss, *Andropogon muricatum,* తెల్లవట్టివేరు. **లఘువు** *laghuvu.* adj. Swift, quick, వడిగల. Light, not heavy; slight, trivial, trifling. Convalescent, better in health. Abating, moderating, as applied to disease, చులకని. తేలికైన, శాంతమైన. n. An abatement, lessening, slackening. A short syllable. A leap, darting. Quick time in music. శాంతము, గురువుకానిది, గంతు, వేగము, తాళములో భేదము. **లఘువుగా** *laghuvu-ga.* adv. Lightly. In good health. Gently, well, softly, slowly. తిన్నగా, స్వస్థముగా. **లఘుశంకకు పోవు** *laghu-sankaku-povu.* v. n. To pass urine. ఉచ్చపోయు.

లచ్చి [from Skt. లక్ష్మి.] n. Same as లక్ష్మి. (q. v.) లచ్చిమగడు same as లక్ష్మీమగడు.

లచ్చేవము Same as లక్షణము. (q. v.)

లజ్జ *lajja.* [Skt.] n. Shame, modesty, bashfulness, shyness, సిగ్గు. **లజ్జాళువు** or **లజ్జాళులుడు** *lajjaluvu.* adj. Bashful, modest. సిగ్గుగలవాడు. **లజ్జించు** *lajjintsu.* v. n. To be ashamed, bashful or shy. సిగ్గుపడు. **లజ్జితము** *lajjitamu.* adj. Abashed. సిగ్గుపడిన.

లటుక్కున laṭakku-na. [Tel. (anuk.)] adv. Suddenly. అకస్మాత్తుగా.

లటుపటు, లటుపటము or లటుపిటు laṭapaṭa. [Tel.] n. Fighting, a quarrel, పోరాటము. "కల్లసత్యములును కపటకృత్యములు, లటుపటంబులును లాలామాలలును." L. vii. 277. Bragging, boasting. డంభాలునరకడము, గప్పాలుకొట్టడము. "నావుడు పరిపూరించెద వీవుండుటయొకిరికార యిదిచేటుగనే గావించితి చేరికదగలావించుకగలిగి నేనిలటుపటలేలా." G. vii. 29.

లటహము laṭahamu. [Skt.] n. A kind of drum. వాద్యవిశేషము. adj. Skilful, attractive. కార్యకుశలము. "ధక్కాపాండుఢక్కారవజాన కలటహాపటహాకమట, అవజనిస్సాన." H. iii. 38.

లట్టు laṭṭu. [Tel.] n. A step, పడియ.

లట్టువ or లటువ్వ laṭṭuva. [Tel.] n. A cudgel. దుడ్డుకర్ర. A small cymbal, చిటితాళము. "చ॥ కరమువమానిలట్టువయు కంబళి మంపము వంచుజంకిటం, దిరిపెపుగూడయుంగొనితదీయని వాసము నిర్గమించి యొవ్వరుతనుజూతురో యనుచు." Vaija. iii. 98.

లటాలున laṭhālu-na. [Tel. (anuk.)] adv. Suddenly, all at once. లటుక్కున.

లడాయి laḍāyi. [H.] n. A fight, battle, యుద్ధము.

లడి laḍi. [H.] n. A skein of lace, &c., నిడుపుగామట్టిన సరిగెలోనగువానిచుట్ట. A skein of gold or silver thread. A string of pearls, flowers, &c.

లడ్డిగ, లడ్డిగె or లడ్డిగము laḍḍiga. [Tel.] n. A kind of bottle used in travelling, బుర్ర, ఒకవిధమైనపాత్ర. "కావడిపైనంటగట్టినకొకావి, కాటికంబళియాత్రసంచియులర, నేతిలడ్డిగనిక్కనించిన సొరకాయ, బుర్రలిర్వంకలపొసగియుండ." H. i. 200. "పంచాకంపుచింతపండు, పెల్లలోవెండికావళ్లకొమ్ములవ్రేలు గిడ్డిముత్తవు నేతిలడ్డిగలును." A. ii. 123. తేనెలడ్డిగ a honey bottle.

లడ్డు laḍḍu. [Tel.] n. A kind of sweetmeat. (Metaphorically,) a scrape, perplexity. లడ్డుకము, లడ్డువము or లడ్వము Same as లడ్డు.

లత or లతిక lata. [Skt.] n. A creeper, a creeping plant, తీగ. A branch, కొమ్మ. ఖడ్గలత a slender sword. తనులత her slender form. లతకూన lata-kūna. n. A sprig, (poetical phrase for a girl.) బాలిక, తీగవంటి ఆడుది. లతాంగి lat-āngi. n. A slender woman; one whose form is slender as a sprig. కన్యక. లతాంతము lat-āntamu. n. A flower (lit: the extremity of a creeper.) లతాంతాస్త్రుడు one who uses blossoms for weapons, i.e., Manmadha, పుష్పాస్త్రుడు. Kalahas. iv. 31. లతాదోల lata-ḍōla. n. A swing formed of twigs. తీగెఉయ్యాల. A. v. 66.

లత్త latta. [Tel.] n. A blow, దెబ్బ. Danger. ఆపద.

లత్తిక lattika. [Tel.] n. A stout and heavy seed of the కచ్చచెట్టు.

లత్తిచేప latti-chēpa. [Tel.] n. A sort of fish, *Drepanus punctatus*. Russell; plate 79.

లత్తుక lattuka. [from Skt. లాక్ష.] n. The red colour called lac, produced like cochineal from insects. లాక్ష లత్తుకదూది cotton steeped in lac liquid and then dried. This by being dipped in water forms red ink. లత్తుకబొత్తులు lattuka-bottulu. n. A certain kind of grain. ధాన్యవిశేషము. H. iv. 158.

లద్ది or లద్దె laddi. [Tel.] n. The dung of horses, asses, elephants, or camels. అశ్వాదులపేడ. లద్దిఆకు trash, the remaining substance of leaves boiled for dye, &c. లద్దిపురుగు laddi-purugu. n. A dung-beetle. The fly that destroys corn, a grub in wood. క్రిమివిశేషము. లద్దెపిప్పి or లద్దిపిప్పి ladde-pippi. n. The blight or murrain that destroys corn. ఒకవిధమైన తెగులు. లడ్డె or లడ్డీడు *ladde*. n. The end of a cloth. నేయువాడు బట్టనేసిన విడిచెడు అంచు.

లపక *lapaka*. [Tel.] n. Money, wealth. ధనము, విత్తము.

లపటాయించు or లప్టాయించు *lapaṭā-y-intsu*. [Tel. anuk.] v. a. To devour, to plunder.

లపనము *lapanamu*. [Skt.] n. The face or countenance. ముఖము. The mouth. నోరు. Voice, talking. మాట్లాడడము. A word, మాట. "కళలేరుకన్నారు తిలకించుబాసనల్ లపన గంధములుకలంచనెసంగ." H. iv. 84. లపితము *lapitamu*. adj. Said, spoken. చెప్పబడిన. n. Voice, speech, a word. మాట.

లప్ప *lappa*. [Tel.] n. A lump (as of sugar or of civet.) ముద్ద గడ్డ. రాశి. "తలము క్లేదముగా తాల్చి మేనులను బొల్పుజవ్వాదిలప్పలు సోడుముట్ట దళముగా నగలుగంధముతోనగలది." Nava. page 58. లప్పము *lappamu*. n. Plaster, cement used to fill up the cracks in wood or the seams of ships, &c. Putty.

లబలబ *laba-laba*. [Tel. anuk. of beating oneself on the mouth, as a mark of distress.] adv. Much, severely.

లభించు *labhintsu*. [Skt.] v. n. To happen, befall, occur, be acquired or gained. ప్రాప్తమగు, ప్రాప్తించు, కలుగు. వాడు చెప్పిన ప్రకారముగా లభించినది it turned out as he prophesied. లబ్ధము *labdhamu*. adj. Gained, acquired, obtained, received, attained. పొందబడిన. n. The quotient in division. భాగహారముచేయగా వచ్చినసంఖ్య. లబ్ధవర్ణుడు *labdha-varṇuḍu*. n. A learned man, పండితుడు. లబ్ధి *labdhi*. n. Profit, gain. లాభము, ప్రాప్తఫలము. కలిమి. "ఇతరమత్స్యములనంగటు తోకాల్చియుండుల లబ్ధిఁబంగమారాధనల్ సల్పుచుం డు." BD. iv. 1822. లభ్యము *labhyamu*. adj. Attainable, procurable. పొందదగిన.

లమిడీ or లమ్డి *lamḍi*. [H.] n. A slave girl, a wretch, scamp. తొత్తు.

లయ *laya*. [Skt.] n. Beating time in music and dancing. తాళము వేయు క్రియ, తాళము. [Tel.] n. Fraud, trick, deceit. మాయ, మోసము. లయకాడు or లయకారి *layakāḍu*. n. A rogue. మోసగాడు. "తే॥ అతని, నిప్పు చెప్పెడిలయకాని దొంగ." Vaijayanti. iv. 81.

లయము *layamu*. [Skt.] n. Loss, destruction, extinction, annihilation, నాశము. The grass called cuss-cuss, వట్టివేరు. ఇంతటితో ఆ ప్రభుత్వమునకు లయకాలము వచ్చినది these were the declining days of the dynasty. లయించు *layintsu*. v. n. To be destroyed. నశించు. To be attached to, be connected with, లగ్నమగు, సక్తమగు. వాని మనసంతా దానియందే లయించియుండగా while his every thought was engrossed by her.

లయ్య *layya*. [Tel.] n. A prostitute.

లలంతిక *lalantika*. [Skt.] n. A necklace hanging as low as the waist. కంఠాభరణము.

లలత్ *lalat*. [Skt.] adj. Shaking, tremulous. చలించే. కదిలే. లలన *lalana*. n. A wanton girl, a beauty. విలాసవతియగుస్త్రీ.

లలాటము *lalāṭamu*. [Skt.] n. The forehead. నుదురు. నొసలు. లలాటలిఖితము or లలాటలిపి *lalāṭa-likhitamu*. n. That which is written on the forehead: (what Mussulmans call 'nasib.') Luck, destiny. (Bramha is imagined to write in crooked lines on the skull, the future events of each life.) లలాటిక or లలాటపట్టము *lalāṭika*. n. A tiara, a fillet ముఖపట్టిక, పాపటబొట్టు.

లలామము *lalāmamu*. [Skt.] n. A sign. గురుతు. A flag, టెక్కెము. A nornament, భూషణము. A coronet of flowers. A mark on the forehead, నుదుటకట్టే పువ్వులదండ కము. తేక, బొట్టు, తిలకము. రమణీలలామములు the loveliest of women. "అద్దంబులా

చినవిశిలలామంబు ప్రతిబింబితంబగుచుండె." B. vii. 416. adj. Chief, principal, excellent, శ్రేష్ఠమైన. Beautiful, agreeable, charming. సుందరమైన. **లలామకము** *lalāmakamu*. n. A coronet of flowers. బాసికము. పురుషశిఖా పుష్పోత్కృష్టమాల్యము. పిల్లజట్టునకట్టినదండ. "సారంగమదంబలదిలలామకమిడి." A. vi. 180. లలాముడు the chief man, ముఖ్యుడు. శ్రేష్ఠుడు. భూపాలలలాముడు the noblest of kings. "మంత్రిలలామా." Ved. Ras. ii. 1. సాధ్వీలలామము the most virtuous of women. "ఈయబలాలలామకెనయేయదుమంచుగాన." T. ii. 105.

లలి *lali*. [Tel.] n. Order, క్రమము. Love. ప్రేమ. Brightness, joy, విలాసము, ఉత్సాహము. Gracefulness, agreeableness. సొగసు, ఒప్పిదము, సమ్మతి, అంగీకారము. adj. Graceful, agreeable. సొగసైన, ఒప్పిదమైన. adv. Gracefully, agreeably. సొగసుగా, ఒప్పిదముగా, అత్యంతము. "లలిమల్లెనిల్లలచుచలిలోచనదీప్తు లడరమంకించి సాగిరాగా." M. IV. iii. 55.

లలితము *lalitamu*. [Skt.] adj. Beautiful, graceful, charming, lovely, gay, cheerful. మనోజ్ఞమైన. సుందరమైన. లలితాంగి a sweet or lovely figure.

లవంగము *lavangamu*. [Skt.] n. A clove. *Caryophyllus aromaticus*. (Watts.) దేవకుసుమము, లవంగపుమొగ్గ. **లవంగపుచెక్క** *lavangapu-chekka*. n. *Cassia lignea* (Ainslie. వరాంగకము. **లవంగపట్ట** *lavanga-patta*. n. Cinnamon. సన్నలవంగపట్ట *Cinnamomum zeylcynicum*. అడవిలవంగపట్ట *Cinnamomum iners* (Watts.)

లవణము *lavanamu*. [Skt.] n. Salt. ఉప్పు. Saltness. ఉప్పన. adj. Salt, saline. ఉప్పగానుండే. సముద్రలవణము sea salt. సైంధవలవణము rock salt. బిడాలవణము salt used in medicine. లవణద్రావకము hydrochloric or muriatic acid, *acidum muriaticum*.

లవణి *lavani*. [Tel.] n. Tightness. బిగువు. "సీ॥ వినేయమైనయొద్దాణంబులవణిచేనక్కళించి పొట్టమక్కళించి." Swa i. 15.

లవనము *lavanamu*. [Skt.] n. Reaping, mowing. పైరుమొదలుకొని కోయుటము.

లవము *lavamu*. [Skt.] n. A small quantity, a very little, a minute particle. కొంచెము. సూక్ష్మము. లేశము. Cutting, plucking, as a flower, &c. కోయుటము. కోత. adj. Little. కొంచెమైన. **లవించు** *lavintsu*. v. a. To cut, reap, mow. కోయు. **లవలేశము** *lava-lēsamu*. adj. Very little. రవంత. లవలేశమైనను ఎరుగనివాడు one who is utterly ignorant.

లవలవ *lava-lava*. [Tel.] adj. Split, divided, broken asunder. ఛేదిల్లిన. చీలిన.

లవలి *lavali*. [Skt.] n. A kind of creeper. ఒకతీగె. Swa. iii. 146. A. v. 80.

లవిటి *laviti*. [Tel.] n. The root of a bird's wing. రెక్కమొదలు.

లవిత్రము *lavitramu*. [Skt.] n. A sickle, a small reaping hook. కొడవలి. "దురితలతాలవిత్ర." Dasaradhi Satakam.

లశునము *lasunamu*. [Skt.] n. Garlic. వెల్లుల్లి. A certain kind of flaw in a gem, రత్నములలోనుండే దోషవిశేషము.

లసత్ *lasat*. [Skt.] n. Bright, brilliant. ప్రకాశమానమైన.

లసుకు *lasuku*. [Tel.] v. a. To destroy, నాశముచేయు.

లష్కరు *laskaru*. [H.] n. An army, దండు. A lascar, సిపాయి. adj. Stout and strong

లస్తకము *lastakamu*. [Skt.] n. The middle of a bow, where it is grasped. ధనుర్మధ్యస్థానము. A. ii. 88.

లహరి *lahari*. [Skt.] n. A large wave or surf, a billow. A flood. మహాతరంగము. ప్రవాహము. పెద్దకెరటము. T. iv. 150.

లా lā

లాంగలము *lāngalamu*. [Skt.] n. A plough. నాగలి. లాంగలి *lāngali*. n. An epithet of Balarāma. బలరాముడు. The forest tree called *Gloriosa superba*. నీరుపిప్పలి. Rox. ii. 143.

లాంగూలము *lāngūlamu*. [Skt.] n. A hairy tail, as a horse's.

లాంఛనము *lānchhanamu*. [Skt.] n. A mark, or sign, చిహ్నము. A name, or appellation. పేరు.

లాకు *lāku*. [Tel.] n. A feather. పక్షియీక. A new shoot from a stalk of corn, &c. జొన్నపైరులాకుపెట్టినది the cholam has sent out fresh shoots. లాకుకట్టు *lāka-kaṭṭu*. n. Pinioning the arms. రెడ్డచేతులు విరిచికట్టు. లాకులు *lākalu*. n. plu. Small pieces of stick, used by weavers. సాలెవాడు పడుగునందుంచే పుల్లలు. "కొలింపు పడుగులు కండెలకప్పెర గోలముల్ లాకులునిలికడప. గంప, డొల్ల. కళాసంబు. కదురు, నెమికి." H. ii. 12. లాకుకట్టె *lāka-kaṭṭa*. n. The unfinished warp of a cloth with pieces of wood still stuck in it. లాకులతో చుట్టియుంచిన నేసిముగియని పడుగు.

లాక్ష *lāksha*. [Skt.] n. Lac, లక్క. లాక్షారసము *laksha-rasamu*. n. The red dye obtained from lac. లత్తుక.

లాక్షణికుడు *lākshaṇikudu*. [Skt. from లక్షణము.] n. One who knows the rules of the various arts, &c. A grammarian. A classical scholar. లక్షణము తెలిసినవాడు, లక్షణజ్ఞుడు.

లాగ *lāga*. [Tel.] n. A burrow, hole. కలుగు, బొరియ, బిలము. "అడవియెల్లెడలంచినవనిసాధ పెల్లెడయుండుతోలాగలమల్లసిల్లు." Swa. iv. 25 "అనివివినిక్కనడి, తనమునోటికిల్లినని ప్రతిబలిఠుండును వేరొకతగులాగనుఱని సముచిత వర్తనము సౌఖ్యముచొందుగా." M. XII. iii. 236. లాగదాగుడు *lāga-dāgudu*. n. A snake, సర్పము. లాగరి *lāg-ari*. (లాగ+అరి) n. The ear. చెవి.

లాగము *lāgamu*. [from Skt. లాఘవము.] n. Same as లాఘవము. (q. v.) లాగి *lāgi*. adj. Light; easy; skilful. లాగమగల, లఘువైన, సులభమైన.

లాగు *lāgu*. [Tel.] v. a. & n. To pull, haul, drag, draw. ఈడ్చు. వాడు ప్రాణముపోవునప్పుడు వానికాళ్లుచేతులు లాగినవి in dying his arms and legs were drawn up, or were contracted. n. Attraction, ఆకర్షించడము. Consent, సమ్మతి. Manner, విధము. A summersault, leap, లంఘనము. Short drawers, reaching only to the middle of the thigh. చెల్లడము. లాగించు *lāgintsu*. v. a. To cause to pull or drag, లాగునట్లుచేయు. లాగుకొను *lāgu-konu*. v. a. To take by force, seize. బలాత్కారముగా తీసికొను. అపహరించుకొను. లాగుబడి *lāgu-baḍi*. n. Expense, cost. లాగులాడు *lāgul-āḍu*. v. n. To struggle, పెనగులాడు. లాగు or లాగున *lāgu*. adv. Like, as, రీతిగా, విధముగా, వలె. "పెలయుమాటిశ్చంద్రుని విధమున, నలునికరణి, పురుకుత్సువాడ్పున, పురూరవునిరీతి, సగరులాగున, కార్తవీర్యుమర్యాదగను, నయమునిక్కి యచ్చు." H. i. 42. ఏలాగున్నది how is it, in what fashion is it? ఈలాగున in this way. ఆలాగున in that manner? అతడు చెప్పినలాగున according to what he said? అది అయ్యేలాగున చేయవలసినది you must manage to get this done. మాకు అందేలాగు so that it may reach us. మొద్దులాగు నిలిచినాడు he stood stock still. వాని ముఖములాగు ఉండెను it looked like his face. ఇట్లు చేసేలాగున చెప్పుము tell him to do so.

లాఘవము lāghavamu. [Skt. from లఘువు.] n. Lightness, slightness, delicacy, easiness, facility, dexterity. లఘుత్వము. Health, ఆరోగ్యము. హస్తలాఘవము or కరలాఘవము sleight of hand. నన్ను లాఘవముచేసిరి or లాఘవపరిచిరి they scorned me.. మాయువారికి లాఘవముగానుండును it will appear contemptible. "మానలంపటలాఘవమున, నీవేటికి బుద్ధిగొంటి." B. X.

లాచారు lāchāru. [H.] adj. Helpless, forlorn, poor.

లాచి or లాచీ lāchi. [Tel.] n. The sack to receive loads, placed upon horses or asses, గుర్రములమీదను గాడిదలమీదను వేసే గోనె. A load carried on a small cart.

లాచు lātsu. [Tel from లాగు.] v. n. To lie in ambush, పొంచు. To oppose, కవియు. v. a. To pull, haul, ఈడ్చిపట్టు, లాగిపట్టు. "వారికధ్వగులులాచి యిడుమవిడియములపేర." A. ii. 69. "దాచినమీమాలధనమెల్లబెట్టి గోచికాదైదానిగోనుచు నేతెంచిలాచియువ్వాడునీలాగోత్తి చూడ." HD. ii. 1051. "కటిసూత్రమున లాచికట్టినగోచి." L. xi. 253.

లాజలు lājalu. [Skt.] n. plu. Fried grain, parched corn. పేలాలు, బొరుగులు.

లాటదేశము lāṭa-dēsamu. [Skt.] n. The ancient name of a part of Southern India: Guzerat or Malayalam.

లాటి lāti. [Tel.] n. The Tailor bird. పిచ్చుక భేదము.

లాటీకర్ర lāti-karra. [Tel. లాఠీ corruption of లావాటి.] n. A staff or club. దుడ్డుకర్ర.

లాడము lāḍamu. [H.] n. A horse shoe. లాడములుకట్టు to shoe a horse.

లాడీ lāḍi. [Tel.] n. A large ulcer, a galled sore, a sore on the back of any animal of burden produced by its load. పెద్దపుండు. లొట్టపుండు. Matter or pus exuding from the ear, చెవిపుంటిలోనుండికారే రసి. "లాడికి మూగుకాకుల బలాయన మొందగజేయు." H. v. 35. A sacrifice, బలి.

లాడె or లాడియ lāḍe. [Tel.] n. Loading a pack ox. ఎద్దుమీదను బరువెక్కించుట.

లాత See లాయు.

లాతము. లాతాము or లాతపుగోల lātamu. [Tel.] n. A stick, staff, rod, a hermit's staff. దండము, సన్యాసిచేతిదండము, చేతికోవ్వ, వంకరకోల. "కకపాలకేదార కటకము త్రికపాటి కురుచలాతముతోడ గూర్చిపట్టి." Swa. i. 15. "ఈబలపవుంగోడుపునిలపైవల సిన దొమ్మిలెక్క లొండెకేఖలొండెవ్రానియా లాతపుంగోలసవ్యహస్తంబునంబట్టి ముట్టించినసన్ని దయునీవుతలంచి ప్రాణులై." G. viii. 116.

లాతి lāti. [Tel.] adj. Other, strange, foreign, అన్యము. n. A stranger, an alien. అన్యపురుషుడు, అన్యస్త్రీ. లాతివాడు a stranger, పరుడు, అన్యుడు. "ఇప్పుడు మగదీర్చుకోవన్నె నేమొగాక యేమిచేసితిలాతి నేపోముసకును." R. vi. 30. "తల్లినచ్చిభక్తిమైనుపచరింపక లాతికై యుటుంటూరకుండుట యుక్తమై" M. XI. ii. 32. Plu. లాతులు.

లాతు lātu. [Tel.] adj. Much, great, అధికము.

లాపరో or లాపరాయి lāpuṟa. [Tel. లాపు+రాయి.] n. A grate over a drain. జలగ్రాహిణి మీదకు కప్పు చొరకుండా నిలిపిన వానిబంధపుపలక, రేక, కండ్లరాయి, చిక్కుపలక. "మగుడిలాపరాయి కాపురాసికడనిలిచి." A. vi. 9.

లాపు lāpu. [Tel. from లాచు.] n. Lying in ambush, &c. See లాచే. లాపోను combination, interference.

లాభము lābhamu. [Skt.] n. Gain, profit, advantage. దొరకడము, ప్రాప్తి. Interest on money. క్రయవిక్రయములవల్లవచ్చినహెచ్చు, వడ్డి. లాభనష్టములు profit and loss.

లామజ్జకము *lāmajjakamu*. [Skt.] n. The root of the *Andropogon laniger*, usually termed Cuss-cuss. The *Juncus ordoratis* of Pharmacy. (Watts.) తెల్లవట్టివేరు, వటి వట్టివేరు.

లాయఖు *lāyakhu*. [H.] adj. Fit, proper, suitable. తగిన. లాయఖుకాదు it is not proper.

లాయము *lāyamu*. [Perhaps from Eng. 'lines'.] n. A stable. అశ్వశాల.

లాయు or లాతిచేయు *lāyu*. [Tel.] v.n. To increase, prosper, be proud. అతిక్రమించు, విజృంభించు. లాతి *lāta*. n. Pride, గర్వము.

లాల or లాలాజలము *lāla*. [Skt.] n. Slaver, saliva, spittle. చొంగ, చొల్లు.

లాలన or లాలనము *lālana*. [Skt.] n. Wheedling, coaxing, flattering. బుజ్జగింపు.

లాలము *lālamu*. [Tel.] n. A certain cloth put on over a saddle cover. జల్లారుక్రింది కోలు. లాలసరి *lālasari*. (లాలము+సరి) n. Scarlet tufts attached to a state saddle. గుర్రపుపల్లాన పక్కలందుగట్టు పట్టుకుచ్చులు.

లాలస *lālasa*. [Skt.] n. Ardent desire, అతికాంక్ష, ఔత్సుక్యము. Soliciting, asking. ప్రార్థన, యాచన. Amorousness, విషయాలంపటము. లాలసము *lālasamu*. adj. Devoted to, attached to. విషయాలంపటులైన, మిక్కిలి కాంక్షగల. లాలసుడు *lālasudu*. n. One who loves, one who is wishing for. మిక్కిలి కాంక్షగలవాడు.

లాలాట *lālāta*. [Skt. from లలాటము.] adj. Relating to the forehead. నొసటి. "లాటప్రద్గాంతిలాలాటఘర్మంబు దీలాటనక్రియలుబాయుం గడోపి." T. ii. 32. టీ॥ లాలాట, లలాటప్రదేశమందుపుట్టిన.

లాలి *lāli*. [Tel.] n. A cradle, ఉయ్యాల. A lullaby sung to children. జోలికనూరి విప్పడునుపదము. "లాలిలాలియటంచుమేలిలాలను లుపాడి." Charu Chandrōd. iii.

లాలించు *lālintsu*. [Skt. from లాలనము.] v. n. To wheedle, coax, lull, soothe. బుజ్జగించు. See లాలన. లాలితము *lālitamu*. adj. Coaxed, wheedled, seduced, loved, desired, Bright, illumined. బుజ్జగింపబడిన. మిక్కిలి కాంక్షింపబడిన, ప్రకాశింపబడ్డ. Beautiful, సుందరమైన. "బాలేందు రేఖరోచిల లాలితమగున లదికృతలాగునదధరిజీ, పాలునిగేహముమెరసెను." B. X.

లాలిత్యము *lālityamu*. [Skt. from లలితము.] n. Beauty. అందము, సొగసు.

లాలు *lālu*. [H.] adj. Red. ఎర్రని. లాలుకుంచెలు *lālu-kunchelu*. n. plu. Scarlet tufts attached to a state saddle. ఎర్రని చిన్నతెల్లులు. "లాలుకుంచెలు." A. v. 55. అనగా, గుర్రముయొక్క పల్లమునకు కట్టే యెర్రని చిన్నచామరములు.

లాలూచి *lālūchi*. [H.] n. Temptation, inducement, bribery.

లావకము Same as లావుకపిట్ట. (q. v.)

లావణము *lāvanamu*. [Skt. from లవణము.] n. A list of soldiers or servants. Enlistment. కొత్తగా కొలువునకువచ్చిన కొలువుడు కానిని పట్టికయందు వ్రాసికొనుట. The profits of a custom house. లావణముచేయు to enlist. లావణి *lāvani*. n. Money advanced for grazing cattle on pasture land.

లావణ్యము *lāvanyamu*. [Skt.] n. Beauty, loveliness. A pearly white color. సౌందర్యము, ముక్తాఫలచ్ఛాయావదంగప్రకాశమానకాంతి, ముఖకాంతివిశేషము.

లావాదేవి *lāvā-dēvi*. [H.] n. Traffic, mercantile transactions, buying and selling, money dealings in general. లావాదేవిచేసినాడు he quarrelled or gave annoyance.

లావిక *lāvika*. [Skt.] n. A female who vends articles. అమ్మునది. పువ్వులావిక a woman who sells flowers.

లావు *lāvu.* [Tel.] n. Bigness, stoutness, corpulence. స్థూలత్వము. Power, strength, సామర్థ్యము, శక్తి, బలము. Greatness, అతిశయము, ఆధిక్యము. Alms, భిక్షము. లావులు large quill feathers, రెక్కలోనుండెడి పెద్దయీకెలు. "వెలవెల బారుమోములు గావులుంచలింప గదలె దిక్కులకున్ గరుడకులము." N. ii. 72. "లలనకో రెయుందునీవికను లావునకుంజనవేల." Vaij. ii. 125. టీ॥ లావునకుం, భిక్షమునకు. adj. Stout, స్థూలము. Difficult, impossible, అశక్యము. లావువాడు a stout man. లావుమంది a great many people. లావుపెట్టు to fertilise (land). లావరి *lāv-ari.* (లావు+అరి.) n. A robust man. బలాఢ్యుడు. "పోరిలో వాడిమిగొంతగాలమిల బ్రాలుటలావరియోటు నిల్పి వావాడిశరంబుచే." A. vi. 24. లావాటి *lāvāṭi.* adj. Big, large, fat. స్థూలమైన. లావుకపిట్ట or లావుకము *lāvuka-piṭṭa.* n. A sort of quail, *Perdix chinensis.* The Courier Plover. *Cursorius coromandelicus.* (F. B. I.)

లాసము *lāsamu.* [Skt.] n. Dancing. ఆట, నాట్యము, నృత్యము. లాసకము *lāsakamu.* n. A peacock. నెమలి. లాసిక *lāsika.* n. An actress, a female dancer, నాట్యముచేయుస్త్రీ. లాసకుడు *lāsakuḍu.* n. A dancer, actor. నాట్యముచేయువాడు. లాస్యము *lāsyamu.* n. Dancing. నాట్యము.

లాహిరి or లాహిరీ *lāhiri.* [Tel.] n. Drunkenness, intoxication. మైకము. "దేహంబులాహిరిగొను తెరంగున." Radha. i.

లి li

లింగము *lingamu.* [Skt.] n. A mark, sign, token, symptom, characteristic. చిహ్నము. An element, principle. The male organ of generation. The phallus, i.e., emblem symbolic of Siva. పాంచభౌతిక ప్రకృతి, శివమూర్తివిశేషము. Nature as an active power in creation. అబ్లింగము hydrogen, the watery element. పృథివీలింగము the earth. తేజోలింగము caloric. Gender, in grammar, as పుంలింగము the masculine gender. స్త్రీలింగము the feminine gender. నపుంసకలింగము the neuter gender. అనియతలింగము or త్రిలింగము common gender. బాణలింగము a cylindrical oblong pebble or crystal worshipped as the emblem of Siva. గురులింగము a father confessor. శివలింగము an image of Siva. జంగమలింగము a man of the Jangam sect. ప్రసాదలింగము what is dedicated to Siva. లింగశరీరము the subtile or atomic body, the active and causative principle in animated creatures, the quintessence or ethereal substance constituting the soul or spirit, మనోబుద్ధి దశేంద్రియ పంచప్రాణములింగల సూక్ష్మదేహము. లింగకట్టుమాత్ర *linga-kaṭṭu-mātra.* n. A particular kind of pill made of factitious cinnabar. లింగాకారముగాచేసిన రసవస్తువులగుళిక. లింగకాయ *linga-kāya.* n. The solitaire or small case usually made of silver to keep the lingam or phallus in and worn on the breast, suspended by a cord round the neck. సజ్జెకాయ. లింగడు *lingaḍu.* n. A name of the god Siva. జంగమయ్య, శివుడు. లింగదొండ *linga-doṇḍa.* n. A creeper with a red conical fruit, *Bryonia laciniosa.* దొండలోభేదము. లింగధారి or లింగవంతుడు *linga-dhāri.* n. One who wears the lingam or phallus. లింగమును కట్టుకొనియుండువాడు. లింగపొట్ల *linga-poṭla.* n. A kind of snake gourd, లింగాకారపు విత్తులుగల ఒకవిధము పొట్ల, శిగ్రుకము. లింగబలిజలు *linga-balijalu.* n. plu. People of the బలిజ caste, who wear the lingam in a case hung round their necks. లింగవంతులైన బలిజవాండ్రు. లింగవృత్తి, లింగవృత్తుడు or లింగి *linga-vritti.* n. A religious hypocrite, one who assumes the dress, &c., of an ascetic in order to get a livelihood. ధర్మధ్వజి, పొట్టపోసికొనుటకు జటలు రుద్రాక్షలు ధరించువాడు.

లికుచము or లకుచము *likuchamu*. [Skt.] n. A lime or lemon. A species of the bread fruit tree. *Artocarpus lacucha.* నిమ్మపండు, కమ్మరేగుపండు.

లిక్కి *likki*. [Tel.] n. A small sickle. గడ్డిము దలైనవానిని కోసే చిన్న కొడవలి

లిక్కుజిట్ట *likku-jitta*. [Tel.] n. The Tailor bird. పక్షివిశేషము.

లిఖించు or లిఖియించు *likhintsu*. [Skt. from లిఖ్ to scratch.] v. a. To write. వ్రాయు. లిఖితము *likhitamu*. n. Writing, వ్రాత. A manuscript. వ్రాసినవ్రాత. A letter, వ్రాయబడిన. adj. Written, drawn, delineated, painted, వ్రాయబడిన. లిఖితవ్యము *likhitavyamu*. adj. Worthy or fit to be written or drawn, వ్రాయదగిన. లిఖితుడు *likhitudu*. n. A witness that signs a document. సంతకముచేసినసాక్షి. A witness, సాక్షి.

లిడ్డి *liddi*. [Tel.] n. A stake driven into a hole that is made in a mortar. The stoppage of the breadth through the nose on account of a cold.

లిపి *lipi*. [Skt. from లిప్ to smear.] n. Writing in general, hand-writing, a written character. వ్రాత. దేవనాగరలిపి the Devanāgari character. లిపికారుడు. లిపికరుడు or లిపికరుడు *lipi-karudu*. n. A scribe, writer or copyist. వ్రాయువాడు. లిప్తము or లిప్తకము *liptamu*. adj. Smeared, anointed, plastered. పూయబడిన. లిప్తకము *liptakamu*. n. A poisoned arrow.

లిప్స *lipsa*. [Skt.] n. Desire, wish. ఇచ్ఛ, కోరిక. లిప్సుడు *lipsudu*. n. One who wishes. ఇచ్ఛగలవాడు.

లిఫాఫా *liphapha*. [H.] n. An envelope, లకోటా.

లిబ్బి *libbi*. [Tel.] n. Wealth, riches. ధనము, నిధి. "నిబ్బరిముకుప్పతిలమేనుప్పబాప. కొబ్బునను నిబ్బరి వులిబ్బులప్పజేసి పెంచుచిదియు చేరమ్ము గత్తించుగాక." Bahulas. § 116. లిబ్బిపడతి Lakshmi, లక్ష్మీదేవి. లిబ్బులు *libbulu*. n. plu. Treasuries, నిధులు, ధనస్థానములు. లిబ్బుల రాయుడు or లిబ్బులదొర Kubēra, కుబేరుడు, ధనాధిపతి.

లిబ్బి Same as లిబి. (q. v.)

లిమ్మ *limma*. [Tel.] n. A twig used as a whisk. మండ. "వాడికి యంగడిపోయ మెంచక, ముకుమున నొక్కమీనమిడి మూసిన యూగిల చేతిలిమ్మతో కొనపుచుదీనిగొండు వెలసొమ్మనియమ్ముచు నున్నవాడనా." Chenna. iv. 344.

లియ్యము Same as లీయము. (q. v.)

లిలిక్ష *liliksha*. [Skt.] n. Inclination to lick. Acquisitiveness. ఆస్వాదించెచ్చి. "గోమేధక ప్రభాంకూర మిథ్యామధుద్రవ లిలిక్షామిళద్భల్ల కము." Parij. ii. 105.

లివ *liva*. [Tel.] n. Agility, lightness. లాఘవము. (Vulgarly), a syllable. రెండు లివలుగలశబ్దము a word of two syllables. "సీ॥ కదుభోకమిరింగ మడమలుదాటించుచును ముందుకై లివచూపిచూపి." KP. iii. 85. లివ లివ *liva-liva*. adv. Easily, సులకనగా, సులభముగా.

లిహాల్ *lihal*. [Skt.] adj. Licking. A word only used in compounds as అభ్రంలిహాల్ sky-high; lit. 'licking the skies,' ఆకాశ మును అంటే.

లీ li

లీక్ష *liksha*. [Skt.] n. A nit. ఈరు.

లీఢము *lidhamu*. [Skt.] adj. Eaten, తినబడిన.

లీనము *linamu*. [Skt.] adj. Absorbed into, swallowed up in. కలిసిపోయిన, లయించిన. Melted, కరగిన. "అంతర్లీనమహేశ్వరుచు" (P. i. 314.) అనగా, తనమనస్సులో దాచుచు.

లియత or లియము liyata. [Skt.] n. Friendship, intimacy. సఖ్యము. లియముగా liyamu-ga. adv. Intimately, in a friendly manner. స్నేహముగా, చెలిమిగా.

లీల lila. [Skt.] n. Play, sport, pastime, diversion. క్రీడ, కేళి, విలాసము. ప్రభులింగలీల the Siva comedy. A deed, work. క్రియ. Manner, mode, fashion, way. విధము, రీతి. ఇట్లీల in this way. అలీల in like manner. "ఇట్లీలనడుచు వారలు." S. iii. 113. లీలాకోపము sportive anger. లీలావతి lilavati. n. A sportive girl. విలాసవతి.

లు lu

లు lu. [Tel.] n. The sign of the plural in Telugu. It is probably a corruption of the Sanskrit word గురు. In the Ujjayani or Middle Indian dialect, as seen, according to Cunningham, in the Girnar, Rupenath and other inscriptions of Asoka, the word గురు (guru) first occurs in the form of గులు (gulu). Cf. కళ్ used in Tamil and గళు in Kanarese. గులు as a plural ending occurs in a few words in Telugu, as కాలగులు. *Vide* Seshagiri Sastri's Notes on Telugu Grammar. Originally there was no sign of the plural in the Dravidian tongues. See Caldwell. The use of లు as a plural sign was finally extended to other than Masculine nouns, as తమ్ములు, స్త్రీలు, చెట్లు, &c.

లుంగ lunga. [Tel.] n. The weight of a cloth, వస్త్రభారము.

లుంగము lungamu. [Skt.] n. The citron. మాతులుంగము. పుల్లమాదీఫలము.

లుంగి lungi. [H.] n. A frock, or petticoat. కుల్లాయి కుప్పసములుచేర్చి కట్టినపావడ.

లుంటాకుడు luntakudu. [Skt.] n. A thief or robber, a plunderer. అపహరించువాడు, దొంగ. R. i. 6.

లుంఠనము or లుఠనము lunthanamu. [Skt.] n. Rolling on the ground. భూమి మీద పొరలుట. లుంఠితము lunthitamu. adj. Rolled on the ground (as a horse).

లుకలుక luka-luka. [Tel. anuk.] n. The noise made in running or by insects boring through wood. లుకలుకమను luka-lukam-anu. v. n. To wriggle, crawl about. మెదలు. లుకలుకలాడు luka-lukaladu, v. n. To totter, తడబడు.

లుక్కు lukku. [Skt.] n. Elision, cutting off, dropping, rejecting. లోపము. కొట్టుట.

లుగచెడు luga-chedu. [Tel.] v. n. To be spoiled, పాడుచెడు. పాడుకొన్న.

లుగుసాను lugu-sanu. [H.] n. Loss. నష్టము

లుచ్చా luchchha. [H.] adj. Mean, base. n. A scoundrel, wretch. లుచ్చాతనము meanness, baseness.

లుప్తము luptamu. [Skt. connected with the root of లోపము.] adj. Disappearing. Cut off, rejected, as a vowel by elision. లోపించినది.

లుబ్ధము lubdhamu. [Skt.] adj. Covetous, greedy, desirous, avaricious. లోభముగల. లుబ్ధకుడు lubdhakudu. n. A selfish man, a miser. పిసినిగొట్టు. A fowler, huntsman. బోయవాడు. లుబ్ధత్వము lubdhatvamu. n. Covetousness, avarice. లోభిత్వము. లుబ్ధు or లుబ్ధుడు lubdhu. n. A miser. లోభి. A huntsman. బోయవాడు.

లులాయము lulayamu. [Skt.] n. A wild male buffalo. కారుదున్నపోతు. లులాయి lulayi. n A female buffalo. అడవిగేదె.

లులి luli. [Tel.] n. Littleness, a little, తక్కువ. లులిపడు to become low or less. హీనమగు.

లుల్లిగాడు, లుల్లిగాడు or లొల్లిగాడు lulligadu. [Tel.] n. A bankrupt, a spendthrift. A man in distressed circumstances. కెడ్డచెడినవాడు. A low man, అధముడు.

లూ lū

లూటి or లూటీ lūṭi. [H.] n. Plunder, loot, sacking కొల్లపెట్టడము. Danger, ఉపద్రవము. A lachrymal abcess, a boil near the eye. చూడకలోనివ్రణము. లూటీచేయు or లూటీచేయు lūṭi-chēyu. v. n. To plunder.

లూత lūta. [Skt.] n. A spider. సాలెపురుగు.

లూనము lūnamu. [Skt.] adj. Cut. కోయబడిన.

లూమము lūmamu. [Skt.] n. A tail. తోక.

లూలామాలము lūla-mālamu. [Tel.] n. Cheating, wheedling, defrauding. మోసము, వంచన. "క॥ లూలామాలపువాటలు, చాలునవినవలిగిలిన నిజంబుగురూపం, బాలోనబలు పవలెనని, నీలగ్రీవుడునిటలనేత్రముజూపక." Kālahasti. iii. 194.

లె le

లెంక lenka. [Tel.] n. A servant. భటుడు, సేవకుడు. "క॥ అవసరమక్కరలంగై, చువకర్జము లందువేటలోటలయందుగా, దవ్వులైనపాతలెంకల, మవ్వుటగాముమరజాడు మోహినవ్వుదెవ్వరైనగా." R. ii. 8.

లెంట lenṭa. [Tel.] n. Alum, పటిక.

లెండి lenḍi. [Tel. from లేచు to rise.] v. imperative plu. Rise ye. A colloquial expression like "To be sure"! you see! of course! you know! "కోలెం జేమిటిమాట వాపయునమాపాస్తినమంబల్కు టో." T. ii. 164.

లెంప lempa. [Tel.] n. A side, a cheek. చెంప, కట్టు, ప్రక్క. లెంపకాయ lempa-kāya. n. A slap on the cheek. చెంపకాయ.

లెక్క lekka. [Tel.] n. Number, సంఖ్య. An account, a sum in arithmetic, reckoning. గణితము. [from Skt. లక్ష్యము.] Esteem, regard. లక్ష్యము. లెక్కలేని numberless. వాడు మంచిలెక్కగాడు he is a good accountant. వాడు లెక్కలు చదువుచున్నాడు or లెక్కలునేర్చుకొనుచున్నాడు he is learning arithmetic. లెక్కతేల్చు to ascertain the balance in an account. లెక్కచూచు to make out or look over an account. వాడు నన్ను లెక్కచేయలేదు he disregarded me. లెక్కగొను, లెక్కచేయు or లెక్కించు lekkagonu. v. a. To esteem, respect. లక్ష్యముచేయు, గౌరవించు. లెక్కపెట్టు or లెక్కించు lekka-peṭṭu. v. a. To reckon, count. To regard, mind, esteem. ఎంచు. లక్ష్యముచేయు.

లెప్ప or లెప్పము leppa. [Tel.] n. An aim, a butt, గురి, లక్ష్యము. "లెప్పమాదనప్రాణిం గొను." Charitra. i. 255.

లెస్స lessa. [Tel.] n. Good, well being, weal, a good state, health, right. శుభము, క్షేమము, బాగు, మంచి. plu. లెస్సలు. adj. Good, క్షేమయుక్తము. Excellent, శ్రేష్ఠము. Proper, యోగ్యము, శ్రేయస్కరము. అంతా లెస్సలా is all right? "దేశభాషలందు తెలుగు లెస్స." A. i. 18. "అనినలెస్సగాకయనిభర్తృహరుడు." (M. XV. ii. 195.) very well, said he. లెస్స or లెస్సగా adv. Well, properly. duly. Severely. దానిని లెస్సగా కొట్టినాడు he beat it soundly. లెస్సవాడు lessa-vāḍu. n. A proper or excellent man, యోగ్యుడు.

లే lē

లే lē [Tel. from లేచు.] v. imperative. Rise. Interj. Go to, you know, of course. పోనీలే పోనియ్యవాడులే let him go, never mind. ఇక్కడ ఉన్నారులే never mind, they are here.

లే lē. [Tel.] adj. A contraction for లేత tender, as లేతెమట, లేగొమ్మ, లేగాడ్పు, లేత దూడ, లేకెలు, &c. లేవయసు tender age.

లేనగవు a slight laugh, a smile. లేతోట a blooming garden. లేగసవు tender grass.

లే lē. [Tel.] The base of the negative forms లేక, లేని, లేదు, &c. లేక lēka. past participle of లేదు. Not being, not being present, without, wanting. అతడు అక్కడ లేకపోవుటవల్ల by his not being there. వానికి రూకలు లేకపోవుటవల్ల by being in want of money. దాన్ని అడిచేవారులేక యిల్లు విడబడి తిరిగినది she played these pranks as there was no one to check her. కూటికిలేక being in want of food. When added to the infinitive, it means Unable. రాలేక unable to come. దానిని చూడలేక unable to look at it, unable to bear the sight of it. లేకుండ or లేకుండా lēk-unḍa. is used in much the same way as లేక; e.g., అతడు లేకుండ వాల్లకాదు I cannot do it without him లేకుండాచేయు lēk-unḍa-chēyu. v. a. To do away, to get rid of, to turn out. నివృత్తిచేయు. వారిని ఆ యింటిలోలేకుండా చేయుము turn them out of the house. అది వాడు ఇవ్వనక్కరలేకుండా చేస్తిని I relieved him from the necessity of giving it. లేకుండు lēk-unḍu. v. n. To be absent, to be wanting. లేదు lēḍu. He is not; he is not present. ఇంటిలోలేడు he is not in the house. చేయలేడు he cannot do it. వీక్షింపగ లేడయ్యె he could not behold it. లేదా lēdā. Is it not? or, or else. అది అక్కడ లేదా is it not there? లేదు lēdu. It is not. అది అక్కడ లేదు. it is not there. లేనట్టు lēn-aṭṭu. As if it is not అతడు లేనట్టున్నది it appears he is not there. అతడు లేనట్టు తెలిసి knowing that he was not there. లేని lēni. adj. Devoid of. తెలివిలేనివాడు he who is devoid of sense. వాడు నోరులేనివాడు he is a dumb creature, a mere fool. తప్పులేని faultless. దారిలేని అడవి a pathless forest. విలువలేనిమాణిక్యము a priceless gem. లేనిపోనివారు nonsense, a fool's errand. లేనిపోనిసౌఖ్యములు vain deluding joys. లేనిమాటలు slanders, falsehoods. లేనిపోనిసాకు a false pretence. పోనులేని పోరుపుట్టి నిష్ఠూర్యము a dispute arose without cause. "అదియునుగాక రాజ్యమును మునుపు భూతంబు సోకినప్పు డెట్టికుమదుకుము లేనిపోనుగ నులేనిమాటగఁ తనము, లేనిచెప్పడు గొంతర్థమునకలదు." K. P. v. 248. లేనివారు the absent; the poor. లేమి lēmi. n. Nullity, not being, absence, want, poverty. కొఱతము, దండము, దారిద్ర్యము. "జనకుడు లేమికింకరుడువిపాదము నొంది." M. X. ii. 17. ధనములేమి want of wealth. కలిమిలేములు gains and losses, riches and poverty. లేమిడి lemiḍi. n. Poverty, want. దారిద్ర్యము. లేరు lēru. v. 3rd. pers. plu. They are not. M. V. i. 342. వారు లేరు they are not here, not living. లేవు lēvu. v. (neuter.) They are not.

లేండ్లు lēnḍlu [Tel. plu. of లేడి] n. Antelopes. జింకలు.

లేక lēka. Conj. Or, else. ఇల్లు లేక తోట a house or a garden. లేక లేక lēka-lēka. adv. At last. లేకలేక వానికి ఒక కొడుకు పుట్టినాడు at last he had a son born to him. లేకపోవు lēka-pōvu. v. n. To be in want of. విహీనముగానుండు. వాడు అప్పుడు తెలివిలేక ఉండినాడు he was then out of his senses.

లేక lēka. [from Skt. లేఖ.] n. A letter of correspondence, జాబు. A row of thick-set trees, ఎడములేక మిక్కిలి దగ్గరగానుండు వృక్షముల వరుస. A multitude, సమూహము.

లేక lēka. [Tel. another form of లెంక.] n. A servant. భటుడు. లెంక.

లేకరి lēk-ari. [from Skt. లేఖ.] n. A writer, a penman. లేఖకుడు. లేఖరి, వ్రాతకాడు

లేకి lēki. [Tel.] n. Grain dropped down on the ground, రాలిన ధాన్యపుగింజలు. A worthless wretch, a vagabond. లే వు రు గొట్టు, పనికి మాలినవాడు, పనికిమాలినది, అప్రయోజకుడు. "లేకులలో కులకాకరఫులకు వాలిచాకని లేలు సందడించెదవు." BD. iv. 101. లేకిచేష్టలు silly doings. లేకిబడియ a rascal, a scoundrel. లేకిబ్రతుకు *lēki-bratuku*. n. A miserable life, a hand to mouth livelihood. లేకివాడు *lēki-vāḍu*. n. One who lives from hand to mouth. A useless person. అప్రయోజకుడు.

లేకుంటే. లేకపోతే or లేకపోయినా *lēk-unṭē*. adv. Or else, otherwise.

లేకునికి *lēk-uniki*. [Tel.] n. The state of being in want of. లేకపోవుట. అతడక్కడ లేకునికి for his being absent there. "ఒడలు ప్రాణములు లేకునికి భావించి." DRA. 331.

లేఖ *lēkha*. [Skt. from లిఖ్ to scratch.] n. A letter, an epistle. జాబు. A line, a row. రేఖ, పఙ్క్తి, వరుస. లేఖకుడు *lēkhakuḍu*. n. A scribe, writer, clerk. వ్రాతకాడు, లేకరి. లేఖనము *lēkhanamu*. n. Writing. వ్రాయడము, వ్రాత. లేఖనవృష్టి empty words, mere rigmarole. ఈ జాబు లో వట్టిలేఖనవృష్టేగాని వేరే యేమిన్ని లేదు this letter is a pack of nonsense and nothing else. లేఖనికుడు *lēkhanikuḍu*. n. One who gets a letter written for him by another and makes a mark on it to show that it is written by himself or under his orders. తనపరుతం పెట్టి ఒకరిచేత వ్రాయించువాడు. లేఖనీయము or లేఖ్యము *lēkhan-iyamu*. adj. Worthy or fit to be written, వ్రాయదగిన. లేఖభామిని *lēkha-bhāmini*. n. A goddess. దేవతాస్త్రీ. "లేఖభామినులరయు." Vasu. v. 4. లేఖహారకుడు *lēkha-hārakuḍu*. A letter carrier, a postman. లేఖర్షభుడు *lēkharshabhuḍu*. n. A title of Indra. వేల్పుదొర, ఇంద్రుడు. లేఖ్యము *lēkhyamu*. n. A business letter. వ్యవహారవిషయమైన వ్రాత. లేఖితము Same as లిఖితము. (q. v.)

లేఖిని or **లేఖని** *lēkhini*. n. A pen. వ్రాసే కలము. లేఖుడు *lēkhuḍu*. n. A god, a deity. దేవత.

లేగ *lēga*. [Tel. లేత+కాను౦పు.] n. A sucking calf. క్రొత్తగాపుట్టినదూడ. A calf, దూడ, వత్సము, మేతపట్టనిదూడ. A delicate chisel used by stone-cutters. సన్న ఉలి. ఆవులావులు పోట్లాడితే లేగలకాళ్లు విరుగుతవి or లేగలు మధ్యను నలిగి పోతవి when the cows quarrel the calves' legs are broken; i.e., when the great fall out the poor suffer. లేగటావు or లేగటిదూడావు *lēga-ṭ-āvu*. n. A cow with a young calf at foot. లేతదూడగల ఆవు.

లేచు *lētsu*. [Tel.] v. n. To rise, get up, arise. ఉత్థితమగు, పొటమరించు, లేవు. To rise from sleep, నిద్రలేచు, మేలుకొను. లేచివస్తిని I came away. కజ్జి లేచినది the itch appeared. లేచిపోవు *lēchi-pōvu*. v. n. To depart, go away. వెళ్లు. లేచిపో be gone! get off! వాడు లేచిపోయినాడు he walked off. లేవ *lēva*. Infinitive of లేచు, వానిని లేవనెత్తినాను. I lifted him up. లేవగొట్టించు *lēva-goṭṭintsu*. v. a. To expel. వానిని ఆ యింటిలోనుంచి లేవగొట్టించినాడు he got them turned out of the house. లేవనెత్తు or లేవదీయు *lēva-n-ettu*. v. a. To lift up, pull out; to turn out; to expel. బయటికీడ్చి విడిచిపెట్టు, వెళ్లగొట్టు. వాణ్ని లేవనెత్తు help the man up.

లేట *lēṭa*. [Tel.] n. A bough or branch. కొమ్మ, శాఖ. లేటమొగముపడు to be turned away, as the face, విముఖమగు.

లేడి or **లేటి** *lēḍi*. [Tel.] n. An antelope. కురంగము, జింక. "ఇట్లు కెవ్వాడి యలసికాచిన మృగంబు నా యరకొ చేయుటగాని నేమాయనుటు కనకపుచుక్కతోరాగాగుకంబు పరపలేటి బా కొమ్మసవికెక్కి పాటుకొనిన." R. v. 160. "కునికెలాగంటన లేన, గినుత్రినిలేదిని బాచి గతిగాసుదుడు, లెవకేనమ్ములసాలం, టిని ద్రళ్లగ

నెనెరవునవునపూదరయంబై." M. I. v. 56. **లేడికంటి** *lēḍi-kanṭi* n. A bright-eyed-girl, a girl or woman with gazelle-like eyes. మృగాక్షి. Plu. లేళ్లు.

లేత *lēta.* [Tel.] adj. Young, tender, soft. తరుణమైన, కోమలమైన. లేతయెండ soft sunshine. లేతవన్నె a light tint. Easy, సులభ. (సౌ. iii.). Small, little, straight, light, thin, soft, కొంచెము, చిన్న, తిన్నని, తేలికైన, పలుచని, మెత్తని, సన్నని. **లేతతనము** or **లేతరికము** *lēta-tanamu.* n. Infancy, youth, tenderness. తరుణత్వము.

లేడు *lēḍu.* [Tel.] n. A bear, ఎలుగుబంటి. **లేడుబంటి** or **లేడుబంటి** *lēḍu-banṭi.* n. A lie, బొంకు.

లేపనము *lēpanamu.* [Skt.] n. Smearing, plastering, anointing. అలకడము, పూయడము, చేరుకడము. **లేపించు** *lēpintsu.* v. a. To smear, చేరుము, పట్టించు. **లేపకుడు** *lēpakuḍu.* n. One who smears, సున్నములోనకువానిని పూయువాడు. **లేపము** *lēpamu.* n. Plastering, smearing, పూయడము, పూత. Plaster, mortar. సుధ, సున్నము. Food. భోజనము.

లేప్యము *lēpyamu.* n. A coating, పూత. adv. Fit to smear, పూయదగిన.

లేపు *lēpu.* [Tel. from లేచు.] v. a. To cause to rise, to raise, లేవజేయు. To rouse, awake, stir up. నిద్రలేపు to arouse from sleep. దుమ్మురేపు to raise dust. అడ్డముగా ఒకగోడ లేపినాడు he raised a wall across. వాణ్ని ఆ యింటిలోనుండి లేపు turn him out of the house. **లేపించు** *lēpintsu.* v. a. To remove, to turn out, వెళ్లగొట్టు, విస్తర్తిచేయు. వారిని ఆ యింటిలోనుంచి లేపించినాడు he turned them out of the house. **లేపు** n. A bed, పెన్తె, పరుపు. "చిల్కలకొల్లనందమా, పు॥ సెల పట్టెమంచమున చాయనగానుతివానుపైదురం, గిరబులికమాలలేపునసొగింకయనించెమనోభవమ్ము భూ." H. i. 73. A mane, జూలు

లేబరము *lēbaramu.* [Tel.] adj. Empty, శూన్యము.

లేమ *lēma.* [Tel.] n. A woman. స్త్రీ. adj. Tender, young., లేత.

లేమి, **లేమిడి** See under లే.

లేలిహానము or **లేలిహానము** *lēli-hānamu.* [Skt.] n. A snake. పాము.

లేవ *lēva.* [Tel.] n. A horse's face, గుర్రపు కిలాటము.

లేవడి *levaḍi.* [Tel. from లే (q. v.)] n. Want, లేమి. Poverty, దారిద్ర్యము. adj. Poor, దరిద్రము. Low, base, vile, mean. నీచమైన, అల్పమైన. "యుగమెంత లేవడి." A. iv. 285. టీ॥ యుగమెంతలేవడి, స్త్రీయెంతోనీచము, అనగా అల్పమైపోవునని భావము. "కులములేవడిర్తైన పుట్టలేదా విలువజెప్పగరానివజ్రంబులులతాంగి." Garuḍāch. 66.

లేవిడి *lēviḍi.* [H.] n. Disgrace. లేవిడికొట్టు to disgrace openly by crying Fie!

లేశము *lēśamu.* [Skt.] n. Littleness, కొంచెపుదనము. A little, a small portion; a particle, atom. adj. Very little. కొంచెము. లేశమైనాలేదు there is not even the least, not a whit, not a jot. **లేసు** *lēsu.* (from లేశము.) adj. Light, సులభ. Easy, సులభము.

లేహనము *lēhanamu.* [Skt.] n. Licking, నాకుట. **లేహము** *lēhamu.* n. Food, భోజనము. **లేహ్యము** *lēhyamu.* adj. That which can be licked, నాకదగిన. n. An electuary, a medicine. Nectar, ambrosia. నాకి భుజింపదగినమందు, నాకి భుజింపదగిన వ్యంజన విశేషము. కల్కద్రవ్యములుచేర్చి ముద్దగాచేసిన మందు. అమృతము.

లొ lo

లొంక *lonka.* [Tel.] n. A dell, a valley. కోన. "ఆ॥ గరబిపాలుడంటరుగొంటునన్పోటు, ‧ కట్టి

వాలుగలబట్టికొనుచు, లొంకలొచ్చెనాత్త గొంకక వాలుండు. కదనితివియబట్టి వెదకుమాద్రి..." G. viii. 45.

లొంగు or **లోగు** *longu.* [Tel.] v. n. To submit, to yield, to be humble. లోకువ. తగ్గు. To withdraw, retreat. వెనుదీయు. **లొంగినంత** *longin-anta.* adj. As much as possible, or practicable. సాధ్యమైనంత. రెండుఏర్లతోను లొంగినంతభూమి దున్నినాడు he tilled as much land as could be done with two ploughs.

లొండు *londu.* [Tel.] n. A pond, tank. జలాశయవిశేషము.

లొంప *lompa.* [Tel.] n. A small house. కొంప.

లొగ్గు or **లొంగు** *loggu.* [Tel.] v. n. To submit, to yield, to be humble. లోబడు. **లొగ్గడి** *loggadi.* n. Confusion, perplexity, కలవరము, క్షోభము. **లొగ్గడిల్లు** or **లొగ్గడిలు** *loggadillu.* v. n. To be confounded or perplexed, క్షోభమునుపొందు, కలవరుదుపడు. క్షోభించు. **లొగ్గడిలజేయు** *logga-dila-jēyu.* v. a. To subdue, make one yield. లోబడునట్లుచేయు. "లోపాపుపెం డొట్లలో లొగ్గడిలజేసి." Pal. 446.

లొచ్చు or **లొజ్జు** *lotstsu.* [Tel.] adj. Inferior, less, deficient. తక్కువ. "మ॥ ఇ. చెలం రెల్లగా మనలచ్చానతికిలొచ్చె నుమ్మ రమ్య కృతిగా." Chamatk. Manj. ii. 9. "ధాత్రిగల పార్థివులెల్లను లొచ్చునిసికా." Chatu. i. 52. line 10. ఎక్కినవానికి ఏనుగులొజ్జు an elephant is nothing when you are upon it.

లొట Same as లొట్ట. (q. v) **లొటకజిట్ట** Same as లొట్టకన్నుజిట్ట. (q. v.)

లొటలొట *lota-lota.* [Tel.] adv. Sounding like a pot when struck. Quickly. చటచట. "ఇటునటునగనానిలోనికి లొటలొటజనిమించ మెక్కి-లొలతఃబిత్తట్టమునగూర్చుండిన" Jagannad. iii. 78. **లొటలొటమను** *lota-lotam-anu.* v. n. To rattle. To dangle about, to be loose, లొటలొటయనుచు ఊగులాడు, పదు లైయుండు.

లొటసచ్చి *lota-sachchi.* [Tel.] n. Carbonate of Soda. (Watts).

లొటారము *lotāramu.* [Tel.] n. A hole, బొక్క, బిలము. adj. Empty, pithless. నిస్సారమైన. "ఈలోకసుఖములు శైలబటా రములోఃలొటారంబు, లో తె రం గి." Rama Satva Rajam. iii. 5. శైలబటారంబులోన లొటారంబు big without, empty within.

లొటిపిట or **లొట్టిపిట్ట** *lotipita.* [Tel. లొట్టి + పిట్ట. Lit: a hollow-eyed object.] n. A camel ఒంటె. **లొటిపిటఅల్లి** *lotipita-alli.* n. A species of rushes, *Scirpus articulatus.* Rox i. 214.

లొటుక్కు *lotukku.* [Tel.] adv. Suddenly, చిడీలున.

లొట్ట *lotta.* [Tel.] n. A smack or cluck with the tongue. Hollowness of the eyes or cheeks. Low ground, a pit. పల్లము. ఆముదపులొట్ట the dried stem of the castor oil plant. adj. Sunken, hollow. Dried up, wasted away (as an eye). అణగియుం టగానుండే. "మిట్టపండ్లును పెనులొట్టకన్న వయును." Jagannad. i. 54. **లొట్టకన్నుజిట్ట** *lotta-kannu-jitta.* n. The bird called *Prinia socialis.* See జిట్ట **లొట్టపోవు** *lotta-pōvu.* v. n. To be sunken, అణగు. To be injured. వానికన్ను లొట్టపోయినది his eye is injured. చావుతప్పి కన్ను లొట్టపోయినది (proverb) he escaped death but his eye is injured. **లొట్టవేయు** *lotta-vēyu.* v. n. To click or smack the tongue against the palate. దేనినైనను తిని నాలుకతో చప్పుడుచేయు. **లొటతాటకత్తె** *lota-tāta-katte.* n. A cunning wench, a deceitful woman. మాయలమారి. "వెదరిపోలాచెరో నేసాలుపన్ని లోకంబులోలేని లొటతాటకత్తె." HD. 1901.

లొట్టి *lotti.* [Tel.] n. The small earthen pot used in drawing toddy from the tree. చెట్టునకల్లుకొలిచేకుండ. "చెలమచ్చుబాన్పనెదలా దానవను బట్టౌకావంబుగానేక, కల్లు మాకేముప లంబు పామధుజమందుం గానికిర్వంకలక, కలు లొట్లాందెడు కల్లనిచ్చిన పిరుందం గొమ్మకాల్బల దముక, కలకొరాముడిగుడ్డయుం దనర్త్రాతు కాలమంజెప్పడుక." Chenu. v. 202. లొట్టి మనిషి a drunkard, తాగుబోతు. లొట్టి పుండు *lotti-pundu.* n. A hollow sore, an ulcer, a sinus.

లొట్టిపిట్ట, లొట్టిపిటు, లొట్టియ or లొట్టియగు *lotti-pitta.* [Tel.] n. A camel. ఉష్ట్రము. See లొటిపిట.

లొడపెట్టు *loda-pettu.* [Tel.] v. a. To stir up, (as a liquid), to rummage. చెయివేసి కందరగోళముచేయు, ద్రవద్రవ్యమును చేతితో కలియబెట్టు.

లొడలొడ or లొడబిడ *loda-loda.* [Tel. anuk.] adj. Loose, వదులైన. adv. Confusedly. తారుమారుగా. Quickly, త్వరగా. లొడలొడ మని నెత్తురుకారెను the blood flowed rapidly. ఆ చొక్కాయచేతిలో చెయిదూరిస్తే లొడలొడమని యున్నది the sleeve very loose.

లొడిత, లొడితిని or లొడుత *lodita* [Tel.] n. The span from the thumb to the fore finger ప్రాదేశము. లొడితెడు *lodit-edu.* adj. Span-long. జెత్తెడు.

లొడుకు or లొడుగు *loduku.* [Tel.] adj. Lean, fallen in, miserable. చిక్కిమాసిన. "బడుగువ్విజాలుకూడి లొడుకుమంత్రములుజదివి ఎడుగుజేసెడనువివరుకొందురు కడుపుదావునకై కావుమన్నట్లుదయా." Vema. 886. n. A kind of bell tied to the neck of a cow, ఆవు మెడను కట్టెడు ఘంటావిశేషము.

లొడ్డ Same as రొడ్డ. (q. v.)

లొడ్డు Same as రొడ్డు. (q. v.) లొడ్డుపులుసు or రొడ్డుపులుసు *loddu-pulusu.* [Tel.] adj. Sharply acid. చెడుపులుపు.

లొత్త *lotta.* [Tel. another form of లొట్ట.] n. Low ground, a pit, పల్లము.

లొద్ద *lodda.* [Tel.] n. A lump. ముద్ద. A heap, పోగు, రాశి. "అమృతంపుముద్ద తియ్యం బులొద్ద." Navanad. 131.

లొద్ది *loddi.* [Tel.] n. A hollow in the ground, a gully, a ravine between hills. కొండలసందునుండే లోయ.

లొద్దుగు or లొద్దిచెట్టు *loddugu.* [from Skt. లోధ్రము.] n. A tree called *Symplocos racemosa*, the bark of which is used in dyeing. గాలవవృక్షము, చిల్లివృక్షము.

లొల్ల *lolla.* [Tel.] n. A drag, a sort of barrow or rake drawn by oxen. పొలము మిట్టపల్లములులేకుండా సరిచేసెబల్ల.

లొల్లి *lolli.* [Tel.] adj. Thick, కరదైన. Heavy, ఘనమైన.

లొళ్లని *lollani.* [Tel. (anuk.)] adv. Fiercely, as the bark of a dog. లొళ్లని కరిచబోయినది the dog rushed on him barking fiercely.

లో lō

లో *lō.* [Tel.] prep. In, within, inside of, amongst, among, of. దారిలో on the road. ఇంటిలో or ఇంట్లో in the house. వచ్చినంతలో on his coming. అంతలో or ఇంతలో in the meantime. The word must be translated to suit the verb with which it is used. Thus, బిళ్లను మెడలో వేసు కొన్నాడు he wore the badge over his shoulder. తలలో పాగా చుట్టుకొన్నాడు he rolled the turban round his head. అత్తలోనుండి విభాగము కాలేదు she is not separated from her mother-in-law's family. ఇంతరాత్రిలో so late at night. తమలోతాము మాటాడుకోలేదు they did not speak to each other. వేలిలోనుండే ఉంగరము the ring on his finger. బిడ్డ నాపక్కలో పండుకొని ఉండినది the child lay down at my side. మాలో అందరు all of us. వాడు అందరిలో మంచివాడు he is the best of them all. (See లోను and లోని.) పనిలో మాట్లాడుట to talk during work, or while at work. చెట్టులో బంక కారుతున్నది gum flows from the tree. అతడు నాచేతిలో కోసినాడు he inflicted a wound on my hand. లో *lō*. adj. Inner, internal, inside. Inferior, or subordinate. లోగది an inner room. లోకాపు a sub-renter or under farmer. లోచెయ్యి the inner hand, i. e., the palm of the hand. లోగొను to take inside, to receive, to contain within itself, లోపల నడుచుకొను. లోమనుష్యుడు a reserved or self-contained man. లోగా *lō-gā*. adv. Within, inside, meanwhile, in the course of, లోపల. పదిదినములకులోగా within ten days. ఈలోగా meantime. ఇది వానికి చేరే లోగా before this reaches him. యాభైయేండ్లకులోగా before he was fifty years old.

లోకము *lōkamu*. [Skt.] n. A world, a division of the universe as heaven, earth, and hell. భువనము. The human race, mankind, జనము. Heaven; (metaphorically) a palace. ఇంద్రలోకము. "ప్రాణిలోకంబు బాధలబరచునపుడు." Swa. iii. 58. దానికి బిడ్డలమీదనే లోకము she gives herself entirely to her children, or her children are all the world to her. లోకత్రయము the universe, lit. the three worlds. లోకాభిరామముగా మాట్లాడుచుండగా while they were talking on various matters. లోకప్రవాదము a common saying, current report, town talk, వదంతి. లోకబాంధవుడు *lōka-bāndhavuḍu*. n. The universal friend i. e, the sun, సూర్యుడు. లోకమాత *loka-māta*. n. An epithet of Lakshmi. లోకాలోకము *lōkā-lōkamu*. n. A mountainous belt bounding the world. చక్రవాళపర్వతము. లోకారాధ్యుడు *lōk-ārādhyuḍu*. n. The universally adored, i. e., God, the Lord. ఈశ్వరుడు. లోకులు *lōkulu*. n. plu. People, folk, the community, జనులు. లోకులేమందురు what will people say? లోకేశుడు *lōk-ēśuḍu*. n. The lord of the world, i. e., Bramha, చతుర్ముఖుడు. A king, రాజు. లోకోక్తి *lōk-ōkti*. n. A proverb, సామెత. లోకోత్తరము *lōk-ōttaramu*. adj. Best in the world. శ్రేష్ఠమైన.

లోకువ *lōkuva*. [Tel.] adj. Subordinate, inferior, subject to, అధీనము. లోనైన. తక్కువైన. బీదవాడు బిచ్చగానికన్నా లోకువ the poor man is beneath even a beggar. నేను అందరికిన్నీ లోకువ I am every man's servant, I am a slave to every body. మాకు లోకువగానుండేవారు those who are subject to us. "కంతునకైన లోకువగాని వాడు ధరలోకలడె." T. iii. 84. వాండ్లను లోకువచేసుకొన్నాడు he got them into his power.

లోగడ *lōgaḍa*. [Tel. లోను+కడ.] n. The intervening space or time, అంతరాళము. The past time, గతకాలము. adv. Formerly, previously. పూర్వము. లోగటి or లోగడి *lōgaṭi*. adj. Former, previous, last. మునుపటి, ముందటి. లోగటిదినము the day before. లోగడి విక్రమనామసంవత్సరమందు in the year Vikrama before the last.

లోగడప *lō-gaḍapa*. [Tel.] n. The inner door, రెండో ద్వారబంధము.

లోగిలి or లోగిడి *logili*. [Tel. లోను+కిలి.] n. A house. బవంతి. The interior of a house, గృహాంతర్భాగము, plu. లోగిళ్లు. Gen. లోగిటి.

లోగు *lōgu*. [Tel.] v. n. To yield, submit, retire, retreat, go back. వెనుకదీయు, లొంగు, లోబడు, లోనగు, అడగు. To enter, చొచ్చు. "లోగవించుమక్కైవరాగతినంబుఁ దోయి వలువవెల్లబాదివాపు." Appa. ii. 36.

లోచనము *lōchanamu*. [Skt.] n. The eye. కన్ను.

లోచెయ్యి, లోచెయి, లోకెయ్యి or లోకెయి *lōcheyyi*. [Tel.] n. The palm of the hand. అరచెయ్యి. "పదనిశ లోచేత గెడచేత వ్రేయుచు." BD. iv. 196. వానిమంత్రి, శత్రువులకు లోచెయ్యిగానున్నాడు his minister is plotting with the enemy.

లోచు *lōtsu*. [Tel. from లోగు.] v. a. To cause to submit, లోగజేయుట.

లోచూపు *lō-tsūpu*. [Tel.] n. Inner vision, spiritual discernment, second sight, జ్ఞానదృష్టి.

లోటు *lōṭu*. [Tel.] n. A well, a pond. ఊటకయువితేనము.

లోటా *lōṭa*. [H.] n. A small drinking vessel ఒకవిధమైన చిన్న పానపాత్రము.

లోటు *lōṭu*. [Tel.] n. Loss, detriment, deficiency. తక్కువ, నష్టము, లోపము. లోటుపోవు *lōṭu-pōvu*. v. n. To become deficient, to prove a loss, నష్టియగు, లోపమగు.

లోడి or లోడీ *lōḍi*. [Tel.] n. Dumb-bells, ముద్గరు, సాముచేర్చువారు త్రిప్పెటిది. Plu. లోడీలు.

లోడు *lōḍu*. [Tel.] n. A cushion to lean on. ఒరుగుదిండు. v. a. To rake up as with a finger, వ్రేలులోనగువానితో కెల్లగించు.

లోతక్కువ *lō-takkuva*. [Tel.] n. The rest, residue, remainder, what is deficient or wanting. మిగత. adj. Remaining, as a balance. కడమ.

లోతు *lōtu*. [Tel.] n. Depth. నిమ్నము. ఈ బావిలో నీళ్లు నిండా లోతుకుపోయినవి the water in the well has sunk very low. పిల్లి నీళ్లకుపోతే బావి లోతుకుపోయినది when the jade goes to the well the water slinks away. Profundity. అది లోతైనమాట that is a deep saying. లోతిడి *lotiḍi*. (లోతు+ఇడి.) adj. Not deep, shallow, లోతులేని.

లోధ్రము *lōdhramu*. [Skt.] Same as లొద్దుగు. (q. v.)

లోను *lōnu*. [Tel.] n. The inside. లోపల, The heart or mind. మనస్సు. "లోనుబదిల పరచి లోనివిరోధుల గెలిచి చెట్టువారు తెలియు నివారు." Vēma 1836. The beginning, మొదలు. adj. Subject to, లోనైన. లోన *lōna*. Inside. adv. Within, inwardly, internally. "లోనదృఢంబులేని పైలోభిన నమ్మి" (Bhask. § 71.) లోనదృఢంబులేని internally weak. "అబ్రహ్మణ్యములోనగాము గాని." A vi. 158. ఈలోన in the meantime. లోని *lōni*. adj. Inner, inside, internal. లోపలి. అందులోని which is therein. లోనిసముద్రము far out at sea. లోనియిల్లు the inner room. లోనగు *lōn-agu*. v. n. To be gained, seduced, brought over. లోబడు. వారిమోసములకు లోనైనాడు he was snared by their guile. అన్యాయమునకు లోనైనాడు he acted unjustly.

లోపము *lōpamu* [Skt.] n. Deficiency; a defect, a flaw, fault; something wanting, a hiatus, omission, disappearance. A passage lost in a poem. Dropping a letter by grammatical rule. అగుపడక పోవడము, హీనత్వము, తక్కువ. పూర్వస్థితికి లోపములేకుండా వారికి జరుగుతున్నది they have not fallen away from their former state. లోపించు *lōpintsu*. v. n. To be dropped, elided, understood, as a syllable. అగుపడకపోవు.

లోపల *lōpala*. [Tel.] n. The inside. లోను, అంతరము. (affix) Among, in, within. మాయింటిలోపల ఉన్నాడు he is now in my house. నన్ను పదిలోపల పదకొండుగా చూచినారు they looked upon me as one of the mob. "తనశిష్యులలోపల నిన్ను దురాచారపరాక్రమాఢ్యుడని." M. X. i. 231. "ఏటిలోపల తీర్థంబులెల్లదిరిగి." N. vi. 162. ఏటిలోపల within one year. లోపలి *lopali*. adj. Inner, interior. లోని. లోపలిసౌధము

the inner chamber. "లోపలిసౌధంబులోన వర్తించుచు." Bhāg. X. లోలోపల lō-lōpala. adv. Secretly. రహస్యముగా, మర్మముగా.

లోప్త్రము lōptramu. [Skt.] n. Plunder, booty, stolen goods, దొంగిలించినసొమ్ము.

లోబడు lō-baḍu. [Tel. లోను+పడు.] v. n. To submit or yield, to consent. To be in one's power, to be subject to one. లొంగు, స్వాధీనమగు, సమ్మతించు, తగ్గు. "లోబడితినీకని బాసకునిల్చె నో యువశా." Swa. vi. 79. లోబరుచుకొను lō-barutsu-konu. v. a. To master, conquer, bring over. స్వాధీనపరచుకొను.

లోభము lōbhamu. [Skt.] n. Covetousness, cupidity, avarice, eagerness; miserliness, stinginess. పిసినితనము. లోభి lōbhi. n. A miser, a covetous or a greedy man. పిసినిగొట్టు, పిసినారిగొట్టు, ఆశాపాతకుడు. లోభిత్వము lōbhitvamu. n. Covetousness. పిసినారితనము.

లోమము Same as రోమము (q. v.)

లోమశము lōmaśamu. [Skt.] n. A polecat. బూతిపిల్లి, పూతిమార్జాలము.

లోయ lōya. [Tel.] n. A pit or hollow place in a hill, a deep crack or opening. పర్వతముమీద మిక్కిలి లోతుగానుండే బిలము. కొండపగులు. A valley.

లోల lōla. [Skt.] n. A crone, beldame, wretch. లోల or లోలము lōla. adj. Trembling, wavering moving, shaking, tremulous, unsteady. చంచలము, కదలునట్టి. Wishing very much, desiring greatly, greedy. ఆశగల, మిక్కిలి ఇచ్ఛగల. లోలత్వము or లౌల్యము lōlatvamu. n. Wish, desire. తృష్ణ, ఆశ. Shaking, moving, చాంచల్యము. "వికేళికేల జనియించుచు లౌల్యమింపుగా." A. iii. 68. టీ. లౌల్యము, తృష్ణ. "మెల్లన నడనందొడంగు ఘనలౌల్యపు చూపుల చూచు." H. ii. 113. లోలలోచన or లోలాక్షి lōla-lōchana. n. A girl with rolling eyes or a swimming glance, చంచలాక్షి. లోలుడు lōluḍu. n. One who loves, is devoted to, is enamoured of. చంచలుడు, ఆసక్తుడు. లోలుపము lōlupamu. adj. Covetous, cupidinous. ఆసక్తిగల.

లోవ lōva. [Tel.] n. A valley, లోయ. The eaves of a house, ఇంటిచూరు. A burrow in the ground, నేలబొరియ. "గాలిమంటచేనుప్రాకారంబులోపలి బోయిలుమట్టులు పొందు పడిన." H. i. 209.

లోవంక lō-vanka. [Tel. లో+వంక.] adj. Bent inwards. లోనికివంగిన. "లోవంకభుజంబులు, గొంకినికలుగావిరుసృట్లుమెప్పు." A. iv. 47.

లోవరి lōvari. [Tel. లోను+అరి.] n. An apartment. కొట్టికట్టు.

లోవి lōvi. [Tel.] n. A large brass water pot. నీళ్లుతెచ్చుకొనే యిత్తడిపాత్ర. A cooking vessel, వంటకుండ. A vessel, స్థాలి.

లోవు lōvu. [Tel.] v. n. Same as లోగు. (q. v.)

లోవయినము or లోవైనము lo-vayinamu. [Tel.] n. That which is past, the past. కడచినదినముయము. adj. Past, former, older.

లోష్టము lōshṭamu. [Skt.] n. A clod or lump of earth. మంటిగడ్డ. హేమలోష్టములందు సమభావముకలవాడు he who looks upon gold as dross. M. XII. vi. 76.

లోహము lōhamu. [Skt.] n. Metal in general, అష్టలోహసామాన్యము. Iron. ఇనుము. పంచలోహములు the five metals, viz., gold, silver, brass, bronze and iron. అష్టలోహములు include lead, tin and another metal called తీవరము. లోహకారకుడు lōha-kārakuḍu. n. A blacksmith. కమ్మరవాడు, కమ్మరి. లోహజిత్తు lōha-jittu. n. A diamond (as "surpassing all metals" in hardness.), వజ్రము.

లోహితము lōhitamu. [Skt.] n. Ruby colour, redness, రక్తవర్ణము. రుధిరము. Blood, నెత్తురు.

adj. Red. ఎర్రని. లోహితకము lôhitakamu. n. A ruby. కెంపు. లోహితాంగుడు or లోహితుడు lôhit-angudu. n. The planet Mars. అంగారకుడు. లోహితాశ్వుడు lôhit-âsvudu. n. Fire. అగ్నిహోత్రుడు. లౌహిత్యము lauhityamu. n. A blush, redness. ఎరుపు.

లౌ lau

లౌకికము laukikamu. [Skt. from లోకము.] (Vulgarly, లౌకికము) n. Business, worldly affairs. ఉద్యోగము, లౌకిక వ్యాపారము. అతనికి ఇప్పుడు లౌకికములేదు he is now unemployed. adj. Secular, mundane, worldly, human, what prevails amongst men or is familiar to mankind. ప్రపంచసంబంధమైన. M. XIII. v. 192. లౌకికుడు laukikuḍu. (vulgarly, లౌకికుడు) n. A layman, a secular Brahmin, a man of the world. ఉద్యోగస్థుడు. నేను వైదికుని లౌకికుడనుగాను I am not a man of the world.

లౌడి, లవుడి, లౌణి or లవుణి lauḍi. [Tel.] n. A club or mace, పరిఘము.

లౌల్యము See under లోలు.

లౌహము lauhamu. [Skt. from లోహము.] adj. Metallic, లోహవికారమైన.

వ va

వ va. [Tel.] The consonant V or W. As with h in English, v is Telugu is sometimes added in places where it does not occur, and dropped in places where it does occur by incorrect speakers or writers; e. g., ఒల్లు is often pronounced and written వల్లు and ఊరు, వూరు; while words like వెర్రి and వెచ్చేము are pronounced and written ఎర్రి and ఎచ్చేము. The initial V is also frequently changed into a vowel or a Y by vulgar speakers; e. g., ఏమ or యేమ for వేమ, ఎట్టి or యెట్టి for వెట్టి.

The initial P (in verse) is sometimes changed into V; thus వోయె (vōye) for పోయె (pōye) he went; వాపె (vāpe) for పాపె (pāpe) he removed.

Sometimes the initial V changes into B, as బలె for వలె 'like.' "దీపాంకురపఙ్క్తులం బలె." Bhanumat. iv. 142. This change is caused by the preceding sunna.

Sometimes in the second syllable G changes into V; as వగడము, వవడము.

In prosody వ stands for వగణము an iambic; more usually written లగము. And in poems వ॥ stands for వచనము prose.

వంక vanka. [Tel. from వంగు.] n. A side, quarter, direction, పక్క, దిక్కు. Crookedness, a bend. A pretence or pretext. వక్రత్వము, వంకర, వంపు. Fault, blame. నేరము. A rivulet or watercourse. వాగు. ఆలివంకవారు relations by the wife's side. కట్టెవంకపొయి తీర్చును fire settles the crookedness of the wood. తాను ఆడలేక మద్దెల మీద వంకపెట్టినాడు he cannot dance so he finds fault with the drum. నావంకచూడు look towards me. నెత్తురు వంకలుకట్టినది the blood flowed in streams. వారిమీద వంకపెట్టి వ్రాసినాడు he wrote laying the blame on them. నెలవంక a half moon. adj. Crooked. వక్రమైన. "పెడతటివంకనికరము." P. iii. 211. టీ॥ వక్రముగావేసుకొన్న జొట్టును. affix. By, through, వల్ల. "పంచనయిప్పుడీ కులువ వంకజనించెజనింపుమాకు." P. iii. 309. "క్రతువువంక గలుగునా మోక్షంబు." Vema. 952. వంకదారి a crooked way, వంకరదారి.

వంకము or వంకోము vankamu. n. A crooked stick used while threshing corn.

వంకర vankara. n. Crookedness, a bend or curve. Blame, a fault. వక్రత్వము, దోషము.

వంకర, వంకరటింకర or వంకరటొంకర vankara. adj. Crooked, distorted. వంకరైన. వంకరమాటలు crooked language, nonsense. వంకరపోవు to become crooked. వంకసన్న

మువు *vanka-sunnamulu*. n. plu. A sort of rice. వడ్లలోభేదము.

వంకాయ *van-kāya*. [Tel. వంక+కాయ.] n. The vegetable called a brinjal or egg plant. *Solanum melongena*. Rox. వార్తాకము. కర్పూరవంకాయ the plant called a love apple. గుజ్జువంకాయ a large sort of brinjal.

వంకి *vanki*. [Tel. from వంకు.] n. An arrow. బాణము. A dagger, బాకు. A sort of hook, కొక్కి. "తిమ్మతుపాకికొండలిరాకువంకి, కమ్మనిగిల్లు చెంగల్వ కేడెయము, బాణపూబాకు గొజ్జగిపెద్దకత్తి." ND. i. 593. వంకీలు *vankius*. A certain musical instrument. వాద్యవిశేషము. A dagger. బాకు. "బూరలును భేరులు పోటు ధారలును కాహళవంకీలు కావికొమ్ములును శంఖ సమూహంబుల్ సన్నాయులెల్లన్." Pal. 257. వంకీ *vanki*. n. An armlet of a crooked shape, స్త్రీలు సందిటధరించే ఒకవిధమైన నగ. వంకె or వంకెయ *vanke*. n. A kind of grain, సస్యవిశేషము. A wooden hook or peg in the wall. మంటిగోడకుచేసిన చిలుక కొయ్య. పులిగోళ్లవంకెలు a certain kind of grain. తెల్లవంకెలు another kind of grain. H. iv. 159. వడ్లవంకెలు a fine species of rice.

వంగ *vanga*. [Tel.] n. The Brinjal or Egg plant, *Solanum melongena*. వార్తాకము. చిరివంగ a small species of this. వంగకాయలు or వంకాయలు brinjals, వార్తాకములు. "వంగకాయలుప్పొంగ తినంబులుట్టె." BD. ii. 807. Also, వంగపండు or వంగపండుగువ్వ the Indian Oriole. *Oriolus kundoo*. కొండవంగపండు the Black-headed Oriole. *Oriolus melanocephalus*. (F. B. I.) "ఎల్లెడపాడిపిట్ట వంగపండుభరతముకోకిల." H. iii 14. వంగరేడు కూర *vanga-rēḍu-kūra*. n. A plant growing on sand hills near the sea. *Crithmus indicus*. Rox. ii. 509.

వంగము *vangamu*. [Skt.] n. Lead, tin. సత్తు, తగరము. వంగభస్మము the calx or ashes of lead. వంగదేశము *vanga-ḍēsamu*. n. The ancient name of Bengal.

వంగసము or వంగడము *vangasamu*. [Skt. from వంశము.] n. A family, race, lineage. వంశము, కులము. "భూమిలో మునుసూర్యచంద్రులవారి వంగడములై పెంపొందువారలు." R. i. 111.

వంగు *vangu*. [Tel.] v. n. To bend, bow, stoop. To become crooked. To become low or humble. వంగు, ఒరగు, నమ్రుడగు. ఒళ్లువంగిపనిచేయు to work hard. ఒళ్లువంగని వాడు one who does not choose to bend his back, a lazy man. వంగదీయు *vanga-diyu*. v. a. To bend, bow down. వంచు. వంగుడు *vanguḍu*. n. A crack, బీటిక. An excrescence, స్ఫోటము. వంగుళ్లు drippings of the eaves. వానవెలిసిన తర్వాత బొట్టుబొట్టుగా పడుచుండేనీళ్లు. "దప్పుల జల్లనిసోకు వంతకనుమసపడి, జల్లనీరూనిమ్మన జల్లుమెదిలి, గాలియెలుగొలుచేకొమ్మగదలిచల్ల. దల యెత్తకమున్న వంగుళ్లదడిపెదరుల." A. iv. 169. వంగులు *vangulu*. n. plu. The ribs or bends of a boat. పడవలోని అడ్డవాసములు.

వంచన *vanchana*. [Skt.] n. Cheating, fraud, craft. ఒకరిని దగాచేయుడము, మోసము, కపటము. ఆత్మవంచన self-deception, wronging oneself. వంచకత్వము *vanchakatvamu*. n. Cheating, fraud. మోసము. "తత్వమంత్రి యువంచకత్వంబునను." Vēma. 2057. వంచకము *vanchakamu*. adj. Cheating. మోసముచేసే. n. A fox. నక్క. వంచకుడు *vanchakuḍu*. n. A rogue, impostor. మోసగాడు. వంచించు *vanchintsu*. v. a. To cheat, defraud, trick, wrong. మోసముచేయు. వంచితము *vanchitamu*. adj. Tricked, deceived, wronged. మోసముచేయబడిన.

వంచె or వంచియ *vanche*. [Tel.] n. A sack, గోనె.

వంచె, వంచేము or **వంచి** *vantsa.* [Tel.] n. The ace, at dice, ఒకటి. A piece of land, place. పట్టు, ప్రదేశము. చేవుటివంచ a spot of salt land. రేగడవంచపొలము a bit of black cotton soil. గరుపువంచపొలము a stony sandy soil. రాతివంచను ఇసుకనేల. నాలువంచె four at dice. తీవంచె three at dice.

వంచాడించు or **వంచాడించు** *vantsādintsu.* [Tel.] v. n. To be frightened or alarmed. బెదరు.

వంచు *vantsu.* [Tel. from వంగు.] v. a. To bend, bow down; to make a thing crooked, to make one stoop; to humble, lower, reduce, వంగజేయు, వంగదీయు. తలవంచి hanging down the head. నీళ్లు వంచివేసినాడు he poured the water off. నావేలువంచేవాడు ఎవడు who can bend my finger? i. e., who can lay a finger upon me?

వంజరము or **వంజేరము** *vanjaramu.* [Tel.] n. The coal-fish, seer-fish or scomber, *Gadus carbonarius*, resembling a very fine haddock.

వంజులము or **వంజుళము** *vanjulamu.* [Skt.] n. A sort of bird with a remarkably sweet whistle. Also, the tree called *Jonesia asoca*: and another tree, called *Dalbergia ougeinensis.* పక్షివిశేషము, అశోకవృక్షము, తినిసెము, 'నెమ్మిచెట్టు, ప్రబ్బచెట్టు.

వంజెరగు *van-jeragu.* [Tel. వంక+చెరగు.] n. The end of a woman's garment. కొంగు.

వంజె *vandza.* [Tel.] n. A barren woman, a sterile cow. గొడ్డావు, గొడ్రాలు. "సీ॥ వంజలనైనను పలకేర్పడగ నాశధింకి జేపగజేసిపాలు గొందు." M. IV. i. 95. వంజెలు the cross pieces that support the ribs of an umbrella.

వంటె or **ఒంటె** Same as వంజరము (q. v.)

వంట *vanta.* [Tel. from వండు.] n. Cooking or dressing food, cookery. వండడము, పాకము. పిండివంటలు flour cakes, pastry. adj. Boiled, cooked. వండబడిన. పచనముచేయబడిన. వంటనూనె or వంటచేమురు oil used in cookery. వంటాముదము boiled castor oil, (opposed to the cold drawn oil.) వంటగుగ్గిలము boiled dammer. **వంటకత్తె** or **వంటలక్క** *vanta-katte.* n. A cook-woman. **వంటకము** *vantakamu.* n. Food. అన్నము. **వంటచెరుకు, వంటచెరకు. వంటకట్టెలు** or **వంటసరకు** *vanta-cheruku.* n. Fuel, firewood, ఇంధనసమూహము. **వంటయిల్లు, వంటసాల** or **వంటశాల** *vanta-y-illu.* n. A kitchen, cookroom. మహానసము. "కుందేళ్లవంటయిల్ చొచ్చినశశముగరుణజేయకగూరిగా వండదగునె." (HD. i. 1199) Is it fair to cook a rabbit that has taken refuge in a kitchen? వంటుప్పు salt extracted by boiling sea-water. **వంటరాయి** *vanta-rāyi.* n. An artificial ruby. కురువిందము. **వంటరి** *vant-ari.* n. A cook, one who knows how to cook. **వంటలు** *vantalu.* n. plu. Dried cow dung, which is used as fuel. పిడకలు. **వంటవాడు, వంటలవాడు** or **వంటకాడు** *vanta-vādu.* n. A cook. పాచకుడు.

వంటి *vanti.* [Tel. from వలె.] adj. Like, similar to. నావంటి like me. బొగ్గువంటి like charcoal. నీవంటి like thee. అటువంటి, ఇటువంటి such.

వంటు *vantu.* [Tel.] n. Convenience, propriety, అనుకూల్యము, అనువు. "వంటుదప్పినతేళ వంటకము విషంబు కంటచూడ గానొకంటగించు." Vema.

వంతెము or **వంటేరుము** *vantemu.* [Tel.] n. A district or taluq. తాలూకా.

వండ *vanda.* n. Danger, ఆపద. Silt, బురద. [Skt.] n. An unchaste woman, రంకులాడు. adj. Stubborn, మొండి. **వండలి** or **వండు** *vandali.* n. Alluvial soil: mud, mire; the muddy deposit of a flood or river. ఎండినబురద. పట్టిపోయినరేగు మొండైనవాటిలోకేసినమట్టి. "నా కి రా ను లు పిండలి

వండులరొమ్ము." Zaco. iv. 52. వండనీళ్లు muddy water.

వండు *vaṇḍu*. [Tel.] v. a. To cook, boil, (food, oil, &c.); distil (spirits); to fuse iron. వంటచేయు, పక్వముచేయు. ఒంటివంట సారాయి spirits only once distilled. **వండించు** *vaṇḍiñtsu*. v. To have food cooked. పచనముచేయించు.

వండుసున్నము *vaṇḍu-sunnamu*. [Tel.] n. Fine lime plaster.

వండ్ర or **వండర** *vaṇḍra*. [Tel.] n. A favourable lease or rent. వండ్రభూమి land unfit for cultivation.

వంత *vanta*. [Tel.] n. Vexation, regret. మనోదుఃఖరూపమైనవిచారము. Sorrow, grief, సంతాపము. Pain, బాధ. A cry, ఏడ్పు. "దవి బానిగాని లెడుపట్టినక్రైవడి వంతనొందె వ్రతులుపతి." R. v. 168. "నావంతయేమిచెప్పదు నావంత యేసుఖములేదు." Bmj. iii. 33. A rivulet. ఏరు, కుల్య, చిన్నకాలువ. "ఎమపోతునప్పుడుకమ్మరి తనయింటికిరాకయున్న తత్పురినిండ్లలో వనముల వంతలడొంకల నసుగోనుచుంగా వచ్చివచ్చికనియె చ్చోటన్." H. v 79. "వంతలక్రంతల చెట్ల గట్లనావార మతింజరించి." P. i. 496.

వంతు *vantu*. [Tel.] n. A share, portion, part. A turn, time, or bout by rotation. పాలు, భాగము, వరుస. Likeness, సామ్యము. "నెలకొక్కరుండుగా, నిలువుడుటంచుబంచెవిధి నీరజమిత్రులవంతుదీరగన్." T. ii. 12. 172. "శ్రాంతిగాడుజావకోంపదనుకబోవు వంతుకింతేగా నివకవలేదు. Vema. Rivalry, పోటి.

వంతుడు *vantuḍu* [Skt.] Affix meaning Possessed of, gifted with, having, possessing. ధైర్యవంతుడు a brave man. విద్యావంతుడు a learned man. ధైర్యవంతుడు a courageous man.

వంతెన *vantena*. [Tel.] n. A bridge.

వంద *vanda*. [Tel.] n. A hundred, శతసంఖ్య, నూరు.

వందనము *vandanamu*. [Skt.] n. An obeisance, salutation, అభివాదనము, నమస్కారము. Praise, స్తుతి. Thanks. **వందనమిడు** or **వందనముచేయు** *vandanam-iḍu*. v. n. To honour, salute, bow to. **వందనమాల** *vandana-māla*. n. A garland hung over a gate or carved in stone trellis. ద్వారమందు కట్టినతోరణము. **వందారువు** or **వందారుడు** *vandāruvu*. n. One who salutes or pays homage. నమస్కారము చేయువాడు. **వంది** *vandi*. n. A herald, bard, panegyrist. ప్రాతఃకాలమందు రాజులను మేలుకొలిపేవాడు, స్తుతిచేసి జీవించువాడు, బట్టువాడు. **వందించు** *vandiñtsu*. v. a. To praise, స్తుతించు. **వందితుడు** *vandituḍu*. n. One who is praised or saluted, స్తుతింపబడినవాడు, నమస్కరింపబడినవాడు. **వంద్యము** *vandyamu*. adj. Honourable, venerable, worthy of regard Lauded or laudable. కొనియాడదగిన, పూజ్యమైన. "సకలలోకైకవంద్యంబు సకలసుజన, చిత్తరంజనకారణంబుత్తమంబు." Vish. i. 31. **వంద్యుడు** *vandyuḍu*. n. One who is worthy to be praised. పూజ్యుడు. లోకవంద్యుడు fit to be praised or extolled by the whole world.

వందర *vandara*. [Tel.] n. A piece, fragment, bit. తునక. Also, a favourable lease or rent. వందరభూమి land unfit for cultivation. **వందరలాడు** *vandaral-āḍu*. v. n. To mangle. ఛిన్నాభిన్నముచేయు. To cut, sever, ఖండించు. "కర యుతుల కులిశనికాతనఖా, వలభిన్నుండు వ్రచ్చివందరలాడెన్." M. I. ii. 100.

వందిలి *vandili* [Tel.] n. Calamity, embarrassment.

వందు *vandu*. [Tel.] v. n. To grieve, sorrow, be afflicted. దుఃఖపడు, విచారపడు, సంతాపించు. "యుక్తకార్యయత్నము ఫలియించుసుక్కి రుడదక్కగజేయగవందనేటికిన్." BRK. 715. **వందురు** *vanduru*. v. n. To grieve, to be vexed or sorrowful. దుఃఖపడు, విచారపడు. "వారలుగట్టి కూరలకనంబుగ నుగ్రవనంబులోని పద్మాకరమునొందిఁయందురినఫల్గుడు నుజ్వలరాజ్యవైభ వోదారులమైకినుంగొని." M. III. v. 373. "చ॥ వనమునకేగి వందురినవారనివారలమీరవక్కు మున్, జెనకదలంతురు." M. III. v. 386.

వందె or వందిరు *vande.* [Tel.] n. A kind of grass, తృణవిశేషము.

వండొందు *randondu.* [Tel.] n. A kind of fish.

వంద్యుడు See under వందనము.

వంధ్య *randhya.* [Skt.] n. A childless woman. గొడ్రాలు. A barren cow. గొడ్డావు. వంధ్యము *vandhyamu.* adj. Barren, as a tree. కాయని (చెట్టులోనగునది).

వంపు *campu.* [Tel. from వంగు.] n. Crookedness; a bend, curve. వక్రత్వము, వంకర. తలవంపులు hanging the head; shame, disgrace. adj. Bent, crooked, వంగిన, వంకరైన.

వంబతాడు *camba-tadu.* [Tel.] n. A certain rope belonging to a waterlift. కపిలకువేసే ఒక తాడు.

వంశము *vamsamu.* [Skt.] n. A race, line, lineage, family, stock, extraction; a dynasty. తండ్రి తాతమొదలైనవారి పరంపర. A bamboo. వెదురు. A multitude, సమూహము. వంశస్థుడు *vamsa-sthudu.* n. A man belonging to a family. కులస్థుడు. వంశానుచరితము *vams-anu-charitamu.* n. A pedigree, genealogy, a chronicle, or genealogical history. వంశచరిత్ర. వంశావళి *vams-avali.* n. Genealogy. వంశక్రమము. వంశవృక్షము *vamsa-vrikshamu.* n. A genealogical tree.

వకవకలు or వకావకలు *vaka-vakalu.* [Tel.] n. plu. Splashings, చెదరుటలు. Pieces, fragments, bits, ఖండలు.

వకాలతు *vakalatu.* [H.] n. Agency, attorneyship, power of attorney. వకీలు *vakilu.* n. An attorney or agent. A vakil or pleader in a law court.

వకుళము *vakulamu.* [Skt.] n. The plant termed *Mimusops elengi.* పొగడచెట్టు.

వక్క *vakka.* [Tel.] n. A bit, fragment, shiver or piece, as of glass, or areca nut. తునక, పోకచెక్క. వక్కలు areca nut bits or fragments. తెల్లవక్కవడ్లు a kind of rice, ఒకవిధమైనవడ్లు.

వక్కణ or వక్కాణ *vakkana.* [from Skt. వచ్ to speak.] n. The heading of a letter, &c. Compliments written at the head of a letter, జాబు మొదలైనవాటికి మొదట వ్రాసే వాడుక మాటలు. "అని యిటు వ్రాయు పద్యమునయందుగ వ్రాసినజాబువక్కణల్ విని తన మంత్రిశేఖరుని." Bmj. iii. 256. Titles, బిరుదావళి, బిరుదాము. A commentary, వ్యాఖ్యానము. వక్కణించు Same as వక్కాణించు (q. v.)

వక్కరము *vakkaramu.* [from Skt. వక్రము.] n. Same as వంకర (q. v.) వక్కరాలు *vakkar-alu.* n. A jade, scold. An impostor. కుటిలస్త్రీ, వంచకురాలు. "పెనురక్కసివక్కరాండ్ల బిలిచి." R. vi. 171. వక్కరించు or వక్కరించు *vakkarintsu.* v. n. To err, go crookedly, to follow an irregular course, వంకరదోవలబోవు. To oppose, rebel, తిరుగబడు. "బుజ్జగింపవుచలం బొక్కించరేనివలదన్న మానవు వక్కరించెదవు." Charitra. ii. 1535.

వక్కాకు or వక్కలాకులు *vakk-aku.* [Tel. వక్క+ఆకు.] n. Betel nut, i. e., betel and nut. తాంబూలము, ఆకువక్క.

వక్కాణించు *vakka-nintsu.* [from Skt. వచ్ to speak.] v. a. To tell, narrate, describe. చెప్పు, వాక్రుచ్చు. "ధర్మశాస్త్రములువక్కాణింపగా జొచ్చినావానేకాక." N. ix. 309. To write a commentary on, to comment on, వ్యాఖ్యానముచెప్పు. వక్కాణము *vakkanamu.* n. News, సమాచారము. See వక్కణ.

వక్కి *vakki.* [Tel.] adj. Lean, fleshless. బక్కయైన, పలచని, కృశము. వక్కిపక్షి, వక్కికట్టె or వక్కివాడు *vakki-pakshi.* n. A starveling, బక్కవాడు. వక్కు vakku. v. n. To become lean. బక్కచిక్కు, కృశించు. "ము [illegible]." Vema. 816. వక్కు, వక్కుకొంగ or వక్కుపులుగు vakku. n. A heron, బకము.

వక్త vakta. [Skt. from వచ్ to speak.] n. One who speaks, మాట్లాడువాడు. A speaker, an orator. సభలయందు నిర్భయముగా మాట్లాడువాడు, వాచాలుడు. A learned man, పండితుడు. వక్తవ్యము vakta-vyamu. adj. Fit or proper to be spoken, or said. చెప్పదగిన, మాటాడదగిన. n. A word, speech, మాట. అవక్తవ్యము unspeakable, unutterable, not to be mentioned.

వక్త్రము vaktramu. [Skt.] n. The mouth, face, countenance, ముఖము, మోము.

వక్రము vakramu. [Skt.] adj. Crooked, awry, bent, curved, twisted. వంకరైన. Cruel, perverse, wicked. క్రూరమైన. "గ్రహము [illegible]." (Vish. viii. 267) all the planets moved in irregular courses. వక్రతమములు vakra-tamamulu. n. Lit. 'Most crooked' ones, In Telugu grammar, this term denotes the diphthongs ఐ and ఔ. వక్రత్వము vakratvamu. n. Crookedness. వంకరతనము. Perversity, cruelty. వక్రములు vakramulu. n. plu. In Telugu grammar this term denotes the vowels ఎ, ఏ, and ఒ, ఓ. వక్రించు vakrintsu. v. n. To err, or go in an irregular course, as planets. To turn, మరలు, మరలుట. వక్రిమ or వక్రిమము vakrima. n. Crookedness, కుటిలత. "[illegible]." H. ii. 109. వక్రోక్తి vakr-ôkti. n. Equivoque, a hint, insinuation, evasion, అలంకారశ్లేషము.

వక్షము or వక్షస్సు vakshamu. [Skt.] n. The chest. రొమ్ము. వక్షోజము or వక్షోరుహము vakshô-jamu. n. A woman's breast. స్తనము.

వక్ష్యమాణము vakshya-mânamu. [Skt.] adj. That which is about to be said, చెప్పబోయెడి.

వగ vaga. [Tel.] Grief, vexation, melancholy, regret, remorse. దుఃఖము, సంతాపము, విచారము, శోకము. Intention, ఆలోచన. Mode, way, manner, విధము, రీతి, తోవ, గతి. Amorous action, శృంగారచేష్ట, విలాసము. మాటికివగలేనివాడు he who has no means of living. "[illegible]." R. v. 87. "[illegible]." M. XI. i. 22. adj. Beautiful, handsome. "[illegible]." T. ii. 98. వగకత్తె or వగలాడి vaga-katte. n. A coquette, belle. శృంగారచేష్టలుగలస్త్రీ, విలాసవతి. A rogue, a deceiver, మాయలాడి. వగకాడు or వగలాడు vaga-kâḍu. n. A fop, a beau, a gallant. వన్నెకాడు, విటకాడు, సొగసుకాడు, విలాసవంతుడు. వగచు vagatsu. v. n. To grieve, sorrow. దుఃఖించు, శోకించు. To regret, repent, పశ్చాత్తాపపడు. To cry, ఏడ్చు. v. a. To consider, think, విచారించు, ఆలోచించు. "[illegible]." R. v. 274. వగతెగు vaga-tegu. v. n. To be settled or decided. తీరు, పరిష్కారమగు, నిశ్చయమగు. వగతెంచు vaga-dentsu. v. a. To decide, settle, determine. వగతెగునట్లుచేయు. తీర్చు, పరిష్కారముచేయు. "[illegible]." S. iii. 509. వగవ or వగవగ vagava. adv. Grievingly, sorrowfully. "[illegible]." M. I. i. 130. వగపు vagapu.

n. Grief. మనోదుఃఖ రూపమైనవికారము, శోకము.

వగరు, వగరము, వగరుపు or **వగర్పు** *vagaru.* [Tel.] n. Hard breathing, panting. శ్వాసరోగము. **వగరుచు** or **వగర్చు** *vagarutsu.* v. n. To breathe hard, to pant. రొప్పు.

వగరు or **ఒగరు** *vagaru.* [Tel.] n. and adj. Astringent.

వగైరా *vagaira.* [H.] adj. Etcetera, and so forth. ఇత్యాది. రామయ్యవగైరాలు Ramayya and others.

వగ్గు or **వఙ్గు** *vaggu.* [Tel.] adj. Lean, skinny, decrepit. ముదిమిచేత ఎండిపరుసుగా నుండే, బక్కచిక్కిన. "వగ్గుకోతికిసీవమువచ్చిన కీతి." HD. iii. 342. "కపులుమునవగ్గు గపవిక టముఁబడగా." Swa. iv. 123. ముసలివగ్గు a decrepit old man.

వచనము *vachanamu.* [Skt. from వచ్ to speak.] n. Speech, speaking. A word, మాట. A sentence. A dictum, an aphorism, a rule. ధర్మశాస్త్రములోని ప్రమాణ వాక్యము. Prose (as distinguished from metre) ఛందోబద్ధము కాకుండా మాటలుగా వ్రాసినది, గద్య. Number, in the grammatical sense, as ఏకవచనము the singular number, ద్వివచనము dual, and బహువచనము plural. వ్యాకరణములో ఏకవచనాదులు. **వచస్సు** *vachassu.* n. Speech, speaking. మాట. **వచించు** or **వచియించు** *vachintsu.* v. a. To say, speak, tell, relate. పలుకు.

వచ్చ *vatstsa.* [Tel.] n. A canker worm or blight which destroys trees. చెట్లకు పట్టి బొత్తిగా నాశముచేసే ఒకవిధమైన చీడ.

వచ్చు *vatstsu.* [Tel.] v. n. To come, arrive. To happen, occur, take place. చేరు, సంభవించు, కాడు, ప్రాప్తమగు. రేపువత్తురు they will come to-morrow. నిన్నవచ్చితిమి we arrived yesterday. నాతోకూడావచ్చినాడు he accompanied me. మనసువచ్చినన్ని కాకితాలు పుచ్చుకొన్నాడు he took as many papers as he pleased. నీ మనసువచ్చినట్టుచెయ్యి do as you please. This verb is used (like Come in all languages), in numerous senses. వచ్చేతేప next time. వచ్చేనెలలో in the next month. వచ్చేకీడుగండ్లు రాకమానవు the evil that must happen will happen. As an auxiliary, it is added to the present participle of any verb to denote long habit or continuance, as చదువుచువచ్చినాడు he continued to read. అట్లుచేయుచువచ్చినాను I have been doing so all along. అక్కడికి పోవుచువచ్చినాడు he used to go there. It is also joined to the past participle of the verb వలయు. ఇట్లు చేయవలసివచ్చినది it became necessary to do so. It is added to the infinitive in A. ఇది మాకు తెలియవచ్చినది it came to our knowledge. నాకు బుద్ధిచెప్పవచ్చినాడు he went so far as to advise me. వచ్చు or వచ్చును (the third person singular aorist of వచ్చు) is used with the infinitive as an auxiliary signifying permission, possibility or probability. నీవు అక్కడికి పోవచ్చును you may go there. మేము రావచ్చునా? may we come? అట్లు కావచ్చును it may be so perhaps. రాదు (the neg. aor. 3rd person singular) means must not or cannot. నీవు అక్కడికి పోరాదు you must not go there. నేను చేయరాదు I cannot do it. అట్లా చెప్పరాదా can you not say so? Added to a dative, వచ్చు is used to mean To be got, gained, acquired, to be available. ఆ భాష వానికి వచ్చినది he has learned the language, he knows that tongue. ఈ బియ్యము నెల దినాలకు వచ్చినవి this rice lasted for one month. వానికేమివచ్చినది what happened to him? ఇయ్య మనసువచ్చినది he was inclined to give it. వానికి బుద్ధివచ్చినది he has learnt sense. వానికి మీసాలువచ్చినవి his whiskers have grown. దానికి

మళ్లీ కండ్లువచ్చినవి she has recovered her sight. ఆ బిడ్డకు పళ్లువచ్చినవి the child has cut its teeth. ఇక్కడ సకారమునకు లోపమువచ్చినది there is here an elision of the letter S. వానికి అన్నానికి లోపము వచ్చినది he is even in want of food. వానికి ఒంటికివచ్చినది he fell sick. ఇది పనికివచ్చును this will do, this will be useful. ప్రాణమునకువచ్చే perilous, hazardous. ఇది నీ ప్రాణమునకువచ్చును this will put your life in peril. నోటికివచ్చినట్టు వారిని తిట్టినాడు he gave them all the abuse he could think of. అతనిపేరు నాకు రాలేదు I cannot recollect his name. ఆ పాఠము వానికి రాలేదు he does not know the lesson. **వచ్చుబడి** *vatstsu-badi*. n. Income. ఆయతి. రాబడి. వానికి నిండా వచ్చుబడి యున్నది he has a large income. **వచ్చేరాములు** *vatstsu-rāmulu*. (వచ్చుట+రాము.) n. Coming and not coming. వచ్చుటయును రామియును.

వజా *vaja*. [H. from Arabic.] n. Deduction, subtraction, మినహాయింపు.

వజీరు, వజీరుడు, వజ్జీరుడు or **వజ్రీరుడు** *vajīru*. [H.] n. A 'vizier' or minister. మంత్రి. A hero, శూరుడు. A commander. సేనాని. "నానా వజీరసేనామాన్యభేదములును." Vasu. (preface.) 24. టీ॥ వజీర, మ్లేచ్ఛప్రధానులయొక్క... "లావుగ నార్చుచుజా గలుగులాయవు తేజీవజీరు దంటశౌర్యా వనజారిపై బరప." T. v. 136. టీ॥ గలుగులాయవు తేజీవజీరు, చొక్కటు స్థానముగాగలిగిన రొంటు కవావటము కలిగినటువంటి విఘ్నేశ్వరుడు. "చిత్రుడుం జేకట్టి జేరుపడ్డ సేయ వచ్చుం డెడా." H. ii. 189. టీ॥ మన్మథుణ్ని లక్ష్యము చేయకుండా ఉండెను. Plu. వజీర్లు "సీ॥ ... త్రేయుమేలై వజీర్లువచ్చి సలాముచేసినిలువ." సా. i. "వనితామరుల్తైపురంటువింటి ... శ్రీదుహ హుండు" Satyabha. iii. 79.

వజ్జరము or **వజ్రము** *vajjaramu*. [Tel.] n. A kind of sea fish. ఒకవిధమైన సముద్రపుమ

త్స్యము. Glue used by carpenters, చెక్కలు అతుకుటకు వేసేబంక.

వజ్రము *vajramu*. [Skt.] n. A diamond, రవ. నవరత్నములలో నొకరత్నము. Adamant: a thunder-bolt; the weapon of Indra. వజ్రాయుధము. వజ్రకుంఠుడు a block head. **వజ్రకీటము** *vajra-kīṭamu*. n. A worm that bores through hard stone. **వజ్రదండము** or **వజ్రదండపురుగు** *vajra-dandamu*. n. An insect engendered in an ulcer. వ్రణములోపుట్టేపురుగు. వజ్రదేహము an adamantine frame, a strong constitution, a constitution of flint. **వజ్రదేహి** *vajra-dēhi*. n. A man of iron constitution. **వజ్రనిర్ఘోషము** *vajra-nirghōshamu*. n. A clap of thunder. పిడుగుచప్పుడు, ఉరుము. **వజ్రపుష్పము** *vajra-pushpamu*. n. The blossom of the sesamum. నువ్వుపువ్వు. **వజ్రవల్లి** *vajra-valli*. n. The plant termed *Cissus quadrangularis*. నల్లేరు. **వజ్రాంగి** or **వజ్రాంగీకము** *vajr-angi*. n. Admantine armour, వజ్రమయకవచము. **వజ్రి** *vajri*. n. One who has or carries a thunder-bolt. వజ్రాయుధముగలవాడు. An epithet of (Indra) as armed with the thunderbolt. ఇంద్రుడు.

వజ్జె *vadzdza*. [Tel.] n. An expedient, ఉపాయము, నెరవు.

వటకము *vaṭakamu*. [Skt.] n. A kind of cake, వడియము. A pill, a bolus. మాత్ర.

వటుగ, వటూరి or **వఠారి** *vaṭaga*. [Tel.] adj. Clever, skilful, నేర్పుగల, సమర్థతగల.

వటము *vaṭamu*. [Skt.] n. The Banyan or Indian fig tree. మర్రిచెట్టు. వటపత్రము a fig leaf.

వటారము or **వఠారము** *vaṭāramu*. [Tel.] n. A lodge. బస. A palace, నగరు. "దివ్యవాహనసముదగ్రోద్దరణవటారమున, కరిసమంద్రులు మందురవాటికలవటి." Navanandha. 306.

వటూరి See under వటుగ.

వటించు *vaṭintsu.* [Tel.] v. n. To starve. కస్తుపడు, ఉపవాసముచేయు. వాడు అన్నానికి లేక వటించినాడు he starved for want of food.

వటుడు, వటువు or **వటుకుడు** *vaṭuḍu.* [Skt.] n. A bachelor, an unmarried Brahmin, a celibate. బ్రహ్మచారి. A boy, బాలకుడు. **వటుత్వము** *vaṭutvamu.* n. Bachelorship, the state of being unmarried, celibacy. బ్రహ్మచర్యము.

వట్ట *vaṭṭa.* [Tel.] n. The bar that turns the centre post of a sugar mill. చెరకుగానుగ కోటేనడిమికోకలికిచేయు అడ్డమాను. **వట్టకాయలు** or **వట్టలు** *vaṭṭa-kāyalu.* n. plu. The testicles. వృషణములు, బీజములు. వట్టలుకొట్టు to castrate. lit: to strike the (bullock's) stones, (which are crushed with a mallet, not cut out.)

వట్టము *vaṭṭamu.* [Tam.] n. The agio allowance, a rate of exchange, abatement.

వట్టి *vaṭṭi* [Tel.] adj. Empty, mere, plain, simple, naked, downright, utter, gross, false, vain: unprofitable, groundless. ఉత్త. ఏమియులేని. ప్రయోజనములేని. వట్టిఆవు a dry cow. వట్టికాలు a shin bone, పిక్కపెలు వటికాలు. వట్టిగోడ a mere wall, a blind wall. వట్టికాళ్లతో వచ్చినాడు he came barefoot. వట్టిమన్ను loose earth. వట్టిగాలి mere wind, without rain. వట్టిప్రయాసము unprofitable labour. వట్టిమాట an untrue word, a meaningless word, లేనిమాట, అపవాదము. వట్టిసరి or వట్టిసరులు, a kind of grain. సస్యవిశేషము. వట్టివాడు an empty fool, వ్యర్థుడు. **వట్టివేరు** *vaṭṭi-vēru.* n. A fragrant grass usually called Cusus. *Andropogon muricatus.* (Watts.) Same as అవురుగడ్డివేరు, అవురువేరు, విడవలివేరు, ఉశీరము లామజ్జకము. **వట్టు** or **వట్టిపోవు** *vaṭṭu.* v. n. To dry, become dry, be drained. నీరు ఇంకు, నీరు ఎండిపోవు. ఇంకు. To become lean, కృశించు. n. Drying up, draining, నీరువట్టిపోవడము. A dried vegetable, వరుగు. A scab, ఎండినపక్కు. A hoop, కొయ్యకుగాని దూలమునకుగాని బలిమిచ్చుటకు వేసిన కట్టు. A limit, మేర. ఇంతవట్టు thus far, ఇంతమట్టుకు. "అనుజాలదనయులమత్సరిజనులను సమయించినవారుసమరోల్లాసంబున మెరయ జాడచేర్తు రెజనసాధున కింతవట్టుసంజయచెపుమా." M. IX. ii. 16.

వట్నము *vaṭnamu.* [Tel.] n. A sack or gunny bag filled with grain. ధాన్యాదులు నించినగోనె. వట్నాలకర్ర. a stick used to carry such a bag.

వత్రు or **వత్రుని** *vatra.* [from Skt. వర్తులము.] n. Roundness. వర్తులము. గుండ్రని. **వత్రు. వత్రుని** or **వత్రుముగానుండే** adj. Round. గుండ్రని. **వత్రుము** *vatramu.* adj. Short, హ్రస్వము. n. A bag in which betel and nut are kept. తక్కాకుతిత్తి. **వత్రుపడు** *vatrapaḍu.* v. n. To become less, to be diminished, decreased, or lessened, తగ్గు. **వత్రుపెట్టు** *vatra-peṭṭu.* v. a. To diminish, decrease, make less, తక్కువపరుచు. తగ్గించు. **వత్రించు. వత్రిల్లు** or **వత్రులు** *vatrintsu.* v. n. To make round, or cut round. గుండ్రనగాచేయు. To turn, తిరుగు. To turn back, పరాఙ్ముఖుడగు. To happen, occur, కలుగు, వచ్చు. సంభవించు. To be agreeable or pleasant. ఒప్పు "నగుబాటు వత్రిల్లెనాతులలోన." BD. v. 103. **వత్రువ** or **వత్రువు** *vatruva.* adj. Round, circular. బటువైన, గుండ్రని. n. Roundness, గుండ్రము, వర్తులము. **వత్రువసుడి** *vatruva-suḍi.* n. Lit: "The round twirl," i. e., the letter ౄ the secondary form of ఋ.

వదర, వదరి or **వదారి** Same as వటూరి. See under వటుగ.

వడ *vaḍa.* [Tel.] n. Heat, వేడిమి, ఎండవెగ. తాపము. Trouble, pain, labour, శ్రమము.

A sort of cake, గారె. A kind of hot cake. adj. Hot, వేడి. వడకొట్టి చచ్చిపోయినాడు or వడతగిలి చచ్చిపోయినాడు he died of sunstroke. "నిప్పులవసంతములాడు సెందిలవడబల్లులుపడమటి వాయువులును." P. i. 304. వడగల్లు vaḍa-gallu. n. A hailstone. "రాలెనొయ్యనవడగండ్లుపాలభండ్లు." A. iv. 118. వడగవ్వ vaḍa-gavva. n. The name of a certain fish, a species of Scomber. Russell, plate 139. వడగాలి or వడగాడ్పు vaḍa-gāli. n. The hot or land wind. నిప్పుగాలి. వడగొను vaḍa-gonu. v. n. To feel hot, తాపమునుపొందు. వడపప్పు vaḍa-pappu. n. A dish of green gram, split and soaked in water, with salt, pepper, assafœtida, &c. ఉపవిశేషదినములకు నానవేసి కొంచెము ఉప్పు ఇంగువకలిపిన పెసరపప్పు. వడపిందె vaḍa-pinde. n. A tender fruit that falls down from a tree through the heat of the weather. వడమూడి vaḍa-mūḍi. n. One who makes it hot for his enemies, శత్రువులకు తాపమును కలుగజేయువాడు. A Telugu name of Bhīma, one of the heroes of the Pāndu race. భీముడు. "కని కదనడ మనితుంతంతంబుడివిబడికరులగమూకు పోరులందు కతనకౌనవనుడియపటిన తెరుకేర్పడినగ వేగవేగ తేరు వరపెంగతిదులా." M. VI. ii. 375.

వడకట్టు Same as వడయబోయు. See under వడియు.

వడకు vaḍaku. [Tel.] n. The North. ఉత్తర దిక్కు. వడకుగుబ్బలి or వడకుకొండ vaḍaku-gubbali. n. The Himalayas. హిమాచలము. వడకుతోవ same as ఉత్తరాయణము.

వడకు or వణకు vaḍaku. [Tel.] v. n. To tremble, shake, quiver, shudder. కంపమును పొందు, కంపించు. n. Trembling, shaking, shuddering. వడకాడు (వడకి+ఆడు.) Same as వడకు. వడకించు or వడికించు vaḍakintsu. v. a. To cause to tremble, to shake, వణుకునట్లుచేయు.

వడకు See వడుకు.

వడదోలు vaḍa-dōlu. [Tel. వడము+తోలు.] n. A leather rope, used by toddy drawers. గనెల్లవాడు నడుమునకు కట్టుకొనేతోలు. A leather hunting-coat. వేటకాడు శరీరమునకు తొడిగికొనేతోలు.

వడప vaḍapa. [Tel.] n. The web which surrounds the lower parts of the stem-leaves of a palm tree. జెడ్డ.

వడపు vaḍapu. [Tel.] n. A den: the spot under a over-hanging cliff.

"మారొల్లతోగలమానిపుతెల్ల చంద్రకాంతకుగూడి గమకించియుండు వాడకాడుడు మహోదుజంబు బోలెడి. వాపోవుతెల్లనవపుఃశేశి సంబరమిత్తురు నతెల్లనగూడి." Pal. 30.

వడపోయు or వడబోయు Same as వడకట్టు. See under వడియు.

వడము vaḍamu. [Tel.] n. A very thick rope. మోకు. A garland, దండ. తేరుమోకు a rope used to drag a car.

వడలు or వాడలు vaḍalu. [Tel.] v. n. To fade, or wither. పుష్పాదులువాడు.

వడవడ vaḍa-vaḍa. [Tel. anuk.] adv. Violently (shaking). గడగడ.

వడసారము or వడారము vaḍasāramu. [Tel.] adv. Totally, entirely, పూర్తిగా.

వడి vaḍi. [Tel.] n. Quickness, briskness, celerity, rapidity; sharpness, violence. తీవ్రము. వేగము. Prowess, courage. శౌర్యము, పరాక్రమము. Time, కాలము. as in ఇంచుకవడి. కొంతవడి. పెద్దవడి. The twist of a cord. దారముపేని. పురిపెనవు, పురిపెనువుచ్చు వడుపుపెన్ను. (In prosody) rhyming syllables. కవిత్వమందు యతి, పద్యయతి. plural వళ్లు. వడికాడు vaḍi-kāḍu. n. A quick or brave man. వేగముకలవాడు. శౌర్యవంతుడు. వడికలతనము courage, bravery, వడికలవాతనము, శౌర్యము. వడికొలుపు vaḍi-kolupu. v. a. To twist.

మెలిపెట్టు. "మొలకమీసలువడిగొల్పుమురువు తళ్కా." T. ii. 73. To hasten, to cause to be quick. వేగముకలుగునట్లుచేయు. **వడిగొను** *vaḍi-gonu.* v. n. To become twisted, మెలిపడు. To be fast, వేగముకలుగు. **వడిగల** *vaḍi-gala.* adj. Quick, brisk, violent, clever, brave, వేగముగల, శూరత్వముగల. వాడు మంచివడిగలవాడు he is very quick or clever. adv. Quickly, freshly, త్వరగా, వుఱిగొని. "వడుచులేచుచుడు నమువడిగొంచొదవెడుకినుకల గడుబెట్టెదనుగ." M. V. ii. 348. **వడిపడు** *vaḍi-paḍu.* v. n. To be troubled, afflicted, oppressed; to toil. **వడిపెట్టు** or **వడివేయు** *vaḍi-peṭṭu.* v. a. To twist. మెలిపెట్టు. మలుచు. "తే॥ కి అలుకచేసుండబుగ్గలనుబిచితిట్టితొడలుబడి పెట్టికోదండమమరగట్టిరెట్టతెగగట్టి." H. ii. 180. To trouble, annoy, persecute. బాధపెట్టు. **వడిసుడి** *vaḍi-suḍi.* n. A whirlpool. ఆవర్తము.

వడికట్టు or వడిగట్టు Same as వడియగట్టు. See under వడియు.

వడియము *vaḍiyamu.* [Tel.] n. A cake made of black gram (split, soaked and ground,) mixed with salt, chillies, and assafœtida; it is dried in the sun and eaten as pickle. సంబారోపేతమైన మినపప్పు మొదలగువాటితో చేసి ఎండబెట్టిన వటకము.

వడియు *vaḍiyu.* [Tel.] v. n. To flow, to drip down or trickle as tears from the eyes, to distil or fall by drops. To decrease, to be diminished, as water in a river, to sink into the ground. స్రవించు, జాఱు, కారు, ఇట్టిపోవు, తరుగు, ఇంకు. చెరువులో నీళ్లన్నియు వడిసిపోయినవి the water in the tank is all dried up. To become lean or thin, కృశించు. చిక్కు. వాని ఒళ్లు మునుపటికంటె ఇప్పుడు మిక్కిలి వడిసిపోయినది his body is now much thinner than before. **వడియగట్టు, వడియబోయు, వడకట్టు, వడబోయు** or **వడికట్టు** *vaḍiya-gaṭṭu.* v. a. To strain or filter. ద్రవద్రవ్యమును శుద్ధిచేయు, వలువలు మొదలగువాని లోనుండా చేయు. **వడియబోత** *vaḍiya-bōta.* n. Filtering, straining. ద్రవద్రవ్యములను శుద్ధి చేయుడము. **వడుచు** *vaḍuchu.* v. a. To cause to be strained or filtered. వడియజేయు. To cause to drip, కార్చు. **వడుపు** *vaḍupu.* n. The state of being emaciated, వడియుట, కృశించుట.

వడిసెల or వడిసె *vaḍi-sela.* [Tel.] n. A sling for throwing stones. వడుమ రాయి పెట్టితిప్పి రువ్వే త్రాటిసాధనము. **వడిసెగడ్డ** *vaḍise-gaḍḍa.* n. A bubo. గజ్జలలోలేచే మేహవ్రణము, పంకటపుబిళ్ల.

వడుకు *vaḍuku.* [Tel.] v. a. To spin thread. రాట్నముమునుతిప్పి పత్తినినూలుగాచేయు. **వడుకుడు** *vaḍukuḍu.* n. The act of spinning cotton into thread.

వడుగు or వడువు *vaḍugu.* [Tel.] n. Mode, manner, style, way. విధము, రీతి. "ఒక సూర్యమండలములోక్కవడువునకూడియున్నవైన జాడవచ్చు." Ellana. iii. 451. The ceremony of initiation into the Dwija or twice-born castes. ఉపనయనము. **వడుగు, వడువు** or **వడుగడు** n. A Brahmin-bachelor. బ్రహ్మచారి.

వడుచు and వడుపు. See under వడియు.

వడుసు *vaḍusu.* [Tel.] n. The act of being torn when a cloth is handled to be ironed or bleached. మోటుతనముగా చలువచేయుట చేత వస్త్రమునందు పడునుపేకలుసందిచ్చి వంకర గాతొలగుట. **వడుసుడి** *vaḍu-suḍi.* (వడుసు+సుడి.) n. A fine (paid to the king). (రాజుకిచ్చు) దండుగ. **వడుసుపోవు** *vaḍusu-pōvu.* v. n. To be torn, as a cloth. వస్త్రము వడుసు కలిగియుండు.

వడె or వడియ *vaḍe.* [Tel.] n. A peg, చిలుకకొయ్య.

వడ్డన See under వడ్డించు

వడ్డి *vaddi*. [from Skt. వృద్ధి.] n. Interest on money. ధనముకు పెరుగుదల. న్యాయవడ్డి legal interest. వడ్డీకివడ్డీ compound interest. వడ్డికిచ్చు to lend on interest. వడ్డిబ్రతుకు *vaddi-bratuku*. n. Living by lending money at interest. వడ్డిభోగ్యము *vaddi-bhogyamu*. n. Usufruct of a field, given in lieu of interest on money borrowed. అప్పుఇచ్చినవారికి వడ్డికి చెల్లగా అనుభవించునది.

వడ్డించు *vaddintsu*. [Tel.] v. a. To help at meals, to serve up a meal. అన్నమిడు. వానిమాటలను నీమీద వేసుకొని వడ్డించుకొనుట ఎందుకు why do you take his words to yourself? "అనుచుదమయంతికి ... వడ్డించుకొనుట ..." Ahal. ii. 46. "అతనివడ్డింపవచ్చి ... గించి." Ila. ii. 11. వడ్డన or వడ్డింపు *vaddana*. n. Serving out, or helping food. ఇడుట, వడ్డించుట. వడ్డనయినది dinner is served. రెండవవడ్డన the second course.

వడ్డె See ఒడ్డె.

వడ్రంగి, వడ్లంగి, వడ్లవాడు or వడ్లబత్తుడు *vadrangi*. [Tel.] n. A carpenter. వడ్రంగము, వడ్లపని. వడ్రము or వడ్లంగితనము *vadrangamu*. n. The trade of a carpenter. వడ్లవానిపని. వడ్రంగిపని. వడ్రంగిపిట్ట or వడ్లంగిపిట్ట *vadrangi-pitta*. n. A woodpecker. దార్వాఘాటము. వడ్లకంకణము *vadla-kankanamu*. n. A curlew. కొల్లంకులలో భేదము. వడ్లత or వడ్లతి *vadlatu*. n. A woman of the carpenter caste.

వడ్లు *vadlu*. [from Skt. వ్రీహి, and plu. of వడి.] n. Paddy, rice in the husk, rice grain. వరిధాన్యము, శాలిధాన్యము. పిచ్చుకవడ్లు a fine sort of paddy. వడ్లచిలుక *vadla-chiluka*. n. A kind of insect that infests rice.

వణకు or వణుకు See వడకు.

వణిక్కు or వణిజ్య *vanikku*. [Skt.] n. Trade, traffic, commerce. వాణిజ్యము, వర్తకము, క్రయవిక్రయములు. వణిక్కు or వణిజుడు *vanikku*. n. A merchant or trader. వర్తకుడు. "వణిజులు లోకప్రవర్తనము ... ." M. XIII. v. 11. వణిక్పతి a mayor or chief merchant. వణిగ్జనము *vanig-janamu*. n. Tradesfolk, merchants as a body. వర్తకులు.

వణితము *vanitamu*. [Tel.] n. A district, country, తాలూకా, సంతము.

వతంసము or అవతంసము *vatamsamu*. [Skt.] n. A crest; an ornament on the head: an earring. శిరోభూషణము, సిగబంతి. చెవిలో నుంచే పువ్వు వెల్లవాడులు, పూగుత్తు. Metaphorically, the crest or chief, as హయావతంసము the noblest of horses.

వత్త *vatta*. [Tel.] n. A dried vegetable, anything that has dried up or withered. వరుగు.

వత్తి *vatti*. [from Skt. వర్తి.] n. A wick. దీపపు వత్తి. మైనపువత్తి a wax candle. వత్తివలె మెత్తనైనది it is as soft as a wick.

వత్తుగా *vattu-ga*. [From Skt. వత్.] adv. Accordingly. ప్రకారముగా. విధివత్తుగా according to rule.

వత్సము *vatsamu*. [Skt.] n. The breast, the chest. రొమ్ము. A year. సంవత్సరము. A calf. ఆవుదూడ. A boy, బాలుడు. వత్సతరము *vatsa-taramu* n. A steer. కోడెదూడ. "... ." M. XII. iv. 40 వత్సలత *vatsalata*. n. Tenderness, affection, love. స్నేహము, విశ్వాసము, వాత్సల్యము. వత్సలము *vatsalamu*. adj. Affectionate, kind. ప్రేమగల, విశ్వాసముగల. వత్సలుడు *vatsaludu*. n. A kind or affectionate man, వాత్సల్యముగలవాడు. వత్సుడు *vatsudu*. n. A little boy. మగశిశువు, బాలుడు.

వత్సనాభము or వత్సనాభి Same as వస నాభి. (q. v.)

వత్సరము *vatsaramu.* [Skt.] n. A year. సంవత్సరము, అబ్దము.

వదంతి *vadanti.* [Skt.] n. Talk, report, rumour. లోకప్రవాదము.

వదనము *vadanamu.* [Skt.] n. The face, countenance, mouth. ముఖము, నోరు. **వదన** *vadana.* adj. Having a face. చంద్రవదన having a face as bright as the moon.

వదనిక or **బదనిక** *vadanika.* [Tel.] n. A parasitic plant, *Epidendron tesseloides* and other species. శీవంతికాప్పతము, వృక్షరుహ.

వదరు or **వదురు** *vadaru.* [Tel.] v. n. To spread. అదరు, వ్యాపించు. To prattle, chatter, jabber. ప్రేలు. "నోరువదలుటకువదరిన." Vema. iii. 305. n. Chattering, prattling. ప్రేలుడు The long gourd, సొరకాయ, అనపకాయ. వదరుతీగె the creeping plant of the long gourd. *Cucurbita lagenaria.* అనపతీగె, సొరతీగె. "ఆ వదరుదైనయాకువరము ననిదిరియుక్క... వదరుపుట్టె పెట్టినది మొయుమనుచుదాని శాకవైవగాను." M. III. iii. 44. **వదరు బోతు, వదురుబోతు** or **వదర** *vadaru-bōtu.* n. A chatterbox, an empty talker. ప్రేలువాడు.

వదలు or **వదులు** *vadalu.* [Tel.] v. n. To be loosened, to be slackened or untied; to cease, depart, disappear. సడలు, ఊడు, విడు. జ్వరము వదిలిపోయినది the fever went off. నా గ్రహచారము వదిలేకాలమువచ్చినది the time has arrived for my ill-luck to come to an end. ఆ కష్టము వదిలిపోయినది that trouble is now over. v. a. To loosen, let go, quit, renounce, abjure, give up, abstain from. విడిచిపెట్టు, విడుచు, మానుకొను. The act of leaving, విడుపు. **వదలించు, వదిలించు** or **వదల్చు** *vadaltsu.* v. a. To loosen, slacken, release, get rid of. విడిపించు, సల్లించు, పోగొట్టు. వారిగర్వమును వదలించినాడు he crushed their pride. **వదలివేయు** or **వదలుకొను** *vadali-vēyu.* v. a. To abandon or leave, to desist from, get rid of, abstain from, మానుకొను, త్యజించు.

వదాన్యము *vadānyamu.* [Skt] adj. Liberal, generous, munificent. బహుప్రదమైన, విక్కలి ఇచ్చునట్టి. Speaking kindly, eloquent. మనోహరముగామాట్లాడే. వదాన్యునైనదికి ...కామధేనువు. Parij. ii. 130. **వదాన్యుడు** *vadānyudu.* n. A liberal man. దాత, కుబేరుడు. One who talks sweetly. మనోజ్ఞముగా మాట్లాడువాడు.

వది *vadi.* [Tel.] n. A pit to catch elephants in. A trap. ఊబి.

వదినె or **వదినియ** *vadine.* [Tel.] n. An elder brother's wife. అన్నభార్య. The daughter of a mother's brother or of a father's sister, if older than one's self. తనకంటె పెద్దదైన మేనత్త మేనమామల కూతురు. The elder sister of a wife or husband. మొగుడి అక్క, లేక పెండ్లానికి అక్క. మీయన్నయు వదినెయు your elder brother and his wife. వాడవదినె a prostitute, which Shakespeare also calls an "aunt." వేశ్య. "వాడవదినెకల వావివర్తనములు చాడిగానికి జాడబుద్ధి, మూఢమతులకెంమదిముతో జ్ఞానంబు." Vema. 1689.

వదుడు *vadudu.* [Skt.] n. One who speaks. మాటలాడువాడు. ప్రియంవదుడు one who uses kind words.

వదులు Same as వదలు. (q. v.) adj. Loose. బిగువుకాని. **వదులుడి** *vaduludi.* (వదులు+ఊడి.) n. A crack. బీటిక.

వదె, వదియ or **వందె** *vade.* [Tel.] n. A kind of grass. తృణవిశేషము.

వద్ద or **ఒద్ద** *vadda.* [Tel.] adj. and affix. Near, with, by, at, to. సమీపము. ఇంటివద్దనున్నాడు he is at home. నావద్దలేదు I have not got it. నీవద్దఉన్నదా have you got it? అతనివద్ద చెప్పిరి they told it to him. తీరమువద్ద close by the shore. వద్ది vaddi. (infl. of వద్ద) adj. Near, which is near. తనవద్దిచెలులు her playmates that were with her. నావద్దిపత్రములు the bonds which are with me, నాయొద్దనున్నపత్రములు.

వద్దు *vaddu.* [Tel. contracted from వలదు the neg. aor. of వలచు to will.] Do not, must not. See వలదు.

వధ or **వధము** *vadha.* [Skt.] n. Killing, slaying, murder. చంపడము, మారణము. **వధించు** or **వధియించు** *vadhintsu.* v. a. To kill, slay. చంపు.

వధువు or **వధూ** *vadhuvu.* [Skt.] n. A woman, lady. ఆడది, స్త్రీ. A wife. భార్య, పెండ్లాము. A daughter-in-law. కోడలు. A bride, పెండ్లికూతురు. వధూవరులు bride and bridegroom, man and wife. వధూమణి the flower of her sex. **వధూజనము** *vadhū-janamu.* n. Women, womankind. **వధూటి** *vadhūti.* n. A woman, వనిత. A virgin, కన్యక. A daughter-in-law, కోడలు.

వధ్యము *vadhyamu.* [Skt. from వధ.] adj. Deserving death, condemned to die. చంపదగిన. "కనుగొనిరివధ్యశృంగారంబుచేసి." (BD. iv. 782.) decking out a victim for sacrifice, or adorning a culprit for the halter. **వధ్యుడు** *vadhyudu.* n. A culprit: one who is condemned to death, చంపదగినవాడు.

వనటు See under వనరు.

వనము *vanamu.* [Skt.] n. A forest, a wood, అరణ్యము, అడవి. An orchard, grove, fruit garden, తోట, తోపు. Water, జలము. చింతవనము a tamarind grove. A multitude, సమూహము. సరసీవనము a group of lakes. **వన** *vana.* adj. Wild, not domesticated or tame, అడవిసంబంధమైన. వనగజము a wild elephant. వనమల్లిక a wild jasmine. వనమక్షిక a gadfly. **వనచరము** *vana-charamu.* n. Lit. a wood rover: i. e., a monkey, వానరము. **వనజము** *vana-jamu.* n. A lotus or water-lily. తామరపువ్వు. A wild elephant. A wild bird. **వనజలోచనుడు** *vanaja-lōchanudu.* n. An epithet of Vishnu, విష్ణువు. **వనజసంభవుడు** *vanaja-sambhavudu.* n. The one who sprang from the lotus, i.e, Brahma, చతుర్ముఖుడు. **వనజాక్షి** *vanaj-akshi.* n. The lotus-eyed: a poetical word for a lady. వనిత. **వనదము** *vanadamu.* n. A cloud. మేఘము. వనదాభ్రము sky blue. **వనదీపము** *vana-dīpamu.* n. The glory of the garden, an epithet of the Champaka flower. సంపెంగపువ్వు. **వనధి** *vana-dhi.* [from వన water + ధి place for.] n. The sea. సముద్రము. "వనధితీరముల నలరించి." R. v. 275. **వనప్రియము** *vana-priyamu.* n. A cuckoo, కోయిల. **వనభూషణము** *vana-bhūshanamu.* n. A bird called the Mocking bird. **వనభోజనము** *vana-bhōjanamu.* n. A picnic. వేడుకగా మిత్రబాంధవులతోకూడ ఒక తోటకుపోయి అక్కడ భోజనముచేయుట. A kind of bird, the Green Bulbul, *Chloropsis jerdoni.* (F. B. I.) **వనమాల** *vana-māla.* n. A chaplet, or garland. **వనమాలి** *vana-māli.* n. An epithet of Krishna. కృష్ణుడు. **వనవిహారము** *vana-viharamu.* n. Rambling in a garden for pleasure. తోటలోవేడుకగా తిరుగడము. **వనశృంగాటము** *vana-sringāṭamu.* n. A plant, *Ruellia longifolia,* గొలుగు. పల్లేరు. **వనస్పతి** *vanaspati.* n. A tree which bears fruit without flowering, పూయకకాచేచెట్టు. **వనాటము** *vanāṭamu.* n. An animal that lives in the woods.

వనరు *vanaru.* [Tel.] v. n. To grieve, pine, sorrow, దుఃఖించు, శోకించు, చింతించు. దీనాలాపములాడు. **వనరు**, **వనపు** or **వనటు** *vanaru.* n. Grief, pining. మనోవ్యథ. కూరిమైనవిచారము, దుఃఖము, శోకము. వగపు. "అనయంబునువనటముని పాపాంబువుల్వినీర్ణముట్టకతోచిన ముంచించి." M. XV. ii. 183.

వని *vani*. [Skt.] n. A forest, వనము, అడవి. **వనిక** *vanika*. n. A forest, అడవి. A park, grove, తోట, తోపు. "అనఘరోపకంఠవని కావనిజాతలతాచరన్మహోవానరయూథ ముద్దవిడి వచ్చి." P. i. 134.

వనిత *vanita*. [Skt.] n. A woman, damsel. స్త్రీ.

వనీపకుడు *vanīpakuḍu*. [Skt.] n. A beggar. యాచకుడు.

వనౌకసము *vanau-kasamu*. [Skt. from వనము.] n. A monkey. కోతి.

వన్నె or **వన్నియ** *vanne*. [from Skt. వర్ణము.] n. Colour, hue. రంగు, వర్ణము. Beauty, అందము. Ornament, అలంకారము, శృంగారము. Brightness, కాంతి. Fame, ప్రసిద్ధి. Manner, విధము. A paint, వర్ణపుపూత. Affected airs, gestures. Touch, quality of precious metals, రత్నాదులకాంతి, బంగారు వెండిలోనగువాని మేలిమి. Honour, esteem, గౌరవము. "లోక మువారుమెచ్చగా, వన్నెకువానికెక్కె." T. ii. 38. ఎనిమిదివన్నెబంగారు gold of the eighth touch (of 8 carats fine,) that is, half pure. పదహారువన్నెబంగారు gold of sixteen carats, that is, quite pure. adj. Coloured. వర్ణముగల. **వన్నెకత్తె** or **వన్నెలాడి** *vanne-katte*. n. An elegant or graceful girl. శృంగారవతి, సొగసుకత్తె. **వన్నెకాడు** or **వన్నెలాడు** *vanne-kāḍu*. n. A beau, a handsome man. శృంగారవంతుడు, సొగసుకాడు. **వన్నెచీర** *vanne-chīra*. n. A coloured cloth, రంగుబట్ట. **వన్నెపులుగు** or **వన్నెల పులుగు** *vanne-pulugu*. n. Lit: The painted bird, i. e., a pheasant, జీవంజీవము.

వన్య *vanya*. [Skt.] n. A multitude of groves or forests. A quantity of water, a flood, a deluge. వనసమూహము, ప్రవాహము. **వన్యము** *vanyamu*. adj. Forest, savage, wild, produced in a wood. అడవిసంబంధమైన, అడవిలోపుట్టిన.

వప *vapa*. [Skt.] n. The mucous, or glutinous secretion of the flesh or bones: a caul of fat. కడుపులో బొడ్డువద్దనుండే బట్ట వంటిపొర.

వపనము *vapanamu*. [Skt.] n. Shaving, ముండనము, గొరుగుట. Sowing, విత్తుట. **వప్త** *vapta*. n. One who sows, విత్తెడువాడు. Father, తండ్రి.

వపువు or **వపుస్సు** *vapuvu*. [Skt.] n. The body. శరీరము.

వప్రము *vapramu*. [Skt.] n. A fort, a citadel. కోట. A mud wall, a rampart, the glacis of a fort, కోటగోడ, పుట్టకోట. కొండచెత్తము, కోటఅడుగున పెట్టినగోడ మట్టిదిన్నె మొదలైనవి. A shore, తీరము. "రాజులో గిలిచుట్టురాలవప్రంబు." Sar. D. 112. **వప్రక్రీడ** *vapra-krīda*. n. Butting, as of an elephant or bull, &c. ఏనుగులు మొదలైనవి కొమ్ములతో ఏటిదరులను పెళ్లగించేఆట.

వమథువు *vamadhuvu*. [Skt.] n. Water ejected from the elephant's trunk. ఏనుగు తొండపుతుంపురు. Vomiting, వాంతి.

వమనము *vamanamu*. [Skt.] n. Vomiting. వాంతి. **వమనకాకి** *vamana-kaki*. n. A bird, the small green-billed Malacua. *Rhopodytis virudirostris*. (F. B. I.)

వమ్ము *vammu*. [Tel.] adj. Vain, fruitless. వ్యర్థము, నిరర్థకము. "రారాజుమన్ననవమ్ముచేసి." M. X. i. 74. "వమ్మగుపుణ్యంబు వచ్చువాపదలు." HD. ii. 250. "సొమ్ములెల్లవమ్మయ్యెను." Kālahas. iv. 56. n. Ruin, wasting. నాశము, పాడుచేయుట. **వమ్ముపోవు** *vammu-pōvu*. v. n. To become useless, వ్యర్థమగు. To be wasted or lost, నష్టమగు. పాడైపోవు.

వమ్రి *vamri*. [Skt.] n. The white ant. చెద. A kind of black ant. చెట్లునకెక్కే పెద్దనల్లచీమ.

వయసు or వయస్సు vayasu. [Skt.] n. Age, time of life, any period of life, ప్రాయము, ఈడు. Youth, యౌవనము. వయసువచ్చినవాడు a full grown boy. వయఃకాలము youth, maturity. వయసువచ్చినచిన్నది a grown girl. వయస్తంభము the art of prolonging youth by finding the philosopher's stone. "పాద వయస్తంభనకౌశలములు." L. vii. 370. వయసుది vayasu-di. n. A young woman. యౌవనవతి. వయసువాడు vayasu-vadu. n. A young man. యౌవనవంతుడు. వయస్థుడు vayas-thudu. n. A man in the prime of life. వయసువాడు. వయస్య vayasya. n. A female friend. చెలికత్తె, సఖి. వయస్యుడు vayasyudu. n. An equal, a friend. స్నేహితుడు. సఖుడు.

వయాళి or వయ్యాళి vayali. [Skt. from వాహ్యాళి.] n. Gallopping, speed, going at a rapid pace. సవారి, పరుగు, విహారము. A car, a chariot. రథము. "మేదురపోయినచోట పొదవెంద్రుకలుపట్టి అరకొయలుః య్యాళిదోలి తోలి." H. v. 47 When the procession called గరుడోత్సవము takes place at great temples there is a custom of advancing and receding alternately; this is called వయ్యాళి.

వయ్యమము or వాయమము vayyama. [Tel. adj. Vain, useless, వ్యర్థము.

వర vara [Tel.] n. A limit. మేర, పర్యంతము. ఇదివరలో before this time. అదివరలో before that time. [for వర.] Kind, sort. ఈ వరబంగారు gold of this kind. A kind of grain, ధాన్యవిశేషము. వర (for వర) n. A scabbard, a sheath. ఖడ్గకోశము. వరదూయు to unsheath or draw out of the scabbard. పోయినది వర ఉండేది కత్తియనిరెంచు what we have lost is the mere sheath but what we have got is the very blade, i. e., he who is dead is nothing to his successor. వరకట్టు vara-kattu. v. n. To test gold by rubbing it on a touchstone. Also, to prepare land for cultivation. వరగొడ్డము vara-goddamu. (వర+గొడ్డము.) n. A crooked word, వంకరమాట. వరకు or వరకును vara-ku. postp. Until, as far as, పర్యంతము. ఇదివరకు until this. అదివరకు so far, until that time. అపరకే పారి పోయియుండిరి they had already fled. ఎంత వరకు to what extent? how far? అతడు చనిపోయేవరకు up to the time of his death. నేను వచ్చేవరకు until I come. వర or వర vara. n. The large circular ring of pottery sunk in a small well, to prevent the earth from falling in. నూతికిపెట్టేది.

వరండము varandamu. [Skt.] n. A hayrick or bundle of hay. గడ్డివామి, గడ్డికట్ట. A pimple on the face. ముఖముమీది మొటిమ.

వరకము varakamu. [Tel.] n. The multiplier in Arithmetic. A rut cut by water. Imprisonment with hard labour. వరకములు, వరగలు or వరిగెలు varakamulu. n. The pulse termed Wild Kidney Beans, See వరిగెలు.

వరకు or వరవు varaku. [Tel.] n. An intricacy, difficulty, చిక్కు, వలపు, కపటపువంచన. A metal plate, రేకు. Gilding, మెరుగు.

వరగచేప varaga-chepa. [Tel.] n A kind of fish. మత్స్యవిశేషము.

వరగలించు varaga-lintsu. v. n. To shine, or glitter. ప్రకాశించు.

వరగలు or వరిగెలు varagalu. [Tel.] n. A kind of grain called Wild Kidney Beans, Panicum miliaceum. అరుగులు.

వరట varata. [Skt.] n. A goose. A female swan. ఆడుహంస. Vasu. ii. 84. వరటు [Tel.] n. A lump of dried cowdung. ఎండిన పేడచెక్క. వరటు varatu. v. n. To pine, to become lean or lank. కృశించు, "జరరాక్షి వెల్లువుల్లార్చి విక్కిలివరటినాడు

ము హొళావవాసములను." Kuchelo. i. 38. వరటినాడు=కృశించినాడు. "మిగులవరటున్న"= మిక్కిలి కుశ్శించియున్న. ib. iii. 10.

వరడు *varadu.* [Tel. Tam. and Mal.] n. An old fox. ముదినక్క. A large kind of fox. పెద్దజాతినక్క. A fox, నక్క. "వరడులంతమ చేరువబెల్లరచుట బిట్టెదురు గాలియుదరుటగ్రద్దల్ దరుముగనాడుట." M. VIII. ii. 126. "క॥ కృతరామ్రునక్ని హొళాత్రా, యుతనంబునవరచెవర డులు." భార. సభా. ii.

వరణము *varaṇamu.* [Skt.] n. An outer building, enclosure, or wall. ప్రాకారము. R. i. 119.

వరత్ర *aratra.* [Skt.] n. A leathern thong or girth. టంగువారు. "పత్రభాగములవెంబడి కుధంబుల్ జారిపోవరత్రల్ ప్రయత్నాలొంగిపొంగి." P. i. 65.

వరద *varada.* [Tel.] n. The overflow of a river, a torrent or flood. An inundation. నదిలోనుంచి వైటికివచ్చిన క్రొత్తనీరు, ప్రవాహము. వరదగుడి *varada-guḍi.* n. A halo round the sun or moon, సూర్యాదిపరివేషము. వరద పారు or వరదలుపారు *varada-pāru.* v. n. To flow in a torrent or torrents.

వరమడు See under వరము.

వరపు *varapu.* [Tel.] n. Drought, want of rain. అనావృష్టి, వానలేమి. "వరపునలతకూన వాడినయట్లు." Abhi. D. 317.

వరము *varamu* [Skt.] n. A boon or blessing sought in prayer, a divine gift. దేవతాదుల వల్ల పడసిన అనుగ్రహము. adj. Best, excellent, noble. శ్రేష్ఠమైన. వరరత్నము an excellent gem. సరోవరము a beautiful lake. వరదుడు *vara-dudu.* n. A benefactor, one who bestows a boon. వరమిచ్చువాడు, కోరికను తీర్చువాడు. వరవర్ణిని *vara-varṇini.* n. An excellent woman, a woman in general. ఉత్తమస్త్రీ. ఆడుది. వరసతి *vara-sati.* n. A fine or excellent woman. నిందా పతివ్రతగానుండేటిది. Vēma. వరాంగము *var-āngamu.* n. The head, శిరస్సు. The organ of generation. వరారోహ *var-āroha.* n. An excellent woman, a lady. ఉత్తమస్త్రీ. వరుడు *varuḍu.* n. An excellent man. శ్రేష్ఠుడు. One who chooses or selects (a wife), వరించువాడు. A husband, మగడు. A bridegroom, పెండ్లికొడుకు.

వరలు *varalu.* [Tel.] v. n. To shine or be splendid. ప్రకాశించు, వెలయు. To continue, to be, to behave. ప్రవర్తిల్లు. To spread, వ్యాపించు. "మెరుగులగన్నులమిరుమిట్లుగొనగ, వరలెడురత్నపర్వతములట్లక్." BD. iv. 2063.

వరవ *varava.* [Tel.] n. A channel of supply to an artificial lake or tank. చెరువునకు నీళ్లు వచ్చుట కేర్పరిచిన కాలువ. వరవచేప *varava-chēpa.* n. A kind of fish. మత్స్యవిశేషము.

వరవడి. వరువడి or ఒరవడి *varavaḍi.* [Tel.] n. The top line, a copy set to school boys learning to write. మేలుబంతి.

వరపు or వరవుడు *varavu.* [Tel.] adj. Slavish, servile. ఊడిగపు. n. A servant or slave. దాసి. సేవకుడు. వరవుడము *varavuḍamu.* n. Service, servitude. దాస్యము. "నీసపత్నికికిన్ వరవుడ వైచరింపుమని వారని శివ్యగ శాపమిచ్చిన." M. XIII. i. 60.

వరస or వరుస *varasa.* [Tel.] n. A line or row, పఙ్క్తి. A series or order, పరంపర. A mode, way, క్రమము, విధము. Relationship, బంధుత్వక్రమము. Usage, వాడుక. A turn, relief, or time, వంతు. ఒకవరుస once. Likeness, similitude, సామ్యము. A present, a donation, a gift solemnly presented by a procession of relations or friends. బంధువులుగాని మిత్రులుగాని వాద్యసహితముగా తీసికొనివచ్చే బహుమానము. "మిముబంటిపెద్దలెరుగు వారిదయిగా వరుసదప్పివచించిన." URK. iv. 273. ఆపని యీవరుసనుండగా when the business was in this state. కేవు అటినివరుస it is his turn to-morrow. నన్ను వాడు బ్రతుకనిచ్చే వరుసకనపడదు there is no chance of his sparing me. వరుసతప్పు to commit incest. ఎప్పుడు చెప్పేవరుసనే చెప్పినారు they talked as they have always done. వరుసజ్వరము remittent or recurring fever such as tertian or quartian. వరసగా or వరుసగా varusa-gā. adv. In a line, in order, regularly. క్రీతిగా, క్రమముగా. అన్నదమ్ములవరుసగానున్నారు they are connected as brothers. వరుసమొగ్గరము varusa-moggaramu. n. A military evolution. ఒంటి వ్యూహము.

వరహా or వరా varahā. [from Skt. వరాహము.] n. The gold coin bearing the impression of a boar (వరాహము), and termed a pagoda, equal to $3\frac{1}{2}$ rupees. కరుకువరహా a coin equal to four rupees. కంఠీరవరాయవరహాలు Kanterai pagodas, 105 of which are equal to rupees 305-7-4. The weight called వరహాయెత్తు is equal to 52·56. grains avoirdupois. తొమ్మిదిచిన్నములయెత్తు బంగారు పుముద్రిక.

వరాటకము or వరాటిక varāṭakamu. [Skt.] n. The small shell called a cowri which is used as a coin. గవ్వ. The seed vessel of the lotus, తామరదుద్దు.

వరాశి or వరాసి varāsi. [Skt.] n. A coarse cloth. ముతకబట్ట.

వరాహము varāhamu. [Skt.] n. A boar or hog. అడవిపంది. వరాహావతారము the third incarnation of Vishnu in the shape of a boar. వరాహకూర్చము (or, vulgarly వరాకట్టె) varāha-kūrchamu. n. A brush made of hog's bristles.

వరి vari. [from Skt. వ్రీహి.] n. Rice in the husk, usually called paddy. వడ్లు. వరిచేను or వరిమాగాణి a rice field. ఎర్రసన్నవరి a small kind of rice with a red husk. తెల్లసన్నవరి a small kind of rice with a white husk. వరుసవరి the crop that rises from grains of paddy that have fallen accidentally. వరిగడ్డి vari-gaḍḍi. n. Rice straw. శాలితృణము. వరిగింజలు vari-ginjalu. n. Rice in the husk. వరిపొట్ట vari-poṭṭa. n. The unopened ear of rice. కలమగర్భము. వరిబీజము vari-bījamu. n. Swelled testicle, orchitis, hydrocele, or hernia. ఒకపక్కవాచిన వృషణము. బుడ్డ. వరిముల్లు vari-mullu. n. The awn or beard of rice in the husk. ధాన్యశూకము.

వరించు or వరియించు varinṭsu. [Skt.] v. a. To desire, wish for, covet. To choose for (one's) husband. పొందు, కోరు, వలచు. "అదితిపద్మినిరతుగానిపతిని వరియింపకోర్లక బ్రహ్మచర్యమున నిరతింబరియుర్యాశ్రమంబున నిలిచె." M. IX. ii. 274. "ఇది నాకుతొల్లి వరియింపబెట్టి భార్య." ib. 1. i. 186.

వరిగెలు Same as వరిగలు. (q. v.)

వరిష్ఠము or వరీయము varishṭhamu. [Skt.] adj. Very excellent, supreme, best, most preferable. మిక్కిలి శ్రేష్ఠమైన. వరిష్ఠుడు or వరీయుడు varishṭhuḍu. n. A chief, a noble man. మిక్కిలి గొప్పవాడు, అతిశ్రేష్ఠుడు.

వరుగు varugu. [Tel.] n. Vegetables, fruit or fish preserved by drying. ఎండబెట్టినకూరలుమొదలైనవి. A kind of Vulture, గృధ్రవిశేషము. వంకాయవరుగు dried brinjals. మామిడివరుగు sun-dried mangoes. వరుగుచేప varugu-chēpa. n. Dried fish. ఉప్పుచేప. వరుగైన varugaina. adj. Dried, dry. ఎండి కృశించిన.

వరుజు varudzu. [Tel.] n. A ridge to retain water in corn fields. మళ్లకుకట్టినగట్టు, గవను. "కని వరుజెబడిరొంపిబ్రొక్కెన్." A. iv. 163.

వరుడు See under వరము.

వరుణుడు varuṇuḍu. [Skt. cf. Gk. Ouranos.] n. Varuna, the Hindu Neptune, who is the god of the waters and regent of the west. పశ్చిమదిక్పాలుడు. నీటిరేడు. వరుణ

వను a prayer offered to Varuna for rain in time of drought. వరుణము *varuṇamu*. n. Water, జలము.

వరువట్టులు or **వరువట్లు** *varu-vaṭṭulu*. [Tel. వట్టులు+వట్టులు.] n. Quite empty or dry (things.) మిక్కిలివట్టులు. **వరువట్లుగొను** or **వరువట్లువట్టు** *varu-vaṭlu-gonu*. v. n. To dry up entirely, బొత్తిగా ఎండిపోవు. MI. V. ii. 94.

వరువాయి *varuvāyi*. [Tel.] n. The dawn, morning, ప్రాతఃకాలము. **వరువాత** (in the locative case.) In the morning, ప్రాతఃకాలమందు.

వరుస See వరస.

వరూథము *varūthamu*. [Skt.] n. Armour, a piece of armour, a coat of mail. కవచము. A sort of wooden fender or ledge round a carriage, as a defence from collision. రథమును సంరక్షించే వ్యాఘ్రచర్మాదికము. A piece of leather inserted in the bush of a carriage wheel to prevent the axle from being worn out, a washer, చక్రరంధ్రము లందు చొప్పించే నెమ్ములు.

వరూథిని *varūthini*. [Skt.] n. An army. సేన. Also, the name of a mountain nymph, ఒక దేవతాస్త్రీయొక్క పేరు.

వరేణ్యము *vareṇyamu*. [Skt.] adj. Chief, noble, principal, pre-eminent. శ్రేష్ఠమైన, ముఖ్యమైన. **వరేణ్యుడు** *vareṇyuḍu*. n. A chief, or pre-eminent man, శ్రేష్ఠుడు, ముఖ్యుడు.

వర్గము *vargamu*. [Skt.] n A class or tribe, a group or set of things, the whole group or body of a number of similar things. సజాతీయసమూహము. A chapter, అధ్యాయము. భూవర్గము the chapter regarding the earth. కవర్గము the class of guttural letters. త్రివర్గము a class of three (objects, as love, duty, and wealth.) మిత్ర వర్గము a body of friends, a band of allies. మీయాశ్రితవర్గములో నున్నానుగనుక as I am one among the number of your dependants. అరిషడ్వర్గము the six classes of foes to good, i. e., the six passions, కామక్రోధ లోభ మోహమదమాత్సర్యములు, desire, wrath, covetousness, lust, arrogance, and envy. కట్టువర్గము a dress, or suit of clothes. **వర్గావర్గి** *vargā-vargi*. [Mahr.] n. Exchange, transfer, income, resources. మార్పుబడి. **వర్గావర్గీచేయు** *vargā-vargī-cheyu*. v. a. To change, or exchange. మార్చు. **వర్గు** or **వర్గువు** *vargu*. n. A square number (in arithmetic), సమసంఖ్య. In accounts, it means a ledger. అసామివారిగా వ్రాసినలెక్క పేరువారుసగా వ్రాసినలెక్క. Change of appointment, ఉద్యోగము లమార్పడము. **వర్గించు** *vargintsu*. v. a. To classify, class, post, arrange. తరగతిగా ఏర్పరచు, వర్గుచేయు

వర్చస్సు *varchassu*. [Skt.] n. Form, figure, shape, రూపము. Light, lustre. ప్రభ, కాంతి, తేజము.

వర్జించు *varjintsu*. [Skt.] v. a. To relinquish, give up, abandon. త్యజించు, విడిచిపెట్టు. "విప్రయనర్జించి యదుకులోత్తమ." M. XIII. ii. 304. **వర్జనము** *vrajanamu*. n. Quitting, abandonment, shunning, avoiding. విసర్జనము, మానుకొనడము. **వర్జనుడు** *varjanuḍu*. n. One who quits, avoids or abandons. విడిచిపెట్టువాడు, మానుకొనువాడు. "అనూయావర్జనుడై తను విప్రకోటి సంభావింపగా." M. XII. ii. 411. **వర్జితము** *varjitamu*. adj. Abandoned, avoided, excepted, excluded. విడిచిపెట్టబడిన, తీసివేయబడిన, త్యజింపబడిన. **వర్జితుడు** *varjituḍu*. n. One who is shunned, cut off, abandoned, త్యజింపబడినవాడు. **వర్జ్యము** or **వర్జనీయము** *varjyamu*. adj. That which should be abandoned, avoided, shunned, renounced, given up. విడిచిపెట్టదగిన, త్యజింపదగిన. **వర్జ్యము** n. An evil hour, an unlucky period of the day. తాత్కాల్యము. దినమునకు నొపయుక్తమైనకాలము.

వర్ణము *varṇamu*. [Skt.] n. Colour, hue, tint. రంగు. A tribe, class, caste, order. కులము, జాతి. A letter of the alphabet. అక్షరము. వర్ణవిభేదము discrimination of caste. వర్ణక్రమము the order of the letters, spelling. వర్ణాచారములు the rules of caste. వర్ణానుగుణ్యముగా conformably to the caste rules. **వర్ణకము** *varṇa-kamu*. n. Sandal paste, చందనము, గంధము. Perfume, ointment. Paint, pigment, as indigo, orpiment, &c. లేపనము. నీల్యాదిలేపనద్రవ్యము. A case ending in Telugu grammar. ప్రత్యయము. **వర్ణన** or **వర్ణనము** *varṇana*, n. Description. A characteristic, feature. Praise, panegyric. స్తోత్రము. వర్ణనాంశము a descriptive passage, a thing that is the subject of description. **వర్ణనీయము** *varṇa-nīyamu*. adj. Fit to be described, delineated, or praised. స్తోత్రముచేయదగిన. నిర్వర్ణనీయము indescribable. **వర్ణమాల** *varṇa-māla*. n. The alphabet. అక్షరసమామ్నాయము. **వర్ణి** *varṇi*. n. An unmarried Brahmin boy. A bachelor, బ్రహ్మచారి, వటుడు. A painter, చిత్రువు వ్రాయువాడు. **వర్ణించు** *varṇinṭsu*. v. a. To praise, describe, depict. స్తోత్రముచేయు, వివరించు. **వర్ణితము** *varṇitamu*. adj. Described, praised, స్తోత్రము చేయబడిన.

వర్తకము *vartakamu*. [Skt.] n. Trade, traffic, commerce. బేరము, వ్యాపారము. A sort of quail, *Perdix oilvacca*. బలిచెపిట్ట, మీనవల్లంకిపిట్ట. **వర్తకుడు** *vartakuḍu*. n. A merchant, or trader. బేరముచేయువాడు.

వర్తనము *vartanamu*. [Skt.] n. Conduct, behaviour, నడవడి. Staying, abiding. ఉనికి, స్థితి. Profession, occupation, livelihood. వృత్తి. వ్యాపారము, జీవనోపాయము. An act, పని. కృత్యము. "ఆధూమకేతువిప్ర నా వర్తనము నీవచెప్పితివింక చేకొప్పవలెవి. KP. iv. 2. "భుజనంబులవర్తనంబులునీకు తేటపడనివిరేవ్వగా వున." M. XII. i. 20. "స్వహస్త్యత్యనర్తనలన్నాంపించు." T. ii. 161. **వర్తన** *vartana*. [from వర్తనము.] n. A fee. **వర్తనుడు** *vartanuḍu*. n. (In composition) One who practises, or behaves, వ్యాపారముగలవాడు. పాపవర్తనుడు an evil doer. సద్వర్తనుడు a well doer, one who acts properly. "నావరుసగనియాపాపవర్తనుండు." Kaluvai. § 134. ఆజ్ఞావర్తనుండై obediently, in obedience or conformity to the command. **వర్తమానము** *varta-mānamu*. n. Situation, condition, circumstance. స్థితి, సంగతి. News, intelligence. సమాచారము, వృత్తాంతము. The present time. The present tense, in Grammar. విద్యమానము, జరుగుచున్న కాలము. "అనాగతవర్తమానంబులు నుచితానుచితకథాసారస్యంబులంతెలుపుమనిన." H. i. 51. **వర్తమానము** adj. Being, existing, living, being present. స్థితమైన, విద్యమానమైన. సర్వత్రవర్తమానమైన omnipresent. Anand. i. 11. **వర్తి** *varti*. n. One who is, behaves or acts, వర్తించువాడు. Sandal, perfume. గాత్రానులేపని, పరిమళద్రవ్యములుకూర్చిన గంధపువిల్ల. The foil placed under a precious stone of the same colour to increase its lustre. మణిరంజకద్రవ్యము. The wick of a lamp, దీపపువత్తి. **వర్తించు**, **వర్తిలు** or **వర్తిల్లు** *vartinṭsu*. v. n. To be, remain, abide; to act, behave. ఉండు, ఎసించు, ప్రవర్తించు. "ఎరుక్యదినివాసంబెందువర్తింతు." URK. ii. 262. ఈశబ్దము మూడు లింగములయందును వర్తించును this word is used in all genders, i. e., it is of the common gender. **వర్తిష్ణువు** *vartishṇuvu*. adj. Staying, abiding, being stationary, or fixed. ఉండేవాడు, నిలుకడగానుండువాడు, వర్తించువాడు.

వర్తులము *vartulamu*. [Skt.] adj. Round, circular, globular, spherical. గుండ్రని, చుట్రైన. పటువైన. "వర్తులాధరరము." వసు. v.

వర్త్మము vartmamu. [Skt.] n. A road, path, way, course. మార్గము, త్రోవ.

వర్దీ vardi. [H.] n. Report, news; an order, warrant. జప్తువర్దీ a warrant of attachment.

వర్ధకి vardhaki. [Skt.] n. A carpenter. వడ్లవాడు.

వర్ధిలు, వర్ధిల్లు or ప్రవర్ధిల్లు vardhilu. [Skt.] v. n. To grow, increase, improve, flourish, thrive, prosper. వృద్ధిపొందు, పెరుగు. "వృద్ధి వినూతేంద్రుండవర్ధిలుమన్న నీవు." Dab. 240. వర్ధించు vardhintsu. v. a. To cause to thrive, to nourish. వర్ధిల్లజేయు, పెంచు. వర్ధిష్ణువు vardhishnuvu. adj. Prosperous, flourishing. వృద్ధిపొందుచున్న. "స్వస్వప్రవర్ధిష్ణుధర ణీరుహా." Swa. i. 32. వర్ధిష్ణుడు or వర్ధిష్ణువు vardhishnudu. n. One who prospers or flourishes. వృద్ధిపొందువాడు. వర్ధనము vardhnamu. adj. Increasing, growing, thriving. పెరిగే, అభివృద్ధిఅయ్యే. మర్దనంగుణవర్ధనం stripes breed virtue. n. Increase, growth, improvement. పెరుగుట, అభివృద్ధి. నందివర్ధనము a shrub called *Nerium coronarium*, నంద్యావర్తము. కుందవర్ధనము a species of this flower. "కుందవర్ధనములుకొండవ గోగులును." L. iii. 33. వర్ధమానము vardha-manamu. adj. Increasing, growing, thriving. అభివృద్ధిఅగుచున్న, పెరిగే. వర్ధమానకము vardha-manakamu. n. A lid. మూకుడు. వర్ధితము vardhitamu. adj. Increased, grown, thriven. వృద్ధిపొందింపబడిన.

వర్మము or వర్మువు varmamu. [Skt.] n. Mail, armour. కవచము. Jaimini ii. 50. వర్మితము varmitamu. adj. Armed, accoutred. కవచాలంకృతమైన.

వర్యము varyamu. [Skt.] adj. Chief, principal. ముఖ్యమైన, శ్రేష్ఠమైన. వర్యుడు varyudu. n. A chief, leader. ముఖ్యుడు, శ్రేష్ఠుడు. మునివర్యుడు a noble sage. కుమారవర్యుడు the noblest of sons. వర్య varya. n. One who chooses her own husband, తనంతట మగని వరించుకొన్నట్టి ఆడుది. A noble or distinguished woman, ముఖ్యురాలు.

వర్ర or ఒర్ర varra. [Tel.] n. A pungent taste. కారము. వర్రమీను varra-minu. n. A kind of fish. మత్స్యభేదము.

వర్రు varru. [Tel.] n. A heap or quantity. అతిశయము. A flood, inundation. వరద, ప్రవాహము. "నెత్తురు వర్రులువారజంపుదురు." M. XIII. v. 63. adj. Much. విస్తారమైన. వర్రొడ్డు varr-oddu. (వర్రు+ఒడ్డు.) v. n. To flow in a stream, ప్రవహించు. వర్రె, వర్రియ or ఒర్రె varre. n. A crack. బీటిక. A rick of corn, చిన్నకుప్ప. A rick of straw. గొడ్డువర్రె.

వర్షము varshamu. [Skt.] n. Rain, a shower, వాన. A year, సంవత్సరము. The state of being a eunuch, షండత్వము. వర్షము వెలిసినది the rain has ceased. వర్షాభావము want of rain. వర్షకాలము or వర్షాకాలము varsha-kalamu. n. The rains or rainy season. వానకాలము. వర్షణము varshanamu. n. Raining, వానకురియుటము. Sprinkling. నీళ్లు చిలకరించడము. వర్షధరుడు or వర్షవరుడు varsha-dharudu. n. A eunuch. కొజ్జావాడు. వర్షాభువు varsha-bhuvu. n. Lit. That which is born in the rainy season, i. e., a frog, కప్ప. A. iv. 113. వర్షాశనము varsh-asanamu. n. An annuity, or yearly maintenance. సంవత్సరమునకొకసారి జీవనార్థముగానిచ్చుసొమ్ము. వర్షించు varshintsu. v. n. To rain. వానకురియు. నెత్తురు వర్షింప while it rained blood. Jaimini. vii. 47. వర్షీయసి varshiyasi. n. A very aged woman. ఏండ్లుచెల్లినది, ముసలిది. "ప్రత్యక్షుల్లంబ్రాత్రి వర్షీయసీపలితపాండురకేశబంధమునన."

వర్షీయుడు *varshīyudu.* n. A very old man.

వర్షోపలము *varsh-ōpalamu.* n. A hail-stone, వడగల్లు.

వర్ష్మము *varshmamu.* [Skt.] n. The body. శరీరము.

వల *vala.* n. A net. జాలము. "వలసూత్రనీటిలో నేయుచుంగ." BD iv. 1818. "నీవలమజిక్కి విశ్వసిలంచు." L. iv. 241. [For వలపు.] Love, కామము. వలకాక *vala-kāka.* n. Amorous desire, మన్మథతాపము. (క్షేత్రయ). వలకాడు *vala-kādu.* n. A lover. కాముకుడు. వసు. iv. వలకారి *vala-kāri.* n. One who causes another to fall in love. వలపించువాడు, లేక వలపించునది. వలకారితనము *vala-kāri-tanamu.* n. Prettiness, gracefulness. శృంగారిత్వము. "అలవోకగానచ్చి యప్పు డప్పటికి సమేలంపు మాటలమేలమాడు, వలరాయునకు బాలకటకిసేతింతోడి వలకారితనమునకస్నె నెట్టు, అన్యాయదేశంబులాడి నెచ్చెలులచే ప్రియమారనేమేని చెట్టింపంపు." Vish. vi. 19. వలకారి వగలు *vala-kāri-vagalu.* n. Airs, graces, pretty ways or gestures. వన్నెలాడిటక్కులు. వలదొర, వలరాజు, వలరాయుడు or వలరేడు *vala-dora.* n. A name of Manmatha, the Hindu Cupid. మన్మథుడు. వలవంత or వల్వంత *vala-vanta.* n. Amorous desire, మన్మథవ్యథ. Emotion, passion, grief, affliction, misery, మనోవ్యథ, దుఃఖము, పరితాపము. "ఆత్మనత్సర్వభూతాని యనుటబొంకె, ముద్దియల కైనవలవంతమువ్చులను, నాటపాటలగతుల గొంతమవముగాని, నోరులేనిజంతువులకె నొప్పిను నము" A. v. 45. టీ॥ వలవంత. పరితాపము. "శోకవిమగ్న మానసాంభోరుహాలైపథంబుగొని పోయెదరివ్వలవంత మీకు నేకారణ జాతమయ్యె." Vedanta Rasayanam iv. 129.

వల *vala.* [Tel. for వలను.] adj. Right, కుడి. వలచేయి or వలకేలు the right hand. "అరుదుగావలచేతన్ తమాలికరము." DR. Aran. 208. "వలకేల్దలక్రిందకేర్చుకొని." P. i. 256. వలకట్టు *vala-kattu.* (వలను+కట్టు.) v. a. To make a thing convenient, అనుకూలపరుచు. వలకడ *valakada.* (వలను+కడ.) n. The South side. దక్షిణపుదిక్కు. వలగొను (వలను+కొను). వలచుట్టు (వలను+చుట్టు) or వలదిరుగు *vala-gonu.* v. n. To walk round, circumambulate. ప్రదక్షిణముచేయు. చుట్టుకొను. "నిదాఘమహీరుహాపార్శ్వభాగమునకె వలగొని మ్రొక్కి." Parij. v. 88. వలచుట్టు *vala-tsuttu.* n. The act of walking round anything. వలగొనుట.

వలంతి See వలతి.

వలకు or వలకువు *valaku.* Same as వలను. (q. v.)

వలగ్నము *va-lagnamu.* [Skt.] n. The middle part of the body, దేహమునొక్క మధ్యము. The waist, నడుము. KP. v. 67.

వలచు or వల్చు *valatsu.* [Tel.] v. n. To smell or emit perfume. వాసనకొట్టు. "గమగమవలచు చొక్కపుజవాది." Swa. ii. 59. "శ్వాసదంబులసదవాత్రిప్పినలచి, పరుసదనువను మురుతోవనరిసియెయుట." A. vi. 18. టీ॥ వలచు. కంపుకొట్టుచుండే. v. a. To love, wish, long for, కామించు, మోహించు, కోరు, ఆశించు. అపేక్షించు. "వానింతవలచియున్నది యుమామోహాదినిగనలతు." P. iii. 308. వలపు or వల్పు *valapu.* n. Love, affection, fondness, మోహము, కామము. A desire. కోరిక. Smell, fragrance, పరిమళము. "పూనికనాటతోట వలపుల్గలకప్రపుకమ్మధూళి." R. iii. 98. వలపుల్గల, వాసనలుగలిగినటువంటి "కసటువోపన్నుటగడిగి పువ్వులతావివలనైనకమ్మజవ్వాది వలపునెరప." T. iii. 131 టీ॥ వలపు, వాసన. వలపించు *valapintsu* v. a. To inveigle, tempt, enamour or cause to love. మోహింపజేయు. వలపించుట *valapintsuta.* n. Enamouring, tempting. మోహింపజేయుడము. "నయ్యాటముల్ వింతలుగాగిరికలల్ వలపించుటల్ నగుటల్." H. i. 293. వలపు

కాడు *valapu-kāḍu.* n. A lover, an amorous person. కాముకుఁడగువాఁడు, కాముకుఁడు. **వలపుకత్తె** or **వలపుకత్తియ** *valapu-katte.* n. An amorous woman, కాముకురాలు, కాముకి. **వలపుటీలు** Same as పొత్తముడి. (q. v.) **వలపుమోపరి** *valapu-mōpari.* n. Lit: The bearer of scents, i. e., the air, వాయువు, గంధవహుఁడు. **వలపులరేఁడు** or **వలపురాయఁడు** *valapula-rēḍu.* n. The god of love. మన్మథుఁడు. **వలవని** or **వల్వని** *valavani.* adj. Not wanted, useless. అక్కఱలేని, కొఱగానిన. adv. Much, very. అతి. అమితమైన. "చేయువలవనికార్యం బునేచేయుకొనెన." Padma. iii. 61. చేయవలవని కార్యము what one ought not to do, చేయరానిపని. "వలవనికీడివన్వు." P. ii. 135. వలవనికీడి, అనగా పనికిమాలిన రాజసము.

వలత్ *valat.* [Skt.] adj. Shaking, moving. చలించే, కదిలే. "వలదుదిదయారుణ ద్యుతులు." T. ii. 66.

వలతి or **వలంతి** *valati.* [Tel.] n. A genius, a skilful person. నేర్పరి. A woman, ఆడుది. A place, చోటు. "నీవడవికరుగ నొడబడి, నీవెను కనెవచ్చినపుడ నిందింతురుమమ్మిా వెఱులితనిమాన్పం గావలతులుగాదెయని జగజ్జనులధిపా." M. XIII. i. 79. "భామకృతిచెప్పవలతులప్ప ద్దముఖులు." A. i. 13. adj. Obtained, got, పొందబడిన, అర్జనమైన. Handsome, elegant, అందమైన. Agreeable. హితమైన, అనుకూలమైన. "మకరందమధుపాన మత్తశిలంబనికరాకారంబైన నీరజాకరము, వలతియైయలాసకోపవరసమిాపమున నెలసిన యొప్పుతో నాకతపోవనము." DRU. 1104. **వలతితనము** *valati-tanamu.* n. Cleverness, skilfulness. నేర్పు, గట్టితనము. "వలతితనంబెలయగవాచెలి కానికిమత్తరంబు చెప్పెచు." Rasica. v. 132.

వలదు *valadu.* [Tel.] adj. Big, great, స్థూలమైన, గొప్పదైన, అధికమైన. n. Greatness, ఆధిక్యము, గొప్పతనము.

వలదు or **వద్దు** *valadu.* [Tel. negative aorist of the verb వలయు.] v. Ought not, must not, do not. అట్లు ఉండవలదా or ఉండవద్దా should it not be so, ought it not to be so? నాకు వలదు or నాకు వద్దు I do not want it. అట్లు ఐద్దండి I pray you not to do so. అట్లు చెప్పవలదు do not say so. నేను రావలదా am I not to come? ఈ రూకలు ఇయ్యవలదా is not this money to be paid? నాతో చెప్పవలదా should you not tell me? నన్ను వలదన (i. e., ఐద్దని చెప్పడమునకు) నీకు న్యాయముకాదు it is not right that you should forbid me? "వలదువిగారలినట వాగ్వాదమంకరింప" it is not right for you to begin a quarrel.

వలన See under వలను.

వలనము *valanamu.* [Skt.] n. Moving, turning. కదిలించడము, తిప్పడము, కంటిపాప తిరుగుట. "లలనాజనాపాంగ వలనావసదనంగ తులనాభికా భంగదోఃప్రసంగ." Vasu. i. 41.

వలను *valanu.* [Tel.] n. A side, direction. వైపు, దిక్కు, పార్శ్వము. A method, manner, విధము, రీతి. Grace, excellence, ఒప్పిదము. Art, skill, a stratagem. ఉపాయము, నేర్పు. A sign or omen. శకునము. "బాలుఁడురాజతో బలికె నిట్లనుచు. వలమజాలచితియయ్యవను భోజరాజ. శకునాలుగాఁపడిసమయముంబుగాదు, మగుడు మునీవనిన మనుజేశుడనిరెు." Pal. 133. Purity, శుచిత్వము. Convenience, practicability, possibility. అనుకూల్యము. "నిరుపమహారమాణిక్యములౌ గరగ, వలనుల ప్రాసినవన్నెచిత్రములు. దలుగదల్పవైనస్తంభాదలి." HD. i. 877. adj. Pertaining to the right hand side, కుడి, దక్షిణము. Proper, యుక్తము. **వలనుగ** *valanu-ga.* adv. Artfully, skilfully, gracefully, agreeably. ఉపాయముగా, ఒప్పిదముగా. "ఒకటిక్రిందనొకటి నొనరబడ్డముబెట్టి వలనుగ గుణియుంపనరుసబెరుగు." Vema. 1242. **వలనైన** *valan-aina.* adj. Agreeable, ఇంపైన. "కసటువోవన్నిట గడిగిపువ్వులతావి, వలనైన కమ్మజవ్వాదివలపు నెఱపి." T. iii. 131. టీ: వల

నైన, ఒప్పగానుండెడి. **వలన** or **వలనన్** *valana.* A postposition used as a case ending in the 5th case. By, by means of, with, from, వల్ల. "నీవలనంబరమప్రీ తుండనైతి." M I. i. 175.

వలపల *valapala.* [Tel. వలను+పల.] n. The right side. కుడిప్రక్క. దక్షిణపార్శ్వము. **వలపలగిలక** *valapala-gilaka.* n. The letter ఱ (r), which is always written on the right side of the syllable before which it is pronounced, as చేయుఱ to join, మారుఱ to change **వలపలించు** *valapalintsu.* v. a. To surround, go round, వలగొను. వలచుట్టు. **వలపట** or **వలపల** *valapata.* adv. On the right side. కుడిపక్కను. "నీవలపటమేము. నీవుదాపటను." BD. iv. 817. **వలపటి** or **వలపలి** *valapati.* adj. Of the right side, or dexter. కుడి.

వలపు See under వలచు.

వలభి *valabhi.* [Skt.] n. The wooden frame of a thatched roof. సోపానవి, అనగా ఇంటి మేలుకప్పు. A temporary building on the roof of a house. చంద్రశాల, ప్రాసాదముపైని యిల్లు. "వైజయంతోపరిస్ఫుటవలభినిభంబు." Parij. iv. 49.

వలమానము *vala-manamu.* [Skt.] adj. Moving. కదలుచుండెడి. చలించుచున్న. "పవమాన వలమానవనమాలికలసోలి." T v. 142.

వలము *valamu.* [Tel.] n. Abundance, విస్తారము. Stoutness, bigness, స్థూలత్వము, లావు. adj. Stout, స్థూలము.

వలమురి *vala-muri.* [Tel. వలను+మురి] n. Lit: That which has its volutes formed from right to left. The conch of Vishṇu. విష్ణుశంఖము. వలమురితాలుపు an epithet of Vishṇu. విష్ణువు. "వలమురిపైనంటు జలధి సంకేమునంగ కశమునైకస్తుతికప్పమెరయు." S iii 407.

వలయము *valayamu.* [Skt.] n. A bracelet, an armlet, any thing round. కడియము, మురుగు, చక్రము, ఉంగరము, మండలము, గుండ్రనిది. A boundary, an enclosure. పొలిమేర, ఆవరణము. వలయవామనముద్ర an image of Vāmana placed as a boundary mark. వలయశాసనము an inscription placed on a boundary. **వలయితము** *valayitamu.* adj. Surrounded, encompassed. చుట్టుకొనబడినది.

వలయు *valayu.* [Tel.] v. n. To be liked, desired or wanted. ఇష్టమగు, ఐపేక్షితమగు. To be needful, or necessary, ఆవశ్యకమగు. To be proper, యుక్తమగు. To be surrounded, వలయితమగు. "మృగమునలయంబోలెన్." పంచ. నా. ii. "స్వబుద్ధిరాజుకు విశేషింపవల యు" (P. i. 391) the use of his own judgment is much needed in a king. "కయ్యమునకు నెయ్యమునకు వియ్యమునకు సమత వలయు." (ib. ii. 47) in combat, in intermarriage, and in friendship equality is wanted; or, there should be a similarity. "లాభాలాభములరయవలయు." (ib. iv. 431) you should look to the chances of gain or loss, of success or failure. **వలె, వలెను, వలసినది** or **వలయును** are added as auxiliaries, to the Root in the Infinitive of any verb; to give the idea of obligation or necessity: నేను ఇంటికి పోవలెను I must go home. నీవు ఇక్కడికి రావలెను you must come here, you should come here, I hope you will come here. తమదయ రావలెను నా దరిద్రము తీరవలెను I hope your favour will come and that my poverty will be removed. ఆయన రేపో ఎల్లుండో రావలెను he must be here tomorrow or the next day, i. e., we expect him here tomorrow or the next day. వాడు దానితమ్ముడుగా ఉండవలెను I suppose he must be her brother. నాకు ఆ పుస్తకము కావలెను I want that book. వాణ్ని చంపియుండవలెను they must have killed him. నీకు అట్లురావలెను this serves you right. నీవు సంశయించవలసినదిలేదు you need not doubt it, there is no occasion to doubt it. వాణ్ని పిలువవలెనని అక్కడికి వెళ్లితిని I went there to call him. ఈ పని చేయవలెనని పోవుచుండగా as I was going there to do this. జగడమాడవలెనని వస్తివా did you come on purpose (or wanting) to quarrel? వలసి (the past p || of వలయు.) ఇవ్వవలసి యిస్తిని I paid it, because I had to. "నిశాచరునకుద్యోగంబుమానుకొనవలసె." Swa. iv. 163. అట్లు చేయవలసివచ్చును it will become necessary to do so. వలసిన (past part. of వలయు) is used as an affix (similar to the Latin-*ibilis* or-*endus*). చెల్లించవలసిన సొమ్ము money due, the sum payable. "వలసినసంపదలోకలుగగా." T. ii. 34. ఈ వలసిన, కావలసినటువంటి. వలసె or వలసెను (the past tense of వలయు) it became necessary, or requisite. వానితో చెప్పవలసె I was obliged to tell him. "వినిపింపరానికార్యము వినిపింపవలసె." Swa. iv. 176. The negative aorist of this, వలవదు, వలదు, see under వలదు.

వలవల or విలవిల *valavala.* [Tel.] adv. Bitterly, much greatly, వెలవెలమని, తోటతోటమని. "తరుకు నిద్దంపుటద్దపు తోముకళపై ప్పైనవలవల కన్నీరునిడుచుకమ్మ." Anirudh. ii. 104. వలవలయేడ్చు to weep bitterly. Flutteringly, as a bird does when it alights on the ground.

వలవలన *valavalana.* [Tel.] adj. Loosened. వదలిన. "వలవలనైన దంతములు."

వలస *valasa.* [Tel.] n. Emigration, fleeing, flight from home for fear of the king or a hostile army, expatriation. స్వదేశములో నుండడమునకు ఉపద్రవమువచ్చి పరదేశమునకు లేచిపోవడము. వలసతీయు or వలసపోవు to fly from home for fear of an enemy. అన్నమునకువలసపోవు to emigrate in search of food. వలసపిట్ట *valasa-piṭṭa.* n. The golden plover.

వలాహకము *valāhakamu.* [Skt.] n. A cloud. మేఘము.

వలి *vali.* [Skt.] n. A fold, ముడుత. See వలిముఖము. [Tel.] n. Cold, coldness, చలి. Shivering through cold, కంపము. "పవనశైత్యంబులు వలిచునదసు." ABA. iii. 92. "వానకుకెండకు వలికిగాడ్పునకు." Pativr. 83. line 8. adj. Cold, chill. చల్లని. "మదిరాక్షి వలిగాడ్పుకొదమనెత్తావినే బొలయుచున్నదుగాని పొలయనెరచు." R. v. 175. వలిగొను *vali-gonu.* v. n. To be chill, to feel very cold, to shiver, చలిపెట్టు. "కలువరేడునెరింగికన్నుల జూచిదివలి గొన్న పెయి తెలవరులాగాకమిని, గడగడ వడకుచుకవుధయుంపడుచు." Sar. D. 475. వలితిప్ప *vali-tippa.* n. A phrase for the Himalaya mountains. హిమపర్వతము. వలిపని *vali-pani.* n. The act of cooling anything, శైత్యోపచారము. నిలా. iii. వలిపిరి *vali-piri.* n. Cold, చలి. A chill, shivering, వణకు. వలిపిరిగొట్టు *valipiri-goṭṭu.* n. One who shivers from cold. చలికువాడు. వలిమల, వలిగట్టు, వలిగుబ్బలి or వలిగొండ *vali-mala.* n. A snow-clad mountain, మంచుకొండ. The Himalayas. వలిమిడి *vali-midi.* n. A kind of foot-rot from which cattle suffer, పశువులకు కాలిమడమలయందు కలిగే రోగవిశేషము. వలిమొలక or వలిమొల్క *vali-molaka.* n. The son of the Wind god, వాయుపుత్రుడు. An epithet of Bhima, భీముడు. వలివెలుగు or వలివెల్గు *vali-velugu.* n. The Moon. చంద్రుడు.

వలికి or వల్కి *valiki.* [Tel.] n. A kind of bird, also called సారసపక్షి or బెగ్గురు.

వలిచేలు *valiṭsalu.* [Tel.] n. plu. Roof laths. పెండేలు.

వలితము *valitamu.* [Skt.] adj. Surrounded. చుట్టబడిన. Shaken, చలనముపొందిన.

వలిదము *validamu*. [Tel.] n. A sort of cloth. వస్త్రవిశేషము. "వలిదంబుసరికిమ్మి తెలుపు దివ్యాంబరంబును, మదియరాగంబు, కేవాంబ రంబు." BD. iii. 119.

వలిపము, వలిపెము or **వల్పము** *valipamu*. [Tel.] n. A fine sort of muslin. సెల్లా, సన్నని తెల్లవస్త్రము. A clean cloth, మడుగుబట్ట. "బంగారుసరిగెలపట్టంచువలిపంబు నెరికమీగాళ్లపై నెరసితూల." Surabha. 44. "తడియొత్తిసన్న వలిపెంబిడి మణిపీఠస్థయైయుంతిమెరుగు చెన్నెదు నమరులార్చి." A. vi. 177. **వలిప, వలిపపు** or **వలిపము** *valipa*. adj. Fine (as muslin,) సన్నని, పాతైన. Pure, clean, శుభ్రమైన. White, తెల్లని. "తేటయాగొజ్జంగినీటమజ్జ నాడి వలిపచెంగావిపావడధరించి. T. iii. 23. టీ॥ వలిప. సన్నపు తెలిగలిగినటువంటి. "తాగకార్ధి శకిరణకదంబకంబు, చిలికెబలుచనివలిపెంపుజేముకు మంచు." Parij. ii. 50. "వల్పపయ్యట," "వల్పపావడ."

వలియు *valiyu*. [Tel.] v. n. To become thin, సన్నగిలు. To be tired or fatigued, డస్యు.

వలీకము *valikamu*. [Skt.] n. The edge of a thatched roof, eaves, ఇంటిచూరు.

వలీముఖము *vali-mukhamu*. [Skt. from వలి a fold, ముఖము.] n. A monkey. వానరము, కోతి.

వలుకు or **వలుకు** *valuku*. [Tel.] n. An intricacy, difficulty. వలకు, చిక్కు. A dispute, తగవు. "అంతరంమెరుగనివలుకులు." Satyabha. iv. 283.

వలుద, వలుంద or **వల్ద** *valuda*. [Tel.] adj. Big, large, stout, స్థూలమైన, గొప్ప. "చాలవలుందదిమీలగ్నకోని." Chenn. iv. 343. "వలుదమత్స్యంబు." BD. iv. 1816.

వలువ, వలువము, వలువు, వల్వము or **వల్వ** *valuva*. [Tel.] n. A fine garment, a cloth. వస్త్రము. "చెలువొందువలువలు వల హెమ్మసొమ్ములు." T. iii. 5.

వలె, వలెను or **వలెనే** *vale*. [Tel. from పోలు.] adv. Like, resembling, according to, as though. రీతిగా, పోలికగా. "నన్నురాధ వలె నేలుము" Ila. ii. 155. **వలె** or **వలెను** [from వలయు.] See వలయు.

వలెవాటు See వల్లెవాటు.

వల్కము *valkamu*. [Skt.] n. The bark of a tree, the fibre of a tree or plant. చెట్టుపై పట్ట, తోక, నార. **వల్కలము** *valkalamu*. n. The bark of a tree, చెట్టుపైనార. A hermit's garb made of bark. నారచీర.

వల్గ *valga*. [Skt.] n. A bridle, a rein. గుర్రపుకళ్లెముతగిలించేవారు, వాగె.

వల్గత్ *valgat*. [Skt.] adj. Moving. కదలు చున్న. **వల్గనము** *valganamu*. n. Galloping, prancing, curvetting. అశ్వగమనభేదము. "కేనుమెమంబుదెక్కి రంటకుని రీతితోడనలవల్గ నుల్ గవాగాల్ చెలంగ." T. v. 75. టీ॥ వల్గనముల్, దుముకుటలు. **వల్గించు** *valgintsu*. v. n. To gallop, to curvet, to bound. (గుర్రము) నరుగెత్తు. "నదన ద్వారమువిచ్చి విట్టుంగరవాగె వల్గింపగాలితో." Vish. vii. 375. **వల్గితము** *valgitamu*. n. A horse's gallop. అశ్వగతిభేదము, ఒకవైపుగానడచుదము. **వల్గువు** *valguvu*. adj. Handsome, beautiful, delicate, tender. సుందరమైన, మృదువైన. n. An eyelash, కనురెప్పమీదివెండ్రుక.

వల్మీకము or **వల్మీకము** *valmikamu*. [Skt]. n. An ant hill, పుట్ట. వల్మీకముల్లో బ్బునమును గలుగు the serpents enter the ant hills.

వల్ల *valla*. [Tel. another form of వలన.] A postposition used as a case ending in the 5th case of nouns and pronouns. By, by means of, from. వానివల్ల తెలిసినది I learned it from him, or of him. ఈ మందువల్ల by means of this medicine. adj. Convenient, feasible, practicable, possible. యుక్తము, అనుకూలము. అది వల్లకాదు it is impossible. అక్కడికి పోవల్లలేదు you cannot go there. ఇది లేకుండే వల్లకాదు I cannot do without this. చెల్లిస్తేగాని వల్లకాదు you cannot avoid paying it. వాడు ఉండేగాని వల్లకాదు I cannot do without him. నీవు వస్తేగాని వల్లకాదు your coming is indispensable, it cannot be done unless you come. చెప్పకపోక వల్లకాదు you cannot avoid explaining this. n. A stratagem, expedient, convenience. ఉపాయము, యుక్తి. వల్లపట్టుతప్పి పడినాడు he lost his hold and fell. ఎడమువల్లవాడు a left handed man, ఎడమచెయి వాటముగలవాడు. వల్లకాని *valla-kāni*. adj. Impracticable, impossible. అసాధ్యమైన. వల్లమాలిన *valla-mālina*. adj. Much, excessive; impracticable, అపరిమితమైన. వల్లగానుండు *valla-ga-n-uṇḍu*. v. n. To be convenient, practicable, possible, feasible. సాధ్యముగానుండు.

వల్లకాడు *valla-kāḍu*. [Tel. వల్లడి+కాడు.] n. A cemetery, a place for burning or burying corpses. శ్మశానము. The inflected form వల్లకాటి like "gallows" is used as a term of scorn. వల్లకాటిఅవాడు that vile Doctor.

వల్లకి *vallaki*. [Skt.] n. The Indian lute. వీణె, విపంచి.

వల్లడి *vallaḍi*. [Tel.] n. A causeless or unaccountable danger or calamity. అకారణమైన ఆపద. Plunder, కొల్ల. వల్లడికాడు *vallaḍi-kāḍu*. n. One who causes danger without a cause. అకారణముగా ఆపదను కలుగచేయువాడు. A plunderer, కొల్లపెట్టువాడు.

వల్లభము *vallabhamu*. [Skt.] n. A horse of a good breed. మేలుజాతిగుర్రము. adj. Dear. ప్రియమైన. వల్లభ *vallabha*. n. A loved woman, a mistress, a wife. ప్రియురాలు. వల్లభుడు *vallabhuḍu*. n. A lover, a husband, a friend, ప్రియుడు. మగడు. A lord, ruler, chief, అధిపతి.

వల్లము or వల్ల *vallamu*. [Tel.] n. A purse. తిత్తి. సంచి. "నిద్దపుదోపతిపట్టిడొల్లిరాదిచిచి పెంపిరివల్లమడి దించి" A. vi. 106.

వల్లరసి *valla-rasi*. [Tel.] n. A tree called *Walsura ternata*. Rox. ii. 389.

వల్లరి *vallari*. [Skt.] n. A tender twig with the sprouting leaves on it. చిగిరించిన లేతకొమ్మ. A bunch of flowers. A compound pedicle, a composite flower; a creeper. పూగుత్తి. చిగురుగుత్తి, తీగె. "వల్లరులంటంబువడిజొట్టుకొనిరెు." L. vii. 50.

వల్లవుడు *vallavuḍu*. [Skt.] n. A cook, వంటవాడు. A herdsman. గొల్లవాడు. వల్లవి *vallavi*. n. A cowherdess, a milkmaid. గొల్లది. Vasu. iv. 16.

వల్లి or వల్లిక *valli*. [Skt.] n. A creeper, or climbing plant. తీగె, లత.

వల్లించు *vallintsu*. [Tel. from వల్లె.] v. a. To learn or get by heart, to repeat from memory or by rote. వల్లెవేయు, పాఠముచేయు. See వల్లె.

వల్లిగము *valligamu*. [Tel.] n. An iron hoop which forms the rim of a leathern bucket. బొక్కెనపైనియినుపవలయము.

వల్లువము Same as వల్లము. (q. v.) "పెనంగ వల్లువము త్రెంచి." ఆము. vi.

వల్లూరము *vallūramu*. [Skt.] n. Dried flesh, a dry rasher or steak. ఎండినమాంసము, కరకుట్టు, కరవాడు. Bacon, pork, పంది మంసోడు.

వల్లె, or వల్లియ *valle*. [Tel.] A noosed rope: a noose for catching cattle. పోవుచున్నదొడ్డును కొమ్ములకువేసి పట్టుకొనే త్రాడు. పాశము. The noose of Varuṇa.

"వల్చిమాయున్న పాలమెల్ల వల్లెవైచుచందిమున వా ట్టుకొనిన." P. ii. 205. టీ॥ వల్లెవైచుచందమున, వల్లెత్రాడువేసినట్లువలెనే. Repetition, చెప్పినది మరల మరల చెప్పుట. adv. Yes, సరే. "క॥ వల్లెయని రాజనందను, లెల్లనుసమకట్టి." భార. ఆది. iii. వల్లెకోలుపు, వల్లెకొల్పు an epithet of Varuna, వరుణుడు. వల్లెవాటు or వలెవాటు valle-vaṭu. n. A scarf, a term for the upper garment, if gracefully arranged round the neck. సాగముగావేసికొన్న ఉత్తరీయము. వల్లెయొక్క వాటువంటివాటు.

వల్వ Same as వలువ. adv. Sweetly. Also, the infinitive form of the verb వలచు. వల్వక or వలువక without wishing. వల్వము same as వల్వ, వలువ or వలువము.

వలక్షము valakshamu. [Skt.] adj. White, తెల్లని.

వలవు or **ఒలవు** valavu. [Kan.] n. A stratagem, trick, device. A secret. ఉపాయము, కుట్ర, మర్మము, బంధించుము, తంత్రము. "దేవ దానవ మహాహవ నాటకసూత్రధారిపై ఘనము గవిసెనిమాటు బయుకాదవునినికి నేర్పెరింగ నే." T. iv. 236. టీ॥ వలవు, అంగా జాడ. వీడు శత్రువులకు వలవుగానుండినాడు he was plotting with the enemy.

వలాగ్రము valāgramu. [Tel.] n. A superior species of the areca (or betel) nut. క్రముకభేదము.

వలావలి valāvali. [Tel.] n. Excessive joy or pride, కుతూహలము, విజృంభణము. Riot, hubbub. అడావుడి, కోలాహలము. "చిలుక కేటికెవలావలియిఁకర్ప" P. iv. 191. "సీ॥ లలితానసేందు మండలపాండురచ్ఛాయ వనరుహ వలివలావలియడంప." Vasu. iii. 160. టీ॥ వలావలి, అడావుడిని.

వలాసము valāsamu. [Tel.] n. A bag, pouch, సంచి.

వలి vali. [Skt.] n. A fold of the skin or fat forming lines across the belly over the navel. కడుపుమీదిముడత. శరీరపుముడత. Any fold, ముడుత. A rhyming letter, యతిస్థానాక్షరము. "వలిలోనంగము లుపొక్కిలినుట్లు." N. ii. 284. వలులు valulu. n. plu. Folds, ముడుతలు. Goods, సరుకులు. "మంచి వలులకు వెలజోసగించువేళ." S. iii. 46.

వలుకు valuku. [Tel.] n. Justice. A dispute, జగడము. A quality, గుణము. ధర్మము.

వశము vaṣamu. [Skt.] n. Possession, custody, charge. Subjection, submission, లోకువ, స్వాధీనము. Ability, authority, power, supremacy, ప్రభుత్వము, అధికత్వము. అతనివశములో ఉన్నది it is in his charge or in his hands. "ధనముపీథమడిన దైవవశంబున నుండదు." సమీరవశంబున carried by the wind, breeze-borne. ఆ యింటిని తనవశము చేసికొన్నాడు he took charge or possession of the house. నన్ను వశపరచుకొనలేకపోయినాడు he was unable to get me into his hands. అది నాకు వశము, లేక. అది నా వశమైనున్నదా is it in my power to do so? కాలవశముచేత in the course of time, by the lapse of time. నాకు ఆకలి వశముకాకుండా ఉన్నది I cannot curb my appetite, I am excessively hungry. నా పుణ్యవశమున by my luck. **వశ** vaṣa. n. A wife, పెండ్లాము. A female elephant, ఆడుఏనుగు. A barren cow, గొడ్డుటావు. **వశంవదము** vaṣam-vadamu. adj. Submissive, obedient. విధేయమైన. **వశంవదుడు** vaṣam-vaḍuḍu. n. One who talks submissively, one who is submissive, విధేయుడు, లోకువయినట్లు మాటలాడువాడు. **వశత్వము** vaṣatvamu. n. Obedience, submissiveness. M. XVI. i. 226. కాలవశత్వంబున by the course of time. **వశపరచుకొను** vaṣa-paratsu-konu. v. t. To take possession of, to take under one's control.
వశాత్ or **వశాత్తుగా** vaṣat. adv. Through, by in consequence of, in

subjection to, over-powered by. గ్రహచా రవశాత్తుగా through his bad luck. దైవవశాత్ by the finger of God. వశి vaṣi. n. A chaste man; one who has subdued his passions. ఇంద్రియ నిగ్రహముకలవాడు. వశీకరణము vaṣī-karaṇamu. n. The act of over-powering, subduing, or inveigling by charms, spells or drugs. మందుమాకుల చేత స్వాధీనముచేసికొనడము, వశ్యముచేసు కొనడము. వశీకరించు vaṣī-karinṭsu. v. a. To subdue or over-power by means of charms, drugs, &c. వశ్యము vaṣyamu. adj. Dependant on, subject to, over-powered by charms, drugs, &c. స్వాధీనమైన, లోబడైన. వశ్యుడు vaṣyuḍu. n. A dependant, one who is submissive, obedient, or subject to, విధేయుడు. వశ్యురాలు vaṣyu-r-ālu. n. She who is submissive. విధేయురాలు. వశ్యౌషధము vaṣy-aushadhamu. n. Any medicine made use of to subject another to one's own will. A love-powder.

వషట్కృతము vashaṭkṛitamu. [Skt.] adj. Burnt as an offering. అగ్నియందు వేల్వ బడిన (హవిస్సు).

వస vasa. [from Skt. వచము.] n. Sweet flag: *Acorus calamus.* (E.P.) వసపోలు the root of this, macerated in milk as pap and given to an infant. చెక్కిలి మీటినవసగారుశిశువు a babe so young that if you touch his cheek it will exude pap. Serum; fat on the kidneys. A thin layer of fat found below the navel. కడుపులో బొడ్డుక్రిందనుండే ఉల్లిపొరవంటి కొవ్వు, వస. వసనాభి vasa-nābhi. n. Indian Aconite, *Aconitum ferox.*

వసంతము vasantamu. [Skt.] n. Spring time. వసంతఋతువు. Water mixed with turmeric and lime powder, which is thrown over people on festive occasions. పసుపు సున్నముకలిపిన ఎర్రనీళ్లు. వసంతమునాడు to fling such water over each other as a frolic in particular feasts. వసంత కడిమి vasanta-kaḍimi. n. A kind of tree. ధూళికదంబవృక్షము. వసంతగంధము vasanta-gandhamu. n. The plant called *Rottleria tinctoria.* కుంకుమవృక్షము. R. iii. 827. వసంతఘోషి vasanta-ghōshi. n. The vernal songster, i. e., the Indian cuckoo, కోకిలము, కోయిల. వసంతద్రుమము vasanta-drumamu. n. Lit. The tree of the spring season, i. e., the mango tree. మామిడి. వసంతుడు vasantuḍu. n. The god of Spring. *Vertumnus.*

వసత్ vasat. [Skt.] adj. Residing in, remaining at, dwelling in. ఉండే. వాసము చేసే.

వసతి vasati. [Skt. from వస్ to dwell.] n. A house, dwelling. ఇల్లు. Convenience. commodiousness, comfort. హాయి. సౌఖ్యము, అనుకూలము. Night, రాత్రి. Also, a pension, an allowance of money, భరణము. వసతి దారుడు a pensioner, a holder of an allowance of rent-free land. A proprietor of land, a landholder. అక్కడ నీళ్లవసతిలే నందున as good water is not easily procurable there. ఆయిల్లు నిండా వసతిగాలేదు the house is not very convenient. వారికి ఆ గ్రామములో వసతులు ఏర్పరిచినాడు, లేక, ఇచ్చినాడు he granted them a living in that village. వసతిగానుండే vasati-ga-n-unḍē. adj. Convenient, commodious. హాయిగానుండే. అక్కడ నీకు వసతిగా నుంటే దిగు if you find a suitable spot you may halt or put up there.

వసనము or వస్నము vasanamu. [Skt. from వస్ to dwell.] n. Staying, living. ఉనికి. A cloth, robe, వస్త్రము. Chenn. iii. 220.

వసము vasamu. [from Skt. వశము.] n. Submissiveness, having under one's control, స్వాధీనత, అధీనత. adj. Submissive, obedient. అధీనము. Possible, శక్యము. వస పడు or వసపోవు vasa-paḍu. v. n. To be controllable. స్వాధీనమగు. వసపోక

irresistibly, uncontrollably, స్వాధీనమవక. **వసమరు** *vasam-aru*. v. n. To fade or fail, తేజముచెడు, రంజుచెడు. "తెనుఁగు జనువసిష్టి చేసి శ్రేయమంటయు, వసమరివాడుర్పైపడి కూలిచచ్చె." DRU. 1146.

వసల or **వసలా** *vasala*. [Tel.] n. A tenon, or piece of wood joined on to another. కొయ్యకు అతుకువేయుకొయ్య.

వసార or **వసారా** *vasāra*. [Tel.] n. A verandah. పంచోడి, పంచేపాళి.

వసి *vasi*. [Tel.] n. A spike, a wooden pin. కొయ్యమేకు. "వసులబెక్కు కురంగివిపదిములను." Paidim. ii. 118. Prefix to certain verbs and nouns: Much, great, మిక్కిలి. **వసిగొను** *vasi-gonu*. v. n. To undertake, attempt. పూను, ఉత్సహించు. "ద్వి॥ వసిగొని పూరించుందే పతిలు నెత్తంగ, ..." BD vi. 1796. **వసిగోడ** or **వసులగోడ** *vasi-gōda*. n. A wall in which stakes are fixed. లోపల కొయ్యలు జేసి కట్టిన గోడ. "వసులగోడలమైన సుధనిచ్చె లేక యొక్క నేరవితేటియు మ్మెరాడి." Suca. i. 63. **వసితాకు** *vasi-tāku*. n. A great or heavy blow. గొప్పదెబ్బ. **వసిమాలు** *vasi-mālu*. v. n. To be quite lost or ruined, మిక్కిలి చెడిపోవు. **వసివారు** *vasi-vāru*. v. n. To run off, మిక్కిలిపారు. **వసివాడు** *vasi-vādu*. v. n. To fade much, to lose the first brilliancy, మిక్కిలి వాడు, కసుగందు. "వసివాడినముద్దుమొగంబు." Suca. i. 114. **వసివాడులు** or **వసివాళ్లు** *vasi-vādulu*. n. plu. Paleness, great fading. మిక్కిలి వాడుటలు, కసుగందులు. "ముసుగుడగ్గరబిగిచిముసు దచందమున, వసివాళ్లువాడుచు వదనంబుపంచి, కాటుకకన్నీరు కడగోరదిద్ది." Navan. 105.

వసించు or **వసియించు** *vasintsu*. [Skt. from వస్ to dwell.] v. n. To dwell, reside, lodge, live. To be, remain. ఉండు, వాసముచేయు, నివసించు.

వసిష్ఠుడు *vasishthudu*. [Skt.] n. The name of a celebrated hermit. బ్రహ్మమానసపుత్రుడు. **వసిష్ఠవాక్యము** *vasishtha-vākyamu*. n. Lit: Vasistha's dictum. A peremptory command.

వసులపాతర *vasula-pātara*. [Tel.] n. A sort of fighting cock. ఒకవిధమైన పందెపు పుంజు. "కత్తులపొదిసింహగాలిచేతాకుండు, వసులపాతర పౌరపపుట్టుచ్చు." H. iii. 268.

వసులు *vasulu*. [Tel.] v. n. To slip out, be dislocated. తొలగు. **వసిలిపోవు** *vasili-pōvu*. v. n. To slip out, or be dislocated. తొలగిపోవు.

వసువు *vasuvu*. [Skt.] n. Gold. బంగారు. Wealth, riches, ధనము. A gem, a jewel, రత్నము. A ray of light, కిరణము. Water, జలము. A kind of demi-god, దివ్యగణదేవతలలో నొకడు. The name of a king, ఒక రాజు పేరు. వసుధారాస్తంభము a pillar out of which a fountain gushes. **వసువులు** or **అష్టవసువులు** *vasuvulu*. n. plu. Eight demi-gods called Vasus. They are ఆపుడు, ధ్రువుడు, సోముడు, అధ్వరుడు, అనిలుడు, ప్రత్యూషుడు, అనలుడు, ప్రభాసుడు. **వసుంధర**, **వసుగర్భ**, **వసుధ** or **వసుమతి** *vasun-dhara*. n. The earth. భూమి. **వసుదేవుడు** *vasu-dēvudu*. n. The father of Krishna. కృష్ణునితండ్రి.

వసూలు *vasūlu*. [H.] n. A collection of money. జమ **వసూలుచేయు** *vasūlu-chēyu*. v. a. To collect money, to realise.

వస్తాదు *vastādu*. [H.] n. A leader, a captain, a tutor.

వస్తి *vasti* [Skt.] n. The abdomen or lower part of the belly పొత్తికడుపు. The end of a cloth, బట్టయొక్క మొదటిపడి.

వస్తువు *vastuvu*. [Skt.] n. A thing, article, matter, substance. పదార్థము, సొమ్ము, సరుకు. "ఆట్టిపురుషుడు మనమునన్నిటినుచు చెప్పరాట్టి

వస్తువులేదు." Vēma. iii. "జీవిపోక ముంజతీవశి వస్తువులిచ్చి, జీవినిలువవలయు జీవముగతి, జీవి తోలగువెనుక జీవవస్తువులేల." ib. v. 61. పరవస్తువు the Supreme Being, Providence, God.

వస్త్రము *vastramu.* [Skt.] n. A cloth, clothes, raiment, dress, చేలము, బట్ట. కట్టువస్త్రముతో నన్ను తెచ్చినారు they brought me in my shirt, they brought me just as I was. అన్నవస్త్రములు food and raiment. వస్త్రగాలితముచేయు to strain a powder through a dry cloth.

వహవ్వా *vahavvā.* [H.] interj. Well done! Bravo!

వహి *vahi.* [from Skt. వహ్ to carry.] n. A book, పుస్తకము. An account book. లెక్కపుస్తకము. A head in accounts. Manner, mode, fashion, రీతి. Celebrity, reputation. ఖ్యాతి, పేరు. "ఈవహిదినదినమర్పిన గాలింపగ." Bhanumad. iv. 29. "మహిమీదనెల్లధర్మరాజాఖ్య వహికెక్కగాధర్మిజాతజ్ఞ సరణి." L. i. 66. వహిలెక్క an account kept in a book. n. One who bears. వహించువాడు.

వహించు or **వహియించు** *vahintsu.* [Skt. వహ్ to carry.] v. a. To bear, support, sustain, assume, undertake. అతడు ఈ ప్రతిష్ఠను వహించినాడు he gained this reputation. నామీద కాన్పొగ్గరమును వహించినాడు he entertained ill will against me. ముష్కరమును వహించు to become obstinate. ఠమజోబును శిరసావహించినాను I have the honor to acknowledge your letter. **వహనము** *vahanamu.* n. Carrying, bearing, వహించుట. Anything that carries. A ship, ఓడ. **వహిత్రము** *vahitramu.* n. A raft, a float, a vessel. నావాభేదము. BD. ii. 509. A. iv. 113. **వహ్ని** *vahni.* n. Fire, the god of fire. అగ్ని.

వా va

వా *vā.* [Tel. Short for వాయి.] n. The mouth, the face. నోరు "కనిముసుమ్మునబూడిదిగిరింతవామూయుటెరిగిన నూతిపాతిరబోరిదులు." A vi. 12. టీ॥ వామూయు నెరిగినదిగిరింత, ఖడ్గముఖమెల్లా మూయుటెరిగిన. The edge of a sword, ఖడ్గధార. **వాకట్టు** *vā-kattu.* n. Gagging, వాగ్బంధనము, నోరు తెరవకుండా చేయుటము. ఈతాకట్టు వాకట్టు అయినది this mortgage is fore-closed. v. a. To gag. నోరెత్తకుండాచేయు. "కుక్కలవాకట్టిన్పొవిగో ధన్యమాభోగంబుల్ ప్రకాశించి." HN. v. 158. **వాకాటు** *vā-kātu.* n. Wrangling, వాగ్వాదము. వాచచ్చినవాడు a dumb animal, i. e., a mere fool. **వాచెరుచు** *vā-cherutsu.* v. a. To spoil the taste of the mouth. **వాచరచు** *vā-tsaratsu.* v. a. Lit: to beat the mouth. To beg alms. (Indian beggars or complainants often slap their open mouth with the open hand in wailing to attract attention.) దీనప్ప త్తిని యాచించు, నోటిమీదకొట్టుకొను. v. n. To cry, మొరపెట్టు. "వాత్రోవకడ్డంబు నిలిచివాచరువకనిలునిలుచదనుచు." BD. v. 1050. బాదరువక. మొత్తుకొకుండా. **వాచవి** *vā-tsavi.* n. Taste or flavour to the mouth. నోటిరుచి. "భూజనకుమారునకు వాచవిగానిద్ధనిరుడు ద్రావించి." Sār. D. 556. **వాతెర** *vā-tera.* (వా+తెర.) n. The lower lip; lit. the screen of the mouth. పెదవి. అధరోష్ఠము. **వాపాఠము** *vā-pāthamu.* n. Recitation, repeating verses by rote. ముఖస్థము గా నుండినది. "ధర్మశాస్త్రంబు వాపాఠంబు నీకు పరిపరివిధముల పలికింపనేర్చు." **వాపుచ్చు** *vā-putstsu.* v. a. To open the mouth. నోరుతెరచు. To say or tell, చెప్పు. **వాపోవు** *vā-pōvu.* v. n. To cry out, to chatter or babble. To cry or bewail, రోదనముచేయు, అక్కరలేనిమాటలాడు, ఏడ్చు.

వాంచు *vāntsu.* [Tel. another form of వంచు.] v. a. To bow down, to decline, to bend. వంకచేయు. "మునిమునినిగపుతో మోమువాంచు" Radha Madh. i. 60.

వాంఛ *vānchha.* [Skt.] n. Wish, desire, attachment. ఇచ్ఛ, కోరిక, కాంక్ష. **వాంఛించు**

vānchhintsu. v. a. To desire, long for, wish, fancy, like. ఇచ్ఛించు, కోరు, కాంక్షించు. వాంఛితము vānchhitamu. adj. Desired, కోరబడిన.

వాండ్రు or వాండ్లు vāndru. [Tel. the third person plural of వాడు he.] n. They, those people. వారు.

వాంతి vānti. [Skt.] n. Vomiting. కక్కడము, వమనము, డోకుకొనడము. వాంతిభ్రాంతి or వాంతిభేది vomiting and purging, cholera. వాంతము vāntamu. adj. Vomited. కక్కబడినది.

వాంశికుడు vāmsi-kudu. [Skt. from వంశము a bamboo.] n. A flute-player, a piper. పిల్లంగ్రోవినూదువాడు.

వాక vāka. [Tel.] n. A side. ప్రక్క. కరవాక the shore side. A river, a stream, ఏరు, నది. "చదలువాకసిటజలకమాడి." Parij. iv. 49. "ప్రవహించెదిని కేనవాకయనగ." Ila. iii. 127. వరికివాక దొరకునూక what avails a crop without a stream? what avails a chief without a troop? వాకతాలుపు or వాకతాల్పు lit. the river-crested; an epithet of Siva, గంగాధరుడు.

వాకకాయ, వాక్కాయ or వాకలిగ్గికాయ vāka-kāya. [Tel.] n. The tree called *Carissa carandas*; also, *Carissa spinarum*, (Watts.) the fruit of which is edible. పెద్దకలివికాయ. "కొలకక్కాయయును వాకలిగ్గికాయయును చిరిసెల్లికాయయును చిల్లకాయ." H. iv. 169.

వాకబు vākabu. [H.] adj. Skilled, versed in, experienced, accustomed to. n. Experience. అనుభవము. వాకబుచేయు to ascertain by making enquiries.

వాకము vākamu. [Tel.] n. Level. సమము. A side, ప్రక్క. Convenience, అనుకూలము.

వాకర vā-kara. [Tel.] n. Retching to vomit. ఓకరింత.

వాకిలి vākili. [Tel. వా + ఇల్లు.] n. A door, a door way, a front yard. తలవాకిలి an entrance into a house, a gate way, ద్వారము, గృహద్వారము. plu. వాకిండ్లు, వాకిళ్లు or వాకిళులు. Gen. వాకిటి. Loc. వాకిట. "అటగోక్కష్టముడువచ్చిననసింకపనిద్రైన, పదలివత్తురుకల వాకిళులకు." N. ix. 293. వాకిటికాండ్లు porters, door-keepers, ద్వారపాలకులు. వాకిలితలుపు the house door. వాకిట నుండు to stop at the door, to be in menses.

వాకుడు vākudu. [Tel.] n. A sort of prickly nightshade, *Solanum jacquini*, కంటకారిక.

వాక్కు or వాకు vakku. [Skt.] n. Speech, speaking. A word, పలుకు, మాట. "పాలవంటి వాకుపన్ను పెక్కడువారు, వాకురుగరువారు." Vēma. 1314. మనోవాక్కాయకర్మంబుల by mind, word, limbs or acts. వాగ్దత్తము a promise. వాగ్దానము giving a promise. వాక్సహాయము interest, recommendation. వాక్పటుత్వము power of speech, eloquence. వాకొను va-konu. v. a. To tell, say, utter, speak. చెప్పు. మాటాడు. To cry out. అరచు. వాక్పతి or వాగీశుడు vāk-pati. n. Lord of speech. A name of Brahma or of Brihaspati, బ్రహ్మ, బృహస్పతి. An eloquent person. మిక్కిలి చతురముగ మాట్లాడువాడు. A poet కవీశ్వరుడు. వాక్యము vākyamu. n. A sentence, కర్తృకర్మ క్రియా సంబంధముగల పదసమూహము. Speech, a word, utterance, dictate. మాట. (In astronomy,) the process for astronomical computations. వాక్రుచ్చు va-krutstsu. (వాకు+ కూర్చు.) v. a. To say, utter. చెప్పు. To name, పేరుచెప్పు. "గారాబుసంతతిగలుగమి మనకుక్షిర మవృత్తస్వగతిర్నా స్తియనుచు వరవేద వాక్యముల్ వాక్రుచ్చుచుండు." L. iii. 105. వాక్సరణి vāk-sarani. n. The course of conversation. వాగ్ధోరణి. వాగ్జాలము vāg-jālamu. n. A mass of words, loquacity. శబ్దచయము. వాగ్దేవత or వాగ్దేవి vāg dēvata.

n. The goddess of speech, Sarasvati, సరస్వతిదేవి. వాగ్ధాటి *vāg-dhaṭi*. n. Readiness of speech, వాక్పటుత్వము. వాగ్బంధనము *vāg-bandhanamu*. n. Silencing, stopping any one's speech. నోరుకట్టుటము. వాగ్మి *vāgmi*. n. A man of eloquence, an orator, one who is talkative, or talks much. సలుగురిలో నిర్భయముగా మాట్లాడేవాడు, యుక్తియుక్తముగా మాట్లాడువాడు, మాటకారి. వాగ్వాదము *vāg-vādamu*. n. A verbal dispute or altercation, an argument. వాక్కలహము. వాఙ్మూలము *vāng-mūlamu*. (from వాక్ mouth and మూలము origin.) n. A deposition, an oral statement. వాచాచెప్పినది. వాచాచెప్పినదానిని వ్రాసినది. వాఙ్మూలము వ్రాయించు or ఇచ్చు *vāng-mūlamu-vrayintsu*. v. n. To depose, to make a deposition. వాఙ్మూలము వ్రాసికొను to take down a deposition. వాఙ్మూలముగా *vāng-mūlamu-gā*. adv. Orally, by word of mouth. నోటిమాటగా.

వాగ Same as వాగె. (q. v.)

వాగడుపు *vā-gaḍupu*. [Tel. వావు+కడుపు.] n. A swollen belly. వాచినకడుపు. "సీ॥ బీద సరాలతో బెరుగువాగడుపులో బల్లనల్లడలంగు ద్రుళ్లిపడగ." S. iii. 37.

వాగర *vā-gara*. [Tel. వ్రాయు + కర్ర.] n. A painting brush. తూలిక.

వాగరత or వాగర్త *vāg-arata*. [Tel. వాగులు+ అరత.] n. The sea-side or shore. సముద్రతీరము.

వాగరా *vāgarā*. [Tel.] n. A channel, or water course by which water comes into a reservoir. చెరువుకు నీళ్లువచ్చేకాలువ.

వాగళ్లము or వాగళము *vā-gallamu*. [Tel. వా+కళ్లము.] n. The circular space round a thrashing floor. కళ్లముచుట్టుఉండుచోటు, కళ్లముయొక్కముందుభాగము.

వాగాడంబరము Same as వాగ్వాదము. See under వాక్కు.

వాగీశుడు See under వాక్కు.

వాగు *vāgu*. [Tel.] v. n. To sound, ring, or emit sound. మోగు. To talk or chatter, అక్కరలేనిమాటలాడు, వదరు. n. A hill stream, a torrent, a channel, a hollow or breach such as that formed by a torrent. కొండమీదనుండివచ్చినకాలువ, సెలయేరు. An army, సైన్యము. "వాగులతో పరదళతతిన్నిరోధించిన బిరుదెవ్వరు?" Bhāskara. § 45. వాగుడు *vāguḍu*. n. Sounding, noise, మ్రోగుడు, మ్రోత, ధ్వని. వాగులు *vāgulu*. n. plu. Waves, అలలు.

వాగుర *vāgura*. [Skt.] n. A net, snare, noose, toils or nets for birds or animals. ఉరి, వల. వాగురికుడు *vāgur-ikuḍu*. n. A hunter, a snarer of birds or animals. ఉరులువలలుపన్ని వేటాడిజీవించేవాడు.

వాగె, వాగ or వాగియ *vāge*. [Skt.] n. The rein of a bridle, గుర్రపుకళ్లెమును తిగిలించేవారు. A painting brush, చిత్తరువువ్రాసేతూలిక. "తురంగంబులవాగెలుపట్టియెత్తి." M. IV. iv. 172. "శ్యామలకపిల, వర్ణములుకూర్చి చిప్పలవాగెలునిచి, చిత్తరువువ్రాయుగుళ్లలో చిత్రనుముడు." H. iii. 7.

వాచ *vācha*. [Skt.] n. Another form of వాక్కు. (q. v.). వాచంయముడు *vācham-yamuḍu*. n. A sage or prophet, మునీశ్వరుడు, మౌని. వాచకము *vāchakamu*. n. A word, a significant sound, శాస్త్రకల్పిత వాక్కు, వాచ్యార్థమును తెలుపుశబ్దము. (Vulgarly) fluency in reading, చదివేవాచకపు శక్తి. వాచస్పతి *vāchas-pati*. n. The lord of speech, i. e., Brihaspati. వాచా *vāchā*. adv. Orally, verbally, viva voce, by word of mouth. అతను వాచాచెప్పినాడు he said it orally. వాచాటుడు or వాచాలుడు

vāchāṭuḍu. n. A talkative man, one who talks idly or blamably, a tattler, వాగుపోతు, స్త్రీలవాడు, మాటకారి. "వాచాటులగు జరకవనితలు." A. iv. 43. వాచాలము vāchālamu. adj. Chattering, talkative, gabbling, talking much. స్త్రీల, వాగే, వదరిమాటిన మాటలాడే. వాచాలత or వాచాలత్వము vāchālatu. n. Talkativeness, readiness or fluency of speech, tattling, స్త్రీలడము, వాగడము, తిరుమాగా మాటలాడడము. "రాజలల్ల ఇలగ వాచాలత్వముబాపె." G. vii. 10. వాచించు vāchiṇtsu. v. a. To tell, చెప్పు. To read, చదువు. వాచికము vāchikamu. n. News, intelligence, tidings. చెప్పిపంపించిన వర్తమానము, సమాచారము. "కాంచన పత్రికావళుల కౌతుకమూనక వాచికంబు ప్రాయుంచినమస్తకేశనము ధేశులకంపిన." Vasu. v. 80. టీ॥ వాచికము, సందేశవాక్య. వాచ్యము vāchyamu. adj. Fit or proper to be spoken or said. చెప్పదగిన. Blameworthy, vile, contemptible, low, out-caste. నిందింపదగిన, నింద్యము. హీనము. In grammar, the voice or mood of a verb. కర్తృవాచ్యము the active voice; కర్మణివాచ్యము the passive voice.

వాచేరము See under వా.

వాచ్చారు vāṭsaru. [Tel.] v. n. To lament, వలవించు, ప్రలాపించు. "పద్మరులపోకి చాలవాపోకలు." Satya. iii. 93. వాచేరము or వాచ్చారపము vāṭsaramu. n. Lamentation, వాపోవుట, పరితేపనము.

వాచు vāṭsu. [Tel.] v. n. To swell. బొప్పిచేరలాడు. To pine, long, be eager. కేపురించు, ఏడుచు. (The Hindus like the Musulmans imagine the face and the legs to swell with desire or want.) వాడు కూటికి వాచియున్నాడు he is perishing for want of food. మేము దానికి వాచినవారముకాము we are not pining for it, we do not care for it. "ఉ॥ మేముస్తి అముగ వాచినవారిమెల్లనిగురువయిన విగ్గాను నెంటె బాప్పభుజా." V. P. vi. 100

వాచూరు vā-ṭsūru. [Tel.] n. The eaves of a house. ఇంటి మూడువాడ, ముంజూరు. వామూగిపట్టె అనగా ఇంటిముంజూరుమూనీటి.

వాజపేయము vājapēyamu. [Skt.] n. A particular kind of sacrifice. యజ్ఞభేదము.

వాజి vāji. [Skt.] n. A horse. గుఱ్ఱము. A bird, పక్షి. An arrow, బాణము. వాజిగంధ vāji-gandha. n. The name of a plant, *Physalis flexuosa*. పెన్నేరు.

వాజీవి vājīvi. [H.] adj. Just, right, reasonable, proper. న్యాయమైన, సరియైన, తగిన.

వాడే vāḍsa. [Tel.] n. Disgust. రోత. adj Disgusting, రోతగల.

వాడేము vāḍsamu. [Tel.] n. A kind of bird. ఒకవిధమైనపక్షి.

వాటము vāṭamu. [Tel.] adj. Handsome, pretty. అందమైన. "వాటములైన సుందరులు." V. P. viii. 108. Convenient. అనుకూలమైన. n. Convenience, అనుకూలము. The slope of the ground, a roof, &c., which allows the water to flow off; sloping, slanting. వాలు, ఏటవాలుగానుండడము. "వాటంబులైన నివాలాయితోనగోళ్లు." Surabha. i. 63. [Skt.] n. A road, way, మార్గము. A street, ఇండ్లవరుస, వీధి. A garden, తోట. The site of a house or building, ప్రదేశము. యజ్ఞవాటము the spot where a sacrifice is made. వాటపడు vāṭa-paḍu. v. n. To be convenient. అనుకూలపడు, జరపడు, వల్లగానుండు.

వాటి or వాటిక vāṭi. [Skt.] n. A garden plot, or orchard. తోట. A place, the site of a house or building. ప్రదేశము, స్థలము. A row of houses, a street ఇండ్లవరుస. స్నానవాటిక a bath. చండాలవాటిక the abode of Pariahs. "ఇల్లాగ్రహైన స్నానవాటియుఖమూలాగోలంబుగా." Bilh. iii. 25.

వాటు vāṭu. [Tel. from వడి and పాటు.] n. The act of throwing. వైచుట. A blow, stroke, దెబ్బ. A mode, manner, way, fashion, విధము, రీతి. Convenience. కత్తివాటు an incision or cut. "మాయదయామాటకు మారుత్తరింబు వారొత్తగాలేక వాటు దప్పినను, జోహారు నమ్మట్లు." L. vii 77. Turning over, upsetting. బండి వాటుపడును the cart will upset. వాటుగాలు vāṭu-gālu. n. A lame leg, a leg that has a convulsive twitch in walking. నడవడినులో పక్కవాటుగా పోయే కాలు. "వాటుగాలును రోలునంటినదును." HK. iv. 143. "వాటుగాలనరాదు చేటు దెచ్చు." S. ii. 20. వాటుగాలు వేసుకొనుచు వచ్చినాడు he came twitching along or limping. వాటురాయి vāṭu-rāyi. n. A stone for slinging, a pebble or stone that could be easily flung at a person, రువ్వడమునకుతగిన రాయి. "ద్విఃబలుకులబూడిదయును వాటురాలు." BD. v. 680. వాటులాడు vāṭul-āḍu. v. n. To fight, కొట్లాడు. వాట్లీడు vāṭl-īḍu. n. A quarrelsome man, కొట్లాడువాడు.

వాడ vāḍa. [Tel. for ఓడ.] n. A ship. నావ. వాడంగి vāḍangi. n. A boat man, ఓడవాడు. The beams of a boat, దోనెకులోతట్టుచేసేదూలము. వాడగన్నేరు vāḍa-gannēru. n. A certain fragrant plant, called Oleander, *Nerium odorum*, కరవీరవృక్షము. వాడగాలి vāḍa-gāli. n. Wind that blows from the sea, a strong wind. వాడముక్కు vāḍa-mukku. n. A small thin long snouted fish. మత్స్యభేదము.

వాడ vāḍa. [Tel.] n. A street, a range or row of houses. వీధి, ఇండ్లవరుస. Fragrance, scent, పరిమళము. "వాడవారిరిగినవాస్న దరుగు." H. i. 138. "వాడకురిలి తిట్టు వలదన్న మెరబెట్టు, ముందుముగి విడిట్టుముకుకుబెట్టు గిడుసురాలు మగని నింపబెట్టుమ్మురా." Vema. 173. వాడకురిలి. విభక్తి. వాడకట్టు vāḍa-kaṭṭu. n. Neighbourhood. వాడవదినె vāḍa-vadine. n. A whore, లంజె, వేశ్య. "వాడవదినె కేలవానివర్తనములు, వాడిగాని కేలజాడబుద్ధి మూఢమతుల కేల ముదముతో జ్ఞానంబు." Vēma. 1869.

వాడి vāḍi. [Tel.] n. Sharpness of weapons or instruments. అయుధాదులకరుకు, పదును. Heroism, శౌర్యము. adj. Sharp. కరుకు, తీక్ష్ణము, నిశితము. Cruel, క్రూరము. "మజ్ఞానము వాడికురియుచేబట్టి." BD. v. 1435. వాడిమగడు vāḍi-magaḍu. n. A hero, శూరుడు. వాడిమి vāḍ-imi. n. Sharpness, కరుకు, తైక్ష్ణ్యము. Brightness, తేజము, ప్రకాశము. Courage, శౌర్యము.

వాడు vāḍu. [Tel. cf. Tam. అవన్. The Drav. base of the word is అ or ఆ= that. The primitive form is అడు he. cf. అది. The sound of వ (V) is added to facilitate the pronunciation.] pron. in the third person masculine singular. He, that man, ఆ పురుషుడు. Gen. వాడి or వాని his. Dative వాడికి or వానికి to him. plu. వారు, వాండ్లు, వారలు or వాండ్రు they. వారు తమతమ యిండ్లకుపోయినారు they all went to their respective houses. వాడికివాడే he himself. వారికివారే they themselves. It is added to the genitive of a noun. ఇంటివాడు the owner of the house, the house-owner. గుర్రపువాడు a horsekeeper. రావిపాటివారు the people of the Ravipati family. తప్పెటవాడు he of the drum, the drummer. అక్కడివారు the people of that place. వాడు నావాడు he is a man of mine, i.e., he is my kinsman, my relation. అతని వారు his relations, his friends, his people. It is also added to verbal participles. పోయేవాడు the man who goes. పాడేవాడు he who sings, the singer. ఆడేవారు those who play, the players. వెళ్లేవాడా O passer-by! Added to adjectives, it forms the corresponding nouns. మంచివాడు a good man. చెడ్డవాడు a bad man. ముసలివాడు

an old man. చిన్నవాడు a boy. పెద్దవారు old folks. చిన్నవారు young folks.

వాడు [Tel.] v. n. To wither or fade. మ్లానమగు. "అరయాసత్వరమునవానవాజ్ఞమువాడ." T. iii. 144. వాడించు or వాడుచు vāḍinṭsu. v. a. To cause to wither, వాడజేయు. వాడబారు, వాడుపారు, వాడువెంచు or వాడుపడు vāḍa-bāru. v. n. To fade. మ్లానమగు, కందు. "సీ॥ లవలీదళములట్ల సవర్ణనచెక్కు-లు వాడ బారగముద్దులాడిరాడి." UR. iv. 287. వాడు or వాడుకొను vāḍu. v. a. To use, to make use of, ఉపయోగపరచు, పను పరచుకొను, వినియోగపరచు. v. n. To be generally talked, or spoken of. పరంతిగా చెప్పుకొను. వారీమాటలనువాడుకొనినారా did they use these words? వాడుదల vāḍu-dala. n. Use, practice, వాడుక, అభ్యాసము. వాడుక or వాడిక vāḍuka. n. Practice, habit, custom. సాధారణప్రసిద్ధి, పను పడ డము, ఉపయోగము, అభ్యాసము, అలవాటు. Business, వ్యవహారము. వాడికకు తెచ్చు to use, make use of. adj. Customary, usual, habitual. అలవాటుగానుండే. వాడుకగా or వాడికగా vāḍuka-gā. adv. Usually, commonly. అలవాటుగా. వాడుకపడు vāḍuka-paḍu. v. n. To be accustomed. పనుపడు, అలవాటుపడు. ఈపనిలో వాడుకపడ్డవారు persons accustomed to this business. వాడికవారు or వాడుకవాండ్రు vāḍika-vāru. n. plu. Customers. వాడికగా వచ్చువారు.

వాడెదవ vāḍe-dava. [Tel.] n. The end of a sugar-cane, చెరుకుదిబ్బ.

వాణి vāṇi. [Skt.] n. Voice, speech, sound, వాక్కు, పలుకు. The name of the Goddess of Speech, సరస్వతి. ఆకాశవాణి or గగనవాణి a voice from heaven, a voice heard from the sky. వాణీశుడు vāṇ-īsuḍu. n. Brahma, the husband of Sarasvati. బ్రహ్మదేవుడు.

వాణిజ్యము vāṇijyamu. [Skt. from వణిక్కు.] n. Traffic, trade, commerce. క్రయవిక్రయములుచేసే వైశ్యవృత్తి. వాణిజుడు vāṇijuḍu. n. A trader, merchant, వర్తకుడు, వణిజుడు.

వాణిని vāṇini. [Skt.] n. An actress, a dancer, a public singer. నాట్యకత్తె, ఆటకత్తె.

వాత vāta. [Tel. from వాయు.] n. A burning, a brand, a cautery, the mark which it produces. కాలినలోహముతో రోగమువచ్చిన పశ్వాదులను కాల్చడము. Also, the 3rd case of వాయి. By or in the mouth, నోటితో లేక, నోటియందు. వాతవేయు vāta-vēyu. v. a. To burn with an iron or apply as the actual cautery. To cauterize, to brand. కాలినలోహముతో రోగముగలపశ్వాదులను కాల్చు. To put in the mouth. నా యింటిని వాడు వాతవేసుకొన్నాడు he devoured my house, i. e, he seized my property. See under వాయి.

వాతము vātamu. [Skt.] n. Air, wind, వాయువు. గాలి. Rheumatism, gout, inflamation of the joints. వాతపోతము vāta-pōtamu. n. An infant breeze, a gentle wind, పిల్లగాలి. వాతపోథము vāta-podhamu. n. The Palasa tree, *Butea frondosa*. మోదుగచెట్టు, కింశుకము. వాతప్రమి, వాతమృగము or వాతాయువు vāta-prami. n. A swift antelope, గాలికెదురుగానడిచే మృగము. వాతాయనము vāt-āyanamu. n. A window, కిటికీ. వాతాశి vātāśi. n. A serpent. సర్పము.

వాతికాసు or వాతిబిరుద్యము See under వాయి.

వాతూలము vātūlamu. [Skt.] n. Wind గాలి. A whirlwind, a gale, a hurricane, సుడిగాలి. "ప్రగండవాతూలవాతంబనియు నగనో డ." Swa. Pref. 3. వాత్య vātya.

n. A whirlwind, or hurricane. సుడిగాలి, వాతూలము.

వాతెర See under వా.

వాత్సల్యము, వాత్సల్యత or వత్సలత vatsalyamu. [Skt. from వత్సలము.] n. Parental love, fondness. విశ్వాసము, పుత్రాదులయందుగలుగుప్రేమ. పుత్రవాత్సల్యము paternal kindness.

వాదనము vādanamu. [Skt.] n. Sound, sounding; beating. వీణాదిధ్వని, వాయించడము.

వాదము vādamu. [Skt. from వద్ to speak.] n. A dispute, discussion, contention. మాటలపూర్వకమైన కలహము, వాగ్వాదము, తగవు. Alchemy, రసవాదము. వాదభ్రష్టో వైద్యశ్రేష్ఠః he who fails in alchemy becomes an excellent doctor. "బధిరుబలె దరిద్రునికతివాదివపరిచినదకఁగాచుదాఁడ్చున." P. Pref. 15. టీ॥ వాదిపగిది, రసవాదివలెను. వాదించు, వాదము చేయు or వాదాడు vādinṭsu. v. a. To argue, debate, dispute, discuss. కలహముచేయు, జగడమాడు, తర్కించు. వాది vādi. n. A speaker. One who argues, వాదించువాడు. A plaintiff or complainant. వ్యాజ్యము తెచ్చినవాడు, తగవునకుపోయినవాడు. ప్రతివాది a defendant. ఏకవాది one who speaks or argues the point alone. "ఏకవాదికెల కచుచలంబు." Vēma. iii. 96. వాదు vādu. (from Skt. వాదము) n. A dispute, contention, fighting. కలహము, యుద్ధము. "స్త్రీల తోడివాదులాపకుము." Sumati. i. "వల దన్న బోవుదువె వాదుకుడిచుక." Ila. iv. 72. వాదుడుకుట, అనగా జగడమునకు పోకుట. "మునుగజాస్యునితో వాదుడుగక దొం నర్చిన పిమ్మట." S. iii. 412. వాదుచేయు or వాదులాడు vādu-chēyu. v. n. To dispute, to contend. వివాదమాడు, పోరుచేయు.

వాదోడు vā-dōḍu. [Tel. వా+తోడు.] n. Assistance in word or in speaking, మాటకు సహాయము. A social companion, a friend to talk with. మాటకుతోడు. An instrument to open and examine the diseased mouth of an animal, a pharingoscope. "వాదోడైనకుకాంగవాటులు, బెల్లం." Charu Chandrod. iv. 85.

వాదర vādara. [Tel. వాడి+ధార.] n. The edge of a sword. ఖడ్గాదితీక్ష్ణధార.

వాదిత్రము vāditramu. [Skt.] n. A kind of musical instrument. నాల్గువిధములైనవాద్యము. Music, వాద్యధ్వని. B. X. 245. B. i. 143.

వాద్యము vādyamu. [Skt.] n. Any musica instrument. మద్దెలడోలుసన్నాయిమొదలైనవాద్యములు మొదలగునవి.

వాన vāna. [Tel.] n. Rain, a shower, వర్షము. Plu. వానలు showers. The rainy season, వర్షాకాలము. వానలేనిపట్టిపిడుగు lit: a thunderbolt without rain: i. e., mere words without deeds. వానకాళ్లు vāna-kāllu. n. Dark or black streaks in the sky, which are a sign of rain, a Nimbus or raincloud, a water spout, వర్షధారలు. "శ్యామలోపరినిబిడచ్ఛదాత్రములకు కాండపండంబాదిగువానకాళ్లు గాగ." Swa. iii. 109. టీ॥ వానకాళ్లు, ఉదకధారలు. "మింటిపైనుండి తనవెంటనంటివచ్చుకాలసర్పంబులన వానకాళ్లుదనర." Paidim. iv. 13. వానకోకిల, వానకోయిల or వానకోవెల vāna-kōkila. n. The Coel or Indian Cuckoo. Also used for a swallow or martin. చాతకపక్షి. A harmless water snake of a brown colour, with two light green stripes down the back. వానకురిసినప్పుడు కైటపడే నీర్లపాము. "పడిగాపి ధిటితో వర్షంబుకాక కోరుచుండెడివానకోయిలభంగి." Pal. 15. వానదేలిపులుగు vāna-deāli-pulugu. n. A swan.

పాంసు. "అనిదయలవానజాలిపులుగావన జాతిని తెరచేడినజా." H. iv. 67. వానతరి *vana-tari*. n. The rainy season. వర్షాకాలము, వర్ష ఋతువు. వానకోయిల an epithet of the cuckoo. **వానపాము** or **వానపేను** *vana-pamu*. n. An earthworm; (lit: a rain worm. గండూపదము, మహీలత, ఎర్రిపాము. వానరాయి *vāna-rāyi*. n. A hailstone. వడగల్లు.

వానప్రస్థుడు *vāna-prasthudu*. [Skt.] n. A hermit, a recluse. కృతీయాశ్రమమందుండువాడు. వానప్రస్థము living in a forest.

వానరము *vānaramu*. [Skt.] n. A monkey, or ape, a "man of the woods." కోతి. వానరుడు a monkey; a mischief-maker, చెడ్డపనిచేయువాడు.

వానస్పత్యము *vānas-patyamu*. [Skt. from వనస్పతి.] n. A tree which bears blossoms and fruit; as the mango, Eugenia, &c. పూచికాచేచెట్టు. A tree which bears fruit without flowering is called వనస్పతి.

వాని *vāni*. [Tel. Possessive of వాడు and another form of వాడి.] pron. Of him, his. వానియొక్క. వానిజా or వానిని (the acc. singular of వాడు or the acc. plu. of అది that.) Him, or them. Those things, వాటిని. "కోరలుగలవాని గోళ్లుగలవాని కొమ్ములుగలవాని నమ్మవలదు." (G. i. 284.) never trust those animals which have tusks, claws, or horns.

వానీరము *vānīramu*. [Skt.] n. A sort of cane or rattan, *Calamus rotang*. వేతసము, ప్రబ్బ.

వాను *vānu*. [Tel.] v.a. To make, as pots, (కుండలు) చేయు. "అజాండభాండముల్ వానను." A. i. 3. "కేవల బ్రహ్మాండవివిధభాండములు గూడవానెడువాడికమ్మరియితడు." BD. iv. 120. వానించు *vānintsu*. v. a. To get (pots) made: to have (bricks) prepared. (కుండలు) చేయించు. (ఇటికెలు) కోయించు. ఇటికెలువానించి ఆ దేవాలయము కట్టించినాడు he got bricks made and had the temple built. వానె *vāne*. The name of a low caste among the Banians. A. iv. 36. వానెత *vāne-ta*. n. A woman of that caste. "అద్వైటికోటియగసాలె, సాలె, పటుసాలె, వానె, జైనాతి." A. iv. 56. వానీడు *vān-īdu*. (వానె + ఈడు.) n. A man of the Banian caste, వానెకులమువాడు. An epithet of Kubēra. కుబేరుడు.

వాపదండము See వాయుదండము.

వాపసు *vāpasu*. [H.] n. Restitution, returning. వాపసుచేయు to return, తిరిగియిచ్చు.

వాపి *vāpi*. [Skt.] n. A large oblong pond, pool, or lake. పెద్దకోనేరు. A well with steps, నడబావి.

వాపితము *vāpitamu*. [Skt.] adj. Sown, as seed. విత్తబడిన. Shaven, గొరగబడిన.

వాపు *vāpu*. [Tel. from వాచు.] n. Swelling, protuberance, intumescence. శోఫ, వాపుట. Pining or longing, ఆశ, దుఃఖించుట, ఏకట. మెంగుడువచ్చినతర్వాత దాని వాపుతీరెను the arrival of her husband put an end to her pining. వాపి *vāpi*. n. One whose body is swollen, వాపురోగముగలవాడు. వాపిరి *vāpiri*. (వాపు+ఇరి.) n. Lamenting, ఏకరట. వాపిరిగొట్టు *vāpiri-goṭṭu*. n. A glutton. తిండిపోతు. A fickle-tongued man, వాక్చాపల్యముగలవాడు. A gloomy looking man, ఏకరువాడు, దుఃఖించుచుండువాడు. వాపు *vāpu*. (for వాయించు.) n. Sounding a drum, &c. వాయించుట. వాపుతెవులు *vāpu-tevulu*. n. The dropsy. వాపురోగము, శోఫ.

వాపుచ్చు *va-putstsu*. [Tel.] v. a. To open the mouth, నోరుతెరచు. To say or tell, చెప్పు. వాపుచ్చని unsaid, that cannot be said.

చెప్పని, చెప్పగూడని. వాపోవు *va-pôvu.* v. a. To cry out, అరచు. To cry, bewail, weep, ఏడ్చు. వాపోక *va-pôka.* n. Crying, అరచుట, ఏడ్చుట.

వామ See under వామము.

వామదేవుడు *vama-dêvudu.* [Skt.] n. A name of Siva. శివుడు.

వామనము *vâmanamu.* [Skt.] adj. Dwarfish, short. పొట్టి. n. A tree termed ఊడుగుచెట్టు. వామనకాకి *vâmana-kaki.* n. The green billed Cuckoo. వామనకాయలు or వామనములు *vamana-kayalu.* n. plu. The name of a certain fruit used as a pickle. ఊరగాయచేసే ఒకవిధమైన కాయలు. Tender tamarind fruit, లేతచింతకాయలు. వామనగుంటలు *vamana-guntalu.* n. A tablet with fourteen holes for playing at a kind of game. గవ్వలుగాని చింతగింజలు మొదలైనవా టినిగాని వేసి ఆడే రెండు వరుసలుగా చేసిన గుంటలుగలపీట. వామనపాటుకాడు *vamana-patu-kadu.* A kind of bird. వామనావతారము *vaman-avataramu.* n. The fifth incarnation of Vishṇu as a dwarf. విష్ణువుయొక్క అయిదవ అవతారము. వామనీకృతము *vamani-kritamu.* adj. Shortened, stunted. పొట్టిగాచేయబడిన. వామనుడు *vamanudu.* n. A dwarf. పొట్టివాడు. An epithet of Vishṇu, విష్ణువు.

వామము *vamamu.* [Skt.] adj. Left, not right. సవ్యము, ఎడమ. Charming, lovely, రమ్యమైన. Crooked, వక్రము. Short, పొట్టి, హ్రస్వము. వామ *vama.* n. A lovely woman, సుందరమైనస్త్రీ. వామకరము *vama-karamu.* The left hand. ఎడమచెయ్యి. వామలోచన *vama-lôchana.* n. Lit: the bright eyed, or fine eyed, i.e., a beautiful eyed woman. సుందరనేత్రములుగలస్త్రీ. వామాన్యకరము the right hand; lit. the hand which is different from the left, కుడిచెయ్యి. KP. vi. 33.

వామలూరము or వామలూరువు *vamalû-ramu.* [Skt.] n. An ant hill, or mole hill, especially the mounds of earth thrown up by the white ant. పుట్ట.

వామి *vami.* [Tel.] n. A heap as of straw, a stack, any heap. రాశి, ప్రోగు, కుప్ప. "వామిగా పడగండ్లువర్షించెననగ, కురిసినమొగు మందుకుంభినిపెల్ల పెరచి." DR. Aranya. 86. వామిగా, కుప్పకుప్పలుగా. "పెరటిలో కప్పు కొలు, మునుగలును, చొప్పపెనువామి, జనుము, రుబ్బురోలు." S. ii. 440. [Skt.] A mare, ఆడగుర్రము. A she-ass. పెసరము, ఆడగాడిద. వామిదొడ్డి *vami-doḍḍi.* n. A stack-yard. గడ్డివేయుచోటు.

వామింటు or వాయింటు *vaminta* [Tel.] n. A small shrub, the leaves of which are used medicinally. *Oleome pentaphylla*, అజగంధిని.

వాము See ఓమము.

వాయ *vaya.* [Tel.] n. A quantity of grain put in a mortar to be pounded at one time; so much grain as the mortar holds at once. దంచుటకు రోటిలో నొకసారిపోయు ధాన్యము. A quantity of rice and curry mixed to be eaten. A crack or valley in a hill, కొండసందిచ్చినచేట.

వాయగొట్టు or వాచగొట్టు *vaya-gottu.* [Tel. from వాచు.] v. a. To beat so as to cause a swelling. To cause to swell. To make one pine for. వాచేటట్లుచేయు, ఏకారునట్లు చేయు.

వాయదండము or వాపదండము *vaya-danḍamu.* [Skt.] n. A loom, సాలెవాడు నేత నరికెట్టెడు పలక.

వాయనము *vayanamu.* [Skt.] n. A cake or cakes offered to the Deity and then given as a present to a Brahmin woman at the commencement of the performance of a vow, వ్రతోద్యాపనకాలమునందు ఉపాయ నముగా నిచ్చెడిమోదకము. చేటవాయనము

cakes so given in a winnowing basket. మూసివాయనము cakes so given covered. ఇచ్చివాయనము పుచ్చుకొంటి వాయనము the like for the like, tit for tat.

వాయము *vāyamu*. [Tel.] adj. Useless, vain, వ్యర్థము. "వాయపుబ్రతుకేల." మార్క. iv.

వాయవ్యము *vāyavyamu*. [Skt. from వాయువు.] adj. Pertaining to the wind, వాయుసంబంధమైన. n. The north-western corner of the earth, the North-west quarter. వాయవ్యదిక్కు.

వాయసము *vāyasamu*. [Skt.] n. A crow, కాకి. వాయసఫలన్యాయము see కాకతాళన్యాయము. **వాయసారాతి** *vāyasārāti*. n. An owl. గుడ్లగూబ. (lit. the foe of the crows.)

వాయి *vāyi*. [Tel.] n. The mouth, నోరు. The face, ముఖము. The edge of any cutting instrument, కత్తియంచు. Wind, వాయువు; as కోరవాయి, మందవాయి. వాయువిళంగము the name of a tree. M. III. vi. 261. వెల్లవాయి a valley or hollow through which a stream sometimes runs, వలుదిక్కులను కురియునీళ్లు వచ్చేదారి. నూతివాయికట్టు a parapet round a well, దపుడుగోడ. పశ్వాదులుపడకుండా బావి చుట్టుకట్టినగోడ. Plu. వాయిలు. వాత *vāta*. (Loc. of వాయి the mouth.) In the mouth. మీరు వచ్చేదాక మాకు వాత తడిలేదు there was no moisture in our mouth until you came, i.e., we were in terror until your arrival. వాణ్ని ఫిరంగివాత పెట్టినారు they blew him up from the mouth of a cannon. **వాతరట్టు** *vāta-rattu*. n. A chatter box, వదరుబోతు. **వాతవాడి** *vāta-vādi*. n. An unpleasant talker. **వాతి** *vāti*. (Gen. of వాయి.) **వాతికాసు** *vāti-kāsu*. n. Hush-money, a bribe. లంచము. **వాతిబియ్యము** or **వాతికాసు బియ్యము** *vāti-biyyamu*. n A few grains of rice put in the mouth of a dead person when lying on the funeral pile. పీనుగునోటవేసేబియ్యము. **వాయోడు** *vāy-ōdu*- v. n. To be unable to open the mouth, to be unable to talk, to be timid in speaking, to be bashful or reserved in speech. వాయోడక frankly, freely నోరు అణుచుకొనకుండా. "అత్తనడిగెల వాయోడకక నరుల బోదువారలతోడక." S. iii. 321.

వాయించు *vāyintsu*. [Tel.] v. a. To beat, strike, sound or play on a drum, a lute, &c. మేళమువుండ్లైనవాటినిగొట్టు, వీణమీటు, సన్నాయిమొదలైనవాటినిఊదు. చదువుకున్నది తెల్లికంటవాయించు to forget what one has learnt. **వాయింపు** *vāyimpu*. n. Sounding a drum, etc. వాయించుట. వాయిదము same as వాద్యము. (q. v.) వాయిద్యము corruption of వాద్యము (q. v.)

వాయింట or **వావింట** *vāyinta*. [Tel.] n. A small shrub, the leaves of which are used medicinally. *Cleome pentaphylla*, ఆవాకంటిని.

వాయిదా *vāyidā*. [H.] n. A stated period for the discharge of a debt or for the payment of a sum of money. గడువు. An adjournment.

వాయిదార *vāyi-dāra*. [Tel.] n. A crooked sword. వంకలుగలకత్తి.

వాయువు *vāyuvu*. [Skt.] n. Air, wind, గాలి. A rheumatic distemper, rheumatism, వాతరోగము. అజీర్ణవాయువు a species of dyspepsia. ఉదరవాయువు flatulency in the stomach. ఊర్ధ్వవాయువు difficult and short respiration, asthma. తిమురువాయువు paralysis, palsy, deprivation of motion and sensation together, i. e., numbness. పక్షవాయువు or పార్శ్వవాయువు hemiplegia. ముద్దవాయువు dead palsy. సెగవాయువు flatulency in the body said to be caused by venereal heat. వాయువునకు పథ్యమైనమందు or వాతహరమైనమందు a medicine that dissipates flatulency. వాతనాడి a flatulent pulse. వాతాతిసారము a flatulent disease of this kind, diarrhœa. వాయునిరోధము the art of stopping the breath, practised with a view to attain length of days. ప్రాణాయామము. వాయుపథము vayu-pathamu. n. The atmosphere. ఆకాశము. వాయువిళంగము vayu-vilangamu. n. A medicinal seed, like a pepper corn, put in the mouth of children in order to assist their speech. చిత్రతండులము. వాయువేగి vayu-vegi. adj. Swift as the wind. వాయుసఖుడు vayu-sakhudu. n. Lit: the friend of the wind, i.e., fire, అగ్ని.

వార vara. [Tel.] n. A skein of thread for weaving, containing eight punjams. ఎనిమిదిపుంజములనూలు. Variance, difference, discrepancy, especially in calculation. (లెక్కలో) ఎక్కువతక్కువలు.

వారక varaka. [Tel.] adv. Constantly, unintermittingly, continually, perpetually. సంతతము, ఎడతెగక, ఎడతెగక.

వారకము varakamu. [Tel.] n. A stipend: pay given in advance: money advanced to cultivators to be received again without interest when the crop is reaped. పొరుబడి కాలములో ఇచ్చి ఫలకాలములో వడ్డీ లేకుండ మళ్లీ రాబట్టుకొనుట.ఒకాని. "వలసి నకతంబువారకంబులు కొలదిమీరగనిచ్చి కూడు గకుండు." L. iv. 113.

వారడ varada. [Tel.] n. A bit of a palmyra leaf, తాటాకు చిప్ప.

వారడి varadi. [Tel.] n. Deficiency, difference in exchange, loss. లోపము, నష్టి. ఆవారడియందులో కలిసివచ్చినది that deficiency is made up by this (gain).

వారడు varadu. [Tel.] v. a. To give up. చాలించు.

వారణము varanamu. [Skt.] n. Resistance. opposition, warding off a blow, guarding, defence: a shield. నివారించడము, వారించుట. ప్రతిషేధము, డాలు. An elephant, ఏనుగు. వారణరాజము the prince of elephants. వారణపుడేగ varanapu-dega. n. A kind of hawk, డేగలలోభేదము. Jerdon No. 33. వారణబుస or వారణప్పుష varana-busa n. The plantain tree. అరటిచెట్టు. వారణ varana. n. An embankment, చెలియలికట్ట.

వారణాసి varan-asi. [Skt.] n. Benares. కాశీపట్టణము.

వారబట్టు va-ra-battu. [Tel. వా+రాగ+పట్టు.] v. a. To drink, ఆరగించు. To dry up. ఇంకించు.

వారము Another form of వారుణము. (q. v.)

వారము varamu. [Skt.] n. A day of the week. దినము. ఆదివారమువొదలైనది. A time, తడవ. ఆవృత్తి. A multitude, a flock or herd, a quantity, a heap. సమూహము. వారము వారము many a time, repeatedly, often. "వివవారత్రయవిజ్ఞానపటిష్ఠము నధ్యకోటిచ ట్టున." A. iv. 289. టీ॥ వారత్రయ, మూడుమార్లైన. వాడువారాలుచేసుకొని తినిందు మన్నాడు every day of the week he gets his dinner at a different house. "అంత సొంకవారమున తినవంతకుట." P. i. 351. వారకాంత, వారాంగన, వారకాముకి. వారసతి or వారస్త్రీ vara-kanta. n. A courtezan, a prostitute, a dancing girl. గణిక, వేశ్య, భోగముది.

వారయాత్రికుడు vara-yatrikudu. [Skt.] n. A relation by marriage, a relation who comes to witness a wedding, పెండ్లిచుట్టము.

వారలు varalu. [Tel. poetical for వారు.] pron. They.

వారవాణము vara-vanamu. [Skt.] n. A piece of armour: a quilted jacket. కవచము, దూది నించినచొక్కాయి.

వారసుడు varasudu. [H.] n. An heir, master, lord, owner. ఉత్తరాధికారి, యజమానుడు.

వారావధి or వారధి *vār-avadhi.* [Tam.] n. A bridge. వంతెన.

వారాహి *vār-āhi.* [Skt.] n. A wild sow. అడవి ఆడుపంది.

వారి *vāri.* [H.] affix. According to, by; as తారీఖువారి according to date. ఆసామివారి man by man వారీనామా *vāri-nama.* n. A bill of lading, a receipt given by a ship captain for goods laden on his vessel.

వారి *vāri.* [Tel. the infl. of వారు.] pron. in the genitive case. Of them, వారియొక్క.

వారి *vāri.* [Skt.] n. Water. జలము, నీళ్లు. వారాశి, వారిరాశి or వారాన్నిధి *vārāṣi.* n. A collection of waters. The ocean, సముద్రము. "మోహవారాశిలోనదామునిగి యుండు." Vema. 393. వారిజము *vāri-jamu.* n. Lit: The water-born, i. e., a lotus or water lily, పద్మము. వారిదము or వారివాహము *vāri-damu.* n. A cloud. మేఘము. వారిధి or వారినిధి *vāri-dhi.* n. The sea. సముద్రము. వారిధికన్య *vāri-dhi-kanya.* n. Lakshmi, the sea-born goddess, లక్ష్మి.

వారించు *vārintsu.* [Skt.] v. a. To do away, drive away, warn off or ward off, avert. To guard, defend, prevent, elude, or oppose. To dissuade, forbid. నివారించు, అడ్డగించు, ప్రతిషేధించు. "దమయంతిని వేశించు ప్రవేశించునప్పుడు నిన్నెవ్వరువారించుగోపరనిన." M. III. ii. 38.

వారిణ or వారిణె *vāriṇa.* [Tel.] n. The cord with which the large iron bucket is fastened to the hanging arm of a picota. బానను ఏతపుగడకు కట్టేదారము. A kind of net used to catch small fish. వారిణపీట *vāriṇa-pīṭa.* n. A stick used in fixing the yoke to the plough.

వారు *vāru.* [Tel.] n. A strap of leather. తోలుపవలె నిడుపుగాకోసిన చర్మపుచీలిక, సన్నగా కోసినతోలు. వారంటువిల్లు *vār-anṭu-villu.* (వారు+అంటువిల్లు.) n. A large bow used by masons, రాతిపనివారి వారుకట్టిన పెద్దవింటిలోకాలు.

వారెన *vārena.* (వారు + ఎన.) n. A piece of leather or rope used to tie the yoke and the pole of a cart together, కాడిలో కాడినిచేర్చికట్టువారులోనగునది. A rope used for a similar purpose in a plough or a waterlift. ఏతిలోతో కాడిని చేర్చికట్టుటకు గాని ముంగిసప్పనితో కడను చేర్చికట్టుటకుగాని ఉపయోగించెడు వారులోనగునది. వారెనపీట *vārena-pīṭa.* n. A piece of wood placed between the yoke and the shaft of a plough.

వారు *vāru.* [Tel. plu. of వాడు he.] pron. They, వాండ్రు. It is also thus used, as equivalent to people, folk. మావారు my people. మీవారు your people. ఈ యూరివారు the people of this village. నేను చూచినవారు the people whom I saw. Added to some nouns it has an honorific sense, as దేవరవారు, దొరవారు your honor. Infl. వారి their. వారు v. n. To flow down, or drain off, as water from boiled rice, వడియు, గంజివెడలనగునది వారు. To be lessened or diminished, తరుగు. v. a. To pare or cut thin, as the ends of a palm leaf. తాటాకు చివరచెక్కు. వారుకొను *vāru-konu.* v. a. To take up by the handful. Metaphorically, to get, gain, possess oneself of. పిడికిళ్లతోడగాఎత్తుకొను, పొందు; చెందు. నన్ను మోసము చేసి వాడేమి వారుకొన్నాడు has he gained any thing by cheating me? వారుచు or వార్చు *vārutsu.* (causal of వారు) v. a. To touch water with the lips and cast it away. ఆచమించు. To cause to flow, వారజేయు. గంజివార్చు to pour off the water from boiled rice by inclining the vessel, వారునట్టుచేయు. To expect, ప్రతీక్షించు, ఉద్దేశించు. సంధ్యవార్చు to offer up prayers: (because while uttering the prayer called సంధ్య they let water run through their fingers.) "హేమకుంభ జలములనువార్చి జలకంబుదీర్చి." DRU. 774. "సంధ్యవార్చువేళ."

G. vi. 17. వారుపు or వార్పు vārupu. n. The act of straining water or letting it flow, ఆవమనము. Water poured off from boiling rice, గంజి.

వారుణి vāruṇi. [Skt. from వరుణ.] n. The West, the region of Varuṇa. పడమటిదిక్కు. Any spirituous liquor, కల్లు.

వారువము or వార్వము vāruvamu. [Tel.] n. A horse. గుర్రము. "వారువముదిగనురికి వసుధగంపించ." Pal. 497.

వార్పు See వారుచు under వారు.

వార్త vārta. [Skt.] n. Tidings, intelligence, news, talk, conversation, a report. వర్తమానము, వృత్తాంతము, మాట, సంభాషణ. వాడు వెళ్లినాడన్న వార్త ఒకటే కాని వాడు నిజముగా వెళ్లలేదు the report is that he went, but in reality he did not go. "కలలోనగన్న వార్తలకింతవలవంతలేమి కారణమనియెంచుకొంటి." Anirudh. ii. 158. వార్తకాడు vārta-kāḍu. n. A talkative person. మాటకారి. "నేర్తునన్న వాడువార్తకాడు." Vēma. 450. వార్తకెక్కు vārta-k-ekku. v. n. To obtain notoriety. ప్రసిద్ధినిపొందు. "నువ్వుగింజమేనగోసిచ్చి శిబిరాజు వార్తకెక్కె చాలవన్నెకెక్కె." Vēma. 289. వార్తలాడు vārtal-āḍu. v. n. To talk, speak, converse. మాట్లాడు, సంభాషించు. వార్తావహుడు or వార్తికుడు vārta-vahuḍu. n. A messenger. వెళ్లి వర్తమానము తెలిసికొని పోయి చెప్పువాడు.

వార్తాకము vārtākamu. [Skt.] n. The Brinjal, Egg plant, *Solanum melongena*, వంగచెట్టు, వంగకాయ. వార్తాకి vārtāki. n. The plant called *Solanum indicum*, ములకచెట్టు.

వార్తికము vārti-kamu. [Skt. from వార్త.] n. A gloss, a commentary. సూత్రవివరణముగాను సంగ్రహముగాను ఉండే వాక్యము, ఉక్తానుక్తార్థములను తెలిపెడి గ్రంథము.

వార్ధకము vārdhakamu. [Skt. from వృద్ధ.] n. Old age, ముసలితనము. An assembly of old men, ముసలివాండ్ర సమూహము. వార్ధక్యము vārdhakyamu. n. Old age. ఏబదియేండ్లకు దాటియుండడం, వృద్ధత్వము.

వార్ధి Same as వారిధి. (q. v.)

వార్ధుషికుడు vārdhu-shikuḍu. [Skt. from వృద్ధి.] n. A usurer. వడ్డిచేత జీవించువాడు.

వార్పు See under వారు.

వార్వము Same as వారువము (q. v.). వార్వపుటగ్గి volcanic fire under a sea, బడబాగ్ని.

వార్షికము vārshikamu. [Skt. from వర్షము.] adj. Pertaining to a year, limited to a year. సంవత్సరకాలపరిమితిగల.

వాలకము vālakamu. [Tel.] n. Deceit. మోసము. Hypocrisy, pretence. వేషము.

వాలధి or వాలహస్తము vāladhi. [Skt.] n. A hairy tail. రోమగుచ్ఛపుచ్ఛము, ఏనుగు గుర్రములోనగువానితోక.

వాలము vālamu. [Skt.] n. A tail, తోక. A sword, ఖడ్గము. [Tel.] A royal tiger, బెబ్బులి.

వాలియించు or వాలాయించు vālayintsu. [Tel.] v. n. To be compelled or forced, నిర్బంధపడు. v. a. To oppress, force, compel, నిర్బంధించు.

వాలరుగుడు vāl-aruguḍu. [Tel. వాలు+అరుగుడు.] n. A tailless monkey, a baboon, వాలిడికోతి.

వాలాయము vālāyamu. [Tel.] n. Force, compulsion, నిర్బంధము. adj. Inevitable, అనివార్యము. Constant, నిరంతరము. వాలాయముగా vālāyamu-gā. adv. Positively, certainly, undoubtedly, అవశ్యము, సిద్ధముగా, రూఢిగా. (Also, less correctly) usually, often, commonly. వాడుకగా. "ఆరాటవాలాయముగా ధరణింబుట్టగలడట." KP. v. 100. "మాయామద బావుము

వాలాయమహోగ్రములు, దుర్వారస్ఫురద్బలంబగా వాయునిచే వేయం బ్రభగ్నములై యక్కడ యక్కడ విన్నినమై..." R. iii. 66.

వాలారు valāru. [Tel. వాలు + అరు.] adj. Sharp, as a sword. Swordlike, resembling a sword, వాడియైనఖడ్గమువంటి. "వాలారుకట్టెరులయందు..." Parij. v. 56. వాలారు ములుకు a sharp arrow.

వాలార్చు vāl-ārtsu. [Tel.] v. a. To brandish a sword, కత్తిఝళిపించు. "నడిగొని..." వాలార్చివాడి." BD. v. 425.

వాలిక vālika. [Tel. from వాలు.] adj. Long. నిడుపైన, దీర్ఘమైన. "నిడువాలికచూపు." Vasu. iii. 59. టీ॥ మిక్కిలి పొడవైనచూపు. Sharp, వాడియైన. "వాలికయమ్ములు" భార. ద్రో. i. [Skt.] n. A pit in the roof of the mouth. అంగిలిగుంట. వాలికనడ vālika-nada. n. A certain pace in horses. అశ్వగమనభేదము. "ఇట్టివ్యయనిపి..." [illegible] G. viii. 74.

వాలు or వ్రాలు vālu. [Tel.] v. n. To bend or weigh down. To light or perch. To hang loose; to fall down. [illegible], చెట్టుమీదవ్రాలినది, కిందికివంగు, దిగబడు, పండు, జారు, పడు. To increase, అతిశయించు. v. a. To transgress, exceed, అతిక్రమించు. వాలి నతిన్కి...మై in the passion which he felt, వచ్చినకోపముచేత. వాలినకృపచేత through the grace that descended on thee, వచ్చిన అనుగ్రహముచేత. అడివాని పాదములమీదవాలెను she fell at his feet. "[illegible]" R. v. 290. "పుష్పవృష్టి వ్రాలుచుండె." T. iii. 111. వాలు vālu. n. A sword, కత్తి. A slope, a descent. అడ్డపాటు. Length, దైర్ఘ్యము. Sharpness, వాడిమి. "అలివిమలతేనియలవాలు అలినివాలు." H. ii. 16. [illegible] వాలు vālu. adj. Long, sloping, slanting, descending, drooping. దీర్ఘమైన, అడ్డకోపాటుగానుండే. వాలుచూపులు drooping glances. Sharp, వాడియైన. Cruel, క్రూరమైన. వాలుమ్ము or వాలు టమ్ము a sharp arrow. వాలుకొంగ vālu-konga. n. A stork, పక్షిభేదము, [illegible]. వాలుగ or వాలుగా vālu-ga. adv. Slantingly, lengthily, అడ్డకపాటుగా, నిడుపుగా. వాలుగంటి or వాల్గంటి vālu-ganti. n. A bright eyed woman; lit: a long-eyed girl. దీర్ఘములైనకన్నులుగల స్త్రీ, ఆయతాక్షి, విశాలాక్షి. వాలుగడుపు or వాల్గడుపు vālu-gaḍupu. n. A projecting or protuberant belly, బొజ్జ. వాలుగొమ్ము a canal or sluice. వాలుచు or వాల్చు vālutsu. v. a. To bend, incline, slant. [illegible]. To cut off, [illegible]. కన్నువాల్చు to droop the eye-lids, i. e., to close the eyes. రాత్రియంతా కన్నులు వాల్చలేదు I did not close my eyes all night. అమంచమును వాల్చినాడు he slanted the couch. "[illegible]" HD. i. 947. టీ॥ వాలిన, వచ్చిన; [illegible], వాలు, దీర్ఘమైన; [illegible] వాలుచుకొనగా, కోసి వేయుట [illegible]. వాలుచుక్క or వాల్చుక్క vālu-tsukka. n. The planet Venus or its regent. శుక్రుడు. "[illegible]" Sar. D. 558. వాలుచేప vālu-chēpa. n. A kind of fish called *Chirocentrus nudus.* మత్స్యభేదము. వాలుడు vāluḍu. adj. Hanging down. వాలుడుకొమ్మలు branches that hang down. n. A kind of tree. ఎర్రవాలుడు the red kind. వాలుడుచెక్క the bark of this tree used in medicine. వాలుడుతైలము the oil extracted from this bark. "[illegible] వాలుడుతైలంబు [illegible]." P. i. 725. వాలుపు or వాల్పు vālupu. n. Bending down, వాల్చుట. వాలుప్రొద్దు vālu-proddu. n. The morning or evening sun,

కతప్రాప్తి, అపరాజ్ఞము. వాలుమగఁడు *vālu-magaḍu.* n. The hero of the sword, i. e., A brave man, శూరుడు.

"క॥ కాలిమియుద్ధృతియుప్రజ్ఞ,
శీలతయు పరాక్రమంబు శేముఖ్యతయున్,
కాలోచితకార్యములను,
వాలుమగండేలు జలధివలయితధరణిన్."

P. iii. 32.

వాలుమెకము, వాల్మెకము, or వాలుమృగము *vālu-mekamu.* n. The sworded beast, i. e., the wild boar. అడవిపంది. "అల్పుపుడు తరువుడికి తెసవలలకు లోబడకపారు వాలుమృగములన్ బలుదూపుల బడ నేయుచు, జాలకన పాలింబంచె తెక్కునూకెరసమితిన్." Padma. i. 55.

వాలుక *vāluka.* [Skt.] n. Sand. ఇసుక.

వాలుగ or వాలువ *vāluga.* [Tel.] n. A kind of fish. A fish in general, చేప. The name *vāluga* is given to two or three kinds of fish, which are scaleless, rank and oily. Thus, వాలుగచేప is a sea-fish, *Trichiurus lepturus.* See Russell, plate 165. Another *vāluga* is a fresh water fish, found in tanks but oftener in rivers. Another is a species of *Silurus* (Russell, plate 165). ముల్లువాలుగ is the Cat fish, which is nearly globular, and is covered with prickles. వాలుగకంటి *vāluga-kanṭi.* n. A beautiful eyed woman, a woman whose eyes are as beautiful as those of a fish. వాలుగ టెంకి a sort of Scale-fish. Russell, plates 3 and 10. *Rhinobatus lævis.* (Jerdon.) వాలుగపాము a certain venomous water snake. "వాలుగమీలుమిట్టిపడగ." S. iii. 291. "క్రొవ్విరిమీనులతేండ్రి కొలువు లెంకలకిచ్చె వాలుగలనుసంగడీలకిచ్చె." G. i. 111. వాలుగటాలు, (మీనకేతనుడు) is a title of Manmatha whose banner is a fish.

వాలూరు *vālūru.* [Tel.] v. n. To delay. అలస్యముగు.

వాలెము Another form of వాలాయము (q. v.)

వాల్మీకి *vālmīki.* [Skt. from వల్మీకము.] n. The name of the author of the Sanskrit Ramayana.

వాల్లభ్యము *vāllabhyamu.* [Skt. from వల్లభ.] n. Authority, rule, అధిపత్యము, దొరతనము. Love, affection. Influence, ప్రీతి, విశ్వాసము, బలము, చొరవ. వానికి రాజునద్ద నిండా వాల్లభ్య మున్నది he has much influence with the king. "వాల్లభ్యలభ్యభద్రక్రమాంబోజ్యజనా శప్తత్రపృతిరూ." A. ii. 105. టీ॥ వాల్లభ్యము, భక్తవత్సలయము. పూజ్యేనప్యమరాగోభక్తియని యున్నది గనుక పెద్దలయందలి విశ్వాసము భక్తియని బడుచున్నది.

వాళి or వాలి *vaḷi.* [Tel.] n. Custom, practice, usage, experience, వాడుక. A cattle-path, పశువులుపోవుదారి. మాయింటివాళి the custom in my family. అది నాకు వాళిలేదు I am not accustomed to it.

వావదూకుడు *vā-vadūkuḍu.* [Skt.] n. An eloquent man, an orator. వక్త, లెస్సగామాట్లాడు శక్తిగలవాడు, యుక్తియుక్తముగా మాట్లాడువాడు, వాగ్మి.

వావాదు *vā-vādu.* [from Skt.] n. An address. ఉపన్యాసము.

వావి *vāvi.* [Tel.] n. Legality, lawfulness, consanguinity, legitimacy. వరుస. Relationship, బంధుత్వము. "వావి కెల్లలుగాని కూతురువంటిది." భా. X. వావితప్పు to commit incest. ఇది వావికాదు this is not right, i. e., this is incest. ఆ పడుచును పెండ్లాడుటము వావికాదు it is unlawful for him to marry that girl.

వావింట or వాయింట *vāvinṭa.* [Tel.] n. A small shrub, which is edible and medicinal, *Cleome pentaphylla.* అజగంధ, బచ్చిరి.

వావిక *vāvika.* [Tel.] n. The pit at the bottom of the throat on the breast bone. కంఠము క్రిందుటుండుగుంట.

వావిరి vāviri. [Tel.] n. Order, series, క్రమము. అనుగతి. Greatness, glory. Patience, quiet, resignation. సహనము. "పతిదయ్యాకుండాపొంది పట్టాయంబునకు. బోవు మనాన్నగిపెా పూజో డిదయునుచు, వావిరిదా జ్ఞానివడివడినరుగ." ND. iv. 600. adj. Great, much, అధికము. Following, అనుగతము. Difficult to obtain, దుష్ప్రాప్యము. "కేవలకల్పవాకధలుక్కృత్రిమరత్నము లాద్యసత్ఫలో, వావిరిపుట్టురత్నములు." Vasu. Pref. 35. adv. Very, exceedingly, much. అత్యంతము. "భావంబురూపంబుభక్తిదయు ప్రియము, వావిరి నర్తించినర్తించివాని, మనమునదయు బుట్టమాటలుంచె ప్పి." ND. i. 612.

వావిలి vāvili. [Tel.] n. The Five leaved Chaste tree, *Vitex negundo* or *Cleone pentaphylla*. Heyne. శేఫాలిక. నిర్గుండి. నల్లవావిలి a shrub called *Justicia gandarusa*. Another species is called కొండవావిలి.

వావురము vāvuramu. Another form of వారువము (q. v.) Also, a conveyance, వాహనము.

వాశితము or వాసితము vāsitamu. [Skt.] n. The chirping of birds, or the cry of animals. మృగపక్షులధ్వని.

వాస Same as వాసము (q. v.)

వాసంతము vāsantamu. [Skt. from వసంత.] adj. Vernal. వసంతఋతుసంబంధమైన. n. A cuckoo. వాసంతి vāsanti. n. A species of wild jasmine, *Jasminum auriculatum*. వసంతకాలపుమల్లె, అడవిమల్లె.

వాసకసజ్జిక vāsaka-sajjika. [Skt.] n. A woman who expects to meet her husband. తాను అలంకరించుకొని మగనికోసరము కనిపెట్టుకొనియుండు స్త్రీ.

వాసన vāsana. [Skt.] n. Smell, scent, odour, fragrance. Flavour. పరిమళము. Notion, recollection from memory. Fancy, imagination. మునుపు అనుభవించినదాని స్మరణ. ఇది పూర్వజన్మవాసన this is the influence of his former birth. వానికి సంస్కృతవాసనలేదు he has not the slightest acquaintance with Sanskrit. "ఉదరార్థకజన్మధుర్యవాసనల్." R. iii. 95. వాసనకొవ్వొత్తి a scented wick, సుగంధవత్తి. వాసనచూచు vāsana-tsūtsu. v. a. To smell. వాసనపట్టు to scent, to catch the scent of, to trace, to track. వాసనవేయు or వాసనకొట్టు vāsana-vēyu. v. n. To smell, to emit an odour: to stink. పరిమళించు, కంపుకొట్టు.

వాసము or వాస vāsamu. [Tel.] n. A rafter of a building. ఇంటికప్పులోనిదూలమీదవేసేవి. వాగవాసము the hook that suspends a swinging cot. వాసపుబియ్యము grains of gum found inside a hollow bamboo. వాసవేయు vāsa-vēyu. v. a. To place the rafters on a building, to rafter it. ఇంటిపైకప్పునకువాసములుకట్టు, వాసాలుపరచు. పెంకుకట్టు.

వాసము vāsamu. [Skt.] n. A house, habitation, abode, dwelling, residence. గృహము. ఆయన మమ్మును తన గర్భవాసములో పెట్టుకొనియుండినాడు he kept us in his bosom, i. e., we were in his protection. వాని గర్భవాసములోపుట్టినవాడు the son of his own body, his son. "కోసలోత్తరాదివాసకులు." Kala. i. 152. వాసము or వాసస్సు n. A cloth: clothes. వస్త్రము. వాసకము vāsakamu. n. A house. ఇల్లు. వాసగృహము vāsa-grihamu. n. A bed chamber, పడకయిల్లు.

వాసరము vāsaramu. [Skt.] n. A day, దినము. వాసరాంతము the close of the day.

వాసరా vāsarā. [Tel.] n. Compensation. చెల్లుగా ఇచ్చినది.

వాసవుడు [illegible] [Skt. from వసువు] n. Indra. ఇంద్రుడు.

వాసి vāsi. [Tel.] n. Difference. తారతమ్యము, భేదము. Greatness, ఆధిక్యము, గొప్పతనము. Profit, లాభము. Fame, renown, ప్రసిద్ధి. Amelioration, improvement in health or quality. స్వస్థము, గుణము. Comparative merits, superiority amongst competitors. Influence. Splendour, glory, celebrity, eminence, honor, lustre. ప్రసిద్ధి. శ్రేయస్సు. "రఘుశేఖరబల్విల్లలకాడవాడు, నీవాసియుండన్న నే డుగనవచ్చు." R. v. 316. "నదినెలు తెలిసినవాసి తేదటు." H. i. 138. "వాసి చెడి నర కము కాంతితో." UR. iv. 297. వానిఒళ్లు వాసిచేసిరి they cured him. ముఖవాసి fascination, personal influence. వానికి చెయివాసి కద్దు he has a lucky hand, he is fortunate in his practice. మాటవాసికిచెప్పినాను I said it without any particular reason. Extent, limit, పరిమితి. This is affixed to words denoting fractions: thus, అరవాసి one half. కాలువాసి one quarter. Advantage gained in measurement, &c., surplus. ధారణవాసి advantage gained by price. "ధారణవా సిక్కినోదల్ పెట్టుము." A. vi. 93. టీ ॥ వాసి, యూర్పురెుక్కువ తక్కువలకొరకు. "మాయక్కతన్న రాధికయేరెుక్కువయైన చానయెరిగింపుమదే యూయుమనాయుమన్నిక ప్రాయమ్మనరాజాబం టువాసిదలంపక." Ila. iii. 179. టీ ॥ రాజా బంటువాసి, అనగా దొరకును సేవకునకును ఉండే తారతమ్యము. వాసి vāsi. adj. Greater, గొప్ప. Better, either in health or in quality. స్వస్థము, బాగు. అది యిప్పుడు నిండావాసి it is much better now. రోగము వాసియైనది the disease is cured. వారికంటెవీరు వాసి these are better than the other men. వాసికెక్కు vāsi-k-ekku. v. n. To rise to celebrity, become great, obtain eminence, attain superiority, ప్రసిద్ధినిపొందు "లోకమువారు మెచ్చగా వన్నెకువాసికెక్కి." T. ii. 38 "వి యముపకారము నుబ్బగించులకా వాసికి నెక్కి." Anirudh.iii. 59. వాసిగా vāsi-ga. adv. Well, properly, fully. తేర్పగా. "కాళిమహీమను మాచేవాసిగదిని సంశయములు వాసితిమిక నీకాను లను." P. iv. 262. వాసిచేయు vāsi-chēyu. v. a. To ameliorate, cure, make better. స్వస్థము చేయు. వాసితనము vāsi-tanamu. n. Propriety, fitness, యుక్తము. "సత్యభామా విధేయుడవలా మరలగొనుటతో వాసితనము." Parij. iv. 16.

వాసి vāsi. [Skt. from వస్ to dwell.] n. A resident, inhabitant, dweller. నివసించు వాడు. నగరవాసులు citizens. గ్రామవాసులు villagers. వనవాసి a hermit.

వాసించు vāsintsu. [Skt.] v. n. To dwell, live. To smell or be fragrant. పరిమళించు. "ఉదయాది సేధనాధుల్లలక్షైన చిక్క ని చిక్కని పెరుగు వాసింపజేర్చి." Krishna § 81.

వాసితము vāsitamu. [Skt.] adj. Perfumed, scented. పరిమళింపజేయబడిన.

వాసుకి vāsuki. [Skt.] n. The name of a king of the Serpents. ఒక సర్పరాజు.

వాసుదేవుడు vāsu-dēvudu. [Skt. from వసు దేవ.] n. Lit. The son of Vāsudēva, i. e., Krishna. కృష్ణుడు.

వాసె, వాసియు or వాసెగోలు vāse. [Tel. వాసె+కోలు.] n. A flute or fife, పిల్లంగ్రోవి. "సన్నగాలేవినెవాసెగోలుడిగోలు." A. iv. 38.

వాసెన vāsena. [Tel.] n. A cloth tied over the mouth of a vessel, particularly of one in which cakes are boiled by steam. కుండమూతికికట్టినగుడ్డ. A cloth bound over the head. అస్వస్థముగానుండేవాండ్రు తలకు కట్టుకొనేగుడ్డ. వాసెనకుడుము a cake boiled in steam. ఇడ్డెన.

వాస్తవము vāstavamu. [Skt.] n. Reality, truth. తథ్యము, యథార్థము. వాస్తవము or వాస్తవికము adj. True, real, genuine, యథార్థమైన, తథ్యమైన. వాస్తవికార్థము the true, real, or literal meaning.

వాస్తుకము or వాస్తూకము vâstukamu. [Skt.] n. A potherb, *Chenopodium album*. చిక్కుడాకుకూర.

వాస్తువు vâsturu. [Skt.] n. The site of a house; a house, a habitation, గృహము వసనిర్మాణయోగ్యమగుభూమి, గృహము. వాస్తవ్యము vâstavyamu. adj. Fit to dwell in, వసింపదగిన. వాస్తవ్యుడు vâstavyudu. n. A dweller, inhabitant, resident. అక్కడి వాస్తవ్యులు those who dwell there. వాస్తోష్పతి vâstôsh-pati. n. A name of Indra. ఇంద్రుడు.

వాహనము vâhanamu. [Skt.] n. A vehicle, or conveyance of any kind; a carriage, car, horse, &c ఎక్కిపోవుటకు సాధనమైనది. వాహము vâhamu. n. A horse. గుర్రము. వాహకుడు vâhakudu. n. A porter, a carrier; a bearer of dead bodies. మోసేవాడు, పీనుగుమోసేవాడు. వాహితము vâhitamu. adj. Borne, carried, supported. వహింపబడిన. వాహిని vâhini. n. A river, a stream. నది. An army, or force. సేన. Eloquence, వాగ్ధోరణి. వాహినీపతి vâhini-pati. n. The leader of an army. సేనానాయకుడు. The ocean, సముద్రుడు. వాహ్యము vâhyamu. n. A carriage, a vehicle, a beast of burden. వాహనము. పరువులు మోయదగినవి. adj. Fit to be carried or borne. మోయతగినది. వాహ్యాళి vâhyâli. n. An excursion, trip. విహారము, సవారి. An expedition.

వాహిత్థము vâhitthamu. [Skt.] n. The part of an elephant's forehead between the frontal lobes. ఏనుగుయొక్క పిన్ననుదుటి బుడుపులకింది స్థానము.

వి vi

వి vi. [Skt.] A particle and prefix, implying intensity, muchness separation as in విభ్రాంతి, వియోగము.

వి vi. [Tel.] An affix, a contraction for అవి or ఇవి. Thus ఇవి నావి those are mine. ఈ బట్టలు అతనివి these clothes are his.

వింగడము or వింగళము vingaḍamu. [Kanarese] adj. Separate, వేరు, ప్రత్యేకమైన. Spacious. విశాలమైన. Beautiful, సుందరము. Strange, విపరీతము. "సీ॥ వింగడంబైనట్టి మంగళకళలొప్పు బృందావనికి ముగ్గుపెట్టుదాన." A. iv. 76. "వింగడమైనరొమ్ముల వానిదిగనుంగొని." ib. v. 3. వింగడముగ vingaḍamu-ga. adv. Separately. వేరుగా, ప్రత్యేకముగా. వింగడించు or వింగళించు vingaḍintsu. v. a. To separate, put asunder, divide. ప్రత్యేకముచేయు, విభజించు, వేరుపరచు.

వింజ vinja. [Tel.] n. Surprise, wonder. విస్మయము. "తనసుఖాలాస్థానంబెల్లసావధానంబు గనువింజమాకీడినట్లు విభుచుండనన్నకేంద్ర చంద్రువనునట్లుని చెప్పుందొరంగె." KP. v. 13.

వింజరము or వింజిరము vinjaramu. [Tel.] n. The seer-fish. Russell plate 134. Ainslie 154.

వింజామర or వింజామరము vin-jâmara. [Tel. వెల్ల+చామర Cf. Tam. వెణ్‌చామర.] n. A white whisk or chowri, the tail of th *Bos grunniens*. తెల్లనిచామరము. "గీ॥ భార్గవింజామరవిభానొప్పుచాలదొరగనిరొ." ఆము. iv వింజామరటపాకాయలు vin-jâmara-ṭ-âvulu. n plu. A sort of firework, బాణవిద్యలో భేదము. "దుక్కమలీలతోలిన చంచాలంబులు పత్తులమించిదూకాళ్ళ బాణములవింజామరటపాకాయలువిరుగులా." Bahulas. iv. 92.

వింజిలి vinjili. [Tel.] n. A certain fish.

వింధ్యము vindzamu. [from Skt. వింధ్యము.] n. The Vindhya mountains.

వింట vinṭa. [Tel.] The ablative of విల్లు a bow. వింటి. The genitive of విల్లు. Of or belonging to a bow. విల్లుసంబంధమైన. వింటి

[illegible] vinṭi-kōla. n. A bow-like instrument used by masons. వింటిపట్టు vinṭi-paṭṭu. n. The part of the bow where the arrow is fixed. వింటిరాశి vinṭi-rāsi. n. The sign called Sagittarius, ధనూరాశి. వింటివాడు vinṭi-vāḍu. n. A bowman, an archer, విలుకాడు. విండ్లు or వింటులు vinḍlu. n. (plu. of విల్లు) Bows, ధనుస్సులు.

వింట vinṭa. [Tel. from విను.] n. Hearing, వినుట. వింటి the same as వింటిని, విన్నాను.

వింటాలము vinṭālamu. [Tel.] n. A certain feat in wrestling.

వింత vinta. [Tel.] n. Curiosity, wonder; oddity, oddness; an odd thing, a rarity, a thing that causes wonder, a marvel, ఆశ్చర్యము. అద్భుతము. మోమువింతవింత చేసి కొని her countenance being changed. adj. Strange, rare, curious, odd, queer, foreign, new. చోద్యమైన, క్రొత్త. Other, అన్యము. వింతచూపులు odd looks. వింతమాటలు strange words. "ఆడంబరవింత విధముని ద్యూతికులాలరికి." Vasu. iv. 100. వింతగా vinta-gā. adv. Rarely, admirably, wonderfully. చోద్యముగా. వింతరాలు vinta-r-ālu. n. A strange woman. అన్యురాలు. వింతవాడు vinta-vāḍu. n. A stranger, a strange man. చోద్యపు మనుష్యుడు, అన్యుడు.

విందు vindu. [Tel. cf. Tam. విరుందు.] n. A treat, entertainment, banquet, feast. An invitation. Hospitality, ఆతిథ్యము, ప్రార్థనా పూర్వక భోజనము. A guest, భోజనమునకు వచ్చినవాడు, భోజనమునకువచ్చినస్త్రీ, అతిథి. A relation, చుట్టము. కన్నులవిందుగానుండె a feast for the eyes, a delicious or alluring sight. "చూడ్కి విందొనరించి." N. ix. 276. మాకు విందులేనికూడు మందు a dinner without a guest is medicine with us, i. e., we seldom dine without friends. "కొండము మున్నవనుమకోతియువిందా." Vema. 1783. తమ్మిపూవిందు the friend of the lotus, i. e., the sun. R. v. 175. విందుచేయు or విందు చేయు vindu-chēyu. v. n. To give a party or a feast. మర్యాదిగాపిలిచి భోజనము పెట్టు. విందుకుపిలుచు vindu-ku-pilutsu. v. a. To invite, to call to a feast. భోజనమునకుపిలుచు. విందుపురుగు vindu-purugu. n. A kind of spider.

విందువు vinduvu. [Skt.] adj. Intelligent, knowing, wise. తెలివైనవాడు, [illegible], తెలిసిన.

వింధ్యము vindhyamu. [Skt.] n. The Vindhya mountains.

వింశతి vimsati. [Skt.] pron. Twenty. ఇరువది సంఖ్య. వింశము vimsamu. adj. Twentieth. ఇరువదవ.

వికచము vikachamu. [Skt.] adj. Expanded blown, open as a flower. వికసించిన.

వికటము vikaṭamu. [Skt.] adj. Large, great, విస్తీర్ణమైన, గొప్ప, వికారమైన. Very crooked, మిక్కిలివంకరైన. Horrible, frightful. Changed in form or appearance. Reverse, contrary. విరుద్ధరూపము గల, విరుద్ధమైన. "భూమిరియుధరాధిప్రవారము వాని వికటబంధములకల్పించదగునె." S. i. 52. వికటకవి vikaṭa-kavi. n. A jester, a buffoon. ఏడాదించే కోడాడిచేవాడు, వికటముగా మాటాడువాడు, హాస్యకరుడు. వికటించు vikaṭintsu. v. n. To contradict. To disagree with the health. విరుద్ధమగు. వికటకొను. "కరిగాములు నమసరించకవికసంబున తిన్నతిండివికటించునుమీ." Sumati. 55. "కరిగాముగా మాధరిగాము, కరిగాముతేన్నె అనుతిక కంతాధరిగా స్వరిగామతమువికటించినమనుమరి కాపులకుమనుల మరిగామునుమతి." ib. 121.

వికత్థనము vikatthanamu. [Skt.] n. Praise, స్తోత్రము. Ironical applause, egotistical boasting, irony, ironical or unmerited praise. మిథ్య. "వరుసావాగ్విస్పవికత్థనము." N. viii. 204.

వికరణిదూలములు *vikarani-dūlamulu.* [Tel.] n. plu. The cross lower beams of a shelving roof. చిప్పపెంకలందు వేసేదూలములు.

వికర్తనుడు *vi-kartanudu.* [Skt.] n. The sun. సూర్యుడు.

వికలము *vikalamu.* [Skt.] adj. Defective, imperfect, mutilated. Decayed, impaired. Confused, agitated. Withered, waning. విచ్ఛిన్నమైన, భగ్నమైన, చెడిన, కలుషమైన. "అన్యూరుదృష్టు జూడనార్తివికలులకుకు." M. XV. i. 166. **వికలత్వము** or **వికలత** *vikalatvamu.* n. Confusion, agitation, decay. కలుషత్వము, శైథిల్యము. "లావరియుష్మదంగవికలత్వముపాటిరి" P. i. 499. **వికలాంగుడు** *vikal-āngudu.* n. A cripple, one who is deformed or maimed. అంగహీనుడు. "ఇట్లువికలాంగుండైపుట్టినయసూరుండు." M. I. ii. 8. **వికలితము** *vikalitamu.* adj. Confused, confounded: decayed, impaired, withered. కలుషమైన, శిథిలమైన. "ఏకరణివికలితాత్ముడు కాకుండుంబతి." B. i. 535. **వికలుడు** *vikaludu.* n. A fool, one who is in confusion. కలత పాటినమనస్సుకలవాడు. "వేరిమనవిరిచిభ్రాంతి వికలుండవకుమీ." P. ii. 152.

వికల్పము *vikalpamu.* [Skt.] n. Confusion, doubt, indecision, ambiguity, an alternative opinion, option. ద్వైవిధ్యము, సందేహము, భ్రాంతి. **వికల్పము** or **వైకల్పికము** adj. Optional, admitting of two forms (in grammar); alternative, ద్వివిధమైన, సందిగ్ధమైన.

వికవిక or **వికావిక** *vika-vika.* [Tel. (anuk.)] adv. Much, aloud (a word used of laughter.) పకపక. "క్రొంగాటి పునికివాటల వికావికనావనిలించినవ్వుచుూ." T. ii. 95. **వికవికనవ్వు** *vika-vika-navvu.* v. n. To laugh out, to laugh loudly. పకపకనవ్వు. "కకవక మందురాగనువికావికనవ్వు." Ha. iii. 71.

వికసించు or **వికసిల్లు** *vikasintsu.* [Skt.] v. n. To open, blow, expand, as a flower. పువ్వు మొదలైనవి విరియు, వికాసముపొందు. **వికసనము** *vikasanamu.* n. Blossoming, expanding, as a flower. Understanding, consciousness. తెలివి. **వికసితము** *vikasitamu.* adj. Expanded, in bloom, as a flower, వికసించిన. **వికాసము** *vikāsamu.* n. Expansion, opening, blowing, bloom. వికసనము. వికసనము. Brightness. ప్రకాశము. "వికసనవికాసము, శ్రీకలరూపమున్న దివ్యుడు." Vish. viii. 395. **వికాసితము** *vikāsitamu.* adj. Opened, expanded, blown, as a flower. వికసించిన, విరిసిన.

వికారము *vikāramu.* [Skt.] n. A change of form, nature or quality, alteration; a transition from the quiescent state of the mind. Disease, sickness. Oddness, queerness, ugliness. వికార్యాగము, ప్రకృతి వ్యత్యాసము, మారురూపము పొందుట, రోగము. "లోకులెంచుచుండి లోకవికారంబులకరికి చేయువాడు." Vema. 2056. వికారములు strange doings or tricks వికృతములైనచేష్టలు. **వికారము** adj. Ugly, unnatural, odd, queer. విరూపమైన, కురూపమైన, వింతైన. **వికారముగా** *vikāramu-ga.* adv. Oddly, queerly, unnaturally. విరూపముగా, కురూపముగా. నాకు ఒళ్లు వికారముగానున్నది I am ailing a little. కడుపులో వికారముగానున్నది I feel nausea. **వికారించు** *vikārintsu.* v. n. To disagree with the health: to ail. ఒడలికి సెట్టక (or పడక) పోవు. **వికారి** *vikāri.* n. The name of a Telugu year.

వికిరము *vikiramu.* [Skt.] n. A bird. పక్షి. A piece, ఖండము. The funeral cake offered for one destitute of surviving relatives to do it for him. కర్తలులేని వారికి చేయుపిండము.

వికీర్ణము *vikirnamu.* [Skt.] adj. Scattered, spread about, dispersed, sprinkled. చెదరిన, విరజల్లబడిన, వ్యాప్తమైన. **వికిరణము** *vikiranamu.* n. Scattering. చెదరజల్లడము.

వికృతము *vikritamu.* [Skt. from వికారము] adj. Changed, altered, transformed.

Imperfect, deformed, faded. వికారమైన, విరూపమైన, వికారితమైన, వికలాంగమైన. "వివిధ పాపాత్ములు వికృతశరీరులై యాతనాబాధ లందుచుండగా." M. XVIII. i. 39. "పరుషడి వికృతరూపమున నరయాధ్యక్షకళ." ND. iv. 496. వికృతి vikriti. n. Change, transformation, metamorphosis; distortion, depravity. వికారము, కించిత్ప్రకృత్యన్యధాభావము, వికారస క్షోభవిక్షేపమనో జాతవికారము. In grammatical treatises this name is applied to the Telugu language, as distinguished from అద్యప్రకృతి the Sanskrit. "వికృతి బాసిన నాకు నేమమేటికి." L. xvii. 64. The name of a Telugu year.

విక్కము vikkamu [Skt.] n. A young elephant, ఏనుగుపిల్ల

విక్కవిరియు vikka-viriyu. See under విరియు.

విక్కు vikku. [Tel.] v. n. To stretch out (as the limbs.) To swell with pride. ఒడలు విరుచుకొను, విక్కుకొను, గర్వించు, విజృంభించు. క॥ "చిక్కెంబో వీడునాడు చేతనటంచున్, విక్కుచు దల్లికడకుజని." Chandra Rek. ii. 4.

విక్రమము vikramamu. [Skt.] n. Heroism, valour, power, might, energy. శక్తి, అధికబలము, ప్రతాపము, సాహసము. A foot, పాదము. A footstep, పాదవిక్షేపము. "విక్రమత్రయిమాధవుడాక్రమించె." A. v. 143. విక్రముడు, విక్రమాదిత్యుడు or విక్రమార్కుడు vikramudu. n. A certain king, the founder of an era wherein the year 1960 is coeval with 1903. A.D. విక్రమించు vikramintsu. v. n. To show prowess, to use one's power, to be energetic. సాహసముచేయు, పరాక్రమించు.

విక్రయము vi-krayamu. [Skt.] n. Selling, sale, vending. అమ్మడము. విక్రయికుడు or విక్రయి vi-krayikudu. n. A seller, vender, dealer, అమ్మేవాడు. విక్రయించు vi-krayintsu. v. a. To sell. అమ్ము. విక్రేత vi-krēta. n. A seller, vender. అమ్మేవాడు. విక్రేయము vi-krēyamu. adj. Vendible, saleable. అమ్మదగిన.

విక్రియ vi-kriya. [Skt.] n. Change, alteration of mind, form or condition. వికారము, కించిత్ప్రకృత్యన్యధాభావము.

విక్రీడితము vi-kriditamu. [Skt.] adj. Well played or danced. మిక్కిలి ఆడబడిన.

విక్షేపము vi-kshēpamu. [Skt.] n. Throwing, propelling, casting. వేయుడము, విసిరివేయుడము, ఎగరవేయుడము. Confusion, perplexity, distress of mind. క్షోభము, కలత. In astronomy, Latitude. విక్షేపించు vi-kshēpintsu. v. a. To toss up, ఎగరవేయు. To throw away. విసిరివేయు. విక్షేపణము vi-kshēpanamu. n. Scattering, dispersing. Throwing. విక్షిప్తము vi-kshiptamu. adj. Tossed up, thrown with force.

విక్షోభము vi-kshōbhamu. [Skt.] n. Agitation, distress of mind, anxiety. వ్యాకులత, చిత్తక్షోభ.

విఖ్యాతి vi-khyati. [Skt.] n. Great fame, celebrity. మిక్కిలి ప్రసిద్ధి. విఖ్యాతము vi-kyatamu. adj. Very famous, celebrated. మిక్కిలి ప్రసిద్ధమైన.

విగడియ vi-gadiya. [from Skt. ఘటిక.] n. The sixtieth part of a గడియ. i. e., of a period of 24 minutes.

విగతము vi-gatamu. [Skt.] adj. Quite gone, disappeared. అంతరించినట్టి, పోయినట్టి. Gloomy, obscure. నిస్తేజస్కమైన. విగతజీవుడు or విగతదేహుడు the deceased. విగతసత్త్వుడై having lost his courage, being deprived of his strength. విగతకల్మషుడై freed from sin, sinless, pure. విగతప్రజ్ఞుడు one who has lost his wits, who is devoid of sense.

విగళితము vi-galitamu. [Skt.] adj. Much fallen, dropped, మిక్కిలి జారిన, పతితమైన.

విగాహించు vi-gāhintsu. [Skt.] v. n. To sink, as in water. మునుగు, క్రుంకు. విగాహితము vi-gāhitamu. adj. Sunk, మునిగిన. విగాహము vi-gāhamu. n. Sinking, మునుగుట.

విగుర్రించు vigurrintsu. [Tel. విరుచు+విరుచు.] v. a. To break well or thoroughly. చెక్కగావిరుచు.

విగ్రహము vigrahamu. [Skt.] n. War, a battle, యుద్ధము. An image, idol, form, shape; the body. ప్రతిమ, శరీరము. విగ్రహించు vigrahintsu. v. n. To quarrel, to fight, కలహించు, పోరు.

విగ్రుడు, విఖ్యుడు or విఖ్రుడు vigrudu. [Skt.] n. A noseless person, ముక్కిడి.

విఘటిక or విఘడియ Same as విగడియ. (q. v.)

విఘట్టనము vi-ghattanamu [Skt.] n. Rubbing, friction, striking. ఒరసికొనుట, కొట్టడము.

విఘసము vi-ghasamu. [Skt.] n. The residue of food offered to the gods, to the manes, to a venerable guest, or to a spiritual preceptor. దేవతాతిథిశిష్టాన్నాదికము.

విఘాతము vi-ghātamu. [Skt.] n. A hindrance, obstacle, impediment, difficulty, stumbling-block. అడ్డంకి, ప్రతిబంధకము. Evil, harm, damage, చెరుపు. A great blow, పెద్దదెబ్బ. విఘాతించు or విఘాతముచేయు vighātintsu. v. a. To impede, hinder, obstruct, అడ్డంకికలుగజేయు. To spoil, injure, ruin, చెరుచు. To kill, చంపు.

విఘూర్ణనము vi-ghūrnanamu. [Skt.] n. A whirl, gyration. గిరగిరతిరుగడము. విఘూర్ణితము vi-ghūrnitamu. adj. Spinning, turning, whirling round. గిరగిరతిరిగే.

విఘ్నము vighnamu. [Skt.] n. A hindrance, impediment, obstacle, obstruction, అడ్డంకి, ప్రతిబంధము. విఘ్నపడు vighna-padu. v. n. To be obstructed or hindered, అడ్డిపడు.

విఘ్నేశుడు, విఘ్నేశ్వరుడు or విఘ్నరాజు vighn-ēsudu. n. The usual name of Ganēsa (corresponding to Janus.) వినాయకుడు. A pot-bellied man, a glutton.

విచక్షణము vi-chakshanamu. [Skt.] adj. Wise, clever, able, skillful. తెలిసిన, సమర్థమైన. విచక్షణుడు vi-chakshanudu. n. One who is wise or skillful. తెలిసినవాడు. సమర్థుడు, నేర్పరి.

విచారణ vi-chārana. [Skt.] n. Investigation, examination, inquiry, search, research. యథార్థనిరూపణము, వివేచన, నిష్పాదనము, ఉచితానుచితములువిచారించడము, పరిశీలన, చర్చ. అతనికి మావిచారణలేదు he takes no notice of us. విచారణకర్త vi-chārana-karta. n. An inquirer, a superintendent, an investigator. విచారించువాడు, విచారణచేయువాడు. విచారము vi-chāramu. n. Thought, investigation, examination, consultation, discussion, disputation, reasoning. ఆలోచన, వివేచన, చర్చ. Grief, sorrow, care, చింత, సంతాపము. విచారపడు vi-chāra-padu. v. n. To be sorrowful, to grieve, వ్యాకులపడు, సంతాపించు. విచారణీయము or విచార్యము vi-chāranīyamu. adj. Fit to be or that which ought to be discussed or investigated. విచారణచేయదగిన, పరిశీలనచేయదగిన. విచారించు or విచారణచేయు vi-chārintsu. v. a. To investigate, examine, inquire into. విమర్శచేయు, పరిశీలనచేయు. v. n. To reflect, consider, deem, suppose, think. ఎంచు, ఆలోచించు. అట్లు విచారించినాడు such was his opinion. To grieve, సంతాపించు. విచారితము vi-chāritamu. adj. Investigated, examined, judged, discussed, tried. పరిశీలనచేయబడిన.

విచికిత్స vi-chikitsa. [Skt.] n. Doubt, uncertainty; an error, mistake. సంశయము, సందేహము.

విచికిలము vichikilamu. [Skt.] n. A kind of Jasmine; a shrub called *Vangueria spinosa*, మల్లెచెట్టు, మల్లెపువ్వు, దనము.

విచిత్రము *vi-chitramu.* [Skt.] n. Surprise, wonder, astonishment. విస్మయము, ఆశ్చర్యము, ఆశ్చర్యము. A variegated color, చిత్రవర్ణము. adj. Wonderful, surprising. Variegated, gaudy, painted, coloured; beautiful, handsome. నానావర్ణమైన, చిత్రవర్ణములుకల, సుందరమైన, విలక్షణమైన, ఆశ్చర్యమైన.

విచేష్ట *vi-chēshṭa.* [Skt.] n. Motionlessness, నిశ్చేష్ట. **విచేష్టించు** *vi-chēshṭintsu,* v. n. To move about much, to be active. మిక్కిలి చేష్టించు. **విచేష్టితము** *vi-chēshṭitamu.* adj. Motionless, immovable, నిశ్చేష్టితము.

విచ్చేయు *vich-chēyu.* [for Skt. విజయముచేయు.] v. n. To come, వేంచేయు. "నీకెల్లకుశలంబులుంగలవు విచ్చేయుండు వేడంచు బల్కిన రాజేంద్రుడు పట్టణంబునకు వేగన్." Vish. vi. 98. To go, పోవు. నీవెచ్చోటికి విచ్చేయుకుము do not go anywhere.

విచ్చ *vitstsa.* [Tel.] n. A small ball of thread. చిన్న నూలుఉండ.

విచ్చలవిడి *vitstsala-viḍi.* [Tel. విచ్చలు+విడి.) n. Independence, freedom, స్వాతంత్ర్యము. adj. Independent, free, స్వతంత్రము. విచ్చలవిడి or విచ్చలవిడిగా *vitstsala-viḍi.* adv. At pleasure, at will, freely, independently. యథేచ్ఛముగా, స్వతంత్రముగా. "ఇన్నాళ్లకేతగా దింతవుండే మితమువిచ్చలవిడిగా మెలగరాదు." NH. v. 17. విచ్చవిచ్చలు *vitstsa-vitstsalu.* (anuk.) n. Dispersion on all sides; scattering about. యథాయథలు. adv. Pell-mell, dispersedly. యథాయథలుగా.

విచ్చాయ *vits-tsāya.* [Tel.] n. A flaw in a precious stone.

విచ్చు *vitstsu.* [Tel.] v. n. To become open or loose, to burst asunder, as a ripe fruit, to be cracked, split or broken, to be dispersed. విరియు, వికసించు. పగులు, చీలు. "మహాప్రకయింపుచుకవిప్పువిచ్చుమొగ్గంబు మరిపొరిపోదురు సమస్తదిశాగతులైనయాధ్వగుల్." A. iv. 170. మొగ్గవిచ్చినది the bud opened. దండువిచ్చి యథాయథలైపోయినది the army broke up and every man went his way. ఆగోడ విచ్చినది a crack has opened in the wall. ఆకుండ విచ్చినది the pot cracked. మూసలో లోహముకరిగి కన్నువిచ్చి ఆడునప్పుడు when the melted metal looks quite clear. v. a. To open, loosen, untie, undo; to spread, expand. విరియజేయు, వికసించు. దాని కొప్పువిచ్చినాడు he untied her knot of hair. కన్నువిచ్చి వారిని చూచినాడు he opened his eyes and looked at them. పాము పడగవిచ్చినది the snake spread or expanded its crest. "మేడిపండుచూడ మేలిమైయుండును పొట్టవిచ్చి చూడ పురుగులుండు." Vema. 174. విచ్చు *vitstsu.* n. The act of being scattered or dispersed. చెల్లాచెదరగుట. adj. Scattered, scattering, చెల్లాచెదరైన. చెల్లాచెదరుచేయునట్టు. **విచ్చుకత్తి** *vitstsu-katti.* n. A drawn sword, ఒరదూసినకత్తి. **విచ్చుటాకు** *vitstsu-ṭ-āku.* n. A coloured palmyra leaf rolled up and put in the pierced ears of women, in order to widen the bore for an earring. చెవ్వాకు. **విచ్చుమొగ్గ** *vitstsu-mogga.* n. An opening bud, విరియుమొగ్గ.

విచ్ఛాయము *vich-chhāyamu.* [Skt.] n. A flying shadow, as that of a flock of birds. పక్షులయొక్క నీడ. Fading, వాడిపోవడము. adj. Faded, నిస్తేజస్కమైన. "మార్గశ్రమంబున విచ్ఛాయములైనభక్తుని పదాంభోజంబులు." G. vi. 117.

విచ్ఛిత్తి *vich-chhitti.* (vulgarly విచ్ఛిత్తు) [Skt.] n. Parting, separation, ఎడబాటు. Loss, destruction, భంగము. Cutting, నరుకుట. గర్భవిచ్ఛిత్తి a miscarriage. **విచ్ఛిన్నము** *vich-chhinnamu.* adj Parted, divided, cut, separated, interrupted. భిన్నమైన. భగ్నమైన, నరకబడిన. అవిచ్ఛిన్నమైన or నిర్విచ్ఛిన్నమైన continual. **విచ్ఛేదము** *vich-chhēdamu.* n. Disjunction, separation, cutting, removal. నరుకుట, వియోగము, భంగము.

విజనము *vi-janamu.* [Skt. వి+జనము.] adj. Solitary, private, lonely, uninhabited. నిర్జనమైన.

విజయము *vi-jayamu.* [Skt.] n. A great conquest, a complete triumph, a great victory. మిక్కిలి గెలుపు. This word is used in the titles of several poems, and can be translated 'Adventures' or 'Tale,' as తారాశశాంకవిజయము the adventures of Tāra and Sasanka, similar to those of Stella and the Genius. **విజయ** *vi-jaya.* n. The name of a Telugu year. **విజయదశమి** *vijaya-dasami.* n. The tenth day of the month Asvayuja, being the day after the festival to Sarasvati, when all books, arms and instruments of trade are worshipped. **విజయముచేయు** or **విజయముచేయు** *vi-jayamu-chēyu.* v. n. To come: వచ్చు. To proceed: deign or condescend to come or go. వేంచేయు, విచ్చేయు, ఎమ్ము, పోవు. ఈవేళ మాయింటికి విజయముచేస్తారా will you do me the honor to come to my house? will you favour me with your company. "దేవదేవుండువిజయంబుచేసినయీస్వప్నంబు." A. pref. 21. "విద్వత్సింహాసనంబునకు విజయంబు చేయుమనుటయు." ib. iv. 111. **విజయస్తంభము** *vijaya-stambhamu.* n. A pillar of victory. జయించినాటిజయస్తంభము. "పొట్టునూరివిజయస్తంభోపలోట్టంకితి." A. iv. 345. **విజయి** *vi-jayi.* adj. Victorious, triumphant. జయమును పొందిన, జయముగల. n. A conqueror. జయించినవాడు. **విజయీభవ** *vijayi-bhava.* interj. Hail to so and so, here's to the health of so and so. Hallelujah. సర్వోత్కృష్టుడవుగా నుండుము. **విజయుడు** *vi-jayudu.* n. A name of Arjuna. అర్జునుడు. విజయవిలాసము a poem in his honour. Jaya and Vijaya are the names of the two porters at the gate of the palace of Vishnu, విష్ణువుయొక్క ద్వారపాలకులు.

విజాతి *vi-jati.* [Skt.] n. A different species, వేరైనజాతి. **విజాతీయము** *vi-jatiyamu.* adj. Of a different species, of a different sort or nature. Strange, queer, odd. విజాతిమైన, భిన్నమైన, వింతైన, అన్యతమైన.

విజిగీష *vi-jigisha.* [Skt.] n. A great desire to conquer, emulation, rivalry. మిక్కిలి జయించనిచ్ఛ. A. pref. 12. **విజిగీషువు** *vi-jigishuvu.* adj. One who is desirous of victory. మిక్కిలి జయేచ్ఛగలవాడు. A. iv. 195. ib. iii. 21.

విజితము *vi-jitamu.* [Skt.] adj. Subdued, overcome, conquered. జయింపబడిన. **విజితుడు** *vi-jitudu.* n. One who is defeated or conquered, జయింపబడినవాడు.

విజృంభణము *vi-jrimbhanamu.* [Skt.] n. Budding, expanding. వికసనము, వ్యాపకత్వము. Pride, మిక్కిలి జృంభణము. **విజృంభించు** *vi-jrimbhintsu.* v. n. To bloom, blossom, flourish, to be in its pride, shine forth, display. వికసించు, సామర్థ్యము ప్రకాశింపజేయు, చెలరేగు. వాడిప్పుడు నిండా విజృంభించియున్నాడు he is now in his pride. నిండా విజృంభింపబోకుము do not hold up your head too high. **విజృంభితము** *vi-jrimbhitamu.* adj. Spread, open, expanded. వికసించిన, వ్యాప్తమైన. A. i. 45. ib. ii. 60. Proud, గర్వించిన.

విజ్ఞప్తి Same as విజ్ఞాపనము and విన్నపము. (q. v.)

విజ్ఞాతము *vi-jnatamu.* [Skt. వి+జ్ఞాతము.] adj. Celebrated, famous, known, understood. ప్రసిద్ధమైన, తెలిసికొనబడిన. "విజ్ఞాతరూపకళాస్ఫురణవిభ్రు." A. iii. 83. **విజ్ఞాతుడు** *vi-jnatudu.* n. A famous man. ప్రసిద్ధుడు.

విజ్ఞానము *vi-jnanamu.* [Skt.] n. Knowledge of science, learning, విశేషజ్ఞానము, శాస్త్రాదులయందలిజ్ఞానము. A. vi. 86. **విజ్ఞుడు** or **విజ్ఞానుడు** *vi-jnanu.* n. A man of great learning. విశేషజ్ఞానముగలవాడు. "ఘనవిజ్ఞానశ్రీనందంబునకాగనిన." A. iii. 20.

విజ్ఞాపనము or విజ్ఞప్తి *vi-jnyapanamu*. [Skt.] n. Representing, informing. విన్నపము. A petition, request, prayer, making a representation. "అరిని చే తవిజ్ఞాపనంబు చేయించి అనుమతిగాంచి." A. vi. 130. విజ్ఞాపించు or విజ్ఞాపనముచేయు *vi-jyna-pintsu*. v. a. To represent, address, request, pray, విన్నపముచేయు, విన్నవించు.

విజ్ఞుడు *vi-jynudu*. [Skt.] n. A skillful man, one who is conversant with (a subject), a wise or learned man. నిపుణుడు, పండితు.

విడ్డు *vidzdzu*. [Tel.] v. n. To spread, వ్యాపించు. n. Kicking about, తన్నుకొనుచుండుట. విడ్డువిడ్డుగ *vidzdzu-vidzdzu-ga*. adv. In a mangled manner, in pieces, piecemeal, ఖండఖండముగా. "విడ్డువిడ్డుగ చిన్నంగనిపడువకిలముకరకుటంపుఖులనింతెంచిరకైగిదల." Swa. iv. 85. టీ॥ విడ్డువిడ్డుగాదన్నంగ, నలి నలిఅగునట్లు తన్నుచున్నప్పటికిని.

విడ్డోడు, విడ్డోడుగానుండే or విడ్డోడైన *vidz-dzodu*. [Tel. విడు+ఓడు.] adj. Odd, not even, not a pair, discordant. జతగా నుండానుండే, జోడుకాని, సరికాని. "సీ॥ శ్రుతు లవిడ్డోడైనచోదంత్ర పెనిచరిడించి కిటికిటిని పెద్రప్ప." Vaijayanti. i. 86. విడ్డోడుపడు *vidzdzodu-padu*. v. n. To become discordant, to differ, భేదపడు.

విటంకము *vitankamu*. [Skt.] n. A dovecote, an aviary. కపోతపాలిక, పక్షులనుండనిమ్మ గూడు.

విటకాడు, or విటకత్తె See విటుడు.

విటతాటము, విటపటము, విటలాటనము or వీటతాటము *vita-tatamu*. [Tel.] n. Confusion, disorder. తారుమారు. adj. Confused, disorderly, తారుమారైన. విటతాటముగ *vita-tatamu-ga*. adv. Topsy-turvy. తారుమారుగా, తలక్రిందులుగాకలిదీపలుండునట్లు. "వెసనైన్య ప్రతిమలవిటతాటముజేసి, వసతులన్నియు బ్రచ్చినైపించెగాక." BD. vi. 202. "కోటలు వ్రిన్నమొనారదనతోటి జల్కాడపోలి యు, కోటు వల్లదలక మాహాగ్రతిగాలడో విడమున్న ను, తర్కా టతోరు: యుద్ధక్రీడ గోపురాట్టకసంఘ తుల్, విటతాటముజేసిరక్కసివీరులాక్కమా త్రలోనా," M. III. vii. 82.

విటపము *vitapamu*. [Skt.] n. A branch of a tree with its new sprouts or shoots చిగిరించినకొమ్మ. A branch, కొమ్మ. A clump, పొదలైనచెట్టు. విటపి *vitapi*. n. A tree. వృక్షము. A banyan tree, మర్రిచెట్టు.

విటుడు, విటకాడు, విటపురుషుడు *vitudu*. [Skt.] n. A lover, a gallant or paramour. వల్లభుడు. విటి, విటకత్తె, విటులాడి or విటురాలు *viti*. n. A belle. వన్నెలాడి, కులటలాడి. విటరాయుడు, విటుపుడు or విటోత్తంసుడు *vita-rayadu*. n. A leader in fashion, a prince of gallants.

విట్చరము *vitcharamu*. [Skt.] n. A domestic pig, సూకరము. ఊరపంది.

విడంబనము *vidambanamu*. [Skt.] n. Imitation, copying. అనుకరించడము. అనుకరణము. "అనేకకోటిమార్తాండమండల ప్రభా డంబరవిడంబనంబైన యారాజాధిష్య తేజంబు." T. v. 84. Deception, మోసపుచ్చుట. విడంబించు *vidambintsu*. v. a. To imitate, copy, అనుకరించు. To broaden, expand, extend. విస్తరించు. To deceive, మోసపుచ్చు. "చంద్రకిరణంబు విడంబింప కుంపులుగోని" P. i. 283. "నిరదంబులమింబు విడంబించుచీకటిమ్రాకులు." T. iii. 29. విడంబితము *vidambitamu*. adj. Imitated, copied, simulated, transformed. అనుకరింప బడిన. Extended, spread. విస్తరింపబడిన. విడంబితుడు *vidambitudu*. n. One who is distressed, mortified, annoyed. పీడితుడు, బాధింపబడినవాడు.

విడక్రొప్పు, or విడనాడు See under విడు.

విడవలి *vidavali*. [Tel.] n. A kind of grass used for thatching the roofs of houses.

Andropogon muricatum. వట్టివేరు కసువు. విడివట్లిల్లు a house thatched therewith.

విడి *viḍi.* [Tel.] n. A red tint, అరుణకాంతి. Clearness, transparency, brilliancy, నైర్మల్యము, స్వచ్ఛత. Heroism, courage, valour, ప్రతాపము, పరాక్రమము. Anger, క్రోధము. The pods in a cotton fruit, ప్రత్తికాయలోని కిడ. "విడికలమానికముంబుత్తడికోడం గూర్చి నట్లు." P. iii. 285. adj. Red, అరుణము. Clear, transparent, స్వచ్ఛమైన, నిర్మలమైన. Separate, distinct. Single, odd, extra, spare, unoccupied, unemployed, loose. ఒంటి, ప్రత్యేకమైన. మిగతగానుండే. పనిఉండి విడిచిన. That can be untied, విడువదగిన. "విడికొంపువడగాడుగులు, కడువేడుకచేపు దూన." N. ix. 219. విడాకు *viḍ-āku.* (విడి+ఆకు.) n. A loose leaf. Divorce. విడిసంజె *viḍi-sandza.* n. The ruddy dawn or evening, ఎర్రసంజె. విడిపువ్వు an unstrung flower. విడిముత్యములు loose pearls. విడిమనిషి a single man, an extra man, one who is unoccupied or unemployed. విడిఆకులు loose leaves, not stitched. విడిపుదంది a single cloth (meaning one of a pair.) విడిపాదరోడు one sandal, an odd shoe. విడిపూస an odd bead. విడిమేను naked, దిసమొల. విడిత్తైదువ a loose woman, లంజె. విడికథ a riddle to be solved, విడువదగినకథ. విడికోడె a bullock that is set free from work, పనినుండివిడిచిన కోడె. విడి *viḍi.* (past p. of the verb విడు.) Setting aside, leaving off. విడిచిపెట్టి. adv. Alone, ఒంటరిగా. విడిగానుండే *viḍi-gā-nuṇḍē.* adj. Single, unoccupied, unemployed, loose. ఒంటరిగానుండే, మిగిలియుండే, ఒకటి సొకటి చేరకుండా ఉండే. విడిగోలు *viḍi-gōlu* adj. Spare, unemployed. మారుపు, పనిలేని. విడిగోలు ఎద్దులు spare bullocks. వాడు విడిగోలుమీద దున్నును he ploughs with different yokes of cattle in turn. విడిదల *viḍi-dala.* (విడిది+తల.) n. A halting place. విడియుచోటు, విడిసినచోటు, దండుదిగినస్థలము. "విడిదలకుపోయినపుడు నీకొడుకులెల్లానాగా నందమునికడకరుగుచుండి." M. VI. iii. 70. **విడిది** *viḍidi.* n. Halting, విడియుట. A lodging, a residence, దిగుబస, విడిసినచోటు. "ఈ విడిదింటిలోనికేలరూయు." L. iv. 240. విడిదిచేయు *viḍidi-chēyu.* v. n. To halt, stay, abide, దిగు, బసచేయు. విడిపట్టు *viḍi-paṭṭu.* (విడిది+పట్టు.) n. A halting place, విడిదిచోటు. A lodging, inn, బస. "అమర విభుండు చేరి వినయానతుడై విడిపట్టునైజయుంతము నకు బెత్తెంపుమన." Parij. iii. 76. విడిమట్టు *viḍi-maṭṭu.* n. A dwelling place, వాసస్థానము, కాపురస్థలము. Also, same as విడిది. విడిమట్టుచేయు *viḍi-maṭṭu-chēyu.* v. n. To halt, stay, lodge, దండుదిగు, బసచేయు. విడివడు or విడిపడు *viḍi-paḍu.* v. n. To separate, విడు, విడబడు. To slip, జారు, To escape, get free, break loose, to shake off (shame), విడిపించుకొను, జంకువిడుచు. విడిపోవు or విడివోవు *viḍi-pōvu.* v. n. To cease or terminate, తనకుతానే పడలు, విడిపడు. విడిముడి *viḍi-muḍi.* n. Wealth, riches, ధనము, ఐశ్వర్యము. విడియుత్తము *viḍi-y-uttamu.* n. The glove or leather worn on the huntsman's arm for the hawk to perch upon. డేగముండలైనవికూర్చుండడమునకై వేటకాని చేతికి కట్టుకొనేచర్మము. "విడియుత్తైమునందల యొత్తి చూచుబలో సాళువముగా వడింబరపొళలు వయిగా విడిచెన్ మహోద్ధతిన్." Swa. iv. 82. విడివేట *viḍi-vēṭa.* n. Falconry, డేగవేట.

విడియ, విడియము. విడెము or **విడ్యము** *viḍiya.* [Tel.] n. Betel and nut, తాంబూలము. "పదికంబుకిందట బసనందుమున్న మడచిన విడియముల్ గొంచి దొమక్కడి విడియ లింతవ్వరు వచ్చిరిక్కడికని దనయింతినిదురుక." BD. v. 589.

విడియు *viḍiyu.* v. n. To halt, alight, stay, lodge, వసించు, (ప్రయాణీకులు దారిలో నొక చోట) దిగు, బసచేయు. To be separated, to become separate, విడు. To slip, జారు. విడియించు *viḍiyintsu*. v. a. To lodge, place, cause to alight, దిగునట్లుచేయు, బసచేయించు. "రథమున నవ్వుష్టికైవాయుదిగి రత్నేలపై విడియించురు గ్రక్కా." A. iv. 170. See విడిది.

విడు *viḍu*. [Tel.] v. n. To separate, become loose, వీడు. To fall asunder, వినకుతానేవదలు, వీడిపోవు, విడిపోవు. "నీళ్లమీదబుగ్గ నిలిచి నప్పుడు కర్లువేనవచ్చితాకుగాక. విడకుండు కింత విశ్రాంతిపడుదురు." Vema. 70. v. a. To relinquish, leave, quit, abandon, give up, loosen, untie, undo, let go, release, separate, త్యజించు, మానుకొను, వదలు, విచ్చు, విప్పు, విడ్చు. విడుగడ or విడుగర *viḍu-gaḍa*. n. Release, liberation. విడుదల, విమోచనము. "ఈ కిత్రి వ్వ గౌకికి యిప్ప డ కారవారనేమనీకు విడుగరవేయం దొరకొనుట నీదుభాగ్యం బరితత్వము దొరకిమైత్రియులమను మదిగా." M. XII. iii. 207. "అన్యదేశ్యన ధర్మవిడుము." A. iv. 257. విడుగు *viḍugu*. v. n. To blow or expand, as a flower, వికసించు. "మడిగెలోగలడగెకెక్కు లు విడిగె పరిమాజమ్ములుడిగె వెన్నెల." S. I. 164. విడకొక్కు or విడద్రొక్కు *viḍa-dokku*. v. a. To allot, set aside, grant, as land. విడుచు, ఇచ్చు. అయూరికెండ నాయూరి పొలములో కొంతభూమి విడదొక్కినారు they allotted some land from one village to that village. విడనాడు *viḍa-n-āḍu*. v. a. To cast off, desert, quit, relinquish, divorce. విడుచు, విడిచిపెట్టు, వదులు. "మూలగూరిమెచ్చు గుణవంతు విడనాడి." Vema. 1752. విడబడు or విడివడు *viḍa-baḍu*. v. n. To escape, get free, break loose, విడు. విచ్చేలవిడికుకు. కట్టువవిడించుకొని విరంకుశముగానుండు, కిX నుండి జేరుపడు. నిర్బంధముమండి తొలగు. To slip, జారు. "ఆతనిమహాలాడ్డండగజము. తన్ను దామరచి మదగ్రస్తయగుచు. కడిదిమావింతుని బడ ద్మూరిచేసి. విడివడిదండెల్ల విరియ దోలచుచు." B.D. iv. 352. అది విడివడిమాట్లాడినది she shook off all shame and spoke.

విడుచు or విడ్చు *viḍutsu*. [Tel.] v. n. & a. To relinquish, leave, quit, abandon, give up, loosen, slacken, untie, undo. To cease, to terminate. చాలించుకొను, మానుకొను, వదలుకొను. ఆ చెట్టు నాలుగుకొమ్మలు విడిచినది that tree has produced four branches. వానవిడిచెను the rain is over. గ్రహణము విడిచినది the eclipse is now over. దీవతవిడిచినది the plague has ceased. అంటువిడిచినది the impurity has passed away. దయ్యమువిడిచినది the demon has quitted him or let him go. క్రోధమునువిడిచినాడు he has laid aside his wrath. చేనిలో ఆవును మేయవిడిచినాడు he let the cow go to graze on the crop. ఆహారమునువిడిచెను he gave up eating. ప్రాణమునువిడిచెను he gave up the ghost. ఆమె కన్నీళ్లువిడిచెను she shed tears. బాణమువిడుచు to discharge a rocket. ఆ కోటను విడిచిపోయిరి they quitted the fort. కర్మమువిడుచు to peform a certain rite. పట్టినపట్టు విడవడు he will never let go his hold. కుమార్తెను అత్తవారిఇంట విడిచినాడు he left his daughter at the house of her mother-in-law. దినమువిడిచిదినము on alternate days, every other day. బట్టలువిడుచు to strip. ఊపిరివిడుచు to breathe. వారిని తెయ్యక విడిచినాడు he abandoned them. "కొంగుకొగామువిడిచిగొబ్బునసేరాడు." Vema. 171. విడిచిపెట్టు *viḍichi-peṭṭu*. v. a. To relinquish, leave, quit, abandon, give up. To loosen, untie, undo, చాలించుకొను. వదలు. విడిపించు *viḍipintsu*. v. a. To loose, let go, release. విడిచిపెట్టు, వదలు, పోనిచ్చు. విడిపించుకొను *viḍipintsu-konu*. v. n. To escape, get free, break loose, విడివడు, వదలించుకొను. విడుత *viḍuta*. n. A time, తడవ. ఒకవిడుత once. రెండువిడుతలు twice. విడుదల, విడుపు, విడ్పు or విడుదుర *viḍu-dala*. n. Release, liberation, setting at liberty, freeing, కడతేరడము, నివృత్తి, విమోచనము. విడుదలపత్రము a deed of surrender or relinquishment. విడుపు also means

Almsgiving, దానము. విడుపరి *vidup-ari*. n. One who abandons a friend, &c. మిత్రత్యాగశీలుఁడు. A liberal man, త్యాగశీలుఁడు. విడుపడు *vidu-padu*. (విడుపు+పడు.) v. n. To separate, to be severed. విడిపోవుచున్నాడు.

విదూరశిల *vidūra-śila*. [Skt.] n. The stone called Cat's eye or Lapis lazuli. వైడూర్యము. "పెళపెళమంచువిచ్చునుమ క్షితి విదూరశిలాంకురచ్ఛటోద్భవశిలాప్లు." A. iv. 138.

విడెము Same as విడియము and విడియము. See under విడి.

విద్దూరము *viddūramu*. [Tel.] n. Obstinacy, stubbornness, enmity, మూర్ఖత్వము, శత్రుత్వము. "విద్దూరములుచ్చెనేకస్సారము నకు." Pal. 334. adj. Obstinate, stubborn, inimical. మూర్ఖమైన, శత్రుత్వమైన. రాజవిద్దూరము the enmity between kings.

విద్యము Same as విడియము. See under విడి.

విద్వరము *vidvaramu*. [Skt.] n. Danger, ఉపద్రవము.

విణ్మయము *viṇ-mayamu*. [Skt.] adj. Covered with dung, filthy, foul, పురీషముతో కూడిన. "ఖరమూత్రవిణ్మయ కర్దమస్థలములు." Surabha. i. 67.

విత See విదా.

వితండము *vitaṇḍamu*. [Skt.] n. Wrangling, controversy, contention. స్వపక్షస్థాపన ముగా వాదించేడువాదము, దుర్వాదము, అడ్డ మాడడము. వాడు నాతో వితండవాదముచేసి నాడు he wrangled or squabbled with me. వితండవాది *vitaṇḍa-vādi*. n. One who wrangles. దుర్వాదము చేయువాడు.

వితంతువు *vi-tantuvu*. [Skt.] n. A widow. విధవ.

వితంసము *vitaṁsamu*. [Skt.] n. A net, a chain or other thing made to confine beasts or birds. మృగపక్షిబంధనోపకరణము, వలలు ఉరులు మొదలైనవి.

వితతము *vitatamu*. [Skt.] adj. Stretched, extended, expanded, spread, diffused. విస్తృతమైన. విరివిచేయబడిన. వితతి *vi-tati*. n. An assemblage, quantity, cluster, సమూహము. "విప్రసమూహవితతివిరించిచేసాడించె." Ila. i. 103.

వితథము *vi-tathamu*. [Skt.] adj. False, untrue. అసత్యమైన. n. A falsehood, అబద్ధపుమాట.

వితము *vitamu*. [from Skt. విధము.] n. Manner, way, mode, kind, sort, విధము. "వితముచెలిసినవారు వేదాంతపెద్దలే." Vēma. ii. 283. వితమరి *vitam-ari*. n. A skilful person, కార్యదక్షుఁడు. A husbandman, a peasant, కాపువాడు.

వితరణము *vitaraṇamu*. [Skt.] n. Bounty, liberality. దానము, ఈవి, త్యాగము. వితరణి *vitaraṇi*. n. A liberal or bountiful man. దాత. ఈవికాడు. "పండితకవులప్రోపైనవితరణులు నిట్లనిరతికి నేకు విద్యలెల్ల." Kālahasti Satakam 77. In another Satakam, "శశిమ కలాభిక్షన్నను, దినదినముకోపితోలు వితరణు లెక్కడ."

వితర్కము *vi-tarkamu*. [Skt.] n. Reasoning, discussion, doubt, deliberation; a conjecture, opinion, inference. ఊహ, తర్కము, తర్కించడము, సందేహము. వితర్కించు *vi-tarkiṁtsu*. v. n. To reflect, ponder hesitate, తలపోయు, డోలాయమానమగు, సందేహించు, ఊహించు.

వితర్డి or వితర్దిక *vitardi*. [Skt.] n. A raised seat, or terrace, usually called a pyal. వేదిక, అరుగు, తిన్నె "వితర్డులవేదికల తర్దుల." L. iii. 41.

వితలము *vitalamu*. [Skt.] n. The name of the second region in Patalam, the infernal or nether world, ద్వితీయాధోలోకము.

వితస్తి *vitasti*. [Skt.] n. A span; twelve fingers' breadth. జేన, పన్నెండు అంగుళముల కొలత.

విటా or విట vita. [from Skt. వ్యర్థ.] adj. Useless, vain, వ్యర్థము, వృథా. విటావిట vita-vita. adj. Quite useless, మిక్కిలి వ్యర్థము.

విటాకు vitaku. [Tel.] n. Horror, confusion, నిశ్చేష్టత, ఎటుమతోచక కలవరపడియుండడము. Forgetfulness, absent-mindedness, పారవశ్యము, పరాకు. విటాకుడు or విటాకుడు n. One who is confused or struck dumb. నిశ్చేష్టితుడు, పరవశుడు. విటాకుపడు vitaku-padu. v. n. To be confused or confounded, to be at a loss, నిశ్చేష్టితుడగు, ఎటుమతోచక కలవరముగానుండు. "మార్గము దప్పికంపలజిక్కి మదిని విటాకుపడిచింతము నుంచుచు." G. iii. 21.

విటాన vitana. [from Skt. విధము.] adv. In the manner of, like. విధముగా, రీతిగా. "నక్కరయునలలోనచిక్కికొన్నవిటాన." Ila. iii. 59.

వితానము vitanamu. [Skt.] n. An awning, tester or canopy, మేలుకట్టు. A heap, a quantity, సమూహము. Extent, వైశాల్యము. "విమత సస్యవితానమునకువాన." Suca. iii. 286. "ధన ద్యుతివితానముచిమలగాలుకొలె." M. v. iii. 364. adj. Empty, శూన్యము. Dull, మందము.

వితీర్ణము vi-tirnamu. [Skt.] adj. Crossed, passed, దాటబడిన. Given, ఇయ్యబడిన.

విత్త vitta. [Tel.] n. A very small sack. మిక్కిలి చిన్నగోనె.

విత్తనము See under విత్తు.

విత్తము vittamu. [Skt.] n. Wealth, riches, ధనము. adj. Known, తెలియబడిన. Obtained, gained, పొందబడిన. Famed, ప్రసిద్ధినొందిన. Investigated, inquired into, విచారింపబడిన.

విత్తు vittu. [Skt. from విద్ to know.] n. He who knows. తెలిసినవాడు. వేదవిత్తు skilled in the Vedas.

విత్తు vittu. [Tel] v. a. To sow, విత్తులుచల్లు, వేయు. "జొన్నలుగలయుదపులుమహిదున్నకవిత్తక ఫలించు." Vish. ii. 156. n. A seed; a testicle, విత్తనము, బీజము. విత్తనము vittanamu. n. A seed. విత్తు, బీజము. విత్తించు vittintsu. v. a. To cause to sow, to get to be sown. ఆ పొలమును విత్తించినాడు he caused the field to be sown.

విదగ్ధము vi-dagdhamu. [Skt.] adj. Skilful, clever. సమర్థమైన, నేర్పుగల. విదగ్ధత vi-dagdhata. n. Cleverness. కౌశల్యము, సమర్థత. విదగ్ధుడు vi-dagdhudu. n. A learned or clever man. కార్యకుశలుడు, నేర్పరి.

విదరము vidaramu. [Skt.] n. Splitting, చీల్చుట.

విదర్భము vi-darbhamu. [Skt.] n. A dry, or desert soil, మరుస్థలము. విదర్భదేశము the country called Vidarbha, a district to the south-west of Bengal, the modern Behar proper. కోశదేశము. విదర్భ a city of that name.

విదలించు or విదల్చు See under విదులు.

విదళనము vi-dalanamu. [Skt.] n. Breaking, rending, splitting, బద్దలుచేయుట. విదళము vidalamu. n. Split pulse. కందులు మొదలైనవాటిపప్పు. Cuttings, chips. పేడ్లు, బద్దలు. adj. Opened, expanded, blown, as a flower. Rent, split. వికసించిన, పగిలిన, బద్దలైన. విదళించు vi-dalintsu. v. a. To split, cut, break, rend. పగులగొట్టు, నరుకు. "కడగినవీరుదారవిలిఖడ్గముచే విదళించిపొమ్మటో." Krishn. Abhyu. ii. 156. విదళితము vidalitamu. adj. Rent, torn, split. Blown, expanded. పగులగొట్టబడ్డ, చించబడ్డ, వికసించిన.

విదారణము vidāranamu. [Skt.] n. Tearing, splitting, severing. చీల్చుట. విదారించు vidārintsu. v. a. To tear, split. పగులగొట్టు, చీల్చు. "దుర్గాదేవికినీకరాతలంబొడ్డోవిదారించి." Sananda Padya ii. 17 విదారితము vidāritamu. adj. Torn, split, dashed to pieces, బద్దలుచేయబడిన. M. VII. iv. 308.

విదాహము *vi-dāhamu.* [Skt.] n. Great thirst. మహాతృష్ణ.

విదిక్కు *vi-dikku.* [Skt.] n. An intermediate point (or half-point) of the compass, as south-east, south-west, north-west, north-east. రెండుదిక్కుల నడుమ, మూల, ఆగ్నేయాది కోణములు.

విదితము *viditamu.* [Skt.] adj. Known, understood, evident, plain. తెలియబడిన, స్పష్టమైన. "విదురదిక్పాలురువిదితులు." M. III. ii. 34. **విదితముగా** *viditamu-ga.* adj. Clearly, plainly, evidently. విశదముగా, స్పష్టముగా. "విదితంబుగశాస్త్రంబులు చదువుచు న్నంతె." Vish. vi. 8. "జనవ్యవిదితముగను." Kuchleo. ii. 47. **విదితుడు** *vidituḍu.* n. A well-known or celebrated man. తెలియబడినవాడు, ప్రసిద్ధుడు.

విదియ *vidiya.* [from Skt. ద్వితీయ.] n. The second day after full moon or new moon. పక్షమందు రెండవ తిథి.

విదీర్ణము *vi-dīrṇamu.* [Skt.] adj. Torn, split, burst. చీల్చబడిన. Expanded, opened, విచ్చిన. "నేమిఘట్టనమున భూమివిదీర్ణమై పాంసు రూపమున పథంబునొరగ." BRY. 3256.

విదుడు *viduḍu.* [Skt.] n. (In composition), one who knows. తెలిసినవాడు, ఎరిగినవాడు.

విదులు or **విదురు** *vidulu.* [Tel.] v. n. To fall or drop down. రాలు. ఆ చెట్టు పండ్లతో విదులు చున్నది the tree is overburdened with fruit. **విదులుచు, విదుల్చు, విదురుచు, విదుర్చు, విదలుచు, విదలించు, విదల్చు, విదిలించు** or **విదిలుచు** *vidulutsu.* v. a. To shake off, get rid of. To reject angrily. శోధించు, దులుపు. నన్ను పట్టుకొని విదిలించి విడిచిపెట్టినాడు he seized me and chastised me. **విదులుపు, విదుల్పు, విదురుపు** or **విదుర్పు** *vidulupu.* n. The act of shaking, విదులుట. **విదిలింపులు** *vidilimpulu.* n. plu. Chastisement, reprimand, చీవాట్లు.

విదుషి *vidushi.* [Skt.] n. A learned woman. పండితురాలు.

విదూరము *vi-dūramu.* [Skt.] adj. Very far or remote. మిగులదూరమైన. వివేకవిదూరుడు he who is wholly devoid of wisdom. "తమతమ్ముల వివేకవిదూరులు." M. I. i. 129.

విదూషకుడు *vi-dūshakuḍu.* [Skt.] A wag, jester, buffoon. హాస్యగాడు, శృంగారనాయకుని సచివులలో నొకడు. "విదూషక పూర్వకము పురాణాదిగోష్ఠివిచార పూర్వకము." A. iv. 321. ఈ విదూషక, పరిహాసకులు. One who is given to fault-finding in others. **విదూషితము** *vi-dūshitamu.* adj. Dirty, ugly. మలీమసమైన, వికారమైన. "మషీవిదూషితాకారము." P. iii. 352.

విదేశము *vi-dēśamu.* n. A foreign country, abroad, any place away from home. పరదేశము, అన్యదేశము. **విదేశస్థుడు** *vi-dēśa-sthuḍu.* n. One who remains abroad, పరదేశమునందుండు వాడు. **విదేశి, విదేశీయుడు** or **విదేశ్యుడు** *vi-dēśi.* n. A foreigner, పరదేశస్థుడు. "విదేశ్యులెరుచు." A. iv. 208. **విదేశగతుడు** *vi-dēśa-gatuḍu.* n. One who is away from home, a pilgrim, emigrant, దేశాంతరగతుడు. **విదేశత** *vi-dēśata.* n. Absence from home, దేశాంతరప్రస్థత్వము. "ఇద్దరి మిద్దరమై విదేశత నొప్పకనొచ్చి మోహమున నూతనమునిం." Ila. iii. 165.

విదేహి *vi-dēhi.* [Skt.] adj. Incorporeal, bodiless, without a body. శరీరవిహీనుడైన.

విద్దె or **విద్దియ** *vidde.* [from Skt. విద్య.] n. Science, knowledge, learning. చదువు. A trick; guile. "అద్దిరభక్తసనియుల గొంటేటినను విద్దెలాడుటగాక విందుమెత్తొల్లి, విపరీతమిందరు వినగబల్కితి." BD. v. 208. **విద్దెము** or **విద్దియము** *viddemu.* n. The tottering gait of an infant. నిలువనేరకుండా పెట్టేవిడ్డ ఆడే ఆట. "జనకుండవ్వల బిడ్డనేతిడువగ్గనేర్ప రాముని విందయుంచునటించు." N. iv. 165. విడ్డెలాడు vidde-l-āḍu. v. n. To juggle, గారడి విద్యలు చేయు.

విద్య vidya. [Skt. from విద్ to know.] n. Knowledge, science, learning, education; an art, తెలువు, జ్ఞానము. Conjuring, juggling. మహావిద్య the great art, i. e., magic. విద్యాధరుడు vidya-dharuḍu. n. A demigod of a particular class, a fairy, or genius, ఖేచరవిశేషము. విద్యార్థి vidy-ārthi. n. A pupil, student, చదువు కోరువాడు, చదువు కొనువాడు. విద్యావంతుడు vidya-vantuḍu. n. A man of learning.

విద్యమానము vidya-mānamu. [Skt.] adj. Existent, present. వర్తమానము, ఉండేటువంటి. n. Condition, state. స్థితి. ఇప్పుడుండేవిద్యమానముచూస్తే if we consider the present state of things.

విద్యుత్తు vi-dyuttu. [Skt.] n. Lightning. మెరుపు. విద్యోతించు vi-dyōtintsu. v. n. To shine, ప్రకాశించు, వెలుగు.

విద్రధి vidradhi. [Skt.] n. A deep seated or internal abscess. కడుపులోపుట్టి వాపిలో పైకెల్లే వ్రణభేదము. A disordered liver, కడుపులోనిబల్ల.

విద్రవము or విద్రావము vi-dravamu. [Skt.] n. Flight, retreat, running away from a battle field. పారిపోవడము. Flowing out, leaking.

విద్రుము Same as విదురుము or విదిలించు. See under విదులు. (q. v.)

విద్రుతము vi-drutamu. [Skt.] adj. Liquified, melted; flown, running, కరిగి విరుగాకారే.

విద్రుమము vi-drumamu. [Skt.] n. Coral. పగడము. A tender or young leaf or shoot. చిగురు.

విద్వాంసుడు vidvāmsuḍu. [Skt.] n. A learned man, a man of letters. పండితుడు. విద్యత్ప్రభువు a patron of learning. విద్వాంసురాలు vidvāmsu-r-ālu. n. A learned woman. పండితురాలు, తెలిసినస్త్రీ.

విద్వేషము vi-dvēshamu. [Skt.] n. Enmity, hatred. పగ. విద్వేషి, విద్విష్టు or విద్వేషుడు vi-dvēshi. n. An enemy, foe. శత్రువు. "ఓరి విద్విష్టయుగారి." Chatu. 36. విద్వేషించు vi-dvēshintsu. v. n. To bear malice or enmity, పగగొను, విరోధించు.

విధ vidha. [Skt.] n. Plenty, సమృద్ధి. విధము vidhamu. n. Kind, sort, way, manner, mode, state. ప్రకారము. Pay, wages, hire, జీతము. ఏవిధముగా how, in what manner? ఈ విధముగా thus. నీవు ఎన్ని విధాలచెప్పినా వినడు whatever you may say he will not listen.

విధవ vi-dhava. [Skt. వి+ధవ.] n. A widow. పెనిమిటిలేనిది. A term of scorn, applied to both sexes.

విధాత or విధాతృడు vidhāta. [Skt.] n. A name of Brahma, the creator. బ్రహ్మ.

విధానము vidhānamu. [Skt.] n. Doing. చేయుట. A command, rule, ordinance, ఆజ్ఞ. Performing prescribed rites, or acts prescribed in the sacred books of the Hindus. విధ్యుక్తప్రకారము చేయుటము. Worship, పూజ. విధాయకము vidhāyakamu. n. An ordinance, order, decree, విధి, ఆజ్ఞ. adj. Binding, enjoined. విధాయకుడు or విధాతు vidhāyakuḍu. n. A director, an authority, particularly in religion. నిర్ణేత, విధించువాడు.

విధి vidhi. [Skt.] n. An order, command, rule, law. నియోగము, విధానము. An act prescribed by the Vedas; an ordinance; duty. వేదశాస్త్రోక్తవిధి, ఏర్పాటు. Providence. Fate, destiny, luck. భాగ్యము. Brahma,

God. విధిలేక వెళ్లినాను having no alternative I went there. పదిదినములు నీవు ఇక్కడ ఉండక విధిలేదు there is no alternative, you must remain here for ten days. నావిధి నేమందును this is my fate, what can I say? విధివశముచే దొరికినది, లేక, చిక్కినది it was found by chance. యథావిధిగా నడిచినది it was done according to rule. **విధించు** *vidhintsu.* v. a. To order, command, ordain, prescribe, allot, adjudge, assign. ఆజ్ఞాపించు, నిర్ణయించు. ఏర్పాటు చేయు, కట్టడచేయు. వానికి ప్రాయశ్చిత్తము విధించినారు they appointed him a penance. శిక్ష విధింపబడినది this punishment was awarded. యాభైరూపాయలు అపరాధము (లేక, జులమానా) విధించినారు they sentenced him to pay a fine of Rs. 50. **విధ్యుక్తము** *vidh-yuktamu.* adj. Prescribed, legal, యథావిధియైన. **విధ్యుక్తముగా** *vidh-yuktamu-gā.* adv. Legally, in proper form or manner, యథావిధిగా.

విధుంతుదుడు *vidhuntududu.* [Skt.] n. A name of Rāhu, రాహువు.

విధురము *vidhuramu.* [Skt.] adj. Agitated, distressed, overcome with anxiety or distress; bewildered, confused. Separate, absent, భయయుక్తమైన, విహ్వలమైన, ఎడబాటు పొందిన, వైకల్యముపొందిన. **విధురుడు** *vidhuruḍu.* n. A widower, భార్యచచ్చినవాడు.

విధువు *vidhuvu.* [Skt.] n. The moon, చంద్రుడు. Vishnu, విష్ణువు.

విధూతము *vi-dhūtamu.* [Skt.] adj. Shaken, కదలింపబడిన. Left, let go, thrown, విడువబడిన. **విధూతి, విధూననము** or **విధూవనము** *vi-dhūti.* n. Shaking, tremor, trembling, కదలించుట.

విధేయము *vi-dhēyamu.* [Skt.] adj. Obedient. చెప్పినట్టువినే. వినయవిధేయముగా with humble obedience. **విధేయత** *vi-dhēyata.* n. Obedience. **విధేయవిశేషణము** *vi-dhēya-viśēshaṇamu.* n. An adjective coming after its noun. **విధేయుడు** *vi-dhēyuḍu.* n. One who obeys; an obedient man. చెప్పినట్టు వినువాడు, వినయముగలవాడు.

విధ్వంసము *vi-dhvamsamu* [Skt. వి+ధ్వంసము.] n. Great ruin, destruction. మిక్కిలి ధ్వంసము, నాశము. **విధ్వంసితము** *vi-dhvamsitamu.* adj. Ruined, destroyed, నాశము చేయబడ్డ.

వినతము *vi-natamu.* [Skt.] adj. Bowed, bent, stooping, humble, modest. Trained, disciplined, వంగిన, నమ్రమైన, సుశిక్షితమైన. **వినతి** *vi-nati.* (వి+నతి.) n. Humility, modesty, reverence, వినయము. A salutation, bowing, నమస్కారము. **వినతుడు** *vi-natuḍu.* n. A humble, modest or unassuming man, వినీతుడు, నమ్రుడు.

వినని *vinani.* [Tel. from విను.] adj. Unheard of, not heard of. శ్రుతముకాని. Not hearing. వినని వాడు a deaf man.

వినమితము *vi-namitamu.* [Skt.] adj. Much bowed down, declined, humbled, conquered, మిక్కిలివంచబడిన, వంగిన, జయింపబడ్డ.

వినమ్రము *vi-namramu.* [Skt. వి+నమ్రము.] adj. Much bent, bowed, humble, modest. మిక్కిలివంగిన, లొంగిన.

వినయము *vi-nayamu.* [Skt. వి+నయము.] n. Humility, modesty, gentleness, mildness, reverence, వినతి, వినమ్రత. వినయపూర్వకముగా or వినయవిధేయముగా humbly. **వినయవంతుడు** *vi-naya-vantuḍu.* n. A humble man, నమ్రతగలవాడు. **వినయవర్తనుడు** *vi-naya-vartanuḍu.* n. One who acts humbly, నమ్రతతో నడుచుకొనువాడు.

వినా or **వినాగా** *vinā.* [Skt.] adv. Save, except, without. తప్ప. **వినాయించు** or **వినాచేయు** *vināyintsu.* v. a. To except, exclude, make an exception of, leave out of account. తప్పునిచ్చు, విడిచిపెట్టు.

వినాయకుడు *vināyakuḍu.* [Skt.] A name of Gaṇesa, విఘ్నేశ్వరుడు.

వినాశము *vi-nāṣamu.* [Skt. వి+నాశము.] n. Great ruin, total loss, destruction, annihilation. మిక్కిలినాశము. నీవు వినాశమునకు వచ్చెదవా are you rushing on destruction? వినాశమునొందు to perish.

వినిందించు *vi-nindintsu.* [Tel.] v. a. To blame much, మిక్కిలి నిందించు.

వినికి, వినికిడి or **వినిపించు** See under విను.

వినిమయము *vi-nimayamu.* [Skt.] n. Barter, exchange. ఒక వస్తువును ఇచ్చి మరొకటిని పుచ్చుకోవడము, వస్తువులమారుపు. A pledge, deposit, security, కుదువ.

వినియోగము *vi-niyōgamu.* [Skt. వి+నియోగము.] n. Using, use, utility, advantage, serviceableness, ఉపయోగము. Sharing any thing sacred, as gifts distributed among Brahmins at a temple. గుడిలో ప్రసాదము పంచి పెట్టడము. అందువల్ల నేమి వినియోగము what is the good of it? వినియోగము లేని మాట an unprofitable statement. **వినియోగించు** or **వినియోగపడు** *vi-niyōgintsu.* v. n. To be used or applied. ఉపయోగపడు. **వినియోగించు** or **వినియోగపరచు** *vi-niyōgintsu.* v. a. To use, apply. ఉపయోగపరచు. నీయావచ్ఛక్తిని వినియోగపరచవలసినది you must use every effort; you must apply or put forth all your strength. దీనిని దేనికి వినియోగపరచవచ్చును to what purpose can this be applied? **వినియుక్తము** *vi-niyuktamu.* adj. Used, ఉపయోగింపబడిన.

వినిర్గతము *vi-nir-gatamu.* [Skt.] adj. Gone out, departed from. అవతలయైన, బయలువెడలిన. "విశ్వప్రతాపి వినిర్గతపాపి." BD. ii. 406.

వినిర్మలము *vi-nir-malamu.* adj. Very pure, or clear. నిష్కల్మషమైన.

వినిర్ముక్తము *vi-nir-muktamu.* [Skt.] adj. Liberated, let loose or free, exempt, free from, విడువబడిన.

వినివారణము *vi-nivāraṇamu.* [Skt. వి+నివారణము.] n. Prevention; an obstacle, hindrance. "తనయాయిచ్చవిహరించు ఋష్యాదిపదసేవలందంబుకుంగావటే వినివారణంబుతఁబొందకే వెరపు నేడి భ్రాంతియుంజెందవు." Bhāg. x. §. ix 9.

వినివేదితము *vi-nivēditamu.* [Skt. వి+నివేదితము.] adj. Offered, as sacrifice. నైవేద్యము చేయబడిన.

వినిష్క్రాంతము *vi-nishkrāntamu.* [Skt. వి+నిష్క్రాంతము.] adj. Going out, setting out. బయలువెడలిన. "మరియువిష్ణుపాద వినిష్క్రాంతయు శశాంకమండలప్లావయునైన యాకాశగంగ." Vish. iii. 37.

వినిష్ఠ్యూతము *vi-nishṭhyūtamu* [Skt. వి+నిష్ఠ్యూతము.] adj. Cast, thrown, sent, directed, despatched, ejected from the mouth, spit. వినిర్గతమైన, ఉమ్మివేయబడిన.

వినీతము *vi-nītamu.* [Skt. వి+నీతము.] adj. Humble, modest, trained. వినయముగల, శిక్షితమైన. **వినీతుడు** *vi-nītuḍu.* n. One who is humble, modest, unassuming; one who is educated or trained. వినయముగలవాడు, చక్కగా శిక్షింపబడినవాడు.

వినీలము *vi-nīlamu.* [Skt. వి+నీలము.] adj. Black. నల్లని. "వినీలకుంతల." Vasu. iv. 147.

విను *vinu.* [Tel.] n. The sky. ఆకాశము. "ఆరథరజీ పరాగము భయంకరమై వినువీధిబర్వ..." Vish. ii. 140. **వినుకెంపు** *vinu-kempu.* n. The Sun, సూర్యుడు, ద్యుమణి. **వినుచూలి** or **విన్నుచూలి** *vinu-tsūli.* n. The wind, గాలి. **వినుద్రిమ్మరి** *vinu-drimmari.* n. An aerial being, ఖచరుడు. **వినుప్రోలు** *vinu-prōlu.* n. Heaven. Lit. a city in the sky. **వినుమ్రాను** *vinu-mrānu.* n. The heavenly tree, కల్పవృక్షము. వినువలను or విన్వలను *vinu-valanu*. n. Heaven. స్వర్గము. వినువాక or విన్నది (విను+వది) *vinu-vāka* n. The heavenly Ganges, ఆకాశగంగ, స్వర్నది. వినుసిగదేవర *vinu-siga-dēvara*. n. Siva.

విను *vinu*. [Tel.] v. a. To hear, to listen to, ఆకర్ణించు. To pay attention to, give heed to, obey. మాటవినని disobedient. విన్నావా did you hear? వింటివా have you heard? do you hear? వినడాయెను he did not listen. పెద్దలమాటవిను listen to the advice of your superiors. స్కాందపురాణమువిన్నాడు he had the Skānda Purana read to him. వినబడు *vina-badu*. v. n. To be heard, వినబడు. నాకు వినబడినది I heard it. వినమి *vinami*. n. Not hearing, not obeying. వినకపోవడము. వినవచ్చు *vina-vatstsu*. v. n. To be heard. వినబడు. ఆ చప్పుడు వినవచ్చినది that noise reached my ears. వినికి, విన్కి or వినికిడి *viniki*. n. Audience, hearing, listening. వినడము. నాకు అట్లావినికి I have heard so. వినిపించు or వినుచు *vinipintsu*. v. a. To cause to hear. వినజేయు. To tell, to read out or aloud. ఆ జాబు నాకు వినిపించినాడు he read the letter to me. v. n. To be heard వినవచ్చు. నాకు వినిపించినది I heard it. తుపాకీగాను వినిపించినది it sounded like a gun. వినుకలి or విన్కలి *vinukali*. n. Hearing. వినికి, వినుట. వినుకలికంటి *vinukali-kanti*. n. A snake. వినువారిమాటలు slander, backbiting, చాడీమాటలు.

వినుతము *vi-nutamu*. [Skt. వి+నుతము.] adj. Laudable, praiseworthy. స్తుతింపదగిన. వినుతి *vi-nuti*. n. Great praise, commendation, applause. స్తోత్రము. వినుతించు *vi-nutintsu*. v. a. To praise greatly, commend. స్తోత్రముచేయు. వినుతుడు *vi-nutudu*. n. One who is praised, lauded. స్తోత్రముచేయబడిన వాడు.

వినూత్నము or వినూతనము *vi-nūtnamu*. [Skt. వి+నూతనము.] adj. Novel, new, fresh. నవీనమైన, క్రొత్త.

వినోదము *vinōdamu*. [Skt.] n. Play, sport, pastime; an interesting pursuit, pleasure. స్త్రీపురుషులు క్రీడాదులచేత కాలయాపనచేయడము, క్రీడ, వేడుక. విలాసము. మృగయావినోదము pleasures of the chase. "ఇమ్మైయి బ్రహ్మాండ ప్రకరంబులనేకములుచనియెనవియెల్లవినోదమ్ములు నారాయణునకు." Vish. i. 54. వినోది *vinōdi*. n. One who is delighted or made happy, one who delights in. ఉల్లాసముగలవాడు. కలహవినోది one who loves quarrelling. "కర్మాకర్మములాకృతికర్మవినోదునకు కర్త్వభునకు తెలియుగా." Vēma. 529. విప్రవినోదులు sham priests, a certain caste of beggars who call themselves Brahmins. వినోదించు *vinōdintsu*. v. n. To revel, play, sport, rejoice, సంతోషించు, క్రీడించు, క్రీడాదులచేత ప్రొద్దుపుచ్చు.

విన్కలి See under విను.

విన్కి Same as వినికి. See under విను.

విన్న *vinna*. [from Skt. ఖిన్న.] adj. Pale. విన్నమైన. విన్నదనము or విన్నన *vinna-danamu*. n. Dejection, sorrowfulness, ఖేదము, ఖిన్నతనము. Paleness, వైవర్ణ్యము. Diminution, wanting, న్యూనత, కొరవపడడము, తక్కువయగుట, లేకపోవుట. "అల్లువిఫలప్రయత్నుడైయడవిశా సివిన్నదనమునజనియెనవ్వేటకాడు." P. ii. 217. విన్నన్గు or విన్ననైన *vinna-n-agu*. adj. Dejected, sorrowful, desponding, ఖిన్నమైన, చిన్నబోయిన, విషణ్ణమైన, వ్యాకులమైన. విన్నవగు. v. n. To be dejected, to be in sorrow. ఖిన్నుడగు, చిన్నబోవు. విన్నబోవు or విన్నబడు *vinna-bōvu*. v. n. To become pale, వివర్ణమగు. To be dejected or sorrowful, వ్యాకులపడు, ఖిన్నుడగు, చిన్నబోవు. "సకింత మాత్రనెవిన్నంబవనేల." Parij. iv. 69. విన్నబోయిన *vinna-bōyina*. adj. Dejected, desponding, downcast. ఖిన్నమైన, విషణ్ణమైన. "విన్నంబోయిన మోముతో హృదయ నిర్వేదంబుతో." Ellana. i. 238. విన్నబాటు vinna-bāṭu. n. Dejection, sorrowfulness. విషణ్ణత. Paleness, వైవర్ణ్యము. "నావుడువిన్నబాటువడదనంబుననింగుకదోచబల్కె." Swa. ii. 58. విన్నయై vinna-yai. adv. Being sorry. విషణ్ణయై, చిన్నబోయినదై. "నాగమువిన్నదైనగవెల్లమాని. Pal. 89.

విన్ననువు vinnanuvu. [Tel.] n. Skill, నేర్పు. Manner, విధము.

విన్నపము vinn-apamu. [from Skt. విజ్ఞాపనము.] n. A petition, request. మనవి, విజ్ఞాపనము. విన్నపత్రిక vinna-patrika. (విన్నప+పత్రిక.) n. A petition, విజ్ఞాపనపత్రిక.

విన్నము vinnamu. [Skt.] adj. Made known, తెలియబడిన. Considered, విచారింపబడిన.

విన్నవించు vinna-vintsu. [from Skt. విజ్ఞాపించు.] v. a. To represent, tell, narrate. మనవిచేయు, విజ్ఞాపనముచేయు, విజ్ఞాపించు.

విన్నాణము vinnāṇamu. [from Skt. విజ్ఞానము.] n. Capacity, skill, dexterity. సామర్థ్యము, నేర్పు, చాతుర్యము. Grace, beauty, అందము. A certain hold in wrestling. కట్టిపట్టు. "విన్నాణంబునబోరనేర్తురుమహాపీర ప్రతాపాదిసంపన్నుల్ వీరలుమేటిమల్లురనగా." B. X. 36. 17. విన్నాణమైనది that which is fine or graceful, నాణెమైనది, సొగసైనది. విన్నాణి vinnāṇi. n. One who is skillful or dexterous, నేర్పరి. An ascetic, a recluse. సన్యాసి. విన్నాణము or విన్నాణపు vinnāṇamu. adj. Skillful, clever, నేర్పుగల. Graceful, handsome, అందమైన, సొగసైన. "విన్నాణపుం బిరుదుల్ దిద్దినవిద్దెమూకౌకయరట్టిసెక్కె." Ranga Rao Charitra. ii. 221. విన్నాణముగా vinnāṇamu-ga. adv. Gracefully, skillfully. సొగసుగా, నేర్పుగా.

విన్ను vinnu. [Tel. another form of మిన్ను.] n The sky.

విన్యసించు vinyasintsu. [Skt.] v. a. To keep to place or put, ఉంచు. విన్యస్తము or న్యస్తము vi-nyastamu. adj. Kept, placed, ఉంచబడిన. విన్యాసము vi-nyāsamu. n. Keeping, placing, ఉంచుట.

విపంచి or విపంచిక vipanchi. [Skt.] n. A lute. వీణ.

విపక్వము vi-pakvamu. [Skt. వి+పక్వము.] adj. Raw, not boiled. పండని, పరిపక్వము కాని.

విపక్షము vi-pakshamu. [Skt.] n. An enemy's side, శత్రుపక్షము. విపక్షుడు vi-pakshuḍu. n. An opponent, enemy, శత్రువు.

విపణము vi-paṇamu. [Skt.] n. Selling, అమ్మకము. విపణి vipaṇi. n. A shop, a stall, a market place. అంగడి, అంగళ్లబజారు, అంగడివీధి. A merchant, వర్తకుడు.

విపత్తి or విపత్తు vi-patti. [Skt.] n. A crisis; a sad event, calamity, misfortune, disaster, ఆపద, ఇడుము. విపద్దశ vipad-daśa. n. The time of calamity. ఆపత్కాలము. విపన్నము vi-pannamu. adj. Luckless, unhappy, unfortunate. ఆపదనొందిన. విపన్నుడు vi-pannuḍu. n. One who is unfortunate. ఆపన్నుడు, ఆపదనొందినవాడు.

విపథము vi-pathamu. [Skt. వి+పథము.] n. A wretched road, a bad path. చెడుత్రోవ.

విపరి vipari. [Tel.] n. Exchange. విపరిదస్తావేజు a deed of exchange.

విపరీతము viparītamu. [Skt.] n. Contrariety, reverse, queerness. Abundance. విపర్యయము, వ్యత్యస్తము. adj. Reverse, inverse, contrary, opposite. Strange, odd, prodigious, unusual, queer, unnatural, విపర్యయమైన, వ్యత్యస్తమైన. విపరీతముగా viparīta-mu-gā. adv. Contrariwise, incongruously unnaturally. Abundantly. విపర్యయముగా, విస్తారముగా. విపర్యయము *viparyayamu.* adj. Reverse, inverse, contrary, queer, strange, unnatural, విపరీతమైన. విపర్యయ మహోగ్రకోపము violent or outrageous anger. విపర్యయము or విపర్యాసము *viparyayamu.* n. That which is opposite, contrary, reverse. Difference, వ్యత్యాసము.

విపశ్చిత్తు or విపశ్చితుడు *vipaschittu.* [Skt.] n. A learned man. విద్వాంసుడు. "తెలంగాణ్యులనంద వాధులవిపశ్చిద్వర్యుల్గలగా." K. P. ii. 29.

విపాకము *vi-pākamu.* [Skt. వి+పాకము.] n. Ripeness, maturity. Result, event. The fruit or consequence of action. The crisis or fulness of time. పరిపాకము, ఫలము. పాకము, భాగ్యము.

విపాటనము *vi-pāṭanamu.* [Skt.] n. Breaking, dashing to pieces. బద్దలుచేయుటము. విపాటితము *vi-pāṭitamu.* adj. Broken, dashed to pieces. బద్దలుచేయబడిన. S. iii. 374.

విపాదిక *vi-pādika.* [Skt.] n. Sores or blisters in the hands and feet. A kibe or ulcerated chilblain. పాదస్ఫోటము.

విపినము *vipinamu.* [Skt.] n. A forest, wood, jungle, అడవి.

విపులము *vipulamu.* [Skt.] adj. Extended, huge, big, vast, large, much, deep. విరివి యైన, విస్తారమైన. "విపులార్థనంతంబున్నతస్తుతు లనతిభక్తియుక్తుడై." M. I. i. 158. "విపులపరాక్రమశాలి." Bobbili ii. 99. విపుల *vipula.* n. The earth. భూమి.

విప్పు *vippu.* [Tel.] v. a. To open, untie, loose. ముడివిప్పు to untie a knot. కథను విప్పు to solve a riddle. ఆ సంగతిని విప్పిచెప్పినాడు he explained the matter clearly. పెండ్లి విప్పేదాకా until the marriage was over. n. Loosing, opening, untying. విదయుట, విప్పుటము, విడుదల. Extension. spreading, విస్తారిత, వైపుల్యము, వైశాల్యము. "సీ. ధరిత్రీ ఖ్యాతి వెలయ... పట్టు తో విప్పుతో బరిగొంచుమాడ." A. iv. 193. adj. Extensive, large, విస్తారమైన. "విప్పుకప్పు కొప్పులుకొప్పున ... తెలుపుమీర." T. iv. 144. విప్పుగా *vippu-ga.* adv. Extensively, greatly, widely. విస్తారముగా. "వింతసుంతి జీవివిప్పుగా దోడి పాయు మంచిపూసల యిరుసుకమ్ము." H. iv. 134. "విప్పుగ విరితేనెలానుచు విడుచుయుగా." ib. ii. 81. విప్పగు *vipp-agu.* adj. Large, great, wide. విశాలమైన. "అప్పను తేనె విధవము విప్పుగుచున్నకరిసతటి వృషగిరిపాదుగా." A. ii. 83.

విప్ర *vipra.* See under విప్రుడు.

విప్రకృష్టము *vi-prakṛishṭamu.* [Skt.] adj. Remote, distant. దూరమైన.

విప్రతిపత్తి *vi-prati-patti.* [Skt.] n. Disbelief, unbelief, want of confidence, అవిశ్వాస. Confusion of mind, కలత. Enmity, విరోధము.

విప్రయోగము *vi-pra-yogamu.* [Skt.] n. Separation, especially of lovers. వియోగము, స్త్రీపురుషులయెడబాటు.

విప్రలంభము *vi-pra-lambhamu.* [Skt.] n. Separation, ఎడబాయుట. Deceiving (by a false affirmation or by not keeping a promise), a quarrel. విసంవాదము, ఒప్పకొని చేయనిపోట్లాడము. విప్రలబ్ధ *vi-pra-labdha.* n. A mistress whose lover is not true to appointment. సంకేతస్థలమునకు ప్రియుడురాక మోసముపోయి దుఃఖపడునాయిక. విప్రలబ్ధము *vi-pra-labdhamu.* adj. Tricked, cheated. వంచింపబడిన.

విప్రలాపము *vi-pra-lāpamu.* [Skt.] n. A self-contradictory expression or statement, nonsense, పూర్వాపరవిరుద్ధవచనము.

విప్రశ్నిక *vi-praśnika.* [Skt.] n. A witch, సోదెకత్తె.

విప్రియము *vi-priyamu.* [Skt.] adj. Disliked, disagreeable, displeasing. అనిష్టమైన, అప్రియమైన.

విప్రుడు *vipruḍu.* [Skt.] n. A Brahmin. బ్రాహ్మణుడు. విప్ర *vipra.* adj. Brahmanical, బ్రాహ్మణ సంబంధమైన. విప్రవినోదులు *vipra-vinōdulu.* n. plu. A certain class of Brahmins who are jugglers. గారడివిద్య గాంచ్రియుండే బ్రాహ్మణులు.

విప్లవము *vi-plavamu.* [Skt.] n. Ruin; a national calamity. దేశోపద్రవము.

విఫలము *vi-phalamu.* [Skt.] adj. Fruitless. నిష్ఫలమైన.

విబుధుడు *vi-budhuḍu.* [Skt.] n. A god, an immortal, వేలుపు, దేవత. A learned man, a teacher, విదుషి.

విబూది *vi-būdi.* [from Skt. విభూతి.] n. Ashes, బూది, భస్మము. విబూదిపత్రి, a plant called *Ocimum basilicum.*

విభ *vibha.* [Skt.] n. Lustre, light. తేజస్సు. విభాకరుడు or విభావసుడు *vibha-karuḍu,* n. The sun, సూర్యుడు.

విభక్తము *vi-bhaktamu.* [Skt.] adj. Divided, proportioned. విభజింపబడిన, పంచబడిన. విభక్తి *vi-bhakti.* n. A share, విభాగము. Any case of a noun. సుప్పు, ప్రథమాది. విభక్తుడు *vi-bhaktuḍu.* n. A co-parcener, one who has received his portion. One of a family that has taken his share of the family estate. పాలుపంచుకొనినవాడు, వేరుపడినవాడు. మీరు విభక్తులా అవిభక్తులా is your family divided or undivided? i. e., have you shared your property or do you live together? విభజనము *vi-bhajanamu.* n. Separation, dividing, allotment, విభాగము, విభజించుట. Details, particulars, వివరము. విభజనగా *vi-bhajanaga.* adv. Particularly, in detail. వివరముగా. విభజించు *vi-bhajinṭsu.* v. a. To divide, share. వేరుచేయు, విభాగించు, పంచు.

విభవము *vibhavamu.* [Skt.] n. Wealth, riches. సంపద, ధనము. ఆ ఉత్సవము విభవముతో జరిగినది the festival was grandly performed. "అప్పుగొని సేయు విభవము." (Sumati. 21) luxury supported by contracting debt. విభవ *vibhava.* n. The name of a Telugu year.

విభాగము *vi-bhāgamu.* [Skt.] n. A share, part, portion. పాలు. Division into shares. పంపకము, పంచుట. విభాగించు *vi-bhāginṭsu.* v. a. To share out, divide. పంచు, భాగించు. విభాజకము *vi-bhājakamu.* adj. That which divides. విభజించునది. n. In Arithmetic, a divisor, విభాగించుసంఖ్య. విభాజితము *vi-bhājitamu* adj. That which is divided. విభజింపబడినది. n. A quotient, భాగహారమందు భాగింపగా ఏర్పడిన మొత్తము. విభాజ్యము *vi-bhājyamu.* adj. That which is to be divided. n. A dividend.

విభాతము *vibhātamu.* [Skt.] n. Dawn, daybreak. ప్రాతఃకాలము.

విభావము *vi-bhāvamu.* [Skt.] n. Acquaintance. Attraction or excitement; that which attracts or excites, as dress or perfumes, పరిచితి, కామోద్దీపనము, రసోత్పాదక కారణము. "విభావము యోగ్యాయోగ్య విభావముగా గానఁబలుకుటుచితబుద్ధిగా." Bilh. iii. 27.

విభావరి *vibhāvari.* [Skt.] n. Night. రాత్రి.

విభావసుడు. See under విభ.

విభాష *vi-bhāsha.* [Skt.] adj. (In Telugu grammar) optional.

విభిన్నము *vi-bhinnamu.* [Skt.] adj. Broken. భగ్నమైన. విభిన్నచిత్తులై with broken hearts. Vish. viii. 407.

విభీతకము *vibhītakamu.* [Skt.] n. A tree called *Beleric myrobalan,* or, *Terminalia belerica.* కర్షఫలము, తాండ్రచెట్టు.

విభీషణము *vi-bhīshaṇamu.* [Skt.] adj. Formidable, fearful, terrific, alarming. మిక్కిలి భయంకరమైన. దారుణమైన. విభీషణ

ణముగా vi-bhīshaṇamu-gā. adv. Formidably, terribly, భయంకరముగా. విభీషణుడు vi-bhīshaṇuḍu. n. The name of Ravana's brother.

విభు vibbhu. [Skt.] adj. Omnipresent, all-pervading, eternal. నిత్యము, సర్వగతము. విభుడు or విభువు vibbhuḍu. n. Lord, master, ruler. స్వామి, ప్రభువు. దైవమే విభువు God is lord alone, God is above all.

విభూతి vi-bhūti. [Skt.] n. Blessedness, divine excellence or power. Happiness, సంపద, ఐశ్వర్యము. A divine attribute. అణిమాదులు. అష్టవిభూతులు the eight divine attributes. These are అణిమ invisibility, లఘిమ buoyancy, ప్రాప్తి omnipresence, ప్రాకామ్యము amplitude, మహిమ gravity, or vastness, ఈశత supremacy, dominion, వశిత్వము omnipotence, and కామావసాయిత miraculous creation, &c., at pleasure. White ashes of cowdung, with which the worshippers of Siva smear themselves, తెల్లనిబూడిద. Hence సొమ్ము విభూతిపాలయినది the money is all gone to ruin: lit. to ashes. విభూతి పండ్లు vibhūti-paṇḍlu. n. Balls of white ashes, తెల్లనిబూడిదఉండలు.

విభూషణము vi-bhūshaṇamu. [Skt.] n. An ornament, decoration. ఆభరణము. విభూషితము vi-bhūshitamu. adj. Adorned. అలంకరింపబడిన.

విభేదము vi-bhēdamu. [Skt.] n. Dividing, breaking, wounding. Difference, discrepancy, distinction, separation. Enmity. విచ్ఛేదము, పృథక్త్వము, వైపరీత్యము, శత్రుత్వము.

విభ్రమము vi-bhramamu. [Skt.] n. Turning round, whirling. An error, mistake; doubt, misapprehension, భ్రాంతి, సంశయము. Female dalliance, love, beauty. శోభ, అలంకారము, విలాసము. "తనూవిభ్రమంబు." T. iii. 41. "అహల్యావిలాసవిభ్రమంబులకునివి." N. vii. 86. టీ॥ విలాస విభ్రమంబులు, శృంగారచేష్టలు. A particular feat or gesture in dancing. అభినయభేదము.

విభ్రాంతి vi-bhrānti. n. Error, confusion, hurry, flurry, precipitation, భ్రమము, ఆతురము. "సంతోషవిభ్రాంతికా." Vedanta Ras. ii. 131. టీ॥ సంతోషమువల్ల కలిగిన తొందరపాటుచేతను.

విభ్రాజిత or విభ్రాజి vi-bhrājita. [Skt.] adj. Splendid, luminous, shining. ప్రకాశితమైన. "త్రివిమలభక్తివిభ్రాజితమహిమ." BD. ii. 1059.

విమతుడు vi-matuḍu. [Skt.] n. A dissenter, one of another opinion, an opposer; one who is malevolent or spiteful, an ill wisher, an enemy, విరుద్ధమైనమతముగలవాడు, అన్యమతస్థుడు, శత్రువు. "విమతులబలమరయక వైరముగొనుజనుడు." P. i. 542.

విమర్దనము vi-mardanamu. [Skt.] n. Grinding, rubbing, pounding, trituration. నూరడము, పూయడము.

విమర్శ, విమర్శము or విమర్శనము vimarṣa. [Skt.] n. Examination, scrutiny, investigation; an inquiry, trial విచారణ. విమర్శించు vimarṣintsu. v. a. To examine, try, enquire into. విచారణచేయు, పరామర్శము చేయు.

విమలము vi-malamu. [Skt.] adj. Pure, stainless, unspotted. Clear, apparent, evident, sound. నిర్మలమైన, ఒప్పిదమైన.

విమాత vi-māta. [Skt.] n. A step mother, సవతితల్లి. విమాతృజుడు vi-mātṛijuḍu. n. A step-mother's son. సవతితల్లికొడుకు.

విమానము vimānamu. [Skt.] n. The chariot of a god, దేవతలు ఆకాశమందు ఎక్కితిరిగెడి రథము. A car, vehicle, carriage. An emperor's palace, చక్రవర్తియొక్క సౌధము. A horse, గుర్రము. The pinnacle or upper dome of a temple over the sanctuary. "నవరత్నోజ్జ్వలదివ్యపుష్పకవిమానంబెక్కి." URK. ii. 262.

విముక్తము *vi-muktamu.* [Skt.] adj. Quite liberated, freed, redeemed. మిక్కిలి విడువబడిన, నివృత్తమైన, విమోచనముచేయబడిన. విముక్తి *vi-mukti.* n. Liberation, release, redemption, especially final emancipation from further transmigration. విమోచనము, మోక్షము, అపవర్గము. విముక్తుడు *vi-muktudu.* n. One who is liberated or redeemed. విమోచనముచేయబడినవాడు, ముక్తుడు.

విముఖుడు *vi-mukhudu.* [Skt.] n. One who has turned away his face, పరాఙ్ముఖుడు.

విమోచనము *vi-môchanamu.* [Skt.] n. Liberation, liberating. విముక్తి. నాకష్ట విమోచనమైనది my troubles are over. విమోచితము *vi-môchitamu.* adj. Liberated, freed, redeemed. విమోచనముచేయబడిన, విడిపింపబడిన.

విమోహము *vi-môhamu.* [Skt.] n. Great or excessive passion or love, మిక్కిలి మోహము. విమోహించు *vi-môhintsu.* v. n. To love excessively, మిక్కిలి మోహించు. విమోహితుడు *vi-môhitudu.* n. One who loves excessively.

వియత్ or వియత్తు *viyat.* [Skt.] n. The sky. ఆకాశము. వియచ్చరుడు *viyach-charudu.* n. A treader of the skyey paths, i.e., a celestial, a god, నభశ్చరుడు, ఖచరుడు. వియత్పథము *viyat-pathamu.* n. The skyey path between earth and heaven. ఆకాశమార్గము. వియదాగారము *viyad-agaramu.* n. The skyey mansion, Heaven. ఆకాశనికేతనము. "అత్యుగ్రభైరవహుంకారరవంబునంవియదాగారంబెల్లభేదిల్ల." M. I. vi. 16. వియద్గంగ *viyad-ganga.* n. The heavenly Ganges, ఆకాశగంగ.

వియమము or వియామము *viyamamu.* [Skt.] n. Pain. బాధ.

వియుక్తము *vi-yuktamu.* [Skt.] adj. Separated, sundered. వియోగముగల. వియుక్తుడు *vi-yuktudu.* n. One who is separated, వియోగి.

వియోగము *vi-yôgamu.* [Skt.] n. Separation, disunion, absence, especially of lovers. Death. ఎడబాయుడము, ఎడబాటు, చావు. నాకు భార్యావియోగమయినతరువాత after I lost my wife.

వియ్యము *viyyamu.* [Tel.] n. Connection by marriage, binding together, వైవాహికసంబంధము, ఇచ్చిపుచ్చుకోవడం, సంబంధము. Also, same as వియ్యంకుడు. వియ్యంకుడు *viyyankudu.* [వియ్యము+అంకుడు] n. The father of one's son-in-law or daughter-in-law. వియ్యపురాలు, వియ్యంకురాలు or వియ్యపురాలు *viyyapu-r-alu.* n. The mother of one's son-in-law, or daughter-in-law, వియ్యమందినావిడ. ఆమె నాకు వియ్యంకురాలు she and I are connections through our children having married. వియ్యమందు *viyyam-andu.* v. a. To form a marriage connection, to intermarry, సంబంధముచేయు, పడుచునిచ్చిపుచ్చుకొను. మేము వారితో వియ్యమందగూడదు they and we cannot intermarry. వియ్యముకాడు *viyyamu-kâdu.* n. A relation by marriage, బంధువు. Also, Same as వియ్యంకుడు.

విరక్తి *vi-rakti.* [Skt.] n. Dislike, aversion, disinclination: a loathing or disgust at earthly enjoyments. విరాగము. సంతానములేనివాని బ్రతుకేమిబ్రతుకని వానికి విరక్తిపుట్టినది he began to feel deep dissatisfaction at the thought that the life of the childless is no life at all. ఇందువల్ల ఆమెమీద అయనకు విరక్తిపుట్టినది this made him dislike her. విరక్తుడు *vi-raktudu.* n. One who dislikes or hates.

విరగడ See under విరుగు.

విరచించు *vi-rachintsu.* [Skt.] v. a. To write much; to make, form, frame, compose, విశేషముగా రచించు, చేయు. విరచితము

vi-rachitamu. adj. Composed, framed, formed. విశేషముగా రచితమైన. చేయబడిన.

విరజ *viraja.* [Skt.] n. The name of the river Styx. వైకుంఠమునొద్ద ఉండే ఒకనది.

విరజాజి. విరజాజి, విరవాజి or విరవాది *vira-daji.* [Tel] n. The Double Jasmine. నవమాలికావృక్షము, జాజిపుష్పము.

విరటుడు *viraṭuḍu.* [Tel.] n. The king of the Virāṭa country.

విరతి *vi-rati.* [Skt.] n. Stopping, ceasing, rest, pause, cessation. The caesura or pause in a verse. విరామము, విశ్రాంతి. **విరతము** *vi-ratamu.* adj. Stopped or ceased, rested. విరమించిన, నిలిచిన, చాలించిన. **విరతుడు** *vi-ratuḍu.* n. One who has rested, stopped or ceased. చాలించుకొన్నవాడు.

విరథుడు *vi-rathuḍu.* [Skt.] n. One who is uncoached or flung from his chariot. రథవిహీనుడు.

విరమించు *vi-ramintsu.* [Skt.] v.n. To cease, to be at an end, to rest, తీరు, ముగిసిపోవు, విశ్రాంతిపొందు.

విరళము or **విరాళము** *viralamu.* [Tel.] n. A certain tax. ఒకవిధమైన పన్ను. (అడిదిని గాలు అని అంటారు.) [Skt.] adj. Separated by an interval, remote, rare, clear as handwriting. ఎడమెడముగానుండే, పలిచగానుండే, అరుదుగానుండే. **విరళముగా** *viralamu-ga.* adv. Distinctly, clearly. స్పష్టముగా. **విరళి** *viraḷi.* adj. Broad, విశాలము.

విరవాయు *vira-vāyu.* [Tel. విర+పాయు.] v. n. To separate, part, divide. త్రెలు, పాయలగు. **విరవారు** *vira-vāru.* (విర+పారు) v. n. To fly dispersedly. చెదరిపారిపోవు. "ధీతిమాయున్న లవిరవారిపోయి, బలిమాటిరాము లోబారచేచెవుము." Pal. 15. **విరవిర** *viravira.* n. Blossoming, వికసనము. Kicking about spasmodically. Paleness. **విరవిరపోవు** or **విరవిరమను** *vira-vira-pōvu.* v. n. To turn pale, to be faint, to be convulsed. To be heated. తెలవెలపోవు, కాళ్లుచేతులుతీయు, చచ్చిపోవు, ఎండదెబ్బ ముచేత దేహము విరవిరలాడు. "పిడుగువిధమునవడు నెత్తిత్రెళ్ళత్రెయుటయు, వెసగాళ్లుచేతులు విరవిరపోవ, వశముగాకిలమీద వ్రాలంగనప్పుడు." DRU. 1024.

విరసము *vi-rasamu.* [Skt.] n. Unpleasantness, bad terms, ill-will, disagreement. కలహము. **విరసించు** *vi-rasintsu.* v. n. To hate, ద్వేషించు.

విరహము *virahamu.* [Skt.] n. Separation, parting, absence of lovers, ఎడబాటు, వియోగము. విరహతాపము or విరహాగ్ని the grief or pain caused by the absence of a lover. **విరహి** *virahi.* n. One who is separated from her whom he loves. నాయికావియోగముగలవాడు. **విరహిణి** *virahiṇi.* n. A woman who is absent from her husband or lover. వియోగిని, ప్రియవియోగముగల స్త్రీ.

విరహితము *vi-rahitamu.* [Skt.] adj. Separated, left, విడువబడిన. Devoid of, లేని. **విరహితుడు** *vi-rahituḍu.* n. One who is without, or devoid of, లేనివాడు. ఆద్యంతవిరహితుడు he who is without origin or end.

విరహోత్కంఠిత *virah-ōtkanṭhita.* n. She whose husband or lover is absent. విరహముచేత వేచినపడేనాయిక.

విరాగము *vi-rāgamu.* [Skt.] n. Indifference to the world and the pleasures of sense; absence of desire or passion; stoicism, విరక్తి. **విరాగుడు** *vi-rāguḍu.* n. One who is indifferent to the pleasures of sense.

విరాజమానము *vi-rāja-mānamu.* [Skt.] adj. Very bright, brilliant, మిక్కిలి ప్రకాశించుచున్న. **విరాజితము** *vi-rājitamu.* adj. Splendid, bright, shining. మిక్కిలి ప్రకాశితము.

విరాట్టు or **విరాట్పురుషుడు** *virāṭṭu.* [Skt.] n. The Deity, God. ఆదిదేవుడు. విరాడ్దేహము the corporeal form of the deity. B. iii. 205

విరామము *virāmamu.* [Skt.] n. Rest, respite, interval, remission, pause. End, conclusion, విశ్రాంతి, విరతి, అవసానము.

విరాలము or **విరాళము**, *virālamu.* [Tel.] n. A tax or impost. ఒకవిధమైనపన్ను. See విరళము. విరాలము, విరాళము or విరాళి *virālamu.* n. Love, fascination, longing. మోహము, వ్యామోహము, వలపు. విరహము, మరులు. విరాళి *virāḷi.* n. Piety, devotion, భక్తి. విరాళిగొలుపు to enamour. విరాళిగొన్న enamoured. "చల మనసునవిష్ణు చింతనలు మానదుపీవివిరాళిఁదొట్టితో." Vish. ii. 299. "మ దయా రి కి విరాళిఁబొందగలిగె." A. vi. 155. టీ॥ విరాళిఁబొందగలిగె, తత్పరతఁజెందగలిగెను. adj. Exciting a longing or desire, alluring. వలపుపుట్టించెడి.

విరావము *vi-rāvamu.* [Skt.] n. Sound. ధ్వని, శ్రుతి.

విరి *viri.* [Tel.] n. A flower, పువ్వు. adj. Blooming, blown, as a flower, వికసించిన. Dispersed, scattered, dishevelled, తొలగిన. Free from, liberated. వీడిన, విముక్తమైన. "లీల నీ ప్రాప్యదాక మ వేళయందు నిందు జాబిల్లిపండువెన్నెలలం దింటి కెడ వెడలగాయ నరికంటి కెరలు, మొగలువిరిదొండమలె దాపమున చెరల్పు." R. vi. 21. విరిపువ్వు a blooming flower. విరిగొందులు flower lanes. A. v. 122. విరిపానుపు a flowery couch. విరివిలుకాడు Manmadha. విరిబోడి or విరిబోణి *viri-bōḍi.* n. A blooming girl, a woman, స్త్రీ.

విరించి, **విరించనుడు** or **విరించుడు** *virinchi.* [Skt.] n. A title of Brahma, the creator. బ్రహ్మ.

విరిగి *virigi.* [Tel.] n. A certain tree called *Cordia myxa.* శ్లేష్మాతకము. H. iv. 18. Also, ground that is cracked, పగుళ్లువారిన నేల.

విరిచికట్టు *virichi-kaṭṭu.* [Tel.] v. a. To pinion (a man) or tie his arms behind his back. వెడరెక్కలుకట్టు, చేతులను వెనుకకు మల్లించికట్టు. n. The act of pinioning a man, చేతులను వెనుకకు మరలించికట్టుట.

విరిదట్టు *viri-daṭṭu.* [Tel. విరి+దట్టు.] adj. Separated. ఎడబాటుపొందిన, వియుక్తము.

విరిపోటు *viri-pōṭu.* [Tel.] n. Grudge, ill-will, enmity, పగ, ద్వేషము, భేదము. విరిపోటు చేయు *viri-pōṭu-chēyu.* v. a. To cause ill-will, disunite, separate, భేదించు. "ఈ చక్రవర్తిపై వెనుకనుకుశ్చి వీడిపోవగబల్కి విరిపోటుచేసి."

విరియు *viriyu.* [Tel.] v. n. To blow, open or expand, as a flower, వికసించు. To burst, crack or open. To be loosed or dishevelled, as hair. To break or disperse, as an army. వీడిపోవు, పగులు, చెదరు. To move away from, to be removed, తొలగు. To rejoice, ఉప్పొంగు. నీళ్లుచల్లగానే సున్నపురాళ్లు విరిసినవి on being sprinkled with water, the burning limestones cracked. "విరిసినూలెడు వెల్లవెండ్రుకలు." B. X. 22. "ఇట్లువిరిసిన సేన" M. VII. ii. 40. "కడుపువిరియంగబడి పండ్లుకొరుకుచుమెల్ల." S. iii. 216. మబ్బు విరిసిపోయినది the cloud is dispelled. విక్క-విరియు *vikka-viriyu.* (విరియు + విరియు.) v. n. To blow or blossom well, as a flower, మిక్కిలి వికసించు. విరియబడు Same as విరియు. విరియబారు *viriya-bāru.* (విరియన్+పారు) v. n To blow, or expand, as a flower, వికసించు. To burst or crack, వీడు, పగులు. To expand, extend, వ్యాపించు. విరియబోయు *viriya-bōyu.* v. a. To hang loose, as hair, తలవెండ్రుకలు వ్రేలాడవిడుచు. To slack lime, సున్నపురాళ్ల మీద నీళ్లుచల్లివిచ్చునట్లుచేయు. తలవిరియబోసికొను to wear one's hair dishevelled. విరియించు *viriyintsu.* v. a. To open a flower, to make it bloom. To break. వికసింపజేయు, విరుచు. "ఇలకుమనోగుణంబు విరియించెదు ప్రాణమటంచు మెంచుచు, మ్మలతుని కే విగోర వలదూరివి." T. iv. 113

విరివాయు viri-vāyu. [Tel. విరి+వాయు.] v. n. To split, separate, part, divide. చీలు, పాయలగు. Vasu. ii. 101.

విరివి or విరివిడి viriri. [Tel.] n. Expanse, width, breadth, extent, విస్తృతి, విశాలత, వెడల్పు. Abundance, విస్తారము. "విద్యలేల భూమి విరివిరేల." Vēma. 1099. adj. Extensive, large, wide, విశాలమైన, విస్తృతము. విరివిగా viriri-gā. adv. Widely, much, abundantly. విస్తారముగా, విశాలముగా. "విరివిగా కొమ్మల విచ్చిసికునుము." Sar. D. 376.

విరుగు virugu. [Tel.] v. n. To break or go to pieces. తునియు, భగ్నమగు. To curdle. To fail, to be defeated, to be counteracted. ఓడు, దండువిరుగు, ఒడిపోవు. To be spoilt, పాకముచెడు. దానిమనస్సు విరిగిపోయినది she is quite disgusted. పాలు విరిగిపోయినవి the milk curdled. వానిదేహములో రక్తము విరిగిపోయినది his blood curdled. ఈ మందువల్ల విషము విరిగిపోయినది this medicine counteracted the poison. ఆ బొమ్మచెయ్యి విరుగగొట్టినాడు he broke the arm of the doll. విరగబండినచెట్టు a tree in full bearing. "మిన్ను విరిగిపడ్డ్చి మీదబడ్డట్లు." Sar. D. 196.

" ఇనుమువిరిగెనేనియినుమారుమువ్మారు,
కాచియతుకనేర్చుకమ్మరీడు,
మనసువిరిగెనేని మరియతుకనేర్చునా."

Vēma. 157.

విరుగుడు virugudu. n. An antidote, a remedy, విరుపు, నివారణము. విరగడ or విరుగడ vira-gaḍa. n. Release, liberation, setting at liberty. విడుదల. నీకు యింకా ఆ తొందర విరగడకాలేదా? are you not yet free from that trouble. నేటితో ఈ కష్టములు విరగడైనవి to-day these ills have ended. విరగబడు or విరుగబడు viraga-baḍu. v. n. To be puffed up or haughty. గర్వపడు, బోర్లపడు. విరుగపాటు or విరగపాటు viru-ga-pāṭu. n. Pride, haughtiness, గర్వము, బోర్లబడుట. విరుచు virutsu. v. a. To cause to break, to break. To counteract poison. విరుగజేయు, భగ్నముచేయు. మాటువేసి రసమును గాని విషమునుగాని విరిగిపోవునట్లుచేయు. నెటికలువిరుచు to crack or snap the finger joints. తోకవిరుచు twist the tail. పెదవివిరుచు to turn up the lip in scorn. మండలువిరిచినాడు he broke the branches off a tree. "వెరిమియెుక్కగాలిచె యూనిన్నంచు వెను కొ_క్కొని విరిచెనొకతె." Ila. iv. 29. విరపనిగొయ్య or విరుగనిగొయ్య virapana-goyya. n. A stubborn wretch. మొండివాడు. విరుపు virupu. n. A break, or the act of breaking. An objection, contradiction, విరుచుట, భగ్నము, అడ్డము, ఆక్షేపణ. మెడవిరుపులు a puzzle, stumbling block. మూతివిరుపులు turning up the lip in scorn. adj. Counteracting, విరుగుడు. విరుచుకొను virutsu-konu. (middle voice, with passive sense.) To be defeated. ఆదండు వెనకకు విరుచుకొని పోయినది the army was broken and retreated. ఒళ్లువిరుచుకొన్నాడు he stretched himself through weariness. ఈ కొంచెముపనికి ఏల యెముకలు విరుచుకొంటావు why do you break your bones, i. e., take so much trouble for this trifling business.

విరుద్ధము vi-ruddhamu. [Skt.] adj. Opposed, opposite, reverse, contrary, inconsistent, contradictory, disagreeing with another, hostile, inimical, unfriendly, విరోధముగల, ప్రతికూలమైన, అసంగతమైన, విపరీతమైన. n. Opposition, contrariety, incongruity, enmity. ప్రతికూలత, అసంగతము, శత్రుత్వము, విరోధము.

విరూపము vi-rūpamu. [Skt.] adj. Deformed, ill-shaped, ugly. కురూపమైన. Crooked, వంకరైన. Odd, బేసి. n. Deformity, ugliness, వికృతరూపము. కురూపము. విరూపాక్షుడు vi-rūp-ākshuḍu. n. A name of Siva. శివుడు.

విరేచనము virēchanamu. [Skt.] n. Evacuation by stool, purging. ప్రవృత్తి, భేది,

పోచనము. వానికి నాలుగుసార్లు విరేచనములు అయినవి he had four motions. విరేచనకారి virēchana-kari. adj. Cathartic, purgative. భేదికారి.

విరోచనుడు vi-rōchanuḍu. [Skt.] n. Lit: one that shines: a name of the sun, the moon, or fire. సూర్యుడు, చంద్రుడు, అగ్ని. Also, the name of Prahlāda's Son.

విరోధము vi-rōdhamu. [Skt.] n. Difference, opposition, contradiction, disagreement, discrepancy, enmity, animosity. Detriment, harm, mischief, misdemeanor. ద్వేషము, పగ, వియ్యము, కీడు, చెరుపు, అడ్డంకి. ఎడబాటు. నేత్రవిరోధము an affection of the eyes. మార్గవిరోధము perils in travelling. ఇది ధర్మశాస్త్రవిరోధము this is at variance with the laws of propriety. దేహమునకు విరోధమైన unhealthy, insalubrious. విరోధనము vi-rōdhanamu. n. The act of opposing, విరోధించుట. విరోధి vi-rōdhi. n. An enemy, or opponent. శత్రువు. The name of a Telugu year. విరోధించు vi-rōdhintsu v. n. To oppose, withstand, contradict, prevent; to hate, be at enmity with, be hostile to. విరోధముచేయు, అడ్డగించు, కీడు కపోవు. ద్వేషించు, పగపట్టు. విరోధికృత్తు vi-rōdhi-krittu. n. The name of a Telugu year.

విఱ్ఱవీగు virra-vigu. [Tel. విఱు+వీగు.] v. n. To be proud, swell, be puffed up. గర్వించు, ఉబ్బు. మిక్కిలి నిక్కు. "బలుమైవిఱ్ఱవీగిపడపోటిగ బూచి పరాగ పుంజముక్కుటగల యింగ." Swa. iii. 98. టీ॥ విఱ్ఱవీగి, విఱుగబడి. "విద్యచేత విఱ్ఱవీగువాడు." Vema. 140. "క్రతువుచే నడమునికమువిఱ్ఱవీగుచు." ib. 1847. "విరిసి సంపదలను విఱ్ఱవీగినవిది." ib. 1521.

విలంఘించు vi-langhintsu. [Skt.] v. a. To cross over, pass, transgress. మిక్కిలి లంఘించు, అతిక్రమించు, దాటు. విలంఘితము vi-langhitamu. adj. Transgressed, overstepped అతిక్రమింపబడిన, దాటబడిన.

విలంబము or విలంబనము vi-lambamu. [Skt.] n. Delay, tardiness, loitering, procrastination. Delaying, retarding. ఆలస్యము చేయుటము. విలంబితము vi-lambitamu. adj. Delayed, slow. n. Slow time in music. ఆలస్యముగాతిరినలయ.

విలక్షణము or విలక్షణత vi-lakshaṇamu. n. Difference. భేదము. "శక్రాదులందు నొకడు గాడనుచుకుఱితియువిలక్షణతదెలిపె." A. iii. 13. టీ॥ విలక్షణత, వైలక్షణ్యము. విలక్షణము vi-lakshaṇamu. adj. Other, different. భిన్నమైన. Handsome, beautiful, elegant, excellent, select. విశేషలక్షణముగల, సుందరమైన, ఉత్తమమైన, దివ్యమైన, యోగ్యమైన. ఇది విలక్షణమైనపడుచు she is a handsome girl. విలక్షణముగా vi-lakshaṇamu-ga. adv. Properly, with propriety, handsomely, excellently. చక్కగా. అందముగా. దివ్యముగా. ఆ పెండ్లి విలక్షణముగా జరిగినది that marriage went off very well. విలక్షణుడు vi-lakshaṇuḍu. n. One who is highly accomplished, a model of excellence. One who differs from the common order, one who has some distinguishing qualities, భిన్నుడు, ఉత్కృష్టుడు. వాడు విలక్షణుడుకాడు he is not a man of strict religious habits. "వివిక్తత్వంబువిలక్షణుండుననుచు దయుండును నట్లగుట నింకియునర్థమూలంబగు." A. iii. 82.

విలక్షము vi-lakshamu. [Skt.] adj. Astonished, surprised, abashed, ashamed. ఆశ్చర్యముగల, సిగ్గుపడ్డ. విలక్షుడు vilakshuḍu. n. One who is astonished or surprised, తెరగుపడ్డవాడు. One who is ashamed, సిగ్గుపడినవాడు.

విలగ్నము vi-lagnamu. [Skt.] n. The waist. నడుము. adj. Well struck or hit. చక్కగా తగిలిన.

విలపించు vi-lapintsu. [Skt.] v. n. To lament, wail; to be in grief or affliction. కలుచుకొని కలుచుకొని ఏడ్చు. వగచు. విలాపము or విలపనము vi-lapamu. Lamentation, weeping, bewailing. కలవరింత, కిలుముకొని యేడ్వడము, దుఃఖముతోడి మాట. విలాపించు vi-lapintsu. v. n. To lament, to be in grief or affliction. ఏడ్చు. విలపించు.

విలయము vi-layamu. [Skt.] n. Dissolution, destruction, ruin, annihilation. కల్పాంతము, ప్రళయము, వినాశము. "విలయసమయసమీర." Sar. D. 408. "ప్రియపుత్రుహితులకొప్పించిరికె హాంబువిడిచిన యూరెండు విలయముల్ గాంచి." B. X. 86. 12.

విలవిల vila-vila. [Tel.] n. Convulsiveness. తన్నుకొనుటయందగు ధ్వన్యనుకరణము, వివ్వలత. adv. Convulsively, గిజగిజ. విలవిలకొట్టుకొను or విలవిలలాడు vila-vila-koṭṭu-konu. v. n. To be convulsed, or in convulsions. గిజగిజ తన్నుకొను. విలవిలపోవు vila-vila-pôvu. v. n. To be convulsed. వివ్వలతనొందు. విలవిలలాడించు vila-vila-l-aḍintsu. v. a. To convulse. గిజగిజలాడించు. విలవిలలాడించే vila-vila-l-aḍinchē. adj. Convulsive. గిజగిజలాడించే.

విలసత్ vilasat. [Skt] adj. Shining, splendid. ప్రకాశమైన. విలసనము vilasanamu. n. Sporting, dallying. విలాసము, క్రీడ. Brightness. ప్రకాశము. "వలదివ్చటనీమాయావిలసనములునవిక్రొత్త విడువుమటన్నన్." Kalahasti. iii. 195. విలసితము vi-lasitamu. adj. Shining, splendid. ప్రకాశమానమైన, ప్రకాశితము. "విలసితభక్తినిశ్చలబలంబెడ." BD. v. 505. "వినుతవీణానాదవిలసితంబైన." DUR. 1045. విలసిల్లు vilasillu. v. n. To shine. ప్రకాశించు. To be fine, pleasing, agreeable. ఒప్పు. "కొండలెల్లపసిండి కొండలైవిలసిల్ల." Paidim. v. 46.

విలాతి vilati. [From Persian Vilayati.] n. A foreign country. దేశాంతరము. A country, దేశము. "వసుమంతుడు నా ప్రసిద్ధిగాంచినయొక పెట్టెయూంతునలపెట్టిన మారువిలాతికేగుచుశా తన ధన రాశిమైనిడిప." P. i. 48. విలాయతి or విలాయతు vilayati. n. An inhabited country, a foreign country. విలాయతి గ్రామము a hamlet or dependant village.

విలాపము vi-lapamu. [Skt.] n. Sorrow, sorrowful speech, దుఃఖముతోడి మాట. విలాపించు Same as విలపించు (q. v.)

విలాసము vi-lasamu. [Tel.] n. A label, direction, the superscription on a letter. పైని వ్రాసిన పేరు, జాబుమీద వ్రాసిన చిరునామా. పైవిలాసము. [Skt.] n. Sport, dalliance, amorous blandishments, affection of coyness. స్త్రీలహావభేదము, లీల, క్రీడ. స్త్రీపురుషుల శృంగారచేష్ట. కృష్ణవిలాసము the adventures of Krishna. విజయవిలాసము the tale of Arjuna. విలాసవతి or విలాసిని vilasa-vati. n. A flirt, a coquette, a playful girl, స్త్రీ, వేడుకగలస్త్రీ. విలాసవంతుడు or విలాసి vilasa-vantudu. n. A sportive person.

విలియ or విలియా viliya. [H.] n. Arrangement, order, distribution, classification. విలియాచేయు to compose, arrange in order, assign. ఈ సొమ్మునుగురించి నన్ను అతనికి విలియాచేసినారు they referred me to him for payment. విలియావారి or వికేవారి arranging according to different heads, శాఖలువారిగా ఏర్పరచడము.

విలు or విల్లు or విల్ vilu. [Tel.] n. A bow, ధనుస్సు. విలుకాడు, విల్కాడు, విలుకాలుడు or విలువాల్పు vilu-kaḍu. n. An archer or bowman, ధనుర్ధరుడు, ధానుష్కుడు. విలుబండి or విల్లుబండి vilu-bandi. n. A carriage built on springs. విల్లులుగల బండి. విలురాసి vilu-rasi. n. The sign Sagittarius. ధనూరాశి. విలువిద్య vilu-vidya. n. Archery, skill in the use of the bow. ధనుర్విద్య. విల్తుడు viltudu. n. An archer, bowman. విలుకాడు.

విలుచు or విల్చు vilutsu. [Tel.] v. a. To buy, purchase, కొను. To sell, అమ్ము. "వేలు

లకనిమున్న విలిచినగొరియ, బాల్పడి తేకున్న బందువనేయు." BD. v. 113. గొలిచితిమా పెర కేల్పుల, విలిచితిమా కూలధరుని విందింము పెదలా, తలచితిమా దుర్వృత్తుల, విలిచితిమా వేదమంత్ర విద్యాకతులా." Chan. v. 428.

విలుప్తము *vi-luptamu.* [Skt.] adj. Obsolete, extinguished, forgotten. erased, wanting. విస్మృతమైన. స్ఖలితమైన, మరచిపోయిన, లోపము చేయబడిన, "క్రూరులువిలుప్తధర్మవిచారులుధృతరాష్ట్రసుతులు." M. I. v. 192.

విలులితము *vi-lulitamu.* [Skt.] adj. Tremulous, shaking, waving. కదిలే, చలించే.

విలువ or **విల్వ** *viluva.* [Tel.] n. Price, cost, value. ధర, వెల, క్రయము. విలువకనుపోటు a market, or place for sale. "ఈచంద్రబింబాస్య నీధూమకేంద్రునకీవుమెండలము విక్రయించుచేశ, నీవిల్వలోని వాడీనందనుడు కాడు." NH. iv. 145. **విలువకాడు** or **విల్వకాడు** *viluva-kāḍu.* n. A buyer, వెలయిచ్చి కొను వాడు, క్రయికుడు.

విలేపనము *vi-lēpanamu.* [Skt.] n. Smearing; rubbing with ointment. అంగలేపనము, పూయుట, చందనాదులపూత. An unguent; ointment. చందనాదితైలము. **విలేపి** *vi-lēpi.* n. Rice gruel, గంజి.

విలోకించు *vi-lōkintsu.* [Skt. వి + లోకించు. cf. Eng. 'look.'] v. a. To see, behold, gaze at, view, observe. చూచు. **విలోచనము** *vi-lōchanamu.* n. Seeing, looking at, observing. The eye. కన్ను.

విలోమము *vi-lōmamu.* [Skt.] adj. The wrong way, the reverse way, the opposite order or course, against the hair, against the grain, ప్రతిక్రమము, క్రమమునకు తలక్రిందు, వ్యత్యయము, విపర్యయము, విపరీతము, ప్రతికూలము, అవరోహక్రమముగల. విలోమముగా contrariwise. అనులోమవిలోమశ్లోకము a palindrome or verse that may be read forwards and backwards.

విలోలము *vi-lōlamu.* [Skt.] adj. Tossed, rolling.

విల్లు or **విలు** *villu.* [Tel.] n. A bow. ధనుస్సు. విల్లునమ్ములు or విల్లంబులు a bow and arrows. "తేతే లక్ష్మణ విల్లునమ్ములనుచు." N. viii. 105. విల్లెక్కుపెట్టు to brace a bow. విల్లెక్కుడించు to unbrace a bow. Gen. sing. వింటి and the nom. plu. విండ్లు. నూరువిండ్లదూరములో a hundred bow-shots off. See విలు.

విళంగము or **విలంగము** *vilangamu.* [Skt.] n. A vegetable and medicinal substance considered of great efficacy as a vermifuge, చిత్రతండులము, వాయువిళంగపుచెట్టు.

విళంబి *vilambi.* [Skt.] n. The name of a Telugu year.

వివక్ష *vi-vaksha.* [Skt.] n. A wish to speak. చెప్పనిచ్ఛ. Intention, the aim of a speaker, desire. (In Telugu) Difference, distinction, భేదము. **వివక్షించు** or **వివక్షచేయు** *vi-vakshintsu.* v. a. To wish to speak. చెప్ప నిచ్ఛయించు. To distinguish, వ్యత్యాసముచూచుకనుగొను. **వివక్షితము** *vi-vakshitamu.* adj. Required, or wished to be spoken, wished, desired. చెప్పనిచ్ఛయించిన, వాంఛితమైన. **వివక్షువు** *vi-vakshuvu.* n. One who wishes to speak, చెప్పనిచ్ఛించువాడు.

వివరణము or **వివరము** *vi-varaṇamu.* [Skt.] n. An explanation, specification, comment: a description, a detailed account, విస్తరించిచెప్పడము, వర్ణనము, టీక, వ్యాఖ్యానము. **వివరము** *vivaramu.* n. A hole, burrow, chasm, cave, recess. రంధ్రము, బిలము. **వివరములు** *ivaramulu.* n. plu. Particulars, details; a specification, description, వైనములు. **వివరముగా** *vivaramu-gā.* adv. With all particulars, in detail. విధజనగా. **వివరించు** *vivarintsu.* v. a. To describe, particularise, state, specify, విస్తరించిచెప్పు. వివరముగాచెప్పు. To explain, tell, చెప్పు. To consider, think, విచారించు. To delay, ఆలస్యముచేయు.

వివర్జితము *vi-varjitamu.* [Skt.] adj. Left, abandoned, shunned. త్యజింపబడ్డ.

వివర్ణము *vi-varṇamu.* [Skt.] adj. Pale, pallid, colourless, వికృతవర్ణమైన, నిస్తేజస్కమైన. **వివర్ణుడు** *vi-varṇuḍu.* n. One who has turned pale, తెల్లబారినవాడు.

వివర్తనము *vi-vartanamu.* [Skt.] n. Revolving, turning round, revolution, going round, circumambulating. కదిలినకాలపు భేదము, పొరలడము, ప్రదక్షిణము, తిరగడము, చుట్టివచ్చుట, తిరిగివచ్చుట. **వివర్తము** *vi-vartamu.* n. Dancing, నృత్యము.

వివర్ధనము *vi-vardhanamu.* [Skt.] n. Increase. అభివృద్ధి. "భక్తివివర్ధనములు." L. xviii. 66.

వివశత *vi-vaśata.* [Skt.] n. Helplessness, ecstasy, a trance, పరవశత్వము. కోపవివశత a fit of fury. ఆనందవివశత an ecstasy of joy. **వివశుడు** *vi-vaśuḍu.* n. One who is helpless, one who is in ecstasy, one who is wild with joy or sorrow, one who is bewildered, పరవశుడు. కలతపొందినవాడు, స్వవశముకాని బుద్ధిగలవాడు. "రజనీచరరాజు రౌద్రరసవివశుండై." R. viii. 97.

వివస్వంతుడు *vivas-vantuḍu.* [Skt.] n. The sun, సూర్యుడు. A god, వేలుపు.

వివాదము or **వివాద** *vi-vādamu.* [Skt.] n. A contest, altercation, dispute or quarrel, వాక్కలహము, తగవు. వివాదపడు to quarrel, altercate.

వివాహము *vi-vāhamu.* [Skt.] n. A marriage, wedding, పెండ్లి, పరిణయము. Eight kinds of marriages are distinguished as బ్రాహ్మము, దైవము, ఆర్షము, ప్రాజాపత్యము, ఆసురము, గాంధర్వము, రాక్షసము, and పైశాచము. **వివాహమగు** or **వివాహముచేసికొను.** *vi-vāham-agu.* v. n. To wed, marry. పెండ్లాడు.

వివిక్తము *vi-viktamu.* [Skt.] adj. Lonely or solitary. రహస్యము, ఏకాంతము.

వివిధము *vi-vidhamu.* [Skt.] adj. Various, varied, of different kinds, multiform, diverse. నానావిధమైన, అనేకవిధములుగల.

వివృతము *vi-vṛtamu.* [Skt.] adj. Open, gaping, expanded, particularized, explained, described. వికసించిన, తెరవబడిన, విప్పబడిన, వివరింపబడిన.

వివేకము *vi-vēkamu.* [Skt.] n. Discrimination, judgment, the faculty of distinguishing, prudence, discretion, సదసద్వివేచన, విభేదజ్ఞానము, తెలివి. 'వినువివేకమనెడు వింతగొడ్డలిచేత నల యవిద్యయనెడునడవినరికి." Vema. 341. "తనవివేకములోకమునాదరించెపొగా". T. ii. 38. వివేకముకలిగియుండు to come to oneself, reflect, be wise. తెలివితెచ్చుకొను. **వివేకి** *vi-vēki.* n. One who is cautious or prudent. తెలివిగలవాడు. **వివేకించు** or **వివేచించు** *vi-vēkintsu.* v. a. To reason, discriminate, distinguish. విమర్శచేయు, విచారించు, వివేచనచేయు. "చదువులన్ని జదివి చాలవివేకించ కపటికెన్న నేలక లుగుముక్తి." Vema. 429. **వివేచన** or **వివేచనము** *vi-vēchana.* n. Discrimination, examination, investigation. విమర్శ, విచారణ. వర్ణవివేచన discrimination of caste.

వివ్వత్సము *vi-vatstsamu.* [from Skt. బీభత్సము.] n. Devastation, destruction. Killing. నాశము. **వివ్వత్సుడు** *vivatstsuḍu.* n. An epithet of Arjuna.

విశంకటము *vi-śankaṭamu.* [Skt.] adj. Great, large, gigantic. గొప్ప. బృహత్తయిన, విరివిగల. Vasu. v. 53.

విశంకితము *vi-śankitamu.* [Skt.] adj. Alarmed, fearful, suspected. భీతిల్లిన.

విశకలితము *vi-śakalitamu.* [Skt.] adj. Disordered, jumbled, shivered. విశకలీకృతమైన.

విశదము *viśadamu.* [Skt.] adj. White; clear, pure, pellucid. తెల్లని, నిర్మలమైన,

పరిస్ఫుటమైన. Evident, apparent, manifest. స్పష్టమైన. విశదదుర్మార్గులు downright villains. Charitra ii. 1673. n. Clearness, స్పష్టము. **విశదపరచు, విశదముచేయు** or **విశదీకరించు** viṣada-paruṭsu. v. a. To particularise, explain, define, manifest. స్పష్టము చేయు. **విశదమగు** viṣadam-agu. v. n. To come to light, become clear or known. స్పష్టమగు. అతనిజాబువల్ల ఆ సంగతులు విశదమవును his letter will explain or make clear those matters. తమకు విశదముకావలెనని వ్రాసినాను I have written this for your information. **విశదములు** viṣadamulu. n. plu. Matters, things, particulars. వివరములు.

విశయము vi-ṣayamu. [Skt.] n. A dwelling place, వాసస్థానము.

విశల్యము vi-ṣalyamu. [Skt.] adj. Boneless. Thornless. Free from care or pain. నిర్గతశూలము, నిష్పీడనము. **విశల్యకరణి** vi-ṣalya-karaṇi. n. A plant, *Echites dichotoma*, (Rox.) సంజీవి. **విశల్యుడు** vi-ṣalyuḍu. n. One who is free from thorns or spikes, one who is released from care or pain. నిర్గతశూలుడు, పెకలబడినశూలముగలవాడు, బాధతీరుండావేయబడ్డవాడు. "అంతరభువరుండు సుగ్రీవాదులందు విశల్యులజేసియలరు మంచె." BRY. i. 925.

విశసనము vi-ṣasanamu. [Skt.] n. Killing, slaying, slaughter. చంపడము. సంహరించడము. **విశసించు** vi-ṣasintsu. v. a. To kill, slay. చంపు. "పరగగద్దితోడు పశువులవిశసించి మనుజాలుతినిభువినిమాలలైరి." Vema. 1530.

విశాఖ vi-ṣākha. [Skt.] n. The name of the 16th lunar mansion. **విశాఖము** vi-ṣākhamu. n. The act of standing with the legs about a foot apart from each other. విలుకాడు రెండుకాళ్లనడుమ జేనెడేడము గలుగ నిలుచుట. A spindle, నూలువడికేకదురు. adj. Branchless, శాఖములేని. **విశాఖుడు** vi-ṣākhuḍu. n. A name of Kumaraswamy. కుమారస్వామి.

విశాయము vi-ṣāyamu. [Skt.] n. Taking rest by turns (as applied to watchmen). A turn, పర్యాయము.

విశారదుడు vi-ṣāraduḍu. [Skt.] n. One who is learned, or wise, బాగా చదువుకొన్నవాడు, విద్యాంసుడు. A clever or skilful, famous, or celebrated man; an adept or expert. ప్రగల్భుడు. ప్రసిద్ధుడు. విబుధుడు, నేర్పరి. "క్ష్మా నమెక్కడకో యుద్ధవిశారదుండవు," Rukmangada. iii. 232.

విశాలము viṣālamu. [Skt.] adj. Large, wide, broad, great, spacious. విస్తీర్ణమైన, విరివైన, గొప్ప. ఆ యిల్లు విశాలముగానున్నది that house is a large one. **విశాలత** viṣāluta. n. Width, breadth, వెడల్పు. **విశాలాక్షి** viṣal-akshi. n. An epithet of Pārvati. Lit. Large-eyed.

విశిఖ vi-ṣikha. [Skt.] n. A high way, or carriage road. వీధి, రాజమార్గము. **విశిఖము** vi-sikhamu. n. An arrow, బాణము.

విశిష్టము vi-ṣishṭamu. [Skt.] adj. (In composition.) Endowed with, possessed of, having. కూడుకొన్న. గల. Excellent, superior, distinguished. ఉత్తమమైన, ఉత్కృష్టమైన. **విశిష్టుడు** vi-ṣishṭuḍu. n. One who is endowed with, or possessed of. గలవాడు, కూడుకొన్నవాడు. సద్గుణవిశిష్టుడు one who is endowed with noble qualities.

విశిరస్కుడు vi-ṣiraskuḍu. [Skt.] adj. Beheaded, headless. తలనరకబడిన. వాన్ని విశిరస్కునిగాజేసిరి they beheaded him.

విశీర్ణము vi-ṣirṇamu. [Skt.] adj. Loosened, that has lost the cohesion, or connection of its parts; that has fallen or is falling to pieces: వదలిన, విచ్చిపోయిన, ఊడిపోయిన, రాలిపోయిన. Withered, decayed. శిథిలమైన, జీర్ణమైపోయిన.

విశుద్ధము vi-ṣuddhamu. [Skt.] adj. Pure, clean, cleansed, purified, pious, holy, virtuous, నిర్మలమైన, పవిత్రమైన. **విశుద్ధి**

vi-suddhi. n. Purity, purification, holiness. పరిశుద్ధి, శుచిత్వము. విశుద్ధుడు *vi-suddhudu*. n. One who is pure or holy. పరిశుద్ధుడు. "సుద్దులుగావు విశుద్ధులై విన్న." L. i. 205.

విశృంఖలము *vi-srinkhalamu*. [Skt.] adj. Unchecked, unrestrained, unfettered. అడ్డములేని, అనర్గళమైన.

విశేషము *vi-sêshamu*. [Skt.] n. Sort, kind, species, variety, భేదము, విధము. A particularity, speciality, peculiarity, singularity. A specific quality, a distinguishing property, a characteristic. A particular thing, an individual, an object distinguished by some attribute or adjunct. Merit, excellence; something noteworthy or distinguished, a remarkable occurrence, news. చూడదగిన యుక్తిమవస్తువు. అతిశయము, వింత, వింతరూపము. A charitable or virtuous action. సత్కార్యము, పుణ్యము. ఈ వైద్యునికి హస్తవిశేషమున్నది this doctor has a fortunate hand. ఓషధివిశేషము a sort of herb. అక్షక్రీడావిశేషము a kind of dice-play. నేడేమివిశేషము what is there particular to-day? what is the matter to-day? ఆయన విశేషజ్ఞుడు he is a great scholar. adj. Extraordinary, eminent, remarkable, unusual. Much, more, abundant, greater, exceeding, surpassing. అతిశయమైన, వింతైన, అత్యంతమైన. విశేషమైనకార్యము a good deed. ఈ శ్లోకమునకు ఒక విశేషార్థమున్నది this verse has a secondary or recondite meaning. విశేషణము *vi-sêshanamu*. n. (In grammar). An adjective. విశేష్యలక్షణములను చెప్పేది. గుణవాచకశబ్దము. విశేషించు *vi-seshintsu*. v. n. To excel. అతిశయించు. విశేషించి or విశేషముగా *vi-sêshinchi*. adv. Abundantly, plentifully, much, exceedingly. అధికముగా, విస్తారముగా, మిక్కిలి, మిగుల. అతనితో విశేషించి సహవాసముచేయవద్దు you should not associate much with him. "ఈ యుత్తమసమాయనింబోషించెదవిశేషించికేటు నుండియు బ్రాహ్మణపదంబు గాగారవించెద." T. ii. 178. విశేష్యము *vi-sêshyamu*. n. (In grammar), a noun or substantive. నామవాచకపదము, వస్తువాచకశబ్దము.

విశ్రమము or విశ్రామము *vi-sramamu*. [Skt.] n. Rest, repose, cessation from fatigue or work. విశ్రాంతి. ఊరట. In Telugu verse, it denotes a certain kind of rhyme. ఛందస్సులో యతి, పద్యవిరామము. విశ్రమించు *vi-sramintsu*. v. n. To rest, repose, or refresh oneself. అలయికతీర్చుకొను. ఊరడిల్లు. విశ్రమింపజేయు *vi-sramimpa-jêyu*. v. a. To place, lay, పరుండబెట్టు. "విశ్వత కృష్ణాజినమునందుగా విశ్రమింపజేసి." Jaimini. Bh. vi. 93. విశ్రాంతము *vi-srântamu*. adj. Rested, reposed, refreshed after fatigue, శ్రమదీరిన, అలయికతీర్చుకొనబడిన, ఊరడిల్లిన. విశ్రాంతి *vi-srânti*. n. Rest, repose, refreshment. ఊరట, అలయికతీర్చుకొనడము. Termination. విరామము, అవసానము. "కల్పవిశ్రాంతి" T. iv. 183.) the end of the world. "తద్విలసన్నిద్ధరవారి దీక్షలలో విశ్రాంతిగావించి." Vish. ii. 220.

విశ్రాణనము *vi-srânanamu*. [Skt.] n. A gift, or donation. త్యాగము, ఈవి.

విశ్రావము or విశ్రుతి *vi-srâvamu*. [Skt.] n. Great fame, మిక్కిలిప్రసిద్ధి, ప్రఖ్యాతి. విశ్రుతము *vi-srutamu*. adj. Famous, well-known, celebrated. విదితమైన, మిక్కిలి ప్రసిద్ధమైన. విశ్రుతుడు *vi-srutudu*. n. A very famous man, a well-known man.

విశ్లథము *vi-slathamu*. [Skt.] adj. Loose, relaxed. విడిపోయిన. R. ii. 59.

విశ్లేషము *vi-slêshamu*. [Skt.] n. Separation (especially of lovers), disunion, disjunction. విరహము, వియోగము, ఎడబాటు.

విశ్వ *visva*. [Skt.] n. The earth. భూమి. విశ్వము *visvamu*. n. The universe or world, లోకము, జగత్తు adj. All, universal, entire. సర్వమైన, సమస్తమైన. విశ్వంభర *viṣvam-bhara*. n. The earth. భూమి. విశ్వంభరుడు *viṣvam-bharuḍu*. n. An epithet of Vishnu or Indra. విష్ణువు, ఇంద్రుడు. విశ్వకర్మ or విశ్వకర్ముడు *viṣva-karma*. n. The name of the artist of the gods, corresponding to Vulcan. దేవతలవడ్లవాడు, దేవతలశిల్పి. విశ్వకేతువు *viṣva-kētuvu*. n. An epithet of Aniruddha. విశ్వజనీనము *viṣva-janīnamu*. adj. Agreeable to all men. విశ్వతోముఖము *viṣvatō-mukhamu*. n. An epithet of Brahma. బ్రహ్మము. adj. All pervading, అంతట వ్యాపించిన. విశ్వనాథుడు *viṣva-nadhuḍu*. n. The Lord of the Universe. A name of Siva, especially as worshipped at Benares, కాశీ విశ్వేశ్వరుడు. విశ్వభేషజము *viṣva-bhēshajamu*. n. Dry ginger, శొంఠి. విశ్వరూపము *viṣva-rūpamu*. adj. Existing in all forms, multiform. నానారూపము గల. n. Multiformity. నానారూపము. "విబుధేంద్రశైలంబు విశ్వరూపము జూపె నన నొప్పు కాంచనస్యందనములు." N. v. 17. విశ్వరూపదర్శనము manifestation or display of one's own real form or hidden majesty, నిజస్వరూపమును అగుపరచడము. విశ్వరూపుడు *viṣva-rūpuḍu*. n. He who exists in all forms; a name of Vishnu. విష్ణువు. "విశ్వరూపునకు వినతులు సేయుము." H. iv. 297. విశ్వసృజుడు. విశ్వస్రష్ట or విశ్వస్రష్టుడు *viṣva-srijuḍu*. n. Brahma, the creator, బ్రహ్మ. విశ్వామిత్రుడు *viṣv-āmitruḍu*. n. The name of a certain sage, the son of Gādhi. గాధిసుతుడు. విశ్వామిత్రము *viṣv-āmitramu*. adj. Worthy of Visvámitra: (that is) fabricated, fictitious, artificial, కల్పితమైన, కృత్రిమమైన. విశ్వామిత్రమైనపత్రము a fabricated bond, a Machiavelian trick. తప్పుసృష్టిచేయబడిన. n. A deed worthy of Visvamitra, that is, a trick, fiction, fabrication. Machiavelianism. మోసము, కృత్రిమము, కల్పన. విశ్వామిత్రసృష్టి *viṣvā-mitra-srishti*. n. The creation of a second series of beings, Visvamitra being represented as having created a mimic world. విశ్వులు or విశ్వదేవతలు *viṣvulu*. n. The name given to certain deities of a particular class.

విశ్వసించు *vi-ṣrasinṭsu*. [Skt.] v. a. To trust, rely on, confide in. నమ్ము. విశ్వసనీయము *vi-ṣvasan-iyamu*. adj. Trustworthy, నమ్మదగిన. విశ్వసితము *vi-ṣrasitamu*. adj. Trusted, confided in, trusty, విశ్వసింపబడిన. విశ్వస్త *vi-ṣrasta*. n. A widow, విధవ, విశ్వసింపబడినది. విశ్వస్తము *vi-ṣrastamu*. adj. Trusted. నమ్మబడిన, విశ్వసింపబడిన. విశ్వాసము *vi-ṣrāsamu*. n. Trust, faith, confidence. Affection, kindness, favour. నమ్మికము, ప్రేమ. విశ్వాసి *vi-ṣrāsi*. n. One who is faithful. నమ్మికముగలవాడు. "హితుడు విశ్వాసియుమతిమంతుడునునగు." UR. vi. 392. "జంగమవిశ్వాసిలింగాభిమాని." BD. v. 348.

విషణ్ణము *vishannamu*. [Skt.] adj. Dejected, sad, sorrowful, pensive. శోకయుక్తమైన, వ్యాకులగ్రస్తమైన. M. XII. 2. 274. విషణ్ణుడు *vishannuḍu*. n. One who is dejected, sorrowful, శోకముగలవాడు. See విషాదము.

విషమము *vishamamu*. [Skt.] adj. Odd, uneven, irregular. Unparalleled, unequalled. Contrary, adverse, unfavourable, evil, bad. బేసి. ఎక్కువతక్కువగానుండే, సమముకాని, విరుద్ధము, దుష్టము. విషమసంఖ్య an odd number. విషమజ్వరము a pestilent fever, a fever difficult of cure. విషమాయుధుడు or విషమశరుడు Manmadha, whose arrows are five (an odd number). విషమనయనుడు Siva who has an odd (or extra) eye in his forehead. విషమబుద్ధి an evil or wicked mind. విషమవిభాగము an unfair or unequal division. "విషమకావ్యముకాదు విచారించిచూడ." L. i. 210. "విషమోపల సంప్లుతము." full of rugged rocks. Sanskrit Harisch. xxi. R. vi. 46. విషమించు *visha-*

mintsu. v. n. To be painful, mortal or difficult of cure (as applied to disease.) దోషించు, విరోధించు.

విషము *vishamu.* [Skt.] n. Poison, venom: anything hurtful or destructive. గరళము. చెరుపైనది. నాశకరమైనది. In poetry it sometimes means water, జలము. అది దీనికి విషము that is poison to this. వాని నిలువెల్లా విషము he is a rogue from head to foot. విషముఎక్కినది the poison took effect. విషము దిగినది the effect of the poison went off. నేనంటే వానికి విషముగావున్నది he hates me like poison. దీన్ని నోట్లోవేసుకొంటే విషముగా వున్నది it is as bitter as gall. విషజ్వరము a malignant fever, typhoid fever. విషభేది virulent diarrhœa. విషపాండువు acute dropsy. విషపునీరు the pus or matter in a boil. విషవాక్యాలు fatal expressions, క్రూరవచనములు. **విషధరము** *visha-dhara-mu.* n. A snake or serpent. సర్పము. A cloud, మేఘము. **విషధరుడు** *visha-dharudu.* n. One who carries poison, an epithet of Siva. శివుడు. **విషపుచ్ఛము** *visha-puchchamu.* n. A scorpion. తేలు. A rogue, తులువ. **విషముష్టి** or **విషవృక్షము** *visha-mushti.* n. A poisonous tree, the nux vomica tree. ముష్టిచెట్టు. **విషరుహము** *visha-ruhamu.* n. A lotus, కమలము. "విషమునుగాంచేలపోవు విషరుహానన యనా." Ila. iv. 9. **విషవైద్యుడు** *visha-vaidyudu.* n. A snake-catcher. అహితుండికుడు. A magician, గారడీడు. **విషోల్బణుడు** *vish-ōlbanudu.* n. One who has an excess of venom. అధికవిషము కలవాడు. "బహువదనులునురుదీర్ఘశరీరులును విషోల్బణులును." **విషాహి** *vish-āhi.* n. A venomous serpent. విషముగలసర్పము.

విషయము *vishayamu.* [Skt.] n. An object, matter, subject, affair, thing. Any peculiarity as colour, form, flavour, odour, sound. Definition, respect, relation, అంశము, సంగతి. ఇంద్రియార్థము, శబ్దాదిపంచభూతగుణము. "విషయములజొచ్చి కోయక విషమంటినగతినిజాయి విధమునగధిలో విషసమమాయా సుఖములవిషయములతో గూడకుంద్రు ఛేత్తలు." Vema. 499. ఆ విషయము నాకు తెలియదు I do not know anything about it. ఈ విషయములో నిండాసొమ్ము వ్యయముచేసినాడు he spent much money on this. సద్విషయములలో తన సొమ్ము వ్యయముచేసినాడు he spent his money on worthy objects. శృంగారవిషయమైనకావ్యము a poem on amorous subjects. ఈవిషయమందు in this respect. ఆ విషయమందు in that respect. అతనివిషయమందు regarding him. ఆ విషయమై regarding that subject. ఏతద్విషయముగా మాట్లాడినాడు he spoke regarding this. మీ విషయములో regarding you. **విషయి** *vishayi.* n. An organ of sense. శ్రోత్రాదియింద్రియము. A man of the world, one who is conversant with or interested in worldly occupations or enjoyments. లోకవ్యవహారవ్యక్తుడు, సంసారిమనుష్యుడు, ప్రాపంచికుడు. **విషయించు** *vishayintsu.* v. n. To have to do with carnally. సంభోగముచేయు. **విషయీకరించు** *vishayi-karintsu.* v. a. To aim at. ఉద్దేశించు.

విషాణము *vishānamu.* [Skt.] n. A horn, కొమ్ము. **విషాణి** *vishāni.* n. A kind of tree. జొట్టువుచెట్టు. An elephant, ఏనుగు. An ox, ఎద్దు.

విషాదము *vishādamu.* [Skt.] n. Sadness, grief, lowness of spirits, dejection. ఖేదము. **విషాదించు** *vishādintsu.* v. n. To be sad, to grieve, ఖేదపడు.

విషువము or **విషువత్తు** *vishuvamu.* [Skt.] n. The equinox. రాత్రియును దినమును సమమైనకాలము. **విషువచ్ఛాయ** *vishu-vach-chāya.* n. The shadow of the gnomon at noon, when the sun is in the equinoctial point.

విషూచి or **విషూచిక** *vishūchi.* [Skt.] n. Cholera. వాంతిభేది, విషూచివిరేచనకటము.

విష్కంభము *vish-kambhamu.* [Skt.] n. A bolt of a door, గడెమాను. An obstacle, అడ్డంకి.

విష్కిరము *vishkiramu.* [Skt.] n. A bird, పక్షి.

విష్టపము *vishṭapamu.* [Skt.] n. The world. లోకము.

విష్టరము *vishṭaramu.* [Skt.] n. A seat, a seat of kusa grass. ఆసనము, పీఠము, కుశాసనము. "తదీయసమీపోదార్యాసనమధ్యంబున కృష్ణాజినంబుల విష్టరంబులుగానిడి కూర్చున్న సప్తమునీశ్వరులు." Vish. ii. 23. విష్టరశ్రవుడు *vish-ṭara-sravuḍu.* n. An epithet of Vishṇu. విష్ణువు.

విష్టి *vishṭi.* [Skt.] n. Wages, hire, కూలి. Forced labour, కూలిలేనిపని. Work, పని.

విష్ఠించు *vishṭhinṭsu.* [Skt.] v. n. To ease oneself, to go to stool, మలవిసర్జనముచేయు.

విష్ణుడు or విష్ణువు *vishṇuḍu.* [Skt.] n. Vishṇu, one of the three principal Hindu deities. విష్ణుపదము *vishṇu-padamu.* n. The sky. ఆకాశము. విష్ణుపది *vishṇu-padi.* n. The Ganges, గంగ. విష్ణురథము *vishṇu-rathamu.* n. The Brahminy kite, గరుత్మంతుడు. విష్ణుక్రాంత *vishṇu-krānta.* n. A medicinal creeping plant, *Evolvulus alsinoides* స్థూలకర్ణభూమ్యా.

విష్వక్సేనుడు *vishvak-sênuḍu.* [Skt.] n. Vishṇu. విష్ణువు. The captain of Vishṇu's forces, విష్ణుసేనాధిపతి.

విసంవాదము *vi-sam-vādamu.* [Skt.] n. Arguing first in favor of a thing and then against it.

విసనకఱ్ఱ, విసినికఱ్ఱ or విసనుకఱ్ఱ *visana-karra.* [Tel.] n. A fan. తాలవృంతము.

విసము *visamu.* [from Skt. విషము.] n. Poison విషము. విసదారి *visa-dāri* (for ...) A snake. పాము. విసపాల *visa-pāla.* n. A kind of tree. విసపాలవిత్తు *visa-pāla-vittu.* n. A destroyer, నాశకుడు. విసపుమేతరి *visapu-mêtari.* n. The eater of poison; an epithet of Siva. విసబొడ్డి *visa-boḍḍi.* n. A kind of tree called పొలవృక్షము.

విసరము *visaramu.* [Skt.] n. A multitude, an assemblage, a flock. సమూహము. విసరణము *visaraṇamu.* n. Spreading, diffusion. విస్తరించడము, వ్యాపించడము.

విసరు or విసురు *visaru.* [Tel.] v. n. To come out, బయలువెడలు. To blow, as the wind, to spread, as a scent. గాలికొట్టు, వీచు, వాసనకొట్టు. లోగా అణిగి ఉన్న రోగమును బైట విసిరేలాగు చేసేమందు a searching medicine, a medicine that makes a hidden disease appear. లోనికాక బైటికివిసిరినది the latent fever came out. v. a. To wave, as a fan, to brandish, whisk, flourish, as a sword or a whip. ఆడించు. వీచు. To throw, fling, hurl, sling, రువ్వు. To turn, to grind. తిరుగలివిసరు to turn a mill. వలవిసరు to cast or let down a net. n. Waving, casting, spreading. ఆడించుట, వీచుట, వేయుట, వ్యాపించడము. కాటకమువిసరుచేత through the spreading of the famine. విసరురాయి *visaru-rāyi.* n. A grindstone. తిరుగలి. విసరియాడు Same as విసరు. విసరికొట్టు or విసిరికొట్టు *visari-koṭṭu.* v. a. To fling, to dash. రువ్వు. To scorn, to huff. కసురు. ఒకడబ్బు ఇమ్మంటే మూతితో ముఖములో విసిరికొట్టుచున్నది he asked for a penny, she gave him a scolding. ఆకుండను గోడమీద విసిరికొట్టినాడు he dashed the pot against the wall. విసరివేయు or విసిరివేయు *visari-vêyu.* v. a. To hurl, fling, రువ్వు. ఊరిబైట విసరివేసినట్టుగానుండే ఒకయిల్లు a house that seemed as if it had been thrown out of the town.

విసర్గ *vi-sarga.* [Skt.] n. The character [ః] or two dots representing H, as in the words ప్రాతఃకాలము *pratah-kalamu* విస

ర్గము vi-sargamu. n Abandoning, relinquishment, letting go, emitting, పరిత్యాగము, వదలుకొనడము, విసర్జనీయము. విసర్జనము vi-sarjanamu. n. Quitting, relinquishing, abandoning, renouncing. పరిత్యాగము. Sending, despatching, ప్రేషణము. A gift, donation, దానము, ఇవ్వడము, ఈవి. కేశవిసర్జనము shaving the head. మలమూత్రవిసర్జనము evacuations. మలమూత్రవిసర్జనముచేయు to evacuate the bowels. విసర్జించు vi-sarjintsu. v. a. To abandon, relinquish, give up, renounce. త్యజించు, విడుచు. విసర్జించబడ్డ భార్య a divorced wife. విసర్జనీయము vi-sarjaniyamu. adj. Fit to be relinquished, or abandoned.

విసర్పణము vi-sarpanamu. [Skt.] n. Spreading, extending. వ్యాపించడము.

విసవిస visa-visa. [Tel.] adj. Spreading, ప్రసరించునది. adv. Fast, quickly, hurriedly. వడిగా, చివచివ. "విసవిసవచ్చుచుజవమున నిసరి వనడిచారుజలపవిసట ముఖంశిలా." Rajasekh. i. 70.

విసుకు, విసుగు or విసువు visuku. [Tel.] v. n. To be fatigued, tired, weary. To be disgusted, to be sick at heart. వేసారు, వానిప్రాణము విసికినది he was sick at heart. "విను సంసారమునకు విసువనిమర్త్యులు." M. XIII. v. 223. n. Disgust, weariness, satiety. వేసట, అలసట, నిర్వేదము. విసిమాలు visi-malu. v. n. To be very disgusted. మిక్కిలి విసుగు. విసికించు visikintsu. (causal of విసుకు.) v. a. To weary, disgust, sicken, sadden. వేసటపుట్టునట్టుచేయు.

విసుమానము visumanamu. [from Skt. విస్మయము.] n. Wonder, ఆశ్చర్యము. adj. Wonderful, ఆశ్చర్యకరమైన.

విసువాసము visuvasamu. [from Skt. విశ్వాసము.] n. Faith, trust, affection, విశ్వాసము, నమ్మకము. విసువాసి visuvasi. n. A faithful man, నమ్మకముగలవాడు.

విసురు See విసరు.

విస్పృతము Same as విస్పృతము. (q. v.)

విస్తరి. విస్తర or విస్తరాకు vistara. [from Skt. విస్తరము.] n. A leaf platter, భోజనము చేసెడి ఆకు. plu. విస్తళ్లు.

విస్తరము vistaramu. [Skt.] n. Spreading, expansion; prolixity, detail, abundance, plenty. శబ్దాదులవిస్తృతి, వ్యాప్తి, ప్రాచుర్యము, బాహుళ్యము. విస్తరించి vistarinchi. (participle used adverbially) Much, abundantly, greatly, considerably. నిండా, మిక్కుటముగా. విస్తరిలు or విస్తరిల్లు vistarilu. v. n. To spread, extend, increase, enlarge, exceed, be prolix, dilate. విస్తారమగు, వ్యాపించు. విస్తరించు vistarintsu. v. a. To extend, spread out, increase, swell; to particularise. విస్తరిల్లజేయు, వివరించు. విస్తారము vistaramu. n. Spreading, extension, expanse, breadth, vastness. Plenty, abundance నిండు, బాహుళ్యము. "తనవాని గాంచియుత్కట్యద్భుతంబుగు ధ్వజమున తెరంగు విస్తారము చెప్పెచెప్పిన." M. XIV.iii. 228. adj. Plentiful, abundant; extended, extensive, large, great, much, extreme. బహుళము, నిండినయైన. విస్తారముగా vistaramu-ga. adv. Plentifully, abundantly, largely, much. బహుళముగా, నిండా, చాలా. విస్తీర్ణత vistirnata. n. Extent, area. విస్తీర్ణము vistirnamu. adj. Great, large, wide, extended, extensive. విస్తారమైన, విశాలమైన.

విస్తు vistu. [Tel.] n. Surprise, wonder. ఆశ్చర్యము. Also, dirt, stench, దేహమునందుగలిగెడు దుర్గంధము. "ద్వి. ॥ కోల, వేమారువిసరుమ విస్తుకంపెసగ, బుసలుచెప్పుచు." పల. 3. భా.

విస్తృతము vistritamu. [Skt.] adj. Wide, broad, extensive, large.

విస్పష్టము vi-spashtamu. [Skt.] adj. Very clear, distinct, definite. స్పష్టమైన, ప్రత్యక్షమైన విస్పష్టముచేయు to particularise or specify.

విస్ఫారము or విష్ఫారము *visphāramu.* [Skt.] n. The twang of a bow-string వింటిమ్రోత. వింటిధ్వని. adj. Very great, మిక్కిలి అధికమైన.

విస్ఫురత్ *vi-sphurat.* [Skt.] adj. Shining. ప్రకాశించే. "వృత్రమునివాక్యవిస్ఫురద్బోధమున కు." H. i. 208. విస్ఫురణము *vi-sphuraṇamu.* n. Trembling, quivering of the lips, throbbing of the eyes, &c. Expansion of mind. Splendour, manifestation. కంపనము, మనోవికాసము, ప్రకాశము. విస్ఫురించు *vi-sphurintsu.* v. n. To shine, ప్రకాశించు. To swell, enlarge, విస్తరింపజేయు. విస్ఫురితము *vi-sphuritamu.* adj. Shaken, tremulous: swollen, enlarged. Shining. కంపితమైన. విస్తరింపబడిన. ప్రకాశించే. విస్ఫూర్జితము *vi-sphurjitamu.* adj. Very bright, మిక్కిలి ప్రకాశము పొందిన. విస్ఫూర్తి *vi-sphurti.* n. Throbbing, palpitating, shaking; shining.

విస్ఫులింగము *vi-sphulingamu.* [Skt.] n. A spark of fire. అగ్నికణము.

విస్ఫోటము *vi-sphōṭamu.* [Skt.] n. A pustule, boil, abscess, sore, పొక్కు, బొబ్బ, వ్రణము. విస్ఫోటములు prickly heat, చెమటకాయలు.

విస్మయము or విస్మితి *vi-smayamu.* [Skt.] n. Surprise, astonishment, wonder, ఆశ్చర్యము, వింత. Perplexity, dismay. Pride, గర్వము. adj. Wonderful, ఆశ్చర్యకరమైన. విస్మయముపొందిన raptured, bewildered. విస్మితము *vi-smitamu.* adj. Raptured, amazed, astonished, dismayed. ఆశ్చర్యపడ్డ. విస్మితుడు *vi-smituḍu.* n. One who is astonished.

విస్మృతి *vi-smṛti.* [Skt.] n. Forgetfulness మరపు. విస్మృతము *vi-smṛitamu.* adj. Forgotten. మరచిన.

విస్రంభము *vi-srambhamu.* [Skt.] n. Trust, confidence, విశ్వాసము, నమ్మకము. Affection, regard. స్నేహము. A sham fight, a lover's quarrel. ప్రణయము, అల్లాటజగడము.

విస్రము *visramu.* [Skt.] n. A smell, stench, a smell like that of blood or raw flesh, పచ్చివాసన. adj. Stinking, అపక్వమైనగంధముగల.

విస్రస *visrasa.* [Skt.] n. Old age, decrepitude. ముదిమి.

విస్వరుడు *vi-svaruḍu.* [Skt.] n. One whose voice is changed, భేదపడినకంఠస్వరముగలవాడు.

విహంగమము *vihan-gamamu* [Skt.] n. A bird. పక్షి.

విహంగిక *vihangika.* [Skt.] n. A pole used as a yoke for bearing burdens on the shoulder. కావడిబద్ద.

విహగము or విహంగము *viha-gamu.* [Skt.] n. A bird, an arrow. పక్షి, బాణము.

విహరణము *vi-haraṇamu.* [Skt.] n. Roaming, a ramble, excursion, a walkfor pleasure or exercise. విహారము, సంచరించడము, పర్యటనము, పరిభ్రమణము. విహరించు *vi-harintsu.* v. n. To take a walk or airing, to wander, to go about, to go about for pleasure or exercise, to roam, ramble, rove. సంచరించు, పర్యటనముచేయు, పరిభ్రమణముచేయు. విహారముచేయు, తిరుగు. విహర్త *vi-harta.* n. One who takes a walk, a rambler, rover, విహరించువాడు.

విహసితము See under విహాసము.

విహస్తము *vi-hastamu.* [Skt.] adj. Lit: Without hands, unable to move one's hands. Perplexed, bewildered, confused, confounded. ఉద్విగ్నమైన, విహ్వలమైన, వ్యాకులమైన.

విహాయసము *vi-hāyasamu.* [Skt.] n. The sky. ఆకాశము.

విహాయితము *vihāyitamu.* [Skt.] n. A gift donation దానము. ఇవ్వడము, ఈవి.

విహారము vi-hāramu. [Skt.] n. A walk for pleasure or exercise, a tour, trip, ramble, roaming, play, pastime, sport, excursion, వేడుకగాతిరుగుట, సంచారము, క్రమణము. కేళి. లీల, యాత్ర. A Buddhist monastery. బౌద్ధాలయము. విహారి or విహారుడు vihāri. n. One who takes a walk for pleasure, సంచారము చువాడు. వారు ఉద్యానవిహారులైయున్న వేళ while they were walking in the park.

విహాసము or విహసితము vi-hāsamu. [Skt.] n. A gentle laugh, a smile. చిరునవ్వు.

విహితము vi-hitamu. [Skt.] adj. Ordered, prescribed, ordained, విధింపబడిన. Fit, proper, right, orderly, necessary. Friendly, intimate. Placed, deposited. Done, made. యుక్తమైన. అనుకూలమైన, ఉంచబడ్డ, చేయుబడ్డ. వారిగ్రామములు దోచుట విహితముకాదని considering that it is not proper for us to plunder their villages. "ఇమ్మహాభారతంబి మ్ములబాయుకవిహితావధానులైవినుచుండువారికి." M. I. i. 114. విహితము vi-hitamu. n. Friendship, intimacy. Propriety, fitness, justice. స్నేహము. యుక్తము, న్యాయము. అది విహితమే that is proper. అది విహితముకాదు that is not proper. విహితముగా vi-hitamu-ga. adv. In a friendly manner, on good terms, స్నేహముగా, అనుకూలముగా. విహితుడు vi-hitudu. n. A friend, companion, ally. స్నేహితుడు, అనుకూలుడు. తమకు విహితులైనవారు those who are your friends.

విహీనము vi-hīnamu. [Skt.] adj. Destitute of, devoid of. లేని. విహీనముగా vi-hīnamu-ga. adv. Without, లేక. బుద్ధివిహీనముగా senselessly. విహీనుడు vi-hīnudu. n. One who is destitute of or devoid of. లేనివాడు. వస్త్రవిహీనుడు he who is devoid of clothes.

విహ్వలము vihvalamu. [Skt.] adj. Disturbed, discomposed, disquieted, agitated, affected with fear, sorrow, &c. భయాదులచేత ఆవయవస్వాధీనతతప్పిన, ఉద్విగ్నమైన. "భయవిహ్వలమతులై." Anirud. iii. 163. విహ్వలత or విహ్వలత్వము vihvalata. n. Disturbance, disquiet, perturbation. ఉద్విగ్నత. విహ్వలించు vihvalintsu. v. n. To be disquieted or affected with fear, sorrow, &c. ఉద్విగ్నమగు. "వెఱచిదిశలుదప్పదంతియు విహ్వలించి అప్పళించుకరయుండె కొలంతిమనను." Vish. vi. 290. విహ్వలుడు vihvaludu. n. One who is disturbed, agitated, disquieted or affected with fear, sorrow, &c. ఉద్విగ్నుడు. "విషాదవిహ్వలులై." P. i. 446. "వివేకశిష్యులు విహ్వలులగుదురు." L. xiii. 146.

వీ vī

వీక or వీగు vīka. [Tel. from విగు.] n. Strength, బలము. Valour, courage, శౌర్యము, ధైర్యము. Joy, exhilaration, enthusiasm, ఉత్సాహము. Pride, haughtiness, విజృంభణము, గర్వము, ఉన్నతి. Running away from a battle, flight, retreat, యుద్ధమువలన పారిపోవుట. Disgrace, అవమానము. Humility, దైన్యము. Similarity, similitude. సామ్యము, పోలిక. Bulk, largeness. స్థౌల్యము. Manner, విధము. "ఘనుడవ్వార్థుడు గాండివంబుగొని వీకన్నాండయుక్కించు బోయిన దోశ్శక్తిదొలంగి." Vish. viii. 290.

వీక్ష vīksha. [Skt.] n. Sight, view. చూపు, దృష్టి. వీక్షణము vīkshaṇamu. n. Seeing. అవలోకనము, చూచుట. వీక్షించు vīkshintsu. v. a. To see, view, look at, observe. చూచు. వీక్షితము vīkshitamu. adj. Seen, beheld, చూడబడిన. వీక్ష్యము vīkshyamu. adj. Visible, perceptible. చూడదగిన. Wonderful, ఆశ్చర్యకరమైన.

వీగు vīgu. [Tel.] v. n. To rejoice, to be enthusiastic, ఉత్సహించు. To be proud, విర్రవీగు. To become large or big, స్థూలమగు. To move or step aside, to get out of the way, to retreat, తొలగు, వెనుకదీయు.

To cease, to go off. నివృత్తియగు. "సకుటుంబముగ వీగిచరమశైలము జేరుకుమీ-సాంకుఘము దారుణోరయుకంగ." Swa. iii. 74. టీ॥ వీగి, తొలగిపోయి.

వీచి or **వీచిక** *vichi.* [Skt.] n. A wave. తరంగము.

వీచు *vitsu.* [Tel.] v. n. To blow, as the wind, to spread, as scent. గాలివిసరు, వాసనకొట్టు. "పొలగాలివీచె." A. vi. 20. v. a. To wave, as a fan, hand, &c. To revile, reproach. విసరు; నిందించు. "తెలిసి తలిదండ్రులేమని కలరుకొట్ట్ర, విన్నబంధువులేమని వీతురొగ్గ్ర." Paidim. iv 185. "పూని రేకుళధకార్యమునకైన యిట్లువీచిపల్కి దరుమాటె మతెంటదగిలి." Dab. 140. **వీచోపు** *vi-chōpu.* [వీచే+చోపు.] n. A chowri, a fly-flap, a whisk, వింజామర. "వీచుచీచోపులచ్ఛమ్ములగుకాముడి కుచ్ఛమ్ములసంతరింప." Swa. v. 83. టీ॥ వీచుచీచోపులు, చేయూముండే వింజామరలు. **వీవ** or **వీవంగ** *viva.* (Root in infinitive of వీచే to wave, to fan.) While they waved, విసరగా.

వీజనము *vijanamu.* [Skt.] n. A fan. విసరుకర్ర. "నవరత్నమయమగువీజనవ్రజంబు." Bhanu. Pari. iv. 119.

వీటపటము, వీటతాటము or **విటతాటము** *viṭa-taṭamu.* [Tel.] adv. Piecemeal. ఛిన్నాభిన్నము. "సూకులరెకటార్చి కేతనంబుల విటతాటముల్ చేసిరథ్యములంగూల్చి." M. VIII. i. 148.

వీటి *viṭi.* [Tel.] n. Plunder, booty, కొల్ల. దోపుడు. **వీటిబోవు** *viṭi-bōvu.* v. n. To become blameworthy. దూషితమగు, నిందితమగు. To be lost, నష్టమగు. To become useless, vain or unprofitable, వ్యర్థమగు. **వీటిబుచ్చు** *viṭi-butstsu.* v. a. To lose, ruin, abandon, baffle, disappoint. కోలుపుచ్చు, పోగొట్టు, విడిచిపెట్టు, వ్యర్థముచేయు. "పొరుగిండ్లకు బోవి చ్చుట, [illegible] జిరకాలముండనిచ్చుట బురుషుడు తినసతినివీటి బుచ్చుటకుమతీ." Sumati. 25. "కుత్సితమతిమి కూడుకనమకూడిననరాజ్యము వీటిబుచ్చ గావచ్చినజాళకమి." P. iii. 139. **వీటివాండ్రు** *viṭi-vāndru.* n. Acrobats, rope-dancers దొమ్మరవాండ్రలో భేదము. వీటిది a female rope-dancer, దొమ్మరిది. "వీటిజానివిబొందు విడువజాలక [illegible]." Vema 1693.

వీటి or **వీని** *viṭi.* [Tel.] The plural inflec. of ఇవి these.

వీటి or **వీటిక** *viṭi.* [Skt.] n. The betel leaf and nut. తాంబూలము. వీటీకరండము *a paun-daun*, or tray.

వీడియము, వీడెము, వీడ్యము, విడియము. విడెము or **విడ్యము** *viḍiyamu.* [from వీటిక.] n. Betel leaf with areca nut, &c. తాంబూలము. "[illegible]." A. ii. 69.

వీడు *viḍu.* [Tel. cf. Tam. ఇవన్.] pron. This man. ఈ మనుష్యుడు. Plu. వీరు; infl. వీని.

వీడు *viḍu.* [Tel.] n. A city, పట్టణము. A remuneration, a complimentary present. పారితోషికము, కట్నము. An army, దండు. A military camp, శిబిరము. A crowd of travellers, పథికుల సమూహము. A camp or troop of rope-dancers. దొమ్మరవాండ్రతండా. "యదువిదర్భాన్వవాయ విధేయబంధువర్గముల్వీడు చదివించిరుచితవృత్తి." Chandra Bhanu Charitra. v. 152. "ఉపకారికినుపకారము విపరీతముకాదుకుమ్మవీడుకుబడే, యుపకారికినుపకారము నెపమెన్నకచేయువాడు." Sumati. 19. "చారుడొకడరుదెంచిజోహారుచేసి, కేటిప్రాద్దునదొమ్మరవీటితో జకాశితాపురికరుగ నంగాంచివాడు." Chenna Basa. Pur. ii. 349. **వీడుపట్టు** or **వీడిపట్టు** *viḍu-paṭṭu.* n. A camp, శిబిరము, దండుదిగినచోటు. An abode, వాసస్థానము. A temporary abode, విడిది. "వనివాకిపందరింబరిగ నుచితింపు పలుకులనొడబడ

బరచివిడ్కొల్పి, విడుపట్టుకపోయి విశ్రాంతుడై నుచు." Pal. 45. "అమ్మకీనదనాదిగలుభవపడి విడుపట్టునకరిగిన." M. XII. ii. 374.

వీడు *vīḍu*. [Tel.] v. n. To be separated, loosened or unfastened, విడిపోవు, విడిచిపెట్టు, వదలు. To become plain or evident, విశదమగు. To be fulfilled, కొనసాగు. To increase, prosper, వర్ధిల్లు. v. a. To cause to be separated, విడజేయు. "జనకసుతుం గొల్చి గొలువడంగ వెలదికి మైదీగ విడదాడగ." BX. **వీడజేయు** *vīḍa-jēyu*. v. a. To do away, to cause to be separated, నివృత్తిజేయు. **వీడదీయు** *vīḍa-dīyu*. v. a. To take off, to separate. తొలిగజేయు. విడదీయు. **వీడదొక్కు** *vīḍa-dokku*. v. a. To apportion, assign. పాలుపంచు. **వీడుకొను** or **వీడ్కొను** *vīḍu-konu*. v. a. To quit, leave, abandon. To take leave or permission, విడుచు. విడిచిపెట్టు, వదలు, పోయివచ్చెదనని చెప్పికొని వదలు, సెలవుపుచ్చుకొను. "పాండుపుత్రులదీవించి పునర్దర్శన మర్యాదమాచు వీడ్కొనినిజనివాసంబులకుంజనిరి." M. IV. i. 54. "ఆరగాముగనిచ్చి సుఖముండుడనుచు దత్తుడబ్జుడువీడ్కొని భార్యతోనరిగెనప్పుడు." T. iv. 195 **వీడుకొలుపు** or **వీడ్కొలుపు** *vīḍu-kolupu*. v. a. To send away, dismiss, పంపించు, సాగనంపు. "బ్రాహ్మణశ్రేష్ఠంబులేక బ్రతుకుండని వీడ్కొలిపినంతోయి." P. iii. 254. **వీడుకోలు** or **వీడ్కోలు** *vīḍu-kōlu*. n. Permission to go. పోవననుజ్ఞ. The act of leaving or quitting, విడుపు. Permission, leave. అనుజ్ఞ, సెలవు. Death, చావు. **వీడుచు** *vīḍuču*. v. a. To cause to be separated, విడజేయు. To let go, give up, విడిచిపెట్టు. **వీడుజోడాడు** *vīḍu-dzōḍ-āḍu*. v. n. To undergo a change, to be changed, మారుపాటుకొందు. To resemble, సరిపోలు. **వీడుజోడు** Same as విజ్జోడు. (q. v.) **వీడుపడు. వీడ్వడు. వీడువడు** or **వీడ్వడు** *vīḍu-paḍu*. v. n. To be changed, మారుపడు. To differ, భేదపడు. To totter, as feet, తడబడు. **వీడుపాటు** or **వీడ్పాటు** *vīḍu-pāṭu*. n. Change, మారుపాటు. Difference, వ్యత్యాసము. A decision, settlement. ఏర్పాటు. "కల్లయనిజముల వీడ్పాటొందగా." KP. iii. 269.

వీడెము Same as విడియము. (q. v.)

వీణ *vīṇa*. [Skt.] n. A kind of musical instrument resembling a lute. **వీణావాదుడు** *vīṇa-vāduḍu*. n. One who plays on the lute. వీణవాయించువాడు.

వీణము or **వీణాము** *vīṇamu*. [Tel.] n. A thin or fine cloth. సన్నవస్త్రము.

వీణియ. వీణె. వీనియ or **వీనె** *vīṇiya*. [Tel.] n. The follicle or bag in which musk is produced, a pod of musk. Also, same as వీణ. కస్తూరిదుండే కస్తురిమృగముయొక్క బొడ్డుకాయ. ముఖవీణ a Jew's harp, మారుచెంబు. రుద్రవీణ a sort of lute. A. iv. 38.

వీతము *vītamu* [Skt.] adj. Gone, past; devoid of; tranquil, quiet. గతమైన, పోయిన, శాంతమైన. వీతనిద్రుడై ceasing from sleep. **వీతరాగుడు** *vīta-rāguḍu*. n. A prudent or moderate man, one who has subdued his passions, or curbed his desires. రజోగుణహీనుడు, జితేంద్రియుడు.

వీతి *vīti*. [Skt.] n. A horse. అశ్వము. Jaimini. vi. 112.

వీతిహోత్రుడు *vīti-hōtruḍu*. [Skt.] n. An epithet of the god of fire. అగ్నిహోత్రుడు.

వీతెంచు *vī-tentsu*. [Tel. వీచు+తెంచు.] v. n. To come, or blow, as the wind. గాలి మొదలైనవివచ్చు, విసరు, వీచు. "అద్రికన్యకనొక్క యపూర్వదురాప ఘోషంబు వీతెంచె నాకర్ణించి" P. i. 185.

వీథి *vīdhi*. [Skt.] n. A street; a road, path, way. గృహపంక్తి, మార్గము. A row, line. వ్యవహారములపంక్తి. కేశవీథి the line or division of the hair, the parting over the forehead, పాపట, సీమంతము. వీథిపాటకము a kind of comedy, a farce. (Note: In some compounds this word is often left untranslated.) మానసవీథి or మనోవీథి the heart. గగనవీథి the sky. వనవీథి the forest. వీధి vidi [from Skt. విధి.] Same as విధి.

వీని vini. [Tel.] The genitive of వీడు this man, or of ఇవి these things. వీనియొక్క. వీనిని acc. of or వీడు or ఇవి. "వీనిప్రవృత్తి ప్రవృత్తిమైగొనిచను." M. XIV. iii. 96.

వీనియ or వీనె See under వీణియ.

వీను vinu. [Tel.] n. The ear. చెవి. Fame, ప్రసిద్ధి. వీనుమిగులు vinu-migulu. v. n. To become famous, ప్రసిద్ధికెక్కు. వీనులకంటి vinula-kanti. n. Lit: One that bears with its eyes, i. e., a snake. పాము, చక్షుశ్శ్రవము.

వీపు vipu. [Tel.] n. The back. పృష్ఠము, చరమాంగము, వెనుకమేను. వీపుచూపు to show one's back, to flee, పారిపోవు.

వీప్స vipsa. [Skt.] n. Reiteration, repetition, ద్విరుక్తి. ఇచ్చియిచ్చి, తినితిని, చెట్టుచెట్టు అనుట. వీప్సగా reiteratedly, frequently. పౌనఃపున్యేన, మళ్లీమళ్లీ.

వీయము Same as వియ్యము. (q. v.)

వీర vira. [Skt.] n. A woman who has a husband and sons. Also, same as వీరము. (q. v.)

వీరణము or వీరాణము viranamu. [Tel.] A double drum, used at weddings, అర్ధపటహము. "వీరణములులేనిపెండ్లివృథరా." Sumati. 65.

వీరము viramu. [Skt. cf. Lat. vir.] adj. Heroic, brave, exalted. శూరమైన, శౌర్యముగల, ఉత్తమమైన. వీరస్వర్గము the Olympus or Elysium of heroes. వీరగోష్ఠి the company of heroes, "వీరకేదారింపుపాన." (Vasu. pref.) అనగా రణరంగోచితమైన శిరస్త్రము. వీరక్షామము a severe famine. వీరపాతివ్రత్యము stern chastity, rigid purity. వీరకత్తియ or వీరకత్తె Same as వియ్యంకురాలు (q. v.) వీరకాడు Same as వియ్యంకుడు. (q. v.) వీరజయంతిక vira-jayantika. n. A war dance. యుద్ధమందలి వీరులనృత్యము. వీరత్వము vira-tvamu. n. Heroism, courage, valor, శూరత్వము. వీరతాయెతు vira-tayetu. n. A charm worn by warriors. వీరపత్ని vira-patni. n. A hero's wife. వీరపానము vira-panamu. n. A drink taken at the beginning or end of a battle. వీరభద్రపళ్లెరము vira-bhadra-pallerumu. n. A very large tray. వీరమద్దెలు. వీరమద్దియలు. వీరముద్దియలు. వీరముద్దెలు. వీరమధ్యమములు or వీరముత్రికెలు vira-maddelu. n. plu. Rings worn on the middle toe. వీరులు పాదమధ్యాంగుళియందుంచే ముద్రికలు. వీరముష్టి vira-mushti. n. An extremely orthodox or very bigoted Saivite, a Jangam beggar, one who goes about begging alms from the Vaisyas with sword and shield. వీరరుద్రవేషము వేసికొని కోమట్లను యాచించు ఒకభిక్షుకుడు. వీరవైష్ణవుడు vira-vaishnavudu. n. An extremely bigoted or orthodox Vaishnavaite, వైష్ణవులలో నిండాపట్టుగలిగియుండేవాడు. వీరశైవము vira-saivamu. n. Ultra-orthodox Sivaism. శివమతములో నిండాకరుకుగానుండుట. వీరశైవుడు vira-saivudu. n. A very orthodox or bigoted Saivite. వీరసువు vir-asuvu. n. The mother of a hero, వీరునికన్నతల్లి. వీరావేశము vir-avesamu. n. Zeal, bravery, madness, fury, శౌర్యము, తెగ్గి. వీరాసనము vira-sanamu. n. Keeping a careful sentry at night. వీరుడు virudu. [Skt. cognate with 'hero.'] n. A hero, warrior, or champion, శూరుడు. An excellent man. శ్రేష్ఠుడు. వీర్యము viryamu. n. Heroism, valour, courage, bravery, శౌర్యము. పరాక్రమము. Semen virile. రేతస్సు.

వీరిడి Same as వేడి. (q. v.)

వీరు viru. [Tel.] pron. These persons. వీండ్రు. వీరికి to these persons. "వారికి వీరికిని దొడ్డవాదయ్యె." BX. viii. 34. వీరువారనక అందరిని తిట్టినాడు he abused them all without distinction.

విరుత్ *virut.* [Skt.] n. A creeper, a tendril. లత, తీగె. విరూఢము *virudhamu.* n. An arbor of vine creepers. A sprouting branch. చిగురుకొమ్మ.

విరూపు, వీర్యము See under వీరము.

విలు *vilu.* [Tel.] v. n. To be of use, ఉపయోగించు. adj. Convenient, practicable, అనుకూలము. n. An expedient, convenience; success, facility, practicability, possibility, వాటము. పొసగుపాటు, అనుకూలము. వీలుచేయు *vilu-chēyu.* v. a. To make convenient. To raise money from ryots in proportion to their kists. వీలుగా *vilu-ga.* adv. Expediently, conveniently, అనుకూలముగా, ఉసులుగా, వాటముగా. "వీలుగానికివేసిపూలదండలుచుట్టి." Jagannadha. ii. 21. వీలుపడు or వీల్పడు *vilu-padu.* v. n. To be convenient, to be practicable, అనుకూలపడు, సరిపడు. వీలుపరచు or వీల్పరచు *vilu-paratsu.* v. a. To bring about, manage. అనుకూలపరచు. వీలుజాబితా *vilu-dzabita.* [H.] n. An account according to the estimate.

వీలు or వ్రీలు *vilu.* [Tel.] v. n. To split, burst asunder, as a ripe fruit. విచ్చు. పగులు. చీలు. "వాకుంచెకూలదువీలదుతునియదైపోదు." HD. ii. 277. "అడుగునబండివీలియసరై మధుపుపుట్టగ్రానతేంట్లుముల్లడిగొనిచుట్టిరా." A. i. 21. "వెలువడిరార్చులవిశలంబులగేయుచుగా." BRY. ii. 77.

వీవన or వీవెన *vivana.* [Tel. from వీచు.] n. A fan. తాలవృంతము. విసనకర్ర. A whisk, కురుచ. వీవలి *vivali.* (from వీచు, formed like కావలి.) n. Wind, గాలి.

వీసము *visamu.* [Tel.] n. The fraction called one sixteenth, the sixteenth part of anything. A grain of gold equal in weight to one grain of rice. వడ్లగింజయెత్తుబంగారము. వీసబడి or వీసుబడి *visa-badi.* (వీసము+బడి.) n. Cess or tax, levied on a town and then divided among several persons each of whom pays his share, a certain tax on the profits of a trade. గ్రామమునందు భాగప్రకారముగనిర్ణయించిన భూసాస్తి అంత్రిక్షము. A ryotwari settlement. A measure of land equal nearly to two acres.

వీసర or వీసరము *visara.* (వీసము+అర.) n. Want, defect, deficiency, diminution. కొరత. వెలితి. వీసరపడు or వీసరపోవు *visara-padu.* v. n. To be lacking, or deficient, వెలితిపడు. To fail, be fruitless. వ్యర్థమగు. కించిత్పుణ్యమగు. "కనికానకచేసినవుణ్యపాపముల్ వీసరపోవు." Dasarathi Satakam.

వీసె or వీసెయు *vise.* [Tel.] n. A weight equivalent to 120 tolas, or ⅛ of a maund.

వు VU

వు *vu.* [Tel.] Affix. A termination added to some nouns and verbs, as ధేనువు, వచ్చెదవు.

వృ VṚI

వృంతము *vrintamu.* [Skt.] n. The foot, stalk or pedicle of a leaf or flower, తొడిమ.

వృకము *vrikamu.* [Skt.] n. A wolf. తోడేలు. వృకోదరుడు *vrik-ōdarudu.* n. Wolf-bellied, voracious as a wolf: an epithet of Bhima. భీముడు.

వృక్షము *vrikshamu.* [Skt.] A tree, చెట్టు. ఇది తమరు పెట్టినవృక్షము this is the tree set by your own hand, i. e., I am a protegé of yours, it is your part to do me good. వృక్షవాటిక *vriksha-vatika.* n. A grove or garden. ఇంటిలోనితోట. వృక్షాదనము *vriksh-adanamu.* n. A chisel; an adze, hatchet, chopper. ఉలి, గొడ్డలి. The Indian Fig tree. రావిచెట్టు.

వృజినము *vrijinamu.* [Skt.] n. Sin. పాపము.

వృతము *vritamu.* [Skt.] adj. Covered, screened. ఆవరింపబడిన. వృతి *vriti.* n. A hedge, a fence. కంచె. A. v. 146.

వృత్తము *vrittamu.* adj. Round, circular, globular, full orbed. గుండ్రని, వట్రువైన. n. Practice, custom. నడవడి, నడత. A circle, మండలము. A kind of metre or verse. పద్యభేదము. **వృత్తాంతము** *vrittantamu.* n. Intelligence, news, tidings, a story, narrative. Detail, particulars. వివరణము, వార్త, జనరవము, సమాచారము, ప్రస్తావము. **వృత్తి** *vritti.* n. Being, existence. Livelihood, means of subsistence, profession, conduct. జీవనోపాయము, జీవనము, వర్తనము, కాయకము, కులకాయకము, నడవడిక. A share in a village, granted to a Brahmin in free gift. శ్రోత్రియములో సొంకపాలు. A certain style of composition, అభిధ, లక్షణ, వ్యంజన, లేక, కైశికి, ఆరభటి, సాత్వతి and భారతి. **వృత్తిదారుడు** *vritti-darudu.* n. A proprietor of small grants of land, made free of rent or at a light rent, to Brahmins only.

వృత్రహుడు *vritrahudu.* [Skt.] n. A name of Indra. ఇంద్రుడు.

వృత్రుడు *vritrudu* [Skt.] n. An enemy. The name of an Asura.

వృథా or **వృథ** *vritha.* [Skt.] adj. Vain, empty, fruitless. adv. In vain, uselessly, వ్యర్థముగా.

వృద్ధ *vriddha.* [Skt. from వృధ్ to increase, to grow.] adj. Increased, extended, improved. Old. వృద్ధకావేరి the main stream of the Kaveri. వృద్ధగోదావరి the main stream of the Godavari. **వృద్ధత్వము** *vriddhatvamu.* n. Old age. వార్ధక్యము. **వృద్ధశ్రవుడు** *vriddha-sravudu.* n. An epithet of Indra. ఇంద్రుడు. **వృద్ధాప్యము** *vriddhapyamu.* Old age. ముసలితనము. **వృద్ధి** *vriddhi.* n. Increase, augmentation, extension, పెరుగుట. అభివృద్ధి. Plenty, abundance, prosperity. సమృద్ధి. Interest on money, వడ్డి. Multiplication, గుణకారము. In Sanskrit grammar, the temporal augment. చక్రవృద్ధి. compound interest. హానివృద్ధులు increase and decrease. దానిహానివృద్ధులకు నేను ఉన్నాను I am answerable for all loss and gain, for all good or ill that happens. **వృద్ధు** or **వృద్ధుడు** *vriddhu.* n. An old man. ముసలివాడు. **వృద్ధురాలు** or **వృద్ధ** *vriddhur-alu.* n. An old woman, వృద్ధస్త్రీ. **వృద్ధ్యాజీవుడు** *vriddhya-jivudu.* n. One who lives by lending money at interest.

వృశ్చికము *vrischikamu.* [Skt.] n. A scorpion. తేలు. The Sign Scorpio of the zodiac.

వృషణము *vrishanamu.* [Skt.] n. A testicle, అండము, వట్ట.

వృషభము *vrishabhamu.* [Skt.] n. A bull. ఆబోతు. The sign Taurus, వృషభరాశి. adj. In compounds, excellent, best of its kind, pre-eminent. ఋషివృషభము a noble saint, an exalted sage. కవివృషభుడు a noble poet. **వృషము** *vrishamu.* A bull, an ox, ఎద్దు. **వృషుడు** *vrishudu.* n. An epithet of Indra. ఇంద్రుడు. **వృషధ్వజుడు** or **వృషభాంకుడు** *vrisha-dhvajudu.* n. A name of Siva. శివుడు.

వృషలుడు *vrishaludu.* [Skt.] n. A Sudra. శూద్రుడు. A wretch, పాపాత్ముడు. **వృషలి** *vrishali.* n. A female Sudra; a wretched woman, a barren woman, a woman who gives birth to still-born children. శూద్రస్త్రీ, పెండ్లికాకమునుపు రజస్వల అయినపడుచు, గొడ్రాలు, మృతప్రసూతి, చచ్చుబిడ్డలుకనెడిది.

వృష్టి *vrishti.* [Skt.] n. Rain. వర్షము, వాన.

వృష్ణి *vrishni.* [Skt.] n. One of the descendants of Yadu. ఒక యాదవుడు. Krishna, కృష్ణుడు. Indra, ఇంద్రుడు.

వె ve

వెంగడము *vengadamu.* [Tel.] adj. Reverse, contrary, opposite. విపరీతమైన, విరుద్ధమైన.

" వంగివమునవడి యుబ్బాడు వెంగిడమైతూతురిచ్చి వింటజూడనకుణా." Vij. VII. ii. 8.

వెంగలి, వెంగళి or **వెకలి** *vengali*. [from Skt. వికల.] n. An ignorant man, మూఢుడు. A stupid man, జడుడు. A mad man, fool, idiot. వెర్రివాడు. అవివేకి. " పొంగిచిమ్మురు కింకబోవు బోతికొంగుసవరించు వెన్వెంగళియట్లు." BD. iii. 2285. **వెంగలితనము** *vengali-tanamu*. n. Folly, madness, వెర్రితనము. **వెంగలివిత్తు** *vengali-vittu*. n. A very stupid person, మూఢాగ్రేసరుడు.

వెంచె *ventsa*. [Tel.] n. A lake or pool. మడుగు. " పొంతిగోంతిరెమ్మవిప్పల రేగడవెంచలో వలకా." G. x. 37.

వెంట *venta*. [Tel. from వెను.] n. Business, కార్యము. An affair, విషయము. A way, మార్గము. Manner, విధము. Hunting, the chase, వేట. adv. and postposition. With, along with, in company with, behind, following after, వెంబడి. ఏ వెంట in what manner or way? ఏరీతిగా. నా వెంటవచ్చినాడు he came along with me. వీధివెంటపరుగెత్తినాడు he ran along the street. ప్రవాహము వెంట కొట్టుకొనివచ్చినమానులు the trees that came down the river. వానినోటివెంట వచ్చినమాటలు the words that slipped out of his mouth. వానిముక్కువెంట నెత్తురుకారుచున్నది he is bleeding at the nose. " కాలువవెంటబూచు మల్లికలవనంబనగ." Swa. ii. 24. **వెంటనంటు** or **వెంటబడు** *venta-n-antu*. v. a. To follow, pursue. వెంబడించు. **వెంటనే** *ventan-ē*. adv. and postposition. Immediately, at once, వెంబడిగానే. వారు వచ్చినవెంటనే as soon as they arrived. **వెంటబెట్టుకొను** *ventu-bettu-konu*. v. n. To take along with.

వెంటము *ventamu*. [Tel.] n. Pleasure, joy, వేడుక, కుతూహలము.

వెంటి *venti*. [Tel.] n. A straw rope. మెలి బెట్టినకసవుదారము, కసవుపేని. **వెంటిగొను** *venti-gonu*. v. n. To be twisted, పెనగొను

వెంటిక *ventika*. [Tel. for వెంట్రుక.] n. A hair. **వెంట్రుక** or **వెండ్రుక** *ventruka*. n. A hair. కేశము.

వెంట్రువ *ventruva*. [Tel.] n. A kind of mongoose. *Viverra ichneumon*, ముంగిసభేదము.

వెండి *vendi*. [Tel.] n. Silver. రజతము. **వెండికొండ** or **వెండిగుండు** *vendi-konda*. n. The silver mountain; a name for Kailasa. రజతాద్రి.

వెండి or **వెండియు** adv. Besides, and, further, మరియు. Again, once more, తిరిగి, మరల. Then, after, పిమ్మట.

వెండ్రుక See under వెంటిక. (q. v.)

వెంపర *vempara*. [Tel.] n. Plague, trouble, annoyance, పీడనము. Killing, హింస. **వెంపరలాడు** *vempara-l-āḍu*. v. a. To destroy, kill, హింసించు, చంపు. To harass, annoy, పీడించు. "అంపరవరంపరల వెంపరలాడక తిరు గను." T. v. 33. "చంపిన వారికి చావు సత్యంబు వెంపరలాడెకి విడువదు యముడు." L. xx. 264. "సీ॥ చెవిదాల్చివిని చీమచిటుకన్న కొకపారసెలవి వెంపరలాడుకెట్టురెల్ల." Swa. iv. 16.

వెంపలి *vempali*. [Tel.] n. The Purple Galega, *Tephrosia purpurea*. A small wild shrub with a pink flower and a leaf resembling that of the Indigo plant. శరపుంఖ. మణి కాచము. It has several species called ముల్లువెంపలి the thorny sort, జిగురువెంపలి the gummy kind, తెల్లవెంపలి the whitish and పెద్దవెంపలి the giant species.

వెంబడి *vem-badi*. [Tel. వెను+బడి.] n. The back part or side. వెంట. **వెంబడి, వెంబడిని** or **వెంబడిగా** adv. and postposition. Behind, after, following, with, along with, through. వెంట, కూడ, గుండా. నా వెంబడి వచ్చినాడు he came with me. ఊళ్లవెంబడి తిరుగుచున్నారు they roam from village to village. వాని నోటివెంబడ వచ్చినమాటలు

the words that dropped from his lips. నాచేనువెంబడిచేను the land bordering on my field. దానివెంబడిపద్యము the next verse, the following verse. ఆయన పోయిన వెంబడినే immediately after he went. "వివరమేర్పరచి యీగా వెంబడి పదములగడచి, నల్వంకలతడవి చూచి." R. iii. 212. "వీర్ల వెంబడి తిరుగుట గొన్నాళ్లు." T. ii. 168. వారి కోరిక వెంబడిని in conformity with their wish. "పోరువెంబడిని పౌర్వ్యములంజరించు." Ila. ii. 15. వెంబడించు *vembad-intsu*. v. a. To follow, accompany. To pursue, hunt, వెంటబడు.

వెంబర or **వెంబరి** *vembara*. [Tel.] n. A fool, అవివేకి. A wicked person, దుష్టుడు, దుష్టురాలు. A mad man, వెర్రివాడు. "ద్వి॥ అమ్మ తెంబుకక్కల కంటిచ్చిపులిసి, నంబల్పిత్రాసము నా కించినట్టి, వెంబరిగాని వివేకిగాదెందు." L. xiii. 458. **వెంబరివిత్తు** *vembari-vittu*. n. A fool, a mad man. వెర్రివాడు, వెర్రిది. A very wicked man, దుష్టాగ్రేసరుడు. A very stupid man, మూఢాగ్రేసరుడు.

వెకలి or **వెక్కలి** *vekali*. [from Skt. వికలు.] n. A foolish woman or man, వెర్రిది, వెర్రివాడు, మూఢుడు. An eager man, ఆసక్తుడు. "ఒకవేళకూనరాగములతోక వేళా వెకలి నవ్వు." Satyabhama iii. 126.

వెక్క *vekka*. [Tel.] n. Heat, వేడిమి.

వెక్కసము *vekkasamu*. [Tel.] n. Excess, an extreme. మిక్కుటము. Satiety, glut, fullness, gorge, plethora. Nausea, loathing, repugnance, disgust, dislike, చీదర, అసహ్యము, దుస్సహత్వము. **వెక్కసములు** *vekkasamulu*. n. plu. Disgusting words. దుస్సహవచనములు. "చలొరికదంబంబుల పుక్కిళ్లకు వెక్కసంబై ముక్కులకు నెక్కి చిక్కంబడి." Swa. iii. 37. adj. Excessive, extreme. అధికము. Loathesome, disgusting, దుస్సహము. Hard to get, దుర్లభము. **వెక్కసపడు** or **వెక్కసమందు** *vekkasa-padu*. v. a. To abhor, to loathe, చీదరపడు, అసహ్యపడు. "వెక్కసమందుచుకురుపతి, రక్కసుతో ననియె." M. VI. iii. 99. **వెక్కసపాటు** *vakkasa-patu*. n. The act of being disgusted, loathing. **వెక్కసించు** or **వెక్కసమగు** *vekka-sintsu*. v. n. To be glutted, or gorged. To exceed, మిక్కుటమగు. "కన్నులకు వెక్కసంబైన చెన్ను మిగిలి." Ellana. ii. 114. To become loathesome, disgusting or unbearable, దుస్సహమగు. **వెక్కసములాడు** *vekkasamu-l-adu*. v. a. To scold, to abuse, తిట్టు. "అందరిమీదబడి వెక్కసములాడి ప్రపంచించి యుల్లంఘించిన." Sar. D. 386. **వెక్కసి** *vekkasi*. n. A loathsome, disgusting or unbearable person, దుస్సహుడు, దుస్సహురాలు.

వెక్కిరించు *vekkir-intsu*. [from Skt. వికారము.] v.n. & a. To jeer, scoff at, ridicule, mimic, అపహసించు, వికారచేష్టలుచేయు. **వెక్కిరింత** or **వెక్కిరింపు** *vekkirinta*. n. Mimicry, jeering, ridicule. అపహాస్యము.

వెక్కిలి or **ఎక్కిలి** *vekkili*. [Skt. from హిక్క. cf. Eng 'Hiccough.'] n. Hiccough, retching, హిక్క. plu. వెక్కిళ్లు.

వెక్కివెక్కియేడ్చు *vekki-vekki-y-edtsu*. [Tel.] v. n. To sob in crying. ఎగఊపిరి విడుచుచు ఏడ్చు.

వెక్కు *vekku*. [from Skt. హిక్క.] v. n. To hiccup. వెక్కివిడుచు. To sob in crying n. Hiccup, వెక్కిలి.

వెక్కుడుతీగె *vekkudu-tige*. [Tel.] n. The vegetable called Heartpea. *Halicacabum cardiospermum.* జ్యోతిష్మతి, జ్యోతిష్మతి.

వెక్కురు *vekkuru*. [from Skt. వికారము.] adj. Ugly, odd, queer. వికారమైన. "వెక్కురుతాపసులకు." HD. i. 1382. n. An ugly person, వికారముపట్టినవాడు. "క॥ చొక్కపు రక్కసికులమున, వెక్కురుజన్మించినాడు." భాగ. vii.

వెగచు *vegatsu*. [Tel.] v. n. To sob in crying, వెక్కు.

వెగటు *vegaṭu*. [from Skt. వికటుః] n. Harshness, or acerbity of taste. Abhorrence, loathing, dislike, repugnance, అనిష్టము, అసహ్యము, చీదర. "వేమభోగములమీద వెగటు బడగ." S. iii. 17. "వికటభోగముల వెగటుగాక." P. iii. 56. "సిగ్గువెగటుము బోడమ నిప్పు పాతి దలంప." Swa. ii. 71. adj. Harsh, bitter, disgusting, విరసము. వెగటించు *vegaṭ-intsu*. v. n. To be distasteful, అసహ్యమగు.

వెగడు *vegaḍu*. [Tel.] n. Torpidity, amazement, astonishment, confusion of mind. నిశ్చేష్టత, కల్లడము, తడబాటు. వెగడుపడు *vegaḍu-paḍu*. v. n. To be confused, to be troubled, కల్లడపడు. "బహిర్నిర్గమంబు బోవరించి వెగడుపడియున్న మృగమును రడించి." B. ii. 179.

వెగ్గలము *veggalamu*. [Tel.] n. Excess, much, మిక్కుటము, అధికము. "అట విందగోష్ఠికి వెగ్గలమాడు బేంట్లు." A. v. 129. "బాగాలు వెసనొక్క పద్మాక్షి యొసగిన వెగ్గలంబని కొన్ని వెడలుమిసి." Swa. iii. 87. వెగ్గలము, వెగ్గలపు, వెగ్గలంపు or వెగ్గలమైన *veggalamu*. adj. Excessive, extreme, too much, మిక్కుటమైన, మించిన, అధికమైన. వెగ్గలపుందాపముమాన్పవా." A. i. 11. "కమల లోచనకు వెగ్గలపుభాగ్యంబు." DB. page 167. వెగ్గలీడు *vegal-iḍu*. n. A great man, అధికుడు.

వెచ్చించు See under వెచ్చము.

వెచ్చ *vetstsa*. [Tel. from వేడి.] n. Heat, warmth, వేడిమి. Fever, జ్వరము, కాక. "వీరి పాథరంబునకా బోడము వెచ్చకు కాంతి తొలునర్పు." A. ii. 60. adj. Hot, warm, వేడియైన. "దేవునకు నువెచ్చనిట్టూర్పుపుక్కిట వెడలకున్న." R. vi. 112. వెచ్చదనము or వెచ్చన *vetstsa-danamu*. n. Warmth, heat. వేడిమి. వెచ్చన or వెచ్చని *vetstsana*. adj. Warm, hot. వేడియైన. వెచ్చనూర్చు *vetstsan-ūrtsu*. v. n. To sigh warmly or deeply, వేడియూపిరి విడుచు. Bobbili. ii. 112. వెచ్చచేయు or వెచ్చబెట్టు *vetstsa-chēyu*. v. a. To warm, to heat a little. రవంత వేడచేయు. వెచ్చలు *vetstsalu*. n. The hot season, గ్రీష్మదివసములు. "వెచ్చలంకరకర కాపరాంగములగి ప్పినరోంపులు." A. ii. 56. టీ. వెచ్చలన్, గ్రీష్మదివసములయందు. వెచ్చు *vetstsu*. v. n. To boil, to be heated, కాగు. n. Heat, వేడిమి.

వెచ్చము *vetstsamu*. [from Skt. విసర్జనం.] n. Expenditure, expense. వ్యయము. Purchasing petty articles for household use on credit. ఇంటికి వాడుకొనుటకు కావలసిన చిల్లరవస్తువుల అప్పు. "సరసుడనైతే అంగడి వెచ్చములాడకు వెంగలితో జెలిమివలవదు వినరా." Sumati. 105. అసువెచ్చము the tax on every "shuttle. "పిసినివానియింట పీనుగు వెడలిన కట్టెకోలలకు నుకాసులిచ్చి వెచ్చమాయెననుచు వెక్కివెక్కి యేడ్చురా." Vēma. i.34. వెచ్చగాడు *vetsa-kaḍu*. n. A spendthrift. మిక్కిలికర్చు చేయువాడు. A gallant or paramour, విటుడు. వెచ్చపెట్టు or వెచ్చించు *vetstsa-peṭṭu*. v. a. To spend, to lay out. వ్యయముచేయు. "కట్టకకుడునకు పరులకు బెట్టక తమతండ్రి గూడ పెట్టినసిరి దాగట్ట యుగుడిచియునోరులకు బెట్టియుదనయిచ్చ వెచ్చపెట్టదలంచెగా." Zacca. ii. "దాతనసుచు సకలధనము పాత్రులకును వెచ్చపెట్టుటదియె వ్రతము." Kuchelo. iii. 140. వెచ్చపోవు, వెచ్చపడు or వెచ్చమగు *vetstsa-pōvu*. v. n. To be spent. వ్యయమగు.

వెజ్జు *vedzdzu*. [from Skt. వైద్యః.] n. A physician or doctor, వైద్యుడు. "నీ దేవిరు జమాన్పుటకు దొరవెజ్జులు." P. iv. 73. వెజ్జుతనము *vedzdzu-tanamu*. n. The work or profession of a physician or doctor. వైద్యధర్మము. "వెజ్జుతనమేలయనిమదిలజ్జవొడిమి." Swa. v. 13. వెజ్జురాలు *vedzdzu-r-ālu*. n. A female doctor, వైద్యురాలు.

వెచ్చు See under వెచ్చ.

వెట్ట *veṭṭa*. [Tel. from వేడి.] n. Warmth, heat, sunshine, heat of the body. వేడిమి, ఎండ. The hot season, ఎండకాలము. Enmity. విరోధము, పగ. "సరియగు నిట్టి వెట్టనివి సర్వమటంచటు

మీదసృష్టికిశా." A. ii. 56. "అట్టివేసవి వెడిదంపు వెట్టకతన." ib. ii. 77. "అనుకూలాట్టములప్పటున వెట్టగాకమ్మ పరువుల్లోపైకొక్కి వదలకమ్మ." P. iv. 408. Also, heat due to inflammation. adj. Hot. నిండాకాక గానుండే, వేడిమైన. "వెక్కసపై వ్రాలు వెట్టవేసవులనసల." P. i. 557. వెట్టకారు or వెట్టదినములు veṭṭa-kāru. n. The hot season. వేసవికాలము. "వెట్టదినముల మడుపు లమట్టికలబలుదబుద్ధ్వని వెడలు." Swa. iv. 17. వెట్టచెవులతపసి an epithet of శుక్రుశ్రవ. నీలా. ii.

వెట్టము veṭṭamu. [Tel.] n. An enemy, a foe, శత్రువు. "సీ॥ కలువలచుట్టంబు కలువలవెట్టంబు తనరెండుకన్నులైరెసరువాని." G. ii. 135.

వెట్టి or వెట్టిపని veṭṭi. [from Skt. విష్టి.] n. Drudgery, unpaid work. కూలిలేకచేయుపని. "రాజిరుంగని వెట్టికిక్రమమయ్యెవకట." L. xx. ii. 23. వెట్టిగొను or వెట్టిచేయించు veṭṭi-gonu. v. a To exact work without paying for it. వెట్టితనము veṭṭi-tanamu. n. Drudgery, unpaid labour, కూలిలేక పనిచేయుడము. "చనుడు వెట్టితనంబు చాలులెండనుచు." Bhag. 123. వెట్టివాడు veṭṭi-vāḍu. n. A serf, drudge, or hereditary public slave. The lowest village servant who performs menial offices (such as porter's work) in consideration of certain fees or privileges. వెట్టీడు veṭṭīḍu. n. One who has to work without pay. The same as వెట్టివాడు.

వెడ veḍa. [Tel.] adj. Trifling, petty, mean, base, అల్పము, తుచ్ఛము. Useless, fruitless, vain, కొరగాని, వ్యర్థమైన. Wrong, erroneous, wicked. Excessive, మిక్కుటమైన. Deformed, వికృతము. adv. Slightly, ఇంచుక. "అట్టిమహాత్మునొక్కనికి పాత్రుకుఁడై వెడ గూడుఁజీరయుం బెట్టగనిర్చి వాని మది ప్రీతినిబ్బైదగువృత్తి నేరుమం." M. IV. ii. 190. "వెడదోవమును జెప్పి, వడివవ్వ, వగలాగ్గవుకొలది." A. iv. 203. వెడదోవ= దుర్మార్గము. "వెడమాయనక్కమాటల." P. iv. 578. వెడవిలుతుడు, వెడవిల్తుడు, వెడవిలుకాడు or వెడవింటి veḍa-vilutuḍu. n. The god with the little bow, i. e., Manmadha. మన్మథుడు. వెడవెడ veḍa-veḍa. adj. Very small or petty, అత్యల్పము, సూక్ష్మము. adv. Gradually, slowly, tardily, gently: again and again, repeatedly, సూక్ష్మముగా, మందముగా, మెల్లమెల్లగా, తిన్నగా, మాటిమాటికి. "వానిమాటలకులోలో వెడవెడనగుచు." P. iv. 526. "నిదువెంద్రుకలగుంపులచి వైచికొ వెడవెడపడిముత్తి విధియుతముగ." A. v. 94. టీ. వెడవెడ, మెల్లమెల్లనే. "వెడవెడనిద్ర బొందికను విచ్చినపాంథులమీద." M. V. ii. 123. "కొం తసేపు వెడవెడజంతించి శిరసాకించియుత్తి సన్నంపు టెలుగుతో విట్టులనియె." Swa. iii. 132.

వెడగు or వెడంగు veḍagu. [Tel.] adj. Foolish. వెర్రి, పిచ్చి, అవివేకమైన. "వెడగుమందుల చేతవిమెట్లడంగు, చెడునొకోసిరాదినపాము కాటు." HD. ii. 213. n. Folly, madness. అవివేకము, వికారము. A fool or mad man. వెర్రివాడు. "చెప్పటయునొప్పకయుండు వెడంగులనుట కార్యవచనంబుల తెరంగెరుంగను." M. V. iii. 233. "వెడగు, భీష్మబుద్ధివిసకవెడిసెను." ib. VII. iv. 83. వెడగుపడు veḍagu-paḍu. v. n. To become foolish, అవివేకమునొందు. To become ugly, వికారమునొందు. వెడగుపాటు veḍagu-pāṭu n. The act of becoming foolish or ugly, వెడగుపడుట. వెడగురుపడు veḍaguru-paḍu. n. To be bewildered, దిగ్భ్రమనొందు, జడత్వమునొందు. "వెక్కసకవికి వెడగుపవక." Chartira. p. 251.

వెడద or వెడంద veḍada. [Tel.] adj. Wide, broad, extensive, large, big. వెడల్పైన, విశాలమైన, స్థూలమైన, లావాటి. "వెడదవైరి కనుపట్టు వీనియురము." Swa. ii. 39. "అన్ని వెడద వాతియమ్ము లద్భుతముగ." M. IV. v. 151. "వెడందవాతియమ్ములక్క." M. VII. iv. 257. "వెడద కన్నులు." Swa. vi. 114. "వెడదగం గాళముననుడుగుడిచిలేచి." P. iv. 485. వెడ

వెడదమోముమెకము veḍada-mōmu-meku-mu. n. The big-mouthed, i. e., a lion, సింహము. వెడదవాతియమ్ము a broad tipped arrow.

వెడలచెట్టు veḍala-cheṭṭu. [Tel.] n. A kind of plant, *Gaertnera racemosa.*

వెడలు veḍalu. [Tel.] v. n. To come out, go out, set out, start, బయలువెళ్లు. "వెడలుమని తేరు దూపిన." M. XII. v. 461. వెడలబడు or వెడలబారు same as వెడలు. వెడలబాటు veḍala-bāṭu. n. The act of going out. వెడలించు. వెడలుచు or వెడల్చు veḍa-lutsu. v. a. To take out, send, send away, despatch, వెడలజేయు, బైటికి వెళ్లదీయు, పంపు, సాగనంపు. "శిలమునాయుడు చేతానిమాలదేశంబు వెడలింపబడియున్నాడు." Pal. 92. "శేవేగమె వాలినవిని వెడలింపుమికన్." R. v. 299. "భుజగకేతను బలంబులతోడనిపుడు, మనపుర వెడలింపు మసలకుమింక." Dab. page. 232. వెడలుపు or వెడల్పు veḍalupu. n. Extent, breadth, width, వైశాల్యము, విశాలత. adj. Broad, extensive. విరివి.

వెడ్డు veḍḍu. [Tel.] n. Cunning, hypocrisy. కపటము. Deceit, వంచన. వెడ్డరి veḍḍ-ari. n. A cunning person, a hypocrite, కపటి, వంచకుడు. వెడ్డుపెట్టు veḍḍu-peṭṭu. v. n. To delude, beguile, cheat. మాయచేయు, వంచించు. "అనవుడుమున్నిట్టులనరతిరిపోవగ నీవుమిమ్మునెందును గడువెడ్డువెట్టితిరి." M. XII. v. 300.

వెణద Same as వెడద. (q. v.)

వెణుతురు Same as వెలుతురుచెట్టు. (q. v.)

వెత or వెతారము veta. [from Skt. వ్యథ.] n. Pain, grief, distress. మనోదుఃఖరూపమైన విచారము, బాధ, దుఃఖము. "నావెతతెరుగనింతేకదయుంచు." N. ix. 273. వెతలజిక్కు vetala-jikku. v. n. To pine with grief.

వెతకు, వెతుకు, వెదకు, వెదుకు, వెతుకులాడు వెదకులాడు or వెదుకులాడు vetaku. [Tel.] v. a. & n. To seek, search for, look for. అన్వేషించు.

వెద veda. [Tel.] n. Sowing of the seed, విత్తుట, విత్తులుచల్లడము. The rutting season, పశువుల ఋతువు, ఫలించుకాలము. వెదబడ్డది the seed is sown. "సీ. పాలతీవి సందోహములకు బలాకికావిసరంబులకు మంచివెదలుదోరెక." A. iv. 160. A woman's tresses, కొప్పు. వెదగొర్రు veda-gorru. n. A drill-plough. విత్తనము వేయుమాదుకర్రు లుగలనాగేలు. వెదచల్లు veda-tsallu. v. a. To scatter, to sow broadcast. పారవెల్లు. "వేడిమిదిక్కులవెదచల్లుకొనుచు." DRY. 1412. To cause to spread, వ్యాపింపజేయు. వెదచిందు veda-chindu. v. n. To spread, వ్యాపించు. వెదపెట్టు veda-peṭṭu. v. a. To scatter, sow, as seed, చల్లు, విత్తు. To impregnate. గర్భాధానము చేయు, బీజావాపముచేయు. వెదావు ved-āvu. n. A cow that is in heat, ఫలపడదానకు అయుక్తముగానుండే ఆవు, పొర్లుటకుకెగియున్న ఆవు.

వెదకు See వెతకు. వెదకుడు vedakuḍu. n. Searching, వెదకుట, అన్వేషణము.

వెదురు veduru. [Tel.] n. The bamboo. పోతువెదురు the male bamboo. పెంటివెదురు the female bamboo. కాకివెదురు a kind of reed. బొంగువెదురు bongu-veduru. n. The Sping Bamboo of Central, South, and West India, *Bambusa arundinacea.* (Watts.) వెదురుకంపజిట్ట veduru-kampa-jiṭṭa. n. The bird called the Grass Warbler, or Meadow Wren Warbler, *Cisticola cursitans.* వెదురుపిచ్చిక veduru-pichchika. n. The bird called the Rose Finch, *Loxia totta.* వెదురుప్పు, or వెదురుపాలు vedur-uppu. n. A medicinal salt exuded from the bamboo called Bamboo manna (Watts.) *Tabaschir.* (Ainslie.) వెదురుబియ్యము veduru-biyyamu. n. The bamboo seed, freed from the husk. వేణుతండులము. వెదురుమిడుత veduru-miḍuta. n. A sort of insect said to bore the bamboo. క్రిమివిశేషము. వెదురువిల్లు veduru-villu. n. A bow made of the bamboo.

వెధవ vedhava. [Tel.] n. Corruption of విధవ. (q. v.)

వెనక Same as వెనుక. (q. v.)

వెనకయ్య venak-ayya. [from Skt. వినాయక.] n. Vināyaka, another name of Gaṇēsa. విఘ్నేశ్వరుడు.

వెనకు Same as వెదకు. (q. v.) వెనకుడు Same as వెదకుడు (q. v.)

వెను Same as వెన్ను. (q. v.) వెనుక, వెనక or వెన్క venuka. [Tel. from వెను.] n. The back part or side, the rear, పశ్చాద్భాగము. The front, ముందు. The west, పడమర. Indifference, ఉపేక్ష. adj. Behind or before (in place, order or time.) పశ్చాద్భాగమునవున్న, ముందరవున్న. adv. and affix. Behind, after (in time or place.) Formerly, పశ్చాద్భాగమందు, తదనంతరము, లోగడ. Afterwards, పిమ్మట. దీనిని నావెనుక నాకొడుకులు అనుభవించవలసినది after me this is to be enjoyed by my sons. ముందువెనుకలువిచారించి మాట్లాడు speak with much caution; lit: looking forwards and backwards. వెనుక ముందుతోచకుండా not knowing which way to turn. వెనుకసారి on the latter occasion. ఆవెనుక (wrongly pronounced అనక) thereafter. వెనుకకు, వెనకకు, వెన్కకు or వెన్క venuka-ku. adv. Backwards, వెనుకతట్టుకు, పశ్చాద్భాగమునకు. వానిని వెనుకకుపడదోసెను he thrust him down backwards. "వెన్కకునీడ్చు పాదములతో" T. iv. 52, stepping forwards reluctantly. వెనుకచిక్కు venuka-chikku. v. n. To hang behind, to lag, fall back. వెనుకబడు. వెనుకచూపులమేకము venuka-tsūpula-mekamu. n. A bear. ఎలుగుబంటి. వెనుకటి or వెనకటి venukaṭi. adj. Former, previous. Subsequent, following, latter, hinder. ముందటి, ఇటీవలి, వెనుకనుండే. వెనుకటికాళ్లు the hind legs. వెనుకటి సంగతులు the former matters; also, the latter particulars. వెనుకటికర్మము or వెనుకటి పని obsequies, funeral ceremonies, అపరకర్మము. వెనుకటివాడు venukaṭi-vāḍu. n. A younger brother, తమ్ముడు. The former man. The latter man, ముందరివాడు, ఇటీవలివాడు. వెనుకటివారు those who precede: also, those who come after. వెనుకదీయు venuka-dīyu. v. n. To retreat, draw off, fall back, hesitate. వెనుకకు మరలు, సంకోచించు. వెనుకద్రొక్కు venuka-drokku. v. n. To fall back, retreat. వెనుదీయు. వెనుకపడు venuka-paḍu. v. n. To hang behind, lag, fall back. వెనుకచిక్కు. To remain on hand, as a remainder or surplus. మిగులు, వ్యయమునకు కుండానిలుచు. వెనుకపాటు venuka-pāṭu. n. The act of lagging behind, or of remaining over, వెనుకపడుట. వెనుకముందగు venuka-mund-agu. v. n. To be topsy-turvy, to be thrown into confusion. తలక్రిందగు. వెనుకమేను venuka-mēnu. n. The back, వీపు, చరమాంగము. వెనుకమ్రాను venuka-mrānu. n. A piece of wood on which the man who works a picota sits. వెనుకల or వెనుకాల venukala. (వెను+కలు) affix. Behind, పశ్చాద్భాగమునందు, వెనుక. వెనుకవేయు venuka-vēyu. v. a. To save, lay up, keep in store. కూడబెట్టు. వెనుకసారి venuka-sāri. adv. The last time, on a former occasion, on a latter occasion, పూర్వమొకప్పుడు, కడపటివర్యాయము. వెనుకొను, వెన్కొను, వెనుచేరు, వెనుతవులు, వెన్తవులు, వెనువవులు or వెన్వవులు venu-konu. v. a. To pursue closely, to follow, వెంబడించు. "సౌమిత్రి వెనుకొని చని పట్టంబుగట్టికొమ్మటమ్మని పనిచిన." R. v. 325. వెనుదన్ను Same as వెన్నుదన్ను. (q. v.) వెనుదీయు venu-dīyu. v. n. To turn back, retreat, వెనుకకుమరలు. "శౌర్యోద్ధురుచండిమల వెనుదీయక కాలువాలునరులు త్రిప్పివదియుంగా." Vema. 450. వెనుబడు or వెన్బడు venu-baḍu. v. n. To be grieved, to be sorrowful, విషాదించు, ఖేదించు. వెనుబాటు or వెన్బాటు venu-bāṭu. n. The act of grieving, the state of being sorrowful, grief, sorrow. వెనుబడుట, విషాదము, ఖేదము. వెనువెంట *venu-venta.* adv. Along with. మిక్కిలి వెంబడి.

వెన్న *venna.* [Tel. వెల్ల+నేయి.] n. Butter, నవనీతము. వెన్నడాయి *venna-dayi.* n. A kind of bird. వెన్నదొంగ or వెన్నముచ్చు *venna-donga.* n. Lit. the butter-stealer; a name of Krishna. కృష్ణుడు. వెన్నపడిదము *venna-padidamu.* n. A kind of sweet cake, ఒకదినుసుపిండివంట. వెన్నపాలకాయ *venna-pāla-kāya.* n. A kind of cake. ఒకవిధమైన భక్ష్యము. వెన్నపూస *venna-pūsa.* n. Butter, నవనీతము: (here పూస means a little or a bit, as a pat or bit of butter.) వెన్నప్పము *venn-appamu.* n. A kind of cake. మధురభక్ష్యవిశేషము. వెన్నమడుగు *vennamadugu.* n. A kind of cloth. వస్త్రవిశేషము. H. v. 406. వెన్నముద్ద *venna-mudda.* n. A lump of butter. వెన్నముద్దలు a superior kind of rice, శాలిధాన్యవిశేషము. "పాలమీగడలు శ్రీరంగాలుకామదార్లు రామబాణాలు రెక్కాములు వెన్నముద్దలుచిట్టి బుడుములుదాళువాలు." H. iv. 176. వెన్నముద్దకోడి *venna-mudda-kōḍi.* n. A bird called the Spotted Crake, *Porzana maruetta* (F. B. I.) వెన్నముద్దరాకు *venna-mudda-r-āku.* n. A plant called *Ommelina bengalensis.* వెన్నమెరుగు *venna-meruguu.* n. A kind of cake. వెన్నయుండ *venna-y-unda.* n. A kind of cake. మధురభక్ష్యవిశేషము. వెన్నవెదురు *venna-veduru.* n. A kind of herb. ఒకవిధమైనకూరాకు, విశల్య.

వెన్ను *vennu.* [Tel.] n. The back. వీపు. An ear of corn, వరిమొదలైనవాటి ఎన్ను. "వెనుకచిక్కితిరో యని వెన్ను చేరచి." Lavan. 30. "చెరుకువెన్నుపుట్టిచెరచదాతీపెల్ల." Vēma. 17. వాడు నా వెన్నుదన్నుకొనిపుట్టెను. వాడు he was born next after me. వరి వెన్ను తీసినది the crop of grain sprouted. వెన్నుకట్టె or వెన్నుగుదియ. *vennu-katte.* n. A backbreaker: that is, a cudgel. నడుమువిరగకొట్టెకర్ర, శింశకము. "మచ్చిరిప్ప్యక్షులకును వెన్నుగుదియ." L. xv. 107. వెన్నాడు or వెన్నడు *venn-āḍu.* v. a. To follow closely, to pursue, వెంబడించు. "ఇట్లు వెన్నాడియలరి కానిరిప్పుగంబుమాయయోయేమి." R. v. 160. v. n. To toss about (supine) on the back. వీపున ఇటుఅటుకదలు. "గుదిగొని వెన్నాడు కుసుమపుంజముతోడ" (Ila. i. 10.) టీ॥ వెన్నాడు, వీపునకదలుచుండే. వెన్నిచ్చు *venn-itstsu.* v. n. To retreat, run away. వెనుకదీయు. "పగతురకు వెన్నియ్యపాటిగాదయ్య." Pal. 419. వెన్నుదంతి *vennu-danti.* n. A kind of harrow. చోడికంకి జొన్నకంకి మొదలైనవి మూర్ఛునప్పుడు బయలుదేరు బూగరిపోవుటకును కొనటకును సాధనమైన గొర్రులెంటె నాలుగైదు పండ్లుగలమాను. వెన్నుదన్ను *vennu-dannu.* v. n. To stand behind, వెనుకనిలుచు. v. a. To follow, pursue, వెంబడించు. వెన్నుపట్టె, వెన్నుగాడి, వెన్నుబద్ద or వెన్నుమ్రాను *vennu-patte.* n. The roof tree, the chief beam or ridge of the roof. మొగటిపాసము, ఇంటినడిమిక్రాసుమ్రాను. వెన్నుపట్టె *vennu-patte* n. The spine or backbone, వీపు నడిమియెముక. వెన్నుపాము *vennu-pāmu.* n. The spinal marrow, కుండలి, వెన్నుఎముకలో నుండేమూలగ. వెన్నుపూస *vennu-pūsa.* n. The spine, వీపునడిమియెముక. One joint of the backbone. వెన్నెముకలోని ఒకగణుపు. వెన్నెముక *venn-emuka.* n. The spine or backbone. కశేరుక. వెన్నంటు or వెన్నంటి పోవు *venn-antu.* v. a. To pursue closely, to follow. వెంబడించిపోవు. వెన్నడి or వెన్నగిని *venn-adi.* adv. Along with. వెంటనే, వెంబడి. "ఇక్కడప్రాణముల్ విడిచియేఁబినకోగాదు నీదు వెన్నడికి నిక్కముకీవు చన్నడిచి." BRK. 340. వెన్నడించు or వెన్నడికొను *vennad-intsu.* v. a. To follow after, వెంబడించు. See వెను and వెనుక.

వెన్నుడు *vennudu.* [from Skt. విష్ణు.] n. Vishṇu, Krishṇa.

వెన్నెల *ven-nela.* [Tel. వెలుగు+నెల.] n. Moonlight. చంద్రిక. A kind of salutation, ఒకవిధమైన నమస్కారము. వెన్నెలకారు *ven-nela-karu.* n. Autumn, the season following the rains. శరదృతువు. వెన్నెల కుప్పలు *ven-nela-kuppalu.* n. plu. A game played by children. పిల్లకాయలాటలో ఒక ఆట. "కామరుగా వెన్నెలకుప్పలాడెదు వేళ." Ila. i. 22. వెన్నెలకోలు *ven-nela-kolu.* n. A bow or salutation. నమస్కారము. వెన్నెల గుత్తి *ven-nela-gutti.* n. A poetical phrase for the moon. చంద్రుడు. వెన్నెలపులుగు or వెన్నెలపిట్ట *ven-nela-pulugu.* n. A kind of fabulous bird, which loves the moonlight and is supposed to feed on the moonbeams. చకోరము. వెన్నెలరేడు or వెన్నెలరాయుడు *ven-nela-rēdu.* n. The lord of moonlight, i.e., the moon.

వెప్పు *veppu.* [Tel.] n. Heat, warmth. వేడిమి. వెమ్ము *vemmu.* v. n. To become heated, to be burnt, to pine with sorrow, తప్తమగు, తాపముకొందు.

వెయ్యి, వెయి or వేయి *veyyi.* [Tel.] n. A thousand. సహస్రము. వెయిమంది a thousand persons. పదివేలు ten thousand: (this in many places means many.) వెళ్లుమని పదివేలమాట్లు చెప్పినా వాడు వెళ్లలేదు though I told him to go a thousand times he did not go away. వెయ్యేల or వెయిమాటలేల why a thousand words? why say more? i.e., in a word, after all. వెయ్యి కాళ్లజెర్రి *veyyi-kalla-jerri.* n. Lit: a thousand-legged centipede. A restless wanderer. వాడు వెయ్యికాళ్లజెర్రి, వానికి ఎక్కడ తీరును he has a thousand jobs in hand, he has no leisure. పదివేలకైనా or పదివేలకున్ను వాణ్ని నమ్మవచ్చును we may trust him in every thing.

వెర *vera.* [Tel.] n. Fear, terror, horror. భయము, భీతి. Weight, heaviness, భారము. Wonder, ఆశ్చర్యము. "ఉరుముబిరిదులొక్కటిని వెరబరచుచుదూరోళపటలి." A. iv. 158. టీ. వెర, భయముచేతను. వెరచు or వెరచేరచు *veratsu.* v. n. To be afraid, to fear, to dread, భయపడు. వెరవకుము fear not. వానికృత్రిమము నకు వెరచి dreading his cunning. అనృతమునకు వెరచి fearing to tell a falsehood. వెరపు *verapu.* n. Fear, భయము, భీతి. వెరపరి *verap-ari.* n. A timid man, భయముకలవాడు, భయశీలుడు. వెరపించు *verapintsu.* v. a. To frighten, alarm, భయపెట్టు. వెరపిడి *verap-idi.* n. A fearless person, భయములేని వాడు, భయములేనిది. వెరబొమ్మ *vera-bomma.* n. A scare crow. దిష్టిబొమ్మ. వెరవేకి *vera-vēki.* n. Fear, horror, terror. భీతి, భయజ్వరము. "నన్నెరింగెదుగాక నావేరుకొలము విన్నవృత్యువృత్తైన నావేకివచ్చు" HD. ii. 1192. "కయ్యంబునందాకంబోటంగాయంబులు దాయంబు లేనివరవేకి గొంటినకాశశత్రునామధేయు చండాలకరాళవేషంబు కన్నులంగట్టినట్లుండ" A. vi. 112. Plu. వెరవేకులు. వెరసొచ్చు *vera-solstsu.* v. n. To be afraid, భయపడు. "వికృతులప్పటరా వెరసొచ్చి యొండిగొడుగనిదుయంబు చాచ్చున." M. viii. 36.

వెరక *veraka.* [Tel.] n. A hair. "సీ మావు వెన్నెరకగుట్టిరహాటిడిపిరిదండె" A. vi. 4. "గాలి నాడెడువెరకల" ib. vi. 17.

వెరగు *veragu.* [Tel. connected with వెర.] n. Surprise, astonishment, wonder, ఆశ్చర్యము. The act or state of being stunned, bewilderment, embarrassment, నిశ్చేష్టత. వెరగొందు or వెరగువడు *verag-ondu.* v. n. To be surprised. ఆశ్చర్యపడు. To be stunned, నిశ్చేష్టతకొందు. వెరగుపాటు *veragu-pātu.* n. Wonderment, surprise, bewilderment, వెరగుపడుట. The act or state of being stunned, bewilderment, embarrassment, నిశ్చేష్టత. వెరవెరపాటు *vera-vera-pātu.* n. The act of being stunned.

వెరజు. వెరజు or వెరజోడు veradzu. [Tel.] v. a. To steal, plunder; to take by large handfuls. దొంగిలించు, ముచ్చిలించు. కొల్లకొను, కొల్లగొను. "వెదకి వెదకి వెన్న వెరజోడుచు న్నాడు." V. P. vii. 130. "కదుమ్మానవిడి, ఘసటార్భటముచెల్లగించుకతిసాంద్రత్రీడగర్వోదం, జాతీత్వాత్తోపిభమ్మభావనలుప్పొమ్మతడ్డ వంచారసా." A. iv. 23.

వెరపు See under వెర.

వెరవడాలు verava-dalu. [Tel.] n. A kind of rice, which requires little irrigation. నింటానీళ్లు అక్కరలేని ఒకవిధమైనవడ్లు.

వెరవు or వెరువు veravu. [Tel.] n. A contrivance, expedient, device. ఉపాయము. Skill, cleverness, నేర్పు. Livelihood, జీవనోపాయము. Manner, mode, way, విధము. అక్కడజీవనముచేయువెరవులేక without the means of living there. "వెరవునులాపులేని ప్రజ వేయునిధంబులదివ్యబాణవిద్యురగము మాడిపోవి." M. VII. v. 444. "కాకిచోపు వాడు కడకిపేడుకతోడపెట్టిరింగి మేసవిడిచె తేని." Vēma. 1018. adj. Proper, యుక్తము. Dependent on, అధీనము. వెరవరి verav-ari. n. A clever, adroit, skillful person; an adept or expert, ఉపాయశాలి. నేర్పరి. వెరవిడి verav-idi. n. An unskillful man. ఉపాయహీనుడు.

వెరసి verasi. [Tel.] n. The total, the sum, the whole, లెక్క. మొత్తము. The last thing, కడపటిది. వెరసిమాట the last word, the final decision, కడపటిమాట. adj. Total, entire. మొత్తము, కడపటి. వెరసి రూపాయిలునూరు total rupees one hundred. ఉభయమువెరసి the grand total.

వెరసు verasu. [Tel.] n. A line or row of figures in Arithmetic. అంకెలలోనిసువాని పఙ్క్తి.

వెరువు See వెరవు.

వెర్రి verri. [Tel.] n. Madness, insanity, పిచ్చి. Folly, frenzy, అవివేకము. A mad man, a fool. పిచ్చివాడు, పిచ్చిది, ఉన్మత్తుడు, అవివేకి, తెలివిలేనివాడు. "అసన్నలకోలసల్యుడుభూతకోటిపైవాడ జనుల వెర్రులై." M. IV. iv. 55. plu. వెర్రులు. adj. Mad, insane, foolish, nonsensical, bad, useless, పిచ్చి, పనికిమాలిన. తలనొప్పి. వెర్రితలనొప్పి a distracting headache, a maddening headache. వెర్రిపడుచు a silly girl. Wild, uncultivated. వెర్రిచెరకు the wild sugarcane, *Saccharum arundinaceum*. వెర్రితుమ్మి *Phlomis zeylanica*. వెర్రినిమ్మ the wild lime. వెర్రిపుచ్చ the bitter wild melon. వెర్రిబచ్చలి a wild kind of Portulac. Similarly, వెర్రిఉల్లి, వెర్రిచీర, వెర్రిమెంతి. వెర్రిదూల, &c. Also used, like the word 'silly, in old English, to mean innocent. వాడు పట్టివెర్రివాడు he is a very innocent person. వెర్రితనము verri-tanamu. n. Madness. ఉన్మత్తత. వెర్రిది verr-idi. n. A foolish, silly or mad woman. ఉన్మత్తురాలు. తెలివిలేనిది. వెర్రినీళ్లు verri-nillu. n. Lit. the water that makes one silly, or mad, i. e., any spirituous liquor. మద్యము. వెర్రిబాగులు verri-bāgulu. n. A foolish man or woman, తెలివిమాలినవాడు, తెలివిమాలినది. వెర్రివాడు verri-vadu. n. A mad man, a fool. ఉన్మత్తుడు, తెలివిలేనివాడు. వెర్రివానిచేతిరాయి lit: a stone in the hand of a mad man, i. e., a dangerous experiment.

వెల vela. [Tel.] n. Price, value, rate. విలువ, మూల్యము. A stake on a race or gamble. పందెము. వెలయాలు. వెలముద్దియ, వెలపడతి or వెలపాప vela-y-alu. n. A courtezan, a harlot. బోగముది. వెలలేని vela-lēni. adj. Invaluable, most precious. అమూల్యమైన.

వెలగ velaga. [Tel.] n. The Wood-apple or Elephant apple. *Feronia elephantum*. కపిత్థము. The thorny species is called ముళ్లువెలగ. పొలగలగ is another species. పుల్లవెలగ is the sour species. వెలగకాయ or వెలక్కాయ *velaga-kāya.* n. The fruit called the wood-apple. కపిత్థఫలము, వెలగపండు.

వెలచు *velatsu.* [Tel.] v. a. To clean, purify, శుద్ధముచేయు, శుద్ధిచేయు, తోము.

వెలది, వెలంది or వెలదుక *veladi.* [Tel.] n. A damsel, maid, lady. స్త్రీ. Brightness, ధావళ్యము. వెలది adj. Pure, నిర్మలము. Kind, ప్రసన్నము. వెలదిగా *veladi-gā.* adv. Clearly, plainly. విశదముగా. "వలనొప్ప బోయివచ్చిన తెరంగెల్ల వెలదిగానంతయుదెలిపింప గోరి." Navanath. 104.

వెలనాడు or వెల్నాడు *vela-nāḍu.* n. The name of a subdivision of the Telugu country in ancient times. The name of a particular subdivision of Brahmins. బ్రాహ్మణులలోనొకతెగవారు.

వెలపర *velapara* [Tel.] n. A shrub with a large coarse fruit.

వెలపల or వెలుపల *velapala.* [Tel. వెలి+పల.] n. The outside, exterior, బహిఃప్రదేశము. adv. Outside, externally, on the right side, బైట, కుడిపక్కను. వెలపలి or వెలుపలి *velapali.* adj. Outer, external, outside. Dexter, on the right hand or side. బాహ్యమైన. బైటి. కుడి. వెలుపలినున్న the "next N" or, the letter n *following* a syllable. See బాపలి.

వెలమ *velama.* [Tel.] n. The name of a caste of ancient hill chieftains. వెలమలు or వెలమవారు people of that caste. వెలమగోటు Cavalier treatment, swaggering haughtiness, lordliness, petulance, domineering insolence.

వెలయు *velayu.* [Tel.] v. n. To shine, be splendid. ప్రకాశించు, ఒప్పు. To be pleased. ప్రసన్నతనొందు. To dwell, as a god in an image. To become famous, ప్రసిద్ధికెక్కు. To become known, బయలుపడు. To appear, to come to light, ప్రత్యక్షమగు. ఈ ఊరిలో దేవివెలసినది the goddess has made her appearance in this village వెలయు. వెలయగ or వెలయగా *velaya.* adv. Splendidly, brightly, pleasingly. ఒప్పుగా, ప్రకాశముతో. "కులములో నొకండు గుణహీనుడుండెనా, కులము చెడును వాని గుణము చేత, వెలయు వనములోన మలయజంబున్నట్లు." Vēma. i. 27. వెలయించు *velayintsu.* v. a. To brighten, adorn. ప్రకాశింపజేయు. To please, సంతోషపరచు.

వెలరు *velaru.* [Tel.] n. Whiteness, తెల్లన. వెలరారు or వెలరుపారు *velar-āru.* v. n To become white, తెల్లనగు. To shine, ప్రకాశించు. "జలధిప్రకరంబు వెలవెలనైతోచె వెలరారిదిక్కులంబికదివుచ్చు." Padma. ix. 234. To turn pale, వెలవెలపోవు.

వెలలు Same as వెదలు (q. v.) వెలలుచు Same as వెదలుచు. (q. v.)

వెలవ *velava.* [from Skt. విలేపి.] n. Rice-water, gruel, కాపుడుగంజి.

వెలవడాలు or వెలువడాలు *velava-ḍālu.* [Tel.] n. A kind of grain, ధాన్యవిశేషము, H. iv. 155.

వెలవెలన *vela-vela-na.* [Tel.] n. Paleness, వైవర్ణ్యము. వెలవెలని *vela-vel-ani.* adj. Pale, colourless, wan, తెల్లబోయిన. "కలికివెలవెలని మొగమునతలగదలిచికరటకుండు." P. i. 693. వెలవెలనగు, వెలవెల్లనగు, వెలవెలబోవు, వెలవెలబారు or వెల్వెలబారు *vela-vela-n-agu.* v. n. To turn pale, to be in despair. తెల్లపోవు. వివర్ణమగు, నిరాశకలిగియుండు. వెలవెలనై turning pale, తెల్లపోయి. వెలవెలపాటు *velavela-pāṭu.* n. Paleness. తెల్లపోవడము, వైవర్ణ్యము. "కించిదవనతాననమైన మొగము వెలవెలపాటు తేటపడ్డవనడంచి." A. v. 75.

వెలారించు, వెలారుచు or వెలార్చు *vela-rintsu.* [Tel. వెలి+అరించు.] v. a. To push out, send out, వెడలించు. To throw away, cast off, get rid off. పోగొట్టు. To make known, to show, బయలుపరుచు. "తొల్లిపడి నహాస్లిల్ల వెలారింతునాథపనీమునమునవార్త మెసగి." M. IX. ii. 316. "ధనార్థులయియాడకు వచ్చి నవారి కెంటకెందరినిటుమోసపుచ్చిరవారెల్లిలమెల్ల వెలాప్తులాడుమిత్తినని." Skand. Puran. ii. 190.

వెలి *veli.* [Tel.] n. Whiteness, తెలుపు. The outside or exterior, బయట, బాహ్యము. The external surface of the body, దేహముయొక్క బహిఃప్రదేశము. Publicity, బయలుపాటు. Excommunication, or exclusion from caste, బహిష్కారము. మాలో వెలిఅనేమాటలేదు excommunication is unknown in our caste. "వెలికిగొయ్య తెల్లఁజేసిపెట్టి." Vema. 791. adj. White, తెల్లని. Outer, outside, external. వెలి. బాహ్యమైన. వెలిగుడారు a tent pitched outside the town. వెలిపొలములు the outlying fields of a village. వెలిగొట్టు to drive out. వెలికత్తెరనేల *veli-kattera-nela.* n. A land mixed with gravel. కంకరమన్ను కలిసిననేల. వెలికిలు *veli-kilu.* v. n. To fall on the back, to touch the ground with the back. వెల్లకిలబడు. To lie on the back, వెల్లకిలగాపరుండు. వెలికిల *velikila.* adv. Supine, lying on the back, ఉత్తానముగా. వెలికిలబడు to lie on the back. వెలిగడ *veli-gada.* n. Dry land. మెట్టనేల. వెలిగారము *veli-garamu.* (వెలి+కారము.) n. Borax. బంగారమునకుకాంతితెచ్చే ఒకరకమైన తెల్లనిఉప్పు. వెలిగిడ్డి *veli-giddi.* n. The fabulous cow that grants all wishes, కామధేనువు. వెలిగుల్ల *veli-gulla.* n. A conch shell, శంఖము. "వెలిగుల్లయు వెమాలయు నలిమియు మానికము మేనగలిగిన వేల్పుల" G. iv. 169. వెలిగొండ *veli-gonda.* n. The distant mountain. Same as వెలితిప్ప. వెలిగారు *veli-gauru.* n. The white elephant of Indra, ఐరావతము. వెలిచేంద్ర *veli-tsandra.* n. The white species of the tree called చేంద్ర. వెలిచేవి *veli-tsavi.* n. Adultery. జారత్వము. వెలితిప్ప *veli-tippa.* n. The silver mountain, Kailasa. వెండికొండ, కైలాసము. వెలితుమ్మ the white species of the తుమ్మచెట్టు. వెలిదుక్కి *veli-dukki.* n. Ploughing land while it is moist with rain. నీళ్లుకట్టకుండావానపడితో దున్నడము. (Opposed to రొంపిదుక్కి.) వెలిపము Same as వలిపము. (q. v.) వెలిపుచ్చు or వెలిపరచు *veli-putstsu.* v. a. To reveal, divulge. బైటపెట్టు, బయలుపరుచు. "వేదశిర్షమెల్ల వెలిబుచ్చగా నేల." Vema. 214. వెలిపెట్టు See వెలివేయు. వెలిబూడిద *veli-budida.* n. The ashes of cowdung fuel. పిడకనిప్పులబూడిద. వెలిచిత్తి a certain feat in wrestling. వెలిమాడు exports. లోమాడు imports, goods received. వెలిమావు *veli-mavu.* n. (Indra's) white horse, (ఇంద్రుని) తెల్లగుర్రము, ఉచ్చైశ్శ్రవము. వెలిమావులు white mares. "విమలాంబుదములబూనిన నిమాఘములఁ దగవెలసి వెలిమావులు." M. VII. i. 228. "వేరొక్క వెలిమావువేల్పుదొరకు." R. i. 46. వెలిమిడి or వెల్మిడి *veli-midi.* (వెలి+మిడుకు.) n. The ashes of cow-dung fuel, ashes, పిడకనిప్పులబూడిద, భస్మము. "తెలుపుల న్నెయము మేలుదరి యంగనిసుక వెలిమిడియొముకలు పెనమువ్వపత్తి." Madhura Puran. D. page. 78. వెలిముట్టె *veli-motta.* n. A sort of fish, the 'white snout.' "వెలిముట్టెలనుదిందునల తలార్లకునిచ్చి కొడిసెలఁబకిమోసములకునిచ్చి." G. i. 111. వెలిమ్రాను *veli-mranu.* n. The fabulous tree that grants all wishes, కల్పవృక్షము. వెలియునికి *veli-y-uniki.* n. Living in a foreign land, పరదేశవాసము. వెలివాడ *veli-vada.* n. The outer "street" or suburb of a town in which the pariahs live. బైటనుండేమాలపల్లె, చండాలవాటిక. వెలివాడపని *veli-vada-pani.* n. Cobblers' work. మాదిగపని. "వెలివాడపనికొర్తిమలక వాల్లాని నూనెయిడితంగెడాకుగట్టె దుతిపాతివ్వ." A. vi. 94. వెలివాడు or వెలివాడవాడు *veli-vadu.* n. An outcaste, a pariah. చండాలుడు. మాలవాడు. "వెలివాండ్రు గెవల్లెకుజేర్చి

దుర్గమా." M. xiii. iii. 270. వెలివారు *veli-varu.* n. A cordon formed round a hunting place. వేటాడునప్పుడు బయటచుట్టుకొనేదెబ్బ. వెలివెలియు Same as వెల్లివిరియు. (q. v.) వెలివిసరు *veli-visaru.* v. n. To come out, be revealed, be made public, బయలుపడు. వెలివేయు or వెలిపెట్టు *veli-peyu.* v. a. To eject or excommunicate from a caste or sect. బహిష్కరించు.

వెలికి *veliki.* [Tel.] n. The name of a tree called *Vangueria spinosa.* కంఠపిండీతకము.

వెలిచె, వెలిచియు or వెల్చె *veliche.* [Tel.] n. A sort of quail, called *Elche* in Hindustani. వర్తకమనేపక్షి.

వెలితి or వెల్తి *veliti.* [Tel.] n. Deficiency, want, looseness, thinness, తక్కువ. లోపము. విరళత్వము, తరుచుదనములేమి. గుడ్డ వెలితిగా నుండుటచేత by the thinness of the cloth. పిడివెలితి రెండుమూళ్లపొడవు a span less than two cubits. "క॥ పదివేలదాలిచియ్యగ నధముండొకడియ్యకున్న నర్థికి వెలితా, పదివేలగోవులియ్యగ వెలితా పెంకటియ్యకున్న." adj. Deficient, thin. Inferior, less; low, vulgar. Open, having interstices. తక్కువైన, నీచమైన, లోపమైన, విరళమైన. వెలితిమాటలు low language. వెలితిమానిసి *veliti-manisi.* n. A mean or petty man or woman. అల్పుడు. అల్పురాలు.

వెలియు *veliyu.* [Tel.] v. n. To stop, cease, go off, as rain. వర్షమువిడుచు. To fade, చేయుపోవు.

వెలిసె or ఎలిసె *velise.* [Tel.] n. That part of a beam which juts out beyond the wall, the eaves. ఇంటిచూరు.

వెలు *velu.* [Tel.] adj. Another form of వెలి. (q. v.) వెలుక *vel-uka.* (వెలి+ఉక.) n. Whiteness. తెల్లన. వెలుకబారు or వెల్కబారు *veluka-baru.* v. n. To turn pale. తెల్లబారు. "తనుచాన నళి దప్పుచనినవెవ్వగబోతలోలిదిక్కుజవరాలు వెలుకబారె." Swa. v. 47. "వెలుకబార నిశాంతనిశాంతదీపముల్." Parij. ii. 76. వెలువడు or వెల్వడు *velu-vadu.* v. n. To come out, become known, be made public, బయలుపడు. To set out, బైలువెళ్లు, బైలుదేరు. వెలువరించు, వెల్వరించు or వెలువరచు *velu-varintsu.* v. a. To send out, to force out, to give vent to, make known, divulge. వెలువడజేయు, బైటికివచ్చునట్లుచేయు, బయలుపుచ్చు. "ఒక్కింతసేపుపలుకు వెలువరింపంజాలకయూరకుండె." M. IX. ii. 12.

వెలుగు or వెలుంగు *velugu.* [Tel.] v. n. To shine or give light. ప్రకాశించు. "వెలిగిరిబలములు తొర్యంబులువార్పులువెలంగ." M. VI. ii. 187. n. Light, splendour, brightness, సూర్యచంద్రాదికాంతి, ప్రకాశము, వెలుతురు. A ray of light, కిరణము. Sunshine, ఎండ. దండివెలుగు the great light, i. e., God, పరంజ్యోతి. "పెద్దకున్నపము చెప్పినగానివినరావు, చేవెలుంగిడకున్నచెడును దృష్టి." Vish. viii. 402. వెలుగురేడు *velugu-redu.* n. The lord of light, i. e., the sun. వెలుగించు *velug-intsu.* v. a. To light, kindle. To cause to shine. రగిలించు, ప్రకాశింపజేయు. వెలుగొందు or వెల్గొందు Same as వెలుగు (verb).

వెలుగు or వెల్గు *velugu.* [Tel.] n. A hedge, fence, enclosure. పెరడు మొదలగువానికి కంపతో వేసిన ఆవరణము.

వెలుచె or వెల్చె *velutsa.* [Tel.] n. A serpent, snake, సర్పము.

వెలుచు *velutsu.* [Tel. for వెడలించు.] v. a. To drive, తోలు. వెలుచు or వెలిపించు v. a. To drive out, వెడలించు. "చ॥ వెలిచిన కన్నునీరు జెడి." ఉ. హరి. v. వెలుచు or వెలలుచు *velutsu.* v. a. To roll up thread, (నూలు) తోడు. వెలుపుడు *velupudu.* n. The act of rolling thread. నూలువెలుచుట.

వెలుతురు or వెల్తురు *veluturu.* [Tel. from వెలుగు.] n. Light, lustre. ప్రకాశము. వెలుతురు మొగులు white clouds, తెల్లనిమేఘములు. వెలుతురుచెట్టు *veluturu-chettu.* n. A small species of Babul with pink flowers.

వెలుపలి *velu-pala.* [Tel. వెలి+పల.] n. Outside. adj. Outside, బయటి. adv. Outside. బయట. **వెలుపరించు** or **వెల్పరించు** *velupu-intsu.* v. a. To reveal, divulge, వెలిపరుచు.

వెలుపు Same as వెడలుపు (q. v.) **వెలుపించు** or **వెలుపుచేయు** *velup-intsu.* v. a. To widen, వెడలుపుచేయు. **వెలువు** *velupu* (from వెలు వే.) v. n. To issue, as a stream. నీరుబయలు వెడలు. వేసవిదినములయందుకొద్దినీరువెలువును a little water flows from it in summer.

వెలుమసంధి *veluma-sandhi.* [Tel.] n. A plant called *Leea hirta* (Rox. i. 656.) కాకజంఘ, దాసీపత్ర, పారావతి.

వెలువడములు or **వెల్వడములు** *velu-vada-mulu.* [Tel.] n. pln. A sort of rice. ధాన్యవిశేషము. H. vi. 659.

వెలువడు, **వెలువరించు** and **వెలువరుచు** See under వెలు.

వెల్కుబాకు See under వెలు.

వెల్చ See వెలంచె.

వెల్చి See వెలిచె.

వెల్తి See వెలితి.

వెల్తిడి See under వెలి.

వెల్ల *vella.* [Tel.] n. Whiteness. తెల్లదనము, ధావళ్యము, శ్వేతవర్ణము. adj. White. తెల్లని, ధవళము. "కుంభభవకృపాచార్యుల యుష్ణీశములు వెల్లలు." భార. విరా. v. **వెల్లగిసె** *vell-agise.* n. Flax, తెల్లఅవిసె. వెల్లగిసెలు linseed or flax-seed. **వెల్లగుర్రము** Same as వెలిమావు. (q. v.) **వెల్లచేరపు** *vella-tsarapu.* n. White-washing, గోడపైని తెల్లసున్నము వేయడము. సున్నముకొట్టడము, సున్నపుపూత. **వెల్లన** or **వెల్లదనము** *vella-na.* n. Whiteness. తెల్లన. Paleness, వెలవెలపాటు, పాండురత్వము. "ఇంద్రరాజ్యలక్ష్మీ ముఖమండలంబున నవించిన వెల్లదనంబు నైనదిగా." Parij. ii. 43. **వెల్లనగు** or **వెల్లనారు** *vella-n-agu.* v. n. To become white, తెల్లనగు. **వెల్లని** *vellani.* adj. White, తెల్లని. వెల్లనికన్నులు white eyes. **వెల్లబాటు** *vella-batu.* n. Becoming white. తెల్లనగుట. **వెల్లిమ్రాను** Same as కల్పవృక్షము. (q. v.) **వెల్లయేనుగు** *vella-yenugu.* n. Indra's elephant. ఐరావతము. **వెల్లసున్నము** *vella-sunnamu.* n. Whitewash, గోడకుకొట్టడమునకై కలుపుకొన్న సున్నము. **వెల్లాటుకత్తె** or **వెల్లాటుపుకత్తె** *vell-ata-katte.* n. An adulteress. జారిణి, వేశ్య. **వెల్లాటము** or **వెల్లాటకము** *vell-atamu.* (వెల్ల+ఆటము.) n. Notoriety, publicity, ప్రసిద్ధి. **వెల్లావు** Same as కామధేనువు. (q. v.) వెల్లచేయు to white-wash. **వెల్లుల్లి** *vell-ulli.* (వెల్ల+ఉల్లి.) n. Garlic. **వెల్లెలుక** *vell-eluka.* n. A white rat.

వెల్లకి or **వెల్లంకి** *vellaki.* [Tel. anuk. to the word వేరు.] n. A root, నడ్డ, వేరు. వెల్లకి గా వేరువెల్లంకులు root and all. "పెకలనగు వేరువెల్లకిరయు ప్రవ్వెదుకర్షకునట్లు." A. iv. 266.

వెల్లకిల or **వెలికిల** *vella-kila.* [Tel.] adv. Supinely, with the face upward, ఉత్తానముగా. వెల్లకిలవేయు to turn on the back.

వెల్లడి *velladi.* [Tel.] n. Openness, publicity, బయలు, ప్రసిద్ధి. Emptiness. శూన్యత. క్రమేణ అరణ్యము వెల్లడియైనందున ఏనుగులు నశించినవి as the forests were cleared away the elephants disappeared. **వెల్లడిచేయు** or **వెల్లడిపరుచు** *velladi-cheyu.* v. a. To publish, to make known.

వెల్లాయి or **వెళ్ళాయి** *vellayi.* [Tam.] n. The steam of water used in bleaching cotton cloth, గంజిపెట్టుట. చలవచేయుట.

వెల్లి, **వెల్లిక** or **వెల్లువ** *velli.* [Tel.] n. A flood, stream, ప్రవాహము. A series, వరుస. Whiteness, తెలుపు. వెల్లివేసినదు as it dawned, అరుణోదయకాలమునాగా. "వెల్లివేసుడు స్వచ్ఛోల్లాసమున." BD. iii 410.

వెల్లికొలుపు, వెల్లికొల్పు or వెల్లిగొలుపు *velli-kolupu.* v. a. To inundate. "వి లోకనప్రభావీచికలందఱను జనుకలకాంబుధి వెల్లి గొల్పుచున్." Swa. ii. 33. వెల్లిగొను *velli-gonu.* v. n. To flow, to run as water, to be spread. ప్రవహించు. పరంపరగా వెడలు. ప్రసిద్ధము. "కనుగవమార్గాశ్రుకణములు వెల్లిగొనన క్కొమ్మపెత్తికొనుచు భక్తుండు." BD. v. 409. వెల్లివిరి *velli-viri.* adj. Made known, made public, ప్రకటితము. వెల్లివిరియు or వెల్లిపాడు *velli-viriyu.* v. n. To break forth, spread; to overflow, teem. వ్యాపించు, వెల్లు వలుగట్టు, పరవశైపారు. To become public or famous, ప్రచురము, ప్రసిద్ధము. To swell, ఉబుకు. "ఇట్టిమారయొవ్వలున్న చోట సత్యంబు మూలబడికల్ల వెల్లివిరియు." P. i. 53.

వెల్లుల్లి See under వెల్ల.

వెల్లువ *velluva.* n. A flood, a stream, an inundation. ప్రవాహము. A number of men, a troop, సేన. "దెబ్బదిరెండు వెల్లువలైన నవచరపతుల భూవరులజయించి." DRY. 1494. "శిశకాలమునవచ్చినమంచువెల్లువల్." Kod. i. 43. వెల్లువకట్టు or వెల్లువలుకట్టు *velluva-kattu.* v. n. To flow in streams, to form a pool, ప్రవహించు, మడుగుకట్టు.

వెల్వడు or వెలువడు *vel-vadu.* [Tel. వెలి + పడు.] v. n. To go out, start, బయలుదేరు. వెల్వరించు *velva-r-intsu.* v. a. To cause to start, బయలుదేరజేయు. See వెలువడుములు.

వెల్వెల్ల *vel-vella.* [Tel. వెల్ల + వెల్ల.] adj. Very pale, మిక్కిలి వైవర్ణ్యము.

వెవ్వేరు See under వేరు.

వెళ్లు *vellu.* [Tel. short for వెడలు.] v. n. To go, proceed, depart. To pass, or elapse. To be emitted. పోవు. కడుపు వెళ్లుచున్నది the bowels are loose. నాలుగుదినములు వెళ్లినతర్వాత after four days passed. కడవెళ్ల చదివినాడు he read it to the end. పొలిమేర వెళ్లదొక్కు to tread the boundary line, i.e., to settle the boundary. వెళ్లగక్కు *vella-gakku.* v. a. To vomit up, disgorge, refund, వమనముచేయు, మళ్లియిచ్చివేయు. వెళ్లజేయు, వెళ్లగొట్టు or వెళ్లించు *vella-jēyu.* v. a. To drive out, chase away, eject, expel, పారదోలు. "తిరిగిపోయిన మరితెలియంగజెప్పి భూమి వెళ్లింపుముపొందైనభంగి." Pal. 449. వెళ్లదీయు *vella-dīyu.* v. a. To take out or extract, బయటికితీయు. వెళ్లిపోవు *velli-pōvu.* v. n. To go away, depart.

వెస *vesa.* [Tel.] n. Haste, speed. శీఘ్రము, త్వర. వెసన్ *vesan.* adv. Hastily, with haste, speedily. గ్రక్కున.

వెసనము Same as వ్యసనము. (q. v.)

వెసల or వెసలె *vesala.* [Tel.] n. A deep saucer, or shallow earthen bowl. అటక. A cooking pot, వంటకుండ.

వే vē

వే *vē* [Tel.] pron. Same as వేయి (q. v.) adj. Thousand, సహస్రము. Many, అనేకము. వేమారులు many times. adv. Quickly, speedily, శీఘ్రముగా. "వేవానిర్గతంబైన వార్త్యంబువేసొచ్చి." G. ii. 80. "రథముచేతా నివాసమ్ము." DRAyo. 127. "వినిన వకించిన వేపధమలు." M. XV. ii. 143. వేగంటి or వేగన్నులసామి *vē-ganti.* n. Lit. the thousand-eyed; a name of Indra. ఇంద్రుడు. "దీనికనుగొన్న వేగంటి దేవరకును. వెచ్చనిట్టూర్పు పుక్కిట వెడలకున్నె." R. vii. 112. వేచుంగులపాగ *vē-tsungula-pāga.* (వేయి + చుంగులు + పాగ.) n. The serpent called శేషుడు. Lit. one who has a thousand-folded turban. వేవెలుగు or వేవెలుంగులదొర *vē-velugu.* n. The sun, సూర్యుడు. "వేవెలుంగులదొర జోడు కేవలుంగు." A. i. 22.

వేంచేయు *vēn-chēyu.* [for Skt. విజయముచేయు.] v. n. To proceed; to deign to come; to condescend to go. వచ్చు, పోవు. To come and take a seat, కూర్చుండు. To live or dwell. ఉండు, నివసించు. మాయింటికి వేంచేస్తారా will you do me the honor to come to my house? ఆయన కంచిలో వేంచేసియున్నారు he lives at Conjevaram.

వేంఁడ్రము vēndramu. [Tel.] n. Heat, either of the sun or of a pungent taste. ఉగ్రము, తాపము. వేంఁడ్రపడు vēndra-padu. v. n. To be hot or angry, మండిపడు. "తల్లికికల నైన దయలేదు నామీద తండ్రియొప్పుడు చూచి కేంఁడ్రపడును." H. iii. 195.

వేకటి or వ్రేకటి vēkati. [Tel.] n. Pregnancy, కడుపు, గర్భము. వేకటిమనిషి vēkati-manishi. n. A pregnant woman.

వేకరము vēkaramu. [Tel.] n. Danger, harm. ఉపద్రవము.

వేకరి vēkari [Tel. వ్రేకము+అరి.] n. A gypsy tribe.

వేకి vēki. [Tel.] n. Fever. జ్వరము. మలవేకి Malaria or hill fever. లోవేకి internal fever. "ఎఱ్ఱవాడు దానియేపాటి జూచిన వెఱ్ఱిపట్టిమిగుల వేకిపుట్టు." Vēma 170.

వేకువ vēkuva. [Tel. from వేగు.] n. The dawn, morning. ప్రభాతము, వేగుజాము. వేకువజాము vēkuva-dzāmu. n. The morning watch. తెల్లవారిజాము. వేకువనే vēkuva-nē. adv. Early in the morning

వేగ vēga. [from Skt. వేగము.] n. Swiftness, speed, haste, వడి, త్వర. వేగ, వేగముగా or వేగమే vēga. adv. Speedily, hastily, quickly. శీఘ్రముగా, త్వరగా. "కుండలంబులు వేగగొనిరమ్ము వాలవవాటికి." M. I. i. 164. వేగము vēgamu. [Skt.] n. Swiftness, celerity, velocity, speed, haste, త్వర. త్వరితము, జవము. A stream, flow, current. ప్రవాహము. వేగపడు vēga-padu. v. n. To make haste, త్వరపడు. వేగపాటు or వేగిరపాటు vēga-pātu. n. Hurry, haste, త్వర, శీఘ్రము. "వేగపాటేలయతడనీ విభుడనుటకు." A. v. 86. వేగవతి vēga-vati n. The name of a river that runs by Conjevaram.

వేగరి See under వేగు.

వేగి vēgi. [from Skt. వ్యాఘ్రము.] n. A tiger, పులి. [Skt.] n. A horse. Lit. that which goes fast.

వేగి or వేగిస vēgi. [Tel.] n. A tree, *Pterocarpus bilobus*. సర్జకవృక్షము, రక్తబీజ. Various kinds are called జట్టువేగి and మల్లువేగి. "వేగివేములు మొదలుగాగలవృక్షముల." P. iv. 545

వేగి, వేఁగి or వేగినాడు vēgi. [Tel.] n. The country round Rajamundry, రాజమహేంద్రవరముచుట్టునుండు దేశము. "జమ్మిలోయుబడి వేగిదహించె." A. preface 43.

వేగించు See under వేగు.

వేగిరము vēgiramu. [from Skt. వేగము.] n. Haste, speed, swiftness, త్వర, శీఘ్రము. adv. Quickly, త్వరితము. వేగిరించు or వేగిరపడు vēgir-intsu. v. n. To hurry or hasten. త్వరపడు. "తామనించినేయు దగకట్టి కార్యంబు వేగిరించనీయుం విషమమగును, పచ్చికాయదెచ్చి పడవేయ ఫలమవునె." Vēma. 103. వేగిరకాడు vēgira-kādu. n. A quick man; a hasty or rash man, త్వరగలవాడు. వేగిరకత్తె vēgira-katte. n. A quick woman, a hasty or rash woman, త్వరగలది. వేగిరపాటు vēgira-pātu. n. Hastening. త్వరపడుట. వేగిరపెట్టు vēgira-pettu. v. a. To cause to hasten, to expedite, త్వరపరుచు.

వేగు vēgu. [Tel.] v. n. To dawn. తెల్లవారు, ఉదయమగు. To watch without sleeping, నిద్రమేలుకొనియుండు, జాగారముచేయు. To fry, or be fried. తపించు, కించెలువేగు. To endure, suffer, grieve. పరితపించు, పడు. "కంటికినిద్రగానకొదుగంబడి వేగెదమిందు." A. iii. 40. వీనితో వేగడముకష్టము I cannot get on with him. "వేదనవేగివేగి, దుర్భరవిచారడోలలదూగితూగి." R. v. 228. "తెలతెలవేగుదు బులుగులు, కలకలబలుకంగ జగముకన్నులదాయై తెలతెలవేగుచుదమ్మునెచెలి యల్లన యుదయ శిఖరిశిఖరంబెక్కెన్." Padma. iii. 34. n. Public news, news. రాజ్యసమాచారము, సమాచారము. Espionage, పొంచి రహస్యముగా

మర్మము కనుక్కొనడము. "వేగుండియూరని విధమెల్లనరసి." BD. iii. 1416. వేగుండి, పొంచుండి. వేగు, వేగువాడు, వేగులవాడు vēgu. n. A spy, scout. చారుడు, హార్కారా. వేగరి vēg-ari. (వేగు+అరి.) n. A messenger, spy, scout, చారుడు, హర్కారా, వేగులవాడు. "ఘనముగా వేగర్లకతన తెలిసింటి." వేగించు vēgintsu. v. n. To keep awake. జాగరము చేయు, మేలుకొనియుండు. To cause to be fried. వేగజేయు. వేగింపు vēgimpu. n. Waking from sleep, జాగరము. The ceremony performed on the consummation of a marriage. శోభనము. వేగుచూచు vēgu-tsūtsu. v. a. To spy out, reconnoitre, to explore, రహస్యముగాపోయి తెలిసి వచ్చి మర్మమును కనుక్కొను. వేగుచుక్క, వేగురు చుక్క or వేగువచుక్క vēgu-tsukka n. The morning star, the planet Venus, శుక్రుడు. వేగుజాము vēgu-dzāmu. n. The morning watch. రాత్రి నాలుగవజాము, వేగు జాము, తెల్లవారుజాము. వేగుప్రొద్దు, వేగు పొద్దు or వేపొద్దు vēgu-proddu. n. Matin hour, the time of dawn. ప్రాతఃకాలము. వేవిన vēvina. adv. At dawn. తెల్లవారగా. "వేవినగుడికేగి వేనవేల్విధుల." BD. v. 284. "వేవినమేడపై." A. v. 15. ib. v. 164.

వేగురు vēguru. [Tel. from వేయి.] n. A thousand persons, వెయ్యిమంది.

వేచు vētsu. [Tel. from వేగు.] v. a. To fry, or grill. To torment, persecute, grieve. To wish for, hope, expect, watch for, వేయించు, వేగజేయు, బాధించు, అపేక్షించు, కనిపెట్టు, ఎదురుచూచు. "పొంచితిరివేచిమిగుల నొప్పించు గాక." A. v. 157. "రుచికపుడువేచియిరుకుడు." M. XIII. ii. 192.

వేట vēṭa. [Tel. from వేయు and వేటు.] n. Hunting, the chase. మృగయ, అడవి లోని మృగపశులను చంపడము. A sheep or goat set apart for slaughter. గొర్రె, మేక, మేకపోతు, పొట్టేలు. "పూజించెనాగం కటు వెలయగా వేటలుబోనముల్ పిడులుగా నించెగా." H. ii. 100. వేటకాడు, వేటగిరి or వేటరి vēṭa-kāḍu. n. A huntsman. మృగయుడు. A slaughterer, సంహారకుడు. వేటకుక్క vēṭa-kukka. n. A hound, a hunting dog. మృగాదులనుపట్టేకుక్క. వేట పల్లె vēṭa-palle. n. A village inhabited by huntsmen, బోయపల్లె. వేటపిట్ట vēṭa-piṭṭa. n. A fowler's decoy bird. దీమపుపిట్ట. వేటపోతు vēṭa-pōtu. n. A ram. పొట్టేలు. వేటాడు or వేటలాడు veṭ-āḍu. v. n. To hunt, to follow the chase. అడవిలో పశువులను మృగము లను చంపు. To kill, slaughter, చంపు, వధించు.

వేటికి or వేనికి vēṭiki. [Tel. from ఏవి which.] n. To which things: the dative plural of ఏవి which things. Also, it is the anuk. of the phrase పోటికి, as పోటికివేటికి in rivalry. "పోటికివేటికిచలము నివ్వలముగా."

వేటు or వ్రేటు vēṭu. [Tel. from వేయు.] n. A blow, a stroke. A shot, the discharge of a gun or cannon, దెబ్బ, తాకు, తుపాకి మొదలైనవాటిని ఒకతేప కాల్చడము. "నీతిగాని మాటరాతివేటు." Vēma. 259. వేటుపాటునడి పించిరి they began to fire. వేటుపాటు fighting, coming to blows. వేటులాడు or వేట్లాడు vēṭu-l-āḍu. v. n. To fight, to deal blows. కొట్లాడు. "పువ్వుబంతులవేట్లాడి." Charu Chandrod. iv. 92.

వేడబము vēḍabamu. [from Skt. విడంబనం.] n. Curiosity, wonder, amusement. వింత, వేడుక, చోద్యము. A trick, trickery, deceit, మాయ, వంచన. A mask, వేషము. "విలయకా లమందు విశ్వంబునీ పెద్ద, కడుపులోన దాచుకడిది మేటి, నటుడమీవునేడు నాగర్భజాడవవుట పరమ పురుష వేడబంబుగాదె." (B. x. iii 27). "అస్త్రంబుధరియించుట, తపస్వియనుట యుట్టివే డబములెయ్యోడగలవే." Kasi. Kan. viii. 66.

వేడము or వేడెము vēḍamu. [from Skt. వేష్ట నము.] n. Riding or running round in a ring, మండలగతి, చక్రాకృతిగా తిరగడము.

"శేడెంబును గాని, శేడెంబున దురగంబు పరపి తెరపిగని." టీ॥ చుట్టుపరుగులోడ నుర్రాన్నినడిపించి. వేడించు vēḍinṭsu. v. n. To go round. చుట్టివచ్చు.

వేడి vēḍi. [Tel.] n. Heat, warmth. వేడిమి, ఉష్ణము, తాపము. Sharpness, చురుకు. Brightness. తేజము. adj. Hot, warm. ఉష్ణమైన. వేడినీళ్లు, వేన్నీళ్లు or వేనీళ్లు hot water. వేడికంటి vēḍi-kanti. n Lit: the hot-eyed; an epithet of Siva. వేడిమి vēḍimi. n. Heat, warmth. వెచ్చన, ఉష్ణత్వము. వెన్నెల వేడిమి the warm beams of the moon. Grief, తాపము. Sharpness, acuteness, చురుకు. వేడివెలుగు vēḍi-velugu. n. The Sun, సూర్యుడు. Sunshine, సూర్యరశ్మి. వేడివేలుపు vēḍi-vēlupu. n. The sun, as being the god of heat. సూర్యుడు. Also, the god of fire, అగ్ని.

వేడు vēḍu. [Tel.] pron. Who? ఎవడు?

వేడు vēḍu. [Tel.] v. a. To pray, beseech, entreat, solicit, beg for, ask for. To wish, desire, బతిమాలుకొను, కోరు, అడుగు, రమించు. "పోయినరంబు వేడుమన." Rama Stava. i. 135. వేడుకొను or వేడికొను vēḍu-konu. v. a. To pray, beg, entreat, solicit. ప్రార్థించు. వేడుకోలు or వేడికోలు vēḍu-kōlu. n. Praying, beseeching. An entreaty, prayer. బతిమాలుకొనడము.

వేడుక or వేడ్క vēḍuka. [Tel.] n. A spectacle, show, display, pomp, feast, festival. Curiosity, interest, joy, glee, delight. కుతూహలము, సంతోషము, వినోదము; సంబరము, ఇచ్ఛ, అభిలాష. వేడుకపడు to be happy or pleased. adj. Novel, curious. Delightful, pleasant, amusing. Happy, pleased. వినోదకరము, కుతూహలమైన. సంబరమైన. నిండావేడుకగా నుండినారు they were much pleased, very merry. వేడుకగా or వేడ్కగా vēḍuka-gā. adv. Pompously, splendidly, in an interesting manner, pleasantly, happily, cheerfully. సంబరముగా, ఆనందముగా. వేడుకకత్తె vēḍuka-katte. n. A belle. A courtezan, a harlot, an adulteress. జారస్త్రీ, వేశ్య. వేడుకకాడు or వేడ్కగాడు vēḍuka-kāḍu. n. A fop, a man of pleasure, a lover, an adulterer. విటుడు. క్రీడాసక్తుడు. One who takes a delight in anything, కుతూహలుడు, ఆపేక్షకుడు, వినోదకుడు. వేడుకజూదము vēḍuka-dzūdamu. n. Gambling for pleasure. వేడుకపడు, వేడ్కపడు, వేడుకచేయు or వేడ్కచేయు vēḍuka-paḍu. v. n. To rejoice, to be delighted, to desire eagerly, కుతూహలపడు, అపేక్షించు.

వేడెము Same as వేడము. (q.v.) వేడెపెట్టు vēḍe-peṭṭu. v. a. To cause to surround, పరివేష్టింపజేయు.

వేణి vēṇi. [Skt.] n. A plait or braid of hair. Plaited tresses. జడ. A stream. నదియొక్కపాయ. A canal or channel, కాలువ. The junction of two or more streams, అనేక ప్రవాహములయొక్క కూడిక. A kind of grass, *Andropogon sorratum*. వేణిక vēṇika. n. A plait or braid of hair, plaited tresses, జడ.

వేణువు vēṇuvu. [Skt.] n. A bamboo. వెదురు. A pipe, a flute. పిల్లంగ్రోవి. వేణులావకుడు vēṇu-lāvakuḍu. n. A basketmaker. మేదరవాడు.

వేన్నీళ్లు See under వేడి.

వేత or వ్రేత vēta. [Tel. from వేయు.] n. Throwing, casting, a toss, a throw, a cast. వేయుడము.

వేతనము vētanamu. [Skt.] Wages, hire. జీతము, కూలి.

వేతసము or వేతసి vētasamu. [Skt.] n. A kind of reed or rattan creeper. నీరువంజి, ప్రబ్బచెట్టు, ప్రబ్బలి.

వేత్త vetta. [Skt. from విద్ to know.] n. One who is versed in or acquainted with.

తెలిసినవాడు. తత్వవేత్త one who has a knowledge of the truth.

వేత్రము vētramu. [Skt.] n. A rattan, cane, stick, staff, బెత్తము. A cane tree, a rattan tree. వేత్రధరుడు vetra-dharudu. n. One who carries a cane in his hand. A mace-bearer, a staff-bearer, a door-keeper. ద్వారపాలకుడు. వేత్రపాణి vētra-pāṇi. n. The leader of a musical band. నాట్యముచేర్పువాడు. "నిలిచిననాట్యమునకు నేర్పరియైన వేత్రపాణికిఁగనియముంబుజేసి." Pal. 284. వేత్రవతి vetra-vati. n. The river Betwa, which rises in the province of Malwa and falls into the Jamna. నదివిశేషము.

వేదండము vēdandamu. [Skt.] n. An elephant, ఏనుగు. వేదండగతి a soft pace.

వేదన vēdana. [Skt.] n. Pain, smart, ache, agony, torment, torture, distress, నొప్పి. కష్టము, వ్యథ, దుఃఖము. Perception, sensation, feeling, knowledge, తెలియడము, తెలివి.

వేదము vēdamu. [Skt. ✓ vid. to know.] n. Knowledge, art, science, విద్య, జ్ఞానము. Divine knowledge or science, the sacred or inspired writings. The Veda or sacred books of the Hindus. బ్రహ్మముఖమందు పుట్టినచదువు, శ్రుతి, శాస్త్రము. వాడు చెప్పినది వేదము all he said was taken for gospel. వేదమూర్తులైన his reverence, his holiness, a title given to learned theologians. ధనుర్వేదము the art of the bow, i. e., archery. వేదశాస్త్రము vēda-śastramu. n. The Vedanta or philosophical portion of the Hindu Scriptures. వేదాంతము. వేదాంగములు vēd-āngamulu. n. plu. The sciences dependant on or auxiliary to the Vēdas. వ్యాకరణాదులైన షట్శాస్త్రములు. They are శిక్ష, the science of pronunciation and articulation, కల్పము the detail of religious ceremonies, వ్యాకరణము grammar, ఛందస్సు prosody, జ్యోతిషము astronomy, నిరుక్తి the explanation of the difficult or obscure words and phrases that occur in the Vedas. వేదాంతము vēd-antamu. n. The theological part of the Vedas, i. e., the Upanishads, ఉపనిషత్తులు. A name given to the Advaita system of philosophy. వేదాంతి vēd-anti. n. A follower of the Vedanta philosophy, వేదాంతశాస్త్రమును చదివినవాడు, వేదాంతము తెలిసినవాడు. A bachelor, బ్రహ్మచారి.

వేది or వేదిక vēdi. [Skt.] n. A terrace, a piece of raised ground, a platform. An altar. యాగాదులు చేయుటకుగాను పరిష్కృతమైన భూమి, అరుగు, తిన్నె. వేది n. One who knows or is acquainted with. ఎరిగినవాడు. An epithet of Brahma. బ్రహ్మ. A man of learning. విద్వాంసుడు. త్రిభువనవేది one who knows all nature.

వేదు vēdu. [Tel.] n. A stench, bad smell, వికటగంధము. A smell, గంధము. Nausea, వెగటు. A disgusting word, వెగటుమాట.

వేదురు vēduru. [Tel.] n. Madness, foolishness. వెర్రి, ఉన్మాదము. "ఏమిదవేదురుగొన్నవానివలెను." HK. ii. 118. "తొలంకతవేదురుగొన్నదుష్టమర్కటము." HD. i. 1385. A madman, fool, ఉన్మత్తుడు, మూఢుడు. "విజయుండువచ్చునే వేదురులార." భార. ఆశ్వ. iv.

వేద్యము vēdyamu. [Skt. విద్ to know.] adj. Fit to be known or evident, knowable, తెలియదగిన. ఇది తమకు వేద్యముగును it will be clear to you. వేద్యుడు vēdyudu. n. One who may be known. తెలియదగినవాడు. ఎరుగదగినవాడు. వేదాంతవేద్యుడు one who may be known through or by means of the Vedanta Philosophy.

వేధ vēdha. [Skt.] n. A name of Brahma, బ్రహ్మ. A learned man, విద్వాంసుడు.

వేధము vēdhamu. [Skt.] n. Pain, grief. బాధ. ఖగ్రహవేధలు. శిక. పార్శ్వవేధలు obstacles, hindrances. H. iv 74. వామపార్శ్వవేధలు or బత్తీలు the evil influence of a star

వేధించు *vēdhintsu.* v. a. To pain, torment, tease. బాధించు, పీడించు. వేధితము *vēdhitamu.* adj. Pained, teased, tormented, బాధింపబడిన.

వేనలి *vēnali.* [from Skt. వేణి.] n. A braid of hair, a woman's hair tied in a tuft, a queue. జడ, కొప్పు. A hair, వెండ్రుక. "వేనలిజారి నిక్కి యునే మేను దూర్పెన సైప్రా లగా." Parij. ii. 11.

వేనవేలు See under వేయి.

వేప *vēpa.* [Tel. from వేము.] n. The Margosa or Neem tree. నింబవృక్షము. వేపాకు the leaves of this tree. వేపనూనె margosa oil. కరివేపచెట్టు a tree called *Bergera kœnigii*, whose aromatic leaves are used in cookery. నేలవేము Colombo-root, *Justicia*. కొండవేము a tree, a beautiful variety of the *Melia azadirachta*. తురక వేపచెట్టు *Olax scandens* or *Melia sempervirens.* Rox. వేపపూపండుగ or సంవత్సరాది పండుగ the feast held at the season when the Margosa tree is in flower. This is the Telugu New Year's Day. See వేము.

వేపథువు *vēpadhuvu.* [Skt.] n. Tremor, trembling, tremulousness, కంపము. స్వర కంపము. The shaking palsy, Paralysis agitans. వైద్య. p. 224. వేపనము *vēpanamu.* n. Shaking, shivering, trembling, nervousness, కంపనము, వణుకుట. వేపితము *vēpitamu.* adj. Quivering, shaking, trembling. కంపితమైన.

వేపి or బేపి *vēpi.* [Tel. from వేగు] n. A dog. కుక్క. "వేట వేపులు పటి వేలుమచ్చిక మీర." Jagann. i. 15. "కొచ్చి వేపులు మానిపికోలలాది గ్రామసిమ్హములు." S. i. 130. "జడలచెక్కచిలి కంబాపోకలాడి సైకొని వేపికడించి లిపిఛిక్తి వనోదయ పోలె." S. ii. 49.

వేపు *vēpu.* [Tel. from వేగు.] v. a. To fry, roast, bake. వేయించు, వేచు. "పడిగింపుచుగా నితప్పి వేపించింపించి." BD. iv. 1942. వేపు or వేపుడు n. The act of frying, వేచుట. వేయించడము. వేపు or వేపుడు adj. Baked. వేయించిన, వేచిన. వేపుడుబియ్యము roasted rice, fried or baked in a pan without ghee. n. A frying pan. వేయించు పెట్టి.

వేబోక Same as వేగుబోక. See under వేగు.

వేమము *vēmamu.* [Skt.] n. A loom. సాలె వాడు నేయుపలక, నేతపలక, మగ్గము.

వేము *vēmu.* [Tel.] n. The Margosa or Neem tree, *Ammyadirachta indica.* నింబవృక్షము. See వేప.

వేమాడు or వేముడు *vēmuḍu.* [Tel.] n. A name used for God. దేవుడు. "అముడకాముడకదవులు, గ్రామములను కొనువుదులకర్తమునెంతే, తామెం దులోపడంగిన, వేముడుతో దగునుచునవచ్చు వెంటనె." Vēma. 2150.

వేయి, వెయి or వెయ్యి *veyi.* [Tel.] pron. A thousand. సహస్రము. Plu. వేలు. వేనవేలు *vena-vēlu.* n. (వేలు+వేలు.) Many thousands. అనేక వేలు. వేమరు or వేమారు *vē-māru.* adv. A thousand times, again and again, over and over, often, constantly. పలుమారు, మాటిమాటికి. వేమాటికి *vē-māṭiki.* adv. Again and again. వేయంచులకైదువు *vey-antsula-kaiduvu.* n. Lit. a thousand edged weapon; an epithet of Vishnu's discus, విష్ణుచక్రము. వేయిచేతులరేడు *veyi-chētula-reḍu.* n. Lit: the thousand handed lord, i. e., the sun, సూర్యుడు. వేవెలుగు the sun. వేయిచేతులవయుకమీడు an epithet of కార్తవీర్యార్జునుడు. వేయునేల or వెయ్యేల *vey-un-ēla.* Why a thousand words? In a word, in short. వేలతరబడి *vēla-tarabaḍi.* adv. Thousands on thousands, అనేకసహస్రములు.

వేయించు *vēyintsu.* [Tel. for వేగించు or వేచు.] v. a. To fry, heat, warm, roast, bake. వేగునట్లు చేయు. [Causative of వేయు.] To cause to throw. వేయునట్లు చేయు.

వేయు *vēyu*. [Tel.] v. a. To throw, cast, or fling. To discharge a missile weapon, or fire arms. To let drop, జారవిడుచు. To place, put, put on, as a dress. తొడుగు. దానిని చెంపమీద ఒక దెబ్బ వేసినాడు he gave her a slap on the cheek. ఆ గుడ్డను బల్లమీద వేసినాడు he put the cloth on the table. నాకూటిలో రాయి వేసినాడు he threw a stone into my food, i.e., he injured my livelihood. మూతవేయు to put a lid on, shut. తలుపు వేసినాడు he shut the door. రాత్రి అంతా నేను రెప్పవేయలేదు I did not close my eyes all last night. కోలాటము వేస్తున్నారు they are dancing a Kolatam. గంతులు వేయు to leap. బండికట్టు or వేయు to make the carriage ready. జల్లము వేయు or జీనికట్టు or వేయు to saddle a horse. ప్రశ్న వేయు to ask a question. గుడిసె వేయు to build a hut. దివిటీలు వేయు to light torches. లెక్క వేయు to add up an account. ఆ ఆవు దూడ వేసినది the cow calved. మబ్బు వేసినది it is now cloudy. మేత వేయు to give fodder. కూతవేయు to give a cry. "వేయ్యనరట్టు ట్టిపొమ్మని వినుక కుబడ త్రొచిపి పు వే సె గా పెలుచగా." Vish. ii. 14. పడమటిగాలి వేసేటప్పుడు when the land-wind blows. నాకు భయము వేస్తున్నది I am afraid. కంపు వేస్తున్నది it is stinking. As an auxiliary added to some past participles, it denotes completeness of action and may be expressed by "up, off, on, down, through, away." కోసివేయు to cut off. మూసివేయు to shut up. తోసివేయు to push away. తీసివేయు to draw out. పీకివేయు to pluck up or out. కొట్టివేయు to strike down or cut off. వ్రాసివేయు to write off. ఇచ్చివేయు to give away. తినివేయు to eat up. It is also used with an infinitive; as పడవేయు to cast down; పారవేయు to throw away. వేసికొను *vēsi-konu*. v. a. To put, place, eat, consume. నా సొత్తును వాని నోటిలో వేసికొన్నాడు he devoured my property. ఆ మాత్రను నోట్లో వేసుకొన్నాడు he put the pill in his mouth. టోపి వేసుకొన్నాడు he put on his hat. మిడతవేసుకొనిపోయిన పంట corn eaten up by the locusts.

వేరియ *vēriya*. [H.] n. A tack in sailing. వేరియఫిరాయించు to make a tack or turn.

వేరు *vēru*. [Tel.] n. Separation, division, విభాగము, విభజన. Difference, distinction. భేదము. adj. Other, another, అన్యము. Separate, distinct, different, other, another. ప్రత్యేకము గానుండే, భేదముగల, వేరే. "మహాదాదులందాత్మకంటె వేరులవియటంచు తలచువాడు." B. iii. 18. వేరిమి or వేరడము *vērimi*. n. Difference, enmity, భేదము. వేరము or వేరము *vērami*. n. Enmity, విరోధము, పగ. వేరుపడు or వేర్పడు *vēru-paḍu*. v. n. To be separated, to differ, భేదపడు. వేరుపాటు or వేర్పాటు *vēru-pāṭu*. n. Separation. భేదపడుట. Enmity, విరోధము. Difference, distinction, భేదము. వేరుపోవు Same as వేరుపడు. వారు వేరుపడినారు they separated. వేరుపుచ్చు *vēru-puṭṭsu*. v. a. To divide, separate. ప్రత్యేకపరచు, ఎడబాపు. వేవ్వేరు *vēv-vēru*. (వేరు+వేరు.) adj. Separate, distinct. వేరువేరుగా, వేర్వేరు or వేరేవేరే *vēru-vēruga*. adv. Separately, differently, distinctly, each by itself. ప్రత్యేకముగా. వేరే *vērē*. adj. Other, another, distinct. ఇతరమైన, భిన్నమైన. వేరొక *vēr-oka*. adj. Another, మరియొక. వేరొకడు another man, మరియొకడు.

వేరు *vēru*. [Tel.] n. A root. మూలము. plu. వేరులు or వేళ్లు. వేరిడి *vēr-iḍi*. [వేరు+ఇడి.] n. A fool, a mad man. అవివేకి, వెర్రివాడు, వెర్రి స్త్రీ. "వృథాబోధకుండు వేరిడి గాడే." P. i. 729. వేరిడించు *vēriḍintsu*. v. n. To cause to become foolish, అవివేకమునుపొందజేయు. వేరుపారు or వేరూతన్ను *vēru-pāru*. v. a. To take root. వేరుపనస *vēru-panasa*. n. That kind of jack tree, the fruit of which springs from the root. A. i. 21. వేరుమల్లె *vēru-malle*. n. A creeper called *Ipomea cymosa*. వేరుసంపెంగ *vēru-sampenga*. n. A plant called *Polyanthes tuberosa*. వేరు సెనగ *vēru-senaga*. n. The ground nut. *Arachis hypogæa* (Watts). వేరుశనగచెనగ లు. వేరువిత్తు *vēru-vittu*. n. A bane, ruin, destroyer. నాశకము, నాశకుడు. "వినవేమీకు ల్లవేరువిత్తనినన్ను." M. VIII. iv. 247. "వంశాలవేరువిత్తు." H. iii. 268.

వేల *vēla*. [Skt.] n. A limit, boundary, the sea-shore, పొలిమేర, సముద్రపుచెలియలికట్ట. An inundation of the sea, ఉప్పెన. Painless death, అనాయాసమరణము.

వేలము *vēlamu*. [from Skt. వేష్టనము.] n. A camp, శిబిరము, పాళెము, దండుదిగియుండు చోటు. "అనివేలమంతయుఁబుడుచాటించి." Pal. 308. "వచ్చినయారుడడి వేలముజొచ్చి." ib. 200. Also, same as వేడము (q. v.)

వేలము or వేలాము *vēlamu*. [H.] n. An auction. వేలముపాడు or వేలము వేయు *vēlamu-pāḍu*. v. a. To auction, to sell by auction. వేలంపాట, వేలముపాట or వేలాముపాట *vēlam-pāṭa*. n. An announcement in an auction sale.

వేలార్చు *vēl-ārtsu*. [Tel.] v. a. To throw away, cast off, get rid of. పోగొట్టు. "తద్వేదనవేలార్పంజాలితి." M. VIII. ii. 241.

వేలిమి *vēlimi*. [Tel.] n. A burnt offering. హోమము. "వేలిమియుఁబూజలురార్చనయు, విప్రసపర్యయుఁజిక్కి." Swa. ii. 57. వేలిమి కట్టెలు firewood used in a burnt sacrifice. వేలిమిబొట్టు a mark made on the forehead with the ashes from a burnt sacrifice, రక్ష. "నొసలివేలిమిబొట్టు మసిమీద మృగనాభితిలకంబుబటువుగాదీర్చవచ్చు." R. ii. 109.

వేలు, వ్రేలు, వేలాడు or వ్రేలాడు *vēlu*. [Tel.] v. n. To hang, to be suspended, to dangle. లంబితమగు. వేలబడు or వ్రేలబడు *vēla-baḍu*. v. n. To hang, be pendent, వేలాడు. వేలవేయు *vēla-vēyu*. v. a To hang, to suspend, వేలాడవేయు. తలవేలవేసికొని యున్నాడు or ముఖము వేలవేసికొనియున్నా డు he is downcast, i. e., hanging down his head. A. iv. 22. వేలుడుబొజ్జ a big paunch.

వేలు *vēlu*. [Tel plu. of వేయి.] pron. Thousands. సహస్రములు. "కొండ్రవేల్పండు." R. i. 111. అనగా చాలుమల్లిండియున్నపది వేలాదిగా పండును.

వేలు or వ్రేలు *vēlu*. [Tel.] n. A finger, a toe, a claw. An inch. అంగుళము. పెను వేలు or బొటనవేలు the thumb or great toe. చిటికెనవేలు the little finger or toe. ఆ విద్యలో వాడు వీనికంటె ఒకటువేళ్లు మించిన వాడు that man is a little above this one in learning. వేలువిడిచినమేనమామ an uncle removed by one step of relationship, lit: by the omission of one finger. ఏమైనా వేలుకు వేలు ఎడమే every two fingers are separate: a proverb, meaning that there is a difference even between those (son, nephews, &c.) who appear to be equally in favour. నోట్లో వేలుపెట్టుకొనిపోయినాడు he went off with his finger in his mouth, i.e., he was disappointed or cheated.

వేలుచు, వేల్చు or వ్రేల్చు *vēlutsu*. [Tel.] v. a. To offer up a burnt sacrifice. హోమముచేయు. infin. వేల్వ. వేల్పించు *vēlpintsu*. v. a. To cause to offer a burnt offering. హోమముచేయించు. "హోమము ల్వేల్పించి." ND. ii. 553.

వేలుపు or వేల్పు *vēlupu*. [Tel.] n. A god or goddess, దేవుడు, దేవత. ఇలవేల్పు a god of this world, i.e., a Brahmin. ఇలువేల్పు a patron saint, a genius or household god. వేలుపుటన్ను a goddess. దేవతాస్త్రీ. T ii. 106. వేలుపుటేలు or వేలుపుటేరు the heavenly stream, the celestial Ganges, ఆకాశగంగ; the river Ganges, గంగ. వేలుపుగాయ a mythological being, a Gandharva, గంధర్వుడు. వేలుపుగిడ్డి or వేల్పుటావు the mythological cow that grants all wishes, కామధేనువు. వేలుపుచెట్టు the divine tree that grants all wishes, కల్పవృక్షము. వేలుపు జెడగాఁడు the divine ascetic or monk. i. e., Narada, నారదుడు. వేలుపుటొజ్జ the divine preceptor or Guru, i. e., Brihaspati, సురాచార్యుడు, బృహస్పతి. వేలుపుదాయ an enemy of the gods, i. e., an Asura. వేలుపు బాస the language of the gods, i. e., Sanskrit. వేలుపుబోనము the food of the gods, i. e., Ambrosia, అమృతము. వేలుపుమల or వేల్పుకొండ the hill of the gods, i. e., Mount Meru. వేలుపుమానికము the diamond of the gods, i. e., the philosopher's stone, a jewel that grants all that may be desired, చింతామణి. వేలుపురేడు or వేల్పుదొర the lord of the gods, i. e., Indra. వేలుపుసాని a fortune teller, సోదెచెప్పునది, దైవజ్ఞ. వేలుపుగోయి the white elephant of the gods, ఐరావతము. వేలుపులత్రోవ the sky, ఆకాశము. వేలుపు టిక్క heaven, స్వర్గము. వేల్పుదళవాయి the general of the gods, i. e., Kumāraswāmi, కుమారస్వామి. వేల్పుపెద్ద Brahma, బ్రహ్మదేవుడు, సురజ్యేష్ఠుడు. వేల్పువెజ్జు the physician of the gods, i. e., Dhanvantari, ధన్వంతరి. వేల్పుడు vēlpudu. n. Worship, పూజ.

వెల్మిడి or వ్రేల్మిడి vēl-miḍi. [Tel.] n. A snap or sound of the thumb and finger, చిటిక. "మృదుపూజ జేసి వ్రేల్మిడిలోన బసిడిబడయుటకు." BD. v 468. వ్రేల్మిడిలోన in a moment. చిటికవేయునంతసేపులో.

వెల్లనము vēllanamu. [Skt.] n. Surrounding, చేష్టనము. Shaking. కదలడము, చలనము, ఊగడము. "డోలావెల్లనసుఖలోలుడై." G. ii. 101. వెల్లితము vēllitamu. adj. Shaken, trembling, tremulous. కదలింపబడిన, వ్రేలాడుచున్న. Crooked, bent, వక్రమైన, వంకి.

వేళ vēḷa. [Skt.] n. Time, a time, period or opportunity. కార్యోచితసమయము. కాలము. తరి. ఈవేళ to day, this time. ఆవేళ that day, that time. ఇంకొకవేళరండి come another time. ఒకవేళ perhaps. గంటవేళ one hour's time. రాత్రివేళ night time. సంధ్యవేళ the evening. ఆవేళను at that time. వేళలు (or సమయములు) కాచుకుండెడివారు they who watch for an opportunity. అట్లుచెప్పేవేళకు on his saying so. వాడు వేళాపాళా చూడడు he does not care for time or season. వేళము vēḷamu. [from Skt. వేళ.] adv. Quickly, త్వరితముగా.

వేళాకోళము vēḷa-kōḷamu. [Tel.] n. Intricacy. చిక్కు. Ridicule, derision, joking, పరిహాసము. వేళాకోళముపొందు to be caught in difficulties, చిక్కులబడు; to be ridiculed, పరిహాసింపబడు. "అలంబిడ్డలకొరకైజాలింబడి ధనముగూర్చిచచ్చినదనుకని వేళాకోళము నొందుచు స్త్రీలోలుండైనవాడుచెడిపోవాడై." Ramestava Raj. ii. 62. వేళాకోళపు vēḷa-kōḷapu. adj. Intricate, puzzling. చిక్కు గా నుండే. "క॥ వేళాకోళపుదిగెలు, తేలికలుగలాసములును తీరజడలుదా, చాలుచుపెట్లాకొమింటికా, లీలాహరి దోలనింత నేగ్వరియయ్యెకా." KP. iii. 79. Ridiculing, joking, derisive, పరిహాసమైన.

వేవిలి or వేవిలిచేను vēvili. [Tel.] n. A field ploughed last year but this year lying fallow. నిరుడుదున్ని నిలిపినపొలము. A field cultivated only at intervals. An uncultivated field, దున్ననిపొలము. A field, పొలము. adj. Occasional, done at intervals.

"క॥ దేవార్చనానిమిత్తము,
దావేరొకతోటసేయుదలచియతండా,
తావుగ్రహస్థులచేతన్,
వేవిలిను క్షేత్రభూమినిలువకుగొనియెన్."

వై. i.

వేవిళ్లు vēviḷlu. [Tel.] n. The longing, sluggishness and other affections of a pregnant woman. గర్భిణీస్త్రీయొక్క వాంత్యాది వికారములు.

వేవు Same as వేగు, to dawn (q. v.) వేవుజాము Same as వేగుజాము or వేకువజాము. See under వేగు.

వేపుడు Same as వేసట. (q. v.)

వేశము *vēśamu*. [Skt.] n. A house in general. గృహము. The abode of harlots. వేశ్యలవాడ. వేశ్మము *vēśmamu*. n. A house. ఇల్లు. H. ii. 220. వేశ్య or వేశ్యాంగన *vēśya*. n. A harlot, a prostitute. భోగముది. వేశ్యాప్రేమము a harlot's love, pretended affection.

వేషము or వేశము *vēshamu*. [Skt.] n. Dress, garb, habit, a fashion or manner of dress, costume, a disguise or guise. వస్త్రభూషణాదులు అలంకరించుకొనడము. మారు వేషము a false garb, a disguise. "తత్కుండ నిక్క వేషధరుడై." M. I. i. 151. వేషము వేయు to put on a disguise. కృష్ణవేషము వేసినాడు or కట్టినాడు he dressed or disguised himself as Krishna. తలనొప్పిగానున్నదని వేషము వేసినాడు he feigned a head-ache. వేషగాడు *vēsha-gāḍu*. n. An actor; an impostor, వేషములువేసేవాడు. వేషధారి *vēsha-dhāri*. n. A person in disguise, a hypocrite, an impostor, మారువేషము వేసు కొన్నవాడు. వేషాలమారి *vēshāla-māri*. n. One who feigns, a pretender, a cheat, మాయలమారి. వేషి *vēshi*. n. One who is disguised. వేషధారి. "ఇంద్రుడు ప్రియుండుగ గాకమవేషియైనవాడని." BRY. v. 37.

వేష్టనము *vēshṭanamu*. [Skt.] n. Surrounding, encompassing. చుట్టుకొనడము. వేష్టించు *vēshṭinṭsu*. v. a. To surround, encompass, encircle; to wrap round, twist round. చుట్టుకొను. చుట్టు. వేష్టితము *vēshṭitamu*. adj. Surrounded, encompassed. చుట్టుకొనబడిన. వేష్టము *vēshṭamu*. n. Gum, resin. బంక. A hedge all round, చెట్టుకంచె. వేష్టువ *vēshṭuva*. (from వేష్టనము.) n. A garment. దోవతి.

వేసంగి, వేసగి or వేసవి *vēsangi*. [from Skt. వైశాఖ.] n. The summer, the hot season, ఎండకాలము, గ్రీష్మఋతువు. వేసంగిసెలవులు midsummer holidays.

వేసట *vēsaṭa*. [Tel. from వేసరు.] n. Fatigue, weariness, vexation. అలయిక, అలసట, శ్రమ ము, విసుకు. "జలము త్రావివేసటదీరనదట." Sar. D. 209.

వేసడము *vēsaḍamu*. [from Skt. వేసరము.] n. A mule. కంచరగాడిద. [Tel.] A kind of hawk, ఒకవిధమైనడేగ. "విడిచెవడిగ్గెజా నొకపెద్ద వేసడంబు." Swa. iv. 85.

వేసము *vēsamu*. [from Skt. వేషము.] Same as వేషము (q. v.) Plu. వేసాలు. "వేసాల గ్లాభువిలో త్రాసాలకొగాకముక్కికలిమికి నేలా." వేసగాడు *vēsa-gāḍu*. n. A person in disguise, a masker, అన్యవేషములువేసికొన్న వాడు. వేసాలమారి *vēsāla-māri*. n. One who feigns, మాయలమారి.

వేసరము *vēsaramu*. [Skt.] A mule. వేసడ ము. [Tel.] n. Fatigue, trouble, vexation, శ్రమము. వేసరి *vēsari*. n. A tormentor, బాధకుడు. వేసరించు *vēsarinṭsu*. v. a. To fatigue, vex, or disgust. విసికించు, అలస టపెట్టించు, శ్రమపెట్టు. వేసరు or వేసారు *vēsaru*. v. n. To be fatigued, vexed, disgusted, విసుగు, అలసటపడు, బడలు. To be troubled or pained, శ్రమపడు. నొచ్చు. To be grieved, విచారముకొను.

వేసవి Same as వేసంగి. (q. v.)

వేస్తము Same as వేసడము. (q. v.)

వై vai

వైకక్షకము or వైకక్ష్యకము *vai-kakshakamu*. [Skt.] n. A garland worn like a sash. జంధెమువలె వేసికొనుపూదండ.

వైకటికుడు *vaikaṭikuḍu*. [Skt.] n. A lapidary. రత్నములసానబట్టేవాడు.

వైకల్పికము *vai-kalpikamu*. [Skt. from వికల్పము.] adj. Doubtful, alternative, optional, వికల్పముచేతకలిగిన, సందిగ్ధమైన, పక్షాంతరమైన.

వైకల్యము *vaikalyamu*. [Skt. from వికలము.] n. Lameness, mutilation. Deficiency, defect. Agitation flurry, confusion, perturbation, వికలత, వికలత్వము, వికృతభావము. అంగ వైకల్యము maimedness or lameness. చిత్తవైకల్యము confusion of mind, blindness of heart.

వైకుంఠము *vaikunṭhamu*. [Skt.] n. The paradise of Vishnu. విష్ణువుండెడిస్థానము. మా తండ్రికి వైకుంఠప్రాప్తిఅయిన తరువాత after the death of my father. వైకుంఠుడు *vaikunṭhuḍu*. n. A name of Vishnu. విష్ణువు. Also, applied to Indra.

వైకృతము *vaikṛitamu*. [Skt. from వికృతి. adj. Changed, modified. వికృతిపొందిన, మారురూపుగల.

వైఖరి *vaikhari*. [Skt.] n. Manner, appearance, way, రీతి, విధము.

వైఖానసుడు *vaikhānasuḍu*. [Skt.] n. A monk. వానప్రస్థుడు.

వైగుణ్యము *vai-guṇyamu*. [Skt. from విగుణము.] n. The state of having no qualities, విగుణత్వము.

వైఘ *vaigha*. [Skt.] n. The name of the stream near Madura.

వైచక్షణ్యము *vaichakshaṇyamu*. [Skt. from విచక్షణం.] n. Discrimination, విచక్షణత.

వైచిత్ర్యము *vai-chitryamu*. [Skt. from విచిత్రము.] n. Strangeness, peculiarity, diversity, విచిత్రత.

వైచు or వయిచు *vaitsu*. [Tel. connected with వేయు.] v. a. To cast, throw, విసరి వేయు. To throw down, పడవేయు.

వైజననము *vai-jananamu*. [Skt.] n. The last month of pregnancy, ప్రసవమగునెల, ఈనేనెల, ప్రాద్దుటనెల. A. iv. 176.

వైజయంతము *vai-jayantamu*. [Skt.] n. Indra's palace. ఇంద్రసౌధము. వైజయంతి *vai-jayanti*. n. A banner, a flag. ధ్వజము. The garland of Vishnu. విష్ణుమాలిక. వైజయంతికుడు *vai-jayantikuḍu*. n. A standard bearer. టెక్కెముపట్టువాడు.

వైజాత్యము *vai-jatyamu*. [Skt. from విజాతి.] n. The state of belonging to a different caste, విజాతిత్వము. వైజాతి or వయిజాతి *vai-jati*. n. A certain low caste among Komatis. కోమట్లలో ఒకవిధమైన నీచకులము. "మఱి అగసాలె, సాలె, మటుసాలె, వాని, వైజాతి." A. iv. 56. వైజాతితొండ *vai-jati-tonḍa*. n. A chameleon. తొండ. "మీరు చెల్లెలి మునకు..." [illegible]

వైజ్ఞానికుడు *vai-gnyāni-kuḍu*. [Skt. from విజ్ఞానము.] n. A skilful person, an expert. నేర్పరి.

వైడము See వైరము.

వైడూర్యము *vaidūryamu*. [Skt. from విదూరము.] n. Lit. Pertaining to a country called విదూరము. The stone called a cat's-eye, lapis lazuli. విదూరజము. పిల్లికన్రతనము.

వైణవము *vainavamu*. [Skt. from వేణువు.] adj. Made of bamboo. Produced by the bamboo, వెదురుతోచేయబడిన, వెదురునపుట్టిన. n. Bamboo rice, వెదురుబియ్యము. వైణవికుడు or వేణుకుడు *vainavikuḍu*. n. A flute-player. పిల్లంగ్రోవియూదువాడు. Vasu. v. 81.

వైణికుడు *vainikuḍu*. [Skt. from వీణ.] n. A player on the *Veena*, వీణవాయించువాడు.

వైతనికుడు *vaitanikuḍu* [Skt. from వేతనము.] n. A hired labourer, a cooly. కూలివాడు, కూలికి పనిచేయువాడు.

వైతరణి *vaitarani*. [Skt. from వితరణి.] n. The river of fire that is said to exist in hell. The Hindu Styx. నరకమందలి నిప్పులనది. The name of the mother of the Rakshasas or giants. రాక్షసులతల్లి.

వైతాళిక *vaitalika*. [Skt. from వితాళము.] n. A melody or tune which is without a marked time. రాగవిశేషము. **వైతాళికుడు** *vaitalikudu*. n. A king's bard. తేకువను or వాలకు మేలుకొలుపులుపాడువాడు, బట్టువాడు. "ఒకవైతాళికుడేసుదించి సభలోను స్తుతిపాఠ్యా ప్రయై." G. xi. 135.

వైదగ్ధి or **వైదగ్ధ్యము** *vai-dugdhi*. [Skt. from విదగ్ధము.] n. Dexterity, subtlety, cleverness, skill. విదగ్ధత, విదగ్ధత్వము, చాతుర్యము, నైపుణ్యము. నేర్పు.

వైదర్భి *vaidarbhi*. [Skt. from విదర్భ.] n. The lady born at Vidarbha, a name of Damayanti wife of Nala or Rukmini the wife of Krishna. నలునిభార్య; రుక్మిణి. Also, a certain style of composition, రీతి విశేషము.

వైదికము *vaidikamu*. [Skt. from వేద.] adj. Pertaining to the Vedas; conformable to the Vedas. Canonical, clerical, sacred. వేదమందు చెప్పబడిన, లౌకికముకాని. n. Conformity to the Vedas; any sacred pursuit. ఈవేళ మాయింట్లో కొంచెము వైదికము a certain religious rite is to be celebrated in my house to-day. వాడు లౌకిక వైదికములందు నిండా సమర్థుడు he is equally skilled in sacred and secular pursuits. వైదికవిద్యలు the sacred studies. వైదికాగ్ని the sacred fire, i. e., fire on an altar, sacrificial fire as distinguished from లౌకికాగ్ని common fire. "విమమింత వైదికంబును లౌకికంబును రెండు విధములు యజ్ఞవిధులు." M. XIII. v. 192. వైదికలిపి or వైదికాక్షరము the clerkly hand, a round antique mode of writing like law-text. వైదికబ్రాహ్మణుడు a Vaidika Brahmin, i. e., one who is set apart for religious duties or studies; **వైదికుడు** *vaidikudu*. n. A Brahmin who knows the Vedas, వేదము తెలిసిన బ్రాహ్మణుడు. One who is engaged in sacred pursuits or studies. లౌకికుడుకానివాడు. One who does not know the world, లౌకికము తెలియనివాడు. ఇతడు శుద్ధవైదికుడు he is a very simple man.

వైదుషి or **వైదుష్యము** *vaidushi*. [Skt. from విదుష.] n. Learning, wisdom. పాండిత్యము, విద్యాంసునితనము, పాండిత్యము, జ్ఞానము.

వైదేహి *vaidehi*. [Skt. from విదేహ.] n. A title of Sita, wife of Rama సీతాదేవి. A female merchant, వర్తకురాలు. వైదేహుడు a merchant.

వైద్యము *vaidyamu*. [Skt. from విద్ to know.] n. The art of medicine, surgery. రోగచికిత్సాశాస్త్రము. **వైద్యుడు** *vaidyudu*. n. A physician or surgeon, a doctor చికిత్సకుడు, వెజ్జు.

వైధవ్యము *vaidhavyamu*. [Skt. from విధవ.] n. Widowhood. విధవాత్వము. ముండమోపితనము.

వైనతేయుడు *vaina-teyudu*. [Skt. from వినత.] n. Lit. The son of Vinata: a name of Garuda, the Brahminy kite. గరుత్మంతుడు.

వైనము or **వయినము** *vainamu*. [from Skt. వివరణము.] n. Particulars, detail, వివరము. A convenience, expedient, ఉపాయము. A cause. కారణము. Order, క్రమము. Manner, way, విధము, మార్గము. దానికి ఒక వైనముచేసెదను I will try a plan regarding it. వైనముగాపట్టుకొన్నాడు he held it cleverly so as to be handy. వాడు రాకుండా ఉండేదేమి వైనము what can be the cause of his not coming?

వైపరీత్యము *vaiparityamu*. [Skt. from విపరీతము.] n. Diversity, contrariety, opposition, adverseness. విపరీతత్వము. విరుద్ధము. ప్రాతికూల్యము. వ్యతిక్రమము. తెడబాటు.

వైపు or **వయిపు** *vaipu*. [Tel.] n. A direction, side, quarter, దిక్కు, ప్రక్క. An expedient.

convenience, way, manner, ఉపాయము, ఒడుపు, లక్ష్యము. ఆ కొండమీదికి ఎక్కుటకు నాకు వైపుచిక్కలేదు I did not find a way to go up the hill. "వైపు తెలిసి పలుకవలయును వేమ." Vema. 107. ఈ వైపువారు people of these parts. "కొనసు వైపుల నవ్వ కొనగోటమువ్వవాక మిమిస్తరింపజేతలిరుబోటి." Sakuntala. iii. 53. వైపుకాడు or వయిపుకాడు vaipu-kadu. n. A skilful contriver. ఉపాయశాలి. A man of resources. "గీ॥ బంగలదూసవంబు, ఎడిదికొని తెచ్చుచున్నట్టి వైపుకాడు." Surabhanda. 45.

వైభవము vaibhavamu. [Skt. from విభవము.] n. Wealth, riches, grandeur, splendour, విభవము, ఐశ్వర్యము, మహిమ. "అవాప్త కోటికమతర్క్య వైభవంబు." Lalito. viii. 27. వైభవుడు vaibhavudu. n. One who is flourishing or blooming. విభవముగలవాడు. "నవయౌవనవైభవుండు." Vish. ii. 87.

వైమనస్యము vai-manasyamu. [Skt. from విమనస్సు.] n. Aversion, dislike, estrangement, ill will, విమనోభావము, దుఃఖముతో మనసునొచ్చుట, పగ, విరుద్ధము, స్నేహభంగము.

వైమాత్రేయుడు vai-matreyudu. [Skt. from విమాత.] n. A half brother by a different mother, సవతితల్లికొడుకు.

వైమానికుడు vaimani-kudu. [Skt. from విమానము.] n. One who rides in a celestial car. విమానమెక్కి సంచరించువాడు.

వైమాలము vaimalamu. [Skt. from విమలము.] adj. Great, much, అధికము. వైమాల పుసిగ్గు great shame. వైమాలపుకోపము great anger.

వైయాకరణుడు vaiyakaranudu. [Skt. from వ్యాకరణము.] n. A grammarian, వ్యాకరణ శాస్త్రము తెలిసినవాడు.

వైయాత్యము vaiyatyamu. [Skt. from వియాతము.] n. Boldness, courage, ధైర్యము.

వైరము vairamu. [Skt. from వీరము.] n. Enmity, hostility, antipathy. శత్రుత్వము. వైరనిర్యాతనము or వైరశుద్ధి vaira-niryatanamu. n. Revenge, retaliation, requital of injury. ప్రతీకారము, పగతీర్చు కొనుట. వైరి vairi. n. An enemy, foe, adversary, శత్రువు, రిపుడు, పగవాడు. కరి వైరి the elephant's foe, i. e., the lion. adj. Hostile, inimical, విరోధమైన. వైరించు vairintsu. v. n. To entertain enmity, పగగొను.

వైరవులు, వైరాలు or వయిరాలు vairavulu. [Tel.] n. Charcoal fire, a burning brand or coal, కట్టెలనిప్పు. అంగారము.

వైరస్యము vairasyamu. [Skt. from విరసము.] n. Ill-will, enmity, విరసత్వము, ద్వేషము.

వైరాగి vai-ragi. [Skt. from విరాగము.] n. An ascetic, a devotee; a monk. విరక్తుడు, బైరాగి. వైరాగ్యము vai-ragyamu. n. Freedom from passion or worldly attachments, విరాగత్వము, విరక్తి. పురాణవైరాగ్యము the self restraint caused by reading pious books. ప్రసూతివైరాగ్యము the continence that impresses the mind of an accouchee. శ్మశానవైరాగ్యము the feelings of repentance caused by a funeral.

వైరి. వైరించు See under వైరము.

వైరూప్యము vai-rupyamu. [Skt. from విరూపము.] n. Ugliness, deformity, వికారత.

వైల or వయిల vaila. [Tel.] n. A kind of hawk.

వైలక్షణ్యము vai-lakshanyamu. [Skt. from విలక్షణము.] n. Contrariety, disparity, a difference. విభేదము. విలక్షణత.

వైలోమ్యము vai-lomyamu. [Skt. from విలోమము.] n. Reversal, reading a magic spell, &c. backwards. విలోమభావము. అనగా కొననుంచి మొదటికిచదవడము మొదలైనది.

వైలము or వైడము *vailamu.* [Tel.] n. Haste, speed. adv. Speedily. శీఘ్రముగా. "వచ్చె నివోరావో వైలంబయితును." HD. ii. 298. "వచ్చినవైలమునకు మెచ్చె నాయందు." Pal. 497. వైలము or వయిలము *vailamu.* n. A certain measure of musical time. తాళవిశేషము. "లాలించుచు వైలంబుతాళంబు. పాలి పెల్లాపెల్లిగాయచుగాయి." BD. iii. 1870.

వైవధికుడు *vaivadhikuḍu.* [Skt.] n. One who carries a కావడి. A hawker or pedlar, a news-bearer, a messenger. వార్తావహుడు, చిల్లరఅంగడివాడు. కావడిమీదిసరుకులమ్ముకొనువాడు.

వైవర్ణ్యము *vai-varṇyamu.* [Skt. from వివర్ణము.] n. Change of colour, becoming pale, వివర్ణత, తెల్లబోవుట.

వైవస్వతుడు *vaivasvatuḍu.* [Skt. from వివస్వత్.] n. A title of Yama. యముడు. The name of a Manu, ఒకమనువు.

వైవాహికము *vaivāhikamu.* [Skt. from వివాహము.] adj. Nuptial, matrimonial, relating to marriage. వివాహసంబంధమైన. "వారిజాక్షులందు వైవాహికములందు ప్రాణవిత్త మానభంగమందు." Bhag. vii.

వైశాఖము *vaiśākhamu.* [Skt. from విశాఖ.] n. The name of the second lunar month, ఒకనెలపేరు. A churning staff. కవ్వము.

వైశారద్యము *vai-śāradyamu.* [Skt. from విశారద.] n. Skill. విశారదత్వము, నేర్పు. Learning, పాండిత్యము.

వైశాల్యము *vaiśālyamu.* [Skt. from విశాలము.] n. Breadth, width, extent. విశాలత్వము, వెడల్పు.

వైశికము *vaiśikamu* [Skt connected with వేశ్య.] n. Harlotry, a courtezan's wiles or allurements, భోగముతనము. Cunning, కపటము. adj. Pertaining to a harlot, భోగముదాని. Blameworthy, దూష్యము. వైశికుడు *vaiśikuḍu.* n. A gallant, శృంగారనాయకులలోనొకడు. A licentious man.

వైశేషికము *vaiśeshikamu.* [Skt.] n. One of the six philosophical systems (Darsanas) of the Hindus, in which seven primeval principles are maintained as existing, సప్తపదార్థములను చెప్పునట్టి తర్కశాస్త్రము, దర్శనభేదము, షట్శాస్త్రములలోనొకటి. వైశేషికశాస్త్రము a treatise explaining this system.

వైశ్యుడు *vaiśyuḍu.* [Skt.] n. A man of the third Hindu caste, a merchant, తృతీయవర్ణస్థుడు, కోమటివాడు.

వైశ్రవణుడు *vaiśravaṇuḍu.* [Skt.] n. A name of Kubera, god of riches. కుబేరుడు.

వైశ్వదేవము *vaiśva-devamu.* [Skt. from విశ్వదేవ.] n. A form of sacrifice or prayers offered to all the gods of the world, పంచయజ్ఞములలోనొకటి, విశ్వదేవతలనుగూర్చిచేయు హోమము.

వైశ్వానరుడు *vaiśva-naruḍu.* [Skt. from విశ్వానర.] n. An epithet of the god of fire. అగ్ని.

వైషమ్యము *vaishamyamu.* [Skt. from విషమము.] n. Unevenness, inequality, విషమత్వము, అసమభావము. Enmity. శత్రుత్వము, వైరము.

వైషయికము *vaishayikamu.* [Skt. from విషయము.] adj. Pertaining to the phenomenal, cognisable by the senses, విషయసంబంధమైన.

వైష్ణవము *vaishṇavamu.* [Skt. from విష్ణు.] adj. Relating or belonging to Vishnu. విష్ణుసంబంధమైన. n. Vaishnavism, విష్ణుసంబంధమైనమతము. వైష్ణవుడు *vaishṇa-vuḍu.* n. A follower of Vishnu, విష్ణుభక్తుడు.

వైసారిణము *vaisāriṇamu.* [Skt.] n. A fish. చేప, మత్స్యము. Chen. iv. 346.

వైసిక or వయిసిక *vaisika.* [from Skt. వేషము.] n. Cunning, hypocrisy, కపటము.

వైస్వర్యము *vaisvaryamu.* [Skt. from విస్వరము.] n. Discordance of the voice. విస్వరత్వము.

వైహాయసము *vaihāyasamu.* [Skt. from విహాయసము.] adj. Ethereal, heavenly. గగనసంబంధమైన. "అటనీకునుమానితదేహుండేగ స్త్రైవాహాయసవిధి వారిదముఖ్యామరసంఘముమిక్కిలి యొప్పై." Parij. iii. 10.

వైహాళి *vaihāḷi.* [Skt.] n. Same as వాహ్యాళి (q. v.) Also, Tumult. సందడి. "భక్తిచయసంగాఢస్వరుండును విజితంబడి విస్తారంబుగాగల గవైహాళిదిక్పులయెల్లజగములంగూర్పుండ నిరుమించిగల ధిలుపుట్టుకుండ నెడనెడందలతరులనిలిచి." G. vii. 63.

వో vo

వోఢ *voḍha.* [Skt.] n. A charioteer, a car-driver తోలునడవువాడు. A carrier మోయువాడు.

వ్య vya

వ్యంగ్యము *vyangyamu.* [Skt.] n. Sarcasm, irony, covert expression of contempt, &c. అపక్షేపము, శ్లేషకథ. వ్యంగ్యోక్తి a sarcastic speech or expression. "కాంతికల్లనిదియొవ్యంగ్యముగానబడక." L. viii. 84. Impropriety, indecency, indelicacy, ఎబ్బెరికము. ఇది వారికి వ్యంగ్యముగాదు among them this is no indecency. వ్యంజకము *vyanjakamu.* adj. Making clear or plain, distinguishing, indicative or expressive of passion or feeling. ప్రకాశకమైన, సూచకమైన, బోధకమైన. వ్యంజనము *vyanjanamu.* n. A mark, sign, token. గురుతు, చిహ్నము. A consonant. (in grammar.) హల్లు, కాదిఅక్షరము. A sauce, or condiment. ఆమిష్టపరిణము. కూర. వ్యంజితము *vyanjitamu.* adj. Made visible, manifested. తెలుపబడిన. "జలధి వ్యంజితకారుదముల్ ప్రకటయుగళ్ల క్షేమసంపాదనల్." N. iv. 40.

వ్యక్తము *vyaktamu.* [Skt.] adj. Apparent, clear, manifest, evident, disclosed, revealed, distinct, specified, తెల్లమైన, స్పష్టమైన, ప్రకాశితమైన, తెలియబడిన. వ్యక్తత or వ్యక్తత్వము *vyaktata.* n. Distinctness, manifestation. స్పష్టత. వ్యక్తి *vyakti.* n. An incarnation, జాతికేర్పైన జాతికి ఆశ్రయమైన స్వరూపము, పృథక్స్వరూపము. An individual, a person, a man, జనుడు. ఒకడు. Manifestation, స్పష్టము. "భక్తిహితార్థమైప్ర థమంబెరిగకు, వ్యక్తిగాచెప్పితి వనజముఖి." BD. i. 477. వ్యక్తిగా, అనగా స్పష్టముగా. "భక్తునకును దోడు పరిచారునిచ్చి, వ్యక్తిసందర్శనాసక్తిని తెంచి." ib. v. 444. వ్యక్తుడు *vyaktuḍu.* n. A man of the world, a man of understanding. తెలిసినవాడు, తెలివిగలవాడు. వ్యక్తురాలు *vyaktu-r-ālu.* n. A clever woman, a woman of understanding. తెలివిగలది.

వ్యగ్రము *vyagramu.* [Skt.] adj. Bewildered, confused, perplexed. Eager, ardent, zealous. వ్యాకులమైన, ఆసక్తిగల. "కామకథర వ్యగ్రాంతరంగుండు." Swa. i. 39. వ్యగ్రత *vyagrata.* n. Perplexity, anxiety. వ్యాకులము. చింత. వ్యగ్రుడు *vyagruḍu.* n. One who is perplexed or anxious, తొందరపడువాడు.

వ్యజనము *vyajanamu.* [Skt.] n. A fan. తాళవృంతము, విసనకర్ర.

వ్యతికరము *vyati-karamu.* [Skt.] n. A misfortune, calamity, reverse, grief, trouble, ఆపద, క్షోభము. వ్యసనము. వినర్గము. Reciprocity, reciprocal action, వ్యతిహారము. పరస్పరక్రియ.

వ్యతిక్రమము *vy-ati-kramamu.* [Skt. వి+అతిక్రమము.] n. Contrariety, irregularity, transgression, wrong, క్రమవిపర్యయము, అతిక్రమము.

వ్యతిరేకము *vy-ati-rēkamu.* [Skt.] n. Contrariety, difference, opposition, disagreement, change, విరోధము, భిన్నత, వేరు, మారు. అన్వయవ్యతిరేకములు తెలియలేదు whether it will succeed or no is uncertain, అనుకూల్య ప్రాతికూల్యములు తెలియలేదు. adj. Contrary, opposed to, negative. విరోధమైన. ఆజ్ఞకు వ్యతిరేకముగా against orders. వ్యతిరేకార్థకము, (in Gram.) the negative form of the verb. **వ్యతిరిక్తము** *vy-ati-riktamu.* adj. Different, distinct, contrary, opposite, excepted, withdrawn, భిన్నమైన, వేరుపడిన, మారుపడిన.

వ్యతీపాతము *vy-atī-pātamu.* [Skt.] n. The seventeenth of the astrological Yogas, ఒక గ్రహయోగము, పంచాంగయోగభేదము. A portent, a prodigy indicating calamity, as a comet, earthquake, &c. అత్యుత్పాతము, ఉపద్రవము. Applied figuratively to a naughty, troublesome, mischievous child. Contempt, అనాదరము. Fleeing from a battle, యుద్ధమున వెనుదీయుట. ఓరోరీ వ్యతీపాత go along, you fool! "అలుకమీరమర్కనిబకిరణాళినించి యామునకాచునూగింప నప్పుడున్ననిత సందోగమునన వ్యతీపాతసంజ్ఞ బొడమెనొక్కడు ముజ్జగంబులయందు." T. v. 120.

వ్యత్యయము or **వ్యత్యాసము** *vyatyayamu.* [Skt.] n. Difference, భేదము. Contrariety, opposition, variation, inverted or retrograde order, విపర్యయము, వ్యతిక్రమము. వ్యత్యయముగా contrarily, విరుద్ధముగా. **వ్యత్యస్తము** *vyatyastamu.* adj. Differing, contrary, opposite, reverse, వ్యత్యాసపడిన.

వ్యథ *vyadha.* [Skt.] n. Pain, soreness, ache, agony, torture, suffering, distress, బాధ, నొప్పి. **వ్యథితము** *vyadhitamu.* adj. Pained, hurt, sore, distressed. పీడింపబడిన, దుఃఖితమైన.

వ్యపదేశము *vy-apa-dēśamu.* [Skt. వి+అపదేశము.] n. A great pretence, a notable fraud, a stratagem, మిక్కిలి కపటము, మిష, వ్యాజము.

వ్యభిచరించు *vy-abhi-char-intsu.* [Skt. వి+అభి+చరించు.] v. n. To go astray, తప్పిచరించు. To commit adultery, రంకుపోవు. **వ్యభిచారము** *vy-abhi-chāramu.* n. Deviation from the common rule: fornication, adultery, తప్పిచరించుట, భ్రష్టాచారము, రంకు. **వ్యభిచారి** or **వ్యభిచారిణి** *vy-abhi-chāri.* n. An adulteress, a harlot, jilt. రంకులాలు. **వ్యభిచారుడు** *vy-abhi-chārudu.* n. An adulterer.

వ్యయము *vyayamu.* [Skt.] n. Spending, expense, expenditure. Ruin, waste, పాడు కావడము, నశించుట, నాశము, అర్థవినియోగము, కర్చుకావడము, వెచ్చము, క్షయము. "చనుటొం కగ ప్రాణవ్యయమున, సర్వధనాపహారణమున." M. I. iii. 246. **వ్యయముచేయు** or **వ్యయించు** *vyayamu-chēyu.* v. a. To spend, expend, వెచ్చించు.

వ్యర్థము *vyarthamu.* [Skt.] adj. Useless, vain, fruitless, ineffectual, నిరర్థకమైన, ప్రయోజనము లేని. **వ్యర్థముచేయు** *vyarthamu-chēyu.* v. a. To make vain, waste, spoil, baffle, పాడుచేయు, నిరర్థకము చేయు. **వ్యర్థుడు** or **వ్యర్థజీవి** *vyarthudu.* n. A worthless man, a fool. నిర్భాగ్యుడు. అప్రయోజకుడు. కుటుంబభరణముచేసికొనలేక వ్యర్థుడనైయున్నాను I am a poor fellow unable to support my family.

వ్యవకలనము *vyava-kalanamu.* [Skt.] n. Subtraction of numbers. ఒక అంకెలలో మరొకదానిని తీసివేయుట. **వ్యవకలితము** *vyava-kalitamu.* adj. Subtracted, వ్యవకలనముచేయబడిన.

వ్యవధానము or **వ్యవధి** *vyavadhānamu.* [Skt.] n. A covering, మరుగు, కప్పు. An intervening space, interval, delay. అవకాశము.

వ్యవసాయము vyavasāyamu. [Skt.] n. Effort, attempt, Industry. ఉద్యోగము, పరిశ్రమము. Cultivation, tillage. కృషి, సేద్యము. వ్యవసాయముచేయు to cultivate, సేద్యముచేయు. వ్యవసాయి or వ్యవసాయకుడు vyavasāyi. n. A cultivator, husbandman, farmer. వ్యవసాయముచేయువాడు.

వ్యవసితము vyavasitamu. [Skt.] adj. Ascertained, settled. నిశ్చయింపబడిన.

వ్యవస్థ vyavastha. [Skt.] n. A decree, a statute, rule, law. A written extract from a code of law, a written legal opinion. An engagement, agreement, contract. శాస్త్రనిరూపితనియమము, విధి, నియమము, కోర్టు పండితుడు వ్రాసియిచ్చే విధానపత్రిక, ఒడంబడిక. వానికి ఒకవ్యవస్థలేదు he goes by no rule. వ్యవస్థలేని illegal, unlawful, నియమములేని. వ్యవస్థితము vyavasthitamu. adj. Arranged, fixed, settled, decreed, నియమింపబడిన.

వ్యవహారము vyava-hāramu. [Skt.] n. Usage, custom. వాడుక. Profession, business, occupation, trade. ఉద్యోగము. Civil administration, management of public affairs. వ్యాపారము, పని. A lawsuit, litigation, వ్యాజ్యము, వివాదము. తగవు, దివాణపుపని. వ్యవహారముచేయు to administer or conduct public affairs, to carry on business. వ్యవహారస్థుడు ryava-hāra-sthuḍu. n. A man in business వ్యాపారముచేయువాడు. A public officer, ఉద్యోగస్థుడు. వ్యవహారి vyava-hāri. n. One engaged in trade, a merchant, a litigant. వ్యవహర్త vyava-harta. n. A judge, న్యాయాధిపతి. వ్యవహరించువాడు. వ్యవహరించు vyava-harintsu. v. a. To use, practise, make use of. ప్రయోగించు. వాడుకచేయు. v. n. To dispute or litigate. వ్యాజ్యమాడు, వివాదముచేయు.

వ్యవహితము vy-ava-hitamu. [Skt.] adj. Covered, concealed, ఆవృతమైన. Parted, separated. Not immediate, not direct వ్యవధానముగల. వ్యవహితుడు vy-ava-hituḍu. n. One afar off. దూరమునవున్నవాడు. "అంతరితుఁడగుచుండ దశిద్యవహితుండనిందు నిందింప గారణంబేమి వాకు." Naish. ii. 160.

వ్యసనము vyasanamu. [Skt.] n. Grief, sorrow, affliction, passion, pain. దుఃఖము, చింత, విచారము. A fault, vice. దోషము. A calamity, విపత్తు. M. V. ii. 42. "వేఁట, జూదంబు, పానంబు. వేట, పలుకుప్రల్లదంబును, దండంబుపరుసదనము, ధనము వమ్ముచేయుట, ఇవి సప్తవ్యసనములు. "నిరతవనుస్యయవ్యసనము." P. i. 825. వ్యసనకరమైన vyasana-karam-aina. adj. Grievous. దుఃఖజనకమైన. వ్యసనపడు vyasana-paḍu. v. n. To sorrow, to suffer grief. చింతపడు, దుఃఖించు. వ్యసనార్తుడు vyasan-ārtuḍu. n. One who is afflicted, or is suffering pain or calamity. విపత్తుగలవాడు. పీడింపబడినవాడు. వ్యసని vyasani. adj. Vicious, unfortunate, distressed. దుష్టుడైన. భ్రష్టుడైన, దుఃఖపడే.

వ్యస్తము vyastamu. [Skt.] adj. Confounded, confused, వ్యాకులమైన. Separated, separate, వేరుపడిన. చెదరిన, భిన్నమైన. వ్యస్తపదము a simple or non-compound word, (Grammar).

వ్యా vyā

వ్యాకరణము vyā-karaṇamu. [Skt.] n. Lit: analysis, విభజనము. The science of Grammar. శబ్దశాస్త్రము.

వ్యాకీర్ణము vyā-kīrṇamu. [Skt.] adj. Scattered, tossed or thrown about or away. చెదచెల్లబడిన, చెదరిన. "శార్దూలముదేశ్వ ఖడ్గ

రథ వ్యాకీర్ణము ల్రాతసౌధ్యార సంచారవిహార ముల్." Kálahasti iii. 200.

వ్యాకులము or వ్యాకులితము vy-ākulamu. [Skt.] adj. Afflicted, sorrowful, confused, perplexed, confounded, bewildered, anxious, దుఃఖితమైన, కలతనొందిన, "మదనభూతావేశ వ్యాకులితమానసాంబుజాక్షై." S. iii. 32. వ్యాకులత or వ్యాకులము vyākulata. n. Grief, sorrow, anxiety, affliction. చింత. విచారము. "అప్పటికప్పటికిఁ మనంబునఁ వ్యాకులతఁ నహింప." T. ii. 79.

వ్యాకృతి vy-ākriti. [Skt.] n. Separation, analysis, వేరుపరుచుట. Explanation, exposition, విశదపరుచుట. Translation into another language, భాషాంతరపరుచుట. Grammar, వ్యాకరణము.

వ్యాకోచము vy-ākōchamu. [Skt.] adj. Blown, opened as a flower. వికసించిన.

వ్యాఖ్య or వాఖ్యానము vy-ākhya. [Skt.] n. A commentary, gloss, note, exposition, explanation, టీక, అర్థవివరణము, అర్థవివరణము చేయుట. వ్యాఖ్యాత vy-ākhyāta. n. A commentator, టీకచెప్పినవాడు. వ్యాఖ్యాతము vy-ākyātamu. adj. Explained, expounded. వివరింపబడిన.

వ్యాఘట్టనము vyā-ghaṭṭanamu. [Skt.] n. Rubbing, friction. సంఘట్టనము, ఒరియుటము. వ్యాఘట్టితము vyā-ghaṭṭitamu. adj. Rubbed, rubbed together. ఒరసికొనబడిన.

వ్యాఘాతము vyā-ghātamu. [Skt.] n. Striking, beating, a blow, దెబ్బ. An obstacle, impediment, hindrance, విఘ్నము, అభ్యంతరము. The thirteenth of the astronomical yogas. పంచాంగయోగభేదము.

వ్యాఘ్రము vyāghramu. [Skt.] n. A royal tiger. శార్దూలము. adj. (In comp.), Best, pre-eminent, శ్రేష్ఠము. పురుషవ్యాఘ్రుడు a noble man, పురుషశ్రేష్ఠుడు. వ్యాఘ్రనఖము vyāghra-nakhamu. n. Lit. a tiger's claw. The name of a plant, *Galedupa arboria*, కరంజము. చక్రశారకము. A sort of perfume. గంధవిశేషము. వ్యాఘ్రాజినము vyāghr-ājinamu. n. The skin of a tiger, used to sit upon at devotions. వ్యాఘ్రాటము vyāghrāṭamu. n. A sky-lark. భరద్వాజము, పత్రింత. వ్యాఘ్రి vyāghri. n. A tigress.

వ్యాజము vyājamu. [Skt.] n. An excuse, pretence, deceit, fraud. మిష, కపటము, కపటము. వ్యాజనింద vyāja-ninda. n. Praise in the guise of blame. A figure of rhetoric. నిందాస్తుతి, అలంకారభేదము. వ్యాజస్తుతి vyāja-stuti. n. Sarcastic praise, ironical commendation. స్తుతినిందు. వ్యాజోక్తి vyāj-ōkti n. Double entendre; words that convey an underhand meaning, a covert expression, an inuendo, ఛలోక్తి.

వ్యాజ్యము or వ్యాజ్యేము vyājyamu. [from Skt. వివాదము.] n. A law-suit, case; dispute, contention, litigation. వివాదము, తగవు. వ్యాజ్యగాడు vyājya-gāḍu. n. A disputant, a contending party in a law-suit. వ్యాజ్యగాండ్రు the parties, plaintiff and defendant. వ్యాజ్యమాడు or వ్యాజ్యపడు vyājyam-āḍu. v. n. To contend, litigate, to be at law. To quarrel, dispute, wrangle. తగవులాడు. వివాదపడు.

వ్యాధి vyādhi [Skt.] n. Disease, sickness, disorder. రోగము. తెవులు. వ్యాధిగ్రస్తుడు or వ్యాధితుడు vyādhi-grastuḍu. n. A sick man, a patient. వ్యాధిగలవాడు, తెవులుగొంటు.

వ్యాధుడు vyādhuḍu. [Skt.] n. A fowler, a hunter. బోయవాడు A wicked or cruel man, దుష్టుడు.

వ్యానము vyānamu. [Skt.] n. That one of the five vital airs, which pervades the whole body, సర్వశరీరవ్యాపిగానుండే వాయువు

వ్యాపకుడు, వ్యాపకము See under వ్యాపించు.

వ్యాపాదము vy-āpādamu. [Skt.] n. Evil design, malice prepense. ద్రోహచింత, ద్రోహపుతలపు. వ్యాపాదనము vy-āpādanamu. n. Killing, slaying. చంపడము. Wishing evil, treacherousness. ద్రోహము తలచుట.

వ్యాపారము vyāpāramu. [Skt.] n. An affair, matter, business, occupation, profession; trade, commerce. పని, వ్యవహారము, వర్తకము, ఉద్యోగము. "పాపపరులకు కోపవ్యాపారంబులేతోచు." Vish. i. 21. దుర్వ్యాపారము misconduct, bad practice, crime. సద్వ్యాపారము good conduct, a good action. మనోవ్యాపారము an act of the mind. వ్యాపారముచేయు vyāpāramu-chēyu. v. n. To trade. వర్తకముచేయు. వ్యాపారి vyāpari. n. One engaged in any business. A man belonging to a certain sect among Brahmins, బ్రాహ్మణులలో నొకశాఖవాడు, మాధ్వుడు. గోలకొండ వ్యాపారులు a subdivision of that sect.

వ్యాపించు vyāpintsu. [Skt.] v. n. To pervade, spread, or extend. అంటుట ప్రసరించు. అతనిబుద్ధి తర్కములో వ్యాపించలేదు his mind cannot comprehend logic. వ్యాపి vyāpi. n. One who pervades, వ్యాపించువాడు. వ్యావృతి Same as వ్యాపారము. (q. v.) వ్యాపకము vyāpakamu. adj. Spreading, extending, diffusive, comprehensive; influential. విస్తరించే, వ్యాపించే. రాజువద్ద అతనికి నిండా వ్యాపకముగానున్నది he has great influence with the king. వ్యాపకత, వ్యాపకత్వము or వ్యాపకము vyāpakata. n. Influence, sway, prevalence. ప్రభుత్వము, ప్రాబల్యము, విస్తారము. వ్యాపకుడు vyāpakudu. n. A man of influence. కార్యశీలుడు. వ్యాపనము vyāpanamu. n. Diffusion, pervading, spreading. వ్యాపించుట. వ్యాప్తము vyāptamu. adj. Pervading, encircled, surrounded, penetrated. ఆక్రమ్యమైన, వ్యాపించిన, ప్రవేశించిన, పొందబడిన. వ్యాప్తి vyāpti. n. Pervading, diffusion, permeation, extension, spread. వ్యాపించడము, పొందుట. వ్యాప్తిమీరుదునన్నాను సంగతిలో as I am engaged in this business. వ్యాప్యము vyāpyamu. adj. Fit to pervade, pervasive, వ్యాపించదగిన.

వ్యామము vyāmamu. [Skt.] n. A fathom, a length of two yards. బార.

వ్యామోహము vyā-mōhamu. [Skt.] n. Inordinate affection, lust, carnal desire. మిక్కిలి ఆశ, అత్యంతమోహము. "వ్యామోహంబున లోభము, కామక్రోధంబులుమదవికారములు దలోప్తభ్రమముసు లేక యాత్మారాముండై ఖేదు డున్నరంజిల్లనుమీ." Vish. iv. 182. వ్యామోహించు or వ్యామోహపడు vyamōhintsu. v. a. To lust, desire, or love inordinately. మిక్కిలి ఆశపడు.

వ్యాయామము vyāyāmamu. [Skt.] n. Perambulation, walking up and down. సంచారము. Exercise, శ్రమము. వ్యాయామోవ్యాధినాశాయ exercise cures disease. వ్యాయామి vyāyāmi. n. One who takes exercise.

వ్యాయోగము vyā-yogamu. [Skt.] n. A certain sort of theatrical entertainment, a kind of drama. నాటకభేదము.

వ్యాలీఢము vy-ālīḍhamu. [Skt.] adj. United, joined, put together. కూడుకొన్న. "కాంతాందోళిత చందనాగరులతా వ్యాలీఢ కేళీవనీజాతంబుల్ భవదీయవిశ్వగృహముల్." Vasu. iii. 232.

వ్యాలోలము vyā-lōlamu. [Skt.] adj. Tremulous, shaking, waving. చంచలమైన, తరళమైన. మిక్కిలి కదిలే.

వ్యాళము or వ్యాడము vyālamu. [Skt.] n. A snake, సర్పము. A tiger, పులి. Any beast of prey, వ్యాఘ్రాదిదుష్టమృగము. A vicious elephant, దుష్టగజము. వ్యాళగ్రాహి or వ్యాళగ్రాహుడు vyāla-grāhi. n. A snake-catcher. పాములవాడు. వ్యాళి *vyāli*. A female snake, పెంటిసర్పము. "రాజసేవామను ష్యాణామసిధారావలేహనం పంచాననపరిష్వంగో వ్యాళీవదనచుంబనం."

వ్యావర్తనము *vy-āvartanamu*. [వి + ఆవర్తనము.] [Skt.] n. Surrounding. చుట్టుట. Retreating, turning back, వెనుకకుమరలుట.

వ్యావలనము *vyā-valanamu*. [Skt.] n. Shaking. చలనము. "కరకీలిట ప్రభావ్యావలనములు." L. ii. 18.

వ్యావహారికుడు *vy-āvahārikuḍu*. [Skt. from వ్యవహారము.] n. A man of business, one in business. ఉద్యోగస్థుడు, వ్యవహారము తెలిసిన వాడు. A counsellor, మంత్రి.

వ్యావృతము *vy-āvritamu*. [Skt.] adj. Covered, screened. ఆచ్ఛాదింపబడ్డ, చుట్టబడిన. **వ్యావృత్తము** *vy-āvrittamu*. adj. Surrounded, చుట్టబడిన. Turned back, వెనుకకుమరలిన. **వ్యావృతి** *vy-āvriti*. n. An *ignis fatuus*, a will of the wisp కొరవిదయ్యము.

వ్యాసంగము *vy-āsangamu*. [Skt.] n. Grief, anxiety. Devotion to study, assiduity in study, diligence. చింత, చదువులో చేయు పరిశ్రమము. "ఆసవపానవిధాన వ్యాసంగతరంగితాంతరంగుండగుచున్." M. iv. ii. 330.

వ్యాసక్తుడు *vy-āsaktuḍu*. [Skt.] n. A very diligent man, మిక్కిలి ఆసక్తికలవాడు.

వ్యాసము *vyāsamu*. [Skt.] n. Expansion, diffusion, విరివి. A dissertation, an essay. ఏవిషయమునైనను విరివిగావ్రాయుట. **వ్యాసుడు** *vyāsuḍu*. n. Vyāsa, the sage who is said to have written the Mahā Bhārata. పరాశరునికొడుకు **వ్యాసఘట్టము** *vyāsa-ghaṭṭamu*. n. Any difficult passage in the Mahā Bhārata; a puzzle or stumbling block; an inextricable difficulty. భారతములో అతికఠినముగానుండేపట్టు. అసాధ్యముగానుండునది.

వ్యాహతము *vy-āhatamu*. [Skt.] adj. Smitten, beaten, repulsed, confused. మిక్కిలి కొట్టబడ్డ, పరాభూతమైన, నిష్ఫలమైన. Useless, వ్యర్థమైన.

వ్యాహారము *vyāhāramu*. [Skt.] n. Voice, speech, a word. వాక్కు, ఉక్తి, వచనము. **వ్యాహృతము** *vya-hritamu*. adj. Uttered, spoken, announced. ఉక్తమైన, కథితమైన, పలుకబడిన, పఠింపబడిన. **వ్యాహృతి** *vyā-hriti*. n. Voice, speech, a word, an articulate sound, a mystical word or sound. శబ్దము, మాట, మాంత్రికశబ్దము, మంత్రవిశేషము, ఓమ్ అనునది.

వ్యు vyu

వ్యుత్క్రమము *vyut-kramamu*. [Skt.] n. Reverse or inverted order, an irregular arrangement. క్రమ విపర్యయము, తలక్రిందు. వ్యుత్క్రమపఠనము reading backwards as a spell or charm.

వ్యుత్పత్తి *vy-utpatti*. [Skt.] n. Production, origin, birth. The origin of words, derivation, etymology, శబ్దసంభవప్రకారము, శబ్దసాధనజ్ఞానము. Science, learning, critical knowledge. తెలివి, పాండిత్యము, నైపుణ్యము, విగ్రహము. వ్యుత్పత్తియగు to be born, పుట్టు; to become instructed in or acquainted with. కావ్యవ్యుత్పత్తి acquaintance with a poem. శాస్త్రవ్యుత్పత్తి skill in an art. ఆవయవవ్యుత్పత్తి acquaintance with etymology. **వ్యుత్పన్నము** *vy-utpannamu*. adj. Derived, formed as a derivative word. పుట్టిన, కలిగిన. (ఇది శబ్దమును గురించిన మాట.) **వ్యుత్పన్నుడు** *vy-utpannuḍu*. n. One who is versed in, proficient or learned. నిపుణుడు, పండితుడు, సాహిత్యముగలవాడు. **వ్యుత్పాదకము** *vy-utpādakamu*. adj. Instructive. పాండిత్యజనకమైన. ఇది మంచి వ్యుత్పాదకగ్రంథము this is a very improving book.

వ్యుష్టము *vyushtamu.* [Skt.] adj. Dawned, become daylight or dawn. తెల్లవారిన, వేగిన. n. Dawn, break of day, వేకువ, ఉదయకాలము.

వ్యూ vyū

వ్యూఢము *vyūḍhamu.* [Skt.] adj. Arranged, arrayed, placed in order or array; compact, firm. వ్యూహముగా నుంచబడిన, క్రమముగా నిలుపబడిన, దృఢమైన, దట్టమైన, విశాలమైన. "కవచితవ్యూఢాంగక." Swa. iv. 107.

వ్యూతి *vyūti.* [Skt.] n. Weaving, texture. నేయడము, నేత.

వ్యూహము *vy-ūhamu.* [Skt.] n. A multitude, flock, సమూహము. A phalanx, array, military evolution, the arrangement of troops in various positions. దండాద్యాకారస్థితచతురంగబలరచన, సేనావిన్యాసము. వ్యూహమేర్పరచు to set in array. అర్ధచంద్రవ్యూహము placing an army in a semi-circular position. "కవివ్యూహాండు." (M. VI. p. 108.) he who is surrounded by poets. T. preface, 95.

వ్యో vyō

వ్యోమము *vyōmamu.* [Skt.] n. The sky, the heaven, ఆకాశము. **వ్యోమకేశుడు** *vyōma-kēsudu.* n. Lit. he who is crowned with the heavens or whose locks are the skies, i. e., Siva. శివుడు. **వ్యోమయానము** *vyōma-yānamu.* n. A divine car, a carriage in which the gods ride. విమానము. A balloon.

వ్ర vra

వ్రంత, **వంత** or **వరత** *vranta.* [Tel.] n. A rivulet, stream, కాల్వ. చిన్నకాలువ, ఏరు. A pit, పల్లము. "ఖండితంబైనవకాలువపారితిమి, పెదవ్రంత యేమునితెల్లి జాగెదవు. BD. v. 1001. "రాజులుపెత్తుటం బరకురాముడు వ్రంత లుచేసి." Parij. i. 10.

వ్రక్క or **వక్క** *vrakka.* [Tel. from వ్రయ్యు.] n. A piece, fragment, bit. తునుక, బద్ద. **వ్రక్కవాయు** *vrakka-pāyu.* v. n. To be cut, తెగు. **వ్రక్కవారు** *vrakka-pāru.* v. n. To be cut or split. చీలు, ఛేదిల్లు. **వ్రక్కలించు** *vrakka-lintsu.* v. a. To split or break in pieces, బద్దలుచేయు. **వ్రక్కలింత** *vrakka-linta.* n. The act of cutting in pieces. **వ్రచ్చు** *vratstsu.* v. a. To tear to pieces. చీల్చు, పగుల్చు, ఛేదించు. "అలబలయులనొచ్చి యురటులువ్రచ్చి, రావులగొట్టివారణముల కట్టి." HD. i. 1112.

వ్రజనము *vrajanamu.* [Skt.] n. Going, travelling, travel. గమనము, పర్యటనము. గయావ్రజనము a pilgrimage to Gaya, **వ్రజము** *vrajamu.* n. A multitude, flock, herd. సమూహము, పసులమంద. A cowpen, పశువుల దొడ్డి, పసులకొట్టము, పశువులమందపట్టు. గోకులము. **వ్రజ్య** *vrajya.* n. Wandering, roaming. కార్యార్థము తిరుగుట. ప్రయాణము. A multitude, సమూహము.

వ్రణము *vraṇamu.* [Skt.] n. A boil, ulcer, abscess, sore, sinus, wound. కురుపు, పుండు, గాయము. రాజవ్రణము the boil called a carbuncle.

వ్రతతి *vra-tati.* [Skt.] n. A creeper or climbing plant. తీగ.

వ్రతము *vratamu.* [Skt.] n. A religious vow, a self imposed task, a religious observance or obligation. ధర్మసాధనోపవాసాది పుణ్యకర్మము. వ్రతముచేయు or వ్రతమును అనుష్ఠించు to observe a vow. ఏకపత్నీవ్రతము conjugal fidelity. శాకవ్రతము abstaining from certain food on special occasions. ఏకాదశీవ్రతము the observance of a religious fast on the eleventh day of either lunar fortnight. **వ్రతకల్పము** *vrata-*

kalpamu. n. A treatise on vows. మొదలైన వ్రతములవిధి. వ్రతి or వ్రతస్థుడు *vrati.* n. One who makes or performs vows, a votary, వ్రతములు ఆచరించేవాడు. One who offers a sacrifice, యజ్ఞముచేయువాడు.

వ్రప్పు *vrappu.* [Tel.] n. A split, crack. చీలిక, పగులు, చీలిక. "నీ॥ తలబద్దలగుటయువ్రప్పులక్రొత్తమకియిడె." A. vi. 110. టీ వ్రప్పుల. అనగా బద్దలయిన గాయములయందు.

వ్రయము *vrayamu.* Corruption of వ్యయము (q.v.) "వలసినంతర్థంబువ్రయమునకిత్తు." BD. v. 110. Vema. 1094. ఆయువ్రయము lapse of years. ఎందుకు వాగ్వ్రయముచేస్తున్నావు why do you waste your breath? నామీద నిండా వాగ్వ్రయముచేసినాడు he has given his tongue great liberty about me. వ్రయమైపోవు *vryam-ai-pōvu.* v. n. To be expended, వ్యయమైపోవు.

వ్రయ్యు *vrayyu.* [Tel.] v. n. To go to pieces, to be split. బద్దలగు. చీలు. "వాడిదుశ్శాసనునిరొమ్ము వ్రయ్యఁజేసె." M. IX. ii. 129. వ్రయ్యబడు or వ్రయ్యపోవు Same as వ్రయ్యు. వ్రయ్య *vrayya.* n. A bit, piece, fragment, splinter. బద్ద, చీలిక, ఖండము. తునక.

వ్రా vrā

వ్రాకుడు or వాకుడు *vrākuḍu.* [from Skt. వ్యాఘ్రి.] n. A sort of night shade, *Solanum jacquini.* కంటకారిక.

వ్రాత See under వ్రాయు.

వ్రాతము *vrātamu.* [Skt.] n. A multitude, an assemblage, a number, a heap, a pile. సమూహము, గుంపు. "రత్నభూషణధన వ్రాతంబులిప్పించి." T. iv. 7. "సమస్తసైనికవ్రాతముతో." Jaimini Bhar. v. 183.

వ్రాత్యుడు *vrātyuḍu.* [Skt.] n. A man of the twice-born caste who is not invested with the sacred thread. ఉపనయనాది సంస్కారహీన బ్రాహ్మణుడులోనగువాడు. (Commonly), a blockhead. శుంఠుడు, భ్రష్టుడు. వ్రాత్యవైశ్యుడు a Vaisya who has lost caste.

వ్రాయు *vrāyu.* [Tel.] v. a. To write, draw, paint. లిఖించు. "నిలుచుండిబోటన వ్రేళ్లవ్రాయుదును." Sar. D. 287. To compose, రచించు. వ్రాయసకాడు or రాయసకాడు *vrāyasa-kāḍu.* n. A writer, clerk, secretary, లేకరి, లేఖకుడు. వ్రాయసము or రాయసము *vrāyasamu.* n. Writing, వ్రాత. A letter, జాబు. వ్రాయి *vrāyi.* n. A letter of the alphabet, అక్షరము. A line, రేఖ. A mark on a die, పాచికమీదిబొట్టు. వ్రాయించు *vrāyinṭsu.* v. a. To cause to be written, get or have (it) written. అతనిచేత నొకజాబు వ్రాయించినాను I had a letter written by him, I got him to write a letter. వ్రాత *vrāta.* n. Writing, handwriting. లిపి. వ్రాత or తలవ్రాత fate, destiny, విధి. "ఫలమిచ్చునన వ్రాత ఫలమింతేయనుచు." Sar. D. 414. నీతలవ్రాత వానికాలి వ్రాతకు సమానమా what is thy prosperity when compared with his? వ్రాతకాడు *vrāta-kāḍu.* n. A writer or clerk, లిపికారుడు, లేఖకుడు. లేకరి, వ్రాయువాడు. వ్రాతపని *vrāta-pani.* n. Writing work. Also, chintz work, అద్దకపుపని. వ్రాతపనివాడు *vrāta-pani-vāḍu.* n. One who paints, i. e., one who makes chintz. అద్దకపుపనివాడు. వ్రాతబల్ల *vrāta-balla.* n. A writing table, a desk. వ్రాలు *vrālu.* n. (plu. of వ్రాయి.) The letters of the alphabet. అక్షరములు. Writing, handwriting, లిపి. వ్రాలు or చేవ్రాలు a signature, హస్తాక్షరి. వ్రాలాకు a signed paper, a letter. Pal. 31. వ్రాసికొను *vrāsi-konu.* v. a. To write down, take down, enrol, take a note of.

వ్రాలు or వాలు *vrālu.* [Tel.] v. n. To alight or come down to the ground, as a bird.

పడి క్రిందికివంగు. To lean on, ఒరగు. "కు లర దంబునిండ వ్రాలిన, ధరణీశ్వరుడేడి" వై. ii. To excel, మీరు. To be diminished, తగ్గు. వ్రాలుచు or వ్రాల్చు vrālutsu. v. a. To cause to alight, వ్రాలజేయు.

వ్రీ vrī

వ్రీడ vrīḍa. [Skt.] n. Modesty, shame, లజ్జ. సిగ్గు.

వ్రీలు vrīlu. [Tel.] v. n. To go to pieces, to be split, బద్దలగు, తునియలగు. చీలు. వ్రీలుపడు vrīlu-paḍu. v. n. To become weak. దౌర్బల్యముపొందు.

వ్రీహి vrīhi. [Skt.] n. Unhusked rice of any kind. ధాన్యసామాన్యము, వడ్లు.

వ్రే vrē

వ్రే vrē. [Tel.] n. The shepherd caste, గొల్లకులము. వ్రేపల్లె or రేపల్లె vrē-palle. n. A shepherd village, గొల్లపల్లె. వ్రేడు vrēḍu. n. A shepherd, గొల్లవాడు, గోపకుడు. వ్రేత vrēta. n. A dairy woman, a woman of the shepherd caste, గోపిక, గొల్లది. "వ్రేతలచేతఁ గృష్ణుడు చేతలన్నియుఁ జెప్పింగి." B. X. vii. 40. "వెరగొప్పవ్రేతల మొరగి వెన్నలమెక్కి." Nila. i. 4.

వ్రేకటి or వేకటి vrēkaṭi. [Tel. వ్రేగు+కట్టు.] n. Pregnancy. వేకటి, గర్భము.

వ్రేకము, వ్రేకద or వ్రేగు vrēkamu. [Tel.] n. Weight, heaviness. భారము. Wonder, marvel. అతిశయము, వింత. "నాదుమాద్యూ లకు నెంతయు వ్రేకయితో." M. IV. i. 178. వ్రేగు or వేగు vrēgu. v. n. To become hot, to be heated, తపించు. వ్రేగుపడు vrēgu-paḍu. v. n. To become heavy, భారపడు. వ్రేగైన or వ్రేకైన vrēg-aina. adj. Heavy. బరువైన, అతిశయమైన. వ్రేచు or వేచు vrētsu. v. a. To cause to be heated, to cause to pine, తపింపజేయు, వ్రేగజేయు.

వ్రేటు or వ్రేత vrēṭu. [Tel. for వ్రేయుట.] n. A blow. దెబ్బ, దెబ్బ. వ్రేటుగొను to beat, strike, కొట్టు.

వ్రేడు or వ్రేత See under వ్రే.

వ్రేపల్లె or రేపల్లె See under వ్రే.

వ్రేపు or వ్రేపుడు Same as వేపు, వేపుడు. See under వేగు.

వ్రేయు or వేయు vrēyu. [Tel.] v. a. To strike, beat, కొట్టు. To throw. To cut, నరకు.

వ్రేలు, వ్రేలాడు or వ్రేలుకాడు vrēlu. [Tel.] v. n. To hang down, dangle. వేలాడు. వ్రేలు v. n. To sink under water, మునుగు. వ్రేలు or వేలు vrēlu. n. A finger. An inch, అంగుళము. వ్రేలుచు, వ్రేల్చు or వ్రేలజేయు vrēlutsu. v. a. To hang down. To wash, కడుగు. వ్రేలుడు vreluḍu. adj. Hanging down. వ్రేల్మిడి or వ్రేలుమిడి vrēl-miḍi. n. A crack of the fingers, i. e., an instant. చిటిక. "వాయుములనాలుగుకొన వ్రేల్మిడిని నిలుపదనే వెలా." M. XIII. i. 296. వ్రేల్మిడుచు vrēl-miḍutsu. v. n. To snap the fingers, చిటికవేయు. "చూచుచుచే వ్రేల్మిడుచుచుఁ దలయూచిచివ్వ్రూచిత్తమై యా చపలాక్షీ ముక్కుపయిఁ నంగుళముంగదియించి." M. IV. ii. 357.

వ్రేల్మి vrēlmi. [Tel. for వేల్మి.] n. A burnt offering, an offering by fire. హోమము. "దర్భలును వ్రేల్మిసమిధలును." T. i. 27. టీ హోమమునకు చిదుగులును.

శ sa

శ sa. [Skt.] The letter s pronounced like the second s in 'Issue.'

శంక sanka. [Skt.] n. Suspicion, doubt. సందేహము. Fear, terror. భయము. Grief, sorrow విచారము. శంకానివృత్తి the solution of a doubt, సందేహనివారణము; a motion of the bowels, an evacuation, పురీష విసర్జనము. శంకానివృత్తికిపోయినాడు he went to stool. **శంకించు, శంకిల్లు, శంకపడు** or **శంకనొందు** *sankintsu*. v. n. To hesitate, doubt, suspect, సందేహించు. To fear, భయపడు. **శంకితము** *sankitamu*. adj. Doubtful, uncertain, suspected. సందేహింపబడిన, అనుమానింపబడిన. Frightened, భయపడిన.

శంకరుడు *sankarudu*. [Skt.] n. Lit. one who causes happiness, సుఖమునుకలుగజేయువాడు; an epithet of Siva. శివుడు. **శంకరాభరణము** *sankar-abharanamu*. n. The name of a certain tune. రాగవిశేషము.

శంకుల *sankula*. [Skt.] n. A chisel. ఉలి. A nut-cracker. పోకత్తి.

శంకువు *sankuvu*. [Skt.] n. A stump. A spike, stake, pole, pin, peg. స్థాణువు, మోడు, మేకు. శంకుస్థాపనము establishing a new village by setting stakes on its boundaries.

శంఖము *sankhamu*. [Skt.] n. A conch shell, a conch used as a horn. The number called 100 billions. కంబువు, నూరుఖర్వములు. దక్షిణావర్తశంఖము a conch the windings of which turn to the right. శంఖచక్రములు the conch and the discus, as weapons of Vishnu. శంఖచక్రాలపోగులు round ear-rings worn by Vaishnavites on which is the form of a conch and of a circle. శంఖమందుపోస్తేతీర్థము (a proverb) lit. any water poured in a conch becomes sacred water; that is, all one says is law! I am to take his word for gospel! జీతముముట్టలేదని శంఖధ్వనిచేయుచున్నాడు he is howling for his pay. **శంఖనఖము** *sankha-nakhamu*. n. A small or base shell. క్షుద్రశంఖము, నత్తగుల్ల. A perfume, ఒకవిధమైన పరిమళద్రవ్యము. **శంఖపాణి** *sankha-pani*. n. Lit. the conch bearer, i. e., Vishnu. **శంఖపాలకులు** *sankha-palakulu*. n. plu. A kind of snake. సర్పవిశేషము. "పొట్టపెంజెఱులను, శంఖపాలకులనునాగుల." G. viii. 101. **శంఖిని** *sankhini*. n. A woman of a certain type. An apparition, a fairy. స్త్రీజాతిభేదము, స్త్రీభూతభేదము.

శంగోలు or **శంగోలము** *sangolu*. [Tam.] n. A royal staff, a sceptre. రాజదండము.

శంప or **సంప** *sampa*. [Skt.] n. Lightning. మెరుపు. శంపావళి a succession of flashes. **శంపాంగి** *samp-angi*. n. Lit. Bright-limbed. A woman having a form (అంగము) as brilliant as (శంప) lightning. మెరుపుతీగెవంటిదేహముగలది.

శంపాకము *sampakmu*. [Skt.] n. A kind of tree, *Cassia fistula*. ఆరగ్వధము, రేలచెట్టు.

శంబము or **సంబము** *sambamu*. [Skt.] n. A thunderbolt. పిడుగు, వజ్రాయుధము. "విభుపాపాఘమహీంద్రశంబ." Raja Sekhara. i. 42.

శంబరము *sambaramu*. [Skt.] n. Water. జలము. A fish. చేప. A sort of deer. ఎఱ్ఱచిన్న జింకపోతు. **శంబరుడు** *sambarudu*. n. The name of a demon. ఒక రాక్షసుడు. **శంబరారి** *sambar-ari*. n. Lit. the slayer of Sambara: an epithet of Manmatha, మన్మథుడు.

శంబలము or **సంబలము** *sambalamu*. [Skt.] n. Batta. Provisions or stock for travelling expenses, దారిబత్తెము. Pay, salary, జీతము.

శంబళి *sambali*. [for Tel. ఇంబళి.] n. The tree called *Vitex negundo*.

శంబాకృతము or **సంబాకృతము** *samba-kritamu*. [Skt.] adj. Twice ploughed.

శంబుకము or **శంబూకము** *sambukamu*. [Skt.] n. A bivalve shell, a conch shell, జలశుక్తి, కప్పచిప్ప

శంభలి *sambhali*. [Skt.] n. A procuress, a bawd. కుంటెనకత్తె. Vaij. iv. 38.

శంభువు ṣambhuvu. [Skt.] n. An epithet of Siva. శివుడు.

శంస ṣamsa. [Skt.] n. A word. మాట. Praise, flattery, స్తోత్రము. Desire, ఇచ్ఛ. శంసనము ṣamsanamu. n. Telling, చెప్పుట. Praising, స్తుతించుట. Desiring, కోరుట. శంసితము ṣamsitamu. adj. Said, declared, praised, celebrated, చెప్పబడ్డ, స్తోత్రముచేయబడ్డ.

శకటము ṣakaṭamu. [Skt.] n. A cart, or carriage. The bishop at chess. బండి, చదరంగములో ఒంటె అనేకాయ. శకటవ్యూహము the "cart-evolution," i. e., troops arranged in the form of a cart. Thus the yoke AB is the covering line of skirmishers. CD (the pegs) flanks of the same. E (the pole) the line of communication with F the column; of which HH, the wheels, are cavalry covering the flanks.

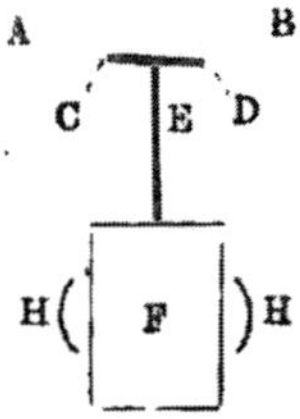

శకటరేఫ ṣakaṭa-repha. n. The name given to the obsolete letter ఱ (R,) also called బండిరేఫ, as its shape is compared to that of 'a cart.'

శకము ṣakamu. [Skt.] n. An epoch or era, particularly the era named after శాలివాహనుడు. A reign, the period of a king's rule. ఒకని పరిపాలనతో చేరిన సంవత్సరము, సంవత్సరసంఖ్యాగణితేమము. ఏలుబడి. వానిశకము ముగిసినది his reign is past, his days are ended. శకాబ్దము ṣak-abdamu. n. A year of an era. ఒకశకములోని సంవత్సరము.

శకలము ṣakalamu. [Skt.] n. A part, a portion, a piece. తునక.

శకుంతము or శకుంతి ṣakuntamu. [Skt.] n. A bird. పక్షి. "ఉద్యచ్ఛకుంతావళీ." Raja Sekhara. i. 11.

శకునము ṣakunamu. [Skt.] n. A bird. An omen or augury, chiefly such as is derived from the flight of birds. "మంచిశకునములను కొంచె పెంచ్లికాదు." Vēma. 1114. శకుని ṣakuni. n. A bird. పక్షి. The name of the uncle of Duryodhana, దుర్యోధనుని మేనమామ.

శకులము, శకులి or శకిలి ṣakulamu. [Skt.] n. A fish. చేప. Swa. v. 62.

శక్తి ṣakti. [Skt.] n. Ability, power, strength, energy, force, బలిమి, బలము, సామర్థ్యము, త్రాణ. The goddess Pārvati, పార్వతీదేవి. The personified energy or wife of a god. శక్తిపూజ worship of the female principle. శక్తుడు ṣaktuḍu. n. One who is able, strong, capable. సమర్థుడు, బలవంతుడు, శక్తిగలవాడు. శక్తము ṣaktamu. adj. Able, capable, సమర్థమైన, దృఢమైన, నిపుణమైన. శక్తత ṣaktata. n. Ability, power, బలము, సామర్థ్యము.

శక్యము ṣakyamu [Skt.] adj. Possible, practicable. సాధ్యమైన.

శక్రుడు ṣakruḍu. [Skt.] n. A name of Indra. ఇంద్రుడు. శక్రగోపము ṣakra-gōpamu. n. The insect called a lady bird. ఇంద్రగోపము, ఆరుద్రపురుగు, చందమామపురుగు. "శక్రగోపముల భావము నొందుచు." Parij. iii. 102. శక్రధనువు ṣakra-dhanuvu. n. The bow of Indra, the rainbow. ఇంద్రధనుస్సు. శక్రభవనము ṣakra-bhavanamu. n. The abode of Indra., i. e., heaven, స్వర్గము.

శచి or శచీదేవి ṣachi. [Skt.] n. The name of the wife of Indra. ఇంద్రునిభార్య.

శఠగోపము ṣaṭha-gōpamu. [Skt.] n. A dish-cover shaped like a cup and on which are two marks like shoes called Vishnu's sandals.

శఠము ṣaṭhamu. [Skt.] adj. Wicked, depraved, deceitful, crafty, దుష్టమైన, దెష్ట, కుటిలమైన. శఠత or శఠత్వము ṣaṭhata. n. Craftiness, deceit, wickedness. ధూర్తత, దుష్టత. శఠన ṣaṭhana. n. Jealousy, envy,

అనుచుడు. శఠించు or శఠించుడు saṭhintsu. v. a. To abuse, revile. దూషించు. "అరిని భటులను వాగార్భటులను శఠించికదిమిరి." Bhanumut. iii. 28. శఠుడు saṭhuḍu. n. A blockhead, fool, cheat, rogue, rascal, జడుడు. మూర్ఖుడు, ధూర్తుడు, కుటిలుడు.

శణము sanamu. [Skt.] n. Hemp. జనుము. శణసూత్రము a hempen cord. జనపనారతో అల్లిన తాడు. "పరిణతశణకణమాణిక్యములు." A. iv. 180.

శతము satamu. [Skt.] n. A hundred. నూరు. శత adj. Hundred, నూరు. అష్టోత్తరశతము a hundred and eight. శతకము satakamu. adj. Hundred. నూరు. n. A collection of one hundred stanzas: a set of 100 verses, on a subject, in the same metre, and having one unvaried chorus. నూరు పద్యములుగల గ్రంథము. భాస్కరశతకము the epigrams of Bhaskara. వేమనశతకము the verses of Vemana. "తన్నుదశశతకంబుకంఠి." M. I. iv. 102. శతకోటి sata-kōṭi. n. One thousand millions. నూరుకోట్లు. A thunderbolt, వజ్రాయుధము. శతఘ్ని sata-ghni. n. A weapon, literally "the slayer of an hundred." శస్త్రభేదము. A club two yards long and fitted with iron spikes, నాలుగుమూరలనిడివిగలయినుపముండ్లకఱ్ఱ. శతదళము or శతపత్రము sata-dalamu. n. Lit: the hundred leafed, i. e., the lotus. తామర. "శతదళమంజరీధవళ." A. iv. 145. శతధృతి sata-dhriti. n. One to whom hecatombs are offered in sacrifice; an epithet of Brahma or Indra, బ్రహ్మ or ఇంద్రుడు. శతపది sata-padi. n. A centipede. కోకటి బండ. కట్లజెర్రి, చెవిగోరుపాము, కర్ణజలూక. శతపుష్ప or శతాహ్వయ sata-pushpa. n. Anise, a sort of dill or fennel. పెద్దసదాపచెట్టు. శతభిషము sata-bhishamu. n. The name of one of the lunar mansions, ఒకనక్షత్రము. శతమన్యుడు sata-manyudu. n. An epithet of Indra. ఇంద్రుడు. శతమానము satamānamu. n. A certain weight, a palam, ఒకపలము. A palam of silver or gold. పలపరిమాణరజతసువర్ణములు. The tāli-boṭṭu, a neck ornament tied on a bride's neck by the bridegroom at the time of marriage, తాళిబొట్టు. A hundred fold, నూటికొలది. శతాంగము sat-āngamu. n. A chariot, a car, స్యందనము, రథము. శతాంశము sat-āmsamu. n. One hundredth part: నూటిలో నొకభాగము. శతానందుడు sat ānanduḍu. n. An epithet of Brahma. బ్రహ్మదేవుడు.

శత్రువు or శత్రుడు satruvu. [Skt.] n. An enemy. విరోధి. పగవాడు. "శత్రుంజయుడనవిపుత్రుడు." Zacc. v. 169. శత్రుత్వము satrutvamu. n. Enmity, hostility, విరోధము.

శనగలు sanagalu. [for Tel. సెనగలు.] n. The chick pea, commonly called Bengal gram, *Cicer arietinum* (Watts.) చణకము, హరిమంథజము. సెనగపులుసు a strong acid collected from this plant by spreading muslin cloths over the field to catch the dew. వేరుసెనగలు the ground nut, earth-nut, pignut, Manila gram, *Arachis hypogæa*.

శని or శనైశ్చరుడు sani. [Skt.] n. The planet Saturn, or its regent. ఛాయాపుత్రుడు. శనిబాధ or శనివేధ the evil influence of Saturn. నా కాలిశని చేత అక్కడికి పోయినాను through the bad luck of my legs I went there. దానినోటిశని అది అట్లు చెప్పినది through the bad luck of her mouth she said so. నా శని విడిచినది my bad luck has left me, i. e., my trouble is over. శనిచారము the evil influence of Saturn. శనివారము sani-vāramu. n. Saturday. మందవాసరము.

శపథము or శపనము sapathamu. [Skt.] n. An oath, a protestation, an asseveration by oath or ordeal. A promise to do a thing. ప్రతిజ్ఞ, ఒట్టు.

శపించు sapintsu. [Skt.] v. a. To curse, imprecate. తిట్టు, శాపమిచ్చు.

శఫరము or శఫరి saphar-amu. [Skt.] n. The silver fish, to the gleam of which in water, poets compare the flash of a glancing eye.

శబర sabara. [Skt.] adj. Barbarous, savage. చెంచుసంబంధమైన. శబరవేషము disguise in the dress of a savage. శబరాలయము a hamlet of a savage tribe, బోయపల్లె. శబరి sabari. n. A woman belonging to a savage tribe, కిరాతస్త్రీ, చెంచుది. "ప్రమథులెరుకలుగా నద్రిరాజతనయ శబరిగా వాల్గువేదములుఁ జాగిలము లుగాఁగ." Kalahasti. iv. 214. శబరుడు sabarudu. n. A savage, a man of the woods, a man of a wild tribe, కిరాతుడు, చెంచువాడు. Siva, శివుడు.

శబలము sabalamu. [Skt.] n. A variegated colour. మిశ్రవర్ణము, చిత్రవర్ణము. శబలి sabali. n. A brindled cow. పైలవర్ణపుఆవు.

శబ్దము sabdamu. [Skt.] n. A sound, noise, roar, report, tone, voice. ధ్వని, నినాదము, స్వనము, మోత. A word, speech, శాస్త్రశిక్షితమైనవాక్యము. శబ్దశాస్త్రము sabda-sastramu. n. Grammar, philology. వ్యాకరణము. శబ్దించు sabdintsu. v. n. To sound. ధ్వనించు, మ్రోగు. శబ్దనుడు sabdanudu. n. One who makes a sound. శబ్దించువాడు. శబ్దప్రమాణము argument based on revelation or authority. శబ్దితము sabditamu. adj. Sounded, శబ్దముచేయబడిన.

శమంతకము samantakamu. [Skt.] n. A certain mythological gem. సత్రాజిత్తునకు సూర్యుడు మెచ్చి తన కంఠభూషణములోనుండి తీసియిచ్చినరత్నము. విష్ణువక్షమందుండునది.

శమము samamu. [Skt.] n. Tranquillity, calmness. శాంతి. శమనము samanamu. n. Tranquillity, peace, calmness; appeasing, soothing, relieving. శాంతి. Killing, వధ. శమనపురి samana-puri. n. Hell. నరకము. A. ii. 4. శమనస్వస samana-svasa. n. A name of the river Jumna. యమునానది. శమనుడు samanudu. n. A name of Yama, యముడు. శమి sami. adj. Peaceful, శమయుతుఁడు. n. A tree called *Prosopis spicigera*, జమ్మిచెట్టు. The husk of peas, &c. కందులు మొదలైనవాటిపొట్టు. శమించు or శమియించు sam-intsu. v. n. To be at rest, to be or become quiet, still, or tranquil, శాంతిపొందు, అడగు. శమితము sam-itamu. adj. Pacified, appeased, still, calm. శాంతిపొందిన. శమించిన.

శయనము sayanamu. [Skt.] n. Lying down, sleeping sleep. నిద్ర. A bed, a couch, పరుపు, మంచము. శయనించు or శయించు sayan-intsu. v. n. To lie down, recline, to go to bed. పండుకొను, పరుండు. శయనీయము sayan-iyamu. n. A bed, a mattress, మంచముమీదపరచిన పరుపు. శయ్య. శయాళువు or శయాళుడు sayaluvu. n. A sleepy, slothful, or sluggish man. నిద్రాళువు. నిదురపోతు. తూగిపడువాడు. అలసుడు, మందుడు. శయ్య sayya. n. A bed, mattress, పడక, పరచినపరుపు. Stringing or tying words together, style, శబ్దగుంఫనము. "గతితంబు వేదశాస్త్ర ప్రసంగము మాని శయ్యగాగ్ర్యకపాటవముపహాగ." T. ii. 72. "అరవిరిశుద్ధశబ్దములు నర్థములుం ధ్వనివైభవంబులుం కరణములుం కవిస్ఫూర్తులును కల్పనాపాకము శయ్యయుం గరసస్ఫురణము." ib. ii. 60. పుష్పశయ్య a bed of flowers.

శయము sayamu. [Skt.] n. The hand. హస్తము. Vasu. vi. "అంజనంబేలశయస్థార్థమునకు." Sar. D. 237.

శరణము saranamu. [Skt.] n. A refuge, shelter, asylum, defence, protection, protector. రక్షకము, రక్షణము. రక్షకుడు, ఆశ్రయము. A house, గృహము. "గంధశరణము." a liquor shop, కల్లంగడి. P. i. 405. "అమహోసురశరణమునకు తామంగకీయనగనోక్షు గానుగలదిసుతుల్ నేమించిబంపగంపంగో ములగతివృత్తులమ్ముకొనఁ జేసెంచెగా." P. ii. 115. ప్రయోగశరణాః వైయాకరణాః grammarians resort to or rely upon usage. శరణాగతుడు saran-agatudu. n. A refugee, one who seeks or takes refuge or shelter with another, one who calls for quarter. శరణుచొచ్చినవాడు. ఆశ్రయించినవాడు. శరణాగతులైరి they threw themselves at his feet, they sought refuge with him. శరణార్థి *saran-arthi*. n. A suppliant, petitioner. "శరణార్థులను గాచుగావున." Swa vi. 113. శరణు *saranu*. (another form of శరణము.) n. A refuge, asylum, shelter, defence, protection. రక్షణము. ఆశ్రయము. A bow, salutation, prostration, obeisance. నమస్కారము. "భయార్తులై శరణు చొచ్చినవారినరక్షించుటకంటె" Vish. v. 244. "విధికృపాతత్వమవిత్తశరణ్యశరణు." A. vi. 147. శరణుచొచ్చు *saranu-tsotstsu*. v. n. To take refuge with. శరణుడు *saranudu*. n. A preserver, a protector. రక్షకుడు, పోషించువాడు. "సకలలంబుదాసై శరణాగతునిగాచువాడు నిలువంగ సారెచోటుకలదె." L. ii. 262. శరణ్యము or శరణీయము *saranyamu*. adj. Fit to be protected or aided. రక్షింపదగిన. Fit to seek refuge under, శరణుచొరదగిన. n. A protection, defence, shelter, రక్షకము. శరణ్యుడు *saranyudu*. n. A protector, defender, saviour, రక్షకుడు. "ఆర్తజనశరణ్యుండు." B. v. 1152.

శరత్తు, శరద. శరత్కాలము or శరదృతువు *saratta*. [Skt.] n. The autumnal or sultry season, the two autumn months after the rains. A year, సంవత్సరము. శరదిందువు *sarad-induvu*. n. The autumnal moon. శరదిందుముఖి she whose face is bright as the harvest moon.

శరభము *sarabhamu*. [Skt.] n. A fabulous monster said to have eight legs. A young camel, ఒంటెపిల్ల, మిగిలినగ్రోమృగము. శరభాంకుడు *sarabh-ankudu*. n. An epithet of Siva. శివుడు.

శరము *saramu*. [Skt.] n. An arrow. బాణము. A sort of reed or grass, రెల్లు. Water, జలము. శరజన్ముడు *sara-janmudu*. n. Lit. born among reeds: an epithet of Kartikeya, కుమారస్వామి. శరధి or శరనిధి *sara-dhi* n. The sea, the ocean. సముద్రము. A quiver, అమ్ములపొది. A sort of cloth, వస్త్రవిశేషము. "సన్నశరంజులయు గొధరయు మేలు బన్నెలయు. సన్నాతుబన్నె కాంభోజ." BD. iii. 144. శరవనము *sara-vanamu*. n. A forest or bed of reeds. రెల్లువనము.

శరవ్యము *saravyamu*. [Skt.] n. A mark or butt. లక్ష్యము, గురి. శరారి or శరాళి *sarari*. n. A sort of bird, probably *Turdus ginginianus*. జలపక్షివిశేషము, ఆడేలు. శరావము *saravamu*. n. A cover, a lid. A shallow cup or dish. మూకుడు. శరాసనము *sar-asanamu*. n. A bow, ధనుస్సు. శరుడు *sarudu*. adj. Possessing arrows. (A word only used in compounds.) పుష్పశరుడు the blossom-arrowed god, i. e., Manmadha.

శరీరము *sariramu*. [Skt.] n. The body. దేహము, గాత్రము. మేను. This word may sometimes be omitted in translation; thus, మీ శరీరములో ఎట్లున్నది how are you? are you in good health? నా శరీరము కుదురుగానున్నది I am well. పొట్టిశరీరముగలవాడు a man of short stature. శరీరసుఖము bodily health. శరీరప్రయాసము hard labour. శరీరసంబంధము consanguinity. శరీరి *sariri*. n. An embodied spirit, a corporeal being, శరీరముగలవాడు. An animal, creature, జంతువు.

శర్కర *sarkara*. [Skt.] n. Sugar. చక్కెర. Gravel, ముదిచినరుసుకు. శర్కరిలము *sarkari-lamu*. n. A gravelly or stony soil. గులకరాళ్లుగలభూమి.

శర్మ or శర్మము *sarma*. [Skt.] n. Joy, happiness. ఆనందము, సుఖము. A name or appellation. నామధేయము, పేరు. A certain title conferred on Brahmins, as గోవిందశర్మ, విష్ణుశర్మ. బ్రాహ్మణుల పట్టపు పేరు. "ధర్మశర్మకరంబని." P. iii. 126. adj. Joyful, సంతోషముకల.

శర్వుడు *sarvudu*. [Skt.] n. An epithet of Siva. శివుడు. **శర్వాణి** *sarvani*. n. An epithet of Pārvati. పార్వతి.

శలభము *salabhamu*. [Skt.] n. A grasshopper or locust, మిడుత. **శలభత్వము** or **శలభత** *salabhatvamu*. n. The locust state: the condition of being a grasshopper. మిడుతలైయుండడము. A ii. 52.

శలము, శలలము or **శలి** *salamu*. [Skt.] n. A porcupine, ఏదుపంది. The quill of a porcupine. ఏదుముల్లు. Sar. D. 459. KP. vi. 7. **శలవిల్లు** *sala-villu*. (for శరవిల్లు.) n. A kind of bow. ధనుర్విశేషము. "శలవిం [illegible]." Bhanumat. ii. 186.

శలాక or **సలాక** *salaka*. [Skt.] n. A thin bar or rod, a ramrod, the rib of an umbrella, one of the bars of a cage, a slip of bamboo, a probe. A pin or peg, a small stake, a fibrous stick used as a brush or pencil. లోహదండము. కమ్మి. పుడక, తూలిక, కుంచెనముచెక్క-ఆయుధము. కనకశలాక a slender rod of gold. పుండులో శలాక వేయు to probe a wound. శలాకపరీక్ష probing, a critical examination.

శలాటువు *salatuvu*. [Skt.] n. An unripe fruit. పండనికాయ. "ఫలశలాటులు." A. v. 134.

శల్యము *salyamu*. [Skt.] n. A bone. A stake, a thorn, an arrow. ఎముక, ముల్లు. బాణము. "పంథిపఖశల్య మెదలో మెదలక." A. iii. 47. [illegible] P. ii. 171. ఇది నాకు హృదయశల్యము గానున్నది this rankles in my mind. వాడు ఎట్టిశల్యమైనాడు he is a mere skeleton.

శల్యుడు *salyudu*. [Skt.] n. A king mentioned in the Mahabharata, యుధిష్ఠిరుని మేనమామ. శల్యసారథ్య a faithless ally. శల్యసారథ్యము double dealing, like that of Salya.

శవము *savamu*. [Skt.] n. A corpse. పీనుగు.

శశము or **శశకము** *sasamu*. [Skt.] n. A hare. చెవులపిల్లి, కుందేలు. "శశవిషాణము" (HN. i. 55.) a hare's horn, కుందేటికొమ్ము, i. e., a natural impossibility, a mere absurdity. **శశధరుడు** or **శశి** *sasa-dharudu*. n. An epithet of the moon, given because the figure in the moon's disc is supposed to resemble a hare. చంద్రుడు. **శశాంకము** *sas-ankamu*. n. Crude camphor. పచ్చకర్పూరము. "ఖండంబులఖండశశాంక ఖండంబులచే." A. v. 98. **శశాంకుడు** *sas-ankudu*. n. Lit: one who has a hare as a sign; an epithet of the moon. చంద్రుడు. తారాశశాంకము the tale of Tara and the moon, like the the story of Stella and the Genius, a very beautiful poem in five books. **శశాదనము** *sas-adanamu*. n. A hawk, falcon. శ్యేనము. డేగ. **శశికాంతము** *sasi-kantamu*. n. A fabulous moon-gem. చంద్రకాంతము. **శశిఖండము** *sasi-khandamu*. n. A phase or portion of the moon. చంద్రకళ. **శశిధరుడు** or **శశిశేఖరుడు** *sasi-dharudu*. n. Lit: one who wears the moon on his head; an epithet of Siva. శివుడు. **శశిరేఖ** *sasi-rekha*. n. A digit or horn of the moon. నెలవంక. **శశివంక** *sasi-vanka*. n. The crescent moon. చంద్రరేఖ.

శశ్వత్ *sasvat*. [Skt.] adv. Again and again, repeatedly. మాటిమాటికి. "శశ్వత్ప్రవర్ధిత [illegible] రతిసౌఖ్య." Mand i. 3.

శష్కులి *sashkuli*. [Skt.] n. A kind of cake. చక్కిలము. The outer ear or opening of the external auditory passage. కర్ణరంధ్రము. బయటిచెవి.

శస్తము *sastamu*. [Skt.] adj. Happy, well. Praised, eulogized. శుభకరమైన, స్తుతింపబడిన. Excellent, best, శ్రేష్ఠమైన. n. Happiness, welfare. శుభము.

శస్త్రము *sastramu*. [Skt.] n. A weapon. A surgical instrument, a knife. ఆయుధము.

శస్త్రవైద్యుడు śastra-vaidyudu. n. A surgeon, one who uses surgical instruments. శస్త్రచికిత్సకుడు. శస్త్రాజీవుడు śastra-jivudu. n. One who lives by his weapons: a man at arms, a soldier, a mercenary. ఆయుధములచే బ్రతుకువాడు, ఆయుధీయుడు, దండువాడు శస్త్రి śastri. n. One who carries a weapon. శస్త్రమును ధరించువాడు.

శా śā

శా śā. [Skt.] A contraction for శార్దూలవృత్తము a kind of metre. Also, a contraction for the "year of Salivahana;" thus; శా॥ శకవర్షంబులు ౧౭౭౨ in the year 1772 of the Salivahana era.

శాంకరి śānkari. [Skt. from శంకర.] n. A name of Kartikēya, of Gaṇēśa, and of fire. కుమారస్వామి, వినాయకుడు. అగ్ని. Kodand. 3. 20.

శాంఖికుడు śānkhikudu. [Skt. from శంఖము.] n. One who blows a conch shell; a shell seller. శంఖమునూదువాడు, శంఖములు అమ్మేవాడు.

శాండిల్యము śāndilyamu. [Skt.] n. The Bael tree, *Aegle marmelos*, మారేడుచెట్టు. శాండిల్యుడు the name of a hermit, ఒక ముని.

శాంతము śāntamu. [Skt.] adj. Calm, patient, tranquil, meek, humble; appeased, calmed, stilled, శమితమైన. n. Patience, mildness, gentleness, tranquillity. ఓర్పు. తాలిమి. సహనము. శాంతి śānti. n. Tranquillity, calmness, quietness, rest, peace, serenity. Stoicism, absence of passion, quietism. Convalescence, cessation or alleviation of disease. A religious rite to avert inauspicious accidents or to procure remission of disease. కామక్రోధాదిరాహిత్యము. ఉపశమనము, రోగాదులుమట్టుపడడము, క్రూరగ్రహాదులకు ఉపశమనముగాచేసేక్రతువు. గ్రామశాంతి a ceremony on completing a village to propitiate evil spirits, &c. ఋతుశాంతి the consummation of a marriage. రోగశాంతి the curing of a disease. తాపశాంతి allaying heat or excitement దాహశాంతి quenching thirst. శాంతించు śāntintsu. v. n. To become calm, to be pacified, శాంతినిపొందు. To improve in health, to become better. మట్టుపడు. కుదురు శాంతిపరచు śānti-paratsu. v. a. To mitigate, alleviate, calm, మట్టుచేయు.

శాంబరి śāmbari. [Skt. from శంబర.] n. The art of conjuring, juggling. మాయ. గారడీ. A female juggler, మాంత్రికురాలు. Also, రతిదేవి. "శాంబరీభిల్లుడు." Swa. preface, 2. టీ॥ మాయాకిరాతుడైన సాంబమూర్తి.

శాంభవి śāmbhavi. [Skt. from శంభువు.] n. An epithet of Parvati. పార్వతి.

శాకటము śākaṭamu. [Skt. from శకటము.] adj. Pertaining to a carriage, బండిది. A yoke ox, బండియెద్దు.

శాకము śākamu. [Skt.] n. A potherb, a vegetable, కూర. శాకవ్రతము abstaining from certain vegetables in certain months. శాకతుంగ śāka-tungu. n. A weed called *Cyperus rotundus*.

శాకిని śākini. [Skt.] n. An elf, imp, fairy, an attendant on Siva and Durga. పార్వతీపరమేశ్వరులను కనిపెట్టుకొనియుండు దేవత. పిశాచవిశేషము.

శాకునము śākunamu. [Skt. from శకునము a bird.] n. Augury, the science of omens. శకునశాస్త్రము. శాకునికుడు śākunikudu. n. A fowler, a bird-catcher. An explainer of omens or dreams. పక్షులను పట్టుకొనిబోయువాడు, శకునస్వప్నఫలములు చెప్పువాడు.

శాక్కరము śākkaramu. [Skt.] n. An ox, ఎద్దు. "శాక్కరసంఘంబుల బెక్కటించాడిచి." హ. పూ. vi.

శాక్తుడు śāktudu. [Skt. from శక్తి.] n. A worshipper of the female principle or Durga, శక్తిమతప్రవర్తకుడు, శక్త్యుపాసకుడు. శాక్తేయము

śâkt-êyamu. n. The worship of Durga. శక్తిమతము, శక్త్యుపాసన. శాక్తేయుడు *śâkt-êyudu*. n. A worshipper of Durga. శక్త్యుపాసకుడు.

శాక్యముని *śâkya-muni*. n. Sakyamuni, a name of Buddha.

శాక్వరము *śâkvaramu*. [Skt.] n. A bullock, [illegible], ఎద్దు. P. i. 200. M. i. 456.

శాఖ *śâkha*. [Skt.] n. A branch, a bough. కొమ్మ. A sub-division of the Vedas. వేదభాగము. A division, a sect. తెగ. శాఖోపశాఖలుగా branch upon branch, i. e., abundantly. ఈ కలహము శాఖోపశాఖలుగా పెరిగినది this quarrel had many ramifications. యజుశ్శాఖ the Yajur Veda. యజుశ్శాఖాధ్యాయుడు a Brahmin who reads the Yajur Veda. శాఖానగరము *śâkha-nagaramu*. n. A suburb. పేట, ఉపనగరము. శాఖామృగము *śâkha-mrigamu*. n. A monkey. కోతి. శాఖి *śâkhi*. n. A tree. చెట్టు.

శాటి or శాటిక *śâṭi*. [Skt.] n. A sheet, a garment, a cloth, దుప్పటి A monk's garment, సన్యాసులబట్ట.

శాఠ్యము *śâṭhyamu*. [Skt. from శఠుడు.] n. Cunning, కపటము, శఠత్వము.

శాద్వలము or శాడ్వలము *śâdvalamu*. [Skt.] n. A meadow or green, a verdant spot, లేతపచ్చికగలభూమి. B. v. 226.

శాణము or శాణి *śâṇamu*. [Skt.] n. A whet stone, grind-stone, hone. సానరాయి. A touch-stone. బంగారుపరీక్షించేరాయి. "శాణసుమ [illegible]." H. ii. 200. శాణచక్రము *śâṇa-chakramu*. n. A cutler's or jeweller's grinding wheel. సాన.

శాతము *śâtamu*. [Skt.] adj. Whetted, sharp, వాడిచేయబడిన, వాడియైన. Feeble, thin, కృశించిన. n. Joy, pleasure, happiness. సుఖము. శాతకుంభము *śâta-kumbhamu*. n. An epithet of gold. బంగారు. శాతోదరి *śât-ôdari*. n. A slender waisted woman. సన్ననడుముగలస్త్రీ.

శాత్రవము *śâtravamu*. [Skt. from శత్రువు.] n. Enmity, hatred. శత్రుత్వము. పగ, ద్వేషము. adj. Appertaining to an enemy. శత్రుసంబంధమైన. శాత్రవుడు *śâtravudu*. n. An enemy. శత్రువు. ద్వేషి, పగవాడు. "శాత్రవమహీశవ్రాతసంహార." Vish. v. 372.

శాదము *śâdamu*. [Skt.] n. Mud, mire, బురద. Fresh grass. [illegible]. లేతపచ్చిక. పచ్చిక.

శానా *śânâ*. [Tel. corruption of చాలా.] adj. Much, plentiful, very, many, long. నిండా, బహు. శానారాత్రిఅయినది it is very late at night. శానామంది or శానాజనము many persons, a great many people. శానాదూరము a great distance. adv. Much, very, greatly. నిండా. విస్తారముగా.

శాపము *śâpamu*. [Skt.] n. A curse, imprecation, malediction, తిట్టు. శాపగ్రస్తము *śâpa-grastamu*. adj. Cursed, lying under a curse. శాపగ్రస్తుడు *śâpa-grastudu*. n. One who is cursed. శాపించు or శపించు *śâpintsu*. v. a. To curse. తిట్టు.

శాబము or శాబకము *śâbamu*. [Skt.] n. The young (of any animal). శిశువు. పిల్ల, కూన.

శాబరము *śâbaramu*. [Skt. from శబర.] adj. Pertaining to a savage, శబరసంబంధమైన. n. The Lodh tree, *Symplocos racemosus*. లోధ్రము, తెల్లలొద్దుగ.

శాబాసు or సెబాసు *śabâsu* [H.] interj. Well done! Bravo! Excellent!

శాబ్దము *śâbdamu*. [Skt. from శబ్దము.] adj. Pertaining to a word, or to sound, శబ్దసంబంధమైన. శాబ్దికుడు *śâbdikudu*. n. One who is skilled in Etymology. శబ్దశాస్త్రముతెలిసినవాడు.

శామనము Same as శాంతి (q. v.)

సాయి *sâyi.* [H.] n. Ink. సిరా, ఇంకి. Duties, tolls, సుంకము. [Skt.] n. One who reclines, పండుకొనియుండువాడు. రంగశాయి he who dwells at Rangam; this is a name of the god at Srirangam close to Trichinopoly.

సాయిరు or **సాయురు** *sâyiru.* [H.] n. Transit duty, custom.

శారద or **శారదాంబ** *sârada.* [Skt. another form of సరస్వతి. See on బ్రహ్మ.] n. An epithet of Sarasvati. సరస్వతి. **శారదము** *sâradamu.* [from శరత్తు.] adj. Produced in the autumn season, autumnal. శరదృతుసంబంధమైన. **శారది** or **శారదము** *sâradi.* n. A tree called *Jussiena repens.* నక్రపద్మము, నీరాకులాటి. T. iii. 29.

శారి *sâri.* [Skt.] n. A Myna, a bird akin to the starlings. గోరువంక, పైనాపిట్ట. A piece or man at draughts, సొగటాలకాయ, జోడమపాశి. An elephant's housings. హస్తిపల్యాణము. ఏనుగుమీదికంబళము, జోడోలు. **శారిక** *sârika.* n. A Myna. గోరువంకపిట్ట. **శారిఫలకము** *sâri-phalamu.* n. A chequered cloth or table for playing draughts, సొగటాలసాళి, జోడుమాడేపలక, చిత్రపలక.

శారీరము *sârîramu.* [Skt. from శరీరము.] adj. Belonging to or produced from the body, corporeal, దేహసంబంధమైన, దేహములోపుట్టిన. "శిథిలకదంబకంబునఁ జొక్కియుశారీర విహీనయుండుమదిఁ దముఁడై, లక్షించిపేల్వగల్గిన సాక్షాదీశ్వరుఁడుగాఁ దెసవాక్సిస్పృహా." Vish. iv. 183. A sweet tone, a modulated sound, melody. మంచికంఠము. కంఠస్వరము. మంచిశారీరముగలవాడు a sweet voiced man. దానిశారీరము బాగానున్నది her tones are fine, her voice is sweet. **శారీరకము** *sârîrakamu.* adj. Corporeal, relating to what is bodily. దేహసంబంధమైన.

శార్కరిలము *sârkarilamu.* [Skt. from శర్కర.] n A gravelly soil. మొరపయినకగల నేల. "సింహాదక్షాంతురచ్ఛిన్న వారిగకుంభజనితముక్తాఫలశార్కరిలము." R. ii. 24.

శార్ఙ్గము *sârngamu.* [Skt. from శృంగము.] n. The name of the bow borne by Vishnu. విష్ణుచాపము. An arrow, విల్లు. **శార్ఙ్గి** *sârngi.* n. An epithet of Vishnu. విష్ణువు.

శార్దూలము *sârdûlamu.* [Skt.] n. A tiger. పులి. adj. (In Composition,) excellent, శ్రేష్ఠము. **శార్దూలవిక్రీడితము** *sârdûla-vikriditamu.* n. The name of a certain metre in prosody.

శార్వరి *sârvari.* [Skt.] n. Night. రాత్రి. The name of a Telugu year. **శార్వరము** *sârvaramu.* n. Thick darkness. కటికచీకటి. adj. Killing. చంపునట్టి.

శాల *sâla* [Skt.] n. A house, edifice; a hall, room, place. గృహము, సభ, చావడి. అశ్వశాల a stable. ఆయుధశాల an arsenal, an armoury. ముద్రాక్షరశాల a printing office. టంకశాల a mint. యాగశాల a place of sacrifice. See సాల. **శాల** n. An avenue or row of trees, a walk or promenade. దోవకు రెండుతట్ల వరుసగా పెట్టిన చెట్లు. తోటలో నడచే పేముగకు వరుసగాకట్టినది.

శాలి *sâli.* [Skt.] n. Rice in the husk, paddy. వరిధాన్యము. An affix denoting "One possessed of." శౌర్యశాలి a brave man. బలశాలి a strong man. పులకితాంగశాలి he who is thrilled or in an ecstasy. **శాలేయము** *sâlêyamu.* n. Land fit for producing a particular rice called Sali. రాజనపువడ్లుపండేభూమి. A sort of dill, or fennel, *Anethum panmorium, Anethum sowa.* Rox. చిన్నసదాపచెట్టు. **శాల్యోదనము** *sâly-ôdanamu.* n. Food prepared from excellent rice.

శాలు or **శాలువ** *sâlu.* [H.] n. A shawl.

శాలూకము or **శాలూరకము** *sâlukamu.* [Skt.] n. The root of the water lily. కలువదుంప. A nutmeg. జాజికాయ.

శాలూరము or **సాలూరము** *sālūramu.* [Skt.] n. A frog. కప్ప.

శాల్మలి *sālmali.* [Skt.] n. The silk-cotton tree, which (like the Sallow) is proverbially big and worthless. బూరుగుచెట్టు. A mere braggart. Also, the name of an island. ఒకద్వీపము.

శావము *sāvamu.* [Skt. from శవము] adj. Relating to a dead body. శవసంబంధమైన. n. Imaginary pollution, proceeding from the death of a relation. శవసంబంధి ఆశౌచము.

శావి *sāvi.* [Ital. and Port. 'Chiavi.'] n. A key, తాళముచెవి.

శాశ్వతము *sāsvatamu.* [Skt. from శశ్వత్.] adj. Eternal, permanent, perpetual, everlasting, నిరంతరమైన. నిత్యమైన. శాశ్వతకౌలు permanent (lease). **శాశ్వతుడు** *sāsvatudu.* n. The Eternal Being, God. నిత్యుడు.

శాసనము *sāsanamu.* [Skt.] n. A command or order, ఆజ్ఞ. Punishment. శిక్షించుట, శిక్ష. An edict, act or command, a charter or royal grant of land, or of villages, &c., usually inscribed on stone or copper. A writing; an inscription, a deed, a contract. Government rule. భూమ్యాదిదానార్థలేఖ్యము. రాజు తాను దానము చేసిన భూమ్యాదులకై వ్రాయించియిచ్చిన కాగితము, అధికారము, రాజ్యపాలనము. Science, శాస్త్రము. శిలాశాసనము a charter inscribed on stone. తామ్రశాసనము a grant or charter inscribed on a copper plate. మరణశాసనము a will. దానశాసనము a deed of gift. "ధారాదత్తమైనతామ్రపుపలకలలావు కొనకరముకలంకసేసి ముడియమీదరాజముద్ర నమరియుండుననదిశాసనంబు." Vema. 1917. "మాయుట్టిపురాణ్యస్తుల శాసనం బెరుగ చేరిమించేవి." Padma. iii. 58. క్రూరశాసనము a tyrannical government. **శాసనికుడు** or **శాసకుడు** *sāsani-kudu.* n. A governor or commander. ఏలేవాడు. **శాసనీయము** or **శాస్యము** *sāsanīyamu.* adj. Fit to be punished, punishable. నిగ్రహార్హము, దండనీయము. **శాసనుడు** *sāsanudu.* n. A ruler, or commander, ఏలువాడు. ఉగ్రశాసకుడు a tyrant. M. III. ii. 43. **శాసించు** *sāsintsu.* v. a. To command. ఆజ్ఞాపించు. To punish, శిక్షించు. **శాసితము** *sāsitamu.* adj. Ordered. ఆజ్ఞాపించబడిన. Governed, ruled, ఏలబడ్డ. **శాసితుడు** *sāsitudu.* n. One who is ordered. "నీవనయము శాసితుండవయియుండుమ వాస్తవమైనావలదే." BRy. iii. 757. **శాస్త** *sāsta.* n. A ruler, governor, one who disciplines, controls or punishes. అధిపతి, శాసించువాడు, శిక్షించువాడు. **శాస్తి** *sāsti.* n. Punishment, chastisement, correction. శిక్ష, దండన. "గానయుం జెక్కిడియమ్మ సూర్యుయుకడికి శాస్తి గావింపకేజనవాచాను వాఘుమంచు." N. vii. 355. **శాస్త్రము** *sāstramu.* n. A science, art, law. విద్యాగ్రంథము. తర్కశాస్త్రము the science of Logic. వ్యాకరణశాస్త్రము the science of grammar. వైద్యశాస్త్రము the science of medicine. జ్యోతిశ్శాస్త్రము the science of Astronomy. వేదాంతశాస్త్రము the science of Theology. ధర్మశాస్త్రము the science of law, a system, or code of ordinances, a code of laws, jurisprudence. శిల్పశాస్త్రము the science of Architecture. అలంకారశాస్త్రము Rhetoric. పాకశాస్త్రము the science of cookery. నీతిశాస్త్రము the science of morals. గణితశాస్త్రము the science of Arithmetic. దోహదశాస్త్రము the science of Agriculture. యోగశాస్త్రము the Yoga Philosophy. ఆయుధశాస్త్రము the science of war, or weapons. **శాస్త్రి** *sāstri.* n. A man of science, a learned man, one skilled in the arts. A title, like "Doctor," assumed by learned Smarta Brahmins. శాస్త్రముతెలిసినవాడు, పండితుడు. The respectful plural is శాస్త్రులు or శాస్త్రులవారు. **శాస్త్రీయము** *sāstrīyamu.* adj. Of or belonging to a science, scientific. శాస్త్ర

సంబంధమైన, శాస్త్రసమ్మతమైన. శాస్త్రీయమర్యాద a prescribed form. శాస్త్రీయమైనశబ్దము a scientific phrase. శాస్త్రోక్తము *sastr-ōk-tamu*. adj. Declared or commanded in the Laws or Codes. Proper, legal, in accordance with scientific usage. శాస్త్రవిహితమైన.

శి si

శింజ *sinja*. [Skt.] n. The twang of a bow, వింటినారిమ్రోత. A tinkle, tinkling sound, jingle, అందెమ్రోత, **శింజానము** *sinjā-namu*. n. Tinkling, jingling. సొమ్ములధ్వని. "మంజుల శింజానమంజీరరవము." DRA. page 244. **శింజితము** *sinji-tamu*. n. Ringing, tinkling. భూషణములమ్రోత. **శింజిని** *sinjini*. n. A bowstring. వింటినారి. A leg ornament, కాలి అందె.

శింబ or **సింబ** *simba*. [Skt.] n. A legume, a pod. పెసలుపొట్టుమొదలైనది.

శింశప or **శింశుప** *simsapa*. [Skt.] n. A tree called *Dalbergia sissoo*. అశోకవృక్షము, ఇరుగుడుచెట్టు.

శింశుమారము *simsu-maramu*. [Skt.] n. A crocodile, మొసలి. A whale, పెద్దమొసలి. The zodiac, సూర్యచంద్రాదులు తిరిగేచక్రము. "అనయంబు శింశుమారాకృతినున్న జ్యోతిశ్చక్రమును ధరధిష్ఠితార్కచంద్రాదులును." Vish. iii. 269. "నీలాంగము శింశుమారమొక యుంగా దెంతే నీవామనా." A. iv. 29. "శింశుమారచక్రవికాశితంబై మేరువునం బురడించు తిర్గెంబున." H. iv. 31. "క్రకచుండను వారు గాశింశుమారమహోగ్రనుండుగా." P. iv. 30. టీ శింశుమారము. మొసలి.

శికస్తు *sikastu*. [H.] adj. Broken, ruined. శిథిలమైన.

శికా or **శిఖా** *sika*. [H. from Skt. శిఖ.] n. A seal. ముద్రశిఖాశుంగరము a ring with a seal, a signet ring.

శిక్యము *sikyamu*. [Skt.] n. The string or loop, suspended from either end of a pole or yoke to receive the burden, the string or loop suspended from the ceiling of a house to hang things on. చిక్కము, కావడిఉట్టి, పాలకుండలుమొదలైనవి పెట్టేఉట్టి.

శిక్ష *siksha*. [Skt.] n. Punishment, correction, chastisement, discipline, శాసనము, శిక్షించుట. Instruction, teaching, అభ్యాసము. విద్యాభ్యాసము. One of the Vēdāngas which deals with the art of pronunciation. **శిక్షించు** or **శిక్షచేయు** *sikshintsu*. v. a. To punish, chastise. To drill, teach, instruct, శాసించు. అభ్యాసముచేయించు. అభ్యాసముచేయు. **శిక్షితుడు** *sikshitudu*. n. One who is taught, drilled, instructed, trained, or punished. అభ్యస్తుడు, శాసితుడు, శిక్షింపబడినవాడు. A skilful man, నేర్పరి.

శిఖ *sikha*. [Skt.] n. The point, top, tip, summit, కొన. A crest, జుట్టు, సిగ. A peacock's crest, నెమలిజుట్టు. A lock of hair left on the crown of the head at tonsure. జుట్టు. A flame, అగ్నిజ్వాల. అందితే శిఖ అందకుంటే కాళ్లు పట్టుకొనేవాడు if it suits he is at the top; if it does not he falls at one's feet: a proverb regarding a timeserver, a beggar on horseback.

శిఖండము or **శిఖండకము** *sikhandamu*. n. The tail of a peacock. మయూరవాలము, నెమలిపురి. Locks left on the crown or the sides of the head at tonsure, చూడము, పిల్లజుట్టు, కాకపక్షము. **శిఖండి** *sikhandi*. n. A peacock, నెమలి. A peacock's tail, నెమలిపురి. An arrow, బాణము. A cock, కోడిపుంజు. The name of the son of Drupada, who being at first a female, the daughter of Drupada, was (by force of tapas) metamorphosed into a man, like Iphis, in Ovid. Commonly, a hermaphrodite. ద్రుపదరాజకొడుకు, ఆడదిగాను మగవాడుగాను ఉభయుండిగానుండేమనిషి. A sort of Boa, commonly called రెండుతలలపాము a thick snake:

(hence) a stubborn person, a pertinacious wretch. మొండి, మూర్ఖుడు. శిఖండికము *sikhandi-kamu.* n. A peacock, నెమలి. A cock, కుక్కుటము. A certain plant called *Abrus precatorius.* గురివెంద. శిఖరము *sikharamu.* n. The point, top, tip, peak, summit. కొన, అగ్రము, పర్వతశృంగము, కొన. శిఖరి *sikhari.* n. A mountain. పర్వతము. A tree, వృక్షము. శిఖరిణి *sikharini.* n. A mixture of plantains or melons in curds with sugar and spices. పెరుగులో అరటిపండ్లు మొదలగునవి చేర్చి చేసినది. The name of a certain melodious metre, వృత్తభేదము. శిఖరిహస్తము *sikhari-hastamu.* n. An attitude in dancing. అభినయభేదము. శిఖామణి *sikha-mani.* n. The gem of a diadem, the crest, the principal jewel, చూడామణి. (As an affix,) the noblest, finest, grandest. నృపశిఖామణి the noblest of kings, the most glorious prince. శిఖావంతుడు *sikha-vantudu.* n. A name of fire, అగ్ని. శిఖావలము *sikha-valamu.* n. A peacock. నెమలి. శిఖి *sikhi.* n. Fire, అగ్ని. A peacock, నెమలి. A cock, కోడి.

శిగ్రువు *sigruvu.* [Skt.] n. A tree called *Hyperanthera morunga.* మునగచెట్టు.

శితము. *sitamu.* [Skt.] adj. Sharpened, whetted. వాడియైన. Thin, weak, feeble, దుర్బలమైన, బక్కయైన.

శితి *siti.* [Skt.] adj. White. తెల్లని. Black, నల్లని. శితికంఠుడు *siti-kanthudu.* n. Lit. the Black-throated one; an epithet of Siva, శివుడు.

శిథిలము *sithilamu.* [Skt.] adj. Slack, loose, flaccid, lax, relaxed, inactive, inert, inattentive, decayed. దృఢముకాని, సడలిన, వదులైన, మందమైన, జడమైన. శిథిలి *sithili.* n. A white ant. వమ్రి. చెద.

శిపివిష్టుడు *sipi-vishtudu.* [Skt.] n. A bald-headed man, బట్టతలవాడు; an epithet applied to Siva, and Vishnu, శివుడు, విష్ణువు.

శిఫ *sipha.* [Skt.] n. A sucker or root growing down from the branches, ఊడ. A branch, కొమ్మ.

శిబిక or శివిక *sibika.* [Skt.] n. A litter, or palanquin. పల్లకి.

శిబిరము *sibiramu.* [Skt.] n. A camp, an encampment, దండువిడిసినస్థలము.

శిర *sira.* [Skt.] n. Any tubular vessel of the body, a nerve, a vein, a tendon, an intestine, ధమని, నరము, ఈనె. శిరము, శిరస్సు or శిరసు *siramu.* n. The head, top. తల. శిరసావహించు *sirasa-vahinchu.* v. a. To place on the head; to acknowledge the receipt of (orders, &c). ఆజ్ఞను శిరసావహించి in submission to your command, obediently, submissively. శిరస్త్రము or శిరస్త్రాణము *siras-tramu.* n. A helmet, ఇనుపగొలుసులతో కట్టినకుల్లాయి, ముకుటము, బొమిడికము. శిరోగృహము *siro-grihamu.* n. A turret, an upper room. చంద్రశాల. శిరోజము or శిరోరుహము *siro-jamu.* n. An hair on the head. తలవెంట్రుక. శిరోధి *sirodhi.* n. The neck, మెడ. శిరోభారము a headache. శిరోమణి *siro-mani.* n. A gem worn in the crest or on the head. చూడామణి.

శిరస్తాదారుడు *sirasta-darudu.* [H.] n. The manager of a Revenue office or of a Civil Court; a Sheristadar.

శిరా or సిరా *sira.* [H.] n. Indian ink, ink.

శిరీషము *sirishamu* [Skt.] n. A kind of tree, *Acacia sirisa.* దిరిసెనము.

శిల *sila.* [Skt.] n. A stone. పాషాణము, రాయి. The stone or plank of wood placed at the threshold of a house, గడపక్రిందిత్రొక్కుడుకమ్మి. శిలామయము built of stone. శిలాక్షరము *sil-aksharamu.* n. Engraving, writing on a rock. (Metaphorically,) an irrevocable promise. రాతిమీదచెక్కిన అక్షరము. One verse says నీలుకొల్ల అమ్మబిసారము. పలుకుల్లశిలాక్షరంబులు. శిలాజతువు or సిలాజిత్తు śila-jatuvu. n. Bitumen; red chalk. పర్వతధాతుభేదము. శిలాపుష్పము śila-pushpamu. n. Storax or benzoin. గుగ్గిలము. సాంబ్రాణి. శిలారసము śila-rasamu. n. A tree called *Altingia excelsa* (Watts.) శిలోచ్చయము śil-ōchchayamu. n. A mountain. పర్వతము. శిలోద్వాసనము śil-ōdvāsanamu. n. A funeral rite, in which a man's ghost is invoked to sit down on a particular stone and తిలోదకములు and వాసోదకములు are offered to it for nine days: on the tenth day they remove it by the rite of expulsion (ఉద్వాసనము), చచ్చినవానికోవాడు పాషాణమును ఎత్తడము సేకర్మము.

శిలము or సిలము śilamu. [Skt.] n. Gleaning, grain gleaned. పరిగెలు ఏరుకొని జీవించుట.

శిలింధ్రము śilindhramu. [Skt.] n. The flower of the plantain tree అరటిపువ్వు. A mushroom, toadstool, fungus, కుక్కగొడుగు.

శిలీముఖము śili-mukhamu. [Skt.] n. A bee; an arrow. అళి, తుమ్మెద, బాణము.

శిల్పము śilpamu. [Skt.] n. An art, any manual or mechanical art. చిత్తరువువ్రాయడము మొదలైనపని. శిల్పి or శిల్పకారుడు śilpi. n. An artist, artisan, artificer, mechanic, handicraftsman. పనివాడు. A painter, మచ్చి. A carpenter, వడ్లంగి. A weaver, సాలెవాడు. (Usually) a stone-cutter, a sculptor, కాసెవాడు. శిల్పశాస్త్రము śilpi-śāstramu. n. A mechanical science; the science of Architecture. చిత్రాదికర్మలను గురించినవిధానము.

శివ śiva. [Skt.] n. A jackal. నక్క. శివ or శివాణి n. An epithet of Durga, the wife of Siva. పార్వతి. శివః or శివుడు śivah. n. The god Siva, the third member of the Hindu Triad. రుద్రుడు. శివంకరుడు or శివతాతి śivan-karudu. n. One who confers happiness or fortune. క్షేమంకరుడు. శుభకరుడు. శివబ్రాహ్మణుడు śiva-brahmanudu. n. A Brahmin of the Siva creed, a Saivite Brahmin, లింగధారి. శివమతము or శైవము śiva-matamu. n. The Saiva sect or religion. శివము śivamu. n. Welfare, happiness, prosperity. శుభము, సుఖము, మాంగల్యము. Inspiration by the deity or by an evil spirit; possession by a demon, ఆవేశము. శివమాడు or శివాలాడు to play pranks as if possessed by an evil spirit. శివముపుట్టించు śivamu-puttintsu. v. a. To spur on, instigate, incite. పురికొలుపు, పుల్లలుపెట్టు. శివరాత్రి śiva-rātri. n. A festival in honor of Siva held on the fourteenth day of the waning moon in the month of Māgha as sacred to Siva. మాఘమాసకృష్ణపక్ష చతుర్దశినాడు వచ్చే శివసంబంధమైన ఉపవాసదినము. శివలింగము śiva-lingamu. n. The phallus worshipped as the emblem of Siva. శివుని పూజచేసేమూర్తి. శివలోకము śiva-lōkamu. n. The abode of Siva. రుద్రుడు ఉండుస్థానము. శివలోకప్రాప్తులైరి, లేక, శివలోకమును పొందిరి they died; (this is a Saivite phrase.) శివవెర్రి śiva-verri. n. Demoniac fury. ఆవేశముచేతవచ్చినపిచ్చి. "మొదలశివవెర్రితలాపై ముదిమదితప్పవది కోపమునవాడిన నీవదిరొయకచేసి కొనిమల్లుదుర." Vaijaianti. iv. 15 శివశివ śiva-śiva. interj. O lord O lord! P. i. 517. శివశక్తి śiva-śakti. n. A holy nun, a female mendicant. ఒక మహాయోగురాలు. శివాలయము śiv-ālayamu. n. A temple of Siva. శివునిగుడి.

శివాయి or సివాయి śivāyi. [H.] adv. Except, extra, separately, besides, తప్ప.

శిశిరము śiśiramu. [Skt.] adj. Cold, frigid, chilly, freezing. చల్లని. n. Dew, frost, హిమము, మంచు. The dewy season, the cold season, winter, మాఘఫాల్గునమాసములు. **శిశిరకరుడు** *sisira-karuḍu.* n. The moon. చంద్రుడు. **శిశిరోపచారము** *sisir-ôpa-chara-mu.* n. Cooling, refrigeration, soothing, refreshment. శైత్యోపచారము.

శిశువు *sisuvu.* [Skt.] n. An infant, babe, baby, a child, the young of any animal, a calf, foal, pup, &c. బిడ్డ, పిల్ల, బాలకుడు, పత్సము. శిశుబాలవృద్ధులు babes, children, and old people; this usually means Men, women, and children, i. e., every body. "శిశుచేంధియుంపకున్న శిశువేదన క్రమ్మరనేలచొప్పడుగా." URT. x. 63. **శిశుత్వము** *sisu-tvamu.* n. Infancy, childhood, boyhood, pupilage. బాల్యము.

శిష్టము *sishṭamu.* [Skt.] adj. Disciplined, trained. శిక్షింపబడిన, ఆజ్ఞాపింపబడిన. Obedient, docile, విధేయతగల, శాంతమైన. సుబుద్ధిగల. Principal, eminent, ప్రధానమైన. "సృష్టిబుట్టినయట్టి శిష్టశివులకు." L. i. 45. **శిష్టాచారము** *sishṭ-âcharamu.* n. A rule, an established line of conduct. తెలిసినపెద్దలనడవడి, సాధువ్యవహారము. **శిష్టి** *sishṭi.* n. An order, command. ఆజ్ఞ. **శిష్టుడు** *sishṭuḍu.* n. One who follows traditional custom; a pious, holy, righteous, good or honest man. సాధువు, సద్వ్యవహారవంతుడు, సదాచారసంపన్నుడు, సజ్జనుడు. One who is commanded, ఆజ్ఞాపింపబడినవాడు.

శిష్యుడు *sishyuḍu.* [Skt.] n. A disciple, pupil, scholar. విద్యాభ్యాసముచేయువాడు. శిష్యదక్షిణ the fees given to a spiritual guide. గురుశిష్యన్యాయము the proper behaviour of a disciple towards his master, docility. అతనికి శిష్యసంపత్తికలదు he has many followers. శిష్యసంచారము a tour among one's pupils, a journey through the villages where one's disciples live.

శిస్తు or **సిస్తు** *sistu.* [H.] n. A land tax, assessment, పన్ను.

శిస్సాల *sissâla.* [H.] adj. Triennial.

శీ ṡî

శీకరము *sî-karamu.* [Skt.] n. A drop of water, a sprinkle, thin rain. అంబుకణము, తుంపర.

శీకు *sîku.* [Eng. 'sick.'] adj. Sick. n. Sickness. అతడు శీకులోనున్నాడు he is unwell.

శీఘ్రము *sîghramu.* [Skt.] n. Speed, quickness. వేగము, త్వర. adj. Quick, speedy, rapid, swift. వేగముగల, త్వరగల. **శీఘ్రముగా** *sîghramu-gâ.* adv. Rapidly, quickly, hastily, త్వరగా, వేగముగా. **శీఘ్రతరము** *sîghra-taramu.* adj. More rapid, quicker. మిక్కిలిత్వరగల.

శీతము *sîtamu.* [Skt.] adj. Cold, chilly, frigid. చల్లని. n. Coldness, chilliness. చల్లన. **శీతకరుడు** or **శీతాంశుడు** *sîta-karuḍu.* n. The moon. చంద్రుడు. **శీతజ్వరము** *sîta-jvaramu.* n. Ague, fever accompanied by shivering. **శీతదుక్కి** *sîta-dukki.* n. Ploughing a field in winter against sowing next spring, ఎండకాలములో విత్తడమునకై వానకాలములో దున్నియుంచడము. **శీతనగము** *sîta-nagamu.* n. The cold mountain, i. e., the Himalaya. **శీతభేది** *sîta-bhêdi.* n. A slimy diarrhoea or dysentery. **శీతలము** *sîtalamu.* n. Coldness, cold, coolness, chilliness, frigidity. చలి, శైత్యము. adj. Cold, చల్లని.

శీధువు *sîdhuvu.* [Skt.] n. Nectar; the juice of flowers; spirit distilled from molasses. అమృతము, మకరందము, మద్యము.

శీర్ణము *sîrṇamu.* [Skt.] adj. Thin, slender, emaciated, lean; dry, withered, decayed. కృశమైన, క్షీణమైన, శుష్కమైన.

శీర్షము *sîrshamu.* [Skt.] n. The head. శిరస్సు, తల. **శీర్షకము** *sîrshakamu.* n. A helmet. శిరస్త్రాణము, ఇనుపగొలుసులతో కుట్టినకుళ్లాయి.

శీలనము *sîlanamu.* [Skt.] n. An examination. పరీక్ష.

శీలము *silamu*. [Skt.] n. Nature, disposition, character; good conduct or disposition, good character; purity. స్వభావము, సద్వృత్తము, పవిత్రచరిత్రము, ఆచారము. **శీలత** or **శీలత్వము** *silata*. n. Disposition, quality, గుణము. భయశీలత timidity. **శీలవంతుడు** or **శీలసంపన్నుడు** *sila-vantudu*. n. A man of good conduct or disposition. సదాచారపరుడు. **శీలించు** *silintsu*. v. a. To accustom, to practise, వాడుకచేయు. To examine, పరిశీలించు. **శీలుడు** *siludu*. n. (In composition,) one who is possessed of, or endowed with, he who practises or is versed in. స్వభావముకలవాడు. భయశీలుడు a timid man.

శు su

శుంఠ or **శుంఠుడు** *suntha*. [Skt.] n. A blockhead. మూఢుడు. వాడు పెద్దశుంఠుడు he is extremely stupid.

శుంఠి *sunthi*. [Skt.] n. Dried ginger. సొంటి. ఉడకవేసి యెండబెట్టిన అల్లపుకొమ్ము.

శుండ *sunda*. [Skt.] n. An elephant's trunk or proboscis. ఏనుగు తొండము. **శుండాలము** *sundālamu*. n. An elephant. ఏనుగు.

శుంభత్ *sumbat*. [Skt.] adj. Shining, splendid. ప్రకాశించే.

శుకము *sukamu*. [Skt.] n. A parrot. చిలుక. **శుకనాసము** *suka-nāsamu*. n. A tree, *Bignonia indica* or *Sesbania grandiflora*, తెల్లఅగిసె. దుండిగము. **శుకవాహుడు** *suka-vāhudu*. n. Lit. he whose steed is a parrot, an epithet of Manmadha.

శుక్కు *sukku*. [Skt.] n. Sorrow, grief, distress, regret. మనోదుఃఖము. శోకము, వగ.

శుక్తము *suktamu*. [Skt]. adj. Pure, clean, bright.

శుక్తి *sukti*. [Skt]. n. A pearl oyster. ముత్తెపుచిప్ప. Any shell. నత్త. **శుక్తిజము** *suktijamu*. n. A pearl. ముత్యము. శుక్తిమంతము the name of a hill.

శుక్రుడు *sukrudu*. [Skt.] n. The planet Venus or its one-eyed regent who was the Guru of the Asuras, దైత్యగురుడు. **శుక్రవారము** *sukra-vāramu*. n. Friday. భృగువాసరము. **శుక్రశిష్యుడు** *sukra-sishyudu*. n. An Asura, అసురుడు.

శుక్ల *sukla*. [Skt]. n. The name of a Hindu year.

శుక్లము *suklamu*. [Skt.] adj. White. తెల్లని. n. Whiteness, తెలుపు. Semen, రేతస్సు. శుక్లనష్టము Spermatorrhoea. **శుక్లవర్ణము** *sukla-varnamu*. n. White colour, శ్వేతవర్ణము. **శుక్లపక్షము** *sukla-pakshamu*. n. The fortnight of the moon's increase. చంద్రవృద్ధికాలము.

శుచి *suchi*. [Skt.] adj. White, pure, purified, cleansed, clean; pious, తెల్లని, పరిశుద్ధమైన, నిర్మలమైన. n. Whiteness. తెలుపు. Purity, purification. పవిత్రత. **శుచికరము** *suchi-karamu*. adj. Cleansing, purifying, పవిత్రముచేసే. **శుచిర్భూతుడు** *suchir-bhūtudu*. n. He who is purified, or free from impurity, పరిశుద్ధుడు.

శుద్ధము *suddhamu*. [Skt.] adj. White, తెల్లని. Pure, clean, stainless, పవిత్రమైన, నిర్దోషమైన. Unmixed, unadulterated; entire, complete. Total, downright, absolute, mere. పరిష్కృతమైన. శుద్ధసంస్కృతము pure Sanskrit. శుద్ధప్రతి a faultless or true copy. శుద్ధఅబద్ధము an utter falsehood. శుద్ధలోభి a perfect miser. In music it means devoid of variations: as శుద్ధకాంభోజి the melody or theme of the Kāmbōdi air. శుద్ధక్రయము absolute sale. శుద్ధక్రయశాసనము a written instrument of absolute sale. n. Whiteness, తెలుపు. The bright lunar fortnight. శుద్ధపంచమి the fifth day of the bright lunar fortnight. **శుద్ధముగా** *suddhamu-gā*. adv. Wholly, entirely, completely, utterly. పూర్తిగా, యావత్తు. శుద్ధాం

ంతము *suddh-āntamu*. n. A harem or seraglio; the private or women's apartments in a palace. అంతఃపురము. The king's wife or concubine. అంతఃపురస్త్రీ. శుద్ధి *suddhi*. n. Purity, cleanness, purification, పవిత్రత, నిర్మలత్వము. వాక్శుద్ధి purity of speech. హస్తశుద్ధి successful practice, as that of a skilful physician. ఆత్మశుద్ధి or భావశుద్ధి spiritual purity, cleanness of heart. చింతమల్లెలు తెప్పించి అతనికి దేహశుద్ధి చేయించినారు they got a cane and purified his body, i. e., gave him a thrashing. శుద్ధీకరింపు *suddhi-karimpu*. n. Cleansing, correction, emendation. పవిత్రీకరణము. శుద్ధుడు *suddhudu*. n. A pure or holy man.

శునకము *sunakamu*. [Skt.] n. A dog. కుక్క. శునకముద్రవేయు to brand one with the figure of a dog. శుని *suni*. n. A bitch, ఆడుకుక్క.

శుభము *subhamu*. [Skt.] adj. Good, happy, lucky, blessed, fortunate, మంగళకరమైన, కళ్యాణమైన. n. Good fortune, welfare, any auspicious ceremony. మంగళము, మంగళమైనకార్యము. శుభకార్యము or శుభప్రయోజనము a happy or auspicious affair, a happy occasion or festival. శుభసూచన a favourable omen. శుభవార్త good news. శుభమస్తు let it prosper. శుభాశుభములు good and evil. శుభకృత్తు *subhakrttu*. n. The name of a Telugu year. శుభరేఖ *subha-rēkha*. n. A letter containing happy news of a wedding.

శుభ్రము *subhramu*. [Skt.] adj. White, fair, bright, shining, pure, clean. తెల్లని, ప్రకాశముగల, పవిత్రమైన. n. Whiteness, purity, cleanliness. శ్వేతవర్ణము, పవిత్రత. శుభ్రముచేయు *subhramu-chēyu*. v. a. To clean, purify, పవిత్రముచేయు. శుభ్రాంశువు *subhr-āmsuvu*. n. The moon. చంద్రుడు.

శుల్కము *sulkamu*. [Skt.] n. A toll, duty, impost, సుంకము. The present bestowed on a bride by her husband. Purchase money given to a bride's parents. Earnest money. ఓలి, కరంకుడ. విద్యాశుల్కము a wager or stake for the victor in an argument.

శుశ్రూష *susrūsha*. [Skt.] n. Service, serving. సేవ.

శుష్కము *sushkamu*. [Skt.] adj. Dry, dried. ఎండిన. Mere, groundless, causeless, unprofitable. వట్టి. కేవలము. శుష్కాన్నము dry bread. శుష్కోపచారములు empty flattery, mere compliments. శుష్కదరిద్రుడు one who is utterly poor, a mere beggar. శుష్కవైరము groundless enmity, mere spite. శుష్కరోదనము mere weeping. శుష్కోపవాసము entire fasting. శుష్కించు *sushkintsu*. v. n. To become dry, lean or poor. ఎండిపోవు.

శూ sū

శూకము *sūkamu*. [Skt.] n. The awn or beard of barley, rice, &c. వరిముల్లు. An insect's bristle or sting. A scorpion's sting, తేలుకొండి. శూకకీటము *sūka-kītamu*. n. A scorpion, నల్లతేలు. శూకజంబుక *sūka-jambuka*. n. A thorny plant, called *guilandina bonducella*, యుఝాకీ, గచ్చచెట్టు. శూకధాన్యము *sūka-dhānyamu*. n. Awned or bearded grain. యవగోధూమాదులు.

శూద్ర *sūdra*. [Skt.] adj. Belonging to the Sudra caste. నాలుగవజాతివారి సంబంధమైన. శూద్రభాష or శూద్రమాట a low word, a vulgar phrase. శూద్రదేవత a rustic god or deity, as Potarazu or Poleramma. శూద్రగ్రంథము a poem written in a mean style, an illiterate book. శూద్రత or శూద్రత్వము *sūdrata*. n. The condition of a Sudra. శూద్రుడు *sūdrudu*. n. A man of the fourth caste, a Sudra. శూద్రురాలు *sūdru-r-ālu*. n. A woman of the Sudra caste. నాలుగవజాతిస్త్రీ.

శూన్యము *sūnyamu.* [Skt.] adj. Empty, void, blank, lonely, deserted destitute of, రిక్తమైన, ఉత్త, నిర్జనమైన, రహితమైన, పాడు. శూన్యహస్తుడై empty handed. శూన్యవిపినము a lonely wilderness. n. A dot, spot, cipher. Vacuum; nothing. సున్న, పూజ్యము, లేమి. Witchcraft, sorcery, చంపు. శూన్యముపెట్టు to injure or kill by sorcery, చంపుచేయు. పిల్లిశూన్యము the black art. **శూన్యకట్టె** *sūnya-katte.* n. A sorceress or witch, చంపుచేసేస్త్రీ. **శూన్యగాడు** *sūnya-gāḍu.* n. A sorcerer, a wizard, an enchanter, చంపుచేసేవాడు. **శూన్యపుబొమ్మ** *sūnya-pu-bomma.* n. An effigy. **శూన్యవాదము** *sūnya-vādamu.* n. Atheism. **శూన్యవాది** *sūnya-vādi.* n. An atheist. నాస్తికుడు. **శూన్యుడు** *sūnyuḍu.* n. (In composition,) one destitute of, విహీనుడు. వాడు జ్ఞానశూన్యుడు he has no wisdom వివేకశూన్యుడు one who has no wit or genius.

శూర *sūra.* [Skt.] adj. Pertaining to a hero. **శూరత్వము** or **శూరత** *sūratvamu.* n. Heroism, courage, bravery, valour. ఆరంభశూరత్వము enthusiasm at the outset. **శూరుడు** *sūruḍu.* n. A hero or champion. రణసాహసముగలవాడు, వీరుడు. ఆరంభశూరుడు he who is vigorous only at starting.

శూర్పణఖ *sūrpaṇakha.* [Skt.] n. The name of a female demon. ఒకరాక్షసి, చుప్పనాక.

శూర్పము *sūrpamu.* [Skt.] n. A winnowing basket. చేట.

శూల or **శూలము** *sūla.* [Skt.] n. A darting or throbbing pain, a racking pain, a twitch, నొప్పి, పోటు. పక్కశూల a stitch in the side. కడుపుశూల the colic. హృదయశూల pain or distress of mind. గ్రహశూల inauspiciousness. **శూలము** *sūlamu.* n. A sharp pointed weapon, a lance, pike, or dart; an iron pin or spit; a stake for impaling. A trident. సలాక, కొఱ్ఱు, త్రిశూలము. "శూలపృథుపటిశ నాగ్యయుధ." A. iv 285. "శూలాంకగ్రస్తపాణి శూర్చుండి." Pal. 374. **శూలపాణి** or **శూలధరుడు** *sūla-pāṇi.* n. Lit. one who bears the trident: an epithet of, Siva, శివుడు. **శూలవ్యాధి** *sūla-vyādhi.* n. Piercing pain in the side, కడుపునొప్పి. **శూలాకృతము** or **శూల్యము** *sūlakritamu.* adj. Roasted on a spit. ఇనుపసలాకయందు గ్రుచ్చి పక్వముచేసిన. **శూలి** *sūli.* n. One who bears a trident; an epithet of Siva, రుద్రుడు.

శృ śri

శృంఖలము *srinkhalamu.* [Skt.] n. A chain or fetter, especially for an elephant; a chain of silver worn as a man's girdle or zone. సంకెల, ఏనుగుసంకెల, మగవానిమొలనూలు. **శృంఖలి** *srinkhali.* n. A certain shrub. కోకిలాక్షము, గొలిమిడిదుబ్బు.

శృంగము *sringamu.* [Skt.] n. A horn, a trumpet. పశువులకొమ్ము, బూర. A peak, the summit of a mountain. కొండకొమ్ము, పర్వతశిఖరము. శృంగభంగముచేయు to crush one's pride. **శృంగి** *sringi.* n. A horned animal. కొమ్ములుగలజంతువు. **శృంగిణి** *sringiṇi.* n. A cow. పశువు.

శృంగబేరము *sringa-bēramu.* [Skt.] n. Ginger. అల్లము

శృంగాటకము *sringāṭakamu.* [Skt.] n. A place where four roads meet. నాలుగుత్రోవలు కలిసినచోటి. An aquatic plant called *Trapa bispinosa,* పరికగడ్డ.

శృంగారము *sringāramu.* [Skt.] adj. Beautiful, handsome. అందమైన. n. Ornament, decoration, beauty. Passion, love. అలంకారము, అందము. లోన వికారము పైశృంగారము inside foul, outside fair. శృంగారభావము love, amorousness. **శృంగారకార్యము** *sringāra-kāryamu.* n. Polite literature, a romance or novel in verse. శృంగారపురుషుడు or శృంగారి *sringāra-purushuḍu*. n. A gallant, a beau, a handsome man. శృంగారవతి *sringāra-vati*. n. A fine or beautiful lady, a belle. శృంగారవనము *sringāra-vanamu*. n. A park, a pleasure garden. ఉద్యానవనము. శృంగారించు *sringārintsu*. v. a. To adorn, decorate. అలంకరించు. ఆ సంగతిని కొంచెము శృంగారించి చెప్పినాడు he told the story with some decorations or improvements.

శృంగి See under శృంగము.

శె ṣe

శెమ్మె or సెమ్మె *semme*. [H.] n. A candlestick, a lampstand, దీపస్తంభము.

శే ṣē

శేఖరము *sēkharamu*. [Skt.] n. A chaplet for the head. సిగదండ, బాసికదండ, శిఖయందు కట్టిగా కట్టిన పూలదండ. చంద్రశేఖరుడు he who is crowned with a crescent, i. e., Siva. శేఖరమగు *sēkharam-agu*. v. n. To be prepared or ready. సిద్ధమగు. అది శేఖరమైనది it is ready. శేఖరించు *sēkharintsu*. v. n. To acquire greatness, గొప్పపడు.

శేఫాలి or శేఫాలిక *sēphāli*. [Skt.] n. A flowering plant called *Nyctanthes arbor tristis*. నల్లవావిలి.

శేముషి *sēmushi*. [Skt.] n. Understanding, intellect. బుద్ధి, మతి.

శేరు or సేరు *sēru*. [H.] n. A *seer*, a weight of eight palams or ten ounces, or about a quart in measure. ఎనిమిదిపలములయెత్తు. కచ్చాశేరు the same more definitely. పక్కాశేరు the large seer which contains three ordinary *seers* or twenty-four *palams*. పావుశేరు one-fourth of a viss.

శేవధి or సేవధి *sēvadhi*. [Skt.] n. A treasury, నిధి.

శేషము *sēshamu*. [Skt.] n. The rest, residue, remainder, remnant, what is left, omitted or rejected, మిగులు. పిత్రుశేషము the remains of a funeral offering. శేషభోజనము eating the leavings of a dinner. అగ్నిశేషము, రోగశేషము, ఋణశేషము, శత్రుశేషము the remnants of fire, of a disease, of a debt, and of a quarrel. శేషంబో పేనపూరటంబు passion supplies the want of argument. శేషపూర్తి చేయు to fill up a deficiency, to supply what is wanting. శేషత or శేషత్వము *sēshata*. n. Obsequiousness, submission. దాస్యము. "నిత్యశేషతనశేషుడు." T. pref. 3. శేషభాగము *sēsha-bhāgamu*. n. The remaining part. మిగత. శేషషష్ఠి *sēsha-shashti*. n. The grammatical phrase for యొక్క "of." It signifies the *superfluous form* because వాడియిల్లు and వాడియొక్కయిల్లు mean the same. శేషించు *sēshintsu*. v. n. To remain as a balance, to be over and above, మిగులు. శేషించిన *sēshinchina*. adj. Remaining, left over, మిగిలిన. శేషించినసొమ్ము the remainder. శేషించినవారు the rest of the people. శేషులు *sēshulu*. n. plu. (In composition,) the rest, the remainder of the people, మిగిలినవారు. హతశేషులు the survivors.

శేషుడు or ఆదిశేషుడు *sēshuḍu*. [Skt.] n. The name of the great dragon, the king of serpents, వెయ్యిపడగలసర్పము, అనంతుడు. శేషవాహనము *sēsha-vāhanamu*. n. A serpent throne used for conveying the image of Vishnu. సర్పాకారముగానుండే వాహనము. శేషశయనుడు *sēsha-sayanuḍu*. n. Lit. one who has Sesha for his bed; an epithet of Vishṇu. శేషాచలము or శేషాద్రి *sēsh-āchalamu*. n. A name of Tirupati. తిరుపతికొండ.

శై sai

శైక్షుడు *saikshuḍu.* [Skt. from శిక్ష.] n. A new disciple. క్రొత్తగా చదువనారంభించిన శిష్యుడు.

శైత్యము *saityamu.* [Skt. from శీతము.] n. Cold, coldness, chilliness, a cold or catarrh. శీతలము. జలుబు. adj. Cold. శీతలమైన. శైత్యముచేయు to take or catch cold. శైత్యోపచారము cooling, refrigeration, the ceremony of offering rosewater, sandal paste, flowers, &c., to alleviate heat. వట్టిశైత్యోపచారములు empty civilities.

శైథిల్యము *saithilyamu.* [Skt. from శిథిలము.] n. Slackness, looseness, flaccidity, dilapidation, ruin. శిథిలత, శిథిలత్వము, దౌర్బల్యము.

శైనేయుడు *saineyuḍu.* [Skt. from శిని.] n. Lit. the son of Saturn. An epithet of Satyaki, the younger brother of Krishna. కృష్ణునితమ్ముడైనసాత్యకి.

శైబికుడు *saibikuḍu.* [Skt. from శిబి.] n. A palanquin bearer. పల్లకిమోయువాడు, బోయ, బెస్త. "పొందుగానందలంబులుపల్లకీలు, దక్షతనాయితముసేయుశైబికులును." KP. viii. 32.

శైలము *sailamu.* [Skt. from శిల.] n. A mountain. పర్వతము. **శైలకన్య** *saila-kanya.* n. Lit. the mountain-born virgin; an epithet of Parvati. పార్వతిదేవి. A. vi. 194. **శైలధన్వుడు** *saila-dhanvuḍu.* n. Lit. one who has a mountain for his bow; an epithet of Siva. **శైలాటము** *sailāṭamu.* n. A lion. సింహము. **శైలేయము** *saileyamu.* n. Rock-salt, రాతియుప్పు.

శైలూషము *sailūshamu.* [Skt.] n. The Bael or Bilva tree, *Ægle marmelos*, బిల్వము, మారేడుచెట్టు.

శైలూషి *sailūshi.* [Skt.] n. An actress, a female performer. ఆటకత్తె. వేషకత్తె. "వాడుమల్లఘంటుడనటుడౌటనిక్కంబు, పెద్దవారిపుట్టపిన్నవారు, గానవరులవిననుగాకయే శైలూషికా." M. iv. ii. 153. "రాత్రిశైలూషికా." Vasu. iv. 22. టీ॥ రాత్రియనెడు నాట్యస్త్రీకి. **శైలూషుడు** *sailūshuḍu.* n. An actor, a dancer. The bandmaster who beats time. నటుడు, నట్టువవాడు, ఆటగాడు, తాళధారకుడు. "ప్రాగ్రంగస్థలమధ్యసంచరచ్ఛైలూషు." P. ii. 415. "అయతశైలూషీశైలూషులు." ib. iv. 357.

శైవము *saivamu.* [Skt. from శివ.] adj. Relating to the god Siva, Saivite, శివసంబంధమైన. n. The Saiva religion or sect. శైవమతము. శైవాచారములు the manners and rites of the Saivites. వీరశైవము the title assumed by the Jangams or Lingayats. **శైవుడు** *saivuḍu.* n. A worshipper of Siva. శివమతస్థుడు. వీరశైవుడు one who belongs to the Jangam creed. ఆదిశైవుడు a Brahmin of that sect.

శైవలము or **శైవాలము** *saivalamu.* [Skt.] n. A kind of aquatic plant or weed. *Vallisneria octandra.* నాచు, నీటిపాచి. **శైవలిని** *saivalini.* n. A river. నది, ఏరు. "శైవలినీరవంబెసగ శైవలినీవినదంబుకన్న మున్నావిలభూరివారి విహారతరంగవిమెచ్చి." Vasu. ii. 183. "గగనశైవలినిందగజొచ్చిరందరుజా." Parij. v. 33.

శైశవము *saisavamu.* [Skt. from శిశువు.] n. Infancy, childhood. శిశుత్వము, బాల్యము. శైశవక్రీడలు childish sports.

శొ so

శొంఠి, శొంటి or **శొంఠికొమ్ము** *sonṭhi.* [from Skt. శుంఠి.] n. Dry ginger.

శో sō

శోకము *sōkamu.* [Skt.] n. Grief, sorrow, affliction, దుఃఖము. పుత్రశోకము grief for the loss of a son. **శోకించు** *sōkintsu.* v. n. To sorrow, grieve, దుఃఖించు. **శోచనము** *sōchanamu.* n. Grieving, దుఃఖించుట.

శోచితము *śōchitamu*. adj. Lamented, grieved, afflicted, దుఃఖితమైన. **శోచనీయము, శోచితవ్యము** or **శోచ్యము** *śōchanīyamu*. adj. Lamentable. దుఃఖింప దగిన.

శోచిస్సు *śōchissu*. [Skt.] n. Splendour, light, lustre. తేజస్సు. **శోచిష్కేశుడు** *śōchish-kēśuḍu*. n. An epithet of the god of fire. అగ్నిహోత్రుడు.

శోణము *śōṇamu*. [Skt.] adj. Red. ఎర్రని, అరుణమైన. n. Redness. **శోణరత్నము** *śōṇa-ratnamu*. n. The ruby. కెంపు. **శోణితము** *śōṇitamu*. n. Blood. రక్తము, నెత్తురు.

శోథము *śōthamu*. [Skt.] n. Swelling, వాపు రోగము.

శోధించు *śōdhintsu*. [Skt.] v. a. To purify, cleanse, refine; to search, examine, investigate, నిర్మలముచేయు, శుద్ధిచేయు, వెదకు. "పరలుగోళ్ళంగ సర్వతముశోధించి." DRK. page 262. **శోధకుడు** *śōdhakuḍu*. n. A searcher, inquirer; a critic, a man of genius: an inquisitive man. చక్కగా విమర్శించువాడు. **శోధనము** or **శోధన** *śōdhanamu*. n. Cleaning, purifying, correcting; a search, trial, investigation, శుద్ధిచేయడము, పరిష్కరించడము, వెదకడము. రాత్రి రాజు నగరశోధనచేసినాడు the king went incognito through the town by night. **శోధనపత్రము** *śōdhana-patramu*. n. A table of errata. శుద్ధపత్రము. **శోధని** *śōdhani*. n. A broom. చీపురుకట్ట, సమ్మార్జని. **శోధితము** *śōdhitamu*. adj. Purified, cleansed, refined. Examined, searched. నిర్మలముచేయబడిన, పరిష్కృతమైన, వెదకబడిన. **శోధ్యము** *śōdhyamu*. adj. Fit to be searched. వెదకదగిన. "శోధ్యస్థానముల్ చూడబంచిన." Anir. iii. 148. శోధ్యస్థానములు places where he is likely to be found.

శోఫ *śōpha*. [Skt.] n. Swelling or intumescence. వాపురోగము. పిత్తశోఫ swelling of the body caused by bile.

శోభ *śōbha*. [Skt.] n. Lustre, radiance, light, splendour, beauty. ప్రభ, కాంతి, సౌందర్యము. **శోభకృత్తు** *śōbha-kṛittu*. n. The name of a year. **శోభనము** *śōbhanamu*. adj. Auspicious, propitious; shining; handsome. మంగళమైన, ప్రకాశమానమైన, అందమైన. n. Happiness, good fortune. The consummation of a marriage. సంగమము, నిషేకము. శోభనముచేయు to finish or complete a marriage. **శోభనములు** *śōbhanamulu*. n. plu. Songs, each foot of which has the word శోభనే as a chorus, మంగళపాటలు. "అక్కరతోసువ్వాలుంశోభనములు ధవళాలుగా మొదలైనపాటలగా దగనేర్పుగా." S. i. 483. శోభనాక్షతలు grains of raw rice, made yellow with turmeric and sprinkled on the heads of persons with a benediction on auspicious occasions. పసుపురాచిన ముక్కువిరగనిబియ్యము. **శోభించు, శోభిల్లు** or **శోభిలు** *śōbhintsu*. v. n. To shine, be splendid. ప్రకాశించు. **శోభితము** *śōbhitamu*. adj. Beautified, decorated. అలంకరింపబడిన, విభూషితమైన. Bright, splendid. **శోభితత్వము** *śōbhitatvamu*. n. Splendor, lustre, ప్రకాశము, తేజస్సు. "శోభితత్వముడిగి." M. XIII. iv. 402. **శోభితుడు** *śōbhituḍu*. n. One who is decorated, అలంకృతుడు. **శోభితురాలు** *śōbhitu-r-ālu*. n. She who is adorned. అలంకృతురాలు. కుంకుమశోభితురాలయిన మా అక్క my sister who is adorned with the red powder on her forehead.

శోష *śōsha*. [Skt.] n. Drying up, ఎండడము. Fainting, faintness. అహారములేనందునగాని శోకముచేతగానివచ్చేసొక్కు. వట్టికంఠశోషగాని ఫలములేదు this is mere waste of breath. **శోషణము** *śōshaṇamu*. n. Drying up. ఎండడము. **శోషము** *śōshamu*. n. Drying, dryness. Fainting, సొమ్మిల్లుట. Pulmonary consumption. Intumescence, swelling. క్షయరోగము, వాపురోగము **శోషించు, శోషిల్లు** or **శోషిలు** *śōshintsu*. v. n. To be dried up, to become dry, lean, thin, poor. ఎండిపోవు, కృశించు. To faint,

అవకాశము లేనందువల్లగాని శోకముచేతగాని మూర్ఛపోవు. శోషింపజేయు śōshimpa-jēyu. v. a. To cause to dry up, ఎండజేయు.

శౌ sau

శౌంఠ్యము saunthyamu. [Skt. from శుంఠ.] n. Blockishness, stupidity. జడత. శుంఠత్వము, మూఢత్వము.

శౌండికుడు saundikudu. [Skt.] n. A dealer in spirits. మద్యజీవి, సారాయి అమ్మేవాడు.

శౌండుడు saundudu. [Skt.] n. One who is able or versed in. సమర్థుడు. జగత్త్రాణశౌండుడు he who is able to rule the universe.

శౌకము saukamu. [Skt. from శుకము.] n. A flock of parrots. చిలుకలగుంపు. A v. 134.

శౌక్తికము sauktikamu. [Skt. from శుక్తి.] adj. Made of oyster shell. ముత్యపుచిప్పతో చేసిన. "శౌక్తికమౌక్తికవిద్రుమముద్రమైలాగరు." M. II. ii. 117.

శౌచము sauchamu. [Skt. from శుచి.] n. Purity, cleanliness, purification, శుద్ధి, పారిశుద్ధ్యము.

శౌరి sauri. [Skt. from శూర.] n. Lit. the hero; an epithet of Krishna, కృష్ణుడు. శౌర్యము sauryamu. n. Heroism, prowess, valour, bravery, courage. శూరత్వము, పరాక్రమము. శౌర్యుడు sauryudu. n. A man of valour, a hero. విపరీతశౌర్యుడు a man of great valour.

శౌల్కుడు or శౌల్కికుడు saulkudu. [Skt. from శుల్కము.] n. A superintendent of tolls or customs, a custom house officer. సుంకరి.

శౌల్బికుడు saulbikudu. [Skt.] n. A copper smith, or brazier. కంచరవాడు, రాగిపనివాడు.

శ్మ sma

శ్మశానము, శ్మశానభూమి or శ్మశానవాటిక smasānamu. [Skt.] n. A cemetery, a place where corpses are burnt or buried. వల్లకాడు, వలికిమిట్ట. శ్మశానవైరాగ్యము "Cemetery-seriousness:" the brief impression made on the mind by the sight of a cemetery.

శ్మశ్రువు smasruvu. [Skt.] n. Beard, whiskers, moustaches. గడ్డము. మీసాలు. రక్తశ్మశ్రువు red whiskers.

శ్యా syā

శ్యామ syāma. [Skt.] n. A girl or maid under sixteen. పదునారేండ్లపడుచు, యౌవనమధ్యస్థురాలు. శ్యామము or శ్యామలము syāmamu. adj. Of a dark tint, dark blue, black, green, నీలమైన, ఆకుపచ్చని. తమాలశ్యామలము growing as a gloomy tree. n. A dark tint, dark blue, black, green, నీలవర్ణము, ఆకుపచ్చన. శ్యామలత్వము syāmalatvamu. n. Blackness, a dark complexion, నైల్యము. శ్యామిక syāmika. n. Blackness. నైల్యము. Darkness, చీకటి. Swa. ii. 29.

శ్యే syē

శ్యేనము syēnamu. [Skt.] n. A hawk, falcon. డేగ.

శ్ర sra

శ్రద్ధ sraddha. [Skt.] n. Wish, desire, care, attention, diligence, zeal. ఆసక్తి. ఇచ్ఛ. Faith, devotion, attachment, విశ్వాసము. వానికి చదువులో శ్రద్ధలేదు he is not diligent in his studies. శ్రద్ధాళువు sraddh-āluvu. n. One who is faithful, zealous, eager, attentive, ఆసక్తిగలవాడు, ఇచ్ఛగలవాడు.

శ్రమ or శ్రమము srama. [Skt.] n. Labour, toil, trouble, distress, hardship, difficulty, fatigue, weariness, అలసట, ప్రయాసము, కష్టము, తొందర. Practice, అభ్యాసము. "శ్రమమున్నచో చేయునని లాంబకంబులెక్కడు కెపకేయు." భార. కర్ణ. ii. Exercise, దేహదార్ఢ్యమునకైచేయు సాము. శ్రమపడు sramapaḍu. v. n. To be troubled, distressed, annoyed; to take pains. శ్రమపెట్టు sramapeṭṭu. v. a. To trouble, pain, plague, torture, annoy. తొందరపెట్టు, బాధించు. శ్రముడు sramuḍu. n. He who is tired or fatigued. అలసినవాడు. Anir. iii. 49.

శ్రవణము sravanamu. [Skt.] n. The ear. Hearing, listening. చెవి, వినడము, వినికిడి. శ్రవణేంద్రియము the sense of hearing. శ్రవస్సు or శ్రవము sravassu. n. The ear. చెవి. P. i. 466. శ్రవణీయము sravaṇīyamu. adj. Worthy to be heard, fit to be heard, audible.

శ్రా srā

శ్రాంతము srāntamu. [Skt.] adj. Refreshed. విశ్రాంతిపొందిన. శ్రాంతి srānti. n. Refreshment, rest, calm, peace, ఊరట, విశ్రాంతి. శ్రాంతుడు srāntuḍu. n. One who is refreshed or at rest, విశ్రాంతిపొందినవాడు.

శ్రాద్ధము sraddhamu. [Skt. from శ్రద్ధ.] n. Funeral ceremonies or obsequies, observed at various fixed periods, consisting of offerings with water and fire, to the gods and manes, and gifts and food to the relations present, and assistant Brahmins. పితృకర్మము, పితృర్థముగా దేశకాలవిధికృత బ్రాహ్మణభోజనము. ఏకోద్దిష్ట శ్రాద్ధము a funeral ceremony observed eleven days after a person's death. నిత్యశ్రాద్ధము daily funeral ceremonies for a year after a person's death. దర్శశ్రాద్ధము the funeral ceremony observed every new moon. మహాలయశ్రాద్ధము a funeral ceremony in the sixth lunar month. సపిండశ్రాద్ధము or సపిండీకరణము a funeral ceremony in which the balls of rice offered to the deceased individually and collectively, are blended together. తీర్థశ్రాద్ధము a funeral ceremony celebrated in a holy place. నాందీశ్రాద్ధము an offering made to the manes of deceased ancestors on solemn occasions. హిరణ్యశ్రాద్ధము money distributed in charity as an offering to the manes. ఆమశ్రాద్ధము uncooked ingredients distributed as above said. అన్నశ్రాద్ధము cooked food served out to guests as aforesaid. ఘటశ్రాద్ధము obsequies performed to a waterjar, which bears the name of a man's living wife, whom he divorces by breaking the jar. వానికి కొంచెము హిరణ్యశ్రాద్ధము చేస్తేగాని ఆ పని అనుకూలపడేటట్టు ఉండలేదు unless you grease his palm, I think that business will not be settled in our favour. శ్రాద్ధదేవుడు sraddha-dēvuḍu. n. Yama, the god of death. యముడు.

శ్రావణము srāvaṇamu. [Tel. for స్రావణము.] n. The pincers or nippers used by goldsmiths. కంసలవాని ఆయుధములలో నొకటి.

శ్రావణము or శ్రావణమాసము srāvaṇamu. [Skt.] n. The fifth lunar month. ఐదవనెల. శ్రావణపౌర్ణిమ srāvaṇa-paurṇima. n. The full moon in the month of Sravana, (July—August.) This is among Hindus the great day of atonement. Certain ceremonies if duly performed on this day are supposed to procure pardon for all the sins of the past year. ఉపాకర్మము. శ్రావణి srāvaṇi. n. A plant called *Sphæranthus indicus*, బోడతరపుచెట్టు called in Tamil కొట్టైక్కరంధై.

శ్రావ్యము srāvyamu. [Skt.] adj. Harmonious, melodious. చెవులకు ఇంపైన.

శ్రి śri

శ్రితము *śritamu.* [Skt.] adj. Dependant on, inherent. ఆశ్రయించియుండే. శ్రితుడు *śritudu.* n. He who is waited upon or served. ఆశ్రితుడు, సేవితుడు.

శ్రీ śrī

శ్రీ *śrī.* [Skt.] n. Lakshmi, the wife of Vishnu, the goddess of plenty and prosperity. లక్ష్మి. Wealth, riches, prosperity, good fortune, సంపద. Beauty, lustre, splendour, glory, శోభ. Also, poison, venom, విషము. విద్యాశ్రీ the glory of learning. ముఖశ్రీ lustre of the face. మాతృశ్రీ a respectful way of mentioning any elderly woman in a letter. adj. Holy, sacred, blessed, venerable, famous, glorious, renowned. Used as an honorific prefix. శ్రీకంఠుడు *śri-kanthudu.* n. An epithet of Siva (lit. poison-throated.) శివుడు, గరకంఠుడు. శ్రీకరము *śri-karamu.* adj. Propitious, happy, blessed. లక్ష్మీప్రదమైన. శ్రీకరుడు *śri-karudu.* n. One who gives wealth, one who grants prosperity, సంపత్కారుడు. శ్రీకాంతుడు or శ్రీపతి *śri-kāntudu.* n. A name of Vishnu, as being the spouse of శ్రీ or Lakshmi. విష్ణువు. శ్రీకారము *śri-kāramu.* n. The letter శ్రీ. The poets compare a beautiful ear to the form of this letter. "కలకంఠకంఠి పీనులకు శ్రీకారముల్ రత్నయంత్రములుగా వ్రాయవచ్చు." Anir. iii. 68. శ్రీకార్యము *śri-kāryamu.* n. Holy duties, i. e., the management of a temple. గుడిపారుపత్తెము. శ్రీకార్యపరుడు *śrikārya-parudu.* n. The manager of a temple. గుడిపారుపత్తి. "శ్రీకార్యపరులగాంచిన లేచి మ్రొక్కి నంజలికొంద్రు జైనశ్రీ లుంటె కో." A. i. 10. శ్రీఖండము *śri-khandamu.* n. A name of mount Malaya. మలయపర్వతము. The sandal tree; sandal wood. చందనవృక్షము. చందనపుచెక్క. "శ్రీఖండశైలగమధ్యాఖండితోచ్చ్రీమంతు." Swa. ii. 1. "శ్రీఖండశిఖరాజు." A. ii. 45. శ్రీ మలయమనే పర్వతశ్రేష్ఠము. శ్రీగంధము *śri-gandhamu.* n. Sandal wood that has a fine scent. వాసనగలగంధము. శ్రీచూర్ణము *śri-chūrṇamu.* n. A yellow paste of turmeric and rice flour, used by the Vaishnavites in marking their foreheads. తిరుచూర్ణము, నామము నడుమ పెట్టుకొనే పసుపుచియ్యముయొక్క పొడి. శ్రీచూర్ణపరిపాలనము a ceremony among Vaishnavites performed when removing a corpse from the house. శ్రీచూర్ణములు *śri-chūrṇamulu.* n. Trumpets, usually blown in pairs before a priest, or in a temple. ఆచార్యులముందరను గుడిలోను ఊదేబూరలు. శ్రీజుడు or శ్రీపుత్రుడు *śri-judu.* n. An epithet of Manmadha, మన్మథుడు. శ్రీతాళము *śri-tālamu.* n. The giant palm tree. *Corypha umbellifera.* బృహద్దళవృక్షము. శ్రీతాళపత్రముల గ్రంథము a book written on the large leaves of this tree. శ్రీతులసి *śri-tulasi.* n. The purple-stalked Basil. తులసిలో భేదము. శ్రీదుడు *śri-dudu.* n. Lit. the wealth giver, an epithet of Kubera. శ్రీధరుడు or శ్రీనివాసుడు *śri-dharudu.* n. A name of Vishnu. విష్ణువు. వేంకటేశ్వరుడు. శ్రీపతి *śri-pati.* n. An epithet of Vishnu. విష్ణువు. A king, రాజు. శ్రీఫలము *śri-phalamu.* n. The Bael fruit tree, *Ægle marmelos*, బిల్వవృక్షము, మారేడు. శ్రీమంతుడు *śri-mantudu.* n. An opulent or wealthy man. భాగ్యవంతుడు. అగర్భశ్రీమంతుడు one born wealthy. శ్రీమత్ *śri-mat.* adj. Prosperous, happy, blessed, holy, noble, glorious: (as a title) "His reverence" శోభనకరమైన, సంపత్కరమైన. The epithet శ్రీమద్రామాయణము is usually given to the celebrated poem written by Valmiki. శ్రీముఖ *śri-mukha.* n. The name of a Telugu year

శ్రీముఖము śrī-mukhamu. n. A pastoral letter, a letter from a Guru or adviser, గురువువ్రాసినజాబు, పెద్దలువ్రాయుజాబు. శ్రీముద్ర śrī-mudra. n. The holy seal; a name given to the stamps used in placing the five marks worn upon the face, &c., by the members of the Madhva sect. శ్రీమూర్తి śrī-mūrti. n. The sacred image, a name given to the సాలగ్రామము (q. v.) శ్రీరంగము śrī-rangamu. n. The name of a holy town situated upon an island close to Trichinopoly, ఉభయకావేరీమధ్యమందు రంగనాయకుల దేవళము ఉండే ఊరు. శ్రీరంగాలు śrī-rangalu. n. The name given to a certain kind of rice. ధాన్యవిశేషము. H. iv. 156. శ్రీరంగాలు or శ్రీరంగకస్తురిపట్టెలు n. A kind of pink flower. పీచుపచ్చిరుపుష్పవర్ణము గలకస్తురిపట్టెలు. శ్రీరస్తు śrī-r-astu. Interj. May it be fortunate, Good luck to it! మంగళమగుగాక. శ్రీశైలము śrī-śailamu. n. The sacred hill, usually called Sri-Sailam, in Kurnool.

శ్రీవత్సము śrī-vatsamu. [Skt.] n. A particular mark, said to be a curl of hair, on the breast of Vishnu, విష్ణువక్షస్థలమందలి మచ్చ. శ్రీవత్సకి, శ్రీవత్సాంకుడు or శ్రీవత్సలాంఛనుడు śrī-vatsaki. n. An epithet of Vishnu. విష్ణువు. శ్రీవాసము śrī-vāsamu. n. Turpentine. గుగ్గిలమువంటి దేవదారుబంక. A lotus. తామరపువ్వు. శ్రీశుడు śrī-śuḍu. n. An epithet of Vishnu. విష్ణువు.

శ్రీశైలము See under శ్రీ.

శ్రు śru

శ్రుతము śrutamu. [Skt.] adj. Heard, reported. వినబడిన. శ్రుతపరచు śruta-paruṭsu. v. a. To represent, state, communicate, తెలియజేయు. శ్రుతి śruti. n. The ear, చెవి. That which is heard, వినబడినది. Revelation. The Vedas, వేదము. A sort of drone corresponding to that used with bagpipes. సంగీతములోనిశ్రుతి. శ్రుతిగూర్చు to put an instrument in tune.

శ్రే śrē

శ్రేణి śrēṇi. [Skt.] n. A line, row, range, rank. Regular order. A multitude, crowd, cluster. పఙ్క్తి, క్రమము, వరుస, సమూహము, సంచయము. "దిగ్గంతావళిశ్రేణి." M. VI. iii. 241. జాలరిశ్రేణి a number of fishermen. P. i. 545. A rafter, ఇంటిపైకప్పుమీద వేసే పట్టె.

శ్రేణిక śrēṇika. [Skt.] n. A tent. డేరా, గుడారము.

శ్రేయము or శ్రేయస్సు śrēyamu. [Skt.] n. Virtue, moral merit, good fortune, prosperity, happiness, beatitude, ధర్మము, పుణ్యము, కళ్యాణము, మంగళము, శుభము, మోక్షము. శ్రేయస్కరము or శ్రేయోవంతము śrēyas-karamu. adj. Prosperous, fortunate, beneficial, producing happiness, లక్ష్మీకరమైన.

శ్రేష్ఠము śrēshṭhamu. [Skt.] adj. Best excellent, superior, chief, eminent, principal. ఉత్తమమైన, ప్రశస్తమైన. శ్రేష్ఠుడు śrēshṭhuḍu. n. An excellent man, a chie man.

శ్రో śrō

శ్రోణి śrōṇi. [Skt.] n. The hip, the loins the posteriors. కటిప్రదేశము, నడుముకింది తొడలమీది భాగము. పిరుదు, మొల.

శ్రోత śrōta. [Skt.] n. A hearer, an auditor. వినేవాడు. M. XII. vi. 188. శ్రోతవ్యము śrōtavyamu. adj. Audible, fit to be heard or listened to. వినదగిన. శ్రోత్రము śrōtramu. n. The ear. చెవి. శ్రోత్రియుడు śrōtriyuḍu. n. A Brahmin well versed in the Vedas. He who is modest, docile, or well behaved. శిష్టుడు. వేదము బాగా వచ్చిన బ్రాహ్మణుడు, ఛాందసుడు. శ్రోత్రియము or శ్రోత్రియగ్రామము *srōtriyamu.* n. A village held at a favourable assessment, a present or donation of a village made to learned men.

శ్రౌ srau

శ్రౌతము *srautamu.* [Skt.] adj. Of or belonging to the Vedas. వేదసమ్మతమైన. వేదమందు విధింపబడిన, వేదోక్తమైన. n. Any observance ordained by the Vedas. A treatise detailing and explaining certain observances. శ్రుతివిహితధర్మాది, వేదచోదితమైన కర్మప్రతిపాదక గ్రంథము.

శ్ల sla

శ్లక్ష్ణము *slakshnamu.* [Skt.] adj. Small, fine, minute, smooth. సూక్ష్మమైన, కృశమైన, సన్నని.

శ్లథము *slathamu.* [Skt.] adj. Slack, loose, lax, relaxed, dishevelled (as hair) జారిన, వదలిన, విడిన.

శ్లా slā

శ్లాఘ or **శ్లాఘనము** *slāgha.* [Skt.] n. Praise, applause, eulogy, flattery, స్తుతి, స్తోత్రము. **శ్లాఘించు** *slāghintsu.* v. a. To praise, applaud, flatter, స్తోత్రముచేయు. **శ్లాఘ్యము** or **శ్లాఘనీయము** *slāghyamu.* adj. Praiseworthy, celebrated, excellent. స్తవనీయమైన, శ్రేష్ఠమైన, దివ్యమైన.

శ్లి sli

శ్లిష్టము *slishṭamu.* [Skt.] adj. Connected, joined, combined, embraced. సంయుక్తమైన, మిళితమైన.

శ్లే slē

శ్లేష *slēsha.* [Skt.] n. Union, combination. సంయోగము. A figure of rhetoric, consisting of the choice, or connection of words, so as to admit of a double interpretation; a species of paranomasia or pun. Double entendre, irony, sarcasm. శబ్దాలంకారవిశేషము, ఏకవాక్యమునకు అనేకార్థము, ద్వ్యర్థము. శ్లేషగావుంచేపద్యము a verse bearing a double meaning.

శ్లేష్మము *slēshmamu.* [Skt.] n. Phlegm, కఫము, తెమడ. శ్లేష్మప్రకృతి a saturnine temperament.

శ్లో slō

శ్లోకము *slōkamu.* [Skt.] n. A verse, a stanza. సంస్కృతపద్యము. Fame, యశస్సు. అర్ధశ్లోకము a hemistich. పుణ్యశ్లోకుడు, ఉత్తమశ్లోకుడు or సుశ్లోకుడు a famous man, one well spoken of.

శ్వ sva

శ్వపచుడు *svapachuḍu.* [Skt.] n. A man of low caste, a pariah. చండాలుడు, మాలవాడు.

శ్వభ్రము *svabhramu.* [Skt.] n. A chasm, hole or gap. రంధ్రము, బొక్క, సందు.

శ్వయథు or **శ్వయథువు** *svayathu.* [Skt.] n. Swelling, dropsy. శోఫ, వాపు.

శ్వవృత్తి *sva-vritti.* [Skt.] n. Service, menial labour. సేవాజీవనము, కొలువు.

శ్వశురుడు *svasuruḍu.* [Skt.] n. A father-in-law. పడుచును ఇచ్చినమామ, భార్యకుతండ్రి. A. v. 102. శంకరశ్వశురశైలము an epithet of the Himalaya, as "father-in-law to Siva." **శ్వశ్రువు** *svasruvu.* n. A mother-in-law. పడుచును ఇచ్చిన అత్తగారు, భార్యకుతల్లి.

శ్వశ్రేయసము *śva-śrēyasamu*. [Skt.] adj. Happy, prosperous. మంగళకరమైన, శుభకరము. n. Prosperity, welfare, happiness. మంగళము, శుభము.

శ్వసనుడు *śvasanuḍu*. [Skt.] n Air, wind; the god of the wind, వాయువు శ్వసనాశనుడు lit. that which feeds on air, i. e., a serpent, సర్పము. శ్వసితము *śvasitamu*. n. Breath, శ్వాసము.

శ్వా śvā

శ్వానము *śvānamu*. [Skt.] n. A dog. కుక్క.

శ్వాపదము *śvā-padamu*. [Skt.] n. Any beast of prey. పులిమొదలైన దుష్టజంతువు. A. vi. 18. A tiger, పులి.

శ్వాసము *śvāsamu*. [Skt.] n. Breath, breathing, respiration, ఊపిరి. Wheezing, asthma. గోజా, ఉబ్బసము. ఉచ్ఛ్వాసము breath inhaled. నిశ్శ్వాసము breath expired or exhaled. వాడు ఎగశ్వాసము విడుచుచున్నాడు or ఊర్ధ్వశ్వాసము విడుచున్నాడు he is gasping or labouring for breath. శ్వాసకాసము *śvāsa-kāsamu*. n. Cough attended with wheezing, asthma, ఉబ్బసముతో దగ్గు.

శ్వి śvi

శ్విత్రము *śvitramu*. [Skt.] n. White spotted leprosy. శ్వేతకుష్ఠము, తెల్లపొడలకుష్ఠు. శ్విత్రి *śvitri*. n. One suffering from this disease.

శ్వే śvē

శ్వేతము *śvētamu*. [Skt.] adj. White, white coloured, fair. తెల్లని. n. White colour. తెలుపు. Silver. వెండి. శ్వేతకుష్ఠువు *śvēta-kushṭhuvu*. n. White leprosy. తెల్లపొడలకుష్ఠు. శ్వేతగరుత్తు or శ్వేతపత్రము *śvēta-garuttu*. n. A swan, హంస. శ్వేతద్వీపము *śvēta-dvīpamu*. n. The White Island, which cannot be identified. సప్తద్వీపములలో నొకటి. శ్వేతపింగళము *śvēta-pingaḷamu*. n. A lion. సింహము. శ్వేతపింగళవర్ణము *śvēta-pingaḷa-varṇamu*. n. Light tawny colour, the colour of a lion. శుక్లకపిలవర్ణము. శ్వేతవాహనుడు *śvēta-vāhanuḍu*. n. An epithet of Arjuna, అర్జునుడు. (Cf. Leucippus.) శ్వేతాద్రి *śvēt-ādri*. n. The white mountain. i. e., the Himalaya mountains, హిమవత్పర్వతము.

ష sha

ష *sha*. The letter *sh* as in *sh*un, shop, &c. It is called కష్టషకారము.

షండము *shaṇḍamu*. [Skt.] n. A multitude, a heap. పద్మాదిసమూహము. A bull, ఆబోతు. "శిరంబులాకశోభిల్లె తరుషండముల మీద." Rukmang. iii. 203. షండుడు *shaṇḍuḍu*. n. A eunuch, an impotent man. భోగ్యహీనుడు. పేడి.

షట్ *shaṭ*. [Skt.] adj. Six. ఆరు. షట్కర్మములు the six acts, or duties enjoined on Brahmins, i. e., అధ్యయన, అధ్యాపన, దాన, ఆదాన, యజన, యాజనములు. షట్కర్ముడు *shaṭ-karmuḍu*. n. A Smarta Brahmin who performs the six acts above enumerated. షడక్షరమంత్రము a spell which has six syllables. షడ్గుణము six-fold, six times as much. ఆరింతలు. "సాహసంబడ్గుణంబైన." షడ్గుణములు అనగా సంధి, కలహించుటము, దండెత్తుటము, యుద్ధానకు సమయము చూచుటము, భేదము పుట్టించుటము, బలవంతునిని చేపట్టుటము. షట్కము *shaṭkamu*. Six. ఆరు. షట్పదము *shaṭ-padamu*. n. Lit. the six-footed, i. e., a bee, the large black bee. అళి, భ్రమరము. షడాననుడు or షణ్ముఖుడు *shaḍ-ānanuḍu*. n. Lit. the six faced; a name of Kumaraswami, the Hindu Mars. కుమారస్వామి. షడ్జము *shaḍjamu*. n. A shrill musical tone like the peacock's cry. The fourth or middle note (tenor) of the Hindu gamut. సప్తస్వరములలో నొక స్వరము. **షడ్భాషలు** *shad-bhashalu.* n. plu. The six languages, i. e., అచ్చ తెనుగు, దేశీయము, గ్రామ్యము, కన్నడి, హాళేకన్నడి, అరవము. **షడ్రసములు** or **షడ్రుచులు** *sad-rasamulu.* n. plu. The six flavours used in cookery: viz., astringent, ఒగరు; sweet, తీపి; salt, ఉప్పు; pungent, కారము; bitter, చేదు; sour, పులుసు. షడ్రసాన్నము a ragout, highly seasoned food. "చలువలుగట్టించు షడ్రసాన్నములంబుల్." lls. i. 87. అనగా మృష్టాన్నము పెట్టును. **షడ్విద్యలు** *shad-vidyalu.* n. plu. The six magic arts; which are called ఆకర్షణము, స్తంభనము, మారణము, విద్వేషణము ఉచ్చాటనము, మోహనము. **షణ్మతములు** *shan-matamulu.* n. The six Schools or doctrines of Philosophy, ఆరుదర్శనములు. They are పాషండ, చార్వాక, బుద్ధ, జైన, వామన, గాణాపత్యములు. But a verse says బౌద్ధంజైనిక, శైవంచ, సౌరంవిష్ణుచశాక్తకం. **షష్టాష్టమము** *shashṭ-ashṭamamu.* n. Enmity, animosity, పగ. విరోధము. వారికి షష్టాష్టమముగానున్నది they are on bad terms. **షష్టి** *shashṭi.* n. Sixty. అరువది. **షష్టిపూర్తి** *shashṭi-pūrti.* n. A feast held on a man's attaining his sixtieth year. అరువదియేండ్లవయసురాగా చేసే చేయు ఉత్సవము. **షష్ఠము** *shashṭhamu.* adj. Sixth. ఆరవది. **షష్ఠి** *shashṭhi.* n. The sixth day of the lunar fortnight, ఆరవతిథి. In grammar, the sixth case. ఆరవ విభక్తి. **షష్ఠికము** or **షష్ఠిక** *shashṭhikamu.* n. A kind of rice of quick growth. వ్రీహిభేదము. **షష్ఠ్యంతములు** *shashṭh-y-antamulu.* n. Dative verses, i. e., a set of verses in the preface of a Telugu poem, having every phrase in the dative thus: To the prince, to the hero, &c., &c. అవతారిక తొలుతచెప్పే షష్ఠీవిభక్తిగల వాక్యములు గల పద్యములు. షష్ఠ్యంతమైన శబ్దము a word in the sixth case. ఆరవ విభక్తియందుండు శబ్దము.

షడ్డకుడు or **షడ్డకుడు** *shaḍḍa-kuḍu.* [Skt.] n. A fellow son-in-law, తోడల్లుడు. వీరు షడ్డకులు these two men are married to two sisters.

షరతు *sharatu.* [H.] n. An agreement, a condition agreed on. ఒడంబడిక.

షరా *shara.* [H.] n. A remark, a post-script, a *nota bene.*

షరాబు *sharābu.* [H.] n. A money changer, a cash-keeper.

షహా *shaha.* [H. Pers. 'Shah.'] n. A king. Interj. Check! (in chess.)

షా shā

షాడబము or **షాడవము** *shāḍabamu.* [Skt.] n. Flavour, taste, savour. రసము, (అనగా ఉప్పు, కారము, పులుసు మొదలైనవి.) Music, singing, గానము, రాగజాతివిశేషము, అనగా షట్స్వరములుగల రాగములు. "నానావిధషాడబములు." A. iv. 331. టీ షడ్రసవిశిష్టభోజనములు.

షాడ్గుణ్యము *shāḍ-guṇyamu.* [Skt. షట్+గుణము.] n. An aggregate of six properties or qualities, such as Greatness (ఐశ్వర్యము). Might (వీర్యము). &c, or Peace (సంధి), Enmity (విగ్రహము). &c. గుణషట్కము.

షాణ్మాతురుడు *shāṇ-māturuḍu.* [Skt.] n. A name of Kartikeya. కుమారస్వామి.

షాణ్మాసము *shāṇ-māsamu.* [Skt.] n. Six months. ఆరునెలలు. **షాణ్మాసికము** *shāṇ-māsikamu.* adj. Of or relating to six months, half yearly. ఆరునెలలకువచ్చే. n. A funeral ceremony performed in the sixth month after death.

షి shi

షికారి or **షికారీ** *shikari.* [H.] n. Sporting, fowling, hunting, వేట. A huntsman a fowler, వేటకాడు. షికారు *shikāru*. n. An airing on foot or horseback, a walk or ride. షికారుకుపోవు to go out for exercise. షికారుకుపోయినాడు he is gone out for a walk or ride.

షిడ్గుడు *shiḍguḍu*. [Skt.] n. A libertine, gallant, paramour. విటుడు.

షు shu

షుమారు [H.] Same as సుమారు (q. v.)

షో shō

షోడశము *shōḍaśamu*. [Skt.] adj. Sixteen, sixteenth. పదునారు, పదునారవ. షోడశోపచారములు sixteen acts of civility. అది వానికి షోడశోపచారములు చేయుచున్నది she does every thing he wants. షోడశకళాపరి పూర్ణుడైనచంద్రుడు the full moon in its splendor. n. A funeral rite celebrated on the twelfth day after a death, in which sixteen Brahmins are fed. చచ్చిన పండ్రెండవనాడు పదహారుగురికి భోజనముపెట్టే కర్మము.

స sa

స *sa*. The letter *s* as in sat, so, &c. It is called వ్యాసనకారము or తలకట్టుసకారము to distinguish it from the other sibilants శ+ష.

స *sa*. [Skt.] (In composition,) with, together with. సకుటుంబముగా together with one's family. సగుణము having (or endowed with) properties or qualities. సజాతీయము of the same tribe, of the same species. సటీక accompanied with a commentary. సదయుడు one who is kind or good. సపక్షము having wings, రెక్కలుగల. సమర్తకముగా in full detail, circumstantially, with all the particulars, minutely, వాచకుండా. సమూలము together with the root, having a root, entire, వేరుతోకూడా, యావత్తు. వారు సమూలముగా నాశమైనారు they are ruined, root and branch. సమేలంపు derisory, satirical. "సమేలంపుమాటల మేలమాడు." Vish. vi. 19. సయుక్తికము reasonable, logical, rational. సరయత with speed, త్వరగా. "సరయతవచ్చి వెల్వడివాకోరము చెంతరథంబుడిగ్గి." T. iv. 193. సలక్షణము classical, beautiful, handsome, లక్షణయుక్తమైన, అందమైన. సలక్షణమైనపడుచు a handsome girl. సలలితము beautiful, lovely. "సలలితకళానిధి." T. Pref. 87. సవిస్తారముగా at full length, extensively, with all the particulars, completely, to the full, వివరముగా. సవినయముగా respectfully. సవినయులై modestly. సహిరణ్యోదకపూర్వకముగా entirely; (lit. with money and water)—a phrase used in making gifts. సహృదయుడు a good hearted man. సహేతుకము reasonable, well grounded. కారణముతోకూడిన. సహేతుకముగా with the reason or the grounds, కారణసహితముగా. సాకూతము significant, అభిప్రాయసహితమైన. సాకూతస్మితము a wanton glance. A. iv. 41. సానుకూలము favour or kindness, success, ఉపకారము. ఆ పని వానికి సానుకూలమైనతరువాత when he succeeded in that affair. అది సానుకూలముకాక పోయినది it did not succeed. సానుకూలము favourable, kind, ఉపకారమైన. సానుకూలమైనమాట favourable word. సానుకూలముగా favourably, kindly, ఉపకారముగా. సాపత్న్యము the condition of a co-wife, the state of being or having a rival wife, సపత్నీభావము, సవతితనము. "నీకమపమసాపత్న్య సంపాదనంబు" A. ii. 24. "సాపత్న్యమునముగాక సైరింపగలదయేకడసపత్ని." N. iii. 122. సాపత్న్యుడు an enemy, శత్రువు; the son of a co-wife. సపత్నీపుత్రుడు. సాపరాధి a culprit, offender, sinner, he who is guilty, నేరస్థుడు. సావకాశము leisure, spare time, an interval, తీరిక, వ్యవధానము. సావధానముగా carefully, diligently, attentively, with due heed, జాగ్రతతో.

సం or సమ్ *sam.* [Skt.] prefix. When used with Skt. nouns and adjectives, it means beautiful, చక్కని. Much, very, మిక్కిలి. Placed before verbs, it means Well, చక్కగా. See సంక్షోభము, సంక్షోభించు, సంఘటిల్లు, సంచరించు, సంచలించు, సంతుష్టి, సందర్శించు, సంపూర్ణము, సంపూర్తి, సంప్రాప్తి, సంప్రీతి, సంయుక్తము, సంయోజితము, సంయోగము, సంరక్షించు, సంస్తుతి, &c. It also means With, together with. సమంచితము worshipped, revered, పూజ్యమైన. సమధికము exceeding, abundant, plentiful, ఎక్కువైన, మిక్కుటమైన, మిక్కిలి అధికమైన. సమన్వితము joined, united, combined, కూడుకొన్న, సంయుక్తమైన. సమర్పించు to give to the great, to offer presents to superiors, పూజ్యులకు ఇచ్చు. సమర్పితము offered, presented, given to superiors, పూజ్యులకు ఇవ్వబడ్డ. సమర్పణ giving to superiors, a thing presented to the great, an offering, పూజ్యులకు ఇయ్యడము. పూజ్యులకు ఇచ్చినవస్తువు. సమవధానంబుతో attentively, జాగ్రతతో. సమాకర్షి far spreading, as scent. సమాకీర్ణము dishevelled, shed, scattered, sprinkled, interspersed. చల్లబడ్డ. వెదచల్లబడ్డ. సమాగతము that which is come right, చక్కగావచ్చిన; got, obtained, పొందిన. సమాగమము union, junction; a coming, arrival, coming together, meeting, assembling. చేరడము. కూడడము, కలియడము. రావడము. సమాదరము respect, esteem, honour, సన్మానము, మర్యాద. సమాదృతము respected, esteemed, సన్మానించబడ్డ. గొప్పచేయబడ్డ. సమాశ్లిష్టము embraced, కౌగిలించుకొన్న. సమాశ్వాసము consolation, condolence, soothing, comforting, సాంత్వనము, ఓదార్చడము. సమిద్ధము shining, glowing, blazing, ప్రకాశమానమైన. "ఏదేవుచాయసమిద్ధకళాంకసంభవులము పద్మజభవులంసేను." BX. 68. సముచితము proper, right, fit, యోగ్యమైన, న్యాయమైన. సముచ్ఛ్రయము height, elevation, ఔన్నత్యత, opposition, విరోధము. సముచ్ఛ్రాయము height, elevation, ఔన్నత్యము. సముచ్ఛ్రితము high, tall, lifted up, raised, పొడుగైన, ఉన్నతమైన. సముచ్ఛ్రితుడు he who is high or elevated. ఉన్నతుడు. సముజ్ఝితము abandoned, left, quitted. త్యజింపబడ్డ, విడువబడ్డ. సముత్కటము much, excessive; drunk, mad, furious; superior, high, మిక్కుటమైన. తాగి మదించిన, కెర్లి. శ్రేష్ఠమైన. ఉన్నతమైన. సముత్తుంగము high, lofty, tall, ఉన్నతమైన. సముత్సుకము zealously active, fond of, attached to, మిక్కిలి అభిలాషగల. సముత్సుకుడు one who is eager, ఆశగలవాడు. యాత్రాసముత్సుకుడై wishing to make a journey. సముదంచితము worshipped; thrown up, tossed. పూజితమైన. విసరబడ్డ, వ్యాపింపబడ్డ. సముదగ్రము high, tall, large, vast, ఉన్నతమైన, స్థూలమైన. సముదగ్రత height, tallness, largeness, ఔన్నత్యము, స్థౌల్యము. సముదీర్ణము generous, great, excellent, intense, దాతలైన. దివ్యమైన. "సముదీర్ణబాహుదర్పోల్లసులైన పుత్రులు." M. XV. ii. 185. సముద్భూతము produced, born, పుట్టిన. ఉత్పన్నమైన. సముద్గమము birth, production, ఉత్పత్తి, కలుగడము. సముద్దండము violent, fierce, ప్రచండమైన. సముద్యతము ready, prepared, సిద్ధమైన. సముద్ధతము rude, ill mannered, misbehaved, పోటు, పెడసరమైన. ధూర్తమైన. సముద్ధతి ill behaviour, effrontery, audacity, misbehaviour, ధూర్తత, దుర్మార్గము. "కనకొమ్ము కరసముద్ధతి గ్రుద్దుకొనుచు." Sar.D. 420. సముద్ధతుడు a boor, a clown, ధూర్తుడు. సముద్ధరణము drawing up, raising, lifting (as water from a well, &c.) నీళ్లుతోడడము; eradicating, వేరుతో పెరకడము. సముద్ధురము heavy, thick, gross, full, గురుమైన. సంపూర్ణమైన. సముద్ధూళించు to smear oneself (with ashes), (విభూతి) పూసికొను. సముద్భాషించు to praise, స్తుతించు. సమున్నద్ధము proud,

గర్వించిన. సమున్నద్ధుడు a proud man, a wiseacre, చదువుగాలికపోయినది తన్ను చదువరిగా నెంచుకొన్నవాడు. సముపస్థితము arrived, present, ready, near at hand, సమాగతమైన, ప్రస్తుతపు. కటస్థమైన. సమూపేతము having, possessed of, కూడుకొన్న. సమ్మిళితము mingled, కలసబడిన. సమ్మేళనము meeting, joining, mixing, చేరడము. కలియడము. సమాపనివాసుడు a by-stander, he who was present, దక్కన ఉండినవాడు. అక్కడనుండినవాడు. సమ్మోదము great pleasure, delight or joy, మిక్కిలి సంతోషము. సమ్మోహము or సమ్మోహనము bewilderment, fascination, stupefaction. విభ్రమము. సమ్మాహింని or సమ్మాహినిగా in common, not separately. పొత్తుగా. సమ్మాహిని ఉన్న కొంతబాడనపొలము a certain boggy spot.

సంకటము sankaṭamu. [Skt.] n. A difficulty, trouble, affliction, danger, calamity. ఇరుకు, బాధ, ఇక్కట్టు. Disease, illness, రోగము. ప్రాణసంకటము mortal peril. సుఖసంకటము a venereal disease. adj. Difficult, unsafe, narrow, కఠినమైన. ఇరుకైన. సంకటపడు sankaṭa-paḍu. v. n. To be in trouble, to be distressed, శ్రమపడు. అన్నవస్త్రములకులేక సంకటపడుచున్నారు they are in trouble for want of food and clothing. సంకటపాటు sankaṭa-pāṭu n. The state of being in trouble, సంకటపడుటు. సంకటపెట్టు sankaṭa-peṭṭu. v. a. To give trouble to, to annoy, harass, బాధపెట్టు, హింసపెట్టు.

సంకటి sankaṭi. [Tel.] n. A coarse pudding made from Cholam or Ragi flour, a thick porridge or pap. సంకటి రాగిపిండితో కడద, ఉడకపెట్టిన పిండి.

సంకరము sankaramu. [Skt.] n. Mixing, blending. Dust, sweepings. మిశ్రమము. ఊడ్చిన కసవుకుప్ప, పెంట. వర్ణసంకరము a mixture of castes. adj. Confusedly mixing or mingling. Mixed, adulterated, of mixed race or caste, of impure origin from intermixture of castes. మిశ్రితమైన, కలియకలుపుగామండే. సంకరజాతి or సంకరకులము a mixed caste. సంకరజాతివాడు a half caste, a person of mixed parentage. సంకరరోగము a complication of diseases. సంకరభాష a mixed language or impure dialect.

సంకర్షణుడు san-karshaṇuḍu. [Skt.] n. A name of Balarāma, బలరాముడు.

సంకలనము san-kalanamu. [Skt.] n. Addition in Arithmetic, సంఖ్యలుకూర్చుట. సంకలితము sankalitamu. adj. That which is added. Added together, as a figure, కూర్చబడిన (సంఖ్య).

సంకల్పము san-kalpamu. [Skt.] n. Resolve, determination, resolution, intention, will. A project, design. A religious or solemn vow, or declaration. మనోవ్యాపారము, మనోనిశ్చయము, ఎన్నిక. దేవుని సంకల్పము providence, the will of God. సంకల్పజుడు or సంకల్పభవుడు sankalpa-juḍu. n. Lit. "The will-born," a name of Manmadha, as "born from the will." మన్మథుడు. సంకల్పించు or సంకల్పముచేసికొను sankalpintsu. v. n. To determine, resolve, project, plan, decree, as Providence does. ఉద్దేశించు, నిశ్చయించుకొను. ఎంచు.

సంకాశము san-kāśamu. [Skt.] adj. Like, similar. సమానమైన, సదృశమైన. Near, సమీపమైన. సంకాశుడు san-kāśuḍu. n. (In composition,) one who is like or similar to, సదృశుడు. సూర్యసంకాశుడు he who is like the sun.

సంకీర్ణము san-kīrṇamu. [Skt.] adj. Crowded, confused. Mixed, impure, miscellaneous. Spread, diffused. ఎడములేకుండా నిండిన. సంకరమైన. అన్నిచోటులకలిసిన, వ్యాపించిన.

సంకీర్తనము san-kīrtanamu. [Skt.] n. Celebration, praising, honour, glorification, స్తోత్రము, గుణకథనము. స్తవనము.

సంకు *sanku*. [from Skt. శంఖము.] n. A shell, a conch. సంకుటుంగరము a ring made of shell. సంకుపూసలు beads made of shell. "సంకుటద్దములు." Pal. 81. **సంకుమూతిగుఱ్ఱము** *sanku-mūti-gurramu*. n. An ass. గాడిద.

సంకుచించు *san-kuchintsu*. [Skt.] v. n. To shrink, shrivel, contract, close up.

సంకుచితము *san-kuchitamu*. adj. Shrivelled, contracted, narrowed, closed. ముడుతలుపడిన, ముడుచుకొన్న, ఇరుకటముగానుండే. ఈ స్థలము సంకుచితముగానున్నందున as this place is not roomy.

సంకుమదము See under సంకువు.

సంకులము *sankulamu*. [Skt.] adj. Spread. వ్యాపించిన. Crowded, perplexed, confused, agitated, ఎడములేక నిండిన. ఒకటితో ఒకటి కలిసిన.

సంకువు *sankuvu*. [Skt.] n. A civet cat. జవ్వాదిపిల్లి. **సంకుమదము** *sanku-madamu*. n. Civet. జవ్వాజి.

సంకెల or **సంకిలియ** *sankela*. [from Skt. శృంఖలము.] n. A fetter, or iron. **సంకెలవాడు** *sankela-vādu*. n. A convict, a prisoner in irons.

సంకేతము *sankētamu*. [Skt.] n. An appointment, agreement, compact, engagement, ఏర్పాటు, ఒడబాటు, నిష్కర్ష, నిర్ణయము. A provision, a matter or point previously arranged. A sign or signal, a token or intimation, generally without words; a nod, wink, beck, indicative gesture. గురుతు, సంజ్ఞ. A name, పేరు. A place of assignation, a rendezvous, ముందుగా మాట్లాడి నిష్కర్షచేసికొన్న స్థలము. A. v. 135. "సంకేతంబులనుండక." Swa. iii. 45. adj. Appointed, fixed, ordained, stipulated, contracted for, agreed upon. నిర్ణీతమైన, నిష్కర్షచేయబడిన, ఏర్పరచుకోబడిన. సంకేతనామము a technical name, a name agreed upon but different from the real name. సంకేతపదము a technical word, a technicality. సంకేతస్థలము or సంకేతస్థానము a place of rendezvous, a place of assignation. నిర్ణయించుకొన్న చోటు. **సంకేతించు** *sankētintsu*. v. a. To appoint, assign, fix, contract for, agree upon. నిష్కర్షచేయు. నిర్ణయించు, ఏర్పాటుచేయు. To give a name to, పేరుపెట్టు. "నానాకసంకేతించిన తెరగున నరయ్యొ దకులుగు దంచు." M. IV. ii. 282. **సంకేతితము** *sankētitamu*. adj. Appointed, fixed, ordained, stipulated, contracted for, agreed upon, నిష్కర్షచేయబడిన, నిర్ణయించబడిన, ఏర్పరచుకొనబడిన.

సంకోచము *san-kōchamu*. [Skt.] n. Shrivelling, contraction, shrinking, shutting, closing, ముడుచుకొనుట, ముకుళించుటము. Narrowness, straitness, ఇరుకు. Backwardness, diffidence, bashfulness, modesty, జంకు, బిడియము. Hesitation, reluctance, సంశయము. **సంకోచించు** *san-kōchintsu*. v. n. To shrivel up or contract. To hesitate, be reluctant, be bashful or timid, ముడుచుకొను. అనుమానించు, వెనుక దీయు. జంకు.

సంక్రందనుడు *san-krandanudu*. [Skt.] n. An epithet of Indra. ఇంద్రుడు.

సంక్రమము *san-kramamu*. [Skt.] n. Difficult progress, advance through difficulties. The transit of a planetary body through the zodiac. గమనము. గతి. సూర్యాదిగ్రహములు ఒకరాశినుండి మరియొకరాశికి పోవడము. A causeway, a bridge, వంతెన. **సంక్రమణము** *san-kramanamu*. n. The passage of the sun or planetary body from one sign of the zodiac into another. సూర్యాదిగ్రహములు ఒకరాశిని విడిచి మరియొకరాశికి పోవడము. **సంక్రమించు** *san-kramintsu*. v. a. To encroach on, ఆక్రమించు. To enter, ప్రవేశించు. **సంక్రాంతి** *san-krānti*. n. The transit of the sun or a planetary body from one sign of the zodiac into another; particularly applied to the passage of the sun from Sagittarius to Capricornus in January when the Hindus celebrate the Pongal (పొంగలి) feast. సూర్యాదిగ్రహములు ఒకరాశిలోనుండి మరియొకరాశికి పోవడము, ముఖ్యముగా సూర్యుడు మకరమునకు ప్రవేశించేది మకరసంక్రాంతి.

సంక్లిప్తము *san-kluptamu.* [Skt.] adj. Brief, short, abridged. n. An abridgment, a summary, సంగ్రహము, సంక్షేపము. సంక్లిప్తముగా briefly, summarily. సంక్లిప్తము చేయు to abridge, to make brief.

సంక్షేపము *san-kshēpamu.* [Skt.] n. An abridgment, a compendium, a summary, సంగ్రహము. సంక్షేపించు *san-kshēpintsu.* v. a. To abridge, abbreviate, contract, సంక్షేపము చేయు, సంగ్రహము చేయు. సంక్షిప్తము *san-kshiptamu.* adj. Abbreviated, abridged, సంక్షేపింపబడిన. సంక్షేపణము *sankshēpanamu.* n. The act of abridging, సంక్షేపపరచుట. సంక్షేపముగా *san-kshēpamu-gā.* adv. Concisely, briefly, సంగ్రహముగా.

సంక్షోభము *san-kshōbhamu.* [Skt.] n. Agitation, alarm, కలత. Distress of mind, sorrow, grief, వ్యాకులత, దుఃఖము, వ్యసనము. సంక్షోభించు *san-kshōbhintsu.* v. n. To be agitated, disturbed, excited, alarmed, కలతపడు. To grieve, sorrow, వ్యాకులపడు. సంక్షుభితము or సంక్షోభితము *san-kshubhitamu.* adj. Agitated, disturbed, grieved, frightened, alarmed, afraid, భిన్నాభిన్నము చేయబడ్డ, వ్యాకులపరచబడ్డ, కలిగిన, భయపడ్డ.

సంఖ్య *sankhya.* [Skt.] n. A number, a numeral. అంక, లెక్క. సంఖ్యలేని numberless. An inquiry, విచారణ. Spiritual knowledge, ఆత్మజ్ఞానము. సంఖ్యము *sankhyamu.* n. War, a battle. యుద్ధము. సంఖ్యాతము *sankhyatamu.* adj. Numbered, counted, reckoned. లెక్కపెట్టబడిన, ఎంచబడిన, గణితము. సంఖ్యావాచకవిశేషణము a definite numeral adjective (cardinal). సంఖ్యావంతుడు *sankhya-vantuḍu.* n. A learned man, పండితుడు, వరుడు. సంఖ్యేయము *sankhy-ēyamu.* adj. Numerable, that which can be counted or numbered, ఎంచదగిన, గణనీయము. సంఖ్యేయార్థకవిశేషణము a definite numeral adjective (ordinal).

సంగడము *sangaḍamu.* [from Skt. సంగతము.] n. Dumb-bells, సాముచేయువారు తిప్పేలోడు. Help, assistance, aid, సహాయము. Friendship, జత, స్నేహము. Meeting, చేరిక. Nearness, సమీపము. A retinue, పరివారము. Service, సేవ. An army, సేన. "అనుపుడు వాడునకును శివిరములనుకునా వెరవు సంగడం బుగాను." M. VII. iv. 59. "తా అంచెలుగట్టి కాలితోదుసైవవసివ్రుగదమ్మప్రోదిరా, యుండ లిపేటి సంగడములయ్యెను." Swa. v. 72. Trouble, annoyance, తొందరము, సంకటము. సంగడమువాడు *sangaḍamu-vāḍu.* n. A friend or companion. చెలికాడు, స్నేహకాడు. సంగడి *sangaḍi.* n. A couple, pair, జంట, జత, జోడు. Friendship, స్నేహము. A friend, a fellow, a playmate, స్నేహకాడు. A raft or boat made of two canoes fastened side by side. రెండుకాలి బొందులు జతగాకట్టిన తెప్ప. Nearness, సమీపము. A side, ప్రక్క. The back, వెనుక. A crowd, సమూహము. Manner, విధము. "ఇ॥ సింగంబులసంగడి నుండదగు దిర ఘటులను." తా. హరి. iv. సంగడిబావులు two wells side by side, జోడు బావులు. సంగడికత్తె *sangaḍi-katte.* n. A female friend or companion. చెలికత్తె. సంగడికాడు or సంగడీడు *sangaḍi-kāḍu.* n. A compeer, fellow, companion, friend, స్నేహితుడు. సంగమడుగు *sanga-maḍugu.* (సంగడి+మడుగు.) n. A lake or pool near a village,

తోటసమీపమందు ఎవరు తవ్వకరయే ఎన్నటికిన్ని నీళ్లు ఉండే మడుగు.

సంగతము *san-gatamu.* [Skt.] adj. Joined, united, come together, coherent, consistent, proper, just, adequate, reasonable, suitable, appropriate, applicable. యుక్తమైన, యోగ్యమైన, సంలగ్నమైన, సంయుక్తమైన. "క మనీయమన్యజ్రసంగతకవాటములు." HD. i. 13. n. Friendship, స్నేహము. Meeting, చేరక. **సంగతి** *san-gati.* n. A circumstance, matter, case, subject, affair, business, event, occurrence: the contents of a writing. Association, junction, union, company, society. Fitness, decorum, propriety. కార్యము, వ్యవహారము. పని, విషయము, సహవాసము, సాంగత్యము, యుక్తము. యోగ్యము, సంపర్కము. అతడు చెప్పిన సంగతి ఏమంటే he stated as follows. ఈ సంగతి నాకు తెలిసి on knowing this. ఆ సంగతి నేను వినలేదు I did not hear of it. అతడు బ్రతికియుండే సంగతి చనిపోయిన సంగతి తెలియలేదు I do not know whether he is alive or dead. **సంగతిని** or **సంగతిగా** *san-gati-ni.* adv. Properly, fitly. యుక్తముగా, తగినట్టుగా. "పట్టు వస్త్రములు భూషణముల్ గలుచందనంబులున్, సంగతిగట్టియుండొడిగి సయ్యనజూచె." ప్రసన్న రాఘవశతకము. **సంగతించు** *san-gatintsu.* v. n. To happen, occur. సంభవించు. ప్రసక్తించు. **సంగతుడు** *san-gatudu.* n. (In composition,) one who is accompanied by, or beset by. కూడుకొన్నవాడు. "అసురాస్త్రసంగతుం డనుతపనుంగని ప్రాద్యుమ్నుంక బడి వేసుదురీరిపులన." M. VI. ii. 341.

సంగమము *san-gamamu.* [Skt.] n. Juncture, union, meeting, the confluence of rivers, sexual intercourse, కలియుటము. మేళనము, సంయోగము. సంగమదోషము any sexual disease, సుఖసంకటము. **సంగము** *sangamu.* n. Junction, meeting, union, intercourse, association, confluence. కూడిక. చేరిక, సంసర్గము. మేళనము, కలియుటము. ఈనదీసాగరసంగమస్థలము the place where this river falls into the sea. నదులసంగము the confluence of rivers. **సంగి** *sangi.* adj. (In composition,) uniting or united with. కూడుకొన్న, మిళితమైన. n. He who is united, he who is attached to. కూడుకొన్నవాడు, మిళితుడు.

సంగరము *sangaramu.* [Skt.] n. War, a battle, combat. యుద్ధము. సంగరావని a battlefield. M. XVI. i. 73.

సంగాతము *san-gātamu.* [from Skt. సంగతమ్.] n. Friendship, స్నేహము. **సంగాతి** or **సంగాతకాడు** *san-gāti.* n. A friend, companion, comrade. స్నేహితుడు. **సంగాతకత్తె** *sangāta-katte.* n. A female friend, స్నేహితురాలు.

సంగీతము *san-gītamu.* [Skt.] n. Music, a song, singing. A choral symphony, గానము. **సంగీతి** *san-gīti.* n. A song. plu. సంగీతులు songs, పాటలు. "సాంగోపాంగసంగీతములగా." G. viii. 163.

సంగోరు *san-gōru.* [Skt. సగము+Tel. కోరు.] n. A half-share. అర్ధభాగము. Half of the gross produce of a crop. సంగోరుపాలు usually means the government share of a crop.

సంగ్రహము *san-grahamu.* [Skt.] n. Seizing, grasping, obtaining, receiving, earning, acquisition, స్వీకారము. స్వీకరించడము. సంపాదించడము. Collecting, amassing, కూడబెట్టడము. పోగుచేయడము. A compilation, abridgment, compendium, సంక్షిప్తగ్రంథము. One verse says కర్తవ్యం ధర్మసంగ్రహం. adj. Short, brief. సంక్షేపమైన. **సంగ్రహించు** *san-grahintsu.* v. a. To seize, grasp, snatch, obtain, acquire, earn, get. సంపాదించు. To abridge, compile, summarize, సంక్షేపించు. సంగ్రహించుకొని వెళ్లు to walk away with anything, లంకించుకొనిపోవు.

సంగ్రామము *sangrāmamu.* [Skt.] n. War, a battle, fighting. యుద్ధము. కలహము, పోరు.

సంగ్రాహము *san-grāhamu.* [Skt.] n. The fist. పిడికిలి. Holding by the fist, పిడికిటపట్టుట. The gripe of a shield, డాలుపిడి, అరిగపిడి.

సంఘటనము *san-ghaṭanamu.* [Skt.] n. Meeting, encountering, happening, occurrence. సంధించడము, సంప్రాప్తముకావడము. **సంఘటించు** or **సంఘటిల్లు** *san-ghaṭintsu.* v. n. To occur, happen. సంభవించు, సంప్రాప్తమగు.

సంఘట్టనము *san-ghaṭṭanamu.* [Skt.] n. Friction, rubbing together, beating, a collision, shock. ఒరసికొనుట. కొట్టడము, తాయించడము. "మే సంఘట్టన మితిమీరియాడె." L. vii. 170.

సంఘము *sanghamu.* [Skt.] n. A collection, heap, multitude, number, assembly, association, society. ప్రాణిసమూహము, గుంపు. **సంఘీభవించు** *sanghi-bhavintsu.* v. n. To become a crowd. గుంపుకూడు. To unite together.

సంఘర్షము or **సంఘర్షణము** *san-gharshamu.* [Skt.] n. Trituration, rubbing. ఒరయుట. Contending. వివాదము, స్పర్థ. Rivalry, పోటి.

సంఘాతము *san-ghātamu.* [Skt.] n. An assemblage, multitude. సమూహము. A hard blow, గట్టిదెబ్బ. సంఘాతమరణము wholesale slaughter, deaths in crowds. కంటకసంఘాతములు a heap of thorns. P. i. 457.

సంచయము *san-chayamu.* [Skt.] n. Heaping, collecting, gathering, కూడబెట్టుట. A heap, multitude, quantity or number. సమూహము, ప్రోగు. **సంచయనము** *san-chayanamu.* n. Collecting, gathering, collecting the ashes or bones of a burnt corpse, పోగుచేయడము, దహనముచేయబడిన శవముయొక్క ఎముకలను పోగుచేయడము.

సంచరించు *san-charintsu.* [Skt.] v. n. To roam, wander, walk. తిరుగు. "సకలజంతువులందు సంచరించు" he pervades or moves in all that lives. **సంచారము** or **సంచరణము** *san-charamu.* n. Traversing, wandering, roaming, travelling, తిరగడము. శిష్యసంచారము a pastoral visitation, or progress made by a Guru. పిశాచసంచారము the walking or haunting of a ghost. **సంచారి** *sanchari.* n. One who wanders about, సంచరించువాడు.

సంచలనము *san-chalanamu.* [Skt.] n. Shaking, moving. కదలడము. **సంచలించు** *san-chalintsu.* v. n. To move, shake, tremble, quake.

సంచి or **సంచీ** *sanchi.* [Tel.] n. A purse, a bag. తిత్తి. గోనెసంచి a sack. మడిసంచి a bag made of woollen cloth or canvas to keep clean clothes in. **సంచికట్టు** *sanchi-kaṭṭu.* n. A physician, సంచికట్టుకొని తిరుగు వైద్యుడు. **సంచిమొదలు** *sanchi-modalu.* n. The capital sum, capital, మూలధనము.

సంచితము *sanchitamu.* [Skt.] adj. Gathered, amassed, accumulated, collected. సంపాదించబడిన, ఆర్జించబడిన, కూడబెట్టబడిన. "పూర్వజన్మసంచితములైన దోషములు." (B. iii. 1001) the sins contracted in a former birth. **సంచిక** *sanchika.* n. A section or part of a book. A few palm leaves or sheets of paper taken out of a volume. ఒక గ్రంథములోనుండి యెత్తికట్టిన కొన్ని పత్రములు. A tract, చేర్చికట్టిన కొన్ని తాటాకులు. లేక కాగితములు. A volume of a Magazine or Journal.

సంచేకరువు, సంచేకరము or **సంచేకారము** *santsa-karuvu.* [from Skt. సత్యంకారః.] n. Earnest money, an advance, బయానా, జట్టీచేసినందుకు గురుతుగా ముందిచ్చినద్రవ్యము.

సంచేము *santsamu.* [Tel.] n. Gold. బంగారు. **సంచేపురేకు** *santsapu-rēku.* n. Gold leaf, bits of gold leaf, బంగారురేకు, "పాలుపుసంచెపురేకు బుక్కాముప్పైబల్లి."

Ila. i. 139. "సంచపు రేకుదుప్పటులుజోరా." H. v. 197.

సంచు *santsu.* [Tel.] n. Manner, way. విధము, రీతి, వైఖరి. An artifice, stratagem, మోసము. A trace, జాడ. Beauty, అందము.

సంఛన్నము *sanchhannamu.* [Skt.] adj. Covered, ఆచ్ఛాదితము. "రేలుపటులసంఛన్న గీర్వాణపదవి." Vish. ii. 135.

సంజనితము *san-janitamu.* [Skt.] adj. Born, produced, become. పుట్టిన, కలిగిన, అయిన. **సంజనితుడు** *san-janitudu.* n. One who is born. పుట్టినవాడు.

సంజయరాయబారము *sanjaya-raya-bharamu.* [Skt.] n. The embassy of Sanjaya; i.e., lukewarm negotiations.

సంజవనము *sanja-vanamu.* [Skt.] n. A cluster of four houses. A house built with four suites of apartments. నాలుగిండ్ల బవంతి.

సంజాతము *san-jatamu.* [Skt.] adj. Born, produced, become. కలిగిన, పుట్టిన, అయిన.

సంజాయిషీ *sanjayisht.* [H.] n. An explanation; conciliation, persuasion, సమాధానము.

సంజీవి *sanjivi.* [Skt.] n. That which gives or revives life, జీవమునుకలుగజేయునది. A medicine which prolongs life. ఆయుస్సును వృద్ధిచేయుమందు. **సంజీవకరణి** *sanjiva-karani.* n. A restorative, a cordial, a reviving medicine, a medicine tending to prolong life, or of sufficient efficacy to raise the dead. మళ్లీ బ్రతికించేమందు. "ఘనతరసంజీవకరణిమోహనను వినితదిగ్గనలేచివచ్చినజాడ." Sar. D. 675. "స్థిరమైనయా యోషధీశైలమెక్కి, కర మొప్పుసంజీవకరణి విశల్య, కరణియు సంధానకరణి సావర్ణ్యకరణినా నాలుగౌషధములుగలవు." DRY. 1504. **సంజీవనము** *san-jivanamu.* adj. Animating, bringing to life. బ్రతికించే.

సంజ్ఞ *sangnya.* [Skt.] n. A gesture, సైగ. A token, sign, గురుతు. A name, appellation, పేరు. A technical name, పరిభాష. Intellect, sense, తెలివి, బుద్ధి. సంజ్ఞావాచకము a noun. **సంజ్ఞప్తి** or **సంజ్ఞపనము** *san-gnyapti.* n. Making known, apprizing, informing. తెలియజేయడము, ఎరుకచేయడము, విన్నవించుట. M. VII. iv. 144.

సంజ్ఞువు *san-gnyuvu.* [Skt.] n. A knock-kneed man. ముట్టికాళ్లవాడు.

సంజ్వరము *san-jvaramu.* [Skt.] n. Heat, burning, scorching. కాక, వేడిమి, ఉష్ణము, కాల్చడము.

సంజె *sandza.* [from Skt. సంధ్య.] n. Twilight, evening. సంధ్యాకాలము. సంజెరాగము, సంజెకెంపు or సంజెకావి the redness of the evening sky. Sar. D. 212. Vasu. v. 96. అరిసంజె అనగా అర్ధాస్తమయకాలము. **సంజెపడు** *sandza-padu.* v. n. To become dusk, సంధ్యాకాలమగు.

సంజోక *san-dzoka.* [Tel. సగము+జోక.] n. The string that strikes the two sides of a double-faced drum, రెండు ముఖములందును తాకే ముడిగల డుబుడక్కనడిమిత్రాడు.

సంత్ర Same as చెంత్ర (q. v.)

సంత *santa.* [Tel.] n. Nearness, చెంత. [from Skt. సంస్థా.] A fair, a market day. చుట్టుపట్ల నుండువారందరును సరుకులమ్మడమునకై ఒకచోటిలో నొకనాడు పెట్టే అంగళ్లవరుస. Recitation of a lesson from the Veda, ఒక్కొకవాక్యముగా నుపాధ్యాయులు చెప్పుచానిని పిల్లకాయలు రెండేసిమారులు చెప్పడము, వేదపాఠము. ఏకసంతగ్రాహి (for ఏకసంధాగ్రాహి) one who is gifted with intuitive perception.

సంతకము *santakamu.* [Tel.] n. A signature, చేవ్రాలు.

సంతతము *santatamu.* [Skt.] adj. Constant, continuous, unceasing. ఎడతెగని, విడువని.

adv. Always, perpetually. నిరంతరము, ఎల్లప్పుడు. వర్షము సంతతధారగా కురిసినది it rained incessantly.

సంతతి *san-tati.* [Skt.] n. Progeny, offspring. సంతానము. పుత్రపౌత్రపారంపర్యము. A series, వరుస. పురుషసంతతి male offspring.

సంతన *santana.* [from Skt. సంధానము.] n. Joining, junction, union. Agreement, concord, suitability, అనుకూలముగా కుదురుడు, కూర్పు, ఇముడిక, పొందిక, చేరిక. "దంతపు రేకు సంతనపని." Satya. ii. 125. **సంతనచేయు** *santana-chēyu.* v. a. To fit, adjust, join, unite. కూర్చు. చేర్చు. ఆ రాళ్లను బాగా సంతన చేసినాడు he fitted the stones together closely. **సంతనకట్టు** *santana-kaṭṭu.* v. n. To be united, చేరు, సంఘటించు. To be prepared, ఆయత్తపడు. **సంతపడు** *santa-paḍu.* (సంతన+పడు.) v. n. To be united, or adjusted. ఒద్దికపడు. **సంతపరుచు** or **సంతపెట్టు** *santa-paruṭsu.* v. a. To unite, adjust, చేర్చు.

సంతన్యమానము *santanya-mānamu.* [Skt.] adj. Spreading, extending. వృద్ధిపొందింపబడిన. "అతఃపురకాంతాకరాంతసంతన్యమాన మణిభాజననీరాజన మంగళంబులంగీకరించి." Swa. v. 65. టీ॥ సంతన్యమాన. మిక్కిలి త్రిప్పబడుచుండే.

సంతప్తము *san-taptamu.* [Skt.] adj. Much heated; pained, grieved, distressed, afflicted. సంతాపితమైన, ఖేదముగల, దుఃఖితమైన. సంతప్తచిత్తుడు he who is much grieved. "సకలదేవమునులు సంతప్తచిత్తులై." Padma. vii. 17. **సంతప్తుడు** *san-taptuḍu.* n. One who is burnt up, or exhausted with heat, hunger or thirst. ఎండ ఆకలి దప్పిచేత పీడింపబడినవాడు.

సంతమసము *san-tamasamu.* [Skt.] n. Total darkness. సర్వత్రపూర్ణాంధకారము, కటికచీకటి. Vasu. iv. 21.

సంతరణము *san-taraṇamu.* [Skt.] n. Crossing or passing over, going across. దాటుడము.

సంతరించు *san-tarintsu.* [Tel.] v. a. To equalise, సరిపరుచు. To earn, get, acquire, సంపాదించు, గడించు. To cause to acquire, కలిగించు. To write, వ్రాయు, రచించు. To protect, support, rear, ధరించు, సంరక్షించు. "చక్కదనమెల్లను ముల్లెగా సంతరించి." H. i. 254. ఆమె నన్ను సాకి సంతరించినది she brought me up and took care of me.

సంతర్జితము *san-tarjitamu.* [Skt.] adj. Threatened, frightened. బెదిరింపబడిన. M. vii. 432.

సంతర్పణము or **సంతర్పణ** *san-tarpaṇamu.* [Skt.] n. Satisfying, satiating. తృప్తిపరుచుట. A feast given to Brahmins. **సంతర్పితము** *san-tarpitamu.* adj. Satisfied, gratified. తృప్తిచేయబడిన. "నిత్యాన్నదాన సంతర్పిత సకలధరాసురుండును." T. Pref. 30.

సంతసము, సంతోసము or **సంతోసము** *santasamu.* [from Skt. సంతోషము.] n. Pleasure, joy, gladness. ప్రమదము, సంతోషము. **సంతసించు, సంతసిల్లు, సంతసిలు, సంతోసిల్లు** or **సంతసపడు** *santasintsu.* v. n. To rejoice, be pleased, be glad, ఉల్లాసపడు, సంతోషించు.

సంతానము or **సంతానవృక్షము** *santānamu.* [Skt.] n. The name of one of the trees of heaven. ఒక కల్పవృక్షము. సప్తసంతానములు:— Digging a tank (తటాకము), building a Brahmin village (అగ్రహారము), building a temple (దేవాలయము), making a garden (వనము), getting a poem written (ప్రబంధము), getting a son (పుత్రుడు), finding treasure (నిధి).

సంతానము *santānamu.* [Skt.] n. A child, బిడ్డ. Offspring, progeny, race. బిడ్డలపరంపర, సంతతి.

సంతాపము *san-tāpamu.* [Skt.] n. Heat, burning heat. కాక, వేడిమి, వెట్ట. Affliction, pain, distress. The fever of desire. సంతాపార్థకము an interjection showing sorrow. సంతాపించు *san-tāpintsu*. v. n. To be afflicted, to be distressed, to be grieved, దుఃఖితుడగు, ఖేదితుడగు, పరితపించు. సంతాపితుడు *san-tā-pituḍu*. n. He who is pained, distressed, or afflicted. ఖిన్నుడు. దుఃఖితుడు. పరితపించువాడు.

సంతు *santu*. [from Skt. సంతతి.] n. Offspring, progeny. సంతానము. మగసంతు male offspring.

సంతులుగొట్టు *santulu-goṭṭu*. [Tel.] v. a. To reproach, blame. నిందించు. "అతిక్రూరుని నన్ను గావటిడి సంతులుగొట్టుచు మోము చేయుచోగా." A. vi. 109.

సంతుష్టము *san-tushṭamu*. [Skt.] adj. Delighted, pleased, satisfied. హృష్టమైన, ఆహ్లాదముగల, ఉల్లసితమైన. సంతుష్టాంతరంగుడై being filled with joy. సంతుష్టి *san-tushṭi*. (సం+తుష్టి.) n. Pleasure, satisfaction, gladness, joy, delight. సంతోషము, హర్షము, ఆహ్లాదము. సంతుష్టుడు *san-tushṭuḍu*. n. He who is delighted, or satisfied. హర్షితుడు.

సంతోషము *san-tōshamu*. [Skt.] n. Pleasure, satisfaction, joy, delight. ప్రమదము, హర్షము. సంతోషపెట్టు *san-tōsha-peṭṭu*. v. a. To gladden, please, gratify. ఉల్లాసపరచు, తుష్టునిగాచేయు. సంతోషించు or సంతోషిల్లు *san-tōshintsu*. v. n. To rejoice, be glad. హర్షించు, సంతోషపడు. సంతోసము Same as సంతోషము. See సంతసము.

సంత్యక్తము *san-tyaktamu*. [Skt.] adj. Deserted, left, quitted, abandoned. విడువబడిన, పరిత్యజింపబడిన.

సంత్రస్తము *san-trastamu*. [Skt.] adj. Frightened, alarmed. భయపడిన.

సంత్రాసము *san-trāsamu*. [Skt.] n. Fear, alarm. భీతి, భయము.

సందంశము *sandamśamu*. [Skt.] n. Pincers, కమ్మరవాని పటుకారు.

సందడి *sandaḍi*. [Tel.] n. A thick crowd, mob. సమ్మర్దము. ఒత్తుడు, గుంపు. Noise, clamour, uproar, a tumult, disturbance. సమ్మర్దధ్వని. "రాజులసందడి రాలినతోడవులు." M. IV. iii. 69. adj. Confused, సంకులము. సందడికయ్యము a noisy or melee fight. సందడించు, సందడిల్లు, సందడిగొను or సందడిపడు *sandaḍintsu*. v. n. To flock, to come in crowds, గుంపులుగొను. To make a noise, సందడిచేయు. To spread, extend. ప్రసరించు, అతిశయించు. "భయవిస్మయంబులు మనంబునసందడింప." P. i. 277. "గలుగదినావె ద మెరుగుపలుమెరుగులు సందడింప." Swa. iv. 106.

సందరము or సంద్రము *sandaramu*. [from Skt. సముద్రము.] n. The sea.

సందర్భము *sandarbhamu*. [Skt.] n. Stringing beads, weaving garlands, etc. Meeting, connection, coherence. Convenience, opportunity, occurrence, context, కూర్పడము, గుచ్చడము, కట్టడము, సంధించడము, క్రమము, ఆనుపూర్వి, అనుకూలము, సమయము, సంఘటించడము. "ప్రయోగసందర్భములు డెందంబు సందడింప." Vish. vii. 148. దీనికిదానికి సందర్భము లేదు. లేక, ఒకటికొకటి సందర్భములేకుండాఉన్నది they disagree, they do not agree. అది ఈ సందర్భములో జరుగదు it cannot be done at this juncture. పూర్వోత్తర సందర్భము ఎరుగక మాట్లాడుచున్నాడు he talks without knowing the circumstances. ఇప్పుడు సందర్భము కాదు it is not convenient now. సందర్భించు *sandarbhintsu*. v. n. To agree, tally, to be convenient, to be opportune, to occur, happen, అనుకూలించు, ఇముడు, సంఘటించు, ప్రాప్తమగు.

సందర్శనము *san-darṡanamu*. [Skt.] n. Seeing, looking, a view. A visit, meeting నిరీక్షణము, చూడడము. సందర్శించు *san-darṡintsu*. v. a. To look at, view, behold, visit. చూచు.

సందష్టము *san-dashtamu.* [Skt.] adj. Bitten, stung. కొరకబడిన.

సందానము *sandānamu.* [Skt.] n. A tether. పలుపు. సందానితము or సందితము *sand-ānitamu.* adj. Tied, bound, కట్టబడిన.

సంది Same as సందు (q. v.)

సందిగ్ధము *sandigdhamu.* [Skt.] adj. Doubtful, questionable. సంశయమైన.

సందిబొందె *sandi-bonde.* [Tel. from సందిలి.] n. An ornament for the arm, an armlet, బాహుపురి. "మేలిమినూలలదండ. కడెములుసంది బొందె విడికమ్మలుమించులమించుమించులన్." H. iv. 101.

సందియము *sandiyamu.* [from Skt. సందేహము.] n. Doubt, uncertainty, suspicion. సందియపడు same as సందేహించు (q. v.)

సందిలి *sandili.* [Tel.] n. The arm from the shoulder to the elbow. దండచెయ్యి. సందిలి దండ, సందిదండ or సందికడియము *sandili-danda.* n. An ornament worn upon the upper part of the arm. An armlet, కేయూరము. Swa. v. 106 సందెడు *sand-edu.* adj. An armful, as much as one can hold in the arms. సందుచేతులుబావిని రొమ్ముకగిలి సంత.

సందు or **సంది** *sandu.* [from Skt. సంధి.] n. A small opening, a fissure, crack, hole, బొక్క, చిల్లి, బీటిక. Space, an interval. ఎడము, మధ్యప్రదేశము, మధ్యకాలము. A lane, a narrow street, చిన్నవీధి, గల్లీ. A nook, corner, మూల. A backyard, పెరడు. A period of time, an opportunity, సమయము, సందర్భము. A direction or quarter. చంకసందు the arm-pit. వేళ్లసందు the space between two fingers. ఇక్కడ సందు విడువు leave a space here. సందిచ్చు to give room or opportunity. వాడు ఎవరికిని సందియ్యకుండా మాట్లాడుతాడు he will let nobody else get a word in, he gives no one an opportunity of speaking. వారిద్దరిసందున వీడు నలిగిపోవుచున్నాడు between the two this man is ruined. సందులు గొందులంతా వెతికినాడు he hunted in every hole and corner. సందుచూచి లోగా చొరబడినాడు he took an opportunity and rushed in. సందువాకిలి the back-door, పెరటిగుమ్మము. సందుముట్టు menses occurring at intervals, that is, at irregular periods. "వేటికి నచ్చెసందు." T. iii. 87. అనగా నేడుసమయమువచ్చెనని. సందిక్రంతజగడములు petty disputes, అల్పమైనజగడములు. **సందుకట్టు** *sandu-kattu.* n. An interval, మధ్యకాలము. గ్రహణపు సందుకట్టు the time that an eclipse lasts. అమావాస్య సందుకట్టు the period of new moon. నేను పోయి వీడు వచ్చేసందుకట్టులో in the interval between my going and his coming. **సందుకొను** *sandu-konu.* v. n. To take or seize an opportunity, సమయము చూచుకొను. To extend, spread, వ్యాపించు. v. a. To unite with, కూడు. To be joined to, to marry, పరిగ్రహించు. **సందుకొట్టు** or **సందుతగులు** *sandu-kottu.* v. n. To be injured by a ghost. **సందుదోషము** *sandu-dōshamu.* n. Demoniac possession. బిడ్డలకు మాససంధియందు కలుగు బాలగ్రహదోషము. ఆ బిడ్డకు సందుదోషముతగిలినది, సందుకొట్టినది or సందుతగిలినది the child is fairy-struck or injured by a ghost that haunts a particular spot. **సందుసాము** *sandu-sāmu.* n. A certain feat in wrestling.

సందుగు *sandugu.* [H.] n. A small box.

సందె *sande.* [from Skt. సంధ్య.] n. Evening, సాయంకాలము. Daily prayers used by Brahmins, &c. సంధ్యావందనము. adj. Vesper; appertaining to the evening, or vesper hour. సాయంకాలపు. సందెచీకటి the evening twilight. సందెదీపమున్నా పెట్టదు she has not so much as a light in the evening. సందెవేళ or సందెకడ at even-tide, in the evening. "అయ్యలుసందెవేళజని యూడగ వింటిని

రాక." H. iii. 69. సందెవార్చు to perform daily prayers. సందెజాము, సందెక్రొత్త or సందెవేళ sande-dzāmu. n. The time of sunrise or sunset, when the night passes into the day or the day into the night. Generally, the evening.

సందేశము sandēsamu. [Skt.] n. A message, news, tidings. వర్తమానము, సమాచారము. సందేశహారుడు sandēsa-hāruḍu. n. A messenger. దూత, హర్కారా, సమాచారమును తీసికొనిపోవువాడు.

సందేహము sandēhamu. [Skt.] n. Doubt, hesitation, suspicion, mistrust, uncertainty. సంశయము. సందేహించు sandēhintsu. v. n. To doubt, suspect, hesitate. సంశయించు, సందేహపడు, అనుమానపడు.

సందోహము sandōhamu. [Skt.] n. An assemblage, multitude. సమూహము.

సంద్రము See సంద్రము. సంద్రుడు Same as సముద్రుడు. (q. v.)

సంధ sandha. [Skt.] n. A vow, promise. Resolution, determination. ప్రతిజ్ఞ, శపథము. Extent, limit. మర్యాద, మేర, అవధి. Parij. v. 52. Also, same as సంధ్య (q. v.)

సంధర్షిణి san-dharsaṇi. [Skt.] n. India rubber.

సంధానము sandhānamu. [Skt.] n. Holding together, joining, uniting, కూర్పుట, సంఘటనము. Reconciliation. బాణసంధానము or శరసంధానము placing an arrow on the bow-string. నాయకీనాయకులకు సంధానముచేసినది she made her master and mistress friends, she reconciled them. "సకలశిష్యులందు సంధానమైయుండి" Vema. 518. సంధానకరణి sandhāna-karaṇi. n. That which heals, reunites or reconciles. వ్రణము చేయు (ఓషధి), మళ్లీకూడునట్లు చేయునది, స్నేహము చేయునది. సంధానించు sandhānintsu. v. a. To join, unite, చేర్చు, కూర్చు. సంధానితము sandh-ānitamu. adj. Joined, united, చేర్చబడిన, కూర్చబడిన. సంధాయకుడు or సంధాత sandhāyakuḍu. n. One who unites. సంధానముచేయువాడు.

సంధి sandhi. [Skt.] n. Connection, union, combination, junction, coalescence. కూడిక, చేరడము, కలియుటము. A joint of the limbs, కీలు. Pacification, peacemaking, conciliation, peace, a treaty, అనుకూలము, సమాధానము. The coalescence of letters in accordance with the laws of euphony. అచ్సంధి the union of vowels. హల్సంధి the union of consonants. ఈయన వారికి సంధి చేసినాడు he made them friends. "దిట్టలిట్లు సంధులు ప్రతిదినగ్రహము." BD. iv. 359. కుసంధి a bad union. సంధివిగ్రహము peace and war. సంధివిగ్రహాధికారము a war ministry, the duty of a war minister. సంధిబంధనము a ligament. సంధించు san-dhintsu. v. a. To cause to meet, to bring together, join, unite. కలుపు, చేర్చు, కూర్చు. సంధించు or సంధిల్లు v. n. To be joined to or united with, కూడు. సంధితము sandhitamu. adj. Joined, united, connected, bound, చేర్చబడిన, కూర్చబడిన, కట్టబడిన. సంధిత్స sandhitsa. n. The desire of joining, an inclination to unite. చేర్చవలెననేయిచ్ఛ. సంధిలు or సంధిల్లు sandhilu. v. n. To happen, occur; to meet. ప్రాప్తమగు, ఎదురుపడు, కలుగు, వచ్చు. "భక్తిగౌరవము విశ్వాసంబు సంధిల్లగా." T. ii. 55. "అచలాత్మజమాటకు శేతవవ్వుసంధిల్ల." Swa. pref. 2. సంధుడు or సంధురాలు sandhuḍu. n. One who is united with. These words are used in compounds; thus సత్యసంధుడు, సత్యసంధురాలు a truthful or veracious man or woman.

సంధుక్షితము sandhu-kshitamu. [Skt.] adj. Lighted, inflamed, kindled. రగిలించబడిన, మండించబడిన.

సంధ్య sandhya. [Skt.] n. Twilight in the morning or evening. సంధ్య or సంధ్యావంద

నము morning or evening prayer. ప్రాతస్సంధ్యావందనము matins. సాయంసంధ్యావందనము vespers. సంధ్యవార్చు to perform matins or vespers. సంధ్యత్రాడు the sacerdotal thread., జందెము. Vema. 380. సంధ్యారాగము *sandhya-rāgamu*. n. The redness of the evening sky. సంజకెంపు.

సంపంగి, సంపగె, సంపగియ or **సంపెగ** *sampangi*. [from Skt. చంపక.] n. The 'gold flower', *Michelia champaka*. చంపకము. A species is కొండసంపంగి. H. iv. 19. (Note: This flower is called by all the synonymes of gold, as సువర్ణపుష్పము, బంగారుపువ్వు, &c., &c. No bee will touch this fragrant flower.) సంపంగినూనె a fragrant oil extracted from this flower. తీగసంపంగి a certain creeper with yellow fragrant blossoms. తెలసంపంగి a kind of long white flowering creeper. ఫలసంపంగి or సకలఫలసంపంగి *Artabotrys odoratissimus*, మనోరంజితము. (Watts). సంపంగిపురుగు *sampangi-purugu*. n. A wasp. కుమ్మెద. సంపంగిపూవడ్లు, సంపగెలు, సంపెగలు or సంపెంగలు *sampangi-pū-vaḍlu*. n. A certain sort of rice. H. iv. 158.

సంపత్తి, సంపత్తు or **సంపద** *sampatti*. [Skt.] n. Fortune, riches, wealth, prosperity. ఐశ్వర్యము, కలిమి, శ్రేయస్సు. "ఇంద్రియంబులకు పాటవసంపదలొంద." M. XII. ii. 158. సంపత్కరము *sampat-karamu*. adj. Causing or bringing prosperity. శ్రేయస్కరమైన. సంపదధికుడు a wealthy man, మిక్కిలి భాగ్యవంతుడు. సంపన్నము *sampannamu*. adj. Wealthy, prosperous, enriched or endowed with, possessed of, సంపదతో కూడుకొనిన, సమృద్ధమైన. సంపన్నుడు *sampannuḍu*. n. A wealthy man. (In composition,) one who is endowed with or possessed of, సమృద్ధుడు, సహితుడు. అర్థసంపన్నుడై being wealthy, ద్రవ్యముగలవాడై.

సంపర్కము *samparkamu*. [Skt.] n. Union, connection, contact, కలయిక, చేరిక, కూడిక.

సంపాకము *sampakamu*. [Skt.] n. A tree, *Cassia fistula*, ఆరగ్వధము, రేలచెట్టు.

సంపాటము *sampaṭamu*. [Tel.] n. Weighing a jewel with all things connected with it.

సంపాతము *sam-pātamu*. [Skt.] n. Descending, falling, coming down, a fall. పతనము, పాటు.

సంపాదనము *sam-pādanamu*. [Skt.] n. Acquisition, earning, getting, acquiring. ఆర్జనము, గడించుట. సంపాదించుట. సంపాదించు *sampā-dintsu*. (or vulgarly సంపాయించు) v. a. To procure, acquire, get, earn. గడించు, ఆర్జించు. సంపాదకుడు *sampādakuḍu*. n. One who earns, or acquires, సంపాదించువాడు. సంపాదితము *sampāditamu*. adj. That which is earned or acquired. సంపాద్యము *sampādyamu*. n. That which is fit to be earned, గడింపదగిన. Also, (colloquially) getting, acquiring, earning. సంపాసారి *sampa-sāri*. n. A merchant, వైశ్యుడు.

"ద్వీప కోటికిబడిగెత్తి కోమవస్తువులు,
పాటించిరెయుసకు సంపాసారులార."

హరిశ్చ. ii.

సంపుటము *sampuṭamu*. [Skt.] n. A casket, a covered box. బరిణె. A volume of a book or magazine. సంపుటించు *sampuṭintsu*. v. a. To close as a flower. To fold the arm. ముకుళించు.

సంపూజనము *sam-pūjanamu*. [Skt.] n. Honouring, veneration, esteem, treating with respect. మిక్కిలి గౌరవించడము, సన్మానము. ఆదరము. సంపూజనీయము *sampūjanīyamu*. adj. Honourable, respected, venerable, గౌరవింపదగిన, ఆదరణీయము. సంపూజితము *sam-pūjitamu*. adj. Honored, respected. గౌరవింపబడిన, మాననీయమైన.

సంపూజ్యము *sam-pūjyamu.* adj. Honourable, adorable. అర్చనీయము.

సంపూర్ణము *sam-pūrnamu.* [Skt.] adj. Complete, finished, whole, entire: filled, full of, perfect. అఖిలము, సమగ్రము.

సంపృక్తము *sam-priktamu.* [Skt.] adj. United, joined, సంయుక్తము.

సంపెంగ See under సంపంగి.

సంపెట *sampeṭa.* [Tel.] n. A sledge-hammer. ఇనుముసాగగొట్టెడు సమ్మెట. "ఉరిమిసంపెట పెట్టుకగిలినయట్లు." Dab. 233.

సంప్రతి *sam-prati.* [Tel.] n. A head accountant. లెక్కలుసరిచూచు పెద్దకరణము. An accountant, కరణము. సంప్రతించు *sam-pratintsu.* v. a. To collate, compare, examine. లెక్కలు మొదలగువానిని సరిచూచు.

సంప్రదానము *sam-pradānamu.* [Skt.] n. Giving, bestowing. ఇవ్వడము. In grammar, the Dative case, చతుర్థీవిభక్తి, షట్కారకములలో నొకటి.

సంప్రదాయము *sam-pra-dāyamu.* [Skt.] n. A rule, routine, method, doctrine, custom, convention, system, practice, tradition, వంశపురీతి, గురుపరంపరచేతవచ్చినది. పరంపరాప్రాప్తధర్మము, వాడుక. adj. Traditional, customary, systematic, వంశపురీతిౖన, గురుపరంపరాగతమైన, పరంపరాప్రాప్తమైన, వాడుకైన. సంప్రదాయకుడు *sam-pra-dāyakudu*, n. (Colloquially), a respectable or well-to-do man. సంప్రదాయముగా *sam-pra-dāyamu-gā.* adv. Systematically, traditionally, in accordance with custom or convention, వంశపురీతిగా, పరంపరాగతముగా, వాడుకగా. సంప్రదాయస్థుడు *sam-pra-dāya-sthudu.* n. An upright or just man, one who walks according to the rules of his caste, క్రమస్థుడు.

సంప్రయోగము *sam-pra-yōgamu.* [Skt.] n. A good use, శ్రేష్ఠమైనప్రయోగము. Association, relation, connection. సంబంధము. Enchantment, an incantation, మూలికలచేతను ఉచ్చాటనాదిక్రియ, వశీకరణాదికర్మము. "స్నానభోజనశయనాది సంప్రయోగ మర్థితులకు మున్నొందునాచరింప." M. III. v. 319. సంప్రయోగమనగా ఆచరించవలెను "సాధులకుఁ సాధుసహవాసమునఁ బాప సంప్రయోగ ముగుట సందియంబె." ib. III. i. 6. సంప్రయోగమగుట అనగా సంప్రాప్తమవుట.

సంప్రసారణము *sam-pra-sāraṇamu.* [Skt.] n. A grammatical term applied to the substitution of ఇ, ఉ, ఋ, ఌ for య, వ, ర, ల in sandhi.

సంప్రహారము *sam-pra-hāramu.* [Skt.] n. War, a battle, a fight, యుద్ధము.

సంప్రాప్తము *sam-prāptamu.* [Skt.] adj. Attained, obtained, gained, become arrived, come. పొందబడిన, వచ్చిన, సంభవించిన, కలిగిన, లభించిన. కలియుగము సంప్రాప్తమైన మీదట after the beginning of the Iron Age.

సంప్రీతి *sam-prīti.* [Skt.] n. Affection, kindness. విశ్వాసము, ప్రేమ.

సంప్రేరణము or సంప్రేరణ *sam-prēraṇamu.* [Skt.] n. An exhortation, instigation. బుద్ధి, బోధన. "దైవసంప్రేరణవడిన." KP. v. 244.

సంప్రేషణము *sam-prēshaṇamu.* [Skt.] n. A funeral ceremony observed on the twelfth day after death.

సంప్రేషము *sam-prēshamu.* [Skt.] n. Sending. An order, command, పనుపు, నిదేశము.

సంప్రోక్షణము *sam-prōkshaṇamu.* [Skt.] n. A ceremonial sprinkling of water. Hallowing, cleansing, consecrating, dedication, lustration, మంత్రోదకముచే చిలకరించడము, దేవాలయాదులను ఉపయోగకరముగా చేయడమునకై మంత్రోదకమును చిలకరించడము, విగ్రహాదులకు కొనప్రతిష్ఠచేయడము. ఆ గ్రహము

పోశపోని సిద్ధముగానున్న దిగాని యింకా సంప్రోక్షణము కాలేదు the idol is all ready and adorned but is not yet consecrated. సంప్రోక్షించు *sam-prōkshintsu.* v. a. To sprinkle with holy water, to consecrate. సంప్రోక్షితము *sam-prōkshitamu.* adj. Sprinkled with, consecrated.

సంఫుల్లము *sam-phullamu.* [Skt.] adj. Well blown, well expanded. తేట్పగా వికసించిన.

సంబంధము *sam-bandhamu.* [Skt.] n. Connection, relation, relationship, relevancy, affinity. సంపర్కము, చుట్టరికము, చేరిక, కూడిక, పొందిక. నీసంబంధమే నాకు కూరాదు I cannot endure having anything to do with you. సంబంధి *sam-bandhi.* n. One who is connected by marriage. ఇచ్చిపుచ్చుకొన్నవాడు. సంబంధముచేసినవాడు. చుట్టము. ఆయన మా సంబంధి he is my kinsman. ఆమె మా సంబంధురాలు she is a connection of ours. సంబంధించు *sam-bandhintsu.* v. n. To be related to or connected with, to have to do with. చేరు, సంబంధము కలిగియుండు.

సంబడము See సంబళము.

సంబరము or సంబ్రము *sambaramu.* [from Skt. సంభ్రమము.] n. Joy, delight. A feast, festival, merry making. సంతోషము, వేడిక, ఉత్సవము. తిరునాళ్లు, పండుగ. సంబరమించు (for సంభ్రమించు.) *sambara-mintsu.* v. n. To be delighted. సంతసిల్లు. Pal. 30.

సంబరి See సంబళి.

సంబరేను or సంబరేణి *samba-rēnu.* [Tel.] n. A kind of shrub. చర్మకష. H. iv. 12 or 14.

సంబళము or సంబడము *sambaḷamu.* [from Skt. శమ్బలమ్.] n. Wages, hire. బత్తెము, Salary, జీతము. Batta, దారిబత్తెము. సంబళపు *sambaḷapu.* adj. Hired, lent. జీతమునకు పెట్టుకొన్న, అద్దెకు తెచ్చిన.

సంబళి, సంబడి, సంబరి or శెంబడి *sambaḷi.* [Tel.] n. A pariah, మాలవాడు. "జడిదయుదు సంబళిసంబళియనుచు, దళముగా మెరపెడి తనమేని కప్పు." KD. ii. 1384.

సంబళించు or సంబడించు *sambaḷintsu.* [Tel.] v. n. & a. To be convenient. వల్లపడు. To manage, furnish, supply. సమకూర్చు, నిర్వహించు, తెప్పించు, పోషించు. "పాడిచినంబునంతం బునకన్న దిరిగితెచ్చురు గక్కుచు సొరగియుంటగాన నసంబళించుకొని పోకుపోకుమనియార్చుచుకొ" Harivamsam, Uttara, ii. 60.

సంబళిక, సంబెల or సంబెళ *sambaḷika.* [Tel.] n. A wallet or sort of pouch, to hold betel leaf, areca-nut and lime. అడపము, వక్కలాకుసంచి. "సంబెలదవలించి తాంబూల దళపూగ నివహంబు చాలంగ నించుమనుబ్బు." A. vi. 94.

సంబవులు See సంబారిగెలు.

సంబాగువు *sambāguvu.* [Tel.] n. A raft to cross a river on. ఏరుదాటే సాధనము.

సంబాధము *sam-bādhamu.* [Skt.] n. Difficulty, trouble; a crowded place. ఇరుకు, సంకటము, ఒత్తుడు, సంకటస్థలము, ఇరుకుస్థలము. adj. Narrow, contracted, impassable, impervious; crowded, ఇరుకైన, ఒత్తుడుగా నుండే, చొరరానటు అసాధ్యమైన.

సంబారము or సంబాము *sam-bāramu.* [from Skt. సంభారము.] n. A mixture of spices for seasoning. Spicery, condiments, curry powder, కూరలలోవేయు రసవర్గము, అవాలు మెంతులు జీలకర్ర మొదలైనవి. సంబారపుచింతపండు tamarind mixed with spicery. "మెంతికూర సంబారంపుచింతపండులు బజ్జాలు." H. i. 113.

సంబాళించు *sam-bāḷintsu.* [from Skt. సంభాళించు.] v. a To comfort, console, ఆదరించు.

"దింబములసంబాళించు గర్భావిదాలు."
పాంచా. ii.

సంబాళిగలు, సమ్మాళిగలు or **సంబుపులు** *samba-ligalu.* [from Skt. సంఫరుపు.] n. Sandals, పావకోళ్లు. Shoes, slippers, పాపోసులు. పాదరక్షలు.

"సీ॥ పట్టంగనీదుసంబాళిగల్
కలనిలోఁజేరవచ్చినమార్తుచేతగాని."
వసు. i.

సంబారులు *sambārulu,* [from Skt. సంభ్రుతులు.] n. plu. A very fine sort of rice కుసుమధాన్యములు. ఉత్తమమైనవడ్లు. గరుడముక్కు సంబారులు another kind.

సంబుద్ధి See సంబోధనము.

సంబెల, సంబెళ or **సంబెలపెట్టె** See సంబళి.

సంబోధనము *sam-bōdhanamu.* [Skt.] n. Addressing, calling to. పిలవడము, ఆమంత్రణము, సంబుద్ధి. In Grammar, the vocative case. **సంబుద్ధి** *sam-buddhi.* n. Calling, పిలవడము ఆమంత్రణము, సంబోధనము.

సంభ్రమము Same as సంబరము (q. v.)

సంభవము *sam-bhavamu.* [Skt.] n. Birth, production. The origin, cause, reason, motive, ఉత్పత్తి. పుట్టుక. హేతువు. adj. Arising from, produced from, descending from. ఉత్పన్నమైన, ఉద్భూతమైన, కలిగిన. పాపసంభవము caused by sin. **సంభవించు** or **సంభవిల్లు** *sambhav-intsu* v. n. To be born, happen, occur. పుట్టు, ప్రాప్తమగు. కలుగు. **సంభవింపజేయు** *sambhav-impa-jēyu.* v. a. To bring about, cause, effect. ప్రాప్తమగునట్లుచేయు.

సంభారము *sam-bhāramu.* [Skt.] n. Provision, preparation. Collection, a multitude, number, quantity, assemblage, సంభృతము, పదార్థసంచయము, సమూహము, సర్వపూర్ణత్వము, గుంపు.

సంభావన or **సంభావనము** *sam-bhāvana.* [Skt.] n. Honor, esteem, respect, worship. A present, reward, prize gift. Vulgarly, alms or money distributed among Brahmins, సన్మానము, గౌరవము, పూజ, దక్షిణ. **సంభావనీయము** *sam-bhāvan-iyamu.* adj. Honorable, worshipful. సన్మానింపదగిన, గౌరవింపదగిన, పూజ్యమైన. **సంభావనీయుడు** *sambhāvan-iyudu.* n. He who is venerable or honored. పూజనీయుడు. లోకసంభావనీయులు all-honoured persons. **సంభావించు** *sam-bhāvintsu.* v. a. To honor, esteem, venerate. గౌరవించు, మర్యాదచేయు, సన్మానించు. **సంభావితము** *sam-bhāv-itamu.* adj. Honored, respected. సన్మానింపబడిన (Colloquially,) Proper, fit, suitable. యుక్తము, వినీతము. **సంభావితుడు** *sam-bhāv-itudu.* n. He who is honored. పూజితుడు. **సంభావ్యము** *sam-bhāv-yamu.* adj. Fit to be praised, honorable, worthy of respect.

సంభాషణ or **సంభాషణము** *sam-bhāshana.* [Skt.] n. Conversation, discourse, talk. చక్కగా మాట్లాడడము. **సంభాషించు** *sam-bhāsh-intsu.* v. n. To converse, talk. చక్కగా మాట్లాడు, సంభాషణముచేయు.

సంభూతము *sam-bhūtamu.* [Skt.] adj. Born, produced, arisen, sprung. ఉత్పన్నమైన, పుట్టిన.

సంభృతము *sam-bhritamu.* [Skt.] adj. Well supported. చక్కగా ధరింపబడిన Gained, got. సంపాదింపబడిన. Possessed of. Filled, full, నిండింపబడిన. "సహస్రబాహుండు అక్షయదోస్తంభసంభృతయుగు వీరత్వంభర." A. iv. 337. **సంభృతి** *sam-bhriti.* n. The act of supporting well. చక్కగా ధరించుట.

సంభోగము *sam-bhōgamu.* [Skt.] n. Coition, sexual intercourse, రతి. **సంభోగించు** or **సంభోగముచేయు** *sam-bōgintsu* v. n. To cohabit, to have sexual intercourse, రమించు.

సంభ్రమము *sam-bhramamu.* [Skt.] n. Passion, emotion, confusion, excitement, agitation, flurry, hurry. తొందర, వేగిర

పాటు, భయము, తొట్రుపాటు, ఆహ్లాదము, ఉత్సాహము. సంభ్రమించు or సంభ్రమమందు sam-bhram-intsu. v. n. To be elated. హర్షించు. To be excited, confused, bewildered, తొందరపడు, తేరిపడు.

సంయమని sam-yamani. [Skt.] n. The name of the capital of Yama. యమునిపట్టణము.

సంయమము sam-yamamu. [Skt.] n. Restraint or control of the passions. Humanity, compassion, the temper that shuns giving pain to others, gentleness. పరపీడాదినివృత్తి. హింసాదులను విడిచిపెట్టుట. సంయమి sam-yami. n. A hermit, or monk. ముని, సంయమముగలవాడు.

సంయుక్తము sam-yuktamu. [Skt.] adj. Combined, joined, united, connected with, possessed of. కూడుకొనిన, కల. సంయుక్తాక్షరము a double letter as *l* in పిల్లి.

సంయుగము sam-yugamu. [Skt.] n. War; a battle, combat. యుద్ధము.

సంయుతము sam-yutamu. [Skt.] adj. Well combined or joined, united, connected with. మిక్కిలి కూడుకొన్న.

సంయోగము sam-yōgamu. [Skt.] n. Union, junction, connection, association with, సంగమము, సంసర్గము, కూడిక. సంయోజితము sam-yōjitamu. adj. Connected, joined, united with. సంలగ్నమైన, మిళితమైన, కూర్పబడిన.

సంరంభము sam-rambhamu. [Skt.] n. Haste, flurry, agitation, trepidation, fear. తొందర, ఇష్టానిష్టకార్యజాతత్వర. తేరిపాటు. తొట్రుపాటు, భయము. Wrath, rage, కోపము. సంరంభి sam-rambhi. n. One who is enraged, or hurried. ఆగ్రహముగలవాడు, తొట్రుపాటుగలవాడు. "భోజపురయాత్రారంభసంరంభిద్రై." A. v. 54. సంరంభించు sam-rambh-intsu. v. n. To be excited or flurried. తేరిపడు. To burst out in rage, fury or pride, ఆగ్రహించు, విజృంభించు.

సంరక్షణ or సంరక్షణము sam-rakshana. [Skt.] n. Sustaining, support, maintenance, nourishment, guardianship, charge, patronage, పోషణ, పాలనము, కాపాడడము. సంరక్షించు sam-rakshintsu. v. a. To support, protect, maintain, patronize, rear. సంరక్షణచేయు, పోషించు, పాలించు, కాపాడు, పెంచు. సంరక్షకుడు sam-rakshakudu. n. A protector, trustee, patron, guardian. పాలకుడు, పోషకుడు.

సంరావము sam-rāvamu. [Skt.] n. Sound, noise. ధ్వని, మ్రోత.

సంరూఢము sam-rūdhamu. [Skt.] adj. Budded, blossomed, grown. అంకురితము, పెరిగిన.

సంరోధము sam-rōdhamu. [Skt.] n. An impediment, hindrance. ఆటంకము, అడ్డగింతము. సంరోధి sam-rōdhi. n. That which causes an impediment. విఘ్నముచేయునది. సంరోధించు sam-rōdhintsu. v. a. To hinder, impede, prevent. అడ్డగించు, ఆటంకపరచు.

సంలాపము sam-lapamu. [Skt.] n. Discourse, conversation, friendly talk. సల్లాపము, ప్రీతితోకూడిన సంభాషణము, ముచ్చట.

సంవత్ samvat. [Skt.] n. A year. అబ్దము, ఏడు. సంవత్సరము samvatsaramu. n. A year. హాయనము, ఏడు. సంవత్సరాది samvatsar-ādi. n. New Year's Day. యుగాది.

సంవర్తకము sam-vartakamu. [Skt.] n. The plough of Balarama. బలరామునినాగలి.

సంవర్తము sam-vartamu. [Skt.] n. A destruction of the universe. ప్రళయము. M. XIV. 150. R. v. 4.

సంవర్తిక sam-vartika. [Skt.] n. The new leaf of a water lily. లేతతామరాకు.

సంవసథము sam-vasathamu. [Skt.] n. A village. గ్రామము.

సంవాదము *sam-vādamu.* [Skt.] n. A conference, discussion, dispute, contention, wrangling. సంభాషణము, కలహము, తర్కించుటము. "అభిముఖ్యంబుసంవాదాత్ప్రమాణ్యం బనుశాస్త్రయంబునంగాని పుట్టమియును." A. iv. 81. సంవాదించు *sam-vādintsu.* v. n. To converse, talk together, discuss, wrangle. సంభాషించు, తర్కించు.

సంవాహనము *sam-vāhanamu.* [Skt.] n. Carrying, తేర్చుగా కొనిపోవుట. Handling, rubbing, pressing the limbs, massage, అంగమర్దనము, ఒళ్లుపిసకడము. సంవాహకుడు *sam-vāhakuḍu.* n. An attendant who shampoos or rubs down the limbs, a massagist, అంగమర్దకుడు, ఒళ్లుపిసికేవాడు.

సంవిత్తు or సంవిత్తి *sam-vittu.* [Skt.] n. Wisdom, understanding, intellect. బుద్ధి, తెలివి, జ్ఞానము.

సంవీతము *sam-vītamu.* [Skt.] adj. Surrounded, enclosed, encompassed. ఆవృతము, ఆవరింపబడిన. n. The sacerdotal thread when hung round the neck like a garland, పేరువలె వేసుకొన్న జందెము.

సంవృతము *sam-vṛtamu.* [Skt.] adj. Covered, concealed, encompassed, clothed with. చుట్టుకొనబడిన.

సంవేగము *sam-vēgamu.* [Skt.] n. Hurry, haste. త్వర, వేగిరపాటు.

సంవేది *sam-vēdi.* [Skt.] n. He who knows. ఎరిగినవాడు, తెలిసినవాడు. "రహస్యసంవేది." M. V. v. 21. సంవేదితము *sam-vēditamu.* adj. Made known. తెలియజేయబడిన.

సంవేశము *sam-vēśamu.* [Skt.] n. Sleep. నిద్ర. A seat, పీఠము.

సంవ్యానము *sam-vyānamu.* [Skt.] n. An upper garment, a cloak. ఉత్తరీయము, పైబట్ట. S. iii. 408.

సంశప్తకుడు *sam-śaptakuḍu.* [Skt.] n. A picked man or soldier, one of a select band sworn never to recede and stationed to prevent the flight of the rest, శపథకృత్యోద్యోగముద్ధారనివృత్తిని, తిరిగిపోవనని ఒట్టుపెట్టుకొని యుద్ధముచేయువాడు. A hero, శూరుడు. M. IX. i. 14. ib. VIII. ii. 321.

సంశయము *sam-śayamu.* [Skt.] n. Doubt uncertainty, suspicion, hesitation. సందేహము. సంశయాళువు *sam-śay-āluvu.* n. A suspicious man, an irresolute man. సంశయించు *sam-śay-intsu.* v. n. To doubt, suspect, hesitate. సందేహించు, అనుమానించు.

సంశ్రయము *sam-śrayamu.* [Skt.] n. A refuge, asylum, protection. ఆశ్రయము, శరణము, అండ. సంశ్రయించు *sam-śrayintsu.* v. a. To flee to, appeal to, resort to, seek protection from, take refuge with, శరణుచొచ్చు, ఆశ్రయించు, అండగొను.

సంశ్లేషము *sam-ślēshamu.* [Skt.] n. An embrace, union, connection, junction, coalescence. కౌగిలింత, ఆలింగనము, సంగమము, సంధి, కలయిక, చేరిక. సంశ్లేషించు *sam-ślēshintsu.* v. n. To coalesce, కలియు.

సంసక్తము *sam-saktamu.* [Skt.] adj. Joined. కలిసిన, చేరిన. Near, adjoining, connected or endowed with, అవ్యవహితమైన, సంయుక్తమైన. సంసక్తి *sam-sakti.* n. Union, adherence; nearness.

సంసత్తు *sam-sattu.* [Skt.] n. An assembly, meeting, audience. కొలువుకూటము, సభ.

సంసరణము *sam-saraṇamu.* [Skt.] n. A highway. రాజమార్గము, బాట. Going, the progress or march of troops. అసంబాధమార్గతి, ఇరుకులేక దండునడుచుట, పురనిర్గమము, రణారంభము. A city gate, గవను, పురద్వారము. Married life, సంసారము. "సంసరణము నిత్తుడు." (P. iv. 451.) టీ. సంసారమునకు అర్హమైనమనస్సుగలవాడు.

సంసరించు *sam-sarinṭsu.* [Skt.] v. n. To be born. జన్మించు. "సంసదవాదులయి ప్రాగ్భవా కల్పంబుల సంసరించుటభావనాబద్ధులే." A. iii. 95.

సంసర్గము *sam-sargamu.* [Skt.] n. Union, connection, intercourse. సంశ్లేషము, సంబంధము, కూడుట.

సంసారము *sam-sāramu.* [Skt.] n. The world, the mundane state. Domestic life, secular life. A family, household. పెండ్లాము బిడ్డలతో కూడియుండడము. Birth, పుట్టుక. వానికి సంసారము తప్పిపోయినది he has lost his wife. సంసారములేనివాడు one who has no wife or children. సంసారతాపత్రయములు family cares. సంసారమునునడిపించు or సంసారమునుసాగించు to support or manage a family. సంసారము చేయు *sam-sāramu chēyu.* v. n. To keep house, to live a family life. కాపురముచేయు. సంసారి *samsāri.* n. A householder, the head or master of a family, a family man; a citizen; an honest man. A secular person as distinguished from a solitary recluse, గృహస్థుడు, గృహపతి. ఆ యూరిసంసారులు the inhabitants (కాపులు) of the village. సంసారి a good or respectable woman, కులస్త్రీ.

సంసిక్తము *sam-siktamu.* [Skt.] adj. Wet, humid. తడిసిన. "రక్తసంసిక్తమైన ధరాతలమున." M. X. i. 15.

సంసిద్ధి *sam-siddhi.* [Skt.] n. Nature. స్వభావము. Perfection, completion, accomplishment. తెన్నుగానలభించడము, చేకూరడము. సంసిద్ధుడు *sam-siddhuḍu.* n. One who is perfect or accomplished. సంపూర్ణుడు. "విశ్రుతగుణసంసిద్ధుడు." P. iii. 35.

సంసృతి *sam-sriti.* [Skt.] n. The world, the mundane state, a domestic life, secular condition; a family, household, సంసారము. M. XII. vi. 212. Swa. i. 33.

సంసృష్టము *sam-srishṭamu.* [Skt.] adj. Connected, united. సంయుక్తమైన, సంశ్లిష్టమైన. సంసృష్టి *sam-srishṭi.* n. Union, connection, సంసర్గము.

సంసేవనము *sam-sēvanamu.* [Skt.] n. Waiting on, serving. పరిచర్యచేయడము, ఉపాసనచేయడము. M. XII. v. 354. సంసేవితము *sam-sēvitamu.* adj. Worshipped, waited on, served, attended. పూజితమైన, ఉపాసితమైన.

సంస్కరించు *sam-skarinṭsu.* [Skt.] v. a. To reform, improve, repair, make better. బాగుచేయు. To purify, sanctify, consecrate, శుద్ధిచేయు, ప్రతిష్ఠించు. To burn a corpse (శవమును) దహనముచేయు. సంస్కారము *sam-skāramu.* n. The act of making better or improving, reformation. చక్కచేయుట. The power of memory, any faculty or capacity. అనుభూతార్థసంస్మృతి. A purificatory or dedicatory rite or ceremony: burning on the funeral pile, దహనము, కాల్చడము. Purification, శోధించడము. పన్నీరు పువ్వులను నీళ్లతో బట్టిలోవేసి అగ్నిసంస్కారము చేసి దించుదురు they put the roses in a still filled with water and by the application of fire make rose water. ఆ శవమును సంస్కారముచేసివేసినారు they burned the corpse. సంస్కృతము *sam-skritamu.* adj. Purified, refined, exquisitely wrought, polished. పరిష్కృతమైన, చక్కచేయబడిన. The Sanskrit language, దేవభాష. సంస్క్రియ *sam-skriya.* n. Funeral ceremonies, such as burning the dead body. దహనము. Any purificatory or dedicatory rite, ఉపనయనాది. "బాలికివాసంస్క్రియలొసరిచి." R. v. 247.

సంస్తంభనము *sam-stambhanamu.* [Skt.] n. The name of a magic arrow which arrests the progress of an enemy. శత్రువుల ప్రసరచేయు అస్త్రవిశేషము. T. v. 113. సంస్తం

స్తంభించు sam-stambh-intsu. v. a. To make firm or rigid. స్థాపించు, సిద్ధము చేయు. KP. iii. 251.

సంస్తవము sam-stavamu. [Skt.] n. Praise, స్తోత్రము, కీర్తి, ప్రస్తుతి. Acquaintance, intimacy, పరిచయము. సంస్తవకారి sam-stava-kari. n. One who praises. స్తోత్రముచేయువాడు. "సంస్తవకారిమునిస్తోమ సామగానంబె సగణా." A. iv. 15.

సంస్థానము sam-sthanamu. [Skt.] n. A state, government, dominion, province. రాజ్యము, సీమ. మైసూరుసంస్థానము the Mysore State. సంస్థానాధిపతి or సంస్థానికుడు sam-sthan-adhi-pati. n. A sovereign or ruler. రాజ్యాధిపతి, ప్రభువు.

సంస్థాపనము sam-sthapanamu. [Skt.] n. Placing, fixing, establishing. నిర్ధారణచేయడము, స్థిరీకరణము. సంస్థాపకుడు sam-sthapa-kudu. n. A founder, author. కల్పించినవాడు, ఏర్పరచినవాడు.

సంస్థితి sam-sthiti. [Skt.] n. Abiding, being, residing with. ఉండడము. సంస్థితము sam-sthitamu. adj. Fixed, established, settled, abiding in. సంస్థితుడు sam-sthitudu. n. One who dwells in. ఉన్నవాడు. "వేదాంతభావసంస్థితుడాదిమపోరుండు" the Supreme Lord who resides in the Scriptures. Suta Samhita. v. 55.

సంస్పర్శ sam-sparsa. [Skt.] n. Touch, contact, feel. తాకడము, చక్కనిస్పర్శము. Vema. 402. సంస్పర్శించు sam-sparsintsu. v. a. To touch. తాకు. B. X. 225. సంస్పృష్టము sam-sprishtamu. adj. Touched, తాకిన, అంటిన.

సంస్పృహ sam-spriha. [Skt.] n. Wish, desire, inclination. మిక్కిలి ఆశ, వాంఛ.

సంస్ఫాలనము sam-sphalanamu. [Skt.] n. Slapping, dashing. చరచడము.

సంస్మరణము sam-smaranamu. [Skt.] n. Recollection, remembrance. తలచడము.

సంహతి sam-hati. [Skt.] n. A flock, assembly, heap, collection, సమూహము, రాశి.

సంహననము sam-hananamu. [Skt.] n. Rubbing the limbs. ఒళ్లుపిసకడము. The body, శరీరము.

సంహరించు sam-harintsu. [Skt.] v. a. To kill, destroy. చంపు. సంహారము or సంహరణము sam-haramu. n. Destruction, annihilation, killing. నాశముచేయుడము, చంపడము. సంహారకుడు or సంహర్త sam-harakudu. n. One who kills. చంపువాడు. సంహృతము sam-hritamu. adj. Destroyed, killed. నాశనముచేయబడ్డ. "అఖిలజనములు సంహృతిమయ్యెనిచట." M. XVI. i. 75. సంహృతి sam-hriti. n. Destruction, loss. సంహారము.

సంహిత sam-hita. [Skt.] n. A peculiar arrangement of the Vedas into short divisions; a collection or compilation of hymns or prayers or legends extracted from a Veda. శాఖ, వేదపరిచ్ఛిన్న వాక్యవిన్యాసము, శాస్త్రము. సంహితము sam-hitamu. adj. Collected, compiled, joined: సంచితమైన, సంయుక్తమైన, కూర్చబడిన.

సకర్మకక్రియ sa-karmaka-kriya. [Skt.] n. An active or transitive verb. కర్మాపేక్షితమైన క్రియావాచకపదము.

సకలము sakalamu. [Skt.] n. The aggregate or whole. సమస్తము, సర్వము, అఖిలము, యావత్తు. adj. All, entire, whole. సమస్తమైన, అఖిలమైన.

సకలాతు, సకలాతు or సగలాతు sakalatu. [H.] n. A kind of woollen cloth మేలైన కంబళిబట్ట.

సకి or సకియ saki. [from Skt. సఖి.] n. A female friend or companion. చెలికత్తె.

A woman, ఆడుది. సకుడు sakudu. n. A friend, companion. చెలికాడు, స్నేహితుడు.

సకిన, సకెన or సగిన sakina. [from Skt. శకునము.] n. An artificial bird, the figure of a bird. కృత్రిమపక్షి, కృత్రిమపక్షి. A doll, బొమ్మ. A chirping noise, కీచుకీచుమనుధ్వని. "తెలిముత్తియంపుబల్, సకినెలతోరణం గిలకల స్నానకుమారవాసకల్యమవాన్నదకా." Vasu. vi. 111. టీ॥ సకినలు=కీచుపిట్టలు. "సకినలకలగడల్ చప్ప కైనమతోనకపకినల్ గొణుగుపావురపుకోళ్లు." N. ix. 482. టీ॥ సకినెలకలగడలు, ఒత్తితే కుంయ్ కుంయ్ అనే బొమ్మపిట్టలుండినదిండ్లు. సకినల మంచము sakinala-mantsamu. n. A bedding formed on a frame of wood, having orifices covered with perforated brass buttons that make a whistling or squeaking sound, గిలకలపట్టెమంచము. కోళ్లు బొమ్మలుగాచేసినమంచము. "తెలికప్రాలిన నందంద యెలుంగులాసకునట్టి, సకినలమంచములు." Swa. vi. 3. "పచ్చలరచించిన చిల్కలకోళ్లనందమౌసకి నెలపట్టెమంచమున." H. i. 73. సకినము sakinamu. [from Skt. శకునము.] n. An omen. సకినంపుపులుగు a bird of omen, an owl. శకునపక్షి, గూబ, పైడికంటె.

సకియ Same as సకి (q. v.)

సకిలించు or సగిలించు sakilintsu. [Tel.] v. n. To neigh. గుర్రముకూయు, గుర్రము హేషారవముచేయు. హేషించు. సకిలింత or సగిలింత sakilinta. n. A neigh, neighing. గుర్రపుకూత, హేష.

సకుటుసుమారుగా sakuṭu-sumaru-ga. [సకుటు (from Skt. సకృత్)+సుమారు (H.)] adv. Here and there, scatteredly, moderately, on an average. సకృత్తుగా.

సకృచ్ఛముగా sa-krichchamu-ga. [Skt.] adv. Without reserve, entirely. సమస్తము, ఏమిన్ని దాచకుండా, యావత్తు. "నీకుసకృచ్ఛంబు గాగచెప్పెద." Sar. D. 539.

సకృత్, సకృత్తు, సకృత్తుగా sakrit. [Skt.] adv. Rarely, seldom, scarcely. ఎప్పుడైనా ఒకమాటు, అరుదుగా, అపరూపముగా. అసకృత్ incessantly.

సక్తము saktamu. [Skt.] adj. Attached, joined, in contact with. అంటుకొన్నదైన, తగులుకొనిన (మనస్సు).

సక్తుచేయు saktu-chēyu [H.] v. a. To use violence. నిర్బంధముచేయు. సక్తుహుకుము a positive order.

సక్తువు saktuvu. [Skt.] n. Flour. పొడిపిండి, పేలపిండి. M. XIII. iv. 106.

సక్థి sakthi. [Skt.] n. The thigh. తొడ, తొడ. సక్థిమూలము the root of the thigh.

సఖి sakhi. [Skt.] n. A female friend. చెలియ, చెలికత్తె. సఖుడు sakhudu. n. A friend, fellow, companion, playmate. స్నేహితుడు. A helper, సహాయుడు. తామరసపఖుడు the lover of the lily, an epithet of the sun. సఖ్యము or సఖ్యత sakhyamu. n. Friendship, intimacy, unanimity, good terms. స్నేహము, చెలిమి. సఖ్యపడు sakhya-padu v. n. To be reconciled, agree, come to terms. సమాధానపడు. సఖ్యపరచు sakhya-paratsu. v. a. To make friends, to reconcile. విరోధముచేయు, సమాధానపరచు. సఖ్యుడు sakhyudu. n. A friend. చెలికాడు. "రాముడు సర్వసఖ్యుడు శరణ్యుడు వాత్సల్యపరుండు." BRK. 529.

సగటు or సగుటు sagaṭu. [H.] n. Average. సరాసరి. సగటున on an average. వారిని సగటున తిట్టినాడు he reviled them at random. వానికి సగటుమాకాలిమట్టు he sets a due value upon no one, he treats no one with proper respect.

సగటు sagaṭu. [from Skt. శకటము.] n. The bishop (in chess).

సగతు sagatu. [H.] n. Embroidery made of wire in patterns. తీగెమాదిగా చేసినసరిగె

పని. "సీ॥ ఉదిరిబంగరుప్రాకహాదని పూపని చోక్క సగకుల పఠోంబట్టు మొగలిపల్లను." Chandranga. ii. 85.

సగము *sagamu*. [Tel.] n. Half. అర్ధము. సగానికిసగము ఎక్కువ ఉన్నది it is half as much again. సగపాలు or సాపాలు *saga-pālu*. n. A moiety, a half share. అర్ధభాగము. Vema. 975. సగరేయి *saga-rēyi*. n. Midnight. అర్ధరాత్రి.

సగలాతు *sagalātu*. [H.] n. A woollen cloth.

సగిన See సకిన.

సగిలించు See సకిలించు.

సగుటు See సకటు.

సగుడము *sa-guḍamu*. [Skt.] adj. Mingled with treacle. బెల్లముతోకలిసిన.

సగుణము *sa-guṇamu*. [Skt.] adj. Having attributes or qualities.

సగోత్రుడు *sa-gōtruḍu*. [Skt.] n. A distant kinsman, a kinsman of the same family name. సమానగోత్రపురుషుడు, జ్ఞాతి, ఏకవంశస్థుడు, దాయ, దాయాది.

సగ్గరి or సగ్గాలము *saggari*. [from Skt. సృగాలము.] n. A jackal, నక్క.

సగ్గిసముగ్గిసలు *saggisa-muggisalu*. [Tel.] n. plu. Suffocation, ఉక్కురుడుపు. "ఎగ్గకుబుట్టు నల్కకుశా సగ్గిసముగ్గిసల్." Mandhat. iii. 252.

సగ్గు or స్రగ్గు *saggu*. [Tel.] v. n. To decrease, grow less, abate, be diminished; to sink, go down. To die, మట్టుపడు, క్షీణించు, అడగు, తగ్గు, చచ్చు. "ఆపత్సంపదలలతుల బ్రాపింపవృథుమలగాని స్రగ్గుకా బొడవై చూపట్టు చంద్రుడు." P. ii. 30. జ్వరముసగ్గినది the fever is subdued. భారముసగ్గినది the load is lightened.

సగ్గుబియ్యము *saggu-biyyamu*. [Malay through Eng.] n. Sago.

సగ్గెడ *saggeḍa*. [Tel.] n. A metal vessel, చెంబు. "ద్వి. బానిసచేతగల్లు. వలసొప్ప చెప్పించి వాడు నిచ్చలును. జలములు గ్రోలెడిసగ్గడనించి." Navanad. 229.

సగ్ధి or సజగ్ధి *sagdhi*. [Skt.] n. Eating together. సహభోజనము, కలసికూడి భోజనము చేయడము, విందు, బంతికుడుపు.

సచివుడు *sachivuḍu*. [Skt.] n. A minister or counsellor. మంత్రి. A friend, companion or associate, చెలికాడు. A helper, సహాయుడు. Vasu. ii. 28. కేళిసచివుడు a playmate, or playfellow.

సచ్చెము *satsemu*. [Tel.] n. A petty loan, చిల్లరరొక్కముప్పు.

సచ్చు Same as చేచ్చు (q. v.) సంపు Same as చంపు (q. v.)

సజగ్ధి Same as సగ్ధి (q. v.)

సజావు *sajāvu*. [H.] adj. Straight, honest. Clear, plain. తిన్నని, స్పష్టమైన, ఆటంకములేని.

సజీవము or సజీవి *sa-jīvamu*. [Skt.] adj. Having life, living, alive. సప్రాణమైన. సజీవుడు or సజీవితుడు *sa-jīvuḍu*. n. One who is alive. ప్రాణవంతుడు. మాతండ్రి సజీవుడైయున్నప్పుడు when my father was living. అతడు సజీవుడైయుండిన మట్టుకు as long as he lived. వారు సజీవులైయున్నారు they are now alive, they are still surviving. "చెచ్చెరనకలి సజీవతుండేని." BD. iv. 308.

సజ్జ *sajja*. [Skt.] n. An armour, a piece of armour, కవచము. Adornment, అలంకారము. సజ్జిక *sajjika*. n. A bed-room, పడకయిల్లు.

• సజ్జనము *sajjanamu*. n. A hedge round a camp. కంపకోట. సజ్జము *sajjamu*. adj. Prepared, got ready, armed. సన్నద్ధమైన, సిద్ధమైయుండే, కవచాలంకృతమైన. సజ్జితము *sajjitamu*. adj. Armed, accoutred, dressed, duly prepared, got ready, కవచయుక్తమైన, అలంకరింపబడిన, సర్వసిద్ధముగానున్న. సజ్జుడు *sajjuḍu*. n. He who is prepared or ready. సన్నద్ధుడు.

సజ్యము sa-jyamu. [Skt.] adj. Strung (as a bow), having a bowstring. అల్లెగల. సజ్య కార్ముకము a bow with the string attached.

సజ్జ sadzdza. [from Skt. సర్జ.] n. A kind of grain. *Holcus spicatus*, గంటెలు. "సజ్జకవ గింపు మేపునం." A. iv. 5. An upper story in a house, కోష్ఠప్రాసాదము. adj. Ready prepared, ఆయుగము. సజ్జ sadzdza. [from Skt. శయ్య.] n. A bed, couch or cot. శయ్య. A box, పెట్టె. A basket, బుట్ట. సజ్జకము sadzdza-kamu. adj. Beautiful, pleasant. మనోజ్ఞము. సజ్జకట్టు sadzdza-kattu. adj. Prepared, ready, అయుతము. సజ్జరసము sadzdza-rasamu. n. The resin or exudation, of the Sal tree. యక్షధూపము, సజ్జక్షారము. సజ్జ గడ్డి sadzdza-gaddi. n. A kind of root like seaweed, the alkali of which is సజ్జక్షారము impure chlorate of soda సజ్జక్షారము. Ainslie i. 395.

సజ్జనకోల sadzdzana-kōla. [from H. saza, punishment.] n. A scourge or whip, a rod. "శిక్షకై తెగ బట్టిపట్టించి కేపుమాపుకొట్టు చెట్టుగ సజ్జనకోలతెగను." H. iii. 180.

సజ్జారము sadzdzāramu. [from Skt. సామజాగారం.] n. A stall or stable for an elephant. శాల, ఏనుగునుకట్టేచోటు.

సట sata. [Tel.] n. An untruth, lie: a trick; cunning, intricacy. అబద్ధము, మాయ, మోసము, కపటము, చిక్కు. సటుపటుమాటలు boasting lies or idle talk, జెల్లిమాటలు. "ద్రోహబుద్ధి నైన దొంగరికమునైన, సటలనైన సాహసములనైన." Vema. iii. 33. "సటలివిమానకోపమా." Parij. iii. 33. సట sata. [Skt.] n. Clotted hair. జెడ, కేసరసమూహము. A mane, జూలు.

సడ sada. [Tel.] n. A thick crop of young sprouts. దట్టముగు నారుపైరు.

సడపు sadapu. [Tel.] v. a. To steal, misappropriate. అపహరించు.

సడలు or సళ్లు sadalu. [from Skt. శ్లథ.] v. n. To become slack or loose, to fall off. వదలు, వీడిపోవు, ఊడు, జారు. n. Loosening, falling, ఊడుట, జారుట. వదలుట. సడలుపడు Same as సడలు. సడలించు, సడలుచు, సడల్చు, సడలజేయు or సళ్లించు sadalintsu. v. a. To untie, unloose, take off. వదలించు, విచ్చు, తీసివేయు.

సడవ sadava. [Tel.] n. A way, త్రోవ. మార్గము.

సడి sadi. [Tel.] n. Infamy, disgrace. అపకీర్తి. Slander, reproach, censure, blame, దూరు, అపవాదము, నింద, దూఱు. A trace, జాడ. "కనినాడనోవినినాడనో చనుదేనామీద నిట్టి సడిమోపంగన్." P. i. 747. సడిసన్న sadi-sanna. adj Celebrated, famous, renowned. ప్రసిద్ధికెక్కిన, పేరుపడ్డ. "మనవలలుందు లావున బంటుతనమున జనులెరుంగగ సడిసన్న వాడు మంచిమగండు దామగ్రంథి యనమునం గ్రామకేళి సాధకారుకుండు." M. IV. iii. 146. "నేర్పును భుజశక్తియుం గలిగి మాధిక దిక్కునను తప్పత్తిపై నని సడిసన్న యేక్షైగబృహన్నలుకంగల దంబుజానన." M. IV. iv. 16. "కార్యాదిగుణముల సడిసన్న యాష్టకరోధుల చెల్లునుర్పుట యుల ఘనీతి." M. XII. ii. 303.

సడించు sadintsu. [Tel.] v. a. To pound, or beat rice. దంచు. సడింపులు or సడింపు బ్రాలు sadimpulu. n. plu. Rice properly beaten, దంపుడుబియ్యము. "ప్రస్తావారిభుజం చమత్కసడింపుబ్రాలు." A. vi. 95.

సడికుడక sadi-kudaka. [Tel.] n. A kind of cake. అపూపవిశేషము. "వెన్న మెరుంగులు, నిడికుడకలు, సడికుడకలు, ముత్తెపుచిప్పలు." H. i. 118.

సడికె or సడికెయ sadike. [Tel.] n. A leash for dogs. కుక్కమెడత్రాడు. "సడికెలదుయ్య మునార మేయుములు, నడరనంకము పోలెవిడిపించు గొనుచు." BD. v. 1391.

సదుగులు *saḍugulu*. [Tel.] n. plu. The joints of the hip. కటిప్రదేశమునందలి కీళ్లు. Crooked or cunning words, వంకరమాటలు.

సద్ద *sadda*. [from Skt. శ్రద్ధ.] n. Care, heed, regard, honor, respect. అక్కర, లక్ష్యము, గౌరవము. "లోకులెమియుగాని సద్దలు సేయరేల్లర." Vish. v. 102. సద్దు *sadda*, adj. Regarded, honored. గౌరవమైన. "ఎవరు సేయుమనుచు సద్దమాటలుగొన్ని యాడిరంతసేమి యురుద్ధనింద్ర" M. XII. iv. 416. **సద్దచేయు** *sadda-chēyu*. v. a. To honor, regard, heed, care for, లక్ష్యపెట్టు, లెక్కచేయు. "తే॥ సద్దచేయుకు కున్నమాజ్ఞగమువారి." N. vii. 179.

సద్దకుడు *sadda-kuḍu*. [from Skt. షడ్డకుడు.] n. A co-son-in-law. తోడియల్లుడు. తన సద్దకుడైన రామస్వామిని పంపినాడు he sent Ramaswami who had married his wife's sister. వీరు సద్దకులు these men are married to sisters.

సణుగు or **సణగు** *saṇugu*. [Tel.] v. n. To grumble, to mutter, to mumble. గొణుగు. n. Grumbling, murmuring, గొణుగుట. Pain, బాధ.

సత్ *sat*. [Skt.] adj. True, good, virtuous. Excellent, venerable, respectable, pure, holy. యథార్థమైన, శుభమైన, మంచి, పావనమైన. One verse says "విదురునివాడక్షుండును చదివినసదసద్వివేక చతురుడగునుగా." సత్కర్మము or సత్కార్యము a good deed. అసత్ not good, evil. సత్కవి a good poet, మంచి కావ్యకర్త. సత్పాత్రము worthy, deserving, fit. యోగ్యమైన, అర్హమైన. సత్పాత్రుడు one who is worthy, deserving or fit, అర్హుడు, తగినవాడు. సత్పురుషుడు a good man, మంచివాడు. సత్పథము a good way, మంచిదోవ. The final letter undergoes the usual phonetic changes when the word is used in composition: e. g. సన్మార్గము a good way, సన్మునీంద్రుడు a holy sage; &c. సచ్చరితుడు a virtuous, honest or upright man, మంచినడతగలవాడు. సచ్చిదానందము God, as the fountain of being, intelligence, and happiness: lit. "it that is good, wise, and happy." నిత్యజ్ఞానానంద స్వరూపపరబ్రహ్మము. సచ్ఛూద్రుడు a pious Sudra, సదాచారముగల శూద్రుడు. సజ్జనత్వము magnanimity, good ness, సత్పురుషత్వము. సజ్జనుడు a respectable man, a good man, సత్పురుషుడు. సదనుష్ఠానము a good practice, సదాచారము. సదమలము pure, spotless, నిర్మలము. సదాచారము virtuous conduct, correct deportment, మంచినడత. సదాచారి a virtuous man. సదాచారులు the wise, the good. సదుత్తరము a proper answer or reply, మంచి ప్రత్యుత్తరము. సదుపాయము an excellent means, a good expedient, మంచిసాధనము. సద్గతి beatitude, salvation, future bliss, ముక్తి. "సద్గతియు చేకుఱు." Swa. ii. 80. సద్గుణము virtue, a good quality, సుశీలము. సద్భక్తి true religion, zeal, strong faith, fidelity, పూజ్యులయందలి మిక్కిలి అనురాగము. సద్భావము goodness, kindness, politeness, విద్యవిూనత, దయ, శిష్టాచారము. సద్వినయము true humility, మంచినమ్రత. సద్వ్యవహారము good behaviour, good conduct, మంచివృత్తి. సద్వ్యాసంగము love of good acts, మంచియిచ్ఛ. సన్నుతము praised, applauded, commended, స్తోత్రముచేయబడ్డ, కొనియాడబడ్డ. సన్నుతి sincere praise, commendation, laud. చక్కనిస్తుతి, స్తోత్రము. సన్నుతించు to praise, applaud, commend, చక్కగా స్తోత్రముచేయు, మెచ్చుకొను. సన్మహత్త్వము greatness, urbanity, గొప్పతనము, శ్రేష్ఠత. Chenn. ii. 77. సన్మార్గము good or virtuous conduct, మంచినడత. సన్మార్గి. or సన్మార్గుడు one of virtuous conduct, one who behaves well. మంచినడతగలవాడు. "సన్మార్గికి కలియుగమున సౌఖ్యము గలదే."

G. v. 69. సత్తుని or సత్తునింద్రుడు a venerable sage or hermit మునిశ్రేష్ఠ. M. I. i. 178.

సత sata. [from Skt. సప్త.] pron. Trois-quatre (seven) at dice or cards. ఆరునొక్కటి, సప్తసంఖ్య. "సతగిల్చిలో." సిం. ii. సతనాల్కలతేజి or సప్తజిహ్వుడు sata-nālkala-tēji. n. Fire, అగ్ని. (ఆన్ర. శా. కాం.)

సతకడము or సతుకుడు satakaḍamu. [Tel. for చదవడము.] n. A scornful expression for the word చదవడము reading. "సతకడముల్ పురాణములు." H. ii. 49.

సతతము satatamu. [Skt.] adj. Eternal, continual. నిరంతరము, ఎడతెగని. adv. Always, ఎల్లప్పుడు. సతము satamu. [from సతతము.] adj. Eternal, permanent. శాశ్వతము, "ఇప్పుడునరులబ్రతుకులికెంతసేపటికో సతములుగావు." Kuchelo. iii. 65. "కలిమియుకేమిలేయున్ సతముకావు." భార. అర. vii.

సతాయించు satāyintsu. [Tel.] v. a. To tease, torment, annoy. పీడించు, బాధించు.

సతి sati. [Skt.] n. A virtuous woman, పతివ్రత. One who burns herself with the corpse of her husband, సహగమనముచేయు స్త్రీ. A woman in general, స్త్రీ. A name of Parvati, పార్వతి.

సతిసప్తమి sati-saptami. [Skt.] n. The ablative case absolute. ప్రథమావిభక్త్యర్థమందు వచ్చే సప్తమీవిభక్తి.

సత్కరించు sat-karintsu. [Skt.] v. a. To worship, honour, treat politely. సన్మానించు. సత్కారము, సత్కృతి, సత్క్రియ or సత్కర్మము sat-karamu. n. A good act, an act of piety or charity, honor, respect, curteous treatment, మంచిపని, సన్మానము. సత్కృతుడు sat-kritudu. n. One who is honoured or reverenced. సన్మానింపబడ్డవాడు.

సత్తా satta. [from Skt. సత్ and సత్త్వం.] n. Essence, sap. సారము. Existence, being. విద్యమానత, ఉనికి. Excellence, goodness, efficacy, మంచితనము, శ్రేష్ఠత్వము, సామర్థ్యము. ఎదిరిసత్తకనిపెట్టెము we will go and spy out the enemy's force. దేవునిదయవల్ల కొంచెము సత్తగానున్నది by the goodness of God, there is a little hope.

సత్తమము sat-tamamu. [Skt.] adj. Best, most excellent, most pure, very holy. మిక్కిలి మంచి, మిక్కిలిశ్రేష్ఠమైన, పూజ్యమైన. సత్తముడు sat-tamuḍu. n. The best or most excellent of men. అందరికంటె మంచివాడు, అందరికంటె పూజ్యుడు, శ్రేష్ఠుడు.

సత్తరువు sattaruvu. [from Skt. సత్రము.] n. A choultry, a lodge or halting place, a hotel or rest house, సత్రము. "జగడపు కూటిసత్తరువుసాకులకోయగువారినిందగినెదు తిండనాలవాడి." KP. iii. 217.

సత్తా sattā. [from Skt. సప్త.] pron. Seven.

"క॥ అత్తినంచిత్తిగదుగ
సత్తాదశ్వాకపంచహాచంచీర
త్తిగయుద్దుగ బద్ధలు
చిత్తముబడలిట్లు చేతికి దచ్చుగా."

ఉ. హరి. iii.

సత్తి satti. [from Skt. శక్తి.] n. Power, ability, energy, strength, force, vigour, శక్తి, బలము, బలిమి. A goddess, కాళికాదేవి, పార్వతి. "ఎలిమిగాల్కొనికలభాషిణికేళికొనకొనలబట్టి వేరొక్కకేల, నొరగత్తివెడలినికొప్పనముడయుంచు సత్తికిగత్తిచెయ్యెత్తిమ్రొక్కె." KP. iii. 131. ఒక్కడే సత్తి అనగా దేవత. The name of Vasishtha's son, వసిష్ఠునికొడుకు. A kind of weapon, సత్తితాలుపు satti-tālupu. n. An epithet of Kumaraswami, శక్తిధరుడు.

సత్తు sattu. [from Skt. సత్త్వం.] n. Essence, sap, strength. సారము, బలము, సారాంశము. Pewter, తగరము. Sediment, refuse. [from Skt. సత్యం.] Truth, సత్యము, తిప్పసత్తు

he extract of the heart-leaved moon-
eed. సత్తుకొప్పెర a vessel made of pewter.
సత్తురూపాయి a counterfeit rupee. సత్తు
Skt. సత్.] n. Being, existence, ఉండుట,
కలిమి. adj. Existing, ఉన్న. Excellent,
శ్రేష్ఠము. True, సత్యము. Meek, సాధువు.
Skt.] n. A star, నక్షత్రము. "హితసద్రత్నాచరి
తుండు." P. i. 83. టీ॥ ఇక్కడ ద్వ్యర్థికాగా
పెద్దలనిన్ని, చంద్రుపదములో నక్షత్రములనిన్ని
అర్థము." సదసత్ sad-asat. n. & adj. Good
and bad Existing and non-existing;
entity and nonentity; being and not
being; true and false. యుక్తాయుక్తమైన,
మంచిచెడులైన, ఉత్తమాధమమైన. సదసద్వివేకము
discrimination between true and false.
B. viii. 263.

సత్తువ or సత్తువు sattuva. [from Skt. సత్త్వ.]
n. Strength, vigour, force, power, energy,
capability. బలము, శక్తి. సత్తువగల భూమి
rich soil.

సత్తెరంగ satte-ranga. [Tel.] n. A kind of grain.
సస్యవిశేషము. "ఊరి సత్తెరంగ చెడంగ సత్తియుక్త."
విష్ణు. పూ. iii.

సత్యము satyamu. [Skt.] n. Truth, veracity,
reality. నిజము, యథార్థము. An oath, ప్రమాణ
ము, ఒట్టు. (Vulgarly,) the miraculous power
of a deity. (మహిమలవారుకలో) మహత్త్వ
ము. adj. True, real, sincere, genuine, truth-
ful. యథార్థమైన, నిజమైన. సత్యప్రవర్తన truth-
ful behaviour, upright conduct. adv. Yes,
verily, truly, indeed. నిజమేను. సత్యముగా
చెప్పు to avow, to vouch for. సత్యముచేయు
to swear. ఈఅమ్మవారు బహుసత్యముకలిగినదేవత
this is a true goddess. భగవత్స్వరూపము
లయందు సత్యముతప్పినది the gods have now
lost their power, the images now ceased
to work miracles. సత్యప్రతిజ్ఞ a sincere
promise or vow. సత్యనిష్ఠ. సత్యయు
గము satya-yugamu. n. The Golden Age.
కృతయుగము. సత్యలోకము satya-lōkamu.

n. One of the fourteen heavens of the
Puranas. సత్యవంతుడు satya-vantuḍu.
n. A truthful or sincere man. సత్యవచ
స్కుడు or సత్యవాది satya-vachaskuḍu. n.
One who speaks the truth, a man of
veracity. నిజస్థుడు. సత్యవతి satya-vati.
n. A truthful woman. సత్యముగలస్త్రీ.
The name of the mother of Vyāsa,
and of the wife of Narada. సత్య
వాక్కు or సత్యవాణి satya-vakku. n. A
true statement. సత్యవ్రతుడు satya-vra-
tuḍu. n. One who is devoted to truth, one
who is sincere or honest. నిజాడికోవాడు
నిజేవాడు, పెద్దమనిషి. సత్యసంధుడు satya-
sandhuḍu. n. An upright man. నిజస్థుడు.
సత్యహరిశ్చంద్రుడు one who is as truthful
as Harischandra, i.e., a very truthful man.
(sometimes used ironically also to mean
a liar.) సత్యాకృతి, సత్యంకారము or
సత్యాపనము saty-ākriti. n. The ratifi-
cation of a bargain, an advance of money,
earnest money, క్రయవిక్రయములు కట్టేమాట,
బయానా, బెట్టి. సత్యానృతము saty-anṛi-
tamu. n. Commerce, trade, traffic. వాణి
జ్యము, వర్తకము.

సత్రము satramu. [Skt.] n. A kind of
sacrifice. యజ్ఞవిశేషము, అనేకదినములుచేసే
యజ్ఞము. Liberality, munificence. సదాదా
నము, నిరంతరము ఇచ్చుటము, ఎడతెగనియీవి.
"నిజచ్ఛాత్రసత్రంబునకు." A. vi. 30.
A choultry or rest house for travellers,
an inn or hotel, అన్నదానగృహము. బాట
సారులు దిగడమునకై కట్టియుండేటిది. See
సత్తిరువు. సత్రశాల satra-sala. n. An
almonry, an apartment in which mendi-
cants are presented with food and gifts.
నిత్యాన్నదానముచేసే యిల్లు.

సత్రాజిత్తు satrā-jittu. [Skt.] n. The name of
the father of Satyabhāma: hence she
is called సాత్రాజితి.

సత్వము satvamu. [Skt.] n. Being, existence. ఉనికి. Essence, nature, స్వభావము. A substance, thing, వస్తువు. Vigour, power, strength. సత్వ, దేహబలము. The quality of excellence or goodness. త్రిగుణములలో సాత్వికి, పృథివ్యాద్యద్రవ్యము. An animal, a being, జంతువు. Mind, మనస్సు. Life, ప్రాణము. An attempt, ప్రయత్నము. "సత్వర జస్తమోగుణవశక్షితి." M. XII. vi. 15. "తన సత్వమెదిరిసత్వముకనుగొనకవ్యాఘ్రసత్వమును." P. iii. 30. "అకలంకాపూర్వసత్వముంజెలియ." Swa. ii. 17.

సత్వరము sa-tvaramu. [Skt.] n. Quickness, celerity. త్వర, వేగము. adj. Quick, త్వరితము. adv. Quickly.

సద sada. [Tel.] n. The hair on a leaf. ఆకు మీదినూగు. సదసత్రు sada-satra. n. Small sticks, etc. చిదుగుచిత్రు. "పూరిబల్లుక్రొత్తదు బజకయూడిగము, సదసత్రు చలివత్రు సరిగచ్చు గత్రు, చెదకియుగానక మదిలిపారించి." BD. 1060. iii.

సదనము sadanamu. [Skt.] n. A house, dwelling, residence. గృహము. బండారుసదనము a treasury, a store-house.

సదమదము or సదసద sada-madamu. [Tel.] n. Destruction, annihilation, death. నాశనము, చావు. "బంధ్యాలరాజాలసదమదము గాను." Pal. 130. సదమదముచేయు to kill, murder, assassinate, destroy, చంపు. సదమదమగు sada-madam-agu. v. n. To be bruised. నలగు.

సదమలము sad-amalamu. [Skt.] adj. Very pure. మిక్కిలి నిర్మలమైన.

సదయుడు sa-dayudu. [Skt.] n. One who is kind. దయతోకూడుకొన్నవాడు.

సదరు or సదరహీ sadaru. [H.] adj. Aforesaid, above-mentioned. పైనచెప్పిన. పైన నుడువబడినది. సదరుకు above, పైన. సదరున చెప్పినప్రకారము is above stated. సదరహీలు the above-said persons, పైనచెప్ప బడినవారు.

సదసద See సదమదము.

సదస్సు, సదసు or సదము sadassu. [Skt.] n. An assembly, a meeting. ధర్మజ్ఞసభ, రాజసభ, సభ. సదస్యుడు sadasyudu. n. An inspector or director of a sacrifice. కర్మానుష్ఠానయజ్ఞాధికవిచారకుడు, సదసద్విశేషకుడు. A councillor, the member of an assembly, సభికుడు. A by-stander, spectator, one present. సాక్షి. A. iii. 58.

సదా sadā. [Skt.] adv. Always, continually. ఎల్లప్పుడు. సదాగతి sadā-gati. n. Lit. a perpetual motion: an epithet of the wind, వాయువు. సదాతనము sadā-tanamu. adj. Eternal, permanent. నిరంతరమైన. సదాతనుడు sadā-tanudu. n. One who is eternal. శాశ్వతుడు. సదారోగి sadā-rōgi. n. A chronic invalid: one who is always ill. రోగిష్ఠుడు, దీర్ఘవ్యాధిగలవాడు. Vani. Vilas. p. 311. సదావృత్తి sadā-vritti. n. Rice, salt, firewood, &c., daily bestowed on travellers or mendicants at a choultry, బైరాగులకును బాటసార్లకును నిత్యము బియ్యముపప్పు ఇచ్చుటము. సదాశివుడు sadā-śivudu. n. Lit. always propitious. An epithet of Siva, రుద్రుడు.

సదాటు sadāṭu. [Tel.] adj. Strong, vigorous, hale. దృఢమైన. "సీ॥ గాటంపుబిగిసదాటైనకుచముల కొరమట్టినిగనికల్ హొయలుమీర." T. ii. 16.

సదాప sadāpa. [from Skt. శతపుష్ప.] n. A sort of fennel, common anise. *Anethum panmorium.* (Rox.) or *Anethum sowa,* మిశ్రేయావృక్షము, శాతేయము. H. ii. 249.

సదాముస్తె sadā-muste. [Tel.] n. A certain plant, a kind of cactus. జెముడు. "పేలతీగలసింధకోలజెముడు బొంతజెముడుబిల్లియుసు సదాముస్తె మునిలు గానిలుఖట్టె నిగి పల్లి గాంచి యుంటు." H. iv. 15.

సమూపాయము See under సత్.

సదృశము or **సదృక్షము** *sa-drisamu.* [Skt.] adj. Similar, like, comparable. సమానమైన, సరి.

సదేశము *sa-dēsamu.* [Skt.] adj. Near, nigh, proximate, adjoining. సమీపమైన, అంతికమైన.

సద్గతి See under సత్.

సద్దు *saddu.* [from Skt. శబ్దః.] n. Sound, noise, tumult, clamour. ధ్వని, సందడి, చప్పుడు. సద్దాతే. interj. Silence! hush, be still, keep quiet.

సద్మము *sadmamu.* [Skt.] n. A house, abode. ఇల్లు.

సద్యః or **సద్యము** *sadyah.* [Skt.] adv. Instantly, momentarily, at the moment, in an instant. తత్కాలమందు, అప్పుడు. భార. స్వ. i. సద్యఃఫలము the immediate result or reward. సద్యఃకాలము present time. సద్యోఘృతము butter just fried, fresh ghee. సద్యోజలము new fallen rain.

సధర్మము *sa-dharmamu.* [Skt.] adj. Accompanied by virtue. ధర్మముతోకూడిన. Equal, సమానము. **సధర్మిణి** *sa-dharmini.* n. A wife. ధర్మపత్ని. Parij. iii. 85.

సధ్యా *sadhya.* [for Skt. సద్యః.] adv. At present, తత్కాలమునకు, ప్రస్తుతమునకు.

సన్, **సన** or **స్న** *san.* [H.] n. A year. సన్‌వారు yearly, annual.

సనగలు, **సెనిగలు**, **సెనగలు** or **శనగలు** *sanagalu.* [from Skt. చణకః.] n. The chick pea, commonly called Bengal gram, *Cicer arietinum.* చణకము. సెనగపులుసు a strong acid collected from this legume by spreading cloths over the field to catch the dew. నేలసెనగలు groundnut, earthnut, pignut, Manilla gram, *Arachis hypogæa.*

సనాతనము *sanatanamu.* [Skt.] adj. Eternal, fixed, permanent. స్థిరమైన, శాశ్వతమైన. **సనాతనుడు** *sanatanudu.* n. The eternal One. శాశ్వతుడు.

సనాథ *sa-natha.* [Skt.] n. A woman who has her lord (or husband) alive. **సనాథము** *sa-nathamu.* adj. That which is accompanied by. కూడుకొనినది. **సనాథుడు** *sa-nathudu.* n. One who is accompanied by his lord or master.

సనాభి *sa-nabhi.* [Skt.] adj. Like, resembling. సదృశమైన, సమానమైన. **సనాభుడు** or **సనాభి** *sa-nabhudu.* n. A cousin, జ్ఞాతి, ఏడుతరములలోని దాయాది.

సని [from Skt. శని.] Same as శని (q. v.)

సనీడము *sa-nidamu.* [Skt.] adj. Near, proximate. సమీపమైన.

సను Same as చను (q. v.)

సనెకలు Same as సన్నికల్లు (q. v.)

సన్న *sanna.* [from Skt. సంజ్ఞ.] n. A sign, gesture, token. సంజ్ఞ. జాడ. కనుసన్న a wink. చేసన్న a sign or motion of the hand. **సన్నకసన్న** *sannaka-sanna.* (సన్నకుగా + అ + సన్న) adv. Gently, idly, జాడగా, మెల్లమెల్లగా. "సన్నకసన్న చేసకొనిగూడియుండెడో మూపాయి బాపరెమూలలారా." Jagann. iii. 9. టీ. సన్నకసన్నకు, చల్లచల్లగా. **సన్నసన** *sanna-sana.* (సన్న + సన్న.) adj. Easy. సులభము.

సన్న See సన్నము.

సన్నదు *sannadu.* [H.] n. A patent of office or nobility. An order. A written grant, instrument or diploma, a charter or letters patent, శాసనము, ఆజ్ఞాపత్రిక.

సన్నద్ధము *san-naddhamu.* [Skt.] adj. Ready, prepared, accoutred, equipped, armed. సిద్ధముగానుండే. **సన్నద్ధుడు** *san-naddhudu.* n. One who is prepared, ready or accoutred. సిద్ధముగానుండువాడు.

సన్నము *sannamu*. [Tel.] adj. Thin, lean, slender, small. పలుచని, కృశమైన. సన్నము, సన్నత or సన్నదనము n. Thinness, leanness. Fineness, smallness. సూక్ష్మత్వము, తనుత్వము, పలుచన, కార్శ్యము. సన్న or సన్నని *sanna*. adj. Thin, lean, fine, small, little, narrow, slight, gentle, soft (not loud), పలుచని, కురుచైన. సన్నగాలి a slight breeze, మందమారుతము. సన్నబట్ట a thin cloth. సన్నబియ్యము fine rice. సన్నకొండ a little hill. సన్నకర్ర a slender stick. సన్నతోవ a narrow passage. సన్నచేపలు small fishes. "అది సన్ననూలువడుకుచున్నది she is spinning a thin thread, i.e., she is pining away. Yayati. v. 52. సన్నయూర్పులు gentle sighs. "సన్నరవళిపాటలు." Swa. vi. 38. టీ॥ సన్నపురక్తిగలిగిన పాటలు. సన్నపురుగు a small insect. **సన్నగాడు** *sanna-gadu*. n. A lean fellow, a little fellow. అల్పుడు. An ant, చీమ. (అప్ప. శాల. కాం). **సన్నగాళె** *sanna-gale*. (సన్నము+గాళె) n. A musical instrument. వాద్యవిశేషము, తిరుచిన్నము. A. iv. 38. **సన్నగించు, సన్నగిల్లు, సన్నగిలు** or **సన్నవారు** *sanna-gintsu*. v. n. To become lean or thin, to pine away, become emaciated. సన్నమగు, కృశించు. **సన్నపాకులగన్నేరు** *sanna-p-akula-ganneru*. n. A species of oleander, శతకుంభము, ఇలసభేదము. **సన్నపాటి** or **సన్నపు** *sanna-pati*. adj. Thin, lean. సన్నని, పలుచని. సన్నపాటివాడు a lean man. సన్నపాటికర్ర a slender stick. **సన్నపిల్లి** *sanna-pilli*. n. A spider. సాలెపురుగు. **సన్నపువాడు** *sannapu-vadu*. n. A poor, weak, low or base man. అల్పుడు. **సన్నమండిగలు** *sanna-mandigalu*. n. A kind of rice. వడ్లలో భేదము. H. iv. 155. **సన్నరాష్ట్రము** or **సన్నరాష్ట్రకము** *sanna-rastamu*. n. A medicinal root. *Alpinia galanga minor.* కులాంజనము.

సన్నయము *sannayamu*. [Skt.] n. A reserve force. వెనుకనుండుదండు. A crowd, సమూహము.

సన్నవిడి *sannavidi*. [Tel. from సన్నము.] adj. Small, fine, (used of species or varieties). సన్నవిడిబియ్యము fine rice.

సన్నహనము *sanna-hanamu*. [Skt.] n. An endeavour, effort. ప్రయత్నము. Hari Vams. II. iv. 126. A breast plate, a piece of armour, కవచము.

సన్నాయి *sannayi*. [H.] n. A clarionet. నాగసరము, వాద్యవిశేషము.

సన్నాసి Same as సన్యాసి (q. v.)

సన్నాహము *sannahamu*. [Skt.] n. Preparation. ప్రయత్నము. Armour, mail, accoutrements, కవచము. సన్నాహముచేయు to prepare, to make ready.

సన్నికర్షము *san-nikarshamu*. [Skt.] n. Proximity, nearness. సమీపము. **సన్నికృష్టము** *san-nikrishtamu*. adj. Near, proximate. సమీపమైన.

సన్నికల్లు, సనికల్లు, సన్నెకల్లు or **సనెకలు** *sanni-kallu*. [Tel.] n. A stone on which articles of food, etc., are bruised. నూరుకొనే రాయి, నూరురాయి.

సన్నిధానము or **సన్నిధి** *sanni-dhanamu* [Skt.] n. Proximity, nearness, vicinity, presence. నికటము, సమీపము. తమ సన్నిధిలో మనవిచేసుకొన్నాను I have informed your honor of this అది తమ సన్నిధానములోనే ఉన్నది it is near your hands. తమ సన్నిధానవర్తులు those who are in your presence, i. e., your servants.

సన్నిపాతము *san-ni-patamu*. [Skt.] n A sort of paralytic disease, delirium, convulsions, hysteria, జెన్ని. A collection assemblage, multitude, సంచయము, కలయిక. ప్రలాపసన్నిపాతము delirium. తాంత్రికసన్ని

పాతము nervous debility. దప్పాపాసన్ని పాతము pains in the body, attended with thirst. అన్నవిషముసన్నిపాతము sudden death or disease caused by eating heartily while convalescent from fever.

సన్నిబద్ధము *san-ni-baddhamu.* [Skt. సం+నిబద్ధము.] adj. Bound firmly, fast tied. బాగాకట్టబడ్డ.

సన్నిభము *san-nibhamu.* [Skt.] adj. Like, resembling. సదృశమైన. సమానము. సన్నిభుడు *san-nibhudu.* n. (In composition,) one who resembles. సదృశుడు. సూర్యసన్నిభుడు bright as the sun.

సన్నివిష్టము *san-ni-vishtamu.* [Skt.] adj. Near, present, at hand, entered into, engrossed in, సమీపమైన, ప్రవేశించిన.

సన్నివేశము *san-ni-vesamu.* [Skt.] n. An open place, either in a town or its vicinity. పట్టణాదివహిప్రదేశము. The backyard of a house. గృహాదులవెనుకస్థలము.

సన్నిహితము *san-ni-hitamu.* [Skt.] adj. Near, neighbouring, close at hand, adjacent. సమీపమందున్న, సమీపించిన. వానికి కాలము సన్నిహితమైనది his last moment approaches, his end is drawing near. వారు మాకు సన్నిహితదాయాదులు they are our nearest kinsmen. సన్నిహితుడు *san-ni-hitudu.* n. One who is near, one who is closely related. సమీపమందుండువాడు.

సన్నీ or **సన్ని** *sanni.* [H.] n. A dagger-like sword, a bayonet తుపాకికొనకు చెక్కియుండే బాకువంటికత్తి.

సన్నుతి, సన్నుతించు See under సత్.

సన్నె or **సన్నెకల్లు** Same as సన్నికల్లు (q. v.)

సన్మానము *san-manamu.* [Skt.] n. Honor, respect. మర్యాద, గౌరవము. సన్మానించు *san-manintsu.* v. a. To honor or pay respect to. గౌరవముచేయు. సన్మాననము *sanmānanamu.* n. The act of honoring. గౌరవించుట. సన్మానితము *san-mānitamu.* adj. Respected, honored. గౌరవింపబడిన.

సన్మోహనవిద్య *san-mōhana-vidya.* n. Glamoury, bewitching, enchantment. భ్రమింపజేయువిద్య. "తనసన్మోహన విద్యచేజనులని ద్రానుగన్నులంతేని." Aniruddh. iii. 53.

సన్న్యస్తము *san-nyastamu.* [Skt.] adj. Left or abandoned, consigned or delivered to. త్యజింపబడ్డ.

సన్న్యసించు *sanyasintsu.* v. a. To renounce the passions or the world. కామ్యకర్మములను విడుచు. To take the vows of an ascetic, to become a monk. To bid farewell to the world. ఆశ్రమస్వీకారముచేయు, కాషాయములు ధరించు. సన్న్యాసము *sanyāsamu.* n. The ascetic state or condition, monachism, asceticism. Abandonment, relinquishment. ఆశ్రమస్వీకారము. చాలించు కొనడము, మానుకొనడము. అస్త్రసన్న్యాసము laying aside weapons, renouncing the use of arms. Vaija. ii. 134. సన్న్యాసి *sanyāsi.* n. A monk, ascetic, hermit. సన్న్యసించిన వాడు.

సపత్ని *sa-patni.* [Skt.] n. A co-wife; one of several wives, a fellow wife, a rival wife. భార్యలలోనొకతె, సవతి. సపత్నీమాత *sa-patni-māta.* n. A step-mother. Vish. v. 227. N. ix. 162. సపత్నుడు *sa-patnudu.* n. An enemy, an adversary. శత్రువు.

సపర్య *saparya.* [Skt.] n. Worship, reverence. పూజ, నమస్య.

సపాటు or **సపాటుము** *sapāta.* [Tel.] adj. Level, level with the ground, మట్టము. "తనమేనిపాదవు తేలసపాటంబుగావించి వింధ్యా చలం బమ్మహాముభావు డెదుర్కొనిరెు." కాశీ. ii.

సపాదము *sa-pādamu* [Skt.] adj. And a quarter. పాతికతో కూడుకొన్న. Thus, ఏకసపాదలక్షము a lac and a quarter. Vasu preface 78.

సపిండుడు *sa-piṇḍuḍu.* [Skt.] n. A kinsman to the seventh generation in a descent from a common ancestor who has a right to partake of the funeral cake. పిండభాగి, సప్త పురుషపర్యంతజ్ఞాతి, ఏడుతరములకులోనిదాయాది. సపిండీకరణము *sa-piṇḍi-karaṇamu.* n. The name of a particular rite celebrated on the 12th day after a death. చచ్చిన పండ్రెండో నాడు చేసే సంవత్సరాంతశ్రాద్ధము.

సప్తము *saptamu.* [Skt. Cf. Eng. 'Seven'.] n. and adj. Seven, the seventh. ఏడు, ఏడవ. సప్త *sapta.* n. A musical instrument with seven strings. సప్తకము *saptakamu.* n. Seven, ఏడు. A ceremony performed on the 12th day after a death. సపిండీకరణము. adj. Seventh, ఏడవ. సప్తకి *saptaki.* n. A woman's girdle or zone. ఏడుపేటలుగల ఆడుదాని మొలనూలు. సప్తజిహ్వుడు *sapta-jihvuḍu.* n. An epithet of fire. అగ్ని. Lit. Seven-tongued, i.e. seven flamed; సప్తతంతువు *sapta-tantuvu.* n. A sacrifice. యజ్ఞము. సప్తతి *saptati.* n. Seventy. డెబ్బది. సప్తపది *sapta-padi.* n. Seven steps. ఏడడుగులు. సప్తపదులు మెట్టించుట a ceremony performed in marriage. "కాళ్ల మెట్టించెను సప్తపదులు." A. vi. 190. "భామకరంబుగ సప్త పదులు త్రొక్కించె." Bhag. 157. సప్తపథ *sapta-patha.* n. The pharynx. సప్తమము *saptamamu.* adj. The seventh. ఏడవ. సప్తమి *saptami.* n. The seventh day after new or full moon. సప్తమీవిభక్తి (in grammar) the seventh or Locative case of the noun. సప్తరాశికము *sapta-rāsikamu.* n. The Rule of Seven, i. e, a species of Compound Proportion, ఏడు పద్దులుగల లెక్క. సప్తసముద్రములు *sapta-samudramulu.* n. The seven oceans of Hindu Cosmology. లవణేక్ష్వాది, ఆరునొక సాగరములు. సప్తార్చి or సప్తార్చుడు *sapt-archi.* n. Fire. అగ్ని హుతాశుడు. సప్తాశ్వుడు *sapt-aśvuḍu.* n. The sun. సూర్యుడు.

సప్తల *saptala.* [Skt.] n. The double jessamine. నవమాలిక, విరజాజి. A. iv. 151.

సప్తి *sapti.* [Skt.] n. A horse. గుర్రము.

సప్పము *sappamu.* [from Skt. సర్పము.] n. A serpent. సప్పపుచుక్క *sappapu-tsukka.* n. The star called ఆశ్లేష.

సప్రయోజనముగా *sa-pra-yōjanamu-gā.* [Skt.] adv. Profitably, advantageously. సఫలముగా.

సప్రాణి *sa-prāṇi.* [Skt.] adj. Living, having life. సజీవి.

సఫణము *sa-phaṇamu.* [Skt.] adj. Crested, hooded. పడగగల. "సఫణాంశైలరాజుసిరాజి." Anir. iii. 125.

సఫరము *sapharamu.* [Skt.] n. The silver fish to the gleam of which in water poets compare the flash of a glancing eye.

సఫలము *sa-phalamu.* [Skt.] adj. Fruitful, advantageous, efficacious, successful. ఫలముతోగూడిన, సార్థకమైన. నా జన్మము సఫలమైనది my life has borne fruit, has been worth living. నా కోరికసఫలమైనది my desire is accomplished. ఈ యుక్తి సఫలమైనది this plan turned out well, this method was successful. నా పూర్వజన్మపుణ్యము సఫలమైనది the merit I acquired in a former birth has now borne fruit. సఫలత *sa-phalata.* n. Benefit, advantage, success, fulfilment. సార్థకత, సాఫల్యము.

సఫేదా *saphēdā.* [H.] n. Whitelead used in painting. adj. White, తెల్లని.

సబబు *sababu.* [H.] n. Reason, ground, cause. కారణము.

సబము *sabamu.* [from Skt. శవము.] n. Same as శవము (q. v.)

సబురు *saburu.* [H.] n. A top-gallant mast. ఓడస్తంభములలోకొనది.

సబలము or సబళము *sabalamu.* [Skt. స+బలము.] n. A sort of spear శక్తి అనే ఆయుధము. ప్రాసము, కుంతము, ఈటె. "సబళ ముద్గరాస్త్రముల తోమరముల క్రూరసోముండ్ల త్రోఁ." M. X. i. 185.

సబాము *sabāmu.* [from Skt. స్వభావము.] Same as స్వభావము. (q. v.) "తే॥ పాలు కడుబెక్కుదాని సబాముతెప్ప." భార. అను. ii.

సబిడి *sabiḍi.* [Tel.] n. A kind of weapon. "సబిడీలవంకుల జేమదాకులను." అచ్చ. యు. కాం.

సబురు *saburu.* [H.] n. A voyage. దరిసబురు sailing along the coast, a coasting trip. లోసబురు sailing far out at sea.

సబ్జా *sabja.* [H.] n. Green or black colour.

సబ్నివీసు *sab-nivīsu.* [H.] n. A writer, paymaster.

సబ్బండు *sabbanḍu.* [Tel.] n. A jumble or *omnium gatherum,* dirt, rubbish. అనేక విధములైన వస్తువులు కలిసినది, ఉచ్చావచము, కన్నకసుమాలము. Filthy language. ఈ బియ్య ములో సబ్బండు కలిసియున్నది this rice is a mass of dirt, mere rubbish.

సబ్బు *sabbu.* [Eng. 'Soap.'] n. Soap. చౌకారము, జిడ్డుపోగొట్టు ఒకవిధమైన చవుటి కారము.

సబ్బుబియ్యము or సగ్గుబియ్యము *sabbu-biyyamu.* [Tel.] n. Sago. ఒకవిధమైన ధాన్యము.

సబ్రహ్మచారి *sa-brahma-chāri.* [Skt.] n. A fellow disciple or student. సతీర్థ్యుడు, సహపాఠి.

సభ *sabha.* [Skt.] n. A convocation, court, an assembly, meeting, levee, council, association, society. A place of meeting, a hall of audience. సమాజము, సమూహము, గృహము, చావడి, కొలువుకూటము. ఉత్తరసభ a superior court or a court of appeal. సభాతాంబూలాదులు betel, etc., served out at a public meeting. సభాకంపము bashfulness in company. సభాపతి *sabhā-pati.* n. The president of an assembly, a chairman at a meeting, సమాజనాయకుడు. సభాసదుడు, సభాస్తారుడు or సభికుడు *sabhā-saduḍu.* n. A member of a council, a councillor, one present at a meeting. One of a company, సభవారిలో నొకడు, సభాస్థిత ధర్మజ్ఞుడు, న్యాయవాది. సభ్యము *sabhyamu.* adj. Polite, polished, genteel, well-bred, fit for or admissible into society. సభారంజకమైన, సౌజన్యమైన, సత్కులప్రసూతమైన. సభ్యత *sabhyata.* n. Politeness, refinement in manners. సజ్జనత్వము. సభ్యత్వము *sabhya-tvamu.* n. Courtiership, councillorship. సభికధర్మము. B. vii. 157. సభ్యుడు *sabhyuḍu.* n. A councillor, a good man, a man of good birth or manners. సభాస్థితధర్మజ్ఞుడు. సభయందుండువాడు, మంచివాడు, సత్కులప్రసూతుడు.

సమ్ *sam.* [Skt.] A particle and prefix implying Union, junction, with, together: as a prefix it corresponds to *con, co, com.* It means also, much, great or well, మిక్కిలి, చక్కగా. సమధికము very great, very much,' మిక్కిలిఅధికమైన. సమాలోకించు to see well. సమావృతము well covered or surrounded. సమాశ్రయము a good support. సమాశ్రితము well supported. సమాసాదితము well got or obtained. సముచితము very proper or suitable. సముత్పన్నము well born. సముత్సుకము very glad or joyful. సముదితము well born. సముద్ధతము very great or proud. సముద్భృతము well raised or supported. సముద్భవించు to be born well. సముద్భూతము well born. సమున్నతము very high See సం.

సమంజసము *sa-manjasamu.* [Skt.] adj. Just, right, proper, fit, correct, accurate, true. సమీచీనమైన, యోగ్యమైన, మంచి, తథ్య

మైన, అవిరోధమైన, న్యాయమైన, ఉపయుక్తమైన. "పూర్వవైరమునమునకోరిక కదుపమంజస స్థితిని." Vish. viii. 440. n. Justice, propriety, fitness, న్యాయము, తనకు ఉచితమైన సర్తమునలన చలిగానకయుండడము.

సమకట్టు sama-kaṭṭu. [Skt.+Tel.] v. n. To get ready, to try, attempt. యత్నపడు, యత్నించు. v. a. To prepare, make ready, సిద్ధపరచు. To arrange, ఏర్పరచు. To make, చేయు. To get, obtain, సేకరించు. "పార్శ్వం బులంగట్టు కంబట్టులాలసరిసమకట్టు తెక్కలం గాయూతు ఖానంఢదను కొండచిలువ నొడిచు." Swa. iv. 166. n. A piece of armour, కవచము.

సమకూడు, సమకూడు or సమకూరు sama-kūḍu. [Skt.+Tel.] v. n. To succeed or take effect, to accrue to, to be got, to be accomplished, to happen, occur. చేకూరు, లభించు, సిద్ధించు, సంభవించు, కలుగు, ప్రాప్తమగు. "సైన్యముచేసమరజయముసమకూరదు." M. XII. iii. 179. సమకూరుచు or సమకూర్చు sama-kūrutsu. v. a. To cause, effect, bring about. చేకూరచేయు.

సమకొను sama-konu. [Skt.+Tel.] v. n. To be got, to be obtained; happen, occur. లభించు, ప్రాప్తమగు, సిద్ధించు, కలుగు. v. a. To attempt, to aim at. యత్నించు. "సకలసద్గ సుఖముసమకొనియుండగా." Swa. ii. 63. "సమకొనిపిరికిద్దరకుసఖ్యముచేయకయున్న సాగదే." P. i. 215. సమకొలుపు or సమకొల్పు sama-kolupu. v. a. To cause to happen. లభింపచేయు, సిద్ధింపచేయు. To make ready, సిద్ధపరచు. To have, bear, endure, కలిగియుండు, సహించు. To induce, incite, persuade. పురికొలుపు, ప్రేరేపించు. "సమకొ ల్పార్థునిజేయవానసురస్తుతికి సమకొల్పితివినన్ను సద్గురుపుత్ర." L. i. 160. సమకోలు sama-kōlu. n. The act of happening, occurrence, accruement. లభించుట, సిద్ధించుట, కలుగుట.

సమక్షము sam-akshamu. [Skt.] n. Presence, sight. ఎదురు. adj. Seen, visible, నయనేంద్రియగోచరమైన. adv. In sight of, in presence of, before. ఎదుట, ముందర.

సమగ్రము sam-agramu. [Skt.] adj Entire, whole, complete. పూర్ణమైన, సమస్తము. సమగ్రత, సమగ్రిమ or సమగ్రిమము sam-agrata. n. Whole, entirety. యావత్తు, అంతయును, సమస్తము.

సమజ్య samajya. [Skt.] n. An assembly, meeting. సభ, పరిషత్తు.

సమత See under సమము.

సమధిగమము sam-adhi-gamamu. [Skt.] n. Obtaining, పొందుట.

సమన్వితము sam-anvitamu. [Skt.] adj. Accompanied by, joined, united, కూడుకొన్న.

సమము samamu. [Skt.] adj. Like, alike, similar, same, equal, even, smooth, level. Impartial, free from passion, equable. సమానమైన, తుల్యమైన, సదృశమైన, అవిషమమైన, తేడకాని, మిట్టపల్లములేకుండా ఉండే. సమసంఖ్య a round or even sum. సమదృష్టిగలవాడు one who is equitable or impartial. n. Equality, evenness, తుల్యత, అవిషమత. A year, సంవత్సరము. "అధూపతియేకషష్టిసమముల్ పూర్ణేందుబింబాస్య తోడా." Vish. vi. 76. సమముచేయు samamu-chēyu. v. a. To level or equalise. మిట్టపల్లములేక పరచు, ఈడుచేయు. సమచతురస్రము sama-chatur-asramu. adj. Four square. చచ్చౌకమైన. సమత or సమత్వము samata. n. Equality, similarity, sameness. తుల్యత. సమదర్శి sama-darsi. n. One who regards all things alike, an impartial man. సర్వభూతములను సమముగా చూచువాడు. సమదృష్టి sama-drishṭi. n. An impartial attitude, considering all things alike. సర్వభూతములను సమముగా చూచుచూపు. సమపదము sama-padamu. n. Standing with the two legs on the same line, as an archer. విలుకాడు రెండుకాళ్లతో సమముగా నిలుచుట. సమరసము *sama-rasamu.* n. Equality, uniformity. Familiarity, fellowship. Kindness, amicableness, సమానరాగము, సమాధానము. వారిప్పుడు సమరసముగా ఉన్నారు they are now on good terms. సమవర్తి *sama-varti* n. One who treats all alike. అంతట సమముగా వర్తించువాడు. A name of Yama the King of Hell. యముడు. P. iv. 398. సమసుప్తి *sama-supti.* n. Lit. an equal or universal sleep. The end of a Kalpa or Age; the destruction of the world, యుగాంతము. "సమసుప్తిబొందించిజగముల ద్రుంచి." BD. v. 27. సమాంశములు *sam-amsamulu.* n. plu. Equality of parts, equal proportions, తుల్యభాగములు. సముడు *samudu.* n. He who resembles, సదృశుడు.

సమయము *samayamu.* [Skt.] n. An opportunity, occasion. An age, period. Time, season, juncture, crisis, కాలము, ఉచితకాలము. Leisure, తీరుబాటు. An oath, imprecation. ప్రతిజ్ఞ, శపథము. An established moral or ceremonial custom, ఆచారము. A settled conclusion, a demonstration, a decision. A contract, engagement, covenant. A sign, సంకేతము. A school of philosophy, దర్శనము, మతము. A doctrine, సిద్ధాంతము. శివసమయము the Saivite sect. విష్ణుసమయము the Vaishnavite sect. సమయముచూస్తూ ఉన్నాడు he is looking for an opportunity. సమయములో సహాయముచేసినాడు he helped me in time of need. సమయపుసందుకట్టు a time of difficulty. సమయములో చెయ్యివిడుచు to forsake a man in the time of need. సమయమైనప్పుడు when an opportunity arises. నేను లేనిసమయమందు when I was absent. నాలుగుగంటలసమయమందు when it was about four o'clock. సమయమునకొక్కమనిషి a time-server, a fickle man. సమయస్ఫూర్తి a quick memory or understanding. సమయస్ఫూర్తిగలవాడు a quick-witted man. సమయమైన or సమయమగు *samayam-aina.* adj. Opportune, seasonable. యుక్తమైన. "సమయంబగుచేత." H. ii. 53. సమయపడు *samaya-padu.* v. n. To attempt, యత్నించు. To watch for an opportunity. To become opportune. To resolve on secrecy, సంకేతించు. "సమయపడి వనవాసంబుచేయవచ్చితిమి." భార. అర. సమయోచితము *samay-ochitamu.* adj. Seasonable, suitable to the occasion, appropriate, కాలోచితమైన. సమయోచితమైనమాట a word in season, an appropriate word.

సమయు *samayu.* [from Skt. శమ్.] v. n. To be ruined or destroyed, to perish, to die. నశించు, చచ్చు. "చేముఱలేనిదివ్వె సమసిపోవు." Vema. 139. "తనవారినెల్లను సమయించితొనుసమసె." M. XIII. v. 466. సమయించు or సమయజేయు *samayintsu.* v. a. To destroy, kill. సంహరించు, నాశముచేయు, చంపు, పెరుచు. "అనుజాల దనయుల మత్సరిజనులను సమయించి వారు సమరోల్లాసంబున." M. IX. ii. 16. సమసిపోవు *samasi-pōvu.* v. n. To be ruined or destroyed, to perish, to die. To be expended, consumed, worn out. నశించు, చచ్చు, అయిపోవు, అలసిపోవు.

సమరము *samaramu.* [Skt.] n. Combat, war, a battle. యుద్ధము.

సమరసము See under సమము.

సమర్త or సమరత *samarta.* [Tel.] n. Puberty. మొదటిముట్టు. సమర్తాడు *samartadu.* v. n. To be grown, arrive at puberty (used of a woman), పుష్పవతియగు, ఋతుమతియగు.

సమర్థనము *sam-arthanamu.* [Skt.] n. Perseverance. పట్టినదిఁ విడువక చేయుట.

Maintaining, establishing, proving, accomplishing, performing, నిర్వాహము, నిర్వహించడము, సాధించడము. సమర్థించు sam-arthintsu. v. a. To master, overcome a difficulty, succeed, accomplish, achieve, పట్టినది తనివట్టు జరగజేయు. సమర్థము sam-arthamu. adj. Able, capable, versed in, master of. Adequate, powerful, strong. శక్తిగల, త్రాణగల, సామర్థ్యముగల. సమర్థత sam-arthata. n. Ability, cleverness, capability. శక్తి, సామర్థ్యము. సమర్థుడు samarthuḍu. A man of ability or talent. శక్తిమంతుడు, గట్టివాడు, నేర్పరి, సామర్థ్యవంతుడు. అట్లు చేయుటకు సమర్థుడనుకాను I have not the ability to do so.

సమర్పించు sam-arpintsu. [Skt.] v. a. To offer a thing (to a god, &c.) సమర్పణము or సమర్పణ sam-arpaṇamu. n. The act of offering any thing (to a god, &c).

సమవర్తి See under సమము.

సమవాయము sama-vāyamu. [Skt.] n. A flock, multitude, collection, heap. సమూహము.

సమవేతము sama-vētamu. [Skt.] adj. Mixed, mingled, united. మిశ్రితము, కూడుకొన్న.

సమష్టి or సమిష్టి samashṭi. [Skt.] n. The whole, the entirety. మొత్తము, సర్వము. సమష్టము, adj. Collected, collective, joint. సమష్టిఆస్తి joint property. సమష్టిగా or సమిష్టిగా samashṭi-gā. adv. Collectively. వారు సమష్టిగానున్నారు they live as one family.

సమస్తము samastamu. [Skt.] adj. All, whole, entire, complete. సకలము, సర్వము, అంతా. n. The whole, all.

సమస్థానము Error for సంస్థానము (q. v.)

సమస్య samasya. [Skt.] n. Part of a stanza proposed by one person to be completed by another as a trial of skill. కవిపరీక్షకొరకు ఇచ్చే పద్యపాదము.

సమాంసమీన samām-samīna. [Skt.] n. A cow which calves every year. ఏటేట ఈను ఆవు. Satyabha. iv. 85.

సమాఖ్య sam-ākhya. [Skt.] n. Fame. కీర్తి. Confederation, convention. బందుకట్టు.

సమాచారము sam-āchāramu. [Skt.] n. News, tidings, intelligence, a report, a message. An occurrence, matter, affair. వర్తమానము, వృత్తాంతము, సంగతి, వ్యవహారము.

సమాజము samājamu. [Skt.] n. A multitude, assembly, గుంపు, సమూహము. A society, association, congregation, church, సభ. సంఘము. సామాజికుడు a member of a society, congregation or church.

సమాధానము sam-ādhānamu. [Skt.] n. Peace, tranquillity, satisfaction, consent, agreement, a treaty. A reason, ground. సమ్మతి, సమ్మతి, అంగీకారము, న్యాయము. సమాధానపడు sam-ādhāna-paḍu. v. n. To agree, consent. సమ్మతిపడు. To be reconciled. సమాధానపరచు sam-ādhāna-paratsu. v. a. To cause one to agree or consent. To reconcile, సమ్మతించునట్టుచేయు.

సమాధి samādhi. [Skt.] n. A grave, or tomb. శవమునుపాతి పైనికట్టినది, గోరీ. Deep meditation on the Deity, devout abstraction, absorption of thought. దేవునియందు తదేకధ్యానముగానుండడము. సమాధిస్థానము a place where a recluse sits when praying or meditating. దేవధ్యానముమీదనుండునప్పుడు కూర్చుండేచోటు. వారు జలసమాధినిపొందిరి they found a watery grave.

సమానము samānamu. [from Skt. సమాధానము.] n. Consent, సమ్మతి. [Skt.] The vital air. నాభియందలి వాయువు. adj. Like, similar, equal, సదృశమైన, తుల్యము. సమానార్థకమైన శబ్దము a synonym or equivalent word. సమానుడు samānuḍu. n. An equal. సంసమానులు equals in all respects.

సమాపకము *samāpakamu*. [Skt.] adj. That which completes. ముగించునది. సమాపకక్రియ *samāpaka-kriya*. n. A finite verb. అసమాపకక్రియ an incomplete verbal form which cannot finish a sentence. సమాపనము *samāpanamu*. n. Finishing, completing. Killing, destroying, ముగించుట చంపడము. సమాప్తము *sam-āptamu*. adj. Finished, completed, ముగిసిన. సమాప్తమగు or సమాప్తియగు *sam-āptam-agu*. v. n. To become finished or completed. ముగింపబడు. సమాప్తి *sam-āpti*. n. The end, completion, close, conclusion, finis. ముగింపు. Death, చావు. సమాప్తించు or సమాప్తిచేయు *sam-āptintsu*. v. a. To finish, end, close, conclude, ముగించు. సమాప్యము *sam-āpyamu*. adj. That which is fit to be ended, terminable. ముగింపదగిన.

సమారాధనము *sam-ārādhanamu*. [Skt.] n. Worship, చక్కని ఆరాధనము.

సమావేశము *sam-āvēṣamu*. [Skt.] n. Being together at one place. ఒకచోటకూడియుండుట. Entrance, ప్రవేశము. Meeting, కలిసికొనుట.

సమాసంజితము *sam-āsanjitamu*. [Skt.] adj. United, combined, connected with. కూడుకొన్న, తగులుకొనిన. "వా పురోవర్తి శాఖాసమాసంజిత సముంజసరత్నపంజరంబున నున్న నన్నుం జూచి." K.P. v. 26.

సమాసము *samāsamu*. [Skt.] n. Composition of words, formation of compound terms. A combination of several words into one, all but the final being devoid of the signs of case, a compound word, రెండుమూడుశబ్దముల నేకపదముగా చేర్చడము. విభక్తి లోపముచేసిన పదము. సమర్థములగు పదముల యేకీభావము. సమాసకము *samāsakamu*. n. A compound word formed out of pure Telugu words, శుద్ధాంధ్రపదములసమాసము. సమాసోక్తి a compound word.

సమాహారము or సమాహరణము *sam-āhāramu*. [Skt.] n. An aggregation, collection, assemblage; contraction, abridgment. సంక్షేపము, చెదరినవి ఒకటిగా పోగుచేయుట.

సమాహితము *sam-āhitamu*. [Skt.] adj. Well placed, settled, assembled, compiled, చక్కగా ఉంచబడిన. Promised, agreed, or assented to, అంగీకరింపబడిన, అంగీకృతమైన. Absorbed in meditation, engaged in devout meditation. Attentive, cautious. సమాధియందున్న, సమాధిస్థము, వినిహితము, సావధానమైన. సమాహితుడు *sam-āhituḍu*. n. One who is well placed. చక్కగా ఉంచబడినవాడు.

సమాహ్వయము *sam-āhvayamu*. [Skt.] n. A name, an appellation. పేరు, నామధేయము. A battle, యుద్ధము.

సమితి *samiti*. [Skt.] n. An assembly, company, సమూహము. War, a battle, యుద్ధము. Union, సంగమము. సమిత్తు *samittu*. n. War, a battle. యుద్ధము.

సమిధ *samidha*. [Skt.] n. Sacrificial fuel, wood for a sacrifice. ఇధ్మము, చిదుగు. Firewood, వంటచెరకు.

సమీకము *samīkamu*. [Skt.] n. War, a combat, a battle, యుద్ధము.

సమీకరణము *samī-karaṇamu*. [Skt.] n. Equalization, making equal to. సమానము చేయుట, ఒకటిగా చేయుట. సమీకరించు *samī-karintsu*. v. a. To equalize, make equal to. సమానముచేయు.

సమీకృతము *samī-kṛitamu*. [Skt.] adj. United. ఒకటిగా చేయబడిన.

సమీక్షణము *sam-īkshaṇamu*. [Skt.] n. The act of looking well, careful inspection, చక్కగాచూచుట. సమీక్ష్యకారి *sam-īkshya-kari*. n. One who does a thing after due consideration, a prudent man. సమీక్ష్య

సమీక్ష్యకారిత్వము *sam-ikshya-kāritvamu.* n. Prudence, forethought. చక్కగా విచారించి చేయడము. అసమీక్ష్యకారిత్వము acting inconsiderately, imprudence. The last book of the Pancha tantram is so styled.

సమీచీనము *samīchīnamu.* [Skt.] adj. True, right, correct, fit, proper. యథార్థమైన, సమంజసమైన, యుక్తమైన, తగిన. n. Truth, సత్యము.

సమీపము *samīpamu.* [Skt.] n. Nearness, proximity, దగ్గర, చేరువ. అతని సమీపమందు నిలిచితిని I stood near him. adj. Near. దగ్గిరనున్న. మధ్యాహ్నము సమీపమైనది it is near noon. సమీపస్థుడు *samīpa-sthuḍu.* n. A bystander. దగ్గిరనున్నవాడు. సమీపించు *samīpintsu.* v. n. To come near, approach, be imminent. దగ్గిరకువచ్చు. వానితండ్రికి కాలము సమీపించేవేళకు when his father was about to die, when death was near at hand.

సమీరణము *samīraṇamu.* [Skt.] n. Going well. చక్కగాపోవుట. సమీరితము *samīritamu.* adj. Gone, చక్కగాపోయిన. Thrown away, పారవేయబడిన. Sent, despatched, పంపబడ్డ. Said, uttered, చెప్పబడ్డ. సమీరుడు *samīruḍu.* n. Wind, air, వాయువు.

సముఖము *sa-mukhamu.* [Skt.] n. Presence, proximity, nearness. ఎదురు, సమక్షము, సామీప్యము. సముఖమునకు వచ్చి రాయభారము చేయు to come into a man's presence and then send an embassy to him, that is, to do an unnecessary thing.

సముచ్చయము *sam-uchchayamu.* [Skt.] n. Connection, collocation, conjunction. A collection, assemblage; (gram.) a conjunction. వేరువేరువాని కొకటిగా పోగుచేయుట, సమూహము, సముదాయము.

సముతు *samutu.* [H.] n. A combination or league, a strike among workmen. కట్టుపాటు. "ఒక రోజూ దాక పాటు లేకుండా సముతు కట్టుకొని కట్టుచేయుకుండా కూర్చున్నారు." Vaij. ii. 87. సముతుకట్టు *samutu-kaṭṭu.* v. n. To strike work, కట్టుకట్టు. సముతుపడు to be caught, to yield, పట్టుపడు. సముతుపరచు to cause to yield. "శా॥ మస్తకమందువిస్ఫులింగాలు కుస్తరించి, సమరసముచూపి కొల్లసే సముతుపరిచి, వాగదికిరించి తక్కినవారల్వాగసడలి, పన్నిపోసిన మందర బరవడయ్యె." చంద్రా. iii.

సముదయము *sam-udayamu.* [Skt.] n. The state or act of being well born. చక్కని ఉదయము. A multitude, assembly, quantity. సమూహము, వయము, గుంపు. సముదాయము *samudāyamu.* n. A multitude. సమూహము, గుంపు. సముదాయపునేల a piece of land which is common to various persons, land held in common. సముదాయపువిన్నపము a general petition.

సముదాయించు *samuday-intsu.* [from Skt. సముదయము.] v. a. To comfort, persuade. To appease, lull, ఓదార్చు.

సముద్గము or సముద్గకము *samudgamu.* [Skt.] n. A casket, a covered box. పెట్టె, సంపుటము, బరిణె.

సముద్దారుడు *samud-dāruḍu.* [H.] n. One who manages a Samut or subdivision of a Taluq. ఒక సముతుయొక్క అధికారి.

సముద్రము or సముద్రము *sa-mudramu.* [Skt.] n. The sea, ocean. అబ్ధి, పారావారము, మున్నీరు, సాగరము, కడలి. There are 7 seas according to Hindu mythology, viz., లవణసముద్రము the sea of salt, ఇక్షుసముద్రము the sea of sugar, సురాసముద్రము the sea of wine, సర్పిస్సముద్రము the sea of ghee, దధిసముద్రము the sea of curds, క్షీరసముద్రము the sea of milk, and జలసముద్రము the sea of waters. సముద్రనవనీతము lit. the butter of the ocean, an epithet of the moon, చంద్రుడు. సముద్రపు చిలుక a flamingo, పూరెంక. సముద్రపచ్చ samudra-patstsa. n. A plant called *Convolvulus speciosus*.

సమూహము samūhamu. [Skt.] n. A crowd, multitude, number, flock, heap, quantity. నివహము, గుంపు.

సమృద్ధము sam-riddhamu. [Skt.] adj. Ample, full, entire; abundant, plentiful, సంపూర్ణమైన. సమృద్ధి sam-riddhi. n. Fulness, plentitude, abundance. Increase, prosperity, success. అభివృద్ధి, మిక్కిలి సంపద. ఆ కుండ సమృద్ధిచేసినాను I filled the pot. సమృద్ధిగా sam-riddhi-gā. adv. Amply, plentifully, fully. సంపూర్ణముగా, విస్తారముగా. సమృద్ధియగు sam-riddhi-y-agu. v. n. To grow full. సంపూర్ణమగు. సమృద్ధుడు sam-riddhudu. n. A wealthy or prosperous man. మిక్కిలి సంపదగలవాడు.

సమేతము samētamu. [Skt.] adj. Having, possessed of, accompanied by. కూడుకొన్న, సహితమైన, కల. సమేతము or సమేతముగా adv. With, together with, along with. సహితముగా, కూడా. సమేతు samētu. [for సమేతము.] adv. Even. సహితము, కూడా. అన్నానికి సమేతులేదు I have not got even food to eat. సమేతుడు samētudu. n. One who is accompanied by, attended by; he who has or is possessed of, సహితుడు, కలవాడు, కూడుకొన్నవాడు. సేనాసమేతుడైవచ్చెను he came with his troops. "అతీతోత్సాహసమేతుడై." M. I. ii. 13. "భూతమగణసమేతుడైమహాభయంబుతోడ." (Vish. ii. 58.) attended by goblins and inspiring fear.

సమేలము sa-mēlamu. [from Skt. సమ్మేళనము.] n. Friendship, familiarity; meeting. ఒద్దిక, చేరిక.

సమ్మతము sam-matamu. [Skt.] adj. Assented to, agreed to, concurred in, approved of, liked, agreeable, సమ్మతియైన, అంగీకృతము. శాస్త్రసమ్మతమైనపని a legal act. అతనికి సమ్మతముకానిది that which is not agreeable to him. సమ్మతముగా sam-matamu-gā. adv. Willingly, agreeably, according to. మనఃపూర్వకముగా, ప్రకారముగా. శాస్త్రసమ్మతముగా according to rule. తమరెట్లు దైవసమ్మతముగా నుండవలసినది you should give such a decision as may be right in the sight of God. సమ్మతి sam-mati. n. Consent approbation, assent. అంగీకారము, ఇచ్ఛ, ఇష్టము, అనుజ్ఞ. సమ్మతివచనము a text adduced in proof. శేషయ్యసమ్మతిని కొమారుడు రంగయ్యవ్రాలు signed by me, Rangaya, on behalf of my father Seshaya. సమ్మతించు, సమ్మతిలు or సమ్మతిల్లు sam-mat-intsu. v. n. To consent or agree. ఒప్పు, అంగీకరించు. సమ్మతుడు sam-matudu. n. One who assented to or agreed to; one who is approved of, అంగీకృతుడు, ఒప్పుకోబడ్డవాడు. సర్వజనసమ్మతుడు he whom all approve.

సమ్మదము sam-madamu. [Skt.] n. Joy, pleasure, happiness. ప్రమోదము, ఆనందము, సంతోషము. సమ్మద sam-mada. n. A gratuity, donation, gift. పారితోషికము, బహుమానము. "అలరిత్రప్రసంగమున కార్థులర్పిన ఛత్రచామరాందోళికలాదిగాగలుగుతోరపు సమ్మదలిచ్చియమ్మహీపాలుడు సత్కరించె." Zace. i. 135.

సమ్మర్దము sam-mardamu. [Skt.] n. A throng, crowd, press. సంకులము, రాయిడి, ఒత్తుడు. War, a battle, యుద్ధము. జనసమ్మర్దము a crowd or press of people. సమ్మర్దముగానుండే sam-mardamu-gā-n-undē. adj. Crowded. ఒత్తుడుగానుండే.

సమ్మాననము sam-mānanamu. [Skt.] n. The act of respecting, గౌరవించుట. సమ్మానము sam-mānamu. n. Respect, గౌరవము.

సమ్మానించు *sam-māninṭsu*. v. a. To respect, treat with respect, honor. గౌరవించు. సమ్మానితము *sam-mānitamu*. adj. Respected. గౌరవింపబడిన.

సమ్మార్జనము *sam-mārjanamu*. [Skt.] n. A search, cleaning. శోధనము. సమ్మార్జని *sam-mārjani*. n. A broom. చీపురు, చీపురుకట్ట.

సమ్మాళిగలు or సంబాళిగలు *sam-māḷigalu*. [from Skt.] n. plu. Sandals. పావుకోళ్లు. Shoes, పాపోసులు. పట్టుసమ్మాళిగలు silk shoes. "సీ॥ అట్టిట్టుదొడిగినయంత్రముల రత్నంపుసమ్మాళిగలుపాదుకొనుచుండ." KP. ii. 23. See సంబాళిగలు.

సమ్ముదము *sam-mudamu*. [Skt.] n. Great joy. మిక్కిలి సంతోషము.

సమ్మె or సమ్మెయు *samme*. [from Skt. సమయము.] n. Confederation, league. సమాఖ్య, కట్టుపాటు. సమ్మెజాబు a letter signed by many.

సమ్మెట *sam-meṭa*. [Tel.] n. A sledge hammer. పెద్దసుత్తి. [from Skt. చర్మయష్టి.] n. A whip. కశ, కొరడా. "కాలుచేసమ్మెటమోయులకాబడక." B. i. 14. సమ్మెటకోల *sam-meṭa-kōla*. n. A javelin, a lance. ఈటె. "అవుడుసమ్మెటకోలలనంకుశములు." M. VII. iii. 57.

సమ్యక్ or సమ్యక్కు *samyak*. [Skt.] adv. All, wholly, properly, duly, fitly. యావత్తు, యుక్తముగా, చక్కగా.

సమ్రాట్టు *sam-rāṭṭu*. [Skt.] n. A paramount sovereign, an emperor. రాజాధిరాజు.

సయాం or సయాము *sayam*. [corruption of Skt. స్వయము.] adj. Own. సొంత. నా సయాంతమ్ముడు my own younger brother.

సయ్యన *sayyana*. [Skt.] adv. Quickly, at once. తెప్పున. "తెవులంసయ్యనవచ్చునా." BD. iv. 841.

సయి *sai*. [from Skt. సహ.] adv. Together with. కూడా. With, తోడ.

సయ్యాట or సయ్యాటము *say-y-āṭa*. [సయి (from Skt. సహ) + Tel. ఆట.] n. A joke. సరసము, పరిహాసము. Sport, కేళి. "తడవాడుజోగా తప్పివిచ్చేయుడు నీసయ్యాటలింక చాలు." P. iv. 724. సయ్యాటించు *say-y-āṭinṭsu*. v. a. To joke. పరిహసించు. సయ్యొద్ద *say-y-odda*. n. Friendship, అనుకూలత, చెలిమి, స్నేహము. సయ్యొద్దగా *say-y-odda-ga*. adv. Amicably, in a friendly manner. వినీతముగా, స్నేహముగా. వారు మిక్కిలి సయ్యొద్దగానున్నారు they are on very good terms.

సయించు *sayinṭsu*. [from Skt. సహనం.] v. n. To be agreeable, to be palatable, to bear, endure, put with, ఓర్చు.

సయిగ Same as సైగ (q. v.)

సయితము *sayitamu*. [from Skt. సహితమ్.] adv. Also, కూడా.

సయిరించు Same as సైరించు (q. v.)

సరంగు *sarangu*. [H.] n. The headman of the sailors in a boat or ship, a boatswain, నావికులపెద్ద, ఓడమాలిమికాడు, నావికుడు.

సరంజాము *saranḍsāmu*. [H.] n. Furniture, things, articles, property. సామాను, వస్తువులు. సరంజాముచేయు to get ready, to supply, కావలసినవస్తువులను సిద్ధముచేయు.

సరంబీ *sarambhi*. [Malay.] n. A porch, gallery, awning; the ceiling in a house, a house made of shingle or board. సరంబీకొట్టు a room with a ceiling, బల్లకూర్పుచేసియుండుగది.

సరకటము *sarakaṭamu*. [Tel.] n. Difficulty, hardship. తొందర. సంకటము. "తెరంగుదప్పినవేళ, మరుంగుపడక, తెరంగుదొలకసరకటంబున నిరకటంబుచేసి." H. K. iv. 85.

సరకట్టు *sara-kaṭṭu*. [Skt. సరము + Tel. కట్టు.] n. A stop on a lute. వీణామెట్టు. "సీ॥ తరుణాం

గుకేచ్చాయదంతపుసరకట్టులింగిలికపువింతరంగు లిన." Swa. i.

సరకు saraku. [Tel.] n. Esteem, regard, care, heed. లక్ష్యము, గౌరవము, "జననాయక నాకుజయముసరకేతలపక." M. VIII. i. 247.

సరకు or సరుకు saraku. [H.] n. An article for sale. అమ్మదగినవస్తువు. An article or thing, వస్తువు. సరకుగొను or సరకుచేయు saraku-gonu. v. a. To esteem, regard, care for, లక్ష్యముచేయు. "అక్కులపతియించుకరయసరకు గొనదవ్విధముగ." M. XIII. ii. 305.

సరగు saragu. [from Skt. స్రాక్.] n. Swiftness, speed. త్వర. సరగ or సరగున saraga. adv. Rapidly, soon, at once, quickly, with speed. శీఘ్రముగా, తెప్పున. "సాగిమొ క్కిలేచిసరగునసొంపలిప్పైకేలుదమ్మిదోయికేలు గొలిచి." B. X. iii. 12.

సరఘ saragha. [Skt.] n. A bee. మధుమక్షిక, తేనెటీగ.

సరటము saratamu. [Skt.] n. A lizard, chamelion. కృకలాసము, తొండ.

సరడు saradu. [from Skt. శరట్టు.] n. A kind of gold necklace worn by women.

సరణి sarani. [Skt.] n. A road, path, way, course. మార్గము, దోవ. A series, order, వరుస. "సరసగాంభీర్యమాధుర్య సరణి తెల్ప." Molli. i. 46.

సరత్ని saratni. [Skt.] n. A short cubit, from the elbow to the extremity of the closed fist. ముష్టిబద్ధహస్తము, పిడికిలిమూర.

సరదా or సర్దా saradā. [H. from Skt. శ్రద్ధ.] n. Fondness, affection.

సరదారు or సర్దారు saradaru. [H. from Skt. శరభాణి.] n. A *Sirdar*, a leader, a superior officer. అధికారి. "సీ॥ హారులుమ్మగ్గిన డిగ్గి యనివీకసరదార్లు సరదార్లుపడిన నోసరిలు వారలు." చంద్ర.

సరదు, సరుదు, సర్దు or సద్దు saradu. [Tel.] v. a. To divide equally. సమముగాపంచు. To arrange, క్రమముగానుంచు.

సరపణి, సరపిణి, సరపెణి or సరభణి sarapani. [Tel.] n. An ornament of gold chains of two or more folds. గొలుసు. "సరపణుల్ జలుల్లిడి పెంపగాబరెఁగ." A. v. 148. "చరణంపుసరపణి మొరపంబువిన్న దంతుల తోడ నెదురునింతులుకుదొలగి." ib. vi 125. టీ॥ పాదములయందలి గొలుసుయొక్క.

సరపువ్వులు or సరపూవులు sara-puvvulu. [Tel.] n. plu. Wreaths, garlands of flowers. పుష్పసరములు. "ఒంటికుచకేరపోచ కుకంటకింపక్రైతి తురిమెడుసరపూవులందరివలు." A. v. 111.

సరబడి sara-badi. [Skt. సరము+Tel. బడి.] n. Friendship. స్నేహము. A passage, an entrance, ద్వారము. "ఇనవంశమణియొద్దకు వ్వారి సరబడిగొలువుకట్టితివి." B. vi. 200.

సరభసము or సరభసముగ sa-rabhasamu. [Skt.] adv. With speed. వేగముగా, త్వరగా. "చనకారణమేమి సరభసంబిది నాతో వినుపింపుమనిన." P. i. 228. సరభసిల్లు or సరభసిలు sa-rabhasillu. v. n. To make haste. త్వరపడు. "పేరువిన్నప్పుడే దూరమైచను భూతచయములు తిరుగలనసరభసిల్లి." H. iii. 89.

సరమ sarama. [Skt.] n. The name of the wife of Ravana's brother. విభీషణునిపత్ని. A bitch, ఆడుకుక్క. The dog of the gods, వేలుపుకుక్క. [From Skt. శ్రమ.] n. Fatigue, trouble. శ్రమము. సరమగొను sarama-gonu. v. n. To be fatigued, to be troubled. శ్రమపడు.

సరము saramu. [Skt.] n. A pond, pool. కొలను. ఇచ్చోటిసరము శరముల్ నిచ్చల్ గొనవిడి." P. iii. 64. A row or string (of pearls), హారము. A wreath (of flowers), (పుష్ప) మాలిక, మాల, చేరు. [From Skt. స్వరు.] n. Breath. శ్వాసము, ముక్కుగాలి.

సరయు *sarayu.* [Skt.] n. The name of a river. సరయూనదము.

సరళము *saraḷamu.* [Skt.] adj. Straight, direct, level. Upright, honest, artless, simple, sincere, candid. తిన్నని, వంకరలేని, ముగ్ధమైన. సరళాచారము proper behaviour. n. (In gram.) a liquid consonant, a soft consonant, as గ, జ, డ, ద, బ. Also, a sort of pine, *Pinus longifolia.* సరళదేవదారు, తెల్లతెగడచెట్టు. H. iv. 19. **సరళత** *saraḷata.* n. Sincerity, uprightness, candour. ఆర్జవము, తిన్నదనము. **సరళముగా** *saraḷamu-ga.* adv. Honestly, uprightly, sincerely, candidly, simply. ముగ్ధముగా, తిన్నగా. **సరళి** *saraḷi.* n. The notes of the gamut in vocal music.

సరవడి *sara-vaḍi.* [Tel.] n. A litter, a palanquin, a sledge.

సరవి *saravi.* [Tel.] n. Regularity, order. వరుస, క్రమము. "వానలు సరవితో వర్షించె." Swa. vi. 127.

సరస *sarasa.* [Tel.] n. Nearness, proximity. సమీపము, దాపు. "సాకెకు చుక్కలసరసకు పోవు." Sar. D. 62.

సరసము *sa-rasamu.* [Skt.] adj. Juicy, tasty. Sapid, soft. Good, virtuous. Charming, agreeable, pleasant, elegant, sweet. Jocose, funny, merry. Easy, cheap. రసయుక్తమైన, సుస్వాదువైన, అందమైన, మనోహరమైన, పరిహాసమైన, లలితమైన; చవుకైన. సరసోక్తి a jocose, amusing or agreeable expression. n. A joke, jest, fun, merriment, amusement, sweetness, pleasantry. Cheapness. పరిహాసము, ఉల్లాసము, వినోదము, సారస్యము; చవుక. సరసమాడు to make jokes, to jest. సరసమాడవద్దు do not jest. సరసము విరసమవును a jest may turn to a strife. సరససల్లాపము jocose talk. ఇప్పుడు బంగారు సరసముగానున్నది now gold is cheap. ఎలుగు సరసము bear's play, a scuffle. "సరసాలంకారముల సౌరస్యమేపార." Ila. i. 2. **సరసత** *sa-rasata.* n. Delicacy, taste, sweetness, elegance, brilliancy of thought, beauty of composition. మాధుర్యము, సారస్యము, లాలిత్యము. ఆ పద్యముయొక్క సరసత the sweetness of the verse. "మేఘరాగాలు సరసతమీర దమ్ము సరళవిద్యుల్లతాదీర్ఘస్వరకటాక్ష." R. vi. 9. సరసత, అనగా సజలత్వము, లాలిత్యము. **సరసముగా** *sa-rasamu-ga.* adv. Jocosely, in joke, humorously. Sweetly, merrily. Cheaply. పరిహాసముగా, సారస్యముగా, ఉల్లాసముగా, చవుకగా. వెల సరసముగానుండినందున as the price was low. **సరసయతి** *sa-rasa-yati.* n. A rhyme not quite precise, but elegant. "అయమాలు చఛజఝశషసలు, సయసన్నుతవర్ణరేఫవసాపురుషగాన, స్త్రీయుయువిధియొండొంటికిని, శ్ర్యయముగవరులయ్యె." Bhima. 71. **సరసుడు** *sa-rasuḍu.* n. A gentleman, a man of good taste, an amiable or well behaved man; one easy of access. రసికుడు. **సరసురాలు** *sa-rasu-r-ālu.* n. A lady, a woman of elegant manners, రసికురాలు.

సరసర *sara-sara.* [సరగ+సరగ from Skt. స్రాక్.] adv. Quickly, rapidly, hastily. చిరచిర, శీఘ్రముగా, మిక్కిలి శీఘ్రముగా. "ద్వారస రసరగానివచ్చి సంభ్రమంబున." BD. iv. 1804.

సరసి, సరస్సు or **సరసు** *sarasi.* [Skt.] n. A pool, pond, lake. మడుగు. కొలను. **సరసి** or **సరసుడు** n. A phrase for an excellent or amiable man. రసికుడు. రసజ్ఞుడు. **సరసిజము** or **సరసీరుహము** *sarasi-jamu.* n. A lotus. పద్మము. **సరసిజనాభుడు, సరసిజాక్షుడు** or **సరసీరుహాక్షుడు** *sarasija-nabhuḍu.* n. Lit. the lotus-born; an epithet of Vishnu, విష్ణువు. **సరసిజభవుడు** *sarasija-bhavuḍu.* n. An epithet of Brahma, బ్రహ్మ. **సరస్వంతుడు** *sa-ras-vantuḍu.* An epithet of Kubera. కుబేరుడు. **సరస్వంతము** *saras-vantamu.* n. Neptune: the sea. సముద్రుడు.

సరసము Same as సరస్సు. (q. v.)

సరస్వతి *sa-ras-vati.* [Skt.] n. Speech. The goddess of speech. A certain river. వాక్కు, వాగ్దేవి, నదివిశేషము. సరస్వతిజెర్రి *sarasvati-jerri.* n. A centipede. కుటురా జము. సరస్వతిపురుగు a name of the shining green lizard with a red tail. రక్తపుచ్ఛి, నలికంఠసర్పము.

సరస్సు Same as సరసి (q. v.)

సరాగము *sa-rāgamu.* [Skt.] n. Friendship, intimacy. ఉల్లాస.

సరాతి *sarati.* [Tel.] n. A chamber, room, apartment. అంతర్గృహము. "మందటిసరాతిదాటి యుటుమంగలిగద్దియ కొంతసేపు సమ్మదమునకాలుస్త తెచి." Satya. iii. 5. A curtain round a tent, గుడారముచుట్టు చేర్పరిచినతెర.

సరాబు or షరాబు *sarabu.* [H.] n. A shroff, banker, money changer, cash-keeper.

సరాళము or సరళము *saralamu.* [Skt.] adj. Easy, free, clear. ధారాళమైన. సరాళముగా *saralamu-ga.* adv. Easily, freely, without difficulty. ధారాళముగా, తిన్నగా. నాకు పాడుటకు గొంతు సరాళముగానుండలేదు my throat is not clear enough to sing.

సరాసరి *sara-sari.* [Tel. సరి+సరి.] n. An average. సగటు, సమత్వము. ఆ పద్దులకు సరాసరి చెయ్యి make an average of the items. adj. Average. సగమైన. ఆ గుర్రములకు సరాసరి వెలయేమి what is the average price of the horses? ఆ గుర్రములకు సరాసరివెల మున్నూరు రూపాయలు అవును the average price of these horses is three hundred rupees. సరాసరి or సరాసరిగా adv. Equally, alike, on an average. సగటుగా. అన్నీ సరాసరిని ఎంతకు ఇస్తావు for what will you sell all together?

సరి *sari.* [from Skt. సదృశ.] n. The end. అంతము. Similarity, likeness. సామ్యము, సమానము, సమము. Propriety, fitness, యుక్తము. [From Skt. సరః.] n. A garland, wreath. హారము. See also సరము. ఆ వంశము అతనితో సరి that family terminates with him. సరిలేనిమాణిక్యము a matchless gem. నెలసరి at the end of the month. ఆ దినముసరి up to that day. నీకు నాకు సరి there is an end of everything between us. సరిగానివారు those who are not equals. "సరిగాని వారితో సరసమాడెడువాని" (Kālahas. §. 66.) he who takes liberties with such as are not his equals. సరిగానిపని improper behaviour or conduct. సరికిసరి tit for tat. గోధుములు బియ్యానికి సరికిసరి ఇస్తారు they barter wheat for an equal quantity of rice. సరికిసరి చేసినాడు he repaid them according to what they had done. సరి adj. Equal, like. సమము, తుల్యమైన. Just, right, proper, fit, correct, suitable, యుక్తమైన, తగిన. Corresponding to. Even, level, not odd, మిట్టపల్లములులేని. Ended, finished, సమాప్తము. అతనికి సరిలేడు he has no equal. రాత్రి అయినా సరే పగలు అయినా సరే be it day or be it night. ఇది సరికాదు this is not right. ఈ ఉత్సవము నేటితో సరి this feast is finished with this day. adv. Equally. సమానముగా, సరిగా. Fully, పూర్ణముగా. "జలధి తో జలధియు సరితూగదు." DRY. 2224. "సరిబల్యముచుకుబల్కు." T. iii. 143. సరి (interj.) Well! Yes! very well! very good! Aha! Aha! Oh! బాగాయెను; అంగీకారార్థము. సరికట్టు *sari-kattu.* v. n. To be equal or similar. దృష్టాంతము. v. a. To attempt, యత్నించు. See సరిపడు below. సరికడచు *sari-kadatsu.* v. n. To exceed, excel. మించుమించు, మీరు, అతిక్రమించు. సరిగా *sari-ga.* adv. Equally, abreast, properly, rightly, correctly, in good order, completely, fully. సమముగా, వేరుగా, పొందుగా, యుక్తముగా, న్యాయముగా, క్రమముగా, సంపూర్ణముగా. ఆ రెండు పల్లకీలు సరిగా వచ్చుచుండెను the two palanquins were coming on abreast. సరిగెల్పులు sari-gelpulu. n. Quits (at dice or games), సమానమైన జయములు. సరిగొను sari-gonu. v. a. To resemble. సమానమగు. To kill, destroy. చంపు, రూపుమాపు. M. VII. iv. 277. సీ॥ "సరియన్న విరిపొన్న సరిగొన్న గరిమచేనంధి రమగునాభిగాంచుదాని." T. iv. 62. సరిచేయు sari-chēyu. v. a. To arrange or put in order, to put straight, to level or make even. To complete, end or finish. To equalize, క్రమపరచు, వంకరలేకుండా చేయు, మిట్టపల్లములులేకుండాచేయు, ముగించు, సమానము చేయు. To ruin, నాశముచేయు. సరిచూచు sari-tsūtsu. v. a. To compare, review, collate. సంప్రతించు, సరిగానున్నదజూచు. సరితూగు sari-tūgu. v. a. To counterbalance, to be equal in weight, to be equal. సమానమగు. సరిపడు, సరితాకు or సరికట్టు sari-paḍu. v. n. To be equal, fit, suit, agree. To be on good terms. To be complete, to be finished, expended, exhausted. సమానమగు, జతపడు, అనుకూలమగు, పొసగు, యుక్తమగు, అయిపోవు. ఆ బియ్యము సరిపడిపోయినవి the rice is all done. మీకు సరిపడితే ఉంచుకొండి keep it if you like it. మేమంటే సరిపడక not being on good terms with us. సరిపడని discontented. సరిపుచ్చు or సరిపెట్టు sari-putstsu. v. a. To equalize, సమముచేయు. To finish, end, complete, consume. ముగించు, కాజేయు, కారాంతముచేయు. సరిపోవు sari-pōvu. v. n. To be equal, become equal, సమానమగు. To fit, suit, agree. To be finished or terminated. To be expended, spent. To be ruined, or destroyed, అయిపోవు, వ్యయమైపోవు, నశించు. To be reconciled, సమాధానమగు. A. vi. 90. నోటికి సరిపోయినట్లు మాట్లాడినాడు he said everything that came to his tongue. అవి నీకు సరిపోవు these will suit you. నీవు తిట్టినదానికిని నేను కొట్టినదానికిని సరిపోయినది the blows I have given are a fair payment for your abuse. ఆ బియ్యము ఆ తపేలాకు సరిపోయినవి the rice was just enough to fill the vessel. సరిపొద్దు or సరిప్రొద్దు sari-poddu. n. Midnight, అర్ధరాత్రి. P. iii. 45. సరిబిత్తరము sari-bittaramu. n. A kind of wrestling. మల్లబంధవిశేషము. సరిబేసులు sari-bēsulu. n. A kind of game played by boys, పిల్లకాయలు ఆడే ఒక ఆట. "గుజ్జనగూళ్ళు ముచ్చిల్లు గోలిపెట్టెలాటలు, సరిబేసులింకా తలాదిగాశైశవక్రీడలాడి." Vish. vii. 212. సరియగు sari-y-agu. v. n. To become equal, సమానమగు, to be destroyed, నశించు. సరియైన sari-y-aina. adj. Equal, like; just, right, proper, fit. Corresponding to. Level, straight; even, not odd. సమమైన, యుక్తమైన, తగిన, మాటిదైన, ఈడైన, అనుమమైన, మిట్టపల్లములు లేని. సరిలేని sari-lēni. adj. Matchless, unequalled. అసమానమైన. సరివచ్చు sari-vatstsu. v. n. To match, be alike, సమానమగు. సరిసమానము sari-samānamu. (a pleonasm.) n. Equality. సమము, తనకు సరిసమానము ఎవరులేరనుకొనుచున్నాడు he imagines that he has no equal. సరేగదా sarē-gada. interj. Very well!

సరించు sarintsu. [Skt.] v. n. To go. వెళ్లు. "సరించెవెంబడిగా." Vaijayanti. iii. 51.

సరిక sarika. [Skt.] n. A necklace of a hundred strands. నూరుపేటలహారము.

సరిగ or సరిగె sariga. [from Skt. స్రక్.] n. A necklace, హారము. Gold lace, silver lace, &c. జెలతారు. సరిగంచుచీర a cloth with gold ends, a cloth trimmed with lace. సరిపట్టు sari-pattu. n. A sort of silk. ఒక విధమైన పట్టుబట్ట. BD. iii. 104.

సరిత్ or **సరిత్తు** *sarit*. [Skt.] n. A river. నది, ఏరు. **సరిత్పతి** *sarit-pati*. n. The lord of rivers, i.e., the sea or ocean. సముద్రుడు.

సరిపణి, సరిపెణి or **సరిపెణ** *saripaṇi*. [Tel. సరి+పెన.] n. A gold or silver chain. బంగారులోనగువానిగొలుసు.

సరియ or **సరి** *sariya*. [Tel.] n. A crack. పగులు, సందు.

సరియించు *sariyintsu*. [Tel.] v. a. To supply, to fill (a lamp) with ghee or oil. అఖండమునకు నూనె సిద్ధముచేయు.

సరీసృపము *sarī-sripamu*. [Skt.] n. A serpent, snake, reptile, సర్పము, పాము.

సరుకు or **సరకు** *saruku*. [H.] n. Wares, goods, commodities, merchandise. వస్తువులు, దినుసులు. సరుకుగాచెల్లించు to pay in kind. See సరకు.

సరుగు *sarugu*. [Tel.] v. n. To increase, grow, improve. పెరుగు, వర్ధిల్లు.

సరుగుడు *sarugudu*. [Tel.] n. A hurdle, sledge, drag. A platform. తడక, తేలుగుడు, కంపకట్టవేసి యీడ్చుకొనివచ్చే చక్రములులేని తడిక.

సరుడు *sarudu*. [Tel.] n. An arrow. బాణము. A blunt arrow, గరిలేనిబాణము.

సరుదు *sarudu*. [Tel.] n. A boundary, ఎల్ల, మేర, సరిహద్దు.

సరుదు or **సర్దు** *sarudu*. [Tel.] v. a. To make even, or level. To eke out or shift with; to make a little go a good way. To arrange, సమముచేయు, చాలీచాలక ఉండే దానిని నలుగురికి సమముగాపంచిపెట్టు, క్రమపరచు. **సరుదుకొను** *sarudu-konu*. v. n. To eke out, or shift with: to make a little go a good way. To make room among themselves, to move a little farther; to get out of the way. To arrange, settle, చాలీచాలక ఉండేదానిని కలుకొంచెము తీసుకొను, ఒత్తు, తొలగు, వారిలోవారు సరుదుకొన్నారు they settled it among themselves. దాన్ని వారే సరుదుకొన్నారు they shared it among themselves. వరద సరుదుకొన్నది it is full tide. కృష్ణ బెజవాడకట్టున సరుదుకొనిపోతున్నది the river Krishna runs by Bezvada.

సరేసు *sarēsu*. [H.] n. A kind of gum, rosin. వజ్రము, వజ్జరము.

సరోజము or **సరోరుహము** *sarō-jamu*. [Skt.] n. A lotus. పద్మము. **సరోజిని** *sarōjini*. n. A bed of lilies, a pond covered with lotus flowers, తామరకొలను. A lotus, తామర.

సరోవరము *sarō-varamu*. [Skt.] n. A pond. దివ్యమైనకొలను.

సర్క *sarka*. [Tel.] n. A kind of cattle disease.

సర్కారు *sarkāru*. [H.] n. The government, Circar. దివానము, దొరతనమువారు. సర్కారు ఉద్యోగము Government employment.

సర్గ or **సర్గము** *sarga*. [Skt.] n. A chapter. అధ్యాయము. **సర్గము** *sargamu*. n. Creation, సృష్టి. Nature, natural property or disposition, స్వభావము. Certainty, నిశ్చయము. "ప్రజాసర్గము." Vish. vi. 196.

సర్జము or **సర్జకము** *sarjamu*. [Skt.] n. The Sal tree, *Shorea robusta*. Also, the resinous exudation of the Sal-tree. సాలవృక్షము. ఏగిచెట్టు, వేగిసచెట్టు. **సర్జరసము** *sarja-rasamu*. n. The resinous exudation of the Sal-tree, resin. యక్షధూపము.

సర్దా or **సరదా** *sardā*. [H. from Skt. శ్రద్ధ.] n. Interest, zeal. ఆసక్తి.

సర్దారుడు or **సర్దారు** *sardārudu*. [H.] n. A chief, captain, leader, ruler. అధికారి, పెద్ద. See సరదారు.

సర్దు Same as సరుదు (q. v.)

సర్పము *sarpamu*. [Skt. Cognate with Eng. 'serpent.'] n. A serpent, snake. పాము. సర్పయాగము a serpent sacrifice.

సర్పరాజు sarpa-rādsu. n. The king of the serpents. వాసుకి, శేషుడు. సర్పాక్షిచెట్టు a kind of tree.

సర్పి sarpi. [Skt.] n. Oil, butter, clarified butter, ghee. ఘృతము, నెయ్యి. Also, a kind of disease.

సర్రున or జర్రున sarru-na. [Tel. (anuk.)] adv. Quickly, as in slipping down.

సర్వము sarvamu. [Skt.] pron. All, the whole. సమస్తము, అంతయు. adj. All, whole, complete, universal, entire, సకలము, అఖిలము. సర్వంసహా sarvam-saha. n. Lit. the all-sustaining, i. e., the earth, భూమి. సర్వంకసప్రజ్ఞగలవాడు a Jack of all trades. సర్వజనీనము sarva-janīnamu. adj. Pertaining to all men, సకలజనులకు సంబంధమైన; agreeable to all men, సమస్తజనులకు హితమైన. సర్వజిత్తు sarva-jittu. n. The name of a Telugu year. సర్వజ్ఞ sarva-gnya. adj. All knowing, omniscient, all-wise. సమస్తము తెలిసిన. సర్వజ్ఞుడు sarva-gnyuḍu. n. An omniscient being. సమస్తము తెలిసినవాడు. సర్వతాపనుడు sarva-tāpanuḍu. n. One who fires all beings; an epithet of Manmatha, మన్మథుడు. సర్వతోముఖము sarvatō-mukhamu. n. Water. నీళ్లు. The sky, heaven, ఆకాశము. Vasu. iv. 13. సర్వతోముఖుడు sarvatō-mukhuḍu. n. A name of Brahma or Siva. బ్రహ్మ, శివుడు. The soul, ఆత్మ. సర్వత్ర sarvatra. adv. Everywhere, in all places, always, at all times. అంతటా, ఎల్లప్పుడు. సర్వత్రయిచ్చు give everywhere. సర్వథా sarvathā. adv. In all ways, by all means, assuredly, at any rate, అన్నివిధాల. సర్వదా sarvadā. adv. Always, at all times. ఎల్లప్పుడు సర్వదుంబాలా sarva-dumbālā. [H.] n. A deed exempting land from all rent. సర్వధారి sarva-dhāri. [Skt.] n. The name of a Telugu year. సర్వనామము [sa]rva-nāmamu. n. A pronoun. సర్వభక్షకుడు sarva-bhakshakuḍu. n. The devourer of all things, an epithet of fire. అగ్ని. సర్వమంగళ sarva-mangala. n. She who is all blessed, most holy or auspicious; an epithet of Parvati, పార్వతి. సర్వమాన్యము sarva-mānyamu. n. Free tenure, land exempt from tax. ఇనాము. సర్వలింగి sarva-lingi. [Skt.] n. A heretic, or free-thinker. పాషండుడు. సర్వశుద్ధిగా sarva-ṣuddhi-ga. adv. Utterly, entirely, every thing being taken into account. సర్వపరిష్కారముగా. వాడికి మాకు సర్వశుద్ధిగా లెక్కలుతీరినవి the accounts between us are finally settled. సర్వస్వము sarvasvamu. n. Entire property, the whole of one's possessions. యావత్తు సొత్తు. సర్వస్వుడు sarvasvuḍu. n. One who possesses all the property, the sole lord. యావదాస్తిగలవాడు. "వదనవనజన్మాంతకు సర్వస్వుడనుచు." Vasu. ii. 54 టీ యావద్ధనముగలవాడనుచు. Swa. vi. 25. సర్వాంగీణము sarv-āng-īṇamu. adj. Appertaining to all the limbs; thorough, entire. యావదంగములసంబంధమైన. "సర్వాంగీణములైన మైమరువులంకావల్లకర్పూరపాంసులు." Parij. iv. 98. సర్వాగ్రహారము sarv-agra-hāramu. n. A village granted to Brahmins free from all tax. పన్నులేకుండా బ్రాహ్మణులకిచ్చిన గ్రామము. సర్వాత్మకము sarv-ātmakamu. adj. All pervading. సర్వవ్యాపకమైన. సర్వాత్మకత్వము sarv-ātmaka-tvamu. n. Omnipresence, the state of pervading all things. సర్వాంతర్యామిత్వము. "అనిలుండేకీభవించినవట్ల నీవు కలసినపిత్రింతుసర్వాత్మకత్వమెప్ప." B. viii. 444. సర్వాత్మనా sarv-ātma-nā. adv. In all ways, by all means, at any rate. సర్వత్ర, కాకేమి, అన్నివిధాల. సర్వాధికారి sarv-adhi-kāri. n. The ruler of all, అన్నిటికియజమానుడు. సర్వేశుడు or సర్వేశ్వరుడు sarv-ēsuḍu. The Lord of all, the Supreme Being, దేవుడు.

సర్వల or **శర్వల** *sarvala*. [Skt.] n. A short spear or lance, an iron spit. చిల్లకోల, తోమరము, శేల.

సర్షపము *sarshapamu*. [Skt.] n. Mustard-seed. ఆవాలు.

సల *sala*. [Tel.] n. A bund or bank raised across a stream to draw off its waters into a different channel.

సలక *salaka*. [Tel.] n. A small sack. One eighth of a putti or 2½ tooms (తూములు). చిన్నగోనె, ఇర్దున్నిరిస. "తొలగ నలాకుకళంక్షములు తండికమ్ముల్ సలకల్ దడేల్ కుతూహలములు." H v. 111.

సలగ, సలుగ or **సలువ** *salaga*. [Tel.] n. or interj. So much! A word used in measuring grain, &c.; one lot of 20 or 100 from which a new reckoning begins. The handful of grain, &c., put down as a mark of reckoning. A fee rated at 16 or 18 మానికలు to the putti, or two rupees per kuchchela (కుచ్చెల). ధాన్యము కొలవడములో కొత్తలెక్క మొదలు పెట్టునప్పుడు అనేమాట, అప్పుడు దోసిలితో ఎత్తి కుప్పగా పోసేధాన్యము, పుట్టికింత అని యిచ్చేరుసుము. నూటికిపొడిచిసల గంటాడు he kills one hundred and cries "That's one lot!"

సలగ, సలగపార or **సలవ** *salaga*. [Tel.] n. A kind of spade or hoe. ఒకవిధమైన పార, పారచిప్ప.

సలవాడి or **సలాడి** *salavadi*. [Tel.] n. A beadle or servant of the Chetty or head-man (పెద్దసెట్టి). A crier, పదిమందికి చావు సమాచారము తెలియజేసేపనివాడు.

సలసల *sala-sala*. [Tel. (anuk. of boiling.)] adv. Loudly, aloud, audibly. కళకళ. "సలసల గ్రాగెడు తైలము." G. vi. 128.

సలహా *salaha*. [H.] n. Advice, counsel.

సలాక or **శలాక** *salaka*. [from Skt. శలాక.] n. A thin bar or rod, a ramrod, the rib of an umbrella, one of the bars of a cage, a slip of bamboo, a probe. A pin or peg, a small stake, a fibrous stick, a fibrous stick used as a brush or pencil. లోహదండము, కమ్మి, పుడక, తూలిక, కుందనము చెక్కే ఆయుధము. కనకశలాక a slender rod of gold. పుంటిలో సలాకవేయు to probe a wound. సలాకపరీక్ష, probing, a critical examination.

సలాకు *salaku*. [Tel.] n. Base metal mixed with gold or silver (a term used by gold-smiths.)

సలాడి See సలవాడి.

సలాపము *salapamu*. [Tel.] n. A pearl fishery.

సలాము *salamu*. [H.] n. A Salaam, a bow or salutation. నమస్కారము. నా సలాములు చెప్పు give my compliments.

సలి *sali*. [Tel.] n. Noise. సందడి. "కరి సలి చేప్పుడు లేదమ్మెయి దొలగిన సైన్యంబు." ఉ. హరి. iii.

సలించు Same as చలించు (q. v.)

సలికము *salikamu*. [Tel.] adj. Small, petty, thin; trembling, అల్పము.

సలిగ *saliga*. [H.] n. Patronage, protection, interest, influence. ప్రాపు, అండ, ఆశ్రయము. "చూతము రాచెలిసలిగ భయంకేలరమ్మ." UH. iv. 152.

సలితము *salitamu*. [Skt.] n. Dismissal from service. కొలువునుండి తీసివేయుట.

సలిలము *salilamu*. [Skt.] n. Water. జలము.

సలుగ or **సలువ** Same as సలగ (q. v.)

సలుగు or **సలువు** *salugu*. [from Skt. శల్యా.] n. A porcupine, ఏదుపంది. "చిల్లరసలుగు లంబిల్లులంజొల్లరంబులపొగనిచ్చి గమికి వెనుకయై." Swa. iv. 51.

సలుగుడు or **చేలుగుడు** *salugudu*. [Tel.] n. A sledge, a vehicle without wheels.

సలుపు, సరుపు, చలుపు or **చేపుపు** *salupu*. [Tel.] n. A throb, a pang, a shooting pain. పోటు. సలుపు or సళుపు v. n. To throb or shoot as a painful boil, to ache, పోట్లుపొడుచు. సలపరము, సలపరింత, సలుపరింత or సళుపరింత salaparamu. n. A pang, throb, pain, ache. సళుపు. సలపరించు, సలుపరించు or సళుపరించు salaparintsu. v. n. To throb or shoot as a boil, to give a shooting pain, as a boil, to ache, సళుపు.

సలుపు salupu. [Tel.] v. a. To do, make, perform, practise. చేయు. "సరసులతోఁ జెల్మి సలుపవలెను." T. ii. 72. "చిందులు సలుపు." to skip about. N. ix. 241. పొత్తుసలుపు to contract friendship. అజ్ఞాతవాసంబుసలిపితిమి we lived in concealment, or incognito. M. V. iii. 272. వ్రతముసలుపు to perform or fulfil a vow. సలిపించు salipintsu. v. a. To get done, to cause to be done or made. చేయించు.

సలువ Same as సలిగె (q. v.)

సలువు Same as సలుగు (q. v.)

సల్లకి sallaki. [Skt.] n. The Gum Olibanum tree, *Boswellia thurifera*. అందుగుచెట్టు.

సల్లాపము or సల్లపనము sal-lapamu. [Skt.] n. Conversation, talk. పరస్పర సంభాషణము. "వాక్యవిస్తరచతురత్వమేర్పడగ సల్లపనం బొనరించునరిత్తోఁ గా." M. iv. i. 197. సల్లాపించు sal-lap-intsu. v. n. To talk or converse. పరస్పరము సంభాషించు.

సల్లోపిల్లో అనియుండు sallō-pillō-ani-y-undu. [Tel.] v. n. To be on good terms. కలిసిమెలిసియుండు. సల్లోపిల్లో అని యుండేవాడు a facetious fellow, a jocose man. కలియగలుపుగా నుండేవాడు, సరసుడు.

సళించు salintsu. [Tel.] v. n. To grieve. దుఃఖించు.

సళుపు See సలుపు.

సళుపరించు See under సలుపు.

సళ్లు or సడలు sallu. [Tel.] v. n. To become slack or loose. సడలు, జారు. వాని ఒళ్లునిండా సళ్లిపోయినది his constitution is much broken down. నడుముసళ్లు to be gone in the loins. "శబరకాంతల కట్టుసళ్లి చెట్టు." Swa. iv. 115. n. Looseness, slackness, సడలు. సళ్లించు sallintsu. (for సడలించు.) v. a. To loosen, slacken. సడలు చేయు A. v. 161. See సడలు.

సవ sava. [Tel.] n. A trace. జాడ. సవసవ sava-sava. n. A slight trace. చాయ. సవసవ, సవసవగా or సవసవలుగా adv. Slightly, indistinctly, half and half. కొద్దికొద్దిగా, జాడజాడగా, చాయచాయగా. "నాడెప్పట్లంబు సవసవగా దెలిసి." Swa. v. 32.

సవడి Same as సవ్వడి (q. v.)

సవతి or సవతాలు sa-vati. [from Skt. సపత్నీ.] n. A fellow wife. సవతికొడుకు a step son. సవతితల్లి a step mother, మారుతల్లి, మారటతల్లి, మారుటతల్లి. సవతిపోరు a quarrel between two wives.

సవతు savatu. [from Skt. సమతా.] n. Equality, likeness, similarity. సామ్యము. adj. Equal, similar. సమానము. "అర్ధంపు మెరుగువాలారుగన్నవమాడ్కి క్రొవ్వనమందనకాంతి సవతుగాగ." A. v. 70. టీ॥ సవతుగాగ, సామ్యమునుపొందగాను. "ఎవ్వరుసవతిందునందు బలవంతుడుపోవిధి." P. ii. 31.

సవదండవల sava-danda-vala. [Tel.] n. A kind of net or snare వాగురాభేదము. Kalahas. iii. 62.

సవదరించు sava-darintsu. [from Skt. ధరించు.] v. a. To wear, put on, hold. ధరించు, వహించు, తాల్చు. "సరిగనిగ్గుగేల నందియల్ సవదరించి." N. vii. 135. To bear, endure, సహించు. సవదరించుటకు దొల్లుజాలరగోళముననందు నవమముపాపనాసనంబుదాక." కాశీ. iv. సవదరి sava-dari. n. A ship's bowsprit.

సవనము *savanamu.* [Skt.] n. A sacrifice. యజ్ఞము. Bathing preparatory to a sacrifice. స్నానము. సవనవిరోధి *savana-virōdhi.* n. The sacrifice-disturber, an epithet of Siva. శివుడు. "సవనవిరోధి కెంగిలిప్రసాదము గొంకకయిచ్చు టొప్పునే." Chenn. ii. 12. సవము *savamu.* n. A sacrifice. అధ్వరము, యజ్ఞము. The honey of flowers, మకరందము. Clear toddy, కల్లుతేట.

సవము Same as సగము (q. v.)

సవర *savara.* [Tel.] adj. Beautiful, fine. చక్కనైన. Level, smooth, చదునైన, నును పైన. సవరచేయు *savara-chēyu.* v. a. To smoothe, to set right, చక్కచేయు. To level, చదునుచేయు. సవరణ, సవరణము, సవరన or సవరనము *savarana.* n. Beauty, elegance, neatness. అందము, సౌమ్యము. Correction, setting right, చక్కపెట్టుట. Adornment, వాహనాద్యలంకరణము. "హయములుచక్కదనంబు నొసపరిసెరకీని సవరణ చెలువంబు సరసకీతి." H. v. 101. Articles or implements for any ceremony or business. సామగ్రి, సరంజామా, పరికరము. "తమ తమ చతురంగ బలంబులకు సవరణంబులుసంఘటింపంజొడంగిన." M. IX. i. 109. సవరణ, సవరన, సవరని, సవరైన or సవరనైన *savarana.* adj. Elegant, neat, graceful. అందమైన. "ఈసవరణరైనమాటలు ప్రసంగము చేసిరిమానినీతిలో." Vish. v. 352. సవరణించు or సవరణచేయు *savaran-intsu.* v. a. To adorn. అలంకరించు. To correct, put in order, చక్కపెట్టు. సవరదనము *savara-danamu.* n. Beauty, elegance, neatness. అందము, సొగసు. "సవరదనంబు లత్కపరాలంచేయు." Sar D. 122. సవరణముగా or సవరణగా *savaranamu-gā.* adv. In good order, in trim. క్రమముగా, చక్కగా. సవరించు, సవరించు or సవరచ్చు *savarintsu.* v. a To adorn, అలంకరించు. To adjust, trim, set right, prepare, కూర్చు. చక్కబరుచు. To rectify, correct, దిద్దు, చక్కపెట్టు, కుదుర్చు, బాగుచేయు. To do, accomplish, చేయు. To bear, carry, తాల్చు. "బహుసాధనంబులు సవరించుకొని మహాటవిని ఁించు." M. XII. iii. 291. "కొప్పుసవరించు." S. iii. 390. సవరింత *savarinta.* n. Trimming as hair or clothes, setting right, arranging. సవరిల్లు *savarillu.* v. n. To be fine, beautiful, or in good order, అందము. సవరు *savaru.* n. Beauty, grace, elegance. అందము, సొగసు. "సవరైననారవాలబవిరి కమ్ములనిత్తునవికీసు మనసురావంటిలేని." H. ii. 42. సవరుపరచు *savaru-parutsu.* v. a. To trim, adjust, set right. దిద్దు.

సవరము *savaramu.* [from Skt. చమరము.] n. The hair of the yak or Tartarian ox, చమరమృగము, which is used by women a queue. False hair used by women. పట్టు సవరము an imitation of this made in silk. సవరపుకుప్పె the gold buckle worn by women on this false hair, చమరమృగసంబంధమైనకుప్పె. సవరపుమేకము *savarapu-mekamu.* n. The yak or Tartarian ox. చమరమృగము.

సవరలు or సవరవాండ్రు *savaralu.* [Tel.] n. plu. The name of a certain tribe in the Vizagapatam District; also, called Thugs or Phaseegars. ఒకవిధమైన చెంచువాండ్లు, ఠగ్గులు, ఫాసీగర్లు. సవరాటకము *savarāṭakamu.* n. The assembly of the Savara people. సవరవాండ్రసంఘము.

సవాయి *savāyi.* [Tel.] n. A venereal disease or eruption.

సవారచేప *savāra-chēpa.* [Tel.] n. A species of Ophi-cephalus or snake headed fish.

సవారీ *savārī.* [from Skt. స్వారి.] n. Riding; any mode of conveyance; a palanquin. గాలిసవారి or గాలిసవారి a walk, an airing. గుర్రపుసవారి riding.

సవాలు *savālu.* [H.] n. A question, proposal. అడ్డసవాళ్లు cross questions, cross examination.

సవి savi. [Tel.] conj. Saying. ఇతి, అని. "పవిపాపివిడువిడువనిభక్తుడ్పైదనర్భు." ABA. iii. 107. "త్వలాదవి పిండీకృతలాఠీతల సవితదాసంబుల్." A. i. 108.

సవిత or సవితృడు savita. [Skt.] n. The sun. సూర్యుడు. A father, తండ్రి. సవిత్రి savitri. n. A mother. తల్లి

సవిధము sa-vidhamu. [Skt.] adj. Near, proximate. సమీపము. R. v. 98.

సవిస్తరము sa-vistaramu. [Skt.] adj. Full, complete. సవిస్తరముగా in full, at length.

సవ్యము savyamu. [Skt.] adj. Left, left hand. వామము, ఎడమ. అపసవ్యము the right. సవ్యకరము the left hand. జెందెమును సవ్యముగా వేసుకొనియుండినాడు he wore the Brahminical thread on the proper shoulder, i.e., the left shoulder. జెందెమును అపసవ్యముగా వేసుకొని యుండినాడు he wore the thread on the wrong shoulder, i. e., the right shoulder. "సవ్యదిశగాత్రిరుమునపసవ్యగతింజాలెంబునవాయం బు తోనిచ్చుచు." Swa. iv. 159. "పిరుకావు లంకట్టినీళ్లదర్భలచేత సవ్యాపసవ్యతల్ చేల్లువారు." Rama Stava. Raj. ii. 74. సవ్యముగా savyamu-ga. adv. Towards the left hand. ఎడముగా. సవ్యసాచి savya-sachi. n. Ambidexter; a title of Arjuna, because he used both hands equally well. అర్జునుడు. సవ్యేష్ఠుడు savyê-shthudu. n. A charioteer, who stands on the proper side, that is, on the left. రథసారథి.

సవ్వడి or సవడి savvadi. [Tel. సవ+వడి.] n. A trace. జాడ.

ససి sasi. [Tel.] n. Soundness, beauty, health, good. బాగు, కుదురు, ఆరోగ్యము. [From Skt. సస్యము.] n. A crop. పరిపండు తైనపంటు. A sprout or shoot, మొలక. "అపమాయముభునిక్తిసమలక్షనడితుల్లిగాకుంజవితతిముగ్గలుతినర్భు." Vaij. i. 56. adj. Good, sound, proper, well, healthy, handsome, బాగైన, కుదురుగానుండే, ఆరోగ్యముగల. "ససిమెరుంగుమొత్తంబుల." Swa. iii. 38. ససేమిరా what is the good of this? ససిగా sasi-ga. adj. Well, properly, in good health. In good order or repair. బాగుగా, క్రమముగా, కుదురుగా. ఆమెకు ఒళ్లు ససిగానుం డలేదు she is unwell or ill. ససువు sasuvu. n. A sprout or shoot. మొలక. "ససువులగ్రొన్ని సువులనడిగి." R. iv. 6. adj. Mild, meek, సాధువు.

సస్కాని sas-kâni. [Tel.] n. A coin worth about eight pies. రెండుడబ్బులనాణెము.

సస్యము sasyamu. [Skt.] n. Produce, a crop, grain. వ్రీహిధాన్యాదిఫలము, పరిపండు తైనపంటు. సస్నెము or ససి sasemu. [from సస్యము.] Same as సస్యము (q. v.)

సహ saha. [Skt.] n. The earth. భూమి. సహా or సహ adv. With, together with, even, also, too. కూడ, సహితము. ప్రస్తుతమునహా even now, and at this very time, and now too. సహకారము saha-kâramu. n. A grafted mango. తియ్యమామిడి చెట్టు. సహకారి or సహకారుడు saha-kâri. n. An assistant, one who helps, సహాయుడు. సహకృతుడు saha-kritudu. n. One who is assisted. ఉపకృతుడు. సహగమనము saha-gamanamu. (sometimes corrupted into సాగమానము.) n. Lit: going with. A widow accompanying her deceased husband, i.e., the immolation of herself on his pyre. Suttee. మగనిశవముతో కూడా దగలబడిపోవడము. సహచరత్వము saha-charatvamu. n. The being a companion. మిత్రత్వము. "విహీనసహచరత్వంబు వికతాయుధత్వంబువావా నాభావంబులొందితి." M. ix. ii. 97. సహచరి saha-chari. n. A female companion or attendant. స్నేహితురాలు, చెలియ. A wife, భార్య. సహచరుడు

saha-charuḍu. n. An attendant, companion, follower, compeer, mate. కూడ తిరుగువాడు, స్నేహితుడు. సహజ *saha-ja*. n. A sister. తోడబుట్టువు. సహజము *saha-jamu*. adj. Lit. Born with. Innate, inherent, natural, proper, true. స్వభావము, కూడబుట్టిన. సహజరేఫ the "common" ర as distinguished from the obsolete ఱ. n. Nature, స్వభావము. Truth, propriety, justice, నిజము, న్యాయము. "సహజమగురాయమం డిసహజంబువలుకక సకలపాతమాడుపాతకుడు." Vema. 1990. సహజన్ముడు or సహజాడు *saha-janmuḍu*. n. A brother. తోడబుట్టిన వాడు. సహదేవిచెట్టు *saha-dēvi-cheṭṭu*. n. Tamarisc; a thorny plant growing in deserts, and fed upon by camels, *Capparis aphylla*. కరీరము, వెలుతురుచెట్టు, దేవ గంధ. H. iv. 12. సహధర్మిణి *saha-dharmiṇi*. n. A lawful wife. ధర్మపత్ని, అగ్నిసాక్షికముగా పెండ్లాడినపెండ్లాము. సహపఙ్క్తిభోజనము, సహభోజనము or సహపఙ్క్తి *saha-pangti-bhōjanamu*. n. Eating together, dining at one table. కూడా భోజనముచేయడము. వారికిని మాకును సహపఙ్క్తిలేదు they and we do not eat together. సహపాఠి *saha-pāṭhi*. n. A fellow-student. కూడా చదివెడి వాడు. సహవాసము *saha-vāsamu*. n. Association, intercourse, friendship. స్నేహము, కూడియుండుట. సహవాసయోగ్యుడుకాడు he is not fit to associate with. సహా *saha*. adv. With, together with, even, too, also, సహితము, కూడా. సహాధ్యాయుడు *sah-ādhyāyuḍu*. n. A fellow-student, brother disciple. సహపాఠి. M. I. i. 216. సహోదరుడు *sah-ōdaruḍu*. n. A brother. తోడబుట్టినవాడు. సహోదరి *sah-ōdari*. n. A sister. సోదరి.

సహనము *sahanamu*. [Skt.] n. Patience, endurance, resignation, quiet, leniency. ఓర్పు. తాలిమి.

సహస్రము *sahasramu*. [Skt.] n. A thousand. వెయ్యి. Also, indefinitely used for many, or any great number, అనేకము. సహస్రదంష్ట్రము *sahasra-damshṭramu*. n. A thousand-toothed animal, i. e., a whale. వేయికోరలుగలచేప, పాఠీనము. సహస్రనామములు *sahasra-nāmamulu*. n. A thousand names. సహస్రనామపూజ a hymn wherein a god is addressed by all his titles. సహస్రపత్రము *sahasra-patramu*. n. A lotus. కమలము. సహస్రపాదుడు or సహస్రాంశువు *sahasra-pāduḍu*. n. Lit. the thousand-rayed, i. e., the sun. సూర్యుడు. సహస్రాక్షుడు *sahasr-ākshuḍu*. n. Lit. the thousand-eyed; an epithet of Indra, ఇంద్రుడు.

సహాయము *sahāyamu*. [Skt.] adj. Auxiliary. ఉపబలమైన. సహాయము, సహాయత or సాహాయ్యము n. Aid, help, assistance, succour, తోడు. నాకు దోవలో సహాయము దొరకలేదు I had no assistance on the way. సహాయముచేయు to aid, to assist. సహాయముగా *sahāyamu-gā*. adv. As an assistant, as an aid, in assistance, తోడుగా, అనుకూలముగా. నాకు సహాయముగా వచ్చినాడు he accompanied me to help me. నాకు సహాయముగా మాట్లాడినాడు he spoke in my favour. అతనికి సహాయముగా వచ్చినవారు those who came to support him. సహాయుడు *sahāyuḍu*. n. An assistant, helper, companion, ally, associate, friend. అనుకూలుడు, తోడైనవాడు, స్నేహితుడు.

సహారువు *sahāruvu*. [Tel.] n. A term used in gambling, జూదమందలి పరిభాష. ఈ. వారి. iii.

సహించు *sahintsu*. [Skt.] v. n. To please, be agreeable. ఇష్టమగు. దానికి కూడు సహించదు food is loathesome to her. అది నాకు సహించదు I do not like it. అది నాకు సహించకుండా to prevent my liking it. v. a. To bear, suffer, tolerate, sustain, endure. తాళు, ఓర్చు, సహించు.

సహితము *sahitamu*. [Skt.] adj. Composed of, accompanied by, in company with. మిళితము, కూడుకొనిన, విషసహితము envenomed. adv. With, along with, even, also, too, into the bargain. కూడా.

సహిష్ణుత *sahishṇuta*. [Skt.] n. Toleration, patience, endurance. ఓర్పు, తాలిమి, సహించడము. సహిష్ణువు *sahishṇuvu*. n. One who is patient, enduring, resigned. ఓర్పుగలవాడు, తాలిమిగలవాడు, సహనుడు.

సహేతుకము *sa-hētukamu*. [Skt.] adj. Having a reason, with a reason. హేతువుతో కూడిన.

సహోదరుడు See under సహ.

సహ్యజ *sahyaja*. [Skt.] n. A name of the river Kaveri. కావేరినది. Vasu. preface 110. A. vi. 119.

సహ్యము *sahyamu*. [Skt.] adj. Sufferable, bearable, endurable, tolerable. తాళగూడిన, సహింపదగిన.

సా sā

సా *sā*. [Tel. short for సాము or సగము.] adj. Half, అర్థము. సామేను half the body, అర్థశరీరము. "అతనిసామేననిలిచినయుగళమూజ." Vasu. preface 8. సాబాలు a half share, అర్థభాగము. "వడివెట్టిలోజలగుడుము సాబాలుప్పతెలను సంబారంపుడింతివండు." A. ii. 111.

సాంకవము *sān-kavamu*. [Skt. from శంకువు.] n. Musk. కస్తూరి, సంకుమదము. A. ii. 26. "తలుకుచెక్కులసాంకవపుతెలముంచి." Ila. ii. 8.

సాంకాలిక *sān-kalika*. [Skt. from కాలము.] n. Interest payable daily, ప్రతిదినమునిచ్చేడి వడ్డీ.

సాంకేతికము *sānkētikamu*. [Skt. from సంకేతము.] adj. Relating to an appointed sign, agreed on, arranged, appointed. నిర్ణీతమైన, సంకేతముచేసికొనిన. సాంకేతికస్థలమునందు in the place agreed on. See సంకేతము.

సాంఖ్యము *sānkhyamu*. [Skt. from సంఖ్య.] n. Ratiocination, the name of a certain school of Philosophy called the Sankhya philosophy, ఒక యోగము.

సాంగత్యము *sāngatyamu*. [Skt. from సంగతి.] n. Association, intercourse. సహవాసము, కూడిక, చేరిక.

సాంగము *s-āngamu*. [Skt. స+అంగము.] adj. Having all the members or parts, comprising all the subdivisions, complete, perfect, full. సంపూర్ణమైన, సావయవమైన. సాంగముగా *s-āngamu-gā*. adv. Completely, at full length. సంపూర్ణముగా. సాంగముచేయు *s-āngamu-chēyu*. v. a. To complete, finish. సాంగోపాంగము *s-āng-ōp-āngamu*. (స+అంగ+ఉప+అంగ) adj. Complete from beginning to end, entire. సంపూర్ణము. సాంగోపాంగముగా *s-āng-ōp-āngamu-gā*. adv. Completely; with all the members and subdivisions, అంగప్రత్యంగములతో కూడా, సవిస్తారముగా.

సాంతపనము *sān-tapanamu*. [Skt.] n. A kind of fast. ఒకవిధమైన ఉపవాసము.

సాంతము *s-antamu*. [Skt.] adj. To the end, full. సాంతముగా to the end, in full. సాంతముచేయు to finish.

సాంటికొంగ *sānti-kongu*. [Tel.] n. The bird called the Cattle-heron. *Bubulcus coromandus* (F. B. I.) Jerdon, No. 308. పక్షివిశేషము.

సాంత్వనము *sāntvanamu*. [Skt.] n. Appeasing, pacification, soothing; urbanity, complaisance. ఆశ్వాసనము, ఓదార్పుట.

సాంత్వము *sāntvamu*. [Skt.] adj. Sweet voiced. మిక్కిలి మధురమైనది (వాక్యం). n. Kindness, favour, దాక్షిణ్యము.

సాంద్రిష్టికము *sān-drishṭikamu*. [Skt.] n. The immediate consequence or result,

అప్పటిఫలము, అప్పుడు కలిగెడుఫలము, సద్యః ఫలము.

సాంద్రము sāndramu. [Skt.] adj. Thick, dense, close, compact, thickset, much, abundant. దట్టమైన, నిబిడమైన, నీరంధ్రమైన. కీర్తిసాంద్ర full of glory. Sar. D. 537.

సాంధ్యము sāndhyamu. [Skt. from సంధ్య.] adj. Evening; produced at evening, or relating to evening. సాయంకాలమందుకలిగిన, సంధ్యాసంబంధమైన. సాంధ్యరాగము the redness of the sky in the evening, సంధ్యారాగము. Also, the name of a sort of silk. BD. iii. 112.

సాంపరాయము, సంపరాయము, సాంపరాయికము or సంపరాయికము sāmparāyamu. [Skt.] n. War, a battle, a combat. యుద్ధము. Vasu. iv. 1. P. iv. 435.

సాంప్రతము sāmpratamu. [Skt.] adv. Now, at this time, at present. ఇప్పుడు, ప్రస్తుతము. Properly, fitly. యుక్తము.

సాంప్రదాయము sām-pra-dāyamu. [Skt. for సంప్రదాయము.] n. Traditional doctrine. గురుపరంపరాగతరహస్యోపదేశము, పరంపరాగతక్రమము. సాంప్రదాయార్థము a traditional meaning. సాంప్రదాయికము sām-pra-dāyakamu. adj. Traditional. సాంప్రదాయికుడు sām-pra-dāyikuḍu. n. (colloquial phrase.) A man of good family, a gentleman, an honest man. మంచివంశస్థుడు, క్రమస్థుడు, యోగ్యుడు, పెద్దమనుష్యుడు.

సాంబశివుడు s-āmba-śivuḍu. [Skt. స+అంబ+శివుడు.] n. An epithet of Siva. అర్ధనారీశ్వరుడు.

సాంబా sāmba. [H.] n. The large red stag called a Sambur. కణితి.

సాంబ్రాణి sāmbrāṇi. [from Skt. సాంబ్రాణి.] n. The fragrant gum called benzoin, సాంబ్రాణిచెట్టువలన గలిగిన ధూపద్రవ్యము. సాంబ్రాణి తైలము an oil extracted from this. సాంబ్రాణివత్తి a perfumed taper or pastille, a candle made of benzoin which produces the fragrance of frankincense. ఊదువత్తి. పరంగిసాంబ్రాణిచెట్టు the Indian Olibanum tree, *Boswellia serrata*, గుగ్గిలపుచెట్టు. (Watts.) సాంబ్రాణి ఆకు a certain herb.

సాంయాత్రికుడు sām-yātrikuḍu. [Skt. from యాత్ర.] n. A sea merchant, ఓడవర్తకుడు.

సాంవత్సరికము sām-vatsarikamu. [Skt. from సంవత్సరము.] n. An anniversary of a death. సంవత్సరాంతమున జరుగునది, తద్దినము, ఆబ్దికము. సాంవత్సరుడు sām-vatsaruḍu. n. An astrologer. జ్యోతిష్కుడు, జోస్యుడు. "సాంవత్సరికదత్తకాల కలావిశేషంబున మంగళతూర్యంబులు మెరసె." M. IV. v. 396.

సాంశయికుడు sāmśayikuḍu. [Skt. from సంశయము.] n. One who has a suspicion or doubt. సంశయముగొనిన మనస్సుగలవాడు.

సాకతము sākatamu. [Tel.] n. Consolation, ఊరడింపు. Favour, అనుగ్రహము.

సాకము sākamu. [Tel.] n. A dispute; a pretext, వ్యాజము. A feast. ఉత్సవము. "సాకమనగను వ్యాజముత్సవముదోచు." ABA. iii. 93.

సాకల్యము sākalyamu. [Skt. from సకలము.] n. The whole, the total, all, entirety, సకలత్వము, సమస్తము, యావత్తు. ఆ కథను సాకల్యముగా (or ససాకల్యముగా) చెప్పుము tell the whole story.

సాకిన్ or సాకీన్ sākin. [H.] adj. Residing. n. An inhabitant.

సాకిరి sākiri. [Skt. from సాక్షి.] n. A witness. సాక్షి. "ఈవిమిత్తముసాకిరిగా వె." ఈ. రా. vi.

సాకు sāku. [Tel.] n. A pretence, pretext, excuse, palliation. నెపము, వ్యాజము. "లాగ్తకునికట్టె సాకుకలద." Balarama i. 106. v. a. To bring up, foster, rear, educate, train up. పెంచు, పోషించు, కాపాడు, విద్యాబుద్ధులుచెప్పు. సాకుకొను sāku-konu. v. a. To adopt, స్వీకారముచేసికొను. పెంచుకొను. సాకుడు sākuḍu. n. Rearing, training.

adj. Reared, trained, adopted, tame. సాకుడుకొడుకు an adopted son. సాకుడు చిలుక a pet or tame parrot.

సాకోటము, శాఖోటము or శాఖోటకము sākōṭamu. [Skt.] n. A certain tree, *Trophis aspera*, గండమాలభఘ్నము, పెద్దబరిక.

సాక్షాత్, సాక్షాత్తు or సాక్షాత్తుగా s-akshat. [Skt.] adv. In sight, in view, in presence of, before. Manifestly, openly, publicly. Very, real, own. సమ్ముఖమందు, ఎదుట, ప్రత్యక్షముగా. సాక్షాద్వాడే or సాక్షాత్తువాడే that very man, the identical person. వాడు సాక్షాత్తుగా వచ్చినాడు he came in person. సాక్షాద్విష్ణువు Vishnu himself. సాక్షాత్సహోదరుడు an uterine brother, an own brother. సాక్షాత్కరించు s-akshat-karintsu. v. n. To manifest oneself, to become manifest or present. ప్రత్యక్షమగు, ఎదుటికివచ్చు. సాక్షాత్కారము s-akshat-kāramu. n. A manifestation of oneself, an appearing in a visible form, ప్రత్యక్షమగుట. సాక్షాత్కృతము s-akshat-kritamu. adj. Made manifest. ప్రత్యక్షమైన. సాక్షాత్కృతి s-akshat-kriti. n. Personal presence; appearance in person, an interview. ప్రత్యక్షముకావడము. సాక్షాత్కృతుడు s-akshat-kritudu. n. One who manifested himself. సాక్షాత్కరించినవాడు.

సాక్షి s-akshi. [Skt. స+అక్షి.] n. An eye witness, a witness, one who testifies to anything, one who gives evidence. ప్రత్యక్షముగా చూచినవాడు, ఎరిగినవాడు. కొంగసాక్షి or అబద్ధపుసాక్షి a false witness. అంతరాత్మసాక్షిగా నేనొకపాపము నెరుగను my heart bears me witness that I did no wrong. అగ్నిసాక్షిగా in the presence of the god of fire. పంచభూతసాక్షిగా నేనెరుగను I swear by the five elements that I am not guilty. ఏకసాక్షిసాక్ష్యము a single witness will not suffice. "తమకుదాండగానె తమవారుకొందరు, వచ్చుకెల్లతమకు సాక్షికాద." (Vema. 1650.) Is not this a proof? సాక్షిభూతుడు s-akshi-bhūtudu. n. One equivalent to a witness, one as good as a witness. చూచుచుండువాడు. సాక్ష్యము s-akshyamu. n. Testimony, evidence ప్రత్యక్షముగా చూడడము, ప్రత్యక్షముగా చూచిన దాన్ని చెప్పడము. సాక్ష్యముగా as an evidence. కొంగసాక్ష్యము or అబద్ధపుసాక్ష్యము false evidence. ప్రత్యక్షసాక్ష్యము direct evidence. సాక్ష్యమిచ్చు or సాక్ష్యముచెప్పు s-akshyam-itstsu. v. n. To give evidence, to bear witness. మనస్సాక్షి the conscience.

సాగ or సాగనారు sāga. [Tel.] n. A sort of hemp, from the fibres of which bowstrings are made. *Sansevieira Zeylanica*, నారట, మూర్వ. సాగనార or సాగనారమట్టు the fibres of this plant.

సాగరము sāgaramu. [Tel.] n. A bullock-load of oil, consisting of a pair of leathern bottles of oil. నెయ్యి నూనె మొదలైనవి నింపిన సిద్దెలజోడు. సాగరము [Skt. from సగర.] n. The sea, ocean. సముద్రము.

సాగు or సొగు sāgu. [Tel.] v. n. To go on, proceed, get on, advance, continue, be current, be usual. To lengthen, to extend, as hot iron under the hammer. To take effect. To begin, నడుచు, జరుగు, దీర్ఘమగు, నిడుపగు, ఆరంభించు. n. A spit or iron lance, a short arrow thrown from the hand, అడుగున త్రాడుకట్టినకటారి, అలుగు వంటి ఆయుధవిశేషము. Cultivation, tillage. కృషి, వ్యవసాయము. దండుసాగుచుండగా when the army was marching. పని సాగలేదు the business does not go on or proceed. అతనిమాట సాగలేదు his word did not take effect. కమ్మి సాగలేదు the wire could not be drawn out or lengthened. ఆ ఉత్సవము సాగుచున్నదా is the feast still kept up? దానికోరిక కొనసాగినది her wish is fulfilled. చెప్పసాగినది she went on to say. ఇది లేకుండా నాకు సాగదు I cannot get on without this. అక్కడ సాగకవచ్చితిని as I could not subsist there I came away. సాగు

సాగుపాటు sāgu-pāṭu. n. Means of getting on, livelihood. జరుగుపాటు. సాగుబడి sāgu-baḍi. n. Cultivation. వ్యవసాయము. plu. సాగుబళ్లు. సాగగొట్టు sāga-goṭṭu. v. a. To hammer out, extend or draw out (by beating a rod of iron, gold, etc.) పొడుగగునట్లుగా కొట్టు. సాగదీయు sāga-dīyu. v. a. To extend, stretch out, draw out, lengthen, పొడుగగునట్లుగా లాగు. To importune, మిక్కిలి ప్రార్థించు. బలిమాలుకొను. వాణ్ని ఎంత సాగదీసినా పోనన్నాడు however much I urged him he said he would not go. సాగనంపు sāga-n-ampu. v. a. To send away, to send one on, to set a traveller on his way, to convey or accompany one for a little distance. పంపించు. సాగబడు or సాగిలబడు sāga-baḍu. v. n. To fall down at full length, flat or prostrate. సాష్టాంగపడు. "సాగబడి మ్రొక్కిన కౌశిక పార్థివుఁ డుక్కి." Parij. v. 48. సాగించు sāgintsu. v. a. To conduct, carry on (a business.) To celebrate (a feast.) జరుపు. సిడ్లసాగించినవారు they performed the swinging feast.

సాగుమానము See సహగమనము.

సాచా sācha. [H.] adj. Faithful, honest, true, real, just. సాచాగా honestly.

సాచివ్యము sāchivyamu. [Skt. from సచివుడు.] n. Ministry, the office of a minister. మంత్రిత్వము. సచివత్వము. "సంజీవక సాచివ్యము నంకేటను." P. i. 386.

సాజము or సాజేము sājamu. [from Skt. సహజము.] adj. Natural, innate, proper, true. "శరముడొనకేరుకొందు సాజంబుగాదు." R. v. 296.

సాజాత్యము sā-jātyamu. [Skt. from సజాతి.] n. Similarity, likeness. సజాతిత్వము, పోలిక.

సాట, సాటా, సాటాకోటి or సాటాబేరము sāṭa. [Tel.] n. Barter, exchange. బేరము, ఒక వస్తువునిచ్చి మరియొకవస్తువు పుచ్చుకొనే బేరము. సాటాయిచ్చు to give in exchange, to barter.

సాటి sāṭi. [Tel.] adj. Like, similar, equal. సమానమైన. తుల్యమైన. నాసాటివారు my equals. సాటి or సాటిక n. Likeness, similarity, equality. సామ్యము. సాటిలేని sāṭi-lēni. adj. Unrivalled, matchless. అసమానమైన. సాటువ sāṭuva. n. Likeness, similitude, comparison. సామ్యము.

సాటించు sāṭintsu. [Tel. for చాటించు.] v. a. To proclaim, to publish by beat of drum. ప్రసిద్ధపరచు.

సాతాని or సాతని sātani. [from Tam. చాత్తాదవర్.] n. Literally, those who do not wear the sacred thread or crown-lock of hair. The Sātānis, a class of Vaishnavites originally formed from various castes, శిఖాయజ్ఞోపవీతములులేని విష్ణుభక్తులు. సాతిన వాండ్లు or చాతినవాండ్లు sātina-vāndlu. n. plu. An epithet of Vaishnava Brahmins, who do not wear the sacred thread and crown-lock of hair. శ్రీవైష్ణవులు. "సాతిని సాతానికులమువారిని." A. ii. 112.

సాతు sātu. [from Skt. సార్థ.] A company of travellers or of merchants. బాటసారుల గుంపు. వర్తకులగుంపు. "దేశాంతరంబున నొకసాతుం గూడి వచ్చి దేశంబునకరుగుచో." M. XII. iii. 450. "వనకరిదొమొక్కటిదుమసాతుకనుంగవిజదనయంబుద్రుంపదొడంగుటయు." ib. XII. iii. 451. "తెరపిడుదుగనకేమిసాతుదిరుగుడుపడియో." A. vi. 98. సాతు sātu. v. a. To put vestments or garlands about an idol. సమర్పించు. "దివ్యాంబరయుగ్మంబుసాతి." BD. i. 814. సాతువాండ్లు or సాతులు sātu-vāndlu. n. plu. The name of a class of people who weave sackcloth. గోనెలు నేయువారివారి. A. vi. 56.

సాత్కరించు sāt-karintsu. [Skt.] v. a. To make over, deliver. అధీనముచేయు. A. iv. 34. సాత్కృతము sāt-kritamu. adj. Delivered, made over, sacrificed. అధీనముచేయబడ్డ. "పివిధసాత్కృతముగఁ జేయుఁ దే." BRY. ii. 1092.

సాత్యవతేయుడు *sātyavu-tēyudu.* [Skt. from సత్యవతి.] n. A name of Vyāsa. వ్యాసుడు.

సాత్రాజితి *satrajiti.* [Skt. from సత్రాజిత్.] A name of Satyabhama, as daughter of Satrājit. సత్యభామ. Parij. xii. 30.

సాత్వతి *satvati.* [Skt.] n. The name of Sisupala's mother.

సాత్వికము *sātvikamu.* [Skt. from సత్వము.] n. Amiability, goodness, sincerity, gentleness. సాధుత్వము, సత్వగుణముచల్లకలిగినది. adj. Virtuous, amiable, good, well disposed, gentle, sincere, సత్వగుణానుబంధియైన. సుశీలముగల. సాధువైన. **సాత్వికపూజ** *sātvika-pūja.* n. A bloodless sacrifice. A bloody rite is called తామసపూజ. గావు ఇయ్యడము మొదలైన జీవహింసలేకుండా చేసే అర్చన. **సాత్వికుడు** *sātvikudu.* n. A peaceable man, a man of gentle temper. తిన్ననివాడు.

సాదన *sādana.* [Skt. from సాధనము.] n. Practice, exercise, అభ్యాసము. Gymnastic exercise. **సాదనకాడు** or **సాదనగాడు** *sādana-kadu.* n. A wrestler, మల్లుడు.

సాదనము or **సదనము** *sādanamu.* [Skt.] n. A house. ఇల్లు. "వ్యాసత్యసాదనమున కరిగా." భార. అర. i.

సాదము *sādamu.* [Tel.] n. Boiled rice. అన్నము (a Vaishnavite word).

సాదరము *s-ādaramu.* [Skt. స+ఆదరము.] adj. Respectful. సన్మానమైన. "సాదరభాషణ సారంగధరుని." Sar. D. 567. **సాదరత** *s-ādarata.* n. Regard, respect, veneration, affection. సన్మానము, ఆదరణ, విశ్వాసము. **సాదరముగా** *s-ādaramu-ga.* adv Respectfully, kindly, సన్మానముగా. **సాదరుడు** *s-ādarudu.* n. One who is gracious. సన్మానముచేయువాడు. "మంత్రాధరుణాసాదరుణా." Balarama. iii. 218.

సాదరు *sādaru.* [H.] adj. Issued, proclaimed, enacted.

సాదర్వారి *sadarvari.* [H.] n. Expenditure and receipts, output and income. Petty charges for pens, ink, paper, &c.

సాదా *sādā.* [H.] adj. Plain, clear, blank.

సాది *sādi.* [Skt.] n. A rider or driver: a coachman, or charioteer, an elephant-driver, a horse-soldier. రథసారథి, మావటీడు. గుర్రపురౌతు. సాదిబలము cavalry. UH. iv. 22. "సాదిబలమెదురేర్పడితోసాదిబలాని." Satya. iv. 114.

సాదు *sādu.* [from Skt. సాధువు.] n. A tame animal. సాధువైనజంతువు. A gentle or good man, మంచివాడు. adj. Tame, mild, gentle, good, మంచి. "క. దుర్జనులగూడి పేదసాదులను గొట్టు." భల్లా. iii.

సాదృశ్యము *sā-drisyamu.* [Skt.] n. Likeness, similarity, resemblance, comparison; an instance, example, illustration. తుల్యత, పోలిక, సామ్యము. దృష్టాంతము, ఉదాహరణము.

సాధకము *sādhakamu.* [Skt.] adj. Completing, effecting, finishing. సాధించునది. n. Practice, exercise. Vouchers in evidence. Instruments, means, medium; authority for the use of a word. అభ్యాసము, ఆలవాటు, దస్తావేజు, ఉదాహరణము. కత్తిసాధకము sword exercise. నీవు చెప్పేమాటకు సాధకముకద్దా have you any means of proving what you say? సాధకబాధకములు the pros and cons of a case. **సాధకముచేయు** *sādhakamu-chēyu.* v. a. To practise, exercise or use. అభ్యాసముచేయు. **సాధకుడు** *sādhakudu.* n. A conqueror, masterer, achiever, సాధించువాడు. నిష్పాదకుడు, సాధనకర్త. A devotee, ఉపాసకుడు. "అభ్యాసయోగసాధకుడుకాడేడు." A. iii. 90. "స్వానుభూతి లేకశాస్త్రవాసనలచే సంశయంబుచెడదుసాధకునకు." (Vema. 115.) **సాధనము** *sādhanamu.* n. A way, means, medium, instrument, agent, contrivance, expedient, tool, implement. Authority, reason. నిష్పాదనము, ఉపకరణము, సామగ్రి, ఉపాయము, హేతువు. సాధనసంపత్తి ways and means. మూలసాధనము the principal means. "చక్రగదాశంఖశార్ఙాది సాధనము." BX. సాధనీయము sādhan-iyamu. adj. That which can be realised or accomplished, practicable. సాధింపదగిన.

సాధర్మ్యము sa-dharmyamu. [Skt.] n. Community, equality or similarity of duty, office or property; likeness, comparison, ఒకటేవిధమైన ధర్మమును కలిగియుండడము, సామ్యము. "ఇటులసాధర్మ్యమించుకయేనిలేని." UR. iv. 256.

సాధారణ sādhārana. [Skt.] n. The name of a Telugu year.

సాధారణము or సాధారణమైన sādhāranamu. [Skt.] adj. Usual, ordinary, customary, common. సామాన్యమైన, సహజమైన. అది వానికి సాధారణము he can very easily master it. "అసాధారణమైనవిద్య" (T. ii. 41.) uncommon learning, profound learning. సాధారణముగా sādhāranamu-gā. adv. Commonly, ordinarily, generally, easily, సామాన్యముగా, అల్పముగా. అనన్యసాధారణము not common to others.

సాధించు sādhintsu. [Skt.] v. a. To achieve, accomplish, effect, master, overcome, conquer. నెరవేర్చు, సమకూర్చు. v. n. To persist in saying, insist upon, affirm. కార్యము సాధించు to obtain a thing by perseverance. "ముక్తిసాధింపగలరు." Vema. 866. ఆ సొమ్మును చెల్లించినాడని సాధిస్తున్నారు they affirm that he paid the money. అడవిని సాధించిరి they subdued the jungle. పగను (or పగ) సాధించినాడు he wreaked his malice. See సాధకము and సాధనము. వాడు లేదని సాధించినాడు he persistently denied the fact. ఆ అమ్మకము జరగలేదని సాధిస్తాడు he makes it out that the sale never took place. సాధు or సాధువు sādhu. adj. Tame, docile, tractable, gentle, good, not vicious. Pleasing, right, correct, fit, proper. Excellent, eminent. దుష్టముకాని, సాత్వికమైన, మనోహరమైన, ఉత్తమమైన, సుబద్ధమైన, మంచి, చక్కని. సాధువైనఆవు a quiet cow. సాధువు sādhuvu. n. A good, meek, harmless or gentle person, a good-natured or virtuous man, a saint. సాత్వికుడు, మంచివాడు, తిన్ననివాడు. "సాధులకుపేదవారికిసెగ్గల్." M. I. i. 130. సాధ్యము sādhyamu. adj. Possible, attainable, practicable, tractable. సాధింపదగిన. n. The twenty second astronomical Yoga. క్రమయోగములలోనొకటి. సాధ్యానుస్వారము sādhy-ānusvāramu. n. The changeable sunna (n) which may be inserted according to circumstances, as in అల్లుడు, అల్లుండు, అతడు, అతండు. సాధ్యుడు sādhyudu. n. One who is easy, docile, gentle or reasonable. సాధింపదగినవాడు, సులభుడు, మెత్తనివాడు. వీడు సాధ్యుడు వారు అసాధ్యులు he may be mastered but they cannot be mastered. An inferior deity, or demigod. సాధ్వసము sādhvasamu. n. Fear, terror. భయము. సాధ్వి sādhvi. n. A good woman, a chaste wife. పతివ్రత. సాధ్వీతుడు sādhvitudu. n. A saint, a chaste or holy man. ముని.

సాన sāna. [from Skt. శాణ.] n. A whetstone or hone, a grind-stone. A stone on which sandal paste is prepared. A piece of stone, metal or wood on which jewels are polished. పదునుపెట్టేరాయి, గంధమునూరే రాయి, రత్నములు చక్కబెట్టేసాధనము. వజ్రాల సాన a machine on which diamonds are cut and polished. సానపట్టడము sāna-pattaḍamu. n. Grinding or polishing. సానపట్టు sāna-pattu. v. a. To grind a knife, razor or sword: to cut and polish gems, పదునుపెట్టు, రత్నములకు మెరుగుపెట్టు. సానపట్టనికెంపు an uncut or unfinished ruby.

సానకత్తి *sāna-katti*. [Tel. for సాదనకత్తి.] n. A sword used in fencing. సాదనచేయు కత్తి.

సాని *sāni*. [from Skt. స్వామిని.] n. A lady, a woman of rank. స్వామిని, అధిపురాలు, పూజ్యురాలు. A wife, భార్య. (Commonly,) a dancing girl, వేశ్య. దొరసాని or ఏలికసాని a lady or queen. రెడ్డిసాని a farmer's wife. మంత్రసాని a midwife. **సానిది** *sānidi*. n. A dancing girl, వేశ్య. **సానిచేప** or **సానిమొయ్య** *sāni-chēpa*. n. A fish, a species of *Labrus*. Russell. **సానివాండ్లు** *sāni-vāndlu*. n. plu. Members of the dancing caste. వ్యభిచారముచేత జీవించే స్త్రీలజాతి.

సానిక *sānika*. [Tel.] n. An earthen vessel, plate or dish మంటికంచము.

సానుకూలము *s-ānukūlamu*. [Skt.] adj. Convenient. అనుకూలమయిన.

సానుమత్తు or **సానుమంతము** *sānumattu*. [Skt.] n. A mountain. పర్వతము.

సానువు *sānuvu*. [Skt.] n. A tableland, even or level ground on the top or edge of a mountain. కొండనెత్తము. "సానుభూములదరుచుగాజదియబడి." Vish. iii. 31. "హిమవత్పర్వతకూటసానువులనుండితెంచు." ib. ii. 336. రత్నసానువు a name of Mount Meru.

సాన్నిధ్యము *sānnidhyamu*. [Skt. from సన్నిధి.] n. Nearness, vicinity, proximity. సామీప్యము.

సాపడు *sāpaḍu*. [Tel.] v. n. To dine. సాపాటుచేయు, భుజించు. **సాపాటు** *sāpāṭu*. n. Food, a meal, భోజనము. Eating, సాపడుట. **సాపాటురాముడు** *sāpāṭu-rāmuḍu*. n. A glutton.

సాపు or **సాఫు** *sāpu*. [H.] adj. Clear, pure, fair, smooth, straight, level, not crooked. సాపుప్రతి a fair copy (of a paper, book, &c.) సాపునాయడము copying out fair. సాపుచేయు to level.

సాప్తపదీనము *sāpta-padīnamu*. [Skt. from సప్తపది.] n. Friendship. సఖ్యము, స్నేహము.

సాఫల్యము *sā-phalyamu*. [Skt. from సఫలము.] n. Fruitfulness, efficacy, success. ప్రయోజనసిద్ధి, ఫలోత్పత్తి. తమదర్శనము కావడమువల్ల నా జన్మసాఫల్యమైనది by seeing you I have accomplished the great end of my life. నా కోరిక సాఫల్యమైనది my object is accomplished, my hopes are fulfilled.

సాఫు See సాపు.

సాబకు *sābaku*. [H.] adj. Former. సాబకు హుకుము a former order.

సాబాలు See under సా.

సామంజస్యము *sāmanjasyamu*. [Skt. from సమంజసము.] n. Fitness, propriety. సమంజసత్వము, యుక్తత.

సామంతుడు *sāmantuḍu*. [Skt.] n. A neighbouring king, a feudatory prince, ఇరుగుపొరుగురాజు. "దొరలుసామంతులుదుర్గాధిపతులు." Sar. D. 592. **సామంతరాగోల** *sāmanta-rāgōla*. n. A kind of weapon. ఆయుధవిశేషము. రాగోల అనగా, పంగలకట్టె. "ద్వి॥ సామంతరాగోలసాచి వేసినను, వలభుజంబున దాకివసుధకుడలిగె." Pal. 418.

సామగ్రి *sāmagri*. [Skt.] n. A thing, article, material, ingredient. A utensil; furniture, goods. ద్రవ్యము, వస్తువు, ఉపకరణము, అస్త్రశస్త్రాదులు.

సామము *sāmamu*. [Skt.] n. The third of the Vedas. తృతీయవేదము. సామగానము the chanting of this Veda. Conciliation, pacification, gentle methods, fair means. శత్రువులను మంచిమాటాడడము, శాంతము, మంచితనము. "సామదానములగాని సమలే." T. iv. 187. Gymnastics such as sword play or wrestling. సాము. "సాముము మానిగొబ్బునసుసందడిదీరినవమ్మ." Chatu. i. 67. **సామగుడు** *sāmaguḍu*. n. A chanter or reciter of the Sama Veda. సామవేదపాఠకుడు. సామజము sāma-jamu. n. Lit. Born from the Sāma Vēda. An elephant, ఏనుగు. సామోద్భవము sām-ōdbhavamu. n. An elephant. ఏనుగు. "మదవత్సామోద్భవస్తోమమర్గ లమై." M. VI. 108.

సామరస్యము. sāma-rasyamu. [Skt. from సమరసము.] n. Equality, friendliness, amicableness. సమభావము, సమరసత్వము.

సామరి See సాము.

సామర్థ్యము sām-arthyamu. [Skt. from సమర్థము.] n. Skill, ability, capacity, adequacy, power, నేర్పు, బలము, శక్తి, యోగ్యత. సామర్థ్యవంతుడు sām-arthya-vantuḍu. n. An able man. బలముగలవాడు. సామర్థ్యవంతురాలు sām-arthya-vantu-r-ālu. n. A skilful woman. నేర్పుగలది.

సామవాయికుడు sāmavāyikuḍu. [Skt.] n. A principal minister or counsellor. The chief of a company or corporation. మంత్రి, ముఖ్యుడు.

సామాజికుడు sāmājikuḍu. [Skt. from సమాజము.] n. A member of an assembly, or society. ధర్మసభాస్థితుడు, సభలోనుండువాడు, సభికుడు.

సామాను sāmānu. [H.] n. Things, baggage, luggage, goods, wares, tools, apparatus. A service or set of things. అంగడిసామానులు bazaar goods. వంటసామానులు cooking ingredients or vessels.

సామాన్యము sāmānyamu. [Skt. from సమానము.] adj. Common, general, usual, ordinary. సాధారణమైన. Middling, inferior, low, base, mean, చులకనైన, జబ్బైన. సామాన్యుడు sāmānyuḍu. n. A common or ordinary person, a base man. తుచ్ఛుడు, అల్పుడు. సామాన్యులు middle class people, common folk. వాడు సామాన్యుడా is he a common man? సామాన్య sāmānya. n. A common woman. సర్వసాధారణ నాయిక.

సామి sāmi. [from Skt. స్వామి.] n. Lord, master. ప్రభువు, యజమానుడు. A king రాజు. A husband, పెనిమిటి. సామిమల a hill on which Kumāraswāmi resides.

సామిత, సామితె or సామెత sāmita. [from Skt. సమతా.] n. A proverb, a common saying, ఒకసంగతికి దృష్టాంతముగా లోకులు వాడుకగా చెప్పేమాట, లోకోక్తి.

సామీప్యము sāmīpyamu. [Skt. from సమీపము.]. n. Nearness, contiguity, proximity, neighbourhood. సమీపత్వము, చాపు.

సామీరి sāmīri. [Skt.] n. Lit. the son of సమీరుడు. An epithet of Hanuman, హనుమంతుడు. Also, of Bhīma, భీముడు.

సాము sāmu. [Tel. short for సగము.] n. A half. అర్థము. "సామసోము సోముగోముగాము." Ila. iii. 170. టీ॥ సాముసోము, సగము చంద్రుని. [from Skt. శ్రమము.] n. Bodily exercise, వ్యాయామము. Fencing or feats of strength, గారిడి. నేలవిడిచి సాముచేయగూడదు if you lose your footing you will lose your power. సాముచేయు to practise gymnastics or feats of strength. సామరి sām-ari. n. A gymnast or fencer. సాము నేర్చినవాడు. సాముకంటిచుక్క sāmu-kanṭi-tsukka. n. The name of a constellation called పుబ్బ or పూర్వఫల్గునీనక్షత్రము.

"ఆ॥ చదువుసాముగలిగి క్షత్రియుల్ సంపూర్ణ,
విద్యలనగవిటవినతికెక్కి,
సాధులనుబరిచ్యుతాధులజేయంగ,
జాలకుండుదురెప్రశంసనేయ."

కవి. i.

సాముద్రికము sāmudrikamu. [Skt. from సముద్రము.] adj. Belonging to the sea. n. Palmistry, the interpretation of spots on the body, and of lines in the hand. దేహములోనుండు మచ్చలను చేతిరేఖలనుచూచి అదృష్టము చెప్పుశాస్త్రము. సాముద్రికుడు

sāmudrikuḍu. n. One who knows palmistry, a palmister. హస్తములు రేఖలుమొదలైనవి చూచి అదృష్టము చెప్పువాడు.

సామిత. See సామిటి.

సామ్యము *sāmyamu.* [Skt. from సమము.] n. Equality, analogy, likeness, similarity, comparison. సమత్వము, పోలిక.

సామ్రాజ్యము *sām-rājyamu.* [Skt. from సమ్రాట్టు.] n. Empire, sway, rule. సమ్రాట్టుతనము, అధికారము, ప్రభుత్వము. నూరు రూపాయల ఇవ్వడము ఒక సామ్రాజ్యమా is it a great thing to give a hundred rupees? సామ్రాట్ or సమ్రాట్టు *sām-rāṭ.* n. An emperor. రాజాధిరాజు.

సామ్రాణి or సాంబ్రాణి *sāmrāṇi* [Tel.] n. Benzoin. సామ్రాణిధూపము incense. సామ్రాణిధూపము వేయు to burn or offer incense. సామ్రాణివత్తి a perfumed taper or candle. A steed, a fine horse, వాజి, గుర్రము, ఉత్తమాశ్వము. "గార్దభంబును వేయు గతులదాటించిన నోజతో సాంబ్రాణి తేజియగునె." Kalahasti §. 49.

సాయకము *sāyakamu.* [Skt.] n. An arrow. బాణము. A sword, ఖడ్గము. సాయము *sāyamu.* n An arrow. బాణము.

సాయము *sāyamu.* [Skt.] n. Evening, the close of the day. సాయంకాలము. సాయంసంధ్య the evening prayer. సాయంకాలము *sāyan-kālamu.* n. Evening. సంధ్యాకాలము. సాయంతనము *sāyan-tanamu.* adj. Belonging to the evening. సాయంకాల సంబంధమైన. సాయంత్రము *sāyan-tramu.* (corruption of సాయంతనము) n. Evening. సాయంకాలము.

సాయము *sāyamu.* [from Skt. సహాయము.] n. Aid, assistance, help. సహాయము. [Tel. anuk.] as అయసాయమ్ములు custom-house duties and the like, సుంకములు సుంకములు. "అయసాయమ్ములు, అవిగావి." Pal. 313.

సాయరు or శాయరు *sāyaru.* [H.] n. A transit duty, customs, tolls. సుంకము.

సాయిల *sāyila.* [Tel.] n. A man belonging to a certain class of mendicants who profess fortune telling. బుడుబుడుక్కల గాడు.

సాయుజ్యము *sā-yujyamu.* [Skt.] n. Identification, intimate union, absorption into the essence of the Deity. దేవునిలో కలిసి పోవడము, సహయోగము.

సారంగము *sārangamu.* [Skt.] n. A deer. దుప్పి. A bee, తుమ్మెద. An elephant, ఏనుగు. A species of Cuckoo, a swallow, a bird of paradise, *Cuculus melanoleucos.* వానకోయిల, చాతకపక్షి. సారంగరాగము *sāranga-rāgamu.* n. A certain tune,. రాగవిశేషము. సారంగి *sārangi.* n. A kind of fiddle with five wires, played with a bow. ఒకవిధమైన వీణె.

సారచెట్టు *sāra-cheṭṭu.* [Tel.] n. A certain jungle tree. సారపప్పు the kernel of the fruit of this tree.

సారణము *sāraṇamu.* [Tel.] n. A kind of hawk. డేగభేదము. "ద్వి॥ సాళువంబులమంచిజల గట్టియలను, పెద్దసారణములబెట్టుగావిడిచి." HD. i. 534.

సారణి *sāraṇi.* [Skt.] n. A sluice, drain, or canal. చెరువుతూము, కాలువ. "సాంద్రమైన మరంద రసప్రవాహ సంతతుల సారణులుపొల్పు సంగుకోట." Vedanta. R. ii. 20.

సారథి *sārathi.* [Skt.] n. A charioteer, a coachman. రథమునడపువాడు.

సారము *sāramu.* [Skt.] n. Essence, substance, the essential or vital part. The pith, sap, marrow. Juice. Vigour. The effect or purport. Riches, wealth. మూలగ, మెదడు, చేవ, బలము, సత్తు, ఫలము, విత్తము, అర్థము, రసము. "సారాస్వాదన, ప్రాణపంచకము

దృష్టింబౌని సంతర్పణంబా." A vi. 29. టీక సారాస్వాదన, మెదడుముఖుంజింపగా. లోహసారము steel. వేదాంతసారము the essence of Theology; (this is the title of a certain Christian book). శూన్యసారము the essence of emptiness. భూసారము the fertility or richness of the earth. ఇందులో సారములేదు in this I see nothing of any worth. సారములేనిమాటలు dry and empty discourse. adj. Excellent, fruitful, rich, శ్రేష్ఠమైన. సారఖండము a rich or fruitful country or soil, "సారాచారము" అనగా, శ్రేష్ఠమైనసరళి. M. XIII. ii. సారతరము *sara-taramu.* adj. More excellent. మిక్కిలిశ్రేష్ఠమైన. సారవంతము *sara-vantamu.* adj. Fruitful, fertile, rich. సారాంశము the essence or purport of any matter. సారవత్తరము *sara-vat-taramu.* adj. Best, most excellent. మిక్కిలిశ్రేష్ఠమైన. సారాంశము *sar-amsamu.* n. The essential part, the pith, gist or purport. An issue framed by a court. సత్త, నిగ్గు, సారస్యము.

సారమేయము *sara-mēyamu.* [Skt.] n. A dog. కుక్క. సారమేయి *sara-meyi.* n. A bitch. ఆడుకుక్క.

సారవ *sarava.* [Tel.] n. A bridge. A scaffolding. వరంజా.

సారసము *sarasamu.* [Skt. from సరస్సు.] n. A lotus or water lily. పద్మము. సారసనేత్ర a lily-eyed or fair-eyed woman. The Siberian or Indian crane, or Cyrus, *Ardea liberica*, బెగ్గురుపక్షి. సారసి *sarasi.* n. The female Indian crane. ఆడుబెగ్గురుపక్షి.

సారస్యము *sarasyamu.* [Skt. from సరసము.] n. Suavity of manners. సరసత్వము.

సారస్వతము *sarasvatamu.* [Skt. from సరస్వతి.] adj. Relating to the goddess Sarasvati. సరస్వతీసంబంధమైన. "ఇతోధికగాథ సారస్వతోద్బోధనంబును." A. pref. 21. అనగా, పాండిత్యమును.

సారా or సారాయి *sara.* [from Skt. సారము or సురా.] n. Arrack, wine, intoxicating liquor, ఎండిసకల్లు, మద్యము.

సారి *sari.* [Tel.] n. A time, turn, occasion. విడప, తేప, మాటు. ఒకసారి once. రెండుసార్లు twice. మూడుసార్లు thrice. ఈసారి this time. నెలకు ఒకసారి once a month. నెలకు నాలుగుసార్లు four times a month. సారి *sari.* [from Skt. స్వారి.] n. A military expedition, యుద్ధయాత్ర. సారె, సారెకు or సారెసారెకు *sare.* adv. Frequently, often, repeatedly, again and again. మాటిమాటికి. "ఘోరంబుగాసారెగుంటకన్నులు త్రిప్ప." S. iii. 91. "సారెపరాకుపొచ్చరిక బలుకు." N. ii. 334.

సారించు *sarintsu.* [Skt.] v. a. To extend, stretch. చాచు. "కరసారించు." To open, తెరచు. "వాకిలిసారించు." To straighten, set right, సరిదీయు, సవరించు. "నారిసారించు." To brandish or flourish a sword, జళిపించు, విసరు. "కుంచెసారించు." To cast a glance. దృష్టిసారించు. To spread, ప్రసరింపజేయు. "వీరలతంత్రుల సారించుచుండురు నారదులను." N. i. 224.

సారు *saru.* [Tel.] n. A kind of dance. నాట్యగతిభేదము.

సారువ *saruva.* [Tel.] n. A scaffolding. A canal. A bridge. A bank or bund, కట్ట, కాలువనిమిద్దెలవని చేయువారికి ఎక్కుటకుంచెడమునకై కొయ్యలతో కట్టినది, రాతితో కట్టిన కాలువ, వంతెన.

సారువా *saruva.* [Tel.] n. A wet crop. నీరుసరాసుపండేపంట.

సారూప్యము *sa-rūpyamu.* [Skt. from స+రూపము.] n. Identity of form, close resemblance, assimilation. సమానరూపముసుకలిగియుండుటము, సమానరూపత్వము.

సారె sāre. [Tel.] n. Presents made to a daughter when sent to her husband's house. పుట్టింటివారు అత్తవారింటికి పంపునప్పుడిచ్చు సరుకు. A potter's wheel, కుమ్మరవాని చక్రము. A stop in a lute, వీణమెట్టు. [From Skt. శారి.] n. A pawn or piece used in games, a die, సోగటాలపావులు, సారిక, జూదసాధనములు, See also under సారి. సారెసత్తు sāre-sattu. n. A sort of cake, అప్పము. "ఉప్పుడుసారె సత్తులు." H. i. 117.

సార్జెంటు or సార్జంటు sārjentu. [Eng. 'serjeant.'] n. A serjeant, బారిబంట్రౌతు. Bobbili. iii. 106.

సార్థకము or సార్థకత s-arthakamu. [Skt.] n. Utility, profit, good, benefit, fruit, use, efficacy. ఫలము, ప్రయోజనము. సార్థకము adj. Having a meaning, significant, to the purpose, well adapted, suitable as an epithet, name or title. Effectual, profitable, useful. అర్థయుక్తమైన, సప్రయోజనమైన, సఫలమైన, అన్వర్థమైన. సార్థకనామము a significant name, a name having its peculiar meaning, as చతుష్పాత్తు a quadruped. సార్థకములేని s-arthakamu-leni. adj. Irrelevant, fruitless, ineffective. నిష్ప్రయోజనమైన.

సార్థము sarthamu. [Skt.] n. A pack, swarm or multitude of animals, a troop or caravan of merchants. జంతుసమూహము, ప్రాణిసమూహము, వణిక్సంఘము. adj. Significant, having a meaning, అర్థముతో కూడిన. సార్థవాహుడు sartha-vahudu. n. A merchant, a trader, a headman or leader, వైదేహకుడు, క్రయవిక్రయకారుడు, వర్తకుడు, ముఖ్యుడు.

సార్లా sarla. [Tel.] n. Success, completion, achievement, good result. కార్యసిద్ధి, అనుకూలత. సార్లాఅగు sarla-agu. v. n. To succeed, to be finished. సఫలమగు, అనుకూలమగు. ఆ పని సార్లాకాలేదు the undertaking did not succeed. సార్లాచేయు sarla-chēyu. v. a. To settle, prepare, get ready, పరిష్కారము చేయు, సిద్ధము చేయు. వాన్ని సార్లాచేసుకొన్నాడు he brought it about, settled it. అది సార్లాఅయినది the thing succeeded well. సార్లాపడు sarla-paḍu. v. n. To be gained, to come to a good result, to prosper, అనుకూలపడు, సఫలమగు. సార్లాపరచు or సార్లాపెట్టు sarla-paratsu. v. a. To bring about, get (a thing) done, get it settled. అనుకూలపరచు, తీర్చు.

సార్వభౌముడు sārva-bhaumuḍu. [Skt. from సర్వభూమి.] n. A universal monarch. సమస్తభూమిని పాలించేరాజు, చక్రవర్తి. పండితసార్వభౌముడు a most celebrated scholar. సార్వభౌమత్వము sarva-bhaumatvamu. n. Universal dominion. సమస్తభూపాలకత్వము.

సాల sāla. [from Skt. శాల.] n. A house, edifice; a hall, room, place. గృహము, సభ, చావడి. చెరసాల a prison. టంకసాల a mint. పురిటిసాల a lying-in apartment. నాటకసాల a theatre. కొలువుసాల an audience-hall.

సాలకము sālakamu. [Skt.] n. A kind of fish. ఒకరకపు చేప.

సాలగ్రామము sala-gramamu. [Skt.] n. The Salagram, a species of ammonite, worshipped by the Vaishnavites as a type of Vishnu. విష్ణుభక్తులు పూజించు రాయి. మత్స్యమూర్తి సాలగ్రామము the Salagram resembling a fish.

సాలభంజిక sāla-bhanjika. n. A doll, a puppet. బొమ్మరాతిక, స్తంభమందుచేసినబొమ్మ.

సాలము sālamu. [Skt.] n. A wall surrounding a building. ప్రాకారము. A tree, వృక్షము. The "Sal-tree," the Umbrella Thorn Tree, *Acacia planifrons*. మద్దిచెట్టు.

సాలస్త్రి sālastri. [H.] n. A farrier, a horse doctor. గుర్రపువైద్యుడు.

సాలారిక sālarika. [Skt.] n. A woman taken captive in war. యుద్ధమందు బంధించి తెచ్చిన స్త్రీ.

సాలావృకము sālā-vrikamu. [Skt.] n. A dog. కుక్క. A wolf, తోడేలు. A jackal, నక్క. A monkey, కోతి.

సాలీడు sālīdu. [Tel. సాలె+ఈడు.] n. A spider. సాలెపురుగు. A weaver, సాలెవాడు.

సాలు sālu. [H.] n. A year. సంవత్సరము. సాలాబాదుగా s ā l ā-b ā d u-g ā. adv. Annually. సాలీనా or సాలీయానా sālīnā. adj. Annual. సాలారు sālāru. n. The end of the year. సాలుబస్సాలు sālu-bassālu. adj. Annual. సాలవాదళవాలెక్క sālavā-dalava-lekka. n. An account regarding the wet and dry grain crops, i. e., for the whole year.

సాలు or సాలువు Same as చాలువు. (q. v.)

సాలె sāle. [from Skt. జాలిక.] n. Weaving. బట్టలు నేయుడము. A caste of weavers, సాలెవాండ్లకులము. సాలెపట్టు sāle-pattu. (from జాలికపటము) n. A spider's web. సాలెపురుగు sāle-purugu. n. A spider. లూతము, ఊర్ణనాభి. సాలెవాడు sāle-vādu. n. A weaver.

సాలోక్యము sā-lōkyamu. [Skt. from స+లోకము.] n. Being in the same world, dwelling in heaven with God, దేవునితో సమాన లోకమందుండుట, సమానలోకత్వము.

సాల్వడు sālvadu. [Tel. సాలు+పడు.] v. n. To become sapless, or lose strength, నిస్సారమగు. To lean to a side, ఒరగు. సాల్వరచు sāl-varatsu. v. a. To cause to lean, &c.

సాళగము sālagamu. [Skt.] n. Harmony in music. తిలతండులన్యాయముగనైన రాగమేళనము. A certain tune, రాగవిశేషము. "లాలితకర్ణసాళగములొప్పెడు." BD. iii. 1364. సాళగించు sālag-intsu. v. n. To be mixed, or mingled, మిళితమగు. సాళగింపు sāla-gimpu. n. Mixing, harmony, మేళనము.

సాళువ, సాళువము, సాళ్వము or సాలువపు గ్రద్ద sāluva. [Tel.] n. A hawk used in hunting. డేగవిశేషము. "వేటసాగించెలరేగిసాళువపుగ్రద్దలు." P. i. 554. అడవినల్లసాళువ the black eagle. కొండనల్లసాళువ and కుంటేటిసాళ్వడేగ are other kinds. సాళ్వడు sālvadu. n. A name given to a dog that hunts like a hawk.

సావకాశము s-āvakāsamu. [Skt.] n. Leisure. సావకాశముగా leisurely.

సావధానము s-ā va-dhā n a m u. [Skt.] n. Attention. సావధానముగా attentively.

సావడచేప sāvada-chēpa. [Tel.] n. A kind of fish of the species called Chimaera, మత్స్యవిశేషము.

సావలి or సావలీడు sāvali. [Tel.] n. A mendicant fortune-teller, డుబుడక్కవాడు.

సావాసము sāvāsamu. [from Skt. సహ-వాసము.] n. Association, companionship, friendship, పొత్తు. సావాసి sāvāsi. n. A friend, an associate, చెలికాడు.

సావి sāvi. [Tel.] n. Time. కాలము. A blasted stalk of withered corn. తీరా పండని మను కంకి యెండిపోయిన పైరు. "ఎరువులెల్లెడుసావిగరువుచల్లగతాళిమామాకైనగంపలతానె తెచ్చి." KP. iv. 84.

సావి Same as సవి (q. v.)

సావిక sāvika [Skt] n. A midwife. మంత్రసాని.

సావిత్రి sāvitri. [Skt.] n. A name of Sarasvati. The gayatri o. sacred hymn to the sun. గాయత్రి. N. v. 79.

సావు Sam as . చావు (q. v.)

సాష్టాంగము s-āsht-āngamu. [Skt.] n. Prostrate adoration. Literally, touching the ground with (స) the eight (అష్ట) limbs

(అంగ), i. e., the hands, knees, shoulders, breast and forehead. సాగిలబడి దండము పెట్టడము. సాష్టాంగదండ ప్రణామముచేయు to do homage. సాష్టాంగదండము or సాష్టాంగ నమస్కారము prostrate homage.

"కరయుగములుచరణంబులు,
నురములలాటస్థలంబు నున్నతభుజముల్,
సరిధరణిమోపిమ్రొక్కిన,
బరువడిసాష్టాంగమండ్రు పరమమునీంద్రుల్."

సాసువులు *sāsuvulu.* [Tel.] n. plu. Mustard seed. ఆవాలు. H. ii. 251.

సాస్న *sāsna.* [Skt.] n. The dewlap of an ox. గంగడోలు.

సాహసము *sāhasamu.* [Skt.] adj. Daring, rash, outrageous, impetuous. తెగువగల. సాహసవృత్తి bold conduct. n. Courage, boldness, daring. Violence, rashness, temerity, impetuosity. Desperate or wild daring, a wild or desperate deed. చొరవ, తెగువ, తెగింపు. సాహసమువహించు to venture, to dare. **సాహసకృత్యము** *sāhasa-kṛityamu.* n. A daring act or deed, a feat, an outrage, తెగువగలపని. **సాహసించు** *sāhas-intsu.* v. n. To dare, venture. తెగించు, సాహసముచేయు. **సాహసికము** *sāhas-ikamu.* adj. Violent, desperate, bold, rash, reckless, hot-brained. తెగువగల. **సాహసికత్వము** *sāhas-ika-tvamu.* n. Daring, rashness, temerity, impetuosity, తెగువ, తెగింపు. **సాహసుడు** or **సాహసికుడు** *sāhasudu.* n. A bold, daring, rash or impetuous man. తెగువరి.

సాహస్రము *sāhasramu.* [Skt. from సహస్రము.] n. Many thousands; a host. వేనవేలు, సహస్రముల సమూహము. **సాహస్రుడు** *sāhasrudu.* n. The commander of a thousand (troops).

సాహాయ్యము *sāhāyyamu.* [Skt. from సహాయము.] n. Aid, assistance, help. సహాయత, సహాయత్వము, సహకారిత, తోడుపాటు.

సాహిణము *sāhiṇamu.* [Tel.] n. A stable. గుర్రపుసాల. **సాహిణి** or **సాహిణీ** *sāhiṇi.* n. A groom, a horsekeeper, రవుతు, గుర్రపువాడు. "పేరంబుముఖాల మెంగపట్ట పన్ని సాహిణులు కండుకొర్రమొదులికిగొనివచ్చి గంధవాహబాంధవంబు గుర్రీక మహాసైంధవంబు." Swa. iv. 37. "చప్పుళ్లుకొట్టి మదల్చుచు సాహిణీలు మావులబరపంగ నైరి." A. iii. 28. "సకలంబుగుర్వురాజభవనంబున సాహిణిరైయొదరింపడే." P. iii. 354.

సాహితి or **సాహిత్యము** *sāhiti.* [Skt.] n. Classical knowledge, scholarship, erudition, అర్థజ్ఞానము. పాండిత్యము. "సాహితీసమరాంగణ సార్వభౌము." A. pref. 54. Association, connection, సంసర్గము, కూడిక. **సాహిత్యజ్ఞాని** or **సాహిత్యజ్ఞానముగలవాడు** *sāhitya-gnyāni.* n. A classical scholar.

సాహు, సాహుకారి or **సాహుకారు** *sāhu.* [H.] n. A rich merchant, a banker.

సాహేబు *sāhēbu.* [H.] n. A sahib, a master. ప్రభువు. దొర. "సాహేబుగారు." రా. వి. v. A Mahomedan, తురకవాడు, మహమ్మదీయమతస్థుడు.

సాహో *sāhu.* [Mahrati.] interj. Behold! Be attentive! An exclamation used by heralds on the approach of a king or on the egress of an idol in a procession. పరాకు, ఎచ్చరిక. "తే॥ గీ॥ స్వామిసాహోపరాకు హెచ్చరికయనుచు, వేత్రిహస్తులు పలుమారు విన్నవింప." Anir. iv. 4.

సి si

సింగము *singamu.* [from Skt. సింహము.] n. A lion. సింహము. **సింగపుపీట** *singapu-pīṭa.* n. A throne, సింహాసనము. "తిమ్మక్షూ సింగపుపీట" పాంచా. i. **సింగడు** *singaḍu.* n. Narsimha. నృసింహుడు. A gypsy, ఎరుకలవాడు. "మాసింగడల్లతికికొండ దరికోతుల మాదితెచ్చినదియిది." S. i. 19. One who is angry.

కోపించినవాడు. **సింగళము** *singalamu*. [from Skt. సింహళము.] n. Ceylon. సింహళదేశము.

సింగి *singi*. n. (fem.) A gypsy woman, ఎరుకలది. **సింగినాదము** *singi-nādamu*. [from సింహనాదము.] n. A horn, a trumpet, కొమ్ము. Nonsense, stupidity, folly, వెర్రితనము. "పరచేతి బెత్తపు మురువుతో కళముఁ దాల్చిన సింగినాదంబులోడ." Chandra Bhānu. Chari. ii. 54.

సింగాణి *singāni*. [from Skt. శార్ఙ్గ.] adj. Made of horn. కొమ్ముతో చేసిన. "సింగాణివిండులు." S. i. 158. **సింగాణి**, **సింగిణి** or **సింగిణీ** [from Skt. శింజిని.] n. A bow. విల్లు. The name of a dog, ఒకకుక్క పేరు. "తిరిగిరిగి సింగిణి వేయుచుండఁజూచుకొనిరా." Swa. iv. 160. "సింగిణీతిరకసంబులు." A. ii. 30.

సింగారము *singāramu*. [from Skt. శృంగారము.] n. Beauty, prettiness, ornament, decoration, embellishment. అందము, అలంకారము, శృంగారము. adj. Ornamented, handsome. అలంకారమైన, అందమైన. **సింగారించు** *singārintsu*. v. a. To adorn, beautify, trim. అలంకరించు. **సింగారి** *singāri*. n. A well-adorned woman, a beautiful woman, శృంగారవతియగు ఆడుది.

సింగి *singi*. [from Skt. సింహము.] n. Irritation. కోపము. వానికి సింగిరగిలినది he is enraged. See also under సింగము.

సింగిణీ See సింగాణి.

సింగిలీకము *singilīkamu*. [Tel.] n. The great black monkey, పెద్ద నల్లకోతి. "ముంగిసవింగిసింగలించింగిలీక కుంపు మానిసికోతులగొన్ని కూడిరము." H. v. 400.

సిందురము *sinduramu*. [from Skt. సిందూరము.] n. Red lead, vermilion, చెందిరము. A sort of tree, వావిలిచెట్టు, సిందువారవృక్షము.

సిందువారము *sindu-vāramu*. [Skt.] n. A kind of tree, *Vitex negundo*. వావిలిచెట్టు

సిందూరము *sindūramu*. [Skt.] n. Same as సిందురము (q. v.)

సింధురము See సింధువు.

సింధువు *sindhuvu*. [Skt.] n. The ocean. A river. The river Indus; the country on its banks, సముద్రము. నది, నదివిశేషము, తన్నికటదేశము. **సింధుశయనుడు** *sindhu-sayanudu*. n. He whose couch is the bed of the sea, i. e., Vishnu. విష్ణువు. **సింధుదేశము** *sindhu-dēsamu*. n. Sindh: the country on the banks of the Indus, the Punjab, సింధునదీప్రాంతభూమి. **సింధుపుత్రి** or **సింధుకన్య** *sindhu-putri*. n. Lit. the daughter of the sea; an epithet of Lakshmi. లక్ష్మి. **సింధురము** *sindhuramu*. n. An elephant. ఏనుగు.

సింహము *simhamu*. [Skt.] n. A lion. The sign Leo. (In composition), Eminent, chief, మృగేంద్రము, అయిదవరాశి. శ్రేష్ఠము. సింహము or సింహపుపలక a large piece of timber, లావాటిమాను. కవిసింహము a noble poet. సింహస్వప్నము (lit. the elephant's dream of his mortal foe the lion.) a killing thought, a dreadful apprehension. సింహలలాటము (corrupted into సింహతలాటము) an ornament in the form of a lion's head, the figure carved on the front of the pole of a Hindu litter. **సింహద్వారము** *simha-dvāramu*. n. The portal or front gate of a house, తలవాకిలి. **సింహనాదము** *simha-nādamu*. n. A loud cry, a war cry or war whoop. Huzzas. క్ష్వేళ, యుద్ధకాలములో భటులు అరచే అరుపు, బొబ్బ. **సింహసంహననుడు** *simha-samhananudu*. n. Lit. one who kills a lion, i.e., a very handsome person, a man of noble presence or figure. సర్వాంగసుందరుడు. **సింహావలోకనము** *simh-āva-lōkanamu*. n. Lit. a lion's look Retrospection. A trick in versification consisting of making each line begin with the last word of the preceding one. వెనుకకు మళ్లిమళ్లి చూచుచుపోవడము, పద్యములో

ముందుచెప్పిన పదమును మళ్లీయెత్తుట రావడము. "ఇదిమహోత్తర కాంతికింపైనదింబంబు, దింబంబు గాదిదిచెంగడుకెంపు, కెంపుగాదిది శేటియుండుదిన మంకెన, మంకెనగాదిదిమందిదిరుగు." T. iii. 63. సింహాసనము simh-asanamu. n. A lion seat, a seat or throne supported by sculptured lions, a throne, నృపాసనము, భద్రాసనము. రాజపీఠము. సింహాసనస్థుడు simh-asana-sthudu. n. One who is enthroned. పట్టాభిషిక్తుడు. సింహి simhi. n. A lioness. ఆడుసింహము. సింహి or సింహిక n. The mother of Rāhu. రాహువుయొక్క తల్లి.

సింహుండము simhundamu. [Skt.] n. The plant called *Euphorbia antiquorum*. వజ్రకంటకము, బొమ్మజెముడు.

సిక sika. [from Skt. శిఖ.] n. A crest, a lock of hair left on the crown. శిఖ, కేశబంధము. సిగ, జుట్టు.

సికతము sikatamu. [Skt.] n. Sand, ఇసుక. A sandy soil, ఇసుకనేల, మొరపనేల. Stone or gravel in the bladder. సికతామేహము sikatā-mēhamu. n. Stone or gravel in the bladder. అశ్మరి. మూత్రకృచ్ఛ్రము. సికతిలము sika-tilamu. adj. Sandy, ఇసుకగల.

సికా or సిక్కా sika. [from Skt. శిఖ.] n. A seal. సికాయుంగరము a ring which is used as a seal, a favourite ring. ముద్దుటుంగరము.

సిక్తము siktamu. [Skt.] adj. Wet, wetted, sprinkled. తడిసిన, తడుపబడిన. మధుసిక్తము moistened with honey, honeyed.

సిక్థకము or సిక్థము sikthakamu. [Skt.] n. Bee's wax. మధూచ్ఛిష్టము, మయినము.

సిక్యము sikyamu. [Skt.] n. The string or loop suspended from either end of a pole or yoke to receive the burden, a string or loop suspended from the ceiling of a house to hang things on. కావడితిట్టి. పాలకుండలు మొదలైనవి పెట్టేతిట్టి, చిక్కము.

సిగ or సిక siga. [from Skt. శిఖ.] n. A lock of hair, left on the crown of the head, at the time of tonsure. సిగబంతి a bouquet or garland of flowers worn on the head.

సిగరము sigaramu. [from Skt. శిఖరము.] Same as శిఖరము (q. v.)

సిగరి or సిగర sigari. [from Skt. శిఖరిణీ.] n. Buttermilk seasoned with spices, మెంతిమజ్జిగ.

సిగినాలు, సికినపువక్కలు or సిగినపువక్కలు siginalu. [Tel.] n. plu. A fine sort of areca nuts, పల్లాలుపల్లాలుగానుండే వాటమైన వక్కలు.

సిగ్గు siggu. [Tel.] n. Shame, shyness, modesty, timidity. లజ్జ. సిగ్గుపడు, సిగ్గుచెందు or సిగ్గుపోవు siggu-padu. v. n. To blush, to be ashamed, to be shy or bashful, లజ్జించు. సిగ్గుపాటు siggu-pāṭu. n. The act of being ashamed or feeling shy, సిగ్గుపడుట. సిగ్గుమాలిన siggu-mālina. adj. Shameless, impudent. లజ్జలేని. సిగ్గరు sigg-aru. (సిగ్గు+అరు) or సిగ్గుచెడు v. n. To lose shame, to become shameless, సిగ్గుపోవు. సిగ్గరి sigg-ari. n. One who is ashamed. సిగ్గుగలవాడు, సిగ్గుగలది. సిగ్గరికత్తె or సిగ్గరికత్తియ sigg-ari-katte. n. A shy or bashful woman. లజ్జగలది. సిగ్గరికాడు sigg-ari-kāḍu. n. One who is ashamed or bashful, సిగ్గుగలవాడు. సిగ్గరితనము sigg-ari-tanamu. n. Shamefacedness, bashfulness. సిగ్గుగానుండడము. సిగ్గిడి sigg-iḍi. (సిగ్గు+ఇడి) n. One who has lost all shame, లజ్జచెడినవాడు, లజ్జచెడినది.

సిచయము sichayamu. [Skt.] n. A cloth, వస్త్రము. An old cloth, జీర్ణవస్త్రము.

సిడము or సిడెము siḍamu. [Tel.] n. A flag, a banner, ధ్వజము. A flagstaff, ధ్వజస్తం

ధము. "నవత్రిస్ఫుటిత్వమైచినవదిరిథ్యంబులకు సూతునరదముసిడముగా జదురుపలుసెదు." M. VII. v. 257. "తిరిగాడుసిడెముగా." M. VI. i. 340. ib. II. ii. 4. ib. VII. ii. 127.

సిడి *siḍi*. [Tel.] n. The cross beam of a picota or water lift. ఏతవుమ్రాను. "క॥ ఏతవుసిడిరా వంగిన, బాతాళపుసిరు దమ్ము." A hook or goad. A machine on which men were formerly suspended in the air by a hook passed through the sinews of the back and swung around in honor of the goddess పోలేరమ్మ. గంపసిడి a basket in which a devotee (instead of being hooked up) is seated and swung about. త్రిప్పి చెల్లించుకొనువారు కొందరు వీపునకొక్కించుకొని ఆడే గాలపుమాను. ఈ దేవతకు ప్రతిసంవత్సరమును మేకపోతు సిడి ఒకటియును నరసిడి ఒకటియును జరుపుచుందురు in honor of this goddess they swing a goat and a man every year. **సిల్లు** or **సిడులు** *sillu*. n. An elephant goad, బరికోల. "ఏనుంగునకుసిల్లుసూపినట్టు." M. IV. v. 92. "కను గొనిసాత్యకి దేమంగునకు సిల్లుసూపినట్లుకోపం బున." ib. VI. ii. 311. "అంగనకుజాలయుగా పేటలు, బోనముల్ సిడులు గావించెగా సుతోత్ప త్తికై." H. ii. 100.

సిత *sita*. [Skt.] n. Sugar. శర్కర. **సితము** *sitamu*. adj. White, bright, light-coloured. తెల్లని. **సితాభము** or **సితాభ్రము** *sitabhamu*. n. Crude camphor. పచ్చకర్పూరము. **సితుడు** *situḍu*. n. One who is white, తెల్లనివాడు.

సిద్దాయము *siddāyamu*. [from Skt. సిద్ధాయము.] n. Saving in expenditure, economy. Embezzlement, pickings. A tax, fee. కర్చుకు ఇచ్చినదానిలో కొంచెముకొంచెముగా తీసికొని కూడబెట్టడము, అపహారించడము, పన్ను, సుంకము.

సిద్దీ *siddī*. [H.] n. An African, a negro, an Abyssinian. నల్లగా మొద్దువలె ఏనుగంత బలముగల కాపూటివవాడు.

సిద్దె or **సిద్దెలు** *sidde*. [Tel.] n. A leather bottle or vessel.

సిద్ధము *siddhamu*. [Skt.] adj. Ready, prepared, ఆయత్తమైన. Accomplished, completed, fulfilled, తీరిన. Cooked, boiled, వండబడిన Constant, eternal, ఎడతెగని, నిత్యమైన. Real, right, true, certain న్యాయమైన, రూఢమైన, యథార్థమైన, ప్రసిద్ధమైన. పడడమునకు సిద్ధమైయుండినందున as it was ready to fall. n. Readiness, accomplishment. Reality, truth. నిష్పన్నముగానుం డడము, సన్నద్ధముగానుండడము, తాత్త్వికత, వాస్తవము. The twenty first of the astronomical Yogas. నిష్కంటకాదియుక్తమైయుండు యోగములలో యిరువైయొకటోది. **సిద్ధపడు** *siddha-paḍu*. v. n. To get ready, to be ready or prepared. **సిద్ధపరచు** *siddha-paraṭsu*. v. a To make ready, prepare. తయారుచేయు, సిద్ధముచేయు. **సిద్ధపురుషుడు** *siddha-purushaḍu*. n. One who by devout abstraction and severe mortification has acquired spiritual perfection and superhuman powers. యోగబలముచేత అణిమాదశక్తిగలవాడు. మహాపురుషుడు. **సిద్ధక్రియ** *siddha-kriya*. n. An action done by a sage or saint. An elixir or miraculous medicine. సిద్ధపురుషునిచేత చెప్పబడ్డమహౌషధము. **సిద్ధముగా** *siddhamu-gā*. adv. In readiness, ready. Actually, verily, doubtlessly. నిజముగా, తాత్త్వికముగా, నిస్సందేహముగా, సన్నద్ధముగా. సిద్ధముగానున్నది it is ready. సిద్ధముగాచెప్పు to tell positively or definitely. **సిద్ధాంతము** *siddh-āntamu*. n. Demonstration. An established truth, a principle. A conclusion, result, decree, doctrine. స్థిరమైనతత్త్వము, స్థాపనము, నిర్ణయము. An astronomical work. నానావిధ జ్యోతిషగ్రంథము. సూర్యసిద్ధాంతము solar astronomy. సిద్ధాంతపంచాంగము an almanac. **సిద్ధాంతి** *siddh-anti*. n. A follower of the Mimamsa philosophy. One who demonstrates or establishes his conclusions. A mathematician or astronomer; one who prepares an almanac. పంచాంగము గుణించువాడు. సిద్ధాంతీకరించు siddh-ānti-kar-intsu. v. a. To lay down as a rule or doctrine, to establish or demonstrate. సిద్ధాంతముచేయు. సిద్ధానుస్వారము siddh-ānu-svāramu. n. The letter N, when an integral part of a word and not merely inserted to save elision, సహజమైనసున్న. సిద్ధార్థి siddh-ārthi. n. The name of a Telugu year. సిద్ధార్థుడు siddh-ārthudu. n. A name of Buddha. సిద్ధి siddhi. n. Fulfilment, accomplishment. The attainment of any object, success: the result, fruit, effect. Ascetic perfection: acquirement of supernatural powers; final beatitude. నిష్పత్తి, ఈడేరుట, ఇరవేరడము, వాంఛితప్రాప్తి, అణిమాదులుచేకూరడము. ఇష్టసిద్ధి, అభీష్టసిద్ధి or మనోరథసిద్ధి the gratification of a wish. క్రియాసిద్ధి the completion of a deed. మంత్రసిద్ధి a charm taking effect. కాయసిద్ధి the state of being invulnerable. "కొట్టిన నదియుకుండుట కాయసిద్ధి." L. xix. 166. ఆయన సిద్ధినిపొందినాడు he died or went to heaven. సిద్ధిరస్తు let (him) be happy, be it successful. సిద్ధించు siddintsu. v. n. To be effected, fulfilled or accomplished; to be gained, acquired, attained, ఈడేరు, సమకూడు, లభించు, ప్రాప్తమగు. ఆయనకు మోక్షము సిద్ధించినది he gained final beatitude. సిద్ధుడు siddhudu. n. A person who has acquired supernatural powers by magic methods; a sort of demigod; a sage, a seer, దేవయోనివిశేషము, అణిమాదిగుణోపేతో విశ్వావసుప్రభృతి, వ్యాసాదులు. సిద్ధురాలు siddhu-r-ālu. n. A female recluse who has acquired supernatural powers by magical methods, అణిమాది సిద్ధిగల స్త్రీ.

సిధ్మము or సిధ్మలము sidhmamu. [Skt.] n. A beauty spot, a bright or golden tint or spot on the body. సిబ్బెము.

సిపాయి sipāyi. [H.] n. A Sepoy, కాలిబంటు.

సిఫారసు sipārasu. [H.] n. A recommendation, a certificate, a testimonial.

సిబ్బంది sibbandi. [H.] n. An army, a retinue, armed peons, సేన, పరివారము.

సిబ్బి or సిబ్బితట్ట sibbi. [Tel.] n. A cullender, a strainer. ఇత్తడిమూకుడు, కంచుపాత్రసున్నప్పుడు కప్పెడిమూదముచేయుటట్ట. చిల్లులసిబ్బి a perforated strainer.

సిబ్బితి sibbiti. [Tel.] n. Bashfulness, modesty. సిగ్గు సిబ్బితికాడు sibbiti-kādu. n. A bashful man, సిగ్గుగలవాడు, బిడియపడువాడు. సిబ్బితికత్తె sibbiti-katte. n. A bashful woman, బిడియముగలది. "కాంతుడుంచి తెచ్చినదైనం, కాంతకు సిగ్గునవ కెల్లగాక కటకటా, కాంతుడుసిబ్బితికాదై, కాంతయునజ్ఞనా సెల్లుకాపురమింకకా." KP. iv. 72.

సిబ్బెము or సిబ్బెరము sibbemu. [from Skt. సిధ్మ.] n. A beauty spot; a damask mahogany tint; a bright or golden tint or spot on the body, సిధ్మలము.

సిర sira. [Skt.] n. Any tubular vessel of the body, a nerve, a vein, a tendon, a gut. ధమని, నాడి, పోలునరము, నరి మెన్నుయొక్క చినర.

సిరంగము si-rangamu. [from Skt. శ్రీరంగము.] n. Srirangam, a sacred town near Trichinopoly. సిరంగడు si-rangadu. (for శ్రీరంగడు). n. The name of the god Sri-Ranga worshipped there.

సిరము siramu. [from Skt. శిరము.] n. The head, తల. Crude camphor, పచ్చకర్పూరము. "తొరగినపచ్చకప్పురపుసిరము." Swa. ii. 59. adj. Cool, చల్లని.

సిరా sirā. [H.] n. Indian ink. మసి, కాటుక, ఇంకి.

సిరాజి or సిరాజీ sirāji. [Perhaps corruption of "Kurachi."] n. A name of a country, సా. ii. adj. Excellent, శ్రేష్ఠము.

సిరాణము *sirāṇamu*. [Tel.] n. A kind of weapon. ఆయుధవిశేషము.

సిరి *siri*. [from Skt. శ్రీ.] n. A name of Lakshmi, the goddess of riches. లక్ష్మీదేవి. Fortune, prosperity, wealth, సంపద. Beauty, splendour, lustre. అందము, శోభ. **సిరిగంధము** Same as శ్రీగంధము (q. v.) **సిరిగట్టు** *siri-gaṭṭu*. n. The name of a hill called శ్రీశైలము. **సిరిచూలి** *siri-tsūli*. n. The son of Lakshmi, i. e., Manmadha. **సిరిమంతుడు** Same as శ్రీమంతుడు (q. v.) **సిరిసింగణావత్తి** *siri-singaṇa-vatti*. n. A certain game played by boys. చిన్నవాండ్రు ఆడే ఒక ఆట.

సిలసిల *sila-sila*. [Tel. (anuk.)] adv. Quickly. త్వరగా. "ఫెళఫెళ వాన్చ మల్లడిగ చేర్చి జనంబున చెట్టుచెట్టునన్ సిలసిల ప్రాకిపూబొదిలు చించి వాళ్ళవాళ్ళిగాఫలావలుల్ జలజలరాల్చి." B. vii. 154.

సిలాజిత్తు *silā-jittu*. [from Skt. శిలాజితు.] n. Bitumen; red chalk. పర్వతధాతుభేదము.

సిలుగు *silugu*. [Tel.] n. Mischief, trouble, inconvenience. ఆపద, చెరుపు, సంకటము, తొందర, ఉపద్రవము. "జలధిగ్రామణీనిశీథము జనని విచ్చలెనే ప్రసంగింపగా సిలుగుల్ చేసెగదిం వళిద్దరహరించెరా." P. i. 626.

సిలువ *siluva*. [H.] n. A cross. కొఱ్ఱు.

సిల్హము or సిల్హకము *silhamu*. [Skt.] n. Incense, gum benjamin or olibanum. పిండికె ము, అందుగుబంక, ధూపద్రవ్యము, చిల్లమడ్డి.

సిల్లి or సిదులు See under సిది.

సివంగి, సివగి, సివ్వంగి or సివ్వగి *sivangi*. [Tel.] n. A cheetah or hunting leopard. చిఱుతపులి. "ఇంచుమించుగ నడిచి మెకి ములగడుమునిదిగోబలుసివంగులు." S. i. 155. "వినుతిశివాచారమనుకుళారి యున జనలోకపథమున సివ్వంగిజంపి." BD. v. 1440. **సివంగితనము** *sivangi-tanamu*. n. Fractiousness, peevishness, a cross or snappish temper. కోపముదోతతనము, చిటచిట.

సివము or సిగము *sivamu*. [from Skt. శివ.] n. Inspiration by the deity or by an evil spirit; possession by a demon. ఆవేశము, దేవతావేశము. సివమాడు or సివాలాడు to play pranks as if possessed by an evil spirit.

సిసలు *sisalu*. [H.] adj. Settled, నిర్ధారమైన.

సిసువు *sisuvu*. [from Skt. శిశువు.] n. An infant. పసిబిడ్డ.

సిసృక్ష *sisṛiksha*. [Skt.] n. A desire to create, సృజింపనిచ్ఛ. **సిసృక్షువు** *sisṛikshuvu*. n. One who desires to create, సృజింపనిచ్ఛగలవాడు.

సిస్తు *sistu*. [Tel.] adj. Pretty, nice, becoming, trim, elegant. అందమైన, సొంపైన. "సిస్తైన దుస్తులు." Bmj. ii. 212. n. Delicacy, fineness. సొంపు. "సీ॥ కస్తూరికాచర్చిసిస్తుగాదనిటులగాతానికుంకుమగందమలది." UR. iv. 237. **సిస్తుగ** or **సిస్తుగా** *sistu-ga*. adv. Gracefully. సొగసుగా, సొంపుగా. **సిస్తుపరచు** *sistu-paratsu*. v. a. To make trim or fine, to deck, to adorn, సొంపుచేయు. చక్కచేయు. "కస్తూరితిలకము సిస్తుపరచి." Ila. i. 80.

సిస్తు or శిస్తు *sistu*. [H.] n. A tax, government rent, charge. పన్ను.

సిస్సాల *sissāla*. [H.] adj. Triennial, మూడేండ్లకొకమారువచ్చే.

సీ sī

సీ *sī*. [from Skt. శ్రీ.] n. Lakshmi. Wealth, సంపద. "సీరాముసేనవాలుమెకంబుల్." స్వా. iv.

సీ or సీ సీ *sī*. [Tel.] interj. Foh! pah! bah! జాగుప్సార్థకము దు చెప్పు మాట "సీయను దివముగాటుటు చేసెననా నగుబాటు

వచ్చెవాకోయుకు." Paidim. v. 108. "తేనెల ధూమమెంగనమిచేదనెలందుమనంబునందు, సీ, బ్రతుకునిరర్థకంబునుమబ్బురుచేసదు.". T. iv. 161.

సీకాయ *si-kaya.* [Tel.] n. The soap acacia, *Acacia concinna.* (E. P.) వాడు సీకాయతీగవలె ఎండిపోయాడు he is become a mere thread-paper.

సీకారి *sikari.* [from Skt. శ్రీకారి.] n. A singer. పాటపాడువాడు, గాయకుడు.

సీగాడు *sigadu.* [Tel.] n. A name given to the Black-bellied Finch Lark, *Myrrhulauda grisea.* (F. B. I.)

సీడు or సిడు *sidu.* [Tel.] n. A skein of thread. పుంజము తక్కువవార. plu. సీడ్లు.

సీత *sita.* [Skt.] n. A furrow, the track of the ploughshare, నాగటిచాలు. The name of Rama's wife, రామునిభార్య. The river Ganges, గంగ. సీతారామార్పణముగా చేసినదానము a gift made in the sacred names of Sita and Rama, a solemn gift. సీతకాటుకలు *sita-katukalu.* n. plu. (Lit. white and black) A sort of rice. ధాన్యభేదము. సీతమ్మపురుగునూలు *sit-amma-purugu-nulu.* n. A certain parasitical plant, *Cuscuta reflexa.* వానకాలములో పొదలమీద అల్లుకొనే ఒకతీగె. సీతాకోకచిలక *sita-koka-chilaka.* n. A butterfly. చిత్రవిచిత్రమైన వర్ణములుగల రెక్కలుగల ఒక పురుగు. సీతాఫలము *sita-phalamu.* n. The white custard apple, *Annona squamosa,* గంధగాత్రము. సీతాభోగములు *sita-bhogamulu.* n. A sort of rice. వడ్లభేదము.

సీతు or సీతువు *situ.* [from Skt. శీతము.] n. Cold, చలి. The cold season, winter, the cold weather, శీతకాలము, చలికాలము.

సీత్కారము, సీత్కృతము or సీత్కృతి *sit-karamu.* [Skt.] n. A sigh: the sound of gushing or spirting: a whispering sound, as in shivering.

సీత్యము *sityamu.* [Skt. from సీత.] n. Land that has been once ploughed, ఒకసారి దున్నినచేలు.

సీదరము or సీత్రము *sidaramu.* [Tel.] n. Poverty, దారిద్ర్యము. లేమిడి. A serpent, a snake, సర్పము. A serpent's skin, కుబుసము. "సీ॥ అనయుంబునసికతప్పనిగో త్రపతుతెవ్వడునసీదరముతోనియునఘభోగులు." Vasu. i. 8. "మాటికినికోకకుసీదరప్రైక్రిందుచుం." P. i. 800.

సీదా *sida.* [H.] n. Right, straight; honest. సీదాగా honestly, rightly, straightly, completely, పూర్తిగా, పొత్తిగా.

సీమ *sima.* [Tel.] n. A country, district: (Colloquially,) a foreign country, as Europe or England. దేశము, (వాడుకగా) యూరోపుఖండము, తెక, ఇంగ్లండుదేశము. A kingdom, రాజ్యము. A limit, boundary, barrier, border, frontier, ఎల్ల, పొలిమేర, హద్దు. A part, place, site, స్థలము, ప్రదేశము. సీమలువిభ్నాములు ఏర్పరచిరి they fixed the boundaries. సీమలుగానిసీమలు countries which are not our home, i. e., foreign lands. మా సీమలు పట్టుకొన్నారు they seized our lands. adj. Foreign, not native. సీమకోడి a turkey. సీమసున్నము white chalk. సీమచింతచెట్టు a kind of tree. సీమకలిచెట్టు a kind of jungle tree.

సీమంతము *simantamu.* [Skt.] n. The parting of the hair on the forehead. కేశవీధి, పాపట. సీమంతము or సీమంతోన్నయనము n. A ceremonial; parting the hair on the forehead at certain periods of first pregnancy. ముదటికర్భవతిగానుండు స్త్రీకి చేయు సంస్కారవిశేషము. సీమంతపుత్రుడు a first born son. సీమంతాస్థి *simant-asthi.* n. The parietal bone. సీమంతిని *simantini.* n. A woman, స్త్రీ.

సీమాతి *simati.* [Tel.] n. An honorable woman, lady, matron. భాగ్యశాలియైన స్త్రీ.

"మా చెలులంటిట్టుమునంత చేరెనటకాసీమాటిసీ మాటికెన్వలదన్న కాదనకేల్పత్రెదరు." Paidi-n. iii. 121.

సీరము *siramu.* [Skt.] n. A plough. నాగలి. P. i. 661. **సీరి** or **సీరపాణి** *siri.* n. An epithet of Balarama. బలరాముడు. **సీరాంగము** *sir-angamu.* n. A plough-share. కర్రు.

సీల or **శీల** *sila.* [Tel.] n. A nail or peg. కీలము. **సీలమండ** or **శీలమండ** *sila-manda.* n. The ankle. గుల్ఫము, మడిమ.

సీవనము *sivanamu.* [Skt. Cf. Eng. 'sew.'] n. Sewing, stitching. (బట్ట) కుట్టడము.

సీవిరి *siviri.* [Tel.] n. A chowri or cow-tail whisk. వింజామరము. "సారథ్యంబువహింప శౌరియును సితచ్ఛత్రంబు గాండీవి చెల్వారం బట్టగ సీవిరుల్ గవలిడగా." M. XII. i. 386.

సీసము or **సీసకము** *sisamu.* [Skt.] n. Lead. సత్తు, నాగము. నల్లసీసము black lead. తెండిసీసము pewter. [From Skt. శీర్షకము.] n. A certain feat in wrestling. మల్లబంధవిశేషము. **సీసకము** *sisakamu.* n. A crown. కిరీటము. **సీసము** *sisamu.* n. A certain metre used in Telugu poetry. పద్యవిశేషము. Irritation, madness. కోపము, వెర్రి. అతనికి సీసముకెక్కినది he was enraged.

సీసా *sisa.* [H.] n. A bottle. బుడ్డి.

సు su

సు *su.* [Skt.] A prefix (like 'Eu' in Greek, meaning) Good, well, శోభనమైన, మంచి. సుముహూర్తము a happy hour. సుదినము a lucky day. Much, very much, thoroughly, మిక్కిలి. సుకరము easy. సుకర్మము a good deed, సత్కార్యము, మంచి పని. సుకృతము a good or righteous deed, righteousness, పుణ్యము. సుఖిమానము happy. **సుగంధి** or **సుగంధపాల** *su-gandhi.* n. A medicinal drug. *Periploca indica.* A perfume, fragrance, మంచి పరిమళముగల వస్తువు. సుగుణము an amiable disposition, a virtue or good quality. వానియందు ఒక సుగుణమున్నది he has one good point or quality. సుగుణుడు or సుగుణి a good man, మంచివాడు, సరసుడు. సుచరిత్రుడు a man of a good character, మంచిశీలముగలవాడు. సుచరిత్ర a woman of a good character. సుజనుడు a good man, మంచివాడు. సుతనువు a handsome woman, శ్రేష్ఠస్త్రీ. సుతనుడు a handsome or well proportioned man, అవయవసౌష్ఠవముగలవాడు. సుదాత a liberal man, దానశీలుడు. సుదారుణము terrible, horrible, భయంకరమైన. సుదూరము very far, మిక్కిలిదూరమైన. సునిశితము acute, very sharp, అతితీక్ష్ణమైన. సునీతుడు a virtuous man, పుణ్యాత్ముడు. సుపథము a path easy to travel, a good road, మంచిత్రోవ, సత్పథము. సుపర్ణుడు an epithet of Garuda, గరుత్మంతుడు. సుప్రలాపము a good word, మంచిమాట; eloquence, elegant discourse, సువచనము. సుప్రసన్నము well pleased, favourable, clear, clean, సుప్రసన్నమైన, నిర్మలమైన, స్వచ్ఛమైన. సుప్రసన్నత delight, clearness, ఉల్లాసము, తేట. "మనమున సుప్రసన్నత సెందగా." Vish. i. 5. సుప్రసిద్ధముగా most celebrated, లోకరూఢిగా. సుబద్ధము correct, true, free from error, నిజమైన; truth, fact, right, నిజము. సుభటుడు a champion, a warrior, శూరుడు. సుభాషితము a good word, eloquence an eloquent word, మంచివాక్కు. "అమృత్వ దాద్యేగాలలోన సుభాషితముంబతింపగన్." సుభిక్షము plenty; prosperous, plentiful. (the opposite is దుర్భిక్షము scarcity.) సుభిక్షముగానుండుకాలము a time of plenty. సుమతి good sense, a sound mind: a wise heart, మంచిబుద్ధి, సద్బుద్ధి. సుమనస్కుడు a good hearted or benevolent man, మంచిమనస్సుగలవాడు. సుమహితము most excellent, దివ్యమైన. సురసము sweet, well favoured, elegant, మధురమైన, సుందరమైన. సురక్షితము well guarded, secure, safe, comfortable, క్షేమమైన, హాయిగానుండే. సురక్షితముగా happily, safely, in a flourishing state, క్షేమముగా, హాయిగా. సురుచిరము beautiful, lovely, engaging, సుందరమైన, రమణీయమైన, మనోజ్ఞమైన. సురూపము handsome, well formed, మనోహరమైన. సుదూపుడు a handsome looking man. సువచనము a good word, మంచిమాట. M. XVI. i. 107. సువాణి a sweet-voiced lady, మంచికంఠము గల స్త్రీ. సువ్రతము a good vow, మంచినోము. సుశ్రావ్యము melodious, చెవులకు మిక్కిలి యింపుగానుండే. సుశ్లోకుడు a celebrated man, సత్కీర్తివంతుడు. M. XIII. iii. 276. సుసంగము good company or society, సత్సహవాసము. సుస్థిరము firm, steady, stable, దృఢమైన, నిలుకడైన. సుస్నాతుడు one who has bathed, స్నానముచేసినవాడు. సుస్నాతుడై having bathed. సుస్నిగ్ధము smooth and soft. మిక్కిలి నున్నని.

సు or సుమ్ము su. [Tel. short for చూడుము.] interj. Indeed! look ye! See సుమి.

సుంకము sunkamu. [from Skt. శుల్కం.] n. A toll, custom, dues, tax. శుల్కము, పన్ను. An obstacle, ప్రతిబంధము. "పంకజాతుని చెల్వొసంగకమునిగి." Swa. iii. 25. కప్పమిమ్మని అనగా, అతిశయించి అని భావము. "చు॥ అతడుతదల్ప పాపఫలమందుటసుంకమువీడిపోయె." A. vi. 55. అనగా, ప్రతిబంధకము నివర్తించిపోయె. "సుంకపు కానులు." S. iii. 207. సుంకమ్మ or సుంకాలమ్మ sunkamma. n. The name of a village goddess. సుంకరి. సుంకరీడు or సుంకీడు sunk-ari. n. A custom house officer; an exciseman. శుల్కవాది, సాయీ సుబారుడు. సుంకము వసూలుచేయువాడు. సుంకరిమెట్టు sunk-ari-mettu. n. A toll or custom-house. సుంకము పుచ్చుకొనేస్థలము.

సుంకు sunku. [Tel.] n. A corn blossom: the yellow flower that comes on each grain in an ear or head of corn, కంకిలోనిగింజ పొలుపుట్టకముందు ప్రతిగింజమీద పచ్చగానుండేపువ్వు. Grain ceremoniously thrown over a married couple. ఒక పళ్లెములో బియ్యముపోసి పైనపళ్లెముమూసి వధూవరులమీదపాటలుపాడుచు చల్లేబియ్యము. "మనయిరామాధవులకుశోభనము టంచుచల్లగాపాడి సుంకులుచేల్లిరపుడు." Ila. i. 114. "విరయుల్ గంటలుగట్టి సుంకువెలయా విం కెంబుతో సెంతిగాకరుకుల్ జాపెమతో తుదలా విరిసిన్ సుక్కిలా వ్రాలుముక్ కంకిగావరులొందలా తెకునింకె కాకలముగర్భింబుల్ తృణప్రాయమై." U.H. iv. 3. 65. సుంకుపోసుకొన్న జొన్న the great-millet in flower. An obstacle or obstruction. ప్రతిబంధము.

సుంకేసలము or సుంకేసరి sunkēsalamu. [Tel.] n. The Tiger-bean-tree, a large tree with white flowers.

సుండీ. సుడీ. సుము, సుడి or సుమండీ sundi. [Tel. for చూడుడు] interj. Look ye, do you know. See సుమి. "మనకిదిసమయము సుండీ." M. vii. 1. 353. "వేమామాటలు వేదముసుండీ." Vema. 2098.

సుంత sunta. [Tel.] adj. Little, small, slight, short, trifling. రవంత, కొంచెము, ఇసుమంత, ఇంచుక. n. A little. కొంచెము. "సుంతయోరుం గబల్మాను." Bmj. ii. 50.

సుందరము sundaramu. [Skt.] adj. Handsome, beautiful, fair, fine. సురూపమైన, విలక్షణమైన, చక్కని. సుందరత sundarata. n. Prettiness, beauty, fairness. చక్కదనము, అందము. "ఏదేవునందిరించేపారుదేవతాతతసభా విభవసుందరతకెందు." B. ii. సుందరి sundari. n. A beauty, a lovely girl. చక్కనిస్త్రీ, అందకత్తె. సుందరుడు sundarudu. n. A handsome man, చక్కనివాడు. సుందారి sundari. n. A certain tree. వృక్షవిశేషము "చిటికారి సుందారి, చీకర్రి, తుమ్మయు." H. iv. 9.

సుకట sukata. [Skt.] n. An untamed cow.

సుకము sukamu. [from Skt. సుఖము.] n. Happiness. సుఖము. సుకవాసి suka-vāsi. n. A happy man, one who leads an easy life, కష్టపడక సుఖముగానుండువాడు.

సుకరము su-karamu. [Skt.] adj. Easy, feasible, practicable. సులభమైన, సుసాధ్యమైన. సుకర su-kara. n. A tame cow.

సుకర్మము See under సు.

సుకారి sukāri. [from H. సికారి.] n. A gypsy tribe. ఊరూరుతిరిగి వర్తకముచేసే ఒక నీచజాతి.

సుకియ sukiya. [from Skt. సుఖము.] n. A sort of cake. ఒకవిధమైన భక్ష్యము.

సుకుమారము su-kumāramu. [Skt.] adj. Comely; young, youthful; soft, smooth, tender, delicate. మృదువు, కోమలమైన. సుకుమారదేహము a delicate form. సుకుమారుడు su-kumārudu. n. A delicate man.

సుకృతము su-kritamu. [Skt.] n. A good work, a good deed, well doing, charity. సుకర్మము, పుణ్యము, శుభము. తనతండ్రికి సుకృతముగా ఈ భూమిని దానముచేసినాడు he made a gift of this land so that his (deceased) father might obtain the fruit of his good deed. సుకృతి or సుకృతవంతుడు sukriti. n. A well doer, a benefactor, పుణ్యవంతుడు, ధన్యుడు. సుకృతాత్ముడు sukrit-ātmudu. n. A man of a good disposition, a virtuous man. పుణ్యవంతుడు

సుక్కాణి or చుక్కాణి sukkāṇi. [H.] n. A rudder, helm.

సుక్కిళ్లు sukkiḷlu. [Tel.] n. plu. Wrinkles, creases. ముదిమిచేత ముఖముగోనుపడుముడతలు.

సుక్కు or సుక్కు sukku. [Tel.] n. Pride. గర్వము. "కోదండుఆచెక్కుచెడసుక్కుగనందు." Pal. 55.

సుక్కురుడు sukkurudu. [from Skt. శుక్రుడు.] n. The planet Venus.

సుఖము sukhamu. [Skt.] n. Happiness, welfare, health, safety, pleasure, enjoyment, delight. ఆనందము, ఆరోగ్యము, సౌఖ్యము, క్షేమము. Heaven, స్వర్గము. నయనసుఖము the delight of one's eyes, the name of a kind of cloth. adj. Pleasing, delightful, agreeable, comfortable, easy, happy, well, cheerful, healthy. ఆనందమైన, ఆరోగ్యమైన, క్షేమమైన. సుఖసత్కథావినోదంబునసుండగా while he was passing his time agreeably in listening to a pious story. సుఖజీవనము sukha-jīvanamu. n. A happy or easy life, కష్టములేనిబ్రతుకు. సుఖజీవి sukha-jīvi. n. A prosperous or happy person. కష్టములేక జీవనముచేయువాడు. సుఖప్రసవము an easy and safe accouchement. సుఖభోగి one who lives at ease. సుఖభోగులు sukha-bhōgulu. n. A sort of grain. ధాన్యవిశేషము. H. iv. 157. సుఖముగా sukhamu-gā. adv. Happily, safely, in good circumstances. సంతోషముగా, క్షేమముగా. మీ తండ్రి సుఖముగానున్నాడా is your father well? సుఖవాసి or సుఖప్రాణి sukha-vāsi. n. A delicate, luxurious person, one who lives at ease. సుకుమారముగానుండేవాడు. సుఖసంకటము or సుఖరోగము sukha-sankaṭamu. n. (lit. the pains of pleasure) Venereal disease. మండలరోగము. సుఖాసీనుడు sukh-āsīnudu. n. One who is seated at his ease. హాయిగా కూర్చున్నవాడు. సుఖి sukhi. n. One who is happy, one who possesses happiness or pleasure, one who is in good health, సుఖముగలవాడు. సుఖించు or సుఖియించు sukhintsu. v. n. To be happy, well or at ease; to be glad, rejoice, be comforted. ఆనందించు, హర్షించు.

సుగంధము su-gandhamu. [Skt.] n. Fragrance. సుగంధపాల su-gandha pāla. n. Indian Sarsaparilla.

సుగతుడు su-gatudu. n. A deified sage, a sage or teacher of the Buddhist sect, బుద్ధదేవు.

సుగమము Same as సుకరము. (q. v.)

సుగుడి or సుగుణి *su-gudi.* [from Skt. సు+గుణి.] n. A good or pleasant man. సరసుడు.

సుగ్గడితనము *suggadi-tanamu.* [Tel.] n. A close texture, as of cloth. సుగ్గడితము or సుగ్గడితపు *suggaditamu.* adj. Thick, close-woven. దట్టముగా నేయబడిన, సొగసు సేరగల, "సుగ్గడితపుటెఱుసేత్రముతో రాణించి." Vasu. v. 96.

సుగ్రీవుడు *su-grivudu.* [Skt.] n. The name of an ally of Râma, who led a host of bears. వాలితమ్ముడు. అక్కడ మహా సుగ్రీవాజ్ఞగా నడుస్తున్నది there matters go on orderly or peaceably. సుగ్రీవాజ్ఞ Draconian law.

సుడాలము *sudalamu.* [Skt.] n. A certain pace in horsemanship. అశ్వధారావిశేషము.

సుడి *sudi.* [Tel.] n. A whirl. ఆవర్తము. A whirlpool. A circlet. A curl or twist in the hair, particularly in the hair of horses. A fold of a leaf. The secondary form [ు] of the letter ఉ. "సుడియనం వట్టుపడయనబుకారశైసెలయు." ABA. ii. 351. ఆ గుర్రానికి సుళ్లు బాగా ఉండలేదు the horse has not good "marks" or curls in its hair. "అనువగుసుళ్లనొప్పములయనిలవాహము లెక్కి." స్వా. vi. (Verb. plu.) Look! behold! "సుడిసుమీసుండి. మాసుమ్మియనంగను విశ్వ యోగ్యముగా నెగడుచుండు." ABA. iii. 109. సుడిగట్టు *sudi-gattu.* n. A hill called చక్రవాళము. సుడిగాలి a whirlwind. సుడిగొట్టు *sudi-gottu.* n. Wind, గాలి. సుడిగొను *sudi-gonu.* v. a. To environ, surround, encompass. చుట్టుకొను. "భామనుడి సుడిగొనవిడికిటలావిచి." R. v. 196. సుడిగోరు *sudi-goru.* n. A ring-like protection for the finger nail used when playing on the lute. సుడిచేందువాచేప *sudi-tsanduva-chêpa.* n. A certain fish, like a small pomfret but with the tail and fins different, a species of *stromateus.* సుడిపోవు *sudi-pôvu.* v. n. To become useless, వ్యర్థమగు. సుడియ *sudiya.* n. Half a bundle of betel leaf. తమలపాకుల మూటలోసగము. A rascal, villain, తులువ. "మాచియల్లనవిప్ప సుడియలుమీరు." Pal. సుడియుడిదము, సుడికొయుదువు or సుడివాలు *sudi-y-adidamu.* n. The short circular missile weapon or discus of Vishnu. చక్రాయుధము, సుదర్శనము. సుడియు *sudiyu.* v. n. To blow like a whirlwind, చుట్టిచుట్టివీచు. To surround, చుట్టుకొను. To appear, పొడచూపు, అగుపడు. To wander, సంచరించు. "సుధజెందుమావిపై సుడియులేనియుపల్కు తీరోదకవ్యాయ సారమె నయు." UH. i. 52. "కడుబెట్టిదపుగాలి సుడి సినసిరిదప్పు దిరిగినమున్నంపుడిగెమార్కి." TUR. vi. 78. సుడివడు or సుడిబడు *sudi-vadu.* v. n. To twist or get entangled, to turn. To hesitate, be puzzled, confused, entangled or ensnared, చీకాకుపడు, కలవరపడు, చలించు, తిరుగు, మెలిపడు. To swoon or faint, సొమ్మసిల్లు, మూర్ఛిల్లు. "ఈతిమిడిసదలి సుడివడుచుమెండలోను సోమరిగాలి." Swa. iii. 38. "నీదుశైన్యముల్ సుడివడ భీష్మదాకుటయు జూచి." M. VI. ii. 294. Plu. సుళ్లు. సుళ్లమారి *sulla-mari.* n. One who has bad marks, చెడ్డ సుడులుగలవాడు; one who whirls about or gives trouble, చుట్లబెట్టువాడు.

సుడీ Same as సుడి (v. plu.) (q. v.)

సుడుము *sudumu.* [Tel.] n. A flock of a hundred sheep. నూరుగొర్రెలగుంపు. A torch దివిటీ. A fagot of firewood or wisp of grass, used as a torch. దివిటీవలె మండెడము నక్కై కట్టినకసవు లేక కట్టెలకట్ట. బోదసుడుము a lighted wisp of straw.

సుణుగు *sunugu.* [Tel.] v. a. To cheat, overreach. మోసపుచ్చు.

సుత *suta.* [Tel.] adv. Since, from. మొదలు కొని. ప్రభృతి, నుండి. Even, also, కూడా. నాటిసుత or అదిసుత ever since that time.

సుత *suta.* [Skt.] n. A daughter. కూతురు.

సుతరాం, సుతరాము or **సుతారము** *sutaram.* [H.] adv. Utterly, totally, at all, in the least. బొత్తిగా.

సుతలము *su-talamu.* [Skt.] n. The sixth of the lower regions, ఆరవపాతాళము.

సుతి *suti.* [from Skt. శ్రుతి.] n. An accompaniment to an air, the drone accompaniment in music, the running bass, the diapason, the tone of a chord. సంగీతశ్రుతి, శ్రుతి. సుతికూర్చు to put an instrument in tune, to harmonise chords. హెచ్చుసుతి a note set too high. తగ్గుసుతి a note that is too low. సుతిగాడు or సుతికాడు a drone-player, one who plays the bag-pipe. సుతిపోయువాడు. "నారద సుతిగూర్చ నేరవు నవ్వులెమ్మని పిగిటెంకటెంకునను మీటు." N. iv. 139. **సుతిమెత్తనివాడు** *suti-mettani-vadu.* n. A meek, soft, patient man. సాత్వికుడు, తిన్ననివాడు.

సుతుడు *sutudu.* [Skt.] n. A son. పుత్రుడు.

సుత్తి, సుత్తె or **సుత్తియ** *sutti.* [Tel.] n. A small hammer. బొరిమీదకొట్టే చినిసుత్తె. సుత్తెపెట్టు or సుత్తెపాటు a dent or mark made by a hammer. **సుత్తియెముక** *sutti-y-emuka.* n. The bone called the Malleus. **సుత్తివర** *sutti-vara.* n. A fish, *Rhinobatus granulatus.*

సుత్రాముడు *sutramudu.* [Skt.] n. An epithet of the god Indra. ఇంద్రుడు.

సుద *suda.* [Tel.] n. The point, end, tip. అగ్రము, కొన, తుది, కడ. "మాతిపోతిన్నులు సుదగొమ్మతెక్కు." HD. p. 255.

సుదతి *su-dati.* [Skt.] n. A woman with beautiful teeth; a woman in general. అందమైన పలువరుసగలది.

సుదర్శనము *su-darsanamu.* [Skt.] n. The city of the gods. అమరావతీపట్టణము. The discus or missile weapon of Vishnu. విష్ణుచక్రము. The Salagram, a species of ammonite, worshipped as a representation of Vishnu, చక్రాకారముగానుండు సాలగ్రామము.

సుద్ద *sudda.* [from Skt. సుధా or శుద్ధ.] n. White pipe-clay. తెల్లమన్ను, శ్వేతమృత్తిక. సుద్దబావి a well sunk in white clay. **సుద్దము** *suddamu.* [from శుద్ధము.] adj. Pure, clean, శుద్ధము. **సుద్దగించు** *sudda-gintsu.* v. a. To smooth by beating with a hammer. మెట్ట పల్లములులేకుండా సుత్తెతో కొట్టు. H. ii. 201. **సుద్ది** *suddi.* adj. Clean, pure, free from pollution. శాతమైన, శుచియైన. "విరాడికిదు సుద్దిగొరకట్టె." Chamatkara Manj. ii. 12. n. Purity, పరిశుద్ధి. Morality, justice, నీతి. [From శ్రుతి.] n. A story; news, tidings, intelligence. మాట, వృత్తాంతము, జనశ్రుతి భేదము. "ప్రొద్దుపోయెను లెమ్మిక సుద్దులేల." Vish. iii. 9. **సుద్దిగాడు** *suddi-gadu.* n. A holy or clean man. పరిశుద్ధుడు. "చూచియు న్నాట్లినటునంటి సుద్దిగాడుకాడటంచుపుకద." Suca. i. 481. **సుద్దిచేయు** *suddi-cheyu.* n. a. To purify, clean. శుద్ధిపరచు.

సుధ *sudha.* [Skt.] n. Nectar, the drink of the gods. అమృతము. Chunam, సున్నము. **సుధాంశువు** or **సుధాంశుడు** *sudh-amsuvu.* n. The moon. చంద్రుడు. సుధాంశురత్నము the poetical amber or noble opal, which is fabled to melt in the moonbeams, చంద్రకాంతము. **సుధాకరుడు** *sudha-karudu.* n. The moon. చంద్రుడు. **సుధాపాణి** *sudha-pani.* n. An epithet of Dhanvantari, the physician of the gods, ధన్వంతరి. **సుధామయూఖుడు** *sudha-mayukhudu.* n. The moon. చంద్రుడు. Vish. ii. 212. **సుధాశనవర్ధకి** *sudh-asana-vardhaki.* n. Visvakarma, the artist of the gods. విశ్వకర్మ. A. iv. 34.

సుధర్మ *su-dharma.* [Skt.] n. The council or assembly of the gods. దేవసభ.

సుధి *sudhi.* [Skt.] n. A learned man, a scholar, విద్వాంసుడు. సుధిజనులు men of sense, learned men, తెలివిగలవారు, విద్వాంసులు.

సునామణి or సుణామణి sunāmaṇi. [H.] n. Reading out, reciting. నా అర్జీ సునామణి అయినదా has my petition been read out?

సునాయాసముగా sun-āyāsamu-gā. [Skt.] adv. Without any difficulty, very easily, మిక్కిలి సులభముగా, అనాయాసముగా.

సునాసీరుడు sunāsīrudu. [Skt.] n. An epithet of the god Indra. ఇంద్రుడు.

సున్న sunna. [from Skt. శూన్యమ్.] n. A cipher. Nothing, nonentity. నాస్తి, అభావము. A dot. The Anusvara or circle used for a nasal letter, as అందము for అ(ం)దము. అనుస్వారము. "నిలుకడసున్న నాదిసహిస్తేముసాస్తి." T. iv. 17. "చూడనికమానప్పార్య ములే సున్న అనుచు." A. v. 163. ఆ పిల్లకాయ సున్నలుచుట్టుచున్నాడు the boy is in round hand. An epigram says, "ఆద్యుడొక్కడున్న సందరుపూజ్యులే లెక్కనిూదసున్న లెక్కిపట్లు, ఆతడుపోవునిమక సందరుపూజ్యులే లెక్కచెంపసున్న లెక్కిసట్లు." సున్నగిలు or సున్నగిల్లు sunna-gilu. v. n. To become round, గుండ్రనగు. సున్నపెట్టు sunna-peṭṭu. v. a. To mark with a cipher, to draw a circlet round a thing; to dupe, elude, cheat. అనుస్వారమునువ్రాయు, వంచించు. "పొరదినిందరి కనుగట్టిసున్న పెట్టిపేసువినుకేర." Ila. iv. 103.

సున్నతి sunnati. [H.] n. Circumcision.

సున్నము sunnamu. [from Skt. చూర్ణం.] n. Lime made of shells or stone. Carbonate of lime. Chunam. కాలుపుసున్నము unslaked lime. సీమసున్నము white chalk. రాతిసున్నము stonelime. గుల్లసున్నము lime made of small shells. పాలసున్నము fine lime. సున్నముకొట్టు or సున్నముపూయు to white-wash. సున్నపుకాయ a small box in which lime, which is used with betel, is kept. వాడు చచ్చి సున్నమైనాడు he was in dreadful trouble. వాళ్ళు సున్నానికి ఎముకలేకుండా కొట్టినారు the ybroke all his bones.

సున్ని sunni. n. Powder. పొడుము. సున్నిపిండి sunni-pindi. n. A paste used as soap in bathing. నలుగుపిండి. శనగసున్ని powdered Bengal gram. సున్నితము sunnitamu. adj. Delicate, susceptible. రవంతైనను హెచ్చినా తగ్గినా తాళని. మీ దేహము నిండా సున్నితము, మోటుదేహముకాదు your constitution is easily affected, it is not tough. రోగులశరీరము మహా సున్నితముగానుండును sick persons are easily affected by any thing. n. Delicacy, susceptibility. రవంత హెచ్చినను తగ్గినను తాళలేకపోవడము.

సుపథము See under సు.

సుపర్ణుడు See under సు.

సుపర్వుడు su-parvudu. [Skt.] n. A god. దేవత, వేలుపు.

సుపాణి or సుప్పాణి sup-āṇi. [Tel. సుప్పు+ఆణి.] n. A clear water (used of a pearl), ముత్యమందలి శుభ్రమైననీరు. A pearl of the first water, శుభ్రమైననీరుగల ముత్యము. "తరుకుసుపాణిముత్యాలపేర్చట్లు." Navanad. page 420.

సుప్తి supti. [Skt.] n. Sleep. నిద్ర. సుప్తుడు suptudu. n. A sleeper. నిద్రించువాడు. సుప్తపాదము a benumbed or paralysed foot.

సుప్రతీకము su-pratīkamu. [Skt.] adj. Handsome, well made. అందగానుండే, మంచి అవయవములుగల. n. The name of the elephant of the north-east quarter. ఈశాన్యపు దిక్కునందలి గజము.

సుబంతము sub-antamu. [Skt. సుప్+అంతము.] n. A technical term in grammar for a noun or substantive, నామవాచకపదము.

సుబాణము su-bāṇamu. [సు (Skt.)+బాణము. Tel.] n. A kind of cannon. ఒకవిధమైన ఫిరంగి. "కోవిఫిరంగిసుబాణముసుంటకోప." ABA ii. 411.

సుబేదారు or **సుబేదారుడు** *subē-dāru.* [H.] n. A Subadar. The governor of a province (సుబా). A serjeant or native captain.

సుబ్బు *subbu.* [Tel.] v. n. To come forth, appear, become manifest. బయలుపడు. "రాముఁడా పట్టముఁగట్టఁగాఁడాదురవార్తల్ సుబ్బినన్ గ్రాఁ." R. v. 2.

సుబ్రహ్మణ్యుడు *su-brahmanyudu.* [Skt.] n. A name of Kumaraswami, the god of war, కార్తికేయుడు.

సుభగ *su-bhaga.* [Skt.] n. A pleasing or happy woman. ఇష్టురాలు, భాగ్యవంతురాలు. The cord is bound on the neck of the bride with a blessing that runs as follows, "మాంగల్యతంతునానేన మమజీవన హేతునా కంఠేబధ్నామి సుభగే త్వంజీవశరదాం శతం." **సుభగము** *su-bhagamu.* adj. Pleasing, gratifying to the eye, beautiful, charming. Beloved, dear; fortunate, auspicious. నేత్రోత్సవమైన, మనోహరమైన, శుభమైన, శోభనమైన. **సుభగత** *su-bhaga-ta.* n. Blessedness, auspiciousness; beauty, charm. శోభనత్వము, మనోహరత, రమణీయత. **సుభగుడు** *su-bhagudu.* n. A fortunate man. భాగ్యవంతుడు.

సుభద్ర *su-bhadra.* [Skt.] n. The sister of Krishna, married to Arjuna. కృష్ణునితోడ బుట్టువు, అర్జునునిభార్య.

సుభిక్షము *su-bhikshamu.* [Skt.] adj. Affording an easy means of subsistence, cheap. సులభభిక్షముగల. The opposite is దుర్భిక్షము.

సుమంగలి *su-mangali.* [Skt.] n. A wife, a spouse, a married woman, one who wears the ornaments of a married woman. ముత్తైదువ, సువాసిని.

సుమనస్సు *su-manassu.* [Skt.] n. A flower. పుష్పము. The great flowered jasmine. మాలతీపుష్పము. A god, an immortal, దేవత, వేలుపు. A learned man, విద్వాంసుడు.

సుమనోరజము *su-manō-rajamu.* n. The pollen or dust of flowers, (lit. flower-dust). పుప్పొడి.

సుమము *sumamu.* [Skt.] n. A flower. పుష్పము. **సుమరసము** *suma-rasamu.* n. The juice of flowers. మకరందము **సుమశరుడు** *suma-śarudu.* n. Lit. one whose arrows are flowers, i. e., Manmatha, మన్మథుడు. **సుమాంజలి** *sum-ānjali.* n. Presenting a nosegay or flowers held in both hands opened and hollowed. పుష్పాంజలి.

సుమా *sumā.* [Tel. short for చూడుమా.] interj. Indeed! సుమీ.

సుమారు or **షుమారు** *sumāru.* [H.] adv. About, nearly. రమారమి.

సుమాళము *sumālamu.* [Tel.] n. Mirth, joy, gaiety, elation, అత్యుత్సాహము, సుఖము. "సామాన్యమానవులంగైకొనక సుమాళంబు చేయంగ బుగా." A. iv. 44. టీ. మనోభావము. **సుమాళి** *sumāli.* n One who is elated with joy. సంతోషముతో ఉప్పొంగువాడు. **సుమాళించు** *sumāl-inṭsu.* v. n. To leap for joy. ఉల్లాసముచేత గంతులువేయు. "తే. గీ. తన్నుఁగని సుమాళించుమధుపునివ్వాఁడయు, నవమయూరముచెలఁ గెనాట్యమాడె." KP. vii. 202. "లీలఁగతుల సుమాళించి యాడె." Vish. vii. 296.

సుమి, సుమీ, సుమ్మి or **సుమ్మీ** *sumi.* [Tel. for చూడుమి.] interj. Look! Verily! Truly! Indeed! నిండా అన్యాయముసుమీ really this is very unjust. plu. సుడీ.

సుముఖము *su-mukhamu.* [Skt.] adj. Pleasing, agreeable. సంతోషకరమైన, రమ్యమైన. n. A fine face, good features. ఉత్తమాస్యము. **సుముఖత** or **సుముఖత్వము** *su-mukhata.* n. Loveliness, prettiness. ప్రసన్నవదనత. "కంటకమెట్టుగాక సుముఖత్వము నొందితివయ్య." Kalahasti. ii. 135. **సుముఖుడు** *su-mukhudu.* n. A handsome or agreeable man. సంతోషకరమైన ముఖముగలవాడు, చక్కనిముఖముగలవాడు.

సుమేరువు *su-mēruvu.* [Skt. cf. 'Sumir.' and 'Merv.'] n. Mount Meru. మేరుపర్వతము.

సుర *sura.* [Tel.] n. A whirlwind. సురగాలి, సుడిగాలి. Wind, గాలి. adj. Large, పెద్ద.

సుర *sura.* [Skt.] adj. Celestial, divine. దేవతలసంబంధమైన. n. A spirituous liquor, toddy, nectar. మద్యము, కల్లు, అమృతము. సురగవి *sura-gavi.* n. The cow of the gods. కామధేనువు. సురజ్యేష్ఠుడు *sura-jyēshṭhuḍu.* n. The eldest of the gods, i.e., Brahma. బ్రహ్మదేవుడు. సురద్విషుడు *sura-dvishuḍu.* n. An enemy of the gods. An Asura. సురనిమ్నగ *sura-nimnaga.* n. The river of the gods, i. e., the heavenly Ganges. సురపతి or సురేశ్వరుడు *sura-pati.* n. The lord of the gods, i. e., Indra. సురలు *suralu.* n. The immortals, the gods. దేవతలు. సురలోకము *sura-lōkamu.* n. Heaven. స్వర్గము. సురవరుడు or సురోత్తముడు *sura-varuḍu.* n. The sun. సూర్యుడు. సురవర్త్మము *sura-vartmamu.* n. The sky, ఆకాశము. సురాచార్యుడు *sur-āchāryuḍu.* n. The priest of the gods; an epithet of బృహస్పతి. సురాలయము *sur-ālayamu.* n. The abode of the gods, i. e., Mount Meru. సురారి *sur-ari.* (సుర+అరి.) n. A foe of the gods, i. e., a demon or fiend. రాక్షసుడు. సురార్చితము *sur-architamu.* adj. Adored by the immortals. దేవతలచేత పూజింపబడిన. సురేజ్యుడు *surējyuḍu.* n. The teacher of the gods. బృహస్పతి. M. V. i. 149.

సురంగము *surangamu.* [Skt.] n. A bore, a hole, a passage dug or excavated. కన్నము, కుహరము, సొరంగము.

సురకత్తి, చురకత్తి or సూరకత్తి *sura-katti.* [from Skt. క్షురికా.] n. A small knife. చిన్నకత్తి.

సురకరువలి, సురగాడ్పు or సురగాలి *sura-karuvali.* [Skt.+Tel.] n. A whirlwind. సుడిగాలి. Bhag. x. 17.

సురకాని *sura-kāni.* [Tel.] n. One-fourth of a quarter of an anna.

సురక్షితము See under సు.

సురటి *suraṭi.* [Skt.] n. The name of a certain tune. రాగవిశేషము. సురటి or సురటీ [Tel. సుర+అటు.] n. A round fan. చట్రపువిసనకర్ర. A whisk for brushing away flies, చామరము, కుంచె. "పువ్వుసురటిని విసరుచుభర్త జనంబు కాంతసేయించె." T. iii. 19. సురటిపట్టతీగెలు *suraṭi-paṭṭa-tīgelu.* n. A drug used in dyeing pink. చేమంతీగెలు.

సురతము *su-ratamu.* [Skt.] n. Coition. స్త్రీపురుషులకలయిక.

సురతాణి *su-ratāṇi.* [Skt.] n. Indra, ఇంద్రుడు. The wife of Indra, ఇంద్రాణి.

సురపొన్న *sura-ponna.* [from Skt. సురపున్నాగ.] n. The tree called *Calophyllum longifolium*, పున్నాగము, దేవవల్లభము.

సురభి *surabhi.* [Skt.] adj. Fragrant, sweet-smelling. సుగంధముగల, పరిమళించే. Beautiful, మనోజ్ఞమయిన. n. A perfume, odour, fragrance. The spring season. The celestial cow, spoken of as granting every wish. సుగంధము, సుర అనే గంధద్రవ్యము, వసంతఋతువు, స్వర్గధేనువు. సురభిళము *surabhiḷamu.* adj. Sweet smelling, మంచివాసనగల. సురభీకరించు *surabhī-karintsu.* v. a. To make fragrant. పరిమళింపజేయు.

సురమాయి or సురమా *suramāyi.* [H. from సురుమా.] adj. Very black. చిక్కనినల్లని.

సురమాలి *suramāli.* [Tel.] n. An air-cushion or pillow. గాలినించినబాలీసు.

సురళించు See సురాళించు.

సురస *surasa.* [Skt.] n. The name of the mother of the Nagas. నాగమాత.

సురసుర *sura-sura.* [Tel. (anuk.)] adv. Bang, slapdash; all at once. This is an adverb used of quickness in taking fire; or of fainting. శీఘ్రముగా. (ఇది నిప్పు అంటుకో

వడము మూర్ఛపోవడముమనుగరించినమాట). " కన లెడుసూడులు కర్ణరంధ్రముల, జొనివినయ ళ్లైనపుర సుర్రుక్కి." HD. ii. 1181. **సుర్రన** or **సుర్రున** *surr-ana.* adv. Aloud, hissingly.

సురామండము *surā-mandamu.* [Skt.] n. The froth of ardent spirits. కల్లుమీదినురుగు. తెత్తె.

సురాళించు or **సురళించు** *surālintsu.* [Tel.] v. a. To wave a lamp or a cup of burning camphor, &c., before an idol, or over a person to avert an evil eye. నీరాజనముచేయు, దృష్టిదోషపరిహారార్థము దిగదుడుచు. To throw away in disdain, నిరాకరించు. " అర్భకుపెట్టుకొని నిఘాతభయనివారణంబు సాగోపృచ్ఛంబు సురాళించి గోమయంబునందిల కంబుపెట్టె." Vish. vii. 109. " కడమపూదండ తెల్ల నొక్కటికబట్టిబాలకపుడు సురాళించిపార వైచె." KP. vii. 76. **సురాళము** *surālamu.* n. Wrathfulness. కోపావేశము. Giddiness, భూతావేశజనితశరో భ్రమణము.

సురిగ *suriga.* [Tel.] n. A sprig, twig, small branch. రెమ్మ.

సురియ or **సురె** *suriya.* [from Skt. ఛురిక.] n. A small knife. చేకత్తి, సూరికత్తి. A. vi. 106. "సుజ్ఞానమను వాడిసురియచేపట్టి." HD. v. 1435. "సురియ బట్టవచ్చుసూరుండుకారాదు." Vema. i. 176. **సురియవాళు** or **సురెయవాళు** *suriyālu.* (సురియ+ఆరు.) n. A Pariah. మాలవాడు.

సూరీ *surī.* [Mahr. 'Surat'.] adj. Made in Surat. సురీదేశోత్పన్నమైన. " సురీపట్టుమపై బరచిరి." Swa. v. 111. టీ॥ సూరత్తుపట్టుతాపి తానుపరచిరి.

సురుగు *surugu.* [Tel.] v. n. To disappear. అదృశ్యమగు. To take flight, retreat, పలాయితుడగు. To wither or fade, వాడిపోవు. To slink away, జోడగాపోవు. To move, shake or tremble, చలించు. " తొలంకి పుత్రునిసెచటికోతొలగనంపి యడవిలోపాము మూరొర్నైన్న దమును మెరిసి, కల్లయేడ్పులనేడ్పు చుకపటవృత్తి, వెదకుసందునసురగజాచెదవునీవు." HN. v. 53. " అట్టినుగతరువు వెనుకకచుట్టపు మూలమున గొందునుసురదుమడినీకట్టుజవించెను." Parij. iv. 68. " శ్రీదిక్పుపకుందనపాత్రముకొని రుక్మిడలాసురిగితిచెప్పమానిజము." M. XIII. ii. 61.

సురుగుడు or **సురుగుడుపట్ట** *surugudu.* [Tel.] n. A tree called *Ventilago madraspatana.* A bark used in dyeing cloth.

సురుడు *surudu.* [Tel.] n. A fire brand, కొంపొయకట్టె.

సురుమా or **షురుమా** *surumā.* [H.] n. Collyrium, antimony.

సురుము *surumu.* [Tel.] n. Powder. చూర్ణము.

సురె See సురియ.

సురేకారము *surē-kāramu.* [Tel.] n. Saltpetre, nitrate of potash. పెట్లుప్పు.

సురేఖత *su-rēkhata.* [Skt.] n. A particular mode in music. గానస్వరభేదము.

సులభము *su-labhamu.* [Skt.] adj. Easy, feasible, attainable, practicable, easy of access. సుఖముగాలభించెడి, కష్టముకాని, సాధ్యమైన, దుర్లభముకాని. **సులభుడు** *su-labhudu.* n. One who is easy, courteous or accessible. గడుసుమనిషికానివాడు. వాడు సర్వసులభుడు he is good or kind to all. భక్తసులభుడు he who is accessible to his worshippers.

సులోచనము *su-lōchanamu.* [Skt.] n. Spectacles, eye glasses. ముక్కద్దము.

సుల్తాను *sultānu.* [H.] n. A Sultan or Mussalman prince.

సులువు or **సులువు** *suluvu.* [from Skt. సులభం.] adj. Light. తేలికైన. Easy, సులభమైన. " సులువుతులగడ చేయూ్యరి." T. iv. 304. n. Facility, lightness. సులభము, తేలిక. **సులువుచేయు** *suluvu-cheyu.* v. a. To facilitate, సులభముచేయు.

[సు]ల్లమారి See under సుడి.

[సు]వర్ణము *su-varṇamu.* [Skt.] n. Gold, బంగారు. సువర్ణకాసులు gold coins. సువర్ణభూపతి a certain medicine. ఔషధవిశేషము. A. iv. 318.

[సు]వారము *suvāramu.* [from Skt. సూపకారము.] n. Cooking, వంట. "చ॥ కొడిమిరి యుంబూగా వెదలిపోయెదుకొండలు వక్కచేసిరొ, క్షుముజలజకులంబోలకుకూరలువండి వెడందచిప్పలం. దుడుకగ కెట్టెముత్తియపుటోగిరముల్ గడుంకున్న రించెన, ద్యొదరఘువీరుసాయకముతెక్కడ చేర్పసువారపుంబసుల్." R. vii. 105. సువారపుటిల్లు *suvārapu-ṭ-illu.* n. A kitchen. వంటయిల్లు. సువారపువాడు *suvārapu-vāḍu.* n. A cook. వంటవాడు.

సువాసిని *su-vāsini.* [Skt.] n. A good woman; one whose husband is alive. పేరంటాలు, ముత్తైదువ.

సువేలము or సువేలాద్రి *su-vēlamu.* [Skt.] n. The name of a certain mountain. పర్వతవిశేషము. R. vii. 141.

సువ్వాలు, సువాలు, సువ్వాల, సువాల, సువ్వలాల or సువ్వి *suvrālu.* [Tel. సువ్వి +అలు.] interj. A word or chorus used in carols, like 'derry down down'. సువ్వి *suvvi.* n. The noise made by persons while pounding rice, దంచుటయందగు ధ్వన్యనుకరణము.

సువ్వో *suvvō.* [Tel.] interj. Behold! చూడుమిరా.

సుషమ *sushama.* [Skt.] n. Exquisite beauty or splendour. అధికకాంతి. మిక్కిలిశోభ. adj. Beautiful, handsome, pleasing. మనోహరమైన, మనోజ్ఞమైన.

సుషి *sushi.* [Skt.] n. A hole. రంధ్రము, బెజ్జము. A. iv. 26. సుషిరము *sushiramu.* n. A hole, orifice. రంధ్రము. A wind instrument, మురళ్యాదివాద్యము, పిల్లనగ్రోవిలోనగు వాద్యము.

సుషీమము or సుశీమము *sushimamu.* [Skt.] adj. Cold, frigid. శీతము, చల్లని.

సుషుప్తి *su-shupti.* [Skt.] n. Sound or deep sleep. మంచినిద్ర, ఒళ్లెరుగనినిద్ర. దీర్ఘసుషుప్తి the long sleep, i. e., death. చావు. సుషుప్తము *su-shuptamu.* adj. Fast asleep, బాగా నిద్రపోవుచుండే.

సుషుమ్న *sushumna.* [Skt.] n. The spinal cord. The name of a particular tubular vessel of the body, spoken of in mystic treatises. The pineal gland.

సుషేణము *sushēṇamu.* [Skt.] n. A cane or reed, the ratan. పేంతసము, ప్రబ్బ. సుషేణుడు *sushēṇuḍu.* n. A name of Vishnu. Also, a name of the physician of the monkey chief Sugriva. విష్ణువు, సుగ్రీవుని వైద్యుడు.

సుష్టు or సుష్ఠు *sushṭu.* [Tel.] adj. Well, good, sound, handsome, healthy. మంచి, బాగైన, అందమైన, ఆరోగ్యమైన. "సుష్టువౌయశనము." Vema. 1238. n. Good condition, a sound state, health, beauty, బాగు, అందము, ఆరోగ్యము. సుష్టుపరచు *sushṭu-paratsu* v. a. To amend, make better. చక్కబెట్టు.

సుసరము or సుసారము *susaramu.* [Skt.] adj. Easy, clear, free, unimpeded. సరళమైన.

సుస్తి or సుస్తీ *susti.* [H.] n. Laziness, idleness.

సుహితము *su-hitamu.* [Skt.] adj. Fit, proper, suitable. తగిన, యుక్తమైన.

సుహృత్తు or సుహృదుడు *su-hṛittu.* [Skt.] n. Lit: a good hearted man. A friend. ఆప్తుడు. సుహృత్కోటి a circle of friends.

సూ sū

సూ or సువ్వో *sū.* [Tel. short for చూడుము.] interj. Behold! చూడుమా. నిశ్చయార్థకము. "ఘనుడిజ్జగములకుకర్తసూబసుమా." L. xvi. 90.

సూకరము *sūkaramu.* [Skt.] n. A hog. అడవిపంది, వరాహము. A pig, పంది. **సూకరి** *sūkari.* n. A sow.

సూక్తము *sūktamu.* [Skt. సు+ఉక్తము.] adj. Well or properly said. చక్కగాచెప్పబడ్డ. n. A hymn in the Rig Veda. వేదములో సూక్తవిషయమునుగురించిన కొన్నిపదసలు. "కన్న సూక్తంబులిత్వాక్షు." L. iii. 52.

సూక్తి *sūkti.* [Skt. సు+ఉక్తి.] n. A good word, a fair or friendly speech. మంచిమాట. Vasu. iv. 8.

సూక్ష్మము *sūkshmamu.* [Skt.] adj. Little, small, minute, atomic, fine, subtle, delicate. Ingenious, subtile, clever, smart, quick. కొంచెము, సన్నమైన, చురుకుగల. సూక్ష్మమైనపని delicate work. సూక్ష్మముగా తెలుపుట to explain in a few words. సూక్ష్మదృష్టి quick sight, సూక్ష్మబుద్ధి a clever or keen intellect. సూక్ష్మశరీరము the spiritual body. సూక్ష్మరూపము the atomic or spiritual form, the ideal body, as distinguished from the bodily shape, the spiritual image. సూక్ష్మావస్థ the invisible or essential condition, spirituality as opposed to corporeal being. **సూక్ష్మము** or **సూక్ష్మత** *sūkshmamu.* n. An atom. Fineness, delicacy, peculiarity, nicety. సూక్ష్మాంత్రములు the small intestines.

సూచకము *sūchakamu.* [Skt.] n. Intimation, information by signs. సూచన, జ్ఞాపకము. adj. Shewing, denoting, intimating, suggesting. అగుపడచేసే, జ్ఞాపకముచేసే. **సూచకుడు** *sūcha-kuḍu.* n. A spy, informer. కొండెగాడు. One who hints or suggests, బోధచేయువాడు. **సూచన** *sūchana.* n. A hint, a suggestion, a slight or faint notice. జాడ. సూచనగాచెప్పు to tell briefly, to give a general idea or outline, to hint. **సూచించు** *sūchintsu.* v. a. To hint, signify, point out, జాడగాతెలియజేయు. "నాచినవో చీనసూచించుచుండితి." Vish. vi. 337. **సూచితము** *sūchitamu.* adj. Hinted at. సూచింపబడిన.

సూచి or **సూచిక** *sūchi.* [Skt.] n. A needle. సూది. An index or sign, తెలియజేయునది. **సూచిముఖము** *sūchi-mukhamu.* n. The point of a needle. సూదిమొన. An arrow. "సూచీముఖంబైనజోవపగరానిచీకటి." BD. v. 383. **సూచిముఖపక్షి** *sūchi-mukha-pakshi.* n. A kind of bird. పక్షివిశేషము. "సూచీముఖపక్షిగాంచి." G. i. 276.

సూటి *sūṭi.* [Tel.] n. An aim, an expedient. గురి, ఉపాయము. Manner, విధము. ఈ పని సూటిపడునా will this business succeed? నీమనసుకు సూటిగా ఉన్నట్టయితే if it seems right to you. adj. Straight, not crooked, right, చక్కని, తిన్నని, తిరుగుల్లలేని, సరియైన. "సూటిమార్గముజూపె కూలధరుడు." Chenna v. 415. **సూటిగా** *sūṭi-ga.* adv. Duly, straight, in a right line. సరిగా. నొసటికి సూటిగా రాయివేసినాడు he threw the stone straight at his forehead. **సూటికాడు** *sūṭi-kāḍu.* n. A marksman, గురికాడు. A handsome person, అందగాడు. **సూటిగొను** *sūṭi-gonu.* v. n. To fit, suit, agree. పొసగు, సరిపడు. "సూటి గొనసాటిపద్య చెక్కినచక్కడించి." Bilh. ii. 194. **సూటిపడు** *sūṭi-paḍu.* v. n. To hit correctly, సరితాకు.

సూడించు *sūḍintsu.* [Tel.] v. n. To be envious. పగగొను. విక్ర. viii.

సూడిగములు *sūḍigamulu.* [Tel.] n. plu. A sort of bracelets. హస్తభూషావిశేషము, గాజులు, చేతికడియములు. "లలనసాహిత్యరంచిన లక్ష్మిహోరె, గౌరవములతో సూడిగములుతాలు." Kasikhandamu. v. 172.

సూడిద or **సూడిదె** *sūḍida.* [Tel.] n. A gift, an offering. కానుక. "కునకంబునకు నెన్ని సూడిదల్ కట్టినా పుట్టినింటికిమల్లగలదు." Miscell. i. 125. line 1.

సూడు *sûḍu*. [Tel.] n. Enmity, pique, spite. పగ, వైరము, విద్వేషము. An enemy, శత్రువు. v. a. To cut, కోయు. "అజ్ఞానమునెడియుడవిని, సుజ్ఞానపు ఖడ్గమున సమ సూడగవలదా." Vema. 2091. "క॥ సూడో క్క టిదియనుమరిదా, కీడొక్క టియును జగంబు క్షింపుటక్కై." UH. iv. 248. "జక్కొనగమినసూడుచక్కనివనగాడు." T. i 44. **సూడుకాడు** *sûḍu-kâḍu*. n. An enemy. వైరి. **సూడువట్టు** or **సూడుకొను** *sûḍu-paṭṭu*. n. To entertain ill will. పగగొను, విరోధించు.

సూతకము *sûtakamu*. [Skt.] n. Ceremonial impurity arising from childbirth or death, జాతాశౌచము, మృతాశౌచము. సూతకముపట్టు to observe the rites of ceremonial impurity. **సూతి** *sûti*. n. Birth, child-bearing. ప్రసవము, కనడము. Offspring, progeny, స్త్రీపురుషరూపసంతానము, బిడ్డ. వ్యాసమునిసూతి the son of Vyasa, i. e., the hermit Suka. "అగ్రసూతి" an elder brother. Ila. ii. 2. "ధనవంతుడగుసర్పసూతికి." Bhanumati. iv. 4. **సూతిక** *sûtika*. n. A lying-in woman, a woman recently delivered. పురిటాలు, నవప్రసూత, బాలెంతరాలు. **సూతికా గృహము, సూతిగృహము** or **సూతీగృహము** *sûtika-gṛihamu*. n. A lying-in chamber. పురిటిల్లు.

సూతము *sûtamu*. [Skt.] n. Mercury, quick-silver. పాదరసము.

సూతము *sûtamu*. [Skt.] adj. Born, engendered. ప్రసూతము, బిడ్డకనిన.

సూతుడు *sûtuḍu*. [Skt.] n. A charioteer. రథసారథి. A carpenter, వడ్లవాడు. A bard an encomiast. కవి, స్తుతిపాఠకుడు, బట్టువాడు. "నయమానసూతగీతలువినంబడ." Mandha. iv. 213.

సూత్రము *sûtramu*. [Skt.] n. A thread, cord, line, yarn, twine. తంతి, నూలు, నూలిపోగు, దారము. A brief rule or precept in grammar, &c., an aphorism. అనేకార్థబోధకసంక్షిప్తవాక్యము. An expedient, contrivance; an artificial piece of work; a machine, ఉపాయము, యంత్రము. కపటసూత్రము a delusive contrivance. కపటనాటకసూత్రధారి "the unseen mover of the world's machine," an epithet of God. జలసూత్రము a water work, a hydraulic engine. వ్యాకరణసూత్రము a concise rule of grammar. ఆపస్తంబసూత్రము the institutes of Apastamba. మీ గోత్రసూత్రములేమి what is your family name? and what is your creed? మంగళసూత్రము the thread with which the marriage badge is tied on the bride's neck. యజ్ఞసూత్రము the sacred thread worn by the three principal classes of the Hindus. "స్మృతిసూత్రసమాజములకు." A. i. 43. **సూత్రగాడు** *sûtra-gaḍu*. n. An artist, a contriver or maker of any machine. యంత్రకాడు. **సూత్రధారకుడు, సూత్రధారుడు** or **సూత్రధారి** *sûtra-dhârakuḍu*. n. The manager or principal actor in a play or drama; the person behind the scenes who pulls the strings of puppets. An instigator, secret agent, or tempter. మేళనాయకుడు, ఆటాడించువాడు, నడిపించువాడు. "జగన్నాటకసూత్రధారికి." T. ii. 77. "జేసూత్రధారిమీరందరుబహురూపులని." B. X. 297. **సూత్రవట్టు** *sûtra-paṭṭu*. v. a. To "lay the line," as a bricklayer does. దారముపట్టు. "ప్రస్తుతసుచేతములోక ప్రపంచమునకు, దారతమ్యంబు దెలుపంగదలచిరొక్కొ, నూటిమింటికి నేలకు సూత్రపట్టు, పికసీరంధ్ర ధారాళవృష్టి కురిసె." R. vi. 3. "పరగువీధులపురిసూత్ర పట్టినట్లు." A. i. 4. **సూత్రపడు** *sûtra-paḍu*. v. n. To match, పొసగు. **సూత్రించు** *sûtrin-tsu*. v. a. To lay down a rule, to enact. సూత్రముగానేర్పరచు, సూత్రపరచు.

సూదనము *sûdanamu*. [Skt.] adj. Destroying, killing. చంపే. n. Killing. చంపుట. **సూదనుడు** *sûdanuḍu*. n. A destroyer.

చంపువాడు. సూదితము sūditamu. adj. Killed, destroyed. చంపబడిన.

సూది sūdi. [from Skt. సూచి.] n. A needle. కుట్టేలుకుట్టుసాధనము. కరికసూదులు a kind of rice. సూదికొమ్ములు slender or sharp horns. సూదివలెవచ్చి దబ్బనమువలెతేలు to enter like a small needle and come out a packing needle. సూదిమల్లిక or సూదిమల్లె sūdi-mallika. n. The eared jasmine, *Jasminum auriculatum*. సూదులవలె సన్నగానుండే మల్లెలు. సూదంటురాయి, సూదిరాయి or అంటు రాయి sūd-antu-rāyi. n. A magnet, a lodestone. కాంతిరాయి, అయస్కాంతము.

సూదుడు sūdudu. [Skt.] n. A cook. వంట వాడు.

సూన sūna. [Skt.] n. A slaughter-house, the shambles. గొర్రెలు మేకలు కోయుస్థలము, కటిలా. See also under సూనుడు. సూన గాడు or సూనరి sūna-gāḍu. n. One who kills. చంపువాడు. A butcher, కటికవాడు. "భక్షులజంపవాల్పుడుసూనగాడు." BD. iv. 1287.

సూనము sūnamu. [Skt.] n. A flower. పువ్వు. సూనశరుడు sūna-śaruḍu. n. Lit. "the god whose darts are flowers," i. e., Manmatha, మన్మథుడు.

సూనుడు sūnuḍu. [Skt. Cf. Eng. 'son.'] n. A son. పుత్రుడు. సూన sūna. n. A daughter. కూతురు.

సూనృతము sūn-ṛtamu. [Skt.] n. Sincerity, veracity, truth. నిజము, సత్యము. adj. True, sincere, యథార్థమైన. సూనృతోక్తి a true word.

సూపము sūpamu. [Skt.] n. Split pease cooked in water. ముద్దపప్పు, వండినపప్పు. సూపకారుడు or సూపుడు sūpa-kāruḍu. n. A cook. వంటవాడు. సూపశాస్త్రము sūpa-śāstramu. n. The science of Cookery. పాకశాస్త్రము.

సూయమానము sūya-mānamu. [Skt.] adj. That which is being offered as a burnt sacrifice. హోమాదులుచేయబడుచుండే. "సూయ మానసోమలతలున్నై." R. iii. 26.

సూయానము sūyāṇamu. [from Skt. సుయానము.] n. A punitive expedition. శత్రుక్షయంకరమైన దండయాత్ర. "శ్రీకరుణాయ్య సూయానముగ నొనరించె మంచిగ నేలనాలుగు చెరగులకును." భార. విరా. v.

సూరకత్తి sūra-katti. [from Skt. ఛురిక.] n. A small knife. అసిపుత్రిక, చురకత్తి.

సూరణము sūraṇamu. [Skt.] n. An esculent root called *Arum campanulatum*. కంద.

సూరపుటము, సూరెపుటము or సూర్య పటము sūra-puṭamu. [Tel.] n. A kind of cloth. వస్త్రవిశేషము. Velvet, మొకమలు. "రగడ ॥ మొకమాలులును సూరెపుటములునా కులును." H. v. 148.

సూరసూతుడు sūra-sūtuḍu. [Skt.] n. The charioteer of the sun. అనూరుడు.

సూరాకారము or సురాకారము sūrā-kāramu. [Tel.] n. Salt-petre. చౌడు వండినది, పెట్లుప్పు.

సూరి sūri. [from Skt. ఛురిక.] n. A knife. ఛురిక. "కేదగిసూరిరొమ్ముదరొమ్ము." A. iv. 151. టీ॥ మొనగలిపువ్వను సూరకత్తి హెచ్చాయును.

సూరి sūri. [Skt.] n. A great scholar: a learned man. విద్వాంసుడు. The sun, సూర్యుడు.

సూరీడు or సూరుడు sūrīḍu. [from Skt. సూర్యుడు.] n. The sun.

సూరెలు sūrelu. [Tel.] n. plu. Sides, flanks. పార్శ్వములు, ఉభయపార్శ్వములు. "అతినిమూరెమున్నవిరిలోకంబులు." M. VII. iii. 185. "అతి నిగానిపోయి వారితల్లిదండ్రులనూరెలనిల్పి." మ. ii. 45. "గాండీవిశస్త్రులనూరెలోజాగి." M. II. i. 138. "మూపింటుకెలదునూరెలకేదమాది

మోహాలంబునబాపున పెసగిఅంటుకొన్నవిధాన." L. ii. 189. సూరెగిల్లు or సూరెగిలు sūre-gillu. v. n. To lean or move aside, ప్రక్క-కొదుగు.

సూరెపాను or సూరెపాము sūre-pānu. [Tel.] n. A triangular perpendicular parasol or fan carried before a prince or an idol.

సూర్మి or శూర్మి sūrmi. [Skt.] n. A metal idol. లోహపుప్రతిమ.

సూర్యుడు sūryuḍu. [Skt.] n. The sun. భాస్కరుడు. సూర్యకాంతము sūrya-kāntamu. n. The sun-gem, tourmaline, అగ్నిశిల, సూర్యరశ్మిగుటుచేత నిప్పుకలిగెడు ఒకవిధమైనరాయి. A well known medicinal herb. సూర్యకాంతిపుష్పము or సూర్యావర్తము sūrya-kānti-pushpamu. n. The sun-flower. *Helianthus annuus*. పొద్దుతిరుగుడుపువ్వు. సూర్యపటము Same as సూరెపటము. (q. v.) సూర్యపాను sūrya-pānu. n. A triangular perpendicular parasol or fan, resembling a fire screen. See సూరెపాను. సూర్యపుటము sūrya-puṭamu. n. Exposure to the sun. ఎండబెట్టడము. సూర్యపుటము పెట్టు to inspissate fluid medicines or extracts by exposure to the sun. సూర్యపుత్రుడు sūrya-putruḍu. n. The son of Helius: an epithet of Śani, of Yama and of Varuna. శనిగ్రహము, యముడు, వరుణుడు. సూర్యప్రభ sūrya-prabha. n. The disc or orb of the sun; also a vehicle or seat with a gilt aureole, సూర్యబింబము, ఒక దేవత వేంచేయు సూర్యాకారమైన వాహనము. సూర్యవాద్యము sūrya-vādyamu. n. A tambourine or small double tabor. పొగామీద కట్టుకొని వాయించే సూర్యాకారమైన చర్మవాద్యము.

సూల [from Skt. శూల.] Same as శూల (q. v.) సూలచేకటులు sūla-chēkaṭulu. n. A kind of bracelet. హస్తభూషణములు. "సూలచేకటులలోకమూలమైదివిరాజ, గనుపులకుండ్ల చేకటులువాల్చి." S. i. 176. సూలలదండ sūlala-daṇḍa. n. A kind of necklace. కంఠభూషణవిశేషము. "చేకటులుమేలిమిసూలలదండ." H. iv. 101.

సూళము sūḷamu. [Skt.] n. A certain tune or song. గీతవిశేషము. "గాదల్ పెంచ్చుగభాధిరింపుచోలకంగాతాళమూంబులతో తీతావాధ. జయాంకసంకలితముల్ సూళాదిగీతావళుల్." NH. ii. 125. "ఆలాపములుచేసియారాజామీది సూళాదులింపులుసొగయబాడుటయు." HD. i. 873.

సూసకము sūsakamu. [Tel.] n. A kind of jewel worn on the head by women. తిరుగుడుబిళ్ల, పిగపువ్వు. "సీ. వెంగల్వపూదండజేర్చి పెందురుమునై, ఘనసారముననూసకముఘటించి." చంద్రా. vi. 5.

సూసరి sūsari. [Tel.] n. A bricklayer, plasterer. గాదెకాడు, సున్నముపూయువాడు, లేపకుడు.

సృ sṛi

సృక్కము or సృక్కి srikkamu. [Skt.] n. A corner of the mouth. నోటిపెలవి. పెదవిమూల.

సృగాలము srigālamu. [Skt.] n. A jackal. నక్క. సృగాలిక srigālika. n. A female jackal. ఆడునక్క.

సృజించు srij-inchu. [Skt.] v. a. To create, make, form, produce. పుట్టించు, కలుగజేయు, సృష్టిచేయు. సృష్టము srishṭamu. adj. Created, made, formed, invented. పుట్టింపబడ్డ, కల్పింపబడ్డ, నిర్మింపబడ్డ, సృజింపబడిన. సృష్టి or సృజన srishṭi. n. Creation, formation, fabrication, invention. production, fabrication, invention. సృజించుట, ఉత్పత్తి, నిర్మాణము, కల్పన. The world, the universe. జగత్తు, చరాచరము. సృష్టించు or సృష్టిచేయు srishṭinchu. v. a. To create, make, form, fabricate, invent. పుట్టించు. కలుగజేయు. కల్పించు. సృష్టికర్త *srishti-karta.* n. The creator, or lord of creation. నిర్మాణముచేయువాడు. సృష్టియగు *srishti-y-agu.* v. n. To be created. పుట్టు, కలుగు.

సృణి *srini.* [Skt.] n. A goad, a hook with which elephants are urged. అంకుశము.

సృతి *sriti.* [Skt.] n. A way, road, path. మార్గము. Going, పోక.

సె se

సెందారులు *sendārulu.* [Tel.] n. plu. An instrument which was apparently used in hunting. మృగయాసాధనవిశేషము. "దీమం బులునిలిపియు, కారులుపొనిపియు, సెందారులు దీర్చియు వలలకుందాచ్చియు." Rukmangada. iii. 90.

సెక or సెగ *seka.* [from Skt. శిఖా.] n. Heat, warmth. ఉష్ణత్వము. సెట్ట, వేడిమి. తాపము. A flame, జ్వాల. "చంద్రరజంబుచేజనియించెసెక లంచు సెగతాకబ్బంతిమంటపిపసేల." Anir. iii. 29. సెకకంటి *seka-kanti.* n. Lit. the flame-eyed, an epithet of Siva. సెకవెలుగు *seka-velugu.* n. An epithet of the sun, సూర్యుడు. సెగగడ్డ *sega-gadda.* n. A boil, pimple, pustule, arising from heat. తాపుచేతపేచినకురుపు. సెగబెట్టు *sega-bettu.* v. a. To warm. నిప్పు తాకనుఉంచు. సెగరేడు *sega-rēdu.* n. Fire, అగ్ని, శిఖావంతుడు. సెగరోగము *sega-rōgamu.* n. Gonorrhœa. మండలరోగము.

సెగ్గు, సెగ్గము or సెగ్గెము *seggu.* [Tel.] n Reproach, censure, a false accusation. అపవాదము, నింద. Disgust, రోత. సెగ్గము *seggamu.* adj. Disgusting, రోతయైన. Blameworthy, నింద్యము. సెగ్గింపు *seggimpu.* n. Disgust. రోత. సెగ్గించు *segginsu.* v. a. To reproach, blame, accuse, to evince disgust or horror at. నిందించు, దూషించు, అసహ్యపడు, రోయు. ఏవగించు. "పీమునగడింపున సెగ్గింపదెవ్వరిట్లునేయుచుతన్నే." Vish. vi. 57.

సెజ్జ *sedzdza.* [from Skt. శయ్యా.] n. A bed, a couch శయ్య. A basket of plaited cocoanut leaves to hold flowers, fruits, &c. The box worn by Jangams, containing the lingam. పూలుమొదలైనవి పెట్టెబుట్ట, సంపుటము, లింగకాయమొదలైనవి ఉంచేసంచి. "రాత్రియుఁగటయు లింగముపెజ్జగాగనితొత్తుడైయుంటి." M. XII. iii. 202.

సెట్టి or శెట్టి *setti.* [from Skt. శ్రేష్ఠి.] n. A merchant, వర్తకుడు. A title assumed by all members of the Beri Komati, or Balija caste who are merchants.

సెనగలు *senagalu.* [from Skt. చణక.] n. The pulse called Bengal gram. *Circer arietinum.*

సెపియించు or సెపించు *sepiyintsu.* [from Skt. శపించు.] Same as శపించు (q. v.)

సెబాసు, సేబాసు or శాబాసు *sebāsu.* [from Tel. చీ+ H. శేక్.] interj. Hollo! What a wonder! well done! bravo! ఆశ్చర్యము!

సెబ్బర, చెబ్బర or సెబ్రు *sebbara.* [Tel.] n. Evil, కీడు. Harm, చెడుగు. మంచిసెబ్బరలు, good and bad.

సెమ్మె *semme.* [from Skt. శమ్యా.] n. A brass lampstand. ఇత్తడిదీపస్తంభము.

సెర *sera.* [Tel.] n. A line or streak in the eye, జీర. "ఎర్రనిసెరలతోడికపిలకన్నుల పెడంకతాల్పులును." Harivamsa. v. 167.

సెరగు *seragu.* [Tel.] n. Danger, ill fortune, evil, harm. ఆపద.

సెరబడి *sera-badi.* [Tel.] n. Friendship. స్నేహము.

సెరింత *serinta.* [Tel.] n. Jest, jeering mimickry. హాస్యము. "పగవునవ్వుసెరింతవానినుపోస్యము." ABA. i. 162.

సెల *sela*. [from Skt. శిల.] n. A fountain head. అంబుప్రదేశము, నదీమూలము. A hill stream or torrent. సెలయేరు. A twig, ఉలి. A burrow, a hole, బొరియ, బొక్క. A line or streak, చీర. The mouth or orifice of an ulcer, వ్రణముననుండు చీముపార్వబించురంధ్రము. The point of an arrow, బాణపుములికి. [from Skt. శలమ.] n. A porcupine's quill, ఏదుపందిముల్లు. [from Skt. శల్యం.] n. A sharp point of a dagger, &c. మునికోలలో నడువాని యునుపముల్లు. An arrow, బాణము. "క॥ ఎరకలు విరుగనరికినయెడల సెలలకు విడిన జలగలపాలు పున." Parij. ii. 112. "సెల నెప్పకొనిరొప్పులిప్పెనదీడించి పడవైరులొప్పి నీపాదమున." Swa. iv. 44. టీ॥ సెలనెప్ప కొని, డొంకలోతావుచేసుకొని. సెలలుపారే పుండు a fistula, a deep sore or ulcer. సెలకట్టె, సెలకట్టియ or సెలగోల *sela-kaṭṭe*. n. A dart, javelin, arrow. A bamboo rod or stake, a slender stick. A shepherd's crook. చెయ్యూతకె, చిరుతకట్టె, సన్నకర్ర, శరము, మూరెడుకట్టె చబుకుకట్టినది. "కట్టినవిలిదిండ్లు సెలకట్టియ విండ్లునువిండ్ల గాసెనల్." Swa. iv. 43. "క॥ మొలచట్టిచెరుగుచిక్కము, బలుదిట్టకొరలుడొకడు పటువగుముష్టిగా, సెలకట్టబట్టి కెరొక, సెలకట్టింగొట్టెనైచె శెకురుంగాశీగా." Swa. iv. 83. "కనిచేశాసెలగోలపట్టికొనుచు కా నిమ్మకానిమ్మరా." BX. 349. సెలపంది *sela-pandi*. n. A porcupine, ఏదుపంది, ముండ్ల పంది. సెలపారు, సెలపడు, సెలవారు or సెలవేయు *sela-paru*. v. n. To fester or run into sinuses; to break into holes as a bad sore or ulcer. పుండిలో బొక్కలుపడి మూలమూలకుపారు. సెలపారినపుండు or సెల పుండు a sinuous ulcer which breaks into holes. ఆ పుండు సెలలుపారుచున్నది the ulcer breaks into holes. "చిరుగోటి పోటులసెలపారునందురు." Ila. ii. 7. సెలయేరు *sela-y-ēru*. n. A waterfall, cascade, mountain torrent. నిర్ఝరము, ధార. సెలయూట *sela-y-ūṭa*. n. A mountain spring. కొండ యూట.

సెలగ, శెలగ, శలగ or సలగ *selaga*. [Tel.] n. or interj. So much! A word used in measuring grain. "One lot;" from which a new reckoning begins. The handful or pinch of grain put down as a mark of reckoning, నూటిసంజ్ఞ. A fee rated at 16 or 18 కూనికలు to the Putti or at two rupees per Kuchchela (కుచ్చెల). ధాన్యము కొలవడములో కొత్తలెక్క మొదలుపెట్టేటప్పుడు ఆ నేమాట, అప్పుడు దోసిలితో యెత్తి కుప్పగాపో యుధాన్యము, పుట్టికింత. అని యుచ్చేరుసుము. నూటికి పాడిచి సెలగంటాడు he kills one hundred and cries "that is one lot."

సెలగ or సెలగొమ్మ *selaga*. [Tel.] n. A branch of a branch. ఉపశాఖ.

సెలగపార *selaga-para*. [Tel.] n. An Indian spade or hoe. ఒకవిధమైనపార, గొడ్డలి.

సెలగు or శెలగు *selagu*. [Tel.] v. a. To cut to pieces. ఖండించు.

సెలగులు *selagulu*. [Tel.] n. plu. Troubles. చిక్కులు. "చిల్లరసిద్ధులసెలగులబాపి." L. xix. 335.

సెలయు *selayu*. [Tel.] v. n. To burst out, to riot. చెలరేగు. "తనక్రొవ్వగనుపట్టు ధర శీఘ్రములగిట్టు సెలనీకొమ్మునగొట్టు కలగబెట్టు." N. i. 144. v. a. To chop, to cut. నరుకు. To scatter, చిమ్ము. "చెలిదాక్చిదిని చీమచిటుకన్న కొకపారి సెలనిసెంపరలాడుబిట్టరెల్ల." Swa. iv. 16.

సెలవి *selavi*. [from Skt. సృక్కి.] n. A corner of the mouth. పెదవిమూల. "సీ॥ సెలవుల నదరశేముఖముగా." Swa. ii. 5. "సెలవుల దిగిండిపేక్రదంష్ట్రికలుమెరయ." ib. iv. 155.

సెలవు *selavu*. [Tel.] n. Leave, permission. An order, ఆజ్ఞ. Expenses, charges, expenditure (Madras Telugu) వ్యయము. Use, ఉపయోగము, Dismissal; a holiday, విడుపు.

సెలవిచ్చు *selav-itstsu.* v. a. To order, command. ఆజ్ఞాపించు. అట్లు సెలవిచ్చినారు he was pleased to say so. To give leave, to permit, allow, give permission. వేసంగి సెలవు the midsummer holidays. సెలవుపుచ్చుకొను take leave, depart. నాకు సెలవుకులేదు I have nothing to live on, నాకు ఖర్చుకులేదు. **సెలవుకాడు** *selavu-kādu.* n. A prodigal, a spendthrift. దూబరదిండి. **సెలవు చేయు** *selavu-chēyu.* v. a. To spend, to expend. వ్యయము చేయు, ఖర్చు చేయు (Madras Telugu).

సెలసు *selasu.* [Tel.] n. A kind of tree. దారువిశేషము. సెలసువిల్లు or సెలవిల్లు *selasu-villu.* n. A bow made of its wood. "వీకగలిగిన విడవిల్లు వెదురువిల్లు సెలసువిల్లును మొదలైనవేగ విండ్లు చులకగాదీసి." Kalahasti. iii. 43.

సెల్లా *sella.* [from Skt. చేలం.] n. Muslin: any cloth without a border. Jaconet. అంచులేని తెల్లనిబట్ట. రవసెల్లా fine muslin.

సెల్లుడు [from Skt. శల్యుడు.] Same as శల్యుడు one of the heroes of the Mahabharata.

సే sē

సేకము or **సేచనము** *sēkamu.* [Skt.] n. Wetting, sprinkling. తడుపుట, చల్లుట. ప్రోక్షణము. సేకముచేయు to smear, పేరము. "ఇవియూడిగామండులన్ని యునూర్చి చెచ్చెరదనువెల్లసేకంబుచేసి." BD. iii. 1162. "భవదీయవిలోకనామృతసేకంబున." M. XII. i. 33. "ఘనబీజములపాదుగావించినాటెజలసేకమునపోషణముగావించి." Sar. D. 375.

సేకము *sēkamu.* [from Skt. శేకా.] n. Heat, warmth. సెగ, కాక. "సీ॥ కుముదములకుంపటిసేకమలర్ గోరువారు." P. i. 725. "సేకపుసరుకులుపోకలువాకులుగొంకళ్లు." ib. i. 722. టీ॥ సేకపుసరుకులు, ఉష్ణవస్తువులు.

సేకరించు *sēkarintsu.* [from Skt. స్వీకరించు.] v. a. To prepare, collect. సిద్ధముచేయు, కూర్చు. సంగ్రహించు. To recover, తెప్పించు. **సేకరము** *sēkaramu.* n. Collecting, preparing anything. సంగ్రహించుట.

సేగి *sēgi.* [Tel.] n. Loss. నష్టి. Evil, harm. calamity, misfortune. కీడు, ఆపద. "నాడెన రగ్యాదిదేవునకుదుకువట్టినగలదె నేడకటసేగి." R. iii. 139. "ఏమనిచెప్పవచ్చువసుధేశ్వరయాబలుసేగి." Vasu. ii. 161. "ఘనులాప్తులసేగికోర్వగాలేరుగదా." P. ii. 40. **సేగిపోవు** *sēgi-pōvu.* v. n. To fail, prove useless, be in vain. వ్యర్థమైపోవు. "నీనిమిత్తముతపమెల్లనుసేగిపోయెను." Vish. ii. 249.

సేచకము *sēchakamu.* [Skt.] adj. Sprinkling. తడిపే. ప్రోక్షణముచేసెడి. n. A cloud, మేఘము. **సేచనము** *sēchanamu.* n. Sprinkling, wetting, తడుపుట, ప్రోక్షణముచేయుటము.

సేడుకర్ర *sēdu-karra.* [Tel.] n. A kind of instrument used by weavers. సాలెవాని సాధనవిశేషము.

సేతువు *sētuvu.* [Skt.] n. A bridge, a causeway, dam, bank or mound. The bridge at Rameswaram. గట్టు, కట్ట. వంతెన. రామేశ్వరమువద్దనున్న వారధి."గతసలిలమునకుసేతువేలా." Bilh. iii. 38.

సేద *sēda.* [from Skt. ఖేదః.] n. Fatigue, weariness, languor, distress. అలయిక, బడలిక, శ్రమము. **సేదగొను** *sēda-gonu.* v. n. To be tired, wearied, fatigued. బడలు, శ్రమమునొందు. సేదదేరు to be calmed or comforted. సేదదీర్చు to comfort. "శైత్యోపచారంబులసేదదీర్పంబెద్దయుం." Ila. iii. 10.

సేద్యము *sēdyamu.* [Tel.] n. Cultivation, tillage, farming. కృషి. **సేద్యగాడు** or **సేద్యకాడు** *sēdya-gādu.* n. A farmer, ploughman, agricultural labourer, సేద్యము చేయువాడు. వ్యవసాయముదారుడు, కాపు.

సేన or శానా *sēna*. [Tel. corruption of చాలా or చాల.] adj. Much, plenty. విస్తారమైన. సేన, సేనా or సేనగ adv. Much, abundantly. విస్తారముగా. "సేనగవాంఛితాన్నముఖు లొందగ." Bhāska. §. 59.

సేన *sēna*. [Skt.] n. An army, forces. చతురంగబలములగలసమూహము, దండు, సైన్యము. సేనాంగము *sēn-angamu*. n. A component part of an army, as elephants, chariots, cavalry or infantry. హస్త్యశ్వరథపదాతిసమూహము. సేనాధిపతి or సేనాపతి *sēn-ādhi-pati*. n. A general, commander; a leader or headman. సేనానాయకుడు, దండునాయకుడు, మొనగాడు. సేనాధిపత్యము or సేనాపతిత్వము *sēn-ādhi-patyamu*. n. Generalship, leadership, command of an army. సేనానాయకత్వము, దండుయొక్క అధిపత్యము. సేనాని *sēnāni*. n. A general. Also, an epithet of Kumaraswami, the god of war. దండునాయకుడు, కుమారస్వామి. సేనాముఖము *sēna-mukhamu*. n. The front or van of an army. సేనయొక్క అగ్రభాగము.

సేపు *sēpu*. [Tel.] n. Time, a period. కాలము. కొంతసేపు some time. జాముసేపు an hour's time. క్షణముసేపటికి for a moment. కొంచెముసేపటికి soon, shortly after. గడియసేపటికి in an hour. ఇంతసేపటికిరాలేదు he has not come till this while.

సేబాసు, శాబాసు or సెబాసు *sēbāsu*. [H.] interj. Well done! Bravo! See సెబాసు.

సేమంతి or సేమంతిక *sēmanti*. [Skt.] n. The flower called *Chrysanthemum indicum*. చేమంతి. "తలమాపెనాగవంక ధళధళత్సేమంతి కాగంధినీవారికగ్రథరములు." Parij. iii. 91.

సేమము *sēmamu*. [from Skt. క్షేమము.] n. Happiness, well being, welfare, health. కుశలము, ఉన్నదిచెడకుండుట, శుభము.

సేరి or శేరి *sēri*. [H.] n. Free land, which, though not Inam, pays no direct tax to Government. Land rented by a farmer from a Zemindar or possessor of a Manyam and free of tax to Government. Land which pays no money rent, but a portion of the crop as payment in kind. Also, land cultivated by the proprietor himself, a home farm.

సేరు or శేరు *sēru*. [H.] n. A *seer*, a measure of weight equal to two pounds: also, a measure of quantity equal to about a quart. (It varies in various parts of the country.) అరువదినాలుగు శేర ఇరువదిడబ్బుల యెత్తు; ఎనిమిదిపలములయెత్తు; ఇరువదినాలుగు తులములయెత్తు. కచ్చాసేరు the same more definitely. పక్కాసేరు the large seer which contains three సేరులు, that is, twenty four పలములు or ninety-six rupees' weight. సవ్వాసేరు a seer of thirty rupees' weight.

సేల *sēla*. [from Skt. చేలము.] n. A cloth, వస్త్రము.

సేళము *sēlamu*. [Tel.] n. A kind of tree. ఒకవిధమైనచెట్టు.

సేవ or సేవనము *sēva*. [Skt.] n. Service, servitude, homage, reverence, worship. పరిచర్య, శుశ్రూష. సేవచేయు to serve, to wait on, attend on. ఏకాంతసేవ solitary adoration. తీర్థసేవ visiting a holy place. ఔషధసేవనము taking medicine. "అమలవాయుసేవనము నిర్మలత్వంబు." M. XII. vi. 2. సేవకవృత్తి *sēvaka-vritti*. n. Servitude, living by service. కొలువుచేసి జీవించడము, నవుకరి. సేవకుడు or సేవి *sēvakudu*. n. A servant, an attendant. దాసుడు. తమసేవకుడైన your obedient servant. సేవించు or సంసేవించు *sēvintsu*. v. a. To serve, to worship, to prostrate oneself, to salute; to eat or drink, as a medicine, &c. కొలుచు, పూజించు, పుచ్చుకొను, తిను, త్రాగు. "కావునసేవించమున సుర సేవింపకయుండుటొప్పు." M. XIII. v. 166. బహుదివ్యదేశములు సేవించినాడు he visited many shrines. సేవితము *sēvitamu*. adj. Served, worshipped. కొలువబడిన, పూజిం

పబడిన, ఉపాసితమైన. **సేవితుడు** *sēvitudu.* n. One who is worshipped or venerated. నమస్కృతుడు. మునిసేవితుడైన యీశ్వరుడు the god who is adored by the hermits. **సేవ్యము** *sēvyamu.* adj. Venerable, worthy of worship, సేవించదగినదగు అర్హమైన, ఉపాస్యమైన. n. Ploughed land. దున్ని సిద్ధము చేసినపొలము. **సేవ్యుడు** *sēvyudu.* n. One who is venerable, one who deserves worship or veneration. సేవింపదగినవాడు.

సేవియ or **సేవె** *sēviya.* [from Skt. సేవిక.] n. A kind of food prepared from wheat flour, sugar and milk.

సేసలు or **సేసబ్రాలు** *sēsalu* [from Skt. శేష.] n. Raw rice thrown on the heads of the bride and bridegroom during the marriage ceremony. మంత్రాక్షతలు, అక్షతలు, తలంబ్రాలు. సేసకొప్పు tresses worn on the wedding day. పెండ్లికొప్పు. కొంగెసిగ. "సేసకొప్పునజారుచెంగల్వమొగడలు జాగరాయిఁకటాక్షములనెనయ." Vasu. iv. 121. "వారలుత్సహించివలకొప్పుదీవించి, సేసలిడిరియు వతిశిరమునందు." B. X.

సై sai

సై or **సయి** *sai.* [from Skt. సహ.] adj. or prefix. Assisting, together with. See సైదోడు.

సైంధవము *saindhavamu.* [Skt. from సింధు.] adj. Born in or belonging to Sind. n. A horse from Sind, సింధుదేశజాతాశ్వము. సైంధవము or సైంధవలవణము n. Salt brought from Sind. సింధుదేశపుదీలవణము.

సైంహికేయుడు *sainhik-ēyudu.* [from Skt. సింహిక.] n. A name of Rahu. రాహువు.

సైకతము *saikatamu.* [from Skt. సికత.] adj. Sandy in general. సికతామయమైన, ఇసుకతో సంబంధించిన. సైకతలింగము an effigy made of sand. n. A hillock or dune of sand. ఇసుకదిబ్బ. సైకతశ్రోణి *saikata-srōṇi.* n. A beautiful woman. Vasu. ii. 146.

సైకము or **సయికము** *saikamu.* [Tel.] n. Thinness. సూక్ష్మత్వము. adj. Thin, light, nice, pretty, trim. సూక్ష్మము, అల్పము. సన్ని, తేలికైన, చక్కని. "సరిగంచుచెంగావిసైకపు దుత్తరిలవక్షుచ్చిత్తల అంధ్రునుశిర." Bmj. iii. 136.

సైగ or **సయిగ** *saiga.* [from Skt. సంజ్ఞ.] n. A sign, gesture. సంజ్ఞ. కనుసైగ a wink. చేయిసైగ a sign with the hand.

సైచు or **సయిచు** *saitsu.* [from Skt. సహనము.] v. n. and a. To bear, endure: to pardon. సహించు, మన్నించు. "ఇంక నాపయి దయ యొట్లుగల్గునో మీకు సైచకయున్న నాబ్రతుకేల." T. iv. 20. "అపరాధశతసహస్రాపహిష్ణువైనది." BD. iv. 516.

సైతము or **సయితము** *saitamu.* [from Skt. సహితమ్.] adv. Even, too, also, కూడా. "మేముసైతముగా, వాదినవారియట్లగరువంబునగర్ణ నుచుంటిమవ్విభుగా." Vish. vi. 100.

సైదము or **సయిదము** *saidamu.* [Tel.] n. Wheat flour. గోధుమపిండి.

సైదోడు or **సయిదోడు** *sai-dōdu.* [Tel. సయి+తోడు.] n. A brother or sister. తోడబుట్టిన వాడు, తోడబుట్టినది, తోడబుట్టువు. "తనసైదోడువలెబ్రోవుము." Satyabha. iii. 165. Vasu. iii. 138.

సైనిక *sainika.* [Skt. from సేన.] adj. Of or relating to an army. దండుసంబంధమైన. సైనికుడు *sainikudu.* n. A soldier, సేనతోసంబంధించినవాడు. బంటు. A general, సేనాధిపతి. సైన్యము *sainyamu.* n. An army. దండు.

సైరంధ్రి *sairandhri.* [Skt.] n. A good woman who being deserted by her husband engages to work in another's house.

సాగడు విడివిపోయినందున పరగృహమందుండి స్త్రీలకు శృంగారించునట్టిస్త్రీ. M. IV. iii. 31. A female guard in a harem, అంతఃపుర ప్రకాపరిక స్త్రీ. సైరంధ్రీత్వము *sairandhritvamu*. n. The state of being a servant maid in another's house. పరగృహమందు ఆడంగులకు శృంగారించేదిగా యుండడము.

సైరించు or సయిరించు *sairintsu*. [from Skt. సహనమ్.] v. a. To endure, suffer. సహించు, తాళు. "సకలాపరాధులసైరించిమమ్ముసుకృతవంతుల జేయుమీ." BD. v. 1149. సైరణ *sairaṇa*. n. Patience. సహనము. "దానులగానమ్ముడలు సర్దరింపు, మీసైరణవార్ధి యింకదో యింక." BD. v. 1068.

సైరికుడు *sairikudu*. [Skt. from సీరము a plough.] n. A ploughman. దున్నెడువాడు.

సైరిభము *sairibhamu*. [Skt.] n. A wild buffalo. కారెనుపోతు.

సొ SO

సొంటి or సొంటికొమ్ము *sonti*. [from Skt. శుంఠి.] n. Dry ginger. తక్కనముచేసి యెండబెట్టిన అల్లము, శృంగబేరము. "తోగికొంగాలకుసొంటికొమ్ము" a mere trick, delusion. S. iii. 24. సొంటు *sontu*. n. A fault, defect. దోషము, తప్పు. దానికొక సొంటుపెట్టినాడు he found fault with it. సొంట్లువెదకు to be captious. ఏపదార్థమును వర్జించినను సొంట్లు వెదకువాడు a very delicate eater, a squeamish person.

సొంతము *sontamu*. [from Skt. స్వతన్త్రమ్.] adj. Own, private. స్వకీయమైన.

సొంపు *sompu*. [Tel.] n. Elegance, grace. సొగసు. అందము. Glee, delight, joy, సంతోషము, ముదము. ఉల్లాసము, వేడుక. Happiness, సుఖము. Brightness, cheerfulness, కాంతి, ప్రసన్నత. Abundance, సమృద్ధి. "మనరథము పరపుమిప్పుడు సునిశితబాణములనతి నిసొంపుగానిందుగా." M. VI. ii. 148. సొంపైన *somp-aina*. adj. Nice, elegant, pretty, trim. మనోజ్ఞము. సొంపారు, సొంపిలు, సొంపెల్లు or సొంపారు *somp-āru*. v. n. To bloom, be lovely, pretty or pleasant. సొగసుగానుండు, ఉల్లాసముగానుండు.

సొక్కు or సోక్కు *sokku*. [Tel.] n. Faintness, stupefaction, intoxication, confusion of mind. మయికము, మత్తు, పరవశత, కలవరము, భ్రమ. సొక్కుపొడి intoxicating powder, love powder, a conjuring drug. సొక్కుమందు an intoxicating drug. "ఇక్కడనై పెక్కింబు సొక్కుదక్కకమున్న గ్రక్కున జనుము." M. IV. v. 212. సొక్కు *sokku*. v. n. To be bewildered, stupefied, deluded. పరవశతను పొందు, మత్తుకమ్ము, భ్రమనుజెందు. "పుష్పపరిమళమానవాసనకార్తిసొక్కుచును." BD. iv. 1605. సొక్కించు or సోక్కించు *sokkintsu*. v. a. To stupefy, intoxicate, enamour. పరవశతను పొందించు, మత్తుకమ్మేటట్లు చేయు.

సొగటము *sogaṭamu*. [Tel. (సొగపు+ఆటము.)] n. A man or piece used in backgammon. సొ. శ. సొగటాలు *sogaṭālu*. (సొగపు+ఆటములు) n. plu. Backgammon. Dice-play. A certain game played with dice on a coloured cloth. The pieces or pawns used in this game. పగడసాలాట, జూదమాడే సాలెలు. సొగటాలగుడ్డ the chequered cloth used in this game. "సొగసుపటికంబుల నమర్చిరిచూడుమీసొగటాలచందము." S. i. 158. "దారదాలుసొగటాలు దాట్రాయిబదరంగములు." H. iii. 191.

సొగటు *sogaṭu*. [Tel.] n. Withering. వాడుట.

సొగయు *sogayu*. [from Skt. సుఖమ్.] v. n. To be bewildered, stupefied, deluded. To languish, fade away; to be charmed or touched with love. మూర్ఛిల్లు. సొక్కు, పరవశమగు. మురియు. "సుఖసత్కథా వినోదములు సొగయుచు మన్నెడ కుద్దికైక మాఃకుండకుము." BD. i. 5. సొగపు or సొగయిక *sogapu*. n. Stupefaction, intoxication, సొక్కు, పారవశ్యము. సొగయించు *sogayintsu*. v. a.

To stupefy, intoxicate, enamour. సొక్కించు. "సొగసిసొగయించి సిరద్రైన చూపులూచి." E.? iii. 111. **సొగసు** or **సొగుసు** *sogasu.* n. Beauty, elegance, prettiness, niceness. శృంగారము, అందము, సౌందర్యము, విలాసము. Stupefaction, పారవశ్యము. adj. Pretty, beautiful, elegant, handsome, nice. అందమైన, సుందరమైన. **సొగసుకాడు** *sogasu-kāḍu.* n. A beau, a handsome man, అందగాడు. A gallant, విటకాడు. **సొగసుకత్తె** *sogasu-katte.* n. A belle, a handsome woman. అందగత్తె, విటకత్తె. **సొగియు** *sogiyu.* v. n. To be pleasant. ఇంపగు. **సొగియించు** *sogiy-intsu.* v. n. To be happy. సుఖించు.

సొచ్చెము *sochchemu.* [from Skt. శోచము.] n. A remainder, overplus. హెచ్చు, అధికము. A fractional quantity. Small change, loose cash. చిల్లర. "... ధనేశులిధుల్ తమ వడ్డికిచ్చుదురు, ఇచ్చినసొచ్చెమెంతయుచు నవ్వుదురు వ్వారిలోని సోమటుల్." T. ii. 19.

సొజ్జె or **సొజ్జి** *sojje.* [Tel.] n. A mess, or dish made of grits of roasted rice or broken rice, boiled after having been heated in a dry state. వియ్యము వేయించి వండిన అన్నము. సొజ్జబూరె a kind of cake.

సొటసొట *soṭa-soṭa.* [Tel.] n. The state of being emaciated. కృశించడము, కార్శ్యము. **సొటసొటపోవు** *soṭa-soṭa-pōvu.* v. n. To become lean, కృశించు. To be dejected, దిగజారిపోవు. "చిట్టచెదర దిగులుగొని సొటసొట పోవక వినుకమందు చూడక." H. v. 218. **సొటసొటలాడు** *soṭa-soṭa-l-āḍu.* v. n. To pine, to be in trouble. నకనకలాడు. వాడు ఆకలిచేత సొటసొటలాడుచున్నాడు he is famishing.

సొట్ట or **సొట్టు** *soṭṭa.* [Tel.] n. Crookedness; a dent, excavation. A bruise made in a metal vessel. సొట్ట, వక్రత, సొట్టు. adj. Lean, emaciated, distorted or crippled. ఈడేరోయిన. సొట్టకన్ను a deformed eye. సొట్టనోరు a wry mouth. సొట్టకాలు a bandy leg. సొట్టచేతులవాడు a man with twisted hands. సొట్టపల్లము concave.

సొడ్డు *soḍḍu.* [from Skt. శోధ్యమ్.] n. A slap on the head of a loser in a game, applied with both the winner's hands. (Metaphorically,) a defect, fault, imputation, ఆటలో ఓడినవాని తలమీదవేయు దెబ్బ, లోపము. న్యూనత, కొరత. సొడ్డువేయు to give such a slap with the open hand, to dupe or to make a fool of. "సోమయాజనియట్టి సొడ్లకత్తె పెనురంభ." Vema. 903. "నిఖిలమున తలకు నెమకమేమునసొడ్డు." ib. 2129. అతడు చేసినపనిలో ఏమి సొడ్డుగలదా is there any defect in the work he has done? **సొడ్లమర** or **సొళ్లమర** *soḍla-mara.* n. The fish called the Angel shark, *Squatina.* మత్స్యవిశేషము.

సొత్తు *sottu.* [from Skt. స్వత్వమ్.] n. Property, goods. సొమ్ము. ఆస్తి.

సొద *soda.* [from Skt. చితా.] n. A funeral pile, the fire used in a funeral pile. చితి. చిచ్చగ్ని, ఒలికి. Grief, sorrow, చింత. "సుదతిరొదటికిసొదచొచ్చెదు." Vish. v. 231. ఏల అగ్నిప్రవేశము చేస్తున్నావు! "సొదవంటియూపుత్రశోకంబునాకు." Sar. D. 632. "తుదిని సెవ్వరైన సొదమున్గుచేవరు." Vema. 950.

సొన *sona.* [Tel.] n. Juice that exudes from plants, the acrid juice or milk of some plants, స్రవించునది. చెట్టు కాయకోసిన వ్వుడు వచ్చేరసము. జీడి. A stream of such juice, ఊటకాలువ. The white of an egg గుడ్డులోనితెలుపు. The hairy covering of a fruit, &c. "సొనచేటపొటమరించిసెనవారినయట్టి." Swa. vi. 31.

సొన్నము or **సొన్న** *sonamu.* [from Skt. స్వర్ణమ్.] n. Gold. బంగారు. A certain gold coin, వరహా. "...సొన్న

టుకొంటిచ్చిన అన్నమిడెడువాడు గలరెయని యు మనుకరీ." Zacc. vi. 114. సొన్నారి sonnāri. (సొన్నము+అరి.) n. A goldsmith, స్వర్ణకారుడు, అగసాలెవాడు, కంసలవాడు.

సొబగు sobagu. [from Skt. శుభగః.] n. Beauty, prettiness. సౌందర్యము, సొగసు. సొబగుడు sobagudu. n. A handsome man, చక్కనివాడు. A lover, sweetheart, విటుడు.

సొబను sobanu. [Tel.] n. The fœtus of a mare. బడబమోలు.

సొమ్మ somma. [from Skt. శ్రమః.] n. Faintness, swoon. మూర్ఛ. Torpidity, lack of sensation, తిమురు. నా కాలు సొమ్మగా నున్నది my leg is asleep. "సొమ్మతెలిసి." అచ్చ. యు. కా. సొమ్మసిలు, సొమ్మసిల్లు, సొమ్మగొను, సొమ్మపోవు or సొమ్మలుపోవు somma-silu. v. n. To faint, to swoon. మూర్ఛపోవు. "క॥ అనిదొంగకుమారుంజని తెచ్చిన సొమ్ములు గాంచి సొమ్మసిలి తెలిసి, దురంతనితాంతచింత మున మునకను గొని." R. v. 279.

సొమ్ము sommu. [from Skt. స్వమ్.] n. Money. ధనము. Property, goods, jewels, అధీన వస్తువు, సొత్తు. భూషణము, అభరణము. ఇది నీసొమ్మా is this your money? "ధృతి కుదిర్ప మహాపతివ్రతాత్వ, సత్యసౌశీల్యశమద మాదిగనిధులు, జానకీదేవిసొమ్ములుగా నికావు సొమ్ములివి కాంతికని పర్కొనూర్యసుతుడు." R. v. 283. Also, cattle (a sense peculiar to the North.) గోసమూహము, గోధనము.

సొయ్యక soyyaka. [Tel.] n. A kind of musical instrument. వాద్యవిశేషము. "తాళ ములో మురజములో గిడిగిల్లసొయ్యకలో కిన్నెర లను." Balaram. v. 24.

సొరంగము sorangamu. [from Skt. సురఙ్గః.] n. A hole in the ground or in a wall. రంధ్రము.

సొర or సొర్ర, sora. [Tel.] n. The Bottle Gourd. *Cucurbita lagenaria.* కుంబి. చేదు సొర the bitter gourd, కటుతుంబి. నల్లసొర a black kind of the same. సొరకాయ the fruit of the gourd, అలాబువు. సొరకాయలు తెగనరుకువాడు a braggart. సొరకాయబుర్ర, the dry shell of a gourd.

సొర sora. [Tel.] n. Grief, sorrow. వ్యాకులత. "సొరసొరదయునగను పరగుచింత." ABA. ii. 454.

సొర or సొర్ర, సొరమీను or చొర sora. [Tel.] n. A shark, a general name for several ravenous fishes. ఝషము. కొమ్ము సొర a swordfish. *Carcharias laticaudus.* (F. B. I.) పేడాడిసొర్ర or కొమ్ముసొర్ర the Hammer-headed Shark. Russell, plate XII. సొర్రకోవ sorra-kōva. n. A shark called *Carcharias macloti* (F. B. I.) పాల సొర్ర the small blue shark. రాతిసొర్ర the brown shark. మట్టసొర్ర the flat shark. తేలుసొర్ర the long tailed shark. (Russell, plates XII. XV. XVI.) సొమ్మసొర and పొక్కిసొర్ర are other species. నీకసొర్ర or కరమూతిసొర్ర a shark called *Carcharias menisorrah* (F. B. I.) సొరపియ్య sora-piyyi. n. Literally "shark's dung. The cuttle bone. సముద్రఫేనము. సముద్రపునురుగు.

సొరగు soragu. [Tel.] n. Swoon, fainting, మూర్ఛ. A dry leaf, ఎండాకు. v. n. To be lost, disappear, లీనము.

సొరదోకి sora-dōki. [Tel.] n. A wicked person. దురాచారుడు.

సొరపు sorapu. [Tel.] adj. Thin, lean, emaciated. కృశము.

సొరము soramu. [from Skt. స్వరః.] n. The voice. కంఠధ్వని. A musical note, షడ్జాది.

సొరిది soridi. [Tel.] n. Order, regularity. వరుస. క్రమము. adv. Regularly, properly, plentifully, much. వరుసగా. క్రమముగా, విశేషముగా, విస్తారముగా.

సొరుగు *sorugu.* [Tel.] n. The drawer of a table or box. పెట్టెలు మొదలయినవాటిలోని అర. A swoon, మూర్ఛ. v. n. To faint, to swoon, మూర్ఛిల్లు. To fade or languish, to fall down. To run away. వాడు, కూలు, పడు, పారిపోవు. "విహారశిఖావాతిచే నెమ్ములు విరిగి సొరిగిజీవముచిడిచెను." P. i. 241. "తోంటత పుత్త్రుని నెదటికి నేలగనంపి. యువవిలోపానము మూర్ఛిల్లన్నదనుచు మెంరిగి. కల్లరేదుబ్బుల సేద్యుము కపటవృత్తి. వెదకుసంచుః సొరిగజాచెదవునీవు." N. H. v. 53.

సొలయు *solayu.* [Tel.] v. n. To languish, faint. సొక్కు. నీరసమొందు, మూర్ఛిల్లు, ఖిన్నము. To hesitate, go back, వెనుదీయు. "సొలపి వంట యుల్లుజొచ్చినకుం జేలుచంద్రమయ్యె." HK. iii. 152. To be tired or disgusted with, వైరస్యముచెందు. **సొలపు** or **సొలయిక** *solapu.* n. Languishment, swooning, faintness. విస్రాంతి, పారవశ్యము. మూర్ఛ, బడలిక. సొలపుమాపు a languishing glance. "సహజంబుగా పధూబముల కాటమాని సొలపున సొరగజారడగా." T. ii. 72. **సొలపు** *solapu.* v. a. To cause to languish, to cause to faint. సొక్కించు. **సొలపుతనము** *solapu-tanamu.* n. Languishment, faintness. సొక్కు, మ్లానభావము, ఖిన్నత. **సొలిమిడి** *solimudi.* n. A swoon, fainting. మూర్ఛ, సొమ్మ.

సొల్లుకట్లులు *sollu-kaṭṭulu.* [Tel.] n. plu. Words or sounds used by the manager of a band of dancers. ఆటకాడింపించుటలో నట్టువుగాడు తధిక్కు. తకత్తైత్తై అని చెప్పేటివి.

సొల్లెము. సొల్లెము or **సొల్లియము** *sollemu.* [Tel.] n. A peacock's feather. A turban in which peacock's feathers are worn. నెమలిరెక్కలు చుట్టినపాగ. "జడలుముల్లి. సొల్లెముగ, సన్నపుసొగలడంగి జుట్టిచిల్లడములుధరిని." Swa. iv. 39. టీ॥ సొల్లెముగ. అనగా పింఛకట్టకేసిన చుట్టగాను.

సొర or **సర** *sora.* [Tel.] n. A whisper. గుసగుస. సొవసొవ or సవసవ whispers. "తే॥ సొవసొవలు విన్నమాత్రమునన్నరుమటంచు." H. v. 190.

సో so

సోకు *sōku.* [Tel.] v. n. To touch, come in contact with. To be communicated by contagion, to affect or catch, as a distemper. తాకు, తగులు. To be possessed by a demon, to be affected by the evil influence of stars or demons. గ్రహావేశించు. n. Touching. A touch, contact; a sensation, తాకుట, స్పర్శము. A blow, దెబ్బ, పోటు. An evil spirit, a demon, రాక్షసుడు, పిశాచము. "ఇక్కడనిమీన నాటెంతునాసోకు." N. ix. 409. "మూర్ఛాభిషిక్తుండు సోకోర్చియల కుడగునలజల్లుదిక్కు." A. iv. 335. "కుమారశిలిముఖాళి సోకులనిజహృత్పుటల్ విరిసి." P. iv. 142. దీనిమీద ఎండ సోకుచున్నది it is exposed to the sun. గాలిసోకకుండా ఉంచు to be screened from the wind's touch. "విష్ణుసోకనక్రియ." Ellana. i. 252. "పరుసముసోకిన బంగారమైనట్టు." Vema. 504. "కమలాక్షునస్త్రసోకి కమలినభంగిన." ib. 1434. నామాటలు వానిచెవిని సోకలేదు my words did not reach or enter his ears. ఆ దెబ్బ వానికి సోకలేదు the blow did not hit him. దానికి గాలిసోకినట్లున్నది she appears to have been touched by a demon. సోకుచుక్క the constellation called మూలానక్షత్రము. **సోకుటొజ్జ** *sōku-ṭ-oḍz-dza.* n. The teacher of the Asuras, దైత్యగురువు. శుక్రుడు. **సోకుడు** *sōkuḍu.* n. Touching, స్పర్శము. An evil spirit. పిశాచము. An Asura or demon, రాక్షసుడు. Demoniacal possession, గ్రహావేశము. **సోకుదయ్యము** or **సోకుమారి** *sōku-dayyamu.* n. Wind, the god of the wind. వాయువు, మారుతము. **సోకులరేడు** *sōkula-rēḍu.* n. The regent of the S. W. region

నైర్మల్యము, మూలలేదు. సోకించు sôkintsu. v. a. To put in contact, to cause to touch. తాకించు.

సోగ sôga. [Tel.] adj. Long, tall, prolonged. దీర్ఘమైన, నిడుపైన. సోగ్గైనకొండ a pyramidal rock, a shaft. Ila. ii. 43. సోగమెడ a long neck. సోగ or సోగతనము n. Length. నిడుపు, దైర్ఘ్యము. "తిరుకుంచేటియువిప్ప సోగ తన మందంబొప్పగా." T. iii. 66.

సోగు sôgu. [from Skt. స్రక్.] n. A garland, a necklace. సరము.

సోడు sôḍu. [Tel.] n. The crown of the head. మాడుపట్టు, బ్రహ్మరంధ్రము. సోడుముట్టు sôḍu-muṭṭu. v. n. To spread, pervade, be diffused throughout. అంతటవ్యాపించు, కలకొన్న, మిన్నుముట్టు. "పుష్పసురభిగంధంబు లు సోడుముట్టె." Parij. v. 53. "శా॥ నీడసుకేసు పునదివ్యా, మోదముసాంద్రముయి సోడుముట్టెడు నత్యా, హ్లాదమవశ్వర్యసముత్పాదియనుచు." M. XIII. ii. 458.

సోఢ sôḍha. [Skt.] n. A clever, able, patient, enduring man. సమర్థుడు, సహించువాడు, ఓర్పువాడు. సోఢము sôḍhamu. adj. Borne, suffered, endured. సహింపబడిన (తప్పుమొద లగునవి).

సోణము sôṇamu. [Tel.] n. The root of the nose. నాసామూలము. "శా॥ సోణాలంటు ఘోణాచ్ఛిదలా." A. v. 5.

సోత్ప్రాసము s-ôt-prāsamu. [Skt. స+ఉత్+ప్రాసము.] n. Irony, sneering, praise which is covert censure. సోల్లుంఠనము, ఎత్తిపొడుపుమాట.

సోద sôda. [Tel.] n. Plaster. గచ్చు, గార.

సోదన sôdana. [from Skt. శోధన.] n. An examination. శోధనము. An omen, శకునము. శకునార్థము రామాయణము మొదలైన గ్రంథము లందు నొకమునకు శోధించుట. సోదించు sôdintsu. v. a. To examine, to scrutinise. శోధనచేయు.

సోదరి s-ôdari. [Skt. స+ఉదర.] n. A sister. తోడబుట్టినపడుచు. సోదరుడు s-ôdaruḍu. n. A brother. తోడబుట్టినవాడు.

సోదా sôdā. [H. from Skt. శోధన.] n. An examination, a search. పరీక్ష, వెదకుట. సోదాచేయు or సోదాచూచు to make a search, to search, to examine. సోదా వారంటు a search warrant.

సోదె or సోదియ sôde. [from Skt. చోద్యమ్.] n. Fortune-telling. రాబోవు అదృష్టమును చెప్పడము, రాగల శుభాశుభములను చెప్పుట. సోదె చెప్పు or సోదెచూచు sôde-cheppu. v. n. To tell fortunes, రాబోవు అదృష్టమును చెప్పు. సోదెకత్తె sôde-katte. n. A female fortuneteller. విప్రశ్నిక, సోదెచెప్పుస్త్రీ, దైవజ్ఞ, రాబోవు అదృష్టముచెప్పునది.

సోద్యము or సోద్దెము sôdemu. [from Skt. చోద్యమ్.] n. Wonder, astonishment. ఆశ్చర్యము. adj. Wonderful. ఆశ్చర్యకరమైన.

సోన sôna. [Tel.] n. A drizzle, a slight shower of rain. అల్పవర్షము, సన్నవాన. Rain, వాన. "పూదేనెసోనలు మంచువిధమున తానముల్ విస్తరిల్ల." UR. vii. 173.

సోపనము [from Skt. సోపానము.] Same as సోపానము (q. v.)

సోపానము or సోపానము sôpanamu. [Skt.] n. A step of a staircase or of a flight of steps. మెట్టు.

సోపు sôpu. [Tel.] n. Anise seed. *Pimpinella anisum, Anethum foeniculum.* మసాలాలోవేయు సంబారవుదినుసు. సీమసోపు the Caraway, *Carum carui.* (Watts).

సోబ sôba. [from Skt. శోఫ.] n. A swelling, tumour. శోఫ.

సోబనము sôbanamu. [from Skt. శోభనమ్.] n. Happiness, good fortune. మంగళము.

సోబాన sôbāna. [from Skt. శోభనమ్.] n. A song, each foot of which has the word

సోభానే as a chorus. "సోభానపాటలు సొగసులుకు." H. v. 31.

సోబె or **సోబియ** *sôbe.* [from Skt. శోభ.] n. A beauty spot; a damask or mahogany tint; a bright or golden tint or spot on the skin. సిబ్బెము.

సోమ or **సోమము** *sôma.* [from Skt. శ్రమ.] n. Toil, fatigue శ్రమము. Courage, పరాక్రమము.

సోమ, సోమలత or **సోమవల్లి** *sôma.* [Skt.] n. The Moon plant, *Asclepias acida*, or *A. aphylla*, పుల్లతీగ, తిప్పతీగ. సోమపానము drinking the juice of the Asclepias. **సోమధార** *sôma-dhāra.* n. The heavenly Ganges, ఆకాశగంగ. **సోమపీథి, సోమపీతి** or **సోమపుడు** *sôma-pīthi.* n. One who drinks the juice of the Asclepias. యజ్ఞములో సోమరసముత్రాగువాడు. **సోమయాజి** *sôma-yāji.* n. A sacrificer, యజ్ఞము చేసినవాడు.

సోమరి *sôm-ari.* [సోము (from Skt. సుఖము)+ Tel. అరి.] adj. Idle, lazy. Slothful. అలసమైన. బద్ధకముగల. మందమైన. "సోమరిగాలి." Satyabh. iv. 195. "కేదములంతట నిద్రసోమరై గ్రక్కున నీటిలోగలిసె." T. ii. 15. n. A sluggard, a lazy person, an idler, అలసుడు, ఒళ్లువంగనివాడు, మందుడు. బద్ధకుడు. **సోమరితనము** *sômari-tanamu.* n. Sluggishness, laziness. ఒళ్లువంగనితనము, బద్ధకము.

సోమవారము *sôma-vāramu.* [Skt. from సోమ the moon.] n. Monday. ఇందువాసరము. See సోముడు.

సోమసూత్రము *sôma-sûtramu.* [Skt.] n. A vessel with a spout. A basin with a spout and handle. The receptacle or pit on the outside of a temple to receive the water with which the idol has been bathed. ముక్కు చెంబు పిడికల చిన్నపాత్ర. సొట్టనుండి నీళ్లుపోవుదారి, లింగాభిషేకజలము పోయి పడుతొట్టి. సోమసూత్రప్రదక్షిణము circumambulation around a temple with such turnings that the circumambulation shall be complete without the *somasûtram* (hole to receive the water,) having been crossed. "ప్రదక్షిణాభివందనంబులు సవ్యాపసవ్యంబులగుచు బదియురెండు గాసించుచటరీతి, శంకరునొద్ద సోమసూత్రముగాటరానివిజము." Vanivilas. page 219.

సోమాసి [from Skt. సోమయాజి.] Same as సోమయాజి (q. v.)

సోమించు *sômintsu.* [from Skt. సుఖమ్ changed into సోము.] v. n. To resemble. పరిపోలు. To be courageous, పరాక్రమించు. To be arrogant, విజృంభించు. To spread, వ్యాపించు.

సోమిద or **సోమిద** *sômida.* [from Skt. సోమమ్. See సోమలత.] n. A tree called *Coronilla sesban, Coronilla picta, Pentaptera tomentosa.* తిప్పతీగ or శంపట్టి. **సోమిదేవమ్మ, సోమిదమ్మ, సోమిదవమ** or **సోమిసాని** *sômi-dêv-amma.* n. A title bestowed upon the wife of a Somayaji (సోమయాజి), యజ్ఞపత్ని. సోమయాజులభార్య. See సోమలత. "చేసినకూరిమి సోమిదమ్మ సౌభాగ్యమహత్వై భవంబు." Swa. i. 7.

సోము *sômu.* [from Skt. సుఖము.] n. Happiness, pleasure, joy, health. సుఖము. adj. Happy, pleasing, ఆసక్తము.

సోముడు *sômuḍu.* [Skt.] n. The moon, the regent of the moon, the god of beauty. చంద్రుడు. See సోమవారము.

సోయగము *sôyagamu.* [Tel.] n. Beauty, elegance, harmony, splendour. సౌందర్యము, అందము, చక్కదనము, కాంతి. "సోయగంబున నిరవాయింప." Vasu. iii. 140. "ప్రార్థించుసోయగముః తెగశిరమువాంచి." P. iv. 345. "కేయూరగాధుంబుల సోయగంబులంగమంగని." Swa. i. 34. **సోయగపు** *sôyagapu.* adj. Handsome, beautiful. అందమైన, సొగసైన. "అలరుమానికంబు సోయగపు దండెలెక్క." H. iv. 84.

సోరంగి *sōrangi*. [Tel.] n. A long snouted fish called the Indian whiting. అరటి కాయ ఆకుచేప.

సోరణగండి, సోర్ణగండి or **సోరణము** *sōraṇa-gaṇḍi*. [Tel.] n. A window, a sky-light. గవాక్షము. A. iii. UR. ii. 312. **సోరణదివియలు** *sōraṇa-diviyalu*. n. plu. Lights kept in the windows. గవాక్షములందలి దీపములు. "పురవప్రఘటిత మణిగణసురుచిరవీథి కులవలనసోరణదివియల్ పరకుగానరెక్కిరాత్రులు." Vikramarka. i. 67.

సోరు or **సోరుప్పు** *sōru*. [Tel.] n. Salt-petre. పెట్లుప్పు, క్షారము. సోరుప్పుద్రావకము nitric acid.

సోల *sōla*. [Tel.] n. A certain dry measure, equal to a seer. పదునారుడబ్బులయెత్తు వస్తువుపట్టేకొలది, శాస్త్రకారుడుచెప్పినది తొమ్మన్నూరుగింజలుపట్టేది. **సోలవెలితిగా** *sōla-veli-ti-gā*. adv. Scornfully, contemptuously. కొంచెముతక్కువగా. "ఏలయూబహుదూపుశేష్టైన మున్న పోలవెలితిగనిన్ను జూచితినయ్య." BD. iv. 1028. "ఈచందమిట్లుతాల్పక యూచందంబున నెయున్న యప్పుడునిన్నుఁ జూచితినిపోలవెలితిగ నీ చుక్కల దగిలికొనగ చేటెకినాకున్." BP. vi. 238. **సోలెడు** *sōl-eḍu*. adj. A small pailful. అరతవ్వెడు.

సోలము See under సోలు.

సోలు *sōlu*. [Tel.] v. n. To reel, stagger, faint; to become stupid. సోకు, వివశత్వము నొందివ్రాలు. **సోలము** or **సోలింత** *sōlamu*. n. Intoxication, stupefaction. మత్తు, చొక్కు. **సోలాడు** *sōl-āḍu*. v. n. To be diffused through. వ్యాపించు. "కటిమండమివిరిదండ ఘుమఘుమల్ పోలాడ." H. iv. 124. **సోలించు** *sōlintsu*. v. a. To make faint, to charm, to fascinate. వివశునిగాచేయు.

సోలుపు *sōlupu*. [Tel.] n. A line, a row. వరుస, పంక్తి. **సోలుపుగా** *sōlupu-gā*. adv. In a line or row. వరుసగా.

సోల్కట్లు *sōl-kaṭlu*. [Tel.] n. Words or sounds used by the manager of a band of dancers. ఆటకొలిపించడములో నట్టువకాడు తధిక్కు, తకతైతై అని చెప్పేటివి. "తుంబురమీటి గీతంబుపాడుచునొక, మనుతోష్ఠిపరిగమపధయుగంగ, జగ్గుసోల్కట్ల నుగ్గడించుచునొక్క చక్కదబొమ్మ రధిక్కుమనగ." Ila. ii. 17.

సోల్లుంఠనము *s-ōl-lunṭhanamu*. [Skt.] n. Irony, taunt, sneer, jeering. సోత్ప్రాసము, ఎత్తిపొడుపుమాటలు. Vish. vii. 21.

సోళాదొప్పి or **సోళాందొప్పి** *sōḷā-doppi*. [Tel.] n. A kind of gambling. ద్యూతవిశేషము.

సోహము *sōhamu*. [Skt. స+అహమ్.] n. I am He, The Deity and I are one. అతడేనేను; అతడు అనగా ఈశ్వరుడు, పరమాత్మ; నేను అనగా జీవుడు, జీవాత్మ. అతడేనేననగా జీవాత్మ పరమాత్మలకు భేదములేదనుట.

సౌ sau

సౌందర్యము *saundaryamu*. [Skt. from సుందరము.] n. Beauty. అందము, చక్కదనము.

సౌకర్యము *saukaryamu*. [Skt. from సుకరము.] n. Health, good condition, comfort. స్వస్థత, అనారోగ్యము. మా అప్పకు ఒళ్లు సౌకర్యములేదు my father is not well. దేహసౌకర్యములేక being unwell. **సౌకర్యముగా** *saukaryamu-gā*. adv. In good health, comfortably, ఆరోగ్యముగా, సుఖముగా, సౌఖ్యముగా.

సౌకుమార్యము *sau-kumāryamu*. [Skt. from సుకుమారము.] n. Delicacy, tenderness, మృదుత్వము, సుకుమారత్వము.

సౌఖశాయనికుడు or **సౌఖసుప్తికుడు** *saukha-śāyanikuḍu*. [Skt.] n. A bard or minstrel, whose duty it is to waken the prince in a morning with music and song. వైతాళికుడు, రాజులను నిద్రమేలుకొలుపు వాడు, సుఖనిద్రయాయని ప్రశ్నముచేయువాడు. A. iv. 320.

సౌఖ్యము *saukhyamu.* [Skt. from సుఖము.] n. Ease, health, relief, comfort. సుఖము, హాయి. ఈ యింట్లో నాకు సౌఖ్యములేదు I am not comfortable in this house. నీకు ఒళ్లు సౌఖ్యముగానున్నదా are you well?

సౌగంధికము *sau-gandhikamu.* [Skt. from సుగంధము.] n. The white waterlily. *Nymphea lotus.* తెల్లగలువ. Sulphur, గంధకము. **సౌగంధ్యము** *sau-gandhyamu.* n. Fragrance, సువాసన.

సౌచికుడు *sauchi-kudu.* [Skt. from సూచి.] n. A tailor. బట్టలుకుట్టువాడు, కుట్రపువాడు, దర్జీ.

సౌజన్యము *sau-janyamu.* [Skt. from సుజనుడు.] n. Good nature, urbanity, kindness, friendship. సుజనత్వము, మంచితనము. వారు సౌజన్యముగానున్నారా are they on good terms?

సౌదామని or **సౌదామిని** *saudāmani.* [Skt.] n. Lightning. మెరుపు.

సౌదాయికము *sau-dāyikamu.* [Skt.] n. A dowry given by the parents or by the brothers of the bride.

సౌధము *saudhamu.* [Skt.] n. A mansion, a palace. రాజగృహము, నగరు, మేడ.

సౌనికుడు *sauni-kudu.* [Skt.] n. A butcher. కటికవాడు.

సౌప్తికము *saupti-kamu.* [Skt. from సుప్తి.] adj. Connected with or relating to sleep. నిద్రాసంబంధమైన. n. A nocturnal combat, a night attack. నిద్రించుటలోనగు సమయము లందు శత్రువులపైబడి చంపుట. The name of a book of the Maha Bharata. మహాభారతములో నొకపర్వముయొక్క పేరు.

సౌభాగ్యము *sau-bhāgyamu.* [Skt. from సుభగము.] n. Auspiciousness, good fortune. మంచి అదృష్టము, సుభగత్వము. "మాకు సౌభాగ్యభిక్షంబు పెట్టవేయుముచు." BD. iv. 1347. **సౌభాగ్యవతి** *sau-bhāgya-vati.* n. A good wife, a good woman. A woman whose husband is living. ముత్తైదువ. This is used as a title in addressing a married woman. సౌభాగ్యవతిరైన మా అక్క my honoured sister.

సౌమనస్యము *sau-manasyamu.* [Skt. from సుమనస్సు.] n. Friendliness, favourableness of mind or disposition. మంచిమనసు కలిగియుండుటను, స్నేహభావము.

సౌమ్యము *saumyamu.* [Skt. from సోమ.] adj. Lunar. Handsome, pleasing. Mild, gentle, placid. చంద్రసంబంధమైన, సుందరమైన. శాంతమైన, తిన్నని. ఆయన నిండా సౌమ్యమూర్తి he is very mild or gentle. ఆయనకు జ్వరము కొంచెము సౌమ్యముగానున్నది his fever is now diminishing. n. Smoothness, gentleness, mildness. శాంతము, తిన్నదనము. **సౌమ్య** *saumya.* n. The name of a year. **సౌమ్యవారము** *saumya-vāramu.* n. Wednesday. బుధవారము. **సౌమ్యుడు** *saumyudu.* n. A name of Budhudu, given for his being the son of Soma by Tara or Venus. బుధగ్రహము. A mild man, తిన్నని వాడు, ఒప్పినవాడు. ఆయన మిక్కిలి సౌమ్యుడు he is very gentle.

సౌర *saura.* [Skt. from సూరుడు the sun.] adj. Solar, of or belonging to the sun. సూర్యసంబంధమైన. సౌరజపము worship of the sun. **సౌరము** or **సౌరమతము** *sauramu.* n. The school of the worshippers of the sun. సూర్యోపాసకుల సిద్ధాంతము. **సౌరమానము** *saura-mānamu.* adj. Measured by the sun, solar. సూర్యగతినిబట్టి యేర్పరచబడ్డ, సూర్యసంబంధమైన.

సౌరభము or సౌరభ్యము *saurabhamu.* [Skt. from సురభి.] n. Odour, fragrance. వాసన, పరిమళము. సౌరభేయము *saura-bhēyamu.* n. An ox. బలీవర్దము, ఎద్దు. A. iv. 83. సౌరభేయి *saura-bhēyi.* n. A cow, ఆవు, గోవు.

సౌరాష్ట్రము *sau-rāshṭramu.* [Skt.] n. The name of a country and of a certain tune. ఒకదేశము, రాగవిశేషము.

సౌరి *sauri.* [Skt.] n. A name of Sani. శనైశ్చరుడు. Also, of Yama, యముడు.

సౌరికుడు *sauri-kuḍu.* [Skt. from సుర.] n. An arrack merchant, a wine-seller. సారాయి అమ్మేవాడు, కల్లు అమ్మువాడు.

సౌరు or సవురు *sauru.* [Tel.] n. Bloom, beauty. చక్కదనము. Manner, విధము. "నిగ్గలేమారు సొగాయుసౌరు" T. iv. 59. adj. Beautiful, మనోజ్ఞము.

సౌవర్చలము *sauvarchalamu.* [Skt.] n. Sochal salt, natron, alkali. ఒకవిధమైన ఉప్పు.

సౌవర్ణి *sau-varṇi.* [Skt. from సువర్ణము.] adj. Golden, made of gold. బంగారుతో చేసిన, బంగారుగల. సౌవర్ణికము *sau-varṇikamu.* n. A weight of gold, a weight of four large *Ratis* or mashas. నిష్కములో నాలు గోపాలు, నాలుగు మినపగింజలయెత్తు. సౌవర్ణకరణి a kind of drug, ఓషధివిశేషము.

సౌవిదల్లుడు or సౌవిదుడు *sau-vidalluḍu.* [Skt.] n. A guard over a harem. అంతఃపురపు కావలివాడు.

సౌవీరము *sauvīramu.* [Skt.] n. Antimony, collyrium. కాటుకరాయి, నీలాంజనము. Sour rice water, పులికడుగునీళ్లు. The fruit of the jujube tree. బదరీఫలము, రేగుపండు. A certain country on the banks of the Indus. సౌవీరపాషాణము *sauvira-pāshā-ṇamu.* n. Antimony. కాటుకరాయి.

సౌశీల్యము *sau-śilyamu.* [Skt. from సుశీలము.] n. Well-disposedness, natural amiability. సుశీలత్వము, సుశీలత, మంచిస్వభావము.

సౌష్ఠవము *saushṭhavamu.* [Skt. from సుష్ఠు.] n. Beauty, goodness, excellence. సుష్ఠుభావము, చక్కదనము, తిన్నదనము. అవయవ సౌష్ఠవముగలవాడు a well made man, a well proportioned man. "గుంతలాదిసౌష్ఠవంబున." R. iv. 64.

సౌహార్దము or సౌహృదము *sau-hardamu.* [Skt. from సుహృత్.] n. Friendship. స్నేహము.

స్క ska

స్కందుడు *skanduḍu.* [Skt.] n. The name of the god of war, Kumaraswami. కుమారస్వామి.

స్కంధము *skandhamu.* [Skt.] n. The shoulder or the head of the humerus. భుజశిరస్సు. The trunk of a tree, కొమ్మలక్రింది మాను, చెట్టుబోదె. A chapter, ప్రకరణము. A battle, యుద్ధము. వారు సమానస్కంధులు or సరిసమానస్కంధులు they are equals. స్కంధశాఖ the first branch springing from the trunk of a tree, మ్రానిమొదటికొమ్మ. స్కంధపట్టిక *skandha-paṭṭika.* n. The lintel of a door, గడపపట్టె. స్కంధావారము *skandhā-vāramu.* n. A camp, a halting place. దండువిడిసినచోటు, శిబిరము. An army, దండు. "స్కంధావారంబుదరితుండోచ్చి." M. V. i. 100.

స్కన్నము *skannamu.* [Skt.] adj. Fallen, fallen down or from; trickling out or down. చ్యుతము, గళితము, జారిన.

స్ఖ skha

స్ఖలనము *skhalanamu.* [Skt.] n. Stumbling, slipping, tripping, dripping, trickling, చ్యుతి. తొట్రుపడడము, జారడము. రేతస్స్ఖలనము

emission of semen. "పదస్ఖలనంబున" by a slip of the foot. Mandhata. iii. 161. స్ఖలించు skhalintsu. v. n. To slip, జారు. To stumble, తొట్రుపడు. స్ఖలితము skhalitamu. adj. Slipped, fallen, gone, shaken. Stuttering. చ్యుతమైన, జారిన, తొట్రుపడిన. "మదస్ఖలితాత్ముడో పుట్టువెర్రియో." KP. vi. 16. అస్ఖలితబ్రహ్మచారి one who has no connection with women. స్ఖలితత్వము skhali-tatvamu. n. An error, omission, trip, slip. తప్పు, పొరపాటు, తొట్రుపాటు, జారడము. స్ఖాలిత్యము skhālityamu. n. An error, omission. తప్పు, పొరపాటు.

స్టా sṭā

స్టాంపు or స్టాంపు sṭāmpu. [Eng. 'stamp'.] n. A stamp. ముద్రస్టాంపుకాగితము a stamped paper.

స్త sta

స్తంబము stambamu. [Skt.] n. A clump of grass. A sheaf of corn. తృణాదిగుచ్ఛము, దుబ్బు. స్తంబేరమము stambē-ramamu. n. An elephant. ఏనుగు. Parij. iv. 44.

స్తంభము stambhamu. [Skt.] n. A pillar, a post, a stalk, stem, trunk, కంబము. Stupidity, stupefaction. Stoppage or suppression of any sense or power caused by magical incantations or drugs, &c. ఊరకుండుట, మ్రాన్పాటు. నిలుపడము. అరటిస్తంభము the stem of a plantain tree. స్తంభనము stambhanamu. n. Stopping, obstruction, hindrance. నిలుపడము, ఆటంకపరచడము. అగ్నిస్తంభనము restraining the power of fire by magical means. జలస్తంభనము continuing a long while under water without inconvenience. వాయుస్తంభనము raising the body in the air and maintaining it in such a position without support. భూతస్తంభనము the laying of ghosts, &c. మృగస్తంభనము restraining wild beasts. ఖడ్గస్తంభనము preventing a sword from doing injury. గతిస్తంభనము stoppage, preventing a man from moving. స్తంభించు stambhintsu. v. n. To stop, to become motionless, stupefied or insensible, నిలిచిపోవు, మ్రాన్పడు. ఈ మాటవిని స్తంభించిపోయినాడు on hearing this he stood stock-still. స్తంభించు or స్తంభింపజేయు stambhintsu. v. a. To strike dead, deprive of the power of moving, make motionless. కదలకుండా నిలిచేటట్టుచేయు, మ్రాన్పడజేయు.

స్తనము stanamu. [Skt.] n. A woman's breast. కుచము, చన్ను. వాడు స్తనశల్యపరీక్ష చేయుచున్నాడు he makes a minute examination; literally, he will even search for a bone in a breast. స్తనంధయుడు stanan-dhayudu. n. A suckling, an infant at the breast. చన్నుకుడిచేముద్దబిడ్డ, చంటిపాప. స్తన్యము stanyamu. n. Milk. పాలు, చనుబాలు. స్తన్యపానము drinking mother's milk.

స్తనయిత్నువు stana-yitnuvu. [Skt.] n. A cloud. మేఘము. A. iv. 123. స్తనితము stanitamu. n. Thunder. మేఘనిర్ఘోషము, ఉరుము, గర్జనము.

స్తబకము stabakamu. [Skt.] n. A cluster of blossoms, a bunch of flowers, a nosegay or bouquet, గుచ్ఛము, పూగుత్తి.

స్తబ్ధము stabdhamu. [Skt.] adj. Firm, stiff, motionless, immovable, paralized, stupefied, stupid, dull. చేష్టారహితమైన, నిశ్చేష్టితమైన, బిగుసుకొనుండే, నిక్కబొడుచుకొన్న. స్తబ్ధరోమము stabdha-rōmamu. n. (lit. stiff haired) A hog. పంది. స్తబ్ధుడు stabdhudu. n. A blockhead. జడుడు. వాడా మాటవిని స్తబ్ధుడుగానుండెను on hearing that he stood as if thunderstruck.

స్తవము stavamu. [Skt.] n. Praise. స్తోత్రము.

స్తి sti

స్తిమితము *stimitamu.* [Skt.] adj. Slow, soft, gentle, dull. మందమైన, తిన్నని. అతని ఒళ్లు స్తిమితముగానున్నది he is a little better. ఇప్పుడు ధర స్తిమితముగానున్నది at present the sale is dull, మందముగానున్నది.

స్తు stu

స్తుతి *stuti.* [Skt.] n. Praise, applause. స్తోత్రము. స్తుతించు or స్తుతియించు *stutintsu.* v. a. To praise, applaud. స్తోత్రముచేయు, పొగడు. స్తుతిపాఠకుడు *stuti-pāṭhakuḍu.* n. A eulogist, a flatterer. బట్టువాడు. స్తుతము *stutamu.* adj. Praised. పొగడబడిన. స్తుత్యము *stutyamu.* adj. Laudable, praiseworthy. పొగడదగిన. స్తోత్రముచేయదగిన.

స్తూ stū

స్తూపము *stūpamu.* [Skt.] n. A mound of earth. దిబ్బ.

స్తే stē

స్తేనుడు *stēnuḍu.* [Skt.] n. A thief, robber, దొంగ. స్తేయము *stēyamu.* n. Theft, robbery. చౌర్యము. స్తేయి *stēyi.* n. A thief. చోరుడు, దొంగ. స్వర్ణస్తేయి a stealer of gold, that is, a goldsmith (in allusion to his work). స్తైన్యము *stainyamu.* n Theft. దొంగతనము.

స్తో stō

స్తోకము *stōkamu.* [Skt.] adj. Little, small, diminutive. అల్పమైన, సూక్ష్మమైన.

స్తోత్రము *stōtramu.* [Skt.] n. Praise, applause. స్తుతి. స్తోత్రించు *stōtrintsu.* v. a. To praise, applaud. స్తుతించు, పొగడు, స్తోత్రముచేయు.

స్తోభము *stōbhamu.* [Skt.] n. False or deceptive encouragement, deceptive promises. తప్పుప్రేరేపణ, కపటవాక్యము, మాయ మాటలు.

స్తోమము *stōmamu.* [Skt.] n. A mass, heap, quantity, assemblage, multitude, crowd, body, troop, company, crew, gang, club, pack, host, army. సమూహము, గుంపు. దండు. Praise, స్తోత్రము. A sacrifice, యజ్ఞము. ధూమస్తోమము a volume of smoke. వారు స్తోమసహితులుగావచ్చినారు they came in crowd with their followers.

స్త్రీ strī

స్త్రీ *strī.* [Skt.] n. A woman. ఆడుది. adj. Female, feminine. స్త్రీలింగము the feminine gender. స్త్రీలోలుడు one who is enamoured by women. స్త్రీబుద్ధి a weak, fickle or effeminate mind. స్త్రీధనము pin-money, the gift bestowed by parents on their daughter after her marriage: the wife's property or private purse. స్త్రీఘోషము *strī-ghōshamu.* n. The dawn. వేకువ, ప్రభాతము. స్త్రీత్వము *strī-tvamu.* n. Womanhood, feminineness. ఆడుతనము. "తాత్త్వికములైన పురుష స్త్రీత్వంబులులేవు పార్వతీ శివునకు." M. XIII. v. 131. స్త్రీరత్నము *strī-ratnamu.* n. An excellent woman. Also, a kind of plant. స్త్రీవిద్య *strī-vidya.* n. The education of woman. స్త్రైణము *straiṇamu.* adj. Female, feminine. ఆడుదానిసంబంధమైన. n. Womanhood. స్త్రీత్వము, ఆడుతనము The nature of woman, స్త్రీస్వభావము. M. I. viii. 188.

స్థ stha

స్థ *stha*. [Skt.] adj. Staying, abiding, being, situated. ఉండే.

స్థండిలము *sthaṇḍilamu*. [Skt.] n. A level square piece of ground, prepared for a sacrifice. అగ్నిస్థాపనార్థము చతురస్రముగా బాగుచేయబడిన ప్రదేశము, అరికిసస్థలము.

స్థగనము *sthaganamu*. [Skt.] n. A covering, concealment. కప్పడము, ఆచ్ఛాదనము. స్థగితము *sthagitamu*. adj. Covered, hidden, concealed. కప్పబడిన. "[illegible] స్థగితద్యుమణికి." Swa. pref. 56.

స్థపతి *sthapati*. [Skt.] n. An architect, a master carpenter or builder. రథకారుడు. An excellent person, శ్రేష్ఠుడు.

స్థలము, స్థళము or స్థలి *sthalamu*. [Skt.] n. A place, spot, locality, region, district, స్థానము, ప్రదేశము, చోటు. Room, space. పరస్థలము a foreign or strange place. పరస్థలపువాడు a person from another place. స్థలపురాణము *sthala-purāṇamu*. n. A legend associated with a particular place, పుణ్యక్షేత్రమాహాత్మ్యము. స్థలమాహాత్మ్యము *sthala-mahatmyamu*. n. The influence of a place. క్షేత్రప్రభావము.

స్థవిరము *sthaviramu*. [Skt.] adj. Old, aged. ముసలి. ఏండ్లుచెల్లిన. స్థవిరుడు *sthavirudu*. n. An old man, ముసలివాడు.

స్థవిష్ఠము *stha-vishṭhamu*. [Skt.] adj. Very big or fat. మిక్కిలి స్థూలమైన.

స్థవీయము *sthavīyamu*. [Skt.] adj. Solid, compact. Very stout; great, respectable. మిక్కిలి స్థూలమైన, గొప్ప, దొడ్డ.

స్థా stha

స్థాణుడు *sthāṇudu*. [Skt.] n. A name of Siva. శివుడు. T. ii. 18. స్థాణువు *sthāṇuvu*. n. A name of Siva. The trunk of a tree; a pollard; a stake. శివుడు, శాఖాపత్రశూన్యవృక్షము, కొయ్య. A nail, మేకు.

స్థాత *sthāta*. [Skt.] n. One who is or resides. ఉండువాడు, నివాసి.

స్థానము *sthānamu*. [Skt.] n. A place, situation, spot, site, ground, space, a home, abode, position, post, dignity, స్థలము, ప్రదేశము, పదము, ఉనికిపట్టు. త్రిస్థానములు three shrines; these are ప్రయాగ, కాశీ, గయ [illegible], శ్రీశైలము. "[illegible] తీర్థంబులు చూచుచు వెలసిన త్రిస్థానములకు [illegible]." G. vi. 124. ఆయన నాకు పితృస్థానమువాడు he is in the place of my father. ఏకస్థానము the unit's place, any number under ten. దశస్థానము the ten's place. శతస్థానము the hundred's place. స్థానికము *sthānikamu*. adj. Local, belonging to a place. స్థలసంబంధమైన. స్థానికుడు *sthānikudu*. n. A warden, a beadle. గుడిమణియగాడు, గుడిపారుపత్తెగాడు. స్థానికులు the servants in a temple. గుడిపరిజనము. "స్థానికవ్యూహంబు వెంటరా నవైష్ణవకుంతు సేవించి." A. iv. 59. "[illegible] స్థానికుడొ సంగిసుమప." A. ii. 109. స్థానీయము *sthānīyamu*. n. A city, a town, పట్టణము.

స్థాపించు *sthāpintsu*. [Skt.] v. a. To set up, erect, found, నిలుపు. To establish, confirm, ప్రతిష్ఠచేయు, ఏర్పరచు, నిర్ధారణచేయు. స్థాపితము *sthāpitamu*. adj. Set up, erected. నిలుపబడిన. Fixed, settled, founded, established. ప్రతిష్ఠితమైన, స్థిరముచేయబడ్డ, ఏర్పరచబడిన, నాటబడిన, నిర్ధారణ

చేయబడిన. స్థాపన or స్థాపనము *sthāpana.* n. Fixing, erecting, placing, establishing, founding, setting up. స్థాపించుట, ప్రతిష్ఠ చేయడము, నిలుపడము, ఏర్పరచడము, నాటడము. భూస్థాపనము burial.

స్థామము *sthāmamu.* [Skt.] n. Bodily strength or vigor, శరీరబలము.

స్థాయి *sthāyi.* [Skt.] n. That which exists. ఉండునది. adj. Existing, ఉన్న. Steady, firm, unchangeable, permanent, lasting. నిలుకడైన, స్థిరమైన, నిరంతరమైన. స్థాయిగానుండే ఉద్యోగము a permanent employment. ఆచంద్రార్కస్థాయిగాను as long as sun and moon endure. స్థాయిభావము *sthāyi-bhāvamu.* n. The characteristics of the amorous passion. స్థాయుకుడు *sthāyu-kuḍu.* n. The overseer of a village. ఏకగ్రామాధికారి.

స్థాలి *sthāli.* [Skt.] n. Any small pot. కుంభము, కుండ. A cooking pot, వంటకుండ. A small drinking vessel, నీళ్లుతాగే చిన్నపాత్ర. స్థాలీపులాకన్యాయము judging of the whole by a part; for the whole pot is boiled if a spoonful is. కుండెడు అన్నమునకు ఒక మెతుకును పట్టిచూచుట అను న్యాయము.

స్థావరము *sthāvaramu.* [Skt.] adj. Fixed, stationary, firm, stable, immovable. స్థాయిగానుండే, ఉన్నచోటనుండి అవతలికి కదలని, స్థిరమైన, అచలమైన. n. Immovable property such as land, houses, &c. a fixed place of abode. తోట దొడ్డి యిల్లు వాకిలి మొదలైన కదలనిసొత్తు. స్థావరజంగమములుగానుండే సొత్తులు property which is partly immovable and partly movable. స్థావరముగా *sthāvaramu-gā.* adv. Permanently. శాశ్వతముగా, నిలుకడగా. వారక్కడ స్థావరముగాను న్నారు they have settled there permanently. స్థావరము ఏర్పరచుకొనుట to have fixed abodes.

స్థాసకము *sthāsakamu.* [Skt.] n. Perfuming, smearing the body with sandal or fragrant unguents. గంధాదులుపైపూత, కుంకుమ మొదలైనవానిపూత.

స్థాస్నువు *sthāsnuvu.* [Skt.] adj. Firm, stable, permanent. నిలుకడైన, స్థిరమైన, బహుకాలము ఉండునట్టి.

స్థి sthi

స్థితము *sthitamu.* [Skt.] adj. Standing, staying, being, situated. ఉన్న, నిలుచున్న. స్థితి *sthiti* n. State, condition. Existence. Property, estate. ఉనికి, దశ, అవస్థ, ఆస్తి. సృష్టిస్థితిసంహారములు creation, existence and destruction. భూస్థితి landed property. స్థితిమంతుడు *sthiti-mantuḍu.* n. A man of property, a well-to-do man, ఆస్తిపరుడు, ధనవంతుడు.

స్థిర *sthira.* [Skt.] n. The earth. భూమి. స్థిరము *sthiramu.* adj. Fixed, firm, stable, steady, steadfast, immovable, permanent, lasting, enduring, కదలని, నిలుకడైన, స్థావరమైన, నిశ్చయమైన, నిర్ణయమైన. స్థిరత or స్థిరత్వము *sthirata.* n. Permanency, durability, firmness, steadiness, స్థైర్యము. మతిస్థిరత steadiness of mind. స్థిరపరచు *sthira-paruṭsu.* v. a. To confirm, ratify. దృఢీచేయు. స్థిరవారము *sthira-vāramu.* n. Saturday. శనివారము, మందవారము. స్థిరాస్తి immovable property.

స్థూ sthū

స్థూణ *sthūṇa.* [Skt.] n. A post, a pillar. An anvil. An iron image. స్తంభము, దాగిలి, ఇనుపప్రతిమ.

స్థూరి *sthūri.* [Skt.] n. A pack horse. బరువు మోయు గుర్రము.

స్థూలము *sthūlamu*. [Skt.] adj. Large, bulky, thick, fat, corpulent. Corporeal, as opposed to spiritual. బృహత్తైన, లావుదైన. స్థూలదేహి a corpulent man. స్థూలనాసికము a large nosed animal. "స్థూలముకనుసుడ్డు సూక్ష్మంబుకప్పాప." Vēma. 593. స్థూలాంత్రము a large intestine.

స్థే sthē

స్థేమము *sthēmamu*. [Skt.] n. Bodily strength. శరీరబలము.

స్థేయుడు *sthēyuḍu*. [Skt.] n. A very steady person. మిక్కిలి స్థిరుడు.

స్థై sthai

స్థైర్యము *sthairyamu*. [Skt. from స్థిరము.] n. Steadiness, steadfastness, stability, firmness. స్థిరత్వము, ధీరత, దార్ఢ్యము.

స్థౌ sthau

స్థౌణేయము *sthauṇēyamu*. [Skt.] n. A sort of perfume, గంధివనము.

స్థౌల్యము *sthaulyamu*. [Skt. from స్థూలము.] n. Bulk, largeness, greatness, fatness, corpulence, thickness. స్థూలభావము, బృహత్త్వము, లావు.

స్న sna

స్నపనము *snapanamu*. [Skt.] n. Bathing, washing, ceremonial ablutions. స్నానము. స్నపనపాత్ర a vessel used in worship.

స్నస *snasa*. [Skt.] n. A very fine artery or vein. సన్న పునరము.

స్నా snā

స్నాతకుడు *snātakuḍu*. [Skt.] n. A Brahmin who is a householder, duly initiated after completing his studies. వివాహార్థముగా స్నాతకవ్రతముచేయువాడు, స్నానశీలవ్రతుడు, సమావర్తనముచేసి గృహస్థు అయినవాడు. If at the end of this period, he has not acquired a knowledge of the Vedas, he is called వ్రతస్నాతకుడు. If he has acquired this knowledge before the end of the period, he is called విద్యాస్నాతకుడు. If he finishes his studies with the expiration of the period, he is termed ఉభయస్నాతకుడు. స్నాతుడు *snātuḍu*. n. One who has bathed, స్నానముచేసినవాడు, నీళ్లుపోసుకొన్నవాడు. "సుస్నాతులై." M. XIII. iii. 102. స్నానము *snānamu*. n. Bathing, ablution, a bath. మునగడము. కంఠస్నానము bathing all but the head. శిరస్స్నానము bathing the whole body. కటిస్నానము bathing up to the middle. స్నానఘట్టము a bathing place. ప్రాతస్స్నానము a morning bath అభ్యంగస్నానము bathing after having anointed the head with oil. స్నాతమైనతరువాత after bathing. కృతస్నానుడై having bathed. జ్ఞానస్నానము Christian baptism.

స్నాయువు *snāyuvu*. [Skt.] n. A tendon, a muscle, described as a tubular vessel attached to the bones at either end, and conveying vital air. సంధిబంధనము, నరము, సన్నపునరము. స్నాయుబంధనము a ligament. స్నాయుచక్రములు muscle rings.

స్ని sni

స్నిగ్ధము *snigdhamu*. [Skt.] adj. Smooth, soft. నున్నని. Thick, సాంద్రమైన, చిక్కని. Amiable, affectionate, kind, స్నేహముగల.

స్ను snu

స్నుష *snusha*. [Skt.] n. A daughter-in-law. కోడలు.

స్నే snē

స్నేహము *snēhamu*. [Skt.] n. Love, affection, fondness, friendship. ప్రేమ, చెలిమి. Oil, unguent, తైలము, చేమురు. ప్రాణస్నేహము intimate friendship. స్నేహించు or స్నేహముచేయు *snēhintsu*. v. a. To cultivate or court another's friendship. హితముచేయు. స్నేహితుడు *snē-hitudu*. n. A friend. నేస్తకాడు. స్నేహితురాలు *snē-hitu-r-ālu*. n. A female friend, నేస్తురాలు. స్నేహోత్పాదకగ్రంథులు sebaceous glands.

స్ప spa

స్పందము *spandamu*. [Skt.] n. Motion, a slight movement, shaking, vibrating, fluttering, quivering, agitation. ఇంచుకకంపము, చలనము, కదలడము, వణకడము. స్పందితము *spanditamu*. adj. Agitated, moved, shaken. కంపితమైన, కదలింపబడిన.

స్పర్ధ *spardha* [Skt.] n. Emulation, jealousy, envy, vying, competition, rivalry. పోటి, బిరప్రతివివాదము, సంఘర్షణ. పరస్పరస్పర్ధలు mutual emulations. స్పర్ధాళువు *spardhāluvu*. n. A competitor, a rival. స్పర్ధగలవాడు. స్పర్ధి *spardhi*. adj. Envious, emulous. పోరాడే, వాదించే.

స్పర్శ or స్పర్శము *sparṣa*. [Skt.] n. Touch, contact. Feeling, the sense of touch, తాకడము, తగలడము. రక్తస్పర్శము contact with blood. జలస్పర్శము the usual phrase for making water: because water must afterwards be touched in purification. స్పర్శనము *sparṣanamu*. n. Touching, coming into contact with. తాకడము, తగలడము. A gift, donation, దానము. "చరణస్పర్శనంబుచేసి." M. XIII. iii. 335. స్పర్శనాడులు sensory nerves. స్పర్శనుడు *sparṣanuḍu*. n. The god of the air or wind. వాయువు. స్పర్శవేధి or స్పర్శమణి *sparṣa-vēdhi*. n. The philosopher's stone, the touch of which changes other metals into gold. తాకగానే ఇనుము మొదలైనవాటిని బంగారుచేయు మణివిశేషము, పరుసవేది. స్పర్శించు *sparṣintsu*. v. a. To touch, to feel. స్పృశించు, తాకు, అంటిచూచు. స్పర్శేంద్రియము *sparṣ-ēndriyamu*. n. The sense of touch.

స్పష్టము *spashṭamu*. [Skt.] adj. Clear, plain, distinct, apparent. విశదమైన. ఇది స్పష్టమైన అబద్ధము this is an evident lie.

స్పృ spri

స్పృక్కు *sprikku*. [Skt.] n. Touching. స్పర్శము. Connection, affinity. సంబంధము. స్పృశించు or సంస్పృశించు *sprisintsu*. v. a. To touch, feel. తాకు. స్పృశ్యము *sprisyamu*. adj. What may be felt or touched. తాకదగిన, స్పృశింపదగిన. స్పృష్టి *sprishṭi*. n. Touch, feeling, contact. తాకడము, తగలడము.

స్పృహ *spriha*. [Skt.] n. Wish, desire, hope. ఇచ్ఛ, ఆశ, కోరిక. నిస్పృహ void of desire. వారు అందునుగురించి నిస్పృహులైయున్నారు they have no hope of it. స్పృహణీయము or స్పృహ్యము *sprihaṇīyamu*. adj. Desirable, fit to be wished for, కోరదగిన, ఆశింపదగిన.

స్ఫ spha

స్ఫటము *sphaṭa*. [Skt.] n A snake's hood. పడగ. A. iv. 214. స్ఫటి *sphaṭi*. n. A snake, పాము.

స్ఫటికము *sphaṭikamu.* [Skt.] n. Crystal, quartz. పటికపురాయి.

స్ఫా sphā

స్ఫాయత్ *sphāyat.* [Skt.] adj. Expanding. విస్తృతమైన. "ఫలస్ఫాయద్వటత్త్వజను." A. vi. 15.

స్ఫారము or **స్ఫారకము** *sphāramu.* [Skt.] adj. Great, large. ఘూయిష్ఠమైన, పెద్ద, అధికమైన. "ప్రకటస్ఫారజటాచ్ఛటాకలితుడై." Bmj. iv. 23. "మంటపపహాప్రస్ఫారక ద్వారక." Anir. iii. 43.

స్ఫి sphi

స్ఫీతము *sphītamu.* [Skt.] adj. Swollen, enlarged, spacious. Much, many. పీనమైన, విశాలమైన, బహుళమైన. A. iv. 41. "అద్దు భుండనురమై స్ఫీతకోపంబున." Vish. vii. 345.

స్ఫు sphu

స్ఫుటనము *sphuṭanamu.* [Skt.] n. Splitting. భేదించుట.

స్ఫుటము *sphuṭamu.* [Skt.] adj. Blown, open, expanded. వికసించిన. Clear, plain, manifest, విశదమైన. గ్రహస్ఫుటము or స్ఫుట గ్రహము the true place of a planet.

స్ఫురణము *sphuraṇamu.* [Skt.] n. Quivering, vibrating, tremulous motion, gleaming, sparkling, glittering, shining, blooming, expanding. కదలుడము, అదురుడము, వికసిడము, తళతళమనడము, మెరయడము, ప్రకాశించడము, విజృంభణము. An idea occurring to the mind. తోచుట. "భీమాయుధస్ఫూర్తిరాజ మండలగ్రాసాకమాగధతమస్ఫురణంబడంచి." N. ix. 532. **స్ఫురత్** *sphurat.* adj. Gleaming, glancing, flashing, sparkling, shining, ప్రకాశించే, తళతళమని మెరిసే. "హారస్ఫురద్గురు ముక్తావళ." A. ii. 11. **స్ఫురించు** *sphurinṭsu.* v. n. To quiver, tremble, shake, gleam, glitter. To occur or come into the mind. చలించు, కదలు. ప్రకాశించు. తోచు, జ్ఞాపకము నకుగచ్చు. అది నాకు స్ఫురించకుండా ఉన్నది, లేక, అది నా మతికి స్ఫురించదు it does not occur to me. **స్ఫురితము** *sphuritamu.* adj. Shaken, trembling. Exposed, outstretched. Shining, gleaming. కదిలే, చలించే, వ్యాపించిన, మెరిసే, తళతళమనే. Occurring to the mind. తోచిన. "శ్రుతికుండల స్ఫురితముక్తాభిముఖ్య." N. vii. 249. **స్ఫురితుడు** *sphuritudu.* n. One who is distinguished. ప్రకాశమానుడు. "సరసప్రోత్సాహ స్ఫురితుడవు." P. ii. 165.

స్ఫులింగము *sphulingamu.* [Skt.] n. A spark of fire. అగ్నికణము, మిణుగురు.

స్ఫూ sphū

స్ఫూర్జిత *sphūrjita.* [Skt.] adj. Thundering "రావలస్ఫూర్జితాననము.." P. iv. 312.

స్ఫూర్తి *sphūrti.* [Skt.] n. Excitation, palpitation, vibration, tremulousness. Manifestation. Excess, fulness; expanding, prevalence. Gleaming, sparkling, shining, ప్రవృత్తి, కంపము, ప్రకాశము, ఉదయము, విజృంభణము, అతిశయము, పరిపూర్ణత. Thinking, తోచుట. "పురితేయల్ మహనీయ జంగమ పదస్ఫూర్తిం గదుక్ రాలఁగా." P. i. 70. "భూసామడిస్ఫూర్తి బ్రోచిసీయ." ib. iv. 368. "కనకగిరిస్ఫూర్తిగల చె గౌకమిస్రాచె." A. i. 43. విగ్రహస్ఫూర్తిగాఁగలవాడు a stout man. సమయస్ఫూర్తిమాట a sudden thought, a repartee on the spur of the moment. అతనికి సమయస్ఫూర్తి కలదు he has a ready wit.

స్ఫో sphō

స్ఫోటము sphōṭamu. [Skt.] n. Breaking, bursting. చిట్లడము, చితకడము, భేదనము, బద్దలుచేయుడము. A boil, a tumour. కురుపు. స్ఫోటకము sphōṭakamu. n. A boil, blain, pustule, blister. కురుపు, బొబ్బ. The small pox, మసూచికము.

స్మ sma

స్మయము smayamu. [Skt.] n. Pride, arrogance, గర్వము. Wonder, అద్భుతము, ఆశ్చర్యము. "భక్తిభూత ప్రతిపక్షస్మయుడౌనతడు." M. IV. v. 20. స్మయమానము smayamanamu. adj. Smiling. చిరునవ్వుగల.

స్మరణము smaraṇamu. [Skt.] n. Memory, recollection, remembering, thought. తలంపు. చింత, జ్ఞప్తి. స్మరించు or స్మరియించు smarintsu. v. a. To think of, recollect. తలచు, స్మరణముచేయు.

స్మరుడు smaruḍu. [Skt.] n. Manmatha, మన్మథుడు, మరుడు. స్మరహరుడు an epithet of Siva, శివుడు.

స్మా smā

స్మారకము smārakamu. [Skt.] adj. That reminds, that refreshes the memory. తలంపుపుట్టించే. n. Consciousness, sense. స్మృతి, తెలివి, బుద్ధిస్వాధీనము. ఆ దెబ్బచేత నాకు స్మారకముతప్పినది the blow made me unconscious. నాకు స్మారకము వచ్చినతరువాత after I cam· to my senses or recovered my consciousness.

స్మార్తము smārtamu. [Skt. from స్మృతి.] adj. Agreeable to or based on the Smṛitis, [illegible] canonical, స్మృతిశాస్త్రసిద్ధమైన.

స్మార్తులు smārtulu. n. The followers of the doctrines of Sankara Chari which inculcate the worship of both Vishṇu and Siva. శంకరాచార్యులవారి మతమును అవలంబించినవారు.

స్మి smi

స్మితము or స్మితి smitamu. [Skt.] n. A smile. చిరునవ్వు. మందస్మితము a gentle smile. స్మితము adj. Smiling. Blown, opened, blooming. చిరునవ్వుగల, వికసితమైన.

స్మృ smṛi

స్మృతి smṛiti. [Skt.] n. Recollection, memory, remembrance, understanding. స్మరణ, తెలివి, తలంపు, బుద్ధి. The code of Hindu law; jurisprudence, a law book or code of laws, ధర్మసంహిత, ధర్మశాస్త్రము.

స్మే smē

స్మేరము smēramu. [Skt.] adj. Smiling, laughing, చిరునవ్వుగల. Blown, opened, వికసించిన. "ప్రియాకేళీస్మేరచిత్తుడై." M. XVI. i. 2.

స్య sya

స్యందనము syandanamu. [Skt.] n. A car, a war chariot. రథము. A tree called *Dalbergia ougeinensis.* తినిశవృక్షము, తినాసము, అతిముక్తకము, నెమ్మిచెట్టు.

స్యందము or స్యందనము syandanau. [Skt.] n. Oozing, trickling, dropping, flowing. స్రవించుట, కారుట. స్యంది syandi. adj. Oozing, trickling. స్రవించే, కారే.

స్యదము syadamu. [Skt.] n. Speed, velocity. వేగము, జడి.

స్యన్నము syannamu. [Skt.] adj. Flowing, dropping, trickling. జారెడు, కారెడు, స్రవించే.

స్యా syā

స్యాలుడు or శ్యాలుడు syāluḍu. [Skt.] n. A wife's brother. భార్యతోడబుట్టినవాడు. స్యాలిక or శ్యాలిక syālika. n. A wife's sister.

స్యూ syū

స్యూతము syūtamu. [Skt.] adj. Sewn, stitched. కుట్టబడ్డ. "సూత్రస్యూత పాళకస్థ లమ్." A. v. 20.

స్ర sra

స్రక్కు srakku. [Skt.] n. A chaplet, wreath, garland. పూదండ.

స్రగ్గు or సగ్గు sraggu. [Tel.] v. n. To go off, diminish, be abated; to pine, to become thin; to die. తగ్గు, క్షీణించు, చచ్చు, నశించు. "అపత్యంపడిలలకుల ప్రాపింపవునుబలగాని స్ర గ్గకాడనైనోపట్టుచుల్రుడు." P. ii. 30.

స్రజము srajamu. [Skt.] n. A chaplet, wreath, garland. పూదండ.

స్రవము, స్రవణము or స్రావము sravamu. [Skt.] n. Oozing, trickling, dripping. కారడము. స్రవంతి sravanti. n. A river, నది. A. iv. 189. B. v. 85. స్రవించు or స్ర వించుచు sravintsu. v. n. To ooze, trickle, flow. కారు.

స్రష్ట srashṭa. [Skt. from సృజ్ to create.] n. The Creator. A name of Brahma. బ్రహ్మ.

స్రస్తము srastamu. [Skt.] adj. Fallen down, dropped. పడిన. జారిన. స్రస్తోత్తరీయము her fallen robe. B. X. 355.

స్రా srā

స్రావకము srāvakamu. [Skt.] adj. Oozing, trickling, flowing. కారునట్టి.

స్రావణము srāvaṇamu. [Tel.] n. The pincers or nippers used by a goldsmith, కంసలవానికారముట్టు.

స్రావము See స్రవము.

స్రావి Same as సరవి (q. v.)

స్రు sru

స్రుక్కు srukku. [Tel.] v. n. To withdraw from. కుదించు. To be afraid of, భయపడు. To close (as a flower), ముడుచు. To be folded, to be crumpled, as skin, ముడతపడు. To be diminished, తగ్గు, క్షీణించు. To be sorrowful, to grieve, దుఃఖించు, చింతించు. To faint, languish, మూర్ఛిల్లు, సొక్కు, సొమ్మసిల్లు. To hesitate, సంకోచించు. To fade, వాడు. To surround, encircle, చుట్టుకొను. n. Entanglement, a tangle. చిక్కు. Sorrow, grief, దుఃఖము, శోకము. A fold of the skin on the stomach, కడుపుమీదిముడత. "కడగా వాతితోరువతేకయేగతిగా స్రుక్కునా." Vasu. ii. 11. "విహాబాదరతగా స్రుక్కు." M. XII. v. 160. స్రుక్కబడు srukka-aḍu. v. n. To grieve, దుఃఖించు. స్రుక్కించు srukkintsu. v. a. To make faint or fatigued, to fatigue, to weaken, సొక్కించు, బలహీన ముచేయు. స్రుక్కుచేప srukku-chēpa. n. A sort of fish. మత్స్యభేదము.

స్రుక్కు or స్రువము srukku. [Skt.] n. The ladle with which ghee is poured into a sacrificial fire. ఆజ్యహోమముచేసే సాధనము.

స్రుతము srutamu. [Skt.] adj. Flowed, dropped, oozed. కలితమైన, జారిన, కారిన. స్రుతి sruti. n. Flowing, dropping. కా

దము. "జలస్రుతిపాటిపాటికిం గరుగుచు." A. iv. 137.

స్రువము *sruvamu.* [Skt.] n. A ladle used at sacrifices. అజ్యహుంతిచేసే మానిగరిటె.

స్రో srō

స్రోతస్సు *srōtassu.* [Skt.] n. A stream, current, the flow of a river. జలప్రవాహము. స్రోతోవేగము the rapidity of the current. M. XII. v. 559. **స్రోతస్విని** *srōtasvini.* n. A river. నది, ఏరు.

స్వ sva

స్వ *sva.* [Skt.] adj. Own, self, individual. ఆత్మీయమైన, తన. స్వకాయకష్టము bodily labour, individual exertions. స్వకపోలకల్పితము lit. invented in one's own head; original, not borrowed, as an idea, apocryphal, as a story made out of one's own head, అబద్ధమైన, లేనిపోని. స్వకార్యము one's own affair, one's own peculiar duty, తనపని. స్వకార్యధురంధరుడు a selfish man. స్వజనము one's own family, dependents, relations, people, friends. బంధువులు, పరిజనము. స్వజనుడు a relation, a friend, బంధువు. జ్ఞాతి, సగోత్రుడు, స్నేహితుడు స్వజాతి one's own class or nation, one's own kind, తనకులము. స్వజాతివైరి an enemy of one's kind. A rhyme says "స్వజాతివైరిని త్యాగి కాస్వ వస్త్రింపు గజద్వజా." స్వదత్తము self-bestowed, given by one's own hand, తనచేతితోనే ఇయ్యబడిన. "స్వదత్తాద్ద్విగుణంపుణ్యం." స్వదేశస్థుడు a fellow countryman, a native, మనదేశపువాడు. స్వధర్మము one's own particular duty, a natural or peculiar characteristic, a peculiarity. తాను చేయవలసినకార్యము, స్వభావము. స్వధర్మత్యాగము apostacy, abandonment of caste or faith, జాతిభ్రంశము. స్వబుద్ధి one's own desire, wish, or will. స్వబుద్ధిగా or స్వబుద్ధిచేత voluntarily, of one's own accord. స్వవశీకృతము taken into his own hands. తనస్వాధీనము చేసుకోబడ్డ. స్వశక్తి one's own power. తన సామర్థ్యము. వానికి స్వశక్తిలేదు he has no power of his own, or in himself. స్వాధికారము one's own right or title, dominion, తన అధికారము, తన ప్రభుత్వము. స్వాధిక్యము self importance, pride, arrogance, తన గొప్పతనము, గర్వము. స్వాధిష్ఠానము the second of the six regions of the human body, the upper part of the abdomen. చక్రవిశేషము. "మూలాధారస్వాధిష్ఠానమణిపూరక అనాహత విశుద్ధాగ్నేయ సహస్రారంబులను చక్రంబులను." H. iii. 235. స్వానుభూతి individual enjoyment, personal experience. ఆత్మీయానుభవము. స్వానుభోగము one's own enjoyment. తన అనుభవము.

స్వంతము *svantamu.* [for Tel. సొంతము.] adj. Own, private, belonging to one's self. స్వకీయమైన. దాన్ని స్వంతానికి కొనుక్కొన్నాడు he bought it on his own account. **స్వంతముగా** *svantamu-gā* adv. Himself, in person. తానే. ఆయనే స్వంతముగా వచ్చినాడు he came in person. **స్వంతగాడు** or **సొంతగాడు** *svanta-gāḍu.* n. A proprietor or owner. యజమానుడు. ఖామందు.

స్వకము *svakamu.* [Skt.] adj. Proper, peculiar, own. స్వకీయమైన, తన. "స్వకదేహంబు లెంగునా." N. iv. 22.

స్వకీయము *svak-iyamu.* adj. Peculiar, own, private, of one's own. సొంతమైన, తన.

స్వచ్ఛందము *svach-chandamu.* [Skt.] adj. Spontaneous, voluntary, uncontrolled, self-willed, independent. స్వేచ్ఛగానుండే. యథేచ్ఛముగానుండే. స్వతంత్రమైన, మనస్సువచ్చినట్టుండే. "స్వచ్ఛందాహారాది లాభంబున." P. i. 106. **స్వచ్ఛందవృత్తి** *svach-chanda-vritti.* n. An independent life. Independence. **స్వచ్ఛందుడు** *svach-chanduḍu.* n. One who is independent, free, uncontrolled, or self-willed. స్వతంత్రుడు, యథేచ్ఛముగానుండేవాడు.

స్వచ్ఛము *svachchamu.* [Skt.] adj. Clear, transparent, pellucid, white, pure, నిర్మలమైన, నిష్కళంకమైన, శుభ్రమైన. **స్వచ్ఛముగా** *svachchamu-ga.* adj. Clearly, purely, transparently, evidently. నిర్మలముగా, శుభ్రముగా, నిష్కళంకముగా, స్పష్టముగా.

స్వజనుడు See under స్వ.

స్వతః *svatah.* [Skt. corrupted into స్వతహాగా in Telugu.] adv. Naturally, of itself, instinctively, personally, spontaneously. స్వభావతః, తనకుతానే. ఆయన స్వతఃవచ్చెను he came in person. స్వతఃప్రకాశమైన naturally bright, lucid in itself, self-bright. **స్వతస్సిద్ధము** or **స్వతస్సిద్ధమైన** *svatas-siddhamu.* adj. Self made or self existent, inherent by nature. సహజమైన. స్వతస్సిద్ధముగానుండే బాధ్యత a natural right, an unalienable title.

స్వతంత్రము *sva-tantramu.* [Skt.] adj. Independent, not subject to any other's will, free, uncontrolled, head-strong, despotic, యథేచ్ఛమైన. ఒకరివిడిగానుండే, పరతంత్రముకాని, పరాధీనముకాని. "స్వతంత్ర సంచారిణై." M. XV. ii. 64. n. Independence, freedom, స్వేచ్ఛ. Hereditary right; a right. మాకు ఇది యేమి స్వతంత్రము you take liberties. స్వతంత్రనాడులు independent nerves. స్వతంత్రకండరములు involuntary muscles. **స్వతంత్రించు** *sva-tantrintsu.* v. n. To do any thing out of one's own head, or, on one's own responsibility, to act for oneself. ఆయన ఆజ్ఞప్రకారము చేసినానుగాని నేను స్వతంత్రించలేదు I did this according to his orders, not independently of him. **స్వతంత్రుడు** *sva-tantrudu.* n. One who is his own master, one who is independent. స్వచ్ఛందుడు, తన మనసువచ్చినట్టు నడిచేవాడు. ప్రాప్తస్వతంత్రులు. **స్వతంత్రురాలు** *sva-tantru-ralu.* n. A woman who is her own mistress. ఒకరికి అణిగియుండనిది.

స్వత్వము *svatvamu.* [Skt.] n. A natural condition of things. ఉన్నదిఉన్నట్టు ఉండడము.

స్వనము *svanamu.* [Skt.] n. Sound, noise, ధ్వని. **స్వనత్** *svanat.* adj. Sounding, మ్రోగెడు. స్వనత్కాహళము a pealing trumpet.

స్వపచుడు or **శ్వపచుడు** *svapachudu.* [Skt.] n. A man of a low caste, a Pariah. చండాలుడు, అంత్యజుడు, మాలవాడు.

స్వప్నము *svapnamu.* [Skt.] n. A dream, vision, dreaming, కల. Sleep, నిద్ర. జాగ్రత్స్వప్నసుషుప్తులు waking, sleep and deep sleep. స్వప్నమగు to dream. రాత్రి నాకొక స్వప్నమైనది I had a dream last night. స్వప్నదోషము *pollutio nocturna.* స్వప్నావస్థ the condition of being asleep.

స్వభాను *sva-bhanu.* [Skt.] n. The name of a Telugu year.

స్వభావము *sva-bhavamu.* [Skt.] n. Nature, natural state, property, disposition, peculiarity, inclination, turn of mind. సహజమైనగుణము. కుటిలస్వభావుడు a man of crooked disposition. వాడు తన స్వభావమును విడనాడలేదు he did not abandon his natural disposition. తనస్వభావము కొద్దీ చేసినాడు he did it according to his own temper. **స్వభావముగా** *sva-bhavamu-ga.* adv. Naturally, frankly, freely, sincerely, without disguise. సహజముగా, నిష్కపటముగా, ధారాళముగా.

స్వము *svamu.* [Skt.] n. Property, wealth. ధనము. "నిజస్వంబిచ్చెనిచో నిష్ప్రయోజనమా." P. i. 98. Self, తాను. adj. Own, తన.

స్వయము *svayamu.* [Skt.] adj. One's own, స్వకీయమైన. **స్వయముగా** *svayamu-ga.* adv. Of one's own self or accord, spontaneously, in person. తానే, తనకుతానే, స్వేచ్ఛగా. ఆయన స్వయముగా వచ్చెను he came in person. స్వయముగా ఆడేయంత్రము an automaton or self-moving machine. స్వయంకృతము svayam-kritamu. adj. Self-done, self-formed. తనకుతానే చేసుకొన్న. స్వయంకృతానర్థము harm brought upon oneself. స్వయంకృతాపరాధము a sin committed voluntarily. స్వయంకృషి svayam-krishi. n. Personal effort, own labour, self-culture. స్వప్రయత్నము, తానే పడిడిపాటు. స్వయంకృషిచేత సంపాదింపబడినసొమ్ము property which is acquired by personal labour. అతని స్వయంకృషికింద నుండు భూమి lands the cultivation of which he kept in his own hands. స్వయంపాకము svayam-pākamu. n. Rice, &c. given to a guest for him to cook and eat. ఒకనికి పూటకయ్యేటట్టు ఇచ్చే వస్తువిస్తుమునుండైనవి. స్వయంపాకమిచ్చు to give rice, &c., to another to be cooked by himself and eaten. ఒక స్వయంపాకము ఇప్పించు to give rice, &c., to a man for one meal. Cooking, particularly if performed with one's own hand: cooking in general, తానేవండుకొనడము, వంట. నేటి స్వయంపాకమెవరిది who has cooked to-day? who has given (you) this day's food? అంతామనసులో స్వయంపాకము చేస్తున్నాడు he keeps his thoughts to himself. స్వయంపాకి svayam-pāki. n. One who cooks for himself. తనకుతానే వంటచేసికొనువాడు. స్వయంభువు svayam-bhuvu. adj. Self existent, self formed, self produced. తనకుతానేపుట్టిన, పుట్టినది పుట్టినట్టుగా ఉండే. స్వయంభూరవ a rough diamond. స్వయంభూలింగము a natural image, a stone uncarved by man. n. The Self-existent One. The Creator, దేవుడు. స్వయంవరము svayam-varamu. n. Choice of a husband by oneself; the public choice of a husband by a princess. తానే మగనినికోరుకొనడము. స్వయంవరోత్సవము a day appointed for the selection of a husband by a princess out of an assembly of suitors. స్వయంవరముచాటించు to proclaim a Swayamvara. స్వయంవ్యక్తము svayam-vyaktamu. adj. Self formed. స్వయంభువైన. స్వయంవ్యక్తమూర్తి a self formed image.

స్వరము svaramu. [Skt.] n. A voice, sound, noise, note, tone, tune. A vowel. An accent. Air breathed through a nostril. కంఠధ్వని, రవము, ధ్వని, తానము, షడ్జాది సంగీతస్వరము, అచ్చు, ఉదాత్తాదివేదస్వరము, నాసాపవనము, ఒకముక్కుగుండా విడువబడినగాలి. సప్తస్వరములు the seven notes of the gamut. స్వరభంగము a fluttering of the voice. అపస్వరము a false note. స్వరమండలము or స్వరమండలి a musical instrument composed of a number of reeds joined together and played on with the finger. "స్వరమండలములు కిన్నెరలు." H. v. 412. స్వరశాస్త్రము a certain mode of fortune-telling, wherein the breath is emitted from one or the other nostril, and this is taken as the basis of a certain calculation. ముక్కుగాలినిపట్టి ప్రశ్నచెప్పే శాస్త్రము. The breath that comes through the right nostril is called సూర్యనాడి and the breath that comes through the left nostril is called చంద్రనాడి. స్వరపేటిక svara-pēṭika. n. The larynx.

స్వరాట్టు or స్వరాట svarāṭṭu. [Skt.] n. An epithet of Brahma. బ్రహ్మము.

స్వరువు svaruvu. [Skt.] n. Indra's thunderbolt. ఇంద్రాయుధము. "మరుత్పతి స్వరుకృతి." A. iv. 141.

స్వరూపము sva-rūpamu. [Skt.] n. The real nature of a thing, an image, one's own proper shape or body, the natural figure or form, the natural state, condition or purpose. Truth, a definition. స్వభావము, యాథార్థ్యము, వివరము, నిజమైన ఆకారము. స్వరూపనాశనము annihilation. పదిస్వరూపములు ten head of cattle. కుమ్మరస్వరూపములు articles of pottery. ధన్యస్వరూపులైన తమరు

you who are the image of justice, you who are equity itself.

స్వర్గము svar-gamu. [Skt.] n. The paradise of Indra, in which mortals receive the reward of their virtuous acts, దేవలోకము. మా తండ్రి స్వర్గస్థులైనతరువాత after my father died. స్వర్నది svar-nadi. n. The Ganges of heaven. ఆకాశగంగ. స్వర్వేశ్య svar-vesya. n. A nymph of heaven. అప్సరసుండగైన వాడు. స్వర్వైద్యులు svar-vaidyulu. n. The physicians of Swarga. అశ్వినీదేవతలు, దేవతలవైద్యులు.

స్వర్ణము svarnamu. [Skt.] n. Gold. కనకము, బంగారు. స్వర్ణరససిద్ధి alchemy. ఆ కవికి స్వర్ణాభిషేకము చేసినాడు he made the poet wallow in wealth. ఆ ధ్వజస్తంభమునకు స్వర్ణాభిషేకము చేయించినాడు he gilt the flagstaff of the temple. స్వర్ణకారుడు svarna-karudu. n. A goldsmith. కంసలవాడు.

స్వర్భానువు or స్వర్భానుడు svar-bhanuvu. [Skt.] n. The personified ascending node. రాహువు.

స్వర్లోకము Same as స్వర్గము (q. v.)

స్వల్పము svalpamu. [Skt.] adj. Very little, small, few, trifling, insignificant. కించిత్తు, సూక్ష్మమైన, మిక్కిలి అల్పమైన. స్వల్పదినములలో in a few days. స్వల్పదూరము a little way off. స్వల్పకార్యము a trifling work or business. ఇవి ఈ దేశములో స్వల్పముగానున్నవి these are rarely met with in this country.

స్వస svasa. [Skt.] n. A sister. తోడబుట్టినది.

స్వస్తి svasti. [Skt.] A Skt. particle meaning Excellent; well done! may good attend you! may it be well with you! So be it; Amen. n. Welfare, క్షేమము, పుణ్యము, మంగళము, శుభము. "స్వస్తి యగుగాక." పా. పూ. iii. "స్వస్తిరేదనుజ వరేణ్య." N. iv. 129. "స్వస్తస్తుసుమనోగస్తు" H. i, 47. స్వస్తివాచనము a blessing or benediction. any benedictory speech. స్వస్తిచెప్పు to wish well. రాజువాస్వస్తి రావణాస్వస్తి అని యుండవలెను (a proverb meaning) Bless them both and keep neutral.

స్వస్తికము svastikamu. [Skt.] n. Any lucky or auspicious object. మంగళవస్తువు. A building or palace facing east. తూర్పు వాకిలిగల మందిరము. The meeting of four roads, చేరుకము.

స్వస్తిముఖము svasti-mukhamu. [Skt.] n. A letter or epistle. జాబు.

స్వస్థము svasthamu. [Skt.] adj. Easy, well, at ease, in good health, sound. నెమ్మదిగానున్న, ఆరోగ్యమైన. స్వస్థచిత్తము a mind at ease. స్వస్థత or స్వస్థము svasthata. n. Health, soundness, convalescence. ఆరోగ్యము. ఆ రోగము స్వస్థమైనది the disease is cured. స్వస్థపరచు or స్వస్థముచేయు svastha-parutsu. v. a. To cure, ameliorate, make better. బాగుచేయు, కుదుర్చు. స్వస్థమగు svastham-agu. v. n. To recover from illness, to become whole. కుదురు. స్వస్థముగానుండు to be at ease, to be well, to be in good health, నెమ్మదిగానుండు, ఆరోగ్యముగానుండు.

స్వా svā

స్వాంతము svāntamu. [Skt.] n. The mind, the faculty of thought and feeling. The heart. మనస్సు.

స్వాగతము sv-āgatamu. [Skt. సు+ఆగతము.] n. Welcome, salutation, receiving. క్షేమము, కుశలము, కుశలప్రశ్నము, సుఖముతోడి రాక. "గద్దియపైనిడియుంపంజేసి స్వాగతంబు ఇడి." H. i. 86.

స్వాతంత్ర్యము svā-tantryamu. [Skt. from స్వతంత్రము.] n. Independence, freedom, liberty. స్వతంత్రభావము, స్వతంత్రత. అస్వాధీ

ము, స్వేచ్ఛాధీనత, విచ్చలవిడిగాతిరుగుట. ఏ స్త్రీ స్వాతంత్ర్యమర్హతి no woman is *sui juris*; no woman can act independently.

స్వాతి *svāti*. [Skt.] n. Arcturus, the fifteenth lunar asterism. చిత్తకు అవతలినక్షత్రము, పదిహేనోనక్షత్రము. స్వాతికార్తి the fifteenth constellation in which the sun happens to be for thirteen days in the month of October or November. స్వాతిచిప్పలు the oysters that gape expecting drops of rain in Swāti. తమరాకకొరకు స్వాతిచిప్పలవలె నోరుతెరుచుకొని యున్నాము we look out with thirsty expectation for your arrival. స్వాతికొంగలు a kind of cranes or storks which emigrate in this month. స్వాతివాన genial showers supposed to impregnate oysters with pearls. "స్వాతిబకంబులుచీకను." H. iii. 52. "స్వాతి వృష్టిగురియుచునుండి." H. ii. 171.

స్వాదనము *svādanamu*. [Skt.] n. Drinking, పానము. స్వాదము *svādamu*. n. Taste; రుచి. Tasting, రుచిచూచుట. స్వాదితము *svāditamu*. adj. Drunk, as a liquid, పానముచేయబడిన. స్వాదు or స్వాదువు *svādu*. n. Sweetness, taste, flavour, fragrance. తీపి, మాధుర్యము, పరిమళము. adj. Sweet, agreeable. తియ్యని, మధురమైన, రమ్యమైన, అందమైన.

స్వాధీనము *sv-ādhīnamu*. [Skt. స్వ+అధీనము.] n. Charge, trust, subjection, possession, power, control. వశము, అధికారము. వారు అతని స్వాధీనములో నున్నారు they are under his control. దాన్ని నీ స్వాధీనముచేస్తిని I gave it into your charge. వానిచెయ్యి వాని స్వాధీనములోలేదు he cannot use his hand. వాడు దానిని స్వాధీనపరచుకొన్నాడు he got it into his possession. ప్రస్తుతము స్వాధీనముకాని సొమ్ము money not available at present. ఆ పని తన స్వాధీనము చేసుకొన్న తరువాత after he undertook the affair or took it into his own hands. స్వాధీనపతిక *sv-ādhīna-patika*. n. A self-willed woman, one who rules her husband. చెప్పినట్లు ఆడే మగడుగల ఆడది. స్వాధీనుడు *sv-ādhīnuḍu*. n. A dependent, an obedient man, one who is subject to another, one who is subservient, docile, or tractable. వశ్యుడు, విధేయుడు. వారు స్వాధీనులుకారు they are disobedient. తనకు స్వాధీనుడుగానుండే తమ్ముని పంపించినాడు he sent his brother who was under his control. స్వాధీనురాలు *sv-ādhīnu-r-ālu*. n. A woman who is subject to, or submissive. విధేయురాలు.

స్వాధ్యాయము *sv-ādhyāyamu*. [Skt. స్వ+అధ్యాయము.] n. Inaudible reading, muttering of prayers, study of the Vedas. జపము, వేదాధ్యయనము. The Vedas, వేదము. స్వాధ్యాయి one who studies the Vedas. వేదాధ్యయనముచేయువాడు.

స్వానము *svānamu*. [Skt. another form of స్వనము.] n. Sound, noise. ధ్వని, రవము.

స్వాపతేయము *svāpatēyamu*. [Skt.] n. Wealth, property. విత్తము, ద్రవ్యము. H. iii. 20.

స్వాపము *svāpamu*. [Skt.] n. Sleep. నిద్ర. Vasu. ii. 50.

స్వాభావికము *svā-bhāvikamu*. [Skt. from స్వభావము.] adj. Natural, innate, inherent, peculiar. స్వభావముచేత కలిగిన, సహజమైన, ప్రకృతి సిద్ధమైన.

స్వాభిమానము *sv-ābhi-mānamu*. [Skt.] n. Favouritism. తనవాడనే విశ్వాసము. వానికి స్వాభిమానమే ముఖ్యము he is guided solely by favouritism.

స్వామి *svāmi*. [Skt. from స్వమ్.] n. A lord, master, sovereign, owner, proprietor, husband, spiritual guide or preceptor. "My lord, Sir." A Brahmin is usually thus addressed by a junior or by a Sudra. ప్రభువు, కర్త, పతి, గురువు, దేవుడు, దేవత. స్వామిపరాకు behold! be attentive. భాగ

స్వామి a share holder, పాలివాడు. స్వామిత *svāmi-ta*. n. Mastership, lordship, ownership. ప్రభుత్వము, యజమానత్వము. స్వామిత్వము *svāmitvamu*. n. Mastership, lordship, ownership, right, title. ప్రభుత్వము, కర్తృత్వము, అధికారము, బాధ్యత. అతనిస్వామిత్వముపోయినది he has lost his ownership. స్వామిద్రోహము *svāmi-drōhamu*. n. Treason, treachery to a master, unfaithfulness to a superior. యజమానునికి చెరుపుచేయుటము. స్వామిద్రోహి *svāmi-drōhi*. n. A traitor. యజమానునికి చెరుపుచేయువాడు. స్వామిని *svāmini*. n. A mistress, a female owner, ఒడయురాలు. స్వామిభోగము *svāmi-bhōgamu*. n. The landlord's share of the produce of land cultivated by a tenant. పాయకారి మిరాశిదారునికి ఇచ్చేభాగము. స్వాములవారు *samula-vāru*. n. His grace, his reverence, his holiness, a minister or father. గురువులు. స్వామ్యము *svāmyamu*. n. Ownership, right, title. స్వాతంత్ర్యము, బాధ్యత.

స్వారస్యము *svā-rasyamu*. [for Skt. సారస్యము.] adj. Pleasing, delicious, good, excellent. స్వారస్యము or సారస్యము *svā-rasyamu*. n. Sweetness, juiciness, savouriness. Pathos, spirit, fire. రసము, సత్తు, గుణము. మీరు అక్కడికి వెళ్లినందువల్ల స్వారస్యములేదు there is no advantage in your going there. "చవిగానిపలుకుల స్వారస్యమేమి." Dab. 141.

స్వారాజ్యము *svā-rājyamu*. [Skt.] n. The celestial region, heaven, స్వర్గరాజ్యము, స్వర్గలోకపుదొరతనము. స్వారాట్టు *svā-rattu*. n. The king of heaven, స్వర్గలోకాధిపతి. A name of Indra. ఇంద్రుడు.

స్వారి *svari*. [Tel.] n. A pleasure excursion. వాహ్యాళి, విహారము.

స్వార్జితము *sv-ārjitamu*. [Skt.] adj. Self-acquired, obtained or accumulated by one's own labour. తనసంపాద్యమైన, స్వకాయకష్టముచేత సంపాదింపబడ్డ. n. Property that has been personally acquired, as distinguished from that which has been inherited. స్వంతసంపాద్యము.

స్వార్థము *sv-ārthamu*. [Skt.] n. Regard to one's self, self-interest, personal benefit. స్వప్రయోజనము. తనమేలు. స్వార్థకము *sv-ārthakamu*. n. The indicative mood in Grammar. స్వార్థపరుడు *sv-ārtha-parudu*. n. A selfish man, he who is devoted to his own interest. స్వప్రయోజనమునే ముఖ్యముగా విచారించేవాడు, స్వసుఖమునే విచారించేవాడు.

స్వాస్థ్యము *sv-āsthyamu*. [Skt.] n. Ease, happiness, comfort, relief, recovery, abundance of food and raiment. A share in a Brahmin village, a share. నెమ్మది, ఆరోగ్యము, వస్త్రాన్నసమృద్ధి. ఉదకస్వాస్థ్యము a supply of water. అయనకు చిత్తస్వాస్థ్యములేదు he is uneasy in mind.

స్వాహా or స్వాహాకు *svāha*. [Skt.] interj. Hail! An exclamation used in making an oblation to the gods. n. The name of the wife of the god of fire, a goddess presiding over burnt offerings, దేవతలకు హవిస్సును అహుతిచేసేటప్పుడు చెప్పేమాట, అగ్నిభార్య. "స్వాహాకారముడొట." Swa. iii. 67.

స్వి svi

స్విన్న *svinna*. [Skt.] adj. Sweating, perspiring. చెమర్చి. ప్రవించే.

స్వీ svī

స్వీకరించు *svī-karin-tsu*. [Skt.] v. a. To adopt, embrace, acknowledge, receive. అంగీకరించు, గ్రహించు, పుచ్చుకొను. స్వీకారము *svī-kāramu*. n. Adopting, appropriating. Acknowledgment, assent, consent. Entering or embracing a new condition of life, ఆశ్రమము, as becoming a married man after being a bachelor. అంగీకరించడము, అంగీకారము, సమ్మతించడము, గ్రహించడము, ఒప్పిక. "ప్రతిపాలకపుత్రాజనస్వీకారసంగ్రహాత్సేకమునకు." P. i. 716. ఆమె పుత్రస్వీకారము చేసికొన్నతరువాత after she has adopted a son. ఆయన ప్రసాదస్వీకారముచేసికొన్నాడు he embraced a monkish life. స్వీకృతము svi-kritamu. adj. Admitted, acknowledged, confessed, promised, accepted, adopted. అంగీకరింపబడ్డ, ప్రతిగ్రహించిన, పెంచుకోబడ్డ. స్వీకృతపుత్రుడు an adopted son. స్వీకృతి svi-kriti. n. Adoption, acknowledgment, అంగీకరించడము, సమ్మతించడము, గ్రహించడము.

స్వీయము sviyamu. [Skt.] adj. Own, one's own, relating or belonging to one's self. ఆత్మీయమైన, ఆత్మసంబంధమైన, తన. స్వీయ sviya. n. A virtuous woman, a wife who is entirely devoted to her husband. పతియందనురాగముగలది అనురాగముగలవారాలు, పతివ్రత, సాధ్వి.

స్వే svē

స్వేచ్ఛ sv-ēchcha. [Skt.] n. One's own will or pleasure, liberty, free will, self-will, స్వతంత్రత, యథేచ్ఛ, ఆత్మేచ్ఛ, తనయిష్టము. స్వేచ్ఛగా sv-ēchcha-gā. adv. Voluntarily, freely, willingly. యథేచ్ఛగా, తనయిష్టాన, తనమనస్సువచ్చినట్టుగా. స్వేచ్ఛాపరుడు sv-ēchchā-parudu. n. He who is uncontrolled, independent or self-willed, స్వతంత్రుడు, యథేచ్ఛముగా నడిచేవాడు, అసాధ్యుడు.

స్వేదని svēdani. [Skt.] n. An iron plate used as a frying pan. పెనము.

స్వేదము svēdamu. [Skt.] n. Sweat, perspiration, warmth, heat. ఘర్మము, చెమట, ఉష్ణశరీరోష్ణము. "చెమ్మ లొప్పై స్వేదము గ్రమ్మ." N. ix. 365. స్వేదజములు svēda-jamulu. n. Worms, insects, maggots, mosquitos, &c., which are supposed to be engendered by heat and damp. క్రిమికీటకాదులు, ఉక్క చెమ్మచేతపుట్టే పురుగులు, దోమలు మొదలైనవి. స్వేదనాళము a sweat duct. స్వేదరంధ్రములు pores of the skin. స్వేదోదకము svēd-ōdakamu. n. Perspiration, చెమట.

స్వై svai

స్వైరము svairamu. [Skt.] adj. Self-willed, pertinacious, obstinate. యథేచ్ఛమైన, స్వతంత్రమైన, మూర్ఖమైన. "మారుడు స్వైరవిహారుడై." Ahalya. iii. 16. "స్వైరగతిని విహరించెను." N. i. 7. స్వైరి svairi. n. An independent man, స్వతంత్రుడు. స్వైరిణి svairini. n. An unchaste wife, an adulteress, a wanton woman, పాంసుల, వ్యభిచారిణి, రంకులాడి.

హ ha

హ ha. The letter H.

హంకరించు han-karintsu. [from Skt. అహంకరించు.] v. n. To be proud, అహంకరించు. హంకారము han-kāramu. (from అహంకారము.) n. Haughtiness, arrogance, self-conceit, అహంకారము, గర్వము. "సీ॥ తలకొండు పెరతనంబులుపుట్టు పుట్టిల్లు హంకారములకెల్లనాటపట్టు." చంద్రా. ii.

హంగామి hangāmi. [H.] adj. Temporary, తాత్కాలికమైన. హంగామిదిబ్బంది a temporary establishment.

హంగు or అంగు hangu. [Tel.] n. Convenience, agreeableness. ఒనరు, పొందిక.

దిగడమునకుహాంగు అనుకూలగున so as to be convenient to get down.

"కేసమునకునైన దాసరిగావచ్చు,
హాంగుదప్పవేళ జంగమగును,
షదియుచేలకైన బాపడుకారాదు."
Vema. 263.

"వచ్చిహాంగువిడిచిసర్వేశుగొలువరా."
ib. 1924.

హాంగుపరచు *hangu-paratsu.* v. a. To make convenient. అనుకూలపరచు. **హాంగైన** *hang-aina.* adj. Convenient, agreeable. ఒనరైన.

హాంజిక *hanjika.* [Skt.] n. A certain medicinal root. బ్రాహ్మణయష్టిక, చిరిలేకు.

హాండ, హాండా or **హాండీ** *handa.* [H.] n. A large wide mouthed vessel.

హాంత *hanta.* [Skt. from హన్ to kill.] n. A murderer, a slayer, a murderess. ఘాతుకుడు, ఘాతుకురాలు. "ధరిత్రినింతహాంతంగను గొంటలేదు." P. i. 286. **హాంతతనము** *hantatanamu.* n. Cruelty, ferocity. క్రూరత్వము, ఘాతుకత్వము. "హాంతతనమునమొగిచెలు మింతలేక పొడిచియాడితివింక నీపొందుచాలు." Abhiman. Padya. i. 154. **హాంతృత** *hantrita.* n. The being a murderer. హననశీలత. "వ్రతహాంతృతార్తకీటక." A. v. 149.

హంతకారము or **హంతాకారము** *hantakaramu.* [Skt.] n. Food to be given to a guest. అభ్యాగతునికి పెట్టవలసిన అన్నము. "అగ్నికార్యంబుదీర్చి యనంతరంబ హంతకారంబు నిష్ఠ జేయుంగవలయు, హంతకారంబొనర్ప బ్రహ్మాదులైన త్రిదశముఖ్యులతృప్తిబొందెదరు సువ్వె." Kasi Khand. v. 275.

హంవీరుడు *ham-virudu.* [Skt.] n. A hero, champion, warrior. క్షత్రియుడు, శూరుడు. "సమరహంవీరుడు." T. v. 116.

హంస or **హంసము** *hamsa.* [Skt.] n. A swan. A certain fabulous bird supposed to be a swan. Also, a water-fowl, probably the Ruddy Shieldrake. శ్వేతగరుత్తువు, నీళ్లువిడిచి పాలుద్రాగే పక్షి. "రాజహంసలుగాని రాజహంసలుకారు." Vasu. pref. 62. The name of one of the vital airs. శారీరవాయువు, ఉచ్ఛ్వాసనిశ్వాసరూపమైన వాయువు. The Divine Spirit, పరమాత్మ. హంసగమనము a decent and modest gait. హంసగమన, హంసగామిని or హంసయాన a woman who walks elegantly. adj. (In composition), Best, excellent. శ్రేష్ఠము. రాజహంస a noble prince. **హంసకము** *hamsakamu.* n. An ornament for the feet. కాలికటకము, కాలికడియము, కాలిఅందె. హంసతూలికాతల్పము a swan's down-bed or couch, a bed stuffed with the wool of the shrub, *Asclepias gigantea* (జిల్లేడు) or of the silk cotton tree (శాల్మలి or బూరుగు.) హంసతూలపరుపు, లేక, బూరుగుదూదిపరుపు. **హంసపాదము** *hamsa-padamu.* n. A star, caret or asterisk. ఇక్కడ తప్పిపోయినది అని తెల వ్రాసియున్నదనేదానికి గురుతు. **హంసపాది** or **హంసపాదిచెట్టు** *hamsa-padi.* n. A creeping plant, *Cissus pedata* or *Coldenia procumbens.* గోధాపది, సువహా, చెప్పుతట్టచెట్టు. **హంసయంత్రము** *hamsa-yantramu.* n. A hinge. మొల, కీలు. "కవాటహంసయన్త్రేణ యథాసంపరివర్తతే, తథాలసస్సశ్య్యాంశయ్యాయాంపరివర్తతే." Sanskrit translation of Proverbs XXVI. 13. **హంసవళి** *hamsa-vali.* n. A kind of cloth. వస్త్రవిశేషము. BD. iii. 105. **హంసవాహనుడు** *hamsa-vahanudu.* n. An epithet of Brahma, because he rides upon a swan. బ్రహ్మ. **హంసి** or **హంసిక** *hamsi.* n. A female swan. ఆడుహంస. **హంసుడు** *hamsudu.* n. The sun, సూర్యుడు. A spiritual preceptor, గురువు. A liberal o moderate prince, one who is not covetous nor ambitious. లోభగుణములేని ప్రభువు.

హంసాయి hamsāyi. [H.] n. A neighbour. హంసాయిగ్రామము a neighbouring village.

హకీకత్తు hakī-kattu. [H.] n. An account, a statement, a representation of occurrences or affairs. వృత్తాంతము.

హక్కాసు hakkasu. [H.] n. Spite, hatred. పగ.

హక్కు hakku. [H.] n. A lawful right or title. బాధ్యత. హక్కుదారుడు hakku-dārudu. n. A rightful owner; an heir, బాధ్యుడు. హక్కుదావా hakku-dāvā. n. A claim. హక్కుసాయి hakku-sāyi. n. A co-parcener.

హజారము, హజారు, హుజూరు or అజారము hazāramu. [H.] n. Presence. ఆస్థానము. A royal hall or chamber of audience. A place where persons of distinction sit. ఆస్థానమంటపము రాజసభ, కొలువుకూటము. నగరికి నెలిదారిది "నిన్నటియట్లనంది యుండిన యవ్వాదుమునంబుతో హజారముచేరగా." S. iii. 191.

హడ్డు or అడ్డు haddu. [Tel.] n. A foot. పాదము. "ఏనుగుహడ్డుతో నెల్ల సర్వంబులు హడ్డుల నడగినయట్లనొరె." M. XII. ii. 260.

హట్టము hattamu. [Skt.] n. A market, a fair. అంగడివీధి. "హట్టస్థిత స్తంభంబులో చెరుగుచున్నది." A. ii. 48.

హఠము hathamu. [Skt.] n. Obstinacy, violence, severity, contumacy. మూర్ఖత, మొండితనము, ముష్కరత, బలాత్కారము. A kind of meditation, యోగభేదము. హఠముసాధించు to persevere in obstinacy. హఠము తీర్చుకొను to pay a grudge. హఠముపట్టు to be obstinate. adj. Stubborn, obstinate, pertinacious, resolute, determined. మూర్ఖమైన, మొండి, పిడివాదముగల. హఠముగా hathambu-gā. adv. Pertinaciously, stubbornly. మూర్ఖముగా, ముష్కరముగా. "స్థైర్యంబైన హఠంబుగా నిలువవమండిరా ద్రోహకులు." T. ii. 18. హఠయోగము hatha-yōgamu. n. Abstract contemplation, whilst suspending the breath. This is generally a method of austere devotion, such as standing on one leg, holding up the arms, inhaling smoke, with the head inverted, &c. It is opposed to Raja yogam. కఠినమైన తపస్సు. హఠవాది hatha-vādi. n. A violent man, a determined or obstinate man. పట్టిన పట్టు విడువనివాడు. హఠాల్, హఠాత్తుగా or హఠాత్తున hathat. adv. Suddenly, unawares. దబ్బున, ఆకస్మాన, అదరిపాటున. హఠాత్కరించు hathat-kar-intsu. v.a. To force, compel, ravish బలాత్కారముచేయు. హఠారంబుగా hatharambu-gā. adv. Violently, fiercely. ఉగ్రముగా. "కఠారంబుల కఠోరంబుగా గ్రుమ్మును, కఠారంబులపాటారంబు గానరుకును." BRY. 647.

హణిగెలు hanigelu. [Kan.] n. Salutations, reverences. వందనములు. "నీలాచలమున నెలకొను పురుషోత్తమునకు హణిగెలు దండిగ జేర్చుము." H. iv. 280.

హతము hatamu. [Skt.] adj. Killed, slain, defeated, struck, hit, destroyed, blasted, blotted out. చంపబడ్డ, కొట్టబడ్డ, నాశము చేయబడ్డ, ధ్వంసముచేయబడ్డ, చెరుపబడ్డ, పోగొట్టబడ్డ. హతశేషులు the survivors. హతశ్రీ having lost fortune, ruined. n. Ruin, destruction, killing, నాశనము, సంహారము. హతముచేయు hatamu-chēyu. v. a. To kill, destroy, demolish. నాశముచేయు, సంహారము చేయు. హతహతముగా, హతహతముగా or హతాహతముగా hata-hatamu-gā. adv. Destructively, violently, outrageously. ధ్వంసమయ్యేటట్టుగా, అపూర్వముగా "హతహతములుగాగ పోటులాడుచు బకువులే." G. vii. 84. "అనిచురగముతొక్కియంత

నేగముస, అశ్వంబుడో లెను హతహతముగాను." Pal. 496. **హతాశుడు** *hat-āsudu*. n. He who is disappointed. విఫలమైన కోరికగలవాడు. **హతాహతము** *hata-hatamu*. n. Destruction, violent contention. ధ్వంసము, మహాత్తైనజగడము. **హతి** *hati*. n. Striking, smiting, a blow. కొట్టడము, దెబ్బ. "విహాంహతిచే." P. i. 241. **హతుడు** *hatudu*. n. One who has been struck, smitten, destroyed, or killed. One who is void of, or bereft of. కొట్టబడ్డవాడు, చంపబడ్డవాడు, విహీనుడు.

హత్త *hatta*. [Tel.] n. Entanglement. తగులుకొనడము, చిక్కుకొనడము.

హత్తి *hatti*. [from Skt. హస్తి.] n. An elephant. ఏనుగు.

హత్తు, అత్తు, హత్తుకొను or **అత్తుకొను** *hattu*. [Tel.] v. n. To adhere to, come in contact with, take to, be attached or addicted to, succeed, attain, approach. అంటుకొను, సక్తమగు, పొందు, కలుగు, చాయు, అంటు, తగులుకొను, సఫలమగు. "హత్తుకొని మొక్కుకొందురుసత్తెరువుంగట్టబనిచి." A. vi. 96. **హత్తించు** *hattintsu*. v. a. To attach, join, touch. అంటుకొనునట్లుచేయు, సక్తముచేయు, లగింపజేయు. "చిత్తమువాహత్తించిన." N. iv. 161.

హత్య *hatya*. [Skt.] n. Killing, slaying, slaughter, murder. వధ, చంపడము. ఆత్మహత్య suicide. గోహత్య the slaughter of a cow. నరహత్య manslaughter, murder. బ్రహ్మహత్య the killing of a Brahmin. పితృహత్య patricide. **హత్యచేయు** *hatya-chēyu*. v. a. To kill, to commit murder. చంపు. **హత్యచేసికొను** *hatya-chēsi-konu*. v. n. To commit suicide. స్వప్రాణహానిచేసికొను.

హదను or **అదను** *hadanu*. [Tel.] n. An opportunity, time. సమయము, కాలము. "అహాదనంబెలంగుజనము." A. iv. 130.

హద్దు *haddu*. [H.] n. A limit, boundary. ఎల్ల, పరిమితి.

హననము *hananamu*. [Skt. from హన to kill.] n. Killing, destroying. చంపడము.

హనువు *hanuvu*. [Skt.] n. The jaw, the upper part of the cheek. చెక్కిలి మీదిభాగము. **హనుమ, హనుమంతుడు, హనుమడు, హనుమానుడు** or **హనుమంతరాయుడు** *hanuma*. n. The name of the chief of the monkeys (now deified) who was an ally and spy of Rama. ఆంజనేయుడు. వాడు హనుమంతునివలె నున్నాడు he has high or great cheek-bones. **హనుమంతబీర** *hanumanta-bīra*. n. A plant, a kind of cucumber. *Cucumis acutangulus*. ఒకవిధమైనబీర.

హబిసీ *habisī*. [Skt. for 'Abysinia.'] n. The name of a country. An Abysinian, an African, a negro, సిద్దీవాడు, నల్లగానుండే ఆఫ్రికాదేశపు మనుష్యుడు. "హబిసీరాతులనంగతుష్కిదలు సాంపారగా." Charu Chandro. iv. 46.

హమేషా *hamēsha*. [H.] adv. Continually, always. ఎల్లప్పుడు.

హయము *hayamu*. [Skt.] n. A horse. గుర్రము. హయమేధము the sacrifice of a horse. **హయగ్రీవుడు** or **హయవదనుడు** *haya-grīvudu*. n. A name of Vishnu as being the god of learning. విద్యాధిదేవత అయిన విష్ణువు. **హయమారకము** *haya-mārakamu*. n. The shrub named *Nerium odorum*. ఓదగన్నేరుచెట్టు. **హయవాహనుడు** *haya-vahanudu*. n. Lit. the "Equestrian," a name of Kubera who rides on a horse. కుబేరుడు. **హయాంఘ్రి** *hay-ānghri*. n. The name of a herb. గుర్రపుగిట్టలాకు. **హయావళి** *hay-āvali*. n. A kind of cloth. వస్త్రవిశేషము. BD. iii. 118.

హయాము *hayāmu*. [H.] n. Period, time, reign, authority, కాలము.

హరణము See under హరించు

హరబ్బి or అరబ్బి *harabbi*. [H. Arab.] n. Arabia. An Arab horse.

హరము *haramu*. [Skt.] adj. Expelling, taking away, removing, counteracting evil effects. Stealing. నివారకమైన, పోగొట్టే, దొంగిలించెడి.

హరామి *harâmi*. [H.] adj. Wicked, vicious. దుష్ట.

హరి *hari*. [Skt.] adj. Green, yellow, bay, tawny. పచ్చని, బంగారువన్నెగల. n. A name given to Vishnu, Indra and Yama, విష్ణువు, ఇంద్రుడు, యముడు. A horse, గుర్రము. A lion, సింహము. An ape, కోతి. A frog, కప్ప. The sun, సూర్యుడు. The moon, చంద్రుడు. Air, వాయువు. A parrot, చిలుక. A snake, పాము. A ray of light, కిరణము. హరిహరి O lord! O lord! హరి హరాదులు all the deities. (Lit:) Vishnu, Siva, &c. హరిచందనము *hari-chandanamu*. n. The yellow and fragrant sort of sandal wood. పసుపువన్నెగలచందనము. హరిప్రియ *hari-priya*. n. The Basil plant, తులసి. హరిబువ్వము *hari-buvvamu*. n. A marriage feast. పెండ్లిలో అడుగారును మగవారును కూడి భోజనము చేయుటము. హరిమంథకము *hari-manthakamu*. n. Chick pea, *Cicer arietinum*. సెనగలు. హరివాణము *hari-vâṇamu*. n. A metal dish of any kind, a dish, a plate, పాత్ర, చిన్న కంచాళము, తట్ట. హరివాసరము *hari-vâsaramu*. n. The eleventh day of each lunar fortnight, which is kept as a fast. ఏకాదశి. హరి హయుడు *hari-hayuḍu*. n. An epithet of Indra. ఇంద్రుడు. హర్యక్షము *hary-akshamu* n. (Lit: Yellow-eyed). A lion. సింహము. హర్యక్షుడు *hary-akshuḍu*. n. An epithet of Kubera.

హరించు or హరియించు *harintsu*. [Skt.] v. n. To be digested, to waste away, to perish, go off or disappear, as a disease, to subside, క్షయించు, క్షీణించు, జీర్ణించు, అడగు. శేషించియుబ్బిన ఔషధము హరించి పోయినది the medicine was carried off, i. e., the medicine did no good. v. a. To counteract, expel, as an antidote does; to carry off. To take by violence, usurp, plunder, rob, steal, kill, destroy. దోచుకొను, దొంగిలించు, చంపు, నాశముచేయు, అడచు. మజ్జిగ మామిడిపండ్లదోషమును హరించును butter-milk counteracts the bad effects of mangoes. "చోరవృత్తిని హరించి తమంగొని పోవుచుండగా." N. i. 239. హరణము *haraṇamu*. n. Seizing, taking away forcibly, removing, carrying or bearing off; as of pain, &c. Stealth, theft, rape. Lapse or passing of time. నివారణము. హరించుట, గ్రహణము. A special gift or bonus: a nuptial present, అరణము. అల్లునికి హరుణిక ఇచ్చినసొమ్ము. భుక్తికైనాహారణభరణశక్తిచూపినాను I did to the best of my power to gain my bread. మిక్కిలి కాలహరణమైనది there has been much loss of time. ఆ సొమ్మును చెల్లించకుండా కాలహరణము చేయుచున్నాడు he is putting off the payment of the money. వాడు ఊరక కాలహరణము చేస్తున్నాడు he is wasting the time. హరింపు *harimpu*. n. Waste, loss, embezzlement, abstraction. నాశము, నష్టము, దోపిడి, అపహరణము. హరింపు లోకి తెచ్చు to digest, జీర్ణించు. హరికుడు *harikuḍu*. n. A thief, a gambler. తస్కరుడు, ద్యూతకారుడు. హారికప్రయోగము gambling, ద్యూతము. "రాజన్యగాథిముఖబంధనంబును హారిక ప్రయోగంబును." G. xi. 177.

హరిగ or అరిగ *hariga*. [Tel.] n. A shield. కేడెము.

హరిగోలు or అరిగోలు *hari-gôlu*. [Tel.] n. A boat made of wicker work covered with hides, a coracle, చిన్న పుట్టి.

హరిణము *hariṇamu*. [Skt.] adj. White. తెల్లని. n. White colour. తెలుపు, శ్వేతవర్ణము. An antelope, కురంగము, లేడి. హరిణక్రీడ or హరిణక్రీడనము *hariṇa-krîḍa*.

n. A certain game played by boys, leap-frog. ఒకవిధమైన ఆట. "ఇరువురు నిరువురు తోడై సెరసి దొంకతిరుంకతిహరిగపెద్దయుదూరుబు నుచుగెల్చుచునోడుచు, హరిణ ... " V. P. vii. 214. హరిణనాభి *hariṇa-nābhi*. n. Musk, the animal perfume so called. కస్తూరి. హరిణాంక మౌళి an epithet of Siva as crowned with the moon. శివుడు. హరిణాక్షి *hariṇ-akshi*. n. A lady; (lit.) gazelle-eyed. ఏణలోచన. హరిణి *hariṇi*. n. A doe, a female antelope. ఆడుజేడి.

హరితము *haritamu*. [Skt.] adj. Green, verdant. ఆకుపచ్చని. n. Green colour, ఆకుపచ్చరంగు. A bay horse, పచ్చగుర్రము. హరితపత్రిక *harita-patrika*. n. A green tree, an evergreen. పచ్చాకుచెట్టు. హరితమంజరి *harita-manjari*. n. A plant, *Acalypha indica*, కుప్పింటచెట్టు. హరిత్తు *harittu*. n. The colour green. ఆకుపచ్చ. A bay horse, పచ్చగుర్రము. A point of the compass. దిక్కు. "హరిదంతము, N. i. 211. హరిదశ్వుడు *harid-asvudu*. n. The sun. సూర్యుడు.

హరిదళము or అరిదళము *hari-daḷamu*. [from Skt. హరితాళమ్.] n. Yellow orpiment, *Arsenicum flavum*. చేమగాంద్రు మూలిక పూసుకొనేటిది. స్వర్ణతాళము gold coloured orpiment, *auri-pigmentum*.

హరిద్ర *haridra*. [Skt.] n. Turmeric. పసుపు. హరిద్రువు *haridruvu*. n. Wood saffron. మ్రానిపసుపు. హరిద్రాభము *haridrābhamu*. n. Yellow colour. adj. Yellow.

హరిన్మణి *harin-maṇi*. [Skt.] n. An emerald. పచ్చ, మరకతము.

హరిబీకెలు or హరిబెయ్యాకెలు *harib-ikelu*. [Tel.] n. Porcupine's quills. ఏదుపంది ముండ్లు. "ఏదికొనిన హరిబీకెలు." H. v. 411. "అపమునొగ్గధురీణాలకునిరుదంచురగ్గలవై హరిబెయ్యాకెలు." S. i. 157. "బురుదుబెంకలు పెను పులులగోళ్లు, హరిబెయ్యాకెలు పెమ్మిపురికొంబు ములు." S. i. 186.

హరుడు *haruḍu*. [Skt.] n. An epithet of Siva. శివుడు. హరాద్రి *har-adri*. n. Mount Kailasa, the favourite resort of Siva. కైలాసము.

హరువు or హరువ్వు *haruvu*. [Tel.] n. Beauty, comeliness, elegance. Skill: a trick. సొగసు, అందము, ఉపాయము, నాణెమైన పని. adj. Fine, pretty, beautiful, clever, excellent. "పన్నిటంచవపుచల్వగట్టిహరువొప్పాం నాదిగంధంబు తేఁకన్ నిందారవలంది." T. iii. 129. "ఒకవింతహరువైన యూర్ధ్వపుండ్రంబుపై" N. v. 89. "పరిమళంబులు కేంప హరువువరచి." N. ix. 124. హరువరి *haruv-ari*. n. A clever man. నేర్పరి, ఉపాయకారి. "శ్రీరామచంద్రుడో హాయూరా హరువరి సెరుంకునంగద ముఖ్యులో." R. vi. 68. హర్వుకాడు *harru-kāḍu*. n. A clever man. కర్పితకుడు.

హరుసము or అరుసము *harusamu*. [from Skt. హర్షము.] n. Gladness. సంతోషము. "హరుసము కెంధివచ్చిరిటయందరుమందరి కేలు గుంపుపై." KUR. ii. 6. హరుసించు *harusintsu*. v. n. To rejoice.

హర్కారా *harkāra*. [H.] n. A messenger, a courier.

హర్త *harta*. [Skt.] n. One who steals or removes. హరించువాడు.

హర్మ్యము *harmyamu*. [Skt.] n. A mansion, palace. రాజగృహము, ధనికుని గృహము. A storeyed house, మిద్దెయిల్లు.

హర్యక్షము See under హరి.

హర్షము *harshamu*. [Skt.] n. Gladness, joy, exultaion. సంతోషము. హర్షకుడు *harshakuḍu*. n. One who causes joy, one who gives pleasure, సంతోషింపజేయువాడు. హర్షణము *harshaṇamu*. n. Pleasure, joy, rejoicing, సంతోషించుట. హర్షకుడు *harshakuḍu*. n. One who rejoices or is glad, సంతోషించువాడు. హర్షమాణము *harsha-māṇamu*. adj. Pleased, happy, cheerful, glad, సంతోషించుచున్న. హర్షి *harshi*. n. One who is joyful or pleased, సంతోషముగలవాడు. హర్షించు *harshintsu*. v. n. To be glad, rejoice, be pleased with, సంతోషించు. ఆయన ఇంత పనికి హర్షించునా will he be pleased with this? హర్షితము *harshitamu*. adj. Delighted, glad, cheerful. సంతోషపెట్టబడిన.

హలము *halamu*. [Skt.] n. A plough, నాగలి. హలరేఖ in palmistry, a mark in the palm, resembling a plough and denoting victory. హలి or హలాయుధుడు *hali*. n. A ploughman, మడకదున్ను వాడు. Also, an epithet applied to Balarama. హలికుడు *halikuḍu*. n. A ploughman. కృషికుడు, దున్నుకొని బ్రతికేవాడు. హల్య *halya*. n. A field once ploughed. హల్యము *halyamu*. adj. Ploughed, tilled. దున్నబడ్డ. n. A collection of ploughs. నాగళ్ల సమూహము. A i. 52.

హలహలము, హాలాహలము or హాలాహలము *hala-halamu*. [Skt.] n. Poison, venom. గరళము.

హల్కా, హల్కి or అల్కి *halka*. [H.] adj Mean, low, inferior. నీచమైన, క్షుద్రమైన, అల్పమైన.

హల్లకము *hallakamu*. [Skt.] n. The red lotus. ఎఱ్ఱతామర. "హల్లకపాణి" rosy fingered. Ila. iii. 8.

హల్లకల్లోలము or అల్లకల్లోలము *halla-kallōlamu*. [Tel.] n. A tumult, confusion, disorder, disturbance. తారుమారు. "మల్లో కముల్ హల్లకల్లోలముల్ శేయు." P. i. 675.

హల్లీసకము *hallīsakamu*. [Skt.] n. A dance performed by women moving in a circle and holding sticks in their hands, అడుగులు వర్తులముగానిలిచి ఆడే ఆట, కోలాటము, చేతులుపొందుగాపెట్టుకొని ఆడే తాండవము. A. iii. 121.

హల్లు *hallu*. [Skt.] n. A consonant. కకారాద్యక్షరము.

హల్లోహల *hallō-hala*. [Skt.] adj. Bewildered, stumbled. తొట్రుపడిన, చీకాకుపడిన. హల్లోహలుడు *hallō-haluḍu*. n. A wanderer; one who is bewildered or confused, తొట్రుపాటుపొందినవాడు. "వాక్ప్రల్లోల హల్లోహలా." N. ix. 543.

హలహలి, హలీహలిక, హాలాహలి or హలాహలి *hala-hali*. [Skt.] n. Haste. త్వర. A confused or tumultuous noise, tumult, uproar. కోలాహలము, కలకలము, సందడి. Violence, oppression, ఔద్ధత్యము. Courage, heroism. శౌర్యము. "అమ్మునివాధు లెక్కి కొండొరులకు వడి శేయూఁతగొని హాళాహళి మీరగా." N. i. 117.

హల్లి *halli*. [Tel.] n. A cipher, సున్న.

హవణించు or హవనించు *havanintsu*. [Kan.] v. a. To wear, to put on, to adorn, to set right. To perform, accomplish. To lay. ధరించు, అలంకరించు, చక్కజేయు, చెల్లించు, ఉంచు, పెట్టు. "కమ్మఁబంగరు చాయ కన్గవల్ హవణించి హంసకన్యాకృతిచే నటించుచుండి." T. iv. 154. "అడినపంతంబు హవణించుకొంటి." L. viii. 95. అనగా, చెల్లించుకొంటిని. హవణిల్లు *havaṇ-illu*. v. n. To shine, bloom, be splendid. విలసిల్లు, వెలయు, ప్రకాశించు. "హవణిల్లుముత్యాల రవికతొడిగి." Ila. i. 80. హవణింపు *havan-impu*. n. Beautification, adorning, అలంకరణము. Vigilance, precaution, జాగరూకత. "అనురూపరుచిసంపదలా హవణింపు సొంపులకా హాళిమియిక గనుంగొని." T. ii. 78. హవణి, హవణిక or హవణు *havaṇi*. n. Beauty. ఒప్పిదము. Carefulness, caution, పదిలము. జాగ్రత్త, ఎచ్చరిక. హవణుగా *havaṇu-ga*. adv. Carefully, cautiously. పదిలముగా. జాగ్రతగా.

హవనము *havanamu.* [Skt.] n. A sacrifice, oblation, burnt-offering. హోమము. హవనీయము *havanīyamu.* adj. Sacrificial, fit for or intended for sacrifice. హోమము చేయదగిన. హవము *havamu.* n. A sacrifice, oblation, యజ్ఞము. A command, ఆజ్ఞ. A call, calling, పిలుపు. హవి. హవిస్సు or హవిష్యము *havi.* n. An oblation of ghee or clarified butter; an article fit to be offered in sacrifice. Any thing fit to be eaten on holy days and on sacred occasions, as wheat, cow's milk, &c. హోమ ద్రవ్యము, ఘృతము, నెయ్యి. పిండి మొదలైన లఘ్వాహారము, వ్రతాదులయందు విహితమైన భోజనీయ ద్రవ్యము. హవ్యము *havyamu.* n. An offering to the gods. దేవతార్థ నియమితాన్నము, హోమీయ ద్రవ్యము. హవ్యకవ్యములు offerings to the deities and the manes of deceased ancestors. దేవతలకును పితృదేవతలకును యోగ్యమైన అన్నము. హవిర్భుక్కు, హవ్యవహుడు, హవ్యవాహుడు or హవ్యవాహనుడు *havir-bhukku.* n. Fire. అగ్నిహోతృడు.

హవుసు Same as హౌసు. (q. v.)

హవేలీ *havelī.* [H.] n. A mansion, a palace. నగరు.

హవ్యము See under హవనము.

హసంతి or హసని *hasanti.* [Skt.] n. A portable furnace or fire pot. కుంపటి.

హసదు, హసాదు or అసాదు *hasadu.* [Tel.] adj. Noble, great, శ్రేష్ఠ.

హసనము or హసము *hasanamu.* [Skt.] n. Laughing, a smile. నవ్వు. హసించు *hasintsu.* v. n. To laugh, smile. నవ్వు. హసితము *hasitamu.* n. A laugh, a smile. నవ్వు. adj. Laughing, smiling, నవ్విన.

హస్తము *hastamu.* [Skt.] n. The hand. చెయ్యి. The arm, భుజము. An elephant's trunk, ఏనుగుతొండము. A cubit, మూర. అది హస్తగతమైనది it came into my possession or power. హస్తదోషము a slip of the pen, an error in writing. హస్తతలము the palm of the hand. హస్తవారణము *hasta-vāraṇamu.* n. Prevention (of beating, &c.) by interposing the hand. హస్తాంతరము *hast-antaramu.* n. Stock; total amount in a treasury: money in hand. బొక్కసములో సిద్ధముగానుండే రూకలు. హస్తాక్షరి *hast-akshari.* n. Handwriting, signature. వ్రాలు. హస్తానక్షత్రము *hasta-nakshatramu.* n. The thirteenth lunar mansion. పదమూడో నక్షత్రము, ఉత్తరకు అవతలి నక్షత్రము. హస్తి *hasti.* n. An elephant. ఏనుగు. హస్తిమశకాంతరము a huge difference, as between an elephant and a fly. హస్తినఖము *hasti-nakhamu.* n. A mound of earth or masonry, screening the access to the gate of a city or fort. పురద్వారకూటము, పట్టణద్వారము ముందటిబురుజు. The glacis of a fortified town. హస్తిని *hastini* n. A she elephant. ఆడయేనుగు. A woman of the stolid type, స్త్రీజాతిభేదము. హస్తిపకుడు *hastipakuḍu.* n. An elephant driver. మావటీడు. హస్తిభారము *hasti-bhāramu.* n. The base or foot; a basis; a foundation. పునాది.

హా hā

హా *hā.* [Skt.] interj. Ah! alas! An interjection expressive of weariness, sorrow, pain, wonder, surprise, or pleasure. "హాయనిపలుకుచు." N. iii. 1290. "హా పుత్రయనుచు." Sar. D. 336. హారవము *hā-ravamu.* n. The exclamation "Ha!" (రవము meaning sound.) హా అనేనినాదము.

హాజరు *hāzaru.* [H.] adj. Present, ready. హాజరుజామీను bail for producing a culprit. గైరుహాజరు absence. హాజరుపట్టీ an attendance register.

హాజీరము Same as హాజారము. (q. v.)

హాటకము *hāṭakamu.* [Skt.] n. Gold. బంగారు. హాటకగిరి or హాటకధరాధరము the hill called Maha Meru. మహామేరువు. హాటకగర్భుడు *hāṭaka-garbhuḍu.* n. An epithet of Brahma. హిరణ్యగర్భుడు, బ్రహ్మ.

హాని *hāni.* [Skt.] n. Loss, damage, detriment, injury, harm, mischief, ruin, peril. తక్కువకుట, నష్టము, చెరుపు, కీడు, చేటు. హానివృద్ధులు adversity and prosperity. హానికరము *hāni-karamu.* adj. Doing injury, pernicious, injurious, harmful, చెరుపైన.

హామిక or అమిక *hāmika.* [from Skt. అహమహమిక.] n. Egotism, pride, vanity. Vigour. గర్వము, కొవ్వు. "నేర్పుగల్గియుండా తెల్లనిహామికల్." Anir. iii. 126.

హామితకావి *hāmi-takāvi.* [H.] n. An advance for cultivation on the responsibility of a third person. జామీనుమీద ఇచ్చే [illegible]

హాయనము *hāyanamu.* [Skt.] n. A year. సంవత్సరము.

హాయి *hāyi.* [Tel.] n. Happiness, peace, quiet, comfort. సుఖము, సౌఖ్యము, నెమ్మది, నిమ్మళము. హాయిగా *hāyi-gā.* adv. Happily, comfortably, at ease. సుఖముగా, నెమ్మదిగా.

హారకుడు *hārakuḍu.* [Skt. from హరించు.] n. A thief, robber, plunderer, ravisher, దొంగ, దోచుకొనువాడు, చోరుడు, నాశకుడు.

హారతి, ఆరతి or మంగళహారతి *hārati.* [from Skt. ఆరాత్రికము.] n. A wave-offering to a deity. An offering of camphor, &c., presented on marriages or such like festivities to prevent the bad effects of an evil eye. దీపహారతి an offering of lights. ధూపహారతి an offering of burning incense. కర్పూరహారతి an offering of lighted camphor. కుంభహారతి an offering of a vase with a lamp on its mouth. హారతిపాటలు songs sung at the time of offering camphor to a deity or on festive occasions, having the phrase హారతులెత్తరే as a chorus.

హారము *hāramu.* [Skt.] n. A necklace, a string of pearls, a garland, a string or row, పేరు. In Arithmetic, the divisor: also the denominator of a fraction. ముత్యాలహారము a string of pearls. హారకము *hārakamu.* n. The divisor. భాజకము [illegible]. హారి *hāri.* adj. Beautiful. రమ్యమైన, సుందరమైన, మనోజ్ఞమైన. Taking, getting. గ్రహించే. R. i. 215. హార్యము *hārya-mu.* n. The dividend. హరింపదగినది.

హాల *hāla.* [Skt.] n. Wine, సుర, మద్యము.

హాలము *hālamu.* [Skt.] n. A plough. నాగలి.

హాలహాలము or హాలాహాలము *hāla-halamu.* [Skt.] n. Deadly poison. విషము.

హాలిక *hālika.* [Skt. from హలు.] adj. Belonging to a plough, appertaining to farming, agricultural. లాంగల సంబంధమైన, కాపువారి సంబంధమైన. "[illegible] హాలిక [illegible]." N. i. 42. హాలికుడు or హాలికుడు *hālikuḍu.* n. A ploughman, a farmer, a cultivator, a husbandman. కృషికుడు, కాపు, దున్నకొని బ్రతికేవాడు, రెడ్డి. "[illegible]" Pururavas Charitra. iv. 35.

హాలు *hālu.* [H.] adj. Current, present. హాలుసాలు or హాల్సాలు *hālu-sālu.* n. The current year, నడిచేసంవత్సరము.

హాలు *hālu.* [Eng. 'Hall'.] n. A hall.

హాళి *hāḷi.* [Tel.] n. Eagerness, desire, ఆసక్తి. Joy, gladness. ఆనందము, సంతోషము, ఉత్సాహము. "[illegible]." R. i. 19.

హావడి, హావళి or ఆవడి *hāvaḍi.* [Kan.] n. Annoyance, trouble, distress, molestation. ఉపద్రవము, బాధ. "[illegible]." Vish. ii. 121. "[illegible]." A iv. 291.

హావము hāvamu. [Skt.] n. An amorous gesture: dalliance, blandishment. స్త్రీల శృంగార రసభావములవల్ల కలిగే క్రియ, నేత్రాది వికారములచేత తెలియదగిన మనోవికారము. "కనకాంగియల్ల మందిరమునకుం జని హావభావములం దనుకొల్పగా." N. iv. 34.

హాశ్శీలు, హాస్సీలు or హాసీలు hāssilu. [H.] n. Duty, customs, a tax. పన్ను.

హాసము or హాస్యము hāsamu. [Skt.] n. Laughter, laughing, merriment, sport, fun. నవ్వు. దరహాసము graceful smile. హాస్యము hāsyamu. n. Joking, jesting. హాసించు hāsintsu. v. n. To laugh, నవ్వు.

హాస్తికము hāstikamu. [Skt. from హస్తి.] n. A herd of elephants. ఏనుగులగుంపు. హాస్తికుడు hāstikuḍu. n. An elephant-driver. మావటివాడు.

హాహా hā-hā. [Skt.] interj. How wonderful! Oh! ఆశ్చర్యోక్తి. Alas! alas! ah me! శోకోక్తి. హాహాకారము hāhā-kāramu. n. Cries of "Ha! Ha!" or "Ah". ఏడ్పు, పెడబొబ్బలు.

హాహూదు hāhuḍu. [Skt.] n. One of a class of singers in the heaven of Indra. ఒకజాతి దేవగాయకుడు.

హి hi

హింగుది, హింగుదము, హింగులి or ఇంగుది hingudi. [Skt.] n. A small kind of egg plant. *Solanum melongena*. బృహతి, నేలములక.

హింగువు hinguvu. [Skt.] n. Asafoetida. ఇంగువ.

హింగుళము hingulamu. [Skt.] n. Vermilion. ఇంగిలీకము.

హిండనము hiṇḍanamu. [Skt.] n. Spread, extension, wandering. వ్యాప్తి, ప్రసరించ డము, తిరుగుట. "నీలకుంభరుచి హిండనమా యున." Kalahasti: 1. 60. హిండితము hiṇḍi-tamu. adj. Extended, spread, wandering. వ్యాపించిన.

హింతాళము hintāḷamu. [Skt.] n. The marshy date tree. నీరుతాడిచెట్టు.

హిందూ hin dū. [Persian through Skt. సింధు.] adj. Hindu. ఇండ్యాదేశసంబంధమైన. "హిందూరాజ్య రమాధురంధర." Swa. iii. 176. హిందువు hinduvu. n. A Hindu.

హిందోళము hindōlamu. [Skt.] n. A certain tune. సంగీతరాగభేదము.

హింస or హింసనము himsa. [Skt.] n. Injury, hurt, harm, evil, torture, mischief, killing. బాధించుట, చంపడము. హింసించు himsintsu. v. a. To plague, torment, do harm, injure, kill, murder. బాధించు, చంపు. హింసకము or హింస్రము himsakamu. adj. Mischievous, hurtful, injurious. బాధించునట్టి. హింసకుడు himsakuḍu. n. An evil-doer, an oppressor, a murderer. బాధించువాడు, చంపువాడు.

హిక్క hikka. [Skt.] n. Hiccup, hiccough. ఎక్కిలి.

హిజారు or ఇజారు hijāru. [H] n. A pair of trousers, short breeches. "పసిడి పట్టుహిజారు." శుక. i.

హితము hitamu. [Skt.] adj. Good, beneficial, friendly, kind, profitable, మంచి, అనుకూలమైన, ప్రియమైన, శుభమైన. హిత శత్రువు a secret enemy. n. That which is good, benefit, welfare. మంచిది, మేలు. హితముగా hitamu-gā. adv. Agreeably, in a friendly manner, అనుకూలముగా, ప్రియముగా. హితవాది hita-vādi. n. He who gives good advice. మేలుచెప్పువాడు. హితుడు hituḍu. n. A friend, an ally. ఇష్టుడు. హితోపదేశము hit-ōpa desamu. n. Friendly advice. The name of a book on morals.

హితవు or ఇతవు [from Skt. హితము.] Same as హితము. హితవరి or ఇతవరి hitav-ari. n. A friend. ఇష్టుడు.

హిమము *himamu.* [Skt.] n. Dew, frost, snow. మంచు. A fragrant grass called *Cyperus.* పొలతూర. Sandal, చందనము. adj. Cold, frigid, chilly, dewy, snowy. శీతలమైన, మంచుమయమైన. **హిమకరుడు, హిమధాముడు, హిమాంశువు, హిమభానుడు** or **హిమరశ్మి** *hima-karuḍu.* n. The moon. చంద్రుడు. **హిమగిరి, హిమవంతము, హిమాద్రి, హిమాచలము, హిమాలయము** or **హిమశైలము** *hima-giri.* n. The snowy mountain, the Himalaya range. మంచుకొండ. **హిమమయూఖుడు** or **హిమమయూఖుడు** *hima-mayūkhuḍu.* n. The moon. చంద్రుడు. "హిమమయూఖకరాదుల." N. ii. 465. **హిమవారి** or **హిమాంబువు** *hima-vari.* n. Rose water. పన్నీరు. "హిమవారిజలకేళులు." A. vi. 176. "కనుదమ్ముల హిమాంబుపులుకుపరాదు." Vasu. iii. 241. Swa. v. 126. **హిమాగమము** *him-āgamamu.* n. The cold season, winter. శీతకాలము. **హిమాని** *himani.* n. Snow, ice, hoar-frost. నీహారము, హిమసమూహము. Swa. v. 135. **హిమిక** *himika.* n. Hoar-frost. నీహారము, మంచు.

హిరణ్యము *hiraṇyamu.* [Skt.] n. Gold. Wealth, money. బంగారు, సొత్తు, ధనము, సొమ్ము. సహిరణ్యోదకదానము a gift of land, &c., with some money and water given to signify that the gift is not retractable. **హిరణ్మయము** *hiraṇ-mayamu.* adj. Golden, made of gold. స్వర్ణమయమైన. **హిరణ్యగర్భుడు** *hiraṇya-garbhuḍu.* n. An epithet of Brahma. బ్రహ్మ.

హిహి, హీహీ, హుంహుం, ఇహిహిహీ *hihi.* [Skt.] interj. Ha! ha! heyday! An expression of surprise, of scorn, or of sorrow. హాస్యోక్తి, ఆశ్చర్యము, తిరస్కారము, వ్యసనము మొదలగువానిని తెలుపుమాట.

హీ hī

హీనము *hīnamu.* [Skt.] adj. Bad, low, mean, vile, base. Left, abandoned. తుచ్ఛమైన, నీచమైన, వర్జితమైన, విడువబడిన, రహితమైన, లేని. In compound words it denotes Bereft of, without, destitute or deprived of, free from. హీనవృత్తి a mean occupation. అతడు హీనదశలోనున్నాడు he is in low circumstances. హీనస్వరము a low voice. హీనజాతియైన degraded, outcast. హీనజాతివాడు an outcast. "హీనప్రజ్ఞుడు." M. XII. iii. 328. **హీనత, హీనత్వము** or **హైన్యము** *hīnata.* n. Lowness, meanness, baseness. Want, defect, నీచత్వము, అల్పత్వము, లోపము, లేమి. బలహీనత weakness, debility. బుద్ధిహీనత foolishness. "హీనస్థానమున నిలిచి హీనత నొందెన్." M. XII. iv. 414. "అనాహీనత ముద్ధము." M. XIII. iv. 305. **హీనరాశి** *hīna-rāsi.* n. The lowest part of a rick or heap. **హీనవాది** *hīna-vadi.* n. The loser in an argument or law suit. ఓడినవాడు. వారు హీనవాదులయిరి they came off losers. **హీనుడు** *hīnuḍu.* n. A low, mean or base man. (In composition) he who is without, destitute of, or deprived of. అల్పుడు, నీచుడు, రహితుడు. అంగహీనుడు he who is defective in a limb, he who is crippled. వస్త్రహీనుడు he who is without clothes. కులహీనుడు a man of low caste. బుద్ధిహీనుడు he who is without wisdom. రూపహీనుడు he who is devoid of beauty. ధనహీనుడు a penniless man, a poor man. లజ్జాహీనుడు he who is without shame.

హీరము *hīramu.* [Skt.] n. A diamond, వజ్రము, రవ.

హు hu

హుంకరించు or **హుంకారించు** *hum-kar-intsu.* [Skt.] v. n. To cry ha! To shout, to yell, to utter a menacing sound. భయంకర ముగా హుమ్మను. **హుంకారము** or **హుంకృతి** *hum-karamu.* n. Uttering a menacing sound. Huzzas, roars, hurrahs, war-whoops. గర్జన, భయంకరముగా హుమ్మని అరచడము, విక్రమసూచకశబ్దము. "ధిక్కారరటిలా చమత్కార హుంకారముల్ భూరిసైమిరి." N. vi. 276. **హుంకారపక్షి** *hum-kāra-pakshi.* n. A Sun-bird or honey-bird, తేనెపిట్ట. **హుంకారి** *hum-kāri.* n. He who shouts or yells. హుంకారముచేయువాడు. ఘనాహుంకార హుంకారులై shouting with pride.

హుంకించు *hum-k-intsu.* [Skt.] v. n. To neigh, to groan in making an effort. హుంకించి దొంకదుముకు దుముకినాడు he drew in his breath and took a leap.

హుండి *hundi.* [H.] n. A bill or cheque on a bank. దర్శనహుండి a bill payable at sight.

హుకుము *hukumu.* [H.] n. An order, ఆజ్ఞ.

హుజూబిక్కొమరుడు *hudzubik-komarudu.* [from 'Uzbeck.'] n. An Uzbeck or Tartar. తురకవాడు. "హుజాబిక్కొమరునిరోజ హి జారుడు బదమిజారదునగళ్ గోషికినాడు." Jagann. i. 90.

హుజూరు *hudzūru.* [H.] n. The presence. Headquarters, Huzur. సముఖము, సన్ని ధము.

హుటాహుటి *huṭa-huṭi.* [Tel.] n. Swiftness, haste వేగము. గమనవేగము. adj. Rapid, quick, శీఘ్రమైన, వడిగలైన. "కదతనలేకరుగు దుము హుటాహుటినడలు." Swa. i. 38. "హుటాహుటినాట్యముసల్ప." H. ii. 191. హుటాహుటి ప్రయాణము a forced march. **హుటాహుటిగా** or **హుటాహుటిగా** *huta-huṭi.* adv. Rapidly, quickly, hurriedly. శీఘ్రముగా, వేగముగా, త్వరగా.

హుడుక్కు, హుడుక్క or **ఉడుక్క** *huḍukku.* [Skt.] n. A small drum shaped like an hour glass. ఢక్క.

హుతభుక్కు, హుతవహుడు or **హుతాశ నుడు** *huta-bhukku.* [Skt.] n. The god who lives on sacrifices; a title of Agni.

హుమా or **హుమాయి** *huma.* [Mahrati] n. A horse. గుర్రము.

హుమ్మను *humm-anu.* [Tel.] v. n. To cry ho! or "avaunt." హుం అని కోపమూర్ఖడు లపేరు అను. "హుమ్మనియలద కొమ్ములగ్రుమ్మనచ్చు." N. x. 37.

హురుమంజి, హురుమంజీ, హురుముంజి or **హుర్మంజి** *hurumanji.* [H.] n. The name of a country. A fine reddish pearl. ఎర్ర నాలుగల దివ్యమైన ముత్తెము. adj. Dark or brown red. రక్తవర్ణమైన. "పచ్చనిహురుమంజి పని వాగెపక్కెరపారసీ పల్లంబు పట్టెయమము." Swa. iv. 36. టీ: హురుమంజిపని, అనగా హు రుమంజి ముత్యాలుకూర్చిన. "మేలైనహురుమంజి ముత్యాలకుల్లాయి మాకచక్యంబులుసందడింప." Bhanumati: iv. 55.

హురుమత్తు or **హుర్మత్తు** *huru-mattu.* [H.] adj. Large, great, much, big. గొప్ప, పెద్ద. n. Honor, esteem.

హుళక్కి, హుళికి, హుళికి, or **ఉళక్కి** *huḷukki.* [Kan.] n. A falsehood, a lie. పట్టిమాట, అబద్ధము. Unreality, nothingness. అభావము. "లేదనదంబు తెప్పడిహుళక్కి సహాయ ము సర్వమంగళంబు." Swa. iv. 145.

హుసారు, హుషారు or **ఉషారు** *husāru.* [H.] n. Care, carefulness, watchfulness, wariness, alertness. జాగరూకత, జాగ్రత్త.

హూ hū

హూ *hū.* [Tel.] n. The sound of a yawn. ఆవులించుటయందలి ధ్వని.

హూణుడు *hūṇudu.* [Skt. from 'Hun.'] n. A Hun, a barbarian, a European. ...

వాడు, తెల్లవాడు. హూణదేశము Europe. హూణులు the Huns, the Europeans. "హూణాఖ్యసర్వదేశములుహూణి." H. iv. 27.

హూతము or ఆహూతము hūtamu. [Skt.] adj. Called, summoned, invited. పిలువబడిన. హూతి or ఆహూతి hūti. n. A call, calling. పిలుచుట, పిలుపు.

హూయమానము hūya-mānamu. [Skt.] adj. Offered as a sacrifice by fire. హోమము చేయబడే. "హూయమానహవిర్వితతులు." R. iii. 26.

హూహువు hūhuvu. [Skt.] n. The name of certain singers in the heaven of Indra. స్వర్గగాయక భేదము.

హూహూ hūhū. [Tel.] n. A cry of "hu, hu" expressive of shivering. చలిచేత హూహూ అనడము. "సీ॥ జనులుహూహూయనుచుచలి చేత కుక్కుకబంటి తోయములలోపల వసించి." B. iv. 838.

హృ hṛi

హృతము or ఆహృతము hṛitamu. [Skt.] adj. Taken, taken away, stolen. హరింపబడిన. హృతి or ఆహృతి hṛiti. n. Taking away by force or fraud. అపహరణము, హరణము.

హృత్తు, హృదయము or హృది hṛittu. [Skt.] n. The heart, the mind, the seat of thought and feeling. అంతఃకరణము, మనస్సు. హృత్పద్మములు the lotus of the heart, the soul or mind. హృత్తాపము mental anguish or distress. హృద్గతము impressed on the heart, remembered. ఆ పద్యము నాకు హృద్గతము కాలేదు I have not got the verse by heart. సుహృదయుడు a good or kind-hearted man. హృదయంగమము hṛidayan-gamamu. adj. Heart-moving, affecting. Pleasant, agreeable. ఇంపైన, మనోహరమైన. "హృదయంగమరావంబును." Swa. v. 88. హృదయాళువు hṛiday-āluvu. n. An affectionate or kind-hearted man. దయాళువు, మంచిమనస్సుగలవాడు. హృద్యము hṛidyamu. adj. Amiable, dear, beloved, affectionate, kind. మనస్సునకింపైన, ప్రియమైన, వాత్సల్యముగల. హృద్యాంగి fair-limbed, lovely. H. iii. 41. హృద్రోగము hṛid-rōgamu. n. Disease of the mind. Grief, మనోవ్యాధి.

హృషితము hṛishitamu. [Skt.] adj. Rejoiced, gladdened, surprised. తుష్టమైన, సంతోషింపబడిన.

హృషీకము hṛishīkamu. [Skt.] n. An organ of sense. ఇంద్రియము. M. XIV. ii. 191. హృషీకాతీతము imperceptible by the organs of sense. హృషీకేశుడు hṛishīk-ēsuḍu. n. A name of Vishnu. విష్ణువు.

హృష్టము hṛishṭamu. adj. Rejoiced, delighted. సంతోషింపబడిన. హృష్టి hṛishṭi. n. Joy. సంతోషము. హృష్టుడు hṛishṭuḍu. n. He who rejoices, he who is pleased. తుష్టుడు, సంతోషించినవాడు. హృష్యత్తు hṛishyattu. adj. Pleasing, rejoicing. సంతోషించే.

హె he

హెగ్గడి or హెగ్గడు heggaḍi. [Kan.] n. A chieftain, a headman. పెద్ద, యజమానుడు, శెట్టి. A man who guards a harem, అంతఃపురపుకావలివాడు. "పాండుగానందలంబులు పల్లకీలు దక్షతనాయితము సేయుచౌలికులను. తగువాహనముల నంతఃపుర కాంతలనిడి, దిండ్లువైపించు హెగ్గడులును." KP. viii. 33. హెగ్గడి, హెగ్గడికత్తె, హెగ్గడీ or హెగ్గాలి heggaḍi. n. A lady in waiting, a maid of honour, a handmaid. సైరంధ్రి, ఆడపాప, పనికత్తె. A woman who guards a harem, అంతఃపురపుకావలికత్తె. "ఆనిడు తెచ్చిన రక్షభూషాంబరములందుకొన హెగ్గడీలతో నానతిచ్చి." Satyabha. iv. 244. హెగ్గడికాడు or హెగ్గడీడు Same as హెగ్గడి.

హెగ్గళ *heggaḷa.* [Kan.] n. A kind of trumpet. ఒక తూరువాద్యము. "త్రాలందిష్టళ కంబు కొట్ట కెరుదలా రాకాసులన్నేళ హెగ్గాళల్ప ట్టె." R. viii. 74.

హెచ్చు or ఎచ్చు *hetstsu.* [Tel.] v. n. To increase, grow, multiply, అధికమగు. n. An increase, augmentation. అధిక్యము. "అరవిం దములగచ్చులడగించుకొని హెచ్చు." Swa. vi. 107. హెచ్చరించు or ఎచ్చరించు *hetstsar-intsu.* v. a. To encourage, hint at, allude to, advert to, call to memory, warn, సూచనచేయు. హెచ్చరిక or ఎచ్చరిక *hetstsar-ika.* n. A hint, intimation, precaution, warning, arousing, encouragement. సూచన, జాగ్రత్త. Joy, సంతోషము. "కుబేరశంకరుల్ సరసమగోల్వ మ్రొక్కులిడ స్వామి పరాకవధారుదేవ, హెచ్చరికయటంచు కంచుకులు." N. i. 177. హెచ్చరిల్లు or ఎచ్చరిలు *hetstsar-illu.* v. n. To increase, grow, improve. అభివృద్ధిపొందు. To be encouraged, to beware, to be on the alert. ఎచ్చరిక కలిగియుండు. "ఏ రయం పా యం బు లేనైన హెచ్చరిలగనిక రాతుసకులము రమేశ్వ రు ం డు తుకుమునమికంక." KP. vi. 26. హెచ్చించు *hechch-intsu.* v. a. To increase, augment, multiply, అధికముచేయు. హెచ్చిల్లు, హెచ్చిలు or ఎచ్చిలు *hechch-illu.* v. n. To augment, increase, multiply, అధికమగు. హెచ్చు, హెచ్చిన or ఎచ్చిన *hetstsu.* adj. Exceeding, much, more, excessive, great, superior. అధి కమైన, పెంపొందునైన. "హెచ్చినమైత్రి." A. iv. 187. నన్ను హెచ్చుతక్కువలుగా మాట్లాడినాడు he reviled me. హెచ్చుతగ్గులుగానుండే భూమి uneven ground, land that is up and down. హెచ్చుగ or హెచ్చుగా *hetstsu-ga.* adv. Much, more, greatly. అధికముగా. "వజ్రములు మగువలు తోడుతలూ హెచ్చుగ గొల్వ వచ్చును." T. ii. 19.

హెజ్జిజ్జి *hejjijji.* [Tel.] n. A certain tune, రాగవిశేషము. "హెజ్జిజ్జివలంబునించుకంక." H. v.

హెడ్డొర *heddora.* [Kan.] n. The name of the river Heddora. నదివిశేషము. "హెడ్డొర యమున నదియులనిండపార." BD. v. 989.

హే hē

హేజీబు *hējību.* [H.] n. A minister. మంత్రి.

హేతి *hēti.* [Skt.] n. A weapon. ఆయుధము. హేతిరాజు the discus or missile weapon of Vishnu. సుదర్శనము. A flame, మంట.

హేతువు *hētuvu.* [Skt.] n. Cause, reason, motive, ground, object, purpose, కారణము. హేతుకము *hētukamu.* n. Reason, cause. కారణము. "కమలాభిరుచి హేతుకంబైన లేబం బు." Ila. i. 69. హేతుభూతము *hētu-bhūtamu.* adj. Being the cause. కారణము గానుండే. A. vi. 133. హేతుభూతుడు *hētu-bhūtuḍu.* n. One who is the cause. కారణ కర్త. "ఎవ్వడఖిల జగత్రా హేతుభూతుడు." N. ii. 90.

హేమంతము or హేమంత ఋతువు *hēmant-amu.* [Skt. from హిమము.] n. The cold season, winter. మంచుకాలము, శీతకాలము, చలికాలము.

హేమము *hēmamu.* [Skt.] n. Gold. బంగారు. "హేమాంగి" the golden maid. T. ii. 75. హేమకారకవిద్య *hēma-kāraka-vidya.* n. Alchemy, the art of making gold. రసవాదము. హేమకారుడు *hēma-kāruḍu.* n. A goldsmith. కంసలవాడు, స్వర్ణకారుడు. హేమపుష్పకము *hēma-pushpakamu.* n. The Gold flower, *Michelia champaka.* సంపంగిచెట్టు, సంపెగచెట్టు. హేమ పుష్పిక *hēma-pushpika.* n. A kind of wild golden Jessamin. పచ్చఅడవిమల్లె. హేమాద్రి *hēm-adri.* n. The golden mountain, i. e., Mount Meru. మహామేరువు, బంగారు కొండ. హేమాహేములు *hēma-hēmīlu.* n. Great men, wealthy men, men of position, superiors. ఘనులు, ధూర్జులు. H. i. 256. పల్లెగొల్లలాలో కాపులు హేమాహే మీలుగానున్నారు the farmers of the

Nellore district are very opulent. హేమించు *hēm-intsu.* v. n. To turn to gold. బంగారమగు. వారివృద్ధు, నిండా హేమించి యున్నారు they are now very wealthy.

హేయము *hēyamu.* [Skt.] adj. That which is to be abandoned, abominable, disgusting, mean, base, vile. త్యాజ్యమైన, తుచ్ఛమైన, అధమమైన, అసహ్యమైన. హేయంబైన సంసారము this vile life. హేయత *hēyata.* n. Vileness, baseness. తుచ్ఛత, అసహ్యత. హేయపడు *hēya-paḍu.* v. n. To be disgusted.

హేరంబుడు *hērambuḍu.* [Skt.] n. A proud hero. శౌర్యముచే గర్వించినవాడు. A title of Ganesa. వినాయకుడు.

హేరవళి or హేరావళి *hēravali.* [Tel.] n. A parti-colored cloth. పొడవస్త్రము.

హేరామి *hērami.* [Tel.] n. Oppression, persecution, annoyance. హింసించుట, ఉపద్రవపరచుట.

హేరాళము *hēraḷamu.* [Tel.] adj. Much, excessive, great, huge. అతిశయమైన, విస్తారమైన, పెద్ద, లావాటి. "హేరాళమగుచు బుగులు కొనియె నవామ్రాత పూర్వకములు పారిజాత మహీజాత పరిమళములు." Parij. v. 54. "పిరంగులగముల్ హేరాళమైపెల్లగా." Bobbili. iii. 79. హేరాళముగా *hēraḷamu-gā.* adv. Much, greatly, abundantly, excessively. అతిశయముగా, విస్తారముగా. "వకులాదిపుష్పముల్ హేరాళముగనుగూర్చి." KP. vii. 63.

హేల or హేళ *hēla.* [Skt.] n. Sport, play, wanton dalliance. విలాసము, శృంగారచేష్ట, లీల. Scorn, తిరస్కారము. "సురేంద్రనందనుడు మునుగొని హేళనమాటు." R. v. 294 హేళనము *hēlanamu.* n. Contempt, disrespect, mockery, ridicule. తిరస్కారము, అలక్ష్యము, పరిహాసము, ఎకసక్కెము. హేలావతి *hēlā-vati.* n. A flirt, a jade, a playful girl. విలాసిని, విలాసవతి.

హేళి *hēli.* [Skt. Cf. Gk. 'Helios'.] n. The sun. సూర్యుడు. హేళితనూభవ the river Kalindi. కాళిందీనది. "హేళియు పడమట వ్రాలెను." BP. iv. 199.

హేవాక or హేవాకము *hēvāka.* [Skt.] n. Sport, dalliance. విలాసము, ప్రౌఢశి, తత్కాల మూన ప్రౌఢశి, స్త్రీలశృంగారభావజ క్రియాభేదము, అభిజ్ఞత.

హేవిళంబి *hē-vilambi.* [Skt.] n. The name of a Telugu year.

హేష or హేషితము *hēsha.* [Skt.] n. Neighing, a neigh. గుర్రపుసకిలింత. హేషారవము or హేషాఘోషము the sound of neighing. హేషమాన *hēsha-māna.* adj. Neighing. సకిలించుచున్న. హేషించు *hesh-intsu.* v. n. To neigh. సకిలించు.

హై hai

హైన్యము *hainyamu.* [Skt. from హీనము.] n. Baseness, meanness. Nonentity, nonexistence. నీచత్వము, అల్పత్వము, హీనత్వము, హీనత, అభావము, లేమి. "దారిద్ర్యంబున ప్రజ్ఞాహైన్యంబువాటిల్లు ప్రజ్ఞారాహిత్యంబున సత్క్రియలుడుగు." P. ii. 142.

హైమము *haimamu.* [Skt. from హేమము.] adj. Golden, made of gold, appertaining to gold. స్వర్ణమయమైన, స్వర్ణసంబంధమైన. [From హిమము.] Cold, frigid, చలిగల. "హైమవస్త్రాంబరంబులను." N. iii. 168. హైమనము or హైమంతము *haimanamu.* adj. Cold, wintry. హేమంతఋతుసంబంధమైన, చలియైన. హైమవతి *haima-vati.* n. An epithet of Parvati or of the Ganges. పార్వతి, గంగ. హైమవతీశుడు an epithet of Siva.

హైయంగవీనము *haiyan-gavinamu.* [Skt.] n. Clarified butter prepared a day before it is used, fresh butter. అప్పుడు తరచిచిలికిన వెన్న, అప్పుడు వెన్నకాచిన నెయ్యి, సద్యోఘృతము.

హైరాను *hairanu*. [H.] n. Trouble, fatigue. ఆయాసము, శ్రమము.

హైసరే *haisare*. [Tel.] interj. Bravo excellent! good! very well! well done. శాబాసు, సరే. "ఔరౌ హైసరే హైసరే సొగసు కేళీవిలాసంబు." T. iii. 41.

హొ ho

హొం *hom*. [from Kan. హొన్ను. Tel. & Tam. పొన్ను.] adj. Golden, made of gold. సువర్ణమయమైన, బంగారపు. హొంగోక a gold brocade. హొన్నంచురథంబు a gilded chariot. హొంబట్టు silk woven with gold. హొంబట్టము gold cloth.

హొంత *honta*. [Tel.] n. Trouble, పరిశ్రమము. adv. With a little trouble, carefully. Melodiously, harmoniously. Artfully, cleverly. ప్రావీణ్యముగా, నేర్పుగా. "కే హొంతబాటలు వనవిహారోత్సవంబు, సలుపు టయము." Anir. ii. 36. హొంతకారి, హొంతకాడు or హొంతకాడు. *honta-kari*. n. A clever man or woman, a genius, a beauty. A fencer, a wrestler. A rogue, a cheat, a juggler, a conjuror నేర్పరి, కట్టివాడు, కట్టిది, సొగసుకత్తె, సాముచేసే నటెట్టి, చూచుమండగా మాయచేయుపురుషుడు. అటువంటి స్త్రీయు. "గరడిలో సరి హొంతకారులై సాములమీరిన రాజకుమారమణులు." H. ii. 9.

హొన్ను *honnu*. [Kan. from Drav. పొన్ను.] n. Gold, the gold coin called a pagoda, సువర్ణము, కాంచనము. వరహా. "హొన్నంచు పక్కెర." N. ii. 81. "హొన్నుగట్టుల మెచ్చుని ఘనరథములు." Swa. v. 50. హొన్నిత్తడి *honu-ittadi*. (హొన్ను+ఇత్తడి.) n. A kind of brass. ఇత్తడిలోభేదము. See also under హొం.

హొమ్ము or ఉమ్ము *hommu*. [Tel.] adj. Big, plump. స్థూలము.

హొయలు *hoyalu*. [Tel.] n. Grace, charm, agreeableness. విలాసము, సొగసు. హొయలుగా *hoyalu-ga*. adv. Gracefully, agreeably, విలాసముగా, సొగసుగా. "కనుబొమల్ జంకించుకొా నెదు హొయలు." H. iv. 241. హొయలుబండి *hoyalu-bandi*. n. An evening carriage. గాడి.

హొరగు or హొరంగు *horagu*. [Tel.] n. Grace, elegance, సొగసు, విలాసము. "దాని కడాని హొరంగుమేనిదాల్." Ila. iii. 199. "పలుకుల హొరంగు." Krishna Raya Vijayam. iv. 58.

హో hō

హో *hō*. [Tel.] interj. "Holloa!" ఓ అనుదానికి మరోకరూపము. "అసమానుబాలాచి హోయని నివారించి." BD. v. 294.

హోడము *hōḍamu*. [Skt.] n. A ship, boat, ఓడ, నావ.

హోత *hōta*. [Skt.] n. A priest who offers a burnt sacrifice, a reciter of the Rig Veda. ఋత్విజుడు, హోమముచేయువాడు, ఋగ్వేద గాయకుడు. హోత్రి *hōtri*. n. A sacrificer. సోమయాజి. "ఋక్షు హోత్రి." P. pref. 11.

హోదా *hōdā*. [H.] n. Office, authority, rank.

హోమము *hōmamu*. [Skt.] n. A burnt offering. అగ్నియందు వేల్చుట. "హోమధేను వు." HD. i. 1810. హోమకుండము a hole in the ground or an altar, for receiving the fire for an oblation. హోమాగ్ని sacrificial fire.

హోర *hōra*. [Tel.] n. An expedient, contrivance: a wit, a person clever at expedients. ఉపాయము, ఉపాయశాలి. హోరగలవా డు or హోరమనిషి a clever man సమర్థుడు, ఉపాయశాలి.

హోర *hōra*. [Skt. Cf. Lat. 'hora.'] n. The twenty-fourth part of a day. An hour. గంటసేపు, సమయము. Part of the duration of a sign, లగ్నమధ్యభాగము, రాశ్యర్థము, లగ్నాంశము, లగ్నభేదము.

హోరాహోరు hōraṭa. [Tel.] n. Excitement, eagerness. ఆతురము.

హోరాహోరి, హోరాహోరిగా or హోరాహోరీగా hōra-hōri. [Tel.] adv. Without intermission, incessantly. ఎడతెగక, తెప్పగా. "హోరాహోరిగా పోరి." Swa. iii. 129. "వారియిద్దరు శమలోపల నీరము గొని రాజ్యకాంక్ష విజిగీషువులై హోరాహోరి చింతోషం." A. iii. 21. హోరాహోరి n. A quarrel, dispute. రచ్చ, మహాక్షయమైనపోరు.

హోరు hōru. [Tel.] adj. Boisterous. n. Boisterousness. A roar. హోరుగాలి a tempestuous wind. హోరున, హోరున or హోరున hōr-una. adv. With a great noise. మహాధ్వనితో. "మహాగి రుల్ హోరన." A. vi. 58.

హోలి, హోలీ or హోలిక holi. [Mahrati.] n. The pile (of wood, grass, &c., arranged to be kindled at the close of the Holi feast. కామునిపండుగ కడపటివాడు తగల బెట్టడమునకై పోగుచేయబడు గడ్డికంపమొదలగు నవి. హోలీపండుగ holi-panduga. n. The Holi feast held about the beginning of March. వసంతోత్సవము, కామునిపండుగ.

హౌ hau

హౌత్రము hautramu. [Skt. from హోతృ.] n. The duty of the reciter of the Rig-Veda at a sacrifice. యజ్ఞములో ఋగ్వేద మెరిగిన ఋత్విజునియొక్క కర్మము. "అత్రివసిష్ఠ దక్ష పులహాంగిరులాది మహా మునీంద్రులౌద్గాత్రము. హౌత్రమాధ్వరము దక్షులుసగర్గినయాగ కర్మముల్ మాత్రవిధానవైఖరిని జొప్పడజేయగ." T. v. 206.

హౌదా or హౌవుదా hauda. [H.] n. A seat fixed on the back of an elephant, a howdah, అంబారి.

హౌసు or హౌవుసు hausu. [H. from Arabic.] n. Beauty, సొగసు, విలాసము. "కొరావి కృదనంబు హౌసుమురిపెంబయ్యాకరియొయ్యార మా." T. iii. 41. హౌసుకాడు or హౌవుసుకాడు hausu-kāḍu. n. A beau, a gallant, సొగసుగాడు. హౌసుతోట or హౌవుసుతోట hausu-tōṭa. n. A park, a garden. ఉపవనము, శృంగారవనము.

హ్ర hra

హ్రదము hradamu. [Skt.] n. A lake, a large sheet of deep water. నదిమధ్యాగాధజలాశయము, లోతుమడుగు.

హ్రస్వము hrasvamu. [Skt.] adj. Short, low in stature, dwarf, little; short, as a vowel; small, less. వామనమైన, పొట్టి, దీర్ఘముకాని, లఘువైన, అల్పమైన. ఆకారోహ్రస్వః యశాస్తు విపులాః short is his stature, great his fame. వారికి నడిచేమాన్యములు హ్రస్వము చేయించినాడు he cut short their livings. n. A short syllable in prosody. ఏకమాత్ర, వర్ణము, లఘ్వక్షరము. హ్రస్వుడు hrasvuḍu. n. A dwarf. పొట్టివాడు.

హ్రా hrā

హ్రాదితము hrāditamu. [Skt.] adj. Delighted. సంతోషింపబడిన.

హ్రాదిని hrādini. [Skt.] n. Lightning, a thunderbolt, మెరుపు, వజ్రాయుధము. A river. ఏరు.

హ్రీ hrī

హ్రీ hrī. [Skt.] n. Shame, modesty, bashfulness, సిగ్గు, లజ్జ. హ్రీణము or హ్రీతము hrīnamu. adj. Ashamed, bashful, modest, సిగ్గుపడిన.

హ్రే hrē

హ్రేష Same as హేష (q. v.)

హ్లా hlā

హ్లాదము or హ్లాదనము hlādamu. [Skt.] n. Joy, pleasure. సంతోషము, సంతోషించుట. హ్లాదితము hlāditamu. adj. Gladdened, delighted, pleased.

APPENDIX.

అనుబంధము.

అ a

అంకుడు *ankudu.* [Tel.] n. A god. దేవుడు.

అంగవస్త్రము *anga-vastramu.* [Skt.] n. A man's lower garment. చిన్నపంచె.

అంగిలిగుంట *angili-gunṭa.* [Tel.] n. The pit of the mouth or palate.

అంగులిత్రాణము *anguli-trāṇamu.* [Skt.] n. Armour for the hand or fingers. హస్త కవచము, అత్తెము.

అంచించు *anchintsu.* [Tel.] v. n. To estimate the value of anything. అంచనా వేయు.

అంటునూనె or **అంటునూనియ** *anṭu-nūne.* [Tel.] n. Oil used in bathing. తలంటుకొను మంచినూనె.

అంటురాయి *anṭu-rāyi.* [Tel.] n. (Correct thus :—) A magnetic stone. సూదంటు రాయి.

అంట్లు *anṭlu.* [Tel.] n. plu. Small lice. అంటుపేలు.

అంతర్జంఘాస్థి *antar-jangh-āsthi.* [Skt.] n. The bone called the Tibia.

అండలము *andalamu.* [Skt.] n. A ledge or ridge half way up the bank of a tank or well.

అంబుదము *ambudamu.* [Skt.] n. A cloud. మేఘము.

అంసఫలకము *amsa-phalakamu.* [Skt.] n The shoulder blade or Scapula.

అక్షయ *a-kshaya.* [Skt.] n. The name of a Telugu year.

అక్షింతలు *akshintalu.* [from Skt. అక్షతలు.] n. A kind of thorny grass which sticks to one's clothes.

అగవు *agavu.* [Tel.] n. A deed, an act. కార్యము, పని.

అగ్నివేంద్రపాకు *agni-vendra-p-āku.* [Skt.+ Tel.] n. A plant used in medicine.

అచ్చులుపోయు *atstsulu-pōyu.* [Tel.] v. n. To bind yarn for weaving.

అటగాడు *aṭa-gāḍu.* [Tel. from అతడు.] pron. He (in contempt.) వాడు.

అడావడి. అడావిడి or **అడావుడి** *aḍāvaḍi.* [Tel.] n. Neglect, carelessness, want of restraint. అడావుడిసంస్థానము a neglected estate. అడావుడిమనిషి a person devoid of self-restraint. "ఇంట్లో పెండ్లి అయితే ఊళ్లో కుక్కలకు అడావుడి" (proverb.)

అదమాయించు *adamāy-intsu.* [Tel.] v. a. To browbeat, to check by frightening.

అనుభవశాలి *anubhava-śāli.* [Skt.] n. A man of experience.

అనుభుక్తము *anu-bhuktamu.* [Skt.] adj. Enjoyed. అనుభవింపబడిన.

అన్నరసము *anna-rasamu.* [Skt.] n. Chyle.

అనామత్తుగా *anāmattu-gā.* [H. corruption of అమానతు.] adj. Separately. ఆ సొమ్మును అనామత్తుగా ఉంచినాను I kept that money apart.

అనుకు *anuku.* [Tel.] (Add) అన్వు-కుకుకు. v. n. (not adv.)

అనుగలము *anugalamu.* [from Skt. అను కూలము.] adj. Convenient. అనుకూలమైన. Equal, సమానము.

అనుష్టానము Same as అనుష్ఠ (q. v.)

అపరంజి *aparanji.* [H. from Arabic *Afranjiya* which means 'foreign' and perhaps originates in that word which is derived from 'foraneus,' external.] n. Fine gold. అపరంజికాసు lit. 'foreign coin.' A Venetian sequin.

అప్పీలు *appilu.* [Eng 'appeal.'] n. An appeal.

అమలు *amalu.* [H.] n. Authority. అమలు లోనికి తెచ్చు to put in force.

అమానీ *amani.* [H.] n. One's own charge. ఆ భూమి అమానీ అయినతరువాత after the land was taken into (the Collector's) own charge.

అయ్యగారు or **అయ్యవారు** *ayya-gāru.* [Tel.] n. A teacher or guru. ఆచార్యుడు. A venerable man, పూజ్యుడు.

అయివజు *ayivajzu.* [H.] n. Value.

అరకొర or **అరగొర** *arakora.* [Tel.] n. Hesitation, doubt.

అరణి *arani.* [Skt.] n. (Add) A plant which supplies the wood for this purpose, *Prunna spinosa.*

అరవ *arava.* [Tel.] n. A troublesome cow. సాధువుకాని ఆవు. adj. Wicked, దుష్టము, దుష్టుడు అరవత *aravata.* n. A Tamil woman. ద్రావిడస్త్రీ

అరి *ari.* [Skt.] 7th line. For 'prid end,' read 'pride and.'

అరిమురి *ari-muri.* [Tel.] n. Confusion. కలత. అరిమురిపడు to be confused or confounded, కలతపడు.

అర్జీ *arji.* [H.] n. A petition. అర్జీదారుడు a petitioner.

అల్లకము *allakamu.* [Tel. from అల్లు.] n. Weaving, twisting. అల్లిక.

అల్లాటప్పా *alla-tappa.* [Tel.] n. Deceit, humbug. A mistake, error, fault.

అళాకు *alaku.* [Tam.] n. A measure of capacity, equal to 12¼ cubic inches.

అవ్వపండు *avva-pandu.* [Tel.] n. The fruit of *Trichosanthes palmata.*

అసలు *asalu.* [H.] adj. Original, first. మొదటి. n. Principal. అసలుకాపీ an original or first copy. అసలుశిస్తు original rent.

అస్థిపంజరము *asthi-pandzaramu.* [Skt.] n. A skeleton.

అహము *ahamu.* [Skt.] n. (In Philosophy), Self consciousness, the sense of individuality.

ఆ ā

ఆక్టింగు *akting.* [Eng. 'acting.'] adj. Acting, not permanent, not confirmed, as in an appointment.

ఆంగీరస *āngīrasa.* [Skt.] n. The name of a Telugu year.

ఆణి *āni.* [Tel.] n. A wen or callosity on the foot.

ఆన్సరు *ānsaru.* [Eng. 'answer.'] n. An answer, a reply. (In a court of justice), a counter petition or counter plea.

ఆబాదు *ābādu.* [H.] n. A big town, a city.

ఆరుద్రపురుగు *ārudra-purugu.* [Skt. + Tel.] n The Cochineal insect.

ఆసుపత్రి or **ఆస్పత్రి** *āsupatri.* [Eng. 'hospital.'] n A hospital

ఇ i

ఇంకి *inki*. [Eng. 'ink.'] n. Ink.

ఇతిగాడు Same as ఇతడు (q. v.) (Used in contempt.)

ఇన్స్పెక్టరు or **ఇనస్పెక్టరు** *inspectaru*. [Eng. 'Inspector.'] n. An Inspector.

ఇరసాలు or **ఇరాసాలు** *irasālu*. [H.] n. Sending, remittance. ఆ సొమ్ము ఖజానాకు ఇరసాలు అయినది the money was remitted to the treasury.

ఇలాకా *ilākā*. [H.] adj. That is connected with. సంబంధించిన.

ఉ u

ఉక్కురోషము *ukku-roshamu*. [Tel. + Skt.] n. Great pride or anger.

ఉత్తమత్వము *ut-tama-tvamu*. [Skt.] n. Excellence.

ఉత్తరసభ *ut-tara-sabha*. [Skt.] n. A court of appeal.

ఉపపత్ని *upa-patni*. [Skt.] n. A concubine.

ఉప్పళము or **ఉప్పలము** *uppalamu*. [Tel. ఉప్పు+పాలము.] n. A salt pan, a salt marsh.

ఉప్పుకోఠారు *uppu-kotharu*. [Tel. + H.] n. A salt depôt.

ఉప్పుమిడత *uppu-midata*. [Tel.] n. The insect called a mole cricket.

ఉబ్బకము *ubbakamu*. [Tel. from ఉబ్బు.] n. Greatness, ఆధిక్యము. Joy, ఉత్సాహము.

ఉబ్బెత్తు *ubb-ettu*. adj. Convex.

ఉమేదువారి *umēdu-vāri*. [H.] n. A candidate for employment, a volunteer. ఉమేదువారిపటాలము a volunteer corps.

ఉల్లంకి *ullanki*. [Tel.] n. A small plover or sandpiper.

ఊ ū

ఊదబొడ్డు Same as ఊదుబొడ్డు. See under ఊదుట.

ఎ e

ఎకాయెకి *ekā-y-eki*. [H.] adv. Suddenly, at once.

ఎగచు *egatsu*. [Tel. from ఎగయు.] v. a. To cause to fly. ఎగచుకొను. To chase, run after, తరుము.

ఎగురు *eguru*. [Tel.] n. Flying, a jump. ఎగురుట, గంతు.

ఎడగడ్డ *eda-gadda*. [Tel.] n. A bank, shore. ఒడ్డు, దరి, గట్టు, తీరము.

ఎత్తుదెంచు *ettu-dentsu*. [Tel.] v. n. To lead an expedition against, to fall upon, as an army, దండెత్తివచ్చు.

ఎవ్వల *ev-vala*. [Tel. ఏ+వల.] n. Which direction or side, ఏవైపు.

ఎస్టిమేటు *estimētu*. [Eng. 'estimate.'] n. An estimate. మదింపు.

ఏ ē

ఏరుపడు Same as ఏర్పడు (q. v.). **ఏరుపాటు** Same as ఏర్పాటు (q. v.)

ఒ o

ఒంటింపు *ontimpu*. [Tel.] n. Distribution of work by arrangement, organisation. ఏదు ఏదు ఈ పని చేయవలెనని చేసిన ఏర్పాటు.

ఒండె *onde*. [Tel. from ఒండు.] conj. Either, or, కాని

ఒగిడిగ *ogi-diga*. [Tel.] n. An ornament worn on the head by women. జడబిళ్ల.

ఒడివిడిప్రాలు *odiviḍi-prālu*. [Tel.] n. A kind of grain. ధాన్యవిశేషము.

ఒలయు olayu. [Tel.] v. n. To meet, unite. కలయు, చేరు.

ఒలవు olavu. [Tel.] n. A secret, a contrivance. మర్మము, ఉపాయము. ఒలవరి one who knows a secret, మర్మజ్ఞుడు; a man of tact, ఉపాయము నెరిగినవాడు.

ఓ ō

ఓటుచేయు ōṭu-chēyu. [Tel.] v. a. To deceive, defeat. భంగపరుచు.

ఓడంగి ōḍangi. [Tel. from ఓడ.] n. A sailor, a boatman, boatswain. ఓడవాడు, పడవ వాడు.

ఓర ōra. [Tel.] n. A side. ఓరగా. adj. Inclined to a side, bent, ఒరగిన, వంగిన.

ఔ au

ఔన్నత్యము aunnatyamu. [Skt. from ఉన్నతము.] n. Height. ఎత్తు.

క ka

కంటివాలు kanṭi-vālu. [Tel. from కల్లు.] n. Lit. A stone-sword. An epithet of Vishnu's discus, చక్రాయుధము.

కంఠమణి kanṭha-maṇi. [Skt.] n. Adam's apple, the pharynx.

కండరము kanḍaramu. [Skt.] n. A muscle.

కండాయము kandāyamu. [Tel.] n. A fixed portion of tax payable at a certain time. Rent paid in money as distinguished from rent paid in kind.

కక్కిరిబిక్కిరి kakkiri-bikkiri. [Tel. (anuk.)] n. Confusion. తారుమారు.

కచేరి kachēri. [H.] n. An office, a Cutchery.

కజానా See ఖజానా.

కటకట kaṭa-kaṭa. [Tel. (anuk)] n. A crackling noise, as in chewing. &c. కొరకుటలో నగు ధ్వన్యనుకరణము. పండ్లు కటకట కొరికెను he gnashed his teeth.

కడుపుమంట kaḍupu-manṭa. [Tel.] n. Heart-burning, indignation.

కదలాడు Same as కదలు (q. v.)

కనాలు kanālu. [Eng. 'canal.'] n. A canal. కాలువ.

కనుపొట్టలు kanu-poṭṭalu. [Tel.] n. The under eyelids. కంటిపై క్రింది రెప్పలు.

కన్నెబావి kanne-bāvi. [Tel.] n. A dry well. నీళ్లులేని బావి. A large well, కోనేటివంటి పెద్ద బావి.

కన్నోటు kann-ōṭu. [Tel. కన్ను+ఓటు.] n. Fear. భయము, బెదరు.

కప్పురభోగి kappura-bōgi. [from Skt. కర్పూరభోగి.] n. A kind of grain.

కమ్మపిల్లి kamma-pilli. [Tel.] n. A Civet cat.

కయిదీ, ఖైదీ or ఖయిదీ kayidī. [H.] n. A prisoner. కయిదు, ఖైదు or ఖయిదు kayidu. n. Imprisonment.

కరటు karaṭu. [Skt.] n. A troublesome milch cow. ప్రయాసముతో పిదుకదగిన ఆవు.

కరవాక kara-vāka. [Tel.] n. Muddy ground on the seashore.

కరారు See ఖరారు.

కర్ణభేరి karṇa-bhēri. [Skt.] n. The tympanum of the ear.

కర్రనూనె karra-nūne. [Tel.] n. Wood oil, vegetable oil.

కలవ kalava. [Tel.] n. A mixture of sand and chunam. ఇసుకయు సున్నమును కలిసినది.

కలింగిరిపండు kalingiri-panḍu. [Tel.] n. A water melon.

కలెక్టరు *kalekṭaru.* [Eng. 'collector.'] n. A collector, the magistrate in charge of a district or of its sub-division.

కల్లరిపిట్ట *kallari-piṭṭa.* [Tel.] n. The snake-bird. *Plotus melanogaster.* (F. B. I.)

కళాయి *kaḷāyi.* [H.] n. Tin. తగరము. కళాయి చేయు to tin a vessel.

కవట *kavaṭa.* [Tel.] adj. Tender, young. లేత. కవటాకు a tender leaf.

కసుగు *kasugu.* [Tel.] v. n. To be bruised, to be vexed in mind. నలుగు. v. a. To bruise, rub, smear, give pain, నలుచు, పులుము, బాధించు.

కస్తూరి *kastūri.* [Skt.] n. A pet name for a dog.

కస్బా *kasbā.* [H.] n. The principal or large town in a district or division of country.

కా kā

కాంచిపండు *kānchi-paṇḍu.* [Tel.] n. The fox grape, *Solanum nigrum* (Ainslie).

కాగుడు *kāguḍu.* [Tel. from కాగు.] n. Boiling. ఉడుకుట.

కాయిలా *kāyilā.* [H.] n. Sickness. వ్యాధి.

కారురాళ్లు *kāru-rāḷḷu.* [Tel. కరుకు+రాళ్లు.] n. plu. Uncut, rough or untrimmed stones used in building.

కి ki

కిరోసినునూనె *kirosinu-nūne.* [Eng. 'kerosine oil.'] n. Kerosine oil. (Sometimes corrupted into కిరస్తానినూనె.)

కివ్వు *kivvu.* [Tel.] v. n. To die. మడియు.

కిస్తు *kistu.* [H.] n. Government tax, *kist.* కిస్తుబందీప్రకారము by instalments.

కు ku

కుక్కగొడుగు *kukka-goḍugu.* [Tel.] n. Lit. a 'dog's umbrella.' A fungus, toad-stool, mushroom, పుట్టగొడుగు.

కుట్టుసురు *kuṭṭ-usuru.* [Tel. కురు+ఉసురు or కుట్టి+ఉసురు.] n. A little life. కొంచెము మిగిలియున్న ప్రాణము.

కుడిపి *kuḍipi.* [Tel.] n. A deformed person. కురూపి.

కుడుప *kuḍupa.* [Tel.] n. Cheating, deceit. వంచన.

కుల్లుపోతు *kuḷḷu-pōtu.* [Tel.] n. An envious or jealous person.

కుసుంభరాగము *kusumbha-rāgamu.* [Skt.] n. Feigned love. బయటికిమాత్రము చెలిముగా కనబడి లోపల పొత్తగాలేని అనురాగము.

కుసూలము *kusūlamu.* [Skt.] n. A hamper, or large high basket for storing grain. గాదె.

కుస్తీ or కుస్తి *kusti.* [H.] n. Gymnastics, physical exercise. కుస్తీచేయు to practise gymnastics.

కూ kū

కూని or ఖూని *kūni.* [H.] n. Murder. నరహత్య.

కే kē

కేజు or కేసు *kēḍzu.* [Eng. 'case.'] n. A case, a law-suit, civil or criminal. నామీద కేసుతెచ్చినాడు he brought a sui against me.

కొ ko

కొఠీ *koṭhī.* [H.] n. A bank where money is kept.

కొప్పరము kopparamu. [Tel.] adj. Great, raging, fiery. విజృంభితము. "కోకములో కొప్పరమైనవో." దాశరథి శతకము.

కో kō

కోటు kōṭu. [Eng. 'coat.'] n. A coat.

కోణము kōnamu. [Skt.] n. An angle. త్రికోణము a triangle. పంచకోణము a pentagon.

కోర్టు kōrṭu. [Eng. 'court.'] n. A court of law, a court of justice, న్యాయసభ.

క్రీ krī

క్రీగడుపు krī-gaḍupu. [Tel.] n. The abdomen. క్రిందికడుపు.

క్రీతొడ krī-toḍa. [Tel.] n. The lower part of the thigh. క్రిందితొడ, తొడయొక్కదిగువ భాగము.

క్రే krē

క్రేణి krēni. [Tel.] n. Ridicule. పరిహాసము. క్రేణిచేయు to ridicule, పరిహాసముచేయు.

క్రేగ్గపాటు Same as క్రేగ్గుపాటు (q. v.)

క్వై kvai

క్వైనా kvainā. [Eng. 'quinine.'] n. Quinine.

క్లో klō

క్లోమకము klōmakamu. [Skt.] n. The diaphragm.

ఖ kha

ఖజానా khajānā. [H.] n. A treasury. ఖజాంచీ a treasurer.

ఖరారు kharāru. [H.] adj. Strict. ఖండితమైన.

ఖి khi

ఖిర్దు ఆబాదుచేసికొను khirdu-ābādu-chēsi-konu. [H.] v. a. To cultivate fully.

గ ga

గంజికాలు ganji-kālu. [Tel.] n. A bent knee. గంజికాలు పట్టుకొనిపోతాము we will catch (your) bent knee and carry you across (the stream).

గంటెలు ganṭelu. [Tel.] n. Spiked millet, *Panicum spicatum*.

గగ్గి gaggi. [Tel.] n. An ear or head of cholam, ragi, &c., from which the grain has been removed by thrashing.

గబ్బుచీకటి gabbu-chīkaṭi. [Tel.] n. Thick darkness. గాఢాంధకారము.

గల్ల galla. [Tel.] n. Phlegm, కల్లె.

గవర్నరు gavarnaru. [Eng. 'governor.'] n. A governor. The Governor of a Presidency.

గా gā

గాంగి gāngi. [Eng. 'gang.'] n. A gang of men.

గాడికలుగు gāḍi-kalugu. [Tel.] v. a. To burn. సంతాపముచేయు.

గాటు gāṭu. [from Skt. ఘాత.] n. A blow. గాటుకలుగు to be split, భేదిల్లు.

గి gi

గిరగిటలు or గిర్గిటలు gira-giṭalu. [Tel.] n. plu. A kind of cymbals. ఆనుకపుడు వాయించెడు తాళము.

గిరస *girasa.* [Tel.] adj. Timid, runaway. పిరికి, సమరభీరువు.

గు gu

గుడుసరి *guḍus-ari.* [Tel. గుడుసు+అరి.] n. A cunning person. కపటముకలవాడు.

గురుపోడుచు *guru-poḍuṭsu.* [Tel.] v. n. To snore. గురకపెట్టు.

గుర్తించు *gurtinṭsu.* [Tel.] v. a. To recognise. గురుతుపట్టు.

గె ge

గెడ్డ *geḍḍa.* [Tel.] n. A water course.

గొ go

గొణిజె or **గొణిజ** *goṇidza.* [Tel.] n. A hook into which a bolt fastens. తలుపు గ్రంథి తగిలించే ఇనుపకొంకి.

గో gō

గోటుకట్టె *gōṭu-kaṭṭe.* [Tel.] n. A belle. నీటుకత్తె.

గోము *gōmu.* [Tel. for గారాబము.] n. Excessive kindness, over-indulgence. పిల్లవానిని గోముచేస్తున్నాడు he is spoiling the child.

గోరుపులు, గోర్పులు or **గోర్పుళులు** *gōru-pulu.* [Tel.] n. plu. Balls to play with. గోరుపులాడు or గోర్పులాడు to play at tossing a ball, to toss up in play. పుట్టచెండ్లాడు, ఎగురవేయు.

గ్ర gra

గ్రండె *granḍe.* [from Skt. గ్రంథి.] n. An iron ring fastened to a door. ద్వార బంధము లోపలనుండి నిలువుగులయందు బిగగొట్టిన మొలలకు తగిలించెడు కీలుపులయందలి ఇనుపకట్టె.

గ్రా grā

గ్రామనత్తము *grāma-nattamu.* [Skt. + Tel.] n. A village site.

ఘ్రా ghrā

ఘ్రాణించు or **ఆఘ్రాణించు** *ghrāṇ-inṭsu.* [Skt.] v. a. To smell. వాసనచూచు, మూర్కొను.

చ cha

చండాలము *chanḍālamu.* [Tel.] n. Filth, a filthy mass.

చక్రవాళము *chakra-vāḷamu.* [Skt.] n. The Brahminy duck or Ruddy Shieldrake. A kind of fabulous bird.

చలామణి *chalāmaṇi.* [H.] n. Acceptance. చలామణిఅగు to be accepted.

చార్జి *charji.* [Eng. 'charge.'] n. A charge. Cost, expense, వెల. కిరీదు. ఎంతచార్జి what is the charge or cost? Anything entrusted to another. An office. చార్జితీసుకొన్నాడు he took charge of the office. చార్జిఅప్పగించి పోయెను he gave over charge and went away. An accusation, a complaint. వానిమీద చార్జిచేసిరి they charged him, they filed a complaint against him.

చి chi

చిక్కుపట్టు *chikka-paṭṭu.* [Tel.] n. A firm hold. Certainty, నిశ్చయము.

చిట్ట *chiṭṭa.* [Tel.] n. A small bush. చిన్నపొద. "పనసపుజెట్లలన." వసు. i. "చిట్టలను చెట్లు." స్వా. iv.

చిన్నరికము chinna-rikamu. [Tel.] n. Infancy, childhood. చిన్నతనము.

చిల్లరవాడు chillara-vadu. [Tel.] n. A common man. సామాన్యుడు.

చీ chī

చీకటి chikati. [Tel. చీకు+కట్టు.] n. Darkness. See under చీకటి.

చీకు chiku. [Tel.] n. Blindness. గుడ్డితనము. చీకురించు to become blind, గుడ్డిదగు.

చె che

చెచ్చెర or చెరచెర chech-chera. [Tel.] adv. Quickly. శీఘ్రముగా.

చెలగు or చెల్గు chelagu. [Tel.] v. a. To cut. ఖండించు, నరుకు.

చెలయు or చెలయు chelayu. [Tel.] v. n. To be proud, to increase. విజృంభించు. v. a. To scatter, చిమ్ము.

చే chē

చేదుకట్టు chēdu-kattu. [Tel.] n. The gall bladder.

చ tsa

చేంకి Same as చంక (q. v.)

చచ్చుడు tsatstsudu. [Tel.] adj. Dead. చచ్చిన. చచ్చుడు బాకీ an irrecoverable debt.

చదరము tsadaramu. [from Skt. చతురస్రమ్.] adj. Equal, సమానమైన. Having no defect, perfect కొరతలేని.

చొ tso

చొలగు, or చొలయు tsolayu. [Tel.] v. n. To faint, మూర్ఛపోవు. To retreat, fall back, వెనుదీయు. To be disgusted with. వైరస్యమునొందు.

జ ja

జఠరాగ్ని jathar-agni. [Skt.] n. The gastric juice.

జడ్జి jadji. [Eng. 'judge.'] n. A judge. న్యాయాధిపతి.

జనానా or జేనానా janana. [H.] n. Apartments appropriated to women. A seraglio, a harem, the women in a harem.

జమాయించు jamayintsu. [H.] v. n. To grow vigorous.

జవాబుదారీ javabu-dari. [H.] n. Responsibility.

జా jā

జాతివాడు jati-vadu. [Skt.+Tel.] n. A European.

జారీచేయు jari-cheyu. [H.] v. a. To enforce, to grant. ఆ భూమిని నాకు జారీచేసినాడు he granted that land to me.

జాస్తి jasti. [H.] n. Excess. జాస్తిపన్ను an additional tax.

జి ji

జిల్లా jilla. [H.] n. A territorial revenue division, a zillah or district, జిల్లేదారుడు a subordinate revenue officer.

జీ jī

జీర్ణరసము jirna-rasamu. [Skt.] n. Gastric juice.

జె dza

జంపె dzampe. [Tel.] n. (correct thus :—) Quick time in Music.

జగా Same as జాగా (q. v.)

జట్టి dzatti. [H.] n. A contract. జట్టిబేరము a wholesale purchase.

జమ dzama. [H.] n. Collection of revenue. జమాఖర్చులు income and expenditure.

జరీ dzari. [H.] n. Lace, ornamental network of silk, flax, cotton, or of gold or silver. సరిగె.

జరూరు dzarūru. [H.] n. Haste. adj. Necessary, urgent.

జల్లిక dzallika. [Tel.] n. Jelly.

జా dzā

జాము dzāmu. [from Skt. యామము.] n. A period of three hours.

జు dzu

జుబ్బా dzubbā. [H.] n. A shirt.

జుమికీలు dzumikīlu. [Tel.] n. plu. A kind of ear ornaments worn by women.

జో dzo

జోరు dzōru. [H.] n. Strength, vigor.

ఝ jha

ఝంకరించు jhan-kar-intsu. [Skt.] v. n. To buzz, as a bee. ఝంకారముచేయు.

ట ta

టలాయించు or తలాయించు talāyintsu. [H.] v. a. To shirk work. v. n. To walk about, ఇటు అటు తిరుగు.

టె te

టెల్లిగ్రాపు telli-grāpu. [Eng. 'telegraph.'] n. Telegraph. టెలిగ్రాము teli-grāmu. n. A telegram, తంతివర్తమానము. టెలిగ్రాపు పంపు to send a telegram. టెలిగ్రాపుకొట్టు to telegraph.

టే tē

టేకు or తేకు tēku. [Eng. 'teak.'] n. Teak, *Tectona grandis* (Linn).

త ta

తండిరి Same as తండ్రి (q.v.)

తడవు tadavu. [Tel.] n. Searching, వెదకుట. తడవులాడు to go about searching, to search by feeling with one's hands in darkness, వెదకు, వెదకులాడు.

తమాయించు tamā-y-intsu. [Tel.] v. n. To stop, cease, ఆగు. తమాయించుకొను to bear, endure, సహించు, ధరించు.

తరంకట్టుల taram-kattula. [H.] n. Classification of soils, &c., తరందారీ a classifier.

తరిమాను tari-mānu. [Tel.] n. A weaver's beam.

తరువాయి taruvāyi. [Tel.] n. A time, తడవ, సారి, మారు.

తలకప్ప tala-kappa. [Tel.] n. A tadpole, the young of a frog.

తసరబు tasarabu. [H.] n. Seizure. తసరబు చేయు to seize. నా చేనిఫలమును బిరు తసరబు చేసినారు they have seized my crop.

తా tā

తాటకత్తె tāta-katte. [Tel.] n. A deceitful woman. మోసకత్తె.

తారుమారు tāru-māru [Tel.] n. Confusion, disorder.

తి ti

తిబ్బి tibbi. [Tel.] n. Backstitching. ముందరి కుట్టుపోనిచ్చుచు వెనుకకు మరలించి మరలించి కుట్టడము కట్టుకుట్టు.

తిరుగుడు *tiruguḍu.* [Tel.] n. A wheel. చక్రము.

తీ tī

తీరు *tīru.* [Tel.] v. n. To be possible. శక్యమగు. To be at leisure. అవకాశపడు.

తు tu

తువర Same as తుంబర (q.v.)

తులామానము *tulā-mānamu.* [Skt.] n. A measure of weight.

తుస్సు *tussu.* [Tel.] adj. Base, inferior. నీచము.

తూ tū

తూగుపలక *tūgu-palaka.* [Tel.] n. A plumb line. తాపివాడు గోడలమట్టమును చూచుటకై రాయి వ్రేలగట్టిన నిడుపాటిపలక.

తె te

తెర *tera.* [Tel.] n. A series. పరంపర.

తెలగబలిజెలు *telaga-balijelu.* [Tel.] n. A certain caste.

తే tē

తేలుకొండిచెట్టు *tēlu-koṇḍi-cheṭṭu.* [Tel.] n. A shrub called *Tragia involucrata*.

తొ to

తొలుబలుకులు or **తొలుపలుకులు** *tolu-balu-kulu.* Tel.] n. plu. Lit. the ancient words, i. e., the Veda, వేదము.

ద da

దండాన్వయము *daṇḍ-ānvayamu.* [Skt.] n. A paraphrase or detailed statement.

దడబడ *daḍa-baḍa.* [Tel. (anuk.)] n. Noise. సందడి. Hurry, త్వర. Excitement, ఆటోపము.

దప్పిక Same as దప్పి (q. v.)

దబ్బర *dabbaru.* [Tel.] n. A fault. తప్పు.

దర్భపోటు *darbha-pōṭu.* [Tel.] n. A cant phrase for a Srāddha or funeral.

దస్తావేజు *dastā-vēḍzu.* [H.] n. Evidence in writing.

దా dā

దాఖలు See దఖలు.

దాణా *dāṇa.* [H.] n. Horse gram. "గుర్రము గుడ్డిదైనను దాణాలో తక్కువయుండదు." (proverb.)

ది di

దిమాకు or **ధిమాకు** *dimaku.* [H.] n. Insolence.

దు du

దుండి *duṇḍi.* [Tel.] n. A lady. దొరసాని.

దె de

దెప్పరము *depparamu.* [Tel.] n. A word of censure, a harsh word. నిష్ఠురవచనము, దుస్సహవచనము.

ద్రా drā

ద్రావిడప్రాణాయామము. *drāviḍa-prāṇa-yāmamu.* [Skt.] n. Intricate and crooked procedure.

ద్వి dvi

ద్విశిరము *dvi-śiramu.* [Skt.] n. The biceps muscle.

ధా dhā

ధార *dhāra.* [Skt.] n. A waterfall.

ధూతు See ధివాతు.

న na

నజ్జు *nandsu.* [Tel.] n. Beri-beri, dropsy.

నంబరు or నెంబరు *nambaru.* [Eng. 'number.'] n. A number. Also, a case or law-suit. సెంబరురాయి a boundary stone.

నక్కు *nakku.* [Tel.] n. A plough-share, నాగటిఱ్ఱు.

నవరసు *navarasu.* [H.] n. A sovereign, a pound sterling.

నా nā

నామరులు *namarulu.* [Tel. నాము+మరులు.] n. Dice. పాచికలు.

ని ni

నిశాని *nisani.* [H.] n. A signature. వ్రాలు, చేవ్రాలు.

నీ nī

నీరాటము *nirāṭamu.* [Skt.] n. An animal that lives in water. నీళ్లయందు చరించు జంతువు. " క: నీరాట వనాటములకు, బోరాటం బెట్లుకలిగె," భాగ. vii.

నీరుమోపరి *niru-mop-ari.* [Tel.] n. A water pot. కుంభము. A cloud, మేఘము.

ను nu

నుసిమిరి or నుశిమిరి *nusimiri.* [Tel.] n. Eczema, a skin complaint.

నో nō

నోటు *nōṭu.* [Eng. 'note.'] n. A note. A currency note. నోటరుబాండు a note or bond.

ప pa

పంచాయితీ or పంచాయతీ *panchayiti.* [H.] n. A Panchayat, a board of arbitration, a jury. పంచాయతీదారులు the members of a Panchayat.

పట్టా or పట్టీ *paṭṭa.* [H.] n. A rail made of iron or other metal. ఇనుములోనగువానికమ్మి.

పడుగు *paḍugu.* [Tel.] n. A heap of un-threshed ears of corn.

పన్నె *panne.* [Tel.] n. A goad attached to a stirrup, అంకెవన్నెకు వెనుకటి ఇనుపముల్లు. A spur.

పబ్లికు *pabliku.* [Eng. 'public.'] adj. Public, బహిరంగము. పబ్లికుగా publicly.

పమ్ము *pammu.* [Tel.] v. a. To stitch, to hem, అంచులుమడిచికుట్టు. పమ్మకము *pammakamu.* n. Hemming, అంచులు మడిచికుట్టెడు కుట్టు.

పర్లాంగు *parlangu* [Eng. 'furlong.'] n. A furlong.

పా pā

పారంపరి Same as పారంపర్యము (q. v.)

పారుపోగు *paru-pōgu.* [Tel.] n. Loose texture, in weaving. దూరదూరముగాపోయు నూలిపోగు.

పాసగు *pās-agu.* [Eng. 'pass.'] v. n. To pass in an examination.

పే pē

పేనసలు or పెన్సిలు *pēnasalu.* [Eng. 'pencil.'] n. A pencil.

పై pai

పైత్యరసము *paitya-rasamu.* [Skt.] n. Bile,

పో pō

పోగుపోయు pōgu-pōyu. [Tel.] v. a. To make a running stitch. సంతనక్కై తిన్నగా పోగు పోసించినట్లు.

ప్ర pra

ప్రగండిక pra-gaṇḍika. [Skt.] n. The humerus.

ప్రలంభము pra-lambhamu. [Skt.] n. Deceitfulness. వంచనము.

ప్రా prā

ప్రావ prāva. [Tel.] n. Way, manner, style. పద్ధతి. adj. Convenient, అనుకూలము. Proper, right. యుక్తము.

బ ba

బచ్చలి batstsali. [Tel.] n. A bathing place; a place for washing vegetables, &c. A certain vegetable. కందకులేని దురద బచ్చలి కేమి? (proverb.)

బస్తి basti. [H. from Skt. వస్ to dwell.] n. A town.

బా bā

బాంకి bānki. [Eng. 'bank.'] n. Bank, a place where money is kept in custody, కొఠి.

బూ bū

బూట్సు būṭsu. [Eng. 'boots.'] n. plu. Boots.

బ్ర bra

బ్రహ్మనాడి brahma-nāḍi. [Skt.] n. The aorta.

బి bi

బింబము bimbamu. [Skt.] n. A lens. నొక్కు నిమ్ము బింబము a concave lens. స్ఫటికాకార బింబము a [illegible]lline lens.

బిల్లు billu. [Eng. 'bill.'] n. A bill or enactment.

బు bu

బుడగ Same as బుగ్గ (q. v.)

బె be

బెకబెక beka-beka. [Tel. (anuk.)] n. The noise made by a frog. కప్పకూత.

బో bō

బోటు bōṭu. [Eng. 'boat.'] n. A boat, పడవ.

బోర్డు bōrḍu. [Eng. 'board.'] n. A board. A black-board used in schools. నల్లబల్ల. A council or meeting of managers convened for business, సభ.

మ ma

మన్య manya. [Skt.] n. The carotid artery.

మా mā

మాంసగ్రంథులు māmsa-granthulu. [Skt.] n. Glands.

మీ mī

మీటింగు mīṭingu. [Eng. 'meeting.'] n. A meeting or an assembly. సభ.

ము mu

మునగ munaga. [Tel.] n. The horse-radish tree, *Moringa pterygosperma*.

మై mai

మైనరు mainaru. [Eng. 'minor.'] n. minor. యుక్తవయస్సురానివాడు.

మైలు *mailu*. [Eng. 'mile.'] n. A mile.

మో mō

మోతుబరు *mōtubari* [H.] n. Support.

యు yu

యునాని *yunāni* [H. from యునస్.] n. A Greek school of medicine, as opposed to Misri or Egyptian.

ర ra

రబ్బరు or లబ్బరు *rabbaru*. [Eng. 'rubber.'] n. India rubber, caoutchouc, gum elastic. పాలుబంక

రా rā

రాజీనామా *rājīnāma*. [H.] n. An agreement, compromising a matter in dispute, reconciliation. Resignation.

రి ri

రివిజన్ *rivijan*. [Eng. 'revision.'] n. Revision (a court term.)

రివిన్యూ *rivinyū*. [Eng. 'revenue.'] n. Revenue.

రివ్యూ *rivyū*. [Eng. 'review.'] n. Review (a court term.)

రై rai

రైటరు *raitaru*. [Eng. 'writer.'] n. A writer, a clerk.

రైలు *railu*. [Eng. 'rail.'] n. A rail or railway train. రైలుబండి a railway carriage. రైలుమార్గము a railway. రైలుమార్గముగా by rail.

ల la

లబ్బరు Same as రబ్బరు (q. v.)

లా lā

లాకు or లాకులు *lāku*. [Eng. 'lock.'] n. A lock in a canal.

లాపోసు-అగు *lāpōsu-agu*. [H.] v. n. To go over to the side of, to collude with.

లో lō

లోటు *lōtu*. [H.] n. Loss. నష్టము.

వా vā

వారంటు *vārantu*. [Eng. 'warrant.'] n. A warrant (a court term).

వె ve

వెలుతురుచెట్టు *veluturu-chettu*. [Tel.] n. The tree called *Dichrostachys cineria* or *Acacia cinerea*.

శా sā

శాంక్షను *sankshanu*. [Eng. 'sanction.'] n. Sanction. ఉత్తరువు, అనుజ్ఞ, సెలవు.

షు shu

షురుమా *shuruma*. [H.] n. Antimony

స sa

సరక *saraka*. [Tel.] n. Rinderpest, a cattle disease.

సి si

సిలిమి *silimi.* [Tel.] n. A large pipe used for smoking *ganja*.

సె se

సెల్లా *sella.* [H.] n. Calico

స్టే sṭē

స్టేషను *sṭēshanu.* [Eng. 'station.'] n. A station. ఠాణాము. A police station or a railway station.

స్లో slō

స్లోపు *slōpu.* [Eng. 'slope.] n. A slope. స్లోపుగా sloping.